HAVE Y[...]
THE FREE[...]

AGE, WEIGHT & DISTANCE TABLE
For use with Chase and Hurdle races

Distance	Age	Jan	Feb	Mar	Apr	May	June
2m	5	12—7	12—7	12—7	12—7	12—7	12—7
	4	11—13	12—0	12—1	12—2	12—3	12—4
2¼m	5	12—7	12—7	12—7	12—7	12—7	12—7
	4	11—12	11—13	12—0	12—1	12—2	12—3
2½m	5	12—7	12—7	12—7	12—7	12—7	12—7
	4	11—11	11—12	11—13	12—0	12—1	12—2
2¾m	5	12—6	12—7	12—7	12—7	12—7	12—7
	4	11—10	11—11	11—12	11—13	12—0	12—1
3m	5	12—6	12—6	12—7	12—7	12—7	12—7
	4	11—8	11—10	11—11	11—12	11—13	12—0

Distance	Age	July	Aug	Sep	Oct	Nov	Dec
2m	5	12—7	12—7	12—7	12—7	12—7	12—7
	4	12—4	12—5	12—5	12—6	12—6	12—7
	3	11—5	11—6	11—8	11—9	11—11	11—12
2¼m	5	12—7	12—7	12—7	12—7	12—7	12—7
	4	12—3	12—4	12—5	12—5	12—6	12—6
	3	11—4	11—5	11—7	11—8	11—9	11—10
2½m	5	12—7	12—7	12—7	12—7	12—7	12—7
	4	12—2	12—3	12—4	12—5	12—6	12—6
	3		11—4	11—6	11—7	11—8	11—9
2¾m	5	12—7	12—7	12—7	12—7	12—7	12—7
	4	12—2	12—3	12—4	12—5	12—5	12—6
	3					11—7	11—8
3m	5	12—7	12—7	12—7	12—7	12—7	12—7
	4	12—1	12—2	12—3	12—4	12—5	12—5
	3				11—5	11—6	11—7

For 6-y-o's and older, use 12-7 in all cases

Note Race distances in the above tables are shown only at ¼-mile intervals. For races of 2m1f use the 2¼-mile table weights; for races of 2m3f use 2½ miles; and so forth. For races over odd distances, the nearest distance shown in the table should be used. Races over distances longer than 3 miles should be treated as 3-mile races.

National Hunt Flat races A separate age, weight & distance table is used for NH Flat races but there is no weight-for-age allowance for 5-y-o's; over 2 miles from January to November the allowance for 4-y-o's is 1 lb less than it is over jumps.

CHASERS & HURDLERS 2016/17

Price £75.00

A TIMEFORM PUBLICATION

A Timeform Publication

Compiled and produced by

Geoff Greetham (Publishing Editor), Paul Muncaster (Managing Editor), John Ingles (Senior Editor, 'Top Horses In France' & Editor for pedigrees), Phil Turner (Handicapper and Consultant Editor), Martin Rigg, Dan Barber, Paul Goodenough (Handicappers), Nic Doggett, Ben Fearnley, Adam Houghton (Essays), Keith Wilkinson, Kris Hilliam, Jake Price (noteforms), David Holdsworth, Wendy Muncaster, Rachel Todd, Chris Wright, Ivan Gardiner, Michael Williamson (Production)

© Timeform Limited 2017   ISBN 978-0-9933900-7-4

CONTENTS

The age, weight and distance table, for use in applying the ratings in races involving horses of different ages, appears on the end paper at the front of the book

Chasers & Hurdlers 2016/17

Introduction

It is now more than fifty years since Arkle made his last appearance on a racecourse but, long after his final season, his astonishing achievements shine as brightly as ever—or cast an ever-lengthening shadow depending on your point of view. As regular readers will know, Arkle's feats crop up regularly in *Chasers & Hurdlers*, and an account of the final race of his extraordinary career, which came to an abrupt end in the 1966 King George VI Chase when he was still in his prime, can be found in the essay on the latest King George winner **Thistlecrack**. While there were hopes that the immensely popular Arkle would race again after his injury at Kempton, his owner Anne, Duchess of Westminster eventually announced his retirement formally on October 9th 1968. But the 1966 King George wasn't the last that Arkle's legion of fans in Britain got to see of him, as he was invited to Wembley for the 1969 Horse of the Year Show (boosting advance bookings by thirty-five per cent) where he took part in the twice-daily Parade of Personalities, sometimes ridden by his old jockey Pat Taaffe. 'All the clapping was right down his street!' said his owner. 'Arkle adored it. There was a costermonger's cart there, piled with apples and pears. And Arkle absolutely stripped it. I wrote to the owner to apologize and he wrote me the most charming letter back, saying he was delighted and honoured that Arkle had eaten all his fruit.'

The passage of time has done little to diminish Arkle's popularity as shown by the result of a *Racing Post* poll in 2004 in which readers were asked to select their favourite racehorse of all time. Even now, few would argue with Arkle's iconic status, or indeed his claims to greatness, though quantifying his brilliance has, inevitably, proved a more contentious topic. Timeform's rating of Arkle was addressed most recently in the essay on Douvan in *Chasers & Hurdlers 2015/16* which gives a comprehensive account of Arkle's best performances and the arguments supporting what, for some, is a scarcely credible rating. Suffice to say here that the 1967 Gold Cup was won in Arkle's absence by Woodland Venture (a faller two out when challenging the labouring Arkle in the King George) who beat Arkle's Hennessy conqueror Stalbridge Colonist by three quarters of a length, with What A Myth (third in receipt of 33 lb in the Hennessy), who went on to win the 1969 Gold Cup, another two lengths back. Stalbridge Colonist, who had been getting 35 lb from Arkle at Newbury, also finished a close third in the 1968 Gold Cup.

Arkle's 'theme music' chosen by his owner for his parades at Wembley was the song 'There Will Never Be Another You.' If there is never to be the like of 'Himself' again, it's a grim prospect, according to the *Racing Post*'s Tom Kerr, who was named Racing Writer of the Year at the fiftieth Horserace Writers & Photographers Association Derby Awards Lunch in December. 'What I have a problem with is the constant comparisons. Comparisons that ensure every champion since is doomed to be judged a distant second best, forever in the shade of the longest shadow in sport.' Writing in the build-up to the latest Cheltenham Festival, Kerr went on: 'This is best epitomised by Timeform's

Sizing John became the first horse to complete the Irish Gold Cup/Cheltenham Gold Cup/Punchestown Gold Cup treble in the same campaign, an achievement that perhaps deserved to be celebrated more than it was at the time; British-bred jumpers are enjoying a rare spell in the limelight and Sizing John was the second British-bred winner of the Cheltenham Gold Cup in three years, following Coneygree

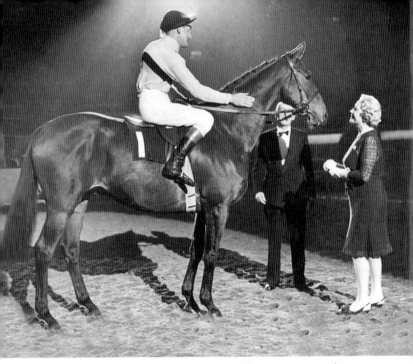

*Horse of the Year Show, Wembley, October 1969—Arkle, now in retirement, makes a
special appearance with his owner Anne, Duchess of Westminster, as the band strikes up
'There Will Never Be Another You'*

212 rating for Arkle, one that makes him nearly two stone ahead of Sprinter
Sacre and Kauto Star, the best of the modern era, and a rating that will never be
challenged. The idea that the sport has formalised the fundamental inferiority
of every horse who will ever live is depressing enough, but there's one thing
that's even worse, and that's the intellectually stunted and ultimately soulless
pastime of comparing horses from one era to those of another.'

As Douvan's essay in last year's Annual conceded, 'comparisons between
past and present champions in any sport are difficult to make, and claims can
never be substantiated to everyone's satisfaction' but 'what is not open to
challenge, and what was fully demonstrated in competition, is that Arkle and
[his contemporary and stable-companion, himself rated 210] Flyingbolt were
capable of conceding almost the full range of the handicap to horses of Gold
Cup standard, horses good enough to win that race or finish close up.' Arkle's
rating, whilst objectively arrived at, is of course not above criticism, but nor
should it be interpreted as a stick with which to beat more recent champions
of their own eras. Besides, it's the difficulty of comparing different eras
which stimulates the far from soulless debate about the relative merits of past
heroes—whether that takes place in pubs, or in the letters pages of the *Racing
Post*, or on social media. This is something which most fans of any sport, not
just racing, will surely recognise. And is Arkle, from the 'sixties, really casting

'the longest shadow in sport'? What about Don Bradman, for example, hailed by *Wisden* as 'the greatest phenomenon in the history of cricket'? He still holds numerous Test match records from the 'thirties and 'forties, most famously his batting average of 99.94 which no-one else has ever rivalled.

Arkle was the first horse to be honoured with having a race named after him at the Cheltenham Festival when, just months after his retirement was announced, what was formerly the Cotswold Chase was run for the first time as the Arkle Challenge Trophy in 1969. Only two other horses, both also Gold Cup winners, have been given the same distinction, though Golden Miller and Dawn Run had to wait a lot longer, until new races were created at the Festival, and even then have their names relegated to brackets after commercial race titles. Fittingly, recent runnings of the Arkle have been won by some outstanding chasers of the current era, the latest edition going to **Altior**, unbeaten in eleven starts over hurdles and fences, and only the third novice to be named Timeform's Horse of the Year. Altior's essay refers to the retirement of another of his stable's now record six Arkle winners Sprinter Sacre, the 2012 winner who went on to record the highest Timeform rating (192p) since the days of Arkle himself (Nicky Henderson's 2013 Arkle winner Simonsig, who never quite fulfilled his own considerable potential, had to be put down after breaking a leg in a fall at Cheltenham on the day Sprinter Sacre's retirement was announced). Sprinter Sacre went on to win two Queen Mother Champion Chases, but the fate of Arkle in the King George should have served as a reminder that even 9/2-on shots are not bombproof. The immensely exciting 2016 Arkle winner **Douvan** lost his unbeaten record at the very same odds when sustaining an injury (apparently not a career-ending one, thankfully, in his case) in the latest running of the Champion Chase, an upset that rather overshadowed the victory of **Special Tiara** who was winning the race at the fourth attempt (coincidentally Sprinter Sacre was also 9/2-on when losing his unbeaten record over fences in the Desert Orchid Chase at Kempton). Also put in the shade somewhat in what has been a golden era of Arkle winners, although another top-class chaser in his own right, was the 2015 winner **Un de Sceaux**, who was kept apart from his stable-companion Douvan but won all three of his starts in Britain, the Tingle Creek, Clarence House and Ryanair Chase.

Arkle was the first horse to have a race named after him at the Cheltenham Festival; the latest edition was won by the brilliant Altior, unbeaten in eleven starts over jumps and only the third novice to be named Timeform Horse of the Year since the start of the Chasers & Hurdlers series

Douvan's owners Susannah and Rich Ricci have enjoyed something of a charmed life as one of the main patrons of Willie Mullins' stable in recent years, but, as Douvan's essay details, their luck took a turn for the worse in the latest campaign, losing another of their top-class chasers Vautour to a freak paddock accident, while neither of their Champion Hurdle winners, Faugheen nor Annie Power (the latter now retired and in foal to Camelot), made it to the track. Dual runner-up **Djakadam** was a beaten favourite when fourth in his latest Gold Cup bid (his essay reminds readers of The Fellow and looks at the career of that horse's trainer Francois Doumen who has announced his retirement), while exciting novice chaser **Min**, favourite to win the Supreme won by Altior at the 2016 Festival, had his campaign curtailed by injury (his essay looks at the strength of the 2016 Supreme field and also reveals Timeform's nomination for the highest-quality contest in Cheltenham Festival history). The Ricci colours were, however, carried successfully at the Festival by **Let's Dance** in the Dawn Run Mares' Novices' Hurdle, her chosen engagement among five possible races during the week—her essay calls for forty-eight-hour declarations to be applied more widely, something which would benefit the promotion of jumping in general, as well as making running plans clearer for punters.

While Ireland's top trainer shared some of the blows sustained by the Riccis, Mullins received a major setback from another quarter before the season proper got under way when another of his biggest supporters, Gigginstown House

The retirement of Sprinter Sacre was announced at Cheltenham's meeting in November; he ran up a stunning sequence of victories in the 2012/13 season, including a nineteen-length win in the Queen Mother Champion Chase, and ended that season rated 192p, the highest rating recorded over jumps in the Chasers & Hurdlers era, just ahead of that achieved by Kauto Star

Still in his thirties, self-made Gordon Elliott has built his County Meath base virtually from scratch over the past few years into one of the most powerful stables in Britain and Ireland; he came very close to wresting the Irish trainers' title from perennial champion Willie Mullins and pipped him to the leading trainer title at the Cheltenham Festival (pictured with the trophy)

Stud, moved sixty of its horses to other Irish stables after a disagreement over training fees. That alone made Mullins' position as perennial champion trainer a little less secure, but the transfer of some of the best Gigginstown horses to his closest rival Gordon Elliott helped turn Mullins' long-standing monopoly of the title into a very live two-horse race. Mullins came out on top, again, in the end, to be Irish champion for the tenth season running, but only after coming from behind in the final week of the season at Punchestown, which, this year, corresponded with the last week of the British season for a welcome change (the sport in Britain and Ireland is so interwoven that it is unfortunate that technical issues are created by the seasons not always running concurrently). Novice hurdlers **Cilaos Emery** and **Bacardys** (whose essay looks at the important role played by Mullins' amateur son Patrick during the final week), along with top Irish juvenile **Bapaume** and dual-purpose performer **Wicklow Brave**, all did their bit, as did unbeaten novice chaser **Great Field** (the least celebrated of a top quintet of novice chasers in the latest season, about which there is more in the essay).

Elliott might have failed narrowly to win his first Irish trainers' championship but he had the bragging rights at Cheltenham where he was top trainer ahead of Mullins (by virtue of more second places), the pair's six wins apiece contributing to a record Irish haul at the Festival of nineteen. Mullins failed to register a winner on the opening day for the first time since 2008, whereas Elliott landed a treble thanks to the mercurial **Labaik** consenting to jump off in the Supreme, **Apple's Jade** beating the Mullins/Ricci pair **Vroum Vroum Mag** and Limini in the David Nicholson, and former Triumph Hurdle winner Tiger Roll landing the first running of the National Hunt Chase as a Grade 2 contest. Apple's Jade had been among the Gigginstown horses Mullins had lost, and her essay looks more closely at the narrowing gap between Ireland's top two trainers and Elliott's successful Cheltenham Festival (a topic also visited in the essay on **Death Duty**). Champion Bumper winner **Fayonagh** (the mount of Ireland's champion amateur Mr Jamie Codd) and **Cause of Causes** (ridden by the same jockey), who achieved the unusual feat of winning his third different race at the Festival in as many years in the Cross-Country Chase (the essay recalls multiple Cheltenham Festival winners), also contributed to Elliott's total, but it was **Champagne Classic**'s success in the Martin Pipe which gave him particular pleasure for reasons explained in his essay. After a slower than usual start to the Festival, Mullins hit back with a four-timer on the Thursday which included a double for the Andrea and Graham Wylie-owned pair **Nichols Canyon** and **Yorkhill** (whose essay, like that on Un de Sceaux, includes interesting insight from eleven times leading jockey at the meeting Ruby Walsh on handling difficult horses). Yorkhill won the Golden Miller and Nichols Canyon the Stayers' Hurdle (a first win for his trainer—but not for his owners—in the race which reverted to its former name), with the four-timer completed by Let's Dance and Un de Sceaux already mentioned. Un de Sceaux's Ryanair win was gained at the chief expense of **Sub Lieutenant** (interesting stats to be found about the Gigginstown string), thus depriving Gigginstown's Michael O'Leary of a first win in the race he sponsors. Mullins also achieved the notable feat of bringing County Hurdle top weight **Arctic Fire** back to win that competitive handicap after more than a year off, while Arctic Fire and Spa winner **Penhill** (whose entry recounts the interesting background of owner Tony Bloom) completed a final-day double for the stable's number two jockey Paul Townend.

While the Mullins monopoly on the Irish title came under serious threat in the latest season, the emergence of Elliott as a second superpower in the Irish training ranks must make competing against both yards even more daunting for middle-ranking and grassroots trainers. This is a topic discussed in the essay on Gigginstown's Troytown winner **Empire of Dirt** who was one of no fewer than eleven horses saddled in the race by Elliott (further evidence of him taking a leaf out of Martin Pipe's book—Pipe ran ten in the 2001 Grand National) on a day when he had a six-timer on the Navan card. Elliott's tremendous record in Ireland's valuable handicap chases is covered in the essay on Paddy Power Chase winner **Noble Endeavor**, though it also raises the question of whether there was an ulterior motive for a mob-handed approach in such races. Gigginstown's thirteen runners in the Irish Grand National raised some eyebrows too (Elliott was responsible for 'only' nine of those) in a concerted but unsuccessful bid to win what is now Ireland's most valuable jumping prize. Gigginstown, who were champion owners in Ireland, were without the services of the Elliott-trained 2016 Gold Cup winner Don Cossack, whose retirement was announced in January without having run again in the meantime. Besides the well regarded Elliott-trained novice hurdler Death Duty, Gigginstown also enjoyed Grade 1 success with **Valseur Lido** in the Champion Chase at Down Royal in Northern Ireland (his essay discusses the potential impact from Brexit on racing in Britain and Ireland), **Outlander** in the Lexus Chase (his teenage jockey Jack Kennedy, whose career features in the essay, also won on Labaik at Cheltenham), **Petit Mouchoir** who did the double at Leopardstown in the Ryanair Hurdle and Irish Champion Hurdle (all three of those formerly with Mullins), and **Road To Respect** who took advantage of a wayward display

Ryanair supremo Michael O'Leary is pictured with wife Anita after the success of Apple's Jade in the David Nicholson Mares' Hurdle at Cheltenham; the essay on Apple's Jade recounts the consequences of O'Leary's decision to remove sixty of his Gigginstown House Stud string from the stable of Willie Mullins at the start of the season

from Yorkhill to win back some more of his owner's sponsorship money in the Ryanair Gold Cup at Fairyhouse. Road To Respect, whose essay examines a controversial Ten Up Novices' Chase, had earlier given his veteran trainer Noel Meade, who had another good novice chaser, **Disko**, for the same owners, a first winner over fences at the Cheltenham Festival in the Plate.

Don Cossack's jockey Bryan Cooper (who suffered a catalogue of injuries during the season) and Sub Lieutenant's former trainer Sandra Hughes (who subsequently announced her impending retirement at the end of the season) were others who found their services were no longer required by the 'results-driven' Gigginstown operation but a beneficiary of theirs was Special Tiara's trainer Henry de Bromhead whose new intake included Valseur Lido, Sub Lieutenant and Petit Mouchoir. A shock retirement from the Irish training ranks in September was that of Colm Murphy, whose Cheltenham successes had included Brave Inca in the 2006 Champion Hurdle and Big Zeb in the 2010 Queen Mother Champion Chase. Murphy enjoyed backing from the likes of Gigginstown (Empire of Dirt had been his final Festival winner in 2016) but claimed 'my accountancy background told me we just can't make it pay any more.' Murphy had only just received more horses from Ann and Alan Potts when they decided to move the horses they had in training with de Bromhead, the latter's biggest loss proving to be **Sizing John** whose new trainer was Jessica Harrington. The 2016 Arkle runner-up had spent much of his career chasing Douvan in vain (second to him again at Leopardstown just after Christmas), but flourished when stepped up in trip to complete what his essay hails as 'one of the finest achievements by an Irish-trained chaser in recent times', a hat-trick of Gold Cups at Leopardstown (Irish Gold Cup), Cheltenham and Punchestown (in which 2015 Cheltenham Gold Cup winner

Ann and Alan Potts (pictured left) made a major breakthrough into the league of big owners in the latest season, though Mrs Potts was able to enjoy it all too briefly, news of her death after a long illness being announced in August; for Sizing John's jockey Robbie Power and trainer Jessica Harrington (second right) it was a season to remember, a treble at the Festival firmly establishing Mrs Harrington as the leading female trainer in Cheltenham Festival history

Coneygree finished third), something that had never been completed before in the same season. Harrington, who won the Queen Mother Champion Chase in 2003 and 2005 with Moscow Flyer and the Champion Hurdle with Jezki in 2014, became the third woman after Jenny Pitman (Burrough Hill Lad and Garrison Savannah) and Henrietta Knight (triple winner Best Mate) to train a Gold Cup winner and, with two other winners at the latest Festival, is now the meeting's most successful female trainer. Sizing John was her very first runner in the Gold Cup but she could be doubly represented in 2018 with **Our Duke**, who put up a stunning performance, especially for a novice, to land the Irish Grand National (a big handicap in Ireland in which 'smaller' owners did get a look-in).

Ann and Alan Potts broke into the league of big owners in the latest season, though sadly the success of Sizing John and others was something Mrs Potts was able to enjoy only briefly with news of her death in August 2017. The couple switched fifteen of their existing horses to Colin Tizzard whilst strengthening their team with the private purchase of **Fox Norton** (third in Douvan's Arkle) who proved a revelation in the spring, beaten only narrowly in the Queen Mother Champion Chase before going on to win the Melling Chase at Aintree before beating Un de Sceaux at Punchestown. Two more Grade 1 wins at Aintree came courtesy of novice hurdlers **Pingshou** and **Finian's Oscar**, the latter an exciting prospect who, as his essay details, is just one of several expensive purchases sourced by Alan Potts from Irish points. Finian's Oscar's essay also refers to the re-opening of Hereford, where he made his Rules debut, after four years of closure, while **Sizing Codelco** was another winner at both Aintree and Punchestown for the same connections. The influx of Potts-owned horses to the Tizzard yard added further strength to a stable that already had at least three live Gold Cup contenders. With the popular **Cue Card** winning his third Betfair Chase, novice Thistlecrack, on just his fourth start over fences, denying Cue Card a second King George victory, and the bold-jumping **Native River** completing the Hennessy Gold Cup-Welsh National double, no wonder their trainer felt like he'd 'got all the toys.' Injury to Thistlecrack ruled him out of the Gold Cup in which Cue Card came down at the third last for the second year running (his essay mentions others who have suffered similar fates, while the essay on Altior looks at further changes made to the positioning of two of Cheltenham's more controversial fences) but Native River ran well to be pipped for second in the Gold Cup by **Minella Rocco** (whose essay suggests a change to the punishment for jockeys found guilty of seriously infringing the whip rules).

Native River will go down as the final winner of the Hennessy after sixty years of sponsorship by the cognac firm (Arkle looms large in the history of the Newbury race, too, as his essay recalls), while **Taquin du Seuil** (whose essay has an interesting story about E.S.B's Grand National) became the first winner of the other big pre-Christmas handicap chase in its latest guise, now the BetVictor Gold Cup, which started life as the Mackeson. Hopefully, the fortunes of those two races won't go the same way as the race that pioneered commercial sponsorship, the Whitbread Gold Cup. The latest renewal of the Sandown race, nowadays the bet365 Gold Cup, was a substandard affair won by rank outsider **Henllan Harri**, though its pulsating finish was at least reminiscent of the 1984 thriller from the race's heyday (the attraction of Sandown for so many jumping followers is examined in the essay which also calls for the confusion over having two winning posts to be sorted out). Alcohol-related sponsorships are running dry as bookmakers take over—Ladbrokes replace Hennessy at Newbury—though the valuable pre-Christmas two-mile handicap hurdle won by **Brain Power** (the essay charts the ups-and-downs of Michael Buckley's involvement in ownership) known simply as 'the Ladbroke' had to be underwritten by Ascot in the latest season (run as the Wessex Youth Trust Handicap Hurdle) after the bookmaker dropped its sponsorship of a contest with which it had been synonymous since its former incarnation at Leopardstown. The previous month, Ladbrokes completed its merger with Coral to become the UK's biggest retail bookmaker, though only after having to sell 359 betting shops to satisfy the competition authorities. The season's most valuable handicap hurdle, the Betfair Hurdle, again fell to a novice when won by the previous season's Champion Bumper winner **Ballyandy**. While the last big handicap chase of the season has lost some of its lustre, the rest of the programme of what is now the 'Finale' meeting of the jumps season at Sandown has been strengthened in recent years so that the best chasers on the card are now much more likely to be seen in the Grade 1 Celebration Chase (Altior beat Special Tiara in the latest renewal). The now Grade 2 Oaksey Chase was won, like its three previous editions, by the durable twelve-year-old **Menorah** whose first big win had come seven years earlier in the Supreme, while the winner of the Select Hurdle (also promoted to Grade 2), the Nicky Henderson-trained **L'Ami Serge**, went on to become the third British-trained winner in a row of France's top hurdle, the Grande Course de Haies d'Auteuil. Menorah's essay contains some interesting reflections by Sir Anthony McCoy on adjusting to retirement and reviews the second championship for Richard Johnson, among the highlights of which was his Cheltenham Festival success aboard **Defi du Seuil** (a third winner of the Triumph Hurdle for Johnson and trainer Philip Hobbs and the undisputed top juvenile hurdler in Britain and Ireland).

For the second year running the trainer's championship was, mathematically at least, still in the balance until the final day of the season. Paul Nicholls had successfully fought off the challenge from Willie Mullins twelve months

The trainers' championship in Britain went to Nicky Henderson for the fourth time; Buveur d'Air gave him a record sixth winner of the Champion Hurdle and his Cheltenham Festival total has now reached fifty-eight (Altior was also a record sixth Arkle winner for him)

earlier, but was unable to repel Nicky Henderson despite **Vicente** keeping him in the hunt by winning the Scottish Grand National the previous weekend for the second year running. While Tizzard had 'all the toys', Nicholls is finding it difficult, as the balance of power changes, to source the Grade 1 horses which not so long ago were much more numerous at Manor Farm Stables. Astute placing contributed to a record total of wins for the yard, exemplified by the likes of novice chasers **Frodon** and **San Benedeto** winning six races apiece (the latter also needed a good slice of luck to land his Grade 1, the Maghull at Aintree). But that wasn't enough to prevent Henderson winning the title for the second time (and fourth in all) since Nicholls first became champion in the 2005/06 season. Although Cheltenham has never been the be-all and end-all for Nicholls, he moved into third ahead of Fulke Walwyn in the all-time trainers' list at the Festival when **Pacha du Polder** gave him his forty-first success at the meeting in the Foxhunter. The previous year's fifth was not attended by the same hype that surrounded his participation under Victoria Pendleton on that occasion, though his success under Bryony Frost meant that all three amateur races at the Festival were won by lady riders. Pacha du Polder's essay draws attention to the anomaly of amateurs being exempt from the stricter requirements being applied to their professional colleagues. There was more publicity over Lizzie Kelly's participation (short-lived, it turned out) in the Gold Cup, though she and her mount **Tea For Two**, whose essay offers support for the idea of a female riding allowance, bounced back to beat Cue Card narrowly in the Bowl at Aintree. Riding at the Festival for the first time was Rachael Blackmore who became the first female to be champion

14

conditional in Ireland, though her age meant she was ineligible to participate in the Festival's conditionals' race, the Martin Pipe. Only the second woman to turn professional over jumps in Ireland, Blackmore went on to ride out her claim in June. She's had no lack of opportunities in Ireland, where her seasonal total matched that of Barry Geraghty from only slightly fewer rides than champion (for the twelfth time) Ruby Walsh. The Festival's leading lady rider Nina Carberry missed much of the latest season whilst expecting her first child, while her brother Peter (winner of the 2007 Champion Hurdle aboard Sublimity), based in France nowadays, where he won the Grand Steeple-Chase de Paris in 2006 and 2008 on Princesse d'Anjou, announced his retirement in May less than a year after elder brother Paul had to call time on his career in the saddle. As reported in the Introduction to last year's Annual, Paul Carberry nominated his Grand National win on Bobbyjo, trained by his father, as his career highlight. Besides training the 1999 Aintree winner, Tommy Carberry, who died in July 2017 aged seventy-five, had ridden the last Irish-trained winner of the race before Bobbyjo when L'Escargot beat Red Rum in 1975. Ten Up's win in the same year's Gold Cup was the third for Carberry, who was Irish champion four times, after L'Escargot's double in 1970 and 1971.

While Paul Nicholls might have a more phlegmatic approach to Cheltenham, his chief rival makes no secret of the Festival's importance to him—'you've had a pretty good idea since Christmas where the A-team is and you're in Cheltenham mode from then on, planning what route you're going to take there.' One member of Henderson's A-team who took an unusual route to the Festival was the Champion Hurdle winner **Buveur d'Air** who began his campaign winning a couple of novice chases. Buveur d'Air and runner-up (for the third time) **My Tent Or Yours** represented the most successful owner in Festival history (Buveur d'Air gave J. P. McManus a fiftieth win at the meeting), as well as its most successful trainer, and the winner's essay gives an overview of the long and successful association both men have had—largely independently of each other—with Cheltenham. **Might Bite**, who won the RSA Chase in the meeting's most dramatic finish and then went on to win at Aintree, was another of Henderson's winners at the Festival and would have won the other Grade 1 staying novice chase, the Kauto Star at Kempton, but for a last-fence fall when clear. Henderson is easily the most successful trainer at Kempton but, as Thistlecrack's essay relates 'one of jumping's irreplaceable assets' is under threat from development which evokes the role of Henderson's father Johnny when both Cheltenham and Aintree came under similar threats in the 'sixties and 'seventies. Buveur d'Air and the Harry Fry-trained **Unowhatimeanharry** were new additions to the McManus string in the latest season, the latter starting favourite for the Stayers' Hurdle, in which he met with his only defeat in the last two seasons before turning the tables on Nichols Canyon at Punchestown. Besides the eventual first two, McManus was also represented in the Champion Hurdle by beaten favourite **Yanworth**, though he too bounced back from his only defeat of the campaign to land the Stayers' Liverpool Hurdle.

There was a bit more to Yanworth's defeat at Cheltenham, though, as he returned a positive test in circumstances which are discussed fully in his essay. Of greater significance than Yanworth's subsequent disqualification from seventh was the fact that the case, heard in July, was the first to be dealt with by the BHA's new-look Disciplinary Panel. Reform of the Disciplinary Panel formed an important part of the twenty-four recommendations made by Christopher Quinlan QC in his report, conducted during the summer of 2016, which was instigated by the BHA's Integrity Review in March of that year. Quinlan criticised the existing process of appointing members of the

Disciplinary Panel as being 'opaque and not formalised' and early in 2017, under former Old Bailey judge Brian Barker QC in the newly-created role of Judicial Panel Chairman, an open competition was held to recruit Panel members from a broader background within the sport, among them former trainers and jockeys—Jenny Pitman and Philip Robinson are among the pool of Panel members which formerly consisted almost entirely of stewards.

Restoring the trust in the fairness of some of British racing's disciplinary processes (an issue covered in the Introduction to last year's Annual) is proving an uphill task for the British Horseracing Authority. The re-hearing in November of the corruption case against trainer Jim Best, in particular, proved a grave embarrassment for the authorities. Best had appealed against a four-year disqualification for various integrity offences, including ordering his then-conditional jockey Paul John to 'stop' two horses in December 2015. The original disqualification, imposed at a disciplinary hearing in April, was quashed on appeal after it emerged that the chairman of the panel which heard the original case had an undisclosed commercial relationship with the BHA, something which Best's lawyers successfully argued gave the appearance of bias. Having decided against simply dropping the case, the BHA staked its credibility on prosecuting Best again and he was found guilty for a second time, by a new independent panel, of giving 'stopping' orders to his jockey John. The resulting punishment, though, was widely seen as farcical, with Best given a six-month suspension from training—just eight months after being disqualified (a more serious punishment though being suspended) for four years for the same offence. Best considered an appeal against the suspension but, in the end, did not do pursue it, his lawyers pointing out that two wildly contrasting penalties handed down by the two different panels showed that BHA disciplinary proceedings were a 'lottery' and their client was not prepared to take 'another expensive roll of the dice'.

The second panel, like the first, accepted the evidence of Paul John against his former employer and concluded that the two rides in question were 'unhesitatingly' stopping rides and that it was 'overwhelmingly likely' that Best had given the instructions. In other words, Best was a cheat, guilty of defrauding racegoers and punters, as well as suborning a young jockey to break the rules (Best denied the charges throughout while John, whose own ban turned out to be just a week or so shorter than Best's, admitted his offence and did a 'deal' with the BHA to give evidence; the second panel, however, ruled that the relevant correspondence between the BHA and John's solicitor should have been disclosed to Best). The independent panel that presided over the re-hearing said that the original four-year disqualification had been 'too substantial to stand' but it clearly sensed that there would be unease over its own adjudication and, in its judgement, it criticised the BHA's guidelines for penalties as being of 'limited assistance'. It amplified its criticism by saying that 'If the BHA regards suspension or disqualification for a longer period as appropriate for such a case as the present, then it would be wise were the guidelines to reflect that policy directly and with clarity.' The BHA had urged the panel to impose 'a significant period of disqualification on Mr Best to preserve the reputation of British horse racing and to maintain public confidence in the integrity and proper regulation of our sport.'

In the immediate aftermath of the Best case, the BHA was keen to highlight the fact that the Disciplinary Panel was an independent body (partly to deflect criticism from the BHA to the Panel itself?). There had been other cases deemed potentially unsound because they had had the same chairman as the original Best hearing, one of them involving Anthony Knott, the former owner of Hunt Ball, and Andrew Callow who had both been banned from racing for three years after being found guilty on inside information charges (laying one of Knott's horses to lose) in 2014. In that case, however, far from stressing the independence of the various Disciplinary Panels and Appeal Boards, the BHA took it upon itself to quash the convictions of Knott and Callow (which were struck from the record), although, under the rules, the BHA does not have the specific powers to overturn decisions made by Disciplinary Panels or Appeal Boards which—be careful lest your sides split—are, according to the BHA's chief regulatory officer Jamie Stier, 'separate from and independent of the BHA.' Riding roughshod over its own rules is no way for the BHA to convince its critics that it can be trusted to handle integrity matters. The BHA's chief executive Nick Rust, who inherited most of the serious problems when he took over in 2015, claimed that the 'deal' with Knott and Callow was 'in racing's best interests', a curious statement which only served to emphasise the BHA's usual preference for silence or obfuscation over clarity (the real reason surely was to save the BHA a further whacking legal bill, figures published in the BHA's annual report and accounts for 2016 showing that the Best case and other related legal charges had already topped £400,000). The Quinlan Report concluded that there was 'urgent need' for reform. Further changes are expected, including a complete rewrite of the Rules of Racing which, according to Nick Rust, will incorporate stiffer punishment for corruption (the penalties hopefully more clearly spelled out this time). Rust said that the BHA 'was learning from its mistakes' and he finally apologised on behalf of the regulator for the costly 'error of judgement' in failing to divulge the work that Matthew Lohn, the chairman of the original Best disciplinary panel, had been doing for the BHA.

Best was a former trainer of Gas Line Boy who showed prominently in the closing stages of the latest Grand National before finishing fifth behind **One For Arthur**, only the second winner of the race to be trained in Scotland. His entry recalls in words and pictures the first Scottish-trained National winner, Rubstic, as well as several more from north of the border who have gone close. Among the reminders displayed at Aintree of other Nationals of the past was one commemorating the fiftieth anniversary of Foinavon's famous 100/1 victory under John Buckingham, later a jockey's valet, who died in December aged seventy-six. Earlier that season, incidentally, Foinavon had taken on Arkle in the King George, finishing a remote fourth behind Dormant, and was an even bigger outsider than at Aintree when tailed off at 500/1 in the Gold Cup. The mayhem of the 1967 pile-up is a far cry from modern Nationals (there were four fallers in the latest edition in which all the runners again returned safely—the same number unseated), though One For Arthur's essay asks if Aintree, in its eagerness to portray the race as being much better regulated and safer than it once was, while celebrating all the old anniversaries with gusto, is trying to have it both ways. The essay questions whether the course is proud of the Grand National's heritage or ashamed of it? Also covered is the row which developed over the weights allotted to some of the Gigginstown-owned entries, while the handicapping of Irish horses in Britain is also covered in the essay on the Pertemps winner **Presenting Percy**, one of seven Irish-trained winners of the ten handicaps at the Cheltenham Festival. As the postscript to the latest National winner mentions, the annual parade of former winners will be much depleted following a spate of recent deaths among retired National heroes, and to their number must be added the 2015 winner **Many Clouds** who collapsed and died after a typically game victory over Thistlecrack in the Cotswold Chase at Cheltenham in January—as well as paying tribute to one

The Grand National weights were revealed at a special event at the Victoria & Albert Museum in London, with the now-retired 2016 winner Rule The World in attendance; Rule The World's owner Michael O'Leary was involved in a war of words with BHA Head of Handicapping Phil Smith over the treatment of some of the Irish entries, which resulted in three of the top weights owned by O'Leary's Gigginstown operation heading a series of Irish withdrawals at the first scratching deadline

of the best National winners of recent years, his essay also puts the record straight over the cause of his demise and recounts others who met their end on the racecourse in the latest season.

The Grand National, the latest renewal included, has provided some rare highlights in a lean decade for northern jumping stables through the victories of the Donald McCain-trained Ballabriggs (owned, like Many Clouds, by Trevor Hemmings in whose colours Vicente won the latest Scottish National) and Auroras Encore trained by Sue Smith, the last woman to train a National winner before Lucinda Russell became the fourth to do so with One For Arthur. The current state of jumping in the North is revisited in the essay on Mr Hemmings' **Cloudy Dream** who finished runner-up in the Arkle and was also a good second in the Manifesto Novices' Chase in which he split **Flying Angel** (whose entry outlines a sharp change in fortunes at the latest Cheltenham Festival for the Twiston-Davies stable) and **Top Notch** (on whom there is background about his owners Simon Munir and Isaac Souede, with more to be found on L'Ami Serge). Cloudy Dream's northern-based jockey Brian Hughes finished runner-up in the latest jockeys' championship, and while it is true that Jonjo O'Neill was the last champion jump jockey based in the North, Yorkshire-born James Reveley made history in December when becoming the first British jockey to be champion over jumps in France. As detailed at the end of this Annual in 'Top Horses In France', which as usual reviews the French season, Reveley went on to win the Grand Steeple-Chase de Paris in May for the second year running on So French. Like One For Arthur's jockey Derek Fox, Reveley had Jack Berry House, the Injured Jockeys Fund's rehabilitation centre in Malton, to thank for aiding his recovery from injury during the season. James Reveley's father Keith retired from the training ranks during the latest season, ending the long association of the Reveley name with northern racing, while another name missing from race cards from now on, principally in the North, both over jumps and on the Flat, will be that of Alan Swinbank who died suddenly in May aged seventy-two. Swinbank's biggest wins came on the Flat, but some of his best horses began their careers in bumpers, Lancashire Oaks winner Turbo Linn being unbeaten in five such races, for example, and the globe-trotting Collier Hill, who won the Hong Kong Vase on his final start, starting out winning a similar event at Catterick! From the same part of the world as Swinbank, Denys Smith, who died in November aged ninety-two, was something of a pioneer of training all year round. 'The attitude at the time was that the Flat was the Flat, and the jumps was the jumps. You didn't mix the two. I was having none of it, and before long, Peter Easterby was following me, and then Mary Reveley [grandmother of James] did too.' Smith trained winners as diverse as the 1972 Middle Park winner Tudenham and the 1968 Grand National winner Red Alligator who had been badly hampered in the melee when third to Foinavon the year before.

Another northern jockey, senior member of the weighing-room Brian Harding, had his final ride at Perth, for Nicky Richards, at the end of April at the age of forty-four. His biggest win came for Richards' father Gordon on One Man in the 1998 Queen Mother Champion Chase, while Paul Moloney, who rode over eight hundred winners and reached the frame in seven consecutive Grand Nationals (including three times on his Hennessy Gold Cup winner State of Play) was another retirement from the saddle. One Man began his career with the late Arthur Stephenson, as did, in his teens, Andrew Thornton, who is only a month younger than Harding and, like fellow Gold Cup-winning jockey Paddy Brennan, reached the landmark of a thousand victories over jumps in Britain in the latest season, the latter winning a bet with Sir Anthony McCoy that he'd be the first of the pair to do so. 'AP said I had no chance of beating Andrew to the thousand winner mark and the bet was a thousand pounds and that thousand pounds will go to Freddy Tylicki's fund,' said Brennan who reached his total in November shortly after the Flat jockey's career-ending accident. Thornton's long-awaited thousandth winner finally came as part of a double at Wincanton on Boxing Day. IJF patron Thornton has had his own

Among the most prominent retirements from the jockeys' ranks were the veteran Brian Harding (left), whose long association with the Richards stable at Greystoke included winning the Queen Mother Champion Chase on One Man (he enjoyed his best season as recently as 2014/15 with 56 wins); Paul Moloney gained his biggest wins in the Hennessy (State of Play) and the Welsh Grand National (Mountainous) and achieved the remarkable feat of finishing in the first four in the Grand National seven years in a row between 2009 and 2015

share of injuries over the years, though probably none quite so bizarre as the one that has kept him out of action since Wincanton, when he twisted his knee turning to speak to connections after reaching that milestone.

Days earlier, Thornton had been successful at Bangor on Barton Gift in the colours of Mercy Rimell, who died in July 2017 at the age of ninety-eight. The same colours were carried by Thornton on Simon who looked sure to play a part in the finish of the 2007 Grand National when falling at second Valentine's. Mrs Rimell's husband Fred trained four Grand National winners (though their training operation was 'very much a joint effort' in his words) and two Gold Cup winners, including the aforementioned Woodland Venture in 1967. Mrs Rimell took over the licence at Kinnersley on her husband's death in 1981 and won the Champion Hurdle two years later with Simon's relative Gaye Brief. At five foot eleven, Thornton wouldn't win any style awards in the saddle, while his wearing of contact lenses has also earned him plenty of mickey-taking in the weighing-room—'I always tell them I'm going down the inner as there's a white rail there!' Less than perfect vision is something Thornton shares with the latest Gold Cup-winning jockey Robbie Power as Sizing John's essay explains. Eyesight problems, though, rather pale into insignificance compared with the handicap overcome by amateur rider Captain Guy Disney, who lost his lower right leg while serving in Afghanistan. Disney completed the double of the Royal Artillery and Grand Military Gold Cups at Sandown on the David Pipe-trained Rathlin Rose.

Exploits such as Captain Disney's, the unusual tale of **Airlie Beach** before she became a Grade 1 winner in the latest season, and the twists and turns of Labaik's campaign, are among the welcome reminders that there are still compelling stories to be told in a sport where the black-and-white footage from the days of Arkle and Foinavon can nonetheless sometimes seem to come from a more colourful era. As usual, the names of horses highlighted in this Introduction are among those covered in essay form in the main body of the book, with the aim of providing more detailed accounts of many of the best horses, as well as discussing current issues, recalling historical achievements and providing pointers to the future. They form part of the comprehensive A to Z of every horse which ran during the British season (April 27th 2016—April 29th 2017), as well as the pick of the Irish (except for some performances in Ireland very early in the season which were covered in *Chasers & Hurdlers 2015/16*). The hundreds of accompanying photographs help to provide a unique record of the jumping year.

October 2017

HIGHEST TIMEFORM RATINGS

Chasers & Hurdlers 1975/76 was the first in the Timeform annual series but the jumping edition of the weekly Timeform Black Book has been published since 1962/3. The following 'annual' ratings are the highest achieved in Britain and Ireland since that time.

Chasers

212 Arkle
210 Flyingbolt
192p Sprinter Sacre
191 Kauto Star
191 Mill House
187 Desert Orchid
186 Dunkirk
184+ Moscow Flyer
184 Burrough Hill Lad, Long Run
183 Don Cossack, Master Oats
182 Azertyuiop, Best Mate, Captain Christy, Carvill's Hill, Douvan, Imperial Commander, Kicking King, See More Business, Well Chief
181 Cue Card, Denman
180 First Gold, Vautour
179 Badsworth Boy, Bobs Worth, Fortria, Master Minded, One Man
178 Imperial Call, Pendil
177 Bregawn, Kinloch Brae, Klairon Davis, Martha's Son, The Dikler
176 Buona notte, Little Owl, Looks Like Trouble, Silviniaco Conti, Suny Bay, Titus Oates
175p Altior
175+ Exotic Dancer
175 Brown Lad, Captain Chris, Djakadam, Flagship Uberalles, Kingscliff, L'Escargot, Night Nurse, Rough Quest, Silver Buck, Wayward Lad
174 Barnbrook Again, Beef Or Salmon, Bula, Finian's Rainbow, Flemenstar, Jodami, Pearlyman, Thistlecrack, Tidal Bay, Un de Sceaux
173 Blazing Walker, Captain John, Cool Dawn, Cyfor Malta, Florida Pearl, Remittance Man, Sir des Champs, Teeton Mill
172 Barton Bank, Big Zeb, Bradbury Star, Brown Chamberlin, Crisp, Gloria Victis, Go Ballistic, Katabatic, Rushing Wild, Sire de Grugy, Sizing Europe, Strong Promise, Valley Henry, Viking Flagship

Hurdlers

182 Night Nurse
180 Istabraq, Monksfield
179 Persian War
178 Comedy of Errors
177 Lanzarote, Limestone Lad
176+ Big Buck's
176 Bird's Nest, Bula, Faugheen, Golden Cygnet
175 Baracouda, Deano's Beeno, Gaye Brief, Salmon Spray, Sea Pigeon
174p Thistlecrack
174 Alderbrook, Dramatist, For Auction, Magic Court, Morley Street
173p More of That
173 Dato Star, Dawn Run, Hurricane Fly, See You Then
172 Anzio, Bannow Rambler, Beech Road, Boreen Prince, Browne's Gazette, Danoli, Flatterer, Iris's Gift, Mighty Man, Prideaux Boy
171 Barnbrook Again, Canasta Lad, Captain Christy, Celtic Gold, Chorus, Daring Run, Grands Crus, Jezki, Le Coudray, Moyne Royal, Pollardstown, Punchestowns, Rock On Ruby

The following ratings for horses in the pre-Timeform era, compiled by Randall and Morris for 'A Century of Champions', were used by Timeform for an exhibit in Cheltenham's Hall of Fame:

190 Easter Hero
188 Golden Miller
183 Pas Seul, Prince Regent
176 Sir Ken

TIMEFORM
CHAMPIONS
OF 2016/17

Altior follows in the footsteps of hurdlers Danoli in 1993/4 and Make A Stand in 1996/7 as only the third novice to be named Timeform Horse of the Year in the forty-two years of Chasers & Hurdlers

HORSE OF THE YEAR
& BEST NOVICE CHASER
RATED AT 175p

ALTIOR

7 b.g High Chaparral – Monte Solaro (Key of Luck)

Owner Mrs Patricia Pugh   Trainer Nicky Henderson

BEST STAYING CHASERS – RATED AT 174
CUE CARD
11 b.g King's Theatre – Wicked Crack (King's Ride)
Owner Mrs Jean R. Bishop   Trainer Colin Tizzard
THISTLECRACK
9 b.g Kayf Tara – Ardstown (Accordion)
Owner John & Heather Snook   Trainer Colin Tizzard

BEST TWO-MILE CHASER – RATED AT 182
DOUVAN
7 b.g Walk In The Park – Star Face (Saint des Saints)
Owner Mrs S. Ricci   Trainer W. P. Mullins

BEST HUNTER CHASE – RATED AT 142
FOXROCK
9 b.g Flemensfirth – Midnight Light (Roselier)
Owner Barry Connell   Trainer T. M. Walsh

BEST TWO-MILE HURDLER – RATED AT 170
BUVEUR D'AIR
6 b.g Crillon – History (Alesso)
Owner Mr John P. McManus   Trainer Nicky Henderson

BEST STAYING HURDLERS – RATED AT 165
NICHOLS CANYON
7 b.g Authorized – Zam Zoom (Dalakhami)
Owner Andrea & Graham Wylie   Trainer W. P. Mullins
UNOWHATIMEANHARRY
9 b.g Sir Harry Lewis – Red Nose Lady (Teenoso)
Owner Mr John P. McManus   Trainer Harry Fry

BEST NOVICE HURDLER – RATED AT 160§
LABAIK
6 gr.g Montmartre – Avanguardia (Choisir)
Owner Mr A. J. O'Ryan   Trainer Gordon Elliott

BEST JUVENILE HURDLER – RATED AT 151p
DEFI DU SEUIL
4 b.g Voix du Nord – Quarvine du Seuil (Lavirco)
Owner Mr John P. McManus   Trainer Philip Hobbs

BEST BUMPER PERFORMERS – RATED AT 118
FAYONAGH
6 b.m Kalanisi – Fair Ina (Taipan)
Owner Mrs M. Gittins   Trainer Gordon Elliott
PALOMA BLUE
5 br.g Stowaway – Court Leader (Supreme Leader)
Owner Mr C. Jones   Trainer Henry de Bromhead

THE TIMEFORM 'TOP 100'
CHASERS AND HURDLERS

Hurdlers
170 Buveur d'Air
166 Camping Ground
165 Nichols Canyon
165 Unowhatimeanharry
164 Yanworth
163 Arctic Fire
163 My Tent Or Yours
162 Lil Rockerfeller
162 Petit Mouchoir
161 L'Ami Serge
161 Ptit Zig
161§ Wicklow Brave
160 Alex de Larredya
160 Diakali
160 Sutton Place
160§ Labaik
159 Footpad
158 Apple's Jade (f)
158 Brain Power
158x The New One
156 Silsol
155p Bacardys
155 Clondaw Warrior
155 Cole Harden
155 Finian's Oscar
155 Modus
154 Agrapart
154 Ivan Grozny
154 Shaneshill
154 Sharp Rise
154 Supasundae
154§ Renneti
153p Campeador
153 Irving
153 Native River
153 Snow Falcon
152 Neon Wolf
152 Ivanovich Gorbatov
152 Penhill
152 Presenting Percy
152 Taquin du Seuil
151p Defi du Seuil
151p Willoughby Court
151 Ballyoptic
151 Garde La Victoire
151 Sceau Royal
151 Vroum Vroum Mag (f)
150 Ch'tibello
150 Limini (f)
150 Melon
150 Thomas Hobson
150x Hidden Cyclone
149 Monalee
149 Old Guard
149 Open Eagle
149 River Wylde
149 Seeyouatmidnight
148+ Mick Jazz

148 Chesterfield
148 Death Duty
148 Lieutenant Colonel
148 One Track Mind
148 Tombstone
147 Champagne Classic
147 De Plotting Shed
147 Jezki
147 Jury Duty
147 Messire des Obeaux
147 Mister Miyagi
147 Monksland
147 Starchitect
147 Thousand Stars
147 Volnay de Thaix
147 Who Dares Wins
147 Wholestone
147 Zarkandar
146p The Worlds End
146 Aux Ptits Soins
146 Bapaume
146 Barney Dwan
146 Clyne
146 Diego du Charmil
146 Rashaan
145p Beyond Conceit
145+ Aubusson
145+ Un Temps Pour Tout
145 Adrien du Pont
145 Ballyandy
145 Bamako Moriviere
145 Brother Tedd
145 Court Minstrel
145 Debece
145 Desert Cry
145 Le Rocher
145 Movewiththetimes
145 Quick Jack
145 Saturnas
145 Shelford
145 Ubak

Chasers
182 Douvan
175p Altior
174 Cue Card
174 Thistlecrack
170p Great Field
170 Fox Norton
170 Sizing John
169 Djakadam
169 Many Clouds
169 Un de Sceaux
168 Coneygree
168 Menorah
168 Valseur Lido
167p Our Duke
167 Minella Rocco
167 Sub Lieutenant
166 Might Bite

166 Native River
166 Special Tiara
166 Tea For Two
165 God's Own
165 Outlander
165 Sire de Grugy
163 Don Poli
163 Empire of Dirt
162 Un Temps Pour Tout
162x Champagne West
161p Yorkhill
161+ Ar Mad
161 Saphir du Rheu
161 Smad Place
161 The Last Samuri
161 Zabana
161? Alary
160P Min
160 Aso
160 Definitly Red
160 Silviniaco Conti
160 Uxizandre
159p Coney Island
159 Ballycasey
159 Bristol de Mai
159 Carlingford Lough
159 Garde La Victoire
159 Irish Cavalier
159 Kylemore Lough
159 More of That
159 Seeyouatmidnight
159 Sir Valentino
159 Top Gamble
159 Vaniteux
159 Village Vic
159 Whisper
158 Blaklion
158 Noble Endeavor
158 Otago Trail
158 Taquin du Seuil
157p One For Arthur
157 Alelchi Inois
157 Devils Bride
157 Disko
157 Rock The World
157 Royal Regatta
157 Sizing Codelco
157 Sizing Granite
157 Top Notch
156p American
156+ Road To Respect
156 Black Hercules
156 Josses Hill
156 Tenor Nivernais
156 Traffic Fluide
155p Buveur d'Air
155 Ballynagour
155 Charbel
155 Dodging Bullets

24

155 Shantou Flyer
155 Vieux Lion Rouge
154 Ball d'Arc
154 Cause of Causes
154 Flying Angel
154 Lord Scoundrel
154 Simply Ned
154§ Vibrato Valtat

153 Cloudy Dream
153 Politologue
153 Roi des Francs
153 San Benedeto
153 Theatre Guide
152+ Kitten Rock
152 Road To Riches
152 Carole's Destrier

152 Clarcam
152 Don't Touch It
152 Double Shuffle
152 Ordinary World
152 Perfect Candidate
152 Sharp Rise
152 Three Musketeers
152 Yala Enki

THE TIMEFORM TOP JUVENILES, NOVICES, HUNTER CHASERS AND NH FLAT HORSES

Juvenile Hurdlers
151p Defi du Seuil
146 Bapaume
145 Mega Fortune
144 Charli Parcs
143 Landofhopeandglory
142 Divin Bere
141p Call Me Lord
139p Cliffs of Dover
139 Master Blueyes
137 Coeur de Lion
137 Ex Patriot
136p Mengli Khan
136 Project Bluebook
135+ Meri Devie (f)
135 Dandy Mag
134p Bedrock
134 Dolos
134 Titi de Montmartre (f)
133 Don Bersy
133 Flying Tiger
133 Forth Bridge
131 Soldier In Action
130 Dinaria des Obeaux (f)
130 Magie du Ma (f)
129 Domperignon du Lys
129 Nietzsche
128 Diable de Sivola
128 Evening Hush (f)
128 Fidux
128 Landin
128 Monsieur Co

Novice Hurdlers
160§ Labaik
155p Bacardys
155 Finian's Oscar
152 Neon Wolf
152 Penhill
152 Presenting Percy
151p Willoughby Court
150 Melon
149 Monalee
149 River Wylde
148+ Mick Jazz
148 Death Duty
147 Champagne Classic
147 Messire des Obeaux
147 Wholestone

146p The Worlds End
145p Beyond Conceit
145 Ballyandy
145 Debece
145 Movewiththetimes
145 Saturnas
144p Captain Forez
144p The Storyteller
144+ Fountains Windfall
144 Cilaos Emery
144 Constantine Bay
143 Elgin
143 No Comment
143 Rather Be
143 West Approach

Novice Chasers
175p Altior
174 Thistlecrack
170p Great Field
167p Our Duke
166 Might Bite
161p Yorkhill
160P Min
159p Coney Island
159 Whisper
157 Disko
157 Top Notch
156p American
156+ Road To Respect
155p Buveur d'Air
155 Charbel
154 Ball d'Arc
154 Flying Angel
153 Cloudy Dream
153 Politologue
153 San Benedeto
152 Don't Touch It
152 Ordinary World
151 Anibale Fly
151 Bellshill
151 Forest Bihan
151 Label des Obeaux
151 Woodland Opera
151§ Tiger Roll
150 Baily Cloud
150 Baron Alco

National Hunt Flat Horses
118 Fayonagh (f)

118 Paloma Blue
116 Getabird
116 Lalor
116 Western Ryder
115p Samcro
115 Claimantakinforgan
115 If The Cap Fits
115 Next Destination
115 Red Jack
114 Debuchet
113 Carter McKay
113 Enniscoffey Oscar
113 Monbeg Worldwide
113 Poli Roi
113 Sam Brown
112 Peculiar Places
111p Ballyward
111 Black Op
111 Settie Hill
110 Catwalk King
110 Ravenhill Road
109p Canardier
109 As You Were
109 Cap Soleil (f)
109 Cause Toujours
109 Crackerdancer (f)
109 Daphne du Clos (f)
109 Sam's Adventure
108 Midnight Stroll
108 Planet Nine

Hunter Chasers
148 First Lieutenant
148 Hurricane Ben
142 Foxrock
137 On His Own
137 Pacha du Polder
136 Wonderful Charm
135 Balnaslow
134 Paint The Clouds
133 Mendip Express
131 Barel of Laughs
131 Dineur
131 Monsieur Gibraltar
130 Black Thunder
129 Darwins Fox
129 On The Fringe
129 Vasco du Mee

2016/17 STATISTICS

The following tables show the leading owners, trainers, jockeys, sires of winners and horses over jumps in Britain during 2016/17. The prize-money statistics, compiled by *Timeform*, relate to win-money and to first-three prize money. Win money has traditionally been used to decide the trainers' championship, though since 1994 the BHB (now the BHA) and the National Trainers' Federation have recognised championships decided by total prize money as determined by the *Racing Post*. The jockeys' championship has traditionally been decided by the number of wins.

	OWNERS (1,2,3 earnings)	Horses	Wnrs	Indiv'l Races Won	Runs	%	Stakes £
1	Mr John P. McManus	142	56	94	538	17.5	2,543,905
2	Mr Simon Munir & Mr Isaac Souede .	26	17	34	112	30.4	805,612
3	Paul & Clare Rooney	86	40	67	314	21.3	700,781
4	Two Golf Widows	2	1	3	5	60.0	610,227
5	Mr Trevor Hemmings	47	18	29	172	16.9	583,190
6	Ann & Alan Potts	14	6	11	54	20.4	544,411
7	Gigginstown House Stud	37	4	4	47	8.5	488,875
8	Mrs Jean R. Bishop	5	5	8	31	25.8	436,654
9	Ann & Alan Potts Partnership	8	2	2	9	22.2	414,846
10	Brocade Racing	14	4	6	67	9.0	384,868
11	S Such & CG Paletta	5	3	6	30	20.0	313,682
12	Mrs S. Rowley-Williams	1	1	2	5	40.0	298,141

	OWNERS (win money)	Horses	Wnrs	Indiv'l Races Won	Runs	%	Stakes £
1	Mr John P. McManus	142	56	94	538	17.5	1,544,253
2	Two Golf Widows	2	1	3	5	60.0	606,517
3	Mr Simon Munir & Mr Isaac Souede .	26	17	34	112	30.4	485,939
4	Paul & Clare Rooney	86	40	67	314	21.3	470,535
5	Mr Trevor Hemmings	47	18	29	172	16.9	411,178
6	Ann & Alan Potts	14	6	11	54	20.4	403,888
7	Ann & Alan Potts Partnership	8	2	2	9	22.2	381,564
8	Mrs Jean R. Bishop	5	5	8	31	25.8	306,585
9	E. O'Connell	1	1	3	3	100.0	296,808
10	Mrs Patricia Pugh	3	3	9	15	60.0	279,855

	TRAINERS (1,2,3 earnings)	Horses	Wnrs	Indiv'l Races Won	Runs	%	Stakes £
1	Nicky Henderson	173	89	154	618	24.9	2,862,983
2	Paul Nicholls	161	87	171	673	25.4	2,551,969
3	Colin Tizzard	86	38	57	405	14.1	2,050,976
4	Nigel Twiston-Davies	109	55	95	586	16.2	1,581,143
5	Philip Hobbs	158	70	111	593	18.7	1,499,770
6	Alan King	128	59	104	490	21.2	1,374,407
7	Dan Skelton	202	81	118	698	16.9	1,325,478
8	Tom George	77	46	71	342	20.8	1,087,219
9	Jonjo O'Neill	156	56	78	689	11.3	1,009,134
10	W. P. Mullins, Ireland	47	7	9	52	17.3	943,394
11	Lucinda Russell	89	28	43	411	10.5	923,477
12	Gordon Elliott, Ireland	94	22	30	170	17.6	899,334

TRAINERS (by win money)	Horses	*Indiv'l Races* Wnrs	Won	Runs	%	*Stakes* £
1 Nicky Henderson	173	89	154	618	24.9	1,903,995
2 Paul Nicholls	161	87	171	673	25.4	1,763,185
3 Colin Tizzard	86	38	57	405	14.1	1,463,028
4 Philip Hobbs	158	70	111	593	18.7	1,006,222
5 Nigel Twiston-Davies	109	55	95	586	16.2	954,707
6 Alan King	128	59	104	490	21.2	940,447
7 Lucinda Russell	89	28	43	411	10.5	801,147
8 Dan Skelton	202	81	118	698	16.9	793,395
9 W. P. Mullins, Ireland	47	7	9	52	17.3	756,258
10 Harry Fry	87	40	67	286	23.4	650,632
11 Neil Mulholland	129	57	108	556	19.4	607,654
12 Tom George	77	46	71	342	20.8	598,750

TRAINERS (with 100+ winners)	Horses	*Indiv'l Races* Wnrs	Won	2nd	3rd	Runs	%
1 Paul Nicholls	161	87	171	92	80	673	25.4
2 Nicky Henderson	173	89	154	100	70	618	24.9
3 Dan Skelton	202	81	118	134	101	698	16.9
4 Philip Hobbs	158	70	111	93	67	593	18.7
5 Neil Mulholland	129	57	108	76	59	556	19.4
6 Alan King	128	59	104	91	79	490	21.2

JOCKEYS (by wins)	1st	2nd	3rd	Unpl	Mts	%
1 Richard Johnson	189	192	139	506	1026	18.4
2 Brian Hughes	144	164	128	430	866	16.6
3 Sam Twiston-Davies	137	103	91	342	673	20.4
4 Aidan Coleman	122	97	90	452	761	16.0
5 Noel Fehily	119	93	60	276	548	21.7
6 Harry Skelton	101	103	75	252	531	19.0
7 Tom Scudamore	100	100	85	469	754	13.3
8 Paddy Brennan	95	66	62	231	454	20.9
9 Daryl Jacob	87	63	53	203	406	21.4
10 Tom O'Brien	81	65	66	371	583	13.9
11 Sean Bowen	79	75	42	236	432	18.3
12 Wayne Hutchinson	74	72	68	171	385	19.2

JOCKEYS (1,2,3 earnings)	*Races* Won	Rides	%	*Stakes* £
1 Richard Johnson	189	1026	18.4	2,327,296
2 Noel Fehily	119	548	21.7	2,210,739
3 Aidan Coleman	122	761	16.0	1,720,216
4 Sam Twiston-Davies	137	673	20.4	1,711,344
5 Brian Hughes	144	866	16.6	1,435,778
6 Tom Scudamore	100	754	13.3	1,293,462
7 Daryl Jacob	87	406	21.4	1,281,286
8 Paddy Brennan	95	454	20.9	1,278,658
9 Harry Skelton	101	531	19.0	1,102,381
10 Barry Geraghty	41	153	26.8	1,068,252

JOCKEYS (by win money)				*Races* Won	Rides	%	*Stakes* £
1	Richard Johnson			189	1026	18.4	1,543,453
2	Noel Fehily			119	548	21.7	1,458,800
3	Sam Twiston-Davies			137	673	20.4	1,134,478
4	Aidan Coleman			122	761	16.0	1,032,492

CONDITIONAL JOCKEYS	*1st*	*2nd*	*3rd*	*Unpl*	*Mts*	%
1 Harry Cobden	63	44	37	182	326	19.3
2 David Noonan	36	37	44	261	378	9.5
3 Harry Bannister	30	26	17	84	157	19.1

AMATEUR RIDERS	*1st*	*2nd*	*3rd*	*Unpl*	*Mts*	%
1 Mr James King	19	11	10	85	125	15.2
2 Mr S. Davies-Thomas	10	7	8	9	34	29.4
3 Mr M. Legg	10	5	5	26	46	21.7

SIRES OF WINNERS (1,2,3 earnings)	*Races* Won	Runs	%	*Stakes* £
1 Kayf Tara (by Sadler's Wells)	156	982	15.9	2,188,732
2 King's Theatre (by Sadler's Wells)	113	852	13.3	2,128,480
3 Milan (by Sadler's Wells)	88	871	10.1	1,556,044
4 Presenting (by Mtoto)	124	942	13.2	1,420,119
5 Midnight Legend (by Night Shift)	121	784	15.4	1,363,552
6 Oscar (by Sadler's Wells)	96	730	13.2	1,079,414
7 Flemensfirth (by Alleged)	81	683	11.9	866,461
8 Beneficial (by Top Ville)	89	781	11.4	768,044
9 Westerner (by Danehill)	71	538	13.2	640,232
10 Authorized (by Montjeu)	44	230	19.1	604,137
11 Shantou (by Alleged)	56	288	19.4	546,541
12 Voix du Nord (by Valanour)	16	98	16.3	527,193
13 Gold Well (by Sadler's Wells)	38	277	13.7	514,268
14 Indian River (by Cadoudal)	28	168	16.7	482,993
15 Kapgarde (by Garde Royale)	32	169	18.9	469,970

SIRES OF WINNERS (by win money)	*Indiv'l* Horses	*Races* Wnrs	Won	*Stakes* £
1 Kayf Tara (by Sadler's Wells)	239	99	156	1,500,428
2 King's Theatre (by Sadler's Wells)	196	74	113	1,312,190
3 Milan (by Sadler's Wells)	222	60	88	1,142,548
4 Midnight Legend (by Night Shift)	176	70	121	986,966
5 Presenting (by Mtoto)	248	79	124	780,656
6 Oscar (by Sadler's Wells)	193	67	96	663,425

LEADING HORSES (1,2,3 earnings)	Won	Runs	£
1 One For Arthur 8 b.g Milan–Nonnetia	3	4	610,227
2 Buveur d'Air 6 b.g Crillon–History	5	5	374,391
3 Sizing John 7 b.g Midnight Legend–La Perrotine	1	1	327,462
4 Native River 7 ch.g Indian River–Native Mo	3	5	302,548
5 Special Tiara 10 b.g Kayf Tara–Special Choice	2	5	298,141
6 Un de Sceaux 9 b.g Denham Red–Hotesse De Sceaux	3	3	296,808
7 Cue Card 11 b.g King'S Theatre–Wicked Crack	2	6	292,142
8 Fox Norton 7 b.g Lando–Natt Musik	3	5	275,700
9 Altior 7 b.g High Chaparral–Monte Solaro	6	6	262,734
10 Cause of Causes 9 b.g Dynaformer–Angel In My Heart	1	3	251,913

EXPLANATORY NOTES

'Chasers & Hurdlers 2016/17' deals individually, in alphabetical sequence, with every horse that ran over jumps or in National Hunt Flat races in Britain during the 2016/17 season, plus a number of foreign-trained horses that did not race here. For each of these horses is given (1) its age, colour and sex, (2) its breeding and, where this information has not been given in a previous Chasers & Hurdlers or Racehorses Annual, usually a family outline, (3) a form summary giving its Timeform rating—or ratings—at the end of the previous season, followed by the details of all its performances during the past season, (4) a Timeform rating—or ratings—of its merit (which appears in the margin), (5) a Timeform commentary on its racing or general characteristics as a racehorse, with some suggestions, perhaps, regarding its prospects for 2017/18 and (6) the name of the trainer in whose charge it was on the last occasion it ran.

The book is published with a twofold purpose. Firstly, it is intended to have permanent value as a review of the exploits and achievements of the more notable of our chasers and hurdlers in the 2016/17 season. Thus, while the commentaries upon the vast majority of the horses are, of necessity, in note form, the best horses are more critically examined. The text is illustrated by posed portraits of the most notable horses (where these are available) and photographs of the major races. Secondly, the book is designed to help the punter to analyse races, and the notes which follow contain instructions for using the data.

TIMEFORM RATINGS

The Timeform Rating of a horse is simply the merit of the horse expressed in pounds and is arrived at by careful examination of its running against other horses using a scale of weight for distance beaten. Timeform maintains a 'running' handicap of all horses in training throughout the season.

THE LEVEL OF THE RATINGS

At the close of each season the ratings of all the horses that have raced are re-examined which explains why some of the ratings may be different from those in the final issue of the 2016/17 Timeform Chasing Black Book series. The 'Chasers & Hurdlers' figure is the definitive Timeform Rating.

RATINGS AND WEIGHT-FOR-AGE

The reader has, in the ratings in this book, a universal handicap embracing all the horses in training it is possible to weigh up, ranging from tip-top performers, with ratings from 170 upwards, down to those rated around the 60 mark. All the ratings are at weight-for-age, so that equal ratings mean horses of equal merit. In using Timeform to assess the prospects of various runners, allowance should be made for any difference specified by the Age, Weight and Distance Table at the front.

Steeplechase ratings, preceded by c, should not be confused with hurdle ratings, preceded by h. Where a horse has raced over fences and also over hurdles its ratings as a chaser and hurdler are printed one above the other, the steeplechase rating (c) being placed above the hurdle rating (h).

Thus with REGALITY c157
                                              h143

the top figure, 157, is the rating to be used in steeplechases, and the one below, 143, is for use only in hurdle races. Where a horse has a rating based on its performance in a bumper it is preceded by 'b'. The procedure for making age and weight adjustments to the ratings (i.e. for the calculation of Race Ratings) is as follows:

A. Horses of the Same Age

If the horses all carry the same weight there are no adjustments to be made, and the horses with the highest ratings have the best chances. If the horses carry different weights, jot down their ratings, and to the rating of each horse add one point for every pound the horse is set to carry less than 12st 7lb, or subtract one point for every pound it has to carry more than 12st 7lb. When the ratings have been adjusted in this way the highest resultant figure indicates the horse with the best chance at the weights.

Example (any distance: any month of the season)

Teucer	5 yrs (11-0) ..	Rating 140 ..	add 21	....	161
Kiowa	5 yrs (10-7) ..	Rating 125 ..	add 28	....	153
Golden Age	5 yrs (10-4) ..	Rating 120 ..	add 31	....	151

Teucer has the best chance, and Golden Age the worst

B. Horses of Different Ages

In this case, reference must be made to the Age, Weight and Distance Table at the front. Use the Table for steeplechasers and hurdlers alike. Treat each horse separately, and compare the weight it has to carry with the weight prescribed for it in the table, according to the age of the horse, the distance of the race and the month of the year. Then, add one point to the rating for each pound the horse has to carry less than the weight given in the table: or, subtract one point from the rating for every pound it has to carry more than the weight prescribed by the table. The highest resultant figure indicates the horse most favoured by the weights.

Example (2¾m steeplechase in January)

(Table Weights: 8-y-o 12-7; 7-y-o 12-7; 5-y-o 12-6)

Black Book	8 yrs (12-8) ..	Rating 140 ..	subtract 1	....	139
Pressman	7 yrs (12-3) ..	Rating 132 ..	add 4	....	136
Copyright	5 yrs (12-7) ..	Rating 150 ..	subtract 1	....	149

Copyright has the best chance, and Pressman the worst

Example (3m hurdle race in March)

(Table Weights: 9-y-o 12-7; 5-y-o 12-7; 4-y-o 11-11)

Oxer	9 yrs (10-12) ..	Rating 110 ..	add 23	....	133
Clairval	5 yrs (10-7) ..	Rating 119 ..	add 28	....	147
Gallette	4 yrs (10-7) ..	Rating 128 ..	add 18	....	146

Clairval has the best chance, and Oxer the worst

C. Horses in bumpers

The procedure for calculating Race Ratings in bumpers is precisely the same as in (A) or (B).

Example (2m bumper in February)

(Table Weights: 6-y-o 12-7; 5-y-o 12-7; 4-y-o 12-1)

Squall	6 yrs (10-12) ..	Rating 88 ..	add 23	....	111
Lupin	5 yrs (11-3) ..	Rating 97 ..	add 18	....	115
Chariot	4 yrs (10-9) ..	Rating 84 ..	add 20	....	104

Lupin has the best chance, and Chariot the worst

The bumper ratings can be used not only within the context of bumper races themselves, but also as an indication of the potential form of such horses in their first few starts over jumps.

JOCKEYSHIP AND RIDERS' ALLOWANCES

For the purposes of rating calculations it should, in general, be assumed that the allowance the rider is able to claim (3 lb, 5 lb, or 7 lb) is nullified by his or her inexperience. Therefore, the weight adju*stments to the ratings should be calculated on the weight allotted by the handicapper, or determined by the conditions of the race,* and no extra addition should be made to a rating because the horse's rider claims an allowance. This is the general routine procedure; but, of course, after the usual adjustments have been made the quality of jockeyship is still an important factor to be considered when deciding between horses with similar chances.

WEIGHING UP A RACE

The ratings tell which horses in a particular race are most favoured by the weights; but complete analysis demands that the racing character of each horse is also studied carefully to see if there is any reason why the horse might be expected not to run up to its rating. It counts for little that a horse is thrown in at the weights if it has no pretensions whatever to staying the distance, or is unable to act on the prevailing going. Suitability of distance and going are no doubt the most important points to be considered, but there are others. For example, the ability of a horse to accommodate itself to the conformation of the track. There is also the matter of a horse's ability and dependability as a jumper and of its temperament: nobody would be in a hurry to take a short price about a horse with whom it is always an even chance whether it will get round or not, or whether it will consent to race.

A few minutes spent checking up on these matters in the commentaries upon the horses concerned will sometimes put a very different complexion on a race from that which is put upon it by the ratings alone. We repeat, therefore, that the correct way to use Timeform, or this annual volume, in the analysis of individual races is, first to use the ratings to discover which horses are most favoured by the weights, and second, to check through the comments on the horses to see what factors other than weight might also affect the outcome of the race.

THE FORM SUMMARIES

The form summaries enclosed in the brackets list each horse's performances in the last season in sequence, showing, for each race, its distance in furlongs, the state of the going and the horse's placing at the finish. Steeplechase form figures are prefixed by the letter 'c', hurdle form figures by the letter 'h' and bumper form figures by the letter 'b'.

The going is symbolised as follows: f–firm, m–good to firm, g–good, d–good to soft/dead, s–soft, v–heavy.

Placings are indicated up to sixth place, by superior figures, an asterisk denoting a win; and superior letters are used to convey what happened to the horse during the race: F–fell (F^3 denotes remounted and finished third); pu–pulled up; ur–unseated rider; bd–brought down; R–refused; rr–refused to race; su–slipped up; ro–ran out; co–carried out; d–disqualified

Thus, [2016/17 h82, b80: h16g h16s* c18g^{pu} h16f^2 c20v^F Apr 10] states that the horse was rated 82 over hurdles and 80 in bumpers at the end of the previous season. In the 2016/17 jumping season the horse ran five times; unplaced in a 2m hurdle race on good going, winning a 2m hurdle race on soft going, being pulled up in a 2¼m steeplechase on good going, running second in a 2m hurdle race on firm going and falling in a 2½m steeplechase on heavy going. Its last race was on April 10th.

Where sale prices are given they are in guineas unless otherwise stated. The prefix $ refers to American dollars and € indicates the euro. Any other currencies are converted into pounds sterling at the prevailing exchange rate.

THE RATING SYMBOLS

The following symbols, attached to the ratings, are to be interpreted as stated:-

p   likely to improve.

P   capable of *much* better form.

+   the horse may be better than we have rated it.

d   the horse appears to have deteriorated, and might no longer be capable of running to the rating given.

§   unreliable (for temperamental or other reasons).

§§   so temperamentally unsatisfactory as to be not worth a rating.

x   poor jumper.

xx   a very bad jumper, so bad as to be not worth a rating.

?   the horse's rating is suspect or, used without a rating, the horse can't be assessed with confidence or, if used in the in-season Timeform publications, that the horse is out of form.

CHASERS & HURDLERS 2016/17

AACHEN 13 b.g. Rainbow Quest (USA) – Anna of Saxony (Ela-Mana-Mou) [2016/17 c146, h–: c25.5d^{pu} c24.2s^{pu} c25.2v^{pu} Feb 1] useful gelding: winning hurdler: smart chaser at best, no form in 2016/17: tried in headgear. *Venetia Williams*   **c–** **h–**

AALY 10 b.g. Milan – Leyaaly (Night Shift (USA)) [2016/17 c–, h70: h25.6s h25.6g^3 h25s^{pu} h25.6d^3 Mar 18] winning pointer: poor handicap hurdler: pulled up both starts in chases: stays 27f: acts on soft and good to firm going: wears hood: has worn tongue tie, including usually in 2016/17. *Lydia Richards*   **c–** **h62**

AAMAN (IRE) 11 gr.g. Dubai Destination (USA) – Amellnaa (IRE) (Sadler's Wells (USA)) [2016/17 h80: h18.5d^4 h19.9g^5 Jul 5] poor handicap hurdler: won novice event at Newton Abbot in June: stays 2½m: acts on good to soft going: in tongue tie last 3 starts. *Bernard Llewellyn*   **h81**

AARYAM (FR) 5 b.g. Dylan Thomas (IRE) – Selinea (FR) (Keltos (FR)) [2016/17 b15.7g b15.8s^5 h15.8g^5 h15.8v h23.1s^{pu} h19.9s^{pu} h21.9v^{pu} Mar 19] no form in bumpers: poor form over hurdles: left Peter Bowen after seventh start: tried in blinkers: in tongue tie last 2 starts. *John Flint*   **h77** **b–**

ABBEYGREY (IRE) 8 b.g. Generous (IRE) – Garw Valley (Mtoto) [2016/17 c20m^{ur} h21.6v* h23.4s^2 c23.8s^2 c29.2v^{pu} Mar 12] fair handicap hurdler: won at Exeter (amateur) in December: fair handicap chaser: stays 3¼m: acts on heavy and good to firm going: often races towards rear/travels strongly. *Evan Williams*   **c108** **h102**

ABBEY LANE (IRE) 12 b.g. Flemensfirth (USA) – Hazel Sylph (IRE) (Executive Perk) [2016/17 c20g c21.5d^4 h16.2d^{pu} Jun 29] strong gelding: multiple winning pointer, including in 2017: useful hurdler at best, pulled up in handicap in June: maiden chaser: stays 3m: acts on good to firm and heavy going. *Colin A. McBratney, Ireland*   **c109** **h–**

ABBEY STORM (IRE) 11 br.g. Presenting – Bobbies Storm (IRE) (Bob Back (USA)) [2016/17 c96, h–: c24.2d^4 c21.2m* May 28] winning hurdler: fair handicap chaser: in first-time cheekpieces, won at Cartmel in May: stays 25f, at least as effective at shorter: acts on good to firm and heavy going. *Micky Hammond*   **c111** **h–**

ABBEYVIEW (IRE) 10 b.g. Misternando – Castle Spirit (IRE) (Clearly Bust) [2016/17 c96: c21.2m* c20g^6 c23.8m^2 Apr 25] multiple winning pointer: fair form in chases: won maiden hunter at Cartmel in May. *Mrs Sheila Crow*   **c103**

ABBOTSWOOD (IRE) 6 b.g. Stowaway – Grove Juliet (IRE) (Moscow Society (USA)) [2016/17 h20g^4 h19.9s h21g* Apr 24] €35,000 3-y-o, £50,000 5-y-o: fifth foal: half-brother to fair chaser Peterbrown (23f/3m winner) and bumper winner Bevnott (both by Shantou): dam no sign of ability: winning pointer: fair form over hurdles: won maiden at Warwick in April: will stay 3m: wears tongue tie. *Charlie Longsdon*   **h109**

ABBREVIATE (GER) 6 b.g. Authorized (IRE) – Azalee (GER) (Lando (GER)) [2016/17 h124: h21.6d^2 h24.4d^2 h23.6v h24d Apr 27] good-topped gelding: fairly useful handicap hurdler: second at Ascot (conditional) in December and Doncaster in February: stays 3m: acts on soft going. *Kim Bailey*   **h125**

ABERTILLERY 5 b.g. Shamardal (USA) – Nantyglo (Mark of Esteem (IRE)) [2016/17 h95: h16m^{ur} h15.8d Dec 4] sturdy gelding: poor maiden on Flat: lightly raced over hurdles, no form in 2016/17. *Michael Blanshard*   **h–**

ABIDJAN (FR) 7 b.g. Alberto Giacometti (IRE) – Kundera (FR) (Kadalko (FR)) [2016/17 h129: c16.3g* c17.4d^2 c21.1g^F h19.8d c16g^5 c21m^4 c16.2g^2 Apr 24] fairly useful hurdler at best: fairly useful form over fences: won maiden at Newton Abbot in May: left Paul Nicholls after fourth start: stays 19f: acts on good to soft going: has worn tongue tie, including in 2016/17. *Dan Skelton*   **c127** **h–**

ABIGAIL LYNCH (IRE) 9 b.m. Oscar (IRE) – Tanit Lady (IRE) (Presenting) [2016/17 c104, h–: h16d c23g^4 Jul 21] well-made mare: winning pointer: fairly useful hurdler at best: maiden chaser: should stay beyond 2m: acts on heavy going: tried in cheekpieces: wears tongue tie. *Kerry Lee*   **c80** **h–**

ABLAZING (IRE) 6 b.g. Mastercraftsman (IRE) – Moore's Melody (IRE) (Marju (IRE)) **h116**
[2016/17 h87, b74: h15.9g^6 h15.8g^3 h15.8g* h15.8g^3 h20g^3 h19.1g^2 h20g* Sep 12] fairly
useful handicap hurdler: won at Uttoxeter (twice) in July and Worcester in September:
stays 2½m: acts on good to soft going: wears blinkers nowadays: strong traveller.
Johnny Farrelly

A BOLD MOVE (IRE) 7 b.g. Shantou (USA) – Sprint For Gold (USA) (Slew O' Gold **h114**
(USA)) [2016/17 h85p, b76: h20s^4 h15.8d^2 Apr 16] dual point winner: fair form over
hurdles: better effort in 2016/17 when second in novice at Ffos Las (in cheekpieces) in
April: trained on reappearance only by Alan King: may prove best at short of 2½m.
Christian Williams

ABOLITIONIST (IRE) 9 b.g. Flemensfirth (USA) – All The Roses (IRE) (Roselier **c147**
(FR)) [2016/17 c129, h111: c20d^2 c24d^2 c24s* c29d^3 Apr 17] workmanlike gelding: fairly **h–**
useful hurdler at best: smart handicap chaser: won Leinster National Handicap Chase at
Naas (by 1¾ lengths from Folsom Blue) in March: third in Irish Grand National Chase at
Fairyhouse (14¾ lengths behind Our Duke) in April: stays 29f: acts on soft and good to
firm going: tried in headgear. *Ellmarie Holden, Ireland*

ABOVE BOARD (IRE) 6 b.g. Mahler – Blackwater Babe (IRE) (Arctic Lord) [2016/17 **h119**
b98p h19.9s^2 h19.3s* h21.4s^{pu} Jan 7] bumper winner: fairly useful form over hurdles: won
novice at Carlisle in December: folded quickly in handicap next time. *Jonjo O'Neill*

A BOY NAMED SUZI 9 b.g. Medecis – Classic Coral (USA) (Seattle Dancer (USA)) **h116**
[2016/17 h19d h16.3g^3 h15.8d^3 h16g h20.6m Apr 17] sturdy gelding: fairly useful handicap
hurdler: best form at 2m: acts on heavy going: tried in cheekpieces. *Lucy Wadham*

ABRACADABRA SIVOLA (FR) 7 br.g. Le Fou (IRE) – Pierrebrune (FR) (Cadoudal **c128**
(FR)) [2016/17 c130, h–: c24.2s^{pu} c23g^5 c26.7s^2 c23d* c30.7d c23.8v^{pu} c28.4g* c28.4g^{pu} **h–**
Apr 15] useful-looking gelding: winning hurdler: fairly useful handicap chaser: won at
Taunton in February and March: stays 3½m: acts on heavy going: wears cheekpieces
nowadays. *David Pipe*

ABRICOT DE L'OASIS (FR) 7 b.g. Al Namix (FR) – La Normandie (FR) (Beyssac **c136**
(FR)) [2016/17 c116p, h125: c19.4g h20.5g^2 c24d^F h24.4g^3 h23.1s^2 c23.8g^2 Apr 9] fairly **h126**
useful handicap hurdler: useful handicap chaser: second at Ffos Las (head behind Upswing)
in April: stays 3m: acts on soft and good to firm going: has worn headgear, including last 2
starts: usually leads. *Dan Skelton*

ABSOLUTE (IRE) 6 b.g. Danehill Dancer (IRE) – Beyond Belief (IRE) (Sadler's Wells **h72**
(USA)) [2016/17 h104: h19.7g h17.1d h15.7d h20.6s^{pu} h16.4s^{pu} h15.7s^3 h21.3d^5 Mar 21]
rather lightly-made gelding: poor maiden hurdler: unproven beyond 17f: acts on heavy
going. *Sue Smith*

ABSOLUTELY BYGONES (IRE) 9 b.g. Alderbrook – Majella (IRE) (Fourstars **c–**
Allstar (USA)) [2016/17 h–: h23.1m^4 c24.2s^6 c25.5d^{pu} c24.2d^{pu} Mar 21] angular gelding: **h89**
fair handicap hurdler at best: no form over fences: stays 25f: acts on heavy going: tried in
cheekpieces: wears tongue tie. *Jackie du Plessis*

ABSOLUTELY FRANKIE 7 ch.g. Zaha (CAN) – La Piazza (IRE) (Polish Patriot (USA)) **h–**
[2016/17 b16v h15.8s h16v^4 Mar 22] no show in bumper/over hurdles. *Martin Bosley* **b–**

ABSOLUTE POWER 6 b.g. Flemensfirth (USA) – Crystal Ballerina (IRE) (Sadler's **b97**
Wells (USA)) [2016/17 b16s^2 b16.3s^3 Jan 18] €32,000 3-y-o: second foal: dam unraced
sister to useful hurdler/fairly useful chaser (2½m/21f winner) Sizing Symphony: fairly
useful form in bumpers: better effort when third at Newbury in January: will stay further
than 2m. *Rebecca Curtis*

ABSOLUTLYFANTASTIC 10 b.g. Alhaarth (IRE) – Persian Walk (FR) (Persian Bold) **c–**
[2016/17 c–, h113: h16.8g^{pu} h20d^6 h22m^6 h18.5m^4 h21.6g Sep 16] rather leggy gelding: **h93**
fair handicap hurdler, below form in 2016/17: winning chaser: stays 2¾m: acts on good to
firm and good to soft going: wears tongue tie. *Martin Hill*

ABYAAT (IRE) 6 b.g. Halling (USA) – Why Dubai (USA) (Kris S (USA)) [2016/17 h104: **h87**
h16m^5 h16.8m Jul 1] modest handicap hurdler: raced around 2m: acts on soft and good to
firm going: in cheekpieces last 3 starts: wears tongue tie. *Victor Dartnall*

ACADEMY GENERAL (IRE) 11 b.g. Beneficial – Discerning Air (Ezzoud (IRE)) **c63**
[2016/17 c–, h77: h21.6g c17m^6 c22.6g^{pu} h21.6g^{pu} h19g h23.1g^{pu} c19.2m^3 Apr 18] won **h55**
twice in points: winning hurdler/maiden chaser, little form in 2016/17: left Patricia Shaw
after fourth start: stays 23f: acts on good to firm and good to soft going: has worn headgear,
including often in 2016/17: has worn tongue tie, including last 3 starts. *Jackie du Plessis*

Ten Up Novices' Chase, Navan—
Acapella Bourgeois and Roger Loughran slip their field for a wide-margin win

ACADIAN (FR) 7 b.g. Sulamani (IRE) – Acarina (IRE) (Desert Story (IRE)) [2016/17 **c82** h76: h21.6g^{ur} h22g^4 c24d^F c23g^{pu} c22.6m^5 h23g^3 h25.6s^2 h23.8v^4 h23.1s^4 h27v^2 h27v^4 Mar **h83** 5] poor maiden hurdler: poor form over fences: stays 27f: acts on heavy going: wears headgear: tried in tongue tie: often races towards rear. *Nigel Hawke*

ACAJOU DES BIEFFES (FR) 7 b.g. Millennium Bio (JPN) – Pietragella (FR) **h88** (Baryshnikov (AUS)) [2016/17 h82, b91: h19.9m* h23.3g h16.8g h20s^{pu} Nov 15] good-topped gelding: modest handicap hurdler: won at Uttoxeter in June: left Anthony Honeyball after second start: best effort at 2½m: acted on good to firm going: in blinkers last 2 starts: in tongue tie last 5 starts: dead. *Alexandra Dunn*

ACAPELLA BOURGEOIS (FR) 7 ch.g. Network (GER) – Jasmine (FR) (Valanjou **c148 +** (FR)) [2016/17 h139: h24d^4 c19d^F c21.5d^3 c19d^4 c20s* c24s* c24.4g^6 c24.5d^5 Apr 25] **h–** lengthy gelding: smart chaser: won maiden at Navan (by 4¾ lengths from Arbre de Vie) in January and Ten Up Novices' Chase at same course (by 32 lengths from Road To Respect, soon well clear) in February: stays 3m: acts on heavy going: has worn hood, including in 2016/17: tried in tongue tie. *Ms Sandra Hughes, Ireland*

ACCESSALLAREAS (IRE) 12 ch.g. Swift Gulliver (IRE) – Arushofgold (IRE) **c83 §** (Alphabatim (USA)) [2016/17 c95, h–: c19.2d c19.4m* c20g^6 c16.3g^2 c21g^{pu} c15.7m^4 **h–** c16g^2 c19.9m^5 c17g^5 c17.2d^3 Apr 27] workmanlike gelding: very lightly raced over hurdles: poor handicap chaser: won at Stratford in July: stays 21f: acts on soft and good to firm going: wears headgear: has worn tongue tie: often leads: temperamental. *Sarah-Jayne Davies*

ACCORDING TO DAN (IRE) 12 ch.g. Accordion – Springwell Sue (IRE) (Naheez **c–** (USA)) [2016/17 c22.6m^{pu} May 20] won 3 times in points: pulled up both starts in hunter chases: in blinkers second time. *P. Foster*

ACCORDING TO HARRY (IRE) 8 b.g. Old Vic – Cassilis (IRE) (Persian Bold) **c126** [2016/17 h105: h23.1m^F h19.4g* h22.5s^3 c25.8m^3 h23g* c23.8g^2 c23.8m* Apr 25] fairly **h117** useful form over hurdles: won novice at Worcester in August: fairly useful form over fences: won novice handicap at Ffos Las in May and handicap at Ludlow in April: left Philip Hobbs after fifth start: stays 3m: acts on soft and good to firm going: often travels strongly. *Nicky Martin*

ACCORDING TO THEM (IRE) 13 ch.g. Quws – Any Old Music (IRE) (Montelimar (USA)) [2016/17 c25.5s^{pu} h19.5v^{pu} c23.5v^{pu} Jan 31] sturdy gelding: maiden hurdler: modest chaser at best, no form in 2016/17: tried in headgear: wore tongue tie: unreliable: dead. *Daniel Steele*   **c– §** **h– §**

ACCORDING TO TREV (IRE) 11 ch.g. Accordion – Autumn Sky (IRE) (Roselier (FR)) [2016/17 c–x, h125: c24.1d c25.5s^3 c20.5m^{ur} Apr 18] good-topped gelding: winning hurdler: useful chaser at best, no form in hunters in 2016/17: has worn headgear/tongue tie. *Alan Hill*   **c–** **h–**

ACCORD (IRE) 7 b.g. Arcadio (GER) – Detente (Medicean) [2016/17 h16g^2 h16.4g^3 h18.6s^3 h16v^3 Feb 4] sturdy, workmanlike gelding: second foal: dam (h83) lightly raced over hurdles: off mark in Irish maiden points at third attempt: fair form over hurdles, placed all 4 starts in novices/maiden. *David Bridgwater*   **h113**

ACDC (IRE) 7 b.g. King's Theatre (IRE) – Always Alert (IRE) (Slip Anchor) [2016/17 b88: b16.2d^3 h16.4d^5 h22s^{pu} h22s^2 h19.4g^6 h20.1s* h24.3d^5 Apr 21] modest form in bumpers: fair form over hurdles: won maiden at Hexham in March: likely to prove best at short of 3m: acts on soft going: in hood last 2 starts: usually races in rear. *Chris Grant*   **h109** **b84**

ACE FIGHTER PILOT 11 b.g. Silver Patriarch (IRE) – Vedra (IRE) (Carlingford Castle) [2016/17 c–, h–: c21d^6 Jun 21] winning hurdler: fairly useful chaser at best, very lightly raced and no form since 2013/14: should stay 3m: acts on good to firm and heavy going. *Jim Best*   **c–** **h–**

ACES OVER EIGHTS (IRE) 8 b.m. Old Vic – Conjure Up (IRE) (Jurado (USA)) [2016/17 c–, h98: c16.5s^2 c16.3g* c16g^6 c20.9g^2 c20s^5 c16s^6 c20d^2 c21.3d^{pu} Feb 21] workmanlike mare: winning hurdler: fair handicap chaser: won at Towcester in May: stays 21f: acts on soft going: usually in cheekpieces in 2016/17. *Kerry Lee*   **c104** **h–**

ACHILL ROAD BOY (IRE) 8 b.g. Morozov (USA) – Presenting Katie (IRE) (Presenting) [2016/17 c24.2s^3 c20.1s^F c21.5s* h20.5s^6 c24.3v^4 c21.6v^3 h20.1s* c20.9d Apr 5] fair handicap hurdler: won novice event at Hexham in March: similar form over fences: won handicap at Ayr in December: stays 3m: acts on heavy going. *Stuart Coltherd*   **c103** **h103**

ACHIMOTA (IRE) 11 b.g. Double Eclipse (IRE) – Tullyfoyle (IRE) (Montelimar (USA)) [2016/17 c117, h92: c22.5v^{pu} c23.6d* c24.2v^{pu} Jan 1] winning hurdler: fairly useful handicap chaser: won at Chepstow in November: should stay beyond 3m: acts on heavy going: in blinkers last 2 starts: has worn tongue tie, including last 2 starts: inconsistent. *Graeme McPherson*   **c123** **h–**

ACROSS THE TWEED (IRE) 11 b.g. Alderbrook – Cash Chase (IRE) (Sexton Blake) [2016/17 h23.9m^{pu} May 11] maiden hurdler, very lightly raced and no form since 2012/13: little above over fences: tried in headgear: usually wears tongue tie: temperamental. *Lisa Harrison*   **c– §** **h– §**

ACT ACCORDINGLY 4 gr.g. Sagamix (FR) – Anns Girl (Newski (USA)) [2016/17 b13.7d ab16g Dec 10] no form in bumpers. *Jimmy Fox*   **b–**

ACT ALONE 8 b.g. Act One – Figlette (Darshaan) [2016/17 h20g^5 Aug 21] leggy, close-coupled gelding: fairly useful hurdler at best, below that only start in 2016/17: stays 21f: acts on good to soft going. *Nicky Henderson*   **h–**

ACT FOUR (IRE) 9 b.g. Old Vic – Quadrennial (IRE) (Un Desperado (FR)) [2016/17 h100: h18.5g^3 h22m h23.1g^5 h20g h21s^5 h25.5s h19.9v^6 h16v* h15.8v^6 h19.5g* h19.5m^6 Apr 28] good-bodied gelding: modest handicap hurdler: won at Warwick (conditional) in March and Chepstow (novice) in April: should stay further than 19f: acts on heavy going: in cheekpieces last 4 starts: wears tongue tie: usually races towards rear. *Matt Sheppard*   **h90**

ACTING LASS (IRE) 6 b.g. King's Theatre (IRE) – Darrens Lass (IRE) (Montelimar (USA)) [2016/17 h19.7s* h21.7s^2 h19.3s^4 Feb 18] fourth foal: dam (c99), 2½m-3m chase winner, half-sister to fairly useful hurdler/fair chaser (stayed 27f) Elzahann: useful form over hurdles: won novice at Hereford on debut in November: best effort when second in similar event there (7 lengths behind Finian's Oscar) in December: will stay 3m: in tongue tie last 2 starts. *Harry Fry*   **h133**

ACTINPIECES 6 gr.m. Act One – Bonnet's Pieces (Alderbrook) [2016/17 h126, b81: c19.4m^{ur} c23.9g^6 c24.2s* c24.2s^{pu} c19.4d^2 c25.2s* c19.9s^3 c22.2g^F Apr 15] workmanlike mare: fairly useful hurdler: useful chaser: won novice at Wetherby in November and mares handicap at Catterick (by 3¼ lengths from Conquer Gold) in February: stays 25f: acts on soft going. *Pam Sly*   **c133** **h–**

ACTIONDANCER (IRE) 6 b.g. Craigsteel – Sudden Action (IRE) (Shardari) [2016/17 h–, b–: h15.8d^5 h15.5g h15.8v^{pu} h16.6d h16v^5 h19.7d^{pu} Mar 26] workmanlike gelding: poor maiden hurdler. *Henry Oliver*   **h74**

ACTION REPLAY (IRE) 6 b.g. Milan – Mary Connors (IRE) (Mandalus) [2016/17 **h115 p** h16.7g⁵ h16s⁶ h15.9d⁴ h15.9v² Jan 2] €70,000 3-y-o: seventh foal: brother to fairly useful hurdler/chaser Crash (2½m-2¾m winner), stayed 25f, and half-brother to 2 winners, including fair hurdler Doesheeverstop (2¾m winner, by Turtle Island): dam (b75) ran twice in bumpers: fairly useful form over hurdles: second in novice at Plumpton in January: bred to stay at least 2½m: open to further improvement. *Philip Hobbs*

ACTIVE IN MILAN (IRE) 8 b.g. Milan – Shirley Venture (Be My Chief (USA)) **c–** [2016/17 c26.2dᵖᵘ Apr 10] winning pointer: pulled up in maiden hunter on chasing debut: wore cheekpieces. *Alan Wight*

ACTIVIAL (FR) 7 gr.g. Lord du Sud (FR) – Kissmirial (FR) (Smadoun (FR)) [2016/17 **c–** c144p, h144: c20.5dᵘʳ c20v⁵ Feb 11] angular gelding: useful hurdler/chaser, went as if **h–** amiss only completed start over fences in 2016/17: stays 21f: acts on heavy going: in tongue tie last 3 starts. *Neil Mulholland*

ACTLIKEACOUNTESS 6 gr.m. Act One – Countess Point (Karinga Bay) [2016/17 b70: **h86** h16d h18.5s h18.5s h20.5g* h23.9gᶠ Feb 21] modest form over hurdles: won conditionals mares handicap at Leicester in January: best effort at 2½m: dead. *Neil Mulholland*

ACT NOW 8 br.m. Act One – Lady Turk (FR) (Baby Turk) [2016/17 h81: h21.6s³ h23v **h106** h25s* h24v² h26v⁴ h25.5d* Mar 26] fair handicap hurdler: won at Plumpton in February and Hereford (mares event) in March: out-and-out stayer: acts on heavy going: wears tongue tie: front runner/races prominently. *Anthony Honeyball*

ACT OF SUPREMACY (IRE) 7 b.g. Presenting – Supreme Touch (IRE) (Supreme **c–** Leader) [2016/17 h95: c20mᵖᵘ h17.7g⁴ h20d⁴ Jun 29] good-topped gelding: modest form **h97** over hurdles: pulled up in novice handicap on chasing debut. *Warren Greatrex*

ACTONETAKETWO 7 b.m. Act One – Temple Dancer (Magic Ring (IRE)) [2016/17 **h–** h–: h19g⁴ h16.5m⁵ Apr 27] sturdy mare: modest/unreliable on Flat, stays 8.5f: no form over hurdles. *Derrick Scott*

ADAM DU BRETEAU (FR) 7 ch.g. Network (GER) – Odelie de Fric (FR) (April Night **c128** (FR)) [2016/17 c107, h89: h23.3g c23g* c23m³ c19.9m* c25.6g³ c25.5d* c24g c24.2g³ **h–** c24.1gᵖᵘ Apr 15] maiden hurdler: fairly useful handicap chaser: won at Worcester in July, Huntingdon (novice) in October and Fontwell in December: stays 25f: acts on good to firm and good to soft going: wears headgear: races prominently. *Jonjo O'Neill*

ADARENNA (IRE) 5 b.m. Nayef (USA) – Adelfia (IRE) (Sinndar (IRE)) [2016/17 h22d⁶ **c101** h17.2g⁴ h22.1d⁴ h20g h16g c16g² c16.1d* c24s⁵ Mar 30] modest maiden on Flat: modest **h88** form over hurdles: fair form over fences: won novice handicap at Towcester in November: unproven beyond 17f: acts on good to soft going: in cheekpieces last 3 starts: has worn tongue tie. *John Joseph Hanlon, Ireland*

ADEENNE DE SEVRES (FR) 7 ch.g. Network (GER) – Gelee Royale (FR) (Royal **h–** Charter (FR)) [2016/17 h65: h15.8g May 14] maiden pointer/hurdler: tried in hood. *Tom Lacey*

ADEPT APPROACH (IRE) 11 b.g. Milan – Musical Approach (IRE) (Dry Dock) **c89** [2016/17 c–: c27.2d⁶ May 12] multiple point winner: won hunter on chase debut in 2013/14, let down by jumping last 2 starts in that grade: stays 3¼m: acts on heavy going: tried in cheekpieces. *P. G. Hall*

ADHERENCE 4 b.g. Sir Percy – Straight Laced (Refuse To Bend (IRE)) [2016/17 h16.7g **h–** Jul 31] fair maiden on Flat, stays 1¾m: behind in juvenile hurdle. *Tony Coyle*

ADIOS ALONSO (IRE) 11 b.g. Saffron Walden (FR) – Rosy Rockford (IRE) **c97** (Beneficial) [2016/17 c91, h–: c22.6mᶠ h23m³ h23.3gᵖᵘ h23.1g Oct 25] poor handicap **h83** hurdler: modest handicap chaser: stays 23f: acts on soft and good to firm going: has worn cheekpieces, including in 2016/17: front runner/races prominently. *Rosemary Gasson*

ADMIRAL BARRATRY (FR) 4 b.g. Soldier of Fortune (IRE) – Haskilclara (FR) **h115** (Green Tune (USA)) [2016/17 h16.4s² h15.7dᵘʳ Feb 18] fourth foal: dam useful 6f/7f winner at 2 yrs in France: fairly useful form over hurdles: second in juvenile at Enghien in May on completed start. *Nick Williams*

ADMIRAL BLAKE 10 b.g. Witness Box (USA) – Brenda Bella (FR) (Linamix (FR)) **c79** [2016/17 c63, h84: c24v³ h23.1s h19.2v⁵ h23.6s⁵ h23.1g Apr 11] poor handicap hurdler: **h65** poor form over fences: stays 3m: raced mostly on soft/heavy going: tried in blinkers. *Laura Young*

ADMIRAL KID (IRE) 6 b.g. Mythical Kid (USA) – English Clover (Tina's Pet) **h105** [2016/17 b96p: h21gᶠ h15.9g⁴ h20gᶠ h16s⁵ Jan 8] third in Irish point: bumper winner: fair form over hurdles: will prove suited by further than 2m: often leads. *Neil Mulholland*

ADMIRAL'S SECRET 6 b.g. Kayf Tara – Bobs Bay (IRE) (Bob's Return (IRE)) **h107**
[2016/17 b85: h15.8s³ h16.8v³ h17.7v Jan 29] fair form over hurdles: third in novice at
Uttoxeter and maiden at Exeter: bred to be suited by further than 2m: wears tongue tie.
Victor Dartnall

ADRAKHAN (FR) 6 b.g. Martaline – Annee de La Femme (IRE) (Common Grounds) **c84**
[2016/17 h108: c20d⁵ h19.9d h19.3g Jan 12] useful-looking gelding: fair hurdler at best, **h–**
well held in 2016/17 including on chasing debut: left Dan Skelton after first start: unproven
beyond 17f: acts on heavy going. *Wilf Storey*

ADRIEN DU PONT (FR) 5 b.g. Califet (FR) – Santariyka (FR) (Saint des Saints (FR)) **h145**
[2016/17 h145p: h16.4g⁴ h19.4v³ h20.3sᵘʳ h19.1sᵖᵘ Feb 26] smart hurdler: third in Prix
Renaud du Vivier at Auteuil (1½ lengths behind Capivari) in November: stays 19f: acts on
heavy going: usually in tongue tie. *Paul Nicholls*

ADRRASTOS (IRE) 5 b.g. Areion (GER) – Laren (GER) (Monsun (GER)) [2016/17 **h115**
b16.8m² b16g³ h15.8m² h16.2g² h15.8v³ h16.3g³ h15.9m* Apr 16] €25,000 3-y-o: lengthy **b80**
gelding: fourth foal: half-brother to fairly useful hurdler L'Aigle Royal (17f-21f winner, by
Sholokhov): dam, 17f-2½m hurdle/chase winner in Germany/Czech Republic, also 11f
winner on Flat: modest form in bumpers: fairly useful form over hurdles: won maiden at
Plumpton in April: left Stuart Kittow after second start: raced around 2m: acts on good to
firm going: sometimes in hood: front runner/races prominently. *Jamie Snowden*

AENGUS (IRE) 7 b.g. Robin des Champs (FR) – Which Thistle (IRE) (Saddlers' Hall **c–**
(IRE)) [2016/17 h19.9v⁵ h19.7s h16.2s h21.2s⁶ h19.7d* h25.3s* h19.9s³ Mar 18] **h121**
3-y-o: fourth foal: half-brother to fairly useful hurdler/useful chaser Irish Thistle (2m-2½m
winner, by Luso) and fair 19f hurdle winner Why Not Thistle (by Flemensfirth): dam
unraced: bumper winner: fairly useful handicap hurdler: won at Wetherby and Catterick in
February: all but fell only start over fences: left Noel Meade after final (2015/16) start:
stays 25f: acts on soft going: in cheekpieces last 4 starts. *Jennie Candlish*

AERIAL (FR) 11 b.g. Turgeon (USA) – Fille Formidable (USA) (Trempolino (USA)) **c129**
[2016/17 c134, h–: c27.2s* c22.3s⁴ c24.2s Jan 7] good-topped gelding: winning hurdler: **h–**
fairly useful handicap chaser: won Southern National at Fontwell (by 2½ lengths from
Fergal Mael Duin) in November after 18-month lay-off: lame final start: stays 27f: acts on
good to firm and heavy going: tried in cheekpieces/tongue tie. *Paul Nicholls*

AERLITE SUPREME (IRE) 10 b.g. Gold Well – Supreme Evening (IRE) (Supreme **c124**
Leader) [2016/17 c127, h127: c24s c19.4d² c19.9g⁴ c22.9s c20.2s⁴ c20s⁶ c20d⁶ c19.9gᵘʳ **h–**
Apr 15] rangy gelding: fairly useful hurdler: fairly useful handicap chaser: second at
Wetherby in November: stays 3m: acts on heavy going: has worn headgear: wears tongue
tie. *Evan Williams*

AFFAIRE D'HONNEUR (FR) 6 ch.g. Shirocco (GER) – Affaire de Moeurs (FR) **h118**
(Kaldounevees (FR)) [2016/17 h129: h19.1s* h17.7d⁵ h22.8vᵖᵘ h19.5s³ h23.1s⁴ Mar 12]
leggy gelding: fairly useful hurdler: won novice at Fontwell in October: stays 19f: acts on
soft going: tried in cheekpieces: usually races close up. *Harry Whittington*

AFIENYA (IRE) 7 gr.m. Tikkanen (USA) – Tullyfoyle (IRE) (Montelimar (USA)) **b–**
[2016/17 b15.6g Nov 3] no form in bumpers. *Simon West*

AFRICAN GOLD (IRE) 9 b.g. King's Theatre (IRE) – Mrs Dempsey (IRE) (Presenting) **c100**
[2016/17 c–, h–: h21.9s⁴ c24.2s c24.1s⁴ Jan 23] big, strong gelding: smart hurdler/useful **h108**
maiden chaser at one time, has deteriorated considerably: stays 3m: acts on heavy going:
tried in headgear: usually wears tongue tie (didn't in 2016/17). *Paul Morgan*

AFRICAN TIGER 6 b.g. Tamure (IRE) – Scarlet Glory (Past Glories) [2016/17 h19.8d **h89**
h18.5s h18.5s h21.4dᶠ h21.6m Apr 15] third foal: dam winning pointer: modest form over
hurdles: running easily best race when fell last in handicap at Wincanton in March, likely
to have won: tried in cheekpieces. *Harry Fry*

AFTER EIGHT SIVOLA (FR) 7 b.g. Shaanmer (IRE) – Eva de Chalamont (FR) (Iron **c108**
Duke (FR)) [2016/17 h123: c16.3g* c16m⁶ c16.4gᵖᵘ c20.2mᵖᵘ h19m⁴ Apr 27] sturdy **h117**
gelding: fairly useful handicap hurdler: fair form over fences: won novice at Newton Abbot
in October: stays 19f: acts on good to firm and heavy going: wears hood: often races
towards rear. *Nick Williams*

AFTER HOURS (IRE) 8 b.g. Milan – Supreme Singer (IRE) (Supreme Leader) **c125**
[2016/17 h115: c18m⁴ c17.5s² c16.4d² c16s c16v² c20.9s² c24s² Mar 30] workmanlike **h–**
gelding: winning Irish pointer: fair hurdler: fairly useful maiden chaser: second in novice
handicap at Hereford and handicap at Warwick last 2 starts: stays 3m: acts on heavy going:
in cheekpieces last 3 starts. *Henry Oliver*

AFTER RAIN (FR) 7 br.g. Al Namix (FR) – La Lorelei (FR) (Passing Sale (FR)) **h130**
[2016/17 h16g h16d h16d³ h16g h16d³ h20.5d⁴ Apr 29] second foal: half-brother to French
1½m bumper winner Ultramaille (by Maille Pistol): dam French 2¼m chase winner: useful
handicap hurdler: again shaped well when fourth in Ballymore Handicap Hurdle at
Punchestown (2¼ lengths behind Open Eagle) in April: stays 2½m: acts on heavy going:
wears hood: usually races nearer last than first. *J. R. Barry, Ireland*

AFTER TONIIGHT (FR) 7 b.g. Lando (GER) – Affair (FR) (Montjeu (IRE)) [2016/17 **h67**
h16.2sᵖᵘ h19.3d⁴ Dec 13] bumper winner: poor form over hurdles after 2-year absence:
placed in maidens on Flat in early-2017: sold £4,500 in March. *Keith Reveley*

AGAMEMMON (IRE) 5 b.g. Getaway (GER) – Oscar Road (IRE) (Oscar (IRE)) **h114**
[2016/17 b15.7d* b15.7d⁴ h19g⁴ h21s² h23.1s³ h19.9s⁴ Apr 1] €35,000 3-y-o: rather **b99**
unfurnished gelding: fifth foal: half-brother to 3 winners, including bumper winner/fairly
useful 2¾m hurdle winner Ballela Boy (by Golan) and fairly useful 19f chase winner
Highbrow Blue (by Blueprint): dam (c78/h91) 2½m hurdle winner: won completed start in
maiden points: fairly useful form in bumpers: won at Southwell in November: fair form
over hurdles: stays 21f: tried in blinkers. *Tom Lacey*

AGATHE ROSALIE (IRE) 4 b.f. Presenting – Agathe du Berlais (FR) (Poliglote) **b–**
[2016/17 b16.3s b16.7g Mar 27] €50,000 3-y-o: first foal: dam French maiden half-sister
to temperamental but very smart hurdler/fairly useful chaser (2m/17f winner) Afsoun and
smart hurdler (2m-2½m winner) Agrapart: no form in bumpers: tried in hood. *Lucy Wadham*

A GENIE IN ABOTTLE (IRE) 6 b.g. Beneficial – Erkindale Miss (IRE) (Supreme **c150**
Leader) [2016/17 h24d⁶ c22.5s³ c21.5d² c24v* c24s² c31.8g⁵ c24.5d³ Apr 25] €36,000 **h–**
3-y-o, £60,000 4-y-o: rangy gelding: fourth foal: half-brother to bumper winner/fairly
useful hurdler Missyspet (2½m winner, by Westerner): dam (b90) bumper winner: bumper
winner: fair form over hurdles: won maiden at Naas in 2015/16: smart form over fences:
won maiden at Fairyhouse (by 5½ lengths from Blazer) in December: second in Grade 3
novice at Naas (¾ length behind Anibale Fly) in January and third in Champion Novices'
Chase at Punchestown (in cheekpieces, 5¾ lengths behind Disko) in April: stays 25f: acts
on heavy going: usually races close up. *Noel Meade, Ireland*

AGENTLEMAN (IRE) 7 b.g. Trans Island – Silvine (IRE) (Shernazar) [2016/17 c95, **c89**
h89, b57: c16.4g⁴ c17.1m⁶ c15.6d c17.2g⁴ h16.7g⁴ h16.8g² h16g h15.7g h18.5d⁴ Sep 26] **h83**
poor maiden hurdler: modest maiden chaser: left Tim Easterby after fourth start: stays 21f:
acts on heavy going: in cheekpieces last 5 starts: usually races towards rear, often travels
strongly. *Roy Brotherton*

AGENT LOUISE 9 b.m. Alflora (IRE) – Oso Special (Teenoso (USA)) [2016/17 h88§: **h73 §**
h24vᶠ h25.3dᵖᵘ h27v⁴ h23.3s³ Mar 18] modest handicap hurdler: below form in 2016/17:
stays 27f: acts on good to firm and heavy going: usually wears headgear: often races
towards rear: unreliable. *Mike Sowersby*

AGE OF DISCOVERY 8 b.g. Nayef (USA) – Magic Tree (UAE) (Timber Country **c–**
(USA)) [2016/17 h96: h19.9g c22.6gᵖᵘ Aug 11] maiden hurdler: pulled up in novice **h–**
handicap on chasing debut: unproven beyond 2m: acts on good to firm going: tried in
blinkers: wears tongue tie. *Dan Skelton*

AGE OF GLORY 8 b.g. Zamindar (USA) – Fleeting Moon (Fleetwood (IRE)) [2016/17 **h92**
h91: h16.4s h17s³ h17d Feb 20] modest handicap hurdler: unproven beyond 17f: acts on
soft going: often races towards rear. *Barbara Butterworth*

AGESILAS (FR) 9 gr.g. Ultimately Lucky (IRE) – Aimessa du Berlais (FR) (Nikos) **h– §**
[2016/17 h57§: h16.4sᵖᵘ h19vᵖᵘ Jan 30] maiden hurdler, no form in 2016/17: wears
headgear nowadays: temperamental. *Andrew Crook*

AGHA DES MOTTES (FR) 7 b.g. Mister Sacha (FR) – Java des Mottes (FR) (Passing **h–**
Sale (FR)) [2016/17 h86: h15.8g h16.7g Jul 31] bumper winner: maiden hurdler, no form
in 2016/17: raced around 2m: acts on good to soft going. *Ian Williams*

AGINCOURT REEF (IRE) 8 b.g. Gold Well – Hillside Native (IRE) (Be My Native **c122 §**
(USA)) [2016/17 c111, h–: c21.1d⁶ c19.2s³ h16.8g⁴ h18.7g³ h20.3d² h21.2d* h21.3s* **h115 §**
h21.4s⁶ h20.5v⁶ c20.3s* h20.5g h19m³ Apr 27] good-topped gelding: fairly useful handicap
hurdler: won at Ludlow in November and Wetherby in December: fairly useful handicap
chaser: won at Southwell in March: left Gary Moore after fourth start: stays 21f: acts on
soft and good to firm going: wears headgear: moody. *Roger Teal*

A GOOD SKIN (IRE) 8 b.g. Presenting – Triaskin (IRE) (Buckskin (FR)) [2016/17 **c136**
c141, h–: c23.6g³ c23.8m⁶ c26g⁴ c26.3s c25g c23.8g⁵ Apr 26] lengthy gelding: maiden **h–**
hurdler: useful handicap chaser: third at Chepstow (2¾ lengths behind Potters Cross) in
October: stays 3¼m: acts on soft going: in headgear last 3 starts. *Tom George*

Dornan Engineering Relkeel Hurdle, Cheltenham—Lizzie Kelly sees in 2017 with a New Year's Day double on Coo Star Sivola and Agrapart (pictured), the latter claiming the scalps of L'Ami Serge (right) and Cole Harden (cheekpieces)

AGRAPART (FR) 6 b.g. Martaline – Afragha (IRE) (Darshaan) [2016/17 h144: h19.4d h21.4s⁴ h20.3s* h22.8d³ h24g Mar 16] good-topped gelding: smart hurdler: won Relkeel Hurdle at Cheltenham (by head from L'Ami Serge) in January: raced freely/jumped sketchily when third in Rendlesham Hurdle at Haydock (4 lengths behind Zarkandar) in February: stays 21f: acts on heavy going: often races prominently. *Nick Williams*   **h154**

AGREEMENT (IRE) 7 b.g. Galileo (IRE) – Cozzene's Angel (USA) (Cozzene (USA)) [2016/17 h–: h23.6d h21s c15.9g² c15.9s⁵ Feb 16] lengthy gelding: fair hurdler at best, no form since 2014/15: beat only one rival each start over fences: stays 2½m: acts on soft going: has worn headgear. *Nikki Evans*   **c–**
h–

AGRICULTURAL 11 b.g. Daylami (IRE) – Rustic (IRE) (Grand Lodge (USA)) [2016/17 c–§, h–§: c20.1mᶠ May 11] winning hurdler: maiden chaser, no form since 2013/14: temperamental. *Lucy Normile*   **c– §**
h– §

A HARE BREATH (IRE) 9 b.g. Alkaadhem – Lady Willmurt (IRE) (Mandalus) [2016/17 h133: h16.4s⁴ c17.4s* c16.4d³ c15.9g h20g Apr 7] well-made gelding: useful handicap hurdler: fourth in Greatwood Hurdle at Cheltenham (2¼ lengths behind North Hill Harvey) on return: useful form over fences: won novice at Bangor (by 5 lengths from Gala Ball) in December: stays 21f: acts on soft going: often races towards rear. *Ben Pauling*   **c139**
h136

AHIO (FR) 6 b.g. Chichi Creasy (FR) – Amalhouna (FR) (Keos (USA)) [2016/17 h16v⁵ h19.3s Feb 18] sturdy gelding: modest form over hurdles, off 2 years before eye-catching return: may yet do better. *Gary Moore*   **h85 +**

AH LITTLELUCK (IRE) 7 b.g. Mahler – Star of Hope (IRE) (Turtle Island (IRE)) [2016/17 h24g* h20.5d* h24g* h22.6d h20vᵖᵘ h24g h24dᶠ h24d Apr 27] second foal: dam unraced half-sister to fairly useful hurdler (2m winner) Scoop The Pot (by Mahler): maiden pointer: useful hurdler: won maiden at Cork and novice at Sligo in May, and handicap at Listowel in June: stays 3m: acts on heavy going: tried in tongue tie: usually races close up. *T. Gibney, Ireland*   **h132**

AHRAAM (IRE) 4 b.g. Roderic O'Connor (IRE) – Simla Sunset (IRE) (One Cool Cat (USA)) [2016/17 h15.9m² h15.8m⁴ h16m⁴ Nov 4] sturdy gelding: fair maiden on Flat, stays 1¼m: modest form over hurdles: best effort when second in juvenile at Plumpton in September. *Harry Whittington*   **h98**

AIAAM AL NAMOOS 8 b.g. Teofilo (IRE) – Deveron (USA) (Cozzene (USA)) [2016/17 h112: c19.3dᵘʳ Nov 8] fair hurdler: unseated second on chasing debut after 17-month absence: stays 3m: acts on good to soft going (won bumper on good to firm). *Chris Grant*   **c–**
h–

40

AIGLE DE LA SEE (FR) 7 gr.g. Al Namix (FR) – Janita de La See (FR) (Useful (FR)) **c–**
[2016/17 c90, h110: h26.4m² May 15] angular gelding: fairly useful handicap hurdler: **h117**
maiden chaser: stays 3¼m: acts on good to firm and heavy going: has worn cheekpieces:
usually races prominently: joined E. Turner. *Nicky Henderson*

AINSLIE (IRE) 5 gr.g. Mastercraftsman (IRE) – Capriole (Noverre (USA)) [2016/17 **h115**
h16g² h18.2dᶠ h16d⁴ h16.5g⁴ h16m³ h16.4g² h16g² h16d² h16d Dec 4] fair on Flat, stays
9.5f: fairly useful maiden hurdler: second in handicap at Navan in November: unproven
beyond 2m: acts on good to firm and good to soft going: wears tongue tie: often travels
strongly. *Gordon Elliott, Ireland*

AIN'T NO LIMITS (FR) 5 b.g. Kapgarde (FR) – Elitiste (FR) (Arctic Tern (USA)) **h98**
[2016/17 b13.7m² b15.7m⁴ h21.6dᵖᵘ h16.7d³ h19.7s⁶ h19.4g h21s h21.2m⁵ Apr 25] **b90**
€26,000 3-y-o: good-topped gelding: eighth foal: dam French 7.5f winner: fair form in
bumpers: better effort when second in maiden at Towcester in October: modest form over
hurdles. *Charlie Longsdon*

AINTREE MY DREAM (FR) 7 b.g. Saint des Saints (FR) – Pretty Melodie (FR) **h139**
(Lesotho (USA)) [2016/17 b102: h20d* h19.8s⁴ h22.8s³ h21v* h15.8sᶠ h19.7s* h23.9g⁴
Apr 26] lengthy gelding: chasing type: point/bumper winner: useful hurdler: won novices
at Carlisle in October, Warwick in February and Hereford (by 37 lengths from Finula) in
March: stays 21f: acts on heavy going: wears tongue tie: usually leads/travels strongly.
Dan Skelton

The Gascoigne Brookes Partnership III's "Agrapart"

AIR

AIR APPROACH 5 b.g. New Approach (IRE) – Grecian Air (FR) (King's Best (USA))   **h98**
[2016/17 b16.5g⁶ b13.6g⁶ h18.5g² Apr 26] fourth foal: half-brother to 2 winners, including   **b–**
fair hurdler Magic Skyline (2m/17f winner, by Refuse To Bend): dam unraced half-sister
to useful hurdler/fairly useful chaser (probably stayed 21f) Desert Air: well held in
bumpers: 25/1, second of 5 in maiden at Exeter (tongue tied, 4½ lengths behind Stealing
Mix) on hurdling debut. *Tim Vaughan*

AIR DE ROCK (FR) 8 b.g. High Rock (IRE) – Onciale (FR) (Ultimately Lucky (IRE))   **h99**
[2016/17 h16.2s³ h15.5g h19.7sᶠ h18.6s h21v⁵ Mar 12] fourth foal: half-brother to 3
winning hurdlers in France, including Cat And Co (2¼m winner) and Bijou Plage (17f-19f
winner) (both by Martaline): dam, French 2¼m hurdle winner, also 11f/13f winner on Flat:
maiden hurdler, fair at best in France in 2015/16: unproven beyond 17f: best form on soft/
heavy going: tried in cheekpieces. *Venetia Williams*

AIR GLIDER (IRE) 7 b.g. Mountain High (IRE) – California Blue (FR) (Pebble (FR))   **h104**
[2016/17 h104: h16.8d³ Apr 28] won 3 times in points, including in 2017: fair maiden
hurdler: in blinkers last 3 starts, in tongue tie last 2. *Dan Skelton*

AIR HORSE ONE 6 gr.g. Mountain High (IRE) – Whisky Rose (IRE) (Old Vic) [2016/17   **h142**
h118, b116: h16.4g⁶ h16.8g⁴ h16.8v* h19g* h19.3s* h16.8g⁴ h20.5d Apr 29] rather
unfurnished gelding: useful hurdler: won maiden at Exeter and novice at Taunton in
January, and handicap at Ascot in February: fourth in County Hurdle at Cheltenham (2½
lengths behind Arctic Fire) in March: should be suited by 2½m: acts on heavy going.
Harry Fry

AIRLIE BEACH (IRE) 7 b.m. Shantou (USA) – Screaming Witness (IRE) (Shernazar)   **h140**
[2016/17 h19.8s* h19.5g* h21.3d* h20g* h16g* h16d* h16.8g h20d⁶ h20d² Apr 29]

Thoroughbred breeders spend a lot of time, thought and money arranging
their matings in the hope of producing the next champion. But given the opportunity,
which they very rarely are, of course, thoroughbreds are no different from other
animals in doing what comes naturally, without human intervention, as Willie
Mullins' stable unexpectedly found out in the spring of 2012. A two-year-old
daughter of Shantou surprised the Mullins team by showing signs of being in foal
despite having been turned out with other fillies, along with what was believed—
wrongly as it turned out—to be the gelded Miguel Angel (a son of Binocular's sire
Enrique), a yearling purchase from France the previous autumn. 'Miguel Angel was
never checked and we just threw him out with our homebreds' explained Mullins'
son Patrick. 'We thought Airlie Beach looked a little large a few months later so
we had her checked and by then it was too late to abort the pregnancy so we had to
follow through with it.'

Three years later, Airlie Beach made a winning debut in a bumper at
Kilbeggan in the summer of 2015, while Miguel Angel, now definitely a gelding,
began his career in a similar event early in the latest season at Ballinrobe before
carrying the colours of Willie Mullins' wife Jackie to victory in a maiden hurdle two
starts later at Tramore in June. Beaten on both starts since, Miguel Angel has shown
just fair form, looking a hard ride, but his former mate Airlie Beach showed no ill
effects from her premature experience of motherhood as she proceeded to win her
first six starts over hurdles, culminating in a Grade 1 success in the Bar One Racing
Royal Bond Novices' Hurdle at Fairyhouse in December. The Royal Bond has an
impressive roll of honour that includes Istabraq, Moscow Flyer, Hardy Eustace,
Hurricane Fly, Jezki and Nichols Canyon, as well as the very good mares Liss A
Paoraigh and Like-A-Butterfly, while the line-up for the latest renewal included
future Cheltenham Festival winners Penhill and Labaik. Neither of those played a
part in the finish, however, with Labaik refusing to start and Penhill, the eventual
fourth, being badly hampered by the fall two out of the favourite Peace News. That
left Airlie Beach clear as she made all the running to beat stable-companion Saturnas
by six and a half lengths with Le Martalin third, giving Willie Mullins a record
seventh win in the race.

On her reappearance back at Kilbeggan in July, Airlie Beach had justified
short odds, as she went on to do on each of her five starts before the Royal Bond,
all of them in races confined to mares. After winning her maiden, she followed up
against just two rivals in a novice at the same track, was impressive in beating her
slightly better-fancied stablemate Retour En France in a minor event at Galway,

42

Bar One Racing Royal Bond Novices' Hurdle, Fairyhouse—'gymslip mum' Airlie Beach makes all to complete a remarkable six-timer over hurdles

gave an authoritative beating to another stable-companion, Daisy's Gift, in a listed contest at Gowran later in September and then gave 7 lb all round when accounting for main market rival Shattered Love by half a length in a Grade 3 contest at Down Royal at the beginning of November. Airlie Beach travelled well through the race for all her wins, and, apart from on her first start over hurdles, made all the running each time. After her busy spell, Airlie Beach was then rested until the Dawn Run Mares' Novices' Hurdle at the Cheltenham Festival for which she started second favourite to her stable-companion Let's Dance who had herself won her last four starts. There was little between the pair on form but, while Let's Dance extended her winning sequence, Airlie Beach proved disappointing after being taken on for the lead by La Bague Au Roi, dropping right out between the last two hurdles and beating only one home after being eased. She was below form again a month later in the Grade 1 mares novice at Fairyhouse, in which Let's Dance was beaten by another stable-companion Augusta Kate. Airlie Beach ran a much better race, although no match for fourteen-length winner Apple's Jade, in the Mares' Champion Hurdle at Punchestown where she fared best of her stable's four runners.

Airlie Beach (IRE) (b.m. 2010)	Shantou (USA) (b 1993)	Alleged (b 1974)	Hoist The Flag / Princess Pout
		Shaima (b 1988)	Shareef Dancer / Oh So Sharp
	Screaming Witness (IRE) (b 1999)	Shernazar (b 1981)	Busted / Sharmeen
		Crazy Rose (b 1981)	Son of Silver / Vieille Phoebe

The sturdy Airlie Beach is the third foal and now the best of four winners, all trained by Mullins, out of her dam Screaming Witness. Airlie Beach was preceded by bumper and two-mile hurdle winner Dr Machini (by Dr Massini) and Valerian Bridge (by Heron Island) who showed smart form when winning all three of his bumpers for Gigginstown in the 2014/15 season but wasn't seen again. Airlie Beach's year-younger half-sister Screaming Rose (by Darsi) showed useful form over hurdles in the latest season, winning twice at Killarney in the summer and running her best race when third in a big field in a three-mile handicap at the Punchestown Festival. Screaming Witness ran just twice in bumpers in Jackie Mullins' colours, providing son Patrick with his very first ride under Rules on her debut and improving

Miguel Angel (left) and Airlie Beach (right) flank their 'lovechild' at Willie Mullins' yard in the summer of 2016

on that when finishing fourth at Punchestown on the second occasion. Airlie Beach's unraced grandam Crazy Rose produced a couple of ordinary winners in France and a winning pointer but she is also the grandam of Irish hurdler Our Girl Salley and staying chaser Loch Ba, both of them useful. Crazy Rose was also a half-sister to La Tarasque, a leading four-year-old hurdler of her generation in France (placed in the Alain du Breil and Renaud du Vivier), and to the dam of the useful hurdler/chaser Sphinx du Berlais who finished fourth in the Grande Course de Haies, the French Champion Hurdle. As for Airlie Beach's own foal, who is now a four-year-old, he was being advertised for sale by the Mullins stable in the summer of 2017. Airlie Beach, who stays twenty-one furlongs and acts on soft ground, has now embarked on a more conventional broodmare career. She was reported to be in foal to Mount Nelson when finishing third on her Flat debut in a maiden at Killarney in July. *W. P. Mullins, Ireland*

AIR NAVIGATOR 6 b.g. Yeats (IRE) – Lox Lane (IRE) (Presenting) [2016/17 b16.8s* Feb 12] fifth foal: dam unraced half-sister to fair hurdler/useful chaser (stayed 3m) Duncliffe: 12/1, won bumper at Exeter (by 1¼ lengths from Harefield) on debut. *Tom George*   **b101**

AIR OF GLORY (IRE) 7 ch.g. Shamardal (USA) – Balloura (USA) (Swain (IRE)) [2016/17 h91: h15.3dpu h16.6g Jan 27] maiden hurdler, no form in 2016/17: unproven beyond 2m: acts on soft going: in headgear last 5 starts: has worn tongue tie. *John Spearing*   **h–**

AIRPUR DESBOIS (FR) 7 b.g. Canyon Creek (IRE) – Hero's Dancer (FR) (Hero's Honor (USA)) [2016/17 h99, b80: h21mpu h25.6g4 h23.8vpu h19.9v2 h20.6vpu c20.9dpu Mar 25] modest maiden hurdler: pulled up in novice handicap on chasing debut: left Charlie Mann after third start: stays 3m: acts on heavy going: usually wears cheekpieces: in tongue tie last 3 starts. *Oliver Greenall*   **c–** **h92**

AISLABIE (FR) 4 gr.g. Soldier of Fortune (IRE) – Someries (FR) (Kendor (FR)) [2016/17 h15.7gur h15.6g3 h16s* h16.7spu Feb 19] dam half-sister to useful French hurdler/fairly useful chaser (2¼m-2½m winner) Trespass: fair maiden on Flat, stays 12.5f: fair form over hurdles: won juvenile at Wetherby in December. *Mark Walford*   **h110**

AKA DOUN (FR) 6 b.g. Smadoun (FR) – Akar Baby (Akarad (FR)) [2016/17 h100: h15.8g May 14] sturdy gelding: maiden hurdler: best effort at 23f: acts on heavy going: often in headgear. *Emma Lavelle*   **h72**

AKAVIT (IRE) 5 b.g. Vale of York (IRE) – Along Came Molly (Dr Fong (USA)) [2016/17 **h–**
h119: h19.9vᵖᵘ h18.5s Dec 15] compact gelding: fairly useful hurdler at best, no form in
handicaps in 2016/17: unproven beyond 2m: acts on soft going: tried in cheekpieces:
usually leads. *Ed de Giles*

AKULA (IRE) 10 ch.g. Soviet Star (USA) – Danielli (IRE) (Danehill (USA)) [2016/17 c–, **c88**
h104x: h15.7v⁴ h15.8s⁶ h15.8v⁵ h15.5g⁴ h16d² h15.7d* h15.7s* h16v c15.2d³ Mar 31] **h103**
angular gelding: fair handicap hurdler: won selling events at Southwell in February and
Catterick in March: maiden chaser, usually let down by jumping in earlier days: unproven
beyond 17f: acts on good to firm and heavy going: has worn headgear, including last 5
starts: tried in tongue tie: front runner/races prominently. *Barry Leavy*

AL ALFA 10 ch.g. Alflora (IRE) – Two For Joy (IRE) (Mandalus) [2016/17 c128, h122: **c131**
c21g⁴ c20g* c21m³ Apr 15] workmanlike gelding: fairly useful hurdler: useful handicap **h–**
chaser: won at Worcester (by ¾ length from Presenting Arms) in May: stays 3m: acts on
heavy going: tried in tongue tie. *Philip Hobbs*

ALAMEDA 6 b.m. Indian Danehill (IRE) – Madge Carroll (IRE) (Hollow Hand) [2016/17 **h88**
b15.8m⁴ b16.3m h21v h21s² Mar 16] second foal: dam (c111/h94) 2½m-25f hurdle/chase **b75**
winner: modest form in bumpers: better effort over hurdles when second in mares novice
at Towcester in March: should be suited by further than 21f. *Henry Daly*

ALAMEIN (IRE) 7 b.g. Beneficial – Lady of Appeal (IRE) (Lord of Appeal) [2016/17 **c134**
h16ᵘʳ h16.5g³ h16s c17v* c20s⁴ c18s³ Mar 25] €45,000 3-y-o: fourth foal: brother to fairly **h119**
useful hurdler/winning pointer Quiet Candid (2m/17f winner) and fair chaser Easyondeye
(21f winner): dam unraced half-sister to useful staying chaser Midnight Caller: bumper
winner: fairly useful hurdler: useful form over fences: won maiden at Fairyhouse (by 8½
lengths from Dicosimo) in February: unproven beyond 17f: best form on soft/heavy going:
wears cheekpieces/tongue tie: front runner/races prominently. *M. F. Morris, Ireland*

ALANJOU (FR) 7 b.g. Maresca Sorrento (FR) – Partie Time (FR) (Nononito (FR)) **c101 §**
[2016/17 c84, h62: c23m³ c21.1dᵖᵘ c23d⁵ c23g² c25.7m⁵ c23.8g³ c23.8gᵖᵘ Nov 28] close- **h–**
coupled gelding: maiden hurdler: fair handicap chaser: stays 3m: acts on heavy going:
usually wears headgear: temperamental. *Henry Tett*

ALARY (FR) 7 ch.g. Dream Well (FR) – Cate Bleue (FR) (Katowice (FR)) [2016/17 **c161 ?**
c23.4s² c29.8s³ c21.4s⁶ c21.9d³ c27.3s² c24.1sᵖᵘ c24.2sᶠ c20.8g⁶ Mar 16] half-brother to **h–**
several winners in France, including winning hurdler/useful chaser Musica Bella (17f-21f
winner, by Bateau Rouge), stayed 27f: dam, winning chaser up to 25f in Italy (also French
bumper winner), half-sister to dam of smart staying chaser Iris Bleu: maiden hurdler: high-
class chaser: third in Grand Steeple-Chase de Paris (9 lengths behind So French) in May
and Prix Heros XII (1¾ lengths behind Milord Thomas) in October, and second in Prix La
Haye Jousselin (½ length behind Milord Thomas) in November, all at Auteuil: left
Francois-Marie Cottin and below best after fifth start: stays 3¾m: acts on soft going: wears
tongue tie. *Colin Tizzard*

ALASKAN POET 5 b.g. Yeats (IRE) – Takotna (IRE) (Bering) [2016/17 b17.7d² b17.7g³ **b86**
Nov 28] fair form when placed in bumpers: dead. *Alan King*

A L'ASSEAU (FR) 5 b.g. Assessor (IRE) – En Piste (FR) (Pistolet Bleu (IRE)) [2016/17 **h–**
b16s h19.5v h16s h16.3g Apr 1] well beaten in maiden bumper/over hurdles: tried in **b–**
tongue tie. *Evan Williams*

A LASTING JOY 6 b.m. Refuse To Bend (IRE) – Sir Kyffin's Folly (Dansili) [2016/17 **b–**
b–: b15.8d Feb 9] no form in bumpers. *Jonathan Geake*

ALBATROS DE GUYE (FR) 7 ch.g. Maille Pistol (FR) – Balibirds (FR) (Bricassar **c60**
(USA)) [2016/17 c86, h–: c22.5vᵖᵘ c25.7d⁴ c23.6dᵖᵘ c23.6sᵖᵘ h19.2v h19.8vᵖᵘ Mar 9] **h–**
sturdy gelding: maiden hurdler: modest handicap chaser: out of sorts in 2016/17: stays
2½m: acts on soft going: has worn headgear, including in 2016/17: usually wears tongue
tie. *Anna Newton-Smith*

ALBEROBELLO (IRE) 9 b.g. Old Vic – Tourist Attraction (IRE) (Pollerton) [2016/17 **c122**
c124, h120: c22.6d* Mar 25] stocky gelding: fairly useful hurdler: fairly useful handicap **h–**
chaser: won at Stratford in March after 12-month absence/change of yard: stays 3½m: acts
on good to firm and heavy going: wears tongue tie: front runner/races prominently.
Nicky Martin

ALBERTA (IRE) 8 ch.g. Choisir (AUS) – Akita (IRE) (Foxhound (USA)) [2016/17 h114: **h113**
h16s⁶ h15.9g² h16g⁶ Nov 7] fairly useful on Flat, stays 1½m: bumper winner: fair maiden
hurdler: should be suited by further than 2m: acts on soft going: in visor last 3 starts.
Jim Best

ALBERT D'OLIVATE (FR) 7 b.g. Alberto Giacometti (IRE) – Komunion (FR) **c112**
(Luchiroverte (IRE)) [2016/17 c–, h110: c24.2s³ c24v⁶ c23.6s⁴ h23.9s h23.1d Feb 24] **h95**
good-topped gelding: fair handicap hurdler, disappointing last 2 starts: fair form over
fences: stays 3m: best form on soft/heavy going: wears headgear: usually races prominently.
Robert Walford

ALBERT HERRING 5 b.g. Tobougg (IRE) – Balsamita (FR) (Midyan (USA)) [2016/17 **h89**
h92: h22mpu h17.7g⁶ h20g Sep 6] modest maiden hurdler: stays 2¼m: best form on good
going: usually races prominently. *Jonathan Portman*

ALBERTO'S DREAM 8 b.g. Fantastic Spain (USA) – Molly's Folly (My Lamb) **c79**
[2016/17 c105, h–: c20.3spu c20.3s² h23v h23.8d⁴ h25d⁶ Feb 9] modest handicap hurdler: **h85**
fair handicap chaser: below best in 2016/17: best up to 21f: acts on heavy going: in
cheekpieces last 4 starts. *Tom Symonds*

AL BOUM PHOTO (FR) 5 b.g. Buck's Boum (FR) – Al Gane (FR) (Dom Alco (FR)) **h142**
[2016/17 h20v³ h16d⁴ h20s* h24d⁵ Apr 26] first foal: dam, unraced, out of half-sister to
Scottish Grand National winner Al Co and to dam of top-class hurdler/high-class chaser up
to 3m Grands Crus: useful form over hurdles: won maiden at Thurles in January and Grade 2
novice at Fairyhouse (by 4 lengths from Stand Up And Fight) in April: trained on debut
(fell) in 2015/16 by Emmanuel Clayeux: should stay further than 2½m: acts on soft going:
often travels strongly. *W. P. Mullins, Ireland*

ALCALA (FR) 7 gr.g. Turgeon (USA) – Pail Mel (FR) (Sleeping Car (FR)) [2016/17 **c134**
h126: h26.5g⁶ c20v³ c20.9vF c20d³ c23.8m* c21.1g³ Apr 21] tall gelding: fairly useful **h115**
handicap hurdler: useful form over fences: won novice handicap at Ludlow in April: stays
3m: acts on good to firm and heavy going: has worn hood, including usually in 2016/17:
wears tongue tie: often races towards rear. *Paul Nicholls*

ALCANAR (USA) 4 ch.g. Teofilo (IRE) – Badalona (Cape Cross (IRE)) [2016/17 h16s³ **h107**
h16s⁴ h16.3s⁴ Mar 3] fair maiden on Flat, stays 1½m: fair form over hurdles: best effort
when fourth in juvenile at Warwick in January: likely to stay further than 2m. *Tony Carroll*

ALCATRAZ (IRE) 5 b.g. Camacho – Spring Opera (IRE) (Sadler's Wells (USA)) **h–**
[2016/17 h15.9gpu Oct 31] fairly useful on Flat, stays 1½m: pulled up in maiden on
hurdling debut. *George Baker*

ALCHIMIX (FR) 7 b.g. Al Namix (FR) – Julie Noire (FR) (Agent Bleu (FR)) [2016/17 **c82**
h79: h19.3m² h22.1m h22.1d⁶ c20.5spu c16.9d⁶ c16.4d⁶ c15.9s⁴ c19.3d² c15.7spu c21.1vF **h87**
c19.3vpu Feb 23] modest maiden hurdler: poor maiden chaser: stays 19f: acts on good to
firm and good to soft going: in cheekpieces last 5 starts: tried in tongue tie. *Micky Hammond*

ALCOCK AND BROWN (IRE) 5 b.g. Oasis Dream – Heart Stopping (USA) (Chester **h119**
House (USA)) [2016/17 h16d² h16m* h16g* h20g³ h17.9s⁴ h16.5g Mar 30] fair on Flat,
stays 1½m: fairly useful form over hurdles: won maiden and novice at Worcester in July:
probably stays 2½m: acts on soft and good to firm going: often travels strongly. *Dan Skelton*

AL CO (FR) 12 ch.g. Dom Alco (FR) – Carama (FR) (Tip Moss (FR)) [2016/17 c127, **c137 d**
h101: c24s⁵ c25g* c26.1gur c24.2s c26spu c31.8g Apr 22] smallish, angular gelding: fair **h–**
hurdler: useful handicap chaser: won at Aintree in May, standout effort in 2016/17: stays
4m: acts on any going: has worn headgear, including last 5 starts. *Peter Bowen*

ALDEBURGH 8 b.g. Oasis Dream – Orford Ness (Selkirk (USA)) [2016/17 h104: h16.5s **h–**
h16.2g Apr 26] compact gelding: fairly useful on Flat, stays 1½m: maiden hurdler, well
held in handicaps in 2016/17. *Nigel Twiston-Davies*

ALDERBROOK LAD (IRE) 11 ch.g. Alderbrook – Alone Tabankulu (IRE) (Phardante **c132**
(FR)) [2016/17 c141, h–: c21.2mur c21.2d² c25.5d² c25.5d c23.8d⁶ c19.4m c19.3d Nov 8] **h–**
winning hurdler: useful handicap chaser: second at Cartmel in June and July: lost form
after: stays 25f: acts on good to firm and heavy going: tried in hood/tongue tie: front
runner/races prominently. *Micky Hammond*

ALDERLEY HEIGHTS 8 b.m. Windsor Heights – Alderley Girl (Footloose Esquire) **h91**
[2016/17 h89: h22g² h21.6gpu Oct 20] modest handicap hurdler: will stay beyond 23f: acts
on heavy going. *Polly Gundry*

AL DESTOOR 7 ch.g. Teofilo (IRE) – In A Silent Way (IRE) (Desert Prince (IRE)) **h104**
[2016/17 h19.9s h15.7s⁵ Dec 17] close-coupled gelding: fairly useful on Flat, stays 11f:
maiden hurdler: stays 19f: acts on heavy going: has worn hood: often in tongue tie.
Jennie Candlish

ALELCHI INOIS (FR) 9 b.g. Night Tango (GER) – Witness Gama (FR) (Take Risks **c157**
(FR)) [2016/17 c149, h124: c22g* c22.5g² c22.5g* c24.9g³ c20d* c20d⁴ c21v⁴ c30.2d **h–**
c30.2gpu c21.1gpu Apr 7] well-made gelding: winning hurdler: very smart chaser: won
minor events at Punchestown (by length from Sadler's Risk) in June and Galway (by 32

lengths from Clarcam) in July, and Clonmel Oil Chase (by 5 lengths from Clarcam) in November: second in Galway Plate (1¼ lengths behind Lord Scoundrel) 4 days before second success: stays 3m: acts on soft and good to firm going: usually races nearer last than first. *W. P. Mullins, Ireland*

ALEXANDER OATS 14 b.g. Insan (USA) – Easter Oats (Oats) [2016/17 c–, h–: c20.1d^{pu} Apr 30] close-coupled gelding: maiden hurdler: fair chaser at best, no show either start in April 2016 after long absence: stays 25f: acts on heavy going: wears headgear: temperamental. *Robert Goldie*   c– §
h–

ALEXANDER THE GREY 6 gr.g. Fair Mix (IRE) – Cadourova (FR) (Cadoudal (FR)) [2016/17 b69p: b13.6d h15.8m^4 h16g^3 h15.8d^4 h19m^4 h18.6m^3 Apr 17] poor form in bumpers: fair form over hurdles: stays 19f: acts on good to firm going: in hood last 5 starts. *Graeme McPherson*   h104
b–

ALEX DE LARREDYA (FR) 7 b.g. Crillon (FR) – Kin d'Estruval (FR) (Panoramic) [2016/17 h21.4s* h21.4s^3 h25.4d^2 h19.4d* h19.4d^2 h23.9s* h24.4d^5 h19.4s^4 h19.4s^4 Apr 17] compact gelding: fourth foal: half-brother to French 13f bumper winner Royal Kin (by Adnaan): dam French 17f/2¼m chase winner: high-class hurdler: successful at Auteuil in Grande Course de Haies de Printemps (Group 3 handicap) in May, Prix de Compiegne (by 7 lengths from Ballotin) in September and Grand Prix d'Automne (by 7 lengths from Solway) in November: second in Grande Course de Haies d'Auteuil (2 lengths behind Ptit Zig) in June 2016 and runner-up again (in first-time blinkers, beaten 1½ lengths by L'Ami Serge) in latest renewal after end of British season: below form in Long Walk Hurdle at Ascot seventh outing: winning chaser: stays 25f: acts on heavy going: has worn tongue tie. *Francois Nicolle, France*   c–
h160

ALF 'N' DOR (IRE) 6 ch.g. Flemensfirth (USA) – Greenflag Princess (IRE) (Executive Perk) [2016/17 b98: h21g^3 h23.1v^3 h20d^2 h23.3v^4 h20.5s^5 h20v* h20v^3 h20d^4 Apr 16] bumper winner: fairly useful handicap hurdler: won at Ffos Las in March: stays 23f: acts on heavy going: usually in cheekpieces/tongue tie: often travels strongly. *Peter Bowen*   h115

ALFIBOY 7 b.g. Alflora (IRE) – Cloudy Pearl (Cloudings (IRE)) [2016/17 h103p: c16.2v^{pu} Dec 31] workmanlike gelding: runner-up in novice in 2015/16, only outing over hurdles: pulled up in novice on chasing debut: in hood last 2 starts: joined Sue Smith. *Paul Webber*   c–
h–

ALFIE'S CHOICE (IRE) 5 b.g. Shantou (USA) – Bally Bolshoi (IRE) (Bob Back (USA)) [2016/17 b84: h19.9s h15.8s^3 h15.8d^5 h23.1d^3 Mar 21] fair form over hurdles: will stay 3m+. *Kim Bailey*   h108

ALFIE SPINNER (IRE) 12 b.g. Alflora (IRE) – Little Red Spider (Bustino) [2016/17 c133, h–: c26.7s* c26.2s^4 c33.4s Mar 18] good-topped gelding: winning hurdler: useful handicap chaser: won at Wincanton (by 3 lengths from Abracadabra Sivola) in January: stays 4m: acts on heavy going: in cheekpieces/tongue tie last 4 starts: often leads. *Kerry Lee*   c131
h–

ALFLORA MUPPET 6 b.m. Alflora (IRE) – She's No Muppet (Teenoso (USA)) [2016/17 b16v b16.6d Jan 28] £600 5-y-o: second foal: dam (h93) unreliable bumper/17f/2½m hurdle winner: well beaten in bumpers: left Gay Kelleway after first start. *Martin Smith*   b–

ALFRED OATS 13 b.g. Alflora (IRE) – Easter Oats (Oats) [2016/17 c–: c21.5s^2 c24.3v^2 Jan 16] modest maiden chaser: stays 25f: best form on soft/heavy going: in tongue tie last 5 starts. *Robert Goldie*   c85

ALFREDO (IRE) 5 ch.g. Arcano (IRE) – Western Sky (Barathea (IRE)) [2016/17 b100: b13.6d Apr 29] won first of 2 starts in bumpers: useful on Flat, stays 16.5f, won 4 handicaps later in 2016. *Seamus Durack*   b–

ALFRED ROLLER (IRE) 5 b.g. Mahler – Cointosser (IRE) (Nordico (USA)) [2016/17 b17.1d h16.7v h16s^5 h15.9d h16s^6 h20.3s^6 h23.1d^{pu} Mar 21] €30,000 3-y-o, £50,000 4-y-o: half-brother to 3 winners, including fair hurdler Spinning Coin (17f winner, by Mujahid) and a winning pointer by Oscar: dam (h104), 2m/17f hurdle winner, also 7f/1m winner on Flat: third in Irish maiden point on debut: tailed off in bumper: modest form over hurdles: unproven beyond 2m: acts on soft going. *Jonjo O'Neill*   h94
b–

AL GUWAIR (IRE) 7 b.g. Shirocco (GER) – Katariya (IRE) (Barathea (IRE)) [2016/17 h67: h21.4m^{pu} h21.6g^{pu} h19.1g Aug 18] maiden hurdler, no form in 2016/17: dead. *Mark Hoad*   h–

ALHAMAREER (IRE) 5 ch.g. Teofilo (IRE) – Ribot's Guest (IRE) (Be My Guest (USA)) [2016/17 h103: h19.6g h19.9g h15.7g Oct 3] angular gelding: maiden hurdler, well held in hood: often races prominently. *Paul Webber*   h–

ALIANDY (IRE) 6 b.g. Presenting – Water Rock (El Conquistador) [2016/17 h106p, b84: h20.3d* h19.4g^2 h23.9s^2 h21.2s^4 Mar 2] good-topped gelding: fair handicap hurdler: won at Southwell in November: stays 3m: acts on soft going: often races in rear. *Kim Bailey*   h114

ALI

ALIBI DE SIVOLA (FR) 7 b.g. Shaanmer (IRE) – Neva de Sivola (FR) (Blushing Flame (USA)) [2016/17 h126p: h21gpu h23.5mpu Apr 2] fairly useful hurdle winner, pulled up both starts in handicaps in 2016/17 after long absence/change of yards. *Nicky Henderson* **h–**

ALI BIN NAYEF 5 b.g. Nayef (USA) – Maimoona (IRE) (Pivotal) [2016/17 h15.8g³ h16m h16.7g⁶ h15.8gpu h20g⁴ Oct 26] modest on Flat, stays 1¾m: similar form over hurdles only on debut: tried in cheekpieces: front runner/races prominently: sold to join John Joseph Hanlon £4,800 in March. *Michael Wigham* **h92**

ALICE OF GLEVUM 5 b.m. Kirkwall – Lady Busted (Almoojid) [2016/17 b15.7d b16g Aug 11] fourth foal: dam (h61) maiden hurdler (stayed 2¾m): no form in bumpers: tried in hood. *Dominic Ffrench Davis* **b–**

ALICE THORNTON 5 b.m. Hurricane Run (IRE) – Alice Alleyne (IRE) (Oasis Dream) [2016/17 b16.2d Jun 11] €1,000 4-y-o: first foal: dam 6f/7f winner: fairly useful on Flat, stays 1m, won twice in 2016: tailed off in bumper on debut. *Martin Todhunter* **b–**

ALISIER D'IRLANDE (FR) 7 br.g. Kapgarde (FR) – Isati's (FR) (Chamberlin (FR)) [2016/17 c151+, h–p: c16g³ c20dur c17d⁵ h16s⁶ c16v* c15.8g Apr 6] good sort: winning hurdler: smart chaser: won Grade 3 event at Naas (by 10 lengths from Pairofbrowneyes) in February: unproven beyond 17f: acts on heavy going: tried in hood: wears tongue tie: front runner/races prominently. *Henry de Bromhead, Ireland* **c149 h–**

A LITTLE MAGIC (IRE) 6 b.g. Kayf Tara – Debut (IRE) (Presenting) [2016/17 h113p: h21.6g h16.3g³ h16.3g⁴ c16gur c16.5g c16.5d* c15.7g* c18.2g³ c21.4m* Apr 9] fairly useful hurdler, below best first 3 starts in 2016/17: useful form over fences: won handicaps at Huntingdon in December, Catterick in January and Market Rasen in April, 2 of them novice events: stays 21f: acts on good to firm and good to soft going: usually wears hood: in tongue tie last 2 starts: front runner/races prominently, often freely. *Jonjo O'Neill* **c135 h103**

ALIZEE DE JANEIRO (FR) 7 b.m. Network (GER) – Katana (GER) (Funambule (USA)) [2016/17 h107: c16d⁴ c21.5gF c15.6vpu h18.1s⁵ h19.4g* h21.4vpu h18.1d³ Apr 10] fair handicap hurdler: won mares event at Musselburgh in March: modest form only completed start over fences: stays 19f: acts on heavy going: in cheekpieces last 3 starts. *Lucinda Russell* **c99 h105**

ALIZEE JAVILEX (FR) 7 b.m. Le Fou (IRE) – Etoile du Lion (FR) (New Target) [2016/17 h98p, b103: h20.6g⁵ h21.2d² h15.5g⁴ h15.8v⁶ h18.6s⁴ h15.8g⁵ Apr 17] bumper winner: modest maiden hurdler: stays 21f: acts on heavy going. *Lucy Wadham* **h96**

ALKAJAZZ (IRE) 7 b.m. Alkaadhem – Northern Jazz (IRE) (Tiraaz (USA)) [2016/17 h22.1g⁴ Jun 1] third foal: dam unraced half-sister to useful hurdler/fairly useful chaser (stayed 3¼m) Cokenny Boy: maiden pointer: 3/1, fourth in mares maiden at Cartmel (31¾ lengths behind Tullyglush) on hurdling debut: wore tongue tie. *Stuart Crawford, Ireland* **h65**

ALLA SVELTA (IRE) 11 b.g. Milan – Miss Greinton (GER) (Greinton) [2016/17 c103, h94: h23.1spu h19.2v h21.2g h21.9dpu Apr 16] sturdy gelding: fairly useful hurdler at best, no form in 2016/17: maiden chaser: has worn headgear, including in 2016/17: has worn tongue tie. *Sheila Lewis* **c– h–**

ALLBARNONE 9 b.g. Alflora (IRE) – What A Gem (Karinga Bay) [2016/17 h110: h22.1m* h22.1d² h20d⁵ h21.1s c19.1s² c20s⁵ c20.3g³ Apr 22] good-topped gelding: fairly useful handicap hurdler: won at Cartmel in May: similar form in small-field events over fences: probably stays 3m: acts on good to firm and good to soft going. *William Kinsey* **c120 h116**

ALLBLAK DES PLACES (FR) 5 b.g. Full of Gold (FR) – Amiraute (FR) (Septieme Ciel (USA)) [2016/17 h143p: h20v⁵ h16g h21.1d h20.5d Apr 29] smallish, angular gelding: useful hurdler at best, no form in 2016/17: tried in tongue tie. *W. P. Mullins, Ireland* **h–**

ALL BUT GREY 11 gr.g. Baryshnikov (AUS) – Butleigh Rose (Nicholas Bill) [2016/17 c101, h–: h18.5m h19.8dpu h16.5g h19s⁵ h19g h19.8v h23.9g⁶ c21m³ Apr 15] compact gelding: poor handicap hurdler/chaser nowadays: stays 21f: acts on good to firm and heavy going: wears tongue tie. *Carroll Gray* **c79 h70**

ALLCHILLEDOUT 8 b.g. Alflora (IRE) – Miss Chinchilla (Perpendicular) [2016/17 h101: c20vpu c23.6s* c23.6s² c24v⁴ c23.6spu Mar 13] sturdy gelding: fair hurdler: fair form over fences: won novice handicap at Chepstow in January: stays 3m: best form on soft/heavy going: in blinkers last 4 starts: wears tongue tie: front runner/races prominently, usually travels strongly. *Colin Tizzard* **c112 h–**

ALL CURRENCIES (IRE) 5 b.m. Getaway (GER) – Splendid Presence (IRE) (Presenting) [2016/17 b15.7d b15.7s³ b15.8s⁶ b16g⁶ Apr 24] €12,500 3-y-o: third foal: dam unraced: won Irish maiden point on debut: fair form in bumpers, standout effort when third at Ascot: left Suzy Smith after first start: tried in hood. *Gary Moore* **b87**

ALL DOLLED UP (IRE) 5 b.m. Aussie Rules (USA) – All On Sugar (GER) (Red **h–** Ransom (USA)) [2016/17 h15.8g^{pu} h15.8d⁶ Apr 16] modest maiden on Flat, stays 1m: no form over hurdles. *Sarah-Jayne Davies*

ALL DOWNHILL (IRE) 7 b.g. Indian Danehill (IRE) – Socialite Girl (Glacial Storm **b81** (USA)) [2016/17 b16.8m b16.8m³ b16.8g Oct 7] second foal: dam, little form, half-sister to fairly useful hurdler/useful chaser (stays 3m) Wizards Bridge: modest form in bumpers: easily best effort when third at Newton Abbot: in tongue tie last 2 starts. *William Reed*

ALLEE BLEUE (IRE) 7 ch.g. Mount Nelson – Murrieta (Docksider (USA)) [2016/17 **h131** h130: h16.8g h16d⁵ h20.5v* h19.6d² h19.9s^{pu} h20g Apr 7] well-made gelding: useful handicap hurdler: won at Leicester in February: stays 2½m: best form on soft/heavy going: front runner/races prominently. *Philip Hobbs*

ALLEGRI (IRE) 8 b.g. Key of Luck (USA) – Bermuxa (FR) (Linamix (FR)) [2016/17 **h–** h–: h15.8m^{pu} Oct 2] maiden on Flat: no show both starts over hurdles. *Alan Coogan*

ALLELU ALLELUIA (GER) 6 b.g. Doyen (IRE) – Anna Spectra (Spectrum **h112 p** (IRE)) [2016/17 h–: h20d* h20g² Jul 26] fair form over hurdles: won maiden at Aintree in June: open to further improvement. *Jonjo O'Neill*

ALLEZ COOL (IRE) 8 ch.g. Flemensfirth (USA) – La Fisarmonica (IRE) (Accordion) **c105** [2016/17 h–: c24.2s^{pu} c24.2d⁶ c24.2s^{pu} c23.4v^{ur} c26.3g⁶ c20.9d* c30.6g⁶ Apr 28] winning **h–** hurdler: fair handicap chaser: won novice event at Carlisle in April: stays 25f: acts on heavy going: in headgear last 4 starts: front runner/races prominently. *George Bewley*

ALLEZ JACQUES (IRE) 5 b.g. Robin des Champs (FR) – Crystal Stream (IRE) (Dr **h92** Massini (IRE)) [2016/17 b17.7g⁴ b16s h18.7g⁴ Mar 25] £62,000 3-y-o: third foal: dam, ran **b86** once in bumper, half-sister to fairly useful hurdlers Native Shore (stayed 2½m) and Bin It (stayed 3m): fair form in bumpers: better effort when fourth at Plumpton: 15/2, fourth in maiden at Stratford (10 lengths behind Cornish Warrior) on hurdling debut. *Emma Lavelle*

ALLEZ SEA (IRE) 5 br.g. Sea The Stars (IRE) – Alizaya (IRE) (Highest Honor (FR)) **b105** [2016/17 b71: b16g³ b16m* h16.4s⁴ Nov 13] sturdy gelding: useful form in bumpers: won maiden at Fairyhouse in October: fourth in listed event at Cheltenham (2¾ lengths behind Poetic Rhythm) month later. *James Leavy, Ireland*

ALLEZ VIC (IRE) 11 b.g. Old Vic – Newgate Fairy (Flair Path) [2016/17 c124, h121: **c100** c21.2g⁵ c22.5s⁴ c23.6d c23.8g⁵ c23.8v⁴ h19.5s h23v⁵ Feb 20] lengthy gelding: fairly useful **h94** hurdler/maiden chaser at best, well below that in 2016/17: stays 3m: acts on heavy going: has worn headgear. *Evan Williams*

ALL FIRED UP (IRE) 10 b.g. Mr Combustible (IRE) – Hannah's Retreat (IRE) **c–** (Houmayoun (FR)) [2016/17 c74, h–: c23.8m^{pu} Oct 20] maiden hurdler: maiden chaser, **h–** lightly raced since 2014/15: usually wears headgear. *Evan Williams*

ALL FOR THE BEST (IRE) 5 b.g. Rip Van Winkle (IRE) – Alleluia (Caerleon (USA)) **h116** [2016/17 h16.7g³ h15.8g⁴ h15.8d* h16m h19.9d* h19.9d* h21.4s⁶ h20.5g² Apr 22] closely related to fairly useful hurdler/fair chaser Tugboat (2½m-3m winner, by Galileo): fairly useful on Flat, stays 16.5f: fairly useful hurdler: won novice at Uttoxeter in July and handicap at Sedgefield in December: stays 2½m: acts on good to soft going: tried in cheekpieces/tongue tie. *Robert Stephens*

ALLFREDANDNOBELL (IRE) 4 b.g. Alfred Nobel (IRE) – Its In The Air (IRE) **h107** (Whipper (USA)) [2016/17 h15.7g³ h16s* h15.7s⁵ h16.8g³ h16g Apr 23] modest maiden on Flat, stays 1¼m: fair form over hurdles: won juvenile maiden at Wetherby in January: raced around 2m: acts on soft going. *Micky Hammond*

ALL GREAT N THEORY (IRE) 11 b.g. Old Vic – Miss Compliance (IRE) (Broken **c92** Hearted) [2016/17 c120, c23.6v⁵ Mar 23] multiple point winner: twice-raced in hunter chases, better effort when second in maiden in 2013/14. *Mrs Julie Wadland*

ALL HELL LET LOOSE (IRE) 8 b.g. Shantou (USA) – Gan Ainm (IRE) (Mujadil **c125** (USA)) [2016/17 c120, h135: h20d⁵ c19.9g* c20.4g^{pu} c24s³ c21.2d^F Apr 9] useful-looking **h–** gelding: useful hurdler: fairly useful form over fences: won maiden at Kilbeggan in June: left Ms Sandra Hughes after first start: barely stays 3m: acts on heavy going: has worn headgear: wears tongue tie: front runner/races prominently. *Henry de Bromhead, Ireland*

ALL IS GOOD (IRE) 5 b.g. Scorpion (IRE) – Peinture Rose (IRE) (Marathon (USA)) **h107** [2016/17 h16.7g² h16.7d³ Apr 27] second foal: dam unraced half-sister to fairly useful hurdler (stays 2½m) Whatsthatallabout: fell in Irish maiden point on debut: fair form when placed in novice hurdles at Market Rasen: likely to stay 2½m: wears hood. *Robin Dickin*

ALL KINGS (IRE) 8 b.g. Milan – Rilmount (IRE) (Roselier (FR)) [2016/17 h111: **h–** §
h23.9g[pu] h23.1d Feb 24] lengthy gelding: placed in Irish maiden points: maiden hurdler,
standout effort when second in novice in 2015/16: stays 23f: tried in tongue tie: ungenuine.
Harry Fry

ALL MY LOVE (IRE) 5 b.m. Lord Shanakill (USA) – Afilla (Dansili) [2016/17 h16s[F] **h115**
h16.7s* h15.7s[2] h16.7g[5] Mar 27] fairly useful from other
hurdles: won mares novice at Market Rasen in February: likely to prove best around 2m.
Pam Sly

ALLOW DALLOW 10 b.g. Gold Well – Russland (GER) (Surumu (GER)) **c118**
[2016/17 c115, h–: c24d[2] c21.1d[2] c24.1d[2] c25.8g c19.9d[3] c19.4g[3] c19.2v[pu] c16s[3] c20v[6] **h–**
c17.4v[3] c16s[pu] h19.5g Apr 17] maiden hurdler: fairly useful handicap chaser: left Jonjo
O'Neill after fifth start: stays 3m: acts on heavy going: usually wears headgear: has worn
tongue tie. *Nikki Evans*

ALL RILED UP 9 b.m. Dr Massini (IRE) – Martha Reilly (IRE) (Rainbows For Life **h80**
(CAN)) [2016/17 h79: h19g* May 2] poor handicap hurdler: won at Warwick (conditional)
in May: stays 2½m: acts on good to firm and good to soft going: usually races close up.
Harry Chisman

ALL SET TO GO (IRE) 6 gr.g. Verglas (IRE) – Firecrest (IRE) (Darshaan) [2016/17 **h142**
h131p: h15.7m[2] h16g[3] h15.8g[4] h16.6g* Dec 10] angular gelding: useful handicap hurdler:
won at Doncaster (by 4 lengths from Eyes of A Tiger) in December: raced around 2m: acts
on good to firm and heavy going: wears tongue tie: usually travels strongly. *Paul Nicholls*

ALL THE ANSWERS 6 br.g. Kayf Tara – Shatabdi (IRE) (Mtoto) [2016/17 h16.5g* **h132**
h16s[3] h16.5d* h16g[3] h16d[F] Dec 4] €30,000 3-y-o: first foal: dam (c124/h136), hurdle/
chase winner up to 2½m, also 1½m winner on Flat, closely related to high-class chaser
(stayed 21f) Rajdhani Express: bumper winner: useful hurdler: won maiden at Galway in
July and handicap there in October: raced around 2m: acts on good to soft going: wears
hood/tongue tie. *Joseph Patrick O'Brien, Ireland*

ALLTHEDOLLARS (IRE) 7 ch.g. Stowaway – Pamsy Wamsy (IRE) (Taipan (IRE)) **c–**
[2016/17 c–, h67: h19.9d[pu] Oct 2] maiden hurdler: pulled up both starts over fences: has **h–**
worn headgear: usually wears tongue tie: usually leads: temperament under suspicion.
Joanne Foster

ALLTHEGEAR NO IDEA (IRE) 10 b.g. Sayarshan (FR) – All The Gear (IRE) **c116**
(Nashamaa) [2016/17 h115: c24.1s[4] c16s[3] c15.9s[2] c20s[3] c23.8g[3] Apr 26] winning hurdler: **h–**
fairly useful form over fences: second in handicap at Leicester in March: stays 27f,
effective at much shorter: acts on heavy going: has worn hood: usually races towards rear.
Nigel Twiston-Davies

ALL THE WINDS (GER) 12 ch.g. Samum (GER) – All Our Luck (GER) (Spectrum **h85**
(IRE)) [2016/17 h–: h16g Sep 23] smallish gelding: fairly useful on Flat, stays 14.5f: fair
hurdler at best, well below that only outing in 2016/17: unproven beyond 2m: acts on soft
and good to firm going: wears tongue tie. *Shaun Lycett*

ALL TOGETHER (FR) 6 ch.g. Zambezi Sun – Mareha (IRE) (Cadeaux Genereux) **c131**
[2016/17 c131, h114: h20g[2] c16.9m[5] c18.8d[F] c20s[2] c20.8g[ur] Mar 16] compact gelding: **h114**
fair form over hurdles: useful handicap chaser: second at Sandown (2 lengths behind
Mercian Prince) in January: stays 2½m: acts on heavy going: usually races prominently.
Johnny Farrelly

ALL WE KNOW 10 b.g. Green Desert (USA) – Anniversary (Salse (USA)) [2016/17 **h–**
h19.8d[pu] Mar 26] unseated rider in point: no form in maidens on Flat/over hurdles.
Susan Gardner

ALL YOURS (FR) 6 ch.g. Halling (USA) – Fontaine Riant (FR) (Josr Algarhoud (IRE)) **c?**
[2016/17 h136: h15.7m[5] c16.5g[2] May 17] smallish, workmanlike gelding: useful handicap **h136**
hurdler: fifth in Swinton Handicap Hurdle at Haydock (6¾ lengths behind Gwafa) in May:
1/5, went as if amiss when second in novice at Huntingdon (20 lengths behind War Singer)
on chasing debut: raced around 2m: acts on good to firm and heavy going: wears hood/
tongue tie. *Paul Nicholls*

ALLYSSON MONTERG (FR) 7 b.g. Network (GER) – Mellyssa (FR) (Panoramic) **h110**
[2016/17 h131p: h25.3s Nov 12] strong gelding: will make a chaser: useful hurdler: well
held in handicap only outing in 2016/17: should stay beyond 2½m: best form on heavy
going: front runner/races prominently. *Richard Hobson*

ALMAGEST 9 br.g. Galileo (IRE) – Arabesque (Zafonic (USA)) [2016/17 h96: h19.9g **h84** §
h23.3g[6] h26.4g[pu] h23g Aug 21] modest maiden hurdler: stays 2¾m: acts on soft going:
usually in headgear/tongue tie: temperamental. *Robert Stephens*

ALMOST GEMINI (IRE) 8 gr.g. Dylan Thomas (IRE) – Streetcar (IRE) (In The Wings) [2016/17 c–, h113: h19.9g^F h19.3s^3 h19.3v^3 Mar 9] fair handicap hurdler: well beaten only outing over fences: stays 3m: acts on soft going: wears headgear. *Kenneth Slack* c– h106

ALONG CAME THEO (IRE) 7 b.g. Vertical Speed (FR) – Kachina (IRE) (Mandalus) [2016/17 h94: h19.3s^4 h19.7s^pu Dec 26] fair in bumpers: lightly raced over hurdles: bred to stay 2½m. *Andrew Crook* h80

ALOOMOMO (FR) 7 b.g. Tirwanako (FR) – Kayola (FR) (Royal Charter (FR)) [2016/17 c139p, h128: h21.6d^3 c20.8s^F Dec 10] well-made gelding: fairly useful maiden hurdler: useful chaser: held when fell 3 out in Grade 3 handicap at Cheltenham in December: stays 2¾m: acts on soft going: tried in cheekpieces: often travels strongly. *Warren Greatrex* c– h119

ALOTTARAIN (IRE) 7 b.m. Zerpour (IRE) – Alottalady (IRE) (Mandalus) [2016/17 h104: h16g h21.6g h18.7d^3 h18.7m^5 h16g^3 h16d^4 c16s^5 c17v^5 c17v^5 c17g^5 c19.2g^3 Apr 12] close-coupled mare: poor handicap hurdler: poor form over fences: stays 19f: acts on good to firm going: tried in cheekpieces: often races in rear. *Seamus Mullins* c72 h83

ALPERTON 4 ch.g. Apple Tree (FR) – Elfailwen (Afzal) [2016/17 b16s b15.8g^6 Apr 17] no form in bumpers: in tongue tie second start. *Mark Rimell* b–

ALPHA DES OBEAUX (FR) 7 b.g. Saddler Maker (IRE) – Omega des Obeaux (FR) (Saint Preuil (FR)) [2016/17 h162: h24d^3 c20s^5 c22g* c20g* c20d^3 c24d^pu c24.4g^4 c29d c24.5d^6 Apr 25] lengthy gelding: high-class hurdler: smart chaser: won maiden at Thurles (by 1½ lengths from Round Tower) in October and Grade 3 novice at Cork (by 3¼ lengths from Westerner Lady) in November: third in Drinmore Novices' Chase at Fairyhouse (4½ lengths behind Coney Island) in December: stays 3m: acts on heavy going: has worn headgear, including last 2 starts: reportedly bled sixth/seventh outings. *M. F. Morris, Ireland* c147 h–

ALPHA INDI (IRE) 6 b.g. Oscar (IRE) – High Park Lady (IRE) (Phardante (FR)) [2016/17 h19.1v h15.8d h18.7g^2 Mar 25] €35,000 3-y-o, £20,000 5-y-o: brother to useful hurdler/winning pointer Clean Sheet (2m-2½m winner) and bumper winner/useful 19f hurdle winner Nelson's Bridge and half-brother to a winning pointer by Karinga Bay: dam (c85), winning pointer, half-sister to dam of Irish Grand National winner Shutthefrontdoor: in frame all 3 starts in Irish maiden points: fair form over hurdles: best effort when second in maiden at Stratford in March: will be suited by 2½m+: open to further improvement. *James Evans* h100 p

ALPHA MALE (FR) 6 b.g. Poliglote – Arzuaga (Alflora (IRE)) [2016/17 b16g h20.5d^3 h21.6d^3 h24.5d^3 h25d^2 Mar 15] €38,000 3-y-o: compact gelding: second foal: dam unraced half-sister to fairly useful hurdler/chaser (stayed 3¼m) Mr Fluffy: mid-division in maiden bumper: fairly useful form over hurdles: seems to stay 25f. *Nicky Henderson* h120 b83

ALPHAMOR (IRE) 7 b.m. Morozov (USA) – Alphablend (IRE) (Alphabatim (USA)) [2016/17 c25.5d^5 May 12] £3,400 5-y-o: sixth foal: half-sister to fairly useful hurdler Laser Hawk (2m winner, by Rashar): dam unraced: maiden pointer: well beaten in mares hunter on chasing debut. *Mrs S. M. McPherson* c–

ALPHA VICTOR (IRE) 12 b.g. Old Vic – Harvest View (IRE) (Good Thyne (USA)) [2016/17 c99§, h113§: h24.1d h26v^pu Dec 31] workmanlike gelding: useful hurdler/chaser at best, has gone wrong way temperamentally: stays 33f: acts on heavy going: has worn cheekpieces: wears tongue tie: one to leave alone. *William Kinsey* c– § h– §

ALPINE SECRET (IRE) 5 br.g. Stowaway – Squaw Valley (IRE) (Saddlers' Hall (IRE)) [2016/17 b67: h21.4d^3 h20.3v^5 h20.5v^6 h16s h15.8g^4 h19g Apr 24] fair form over hurdles: stays 21f: acts on heavy going: often races freely. *Ben Pauling* h102

AL REESHA (IRE) 6 b.m. Kayf Tara – Simply Kitty (IRE) (Simply Great (FR)) [2016/17 b93: h16g* h21s^4 h16.2v^5 h20.7d c16.4g^F Mar 29] fair form over hurdles: won novice at Fakenham in October: fell fatally on chasing debut: best effort at 2m: in tongue tie last 2 starts: front runner/raced prominently. *Dan Skelton* c– h100

ALRIGHT CHIEF (IRE) 5 b.g. Daylami (IRE) – Lee Valley Native (IRE) (Be My Native (USA)) [2016/17 b16.8g^6 Apr 26] maiden pointer: well beaten in maiden bumper. *Mrs Jane Price* b56

ALRIGHT JOHN 10 b.g. Relief Pitcher – Sovereign's Gift (Elegant Monarch) [2016/17 c26g Apr 27] won 3 times in points: little impact in hunter chases. *Mrs Janet Ackner* c–

AL SHAHIR (IRE) 5 b.g. Robin des Champs (FR) – Sarah Massini (IRE) (Dr Massini **b104**
(IRE)) [2016/17 b17.1d² b15.7d² b16.4v* Feb 15] €38,000 3-y-o: third foal: half-brother to
bumper winner/fairly useful hurdler Mr Boss Man (2m winner, by Beneficial), stays 2½m:
dam unraced half-sister to useful hurdler/smart chaser (stays 4m) Measureofmydreams:
fairly useful form in bumpers: won maiden at Newcastle in February: bred to stay at least
2½m. *Dan Skelton*

ALTAAYIL (IRE) 6 br.g. Sea The Stars (IRE) – Alleluia (Caerleon (USA)) [2016/17 **h– p**
h16.3d h16.3s h16v⁶ Feb 4] good-topped gelding: closely related to fairly useful hurdler/
chaser Tugboat (2½m-3m winner, by Galileo): useful on Flat, stays 1¾m: left Sir Michael
Stoute £19,500/off 21 months, well held all 3 starts over hurdles: may yet do better in
handicaps. *Gary Moore*

ALTA ROCK (IRE) 12 b.g. Luso – Princess Lulu (IRE) (Carroll House) [2016/17 c92x, **c– x**
h–: h17.2g Aug 27] placed in points in 2017: fair hurdler at best: winning chaser: stays **h–**
3¼m: acts on heavy going: often let down by jumping over fences. *Sue Smith*

ALTERNATIF (FR) 7 b.g. Shaanmer (IRE) – Katerinette (FR) (Video Rock (FR)) **c129**
[2016/17 c135, h133: c25.8g⁴ c25g⁴ c23.8d c23.5g³ Dec 10] strong gelding: winning **h–**
hurdler: useful handicap chaser: regressed in 2016/17: stays 25f: acts on heavy going:
wears headgear: has worn tongue tie: temperament under suspicion. *David Pipe*

ALTESSE DE GUYE (FR) 7 ch.m. Dom Alco (FR) – Mascotte de Guye (FR) (Video **c116**
Rock (FR)) [2016/17 h116: h21.2m³ h21.1g⁵ h21.1s⁵ c20.9s² c23g² Dec 30] angular mare: **h111**
fair handicap hurdler: fairly useful form over fences when runner-up in novice handicaps:
stays 3m: acts on soft going: has worn hood, including in 2016/17: usually races nearer last
than first. *Martin Keighley*

ALTIEPIX (FR) 7 ch.g. Fragrant Mix (IRE) – Naltiepy (FR) (Dom Alco (FR)) [2016/17 **c120**
c20g³ c25g³ c25.5g³ c23.6s³ c20s³ c22.6sᵖᵘ c19.4g² Apr 23] fifth foal: dam unraced half- **h–**
sister to fairly useful hurdler/useful chaser (stayed 3¾m) Pomme Tiepy: winning hurdler:
fairly useful handicap chaser: placed all completed starts in 2016/17: left Gordon Elliott
after third one: stays 25f: acts on heavy going: usually wears headgear nowadays: in tongue
tie last 4 starts: often travels strongly. *Kerry Lee*

ALTIOR (IRE) 7 b.g. High Chaparral (IRE) – Monte Solaro (IRE) (Key of Luck **c175 p**
(USA)) [2016/17 h167p, b115: c18s* c15.5d* c16g* c16.4d* c15.9g* c15.5g* **h–**
Apr 29]

Since the start of the *Chasers & Hurdlers* series, the first of which covered
the 1975/76 season, Timeform has selected a Horse of the Year (until 2007/08 the
annual award went to the 'Timeform Champion Jumper'). The title mostly goes to
the highest rated horse in the Annual and, for much of the latest season, until he
suffered a pelvic fracture when well beaten in the Queen Mother Champion Chase,
Douvan seemed destined to pick up the award. However, Douvan's unfortunate
injury at jumping's most prestigious fixture, and his absence from the other
important spring festivals, left the door open for others. The outstanding staying
novice chaser Thistlecrack also had his campaign curtailed by injury and he was
one of several notable absentees from the Cheltenham Gold Cup which was won
by Douvan's old sparring partner Sizing John who found himself making his own
headlines after being stepped up in trip. Sizing John's unique treble in the Irish Gold
Cup, the Cheltenham Gold Cup and the Punchestown Gold Cup is celebrated on the
dust jacket of this edition of *Chasers & Hurdlers* and was one of the season's most
memorable achievements. In the end, though, the title of Timeform Horse of the
Year went to a novice for only the third time in forty-two years, with the impressive
Altior, unbeaten in six starts, following in the footsteps of Danoli in 1993/4 and
Make A Stand in 1996/7. Irish-trained Danoli famously lived up to his billing as
'one of Ireland's biggest Cheltenham bankers for many a long day' when winning
the Sun Alliance Novices' Hurdle (now officially registered as the Baring Bingham
and branded in recent times as the Neptune Investment). Danoli's standing among
the season's best hurdlers wasn't so clear after his Cheltenham win as it became
when he slammed a good line-up, including six of the Champion Hurdle field, in the
Aintree Hurdle, recording the top performance by a hurdler that season and showing
a level of form seldom attained by a novice (he was rated 172p, 1 lb in front of that
season's top-rated chaser the durable The Fellow who had won the Cheltenham Gold
Cup at the fourth attempt). Make A Stand wasn't unique in winning the Champion

Hurdle while still a novice—Royal Gait and Alderbrook had done it earlier in the 'nineties, for example—and he couldn't be rated a great champion hurdler, but his was a great story, that of a disappointing four-year-old bought out of a claimer on the Flat by trainer Martin Pipe and transformed over the next two seasons into the best hurdler in the land, an exciting jumper who usually set a scorching gallop that looked impossible to keep up with and frequently had his rivals at full stretch some way from home (he never saw another horse when winning the Champion Hurdle in which none of his opponents even got a close look at him).

The nascent chasers Sprinter Sacre and Douvan both earned exceptionally high ratings in their novice seasons, 175p and 180p respectively, the highest ratings attained by a novice chaser in the *Chasers & Hurdlers* era—until Altior joined them on the podium in the latest season. Sprinter Sacre was the best two-mile chaser in 2011/12, as well as being the best novice chaser, but the Horse of the Year award went to the staying hurdler Big Buck's who, in another unbeaten campaign, achieved his fourth win in the World [now Stayers'] Hurdle. Douvan too was the best two-mile chaser in the same year that he was best novice chaser but he was pipped to the Horse of the Year award in a vintage 2015/16 season by the best staying chaser Don Cossack, who joined Night Nurse, Monksfield, Dawn Run, Desert Orchid, Istabraq, Moscow Flyer and Kauto Star on a very select list who have been Timeform Horse of the Year over the jumps more than once.

Altior's claims to the title in the latest season were enhanced by his unbeaten record which, like those of Sprinter Sacre and Douvan in their novice season, included an impressive victory in the top race for the two-mile novice chasers, the Arkle Trophy at the Cheltenham Festival. All of Douvan's performances as a novice came against fellow novices—he completed a notable spring festival treble when adding further wins at Aintree and Punchestown—but, like Sprinter Sacre, Altior also contested races in open company, emulating his illustrious stablemate by winning the Game Spirit Chase on Betfair Hurdle day at Newbury (winning by thirteen lengths from Fox Norton who was just touched off in the Queen Mother Champion Chase before going on to win the Melling Chase at Aintree and the Champion Chase, from Un de Sceaux, at Punchestown). More significantly, long odds-on Altior rounded off his campaign with an eight-length victory over the winner of the Queen Mother Champion Chase, Special Tiara, in the Celebration Chase at Sandown's Finale meeting, arguably his best display so far and one that left the impression that even better performances are on the cards when he runs regularly in open company in the next season. Rated just superior to the season's top staying novice chaser Thistlecrack, who won the King George VI Chase, and ranked behind only Douvan in the complete list of jumpers, Altior has clearly already arrived in the top rank. Still only seven, however, he remains the sport's top prospect, though the careers of both Sprinter Sacre and Douvan have provided reminders that top performers are not immune to the all-too-prevalent injury, illness and loss of form which decimates the ranks of the jumpers each season. That said, Altior could, all being well, enrich the sport for many seasons to come, perhaps joining the illustrious list of those who have won the title of Timeform Horse of the Year more than once. He will certainly remain very hard to beat in the short term.

Altior was unbeaten in five novice hurdles in 2015/16, including the Supreme Novices' Hurdle at Cheltenham where he upset the Mullins-trained favourite Min, who was attempting to give owners Rich and Susannah Ricci their fourth successive win in the race. Like Altior and Min, Altior's stablemate Buveur d'Air was also unbeaten over hurdles and started third favourite behind that pair. Altior's seven-length victory over Min, with Buveur d'Air third, looked very strong form at the time. It looks even better now, rivalling the famous edition of 2011 which Al Ferof won from Spirit Son and the subsequent Arkle first and second Sprinter Sacre and Cue Card. There is more about the strength of the 2016 Supreme field in the essay on Min but the first three went unbeaten in the latest season, collectively winning thirteen races, and all bar one of the fourteen runners has won at least once since. The decision to send Altior chasing came as something of a surprise—he stood out as a Champion Hurdle contender—but he had been schooled over fences before being turned out for the summer, his jumping reportedly 'absolutely excellent', according to his trainer who said that the performance had given Altior's connections 'plenty of food for thought'. When Altior returned to action in the autumn, it was as a novice chaser with trainer Nicky Henderson summing him up as 'having so much scope and that's why we are chasing and not hurdling ... He's got the physique to do it and he's been exceptionally good at home.' Altior passed his early tests with flying colours, beating a sole rival in a novice event at Kempton in November on his debut and then beating Charbel, another who had run in the 2016 Supreme, impressively in the Racing Post Henry VIII Novices' Chase at Sandown in early-December, surviving a blunder at the fourth but jumping much better as the race went on. Altior completed his hat-trick in novice events in the 32Red.com Wayward Lad Novices' Chase at Kempton's Christmas meeting when his jumping was much more assured than it had been at Sandown.

Altior won his first three races over fences by a cumulative winning distance of eighty-seven lengths, facing a total of only six opponents (Marracudja contested both the Henry VIII and the Wayward Lad) and starting long odds on each time. It went without saying that he had all the attributes to go right to the top over fences and more substance was given to that view when he justified short odds in breathtaking fashion in the Game Spirit, a race branded as the Betfair Exchange Chase. As well as Fox Norton, the four-runner line-up included the former Queen

Betfair Exchange Chase (Game Spirit), Newbury—Nico de Boinville takes over after injury as Altior thumps established graded performers Fox Norton (noseband) and Dodging Bullets

Racing Post Arkle Challenge Trophy Novices' Chase, Cheltenham—Altior is left clear two out by the fall of old rival Charbel; the grey Cloudy Dream and Ordinary World fill the places

Mother Champion Chase winner Dodging Bullets, running in first-time cheekpieces in an attempt to rekindle his enthusiasm after a lengthy spell below form. Fox Norton had had three months off since winning the Grade 2 Shloer Chase (Cheltenham) in November from Simply Ned and Special Tiara on his first start for new owners Ann and Alan Potts and for trainer Colin Tizzard. Fox Norton had plenty on conceding 5 lb to Altior, but Altior could not have been more impressive, some of his jumping simply magnificent under regular jockey Nico de Boinville (Noel Fehily had deputised for the sidelined de Boinville on Altior's first three outings over fences). Altior cruised clear from four out after making the running, his wide-margin victory showing him—strictly on form—even better over fences than he had been over hurdles. There was speculation in some quarters that Altior might go for the Queen Mother Champion Chase instead of the Arkle, but—although Altior had been entered—connections passed up the prospect of a duel with Douvan, Nicky Henderson saying 'We don't see the need to go for the Champion Chase this year and the one horse you'd avoid at all costs is Douvan—though it's a lovely thought that we could be taking him on in a year's time'.

The Racing Post Arkle Trophy has had some excellent winners in the last few years including Sprinter Sacre, Simonsig, Un de Sceaux and Douvan, all of whom obliged at odds on. Altior made it five odds-on winners of the race in the last six years—he started at 4/1-on (the same odds as Douvan when he won) and also gave his trainer a record sixth win in the race (one more than Tom Dreaper). Altior won by six lengths and nine lengths from northern raider Cloudy Dream and 25/1-shot Ordinary World after being left in front by the fall of Charbel who crumpled on landing over the second last. Charbel hadn't been seen since finishing six lengths second to Altior in the Henry VIII Chase, the closest any horse had finished to Altior over fences until the Arkle. The pace-setting Charbel's advantage was being reduced when he departed and the bold-jumping Altior already looked set to take his measure. The Arkle wasn't anything like so strongly run as it can be sometimes and Altior's superiority over his closest rivals was not accurately reflected in the distances between them on the day. There was no mistaking the winner's dominance, though, as he stormed home from a staying-on Cloudy Dream, putting a further five lengths between himself and that opponent inside the final furlong alone. Altior's strength in the closing stages and at the finish has been a feature of his career so far.

Charbel's fall in the Arkle came at the sometimes-controversial second last on the Old Course which was repositioned again in the latest season. The Old Course is tighter than the New Course and used to have just the one fence in the

55

final straight, with the second last positioned on the downhill section approaching the home turn, at a point where the tempo is really being stepped up in most races. In its traditional form, it was a feared fence, one that claimed more than its share of casualties, departures often caused because the ground drops away, rather than by the fence itself. After various attempts had been made over the years to make the ground more level before and after the obstacle, the decision was taken after the 2010 Festival to move the obstacle on the grounds of safety after Citizen Vic's fatal fall at the fence (which he jumped well) when leading the field in the RSA Chase. Having two fences rather than one in the home straight on the Old Course meant that there was only a short run from the final bend to the second last, and a distance of only 133 yards between the last two fences (it is 169 yards on the New Course), which changed the character of the Old Course to a degree, presenting a different challenge for horse and rider. The re-siting of the second last hasn't been so successful as the Cheltenham management must have hoped, with seven horses at the 2016 Festival—including Vaniteux who looked like being placed in the Arkle—departing at the fence in the four steeplechases on the first day (the tally on the Tuesday at the latest Festival was four). The Cheltenham management's latest change was to move the second last ten yards or so closer to the final fence in order to give the runners a fraction longer before jumping it, though it still comes almost immediately as the runners have straightened up after rounding the home bend. There were five casualties at the newly re-sited fence at Cheltenham's first two-day meeting of the season but the change has the support of the Professional Jockeys Association and the BHA, while Cheltenham says it will continue to monitor the fence. Another change made in the latest season was to move the notorious fourth last on the New Course ten yards or so further back, closer to the left-hand bend at the top of the hill (the fence had first been moved—also nearer to the turn—eight years earlier). The races staged on the New Course include the Gold Cup, and Kauto Star fell at the troublesome fence in spectacular fashion in the 2010 edition. The third-last on the New Course, another downhill fence, has been in the news in the last two years with Cue Card falling there in the Gold Cup both years (and Silviniaco Conti fell there in the 2013 Gold Cup), but jockeys have always had more of an issue with the fourth last which is probably a little more tricky.

From the early appearances over fences of Altior, trainer Nicky Henderson was asked whether he regarded the horse as the heir apparent to Sprinter Sacre ('He's got a long way to go to fill his shoes,' Henderson had said in the run-up to the Arkle). Sprinter Sacre ran up a stunning sequence of wins in the 2012/13 season, including a nineteen-length victory in the Queen Mother Champion Chase over the 2011 winner Sizing Europe, followed by wins in the Melling Chase at Aintree and the Champion Chase at Punchestown (he was the first since Istabraq in 1999 to win championship races in the same season at the three major spring festivals, something Douvan also went on to achieve—though he did it as a novice). Sprinter Sacre ended the 2012/13 season rated 192p, the highest rating recorded over jumps in the *Chasers & Hurdlers* era, just ahead of that achieved by Kauto Star. There looked to be the prospect of even better to come, but Sprinter Sacre's career was suddenly halted by a heart condition which put him in the wilderness for a time. Against general expectation, he made a remarkable comeback in the 2015/16 season and regained the Queen Mother Champion Chase, going through the season unbeaten in four appearances. The first signs that the old Sprinter Sacre might indeed be on the way back came when he ran away with the Shloer Chase at Cheltenham on his seasonal debut. It was just two hours before the latest running of that race—in which, sadly, Sprinter Sacre's dual Cheltenham Festival-winning contemporary Simonsig broke a leg—that Sprinter Sacre's retirement was announced. Nicky Henderson explained that heat had been found in the ten-year-old's near-fore after he had worked earlier in the week and 'at his age, and where we have been, we couldn't ask him to come back next season at eleven, rising twelve'. Sprinter Sacre was paraded on the racecourse and received a tumultuous reception, the cheers having barely subsided when the stable suffered the blow of losing Simonsig.

bet365 Celebration Chase, Sandown—reigning Queen Mother Champion Chase winner Special Tiara (stars) proves no match for the outstanding novice Altior

The retirement of Sprinter Sacre, in particular, robbed Seven Barrows of one of its potential big money earners, but Nicky Henderson still ended the season as champion trainer (for the fourth time), dethroning ten-times champion Paul Nicholls after passing him at the Cheltenham Festival and never being in serious danger of being caught afterwards. After Altior's Arkle win, Buveur d'Air (who had begun the season over fences) gave Henderson a sixth winner of the Champion Hurdle, another record, while Might Bite won the following day's RSA Chase to take his trainer's total number of Cheltenham Festival wins to fifty-eight, four ahead of Willie Mullins. The latest Festival, incidentally, featured two performances that provided further testament to the brilliance of the absent Sprinter Sacre: Un de Sceaux, runner-up to Sprinter Sacre twelve months earlier in the Queen Mother Champion Chase, won the Ryanair Chase, while Special Tiara, third in that Champion Chase, won the Queen Mother Champion Chase itself. Sprinter Sacre had gone on to beat Un de Sceaux again—by fifteen lengths—in the Celebration Chase at Sandown's Finale meeting (it also turned out to be Sprinter Sacre's finale) and he featured in a parade of past and present stars at the same fixture twelve months on. Altior was the Seven Barrows representative this time in the Celebration Chase and he was one of the three winners on the card for Nicky Henderson who extended his lead to give him what was ultimately a comfortable win in the trainers' championship (although, technically, the title battle went down to the final day). Altior started at 100/30-on to beat Special Tiara, the prolific winning novice San Benedeto, and Vaniteux. In reality, the race was a match between Altior and Special Tiara but it turned out to be very one-sided, Altior sweeping aside the front-running Special Tiara between the last two fences and finishing well on top, with San Benedeto and Vaniteux hardly getting in a blow at any stage. Special Tiara might not have been quite at his very best on the day but Altior's striking display—he again jumped superbly and showed a fine turn of foot—whetted the appetite for his reappearance in the next season, presumably in the Tingle Creek Chase at Sandown. If Douvan doesn't return to action in the two mile division, his stable should be able to mount a competitive challenge to the peerless Altior with the exciting Great Field and a fully fit Min (who had to miss an intended clash with Altior in the Arkle after a setback). Neither of those has met Altior yet over fences but the essay on Great Field emphasises the

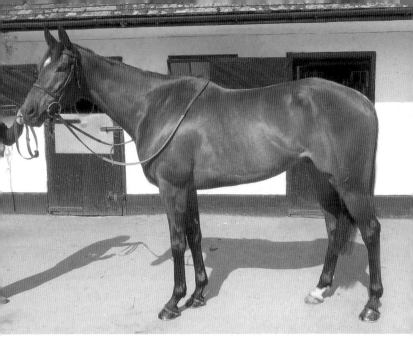

Mrs Patricia Pugh's "Altior"

strength in depth among the latest batch of novice chasers who look like proving more than a match for the older established stars who will have a tough fight on their hands to hold them off in the open championship events.

				Northern Dancer
		Sadler's Wells		
	High Chaparral (IRE)	(b 1981)		Fairy Bridge
	(b 1999)	Kasora		Darshaan
Altior (IRE)		(b 1993)		Kozana
(b.g. 2010)		Key of Luck		Chief's Crown
	Monte Solaro (IRE)	(b 1991)		Balbonella
	(br 2000)	Footsteps		Broken Hearted
		(br 1991)		Remoosh

The good-topped Altior has always had enough size and scope to suggest he would make a chaser, but he does not quite fill the eye in the same way as the commanding Sprinter Sacre, though few chasers would (the imposing Sprinter Sacre stood over seventeen hands and would have been difficult to fault in the show-ring). Altior's sire, the now-deceased Sadler's Wells stallion High Chaparral, wasn't the perfect specimen either, being an angular, good-topped individual who was not the best of movers, but it didn't stop him winning the Derby and the Irish Derby before establishing himself in championship races on both sides of the Atlantic as a four-year-old when he won the Irish Champion and dead-heated in the Breeders' Cup Turf, a race he had also won as a three-year-old. High Chaparral's only defeats in a thirteen-race career came on his debut and in the two editions of the Prix de l'Arc de Triomphe which he contested (third both times). High Chaparral's record at stud includes some notable Flat winners in both hemispheres, So You Think, Toronado, Free Eagle and It's A Dundeel among them, but his fee had fallen to €10,000 by 2009, after he had been retired in 2004 at €35,000. High Chaparral's book of mares in 2009 contained a number with a jumping background, including the bumper winner and fair winning hurdler Monte Solaro (one of her two wins came under bottom weight in a handicap hurdle at Tralee which had Grade 3 status, her performance earning her some flattering 'black type' which probably helped in getting a nomination to High Chaparral. Altior is the third of four winners out of Monte Solaro, the two that preceded him being his year-older half-sister the useful two-mile hurdler Princess Leya (by Old Vic) and the three-years-older fairly useful hurdler and useful chaser Key To The West (by Westerner) who stays two and a half miles but seems to have lost his way in the last couple of seasons. Monte Solaro produced a brother to Altior between Key To The West and Princess Leya, but the short-lived Cestus ran only once, showing promise when second in a bumper. Altior's year-younger half-brother Silverhow (by Yeats) also raced for Altior's connections (he has since been sold and will be with Colin Tizzard in the next season). Silverhow showed fairly useful form at up to two and a half miles over hurdles in the latest season, winning handicaps at Sandown and Cheltenham. Further back, this is the family of the Triumph Hurdle runner-up Moorish (a half-brother to Altior's grandam Footsteps) and of the Sweeps Handicap Hurdle winner Decent Fellow, also runner-up in the Triumph incidentally and a good dual-purpose performer (Decent Fellow is a brother to Altior's fourth dam Rivers Maid). Monte Solaro has an unraced four-year-old filly by Milan, a two-year-old colt by the same sire and she visited Douvan's sire Walk In The Park in 2016. Altior, who wore ear plugs at Cheltenham, stays two and a quarter miles and acts on soft going, though he doesn't need the mud. He often travels strongly in his races and can produce a good turn of finishing speed, and it bears repeating that he is a fine jumper. *Nicky Henderson*

ALTO DES MOTTES (FR) 7 b.g. Dream Well (FR) – Omance (FR) (Video Rock (FR)) [2016/17 c129, h104: h22.8s^{pu} c30g^6 c23.4s* c32.6s^F c26.2s^{pu} Mar 25] rather sparely-made gelding: fair hurdler: fairly useful handicap chaser: won at Newcastle in January: stays 3¾m: acts on heavy going: wears cheekpieces nowadays: tried in tongue tie. *Henry Hogarth* c122 h–

ALTRUISM (IRE) 7 b.g. Authorized (IRE) – Bold Assumption (Observatory (USA)) [2016/17 h125: c17.3m* h17.2m* c17.3g^2 Jul 18] workmanlike gelding: useful handicap hurdler: won at Cartmel in June: similar form over fences: won maiden at Cartmel in May, and likely to have landed handicap there in July had saddle not slipped: raced around 2m: acts on soft and good to firm going: tried in hood: front runner/races prominently. *James Moffatt* c135 h135

AL VALIENTE 6 br.g. Alflora (IRE) – Barton Flower (Danzero (AUS)) [2016/17 h18.5g h15.3d h19.7s h20v^{pu} c21.2s^{pu} Jan 1] no form in varied events, including points: tried in tongue tie. *Tim Vaughan* c– h–

ALVARADO (IRE) 12 ch.g. Goldmark (USA) – Mrs Jones (IRE) (Roselier (FR)) [2016/17 c139§, h–: c27.3s^6 c25.5d^F c32.8g^6 c26g^{pu} c31.8g^4 Apr 22] tall gelding: winning hurdler: useful handicap chaser: slipped in weights before 2½ lengths fourth of 30 to Vicente in Scottish Grand National at Ayr (runner-up to same horse in race previous year): stays 35f: acts on good to firm and heavy going: one to be wary of (has refused twice). *Fergal O'Brien* c132 § h–

ALWAREED 5 ch.g. Makfi – Sinduda (Anabaa (USA)) [2016/17 b–: b16.8s^4 h16.2m May 29] poor form in bumpers: tailed off in novice on hurdling debut. *John Wade* h– b67

ALWAYS ARCHIE 10 b.g. Silver Patriarch (IRE) – Angel Dust (FR) (Cadoudal (FR)) [2016/17 h–: c22.6g* Apr 23] dual winning pointer: winning hurdler: 5/1, also won hunter at Stratford (by 20 lengths from Bound For Glory) on chasing debut: stays 3m: raced only on good going or softer: tried in tongue tie. *Tim Vaughan* c120 h–

ALWAYS ON THE RUN (IRE) 7 br.g. Robin des Pres (FR) – Kerrys Cottage (IRE) (Leading Counsel (USA)) [2016/17 c132, h111: c17.1d* c15.9g c21.7g^3 c19.1g^2 c20.5d^5 c20.2s^2 Feb 16] fair hurdler: useful handicap chaser: won at Kelso (by 1¼ lengths from Special Catch) in May: stays 2½m: acts on soft and good to firm going: has worn hood, including last 4 starts. *Tom George* c134 h–

ALWAYSRECOMMENDED (IRE) 8 ch.g. Gamut (IRE) – Awbeg Beauty (IRE) (Supreme Leader) [2016/17 h64: h16.2d h19.9g^3 h25.3s^5 h19.7d h24g^5 Apr 8] poor maiden hurdler: probably stays 3m: best form on good going: tried in hood. *Jane Walton* h63

ALWAYS TIPSY 8 b.g. Dushyantor (USA) – French Pick (USA) (Johannesburg (USA)) [2016/17 h115: h20.2m^F h20.1d^{ur} h20.7d^6 c19.9g^2 Mar 1] smallish, lengthy gelding: unbeaten in 4 points: fair handicap hurdler: 15/8, second in hunter at Musselburgh (8 lengths behind Top Cat Henry) on chasing debut: left N. W. Alexander after third start: should stay 3m+: acts on good to firm and heavy going. *Alan Wight* c102 h111

ALYASAN (IRE) 6 ch.g. Sea The Stars (IRE) – Alaya (IRE) (Ela-Mana-Mou) [2016/17 **h105** h96p, b101: h15.8g^{pu} h16.8m^4 h18.7m* h16.3m^2 h16g^2 h16.8g^3 h16g^3 h15.6g^6 h16.6g^4 h19.7s^6 h15.7d^5 h15.6g h16g^{pu} Apr 17] sturdy gelding: fair hurdler: won seller at Stratford in July: left Seamus Durack after third start, Dan Skelton after seventh: stays 19f: acts on good to firm going: usually wears headgear/tongue tie. *David Thompson*

ALYS ROCK (IRE) 8 gr.m. Medaaly – Rock Slide (IRE) (Bob Back (USA)) [2016/17 **c97 p** h94, b–: h15.7g h16.3m^4 h16s h16.8s* h19.9g c16.4m* Apr 19] rather sparely-made mare: **h77** poor handicap hurdler: won mares event at Sedgefield (left in front run-in) in January: 3/1, also won novice handicap there (easily by 10 lengths from Leading Score) on chasing debut: stays 21f: acts on soft and good to firm going: often travels strongly: inconsistent, but open to improvement over fences. *Michael Appleby*

ALZAMMAAR (USA) 6 b.g. Birdstone (USA) – Alma Mater (Sadler's Wells (USA)) **h133** [2016/17 h125: h24.7m* h24g h26.5g h19.3d^2 h26.1g^5 h24g Mar 16] good-topped gelding: useful handicap hurdler: won at Aintree in May: second at Catterick (½ length behind Nietzsche) in January: left Warren Greatrex after third start: stays 3¼m: acts on good to firm and heavy going: wore headgear/tongue tie for previous yard. *Sam England*

AMALFI DOUG (FR) 7 gr.g. Network (GER) – Queissa (FR) (Saint Preuil (FR)) **h98** [2016/17 b77: b17.7d^5 h16.3m^3 h16g^5 Nov 7] modest in bumpers: similar form over **b–** hurdles: better effort when third in maiden at Stratford: left Michael Blanshard after first start: has raced freely. *Tom Lacey*

AMANTIUS 8 b.g. Multiplex – Ghana (GER) (Bigstone (IRE)) [2016/17 h18.5m^6 h15.8v^2 **h100** h15.5g* h21.4d^4 h20.3s h21.4d^{pu} h23.9g^F Mar 2] sturdy gelding: fair handicap hurdler: won at Leicester and Wincanton in December: stayed 21f: acted on good to firm and heavy going: wore blinkers: usually raced nearer last than first: dead. *Johnny Farrelly*

AMANTO (GER) 7 b.g. Medicean – Amore (GER) (Lando (GER)) [2016/17 h118: **c122** c16.5g^2 c21m^{pu} h17.7s^4 h19.3d Jan 25] good-topped gelding: fairly useful on Flat, stays **h117** 2m: fairly useful maiden hurdler: similar form over fences: better effort when second in novice handicap at Worcester in June: left Paul Nicholls after second start: stays 19f: acts on soft going: usually wears headgear: in tongue tie last 3 starts. *Ali Stronge*

AMARILLO ROSE (IRE) 5 ch.m. Flemensfirth (USA) – Compton Fair (Compton **h–** Place) [2016/17 b17m^6 b16g b18.2d^{ur} b16g^6 b18.2g^5 b16g^3 h16s h16m b17.3g^3 Mar 26] **b77** fourth foal: dam no form on Flat: modest bumper performer: well held completed start over hurdles. *Liam Lennon, Ireland*

AMATEUR (IRE) 4 ch.g. Giant's Causeway (USA) – Adja (IRE) (Rock of Gibraltar **b98** (IRE)) [2016/17 ab16g^2 b15.6g^3 b16s* b17g Apr 7] second foal: half-brother to useful French/US 1m winner Amboseli (by Medaglia d'Oro): dam, French maiden (stayed 10.5f), half-sister to fair hurdler/fairly useful chaser (stayed 2½m) Authinger: fairly useful form in bumpers: won at Chepstow in March: left Olly Williams after first start, Geoffrey Harker after second: in cheekpieces last 2 starts. *John Flint*

AMAZING COMEDY (FR) 7 b.g. Great Pretender (IRE) – Comedie Divine (FR) **c140** (Lesotho (USA)) [2016/17 c36.3g^5 c24.9v^{pu} c23.9g^4 c25.4g^3 c29.8v^{pu} c22.9d^{ur} c27.8s^5 **h–** c22.9s* c30.8v^F c24.9d* c30.2g^5 Mar 15] good-topped gelding: winning hurdler: useful chaser: won cross-country events at Pau in January and February: best effort when fifth in Glenfarclas Cross Country Chase at Cheltenham (16 lengths behind Cause of Causes) in March: stays 3¾m: acts on soft going: wears headgear: has worn tongue tie. *Phillippe Cottin, France*

AMBER FLUSH 8 b.m. Sir Harry Lewis (USA) – Sari Rose (FR) (Vertical Speed (FR)) **c–** [2016/17 c94, h99: h25g^5 h21.6d^2 h24d^4 h23.3g^5 h23m c25.7m^{pu} h25m h24d^{pu} h24.1s^{pu} Jan **h86** 24] modest handicap hurdler: maiden chaser: left Martin Smith after seventh start: stays 25f: acts on good to firm and good to soft going: tried in cheekpieces/tongue tie: usually races close up. *Clare Ellam*

AMBER GAMBLER (GER) 7 b.g. Doyen (IRE) – Auenglocke (GER) (Surumu **c113** (GER)) [2016/17 h62: h19d c23.8v^{pu} h20.6d^4 c21.2s* c24.2s* c21.7g* c23.8s^{pu} Feb 22] **h96** modest form over hurdles: won novice handicap at Market Rasen in December: fair form over fences: won handicaps at Fakenham (novice), Wetherby (amateur) and Taunton in January: stays 3m: acts on soft going: often travels strongly. *Ian Williams*

AMBERJAM (IRE) 7 b.g. Duke of Marmalade (IRE) – Makarova (IRE) (Sadler's Wells **c102** (USA)) [2016/17 h23.3v* c24v* c28s^{pu} c24s^{pu} Apr 1] modest hurdler: won handicap at **h99** Uttoxeter in December after 2-year absence/change of yards: fair form over fences: won novice handicap at same course in January: lacklustre efforts after: stays 27f: best form on heavy going: has worn tongue tie. *Oliver Sherwood*

AMBER SPYGLASS 7 ch.g. Act One – Northern Bows (Bertolini (USA)) [2016/17 h–, b96: h16.3g⁵ h15.7v⁴ h16.3v⁴ h18.7m⁴ h15.8vᵖᵘ Dec 16] bumper winner: poor form over hurdles. *David Bridgwater* — **h84**

AMBION LANE (IRE) 7 b.g. Scorpion (IRE) – Thrilling Prospect (IRE) (King's Ride) [2016/17 h109, b79: h19.9s c23.8vᵖᵘ c30.7dᵖᵘ h23.6v² Mar 23] fair maiden hurdler: pulled up both starts over fences: stays 3m: acts on heavy going: wears headgear. *Victor Dartnall* — **c–** **h103**

AMBITIOUS PURSUIT (IRE) 9 b.g. Cloudings (IRE) – Gladriels Jem (IRE) (Mister Lord (USA)) [2016/17 c65: c16.3g c23gᵖᵘ Apr 6] multiple winning pointer: maiden chaser, no form in 2016/17: in cheekpieces last 2 starts. *Mrs L. Glanville* — **c–**

AMBIVALENT ABOUT 6 b.m. Josr Algarhoud (IRE) – Peppermint Plod (Kinglet) [2016/17 h20.7sᵖᵘ h15.9s h15.7m³ Apr 13] second foal: half-sister to bumper winner/useful hurdler The Strawberry One (19f-21f winner, by Kadastrof): dam unraced: poor form over hurdles. *David Arbuthnot* — **h59**

AMBLE INN 5 b.m. Sulamani (IRE) – Distant Florin (Medicean) [2016/17 b15.7g⁴ b15.7g b15.8v⁵ b15.8d⁶ h16mᵘ⁴ Apr 18] first foal: dam (b81) bumper winner: poor form in bumpers/ on hurdling debut. *Anthony Carson* — **h76** **b67**

AMERICAN (FR) 7 b.g. Malinas (GER) – Grande Sultane (FR) (Garde Royale) [2016/17 h128p: c24.2s* c24s* c24s* Mar 18] tall, useful-looking gelding: fairly useful form over hurdles: very smart form over fences, unbeaten in 3 starts: won novice at Exeter (by 2¼ lengths from Label des Obeaux) in November, listed novice at Warwick (by 4½ lengths from Champers On Ice) in January and novice handicap at Uttoxeter (by 8 lengths from Rock The Kasbah) in March: stays 3m: acts on soft going: usually races close up: open to yet more improvement. *Harry Fry* — **c156 p** **h–**

AMERICAN GIGOLO 5 b.g. Azamour (IRE) – Sadie Thompson (IRE) (King's Best (USA)) [2016/17 b71: b15.3m* h16sᵘʳ h16.6d² h16.5g Apr 7] rather unfurnished gelding: fair form in bumpers: won at Wincanton in November: fair form over hurdles: second in novice at Doncaster (9 lengths behind Stowaway Magic) in January. *Charlie Mann* — **h109** **b90**

The Jago Family Partnership's "American"

AMERICAN LEGEND (IRE) 9 b.g. Presenting – Coole Eile (IRE) (King's Ride) **c106 §**
[2016/17 c119§, h–: c23m⁴ May 19] winning hurdler: fairly useful handicap chaser: won **h–**
point in April: stays 27f: acts on soft and good to firm going: wears headgear: often races
towards rear: unreliable. *Jonjo O'Neill*

AMERICAN LIFE (FR) 10 b.g. American Post – Poplife (FR) (Zino) [2016/17 h108: **h93 §**
h21g h24.6d h23.1g h20.7g h19.9v⁵ h25d^F h23.3v⁴ h25v⁴ h23v² h27v^pu h23.9g² Apr 26]
close-coupled gelding: modest handicap hurdler: stays 27f: acts on heavy going: wears
headgear/tongue tie: temperamental. *Sophie Leech*

AMERICAN TOM (FR) 6 b.g. American Post – Kirkla (FR) (Bikala) [2016/17 c16d* **c140 p**
c16s^F Jan 8] closely related to 2 winners, including Shy (French 2m-19f hurdle/chase **h–**
winner, by Signe Divin), and half-brother to 2 winners, including Two Be K (French 19f
chase winner, by King's Theatre): dam unraced: winning hurdler: useful form over fences:
won maiden at Punchestown in December, digging deep: struggling when falling next time
(reportedly coughing post-race): likely to stay 2½m: remains with potential. *W. P. Mullins,
Ireland*

AMERICAN WORLD (FR) 13 b.g. Lost World (IRE) – Rose Laura (FR) (Rose Laurel) **c– x**
[2016/17 c68, h–: c24.1g^F c22.6m c23m^F c23g^pu h23.8d^pu Jan 25] lengthy gelding: winning **h–**
hurdler/chaser, no form in 2016/17: tried in headgear: has worn tongue tie: often let down
by jumping over fences. *Lady Susan Brooke*

AMERICARNO (IRE) 4 b.g. Arcano (IRE) – Cafe Creme (IRE) (Catrail (USA)) **b–**
[2016/17 ab16g Dec 10] tailed off in junior bumper. *Chris Down*

AMERTON LANE 5 b.g. Multiplex – Sunisa (IRE) (Daggers Drawn (USA)) [2016/17 **h–**
b16.7s h16.7g³ Mar 25] sturdy gelding: well beaten in bumper/novice hurdle. *Evan Williams* **b–**

AMI DESBOIS (FR) 7 b.g. Dream Well (FR) – Baroya (FR) (Garde Royale) [2016/17 **h142**
h125, b76: h23.3d* h22.8v* h24s² h20.5d³ h24.1s* h24g⁵ h20.6g* Apr 8] good-topped
gelding: useful hurdler: won maiden at Hexham in May, handicaps at Haydock in
November and Wetherby (by 3 lengths from Sam Red) in February, and novice at
Newcastle in April: second in Albert Bartlett Novices' Hurdle (Bristol) at Cheltenham
(length behind Wholestone) and third in Challow Novices' Hurdle at Newbury (6½ lengths
behind Messire des Obeaux): stays 3m: acts on heavy going: wears tongue tie: usually
leads. *Graeme McPherson*

AMIDON (FR) 7 b.g. Dom Alco (FR) – Immage (FR) (Bad Conduct (USA)) [2016/17 **c108**
c119, h97: c23.9s^pu c24.5d⁴ c27.6d Dec 26] good-topped gelding: maiden hurdler: fairly **h–**
useful handicap chaser: below form in 2016/17: stays 3¼m: acts on heavy going: has worn
headgear, including in 2016/17. *Lucy Wadham*

AMIGO (FR) 10 b.g. Ballingarry (IRE) – Allez Y (FR) (Pistolet Bleu (IRE)) [2016/17 **c111 §**
c131§, h106: h26.5m c23m^pu c25.8g⁵ c24.2g² Apr 17] dual point winner: useful hurdler/ **h–**
chaser at best, no longer same force: left David Pipe after third start: stays 4m: acts on good
to firm and heavy going: usually wears headgear/tongue tie: unreliable. *Mrs L. Braithwaite*

AMILLIONTIMES (IRE) 9 b.g. Olden Times – Miss Million (IRE) (Roselier (FR)) **c116**
[2016/17 c92, h94: c21.3g² c20.1m* c20.1d* c21.6d* c20.9d* c20.5g³ c20g⁵ Nov 7] **h–**
winning hurdler: fairly useful handicap chaser: won at Perth in May and June, Kelso in
September and Carlisle in October, 2 of them novice events: stays 4m: acts on good to
firm and good to soft going: wears tongue tie: often races towards rear. *Jackie Stephen*

AMINABAD (FR) 7 b.g. Singspiel (IRE) – Amenapinga (FR) (Spinning World (USA)) **c121**
[2016/17 c17m c21.5d³ c19.9g c15.5v⁴ c19.2d* c16.3s³ h16.5g c16.3g^F c20.1g⁶ Apr 28] **h–**
fairly useful hurdler: fairly useful chaser: won novice at Catterick in January: left Gordon
Elliott after third start: stays 21f: acts on heavy going: in cheekpieces last 2 starts: wears
tongue tie. *Patrick Griffin, Ireland*

AMIRAL COLLONGES (FR) 7 ch.g. Dom Alco (FR) – Idole Collonges (FR) (Brezzo **c107 §**
(FR)) [2016/17 c–, h119: h20d c23.9s^pu c24s⁶ c27.6d² c25.5v⁵ c23.8s^pu c24g³ Mar 28] **h–**
sturdy gelding: fairly useful hurdler: fair handicap chaser nowadays: stays 3½m: acts on
soft and good to firm going: has worn cheekpieces, including last 5 starts: often races
prominently: temperamental. *James Evans*

AMIRLI (IRE) 6 ch.g. Medicean – Amenapinga (FR) (Spinning World (USA)) [2016/17 **h62**
h–: h19.9g Aug 25] fair on Flat, barely stays 2m: poor maiden hurdler: in cheekpieces last
2 starts: usually in tongue tie. *Alistair Whillans*

AMITIE WALTZ (FR) 5 b.g. Sinndar (IRE) – Lia Waltz (FR) (Linamix (FR)) [2016/17 **h72** b15.8m[4] b16.7d[3] h16.3d[3] Jun 14] second foal: half-brother to 1m-1¼m winner Koliakhova **b91** (by Literato): dam ran once on Flat: fair form in bumpers: 16/1, third in novice at Stratford (34 lengths behind Bleu Et Noir, not fluent) on hurdling debut: second in maiden on Flat in April for Richard Hughes. *Dan Skelton*

AMONIT (IRE) 5 b.g. Yeats (IRE) – Sinnaja (Sinndar (IRE)) [2016/17 b16g b16.2f[4] **b63** Jun 5] failed to complete all 3 starts in points: poor form in bumpers: left Stuart Crawford after first start (tongue tied). *Lucinda Russell*

A MONTMARTRE (FR) 5 b.m. Montmartre (FR) – Stefania (IRE) (Monsun (GER)) **h104** [2016/17 h18.5s h16.2s h15.9s[5] h17.7s[3] h21m[5] h16.5m* Apr 27] closely related/half-sister to winning jumpers abroad by Motivator and Alzao: fairly useful on Flat, stays 1¼m: fair form over hurdles: won mares handicap at Taunton in April: stays 2¼m: acts on soft and good to firm going. *Nick Mitchell*

AMOOLA GOLD (GER) 4 b.g. Mamool (IRE) – Aughamore Beauty (IRE) (Dara **b93** Monarch) [2016/17 b16s[2] Feb 10] closely related/half-brother to numerous winners, including Austrasien (2¼m hurdle winner) and Athenry (17f/2¼m hurdle/chase winner) (both in France, by Nicaron): dam unraced: 14/1, second in maiden bumper at Kempton (1¼ lengths behind Haafapiece) in February. *Dan Skelton*

AMORE ALATO 8 b.g. Winged Love (IRE) – Sardagna (FR) (Medaaly) [2016/17 c140, **c135** h–: c24.2d* c24g[3] c20v[4] Feb 4] strong gelding: winning hurdler: useful chaser: won listed **h–** event at Sandown (by 7 lengths from Ballybolley) in November: stays 3m: acts on soft going: tried in cheekpieces. *Johnny Farrelly*

AMOUR DE NUIT (IRE) 5 b.g. Azamour (IRE) – Umthoulah (IRE) (Unfuwain (USA)) **h124** [2016/17 h16.5g[2] h21.2s h19g[3] h16.5g* h16.5g[2] h16.8m* Apr 15] half-brother to fairly useful hurdler El Massivo (2m winner, by Authorized): smart on Flat, stays 17.5f: fairly useful form over hurdles: won handicap at Taunton in March and novice at Newton Abbot (8/1-on) in April: should be suited by 2½m: acts on good to firm going: front runner/races prominently, often travels strongly. *Paul Nicholls*

AMOUR D'OR 6 b.m. Winged Love (IRE) – Diletia (Dilum (USA)) [2016/17 h102: **h–** h17.4s h17.4m[pu] h19.7v[pu] h23.9g[pu] h23.9m[5] Apr 20] sturdy mare: fair hurdler at best, no form in 2016/17: left Nick Williams after second start: in tongue tie last 2 starts: usually races close up, tends to find little. *Jess Westwood*

AMRON KALI (IRE) 7 b.m. Kalanisi (IRE) – Glacial Snowboard (IRE) (Glacial Storm **h100** (USA)) [2016/17 h20g h24g[pu] h16g h20g[ur] h16d h17.7v* h19.4d[3] h20.5s[3] h20.5s[3] h21.2g[4] h23.4g[2] Apr 17] third foal: half-sister to fairly useful hurdler Dont Tell Pa (2m-2¼m winner, by Oscar): dam unraced half-sister to fairly useful hurdler/useful chaser (stayed 3m) The Vicar and useful hurdler/chaser (stayed 25f) Warden Hill: fair handicap hurdler: won at Fontwell in January: left J. D. Motherway after fifth start: stays 23f: acts on heavy going: tried in cheekpieces: wears tongue tie: patiently ridden. *Paul Henderson*

AMRON KRIS (IRE) 9 b.g. Kris Kin (USA) – Gleann Alainn (Teenoso (USA)) [2016/17 **c95** c26g[5] c23.6g[4] May 17] dual winning pointer: modest form in chases: better effort when fifth in hunter at Cheltenham. *J. M. Ridley*

AMUSE ME 11 gr.g. Daylami (IRE) – Have Fun (Indian Ridge) [2016/17 c105, h116: **c106** h25.4m h22.1m[3] c21.2d[3] c21.2d[4] c21.5g[6] c20.1d[5] c19.9d[2] c19.9g[5] c21.1m[4] Apr 19] sturdy **h111** gelding: fair handicap hurdler/chaser: stays 2¾m: acts on good to firm and heavy going: has worn cheekpieces/tongue tie, including last 3 starts. *James Moffatt*

ANCHOR MAN (IRE) 5 b.g. Stowaway – False Note (IRE) (Accordion) [2016/17 **h120** h21.6g* h24s[6] h21.4s[2] h20.6s[pu] h21.4m[3] Apr 5] smallish gelding: runner-up in Irish maiden point: fairly useful form over hurdles: won novice at Exeter in November: stayed 2¾m: acted on soft going: dead. *Paul Nicholls*

ANCHORS AWAY 6 b.g. Black Sam Bellamy (IRE) – School Days (Slip Anchor) **b–** [2016/17 b16.8m[pu] Jul 1] pulled up in bumper: dead. *Martin Hill*

ANCIENT SANDS (IRE) 9 b.g. Footstepsinthesand – Antiguan Wells (IRE) (Sadler's **c94** Wells (USA)) [2016/17 h16d[2] h17m* h16g[3] h17m[3] h16.1g[6] h16d[5] c16d c20v c20g[4] Apr 16] **h134** useful handicap hurdler: won at Killarney in May: maiden chaser, fair form at best: best form around 2m: acts on good to firm and heavy going: has worn tongue tie. *John E. Kiely, Ireland*

AN DEARG MOR (IRE) 7 ch.g. Robin des Champs (FR) – Johnston's Flyer (IRE) **h** (Orchestra) [2016/17 b16g[2] Nov 4] useful form in bumpers: second at Down Royal (3¼ **b106** lengths behind Joey Sasa) on sole start in 2016/17: fourth in maiden only outing over hurdles. *Emmet Mullins, Ireland*

ANDHAAR 11 b.g. Bahri (USA) – Deraasaat (Nashwan (USA)) [2016/17 h104: h23.9d⁵ **h85 §** h23.9s h24.3d h23.8g⁴ h24d⁶ h23.8g⁴ h23.8g⁵ h23.8g³ h20.5v³ h25.8s⁵ h23.9g Apr 26] rather leggy gelding: modest handicap hurdler: stays 3m: acts on soft going: has worn headgear, including in 2016/17: tried in tongue tie: none too genuine. *N. W. Alexander*

AND THE NEW (IRE) 6 b.g. Kalanisi (IRE) – Wheredidthemoneygo (IRE) (Anshan) **b112** [2016/17 ab16g³ b16.4g b17g⁶ Apr 7] €13,000 3-y-o: rather unfurnished gelding: fifth foal: half-brother to fair hurdler Apachee Prince (2¼m winner, by Indian Danehill), stays 3m: dam (h89), maiden hurdler (stayed 3m), half-sister to fairly useful hurdler (stayed 25f) Blue Ride: useful form in bumpers: 33/1, improved again when 3½ lengths sixth of 19 to Lalor in Grade 2 event at Aintree: left Stuart Crawford after only 2015/16 start. *Johnny Farrelly*

ANDY KELLY (IRE) 8 ch.g. Flemensfirth (USA) – Fae Taylor (IRE) (Desert Style **c129** (IRE)) [2016/17 c133p, h–: c20.5sᵘʳ c18.8d⁵ Dec 17] lengthy gelding: winning hurdler: **h–** useful handicap chaser: stayed 2¾m: acted on heavy going: dead. *Emma Lavelle*

AN FEAR CIUIN (IRE) 6 b.g. Galileo (IRE) – Potion (Pivotal) [2016/17 h21.3dᵘʳ **h92** h16.2g³ Apr 27] brother to fair/ungenuine hurdler Mad For Road (17f winner): fairly useful on Flat, stays 2m: modest form over hurdles: trained on reappearance only by Richard Ford: tried in cheekpieces. *R. Mike Smith*

ANGE DES MALBERAUX (FR) 7 b.g. Michel Georges – Petite Baie (FR) (Alamo **h90** Bay (USA)) [2016/17 h79, b–: h16.2g⁵ h22.1d⁵ h19.6d² h19.9g* h18.1m⁶ h18.1s⁶ h16.8s³ h16.4sᵖᵘ h19.9g Mar 29] modest handicap hurdler: won novice event at Sedgefield in September: stays 2½m: acts on good to soft going: wears headgear. *James Ewart*

ANGEL FACE 6 b.m. Kayf Tara – Safari Run (IRE) (Supreme Leader) [2016/17 h100: **h103** h20g³ h19.9g² h19.6g³ h16g² h20g⁵ Nov 6] fair maiden hurdler: stays 2½m: acts on soft going: usually in tongue tie. *Paul Morgan*

ANGEL IN THE SNOW 4 ch.g. Haafhd – Chilly Filly (IRE) (Montjeu (IRE)) [2016/17 **h–** h15.6gᶠ h16s h18.6s h16.6g Jan 27] modest maiden on Flat, stays 12.5f: no form over hurdles. *Brian Ellison*

ANGEL OF HARLEM 4 b.f. Presenting – Whoops A Daisy (Definite Article) [2016/17 **b–** b15.8v Mar 1] £43,000 3-y-o: first foal: dam (h131), bumper/2m-3m hurdle winner, half-sister to fairly useful hurdler/useful chaser (stayed 19f) Dick Dundee: tailed off in bumper. *Mark Bradstock*

ANGEL'S ENVY 5 b.m. Yeats (IRE) – Caoba (Hernando (FR)) [2016/17 b16.8g⁵ b15.6g **h–** b16.6d h19.9g h19.3g⁶ Apr 15] second foal: closely related to fair hurdler Hag Stone (2m **b64** winner, by Kayf Tara): dam (h121), 19f-2¾m hurdle winner, also 2m winner on Flat: little sign of ability: tried in hood. *Iain Jardine*

ANGLINGFORCHARLIE 8 b.g. Catcher In The Rye (IRE) – Annies Valentine (My **c91** Best Valentine) [2016/17 c87, h–: c21gᵖᵘ c16.1g⁴ Feb 21] winning pointer: once-raced over **h–** hurdles: modest form in hunter chases: stays 2½m: acts on heavy going. *Miss Beth Childs*

ANGUS GLENS 7 gr.g. Dalakhani (IRE) – Clara Bow (IRE) (Sadler's Wells) **h113** [2016/17 h115: h19.7g² h23.1d³ h24.7d⁶ h20.3g⁴ h16.3m³ h16m* h15.7g⁴ Nov 10] fair handicap hurdler: won at Warwick in November: left David Dennis after fifth start: stayed 2½m: acted on good to firm going: wore cheekpieces: usually raced prominently: dead. *Grace Harris*

ANGUS MILAN (IRE) 8 b.g. Milan – Lasado (IRE) (Jurado (USA)) [2016/17 c17d c17d **c124** c20d⁵ c21.6s* c23.4s³ c20.5v² c28.5g Mar 26] winning hurdler: fairly useful handicap **h–** chaser: won novice event at Kelso in December: stays 2¾m: acts on heavy going: wears tongue tie. *Noel C. Kelly, Ireland*

ANIBALE FLY (FR) 7 b.g. Assessor (IRE) – Nouba Fly (FR) (Chamberlin (FR)) **c151** [2016/17 h145p: h20d* c17d* c20d² c24gᵖᵘ c24s* c24s⁴ c24.5d² Apr 25] lengthy gelding: **h–** useful hurdler: smart form over fences: won maiden at Navan (by ¾ length from Martello Tower) in November and Grade 3 novice at Naas (by ¾ length from A Genie In Abottle) in January: second in Drinmore Novices' Chase at Fairyhouse (2¼ lengths behind Coney Island) in December and Champion Novices' Chase at Punchestown (5 lengths behind Disko) in April: stays 25f: acts on heavy going: wears tongue tie: usually races towards rear. *A. J. Martin, Ireland*

ANITOPIA 12 gr.g. Alflora (IRE) – The Whirlie Weevil (Scallywag) [2016/17 h–: c17.1sᵖᵘ **c75** c20.5s⁶ c15.5s² c20.1vᵖᵘ h16vᵖᵘ Feb 27] maiden hurdler: poor form over fences: stays **h–** 2½m: acts on heavy going. *Linda Perratt*

AN LAOCH (IRE) 5 b.g. Flemensfirth (USA) – Petite Ballerina (IRE) (Oscar (IRE)) **h97**
[2016/17 h20.6g³ h23.3g⁵ Apr 25] £15,500 3-y-o: second foal: dam (h80), maiden hurdler,
closely related to fairly useful hurdler/staying chaser Gripit N Tipit: off mark in maiden
points at fourth attempt: modest form over hurdles: better effort when third of 4 in steadily-
run novice at Newcastle: wears tongue tie. *Chris Grant*

ANNACOTTY (IRE) 9 b.g. Beneficial – Mini Moo Min (Ardross) [2016/17 c153, h–: **c140**
c20.4sᵖᵘ c23.8d c20.8sᵘʳ c24g c25g Mar 14] good-topped gelding: winning hurdler: smart **h–**
handicap chaser: largely well below form in 2016/17 (reportedly hobdayed before
reappearance): stays 3m: acts on heavy going: wears headgear: usually races close up.
Alan King

ANNA MILAN 9 b.m. Milan – Glass Note (IRE) (Spectrum (IRE)) [2016/17 h21sᵖᵘ **h–**
Mar 30] first foal: dam 1½m winner: pulled up in maiden hurdle. *Alan Phillips*

ANNAMULT (IRE) 9 ch.m. Beneficial – Summer Smile (IRE) (Hollow Hand) [2016/17 **c79**
c75, h–: c20.3v* h20.3m c22.6mᵖᵘ c24d² c24d⁶ c20.3g Apr 21] point winner: maiden **h–**
hurdler: poor handicap chaser: won at Southwell in May: stays 3m: acts on heavy going:
tried in visor. *Alan Phillips*

ANNIE ALAINN (IRE) 10 ch.m. Beneficial – Hurst Flyer (Neltino) [2016/17 h17.8g³ **h116**
h16d³ h16.3v⁴ h19.9g h16g h15.8d⁴ h19.7g* h16.4s* h19.9v* h16s³ h16v* Jan 31] sixth
foal: sister to bumper winner/fairly useful chaser Arctic Ben (2m-2½m winner) and half-
sister to winning pointers by Dr Massini and Presenting: dam (c97/h96) 2½m/21f hurdle/
chase winner: fairly useful handicap hurdler: won at Hereford in October, Newcastle and
Uttoxeter in December, and Lingfield in January: left Thomas Mullins after second start:
stays 2½m: acts on heavy going: has worn headgear: front runner/races prominently.
Fergal O'Brien

ANNIE'SBOYDAVE 7 b.g. Passing Glance – Earcomesannie (IRE) (Anshan) [2016/17 **h–**
b–: h19d⁶ h19dᵖᵘ h19.2gᵖᵘ h19.7gᵖᵘ h23.8dᵖᵘ h23.9g h21g Apr 24] no form over hurdles: in
tongue tie last 2 starts. *Peter Pritchard*

ANN MARIES REJECT (IRE) 8 br.m. Sendawar (IRE) – Charlestown Lass (Bob **h74**
Back (USA)) [2016/17 h69: h23.3m⁴ h16d⁵ h23m⁵ h23.3g Jul 22] failed to complete both
starts in points: poor maiden hurdler: best effort at 23f: acts on good to firm going: often
races towards rear. *Brian Barr*

ANOLYSSE MORINIERE (FR) 7 b.g. Network (GER) – Onolyssa (FR) (Nononito **c76**
(FR)) [2016/17 h17.4g⁵ h17.4d² c18.9g⁶ h17.9g* h18.9g⁵ h17.9g³ h18.9g⁴ h16m Nov 2] **h111**
first foal: dam (c114/h115), French 17f-2½m hurdle/chase winner, half-sister to useful
hurdler (stayed 23f) Hulysse Royal: bumper winner: fair hurdler: won minor event at
Cazaubon-Barbotan-les-Thermes in July: poor form on chasing debut: left J-P. Daireaux
after seventh start: stays 19f: has worn headgear. *Martin Hill*

ANOTHER BILL (IRE) 7 ch.g. Beneficial – Glacier Lilly (IRE) (Glacial Storm (USA)) **h124**
[2016/17 h115p: h20.1g* h23.3d⁵ h22.7d* h22.7s* h23.1sᶠ h22.8d⁶ Feb 18] fairly useful
hurdler: won maiden at Hexham in May, and novices at Kelso in October and November:
stays 23f: acts on good going. *Nicky Richards*

ANOTHER COBBLER (FR) 7 gr.m. Fragrant Mix (IRE) – Qualine du Maquis (FR) **h–**
(Video Rock (FR)) [2016/17 h–: h19.6gᵖᵘ May 14] little sign of ability: dead. *Henry Daly*

ANOTHER CRICK 4 b.g. Arcadio (GER) – Suetsu (IRE) (Toulon) [2016/17 b15.7g⁴ **b88**
Mar 28] €9,000 3-y-o: fifth foal: half-brother to a winning pointer by Dapper: dam winning
pointer: 16/1, fourth in bumper at Southwell (6¾ lengths behind Royal Ruby) on debut.
Noel Williams

ANOTHER DARK RUM 13 br.g. Beat All (USA) – Gourmet (IRE) (Homo Sapien) **c– §**
[2016/17 c19.9gᵖᵘ Mar 1] close-coupled gelding: dual winning pointer: maiden hurdler: **h– §**
modest chaser at best: stays 25f: acts on soft going: tried in cheekpieces: temperamental. *S.
J. Leadbetter*

ANOTHER DIMENSION (IRE) 11 b.g. Overbury (IRE) – Freshwater (IRE) **c–**
(Commanche Run) [2016/17 c–, h91: h23.9m² h22.1g⁴ h23.9s h23.1g⁵ Aug 13] fair hurdler **h79**
at best, poor by the end: maiden chaser: stayed 25f: acted on soft and good to firm going:
tried in blinkers: wore tongue tie: dead. *Rose Dobbin*

ANOTHER FRONTIER (IRE) 6 b.g. Darsi (FR) – Scent With Love (IRE) (Winged **h118**
Love (IRE)) [2016/17 h112, b–: h24.7g⁴ h21.2v² h23.3v h23.9s* h21.4s³ h26s h25g⁴
Apr 24] fairly useful handicap hurdler: won at Taunton in February: stays 25f: acts on
heavy going: tried in visor: often races prominently. *Nigel Twiston-Davies*

ANOTHER HERO (IRE) 8 b.g. Kalanisi (IRE) – Storm Front (IRE) (Strong Gale)   **c135**
[2016/17 c138p, h–: c23.6g⁶ c23.8d⁴ c24d³ c26g c31.8g Apr 22] workmanlike gelding: **h–**
winning hurdler: useful handicap chaser: fourth in Silver Cup at Ascot (2½ lengths behind
Regal Encore) in December and third in Sky Bet Chase at Doncaster in January: stays 3m:
acts on good to firm and heavy going: tried in cheekpieces/tongue tie: often races towards
rear. *Jonjo O'Neill*

ANOTHER JOURNEY 8 b.g. Rail Link – Singasongosixpence (Singspiel (IRE))   **c–**
[2016/17 c99, h111: c16m⁵ May 8] big gelding: fair hurdler: maiden chaser: raced mainly   **h–**
around 2m: acts on good to soft going: often races prominently. *Sarah-Jayne Davies*

ANOTHER MATTIE (IRE) 10 b.g. Zagreb (USA) – Silver Tassie (FR) (Kaldounevees   **c–**
(FR)) [2016/17 c–, h119: h25.8s⁵ h24.3sᵖᵘ h20.6s³ h24.3s³ h24.3v* h20.9s⁶ Apr 3]   **h115**
workmanlike gelding: fairly useful handicap hurdler: won at Ayr (amateur) in March:
maiden chaser: stays 3m: acts on heavy going: tried in cheekpieces: wears tongue tie: often
leads: signs of temperament. *N. W. Alexander*

ANOTHER NUDGE (IRE) 5 b.m. Getaway (GER) – Another Shot (IRE) (Master   **h–**
Willie) [2016/17 b–: b15.8m b17.7d⁵ b15.8d h20.7sᵖᵘ h15.8s Jan 19] no form in bumpers/   **b–**
over hurdles: tried in blinkers. *David Dennis*

ANOTHER SQUEEZE 9 gr.m. Proclamation (IRE) – Tight Squeeze (Petoski) [2016/17   **h–**
h15.7dᵖᵘ Nov 15] modest maiden on Flat, stays 1¼m: pulled up in mares novice on
hurdling debut: wore hood. *Peter Hiatt*

ANOTHER STOWAWAY (IRE) 5 b.g. Stowaway – Another Pet (IRE) (Un Desperado   **b92**
(FR)) [2016/17 b15.7v⁵ b15.6g⁴ b16v² Mar 12] €20,000 3-y-o, £80,000 4-y-o: sixth foal:
half-brother to modest hurdler Aurora's Dream (2¼m winner, by Kutub) and a winning
pointer by Old Vic: dam, ran once in bumper/point, half-sister to smart chaser (stayed
3m) Super Tactics: third in Irish maiden point: fair form in bumpers: second at Warwick in
March: will be suited by further than 2m. *Tom George*

ANOTHER SUNSHINE 6 b.m. Kayf Tara – Sunshine Rays (Alflora (IRE)) [2016/17   **b78**
b62: b16g⁵ Aug 11] modest form on second of 2 starts in bumpers: tried in hood.
Warren Greatrex

ANOTHER VENTURE (IRE) 6 ch.g. Stowaway – Hard Luck (IRE) (Old Vic)   **h120**
[2016/17 h21.2v² h21d² h19.8v* Mar 11] €10,000 4-y-o, £32,000 5-y-o: tall
gelding: first foal: dam unraced half-sister to fairly useful chaser (stayed 25f) Monty's
Quest: runner-up in Irish maiden point on debut: fairly useful form over hurdles: won
novice handicap at Sandown in February: will stay 3m: acts on heavy ground. *Kim Bailey*

AN POC AR BUILE (IRE) 8 ch.g. Mountain High (IRE) – Miniconjou (IRE) (Be My   **c104 §**
Native (USA)) [2016/17 c117§, h103: c21.4g² c19.2v⁴ c25.6d³ Jan 25] good-topped   **h–**
gelding: winning hurdler: fair handicap chaser: stays 25f: acts on heavy going: has worn
cheekpieces: usually races nearer last than first: temperamental. *Sophie Leech*

ANSAAB 9 b.g. Cape Cross (IRE) – Dawn Raid (IRE) (Docksider (USA)) [2016/17 h16gᵖᵘ   **h–**
h16g Oct 29] fairly useful on Flat, stays 1½m: no form in novice hurdles: tried in tongue
tie. *Laura Morgan*

AN SCAIRP (IRE) 5 b.g. Scorpion (IRE) – Stepping Out Well (IRE) (Zaffaran (USA))   **b–**
[2016/17 b16g b16.3d Mar 13] no form in bumpers: left Dan Skelton after first start.
Roy Brotherton

AN SILTEAN (IRE) 6 b.g. Milan – Shatani (IRE) (Shahrastani (USA)) [2016/17 b16s   **h105 p**
h21.4s⁶ h19.1v⁴ h21.4s⁵ h23.1g² Apr 11] €30,000 3-y-o, £68,000 5-y-o: lengthy, rather   **b–**
unfurnished gelding: fourth foal: half-brother to fairly useful hurdler/chaser Guiding
George (19f-3m winner, by Flemensfirth): dam, ran once in a bumper, half-sister to useful
hurdler/smart chaser (stays 4m) Measureofmydreams: won Irish maiden point on debut:
tailed off in bumper: fair form over hurdles: best effort at 23f: tried in cheekpieces: often
races towards rear: open to further improvement. *Harry Fry*

ANTARTICA DE THAIX (FR) 7 gr.m. Dom Alco (FR) – Nouca de Thaix (FR)   **c145**
(Subotica (FR)) [2016/17 h122, b87: h21.4m² c20s² c20.2sꟳ c20.3s* c19.9s* c20.2d*   **h123 +**
c20.8g⁴ Apr 20] good-topped mare: fairly useful form over hurdles: smart form over
fences: won mares novice at Bangor in February, and listed mares event at Huntingdon (by
9 lengths from Desert Queen) and novice at Wincanton (by 22 lengths from Charmix) in
March: stays 21f: acts on good to firm and heavy going: wears hood/tongue tie: front
runner/races prominently, often travels strongly. *Paul Nicholls*

ANTEMIO (FR) 4 b.g. Rip Van Winkle (IRE) – Peinture d'Or (IRE) (Peintre Celebre (USA)) [2016/17 h15.8m h15.8d⁴ h16m h19gᵖᵘ h15.8vᵖᵘ Dec 31] angular gelding: maiden on Flat in France: poor form over hurdles: tried in cheekpieces: in tongue tie last 3 starts. *Nigel Hawke* **h71**

ANTEROS (IRE) 9 b.g. Milan – Sovereign Star (Taufan (USA)) [2016/17 c98p, h130: c20.3v³ c21.2g² c21.2m³ c21.4gᵖᵘ h23.9g h25.3s* h24g⁵ h23.6sᵖᵘ h22.8d⁵ h23.6v Feb 25] lengthy gelding: fairly useful handicap hurdler: won listed event at Cheltenham in November: fairly useful form over fences: second in maiden at Cartmel in June: stays 25f: acts on heavy going: has worn cheekpieces: wears tongue tie: often races towards rear: temperamental. *Sophie Leech* **c120 §** **h127 §**

ANTI COOL (IRE) 8 b.g. Heron Island (IRE) – Youngborogal (IRE) (Anshan) [2016/17 h–, b82: h15.7g⁴ c20gᵖᵘ c16.3gᵖᵘ c17g* c15.7g* c16.4g* Sep 1] off mark in Irish points at sixth attempt: poor form over hurdles: modest form over fences: won handicaps at Stratford and Southwell in August, and at Sedgefield in September, last 2 novice events: should be suited by 2½m+: best form on good going: in headgear last 4 starts. *Robin Dickin* **c93** **h77**

ANTIPHONY (IRE) 6 b.g. Royal Anthem (USA) – Hazel's Glory (IRE) (Mister Lord (USA)) [2016/17 h103: h16.8g h16.5v³ h16g³ h16g² h18.2g⁵ c17.4v² c18.5d Oct 14] rangy gelding: fair maiden hurdler: similar form over fences: better effort when second in maiden at Sligo: won point in April: left Philip Hobbs after first start: stays 2¼m: acts on heavy going: wears hood. *Gordon Elliott, Ireland* **c100** **h100**

ANTON DOLIN (IRE) 9 ch.g. Danehill Dancer (IRE) – Ski For Gold (Shirley Heights) [2016/17 h97: h15.8g² h17.2g h15.8g² h15.8d h16.3g⁴ h16gᵘʳ h15.8d³ h15.8d⁴ h15.8d⁵ h15.5g h16.8d⁶ h15.8m* Apr 18] modest handicap hurdler: won at Ludlow (amateur) in April: stays 2½m: acts on soft and good to firm going: has worn headgear: unreliable. *Michael Mullineaux* **h91 §**

ANTONY (FR) 7 b.g. Walk In The Park (IRE) – Melanie du Chenet (FR) (Nikos) [2016/17 c126, h116: c21.1s* c23.8m* c22.4g c24.2vᵖᵘ Feb 4] good-topped gelding: fairly useful hurdler: useful handicap chaser: won at Fontwell and Grade 3 event at Ascot (by 4½ lengths from Junction Fourteen) in October: stays 3m: acts on soft and good to firm going. *Gary Moore* **c131** **h–**

ANY CURRENCY (IRE) 14 b.g. Moscow Society (USA) – Native Bavard (IRE) (Be My Native (USA)) [2016/17 c145, h–: c27.3s c26.3sᵖᵘ c30.2d³ c30.2g c28.1g⁵ Apr 19] rather leggy gelding: maiden hurdler: useful handicap chaser: below best in 2016/17, even when third in cross-country event at Cheltenham (24 lengths behind Urgent de Gregaine) in January: stays 4m: acts on good to firm and heavy going: wears headgear: has worn tongue tie: front runner/races prominently. *Martin Keighley* **c133** **h–**

ANY DRAMA (IRE) 6 b.g. Gamut (IRE) – Oak Lodge (IRE) (Roselier (FR)) [2016/17 b106: h20.5d⁴ h20.6s* h18.5d* h24gᵖᵘ Mar 17] medium-sized gelding: useful bumper performer: useful form over hurdles: won novices at Market Rasen (by 38 lengths from Bally Gilbert) and Exeter in February: should stay 3m: tried in cheekpieces: front runner/races prominently. *Harry Fry* **h136**

ANY SECOND NOW (IRE) 5 b.g. Oscar (IRE) – Pretty Neat (IRE) (Topanoora) [2016/17 h16d* h16v* h16v³ h20sᵘʳ Apr 2] fourth foal: dam, second in bumper from 2 starts, half-sister to fair hurdler/fairly useful chaser (stayed 31f) Rate of Knots: useful form over hurdles: won maiden at Navan (66/1) in December and Moscow Flyer Novices' Hurdle at Punchestown (by 1¼ lengths from Crack Mome) in January: bred to stay at least 2½m: remains open to improvement. *T. M. Walsh, Ireland* **h138 p**

Sodexo Gold Cup Handicap Chase, Ascot—Antony is poised to take over from runner-up Junction Fourteen (No.4) two out; the grey Saphir du Rheu takes third, whilst top weight Tea For Two (star on cap) fades into fifth

ANYTHINGMAYHAPPEN (IRE) 6 b.g. Publisher (USA) – Wild Coast (IRE) **h89**
(Gothland (FR)) [2016/17 b75: b15.3m⁴ h20g⁵ h15.3d h17.7s h19g⁶ h21.4d* Mar 26] poor **b64**
form in bumpers: modest form over hurdles: won handicap at Wincanton in March: will
stay 3m: acts on good to soft going. *Jeremy Scott*

ANYWAYTHEWINDBLOWS 5 ch.g. Shirocco (GER) – Welanga (Dansili) [2016/17 **b67**
b16.4v³ b16.2g⁶ Apr 28] poor form in bumpers. *Nicky Richards*

APACHEE PRINCE (IRE) 8 b.g. Indian Danehill (IRE) – Wheredidthemoneygo (IRE) **c98**
(Anshan) [2016/17 h113: h21.4s c15.6vᵖᵘ c23.8g⁴ c19.9gᵖᵘ h23.8gᵖᵘ h19.7dᵖᵘ h24.3dᵖᵘ Apr **h–**
21] fair hurdler, no form in 2016/17: modest form only completed start over fences: stays
3m: acts on good to soft going: has worn headgear/tongue tie. *Alistair Whillans*

APACHE OUTLAW (IRE) 8 b.g. Westerner – Bermuda Bay (IRE) (Be My Native **h96**
(USA)) [2016/17 h104, b88: h16v h15.8d⁴ h20sꟳ h24s h16s Jan 28] fell in Irish maiden
point: modest handicap hurdler: stays 19f: acts on soft going: races prominently. *John
Joseph Hanlon, Ireland*

APACHE PEARL (IRE) 6 br.g. Indian Danehill (IRE) – Pearl Buttons (Alflora (IRE)) **h72**
[2016/17 h–, b–: h15.8m⁴ h15.9g May 28] little form over hurdles: tried in tongue tie: front
runner/races prominently. *Warren Greatrex*

APACHE PILOT 9 br.g. Indian Danehill (IRE) – Anniejo (Presenting) [2016/17 c81, h–: **c86**
c24.2d⁵ c23.8mᵖᵘ c24.2g³ c24.2g² c20.1d* c24.2d c20.1g⁴ c23.4s⁵ c26.3s c20.5s⁵ c20.1s⁵ **h–**
c23.8g⁶ c25.2d c24.2g* Apr 25] maiden hurdler: modest handicap chaser: won at Hexham
in June and April: stays 25f: acts on soft going: usually wears headgear: wears tongue tie.
Maurice Barnes

APACHE SONG 4 ch.f. Mount Nelson – Pantita (Polish Precedent (USA)) [2016/17 **h106**
h16.6g² h16.3g³ Mar 25] half-sister to modest hurdler Hija (17f/3m winner, by Avonbridge):
fair maiden on Flat, stays 1¼m: fair former over hurdles: better effort when second in
juvenile at Doncaster in February. *James Eustace*

APALIS (FR) 5 gr.m. Mastercraftsman (IRE) – Parcimonie (Nombre Premier) [2016/17 **h–**
h19.7sᵖᵘ h16vᵖᵘ h19g h21.2s⁴ Mar 23] fair on Flat in France, stays 1½m: no form over
hurdles: in headgear last 2 starts: usually wears tongue tie. *Charlie Mann*

APASIONADO (GER) 6 ch.g. Mamool (IRE) – Api Sa (IRE) (Zinaad) [2016/17 b16g³ **h130**
b16g³ b16.7g* h15.8d* h15.8g* h19.8s h16.6g² h16g² Mar 18] sturdy gelding: brother to 2 **b97**
winners in Germany and half-brother to 2 winners there by Areion, including useful winner
up to 11f Ashantee: dam useful German 1m/9f winner: fairly useful form in bumpers: won
at Market Rasen in September: useful form over hurdles: won novices at Uttoxeter in
October and Huntingdon in November: left Mervyn Torrens after second start: best form at
2m: acts on good to soft going. *Stuart Edmunds*

A PLEIN TEMPS (FR) 7 b.g. Alberto Giacometti (IRE) – Flower des Champs (FR) **h–**
(Robin des Champs (FR)) [2016/17 h109: h23.1s Nov 20] winning Irish pointer: fair
hurdler: shaped as if amiss only start in 2016/17: stays 3m: acts on heavy going: in
cheekpieces last 2 starts: in tongue tie last 3: usually races close up. *Harry Fry*

APOLLO CREED (IRE) 5 b.g. Vinnie Roe (IRE) – Just Cassandra (IRE) (Eurobus) **b98**
[2016/17 b15.8v⁶ b16.2v² Feb 7] €20,000 3-y-o: second foal: closely related to fair hurdler
Rodger Roo (19f winner, by Definite Article): dam (c103) 3m/25f chase winner: fairly
useful form in bumpers: better effort when second at Hereford in February: will stay at
least 2½m. *Evan Williams*

APPLAUS (GER) 5 b.g. Tiger Hill (IRE) – All About Love (GER) (Winged Love (IRE)) **h108**
[2016/17 b89: h16.4d⁴ h16.4s³ h22.7s h16.4v* h16.4v² h16.4g⁴ h16.2g* Apr 25] bumper
winner: fair hurdler: won novices at Newcastle in February and Hexham in April: should
stay at least 2¼m: acts on heavy going: in cheekpieces/tongue tie. *Micky Hammond*

APPLE OF OUR EYE 7 b.g. Passing Glance – Apple Anthem (True Song) [2016/17 h115: **h119**
h20g² h19.7g³ h19.4g h21gᵖᵘ Feb 25] fairly useful handicap hurdler: third at Wetherby in
October: stays 21f: acts on good going: often races prominently. *Charlie Longsdon*

APPLE POPS 7 b.m. Apple Tree – Rio Pops (Broadsword (USA)) [2016/17 h–: **h–**
h19.8dᵖᵘ Nov 17] no form: dead. *Neil Mulholland*

APPLESANDPIERRES (IRE) 9 b.g. Pierre – Cluain Chaoin (IRE) (Phardante (FR)) **c– p**
[2016/17 h113p: h16d h16.6g h15.8s* h19.7d³ c16.4sꟳ h15.8sꟳ h17.7d² h19.7m* Apr 13] **h129**
won 2 of 4 starts in Irish points: fairly useful handicap hurdler: won at Uttoxeter in
December and Wetherby in April: fell eighth in novice handicap at Sedgefield on chasing
debut: stays 2½m: acts on soft and good to firm going: in headgear last 3 starts: often
travels strongly. *Dan Skelton*

APPLE'S JADE (FR) 5 b.m. Saddler Maker (IRE) – Apple's For Ever (FR) (Nikos) **h158**
[2016/17 h157p: h16d* h16g^2 h16.4s^2 h20d* h20v^2 h19.9g* h20d* Apr 29]

Ten years after first making his name by winning the Grand National with Silver Birch, when he had still to train a winner under Rules in his own country, Gordon Elliott went close in the latest season to ending Willie Mullins' seemingly impregnable reign as Ireland's champion jumps trainer. Going into the Punchestown Festival in the last week of the Irish season, Elliott still held a lead of around €400,000 but, despite Elliott's five wins at Punchestown, three of them in Grade 1 contests, it was Mullins who again emerged on top, to the tune of around €200,000, securing his tenth consecutive title and his fifth in a row with Elliott as runner-up. Mullins has enjoyed a period of overwhelming dominance in Ireland, but Elliott has been closing the gap on him each season, mainly thanks to an ever-expanding string. In the first season in which Elliott finished runner-up to Mullins, 2012/13, Elliott ran only around half the number of horses which Mullins sent out. However, by 2015/16, Elliott had more than doubled the size of his string and saddled more individual horses in an Irish season than Mullins for the first time, as well as reaching a century of winners (123) and passing the equivalent of more than a million pounds in prize money, both for the first time too.

There was little to suggest Mullins' monopoly was under any immediate threat, though, as he ended the 2015/16 season with a prize-money total still more than twice that of his closest rival and with the prospect of the likes of Douvan, Vautour, Djakadam, Annie Power and a fit-again Faugheen to represent him in the latest season. Besides those established stars owned by Rich and Susannah Ricci, an array of promising younger horses included the filly Apple's Jade, the top juvenile hurdler who had won so impressively at Aintree and then followed up at Punchestown in the colours of another of Mullins' biggest supporters Gigginstown House Stud. But in a season in which so much went wrong for Mullins and a lot went right for Elliott, it was only in the last days of the season that Mullins managed to claw back the lead which Elliott had opened up in the autumn, before the better horses in the Mullins string had started appearing. Despite having the upper hand almost throughout, Elliott played down his chances of winning the title for most of the season, justifiably so as it turned out, but he did admit to being 'heartbroken' at losing his advantage so late in the day. Another huge increase in stable strength

Bar One Racing Hatton's Grace Hurdle, Fairyhouse—Apple's Jade gets the better of former stable-companion Vroum Vroum Mag (white face) in a grandstand finish

undoubtedly helped to put Elliott in with a chance, so that even with a strike-rate only half that of Mullins', Elliott sent out the greater number of winners, eventually matching the record total of one hundred and ninety-three which Mullins had set in 2012/13. A colossal two hundred and eighty-five individual horses ran for Elliott at one time or another during the latest Irish season (exactly two hundred more than four years earlier), which was over a hundred more than Mullins could muster.

Part of that increased string was accounted for by the shock announcement in September that Gigginstown was moving sixty of its horses from Mullins over a reported disagreement about an increase in training fees. Elliott was the chief beneficiary as the sixty horses were dispersed. Among his intake of twenty were the top-class chasers Outlander and Don Poli who finished first and second (ahead of their former stablemate Djakadam) in the Lexus Chase later in the season, and, potentially the most exciting recruit of all, the possible Champion Hurdle contender Apple's Jade. As it happened, all three of Apple's Jade's victories for her new stable, each of them in Grade 1 contests, came at the chief expense of Mullins-trained rivals. The first of those came in a thrilling edition of the Bar One Racing Hatton's Grace Hurdle at Fairyhouse at the beginning of December. By then, though, Apple's Jade had already been beaten in her first two starts for her new yard the previous month. She was upset at short odds by fellow four-year-old Rashaan in the WKD Hurdle at Down Royal on her first start for six months and then went down by just a nose to Irving when favourite again for the 'Fighting Fifth' Hurdle at Newcastle, but only after being hampered by the fall of the other Gigginstown representative Petit Mouchoir three out. The step up in trip for the Hatton's Grace promised to suit Apple's Jade who received weight all round in a field of seven, in which Vroum Vroum Mag, unbeaten in ten starts for Mullins and having her first start since the Punchestown Champion Hurdle the previous spring, started at odds-on. The fact that Apple's Jade was reunited with regular jockey Bryan Cooper was also in her favour as the pair have struck up a really good partnership (Cooper had been injured when Apple's Jade ran at Down Royal and had chosen to ride Petit Mouchoir instead at Newcastle). Ridden prominently as usual, Apple's Jade got first run when Cooper kicked on entering the straight before the more patiently ridden Vroum Vroum Mag moved up smoothly to edge ahead at the final flight, only for Apple's Jade to find plenty and regain the lead in the final strides. There was a short head in it, with seven lengths back to the Mullins second string Shaneshill in third.

While the Champion Hurdle was apparently off the agenda for Apple's Jade by now, Cheltenham certainly wasn't and her new target was the David Nicholson Mares' Hurdle which Vroum Vroum Mag had won the season before. Apple's Jade met with another surprising defeat on her only run in the interim when beaten at 5/2-on by the Mullins-trained Limini, winner of the Dawn Run at Cheltenham the previous season, in the listed Quevega Mares Hurdle at Punchestown in February, the race which had been scheduled for the return of the previous year's winner Annie Power. Possibly more in need of the race than expected after an eleven-week break (the same excuse had been cited after her Down Royal defeat), Apple's Jade couldn't match the winner's turn of foot from the last. Willie Mullins has dominated the David Nicholson Mares' Hurdle for most of its existence, Vroum Vroum Mag proving in a different league to her rivals in 2016 much as six-times winner Quevega had been before her, but the latest renewal, branded again as the OLBG Mares' Hurdle, looked a much more competitive affair, pitting Apple's Jade against both Vroum Vroum Mag and Limini. Mares races in general tend to be unpopular as a betting medium but punters cannot have found much fault with this contest which, while still attracting the usual large number of mares who were no better than useful, was one of the top ten races at the Festival by betting turnover. Apple's Jade, tongue tied for the first time, was third choice in the betting at 7/2 behind Limini at 6/4 and Vroum Vroum Mag at 11/4. Ruby Walsh had chosen Limini over Vroum Vroum Mag although the previous year's winner had added to her prolific record, since her narrow defeat in the Hatton's Grace, by winning Leopardstown's Christmas Hurdle over three miles, after which she only scrambled home at 5/1-on over two miles in the Doncaster Mares' Hurdle. The finish at Cheltenham duly concerned the first three in the betting, though another Irish mare, Jer's Girl, a 14/1-shot, was creeping into

OLBG Mares' Hurdle (David Nicholson), Cheltenham—the highest-quality renewal in this race's ten-year history, with Apple's Jade (centre) again digging deep to hold off 2016 winner Vroum Vroum Mag (No.18) and the same connections' Limini (right)

it and going well when falling three out, in the process bringing down a couple of others. The principals avoided the melee, but, in the end, the Mullins pair were both disadvantaged by being held up in a muddling race as Apple's Jade benefited from another astute ride by Cooper who kept his mount much closer to the pace. All three jumped the last together, with Apple's Jade challenged on both sides and Vroum Vroum Mag even edging ahead briefly on touching down before Apple's Jade pulled out more to win by a length and a half, with Vroum Vroum Mag getting the better of Limini by just a nose for second.

It was the first time the David Nicholson had gone to a trainer other than Willie Mullins since the inaugural edition in 2008 won by the Donald McCain-trained Whiteoak. Apple's Jade formed part of a first-day treble for Elliott at the Festival, along with Labaik in the Supreme Novices' and the Gigginstown-owned Tiger Roll in the National Hunt Chase, while three more winners later at the meeting, including Champagne Classic in the same colours in the Martin Pipe, made Elliott leading trainer at the Festival (Mullins also had six winners but two seconds to Elliott's three). Elliott's first Festival success had come in the 2011 National Hunt Chase with Chicago Grey, five years after he also had his very first runner under Rules (Ireland or Britain) at the Festival with 100/1-shot Brandon Mountain who was pulled up in the Fred Winter. Straight after the latest Festival, Elliott was soon back down to business at home when landing a five-timer at his local track Navan on the Sunday after Cheltenham, his victories including the Grade 2 Webster Cup Chase with A Toi Phil, another of the Gigginstown horses formerly trained by Mullins. At that stage of the season, Elliott was 4/1-on with Betfair to be champion, with Mullins at 5/2. By the final day of the season the picture looked very different, however, and Apple's Jade's victory over a four-strong Mullins team in the Irish Stallion Farms European Breeders Fund Mares Champion Hurdle on the last day of the Punchestown Festival was not enough to stop another championship going the way of Mullins. This was another race in which the by now in-foal Annie Power,

Gigginstown House Stud's "Apple's Jade"

twice successful in it in the past, had been due to make a possible belated return and, in her absence, the Mullins quartet had a 'B-team' look about it, even though it included the previous year's winner Whiteout, as well as Augusta Kate who had won the Grade 1 novice for mares at Fairyhouse. Apple's Jade stood out on form and won accordingly by fourteen lengths from another of the Mullins runners, the novice Airlie Beach, whose stable companions took the next three places as well.

	Saddler Maker (IRE) (b 1998)	Sadler's Wells (b 1981)	Northern Dancer / Fairy Bridge
Apple's Jade (FR) (b.m. 2012)		Animatrice (b 1985)	Alleged / Alexandrie
	Apple's For Ever (FR) (b 2000)	Nikos (b or br 1981)	Nonoalco / No No Nanette
		Apple's Girl (b 1989)	Le Pontet / Silver Girl

Interviewed immediately afterwards about future plans for Apple's Jade, her connections seemed to have different views. Owner Michael O'Leary outlined a similar campaign in mares races, but Gordon Elliott suggested a bolder policy, involving Apple's Jade's stepping up in trip and into open competition, saying 'She could be one for three miles and the World [Stayers'] Hurdle.' Two and a half miles certainly suits Apple's Jade better than two, and her strong finishes over the longer trip point to her staying further still, something backed up by her breeding. Her sire Saddler Maker is responsible for other leading jumpers in the British Isles, Alpha des Obeaux, Bristol de Mai and Label des Obeaux, and all of them are stayers,

Alpha des Obeaux runner-up in a World Hurdle for Gigginstown. Apple's Jade's pedigree on the distaff side was dealt with in last year's Annual. To summarise, she is a granddaughter of a good French hurdler Apple's Girl, whose wins included the Prix La Barka. Apple's Jade's dam Apple's For Ever won five times at up to around two and a half miles over hurdles and fences and has produced two other winners in France who are sisters to Apple's Jade. Apple's Jade is a tall, unfurnished mare who acts on heavy going and races prominently. She is a good jumper too, something that stood her in good stead in particular in the closing stages of the David Nicholson at Cheltenham. She was tongue tied again for her last two starts. *Gordon Elliott, Ireland*

APPLESOLUTELY 6 b.m. Apple Tree (FR) – Allerford Annie (IRE) (Oscar (IRE)) **b–** [2016/17 b15.8d May 5] first foal: dam unraced sister to fairly useful/unreliable staying hurdler What An Oscar: dual point winner, placed twice in 2017: tailed off in mares bumper. *Philip Hobbs*

APPLE'S QUEEN (FR) 7 gr.g. Saddler Maker (IRE) – Queenhood (FR) (Linamix (FR)) **c58** [2016/17 c20.2s² Mar 1] multiple point winner: lightly raced over hurdles: maiden chaser: **h–** left Emmanuel Clayeux after final start in 2015/16: stays 19f: has worn cheekpieces. *Mrs S. Alner*

APPLETREE LANE 7 b.m. Croco Rouge (IRE) – Emmasflora (Alflora (IRE)) [2016/17 **h92** h86: h15.8v⁵ h18.6s² h19.9v³ Mar 5] modest maiden hurdler: stays 2½m: acts on heavy going. *Tom Gretton*

APPROACHING STAR (FR) 6 ch.m. New Approach (IRE) – Madame Arcati (IRE) **h68** (Sinndar (IRE)) [2016/17 h83: h16.3m³ h15.9g⁶ Jun 2] sparely-made mare: modest maiden on Flat, stays 1¼m: poor form over hurdles. *Dai Burchell*

APPROPRIATE (FR) 7 b.m. Kapgarde (FR) – Oreli (FR) (Robin des Pres (FR)) **c–** [2016/17 c–, h–: h22g h18.5d h19.1g c25.5g^pu Aug 25] of no account: wears hood/tongue **h–** tie. *Paul Henderson*

APPY DAYS (IRE) 7 b.m. King's Theatre (IRE) – A-To-Z (IRE) (Ahonoora) [2016/17 **h106 p** b16d² b16g ab16g* b15.8d³ h16.5g⁴ h15.6g* Jan 20] sister to useful hurdler/fairly useful **b88** chaser Royal Alphabet (2m winner) and bumper winner/fairly useful hurdler Queen Alphabet (2m winner) and closely related/half-sister to 3 winners: dam useful 7f/1m performer: fair form in bumpers: won at Lingfield in November: fair form over hurdles: won mares novice at Musselburgh in January: later placed on Flat: left Peter Fahey after second start: open to further improvement. *Ian Williams*

APSATOU (FR) 6 b.m. Astarabad (USA) – Touques (FR) (Tip Moss (FR)) [2016/17 **h–** h16g^pu Dec 27] won juvenile at Cagnes in 2014/15 on first of 2 starts over hurdles: dead. *Dan Skelton*

APTERIX (FR) 7 b.g. Day Flight – Ohe Les Aulmes (FR) (Lute Antique (FR)) [2016/17 **c142** h131: h15.7m⁶ c15.2g⁴ c19.3d* c15.2d* c15.2s^ur c19.9g³ c19.1s* c15.5g⁶ Apr 22] **h122** workmanlike gelding: fairly useful handicap hurdler: useful chaser: won handicaps at Sedgefield in November and Wetherby in December, and novice at Doncaster in March: stays 19f: acts on soft going. *Brian Ellison*

AQALIM 7 b.g. Raven's Pass (USA) – Aviacion (BRZ) (Know Heights (IRE)) [2016/17 **c135 §** h147§: c24.1g² c23.6d² c24.4s^pu c23.4d³ c28.4d^pu Feb 18] good-topped gelding: smart **h– §** hurdler: useful form over fences: standout effort when second in novice at Chepstow (4 lengths behind easy winner Thistlecrack) in October: stayed 3m: acted on heavy going: wore headgear: ungenuine: dead. *Tim Vaughan*

AQUA DUDE (IRE) 7 br.g. Flemensfirth (USA) – Miss Cozzene (FR) (Solid Illusion **c138** (USA)) [2016/17 h134p: c21.6v^pu c16.3s³ c22.4d^ur c19.9s³ c19.9d² c19.9g Mar 25] well- **h–** made gelding: won Irish maiden point on debut: useful hurdler: useful form over fences: second in novice handicap at Haydock (short head behind Captain Redbeard) in February: stays 2½m: acts on soft going. *Evan Williams*

ARABIAN OASIS 5 b.g. Oasis Dream – Love Divine (Diesis) [2016/17 h102: h16.2d³ **h95** h15.7s^pu h16.6s h16.8d⁴ h18.6m* h20.2g³ Apr 27] modest handicap hurdler: won at Market Rasen (conditional) in April: stays 2½m: acts on good to firm going: sometimes in cheekpieces: often races in rear. *Philip Kirby*

ARAKHAN 4 b.g. Malinas (GER) – Mays Dream (Josr Algarhoud (IRE)) [2016/17 b13g⁵ **b96** b15.6g³ b17d* b16.3g⁴ Apr 1] fifth foal: half-brother to smart 7f/1m winner Fire Ship (by Firebreak): dam ran once on Flat: fairly useful form in bumpers: won at Carlisle in February. *Richard Fahey*

ARAMADYH 6 gr.m. Authorized (IRE) – Swift Dispersal (Shareef Dancer (USA)) **h91** [2016/17 h84: h16.8m h18.5d* h16.8g h16v^F Mar 23] modest handicap hurdler: won selling event at Newton Abbot in September: stayed 2¼m: acted on good to soft going: tried in visor: dead. *Jimmy Frost*

ARAMIST (IRE) 7 gr.g. Aussie Rules (USA) – Mistic Sun (Dashing Blade) [2016/17 **h89 p** h19.9s^3 Nov 22] fairly useful on Flat, stays 16.5f: 3/1, third in conditionals novice at Sedgefield (17½ lengths behind The Bay Oak) on hurdling debut: should do better. *Alan Swinbank*

ARANTES 6 b.g. Sixties Icon – Black Opal (Machiavellian (USA)) [2016/17 h97: h16.2g^6 **c67** h17.1d h18.1s^4 h16.4d^5 h19s^6 h15.6g^4 h19.4g c15.7s^6 c16.4v^4 h21.4v^F h20.6g c21.6d^5 Apr **h84** 10] poor maiden hurdler: poor form over fences: left R. Mike Smith after first start: unproven beyond 2¼m: acts on heavy going: has worn headgear. *Andrew Hamilton*

ARBEO (IRE) 11 b.g. Brian Boru – Don't Waste It (IRE) (Mister Lord (USA)) [2016/17 **c95 §** c110§, h–: c24.2s^6 c26d^{pu} c23.6s^3 c25.7v^5 c28s^{pu} c25.1m^{pu} Apr 5] useful-looking gelding: **h–** maiden hurdler: modest handicap chaser: stays 29f: acts on heavy going: tried in blinkers: usually races close up: temperamental. *Diana Grissell*

ARBORETUM 9 b.g. Kayf Tara – Step Lively (Dunbeath (USA)) [2016/17 c19.3s^4 **c80** c23.6g c21.2m^4 h15.8g c24g^4 c19.3g^3 c19.3g^4 c24d^{pu} c23.8g^4 Nov 2] dual winning pointer: **h–** well held only outing over hurdles: poor maiden chaser: stays 3m: has worn tongue tie: often races towards rear. *Mike Sowersby*

ARBRE DE VIE (FR) 7 b.g. Antarctique (IRE) – Nouvelle Recrue (FR) (Ragmar (FR)) **c149** [2016/17 c140p, h149: h20d c21.5v^2 c20s^2 c31.8g^{ur} c29d^{bd} c21d^2 Apr 28] angular gelding: **h–** smart hurdler: smart form over fences: second in novice handicap at Punchestown (¾ length behind Woodland Opera) in April: stays 3m: acts on heavy going: tried in hood: usually races nearer last than first. *W. P. Mullins, Ireland*

ARCADIANA (IRE) 7 b.m. Arcadio (GER) – Sovana (FR) (Kadounor (FR)) [2016/17 **b–** b–: b15.7g May 24] no form in bumpers. *John Gallagher*

ARCAMANTE (ITY) 6 b.g. High Chaparral (IRE) – Caractere (IRE) (Indian Ridge) **h76** [2016/17 h101: h19.6g h22g^5 h23g h23m^6 h20g^{ur} h23.3g^5 h23.1g^{bd} h26.4g^3 h27g^{pu} h20.3m^5 h19.9d^6 h25.6g Nov 4] poor maiden hurdler: stays 23f: acts on good to soft going: wears headgear. *Mike Hammond*

ARCHANGEL RAPHAEL (IRE) 5 b.g. Montjeu (IRE) – La Sylvia (IRE) (Oasis **h107** Dream) [2016/17 h17.7d^6 h15.7m^4 h17.7s^6 Dec 26] good-bodied gelding: fairly useful on Flat, stays 1½m: fair form over hurdles: best effort when fourth in novice at Ascot in October: in cheekpieces last 2 starts. *Amanda Perrett*

ARCHIE BOY (IRE) 15 b.g. Basanta (IRE) – Darial Mill (IRE) (Salluceva) [2016/17 **c–** c100, h–: c20.2m^{pu} May 10] winning hurdler: smart chaser at best, pulled up in hunter in **h–** early-2016/17: stays 23f: acts on firm and good to soft going: has worn headgear: has worn tongue tie, including last 3 starts: usually races nearer last than first. *Miss E. H. Yardley*

ARCHIE RICE (USA) 11 b.g. Arch (USA) – Gold Bowl (USA) (Seeking The Gold **c–** (USA)) [2016/17 h100: h21.6m^4 h26.5m* h21.6g^3 h26.5g^6 c19.2g^4 Nov 9] good-topped **h98** gelding: multiple point winner: modest handicap hurdler: won at Newton Abbot in July: well beaten in novice on chasing debut: stays 3¼m: acts on soft and good to firm going. *Jimmy Frost*

ARCHIPELIGO 6 b.g. Archipenko (USA) – Red Slew (Red Ransom (USA)) [2016/17 **h85** h93: h16g^3 h16.2f^4 Jun 5] fair on Flat, stays 1½m, below form in 2017: modest maiden hurdler: unproven beyond 2m: acts on good to soft going: in cheekpieces last 2 starts. *Iain Jardine*

ARCO (IRE) 6 b.m. Flemensfirth (USA) – Babygotback (IRE) (Amilynx (FR)) [2016/17 **h–** b–: h16.8g^5 h21.2g^{pu} h16.2s Nov 4] lengthy mare: no form over hurdles. *Philip Kirby*

ARCTIC BEN (IRE) 13 gr.g. Beneficial – Hurst Flyer (Neltino) [2016/17 c79, h–: **c96 §** c20.8g^5 c20.9m^3 c24m^{pu} c20g^4 c21.2s^3 c21m^{pu} Apr 15] quite good-topped gelding: maiden **h–** hurdler: fairly useful handicap chaser at best, very much on downgrade: stays 21f: acts on heavy going: front runner: temperamental. *Henry Daly*

ARCTIC CHIEF 7 b.g. Sleeping Indian – Neiges Eternelles (FR) (Exit To Nowhere **h–** (USA)) [2016/17 h15.8s^{pu} h16.6g^{pu} Feb 22] placed in bumpers: no form over hurdles after long absence: tried in tongue tie. *Richard Phillips*

ARCTIC DESTINATION (IRE) 6 b.g. Dubai Destination (USA) – Arctic Scale (IRE) **h106 p** (Strong Gale) [2016/17 b94p: b16.2d^4 h22.7d^2 Oct 22] Irish point winner: fair form in **b92** bumpers: evens, second in novice at Kelso (1¼ lengths behind Another Bill) on hurdling debut: should do better. *Donald McCain*

ARCTIC DIXIE 9 ch.m. Desideratum – Arctic Oats (Oats) [2016/17 h99: h19.9g³ h23m **h88** h22g⁵ h23.3g Sep 18] modest maiden hurdler: stays 23f: acts on good to soft going: wears headgear/tongue tie. *Rob Summers*

ARCTIC FIRE (GER) 8 b.g. Soldier Hollow – Adelma (GER) (Sternkoenig (IRE)) **h163** [2016/17 h165: h16.8g* h16g³ Apr 28]

Quevega proved year after year that a lengthy absence beforehand was no bar to winning at the Cheltenham Festival. Of her six wins in the David Nicholson Mares' Hurdle, the last four were all gained without a run since Punchestown the previous spring, while the one before that had come on her first start since a run at Auteuil the previous May. Quevega was head and shoulders above most of the mares she met at Cheltenham each year, and her absences beforehand were not always enforced ones. It was, therefore, a still greater feat of training on Willie Mullins' part when he brought Arctic Fire back to win the latest County Hurdle. The former Champion Hurdle runner-up not only made a successful return from over a year off—four hundred and eighteen days to be exact—following an injury (a chip to a sesamoid bone), but did so carrying top weight against twenty-four rivals in one of the most competitive handicap hurdles of the whole season, let alone the Festival. It brought to mind a similar feat at the 1991 Festival accomplished by Martin Pipe with the injury-prone Omerta who returned from almost as long an absence, more than twelve months, to win the Kim Muir on his first start for the trainer. Pipe, of course, produced numerous similar training feats during his pioneering career, including when saddling Cyborgo to win the 1996 Stayers' Hurdle on his first start since finishing runner-up in the 1995 renewal. Old school methods worked too sometimes, though, as Martha's Son was effectively having his first run for nearly sixteen months (he had fallen at the second on a recent comeback) when winning the Queen Mother Champion Chase in 1997 for Captain Tim Forster (Forster's protege Henry Daly also came close to winning the 2007 Plate with Palarshan, who was runner-up in that race on his first outing in two years).

Arctic Fire's only previous appearance in a handicap had come when finishing second to Lac Fontana in the County Hurdle as a novice three years earlier. Although he was racing from a BHA mark 17 lb higher this time, an assessment of 158 represented some leniency on the official handicapper's part, given that Arctic Fire had been 8 lb higher still when last seen. That was in the Irish Champion Hurdle at Leopardstown in January 2016 when he had been beaten fifteen lengths by stable-companion Faugheen who also sustained an injury after the same race and has not been seen at all on a racecourse since. Arctic Fire finished much closer to Faugheen when runner-up to him in the 2015 Champion Hurdle, though it wasn't until the Hatton's Grace Hurdle at Fairyhouse towards the end of that year that he was finally able to record a Grade 1 win. The fact that Arctic Fire, a 20/1 chance, was ridden by Paul Townend in the County Hurdle signalled that he wasn't the stable's first string. In fact, Mullins related afterwards that he had thought Arctic Fire 'could be a social runner rather than a fancied one.' Although for so long an understudy to Ruby Walsh, Townend has now won six races at the Cheltenham Festival, four of

Randox Health County Handicap Hurdle, Cheltenham—
Paul Townend repeats his 2015 win for the same connections as Arctic Fire (hood) swoops wide to
beat L'Ami Serge (extreme right) and the leader Ozzie The Oscar

Wicklow Bloodstock (Ireland) Ltd's "Arctic Fire"

those wins coming for the Mullins stable on occasions when it has turned out that, for one reason or another, Walsh has been on the 'wrong' one. Townend profited from Walsh's last-flight fall on hot favourite Annie Power to win the 2015 David Nicholson Mares' Hurdle on Glens Melody and he won the County Hurdle at the Festival that year on 25/1 outsider Wicklow Brave (in the same colours as Arctic Fire) when Mullins fielded five runners. Townend completed a quick long-priced double for his stable when Arctic Fire's win was followed by Penhill's 16/1 success in the Spa in which Mullins had four runners.

Mullins was responsible for just two runners in the latest County Hurdle, with Ruby Walsh taking the ride on Renneti who was sent off at 11/1. With Grand National sponsors Randox Health adding their name to the race, the name of Vincent O'Brien, first appended to the race title in 1995 following the trainer's retirement, was dropped, raising adverse comment in some quarters, considering the significant part played by O'Brien in the immediate post-war history of what was then known as the National Hunt meeting. Favourite for the County at 5/1 was the previous season's Triumph Hurdle winner Ivanovich Gorbatov, the subject of a gamble wearing blinkers for his first start in a handicap, after failing to make much of an impact in Grade 1 company in Ireland. The gallop was strong, though those in the main pack were content to let outsider Wakea race into a clear lead before pegging him back in the straight. Arctic Fire typically travelled well under a patient ride and, in a relatively trouble-free race given the size of the field, Townend was able to make good progress wide on the home turn and move across to the stand rail, steering a near-identical path to the one he had taken on Wicklow Brave, on whom he had the race sewn up much further from home. Close up jumping the last, Arctic Fire stayed on to lead in the closing stages and he prevailed in a finish of necks with the even longer-priced pair L'Ami Serge and Ozzie The Oscar. Ivanovich Gorbatov wasn't beaten far in sixth, after holding every chance at the last, while the far from straightforward Renneti ran on strongly after the final flight to finish eighth. Things didn't work out quite so well for Arctic Fire—again ridden by Townend—in the following month's Punchestown Champion Hurdle but he still ran creditably to be a never-nearer third to Wicklow Brave, beaten under two lengths.

		⎧ In The Wings	⎧ Sadler's Wells
	⎧ Soldier Hollow	⎪ (b 1986)	⎩ High Hawk
	⎪ (br 2000)	⎩ Island Race	⎧ Common Grounds
Arctic Fire (GER)	⎪	(b 1995)	⎩ Lake Isle
(b.g. 2009)	⎨	⎧ Sternkoenig	⎧ Kalaglow
	⎪ Adelma (GER)	⎪ (gr 1990)	⎩ Sternwappen
	⎩ (gr 1999)	⎩ Alke	⎧ Konigsstuhl
		(b 1988)	⎩ Astra

The pedigree of the rather leggy Arctic Fire, by the very smart performer around a mile and a quarter Soldier Hollow out of a German eleven-furlong winner, was discussed in *Chasers & Hurdlers 2014/15*. The only update from his family comes from the Czech Republic where Ange Guardian, who is out of a half-sister to Arctic Fire's dam, finished second in the Velka Pardubicka in October. Arctic Fire stays two and a half miles (he was reportedly suffering from a respiratory infection when well beaten on his only try over three miles) and he acts on heavy ground, though he certainly doesn't need the ground to show his form. A plan was announced to try him again on the Flat after Punchestown, a sphere in which he had previously run only twice, winning on his debut in France in 2012. *W. P. Mullins, Ireland*

ARCTIC GOLD (IRE) 6 b.g. Gold Well – Arctic Warrior (IRE) (Arctic Lord) [2016/17 h132, b–: h21.1s[6] h23.4s* h23.6spu c25.2vur c24v[2] h24g h20.3g[3] h20.2g[3] Apr 28] good-topped gelding: useful handicap hurdler: won at Sandown in December: second in novice at Warwick won by Belami des Pictons on completed start over fences, blundering 5 out and eased run-in: stays 3m: acts on heavy going: front runner/races prominently. *Nigel Twiston-Davies*   **c134 h132**

ARCTIC LADY (IRE) 6 b.m. Milan – Arctic Rose (IRE) (Jamesmead) [2016/17 b78p: b15.7g[3] h18.5s h21.7v[3] h25.3s[3] c20v[6] c25.1m[5] Apr 5] won Irish mares maiden point on debut: modest form in bumpers/over hurdles: well held both starts in handicap chases: stays 2¾m: acts on heavy going: wears tongue tie: races prominently. *Tom George*   **c– h96 b84**

ARCTIC SKIPPER (IRE) 8 b.g. Flemensfirth (USA) – Coco Opera (IRE) (Lafontaine (USA)) [2016/17 c16d* c24d Dec 28] half-brother to fair 2m hurdle winner Smokey Mountain (by Saddlers' Hall), modest hurdler/chaser Star Tenor (2m-19f winner, by Fourstars Allstar) and a winning pointer by Milan: dam (h110), 2m-2¼m hurdle winner, half-sister to high-class chaser (best around 2m) Mulligan: winning hurdler: useful chaser: won Fortria Chase at Navan (by short head from Gilgamboa) in November: effective at 2m and probably stays 3m: acts on heavy going: front runner/races prominently. *Vincent Laurence Halley, Ireland*   **c144 h–**

ARCTIC VODKA 5 gr.g. Black Sam Bellamy (IRE) – Auntie Kathleen (Terimon) [2016/17 h17.1g[4] b16.4s b16s h19.3g Apr 15] poor form in bumpers: tailed off in novice on hurdling debut. *Sharon Watt*   **h– b73**

ARDAMIR (FR) 5 b.g. Deportivo – Kiss And Cry (FR) (Nikos) [2016/17 h123: h16.6g[5] Dec 10] good-topped gelding: fairly useful maiden on Flat, stays 16.5f: fairly useful hurdler: well below form only start in 2016/17: raced around 2m: acts on good to firm going: usually races towards rear. *Alan King*   **h90**

ARDEA (IRE) 9 b.g. Millenary – Dark Dame (IRE) (Norwich) [2016/17 c105p: c24.2d* c24.2s[2] c26g[2] c24.2d* c24.2g* Apr 25] multiple point winner: fairly useful form in chases: won hunters at Hexham (maiden) very early in season, Wetherby in March and Hexham again in April: second at Wetherby and Doncaster other 2 starts in 2016/17: stays 3¼m: acts on soft going: often races towards rear: has idled. *Justin Landy*   **c123 h–**

ARDEN DENIS (IRE) 8 ch.g. Generous (IRE) – Christian Lady (IRE) (Mandalus) [2016/17 h20v[4] h23v[3] h21.4d* h21.7s[3] Mar 11] good-topped gelding: winning pointer: modest handicap hurdler: won at Wincanton in February: likely to stay 3m: acts on heavy going. *Neil Mulholland*   **h99**

ARDESIA (IRE) 13 b.g. Red Sunset – Lowtown (Camden Town) [2016/17 h68: h16.2d³ h16.7g⁵ h22.1gᵖᵘ Jul 18] close-coupled gelding: poor handicap hurdler: stayed 2½m: acted on heavy going: often wore cheekpieces: tried in tongue tie: usually raced prominently: dead. *Tina Jackson* **h66**

ARDKILLY WITNESS (IRE) 11 b.g. Witness Box (USA) – Ardkilly Angel (IRE) (Yashgan) [2016/17 c130, h–: c25.1m⁴ c24.5dᵖᵘ c24.2s³ h21.4s c24.2s² c24.2dᵘʳ Mar 10] strong gelding: winning hurdler: fairly useful chaser: second in Royal Artillery Gold Cup (Amateur Riders) at Sandown in February: stays 25f: acts on heavy going: has worn headgear, including in 2016/17: has worn tongue tie. *Jamie Snowden* **c125 h–**

ARDMAYLE (IRE) 5 ch.g. Whitmore's Conn (USA) – Welsh Connection (IRE) (Welsh Term) [2016/17 b16.7s⁵ h20g³ h15.7v⁴ c20.2s* c16v* c24.2g⁴ Apr 17] £50,000 4-y-o: seventh foal: brother to fairly useful hurdler/chaser Ink Master (2m winner) and fairly useful hurdler/winning pointer Conal (2¾m winner): dam, lightly raced in points, half-sister to fairly useful hurdler/useful chaser (stayed 3¼m) Ballytrim: off mark in Irish points at second attempt: fifth in bumper: fair form over hurdles (open to improvement): fairly useful form over fences: won novice handicaps at Leicester in February and Lingfield in March: stays 2½m: acts on heavy going. *Ali Stronge* **c120 h102 p b–**

ARDMILLAN (IRE) 9 b.g. Golan (IRE) – Black Gayle (IRE) (Strong Gale) [2016/17 c18sᵖᵘ c20s⁶ c24sᵘʳ c20.1vᶠ h20.5v⁴ c20vᵖᵘ Apr 1] 25/1, last of 4 finishers in novice at Ayr (5¾ lengths behind Progress Drive) on hurdling debut, very much having run of race: fair handicap chaser: little form in 2016/17: stays 3m: acts on heavy going. *Stuart Crawford, Ireland* **c88 h103**

ARDVIEW BOY (IRE) 8 b.g. Tamayaz (CAN) – Cill Uird (IRE) (Phardante (FR)) [2016/17 h16g⁵ h16g³ h20g h16.2s h16s h20v h16v Apr 1] modest maiden hurdler: unproven beyond 2m: acts on soft going: usually leads. *Anthony Mulholland, Ireland* **h93**

AREEMA (IRE) 7 b.g. Desert King (IRE) – Old Glenort Daragh (IRE) (Entrepreneur) [2016/17 h16g h19.5s h23.8g² h22s h20.2g⁵ Apr 27] placed on second start in maiden points: fair maiden hurdler: stays 3m: acts on soft going: tried in cheekpieces/tongue tie. *Ian Ferguson, Ireland* **h105**

AREGRA (FR) 7 gr.g. Fragrant Mix (IRE) – Elisa de Mai (FR) (Video Rock (FR)) [2016/17 c82, h62: c16.4gᵖᵘ c19.2d³ c20.1d c20g⁴ c20.3gᵖᵘ h19.9g⁴ Aug 25] poor maiden hurdler: poor handicap chaser: stays 19f: acts on good to firm and good to soft going: wears headgear: front runner/races prominently: temperamental. *Peter Niven* **c74 § h61**

ARE THEY YOUR OWN (IRE) 9 b.g. Exit To Nowhere (USA) – Carioca Dream (USA) (Diesis) [2016/17 h118: c21.2gᶠ Apr 17] sturdy gelding: fairly useful hurdler: clear when fell last in novice hunter at Fakenham on chasing debut after 17-month absence: stays 21f: acts on good to firm and good to soft going: has worn tongue tie, including last 5 starts: front runner. *Mrs A. Slatter* **c116 h–**

ARGANTE (FR) 8 b.g. Singspiel (IRE) – Abyaan (IRE) (Ela-Mana-Mou) [2016/17 h120p: h15.7d⁶ h20g* h21gᵖᵘ Feb 25] sturdy gelding: fairly useful on Flat, stays 16.5f: fair form over hurdles: won maiden at Fakenham in December. *Nicky Henderson* **h114**

ARGOT 6 b.g. Three Valleys (USA) – Tarot Card (Fasliyev (USA)) [2016/17 h111: h19.1gᵖᵘ c24g c21g c21.1d* Sep 4] lengthy gelding: fair hurdler: fairly useful form over fences: won handicap at Fontwell in September: stays 21f: acts on heavy going: has worn headgear, including in 2016/17: usually races close up: signs of temperament. *Charlie Longsdon* **c118 h–**

ARGUS (IRE) 5 b.g. Rip Van Winkle (IRE) – Steel Princess (IRE) (Danehill (USA)) [2016/17 h16.8v⁶ h16.8s⁶ h16.3d Feb 11] rather leggy gelding: fairly useful on Flat, stays 1¾m: poor form in maiden/novice hurdles: tried in hood: capable of better. *Alexandra Dunn* **h81 p**

ARGYLE (IRE) 4 gr.g. Lawman (FR) – All Hallows (IRE) (Dalakhani (IRE)) [2016/17 h15.9v⁴ h15.9v³ h16m Apr 4] fair maiden on Flat, stays 2m: modest form over hurdles: best effort when third in maiden at Plumpton in February. *Gary Moore* **h97**

ARIAN (IRE) 5 b.m. King's Theatre (IRE) – Brave Betsy (IRE) (Pistolet Bleu (IRE)) [2016/17 b57p: ab16g⁵ b16.7s* h19.5vᶠ Feb 20] fair form in bumpers: won mares maiden at Bangor in December: held in third when fell 2 out in mares novice won by Hitherjacques Lady at Lingfield on hurdling debut. *John Flint* **h103 b93**

ARISTOCLES (IRE) 4 b.g. High Chaparral (IRE) – Amathusia (Selkirk (USA)) [2016/17 h16.1mᵐ h17.7d⁵ h16s⁶ h19.1v⁵ h21.9vᵖᵘ Mar 19] half-brother to modest hurdler Maria's Choice (2¼m winner, by Oratorio): fair on Flat, stays 1¾m: modest form over hurdles: left Stuart Edmunds after second start: stays 19f: in cheekpieces last 3 starts. *Nikki Evans* **h95**

ARISTO DU PLESSIS (FR) 7 b.g. Voix du Nord (FR) – J'aime (FR) (Royal Charter (FR)) [2016/17 h145: c15.9g⁵ h15.3m³ h18.9v⁵ h16.6g h16.2v⁴ h15.6gᵖᵘ Feb 4] angular gelding: useful handicap hurdler: largely out of sorts in 2016/17: tailed off in novice on chasing debut: stays 19f: acts on soft going: sometimes in headgear in 2016/17: front runner/races prominently. *James Ewart* **c–ᴴ121**

ARKADIOS (FR) 6 b.g. Elusive City (USA) – Blue Card (FR) (Trempolino (USA)) [2016/17 h19.7sᵖᵘ h16.8sᵖᵘ h16.5g h21.4sᵖᵘ h15.3vᵇᵈ h20.6mᵖᵘ h21.6mᶠ Apr 15] half-brother to French 17f hurdle winners Blue Boy (by Falco) and Viguria (by Green Tune): fairly useful on Flat in France, stays 12.5f: modest maiden hurdler: in lead when held 2 out in novice handicap at Newton Abbot, standout effort: tried in blinkers: in tongue tie last 5 starts. *David Pipe* **h97**

ARKOSE (IRE) 13 b.g. Luso – Endless Patience (IRE) (Miner's Lamp) [2016/17 c26g⁴ Feb 22] well-made gelding: won 3 times in points: fairly useful hurdler/chaser at one time: well held on hunter debut: stays 3¾m: acts on soft and good to firm going: wears headgear. *Tim Thirlby* **c79 h–**

ARMAANS WISH (IRE) 6 ch.g. Presenting – Pretty Puttens (IRE) (Snurge) [2016/17 b15.8m* b16.8g² b16m² Jul 4] €27,000 3-y-o: second foal: dam unraced half-sister to Cheltenham Gold Cup winner Denman (by Presenting): fairly useful maiden in bumpers: won maiden at Ludlow in May: will stay at least 2½m. *Nicky Henderson* **b98**

AR MAD (FR) 7 b.g. Tiger Groom – Omelia (FR) (April Night (FR)) [2016/17 c157+, h–: c15.5d³ Dec 3] lengthy gelding: winning hurdler: high-class form over fences: completed 4-timer as novice in 2015/16: off 10 months, 9/2, better than ever when 3½ lengths fourth of 6 to Un de Sceaux in Tingle Creek Chase at Sandown, only outing in 2016/17: stays 21f: acts on heavy going: has worn hood: front runner, often travels strongly. *Gary Moore* **c161 + h–**

ARMEDANDBEAUTIFUL 9 b.m. Oscar (IRE) – Grey Mistral (Terimon) [2016/17 h20.6d c23.8g⁵ Apr 9] maiden hurdler/chaser, no form in 2016/17: stays 3m: acts on good to soft going. *Tom Gretton* **c– h–**

ARMEDANDDANGEROUS (IRE) 12 b.g. Kris Kin (USA) – Lucky Fountain (IRE) (Lafontaine (USA)) [2016/17 c104, h–: h21d c27.6d⁴ c28sᵖᵘ c29.2vᵖᵘ Mar 22] good-topped gelding: winning hurdler: fair handicap chaser: stays 3½m: acts on heavy going: has worn headgear, including in 2016/17: in tongue tie last 4 starts: unreliable. *Tom Gretton* **c104 § h–**

ARMEMENT (FR) 6 b.g. Smadoun (FR) – Apparement (IRE) (Anabaa (USA)) [2016/17 b–: b16.4g h19.7gᵖᵘ h16dᵖᵘ Nov 16] no form in bumpers/over hurdles. *James Grassick* **h– b–**

ARMOROUS 6 b.g. Generous (IRE) – Armorine (FR) (Jeune Homme (USA)) [2016/17 h18.6dᵖᵘ h16.2d² h19.6d³ h16s Nov 23] poor form over hurdles: in hood last 3 starts: often races in rear. *Joanne Foster* **h77**

AROUSAL 5 b.m. Stimulation (IRE) – Midnight Mover (IRE) (Bahamian Bounty) [2016/17 h16.8g⁴ h16.2d h24m³ h16.2g⁶ Oct 8] poor maiden on Flat: no form over hurdles. *Tina Jackson* **h–**

ARPEGE D'ALENE (FR) 7 gr.g. Dom Alco (FR) – Joliette d'Alene (FR) (Garde Royale) [2016/17 c134+, h148: c23.6g⁵ c25d* c25.3g² c26.3s³ c23.8s⁴ c31.8g⁴ c31.8gᵖᵘ Apr 22] tall gelding: smart form over hurdles: second to Mall Dini in Pertemps Final at Cheltenham in 2015/16: smart chaser: won 2-finisher novice at Aintree (by 10 lengths from Wotzizname) in November: fourth to Tiger Roll in National Hunt Chase at Cheltenham: stayed 4m: acted on soft going: wore headgear/tongue tie: dead. *Paul Nicholls* **c145 h–**

ARQUEBUSIER (FR) 7 bl.g. Discover d'Auteuil (FR) – Djurjura (FR) (Akarad (FR)) [2016/17 c102, h103: c20s³ c20s* c20v³ c22.7g⁵ h16.7s c20.9s⁶ Mar 11] sturdy gelding: fair hurdler: modest handicap chaser: won at Warwick in December: stays 21f: acts on heavy going: wears headgear. *Emma Baker* **c99 h–**

ARSENALE (GER) 6 b.m. Nicaron (GER) – Alte Rose (GER) (Monsun (GER)) [2016/17 h–: h16.8d Apr 28] modest on Flat, stays 1½m: no form in maiden hurdles: tried in cheekpieces. *Michael Appleby* **h–**

ARTHAMINT 9 b.g. Passing Glance – Araminta (Carlingford Castle) [2016/17 c100§, h95: c23.9g³ c19.5vᵖᵘ c21.3s⁴ c20vᵖᵘ Apr 1] maiden hurdler: modest handicap chaser: left Dan Skelton after first start: stays 3¼m: acts on heavy going: has worn headgear, including in 2016/17: wears tongue tie: irresolute. *Eoin Christopher McCarthy, Ireland* **c96 § h–**

ARTHINGTON 4 b.g. Haafhd – Pequenita (Rudimentary (USA)) [2016/17 b16s ab16g³ b15.7m³ Apr 13] £3,500 3-y-o: fifth foal: half-brother to fairly useful hurdler In On The Act (2m winner, by Act One), stays 2½m: dam (c108/h94), temperamental 2m-21f hurdle/ chase winner, also 11f winner on Flat: modest form in bumpers. *Seamus Mullins* **b83**

ARTHUR BURRELL 8 ch.g. With The Flow (USA) – Kingsmill Quay (Noble Imp) **h99** [2016/17 h93, b89: h16.8d² h21.6m³ h21.6m Apr 15] bumper winner: modest form over hurdles. *Jackie du Plessis*

ARTHUR MC BRIDE (IRE) 8 b.g. Royal Anthem (USA) – Lucky Diverse (IRE) **c–** (Lucky Guest) [2016/17 c–, h101x: h24g³ h22.1m² h23.3d* h23g⁴ Jul 26] useful-looking **h109 x** gelding: fair handicap hurdler: won at Uttoxeter in July: pulled up only start over fences: stays 3m: acts on good to firm and heavy going: tried in tongue tie: often let down by jumping. *Nigel Twiston-Davies*

ARTHUR'S LEGEND (FR) 5 b.g. Flying Legend (USA) – Strawberry (IRE) **h–** (Beneficial) [2016/17 b15.8g b16.7s h20.3vᵖᵘ Dec 11] no form in bumpers/maiden hurdle: **b–** left Denis Quinn after first start: tried in visor: has worn tongue tie. *Amy Murphy*

ARTHUR'S OAK 9 b.g. Kayf Tara – Myumi (Charmer) [2016/17 c152, h–: c15.2s⁵ **c131** Dec 27] strong gelding: winning hurdler: smart handicap chaser: below form only start in **h–** 2016/17: best form at 2m: acts on heavy going: usually leads, often travels strongly. *Venetia Williams*

ARTHUR'S REUBEN 4 b.g. Malinas (GER) – Ambitious Annie (Most Welcome) **b60** [2016/17 b15.7d⁶ Feb 26] well held in bumper. *Jennie Candlish*

ARTHURS SECRET 7 ch.g. Sakhee's Secret – Angry Bark (USA) (Woodman (USA)) **h119** [2016/17 h115: h16.2m² h19.4g³ h19.4g² h23.8g² h26.1g² h24.4s h22.8g⁴ Apr 15] fairly useful handicap hurdler: second at Musselburgh in January/February: left John Quinn after first start: stays 3¼m: acts on good to firm going: tried in cheekpieces. *Sandy Thomson*

ARTHUR'S SECRET (FR) 7 b.g. Secret Singer (FR) – Luna Park (FR) (Cyborg (FR)) **c127 p** [2016/17 c–, h98: c20.9s* Mar 13] easily won all 5 starts in points: winning hurdler: fairly **h–** useful form in chases: won novice hunter at Stratford in March: stays 21f: acts on soft going: tried in tongue tie: open to further improvement over fences. *Martin Weston*

ARTIFICE SIVOLA (FR) 7 gr.g. Dom Alco (FR) – Kerrana (FR) (Cadoudal (FR)) **c124** [2016/17 c123, h117: h16.3g* h20s* c16.2s² c15.5d⁴ Mar 10] compact gelding: fairly **h121** useful hurdler: won novice at Stratford in October and handicap at Fakenham in January: fairly useful handicap chaser: second at Warwick in January: stays 2½m: acts on soft going: wears hood: usually leads, often travels strongly. *Lucy Wadham*

ARTISTE DU GOUET (FR) 7 b.g. Lavirco (GER) – Newhaven (FR) (Subotica (FR)) **c–** [2016/17 h–, b–: h19.2g³ c20gᵖᵘ c23g⁶ h15.3d⁴ h21.4d⁵ Dec 13] big, lengthy, workmanlike **h72** gelding: poor form over hurdles: no promise over fences: left Heather Dalton after third start: tried in tongue tie: temperament under suspicion. *Barry Brennan*

ART LOOKER (IRE) 5 b.g. Excellent Art – Looker (Barathea (IRE)) [2016/17 h19.7s **h87** h16.8m⁵ h16.5m³ Apr 27] no show in Flat maidens: limited promise in novice/maiden hurdles: wears tongue tie. *Tracey Barfoot-Saunt*

ART MAURESQUE (FR) 7 b.g. Policy Maker (IRE) – Modeva (FR) (Valanour (IRE)) **c149** [2016/17 c147, h–: c21g* c19.4g* c20.4s c20.8g c20.8g c22.7gᵖᵘ Apr 29] rangy gelding: **h–** has reportedly had breathing operation: winning hurdler: smart handicap chaser: won at Newton Abbot in May and Chepstow (by head from Double Shuffle) in October: found things tougher after: stays 21f: acts on good to firm and heavy going: has worn headgear, including final start. *Paul Nicholls*

ART OF LOGISTICS (IRE) 9 b.g. Exit To Nowhere (USA) – Sanadja (IRE) (Slip **c134** Anchor) [2016/17 c139, h–: c19.2g c21.4d² c22.6gᵘʳ c19.4m⁴ Oct 12] strong gelding: **h–** winning hurdler: useful handicap chaser: probably stays 23f: acts on soft and good to firm going: wears headgear: in tongue tie last 2 starts. *Philip Hobbs*

ART OF PAYROLL (GER) 8 b.g. Shirocco (GER) – Anna Maria (GER) (Night Shift **c133** (USA)) [2016/17 c129p, h134: h16d c16g² c19.5g² c22s² c17d³ c20s⁴ c22s³ c24.7dᵖᵘ Apr **h–** 17] useful handicap hurdler/maiden chaser: stays 2¾m: acts on good to firm and heavy going: wears tongue tie. *Ms Sandra Hughes, Ireland*

ARTY BELLA 6 b.m. Overbury (IRE) – Gertrude Webb (Central Park (IRE)) [2016/17 h–: **h–** h18.5g May 25] winning pointer: no form over hurdles. *Jimmy Frost*

ARTY CAMPBELL (IRE) 7 b.g. Dylan Thomas (IRE) – Kincob (USA) (Kingmambo **h99** (USA)) [2016/17 h103p: h16.8g³ h19.3m⁴ h16.4g h19.4g⁵ Nov 25] workmanlike gelding: fairly useful on Flat, stays 21f: modest maiden hurdler: should stay beyond 19f: acts on good to firm and good to soft going: in cheekpieces last 4 starts. *Bernard Llewellyn*

AS AND WIIEN (IRE) 6 br.g. Presenting – Coole Eile (IRE) (King's Ride) [2016/17 **h–** b15.3m² h19.8d h15.7g h19.3d Jan 25] €58,000 3-y-o: good-topped gelding: brother to fair **b85** hurdler/fairly useful chaser American Legend (2½m-27f winner) and half-brother to 2 winners, including smart 2½m bumper winner/fairly useful 23f hurdle winner Snow Tern (by Glacial Storm): dam unraced sister to useful hurdler/staying chaser Tullymurry Toff out of half-sister to top-class staying chaser Marlborough: second in bumper at Wincanton: no form over hurdles: left Paul Nicholls after second start: has worn tongue tie. *Ben Haslam*

ASCENDANT 11 ch.g. Medicean – Ascendancy (Sadler's Wells (USA)) [2016/17 c–, h125: h20d^{pu} h15.8d^2 h16.5g^5 h19.9s^F Jan 29] well-made gelding: fairly useful handicap hurdler: unseated early only outing over fences: trained first 2 starts in 2016/17 by Alan Jones: stays 21f: acts on good to firm and heavy going: has worn blinkers/tongue tie. *Johnny Farrelly* — c–, h119

ASCOT DE BRUYERE (FR) 7 b.g. Kapgarde (FR) – Quid de Neuville (FR) (Le Balafre (FR)) [2016/17 c108, h113: c16.4g^3 c19.3d^3 c21.5s^4 c21.6s^2 c20.5v^4 c21.6s* c23.4s^{pu} Apr 3] fair hurdler: fair handicap chaser: in front when left alone last in novice event at Kelso in March: stays 2¾m: acts on soft going: wears headgear: front runner/races prominently. *James Ewart* — c113, h–

ASCOTDEUX NELLERIE (FR) 7 ch.g. Network (GER) – Jumper Nellerie (FR) (Panoramic) [2016/17 h122, b97: c20m^{pu} h21d^4 h21.6m^6 Apr 15] useful-looking gelding: bumper winner: fairly useful hurdler: pulled up in novice handicap on chasing debut: will stay 3m: acts on good to soft going. *Kim Bailey* — c–, h116

AS DE FER (FR) 11 b.g. Passing Sale (FR) – Miss Hollywood (FR) (True Brave (USA)) [2016/17 c126, h–: c20d^5 c22.9s^{ur} c26.7s^4 c24.2s c22.9v^{pu} Mar 22] maiden hurdler: fairly useful handicap chaser: stays 27f: acts on heavy going: has worn headgear: wears tongue tie: front runner/races prominently: unreliable. *Anthony Honeyball* — c119 §, h–

AS DE MEE (FR) 7 b.g. Kapgarde (FR) – Koeur de Mee (FR) (Video Rock (FR)) [2016/17 c141, h–: c19.2d* c20.4s c21.1d* c20.8s^{pu} c17.4s^2 c21.1g^5 c20g^4 Apr 29] rangy gelding: winning hurdler: useful chaser: won maiden at Fontwell in October and Grand Sefton Chase at Aintree (by 5 lengths from Seefood) in December: fourth in novice handicap at Sandown (3½ lengths behind Shantou Village) final start: stays 21f: acts on heavy going: has worn headgear: front runner/races prominently, often travels strongly: not straightforward (carries head awkwardly under pressure). *Paul Nicholls* — c143, h–

ASHCOTT BOY 9 ch.g. Lahib (USA) – Last Ambition (IRE) (Cadeaux Genereux) [2016/17 c121, h–: c19.9g* c20d^2 c20g^F c20g c19.4m c19.4d^6 c20.2f^4 Apr 23] lengthy gelding: winning hurdler: fairly useful handicap chaser: won at Aintree in May: below form after next start: stays 2½m: acts on good to firm and heavy going: has worn headgear, including last 3 starts. *Neil Mulholland* — c124, h–

ASHES CORNER (IRE) 7 b.g. Marienbard (IRE) – Up Thyne Girl (IRE) (Good Thyne (USA)) [2016/17 h–§: h16.2d^4 h22.1m^3 May 30] third on completed start in Irish points: modest form over hurdles: best effort at 2¾m: acts on good to firm going: tried in cheekpieces: temperamental. *Julia Brooke* — h85 §

ASHFORD WOOD (IRE) 9 b.g. Stowaway – Shambala (IRE) (Imperial Ballet (IRE)) [2016/17 c90, h–§: c24g^{pu} c26.2d c26.3d^R c23.5v^3 c25.6d^{pu} Feb 26] lengthy gelding: winning hurdler: poor maiden chaser: stays 3m: best form on heavy going: has worn headgear, including in 2016/17: often races prominently: temperamental. *Tim Vaughan* — c82 §, h– §

ASHJAN 4 b.g. Medicean – Violet (IRE) (Mukaddamah (USA)) [2016/17 h16g^5 h16.2v^2 h16.8g Apr 10] lightly raced on Flat: well held in juvenile/maiden hurdles: tried in blinkers/tongue tie. *Mark McNiff, Ireland* — h–

ASHKOUN (FR) 6 b.g. Sinndar (IRE) – Ashalina (FR) (Linamix (FR)) [2016/17 h92: h19.9g^{pu} h19.5m^4 Apr 28] maiden hurdler, modest at best: stays 19f: acts on good to firm and heavy going: wears hood: has worn tongue tie, including last 4 starts: usually leads. *Tim Vaughan* — h74

ASHOKA (IRE) 5 gr.g. Azamour (IRE) – Jinskys Gift (IRE) (Cadeaux Genereux) [2016/17 h120: h16d^{pu} h15.8v^{pu} h16s h15.8s^6 h18.7g* h18.5m* Apr 18] well-made gelding: fairly useful handicap hurdler: won at Stratford and Exeter in April: stays 19f: acts on good to firm and heavy going: has worn cheekpieces, including last 3 starts: in tongue tie last 2. *Dan Skelton* — h116

ASH PARK (IRE) 9 b.g. Milan – Distant Gale (IRE) (Strong Gale) [2016/17 h104: h16.2d* h16.2d^2 h17.2g* h20.1d* h17.2m^2 c20d^2 c16.3s^{ur} c20.1s^2 c19.9g^3 c21.6v^{ur} c16.4s^3 c17.1v^4 c19.9g* c21.4m^2 c15.5d^4 Apr 21] fairly useful handicap hurdler: won at Kelso (conditional) in May, and Cartmel (conditional) and Hexham in June: useful chaser: won novice at Musselburgh in March: stays 2½m: acts on soft and good to firm going. *Stuart Coltherd* — c133, h118

coral.co.uk Best Price Guaranteed On Horse Racing Handicap Chase, Chepstow—
a deserved win for Aso in a consistent campaign

ASHTOWN (IRE) 10 b.g. Westerner – Christmas River (IRE) (Be My Native (USA)) **h–**
[2016/17 h96: h20g^{pu} h15.8v^{pu} Dec 21] maiden Irish pointer: maiden hurdler, no form in
2016/17: stays 2½m: acts on soft going. *Malcolm Jones*

ASK ALICE 4 b.f. Robin des Champs (FR) – Viva Victoria (Old Vic) [2016/17 b15.7s^6 **b–**
Mar 20] first foal: dam unraced out of fairly useful chaser (winner up to 3½m) Rosie
Redman: tailed off in bumper. *Martin Keighley*

ASKAMORE DARSI (IRE) 8 b.g. Darsi (FR) – Galamear (Strong Gale) [2016/17 c117, **c113 §**
h–: c24.5d^3 c26.2d^5 c28.4v^{pu} c24.1s^{pu} h25.3s^5 h27v* h25g^3 Apr 15] good-bodied gelding: **h115 §**
fairly useful handicap hurdler: won at Sedgefield in March: fairly useful handicap chaser:
stays 27f: acts on heavy going: wears headgear: temperamental. *Donald McCain*

ASKCOLIN (IRE) 8 ch.g. Ashkalani (IRE) – Wild Bramble (IRE) (Deep Run) [2016/17 **h–**
h20d^{pu} Jun 22] pulled up in novice hurdle. *Seamus Mullins*

ASKER (IRE) 9 b.g. High Chaparral (IRE) – Pay The Bank (High Top) [2016/17 h68§: **h– §**
h19.5d Oct 25] angular gelding: maiden hurdler: usually wears headgear: in tongue tie last
3 starts: temperamental. *Nick Lampard*

ASKGARMOR (IRE) 5 b.g. Ask – Karmafair (IRE) (Always Fair (USA)) [2016/17 **h61**
b16.8d^4 h16.8d^5 h16.2v h16.2v Mar 4] off mark in maiden points at fourth attempt: **b77**
fourth in bumper at Sedgefield: well held in novice hurdles: will be suited by 2½m+.
Tristan Davidson

ASKING QUESTIONS (IRE) 5 b.g. Ask – Just Sara (IRE) (Insan (USA)) [2016/17 **b84**
b16.7g^2 Apr 22] €37,000 3-y-o: seventh foal: dam unraced half-sister to useful chasers up
to 25f Present Man and Caim Hill: Irish maiden point winner: 7/1, second in conditionals/
amateur bumper at Bangor (15 lengths behind Juge Et Parti) in April: will stay at least
2½m. *Oliver Greenall*

ASKNOTWHAT (IRE) 6 ch.g. Dylan Thomas (IRE) – Princess Roseburg (USA) **h99**
(Johannesburg (USA)) [2016/17 h90: h20.6g^4 h21.6m^4 h18.7m^F Aug 24] fair maiden
hurdler: may prove best at short of 21f: acts on soft and good to firm going: tried in
cheekpieces. *David Bridgwater*

ASK PADDY (IRE) 5 ch.g. Ask – Dalzenia (FR) (Cadoudal (FR)) [2016/17 h–, b–: **h101**
h15.7g h17.2m h15.7g^5 h22s^4 h24.1s^5 h19.3s* h19.9s* h19.9d* h19.7d^6 Mar 21] sturdy
gelding: fair handicap hurdler: won at Catterick (conditional) and Sedgefield in February,
and at Sedgefield again in March: stays 2½m: acts on soft going: tried in tongue tie: usually
leads. *Sam England*

82

ASK THE WEATHERMAN 8 b.g. Tamure (IRE) – Whatagale (Strong Gale) [2016/17 **c127 p**
c25.1v* c26.3g Mar 17] £19,000 4-y-o: closely related to useful hurdler/chaser Tot
O'Whiskey (2m-3m winner, by Saddlers' Hall): dam (c109) 21f-25f chase winner: prolific
winning pointer: useful form in chases: won hunter at Wincanton in February: seventh in
Foxhunter Chase at Cheltenham (5¾ lengths behind Pacha du Polder, novicey mistakes)
following month: wears cheekpieces: remains open to improvement. *Jack R. Barber*

ASOCKASTAR (IRE) 9 b.g. Milan – Baie Barbara (IRE) (Heron Island (IRE)) [2016/17 **c90 §**
c–, h70: h15.8m² h20d⁵ h19.4g² h20s⁵ c16.4d³ Mar 14] modest handicap hurdler: maiden **h96 §**
chaser: stays 23f: acts on soft and good to firm going: has worn headgear: tried in tongue
tie: unreliable. *Tim Vaughan*

ASO (FR) 7 b.g. Goldneyev (USA) – Odyssee du Cellier (FR) (Dear Doctor (FR)) [2016/17 **c160**
c145, h–: c20.4s⁴ c20.8s² c19.4s* c20.8s c24g⁴ c20.8g³ c25g⁴ Apr 6] useful-looking **h–**
gelding: winning hurdler: high-class chaser: won handicap at Chepstow (by 4 lengths
from Drumlee Sunset) in December: career-best third in Ryanair Chase at Cheltenham
(7½ lengths behind Un de Sceaux) in March: stays 3m: acts on heavy going: has worn
cheekpieces, including last 2 starts: often races towards rear. *Venetia Williams*

ASPECIALPRESENT (IRE) 7 br.g. Presenting – Escrea (IRE) (Oscar (IRE)) [2016/17 **h–**
b71: h21m⁵ Apr 4] poor form in bumpers: well beaten in novice on hurdling debut.
Adrian Wintle

ASPERGILLUM 5 b.g. Midnight Legend – Rosita Bay (Hernando (FR)) [2016/17 b–p: **b65**
b16.7d³ b15.7d Nov 15] poor form in bumpers: left Tom Lacey after first start: tried in
tongue tie. *Peter Bowen*

ASTAROLAND (FR) 7 b.g. Astarabad (USA) – Orlandaise (FR) (Goldneyev (USA)) **h109**
[2016/17 h111: h16.5d⁵ h16.2d⁵ h19.6g² Jul 29] fair handicap hurdler: stays 2½m: acts on
good to firm and heavy going: has worn tongue tie: often races towards rear, usually travels
strongly. *Jennie Candlish*

AS THE CROW FLIES (IRE) 6 b.g. Presenting – Regle d'Or (FR) (Robin des Champs **b81**
(FR)) [2016/17 b16.2s⁴ Jul 10] €28,000 3-y-o: third foal: half-brother to useful hurdler
Little King Robin (2m-23f winner, by King's Theatre): dam unraced sister to fairly useful
chaser (stayed 2¾m) Robin de Sherwood and fairly useful hurdler/useful
chaser (stayed 3m) Exit To Wave: multiple point winner, including all 3 starts in 2017: 9/2,
fourth in bumper at Perth (9½ lengths behind Toberdowney) in July. *Sean McParlan,
Ireland*

ASTHURIA (FR) 6 b.m. Sagacity (FR) – Baturia (FR) (Turgeon (USA)) [2016/17 h20s* **h138**
h16sF h18vF h16.8g⁵ h16.3d* Apr 27] smallish mare: fifth foal: half-sister to French 17f
hurdle winner Bat Driver (by Domedriver) and French 2½m-21f chase winner Rolibat (by
Roli Abi): dam ran once over hurdles in France: useful hurdler: won mares maiden at
Fairyhouse in November and mares novice at Punchestown (by 5 lengths from Pravalaguna)
in April: stays 2½m: acts on soft going: in hood last 2 starts: front runner/races prominently,
usually travels strongly. *W. P. Mullins, Ireland*

ASTIGOS (FR) 10 b.g. Trempolino (USA) – Astonishing (BRZ) (Vacilante (ARG)) **c66 §**
[2016/17 c119§, h–: c20.3d c16v³ c16vᵖᵘ c21.1s⁶ c24.1gᵖᵘ h26.4gᵖᵘ Apr 23] sturdy gelding: **h– §**
fairly useful hurdler/chaser at best, has lost way: stays 3m: best form on soft/heavy going:
wears headgear: tried in tongue tie: ungenuine. *Tom Gretton*

ASTON CANTLOW 9 b.g. Hurricane Run (IRE) – Princess Caraboo (IRE) (Alzao **c–**
(USA)) [2016/17 h117: h16.8m⁴ c16.5g⁵ Jun 4] maiden hurdler, fair at best: well beaten in **h80**
novice handicap on chasing debut, and pulled up in Irish points later in 2016: unproven
beyond 2m: best form on soft/heavy going: wears tongue tie. *Philip Hobbs*

ASTRACAD (FR) 11 br.g. Cadoudal (FR) – Astre Eria (FR) (Garde Royale) [2016/17 **c133**
c134, h–: c21g c20.4g* c21.1d c19.4s² c24.2s c24g⁴ Feb 22] sturdy gelding: winning **h–**
hurdler: useful handicap chaser: won veterans event at Cheltenham (by 1½ lengths from
Ericht) in November: stays 21f: acts on soft going: has worn headgear: has worn tongue tie,
including in 2016/17. *Nigel Twiston-Davies*

ASTRAPAIOS (IRE) 5 b.g. Stowaway – Janet Lindup (Sabrehill (USA)) [2016/17 **b96**
b15.8v³ b15.7v Feb 15] half-brother to bumper winner/winning hurdler Blackson Zulu
(2½m winner, by Supreme Leader): dam, maiden on Flat (stayed 1¾m), half-sister to
useful hurdlers Hopscotch (2m/17f winner) and Sheriffmuir (2m-2½m winner): fairly
useful form in bumpers: easily better effort when third in maiden at Ffos Las in December.
Harry Whittington

ASTRE DE LA COUR (FR) 7 b.g. Khalkevi (IRE) – Gracieuse Delacour (FR) (Port Etienne (FR)) [2016/17 c74P, h–: h15.7m h15.8s⁴ h16.3g⁵ c18.2m* c15.7v² c15.7d² Feb 18] good-topped gelding: useful handicap hurdler at best: useful form over fences: won 3-runner handicap at Taunton in December: second in handicaps at Wincanton in February: stays 2¼m: acts on good to firm and heavy going: front runner/races prominently. *Robert Walford* **c140 h115 +**

ASTRUM 7 gr.g. Haafhd – Vax Star (Petong) [2016/17 h102§: h16.8d* h19.6dᵖᵘ h17.2d⁴ h18.6g⁵ h16.2dᵘʳ h16.8s⁴ h16.8v² h18.7g* h18.7g Apr 15] angular gelding: fair hurdler: won conditionals maiden at Sedgefield very early in season and seller at Stratford in April: left Donald McCain after eighth start: stays easy 19f: acts on heavy going: wears headgear: tried in tongue tie: front runner/races prominently: temperamental. *Phil Middleton* **h105 §**

ASUM 6 b.g. Kayf Tara – Candy Creek (IRE) (Definite Article) [2016/17 b95p: h16d⁴ h16.5g* h19.4d h16.3gꟳ Apr 1] fairly useful form over hurdles: won maiden at Taunton in December: likely to prove best around 2m: tried in hood: in tongue tie last 3 starts: often races towards rear. *Dan Skelton* **h118**

ASUNCION (FR) 7 b.m. Antarctique (IRE) – Liesse de Marbeuf (FR) (Cyborg (FR)) [2016/17 c84, h–: c16m h17.1d c15.8g⁵ c19.2s* c15.5s³ c20.5v⁵ c19.2s⁴ c20.1v² Mar 7] maiden hurdler: poor handicap chaser: won at Market Rasen in December: stays 2½m: best form on soft/heavy going: wears headgear: front runner/races prominently: unreliable. *Rebecca Menzies* **c81 § h–**

ASYLO (IRE) 5 b.g. Flemensfirth (USA) – Escrea (IRE) (Oscar (IRE)) [2016/17 b16g* b16s b16s⁴ Mar 13] €36,000 3-y-o: fourth foal: brother to fairly useful hurdler McKenzie's Friend (2m-2½m winner): dam (c116/h124) 2m-2½m hurdle/chase winner: fair form in bumpers: won at Chepstow in December. *Dan Skelton* **b87**

AS YOU LIKE (IRE) 6 b.g. Beneficial – Rubys Shadow (IRE) (Supreme Leader) [2016/17 h20d² h21.6m³ h19.9g⁵ Sep 18] €120,000 3-y-o: brother to several winners, including useful hurdler/fair chaser Shadow Eile (2m-2½m winner) and fairly useful hurdler/chaser Corskeagh Royale (2½m-2¾m winner): dam unraced: fair form over hurdles: best effort when second in novice at Ffos Las on debut: remains with potential. *Jonjo O'Neill* **h101 p**

AS YOU WERE (FR) 5 b.g. Azamour (IRE) – Princess Skippie (USA) (Skip Away (USA)) [2016/17 b16s* Mar 9] fifth foal: half-brother to 3 winners on Flat in Italy, including useful 7f-1½m winner Pentagono (by Oratorio): dam maiden on Flat in USA: 4/1, won maiden bumper at Thurles (by 16 lengths from Judgement Day) on debut. *Emmet Mullins, Ireland* **b109**

A TAIL OF INTRIGUE (IRE) 9 b.g. Tillerman – Princess Commanche (IRE) (Commanche Run) [2016/17 c21.2dᵖᵘ c24.2d³ c24sᵖᵘ Apr 1] workmanlike gelding: winning hurdler: fairly useful chaser at best, below that only completion in 2016/17 after long absence: stays 3m: acts on good to firm and heavy going. *Nicky Henderson* **c113 h–**

Florida Pearl Novices' Chase, Punchestown—the recently-announced split between Gigginstown and Willie Mullins doesn't include Closutton's jockey Ruby Walsh, who picks up a nice winning spare ride on A Toi Phil

AT FIRST LIGHT 8 b.m. Echo of Light – Bisaat (USA) (Bahri (USA)) [2016/17 h113: h20m^pu h19.9g^2 h25.6g^4 h21.6g^6 h20v^4 h19.5s^4 h24.2s^pu Mar 3] lengthy mare: fair handicap hurdler: stays 2¾m: acts on heavy going: temperamental. *David Weston* **h105 §**

ATHOU DU NORD (FR) 7 b.g. Voix du Nord (FR) – Orathou du Plaid (FR) (Lute Antique (FR)) [2016/17 h111: h20.6g^pu h19.9s^5 h16.3g^4 c18g^2 c17g^2 c19s Nov 6] fair hurdler at best, below that in early-2016/17: left Ali Stronge, second twice over fences in Germany after: stays 2½m: acts on heavy going: has worn tongue tie. *C. von der Recke, Germany* **c?** **h87**

ATHY RIVER (IRE) 5 b.m. Oscar (IRE) – Athy Princess (IRE) (Over The River (FR)) [2016/17 b16.2s^4 b15.8m^3 ab16g^6 h15.8g^3 h19.5g^4 Apr 17] rather unfurnished mare: sister to bumper winner/fairly useful hurdler Call Oscar (17f winner): dam, winning pointer, half-sister to Cheltenham Gold Cup winner Imperial Call: modest form in bumpers/over hurdles. *Fergal O'Brien* **h93** **b78**

ATIRELARIGO (FR) 7 b.g. Puit d'Or (IRE) – Ouchka (FR) (April Night (FR)) [2016/17 c–, h108: c20.5s^ur c19.4g^* c20s^F c19.4s^F h19.9s^* h21.2g^3 Apr 3] fairly useful form over hurdles: won novice at Uttoxeter in March: fairly useful handicap chaser: won at Chepstow in December, only completion over fences in 2016/17: will stay 3m: acts on soft going: usually races towards rear: often let down by jumping. *Philip Hobbs* **c123 x** **h121**

ATLANTA ABLAZE 6 b.m. Kayf Tara – Rocheflamme (FR) (Snurge) [2016/17 h99p, b96: h21.2m^* h21s^3 h18.9s^4 h19.5s^5 h20.5g Mar 25] well-made mare: fair form over hurdles: won mares novice at Ludlow in October: likely to stay further than 21f: acts on soft and good to firm going. *Henry Daly* **h113**

ATLANTIC GOLD (IRE) 7 b.g. Robin des Pres (FR) – Marys Isle (IRE) (Erins Isle) [2016/17 h129: c24.2g^3 c24.1g^pu Sep 28] Irish point winner: useful hurdler: fairly useful form in novice chases: stayed 25f: acted on good to firm and heavy going: front runner/raced prominently: dead. *Charlie Longsdon* **c119** **h–**

ATLANTIC GREY (IRE) 4 gr.g. Acambaro (GER) – Clooney Eile (IRE) (Definite Article) [2016/17 b13.7g b14s b16.7s^2 b16g Apr 24] smallish, lengthy gelding: modest form in bumpers: will stay beyond 2m: in tongue tie last 2 starts. *Nigel Twiston-Davies* **b79**

ATLANTIC HIGH (GER) 4 b.g. King's Best (USA) – Atlantic High (Nashwan (USA)) [2016/17 h16.2d^5 h15.8d^3 h16m^6 h19.9s^pu h19g Dec 30] fair form on Flat for J. E. Hammond: poor form over hurdles: tried in cheekpieces: in tongue tie last 4 starts. *Nigel Hawke* **h82**

ATLANTIC ROLLER (IRE) 10 b.g. Old Vic – Tourist Attraction (IRE) (Pollerton) [2016/17 c124§, h–: c24.1g^2 c21g^4 c20.1s^3 Jul 10] well-made gelding: winning hurdler: fair maiden chaser nowadays: stays 3m: acts on heavy going: wears cheekpieces: tried in tongue tie: usually leads: ungenuine. *Chris Gordon* **c110 §** **h–**

ATLANTIC SPLASH 7 ch.g. Dreams End – Atlantic Lady (GER) (Dashing Blade) [2016/17 b15.9g May 28] tailed off in bumper/Flat maiden. *Nikki Evans* **b–**

ATLANTIC STORM (IRE) 5 b.g. September Storm (GER) – Double Dream (IRE) (Double Eclipse (IRE)) [2016/17 b18d h15.8g^6 h15s^4 h16.3d h16.7g^* h19g^4 Apr 24] €36,000 3-y-o: good-topped gelding: fifth foal: half-brother to useful hurdler/chaser Tagrita (17f-23f winner, by King's Theatre): dam unraced half-sister to top-class staying chaser Grey Abbey: well beaten in maiden bumper: fairly useful form over hurdles: won handicap at Bangor in March: left Adrian Maguire after first start: will be suited by 2½m+: tried in hood: usually races towards rear: remains open to improvement. *Dan Skelton* **h118** **b–**

A TOI PHIL (FR) 7 b.g. Day Flight – Lucidrile (FR) (Beyssac (FR)) [2016/17 h140: h20s^pu c19.5g^* c22.5d^* c20d^6 c24d^5 c21g^* c21.3s^5 c20v^* c24g^2 c24.5d^4 Apr 25] sturdy gelding: useful hurdler: smart chaser: won maiden at Down Royal and Florida Pearl Novices' Chase at Punchestown (by 7 lengths from Jetstream Jack) in November, Leopardstown Handicap Chase (by neck from Stellar Notion) in January and Webster Cup Chase at Navan (by 8 lengths from Nearly Nama'd) in March: left W. P. Mullins after first start: stays 3m: acts on heavy going. *Gordon Elliott, Ireland* **c148** **h–**

coral.ie Leopardstown Handicap Chase, Leopardstown—A Toi Phil (extreme left) pounces very late to pip Stellar Notion (white face) and Rolly Baby (second right)

Irish Stallion Farms European Breeders Fund Mares' Novices' Hurdle Championship Final, Fairyhouse—Augusta Kate overcomes a mistake at the last to lower the colours of stable first string Let's Dance

ATOMIC RUMBLE (IRE) 4 b.g. Oscar (IRE) – Atomic Betty (IRE) (Anshan) [2016/17 b15.8v⁴ b15.8m² Apr 25] modest form in bumpers. *Peter Bowen* **b77**

ATOMIX (GER) 6 b.g. Doyen (IRE) – Aloe (GER) (Lomitas) [2016/17 b95: h15.8d⁵ h16.4d³ h15.6gᶠ h19.4g h20.8d h20.6m² h20.6m Apr 17] leggy gelding: bumper winner: fair maiden hurdler: may prove best short of 2½m: acts on good to firm and good to soft going: often races freely. *Peter Niven* **h105**

A TOUCH OF SASS (IRE) 7 b.m. Mahler – Lwitikila (Denel (FR)) [2016/17 h70, b81: h16.3mᵖᵘ May 15] winning pointer: poor form over hurdles: tried in hood: usually races freely. *John Spearing* **h–**

ATTENTION PLEASE (IRE) 7 b.g. Kalanisi (IRE) – Dangerous Dolly (IRE) (Jurado (USA)) [2016/17 c67, h76: c25.5m³ c25.5g² Jul 18] maiden hurdler: poor form over fences: stays 25f: acts on soft and good to firm going: tried in blinkers: often races towards rear. *Rose Dobbin* **c81 h–**

ATTEST 4 b.g. Cacique (IRE) – Change Course (Sadler's Wells (USA)) [2016/17 h15.8v⁵ h16.6g⁶ h16.3s h18.7d* Mar 13] placed on first of 3 starts in maidens on Flat: fair form over hurdles: won juvenile at Stratford in March. *Warren Greatrex* **h104**

ATTIMO (GER) 8 ch.g. Nayef (USA) – Alanda (GER) (Lando (GER)) [2016/17 c112, h–: c24sᶠ c15.2mᵖᵘ c22.5vᵖᵘ c26.3s⁵ c20.3v⁵ c19.3d* c21.4s⁴ c21.1s⁴ c24.2d³ c19.2sᵖᵘ c21.3dᵖᵘ c21.1m Apr 19] big gelding: maiden hurdler: fair handicap chaser: won at Sedgefield in December: stays 3m: acts on soft going: wears headgear/tongue tie: often races towards rear. *Sam England* **c112 h–**

ATTRACTION TICKET 8 b.g. Selkirk (USA) – Trick (IRE) (Shirley Heights) [2016/17 h16.7g h16.7dᵖᵘ Aug 19] fair at one time on Flat, stays 1½m: maiden hurdler, no form in 2016/17: raced around 2m: has worn headgear, including in 2016/17: in tongue tie last 4 starts: often races prominently. *Joanne Foster* **h–**

ATTRIBUTION 7 ch.g. Alhaarth (IRE) – Competa (Hernando (FR)) [2016/17 c16m² c16g* c16d³ c17d* c19.5v³ c20d⁵ Apr 16] €97,000 3-y-o: half-brother to 2 winners, notably Champion Hurdle winner Punjabi (by Komaite): dam unraced: winning pointer: winning hurdler: useful form over fences: won maiden at Naas in November and Grade 3 novice at Navan (by ½ length from Briar Hill) in December: third in Craddockstown Novices' Chase at Punchestown (4 lengths behind Identity Thief) and Grade 2 novice at Limerick (5¼ lengths behind Bellshill): stays 2½m: acts on heavy going: tried in cheekpieces: front runner/races prominently. *Henry de Bromhead, Ireland* **c143 h–**

AUBUSSON (FR) 8 b.g. Ballingarry (IRE) – Katioucha (FR) (Mansonnien (FR)) [2016/17 c130p, h151: h21.4s⁵ h25.4d⁴ h23.9s⁴ c26g c26.3s h26.1g⁶ h24g c27.9d⁴ Apr 16] tall, good-topped gelding: smart hurdler: useful form over fences: stays 3¼m: acts on heavy going: tried in cheekpieces. *Nick Williams* — **c136 +** **h145 +**

AUDACIOUS PLAN (IRE) 8 b.g. Old Vic – North Star Poly (IRE) (Presenting) [2016/17 c130, h–: c23.6gᵖᵘ h23.6d³ c24.1s³ c23.4s c30.7dᵖᵘ h20v Mar 19] good-topped gelding: fair handicap hurdler: fairly useful handicap chaser: third at Bangor in December: stays 3¾m: acts on soft going: wears headgear. *Rebecca Curtis* — **c120** **h108**

AUENWIRBEL (GER) 6 b.g. Sholokhov (IRE) – Auentime (GER) (Dashing Blade) [2016/17 c112, h127: h16.3g⁴ h16.5g h18.5s Dec 15] angular gelding: fairly useful hurdler at best, well below that level in Britain: winning chaser: stays 19f: acts on heavy going: tried in blinkers: has worn tongue tie. *Laura Young* — **c–** **h96**

AUGHCARRA (IRE) 12 b.g. High Chaparral (IRE) – Pearly Brooks (Efisio) [2016/17 h64§: h18.7m May 20] poor hurdler: stays 2½m: acts on good to firm and good to soft going: has worn cheekpieces: unreliable. *Harry Chisman* — **h– §**

AUGUSTA KATE 6 b.m. Yeats (IRE) – Feathard Lady (IRE) (Accordion) [2016/17 b114: b16d* h23.1d* h20sᶠ h24g⁶ h20d* h20d⁵ Apr 29] neat mare: useful bumper performer: useful form over hurdles: won mares maiden at Thurles in November and Irish Stallion Farms EBF Mares' Novices' Hurdle Championship Final at Fairyhouse (by ½ length from Let's Dance) in April: has won at 23f, but at least as effective at shorter: acts on soft going: usually races nearer last than first, often travels strongly. *W. P. Mullins, Ireland* — **h142** **b–**

AUNTY ANN (IRE) 6 b.m. Vinnie Roe (IRE) – On Good Advise (IRE) (Taipan (IRE)) [2016/17 h18.5g* h21.6g² h23.3d⁵ h20.6sᵖᵘ h21.2d³ h18.5dᵖᵘ h23.9g⁶ h21.6m³ Apr 15] €1,600 3-y-o, £10,000 5-y-o: second foal: dam unraced half-sister to fairly useful hurdler/useful chaser (stayed 25f) Steel Summit out of half-sister to Grand National winner Earth Summit: winning Irish pointer: fair hurdler: won mares novice at Newton Abbot in May: left Kim Bailey after sixth start: stays 2¾m: acts on good to firm and good to soft going: tried in tongue tie: usually races close up. *Charlie Longsdon* — **h111**

AUPCHARLIE (IRE) 11 b.g. Daliapour (IRE) – Lirfa (USA) (Lear Fan (USA)) [2016/17 c130, h–: c25s c21.5v* c26.3g Mar 17] workmanlike gelding: winning hurdler: fairly useful chaser: won hunter at Fairyhouse in February: left Henry de Bromhead after first start: barely stays 3¼m: acts on heavy going: tried in cheekpieces/tongue tie: often races towards rear. *J. T. R. Dreaper, Ireland* — **c124** **h–**

AURILLAC (FR) 7 gr.g. Martaline – Ombrelle (FR) (Octagonal (NZ)) [2016/17 h124, b112: c23.6g² c23.8d³ c23.4d² c22.4d² c25.2vᵖᵘ c24.4gᵖᵘ Mar 15] good-topped gelding: fairly useful hurdler: useful form over fences: placed first 4 starts, including when second in novice handicaps at Newbury in December: should stay beyond 3m: acts on soft going: has worn headgear, including usually in 2016/17. *Rebecca Curtis* — **c135** **h–**

AUSTIN FRIARS 5 b.g. New Approach (IRE) – My Luigia (IRE) (High Estate) [2016/17 h–: h15.9m h15.9g* Oct 17] angular gelding: modest hurdler: won novice handicap at Plumpton in October: raced only at 2m: tried in visor: temperamental. *Jim Best* — **h92 §**

AUSTRALASIA (IRE) 7 b.g. Zerpour (IRE) – Leachestown (IRE) (Insatiable (IRE)) [2016/17 h–, b94: h19.3mᵖᵘ h20.1d* h20.1s* h27gᵖᵘ Oct 27] sturdy gelding: fair form over hurdles: won novice and handicap at Hexham in September: stayed 2½m: acted on soft going: usually wore headgear: dead. *Karen McLintock* — **h112**

AUTHORIZED CADEAUX 5 b.g. Authorized (IRE) – Nord's Cadeaux (Cadeaux Genereux) [2016/17 h24m⁶ h22d⁵ h23.7mᵖᵘ h24.4vᵖᵘ h21gᵖᵘ h23.9g⁶ Aug 20] 8.5f/9f winner on Flat in Italy at 2 yrs: modest maiden hurdler: stays 3m: acts on good to firm and good to soft going: wears headgear: often in tongue tie: temperamental. *Gordon Elliott, Ireland* — **h89 §**

AUTHORIZED TOO 6 b.g. Authorized (IRE) – Audaz (Oasis Dream) [2016/17 h117: h16g* h20g⁴ c16m c16m* c16.4g⁶ c20.2m³ c22.7gᵖᵘ h21.2s h15.7s² h20.5g³ Mar 27] rather leggy gelding: fairly useful handicap hurdler: won at Worcester in July: similar form over fences: won handicap at Lingfield in November: stays 21f: acts on good to firm and heavy going: wears cheekpieces. *Noel Williams* — **c121** **h119**

AUTO MAC 9 b.g. Auction House (USA) – Charlottevalentina (IRE) (Perugino (USA)) [2016/17 h72: h15.8m Jun 9] poor hurdler: best around 2m: acted on good to firm and heavy going: dead. *Mike Sowersby* — **h–**

AUTOMATED 6 b.g. Authorized (IRE) – Red Blooded Woman (USA) (Red Ransom (USA)) [2016/17 h129: h16d h16.1g h22d³ h20g⁴ h16d⁵ h20s* h21.1g h20.5d⁵ Apr 29] smallish, sturdy gelding: useful handicap hurdler: won at Navan in December: stays 2¾m: acts on heavy going: tried in cheekpieces/tongue tie: often races towards rear/travels strongly. *Gordon Elliott, Ireland* **h138**

AUTUM RAIN (IRE) 5 b.m. Arcadio (GER) – Liberty Miss (IRE) (Flemensfirth (USA)) [2016/17 h15.8d h15.8s³ h19.7s h22g Apr 1] first foal: dam failed to complete in 2 points: runner-up on second of 2 starts in Irish maiden points: poor form over hurdles: should stay beyond 2m. *Tom Weston* **h70**

AUVERGNAT (FR) 7 b.g. Della Francesca (USA) – Hesmeralda (FR) (Royal Charter (FR)) [2016/17 c126, h–: c22.6m⁵ h21.6s c24s³ c30.2dᵘʳ c24s* c30.2g⁴ Mar 15] workmanlike gelding: winning hurdler: useful chaser: won cross-country event at Punchestown in February: fourth in Glenfarclas Cross Country Chase at Cheltenham (11½ lengths behind Cause of Causes) in March: left Jonjo O'Neill after first start: stays 3¼m: acts on heavy going: tried in cheekpieces/tongue tie: often travels strongly. *Enda Bolger, Ireland* **c143** **h–**

AUX PTITS SOINS (FR) 7 gr.g. Saint des Saints (FR) – Reflexion Faite (FR) (Turgeon (USA)) [2016/17 h130+: c19.2g² c23.4s* c24g⁴ h22.8d² h24.7g Apr 8] tall, useful-looking gelding: smart form over hurdles: second in Rendlesham Hurdle at Haydock (3¾ lengths behind Zarkandar) in February: useful form over fences: won novice at Kelso in December: stays 23f: acts on soft going: often races prominently. *Paul Nicholls* **c138** **h146**

AVEALITTLEPATIENCE (IRE) 4 b.f. Dubai Destination (USA) – Adjisa (IRE) (Doyoun) [2016/17 b12.4d ab16g Feb 20] stocky filly: half-sister to several winners, including useful hurdler/fairly useful chaser Spirit of Adjisa (2½m/21f winner, by Invincible Spirit) and fair hurdler Veronica's Napkin (2m winner, by Yeats): dam unraced: poor form in bumpers: wears tongue tie. *Fergal O'Brien* **b73**

AVEL VOR (IRE) 6 ch.g. Green Tune (USA) – High Perfection (IRE) (High Chaparral (IRE)) [2016/17 c63, h92: h19g h23g c23mᵖᵘ h18.7m² h16.3g² h16.7g³ h21.6m h23g⁴ h16g⁶ h18.7g⁶ Oct 27] short-backed gelding: modest hurdler: little form over fences: stays 19f: acts on good to firm and good to soft going: has worn headgear, including in 2016/17: has worn tongue tie: often races towards rear. *Nigel Hawke* **c–** **h91**

AVIDITY 8 b.g. Passing Glance – Epicurean (Pursuit of Love) [2016/17 h129: c15.9m⁴ c17.4g* h15.6gᵖᵘ c15.5d⁵ Apr 21] rather leggy, workmanlike gelding: fairly useful hurdler: similar form over fences: won novice at Bangor in May: stays 2½m: acts on good to firm and heavy going: tried in cheekpieces: has worn tongue tie. *James Ewart* **c128** **h–**

AVIDIUS CASSIUS (IRE) 9 b.g. Flemensfirth (USA) – Rixdale (FR) (Riverquest (FR)) [2016/17 c26g⁶ Apr 27] winning pointer: lightly-raced hurdler: 33/1, sixth in hunter at Cheltenham (12¼ lengths behind Lilbitluso) on chasing debut. *Miss H. Brookshaw* **c90** **h–**

AVISPA 8 b.m. Kayf Tara – Ladylliat (FR) (Simon du Desert (FR)) [2016/17 h118: h18.5m² h15.7s* h16.8d² h16.3m* h15.8g² Apr 3] lengthy, rather sparely-made mare: fairly useful hurdler: won novices at Southwell (mares) in May and Stratford in July: stays 19f: acts on soft and good to firm going (won bumper on heavy): tried in hood: usually races prominently/travels strongly, though hasn't always found so much as seemed likely. *Alan King* **h118**

AVITHOS 7 b.m. Kayf Tara – Digyourheelsin (IRE) (Mister Lord (USA)) [2016/17 b16d h21.6mᶠ h16.8gᵖᵘ h21.6m⁵ h21.6g⁴ h18.5g⁶ h19.5d³ h21.6s⁶ h15.8v⁶ h16.5g⁶ h23.9g² h23.9g* h23.9g⁴ h23.9g Mar 30] fourth foal: dam (h94) 2½m hurdle winner: well beaten in mares bumper: modest handicap hurdler: won mares event at Taunton in February: stays 3m: acts on good to soft going. *Mark Gillard* **h92** **b–**

AVON CONQUEST 5 br.m. Avonbridge – Another Conquest (El Conquistador) [2016/17 b16.2s h19.1vᵖᵘ Jan 29] third foal: dam (c96/h85), 3m chase winner, sister to fair hurdler/fairly useful chaser (stayed 25f) Kellys Conquest: no show in bumper/novice hurdle. *Seamus Mullins* **h–** **b–**

AWAKE AT MIDNIGHT 5 b.g. Midnight Legend – Wakeful (Kayf Tara) [2016/17 b15.7v b14d⁵ Dec 21] poor form in bumpers. *Philip Hobbs* **b70**

AWAY DOWN WEST (IRE) 7 b.g. Stowaway – Western Starlight (IRE) (Shahanndeh) [2016/17 c23dᵖᵘ c24dᵖᵘ c24.5vᶠ c23.5vᵖᵘ Mar 6] maiden hurdler: no form over fences: in cheekpieces last 3 starts. *Nikki Evans* **c–** **h–**

AWAYINTHEWEST (IRE) 5 b.m. Getaway (GER) – Sarah's Hall (IRE) (Saddlers' Hall (IRE)) [2016/17 b16g b16.5d⁵ b16s⁵ b16s³ h16s b16v* h16v³ h16g⁴ h18.5v² h16.8g⁶ h16.3d⁵ Apr 27] third foal: dam unraced half-sister to smart hurdler/fairly useful chaser (stayed 25f) Celtic Native: fair form in bumpers: won maiden at Fairyhouse in December: fairly useful form over hurdles: second in mares maiden at Clonmel in February: will be suited by 2½m+: acts on heavy going. *P. A. Fahy, Ireland* **h125 b89**

AWAYWITHTHEGREYS (IRE) 10 gr.g. Whipper (USA) – Silver Sash (GER) (Mark of Esteem (IRE)) [2016/17 c108§, h123§: h21.9s h23.6gᵖᵘ h23.6s⁴ h26s³ h23.5s h26s Mar 30] angular gelding: fairly useful handicap hurdler: maiden chaser: stays 3¼m: acts on heavy going: usually wears headgear: tried in tongue tie: unreliable. *Peter Bowen* **c– § h116 §**

AWBEG MASSINI (IRE) 11 b.g. Dr Massini (IRE) – Awbeg Flower (IRE) (Alphabatim (USA)) [2016/17 c25.3g Apr 27] workmanlike gelding: winning Irish pointer: maiden hurdler: no form in chases: stays 2½m: best form on soft/heavy going: has worn tongue tie. *K. M. Hanmer* **c– h–**

AWESOME ROSIE 6 b.m. Midnight Legend – Awesome Aunt (IRE) (Vestris Abu) [2016/17 h117, b91: h20m⁵ h15.8d⁶ h19.4g² h20.6s³ h18.9g Apr 15] compact mare: bumper winner: fairly useful handicap hurdler: will prove best up to 21f: acts on soft going: often travels strongly. *Alan King* **h117**

AWESOME TUNES (IRE) 7 b.g. Milan – Europet (IRE) (Fourstars Allstar (USA)) [2016/17 h19.9g⁴ h23g⁴ c23.4m⁴ h21.6gᶠ h20.5g⁵ Oct 31] €32,000 3-y-o, £14,000 6-y-o: sixth foal: brother to fair hurdler Mother Meldrum (17f-2¼m winner) and a winning pointer: dam unraced half-sister to useful 2m hurdle winner Scenic Route: winning Irish pointer: modest form over hurdles: 2/1, sixth in novice handicap at Kelso (17½ lengths behind Mister Don) on chasing debut: may prove best around 2½m for time being: wears tongue tie. *David Pipe* **c84 h87**

AYE AYE CHARLIE 5 b.g. Midnight Legend – Trial Trip (Le Moss) [2016/17 b17d³ b16s⁶ b15.7s* b16g⁴ Apr 22] sixth foal: half-brother to fair hurdler/useful chaser Chase The Spud (2½m-33f winner, by Alflora): dam winning pointer: fairly useful form in bumpers: won maiden at Southwell (dead-heated with The Last Day) in January: will be suited by 2¼m+. *Fergal O'Brien* **b97**

AYELYA (IRE) 5 b.m. Nayef (USA) – Aliyama (IRE) (Red Ransom (USA)) [2016/17 h20v h16g h20.2d h16.2d⁴ h16dᵘʳ h20s h16.4v Feb 2] €1,000 3-y-o: first foal: dam unraced half-sister to smart 2m hurdle winner Alaivan: poor maiden hurdler: stays 21f: acts on good to soft going: has worn headgear/tongue tie. *John Joseph Hanlon, Ireland* **h77**

AYE WELL 12 b.g. Overbury (IRE) – Squeeze Box (IRE) (Accordion) [2016/17 c126, h–: c17.1d⁴ c17.1s⁵ c15.2s* c15.2s⁶ Dec 27] strong gelding: winning hurdler: fairly useful handicap chaser: won at Wetherby in November: stays 2½m: acts on heavy going: often races prominently. *Stuart Coltherd* **c126 h–**

AYLA'S EMPEROR 8 b.m. Holy Roman Emperor (IRE) – Ayla (IRE) (Daylami (IRE)) [2016/17 h101: h20g* h20d² h19.9g⁴ h19.1g³ h21.6d h20v⁶ h19.5g Apr 17] sturdy mare: modest handicap hurdler: won mares event at Fakenham in May: stays 2½m: acts on soft going: wears cheekpieces. *John Flint* **h99**

AY UP MRS 4 b.f. Monsieur Bond (IRE) – Smiddy Hill (Factual (USA)) [2016/17 b12.4d b12.4d Jan 14] lengthy, workmanlike filly: fourth foal: dam 5f winner: no form in bumpers/ Flat maiden. *Rebecca Bastiman* **b–**

AZARI 5 b.g. Azamour (IRE) – Atasari (IRE) (Whipper (USA)) [2016/17 h15.3d⁶ h18.5gᵘʳ h15.8g⁶ Apr 28] useful on Flat (stays 9f) in Italy: poor form over hurdles: in tongue tie last 2 starts. *Paul Nicholls* **h80**

AZA RUN (IRE) 7 b.g. Hurricane Run (IRE) – Aza Wish (IRE) (Mujadil (USA)) [2016/17 h87: h16g⁶ h15.8v² h15.8v h15.5v* h15.8v³ h18.6m³ Apr 17] modest handicap hurdler: won at Leicester in February: stays 19f: acts on good to firm and heavy going: tried in tongue tie: often races towards rear. *Shaun Harris* **h90**

AZBO 5 b.g. Azamour (IRE) – Sularina (IRE) (Alhaarth (IRE)) [2016/17 b16.8d Mar 21] tailed off in bumper. *Seamus Mullins* **b–**

AZERT DE COEUR (FR) 7 b.g. Tiger Groom – Eden de Coeur (FR) (Lampon (FR)) [2016/17 c116, h–: c24sᵖᵘ c19.4d* c19.1d⁵ c25.6dᵘʳ c22.6s² c24gᵖᵘ Mar 28] good-topped gelding: winning hurdler: fair handicap chaser: won at Chepstow in November: stays 19f: acts on heavy going. *Venetia Williams* **c112 h–**

AZURE FLY (IRE) 9 br.g. Blueprint (IRE) – Lady Delight (IRE) (Be My Native (USA)) **c123**
[2016/17 c131§, h–§: c25.1m² c23.8g³ c25.6m² c25g² c24.2s² c28.5s³ c32.8g³ c24s^pu **h–**
c28.1g⁴ Apr 19] good-topped gelding: winning hurdler: fairly useful handicap chaser: stays
33f: acts on good to firm and heavy going: wears headgear/tongue tie. *Charlie Longsdon*

AZURE GLAMOUR (IRE) 8 br.g. Golan (IRE) – Mirazur (IRE) (Good Thyne (USA)) **h–**
[2016/17 h96: h16.8s Apr 28] modest hurdler: went as if amiss only start in 2016/17: stays
2½m: acts on heavy going: wears headgear nowadays: usually leads: signs of temperament.
Kenneth Slack

AZZERTI (FR) 5 b.g. Voix du Nord (FR) – Zalagarry (FR) (Ballingarry (IRE)) [2016/17 **h127**
b83: h17.7d² h16d³ h15.7d* h16.3d² h16s* h20.3g³ Apr 19] rather leggy gelding: fairly
useful form over hurdles: won maiden at Towcester in December and novice at Sandown
in March: placed in stronger races all other starts: stays 2½m: acts on soft going: tried in
hood: often races towards rear/travels strongly. *Alan King*

AZZURI 5 b.g. Azamour (IRE) – Folly Lodge (Grand Lodge (USA)) [2016/17 h133: h16s² **h126**
h15.8s* h15.3d² h16d² Apr 21] sturdy gelding: fairly useful hurdler: won maiden at
Huntingdon in March: raced around 2m: acts on soft going: often in tongue tie: front
runner/races prominently, often freely. *Dan Skelton*

B

BABENY BRIDGE (IRE) 8 b.g. Exit To Nowhere (USA) – Rose of Clare (Bob Back **c–**
(USA)) [2016/17 c–, h107: h23g² h23.9d* Nov 30] multiple point winner: fair form over **h110**
hurdles: won handicap at Ffos Las in November, suited by emphasis on stamina: poor form
only chase start: will stay beyond 3m. *Nick Williams*

BABY BACH (IRE) 7 gr.g. Bach (IRE) – Anns Island (IRE) (Turtle Island (IRE)) **c121**
[2016/17 h126: c17d⁴ c20s⁵ c20.5v^pu c28.5g⁶ c24.3g Apr 22] Irish point winner: fairly **h–**
useful hurdler: fairly useful form in chases: stays 29f, effective at much shorter: acts on
heavy going: tried in cheekpieces: often races towards rear. *Stuart Crawford, Ireland*

BABY JAKE (IRE) 8 b.g. Morozov (USA) – Potters Dawn (IRE) (Talkin Man (CAN)) **c114**
[2016/17 h114: h16g h16g⁴ h16m^F h17.2d* h16.1g⁵ h17.2g⁴ h16s³ h20g⁵ c16g⁴ h15.8d* **h124**
Nov 19] fairly useful handicap hurdler: won lady riders events at Cartmel in July and
Huntingdon in November: 14/1, some encouragement when fourth in maiden at Wexford
(11½ lengths behind Ball d'Arc) on chasing debut: stays 2½m: acts on soft and good to firm
going: tried in hood: often races towards rear. *John Joseph Hanlon, Ireland*

BABY KING (IRE) 8 b.g. Ivan Denisovich (IRE) – Burn Baby Burn (IRE) (King's **c135**
Theatre (IRE)) [2016/17 h125: h15.7v³ c15.7v* Feb 2] good-topped gelding: fairly useful **h124**
handicap hurdler: 9/4, useful form on chasing debut when winning novice handicap at
Wincanton by neck from Astre de La Cour: stays mainly around 2m: acts on heavy going:
wears tongue tie: usually races towards rear. *Tom George*

BABY SHERLOCK 6 ch.g. Shirocco (GER) – Lady Cricket (FR) (Cricket Ball (USA)) **h66 p**
[2016/17 h69, b88: h15.8s h16g Sep 12] modest form in bumpers: poor form in novice/
maiden hurdles: type to do better in handicaps. *David Pipe*

BABY TICKER 8 ch.m. Endoli (USA) – Baby Gee (King Among Kings) [2016/17 h83, **h95**
b78: h20d h16.8s^ur h16.4v² h16.4g⁵ Mar 24] modest maiden hurdler: should be suited by at
least 2½m: acts on heavy going. *Donald Whillans*

BABY TWIG (FR) 6 b.m. Network (GER) – Natty Twigy (FR) (Video Rock (FR)) **b105 p**
[2016/17 b16g* Oct 12] €57,000 3-y-o: fourth foal: half-sister to 2 winners by Martaline,
including useful ½m hurdle winner Twigline: dam French 17f chase winner: 5/6, created
very good impression when winning mares maiden bumper at Punchestown on debut by 16
lengths from Good To Flow, travelling strongly, leading over 1f out and forging clear:
useful prospect. *Gordon Elliott, Ireland*

BACARDYS (FR) 6 b.g. Coastal Path – Oasice (FR) (Robin des Champs (FR)) **h155 p**
[2016/17 b121: b16d³ h16v^F h16d* h18s* h21.1g^pu h20g* Apr 28] **b–**
'Reliable sources tell me I'm reminiscent of Mr J. Wayne at times, but seeing
as *The Searchers* is one of my favourite films, I take that as a compliment!' It was Mr
P. W. Mullins, not John Wayne, who rode to the rescue and helped to secure a tenth
consecutive Irish trainers' championship for his father Willie, a title which hung in
the balance until the final days of the season at the Punchestown Festival. Mullins'
amateur son Patrick proved something of an unlikely hero given his position in the

Deloitte Novices' Hurdle, Leopardstown—Bacardys comes out best of the Willie Mullins-trained sextet as he pegs back stablemate Bunk Off Early (No.7)

pecking order among the posse of jockeys at Closutton. That said, Mr Mullins found himself on four of the stable's nine winners at the Festival—from just eight rides for his father at the meeting—and those four proved crucial to pipping Gordon Elliott in the championship. Stable jockey Ruby Walsh rode just two of the stable's nine winners, with his main understudy Paul Townend riding only one, as did nephew David Mullins and Jody McGarvey. Three of the wins for Mr Mullins resulted in his landing a memorable treble on the Friday, with Montalbano's win in the two-mile novice hurdle supplementing Grade 1 successes earlier on the card for Wicklow Brave in the Punchestown Champion Hurdle and Bacardys in the Tattersalls Ireland Champion Novices' Hurdle. Mullins senior saddled four runners in each of the three races won by his son whose other winner came on the final day of the meeting when 20/1-shot Open Eagle was one of seven runners for the yard in the valuable Ballymore Handicap Hurdle. As well as contributing to his father's title challenge, Mr Patrick Mullins was motivated by having his own champion amateur title to defend but, in the end, he fell just one short of catching Jamie Codd in his bid to be champion Irish amateur for the tenth time. Being the son of Ireland's perennial champion trainer gives Mr Mullins better opportunities than most amateurs, but, as his father says, 'he wouldn't be riding these horses if I didn't think he was up to it, I wouldn't let him if he wasn't good enough.'

Mr Mullins and Bacardys were already well acquainted before the latest Punchestown Festival. They had teamed up successfully for bumper wins the previous season at Leopardstown and in the Grade 2 contest at Aintree (Ruby Walsh rode Bacardys when third at Cheltenham in between behind Ballyandy and Battleford, both of whom he had behind him at Aintree). Mr Mullins had also finished third on Bacardys in the Champion INH Flat Race at the 2016 Punchestown Festival and was reunited with him successfully when one of six runners for the stable in a ten-runner field for the Deloitte Novices' Hurdle at Leopardstown in February. Walsh's mount Saturnas was all the rage in the betting at 5/4 but shaped as though amiss and finished tailed off last as 12/1-shot Bacardys got the better of the stable's apparent second string Bunk Off Early by three quarters of a length. Bacardys still had some work to do two out but made good progress going to the final flight and found plenty to lead on the run-in, plainly suited by the longer trip and leaving the strong impression that he would be suited by further still. However, when sent off the 4/1 second favourite for the Baring Bingham over another three furlongs at the Cheltenham Festival (where he wore ear plugs), Bacardys never got the chance to show what he could do as his race was effectively over before halfway when he was badly hampered by the fatal fall of Consul de Thaix at the fifth flight. Prior to the Deloitte, Bacardys had got off the mark over hurdles at the second attempt in a maiden at Leopardstown just after Christmas. He overcame a mistake two out to land the odds on that occasion, after coming down three out when poised to make a winning hurdling debut at Cork the previous month.

Willie Mullins had won the Tattersalls Ireland Champion Novices' Hurdle eight times previously, most recently with Vautour in 2014 and Nichols Canyon in 2015. Vautour landed the odds against just three rivals and Nichols Canyon against five but the latest renewal attracted a more competitive field of nine, in which Bacardys was only fifth in the betting at odds of 10/1. As it turned out, it arguably took a better performance from Bacardys to win at Punchestown than it had for Willoughby Court to land the Baring Bingham at Cheltenham. Finian's Oscar, unbeaten in four starts over hurdles for Colin Tizzard, had had to miss Cheltenham but confirmed himself one of the most exciting novice hurdlers around with a Grade 1 win in the Mersey Novices' Hurdle at Aintree. Another of the Champion Novices' runners, Death Duty, was held in particularly high regard by his trainer Gordon Elliott, though he was already beaten when unseating his jockey at the last in the longer-distance Spa Novices' Hurdle at Cheltenham where he had been sent off a short-priced favourite. Jockey bookings pointed to Let's Dance and Bleu Berry being the pick of the Mullins quartet, with Let's Dance having won the Dawn Run Mares' Novices' Hurdle at Cheltenham (before being beaten by stable-companion Augusta Kate in the Grade 1 mares novice at Fairyhouse) and the progressive Bleu Berry having completed a hat-trick in a Grade 2 novice contest at Fairyhouse. Finian's Oscar headed the betting at 13/8, ahead of Let's Dance on 3/1, Death Duty at 9/2 and Bleu Berry on 8/1. Let's Dance and the other Mullins-trained runner Kemboy disputed much of the running before Finian's Oscar took over entering the straight and soon quickened clear. However, after looking all set for a clear-cut success, Finian's Oscar lost some momentum at the last and Bacardys, staying on all the time, collared him in the final fifty yards to snatch the verdict by a short head, in another of the week's thrilling finishes. Death Duty finished another seven lengths back in third, just ahead of Let's Dance, with a gap back to Bleu Berry in fifth.

Tattersalls Ireland Champion Novices' Hurdle, Punchestown—ample compensation for a luckless Cheltenham experience as Bacardys collars British raider Finian's Oscar; Death Duty (right) and Let's Dance (left) complete the frame

Shanakiel Racing Syndicate's "Bacardys"

Bacardys (FR) (b.g. 2011)	Coastal Path (b 2004)	Halling (ch 1991)	Diesis / Dance Machine
		Coraline (b 1994)	Sadler's Wells / Bahamian
	Oasice (FR) (ch 2002)	Robin des Champs (b 1997)	Garde Royale / Relayeuse
		Judice (ch 1997)	Agent Bleu / Herenice

The angular Bacardys is the first foal out of his dam Oasice, a daughter of Robin des Champs whose best jumpers include such Mullins stars as Vautour, Quevega and Sir des Champs. Oasice raced only on the Flat in AQPS races, winning six times at a mile and a half to thirteen furlongs. She is a half-sister to six winning jumpers in France, though, including Visionice, a useful chaser and fairly useful hurdler at up to two and a half miles. The grandam of Bacardys, Judice, was also campaigned exclusively on the Flat, winning once over a mile and a half, but she too had several winning siblings over jumps, notably Arenice, the 1996 Grand Steeple-Chase de Paris winner who was Guillaume Macaire's first winner of France's biggest jumps race. Arenice also made an appearance in Britain the year before when coming last of five finishers behind Master Oats in the Pillar Property Chase (now the Cotswold) at Cheltenham. Bacardys won the second of his two starts in points as a four-year-old (fell on debut) and looks sure to stay a good deal further than two and a half miles when sent over fences in the next season. He has raced only on good ground or softer, and won his first bumper on heavy. *W. P. Mullins, Ireland*

BACCALAUREATE (FR) 11 b.g. High Chaparral (IRE) – Rose d'Or (IRE) (Polish **c–** Precedent (USA)) [2016/17 h20v h16.5m⁴ h16g c17m h20d h18.5m h19g h21.6v⁴ h16.8d* **h90** h16.8s² h18.5d h16.8g⁵ Apr 26] rather leggy gelding: modest handicap hurdler: won at Exeter in February: maiden chaser: left Turlough O'Connor after fifth start: stays 3m: acts on firm and soft going: wears headgear: has worn tongue tie: often races prominently. *Jimmy Frost*

BACCHANEL (FR) 6 b.g. Vendangeur (IRE) – Pardielle (FR) (Robin des Champs (FR)) **c111** [2016/17 h102p, b91: h23.9s⁵ h23.1v⁶ c24.2sᵖᵘ c24v² c24.2d² Mar 21] rangy gelding: **h76** lightly-raced maiden hurdler: best effort (fair form) over fences when second in novice handicap at Exeter: stays 3m: acts on heavy going. *Philip Hobbs*

BACHASSON (FR) 6 gr.g. Voix du Nord (FR) – Belledonne (FR) (Shafoun (FR)) **c147 p** [2016/17 h142: c18dᶠ c20v² c20v* Feb 18] smallish gelding: useful hurdler: smart form **h–** over fences: won maiden at Gowran on final start by 6½ lengths from General Principle, with plenty in hand: should stay beyond 2½m: acts on heavy going: often races prominently, usually travels strongly: should do better still as a chaser. *W. P. Mullins, Ireland*

BACH DE CLERMONT (FR) 6 b.g. Della Francesca (USA) – Fleur de Princesse (FR) **h116** (Passing Sale (FR)) [2016/17 h15.8d⁴ h16g⁴ h20s³ h19g² Mar 30] £170,000 4-y-o: fourth foal: half-brother to smart French hurdler/fairly useful chaser Perly de Clermont (17f-19f winner, by Ultimately Lucky): dam French maiden (placed at 2m over hurdles): Irish point winner: fairly useful form over hurdles: best effort when second in maiden at Taunton: stays 19f. *Evan Williams*

BACK BY MIDNIGHT 8 ch.g. Midnight Legend – Roberta Back (IRE) (Bob Back **c115** (USA)) [2016/17 h104: c16m³ c15.5s* c16.9d⁶ c16.3s⁴ c15.7d⁴ c18.2g* Mar 20] sturdy **h–** gelding: fair hurdler: fairly useful chaser: won handicaps at Sandown in December and Taunton in March: stays 2½m: acts on heavy going: has worn hood: wears tongue tie: usually leads. *Emma Baker*

BACKINTHESADDLE (IRE) 9 ch.g. Rudimentary (USA) – Grangeclare Lodge (IRE) **h95** (Top of The World) [2016/17 h20.5d⁵ h16s h16d* h16s³ h16d h16v³ h19.5s⁵ h20.6g⁶ Apr 8] modest handicap hurdler: won at Down Royal in December: stays 2½m: acts on soft going: wears tongue tie. *Benjamin Arthey, Ireland*

BACK TO BALLOO (IRE) 11 gr.g. Jimble (FR) – Fleur du Chenet (FR) (Northern **c–** Fashion (USA)) [2016/17 c–, h105: c16m h16d h18.2g⁶ h18.6g h16.6g² h16g h16.6d⁶ **h97** h15.8s³ h15.7g⁵ Apr 21] modest handicap hurdler: winning chaser: left Colin A. McBratney after third start: stays 2¾m: acts on heavy going: has worn headgear: tried in tongue tie: usually races prominently, often freely. *Peter Winks*

BACK TO BRACKA (IRE) 10 b.g. Rudimentary (USA) – Martha's Glimpse (IRE) **c101** (Tidaro (USA)) [2016/17 c133, h–: h20.1dᵖᵘ c25.5d c20.1g³ c24.3sᵖᵘ c15.2s⁶ h21.4sᵖᵘ Jan **h–** 2] winning hurdler: useful handicap chaser, well below best in 2016/17: should stay 2¾m: acts on soft going (won bumper on heavy): tried in tongue tie: often leads. *Lucinda Russell*

BACK TO THE THATCH (IRE) 5 b.g. Westerner – Melville Rose (IRE) (Phardante **h120** (FR)) [2016/17 h22g⁵ h25.5s⁶ h23.1s* h23.1s² h23.3v⁴ h24g Apr 20] £37,000 4-y-o: seventh foal: half-brother to fairly useful hurdler/useful chaser Lucky Landing (2m-2½m winner) and a winning pointer (both by Well Chosen): dam (h89) maiden hurdler (stayed 2½m): placed on both starts in Irish maiden points: fairly useful form over hurdles: won novice at Bangor in December: stays 23f: acts on soft going. *Henry Daly*

BACT TO BLACK 5 b.g. Black Sam Bellamy (IRE) – Linagram (Classic Cliche (IRE)) **h76** [2016/17 h19.5m⁶ Nov 8] 20/1, badly needed experience when sixth in novice hurdle at Lingfield (35½ lengths behind Phobiaphiliac) on debut. *Robert Walford*

BADBAD LEROY BROWN 5 gr.g. Lucarno (USA) – Leroy's Sister (FR) (Phantom **h105** Breeze) [2016/17 b76: b16.8s⁵ h23.1s h21.2s h15.8v⁶ h19.7d⁴ h22g³ Apr 1] winning **b72** pointer: poor form in bumpers: fair form over hurdles: won handicap at Hereford in March: stays 2¾m: acts on good to soft going: wears tongue tie. *Oliver Greenall*

BAD BOY DU POULDU (FR) 6 b.g. Loup Solitaire (USA) – Wild Flush (USA) (Pine **h110** Bluff (USA)) [2016/17 h107: h16d h19.1d³ h16g h17.7g* Apr 21] good-topped gelding: fair form over hurdles: won handicap at Fontwell (in first-time blinkers) final start: stays 2¼m: acts on soft going: often races towards rear. *Gary Moore*

BADEN (FR) 6 gr.g. Martaline – Ma Sonate (USA) (Val de L'Orne (FR)) [2016/17 h130p: **h122** h20d³ h21.1g⁵ h21.3d* h20.3sᵖᵘ h24g h20d⁵ Apr 26] deep-girthed, well-made gelding: winning pointer: fairly useful hurdler: won novice at Wetherby in December: stays 21f: acts on soft going. *Nicky Henderson*

BADGED 8 b.g. High Chaparral (IRE) – Meshhed (USA) (Gulch (USA)) [2016/17 c–x, h105: h20.2d h20.2s^{pu} h20.2g^{pu} Aug 20] maiden hurdler/chaser: has worn headgear, including in 2016/17: tried in tongue tie: often races towards rear: often let down by jumping. *Lucy Normile* — **c– x** **h–**

BADGER RUN (IRE) 6 gr.g. Acambaro (GER) – Charannah (IRE) (Red Sunset) [2016/17 h–, b–: h21.4m^4 h22g h23.9g^F h21m^{pu} Apr 4] little form in bumpers/over hurdles. *Pat Murphy* — **h59**

BADGERS RETREAT 11 b.g. Elusive City (USA) – Heuston Station (IRE) (Fairy King (USA)) [2016/17 c98, h–: c20s^{pu} c21.1g^{pu} c19.4m^2 c19.4g^{pu} c21g^5 c21g^{pu} c20g c20g^{pu} Sep 29] maiden hurdler: modest handicap chaser: stays 2¾m: acts on soft and good to firm going: wears headgear. *Nick Mitchell* — **c90** **h–**

BADGER WOOD 8 b.g. Overbury (IRE) – Parlour Game (Petoski) [2016/17 c104, h90: h23.3v^{pu} c23.9d^{pu} May 25] maiden hurdler: winning chaser: stays 23f: acts on heavy going: has worn cheekpieces, including when pulled up both starts in 2016/17: usually races close up. *Giles Smyly* — **c–** **h–**

BADILOU (FR) 6 b.g. Ballingarry (IRE) – Doumia (FR) (Dounba (FR)) [2016/17 h100: h15.3m h18.5g h20g^{pu} h21.4d^6 h16.5g Dec 30] angular gelding: winning hurdler, limited impact in handicaps in Britain: stays 19f: acts on good to firm going. *Martin Hill* — **h70**

BAFANA BLUE 6 b.g. Blueprint (IRE) – Anniejo (Presenting) [2016/17 b17.1g^6 b16.4d h22.7s^{pu} Dec 29] showed little in bumpers/maiden hurdle. *Chris Grant* — **h–** **b–**

BAFANA CHOICE 11 b.g. Bollin Eric – Lorna's Choice (Oats) [2016/17 c26.2d^2 Apr 10] multiple point winner: modest maiden chaser: stays 3¼m: acts on soft and good to firm going: sometimes in cheekpieces. *Mrs S. E. Grant* — **c93**

BAGAD BIHOUE (FR) 6 b.g. Nickname (FR) – Lann Bihouee (FR) (Video Rock (FR)) [2016/17 b–: b16.8m* h21.6m* h18.7g* h18.7g* h19.5g^6 h15.3m* h15.7m^2 Oct 29] useful-looking gelding: fairly useful form in bumpers: won at Newton Abbot in July: fairly useful form over hurdles: won maiden at Newton Abbot in July, 2 novices at Stratford in August and novice at Wincanton in October: stays 2¾m: acts on good to firm going: front runner. *Paul Nicholls* — **h129** **b102**

BAGGING TURF (IRE) 7 b.m. Scorpion (IRE) – Monica's Story (Arzanni) [2016/17 h102: c19.9d* c20.2s^F c19.7v^{pu} c19.9g^2 Apr 3] winning hurdler: fairly useful form over fences: won novice handicap at Huntingdon in December: stays 21f: acts on heavy going: in cheekpieces last 2 starts. *Gary Moore* — **c116** **h–**

BAGS GROOVE (IRE) 6 b.g. Oscar (IRE) – Golden Moment (IRE) (Roselier (FR)) [2016/17 b111: h16.3d^2 h18.8d^2 h19g* h19.6d^5 h19g* Mar 20] good-topped gelding: useful bumper performer: fairly useful form over hurdles: won novices at Taunton in January and March: will stay 2½m+: acts on heavy going: tried in cheekpieces: wears tongue tie. *Harry Fry* — **h128**

BAHATI BOY (IRE) 10 b.g. King's Theatre (IRE) – Carrigmorna Flyer (IRE) (Bob Back (USA)) [2016/17 h20g h18.5d h16.8g Oct 20] maiden pointer/chaser: one-time fair hurdler, no form in 2016/17: left Katie Stephens after second start: has worn hood: tried in tongue tie: usually races close up. *Steven Dixon* — **c–** **h–**

BAH LAMB 6 ch.m. Sakhee (USA) – Lucinda Lamb (Kayf Tara) [2016/17 b16.8s^5 Apr 28] second foal: half-sister to bumper winner Tom Lamb (by Central Park): dam (h69), placed in bumpers/twice-raced over hurdles, half-sister to useful hurdler/fairly useful chaser (stayed 25f) Lord Lamb and useful 2m hurdler Mr Lamb: 6/1, fifth in bumper at Sedgefield (25 lengths behind Royal Supremo) on debut. *Andrew Crook* — **b–**

BAHRIKATE 4 b.f. Bahri – Dispol Katie (Komaite (USA)) [2016/17 h16s^5 h16.4v^5 h19.4g h16.2s^5 h16.2g* Apr 27] poor maiden on Flat, stays 1m: modest form over hurdles: won handicap at Perth in April: may prove best around 2m: in tongue tie last 3 starts: usually races towards rear. *Susan Corbett* — **h91**

BAHUMBUG 7 b.g. Bahamian Bounty – Stan's Smarty Girl (USA) (Smarty Jones (USA)) [2016/17 c16s^4 c15.7d^6 c17.4v^{pu} c16s^4 c16s c17.4d^4 Mar 18] sturdy gelding: maiden hurdler: no form in chases: in headgear last 4 starts. *Seamus Mullins* — **c–** **h–**

BAIE DES ILES (FR) 6 gr.m. Barastraight – Malownia (FR) (Smadoun (FR)) [2016/17 c138, h118: h22.6d c29.5s^5 c28s* c25v^3 Feb 25] useful hurdler at best: useful chaser: won handicap at Punchestown in February by 4¾ lengths from Sambremont: thorough stayer: acts on heavy going: has worn cheekpieces, including last 3 starts. *Ross O'Sullivan, Ireland* — **c143** **h–**

BAILEYS CONCERTO (IRE) 11 b.g. Bach (IRE) – None The Wiser (IRE) (Dr **c125** Massini (IRE)) [2016/17 c124, h–: c23.8d² c21.2d⁶ c25g⁴ c19.9d⁵ c19.9s² c22.9sᵖᵘ c24.2s **h–** c20g² c20.1g⁴ Apr 27] winning hurdler: fairly useful handicap chaser: stays 3m: acts on heavy going: has worn headgear/tongue tie, including in 2016/17. *Dianne Sayer*

BAILY CLOUD (IRE) 7 ch.g. Touch of Land (FR) – Cap The Rose (IRE) (Roselier **c150** (FR)) [2016/17 h20s c16g* c19.9g⁵ c22.7g⁵ c18.2g⁵ c20.5g* c18.2d³ c20sᶠ c16d³ c18g⁵ **h–** c17d⁴ c19gᵘʳ c19.9gᶠ c20d⁴ c16dᵘʳ Apr 27] €24,000 3-y-o: good-topped gelding: seventh foal: half-brother to bumper winner/fair chaser Capilla (2m/2½m winner) and poor hurdler/ fair chaser Amethyst Rose (2m-21f winner) (both by Beneficial): dam unraced sister to fairly useful hurdler/smart chaser (2m-2¼m winner) Alcapone: fairly useful hurdler: smart chaser: won maiden at Tramore in June and novice at Killarney (by 1½ lengths from Tiger Roll) in August: seemed to excel himself when fourth of 6 to Road To Respect in Ryanair Gold Cup Novices' Chase at Fairyhouse penultimate start: stays 21f: acts on heavy going: wears cheekpieces: usually wears tongue tie. *M. F. Morris, Ireland*

BAJARDO (IRE) 9 b.g. Jammaal – Bit of Peace (IRE) (Le Bavard (FR)) [2016/17 h–: **c97** c16g c17.2g² c16.1g* Mar 20] raw-boned gelding: maiden hurdler: modest form over **h–** fences: in tongue strap, very fortunate winner of handicap at Taunton final start, held when left in lead final 100 yds: stays 2¼m: acts on heavy going. *Emma Baker*

BAKMAJ (FR) 5 b.g. Balko (FR) – Myralienne (FR) (Myrakalu (FR)) [2016/17 b16d² **b104** b16g* b16.4g Mar 15] €18,000 3-y-o: lengthy gelding: third foal: dam French maiden: fairly useful form in bumpers: left Peter Fahey, won maiden at Leopardstown in January by 5 lengths from Imperial Way: 12/1, run best excused when 16½ lengths fourteenth of 22 to Fayonagh in Champion Bumper at Cheltenham final start, meeting trouble. *Alan Fleming, Ireland*

BAKO DE LA SAULAIE (FR) 6 b.g. Balko (FR) – Krickette (FR) (Passing Sale (FR)) **h116** [2016/17 h85p, b–: h17.1d⁵ h16d⁶ h22.7s* h24.1s* Dec 27] second in Irish maiden point on debut: well held in bumper: fairly useful form over hurdles: won novice handicap at Kelso and handicap at Wetherby, both in December: stays 3m: acts on soft going. *Rose Dobbin*

BAKU BAY (IRE) 9 b.g. Flemensfirth (USA) – The Girlfriend (IRE) (Glacial Storm **c120** (USA)) [2016/17 c119, h–: c23.9g* May 15] strong gelding: winning hurdler: fairly useful **h–** chaser: won novice handicap at Market Rasen in May: stayed 3m: acted on heavy going: in cheekpieces final 2 starts: often raced prominently: dead. *Ali Stronge*

BALACH MOR (IRE) 5 b.g. Robin des Champs (FR) – Silver Skirt (IRE) (Silver **b–** Patriarch (IRE)) [2016/17 b16g Apr 24] tailed off in bumper. *Michael Scudamore*

BALBIR DU MATHAN (FR) 8 b.g. Saint des Saints (FR) – Jeapano (FR) (Panoramic) **c123** [2016/17 c133, h–: c20d c26gᵖᵘ c20v³ c20g³ Apr 16] good-topped gelding: winning **h–** hurdler: fairly useful maiden chaser: stays 2¾m: acts on heavy going: tried in cheekpieces: wears tongue tie: front runner/races prominently. *Alan Fleming, Ireland*

BALDADASH (IRE) 12 b.g. Beneficial – Balda Girl (IRE) (Mandalus) [2016/17 c–, **c–** h102: h21.6d³ h19.2g⁵ h21.4d h23.6sᵖᵘ h20.3s⁴ h21m* h21.9d h23.9m Apr 27] rather leggy **h90 §** gelding: winning pointer: modest handicap hurdler: won at Kempton in April: maiden chaser: stays 2¾m: acts on soft and good to firm going: wears cheekpieces: front runner/ races prominently: temperamental. *Jose Santos*

BALGEMMOIS (FR) 4 ch.g. Balko (FR) – Venise Doree (FR) (Starborough) [2016/17 **h99** b13.7d⁶ h16.3s³ h16.7s³ Feb 7] £27,000 3-y-o: rather unfurnished gelding: third foal: dam, **b73** French hurdler/chaser (17f winner), half-sister to useful hurdler/fairly useful chaser (2½m-2¾m winner) Mirage Dore: sixth in junior bumper at Towcester: modest form in juvenile hurdles: will stay further than 2m. *Ali Stronge*

BALIBOUR (FR) 5 b.g. Policy Maker (IRE) – Saintheze (FR) (Saint des Saints (FR)) **b–** [2016/17 b16g b16.8v b16.6g Feb 22] no form in bumpers: tried in tongue tie. *Emma Lavelle*

BALINROAB (IRE) 10 b.g. Milan – Gentle Eyre (IRE) (Aristocracy) [2016/17 c108§, **c– §** h–: h23.3gᵖᵘ Sep 7] big, workmanlike gelding: maiden hurdler: fair chaser: stays 25f: acts **h–** on good to firm and heavy going: usually wears headgear: tried in tongue tie: sometimes finishes weakly: unreliable. *Mark Bradstock*

BALKO DES FLOS (FR) 6 ch.g. Balko (FR) – Royale Marie (FR) (Garde Royale) **c149** [2016/17 h131, b109: h20d c20d² c21.5v* c24s³ c21.3s³ c19.9gᶠ c21d³ Apr 28] good- **h–** topped gelding: useful form over hurdles for W. P. Mullins: even better over fences: won maiden at Fairyhouse (by 16 lengths from Arbre de Vie) in January: resumed progress when 2 lengths third of 15 to Woodland Opera in novice handicap at Punchestown final start: stays 25f: acts on heavy going: front runner/races prominently. *Henry de Bromhead, Ireland*

BALLASALLA (IRE) 5 br.g. Presenting – Papoose (IRE) (Little Bighorn) [2016/17 b16.4v Feb 15] brother to Grand National winner Ballabriggs: tailed off in maiden bumper. *Donald McCain* **b–**

BALL D'ARC (FR) 6 b.g. Network (GER) – Pretty Moon (FR) (Moon Madness) [2016/17 h138, b101: h16d⁶ c17v² c16mᵘʳ c18g² c16g* c16d⁴ c20d² c17d³ c17s* c17s* c20s* c17s² c20d³ c16d³ Apr 27] sturdy gelding: useful hurdler: smart chaser: won maiden at Wexford in October, Dan Moore Memorial Handicap Chase at Fairyhouse (by 9 lengths from Pairofbrowneyes) in January, Flyingbolt Novices' Chase at Navan (by 19 lengths from Tully East) in February and Grade 3 novice at Naas (by 15 lengths from Gangster) in March: subsequently second in Normans Grove Chase at Fairyhouse (½ length behind Ballycasey) and third in Ryanair Gold Cup Novices' Chase at Fairyhouse (5¼ lengths behind Road To Respect) and Ryanair Novices' Chase at Punchestown (13¼ lengths behind Great Field): stays 2½m: acts on heavy going: has worn hood. *Gordon Elliott, Ireland* **c154 h–**

BALLELA MAGIC (IRE) 6 b.m. Kalanisi (IRE) – Glen's Magic (IRE) (Jurado (USA)) [2016/17 h19.2vᵖᵘ h19.4s³ h20.3g⁵ h21.2m³ Apr 18] €2,200 3-y-o, £15,000 5-y-o: fourth foal: dam lightly-raced half-sister to useful hurdler/fairly useful chaser (stayed 2½m) Glens Music, herself dam of smart hurdler (stayed 2¾m) Glens Melody: off mark in Irish points at second attempt: fair form over hurdles: stays 21f. *Ben Case* **h110**

BALLET MARBLELESS 11 b.g. Baryshnikov (AUS) – Lost Your Marbles (IRE) (Mandalus) [2016/17 c21.1dᵖᵘ May 12] long-standing maiden pointer: pulled up in maiden hunter on chasing debut. *John Mead* **c–**

BALLINALACKEN (IRE) 9 b.g. Fruits of Love (USA) – Miss Daisy (Daylami (IRE)) [2016/17 h99§: h23.3d³ May 5] modest handicap hurdler: stays 21f: acts on good to firm and heavy going: wears headgear: races towards rear: weak finisher. *Clare Ellam* **h89 §**

BALLINTARA (IRE) 5 b.g. Getaway (GER) – Miltara (IRE) (Milan) [2016/17 b17.7g³ b16g Apr 24] first foal: dam once-raced close relative to fairly useful hurdler/chaser (stays 19f) Oscatara: fell in point on debut: fair form in bumpers. *Diana Grissell* **b87**

BALLINURE (IRE) 7 b.g. Alkaadhem – Christy's Pride (IRE) (Kambalda) [2016/17 h108, b99: h19.9g* h20.3d⁵ h21.6d* h21.1g⁴ h16.4g h23.5d² Dec 17] compact gelding: placed in Irish maiden points: bumper winner: fairly useful handicap hurdler: won at Uttoxeter in May and Newton Abbot in September: stays 3m: acts on good to soft going: tried in cheekpieces. *Nicky Henderson* **h119**

BALLINVARRIG (IRE) 10 b.g. Beneficial – Leos Holiday (IRE) (Commanche Run) [2016/17 c128§, h–: c19.9gᵖᵘ c25gᵖᵘ c19.2v⁵ c19.2v⁴ c20.2s* c20.2s* c20.2s² Mar 10] big, strong gelding: maiden hurdler: useful handicap chaser: won at Leicester in February and Wincanton in March: stays 3m: acts on heavy going: wears headgear: races prominently, strong traveller: temperamental. *Tom George* **c132 § h–**

BALLINVEGGA (IRE) 7 gr.g. Royal Anthem (USA) – Gill's Honey (IRE) (Celio Rufo) [2016/17 h111p, b86: h23.9m h23.9d h20.2s⁵ h20.2g c19.9g⁵ c23.8g⁵ Dec 14] winning pointer/hurdler: modest form in chases: stays 2½m: acts on soft going: tried in blinkers. *Jackie Stephen* **c90 h96**

BALLYANDREW (IRE) 6 b.g. Westerner – Royale Acadou (FR) (Cadoudal (FR)) [2016/17 b–: h15.7g⁵ h16g Nov 7] behind in bumper and 2 novice hurdles. *Nigel Twiston-Davies* **h–**

BALLYANDY 6 b.g. Kayf Tara – Megalex (Karinga Bay) [2016/17 b123: h16.2s² h16.4s³ h19.8s² h16.3d* h16.4g⁴ Mar 14]
The latest Betfair Hurdle, the season's most valuable handicap hurdle on British soil, fell to yet another novice. Ballyandy became the sixth to win in the last eight runnings, following the victories of Get Me Out of Here, Recession Proof, My Tent Or Yours, Splash of Ginge and Agrapart. He was a popular winner, too, sent off the clear 3/1 favourite in a smaller than usual field of sixteen for the Betfair (Recession Proof's renewal attracted fifteen runners, the only other time the field has dipped below twenty since 2002). Ballyandy's hurdling experience beforehand amounted to just three starts (like the first three aforementioned winners), none of which he had won, with a BHA mark of 135 for his handicap debut not making him look especially well treated. The pick of the weights in the early-closing contest **h145**

*Betfair Hurdle (Handicap), Newbury—well-backed favourite Ballyandy
holds off Movewiththetimes (hoops) to become the sixth novice in the current decade
to win the richest handicap hurdle in Britain*

looked to be the in-form Clyne who had seemed to excel himself when running Ballyandy's stable-companion The New One to a length in the Champion Hurdle Trial at Haydock after the Betfair weights had been published. However, Ballyandy had more behind him than just a truncated hurdling record. He had been one of the best bumper horses of the previous season with his four wins including the Champion Bumper at Cheltenham, which had been preceded by the listed bumper which concludes the Betfair Hurdle card. There was every chance that the best of Ballyandy had still to be seen over hurdles.

For the first time since his bumper days, Ballyandy found himself back in a big field at Newbury in a race run at a proper gallop and he duly proved a different proposition in a race in which a good pace was set by his stable-companion Ballyhill, another novice. Though making smooth headway from mid-division early in the straight, Ballyandy wasn't the only one travelling like a winner, with a similar move being made by the Paul Nicholls-trained Movewiththetimes, another novice with just three runs over hurdles (of which he had won two, as well as his only start in bumpers). Ballyandy and Movewiththetimes began to draw away from the remainder on the run to the final flight, Sam Twiston-Davies on Ballyandy and Barry Geraghty on Movewiththetimes both appearing to have plenty of horse under them as they did so. It was only jumping the last that both jockeys really began to ask their mounts for maximum effort. Ballyandy was fractionally the quicker away and responded to his rider's urgings all the way to the line to hold off the persistent Movewiththetimes by three quarters of a length. Clyne, who had led three out, kept on well to finish another six lengths away in third, the first three in the betting taking the first three places, with the Greatwood third Song Light completing the frame. Ballyandy was a first Betfair Hurdle winner for Sam Twiston-Davies as his father's other winner, the 33/1-shot Splash of Ginge in 2014, had been partnered by the stable's then 7-lb claimer Ryan Hatch. Sam Twiston-Davies is tied principally to the Nicholls stable (and was able to ride Ballyandy because Barry Geraghty was riding Movewiththetimes for owner J. P. McManus by whom he is retained).

Ballyandy's three defeats before the Betfair all came at short odds in novices before the turn of the year. His reappearance came in an early-season treat for Perth racegoers at the track's final meeting of the year in late-September in an otherwise ordinary novice which was also chosen for the hurdling debut of the 2015 Champion Bumper winner Moon Racer. The David Pipe-trained Moon Racer shaded favouritism at the off and there was little between the two principals in the closing stages, Ballyandy just coming off worse by three quarters of a length. Incidentally, Ballyandy's stable-companion Flying Angel (third in the 2016 Betfair while still a novice) made a winning chasing debut on the same card, while another in the stable's Scottish raiding party to go on to much better things in the core part of the season was Foxtail Hill who fell in the handicap chase. Ballyandy and Moon Racer met again in a Grade 2 novice at Cheltenham's Open meeting in November, Ballyandy finishing third despite being weighted to turn the tables (he was reportedly distressed afterwards), while a step up in trip failed to bring about any immediate improvement when he went down by half a length to Messire des Obeaux in another Grade 2 contest at Sandown the following month when receiving 7 lb from the winner. Ballyandy's jumping lacked fluency at Sandown, and that remained something of a worry after Newbury when he was sent off joint favourite for the Supreme Novices' at Cheltenham. Although he ended up matching his Betfair form in finishing a staying-on fourth to Labaik, Ballyandy had an unfortunate experience early on and never looked comfortable after being baulked on landing over the second flight and dropping back a number of places.

		Kayf Tara		Sadler's Wells		Northern Dancer
Ballyandy		(b 1994)		(b 1981)		Fairy Bridge
(b.g. 2011)				Colorspin		High Top
				(b 1983)		Reprocolor
		Megalex		Karinga Bay		Ardross
		(ch 1998)		(ch 1987)		Handy Dancer
				Flaming Rose		Roselier
				(b 1990)		Little Flame

The well-made Ballyandy, actually registered as a non-thoroughbred by Weatherbys, is the best of six winners out of his dam Megalex, five of them by Kayf Tara. Her other winner, Bert The Alert (by Proclamation), was successful three times on the polytrack at Lingfield at up to two miles. Like Ballyandy, all four of his winning siblings by Kayf Tara made a successful debut in bumpers, though the only one to enjoy anything like so much success afterwards as Ballyandy was Megastar, who won the Grade 2 bumper at Aintree and showed useful form over hurdles (second in the Tolworth) before ultimately losing his way and proving ungenuine. Most of Megalex's foals have been trained by Gary Moore, including her latest offspring to reach the track, Kaveman (also by Kayf Tara), who was even money to keep up the family record on his bumper debut at Warwick in January but finished well beaten, albeit showing some promise. Megalex won on her first start after joining Moore in a two and a half mile mares novice hurdle at Fontwell after which she was reportedly lame and never ran again. Moore also trained the sire of Megalex, the smart Flat horse Karinga Bay, in the latter part of his career. Ballyandy's grandam Flaming Rose showed no ability in bumpers or over hurdles but she has now bred three winners, including the fairly useful staying hurdler Luccombe Down who completed an early hat-trick in the latest season. Whilst he travels strongly in his races, Ballyandy should prove just as effective over at least two and a half miles, and he looks the type to do well over fences too. He put up one of his best bumper performances on heavy ground but is also effective under much less testing conditions. He has, incidentally, been ridden by Sam Twiston-Davies on nine of his eleven starts, with Ryan Hatch (who missed the rest of the latest season after a very bad fall at Cheltenham in December) taking the mount for the other two, on his winning bumper debut and for that below-par third at Cheltenham in the autumn. *Nigel Twiston-Davies*

BALLYANTICS (IRE) 6 b.g. Marienbard (IRE) – Ballindante (IRE) (Phardante (FR))   **h–**
[2016/17 h20g Apr 9] tailed off in novice hurdle on debut. *Neil Mulholland*

BALLYARTHUR (IRE) 7 b.g. Kayf Tara – Ariels Serenade (IRE) (Presenting) [2016/17   **h126**
h113p: h20d² h21.1s⁴ h21.6dᶠ h20.5g* h22.8d³ h19.9s² Apr 9] tall gelding: Irish point winner: fairly useful hurdler: won novice at Leicester in January: creditable efforts last 2 starts: stays 2½m: acts on soft going: wears tongue tie. *Nigel Twiston-Davies*

BALLY BEAUFORT (IRE) 9 b.g. Old Vic – Miss Compliance (IRE) (Broken Hearted)   **c–**
[2016/17 c137, h–: c24sᵖᵘ Apr 30] sturdy gelding: winning hurdler: useful chaser at best: **h–**
stays 25f: acts on heavy going: in cheekpieces last 3 starts: usually races close up. *Nigel Twiston-Davies*

BALLYBEN (IRE) 9 ch.g. Beneficial – I'm Maggy (NZ) (Danseur Etoile (FR)) [2016/17   **c127**
c116, h–: c24.2d⁵ c26.2d* c24.3s² c26.2s² c30g c26.2d Apr 10] winning hurdler: fairly   **h–**
useful handicap chaser: won at Carlisle in October: good second at Ayr and Carlisle: stays 3¼m: acts on heavy going: has worn cheekpieces. *Malcolm Jefferson*

BALLYBILL (IRE) 7 ch.g. Presenting – Corrieann (IRE) (Anshan) [2016/17 h16.2dᵖᵘ   **h–**
h20.2m May 11] no form in bumper/over hurdles: tried in cheekpieces. *Lucinda Russell*

BALLYBOGEY (IRE) 11 b.g. Definite Article – Beenaround (IRE) (King's Ride) **c118**
[2016/17 c116, h–: c19m² c15.8d^pu c21.4g⁶ c17.3g⁴ c19.4d^pu c24g³ Jan 27] big gelding: **h–**
winning hurdler: fairly useful handicap chaser: stays 2½m: acts on soft and good to firm
going: has worn cheekpieces. *Charles Pogson*

BALLYBOKER BREEZE (IRE) 9 b.g. Gold Well – Ballyboker Lady (IRE) (Rashar **c137**
(USA)) [2016/17 c129p, h–: c23.4d² c24.1s* c24d Jan 28] winning Irish pointer: winning **h–**
hurdler: useful chaser: won handicap at Bangor (by 4½ lengths from Kaki de La Pree) in
December: likely to stay further than 3m: acts on heavy going. *Nicky Richards*

BALLYBOKER BRIDGE (IRE) 10 b.g. Gold Well – Ballyboker Lady (IRE) (Rashar **c139**
(USA)) [2016/17 c133, h–: c33g³ c24s² c24s³ c30.2g⁶ c24m^ur Apr 29] workmanlike **h–**
gelding: modest form from only start over hurdles: useful chaser: good effort when 17¼ lengths
sixth of 16 to Cause of Causes in Glenfarclas Cross Country Chase at Cheltenham in
March: stays 33f: acts on heavy going: wears cheekpieces: usually leads. *Peter Maher,
Ireland*

BALLYBOLLEY (IRE) 8 b.g. Kayf Tara – Gales Hill (IRE) (Beau Sher) [2016/17 c143, **c148**
h–: c16.3g² c19.4m* c19.9m* c24.2d² h22.8v^pu c20.1s³ c20.5g⁴ c19.9g* Apr 15] tall **h–**
gelding: useful hurdler at best: smart chaser: won novices at Wetherby and Huntingdon in
October: better than ever when also winning handicap at Haydock (for second year
running) final start by 17 lengths from Captain Redbeard: stays 3m: acts on heavy and good
to firm going: has worn hood: usually tongue tied. *Nigel Twiston-Davies*

BALLYBROWNEYBRIDGE (IRE) 7 b.m. Kalanisi (IRE) – Ballybrowney Hall **h74**
(IRE) (Saddlers' Hall (IRE)) [2016/17 h91, h89: h21.2d⁵ Dec 21] lightly-raced novice
hurdler, modest form at best: bred to stay 3m+. *Venetia Williams*

BALLYCAMP (IRE) 8 br.g. Kayf Tara – All Our Blessings (IRE) (Statoblest) [2016/17 **c117**
h115: h20.6g³ h20d⁴ h16.7g² c15.7g² Aug 14] winning pointer: fair maiden hurdler: fairly **h111**
useful form when second in novice at Southwell (9 lengths behind Stephanie Frances) on
chasing debut: stays 21f: acts on good to soft going: wears tongue tie: front runner/races
prominently. *Charles Pogson*

BALLYCASEY (IRE) 10 gr.g. Presenting – Pink Mist (IRE) (Montelimar (USA)) **c159**
[2016/17 c149, h–: c22g^F c22.5g³ c20.5d* c24v⁵ c20d* c16d³ c20v* c17s* c16d⁵ Apr 25] **h–**
good-topped gelding: winning hurdler: very smart chaser: won handicap at Killarney (by
3¾ lengths from Rightville Boy) in August, PWC Champion Chase at Gowran (by 11
lengths from Road To Riches) in October, Red Mills Chase at Gowran (by 4¼ lengths from
Clarcam) in February and Normans Grove Chase at Fairyhouse (by ½ length from Ball
d'Arc) in April: best at up to 2½m nowadays: acts on heavy going: has worn cheekpieces:
usually races close up. *W. P. Mullins, Ireland*

BALLYCASH (IRE) 6 b.g. Kalanisi (IRE) – Waterlily (IRE) (Revoque (IRE)) [2016/17 **c–**
h–, b85: h20g⁵ h20g⁵ h20.7g^ur h20.3d⁴ h20.7d³ h19.7s^F h16.7s³ c17g^pu Apr 23] good- **h103**
topped gelding: winning pointer: fair maiden hurdler: pulled up in novice handicap on
chasing debut: may prove best at shorter than 2½m: acts on good to soft going: tried in
hood. *Nigel Twiston-Davies*

BALLYCASSEL (IRE) 12 ch.g. Presenting – Sara's Gold (IRE) (Ashkalani (IRE)) **c–**
[2016/17 c16.3g Apr 27] sturdy gelding: winning pointer: maiden hurdler/chaser: **h–**
seemingly stays 23f: acts on good to firm and good to soft going: has worn headgear: has
worn tongue tie, including only outing in 2016/17. *Mrs Sarah Stafford*

BALLYCOE 8 b.g. Norse Dancer (IRE) – Lizzy Lamb (Bustino) [2016/17 c109, h–: **c112**
c20.3g* c20.3s⁴ c19.9s⁴ c20s c20.5g³ c19.4g^F Apr 1] tall gelding: winning hurdler: fair **h–**
handicap chaser: won novice event at Bangor in April: stays 23f: acts on soft going: wears
tongue tie. *Chris Gordon*

BALLYCOOL (IRE) 10 b.g. Helissio (FR) – Carnoustie (USA) (Ezzoud (IRE)) [2016/17 **c100 §**
c108§, h–: c21.2m⁵ c21.2d⁶ c20.3d* c17.3d^ur c19.3g³ c17.4g Oct 25] maiden hurdler: fair **h–**
handicap chaser: won at Bangor in August: stays 2½m: acts on heavy going: wears tongue
tie: usually races towards rear: unreliable. *Lucinda Russell*

BALLYCROSS 6 b.g. King's Theatre (IRE) – Ninna Nanna (FR) (Garde Royale) **c132**
[2016/17 h126: c20d² c24.4s³ c23.6g⁴ c23.6s³ c29.2s^pu c31.8g Mar 14] sturdy gelding: **h–**
Irish point winner: useful hurdler: similar form in chases: best effort when 5¾ lengths third
of 8 to Pobbles Bay in novice handicap at Chepstow on fourth start: stays 3m: acts on heavy
going: usually races prominently. *Nigel Twiston-Davies*

BALLYCRYSTAL (IRE) 6 b.g. Oscar (IRE) – Musical Madam (IRE) (Musical Pursuit) **h121**
[2016/17 h97: h21.2g* h20.8g² h22s* h23.8g⁵ h19.9v⁴ Mar 5] useful-looking gelding:
winning Irish pointer: bumper winner: fairly useful form over hurdles: won novices at

Sedgefield in October and Newcastle in December: bled last 2 starts: should prove suited by 3m+: acts on soft going: often races prominently. *Brian Ellison*

BALLYCULLA (IRE) 10 b.g. Westerner – Someone Told Me (IRE) (Saddlers' Hall (IRE)) [2016/17 c135x, h–: c24.2s¹ c30gᵖᵘ h23.4v⁴ h23.6v h26s Mar 30] leggy gelding: fairly useful handicap hurdler: handicap chaser, useful at best: stays 4m: acts on heavy going: has worn headgear, including in 2016/17. *Warren Greatrex* **c106** **h120**

BALLYDAGUE LADY (IRE) 10 b.m. Luso – Cottstown Belle (IRE) (Flemensfirth (USA)) [2016/17 c112, h86: c23g* c20m* c20.3dᵖᵘ Nov 29] workmanlike mare: modest maiden over hurdles: fairly useful handicap chaser: won at Worcester (mares event) in October and Warwick in November: stayed 23f: acted on good to firm and heavy going: wore cheekpieces: dead. *Neil Mulholland* **c115** **h–**

BALLYEGAN (IRE) 12 b.g. Saddlers' Hall (IRE) – Knapping Princess (IRE) (Prince of Birds (USA)) [2016/17 c92x, h–: c20m⁵ c18.9s³ c18.9s⁵ c19.4s⁶ c18.2g⁵ Apr 6] workmanlike gelding: dual point winner: maiden hurdler: poor handicap chaser nowadays: stays 3¾m: acts on heavy going: has worn tongue tie: front runner/races prominently: often let down by jumping. *Bob Buckler* **c80 x** **h–**

BALLYGARVEY (FR) 11 b.g. Laveron – Vollore (FR) (Cadoudal (FR)) [2016/17 c126, h–: c20.2s³ c20.2vᵖᵘ c20v⁵ Feb 24] smallish, compact gelding: winning hurdler: useful chaser at best: little impact in 2016/17: stays 2½m: acts on heavy going: usually races close up. *Philip Hobbs* **c101** **h–**

BALLY GILBERT (IRE) 6 ch.g. Stowaway – Reedsbuck (FR) (Cyborg (FR)) [2016/17 b101: h21.1g h19.7s⁵ h20.6s² h24.2sᵖᵘ Mar 3] tall, good sort: placed both starts in points: fair form over hurdles: breathing problem final start: should prove suited by 2¾m+: front runner/races prominently. *Ben Pauling* **h112**

BALLYGOWN BAY (IRE) 4 b.g. Flemensfirth (USA) – Star Shuil (IRE) (Soviet Star (USA)) [2016/17 b16s³ h16v³ Mar 12] €60,000 3-y-o: second foal: dam, ran twice in bumpers, out of Stayers' Hurdle winner Shuil Ar Aghaidh: fair form when third in bumpers at Warwick. *Philip Hobbs* **b87**

BALLYGROOBY BERTIE (IRE) 9 b.g. King's Theatre (IRE) – Vigna Maggio (FR) (Starborough) [2016/17 c108, h73: h18.4dᵖᵘ h19.3g⁵ c23.8g² h20.2g Apr 28] poor handicap hurdler: maiden chaser, fair form at best: probably stays 2½m: acts on good to firm and good to soft going: wears headgear: has worn tongue tie. *R. A. Curran, Ireland* **c96** **h78**

BALLYHEIGUE BAY (IRE) 10 b.g. Rudimentary (USA) – Terinka (IRE) (Erins Isle) [2016/17 c128, h–: c24g² c27.2sᶠ h25v⁴ h23.5s h25s* h24.2d Mar 24] good-topped gelding: fair handicap hurdler: won at Plumpton in March: fairly useful handicap chaser: stays 29f: acts on heavy going: has worn headgear, including last 2 starts: wears tongue tie: front runner/races prominently. *Chris Gordon* **c123** **h110**

BALLYHEIGUE (IRE) 8 b.g. High Chaparral (IRE) – Lypharden (IRE) (Lyphard's Special (USA)) [2016/17 h16d Jun 19] modest on Flat, stays 1¾m: no form over hurdles: sometimes in headgear. *Seamus Mullins* **h–**

BALLYHENRY (IRE) 7 br.g. Presenting – Afarka (IRE) (Kahyasi) [2016/17 h116: c24d³ c23.5g h24.4dᵖᵘ Mar 6] rangy gelding: fairly useful hurdler at best: better effort (fairly useful form) over fences when third in novice handicap at Southwell in November: stays 3m: acts on soft going: tried in cheekpieces/tongue tie. *Ben Pauling* **c121** **h–**

BALLYHILL (FR) 6 b.g. Al Namix (FR) – Laly Light (FR) (Start Fast (FR)) [2016/17 b88: b15.7g h16.2g* h21.2g* h15.7v⁴ h16.8g⁴ h16g³ h21s⁵ h16.3d h20.3g Mar 17] good-topped gelding: promise when fell in Irish maiden point: fair form at best in bumpers: fairly useful hurdler: won novice at Hereford in October and minor event at Ludlow in November: stays 21f: acts on heavy going. *Nigel Twiston-Davies* **h126** **b82**

BALLYKAN 7 b.g. Presenting – La Marianne (Supreme Leader) [2016/17 c135, h117: c26.1g⁶ c22.6mʳᵒ c20.1s* c20.3g* c21.4g³ c24.1v⁴ c24g⁵ c20.8g⁶ c21.1gᶠ c23.8g⁴ Apr 26] lengthy, useful-looking gelding: fairly useful hurdler: useful handicap chaser: won at Perth in July and Southwell in August: stays 3m: acts on soft and good to firm going: wears cheekpieces/tongue tie. *Nigel Twiston-Davies* **c138** **h–**

BALLYKNOCK LAD (IRE) 8 b.g. Bach (IRE) – Ballyknock Lass (IRE) (Electric) [2016/17 c–, h115: c25.1m* h23g* c24.1g² c23m* Aug 17] fairly useful handicap hurdler: won at Worcester in July: fairly useful form in chases: won handicaps at Wincanton in May and Worcester in August: stays 25f: acts on good to firm going: wears tongue tie: often races prominently, usually responds generously to pressure. *Kim Bailey* **c126** **h119**

BALLY LAGAN (IRE) 9 gr.g. Kalanisi (IRE) – Rose Palma (FR) (Great Palm (USA)) [2016/17 c81, h–: c24d^{ur} c20.5m c20.3g^3 c20.9g^5 c20g^3 c15.6g^4 c23g^6 c20.2g* c18.2g* c18.2g* c17.2m^{pu} Apr 17] stocky gelding: maiden hurdler: modest handicap chaser: won at Leicester in January, and at Taunton in March and April: best around 2½m: acts on soft and good to firm going: wears headgear: has worn tongue tie. *Robin Dickin*   **c98 h–**

BALLY LONGFORD (IRE) 9 b.g. Gold Well – Stay On Line (IRE) (Over The River (FR)) [2016/17 c136, h–: c16g^4 c18.2g^6 c15.9g^3 c26g^3 c24g^6 Dec 27] lengthy gelding: winning hurdler: useful handicap chaser: left Henry de Bromhead, third at Cheltenham in November (3¾ lengths behind Un Beau Roman) and December (Grade 3 event. 3¾ lengths behind Theatre Guide): likely to prove best up to 3m: acts on soft and good to firm going: in tongue tie last 2 starts. *Colin Tizzard*   **c134 h–**

BALLYMALIN (IRE) 7 b.g. Presenting – Murrurundi (IRE) (Old Vic) [2016/17 b105: h23.9s* h23.9g^3 h24d* h21.9v* h24.5d* h23.1s^3 h24g h24.7g^5 Apr 7] medium-sized gelding: winning pointer: useful bumper performer: also useful over hurdles: won novices at Perth in September, Southwell in November, Ffos Las in December and Kempton in January: good fifth of 11 to The Worlds End in Sefton Novices' Hurdle at Aintree final start: stays 25f: acts on heavy going: front runner/races prominently. *Nigel Twiston-Davies*   **h136**

BALLYMOUNTAIN BOY (IRE) 6 b.g. Mountain High (IRE) – Minoras Return (IRE) (Bob's Return (IRE)) [2016/17 b16.8g^5 b16.4s b15.8s^2 b15.8d* h15.8d^3 h21s^4 h15.7s^3 Mar 16] €15,000 3-y-o: useful-looking gelding: second foal: dam, unraced, out of half-sister to high-class chaser Observe: won Irish maiden point: fairly useful form in bumpers: won at Huntingdon in December: fair form over hurdles: stays 21f: usually races close up. *Martin Keighley*   **h111 b100**

BALLYNAGOUR (IRE) 11 b.g. Shantou (USA) – Simply Deep (IRE) (Simply Great (FR)) [2016/17 c161, h145: h21.4s c26.1g^2 c21.4g^2 c20.4s^{pu} c26g^{pu} c20.8s^{pu} c34.3d Apr 8] sturdy gelding: very smart hurdler and high-class chaser in his prime: runner-up in 2 chases early in season, namely Summer Cup at Uttoxeter (2 lengths behind Drop Out Joe) and Summer Plate at Market Rasen (8 lengths behind Long House Hall): completed only once subsequently, when well-beaten eleventh of 40 to One For Arthur in Grand National at Aintree: stays 3¼m: acts on heavy going: wears hood/tongue tie: usually races nearer last than first: has bled. *David Pipe*   **c155 d h–**

BALLYNORTH BENNY (IRE) 5 ch.g. Beneficial – Maslam (IRE) (Robellino (USA)) [2016/17 b15.7v h23.1v h20.8d^5 h20.6s^{pu} Mar 12] won Irish maiden point on debut: well held in bumper: modest form at best over hurdles: dead. *Graeme McPherson*   **h98 b–**

BALLYOISIN (IRE) 6 b.g. Presenting – Regal Force (IRE) (King's Ride) [2016/17 c21.5v^F c17s* c17s^F c16d^F Apr 27] second foal: dam (h97), maiden hurdler (stayed 19f), half-sister to fairly useful hurdler/chaser (winner up to 2¾m) Nor'nor'east: winning pointer: fairly useful hurdler: smart form on only completed start in chases, when winning maiden at Fairyhouse in January by 6 lengths from Townshend: bred to stay 2½m+: acts on soft going: front runner/races prominently. *Enda Bolger, Ireland*   **c147 h–**

BALLYOLIVER 13 b.g. Kayf Tara – Macklette (IRE) (Buckskin (FR)) [2016/17 c123§, h–: c24g^{pu} May 14] strong gelding: maiden hurdler: fairly useful chaser at best: stays 3¼m: acts on heavy going: has worn headgear, including last 2 starts: often races lazily: inconsistent. *Venetia Williams*   **c– § h–**

BALLYOPTIC (IRE) 7 b.g. Old Vic – Lambourne Lace (IRE) (Un Desperado (FR)) [2016/17 h144p, b67: h19.5g* h24.1g^F h24.2d^2 h24.4d^F h24s^4 h24g^{pu} h24.7g^5 Apr 8] well-made gelding: winning pointer: smart hurdler: won Silver Trophy at Chepstow (by 1¼ lengths from Crimson Ark) in October: second in Long Distance Hurdle at Newbury (6 lengths behind Unowhatimeanharry) in November and running well when falling last (would have been placed) in Long Walk Hurdle at Ascot in December: creditable fifth of 11 to Yanworth in Stayers' Liverpool Hurdle at Aintree final start: stays 25f: acts on heavy going: tried in tongue tie. *Nigel Twiston-Davies*   **h151**

BALLYPOINT (IRE) 6 b.g. Mahler – Angel Trix (IRE) (Un Desperado (FR)) [2016/17 h118, b–: h23.9g h23.1s^6 c21.7d c24.2s c23.8m^4 Apr 25] tall gelding: fairly useful hurdler at best, no form in 2016/17: best effort (fairly useful form) in chases when seventh in novice handicap at Towcester: stays 2½m: acts on heavy going: in tongue tie last 3 starts. *Nigel Twiston-Davies*   **c116 h–**

BALLYRATH (IRE) 7 b.g. Flemensfirth (USA) – Rose Wee (IRE) (Roselier (FR)) [2016/17 c117, h91: h23.3s^2 Apr 30] sturdy gelding: fair maiden over hurdles: fairly useful chaser: should be suited by 3m+: best form on soft/heavy going: wears headgear. *Nigel Twiston-Davies*   **c– h111**

BALLYROCK (IRE) 11 b.g. Milan – Ardent Love (IRE) (Ardross) [2016/17 h121: c119 §
c20.3v⁴ c26.1sᵖᵘ c24g* c26.2dᵖᵘ c23.5g⁵ c23.6s⁶ h25.5s⁴ h20g* Apr 17] useful-looking h109 §
gelding: fair hurdler: won seller at Fakenham final start: fairly useful form over fences:
won novice handicap at Southwell in October: stays 3m: acts on heavy going: has worn
headgear, including in 2016/17: wears tongue tie: one to be wary of. *Tim Vaughan*

BALLY SANDS (IRE) 13 b.g. Luso – Sandwell Old Rose (IRE) (Roselier (FR)) [2016/17 c–
c–, h–: h25g⁴ h23.3s² h23.3g Jul 5] tall, good-topped gelding: point winner: winning h82
hurdler/chaser, poor nowadays: stays 29f: acts on heavy going: has worn headgear,
including last 3 starts. *Robin Mathew*

BALLYTHOMAS 10 b.g. Kayf Tara – Gregale (Gildoran) [2016/17 c–, h96: h24v c102
c24.2sᵖᵘ c24.2s⁶ c23.8g* c23.8g* c23.9m² c23.8gᵖᵘ Apr 26] fair hurdler at best: fair h–
handicap chaser: won at Musselburgh in February and March: stays 25f: acts on good to
firm and heavy going: has worn cheekpieces: often leads. *David Thompson*

BALLYTOBER 11 b.g. Kahyasi – Full of Birds (FR) (Epervier Bleu) [2016/17 c121, h–: c114
c16.1g⁶ c23.4d² Mar 24] tall gelding: has reportedly had breathing operation: winning h–
pointer/hurdler: fairly useful hunter chaser: stays 25f: acts on good to firm and heavy
going: has worn headgear, including last 4 starts: wears tongue tie. *Ian Prichard*

BALLYVAUGHN (IRE) 7 b.g. Robin des Pres (FR) – Countessdee (IRE) (Arctic Lord) c88
[2016/17 c101, h80: c16g c19.9g⁵ c20.9s⁴ c20g⁴ h22g⁵ Jul 28] poor maiden hurdler: h63
modest handicap chaser: likely to prove best up to 2½m: acts on soft going: tried in tongue
tie. *Caroline Bailey*

BALLYVESEY (IRE) 12 ch.g. Anshan – Bridgequarter Lady (IRE) (King's Ride) c– §
[2016/17 c23.8m⁶ May 11] sturdy gelding: multiple point winner: winning hurdler: one- h–
time fairly useful chaser: stays 3¼m: acts on soft and good to firm going: often in headgear/
tongue tie: temperamental. *D. Holmes*

BALLYVIC BORU (IRE) 5 b.g. Brian Boru – Thedoublede (IRE) (Deploy) [2016/17 b99
b16.8d² b15.6g* b16g³ Apr 22] first foal: dam tailed off in bumper only start: off mark in
Irish maiden points at second attempt: fairly useful form in bumpers: won at Musselburgh
(by ¾ length from Beyond The Clouds) in February: 8½ lengths third of 12 to Pym at Ayr
final start. *Brian Ellison*

BALLYVOQUE (IRE) 11 b.g. Revoque (IRE) – Timissa (IRE) (Kahyasi) [2016/17 c110
c107, h99: c16.4g⁴ Aug 25] leggy gelding: winning hurdler: fair maiden chaser: stays h–
2¾m: acts on soft going. *George Charlton*

BALLYWARD (IRE) 5 b.g. Flemensfirth (USA) – Ifyoucouldseemenow (IRE) b111 p
(Saddlers' Hall (IRE)) [2016/17 b20d* Dec 27] second foal: dam fair hurdler/fairly useful
chaser (2½m-2¾m winner) out of smart hurdler/fairly useful chaser (stayed 25f) Sallie's
Girl: runner-up in point: 9/10, won maiden bumper at Leopardstown by 16 lengths from
Drumconnor Lad, storming clear: looks smart prospect. *W. P. Mullins, Ireland*

BALLYWILLIAM (IRE) 7 b.g. Mahler – Henrietta Howard (IRE) (King's Ride) c–
[2016/17 h121: c23.4dᵖᵘ h26sᵖᵘ h26sᵖᵘ Mar 30] rangy gelding: fairly useful hurdler at best: h–
out of sorts in 2016/17, pulled up in novice handicap on chasing debut: in headgear last 5
starts: usually races towards rear. *David Pipe*

BALMORAL PRINCE 6 b.g. Multiplex – Balmoral Princess (Thethingaboutitis (USA)) h–
[2016/17 b–: b16d⁵ b16.7g⁴ h20m⁴ h16m h19.9g h25.5g⁴ Oct 6] poor form in bumpers: no b61
form over hurdles. *Shaun Lycett*

BALMUSETTE 8 b.m. Halling (USA) – Tcherina (IRE) (Danehill Dancer (IRE)) h–
[2016/17 h124: h22.1dᵖᵘ Jul 16] useful hurdler at best: stays 3m: acts on soft and good to
firm going: held up. *Keith Reveley*

BALNASLOW (IRE) 10 b.g. Presenting – Noble Choice (Dahar (USA)) [2016/17 c134, c135
h–: c25sᵖᵘ c22.6s² c26.3g⁵ c21.1g² c24.5d* Apr 28] tall gelding: winning hurdler: useful h–
chaser: won Champion Hunters Chase at Punchestown final start by neck from Mendip
Express: fell before Gordon Elliott after reappearance: stays 3¼m: acts on soft and good to firm
going: has worn tongue tie. *Graham McKeever, Ireland*

BALTAZAR D'ALLIER (FR) 6 br.g. Malinas (GER) – Kinoise d'Allier (FR) (Roi de h131 p
Rome (USA)) [2016/17 h19d* h20.5d² h22.5vᶠ Mar 19] €30,000 3-y-o: rangy, raw-boned
gelding: second foal: dam placed over hurdles in France at around 2m: won maiden on
point debut: useful form over hurdles: won maiden at Naas (by 16 lengths from Mighty
Stowaway) in November: 2 lengths second of 8 to Messire des Obeaux in Challow
Novices' Hurdle at Newbury in December: stumbled and fell fifth in novice at Navan final
start: will stay 3m: remains open to improvement. *Gordon Elliott, Ireland*

BALTHAZAR (IRE) 5 gr.g. Dark Angel (IRE) – Engraving (Sadler's Wells (USA)) [2016/17 h16.2v⁶ h17d Apr 5] well held in 2 Flat maidens/novice hurdles. *Hugh Burns* **h–**

BALTIC STORM (IRE) 6 b.g. Kandahar Run – Born Wild (GER) (Sadler's Wells (USA)) [2016/17 h125: h17.7m* Sep 18] fairly useful form over hurdles: won 3-runner novice at Plumpton only outing in 2016/17: stays 2¼m: acts on good to firm and good to soft going: usually travels strongly. *Charlie Mann* **h125**

BALTIMORE BUZZ (IRE) 8 b.g. Beneficial – Supreme Dancer (IRE) (Supreme Leader) [2016/17 h16m b20.5d* h16.5v² h21.3d⁶ h16vᵖᵘ Mar 10] maiden pointer: won bumper at Roscommon in July: fair form over hurdles: left Aidan Anthony Howard/off 6 months, breathing problem final start. *Noel C. Kelly, Ireland* **h102 b91**

BALTIMORE ROCK (IRE) 8 b.g. Tiger Hill (IRE) – La Vita E Bella (IRE) (Definite Article) [2016/17 c142, h–: c16d⁴ c16d⁴ c17sᵖᵘ c15.8g⁵ h16.8g h16g Apr 22] rather leggy gelding: fairly useful handicap hurdler/chaser: raced around 2m: acts on heavy going: has worn cheekpieces, including in 2016/17: wears tongue tie: usually races nearer last than first. *Neil Mulholland* **c127 h126**

BAMAKO MORIVIERE (FR) 6 b.g. Califet (FR) – Halladine (FR) (Passing Sale (FR)) [2016/17 h135p: h16d⁴ h20d⁶ h16g* h20s* h16.1g h16g* Aug 28] smart hurdler: won handicap at Punchestown (by 2¼ lengths from Princely Conn) in June and minor events at Bellewstown (by 7 lengths from Clarcam) in July and Cork (by 5½ lengths from My Painter) in August: stays 2½m: acts on heavy going: in tongue tie last 4 starts: usually leads. *W. P. Mullins, Ireland* **h145**

BAMBI DU NOYER (FR) 6 b.g. Sageburg (IRE) – Zouk Wood (USA) (Woodman (USA)) [2016/17 c115, h117: h16.2d h17.2g h20.1dᵖᵘ h15.8d⁴ Apr 16] handicap hurdler/chaser, fairly useful at best: left Simon Waugh after third start: stays 19f: acts on soft going. *David Pipe* **c– h97**

BANCO DE LOGOS (FR) 6 b.g. Laverock (IRE) – Funkia (FR) (Royal Charter (FR)) [2016/17 b16.8m⁶ h15.3m³ b16g h18.5s⁵ h15.3d⁴ h19.8d⁴ Mar 26] €13,000 3-y-o: workmanlike gelding: half-brother to several winners, including fairly useful hurdler/useful chaser Requin (17f-19f winner, by Video Rock), stayed 2¾m: dam, French 17f chase winner, also 11f winner on Flat: modest form in bumpers: fair form over hurdles: likely to prove best at around 2m: usually races close up. *Charles Whittaker* **h102 b83**

BANDIT COUNTRY (IRE) 8 b.g. Flemensfirth (USA) – Calomeria (Groom Dancer (USA)) [2016/17 c–, h102§: h18.6d² h20d² h24gᵖᵘ Aug 23] fair maiden hurdler: winning chaser: stays 2¾m: acts on soft going: usually in headgear: wears tongue tie: irresolute. *Sophie Leech* **c– h103 §**

BANDITRY (IRE) 5 b.g. Iffraaj – Badalona (Cape Cross (IRE)) [2016/17 h15.7d⁵ h17s³ Dec 3] sturdy gelding: useful on Flat, stays 10.5f: fair form when fifth in introductory hurdle at Ascot and third in novice at Aintree: will prove best at sharp 2m: wears hood: capable of better. *Ian Williams* **h108 p**

BAND OF THUNDER 9 ch.g. Shirocco (GER) – Black Opal (Machiavellian (USA)) [2016/17 h81: h21.6g⁵ h24d⁶ Jul 10] winning hurdler, modest at best: stays 25f: acts on soft going: has worn headgear, including last 5 starts: temperamental. *Martin Smith* **h– §**

BANDOL (IRE) 9 b.g. Zagreb (USA) – Formal Affair (Rousillon (USA)) [2016/17 h19g² h18.7m h20g c15.7gᵘʳ c16.5g* c15.7gᶠ c18.9s* c16.4v* c15.7s³ c19.3dᶠ c20.1vᵖᵘ Mar 28] rather lightly-built gelding: poor maiden hurdler: modest handicap chaser: won at Worcester in September, Hereford (conditional) in December and Sedgefield in February: left Henry Oliver after seventh start: stays 19f: acts on heavy going. *Simon West* **c92 h73**

BANDON BRIDGE (IRE) 7 br.g. Presenting – Karen Mag (IRE) (Oscar (IRE)) [2016/17 h19.7s h21.6s⁵ h23.6s² c24s* c25.5g⁶ Apr 12] first foal: dam (h99), 2½m hurdle winner/winning pointer, sister to useful chaser (stayed 3¼m) Oscar Delta: dual Irish point winner: modest form over hurdles: modest form over fences: won novice handicap at Warwick in March: stays 3m: acts on soft going: front runner/races prominently. *Katy Price* **c96 h89**

BANDON ROC 6 b.g. Shirocco (GER) – Azur (IRE) (Brief Truce (USA)) [2016/17 h90: h19g h19s* h25d* h19.2v* Feb 15] fairly useful handicap hurdler: much improved, and won at Taunton (conditional), Huntingdon and Towcester in February: stays 25f: acts on heavy going. *Kim Bailey* **h116**

BANDSMAN 6 b.g. Bandmaster (USA) – Soleil Sauvage (Loup Sauvage (USA)) [2016/17 b98: b16.7g² b16.7g² h16g² h18.6s* h16.7d* h21g Mar 18] good-topped gelding: fairly useful form in bumpers: also showed fairly useful form when winning 2 novice hurdles at Market Rasen in December: stays 2¼m: jumps none too fluently. *Dan Skelton* **h125 b96**

BANFF (IRE) 4 b.g. Papal Bull – Hugs 'N Kisses (IRE) (Noverre (USA)) [2016/17 **h–** h16.2v⁶ h16s h15.8s Feb 8] modest maiden on Flat, stays 12.5f: no form over hurdles. *Anabel K. Murphy*

BANG ON FRANKIE (IRE) 5 br.g. Kalanisi (IRE) – Shuil Abbey (IRE) (Saddlers' Hall **b101** (IRE)) [2016/17 b15.7d³ b16.3s⁵ Jan 18] €40,000 3-y-o: strong gelding: third foal: dam, (h105) maiden hurdler (raced around 2m), half-sister to dam of smart hurdler/chaser (winner up to 2½m) Bright New Dawn: better effort (fairly useful form) in bumpers when 5¼ lengths third to Western Ryder in listed event at Ascot in December. *Colin Tizzard*

BANG ON TIME (IRE) 11 b.g. Chevalier (IRE) – Dysart Lady (King's Ride) [2016/17 **c–** c117x: c23.4vᵖᵘ Feb 16] multiple point winner: fairly useful chaser at best: stays 3¼m: acts on any going: wears cheekpieces. *Lynsey Kendall*

BANJO GIRL (IRE) 5 ch.m. Presenting – Oh Susannah (FR) (Turgeon (USA)) [2016/17 **h112** b–: h20.6g⁴ h19.4g³ h15.7v³ h20.3s² Mar 20] well held in bumper: fair form over hurdles: stays 2½m: tried in tongue tie: often races prominently. *Lucy Wadham*

BANK BONUS 8 b.g. Motivator – Small Fortune (Anabaa (USA)) [2016/17 h117: h20d **c84** h20m c21.5d⁵ h21g h16.8d⁴ h19.3g² h19.4d Jan 28] fair handicap hurdler: fifth of 8 in **h112** maiden at Downpatrick on chasing debut: left Gordon Elliott after fourth start: stays 3m: acts on soft and good to firm going: often in hood. *Brian Ellison*

BANKHALL (IRE) 6 b.g. Trans Island – Agena d'Auteuil (FR) (Persian Combat (USA)) **c93 §** [2016/17 h20.1g⁴ h20.2f⁴ h16.2d h19.9dᵖᵘ h21.3g⁴ h23.1s² h25.3d² c24.2s* c25.2dᵖᵘ **h97 §** c24vᵖᵘ h25.3s² c23.4vᵖᵘ h24.1m* Apr 13] €9,500 3-y-o: close-coupled gelding: fifth foal: dam unraced half-sister to fairly useful hurdler/high-class chaser (stayed 21f) Le Roi Miguel: modest handicap hurdler: won at Wetherby in April: modest form over fences: won novice handicap at Wetherby in December: left Stuart Crawford after second start: stays 25f: acts on soft and good to firm going: wears headgear: temperamental. *Mark Walford*

BANK MAN (IRE) 9 b.g. Luso – Lost Prairie (IRE) (Be My Native (USA)) [2016/17 **c–** h17m h21.4d Oct 29] maiden handicap hurdler: showed little only outing over fences: best **h73** effort at 2m: acts on good to soft going: tried in hood. *Michael O'Hare, Ireland*

BANNOW STORM (IRE) 6 b.m. Presenting – Bannow Girl (IRE) (Glacial Storm **h–** (USA)) [2016/17 b85: b16.2m³ b16.2d⁶ b16.2g⁵ h16.2gᵖᵘ Oct 8] modest form in bumpers: **b75** pulled up in mares novice on hurdling debut: tried in hood: often races in rear/freely. *George Bewley*

BANNY'S LAD 8 ch.g. Osorio (GER) – Skytrial (USA) (Sky Classic (CAN)) [2016/17 **c105 x** c–, h109: h23.1g⁴ h23.1g⁶ h21.6m* h22m h19.6g c25.2dᵖᵘ c21.4d c19.9d⁶ c19.3v* c19.1s² **h109** c21.3d⁵ Mar 21] fair hurdler: won maiden at Newton Abbot in July: fair handicap chaser: won at Sedgefield in February: stays 25f: acts on good to firm and heavy going: often races towards rear: often let down by jumping over fences. *Michael Easterby*

BANTAM (IRE) 7 b.m. Teofilo (IRE) – Firecrest (IRE) (Darshaan) [2016/17 h124: **c–** c16.2mᶠ c17.4sᵘʳ Nov 9] lengthy mare: fairly useful hurdler: failed to complete both starts **h–** over fences: likely to prove best at short of 2½m: acts on good to firm and good to soft going. *Henry Daly*

BANYU (FR) 6 b.g. Dylan Thomas (IRE) – Banyu Dewi (GER) (Poliglote) [2016/17 **h137** h133: h17.7d* Apr 29] good-topped gelding: useful form over hurdles: won handicap at Fontwell (by 10 lengths from Maestro Royal) only outing in 2016/17: stays 2¼m: acts on heavy going: often leads/travels strongly. *Philip Hobbs*

BAPAUME (FR) 4 b.g. Turtle Bowl (IRE) – Brouhaha (FR) (American Post) **h146** [2016/17 h16d² h16d* h16s² h16.8g³ h16d* Apr 29]

The competition to become the season's best juvenile hurdler in Ireland was a much less clear-cut affair than it was in either Britain or France. Defi du Seuil proved much the best juvenile trained in Britain, while the filly De Bon Coeur likewise looked head and shoulders above her contemporaries at Auteuil. Ireland's Bapaume came up against both of these champions, finishing third when Defi du Seuil took his unbeaten run over hurdles to six in the Triumph Hurdle, while, at Auteuil, Bapaume would also have probably finished third behind De Bon Coeur in the Prix Alain du Breil had she herself not fallen when looking all set to take her unbeaten record to seven. In between these good efforts, Bapaume won Ireland's big end-of-season juvenile hurdle the Champion Four Year Old Hurdle at Punchestown, in the process accounting for the only two home-trained horses who had beaten him earlier in the season.

AES Champion Four Year Old Hurdle, Punchestown—
Bapaume extends his head-to-head record against Landofhopeandglory (hoops) to three-one;
Meri Devie (right) and Mega Fortune (left) complete the frame

Bapaume didn't make his debut for Willie Mullins until early-December when faced straight away with Landofhopeandglory and Mega Fortune, the pair who went on to prove the two other candidates for the title of top Irish juvenile. The trio met in the Bar One Racing Juvenile Hurdle at Fairyhouse in which Landofhopeandglory, a useful recruit from the Flat, successfully conceded weight to both Bapaume and Mega Fortune in a muddling race. Bapaume made most of the running but a mistake at the last proved costly and he went down by a length, finishing a length and a quarter in front of third-placed Mega Fortune. The same three dominated the Knight Frank Juvenile Hurdle at Leopardstown later in the month, though the order was different this time, with Bapaume showing improved form to run out a game winner. Though again untidy at the last, he stuck to his task on the run-in to beat Landofhopeandglory by a length and three quarters with Mega Fortune just a short head away in third. It was Landofhopeandglory's first defeat in four starts over hurdles, and he was an absentee when Bapaume and Mega Fortune had their next encounter in the Grade 1 Spring Juvenile Hurdle back at Leopardstown in February. Bapaume's tenure as the top Irish four-year-old didn't last long as, on this occasion, it was Mega Fortune who came out on top, by three and a half lengths, the winner ridden more enterprisingly than in his two previous meetings with Bapaume (he was also wearing cheekpieces for the first time over hurdles). Collectively, the Irish-trained juveniles performed well in the following month's Triumph Hurdle, though none could hold a candle to five-length winner Defi du Seuil. They took the next four places behind him, though, Bapaume going second on the run-in but just losing out to the rallying Mega Fortune by a short head for the runner-up spot, with Ex Patriot (fifth in the Spring Juvenile) and Landofhopeandglory took the next two places.

Unusually, the Triumph proved the only occasion when the top British and Irish four-year-olds met. There were no Irish runners in the Anniversary Hurdle at Aintree, which Defi du Seuil went on to win, while, more surprisingly perhaps given Defi du Seuil's absence, there were no British visitors among a field of just seven for the AES Champion Four Year Old Hurdle at Punchestown. The line-up had a familiar look, with Bapaume heading the betting at 2/1, then Mega Fortune at 9/4 and Landofhopeandglory at 4/1. As well as Bapaume, Willie Mullins was represented by the filly Meri Devie, who had finished fourth in the Spring Juvenile, and by Vroum Vroum Mag's half-brother Dandy Mag, runner-up in a Grade 2 contest at Fairyhouse since finishing in rear in the Triumph. Gordon Elliott also had more than one contender, with Mega Fortune being joined by Dinaria des Obeaux, though she had a bit to find with the principals, having finished third in the

Spring Juvenile and down the field in the Triumph. The 66/1 outsider On The Go Again completed the field. Mullins had won the last four editions of the Champion Four Year Old Hurdle and Bapaume made it five under Ruby Walsh for whom the Punchestown Festival was a frustrating meeting, as he rode only one other winner all week. Among no fewer than eight runners-up partnered by Walsh were Djakadam and Nichols Canyon who suffered very narrow defeats in Grade 1 races, while on several other occasions Walsh found himself on the 'wrong' Mullins horse. With the emphasis on speed rather than stamina, underfoot conditions at Punchestown suited Bapaume more than they did Mega Fortune, who had been shaping like a stayer. Always going well, Bapaume was produced to lead at the last after Mega Fortune had gone for home entering the straight. Bapaume won ridden out by a length and a quarter from a back-to-form Landofhopeandglory, with another length back to Meri Devie who just deprived Mega Fortune of third.

The Prix Alain du Breil in June is the top four-year-old hurdle of the first half of the year at Auteuil and is a race that Mullins has long targeted with some of his best juvenile hurdlers. Hurricane Fly and Quevega were both placed in 2008, while more recently Mullins won it with Diakali (winner at Punchestown beforehand) in 2013 and Footpad in 2016. Bapaume's chances of joining them improved greatly when De Bon Coeur, winner of her six other starts over hurdles, took a crashing fall two out when looking well in control. Bapaume was tracking her at the time and was lucky to suffer nothing worse than very minor interference, but in the end he had to give best on the run-in to the other main French hope Prince Ali and went down by half a length, having reportedly lost a shoe at some stage. Stable-companion

Mrs S. Ricci's "Bapaume"

BAR

Dandy Mag also picked up place money in third. Bapaume had begun his career in France the previous spring, winning at Fontainebleau on the second of two starts over hurdles for Augustin Adeline de Boisbrunet.

Bapaume (FR) (b.g. 2013)	Turtle Bowl (IRE) (b 2002)	Dyhim Diamond (ch 1994)	Night Shift
			Happy Landing
		Clara Bow (b 1990)	Top Ville
			Kamiya
	Brouhaha (FR) (b 2006)	American Post (br 2001)	Bering
			Wells Fargo
		Balouchina (b 1990)	Rainbow Quest
			Bamieres

The useful-looking Bapaume is the second good hurdler sired by Turtle Bowl to represent the Mullins stable after the smart Ivan Grozny, winner of two graded events at Tipperary in the latest season. Turtle Bowl, who died at stud in Japan in June, was a very smart miler whose biggest win for Pau trainer Francois Rohaut came in the Prix Jean Prat, though he was also beaten just two short heads in the Queen Anne Stakes on his only start in Britain. Rohaut also trained Bapaume's dam Brouhaha whose only win came in a mile and a half maiden at La Teste, though the trainer's connection with the dam's side of Bapaume's family runs a lot deeper than that. Brouhaha (and Bapaume before his sale to Ireland) carried the colours of Rohaut's mother and are members of a family, all of whom have names beginning with the letter 'B', which has been developed by Rohaut's parents over several generations. The most celebrated member to have carried the Rohaut colours is Balbonella, the 1986 Prix Robert Papin winner, a half-sister to Bapaume's grandam. Francois Rohaut still trained Balbonella at the time of her biggest win as a speedy two-year-old, but she had been bought, reportedly for the equivalent of around half a million pounds, by Maktoum Al Maktoum shortly beforehand. Balbonella subsequently joined Criquette Head and went on to win a total of nine races, ending her racing career in the States (where she won the Grade 3 Dahlia Handicap over an extended mile). She went on to achieve even greater fame as a broodmare and, as well as being the dam of the top-class sprinter Anabaa, the sire of Goldikova, she also produced the Poule d'Essai des Pouliches winner Always Loyal, the Dubai Duty Free winner Key of Luck and the dam of the Gimcrack winner Country Reel. Balbonella clearly passed on plenty of speed but, not surprisingly, that wasn't the main attribute of her Rainbow Quest half-sister Balouchina, Bapaume's grandam, a winner over an extended eleven furlongs at Dax. Bapaume's dam Brouhaha was one of four winners out of Balouchina, while Bapaume is Brouhaha's third foal and only runner to date. Although he enjoyed plenty of success as a juvenile, Bapaume will need to improve to trouble the best hurdlers in open company in the next season. He stays nineteen furlongs and acts on soft ground. *W. P. Mullins, Ireland*

BARABOY (IRE) 7 b.g. Barathea (IRE) – Irina (IRE) (Polar Falcon (USA)) [2016/17   **c96** h100: h17m⁶ h17.2g⁴ h16.2d h15.8g² h15.8d* h15.8g⁴ h15.7g c16.4gᵘʳ c15.5g⁵ c16.9d⁴   **h100** c15.5s* c15.5s⁵ h16.6d h16.8v³ h15.8s⁵ Apr 1] fair handicap hurdler: won at Uttoxeter in July: modest form over fences: won handicap at Ayr in December: raced around 2m: acts on heavy going: has worn headgear, including last 2 starts: has worn tongue tie. *Barry Murtagh*

BARACALU (FR) 6 gr.g. Califet (FR) – Myragentry (FR) (Myrakalu (FR)) [2016/17   **b105** b92: b16.2v* b16g Apr 22] runner-up completed start in Irish points: useful form in bumpers: won maiden at Hexham in March by 30 lengths from Teescomponents Lad: well held final start. *Sandy Thomson*

BARAFUNDLE (IRE) 13 ch.g. Flemensfirth (USA) – Different Dee (IRE) (Beau Sher)   **c– §** [2016/17 c126§, h–§: c28.4vᵖᵘ h23.1sᵖᵘ Dec 9] tall, leggy gelding: one-time smart hurdler/   **h– §** useful chaser: stays 25f: acts on any going: usually in headgear nowadays: tried in tongue tie: front runner/races prominently: temperamental. *Jennie Candlish*

BAR A MINE (FR) 8 b.g. Martaline – Treekle Toffee (FR) (Cadoudal (FR)) [2016/17 c–,   **c–** h100: h22m May 15] maiden hurdler/chaser: stays 21f: acts on heavy going: wears visor: **h–** front runner/races prominently. *Nigel Twiston-Davies*

BARATINEUR (FR) 6 ch.g. Vendangeur (IRE) – Olmantina (FR) (Ragmar (FR)) **h119 §**
[2016/17 h123: h15.8g⁴ h15.7v⁵ h15.7s³ h16.5g⁴ h20.6m Apr 17] fairly useful handicap
hurdler: likely to prove best at around 2m: best form on soft/heavy going: often races
freely: unreliable. *Nicky Henderson*

BAR A VILORBAINE (FR) 6 b.g. Mister Conway (FR) – Pessac Leognan (FR) (Video **h–**
Rock (FR)) [2016/17 b16.8g⁴ h19.1s⁵ Oct 1] well held in bumper/novice hurdle: wears **b–**
tongue tie. *Nigel Hawke*

BARAYMI (FR) 5 b.g. Makfi – Brusca (USA) (Grindstone (USA)) [2016/17 h112: **h105 §**
h17.7s³ h20.5vᶠ h16sᵖᵘ h26vᵖᵘ h19.8f³ Apr 23] sturdy gelding: fair maiden hurdler: stays
2½m: probably acts on any going: usually wears headgear: temperamental. *Jamie Snowden*

BARAZA (FR) 6 gr.g. Smadoun (FR) – Gerbora (FR) (Art Bleu) [2016/17 h90: h18.5m⁴ **c113**
h19.9s c15.9g* c19.1g³ c16g² c17g* Apr 23] good-topped gelding: modest form over **h99**
hurdles: fair chaser: won novice handicaps at Leicester in January and Stratford on final
start: should stay 2½m: acts on good to firm going: tried in blinkers: in tongue tie last 4
starts: front runner/races prominently. *Tom George*

BARBROOK STAR (IRE) 5 b.g. Getaway (GER) – Fille de Robin (FR) (Robin des **h–**
Champs (FR)) [2016/17 b16g⁴ b15.7d h19.7s Mar 11] useful-looking gelding: second foal: **b82**
dam raced half-sister to fairly useful chaser Spock (stayed 21f) and fairly useful hurdler
Blackthorn Prince (stays 3m): modest form in bumpers: tailed off in novice on hurdling
debut. *Philip Hobbs*

BARDD (IRE) 5 b.g. Dylan Thomas (IRE) – Zarawa (IRE) (Kahyasi) [2016/17 b96: **h113**
b16d* h16s⁴ h16s² h19.9s² h15.9m² Apr 16] compact gelding: fair form in novice/maiden hurdles: stays 2½m. *Nicky Henderson* **b94**
at Sandown in November: fair form in novice/maiden hurdles: stays 2½m. *Nicky Henderson*

BAR DE LIGNE (FR) 11 b.g. Martaline – Treekle Toffee (FR) (Cadoudal (FR)) [2016/17 **c114 §**
c126, h–: c19.2g c21.2m c21.4d³ c21.4g² c23.9g⁵ c23.9g² c21.7g⁴ Nov 10] rather leggy **h–**
gelding: winning hurdler: fair handicap chaser nowadays: stays 3m: acts on soft going: has
worn cheekpieces: temperamental. *Brian Ellison*

BAREL OF LAUGHS (IRE) 11 b.g. Milan – Danette (GER) (Exit To Nowhere (USA)) **c131**
[2016/17 c97, h–: c26.3g² c23g* c26.3g³ Mar 17] workmanlike gelding: point winner: **h–**
maiden hurdler: useful chaser: won hunter at Taunton in January by ¾ length from
Grandioso: 100/1, best effort when ½-length third of 23 to Pacha du Polder in Foxhunter
Chase at Cheltenham final start: stays 3¼m: acts on soft going: in cheekpieces last 4 starts:
tried in tongue tie: often races prominently. *Philip Rowley*

BARELY BLACK (IRE) 5 b.m. Urban Poet (USA) – Downtown Rosie (IRE) (Good **b–**
Thyne (USA)) [2016/17 b16g Apr 23] seventh foal: half-sister to fairly useful hurdler/
chaser Takingrisks (2¾m-25f winner, by Golden Tornado): dam poor maiden jumper: well
beaten in mares bumper. *Julia Brooke*

BARE NECESSITIES (IRE) 7 b.g. Sandmason – Marquante (IRE) (Brief Truce **h–**
(USA)) [2016/17 h108, b83: h15.8gᶠ h16.7dᵖᵘ Apr 27] winning Irish pointer: maiden
hurdler, fair at best: likely to prove best at further than 2m. *Shaun Lycett*

BARENICE (FR) 6 b.g. Denham Red (FR) – Delice du Soleil (FR) (Altayan) [2016/17 **h95**
h104: h23.3v⁵ h25d⁵ Dec 26] useful-looking gelding: runner-up in Irish point: modest
maiden hurdler: best effort at 2½m: acted on heavy going: in tongue tie last 5 starts: dead.
Alex Hales

BARIZAN (IRE) 11 b.g. Kalanisi (IRE) – Behra (IRE) (Grand Lodge (USA)) [2016/17 **c–**
c–, h133§: h16.3g³ h19.4g⁶ h22.8sᵖᵘ h20.5d h19s Feb 5] sturdy gelding: fairly useful **h119 §**
handicap hurdler: winning chaser: stays easy 3m, effective at much shorter: acts on good
to firm and heavy going: wears headgear: has worn tongue tie, including in 2016/17:
temperamental. *Brendan Powell*

BARKIS 8 ch.g. Selkirk (USA) – Batik (IRE) (Peintre Celebre (USA)) [2016/17 h16g³ **h104**
h20g² h19.4gᶠ h19.6s Jan 13] useful on Flat, stays 15f: fair form in novice hurdles.
Nicky Henderson

BARLOW (IRE) 10 br.g. Beneficial – Carrigeen Kerria (IRE) (Kemal (FR)) [2016/17 **c82**
c94, h–: c32.5g c21.1d³ May 12] sturdy gelding: winning hurdler: poor hunter chaser **h–**
nowadays: stays 25f: acts on soft going: usually wears cheekpieces: tried in tongue tie.
Miss Chloe Roddick

BARMAN (FR) 6 b.g. Racinger (FR) – Koscina (FR) (Dress Parade) [2016/17 h–, b–: **h120**
h16g⁵ h16m* h15.8g* h16m* h16.3m³ h16g* h16gᶠ h16.3g⁶ Nov 3] sturdy gelding: fairly
useful hurdler: won maiden at Worcester in May, novice at Uttoxeter in June, and handicaps
at Worcester in July and Warwick in September: raced around 2m: acts on good to firm
going: tried in cheekpieces. *Nicky Henderson*

BARNEY BOY 9 b.g. Septieme Ciel (USA) – Keysmith (Greensmith) [2016/17 h21.4s^pu h23.6s^ur h21v^pu Feb 11] runner-up in point: no form in bumpers/over hurdles, bled final start. *Nick Lampard* — **h–**

BARNEY DWAN (IRE) 7 b.g. Vinnie Roe (IRE) – Kapricia Speed (FR) (Vertical Speed (FR)) [2016/17 h135, b65: c24g^2 c20.2d^bd h26s^ur h23.1s^4 h24g^2 h24.7g Apr 8] compact gelding: smart hurdler: good effort when 3¾ lengths second of 24 to Presenting Percy in Pertemps Final at Cheltenham in March: useful form over fences (remains with potential): in control when all but coming to grief at final fence in novice won by Potters Legend at Kempton in November: stays 3m: acts on heavy going: usually races towards rear. *Fergal O'Brien* — **c138 p h146**

BARNEY FROM TYANEE (IRE) 6 b.g. Milan – Miss Opera (Alflora (IRE)) [2016/17 h19.5d h21.4d^5 h19.5g^6 h19.5v^2 h23.4d^5 h23.1d Mar 21] £13,000 5-y-o: third foal: dam unraced half-sister to useful hurdler/smart chaser (2m-21f winner) Woodland Opera out of very smart chaser (2m-3m winner) Opera Hat: placed in Irish maiden points: modest form over hurdles: stays 23f: acts on heavy going. *Michael Blake* — **h94**

BARNEY'S CAULKER 6 b.g. Captain Gerrard (IRE) – Little Cascade (Forzando) [2016/17 b16.2d^4 b16.2g^6 b16.8d Dec 2] poor form in bumpers. *Maurice Barnes* — **b73**

BARON ALCO (FR) 6 ch.g. Dom Alco (FR) – Paula (FR) (Network (GER)) [2016/17 h136: c15.9g^3 c19.7d* c20.8d^2 c17s* c20v^2 c20.8g^2 Mar 16] sturdy gelding: useful hurdler: smart form over fences: won novices at Plumpton in November and January, latter by 2½ lengths from Solatentif: second in Scilly Isles Novices' Chase at Sandown (5 lengths behind Top Notch) and 24-runner Brown Advisory & Merriebelle Stable Plate at Cheltenham (6 lengths behind Road To Respect) last 2 starts: stays 21f: acts on heavy going: usually leads: sound jumper: genuine. *Gary Moore* — **c150 h–**

BARON DE LIGNIERE (FR) 6 b.g. Balko (FR) – Madame La Comtesse (FR) (Adieu Au Roi (IRE)) [2016/17 h–p, b82: h17.7d h16.3d^pu Dec 14] well-made gelding: modest form in bumpers: showed nothing over hurdles: tried in hood: dead. *Chris Gordon* — **h–**

BARON DU PLESSIS (FR) 6 b.g. Network (GER) – Larme A L'Oeil (FR) (Luchiroverte (IRE)) [2016/17 h100, b–: h19d^5 h19.5d h21.1s h21s^2 h19.4g h21.2s^2 h24.2d^5 h24g^2 Apr 19] second on first of 2 starts in Irish maiden points: fair maiden hurdler: stays 21f: acts on soft going: often races prominently/travels strongly. *Ian Williams* — **h100**

BAROQUE STYLE (IRE) 11 b.g. Old Vic – Chasing The Blues (IRE) (Bob Back (USA)) [2016/17 h17.2g c20g^5 c16d^ur h16.5g h20.3s^pu Jan 31] point winner: fair hurdler at best: no form in 2016/17, including over fences: left Gordon Elliott after third start: has worn cheekpieces, including in 2016/17. *Dai Burchell* — **c– h–**

BARRA (FR) 6 b.m. Vendangeur (IRE) – Oasaka (FR) (Robin des Champs (FR)) [2016/17 h16d^2 h18d^2 h18s* h18s^5 h16.8g^2 h20d^3 h16.3d^6 h20d^6 Apr 29] lengthy mare: second foal: dam unraced: won 4 bumpers in France in 2015/16 for E. Vagne: useful hurdler: won mares maiden event at Fairyhouse in January: second in Dawn Run Mares' Novices' Hurdle at Cheltenham (2¾ lengths behind Let's Dance) in March and third in Irish Stallion Farms EBF Mares' Novices' Hurdle Championship Final at Fairyhouse (7 lengths behind Augusta Kate) in April: stays 2½m: acts on soft going: has worn cheekpieces: in tongue tie last 4 starts: often travels strongly. *Gordon Elliott, Ireland* — **h133**

BARRA HOOLEY (IRE) 6 b.m. King's Theatre (IRE) – Dawn Bid (IRE) (Mazaad) [2016/17 b19.8s^2 b18v^4 b16d^6 h19.5g h21d h16.2s h19.4g h23.9g^pu Feb 21] €21,000 3-y-o: sister to bumper winner Megabill, closely related to bumper winner No No Manolito (by High Chaparral) and half-sister to bumper winner/useful 3m hurdle winner On Raglan Road (by Flemensfirth): dam unraced half-sister to useful hurdler/very smart chaser (stayed 27f) Therealbandit and useful hurdler/chaser (stayed 3¼m) The Bajan Bandit: modest form in bumpers: poor form over hurdles: left Gordon Elliott after fourth start: tried in blinkers. *Tom Weston* — **h55 b81**

BARRAMUNDI (IRE) 7 b.g. King's Theatre (IRE) – Lillies Bordello (IRE) (Danehill Dancer (IRE)) [2016/17 h21.2g^4 h24.1d^4 Nov 12] workmanlike gelding: winning pointer: modest form over hurdles: dead. *Sue Smith* — **h92**

BARRA ROTHA (IRE) 10 ch.g. Perugino (USA) – That's Magic (IRE) (Lord Americo) [2016/17 c–, h89: h19.2g^pu May 9] maiden hurdler/chaser: has worn headgear, including last 3 starts. *Laura Hurley* — **c– h–**

BARRICK'S HILL (IRE) 12 b.g. Oscar (IRE) – Lisnacunna Lord (IRE) (Mister Lord (USA)) [2016/17 c110: c24.2d c23.8m^ur c26.2m^pu c23.4v^pu Jan 15] dual winning pointer: maiden chaser, no form in 2016/17: tried in tongue tie. *Gary Rutherford* — **c–**

BARRYS JACK (IRE) 7 b.g. Well Chosen – Theatre Fool (IRE) (King's Theatre (IRE)) **h101**
[2016/17 h16.7g h17.3g⁴ h20g⁵ h23g h19.5g⁶ h16v h21s* h16s h16.3d⁵ h20.1v² h20.6m
Apr 17] €800 4-y-o: first foal: dam unraced half-sister to smart Flat stayer Jardines
Lookout: maiden pointer: fair handicap hurdler: won at Limerick in December: left Pat
Coffey after eighth start: stays 21f: acts on heavy going. *Brian Ellison*

BARTERS HILL (IRE) 7 b.g. Kalanisi (IRE) – Circle The Wagons (IRE) (Commanche **c– p**
Run) [2016/17 h143: c20.4gᵖᵘ Nov 11] strong, lengthy gelding: useful hurdler: off 8 **h–**
months, 11/8, pulled up early in novice won by O O Seven at Cheltenham on chasing
debut, suffering tendon injury: stays 3m: acts on soft going: front runner. *Ben Pauling*

BARTON GIFT 10 b.g. Alflora (IRE) – Marina Bird (Julio Mariner) [2016/17 c112§, h–: **c122 §**
c23.6d c24s c29.6s* c26.7s⁶ c29.6s* c30.7dᵖᵘ Feb 24] strong gelding: winning hurdler: **h–**
fairly useful handicap chaser: won at Bangor in December and February: stays 31f:
acts on heavy going: wears headgear: front runner/races prominently: temperamental.
John Spearing

BARTON KNOLL 5 b.g. Midnight Legend – Barton Flower (Danzero (AUS)) [2016/17 **h104**
b16.7d⁶ b15.7v h19.3g² Apr 15] fourth foal: brother to fair hurdler/chaser Barton Rose **b–**
(2m-21f winner) and fair hurdler Midnight Gem (21f winner): dam (c115/h104), 2m-19f
hurdle/chase winner, half-sister to fair hurdler/useful chaser (stayed 4m) Jass: no form in
bumpers: 16/1, 2 lengths second to Officer Hoolihan in novice at Carlisle on hurdling
debut. *John Mackie*

BARTON ROSE 8 b.m. Midnight Legend – Barton Flower (Danzero (AUS)) [2016/17 **c106**
c–, h109: h21.6g⁴ h20g³ h21.6m² h19.9d³ h19.7g² h19.7s⁶ c18.9s⁴ c15.9s* c15.9sᵖᵘ **h100**
c19.4dᵖᵘ Apr 16] rather leggy mare: fair handicap hurdler: fair chaser: won handicap at
Leicester in February: left Michael Blake after third start: stays 3m: acts on good to firm
and heavy going: has worn cheekpieces. *Charlie Longsdon*

BARTON STACEY (IRE) 12 b.g. Snurge – Life's Treasure (IRE) (Brush Aside (USA)) **c–**
[2016/17 c20.8gᶠ Apr 27] winning hurdler: fairly useful chaser at best: stays 3m: acts on **h–**
good to firm and heavy going: wears headgear: tried in tongue tie. *Mrs O. C. Jackson*

BARWICK 9 b.g. Beat Hollow – Tenpence (Bob Back (USA)) [2016/17 h16.8g⁵ h16m* **h111**
h16g² h16.8mᵘʳ h16.7g³ Oct 25] useful on Flat, stays 1½m: fair form over hurdles: won
maiden at Worcester in August: raced around 2m: acts on good to firm going. *George Baker*

BASFORD BEN 9 b.g. Trade Fair – Moly (FR) (Anabaa (USA)) [2016/17 c105§, h–: **c106 §**
c26.2m* c26.2d³ c25.6gᵖᵘ c26.2s c24v c26.2g³ Apr 15] smallish, well-made gelding: **h–**
maiden hurdler: fair handicap chaser: won at Carlisle in May: stays 3¼m: acts on good to
firm and heavy going: has worn headgear, including in 2016/17: tried in tongue tie: front
runner: temperamental. *Jennie Candlish*

BASSARABAD (FR) 6 b.g. Astarabad (USA) – Grivette (FR) (Antarctique (IRE)) **c107**
[2016/17 h104: h22.7d⁴ h22.7s* h22d² c24.1s³ c24v* c23.4v⁴ c23.6g⁵ Apr 8] tall, useful- **h100**
looking gelding: fair handicap hurdler: won at Kelso (conditional) in October: fair form
over fences: won novice handicap at Warwick in February: stays 3m: acts on heavy going:
usually in visor: often races lazily. *Tim Vaughan*

BASTIEN (FR) 6 b.g. Panoramic – Que du Charmil (FR) (Grand Seigneur (FR)) [2016/17 **h126**
b87p: b16.7g⁶ h17.7s* h15.9v* h20.6s³ Feb 7] sturdy gelding: fair form in bumpers: fairly **b87**
useful form over hurdles: won novices at Fontwell in December and Plumpton in January:
should stay 2½m. *Alan King*

BATAVIR (FR) 8 ch.g. Muhtathir – Elsie (GER) (Barathea (IRE)) [2016/17 h122: c20s **c118**
h22.8s³ c23.4s⁶ c25.2s² c20.9vᵘʳ Mar 1] lengthy gelding: fairly useful handicap hurdler/ **h119**
maiden chaser: stayed 25f: acted on soft going: usually wore headgear/tongue tied: dead.
David Pipe

BAT SHEVA (IRE) 5 b.m. Kalanisi (IRE) – Bathsheba (Overbury (IRE)) [2016/17 b16d **h68**
b16d⁶ b16v h15.6g h16v⁵ h16.8gᵖᵘ Mar 29] sixth foal: half-sister to fair hurdler Baths Well **b67**
(2m winner, by Beat All), stayed 21f: dam, no sign of ability, half-sister to fairly useful
hurdler/fair chaser (2m-21f winner) Tout Regulier: poor form in bumpers/over hurdles: left
Alan A. H. Wells after third start: in hood last 2 starts. *Dianne Sayer*

BATTLE BORN 8 b.g. Kayf Tara – Realms of Gold (USA) (Gulch (USA)) [2016/17 **h–**
h20.5dᵖᵘ Nov 26] lengthy gelding: runner-up in Irish maiden point: useful winner in
bumpers/over hurdles: off 26 months, pulled up only outing in 2016/17: should stay 2½m.
Charlie Longsdon

BATTLEDANCER 11 b.g. Baryshnikov (AUS) – Cede Nullis (Primitive Rising (USA)) **h–**
[2016/17 h16.7d h15.8gᵖᵘ h15.7g h19.9g h15.8d⁶ Oct 13] poor maiden hurdler: in tongue
tie last 2 starts: dead. *Peter Maddison*

BATTLE DUST (IRE) 8 b.g. Portrait Gallery (IRE) – Katie O'Toole (IRE) (Commanche **c107 §** Run) [2016/17 h118§: c21.7d^{pu} c29.6s^6 c28s^{pu} Feb 20] Irish point winner: fairly useful **h– §** hurdler: fair form only completed start in chases: stays 3¾m: best form on soft/heavy going: wears headgear: temperamental. *Kim Bailey*

BATTLEFIELD (IRE) 5 b.g. Central Park (IRE) – Silly Mille (IRE) (Luso) [2016/17 **b–** b16g Apr 8] tailed off in bumper on debut. *John Groucott*

BATTLEFORD 6 b.g. Midnight Legend – Well Maid (Saddlers' Hall (IRE)) [2016/17 **h136** b120: h16d^4 h20d* h22.7d^2 h24v^2 h20.3g h20d^2 Apr 26] compact gelding: fell in point: smart bumper performer: useful form over hurdles: won maiden at Leopardstown in December: second in novice at Thurles (9 lengths behind The Storyteller) in January, Surehaul Mercedes-Benz Novices' Hurdle at Clonmel (4¾ lengths behind Monalee) in February and minor event at Punchestown (3½ lengths behind C'est Jersey) final start: stays 3m: acts on heavy going. *W. P. Mullins, Ireland*

BATTLE OF IDEAS (IRE) 4 ch.g. Fracas (IRE) – Haven't A Notion (Definite Article) **b82** [2016/17 b16s^4 b16g^2 Apr 8] €16,000 3-y-o: first foal: dam, ran once over hurdles, half-sister to useful hurdler (2m-21f winner) Kells Belle: modest form in bumpers, better effort when second at Chepstow: will be suited by 2½m. *Colin Tizzard*

BATTLE OF SHILOH (IRE) 8 b.g. Shantou (USA) – Realt Na Ruise (IRE) (Soviet **c139** Star (USA)) [2016/17 h113p: h23.3s* c22.5d* c23.4s* c23.6s^F c31.8g Apr 22] won both **h116 p** starts in Irish points: fairly useful winner of both starts over hurdles, including handicap at Uttoxeter very early in season: useful form over fences: won novice handicaps at Uttoxeter in October and Newcastle (by 2½ lengths from Hainan) in December: stays 23f (possibly failed to stay when fourteenth of 30 to Vicente in Scottish Grand National at Ayr final start): acts on heavy going: often races prominently/travels strongly: remains open to improvement over hurdles. *Tom George*

BATTLE RANGE 10 ch.g. Selkirk (USA) – Pongee (Barathea (IRE)) [2016/17 c21.2g^{pu} **c–** Jul 18] multiple point winner: pulled up lame after fourth in maiden on chasing debut. *Jacqueline Coward*

BATTLESHIP BOY (IRE) 9 b.g. Kaieteur (USA) – Battle On (Blakeney) [2016/17 c–, **c–** h–: c16g^{pu} Sep 18] little show in novice hurdles/handicap chases. *Sarah-Jayne Davies* **h–**

BATU FERRINGHI (FR) 11 b.g. Numerous (USA) – Dara (IRE) (Danehill (USA)) **c–** [2016/17 c94, h–: c21g^{pu} May 5] prolific winner in points in Britain: winning hurdler: **h–** maiden chaser: stays 3¼m: best form on heavy going: wears headgear. *Mrs C. Hitch*

BAWDEN ROCKS 8 b.g. Anabaa (USA) – Late Night (GER) (Groom Dancer (USA)) **c69** [2016/17 c101, h–: c25.7g^5 May 8] winning hurdler: maiden chaser, fair at best: stays **h–** 2¾m: acts on heavy going: sometimes in cheekpieces: temperament under suspicion. *David Bridgwater*

BAYFIRTH (IRE) 14 b.g. Flemensfirth (USA) – Baylough Lady (IRE) (Lancastrian) **c– §** [2016/17 c76§, h–: c20.1m^F May 11] workmanlike gelding: point winner: maiden hurdler: **h–** poor handicap chaser: stays 25f: acts on good to firm and good to soft going: unreliable. *Andrew Hamilton*

BAY FORTUNA 8 b.g. Old Vic – East Rose (Keen) [2016/17 h95: h15.8g^5 Apr 28] sturdy **h80** gelding: handicap hurdler, modest at best: stays 2½m: best form on good going: tried in cheekpieces. *Mark Usher*

BAYLEY'S DREAM 8 b.g. Presenting – Swaythe (USA) (Swain (IRE)) [2016/17 c–, **c60 §** h101§: c24.2s^4 Feb 17] short-backed gelding: winning pointer: fair hurdler: maiden chaser, **h– §** fair at best: stays 3m: acts on good to firm and good to soft going: has worn headgear/ tongue tie: untrustworthy. *John Aprahamian*

BAY OF FREEDOM (IRE) 8 b.g. Heron Island (IRE) – Kate Gale (IRE) (Strong Gale) **c131** [2016/17 h20.5d^3 h20d^6 h24.2g^{pu} c22s* c23g* c24g^4 c24s^{pu} Jan 28] angular gelding: **h106** bumper winner: fair handicap hurdler: useful chaser: won maiden at Listowel in September and listed event at Wexford (by 8 lengths from Presenting Mahler) in October: stays 23f: acts on heavy going. *Peter Fahey, Ireland*

BAYSBROWN (IRE) 7 b.g. Fruits of Love (USA) – Whenever Wherever (IRE) **c81 p** (Saddlers' Hall (IRE)) [2016/17 h87, b83: h23.9m^3 h23.9s^2 h23.9g^2 h23.9g* h24.6d^2 **h106** h24.3s^5 c23.8g^6 Apr 26] fair handicap hurdler: won at Perth (amateur) in September: off 6 months, probably needed run when sixth of 10 in novice handicap at Perth on chasing debut: stays 25f: acts on soft and good to firm going: front runner/races prominently: capable of better over fences. *Nicky Richards*

BAY TO GO (IRE) 11 b.g. Moscow Society (USA) – Lily Langtry (IRE) (Duky) **c81** [2016/17 c94, h–: c24.2g⁴ c19.7g⁴ c21.2g⁴ Oct 26] lengthy gelding: multiple winning **h–** pointer: maiden hurdler: winning chaser, only poor nowadays: left Miss L. Horsfall after first start: stays easy 3m: acts on soft and good to firm going: has worn headgear, including last 4 starts. *Conrad Allen*

BAYWING (IRE) 8 br.g. Winged Love (IRE) – Cerise de Totes (FR) (Champ Libre (FR)) **c145** [2016/17 h131: c24.2s⁴ c24.2s* c26.2s⁴ Mar 25] useful hurdler: smart form over fences: **h–** 33/1, won Towton Novices' Chase at Wetherby in February by 22 lengths from Calett Mad: shaped better than result when 10¾ lengths fourth of 7 to Yala Enki in handicap at Kelso final start: will stay long distances: acts on heavy going: often races towards rear, usually responds generously to pressure. *Nicky Richards*

BAZOOKA (IRE) 6 b.g. Camacho – Janadam (IRE) (Mukaddamah (USA)) [2016/17 **h106** h16.8s⁴ h16v⁴ h16g⁵ Feb 25] angular gelding: fairly useful on Flat, stays 2m: fair form over hurdles: best effort second start when 13¾ lengths fourth of 9 to Coeur de Lion in novice at Sandown in February. *David Flood*

BEACH BAR (IRE) 6 b.g. Azamour (IRE) – Toasted Special (USA) (Johannesburg **h–** (USA)) [2016/17 h16.3gᵖᵘ Mar 25] good-topped gelding: useful on Flat, stays 1¼m: in hood, refused to settle when pulled up in novice on hurdling debut. *Brendan Powell*

BE A DREAMER 9 ch.g. Dreams End – Miss Fahrenheit (IRE) (Oscar (IRE)) [2016/17 **c– §** c87§, h80: c21.2mᵖᵘ h24dᵖᵘ Jul 10] workmanlike gelding: maiden hurdler/chaser, modest **h–** at best: won point in April 2017: stays 2¾m: best form on soft/heavy going: tried in tongue tie: temperamental. *Mike Sowersby*

BEALLANDENDALL (IRE) 9 b.g. Beneficial – Railstown Lady (IRE) (Supreme **c–** Leader) [2016/17 c–, h122: h21.6gᵖᵘ c16.5gᵖᵘ h16.3g⁵ h16g³ h15.8m³ h16d⁵ h15.8v h16gᶠ **h109** Apr 8] compact gelding: won twice in points: fair handicap hurdler: pulled up both starts in chases: left Matt Sheppard after third start: stays 19f: acts on heavy going: has worn hood. *Deborah Faulkner*

BEARLY LEGAL (IRE) 11 b.g. Court Cave (IRE) – Fair Size (IRE) (Jurado (USA)) **c125** [2016/17 c130, h108: c30d c25g³ c28g h24d⁶ c21g⁴ c21.3s³ h22s² Mar 17] fair handicap **h111** hurdler: fairly useful handicap chaser: stays 29f: acts on heavy going: wears tongue tie. *Karl Thornton, Ireland*

BEAR RIVER (IRE) 7 b.g. Gold Well – Obligee de Sivola (FR) (Video Rock (FR)) **h–** [2016/17 h21.3dᵖᵘ Mar 21] fourth when fell last only start in Irish points: pulled up in seller only outing over hurdles: dead. *Sam England*

BEAR'S AFFAIR (IRE) 11 br.g. Presenting – Gladtogetit (Green Shoon) [2016/17 c148, **c123** h126: c20s² c24.1d³ c21.1g c25.5g* Apr 24] sturdy gelding: one-time smart hurdler/chaser: **h–** fairly useful form in hunter chases in 2016/17, easily landing odds at Warwick final start: stays 25f: acts on good to firm and heavy going. *Philip Rowley*

BEARS RAILS 7 b.g. Flemensfirth (USA) – Clandestine (Saddlers' Hall (IRE)) [2016/17 **c114 §** c116, h55: c23.6m⁴ c24s⁴ c25.5v* c29.6s c25.1vᵖᵘ Mar 9] big, workmanlike gelding: **h–** maiden hurdler: fair handicap chaser: won at Fontwell in January: stays 25f: acts on heavy going: in blinkers last 3 starts: front runner/races prominently: untrustworthy. *Colin Tizzard*

BEAST OF BURDEN (IRE) 8 ch.g. Flemensfirth (USA) – Nuit des Chartreux (FR) **c82** (Villez (USA)) [2016/17 c138, h–: c23.8d³ h20.5dᵖᵘ Nov 26] big, lengthy gelding: winning **h–** hurdler/maiden chaser, useful at best: shaped as if amiss both starts in 2016/17: stays 3m: acts on heavy going: tried in tongue tie: front runner/races prominently. *Rebecca Curtis*

BEATABOUT THE BUSH (IRE) 6 b.g. Bushranger (IRE) – Queen of Fibres (IRE) **h87** (Scenic) [2016/17 h101: h16d⁶ h16m⁶ h20.3d h19g⁶ Dec 20] handicap hurdler, modest nowadays: unproven beyond 17f: acts on heavy going: tried in blinkers/tongue tie: usually races nearer last than first. *Graeme McPherson*

BEAT STREET 6 b.m. Beat All (USA) – Compton Chick (IRE) (Dolphin Street (FR)) **b–** [2016/17 b16.5m Apr 27] sixth foal: sister to fairly useful chaser Lydstep Point (19f winner); dam (c90/h97), 2½m chase winner (stayed 3¼m), half-sister to useful hurdler (2m winner) What's The Verdict: tailed off in mares bumper on debut. *Bob Buckler*

BEAT SYDNEY 6 b.g. Beat Hollow – Sydney Star (Machiavellian (USA)) [2016/17 **b–** b15.7g Oct 3] well beaten in maiden bumper on debut. *Jennie Candlish*

BEAT THAT (IRE) 9 b.g. Milan – Knotted Midge (IRE) (Presenting) [2016/17 h21.5g⁶ **h136 ¡** Apr 29] tall gelding: smart hurdler at best: shaped as if retaining ability when sixth of 8 to L'Ami Serge in Select Hurdle at Sandown only outing in 2016/17: stays 3m: acts on soft going. *Nicky Henderson*

113

BEAT THE TIDE 7 b.g. Black Sam Bellamy (IRE) – Sablonne (USA) (Silver Hawk (USA)) [2016/17 h102: h18.6g* h18.5m⁶ h19.8m⁴ c19.3d⁶ Nov 8] modest handicap hurdler: won at Market Rasen in August: 66/1, sixth in novice handicap at Sedgefield (24 lengths behind Drumlee Lad) on chasing debut: stays 2¾m: acts on soft going: in cheekpieces last 2 starts: open to improvement over fences. *Tim Vaughan* **c89 p**
h95

BEATU (IRE) 8 b.g. Beat All (USA) – Auntie Bob (Overbury (IRE)) [2016/17 h110: h16.7g³ h16.7g⁵ h16.2m³ c16.5g⁴ c16g⁴ Sep 20] fair handicap hurdler: modest form in novice handicap chases: raced around 2m: acts on good to firm and good to soft going. *Donald McCain* **c94**
h107

BEAU BAY (FR) 6 b.g. Bernebeau (FR) – Slew Bay (FR) (Beaudelaire (USA)) [2016/17 h110: h15.8s⁵ Mar 5] fair hurdler at best: stays 2¼m: acts on soft going: usually in tongue tie: often leads. *Alan Jones* **h–**

BEAUBOREEN (IRE) 10 b.g. Revoque (IRE) – Roseboreen (IRE) (Roselier (FR)) [2016/17 c115, h97: c22.5v³ c24.1s⁴ c29.6sᵖᵘ c21.5v⁶ h26vᵖᵘ Feb 11] lengthy gelding: winning hurdler: fairly useful handicap chaser: stays 3¼m: acts on heavy going: wears headgear: has worn tongue tie: front runner/races prominently. *Jennie Candlish* **c116**
h–

BEAUCHAMP VIKING 13 b.g. Compton Admiral – Beauchamp Jade (Kalaglow) [2016/17 c74, h–: c16.3g May 5] maiden hurdler: poor handicap chaser: stays 2¼m: acts on firm and good to soft going: has worn headgear: wears tongue tie: usually leads. *Hugo Froud* **c–**
h–

BEAU DU BRIZAIS (FR) 5 gr.g. Kapgarde (FR) – Belle du Brizais (FR) (Turgeon (USA)) [2016/17 b78p: h15.8s⁵ h16.2g⁴ h16.3m⁴ h16mᶠ h16.5g⁴ h19g* h19g⁴ h20.5g⁴ h19m* Apr 27] compact gelding: fairly useful handicap hurdler: won at Taunton in December (conditionals/amateur event) and April: will stay beyond 2½m: acts on good to firm going: often races prominently. *Philip Hobbs* **h117**

BEAUFORT BOY (IRE) 8 b.g. Heron Island (IRE) – What A Mewsment (IRE) (Persian Mews) [2016/17 h16v⁶ h19.5g Dec 10] very lightly raced and little form in bumpers/over hurdles: in hood last 2 starts. *Zoe Davison* **h–**

BEAUJOLAIS BOB 9 gr.g. Grape Tree Road – Charliebob (Nomadic Way (USA)) [2016/17 c82, h–: c19.8dᵖᵘ c21.1vᵖᵘ Jan 29] maiden hurdler: winning chaser, poor at best: stays 2½m: best form on soft/heavy going: wears blinkers/tongue tie. *Richard Hawker* **c–**
h–

BEAU KNIGHT 5 b.g. Sir Percy – Nicola Bella (IRE) (Sadler's Wells (USA)) [2016/17 h–: h16g May 4] no form over hurdles. *Alexandra Dunn* **h–**

BEAU LAKE (IRE) 13 b.g. Heron Island (IRE) – Brennan For Audits (IRE) (Creative Plan (USA)) [2016/17 h87: h16d⁶ h15.9v h16v Jan 10] strong gelding: modest handicap hurdler: stays 19f: best form on soft/heavy going: tried in cheekpieces. *Suzy Smith* **h89**

BEAUMONT'S PARTY (IRE) 10 b.g. High Chaparral (IRE) – Miss Champagne (FR) (Bering) [2016/17 h96: h16.8s³ h16.8s⁴ h16.8s⁴ h15.7s⁶ h16.8m⁴ Apr 19] good-topped gelding: modest handicap hurdler: left Chris Grant after fourth start: raced around 2m: acts on heavy going: has worn hood, including in 2016/17: often races towards rear. *Laura Morgan* **h91**

BEAU PHIL (FR) 6 ch.g. Cachet Noir (USA) – Neyrianne (FR) (Sheyrann) [2016/17 h104: h18.5g³ h21.6d³ h21.6m² h21.6g⁴ h21.6g* Sep 16] fair hurdler: won maiden at Newton Abbot final start: stays 2¾m: acts on good to firm going: has worn hood, including at Newton Abbot: wears tongue tie: often races prominently/travels strongly: temperament under suspicion. *Paul Nicholls* **h111**

BEAU SANCY (FR) 5 b.g. Blue Bresil (FR) – Touquette (FR) (Phantom Breeze) [2016/17 b16d b17d Apr 5] well held both starts in bumpers. *Kenny Johnson* **b–**

BEAUTIFUL MIX 5 b.m. Fair Mix (IRE) – Just Beautiful (FR) (Mansonnien (FR)) [2016/17 b16.7g² May 14] seventh foal: half-sister to a winning pointer by Exit To Nowhere: dam French 1½m winner: 22/1, 7 lengths second of 9 to Tara View in mares bumper at Bangor on debut, having run of the race. *Neil Mechie* **b87**

BEAUTIFUL PEOPLE (FR) 6 b.m. Early March – Night Fever (FR) (Garde Royale) [2016/17 h–, b82: h16d⁶ h18.7m⁴ h19.9g³ h21s h16.5g h23.9g³ h23.9g h24.5m⁴ Apr 4] modest maiden hurdler: stays 3m: best form on good going: usually races in rear. *Richard Phillips* **h88**

BEAUTIFUL STORM 6 b.m. Great Palm (USA) – Sevenminutesilence (Master Willie) [2016/17 b16.2d⁴ Jun 4] second foal: dam (b74) third in bumper on only start: 50/1, well-held fourth of 10 in bumper at Hexham on debut. *Susan Corbett* **b–**

BEAU TRAVELLER 14 b.g. Beauchamp King – Steady Woman (IRE) (Aristocracy) [2016/17 c21.6d^pu May 4] winning pointer: modest maiden hunter chaser: stays 25f: acts on good to firm going. *Miss Bianca Dunk* — c–

BECAUSESHESAIDSO (IRE) 9 b.g. Winged Love (IRE) – Huit de Coeur (FR) (Cadoudal (FR)) [2016/17 h112: h18.5s^F h23.1d Jan 3] fair maiden hurdler: stays 2½m: acts on good to soft going: often in hood. *Venetia Williams* — h105

BECKY THE THATCHER 4 b.f. Mastercraftsman (IRE) – Fairmont (IRE) (Kingmambo (USA)) [2016/17 h16.4d* h15.6g^ur h15.7g² h16s² h15.7s* Mar 8] close-coupled, rather lightly-built filly: fair maiden on Flat, stays 1½m: fairly useful form over hurdles: won fillies juvenile event at Musselburgh in November and mares novice event at Catterick final start: raced only at 2m: acts on soft going. *Micky Hammond* — h115

BE DARING (FR) 6 gr.g. Dom Alco (FR) – Quinine (FR) (Network (GER)) [2016/17 b72: h19d^F h19.4s⁵ h17.7g⁵ Apr 12] good-topped gelding: lightly raced in bumpers/over hurdles, fair form at best: tried in hood. *Paul Nicholls* — h105

BEDROCK 4 b.g. Fastnet Rock (AUS) – Gemstone (IRE) (Galileo (IRE)) [2016/17 h16g⁵ h17g³ Apr 6] sturdy gelding: fairly useful on Flat, stays 1¼m: useful form over hurdles: 25/1, much better effort when 5¾ lengths third of 8 to Defi du Seuil in Anniversary Hurdle at Aintree: wears tongue tie: should continue to progress. *Dan Skelton* — h134 p

BEDROCK FRED 11 ch.g. Monsieur Bond (IRE) – Sea Mist (IRE) (Shalford (IRE)) [2016/17 c61: c25.1m⁴ h20m^pu c25.8m^pu c21g^pu Aug 10] leggy gelding: multiple winning pointer: showed nothing on hurdling debut: modest maiden chaser: stays 25f: acts on good to firm going: tried in cheekpieces. *David Weston* — c87 h–

BEEN DECIDED (IRE) 7 b.g. Flemensfirth (USA) – Laboc (Rymer) [2016/17 h–, b81: h20d⁶ h23.3s^pu h22.7s^pu Dec 4] poor form over hurdles: front runner/races prominently. *N. W. Alexander* — h66

BEENO (IRE) 8 b.g. Exit To Nowhere (USA) – Kay Theatre (IRE) (King's Theatre (IRE)) [2016/17 b17.8g h19.9g h20.5d h16s⁴ h18.1s⁴ h16.4s² h15.7s² Feb 13] fourth on completed start in points: tailed off in maiden bumper: fair form over hurdles: left Stephen Francis Magee after first start: unproven beyond 2m: acts on soft going: in hood last 5 starts. *Kenneth Slack* — h104 b–

BEER GOGGLES (IRE) 6 br.g. Oscar (IRE) – Tynelucy (IRE) (Good Thyne (USA)) [2016/17 h108: c20.9v³ c23.6s^pu c25.6d^F h23.1d³ h24.2d* h24.3d* Apr 21] fairly useful handicap hurdler: improved form each time when winning at Newbury in March and Ayr in April, beating Silent Steps 8 lengths in latter: fair form over fences: best effort when third in novice handicap at Ffos Las in December: stays 27f: acts on heavy going: in tongue tie last 4 starts: often travels strongly. *Richard Woollacott* — c101 h129

BEEVES (IRE) 10 b.g. Portrait Gallery (IRE) – Camas North (IRE) (Muharib (USA)) [2016/17 c131§, h–: c24g⁵ c24.2d* c25.5d c24g⁵ c32.8g⁵ c24.2g* c23.8g* Apr 26] lengthy gelding: winning hurdler: useful handicap chaser: much improved and won at Hexham in June, Fakenham in March and Perth (by ½ length from Cultram Abbey) on final start: barely stays 4m: acts on heavy going: wears headgear: usually leads. *Jennie Candlish* — c143 h–

BEFOREALL (IRE) 9 b.g. Spadoun (FR) – Maggie Howard (IRE) (Good Thyne (USA)) [2016/17 c126§, h–: c24.2s c28.5s^ur c23.8s⁶ c29.2v^pu Mar 12] good-topped gelding: winning hurdler: fairly useful chaser at best, no form in 2016/17: tried in headgear: has worn tongue tie: temperamental. *Oliver Sherwood* — c– § h–

BEGGARS CROSS (IRE) 7 b.g. Presenting – Ballygill Heights (IRE) (Symboli Heights (FR)) [2016/17 h127: h19d⁴ c25g⁵ c24d⁴ c24d⁴ c24d* c22.4s^F c23.6g³ Apr 8] sturdy gelding: fair hurdler: fairly useful chaser: won handicap at Doncaster in February: stays 3m: acts on soft going: tried in cheekpieces: often races lazily. *Jonjo O'Neill* — c118 h112

BEGGAR'S VELVET (IRE) 11 b.g. Dr Massini (IRE) – Lakelough (IRE) (Mandalus) [2016/17 c105, h–: c26.2m³ c23.8m³ Apr 25] sturdy gelding: multiple winner in points: winning hurdler: fair hunter chaser: left D. Holmes after first start: stays 27f: acts on good to firm and heavy going: in cheekpieces last 5 starts. *Mrs Amy Cox* — c101 h–

BEGGAR'S WISHES (IRE) 6 b.g. Oscar (IRE) – Strong Wishes (IRE) (Strong Gale) [2016/17 b85: b16d⁴ h19d¹ h23.3g² h26.5d⁶ h20g^m h16.7s* h15.7s* h20.5g Mar 27] sturdy gelding: modest form in bumpers: fair handicap hurdler: won at Bangor in February and Southwell in March: unproven beyond 17f: acts on soft going: has worn headgear: wears tongue tie: usually races close up. *Peter Bowen* — h112 h77

BEG TO DIFFER (IRE) 7 ch.g. Flemensfirth (USA) – Blossom Trix (IRE) (Saddlers' **c140** Hall (IRE)) [2016/17 c143p, h–: c27.3s^{pu} c23.6g c29.5s^4 c24.2v^{ur} c24.5d^{pu} Feb 20] useful-looking gelding: useful hurdler in 2014/15: useful handicap chaser: stayed 29f: best form on soft/heavy going: wore headgear: often raced prominently: dead. *Jonjo O'Neill* **h–**

BEHIND THE WIRE (IRE) 6 b.g. Mahler – Mujavail (IRE) (Mujadil (USA)) [2016/17 **c127** h104, b75: c20.9s c23g* c24g^2 c22.4s* c24.1g Apr 15] well-made gelding: maiden hurdler: **h–** fairly useful form in chases: won novice handicaps at Taunton in December and Newbury in March: stays 3m, at least as effective at shorter: acts on soft going: races prominently. *Tom George*

BEHIND TIME (IRE) 6 b.g. Stowaway – She's Got To Go (IRE) (Glacial Storm (USA)) **h129** [2016/17 h108p: h21.1s* h24.2d^4 h23.4v^6 Feb 4] good-topped gelding: fairly useful form over hurdles: won conditionals handicap at Cheltenham in November: should stay 3m: acts on heavy going. *Harry Fry*

BEING GLOBAL (FR) 6 b.g. Epalo (GER) – Haida Iv (FR) (Passing Sale (FR)) **h99** [2016/17 h107: h16.7g^2 h20.3g^3 h15.8d h16g Dec 18] handicap hurdler, just modest form in 2016/17: stays 21f, effective at shorter: acts on soft going. *Caroline Bailey*

BEL AMI DE SIVOLA (FR) 6 b.g. Network (GER) – Notting Hill (FR) (Garde Royale) **h127** [2016/17 b16g* h16g* h20d* h20s^5 h20g^{pu} h20.5d Apr 29] €105,000 3-y-o: well-made **b103** gelding: chasing type: half-brother to several winners, including fairly useful hurdlers/useful chasers Turn Over Sivola (2m winner, by Assessor) and Surgeon de Sivola (French 17f-2½m winner, by Turgeon): dam unraced half-sister to fairly useful hurdler/chaser (2m-2½m winner) Sobers: fairly useful form in bumpers: won maiden at Punchestown in October: fairly useful hurdler: won maiden at Down Royal in November and novice at Fairyhouse in December: stays 2½m: acts on heavy going. *Noel Meade, Ireland*

BELAMI DES PICTONS (FR) 6 b.g. Khalkevi (IRE) – Nina des Pictons (FR) **c148 p** (Denham Red (FR)) [2016/17 h127p, b–: c21.1s^4 c22.4d* c24v* c22.7s* Feb 28] strong, **h–** compact gelding: fairly useful winner of last 3 starts over hurdles in 2015/16: took well to chasing and won novice handicap at Newbury (by ¾ length from Aurillac) in December, and novice events at Warwick (by 22 lengths from Arctic Gold) and Leicester (simple task) in February: stays 3m: acts on heavy going: usually races close up/travels strongly: already smart over fences, and capable of better still. *Venetia Williams*

BELCANTO (IRE) 7 b.m. Bach (IRE) – Love Divided (IRE) (King's Ride) [2016/17 **h96** h90, b88: h21.6d^4 h21.6s^3 h17.2d^4 h23g h21.6d^2 Sep 4] bumper winner: modest handicap hurdler: won at Fontwell (conditionals event) in June: stays 2¾m: acts on good to soft going: in tongue tie last 3 starts: usually leads. *Jamie Snowden*

BEL ESPRIT (IRE) 8 b.m. Presenting – D Judge (IRE) (Strong Gale) [2016/17 h15.3s **h88** h16.8s^4 h23.9g^6 h22g^2 Apr 1] modest maiden hurdler: should stay 3m. *Robert Stephens*

BELIZE 6 b.g. Rail Link – Costa Rica (IRE) (Sadler's Wells (USA)) [2016/17 h110: **h119** h20.3v* h19.1s^5 h23.3v^3 h20.6s^4 Jan 23] workmanlike gelding: fairly useful handicap hurdler: won at Southwell in May: stays 2¾m: best form on heavy going. *Tim Vaughan*

BELLA (FR) 6 b.m. Johann Quatz (FR) – Hasta Manana (FR) (Useful (FR)) [2016/17 **h114** h115: h20m^{ur} h19.2g^2 h16g^5 h16v^4 h16s^F Feb 17] fair handicap hurdler: stays 19f: acts on heavy going: has worn headgear, including final start: wears tongue tie: usually races prominently. *David Pipe*

BELLA GIRINO 5 b.m. Yeats (IRE) – Dancingwithbubbles (IRE) (Supreme Leader) **b70** [2016/17 b–: b15.8d^4 b17.7d^5 Sep 4] poor form in bumpers. *Dan Skelton*

BELLAMY 6 ch.g. Black Sam Bellamy (IRE) – Bonne Anniversaire (Alflora (IRE)) **h115 p** [2016/17 b16.8d^6 h19.1v^4 h19.8d^2 Mar 26] €25,000 3-y-o: seventh foal: brother to fair **b– p** hurdler Samedi Soir (2½m winner) and half-brother to 2 winners, including fair hurdler Grey Missile (21f winner, by Terimon): dam unraced sister to useful hurdler (stayed 19f) Alph and half-sister to top-class hurdler (2m winner) Royal Derbi: won completed start in Irish maiden points: well beaten in bumper: much better effort (fairly useful form) over hurdles when 1½ lengths second to Winningtry in maiden at Wincanton: open to further improvement. *Neil Mulholland*

BELLANEY KNIGHT (IRE) 7 bl.g. Marienbard (IRE) – Bellaney Jewel (IRE) **h113** (Roselier (FR)) [2016/17 h23.3d^2 h22.1d* h22.1d^3 h23.3g^3 h27g Oct 27] chasing sort: first foal: dam (c114/h105) hurdle/chase winner up to 4m: fair form over hurdles: won novice at Cartmel in July: will be suited by 3m+: acts on good to soft going: tried in tongue tie. *John Quinn*

BELLAS TOUCH 6 b.m. Overbury (IRE) – Sesame Squeeze (IRE) (Accordion) [2016/17 **b–**
b16.8g Apr 26] fourth foal: dam unraced half-sister to fairly useful hurdler/useful chaser
(19f-3m winner) Mr Cracker: placed completed start in points: tailed off in maiden bumper.
Patrick Langdown

BELLATRIX 7 b.m. Motivator – Haladiya (IRE) (Darshaan) [2016/17 ab16g⁵ b15.8vᵖᵘ **b–**
Dec 31] half-sister to several winners, including fairly useful/untrustworthy hurdler
Haldibari (3m-27f winner, by Kahyasi) and modest/unreliable hurdler Balustrade (2¾m
winner, by Barathea): dam ran once on Flat in France: showed nothing in bumpers.
Tony Carroll

BELLE EN NOIR 5 b.m. Black Sam Bellamy (IRE) – Miss Holly (Makbul) [2016/17 **b–**
b15.8v⁶ Dec 31] fifth foal: dam (h96), 17f hurdle winner, also 11f-2m winner on Flat, sister
to useful hurdler/chaser (2m winner) Makari: tailed off in mares maiden bumper.
Steph Hollinshead

BELLOW MOME (FR) 6 b.g. Honolulu (IRE) – Oll Mighty Fellow (FR) (Ungaro **c134**
(GER)) [2016/17 h124: c18d⁴ c24d c19g⁴ c24s⁶ c21.2dᵘʳ Apr 9] useful-looking gelding: **h–**
fairly useful form over hurdles: useful form in chases: won maiden at Thurles by 4½
lengths from General Principle in November: 8/11, unseated rider 2 out (held narrow
advantage) in minor event won by Akito at Tramore final start: stays 2½m: acts on heavy
going: usually races close up. *W. P. Mullins, Ireland*

BELLSHILL (IRE) 7 b.g. King's Theatre (IRE) – Fairy Native (IRE) (Be My Native **c151**
(USA)) [2016/17 h146, b126: h24dⁿ c20d* c19.5v* c21.3sꟳ c24.4g³ Mar 15] workmanlike **h–**
gelding: smart hurdler: already as good over fences: won novice handicaps at Gowran in November
and Shannon Airport Novices' Chase at Limerick (by 3¼ lengths from Haymount) in
December: respectable 10 lengths third of 12 to Might Bite in RSA Chase at Cheltenham
final start: stays 25f: acts on heavy going: often races towards rear/travels strongly.
W. P. Mullins, Ireland

BELLS 'N' BANJOS (IRE) 7 b.g. Indian River (FR) – Beechill Dancer (IRE) (Darnay) **c133**
[2016/17 h126: h23.1g h19.5v c22.7g* c22.7s* c31.8g c24.3g⁵ Apr 22] rangy gelding: **h–**
fairly useful hurdler at best, no form in 2016/17: useful form over fences: won novice
handicaps at Leicester in January and February, latter by 1¼ lengths from Dueling Banjos:
left Warren Greatrex after second start: should stay 3m: acts on heavy going: tried in
cheekpieces: has suspect attitude. *Fergal O'Brien*

BELLS OF AILSWORTH (IRE) 7 b.g. Kayf Tara – Volverta (FR) (Green Tune **c121**
(USA)) [2016/17 h106: h23.3g² h25m* c26.2d c23m* c21.4dᵘʳ c23g* c23.4d³ c25.3gꟳ **h112**
Apr 20] good-bodied gelding: fair handicap hurdler: won at Huntingdon in October: fairly
useful form in chases: won novice handicaps at Taunton in December and February: stays
25f: acts on soft and good to firm going: wears tongue tie. *Tim Vaughan*

BELLS OF SUTTON (IRE) 5 b.g. Kalanisi (IRE) – Out Performer (IRE) (Persian Bold) **h–**
[2016/17 h16gᵖᵘ h15.8mᵖᵘ Oct 2] showed nothing in 2 novice hurdles. *Tim Vaughan*

BELLS ON SUNDAY 6 br.m. Black Sam Bellamy (IRE) – Lago d'Oro (Slip Anchor) **h108**
[2016/17 b96: h19.5g⁴ h23.9s³ h20.6s* h19.5sᵖᵘ Jan 20] unfurnished mare:
winning pointer: bumper winner: fair form over hurdles: won mares handicap at Newcastle
in December: stayed 3m: acted on soft going: front runner/raced prominently: dead.
Tom Lacey

BELL WEIR 9 gr.g. Tobougg (IRE) – Belly Dancer (IRE) (Danehill Dancer (IRE)) **c–**
[2016/17 h100: c20mꟳ h22.1m h24.7g⁶ h19.3s² h19.9v³ h20.1g⁴ Apr 25] lengthy gelding: **h98**
modest handicap hurdler: fell first on chasing debut: left Dianne Sayer after third start:
stays 2½m: acts on soft and good to firm going: has worn headgear/tongue tie, including in
2016/17. *Kenneth Slack*

BELMONT PARK (FR) 6 br.g. Al Namix (FR) – Goldoulyssa (FR) (Cadoudal (FR)) **h–**
[2016/17 b–: h19.5d h21s h25.5s⁵ Mar 11] little impact in bumpers/over hurdles.
David Bridgwater

BELMOUNT (IRE) 8 b.g. Westerner – Artist's Jewel (Le Moss) [2016/17 c127, h–: **c127**
c24g³ c25d⁴ c25.8g* c25.2g* c26.2d⁶ c28.8d⁶ c26.3s c25.2vᵖᵘ c23.8s⁵ c26g² Apr 20] well- **h–**
made gelding: winning hurdler: fairly useful handicap chaser: won at Newton Abbot in
September and Hereford in October: stays 3¼m: acts on good to firm and heavy going:
sometimes wears cheekpieces. *Nigel Twiston-Davies*

BEL SAS (FR) 6 b.g. Balko (FR) – Pashka (FR) (Passing Sale (FR)) [2016/17 b16d² b20g² **h124**
h24s* h20.7g* h22d² h16s² h16sꟳ Oct 2] runner-up in maiden on Irish point debut: useful **b105**
form in bumpers: fairly useful form over hurdles: won maiden at Bellewstown and novice

at Galway in July: left W. P. Mullins after sixth start: stayed 3m: acted on soft going: tried in tongue tie: front runner: dead. *Joseph Patrick O'Brien, Ireland*

BELTOR 6 b.g. Authorized (IRE) – Carahill (AUS) (Danehill (USA)) [2016/17 h–: h15.7m h16.3g⁵ h15.8g⁶ h16g³ h16.3d h16.5g³ Mar 20] leggy gelding: useful handicap hurdler: third at Kempton in December, best effort of 2016/17: raced around 2m: acts on soft going: tried in hood: often races freely. *Robert Stephens* **h131**

BE MY SEA (IRE) 6 b.g. Sea The Stars (IRE) – Bitooh (Diktat) [2016/17 h21.2s⁶ h15.8s² Mar 2] fairly useful on Flat, stays 21f: lightly-raced maiden over hurdles, fair form: tried in cheekpieces/tongue tie. *Tony Carroll* **h102**

BENABILITY (IRE) 7 b.g. Beneficial – Whataliability (IRE) (Leading Counsel (USA)) [2016/17 c–, h89: h23.1s⁴ c21.2s⁴ h19.2v⁴ c19.9d* Mar 15] poor handicap hurdler: modest chaser: won handicap at Huntingdon final start: stays 21f: acts on heavy going: in headgear last 3 starts. *Tim Vaughan* **c85 h77**

BEN ARTHUR (IRE) 7 b.g. Marienbard (IRE) – Oscartrainer (IRE) (Oscar (IRE)) [2016/17 h15.8v h15.5g⁵ h16.7d h20s* h23.1sᵖᵘ Mar 7] £8,500 6-y-o: first foal: dam winning pointer: off mark in Irish maiden points at fifth attempt: modest form over hurdles: won handicap at Ffos Las in February: best effort at 2½m: acts on soft going. *Kim Bailey* **h99**

BENARTY HILL (IRE) 7 b.g. September Storm (GER) – Crossmacahilly (IRE) (Executive Perk) [2016/17 h92: h19.3m h22d h22d⁴ h20s⁵ h23d² h23g² c22.6sᵘʳ Dec 26] point winner: modest maiden hurdler: unseated rider second in hunter at Down Royal on chasing debut: stays 3m: acts on good to firm and heavy going: usually wears tongue tie. *Liam Lennon, Ireland* **c– h86**

BENATAR (IRE) 5 b.g. Beneficial – Carrigeen Lily (IRE) (Supreme Leader) [2016/17 h19.1v* h19.6d⁴ h20.5s² h20g⁴ Apr 8] sturdy gelding: brother to 2 winners, including fairly useful chaser Carrigeen Lechuga (2¾m-3m winner), stayed 29f, and half-brother to bumper winner/winning pointer Carrigeen Lonicera (by Old Vic): dam (c121) 19f/21f chase winner: winning Irish pointer: useful form over hurdles: won maiden at Fontwell (by 10 lengths from Groundunderrepair) in January: 33/1, best effort when 8¼ lengths fourth of 13 to Finian's Oscar in Mersey Novices' Hurdle at Aintree final start: will stay beyond 2½m. *Gary Moore* **h138**

BENBECULA 8 b.g. Motivator – Isle of Flame (Shirley Heights) [2016/17 h112: h19d⁵ h15.3m⁴ c15.7dᵖᵘ h17.7d h15.5d h18.5m⁵ Apr 18] angular gelding: handicap hurdler, modest nowadays: pulled up in novice handicap on chasing debut: stays 2¼m: acts on heavy going: usually wears blinkers: usually races close up: temperamental. *Richard Mitchell* **c– h91 §**

BENBENS (IRE) 12 ch.g. Beneficial – Millicent Bridge (IRE) (Over The River (FR)) [2016/17 c140, h–: c33.4sᵖᵘ c31.8g³ c28.8g⁴ Apr 29] workmanlike gelding: winning hurdler: useful handicap chaser: back to best when 2¼ lengths third of 30 to Vicente in Scottish Grand National at Ayr in April: creditable ½-length fourth of 13 to Henllan Harri in bet365 Gold Cup at Sandown just week later: stays 4m: acts on good to firm and heavy going: often races towards rear. *Nigel Twiston-Davies* **c139 h–**

BEN CEE PEE M (IRE) 12 ch.g. Beneficial – Supreme Magical (Supreme Leader) [2016/17 h109: h23.3d h19.9g⁵ h19.6g³ h19.9g³ h19.9g³ Sep 18] good-topped gelding: fair handicap hurdler: stays 2¾m: acts on soft and good to firm going: wears headgear: one to treat with caution. *Brian Ellison* **h103 §**

BENDOMINGO (IRE) 6 b.g. Beneficial – Bobbies Storm (IRE) (Bob Back (USA)) [2016/17 h97, b90: h21dᵖᵘ h16g⁶ h20d² h23.1g² h21.2d³ h25d² h24.4g⁴ h20.5s⁴ h26.4g³ Apr 15] fair maiden hurdler: stays 25f: acts on good to soft going: has worn tongue tie. *Nigel Twiston-Davies* **h109**

BENEAGLES (IRE) 5 b.g. Milan – Liss Rua (IRE) (Bob Back (USA)) [2016/17 h19.9sᵖᵘ h24.5d² h21.2s² h25d* h23.5m⁵ Apr 2] £50,000 4-y-o: useful-looking gelding: closely related to bumper winner God of The Kop (by Old Vic) and fairly useful 3m hurdle winner Minella Aris (by King's Theatre): dam (h97), bumper winner (placed up to 3m over hurdles), half-sister to very smart hurdler (winner up to 2½m) Liss A Paoraigh: runner-up in Irish maiden point: fairly useful form over hurdles: won 2-runner maiden at Huntingdon in March: stays 25f: acts on soft and good to firm going: often races towards rear: remains with potential. *Alan King* **h123 p**

BENECHENKO (IRE) 5 br.g. Beneficial – Beann Ard (IRE) (Mandalus) [2016/17 b15.8v* b16v⁵ b16.8s h16s⁴ Mar 10] €18,000 3-y-o, £36,000 4-y-o: half-brother to 3 winners, including fair hurdler Freedom Statue (2½m winner, by Presenting) and fair chaser Buckland Gold (2m-2½m winner, by Lord Americo): dam unraced: won Irish maiden point on debut: fairly useful form in bumpers: won at Uttoxeter in November, **h86 p b98**

battling well: 7/1, shaped as if needed experience when fourth in novice at Sandown (19¾ lengths behind Azzerti) on hurdling debut: will be suited by 2¼m: capable of better. *Fergal O'Brien*

BENEFICIAL JOE (IRE) 7 b.g. Beneficial – Joleen (IRE) (Bob's Return (IRE))   **h118**
[2016/17 h79: h20.1g^{ur} h19.9g^F h20.6g³ h19.9g⁴ h23g* h26g² h23.3g* h23.1g⁴ Apr 22] sturdy gelding: fairly useful hurdler: won conditionals maiden at Worcester in August and handicap at Hexham in October: stays 3¼m: best form on good going: wears hood: often races in rear/travels strongly. *Graeme McPherson*

BENEFIT IN KIND (IRE) 9 b.g. Beneficial – She's So Beautiful (IRE) (Bluebird   **c77**
(USA)) [2016/17 c86, h–: c23.4d³ c24.2g c24.2d⁵ c20.5s⁴ c21.5s⁵ c24.2s^{pu} c23.8g* Jan 20]   **h–**
maiden hurdler: poor handicap chaser nowadays: won at Musselburgh in January: stays 25f: acts on heavy going: wears headgear/tongue tie: usually races prominently. *Katie Scott*

BENEFIT OF LUCK (IRE) 5 ch.g. Beneficial – Shamrock Miss (IRE) (Bob's Return   **h95 §**
(IRE)) [2016/17 b15.7v⁴ b15.8g^{pu} h20.3s⁵ h19.3m h16m² Apr 28] €54,000 3-y-o: rather   **b84 §**
unfurnished gelding: first foal: dam unraced sister to useful chaser (stayed 2½m) Sizing Africa: modest form in bumpers/over hurdles: left Chris Bealby after second start: temperamental. *Harry Whittington*

BENENDEN (IRE) 9 b.g. Moscow Society (USA) – Ashanti Dancer (IRE) (Dancing   **c– x**
Dissident (USA)) [2016/17 c125x, h–: c23.9g⁵ h24v* h24.6d⁵ h25.5g² h24.1d⁶ h23.1d³ Apr   **h117**
27] useful-looking gelding: fairly useful handicap hurdler: won at Southwell in June: fairly useful chaser at best: stays 3¼m: acts on heavy going: tried in cheekpieces/tongue tie: often let down by jumping over fences. *Michael Scudamore*

BENGALI SONG 7 b.g. Tiger Hill (IRE) – Garabelle (IRE) (Galileo (IRE)) [2016/17   **b94**
b15.7g* Oct 3] backed from long odds into 11/1, won maiden bumper at Southwell on only start: dead. *Neville Bycroft*

BENIDORM 9 b.g. Bahamian Bounty – Famcred (Inchinor) [2016/17 h15.8g h15.8g^{pu}   **h–**
h15.7g h20.3m h15.7d^{pu} Nov 29] no form over hurdles: wears headgear: in tongue tie last 3 starts. *Mairi Wilson*

BENIE DES DIEUX (FR) 6 b.m. Great Pretender (IRE) – Cana (FR) (Robin des   **c134 P**
Champs (FR)) [2016/17 c19.5s* Dec 29] dam half-sister to fairly useful hurdler/useful   **h–**
chaser (stayed 3m) Caribou and useful hurdler (15f winner) Choeur du Nord: 1¾m winner on Flat: fairly useful winner over hurdles in France for Mme I. Gallorini: 4/6, impressive debut over fences when winning mares maiden at Limerick by 30 lengths from Leaders Questions, making running and jumping soundly: stays 2½m: acts on soft going: tried in cheekpieces: exciting prospect. *W. P. Mullins, Ireland*

BENI LIGHT (FR) 6 b.g. Crossharbour – Or Light (FR) (Sleeping Car (FR)) [2016/17   **h62**
b88p: b16.8v⁴ h21.2s⁵ h21.4s⁶ h20v⁵ Mar 19] has shown only a little ability in bumpers/   **b74**
over hurdles. *Tom George*

BENISSIMO (IRE) 7 b.g. Beneficial – Fennor Rose (IRE) (Kotashaan (FR)) [2016/17   **c100**
h113: h15.7g* h16d⁶ c21.4g c16.5g³ c20d⁶ c20v⁵ c20v⁶ h19.9s Apr 1] fair handicap   **h112**
hurdler: won at Southwell in May: fair maiden chaser: left Dan Skelton after fourth start: stays 21f: acts on heavy going: usually races nearer last than first. *Tony Forbes*

BENNACHIE (IRE) 8 b.g. Milan – Stormy Lady (IRE) (Glacial Storm (USA)) [2016/17   **c106 §**
h105: c20.3d² h20d⁴ c19.3g⁵ c23.8m^{pu} c20g⁶ c16.5d³ c19.4s^{pu} h19s Feb 5]   **h85 §**
workmanlike gelding: modest handicap hurdler: fair maiden chaser: stays 2½m: acts on good to firm and good to soft going: usually wears tongue tie: usually races in rear: temperamental. *Tim Vaughan*

BENNY IN MILAN (IRE) 6 b.g. Milan – Chaparral Lady (IRE) (Broken Hearted)   **h107**
[2016/17 b17.8d³ b18g* h16.5g h20g h21.3d⁴ h20d⁵ h20.5d³ h20.8g² h19.5s h18.8g   **b95**
h16s Apr 6] €20,000 3-y-o: brother to useful 1¾m-2¼m winner Bernie The Bolt: dam, (h102) bumper winner, also 1½m-1¾m winner on Flat: maiden pointer: fairly useful form in bumpers: won maiden at Wexford in July: fair maiden hurdler: stays 21f: acts on good to soft going: has worn headgear: often races in rear. *Peter Fahey, Ireland*

BENNYS GIRL (IRE) 9 b.m. Beneficial – Be My Flower (IRE) (Be My Native (USA))   **c80**
[2016/17 c23g^{pu} c25.8g c25.5g^{pu} c17.4m³ c19.7m³ c25.8g³ c25.8g⁴ c25.7g^F h21.6v⁶   **h–**
h19.2v⁶ c20.9d³ c23.8g² c22.6g³ Apr 15] half-sister to fair hurdler/modest chaser Waterloo Chateau (2½m-23f winner, by Presenting): dam unraced: multiple winning pointer: maiden hurdler, no form in 2016/17: poor maiden chaser: stays 3¼m: acts on good to firm and heavy going: usually races close up. *Dai Williams*

BENNYS KING (IRE) 6 b.g. Beneficial – Hellofafaithful (IRE) (Oscar (IRE)) [2016/17 **h124**
h112p: h19.6g² h15.8v² h19.9v* h21d h20.9s⁴ Apr 3] good-topped gelding: fairly useful
handicap hurdler: won at Uttoxeter in December: stays 2½m: acts on heavy going: usually
races prominently. *Venetia Williams*

BENNYS MIST (IRE) 11 b.g. Beneficial – Dark Mist (IRE) (Mister Lord (USA)) **c–**
[2016/17 c144, h–: c20.4g c21.1dᵖᵘ c24.2sᵖᵘ c20.2vᵖᵘ Feb 2] strong gelding: winning **h–**
hurdler: useful chaser at best, out of sorts in 2016/17: has worn headgear, including in
2016/17: front runner/races prominently. *Venetia Williams*

BENNY'S SECRET (IRE) 7 br.g. Beneficial – Greenhall Rambler (IRE) (Anshan) **h92**
[2016/17 h106, b89: h17.1d h19.9vᵖᵘ h16v³ h18.1dᵖᵘ Apr 10] bumper winner: modest
handicap hurdler: stays 2¼m: acts on soft going: has worn hood, including in 2016/17:
sometimes in tongue tie: often races towards rear. *N. W. Alexander*

BENNYS WELL (IRE) 11 b.g. Beneficial – Alure (IRE) (Carroll House) [2016/17 **c– §**
c107§, h–§: c21.3g c24.2gᵖᵘ c26.3sᵖᵘ Nov 22] strong gelding: maiden hurdler: fair chaser **h– §**
at best, no form in 2016/17: has worn headgear/tongue tie: front runner/races prominently:
not one to trust. *Sue Smith*

BENNY THE MIXER 7 gr.g. Fair Mix (IRE) – See My Girl (Terimon) [2016/17 b16.2s **b–**
Sep 22] tailed off in bumper on debut. *Iain Jardine*

BENSACHUINE (IRE) 6 b.g. Beneficial – Almnadia (IRE) (Alhaarth (IRE)) [2016/17 **h102**
b15.8g b16g³ b16g² b17g² b16.6g b16g⁶ h16g² Nov 6] failed to complete both starts in **b92**
points: fair bumper performer: fair form also when second in maiden at Cork on hurdling
debut: usually in hood: often leads. *Denis Hogan, Ireland*

BENTELIMAR (IRE) 8 ch.g. Beneficial – Montel Girl (IRE) (Montelimar (USA)) **c135**
[2016/17 h140: h20d⁴ h16.1g h17d⁴ h16s⁵ h16s² h16g⁶ h22.5g² c16d⁵ c16d³ c25.4s³ c21gᶠ **h140**
Jan 27] sturdy gelding: useful hurdler: good effort when 4¾ lengths second of 5 to Ivan
Grozny in Istabraq Hurdle at Tipperary in October: useful form over fences: running well
in fifth when falling last in Leopardstown Handicap Chase final start: stays 25f: acts on
good to firm and heavy going: tried in hood. *J. R. Barry, Ireland*

BEN THE BOYO (IRE) 6 ch.g. Beneficial – Dyrick Daybreak (IRE) (Ali-Royal (IRE)) **h98**
[2016/17 h23.1v⁴ h23.1s⁵ Dec 22] placed 4 of 5 starts in Irish maiden points: modest form
in maiden/novice hurdles at Bangor: dead. *Harry Fry*

BENTONS LAD 6 br.g. Bollin Eric – Spirit of Ecstacy (Val Royal (FR)) [2016/17 h95: **c98**
h20.2d⁴ h18.2d⁵ h20.2s⁵ h23gᶠ c18.5g⁶ Aug 29] modest maiden hurdler: sixth in maiden at **h88**
Downpatrick on chasing debut: won point in February: stays 2¼m: acts on good to soft
going: tried in hood: has worn tongue tie. *Colin A. McBratney, Ireland*

BENTWORTH BOY 6 b.g. Archipenko (USA) – Maria di Scozia (Selkirk (USA)) **h–**
[2016/17 h–, b101: h16g h16.3m⁵ May 15] bumper winner: no form over hurdles: tried in
hood. *Patrick Chamings*

BENVOLIO (IRE) 10 b.g. Beneficial – Coumeenoole Lady (The Parson) [2016/17 c143, **c105**
h–: c24s c23.6v⁴ Mar 23] workmanlike gelding: point winner: winning hurdler: useful **h–**
chaser at best: just fair form in hunters in 2016/17: stays 29f: acts on heavy going: wears
headgear. *Dr Charles Levinson*

BENZEL (IRE) 9 b.g. Beneficial – Jezel (IRE) (Accordion) [2016/17 h101p: c24s² **c123**
c22.5s* c23g⁴ c24g* c24gᵘʳ c26.2d⁶ c24.1s⁵ c19.2v⁶ c20.3d Jan 3] strong gelding: maiden **h–**
hurdler: fairly useful handicap chaser: won novice events at Uttoxeter in June and
Southwell in August: stayed 3m: acted on heavy going: dead. *Jonjo O'Neill*

BE ON TIME (FR) 6 b.g. Linda's Lad – One More Time (FR) (Le Balafre (FR)) [2016/17 **c– §**
c112, h–: c24.1dᵖᵘ h20dᵖᵘ h20.3d⁵ Jul 10] lightly-raced maiden hurdler: handicap chaser, **h– §**
fair at best: usually wears headgear: tried in tongue tie: ungenuine. *Jamie Snowden*

BEREA BORU (IRE) 9 b.g. Brian Boru – Wayward Venture (IRE) (Mister Mat (FR)) **c103**
[2016/17 c136, h122: c22.9sᵖᵘ c24.1s⁵ c32.6sᵖᵘ Feb 25] fairly useful hurdler: useful chaser **h–**
at best, disappointing in 2016/17: stays 3m: acts on good to firm and heavy going: in
headgear last 4 starts: wears tongue tie. *Peter Bowen*

BERING UPSUN 6 b.g. And Beyond (IRE) – Bering Up (IRE) (Bering) [2016/17 b79: **h75**
b16.8s⁴ h16v⁵ h16.8v⁴ h19.4g Mar 1] rather unfurnished gelding: modest form in bumpers: **b80**
poor form over hurdles: wears hood: front runner/races prominently. *James Ewart*

BERKELEY BARRON (IRE) 9 b.g. Subtle Power (IRE) – Roseabel (IRE) (Roselier **c–**
(FR)) [2016/17 c100, h–: h24.4gᵖᵘ Jan 27] tall, useful-looking gelding: useful hurdler at **h–**
best: maiden chaser: stays 2¾m: acts on soft going: in cheekpieces last 2 starts: usually in
tongue tie. *Richard Phillips*

BERKSHIRE DOWNS 7 b.m. Tiger Hill (IRE) – Cut Corn (King's Theatre (IRE)) **c87**
[2016/17 h101, b83: c20.5d⁴ h20.6d² c20.1s h20.6s² h22.7s² h20.9sᵖᵘ h18.1d⁴ Apr 10] fair **h101**
maiden hurdler: modest form in 2 chases: will stay 3m: acts on heavy going: in cheekpieces
last 3 starts: tried in tongue tie. *Sandy Thomson*

BERMEO (IRE) 6 b.g. Definite Article – Miss Blueyes (IRE) (Dushyantor (USA)) **c95**
[2016/17 h81, b–: h23.3v⁵ h18.5g h23.3s⁶ h23m* c24d² Jul 13] modest handicap hurdler: **h94**
won novice event at Worcester in July: head second to Right Enough in novice handicap at
Uttoxeter on chasing debut: stays 3m: acts on good to firm and good to soft going: in
blinkers last 2 starts: often races in rear. *Johnny Farrelly*

BERNARDELLI (IRE) 9 b.g. Golan (IRE) – Beautiful Blue (IRE) (Xaar) [2016/17 **c137 x**
c134, h–: c24.3s³ c20.1s⁴ c21.6v* c23.4v³ c23.4vᵖᵘ c23.8gᵖᵘ Apr 26] winning hurdler: **h–**
useful handicap chaser: won by 9 lengths from Spanish Fleet at Kelso in January: stays 3m:
acts on heavy going: often let down by jumping. *Nicky Richards*

BERNISDALE 9 ch.m. Bertolini (USA) – Carradale (Pursuit of Love) [2016/17 h74: **h85**
h18.7m⁴ h18.5g* h18.7m⁶ h18.5d⁵ h19.7g³ Oct 31] modest handicap hurdler: won at
Newton Abbot in May: stays 19f: acts on soft and good to firm going. *John Flint*

BERRY DE CARJAC (FR) 6 ch.g. Epalo (GER) – Miria Galanda (FR) (Chef de Clan **c98**
(FR)) [2016/17 h106: h17.7g h18.6g³ c20g⁴ c23.8dᵖᵘ c17gᶠ h20.5g³ h15.5g h16.5g⁴ **h92 §**
h20g⁴ Apr 17] workmanlike gelding: modest maiden hurdler/chaser: stays 2½m: raced
mainly on good going: has worn headgear/tongue tie, including in 2016/17: temperamental.
Nigel Hawke

BERTALUS (IRE) 8 b.g. City Honours (USA) – Deep Dalus (IRE) (Mandalus) [2016/17 **c98 §**
h106: c20.1s⁴ c24.2gᵖᵘ h24.3sᵖᵘ h24.3s⁶ h25.8sᵖᵘ Apr 3] winning pointer: handicap hurdler, **h66 §**
fair at best: modest form on completed start in chases: stays 3m: best form on soft/heavy
going: tried in visor: lazy. *N. W. Alexander*

BERTENBAR 13 b.g. Bertolini (USA) – Ardenbar (Ardross) [2016/17 c108, h–: c16.3sᶠ **c105**
c19.2s³ c17.4s³ c19.9d c17.4d* Mar 18] tall, lengthy gelding: maiden hurdler: fair handicap **h–**
chaser: won at Fontwell final start: stays 2½m: acts on heavy going: in cheekpieces last 4
starts. in tongue tie last 5: front runner. *Dan Skelton*

BERTHA BURNETT (IRE) 6 gr.m. Verglas (IRE) – Starsazi (Observatory (USA)) **h–**
[2016/17 h20.8d h16.8sᵖᵘ Jan 29] no form over hurdles. *Brian Rothwell*

BERTIE BARNES (IRE) 6 b.g. Craigsteel – Mahon Rose (IRE) (Roselier (FR)) **h90**
[2016/17 h75: h16.3m⁶ h15.8v⁵ h19v h21s² Feb 10] modest form over hurdles: best effort
at 21f: acts on soft going. *Richard Phillips*

BERTIE BLAKE (IRE) 4 b.g. Beneficial – Diandrina (Mondrian (GER)) [2016/17 b16s **b–**
b16v Mar 11] well held in bumpers. *Philip Kirby*

BERTIE BORU (IRE) 10 b.g. Brian Boru – Sleeven Lady (Crash Course) [2016/17 **c127 §**
c128§, h–: c25g⁵ c30.2mᵘʳ c24.2vᵖᵘ c24.2d* c28.4g³ c28.4g³ Apr 15] strong, workmanlike **h–**
gelding: maiden hurdler: fairly useful handicap chaser: won at Exeter in March: stays
3½m: acts on heavy going: wears cheekpieces: usually races nearer last than first:
temperamental. *Philip Hobbs*

BERTIE LUGG 9 b.g. Beat All (USA) – Flakey Dove (Oats) [2016/17 h90: h23.3d* **c99**
c20.9s⁵ c24dᵖᵘ h21.2s c23.6g⁵ Apr 17] modest handicap hurdler: won at Uttoxeter in May: **h98**
modest form in novice handicap chases: stays 23f: acts on heavy going: tried in tongue tie.
Henry Oliver

BERTIE MOON 7 b.g. Bertolini (USA) – Fleeting Moon (Fleetwood (IRE)) [2016/17 **h–**
h100: h19.9g Sep 18] handicap hurdler, fair at best: should stay beyond 17f: acts on good
to firm and heavy going: has worn cheekpieces, including final start. *Lydia Pearce*

BERTIE MY BOY (IRE) 8 b.g. Millenary – Slievemhuire (IRE) (Beneficial) [2016/17 **h–**
h20g⁶ Jun 2] tailed off in selling hurdle on debut. *Grant Cann*

BERTIMONT (FR) 7 gr.g. Slickly (FR) – Bocanegra (FR) (Night Shift (USA)) [2016/17 **c–**
h15.7d h16sᶠ h16g h16.5s² h16.5g² h16.8g h16g Apr 22] smallish gelding: useful handicap **h135**
hurdler: missed 2015/16, best efforts in 2016/17 when second twice at Taunton in February:
maiden chaser: unproven beyond 17f: acts on soft going: wears tongue tie: often races
towards rear. *Dan Skelton*

BERWICK BASSETT 8 b.g. Beat All (USA) – Hottentot (Sula Bula) [2016/17 h16.2dᵖᵘ **h–**
h20.2d h22.1g Jul 18] maiden pointer: no form over hurdles. *Andrew Hamilton*

BERWIN (IRE) 8 b.m. Lawman (FR) – Topiary (IRE) (Selkirk (USA)) [2016/17 h–: h18.5g May 25] no form over hurdles. *Sarah Robinson* — **h–**

BESCOT SPRINGS (IRE) 12 b.g. Saddlers' Hall (IRE) – Silver Glen (IRE) (Roselier (FR)) [2016/17 c89§, h98§: c23.4d⁵ h24.3g h23.3g⁶ h24.3d² h23.3s* h23.3v⁵ h22.7s⁶ h25.8v* h24.3s⁴ h23.3s* h25.8s³ h23.9g Apr 26] strong, good-bodied gelding: fair handicap hurdler: won at Hexham in November, Kelso in January and Hexham in March: handicap chaser, fairly useful in his prime: stays 3¼m: acts on good to firm and heavy going: wears headgear: temperamental. *Lucinda Russell* — **c75** **h101 §**

BE SEEING YOU 6 ch.g. Medicean – Oshiponga (Barathea (IRE)) [2016/17 h114: h20d h20d h20.2g⁶ c19.9g h23g² h23.6m⁵ h23.1d h19.2v h21.2g h21.9d⁴ Apr 16] fair handicap hurdler: well beaten in maiden on chasing debut: left Gordon Elliott after fifth start: stays 2¾m: acts on good to firm going: wears headgear/tongue tie. *Trevor Wall* — **c65** **h100**

BESPOKE LADY (IRE) 8 ch.m. Presenting – Coole Alainn (IRE) (Glacial Storm (USA)) [2016/17 c–, h–: c23.9g⁵ c24.2g^pu Jun 4] winning hurdler: no form in chases: stays 3m: acts on good to soft going: sometimes in cheekpieces: temperament under suspicion. *Micky Hammond* — **c–** **h–**

BEST BOY BARNEY (IRE) 11 b.g. Rashar (USA) – Graigue Lass (IRE) (Phardante (FR)) [2016/17 c127, h–: c22.5d² c23d c24g⁶ c22.6g³ c24g⁴ c24m* c23.8g⁵ c25.1m³ c25.1f² Apr 23] rangy gelding: maiden hurdler: handicap chaser, fair nowadays: won at Kempton in October: stays 3¼m: acts on any going: wears headgear/tongue tie: usually leads: quirky sort. *Jeremy Scott* — **c105** **h–**

BEST DIRECTOR (IRE) 9 ch.g. Oscar (IRE) – Taneys Leader (IRE) (Supreme Leader) [2016/17 h–: h23.3v^pu Apr 30] winning pointer: lightly-raced maiden over hurdles. *John Groucott* — **h–**

BESTIARIUS (IRE) 5 b.g. Vinnie Roe (IRE) – Chione (IRE) (Mandalus) [2016/17 b96: h16.4d² h19.6g^ur Mar 25] successful on only start in bumpers: fair form over hurdles: better effort when second in novice at Newcastle in November: should prove suited by 2½m+. *Nicky Richards* — **h107**

BEST PRACTICE (IRE) 6 br.g. Beneficial – Lemon Cello (IRE) (Accordion) [2016/17 h19.9s Nov 12] tailed off in maiden hurdle on debut. *Jonjo O'Neill* — **h–**

BEST SERVED COLD 11 b.g. King's Theatre (IRE) – Mirana (IRE) (Ela-Mana-Mou) [2016/17 c24.2s Jan 1] strong gelding: winning pointer: winning hurdler: maiden chaser, fair at best: stays 25f: best form on good going or softer (acts on heavy): has worn headgear/tongue tie, including only outing in 2016/17. *Lawney Hill* — **c–** **h–**

BEST VALUE (IRE) 10 b.g. Helissio (FR) – Upper Mount Clair (Ela-Mana-Mou) [2016/17 h24g h20g h19.8m⁶ h24.2s c22d h19.7s c24d Feb 9] handicap hurdler/chaser, out of sorts in 2016/17: left T. J. Nagle Jnr after fifth start: stays 25f: acts on good to firm and heavy going: has worn headgear, including in 2016/17: in tongue tie last 3 starts: often leads. *Rebecca Menzies* — **c–** **h78**

BESTWORK D'OLIVATE (FR) 6 b.m. Network (GER) – Komunion (FR) (Luchiroverte (IRE)) [2016/17 c103, h103: h18.5g⁶ h21.6g⁵ h20g⁴ h19.5d^pu c18.2g^pu Apr 6] maiden hurdler/winning chaser: little impact in 2016/17: stays 2¾m: acts on good to firm and good to soft going: has worn headgear, including final start: in tongue tie last 3 starts: usually races nearer last than first. *Martin Hill* — **c–** **h75**

BESTWORK (FR) 6 bl.g. Network (GER) – Harmony (FR) (Lute Antique (FR)) [2016/17 h93, b–: h15.8d⁴ h15.8g h19.9d³ h18.1s^pu c16s c19.2m² Apr 18] modest maiden hurdler: modest form over fences: better effort when second in handicap at Exeter: stays 2½m: acts on good to firm going: has worn hood: tried in tongue tie. *Charlie Longsdon* — **c86** **h86**

BETSY BOO BOO 8 b.m. King's Theatre (IRE) – Quark Top (FR) (Perrault) [2016/17 h77, b–: h20.5g Oct 17] little form over hurdles: in cheekpieces last 2 starts: tried in tongue tie: dead. *Michael Roberts* — **h–**

BETTATOGETHER 8 b.g. Fair Mix (IRE) – Ella Falls (IRE) (Dancing Dissident (USA)) [2016/17 h15.8s^F h15.8g⁵ h16m³ Apr 28] runner-up on first of 2 starts in bumpers in 2014/15: off 25 months, modest form at best in 3 runs over hurdles. *Alan King* — **h95**

BETTER BACK BRACKA (IRE) 6 b.m. Flemensfirth (USA) – Merrill Gaye (IRE) (Roselier (FR)) [2016/17 b85: b17.1d h16d h20d⁵ h22.7s² h21.4v³ h22v⁵ Feb 22] fair at best in bumpers: modest form over hurdles: should stay 2¾m+: acts on heavy going: tried in hood: often in tongue tie. *Noel C. Kelly, Ireland* — **h99** **b–**

BETTER B QUICK (IRE) 11 b.g. Overbury (IRE) – Snow Shine (IRE) (Rainbows For **c84** Life (CAN)) [2016/17 c104, h–: c20.5m⁵ c24.2d⁶ c20g Jul 1] maiden hurdler: handicap **h–** chaser, just poor form in 2016/17: barely stays 3m: acts on heavy going: wears headgear. *Paul Stafford, Ireland*

BETTER DAYS (IRE) 6 gr.g. Daylami (IRE) – Miss Edgehill (IRE) (Idris (IRE)) **c113** [2016/17 h79, b–: h23g* h23.3s⁶ h23.3g c23.8vᶠ c20g* c19.9d⁵ c20v⁵ c23g* c23.8s⁴ **h84** c25.1m* c25.3g² Apr 20] poor handicap hurdler: won at Worcester in May: fair handicap chaser: won at Lingfield in December, Taunton (novice event) in January and Wincanton in April: stays 25f: acts on good to firm going: has worn tongue tie, including in 2016/17: none too reliable. *Nigel Twiston-Davies*

BETTER GETALONG (IRE) 6 b.g. Gold Well – Arequipa (IRE) (Turtle Island (IRE)) **b100** [2016/17 b99: b16s* b16.2v* b16.4g Mar 15] fairly useful form in bumpers: won at Ayr (conditionals/amateur event) in December and Kelso in February: 50/1, 14¼ lengths twelfth of 22 to Fayonagh in Champion Bumper at Cheltenham final start: will be suited by further than 2m. *Nicky Richards*

BETTERLATETHANNEVA (IRE) 6 b.m. Albano (IRE) – Acqua Pesante (IRE) **h84** (Distinctly North (USA)) [2016/17 b17g b15.8m² b16g h15.8d h15.8s h20.5s⁵ h21m³ **b79** h20.3g Apr 21] sixth foal: half-sister to 3 winners on Flat by dam Italian 6f-9f winner: modest form in bumpers: poor form over hurdles: left Francesca Nimmo after first start: stays 21f: acts on good to firm going. *Robin Dickin*

BETWEEN THE WATERS (IRE) 6 ch.g. Indian River (FR) – Catch Ball (Prince **c86 p** Sabo) [2016/17 b16.2g² b15.7m⁵ h24d⁶ h20.5g³ h19.3d⁴ c19.9g⁵ c25.1f⁴ Apr 23] £25,000 **h96** 5-y-o: sturdy gelding: seventh foal: brother to modest hurdler TB Broke Her (2m-23f **b87** winner) and half-brother to fair hurdler Keltic Crisis (3m winner, by Needle Gun): dam (h134), 2½m-3m hurdle winner, also 1½m/13f winner on Flat, half-sister to smart hurdler (2m/17f winner) Satin Lover: Irish point winner: fair form in bumpers: modest form in novice hurdles: modest form in chases, better effort when fourth in handicap at Wincanton: stays 25f: acts on firm going: remains with potential as a chaser. *Jamie Snowden*

BEWARE THE BEAR (IRE) 7 b.g. Shantou (USA) – Native Bid (IRE) (Be My Native **c145** (USA)) [2016/17 h119: h24s* c23.8d* c23.4d* c31.8g c24.3g⁴ Apr 22] strong, workmanlike **h127 +** gelding: fairly useful form over hurdles: won novice at Southwell in May: smart form in chases, winning novice handicaps at Ascot (by 2¾ lengths from Singlefarmpayment) in November and Newbury (by length from Aurillac) in December: creditable fourth in novice handicap at Ayr final start: should stay beyond 3m (never going well after bad mistake fifth when tried at 4m): acts on heavy going: often races towards rear/travels strongly. *Nicky Henderson*

BEYEH (IRE) 9 b.m. King's Best (USA) – Cradle Rock (IRE) (Desert Sun) [2016/17 **c111** c16s² Mar 23] small mare: fairly useful hurdler: off 29 months, second in novice at Ludlow **h–** (5 lengths behind Gino Trail) on chasing debut: stays 2¾m: acts on heavy going. *Michael Appleby*

BEYOND CONCEIT (IRE) 8 b.g. Galileo (IRE) – Baraka (IRE) (Danehill (USA)) **h145 p** [2016/17 h16.3s* h19.3s* h16.4g⁶ h24.7g² Apr 7] good-topped gelding: useful on Flat for Andrew Balding in 2013, stays 21f: smart form over hurdles: won novices at Newbury in January and Ascot (by neck from Topofthegame) in February: in hood, ½-length second of 11 to The Worlds End in Sefton Novices' Hurdle at Aintree final start, good progress between 4 out and 3 out but mistakes last 2: stays 3m: remains with potential. *Nicky Henderson*

BEYOND MEASURE (IRE) 6 ch.m. Flemensfirth (USA) – Faucon (Polar Falcon **c–** (USA)) [2016/17 b89: h21.2m⁶ h15.8v⁴ h16g² h19.4d⁴ c20.3sᵖᵘ h15.7m⁴ Apr 13] angular **h95** mare: bumper winner: modest form over hurdles: pulled up in mares novice on chasing debut: stays 19f: acts on heavy going: tried in hood: front runner/races prominently. *Oliver Sherwood*

BEYOND SUPREMACY (IRE) 5 ch.g. Beneficial – Slaney Athlete (IRE) (Warcraft **b–** (USA)) [2016/17 b16.6g b16.8d Mar 21] well held in 2 bumpers: sold £8,000 in May. *Kim Bailey*

BEYONDTEMPTATION 9 ch.m. And Beyond (IRE) – Tempted (IRE) (Invited (USA)) **h112** [2016/17 h111: h23.3d² h20.1gᵖᵘ h20.1dᶠ h20.1sᵖᵘ h16gᵖᵘ h16.8d³ h16.8dᵖᵘ h20.6sᵖᵘ h16v² h16.4v* h19.9v² h20.1v⁵ h18.9g h20.1g* Apr 25] fair handicap hurdler: won at Hexham very early in season, Newcastle (mares event) in February and at Hexham again on final start: stays 23f, also effective over much shorter: acts on heavy going: wears hood/tongue tie: front runner. *Jonathan Haynes*

BEYOND THE CLOUDS 4 ch.g. Peintre Celebre (USA) – Evening (Mark of Esteem **b100**
(IRE)) [2016/17 b15.6g* b15.6g² Feb 5] fourth foal: half-brother to 2 winners on Flat,
including 5f-8.6f winner Beautiful Day (by Piccolo): dam maiden on Flat (stayed 1¼m):
fairly useful form in bumpers, both at Musselburgh: won by 12 lengths from Hattaab in
January, then staying-on ¾-length second of 6 to Ballyvic Boru month later. *Kevin Ryan*

BEYONDTHEFLAME 7 b.m. And Beyond (IRE) – Flame of Zara (Blushing Flame **h–**
(USA)) [2016/17 b–: h17.2dᵖᵘ h16.2sᵖᵘ h20.1d⁵ h16.2vᵖᵘ h19.9sᵖᵘ h16.4v³ h20.6vᵖᵘ h24g⁶
h19.7g⁵ Apr 23] no form over hurdles. *Jonathan Haynes*

BHAKTI (IRE) 10 b.g. Rakti – Royal Bossi (IRE) (Spectrum (IRE)) [2016/17 h–: **h93 §**
h20.7dᵖᵘ h21.9d* Apr 16] strong, deep-girthed gelding: modest handicap hurdler: won at
Ffos Las in April: left Mark Rimell after first start: stays 2¾m: acts on good to soft going:
temperamental. *Tom Lacey*

BIBI D'EOLE (FR) 6 ch.g. Storm Trooper (GER) – Bibi Star (FR) (Sinjar (FR)) [2016/17 **c–**
c–, h96: h16.8gᵖᵘ May 5] maiden hurdler: modest form at best: fair form only start over **h–**
fences: unproven beyond 17f: acts on soft going. *Graeme McPherson*

BIDDY BLACK 5 ch.m. Black Sam Bellamy (IRE) – Cosavita (FR) (Comte du Bourg **b–**
(FR)) [2016/17 b16.4sᵖᵘ Jan 7] £1,700 3-y-o: first foal: dam (h121) French 15f/2m hurdles
winner: showed nothing in mares bumper. *Simon West*

BIG BAD DREAM (IRE) 5 b.g. Mountain High (IRE) – Stay At Home (IRE) (Blueprint **b86**
(IRE)) [2016/17 b16v³ b16.2g⁵ Apr 25] €3,500 3-y-o: third foal: dam unraced half-sister to
fairly useful hurdler (stayed 25f) Green Light: better effort in bumpers when third at Ayr in
January: bred to be suited by 2½m+. *Donald Whillans*

BIG BAD DUDE (IRE) 8 ch.g. Blueprint (IRE) – Cathedral Ave (IRE) (Darazari (IRE)) **h–**
[2016/17 b–: h19.9g May 14] won Irish maiden point on debut (May 2014): well held in
bumper/novice hurdle. *Tom George*

BIGBADJOHN (IRE) 8 br.g. Vinnie Roe (IRE) – Celtic Serenade (IRE) (Yashgan) **c143**
[2016/17 h123, b95: h24dᵖᵘ c20d³ c22.4g* c23.4g² c24dᶠ c23.8s* c31.8gᵖᵘ Mar 14] tall **h–**
gelding: point/bumper winner: fairly useful hurdler: useful form in chases: won maiden at
Newbury (by 6 lengths from Our Kaempfer) in November and Reynoldstown Novices'
Chase at Ascot (by short head from Flintham) in February: creditable second in Worcester
Novices' Chase at Newbury (8 lengths behind Thistlecrack) in between: stays 3m: acts on
heavy going. *Rebecca Curtis*

BIG BROTHER GEORGE (IRE) 5 b.g. Milan – Jade River (FR) (Indian River (FR)) **h108**
[2016/17 b15.8v⁵ h22s³ h21.6s h19.9s³ Apr 1] €32,000 3-y-o: brother to bumper winner **b85**
New To This Town, closely related to 2 winners by High Chaparral, including bumper
winner/fairly useful hurdler (19f-21f winner) Thumb Stone Blues, and half-brother to
bumper winner Blue Article (by Definite Article): dam (h92) French 17f hurdle winner:
fifth in bumper at Uttoxeter on debut: fair form over hurdles: tried in blinkers: in tongue tie
last 2 starts. *Oliver Greenall*

BIG CASINO 11 b.g. Court Cave (IRE) – Migsy Malone (Afzal) [2016/17 c127, h–: **c123 §**
c19m⁴ c23.8g⁴ c24d² c22.6g* c25.6gᶠ c24g⁶ c23.4s c24d⁴ c22.4d⁶ c29.2g* Apr 24] tall **h–**
gelding: winning hurdler: fairly useful handicap chaser: won at Stratford in October and
Warwick on final start: stays 29f: acts on heavy going: has worn headgear, including in
2016/17: inconsistent. *Nigel Twiston-Davies*

BIG CHIEF BENNY (IRE) 6 ch.g. Beneficial – Be Airlie (IRE) (Lord Americo) **h127**
[2016/17 h129, b100: h20.6s⁶ h19.4g² h21g Dec 26] stocky gelding: fairly useful handicap
hurdler: second at Doncaster in December: stays 21f: acts on soft going. *Alan King*

BIG CHIP AND PIN 5 b.g. Generous (IRE) – Supreme Cove (Supreme Leader) [2016/17 **h94**
h16gᵘ h15.8s h19.7s h19.5s³ h16s⁴ h15.8d⁴ Apr 16] fourth foal: brother to bumper winner/
winning pointer First Drift, and half-brother to fairly useful hurdler/chaser Destroyer
Deployed (2½m-3m winner, by Deploy) and a winning pointer by Runyon: dam unraced:
modest form over hurdles: stays 19f: acts on soft going. *Dai Burchell*

BIG DAWG (IRE) 6 ch.g. Presenting – Supreme Sales (IRE) (Supreme Leader) [2016/17 **h89**
h17.7d⁵ Sep 4] €30,000 3-y-o, £18,000 5-y-o: fourth foal: dam unraced sister to useful
chaser (winner up to 3m) Can't Buy Time and half-sister to Galway Plate winner Stroll
Home: 8/1, 27 lengths fifth of 11 to Canton Prince in novice hurdle at Fontwell on debut,
making mistakes: sold £800 in May. *Gary Moore*

BIG DIAMOND (IRE) 6 b.g. Royal Anthem (USA) – Barrys Best (IRE) (King Luthier) **h60**
[2016/17 h18.5s h21.6s⁶ h16.5s h19g Feb 21] maiden pointer: poor form over hurdles: in
hood last 3 starts, in tongue tie last 2. *Jackie du Plessis*

BIG EASY (GER) 10 b.g. Ransom O'War (USA) – Basilea Gold (GER) (Monsun (GER)) **h–**
[2016/17 h23.1spu h24g Apr 20] good-topped gelding: useful hurdler at best, no form in 2 starts in 2016/17: stays 25f: acts on heavy going: wears cheekpieces. *Philip Hobbs*

BIG FELLA THANKS 15 b.g. Primitive Rising (USA) – Nunsdream (Derrylin) [2016/17 **c128**
c120, h–: c20.8g* c20s² c21.1g³ Apr 6] workmanlike gelding: winning hurdler: useful **h–**
hunter chaser nowadays: won at Cheltenham (by neck from Foynes Island) very early in 2016/17: best effort of season when 3¼ lengths third of 28 to Dineur in Foxhunters' Chase at Aintree: stays 3m: acts on good to firm and heavy going: has worn headgear: wears tongue tie. *Tom George*

BIG GENERATOR 11 ch.g. Generous (IRE) – Frizzball (IRE) (Orchestra) [2016/17 c–, **c–**
h120: h20g h15.7g³ Aug 23] fair hurdler nowadays: winning chaser: stays 2½m: acts on **h102**
good to firm and good to soft going: has worn headgear: has worn tongue tie, including in 2016/17: often races prominently. *Caroline Bailey*

BIG GEORGIE (IRE) 10 b.g. Exit To Nowhere (USA) – Afreen (IRE) (Entrepreneur) **c88**
[2016/17 c102: c24.2s⁶ c24.1spu c24v⁶ c25.7v³ c25.7spu c24.1g⁴ Mar 25] winning pointer: modest maiden chaser: stays 3¼m: best form on heavy going: tried in headgear: often races towards rear, lazy. *Katy Price*

BIGINDIE (IRE) 7 ch.g. Indian Haven – Graceful Air (IRE) (Danzero (AUS)) [2016/17 **h103**
h113: h19.7g⁴ h20.3g⁴ h20.3g⁶ Aug 31] fair handicap hurdler: stays 2½m: acts on good to soft going: often races prominently. *John Weymes*

BIGIRONONHISHIP (IRE) 6 b.g. Beneficial – Portobello Lady (IRE) (Broken **c127**
Hearted) [2016/17 h127: c23.4s² c23.4s² c23.4srr c26.2s³ Feb 8] tall gelding: winning **h–**
pointer: fairly useful hurdler: fairly useful form in handicap chases: stays 3¼m: raced only on soft/heavy going: tried in tongue tie. *Rose Dobbin*

BIG JIM 8 b.g. Revoque (IRE) – Chilly Squaw (IRE) (Commanche Run) [2016/17 c128, **c104**
h–: c15.7s⁶ Dec 17] good-topped gelding: maiden hurdler: fairly useful handicap chaser in **h–**
2015/16. shaped as if in need of race only outing in 2016/17: stays 21f: acts on heavy going: front runner/races prominently. *Alex Hales*

BIG LITTLE MAN (IRE) 7 ch.g. Beneficial – Drama Chick (Riverwise (USA)) **h59**
[2016/17 b16.3g h20g⁶ h23g Jul 12] showed little in points/bumper/maiden hurdles: in **b–**
headgear last 2 starts: dead. *Alastair Ralph*

BIGMARTRE (FR) 6 b.g. Montmartre (FR) – Oh La Miss (FR) (Le Balafre (FR)) **c–**
[2016/17 c–, h132: h16g* h16.8s h16d⁶ h20g Apr 7] lengthy gelding: useful handicap **h130**
hurdler: won at Kempton (by length from Drumcliff) in December: second on completed start over fences in 2014/15: stays 19f: acts on heavy going: front runner/races prominently. *Harry Whittington*

BIG MCINTOSH (IRE) 5 b.g. Bushranger (IRE) – Three Decades (IRE) (Invincible **h–**
Spirit (IRE)) [2016/17 h114: h15.8m h15.6g⁵ h16.2spu Dec 4] sturdy gelding: fair hurdler at best, no form in 2016/17: left John Ryan after second start: has worn tongue tie: usually leads. *Lucinda Russell*

BIG MEADOW (IRE) 6 br.g. Marienbard (IRE) – Lakyle Lady (IRE) (Bob Back **h118**
(USA)) [2016/17 b103: h23.6g³ h23.1v³ h19.9v² h23.6v³ Mar 23] won Irish maiden point on debut: bumper winner: fairly useful form over hurdles: second in handicap at Uttoxeter in February: may prove best at short of 3m. *Neil King*

BIG MIKE (IRE) 9 b.g. Flemensfirth (USA) – Minoras Return (IRE) (Bob's Return **h–**
(IRE)) [2016/17 h20.3spu Mar 20] placed in points/bumpers: fair form on first of 2 starts over hurdles: dead. *Sarah Humphrey*

BIG NIGHT OUT 11 b.m. Midnight Legend – Big Decision (Arzanni) [2016/17 c–, h84: **c–**
h21gpu May 9] winning pointer: maiden hurdler/chaser: stays 19f: acts on good to soft **h–**
going: sometimes in hood: wears tongue tie. *Laura Hurley*

BIG OCCASION (IRE) 10 b.g. Sadler's Wells (USA) – Asnieres (USA) (Spend A Buck **c–**
(USA)) [2016/17 c–, h–: h23.6spu Dec 27] smallish, leggy gelding: fairly useful hurdler/ **h–**
useful chaser at best: pulled up only 2 starts since 2012/13: usually wears blinkers. *Oliver Sherwood*

BIG PENNY (IRE) 5 b.m. Oscar (IRE) – Lady Marnay (IRE) (Darnay) [2016/17 h25.3s² **h97 p**
Feb 13] €14,500 3-y-o, £70,000 4-y-o: second foal: half-sister to bumper winner Lockeen Girl (by Beneficial): dam twice-raced half-sister to smart hurdler (winner up to 21f)

125

Coolnagorna: off mark in Irish mares maiden points at second attempt: 4/1, 13 lengths second to Same Circus in mares novice at Catterick on hurdling debut: should improve. *Jonjo O'Neill*

BIGPIPENOTOBACEE (IRE) 6 b.g. King's Theatre (IRE) – Another Dollar (IRE) (Supreme Leader) [2016/17 h110p, b–: h16.4g⁴ c19.1gᶠ Nov 26] third on both completed starts in Irish points: fair maiden hurdler: fell ninth in novice handicap on chasing debut: remains with potential. *Tom George* — **c– p / h109 p**

BIG RIVER (IRE) 7 b.g. Milan – Call Kate (IRE) (Lord Americo) [2016/17 h106p: h16.2d² h21.4s* h23.8g⁵ h22.8d² h25.8s* Mar 25] runner-up sole start in Irish points: useful form over hurdles: progressed well in 2016/17 and won handicaps at Ayr in December and Kelso (by 10 lengths from Seeyouatmidnight) on final start: stays 3¼m: acts on soft going: in tongue tie last 4 starts. *Lucinda Russell* — **h136**

BIG ROBIN (IRE) 5 b.m. Robin des Champs (FR) – Melodique (Kahyasi) [2016/17 b17g h21.2sᶠ Mar 23] £70,000 4-y-o: first foal: dam unraced daughter of fairly useful French hurdler/winning chaser (15f-2¼m winner) Symphonique: off mark in Irish maiden points at second attempt: eighth of 10 in mares maiden at Aintree in October: 11/4, fell third in mares novice at Ludlow on hurdling debut. *Nicky Henderson* — **h– / b–**

BIG SMILE (IRE) 9 b.g. Zagreb (USA) – Pretty Buckskin (IRE) (Supreme Leader) [2016/17 h–: h16mᵖᵘ Jul 4] unseated both starts in points: no form over hurdles: tried in hood. *John Groucott* — **h–**

BIG SOUND 10 b.g. Supreme Sound – Tarbolton Moss (Le Moss) [2016/17 c112, h–: c24.2d² c23.9d² c24m* h23.3g⁴ c24g* c24.1d⁴ Aug 19] close-coupled gelding: modest handicap hurdler: fairly useful handicap chaser: won at Uttoxeter in June and July: stays 25f: acts on soft and good to firm going: wears cheekpieces: tried in tongue tie: front runner/races prominently. *Mark Walford* — **c118 / h95**

BIG THUNDER 7 gr.g. Dalakhani (IRE) – Charlotte O Fraise (IRE) (Beat Hollow) [2016/17 h88p: h16.7g⁶ h20.5s³ Nov 9] fairly useful on Flat, stays 2¼m: lightly-raced maiden over hurdles, fair form when third at Ayr: sold £11,000 in January. *Micky Hammond* — **h108**

BIG WATER (IRE) 9 ch.g. Saffron Walden (FR) – Magic Feeling (IRE) (Magical Wonder (USA)) [2016/17 c–, h–: h23.1g⁶ h22.8vᵖᵘ h24d⁴ h19.9d⁴ h25.3gᵖᵘ Jan 12] tall gelding: fair handicap hurdler: winning chaser: stays 3m: acts on heavy going. *Alan Swinbank* — **c– / h113**

BIG WINDMILL (IRE) 6 b.g. Stowaway – Neighbours Wager (IRE) (Darazari (IRE)) [2016/17 b70: h15.8v³ h18.8d h16s c16dᵘʳ c18.2d³ Feb 5] tall gelding: off mark in Irish points at second attempt: modest form over hurdles/in chases: best effort at 2m on heavy going: remains with potential as a chaser. *Tom George* — **c85 p / h97**

BILBROOK BLAZE 7 b.g. Kayf Tara – Za Beau (IRE) (Beneficial) [2016/17 c119, h112: c21gᵖᵘ c20.9mᵖᵘ h20g Jun 4] useful-looking gelding: maiden hurdler/chaser, no form in 2016/17: tried in cheekpieces/tongue tie: dead. *Philip Hobbs* — **c– / h–**

BILIDN 9 b.m. Tiger Hill (IRE) – Brightest Star (Unfuwain (USA)) [2016/17 h20.3dᵖᵘ h23.9m Dec 8] lengthy mare: maiden hurdler, no form in 2016/17: stays 2¾m: acts on soft going: has worn blinkers (including in 2016/17)/tongue tie. *Laura Young* — **h–**

BILKO'S BACK (IRE) 5 b.g. Big Bad Bob (IRE) – Chica Roca (USA) (Woodman (USA)) [2016/17 b79: h16.8g⁵ b16.7d⁶ b16.2sᵖᵘ Jul 10] little form on Flat/in bumpers. *Susan Corbett* — **b–**

BILL AND BARN (IRE) 6 br.g. Presenting – Forgotten Star (IRE) (Don't Forget Me) [2016/17 b83p: b17g⁴ May 13] won both starts in points: modest form in 2 bumpers, staying-on fourth of 14 at Aintree only outing in 2016/17. *Paul Nicholls* — **b83**

BILLBUSHAY (IRE) 8 b.g. Westerner – Oscareen (IRE) (Oscar (IRE)) [2016/17 h16d h17m h16.3m⁴ h18.5g² Jul 25] fairly useful handicap hurdler: left Sean Byrne after second start: stays 2¼m: acts on good to firm and good to soft going: tried in cheekpieces/tongue tie. *David Bridgwater* — **h121**

BILL D'ARON (FR) 6 ch.g. Dom Alco (FR) – Nobless d'Aron (FR) (Ragmar (FR)) [2016/17 h–: h19.3m³ May 5] thrice-raced hurdler, first form when third in novice at Carlisle on sole outing in 2016/17: tried in hood. *James Ewart* — **h94**

BILLERAGH MILAN (IRE) 10 b.g. Milan – Billeragh Thyne (IRE) (Good Thyne (USA)) [2016/17 c20.9g⁵ c16dᵖᵘ Jun 16] lightly-raced maiden hurdler/chaser, little form: in headgear last 2 starts. *David Bridgwater* — **c– / h–**

BILLINGSLEY (IRE) 5 b.g. Millenary – Retain That Magic (IRE) (Presenting) **b88**
[2016/17 b16.3d³ b16s⁴ Dec 27] €23,000 3-y-o: second foal: dam (h87) winning pointer/
maiden hurdler (stayed 2½m): fair form in bumpers: better effort when fourth at Chepstow.
Alastair Ralph

BILLY BILLY (IRE) 7 b.m. Darsi (FR) – Mrs Gordi (Classic Cliche (IRE)) [2016/17 **c104**
h113, b101: c16s⁴ c17s^F c23.4v³ c18v⁶ c23.8g^pu Apr 26] point/bumper winner: fair winning **h–**
hurdler: fair form over fences: stays 3m: acts on heavy going: tried in tongue tie. *Stuart
Crawford, Ireland*

BILLY BRONCO 6 ch.g. Central Park (IRE) – Nan (Buckley) [2016/17 b105: h18.9v³ **h118**
h21.9v² h24.3v* h21.5s⁴ Mar 10] useful form when successful on only start in bumpers:
fairly useful form over hurdles: won maiden at Ayr in January, left in lead 2 out: stays 3m:
raced only on soft/heavy going. *Evan Williams*

BILLY CONGO (IRE) 10 b.g. Zagreb (USA) – Delicate Child (IRE) (Son of Sharp Shot **h–**
(IRE)) [2016/17 h108: h20m May 19] winning pointer: handicap hurdler, fair at best: stays
27f: acts on good to firm and good to soft going: wears tongue tie: often races towards rear.
Richard Hawker

BILLY CUCKOO (IRE) 11 b.g. Alderbrook – First Battle (IRE) (Un Desperado (FR)) **c– §**
[2016/17 c19.4g May 4] big gelding: multiple point winner: maiden hurdler: fairly useful **h–**
chaser at best: stays 2½m: acts on heavy going: wears headgear: tried in tongue tie: not
straightforward (often races lazily). *T. H. Messenger*

BILLY ELLIOTT 5 gr.g. Schiaparelli (GER) – Ladylliat (FR) (Simon du Desert (FR)) **b–**
[2016/17 b15.7d b15.8g⁵ Apr 17] showed little in 2 bumpers. *Kim Bailey*

BILLY HICKS 6 b.g. Kayf Tara – Michelle's Ella (IRE) (Ela-Mana-Mou) [2016/17 h16s **h110**
h21v⁶ h15.8s* h19.5v* Mar 23] brother to fairly useful chaser Like It A Lot (2m winner),
stayed 2½m, and a winning pointer, and half-brother to winner on Flat in Italy by Ishiguru:
dam well beaten on Flat: runner-up in point on debut: fair form over hurdles: won novice
at Ludlow and novice handicap at Chepstow, both in March: should stay beyond 19f: in
hood last 2 starts. *Samuel Drinkwater*

BILLY MY BOY 8 b.g. Volochine (IRE) – Key West (FR) (Highest Honor (FR)) [2016/17 **h108**
h100: h16.8m^ur h16g² h16.8m³ h15.3m* h19s⁴ h16.5g³ h16.5m² h19g⁶ h16g h16m* Apr
28] fair handicap hurdler: won at Wincanton in October and Chepstow in April: stays 19f:
acts on soft and good to firm going: has worn headgear, including last 4 starts: tried in
tongue tie: front runner/races prominently. *Chris Down*

BILLY NO NAME (IRE) 9 b.g. Westerner – Just Little (Mtoto) [2016/17 c–, h130: **c–**
h21.6d⁶ h19.5v* h23.6s⁵ h23.4v h23.5m Apr 2] neat gelding: useful handicap hurdler: won **h130**
at Lingfield (by 2½ lengths from Earls Fort) in November: let down by jumping only start
in chases: stays 3m: acts on heavy going. *Colin Tizzard*

BILLY'S HOPE (IRE) 6 b.m. King's Theatre (IRE) – Lady Bellingham (IRE) (Montelimar **h130**
(USA)) [2016/17 h19d* h16.5g⁵ h19.5g³ h20g³ h20d³ h23.1d* h24d⁶ h22.7d⁴ h24d² h24d
Apr 27] closely related to several winners by Old Vic, including useful hurdler/smart
chaser In Compliance (2m-2¾m winner) and fair hurdler/smart chaser One Cool Cookie
(19f-3¼m winner), and half-sister to 21f chase winner Wish In A Well (by Gamut): dam
unraced: bumper winner: useful hurdler: won mares maiden at Limerick in May and novice
at Thurles in November: good second in novice handicap at Fairyhouse (4½ lengths behind
Returntovendor) in April: stays 3m: acts on heavy going: in tongue tie last 5 starts: often
travels strongly. *Mrs J. Harrington, Ireland*

BILLY TWO TONGUES 9 b.g. Heron Island (IRE) – Ranahinch (IRE) (Persian Mews) **c119**
[2016/17 c22.5d⁴ c25.5g* c24g² c27.5g^pu Aug 18] winning hurdler: fairly useful form in **h–**
chases: won novice handicap at Uttoxeter in May and handicap at Fontwell in June: stays
25f: acts on heavy going. *Jeremy Scott*

BILZIC (FR) 6 b.g. Axxos (GER) – Izellane (FR) (Funny Baby (FR)) [2016/17 h86p, b94: **h–**
h19.6g⁵ Apr 29] angular gelding: lightly-raced maiden hurdler: placed in points in
December/April: in tongue tie last 4 starts. *Dan Skelton*

BIM BAM BOUM (FR) 6 b.g. Crossharbour – Quobalt (FR) (Ragmar (FR)) [2016/17 **h–**
h116: h19.6v^pu Nov 9] maiden hurdler, fairly useful at best: stayed 19f: acted on heavy
going: dead. *Harry Fry*

BINCOMBE 9 gr.g. Indian Danehill (IRE) – Siroyalta (FR) (Royal Charter (FR)) [2016/17 **c120**
c117, h–: c21d⁴ c23g* c23m^pu Aug 17] tall gelding: maiden hurdler: fairly useful handicap **h–**
chaser: won at Worcester in July: stays 23f: acts on heavy going: has worn blinkers/tongue
tie. *Philip Hobbs*

BINDON MILL 8 b.g. Tamure (IRE) – Singing Cottage (Greensmith) [2016/17 h110, b91: h19.5d⁴ h23.1v² c19.2v⁵ c24.2s* c24.2d⁴ Mar 21] fair maiden hurdler: fairly useful form in chases: won novice handicap at Exeter in January: will stay long distances: raced only on ground softer than good: often races towards rear. *Victor Dartnall* **c120 h106**

BINGE DRINKER (IRE) 8 b.g. Spadoun (FR) – Our Honey (IRE) (Old Vic) [2016/17 c19.4g* Nov 6] useful hurdler: off 19 months, 11/4, useful form when winning 3-runner novice at Ffos Las on chasing debut by 4 lengths from Might Bite: stays 3m: acts on heavy going: has joined Paul Nicholls: capable of better over fences. *Rebecca Curtis* **c140 p h–**

BINGO CONTI (FR) 6 b.g. Coastal Path – Regina Conti (FR) (Lavirco (GER)) [2016/17 b18s b16.2f* h22.1m² h24g⁵ h19.9g h25.3s^F Feb 28] €46,000 3-y-o: first foal: dam, French 1½m bumper winner, half-sister to dam of Silviniaco Conti: fair form in bumpers: won at Perth in June: fair form over hurdles: running well when falling last (likely to have finished second) in handicap at Catterick final outing: left Gordon Elliott after third start: stays 25f. *Richard Ford* **h105 b89**

BINGO D'OLIVATE (FR) 6 b.g. Laverock (IRE) – Ombrelle de L'Orme (FR) (Marchand de Sable (USA)) [2016/17 h120: h16d⁵ h15.8v^pu h19g^pu h15.8s c20s^F Apr 1] angular gelding: fairly useful handicap hurdler: lost form after reappearance: hampered and fell first on chasing debut: unproven beyond 2m: acts on heavy going: has worn headgear, including in 2016/17. *Noel Williams* **c– h117**

BINOWAGH BAY (IRE) 9 b.m. Flemensfirth (USA) – Sarah O'Malley (IRE) (Bob Back (USA)) [2016/17 h102: h20d h18.2g h20d h22.5d h22.7s² h22.2g h23.3v⁵ Nov 20] well held completed start in points: modest handicap hurdler: stays 25f: acts on soft going: has worn cheekpieces. *Brian M. McMahon, Ireland* **h97**

BIRCH BANK 4 b.g. Multiplex – Dolly Duff (Alflora (IRE)) [2016/17 b16d Mar 21] tongue tied when well held in bumper. *William Kinsey* **b–**

BIRCH HILL (IRE) 7 b.g. Kalanisi (IRE) – Miss Compliance (IRE) (Broken Hearted) [2016/17 h122: h16.7g* h20.6g* h19.5g^pu Oct 9] well-made gelding: won completed start in Irish points: fairly useful hurdler: won maiden at Market Rasen in July and novice there in August: reportedly lame final outing: stays 21f: acts on good to soft going: in tongue tie last 3 starts: usually races close up. *Sophie Leech* **h122**

BIRCH VALE (IRE) 5 br.m. Presenting – Oscar Rebel (IRE) (Oscar (IRE)) [2016/17 b16d⁶ b15.8s Apr 1] £14,000 3-y-o: first foal: dam (h140) 2¼m/2½m hurdle winner: modest form on first of 2 starts in bumpers. *Donald McCain* **b76**

BIRETTA 6 ch.m. Kirkwall – Burqa (Nashwan (USA)) [2016/17 h95, b79: h19.9g h16.7d^pu h15.8g h15.8d h21.2g^pu Nov 10] poor maiden hurdler: unproven beyond 2m: acts on good to soft going: in blinkers last 3 starts: has worn tongue tie: temperamental. *Oliver Greenall* **h55 §**

BISCUIT 6 ch.m. Black Sam Bellamy (IRE) – Falcon's Gunner (Gunner B) [2016/17 b15.7g² b15.7d⁴ b16.7g³ Mar 25] first foal: dam (b85), third both starts in bumpers/well held only start over hurdles, half-sister to fairly useful hurdler/chaser (stays 3m) Kilronan High: fair form in bumpers: left John Weymes after first start: should be suited by further than 2m. *Kim Bailey* **b86**

BISE D'ESTRUVAL (FR) 6 b.m. Kingsalsa (USA) – Option d'Estruval (FR) (Epervier Bleu) [2016/17 h20v^ur c16d^pu c18.2g^F Mar 20] third foal: half-sister to useful hurdler Aurore d'Estruval (2m-2½m winner, by Nickname): dam French 17f hurdle winner: maiden hurdler, modest form for Guillaume Macaire in 2015/16: failed to complete both starts over fences: stays 2¼m: acts on good to soft going: in tongue tie final start: sold £6,500 in May. *Nigel Twiston-Davies* **c– h–**

BISHOP OF BLING (IRE) 4 b.g. Big Bad Bob (IRE) – Convent Girl (IRE) (Bishop of Cashel) [2016/17 h16.8s h16.6g⁴ h16.2v⁴ Jan 11] fair maiden on Flat, stays 1½m: modest form in juvenile hurdles. *Dr Richard Newland* **h96**

BISHOPS COURT 7 b.g. Helissio (FR) – Island of Memories (IRE) (Beneficial) [2016/17 h106, b–: h23s⁴ h20d³ c19.3d^F c16.5d⁴ c17.4s* c19.2v* c20.2s* c20.2d* c21.1v⁵ Mar 5] tall gelding: fair maiden hurdler: useful handicap chaser: won at Fontwell in December and January, and at Wincanton later in January (novice event) and in February: likely to prove best up to 21f: acts on heavy going: wears headgear/tongue tie: usually travels strongly. *Neil Mulholland* **c132 h103**

BISHOPS ROAD (IRE) 9 b.g. Heron Island (IRE) – Nice Resemblance (IRE) (Shernazar) **c146**
[2016/17 c150, h–: c23.4s⁴ c29.5s c24.1s³ c34.3dᵖᵘ Apr 8] compact gelding: winning **h–**
hurdler: smart handicap chaser: best effort of 2016/17 when 9 lengths fourth to Otago Trail
in Rehearsal Chase at Newcastle in November: stays 3½m: acts on heavy going: has worn
cheekpieces: usually races nearer last than first. *Kerry Lee*

BISHOP WULSTAN (IRE) 6 b.g. Oratorio (IRE) – Laurentine (USA) (Private Account **h– §**
(USA)) [2016/17 h97§: h23g Jul 21] sturdy gelding: modest handicap hurdler nowadays:
won point in April: stays 2¾m: acts on good to firm and heavy going: wears headgear:
usually in tongue tie: best treated with caution. *Peter Bowen*

BISOUBISOU 5 b.m. Champs Elysees – Marathea (FR) (Marathon (USA)) [2016/17 **h–**
b17.7d h16s Nov 21] fifth foal: half-sister to bumper winner Madame Trigger (by Double **b–**
Trigger): dam (h89), 19f-3m hurdle winner, also 9.5f/1¼m winner on Flat, half-sister to
useful hurdler up to 2½m Zanir: well beaten in mares bumper and novice hurdle.
Dan Skelton

BISTOURI D'HONORE (FR) 5 b.g. Ballingarry (IRE) – Elivette (FR) (Arvico (FR)) **h109**
[2016/17 b16.8g⁶ h21.6m* h23.9m³ h23.8g⁶ h23.9gᵖᵘ h19.8fᵖᵘ Apr 23] €48,000 3-y-o: **b85**
well-made gelding: second foal: half-brother to bumper winner Calva d'Honore (by
Khalkevi): dam, ran once on Flat in France, half-sister to fairly useful French hurdler/fair
chaser (17f/2¼m winner) Eliga: runner-up on completed start in maiden points: sixth in
bumper at Newton Abbot: fair form over hurdles: won novice at Exeter in November: stays
2¾m: acts on good to firm going: usually races close up. *Paul Nicholls*

BITE THE BISCUIT (IRE) 5 b.g. Getaway (GER) – Kiltoome Scot (IRE) (Oscar **h85**
(IRE)) [2016/17 b15.7s⁴ h19.5v h19g h19g² Apr 6] €10,000 3-y-o: third foal: half-brother **b82**
to a winning pointer by Beneficial: dam, failed to complete in points, half-sister to smart
hurdler/chaser (stayed 3¼m) Boss Doyle: third in Irish maiden point: modest form in
bumper/over hurdles. *Philip Hobbs*

BIT OF A BARNEY (IRE) 14 b.g. Heron Island (IRE) – Soft Tone (IRE) (Buckskin **c–**
(FR)) [2016/17 c20.2sᵖᵘ Feb 28] dual winning pointer: pulled up in maiden hunter on
chasing debut. *C. W. Loggin*

BIT SPICY (IRE) 6 gr.m. Tikkanen (USA) – Like A Bolt (IRE) (Lahib (USA)) [2016/17 **h–**
b17.7g b16d⁵ b16.8g⁶ h15.9g⁶ h15.9m⁴ Apr 16] first foal: dam unraced: poor form in **b62**
bumpers: no form over hurdles. *Steve Woodman*

BITTER VIRTUE 6 b.m. Lucarno (USA) – Avoine (IRE) (Saddlers' Hall (IRE)) [2016/17 **h94**
b83: h16d⁵ h15.7s⁴ h20.3g⁴ h18.7m h18.7m h20m⁵ h20.3m³ h20.3g Apr 21] rather leggy
mare: modest maiden hurdler: stays 2½m: acts on good to firm going: in tongue tie last 4
starts. *David Dennis*

BITUMEN BELLE (IRE) 5 b.m. Oscar (IRE) – Midnight Pond (IRE) (Long Pond) **b–**
[2016/17 b16.4s Jan 7] €25,000 3-y-o: half-sister to several winners, including useful
hurdler My Wigwam Or Yours (21f winner, by Beneficial) and fairly useful hurdler Hidden
Agent (2¼m-3m winner, by Pistolet Bleu): dam unraced: tailed off in mares bumper.
Philip Kirby

BIVOUAC (FR) 6 b.g. Califet (FR) – Pazadena (FR) (Ragmar (FR)) [2016/17 h135: **c127**
c19.2s² c15.9s* c24m² Apr 4] lengthy, good sort: useful hurdler: fairly useful form over **h–**
fences: won maiden at Leicester in March: stays 2½m: acts on heavy going, probably on
good to firm: tried in cheekpieces. *Nicky Henderson*

BLACKADDER 5 b.g. Myboycharlie (IRE) – Famcred (Inchinor) [2016/17 h73: h15.3m⁴ **h76 x**
h15.9g h16d Jun 19] poor maiden hurdler: will prove best at sharp 2m: acts on good to firm
going: has worn hood, including last 5 starts: often races in rear: often let down by jumping.
Mark Gillard

BLACK ANTHEM (IRE) 5 b.g. Royal Anthem (USA) – Rockababy (IRE) (King's **h105**
Ride) [2016/17 b16s h15.3v⁶ h15.3d⁵ h18.5d³ h15.7s⁵ Mar 16] €22,000 3-y-o: half-brother **b–**
to several winners, including useful hurdler/chaser Horizontal Speed (17f-2½m winner, by
Vertical Speed), stays 3m, and useful chaser Florida Express (3m winner, by Florida Son):
dam unraced half-sister to smart staying chaser D'Argent: in frame twice from 4 starts in
Irish maiden points: behind in bumper: fair form over hurdles: front runner/races
prominently. *Brian Barr*

BLACK ART 5 ch.g. Black Sam Bellamy (IRE) – Art Series (Kalanisi (IRE)) [2016/17 **b85**
b16g b16v³ Mar 23] third foal: dam unraced: fair form in bumpers: left Simon Hodgson/off
7 months, showed more than on debut when third of 5 to Dessinateur at Chepstow: sold
£16,000 in May. *Emma Lavelle*

BLACKBERRY WINE (FR) 4 b.g. Naaqoos – Khadidja (FR) (Trempolino (USA)) **b–**
[2016/17 b16.3g Mar 25] collapsed and died after well held in bumper. *Oliver Sherwood*

BLACK BUBLE (FR) 4 b.g. Valanour (IRE) – Miss Bubble Rose (FR) (Sevres Rose **h94**
(IRE)) [2016/17 b16s h16s h15.8s h19.7d h18.7g³ Apr 15] first foal: dam, ran 3 times over
hurdles in France, sister to fairly useful French hurdler/chaser (17f/2¼m winner) Tigresse
Rose: modest form over hurdles: best effort at 19f: front runner/races prominently, often
races freely. *Tony Carroll*

BLACK CAESAR (IRE) 6 b.g. Bushranger (IRE) – Evictress (IRE) (Sharp Victor **h–**
(USA)) [2016/17 h15.9dᵘʳ h15.9gᵘʳ Nov 28] fair on Flat, stays 1m: unseated first both starts
in novice hurdles. *Philip Hide*

BLACK CORTON (FR) 6 br.g. Laverock (IRE) – Pour Le Meilleur (FR) (Video Rock **c– p**
(FR)) [2016/17 h116p, b–: h16.8g³ h18.5g* h16m* c18s² h19g* h19.8g⁴ Apr 29] bumper **h135**
winner: useful hurdler: won novice at Newton Abbot and listed novice at Kempton (by 10
lengths from New Agenda) in October, and handicap at Taunton (by 1¼ lengths from Space
Oddity) in April: tailed off in novice on chasing debut: stays 2½m: acts on good to firm
going: wears hood/tongue tie: should do better over fences. *Paul Nicholls*

BLACKDOWN HILLS 7 b.m. Presenting – Lady Prunella (IRE) (Supreme Leader) **h57**
[2016/17 h–, b83: h20g⁴ Jul 21] bumper winner: little impact in 2 novice hurdles: should
stay at least 2½m. *Mark Bradstock*

BLACKFIRE (FR) 6 b.g. Kingsalsa (USA) – Sister Celestine (Bishop of Cashel) **h94**
[2016/17 h104: h16.7g³ h15.9dꟳ h19.7s h16s h16.2v h16.8s⁵ h19g⁵ Mar 30] rather leggy
gelding: modest maiden hurdler: left Jonjo O'Neill after second start: unproven beyond
17f: acts on soft going: has worn headgear: usually races nearer last than first. *Tom Symonds*

BLACK HAWK (IRE) 8 b.g. Craigsteel – Coolharbour Lady (IRE) (Lord Americo) **h79**
[2016/17 h–: h20.6g⁴ h20.3gᵖᵘ h16g⁴ h21mᵖᵘ Oct 5] poor form over hurdles: tried in hood.
Fergal O'Brien

BLACK HERCULES (IRE) 8 b.g. Heron Island (IRE) – Annalecky (IRE) (Bob's **c156**
Return (IRE)) [2016/17 c154p, h–: c20d⁵ c17d⁴ c20d³ Jan 19] well-made gelding: winning **h–**
hurdler: very smart chaser: back to form when 14½ lengths third of 6 to Sizing John in
Kinloch Brae Chase at Thurles final start: stays 3m: acts on heavy going. *W. P. Mullins,
Ireland*

BLACK ICEMAN 9 gr.g. Iceman – Slite (Mind Games) [2016/17 h98: h18.7m h15.7gᵖᵘ **h–**
Oct 3] modest hurdler at best, no form in 2016/17: should stay beyond 2m. *Lydia Pearce*

BLACK INK 6 b.g. Black Sam Bellamy (IRE) – Incony (Daggers Drawn (USA)) [2016/17 **h–**
b92: h16.2dᵖᵘ Apr 30] fair form in bumpers: in cheekpieces, pulled up in seller on hurdling
debut. *Michael Smith*

BLACK IS BLACK (IRE) 4 b.g. Big Bad Bob (IRE) – Dazzling Dancer (Nashwan **b–**
(USA)) [2016/17 b14d Oct 30] well held in junior bumper/maiden on Flat. *Michael Easterby*

BLACK IVORY 5 b.g. Revoque (IRE) – Annie's Gift (IRE) (Presenting) [2016/17 b82: **h113**
b16.7g³ b16.2d* h20.1d³ h20.1g* h19.9v* h18.1s² h20.2g⁴ Apr 27] useful-looking gelding: **b95**
fairly useful form in bumpers: won at Hexham in June: fair form over hurdles: won maiden
at Hexham in October and handicap at Uttoxeter in November: stays 2½m: acts on heavy
going: front runner/races prominently, often travels strongly. *Malcolm Jefferson*

BLACK JACK JAXON 5 gr.g. Fair Mix (IRE) – No Virtue (Defacto (USA)) [2016/17 **b–**
b14d b15.7s Jan 31] well held in 2 bumpers. *Steve Flook*

BLACK MISCHIEF 5 b.g. Black Sam Bellamy (IRE) – Miss Mitch (IRE) (King's **h121 p**
Theatre (IRE)) [2016/17 b94p: h17.7d³ h14d³ h15.3sꟳ Jan 19] fair form in bumpers: in **b93**
control when fell last in novice won by Monsieur Co at Wincanton on hurdling debut, 3
lengths up and going further clear at time: open to improvement. *Harry Fry*

BLACK NARCISSUS (IRE) 8 b.m. Westerner – Arcanum (IRE) (Presenting) [2016/17 **c105**
c94, h100: c24.2s³ h25.5s⁵ c20.2s² c25.2s* c25.1dʳᵒ h26v³ c22.2gᵖᵘ Apr 15] fair handicap **h102**
hurdler: fair handicap chaser: won at Catterick in February: stays 3¼m: acts on heavy
going: usually races nearer last than first: temperament under suspicion (has run out).
Alexandra Dunn

BLACK NIGIIT (IRE) 5 b.h. Excellent Art – Starfish (IRE) (Galileo (IRE)) [2016/17 **h89**
h15.3v⁵ h21v Feb 11] half-brother to fair hurdler Next Edition (17f winner, by Antonius
Pius), stays 21f: useful on Flat, stays 1½m: modest form in novice hurdles: better effort
when fifth at Wincanton in February. *James Moon, Jersey*

BLACK OP (IRE) 6 br.g. Sandmason – Afar Story (IRE) (Desert Story (IRE)) [2016/17 **b111** b16.6g* b17g Apr 7] £210,000 5-y-o: good-topped gelding: fourth foal: dam, pulled up all 4 starts in points, half-sister to useful hurdler (stays 3m) Younevercall: won Irish maiden point on debut: useful form in bumpers: won at Doncaster (by 2¼ lengths from Claimantakinforgan) in February: well-backed 10/3, below expectations when 9 lengths ninth of 19 to Lalor in Grade 2 event at Aintree. *Tom George*

BLACK SAM 7 ch.m. Black Sam Bellamy (IRE) – Amaretto Rose (Alflora (IRE)) **b87** [2016/17 b16g² b17gᵖᵘ Oct 23] fair form in bumpers: pulled up lame final start. *Alan King*

BLACK SAM BELLA 5 b.m. Black Sam Bellamy (IRE) – Newton Mo (Homo Sapien) **b98** [2016/17 b15.8s² Apr 1] £35,000 5-y-o: fifth foal: dam, pulled up in maiden point, half-sister to Champion Bumper winner/smart chaser (17f-21f winner) Missed That and fairly useful hurdler/useful chaser (stayed 3m) Kia Kaha: won point on debut: 6/1, shaped well when 1¼ lengths second of 12 to Urca de Lima in mares bumper at Uttoxeter: will be suited by 2½m. *Dan Skelton*

BLACK SAM THE MAN 7 b.g. Black Sam Bellamy (IRE) – Sonda (IRE) (Dolphin **c106** Street (FR)) [2016/17 h103, b83: h20v c20.2m⁴ c20d⁵ c25g* c25d⁶ c25.5gᵖᵘ Aug 27] **h82** winning pointer: poor maiden hurdler: fair form over fences: won handicap at Kilbeggan in August: stayed 25f: acted on soft going: sometimes wore tongue tie: dead. *John Joseph Hanlon, Ireland*

BLACK THUNDER (FR) 10 bl.g. Malinas (GER) – Blackmika (FR) (Subotica (FR)) **c130** [2016/17 c–, h–: c23.4v* c23.4v² c26.3gᵖᵘ c21.1gᶠ Apr 6] good-topped gelding: winning **h–** hurdler: useful chaser: won hunter at Kelso in January by 1¼ lengths from Dolatulo: stays 27f: acts on heavy going: in cheekpieces last 2 starts: has worn tongue tie. *Warren Greatrex*

BLACK TULIP 5 ch.m. Black Sam Bellamy (IRE) – Combe Florey (Alflora (IRE)) **h88** [2016/17 b15.7d h16.8s⁴ h18.5m⁴ Apr 15] fourth foal: closely related to bumper winner/ **b–** fairly useful hurdler Kayfleur (2½m-21f winner, by Kayf Tara) and half-sister to bumper winner/useful hurdler Meet The Legend (2m winner, by Midnight Legend): dam (h87), maiden hurdler (stayed 2½m), half-sister to smart hurdler/chaser (stayed 25f) Young Spartacus: well beaten in mares bumper: modest form in mares novice hurdles. *Henry Daly*

BLACK VALENTINE (IRE) 6 b.g. Stowaway – Kavolan (IRE) (Supreme Leader) **h116** [2016/17 h21.4d* h21.4s³ h23.9s h25.6g³ Apr 12] €19,000 3-y-o: first foal: dam of little account: point winner: fairly useful form when winning novice at Wincanton in November on hurdling debut: disappointing subsequently: should stay at least 3m: tried in cheekpieces. *Paul Nicholls*

BLACK WARRIOR (IRE) 7 b.g. Trans Island – Faeroe Isle (IRE) (Erins Isle) [2016/17 **h129** h19.5g* h21m* h20.7g⁴ h20g* h21.1g² h21gᵖᵘ Nov 6] €17,000 4-y-o: fourth foal: half-brother to fair hurdler/chaser Presence Felt (23f-25f winner, by Heron Island): dam placed in bumpers/poor maiden hurdler: fairly useful hurdler: won maiden at Clonmel in May, novice at Limerick in June and handicap at Cork in August: should stay 3m: acts on good to firm going: wears cheekpieces: often travels strongly. *Charles Byrnes, Ireland*

BLACKWATER KING (IRE) 9 b.g. Beneficial – Accordian Lady (IRE) (Accordion) **c–** [2016/17 c–§, h118§: h20.3vᵖᵘ c16g Jul 5] Irish point winner: fairly useful hurdler/fair **h– §** chaser at best: stays 2½m: acts on heavy going: in hood last 5 starts: tried in tongue tie: one to treat with caution. *Johnny Farrelly*

BLACKWELL SYNERGY (FR) 11 b.g. Antarctique (IRE) – Pyu (GER) (Surumu **c– x** (GER)) [2016/17 c–x, h101: h23.3sᵖᵘ h25g⁴ h23.3s⁵ h23.3g h24.5s h25gᵖᵘ Apr 28] **h95** angular gelding: modest handicap hurdler: winning chaser (sketchy jumper): stays 3m: acts on soft and good to firm going: has worn headgear: often races lazily. *Tracey Leeson*

BLACKWOOD ROVER (IRE) 9 b.g. Turtle Island (IRE) – Lady of Fleet (IRE) **c73** (Buckskin (FR)) [2016/17 c93, h–: h19.5v h15.9sᵖᵘ c19.9d³ c15.7g³ c19.9gᵖᵘ Apr 28] point **h–** winner: maiden hurdler, no form in 2016/17: poor maiden chaser: stays 3m: acts on heavy going: usually races towards rear. *J. R. Jenkins*

BLADES LAD 8 ch.g. Haafhd – Blades Girl (Bertolini (USA)) [2016/17 c110, h–: h16.7g **c–** May 6] sturdy gelding: maiden hurdler: fair handicap chaser: raced around 2m: acts on soft **h–** going: in cheekpieces last 5 starts. *Peter Niven*

BLADOUN (FR) 9 gr.g. Smadoun (FR) – Blabliramic (FR) (Panoramic) [2016/17 h109: **c100** c16.3g² c17g c16g⁵ c20v³ c15.7sᵖᵘ Feb 3] fair winning hurdler/maiden chaser: probably **h–** stays 19f: acts on heavy going: has worn headgear/tongue tie. *Michael Blake*

BLAGAPAR (FR) 6 b.g. Al Namix (FR) – Samarkand Bleue (FR) (Sleeping Car (FR)) **h117 p**
[2016/17 h15.7v* h18.7m* h20g⁴ Aug 11] first foal: dam unraced half-sister to useful
hurdler/fairly useful chaser (stayed 2¾m) Queiros Bleu: fourth on completed start in
maiden points: fairly useful form over hurdles: won maiden at Southwell in June and
novice handicap at Stratford in July: should stay 2½m: remains with potential. *Dr
Richard Newland*

BLAIRS COVE 5 b.g. Presenting – Raitera (FR) (Astarabad (USA)) [2016/17 b16d³ **h129 p**
b16d³ b16g⁵ h20.3g² Apr 19] €24,000 3-y-o: second foal: dam unraced half-sister to top- **b93**
class chaser (best around 2m) Golden Silver: fair form in bumpers for P. Twomey: 40/1, 6
lengths second to William Henry in novice at Cheltenham on hurdling debut: in tongue tie
last 2 starts: open to improvement. *Dan Skelton*

BLAKE DEAN 9 b.g. Halling (USA) – Antediluvian (Air Express (IRE)) [2016/17 c–, **c91**
h86§: h22.1g h20.2d³ h20g³ h16.2s* h20.2s⁴ c16.4g² h16.2g* c20.1d⁴ c17.4g⁴ h17.7d **h95**
c17.4sᵖᵘ h17.7vᵖᵘ h17.7g⁴ Apr 21] rather sparely-made gelding: modest handicap hurdler:
won at Perth in July and September: modest form over fences: left Gordon Elliott after
ninth start: stays 2½m: acts on heavy going: usually wears headgear/tongue tie: none too
reliable. *Chris Gordon*

BLAKEMOUNT (IRE) 9 br.g. Presenting – Smashing Leader (IRE) (Supreme Leader) **c133**
[2016/17 c131, h–: c19.3d² c24g⁵ c19.4s³ c21.4s⁴ c26.2s* c24.5d² c33.4s⁵ c31.8g⁶ Apr 22] **h–**
compact gelding: winning hurdler: useful handicap chaser: won at Carlisle in February:
creditable efforts most other starts, on last 2 fifth of 20 to Chase The Spud in Midlands
Grand National at Uttoxeter and sixth of 30 to Vicente in Scottish Grand National at Ayr:
stays 33f: acts on heavy going: front runner/races prominently. *Sue Smith*

BLAKERIGG (IRE) 6 b.g. Presenting – Azalea (IRE) (Marju (IRE)) [2016/17 b90p: **h–**
h16d⁵ h22.7sᵖᵘ Dec 29] fairly useful form only start in bumpers: disappointing in 2 runs
over hurdles. *Nicky Richards*

BLAKLION 8 b.g. Kayf Tara – Franciscaine (FR) (Legend of France (USA)) [2016/17 **c158**
c150, h–: c24.2g⁴ c26g⁵ c24.2s³ c28.4d² c34.3d⁴ Apr 8] angular gelding: winning hurdler: **h–**
very smart handicap chaser: good 3¼ lengths second to Vieux Lion Rouge in Grand
National Trial at Haydock in February: 8/1, better than result when 8¾ lengths fourth of 40
to One For Arthur in Grand National at Aintree final start, doing too much too soon (went
on 4 out and briefly clear after next): stays 4¼m: acts on heavy going: tried in hood: often
travels strongly. *Nigel Twiston-Davies*

BLAKOLIVE (IRE) 5 br.m. Kalanisi (IRE) – Senorita Rumbalita (Alflora (IRE)) **h–**
[2016/17 b15.7d h16d h19.7d h16.2s⁴ h20.3g h24.1m Apr 13] €33,000 3-y-o: third foal: **b–**
half-sister to fair hurdler/chaser Havana Dancer (2m-21f winner, by Flemensfirth): dam
(c115/h124) 2m-21f hurdle/chase winner: well held in bumper/over hurdles: in headgear
last 2 starts. *Mark Walford*

BLAMEITALONMYROOTS (IRE) 7 b.m. Turtle Island (IRE) – Makingyourmindup **c123**
(IRE) (Good Thyne (USA)) [2016/17 c128, h–p: c23.8d³ c26dᵖᵘ c24s* c30.7s⁴ Mar 5] **h–**
angular mare: winning hurdler: fairly useful handicap chaser: won at Kempton in February:
should stay beyond 3m: best form on soft/heavy going. *Oliver Sherwood*

BLAMEITONTHEGOOSE 6 b.m. Dr Massini (IRE) – Senna da Silva (Prince of Birds **b–**
(USA)) [2016/17 b16g Sep 12] fifth foal: half-sister to useful/unreliable hurdler/chaser My
Brother Sylvest (2m-2¾m winner, by Bach): dam (h94) 2m/17f hurdle winner: tailed off in
bumper on debut. *John Flint*

BLANDFORDS GUNNER 8 b.g. Needle Gun (IRE) – Miss Millbrook (Meadowbrook) **c117**
[2016/17 c126, h110: c19.4d⁴ c15.7d⁴ c15.5d⁵ c17.4g² c19.4g⁵ Apr 23] rangy gelding: **h–**
maiden well held over hurdles: fairly useful handicap chaser: stays 19f: acts on soft and good to firm
going. *Harry Whittington*

BLANVILLE (FR) 6 gr.g. High Rock (IRE) – Paricolombieres (FR) (Lute Antique (FR)) **b–**
[2016/17 b15.3m⁵ b15.3vᵖᵘ Feb 2] no form in 2 bumpers. *Steven Dixon*

BLAZER (FR) 6 ch.g. Network (GER) – Juppelongue (FR) (Trebrook (FR)) [2016/17 **c136 p**
c110p, h141: c24v² c20v³ Jan 7] sturdy gelding: useful hurdler: better effort (useful form) **h–**
in maiden chases when 5½ lengths second to A Genie In Abottle at Fairyhouse in
December: stays 3m: acts on heavy going: often races prominently: remains with potential.
W. P. Mullins, Ireland

BLAZING BUCK 11 ch.g. Fraam – Anapola (GER) (Polish Precedent (USA)) [2016/17 **h95 §**
h26.5d² Jun 21] small gelding: handicap hurdler, modest nowadays: stays 3¼m: acts on
heavy going: tried in cheekpieces: temperamental. *Adrian Wintle*

BLAZING GLEN (IRE) 9 ch.g. Beneficial – Kofiyah's Rose (IRE) (Roselier (FR))   c–
[2016/17 c20s^{pu} c20d^{pu} h20g Jul 26] maiden hurdler/chaser: no form in 2016/17: stays   h–
2½m: acts on soft going. *Alan Jessop*

BLAZING WHALE 12 b.g. Classic Cliche (IRE) – Baby Whale (IRE) (Supreme Leader)   c100
[2016/17 c105: c25.5d^2 May 12] multiple winning pointer: fair maiden chaser: stays 25f:
acts on heavy going: in tongue tie last 2 starts. *E. Walker*

BLAZON 4 b.g. Dansili – Zante (Zafonic (USA)) [2016/17 ab16g* b15.8d^2 Mar 15]   b101
£13,500 3-y-o: brother to useful 6f/7f winner Top Offer, closely related to 11.5f-13f winner
Heart Locket and half-brother to 1¼m winner Kefalonia (by Mizzen Mast): dam useful
1m-1¼m winner: fairly useful form in bumpers: won junior event at Lingfield (by ¾ length
from Amateur) in December: neck second to Maria's Benefit at Huntingdon only other
start. *Kim Bailey*

BLENHEIM BROOK (IRE) 12 br.g. Alderbrook – Blenheim Blinder (IRE) (Mandalus)   c– §
[2016/17 c–§, h–: c24.2d h23.9d^{pu} Jun 29] strong, deep-girthed gelding: winning hurdler/   h–
chaser: stays 3½m: acts on heavy going: tried in cheekpieces: wears tongue tie: unreliable.
Lucinda Russell

BLESSED KING (IRE) 7 b.g. Desert King (IRE) – Lady Max (IRE) (Mandalus)   c–
[2016/17 h112, b99: h20.3m^3 c23m^4 h20g^2 h23d* Jul 13] placed in points/bumpers: fair   h103
hurdler: won maiden at Downpatrick final start: tailed off in maiden on chasing debut: stays
23f: acts on heavy going: often in headgear. *Gordon Elliott, Ireland*

BLESS THE WINGS (IRE) 12 b.g. Winged Love (IRE) – Silva Venture (IRE)   c145
(Mandalus) [2016/17 c143, h–: c33g h24d^6 c24d c30.2m^2 c24.5d c25d c30.2g^2 c29d^2 c30d^6 h115 +
Apr 29] sturdy gelding: fairly useful hurdler: useful chaser: good efforts when runner-up in
cross-country events at Cheltenham in December (handicap, beaten 9 lengths by Cantlow)
and March (9 lengths behind Cause of Causes): also ran well when runner-up for second
successive year in Irish Grand National (Handicap) at Fairyhouse in April (beaten 14
lengths by impressive Our Duke): stays 3¾m: acts on good to firm and heavy going: wears
headgear: has worn tongue tie, including final start: usually races towards rear. *Gordon
Elliott, Ireland*

BLETCHLEY CASTLE (IRE) 8 b.g. Dylan Thomas (IRE) – Zaafran (Singspiel (IRE))   h109
[2016/17 h96: h16.6s^2 h17.7g* h19.5g^2 Apr 8] point winner: fair handicap hurdler: won at
Fontwell in March: will prove best up to 19f: acts on soft going: in tongue tie last 3 starts:
front runner, strong traveller. *Seamus Durack*

BLEU BERRY (FR) 6 b.g. Special Kaldoun (IRE) – Somosierra (FR) (Blushing Flame   h143
(USA)) [2016/17 h109p, b–: h16v* h16s* h16s* h20g^5 Apr 28] bumper winner: useful
form over hurdles: won maiden at Fairyhouse in February, listed novice at Naas (by short
head from Outspoken) in March and Rathbarry & Glenview Studs Novices' Hurdle at
Fairyhouse (by 2¼ lengths from Outspoken) in April: may prove best at shorter than 2½m:
best form on soft/heavy going: tried in cheekpieces: often travels strongly. *W. P. Mullins,
Ireland*

BLEU ET NOIR (FR) 6 b.g. Enrique – Gastina (FR) (Pistolet Bleu (IRE)) [2016/17 h103, b78:   h125
h16.8s* h16.3d* h18.7g^2 h16.8g* h16g^F h16.3d^6 h15.9m^{pu} Apr 16] fairly useful hurdler:
won novices at Sedgefield in May, Stratford in June and Newton Abbot in August: stays
19f: acts on heavy going: wears hood: front runner, often races freely. *Tim Vaughan*

BLEU ET ROUGE (FR) 6 gr.g. Charming Groom (FR) – Lady du Renom (FR) (Art   c142
Francais (USA)) [2016/17 h145: c19d* c17g^{ur} c21.3s^4 Feb 12] lengthy gelding: smart   h–
hurdler: useful form when winning maiden at Leopardstown (by ¾ length from Gangster)
in December on chasing debut: let down by jumping at same course both subsequent starts:
should stay at least 2½m: acts on heavy going. *W. P. Mullins, Ireland*

BLINDING LIGHTS (IRE) 12 b.g. Snurge – Tender Return (IRE) (Strong Gale)   c98
[2016/17 c98: c20.2m^3 c25.1m^2 c22.6g^4 Apr 23] winning pointer: modest chaser: stays 25f:
acts on firm going: usually in cheekpieces: wears tongue tie. *Mary Sanderson*

BLOOD CRAZED TIGER (IRE) 6 b.g. King's Theatre (IRE) – Mardi Roberta (IRE)   h136
(Bob Back (USA)) [2016/17 b20g* h20d* h24d* h24g* h20s^3 h20g^F h18s^4 Feb 12]   b99
£82,000 3-y-o: third foal: dam (b93), 1¾m bumper winner, sister to fair hurdler/fairly
useful chaser up to 3m Big Rob: fairly useful bumper performer: won maiden at
Roscommon in May: useful form over hurdles: won maiden at Gowran and novice at Cork

in October, and listed novice at Cork (by 1¼ lengths from Screaming Rose) in November: third in Lawlor's Hotel Novices' Hurdle at Naas (9½ lengths behind Death Duty) in January): stays 3m: acts on soft going: wears hood: in tongue tie last 2 starts: front runner. *Gordon Elliott, Ireland*

BLOODY MARY (FR) 6 gr.m. Fragrant Mix (IRE) – Sacade (FR) (Robin des Champs (FR)) [2016/17 h132, b–: h16.3v⁶ Mar 4] smallish mare: bumper winner: useful hurdler in 2015/16, ran poorly only outing in 2016/17: will stay 2½m: often races prominently. *Nicky Henderson* **h—**

BLOODY NOSE (IRE) 5 b.g. Kalanisi (IRE) – Renvyle Society (IRE) (Moscow Society (USA)) [2016/17 b16d⁵ b16.6g Nov 25] no form in bumpers. *Mark Bradstock* **b—**

BLOSSOM AGAIN 6 b.m. Apple Tree (FR) – Millkom Elegance (Millkom) [2016/17 b–: b15.3m May 10] rather unfurnished mare: no form in bumpers. *Laura Young* **b—**

BLOTTOS (IRE) 5 b.g. Westerner – Autumn Beauty (IRE) (Darnay) [2016/17 b16.4s³ b16.8d³ b17d b16d⁶ Mar 31] €18,000 3-y-o: fifth foal: half-brother to fair hurdler Glowinginthedark (2¾m winner, by Dr Massini): dam unraced half-sister to useful hurdler/fairly useful chaser (stayed 3¼m) Prominent Profile: modest form in bumpers: will be suited by 2½m+. *Sue Smith* **b84**

BLUE APRIL (FR) 6 b.g. Blue Bresil (FR) – Royale Little (FR) (Garde Royale) [2016/17 h99§: h22mᵖᵘ h20.5g⁶ h23.9gᵖᵘ h19v h16.8d² Feb 24] compact gelding: poor maiden hurdler: unproven beyond 17f: acts on soft going: wears headgear: one to treat with caution (has refused). *Jeremy Scott* **h84 §**

BLUE BAY BOY 6 b.g. Blueprint (IRE) – Freydis (IRE) (Supreme Leader) [2016/17 h19.5gᵖᵘ h18.5sᵖᵘ h16.8s h19.7vᵖᵘ Feb 1] no form over hurdles: tried in tongue tie. *Richard Woollacott* **h—**

BLUE BICYCLE (USA) 11 b.g. Put It Back (USA) – Funicello (USA) (Anet (USA)) [2016/17 h16.2d⁴ Jun 4] maiden hurdler/chaser, fairly useful at one time: stays 2½m: acts on soft going: tried in tongue tie. *John Joseph Hanlon, Ireland* **c—**
h—

BLUE BULLET (FR) 6 b.g. Le Fou (IRE) – Jiletta (FR) (Passing Sale (FR)) [2016/17 b15.8g b15.7d² b13.6v² h17.7g Apr 12] €25,000 3-y-o, £15,000 4-y-o: third foal: half-brother to useful chaser Rileyev (2m-17f winner, by Goldneyev), stayed 2½m, and fairly useful French chaser Quakhdari (17f winner, by Akhdari): dam French 17f-19f chase winner: fair form in bumpers: well held in maiden at Fontwell on hurdling debut: tried in tongue tie. *Jamie Snowden* **h—**
b89

BLUE CANNON (IRE) 9 b.g. High Chaparral (IRE) – Blushing Barada (USA) (Blushing Groom (FR)) [2016/17 c–, h–§: h23.3dᵖᵘ h20.2dᵖᵘ Jun 30] winning hurdler/chaser: stays 2½m: acts on soft and good to firm going: has worn headgear: temperamental. *Valerie Jackson* **c—**
h— §

BLUE COMET 6 br.g. Blueprint (IRE) – Be My Valentine (IRE) (Be My Native (USA)) [2016/17 b65: b14d⁴ h21.2s⁴ h19g⁴ Mar 2] poor form in bumpers: fair form over hurdles: better effort, despite drop in trip, when fourth in novice at Taunton final start. *Fergal O'Brien* **h106**
b71

BLUE COURT (IRE) 6 b.m. Court Cave (IRE) – Bobazure (IRE) (Bob's Return (IRE)) [2016/17 h68: h21.2m⁵ h15.8g⁴ h15.7v⁴ h16sᵖᵘ Jan 8] modest form in mares events over hurdles. *Evan Williams* **h91**

BLUE COVE 12 ch.g. Karinga Bay – Meadow Blue (Northern State (USA)) [2016/17 h67: h20.6s h24.4d h27s h25.3s³ h27g³ Mar 29] workmanlike gelding: poor maiden hurdler: stays 3m: acts on heavy going: tried in cheekpieces: has worn tongue tie. *Lynn Siddall* **h65**

BLUE HERON (IRE) 9 b.g. Heron Island (IRE) – American Chick (IRE) (Lord Americo) [2016/17 c17.2g² c15.2d⁴ Nov 12] lengthy gelding: very smart hurdler in 2014/15, missed 2015/16: fairly useful form in novice chases at Market Rasen and Wetherby: stays 2½m: acts on soft going. *Dan Skelton* **c127**
h—

BLUE HUSSAR (IRE) 6 b.g. Montjeu (IRE) – Metaphor (USA) (Woodman (USA)) [2016/17 h18.6sᵖᵘ h16.6s² h16d* h18.1d* h16g² Apr 23] fairly useful on Flat, stays 1½m: fairly useful form over hurdles: won novices at Wetherby (conditionals) in March and Kelso in April: stays 2¼m: acts on good to soft going: usually races prominently/travels strongly. *Micky Hammond* **h118**

BLUE KANGAROO (FR) 4 b.g. Blue Bresil (FR) – Mascotte du Maine (FR) (Maresca Sorrento (FR)) [2016/17 b16.3g Mar 25] sturdy gelding: well held in Goffs UK Spring Sales Bumper at Newbury. *Paul Morgan* **b—**

BLUE KASCADE (IRE) 10 ch.g. Kaieteur (USA) – Lydia Blue (IRE) (Eve's Error)   **c116**
[2016/17 c112, h–: c26.2d⁵ c26.2m⁴ c20.1s⁵ c24.2g* c23.8d* c26.2s c24g⁶ c22.9vᵖᵘ   **h–**
c24.1gᵖᵘ Apr 15] winning hurdler: fairly useful handicap chaser: won at Wetherby in
October and Musselburgh in November: stays 3m: acts on soft going: usually in headgear.
Sandy Thomson

BLUE RAMBLER 7 b.g. Monsun (GER) – La Nuit Rose (FR) (Rainbow Quest (USA))   **h128**
[2016/17 h119: h19.7g* h24.4g² Dec 10] smallish, angular gelding: fairly useful form over
hurdles: won handicap at Wetherby in October: will prove best around 2½m: acts on soft
going. *Ian Williams*

BLUE RHYTHM (IRE) 5 b.g. Milan – Madame Jean (FR) (Cricket Ball (USA))   **h63**
[2016/17 h15.3s h15.8s⁵ h21.7d⁴ h21.9d⁶ Apr 16] well beaten in bumper: poor form in   **b–**
novice hurdles. *Evan Williams*

BLUESIDE BOY (IRE) 9 b.g. Blueprint (IRE) – Asidewager (IRE) (Brush Aside   **c63**
(USA)) [2016/17 c63, h–: c24.2g⁶ c25.5m Jun 24] sturdy gelding: winning Irish pointer: **h–**
poor maiden hurdler/chaser: stays 2¾m: acts on heavy going: has worn tongue tie: often
races prominently. *Harriet Graham*

BLUE SIRE (FR) 6 b.g. Day Flight – Hirlish (FR) (Passing Sale (FR)) [2016/17 b–:   **h103**
h17m⁶ h21.6dᵘʳ Jun 1] compact gelding: well held in bumper: 25/1, unseated rider 2 out
(looked likely to finish third) in novice won by El Bandit at Fontwell, better effort over
hurdles (returned lame). *Gary Moore*

BLUE SURF 8 ch.g. Excellent Art – Wavy Up (IRE) (Brustolon) [2016/17 h15.8m²   **h116**
h15.9g* h15.7d⁶ Dec 16] sturdy gelding: useful on Flat, stays 16.5f: fairly useful form over
hurdles: won maiden at Plumpton in October: stiff task final start. *Amanda Perrett*

BLUE TOP 8 b.g. Millkom – Pompey Blue (Abou Zouz (USA)) [2016/17 h76: h15.8g   **h69**
h16.7s⁶ h15.8d⁴ Mar 15] poor maiden hurdler: unproven beyond 17f: acts on soft going:
has worn cheekpieces, including in 2016/17: tried in tongue tie. *Dai Burchell*

BLYTHE PRINCE 5 b.g. Dutch Art – Arculinge (Paris House) [2016/17 h15.8vᵖᵘ Jan 28]   **h–**
poor maiden on Flat: showed nothing in conditionals maiden on hurdling debut.
Christopher Kellett

BLYTHE STAR (IRE) 5 b.g. Thewayyouare (USA) – Run To Jane (IRE) (Doyoun)   **h–**
[2016/17 h19.9gᵖᵘ Jun 26] poor maiden on Flat, stays 1¾m: showed nothing in maiden on
hurdling debut (wore blinkers). *Christopher Kellett*

BOAGRIUS (IRE) 5 ch.g. Beneficial – Greenhall Rambler (IRE) (Anshan) [2016/17   **h113**
b15.7d* h21.2s³ h19.4s² h16.5g² h20.6m⁴ Apr 9] €40,000 3-y-o, £50,000 4-y-o: fourth   **b104**
foal: brother to bumper winner/modest hurdler Benny's Secret (2¼m winner) and a
winning pointer: dam (c108/h115), 2¼m/2½m hurdle/chase winner, also 1¾m winner on
Flat: won completed start in points: also won bumper at Catterick (by 12 lengths from Blue
Bullet) in December: fair form over hurdles: usually leads: whipped round at start
penultimate outing. *Warren Greatrex*

BOA ISLAND (IRE) 7 b.g. Trans Island – Eskimo Kiss (IRE) (Distinctly North (USA))   **c126**
[2016/17 h100: h21.2g² c20.2m* c20.2m* c24.2gᶠ c23.6g³ c23g⁶ c23.4d⁶ c23.6g*   **h106**
c28.4mᵖᵘ Apr 27] strong gelding: won both starts in points: fair maiden over hurdles: fairly
useful handicap chaser: won at Wincanton in October (novice event) and November
(conditionals race), and at Chepstow (novice event) in April: stays 3m: acts on good to firm
going: tried in cheekpieces: wears tongue tie. *Paul Nicholls*

BOARD OF TRADE 6 ch.g. Black Sam Bellamy (IRE) – Realms of Gold (USA) (Gulch   **h122**
(USA)) [2016/17 h122: h21.6d² h21.1sᶠ h24.2d⁶ Nov 25] fairly useful handicap hurdler:
stays 3m: acts on soft going. *Alan King*

BOARDWALK EMPIRE (IRE) 10 b.g. Overbury (IRE) – Mighty Mandy (IRE)   **c–**
(Mandalus) [2016/17 c103, h–: c23.4dᵖᵘ Mar 24] good-bodied gelding: dual point winner: **h–**
winning hurdler: maiden chaser: stays 3m: acts on heavy going: tried in cheekpieces: in
tongue tie last 5 starts: often races prominently. *Kate Buckett*

BOBABOUT (IRE) 4 b.g. Big Bad Bob (IRE) – Chaperoned (IRE) (High Chaparral   **h123**
(IRE)) [2016/17 h16gᵘʳ h16s* h16dᵘʳ h16g² h16s⁵ h16s³ h16v h16.3d* Apr 27] fair maiden
on Flat, stays 13f: fairly useful hurdler: won juvenile at Listowel in September and
handicap at Punchestown on final start: raced only at 2m: acts on soft going: sometimes in
hood: often races freely. *Mrs J. Harrington, Ireland*

BOBBITS WAY 12 b.g. Overbury (IRE) – Bit of A Chick (Henbit (USA)) [2016/17 c86§,   **c– §**
h–: c19.7sᶠ Jan 2] workmanlike gelding: winning pointer: maiden hurdler: modest handicap   **h–**
chaser at best: stays 2½m: best form on soft/heavy going: wears cheekpieces: tried in
tongue tie: unreliable. *Alan Jones*

BOBBLE BORU (IRE) 9 b.m. Brian Boru – Balreask Lady (IRE) (Shardari) [2016/17 **c96 x** c105, h–: c20.3g^{ur} c16.3g^5 c20d^2 c16g^5 h15.8g^3 h15.8d^4 h19.7g h16d* h15.5g^2 h15.8d^3 **h103** h16s* h16.8s^3 h15.8s^4 h18.5d^5 h15.8s^4 h15.3m^3 h19.5g^5 h16m^5 Apr 28] angular mare: fair handicap hurdler: won mares events at Chepstow in November and January: handicap chaser, just modest form in 2016/17: left Venetia Williams after fourth start: stays 2½m: acts on heavy going: has worn headgear: usually leads: often let down by jumping over fences. *Matt Sheppard*

BOBBLE EMERALD (IRE) 9 ch.g. Rudimentary (USA) – Aunt Emeralds (IRE) **c–** (Roselier (FR)) [2016/17 c–, h112: h25d^{pu} h16.2d^4 h19.1g^{pu} h15.8m* h16m* h16.8g^3 **h112** h16.2s h16.5g^6 h16.3g^3 Apr 1] lengthy gelding: fair handicap hurdler: won at Ludlow in October and Lingfield in November: pulled up only start in chases: stays 3m, at least as effective at 2m: acts on good to firm and heavy going: wears headgear: has worn tongue tie: front runner/races prominently. *Martin Keighley*

BOBBY CULLEN (IRE) 11 ch.g. Bob Back (USA) – Peggy Cullen (IRE) (Presenting) **c–** [2016/17 c19.9m^{pu} Oct 30] dual winning pointer: in cheekpieces, pulled up in novice on chasing debut: dead. *Dai Williams*

BOBBY'S BABE 4 b.f. Big Bad Bob (IRE) – Express Logic (Air Express (IRE)) [2016/17 **h–** h16.2m^{pu} h16.7g^{pu} Jul 16] fair on Flat, stays 6f: pulled up both starts over hurdles. *Tim Easterby*

BOB FORD (IRE) 10 b.g. Vinnie Roe (IRE) – Polar Lamb (IRE) (Brush Aside (USA)) **c121 §** [2016/17 c135§, h–: h23.9g^4 c25.5d c29.2s^{pu} c23.8s^4 c23.8v^{pu} Mar 19] tall gelding: **h124 §** handicap hurdler/chaser, fairly useful nowadays: out-and-out stayer: acts very well on heavy going: has worn headgear, including final start: tried in tongue tie: temperamental. *Rebecca Curtis*

BOB LEWIS 11 b.g. Sir Harry Lewis (USA) – Teelyna (Teenoso (USA)) [2016/17 c94, **c91** h84§: h23g^5 c20d^5 c20g^3 c21g^4 h23m^4 Aug 17] winning pointer: modest maiden hurdler/ **h85** chaser: stays 3m: acts on soft and good to firm going: has worn headgear/tongue tie: usually races nearer last than first. *Stuart Kittow*

BOB MAHLER (IRE) 5 b.g. Mahler – Cooladurragh (IRE) (Topanoora) [2016/17 **h112** b15.8s^3 h20.5v^3 h19.7v^3 h20v^{ur} h24d^F Apr 27] €25,000 3-y-o: useful-looking gelding: **b92** second foal: dam unraced half-sister to fairly useful hurdler/chaser (stayed 3m) A Fine Young Man: third in bumper on debut: fair form over hurdles: should be suited by 3m: temperament under suspicion. *Warren Greatrex*

BOBO MAC (IRE) 6 gr.g. Whitmore's Conn (USA) – Blazing Love (IRE) (Fruits of **h123** Love (USA)) [2016/17 b16s^5 h16.5d^F b16d^3 b16d^3 h19v^2 h15.8d^2 h20.3s* Mar 20] second **b94** foal: dam unraced: fair bumper performer: fairly useful form over hurdles: won maiden at Southwell final outing: left M. Hourigan after fifth start: likely to stay further than 2½m: best form on soft/heavy going. *Tom Symonds*

BOBONYX 7 b.g. Phoenix Reach (IRE) – Twist The Facts (IRE) (Un Desperado (FR)) **c73** [2016/17 c–, h62: h19.9s^{pu} h23.9m^5 h20.6d h23v c21.1v^3 c24.5v^3 c21.7g^2 c23.6d^{pu} Mar 15] **h56** poor maiden hurdler/chaser: stays 3m: acts on heavy going: has worn headgear: tried in tongue tie: often races prominently. *Dai Williams*

BOB'S BOY 4 b.g. Showcasing – Tech Zinne (Zinaad) [2016/17 h16s^3 h16.7s^5 h15.8s^3 **h101** h16m^4 Apr 13] fair on Flat, stays 11.5f: fair form in juvenile hurdles. *Warren Greatrex*

BOB TUCKER (IRE) 10 b.g. Brian Boru – Acumen (IRE) (Phardante (FR)) [2016/17 **c127** c124, h–: c24g* c25.5g^5 c24.5d^5 c25.1m^4 c28.8d^4 c26d^5 c23.4s c23.8m^2 c24.1g^{pu} Apr 15] **h–** workmanlike gelding: winning handicap chaser: fairly useful handicap chaser: won at Kempton in May: stays 29f: acts on good to firm and heavy going: has worn headgear, including final start: tried in tongue tie. *Charlie Longsdon*

BOCASIEN DESBOIS (FR) 6 gr.g. Smadoun (FR) – Quocasienne (FR) (Ungaro **h71** (GER)) [2016/17 h19.3d h19.3d^6 h15.7g h16d Jan 24] off mark in Irish maiden points at fifth attempt: poor form in novice hurdles. *Martin Todhunter*

BODEGA 9 b.g. Grape Tree Road – Gurleigh (IRE) (Pivotal) [2016/17 c120, h111: h19.9s **c124** h26v^5 h24.4g* h24.4g^4 c26g* Mar 25] compact gelding: fair handicap hurdler: won at **h107** Doncaster in January: fairly useful handicap chaser: in tongue tie, won at Newbury final start: stays 3¼m: acts on heavy going: has worn cheekpieces, including in 2016/17. *Ian Williams*

BODEKIN POINT (IRE) 6 br.g. Robin des Pres (FR) – Countessdee (IRE) (Arctic **h88** Lord) [2016/17 b–: h19.9g h20g h19.6m^3 h23.8d^{pu} Nov 28] well held in bumper: modest form over hurdles. *Charlie Longsdon*

BODYSWERVE (IRE) 5 b.g. Getaway (GER) – Madame Martine (IRE) (Spadoun (FR)) [2016/17 b16g h16.7v h15.8v⁵ h16.7s⁴ Dec 9] €52,000 3-y-o: first foal: dam unraced half-sister to fairly useful hurdler/useful chaser (stayed 3½m) That's Rhythm: well beaten in maiden bumper: fair form over hurdles: best effort when fifth in maiden at Ludlow. *Jonjo O'Neill* **h102** **b–**

BOETHIUS 4 b.g. Manduro (GER) – Perfect Note (Shamardal (USA)) [2016/17 h15.8g⁵ h15.7g⁸ h15.8v⁴ h17.7s⁵ h16.8vᵖᵘ h15.8d Mar 15] fair maiden on Flat, stays 8.5f: modest form over hurdles: raced around 2m. *Tim Vaughan* **h88**

BOGARDUS (IRE) 6 b.g. Dalakhani (IRE) – Sugar Mint (IRE) (High Chaparral (IRE)) [2016/17 h16.2m³ Oct 2] fair on Flat, stays 12.5f: 8/1, third in maiden at Kelso (5½ lengths behind Spectator) on hurdling debut. *Patrick Holmes* **h96**

BOGOSS DU PERRET (FR) 6 b.g. Malinas (GER) – Lady Paques (FR) (Lights Out (FR)) [2016/17 h99: h16.8g⁴ h18.5g c16.3gᵖᵘ Sep 16] angular gelding: poor maiden hurdler: showed nothing on chasing debut: unproven beyond 17f: best form on good going: tried in blinkers. *Jimmy Frost* **c–** **h81**

BOHEMIAN RHAPSODY (IRE) 8 b.g. Galileo (IRE) – Quiet Mouse (USA) (Quiet American (USA)) [2016/17 h119: h20g⁵ h20g h19.5g⁴ h16d h15.5g³ Dec 7] sturdy gelding: handicap hurdler, modest nowadays: effective at 2m to 21f: acts on good to firm and heavy going: wears headgear: front runner/races prominently. *Brendan Powell* **h97**

BOHER LAD (IRE) 10 b.g. Gold Well – Shindeesharnick (IRE) (Roselier (FR)) [2016/17 h69: h22g² h23m h22m² c25.1m⁴ h23.8v* h23.8d² h23.1sᶠ h23.9g h25.6s² h24d* h25gᵘʳ h24g* h23.4g³ Apr 17] winning pointer: fair handicap hurdler: won at Ludlow (conditionals event) in November, and at Southwell in February and March: poor form when fourth of 6 in novice handicap at Wincanton on chasing debut: stays 3¼m: acts on good to firm and heavy going: has worn headgear/tongue tie. *Alan Phillips* **c67** **h101**

BOHERNAGORE (IRE) 8 b.g. Tajraasi (USA) – Brownies Haven (IRE) (Bob Back (USA)) [2016/17 h20gᵖᵘ h16m⁶ h15.8s⁶ h17.7d⁶ h17.7d* h17.7v h16dᶠ h17.7g Mar 31] maiden pointer: modest handicap hurdler: won at Fontwell in December: best effort at 2¼m: acts on good to soft going: has worn headgear, including last 5 starts: front runner/races prominently. *Zoe Davison* **h91**

BOITE (IRE) 7 b.g. Authorized (IRE) – Albiatra (USA) (Dixieland Band (USA)) [2016/17 h131: h16d* h20.5d⁵ h16.3d h16.8g h21.4g³ Apr 22] rather leggy gelding: useful handicap hurdler: won at Wetherby (by 5 lengths from William of Orange) in December: stays 21f: acts on heavy going: tried in cheekpieces. *Warren Greatrex* **h138**

BOLD ADVENTURE 13 ch.g. Arkadian Hero (USA) – Impatiente (USA) (Vaguely Noble) [2016/17 h25d² h25.6d³ h24d² h25m Oct 11] sturdy gelding: modest handicap hurdler: left Willie Musson after third start: stays 25f: acts on soft going. *Joanne Thomason-Murphy* **h93**

BOL D'AIR (FR) 6 b.g. Blue Bresil (FR) – Holding (FR) (Useful (FR)) [2016/17 h–, b82: h16g h15.9v* h16.3v* Mar 4] good-bodied gelding: bumper winner: fair form over hurdles: won handicap at Plumpton in January and novice handicap at Newbury (idled markedly run-in) final start: raced around 2m: best form on heavy going: usually in hood: often leads/races freely. *Chris Gordon* **h108**

BOLDBOB (IRE) 5 gr.g. Verglas (IRE) – Special Park (USA) (Trempolino (USA)) [2016/17 h100: h17.2g Jun 1] fair winner over hurdles early in 2015/16, disappointing since: raced around 2m: acts on heavy going: tried in cheekpieces. *Micky Hammond* **h–**

BOLD CONQUEST (IRE) 9 b.g. Oscar (IRE) – Massappeal Supreme (IRE) (Supreme Leader) [2016/17 c–, h114: h23.3s h26g h23.6d² h23.6dᵖᵘ Nov 16] fair handicap hurdler: maiden chaser: stayed 3¼m: acted on heavy going: sometimes wore cheekpieces, including last 3 starts: dead. *Stuart Edmunds* **c–** **h107**

BOLD DUKE 9 b.g. Sulamani (IRE) – Dominant Duchess (Old Vic) [2016/17 h114: h16v h15.8s h19.5s⁴ h21.2g Apr 3] rather sparely-made gelding: handicap hurdler, just modest form in 2016/17: stays 19f: acts on heavy going: wears hood. *Edward Bevan* **h87**

BOLD HENMIE (IRE) 6 b.g. Henrythenavigator (USA) – Seminole Lass (USA) (Indian Charlie (USA)) [2016/17 h102: h21.2d⁶ h18.6g² h17.2m⁴ h15.8d⁶ h15.8g* h16.7g² h18.6g⁴ h15.8g Sep 18] modest handicap hurdler: won at Uttoxeter in July: stays 19f: best form on good going: in cheekpieces last 4 starts: usually races towards rear. *Philip Kirby* **h90**

BOLD HENRY 11 b.g. Kayf Tara – Madam Min (Overbury (IRE)) [2016/17 c144, h–: **c138** c16d^{pu} c15.9g⁶ c15.5s² c15.5v⁴ c16v² c16.3g c16d^{pu} Apr 27] strong gelding: winning **h–** hurdler: useful handicap chaser: second at Sandown (2 lengths behind Garde La Victoire) in January and Chepstow (1½ lengths behind Sew On Target) in February: raced mostly at 2m: acts on good to firm and heavy going: usually races towards rear. *Philip Hobbs*

BOLD IMAGE (IRE) 6 b.m. Milan – Golden Bay (Karinga Bay) [2016/17 b17.7d* Oct **b81 p** 19] £10,000 4-y-o: fourth foal: half-sister to fairly useful chaser Old Pals Act (2½m-25f winner, by Presenting) and bumper winner Watcombe Heights (by Scorpion): dam (h131) bumper/21f-2¾m hurdle winner: 8/1, won mares bumper at Fontwell on debut by 6 lengths from Ruby Russet: bred to stay at least 2½m: should improve. *Suzy Smith*

BOLD PRINCE RUPERT (IRE) 7 br.g. Royal Anthem (USA) – Fortune And Favour **h63** (IRE) (Homo Sapien) [2016/17 h–: h16.2d⁵ h20.3s^{pu} h16.2d^{pu} h22.1g^{pu} h24g² h27g⁶ Aug 25] poor maiden hurdler: has worn headgear, including last 2 starts: signs of temperament. *Sara Ender*

BOLD RUNNER 6 ch.g. Mount Nelson – Music In Exile (USA) (Diesis) [2016/17 h118: **h105** h19.1d⁵ h19s h19.8d h19.5s⁶ h24.2d^F Mar 24] rather leggy gelding: maiden hurdler, fairly useful at best: stayed 21f: acted on good to soft going: wore cheekpieces: front runner/ raced prominently: dead. *Jose Santos*

BOLD SIR BRIAN (IRE) 11 b.g. Brian Boru – Black Queen (IRE) (Bob Back (USA)) **c–** [2016/17 c–, h121: c23.8d^{pu} Jun 29] lengthy gelding: fairly useful hurdler in 2015/16: one- **h–** time smart chaser, no encouragement only outing in 2016/17: stays 3m: acts on heavy going: in tongue tie last 4 starts: often races towards rear: weak finisher. *Lucinda Russell*

BOLERO COLLONGES (FR) 6 gr.g. Fragrant Mix (IRE) – Katy Collonges (FR) **c–** (Lute Antique (FR)) [2016/17 c–, h–: h19.9g⁵ h23.9g Apr 26] maiden hurdler/chaser: little **h56** form in Britain: has worn headgear: in tongue tie last 2 starts. *Simon Waugh*

BOLISTER (FR) 6 b.g. Le Balafre (FR) – Girlish (FR) (Passing Sale (FR)) [2016/17 h88, **h100** b–: h15.9g² Oct 17] sturdy gelding: fair maiden hurdler: raced mainly at 2m: often races towards rear. *Gary Moore*

BOLLIN ACE 6 b.g. Bollin Eric – Bollin Annabel (King's Theatre (IRE)) [2016/17 h110: **h129** h16.8d⁴ h19.4g⁶ h19.7s³ h21.2v* h19.9v* h22v^F h19.9g² Mar 29] fairly useful hurdler: won novices at Sedgefield in February and March: good second in handicap there final start: stays 21f: acts on heavy going: wears headgear: tried in tongue tie: usually races close up. *Tim Easterby*

BOLLIN BUSTER 7 b.g. Bollin Eric – Westie (Primitive Rising (USA)) [2016/17 c23.8g^{pu} **c–** Apr 28] dual winning pointer: pulled up in hunter on chasing debut. *Ms Jackie Williamson*

BOLLIN JULIE 10 b.m. Bollin Eric – Bollin Nellie (Rock Hopper) [2016/17 h23.3v^{pu} **h78** h22s h23.8g h19.9v* h21.4v³ h23.8g Mar 24] poor handicap hurdler: won mares event at Sedgefield in February: stays 25f: acts on heavy going. *Donald Whillans*

BOLLIN LINE 10 b.g. Bollin Eric – Leading Line (Leading Man) [2016/17 c95, h–: **c87** c17.3g³ c15.6d⁶ c20g h19.3d^{pu} Dec 13] maiden hurdler: modest handicap chaser: has form **h–** at 27f, effective at much shorter: acts on soft going: tried in hood: usually races nearer last than first. *Lucinda Egerton*

BOLLYWOOD BOY 6 b.g. Indian Danehill (IRE) – Little Miss Prim (Gildoran) **b–** [2016/17 b15.8g Apr 17] showed nothing in bumper on debut. *John O'Neill*

BOLTON BLUE (IRE) 8 b.g. Blueprint (IRE) – Ebony Countess (IRE) (Phardante (FR)) **h–** [2016/17 h75: h19.3m^{pu} May 5] little form over hurdles: in tongue tie last 5 starts. *Katie Scott*

BOLVING (IRE) 6 b.g. Stowaway – Kiniohio (FR) (Script Ohio (USA)) [2016/17 b101: **h81** h17.7v⁴ Jan 29] useful-looking gelding: fairly useful bumper winner: 6/4, in tongue tie, fourth in novice at Fontwell (33½ lengths behind Solighoster) on hurdling debut: tried in hood. *Victor Dartnall*

BOMBER COMMAND (FR) 5 gr.g. Al Namix (FR) – Ballade Nordique (FR) (Royal **h98 p** Charter (FR)) [2016/17 b15.7g⁴ h15.8s h16.6g h16.3g⁶ Apr 1] fifth foal: dam French **b79** 2m-19f hurdle/chase winner: fourth in bumper at Southwell: modest form over hurdles: will prove suited by 2½m: remains with potential. *Tom George*

BOMBER'S MOON 6 b.g. Erhaab (USA) – Flaviola (IRE) (Moscow Society (USA)) **b95** [2016/17 b16s² b17g Apr 7] sturdy gelding: fourth foal: dam, no sign of ability, sister to fairly useful hurdler/fair chaser (stayed 2½m) Hot Port: fairly useful form when neck second to Mance Rayder in maiden bumper at Warwick in March: out of depth only other start. *Nigel Twiston-Davies*

BONBON AU MIEL (FR) 6 b.g. Khalkevi (IRE) – Friandise Ii (FR) (Mistigri) [2016/17 **h139** h18.1v² h16v* h20.5dᵖᵘ Apr 29] brother to fairly useful hurdler/useful chaser Upepito (2m-2¼m winner) and half-brother to several winners, including winning hurdler/fairly useful chaser Lulumar (2m-2½m winner, by Beyssac): dam ran twice in France (third in 2m hurdle only start over jumps): useful form over hurdles: successful in juvenile for Guillaume Macaire in 2014/15, missed 2015/16: won minor event at Cork (by short head from Lilshane) in March: better form when ¾-length second to Hidden Cyclone in minor event at Leopardstown on return: possibly amiss final outing: stays 2¼m: acts on heavy going. *W. P. Mullins, Ireland*

BONCHESTER 6 b.g. Tikkanen (USA) – Golden Aureole (Gildoran) [2016/17 b16v⁶ **b–** b16.2v⁶ Mar 28] little impact in 2 bumpers. *George Charlton*

BON CHIC (IRE) 8 b.m. Presenting – Homebird (IRE) (Be My Native (USA)) [2016/17 **c124** c124, h–: c21.2g² h24g* h22.1dᵖᵘ h24g⁵ h19.9gᵖᵘ h24.3d Apr 21] useful-looking mare: fair **h113** handicap hurdler: won at Southwell in June: fairly useful handicap chaser: left Dan Skelton after third start: best around 2½m: acts on soft and good to firm going: tried in cheekpieces. *James Moffatt*

BONDI MIST (IRE) 8 gr.m. Aussie Rules (USA) – Akoya (IRE) (Anabaa (USA)) **h70** [2016/17 h82: h18.7m h20m⁵ h21.6g⁶ h20.5g⁵ h19.7g⁶ h19.1d⁴ Dec 6] poor maiden hurdler: stays 19f: acts on soft and good to firm going: has worn headgear, including last 4 starts. *Jonathan Geake*

BONDS CONQUEST 8 ch.g. Monsieur Bond (IRE) – Another Conquest (El **c72** Conquistador) [2016/17 c72, h–: c25.8gᵖᵘ c21.1s² c19.7d³ c25.5s³ Dec 26] maiden hurdler: **h–** poor maiden handicap chaser: stays 25f: best form on soft/heavy going: often in headgear: usually races close up. *Seamus Mullins*

BON ENFANT (FR) 6 gr.g. Saint des Saints (FR) – Montanara Paris (FR) (Turgeon **h121** (USA)) [2016/17 h128, b–: h19.8d h21.3s h26s³ h23.5s Feb 18] angular gelding: bumper winner: fairly useful handicap hurdler: stays 3¼m: acts on soft going: in headgear last 3 starts. *Warren Greatrex*

BON GENRE (IRE) 6 b.g. Fruits of Love (USA) – Cobblers Hall (IRE) (Saddlers' Hall **h–** (IRE)) [2016/17 b88: h19.6gᵖᵘ Apr 29] fair form in bumpers: 50/1, bled when pulled up in novice on hurdling debut. *Robert Stephens*

BONNE QUESTION (FR) 8 gr.g. Tagula (IRE) – Amonita (GER) (Medaaly) [2016/17 **h115** h115: h15.7v* May 10] sturdy gelding: fairly useful hurdler: won maiden at Southwell only outing in 2016/17: unproven beyond 17f: raced only on soft/heavy going: usually races close up, often travels strongly. *Venetia Williams*

BONNET'S VINO 9 b.m. Grape Tree Road – Bonnet's Pieces (Alderbrook) [2016/17 **c110** c99, h107: h20.6s* h19.8s³ c21.2g* c19.4d⁴ c21.2d* h20.6mᵖᵘ Apr 9] lengthy, **h108** medium-sized mare: fair handicap hurdler: won mares event at Market Rasen in November: fair chaser: won novices at Fakenham in December (handicap) and February: stays 23f: acts on heavy going. *Pam Sly*

BONNIE LIZZIE 6 ch.m. Alflora (IRE) – Caitlin Ash (Karinga Bay) [2016/17 b–: b16s⁶ **h–** h20.9sᵖᵘ Dec 4] no sign of ability in bumpers and mares novice hurdle: in cheekpieces last **b–** 2 starts. *Dianne Sayer*

BONNIE MAJOR 7 ch.m. Apple Tree (FR) – Carly Bay (Carlton (GER)) [2016/17 **c–** h20.5d h20.5v c17vᶠ c19.7s c25.7sᵖᵘ Mar 13] no sign of ability: tried in cheekpieces/ **h–** tongue tie. *Anna Newton-Smith*

BONNY KATE (IRE) 7 ch.m. Beneficial – Peppardstown (IRE) (Old Vic) [2016/17 **c142** c139, h–: c21s⁶ c24d³ c25d³ c28s³ c24sᵖᵘ c29dᵖᵘ Apr 17] winning hurdler: useful handicap **h–** chaser: good 5¼ lengths third of 25 to Empire of Dirt in Troytown Chase at Navan in November: stays 3½m: acts on heavy going: usually races prominently. *Noel Meade, Ireland*

BONOBO (IRE) 10 b.g. Quws – Better Folly (IRE) (Rhoman Rule (USA)) [2016/17 c–, **c99** h97: h16.8g* h16s⁵ c16.5g⁴ c15.7vᵖᵘ Jun 20] fairly useful handicap hurdler: won at Newton **h116** Abbot (conditionals event) in May: maiden chaser, fair form at best: stays 21f: acts on good to firm and heavy going: in headgear last 2 starts. *Evan Williams*

BON PAPA (FR) 6 br.g. Network (GER) – Gibelotte (FR) (Royal Charter (FR)) [2016/17 **h116** b16d* h24vᶠ h16d* h21.1gᵖᵘ h24d Apr 26] C150,000 3 y o: good sort: chasing type: **h107** closely related to French hurdler/chaser Au Saut du Lit (17f-21f winner, by Gentlewave) and half-brother to several winners in France: dam unraced half-sister to dam of top-class French hurdler up to 19f Rendons Grace and very smart French hurdler/useful chaser up to

2¾m Homme du Jour: useful form when winning bumper at Fairyhouse (by 6½ lengths from Broken Soul) in December on debut: fairly useful form over hurdles: won maiden at Gowran in January by 4½ lengths from Giant Spirit: subsequently pulled up in Baring Bingham Novices' at Cheltenham and well held in Irish Daily Mirror Novices' at Punchestown. *W. P. Mullins, Ireland*

BONVILSTON BOY 6 b.g. Martaline – Lisa du Chenet (FR) (Garde Royale) [2016/17 **h89** h94, b–: h16d^{pu} h15.8d^5 h18.5m h16g h19s^3 h19.3s^3 h19.6g Apr 22] compact gelding: modest maiden hurdler: stays 19f: acts on heavy going: in headgear last 3 starts, in tongue tie last 4: often races towards rear. *Tim Vaughan*

BONZO BING (IRE) 9 b.g. Gold Well – She's A Dreamer (IRE) (Safety Catch (USA)) **c103 §** [2016/17 c107§, h–: h20d c25.2g^2 c26.9v^{pu} Jan 17] useful hurdler at best, no form in **h–** 2016/17: fair maiden chaser: stays 25f: acts on heavy going: has worn cheekpieces, including in 2016/17: often races towards rear: unreliable. *Martin Todhunter*

BOOGIE LIFE 6 b.m. Tobougg (IRE) – Life Is Life (FR) (Mansonnien (FR)) [2016/17 **h67 p** b93: b17g h16.2g^6 Apr 28] lengthy mare: fair at best in bumpers: 16/1, sixth in mares **b–** novice at Perth (34½ lengths behind Miss Night Owl) on hurdling debut: should do better. *Jim Goldie*

BOOGILY LANE (IRE) 6 gr.g. Tikkanen (USA) – Ninaprettybalerina (IRE) (Rashar **h83** (USA)) [2016/17 b16s h16g h16g h16d h20.5s h24v^5 h20v^6 Mar 23] second foal: dam **b–** winning pointer: failed to complete both starts in points: well beaten in maiden bumper: poor form over hurdles. *S. McConville, Ireland*

BOOK AT BEDTIME 6 b.m. Midnight Legend – Northern Native (IRE) (Be My Native **h101** (USA)) [2016/17 b85p: b16.2d* b15.8m^3 b15.7d^3 h19.9g^3 h20.3g^2 h23.3d^3 h20.6d* **b85** h20.6s^{pu} h16g Apr 21] fair form in bumpers: won mares event at Hexham in May: fair form over hurdles: won mares maiden at Newcastle in November: left Keith Reveley after eighth start: stays 23f: acts on good to soft going: usually races nearer last than first. *Gordon Elliott, Ireland*

BOOK DIRECT (IRE) 6 b.g. Kayf Tara – Sinnaja (Sinndar (IRE)) [2016/17 h18.5g^2 **h117 p** h19.7s^2 Nov 23] €15,500 3-y-o: third foal: half-brother to fair hurdler Kealshore Again (2m winner, by Exit To Nowhere): dam unraced: third in Irish maiden point in May 2015: fairly useful form when second in novice hurdles at Newton Abbot and Hereford: should do better. *Philip Hobbs*

BOOK OF GOLD (IRE) 5 b.g. Flemensfirth (USA) – Ballerina Queen (IRE) (Be My **b92** Native (USA)) [2016/17 b16s^2 b16s^5 Feb 10] £30,000 3-y-o: sturdy gelding: ninth foal: dam unraced half-sister to smart staying chasers Calling Brave and Ottowa: fair form in bumpers: better effort when second at Warwick in December. *Oliver Sherwood*

BOONDOOMA (IRE) 10 b.g. Westerner – Kissantel (IRE) (Broken Hearted) [2016/17 **c–** c155, h–: c15.9g^{pu} Oct 22] well-made gelding: winning hurdler: very smart chaser at best: **h–** stayed 2½m: acted on heavy going: tried in hood: dead. *Dr Richard Newland*

BOOTED EAGLE (IRE) 7 b.g. Oscar (IRE) – Warmley's Gem (IRE) (Phardante (FR)) **h–** [2016/17 b–: h19d^6 h19.9g Jun 26] well held in bumper/over hurdles. *Anabel K. Murphy*

BOOYAKASHA (IRE) 5 b.g. Presenting – Land of Honour (Supreme Leader) [2016/17 **b79 p** b15.6g^6 Jan 3] €120,000 3-y-o: fifth foal: brother to useful/unreliable chaser Fort Smith (21f-23f winner) and half-brother to useful/untrustworthy hurdler/chaser Splash of Ginge (2m-23f winner, by Oscar): dam unraced half-sister to Cheltenham Gold Cup winner See More Business: 4/1, some encouragement when 21¼ lengths sixth of 12 to Beyond The Clouds in bumper at Musselburgh on debut: entitled to do better. *Nicky Richards*

BOP ALONG (IRE) 10 b.g. Double Eclipse (IRE) – Bob Girl (IRE) (Bob Back (USA)) **h112** [2016/17 h104: h23.3d* h25.4m^2 May 28] fair handicap hurdler: won at Hexham in May: stays 25f: acts on good to firm and heavy going: wears headgear: front runner/races prominently. *Alistair Whillans*

BORAK (IRE) 5 b.g. Kodiac – Right After Moyne (IRE) (Imperial Ballet (IRE)) [2016/17 **h101** h123: h16g h15.3m^2 h16.8g^3 h16.5g h15.8s h16.5g^3 h15.8s h16.3g^5 h16m^6 Apr 28] fair handicap hurdler: will stay 2½m: acts on good to firm and heavy going: tried in cheekpieces: has worn tongue tie: often races towards rear. *Bernard Llewellyn*

BORDEAUX BILL (IRE) 6 b.g. Craigsteel – Laura Croft (IRE) (Mister Lord (USA)) **h128 p** [2016/17 b16s^3 h19.9s* h19.9g* h20g^{pu} Apr 8] €4,000 3-y-o, £30,000 5-y-o: lengthy **b90** gelding: fifth foal: dam (h70) winning pointer: Irish maiden point winner: third at Wetherby only start in bumpers: useful form over hurdles: won novices at Sedgefield in January and March (by 15 lengths from Helmsley Lad): 20/1, pulled up in Mersey Novices' Hurdle at Aintree final start: will stay beyond 2½m: remains with potential. *Brian Ellison*

BORDER BREAKER (IRE) 8 br.g. Indian Danehill (IRE) – Flying Answer (IRE) **c–**
(Anshan) [2016/17 c126, h109: c21.2g^pu c24.2d^ur Jun 19] winning pointer/hurdler: fairly **h–**
useful chaser at best: failed to complete in 2016/17: stays 3m: acts on soft going: wears
headgear/tongue tie. *Simon Waugh*

BORDER STATION (IRE) 11 b.g. Shantou (USA) – Telemania (IRE) (Mujtahid **c–**
(USA)) [2016/17 h18.5g h20g^pu h17.7g^5 Aug 18] good-topped gelding: fair hurdler at best, **h–**
no form in 2016/17: maiden chaser: tried in tongue tie. *Laura Young*

BORDER VICTOR 5 b.g. Beat All (USA) – Sambara (IRE) (Shardari) [2016/17 b16.2d **h91**
h20.5s h20.5s^5 h21.4v^5 h19.4s^4 h19.7d^4 h24.1m Apr 13] £8,000 3-y-o: half-brother to 3 **b–**
winners, including fair hurdler/useful chaser Equus Maximus (19f-3m winner, by
Flemensfirth) and fairly useful hurdler Ball of Blue (3m winner, by Presenting): dam
(h131), 2m/2¼m hurdle winner, also 1¾m-2m winner on Flat: tailed off in bumper: modest
form over hurdles: stays 2½m: acts on good to soft going: often races towards rear.
Barry Murtagh

BORED OR BAD (IRE) 5 b.g. Oscar (IRE) – Siberiansdaughter (IRE) (Strong Gale) **h–**
[2016/17 h85: h19.9d^6 h19.5d h23.8v^pu h23.9m h24.4d Jan 9] maiden hurdler, no form in
2016/17: tried in tongue tie. *David Dennis*

BOREHAM BILL (IRE) 5 b.g. Tikkanen (USA) – Crimond (IRE) (Zaffaran (USA)) **b105**
[2016/17 b16.7g* b16.4s^2 b15.7d b15.8d^5 Mar 15] €13,500 3-y-o: workmanlike gelding:
fourth foal: half-brother to fair hurdler/chaser Rosa Fleet (17f-3m winner, by Alflora): dam
(h91), lightly-raced maiden in bumpers/over hurdles (stayed 3m), half-sister to useful
chaser (stayed 3¼m) Royale de Vassy: useful form in bumpers: won at Market Rasen (by
3½ lengths from Bandsman) in October: best effort when length second to Poetic Rhythm
at Cheltenham in November: bred to be suited by 2½m+. *Ben Pauling*

BORIC 9 b.g. Grape Tree Road – Petrea (St Ninian) [2016/17 c109, h–: c24.2g^pu c20.1s^3 **c110**
c20.1s^5 c19.2d^5 c24.2s^3 c24dp^u c26.3g* c24.2m c30.6g* Apr 28] maiden hurdler: fair **h–**
handicap chaser: won at Sedgefield in March and Perth in April: stays 31f: acts on soft
going: wears headgear: often leads. *Simon Waugh*

BORN FOR WAR (IRE) 5 ch.g. Wareed (IRE) – Oscar Bird (IRE) (Oscar (IRE)) **b88**
[2016/17 b16.8s^3 b16.2v^3 Feb 1] €11,000 3-y-o, £40,000 4-y-o: first foal: dam, unraced,
closely related to fairly useful hurdler/chaser (2m-2½m winner) Noras Fancy: runner-up
in Irish maiden point: fair form when third in bumpers at Sedgefield and Hereford.
Tom George

BORN NAUGHTY 5 b.g. Notnowcato – Tremiere (FR) (Anabaa (USA)) [2016/17 **h–**
b16.7d h19.5v h21s^pu Mar 30] no form in bumper/maiden hurdles. *Jamie Snowden* **b–**

BORN OF A TUESDAY (IRE) 10 b.m. Shantou (USA) – Miss Di (IRE) (Phardante **h–**
(FR)) [2016/17 h20.2m h16.2g^pu May 24] maiden pointer: no form in bumper/over hurdles.
Stuart Coltherd

BORN SURVIVOR (IRE) 6 b.g. King's Theatre (IRE) – Bob's Flame (IRE) (Bob Back **h142**
(USA)) [2016/17 h131p: h20g^2 h20.5d^4 h20.5d^3 h18.1v^F h20.3g^6 h16.5g Apr 8] useful-
looking gelding: winning Irish pointer: useful hurdler: good effort when 6 lengths sixth of
23 to Champagne Classic in Martin Pipe Conditional Jockeys' Handicap Hurdle at
Cheltenham in March: stays 21f: acts on heavy going: often travels strongly. *Dan Skelton*

BORN TO FLY (IRE) 6 b.m. Kodiac – Cayambe (IRE) (Selkirk (USA)) [2016/17 **h–**
h15.8g^pu May 30] fair on Flat, stays 1m: in hood, showed nothing in maiden on hurdling
debut. *Christine Dunnett*

BORUMA (IRE) 7 b.g. Brian Boru – Itlallendintears (IRE) (Lil's Boy (USA)) [2016/17 **c–**
c–, h109: h19.7g h24.7m h17.2m^2 h17.2d^2 h22.1d^3 h25.4d^2 h21.3g^3 h22.8v h23.8g^6 h22.8g **h109**
Apr 15] fair handicap hurdler: maiden chaser (likely to have won both starts over fences in
2014/15 but for falling): left Dianne Sayer after second start: stays 3m: acts on good to firm
and heavy going: tried in hood: often races towards rear. *James Moffatt*

BOSS DES MOTTES (FR) 6 b.g. Califet (FR) – Puszta des Mottes (FR) (Ut*Useful **c123**
(FR)) [2016/17 h120: h16.2d^6 c19.2d^4 c16.5g* h16g c15.2m c16.3d^3 c16.4s^5 c16.3s^5 **h–**
c15.7d^6 c19.2s^4 c15.2m^5 Apr 13] rather slightly-built gelding: fairly useful hurdler at best,
no form in 2016/17: fairly useful handicap chaser: won novice event at Worcester in July:
left Dan Skelton after fourth start: stays 2¼m: acts on soft going: usually wears headgear:
has worn tongue tie. *Henry Hogarth*

BOSS IN BOOTS (IRE) 9 gr.g. King's Theatre (IRE) – Grey Mo (IRE) (Roselier (FR)) **c95 §**
[2016/17 c113, h–: c16g c16.3g⁵ c23.8g^F c19.9d⁶ c23.6d^{ur} c23.8g^{pu} c19.2s⁴ h21.6g² Apr **h85 §**
26] angular gelding: handicap hurdler/chaser, modest nowadays: stays 21f: acts on good to
firm and heavy going: wears headgear: usually races towards rear: not one to rely on.
Tim Vaughan

BOSTIN (IRE) 9 ch.g. Busy Flight – Bustingoutallover (USA) (Trempolino (USA)) **h86**
[2016/17 h65: h20.5v h19.5v h25v⁴ h25s³ h22g h21.6g* Apr 21] winning pointer: modest
handicap hurdler: won at Fontwell final start: stays 2¾m: acts on soft going. *Daniel
O'Brien*

BOSTON BLUE 10 b.g. Halling (USA) – City of Gold (IRE) (Sadler's Wells (USA)) **c102 §**
[2016/17 c76, h101§: c18m³ h18.7m⁴ Jul 17] quite good-topped gelding: winning hurdler, **h89 §**
fair at best: better effort (fair form) over fences when third in novice handicap at Kempton:
stays 2¼m: acts on good to firm and heavy going: often races lazily/looks reluctant.
Tony Carroll

BOSTON DE LA ROCHE (FR) 6 b.g. Malinas (GER) – Quesland de La Roche (FR) **h97**
(Arnaqueur (USA)) [2016/17 h106, b–: h19.1g⁴ h16.3g⁴ Apr 23] lengthy gelding: bumper
winner: maiden hurdler, just modest form in 2016/17: likely to stay 2½m: best form on
good going. *Dan Skelton*

BOUDRY (FR) 6 b.g. Crosshairbour – Lavande (FR) (Iris Noir (FR)) [2016/17 b102: **h85**
h15.9d³ h16.3d h16.6d^{pu} h17.7v⁴ Feb 14] workmanlike gelding: bumper winner: maiden
hurdler, modest form at best: usually races nearer last than first: has joined Gordon Elliott.
Warren Greatrex

BOUGGIETOPIECES 7 b.g. Tobougg (IRE) – Bonnet's Pieces (Alderbrook) [2016/17 **c96 §**
c105§, h92: c20.8g^{pu} c16.1m⁴ Apr 27] winning hurdler/chaser: left A. B. Leyshon, just **h–**
modest form on completed start in 2016/17: stays 3m: acts on soft and good to firm going:
tried in cheekpieces/tongue tie: often races towards rear: temperamental. *Tim Vaughan*

BOUGHTBEFORELUNCH (IRE) 4 b.g. Dubai Destination (USA) – Anie (IRE) **b90**
(Saffron Walden (FR)) [2016/17 b16g² Apr 24] £15,000 3-y-o: first foal: dam, unraced, out
of sister to useful 2m hurdler Spirit Leader, herself dam of high-class staying hurdler Prince
of Scars: 20/1, 8 lengths second to World Premier in bumper at Warwick, keeping on well.
Paul Webber

BOUND FOR GLORY (IRE) 11 b.g. Witness Box (USA) – Musical View (IRE) **c105**
(Orchestra) [2016/17 c114, h–: c16.3g³ c22.6m⁵ c23g c22.6g² Apr 23] lengthy gelding: **h–**
multiple winning pointer: winning hurdler: fair chaser: stays 23f: acts on good to firm and
good to soft going: tried in blinkers. *D. M. G. Fitch-Peyton*

BOUND HILL 8 b.g. Kayf Tara – Ardent Bride (Ardross) [2016/17 h90, b66: h21.4m⁴ **c93**
h23g⁶ c20v^{pu} c25.5d⁵ h23.1s⁴ h19.1v* h19.1d* Mar 18] strong gelding: fair handicap **h101 §**
hurdler: won at Fontwell in February and March: shaped much better than result suggests
when fifth in novice handicap at Fontwell on completed start in chases, still in front when
all but falling 2 out: should stay beyond 19f: acts on heavy going: usually in headgear: front
runner/races prominently: temperamental. *Fiona Shaw*

BOURBON PRINCE 6 ch.g. Aqlaam – Good Enough (FR) (Mukaddamah (USA)) **c82**
[2016/17 h84: h18.7g^{pu} c16.4m³ Apr 19] poor maiden hurdler: poor form when third in **h–**
novice handicap at Sedgefield on chasing debut: unproven beyond 17f: acts on good to soft
going: has worn hood: has worn tongue tie, including in 2016/17: often leads. *Sam England*

BOURDELLO 8 b.m. Milan – Haudello (FR) (Marignan (USA)) [2016/17 h95: h20g^{pu} **h–**
h20.5g Nov 27] maiden hurdler, no form in 2016/17: best effort at 19f: acts on soft going.
Emma Baker

BOURNE 11 gr.g. Linamix (FR) – L'Affaire Monique (Machiavellian (USA)) [2016/17 **h111 §**
h85§: h23.3g³ h26.5d⁴ h22.1g* h23.1g* h23.1g² h25.4d³ h24.6d* h25.8s³ h23.1s⁴ h24.3v²
h24.3s⁵ h24.3v² Mar 10] close-coupled gelding: fair handicap hurdler: won at Cartmel and
Bangor (conditionals event) in July, and Carlisle in October: stays 3¼m: acts on heavy
going: wears headgear: temperamental. *Donald McCain*

BOUTAN 4 gr.f. Tobougg (IRE) – High Tan (High Chaparral (IRE)) [2016/17 h15.8v² **h96**
h16.2v⁵ h15.8d⁴ h15.8s⁴ h16.2d⁴ h15.3m⁵ Apr 5] fair on Flat, stays 1¼m: modest form over
hurdles: raced only at 2m: acts on good to soft going: tried in cheekpieces. *Bernard Llewellyn*

BOUVREUIL (FR) 6 b.g. Saddler Maker (IRE) – Madame Lys (FR) (Sheyrann) [2016/17 **c147**
c142, h–: c20.4s⁵ c20.8s⁶ c20.8g³ c21.1g Apr 7] useful-looking gelding: useful hurdler: **h–**
smart chaser: good effort when 7¾ lengths third of 24 to Road To Respect in Brown

Advisory & Merriebelle Stable Plate at Cheltenham in March: much better than result when 29 lengths tenth of 29 to Ultragold in Topham Chase at Aintree final start, badly hampered third and again twelfth: stays 21f: acts on heavy going: wears hood/tongue tie: can look tricky ride (has high head carriage). *Paul Nicholls*

BOWBERRY 6 b.m. Cockney Rebel (IRE) – Blaeberry (Kirkwall) [2016/17 h–: h16.3m[6] h20g[4] Jun 2] poor form over hurdles: in blinkers last 2 starts. *Ali Stronge*   **h71**

BOWDLER'S MAGIC 10 b.g. Hernando (FR) – Slew The Moon (ARG) (Kitwood (USA)) [2016/17 h112: h19.7g[2] h20.1d[6] h20g[5] h19.9g[5] h19.9d h20s* h20.6s h17s[2] h17d[F] h21.3d Mar 31] rather leggy gelding: fair hurdler: won seller at Fakenham in January: stays 2¾m: acts on good to firm and heavy going: has worn tongue tie: often races prominently. *David Thompson*   **h105**

BOWIE (IRE) 10 br.g. Pelder (IRE) – La Fenice (IRE) (Krayyan) [2016/17 h118: h23.3d[pu] c16.1g[pu] h18.6d[5] h18.6s[5] h23.8g[3] h18.6s* h23.1g[4] h23.1d Apr 27] smallish gelding: fair handicap hurdler: won at Market Rasen (conditionals event) in March: reportedly bled when pulled up on chasing debut: stays 21f: acts on good to firm and heavy going: tried in cheekpieces. *Nick Kent*   **c–** **h108**

BOXER BEAT (IRE) 10 b.g. Xaar – Pantoufle (Bering) [2016/17 c17m May 20] maiden hurdler: fairly useful handicap chaser in 2014/15 for Paul W. Flynn, poor form in hunter only outing since: stays 2½m: acts on soft and good to firm going: usually in headgear/tongue tie. *Tim Bryce*   **c74** **h–**

BOX OFFICE (FR) 6 b.g. Great Pretender (IRE) – Quelle Mome (FR) (Video Rock (FR)) [2016/17 h130: c19.2d[5] c16.5g c16.3g[6] c16.5g[6] c19.2g* c20.3g[4] Apr 22] good-topped gelding: useful hurdler: fairly useful chaser: won handicap at Market Rasen in March: should stay 3m: acts on soft going: has worn tongue tie: often races towards rear. *Jonjo O'Neill*   **c117** **h–**

BOYFROMNOWHERE (IRE) 10 br.g. Old Vic – Eist Do Gale (IRE) (Strong Gale) [2016/17 c–, h–: c25.5d[2] c24.1g[5] c24d[6] Oct 2] sturdy gelding: multiple point winner: winning hurdler: handicap chaser, just fair form in 2016/17: stays 3½m: acts on heavy going: has worn headgear: in tongue tie last 5 starts: temperamental. *Adrian Wintle*   **c108 §** **h–**

BOYGOJUMPING 5 ch.g. Midnight Legend – Maisie Malone VII (Damsire Unregistered) [2016/17 b87: c20.9v[pu] c15.9s[6] Mar 10] winning pointer: runner-up only start in bumpers: showed little in 2 hunter chases. *Martin Peaty*   **c–**

BOYHOOD (IRE) 6 b.g. Oscar (IRE) – Glen Dubh (IRE) (Supreme Leader) [2016/17 b98: h20g[2] h20d[2] h19.4g* h23.1g[4] Mar 25] unplaced in Irish maiden point: fairly useful bumper winner: also fairly useful over hurdles: won novice handicap at Doncaster (by 2¾ lengths from Indian Brave) in November: shaped well when fourth in handicap at Bangor final start (lost shoe): should be suited by 2¾m+: remains with potential. *Tom George*   **h123 p**

BOY IN A BENTLEY (IRE) 7 b.g. Kayf Tara – All Our Blessings (IRE) (Statoblest) [2016/17 h113, b92: h21g[ur] h24s[3] h20.1g[5] h19.6g[pu] c19.9d[6] h18.5d[2] h19g[3] Apr 24] lengthy gelding: fair maiden hurdler: well beaten in novice handicap on chasing debut: stays 23f: acts on soft going: in visor last 2 starts: often races prominently: temperament under suspicion. *Kim Bailey*   **c–** **h109**

BRAAVOS 6 br.g. Presenting – Tatanka (IRE) (Lear Fan (USA)) [2016/17 h128, b93: h21.6g[2] h19.5g h19.8d[5] h23.6g[pu] Dec 3] well-made gelding: bumper winner: fairly useful handicap hurdler: stays 2½m: acts on heavy going. *Philip Hobbs*   **h122**

BRACING 8 ch.m. Alflora (IRE) – Sports Express (Then Again) [2016/17 h86: h24.3d[5] h24d[5] h23.8g[4] Jan 3] handicap hurdler, just poor form in 2016/17: stays 3m: acts on good to soft going. *N. W. Alexander*   **h79**

BRACKENMOSS RORY 5 b.g. Overbury (IRE) – Thorterdykes Lass (IRE) (Zaffaran (USA)) [2016/17 b72: h20d[5] h16.2s h16.4s h20.6s h20.5s h25.8v[pu] h19.3d[pu] h22.7d[pu] h23.9g Apr 26] modest maiden hurdler: best effort at 2m: acts on soft going: tried in visor. *Alistair Whillans*   **h85**

BRADFORD BRIDGE (IRE) 5 b.g. Milan – Isis du Berlais (FR) (Cadoudal (FR)) [2016/17 h77p: h18.5g[3] h19.7s[2] h21.4s[4] h19g[6] h21g[3] Apr 24] fair maiden hurdler: will stay 3m: acts on soft going. *Philip Hobbs*   **h112**

BRAE ON (IRE) 9 ch.g. Presenting – Raphuca (IRE) (Be My Native (USA)) [2016/17 c–, h91: c23.4d[6] c25.8v[4] h25d[5] h25.3s[4] Mar 8] small gelding: poor handicap hurdler/maiden chaser nowadays: stays 27f: acts on heavy going. *George Bewley*   **c–** **h68**

BRAES OF LOCHALSH 6 b.g. Tiger Hill (IRE) – Gargoyle Girl (Be My Chief (USA)) **h–**
[2016/17 h20.5d h16s Dec 19] fairly useful on Flat, stays 17.5f: well held in 2 maiden hurdles at Ayr. *Jim Goldie*

BRAHMS DE CLERMONT (FR) 6 b.g. Califet (FR) – Colline de Clermon (FR) **h106**
(Vertical Speed (FR)) [2016/17 b114p: b16.4g* b16.4s⁶ h15.8d⁴ h18.5d² Feb 24] useful **b109**
form in bumpers: won at Cheltenham (by neck from Brillare Momento) in October: fair form over hurdles: better effort when fourth in maiden at Ludlow in December: should be suited by further than 2m. *Paul Nicholls*

BRAIN POWER (IRE) 6 b.g. Kalanisi (IRE) – Blonde Ambition (IRE) (Old Vic) **h158**
[2016/17 h146: h16d³ h16.4s h16s* h15.7d* h16.4g h16g⁵ Apr 28]

    Few owners have experienced the extreme highs and lows of National Hunt racing more than Michael Buckley. The first notable big-race performer to carry Buckley's colours was the 1976 Hennessy Gold Cup winner Zeta's Son, who lost his life just over four months later when breaking a leg at second Valentine's in the Grand National—a freak injury believed to have been caused by stepping in a hole. More ill fortune followed a few years into Buckley's long-running association with champion trainer Nicky Henderson, which began in the 'eighties, as his highly-regarded trio of chasers The Proclamation (whom Buckley still rates as 'probably the best jumper I've owned'), Black Amber and Mutare were all fatally injured on the racecourse within a three-year period in the early-'nineties. Coinciding with a brief dip in numbers, this also prompted a redesign of the Buckley silks (from black and white quartered colours—carried to victory in the County Hurdle in 1993 by Thumbs Up—to plain white with a black cap) in the hope of bringing about a change of luck. Buckley has since enjoyed a lucrative foray into the Flat ranks (notably with his 2014 UAE Derby win with Toast of New York who went on to finish second in the Breeders' Cup Classic) and has had several good National Hunt campaigns, which have yielded some notable successes, including three more Cheltenham Festival wins (the latest with Rock The World in the 2017 Grand Annual Chase).

    The new silks certainly did not eradicate the bad luck altogether, though. The well-touted Lush Life was fatally injured when among the favourites for the 2011 Pertemps Final, while Buckley's 2012 Queen Mother Champion Chase winner Finian's Rainbow had his career ended after sustaining a serious injury in the following year's Paddy Power Gold Cup. In addition, a series of frustrating training setbacks have restricted Beat That to just two below-form runs over hurdles since he beat Don Poli in a Grade 1 novice at the 2014 Punchestown Festival (Beat That did embark on a belated novice chasing career in early-2017/18). Perhaps most galling of all, however, was the fate of Spirit Son who seemed destined for the very top when running away with the 2011 Mersey Novices' Hurdle in which he beat Cue Card by thirteen lengths, with a further eight lengths back to the following year's Champion Hurdle winner Rock On Ruby in third. Alas, Spirit Son never raced again, retired after a life-threatening neck fracture sustained due to a rare virus attacking his neurological system, which ultimately led to his premature death (aged just eight) at the Greatwood charity centre for racehorses. Buckley may not have a potential superstar in the mould of Spirit Son running in his colours at present, but the highest rated of his current team, the very smart hurdler Brain Power, has stood up well to regular racing so far and appeals as an exciting novice chasing prospect for 2017/18.

    That said, Brain Power will do well to match his 2016/17 prize money haul, gained when claiming back-to-back wins in valuable handicap company. Some punters also swelled their coffers on the first occasion, as Brain Power landed a substantial gamble when winning the Jumeirah Hotels And Resorts December Handicap Hurdle at Sandown, beating his stable-companion Consul de Thaix by three quarters of a length in a field of ten under stand-in jockey Sam Twiston-Davies (Henderson's stable jockey Nico de Boinville was injured at the time, though it is worth noting that he didn't ride any of Buckley's horses during the second half of 2016/17). Irish-based David Mullins took the mount on Brain Power for the remainder of the campaign, the undoubted highlight being an impressive win in the Wessex Youth Trust Handicap Hurdle at Ascot later in December, a race Henderson had won three times under its old title when it was run as the Ladbroke.

Wessex Youth Trust Handicap Hurdle, Ascot—Brain Power emerges from the gloom to land an authoritative success; outsider Fergall (left) takes third

Although it was an unsatisfactory race in some respects because it was staged in dense fog, racegoers did not need X-ray vision to appreciate that Brain Power put up a very smart performance under top weight to spreadeagle a competitive-looking field, cruising clear in the latter stages to beat Consul de Thaix again (this time by five lengths), with the enterprisingly-ridden outsider Fergall in third. Brain Power entered the Champion Hurdle picture after this impressive display and was sent off 13/2 fourth choice in a field of eleven at Cheltenham. However, he failed to give his running, finishing a disappointing ninth, and it is possible Cheltenham isn't the ideal track for him (he also finished down the field in the Greatwood Hurdle there in November, though that came after seven months off). The manner in which Brain Power faded out of things from two out in the Champion does, however, suggest that something might have been amiss. A close fifth to Wicklow Brave in the Punchestown Champion Hurdle on his final start was much more like his true form and he would probably have run into a place but for a couple of uncharacteristic mistakes (notably at the last).

Brain Power is by Kalanisi and is the second foal out of Blonde Ambition, a dual winning Irish pointer who showed just modest form under Rules, when placed over hurdles and fences at distances ranging from two and a half miles to twenty-three furlongs. Those sort of trips were in keeping as Brain Power's grandam Titian Blonde was a fairly useful hurdler/chaser who stayed very well and has been an influence for stamina since being retired to the paddocks, also being the grandam of the 2016 Grand National third Vics Canvas, who is out of an unraced half-sister to Blonde Ambition and shares the same sire (Old Vic) as the latter. By contrast, Blonde Ambition's first foal Degooch (by Gamut) seemed to find his stamina stretched when tried over three miles during the latest season, a performance which was sandwiched between chase wins at Uttoxeter and Sedgefield, both at around two and a half miles. Trained by Johnny Farrelly, Degooch is a fairly useful performer who has now won eight times, but he had registered just two of those successes (in a point and bumper) when Brain Power passed through the sale-ring as a three-year-old for €30,000. Brain Power's three-years younger brother (as yet unnamed) made €20,000 as a yearling in the autumn of 2015, but the chances are that representatives from this family will attract considerably more interest from now on—these could include a 2012 Gamut filly and a 2015 Califet colt, Blonde Ambition's only other offspring to date. Brain Power probably changed hands for a much more significant sum himself when joining Henderson and Buckley after landing a gamble in a Newcastle bumper on his debut in February 2015 (his only start for small Irish trainer James Jenkins).

Mr Michael Buckley's "Brain Power"

Brain Power (IRE) (b.g. 2011)	Kalanisi (IRE) (b 1996)	Doyoun (b 1985)	Mill Reef
			Dumka
		Kalamba (b 1991)	Green Dancer
			Kareena
	Blonde Ambition (IRE) (ch 1999)	Old Vic (b 1986)	Sadler's Wells
			Cockade
		Titian Blonde (ch 1988)	Callernish
			Flashey Blond

As his pedigree suggests, the rangy Brain Power should stay beyond two miles in due course, though he is a strong-travelling sort (wears cheekpieces nowadays) and has been raced exclusively at the minimum trip to date, something which is likely to continue, at least in the short term, should connections opt to send him chasing. Despite those fears about the suitability of Cheltenham for him, Brain Power still makes some ante-post appeal at 20/1 for the 2017 Arkle, a race which Nicky Henderson has already won a record-breaking six times. It probably won't be a surprise, however, to learn that his owner is due a change of luck in the race—Thumbs Up was travelling well when brought down three out in the 1994 renewal, and both Tinryland (1992) and Finian's Rainbow (2011) had to settle for the runner-up spot. The Proclamation was a short-priced ante-post favourite for the 1990 Arkle before he fell fatally at Ascot on his final preparatory run. *Nicky Henderson*

BRAMBLE BROOK 7 b.g. Kayf Tara – Briery Ann (Anshan) [2016/17 h99p, b–: h21.6g⁴ h17.1d² h23.6d² c20.9v² c24.2vᵖᵘ c24.2s⁵ c24.2sᵖᵘ Mar 7] strong gelding: fair maiden hurdler: easily best effort (fairly useful form) in chases when second in novice handicap at Ffos Las in December: stays 21f: acts on heavy going. *Colin Tizzard* **c115 h107**

146

BRAND AMBASSADOR (IRE) 9 b.g. Heron Island (IRE) – His Fair Lady (IRE) (In The Wings) [2016/17 c20g h23.9d² h21g⁶ h21.5g⁵ h23.9d h20g h23d Nov 13] winning pointer: fair handicap hurdler: tailed off in maiden on chasing debut: left Gordon Elliott after third start: stays 3m: acts on heavy going: wears headgear. *Gavin Patrick Cromwell, Ireland*   c– h113

BRANDENBURG GATE (IRE) 6 b.g. Germany (USA) – Miss Anchor (IRE) (Slip Anchor) [2016/17 b90: h15.8s⁶ h16.7g⁴ h20d Nov 30] sturdy gelding: modest form at best in maiden hurdles: left Charlie Longsdon after second start: tried in hood. *Jan Mathias*   h92

BRANDON HILL (IRE) 9 b.g. Beneficial – Annesbanker (IRE) (Anshan) [2016/17 c20s⁶ c24s* c23.4s* c24s⁴ Feb 10] lengthy gelding: fairly useful hurdler: useful form when successful in handicap chases at Warwick in December and Newbury (by neck from Potters Corner) in January: stays 3m: raced mainly on soft/heavy going. *Tom Lacey*   c132 h–

BRANDY AND PEP (IRE) 13 b.g. Lord Americo – Furry Hope (Furry Glen) [2016/17 c24.1g² h22g⁵ May 21] poor maiden hurdler/chaser: suited by 3m+: acts on good to firm and good to soft going: has worn cheekpieces. *W. J. Martin, Ireland*   c69 h–

BRANDY BURN 6 b.m. Indian Danehill (IRE) – Kingennie (Dunbeath (USA)) [2016/17 b15.7g Nov 30] sixth foal: half-sister to bumper winner/useful hurdler Clova Island (17f-21f winner, by Turtle Island) and fair hurdler Rev Up Ruby (2½m-25f winner, by Revoque): dam (h89) 2½m hurdle winner: no promise in bumper on debut. *Peter Niven*   b–

BRAQUEUR D'OR (FR) 6 b.g. Epalo (GER) – Hot d'Or (FR) (Shafoun (FR)) [2016/17 b–: b16d h25.5g² h20g⁵ h20d Nov 30] poor form in bumpers: fair form over hurdles: best effort when second in maiden at Hereford in October. *Rebecca Curtis*   h101 b69

BRASS MONKEY (IRE) 10 b.g. Craigsteel – Saltee Great (IRE) (Fourstars Allstar (USA)) [2016/17 c–, h109: h21.2g Apr 3] handicap hurdler, fair at best: maiden chaser: stays 3m: acts on good to firm and heavy going: usually wears headgear. *Martin Keighley*   c– h95

BRAVE BUCK 9 b.g. Bollin Eric – Silken Pearls (Leading Counsel (USA)) [2016/17 c78, h–: h23.8dᵖᵘ Nov 28] plain, quite good-topped gelding: winning hurdler/chaser, fair at best: stays 25f: best form on soft/heavy going. *Henry Daly*   c– h–

BRAVE DEED (IRE) 11 b.g. Kadeed (IRE) – Merlins Return (IRE) (Torenaga) [2016/17 c–p, h97: h21.6s⁴ h21.6v h16.8s* Mar 7] sturdy gelding: winning pointer: modest handicap hurdler nowadays: won at Exeter in March: seemed amiss only start in chases: stays 2¾m: best form on soft/heavy going: in cheekpieces last 3 starts. *Jeremy Scott*   c– h96

BRAVE EAGLE (IRE) 5 b.g. Yeats (IRE) – Sinful Pleasure (IRE) (Sinndar (IRE)) [2016/17 h15.8d* h19.1g* Mar 31] €30,000 3-y-o: second foal: dam 1½m winner: third both starts in Irish maiden points: fairly useful form when successful on both starts over hurdles, in maiden at Ludlow in January and novice at Fontwell, latter 3-runner event by 9 lengths from Mister Serious: will stay at least 2½m: will go on improving. *Nicky Henderson*   h123 p

BRAVE ENCOUNTER 9 br.g. Indian Danehill (IRE) – Dartmeet (IRE) (Presenting) [2016/17 c22.6m³ c25.5g* c25.8g* Oct 20] 3-time winning pointer: maiden hurdler: modest form over fences: won handicaps at Fontwell in August and Newton Abbot (conditionals event) in October: stays 3¼m: best form on good going. *Jamie Snowden*   c94 h–

BRAVE HELIOS 7 b.g. High Chaparral (IRE) – Renowned (IRE) (Darshaan) [2016/17 h115: c16s³ c20m⁵ c23dᵖᵘ h20g c23.8m² c24d³ h19.9s h19.5m Apr 28] rather leggy gelding: handicap hurdler, fairly useful at best (showed little in 2016/17): fair maiden chaser: stays 25f: acts on good to firm and heavy going: tried in hood/tongue tie: usually races towards rear. *Richard Phillips*   c111 h–

BRAVE JAQ (FR) 6 ch.g. Network (GER) – Galaxie (FR) (Useful (FR)) [2016/17 h107p: h15.8d h15.8vᵖᵘ h16.8dᵖᵘ Mar 14] lightly-raced maiden hurdler, showed nothing in 2016/17: in hood last 4 starts: tried in tongue tie. *Tim Vaughan*   h–

BRAVENTARA 6 b.m. Kayf Tara – L'Aventure (FR) (Cyborg (FR)) [2016/17 b71: h21.7g³ h26m* h23.6g h24.4sᶠ h16.5mᶠ Apr 20] lengthy, rather unfurnished mare: fair form over hurdles: won novice at Warwick in November: stays 3¼m: acts on good to firm going: front runner/races prominently. *Nick Williams*   h112

BRAVE SPARTACUS (IRE) 11 b.g. Spartacus (IRE) – Peaches Polly (Slip Anchor) [2016/17 c143, h116: c19.2g h16.2dᵖᵘ h19.9v⁴ h16.8d² h16.4gᵘʳ Apr 8] good-topped gelding: fairly useful handicap hurdler: useful chaser at best, well held on reappearance in 2016/17: stays 21f: acts on good to firm and heavy going: has worn hood: usually leads. *Gillian Boanas*   c– h116

BRAVISSIMO (FR) 6 gr.g. Al Namix (FR) – Mimi Valley (FR) (Cyborg (FR)) [2016/17 **h126** h19v* h18s h21.1g h19g h16g⁶ Apr 28] lengthy gelding: fifth foal: half-brother to 3 winners in France, including winning hurdler/fairly useful chaser Dashing Rose (17f-23f winner, by Varese): dam placed over hurdles in France at around 2m: fairly useful form over hurdles: won maiden at Limerick in December by 3 lengths from Bobo Mac: subsequently disappointing: stays 19f: acts on heavy going. *W. P. Mullins, Ireland*

BRAW ANGUS 7 b.g. Alflora (IRE) – Suilven (Teenoso (USA)) [2016/17 h15.8d h15.5g **h108** h15.8v h15.8s h20.7s* h19.5v² Mar 23] sixth foal: half-brother to fair hurdler Ruby Crown (2m/17f winner, by Rakaposhi King): dam (b76) lightly raced in bumpers/over hurdles: fair form over hurdles: won handicap at Huntingdon in March: will be suited by 2¾m+: best form on soft/heavy going: usually races towards rear. *Kim Bailey*

BREAKING BITS (IRE) 10 br.g. Oscar (IRE) – Lantern Lark (IRE) (Be My Native **h108** (USA)) [2016/17 h111: h19.8m² h19.6d² h20d h22m⁵ h21.6g² h19.1d⁴ h21g h21.2g h21.4f² Apr 23] workmanlike gelding: fair handicap hurdler: stays 2¾m: acts on firm and good to soft going: tried in cheekpieces: front runner/races prominently. *Jamie Snowden*

BREAKING THE BANK 8 ch.g. Medicean – Russian Dance (USA) (Nureyev (USA)) **c– §** [2016/17 c115§, h–: h20.3g³ h23.3g h23.1g h19.9g⁴ h20.7g h21.6v Dec 15] handicap **h91 §** hurdler, modest nowadays: maiden chaser, fairly useful form in 2015/16: stays 2½m: acts on good to firm and good to soft going: has worn cheekpieces/tongue tie: temperamental. *Ben Case*

BREAN GOLF BIRDIE 5 br.m. Striking Ambition – Straight As A Die (Pyramus **h81** (USA)) [2016/17 h16.8m h15.3d h16.8s h15.3f⁴ Apr 23] stocky, plain mare: poor maiden on Flat, stays 1¼m: poor form over hurdles: wears hood. *Carroll Gray*

BREAN SPLASH SUSIE 6 b.m. Tobougg (IRE) – Straight As A Die (Pyramus (USA)) **h–** [2016/17 h–: h16gᵖᵘ May 22] no form in 3 maiden hurdles. *Bill Turner*

BREATH OF BLIGHTY (FR) 6 b.g. Policy Maker (IRE) – Nosika d'Airy (FR) (Oblat **c120** (FR)) [2016/17 h110, b76: h16m³ h16.3m⁵ c21.4s⁴ c16g c16d³ c19.9gᶠ c20.5m* Apr 18] **h102** good-topped gelding: point winner: fair maiden hurdler: fairly useful chaser: won novice handicap at Kempton final start: stays 21f: acts on good to firm and good to soft going: in tongue tie last 2 starts: often races prominently/travels strongly. *Paul Webber*

BRECON HILL (IRE) 4 b.g. Arcano (IRE) – Bryanstown Girl (IRE) (Kalanisi (IRE)) **b92** [2016/17 b15.7s* Feb 13] fifth foal: half-brother to 2 winners on Flat, including useful 1¼m/11f winner Double Discount (by Invincible Spirit): dam unraced half-sister to fairly useful hurdler/chaser (stayed 25f) Julius Caesar: 17/2, won conditionals/amateur maiden bumper at Catterick on debut by 1¼ lengths from Teescomponents Lad. *Alan Swinbank*

BREDON HILL LAD 10 ch.g. Kirkwall – Persian Clover (Abutammam) [2016/17 c102, **c98** h–: c15.7d⁴ c20v³ c20v² c19.4s⁵ c21.1vᶠ c17.4g* c19.4g⁴ Apr 8] lengthy gelding: winning **h–** hurdler: handicap chaser, modest nowadays: won at Fontwell in March: stays 3m: acts on heavy going: wears cheekpieces: in tongue tie last 5 starts: usually leads. *Susan Gardner*

BREDON HILL POPPY 8 b.m. Kayf Tara – Persian Clover (Abutammam) [2016/17 b–: **h–** h16d Jun 19] well held in bumper/novice hurdle. *Susan Gardner*

BREEZE ALONG 7 ch.g. Denounce – Briery Breeze (IRE) (Anshan) [2016/17 b–: **h–** h20gᵖᵘ h16.8d⁴ h16.8g⁶ h16.8g h18.5m Nov 1] lengthy gelding: no form in bumpers/over hurdles. *Susan Gardner*

BREEZY KIN (IRE) 9 ch.g. Kris Kin (USA) – Presentbreeze (IRE) (Presenting) **c85 §** [2016/17 c91, h82: h23.3d h24s³ c25.5g⁴ c22.6m h22gᵘʳ c25.5g² h23.9g⁶ Sep 5] poor **h71 §** maiden hurdler: modest handicap chaser: stays 25f: acts on soft going: wears headgear: front runner/races prominently: one to treat with caution. *Sally Randell*

BRELADE 5 b.g. Presenting – Polivalente (FR) (Poliglote) [2016/17 b16d⁴ b16.5d² b16g* **h139** h16d* h16d² h18s³ h21.1g⁶ h16s Apr 2] €85,000 3-y-o: sturdy gelding: fourth foal: half- **b108** brother to French 15f hurdle winner Grasica (by Bonbon Rose): dam (c125/h114) French 2m-2¾m hurdle/chase winner (including Prix Maurice Gillois): useful form in bumpers: won maiden at Naas in November: useful form over hurdles: won maiden at Navan later in November by neck from Joey Sasa: good efforts next 3 starts, second in Future Champions Novices' Hurdle at Leopardstown (2 lengths behind Saturnas), third in Deloitte Novices' Hurdle at Leopardstown (3 lengths behind Bacardys) in February and sixth of 15 to Willoughby Court in Baring Bingham Novices' at Cheltenham in March: stays 21f: acts on soft going. *Gordon Elliott, Ireland*

BRELAN D'AS (FR) 6 b.g. Crillon (FR) – Las de La Croix (FR) (Grand Tresor (FR)) **h139 p**
[2016/17 h119, b–: h19.8d* Nov 17] bumper winner: useful form over hurdles: in tongue
strap, won handicap at Wincanton by 6 lengths (with plenty in hand) from Winning Spark,
only outing in 2016/17: stays 2½m: acts on good to soft going: in hood last 2 starts: open
to further improvement. *Paul Nicholls*

BRERETON (IRE) 6 b.g. Kalanisi (IRE) – Westgrove Berry (IRE) (Presenting) [2016/17 **h81**
b–: h19.5gF h21.6s4 h18.5s h19.8v4 Mar 9] useful-looking gelding: in tongue tie, poor form
over hurdles. *Richard Woollacott*

BRIAC (FR) 6 b.g. Kapgarde (FR) – Jarwin Do (FR) (Grand Tresor (FR)) [2016/17 h69p, **h99**
b92: h20d2 h23.3g Jul 5] modest maiden hurdler: stays 2½m: acts on good to soft going:
tried in visor. *Jim Best*

BRIAN BORANHA (IRE) 6 b.g. Brian Boru – Tapneiram (IRE) (Kahyasi) [2016/17 **h108**
h102p, b–: h17.1d4 h19.7g h19.9d4 h24.1d2 h25.3d4 h23.1s3 h25.3s3 h23.1d* Apr 27] rather
lightly-built gelding: fair handicap hurdler: won at Market Rasen in April: also first past
post at Catterick in December, but disqualified after jockey weighed in 2 lb light: stays 25f:
acts on soft going: often races prominently. *Peter Niven*

BRIAR HILL (IRE) 9 b.g. Shantou (USA) – Backaway (IRE) (Bob Back (USA)) **c135**
[2016/17 h131: c18.2g2 c20.5d* c17d2 c24dF c24s6 Jan 28] good-topped gelding: very **h–**
smart chaser at best: useful chaser: won maiden at Killarney in August by 2¾ lengths from
Marinero: ½-length second to Attribution in Grade 3 novice at Navan in December: stays
21f: acts on soft going: often races prominently. *W. P. Mullins, Ireland*

BRICBRACSMATE 9 b.g. Revoque (IRE) – Blissphilly (Primo Dominie) [2016/17 h–: **h100**
h15.7dpu h16.7m2 Apr 9] very lightly-raced maiden hurdler: in cheekpieces, first form when
second in novice at Market Rasen. *Michael Mullineaux*

BRICE CANYON (FR) 6 b.g. Kapgarde (FR) – Fille Formidable (USA) (Trempolino **c102**
(USA)) [2016/17 c21.1d2 c20g3 c19.2s4 c19.7s2 c20.2s3 c19.7s3 Mar 13] half-brother to 3 **h–**
winners, including fairly useful hurdler/smart chaser Aerial (2¼m-27f winner, by Turgeon):
dam French 7f/11f winner: won twice in points: maiden hurdler: fair maiden chaser: stays
2½m: acts on soft going: has worn headgear, including last 4 starts: often leads. *Giles Smyly*

BRIDAL SUITE (IRE) 8 b.g. Craigsteel – Selinda Spectrum (IRE) (Spectrum (IRE)) **c–**
[2016/17 c–, h87: h23gpu May 19] point winner: handicap hurdler, modest at best: pulled **h–**
up on chasing debut: stays 27f: acts on heavy going: usually in cheekpieces/tongue tie.
Anabel K. Murphy

BRIDGE END (IRE) 9 br.g. Jimble (FR) – Canny Fathomit (IRE) (Over The River (FR)) **c97**
[2016/17 c23s5 c20s4 c23.8g3 c23.8g3 Mar 1] point winner: modest form over fences: stays
3m: acts on soft going: in cheekpieces last 2 starts: tried in tongue tie. *Ian Ferguson,
Ireland*

BRIDGE OF CALLY (IRE) 4 b.g. September Storm (GER) – Cathy's Pal (IRE) **b69**
(Exit To Nowhere (USA)) [2016/17 b15.8s5 b15.7g3 Apr 21] little impact in bumpers.
Harry Whittington

BRIDGE OF SPIES (IRE) 6 ch.g. Indian River (FR) – Killerig Park (I'm Supposin **h85 p**
(IRE)) [2016/17 h20g5 Oct 19] €5,800 3-y-o: fifth foal: dam unraced half-sister to fairly
useful hurdler/chaser (stayed 25f) Marblehead: off mark in Irish maiden points at third
attempt: 11/10, fifth in maiden at Worcester (16¼ lengths behind Hey Bill) on hurdling
debut: should do better. *Philip Hobbs*

BRIERY BELLE 8 b.m. King's Theatre (IRE) – Briery Ann (Anshan) [2016/17 h134: **c139**
c20g* c20s* c20.8s3 c24.4gpu c20.8gpu Apr 20] strong mare: useful hurdler: also useful **h–**
form on first 2 starts in chases, winning novice at Carlisle in November by 8 lengths from
Vintage Clouds and listed mares novice at Warwick in December by 6 lengths from Desert
Queen: only completion subsequently when third of 4 in Dipper Novices' Chase at
Cheltenham (20½ lengths behind Whisper) in January: stays 3m: acts on heavy going: front
runner/races prominently. *Henry Daly*

BRIERY QUEEN 8 b.m. King's Theatre (IRE) – Briery Gale (Strong Gale) [2016/17 **h140**
h128: h20.3s* h19.8s3 h19.9g5 h24.7g Apr 8] useful-looking mare: useful hurdler: won
mares handicap at Cheltenham in December by 3½ lengths from On Demand: good effort
when 5¾ lengths fifth of 17 to Apple's Jade in David Nicholson Mares' Hurdle at
Cheltenham in March: stays 21f: acts on soft going: wears hood. *Noel Williams*

BRIGADOON 10 b.g. Compton Place – Briggsmaid (Elegant Air) [2016/17 h106: **h68**
h18.7mpu h16.7g4 Aug 13] maiden hurdler, fair at best: may prove best at short of 2½m:
acts on good to firm going: usually races prominently, tends to find little. *Michael Appleby*

*Peter Marsh Chase (Limited Handicap), Haydock—an improved performance by Bristol de Mai,
who is about to be left clear by a mistake from runner-up Otago Trail*

BRIGHT ABBEY 9 ch.g. Halling (USA) – Bright Hope (IRE) (Danehill (USA)) [2016/17
c25.5d Jun 26] winning hurdler: maiden chaser: stays 21f: acts on good to firm going.
Dianne Sayer — **c– h–**

BRIGHT NEW DAWN (IRE) 10 br.g. Presenting – Shuil Dorcha (IRE) (Bob Back
(USA)) [2016/17 c154§, h133: c16d³ h20m³ c18g³ c17g c22.5g h24d³ c15.5s⁴ c15.5v³
c16v⁴ c16.4s³ c16.3g c21.1gᶠ Apr 7] rangy, useful-looking gelding: fairly useful hurdler
nowadays: smart handicap chaser: left Gordon Elliott after sixth start: has form at 3m but
better at shorter: acts on heavy going: usually in headgear/tongue tie prior to joining
present trainer: temperamental. *Venetia Williams* — **c145 § h127 §**

BRIGHT PROSPECT (IRE) 8 b.g. Kutub (IRE) – Bright Future (IRE) (Satco (FR))
[2016/17 h112: h20.2m⁶ c16f³ c16d⁴ c20.1g* c20.1s³ c20.5d² c19.9g⁴ c21.6sᵖᵘ c21.3dᵖᵘ
c23.8g² Apr 26] handicap hurdler, fair at best: fairly useful handicap chaser: won novice
event at Perth in August: stays 3m: acts on soft going: wears cheekpieces. *Jackie Stephen* — **c116 h87**

BRILLARE MOMENTO (IRE) 6 b.m. Milan – Sunshine Leader (IRE) (Supreme
Leader) [2016/17 b20m³ b16.4g² b16.4s⁶ h21.2dᵘʳ h20.3g* h20.3g* Apr 20] well-made
mare: fifth foal: half-sister to a winning pointer by Turtle Island: dam (c95/h96) 2½m
bumper/hurdle winner: fairly useful form in bumpers: useful form in novice hurdles: won
mares event at Southwell in March and listed mares race at Cheltenham (by neck from
Dusky Legend) in April: left J. Culloty after first start: will stay at least 2¾m: often races
prominently/travels strongly: open to further improvement. *Martin Keighley* — **h136 p b95**

BRIN D'AVOINE (FR) 6 b.g. Califet (FR) – Nemenchka (FR) (Turgeon (USA))
[2016/17 h69, b–: h19.9g h18.5dᵖᵘ h20gᵖᵘ Jul 12] well held in bumper and over hurdles: in
cheekpieces final start: often races freely. *Neil Mulholland* — **h–**

BRINESTINE (USA) 8 b.g. Bernstein (USA) – Miss Zafonic (FR) (Zafonic (USA))
[2016/17 h98: h19g⁶ h15.8g h16.7g⁶ h16.8g⁶ h16.8m⁵ h16.8g⁴ c16g³ c15.9g² c15.9sᶠ
c18.2g Mar 30] angular gelding: modest handicap hurdler/maiden chaser: unproven
beyond 17f: best form on good going: has worn headgear, including last 3 starts: wears
tongue tie. *Emma Baker* — **c89 h86**

BRING BACK CHARLIE 7 b.g. Green Card (USA) – Nafertiti (IRE) (Bob Back
(USA)) [2016/17 h86: h15.8d² h15.8d* h21.2g h16.7s⁵ h19.7v⁴ h16.6d⁵ Feb 9] modest
handicap hurdler: won at Uttoxeter in October: best effort at 2m: acts on good to soft going:
tried in cheekpieces: often races towards rear. *Nigel Twiston-Davies* — **h85**

BRINGEWOOD BLUE (IRE) 10 br.m. Blueprint (IRE) – Carramore (IRE) (Topanoora) **h–**
[2016/17 h87: h23.3d^{pu} May 5] little impact in 3 runs over hurdles. *John Needham*

BRIO CONTI (FR) 6 gr.g. Dom Alco (FR) – Cadoulie Wood (FR) (Cadoudal (FR)) **h140 p**
[2016/17 b95: b16.3g* h16.2d^F h18.9v^2 h16.8g h19.4g* h21g* h20g^5 Apr 8] good-topped **b97**
gelding: fairly useful form in bumpers: won maiden at Stratford in May: useful hurdler:
won maiden at Doncaster in January and handicap at Kempton (by 3½ lengths from Divine
Spear) in March: good fifth to Finian's Oscar in Mersey Novices' Hurdle at Aintree final
start: stays 21f: all wins on good ground, probably acts on heavy: strong traveller: remains
with potential. *Paul Nicholls*

BRISE COEUR (FR) 6 b.g. Daramsar (FR) – Rose Bombon (FR) (Cadoudal (FR)) **c76**
[2016/17 c–, h91: h20s^5 c16.1d^4 c16s Dec 19] maiden hurdler, modest form at best: poor **h–**
novice chaser: stayed 21f: acted on heavy going: tried in blinkers: dead. *Nick Williams*

BRISTOL DE MAI (FR) 6 gr.g. Saddler Maker (IRE) – La Bole Night (FR) (April Night **c159**
(FR)) [2016/17 c150, h–: c20d^2 c23.4s^2 c24.1s* c23.4d^3 c26.3g c25g^5 Apr 6] tall gelding: **h–**
winning hurdler: very smart chaser: impressive when winning Peter Marsh Chase
(Handicap) at Haydock in January by 22 lengths from Otago Trail: below form after, only
placing when last of 3 in Denman Chase at Newbury (9¼ lengths behind Native River) in
February: stays 3m: acts on heavy going: usually races close up/travels strongly. *Nigel
Twiston-Davies*

BRITANIO BELLO (FR) 6 b.g. Irish Wells (FR) – Tchi Tchi Bang Bang (FR) (Perrault) **c–**
[2016/17 h120: c16g c20.3d^6 c16.4s^F Jan 18] tall, angular gelding: fairly useful hurdler: **h–**
well held both completed starts over fences: best effort at 2m: acts on heavy going.
Gary Moore

BRITISH ART 5 b.g. Iffraaj – Bush Cat (USA) (Kingmambo (USA)) [2016/17 h16d h16d **h92**
h18.8g^5 h16.8g^4 h16g Apr 21] dam closely related to smart hurdler (stayed 2½m) Drive
Time: modest maiden on Flat, stays 1m: modest form over hurdles: bred to stay 2½m: tried
in cheekpieces. *R. K. Watson, Ireland*

BROAD SPECTRUM (IRE) 6 b.g. Gamut (IRE) – Knock Na Brona (IRE) (Oscar **c–**
(IRE)) [2016/17 h88, b–: h20d^4 c23.4s^{pu} c26.2g^{pu} Apr 15] winning pointer: modest form **h89**
over hurdles: pulled up both starts in chases: should prove suited by further than 2½m: acts
on heavy going: tried in cheekpieces/tongue tie. *Chris Grant*

BROADWAY BELLE 7 b.m. Lucarno (USA) – Theatre Belle (King's Theatre (IRE)) **h73**
[2016/17 h81: h19.3s^F h16d h20.6v^3 h19.7d^3 h27m^2 Apr 19] poor maiden hurdler: stays
easy 27f: acts on good to firm and good to soft going. *Chris Grant*

BROCKTON GANDT 5 b.m. Erhaab (USA) – Oyster Bay (Mandalus) [2016/17 b15.7s **b–**
Mar 20] fourth foal: dam (h62) bumper winner: tailed off in bumper. *Mike Hammond*

BRODY BLEU (FR) 10 b.g. Kotky Bleu (FR) – Brodie Blue (FR) (Agent Bleu (FR)) **c118**
[2016/17 c128, h–: c21.1d^4 c23m* c23.8g^5 c21m^3 c23.8m^6 Apr 25] strong gelding: winning **h–**
pointer: maiden hurdler: fairly useful chaser: won handicap at Worcester in May: left
Robert Walford after third start: stays 3m: acts on good to firm and heavy going: tried in
cheekpieces. *Miss L. Wallace*

BROKEN EAGLE (USA) 9 b.g. Broken Vow (USA) – Tricky Bird (USA) (Storm Bird **c106**
(CAN)) [2016/17 c–, h–: c16.3g^2 c27.5m^4 c21.1g^F Apr 6] leggy, close-coupled gelding: **h–**
prolific winning pointer: maiden hurdler: best effort in chases when second in hunter at
Cheltenham very early in season: should stay beyond 2½m: acts on good to firm going:
wears tongue tie. *Alan Hill*

BROKETHEGATE 12 b.g. Presenting – Briery Ann (Anshan) [2016/17 c77§, h–: c24d^{pu} **c– §**
Jul 13] good-topped gelding: maiden hurdler/chaser: stayed 25f: acted on soft going: **h–**
temperamental: dead. *Chris Grant*

BRONCO BILLY (IRE) 7 b.g. Flemensfirth (USA) – La Fisarmonica (IRE) (Accordion) **c110**
[2016/17 h117: c23g^5 c23.6d^3 c24m c30.7m^2 c23.6g* Apr 28] well-made gelding: **h–**
fairly useful hurdler: fair form in handicap chases, winning at Huntingdon final start: stays
25f: acts on good to soft going: often in cheekpieces: wears tongue tie: often races
prominently: temperament under suspicion. *Jonjo O'Neill*

BROOK (FR) 6 ch.g. Kandidate – Ninon de Ré (Denham Red (FR)) [2016/17 c111, **c109**
h–: c24.5g^2 c23m^F c26.1s^{pu} c23d^6 Jun 29] workmanlike gelding: winning hurdler: fair **h–**
handicap chaser: stays 3m: acts on heavy going: wears headgear/tongue tie: often travels
strongly, tends to find little. *David Pipe*

BROOME LANE 8 b.m. Kayf Tara – Aranga (IRE) (Supreme Leader) [2016/17 c91p, h–: **c55** c25.5d⁵ h19.5dᵖᵘ c23.8g⁶ h23.3v Dec 31] maiden hurdler: poor handicap chaser: stays **h–** 3¼m: acts on soft going: in headgear last 5 starts: usually races close up. *Tim Vaughan*

BROOM TIP (IRE) 5 b.g. Flemensfirth (USA) – Norabelle (FR) (Alamo Bay (USA)) **h98 p** [2016/17 b16g b15.8s h19.5v⁶ h21s³ Mar 30] fourth foal: brother to useful bumper/2m **b–** hurdle winner Invitation Only, stays 2½m, and half-brother to a winning pointer by Presenting: dam, French 15f hurdle winner, also 10.5f-13f winner on Flat: no form in bumpers: modest form over hurdles: better effort when third in maiden at Warwick: likely to stay 2¾m+: capable of better again. *Tom George*

BROTHER BENNETT (FR) 7 gr.g. Martaline – La Gaminerie (FR) (Cadoudal (FR)) **c88** [2016/17 h88: h16m⁵ h16s⁵ c16g⁴ c16v³ c17sᵘʳ c17g⁴ Mar 27] well-made gelding: maiden **h–** hurdler, fair at best: modest maiden chaser: unproven beyond 17f: acts on heavy going: tried in visor: wears tongue tie. *Zoe Davison*

BROTHER GOLD (IRE) 8 gr.g. Generous (IRE) – Glenmoss Rosy (IRE) (Zaffaran **h–** (USA)) [2016/17 h16d h19d h22d Dec 10] bumper winner: maiden hurdler, no form in 2016/17: has worn tongue tie. *Michael O'Hare, Ireland*

BROTHERLY COMPANY (IRE) 5 b.g. Fast Company (IRE) – Good Lady (IRE) **h119** (Barathea (IRE)) [2016/17 h110p: h16g* h16.3m² h16.2g⁵ h15.9m⁵ h16.3d² h15.7g Apr 15] angular gelding: fairly useful handicap hurdler: won at Kempton (amateurs event) in May: raced around 2m: acts on good to firm and good to soft going. *Harry Fry*

BROTHER NORPHIN 5 b.g. Norse Dancer (IRE) – Orphina (IRE) (Orpen (USA)) **h–** [2016/17 b79: b16g h15.3mᵖᵘ h21.4sᵖᵘ h18.5s h19.8v h21.4d⁵ Mar 26] rather unfurnished **b–** gelding: little impact in bumpers/over hurdles: has worn cheekpieces: in tongue tie last 3 starts. *Simon Hodgson*

BROTHER SCOTT 10 b.g. Kirkwall – Crimson Shower (Dowsing (USA)) [2016/17 **c88** c100, h–: c24.2g c20.1d⁴ c24vᵖᵘ c21.2g⁵ c20.1g² c23.4s⁴ c20.1s³ Nov 4] winning hurdler: **h–** modest handicap chaser: stays 23f: acts on good to firm and heavy going: front runner/races prominently. *Sue Smith*

BROTHER TEDD 8 gr.g. Kayf Tara – Neltina (Neltino) [2016/17 h148: h22.8m⁵ c21g² **c135** c19.8g⁴ c18.8d² c20.2d⁴ c21m³ c20g² Apr 29] well-made gelding: smart handicap hurdler: **h145** useful form in chases: runner-up in intermediate event at Newton Abbot, maiden at Ascot (6 lengths behind Different Gravey) and novice handicap at Sandown (neck behind Shantou Village): will stay 3m: acts on good to firm and heavy going. *Philip Hobbs*

BROUGHTONS BANDIT 10 b.g. Kyllachy – Broughton Bounty (Bahamian Bounty) **c90** [2016/17 c116, h100: c21.1d³ c25.7m³ c24m⁵ c19.7g⁵ Oct 31] fair hurdler: handicap **h–** chaser, modest form at best in 2016/17: stays 3m: acts on good to firm and good to soft going: has worn headgear/tongue tie. *Phil York*

BROUGHTONS RHYTHM 8 b.g. Araafa (IRE) – Broughton Singer (IRE) (Common **h114** Grounds) [2016/17 h110: h16mᵖᵘ h16.3d⁵ h18.6s⁴ h15.8v³ h15.8s* Mar 18] lengthy gelding: fair form over hurdles: improved to win novice handicap at Uttoxeter final outing: best form at 2m: acts on soft going. *Henry Spiller*

BROUGHTONS STAR 10 ch.g. Starcraft (NZ) – Marrakech (IRE) (Barathea (IRE)) **h103** [2016/17 h16.3d⁴ h19.5g⁵ h20g⁴ h16d² h20sᶠ h16d² h16vᵘʳ h16vᵘʳ h21d⁴ h20g⁶ Apr 20] workmanlike gelding: fair maiden hurdler: left Willie Musson after first start: stays 21f: acts on soft and good to firm going: wears tongue tie: often travels strongly. *Gordon Elliott, Ireland*

BROWN BEAR (IRE) 6 b.g. Yeats (IRE) – Moray Firth (UAE) (Halling (USA)) **c96** [2016/17 h81, b78: c16.1d³ c19.8d⁴ c19.7s⁶ h21.6v³ h19.1v⁴ c21.1g⁴ c17.4g* Apr 21] **h92** useful-looking gelding: modest maiden hurdler: modest form over fences: won handicaps at Towcester in December and Fontwell final start: stays 2¾m: acts on heavy going: in cheekpieces last 3 starts. *Nick Gifford*

BROWN PADDY (IRE) 7 b.g. Morozov (USA) – River Breeze (IRE) (Sharifabad **h–** (IRE)) [2016/17 b16d⁶ h19.5vᵖᵘ h15.8d h20.6m⁵ Apr 9] maiden hurdler: showed nothing in **b–** bumper/maiden hurdles: left Daniel O'Brien after first start. *Laura Hurley*

BROWN TRIX (IRE) 7 b.g. Flemensfirth (USA) – Five Trix (Minster Son) [2016/17 **c–** c17.3m c20.1gᵖᵘ Jun 4] maiden pointer: showed nothing in 2 chases. *Victor Thompson*

BROWNVILLE 8 b.g. Kayf Tara – Cool Spice (Karinga Bay) [2016/17 c110, h108: c24s* **c116** c24m⁴ c25g⁴ c25.5m² c24v² c23.6s⁴ c29.6s⁴ c23.8g⁶ Apr 9] winning hurdler: fairly useful **h–** handicap chaser: won novice event at Uttoxeter very early in season: stays 3¼m: acts on heavy going: often wears cheekpieces: usually in tongue tie. *Nigel Twiston-Davies*

BRUCE ALMIGHTY (IRE) 6 b.g. Yeats (IRE) – Lady Rolfe (IRE) (Alzao (USA)) **h105**
[2016/17 h117: h23.3s⁵ h19.9vᵖᵘ h19.9d³ h19.7d⁵ h25.3s⁵ h21.3d h23.1g⁶ Apr 22] stocky
gelding: fair handicap hurdler: stays 21f: acts on good to soft going: often in cheekpieces
nowadays: often leads. *Donald McCain*

BRUCE OF CRIONAICH (IRE) 7 b.g. Flemensfirth (USA) – Sommer Sonnet (IRE) **h57**
(Taipan (IRE)) [2016/17 b77: h20g⁶ h21.6vᵖᵘ Feb 14] pulled up in point on debut: modest
form only start in bumpers: in tongue tie, showed nothing in 2 runs over hurdles: left Dan
Skelton after reappearance. *Michael Attwater*

BRUICHLADDICH 5 b.g. Westerner – Highland Cherry (Milan) [2016/17 b16s b16v **h100**
h17s⁵ h16v⁴ h16.2v* Mar 28] first foal: dam unraced: little impact in bumpers: fair form **b60**
over hurdles: suited by way race developed when winning novice at Hexham on final start:
will stay 2½m: raced only on soft/heavy going. *Iain Jardine*

BRUNEL WOODS (IRE) 5 b.g. Oscar (IRE) – Golden Bay (Karinga Bay) [2016/17 **b93**
b88: b15.8v b15.6g³ b16.7m³ Apr 17] fair form in bumpers: third at Musselburgh and
Market Rasen last 2 starts. *David Dennis*

BRUNTON BLUE 12 b.m. Compton Place – Persian Blue (Persian Bold) [2016/17 **h85**
h15.8g* h15.8gᵖᵘ Sep 18] modest handicap hurdler: off over 3 years, won at Uttoxeter in
June: stays easy 2½m: acts on good to firm going. *Caroline Bailey*

BRYDEN BOY (IRE) 7 b.g. Craigsteel – Cailin Vic Mo Cri (IRE) (Old Vic) [2016/17 **h127**
h111: h20.3v⁵ h19.9d³ h19.5d³ h23.3v* h25.5v² h24.3v* h24.2d⁴ h24.4s* h25.8s⁵ Mar 25]
workmanlike gelding: fairly useful handicap chaser: won at Uttoxeter in December, Ayr in
January and Doncaster in March: stays 3¼m: acts on heavy going: has worn cheekpieces:
tried in tongue tie: usually races towards rear. *Jennie Candlish*

BRYNMAWR 7 b.g. Double Trigger (IRE) – Little Feat (Terimon) [2016/17 h19.5s **h112**
h21.4s⁴ h19.1v² h21.4s² Mar 1] fifth foal: half-brother to bumper winner/fairly useful
hurdler Too Generous (2½m/21f winner, by Generous), stayed 3m, and modest/unreliable
hurdler Azione (2m/17f winner, by Exit To Nowhere), stayed 21f: dam (b95) bumper
winner: failed to complete all 3 starts in points: fair form over hurdles, runner-up in novices
at Fontwell and Wincanton. *Colin Tizzard*

BUACHAILL ALAINN (IRE) 10 b.g. Oscar (IRE) – Bottle A Knock (IRE) (Le Moss) **c128 §**
[2016/17 c132§, h–: c24.2d³ c23.6g⁵ c29.2g* c27.2s⁵ c27.9d Apr 16] good-topped gelding: **h–**
has reportedly had breathing operation: winning hurdler: fairly useful handicap chaser
nowadays: won at Sedgefield in October: stays 29f: acts on good to firm and heavy going:
wears headgear: has worn tongue tie, including in 2016/17: temperamental. *Peter Bowen*

BUACHAILL BEAG 6 gr.g. And Beyond (IRE) – Bon Enfant (IRE) (Roselier (FR)) **h– §**
[2016/17 b60: b16m³ h19.2gʳᵒ May 31] poor form in bumpers: ran out sixth on hurdling **b60**
debut: usually in hood/tongue tie: one to treat with caution. *Fergal O'Brien*

BUACHAILLNAHEIREAN (IRE) 4 b.g. Desert Millennium (IRE) – Run Sweetheart **h–**
(USA) (Bold Run (FR)) [2016/17 h15.9m⁴ Sep 18] half-brother to fair 2m hurdle winner
Mind The Steps (by Tamayaz): poor maiden on Flat: well held in juvenile at Plumpton on
hurdling debut. *Neil King*

BUBBA N SQUEAK (FR) 6 ch.g. Dom Alco (FR) – Naiade du Moulin (FR) (Ragmar **h104**
(FR)) [2016/17 b16d⁵ h21gᵖᵘ h20.6g² h23.1d³ h23.9sᵖᵘ h21.3d Mar 31] fifth foal: brother **b75**
to bumper winner All Force Majeure: dam unraced: fifth in bumper on debut: fair form
when placed in novice/maiden hurdles: should stay 3m: acts on good to soft going: tried in
blinkers: often races towards rear. *Dan Skelton*

BUBLE (IRE) 8 b.g. Milan – Glorious Moments (IRE) (Moonax (IRE)) [2016/17 h18.5g⁴ **h108**
h21.2v⁵ h16.7d² Apr 27] runner-up 3 of 4 starts in Irish points: fair form over hurdles: best
effort when second in novice at Market Rasen: should stay at least 2½m. *David Bridgwater*

BUBSY BURBIDGE 6 b.g. Helissio (FR) – Twin Time (Syrtos) [2016/17 h15.9d² h17sᵖᵘ **h95**
h16.3g h15.8d Apr 16] half-brother to several winners, including useful hurdler/chaser
Pass The Time (2m-19f winner, by Passing Glance) and fairly useful hurdler Mr Burbidge
(2m winner, by Midnight Legend): dam (h75), maiden hurdler, 7f-1¼m winner on Flat:
second at Plumpton on debut, well beaten in novice hurdles. *Neil Mulholland*

BUCKBORU (IRE) 9 b.m. Brian Boru – Buckland Filleigh (IRE) (Buckskin (FR)) **h–**
[2016/17 h77: h23mᵖᵘ Jul 4] lengthy mare: poor maiden handicap hurdler: stays easy 3m:
acts on heavy and good to firm going: has worn cheekpieces, including in 2016/17.
Laura Young

BUCKBY BOY 4 br.g. Shirocco (GER) – Fair View (GER) (Dashing Blade) [2016/17 **b85** b15.8g⁴ Apr 3] £40,000 3-y-o: fifth foal: half-brother to fairly useful hurdler Halling's Wish (2¼m winner, by Halling), stays 2¾m: dam, ungenuine maiden hurdler (7f winner on Flat in Germany), half-sister to very smart hurdler/smart chaser (stayed 3¼m) Fair Along: 9/1, 7½ lengths fourth to Cresswell Legend in conditionals/amateur bumper at Huntingdon. *Dan Skelton*

BUCKERS BRIDGE (IRE) 11 b.g. Pelder (IRE) – La Fiere Dame (IRE) (Lafontaine **c122** (USA)) [2016/17 c137: c22.6s³ c26.3gᵖᵘ Mar 17] strong gelding: winning pointer: smart chaser at best: fairly useful form when third in hunter at Down Royal in December: in cheekpieces, pulled up ninth in Foxhunter Chase at Cheltenham final start: stays 25f: acts on heavy going. *M. F. Morris, Ireland*

BUCKHORN TIMOTHY 8 b.g. Tamure (IRE) – Waimea Bay (Karinga Bay) [2016/17 **c134** c132, h–: c23.6g² c23.8m c23.6g Dec 3] winning hurdler: useful handicap chaser: second **h–** at Chepstow (length behind Potters Cross) in October, easily best effort of season: stays 3m: acts on heavy going. *Colin Tizzard*

BUCKHORN TOM 9 b.g. Tamure (IRE) – Waimea Bay (Karinga Bay) [2016/17 c102§, **c97 §** h–: c25.5g³ c25.8dᵖᵘ Jun 21] winning hurdler: modest handicap chaser: stays 3¼m: acts on **h–** heavy going: wears headgear: in tongue tie last 2 starts: temperamental. *Colin Tizzard*

BUCKING THE TREND 9 b.g. Kayf Tara – Macklette (IRE) (Buckskin (FR)) [2016/17 **c130** c131, h–: c25g² h23.3d* Oct 2] good-topped gelding: fairly useful handicap hurdler: **h127** in tongue tie, won at Uttoxeter in October by 1¼ lengths from Some Are Lucky: useful handicap chaser: good second at Aintree in May: stays 25f: acts on heavy going: in cheekpieces last 4 starts in chases: usually races close up, often travels strongly. *Tim Vaughan*

BUCKLED 7 b.g. Midnight Legend – Mulberry Wine (Benny The Dip (USA)) [2016/17 **c–** h90: h20.2f* h20.1dᵖᵘ h20.2sᵖᵘ c23.8g⁵ c23.8gᶠ h23.8g* h22.7d⁵ h20.2g Apr 27] fair **h107** handicap hurdler: won at Perth in June and Musselburgh in March: showed little on completed start in chases: stays 3m: acts on firm and good to soft going: has worn hood. *Sandy Thomson*

BUCKLE STREET 4 br.g. Cacique (IRE) – Rose Row (Act One) [2016/17 h16s² h16.5g³ **h114** h16.2v³ h15.7d* h18.8g⁵ Mar 25] compact gelding: fair maiden on Flat, stays 2m: fair form over hurdles: won novice at Southwell in February: should stay beyond 2m: acts on good to soft going: tried in cheekpieces: wears tongue tie: usually races prominently. *Martin Keighley*

BUCK MULLIGAN 12 b.g. Robellino (USA) – Music Park (IRE) (Common Grounds) **c–** [2016/17 c121, h–: c24.1dᵖᵘ May 26] sturdy gelding: winning hurdler: fairly useful chaser **h–** in 2015/16: in cheekpieces, showed nothing only outing in 2016/17: stays 3m: acts on soft and good to firm going: often races towards rear. *Evan Williams*

BUCKONTUPENCE (IRE) 9 b.g. Brian Boru – Miss Od (IRE) (Good Thyne (USA)) **h99** [2016/17 h102: h25m² h19.7dᵖᵘ h24s⁵ Mar 16] Irish point winner: modest maiden handicap hurdler: stays 23f: acts on soft and good to firm going: often races towards rear. *James Evans*

BUCKSKIN BOULTA (IRE) 9 b.g. Vertical Speed (FR) – Ballymartin Trix (IRE) **c75** (Buckskin (FR)) [2016/17 h111: h24.6g⁵ h23.3d* h23d² h24s c20.1v⁵ c26.3sᵖᵘ h24.4dᵖᵘ **h108** Feb 9] pulled up all 3 starts in points: fair hurdler: won novice at Hexham in June: poor form on completed start in chases: stays 23f: acts on heavy going: wears tongue tie: often leads. *Mark McNiff, Ireland*

BUCK'S LAD 7 b.g. Double Trigger (IRE) – April Attraction (FR) (Mark of Esteem **h96** (IRE)) [2016/17 b15.8s b15.3s h18.5m² Apr 18] first foal: dam (h76), maiden hurdler, **b–** 10.5f-1½m winner on Flat in France, half-sister to useful hurdler (stayed 3m) April Allegro: no form in bumpers: 12/1, second of 6 in maiden at Exeter (8 lengths behind Trevisani) on hurdling debut. *Victor Dartnall*

BUDARRI 4 b.g. Supreme Sound – Amtaar (Nayef (USA)) [2016/17 b14.6s b15.6g Jan **b–** 20] well held both starts in bumpers. *Stuart Coltherd*

BUDDY BOLERO (IRE) 11 b.g. Accordion – Quinnsboro Ice (IRE) (Glacial Storm **c–** (USA)) [2016/17 c24g h16sᵖᵘ h16v c33mᵖᵘ Apr 27] tall gelding: smart hurdler/useful **h–** chaser at best: missed 2015/16, no form in 2016/17: left Mark Pitman after second start: has worn headgear: tried in tongue tie. *A. J. Martin, Ireland*

BUENO RICA (FR) 6 br.g. Cal*fet (FR) – Infante de Rica (FR) (Garde Royale) [2016/17 **h–** b–: h15.7s Jan 31] no show in bumpers/novice hurdle. *Samuel Drinkwater*

BUFFALO BALLET 11 b.g. Kayf Tara – Minora (IRE) (Cataldi) [2016/17 h21.4s⁴ c21.5s³ c24.2s⁶ c20.5v² c21.6sᵘʳ Mar 25] winning hurdler, fair at best: fair form when placed in 2 novice handicap chases: stays 21f: raced mainly on soft/heavy going. *N. W. Alexander* **c109 h99**

BUFFALO SABRE (FR) 5 b.g. Turgeon (USA) – Kerry Rose (FR) (Tel Quel (FR)) [2016/17 h–: h20d³ h21dᵖᵘ h18.5s⁶ c23.6gᵖᵘ Apr 17] modest form in novice hurdles: pulled up in novice handicap on chasing debut: stays 2½m: acts on good to soft going: in cheekpieces last 4 starts: sometimes in tongue tie. *Nigel Hawke* **c– h99**

BUGGI (IRE) 6 b.m. Scorpion (IRE) – Luck of The Deise (IRE) (Old Vic) [2016/17 b16.8g⁴ b16.8g⁶ h19.5mᵖᵘ h19.7s Jan 14] £1,500 5-y-o: fifth foal: half-sister to bumper winner/fairly useful hurdler Joe Farrell (2½m winner, by Presenting), stays 3m: dam unraced half-sister to fairly useful hurdler up to 3m Bondi Storm: modest form in bumpers: no form in novice hurdles: in cheekpieces/tongue tie final start. *Brian Barr* **h– b75**

BUGSIE MALONE (IRE) 7 b.g. Mahler – The Irish Whip (Presenting) [2016/17 h115p: h21g² h23.6d⁴ h23.4s⁴ c23.4d⁴ c23.6s⁵ c24g* c24m² c25.5g² Apr 21] big gelding: winning pointer: fairly useful maiden hurdler: fairly useful chaser: won handicap at Kempton in March: stays 3m: acts on soft and good to firm going: front runner/races prominently. *Chris Gordon* **c120 h118**

BULFIN ISLAND (IRE) 8 b.g. Milan – Tournore Court (IRE) (Insan (USA)) [2016/17 h20.5v⁴ h21s h24.2s³ Mar 3] well-made gelding: won completed start in Irish maiden points: lightly-raced maiden hurdler, stays 3m: acts on soft going. *Alan King* **h100**

BULKOV (FR) 5 b.g. Zambezi Sun – Say Say (FR) (Garde Royale) [2016/17 h17.9s h17.9s³ h17.9v³ h16.5g Apr 7] tall gelding: fourth foal: dam (h117), French 17f/19f hurdle winner, also 11.5f/12.5f winner on Flat: fair maiden on Flat, stays 1¼m: fairly useful maiden hurdler: third at Enghien in listed event (12 lengths behind Isabe) in October and claimer in November: out of depth final outing: maiden chaser: left J-P. Gallorini after third start: probably stays 2¼m: acts on heavy going. *Micky Hammond* **c– h123**

BULL AND BUSH (IRE) 8 br.m. Presenting – Sound of The Crowd (IRE) (Accordion) [2016/17 h25g³ c23.4d h24.1s⁵ Jan 6] useful-looking mare: lightly-raced handicap hurdler, just fair form in 2016/17: tailed off in novice handicap on chasing debut: stays 25f: acts on good to soft going: should do better over fences. *Charlie Mann* **c– p h101**

BULLETPROOF (IRE) 11 b.g. Wareed (IRE) – Laura's Native (IRE) (Be My Native (USA)) [2016/17 c–, h101§: h16.8g⁵ h16m* h18.5m h17.7d h16.5g h16g² h15.8g³ Apr 28] winning pointer: fair handicap hurdler: won at Kempton in May: maiden chaser: stays 2¼m: acts on good to firm and good to soft going: wears headgear: has worn tongue tie: often races in rear: unreliable. *Ken Cunningham-Brown* **c– h106 §**

BULLIONAIRE (IRE) 4 b.g. Gold Well – Dontcallerthat (IRE) (Anshan) [2016/17 b16.3g* Mar 25] £37,000 3-y-o: well-made gelding: first foal: dam (h71) winning pointer/maiden hurdler: 11/2, won 20-runner Goffs UK Spring Sales Bumper at Newbury impressively by 3½ lengths from Midnight Stroll: exciting prospect. *Harry Fry* **b105 p**

BUMBLE BAY 7 b.g. Trade Fair – Amica (Averti (IRE)) [2016/17 h99: h15.9g² h16.8s* h16.7g³ h16m⁶ h16m Apr 28] fair handicap hurdler: won at Newton Abbot in June: raced around 2m: acts on soft going: wears hood/tongue tie: usually races towards rear, often travels strongly. *Robert Stephens* **h100**

BUMBLES BABE 4 b.f. Paco Boy (IRE) – Brooklyn's Sky (Septieme Ciel (USA)) [2016/17 b17g⁴ Apr 15] half-sister to several winners on Flat: dam French 7f winner: well beaten in mares bumper. *Tim Reed* **b–**

BUN DORAN (IRE) 6 b.g. Shantou (USA) – Village Queen (IRE) (King's Theatre (IRE)) [2016/17 h124, b111: c20s³ c20.1s* c19.9s⁶ c20.4g⁶ c15.8g³ Apr 6] useful-looking gelding: fairly useful form over hurdles: useful form in handicap chases: won at Newcastle in December by 5 lengths from Ash Park: creditable 4¾ lengths third to Double W's in Red Rum Chase at Aintree final start: stays 2½m: acts on heavy going: tried in tongue tie: front runner/races prominently, often travels strongly. *Tom George* **c140 h–**

BUNK OFF EARLY (IRE) 5 ro.g. Zebedee – Ctesiphon (USA) (Arch (USA)) [2016/17 h16d* h18s² h16.4g h16.5d⁵ Apr 25] compact gelding: fairly useful on Flat, stays 1½m: useful form over hurdles: won maiden at Leopardstown (by 5½ lengths from Outspoken) in December: best effort when ¾-length second to Bacardys in Deloitte Novices' Hurdle at same course in February: well below form in Grade 1 events last 2 starts (wore ear plugs on first of them): likely to prove best at around 2m. *W. P. Mullins, Ireland* **h141**

BUNNIE OSCAR (USA) 4 b.g. Hard Spun (USA) – Shimmer (USA) (Pulpit (USA)) **b–**
[2016/17 b13.7m Oct 2] tailed off in junior bumper: dead. *Conor Dore*

BUONAROTTI BOY (IRE) 5 b.g. Galileo (IRE) – Funsie (FR) (Saumarez) [2016/17 **h108**
h16g h16g* h16g² h16g² h17.5d⁴ h16g⁶ h20.2g² h16.2s² h16g Oct 13] modest maiden on Flat,
stays 1½m: fair handicap hurdler: won at Kilbeggan in June: stays 2½m: acts on soft going:
in headgear last 5 starts. *Gordon Elliott, Ireland*

BURBANK (IRE) 5 b.g. Yeats (IRE) – Spring Swoon (FR) (Highest Honor (FR)) **h135 p**
[2016/17 b16.3g* h15.8d² h15.8s* h19.4g² h20.5d² Apr 21] €140,000 3-y-o: third **b98**
foal: dam, French 2¼m hurdle winner, also 11.5f winner on Flat, half-sister to high-class
hurdler/very smart chaser (2m-2½m winner) Wahiba Sands: fairly useful form when
winning at Newbury in November, only start in bumpers: useful form over hurdles: won
maiden at Huntingdon (by 7 lengths from Man From Mars) in January: best effort when
7¾ lengths fourth of 15 to Willoughby Court in Baring Bingham Novices' Hurdle at
Cheltenham in March: stays 21f: acts on soft going: remains with potential. *Nicky Henderson*

BURGAS (FR) 6 b.g. Protektor (GER) – Tyrolienne Bleue (FR) (Sunshack) [2016/17 **c128**
c104p, h125: h24d³ c16v² c20s³ c20s⁴ h24s³ h19g h20d³ Apr 26] useful hurdler: creditable **h132**
4¾ lengths third to C'est Jersey in minor event at Punchestown final outing: fairly useful
form over fences: best effort when 3¾ lengths third to Last Goodbye in maiden at Down
Royal in December: stays 3m: acts on heavy going: in tongue tie last 2 starts. *Noel Meade,
Ireland*

BURGESS DREAM (IRE) 8 b.g. Spadoun (FR) – Ennel Lady (IRE) (Erin's Hope) **c67**
[2016/17 c86, h86: h19.1d⁴ h21.6s⁴ c25.7g⁵ h23v* c23.5v² h23v* h23v⁶ Mar 6] tall, **h85**
workmanlike gelding: modest handicap hurdler: won at Lingfield in January and February:
poor maiden chaser: stays 3¼m: acts on heavy going: has worn cheekpieces. *Anna Newton-
Smith*

BURLINGTON BERT (FR) 6 b.g. Califet (FR) – Melhi Sun (FR) (Mansonnien (FR)) **h87**
[2016/17 b101: b16.3m* h16.7s³ Nov 26] rather unfurnished gelding: fairly useful form in **b101**
bumpers, second win at Stratford in May: 11/10, 26 lengths third of 6 to Mr McGo in
novice at Bangor on hurdling debut: tried in tongue tie: sold £2,000 in May. *Warren Greatrex*

BURNING DESIRE (IRE) 6 b.g. Galileo (IRE) – Flames (Blushing Flame (USA)) **h–**
[2016/17 h97: h16g h21.4d Dec 13] lengthy gelding: maiden hurdler, no form in
2016/17: best effort at 2m on soft going: tried in cheekpieces: in tongue tie last 3 starts.
Richard Hughes

BURNING HEAT (IRE) 4 b.g. Rock of Gibraltar (IRE) – Burning Damask (USA) **h109**
(Thunder Gulch (USA)) [2016/17 h15.8d² h16m² h15.8g³ Apr 28] fair maiden on Flat,
stays 2m: fair form in maiden/novice hurdles: should prove suited by further than 2m.
James Eustace

BURNING LOVE (IRE) 4 b.f. Kodiac – Think (FR) (Marchand de Sable (USA)) **h–**
[2016/17 h15.8d Oct 28] modest maiden on Flat, stays 9f: tailed off in mares maiden on
hurdling debut. *Adam West*

BURNSIDE (FR) 4 gr.g. Kendargent (FR) – Tishkara (FR) (Xaar) [2016/17 h15.8m⁴ Oct **h78**
30] fairly useful on Flat, stays 2m: 33/1: didn't jump well when fourth in juvenile at
Huntingdon (21½ lengths behind Hollywood Road) on hurdling debut. *Ian Williams*

BURNT SIENNA (IRE) 7 ch.m. Papal Bull – Lucky Achievement (USA) (St Jovite **h91**
(USA)) [2016/17 h85: h16.2dᵖᵘ h24m h23.3m* h22.1g² h22.1d⁶ h23.3g⁶ h22.5d h23.8g Jan
3] modest handicap hurdler: won mares event at Uttoxeter in June: stays 23f: acts on good
to firm and good to soft going: has worn cheekpieces: wears tongue tie: often races towards
rear. *Noel C. Kelly, Ireland*

BURRENBRIDGE HOTEL (IRE) 6 b.g. Ivan Denisovich (IRE) – Hearthstead **h101**
Dancer (USA) (Royal Academy (USA)) [2016/17 b20g b20g h16v³ h16.7gᶠ h16m* Apr **b–**
28] €1,800 3-y-o: first foal: dam (h79), lightly raced over hurdles, 7f winner on Flat: point
winner: no form in bumpers: easily best effort (fair form) over hurdles when winning
maiden at Chepstow on final outing: left Kieran Purcell after second start: sometimes in
headgear. *Henry Oliver*

BURROWS LANE (FR) 6 b.g. Astarabad (USA) – Condoleezza (FR) (Mansonnien **h114**
(FR)) [2016/17 b16g² b16.5g⁵ b17.8d² b16g* h19.9g² h19.9d³ h22g⁴ Oct 27] first foal: **b93**
dam, French maiden, sister to very smart French chaser Lagunak (stayed 27f): fair bumper

performer: won maiden at Kilbeggan in August: fair form in maiden hurdles: left Miss Elizabeth Doyle after fourth start: stays 2½m: tried in cheekpieces/tongue tie. *Charlie Longson*

BURROWS PARK (FR) 5 b.g. Astarabad (USA) – La Vie de Boitron (FR) (Lavirco (GER)) [2016/17 h15.9g² h16.7s³ h19.1vᵖᵘ h19.3mᵖᵘ Apr 2] good-topped gelding: dam half-sister to fairly useful hurdler/smart chaser (stayed 25f) De Boitron: useful on Flat, stays 1½m: fair form when placed in 2 novice hurdles: saddle slipped final outing. *Venetia Williams* **h113**

BURST YA BUBBLE (IRE) 5 b.g. Spadoun (FR) – Accordian Lady (IRE) (Accordion) [2016/17 b–: b15.8g⁶ h19.5m⁴ h15.7d⁴ h21.6d⁵ h21v Mar 22] rangy gelding: poor form in bumpers: fair form over hurdles: should stay 2½m: often races towards rear. *Seamus Mullins* **h109 b67**

BURTON BORU (IRE) 5 b.g. Brian Boru – Tiffiny Gale (IRE) (Glacial Storm (USA)) [2016/17 h77: h19.5m⁴ Nov 2] rangy gelding: modest form in bumpers: won maiden at Chepstow on hurdling debut by short head from Waterloo Warrior: would have been suited by 2¾m+: dead. *Colin Tizzard* **h105**

BURTONS WELL (IRE) 8 b.g. Well Chosen – Despute (IRE) (Be My Native (USA)) [2016/17 c16.4s² c20v* c20.8s⁴ c20.4gᶠ Mar 14] rangy gelding: fairly useful hurdler: useful from when winning novice handicap chase at Uttoxeter in December by 1¼ lengths from Pistol Park: shaped much better than result next time, then fell ninth in Close Brothers Novices' Handicap Chase won by Tully East at Cheltenham final outing: stays 2½m: raced mainly on soft/heavy going: remains open to improvement. *Venetia Williams* **c134 p h–**

BURY THE EVIDENCE 4 b.f. Phoenix Reach (IRE) – Madam Bijou (Atraf) [2016/17 b15.7s b15.8s⁵ b16.7g⁴ Mar 27] fifth foal: half-sister to smart hurdler/useful chaser Killala Quay (2½m-3m winner, by Karinga Bay): dam unraced: poor form in bumpers: in hood last 2 starts. *Derek Shaw* **b63**

BUS NAMED DESIRE 9 b.m. Alflora (IRE) – Arctic Ring (Karinga Bay) [2016/17 c97, h82: c23gᵖᵘ c25.2sᵖᵘ h25.5vᵖᵘ h24d c25.5dᵖᵘ Mar 7] winning hurdler/chaser, no form in 2016/17: wears headgear/tongue tie. *Matt Sheppard* **c– h–**

BUSTER THOMAS (IRE) 6 b.g. Westerner – Awesome Miracle (IRE) (Supreme Leader) [2016/17 h19.5g* h21v² Feb 11] fifth foal: half-brother to useful hurdler/smart chaser Shotgun Paddy (2½m-29f winner, by Brian Boru), stays 33f, and fair hurdler Fingers Crossed (2m winner, by Bach): dam unraced half-sister to fairly useful hurdler/fair chaser The Parishioner, stayed 3½m: runner-up in Irish maiden point on debut: fairly useful form in novice events both starts over hurdles, winning at Lingfield in December then 12 lengths second to Aintree My Dream at Warwick: bred to stay 2¾m+. *Emma Lavelle* **h121**

BUSY LILLY 8 b.m. Bollin Eric – Princess Derry (Derrylin) [2016/17 b–: h24m⁴ Sep 27] showed nothing in 2 bumpers/novice hurdle. *Charles Pogson* **h–**

BUTLERGROVE KING (IRE) 8 b.g. King's Theatre (IRE) – Sanadja (IRE) (Slip Anchor) [2016/17 c114, h87: c21.1d² c24m² c23g c23.6d c25.1d⁵ c25.6dᵖᵘ c22.6d³ c25.1m⁴ Apr 5] maiden hurdler: fair handicap chaser: stays 3m: acts on good to firm and good to soft going: tried in cheekpieces/tongue tie: often races in rear. *Dai Burchell* **c113 h–**

BUTLERSBRIDGE (IRE) 8 b.g. Heron Island (IRE) – Vivre Aimer Rire (FR) (Cyborg (FR)) [2016/17 h15.8v h19.7s Mar 11] placed once from 4 starts in Irish maiden points in 2013: showed nothing in 2 novice hurdles. *Malcolm Jones* **h–**

BUTNEY ISLAND (IRE) 7 b.g. Trans Island – Tash McGarry (IRE) (Publisher (USA)) [2016/17 h105: h18.5g⁴ h21.6d³ c24.5g⁴ h23.5d h19.8vᵖᵘ h21.4m⁶ Apr 5] sturdy gelding: fair hurdler: won maiden at Newton Abbot in May: tailed off in novice handicap on chasing debut: best effort at 2¼m: acts on heavy going: tried in headgear. *Nick Mitchell* **c– h105**

BUTTERCUP (FR) 6 b.m. Limnos (JPN) – Paranoia (FR) (Esprit du Nord (USA)) [2016/17 c108, h121: c20.9s³ c20.3dᶠ c20.2s⁵ c21.7v* c20v* c20.6v* c20s² Apr 1] maiden hurdler: fairly useful chaser: won novice handicaps at Towcester in February, and at Warwick and Haydock in March: creditable second in similar event at Uttoxeter final outing: stays 2¾m: best form on soft/heavy going: often races towards rear. *Venetia Williams* **c126 h–**

BUVEUR D'AIR (FR) 6 b.g. Crillon (FR) – History (FR) (Alesso (USA)) [2016/17 h152p: c15.7s* c16.2v* h16v* h16.4g* h20g* Apr 6] **c155 p h170**

Buveur d'Air's win in the Champion Hurdle added yet another major prize to the long list of successes compiled by the Cheltenham Festival's most successful owner J. P. McManus and its most successful trainer Nicky Henderson. It was a record sixth win in the race for both men, Henderson having previously shared that distinction with five-times winner Peter Easterby whose wins included two each with Night Nurse and Sea Pigeon. For McManus, Buveur d'Air had the additional significance of being the fiftieth Festival winner in his emerald green, yellow hoops. By the end of the latest Festival, Henderson's career total at the meeting stood at fifty-eight and McManus' at fifty-two, their individual tallies largely gained independently of each other. Apart from sharing another Champion Hurdle winner, Binocular in 2010, the only other Festival winner trained by Henderson for McManus has been Bellvano in the 2012 Grand Annual.

McManus and Henderson began compiling their respective record Festival totals in the 'eighties, with the Edward O'Grady-trained Mister Donovan getting McManus off the mark at Cheltenham in the 1982 Sun Alliance Novices' Hurdle. That was something of a belated first success for an owner whose reputation for tilting at the ring when still in his twenties—a Hugh McIlvanney article in *The Observer* had christened him 'The Sundance Kid'—was already well-founded by then. Gambles on the O'Grady-trained pair Jack of Trumps and Deep Gale in successive runnings of the National Hunt Chase in 1978 and 1979 came unstuck when both horses were fallers, but Mister Donovan, who had been beaten in all four of his races over hurdles in Ireland, before being backed from 6/1 to 9/2, was a successful coup, though not quite so successful as McManus had been hoping for. 'I did not have a very good first day but did not mind too much, as I felt I would get it all back and more on the first race on the Wednesday. I expected we might get 12/1 to 14/1 to our money but word got out about Mister Donovan's ability and I had to take far less than those odds.' O'Grady went on to train four of McManus' first five Festival winners, including Bit of A Skite who changed his owner's luck in the National Hunt Chase when winning the 1983 renewal, though ironically he went unbacked by McManus at Cheltenham after fears that a hoof infection might have scuppered his chances (McManus has since won the National Hunt Chase five more times). There was a hiatus of eight years before McManus recorded his next Festival winner, when Danny Connors gave Jonjo O'Neill his first success at the meeting as a trainer, landing another gamble in the process in the 1991 Coral Golden Hurdle Final. However, since 1994, the McManus colours have been carried to victory at least once at every Festival with the exception of 2011. The Aidan O'Brien-trained Istabraq provided McManus with his first three wins in the Champion Hurdle between 1998 and 2000, followed by Binocular in 2010 and the Jessica Harrington-trained Jezki (who narrowly beat the same owner's My Tent Or Yours, trained by Henderson) in 2014. Like Buveur d'Air, Jezki had finished third in the Supreme Novices' the year before his Champion Hurdle victory.

Read Paddy Brennan At 32Red.com Novices' Chase, Haydock—
Buveur d'Air easily overhauls the grey Cloudy Dream to make a winning start over fences

Nicky Henderson's first Festival winner came three years after that of McManus when See You Then won the first of what was to be three consecutive Champion Hurdles. The Tsarevich, in the Mildmay of Flete, and First Bout, in the Triumph Hurdle, gave Henderson two more Festival winners in 1985. Binocular's Champion Hurdle win in 2010, his trainer's fifth success in the race, came a year after stable-companion Punjabi had beaten him into a close third in the race. Henderson has been successful at every Festival since 2009, with other highlights being the Gold Cup successes of Long Run in 2011 and Bobs Worth (the trainer's fiftieth Festival winner) in 2013. Altior was a record sixth winner of the Arkle for Henderson earlier on the latest Champion Hurdle card, matching the trainer's total in the Triumph Hurdle which is also a record. Altior had beaten Buveur d'Air into third in the previous season's Supreme Novices' Hurdle. If one of the pair was going to be a Champion Hurdle horse then it looked much more likely at the time to be Altior, by High Chaparral from a family of Flat and hurdle winners, rather than the French AQPS Buveur d'Air. To begin with, however, both horses embarked on novice chasing campaigns in the autumn. Buveur d'Air had won the Top Novices' Hurdle at Aintree after his third in the Supreme, though that success proved to be his final one in the colours of Potensis Bloodstock, as he was acquired privately over the summer by McManus. Buveur d'Air's new owner had other potential Champion Hurdle candidates in the autumn, notably the Baring Bingham runner-up Yanworth and the Triumph Hurdle winner Ivanovich Gorbatov, in addition to My Tent Or Yours who had finished second again in the 2016 Champion Hurdle.

Buveur d'Air made a good start over fences with impressive wins at Haydock and Warwick in December, the first from Cloudy Dream and the second from another smart novice Gino Trail, on both occasions in receipt of weight. Jumping well in the main, Buveur d'Air looked well on his way towards the Arkle, but so too did Altior who had made an even bigger impression when winning his three novice chases, including the Grade 1 Henry VIII at Sandown, before the turn of the year. Early in the New Year, however, the Champion Hurdle scene, which had long looked like being dominated by Willie Mullins' candidates, began to take on a very different aspect. With the last two winners Faugheen and Annie Power still to appear—before eventually, further down the line, being announced as absentees—the race suddenly began to look much more open. Another development, which had no doubt not gone unnoticed in the McManus camp, was that Petit Mouchoir, whom Buveur d'Air had beaten at Aintree the previous spring, had won the Ryanair Hurdle and the Irish Champion Hurdle in the absence of either of the dominant Ricci-owned pair. As for McManus' own contenders, Yanworth had won the Ascot Hurdle and the Christmas Hurdle at Kempton without entirely convincing as a potential Champion Hurdle winner. A day after the *Racing Post* had carried the headline on January 31st 'Geraghty: Yanworth must jump into picture', above a story in which McManus' jockey stressed that his mount would need to jump better on his intended appearance in Sandown's Contenders Hurdle that weekend to advance his Champion Hurdle claims, it was announced that Buveur d'Air, already entered in the Scilly Isles Novices' Chase on the same card, was to wait instead for the following week's Morebattle Hurdle at Kelso with a view to his contesting the Champion Hurdle alongside Yanworth. As it turned out, Buveur d'Air went to Sandown after all, replacing Yanworth in the Contenders Hurdle line-up when the latter met with a minor setback.

On heavy ground, Buveur d'Air had only three rivals to beat in the Contenders Hurdle, one of them the outclassed Hurry Henry, and he started at 4/1-on in receipt of 4 lb from the 'Fighting Fifth' winner Irving and the previous season's Kingwell winner Rayvin Black, who was himself returning to hurdling after a belated but unsuccessful chasing debut. Buveur d'Air made the most of the opportunity and ran out an easy length and a half winner from Rayvin Black (also runner-up in 2016) after Irving weakened after the last. The bare form was not anywhere near Champion Hurdle-winning standard, but Buveur d'Air won impressively (Binocular had warmed up for his Champion Hurdle win with a workmanlike success in a three-runner renewal of the same race at 7/1-on). Henderson revealed that he had apparently had switching Buveur d'Air back to hurdles in mind for a while. 'At this

Stan James Champion Hurdle Challenge Trophy, Cheltenham—
a record sixth win in the race for trainer Nicky Henderson as Buveur d'Air beats
stable-companion My Tent Or Yours (hood) who is second in the race for the third time;
Irish raiders Petit Mouchoir (grey) and Footpad (left) complete the frame

stage of his life I think he might just be a sharper hurdler than he is a chaser,' he said after Sandown. 'Barry said he can make a length at his hurdles but he can't do that over fences. He's very quick, very slick over his hurdles, and very speedy too.' With Faugheen missing the previous weekend's Irish Champion Hurdle but (unlike Annie Power) yet to be ruled out of Cheltenham, an announcement that came days later, the 2015 winner still headed the Champion Hurdle betting for which Buveur d'Air was now vying for second favouritism with Yanworth and Petit Mouchoir at odds as low as 7/2.

The last two Champion Hurdle winners to have been switched from chasing earlier the same season had been the Toby Balding-trained Beech Road, successful in 1989, and his stable-companion Morley Street who won two years later. Both had had far unhappier experiences over fences than Buveur d'Air. Beech Road failed to complete in a couple of tries at Newton Abbot and Cheltenham, though he showed some promise when challenging the future Arkle winner Waterloo Boy before taking a crashing final-fence fall at the latter course (it was ten minutes before he got to his feet and emerged from behind the green screens that had been erected around him). Morley Street was an easy winner at Worcester in his first race over British fences (he had earlier won the Breeders' Cup Chase over brush obstacles in the States) but he was let down by his jumping in better company, also coming up against a future Arkle winner in Remittance Man at Ascot, before being pulled up after bleeding from the nose when favourite for the Feltham Novices' at Kempton. Further back, the 1966 Champion Hurdle was won by Salmon Spray who had begun that season by finishing third over fences at Ascot in the Black & White Gold Cup before being returned to hurdles. Salmon Spray had successfully mixed hurdling and chasing the season before, when he fell at an early flight in the Champion Hurdle. The 1966 Champion Hurdle favourite, by the way, was Arkle's brilliant stablemate and contemporary Flyingbolt who had been an impressive winner of the Black & White Gold Cup. He finished third in the Champion Hurdle a day after winning the Two-Mile Champion Chase in a canter.

Without either of its last two top-class winners in the line-up, the latest Stan James Champion Hurdle was open to perceptions beforehand of looking a substandard renewal, though in Buveur d'Air and Yanworth it certainly had at least two contenders who still had the potential to prove themselves champion hurdlers worthy of the name. Yanworth had taken his record to seven out of eight over hurdles in the Kingwell Hurdle at Wincanton but, wearing cheekpieces this time, he did not really win over those critics who expected a more polished performance from a potential Champion Hurdle winner. Buveur d'Air wasn't the only runner in the eleven-strong field to have been lured away from a different original target by the prospect of a more 'winnable' Champion Hurdle than usual. The fragile 2015 Champion Bumper winner Moon Racer, who had won his only two starts over hurdles, made a late switch from the Supreme Novices'. Among the outsiders, the Morebattle Hurdle winner Cyrus Darius, himself a former Top Novices' Hurdle winner who made a successful start over fences before getting injured, and Willie Mullins' 2015 County Hurdle winner Wicklow Brave, who hadn't run over hurdles for nearly eighteen months and was last seen finishing in rear in the Melbourne Cup, were others who might not have ordinarily been given their chance. Handicaps are not orthodox routes to Champion Hurdle success, either, though Henderson's progressive Brain Power looked a leading contender after winning two such races in December, including what was formerly the Ladbroke at Ascot under a big weight, and at 13/2 he completed the first four in the betting behind 2/1 favourite Yanworth, Buveur d'Air on 5/1 and Petit Mouchoir at 6/1. Despite twice finishing runner-up, My Tent Or Yours was the outsider in the respective teams of Henderson and McManus, while The New One was another race regular (third, fifth and fourth in his previous attempts) who had won both the International Hurdle at Cheltenham and the Champion Hurdle Trial at Haydock for a third time earlier in the season. Mullins' depleted challenge was headed by the Irish Champion Hurdle runner-up Footpad whose owners Simon Munir and Isaac Souede were additionally represented by Yanworth's stable-companion Sceau Royal who had finished third behind him at Wincanton.

Turning for home in the Champion Hurdle, only Moon Racer, pulled up three out, and the tailed-off Cyrus Darius were out of the picture, the nine other runners still quite closely grouped. The writing was on the wall, however, for Yanworth, labouring at the back of the pack after being one of the first in trouble, and for Brain Power who dropped out quickly, having still seemingly been going well two out. In contrast, Buveur d'Air, who had travelled strongly under a patient ride before making smooth headway at that stage of the race, took the lead from Petit Mouchoir soon after the home turn and jumped the last with a couple of lengths to spare before pulling further clear on the run-in to win readily by four and a half lengths. The 16/1-shot My Tent Or Yours could make no impression on the winner but belied his years by keeping on well to complete a one, two for his connections, pulling three lengths clear of Petit Mouchoir in third to finish runner-up in a third Champion Hurdle, a position he had also filled in the Supreme as a novice. Footpad, The New One and Sceau Royal were the next three home, ahead of a disappointing Yanworth who was subsequently disqualified after testing positive for a prohibited substance. With Geraghty injured and his understudy getting the call for Yanworth, the ride on Buveur d'Air had gone to Noel Fehily who had also ridden the most recent British-trained winner, Rock On Ruby, in 2012. Fehily knew Buveur d'Air well, having ridden him in all his races the previous season as well as on his two starts for Henderson in bumpers before that. Forty-two-year-old freelance Fehily enjoyed a fine spring and went on to win the following day's Queen Mother Champion Chase on Special Tiara for Henry de Bromhead and was placed in the McManus colours on

Betway Aintree Hurdle, Aintree—
Barry Geraghty returns from injury to do the steering as Buveur d'Air (right) again proves far too
strong for My Tent Or Yours and 2014 winner The New One (left)

Mr John P. McManus' "Buveur d'Air"

Unowhatimeanharry in the Stayers' Hurdle and on Minella Rocco in the Gold Cup to complete a fine run in the Festival's four most important feature races. He also went on to finish in the frame on Blaklion for Nigel Twiston-Davies in the Grand National.

Barry Geraghty was fit again for Buveur d'Air's appearance in the Betway Aintree Hurdle in which he started at 9/4-on against five others, of whom My Tent Or Yours and The New One looked his main rivals, although they had been put firmly in their place at Cheltenham. The New One started the 11/2 second favourite, however, probably because he was a past winner of the race in 2014, whereas the longer trip looked less likely to suit My Tent Or Yours who had finished much further behind Annie Power at Aintree the previous season than he had at Cheltenham. The field was completed by outsiders Old Guard, Rashaan and Identity Thief, the last-named reverting to hurdles having disappointed in recent starts over fences after a very promising beginning to his chasing career (Old Guard had also had a short-lived stab at novice chasing in early 2016/17). The longer trip proved no problem for Buveur d'Air and he put up another smooth, top-class display after The New One had tried to exploit any chinks in his stamina by forcing the pace and pressing on in earnest after the third last. Buveur d'Air headed him going to the final flight and eased clear for a five-length win, with My Tent Or Yours keeping on to snatch second from The New One, who had jumped badly right in the closing stages, with the three others well held. While the last two Champion Hurdle winners have now followed up in the Aintree Hurdle, it is a double that has not been achieved particularly regularly in recent decades. Before Annie Power, McManus' Istabraq in 1999 was the last to land the double in the same season, though that was after a failed attempt the year before when he was beaten in heavy ground by the Champion Hurdle fourth Pridwell at Aintree. The aforementioned Beech Road and Morley Street were the other Champion Hurdle winners to follow up in the Aintree Hurdle in the 'nineties. Beech Road showed his 50/1 win at Cheltenham was no fluke when winning at 10/1 at Aintree, while Morley Street ended up winning the Aintree Hurdle in four successive years. Henderson's triple champion See You Then met with a surprising defeat (to Aonoch) in the Aintree race in 1986, and the only others to complete the Cheltenham/Aintree double are Dawn Run (1984), Gaye Brief (1983), Monksfield (1979 and 1978) and Night Nurse (in 1977, courtesy of his dead-heat at Aintree with Monksfield).

Buveur d'Air (FR) (b.g. 2011)	Crillon (FR) (br 1996)	Saumarez (b or br 1987)	Rainbow Quest / Fiesta Fun
		Shangrila (b 1978)	Riverman / Garden Green
	History (FR) (b 1995)	Alesso (b or br 1983)	Alleged / Leandra
		Clair Deux Lune (ch 1990)	Altayan / Lili Dancer

Buveur d'Air became the first French-bred winner of the Champion Hurdle since Binocular, though McManus' previous winner of the Champion Hurdle was a thoroughbred recruit from the Flat. As explained in his essay in last year's Annual, where his breeding was covered in full, Buveur d'Air's name betrays his AQPS origins and he became the first non-thoroughbred winner of the Champion Hurdle since Hors La Loi III in 2002, the year of Istabraq's short-lived attempt at a fourth win in the race. Hors La Loi was a brother to the 1996 Stayers' Hurdle winner Cyborgo and Buveur d'Air is a half-brother to Punchestowns (by Morespeed) who found only Big Buck's too strong in the 2009 World Hurdle. Big Buck's was himself the best-known and most successful recent example of a chaser reverting to hurdling prior to Buveur d'Air, dominating the staying hurdling scene for another three seasons after unseating his jockey in the 2008 Hennessy Gold Cup which prompted the switch. A 171-rated hurdler, Punchestowns faced a tall order to reach the same heights over fences and he ultimately fell short, often let down by his jumping, including when sent off 2/1 favourite for the RSA Chase in which he finished lame. On the other hand, Punchestowns did win three of his seven chases, including the Scilly Isles. How far up the ladder Buveur d'Air would have gone over fences—the horse he beat on his chasing debut, Cloudy Dream, went on to finish second to Altior in the Arkle—is probably academic now, as he will be the one to beat in all the top hurdles in the next season and is clear favourite in the ante-post lists to retain his Champion Hurdle crown. Buveur d'Air stays two and a half miles and acts on heavy ground. He wore ear plugs at Cheltenham. *Nicky Henderson*

BUYER BEWARE (IRE) 5 br.g. Big Bad Bob (IRE) – Adoring (IRE) (One Cool Cat (USA)) [2016/17 h114p: h16.5g^F h16g^2 h17d^2 h16.6g^4 h17.3g^4 h17.2g^2 c19.9g^3 h16.3d Apr 27] fair hurdler: failed to stay when third in maiden at Kilbeggan on chasing debut: left Gordon Elliott after seventh start: stays 2¼m: acts on good to soft going: usually wears hood: should do better over fences. *Patrick Holmes*   **c87 p** / **h113**

BUY ME OUT 7 gr.m. Fair Mix (IRE) – Maid Equal (Pragmatic) [2016/17 h96, b60: h16.7d^3 h21.6s^2 h18.7m^5 h21.6g^3 h16g^{pu} h19g^5 h21.2g h19.9s^{pu} h15.8v^4 h19.5g Apr 8] modest maiden hurdler: left Grace Harris after ninth start: stays 2¾m: acts on soft and good to firm going: has worn headgear, including in 2016/17: in tongue tie last 3 starts: hasn't always looked straightforward. *Tim Vaughan*   **h93**

BUYWISE (IRE) 10 b.g. Tikkanen (USA) – Greenogue Princess (IRE) (Rainbows For Life (CAN)) [2016/17 c151x, h–: h20g^4 c20.4s^3 c20.8s h21.4s c20.8s^{pu} c24.2s c25g^4 Mar 14] lengthy gelding: useful hurdler: smart handicap chaser: best efforts in 2016/17 when 2¼ lengths third of 17 to Taquin du Seuil in BetVictor Gold Cup at Cheltenham and 10½ lengths fourth of 23 to Un Temps Pour Tout in Ultima Handicap there: stays 25f: acts on good to firm and heavy going: tried in visor: waited with: often let down by jumping over fences. *Evan Williams*   **c146 x** / **h132 +**

BUZ BARTON (IRE) 9 b.g. Bach (IRE) – Cronin's Girl (IRE) (Oscar (IRE)) [2016/17 h21.6m^{bd} h16.8g h21.6m h21.6g^2 h21m^6 h21.6s h16.8g^5 Apr 26] point winner: poor maiden hurdler: stays 2¾m: acts on good to firm going: has worn cheekpieces. *Jimmy Frost*   **h80**

BYGONES FOR COINS (IRE) 9 ch.m. Danroad (AUS) – Reservation (IRE) **c–**
(Common Grounds) [2016/17 h–: h16.2d³ h16.2gF c15.6dpu h17.2d⁴ h17.2dF h15.7g⁶ **h82**
h17.2g Aug 27] poor maiden hurdler: pulled up in novice on chasing debut: unproven
beyond 17f: acts on good to soft going: front runner/races prominently. *Kenny Johnson*

BYRESTEADS FARM 10 b.m. Beat All (USA) – Kinnahalla (IRE) (Lancastrian) **h–**
[2016/17 h16dpu h16.2spu Dec 4] no form in bumpers/novice hurdles: tried in tongue tie.
Katie Scott

BYRON BLUE (IRE) 8 br.g. Dylan Thomas (IRE) – High Society (IRE) (Key of Luck **h101**
(USA)) [2016/17 h119: h20g² h21.6d³ h21.1g h19.5g³ h23.9dpu h23.9s h23.4g⁴ Apr 17]
small gelding: handicap hurdler, just fair form at best in 2016/17: stays 3m: acts on good to
firm going: wears hood/tongue tie. *Brian Barr*

BYRONEGETONEFREE 6 b.g. Byron – Lefty's Dollbaby (USA) (Brocco (USA)) **h66**
[2016/17 h–: h18.1s h16.8s⁶ h16.4s h16.8d h16.2g⁶ Apr 27] poor maiden hurdler: raced
mainly at 2m: best form on good going: has worn headgear. *Stuart Coltherd*

BYRON FLYER 6 b.g. Byron – Nursling (IRE) (Kahyasi) [2016/17 h104p, b90: h20.5g* **h130**
h20.6g* h20d* h20.6g h19.5g h19.4g* h20s⁵ h20g² Apr 7] compact gelding: useful handicap
hurdler: won at Plumpton (conditionals event) and Market Rasen in May, Worcester in June
and Doncaster (by 1¾ lengths from Only Orsenfoolsies) in November: creditable fifth of
22 to Rather Be in Grade 3 event at Aintree final outing: stays 21f: acts on heavy going:
often races towards rear. *Ian Williams*

BY THE BOARDWALK (IRE) 9 br.g. Presenting – Peripheral Vision (IRE) (Saddlers' **c125**
Hall (IRE)) [2016/17 c124, h–: c25.1m³ c23.8d⁵ c23.9g* c24.2m⁴ c25.6g² c23g⁴ c23.8g³ **h–**
c23.8m² Apr 25] strong gelding: has had breathing operation: maiden hurdler: fairly useful
handicap chaser: won at Market Rasen in October: stays 3¼m: acts on good to firm and
good to soft going: wears tongue tie: often races towards rear/travels strongly, tends to find
little. *Kim Bailey*

BY THE FIRESIDE 6 b.g. Dr Massini (IRE) – Dew Drop Inn (IRE) (Saddlers' Hall **b66**
(IRE)) [2016/17 b17.7g⁵ Mar 27] well beaten in bumper on debut. *Jo Davis*

C

CABARET QUEEN 5 b.m. King's Theatre (IRE) – La Dame Brune (FR) (Mansonnien **b87**
(FR)) [2016/17 b15.7g³ Mar 28] third foal: closely related to a winning pointer by Kayf
Tara: dam (h113), unreliable 2½m/21f hurdle winner, half-sister to fairly useful hurdler/
useful chaser (2m-21f winner) Nikos Extra: won completed start in Irish maiden points:
5/2, some encouragement when third in bumper at Southwell (3½ lengths behind Royal
Ruby) in March. *Dan Skelton*

CABERNET D'ALENE (FR) 5 b.g. Day Flight – Haifa du Noyer (FR) (Video Rock **h101**
(FR)) [2016/17 h107p: h18.5g⁶ h16.2g h19sF h16.5m³ h16.5m* Apr 27] rather unfurnished
gelding: fair hurdler: won maiden at Taunton in April: unproven beyond 2m: acts on good
to firm going. *Nick Williams*

CABIN BOY (IRE) 4 b.g. Stowaway – Option (IRE) (Red Ransom (USA)) [2016/17 **b62 p**
b16.7m⁶ Apr 9] £8,500 3-y-o: half-brother to 3 winners, including fairly useful hurdler
Right Option (21f/2¾m winner, by Daylami), stayed 3m: dam, maiden on Flat (stayed
1½m), half-sister to useful hurdler/fairly useful chaser (2m/21f winner) Manorson: 11/2,
very green when sixth in bumper at Market Rasen: open to improvement. *Malcolm Jefferson*

CABLE CAR 6 gr.g. Pastoral Pursuits – Nina Fontenail (FR) (Kaldounevees (FR)) **b78**
[2016/17 b16m² Aug 17] 25/1, second in bumper at Worcester (11 lengths behind Potters
Story) in August. *Debra Hamer*

CAB ON TIMES (IRE) 8 b.g. Indian Danehill (IRE) – Evening Fashion (IRE) (Strong **c–**
Gale) [2016/17 c–, h–: c22.6gpu Apr 23] dual winning pointer: lightly raced over hurdles: **h–**
no form in hunter chases. *S. Rea*

CABRAGH (IRE) 8 b.g. Old Vic – Satco Street (IRE) (Satco (FR)) [2016/17 h15.8s **c114**
h15.7v⁵ h16g h16.8d⁶ c26.3d* c20.1s⁴ c24.1d* c24.1spu c24d³ c21.1v³ c24.2g² Mar 17] **h60**
maiden hurdler: fair handicap chaser: won at Sedgefield (novice event) in December and
Bangor in January: stays 3¼m: acts on soft going: in cheekpieces last 3 starts: usually races
close up. *Sam England*

CAI

CACTUS VALLEY (IRE) 8 b.g. Lawman (FR) – Beech Gardens (Sadler's Wells **c101**
(USA)) [2016/17 h108p: h15.5g h19.4g[6] h16s[6] c19.2d[4] c19.2s[pu] Feb 28] fair handicap **h90**
hurdler, below best in 2016/17: fair form when fourth in novice at Catterick on completed
start over fences: stays 19f: acts on heavy going: wears tongue tie: usually races nearer last
than first. *Michael Easterby*

CADEAU GEORGE 8 b.g. Relief Pitcher – Sovereign's Gift (Elegant Monarch) **c–**
[2016/17 h23.1s[3] h25d* h25.5v h24.2d h24.2d Mar 24] lengthy gelding: fair handicap **h110**
hurdler: won at Huntingdon (conditional event) in December: winning chaser: stays 25f:
acts on heavy going: has worn cheekpieces, including in 2016/17: usually races close up.
Ben Pauling

CADEAUX'S FIRE 4 ch.f. Major Cadeaux – Confetti (Groom Dancer (USA)) [2016/17 **b64**
b15.7s[6] b16.5m[4] Apr 27] sixth foal: half-sister to 6f winner Wedding List (by Pivotal): dam
ran twice on Flat: poor form in bumpers. *Alan King*

CADELLIN 6 b.g. Black Sam Bellamy (IRE) – Clotted Cream (USA) (Eagle Eyed (USA)) **h88**
[2016/17 b–: b16.6g h21.2s[6] h20.1s[4] h17d[5] Apr 5] well held in bumpers: modest form over **b–**
hurdles. *Donald McCain*

CADEYRN (IRE) 5 b.g. Flemensfirth (USA) – Kapricia Speed (FR) (Vertical Speed **b95**
(FR)) [2016/17 b15.7v[3] b16s* b15.7v[5] Feb 15] sixth foal: half-brother to 3 winners,
including smart hurdler Barney Dwan (17f-2½m winner, by Vinnie Roe): dam (c88/h104),
French maiden hurdler/chaser, half-sister to high-class hurdler/smart chaser (stayed 2½m)
Geos and useful French hurdler/chaser (15f-2¼m winner) Kapgarde: won Irish maiden
point on debut: fairly useful form in bumpers: won at Chepstow in December, suited by
emphasis on stamina: will be suited by 2½m+. *Michael Scudamore*

CADGERS HOLE 10 b.g. Helissio (FR) – Not So Prim (Primitive Rising (USA)) [2016/17 **h70 §**
h70§: h23.3v[3] h19.9g[4] May 14] poor maiden hurdler: stays 21f: acts on soft going: wears
hood: has worn tongue tie: usually races towards rear: temperamental. *Lynn Siddall*

CADIRA BEECHES 7 b.m. Lucarno (USA) – Gipsy Girl (Motivate) [2016/17 h21.2s[pu] **h–**
Mar 23] second foal: dam (c96/h72), winning pointer, maiden hurdler/chaser: pulled up in
mares novice hurdle on debut. *Robert Stephens*

CADORE (IRE) 9 b.g. Hurricane Run (IRE) – Mansiya (Vettori (IRE)) [2016/17 h93: **h72**
h16.2s[6] h16.8g[5] h16.2s h20.5s h16.4v[6] h23.8g[4] Mar 24] leggy gelding: poor handicap
hurdler nowadays: stays 2½m: acts on heavy going: wears cheekpieces. *Lucy Normile*

CADOUDOFF (FR) 7 gr.g. Davidoff (GER) – Hera du Berlais (FR) (Cadoudal (FR)) **c–**
[2016/17 c129, h125: c19.9g[F] c21d c23.8d[pu] h21.4s[5] h25.3s[2] h24.2s[2] h26s[F] Mar 30] fairly **h121**
useful handicap hurdler: second at Catterick in February and Newbury in March: fairly
useful chaser at best, no form in 2016/17: stayed 25f: acted on good to firm and heavy
going: tried in cheekpieces/tongue tie: dead. *Charlie Longsdon*

CAERLEON KATE 5 ch.m. Medicean – Towaahi (IRE) (Caerleon (USA)) [2016/17 **h93**
h16s h16g h20s h16d[d] h15.6g[4] h19.5s[4] h20.2g Apr 26] half-sister to fair/ungenuine hurdler/
winning chaser Kristoffersen (2½m-27f winner, by Kris): poor maiden on Flat: modest
maiden hurdler: stays 19f: acts on soft going. *Colin A. McBratney, Ireland*

CAFE AU LAIT (GER) 7 b.g. Nicaron (GER) – Cariera (GER) (Macanal (USA)) **h84**
[2016/17 h15.8m h15.7g h15.8m h15.8g h16.8g h19.1s[2] h15.8v[2] h15.9v[4] h16d* h19.3s[2]
h16v[3] h19.7d Mar 26] sturdy gelding: poor handicap hurdler nowadays: won at Wetherby
(conditional event) in February: stays 19f: acts on good to firm and heavy going: wears
headgear/tongue tie: often travels strongly. *Sophie Leech*

CAFE DE PARIS (FR) 12 b.g. Fly To The Stars – Saint Patricia (FR) (Assert) [2016/17 **c110**
c29.8s[pu] c20.4g[6] c21.9s h23.6d[5] c20d[4] c25.1d c24.1d[pu] Jan 3] fair handicap hurdler/chaser: **h105**
left Francois-Marie Cottin after third start: stays 23f: acts on heavy going: usually wears
headgear: wears tongue tie. *David Pipe*

CAID DU BERLAIS (FR) 8 b.g. Westerner – Kenza du Berlais (FR) (Kahyasi) [2016/17 **c143**
h19.5g h24.7d* h22.8v[pu] c21d[4] c24d[5] c25g[F] h24g Mar 16] leggy gelding: useful handicap **h143**
hurdler: won at Aintree (by 3¾ lengths from Goodbye Dancer) in November: useful
handicap chaser: stays 25f when conditions aren't testing: acts on heavy going: wears
tongue tie: often races towards rear. *Paul Nicholls*

CAID DU LIN (FR) 5 gr.g. Della Francesca (USA) – Asia du Lin (FR) (Agent Bleu (FR)) **h124**
[2016/17 h18.9m[pu] h18.9m[2] h18.9g* h19.1v[pu] h16.5s[3] h17.7d[3] h15.8g[ur] h15.9m[pu] Apr 16]
fifth foal: dam French 21f chase winner: fairly useful hurdler: won 4-y-o event at Niort in

October: left J. P. Trinquier after third start: stays 19f: acts on soft going: usually wears headgear: in tongue tie last 3 starts: front runner/races prominently: signs of temperament (hung badly right sixth start). *Dr Richard Newland*

CAILIN (IRE) 9 b.m. Golan (IRE) – Castle Arms Cailin (IRE) (Be My Native (USA)) [2016/17 h18.5d^pu h21.6s^pu Nov 13] maiden hurdler, no form in 2016/17: best effort at 2m. *Grant Cann* h–

CAILLEACH ANNIE (IRE) 8 b.m. Blueprint (IRE) – Graineuaile (IRE) (Orchestra) [2016/17 h109: c26.2d^4 c24.2s^ur c24v^3 c28.5s c24v^5 c23.6v^3 Mar 23] winning pointer: winning hurdler: fair form over fences: should be suited by long distances: acts on heavy going: in cheekpieces last 4 starts: has worn tongue tie: temperamental. *Jackie du Plessis* c108 § h–

CAIRNSHILL (IRE) 6 gr.g. Tikkanen (USA) – Ilikeyou (IRE) (Lord Americo) [2016/17 h63, b–: h22.1m^5 h23.3g^3 h27g^2 h23.3s^2 h22.5d Oct 14] modest maiden hurdler: stays 27f: acts on soft going: wears tongue tie: usually races in rear. *Mark McNiff, Ireland* h92

CAIUS MARCIUS (IRE) 6 b.g. King's Theatre – Ain't Misbehavin (IRE) (Trempolino (USA)) [2016/17 h105p, b98: h16.2d* h16.2d^2 h16.2d* h16.2s^2 h15.6g^ur h16.7s^4 h16d* h15.7g Apr 15] good-topped gelding: bumper winner: fairly useful hurdler: won novices at Hexham/Perth early in season and handicap at Wetherby in March: raced around 2m: acts on soft going. *Nicky Richards* h122

CAJUN FIDDLE (IRE) 6 b.m. Robin des Champs (FR) – Silk Style (Polish Precedent (USA)) [2016/17 b90: h15.8d^2 h15.7d* h18.5s^4 h19.4d^2 h19g^3 h20.5g^5 h24.3d^pu Apr 21] lengthy mare: fairly useful hurdler: won mares novice at Southwell in November: second in mares handicap at Doncaster in January: stays 21f: acts on soft going: often travels strongly. *Alan King* h118

CAKE DE L'ISLE (FR) 5 b.g. Fragrant Mix (IRE) – Taiga de L'Isle (FR) (Ragmar (FR)) [2016/17 b15.8v h20.6s^pu h20.6m* Apr 9] £32,000 3-y-o: rangy gelding: second foal: dam unraced half-sister to fairly useful French hurdler/smart chaser (stayed 2¾m) Moka de L'Isle): well beaten in bumper: fairly useful form over hurdles: won maiden at Market Rasen in April. *Jonjo O'Neill* h116 b–

CALACH (FR) 5 gr.g. Fragrant Mix (IRE) – Nobless d'Aron (FR) (Ragmar (FR)) [2016/17 b17m^4 May 5] 7/1, fourth in bumper at Carlisle (15½ lengths behind Lieutenant Gruber) in May. *James Ewart* b72

CALARULES 4 gr.g. Aussie Rules (USA) – Ailincala (IRE) (Pursuit of Love) [2016/17 h15.7g^5 h16s^6 h16s^4 h16.6g^2 h16d^4 h19.9d^6 h19.9g Mar 29] half-brother to fairly useful hurdler Getabuzz (19f/2½m winner, by Beat Hollow) and a winning chaser in Italy by Observatory: modest maiden on Flat, stays 1¼m: modest maiden hurdler: should stay 2½m: acts on soft going: in headgear last 3 starts. *Tim Easterby* h92

CALCULATED RISK 8 ch.g. Motivator – Glen Rosie (IRE) (Mujtahid (USA)) [2016/17 c–, h112§: h20s^3 h20m^6 h20g^5 h20g h15.8v^3 h19.5s^5 h19.9v h20v^4 h20v h15.8d^6 Apr 16] rather leggy gelding: modest handicap hurdler nowadays: lightly-raced maiden chaser: stays 2½m: acts on heavy going: has worn cheekpieces, including final start: temperamental. *Debra Hamer* c– h95 §

CALEDONIA 10 b.g. Sulamani (IRE) – Vanessa Bell (IRE) (Lahib (USA)) [2016/17 h123: c20d^F Oct 30] fairly useful hurdler: fell fatally on chasing debut: stayed 3m: acted on heavy going. *Jim Goldie* c– h–

CA LE FERRA (FR) 7 b.g. Turgeon (USA) – Branceilles (FR) (Satin Wood) [2016/17 h–: h16.8d^2 h19.4g Mar 1] placed in bumpers: fair form over hurdles: better effort in 2016/17 when second in novice at Sedgefield in November: shaped as if amiss next time: tried in hood. *James Ewart* h101

CALETT MAD (FR) 5 b.g. Axxos (GER) – Omelia (FR) (April Night (FR)) [2016/17 c23.4s* c23.8d^2 c23g* c24.2s^2 c31.8g c25g^5 c24.3g^2 Apr 22] tall gelding: third foal: half-brother to fairly useful hurdler/high-class chaser Ar Mad (2m-21f winner, by Tiger Groom): dam French 17f/2¼m chase winner: maiden hurdler: smart handicap chaser: won at Newcastle (novice event, by 1¼ lengths from Bigirononhiship) in November and Taunton (by 6 lengths from Roc d'Apsis) in January: second at Wetherby in Towton Novices' Chase (22 lengths behind Baywing) in February and Ayr (novice event, head behind Label des Obeaux) in April: stays 3m: acts on soft going: wears tongue tie: often travels strongly. *Nigel Twiston-Davies* c145 + h–

CALIN DU BRIZAIS (FR) 6 b.g. Loup Solitaire (USA) – Caline du Brizais (FR) **c112** (Turgeon (USA)) [2016/17 c112p, h109: c20s² c21g⁵ h23.1g⁵ c23.6d⁴ c23.9s⁵ c20.2sᶠ **h100** h23.8gᵘʳ h21.2s⁵ h19.5g Apr 17] fair handicap hurdler: fair maiden chaser: stays 21f: acts on soft going: in headgear last 5 starts: has worn tongue tie, including in 2016/17. *Nigel Hawke*

CALIPTO (FR) 7 b.g. Califet (FR) – Peutiot (FR) (Valanour (IRE)) [2016/17 c140, h–: **c136** c16.3g⁶ c20.5dᶠ Apr 21] has reportedly had breathing operation: winning hurdler: useful **h–** chaser: sixth in Grand Annual at Cheltenham (7 lengths behind Rock The World) in March after long absence/trainer change: should stay 2½m: acts on heavy going: has worn hood/ tongue tie. *Venetia Williams*

CALIVIGNY (IRE) 8 b.g. Gold Well – Summer Holiday (IRE) (Kambalda) [2016/17 **c117** h117: c20d⁵ c21.5s² c21.6spu c20.5v⁶ c20d² c20d⁴ c23.8g Apr 26] winning hurdler: **h–** fairly useful maiden chaser: second in handicaps at Ayr (novice event) in December and Carlisle in February: stays 3m: acts on heavy going: has worn hood, including in 2016/17: temperament under suspicion. *N. W. Alexander*

CALIX DELAFAYETTE (FR) 5 b.g. Caballo Raptor (CAN) – Obepinedelafayette **b93** (FR) (Sleeping Car (FR)) [2016/17 b16v* Mar 11] second foal: dam French maiden (third in 19f chase): in hood, 11/2, won bumper at Ayr (by 3¼ lengths from Indian Harbour) in March. *James Ewart*

CALLAGHAN (GER) 4 b.g. Cacique (IRE) – Cent Cheveux Blanc (GER) (Pentire) **h–** [2016/17 h16.3mpu h16m h15.8m h15.8m⁵ h15.5g Dec 1] lengthy gelding: fair maiden on Flat: no form over hurdles: in headgear last 4 starts: wears tongue tie. *Tom Gretton*

CALL CLAUDE (FR) 4 b.g. Martaline – Aisyacall (FR) (Kahyasi) [2016/17 b16.3v⁴ **b71** b16s⁵ Mar 30] poor form in bumpers. *Kim Bailey*

CALLHIMWHATYOUWANT (IRE) 12 b.g. Old Vic – Jaynes Supreme (IRE) **c–** (Supreme Leader) [2016/17 c63, h–: c17m May 20] multiple point winner: maiden hurdler: **h–** fair chaser at best, well held in hunter in May: stays 2½m: acts on heavy going: has worn blinkers. *Miss S. L. Klug*

CALLING DES BLINS (FR) 5 b.m. Konig Turf (GER) – Quelye des Blins (FR) (Silver **h73 p** Rainbow) [2016/17 b86: h16.5g h15.8d h18.7g⁶ Apr 15] bumper winner: poor form over hurdles: in tongue tie last 3 starts: often races towards rear: type to do better in handicaps. *Dan Skelton*

CALL IT ON (IRE) 11 ch.g. Raise A Grand (IRE) – Birthday Present (Cadeaux **c–** Genereux) [2016/17 c–, h112: h24.7d³ Jun 10] fair handicap hurdler, excuse sole outing in **h98** 2016/17: winning chaser: stays 3¼m: acts on good to firm and heavy going: usually wears cheekpieces/tongue tie. *Philip Kirby*

CALL ME BEN (IRE) 7 ch.g. Beneficial – Good Foundation (IRE) (Buckskin (FR)) **c–** [2016/17 h–, b76: h24vpu c20.9spu Jan 4] off mark in Irish maiden points at third attempt: **h–** no form over hurdles/on chasing debut: in cheekpieces last 2 starts. *James Evans*

CALL ME DYLAN 7 gr.g. Act One – Flinders (Henbit (USA)) [2016/17 h16.3d Nov 25] **h–** tall gelding: failed to complete all 3 starts in points: tailed off in maiden on hurdling debut. *Brendan Powell*

CALL ME LORD (FR) 4 b.g. Slickly (FR) – Sosa (GER) (Cape Cross (IRE)) [2016/17 **h141 p** h16.4d⁵ h16.4s* h17.9v* h16g* Apr 29] fifth foal: half-brother to 3 winners on Flat in France, including 7.5f-10.5f winner Dry Martiny (by Meshaheer): dam unraced: useful form over hurdles: won juvenile events at Cagnes-sur-Mer in December, Compiegne in March and Sandown (handicap, by 3¾ lengths from Dolos) in April: left M. Seror after third start: smart prospect. *Nicky Henderson*

CALL ME SID 5 b.g. Schiaparelli (GER) – Zolotaya (Kayf Tara) [2016/17 b16.3v⁶ Mar **b–** 4] runner-up in point bumper on debut: well beaten in bumper at Newbury. *Jennifer Mason*

CALL ME VIC (IRE) 10 b.g. Old Vic – Call Me Dara (IRE) (Arapahos (FR)) [2016/17 **c136** c133, h–: c24g c25d² c23.8d⁴ c24.1vᶠ c19.9s* c26g² Mar 25] good-topped gelding: **h–** winning hurdler: useful handicap chaser: won at Aintree (by 2½ lengths from Baileys Concerto) in December: stays 3¼m: acts on good to firm and heavy going: usually races prominently. *Tom George*

CALL ME WESTIE 5 b.g. Westerner – Popsie Hall (Saddlers' Hall (IRE)) [2016/17 **b–** b16g Apr 8] tailed off in bumper. *Victor Dartnall*

CALL THE COPS (IRE) 8 b.g. Presenting – Ballygill Heights (IRE) (Symboli Heights (FR)) [2016/17 h–: h23.9g c23.8d^R h25s h26.1g h19.9s h20.2g Apr 28] sturdy gelding: useful handicap hurdler at best, little impact in 2016/17: behind when refused last on chasing debut: left Nicky Henderson after second start: stays 3m: acts on good to firm and heavy going: in headgear on 3 of last 5 starts. *Ben Haslam*   **c–** **h109**

CALL TO ORDER 7 b.g. Presenting – Theatre Girl (King's Theatre (IRE)) [2016/17 h116p, b103: h16g^5 h19.5d^3 h21.1s^3 h24g* h22.8d^5 Feb 18] well-made gelding: fairly useful form over hurdles: won handicap at Cheltenham in December: stays 3m: acts on soft going: in cheekpieces last 2 starts: usually races prominently, often travels strongly. *Jonjo O'Neill*   **h123**

CALL ZAC (IRE) 8 b.g. Zerpour (IRE) – Dolly of Dublin (IRE) (Be My Native (USA)) [2016/17 c19.9g^5 Mar 24] pulled up all 4 starts in points in 2016: well held in novice on chasing debut (tongue tied). *Iain Jardine*   **c–**

CALTON ENTRY (IRE) 8 b.g. Bahri (USA) – Gaybrook (IRE) (Shernazar) [2016/17 c95, h103: h16.2m May 12] fair hurdler at best, well held sole outing in 2016/17: maiden chaser: unproven beyond 2m: acts on good to firm going. *Katie Scott*   **c–** **h–**

CALVA D'HONORE (FR) 6 b.g. Khalkevi (IRE) – Elivette (FR) (Arvico (FR)) [2016/17 b15.7g* b16g^3 h15.8d^2 h17.7s h15.8s^4 h15.8d Mar 15] first foal: dam, ran once on Flat in France, half-sister to fairly useful French hurdler/fair chaser (17f/2¼m winner) Eliga: fair form in bumpers: won at Southwell in June: fair form over hurdles: front runner. *Ben Pauling*   **h107** **b94**

CALYPSO DELEGATOR (IRE) 4 b.g. Lilbourne Lad (IRE) – Amber Nectar (IRE) (Barathea (IRE)) [2016/17 h15.8d^pu Oct 13] modest maiden on Flat, stays 11f: pulled up in juvenile maiden on hurdling debut. *Micky Hammond*   **h–**

CAMACHOICE (IRE) 7 b.g. Camacho – Nouvelle Reve (GER) (Acatenango (GER)) [2016/17 h77: h16.6g h20.3d Nov 15] fair hurdler at best, well below form since 2014/15: unproven beyond 2m: best form on good going: has worn headgear, including in 2016/17: tried in tongue tie. *Joanne Foster*   **h–**

CAMAKASI (IRE) 6 b.g. Camacho – Innocence (Unfuwain (USA)) [2016/17 h87: h16.8g h17.9g^pu h16.8m Oct 6] sturdy gelding: fairly useful on Flat, stays 11f: little form over hurdles: in headgear last 3 starts: wears tongue tie. *Ali Stronge*   **h–**

CAMAPLU (FR) 5 gr.m. Turgeon (USA) – Line Tzigane (FR) (Bonnet Rouge (FR)) [2016/17 h16.8d^F Sep 26] second foal: dam (b85), bumper winner, out of half-sister to high-class French hurdler/chaser Or Jack: tailed off when fell 2 out in mares novice hurdle at Newton Abbot. *David Bridgwater*   **h–**

CAMPEADOR (FR) 5 gr.g. Gris de Gris (IRE) – Royale Video (FR) (Video Rock (FR)) [2016/17 h143p: h16d^F Dec 4] useful-looking gelding: smart form over hurdles: in control when fell heavily last in handicap at Fairyhouse on sole outing in 2016/17: raced around 2m: acts on heavy going: tried in hood: likely to progress further. *Gordon Elliott, Ireland*   **h153 p**

CAMPING GROUND (FR) 7 b.g. Goldneyev (USA) – Camomille (GER) (Pennekamp (USA)) [2016/17 c156, h156: c20.5g^2 c23.4d^F h20.3s^5 h19.1s* Feb 26] lengthy, useful-looking gelding: top-class hurdler: left Robert Walford, won National Spirit Hurdle at Fontwell (by 29 lengths from Le Rocher) in February: smart chaser: stays 2½m: acts on heavy going: has worn tongue tie, including in 2016/17 (left off at Fontwell). *Gary Moore*   **c148** **h166**

CAMRON DE CHAILLAC (FR) 5 br.g. Laverock (IRE) – Hadeel (Polish Precedent (USA)) [2016/17 h67: h16.2g h18.5g h16m^5 h16g^3 h19.6s^6 h15.9v^2 h15.7s Mar 20] close-coupled gelding: fair maiden hurdler: stays 19f: acts on good to firm and heavy going: in blinkers last 2 starts: often races towards rear. *Nigel Hawke*   **h105**

CANADIAN DIAMOND (IRE) 10 ch.g. Halling (USA) – Six Nations (USA) (Danzig (USA)) [2016/17 c–, h117: h16d^4 h15.8s h17.7g^ur Apr 21] rather leggy gelding: fairly useful handicap hurdler at best: once-raced chaser: seemed best around 2m: acted on good to firm and heavy going: wore cheekpieces: dead. *Richard Rowe*   **c–** **h101**

CANARDIER (FR) 5 b.g. Crillon (FR) – Idylle du Marais (FR) (Panoramic) [2016/17 b18g* Apr 28] half-brother to several winners, including very smart chaser around 2m Oiseau de Nuit (by Evening World) and smart French chaser Upwelling (17f winner, by Robin des Pres), stayed 2¾m: dam French maiden: gambled-on 8/1, won maiden bumper at Punchestown (by ¾ length from Its All Guesswork) in April: wore hood sole start: sure to progress. *Dermot Anthony McLoughlin, Ireland*   **b109 p**

CANDELITA 10 b.m. Trade Fair – Gramada (IRE) (Cape Cross (IRE)) [2016/17 c–, h–: h15.8g c20.1g^F h15.8g Jul 24] fair hurdler at best, no form since 2014/15: maiden chaser, fell sole outing in 2016/17: has worn headgear, including last 5 starts. *Clare Ellam*   **c–** **h–**

CANDIDE (IRE) 10 ch.g. Albano (IRE) – Sweet Cicely (IRE) (Darshaan) [2016/17 c91, h–: h25d^{pu} c24d^4 May 18] lengthy gelding: fair hurdler at best, pulled up on return: fair handicap chaser, below form sole outing over fences in 2016/17: stayed 3¼m: acted on heavy going: wore cheekpieces: dead. *Sally Randell* **c88** **h–**

CANDY BURG (FR) 4 b.g. Sageburg (IRE) – Candinie (USA) (Bernardini (USA)) [2016/17 h17.4g* h16.9s^{ur} h16.8d^5 h16.4g Mar 15] well-made gelding: fair on Flat, stays 9f: fair form over hurdles: won juvenile at Marseilles Borely very early in season: left Mme J. Laurent-Joye Rossi after first start, S. Culin after second: best effort at 17f: tried in tongue tie: has rejoined former trainer. *Venetia Williams* **h114**

CANFORD CHIMES (IRE) 4 b.g. Canford Cliffs (IRE) – Appleblossom Pearl (IRE) (Peintre Celebre (USA)) [2016/17 b16.6g^3 b16.8d^2 Mar 21] fourth foal: half-brother to 2 winners, including Italian 2m hurdle winner Silent Footsteps (by Footstepsinthesand): dam, 7f winner who stayed 1¼m, half-sister to smart hurdler/fairly useful chaser (stayed 3½m) Kawagino: fair form in bumpers: better effort when second at Exeter in March. *Alan King* **b90**

CANFORD KILBEY (IRE) 4 b.f. Canford Cliffs (IRE) – Sweet Namibia (IRE) (Namid) [2016/17 h15.8d^3 h15.8m^6 Oct 30] modest on Flat, stays 7f: no form over hurdles. *Michael Easterby* **h–**

CANFORD THOMPSON 4 b.g. Canford Cliffs (IRE) – Sadie Thompson (IRE) (King's Best (USA)) [2016/17 h17.2d^5 h16.2d^6 h16g* h16g^5 Oct 28] half-brother to useful hurdler Daneking (2m winner, by Dylan Thomas), stayed 21f, and fair hurdler Scoppio Del Carro (2m winner, by Medicean): fair maiden on Flat, stays 12.5f: modest form over hurdles: won juvenile maiden at Wetherby in October: tried in hood. *Micky Hammond* **h98**

CANICALLYOUBACK 9 b.g. Auction House (USA) – Island Colony (USA) (Pleasant Colony (USA)) [2016/17 c–, h117: c16g c19.4g^4 c19.4d^3 c16g* c16.3g* c16.5g^2 c16.5m^3 c16.3g^2 c16m^4 c16v^F c16s^{pu} h15.8g^3 Apr 3] fair handicap hurdler: fairly useful handicap chaser: won at Uttoxeter and Newton Abbot (novice event) early in season: second at Worcester in August: stays 19f: acts on good to firm and good to soft going. *Evan Williams* **c126** **h104**

CANIVER QUEEN (IRE) 7 ch.m. Sendawar (IRE) – Sharp Dancer (Danehill Dancer (IRE)) [2016/17 h–, b–: h21.6d^5 h22v h21.6m^{pu} Jul 1] modest form over hurdles: stays 2¾m: acts on good to soft going: tried in cheekpieces: often races towards rear. *Brian Barr* **h90**

totepool National Spirit Hurdle, Fontwell—double take needed as Camping Ground routs his field in rain-softened conditions to make a hugely impressive start for a new stable

CANNY TOM (IRE) 7 b.g. Jimble (FR) – Tombazaan (IRE) (Good Thyne (USA)) **h102**
[2016/17 h90, b81: h20v⁵ h24g h20gᵘʳ h17.2g⁴ h18.5g³ h20.2sᶠ h17.8d² h16g³ h16d²
h16.2d Dec 1] fair maiden hurdler: left Shane Donohoe after first start: stays 2½m: acts on
heavy going: tried in hood: often races towards rear/travels strongly: weak finisher. *Gordon
Elliott, Ireland*

CANOODLE 5 b.m. Stimulation (IRE) – Flirtatious (Generous (IRE)) [2016/17 b95: **h109**
b16.4s h15.8s² h16.2s⁵ h15.8gᶠ h16m² h16.5m* Apr 20] leggy mare: bumper winner: fair **b85**
form over hurdles: won mares novice at Taunton in April: raced only at 2m: acts on soft and
good to firm going: has worn headgear, including last 3 starts: often races towards rear.
Hughie Morrison

CANOVA (IRE) 6 ch.g. Art Connoisseur (IRE) – Rain Dancer (IRE) (Sadler's Wells **h85**
(USA)) [2016/17 h96: h18.5g h18.2g⁶ h16v⁵ h18.8g⁴ h16vᵖᵘ Apr 1] modest maiden
hurdler: stays 19f: acts on good to soft going: wears tongue tie. *Gordon Elliott, Ireland*

CANTLOW (IRE) 12 b.g. Kayf Tara – Winnowing (IRE) (Strong Gale) [2016/17 c135§, **c147**
h–: c33g² c26m* c25s c22.5g h21.6s c24s* c30.2m* c30.2d² c30.2g³ c33m² Apr 27] **h122 +**
well-made gelding: useful hurdler at best: smart chaser: won handicap at Killarney (by
½ length from Your Busy) early in season, and cross-country events at Punchestown (by
2¾ lengths from Ballyboker Bridge) in November and Cheltenham (handicap by 9 lengths
from Bless The Wings) in December: second in another cross-country handicap at
Cheltenham (3 lengths behind Urgent de Gregaine) in January: stays 3¾m: acts on good to
firm and heavy going: has worn cheekpieces/tongue tie: usually travels strongly. *Enda
Bolger, Ireland*

CANTON PRINCE (IRE) 6 b.g. Shantou (USA) – Hasainm (IRE) (Grand Lodge **h124**
(USA)) [2016/17 b85: b16.8g* h17.7d* h20g* h19.5gᵖᵘ h15.6g⁴ h19.9sᵖᵘ Mar 18] fairly **b96**
useful form in bumpers: won at Newton Abbot in August: fairly useful form over hurdles:
won novices at Fontwell and Worcester in September: stays 2½m: acts on good to soft
going. *Tim Vaughan*

CAPARD KING (IRE) 8 b.g. Beneficial – Capard Lady (IRE) (Supreme Leader) **c127**
[2016/17 c138, h–p: c24s c25g⁴ c23.6g c26.3sᵖᵘ c23.8d³ c23.8gᵘʳ h24.3d Apr 21] sturdy **h–**
gelding: fairly useful chaser: fairly useful handicap chaser: stays 3¼m: acts on heavy going: in cheekpieces last 2 starts: tends
to jump left. *Jonjo O'Neill*

CAPATOSTA (USA) 5 ch.g. Flashy Bull (USA) – Da River Hoss (USA) (River Special **h–**
(USA)) [2016/17 h–: h19.6m h15.5vᵖᵘ h16g⁵ h16.3g Mar 25] good-topped gelding: lightly
raced on Flat: no form over hurdles: left Charlie Mann after first start: in cheekpieces/
tongue tie last 2 starts. *Sarah-Jayne Davies*

CAP D'AUBOIS (FR) 5 br.g. Snow Cap (FR) – Caline Grace (FR) (Marmato) [2016/17 **h136**
h16d⁵ h16s² h16g Jan 22] half-brother to French hurdler Calin d'Aubois (2½m winner, by
Crillon): dam French 15f-17f hurdle/chase winner: modest maiden on Flat, stays 14.5f:
useful form over hurdles: won newcomers race at Cagnes-sur-Mer in 2015/16 for L. Postic:
second in listed event at Limerick (6½ lengths behind Missy Tata) in December.
W. P. Mullins, Ireland

CAPE ARROW 6 b.g. Cape Cross (IRE) – Aiming (Highest Honor (FR)) [2016/17 h72: **h–**
h20d Oct 20] modest hurdler at best, well held sole outing in 2016/17: barely stayed 2¾m:
acted on heavy going: dead. *Barry Murtagh*

CAPE CASTER (IRE) 6 br.g. Cape Cross (IRE) – Playboy Mansion (IRE) (Grand **c115**
Lodge (USA)) [2016/17 h116: h15.8m² h17.2g³ h20d⁴ c16.5gᵖᵘ c16.3g³ c16v* c16vᵖᵘ **h117**
c16mᵘʳ Apr 18] rangy leggy gelding: fairly useful handicap hurdler: second at Ludlow
early in season: fairly useful form over fences: won handicap at Ffos Las in December:
unproven beyond 17f: acts on good to firm and heavy going. *Evan Williams*

CAPE HIDEAWAY 5 b.g. Mount Nelson – Amiata (Pennekamp (USA)) [2016/17 **h98**
h16.7d⁶ h16.8g³ h16.2s⁴ h19.9d² h19.3gᶠ h19.3d³ h18.6m² Apr 17] fair on Flat, stays 2m:
modest maiden hurdler: in frame on 5 of 6 completed starts: stays 19f: acts on soft and good
to firm going: wears cheekpieces: often races prominently. *Mark Walford*

CAPELAND (FR) 5 b.g. Poliglote – Neiland (FR) (Cyborg (FR)) [2016/17 b94: h16g² **h121**
h18.5g* h18.5s⁶ h19g² Mar 20] bumper winner: fairly useful form over hurdles: won
novice at Newton Abbot in October: second in novice at Taunton in March: often races
freely. *Paul Nicholls*

CAPE OF GLORY (IRE) 4 br.g. Cape Cross (IRE) – Stairway To Glory (IRE) (Kalanisi **h110**
(IRE)) [2016/17 h15.6g* h15.7d³ Dec 13] fairly useful on Flat, stays 1½m: fair form over
hurdles: won juvenile at Musselburgh in November: third in similar event at Catterick:
wears cheekpieces. *Keith Dalgleish*

CAP HORNER (FR) 5 gr.g. Apsis – Rapsodie Sea (FR) (April Night (FR)) [2016/17 **h96**
b16d² b16m⁵ b15.8d⁴ b16s⁶ h20.5m³ Apr 16] second foal: half-brother to French 1½m-1¾m **b63**
bumper winner Bubble Sea (by Great Pretender): dam ran twice in France (third at 1½m):
poor form in bumpers: 18/1, third in novice at Plumpton (4¼ lengths behind Peak To Peak)
on hurdling debut. *Seamus Mullins*

CAPILLA (IRE) 9 gr.g. Beneficial – Cap The Rose (IRE) (Roselier (FR)) [2016/17 c114, **c–**
h–: c20vᵖᵘ c16v⁴ c16sᵘʳ c17.4vᵖᵘ c16sᵖᵘ Feb 20] sturdy gelding: maiden hurdler: fair chaser **h–**
at best, no form in 2016/17: has worn headgear, including in 2016/17: wears tongue tie:
usually leads. *Evan Williams*

CAPISCI (IRE) 12 br.g. Tikkanen (USA) – Dolce Notte (IRE) (Strong Gale) [2016/17 **c71**
c94, h–: c16.5g⁵ c17g⁵ c20.3d⁵ c17g³ c16.5g Sep 12] lengthy gelding: maiden hurdler: **h–**
modest handicap chaser, below best in 2016/17: stays 2½m: acts on good to firm and heavy
going: has worn headgear: has worn tongue tie, including in 2016/17: front runner/races
prominently. *Sarah-Jayne Davies*

CAPITAINE (FR) 5 gr.g. Montmartre (FR) – Patte de Velour (FR) (Mansonnien (FR)) **h139**
[2016/17 b114: h15.3m* h15.7v² h15.7d* h16s² h16g⁴ h18.1vᵖᵘ h15.3f* Apr 23] good-
topped gelding: bumper winner: useful hurdler: won novices at Wincanton in November,
Ascot (Kennel Gate Novices' Hurdle, by 3½ lengths from Captain Forez) in December and
Wincanton again in April: second in Tolworth Novices' Hurdle at Sandown (5 lengths
behind Finian's Oscar) in January: unproven beyond 2m: acts on any going: usually wears
hood: front runner/races prominently. *Paul Nicholls*

CAPITAL FORCE (IRE) 6 b.g. Kayf Tara – Watson River (IRE) (Presenting) [2016/17 **h122**
h18d² h16d⁴ h18g³ h16s* h16.4g Mar 14] €58,000 3-y-o: useful-looking gelding: third
foal: half-brother to fairly useful hurdler Dallas Cowboy (2½m winner, by Beneficial): dam
unraced half-sister to useful hurdler/smart chaser (stayed 2½m) Watson Lake: fairly useful
form over hurdles: won maiden at Thurles in February: stays 2¼m: acts on soft going: often
travels strongly. *Henry de Bromhead, Ireland*

CAPITOUL (FR) 5 b.g. Enrique – Ranavalo (FR) (Ungaro (GER)) [2016/17 b11.4g⁴ **h119**
b11.9g² b13.2g³ b11.9g³ h17.4d² h17.1g³ h16s* h19.7dᶠ Jan 14] third foal: dam unraced **b?**
half-sister to winning hurdler/useful chaser (stayed 3m) Jakari: placed in bumpers: fairly
useful form over hurdles: won maiden at Ayr in December: left J-D. Marion after sixth
start. *Dr Richard Newland*

CAPORALI 4 b.g. Champs Elysees – Pnyka (IRE) (Montjeu (IRE)) [2016/17 b15.7s **b–**
b15.7g Mar 28] well beaten in 2 bumpers. *J. R. Jenkins*

CAPPIELOW PARK 8 b.g. Exceed And Excel (AUS) – Barakat (Bustino) [2016/17 **c–**
c116, h–: h20.5d⁴ h15.8s² Mar 2] sturdy gelding: fair hurdler: fairly useful chaser: stays **h104**
2½m: acts on heavy going: wears headgear/tongue tie. *Ali Stronge*

CAPRICE D'ANGLAIS (FR) 5 gr.g. Kapgarde (FR) – Odile de Neulliac (FR) (Turgeon **c105**
(USA)) [2016/17 c16.9s⁵ c20dᶠ c21.4v h20.7g⁶ h19.7sᵖᵘ h15.5g³ c15.9fᵘʳ c16s* c16.5d* **h105**
c15.9g⁵ c15.7s⁵ h16g* h16g³ Apr 17] leggy gelding: fourth foal: half-brother to French 21f
chase winner Asti du Domaine (by Silver Cross): dam lightly raced in France: fair form
over hurdles: won seller at Fakenham in March: fair handicap chaser: won at Hereford
(novice event) and Huntingdon in December: left Emmanuel Clayeux after third start,
Richard Hobson after twelfth: best around 2m: acts on firm and soft going: wears headgear:
keen-going front runner. *Sam Thomas*

CAPSIS DESBOIS (FR) 5 b.g. Apsis – Gesse Parade (FR) (Dress Parade) [2016/17 b73: **h100**
b17.7g⁵ h19.5m³ h19.5g⁴ h19.6sᵖᵘ h21.6sᵖᵘ Feb 26] poor form in bumpers: fair form over **b64**
hurdles. *Gary Moore*

CAP SOLEIL (FR) 4 b.f. Kapgarde (FR) – Move Again (FR) (Noir Et Or) [2016/17 **b109**
b12.6d* b14s* b16d* Mar 11] good-topped filly: sister to fairly useful French hurdler/
chaser Miss Bailly (2m-2¼m winner) and half-sister to several winners in France,
including fairly useful hurdler Prince Picard (2¼m/19f winner, by Sleeping Car): dam,
French 15f/19f hurdle winner, also 9f-10.3f winner on Flat: useful form in bumpers: won
fillies junior at Newbury (by 2½ lengths from Reel Leisure) in December, listed 4-y-o
event at Cheltenham (by head from Daphne du Clos) in January and listed mares event at
Sandown (by ½ length from Petticoat Tails) in March. *Fergal O'Brien*

CAP ST VINCENT (FR) 4 b.g. Muhtathir – Criquetot (FR) (Epervier Bleu) [2016/17 **b–** b16g Apr 22] winning pointer: tailed off in bumper. *Paul Nicholls*

CAPSY DE MEE (FR) 5 b.g. Apsis – Koeur de Mee (FR) (Video Rock (FR)) [2016/17 **h102** b11.9g* h16.3d h15.8s⁵ h16g³ Mar 17] rather unfurnished gelding: fourth foal: half-brother **b?** to useful hurdler/chaser As de Mee (2m-2½m winner, by Kapgarde): dam French 11.5f/12.5f bumper winner: won Group 3 bumper at Saint-Cloud early in season: fair form over hurdles: best effort when third in conditionals maiden at Fakenham in March: left J. Planque after first start: tried in tongue tie. *Jamie Snowden*

CAPTAIN BONSAI 8 b.g. Morpeth – Fire Ranger (Presidium) [2016/17 h21.6gᵖᵘ h21.6d³ **h–** h16.8m⁴ h16.8m h21.6s Nov 20] compact gelding: no form over hurdles. *Susan Gardner*

CAPTAIN BROWN 9 b.g. Lomitas – Nicola Bella (IRE) (Sadler's Wells (USA)) [2016/17 **c– x** c–x, h121: h22.1m h17.2m⁴ h17.2d⁵ h17.2g* h16d³ h19.4g⁵ h15.6g h16dᶠ Apr 21] **h118** rather leggy, lengthy gelding: fairly useful handicap hurdler: won at Cartmel in August: maiden chaser: stays 2¾m, effective at shorter: acts on soft and good to firm going: tried in headgear/tongue tie: often races towards rear: often let down by jumping over fences. *James Moffatt*

CAPTAIN BUCK'S (FR) 5 b.g. Buck's Boum (FR) – Ombre Jaune (FR) (Brier Creek **h117** (USA)) [2016/17 b105: h19g² h21s* h16.3d⁴ h23.1g* Apr 26] bumper winner: fairly useful form over hurdles: won novices at Kempton in February and Exeter in April: will stay 3m: wears tongue tie. *Paul Nicholls*

CAPTAIN CAMELOT (IRE) 8 b.g. Urban Ocean (FR) – Harneyspet (IRE) (Sharifabad **c73** (IRE)) [2016/17 c95: c23.6m Apr 28] multiple winning pointer: poor form in novice hunter chases: wears hood/tongue tie. *Miss C. Packwood*

CAPTAIN CANADA 10 br.g. Tamayaz (CAN) – Hattie (Sylvan Express) [2016/17 c–, **c–** h82: h25gᵖᵘ May 30] workmanlike gelding: dual winning pointer: poor hurdler: maiden **h–** chaser: stayed 2¾m: acted on heavy going: tried in tongue tie: often raced in rear: dead. *Tim Vaughan*

CAPTAIN CHAOS (IRE) 6 ch.g. Golan (IRE) – Times Have Changed (IRE) (Safety **c133 p** Catch (USA)) [2016/17 h134: c21d⁴ c24s³ c24.2sᶠ Feb 4] lengthy, raw-boned gelding: **h–** winning hurdler: useful form over fences: best effort when third in listed novice at Warwick (6¾ lengths behind American) in January: stays 3m: acts on heavy going: should do better over fences. *Dan Skelton*

CAPTAIN CLAYTON (IRE) 10 b.g. Subtle Power (IRE) – Dont Hurry (IRE) (Muroto) **h107** [2016/17 h19.9g⁵ h21.4d h16.4s⁵ h20.6s² Jan 23] fair handicap hurdler: stays 2¾m, effective at much shorter granted good test: acts on heavy going: has worn tongue tie. *Simon West*

CAPTAIN CONAN (FR) 10 b.g. Kingsalsa (USA) – Lavandou (Sadler's Wells (USA)) **c133** [2016/17 c136, h113: c20d⁶ c18.8dᵖᵘ Dec 17] big, lengthy gelding: fair hurdler: useful chaser **h–** nowadays: sixth in Guinness Handicap Chase at Punchestown (15 lengths behind Irish Cavalier) in April: stays 2½m: acts on heavy going: tried in cheekpieces. *Nicky Henderson*

CAPTAIN FELIX 5 b.g. Captain Gerrard (IRE) – Sweet Applause (IRE) (Acclamation) **h105** [2016/17 h16g² h15.8g h15.8d⁴ h16s² h19.8vᵖᵘ Feb 4] leggy gelding: fair on Flat, stays 1¼m: fair form over hurdles: will prove best at 2m: acts on good to soft going. *James Eustace*

CAPTAIN FLASH (IRE) 8 b.g. Indian River (FR) – Westgate Run (Emperor Jones **c79** (USA)) [2016/17 c98, h90, b–: c24d⁵ c24vᵖᵘ Feb 11] maiden hurdler: modest chaser at best, **h–** below form both starts in 2016/17: stays 3m: acts on heavy going: in cheekpieces last 4 starts: tried in tongue tie: front runner/races prominently. *Jo Davis*

CAPTAIN FOREZ (FR) 5 b.g. Network (GER) – Pourkoipa du Forez (FR) (Robin des **h144 p** Champs (FR)) [2016/17 h16.3d³ h15.7d² h20g² Apr 8] well-made gelding: fifth foal: half-brother to 2 winners in France, including Twist du Forez (17f hurdle winner, by Without Connexion): dam unraced: useful form over hurdles: second in Kennel Gate Novices' Hurdle at Ascot (3½ lengths behind Capitaine) in December and Mersey Novices' Hurdle at Aintree (3 lengths behind Finian's Oscar) in April: will stay beyond 2½m: open to further improvement. *Dan Skelton*

CAPTAIN GEORGE (IRE) 6 b.g. Bushranger (IRE) – High Society Girl (IRE) (Key of **h55** Luck (USA)) [2016/17 h15.3v⁴ Mar 9] fair on Flat, stays 1¾m: well beaten in novice on hurdling debut. *Michael Blake*

CAPTAIN HOX (IRE) 8 b.g. Danehill Dancer (IRE) – Shangri La (IRE) (Sadler's Wells (USA)) [2016/17 c124, h–: c15.6d h16d c16.3s³ c15.5s⁵ c18s⁵ c19.9g⁵ Apr 21] fairly useful hurdler at best, below form sole outing over hurdles in 2016/17: fair handicap chaser: stays 2½m: acts on heavy going: has worn headgear, including in 2016/17: wears tongue tie: has hung right/looked half-hearted. *Patrick Griffin, Ireland* — **c112 §**
h–

CAPTAIN JACK 4 b.g. Mount Nelson – Court Princess (Mtoto) [2016/17 b13.7g b16s b16.6g b16s⁶ Mar 30] no form in bumpers. *Richard Price* — **b–**

CAPTAIN MCGARRY (IRE) 5 b.g. Oscar (IRE) – Garryduff Princess (IRE) (Husyan (USA)) [2016/17 b16g* Mar 18] €32,000 3-y-o: lengthy, useful-looking gelding: has scope: seventh foal: half-brother to fairly useful hurdler/useful chaser Court By Surprise (2½m-25f winner, by Beneficial), stays 29f, and fair hurdler/chaser Drive On Jim (19f-3m winner, by Alderbrook): dam little sign of ability over hurdles: 16/1, green but won maiden bumper at Kempton (by 4 lengths from Colonial Dreams) in March. *Graeme McPherson* — **b105**

CAPTAIN MCGINLEY (IRE) 7 bl.g. Robin des Pres (FR) – Rocella (GER) (Goofalik (USA)) [2016/17 h100: h23.1g c22.7fᵘʳ c26.3gᵖᵘ c25.1s Jan 7] maiden hurdler: no form over fences: wears headgear: often races prominently. *Rebecca Curtis* — **c–**
h–

CAPTAIN MORLEY 6 b.g. Hernando (FR) – Oval Office (Pursuit of Love) [2016/17 h16.3d⁵ Dec 31] well-made gelding: fair chaser, runner-up at flat, stays 12.5f: 11/2, caught eye when fifth in introductory event at Newbury (12½ lengths behind William Henry) on hurdling debut: should make considerable progress. *David Simcock* — **h95 P**

CAPTAIN MOWBRAY 6 ch.g. Shami – Some Like It Hot (Ashkalani (IRE)) [2016/17 h78, b81: h16g h19.9m⁵ h20.2dᵖᵘ h16.8g² h16s⁴ h19.7s² h19.7s³ h19.7d² h20.6g² Apr 8] fair maiden hurdler: stays 21f: acts on soft and good to firm going: held up. *Rebecca Menzies* — **h101**

CAPTAIN OCANA (IRE) 12 b.g. Karinga Bay – Jaystara (IRE) (Jurado (USA)) [2016/17 c21g⁵ c24.2g⁵ c20.9gᵖᵘ c20dᵖᵘ c23mᵖᵘ Aug 17] winning pointer: maiden hurdler: fair handicap chaser at best, on downgrade: stays 25f: acts on soft and good to firm going: tried in cheekpieces. *Mark Gillard* — **c75**
h–

CAPTAINOFINDUSTRY (IRE) 8 b.g. Definite Article – Talk of Rain (FR) (Turgeon (USA)) [2016/17 h113: h19.9spᵘ h23.5s c22.4sᵘʳ c24.5sᵖᵘ Mar 16] rangy gelding: fair hurdler at best, below form in 2016/17: failed to complete both starts over fences: wears headgear: front runner/races prominently. *Mark Pitman* — **c–**
h–

CAPTAINOFTHEFLEET (IRE) 10 ch.g. Refuse To Bend (IRE) – Darabaka (IRE) (Doyoun) [2016/17 h135: h24d⁶ h20v h24s⁵ h24v h19s⁴ h24v² h24d Apr 27] useful handicap hurdler: second at Cork (2¾ lengths behind Westerner Point) in March: stays 3m: acts on heavy going: usually races nearer last than first. *Eamon O'Connell, Ireland* — **h134**

CAPTAIN REDBEARD (IRE) 8 ch.g. Bach (IRE) – Diesel Dancer (IRE) (Toulon) [2016/17 h131: c23.4d⁴ c21.6s³ c20.9s⁴ c19.4s³ c19.4s* c19.9d* c20.4gᵖᵘ c19.9g² Apr 15] sturdy gelding: won both starts in points: winning hurdler: useful handicap chaser: won at Wetherby in January and Haydock (novice event, by short head from Aqua Dude) in February: stays 21f: acts on heavy going. *Stuart Coltherd* — **c139**
h–

CAPTAIN SAM 5 b.g. Black Sam Bellamy (IRE) – Grande Terre (IRE) (Grand Lodge (USA)) [2016/17 b89: h16.7g⁶ h16.7g⁶ Oct 24] poor form in bumpers. *Malcolm Jefferson* — **b63**

CAPTAIN SHARPE 9 ch.g. Tobougg (IRE) – Helen Sharp (Pivotal) [2016/17 c77§, h–: c15.6gᵖᵘ c20.1sᵖᵘ h16.4sᵖᵘ h16.4s³ c16.4d³ h16.4s⁶ c16.4s⁵ h16.4v⁴ c19.3v³ c16.4d⁴ c20.1v⁵ h20.6g c26.3m² Apr 19] sturdy gelding: poor handicap hurdler/chaser: stays 3¼m: acts on good to firm and heavy going: wears headgear: has worn tongue tie: temperamental. *Kenny Johnson* — **c75 §**
h67 §

CAPTAINS HORSE (FR) 5 b.g. Mister Conway (FR) – Laureine (FR) (Sleeping Car (FR)) [2016/17 h19.9g h19.5mᵖᵘ h23.1v h23.1s c23gᶠ c23.8gᵖᵘ c20.9dᵖᵘ Mar 25] no form over hurdles/fences: sometimes in cheekpieces. *Nigel Hawke* — **c–**
h–

CAPTAIN SIMON (IRE) 5 b.g. Dubai Destination (USA) – Gayephar (Phardante (FR)) [2016/17 b16.5g* Apr 6] £28,000 3-y-o: half-brother to useful hurdler/chaser Slieveardagh (2m-2½m winner, by King's Theatre): dam twice-raced half-sister to smart staying chaser Simon: won maiden point on debut: 5/2, also won bumper at Taunton (by neck from Take Em Out) in April, keeping on gamely: will stay at least 2¼m. *Dan Skelton* — **b95**

CAPTAIN WOODIE (IRE) 5 b.g. Presenting – Lasado (IRE) (Jurado (USA)) [2016/17 b16.5m⁵ b15.6g⁴ b16d* Mar 21] €125,000 3-y-o: fifth foal: half-brother to 3 winners, including fairly useful hurdler/useful chaser Coverholder (2m-23f winner, by Oscar) and fairly useful hurdler/chaser Angus Milan (2m-2¾m winner, by Milan): dam unraced half-sister to top-class chaser Harbour Pilot, stayed 3¼m: fairly useful form in bumpers: won at Taunton in December and Wetherby in March. *Nicky Henderson* — **b104**

CARACCI APACHE (IRE) 7 b.g. High Chaparral (IRE) – Campanella (GER) (Lomitas) [2016/17 c121p, h–: c23.4d^F c24g^{pu} Dec 26] tall gelding: winning hurdler: maiden chaser, no form in 2016/17: stays 3m: acts on heavy going. *Nicky Henderson* **c–** **h–**

CARA COURT (IRE) 11 b.g. Court Cave (IRE) – Tarasandy (IRE) (Arapahos (FR)) [2016/17 c77, h–: c24.2d Jun 19] winning hurdler: modest chaser at best, well held sole outing in 2016/17: stays 27f: acts on heavy going: wears headgear: front runner/races prominently. *Joanne Foster* **c–** **h–**

CARALINE (FR) 6 b.m. Martaline – Vie Ta Vie (FR) (Villez (USA)) [2016/17 c117, h79: c16.3s^4 c17.1s^4 c19.3s^3 c20.1s^2 c20.1v^{pu} Mar 10] winning hurdler: fairly useful handicap chaser: second at Newcastle in February: stays 2½m: acts on heavy going: has worn headgear: often races towards rear. *Micky Hammond* **c116** **h–**

CARD GAME (IRE) 8 b.m. Scorpion (IRE) – Cardona (Dashing Blade) [2016/17 h132, b71: h19d^2 h20.6g^2 h16g^5 h20.3s^{pu} h22.8s^{pu} h21.2s^5 h16.8g^3 h20.6m^4 Apr 17] small, compact mare: fairly useful handicap hurdler: second at Warwick and Market Rasen early in season: stays 19f: acts on soft going. *Malcolm Jefferson* **h121**

CARDINAL ROSE 10 ch.g. Karinga Bay – Miniature Rose (Anshan) [2016/17 c103, h59: c24.1g^{pu} h24d^4 Dec 15] close-coupled gelding: maiden hurdler: fair chaser at best, pulled up sole outing over fences in 2016/17: stays 3¼m: acts on good to soft going: has worn headgear: usually races prominently. *Mark Wall* **c–** **h–**

CARDINAL WALTER (IRE) 8 br.g. Cape Cross (IRE) – Sheer Spirit (IRE) (Caerleon (USA)) [2016/17 h133: h20g Oct 23] well-made gelding: useful hurdler at best, well held sole outing in 2016/17: stays 19f: acts on soft and good to firm going: wears hood. *Nicky Henderson* **h–**

CARINENA (IRE) 8 b.m. Shantou (USA) – Dinny Kenn (IRE) (Phardante (FR)) [2016/17 h112, b89: h16.2d^F h16.2d^4 h16.2g^u h16.2s^4 h16.3m^5 Oct 15] bumper winner: fair handicap hurdler: won at Perth in August: stays 2½m: best form on good going: often races prominently. *Nicky Richards* **h114**

CARLI KING (IRE) 11 b.g. Witness Box (USA) – Abinitio Lady (IRE) (Be My Native (USA)) [2016/17 c27.2s c26.2s c24v c24d^2 c29.2v^4 c28.4g^6 Apr 15] fairly useful handicap chaser: second at Doncaster in February: stays 29f: acts on heavy going: wears headgear: front runner/races prominently. *Caroline Bailey* **c119**

CARLINGFORD LOUGH (IRE) 11 b.g. King's Theatre (IRE) – Baden (IRE) (Furry Glen) [2016/17 c167, h–: c25d* h16s^4 c24.3s^4 Feb 12] lengthy gelding: useful hurdler at best: top-class chaser: fourth in Irish Gold Cup at Leopardstown in February: stays 3¼m: acts on heavy going: usually races towards rear. *John E. Kiely, Ireland* **c159** **h121 +**

CARLINGFORD PRINCE (IRE) 8 ch.g. Definite Article – Castle Hope (IRE) (Old Vic) [2016/17 h20.2m^4 May 11] placed in points: modest form over hurdles: in hood, fourth in maiden at Perth on sole outing in 2016/17: will stay further than 2½m. *Tim Reed* **h94**

CARLITA MORIVIERE (FR) 5 b.m. Balko (FR) – Halladina (FR) (Passing Sale (FR)) [2016/17 b17g^3 b16.4s b16.7s Dec 22] good-topped mare: fourth foal: half-sister to bumper winner/smart hurdler Bamako Moriviere (2m-2½m winner, by Califet): dam French maiden: modest form in bumpers. *Rebecca Curtis* **b76**

CARLO ROCKS (IRE) 7 b.g. Carlo Bank (IRE) – Rock Garden (IRE) (Bigstone (IRE)) [2016/17 h102: c24d^4 c24.2s Dec 26] compact gelding: fair hurdler: poor form over fences: stays 3m: best form on soft/heavy going: tried in hood: should still improve over fences. *Caroline Bailey* **c77 p** **h–**

CARLOS DU FRUITIER (FR) 5 b.g. Diableneyev (USA) – Odyssee Madrik (FR) (Antarctique (IRE)) [2016/17 b16s* b16.4v^2 b17g Apr 7] useful-looking gelding: third foal: dam, French maiden, half-sister to useful chaser (stayed 27f) Galant Nuit: in frame both starts in Irish points: fairly useful form in bumpers: won at Warwick in January: second at Newcastle in February: will stay at least 2½m. *Ben Pauling* **b99**

CARLOSWAYBACK (IRE) 12 b.g. Bob Back (USA) – Mandysway (IRE) (Mandalus) [2016/17 c20d^3 c25.1d* c28.5s^6 c24d Jan 14] lengthy gelding: winning hurdler: fairly useful handicap chaser: won at Wincanton in December: stays 25f: acts on heavy going: tried in hood: has worn tongue tie. *Chris Gordon* **c123** **h–**

CARLTON RYAN (IRE) 9 b.g. Morozov (USA) – Dante's Arrow (IRE) (Phardante (FR)) [2016/17 c111p: c26.6g^2 c24.2d* c26.2s^2 Mar 25] multiple winning pointer: fairly useful form in hunter chases: won at Fakenham in February: second at Musselburgh and Kelso on other 2 starts: stays 27f: acts on heavy going: tried in cheekpieces: usually races towards rear. *Michael Easterby* **c116**

CARNAROSS 8 b.g. Norse Dancer (IRE) – Miss Lewis (Sir Harry Lewis (USA)) **c–** [2016/17 c95, h95: h16.8d⁶ Dec 26] modest handicap hurdler, below form sole outing in **h70** 2016/17: maiden chaser: raced mainly around 2m: acts on heavy going: has worn tongue tie. *Julia Brooke*

CARNGLAVE CAT (IRE) 11 ch.g. Moscow Society (USA) – Time O'Day (IRE) (Tale **c66** Quale) [2016/17 c89, h–: c21.1d⁴ May 12] multiple point winner: maiden hurdler: poor **h–** maiden chaser: stays 2¾m: acts on heavy going: in headgear last 5 starts: usually in tongue tie. *T. D. B. Underwood*

CARNINGLI (IRE) 8 b.g. Old Vic – Name For Fame (USA) (Quest For Fame) [2016/17 **c79** c124p, h–: c22.7s⁶ Feb 1] lengthy gelding: useful hurdler: fairly useful maiden chaser, well **h–** below that level sole outing in 2016/17: stays 3m: acts on good to firm and heavy going: temperament under suspicion. *Jamie Snowden*

CARNSPINDLE (IRE) 5 b.m. Ask – Whistling Gypse (IRE) (Good Thyne (USA)) **h118** [2016/17 b18d⁴ b15.7d⁵ b15.8v* h15.5g⁶ h19.5v² h16.8s* h21.6g* h20.3g² Apr 20] €5,000 **b94** 3-y-o: second foal: dam (c88/h74) maiden chaser/hurdler (stayed 25f): fair form in bumpers: won mares maiden at Uttoxeter in December, suited by emphasis on stamina: fairly useful form over hurdles: won mares novice at Exeter and handicap at Fontwell in March: second in listed mares handicap at Cheltenham in April: left Stuart Crawford after first start: will stay 3m: acts on heavy going: usually races close up. *Warren Greatrex*

CAROBELLO (IRE) 10 b.g. Luso – Vic's Queen (IRE) (Old Vic) [2016/17 c79§, h–: **c72 §** c16.3g⁵ c17.4g⁵ c20m⁶ c20m² c23g³ c23g Dec 20] maiden hurdler: poor handicap chaser: **h–** stays 23f: acts on soft and good to firm going: has worn headgear, including last 3 starts: wears tongue tie: front runner/races prominently: temperamental. *Martin Bosley*

CAROLE'S DESTRIER 9 b.g. Kayf Tara – Barton May (Midnight Legend) [2016/17 **c152** c147, h–: c26g² c29.5s Dec 27] well-made gelding: winning hurdler: smart handicap **h–** chaser: second in Hennessy Gold Cup at Newbury (½ length behind Native River) in November: stays 29f: acts on heavy going. *Neil Mulholland*

CARQALIN (FR) 5 gr.g. Martaline – Mica Doree (FR) (Video Rock (FR)) [2016/17 **c61** h89p, b–: h23.4g⁶ h19.5d h19.8d h19g h16.5g꭪ʳ c19.7sᵖᵘ c24.2d⁶ h16.5g Apr 6] maiden **h–** hurdler, no form in 2016/17: poor form over fences: best effort at 17f: acts on good to soft going: has worn headgear, including in 2016/17: tried in tongue tie: often races prominently. *David Pipe*

CARRAIG MOR (IRE) 9 b.g. Old Vic – Lynrick Lady (IRE) (Un Desperado (FR)) **c–** [2016/17 c24.2sꟳ Feb 12] lengthy, useful-looking gelding: winning hurdler: useful chaser **h–** at best, fell sole outing in 2016/17: stays 25f: acts on soft going. *Alan King*

CARRE NOIR (FR) 8 b.g. Clety (FR) – Luella (FR) (Bois Mineau (FR)) [2016/17 h111: **h112** h23.1m³ h19.9g⁴ h19.9g³ h24.2g² Nov 3] fair handicap hurdler: stays 3m: acts on good to firm and heavy going: tried in cheekpieces: often races towards rear. *Martin Hill*

CARRIE ON DUBAI 4 b.g. Dubai Destination (USA) – Carrie On (Shambo) [2016/17 **b– §** b15.7vᵘʳ b17.7s⁶ b17.7g Mar 27] no form in bumpers: temperamental. *Clare Hobson*

CARRIGANOG (IRE) 8 ch.g. Shantou (USA) – Penny Fiction (IRE) (Welsh Term) **c133** [2016/17 c135, h127: c23m² c25s² Jul 15] good-topped gelding: winning hurdler: useful **h–** handicap chaser: second at Ballinrobe and in Midlands National Handicap Chase at Kilbeggan early in season: stays 25f: acts on soft and good to firm going: has worn cheek-pieces, including in 2106/17: in tongue tie last 3 starts. *Joseph Patrick O'Brien, Ireland*

CARRIG CATHAL 6 b.g. Fair Mix (IRE) – Blackwater Bay (IRE) (Supreme Leader) **h140** [2016/17 b16g³ h20m* h18.2d* h20v* h21d⁴ h24sᵇᵈ h20sᵘʳ h20v³ h19s² h19g⁴ h20.5d **b96** Apr 29] £40,000 4-y-o: half-brother to fairly useful/unreliable hurdler/chaser Award Winner (19f-3m winner, by Alflora): dam (h97), 2m hurdle winner (stayed 2½m), half-sister to useful hurdler/smart chaser (winner up to 3m) Razor Royale: winning pointer: fairly useful form in bumpers: useful hurdler: won maiden at Ballinrobe, minor event at Downpatrick and novice at Listowel in first half of season: second in handicap at Naas (1½ lengths behind Rathpatrick) in March: should stay 3m: acts on good to firm and heavy going. *Gordon Elliott, Ireland*

CARRIGDHOUN (IRE) 12 gr.g. Goldmark (USA) – Pet Tomjammar (IRE) (Accordion) **c129** [2016/17 c129, h–: c24.5d* c26.2d* c32.4s² c22.9sᵖᵘ c30g⁵ c24.5d* c26.2d⁶ Apr 10] **h–** lengthy gelding: winning hurdler: fairly useful handicap chaser: won at Carlisle (twice) in ctober and there again in February: second at Kelso in December: stays 4m: acts on good to firm and heavy going: wears headgear/tongue tie. *Maurice Barnes*

CARRIGKERRY (IRE) 10 br.g. Pilsudski (IRE) – Lady Lorraine (IRE) (Oscar (IRE)) **c98**
[2016/17 c–: c16.3g c21g² h20m^d h20.3g* h23.9g h20m³ h22.1d² h20m³ h20.3g² Aug 31] **h116**
multiple winning pointer: fairly useful hurdler: first past post in handicaps at Worcester
(later disqualified as found to be ineligible) and Southwell in May: modest form over
fences: left Mrs R. Fuller after second start: stays 2¾m: acts on good to firm and good to
soft going: tried in cheekpieces: usually leads. *Jamie Snowden*

CARRIGMORNA KING (IRE) 11 b.g. King's Theatre (IRE) – Carrigmorna Flyer **c124 x**
(IRE) (Bob Back (USA)) [2016/17 c140x, h–: c21g⁵ c20g c20g Jul 24] well-made gelding: **h–**
winning hurdler: useful handicap chaser, below form in 2016/17: stays 3m: acts on soft and
good to firm going: wears tongue tie: often let down by jumping. *Philip Hobbs*

CARRUTHERS 14 b.g. Kayf Tara – Plaid Maid (IRE) (Executive Perk) [2016/17 c32.5g **c107**
c27.2d⁴ May 12] strong, compact gelding: successful once in points in 2016: winning **h–**
hurdler: fair hunter chaser nowadays: stays 29f: acts on heavy going: tried in blinkers:
wears tongue tie. *Mrs Sara V. Bradstock*

CARRY ON ARCADIO (IRE) 5 b.g. Arcadio (GER) – Carryonharriet (IRE) (Norwich) **b83 p**
[2016/17 b16d⁴ Oct 24] €75,000 3-y-o: fourth foal: brother to fairly useful hurdler/chaser
Walk To Freedom (2m-2½m winner): dam unraced half-sister to useful hurdler (winner
up to 3m) Holland Park and fairly useful chaser (stayed 25f) Carryonharry: 9/2, promise
when fourth in bumper at Ayr (14 lengths behind Loud And Clear) in October: open to
improvement. *Nicky Richards*

CARRY ON NANDO (IRE) 10 b.g. Misternando – Carry On Pierre (IRE) (Pierre) **c80**
[2016/17 c61: c24.2m⁴ May 3] dual winning pointer: poor form in hunter chases: tried in
cheekpieces. *G. Chambers*

CARRY ON SYDNEY 7 ch.g. Notnowcato – River Fantasy (USA) (Irish River (FR)) **h105**
[2016/17 h109: h20.3v³ h24.1d² h23.3v⁵ h19.6s⁵ h21.7s⁵ Mar 11] rather leggy gelding: fair
handicap hurdler: stays 3m: acts on soft going: usually wears headgear. *Oliver Sherwood*

CARTER MCKAY 6 gr.g. Martaline – Saxona (USA) (Jade Robbery (USA)) [2016/17 **b113**
b16d* b19s* b16.4g b16d* Apr 26] £160,000 5-y-o: workmanlike gelding: first foal: dam,
(b87) bumper winner, also 17f winner on Flat: off mark in points at second attempt: useful
form in bumpers: won at Leopardstown in December and Naas in February. *W. P. Mullins,
Ireland*

CARTERS REST 14 gr.g. Rock City – Yemaail (IRE) (Shaadi (USA)) [2016/17 c100, h–: **c80**
c19.3g⁵ c17.3g⁵ c17.3d⁵ h16.2s⁵ Jul 26] winning hunter: modest handicap chaser at best, **h–**
below form in 2016/17: stays 2½m: acts on heavy going: has worn headgear, including in
2016/17: has worn tongue tie: usually leads. *Alison Hamilton*

CARTHAGE (IRE) 6 b.g. Mastercraftsman (IRE) – Pitrizzia (Lando (GER)) [2016/17 **h76**
h105: h16.8d^{ur} Apr 28] fair maiden hurdler, below form sole outing in 2016/17: unproven
beyond 17f: acts on soft going. *Brian Ellison*

CARUMBA (IRE) 7 b.g. Gold Well – Sarah Marshall (IRE) (Flemensfirth (USA)) **c–**
[2016/17 c23g^{ur} Apr 6] winning pointer: unseated first on chasing debut: wore cheekpieces.
Mrs G. Welch

CASABLANCA MIX (FR) 5 ch.m. Shirocco (GER) – Latitude (FR) (Kadalko (FR)) **h123**
[2016/17 h17.9g* h17.9s* h17.9s⁴ b16.4g⁵ h17.9s* h17.9s³ h17.9s^{pu} h20.3g⁴ Apr 20] **b?**
half-sister to several winners, including very smart French chaser Vanilla Crush (17f-23f
winner, by Martaline) and fairly useful hurdler Arkwrisht (21f/2¾m winner, by Lavirco):
dam, (c121/h116) 2¼m-2¾m hurdle/chase winner, half-sister to useful staying chaser
Raz de Maree and to dam of very smart French chaser (stays 27f) Vezelay: dual bumper
winner: fairly useful hurdler: won juvenile events at Moulins and Auteuil (twice) in first
half of season: also in frame in Group 3 and listed event at Auteuil: left Emmanuel Clayeux
after seventh start: bred to stay at least 2½m: acts on soft going: tried in cheekpieces.
Nicky Henderson

CASCAYE (FR) 5 br.m. Merlino Mago – Castyana (IRE) (Anabaa (USA)) [2016/17 **h105**
b15.8d^{ur} b16s² b15.8d h19.2v³ h16.8d* h16v³ Mar 23] £16,000 3-y-o: fourth foal: half- **b81**
sister to French winner unraced on 11.5f Grey Knight (by Take Risks): dam unraced: modest
form in bumpers: fair form over hurdles: won mares novice at Exeter in February: in
cheekpieces last 5 starts: front runner/races prominently. *Kim Bailey*

CASH AGAIN (FR) 5 br.g. Great Pretender (IRE) – Jeu de Lune (FR) (Useful (FR)) **h110**
[2016/17 h109: h19.9d⁴ h20s⁴ h20d³ h19.8d Mar 11] rather unfurnished gelding: useful
bumper performer: fair form over hurdles: likely to prove suited by further than 2½m.
Paul Nicholls

CASHANOVA (IRE) 6 b.g. Arcadio (GER) – Starshade (IRE) (Oscar (IRE)) [2016/17 **h105** h61, b89: h15.9g h16g⁴ h17.7d³ h23.5d h16s⁴ Feb 10] workmanlike gelding: fair maiden hurdler: should stay beyond 2¼m: acts on soft going. *Nick Gifford*

CASINO MARKETS (IRE) 9 br.g. Fruits of Love (USA) – Vals Dream (IRE) (Pierre) **c138** [2016/17 c110p, h–: c20.9m* c20m² c20m* c16.5g⁴ c15.9g³ c19.9g⁴ c20.8g³ c20g³ **h–** Apr 29] tall gelding: winning hurdler: useful handicap chaser: won at Stratford and Worcester (twice) early in season: third in Silver Trophy Chase (Limited Handicap) at Cheltenham (4¾ lengths behind Henryville) and in novice event at Sandown (1½ lengths behind Shantou Village), both in April: probably stays 3m: acts on soft and good to firm going. *Emma Lavelle*

CASPER KING (IRE) 6 b.g. Scorpion (IRE) – Princess Supreme (IRE) (Supreme **h123** Leader) [2016/17 h118p, b94: h16g* h16.4g⁶ h16.5g² h16.8s* h17.7v* h21g h20.3g⁴ Apr 19] lengthy gelding: fairly useful hurdler: won maiden at Exeter in January and novice at Fontwell in February: also awarded novice at Chepstow earlier in season: stays 2¼m: acts on heavy going. *Philip Hobbs*

CASPIAN PIPER (IRE) 10 b.g. Millenary – Pepsi Starlet (IRE) (Heavenly Manna) **c102** [2016/17 c96, h–: c19.2d c20d⁴ c22.6g⁴ c23.9g² c23g* c23.6g c23.8m³ Oct 20] maiden **h–** hurdler: fair handicap chaser: won at Worcester in September: stays 3m: acts on good to firm and heavy going: usually wears headgear. *Tim Vaughan*

CASSANDANE (IRE) 5 br.m. Jeremy (USA) – Princess Atoosa (USA) (Gone West **h64** (USA)) [2016/17 h17.2m⁶ h15.8g⁴ h16.8gʳᵒ Sep 1] modest on Flat, stays 1½m: poor form over hurdles: tried in cheekpieces. *Shaun Harris*

CASSE TETE (FR) 5 b.g. Poliglote – Ellapampa (FR) (Pampabird) [2016/17 h17.9m² **c137** h16.9d² c21.4s* c23.5vᶠ c15.7v⁴ c19.9d³ c20d* Mar 11] lengthy gelding: brother to fairly **h115** useful French hurdler/useful chaser Saccageur (17f-2¾m winner) and half-brother to several winners, including useful French chaser Veleha (17f-21f winner, by Saint des Saints): dam, winning French hurdler/chaser up to 19f, half-sister to outstanding 2m chaser Azertyuiop: fairly useful form over hurdles: useful form over fences: won 4-y-o event at Auteuil in October and novice handicap at Sandown (by 27 lengths from The Fresh Prince) in March: left Guillaume Macaire after third start: should stay 3m: acts on soft going. *Gary Moore*

CASSIVELLAUNUS (IRE) 5 b.g. Danehill Dancer (IRE) – Celtic Heroine (IRE) **b–** (Hernando (FR)) [2016/17 b65: b16.3m May 15] poor form on first of 2 starts in bumpers. *Daniel Steele*

CASTAFIORE (USA) 4 b.f. Street Cry (IRE) – Showlady (USA) (Theatrical) [2016/17 **h112** h16m² h17s² h15.6gᶠ h15.8d* h16.7s⁶ h18.8gᵖᵘ Mar 25] tall, angular filly: fairly useful form on Flat for A. Fabre, stays 1½m: fair form over hurdles: won fillies juvenile at Ludlow in January: unproven beyond 2m: acts on soft and good to firm going. *Charlie Longsdon*

CASTARNIE 9 b.g. Alflora (IRE) – Just Jenny (IRE) (King's Ride) [2016/17 c77, h–: **c115** c24.2s² c19.2vᵖᵘ c24.2v² c23.6sᵖᵘ c25.1dᶠ c25.2s* Mar 11] maiden hurdler: fairly useful **h–** handicap chaser: won at Hereford (conditional event) in March: stays 25f: best form on soft/heavy going: wears cheekpieces. *Robert Walford*

CASTELLO SFORZA (IRE) 6 b.g. Milan – Young Elodie (FR) (Freedom Cry) **h126** [2016/17 b116p: h18d³ h18d³ h20v² h20.3g Mar 17] good-topped gelding: smart bumper performer: fairly useful form over hurdles: second in maiden at Punchestown in February: usually races prominently, often travels strongly. *W. P. Mullins, Ireland*

CASTERLY ROCK (IRE) 5 b.g. King's Theatre (IRE) – Alderbrook Girl (IRE) **h106 p** (Alderbrook) [2016/17 b16.5g h16g⁴ Mar 18] €95,000 3-y-o: tall gelding: second foal: dam **b–** (c89/h79) ungenuine 3m/25f hurdle/chase winner: tailed off in bumper: 50/1, showed lot more when fourth in novice at Kempton (5¾ lengths behind Excellent Result) on hurdling debut: sure to improve. *Philip Hobbs*

CASTLE CAVALIER 5 b.g. Nayef (USA) – Jardin (Sinndar (IRE)) [2016/17 b–: h21.6m **h–** Jul 1] well held in bumpers: tailed off in maiden on hurdling debut. *Robert Stephens*

CASTLEGRACE PADDY (IRE) 6 b.g. Flemensfirth (USA) – Thunder Road (IRE) **h133** (Mtoto) [2016/17 b16d⁴ h20v² b18s⁴ h16v* h16g⁵ Apr 28] €75,000 5-y-o: fourth foal: half- **b78** brother to bumper winner/fairly useful 2m hurdle winner Frontline (by King's Theatre): dam (h112), 2m hurdle/Flat winner, half-sister to fairly useful hurdler/useful chaser (stayed 25f) Undeniable: runner-up in maiden point: modest form in bumpers: useful form over hurdles: won maiden at Gowran (by 9 lengths from Sizinguptheamazon) in March: front runner/races prominently, often travels strongly. *P. A. Fahy, Ireland*

CASTLEMORRIS KING 9 br.g. And Beyond (IRE) – Brookshield Baby (IRE) **c129** (Sadler's Wells (USA)) [2016/17 h–: c16.3g⁴ h20m* h20g* c20m² c21.4g⁵ Jul 16] lengthy **h120** gelding: fairly useful hurdler: won claimer and handicap at Worcester early in season: fairly useful form over fences: best effort when second in handicap at same course: left Brian Barr after second start: stays 2½m: acts on good to firm and good to soft going: in cheekpieces last 3 starts: tried in tongue tie: front runner/races prominently: genuine. *David Pipe*

CASTLERIGG 4 b.g. Canford Cliffs (IRE) – Persian Star (Shamardal (USA)) [2016/17 **h–** b13.2g⁶ h16.7vᵖᵘ h16.8s Nov 20] no form in bumper/over hurdles: tried in blinkers: in **b–** tongue tie last 2 starts. *Colin Tizzard*

CASTLETOWN BRIDGE (IRE) 10 ch.g. Bienamado (USA) – Midnight Orchid **c104** (IRE) (Petardia) [2016/17 h23.9s⁵ c22gᵖᵘ h23.9g² h23.9dᶠ c22.5d⁵ c26.6g* c23.8g⁴ c26ˢᵘʳ **h114** c25.5sᵖᵘ c30.6gᵘʳ Apr 28] fair handicap hurdler: fair handicap chaser: won novice at Musselburgh in November: stays 27f: acts on heavy going: has worn tongue tie, including last 5 starts. *Paul Stafford, Ireland*

CASTLETOWN (FR) 5 gr.g. Poliglote – Message Personnel (FR) (Mansonnien (FR)) **c118** [2016/17 c17.9s³ c17.4s c17.4s⁵ h22.1d³ h20.2s⁵ c15.9d c19.9g⁶ c21.6s⁴ Dec 29] second **h105** foal: dam (c129), French 15f-19f hurdle/chase winner, half-sister to smart French chaser (stayed 2¾m) Still Loving You (by Poliglote): fair form over hurdles: fairly useful maiden chaser: left Guillaume Macaire after third start: stays 2¼m: acts on soft going: in hood last 3 starts. *Pauline Robson*

CASTLETOWN (IRE) 9 b.g. Oscar (IRE) – Closing Thyne (IRE) (Good Thyne (USA)) **c81 §** [2016/17 c73, h–: c20.9v* c22.5g² May 14] tall gelding: maiden hurdler: poor handicap **h–** chaser nowadays: won at Uttoxeter very early in season: stays 2¾m: acts on heavy going: usually in headgear: has worn tongue tie, including last 2 starts: temperamental. *Sheila Lewis*

CASTLEY LANE 11 b.g. Dapper – Holly (Skyliner) [2016/17 c74, h–: h20.6g c24.2gᵖᵘ **c–** Apr 25] winning pointer: maiden hurdler/chaser, no form in 2016/17: best effort at 3m: **h–** often in headgear/tongue tie: often races prominently. *Sara Ender*

CASUAL CAVALIER (IRE) 9 br.g. Presenting – Asklynn (IRE) (Beau Sher) [2016/17 **c115** c95, h–: c17.1s* c20.1s³ c15.5s* c16.3s* c15.5s² c17.1s³ Mar 25] maiden hurdler: fairly **h–** useful handicap chaser: won at Kelso (novice event) in November, and at Ayr and Newcastle (novice event) in January: second at Ayr in February: stays 2½m: best form on soft/heavy going: usually wears headgear: front runner/races prominently. *George Bewley*

CATACLYSM (IRE) 7 b.g. Captain Rio – Marilaya (Shernazar) [2016/17 h16.2vᵖᵘ **h–** Mar 28] maiden hurdler, pulled up sole outing in 2016/17 (wore hood). *Kevin Hunter*

CATAMARAN DU SEUIL (FR) 5 b.g. Network (GER) – Fleur du Tennis (FR) (Video **c121** Rock (FR)) [2016/17 h18.9g² c17.4s² h18.9s² c21.9s² h21.4s* h21.3s⁶ h19.3d* h20.3g Mar **h122** 17] sixth foal: half-brother to 3 French bumper winners, including 1¼m/1½m winner Quarvine du Seuil (by Lavirco), herself dam of Triumph Hurdle winner Defi du Seuil: dam, French 1½m/15f winner, sister to useful chaser (stayed 25f) Jimmy Tennis: fairly useful hurdler: won novices at Wincanton in January and Carlisle in February: fairly useful form over fences: second in handicap at Auteuil in October: left Emmanuel Clayeux after fourth start: stays 2¾m: acts on soft going: often wears headgear: front runner/races prominently. *Dr Richard Newland*

CATCH A LUCKY STAR (IRE) 8 b.g. Luso – Badia Dream (IRE) (Old Vic) [2016/17 **h–** b18s h19.7d h20s h16v h16v Apr 1] maiden pointer: placed in bumpers: little impact **b–** over hurdles: left J. G. Cosgrave after first start: tried in hood: usually races nearer last than first. *Mark McNiff, Ireland*

CATCHAMAT 8 b.m. Overbury (IRE) – More Flair (Alflora (IRE)) [2016/17 c24.2dᵖᵘ **c–** h16.2v⁵ h20.6s* h22s* Jan 23] second foal: half-sister to useful hurdler Central Flame **h125** (19f/2½m winner, by Central Park): dam winning pointer: won 3 times in points: fairly useful form over hurdles: won novices at Newcastle (twice) in January: pulled up in maiden hunter on chasing debut: should stay at least 3m. *James Walton*

CATCH ANOTHER (IRE) 8 b.g. Kutub (IRE) – Lady Dane (IRE) (Danetime (IRE)) **h–** [2016/17 h16.3gᵖᵘ h20.3g h15.5vᵖᵘ h19.7sᵖᵘ Mar 11] pulled up all 4 starts over hurdles: tried in headgear. *Laura Hurley*

CATCH A THIEF (IRE) 6 b.g. Darsi (FR) – Geray Lady (IRE) (Roselier (FR)) [2016/17 **c–** h–: h19.5d⁵ h20v c25.1s c19.4s Jan 20] lengthy gelding: poor form over hurdles: well held **h72** both starts over fences: should prove best at 2½m+: acts on heavy going. *Evan Williams*

CATCHING ON (IRE) 9 b.g. Milan – Miracle Lady (Bob's Return (IRE)) [2016/17 c–, **c–** h–: h23.1s⁵ c24.2vᵖᵘ h26s h26v* h26s⁵ Mar 30] winning pointer: fairly useful handicap **h119** hurdler: won at Warwick in February: useful chaser at best, pulled up sole outing over fences in 2016/17: stays 3¾m: acts on heavy going: in tongue tie last 2 starts: often races towards rear/travels strongly. *Jonjo O'Neill*

CATCHING SHADOWS (IRE) 8 b.g. Catcher In The Rye (IRE) – Castletown Girl **h102** (Bob Back (USA)) [2016/17 h102p, b103: h20d³ h16s⁵ h16d⁵ h16.4v² Mar 7] pulled up in Irish point: bumper winner: fair form over hurdles: stays 2½m: acts on good to firm and heavy going. *James Ewart*

CATCHIN TIME (IRE) 9 b.g. Chineur (FR) – Lady Dane (IRE) (Danetime (IRE)) **h110** [2016/17 h107: h16g h15.8d⁵ h15.9v⁵ h15.9v* h16v* h16v⁴ h15.3v³ Mar 9] lengthy gelding: fair handicap hurdler: won at Plumpton in January and Warwick in February: unproven beyond 17f: acts on heavy going: has worn headgear: wears tongue tie: usually races towards rear. *Laura Hurley*

CATCH TAMMY (IRE) 11 br.g. Tamayaz (CAN) – Bramble Orchard (IRE) (Orchestra) **c77** [2016/17 c88, h–: c17m⁶ May 20] lengthy gelding: maiden pointer: maiden hurdler: fairly **h–** useful chaser at best, stiff task sole outing in 2016/17: stays 2½m: acts on soft going: has worn headgear: tried in tongue tie. *Mrs I. Barnett*

CATCHTHEMOONLIGHT 9 b.m. Generous (IRE) – Moon Catcher (Kahyasi) **h95** [2016/17 h78: h16.2s² h17.2g² h15.8g³ h18.1m³ h16.2s* h15.8vᵘʳ h20.5g² h16.4s⁴ h16.4g³ h17g* h20.2gᵘʳ Apr 26] modest handicap hurdler: won at Hexham in November and Carlisle (mares event) in April: stays 2¾m: acts on soft and good to firm going: has worn hood: usually races towards rear. *Lucinda Russell*

CATENA ALTA (IRE) 6 br.g. Kalanisi (IRE) – Solar Quest (IRE) (King's Ride) [2016/17 **b73** b–: b15.8g⁶ b16.7g Jul 31] poor form in bumpers. *Seamus Durack*

CATHERINES WELL 8 b.m. Kayf Tara – Dudeen (IRE) (Anshan) [2016/17 h122: **h–** h21.6d Oct 19] fairly useful hurdler, well held sole outing in 2016/17: stays 21f: acts on good to soft going. *Philip Hobbs*

CATSKILL MOUNTAINS (IRE) 4 b.g. Rip Van Winkle (IRE) – Cawett (IRE) **h82** (Danehill Dancer (IRE)) [2016/17 h17.7gᶠ h15.8m h16s⁶ h16.7s⁶ h19v Dec 31] sturdy gelding: half-brother to French 19f hurdle winner Race To Glory (by Montjeu): fair maiden on Flat, stayed 1m: poor form over hurdles: tried in cheekpieces: wore tongue tie: dead. *David Dennis*

CATWALK KING (IRE) 5 b.g. Kutub (IRE) – Queen of Catwalk (IRE) (Un Desperado **b110** (FR)) [2016/17 b16s⁴ b16v* b16d⁶ Apr 27] seventh foal: dam, ran twice in points, half-sister to fairly useful hurdler/useful chaser (stayed 3m) Pennybridge: useful form in bumpers: won ladies maiden event at Cork (by 22 lengths from Cluan Dara) in March. *Miss Elizabeth Doyle, Ireland*

CAULFIELDS VENTURE (IRE) 11 b.g. Catcher In The Rye (IRE) – Saddlers' **c130 §** Venture (IRE) (Saddlers' Hall (IRE)) [2016/17 c128§, h–: c25.1mᵖᵘ c24.2g³ c24.2m* **h–** c22.7f² c24m⁵ Apr 18] good-topped gelding: maiden hurdler: useful handicap chaser: won at Exeter (by neck from Dancing Shadow) in November: stays 3¼m: acts on firm and soft going: wears headgear: usually races close up: temperamental. *Emma Lavelle*

CAUSE OF CAUSES (USA) 9 b.g. Dynaformer (USA) – Angel In My Heart (FR) **c154** (Rainbow Quest (USA)) [2016/17 c152, h–: c16d⁵ c24dᵖᵘ c24.5d c30.2d⁵ c30.2g* **h–** c34.3d² Apr 8]

Asked to reveal his 'most embarrassing moment', Gordon Elliott cites being 'made to stand at the back of the class in the dunce corner.' The self-made Elliott, who has built his powerful County Meath base virtually from scratch over the past few years, isn't the first—and won't be the last—to make a great success of his life after coming up short in his school days. Elliott won the Grand National as a virtually unknown trainer with his first runner in the race (Silver Birch) at the age of twenty-nine and also won the Cheltenham Gold Cup with his first runner in that event too (Don Cossack). Still in his thirties, there is no telling where Elliott's rapid ascent in the training ranks will eventually take him. As outlined elsewhere in this Annual, Elliott came very close to taking the Irish trainers' title from the pre-eminent

Willie Mullins—'Just to be in the shadow of Willie is something special'—and he wrested the trophy for leading trainer at the Cheltenham Festival from Mullins, who had been made odds-on to win it for the fifth year running and the sixth time in seven years. The Elliott string landed an opening day treble, followed by a double on the second day, and finished with a tally of six winners (the same as Mullins whom Elliott pipped by virtue of more second places). The successes of Elliott and Mullins contributed to Irish trainers winning nineteen of the twenty-eight races at the Cheltenham Festival, a record haul which, for the second successive year, secured the BetBright Prestbury Cup, the prize in an Anglo-Irish competition instituted in 2014, the trophy going to the country sending out the most winners.

The first leg of the Cullentra House double on the second day of the Festival came in the Glenfarclas Chase, the cross country event in which, coincidentally, Elliott's Grand National winner Silver Birch had finished second when being warmed up for his tilt at Aintree in 2007. There have been calls in some quarters for a veterans chase to be included in the Cheltenham Festival programme but the cross country chase, which had its second running as a conditions event rather than a handicap, seems to be turning into something resembling a veterans chase itself—usually dominated by Irish-trained challengers (there were only five home-trained runners in the latest edition). Fourteen-year-old Any Currency, a stalwart of the home defence in recent years, was making his fifth appearance in the race (he had been disqualified, following a failed drugs test, after finishing first past the post twelve months earlier). Four twelve-year-olds in the line-up included the Elliott-trained Bless The Wings and the evergreen Quantitativeeasing (making his eighth Festival appearance), the pair that had been promoted to second and third the previous year after the disqualification of Any Currency. Cause of Causes and Quantitativeeasing were among five runners in the race carrying the colours of jumping's biggest owner J. P. McManus who was inducted into the Cheltenham Hall of Fame (along with Big Buck's and Quevega) in the latest season. McManus topped the owners' table in Britain for the tenth time (he lost out to Gigginstown House Stud in the battle to be leading owner in Ireland) and three more winners at the Cheltenham Festival extended his record number of victories at jumping's most prestigious meeting to

Glenfarclas Chase (Cross Country), Cheltenham—Cause of Causes and Mr Jamie Codd team up for a third Cheltenham Festival win in successive years, all in different races; 2016 runner-up Bless The Wings (left) and Cantlow (white cap) chase them home

fifty-two. Istabraq, who landed the Champion Hurdle three times (Buveur d'Air gave McManus his sixth victory in the Champion Hurdle), won four times at the Festival in the famous McManus silks, but Cause of Causes is now just one behind him, having provided McManus with victories in successive years in the National Hunt Chase, the Fulke Walwyn Kim Muir and now the Glenfarclas Chase (ridden on all three occasions by the leading Irish amateur Mr Jamie Codd).

The cross country chase was chosen for Cause of Causes at the latest Festival because his BHA handicap mark was too high to attempt a repeat of his twelve-length win in the 0-145 Kim Muir (in which he had also been runner-up, after clouting the last, in 2014). The Glenfarclas Chase was his only entry at the meeting, though he would have qualified for the open handicap over an extended three miles that is run just before the Champion Hurdle on the opening day (the Foxhunter Chase would be another possibility in the future). All roads lead to Cheltenham nowadays for Cause of Causes and he showed little on his first three outings in Ireland in the latest season before tackling cross country fences for the first time in the Glenfarclas Handicap which had to be rescheduled from the autumn and was run at Cheltenham's Trials meeting at the end of January. Dropped out as usual, Cause of Causes was left with an impossible task before making some late headway to finish fifth behind the 50/1 French-trained winner Urgent de Gregaine, the McManus-owned favourite Cantlow (hampered at a vital stage) and Any Currency. Cause of Causes crossed the Irish Sea again to be schooled over Cheltenham's cross country course between his January appearance and the Glenfarclas Chase at the Festival and he was sent off a well-backed second favourite to Cantlow (whose jockey wore the McManus first colours with the white cap).

Back at concert pitch for the first time since the previous year's Festival, Cause of Causes was always travelling well and storming clear, after leading at the last, to win by nine lengths and a length and a quarter from Bless The Wings (giving the Elliott stable a one, two) and Cantlow. Auvergnat, the joint-youngest horse in the field at only seven, and a stablemate of Cantlow, gave McManus three of the first four and Ireland a clean sweep; Quantitativeeasing ran poorly and was pulled up, while Any Currency managed only ninth and was retired after his next start. Bobs Worth and Vautour were the last horses before Cause of Causes to win different races at three successive Cheltenham Festivals but Cause of Causes is the only horse to achieve the feat in the *Chasers & Hurdlers* era in three different steeplechases, though the cross country is hardly a conventional chase and was described in these pages, when it was introduced in 2005, as the 'crowning insult to those who have reservations about jumping's premier meeting becoming four days'. Silver Fame and Arctic Gold won three different chases in separate years at the meeting in the period immediately following World War II, though they did not do so in successive seasons.

Looking ahead to the next appearance of Cause of Causes at the Festival, ten horses have won at least four times at the meeting including Golden Miller (five Gold Cups in the 'thirties) and the war-time Gold Cup winner Medoc II, and, before them, Dudley whose wins all came at two miles, two of them in the Grand Annual. In addition to the steeplechasing achievements of Golden Miller, Medoc II and Dudley, the hunter chaser Baulking Green (whose wins came in races no longer part of the Festival) and the mighty Arkle also gained their four Festival victories over fences; triple Champion Hurdle winner Sir Ken won the Cotswold Chase afterwards to complete his four-timer, while the very popular staying handicapper Willie Wumpkins (with whom Cause of Causes has been compared), Big Buck's and the mare Quevega (who won six times at the Festival) achieved all their Festival wins over hurdles, like Istabraq.

Next on the agenda for Cause of Causes after Cheltenham was the Grand National, a race in which he had missed the cut by some way the previous year. Cause of Causes had contested the 2015 Grand National in his second season over fences, finishing eighth when arguably not seen to best effect under a patient ride from Paul Carberry, making rapid headway two out before finding no extra on the run-in. Mr Codd was in the saddle in the latest edition, with McManus' retained jockey Barry Geraghty having opted for fellow 16/1-shot More of That, and the chaser he describes as 'an idle little horse who will only do what he has to do' produced the best performance of his career, kept a little closer to the pace than customary before staying on strongly, holding every chance from the home turn, to finish four and a half lengths second to One For Arthur—Cause of Causes had been first past the post in the Virtual Grand National, a mocked-up event broadcast on ITV4 on the eve of the National itself. Irish trainers, incidentally, drew a blank at the Grand National meeting, after dominating the Cheltenham Festival, though the stables of Mullins and Elliott, battling for the trainers' title in Ireland, kept most of their powder dry for the Easter fixture at Fairyhouse—featuring a very richly-endowed Irish Grand National—and the Punchestown Festival. The Coral Cup winner Supasundae, the Ryanair Chase runner-up Sub Lieutenant and the Foxhunter fifth Balnaslow were others who finished second for Ireland in their selected races at Aintree.

There couldn't have been many runners—if any—at the Cheltenham and Aintree festival meetings with more illustrious pedigrees than Cause of Causes and Supasundae. The last-named is a son of Galileo out of a half-sister to the King George VI and Queen Elizabeth Stakes winner Nathaniel and other good performers on the Flat; Cause of Causes is closely related to the 2003 Derby winner Kris Kin (the pair share the same grandsire and are both out of Angel In My Heart, a smart filly, firstly in France and then in the States, where she was runner-up three times in Grade 1 company). While Supasundae was picked up for only £5,000 as a three-year-old and began his racing career in bumpers, Cause of Causes, a Niarchos home-bred, ran on the Flat as a three-year-old for Pascal Bary, winning over eleven furlongs in the French Provinces, before being weeded out and joining Gordon Elliott at the end of that season for €52,000, initially carrying the cerise, white circle colours of Timeform's founder Phil Bull which were revived, under lease, for use by the Timeform Betfair Racing Club. Cause of Causes won the Ladbroke at Ascot, among other races, for the club and was sold privately as a five-year-old to J. P. McManus when that operation was wound up (after five years and a total of thirty-four victories). Cause of Causes, by the way, is not unique among multiple Cheltenham Festival winners in boasting a Derby-winning sibling: Istabraq himself was closely related to the 1984 Derby winner Secreto and was also bought off the Flat. Further details of the pedigree of the good-topped Cause of Causes can be found in the previous extended entries on him in *Chasers & Hurdlers*. The grandam of Cause of Causes, Sweetly, a winner three times in North America, is a half-sister to Gay France, the grandam of two very smart middle-distance performers on the Flat, Needle Gun and Luso, both of whom went on to enjoy careers as jumps sires. The great grandam of Cause of Causes, Sweet And Lovely II, produced eleven winners, also among them Syndaar, the great grandam of another of the Champion Hurdle winners to carry the McManus colours, Binocular (Syndaar and the grandam of Cause of Causes, Sweetly, were sisters). Cause of Causes, who is usually waited with, stays four and a quarter miles and acts on good to firm and heavy going. He wears headgear—cheekpieces over the past two seasons—and has his tongue tied down. *Gordon Elliott, Ireland*

CAUSE TOUJOURS (FR) 5 b.g. Khalkevi (IRE) – Viana (FR) (Signe Divin (USA)) **b109**
[2016/17 b16s* b16.4g Mar 15] compact gelding: fifth foal: brother to fairly useful French hurdler/chaser Vif d'Esprit (17f-21f winner) and half-brother to useful hurdler Analifet (2m winner, by Califet), stayed 2½m: dam French 17f hurdle/chase winner: every chance when unseated last in Irish maiden point: useful form in bumpers: won at Warwick (by 7 lengths from Book of Gold) in December. *Dan Skelton*

CAUTIOUS KATE (IRE) 10 b.m. Witness Box (USA) – Cautious Leader (Supreme **h79**
Leader) [2016/17 h21.4v⁵ h23.9g⁴ Feb 21] runner-up both completed starts in maiden
points: poor maiden hurdler: stays 3m: acts on good to soft going. *Carroll Gray*

CAUTIOUS MAN (IRE) 5 b.g. Golan (IRE) – Hackler Poitin (IRE) (Little Bighorn) **h—**
[2016/17 h20d Oct 30] well beaten in novice hurdle on debut. *Donald McCain*

CAUTORILLO 5 ch.m. Black Sam Bellamy (IRE) – Cent Prime (Hernando (FR)) **b—**
[2016/17 b17.7d⁶ Sep 4] seventh foal: half-sister to fairly useful hurdler/useful chaser
Centasia (2m-2½m winner, by Presenting): dam (h109), French 15f-2¼m hurdle winner,
sister to useful hurdler/fairly useful chaser (stayed 25f) De Soto and fairly useful hurdler
(stayed 3m) Caledonia: tailed off in mares bumper. *Jamie Snowden*

CAVE HUNTER (IRE) 10 b.g. Court Cave (IRE) – Beasty Maxx (GER) (Keen) **c113**
[2016/17 c112: c26.2m* c26.6g c24.2gᵘʳ Apr 25] multiple point winner: fair hunter chaser:
won at Kelso early in season: stays 3¼m: acts on good to firm and good to soft going: wears
headgear/tongue tie: front runner/races prominently. *Mrs Wendy Hamilton*

CAVENTARA 5 b.g. Kayf Tara – L'Aventure (FR) (Cyborg (FR)) [2016/17 b15.8d⁶ **h—**
h21vᵖᵘ Feb 11] no show in bumper/novice hurdle. *Nick Williams* **b—**

CAVE TOP (IRE) 5 b.g. Court Cave (IRE) – Cyrils Top Girl (IRE) (Top of The World) **h109**
[2016/17 b17.1d⁵ h19.9s⁶ h19.9v³ h25.3d³ h16d⁵ Mar 21] €12,000 3-y-o, £25,000 4-y-o: **b—**
second foal: dam (h96), 2½m hurdle winner, half-sister to fairly useful hurdler (2m winner)
Miriam's Dream: maiden Irish pointer: tailed off in bumper: fair form over hurdles: stays
2½m. *Oliver Greenall*

CAWDOR HOUSE BERT 10 b.g. Kayf Tara – Lady Shanan (IRE) (Anshan) [2016/17 **c94**
c20dᵖᵘ c19.4gᵖᵘ c20.9v² c19.4dᵖᵘ Apr 16] winning hurdler: modest form completed start **h—**
over fences: stays 21f: acts on heavy going: tried in cheekpieces. *David Rees*

CEANN SIBHEAL (IRE) 8 b.g. Flemensfirth (USA) – Imperial Award (IRE) (Oscar **c65**
(IRE)) [2016/17 h112: c20.9v⁶ c22.6dᵖᵘ Mar 25] lengthy gelding: runner-up in Irish point: **h—**
fair hurdler: little impact over fences: will stay long distances: acts on heavy going: has
worn cheekpieces, including in 2016/17. *Warren Greatrex*

CEARA BE (IRE) 4 b.f. Oscar (IRE) – Pearl's A Singer (IRE) (Spectrum (IRE)) [2016/17 **b70**
b16.3s⁵ Mar 3] second foal: dam, 2m/2¼m hurdle winner, also 1½m/1¾m winner on Flat:
16/1, fifth in mares bumper at Newbury (18¼ lengths behind Lady Mix) in March.
Alex Hales

CEASAR MILAN (IRE) 9 br.g. Milan – Standfast (IRE) (Supreme Leader) [2016/17 **c119**
c115, h—: c24.2d⁴ c20.5m² Apr 18] useful-looking gelding: has reportedly had breathing **h—**
operation: dual winning pointer: winning hurdler: fairly useful chaser nowadays: fourth in
Grand Military Gold Cup (Amateur Riders) at Sandown in March: stays 3m: acts on heavy
going: wears cheekpieces/tongue tie. *Paul Nicholls*

CECIL CORBETT 10 b.g. Bollin Eric – Cadoutene (FR) (Cadoudal (FR)) [2016/17 **c123**
c25.5g³ c22s* c18.2g c25g³ c22g* c25g⁶ c22s c20v c22dᶠ Apr 18] winning hurdler: fairly **h—**
useful chaser: won maiden at Kilbeggan early in season and handicap at Punchestown in
October: stays 2¾m: acts on soft going: tried in tongue tie: often races in rear. *Gordon
Elliott, Ireland*

CEEGEM (IRE) 5 b.g. Kalanisi (IRE) – Aboo Who (IRE) (Aboo Hom) [2016/17 b16s⁴ **h93**
h16v h18.1s⁵ h16.2g Apr 25] first foal: dam 3m hunter chase winner: well beaten in **b—**
bumper: modest form over hurdles: best effort when fifth in maiden at Kelso in April.
Lucinda Russell

CELEBRE D'ALLEN (FR) 5 ch.g. Network (GER) – Revoltee (FR) (Grand Seigneur **b100**
(FR)) [2016/17 b16.7d³ b15.3v³ Feb 2] £100,000 4-y-o: first foal: dam, French 11.5f-14.5f
bumper winner, half-sister to fairly useful hurdler (stayed 2½m) Trop Fort: challenging
when fell last in Irish maiden point on debut: fairly useful form in bumpers: better effort
when third at Wincanton in February. *David Pipe*

CELESTIAL CHIMES (IRE) 6 ch.m. Mahler – Celestial Rose (IRE) (Roselier (FR)) **h—**
[2016/17 h16m h15.8g⁶ Apr 3] half-sister to several winners, including fairly useful **b—**
hurdler/useful chaser Richard's Sundance (21f-3¼m winner, by Saddlers' Hall) and fairly
useful hurdler/chaser Rossmore Lad (3m winner, by Beneficial): dam unraced: tailed off in
mares bumper/novice hurdle. *Robin Dickin*

CELESTIAL DANCER (FR) 5 b.m. Dr Fong (USA) – Rabeera (Beat Hollow) [2016/17 **h74**
h19.7g² Apr 23] modest maiden on Flat, stays 1¾m: in tongue tie, 6/1, second in maiden at
Wetherby (22 lengths behind Sheneededtherun) on hurdling debut. *Nigel Twiston-Davies*

CELESTIAL MAGIC 5 b.g. Black Sam Bellamy (IRE) – Mighty Merlin (Royal **h116** Applause) [2016/17 h110: h16.8d^{pu} h15.7s^4 h16s* h16v^2 h15.7s^4 h19.5g^4 Apr 17] fairly useful handicap hurdler: won at Warwick (novice event) in January and Towcester in March: stays 19f: acts on soft going. *Richard Phillips*

CELESTIAL PATH (IRE) 5 br.g. Footstepsinthesand – Miss Kittyhawk (IRE) (Hawk **h88** Wing (USA)) [2016/17 h16s^{pu} h16.5g^4 Jan 27] smart on Flat, stays 1m: modest form over hurdles: in hood, better effort when fourth in novice at Taunton in January. *David Pipe*

CELESTINO (FR) 6 b.g. Leeds (IRE) – Evamoon (FR) (River Bay (USA)) [2016/17 **c94** c104, h83: c16m^2 May 11] compact gelding: maiden hurdler: modest maiden chaser: stays **h–** 19f: acts on heavy going: often in headgear/tongue tie. *N. W. Alexander*

CELLDOMFED (IRE) 7 b.g. Beneficial – Eyebright (IRE) (Zaffaran (USA)) [2016/17 **h–** h113: h15.7g^{pu} May 24] fair hurdler, fatally injured sole outing in 2016/17: stayed 21f: acted on soft going. *Jonjo O'Neill*

CELMA DES BOIS (FR) 5 b.g. Ballingarry (IRE) – Palafixe (FR) (Valanour (IRE)) **h78** [2016/17 b17m b16.4m^3 b16g^5 h16.3s^{pu} h16s h16m Apr 4] well-made gelding: third foal: **b86** dam runner-up in French chase at 2¼m: third in Irish maiden only start in points: fair form in bumpers for Paul Nolan: best effort when third in maiden at Ballinrobe early in season: poor form over hurdles. *Richard Rowe*

CELTIC ARTISAN (IRE) 6 ch.g. Dylan Thomas (IRE) – Perfectly Clear (USA) **h93** (Woodman (USA)) [2016/17 h95: h16.8g^4 h15.8m h15.7g Aug 14] modest handicap hurdler: unproven beyond 17f: acts on good to firm going: wears cheekpieces: tried in tongue tie. *Rebecca Menzies*

CELTIC FELLA (IRE) 10 gr.g. Kahtan – Mens Business (IRE) (Buckskin (FR)) **c69 §** [2016/17 c65§, h–: c20.9g^{pu} c23m^4 c23g^4 c23g^4 Nov 24] enterprisingly-ridden winner of **h–** point: maiden hurdler: poor maiden chaser: best effort at 3¼m: acts on good to firm going: wears headgear: often wears tongue tie: unreliable. *Debra Hamer*

CELTIC INTRIGUE (IRE) 10 b.g. Celtic Swing – Macca Luna (IRE) (Kahyasi) **c108** [2016/17 c109, h–: c24g^4 c25.8g^2 Jul 25] point winner: maiden hurdler: fair handicap **h–** chaser: stays 3¼m: acts on soft going: wears headgear: has worn tongue tie: often races prominently. *Kerry Lee*

CELTIC MONARCH (IRE) 8 b.g. Celtic Swing – Trim (IRE) (Ela-Mana-Mou) **h104** [2016/17 h105: h16.2d^2 h22.1m h20.1d^2 h20.5s^2 h20.5v^4 h21.3d^2 h20.1s^3 h21.6s h20d h16v h16d Dec 26] fair handicap hurdler: stays 21f: acts on soft and good to firm going: usually races in rear. *Mark McNiff, Ireland*

CELTIC PARK 7 b.g. Central Park (IRE) – Irish Ferry (Overbury (IRE)) [2016/17 **c88** h19.9s^{pu} h19.7s^6 h21s h23.3v^6 c24v^2 c24v^2 Feb 24] workmanlike gelding: fourth foal: half- **h67** brother to fair hurdler/fairly useful chaser Come On Annie (2m-19f winner, by Karinga Bay): dam unraced half-sister to fairly useful hurdler/useful chaser Europa: winning pointer: lightly-raced hurdler: modest form over fences: third when fell heavily 3 out in novice handicap won by Bassarabad at Warwick in February: stays 3m: best form on heavy going. *Tom Weston*

CELTIC PASSION (IRE) 9 ch.m. Flemensfirth (USA) – Still Bubbly (IRE) (Hubbly **h94** Bubbly (USA)) [2016/17 h21.6g h23m^2 h23.3g* h23g^3 Aug 11] second foal: dam (h72), winning pointer, half-sister to useful hurdler/very smart chaser (stayed 4½m) Nil Desperandum and to dam of smart 21f hurdle winner Willoughby Court: winning pointer: modest handicap hurdler: won at Uttoxeter early in season: will stay at least 3m: acts on good to firm and good to soft going: has worn headgear: often wears tongue tie: usually races nearer last than first. *Emma Lavelle*

CELTIC STYLE (IRE) 4 b.f. Craigsteel – Kissangel (IRE) (Namaqualand (USA)) **b–** [2016/17 b16.8g^6 Apr 26] sixth foal: half-sister to fair hurdler/fairly useful chaser Kellystown Lad (2½m winner, by Old Vic): dam (h84) maiden hurdler (stayed 2½m): well beaten in maiden bumper. *Linda Blackford*

CELTIC SUNLIGHT 7 ch.g. Sakhee (USA) – For Love (USA) (Sultry Song (USA)) **h–** [2016/17 h15.9d^{pu} Dec 12] poor maiden on Flat: pulled up in novice on hurdling debut. *Pat Phelan*

CELTIC SYMPHONY (IRE) 5 b.g. Waky Nao – Coco Honey (IRE) (Leading Counsel **h–** (USA)) [2016/17 b16g^6 b15.8s^6 b16d h16s Mar 17] poor form in bumpers: well held in **b74** maiden on hurdling debut: tried in hood: wears tongue tie. *Seamus Fahey, Ireland*

CELTIC THUNDER (IRE) 8 b.g. Definite Article – Clash Princess (IRE) (Supreme Leader) [2016/17 c96: c19.5g^pu h19.7d^pu c26.3g^pu Apr 7] dual winning pointer: pulled up in maiden on hurdling debut: modest maiden chaser, pulled up both starts over fences in 2016/17: has worn cheekpieces, including in 2016/17: in tongue tie last 4 starts. *R. K. Watson, Ireland*

c–
h–

CELTIC TUNE (FR) 6 b.g. Green Tune (USA) – Kerry Rose (FR) (Tel Quel (FR)) [2016/17 h96p: h21.6g^pu h16.4g h21s³ h25.5s² c24.5s³ c25.6d⁴ c23.6d² c23.6g³ Apr 3] good-topped gelding: modest maiden hurdler: fair form over fences: stays 3¼m: acts on soft going: in cheekpieces last 2 starts: wears tongue tie. *Jonjo O'Neill*

c103
h99

CENTASIA 10 b.m. Presenting – Cent Prime (Hernando (FR)) [2016/17 c129, h–: c21s^pu Apr 29] sturdy mare: winning hurdler: fairly useful chaser at best, pulled up sole outing in 2016/17: best form around 2½m: best form on soft/heavy going: wears tongue tie. *Neil Mulholland*

c–
h–

CENTRAL FLAME 9 ch.g. Central Park (IRE) – More Flair (Alflora (IRE)) [2016/17 c137, h–: c20.1d⁴ Apr 30] big, strong gelding: winning hurdler: useful chaser, excuses when well beaten sole outing in 2016/17: stays 2½m: acts on heavy going. *James Walton*

c–
h–

CENTRAL SQUARE (IRE) 5 b.g. Azamour (IRE) – Lucky Clio (IRE) (Key of Luck (USA)) [2016/17 h15.8d Dec 4] smart on Flat, stays 10.5f: 4/1, looked non-stayer when eighth in novice at Huntingdon (26 lengths behind Glaring) on hurdling debut. *Roger Varian*

h83

CENTREOFEXCELLENCE (IRE) 6 b.g. Oscar (IRE) – Calm Approach (IRE) (Anshan) [2016/17 h96p: h21.6d Apr 29] sturdy gelding: third on completed start in Irish points: modest hurdler, excuses sole outing in 2016/17: unproven beyond 2m: acts on good to soft going: usually races freely. *Gary Moore*

h68

CENTURIUS 7 ch.g. New Approach (IRE) – Questina (FR) (Rainbow Quest (USA)) [2016/17 h112p: h16d⁴ h16.2s⁶ h16s² h15.8s* h16s⁵ h16.3g⁴ Apr 1] tall, good-topped gelding: fairly useful handicap hurdler: won at Ludlow (conditional event) in March: raced only at 2m: acts on heavy going: often travels strongly. *Venetia Williams*

h116

CENTURO (USA) 4 ch.g. Cape Blanco (IRE) – Cats Copy (USA) (Cat's Career (USA)) [2016/17 h15.8m⁶ h15.8d* Oct 13] compact gelding: fair maiden on Flat, seemingly stays 1¾m: modest form over hurdles: won juvenile maiden at Uttoxeter in October: wears cheekpieces/tongue tie. *Jonjo O'Neill*

h97

CEPAGE (FR) 5 b.g. Saddler Maker (IRE) – Sience Fiction (FR) (Dom Alco (FR)) [2016/17 c16.9g⁴ c21.4s* c17.4d⁴ c16.4d* c16.4d^F c15.5s³ c19.9s³ Mar 4] stocky gelding: first foal: dam, placed in 13f French bumper, half-sister to high-class hurdler/smart chaser (stayed 2¾m) Osana and to dam of high-class staying chaser Notre Pere: winning hurdler in France: useful chaser: won 4-y-o event at Lignieres early in season and handicap at Newbury in December: left Emmanuel Clayeux after third start: stays 21f: acts on heavy going: has won when sweating badly: sketchy jumper. *Venetia Williams*

c135 x
h–

CEPORINE (FR) 5 gr.g. Cachet Noir (USA) – Cyclosporine (FR) (Mansonnien (FR)) [2016/17 h20g* h16.4g^ur Oct 22] fourth foal: dam French maiden (placed over hurdles/fences at 2¼m): fairly useful form when won novice hurdle at Fakenham on debut: unseated rider at start next time: best treated with caution. *Richard Hobson*

h120 §

CERNUNNOS (FR) 7 b.g. Della Francesca (USA) – Jackette (USA) (Mr Greeley (USA)) [2016/17 c134, h–: c21.4g^F c20.3g⁵ c21.4g c26.7m³ c19.9s⁶ c23.8d⁶ c19.9g^pu Apr 15] useful-looking gelding: winning hurdler: useful handicap chaser: stays 2½m: acts on soft going: wears headgear/tongue tie: held up: temperamental. *Tom George*

c133 §
h–

CERTAIN TIME 5 b.g. Cape Cross (IRE) – Copperbeech (IRE) (Red Ransom (USA)) [2016/17 b16.3m b15.8g Jul 22] no form in bumpers/2 starts on Flat. *Peter Hiatt*

b–

CERVIN (FR) 5 b.g. Network (GER) – Outre Mer (FR) (Sleeping Car (FR)) [2016/17 ab11.9g² b12.9d⁵ ab11.9g⁵ h17.1g⁵ h19.4g⁴ h15.8v Feb 11] sixth foal: half-brother to fairly useful French hurdler/very smart chaser Vezelay (19f-2¾m winner), stays 27f, and useful French chaser Bob And Co (17f-21f winner) (both by Dom Alco): dam unraced half-sister to useful staying chaser Raz de Maree: placed once in French bumpers: modest form over hurdles: left Alain Couetil after fifth start: tried in cheekpieces. *Tim Vaughan*

h96
b?

CESAR COLLONGES (FR) 5 ch.g. Fragrant Mix (IRE) – Prouesse Collonges (FR) (Apple Tree (FR)) [2016/17 b16.7s⁵ Dec 9] won Irish maiden point on debut: well beaten in bumper. *Evan Williams*

b–

CESAR ET ROSALIE (FR) 5 ch.g. Network (GER) – Regle de L'Art (FR) (Video Rock (FR)) [2016/17 b17m⁵ ab16g* b15.3s h15.6g³ h16g² h16.8g* h16.8m² Apr 19] €68,000 3-y-o: first foal: dam French 19f chase winner: fairly useful form in bumpers: won at Lingfield in November: fairly useful form over hurdles: won novice at Sedgefield in April: left Adrian Maguire after first start: tried in hood: in tongue tie last 4 starts: front runner/races prominently. *Neil Mulholland* **h117 b95**

C'EST JERSEY (FR) 5 b.g. Protektor (GER) – Myrtille Jersey (FR) (Murmure (FR)) [2016/17 h16d² h20v³ h20s* h24g h20d* Apr 26] smallish gelding: useful form over hurdles: won maiden at Navan (by 4¼ lengths from Black Key) in January: off 6 weeks and in blinkers, 7/1, improved further when also won 10-runner minor event at Punchestown final start by 3½ lengths from Battleford: stays 2½m: acts on soft going: has worn cheekpieces: often travels strongly. *W. P. Mullins, Ireland* **h137**

C'EST NO MOUR (GER) 4 b.c. Champs Elysees – C'est L'Amour (GER) (Whipper (USA)) [2016/17 b13.6v³ b15.3v Mar 9] modest form up to 1¼m on Flat: poor form in bumpers. *Peter Hedger* **b71**

CEST NOTRE GRIS (IRE) 7 gr.g. Verglas (IRE) – Alikhlas (Lahib (USA)) [2016/17 h16g⁶ h16.3vᵖᵘ Jun 28] fair on Flat, stayed 1¼m: fair maiden hurdler at best: left Miss Elizabeth Doyle after first start: unproven beyond 2m: best form on soft/heavy going: tried in blinkers/tongue tie: usually raced prominently: dead. *Matt Sheppard* **h95**

CHAIN GANG 6 b.g. Midnight Legend – Gaspaisie (FR) (Beyssac (FR)) [2016/17 h24s h22.8d h19s³ h22d Apr 17] £70,000 3-y-o: half-brother to numerous winners, including smart 2m-2½m hurdle winners Mr Thriller (by Kapgarde) and Gaspara (by Astarabad): dam French 17f-2½m hurdle/chase winner: bumper winner: fairly useful form over hurdles: won maiden at Leopardstown in 2015/16: third in handicap at Naas in March: likely to prove best up to 2½m: best form on soft/heavy going. *Alan Fleming, Ireland* **h125**

CHAIN OF BEACONS 8 b.g. Midnight Legend – Millennium Girl (Skyliner) [2016/17 h99: h20.2s h20.2g⁵ h16.2g⁴ c16.4g⁶ c20.1g² c17.1s⁴ c19.9g² c23.8g² c20.1v⁶ c16.3g* c17.1d² c16g³ Apr 27] modest maiden hurdler: fair handicap chaser: won at Newcastle in April: left Iain Jardine after fifth start: effective at 2m to easy 3m: acts on good to soft going: wears tongue tie: often races towards rear/travels strongly. *Sandy Thomson* **c108 h87**

CHAKISTO (FR) 9 b.g. Discover d'Auteuil (FR) – Chattawakie (FR) (Nikos) [2016/17 h95: h15.8d* c17g³ c16g⁴ h15.3s* h16.4v* c16.4vF Feb 23] fair handicap hurdler: won at Uttoxeter in October, Wincanton (novice event) in December and Newcastle in February: modest form over fences: second when fell last in handicap won by Bandol at Sedgefield in February: best around 2m: acted on heavy going: wore headgear: usually raced nearer last than first/travelled strongly: dead. *Tim Vaughan* **c94 h105**

CHALLICO 5 ch.g. Presenting – Blue Ride (IRE) (King's Ride) [2016/17 b16.8m* May 3] €10,000 3-y-o: fifth foal: half-brother to fair hurdler/fairly useful chaser Sartorial Elegance (2¾m/3¼m winner) and bumper winner Blu Cavalier (both by Kayf Tara): dam (h129) bumper/2m-2¾m hurdle winner (stayed 25f): 16/1, green but won bumper at Exeter (by 2½ lengths from Adrrastos) early in season. *Alexandra Dunn* **b87**

CHALONNIAL (FR) 5 ch.g. Protektor (GER) – Kissmirial (FR) (Smadoun (FR)) [2016/17 b99: h16.7s* h16s³ h18.1v² Mar 4] bumper winner: fairly useful form over hurdles: won novice at Bangor (by 2¾ lengths from Santo de Lune) in December: third in Tolworth Novices' Hurdle at Sandown in January: front runner/races prominently. *Harry Fry* **h123**

CHAMBORD DU LOIR (FR) 7 b.g. Ange Gabriel (FR) – Etoile de Loir (FR) (Lost World (IRE)) [2016/17 c105, h–: h20sᵖᵘ h19.9mᵖᵘ Jun 9] maiden hurdler, no form in 2016/17: winning chaser: stays 19f: in headgear last 4 starts: front runner/races prominently, tends to find little. *Sarah Humphrey* **c– h–**

CHAMPAGNE AT TARA 8 gr.g. Kayf Tara – Champagne Lil (Terimon) [2016/17 h133§: h20d c20s c16.9d² c16.4s³ c15.9s* c20.8gᵖᵘ c16.9m³ Apr 2] rangy gelding: useful handicap hurdler: useful form over fences: won novice handicap at Leicester in February: stays 2½m: acts on soft going: has worn hood: usually races towards rear/travels strongly: faint-hearted, and best treated with caution. *Jonjo O'Neill* **c134 § h– §**

CHAMPAGNE BENEFIT (IRE) 8 b.g. Beneficial – Gorrie Vale (IRE) (Saddlers' Hall (IRE)) [2016/17 h16.2g h15.8s h16.7s h19.6sᵖᵘ c19.2g⁶ c16.1m⁶ Apr 27] won 3 times in points: poor form over hurdles: little impact in 2 chases: in tongue tie last 3 starts: usually leads. *Katy Price* **c– h58**

CHAMPAGNE CHASER 7 b.g. Tobougg (IRE) – Champagne Lil (Terimon) [2016/17 **h103**
h113: h21g h23.4g⁵ h23.8d³ h23v⁴ Feb 20] lengthy gelding: fair handicap hurdler: stays
3m: acts on heavy going. *Tim Vaughan*

CHAMPAGNE CLASSIC (IRE) 6 b.g. Stowaway – Classical Rachel (IRE) **h147**
(Shahanndeh) [2016/17 b16.2d² b20s* h20d² h19v³ h24.5s² h22.3s* h20.3v³ **b106**
h20.3g* h24d* Apr 26]

     Gordon Elliott's name first appeared in a Cheltenham Festival programme
in 1996 when Mr G. Elliott (7) survived a shocking blunder on 40/1-shot Visaga to
finish seventh in the Kim Muir from 5 lb out of the handicap. That was for Nigel
Twiston-Davies who also provided Elliott with the biggest of his forty-six successes
as a jockey under Rules when future Hennessy Gold Cup winner King's Road won
the Champion INH Flat Race at the 1998 Punchestown Festival. However, it was
another British stable, Martin Pipe's, whom Elliott joined in the 1997/98 season, and
while that stay at Pond House resulted in only a few winners, including on James
Pigg in an amateur riders handicap chase at Cheltenham's October meeting, it was
no doubt a hugely informative experience to draw on when the time came for Elliott
to take out his own training licence. Like Pipe, Elliott started from scratch to reach
the top of his profession, culminating in Don Cossack's win in the 2016 Gold Cup,
a race which Pipe himself never won, saddling three placed runners, although his
Gold Cup record also included those high-profile defeats suffered by Carvill's Hill
and the ill-fated Gloria Victis.

     Elliott's six winners at the latest Cheltenham Festival made him leading
trainer there for the first time. Three of those winners came in the Don Cossack
colours of Gigginstown House Stud, and while Apple's Jade and Tiger Roll gained
their wins in more prestigious races, Champagne Classic's success in the Martin
Pipe Conditional Jockeys' Handicap Hurdle—the Festival's penultimate race in
which Elliott clinched the meeting's leading trainer award— understandably gave
him particular pleasure. Elliott had gone close twice in the race before with Toner
d'Oudairies (beaten a neck in 2012) and Noble Endeavor (beaten a head in 2015).
'Apple's Jade was sweet, Cause of Causes [winning his third Festival race] was
special, but to win the Martin Pipe after working for Martin—he's a very good friend
of mine—that was very special.' As well as receiving the race trophy from his former
boss, Elliott invited Pipe up to the winner's rostrum when collecting the award for
leading trainer at the Festival.

     Reminiscent of how Pipe tended to campaign his horses, Elliott keeps his
string busy and Champagne Classic was having his eighth start of the season at
Cheltenham having made his debut under Rules in a bumper at Galway at the end
of October. He hadn't finished out of the first three in any of those races, which
included impressive wins in a bumper at Fairyhouse in November on his second start
and in a maiden hurdle at Thurles in February in which he'd shown form verging

Martin Pipe Conditional Jockeys' Handicap Hurdle, Cheltenham—
Champagne Classic (second right) helps Gordon Elliott to be crowned leading trainer
at the 2017 Cheltenham Festival; outsider Verni (right) and stable-companion
Runfordave (other noseband) fill the places

Irish Daily Mirror Novices' Hurdle (War of Attrition), Punchestown—
Champagne Classic springs a surprise after getting first run on hot favourite Penhill (right);
Tin Soldier (cheekpieces) fills third

on useful. It might not have made him one of the stars of the huge and high-class Gigginstown string, but, contrary to what his owner Michael O'Leary said after the Martin Pipe, it didn't make Champagne Classic anything like deserving of the label 'probably the worst horse we own.' O'Leary's opinion was perhaps coloured by Champagne Classic's disappointing effort when third in a Grade 3 novice hurdle back at Thurles on his final start before Cheltenham, though in hindsight he may not have been suited by the heavy ground on that occasion and the winner Tin Soldier had already beaten him, albeit on better terms, in a maiden at Fairyhouse the previous month. Contesting his first handicap, and running on good ground for the first time, Champagne Classic was always going strongly in touch in the Martin Pipe, led soon after two out and stayed on well after being tackled approaching the last. In a race in which the pace wasn't strong, despite the size of the field, he won by two and a quarter lengths from Verni, with shorter-priced stable-companion Runfordave a length and a quarter back in third and second favourite Coo Star Sivola completing the frame. Champagne Classic was a first Cheltenham Festival win for the promising J. J. Slevin, having his first ride for Elliott.

Champagne Classic's owner had to eat his words again when one of his so-called 'duds' went further to living up to his six-figure price tag by improving a bit more to win the Grade 1 Irish Daily Mirror Novices' Hurdle (registered as the War of Attrition) at the Punchestown Festival where his rivals included not only Tin Soldier again but fellow Cheltenham winners Penhill and Presenting Percy who had won the Spa Novices' and Pertemps Final respectively. The latter pair headed the betting at 2/1 and 5/2, ahead of the Spa runner-up Monalee on 4/1. The 14/1-shot Champagne Classic ran much better back at three miles than he had on a previous try under more testing conditions during the winter and he stayed on to lead before the final flight and, knuckling down really well under firm pressure, kept on to beat the Willie Mullins stable-companions Penhill, who was arguably left with too much to do, and Tin Soldier by two and a quarter lengths and half a length, with Monalee a below-form fourth. Champagne Classic's double at Cheltenham and Punchestown made up for the eclipse at both meetings of the same connections' apparently much more highly-regarded staying novice hurdler Death Duty.

Champagne Classic (IRE) (b.g. 2011)	Stowaway (b 1994)	Slip Anchor (b 1982)	Shirley Heights
			Sayonara
		On Credit (ch 1988)	No Pass No Sale
			Noble Tiara
	Classical Rachel (IRE) (b 2000)	Shahanndeh (b 1987)	Assert
			Shademah
		Alzena (b 1984)	Persian Bold
			Lady Wise

The big, rangy Champagne Classic is a chasing sort on looks and he wouldn't be the first Gigginstown-owned Martin Pipe winner to go on to much better things over fences, with both Sir des Champs and Don Poli being placed in Gold Cups for Willie Mullins after registering further successes at Cheltenham as novice chasers. First, though, he'll need to recover from a leg injury which will reportedly cause him to miss the 2017/18 season. Champagne Classic's sire Stowaway was responsible for Gigginstown's latest participant in the Gold Cup, Outlander, though he proved disappointing at Cheltenham after beating Don Poli in the Lexus Chase. All five foals out of Champagne Classic's unraced dam Classical Rachel to have run are by Stowaway, her other winners being the fair hurdler at around two miles Admiral Hawke and the pointer Stoney. Grandam Alzena was placed at a mile and a half on the Flat and her winners included the fairly useful pair over jumps Tuppenny Cody, a two-mile hurdler, and Waltons Mountain, a chaser who stayed two and a half miles. Alzena was a half-sister to the useful juvenile hurdler Majestic Man. Champagne

Gigginstown House Stud's "Champagne Classic"

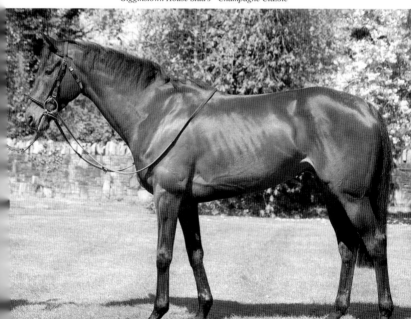

Classic originally changed hands for only €20,000 at Goffs Land Rover NH Sale as a three-year-old, though he had won his only start in points by the time he was resold to Gigginstown for €100,000 at Goffs Punchestown NH Sale in April 2015. Champagne Classic stays three miles and gained his first two wins on soft ground, though his improved efforts in the spring came under less testing conditions. *Gordon Elliott, Ireland*

CHAMPAGNE FEVER (IRE) 10 gr.g. Stowaway – Forever Bubbles (IRE) (Roselier (FR)) [2016/17 c22d* Nov 24] tall gelding: winning hurdler: top-class chaser at one time: won listed event at Thurles (by head from Lord Windermere) in November, sole outing in 2016/17: stays 2¾m: acts on good to firm and heavy going. *W. P. Mullins, Ireland*
   c146 +
   h–

CHAMPAGNE HARMONY (IRE) 7 b.g. Stowaway – L'Harmonie (USA) (Bering) [2016/17 h121, b107: h20s h16.4s⁴ h20.5d⁴ h20.7g² c20v c18v⁴ c20v* c21d⁵ Apr 28] fairly useful form over hurdles: second in novice at Galway early in season: useful form over fences: won maiden at Navan (by 6½ lengths from Crest) in April: stays 21f: acts on heavy going: tried in tongue tie. *S. J. Mahon, Ireland*
   c130
   h121

CHAMPAGNE N CAVIAR (IRE) 9 b.g. Tiger Hill (IRE) – Leukippids (IRE) (Sadler's Wells (USA)) [2016/17 h18.6d⁴ May 25] lengthy, angular gelding: fair maiden hurdler, excuses sole outing in 2016/17: maiden chaser: should stay 2½m: best form on soft/heavy going. *Sophie Leech*
   c–
   h73

CHAMPAGNE RANSOM (FR) 5 gr.m. Mastercraftsman (IRE) – Linorova (USA) (Trempolino (USA)) [2016/17 h80: h19.3m h22.1mᵖᵘ May 30] maiden hurdler, no form in 2016/17: tried in cheekpieces: temperamental. *Micky Hammond*
   h– §

CHAMPAGNE TO GO (IRE) 7 b.m. Beneficial – Terre d'Orient (FR) (Kabool) [2016/17 b100: h19.7g³ h15.8v⁶ h16d² h16.2v³ Dec 7] off mark in Irish mares maiden points at second attempt: bumper winner: fair form over hurdles: tried in cheekpieces: front runner/races prominently. *Kim Bailey*
   h100

CHAMPAGNE WEST (IRE) 9 b.g. Westerner – Wyndham Sweetmarie (IRE) (Mister Lord (USA)) [2016/17 c153x, h–: c20d³ c21v* c25d* c26.3g c24.5d⁴ Apr 26] well-made gelding: winning hurdler: high-class chaser: won listed event at Tramore (by 12 lengths from Roi des Francs) and Thyestes Handicap Chase at Gowran (by 7½ lengths from Ucello Conti) in January: stays 25f: acts on heavy going: front runner/races prominently: often let down by jumping. *Henry de Bromhead, Ireland*
   c162 x
   h–

CHAMP DES REVES (IRE) 5 b.m. Robin des Champs (FR) – Rachel's Choice (IRE) (Ela-Mana-Mou) [2016/17 b16.7gᶠ May 6] fatally injured in bumper. *Fergal O'Brien*
   b–

CHAMPERS ON ICE (IRE) 7 gr.g. Robin des Champs (FR) – Miss Nova (Ra Nova) [2016/17 h142, b112: c24s* c24s² c20.8s⁶ c31.8gᵖᵘ Mar 14] tall, good-topped gelding: useful hurdler: similar form over fences: won novice at Uttoxeter in December: second in listed novice at Warwick (4½ lengths behind American) in January: should stay beyond 3m: acts on heavy going: tried in cheekpieces/tongue tie: often races prominently/lazily. *David Pipe*
   c139
   h–

CHAMPION CHASE (FR) 5 b.g. Voix du Nord (FR) – Darling Frisco (FR) (Trebrook (FR)) [2016/17 h15.8s h15.8d h16v³ h20.3g³ h20.3g⁵ Apr 21] €34,000 3-y-o, £45,000 4-y-o: half-brother to French 17f/21f chase winner Queen Frisco (by Dark Moondancer) and French 19f chase winner Kubana (by Quart de Vin): dam French 13.5f winner: runner-up in Irish maiden point: fair form over hurdles: may prove best at around 2m: acts on heavy going: remains capable of better. *Kim Bailey*
   h100 p

CHAMP (IRE) 5 b.g. King's Theatre (IRE) – China Sky (IRE) (Definite Article) [2016/17 b15.7s* b16g² Feb 25] first foal: dam (h75), lightly raced in bumpers/over hurdles, half-sister to triple Cheltenham Gold Cup winner Best Mate: useful form in bumpers: won maiden at Southwell (by 3½ lengths from Grey Warbler) in January: second at Kempton (2¼ lengths behind Irish Prophecy) following month. *Nicky Henderson*
   b105

CHANCEITON (IRE) 6 b.g. Vinnie Roe (IRE) – Lissnabrucka (IRE) (Lord Americo) [2016/17 h20.5vᵖᵘ h23.3vᵖᵘ Mar 28] runner-up in point: no form in bumpers/over hurdles: in tongue tie last 3 starts. *Lucinda Russell*
   h–

CHANCEOFA LIFETIME (IRE) 10 ch.g. Beneficial – Bounty Queen (IRE) (King's Ride) [2016/17 c109, h–: c24.2dᵖᵘ c20dᵖᵘ c23.9g³ c20.1s⁶ c23.8g Dec 14] maiden hurdler: fair handicap chaser: stays 3¼m: acts on heavy going. *Victor Thompson*
   c103
   h–

Mr R. S. Brookhouse's "Champagne West"

CHANCE TAKEN 9 b.m. Overbury (IRE) – New Dawn (Rakaposhi King) [2016/17 h86: **c65 p** h20.3d² c16s h16.8s² h16.8s³ h16.8d Feb 24] sturdy mare: runner-up in maiden point: **h91** modest maiden hurdler: 10/1, eighth in novice handicap at Hereford (29 lengths behind Caprice d'Anglais) on chasing debut, finding less than looked likely: stays 21f: acts on soft going: has worn headgear, including last 2 starts: should do better over fences. *Noel Williams*

CHANDOS BELLE (GER) 4 b.f. Mamool (IRE) – Chandos Rose (IRE) (Mull of **h97** Kintyre (USA)) [2016/17 h16.6g³ h15.9s² h18.7d⁵ Mar 13] fairly useful on Flat for C. von der Recke, stays 12.5f: modest form over hurdles: best effort when second in mares novice at Plumpton in February. *Stuart Edmunds*

CHANGE OR GO (IRE) 5 b.g. Kalanisi (IRE) – Teffia Rose (IRE) (Old Vic) [2016/17 **h–** h–: h22g Apr 1] no form over hurdles: tried in cheekpieces/tongue tie: dead. *David Dennis*

CHANGING THE GUARD 11 b.g. King's Best (USA) – Our Queen of Kings (Arazi **c107 x** (USA)) [2016/17 c–x, h110: h16g⁴ h15.7g⁵ h15.7g⁴ h16g⁴ h15.8d³ c16m⁴ h15.9g h16d⁵ **h92 §** h20g² Apr 17] sturdy gelding: modest handicap hurdler nowadays: one-time useful chaser, below form sole outing over fences in 2016/17: stays 21f: acts on good to firm and heavy going: wears cheekpieces/tongue tie: temperamental, and often let down by jumping. *Barry Brennan*

CHANKILLO 8 ch.g. Observatory (USA) – Seasonal Blossom (IRE) (Fairy King (USA)) **c100 §** [2016/17 c105§, h80§: c16m³ c16g c17.4g³ c20m³ c18.9s⁵ h23.1s³ h20.5vᴾᵁ h24d⁵ **h89 §** c19.4d² Apr 16] compact gelding: modest maiden hurdler: fair handicap chaser: barely stays 23f: acts on heavy going: wears headgear: often races prominently: unreliable. *Sarah-Jayne Davies*

CHANTARA ROSE 8 br.m. Kayf Tara – Fragrant Rose (Alflora (IRE)) [2016/17 h111: c109
h23.3s h23.3g c23.8d^{pu} c20s^{ur} c20.3v^3 Dec 11] fair handicap hurdler: fair form when third **h101**
in handicap at Southwell in December on completed start over fences: stays 3m: acts on
heavy going: wears cheekpieces: has worn tongue tie, including final start. *Neil Mulholland*

CHANTECLER 6 b.g. Authorized (IRE) – Snow Goose (Polar Falcon (USA)) [2016/17 **h97 x**
h–p: h16.8m^5 h16d^4 h16s Dec 2] lengthy gelding: fair on Flat, stays 1½m: modest form
over hurdles: likely to prove best around 2m: acts on good to soft going: has worn hood: in
tongue tie last 3 starts: usually races freely: often let down by jumping. *Neil Mulholland*

CHAP 7 ch.g. Midnight Legend – Silver Solace (Silver Patriarch (IRE)) [2016/17 h63p, **h88**
b97: h20g^6 h16g^5 h15.8d Nov 19] strong gelding: won maiden point on debut: bumper
winner: modest form over hurdles. *Dan Skelton*

CHAPEL STILE (IRE) 5 b.g. Scorpion (IRE) – Peggy Cullen (IRE) (Presenting) **h82 p**
[2016/17 h16s h16v^6 h16.4v^6 h16v^5 Mar 10] €21,000 3-y-o: sixth foal: half-brother to
useful bumper winner/smart hurdler Rathvinden (2m winner, by Heron Island), stays 21f,
and bumper winner/fairly useful hurdler Savingforvegas (21f winner, by Beneficial): dam
unraced: poor form over hurdles: bred to stay at least 2½m: still unexposed. *Nicky Richards*

CHAPOLIMOSS (FR) 13 ch.g. Trempolino (USA) – Chamoss (FR) (Tip Moss (FR)) c–
[2016/17 c24.5g^{pu} c23m Jul 4] good-topped gelding: maiden hurdler: fairly useful chaser h–
at best, no form in 2016/17: stays 3¾m: acts on good to firm and heavy going: in headgear
last 3 starts: wears tongue tie. *Lawney Hill*

CHARBEL (IRE) 6 b.g. Iffraaj – Eoz (IRE) (Sadler's Wells (USA)) [2016/17 h150, h111: **c155**
h16d^5 c16d* c15.5d^2 c15.9g^{pl} c15.8g^3 Apr 8] tall, useful-looking gelding: smart hurdler: **h–**
very smart form over fences: won maiden at Uttoxeter by ¾ length from Le Prezien) in
October: placed in Henry VIII Novices' Chase at Sandown (6 lengths behind Altior) in
December and Maghull Novices' Chase at Aintree (13 lengths behind San Benedeto) in
April: still in front when fell 2 out in Arkle Chase at Cheltenham, looking sure to be placed:
raced around 2m: acts on soft going: wears tongue tie: usually leads. *Kim Bailey*

CHARIN' CROSS 5 ch.g. Cockney Rebel (IRE) – Lush Lady (IRE) (Kris Kin (USA)) h–
[2016/17 b16s b17v^3 h16.2g Apr 25] well held in bumpers/novice hurdle. *Micky Hammond* b–

CHARLEMAR (FR) 5 b.g. Ballingarry (IRE) – Passemare (FR) (Useful (FR)) [2016/17 **h120**
b11.4g^2 b11.4g* h16m* h17s* h16s^5 h16.6d^4 h21g^{pu} Mar 18] useful-looking gelding: third **b?**
foal: half-brother to French 21f chase winner Beaumar and French 19f-21f chase winner
Asdesmar (both by Khalkevi): dam unraced half-sister to high-class hurdler/useful chaser
(17f-21f winner) Ilnamar: French bumper winner: fairly useful form over hurdles: won
maiden at Chepstow in November and novice at Aintree in December: left J. Planque after
second start: unproven beyond 17f: acts on soft and good to firm going. *Harry Whittington*

CHARLES BRUCE (IRE) 14 br.g. Lord Americo – Lissanuhig (Le Bavard (FR)) [2016/17 c– §
c–§: c32.5g c27.2d^{pu} May 12] angular gelding: fair hunter chaser at best, little form since
2013/14: best effort at 33f: acts on good to soft going: temperamental. *A. Campbell*

CHARLIE BREEKIE (IRE) 8 b.g. Alkaadhem – Highland Breeze (IRE) (Kotashaan **h104**
(FR)) [2016/17 h–: h20.3g^2 h20.3d^3 h23g^{pu} Jul 26] lengthy gelding: fair maiden hurdler:
stays 2½m: acts on good to soft going. *Ben Pauling*

CHARLIE COOK (IRE) 8 b.g. Royal Anthem (USA) – Supreme Baloo (IRE) (Supreme **h116**
Leader) [2016/17 h107: h20m* May 19] well-made gelding: fairly useful handicap hurdler:
awarded race at Worcester early in season: stays 2½m: acts on soft and good to firm going:
often races prominently. *Graeme McPherson*

CHARLIE MON (IRE) 8 ch.g. Presenting – Prowler (IRE) (Old Vic) [2016/17 c20g **c103 §**
c16.5g^2 c20g^{pu} c20.9s^4 c21.2g^2 c23.6g^3 c23.8v^{pu} c22.7f^2 c23.6g^3 c26.2m^3 Apr 28] point **h–**
winner: maiden hurdler: fair maiden chaser: left George Stewart after first start: stays 3m:
acts on firm and soft going: in cheekpieces last 4 starts: front runner/races prominently:
temperamental. *Mike Hammond*

CHARLIE MY DARLING 4 b.g. Malinas (GER) – Somethingaboutmary (IRE) **b66**
(Fayruz) [2016/17 b15.8v^4 b15.8g Apr 9] poor form in bumpers. *Brian Eckley*

CHARLIE PAPA LIMA (IRE) 6 b.g. Winged Love (IRE) – Fairylodge Scarlet (IRE) **b88**
(Mister Lord (USA)) [2016/17 b16g^4 b13.6g^7 Apr 21] €1,500 3-y-o, £15,000 5-y-o: fifth
foal: brother to fairly useful hurdler/useful chaser Firm Order (2½m-25f winner): dam
unraced: off mark in Irish maiden points at fourth attempt: fair form in bumpers: better
effort when second at Fontwell in April. *Harry Whittington*

CHARLIE PARKER (IRE) 4 b.g. Myboycharlie (IRE) – Solaria (IRE) (Desert Prince **h82**
(IRE)) [2016/17 h16m⁶ h15.8m⁵ h15.8g⁴ h19vᵘʳ h19.2v⁵ h16.8d Feb 24] plain gelding:
poor maiden on Flat: poor form over hurdles: stays 19f: acts on good to firm and heavy
going. *Dominic Ffrench Davis*

CHARLIE'S CHARM (IRE) 5 b.g. Golan (IRE) – Ben's Turn (IRE) (Saddlers' Hall **b79**
(IRE)) [2016/17 b16.6g b16.7g⁴ Apr 22] modest form on second of 2 starts in bumpers.
Tim Fitzgerald

CHARLIE STOUT (IRE) 6 br.g. Spadoun (FR) – Full of Elegance (FR) (Cadoudal **h126**
(FR)) [2016/17 b16d⁴ b15.9g b18.3g h21g⁵ h16.5d⁵ h16.5d⁵ h22s h18.4d² h16d³ h20d² **b78**
h16s* h16d³ h16s* h19.5s* h22.8dᵖᵘ h16d² Mar 30] €14,000 3-y-o: half-brother to fairly
useful hurdler/useful chaser Relentless Dreamer (19f-23f winner, by Kayf Tara) and a
winning pointer by King's Theatre: dam unraced half-sister to dam of Cheltenham Gold
Cup winner Long Run: modest form in bumpers: fairly useful hurdler: won handicaps at
Thurles in December and Naas in January, and novice at Down Royal later in January:
second in handicap at Limerick in March: stays 2½m: acts on soft going: wears tongue tie:
often races in rear. *Shane Nolan, Ireland*

CHARLIE WINGNUT (IRE) 10 br.g. Westerner – Back To Stay (IRE) (Supreme **c97**
Leader) [2016/17 h95: h21.3g⁶ h24d³ c24.2s³ Dec 26] dual point winner: modest maiden **h96**
hurdler: 7/1, third in novice handicap at Wetherby (6¾ lengths behind Bankhall) on chasing
debut: stays 3m: acts on soft going: usually races close up/travels strongly. *Sue Smith*

CHARLI PARCS (FR) 4 b.g. Anabaa Blue – Ella Parcs (FR) (Nikos) [2016/17 h17.4s* **h144**
h16g* h16gᶠ h16.8g⁶ Mar 17] tall, useful-looking gelding: sixth foal: half-brother to 3
winners in France, including hurdler/chaser Blue Parcs (15f-2¾m winner, by Maille Pistol)
and chaser Wood Parcs (19f-23f winner, by Sunshack): dam, French 17f chase winner,
half-sister to fairly useful French hurdler/useful chaser (17f-19f winner) Sirius Parcs:
useful form over hurdles: won newcomers race at Enghien in November and juvenile at
Kempton (by 8 lengths from Master Blueyes) in December: left A. Chaille-Chaille after
first start. *Nicky Henderson*

CHARMANT (FR) 5 b.g. Balko (FR) – Ravissante (FR) (Mad Tax (USA)) [2016/17 **h101**
b17m³ b17.1d³ h16s⁶ h16.2v⁵ h17s³ h17v² h16d⁴ Mar 31] second foal: brother to French **b76**
1¾m bumper winner Banal: dam ran once: fell in maiden point on debut: modest form in
bumpers: fair form over hurdles: left Graham McKeever after first start: unproven beyond
17f: acts on heavy going: wears hood: tried in tongue tie: often travels strongly. *James Ewart*

CHARMING LAD (IRE) 12 b.g. Dushyantor (USA) – Glens Lady (IRE) (Mister Lord **c–**
(USA)) [2016/17 c99, h–: h23g c24vᵖᵘ c23mᶠ h25dᵖᵘ Nov 19] rangy gelding: fair maiden **h–**
hurdler/chaser at best, no form in 2016/17: wears headgear/tongue tie. *Anthony Day*

CHARMING ZEN (FR) 5 gr.g. Youmzain (IRE) – Nioumoun (FR) (Dadarissime (FR)) **h136 p**
[2016/17 h17.1g* h16.6g* Feb 22] second foal: half-brother to French 2¾m chase winner
Battinga (by Le Fou): dam French 2¾m chase winner: useful form over hurdles: won 4-y-o
event at Les Sables-d'Olonne in October and novice at Doncaster (by 5 lengths from
Apasionado) in February: left Patrice Quinton after first start: will stay further than 17f:
open to further improvement. *Dan Skelton*

CHARMIX (FR) 7 br.g. Laveron – Open Up (FR) (Fabulous Don (SPA)) [2016/17 h131, **c139**
b–: c19.2d⁴ c20.3s⁴ c20.9s* c19.2sᵘʳ c20.5g³ c20.2d² Mar 26] well-made gelding: won **h–**
maiden point on debut: winning hurdler: useful form over fences: won novice at Hereford
in January: would probably have followed up in novice at Exeter but for unseating 2 out:
stays 21f: acts on heavy going: in cheekpieces last 2 starts: front runner/races prominently.
Harry Fry

CHARTBREAKER (FR) 6 b.g. Shirocco (GER) – Caucasienne (FR) (Galileo (IRE)) **h–**
[2016/17 h121: h21.6d h23.4s Dec 3] angular gelding: fairly useful hurdler in 2015/16, no
form in 2016/17: best effort at 21f: in headgear last 2 starts. *Chris Gordon*

CHARTREUX (FR) 12 gr.g. Colonel Collins (USA) – Ruaha River (FR) (Villez (USA)) **c– x**
[2016/17 c77x, h–: c25.5gᵖᵘ Jun 1] good-topped gelding: winning pointer/hurdler: useful **h–**
chaser at best, no form since 2014/15: stays 27f: acts on heavy going: has worn cheekpieces:
wears tongue tie: often let down by jumping. *Mrs Julie Marles*

CHASE END CHARLIE (IRE) 6 b.g. Scorpion (IRE) – Artist's Muse (IRE) (Cape **c119**
Cross (IRE)) [2016/17 h129, b92. c24g³ c24.1sᶠ h21.6d h21.4a* h24.4d⁵ h21.5p⁶ Mar 10] **h120**
lengthy gelding: failed to complete both starts in points: fairly useful handicap hurdler:
won at Wincanton in January: similar form completed start over fences: should stay 3m:
acts on soft going: in cheekpieces last 3 starts. *Tom Lacey*

Betfred Midlands Grand National (Listed Handicap Chase), Uttoxeter—
stamina is tested to the full as Chase The Spud (left) edges out Mysteree

CHASE ME (IRE) 6 b.g. Mahler – Collatrim Choice (IRE) (Saddlers' Hall (IRE)) **b61**
[2016/17 b16s⁶ Jan 26] maiden pointer, runner-up 4 of 5 starts: in hood, 40/1, sixth in
bumper at Warwick (24½ lengths behind Carlos du Fruitier) in January. *Sarah Hollinshead*

CHASE THE SPUD 9 b.g. Alflora (IRE) – Trial Trip (Le Moss) [2016/17 c134, h–: **c135**
c26.2d c28.4v² c26.3s c26.2s⁵ c33.4s* Mar 18] workmanlike gelding: winning hurdler: **h–**
useful handicap chaser: won Midlands Grand National at Uttoxeter (by 1½ lengths from
Mysteree) in March: stays 33f: acts on heavy going: tried in hood/tongue tie. *Fergal
O'Brien*

CHASE THE WIND (IRE) 8 ch.g. Spadoun (FR) – Asfreeasthewind (IRE) (Moscow **c125**
Society (USA)) [2016/17 c117, h–: c24.2g* c21.2m⁵ May 30] lengthy gelding: winning **h–**
hurdler: fairly useful chaser: won novice at Wetherby early in season: stays 3m: acts on
good to firm and good to soft going: has worn hood/tongue tie: usually leads. *Joanne Foster*

CHASING FAIRIES 6 gr.m. Fair Mix (IRE) – Trial Trip (Le Moss) [2016/17 h–, b–: **h–**
h15.8gᵖᵘ h21vᵖᵘ Dec 31] maiden hurdler, failed to complete both starts in 2016/17.
Alexandra Dunn

CHASMA 7 b.m. Kayf Tara – Luneray (FR) (Poplar Bluff) [2016/17 h91: h19.9g h20.5g⁶ **c97**
h19.3d² h24.1s⁴ c19.2dᵘʳ c21.3d² c19.3d* Mar 14] modest handicap hurdler: modest form **h90**
over fences: won novice handicap at Sedgefield in March: stays 21f: acts on heavy going:
tried in cheekpieces: wears tongue tie. *Michael Easterby*

CHASSEUR DE TETE (FR) 5 b.g. Coastal Path – Escomptee (FR) (Roi de Rome **b–**
(USA)) [2016/17 b16.4s Dec 8] tailed off in bumper. *Lucinda Russell*

CHATEAU CHINON (FR) 5 b.g. Dream Well (FR) – Liesse de Marbeuf (FR) (Cyborg **h96**
(FR)) [2016/17 b15.8v⁶ h15.8d h16s h15.8d Mar 15] €55,000 3-y-o: fifth foal: closely **b83**
related to unreliable 2m/19f chase winner Asuncion (by Antarctique) and half-brother to
useful hurdler/chaser Virgilio (17f-2½m winner, by Denham Red), stays 3m: dam (c118/
h121), French 17f hurdle/chase winner, also 12.5f winner on Flat: green when sixth in
bumper at Uttoxeter: modest form over hurdles. *Dan Skelton*

CHATEAU ROBIN (IRE) 6 br.g. Robin des Pres (FR) – Bella With A Zee (IRE) **h97 p** (Persian Bold) [2016/17 b94: h21d⁵ h19.6d h19v² h21v² Mar 12] modest form over hurdles: remains with potential. *Kim Bailey*

CHATO (FR) 5 ch.g. Malinas (GER) – Queen Bruere (FR) (Mansonnien (FR)) [2016/17 **h88 p** b15.8d* b16g² b15.7d h19g⁶ Mar 2] £13,000 3-y-o: good-topped gelding: second foal: dam **b99** unraced half-sister to fairly useful chaser (stayed 2½m) Speedy Bruere: fairly useful form in bumpers: won maiden at Uttoxeter early in season: 4/1, sixth in novice at Taunton (29¼ lengths behind Spiritofthegames) on hurdling debut: entitled to progress. *Alan King*

CHAVOY (FR) 12 br.g. Saint des Saints (FR) – Dictania (FR) (Iron Duke (FR)) [2016/17 **c–** c115, h–: h20d Oct 20] fairly useful hurdler at best, well below form sole outing in **h–** 2016/17: fairly useful chaser: stays 27f: acts on heavy going: usually in headgear: wears tongue tie: often races in rear. *Rebecca Menzies*

CHEAT THE CHEATER (IRE) 10 b.g. Flemensfirth (USA) – Ballyclough Gale **c92 §** (Strong Gale) [2016/17 c97§, h–: c23.6d c25.3v³ c24v c24.5vF c23.5v⁵ Mar 6] winning **h–** hurdler: modest handicap chaser: stays 3¼m: acts on heavy going: wears headgear/tongue tie: temperamental. *Claire Dyson*

CHEBSEY BEAU 7 b.g. Multiplex – Chebsey Belle (IRE) (Karinga Bay) [2016/17 h122: **h109** h19.7g⁵ h21.1s h20sᵖᵘ Dec 3] fair handicap hurdler: stays 2½m: acts on good to firm and good to soft going. *John Quinn*

CHEENYS VENTURE 5 b.m. King's Theatre (IRE) – Daisies Adventure (IRE) **b–** (Flemensfirth (USA)) [2016/17 b16.8d b17g Apr 15] first foal: dam, unraced, out of half-sister to dam of very smart hurdler/top-class chaser (stayed 25f) Menorah (by King's Theatre): no form in bumpers. *Bruce Mactaggart*

CHEF DES OBEAUX (FR) 5 b.g. Saddler Maker (IRE) – O Dame de Gene (FR) **b105** (Passing Sale (FR)) [2016/17 b16.3v² Mar 4] tall gelding: fourth foal: half-brother to French 17f chase winner Trinite des Obeaux (by Adnaan): dam unraced: useful form in bumpers: raced twice for N. Devilder in 2015/16: second at Newbury (¾ length behind Sam Brown) on sole start in 2016/17: will be suited by further than 2m. *Nicky Henderson*

CHEF D'OEUVRE (FR) 6 b.g. Martaline – Kostroma (FR) (Lost World (IRE)) [2016/17 **c131 x** h129, b93: c21.1sᵘʳ c25.2s² c24s⁴ c25.2v* c23.8sᵘʳ c25.2d³ Mar 26] useful-looking **h–** gelding: fairly useful hurdler: useful form over fences: won maiden at Hereford (by 30 lengths from Weststreet) in February: stays 25f: best form on soft/heavy going: in cheekpieces last 4 starts: front runner/races prominently: has been let down by attitude/jumping. *Warren Greatrex*

CHELSEA FLYER (IRE) 6 b.g. Westerner – Aktress (IRE) (Oscar (IRE)) [2016/17 **h133** b106: h19.9d³ h16.3d² h20.5v⁵ h16.6d* h20g h19.8g Apr 29] well-made gelding: useful bumper performer: useful form over hurdles: won novice at Doncaster in February: stays 2½m: acts on good to soft going: has worn hood. *Emma Lavelle*

CHELTENAM DE VAIGE (FR) 5 b.g. Forestier (FR) – Ratina de Vaige (FR) (April **h93** Night (FR)) [2016/17 b82: b15.7d h16.7s h16.5g h20.3sF h19g h19.2v³ h19.8v³ h22gᵖᵘ Apr **b66** 1] rather unfurnished gelding: poor form in bumpers: modest maiden hurdler: left Giles Smyly after seventh start: should be suited by 2¾m+: acts on heavy going. *Mark Wall*

CHELTENIAN (FR) 11 b.g. Astarabad (USA) – Salamaite (FR) (Mansonnien (FR)) **c–** [2016/17 c–, h149: h15.7mᵖᵘ May 7] well-made gelding: smart hurdler at best, fatally **h–** injured in Swinton Handicap at Haydock sole outing in 2016/17: once-raced chaser: stayed 2½m: acted on good to firm and heavy going: wore hood. *Philip Hobbs*

CHEQUE EN BLANC (FR) 5 b.g. Bernebeau (FR) – Necossaise (FR) (Michel **h97** Georges) [2016/17 b103: h16.7v h15.8s⁶ h20d h19.6s⁴ h19.8vᵖᵘ h19.7dᵖᵘ h21.9d Apr 16] lengthy gelding: bumper winner: modest maiden hurdler: stays 2½m: acts on soft going: tried in cheekpieces: wears tongue tie: often races towards rear. *Tom Symonds*

CHEROKEE PRINCE (IRE) 5 b.g. Westerner – Ara Blend (IRE) (Persian Mews) **b89 p** [2016/17 b16.7g⁵ Oct 25] €35,000 3-y-o: half-brother to several winners, including fairly useful hurdler/chaser Topsham Belle (21f-23f winner, by Presenting) and fair hurdler/ chaser Bellaboosh (17f-2¾m winner, by Dushyantor): dam, lightly raced in points, half-sister to smart chaser (3m-29f winner) Topsham Bay: 3/1, fifth in bumper at Bangor (10½ lengths behind Mr One More) on debut, not ideally placed: capable of better. *Ronald O'Leary, Ireland*

CHERRY PRINCESS 7 gr.m. Act One – Francia (Legend of France (USA)) [2016/17 **h76** h72: h16.2d⁶ h16.2g⁵ h16.8g⁶ h16.2sᵖᵘ Nov 4] poor maiden hurdler: stays 2¾m: acts on good to soft going: sometimes in cheekpieces. *Barbara Butterworth*

CHESHAM ROSE (IRE) 4 gr.f. Mastercraftsman (IRE) – Rose's Destination (IRE) h–
(Dubai Destination (USA)) [2016/17 h16.3m h15.8m⁵ Apr 18] modest maiden on Flat,
stays 1m: well held both starts over hurdles. *Dave Roberts*

CHESTERFIELD (IRE) 7 ch.g. Pivotal – Antique (IRE) (Dubai Millennium) [2016/17 h148
h15.7d h21d h16.3v² h16.5g* h16g* Apr 22] compact gelding: smart handicap hurdler:
won conditionals/amateur event at Aintree (by 5 lengths from Chieftain's Choice) and
Scottish Champion Hurdle at Ayr (by short head from Zubayr) in April: unproven beyond
17f: acts on heavy going. *Seamus Mullins*

CHESTERMAN (IRE) 5 b.g. Westerner – Cherry Pie (FR) (Dolpour) [2016/17 b15.7g² b96
Mar 28] sixth foal: half-brother to bumper winner/fairly useful hurdler Great Try (17f
winner, by Scorpion), stayed 2½m: dam, French maiden (second at 1½m), half-sister to
useful hurdler/high-class chaser (2¼m-2½m winner) The Nightingale: 7/1, second in
bumper at Southwell (1½ lengths behind Royal Ruby) in March. *Sue Smith*

CHESTNUT BEN (IRE) 12 ch.g. Ridgewood Ben – Betseale (IRE) (Step Together c111
(USA)) [2016/17 c119, h–: c16.4d² c15.6d⁴ c17.2d⁴ c19.4d c15.5s⁶ c15.7d⁶ c15.9m² h–
c19.9g⁵ c16.4s* c15.2d⁴ c17.2s³ c15.2d* c17.2m³ c15.7g* Apr 21] lengthy gelding:
winning hurdler: fair handicap chaser nowadays: won at Sedgefield in February, Wetherby
in March and Southwell in April: stays 2½m: acts on good to firm and heavy going: tried
in headgear: has worn tongue tie. *Peter Winks*

CHESTNUT STORM (IRE) 4 ch.f. Rip Van Winkle (IRE) – Always Attractive (IRE) h–
(King's Best (USA)) [2016/17 h19.5vᵖᵘ Feb 25] fair on Flat, stays 16.5f: pulled up in
maiden on hurdling debut. *Brian Barr*

CHEVALGRIS 7 gr.g. Verglas (IRE) – Danzelline (Danzero (AUS)) [2016/17 h19.7s h97
h19.7v h15.8v³ h21.9d² h19.5m² Apr 28] modest maiden hurdler: stays 2¾m: acts on good
to firm and heavy going. *Dai Burchell*

CHEZ CASTEL MAIL (FR) 5 ch.g. My Risk (FR) – Queenly Mail (FR) (Medaaly) b103
[2016/17 b16.7g² b15.8d² b13.6v* b16.3g⁶ Mar 25] tall gelding: first foal: dam, French
maiden, half-sister to useful French hurdler/winning chaser (17f-21f winner) True Love
Mail: fairly useful form in bumpers: won conditionals/amateur event at Fontwell in
February. *Ali Stronge*

CHICAGO OUTFIT (IRE) 12 b.g. Old Vic – Lambourne Lace (IRE) (Un Desperado c117
(FR)) [2016/17 c121, h–: c24.2d* c27.5gᵖᵘ c24.2d⁵ c23.4vᵖᵘ c26.6gᵘʳ c24.2g⁴ Apr 25] h–
lightly-raced hurdler: fairly useful chaser: won handicap at Hexham very early in season:
left George Bewley after third start: stays 25f: acts on soft and good to firm going: wears
headgear: front runner/races prominently. *L. Kerr*

CHICKSGROVE SPRITE (IRE) 6 b.m. Scorpion (IRE) – Homebird (IRE) (Be My h72
Native (USA)) [2016/17 b–: h21.6d⁶ h19g⁵ h19.9d⁵ Mar 14] poor form over hurdles: in
tongue tie last 3 starts. *Neil Mulholland*

CHIC NAME (FR) 5 b.g. Nickname (FR) – Vuelta Al Ruedo (FR) (Ballingarry (IRE)) c128
[2016/17 h141?: h19.4d⁴ h17.9s⁴ h19.4v⁵ c15.7s³ c20vᵖᵘ c19.4d³ c16.2v⁴ c23.6s⁴ c23.4d* h141
h19.4s Apr 17] good-topped gelding: useful hurdler: fairly useful form over fences: won
novice handicap at Newbury in March: stays 23f: acts on heavy going: wears headgear:
front runner/races prominently. *Richard Hobson*

CHIC THEATRE (IRE) 7 gr.g. King's Theatre (IRE) – La Reine Chic (FR) (Balleroy h112
(USA)) [2016/17 h113, b–: h15.7m⁵ h21.1s h20.6s* h22.8g h19g⁶ Apr 24] lengthy gelding:
bumper winner: fair handicap hurdler: won at Market Rasen in December: stays 21f: acts
on heavy going: in cheekpieces on 4 of last 5 starts: in tongue tie last 4 starts. *David Pipe*

CHIDSWELL (IRE) 8 b.g. Gold Well – Manacured (IRE) (Mandalus) [2016/17 h23.1g² c126
c15.9d² c16.3d⁴ c16.3s² c19.3v* c20.5v* c17.1s³ c20.1g⁵ Apr 28] rangy gelding: fairly h122
useful hurdler: fairly useful chaser: won novice at Sedgefield and novice handicap at Ayr
in February: stays 2¾m, effective at shorter: acts on heavy going: front runner/races
prominently. *Nicky Richards*

CHIEF BOTTLEWASHER (IRE) 6 b.g. Moss Vale (IRE) – Edwina (IRE) (Caerleon c–
(USA)) [2016/17 h19.1d* h19g h15.8s c19.2g Apr 11] poor form over hurdles: well held h79
when left alone last in conditionals novice at Fontwell in November: tailed off in novice
handicap on chasing debut: left Charlie Mann after first start: tried in hood. *Aytach Sadik*

CHIEF BRODY 6 b.g. Phoenix Reach (IRE) – Cherry Plum (Medicean) [2016/17 h101, h96
b84: h16.5g² h16.5gᶠ h16.2vᵖᵘ Feb 1] modest maiden hurdler: unproven beyond 2m: acts
on good to soft going: tried in cheekpieces. *Grace Harris*

CHIEF SITTINGBULL 4 ch.g. Indian Haven – Saharan Song (IRE) (Singspiel (IRE)) b73
[2016/17 ab16g⁶ b15.3v⁶ Feb 2] poor form in bumpers. *Emma Lavelle*

QTS Scottish Champion Hurdle (Limited Handicap), Ayr—a mistake at the last by leader Zubayr (centre) proves costly as he just loses out to the other nosebanded runner Chesterfield (left)

CHIEFTAIN'S CHOICE (IRE) 8 b.g. King's Theatre (IRE) – Fairy Native (IRE) (Be My Native (USA)) [2016/17 h123: h16.7g h16d⁶ h15.5g⁵ h15.7s⁴ h16s² h16s* h16d h16.5g² Apr 8] rather leggy gelding: fairly useful handicap hurdler: won at Sandown (conditionals event) in February: stays 19f: acts on heavy going: tried in cheekpieces: usually races towards rear/travels strongly: has found little in the past. *Kevin Frost*   **h117**

CHILDRENS LIST (IRE) 7 b.g. Presenting – Snipe Hunt (IRE) (Stalker) [2016/17 h135: h24d c21.5d⁵ c25.4s* Dec 31] good-topped gelding: point/bumper winner: useful handicap hurdler, below best on return in 2016/17: useful form over fences: won maiden at Punchestown in December: stays 25f: acts on heavy going: open to further improvement over fences. *W. P. Mullins, Ireland*   **c138 p**
h123

CHILL FACTOR (IRE) 8 b.g. Oscar (IRE) – Glacial Princess (IRE) (Glacial Storm (USA)) [2016/17 c129, h–: c25.5g* c24d⁵ c23d² Feb 5] winning hurdler: useful form over fences: won handicap at Fontwell (by ½ length from Saint Roque) early in season: second in similar event at Taunton (2½ lengths behind Abracadabra Sivola) in February: stays 3¼m: acts on soft and good to firm going: has worn headgear: wears tongue tie: usually races prominently. *Anthony Honeyball*   **c137**
h–

CHILLI FILLI 4 ch.f. Presenting – Daprika (FR) (Epervier Bleu) [2016/17 b16.7g Mar 25] £34,000 3-y-o: sister to bumper winner/fairly useful hurdler Fabrika (21f winner) and half-sister to bumper winner Chasing Aces (by Definite Article): dam, French 17f chase winner (also 11f winner on Flat), half-sister to high-class hurdler/smart chaser (stayed 2½m) Geos: needed experience when well beaten in maiden bumper: should do better. *Henry Daly*   **b– p**

CHILL (IRE) 9 b.g. Diamond Green (FR) – Time To Relax (IRE) (Orpen (USA)) [2016/17 c–, h–: h20.5g⁶ May 8] fairly useful hurdler at best, below form since 2014/15: maiden chaser: stays 2½m: wears headgear: has worn tongue tie, including in 2016/17: often races prominently: temperament under suspicion. *Zoe Davison*   **c–**
h–

CHILLI ROMANCE (IRE) 6 b.m. Flemensfirth (USA) – Blue Romance (IRE) (Bob Back (USA)) [2016/17 h89: h16g⁶ h16.3g² h16.7v² h19.7s h16v⁴ h15.8s⁵ h20.3sᵖᵘ Mar 20] modest maiden hurdler: unproven beyond 17f: acts on heavy going: often in hood: tried in tongue tie. *Fergal O'Brien*   **h95**

CHILLY MISS 8 b.m. Iceman – Fairlie (Halling (USA)) [2016/17 h110: h20.6g³ h16.2d³ h20.1d³ Jun 11] fair handicap hurdler: unproven beyond 17f: acts on good to firm and good to soft going. *Malcolm Jefferson*   **h104**

CHINA GREY (FR) 5 gr.m. Slickly (FR) – Dona Bella (FR) (Highest Honor (FR)) [2016/17 b15.8d b16.4s h15.7vᵖᵘ Dec 11] £80,000 3-y-o: has scope: sister to 2 winners, including useful hurdler/fairly useful chaser Olofi (2m-23f winner), and half-sister to 2 winners in France, including hurdler/chaser Dayde (17f/2¼m winner, by Vettori): dam useful French 10.5f/13.5f winner: well held in bumpers: pulled up in mares maiden on hurdling debut: in tongue tie last 2 starts. *Jonjo O'Neill*   **h–**
b–

CHINATOWN BOY (IRE) 9 ch.g. Presenting – Asian Maze (IRE) (Anshan) [2016/17   **c–** c118, h–: h21.4s^{pu} Mar 1] well-made gelding: point winner: fair maiden hurdler, pulled up **h–** sole outing in 2016/17: twice-raced chaser: stays 25f: acts on soft and good to firm going: tried in cheekpieces. *Charles Whittaker*

CHITA'S GAMBLE 7 gr.m. Proclamation (IRE) – Chita's Flight (Busy Flight) [2016/17   **h–** h20g h21.6d h16.3v h20g^{pu} Jul 21] no form, including in points: in hood last 4 starts. *Caroline Keevil*

CHITU (IRE) 7 b.g. Desert King (IRE) – Polly's Joy (IRE) (Oscar (IRE)) [2016/17 h112,   **c132** b101: h20m h19.5g h17s h16s* c19.9g³ c20s² c15.5d* Apr 21] bumper winner: fairly **h126** useful form over hurdles: won handicap at Kilbeggan early in season: useful form over fences: won novice handicap at Ayr (by length from Fair Loch) in April: left Stuart Crawford after sixth start: stays 2½m: acts on soft going: tried in cheekpieces: has worn tongue tie, including final start: often travels strongly. *Patrick Griffin, Ireland*

CHIVERS (IRE) 6 b.g. Duke of Marmalade (IRE) – Thara (USA) (Hennessy (USA))   **h89** [2016/17 h15.9g^{pu} h15.3s⁴ h15.5v³ h19.1v h15.3s h15.9s Mar 13] modest maiden hurdler: unproven beyond 17f: acts on heavy going: has worn cheekpieces, including in 2016/17. *Daniel Steele*

CHLOE'S IMAGE 7 b.m. Lucky Story (USA) – Iwunder (IRE) (King's Best (USA))   **h–** [2016/17 h21.3g Oct 28] good-topped mare: modest on Flat, stays 1¾m: no form over hurdles. *Philip Kirby*

CHOCALA (IRE) 7 b.g. Rock of Gibraltar (IRE) – Arbella (Primo Dominie) [2016/17   **h126** h20.5d² h19.8d² h16s³ Jan 7] compact gelding: useful on Flat, stays 2m: fairly useful form over hurdles: second in novice at Newbury in November: stays 21f: acts on good to soft going. *Alan King*

CHOIX DES ARMES (FR) 5 b.g. Saint des Saints (FR) – Kicka (Shirley Heights)   **b–** [2016/17 b15.7d Nov 19] good-topped gelding: 4/1, seventh in bumper at Ascot (23½ lengths behind King of Realms) in November. *Paul Nicholls*

CHOOCHOOBUGALOO 5 b.m. Rail Link – Charmante Femme (Bin Ajwaad (IRE))   **h–** [2016/17 b–: b16.3g h15.3d^{pu} h15.3d h15.3s Dec 26] lengthy, rather unfurnished mare: no **b–** form in bumpers/over hurdles: often races towards rear. *Laura Young*

CHORAL BEE 8 b.m. Oratorio (IRE) – Chief Bee (Chief's Crown (USA)) [2016/17 h–:   **h–** h21.6d⁴ h20d h16.7g h21.6g^{pu} Apr 12] little form over hurdles: in cheekpieces last 3 starts: has worn tongue tie, including in 2016/17. *Alan Jessop*

CHORLTON HOUSE 5 ch.g. Compton Place – Really Ransom (Red Ransom (USA))   **h85** [2016/17 h–: h16g h15.8g⁴ h16d h15.8g Sep 7] smallish gelding: fair on Flat, stays 1¼m: modest form over hurdles: raced only at 2m: in cheekpieces last 2 starts: usually races towards rear. *Ian Williams*

CHORUS OF LIES 5 b.g. Teofilo (IRE) – Cherry Orchard (IRE) (King's Best (USA))   **h100** [2016/17 h16.2m² h16.4d⁶ h16.2s⁴ h15.7d⁴ Jan 1] modest maiden on Flat, stays 1¾m: fair form over hurdles. *Tracy Waggott*

CHOSEN ROSE (IRE) 5 b.m. Well Chosen – Ambermaryrose (IRE) (Cape Cross (IRE))   **b–** [2016/17 b17.7d Oct 19] £8,000 4-y-o: third foal: dam (b68) lightly raced in bumpers/on Flat: maiden Irish pointer: tailed off in mares bumper. *Sarah Humphrey*

CHOSEN TRIBE (IRE) 5 ch.g. Stowaway – Native Kin (IRE) (Be My Native (USA))   **h106** [2016/17 h21m⁴ h22g⁶ h22g² Apr 23] £6,000 4-y-o: half-brother to 3 winners, including useful chaser Smiles For Miles (2¾m-3m winner, by Oscar) and fairly useful hurdler/ winning pointer Doitforjoe (3m winner, by Vinnie Roe): dam (h101), 2m hurdle winner, half-sister to fairly useful hurdler/chaser (stayed 2¾m) Kickham and fairly useful chaser (stayed 2½m) Knocknagow Leader: placed in Irish maiden point: fair form over hurdles: best effort when second in novice at Stratford in April: left Charlie Mann after second start. *Henry Oliver*

CHOWDER (IRE) 7 br.g. Craigsteel – Little And Often (IRE) (Roselier (FR)) [2016/17   **h–** h20d^{pu} Oct 20] maiden pointer: pulled up in novice on hurdling debut. *Victor Thompson*

CHRISTMAS IN APRIL (FR) 5 b.g. Crillon (FR) – Similaresisoldofa (FR) (Kapgarde   **h105 p** (FR)) [2016/17 b16.7d* h20g⁴ h16.3d³ h15.8d⁵ Mar 15] €60,000 3-y-o: good-topped **b87** gelding: first foal: dam, lightly raced over hurdles/fences in France, half-sister to fairly useful hurdler/chaser (2m winner) All You Need (by Crillon): won bumper at Market Rasen (by 7 lengths from Mortens Leam) early in season: fair form over hurdles: in hood, best effort when fifth in maiden at Huntingdon in March: open to further improvement. *Nicky Henderson*

Betfair Price Rush Hurdle, Haydock—Ch'Tibello lowers the colours of My Tent Or Yours (hoops) in a tactical affair; 2014 and 2015 third Melodic Rendezvous (blinkers) goes one place better this time

CHRISTMAS IN USA (FR) 5 b.g. Shaanmer (IRE) – Diamond of Diana (FR) (Kapgarde (FR)) [2016/17 h20.2m⁵ h22.7s h16.4s⁵ h16sᶠ h20.5vᵖᵘ h18.1s⁴ h16.2g Apr 27] first foal: dam unraced sister to fairly useful French 2¼m hurdle winner Boston Paris: runner-up on completed start in points: fair maiden hurdler for Guillaume Macaire in 2015/16, below that level in 2016/17: twice-raced chaser: probably stays 2¼m: acts on heavy going: tried in hood: wears tongue tie: often races towards rear. *N. W. Alexander* — c– h94

CHRISTMAS TWENTY (IRE) 7 br.g. Zagreb (USA) – Celestial Gale (IRE) (Presenting) [2016/17 h111, b72: h21g c15.9sᵖᵘ c21.6sᵘʳ c21.1g⁶ c21.3gᵖᵘ Apr 23] angular gelding: maiden Irish pointer: fair maiden hurdler, below form on return in 2016/17: little impact over fences: left Stuart Edmunds after first start: usually wears headgear. *Micky Hammond* — c– h–

CHTI BALKO (FR) 5 br.g. Balko (FR) – Ina Scoop (FR) (Murmure (FR)) [2016/17 b13.7d⁵ h16.6d³ h15.7s* h15.7v* h16.5g Apr 7] £25,000 4-y-o: angular gelding: fourth foal: dam French maiden half-sister to dam of useful hurdler/very smart chaser (stayed 2½m) Arzal: third in Irish maiden point on debut: poor form in maiden bumper: fairly useful form over hurdles: won maiden at Catterick in February and novice at Haydock in March: front runner/races prominently. *Donald McCain* — h120 b74

CH'TIBELLO (FR) 6 b.g. Sageburg (IRE) – Neicha (FR) (Neverneyev (USA)) [2016/17 h139p: h15.7m³ h15.7m⁵ h16.2v* h16g³ h15.3d² Feb 18] useful-looking gelding: smart hurdler: won minor event at Haydock (by 2¼ lengths from Melodic Rendezvous) in November: placed in Christmas Hurdle at Kempton (5½ lengths behind Yanworth) in December and Kingwell Hurdle at Wincanton (length behind Yanworth) in February: raced around 2m: acts on good to firm and heavy going: usually races nearer last than first, often travels strongly. *Dan Skelton* — h150

CHU CHU PERCY 6 b.g. Tobougg (IRE) – First Katoune (FR) (Poliglote) [2016/17 b18s h20.1sᵖᵘ h22s h22.7s⁵ Dec 29] winning pointer: poor form in bumpers/over hurdles: left W. Harney after first start: in headgear last 2 starts: tried in tongue tie. *Alistair Whillans* — h61 b66

CHURCH FIELD (IRE) 9 b.g. Heron Island (IRE) – Dante's Thatch (IRE) (Phardante (FR)) [2016/17 c–, h117: h21g² h21d⁵ h20d⁵ h24d⁵ h21.6g⁵ Aug 25] workmanlike gelding: fair handicap hurdler: once-raced chaser: stays 23f: acts on good to firm and heavy going: wears headgear: in tongue tie last 5 starts: front runner/races prominently. *Phil Middleton* — c– h113

CHURCH HALL (IRE) 9 b.g. Craigsteel – Island Religion (IRE) (Religiously (USA)) [2016/17 h90: h24.4g⁴ Nov 25] workmanlike gelding: fairly useful handicap hurdler at best, raced too freely sole outing in 2016/17: stays 3m: acts on soft going: tried in tongue tie. *Emma Baker* — h102

CHURCH LEAP (IRE) 6 gr.g. High Chaparral (IRE) – Alambic (Cozzene (USA)) [2016/17 h108p: h16s⁶ Mar 10] tall, useful-looking gelding: useful bumper winner: fair form over hurdles, excuses sole outing in 2016/17. *Patrick Chamings* h–

CHURCHTOWN CHAMP (IRE) 7 b.g. Robin des Champs (FR) – Annagh Lady (IRE) (Dr Massini (IRE)) [2016/17 h122, b93: c23g² c24d* c24g⁵ Dec 26] strong gelding: winning hurdler: useful form over fences: won novice handicap at Southwell in November: stayed 3m: acted on heavy going: tongue tied last 3 starts: dead. *Dan Skelton* c140 h–

CIAO CIELO (GER) 5 br.g. Lord of England (GER) – Celebration Night (IRE) (Hawk Wing (USA)) [2016/17 h16g² h17.2m³ h16g h16g⁶ Apr 21] fairly useful at best on Flat, stays 1m: modest form over hurdles: raced around 2m: best form on good going: tried in hood/tongue tie: front runner/races prominently, often races freely. *Mark McNiff, Ireland* h98

CIBOIR (FR) 5 gr.g. Fragrant Mix (IRE) – Fleche Noir II (FR) (Quart de Vin (FR)) [2016/17 b16.7d Apr 27] in hood, 66/1, looked ungenuine when well held in bumper. *Nick Kent* b–

CICERON (IRE) 11 b.g. Pivotal – Aiglonne (USA) (Silver Hawk (USA)) [2016/17 c87, h–: c19.3g² c20.3g² c23.8dᵖᵘ c17.2g* c17.2g² c19.2g c21.1dᵖᵘ h18.6g h16g h16.8g⁵ Oct 18] tall gelding: useful handicap hurdler at best, well below form in 2016/17: fair handicap chaser nowadays: won at Market Rasen early in season: stays 2½m: acts on heavy going: usually in headgear: wears tongue tie: unreliable. *Neil King* c107 § h88 §

CIGARISI (IRE) 5 b.g. Kalanisi (IRE) – Eileens Dream (IRE) (Oscar (IRE)) [2016/17 b15.7d⁴ h16.5g⁵ h16.8s³ h15.9v* h16.5g⁶ Mar 30] €17,000 3-y-o: lengthy gelding: second foal: half-brother to a winning pointer by Alflora: dam unraced: fourth in bumper at Ascot: fair form over hurdles: won maiden at Plumpton in February: will stay 2½m: acts on heavy ground: races prominently. *Philip Hobbs* h112 b88

CILAOS EMERY (FR) 5 b.g. Califet (FR) – Queissa (FR) (Saint Preuil (FR)) [2016/17 b104+: b16d* h16s* h16s² h16.4g⁵ h16.5d* Apr 25] h144 b102

The long-running American musical 42nd Street tells the story of chorus girl Peggy Sawyer who is thrust into the spotlight; but the M9 in County Carlow is the thoroughfare down which racing's followers are most likely to come across the unheralded understudy. For that is where Willie Mullins' Closutton Stables are located, the source of a number of winners who emerged from the shadows of better-fancied stablemates to win high-profile races in 2016/17. The County Hurdle winner Arctic Fire, ridden by Paul Townend, was at longer odds than stable jockey Ruby Walsh's mount Renneti at the Cheltenham Festival, but there were much more notable examples at the Punchestown Festival five weeks later. Wicklow Brave, ridden by the trainer's son Patrick, won the Punchestown Champion Hurdle, with 6/4 favourite Vroum Vroum Mag only seventh, and Bacardys was a 10/1 winner of the Champion Novices' Hurdle, with stablemate Let's Dance (3/1) a well-beaten fourth. The most startling example, though, from the five-day festival, was the success of Cilaos Emery who beat his much better fancied stablemate Melon into second when winning the similarly-titled—but half a mile shorter—Champion Novices' Hurdle on the opening day of the meeting.

Cilaos Emery made a successful debut on his only start in bumpers, winning the final race on the first day of the 2016 Punchestown Festival (which took place shortly after the beginning of the 2016/17 British season), and he again accounted for a big field when winning a twenty-four-runner maiden hurdle on his reappearance at Navan in December, a race won the previous season by the smart Anibale Fly. The runner-up to Cilaos Emery, Joey Sasa, went on to finish second in a Grade 2 at Naas in February, while the fifth Showem Silver made the frame in a competitive staying handicap at Punchestown, and Cilaos Emery confirmed the good impression he had made when improving again, despite being beaten at 9/4-on, when a neck second to Mick Jazz in a seven-runner listed novice hurdle at Punchestown in February. All seven of the runners had either won or shaped well last time out and the form of the pair that came clear was viewed in a positive light. Unfortunately, the winner Mick Jazz wasn't seen afterwards, suffering an eleventh-hour injury when a leading fancy for the County Hurdle. Cilaos Emery's own Cheltenham Festival date came three days earlier, in the very first race of the meeting the Supreme Novices' Hurdle, in which he was a respectable fifth to the Gordon Elliott-trained Labaik. Sporting a hood for the first time, Cilaos Emery led from the flag and possibly had too much use

Herald Champion Novices' Hurdle, Punchestown—mid-race exertions take their toll on Melon (checks), who is unable to hold off lesser-fancied stable-companion Cilaos Emery

made of him, eventually beaten around sixteen lengths after being headed turning for home. Cilaos Emery produced a better performance—with different tactics used—when winning the Herald Champion Novices' Hurdle at Punchestown at 8/1 six weeks later. His stablemate Melon, sent off the 5/4 favourite, had found only Labaik too good in the Supreme, and his chance appeared to have been improved when Labaik refused to line up at the start. As discussed in Labaik's essay, his rivals' jockeys did Labaik no favours by approaching the tape early so that the runners had to be sent back to take a turn. However, in the race itself, Melon and Pingshou took each other on from halfway, leaving themselves vulnerable to a strong finisher, unintentionally playing into the hands of jockey David Mullins who employed much more patient tactics on Cilaos Emery than at Cheltenham. Having restrained Cilaos Emery when the two 'big guns' went on, Mullins produced him to challenge before the last, where he wasn't fluent but still had enough to beat Melon by a length, with Pingshou three and a quarter further back in third. The winning performance was a clear career best for Cilaos Emery, though not in the same league as those of the race's three most recent winners Don't Touch It, Douvan and Faugheen, and 20 lb below the rating achieved in the race by Jezki in 2013.

Cilaos Emery (FR) (b.g. 2012)	Califet (FR) (b 1998)	Freedom Cry (b 1991)	Soviet Star
			Falling Star
		Sally's Room (b 1991)	Kendor
			Square Room
	Queissa (FR) (gr 2004)	Saint Preuil (gr 1991)	Dom Pasquini
			Montecha
		Fleurissa (b 1993)	Dress Parade
			Pontiany

Cilaos Emery is owned by the bookmaker Luke McMahon, whose family has had horses with Willie Mullins for years; McMahon's son Aubrey had a handful of rides as an amateur while working for Mullins in 2014, recording two bumper wins on Rio Treasure. The family's horses include 2011 Baring Bingham third So Young, the dual La Touche Cup winner Uncle Junior, and 2016 Clonmel Oil Chase winner Alelchi Inois. While that trio are in the autumn of their careers or retired (Uncle Junior had his final start in April 2016 aged fifteen), as well as Cilaos Emery, McMahon has the year-older Bleu Berry to look forward to in the coming seasons. Bleu Berry won three races in 2016/17, including the listed Kingsfurze

Luke McMahon's "Cilaos Emery"

Novices' Hurdle at Naas in March and the Grade 2 Rathbarry Glenview Studs
Novices' Hurdle at Fairyhouse in April. Like Bleu Berry, Cilaos Emery is French-
bred, a son of Califet picked up for just €7,200 as a foal at Tattersalls Ireland in
2012. Since then, Califet, who was fourth in the 2002 Prix de l'Arc de Triomphe
when trained by Guy Cherel, has moved from Haras du Chene Vert in France to
Boardsmill Stud in Ireland, his fee doubling to €6,000 since 2014; he has been fully
booked since standing in Ireland, the exploits of the fellow Cherel-trained Blue
Dragon—France's highest-rated hurdler whose career has been covered in full in the
'Top Horses In France' section—no doubt going a long way to ensuring his ongoing
popularity. Clarcam, winner of the Racing Post Novices' Chase at Leopardstown and
the Manifesto at Aintree, and Ziga Boy, winner of the Sky Bet Chase at Doncaster in
January for the second time, have been important winners in Britain and Ireland for
Califet, especially as the likes of Analifet, Adrien du Pont and Calipto, who were all
high-profile examples of promising young horses by the same sire, didn't keep their
form. Cilaos Emery is the third foal out of Queissa, a maiden half-sister to the fairly
useful Venetia Williams-trained staying chaser Rydalis, and is a half-brother to the
French bumper winner Berry Emery (by Racinger). The sire of Queissa, Saint Preuil,
is the sire of the high-class chaser of a few years ago, My Will, and is also the sire
of the dam of Alpha des Obeaux. Though Cilaos Emery is a strong traveller who has
only raced over two miles to date, he shapes as if he will stay two and a half miles.
He wore a hood on his last two starts. *W. P. Mullins, Ireland*

CILLIAN'S WELL (IRE) 7 b.g. Trans Island – Live A Lot (IRE) (Saddlers' Hall (IRE)) **h98**
[2016/17 h16.5g h16g h16g⁵ h16.6g h16d⁴ h16g h16g h19.5g Apr 17] first foal: dam (h89)
winning pointer: modest handicap hurdler: won maiden at Tramore in 2015/16: left Miss
Elizabeth Doyle after seventh start: raced mainly around 2m: acts on good to soft going:
usually wears headgear: tried in tongue tie. *John Flint*

202

CINDER RUA (IRE) 10 ch.m. Carroll House – Scree (IRE) (Broken Hearted) [2016/17 **c–** c101, h102: c21.2m^{pu} h16d c20d h24.3s^{pu} c16.2s^6 h20v h19.5s Mar 17] fair hurdler/chaser **h–** at best, no form in 2016/17: tried in headgear. *Miss Nicole McKenna, Ireland*

CIRANO DE SIVOLA (FR) 5 gr.g. Vendangeur (IRE) – Wild Rose Bloom (FR) **h96** (Kaldounevees (FR)) [2016/17 b16s^2 b16s* h18.7g^3 Mar 25] £60,000 4-y-o: third foal: **b95** half-brother to useful French hurdler/chaser Attila de Sivola (17f-21f winner, by Kapgarde): dam unraced: winning pointer: fairly useful form in bumpers: in hood, won at Warwick in January: 5/6, third in maiden at Stratford (6¾ lengths behind Cornish Warrior) on hurdling debut. *Warren Greatrex*

CIRCUS CLOWN (IRE) 12 b.g. Vettori (IRE) – Comic (IRE) (Be My Chief (USA)) **c–** [2016/17 h17.2g h22.1d^{pu} Aug 29] fair hurdler at best, no form in 2016/17: maiden chaser: **h–** stays 2¾m: acts on heavy going: has worn headgear, including in 2016/17: lazy. *Andrew Hamilton*

CIRCUS STAR (USA) 9 b.g. Borrego (USA) – Picadilly Circus (USA) (Fantastic Fellow **h96** (USA)) [2016/17 h105: h16.2d^{pu} h19.7s^3 h16d^4 h16.4s^{pu} h16v^{pu} Mar 10] tall gelding: fair handicap hurdler, below best in 2016/17: best at 2m: acted on heavy going: tried in tongue tie: front runner/raced prominently: dead. *John Dixon*

CITADEL 4 ch.g. Haafhd – Preference (Efisio) [2016/17 h16.3m^{pu} Jul 10] poor maiden on **h–** Flat: in cheekpieces, pulled up in juvenile on hurdling debut. *John Wainright*

CITADEL (FR) 5 b.g. Al Namix (FR) – Oreli (FR) (Robin des Pres (FR)) [2016/17 h19.1d **c–** h17.7g^5 h15.9g h25s^{pu} c19.7s^{pu} c25.7s^{pu} c17g^{pu} Mar 27] little form over hurdles, including **h–** for Francois Nicolle in 2015/16: pulled up all 3 starts over fences: tried in tongue tie. *Diana Grissell*

CITRUS (FR) 5 b.g. Great Pretender (IRE) – Kelle Home (FR) (Useful (FR)) [2016/17 **h96** b11.4g^2 h20g^{pu} h19.5d^6 h16.4m^4 h15.9d* h19.8d^6 h19g h19.7d^5 h15.8v Mar 19] **b–** lengthy gelding: sixth foal: half-brother to 3 winners, including bumper winner/fairly useful hurdler Aniknam (2m winner, by Nickname), stays 2½m, and French 21f cross-country chase winner Veilleur (by Maximum Security): dam unraced: placed in bumpers: modest hurdler: won novice at Plumpton in November: left A. Lefeuvre after first start: best around 2m: acts on good to soft going: has worn headgear, including last 3 starts: wears tongue tie: weak finisher. *David Pipe*

CITY DREAMS (IRE) 7 b.m. Rakti – Attymon Lill (IRE) (Marju (IRE)) [2016/17 h66: **h–** h18.7d^{bd} Jun 14] twice-raced hurdler, fatally injured sole outing in 2016/17. *Philip Kirby*

CITY NEVER SLEEPS (IRE) 5 b.g. Central Park (IRE) – Goodnightmrskelly (IRE) **h98** (Bigstone (IRE)) [2016/17 h16.3g^3 h16.4g h16d h16.5g h16.8g^{pu} h19g h19.2s^2 Mar 16] **b75** €10,000 3-y-o: rather unfurnished gelding: first foal: dam (h72) lightly raced: modest form in bumpers/over hurdles: left S. Curling after first start: stays 19f: acts on soft going: in headgear last 5 starts. *Martin Keighley*

CITY SUPREME (IRE) 7 b.g. Milan – Run Supreme (IRE) (Supreme Leader) [2016/17 **c117** h111: h23.9g h24.4g^3 h21.6d^3 h26s^4 h25v^2 c19.7v* c25.5d^4 h22.8g Apr 15] good-topped **h115** gelding: fairly useful handicap hurdler: placed in conditionals events at Ascot in December and Plumpton in January: fairly useful form over fences: won novice handicap at Plumpton in February: stays 3¼m: acts on heavy going: often wears headgear/tongue tie. *Anthony Honeyball*

CIVIL UNREST (IRE) 11 ch.g. Blueprint (IRE) – Yore (IRE) (Ore) [2016/17 c–x, h–: **c107 x** c15.6d h15.8g^3 h19.6d^3 h16.2d^3 c15.6g* h15.6g^6 h19.3g^5 c19.9g^3 h16.4g* h20.6g^5 **h102** h16.8m* Apr 19] fair handicap hurdler: won at Musselburgh in March and Sedgefield in April: fair handicap chaser: won at Hexham in October: stays 2½m: acts on soft and good to firm going: wears headgear: usually races close up: often let down by jumping over fences. *James Ewart*

CIVIL WAR (IRE) 8 b.g. Scorpion (IRE) – Silvestre (ITY) (Unfuwain (USA)) [2016/17 **h65** h19.1g^4 h15.8m^{pu} Oct 11] fair maiden hurdler, below form both outings in 2016/17: should stay 19f: best form on soft/heavy going: in visor last 4 starts. *Gary Moore*

CIVITESSES (FR) 5 b.m. Prince Kirk (FR) – Glenn Rose (FR) (Scooter Bleu (IRE)) **h75** [2016/17 b16.2s ab16g h16.8d^6 h15.3s h21s^3 h21.6m^5 h23.9m^4 h21.6g^6 Apr 26] €9,000 **b–** 3-y-o: half-sister to useful French hurdler/fairly useful chaser Ultimiste (2¼m/19f winner, by Assessor): dam unraced: maiden Irish pointer: no form in bumpers: poor form over hurdles: stays 2¾m: acts on soft and good to firm going: in blinkers last 3 starts. *Brian Barr*

CKALCO DES LOGES (FR) 5 b.g. Balko (FR) – Olla des Loges (FR) (Sleeping Car **h120** (FR)) [2016/17 h16d³ h19.3d² h20d² h16s* h21.2g⁴ Apr 3] second foal: dam French 21f/2¾m cross-country chase winner: won maiden point on debut: fairly useful form over hurdles: won maiden at Chepstow in March: should stay beyond 2½m: acts on soft going: in tongue tie last 3 starts. *Dan Skelton*

CLAIMANTAKINFORGAN (FR) 5 b.g. Great Pretender (IRE) – Taquine d'Estrees **b115** (FR) (Take Risks (FR)) [2016/17 b15.7v* b15.7d⁶ b16.6g² b16.4g³ b17g⁵ Apr 7] £18,000 3-y-o, £110,000 4-y-o: good-topped gelding: eighth foal: dam maiden on Flat in France: Irish point winner: smart bumper performer: won at Haydock in November: second at Doncaster (2¼ lengths behind Black Op) in February and third in Champion Bumper at Cheltenham (2¾ lengths behind Fayonagh) in March: will stay at least 2½m. *Nicky Henderson*

CLAIRE PET (IRE) 10 b.g. Pierre – Babs Girld (IRE) (Cataldi) [2016/17 c–, h100: **c–** h22mᵖᵘ Jul 17] runner-up on second of 2 completed starts in points: fair hurdler at best, **h–** pulled up sole outing in 2016/17: twice-raced chaser: stays 3m: acts on heavy going: tried in hood. *Dr Richard Newland*

CLAN CHIEF 8 ch.g. Generous (IRE) – Harrietfield (Nicholas Bill) [2016/17 c91x, h97: **c77 x** c15.6vᵖᵘ c15.5s⁴ c16.4sᵖᵘ c17.1d⁵ Apr 10] winning hurdler: poor maiden chaser: unproven **h–** beyond 17f: acts on heavy going: has worn hood/tongue tie, including in 2016/17: often let down by jumping over fences. *N. W. Alexander*

CLANCY'S CROSS (IRE) 8 b.g. Oscar (IRE) – Murphy's Lady (IRE) (Over The River **c–** (FR)) [2016/17 h110: c24.2gᵖᵘ c24d⁵ h25.5vᵖᵘ h25.3s⁶ h22.8v⁴ Mar 22] fair hurdler at best, **h–** no form in 2016/17, including 2 starts over fences: has worn cheekpieces: tried in tongue tie. *Kevin Frost*

CLAN DES OBEAUX (FR) 5 b.g. Kapgarde (FR) – Nausicaa des Obeaux (FR) (April **c148** Night (FR)) [2016/17 h141p: c19.4g⁴ c19.9g* c20.8s² c20v⁵ c19.2d* c20.5g⁴ Apr 22] **h–** well-made gelding: winning hurdler: smart form over fences: won Fuller's London Pride Novices' Chase (Berkshire) at Newbury (by 10 lengths from Virgilio) in November and novice at Exeter (by 11 lengths from Drumlee Sunset) in March: second in Dipper Novices' Chase at Cheltenham (½ length behind Whisper) in January: stays 21f: acts on heavy going: tried in tongue tie: often travels strongly. *Paul Nicholls*

CLAN LEGEND 7 ch.g. Midnight Legend – Harrietfield (Nicholas Bill) [2016/17 h113: **c122** c15.6v* c15.5v⁵ c16.3v³ c17.1v* c20.6v⁴ Mar 22] winning hurdler: fairly useful form over **h–** fences: won novice handicaps at Hexham in December and Kelso in March: stays 2¼m: best form on heavy going: in tongue tie last 2 starts: usually leads. *N. W. Alexander*

CLANVILLE LASS 5 b.m. Tobougg (IRE) – Mulberry Wine (Benny The Dip (USA)) **h–** [2016/17 b74: b15.8d h16.8d Jun 10] compact mare: poor form at best in bumpers: tailed **b–** off in mares novice on hurdling debut. *Ali Stronge*

CLARAGH NATIVE (IRE) 12 ch.g. Beneficial – Susy In The Summer (IRE) (Be My **c93 §** Native (USA)) [2016/17 c111§, h–§: c19.3d⁴ h17m⁵ c17.3m c16d⁵ Jun 30] smallish, leggy **h87 §** gelding: fair handicap hurdler/chaser at best, below form in 2016/17: stays 21f: acts on soft and good to firm going: has worn cheekpieces, including in 2016/17: has worn tongue tie: unreliable. *Martin Todhunter*

CLARA PEGGOTTY 10 b.m. Beat All (USA) – Clair Valley (Ardross) [2016/17 c–, **c–** h85§: h23.3m³ h24d³ h20.3d⁶ h23.1sᵖᵘ Dec 22] poor maiden hurdler nowadays: twice- **h79 §** raced chaser: stays 23f: best form on soft/heavy going: wears cheekpieces: front runner/ races prominently: one to treat with caution. *Tom Gretton*

CLARCAM (FR) 7 b.g. Califet (FR) – Rose Beryl (FR) (Lost World (IRE)) [2016/17 **c152** c156, h–: c16d⁵ c20.5m* h20g* h20s² c22.5g⁵ c22.5g² c24v c25g⁵ c20d² h20s c21v³ c21g **h129 +** c25d c20.4v* c20v² c16v⁶ c25g c21.1g c29d Apr 17] good-topped gelding: fairly useful hurdler nowadays: won minor event at Down Royal in June: smart chaser: won Grade 3 event at Killarney (by 2¼ lengths from The Game Changer) early in season and minor event at Clonmel (by 2 lengths from Val de Ferbet) in February: second in Clonmel Oil Chase (5 lengths behind Alelchi Inois) in November and Red Mills Chase at Gowran (4¼ lengths behind Ballycasey) in February: stays 2¾m: acts on good to firm and heavy going: wears headgear/tongue tie. *Gordon Elliott, Ireland*

CLASSICAL MILANO (IRE) 6 b.g. Milan – Miss Baden (IRE) (Supreme Leader) **h104** [2016/17 h17d h19.3g⁴ h23.3g* Apr 25] €120,000 3-y-o, €4,500 6-y-o: second foal: closely related to a winning pointer by Kayf Tara: dam, unraced, out of sister to high-class chaser (stayed 21f) Thisthatandtother and half-sister to top-class staying chaser Carlingford Lough: in frame completed start in maiden points: fair form over hurdles: won maiden at Hexham in April. *George Bewley*

CLASSICAL SOUND (IRE) 5 b.g. Mahler – Sovienne (IRE) (Soviet Star (USA)) **h71**
[2016/17 h16s h16.2v^pu h16.2v^f h15.7s^F h23.8g h20.6g^pu Apr 8] poor form over hurdles. *Rose Dobbin*

CLASSIC COLORI (IRE) 10 b.g. Le Vie dei Colori – Beryl (Bering) [2016/17 h–: **h–**
h16.2d^5 h18.7m^pu h16.8m^pu Aug 31] fair hurdler at best, no form since 2014/15: often in headgear nowadays. *Martin Keighley*

CLASSICO DAIS (FR) 5 br.g. Al Namix (FR) – Fabema (FR) (Pure Hasard (FR)) **h99**
[2016/17 h20.5d h18.8d h20.5d h25.6s^5 h24d^2 Feb 26] rangy, raw-boned gelding: fourth foal: dam 15f-21f hurdle/chase winner: modest form over hurdles: best effort at 3m: acts on good to soft going: in cheekpieces last 2 starts. *Dan Skelton*

CLASSIC PALACE (IRE) 8 b.m. Classic Cliche (IRE) – Winconjon (IRE) (Oscar **c–**
(IRE)) [2016/17 c–, h96: c16.5g^6 Jul 12] winning pointer: fairly useful hurdler: little **h–**
impact in 2 starts over fences: stays 23f: acts on good to firm going: tried in cheekpieces/ tongue tie. *Patrick Griffin, Ireland*

CLASSIC TUNE 7 b.g. Scorpion (IRE) – Classic Fantasy (Classic Cliche (IRE)) [2016/17 **h114**
h105, b86: h21s h16.6s^5 h19.9s* Apr 1] fair form over hurdles: won handicap at Uttoxeter in April. *Claire Dyson*

CLASSI MASSINI 6 b.m. Dr Massini (IRE) – Classi Maureen (Among Men (USA)) **h90**
[2016/17 b–: b15.8m^5 b16.3m^5 h16.3m^5 h19.6g^2 h20.3g^5 h16d h15.8v h21.6s^pu Dec 26] modest **b79**
form in bumpers/over hurdles: stays 2½m: usually races prominently. *Peter Bowen*

CLASSINAGLASS 10 b.g. Grape Tree Road – Sounds Familiar (IRE) (Orchestra) **c93**
[2016/17 c108: c19.9g^4 c17.2g^5 Jul 16] prolific point winner: fair handicap chaser, below form both outings in 2016/17: stays 3m: acts on soft and good to firm going. *Michael Easterby*

CLASSULA 5 b.g. Sulamani (IRE) – Classic Fantasy (Classic Cliche (IRE)) [2016/17 **b–**
b14d b16s Feb 10] no form in bumpers. *Claire Dyson*

CLAUDE CARTER 13 b.g. Elmaamul (USA) – Cruz Santa (Lord Bud) [2016/17 c–, **c–**
h103: h20.2f h20.2d^4 h17.2g^3 h16.7g* h19.9g^5 h16.2d* h16.2m^5 h15.6g h19.4d h19.3g **h96**
h15.6g Jan 3] neat gelding: modest hurdler nowadays: won conditional/amateur seller at Market Rasen in August and claimer at Perth in September: fell sole outing over fences: stays 2½m: acts on good to firm and good to soft going: wears headgear: front runner/races prominently. *Alistair Whillans*

CLAYTON 8 b.g. Peintre Celebre (USA) – Blossom (Warning) [2016/17 h124: h16.3g^2 **h116**
Nov 3] lengthy gelding: fairly useful hurdler: will prove best at 2m: acts on heavy going: in tongue tie last 3 starts: usually travels strongly. *Gary Moore*

CLEAN SHEET (IRE) 8 b.g. Oscar (IRE) – High Park Lady (IRE) (Phardante (FR)) **c118**
[2016/17 h118p: c21.1g^2 c22.5d^4 c20g^4 Apr 15] tall gelding: winning pointer: winning **h–**
hurdler: fairly useful form over fences: best effort when second in novice at Fontwell in September: left Nicky Henderson after second start: stays 21f: acts on soft going. *Ben Haslam*

CLEAR SPELL (IRE) 6 b.g. Tamayuz – Beat The Rain (Beat Hollow) [2016/17 h16.2g **h– §**
h16.2g^rr Sep 6] fair on Flat, stays 13f: no form over hurdles: most temperamental (refused to race final start). *Alistair Whillans*

CLEEVE HILL LAD 9 b.g. Overbury (IRE) – Lady Prunella (IRE) (Supreme Leader) **c–**
[2016/17 h–: h19.4g c24v^pu Jun 20] maiden hurdler: little impact over fences: best effort at **h–**
21f: acts on heavy going: in headgear last 2 starts: tried in tongue tie. *David Bridgwater*

CLEMENCY 6 b.m. Halling (USA) – China Tea (USA) (High Chaparral (IRE)) [2016/17 **h106**
h110: h21d^pu h20.6g^4 h19.8d^4 h20.5g^3 h19.4g^3 Dec 29] tall, unfurnished mare: fair handicap hurdler: stays 21f: acts on heavy going. *Nicky Henderson*

CLEMENTINA (FR) 4 b.f. Walk In The Park (IRE) – Venexia (FR) (Verpone (IRE)) **b–**
[2016/17 b16.3d^6 Mar 13] first foal: dam unraced half-sister to useful French hurdler (15f-2½m winner) Malone: 6/1, needed experience when sixth in maiden bumper at Stratford. *A. J. Martin, Ireland*

*Weatherbys Stallion Book Wensleydale Juvenile Hurdle (Listed), Wetherby—
the fifth of six wins in a prolific—if curtailed—juvenile campaign for Cliffs of Dover*

CLENAGH CASTLE (IRE) 7 b.g. King's Theatre (IRE) – Orwell's Marble (IRE) **c73**
(Definite Article) [2016/17 c–, h–: c23.4d⁴ c24.2g⁵ May 24] maiden hurdler: poor form **h–**
over fences: stays 2¾m: acts on heavy going: tried in cheekpieces. *Chris Grant*

CLENI WELLS (FR) 6 b.g. Poliglote – Kailasa (FR) (R B Chesne) [2016/17 c102, h99: **c–**
h18.5g h16.8d⁵ h18.5mᵖᵘ h19g h19g² h16s* h16s³ Feb 17] fairly useful handicap hurdler: **h112**
won at Kempton (conditional) in February: maiden chaser: stays 19f: acts on soft going:
has worn headgear, including last 3 starts. *Martin Hill*

CLEVE COTTAGE 9 ch.g. Presenting – Reverse Swing (Charmer) [2016/17 h86: **c79**
h23.3v* h24.7d h21.3g h24.1d h23.3vᵖᵘ c24.2s c24.3vᵖᵘ c24v⁴ c25.6d* c24.2vᵖᵘ Mar 28] **h91**
modest handicap hurdler: won novice at Uttoxeter early in season: poor form over fences:
won novice handicap at Southwell in February: stays 3¼m: acts on heavy going: in
headgear last 5 starts: tried in tongue tie: front runner/races prominently. *Philip Kirby*

CLIC WORK (FR) 5 b.g. Network (GER) – Qape Noir (FR) (Subotica (FR)) [2016/17 **c135**
h107: h16.3m² h19.3m h16.5g* h19m³ c16.4g* c16.1g* c16g³ c16.9mᵖᵘ Apr 2] tall, useful- **h117**
looking gelding: fairly useful handicap hurdler: won at Taunton in November: useful form
over fences: won handicaps at Doncaster (novice) in December and Taunton in January:
stays 19f: acts on good to firm going: tried in hood: wears tongue tie. *Paul Nicholls*

CLIFF HOUSE (IRE) 7 b.g. Mustameet (USA) – Babble On (IRE) (Anita's Prince) **h140**
[2016/17 h134: h17m⁵ h20m² h17m² h16.1g h20v³ h16d h20v Jan 7] useful handicap
hurdler: placed at Ballinrobe and Killarney early in season and at Cork (beaten ½ length by
Emcon) in November: stays 2½m: acts on good to firm and heavy going. *John J. Walsh,
Ireland*

CLIFFS OF DOVER 4 b.g. Canford Cliffs (IRE) – Basanti (USA) (Galileo (IRE)) **h139 p**
[2016/17 h16m* h16.7g³ h15.3m* h16m* h16.4g* h16g* h16.6g* Dec 10] half-brother to
fair 2m hurdle winner Man From Seville (by Duke of Marmalade): fair maiden on Flat,
stays 1½m: useful hurdler: won juvenile maiden at Worcester in August, and completed
5-timer in handicap at Wincanton, juvenile at Kempton, handicap at Cheltenham
(conditional), Wensleydale Juvenile Hurdle at Wetherby (by 9 lengths from Nietzsche) and
Summit Juvenile Hurdle at Doncaster (by 2¾ lengths from Lord Justice) between October
and December: raced around 2m: acts on good to firm going: often travels strongly:
remains open to improvement. *Paul Nicholls*

CLIVE CLIFTON (IRE) 4 b.g. Wootton Bassett – Dearest Daisy (Forzando) [2016/17 **h81** h17.7d⁴ h16m³ h15.8m⁵ Oct 30] fair on Flat, stays 1¼m: poor form over hurdles. *Phil York*

CLOCK ON TOM 7 b.g. Trade Fair – Night Owl (Night Shift (USA)) [2016/17 h106: **h91** h16g⁶ h15.8gᵖᵘ h15.8mᵖᵘ h20s⁴ h15.5d Jan 12] compact gelding: fair handicap hurdler, below best in 2016/17: unproven beyond 2m: acts on good to soft going. *Denis Quinn*

CLOGHOUGE BOY (IRE) 7 b.g. Westerner – Back To Cloghoge (IRE) (Bob Back **b—** (USA)) [2016/17 b17g May 13] off mark in maiden points at fourth attempt: in tongue tie, tailed off in bumper. *Gillian Boanas*

CLONALIG HOUSE (IRE) 7 b.g. Rakti – Balakera (FR) (Lashkari) [2016/17 h21s **c123** h20m h16.7g h20g* h20s⁵ h19.4g* h20d⁵ h20d⁴ c17s³ c20g² Apr 16] fairly useful handicap **h115** hurdler: won at Tipperary in August and Musselburgh in November: fairly useful form over fences: better effort when second in maiden at Cork in April: stays 2½m: acts on good to soft going: wears tongue tie. *A. J. Martin, Ireland*

CLONDAW BANKER (IRE) 8 b.g. Court Cave (IRE) – Freya Alex (Makbul) [2016/17 **c118** h116: c20.2sᵖᵘ c21.1g⁶ c20.5m² Apr 18] useful-looking gelding: winning hurdler: fairly **h—** useful form over fences: best effort when second in novice handicap at Kempton in April: stays 2½m: acts on soft and good to firm going. *Nicky Henderson*

CLONDAW BISTO (IRE) 6 b.g. September Storm (GER) – Solo Venture (IRE) **h108** (Abednego) [2016/17 h102: h19.1s² h21d³ h21.4sᵖᵘ h20.5v⁶ h19.1s⁴ Feb 26] won Irish maiden point on debut: bumper winner: fair form over hurdles: stays 21f: acts on soft going. *Suzy Smith*

CLONDAW CASTLE (IRE) 5 b.g. Oscar (IRE) – Lohort Castle (IRE) (Presenting) **b105** [2016/17 b16.3d* b17g Apr 7] useful-looking gelding: fifth foal: brother to useful hurdler/ winning pointer Red Devil Boys (19f winner) and closely related to fair hurdler/chaser Kara Loca (17f-2½m winner, by Kayf Tara), stays 2¾m: dam (h76) bumper winner: won completed start in Irish maiden points: useful form in bumpers: won maiden at Stratford (by 1½ lengths from Hatcher) in March: eighth in Grade 2 at Aintree (9 lengths behind Lalor) in April. *Tom George*

CLONDAW CIAN (IRE) 7 br.g. Gold Well – Cocktail Bar (IRE) (Hubbly Bubbly **h133** (USA)) [2016/17 h124, b97: h21.1s* h26s h23.1s⁵ h24g Mar 16] lengthy gelding: point/ bumper winner: useful handicap hurdler: won at Cheltenham (by 3½ lengths from Solatentif) in November: stays 23f: best form on soft/heavy going: tried in cheekpieces. *Suzy Smith*

CLONDAW CRACKER (IRE) 6 b.g. Court Cave (IRE) – Twelve Pence (IRE) (Bob **h—** Back (USA)) [2016/17 b96: h19.7gᵖᵘ h19.3m Apr 2] good-topped gelding: won Irish maiden point on debut: bumper winner: little promise over hurdles. *Neil Mulholland*

CLONDAW DRAFT (IRE) 9 b.g. Shantou (USA) – Glen Ten (IRE) (Mandalus) **c122** [2016/17 c20.3d⁵ c20.3g* Apr 22] lengthy, useful-looking gelding: winning hurdler: fairly **h—** useful form over fences: won novice handicap at Bangor in April: stays 21f: acts on soft and good to firm going. *Donald McCain*

CLONDAW ISLAND (IRE) 9 b.g. Heron Island (IRE) – Lady Carew (IRE) (Supreme **c—** Leader) [2016/17 c19.3sꟳ Apr 28] point winner: in hood/tongue tie, weakening when fell heavily 2 out in hunter won by Play The Ace at Sedgefield on chasing debut. *Francesca Nimmo*

CLONDAW KAEMPFER (IRE) 9 b.g. Oscar (IRE) – Gra-Bri (IRE) (Rashar (USA)) **c—** [2016/17 c—, h90: h19.6v³ h20s⁴ h23.8g** h26.1g h20g Apr 7] rangy gelding: useful **h132** handicap hurdler: won at Musselburgh in January: ran twice over fences in 2014/15, would have won but for unseating last on chasing debut: stays 3m: acts on heavy going: tried in headgear: wears tongue tie: usually races prominently. *Donald McCain*

CLONDAW KNIGHT (IRE) 9 b.g. Heron Island (IRE) – Sarah Supreme (IRE) **c—** (Supreme Leader) [2016/17 c23.4sᵖᵘ Nov 26] good-topped gelding: winning pointer: **h—** lightly-raced hurdler: useful chaser at best, pulled up sole outing in 2016/17: stays 25f: acts on heavy going: in tongue tie last 2 starts. *Lucinda Russell*

CLONDAW RIGGER (IRE) 5 b.g. Stowaway – Daytona Lily (IRE) (Beneficial) **h—** [2016/17 b16.7s⁵ h25.5s⁶ h21v h21.9d⁵ Apr 16] rather unfurnished gelding: off mark in **b63** Irish maiden points at fifth attempt: fifth in bumper at Bangor: no form over hurdles. *Katy Price*

CLONDAW SHANE 5 b.g. Black Sam Bellamy (IRE) – Miss Chinchilla (Perpendicular) **h117** [2016/17 h21.4d² h19.8d⁴ h19.8v⁴ h19.5gꟳ Apr 17] runner-up in Irish maiden point: fairly useful form over hurdles: second in novice at Wincanton in November: in tongue tie last 2 starts: dead. *Philip Hobbs*

Guinness Galway Hurdle Handicap, Galway—Ruby Walsh produces
Clondaw Warrior (second right) to land the bumper prize for a syndicate of female owners,
which includes his wife Gillian

CLONDAW WARRIOR (IRE) 10 b.g. Overbury (IRE) – Thespian (IRE) (Tiraaz (USA)) [2016/17 h144: h16.1g* h24s* h24d² h24d³ h24g⁶ h24d Apr 27] lengthy gelding: smart hurdler: won Galway Hurdle (by ½ length from Hidden Cyclone) early in season and minor event at Clonmel (by 5½ lengths from Val de Ferbet) in December: placed in Christmas Hurdle at Leopardstown (1¼ lengths behind Vroum Vroum Mag) later in December and John Mulhern Galmoy Hurdle at Gowran (2¼ lengths behind Shaneshill) in January: stays 3m: acts on soft going: has worn hood, including last 5 starts: often races towards rear/travels strongly. *W. P. Mullins, Ireland*   h155

CLONDAW WESTIE (IRE) 6 b.g. Westerner – You're A Native (IRE) (Saddlers' Hall (IRE)) [2016/17 b–: h21.4s h15.9v h16v⁵ Feb 20] smallish, angular gelding: off mark in Irish maiden points at fourth attempt: no form over hurdles: wears tongue tie. *Lawney Hill*   h–

CLONUSKER (IRE) 9 b.g. Fasliyev (USA) – Tamburello (IRE) (Roi Danzig (USA)) [2016/17 h84: h15.9g⁵ h15.9v³ c17vᶠ c19.7s* c16s² c19.7s² Mar 13] good-topped gelding: poor handicap hurdler: modest form over fences: won novice handicap at Plumpton in February: stays 2½m: best form on soft/heavy going: wears tongue tie: often races prominently. *Linda Jewell*   c94   h70

CLOONACOOL (IRE) 8 b.g. Beneficial – Newhall (IRE) (Shernazar) [2016/17 c142, h131: h16.7gᶠ h15.7m h16g h16s⁴ c16.4d Jan 28] sturdy gelding: useful handicap hurdler, below form in 2016/17 after reappearance fall: useful chaser, well held final outing: stays 2½m: acts on heavy going: tried in blinkers. *Stuart Edmunds*   c–   h128

CLO SACRE (FR) 5 b.g. Network (GER) – Legende Sacree (FR) (Hawker's News (IRE)) [2016/17 b16g h19gᶠ Dec 30] runner-up on completed start in points: tailed off in bumper: fell 2 out in novice at Taunton on hurdling debut, would have finished well beaten. *Paul Nicholls*   h66   b–

CLOSE ESCAPE (IRE) 6 b.g. Robin des Pres (FR) – Music School (IRE) (Saddlers' Hall (IRE)) [2016/17 b–: h15.7g² h20.2dᵖᵘ h16.2s⁴ h15.7g Aug 31] good sort: second in Irish point on debut: modest form over hurdles: should stay further than 2m: tried in hood: temperament under suspicion. *Keith Dalgleish*   h89

CLOSE HOUSE 10 b.g. Generous (IRE) – Not Now Nellie (Saddlers' Hall (IRE)) [2016/17 c23.8g* Apr 28] tall, sparely-made gelding: winning hurdler: fair chaser nowadays: fit from points, won hunter at Perth in April: stays 3m: acts on heavy going: in headgear last 3 starts: has worn tongue tie. *Philip Kirby*   c110   h–

CLOSEST FRIEND 8 b.g. Kayf Tara – Princess of War (Warrshan (USA)) [2016/17 **c121** h115: h18.6g² c16.5g² h16.3m c16.4g³ c16.1m² c20.2mᵖᵘ Oct 14] lengthy gelding: fairly **h110** useful hurdler: fairly useful form over fences: second in novices at Huntingdon early in season and Towcester in October: should stay 2½m: acts on good to firm and good to soft going: wears tongue tie. *Dan Skelton*

CLOTH CAP (IRE) 5 b.g. Beneficial – Cloth Fair (IRE) (Old Vic) [2016/17 b16g **b94** b16.7d⁴ Apr 27] €46,000 3-y-o: first foal: dam, 2m hurdle winner (stayed 3m), half-sister to fair hurdler/fairly useful chaser (stayed 25f) Askmeroe: fair form on second of 2 starts in bumpers: bred to be suited by 2½m+. *Jonjo O'Neill*

CLOUD CREEPER (IRE) 10 b.g. Cloudings (IRE) – First of April (IRE) (Presenting) **c143** [2016/17 c146, h–: c21g³ c20g h24g⁶ Aug 14] useful-looking gelding: fairly useful **h–** hurdler at best, seemed amiss final outing: useful handicap chaser: third at Newton Abbot (5 lengths behind Art Mauresque) early in season: stays 2¾m: acts on heavy going. *Philip Hobbs*

CLOUD MONKEY (IRE) 7 b.g. Marju (IRE) – Sweet Clover (Rainbow Quest (USA)) **h100** [2016/17 h16.2m h15.8m⁴ h16.2d² h19.7g² h16g⁵ h19.3g² h19.7s⁵ h19.3g⁶ h16.4g⁶ Mar 24] fair on Flat, stays 1½m: fair maiden hurdler: stays 19f: acts on good to soft going. *Martin Todhunter*

CLOUDY BOB (IRE) 10 gr.g. Cloudings (IRE) – Keen Supreme (IRE) (Bob Back (USA)) **c121 §** [2016/17 c124, h–: c23.9gᵖᵘ c25gᵖᵘ c23.8d⁵ c20gᵖᵘ c23g c20.5d³ c24s⁶ c24g² c24m* c24m³ **h–** Apr 18] lengthy gelding: winning hurdler: fairly useful handicap chaser: won at Kempton in April: stays 3m: acts on good to firm and heavy going: unreliable. *Pat Murphy*

Act D Wagg Syndicate's "Clondaw Warrior"

CLO

CLOUDY COPPER (IRE) 10 gr.g. Cloudings (IRE) – Copper Supreme (IRE) (Supreme **c– §**
Leader) [2016/17 c130, h110: c27.2s^{ur} c23.5v^{pu} c23.5g^{pu} h19.9v^{pu} Dec 31] sturdy gelding: **h– §**
useful hurdler/chaser at best, failed to complete in 2016/17: wears headgear/tongue tie:
usually races towards rear: temperamental. *Jonjo O'Neill*

CLOUDY DREAM (IRE) 7 gr.g. Cloudings (IRE) – Run Away Dream (IRE) **c153**
(Acceglio) [2016/17 h138p, b108: c15.9d* c16.3v* c15.7s² c16.4d² c15.9g² c19.9g² **h–**
c20.5g* Apr 22]

The Cheltenham Festival is one of the success stories of British racing, but its
dominance is in danger of making the four-day meeting almost the be-all and end-all
of the jumps season. Victories there are used as a barometer of accomplishment and,
when a third successive year went by without a northern-trained winner, it revived
discussion about the overall quality of jumpers trained in the North and in Scotland
nowadays. There was plenty of harking back to thirty or forty years ago, to the
days of powerful northern yards run by such as Peter Easterby, Gordon Richards,
Jimmy FitzGerald, Arthur Stephenson and the Dickinsons (and before them Neville
Crump and Scotland's Ken Oliver). Easterby and Michael Dickinson were the last
northern-based trainers to win the trainers' championship—both won it three times
in a six-year period between 1978/9 and 1983/4—and there hasn't been a champion
jockey based in the North since the days of Ron Barry, Tommy Stack and Jonjo
O'Neill in the 'seventies.

A BHA review of the jumping game published in December 2015 pinpointed
jump racing in the North as requiring special attention and there have been several
initiatives designed to address the issue, including the Northern Lights Series for
mid-tier horses which got under way in January, comprising seventy-five qualifying
races (mostly class 4 handicaps) at fourteen northern courses which will lead to five
£25,000 finals at Carlisle in December 2017 (horses have to contest at least two
qualifiers and finish in the first eight in one of them to be eligible for the finals).
Whether this additional grassroots support will help to arrest the decline in the
number of jumpers trained at northern yards (down by twenty per cent or more since
2010) remains to be seen. An earlier initiative, the Challenger Series, also aimed
at boosting northern jumping, has been successful up to a point but not a single
winner on 'finals day' at Haydock in April hailed from a northern or Scottish yard.
Edward Gillespie, the former Cheltenham supremo who chaired the BHA's review
into jumping, ranks the initial results of the exercise at 'six out of ten', saying there
is still a 'heck of a lot of work to do before it can be hailed a success.' The grassroots
of British racing as a whole—jumping and Flat—has been earmarked to receive
£8m in additional prize money from the money generated by reforms to the betting
levy which now also applies to bookmakers based offshore who have previously
not had to pay.

Scottish-based Lucinda Russell finished eleventh in the trainers' table in
Britain (largely thanks to One For Arthur's win in the Grand National) and other
northern trainers Donald McCain, Malcolm Jefferson, Brian Ellison, Sue Smith and
Nicky Richards were all in the top thirty-five. The axis of power in the National
Hunt training ranks is certainly in the South, though Brian Ellison, whose juvenile
Nietzsche was among the horses to make the frame for the North at the Cheltenham
Festival (in the Fred Winter, a race that provided the North's last winner, Hawk High
in 2014), pointed to the fact that there were only nine British-trained winners in
all at jumping's most prestigious meeting—'These days you've got Willie Mullins
and Gordon Elliott, most trainers find it difficult to compete with them, not just
the northern trainers.' By contrast, the leading jockey in the North, Brian Hughes,
reached a century for the third year in a row and, in a campaign liberally sprinkled
with hat-tricks and four-timers, finished a very creditable second to Richard Johnson
in the championship, ending the season with one hundred and forty-four wins (he
completed his century before the end of January, two months earlier than he had
done before). Hughes says that those who believe he could be champion one day are
'getting a bit carried away', pointing to the fact that his biggest source of winners,

Jordan Electrics Ltd Future Champions Novices' Chase, Ayr—
the grey Cloudy Dream rallies to overhaul Theinval, who finishes runner-up
for the second time in under twenty-four hours

Malcolm Jefferson's Newstead Cottage Stables at Malton (which gave him thirty-six wins) houses a string of around fifty, a long way short of the numbers in the big southern yards.

Malcolm Jefferson has saddled four Cheltenham Festival winners, including landing a handicap double with Cape Tribulation and Attaglance in 2012, when both went on to win at Aintree as well, and his achievements in the latest season, particularly with young horses like Cloudy Dream, Double W's, Waiting Patiently and Mount Mews, provided a reminder, if one were needed, that there are probably more rising stars to look forward to in the northern ranks than for a few years. One For Arthur, already very smart, looks open to further improvement, while the Ellison-trained pair, the high-class Definitly Red (one of the Grand National hard-luck stories) and the smart novice chaser Forest Bihan, are among others who should continue to make their mark. The famous emerald green and yellow quartered colours of three times Grand National-winning owner Trevor Hemmings are carried by Cloudy Dream and Mount Mews, both 'typical of the very nice unraced types that Trevor is sending us now,' according to Jefferson. The Hemmings success stories have tended to come from staying chasers but in Cloudy Dream and Mount Mews he has a couple of good prospects capable of making their names over shorter distances.

Cloudy Dream has been brought along steadily, showing fair form in bumpers (winning twice) as a five-year-old before progressing into a useful hurdler and ending his second season on the track with an unlucky second in the Scottish Champion Hurdle (in which Noel Fehily stood in for the injured Hughes, the only time Hughes hasn't ridden Cloudy Dream). Cloudy Dream looked one to follow over fences in the latest season and landed the odds with plenty in hand in small fields on his first two outings at Carlisle and Haydock. He looked destined for better things but had to settle for second behind Buveur d'Air (to whom he conceded 8 lb) at Haydock in December and behind Forest Bihan (to whom he conceded 3 lb) in the Lightning Novices' Chase at Doncaster in January, running well both times. Doncaster's late-January fixture provides one of northern jumping's best days, featuring two other Grade 2s (in addition to the Lightning), and also the valuable Sky Bet Handicap Chase (formerly known as the Great Yorkshire Chase). Such cards are rare in the North in mid-winter nowadays and it is unfortunate that the meeting takes place on the same day as Cheltenham's Trials meeting. There are signs, by the way, that the one-time mecca of northern jumping Wetherby, where only three northern-trained runners won at the two-day Charlie Hall meeting in October, might be preparing the ground for a much needed, gradual revival of its jumping programme which has been somewhat downgraded in recent times.

Cloudy Dream's next appearance after Doncaster came in the Arkle at the Cheltenham Festival where he turned the tables on Forest Bihan (fifth) when having to settle for minor honours again, this time behind Altior who beat him by six lengths into second, though Cloudy Dream would have run out a clear-cut winner without that outstanding rival in the line-up (Cloudy Dream's run against Buveur d'Air at Haydock, incidentally, was made to look even better when that horse won the Champion Hurdle later on the Cheltenham card). Cloudy Dream was stepped up to two and a half miles on his last two starts and held his form to finish second again—beaten a length by Flying Angel—in a good renewal of the Manifesto at Aintree, before rounding off a very successful campaign with victory in the Jordan Electrics Ltd Future Champions Novices' Chase at Ayr where he stayed on strongly to head Theinval on the flat, going on to win by two lengths, repeating his Cheltenham and Aintree form (Flying Angel started favourite but ran poorly after blundering badly five from home).

		⎧ Sadler's Wells	⎧ Northern Dancer
	⎧ Cloudings (IRE)	⎨ (b 1981)	⎩ Fairy Bridge
	⎪ (gr 1994)	⎩ Ispahan	⎧ Rusticaro
Cloudy Dream (IRE)	⎨	(gr 1981)	⎩ Royal Danseuse
(gr.g. 2010)	⎪	⎧ Acceglio	⎧ English Prince
	⎪ Run Away Dream (IRE)	⎨ (b 1981)	⎩ Arnaz
	⎩ (gr 1992)	⎩ Lisa's Music	⎧ Abwah
		(gr 1981)	⎩ Dancing Song

The good-topped Cloudy Dream is by Cloudings, a sire who has given Trevor Hemmings plenty of success (sire of ill-fated Many Clouds, among others), and he is the sixth foal produced by unraced Run Away Dream who is yet to have another winner under Rules (her daughter by Supreme Leader, Dream Leader, was placed twice in points but was well held in two novice hurdles for Paul Nicholls in the 2009/10 season). Run Away Dream's main claim to fame before producing Cloudy Dream was that she is a half-sister to the high-class two-mile chaser Get Real who won the BMW Chase at the Punchestown Festival meeting. The family is essentially a Flat one, though, whose background is in Belgium where Cloudy Dream's grandam Lisa's Music won both her starts and his great grandam Dancing Song won three times after being successful in a five-furlong maiden at Beverley. Cloudy Dream stays two and a half miles and acts on heavy going. Usually waited with, he is a sound jumper who looks bound to win more good races. Valuable open handicaps should suit him well, with the BetVictor Gold Cup at Cheltenham appealing as an early-season option—despite the fact that the North has won it just once in the past thirty-four years (with L'Antartique saddled by Ferdy Murphy in 2007). *Malcolm Jefferson*

CLOUDY JOKER (IRE) 9 gr.g. Cloudings (IRE) – Rosa View (IRE) (Roselier (FR)) **c–** [2016/17 c120, h106§: h18.6d³ May 25] leggy gelding: fair maiden hurdler: fairly useful **h97 §** chaser: stays 21f: acts on good to firm and heavy going: tried in cheekpieces: front runner/ races prominently: temperamental. *Donald McCain*

CLOUDY TOO (IRE) 11 b.g. Cloudings (IRE) – Curra Citizen (IRE) (Phardante (FR)) **c135** [2016/17 c146, h–: c24.1v h23.3v* c22.3s² c24.2s⁵ c23.8s⁴ c26g³ Mar 25] tall gelding: **h121** fairly useful handicap hurdler nowadays: won at Uttoxeter in November: useful handicap chaser nowadays: placed at Kelso (11 lengths behind Gas Line Boy in veterans event) in December and Newbury in March: stays 3¼m: acts on heavy going: usually races close up. *Sue Smith*

CLOVELLY 7 b.m. Midnight Legend – Chantilly Rose (Primitive Rising (USA)) [2016/17 b16.4d h20.6s³ h19.3s⁴ h20.6v⁵ h22.7s³ Apr 3] fourth foal: dam (h79) maiden hurdler (stayed 2¾m): well beaten in maiden hurdler: modest form over hurdles. *Rhona Brewis*   **h85** **b–**

CLOWN IN THE MOON 7 b.m. Kayf Tara – Con's Nurse (IRE) (Crowning Honors (CAN)) [2016/17 h15.8v Dec 21] fifth foal: sister to 2 winning pointers: dam winning pointer: pulled up in maiden point: tailed off in novice on hurdling debut. *James Evans*   **h–**

CLUBS ARE TRUMPS (IRE) 8 b.g. Flemensfirth (USA) – Pairtree (Double Trigger (IRE)) [2016/17 c112, h–: c26.1d⁴ c26.1sᵖᵘ c23d c23.9g² c24gᵖᵘ c24d⁴ c23.6m³ c20.9d⁶ c20vᵘʳ c20v⁵ c23.6g* c23.9d⁵ Apr 27] maiden hurdler: fair handicap chaser: won at Chepstow in April: stays 3¼m: acts on good to firm and good to soft going: usually wears headgear: tried in tongue tie: temperamental. *Jonjo O'Neill*   **c110 §** **h–**

CLUES AND ARROWS (IRE) 9 b.g. Clerkenwell (USA) – Ballela Girl (IRE) (Mandalus) [2016/17 c105, h75: c17.1d c25.5m² c21.3dᵖᵘ c21.1g⁴ c21.1m⁵ Apr 19] winning hurdler: fair maiden chaser: left John Wade after second start: stays 25f: acts on soft and good to firm going: tried in cheekpieces. *Rebecca Menzies*   **c110** **h–**

CLYNE 7 b.g. Hernando (FR) – Lauderdale (GER) (Nebos (GER)) [2016/17 h130: h15.7v* h18.9s* h15.7s² h16.3d³ Feb 11] tall, angular gelding: smart handicap hurdler: won at Haydock at November (by 7 lengths from Verni) and December: second in Champion Hurdle Trial there (length behind The New One) in January: stays 19f: best form on soft/heavy going: usually races prominently/responds generously to pressure. *Evan Williams*   **h146**

COARSE CUT (IRE) 4 b.g. Duke of Marmalade (IRE) – Keladora (USA) (Crafty Prospector (USA)) [2016/17 h15.8g⁵ Jul 24] fair form on Flat, stayed 1¾m: well beaten in juvenile on hurdling debut: dead. *Eve Johnson Houghton*   **h–**

COASTAL TIEP (FR) 5 b.g. Coastal Path – Jaltiepy (FR) (Monjal (FR)) [2016/17 b16g* h21g* h21.6d⁴ h21g² h20.5d³ Apr 19] €60,000 3-y-o: good-topped gelding: half-brother to 3 winners in France, including fairly useful hurdler/chaser Alpha Tiep (17f-21f winner, by Anzillero): dam, French 1½m winner, half-sister to fairly useful hurdler/useful chaser (stayed 3¾m) Pomme Tiepy: won completed start in points: also won bumper at Chepstow (by ¾ length from Waterloo Warrior) in October: useful form over hurdles: won novice at Kempton in November: second in handicap there (1¼ lengths behind River Frost) in February: will be suited by 2¾m+: best form on good going: tried in cheekpieces: usually races close up. *Paul Nicholls*   **h133** **b103**

COBAJAYISLAND (IRE) 9 b.g. Heron Island (IRE) – Shinora (IRE) (Black Minstrel) [2016/17 c113, h–p: c26.2d³ c24.2d⁴ c24g² c24d* Oct 2] lightly-raced hurdler: fairly useful handicap chaser: won at Uttoxeter in October: left Lucinda Russell after second start: stays 3¼m: acts on heavy going: often races towards rear/travels strongly. *Michael Scudamore*   **c122** **h–**

COBALT MARTHEN (FR) 5 b.g. Balko (FR) – Hellen Marthen (FR) (Passing Sale (FR)) [2016/17 b16g⁵ Apr 8] 12/1, showed a bit when fifth in bumper at Chepstow (20½ lengths behind Truckers Lodge) in April. *Richard Hobson*   **b74**

COBHAM'S CIRCUS (IRE) 6 ch.g. Hernando (FR) – Protectorate (Hector Protector (USA)) [2016/17 h88: h15.3m⁴ h17.7g May 29] modest form on second of 2 starts in 2015/16, standout effort over hurdles: tried in tongue tie. *Robert Walford*   **h57**

COBOLOBO (FR) 5 br.g. Maresca Sorrento (FR) – Nanou des Brosses (FR) (Saint Cyrien (FR)) [2016/17 h19.1s h20.5g⁵ h19.9v⁴ h19.5s* h20.5s² Feb 13] €40,000 3-y-o: second foal: dam, French 1½m bumper winner (second in 21f chase), half-sister to useful French chaser (stayed 2¾m) Sarah des Brosses: fairly useful form over hurdles: won handicap at Chepstow in January: second in similar event at Plumpton in February: will be suited by 3m: acts on soft going: usually races towards rear. *Jonjo O'Neill*   **h116**

COBRA DE MAI (FR) 5 b.g. Great Pretender (IRE) – Miria Galanda (FR) (Ut*Chef de Clan (FR)) [2016/17 h111, b–: h16g⁴ h19.4g⁵ h19.9s⁴ h18.6d⁴ h15.8m² Apr 18] angular gelding: bumper winner: fairly useful handicap hurdler: stays 2½m: acts on good to firm and heavy going: tried in cheekpieces/tongue tie. *Dan Skelton*   **h116**

COCHINILLO (IRE) 8 b.g. Shantou (USA) – Nut Touluze (IRE) (Toulon) [2016/17 h118: h21.2d⁵ Nov 28] fair hurdler, below form sole outing in 2016/17: should prove suited by further than 2½m. *Ben Case*   **h88**

COCKER 5 b.g. Shirocco (GER) – Treble Heights (IRE) (Unfuwain (USA)) [2016/17 h95: h20g⁵ h20g³ h19.6m⁵ Oct 11] modest maiden hurdler: stays 2½m: acts on good to soft going. *Alan Blackmore*   **h93**

COCKLEY BECK (IRE) 5 b.m. Westerner – Bobnval (IRE) (Bob Back (USA)) **b90**
[2016/17 b16d b16.8d* Mar 14] €15,500 3-y-o: sixth foal: half-sister to fair hurdler/chaser
Moncherie (2m-2¼m winner, by King's Theatre): dam unraced half-sister to high-class 2m
hurdler Valiramix: fair form in bumpers: won mares event at Sedgefield in March.
Nicky Richards

COCKNEY WREN 4 b.f. Cockney Rebel (IRE) – Compose (Anabaa (USA)) [2016/17 **b94**
b16.5m² b12.4d³ b15.8g² b16.5m* Apr 27] medium-sized, rather sparely-made filly: sister
to smart hurdler Cockney Sparrow (2m winner) and half-sister to 3 winners, including
fairly useful hurdler Dino Mite (17f-19f winner, by Doctor Dino): dam French maiden
(second at 11f): fair form in bumpers: won mares event at Taunton in April. *Harry Fry*

COCKTAILS AT DAWN 9 b.g. Fair Mix (IRE) – Fond Farewell (IRE) (Phardante (FR)) **c – x**
[2016/17 c147, h–: c25gᵖᵘ c25s⁴ c24gᶠ c20.8gᵖᵘ c34.3dᶠ c23.8g⁶ Apr 26] lengthy gelding: **h–**
winning hurdler: smart handicap chaser at best, no form in 2016/17: stays 21f: acts on good
to soft going: often let down by jumping. *Nicky Henderson*

COCO DES CHAMPS (IRE) 7 br.m. Robin des Champs (FR) – American Chick (IRE) **c86 p**
(Lord Americo) [2016/17 h109: h23.3g c20s⁶ c19.2v⁴ Dec 15] lengthy mare: fair maiden **h100**
hurdler: modest form over fences: left Oliver Sherwood after first start: stays 21f: acts on
soft going: tried in tongue tie: should do better over fences. *Kim Bailey*

COCO FLOWER (FR) 5 ch.m. Born King (JPN) – La Fleur du Roy (FR) (Sleeping Car **h–**
(FR)) [2016/17 h–, b64: h19.9dᵖᵘ h19.7gᵖᵘ Oct 31] neat mare: no form over hurdles: tried
in cheekpieces. *Alex Hales*

COCO LIVE (FR) 5 b.g. Secret Singer (FR) – Iona Will (FR) (Kadalko (FR)) [2016/17 **c–**
c20.3sᵖᵘ h20.3vᵖᵘ h19.9s⁴ Apr 1] €20,000 3-y-o, £33,000 4-y-o: brother to modest chaser **h86**
Very Live (2m/17f winner), and half-brother to bumper winner Paddy Love (by Brier
Creek) and a winning pointer by Subotica: dam unraced: won Irish maiden point on debut:
modest on completed start over hurdles: pulled up in novice on chasing debut: tried in
cheekpieces/tongue tie. *Seamus Mullins*

COCO SHAMBHALA 9 b.m. Indian Danehill (IRE) – Kohinor (Supreme Leader) **c–**
[2016/17 h96p: c23.6gᵖᵘ h25.5s h25.5dᵖᵘ Mar 26] useful-looking mare: maiden hurdler, no **h–**
form in 2016/17: pulled up in novice handicap on chasing debut. *Oliver Sherwood*

CODE BLUE 14 b.g. Sir Harry Lewis (USA) – Nevermind Hey (Teenoso (USA)) **c74**
[2016/17 c–, h–: c19.3s³ Apr 28] dual winning pointer: winning hurdler: poor hunter **h–**
chaser: stays 3m: best form on heavy going: in visor last 4 starts. *R. Tate*

CODE OF LAW 7 ch.g. Papal Bull – Fyvie (Grand Lodge (USA)) [2016/17 h15.8dᵖᵘ **c92**
h20g⁶ h20g c21.1g² h17.7d h25.6s⁵ c19.7g² c20.2m² c19.7gᵘʳ c19.7m² Apr 16] third **h81**
foal: half-brother to a winning pointer by Kheleyf and a winner on Flat in USA by
Singspiel: dam 1½m winner: maiden Irish pointer: poor form over hurdles: modest form
over fences: stays 21f: acts on soft and good to firm going: front runner/races prominently.
Neil Mulholland

CODESHARE 5 b.g. Dansili – Clepsydra (Sadler's Wells (USA)) [2016/17 b–: b17.1g² **b88**
b16.8s Nov 22] fair form in bumpers: best effort when second at Carlisle in November:
won twice on Flat in 2017. *Alan Swinbank*

CODY WYOMING 11 b.g. Passing Glance – Tenderfoot (Be My Chief (USA)) [2016/17 **c122 §**
c123§, h–: c20.3s⁶ c19.4g⁴ c20.4g⁴ c20d* c21.2g⁴ c24.2s c24.2sᵖᵘ c22.9vᵖᵘ Mar 22] big, **h–**
good-topped gelding: winning hurdler: fairly useful handicap chaser: won veterans event
at Lingfield in November: stays 21f: acts on heavy going: wears cheekpieces/tongue tie:
temperamental. *Charlie Mann*

COEUR BLIMEY (IRE) 6 b.g. Winged Love (IRE) – Eastender (Opening Verse (USA)) **h114**
[2016/17 b115: b16d h19.8s⁵ h19.3s² h16.8v² Jan 1] workmanlike gelding: smart bumper **b–**
winner: fair form over hurdles: runner-up on last 2 starts. *Susan Gardner*

COEUR BRULE (FR) 11 b.g. Polish Summer – Sally's Cry (FR) (Freedom Cry) **c–**
[2016/17 c92, h–: c21.1d⁵ May 12] angular gelding: dual point winner: maiden hurdler: **h–**
modest hunter chaser, below form sole outing in 2016/17: stays 3m: acts on any going:
tried in cheekpieces. *David Turner*

COEUR DE FOU (FR) 12 ch.g. Limnos (JPN) – Folly Lady (FR) (Saint Estephe (FR)) **c100 §**
[2016/17 c104§, h–: c24dᵖᵘ c20m³ h21.2g Nov 10] angular gelding: fair handicap hurdler **h74 §**
at one time, below form final outing: fair handicap chaser: stays 21f: acts on good to firm
and heavy going: usually wears headgear: has worn tongue tie: temperamental. *Tom George*

COEUR DE LION 4 b.g. Pour Moi (IRE) – Hora (Hernando (FR)) [2016/17 h16s* **h137**
h16.8d² h16s² h16v* h16.8g Mar 17] useful-looking gelding: closely related to fairly
useful hurdler Magna Cartor (2m winner, by Motivator) and half-brother to useful hurdler

Thomas Campbell (2m winner, by Yeats): dam (h148) 2½m-3m hurdle winner: fairly useful maiden on Flat, stays 17f: useful form over hurdles: won juvenile maiden at Wetherby in November and novice at Sandown in February: second in juveniles at Cheltenham and Sandown in between: should be suited by further than 2m: acts on heavy going. *Alan King*

COEUR TANTRE (IRE) 6 ch.g. Fruits of Love (USA) – Ding Dong Belle (Minster **h109**
Son) [2016/17 h104: h19.1g² h18.5m* h18.5m² h15.3mᵘʳ h16.5g⁵ h16g² h16v⁶ h19.4d h21s
Feb 10] fair handicap hurdler: won at Newton Abbot in August: best form up to 19f: acts on good to firm going: tried in hood: often races towards rear, tends to find little. *Hugo Froud*

COGBURN 5 ch.g. Black Sam Bellamy (IRE) – Realms of Gold (USA) (Gulch (USA)) **b91**
[2016/17 b16s³ b15.3v b15.8g² Apr 17] useful-looking gelding: brother to bumper winner/ fairly useful hurdler Board of Trade (21f winner), closely related to bumper winner/useful 2m hurdle winner Battle Born (by Kayf Tara) and half-brother to several winners: dam little form on Flat: fair form in bumpers: in eyeshields, best effort when second at Huntingdon in April. *Alan King*

COGRY 8 b.g. King's Theatre (IRE) – Wyldello (Supreme Leader) [2016/17 c137, h–: **c135 x**
c25gᶠ c27.3sᵇᵈ c25.5dᵘʳ c26gᶠ h24s* h26sᵖᵘ c24.2s³ c33.4s⁶ c27.9d² c31.8g² Apr 22] sturdy **h128**
gelding: fairly useful handicap hurdler: won at Cheltenham in January: useful handicap chaser: second at Ffos Las (4 lengths behind The Bay Oak) and in Scottish Grand National at Ayr (neck behind Vicente) in April: stays 4m: acts on heavy going: usually in headgear nowadays: front runner/races prominently: often let down by jumping. *Nigel Twiston-Davies*

COILLTE LASS (IRE) 6 b.m. Beneficial – Black Mariah (IRE) (Bob's Return (IRE)) **h133**
[2016/17 h21.7g* h21.2d* h16.5g* h16.6d³ h16.8g h20.3gᵖᵘ Apr 20] €7,500 3-y-o: useful-looking mare: first foal: dam (b76), ran once in bumper, half-sister to very smart hurdler/ useful chaser (stayed 3¼m) Classified: Irish maiden point winner: useful form over hurdles: won maiden at Hereford in October, mares novice at Ludlow in November and listed mares novice at Taunton (by 4½ lengths from Dusky Legend) in December: third in Doncaster Mares' Hurdle (7 lengths behind Vroum Vroum Mag) in January: stays 2¾m: acts on good to soft going: tried in tongue tie: usually races close up. *Paul Nicholls*

COLBERT STATION (IRE) 13 b.g. Witness Box (USA) – Laurenca's Girl (IRE) **c117**
(Commanche Run) [2016/17 h24d h20d h24.2g⁶ h24g⁶ c17d³ c20s c23g⁶ c24s⁴ c20.3s³ **h110**
c20s² c20gᵘʳ c25.8m² Apr 15] strong gelding: fair handicap hurdler/chaser nowadays: left T. M. Walsh after sixth start: stays 3¼m: acts on good to firm and heavy going: has worn headgear, including in 2016/17: wears tongue tie: often travels strongly. *Jonjo O'Neill*

COLD AS ICE (FR) 5 gr.g. Montmartre (FR) – Turiama (FR) (Ashkalani (IRE)) [2016/17 **h95 p**
h16d⁵ Nov 16] fourth foal: half-brother to fairly useful French hurdler Turiamix (17f winner, by Al Namix) and French 19f chase winner Uriama du Houx (by Network): dam, French maiden (placed at 1½m), half-sister to useful French hurdler/chaser (stays 23f) Djagble: 20/1, green when fifth in novice hurdle at Chepstow (11½ lengths behind Utility) on debut: open to improvement. *Venetia Williams*

COLD FUSION (FR) 4 b.f. Frozen Power (IRE) – Tuscania (USA) (Woodman (USA)) **h– §**
[2016/17 h16mᵖᵘ h16.8dᵖᵘ Mar 21] half-sister to fair hurdler Maid of Tuscany (2m-2¼m winner, by Manduro): modest on Flat, stays 16.5f: pulled up both starts over hurdles, in headgear on first occasion: hard ride. *David Flood*

COLD KNIGHT 11 b.g. Sir Harry Lewis (USA) – Arctic Chick (Henbit (USA)) [2016/17 **c98**
c100, h–: c16.3g⁴ c19.4m* c19.9g⁵ c19.4vᵖᵘ c19.4g⁵ c18.2m⁵ Apr 20] lengthy, useful- **h–**
looking gelding: multiple winning pointer: maiden hurdler: modest handicap chaser: won novice event at Stratford early in season: stays 2½m: acts on soft and good to firm going: wears cheekpieces: front runner. *Tom Weston*

COLD MARCH (FR) 7 b.g. Early March – Tumultueuse (FR) (Bering) [2016/17 c150, **c148**
h–: c16.9d⁵ c16.3d⁵ c19.9g* c20.8gᵖᵘ c16g³ Apr 17] good-topped gelding: maiden hurdler: **h–**
smart handicap chaser: won at Musselburgh (by 2½ lengths from Upsilon Bleu) in January: stays 2½m: acts on good to firm and heavy going: has worn headgear, including last 3 starts. *Venetia Williams*

COLE HARDEN (IRE) 8 b.g. Westerner – Nosie Betty (IRE) (Alphabatim (USA)) **c123 p**
[2016/17 h156: h19.4d² h20.3s³ h24s² h24g⁴ h24.7gᵖᵘ Apr 8] sturdy gelding: has reportedly **h155**
had breathing operation: very smart hurdler: placed in Relkeel Hurdle (7 lengths behind Agrapart) and Cleeve Hurdle (1¼ lengths behind Unowhatimeanharry), both at Cheltenham in January: 4/6, second in novice at Wetherby (7 lengths behind Its'afreebee) on chasing debut: stays 25f: acts on good to firm and heavy going: in headgear last 4 starts: usually wears tongue tie: front runner: should do better over fences. *Warren Greatrex*

COLIN'S BROTHER 7 b.g. Overbury (IRE) – Dd's Glenalla (IRE) (Be My Native **c125** (USA)) [2016/17 c115, h119: c17.4s* c16d* c20.9v^pu c20s³ Mar 2] angular gelding: **h–** winning hurdler: fairly useful handicap chaser: won at Bangor in November and Ludlow in December: stays 21f: acts on heavy going. *Nigel Twiston-Davies*

COLIN'S SISTER 6 b.m. Central Park (IRE) – Dd's Glenalla (IRE) (Be My Native **h133 p** (USA)) [2016/17 b108: h19.5g* h21s* h18.9s* h19.8s* h20d⁵ Apr 16] long-backed mare: useful bumper performer: useful form over hurdles: won mares novices at Chepstow in October, Warwick in November, Haydock (listed event, by 6 lengths from My Khaleesi) in December and Sandown (Jane Seymour Mares' Novices' Hurdle, by 9 lengths from Happy Diva) in February: stays 21f: acts on soft going: often races prominently/travels strongly: remains with potential. *Fergal O'Brien*

COLLA PIER (IRE) 8 b.m. Hawk Wing (USA) – Medalha Milagrosa (USA) (Miner's **c125** Mark (USA)) [2016/17 h119: h17s⁶ h17.2g² h15.9m* c16d⁴ c18g³ h15.7m c20.5g² c20d⁵ **h125** c19.9s⁵ c15.8g⁴ c16d Apr 27] angular mare: fairly useful handicap hurdler: won at Plumpton in September: fairly useful maiden chaser: placed in Buck House Novices' Chase at Punchestown (4¼ lengths behind Three Stars) in October and listed mares event at Doncaster (5 lengths behind Kalane) in December: stays 21f: acts on soft and good to firm going: has worn hood/tongue tie: often races in rear. *David Peter Dunne, Ireland*

COLLEY ROW (IRE) 9 b.g. Vinnie Roe (IRE) – Sliabhin Hall (IRE) (Saddlers' Hall **h–** (IRE)) [2016/17 h94: h23.3g h16.8g⁶ h21.6s Nov 20] dual winning pointer: modest hurdler at best, no form in 2016/17: has worn headgear, including in 2016/17. *David Rees*

COLLODI (GER) 8 b.g. Konigstiger (GER) – Codera (GER) (Zilzal (USA)) [2016/17 **c–** c–, h121x: h16.3g* h16.2g⁴ h16d⁴ h16.6g Dec 10] compact gelding: fair hurdler **h110** nowadays: won seller at Stratford in July: fell only start over fences in 2015/16: left David Bridgwater after first start: raced around 2m: acts on good to firm and good to soft going. *Neil Mulholland*

COLONEL FORSTER 5 b.g. Strategic Prince – Forsters Plantin (Muhtarram (USA)) **b–** [2016/17 b16.2f⁵ b16.2d Jun 30] last in 2 bumpers. *Chris Grant*

COLONIAL DREAMS (IRE) 5 b.g. Westerner – Dochas Supreme (IRE) (Supreme **b104** Leader) [2016/17 b13.7d⁴ b15.8d b16g² b15.7g* Apr 21] €55,000 3-y-o: sturdy gelding: fourth foal: half-brother to fairly useful hurdler Lightentertainment (17f-2½m winner, by King's Theatre): dam unraced half-sister to fairly useful hurdler (stayed 3m) Thames: fairly useful form in bumpers: won conditionals/amateur event at Southwell in April. *Nicky Henderson*

COLORADO KID (IRE) 11 b.g. Presenting – Silent Orders (IRE) (Bob Back (USA)) **c79** [2016/17 c–, h–: c21.2m³ c25.5m* c20.1g⁶ c23.4s^pu c23.8g⁵ Nov 2] point winner: twice- **h–** raced hurdler: poor form over fences: won handicap at Cartmel early in season (for John Wade): stays 25f: acts on good to firm going: in headgear last 2 starts. *Rebecca Menzies*

COLOUR MY WORLD 7 gr.g. With Approval (CAN) – Nadeszhda (Nashwan (USA)) **h–** [2016/17 h16m Jul 4] fair on Flat, stays 1m: 50/1, tailed off hurdling debut. *Ed McMahon*

COLOUR SQUADRON (IRE) 11 b.g. Old Vic – That's The Goose (IRE) (Be My **c138 §** Native (USA)) [2016/17 c24s⁴ c30.2g c24m⁴ Apr 29] workmanlike gelding: winning **h–** hurdler: useful chaser nowadays: stays 21f: acts on heavy going: tried in blinkers/tongue tie: often travels strongly: irresolute. *Enda Bolger, Ireland*

COMANCHE CHIEFTAIN (CAN) 5 b.g. Broken Vow (USA) – Platinum Preferred **h107** (CAN) (Vindication (USA)) [2016/17 h15.9v² h15.8s² Mar 23] fair on Flat, stays 1½m: in hood, runner-up both starts over hurdles: better effort (fair form) when beaten 3½ lengths in maiden at Plumpton in February. *Neil King*

COMBUSTIBLE KATE (IRE) 11 b.m. Mr Combustible (IRE) – Aussie Hope (Gran **c–** Alba (USA)) [2016/17 c78, h77: h19.2g May 9] modest hurdler at best, well held sole **h–** outing in 2016/17: maiden chaser: stays 3¼m: acts on good to firm and good to soft going: has worn headgear. *Nick Kent*

COMEDINEWITHME 9 b.m. Milan – Skipcarl (IRE) (Carlingford Castle) [2016/17 **c95** c98p, h–: c25.3g³ c25.2s⁴ Mar 8] multiple winning pointer: lightly-raced hurdler: modest **h–** form in hunter chases: better effort in 2016/17 when third in mares event at Cheltenham early in season: stays 25f: acts on heavy going. *I. M. Mason*

COMEDY HOUSE (IRE) 9 b.g. Auction House (USA) – Kyle Akin (Vettori (IRE)) [2016/17 **h–** h–: h15.9g h21m^pu Apr 4] medium-sized gelding: maiden hurdler, no worthwhile form since 2014/15: stays 2¼m: acts on good to firm and good to soft going: wears headgear. *Michael Madgwick*

COMELY 5 b.m. Midnight Legend – Belle Magello (FR) (Exit To Nowhere (USA)) **h94**
[2016/17 b15.8d³ b16g⁴ h16g³ h20.6s² Mar 12] £36,000 3-y-o: half-sister to several **b86**
winners, including useful hurdlers/chasers Banjaxed Girl (2m-21f winner, by King's
Theatre) and Mountain King (2m-2½m winner, by Definite Article): dam unraced: fair
form on bumper debut: modest form over hurdles: better effort when second in novice at
Market Rasen in March. *Nicky Henderson*

COMEONGINGER (IRE) 10 b.g. King's Theatre (IRE) – Miss Poutine (FR) **c112**
(Chamberlin (FR)) [2016/17 c122, h–: c20g³ c19.4g³ c22.6s² c19.7d⁵ c20g⁴ c19.2vᵖᵘ **h–**
c20.2mᶠ Apr 5] tall, useful-looking gelding: lightly-raced hurdler: fairly useful handicap
chaser, not at best in 2016/17: stayed 3m: acted on soft and good to firm going: wore tongue
tie: often led: dead. *Chris Gordon*

COME ON JOEY (IRE) 6 b.g. Trans Island – Thousand Springs (IRE) (King's Ride) **b–**
[2016/17 b16.8g Apr 26] point winner: well beaten in maiden bumper. *R. C. Smith*

COME ON LAURIE (IRE) 9 b.g. Oscar (IRE) – Megan's Magic (Blue Ocean (USA)) **c–**
[2016/17 c117p, h–: c26.1dᵖᵘ h21g⁴ h24.2g h21.6s⁴ h22g⁵ Mar 25] fair handicap hurdler: **h101**
maiden chaser, pulled up on return in 2016/17: best at short of 3m: acts on heavy going:
tried in hood. *Oliver Sherwood*

COME ON LOUIS 9 b.g. Grape Tree Road – Seamill (IRE) (Lafontaine (USA)) [2016/17 **h–**
h15.8d h16.7g h16.7s h23.1sᵖᵘ Dec 22] maiden point winner: no form over hurdles.
Oliver Greenall

COME ON LULU 6 ch.m. Calcutta – Flashing Floozie (Muhtarram (USA)) [2016/17 **h69**
h16.8vᵖᵘ h15.7s⁴ h16.8g⁶ h19.7g⁴ Apr 23] poor maiden on Flat, stays 1¾m: poor form over
hurdles. *David Thompson*

COME ON YOU (IRE) 9 ch.g. Presenting – Dreamy Run (IRE) (Commanche Run) **c–**
[2016/17 c–, h–: c23mᶠ Jul 4] multiple point winner: maiden hurdler: maiden chaser, fell **h–**
heavily sole outing in 2016/17: often in headgear: in tongue tie last 2 starts. *Gary Moore*

COME TO ME (FR) 5 b.g. Spanish Moon (USA) – Hasta Manana (FR) (Useful (FR)) **b106 p**
[2016/17 b16d* Dec 11] €44,000 3-y-o: half-brother to several winners, including smart
hurdler/useful chaser Sweet My Lord (2m-2¾m winner, by Johann Quatz) and useful
hurdler/winning pointer Vivant Poeme (2¾m winner, by Early March): dam, French
17f/2¼m hurdle/chase winner (stayed 21f), also 1¼m-1¾m winner on Flat: 7/2, created
good impression won maiden bumper at Punchestown (by 4¾ lengths from Burren
Life) on debut: open to improvement. *W. P. Mullins, Ireland*

COMICAL RED 9 ch.g. Sulamani (IRE) – Sellette (IRE) (Selkirk (USA)) [2016/17 c–§, **c93 §**
h70§: c19.2g³ c23gᶠ c25.1s c23g c20.9vʳ h21.4d h25v³ h23.6s h23.1g² h23.9m³ Apr 27] **h68 §**
workmanlike gelding: poor handicap hurdler nowadays: modest maiden chaser: stays 27f:
acts on good to firm and heavy going: usually wears headgear: has worn tongue tie: often
races prominently: moody. *Mark Gillard*

COMMANDING SPIRIT (IRE) 5 ch.g. Presenting – Park Athlete (IRE) (Supreme **h–**
Leader) [2016/17 b15.8g h20g h20g h15.8d h16.7s⁶ h25g⁵ Apr 3] €60,000 3-y-o: brother to **b65**
a winning jumper in Switzerland and half-brother to 3 winners, including bumper winner/
useful hurdler Vieux Lille (17f-23f winner, by Robin des Champs) and fairly useful chaser
Bon Accord (25f winner, by Accordion): dam unraced half-sister to top-class chaser
(stayed 25f) The Listener and to dam of high-class hurdler/chaser (stays 21f) Yorkhill (by
Presenting): needed experience in bumper: no form over hurdles: tried in tongue tie. *Jonjo
O'Neill*

COMMIS D'OFFICE (FR) 5 b.g. Califet (FR) – Pas de Bal (FR) (Le Balafre (FR)) **c120**
[2016/17 c16.9g* c17.4d⁵ c17.4s² c19.9dᵖᵘ Feb 18] third foal: half-brother to 2 winners in **h–**
France, including 2¾m chase winner Uncontrix (by Al Namix): dam unraced half-sister to
smart French chaser (stayed 23f) Lord Mirande: bumper winner: lightly-raced hurdler:
fairly useful form over fences: won 4-y-o event at Le Lion-d'Angers early in season: left
Mme I. Pacault, shaped as if amiss final start: stays 2¼m: acts on soft going: in hood first
3 starts. *Venetia Williams*

COMMON PRACTICE (IRE) 6 b.g. Gold Well – Satalda (IRE) (Satco (FR)) [2016/17 **c–**
h81, b–: h18.5g c20.3dᵖᵘ May 26] maiden hurdler, no form in 2016/17, including on **h–**
chasing debut: tried in blinkers: dead. *Jonjo O'Neill*

COMPADRE (IRE) 6 b.g. Yeats (IRE) – Julivia (FR) (Dernier Empereur (USA)) **c113**
[2016/17 b102: h16d⁶ h17s² h15.5d⁴ h20.6s⁶ c19.9gᶠ c17.2m³ Apr 17] useful-looking **h112**
gelding: bumper winner: fair form over hurdles/fences: unproven beyond 17f: acts on soft
going: in hood last 5 starts, tongue tied last 2: often races prominently. *Jonjo O'Neill*

COMPETITION 5 b.g. Multiplex – Compolina (Compton Place) [2016/17 b85: b16s **b–**
b15.6g⁶ b16d Mar 21] runner-up in bumper on debut in 2015/16, no other form: in tongue
tie last 2 starts. *Brian Rothwell*

COMRAGH (IRE) 7 br.m. Desert King (IRE) – Akica (IRE) (Oscar (IRE)) [2016/17 h97: **h–**
h20.3gᵖᵘ Jun 7] modest form over hurdles, pulled up sole outing in 2016/17: bred to stay
further than 2½m. *Jeremy Scott*

CONA RIVER (IRE) 7 b.g. Robin des Champs (FR) – Raishah (GER) (Motley (USA)) **h106**
[2016/17 b16s h21.7s⁵ h20.3v⁶ Mar 6] rangy gelding: fifth foal: half-brother to bumper/2m **b–**
hurdle winner Maid From Milan (by Milan): dam unraced half-sister to fairly useful
hurdler (stayed 21f) Radanpour: tailed off in bumper: better effort over hurdles (fair form)
when fifth in novice at Hereford in December: in tongue tie last 2 starts. *Jonjo O'Neill*

CONAS TAOI (IRE) 8 b.g. Exit To Nowhere (USA) – Zudika (IRE) (Ezzoud (IRE)) **c119**
[2016/17 c122p, h73: c25g c28.8d⁵ c26d³ Dec 31] good-topped gelding: lightly-raced **h–**
hurdler: fairly useful handicap chaser: fifth in Betfair London National at Sandown and
third at Newbury in December: stays 29f: acts on heavy going: has worn cheekpieces.
Paul Morgan

CONEYGREE 10 b.g. Karinga Bay – Plaid Maid (IRE) (Executive Perk) [2016/17 **c168**
c171p, h–: c24.1v² c24.5d³ Apr 26] **h–**
    When Coneygree became the first novice for forty years to win the
Cheltenham Gold Cup—after just three starts over fences—the world seemed at his
feet. A fine, accurate jumper, he still looked to have further improvement in him over
fences. Unfortunately, he has made only three appearances since earning his place
in Gold Cup history in 2015, and medical bulletins have largely replaced media
coverage of racecourse triumphs and new records. 'Coneygree out', 'Coneygree will
not run', 'No-show Coneygree' … have been the headlines over stories about him
in the past two seasons as injuries and training troubles have dogged his progress.
A hock injury sustained just before Christmas kept him off the course for the
remainder of the 2015/16 season after he proved far too good for his rivals in an
intermediate chase at Sandown on his reappearance (he was 9/2 ante-post favourite
at that time for the Hennessy Gold Cup which he had to miss because of a minor foot
injury, after being pricked by a nail). After recovering and working his way back
to fitness, Coneygree had the Betfair Chase at Haydock as his first main objective
in the latest season. A planned trip to the course for a gallop in advance of Betfair
Chase day was called off on account of firmish going and the dry autumn which held
up his preparation at home. The Charlie Hall Chase at Wetherby had been pencilled
in as a possible starting point but, in the end, Coneygree went to Haydock without
a prep run.
    For a horse returning after more than a year off, he ran very well, jumping
fluently in the lead before eventually finding an on-song Cue Card, winning the
race for the third time, too good on the day, going down by fifteen lengths and
losing his unbeaten record over fences. 'We'll be back and Cue Card won't beat us
again,' was the defiant response of Coneygree's trainer. 'We couldn't have asked
for more, there's been no soft ground to train him on.' Richard Johnson, standing
in for Coneygree's regular jockey Nico de Boinville who was injured, reported that
his mount 'got tired three out and the race will bring him on for the King George
if they choose to go there.' Connections considered the possibility of going instead
to Leopardstown for the Lexus Chase over Christmas, but a poor workout, thought
to have been caused by a fresh injury which is believed to have been picked up
in the Betfair, ruled Coneygree out of Kempton and Leopardstown, ironically just
days after an upbeat bulletin had been issued about his prospects. In early-January,
Coneygree was ruled out of the Gold Cup for the second year running as well. 'His
injury is not so severe as last year but he needs to be completely comfortable before
we can start to train him again,' reported Sara Bradstock, wife of the trainer.
    Coneygree made his only other appearance right at the end of the season in
the Punchestown Gold Cup, connections reported to have been 'over the moon' after
he schooled 'brilliantly' over nine fences at Ffos Las on the Sunday after the Grand
National. Coneygree came up against reigning Cheltenham Gold Cup winner Sizing
John at Punchestown, as well as dual Gold Cup runner-up Djakadam (who had
finished fourth to Sizing John in the latest running). He didn't beat either but gave

A rare action shot of Coneygree, having just his third start—in the Punchestown Gold Cup—since winning the 2015 Cheltenham Gold Cup

them a real run for their money, showing that he is still a force to be reckoned with in the top races when connections have him right. Coneygree went down by a short head and a length and a half (the first three finished well clear) and might have gone even closer had he not made an uncharacteristic mistake at the second last, just as the race was beginning in earnest. There was some talk immediately after Punchestown of a possible tilt at the Grande Course de Haies (French Champion Hurdle) at Auteuil, but some swelling was reportedly found in a hind leg the following day and, although he was soon given the 'all clear', Coneygree wasn't seen again.

			Ardross	Run The Gantlet
Coneygree (b.g. 2007)	Karinga Bay (ch 1987)		(b 1976)	Le Melody
		Handy Dancer (ch 1977)	Green God
			Miss Golightly
	Plaid Maid (IRE) (b 1992)	Executive Perk (b 1985)	Lord Gayle
			Areola
		Tipperary Tartan (b 1980)	Rarity
			Colourful

A strong gelding, Coneygree is one of six foals produced by Plaid Maid, a useful racemare over jumps who stayed three and three quarter miles. Plaid Maid, who is also the dam of the 2011 Hennessy Gold Cup winner Carruthers (by Kayf Tara), died three weeks after foaling a brother to Carruthers, Flintham, who upheld the family name in his first campaign over fences in the latest season, putting up a very useful performance when beaten a short head after attempting to make all in the Reynoldstown Chase at Ascot, a race that Carruthers won. Flintham is an exuberant front runner like his siblings and he is still qualified for novice chases in the next season. The bold-jumping Coneygree will stay further than three and a quarter miles and he acts on heavy going. The Hennessy—under new sponsorship as the Ladbrokes Trophy—is said to be Coneygree's first aim in the next season, with talk of a warm-up in the Kerry National at Listowel in September when, if it happens, it will make Coneygree the first Cheltenham Gold Cup winner to contest that race since L'Escargot was narrowly beaten over forty years ago on his final racecourse appearance before being taken back by his owner Raymond Guest (less than pleased about the Listowel run as he thought L'Escargot had already been retired!) to spend his retirement in the States. *Mark Bradstock*

219

CONEY ISLAND (IRE) 6 b.g. Flemensfirth (USA) – Millys Gesture (IRE) (Milan) c159 p
[2016/17 h142: h24d² h24s² c20s² c20d* c24d² Dec 29] h–

Brooklyn's coastal resort Coney Island was once the largest amusement area in the States, comprising three major theme parks and attracting several million visitors each year, its heyday captured during a memorable sequence in the 1928 blockbuster *Speedy*, the final silent film made by Harold Lloyd. However, the resort has been in decline since World War II, with most of its former attractions either long gone or closed, or in urgent need of repair, with a damning travel article *Little Amusement in Coney Island* illustrating just how far removed it is from those glory days. Coney Island's equine namesake also ended 2016/17 in need of some repair, but the future looks more rosy for him as his glory days still look ahead of him. Although forced to sit out the big spring festivals with a badly-bruised foot, Coney Island had his own reputation enhanced at them by others and he is definitely one of the leading performers that racegoers should most be looking forward to seeing again from the latest crop of novice chasers.

A satisfactory novice hurdling campaign yielded two wins in 2015/16, but it was Coney Island's narrow second to Bellshill in the War of Attrition Novices' Hurdle at Punchestown (run just after the start of Britain's 2016/17 season) which encouraged trainer Eddie Harty the most. 'At least we knew we had a Grade 1 horse then and it's a while since we've had one—you've got to treat them right when you get them.' Having begun his chasing career with an eye-catching second (after seven months off) to Haymount in a very hot beginners event at Punchestown in November, Coney Island opened his account at Grade 1 level in the Bar One Racing Drinmore Novices' Chase over two and a half miles at Fairyhouse early the following month. It looked a strong renewal, with all bar one of the seven runners representing powerhouse owners Gigginstown House Stud (four) and J. P. McManus (two). Coney Island was fifth in the betting at 8/1 and the McManus second string behind Anibale Fly, who was the mount of the owner's retained jockey Barry Geraghty. That isn't always a negative sign, however, as Geraghty's understudy Mark Walsh is a more than able deputy—Walsh provided McManus with the majority of his wins (fifty-one compared to Geraghty's twenty-six) on Irish soil during the latest season. 'He was electric and never missed a beat,' was Walsh's post-race verdict after Coney Island had travelled supremely well in a handy position from the off before taking it up between the last two fences. Coney Island didn't need to be fully extended to beat Anibale Fly cosily by two and a half lengths, with the same distance back to the front-running Alpha des Obeaux in third. Fourth-placed Road To Respect went on to win at both the Cheltenham and Punchestown Festivals, while the disappointing sixth A Toi Phil (the shortest-priced of the Gigginstown quartet in the Drinmore) also landed two valuable prizes later in the campaign.

Bar One Racing Drinmore Novices' Chase, Fairyhouse—Mark Walsh steers home the J. P. McManus 'second string' Coney Island in a good renewal of this Grade 1

Coney Island had to settle for second on his only subsequent appearance, when splitting Our Duke and Disko in a three-way finish to the Neville Hotels Novices' Chase (registered as the Fort Leney) over three miles at Leopardstown later in December, but it says plenty for him that he shaped like the best horse for much of that race. A strong late rally by the thorough stayer Our Duke saw him account for Coney Island by half a length in the end, with the same distance back to Disko, the trio having pulled over twenty lengths clear of the remainder. Our Duke subsequently put up a top-class performance when running away with the Irish Grand National in April, and Disko went on to win twice (including a victory over Our Duke) in Grade 1 company. Coney Island was prominent in the betting for both the Golden Miller and the RSA Novices' Chase when news of his injury was announced in early-March. He seems to have been overlooked by punters since then due to his absence and, at the time of writing, he is 40/1 in the ante-post betting for the 2018 Cheltenham Gold Cup, in which Our Duke and Disko feature at 12/1 and 33/1 respectively.

Coney Island is from a family that has served McManus very well down the years, so it was hardly surprising that connections were prepared to fork out €34,000 to secure him as a foal. His unraced dam Millys Gesture is closely related to the smart staying hurdler/chaser Wichita Lineman (who twice carried the McManus colours to victory at the Cheltenham Festival) and a half-sister to the top-class hurdler Rhinestone Cowboy, who showed his form at two miles (third in the Champion Hurdle) to three miles. There are Flat and National Hunt performers further back in the family, with Coney Island's grandam Monumental Gesture among those who won under both codes, her two wins over hurdles both coming at two miles; she was also a half-sister to the 1990 Triumph Hurdle winner Rare Holiday and to the useful two-mile hurdler/chaser Blazing Spectacle. Coney Island's great grandam Temporary Lull was an unraced sister to the 1987 Nell Gwyn Stakes winner Martha Stevens. Coney Island's year-younger brother Give Me A Minute (also owned by McManus) is the only one among Millys Gesture's other progeny to reach the racecourse so far, and has shown just modest form to date over hurdles for Enda Bolger. Millys Gesture's first foal Ile En Crise (a sister to Coney Island) and her fourth foal Queens Gesture (by Getaway) are both likely to have been sent straight to the paddocks given their pedigree. Millys Gesture has since produced a 2014 filly by Getaway, a 2015 colt by Fame And Glory and a 2016 colt by Leading Light, all as yet unnamed (Fame And Glory fetched €55,000 as a foal).

		Alleged (b 1974)	Hoist The Flag / Princess Pout
	Flemensfirth (USA) (b 1992)	Etheldreda (ch 1985)	Diesis / Royal Bund
Coney Island (IRE) (b.g. 2011)		Milan (b 1998)	Sadler's Wells / Kithanga
	Millys Gesture (IRE) (b 2006)	Monumental Gesture (b 1987)	Head For Heights / Temporary Lull

As some of those names in his pedigree imply, Coney Island certainly isn't short of speed but he is clearly fully effective at around two and a half miles, which should give connections plenty of options. Coney Island was also a winner on soft ground over three miles in his hurdling days (when he also won on heavy), so it could be unwise to draw hard and fast conclusions about the limit of his stamina from his Leopardstown defeat. His form actually improved over hurdles when he was stepped up to staying trips and the chances are that he will stay beyond three miles. Harty certainly has high hopes for him in this regard: 'You'd like to think he's a Gold Cup horse, but you hate to say those things—you need a lot of luck for it to go right!' *Edward Harty, Ireland*

CON FORZA (IRE) 8 b.g. Milan – Classic Track (Distant Music (USA)) [2016/17 c16.5m⁵ c15.7d* c19.4g⁶ c15.7g⁶ h18.7g³ Sep 3] modest handicap hurdler: modest form over fences: won handicap at Southwell in July: stays 19f: acts on good to firm and good to soft going: usually in headgear: wears tongue tie. *Phil Middleton*   **c91 h99**

CONISTON COLD 5 b.g. Captain Rio – Returning (Bob's Return (IRE)) [2016/17 h–: h16.2d⁶ h20.7g^pu May 17] poor form over hurdles: dead. *Michael Easterby*   **h60**

CONNETABLE (FR) 5 b.g. Saint des Saints (FR) – Montbresia (FR) (Video Rock (FR)) **c125** [2016/17 h136: h18.9v⁴ c20.2d* c22.4d h23.4v h19.3s h21.4g⁶ Apr 22] compact gelding: **h137** useful handicap hurdler: fourth at Haydock (5¼ lengths behind El Terremoto) in November: fairly useful form over fences: won maiden at Wincanton in December: stays 2½m: acts on heavy going: has worn headgear, including in 2016/17: lazy. *Paul Nicholls*

CONNIE MARKIEVICZ (IRE) 5 ch.m. Mountain High (IRE) – Bayloughbess (IRE) **b–** (Lancastrian) [2016/17 b15.7g b16d Jun 29] €4,500 3-y-o: seventh foal: half-sister to fairly useful hurdler/useful chaser Some Target (2½m-3½m winner, by Witness Box) and 21f hurdle winner Thehossbehind (by Mahler): dam (b65) winning pointer: well held in 2 bumpers. *Sophie Leech*

CONNIES CROSS (IRE) 10 b.g. Windsor Castle – Rockon-Beauty (IRE) (Mister Lord **c–** (USA)) [2016/17 c118: c27.5mᵖᵘ May 20] multiple winning pointer: maiden chaser: pulled up only outing in 2016/17. *Mrs Sheila Crow*

CONQUER GOLD (IRE) 7 b.m. Gold Well – Ballinamona Wish (IRE) (Kotashaan **c124** (FR)) [2016/17 h99p, b88: h21.4s h24.3s⁵ c23.4v² c25.2s² c24.1g* c22.2g⁴ Apr 15] fair **h114** form over hurdles: fairly useful form over fences: won mares handicap at Bangor in March: stays 25f: acts on heavy going: front runner/races prominently. *Nicky Richards*

CONSTANTINE BAY 6 b.g. Kayf Tara – Alina Rheinberg (GER) (Waky Nao) [2016/17 **h144** h18.9v* h19.5s* h24.4d* h24g⁴ h24.7g⁴ Apr 7] €45,000 3-y-o, £40,000 5-y-o: well-made gelding: will make a chaser: second foal: brother to modest chaser Pandy Wells (2½m-3m winner): dam (c97/h91), 2m-2¼m hurdle/chase winner, also 1¼m winner on Flat: off mark in points at second attempt: smart form over hurdles: won novices at Haydock (by ½ length from Brio Conti) in November, at Chepstow (by 6 lengths from Prime Venture) and Doncaster (River Don Novices' Hurdle, by head from No Hassle Hoff) in January: fourth in Grade 1 events at Cheltenham and Aintree last 2 starts: stays 3m: acts on heavy going: usually responds generously to pressure. *Nicky Henderson*

CONSUL DE THAIX (FR) 5 b.g. Loxias (FR) – Mange de Thaix (FR) (Mont Basile **h132** (FR)) [2016/17 h128p: h16s² h15.7d² h21.1gᶠ Mar 15] well-made gelding: useful form over hurdles: second in Wessex Youth Trust Handicap Hurdle at Ascot (5 lengths behind Brain Power) in December: should have stayed 2½m: acted on heavy going: usually raced towards rear: dead. *Nicky Henderson*

CONTEUR D'HISTOIRE (FR) 5 b.g. Le Fou (IRE) – Page d'Histoire (FR) (Video **h109** Rock (FR)) [2016/17 b15.7g h16.7g⁶ h16.7v h16s² h20.3v⁶ h16.2s h15.8sᵖᵘ h20.7g² h25g⁴ **b–** Apr 28] £63,000 3-y-o: second foal: half-brother to French 19f/2½m chase winner Brasilia (by Enrique): dam French 17f/2¼m hurdle winner: green when down the field in bumper: fair maiden hurdler: stays 21f: acts on soft going: usually in tongue tie: often races prominently. *Jonjo O'Neill*

CONTRE TOUS (FR) 5 b.g. Forestier (FR) – Orphee de Vonnas (FR) (Jimble (FR)) **c126** [2016/17 h16.8s⁵ c18.2d⁵ c17.2g* c17.2m* c16.2g³ Apr 24] fifth foal: half-brother to **h87** useful French hurdler/fairly useful chaser Ballotin (17f-2¾m winner) and bumper winner/fairly useful hurdler Voluptueux (2m winner) (both by Enrique): dam, French 2m-19f hurdle/chase winner, half-sister to dam of top-class French hurdler (stays 21f) Blue Dragon: bumper winner: fair form over hurdles for Guillaume Macaire in 2015/16: fairly useful form over fences: won novice handicap at Market Rasen in March and handicap there in April: stays 2¼m: acts on good to firm and good to soft going: wears tongue tie: often races prominently. *Paul Nicholls*

CONVOI EXCEPTIONAL (IRE) 5 b.g. Dubai Destination (USA) – Marble Sound **h–** (IRE) (Be My Native (USA)) [2016/17 h15.6gᶠ h16.6d h16vᶠ Jan 30] no form over hurdles. *Nicky Richards*

COOKING FAT 6 ch.g. Tobougg (IRE) – Ostfanni (IRE) (Spectrum (IRE)) [2016/17 **h131** h114: h21.4s² h19.7s* h18.9s h25.3s* h22.8gᶠ Apr 15] useful handicap hurdler: won at Wetherby in November and Catterick in February: stays 25f: acts on soft going: often races towards rear. *Dianne Sayer*

COOLADERRY KING (IRE) 9 b.g. King Cheetah (USA) – Daly Lady (IRE) (Lord of **c106** Appeal) [2016/17 c100: c24.1g² c27.5m⁶ c24.2d⁶ Mar 10] dual winning pointer: fair maiden chaser: left Mrs Sheila Crow after second start: stays 3m: acts on good to soft going: has worn hood, including in 2016/17. *Miss Rose Grissell*

COOLANURE (IRE) 8 b.m. Portrait Gallery (IRE) – Aiguille (IRE) (Lancastrian) **c– x** [2016/17 c–, h–: c20.1gᵖᵘ h20.6dᵖᵘ c26gᵘʳ c20.1sᵘʳ c25.6vᵖᵘ c20.1sᵖᵘ h19.7m h19.7g³ **h71** Apr 23] poor maiden hurdler: maiden chaser, no form in 2016/17: stays 25f: acts on good to soft going: usually in headgear: front runner/races prominently: often let down by jumping over fences. *Kenny Johnson*

COOL BARANCA (GER) 11 b.m. Beat Hollow – Cool Storm (IRE) (Rainbow Quest (USA)) [2016/17 h101: h17.2g h20.2s⁶ h20.6g³ h16.2d* h16.2s h19.4g h16.8s Jan 29] sparely-made mare: modest handicap hurdler nowadays: won at Kelso in October: stays 2½m: has won on good to firm going, but best efforts on good or softer: usually races in rear. *Dianne Sayer* **h93**

COOLE CHARMER (IRE) 8 ch.g. Flemensfirth (USA) – Ericas Charm (Alderbrook) [2016/17 h55, b–: c23.6d⁵ c19.7d² h20d c20.3s² c20vᵖᵘ c19.2sᶠ c21.1vᵖᵘ h20.3g h21.9d² Apr 16] rangy, good sort: bumper winner: modest form over hurdles: fair form over fences: stays 2¾m: acts on soft going: tried in cheekpieces. *Neil Mulholland* **c108** **h96**

COOLE CODY (IRE) 6 b.g. Dubai Destination (USA) – Run For Cover (IRE) (Lafontaine (USA)) [2016/17 h19.9s h18.5s² h21.6s² h20.6sᶠ h19.8v* h21.7d² Mar 26] £5,200 5-y-o: lengthy gelding: seventh foal: half-brother to useful but unreliable chaser Fine Parchment (2½m-3¼m winner, by Presenting) and to winning pointers by Presenting and Blueprint: dam (c109), 2m/17f chase winner (stayed 2½m), half-sister to smart hurdler/chaser (stayed 25f) Fundamentalist and to dam of smart hurdler (stays 3m) Barters Hill: Irish maiden point winner: fairly useful form over hurdles: won maiden at Wincanton in March: second in novices at Exeter and Hereford: stays 2¾m: raced only on ground softer than good: in hood since debut: front runner. *Michael Blake* **h118**

COOLE HALL (IRE) 5 b.g. Flemensfirth (USA) – Coole Assembly (IRE) (Saddlers' Hall (IRE)) [2016/17 h20.2g² Apr 26] £42,000 5-y-o: sixth foal: brother to a winning pointer: dam unraced half-sister to smart 2½m bumper winner/fairly useful 23f hurdle winner Snow Tern and fair hurdler/fairly useful chaser (stays 27f) American Legend: off mark in Irish maiden points (dead-heated) at second attempt: 12/1, second in maiden at Perth (nose behind Royal Village) on hurdling debut: will be suited by 2¾m+: sure to progress. *Rose Dobbin* **h115 p**

COOLKING 10 b.g. King's Theatre (IRE) – Osocool (Teenoso (USA)) [2016/17 c–, h108: c25.7d⁵ c23.5v* c28s* c25.7v* c26gᵖᵘ Mar 25] tall gelding: winning hurdler: fairly useful handicap chaser: won at Lingfield in January and February, and at Plumpton (amateur event) later in February: left Chris Gordon after second start: stays 3¾m: acts on heavy going: has worn headgear, including in 2016/17: tried in tongue tie: usually leads. *Gary Moore* **c119** **h–**

COOL MACAVITY (IRE) 9 b.g. One Cool Cat (USA) – Cause Celebre (IRE) (Peintre Celebre (USA)) [2016/17 h128: h16d h16.3g⁴ May 21] fairly useful handicap hurdler, below form both starts in 2016/17: unproven beyond 17f: acts on good to firm going. *Nicky Henderson* **h111**

COOL MIX 5 gr.g. Fair Mix (IRE) – Lucylou (IRE) (Bob Back (USA)) [2016/17 b15.6g⁶ b16g² Apr 22] £9,000 3-y-o: seventh foal: brother to a winning pointer: dam, unraced, out of half-sister to useful hurdler up to 2½m Maysata, herself dam of Cheltenham Gold Cup winner Synchronised: fairly useful form in bumpers: better effort when second at Ayr in April: in hood first start. *Iain Jardine* **b99**

COOLOGUE (IRE) 8 b.g. Helissio (FR) – Scolboa (IRE) (Bob's Return (IRE)) [2016/17 c140, h–: c25g* c26gᵖᵘ c23.4d² c24d c25gᵖᵘ c26g³ Apr 20] good-topped gelding: winning hurdler: useful handicap chaser: won Randox Handicap Chase at Cheltenham in October: stays 25f: acts on heavy going: tried in tongue tie: usually races close up. *Charlie Longsdon* **c141** **h–**

COOL SKY 8 b.g. Millkom – Intersky High (USA) (Royal Anthem (USA)) [2016/17 h116: h15.8d h17.7s² h16d² h15.6g⁶ h17.7d* h20d³ Apr 16] angular gelding: fairly useful handicap hurdler: won at Fontwell in March: stays 2½m: acts on soft and good to firm going: often races towards rear. *Ian Williams* **h118**

COOPER'S FRIEND (IRE) 8 b.g. Kayf Tara – Graphic Lady (IRE) (Phardante (FR)) [2016/17 h111: c16g⁴ c20d³ h19.9g c19.2g² c19.3g* c20g² c21.6sᵖᵘ c20.5v³ c15.5d⁶ Apr 21] strong gelding: fair hurdler, below form sole outing in 2016/17: fairly useful handicap chaser: won at Sedgefield in August: left Charlie Longsdon after sixth start: stays 2½m: acts on good to soft going: wears cheekpieces/tongue tie. *R. Mike Smith* **c119** **h86**

COOPERS SQUARE (IRE) 6 b.g. Mahler – Jessaway (IRE) (Dr Massini (IRE)) [2016/17 h15.8sᵖᵘ h19.7s⁵ h18.7g⁵ Mar 25] maiden Irish pointer: no form over hurdles. *Tom Weston* **h–**

COO STAR SIVOLA (FR) 5 b.g. Assessor (IRE) – Santorine (FR) (Della Francesca (USA)) [2016/17 h133: h19.5g² h19.4v h20.3s* h20.3s⁶ h19v* h20.3g⁴ Mar 17] rangy gelding: will make a chaser: useful hurdler: won novices at Cheltenham (listed event, by 4½ lengths from Report To Base) in January and Warwick in February: second in Persian **h139**

War Novices' Hurdle at Chepstow (length behind El Bandit) in October and fourth in Martin Pipe Conditional Jockeys' Handicap Hurdle at Cheltenham (4 lengths behind Champagne Classic) in March: likely to stay 3m: acts on heavy going. *Nick Williams*

COOTE STREET (IRE) 9 b.g. Winged Love (IRE) – Unknown Quality (Sabrehill (USA)) [2016/17 c–, h–: c21.6d⁶ c20.1g^pu Oct 8] point winner: pulled up sole outing over hurdles: no form in chases: tried in cheekpieces. *F. Jestin* — c– h–

COOZAN GEORGE 8 b.g. Bollin Eric – Pasja (IRE) (Posen (USA)) [2016/17 c102, h94: c21.3g⁴ c21.4g^pu May 15] strong gelding: maiden hurdler: fair maiden chaser, below form both starts in 2016/17: stays 2½m: acts on heavy going: often in tongue tie: usually races towards rear: temperament under suspicion. *Malcolm Jefferson* — c91 h–

COPAIN DE CLASSE (FR) 5 b.g. Enrique – Toque Rouge (FR) (Loup Solitaire (USA)) [2016/17 h–p, b–: h19.5d³ h16d* h19.8v^pu h15.3d* Mar 26] well-made gelding: bumper winner: useful form over hurdles: won novices at Chepstow in November and Wincanton (by 8 lengths from Azzuri) in March: unproven beyond 2m: acts on good to soft going: open to further improvement. *Paul Nicholls* — h130 p

COPERNICUS (IRE) 5 ch.g. Teofilo (IRE) – Nick's Nikita (IRE) (Pivotal) [2016/17 b16m⁴ b17m⁴ b17g⁴ b16.4g Mar 15] sturdy, lengthy gelding: third foal: half-brother to useful 1½m-2m winner Asbury Boss (by Dalakhani): dam useful 1m-1½m winner: fair form in bumpers: won maiden at Killarney in August: left M. Halford after third start: wears tongue tie. *Charlie Longsdon* — b90

COPPER BIRCH (IRE) 9 ch.g. Beneficial – Givehertime (IRE) (Commanche Run) [2016/17 c109, h–: c23.8g* c18.9s* c20.9d⁵ c24.1d⁴ c15.9s⁴ c19.4d^pu Apr 16] rangy, useful-looking gelding: winning hurdler: fair handicap chaser nowadays: won at Ffos Las (dead-heated) and Hereford (conditional event) in November: stays 3¾m: acts on heavy going: often in headgear nowadays. *Evan Williams* — c107 h–

COPPERFACEJACK (IRE) 7 b.g. Robin des Pres (FR) – Leone des Pres (FR) (Tip Moss (FR)) [2016/17 c87, h–: c22.5d³ c24d⁶ c20g² c24d² c25.5s² c23.6d² c23.6g² c23.6g² Apr 17] maiden hurdler: modest maiden chaser: placed on 7 of 8 starts in 2016/17: stays 25f: acts on soft going: has worn cheekpieces, including final start: wears tongue tie: races prominently, often travels strongly: hard to win with. *Paul Webber* — c93 § h–

COPPER KAY 7 b.m. Kayf Tara – Presenting Copper (IRE) (Presenting) [2016/17 b107: b16d⁵ h15.8d* h16.3g² h16.3d³ h21v² h19.4s* h20.5g² h19.5g* Apr 17] useful-looking mare: useful bumper winner: useful hurdler: won mares maiden at Ffos Las in October, and mares novices at Doncaster in March and Chepstow in April: second in Mares 'National Hunt' Novices' Hurdle Finale at Newbury (4 lengths behind Snow Leopardess) in March: will stay 3m: acts on heavy going. *Philip Hobbs* — h130 b96

COPT HILL 9 b.g. Avonbridge – Lalique (IRE) (Lahib (USA)) [2016/17 h79: h16.8d³ h16.4s h15.7d⁴ h16.8s h19.9g³ h19.7m^pu Apr 13] poor handicap hurdler: unproven beyond 17f: acts on heavy going: usually wears headgear: front runner/races prominently. *Tracy Waggott* — h69

CORAL POINT (IRE) 11 ch.g. Hawkeye (IRE) – Green Crystal (Green Dancer (USA)) [2016/17 c23.6g⁵ May 17] multiple winning pointer: lightly-raced hurdler: poor form in hunter chases. *B. Dowling* — c82 h–

CORBETT COURT (IRE) 5 br.g. Court Cave (IRE) – Stefphonic (IRE) (Orchestra) [2016/17 h20v^pu h20g⁶ Apr 9] maiden pointer: poor form over hurdles. *Debra Hamer* — h61

CORDEY WARRIOR 7 b.g. Tobougg (IRE) – Aquavita (Kalaglow) [2016/17 b–: b16.8g³ b16.8g³ h16.8v h19g^pu Mar 2] modest form in bumpers: no form over hurdles: left Victor Dartnall after second start: in headgear last 4 starts, tongue tied last 2: temperament under suspicion. *Karen George* — h– b77

CORINDA 6 b.m. Midnight Legend – Conchita (St Ninian) [2016/17 b16s⁴ b16.2v⁴ b17g Apr 15] third foal: half-sister to modest hurdler Conjola (2½m winner, by Grape Tree Road), stayed 3m: dam, bumper winner, half-sister to fairly useful but temperamental staying chaser Crackadee: no form in bumpers: left Simon Waugh after first start. *Rhona Brewis* — b–

CORK CITIZEN 9 b.g. Overbury (IRE) – Peach of A Citizen (IRE) (Anshan) [2016/17 c122: c24g⁴ c23.8g* c24.2d⁶ Jun 19] fairly useful handicap chaser: won at Ffos Las in June: stays 25f: acts on heavy going: wears headgear/tongue tie: unreliable. *David Pipe* — c123 §

CORNBOROUGH 6 ch.g. Sir Percy – Emirates First (IRE) (In The Wings) [2016/17 **h125** h116: h16.7g* h16.5d* h16.7g h16.2g⁶ h16d³ h16.6g² h16.6g⁴ Dec 10] fairly useful handicap hurdler: won at Bangor and Aintree early in season: placed at Wetherby and Doncaster (intermediate) in November: raced around 2m: acts on good to soft going: often races towards rear. *Mark Walford*

CORNER CREEK (IRE) 7 b.g. Presenting – No Moore Bills (Nicholas Bill) [2016/17 **c–** h94: h19.7v⁶ c23.6gᵖᵘ Apr 17] point winner: maiden hurdler: pulled up in novice handicap **h–** on chasing debut. *Michael Scudamore*

CORNISH WARRIOR (IRE) 6 b.g. Oscar (IRE) – Ballylooby Moss (IRE) (Supreme **h104** Leader) [2016/17 b–: b15.9g³ b16.7g⁴ h20s³ h21.4s⁴ h18.7g* h19.1g³ Apr 12] fair form in **b90** bumpers: fair form over hurdles: won maiden at Stratford in March: left Rebecca Curtis after third start: stays 2½m: tried in cheekpieces: usually races prominently. *Neil Mulholland*

CORONER'S REPORT (IRE) 6 b.g. Coroner (IRE) – My Linda (IRE) (Bob Back **h93** (USA)) [2016/17 b16.4g h23.9sᵖᵘ h23.9m⁴ h19gᵘʳ h19.7v⁴ h20sᵖᵘ Feb 19] €3,400 4-y-o, **b–** £23,000 5-y-o: second foal: dam unraced half-sister to useful hurdler/chaser (stayed 25f) Ross Moff: off mark in Irish maiden points at second attempt: well beaten in bumper: modest form over hurdles: best effort at 2½m: acts on heavy going: in hood last 4 starts: tends to find little. *Rebecca Curtis*

CORREGGIO 7 ch.g. Bertolini (USA) – Arian Da (Superlative) [2016/17 h16gᵘʳ Oct 29] **h–** fairly useful at best on Flat, stays 1½m: no form over hurdles. *Micky Hammond*

CORRIE LOCH 5 b.m. King's Theatre (IRE) – Penneyrose Bay (Karinga Bay) [2016/17 **h91** b16.7s⁴ h19.1d⁶ h19.5g⁵ Apr 17] angular mare: fourth foal: half-sister to fairly useful **b75** hurdler/useful chaser Generous Ransom (19f-2¾m winner, by Generous) and fairly useful hurdler/chaser Imperial Presence (2m winner, by Presenting): dam (c121/h130), 19f-2¾m hurdle/chase winner, half-sister to fair hurdler/useful chaser (stayed 3¼m) Latimer's Place: fourth in bumper at Market Rasen: modest form on second of 2 starts over hurdles. *Alan King*

CORRIN WOOD (IRE) 10 gr.g. Garuda (IRE) – Allstar Rose (IRE) (Fourstars Allstar **c105 §** (USA)) [2016/17 c112, h–: c25gᵖᵘ h25.3s² h23.6g³ c22.9s⁴ c23.4s⁵ Jan 7] workmanlike **h121** gelding: fairly useful handicap hurdler: third at Chepstow in December: smart chaser at best, just fair nowadays: left Donald McCain after first start: stays 25f: acts on heavy going: has worn cheekpieces, including in 2016/17: has worn tongue tie: usually races close up: let down by attitude over fences. *Dan Skelton*

CORSKEAGH EXPRESS (IRE) 6 gr.g. Daylami (IRE) – Zara's Victory (IRE) (Old **h–** Vic) [2016/17 h21.5g h16d h19.9s Nov 22] point winner: no form over hurdles. *Mark McNiff, Ireland*

COR WOT AN APPLE 6 b.g. Apple Tree (FR) – Chipewyas (FR) (Bering) [2016/17 **c84** h78, b75: h15.3m³ h15.3m h17.7g³ c20mᵘʳ c16.1d c19.7d⁴ c20.2g⁶ h19s h20.3s⁵ h17.7m² **h93** Apr 17] modest maiden hurdler: poor form over fences: left Colin Tizzard after third start: stays 2½m: acts on good to firm and good to soft going: tried in cheekpieces: wears tongue tie. *Neil Mulholland*

CORZEAM (FR) 5 gr.g. Early March – Night Fever (FR) (Garde Royale) [2016/17 **b82 §** b15.7vʳʳ b16g⁴ b16sʳʳ Mar 30] sixth foal: dam French 2¾m chase winner: modest form completed start in bumpers: refused to race other 2 starts: wears hood/tongue tie: one to avoid. *Nigel Twiston-Davies*

COSETTE (IRE) 6 b.m. Champs Elysees – Luanas Pearl (IRE) (Bahri (USA)) [2016/17 **h97** h16.8d² h19.9d⁵ Nov 8] fair on Flat, stays 17f: modest form over hurdles: better effort when second in mares novice at Newton Abbot in September: should stay 2½m: wears cheekpieces. *Bernard Llewellyn*

COSMEAPOLITAN 4 b.g. Mawatheeq (USA) – Cosmea (Compton Place) [2016/17 **h105 P** h16.3d* Dec 14] good-topped gelding: dam fairly useful 2m hurdle winner: useful on Flat, stays 1½m: 1/3, won juvenile at Newbury (readily by 7 lengths from Fixed Rate) on hurdling debut: open to significant improvement. *Alan King*

COSMIC DIAMOND 7 b.m. Multiplex – Lucy Glitters (Ardross) [2016/17 h–: h15.9s⁵ **c–** h17.7v⁶ h15.8d h21m⁴ c17m⁴ Apr 16] poor maiden hurdler: well beaten in novice handicap **h73** on chasing debut: should stay 2½m: acts on soft going: in tongue tie last 4 starts: usually races nearer last than first. *Paul Webber*

COSMIC KING (FR) 5 b.g. Kingsalsa (USA) – Kikinda (FR) (Daliapour (IRE)) **h103**
[2016/17 b–: b16.3d² b15.8g h15.8s h15.8s⁵ h15.8g⁶ Apr 3] lengthy gelding: modest form **b83**
in bumpers: best effort when second at Stratford early in season: fair form on last of 3 starts
over hurdles: in hood last 5 starts. *Richard Phillips*

COSMIC STATESMAN 5 ch.g. Halling (USA) – Cosmic Case (Casteddu) [2016/17 **h89**
h102: h18.6g⁶ h15.8dᵖᵘ h19.4g h15.8vᵖᵘ h17.7g⁶ h20.5m² Apr 16] strong gelding: modest
maiden hurdler: stays 21f: acts on soft and good to firm going: in headgear last 4 starts.
Neil King

COSMOS DES OBEAUX (FR) 5 b.g. Spanish Moon (USA) – Kore des Obeaux (FR) **h119 p**
(Saint Cyrien (FR)) [2016/17 h17.9s⁵ h17.9s³ h17.4v* h16.7s³ Feb 10] good-topped
gelding: half-brother to fair hurdler/winning chaser Sophonie (2m/17f winner, by
Kapgarde) and French 21f chase winner Rosaire (by Grand Tresor): dam unraced: fairly
useful form over hurdles: won 4-y-o event at Auteuil in November: third in novice at
Bangor in February: left N. Devilder after third start: capable of better. *Dan Skelton*

COSMO'S MOON (IRE) 4 b.g. Morozov (USA) – She's A Dreamer (IRE) (Safety **b89**
Catch (USA)) [2016/17 b16s⁵ b16.3d Feb 11] €11,000 3-y-o: rather unfurnished gelding:
seventh foal: closely related to useful but unreliable hurdler Bonzo Bing (2m winner,
by Gold Well), stays 2½m: dam unraced: fair form on first of 2 starts in bumpers.
R. P. McNamara, Ireland

COSTANTE VIA (IRE) 6 b.m. Milan – Spirit Rock (IRE) (Rock Hopper) [2016/17 b89: **b89**
b17g² Oct 23] fair form in bumpers: second in mares event at Aintree on sole start in
2016/17. *Nigel Twiston-Davies*

COSTLY DREAM (IRE) 5 b.g. Yeats (IRE) – What Price Love (USA) (Repriced **b80**
(USA)) [2016/17 b15.7v⁶ Nov 18] 20/1, sixth in bumper at Haydock. *Philip Hobbs*

COTILLION 11 b.g. Sadler's Wells (USA) – Riberac (Efisio) [2016/17 h130: h20.1s² Sep **h103**
30] close-coupled, quite good-topped gelding: useful hurdler, beaten in seller sole outing in
2016/17: stays 2½m: acts on heavy going: has worn cheekpieces, including last 4 starts:
has worn tongue tie: often travels strongly. *Ian Williams*

COTSWOLD ROAD 7 b.g. Flemensfirth (USA) – Crystal Ballerina (IRE) (Sadler's **h– §**
Wells (USA)) [2016/17 h107, b83: h25.5v* h23v⁶ h21.6gᶠ Apr 11] maiden hurdler, no form
in 2016/17: in blinkers last 2 starts: often in tongue tie: temperamental. *Colin Tizzard*

COTTAGE OAK (IRE) 14 ch.g. Flemensfirth (USA) – Native Thistle (IRE) (Ovac **c–**
(ITY)) [2016/17 c112, h–: c26.3gᵖᵘ Mar 17] workmanlike gelding: multiple winning **h–**
pointer: winning hurdler: fairly useful chaser at best, out of depth sole outing in 2016/17:
stays 25f: acts on good to firm and heavy going: has worn headgear. *J. J. O'Shea*

COTTERSROCK (IRE) 7 b.g. Robin des Pres (FR) – Toasted Oats (IRE) (Be My **c129**
Native (USA)) [2016/17 h128, b96: h23.3dᵘʳ c20d* c24.4g⁴ c23g³ c20d³ h21gᵖᵘ Mar 18] **h–**
strong gelding: bumper winner: fairly useful hurdler at best, failed to complete both outings
in 2016/17: fairly useful form over fences: won maiden at Uttoxeter in October: should be
suited by 3m: acts on good to soft going: in headgear last 2 starts. *Martin Keighley*

COTTESLOE (IRE) 8 b.g. Teofilo (IRE) – Vignelaure (IRE) (Royal Academy (USA)) **h101**
[2016/17 h16.2d⁴ h15.8m⁴ h16.5m⁵ Dec 8] fair on Flat, stays 2m: fair form on second of 3
starts over hurdles (wore cheekpieces): left John Berry after that. *Neil Mulholland*

COTTONWOOL BABY (IRE) 6 b.m. Gold Well – Golden Steppes (IRE) (Titus Livius **h–**
(FR)) [2016/17 h98, b–: h21g⁴ h23.3sᵖᵘ h21.6g Apr 12] in frame on second of 2 starts in
Irish maiden points: maiden hurdler, no form in 2016/17: tried in cheekpieces: usually
races nearer last than first. *Michael Scudamore*

COUDEFOUDRE (FR) 5 gr.g. Martaline – Chamoss World (FR) (Lost World (IRE)) **h–**
[2016/17 h15.8dᵖᵘ h19.7vᵖᵘ h16s h19.9s⁶ Apr 1] no form over hurdles. *Venetia Williams*

COUGAR KID (IRE) 6 b.g. Yeats (IRE) – Western Skylark (USA) (Westerner) [2016/17 **h96**
h108, b–: h17.7gˢᵘ h18.7m³ h16.3g² h15.7g h19g h19.7v³ h19.2v h19.3s* h20.1sᵖᵘ h19.5g
h21.6g² Apr 21] lengthy gelding: bumper winner: modest handicap hurdler nowadays: won
lady amateur event at Catterick in February: left Philip Hide after fourth start: stays 2¾m:
acts on good to firm and heavy going: has worn headgear. *John O'Shea*

COUGAR'S GOLD (IRE) 6 b.g. Oscar (IRE) – Top Her Up (IRE) (Beneficial) [2016/17 **h–**
b88: b16.7g* h19.4g Jan 27] fairly useful form in bumpers: won at Market Rasen early in **b96**
season: well beaten in maiden on hurdling debut. *Peter Bowen*

COUNTDOWN (GER) 9 b.g. Monsun (GER) – Catella (GER) (Generous (IRE)) **h–**
[2016/17 h22sᵖᵘ Jan 7] runner-up in bumper in 2014/15: no form over hurdles: wears
tongue tie. *Chris Grant*

COUNTERFEITER 7 b.g. Singspiel (IRE) – Grain of Truth (Gulch (USA)) [2016/17 **h102**
h96p: h16g⁴ h16.4g⁶ h19.4g⁶ h20s⁴ Jan 1] good-topped gelding: fair form over hurdles:
unproven beyond 2m: best form on good going. *Martin Bosley*

COUNTER SHY (IRE) 4 b.g. Galileo (IRE) – Cross The Flags (IRE) (Flemensfirth **b94**
(USA)) [2016/17 b16.7m³ Apr 9] first foal: dam (h130), 21f/2¾m hurdle winner, half-sister
to Cheltenham Gold Cup winner Synchronised: 7/2, shaped well when third in bumper at
Market Rasen (head behind Who's My Jockey) on debut. *Jonjo O'Neill*

COUNTERSIGN 8 b.g. Authorized (IRE) – Circle of Love (Sakhee (USA)) [2016/17 **h–**
h105: h18.6g Jun 21] fair hurdler: unproven beyond 17f: acted on good to soft going: usually
wore hood: often raced freely: dead. *Charles Pogson*

COUNT MERIBEL 5 ch.g. Three Valleys (USA) – Bakhtawar (IRE) (Lomitas) [2016/17 **h122**
b80: b15.8g⁵ b17.7d² h15.7d³ h15.9v³ h15.7v² h20d² Apr 16] fairly useful form **b95**
when second on last of 3 starts in bumpers: fairly useful form over hurdles: second in
novice at Towcester in February and handicap at Ffos Las in April: stays 2½m: acts on
heavy going: front runner/races prominently. *Nigel Twiston-Davies*

COUNTRY LEGEND 5 b.m. Midnight Legend – Sylroy (Silver Patriarch (IRE)) **b–**
[2016/17 b16.8g⁵ Apr 26] first foal: dam (h89) 2½m hurdle winner: third in maiden point
on debut: well beaten in maiden bumper. *Miss Harriet Brown*

COUNTRY'N'WESTERN (FR) 5 b.g. Samum (GER) – Cracking Melody (Shamardal **b95**
(USA)) [2016/17 b109p: b16.7d⁵ Apr 27] fairly useful form in bumpers: not seen to best
effect when fifth at Market Rasen on sole start in 2016/17. *David Elsworth*

COUNT SALAZAR (IRE) 12 b.g. Revoque (IRE) – Cherry Sent (IRE) (Presenting) **c78**
[2016/17 c118, h114: c20.1d h23.3dᵖᵘ h23.1g⁴ h23.1g⁴ c23.8g³ Sep 6] lengthy gelding: fair **h65**
handicap hurdler/useful handicap chaser at best, well below that level in 2016/17: stays
25f: acts on good to firm and heavy going: wears headgear: in tongue tie last 3 starts: front
runner/races prominently. *Sally Randell*

COUNTY ROAD (IRE) 6 b.g. Robin des Pres (FR) – Volverta (FR) (Green Tune (USA)) **h85**
[2016/17 h16g⁶ h24d h20g⁴ h24.4d⁵ Jan 9] £15,000 5-y-o: second foal: half-brother to
fairly useful hurdler/chaser Bells of Ailsworth (21f-25f winner, by Kayf Tara): dam, French
2m hurdle winner (1¼m-12.5f winner on Flat), half-sister to useful hurdler/smart chaser
(stayed 2½m) Vol Solitaire: placed both starts in maiden points: modest form over hurdles.
Caroline Bailey

COUP DE GRACE (IRE) 8 b.g. Elusive City (USA) – No Way (IRE) (Rainbows For **c–**
Life (CAN)) [2016/17 c–, h72: c21.1dᵖᵘ h24.8d h20d Jul 17] rather leggy gelding: fair **h–**
maiden hurdler, little form since 2014/15: no form over fences: left Pat Phelan after first
start: tried in visor. *Charles Byrnes, Ireland*

COUP DE PINCEAU (FR) 5 b.g. Buck's Boum (FR) – Castagnette Iii (FR) (Tin Soldier **h114 p**
(FR)) [2016/17 b99p: b15.7m⁸ h16s² Nov 21] good-topped gelding: fairly useful form in **b95**
bumpers: won at Ascot in October: 9/4, second in novice at Kempton (3½ lengths behind
Lough Derg Spirit) on hurdling debut: open to improvement. *Paul Nicholls*

COURT AFFAIRS (IRE) 5 b.g. Court Cave (IRE) – Rock Money (IRE) (Deploy) **b97**
[2016/17 b17d* Apr 5] €13,000 3-y-o: fourth foal: dam unraced half-sister to fairly useful
hurdler/fair chaser (stayed 2¾m) Wouldn't You Agree: 18/1, won bumper at Carlisle (by
6 lengths from Luckime) on debut, soon clear. *Seamus Mullins*

COURT BALOO (IRE) 6 b.g. Court Cave (IRE) – Tremplin (IRE) (Tremblant) [2016/17 **h85**
h56, b73: h23.1g* h23.1d³ h23.1gᵖᵘ h22.7v³ h24g Apr 8] modest handicap hurdler: won
at Bangor early in season: stays 23f: acts on good to soft going: often in cheekpieces.
Alistair Whillans

COURT BY SURPRISE (IRE) 12 b.g. Beneficial – Garryduff Princess (IRE) (Husyan **c124 §**
(USA)) [2016/17 c135, h–: c24g c23.6gᵖᵘ c24.2d² c28.8d c26g⁴ c24.2s⁶ c24g⁵ c23.8m⁴ Apr **h–**
2] well-made gelding: winning hurdler: fairly useful handicap chaser nowadays: second in
veterans event at Sandown in November: stays 29f: acts on soft going: tried in cheekpieces:
temperamental. *Emma Lavelle*

COURT CHALLENGE (IRE) 8 b.m. Court Cave (IRE) – Legal Challenge (IRE) (Strong Gale) [2016/17 h16m h20.3g² h20v³ h20v⁴ Feb 25] half-sister to 3 winners, including fairly useful hurdler Like A Hurricane (2¼m/19f winner, by Simply Great) and fair/ungenuine chaser Adare Prince (2½m-25f winner, by Supreme Leader): dam (h109) 2m-2½m hurdle winner: fair handicap hurdler: won mares event at Gowran in 2015/16: stays 2¾m: acts on heavy going: in tongue tie last 4 starts. *Shane Crawley, Ireland* **h114**

COURT DISMISSED (IRE) 7 b.g. Court Cave (IRE) – Carramanagh Lady (IRE) (Anshan) [2016/17 c116§, h116: c26.2m³ c20.3g² c26.3g³ c23.9s³ c20v⁵ c19.4d c20v³ c20sᵖᵘ Mar 18] compact gelding: winning hurdler: fair handicap chaser: stays 25f: acts on soft going: tried in cheekpieces: temperamental. *Donald McCain* **c110 §** **h–**

COURT DUTY (IRE) 5 b.g. Court Cave (IRE) – Easter Duties (IRE) (Aristocracy) [2016/17 b15.8d Nov 28] well beaten in bumper. *Rebecca Curtis* **b–**

COURTESY CALL (IRE) 8 br.g. Manduro (GER) – Three Wrens (IRE) (Second Empire (IRE)) [2016/17 h16g⁵ h20g⁴ Oct 14] lightly-raced hurdler, modest form in 2016/17: stays 19f: acts on good to firm and good to soft going. *Nicky Henderson* **h96**

COURT FRONTIER (IRE) 9 b.g. Court Cave (IRE) – Dame En Rouge (IRE) (Imperial Frontier (USA)) [2016/17 c24.1g c21g c20.9s² c23.6dᵖᵘ c23.6s* h26s* c30.7s* c33.4sᵖᵘ c27.9d⁵ Apr 16] fair handicap hurdler: won at Warwick in January: fairly useful handicap chaser: won at Chepstow earlier in January and Huntingdon in March: stays 31f: acts on good to firm and heavy going: has worn cheekpieces: often races in rear. *Christian Williams* **c128** **h113**

COURTING HARRY 6 b.g. Lucarno (USA) – Harry's Bride (Sir Harry Lewis (USA)) [2016/17 b–: b15.8m⁴ Apr 25] no form in bumpers. *Sarah-Jayne Davies* **b–**

COURT IN SESSION (IRE) 12 b.g. Court Cave (IRE) – Dangerous Dolly (IRE) (Jurado (USA)) [2016/17 c16m⁴ c16.1g³ c15.9s⁵ c19.2g⁶ Apr 11] useful-looking gelding: multiple point winner: winning hurdler: modest chaser nowadays: unproven beyond 2m: acts on good to firm and good to soft going: has worn headgear: has worn tongue tie, including last 4 starts: one to treat with caution (often reluctant/led in at start). *Mrs Annabel Brook* **c91 §** **h– §**

COURTINTHEMIDDLE (IRE) 6 b.g. Court Cave (IRE) – Kilmessan (IRE) (Flemensfirth (USA)) [2016/17 h20g h19.5s h19.5s h19.7v h20s h21m* h21.6m⁴ Apr 15] £27,000 5-y-o: second foal: dam, unraced, closely related to fairly useful hurdler/useful chaser (winner up to 25f) Takagi and half-sister to fairly useful hurdler/chaser (stayed 31f) Victrix Gale: runner-up in Irish maiden point: poor hurdler: won handicap at Kempton in April: stays 21f: acts on good to firm going. *Deborah Faulkner* **h82**

COURT KING (IRE) 6 b.g. Indian River (FR) – Eliza Everett (IRE) (Meneval (USA)) [2016/17 h75, b–: h20d⁶ h23.3g⁴ h23m⁵ h22.1d⁵ h23.3g* h23.1g* h21.6m⁴ h23.1g² h23.6d* h23.6s Dec 27] fair handicap hurdler: won at Uttoxeter and Bangor in September, and at Chepstow in November: stays 3m: acts on good to firm and good to soft going: wears headgear: has worn tongue tie, including in 2016/17: often races prominently. *Peter Bowen* **h108**

COURTLANDS PRINCE 8 b.g. Presenting – Bathwick Annie (Sula Bula) [2016/17 h70: h15.3m² h16d* h16.8m* h16.7g² h15.3m³ h16m³ Nov 4] fair handicap hurdler: won at Worcester (conditional early) and Newton Abbot early in season: should stay 2½m: acts on soft and good to firm going: wears tongue tie. *Neil Mulholland* **h112**

COURT MINSTREL (IRE) 10 b.g. Court Cave (IRE) – Theatral (Orchestra) [2016/17 c–, h155: h16m² h19.3d⁴ h16.8s⁵ h20.5d h16.8s h16.8g Mar 17] lengthy gelding: smart hurdler: second in listed event at Kempton (neck behind Hargam) in October: winning chaser: stays 19f: acts on good to firm and good to soft going: often races in rear. *Evan Williams* **c–** **h145**

COURT OF LAW (IRE) 9 b.g. Court Cave (IRE) – Divine Dancer (IRE) (Carmelite House (USA)) [2016/17 c97, h69§: c24d² c24.2g⁴ c19.4g⁵ c23m⁵ c15.7m Sep 27] maiden hurdler: modest handicap chaser, below form in 2016/17: stays easy 3m: acts on good to soft going: wears headgear: front runner/races prominently: temperamental. *Donald McCain* **c75 §** **h– §**

COURTOWN OSCAR (IRE) 8 b.g. Oscar (IRE) – Courtown Bowe VII (Damsire Unregistered) [2016/17 c124, h113: h22.8v⁴ c22.9sᵖᵘ h25.5v* c24.3v² c28.4g² c30d⁴ Apr 29] fairly useful handicap hurdler: won at Hereford in January: fairly useful handicap chaser: second at Ayr in March and Haydock in April: stays 3½m: acts on heavy going: tried in cheekpieces: usually leads. *Philip Kirby* **c125** **h125**

COURT PAINTER (IRE) 7 b.g. Court Cave (IRE) – Comings (IRE) (Grand Lodge (USA)) [2016/17 c19.3sᵘʳ c19.3g⁴ c21.2m May 30] point winner: no form in chases. *Victor Thompson* **c–**

COUSIN KHEE 10 b.g. Sakhee (USA) – Cugina (Distant Relative) [2016/17 c100, h125: h22.1m h20.5g⁴ h15.5d⁴ h19.4d⁵ h21.4m⁴ h19.8f² Apr 23] good-topped gelding: fairly useful handicap hurdler: second at Wincanton (amateur) in April: once-raced chaser: stays 2½m: acts on firm and soft going: tried in cheekpieces: temperamental. *Hughie Morrison*   **c–** **h115 §**

COUSIN OSCAR (IRE) 5 b.g. Oscar (IRE) – On The Jetty (IRE) (Be My Native (USA)) [2016/17 b16.8d³ h19.9d³ h16d² h16.7s* h16.2g* h16.5gᵖᵘ Apr 8] €12,000 3-y-o, £30,000 4-y-o: sturdy gelding: third foal: dam (h103) 19f hurdle winner: second on completed start in Irish maiden points: encouragement when third in bumper: fairly useful form over hurdles: won novices at Bangor in February and March: unproven beyond 17f: acts on soft going: usually races close up. *Donald McCain*   **h122** **b81**

COUSIN PETE 9 b.g. Kayf Tara – Leachbrook Lady (Alderbrook) [2016/17 c25.3g* Apr 27] second foal: dam winning pointer: won all 4 completed starts in points: in tongue tie, 4/1, also won hunter at Cheltenham (by 2 lengths from High Hatton) on chasing debut. *Mrs Elizabeth Brown*   **c110**

COWARDS CLOSE (IRE) 10 br.g. Presenting – Parsee (IRE) (Persian Mews) [2016/17 c117, h–: c20.1f c24m³ c24.2gᵖᵘ c23.6s⁵ c23.6g⁶ Apr 3] winning hurdler: fairly useful handicap chaser, below best in 2016/17: stays 25f: acts on heavy going: tried in visor: usually wears tongue tie: often races lazily: temperamental. *Chris Gordon*   **c105 §** **h–**

COWSLIP 8 b.m. Tobougg (IRE) – Forsythia (Most Welcome) [2016/17 h115: h20m h20d⁴ h22.1g* h23.3d² h20.6g⁶ h23.3v⁴ h23.1d⁵ h23.8s⁵ c18v⁵ c24.1gᵖᵘ Mar 25] fair handicap hurdler: won mares event at Cartmel in August: little impact in 2 starts over fences: stays 25f: acts on soft going: wears cheekpieces. *Donald McCain*   **c–** **h106**

COYABA 7 b.g. Midnight Legend – Peel Me A Grape (Gunner B) [2016/17 h20.7d⁶ h19vᵖᵘ Dec 31] sturdy gelding: maiden hurdler, no form in 2016/17: stays 21f: acts on soft going. *Richard Phillips*   **h–**

COYOACAN (FR) 5 b.g. Al Namix (FR) – Jetty Dancer (FR) (Smadoun (FR)) [2016/17 b66: b15.8d³ ab16g⁴ h15.8d³ h15.8g⁵ Apr 3] fair form in bumpers: best effort when third at Huntingdon in December: fair form over hurdles: fair effort when third in maiden at Huntingdon in March: will prove suited by further than 2m: front runner/races prominently. *Warren Greatrex*   **h110** **b94**

CRACKDELOUST (FR) 5 b.g. Daramsar (FR) – Magic Rose (FR) (Manninamix) [2016/17 b97: h15.6g⁴ h16.4v³ h16.8v² h19.9g⁵ h16.8m* Apr 19] bumper winner: fair form over hurdles: won novice at Sedgefield in April: unproven beyond 17f: acts on good to firm and heavy going: often travels strongly. *Brian Ellison*   **h111**

CRACK DU TAY (FR) 5 b.g. Ballingarry (IRE) – Bonjour Jandrer (FR) (Pennekamp (USA)) [2016/17 b15.7v³ b15.9g⁶ h15.8d h16.3d⁶ h15.7d Feb 26] €22,000 3-y-o: first foal: dam, French 2m/17f hurdle/chaser winner, also 11.5f winner on Flat: modest form on first of 2 starts in bumpers: modest form over hurdles. *Mark Wall*   **h98** **b84**

CRACKERDANCER (IRE) 7 b.m. Robin des Champs (FR) – Katie's Cracker (Rambo Dancer (CAN)) [2016/17 b17v² b16v* b16v* Apr 1] €39,000 3-y-o: sixth foal: half-sister to 3 winners, including useful hurdler/chaser Saludos (2m/2¼m winner, by Bob Back): dam (h71), maiden hurdler, 11f-1¾m winner on Flat: useful form in bumpers: won at Limerick in March and Navan (mares event, by 20 lengths from Shimmer's Rock) in April: will stay 2½m: in tongue tie last 3 starts. *Ray Hackett, Ireland*   **b109**

CRACKING FIND (IRE) 6 b.g. Robin des Pres (FR) – Crack The Kicker (IRE) (Anshan) [2016/17 b–: h19.9d⁴ h18.9v⁴ h21.3s h19.3d⁴ h25.3s⁶ h18.9v³ h18.6m² Apr 17] point winner: fairly useful hurdler: won novices at Uttoxeter (awarded race after dead-heating with One Forty Seven) in October and Catterick in January: stays 2½m: acts on good to firm and heavy going: usually leads. *Sue Smith*   **h117**

CRACKING HABIT 10 b.g. Erhaab (USA) – Monty's Lass (IRE) (Montelimar (USA)) [2016/17 c24.2m May 3] dual winning pointer: in blinkers/tongue tie, tailed off in hunter on chasing debut. *Mrs S. Prouse*   **c–**

CRACKING SMART (FR) 5 b.g. Great Pretender (IRE) – Maya du Frene (FR) (Le Pommier d'Or) [2016/17 h16.9d h19s² b16d* Apr 18] third foal: half-brother to French 1½m-1¾m bumper winner Barbarella Smart (by Hurricane Cat): dam (h104), French 17f/2¼m hurdle winner, also 1½m winner on Flat: won maiden bumper at Fairyhouse (by 13 lengths from Narcissistic) in April: fairly useful form over hurdles: better effort when second in maiden at Naas in February: left D. Sourdeau de Beauregard after first start: should prove suited by 2½m+: in tongue tie last 2 starts: should improve further over hurdles. *Gordon Elliott, Ireland*   **h123 p** **b108**

CRACK MOME (FR) 5 ch.g. Spanish Moon (USA) – Peche Mome (FR) (April Night   **h141**
(FR)) [2016/17 h16.8s* h16v² h16.4g Mar 14] rangy, rather unfurnished gelding: first foal:
dam, French 12.5f-1¾m bumper winner, half-sister to fairly useful hurdler/useful chaser
(stayed 2½m) Kalca Mome: French bumper winner: useful form over hurdles: won maiden
at Clonmel in December: best effort when second in Moscow Flyer Novices' Hurdle at
Punchestown (1¼ lengths behind Any Second Now) in January. *W. P. Mullins, Ireland*

CRACK ON JACK 6 b.g. Fair Mix (IRE) – Indian Flag (IRE) (Indian Ridge) [2016/17   **b–**
b16.8g Apr 26] maiden pointer: tailed off in maiden bumper. *A. J. Evans*

CRACK ON MAISIE 6 ch.m. Gold Away (IRE) – Maisie Daisie (FR) (Califet (FR))   **b–**
[2016/17 b15.8d May 5] first foal: dam unraced half-sister to high-class hurdler/smart
chaser (stayed 25f) Crack Away Jack (by Gold Away) and smart 2m hurdler Jolly's
Cracked It: well held in mares bumper. *Emma Lavelle*

CRACK ON TOM (IRE) 8 ch.g. Great Exhibition (USA) – Nordic Cloud (IRE) (Lure   **h–**
(USA)) [2016/17 h58: h19.9g⁶ May 14] chunky gelding: no form in novice hurdles.
Emma Lavelle

CRAFTY ROBERTO 9 ch.g. Intikhab (USA) – Mowazana (IRE) (Galileo (IRE))   **c105**
[2016/17 c110, h–: c16.3g² c19.9d⁴ h16.7s* h16.6g⁵ c17.2d⁵ c17.2s² c20d c17.2m² c17.2d²   **h110**
Apr 27] leggy gelding: fair handicap hurdler: won at Market Rasen (conditional) in
December: fair maiden chaser: best at short of 2½m: acts on good to firm and heavy going:
usually wears headgear: wears tongue tie: front runner/races prominently. *Alex Hales*

CRAGGAKNOCK 6 b.g. Authorized (IRE) – Goodie Twosues (Fraam) [2016/17 h16s*   **h121**
h16s* h15.7s⁵ h20g Apr 7] good-topped gelding: dam half-sister to smart chaser (stayed
25f) Three Mirrors: fairly useful on Flat, stays 14.5f: fairly useful form over hurdles: won
novices at Wetherby in November and December: wears cheekpieces. *Mark Walford*

CRAIGANBOY (IRE) 8 b.g. Zagreb (USA) – Barnish River (IRE) (Riverhead (USA))   **c109**
[2016/17 h104: h20.5s⁵ h16s h16v⁴ c15.9s⁵ c18v* c17.1s⁴ Mar 25] fair maiden hurdler,   **h77**
below form in 2016/17: fair form over fences: won novice handicap at Ayr in February:
stays 21f: best form on heavy going: usually wears hood: often in tongue tie in 2016/17:
races well off pace. *N. W. Alexander*

CRAIGANEE (IRE) 10 b.g. Craigsteel – Hows She Going (IRE) (Strong Statement   **c–**
(USA)) [2016/17 h100: h22m³ h23.6d* c20.9s c24spu h25.5vpu h23.9s h19g⁴ h16.8d⁴   **h99**
h23.1g⁴ Apr 11] tall gelding: fair handicap hurdler: won at Chepstow in October: no form
over fences: stays 3m: acts on heavy going: wears hood/tongue tie: front runner/races
prominently. *Chris Down*

CRAIG STAR (IRE) 7 b.g. Craigsteel – Different Dee (IRE) (Beau Sher) [2016/17   **h106**
h24.6g h23d³ h24g⁴ h21g* h20g* h16.5g³ h20g h21d³ h22.7s⁵ h21.2s h16.4g³ Mar 24]
half-brother to several winners, including winning hurdler/top-class chaser (2m-2½m
winner) Flemenstar, stays 3m, and smart hurdler/useful chaser (2¾m-25f winner)
Barafundle (both by Flemensfirth): dam unraced: fair handicap hurdler: won at Tramore
and Roscommon (dead-heated) in August: left Sean Thomas Doyle after eighth start: stays
3m: acts on good to soft going: often races towards rear. *Donald McCain*

CRAKEHALL LAD (IRE) 6 ch.g. Manduro (GER) – My Uptown Girl (Dubai   **h102**
Destination (USA)) [2016/17 h16.8s² h16.2dur h17.2g* h19.9g² h15.7d h15.6g Feb 4]
modest on Flat, stays 16.5f: fair form over hurdles: won maiden at Cartmel in July: barely
stays 19f: acts on soft going: in blinkers last 2 starts. *Andrew Crook*

CRANK EM UP (IRE) 6 b.g. Royal Anthem (USA) – Carrawaystick (IRE) (Old Vic)   **h110**
[2016/17 h98: h20.5d⁴ h21.2g³ h23.6g⁴ h23.3v* h24.4g⁵ h23.1d⁶ h22v⁵ Mar 18] won Irish
maiden point on debut: bumper winner: fair hurdler: won maiden at Uttoxeter in December:
stays 23f: acts on heavy going: tried in cheekpieces: often races prominently. *David Dennis*

CRAZY JACK (IRE) 9 b.g. Royal Anthem (USA) – Cindy's Fancy (IRE) (Shernazar)   **c109**
[2016/17 c–, h118: h23.9d⁶ c20g⁴ c23.8m⁴ Apr 25] tall gelding: winning pointer: fairly   **h104**
useful handicap hurdler, below form on return in 2016/17: fair hunter chaser nowadays: left
Kim Bailey after first start: stays 3m: acts on heavy going: has worn cheekpieces: often
races prominently. *Mrs A. R. Hewitt*

CRAZY QUEEN 5 ch.m. Le Fou (IRE) – Queen of Norway (USA) (Woodman (USA))   **h73**
[2016/17 b–: h15.7v⁴ h16.7d h16g⁵ h16d Nov 14] smallish, angular mare: poor form over
hurdles: left Anthony Carson after first start. *Denis W. Cullen, Ireland*

CRAZY TRAIN 8 ch.m. Sir Harry Lewis (USA) – Vent d'Aout (IRE) (Imp Society   **h81**
(USA)) [2016/17 h–: h15.3m⁴ h16.8m⁴ h16.3g* h15.8g⁶ Sep 18] poor form over hurdles:
won handicap at Stratford (amateur) in August: raced around 2m: acts on good to firm
going: tried in hood: has worn tongue tie: usually leads. *Robert Walford*

CREATEUR (IRE) 6 b.g. Muthatir – Cracovie (Caerleon (USA)) [2016/17 h102: h15.9g Nov 28] maiden hurdler, modest at best: best effort at 17f: acts on soft going: in hood last 2 starts, tongue tied last 5. *Tim Vaughan* **h–**

CREATIVE BORU (IRE) 9 b.g. Brian Boru – Ruths Rhapsody (IRE) (Creative Plan (USA)) [2016/17 h21.6v c19.4s^{pu} c23g^{pu} Jan 27] Irish maiden point winner: maiden hurdler/chaser, no form in 2016/17: has worn tongue tie, including in 2016/17. *Laura Young* **c– h–**

CREATIVE INERTA (IRE) 7 br.g. Balakheri (IRE) – Rambling Liss (IRE) (Presenting) [2016/17 b17g^3 May 13] third foal: dam unraced half-sister to fairly useful 3m hurdle winner Minella Aris out of half-sister to very smart hurdler (winner up to 2½m) Liss A Paoraigh: dual point winner: in hood/tongue tie, 40/1, third in conditionals/amateur bumper at Aintree (3 lengths behind Gustave Mahler) in May, needing stiffer test. *Miss Harriet Brown* **b83**

CREEP DESBOIS (FR) 5 b.g. Great Pretender (IRE) – Brigade Mondaine (FR) (Arnaqueur (USA)) [2016/17 b17.7g* b16m^3 h18.8d^5 h19.7d^4 h20.8d* h21m^3 Apr 18] €29,000 3-y-o: good-topped gelding: third foal: dam French maiden hurdler (placed at 17f): fairly useful form in bumpers: won at Plumpton early in season: fairly useful form over hurdles: won novice at Doncaster in February: third in handicap at Kempton in April: left Oliver Sherwood after second start: races prominently. *Ben Pauling* **h119 b96**

CREEPY (IRE) 9 b.g. Westerner – Prowler (IRE) (Old Vic) [2016/17 c113, h–: c24m^{pu} Jun 9] lengthy gelding: winning hurdler: useful chaser at best, pulled up sole outing in 2016/17: stays 25f: acts on good to soft going: tried in hood. *Martin Keighley* **c– h–**

CREEVYTENNANT (IRE) 13 b.g. Bob's Return (IRE) – Northwood May (Teenoso (USA)) [2016/17 c96: c20g^2 Apr 3] rangy gelding: useful chaser at best: second in hunter at Ludlow in April: stays 25f: acts on soft and good to firm going: in tongue tie last 3 starts: front runner. *Fergal O'Brien* **c116**

CREOLE DANCER 5 b.m. Norse Dancer (IRE) – Floral Rhapsody (Alflora (IRE)) [2016/17 b16.7g Mar 27] fourth foal: half-sister to fair hurdler Flower Power (2½m winner, by Bollin Eric): dam lightly-raced half-sister to fairly useful 2¾m hurdle winner Maybe The Business: well beaten in mares maiden bumper. *Tony Coyle* **b–**

CRESSWELL BREEZE 7 b.m. Midnight Legend – Cresswell Willow (IRE) (Witness Box (USA)) [2016/17 c132, h–: c21s^3 c23.9g^5 c22.7g^2 c28.4d^5 c24.1g^2 c21d c30d Apr 29] tall, lengthy mare: winning hurdler: useful handicap chaser: second in listed mares event at Leicester in January and mares event at Bangor in March: seems to stay 3¼m: acts on heavy going: wears tongue tie. *Anthony Honeyball* **c132 h–**

CRESSWELL LEGEND 6 b.g. Midnight Legend – Cresswell Willow (IRE) (Witness Box (USA)) [2016/17 b15.7d^3 b15.8g* Apr 3] €75,000 4-y-o: second foal: brother to fairly useful hurdler/useful chaser Cresswell Breeze (2½m-3m winner): dam (c123/h104) 2¾m-3¼m chase winner: won Irish maiden point on debut: fairly useful form in bumpers: won conditionals/amateur event at Huntingdon in April. *Kim Bailey* **b98**

CRESUS D'ARTHEL (FR) 5 b.g. Network (GER) – La Fee d'Arthel (FR) (Ragmar (FR)) [2016/17 b15.9g^2 May 28] 8/1, second in bumper at Ffos Las (7 lengths behind Western Ryder) in May: dead. *Paul Morgan* **b92**

CRICKEL WOOD (FR) 7 b.g. Muthatir – Tanguista (FR) (War Chant (USA)) [2016/17 h115: h16g^3 c17g^5 c20.3d c20.2m^6 h16d Mar 21] good-topped gelding: fair handicap hurdler: fair form over fences: unproven beyond 17f: acts on good to soft going: wears tongue tie. *Charlie Longsdon* **c108 h109**

CRIEVEHILL (IRE) 5 b.g. Arcadio (GER) – Ma Douce (IRE) (Mansonnien (FR)) [2016/17 h15.8v^2 h15.8v^4 h16v* h15.7s^3 h16.8g h20g h20.5g Apr 22] lengthy gelding: second foal: dam lightly-raced daughter of Prix Maurice Gillois winner Madalka: last of 6 finishers in Irish maiden point on debut: fairly useful handicap hurdler: won at Lingfield in January: third in Rossington Main Novices' Hurdle at Haydock (11 lengths behind Neon Wolf) later in month: should stay further than 2m: acts on heavy going: in hood last 5 starts. *Nigel Twiston-Davies* **h129**

CRIMSON ARK (IRE) 7 b.g. Arcadio (GER) – Crimson Flower (IRE) (Soviet Lad (USA)) [2016/17 h125, b84: h19.1d* h19.5g^2 c18.8m^{pu} h21g^6 h21g^F Mar 18] good-topped gelding: won Irish maiden hurdle on debut: useful handicap hurdler: won at Fontwell in September: second in Silver Trophy at Chepstow (1¼ lengths behind Ballyoptic) in October: pulled up in novice handicap on chasing debut: stayed 21f: acted on good to soft going: wore hood: dead. *Emma Lavelle* **c– h130**

CRIN AU VENT (FR) 5 b.g. Laveron – Tentative (FR) (Blushing Flame (USA)) **h–**
[2016/17 h126, b–: h17.7s Nov 13] fairly useful form on hurdling debut in France,
disappointing in 2 starts since (in hood): tried in tongue tie. *Paul Nicholls*

CRINKLE CRAGS (IRE) 7 ch.g. Trans Island – Ashanti Dancer (IRE) (Dancing **c65 §**
Dissident (USA)) [2016/17 h84: h19.3m h20.2d^{pu} h23.3g h25.3d^6 c19.9g^{pu} c15.6g^6 Apr 25] **h– §**
modest hurdler at best, no form in 2016/17: little form over fences: stays 2½m: best form
on good going: temperamental. *Nicky Richards*

CRINKLEY BOTTOM 4 b.f. Dick Turpin (IRE) – Crinkle (IRE) (Distant Relative) **b–**
[2016/17 b15.7s b15.8d Feb 9] half-sister to several winners on Flat, including useful 6f-
1m winner Steed (by Mujahid): dam unraced: soundly beaten in 2 bumpers, in cheekpieces
on second occasion. *Derek Shaw*

CRIQ ROCK (FR) 6 ch.g. Kap Rock (FR) – Criquetot (FR) (Epervier Bleu) [2016/17 **h121**
b115: h16m^3 h15.7d^2 h21.6d^2 h19.3s Feb 18] compact gelding: smart bumper winner:
fairly useful form over hurdles: second in maiden at Ascot in December: usually races
towards rear. *Alan King*

CRISTAL DE SIENNE (FR) 5 b.g. Montmartre (FR) – Heroine de Sienne (FR) **b90**
(Beyssac (FR)) [2016/17 b16.3g^2 b16.8v^5 Jan 1] €8,000 3-y-o: sixth foal: half-brother to 3
winners in France, including chasers Quimte (2¼m/19f winner, by Antarctique) and Saveur
de Sienne (21f winner, by Caballo Raptor): dam useful French 2½m chase winner: fair
form when second at Newbury on first of 2 starts in bumpers: will stay further than 2m.
Harry Whittington

CRIXUS'S ESCAPE (IRE) 4 ch.g. Beneficial – Tierneys Choice (IRE) (Oscar (IRE)) **b70**
[2016/17 b16.4g Mar 24] 5/1, very green when seventh in bumper at Musselburgh (15¼
lengths behind Kelpies Myth) in March. *Gillian Boanas*

CROAN ROCK (IRE) 12 b.g. Milan – Fiddlers Bar (IRE) (Un Desperado (FR)) **c72 §**
[2016/17 c110§, h–: c24.1g^5 Apr 29] well-made gelding: multiple point winner: maiden **h–**
hurdler: fair chaser at best, lightly raced since 2013/14: stays 3¼m: acts on good to soft
going: has worn cheekpieces: has worn tongue tie, including last 2 starts: ungenuine.
R. A. Owen

CROCKERY 7 b.m. Croco Rouge (IRE) – Always Forgiving (Commanche Run) [2016/17 **h78**
h102, b77: h23.1d^6 May 26] placed all 3 starts in maiden points: modest maiden hurdler,
below form sole outing in 2016/17: stays 21f: acts on soft going. *Dan Skelton*

CROCKETT 6 b.g. Rail Link – Tarocchi (USA) (Affirmed (USA)) [2016/17 h–: h18.6s^{pu} **h–**
h16.7d Dec 26] no form over hurdles. *Steve Gollings*

CROCO BAY (IRE) 10 b.g. Croco Rouge (IRE) – April Thistle (IRE) (Alphabatim **c142**
(USA)) [2016/17 c146, h–: c20d^4 c16.5g* c21.4g c15.9g^{ur} c16.9m c16.9d c15.7d^3 c16.3g^5 **h–**
Mar 17] close-coupled gelding: winning hurdler: useful handicap chaser nowadays: won at
Worcester (by head from Canicallyouback) in August: stays 19f: acts on good to firm and
heavy going: tried in cheekpieces. *Ben Case*

CROCODILE DANCER 7 b.g. Croco Rouge (IRE) – She Likes To Boogy (IRE) (Luso) **h68**
[2016/17 h16.4v^{pu} h16d h16.8g h19.9m^4 Apr 19] poor form over hurdles: should stay at
least 23f. *Sam England*

CROOKOFDEVON 8 b.g. Desideratum – Blue Morning (Balnibarbi) [2016/17 b–: **h–**
h16.2d h22.7s^{pu} h22d^{pu} h16.2s^{pu} h18.1d^{pu} Apr 10] no form. *Jean McGregor*

CROOKSTOWN (IRE) 10 b.g. Rudimentary (USA) – Millview Lass (IRE) (Jurado **c117 x**
(USA)) [2016/17 c112x, h114: h19.8m* h20g h21.3g^4 h19.7g h19s^{pu} h20.6s^2 c20.2s **h115**
c20.2s^4 c16.4g^4 c21.3g^4 Apr 23] rangy gelding: fairly useful handicap hurdler: won at
Wincanton early in season: useful handicap chaser, below best in 2016/17: stays 21f: acts
on good to firm and heavy going: wears headgear: often let down by jumping. *Ben Case*

CROPLEY (IRE) 8 gr.g. Galileo (IRE) – Niyla (IRE) (Darshaan) [2016/17 h92: h16.8s **h–**
Nov 20] medium-sized gelding: modest hurdler, excuses sole outing in 2016/17: stays 3m:
acts on heavy going: tried in blinkers. *Dai Burchell*

CROSSHUE BOY (IRE) 7 b.g. Brian Boru – Gluais Linn (IRE) (Supreme Leader) **c111**
[2016/17 b20g^3 h24m* h21m^4 h24g^5 h19.5g* h24g^5 h16.5d^{ur} h20g^{bd} h21.1g h16v c20v^2 **h125**
h20.3s* c20d h21d Apr 26] €8,200 4-y-o: useful-looking gelding: eleventh foal: dam, **b86**
maiden pointer, half-sister to useful hurdler/fairly useful chaser (best up to 21f) Yellow
Spring: point winner: fair form in bumpers: fairly useful hurdler: won maiden at
Punchestown early in season, conditionals/amateur handicap at Kilbeggan in September
and minor event at Wexford in March: fair form when second in maiden at Navan on first
of 2 starts over fences: stays 3m: acts on good to firm and heavy going. *Sean Thomas
Doyle, Ireland*

CROSSPARK 7 b.g. Midnight Legend – Blue Shannon (IRE) (Be My Native (USA)) [2016/17 h120: c20.3v* c20s² c19.1g⁶ c24.2s² c22.7sᵘʳ c20.3s* c24s³ Mar 18] sturdy gelding: winning pointer/hurdler: useful handicap chaser: won at Southwell (novice event) early in season and Leicester (by 3¼ lengths from Always On The Run) in February: stays 3m: best form on soft/heavy going: often races prominently. *Caroline Bailey*   c136 h–

CROSS TO BOSTON (IRE) 11 b.g. Oscar (IRE) – Collopy's Cross (Pragmatic) [2016/17 c75§, h75: c20.1g c24d⁴ c20.1sᶠ Jan 7] maiden hurdler: modest handicap chaser, below form since 2014/15: stays 25f: acts on soft going: has worn headgear/tongue tie: usually races close up: tends to finish weakly. *Sue Smith*   c77 § h–

CROWD CONTROL (IRE) 8 b.g. Oscar (IRE) – Apollo Lady (Alflora (IRE)) [2016/17 h104: c16s⁴ c23.8mᵖᵘ Apr 18] maiden hurdler: little impact in 2 starts over fences: stays 21f: best form on heavy going: tried in cheekpieces: front runner/races prominently. *Lady Susan Brooke*   c– h–

CROWN AND GLORY (IRE) 10 b.g. Turtle Island (IRE) – Monteleena (IRE) (Montelimar (USA)) [2016/17 c94, h–: h19.9gᵖᵘ Oct 27] little form over hurdles: winning chaser: stays 19f: acts on soft going. *Chris Fairhurst*   c– h–

CROWN HILL (IRE) 7 b.g. Definite Article – Silver Prayer (IRE) (Roselier (FR)) [2016/17 h16g² h16g⁴ h16.3m³ h20m³ c16d³ h20.2s* c21.7d⁵ c15.9s* c20.9s* h21.2g⁵ Apr 3] €9,500 3-y-o: fifth foal: half-brother to fairly useful chaser Ruapehu (25f/3¼m winner, by Presenting): dam unraced half-sister to fairly useful 2½m hurdle winner Mary's Manna: fair hurdler: won handicap at Perth in September: fairly useful form over fences: won novice handicaps at Leicester in February and Hereford in March: left Henry de Bromhead after second start, Fergal O'Brien after sixth: stays 21f: acts on soft and good to firm going: has worn hood. *Johnny Farrelly*   c124 h109

CROWN THEATRE (IRE) 8 b.g. King's Theatre (IRE) – Palesa's Legacy (IRE) (Montelimar (USA)) [2016/17 c134, h112: h16d⁶ c16m⁴ h16m c22m h16.7g Jul 31] rather leggy gelding: fair handicap hurdler: useful handicap chaser, below form in 2016/17: stays 2¼m: acts on soft going: wears tongue tie: often races in rear: sometimes finishes weakly. *Henry de Bromhead, Ireland*   c111 h111

CRUACHAN (IRE) 8 b.g. Authorized (IRE) – Calico Moon (USA) (Seeking The Gold (USA)) [2016/17 h92: h23.9m⁵ h20.2s³ h20d⁵ h24.3s⁶ h19s⁵ h23.8g h20.5v² h20.9s⁶ Mar 25] modest handicap hurdler nowadays: stays 3m: acts on heavy going: wears headgear. *Lucy Normile*   h86

CRUCHAIN (IRE) 14 ch.g. Shernazar – Mack Tack (IRE) (Shardari) [2016/17 c109, h–: c21.2m⁴ c20.9v* c19.2g⁵ c21.2d² c20g⁵ c22.6g⁴ Oct 27] useful-looking gelding: winning hurdler: fair handicap chaser nowadays: won at Stratford early in season: stays 2¾m, effective at shorter: acts on good to firm and heavy going: wears headgear: tried in tongue tie: often let down by jumping. *Dai Burchell*   c105 x h–

CRUCIAL ROLE 5 b.g. Westerner – The Lyme Volunteer (IRE) (Zaffaran (USA)) [2016/17 b15.8d⁴ b16v³ b15.8s⁴ Mar 23] third foal: dam (c105/h108) 3m/3¼m hurdle/chase winner: fair form in bumpers: best effort when third in conditional/amateur maiden at Chepstow in February: will stay at least 2½m. *Henry Daly*   b86

CRUISEAWEIGH (IRE) 6 b.g. Oscar (IRE) – Triptoshan (IRE) (Anshan) [2016/17 b100: b17d* h16sᵖᵘ h16.3d h20.3v³ Mar 6] deep-girthed gelding: fairly useful form in bumpers: won at Aintree in November: fair form when third in novice at Southwell (in hood) on last of 3 starts over hurdles. *Tom George*   h113 b99

CRUISE IN STYLE (IRE) 11 b.m. Definite Article – Henrietta Street (IRE) (Royal Academy (USA)) [2016/17 c–§, h99§: h16dᶠ h19.1g h16.8m h18.5m h16g⁶ h15.8g h15.8d⁵ h19.7g h19.7s c19.2m⁵ Apr 18] workmanlike mare: modest hurdler/chaser at best, below form in 2016/17: stays 2½m: acts on any going: usually wears headgear: wears tongue tie: usually races nearer last than first: temperamental. *Kevin Bishop*   c– § h82 §

CRUISING BYE 11 b.g. Alflora (IRE) – Althrey Flame (IRE) (Torus) [2016/17 c75x, h–: c22.5g h24.7dᵖᵘ h23.1s c19.9d⁵ c24.1g² c26.3g Apr 7] modest hurdler at best, no form in 2016/17: modest handicap chaser nowadays: stays 29f: acts on good to firm and heavy going: has worn headgear/tongue tie, including last 3 starts: often let down by jumping. *Gary Hanmer*   c93 x h–

CRY FURY 9 b.g. Beat Hollow – Cantanta (Top Ville) [2016/17 h90: h15.3m³ h17.2g⁶ h16.7d³ h22m h19.5g h16.5m Apr 20] useful-looking gelding: modest maiden hurdler: left Sophie Leech after fourth start: stays 2¾m: acts on good to firm going: in tongue tie last 2 starts. *Matt Sheppard*   h87 ?

CRYSTAL LAD (FR) 5 ch.g. Kapgarde (FR) – Qrystale Mag (FR) (Vertical Speed (FR)) **h128**
[2016/17 b16.3g⁴ h16d² h16s² h18.8d⁶ h15.8s³ h19.1s* h19.8d⁴ h20g Apr 7] €37,000 **b90**
3-y-o: rather unfurnished gelding: second foal: dam, French 17f hurdle winner, half-sister
to smart French hurdler/fair chaser (winner up to 2½m) Crylza Royal and smart hurdler/
useful chaser (stayed 4m) Royal Rosa: ran twice in Irish points, fourth on completed start:
encouragement when fourth in maiden bumper at Stratford (4¼ lengths behind Brio Conti):
fairly useful hurdler: won novice at Fontwell in February: left S. Curling after first start:
stays 2½m: acts on soft going: front runner/races prominently. *Gary Moore*

CRYSTAL PEARL 6 b.m. Beat Hollow – Missouri (Charnwood Forest (IRE)) [2016/17 **h118**
h16d h16.5g⁶ h16s⁶ h16d* h16.4g h20g Nov 6] half-sister to 2m-19f hurdle winner Dee
Cee Elle (by Groom Dancer): fairly useful on Flat, stays 2m: fairly useful handicap hurdler:
won mares event at Limerick in October: stays 19f: acts on heavy going: has worn tongue
tie. *Charles Byrnes, Ireland*

CRY WOLF 4 ch.g. Street Cry (IRE) – Love Charm (Singspiel (IRE)) [2016/17 h16s⁵ **h90**
h16.7s⁴ h16.7s⁶ Feb 7] workmanlike gelding: fair maiden on Flat, stays 1½m: modest form
on first of 3 starts in juvenile hurdles: tried in cheekpieces. *James Evans*

CUCKLINGTON 6 b.g. Kayf Tara – Ardrom (Ardross) [2016/17 h98, b90p: h18.5g **c93**
h24.2g⁵ h21s c25.1s⁵ c21.1v⁶ c26.7dᵘʳ c25.1m² Apr 5] lengthy gelding: poor maiden **h78**
hurdler: modest form over fences: stays 25f: acts on good to firm and good to soft going:
usually wears tongue tie. *Colin Tizzard*

CUE CARD 11 b.g. King's Theatre (IRE) – Wicked Crack (IRE) (King's Ride) **c174**
[2016/17 c181, h–: c25d⁴ c24.2g³ c24.1v* c24g² c21s* c26.3gᶠ c25g² Apr 6] **h–**

Father Time is having a job catching up with the seemingly ageless Cue Card
who added two more Grade 1s to his haul in the eighth season of an illustrious career
stretching back to 2010 when he first hit the headlines after winning the Champion
Bumper as a four-year-old at the Cheltenham Festival at odds of 40/1, forging clear
of another who developed into a top-class performer, Al Ferof, who was retired
in the autumn with a tendon injury. That was the year that Kauto Star, the finest
steeplechaser of his time, and one of steeplechasing's greats, took a heavy fall at
the notorious fourth last in a Gold Cup that had been hyped so much beforehand—
Kauto Star v Denman: The Decider—that it was left wide open to producing
disappointment (the so-called two-horse race provided a different story from the
one anticipated, with third favourite Imperial Commander a deserving winner on
the day). Kauto Star's fall was his second in a total of seven successive appearances
at the Cheltenham Festival—he also departed at the third in the Queen Mother
Champion Chase in 2006—and Cue Card, essentially a fine jumper and a thoroughly
genuine racehorse like Kauto Star, has also now fallen twice at the Festival.

Before missing the 2014 Gold Cup because of injury, Cue Card made four
consecutive appearances at the meeting in four different races, finishing in the
frame in the Supreme Novices' and the Arkle before winning for the second time,
in the 2013 Ryanair Chase. A breathing operation forced Cue Card to miss the 2015
Cheltenham Festival as well, and in both subsequent seasons he has crashed out at
the third last in the Gold Cup. On the first occasion he was chasing the million-pound
bonus on offer for any horse that could win the Betfair Chase, the King George
VI Chase and the Gold Cup in the same season, and he had just moved up eye-
catchingly between the two leaders, eventual winner Don Cossack and Djakadam.
The three of them looked set to fight it out when Cue Card, barely taking off at all,
went from looking at one moment a potential winner to hitting the deck just seconds
later. Cue Card would certainly have been involved in the finish that year had he
not fallen, but the same could not be said with confidence after his latest Gold Cup
fall which came at the same obstacle on the downhill stretch approaching the home
straight. He was still in touch but being pushed along and, on this occasion, was not
travelling so well as some of those around him, though he was alongside eventual
winner Sizing John (and ahead of runner-up Minella Rocco) at the time. The third-
last on Cheltenham's New Course has acquired something of a reputation over the
years for requiring precision, though it is probably not quite so tricky as the fourth
last, on the same downhill stretch.

Betfair Chase (Lancashire), Haydock—a third win in the race for Cue Card who pulls fifteen lengths clear of 2015 Cheltenham Gold Cup winner Coneygree

Cue Card's misfortunes at the third last in the Gold Cup can probably be put down to coincidence (he seemed to be unsighted on the latest occasion) but they bring to mind other occasions when big-race contenders have come a cropper twice or more at the same fence. The five-times Gold Cup winner Golden Miller ran in five Grand Nationals and failed to complete on four occasions (he won on his second appearance in the race). His most infamous exit came when he unseated his rider, in a controversial incident, two fences after Valentine's when starting 2/1 favourite the year after winning. He refused at the same open ditch twelve months later after being remounted when brought down at the first, and refused again at the same fence on his last appearance in the National. Golden Miller incidentally was ridden by a different jockey each time. One of the most enduring memories from the Cheltenham Festival in relatively recent times is of the young claimer Vinnie Keane beating the ground with his whip and throwing himself headlong on to the turf, where he buried his face between his forearms. The cause of Keane's frustration was the virtually identical mishap that had befallen him and his mount Latalomne twelve months earlier at the second last in the Queen Mother Champion Chase. Latalomne was close up on both occasions—which were the only times he fell in his career—and when he came to grief he had yet to be asked for absolutely everything and would have been at least placed on both occasions (he was certainly in the process of running a clear lifetime best both times). 'He was usually quite a good jumper,' recalls Latalomne's trainer Brian Ellison, 'but the first time he didn't get high enough and clipped it, and the second time he jumped it all right but folded on landing … Not much was said afterwards on either occasion, Vinnie said he would have won, the usual jockey stuff, but it was too early to say. We were all gutted but there was no blame attached to Vinnie—better jumpers than Latalomne have come down there travelling at that kind of pace.'

The Cheltenham steeplechase courses provide a stiff examination of a horse's jumping and the original second-last fence on the Old Course is one that proved particularly trappy over the years, being a downhill obstacle which became known for horses knuckling over on landing after jumping the fence well. Work was carried out over a number of years to make the ground around the fence more

Betfair Ascot Chase, Ascot—
Cue Card repeats his 2013 win; Royal Regatta fades into third

level, adjustments made on both the take-off and landing sides. Eventually, however, concerns about the fence's safety record led to it being moved in 2010/11 to a new position in the home straight where, previously, there had been just one fence. A further small change was made in the latest season which is outlined in the essay on Altior which also covers the changes made at the same time to the fourth last fence on the New Course which is used for the Gold Cup. Another top race at the Festival, the Champion Hurdle, produced a similar incident to Latalomne's when Land Afar was found out, first by the second-last flight in 1994 and then by the third-last in 1995, up with the leaders when coming down both times (travelling particularly well in 1994). The 1981 Grand National third Royal Mail fell at first Becher's in the two following years and Travado fell seven out in both the 1993 and the 1994 King George VI Chase.

Cue Card's emotionally-charged 'million-pound' fall, in particular, will always be recalled when his career is recounted in years to come, as will the absence of a Cheltenham Gold Cup victory from his record (he will be twelve by the time of the next Cheltenham Festival and time is surely running out for him to win a Gold Cup now). Cue Card's overall record, though, clearly entitles him to take very high rank among the top-class staying chasers of recent generations, and the substance of that claim should not be questioned just because he hasn't won a Gold Cup, a race won twice by Kauto Star and one regarded almost universally as providing the acid test for the top staying chasers in Britain and Ireland. Although the Gold Cup is missing, Cue Card numbers the three other Grade 1 staying chases in Britain, the Betfair Chase, the King George VI Chase and the Aintree Bowl, among his nine victories at the top level. The latest season saw him win the Betfair Chase at Haydock for the third time in the past four seasons, leaving him just one short of Kauto Star's record four wins in that race.

The Betfair, registered as the Lancashire Chase, has now been run twelve times and just six horses have won it, also among them the dual winner Silviniaco Conti who was in the line-up again for the latest running, along with the returning 2015 Cheltenham Gold Cup winner Coneygree. The field of six was completed by Irish Cavalier, who had beaten Cue Card into third in the Charlie Hall Chase at Wetherby, the very smart Seeyouatmidnight, who attracted plenty of support because of the prevailing heavy ground, and French challenger Vezelay (the race failed for the third year in a row to attract an Irish-trained chaser). Cue Card's defeat in the Charlie Hall, in which he stood out on form and started odds on, undermined confidence in his attempt to win a third Betfair (connections blamed themselves for the defeat, though the fact that Cue Card pressed on—by design—from a long way out was not, in itself, the reason for his below-par performance). A different Cue Card showed up at Haydock, a Cue Card much closer to the one who had enjoyed a vintage season in 2015/16 when, after winning the Charlie Hall, he had recorded an easy seven-length win in the Betfair Chase over Silviniaco Conti and then got the better of Vautour in a rousing finish (the pair clear) to the King George VI Chase. Cue Card and the ill-fated Vautour produced two of the best performances in the King George in the past quarter of a century and Cue Card, clearly as good as ever, was sent off second favourite for that year's Gold Cup. He showed himself none the worse for his fall at Cheltenham when bouncing back to win the Aintree Bowl, cruising home by nine lengths and eight from the placed horses in the Gold Cup, Don Poli and Djakadam. Having been on the go since October, and taken in all four of Britain's open Grade 1s for staying chasers, Cue Card could perhaps be forgiven for managing only fourth in the Punchestown Gold Cup which took place just after the end of the British season, technically at the start of the 2016/17 campaign. Those who doubted Cue Card after his defeat in the Charlie Hall, on his return from a summer break, were made to eat their words when he ended Coneygree's unbeaten record over fences with a fifteen-length triumph in the Betfair Chase, travelling strongly and jumping well all the way and forging clear after taking the lead four from home. The distances back to Vezelay and Silviniaco Conti, who completed the frame, were thirteen lengths and fourteen lengths.

Timico Cheltenham Gold Cup, Cheltenham—
an unsighted Cue Card crashes out at the third last again

Mrs Jean R. Bishop's "Cue Card"

Five weeks later, in the King George VI Chase, Cue Card had no Vautour or Don Cossack (a faller two out when rallying and just in front of Cue Card) to contend with this time. But he didn't show the same form at Kempton as he had at Haydock and was all out to hold on to second from Silviniaco Conti and Tea For Two after giving best in the home straight to his exciting stablemate Thistlecrack, who produced an outstanding performance for a novice chaser on just his fourth start over fences to beat Cue Card by three and a quarter lengths. Give in the ground provides optimum conditions for Cue Card nowadays and the good going at Kempton was probably not soft enough for him. Back on soft in the Betfair Ascot Chase in February, Cue Card won that race for the second time, running away with it by fifteen lengths from Shantou Flyer and confirming himself as probably the standard-setter for the Cheltenham Gold Cup, especially with Thistlecrack being forced to miss Cheltenham through injury. Cue Card's popularity had never been higher than after those Haydock and Ascot wins, yet he actually started only third favourite on Gold Cup day, behind Djakadam and another of his own stablemates, Native River, the three of them and Irish Gold Cup winner Sizing John the only runners to start at single-figure odds. In truth, things started to go wrong for Cue Card long before his fall, as he struggled to find daylight in a tightly-packed field (resulting from a slower than usual pace for the race) from early on the final circuit. Ground conditions weren't ideal for Cue Card at Cheltenham and nor were they when Tea For Two, another faller in the Gold Cup, beat him by a neck in a stirring finish to the Betway Bowl at Aintree. Cue Card has now run five times at the Grand National meeting and never been out of the first two. Typically, he went with plenty of zest, and led from the thirteenth before being headed between the last two; he staged a rally on the run-in but was always being held by Tea For Two, the pair pulling fifteen lengths ahead of third-placed Smad Place in a race that proved to be Silviniaco Conti's last, as his retirement was announced after he trailed in last of six finishers.

		King's Theatre (IRE) (b 1991)	Sadler's Wells (b 1981)	Northern Dancer / Fairy Bridge
Cue Card (b.g. 2006)			Regal Beauty (b or br 1981)	Princely Native / Dennis Belle
		Wicked Crack (IRE) (b 1993)	King's Ride (b 1976)	Rarity / Ride
			Mighty Crack (b 1979)	Deep Run / Treize

The pedigree of the big, lengthy Cue Card has been covered in detail in previous Annuals (this is the seventh essay to have appeared on him). His sire King's Theatre, about whom there is more in the entry on Henllan Harri, was champion jumps sire in Britain and Ireland for the fifth time in the last six years. Cue Card's dam the useful hurdler/chaser Wicked Crack, a €120,000 purchase in 2002 carrying her first foal, was a tough racemare but she has had an in-and-out record at stud, once going five years without any progeny, though she is still active and has produced a foal each year since 2013, with a yearling filly by Leading Light following colts by Beneficial (who made €150,000 at the 2016 Derby Sale and is now named Sidetracked) and by Gold Well, and another filly by Milan. Twenty-four-year-old Wicked Crack's latest assignation was with Douvan's sire Walk In The Park who reportedly covered her successfully. The only filly produced by Wicked Crack before her recent revival at stud, The Wicked Kipper, a younger sister to Cue Card who showed only modest form in bumpers and over hurdles, was retained by Wicked Crack's Welsh-based breeder Roland Crellin and she has a two-year-old filly by Flemensfirth and was carrying to Leading Light in the latest season. For all that Wicked Crack has had a lengthy career as a broodmare, she has produced just one other winner so far, the fair hurdler and fairly useful chaser Hidden Crack (by Lahib) who was her second foal (Cue Card was her third). Cue Card, a strong traveller who often makes the running, wears a tongue tie (he was tried once in cheekpieces). He stays twenty-five furlongs and acts on heavy going and has never raced on anything firmer than good. Though he has a high head carriage and wears a sheepskin noseband in his races, Cue Card is a most genuine racehorse who must have been a pleasure to own over the years. His longevity has helped to make him a real favourite with the racing public who may yet have more wins to cheer in the twilight of his outstanding career. Connections say they have no thoughts of retiring him while he can still produce performances like some of those in the latest season. *Colin Tizzard*

CUIL ROGUE (IRE) 9 b.g. Presenting – Coolshamrock (IRE) (Buckskin (FR)) [2016/17 h–: h20.2g h17.1d h21.4d⁵ h19s h20.2g² Apr 28] winning pointer: modest maiden hurdler: stays 21f: acts on heavy going: has worn hood: tried in tongue tie: usually races towards rear. *Nicky Richards* **h97**

CUIRASSIER DEMPIRE (FR) 5 ch.g. Network (GER) – Juventhura (FR) (Video Rock (FR)) [2016/17 h19.9d⁵ h20g³ h23.1v⁵ Nov 9] £13,000 3-y-o: fifth foal: half-brother to 2 winners in France, including 17f hurdle winner Vent d'Eire (by Assessor): dam unraced: won maiden on completed start in points: fair form when third in maiden at Worcester on second of 3 starts over hurdles. *Tom George* **h100**

CULLENTRY ROYAL 9 b.g. Royal Applause – Fleur A Lay (USA) (Mr Greeley (USA)) [2016/17 h16gᶠ h16g h19.8m h24.2s h20.2s² Jul 27] fairly useful on Flat, stayed 2¼m: fair maiden hurdler: stayed 2½m: acted on soft and good to firm going: tried in cheekpieces: dead. *Gordon Elliott, Ireland* **h101**

CULLY MAC (IRE) 6 b.g. Coroner (IRE) – Catch Those Kisses (Deploy) [2016/17 b–: h16.8d h16.2m h16.2m h19.3gᵖᵘ Nov 30] no form. *Andrew Wilson* **h–**

CULM COUNSELLOR 8 ch.g. Erhaab (USA) – Miss Counsel (Leading Counsel (USA)) [2016/17 h62§: h16.8g⁶ h19.9gᵖᵘ h16.8s⁴ h18.5d⁵ h16.8g⁵ h16.3gᵘʳ h16.8m² h18.5m* h23.9g* h23.9m c23.6g h21.6g⁴ Apr 26] workmanlike gelding: poor handicap **c– h81**

hurdler: won at Exeter and Taunton (novice event) in November: tailed off in novice handicap on chasing debut: stays 3m: acts on good to firm going: wears headgear: usually races towards rear: has looked hard ride. *Chris Down*

CULMINATION 5 b.g. Beat Hollow – Apogee (Shirley Heights) [2016/17 h15.7g⁴ h15.8v⁴ h16.8v² h16v* Mar 10] closely related to smart hurdler Summit Meeting (2m-2½m winner, by Sadler's Wells), stayed 3m: won maiden on Flat for A. Fabre in 2015: fair form over hurdles: won maiden at Ayr in March: should stay further than 2m. *Donald McCain* **h105**

CULTIVATOR 6 b.g. Alflora (IRE) – Angie Marinie (Sabrehill (USA)) [2016/17 b98: h16m² h15.7m* h19.8s³ h20.5d⁶ h21g* h20g Apr 8] unfurnished gelding: bumper winner: useful form over hurdles: won novices at Ascot in October and Kempton in March: third in Winter Novices' Hurdle at Sandown (2¾ lengths behind Messire des Obeaux) in December: stays 21f: acts on soft and good to firm going: has worn hood, including in 2016/17. *Nicky Henderson* **h136**

CULTRAM ABBEY 10 br.g. Fair Mix (IRE) – Kansas City (FR) (Lute Antique (FR)) [2016/17 c129, h–: c26.2d² c32.4s h22.8s⁵ c24.5dᶠ c23.8g² Apr 26] useful-looking gelding: fairly useful handicap hurdler: useful handicap chaser: second at Perth (½ length behind Beeves) early in season: should stay long distances: acts on heavy going: tried in cheekpieces. *Nicky Richards* **c141 h119**

CULTURE DE SIVOLA (FR) 5 b.m. Assessor (IRE) – Neva de Sivola (FR) (Blushing Flame (USA)) [2016/17 h118, b73: h16d⁴ h17.9s³ h19.1gᶠ h20v⁵ h19.5s² h18.9g Apr 15] unfurnished mare: fairly useful handicap hurdler: third in minor event at Compiegne in September: stays 19f: acts on heavy going. *Nick Williams* **h115**

CUMBRIAN FARMER 10 ch.g. Alflora (IRE) – Quark Top (FR) (Perrault) [2016/17 c–, h74: h21.2d³ Apr 28] poor handicap hurdler: failed to complete all 4 starts over fences: stays 25f: acts on good to firm and heavy going: wears headgear: usually wears tongue tie: front runner/races prominently. *Kenneth Slack* **c– h71**

CUP FINAL (IRE) 8 ch.g. Presenting – Asian Maze (IRE) (Anshan) [2016/17 h142: h24d* h26.1g h16.2s⁴ c15.7g* Apr 21] well-made gelding: useful handicap hurdler at best: 30/100, won 2-runner novice at Southwell by 2½ lengths from Spoilt Rotten) on chasing debut: left Nicky Henderson after second start: stays 3¼m: acts on soft going: should do better over fences. *Ben Haslam* **c120 p h122 +**

CUPID'S QUEST (IRE) 5 b.m. Jeremy (USA) – Lovers Nest (Groom Dancer (USA)) [2016/17 h94, b–: h16.2dᵘʳ h20.1g⁵ h16.2d³ h16.2d³ h17.1dᵖᵘ h20.6dᵖᵘ h19.4g Mar 1] modest maiden hurdler: may prove best at 2m with emphasis on speed: acts on good to soft going: usually in hood: wears tongue tie. *Susan Corbett* **h91**

CUP OF AMBITION (IRE) 5 b.g. Vinnie Roe (IRE) – Sparkling Gem (IRE) (Revoque (IRE)) [2016/17 b16s h15.7g⁴ h16g² Apr 17] €3,000 3-y-o, £40,000 4-y-o: fifth foal: brother to fairly useful hurdler Show Court (2m/17f winner): dam unraced: off mark in Irish maiden points at fourth attempt: tailed off in maiden bumper: modest form when second in novice at Chepstow on second of 2 starts over hurdles: in tongue tie last 2 starts. *Martin Keighley* **h99 b–**

CURIOUS CARLOS 8 b.g. Overbury (IRE) – Classi Maureen (Among Men (USA)) [2016/17 h126: h16.2m² h15.9g* h20d³ h16.7g⁶ h15.8s³ h20g h17.7d⁶ h16.5g h19.8g Apr 29] stocky gelding: has reportedly had breathing operation: fairly useful handicap hurdler: won at Ffos Las early in season: sixth in Summer Hurdle at Market Rasen in July: stays 2½m: acts on heavy going: has worn hood: tried in tongue tie: usually races nearer last than first. *Peter Bowen* **h128**

CURRAIGFLEMENS (IRE) 9 b.g. Flemensfirth (USA) – Curraig Monashee (IRE) (Monashee Mountain (USA)) [2016/17 c–: c25.5d* c27.5m⁵ May 20] multiple point winner: fair form in hunter chases: won novice event at Fontwell early in season: tried in tongue tie. *David Kemp* **c103**

CURRENT EVENT (FR) 10 b.g. Muhtathir – La Curamalal (IRE) (Rainbow Quest (USA)) [2016/17 c134, h–: c26.3g⁵ c26.3g Mar 17] compact gelding: prolific winning pointer: winning hurdler: useful chaser at best, well below form in 2016/17: stayed 27f: acted on soft and good to firm going: tried in cheekpieces: usually raced towards rear: dead. *Mrs Rose Loxton* **c95 h–**

CURRENT EXCHANGE (IRE) 12 ch.g. Beneficial – Musical Millie (IRE) (Orchestra) [2016/17 c122: c33gᵖᵘ c25.5s² Feb 26] small gelding: prolific winning pointer: fairly useful chaser, not at best in 2016/17: left Gordon Elliott after first start: stays 3¼m: acts on heavy going: wears headgear/tongue tie: usually races close up. *Francesca Nimmo* **c98**

CUSHEEN BRIDGE (IRE) 9 b.g. Oscar (IRE) – One Hell Ofa Woman (IRE) (Fourstars **c128**
Allstar (USA)) [2016/17 h122: c21.4g⁵ c19.2d³ c21.4g* c20.3gᵘʳ h20.3g⁴ c20g⁶ c23.9g² **h108**
c21.4s* c19.9s⁵ c21.4sᵖᵘ c20.3sᵖᵘ Jan 31] sturdy gelding: fairly useful handicap hurdler,
below form sole outing in 2016/17: fairly useful handicap chaser: won novices at Market
Rasen in July and November: stays 3m: acts on soft going: wears tongue tie. *Charles Pogson*

CUSHY BUTTERFIELD (IRE) 5 b.m. Fruits of Love (USA) – Colleen Ard (IRE) **b–**
(Turtle Island (IRE)) [2016/17 b16.4s Dec 8] €3,200 3-y-o: first foal: dam unraced half-
sister to fair hurdler/very smart chaser (stayed 3¼m) Macgeorge and smart hurdler/chaser
(stayed 4m) Chief Dan George: tailed off in bumper. *Sheena Walton*

CUT THE CORNER (IRE) 9 br.g. Vinnie Roe (IRE) – Snipe Victory (IRE) (Old Vic) **c121 §**
[2016/17 c127§, h117§: h20.5g⁴ h20m⁵ h20.3g c20d⁴ c21.4g* c21.4g⁶ c20g c20.3gᵘʳ **h100 §**
c21.2d⁵ Aug 29] fairly useful handicap hurdler, below form in 2016/17: fairly useful
handicap chaser: won at Market Rasen in July: acts on good to firm and good to
soft going: has worn headgear: temperamental. *Dr Richard Newland*

CYBELLE COLOMBE (FR) 5 b.m. Network (GER) – Sismaelle (FR) (Alberto **b–**
Giacometti (IRE)) [2016/17 b16.2s b16g Apr 17] £20,000 3-y-o: first foal: dam unraced
half-sister to fairly useful French hurdler/chaser (17f-19f winner) Une Destine: well held
in 2 bumpers. *Alan King*

CYCLOP (IRE) 6 b.g. King's Theatre (IRE) – Tasmani (FR) (Turgeon (USA)) [2016/17 **c118**
c127, h–: c26.2d⁵ c27.2s³ c26.2s³ c26.7sᶠ c26.2s⁶ c30.7s² c24s⁴ Mar 30] good-topped **h–**
gelding: winning hurdler: fairly useful handicap chaser: third in Southern National at
Fontwell in November: stays 3½m: acts on heavy going: wears headgear/tongue tie.
David Dennis

CYGNET 11 b.g. Dansili – Ballet Princess (Muhtarram (USA)) [2016/17 c117, h–: h23.3d⁴ **c–**
Jun 19] compact gelding: fairly useful hurdler at one time, well below form sole outing in **h56**
2016/17: fairly useful chaser: stays 3¼m: acts on good to firm and heavy going: tried in
cheekpieces: wears tongue tie. *Peter Bowen*

CYRANO STAR (FR) 5 gr.g. Martaline – Quezac du Boulay (FR) (Useful (FR)) **h84**
[2016/17 b16.7g h19.7d h19.3d⁴ h16.4vᵘʳ Mar 7] €40,000 3-y-o: first foal: dam French **b–**
12.5f-2m winner: tailed off in bumper: poor form over hurdles. *Andrew Crook*

CYRIEN STAR 10 b.g. Bollin Eric – Sainte Etoile (FR) (Saint Cyrien (FR)) [2016/17 **c– §**
c112, h–: c26.1dᵖᵘ c25gʳʳ c22.6g⁵ Oct 27] winning hurdler: fair chaser at best, no form in **h–**
2016/17 (refused to race once and virtually did so other 2 starts): tried in cheekpieces: most
temperamental. *Henry Daly*

CYRIUS MORIVIERE (FR) 7 b.g. Vendangeur (IRE) – Sagesse Moriviere (FR) **c135**
(Vaguely Pleasant (FR)) [2016/17 h138: h16.4g h16.4s c19.1gᶠ c20dᵘʳ c19.1dᵘʳ c16.4dᵖᵘ **h90**
c19.9g⁶ Apr 6] lengthy gelding: useful hurdler, below best in 2016/17: well beaten
completed start over fences, though in process of showing useful form when departing 2
out after saddle slipped in novice at Doncaster in January (would have won): should stay
19f: acts on good to soft going: wears tongue tie: usually races close up. *Ben Pauling*

CYRNAME (FR) 5 b.g. Nickname (FR) – Narquille (FR) (Passing Sale (FR)) [2016/17 **h115**
h15.7d⁵ h19.3s⁶ Feb 18] good-topped gelding: fourth foal: half-brother to 2 winners in
France, including 17f hurdle winner Vakina (by Arvico): dam, French 17f hurdle/chase
winner, also 1½m winner on Flat: fairly useful form over hurdles: won juvenile at Pau for
Patrice Quinton in 2015/16: in hood/tongue tie last 2 starts. *Paul Nicholls*

CYRUS DARIUS 8 b.g. Overbury (IRE) – Barton Belle (Barathea (IRE)) [2016/17 **c–**
c140p, h–: h15.7s⁴ h18.1v* h16.4g Mar 14] good-topped gelding: very smart hurdler at **h143**
best, lightly raced: won Timeform Morebattle Hurdle at Kelso (by 7 lengths from One For
Harry) in February: useful form when won sole outing over fences in 2015/16: stays 2½m:
acts on heavy going. *Malcolm Jefferson*

D

DA BABA ELEPHANT (IRE) 8 b.g. Subtle Power (IRE) – Queenofbenitstown (IRE) **c–**
(Presenting) [2016/17 c16g c17d c17d h16s h20.5sᵖᵘ c20v c19.5s Jan 28] placed on point **h–**
debut: no form in varied events under Rules. *Ronan M. P. McNally, Ireland*

DA BUS BAR (IRE) 7 b.g. Marienbard (IRE) – Carrig Tune (IRE) (Flemensfirth (USA)) **h58**
[2016/17 h16.2d⁶ h16.2dᵖᵘ Jun 19] little show in maiden points/novice hurdles: wore
tongue tie: dead. *Patrick Griffin, Ireland*

DADDY'S FAVOURITE 5 b.g. Hellvelyn – Wavet (Pursuit of Love) [2016/17 b–: b15.8g Jul 22] showed nothing in point/bumpers. *Bill Turner*

    b–

DADSINTROUBLE (IRE) 7 b.g. Presenting – Gemini Lucy (IRE) (Glacial Storm (USA)) [2016/17 h112p: h21.6g³ h21.1gᶠ h22.8s* h22.8d* h20.3g h24.7g³ Apr 8] sturdy gelding: useful handicap hurdler: won at Haydock in January and February: best effort when third in Grade 3 at Aintree (8¾ lengths behind Fountains Windfall) in April: stays 25f: acts on soft going. *Tim Vaughan*

    h135

DAIDAIDAI (FR) 7 b.g. Lando (GER) – Noble World (GER) (Winged Love (IRE)) [2016/17 h–: c17.4d⁵ May 12] sturdy gelding: won 3 of 5 point starts: maiden hurdler: well beaten in hunter on chasing debut: unproven beyond 17f: acts on heavy going: tried in cheekpieces. *W. Russell*

    c54
    h–

DAINTY DIVA (IRE) 9 b.m. Indian Danehill (IRE) – She's So Dainty (IRE) (Great Commotion (USA)) [2016/17 h98: h19.1vᵖᵘ h20.5vᵖᵘ h17.7g Mar 31] sturdy mare: modest handicap hurdler, no form in 2016/17: tried in blinkers/tongue tie: temperamental. *Daniel Steele*

    h– §

DAISY DE SIVOLA (FR) 4 b.f. Assessor (IRE) – Kerrana (FR) (Cadoudal (FR)) [2016/17 h14.9s h16.9s* h17.4s² h17s⁶ h15.8s² c16.9g Apr 4] sister to fairly useful French 17f-19f hurdle/chase winner Task Force Sivola and half-sister to several winners, including useful hurdler Ut de Sivola (2m winner, by Robin des Champs) and useful hurdler/fairly useful chaser Sivola de Sivola (19f-25f winner, by Martaline): dam, French 17f/2¼m hurdle winner, also won 11f bumper: fairly useful form over hurdles: won fillies juvenile at Dieppe in June: 55/10, seventh in minor event at Compiegne on chasing debut: raced around 2m: acts on heavy going: usually races close up. *Nick Williams*

    c–
    h118

DAISY'S GIFT (IRE) 10 b.m. Presenting – Daizinni (Dr Massini (IRE)) [2016/17 h131: c22sᶠ c22.5g h20g² c16s* c17sᶠ h20d⁴ c20d² c24.8vᶠ c22.5v* Mar 19] fairly useful hurdler: second in listed mares event at Gowran in September: useful chaser: won mares maiden at Wexford in November and Grade 2 mares novice at Limerick (by 1½ lengths from Slowmotion) in March: stays 3m: acts on heavy going: in cheekpieces last 3 starts: often races towards rear: often let down by jumping. *W. P. Mullins, Ireland*

    c134 x
    h129

DAIZY (IRE) 8 ch.g. Presenting – I Remember It Well (IRE) (Don't Forget Me) [2016/17 h82: h15.7d c16sᶠ h21.6v⁵ h23.3v⁵ Dec 31] poor handicap hurdler: fell seventh in novice handicap on chasing debut: stays 2½m: acts on heavy going: wears headgear: in tongue tie last 3 starts: often races towards rear. *Matt Sheppard*

    c–
    h60

DAKLONDIKE (IRE) 5 b.g. Gold Well – Strong Irish (IRE) (Corrouge (USA)) [2016/17 b16.2d⁴ h16.2g³ h16v* h16.5s⁶ h23.9g⁴ Apr 6] €46,000 3-y-o, £140,000 4-y-o: tall, rather unfurnished gelding: half-brother to useful hurdler/high-class chaser Great Endeavour (2½m-2¾m winner, by Great Palm): dam unraced half-sister to smart hurdler/chaser up to 3m Full Irish: won Irish maiden point on debut: modest form only start in bumper: fair form over hurdles: won novice at Lingfield in November: should be suited by further than 2m: front runner/races prominently, often races freely. *David Pipe*

    h114
    b77

DAKOTA GREY 6 gr.g. Fair Mix (IRE) – Miss Sassi (Terimon) [2016/17 h115: c16.3sᵖᵘ c15.5vᵖᵘ h16.4vᵖᵘ h16.8gᵖᵘ Apr 7] fair hurdler: pulled up all 4 starts in 2016/17, over fences first 2 occasions: tried in tongue tie. *Micky Hammond*

    c–
    h–

DAKOTA MOIRETTE (FR) 4 b.g. Voix du Nord (FR) – Rahana Moirette (FR) (Dom Alco (FR)) [2016/17 b11.9g² h16dᶠ h16d⁴ h16v² h16d* h16s² h16.4g h16.5d Apr 25] sturdy gelding: second foal: dam, French 1½m/13f bumper winner, half-sister to fairly useful French chaser (stayed 21f) Tikawa Moirette: second in bumper at Nancy for Y. Fouin: fairly useful hurdler: won juvenile maiden at Punchestown in December: raced around 2m: acts on heavy going: front runner/races prominently. *Gordon Elliott, Ireland*

    h120
    b?

DALAKI (IRE) 6 b.g. Dalakhani (IRE) – Lunda (IRE) (Soviet Star (USA)) [2016/17 h115: h16s h16g h20.5g* c17sᵘʳ Jan 15] modest hurdler: won conditionals seller at Leicester in December: unseated rider fifth in maiden on chasing debut: stays 2½m: acts on soft going: tried in blinkers. *Des Donovan, Ireland*

    c–
    h99

DALAMAN (IRE) 6 b.g. Duke of Marmalade (IRE) – Crimphill (IRE) (Sadler's Wells (USA)) [2016/17 h–p: h15.8s h20.9d⁴ h19.9d Oct 13] lengthy gelding: bumper winner: poor form over hurdles: in cheekpieces last 2 starts: sometimes in tongue tie. *Tim Vaughan*

    h68

DALBY SPOOK (IRE) 7 b.m. Jeremy (USA) – Lamassu (IRE) (Entrepreneur) [2016/17 h72: h21.2d h19.3m³ h19.6g⁴ May 14] poor maiden hurdler: stays 21f: acts on good to firm and heavy going: in cheekpieces last 2 starts. *Dianne Sayer*

    h68

DALIANCE (IRE) 8 ch.g. Dalakhani (IRE) – Everlasting Love (Pursuit of Love) **c– §**
[2016/17 c93§, h106§: h20d h23.4g* h23.1s h23.4g³ h23.1s⁴ h25vᵖᵘ Jan 30] sturdy **h102 §**
gelding: fair handicap hurdler: won at Fakenham in October: winning chaser: stays 23f:
acts on heavy going: wears headgear: temperamental. *Noel Williams*

DALI MAIL (FR) 4 gr.g. Satri (IRE) – Queenly Mail (FR) (Medaaly) [2016/17 b16.4v⁴ **b– p**
Feb 15] £11,000 3-y-o: second foal: half-brother to 1¾m bumper winner Chez Castel Mail
(by My Risk): dam, French maiden, half-sister to useful French hurdler/winning chaser
(17f-21f winner) True Love Mail: shaped as if needing run when well held in maiden
bumper: should do better. *Donald Whillans*

DALKADAM (FR) 6 gr.g. Martaline – Cadoudame (FR) (Cadoudal (FR)) [2016/17 c109, **c88**
h104: h19.3d⁵ h19.9s⁴ h15.8v* h15.8v⁴ c16s³ c17.4d² h20.3g³ Apr 21] strong, workmanlike **h94**
gelding: modest handicap hurdler: won novice event at Uttoxeter in December: modest
maiden chaser: unproven beyond 17f: acts on heavy going: usually wears headgear: often
in tongue tie. *J. R. Jenkins*

DALMARELLA DANCER (IRE) 6 gr.m. Mastercraftsman (IRE) – Ting A Greeley **h90 §**
(Mr Greeley (USA)) [2016/17 h19.6s⁵ h16v h16d Apr 16] half-sister to King Ting (2½m
hurdle winner in USA, by Holy Roman Emperor): fair on Flat, stays 1¼m, refused to race
on 2 of last 3 starts in 2016: modest form over hurdles: temperamental. *David Peter Dunne,
Ireland*

DALMATIA (IRE) 6 gr.m. Cape Cross (IRE) – Dalataya (IRE) (Sadler's Wells (USA)) **h121**
[2016/17 h16.5g h16d* h20.3s h18s Feb 12] half-sister to useful hurdler Dispour (2m/17f
winner, by Monsun) and fairly useful hurdler Dalasiri (2m winner, by Dylan Thomas),
stayed 21f: fair maiden on Flat, stays 1¾m: fairly useful handicap hurdler: won at
Punchestown in November: unproven beyond 2m: acts on good to soft going: has worn
tongue tie. *Edward Harty, Ireland*

DALMO 8 b.g. Dalakhani (IRE) – Morina (USA) (Lyphard (USA)) [2016/17 h18f² h17gᵘʳ **c–**
h17g⁶ h16g² h20g³ h16f³ h18m⁴ h23.1g h23.3s⁵ c20.5sᵖᵘ c16.1d Nov 24] plain gelding: **h87**
modest handicap hurdler: no form over fences: left K. Kukk after seventh start: stays 2½m:
acts on good to firm and heavy going: usually wears headgear. *Clare Ellam*

DALTON GLANCE 7 b.m. Passing Glance – Catzybaby (IRE) (Darazari (IRE)) **c–**
[2016/17 b80: b15.8d⁵ h19.5gᵘʳ h16.3m h15.8d h16d h20v h16.5g h20.3sᵖᵘ c22.6gᵖᵘ Apr **h77**
15] angular mare: unplaced in bumpers: poor form over hurdles: pulled up in novice **b65**
handicap on chasing debut: sometimes in headgear. *Martin Keighley*

DAMBY'S STAR (IRE) 7 b.g. Kayf Tara – She Took A Tree (FR) (Sri Pekan (USA)) **h79**
[2016/17 h19.9g⁵ h21.6d⁶ h20g⁴ h25d h23.1gᶠ Apr 11] poor form over hurdles: tried in
cheekpieces: front runner/races prominently. *Mark Bradstock*

DAME ROSE (FR) 4 b.f. Network (GER) – Ile Rose (FR) (Le Riverain (FR)) [2016/17 **b106**
b16g⁵ b16.6d* b16.3v⁵ b17g* Apr 6] angular filly: seventh foal: sister to French 2¼m
hurdle winner Cristal de Roses and half-sister to 2 winners in France, including fairly
useful hurdler/fair chaser Prime Rose (2¼m/19f winner, by Video Rock): dam French

*Goffs Nickel Coin Mares' Standard Open National Hunt Flat Race, Aintree—
outsiders Dame Rose (noseband) and Oscar Rose fight out the finish, with Petticoat Tails and
Shearling (star on cap) completing the frame*

Mr Carl Hinchy's "Dame Rose"

11f/1½m bumper winner: useful form in bumpers: won mares event at Doncaster in January and Nickel Coin Mares' National Hunt Flat Race at Aintree (by ½ length from Oscar Rose) in April: bred to stay further than 17f. *Richard Hobson*

DAMIENS DILEMMA (IRE) 9 b.g. Wareed (IRE) – Olympos Belle (IRE) (Shahrastani (USA)) [2016/17 c95: c24.2d² c26.2m⁴ c24.2d* c26.6g⁶ c24.1d⁶ c21.1g c24.2gᵘʳ Apr 25] workmanlike gelding: multiple point winner: modest chaser: won handicap at Hexham in June: stays 3¼m: acts on good to firm and good to soft going. *Mrs L. A. Coltherd* **c99**

DANBY'S LEGEND 10 b.g. Midnight Legend – Miss Danbys (Charmer) [2016/17 c–, h–: h15.8gᵖᵘ May 17] lengthy, quite good-topped gelding: maiden hurdler, pulled up last 3 starts: winning chaser: has worn hood: tried in tongue tie. *Olly Williams* **c–
h–**

DANCE AND ROMANCE 5 b.m. Kayf Tara – Sweetheart (Sinndar (IRE)) [2016/17 h72p, b62: h16.8d h27s³ h27v⁶ h24g⁴ Apr 8] poor maiden hurdler: best effort at 27f: acts on soft going: in tongue tie last 3 starts. *Tim Easterby* **h80**

DANCE FLOOR KING (IRE) 10 b.g. Generous (IRE) – Strawberry Fool (FR) (Tel Quel (FR)) [2016/17 c–, h–: c16.5g c17.5s³ c19.2v² c19.2s* c20.2d² c20d² c20.2m* Apr 5] lengthy gelding: maiden hurdler: fairly useful handicap chaser: won at Exeter in January and Wincanton in April: stays 2½m: acts on good to firm and heavy going: front runner/races prominently, often travels strongly. *Nick Mitchell* **c121
h–**

DANCE IN THE DUST (IRE) 6 b.g. Scorpion (IRE) – Samotracia (IRE) (Rock of **h104** Gibraltar (IRE)) [2016/17 b–: h19.1d h19.9g⁶ h21spu h16g² h16m³ Apr 28] runner-up in Irish point on debut: fair form over hurdles: unproven beyond 2m. *Jonjo O'Neill*

DANCEINTOTHELIGHT 10 gr.g. Dansili – Kali (Linamix (FR)) [2016/17 c88, h107: **c–** h16.7g h23.1d h20.6g⁴ h17.2g h20g² h20.9d² h19.6g³ h19.3g³ h19.3d* h15.8d⁶ h19.4g* **h108** h19.3s⁴ h16.6s³ h15.8m⁴ Apr 18] sturdy gelding: fair handicap hurdler: won at Catterick (amateur) in December and Musselburgh in January: fell both starts over fences: stays 21f: acts on good to firm and heavy going: tried in cheekpieces: wears tongue tie: usually leads. *Donald McCain*

DANCE OF FIRE 5 b.g. Norse Dancer (IRE) – Strictly Dancing (IRE) (Danehill Dancer **h96** (IRE)) [2016/17 h16.2spu h15.6g h19.4g⁵ h18.1d⁶ h16.2g⁶ Apr 27] useful on Flat for Andrew Balding, stays 10.5f: modest form over hurdles: stays 19f: acts on good to soft going. *N. W. Alexander*

DANCE WITH KATE 6 b.m. Hamairi (IRE) – Vercheny (Petoski) [2016/17 h15.8m⁴ **h–** Apr 25] well held on Flat/hurdling debut. *Bill Turner*

DANCING CONQUEST 7 b.m. Imperial Dancer – Another Conquest (El Conquistador) **c–** [2016/17 b–: h18.5g⁵ c17.5v⁴ c23.5v⁴ Jan 10] well held in bumper/hurdle/chases. *Seamus* **h–** *Mullins*

DANCING DIK 12 b.g. Diktat – Maureena (IRE) (Grand Lodge (USA)) [2016/17 c86, **c– §** h–: h21.6dpu h22m h21.6gpu c16d⁶ c15.7d c21.1vpu c16vpu h23.6s h19g Mar 30] big **h– §** gelding: winning hurdler: poor handicap chaser: has worn headgear, including last 2 starts: front runner/races prominently: temperamental. *Steven Dixon*

DANCING MEADOWS (IRE) 7 ch.m. Alhaarth (IRE) – Kylebeg Dancer (IRE) **c–** (General Monash (USA)) [2016/17 c111, h118: c23.8mpu h19.5gpu Jun 5] lengthy mare: **h–** fairly useful hurdler: let down by jumping both starts over fences: stays 21f: acts on good to soft going: usually in hood. *Gordon Elliott, Ireland*

DANCING OLGA 12 b.m. Baryshnikov (AUS) – Polly Leach (Pollerton) [2016/17 **c71** c19.2g⁴ Apr 11] winning pointer: maiden hurdler: well held in hunter in April on sole start **h–** under Rules since winning on chasing debut in 2014/15: stays 21f: tried in hood. *R. C. Pudd*

DANCING SHADOW (IRE) 8 br.g. Craigsteel – Be My Shadow (IRE) (Torus) **c134** [2016/17 c117, h–: c24m³ h26.5m⁶ c24.2m² c24.2s⁴ c26g* c32.8g* c31.8gpu c31.8g Apr **h83** 22] tall, angular gelding: fairly useful maiden at best over hurdles: useful handicap chaser: won at Doncaster in December and Musselburgh in February: stays 33f: acts on good to firm and heavy going: wears cheekpieces: usually races towards rear. *Victor Dartnall*

DANDAN (IRE) 9 b.g. Zagreb (USA) – Temporary Setback (IRE) (Moonax (IRE)) **c91** [2016/17 c–: c16.3g⁵ Apr 27] multiple winning pointer: modest form over fences: fifth in hunter at Cheltenham very early in season. *Miss Francesca Moller*

DANDRIDGE 8 ch.g. Doyen (IRE) – Arantxa (Sharpo) [2016/17 c143, h–: h19.5g c16g⁴ **c143** c17d⁵ c17d⁶ h16s⁵ c16.3g⁴ c15.8g Apr 6] big, robust gelding: fair handicap hurdler: useful **h113** handicap chaser: fourth in Grand Annual at Cheltenham (4½ lengths behind Rock The World) in March: stays 2½m: acts on soft and good to firm going: wears tongue tie: usually races towards rear. *A. L. T. Moore, Ireland*

DANDY MAG (FR) 4 br.g. Special Kaldoun (IRE) – Naiade Mag (FR) (Kadalko (FR)) **h135** [2016/17 b11.9g² b11.9g² h16v* h16.8g h16d² h16d⁶ Apr 29] neat gelding: fifth foal: half- **b?** brother to smart hurdler/chaser Vroum Vroum Mag (2m-3m winner, by Voix du Nord) and French bumper winner/fairly useful 2¼m hurdle winner Cabriole Mag (by Gris de Gris): dam, French 21f chase winner, half-sister to smart staying chaser Saint Are: runner-up in bumpers for E. & G. Leenders: useful form over hurdles: won maiden at Gowran in February: best effort when second in Grade 2 juvenile at Fairyhouse (½ length behind Project Bluebook) in April. *W. P. Mullins, Ireland*

DANEHILLS WELL (IRE) 9 b.g. Indian Danehill (IRE) – Collatrim Choice (IRE) **c91** (Saddlers' Hall (IRE)) [2016/17 c65, h89: c21.6d² c21.2m⁶ c20.5s³ c20.5s² c24.2spu **h–** c20.5vur h20.5s⁵ c21.6vpu c20.9d Apr 5] winning pointer: modest maiden handicap hurdler/ chaser: stays 2¾m: acts on soft going: usually wears headgear: front runner/races prominently. *Alison Hamilton*

DAN EMMETT (USA) 7 ch.g. Flower Alley (USA) – Singing Dixie (USA) (Dixieland **c–** Band (USA)) [2016/17 h126: c23.4sF h23.6sF h26s Jan 14] fairly useful hurdler at best: **h–** little impact in 2 starts in 2016/17: beaten when fell 5 out in novice handicap won by Calett Mad at Newcastle on chasing debut: in cheekpieces final start. *Michael Scudamore*

DANIELLE'S JOURNEY 7 b.m. Presenting – Harringay (Sir Harry Lewis (USA)) **c–**
[2016/17 h112, b88: h22g² c16.3d⁵ c16s Nov 22] leggy mare: bumper winner: fair hurdler: **h112**
well held both starts over fences: stays 2¾m: acts on heavy going: wears tongue tie. *Stuart Crawford, Ireland*

DANIMIX (IRE) 12 b.g. Dr Massini (IRE) – Spring Blend (IRE) (Persian Mews) **c–**
[2016/17 c135x, h–: c26.1gᵖᵘ c25.5d c20.4g c26.2sᵖᵘ Dec 11] sturdy gelding: winning **h–**
hurdler: useful chaser, no form in 2016/17: in cheekpieces last 2 starts: wears tongue tie:
often races towards rear. *Neil Mulholland*

DANSEUR DU LARGE 4 gr.g. Martaline – Antagua (FR) (Cadoudal (FR)) **h–**
[2016/17 b16d h15.8g Apr 28] well held in bumper/hurdling debut. *Charlie Longsdon* **b–**

DANS LE VENT (FR) 4 b.g. Skins Game – Boreade (FR) (Lost World (IRE)) [2016/17 **b104**
b13.7m* b16.3d³ b16.4g⁶ b15.8m* Apr 18] sturdy gelding: half-brother to fairly
useful hurdler/useful chaser Chancol (2m-2½m winner, by Vangelis): dam, French 1m
winner, half-sister to smart/temperamental hurdler/chaser (stayed 2½m) Takeroc: fairly
useful form in bumpers: won at Towcester (maiden) in October and Ludlow in April: third
in listed event at Newbury (5 lengths behind Daphne du Clos) in February and sixth in
Champion Bumper at Cheltenham in March: left Paul Morgan after first start.
Jamie Snowden

DAN'S QUEST 7 b.g. Kalanisi (IRE) – Piedmont (UAE) (Jade Robbery (USA)) [2016/17 **h65**
h81: h19.7sᵖᵘ h19v Dec 31] useful-looking gelding: poor maiden hurdler: stays 2½m.
Robin Dickin

DANTES KING (IRE) 12 b.g. King's Theatre (IRE) – Forecast Rain (IRE) (Phardante **c60**
(FR)) [2016/17 c25sᵖᵘ c20gᵘʳ c24.7d⁴ c24.5dᵖᵘ Apr 28] big gelding: multiple winning **h–**
pointer: winning hurdler: poor chaser nowadays: stays 25f: acts on good to firm and heavy
going: tried in headgear: has worn tongue tie: usually races nearer last than first: has joined
Ms M. M. Gannon. *Ross O'Sullivan, Ireland*

DANTE'S WAY (IRE) 8 b.g. Scorpion (IRE) – Benedicta Rose (IRE) (Beneficial) **h85**
[2016/17 h100p, b91: h23.3d⁵ h19.9g⁶ h24.6d³ h24d h22.7s h22.7sᵖᵘ h19.3g Jan 12]
bumper winner: modest maiden hurdler, has lost way: left Malcolm Jefferson after first
start: best effort at 2½m: acts on good to soft going: has worn cheekpieces. *Dianne Sayer*

DANVINNIE 8 b.g. Midnight Legend – Top Gale (IRE) (Topanoora) [2016/17 h110: **c90**
c20.9s c22.7g c23g⁵ Feb 21] maiden hurdler: modest form over fences: stays 19f: best form **h–**
on soft/heavy going: in headgear last 2 starts. *Oliver Sherwood*

DAPHNE DU CLOS (FR) 4 b.f. Spanish Moon (USA) – Katarina du Clos (FR) **b109**
(Panoramic) [2016/17 b11.9g* b14s² b16.3d* Feb 11] medium-sized filly: half-sister to
French bumper winners Alyse du Clos (11f winner, by Honolulu) and Solenne du Clos
(1½m winner, by Freedom Cry): dam ran twice in France: useful form in bumpers: won at
Saint-Brieuc (by ¾ length from Della Perla) in October and listed event at Newbury (by 3¼
lengths from Western Ryder) in February: left J. Merienne after first start. *Nicky Henderson*

DARA'S PRESENT (IRE) 6 b.g. Presenting – Ginandit (IRE) (Definite Article) **h102 p**
[2016/17 h19.4g⁶ Jan 27] fourth foal: dam (h83), maiden hurdler (stayed 2½m), half-sister
to useful hurdlers Raise Your Heart (stayed 2¼m) and More Dash Thancash (best around
2m): off mark in Irish points at third attempt: 3/1, sixth in maiden at Doncaster on hurdling
debut: sure to do better. *Harry Whittington*

DARDANELLA 10 b.m. Alflora (IRE) – Ella Falls (IRE) (Dancing Dissident (USA)) **h94**
[2016/17 h91§: h19g* h20g² May 28] modest handicap hurdler: won at Warwick
(conditional) in May: stays 3m: acts on any going: tried in cheekpieces/tongue tie: usually
races close up. *Hugo Froud*

DAREBIN (GER) 5 ch.g. It's Gino (GER) – Delightful Sofie (GER) (Grand Lodge **h119**
(USA)) [2016/17 h118: h16d⁶ h16d* h17.7s⁶ h16d³ h16.5g Apr 8] lengthy gelding: fairly
useful handicap hurdler: won at Lingfield in November: third in Imperial Cup at Sandown
in March: stays 2¼m: acts on heavy going: usually in headgear: usually races prominently.
Gary Moore

DARE ME (IRE) 13 b.g. Bob Back (USA) – Gaye Chatelaine (IRE) (Castle Keep) [2016/17 **c–**
c144, h–: c20g May 29] lengthy gelding: winning hurdler: useful handicap chaser, well **h–**
below form sole start in 2016/17: stays 21f: acts on heavy going. *Venetia Williams*

DARE TO ENDEAVOUR 10 b.g. Alflora – Miss Chinchilla (Perpendicular) **c124 §**
[2016/17 c130§, h–: h20s c24d⁵ c25.5dᵘʳ h24v c30dᵖᵘ Apr 29] tall gelding: maiden hurdler: **h–**
fairly useful handicap chaser: fifth in Munster National Handicap Chase at Limerick in
October: stays 3¼m: acts on heavy going: tried in headgear: often races towards rear:
temperamental. *Eric McNamara, Ireland*

DARING ARTICLE (IRE) 11 br.g. Definite Article – Daring Hen (IRE) (Henbit (USA)) [2016/17 c25d^{pu} c20s^6 c23.8s^{pu} h27g^{pu} Apr 7] winning hurdler: fairly useful chaser at best: left Robert Tyner after first start: stays 3m: acts on soft going: wears headgear: usually in tongue tie. *Oliver Greenall* **c78 h–**

DARING KNIGHT 4 b.g. Dick Turpin (IRE) – Fairy Slipper (Singspiel (IRE)) [2016/17 h16.7d^5 h16.7g^5 h16.7g^4 h20.5g^6 h20.7s^{pu} h15.9s h19.6g^{pu} Apr 22] fair maiden on Flat, stays 1m: modest maiden hurdler: left Martin Smith after sixth start: best effort at 17f: tried in blinkers. *Clare Ellam* **h87**

DARK AND DANGEROUS (IRE) 9 b.g. Cacique (IRE) – Gilah (IRE) (Saddlers' Hall (IRE)) [2016/17 c–, h75: c15.8g^{pu} h19.3d h16.8d* h16.4s^5 h16.8s* h16.8v* h16.8v* h16.8d^F h16.8g^{pu} Apr 7] compact gelding: fair handicap hurdler: won 4 times at Sedgefield in 2016/17: fairly useful chaser at best: unproven beyond 17f: acts on heavy going: usually wears headgear: tried in tongue tie: usually races close up. *Simon Waugh* **c– h104**

DARK DIAMOND (IRE) 7 b.g. Dark Angel (IRE) – Moon Diamond (Unfuwain (USA)) [2016/17 h–: h16.8d^2 h18.6g^4 h22.1m h22.1m^3 h20.6g* h22.1g^4 h23.1g^6 h17.2g^6 h18.6g^F Sep 24] modest handicap hurdler: won at Market Rasen (conditional) in July: stayed 21f: acted on good to soft going: wore headgear: unreliable: dead. *Michael Chapman* **h91 §**

DARK ENEMY (IRE) 4 b.g. Dark Angel (IRE) – Headborough Lass (IRE) (Invincible Spirit (IRE)) [2016/17 h16s h16g h16.3d^{ur} h16s Jan 7] sturdy gelding: little impact in maidens on Flat/juvenile hurdles: tried in cheekpieces: in tongue tie last 3 starts. *Brendan Powell* **h–**

DARKESTBEFOREDAWN (IRE) 10 br.g. Dr Massini (IRE) – Camden Dolphin (IRE) (Camden Town) [2016/17 c86, h100: c25.5d^2 Apr 29] workmanlike gelding: fair hurdler: similar form over fences: stays 25f: acts on heavy going: in headgear last 2 starts. *Caroline Keevil* **c102 h–**

DARK FLAME (IRE) 8 b.g. Gold Well – Glorys Flame (IRE) (Flemensfirth (USA)) [2016/17 h118: c20d* c18.8d^3 c20.8s c20.2s^6 c21m^2 Apr 2] strong gelding: fairly useful hurdler: useful form over fences: won novice chase at Sandown in November: stays 21f: has form on heavy going, possibly better suited by less testing conditions: often races in rear. *Richard Rowe* **c136 h–**

DARK FORCE (FR) 4 gr.g. Gris de Gris (IRE) – Maciga (FR) (Gunboat Diplomacy (FR)) [2016/17 b16s^4 Mar 30] first foal: dam, French 13f bumper winner, placed up to 19f over jumps: 10/1, fourth in maiden bumper at Warwick (21 lengths behind Mance Rayder) in March: likely to improve. *Venetia Williams* **b64 p**

DARK INVADER (FR) 5 b.g. Saint des Saints (FR) – Minirose (FR) (Mansonnien (FR)) [2016/17 b15.3v^4 b15.3f^2 Apr 23] sturdy gelding: fifth foal: brother to smart hurdler/chaser Irish Saint (2m-21f winner) and French 19f hurdle winner Celtic Saint: dam French 2m hurdle winner: fair form in bumpers: better effort when second at Wincanton in April. *Paul Nicholls* **b91**

DARK LOVER (GER) 12 b.g. Zinaad – Dark Lady (GER) (Lagunas) [2016/17 c118, h–: h20.3g^6 h23.1s^4 Nov 20] good-topped gelding: fair handicap hurdler: fairly useful chaser: stays 3m: acts on heavy going: has worn cheekpieces. *Jamie Snowden* **c– h111**

DARK MAHLER (IRE) 6 b.g. Mahler – Aries Rambler (IRE) (Shernazar) [2016/17 h23.1v^{pu} h15.8s^6 h16.3g^4 Apr 1] second foal: dam unraced half-sister to fairly useful hurdler/fair chaser (stayed 2½m) Greenhall Rambler: third in Irish point on debut: modest form over hurdles: best effort when sixth in maiden at Huntingdon in January: will be suited by 2½m: tried in tongue tie. *Emma Lavelle* **h94**

DARLOA (IRE) 8 br.g. Darsi (FR) – Lady Lola (IRE) (Supreme Leader) [2016/17 h15.8g^3 h18.7g^{pu} h15.8g h19.9d h16.8g^{pu} h19s^{pu} Feb 5] poor maiden hurdler: unproven beyond 2m: tried in cheekpieces: wears tongue tie. *Victor Dartnall* **h76**

DARNITNEV 7 b.g. Darnay – Lavender Della (IRE) (Shernazar) [2016/17 h93: h20s^{pu} May 11] modest hurdler: stays 23f: best form on good going: wears headgear. *Martin Keighley* **h–**

DARSI DANCER (IRE) 9 b.g. Darsi (FR) – Jaystara (IRE) (Jurado (USA)) [2016/17 c67§, h91§: h27s^2 h23.3g^2 h23.3d^3 h23.3d* h25.4d^2 h23.9s c26.3d^{pu} h27v^3 h23.3s^3 h27g^{pu} Mar 29] winning pointer: modest hurdler: won conditionals seller at Hexham in June: maiden chaser: stays 27f: acts on soft going: has worn cheekpieces: temperamental. *Stuart Coltherd* **c– § h89 §**

DARTFORD WARBLER (IRE) 10 b.g. Overbury (IRE) – Stony View (IRE) (Tirol) [2016/17 c121, h118: h19.7g h19.9v^4 h22.8s^4 h19.9v^4 c19.4s^4 h23.5s c20v^3 c20s^4 c21.3g^5 Apr 23] compact gelding: fair handicap hurdler/chaser: stays 23f: acts on heavy going: tried in cheekpieces: front runner/races prominently. *Sue Smith* **c108 h103**

DARWINS FOX (FR) 11 b.g. Kahyasi – Parcelle de Sou (FR) (Ajdayt (USA)) [2016/17 c143, h–: c17d6 c19.9g3 c15.9s* c21.1g6 c20g4 Apr 17] sturdy gelding: maiden pointer: winning hurdler: fairly useful chaser: won hunter at Leicester in March: sixth in Foxhunters' Chase at Aintree in April: left Henry de Bromhead after first start: best up to 2½m: acts on good to firm and heavy going: tried in cheekpieces: has worn tongue tie, including last 4 starts: often races prominently. *David Christie, Ireland* **c129 h–**

DARWINS THEORY (IRE) 9 b.g. Montjeu (IRE) – Thrift (IRE) (Green Desert (USA)) [2016/17 c81, h107: h19.5v3 h16v2 h16v3 h15.3v4 Mar 9] fair handicap hurdler: maiden chaser: stays 2¾m: acts on good to firm and heavy going: has worn headgear: wears tongue tie. *Fiona Shaw* **c– h107**

DASHING OSCAR (IRE) 7 b.g. Oscar (IRE) – Be My Leader (IRE) (Supreme Leader) [2016/17 h114: h16.7v* h16s* h19g3 h16.7s2 h20g Apr 7] lengthy gelding: fairly useful hurdler: won novices at Bangor in November and Sandown in December: stays 19f: acts on heavy going: wears tongue tie: front runner/races prominently. *Harry Fry* **h126**

DASHING PERK 6 b.g. Kayf Tara – Dashing Executive (IRE) (Executive Perk) [2016/17 b15.7d5 b15.3s3 h23.6s2 Jan 20] £8,000 3-y-o, £50,000 5-y-o: big, strong gelding: fourth foal: half-brother to fair hurdler/fairly useful chaser Double Dash (2m-3m winner, by Sir Harry Lewis): dam unraced half-sister to fairly useful hurdler/fair chaser (19f-21f winner) She's Our Native: won Irish point on debut: fair form in bumpers: 7/2, shaped well when second in maiden at Chepstow (4 lengths behind Imperial Bay) on hurdling debut: will improve. *Dr Richard Newland* **h113 p b94**

DASSETT GOLD (FR) 4 b.g. Full of Gold (FR) – Marsavrile (FR) (April Night (FR)) [2016/17 b15.8g4 Apr 17] £10,000 3-y-o: fourth foal: dam French maiden (second in 13.5f bumper): 16/1, fourth in bumper at Huntingdon (8¼ lengths behind Hatcher) in April. *Paul Webber* **b85**

DAULYS ANTHEM (IRE) 9 br.g. Royal Anthem (USA) – Over Dubai (Overbury (IRE)) [2016/17 h90: h23d c24d2 c22.6g3 c22.6g2 c25.5g5 c20g4 c22.6m3 Oct 15] workmanlike hurdler: similar form over fences: likely to prove best up to 3m: acts on heavy going: has joined Dan Skelton. *David Dennis* **c94 h–**

DAUPHINE EREINE (FR) 5 b.m. Saint des Saints (FR) – Bellissima de Mai (FR) (Pistolet Bleu (IRE)) [2016/17 c20d* c18d* c19.5g* c21.2d3 Aug 29] fourth foal: half-sister to very smart hurdler/top-class chaser Dynaste (19f-25f winner, by Martaline): dam French maiden (second in 17f chase): once-raced over hurdles: fair form over fences: won minor events at Paray-Le-Monial and Cluny in May, and Avignon in June for A. Adeline de Boisbrunet: stays 2½m: acts on good to soft going: remains open to improvement. *David Pipe* **c109 p h–**

DAUPHINESS 5 b.m. Lucarno (USA) – Princess Angelique (FR) (Sagacity (FR)) [2016/17 b16d Feb 17] second foal: dam (b76) well held in bumper: 25/1, seventh in mares maiden bumper at Fakenham. *Henry Daly* **b–**

DAVERON (IRE) 9 b.g. Winged Love (IRE) – Double Doc (IRE) (Moonax (IRE)) [2016/17 c128, h106: c23.8d c23.8dpu c20s6 c20.2dF h19.9s6 h23.1g5 Apr 22] workmanlike gelding: modest handicap hurdler: fair handicap chaser: stays 21f: acts on heavy going: tried in cheekpieces: usually races close up. *Ben Pauling* **c114 h94**

DAVID CRICKET 5 b.g. Shirocco (GER) – Lady Cricket (FR) (Cricket Ball (USA)) [2016/17 b16d2 b17.7d3 h19.7s5 Nov 23] brother to useful bumper winner/smart hurdler Red Sherlock (2½m winner) and half-brother to bumper winner/useful hurdler Swing Bowler (2m/17f winner, by Galileo): dam (c165/h153) 17f-21f hurdle/chase winner (stayed 25f): fair form in bumpers: 8/1, some encouragement when fifth in novice at Hereford on hurdling debut: should do better. *Alan King* **h88 p b87**

DAVID JOHN 6 b.g. Overbury (IRE) – Molly's Secret (Minshaanshu Amad (USA)) [2016/17 h96: h19.9g* h20dpu h23.6mpu h21.2v Nov 21] sturdy gelding: modest handicap hurdler: won at Uttoxeter in September: stays 2½m: best form on good going: tried in hood/tongue tie: often races towards rear. *Tony Carroll* **h96**

DAWNIERIVER (IRE) 7 br.m. Indian River (FR) – In Sin (IRE) (Insan (USA)) [2016/17 c92, h74: c22.5g3 c21.1gpu c23m2 c22.6g c21.2g* c22.5d* c25.7g4 c24.2s2 c20.8g4 c24g* c22.2g Apr 15] lengthy, rather sparely-made mare: maiden hurdler: fair handicap chaser: won at Cartmel in August, Uttoxeter and Plumpton in October, and Southwell in March: stays 3¼m: acts on soft and good to firm going: wears cheekpieces: often races towards rear, usually travels strongly. *Michael Scudamore* **c111 h–**

DAWN MISSILE 5 b.g. Nayef (USA) – Ommadawn (IRE) (Montjeu (IRE)) [2016/17 **h110** h21s h19.6d³ h15.5d⁵ h19.4d Jan 28] good-topped gelding: useful on Flat, stays 16.5f: fair form over hurdles: in tongue tie final start. *Nigel Twiston-Davies*

DAWNS BACH (IRE) 8 b.m. Bach (IRE) – Dakani (IRE) (Anshan) [2016/17 h19.9sᵖᵘ **h–** Jun 15] maiden pointer: little impact over hurdles: usually wore hood: tried in tongue tie: dead. *Barry Brennan*

DAWSON CITY 8 b.g. Midnight Legend – Running For Annie (Gunner B) [2016/17 **c131** c131, h–: c23.8d⁵ c28.5s² c25.2v³ c25.1v* c31.8gᵖᵘ Apr 22] sturdy gelding: winning **h–** hurdler: useful handicap chaser: won at Wincanton (by 32 lengths from Top Wood) in March: stays 3½m: best form on soft/heavy going: tried in cheekpieces: front runner/races prominently. *Polly Gundry*

DAYDREAM ISLAND (IRE) 7 b.g. Trans Island – Ring Hill (Bering) [2016/17 h20d **c61** h20.1gᵖᵘ h16.2d h22sᵖᵘ c19.9g⁴ c19.9g⁴ c20g⁵ c24.2gᶠ Apr 25] failed to complete both **h–** starts in points: maiden hurdler: poor form over fences: left M. Hourigan after first start: best effort at 2½m: acts on heavy going: tried in hood. *Sheena Walton*

DAY IN PARADISE 6 b.m. Tobougg (IRE) – Sunnyland (Sovereign Water (FR)) **h–** [2016/17 h23.8sᶠ h25.6gᵖᵘ Apr 12] second foal: half-sister to 2½m hurdle winner East Hill (by Lucarno): dam (h104), 2m hurdle winner, half-sister to fair hurdler/fairly useful chaser (stayed 2½m) Brown Teddy: failed to complete both starts over hurdles. *Robert Stephens*

DAYLAMI DAYS (IRE) 6 gr.g. Daylami (IRE) – Euro Gypsy (IRE) (Eurobus) [2016/17 **h81 p** h19g³ Apr 6] €6,000 3-y-o: second foal: dam (c80), winning pointer, closely related to fairly useful hurdler/chaser (stayed 2¾m) Hampshire Express and half-sister to fairly useful hurdler/useful staying chaser Tinker Time: runner-up completed start in maiden points: 7/1, third in novice at Taunton (11½ lengths behind Garo de Juilley) on hurdling debut: open to improvement. *Philip Hobbs*

DAYLAMI KIRK (IRE) 6 b.g. Daylami (IRE) – Uptothefrontkirk (IRE) (Bob Back **b81** (USA)) [2016/17 b16g³ b16.3s b15.3v² b16g Apr 8] €23,000 3-y-o, £23,000 4-y-o: tall, good-topped gelding: second foal: dam, unraced, out of half-sister to dam of Cheltenham Gold Cup winner Synchronised: modest form in bumpers. *Ron Hodges*

DAYMAR BAY (IRE) 11 b.g. Oscar (IRE) – Sunset View (IRE) (Good Thyne (USA)) **c94** [2016/17 c119, h–: c20.8g⁶ c20gᵖᵘ Apr 3] tall, useful-looking gelding: maiden pointer: **h–** maiden hurdler: modest chaser: left Gareth Thomas after first start: stays 2½m: acts on soft and good to firm going: has worn headgear: tried in tongue tie. *S. J. Sampson*

DAY OF ROSES (IRE) 8 b.g. Acambaro (GER) – Dan's Choice (IRE) (Spanish Place **c–** (USA)) [2016/17 h–: h18.5s h21.6v² h19.1vᵖᵘ c24.2d Mar 21] Irish maiden point winner: **h80** poor form over hurdles: well beaten in novice handicap on chasing debut: best effort at 2¾m: acts on heavy going. *Jeremy Scott*

DAYS AHEAD (IRE) 10 ch.g. Kheleyf (USA) – Hushaby (IRE) (Eurobus) [2016/17 **c88** c115, h–: c24mᵖᵘ c19.7d⁶ c15.9f³ c19.9dᵖᵘ c21.7g³ Mar 2] good-topped gelding: winning **h–** hurdler: modest handicap chaser: stays 25f: acts on soft and good to firm going: wears headgear: tried in tongue tie. *Richenda Ford*

DAYS HOTEL (IRE) 12 b.g. Oscar (IRE) – Call Catherine (IRE) (Strong Gale) [2016/17 **c147** c153, h–: c16d⁶ c20d⁵ c17s² Dec 11] tall, well-made gelding: winning hurdler: smart **h–** chaser: second in Hilly Way Chase at Cork (22 lengths behind Douvan) in December: unproven beyond 17f: acts on heavy going: tried in cheekpieces. *Henry de Bromhead, Ireland*

DAYS OF HEAVEN (FR) 7 b.g. Saint des Saints (FR) – Daramour (FR) (Anabaa Blue) **c143 p** [2016/17 h–: c20.5g* h20gᵘʳ h21f⁵ h22f³ c16g* Mar 18] sturdy gelding: fairly useful **h122 +** hurdler: third in Grade 1 at Camden (11¾ lengths behind Top Striker) in November: useful form over fences: won novice at Kempton in May and novice handicap there (by 8 lengths from Holly Bush Henry) in March: stays 2½m: acts on soft going: usually wears hood: signs of temperament (edgy sort and has given trouble at start). *Nicky Henderson*

DAYTIME AHEAD (IRE) 6 gr.m. Daylami (IRE) – Bright Times Ahead (IRE) **h85** (Rainbows For Life (CAN)) [2016/17 h82: h19.9g⁵ h16d⁶ h15.3s h19.5v⁴ h19.5v⁶ h16.8d⁶ h19.8v* h19.2s⁶ h21.6g⁴ Apr 12] modest handicap hurdler: won at Wincanton in March: left Oliver Sherwood after first start: stays 2¾m: acts on heavy going: usually races towards rear: has joined Seamus Mullins. *Simon Hodgson*

DAYTRIPPER 6 gr.m. Daylami (IRE) – Stravaigin (Primitive Rising (USA)) [2016/17 **h103 p** h101, b–: h20.1g⁶ h19s* Dec 5] fair form over hurdles: won handicap at Ayr in December: left Lucinda Russell after first start: stays 19f: acts on soft going: likely to progress further. *Iain Jardine*

DAZINSKI 11 ch.g. Sulamani (IRE) – Shuheb (Nashwan (USA)) [2016/17 h112: h20.3v² **h109** May 10] fair handicap hurdler: possibly best around 2½m: acts on good to firm and heavy going: often in tongue tie: usually races towards rear. *Henry Oliver*

DAZZLING RITA 11 b.m. Midnight Legend – Pytchley Dawn (Welsh Captain) [2016/17 **c–** c–, h–: h21.2d h20.3s² h23.3m⁵ h19.9s⁶ h22v Jun 28] poor handicap hurdler: pulled up both **h67** starts over fences: stays 3¼m: acts on good to soft going: wears tongue tie: front runner/races prominently, usually travels strongly. *Sam England*

DAZZLING TIMES (USA) 5 gr.g. Street Cry (IRE) – Blue Dress (USA) (Danzig **b–** (USA)) [2016/17 b16.2d b16g Jun 20] pulled up in point: last in 2 bumpers. *John Joseph Hanlon, Ireland*

DEADLINE DAY (IRE) 6 b.g. Montjeu (IRE) – Madame Cerito (USA) (Diesis) **h80** [2016/17 h19.9g h15.8g⁵ h15.8g h16.3gᵖᵘ h15.8mᵖᵘ Oct 30] modest maiden on Flat, stays 16.5f: poor from over hurdles: in blinkers in 2016/17. *Michael Mullineaux*

DEADLY APPROACH 6 b.g. New Approach (IRE) – Speirbhean (IRE) (Danehill **c125** (USA)) [2016/17 h105: h16d³ c16.2s³ c16sᵘʳ c16dᵘʳ c16d⁴ c16g⁴ c16.3g³ Apr 19] maiden **h86** hurdler: fairly useful form over fences: won handicap at Ludlow in February: raced around 2m: acts on good to soft going: has worn hood: usually wears tongue tie: front runner/races prominently. *Sarah-Jayne Davies*

DEADLY MOVE (IRE) 8 b.g. Scorpion (IRE) – Sounds Attractive (IRE) (Rudimentary **c111** (USA)) [2016/17 h102: h21g⁶ c19.4g² c19.4d⁴ c23.6m² c20.9s⁵ c24vᵖᵘ Dec 31] strong **h100** gelding: fair maiden hurdler: similar form over fences: stays 3m: acts on good to firm and heavy going: tried in visor: often wears tongue tie. *Peter Bowen*

DEADLY STING (IRE) 8 b.g. Scorpion (IRE) – Gaza Strip (IRE) (Hamas (IRE)) **c–** [2016/17 c125, h–: c25gᵖᵘ May 13] lengthy gelding: winning hurdler: fairly useful chaser **h–** at best: likely to stay long distances: acts on good to soft and good to firm going: wears cheekpieces: in tongue tie last 2 starts. *Neil Mulholland*

DEAD RIGHT 5 b.g. Alflora (IRE) – April Queen (Midnight Legend) [2016/17 b15.8v² **h– p** h16.3d b16d* Apr 27] tall, useful-looking gelding: first foal: dam unraced: useful form **b114** in bumpers: won conditionals/amateur event at Punchestown (by 4½ lengths from Next Destination) in April: 6/1, shaped as if needed experience when eighth in novice at Newbury (25½ lengths behind High Bridge) on hurdling debut: should do better. *Neil Mulholland*

DEALING RIVER 10 b.g. Avonbridge – Greensand (Green Desert (USA)) [2016/17 **c111** c16.5s³ c19.9g⁴ c15.7v⁵ c15.7d³ c16.5g* h16.7g⁵ c16.5g* c16.5g Oct 19] modest handicap **h85** hurdler: fair handicap chaser: won at Worcester in July and September: best around 2m: acts on good to firm and good to soft going: often wears cheekpieces: tried in tongue tie: front runner/races prominently. *Caroline Bailey*

DEANS ROAD (IRE) 8 ch.g. Golan (IRE) – Close To Home (IRE) (Be My Native **c136** (USA)) [2016/17 c19.5d* c22.7g³ c20.5g⁴ c20s* c20s² c20.4g Mar 14] workmanlike **h–** gelding: fifth foal: half-brother to 2 winning pointers by Moscow Society: dam (h85) maiden hurdler: maiden point winner: winning hurdler: useful form over fences: won maiden at Limerick in May and novice at Listowel in September: second in Grade 3 novice at Tipperary (15 lengths behind Westerner Lady) in October: stays 23f: acts on heavy going: usually races close up. *Henry de Bromhead, Ireland*

DEAR SIRE (FR) 5 gr.g. Al Namix (FR) – Polismith (FR) (Poliglote) [2016/17 b76: b16d **h121** b16.8s³ b16.8d² h16.8d² h16.2v⁴ h15.6g* h19.4g* h19.9g⁴ h16g* Apr 22] fairly useful form **b95** in bumpers: similar standard over hurdles: won maiden at Musselburgh in March and handicap at Wetherby (conditional) in April: left Stuart Crawford after third start: stays 2½m: acts on good to soft going: usually wears hood. *Donald McCain*

DEATH DUTY (IRE) 6 b.g. Shantou (USA) – Midnight Gift (IRE) (Presenting) **h148** [2016/17 h110: h20v* h20d* h20s* h20s* h24gᵘʳ h20g³ Apr 28]

The story of how Gordon Elliott claimed the scalp of Willie Mullins in a notably tense battle to be leading trainer at the Cheltenham Festival was bound to be a recurring theme in this edition of *Chasers & Hurdlers* (both trainers finished on six winners—taking twelve of the meeting's twenty-eight races between them—but Elliott saddled three seconds, one more than Mullins). One angle that might be missed, however, is the contrast in the starting prices of the pair's winners. The 25/1 victory of the enigmatic Labaik in the Supreme Novices' Hurdle set the tone for Elliott's week, in which he had other good-priced winners including Tiger Roll (16/1) in the National Hunt Chase, Fayonagh (7/1) in the Champion Bumper and

Lawlor's Hotel Novices' Hurdle (Slaney), Naas—
Death Duty (noseband) is left clear by the final-flight fall of Augusta Kate

Champagne Classic (12/1) in the Martin Pipe. Apple's Jade started at 7/2 when winning the David Nicholson, but the Mullins/Ricci pair of Vroum Vroum Mag (11/4) and Limini (6/4), whom she beat into second and third, were preferred in the betting. Cause of Causes was Elliott's other winner, returned at 4/1 when winning the Cross Country.

On the whole, Elliott's runners were afforded significantly less respect by the betting market than those of Mullins, who had five horses start at shorter than 2/1. Elliott only had one runner who fell into that category, Death Duty, who started at 13/8 for the Spa Hurdle. Death Duty had been the long-term ante-post favourite for the Spa, with Elliott very clear that it was his Festival target, describing the race—in which Death Duty faced a half-mile step up in trip—as being 'made for him' while he also compared the horse to his Gold Cup winner Don Cossack. 'He's a big three-mile chaser in the making, probably a better hurdler than Don Cossack was at the same stage. But he still has to go and do it when he goes chasing.' Elliott's close partnership with owners Gigginstown House Stud means that many well-bred, expensive chasing prospects come through his hands nowadays, and the fact that he was even mentioning Death Duty in the same sentence as the highest-rated horse that he has ever trained—a horse that was Timeform's best bumper performer in *Chasers & Hurdlers 2011/12* and Timeform's Horse of The Year in both 2014/15 and 2015/16—had plenty of punters pricking up their ears. Don Cossack had also been a much-touted horse in his early days, being described by his first trainer Eddie Hales as 'the best horse I have laid my hands on', and by Elliott as 'the best horse I have ever had, the apple of my eye' after his bumper season. That season included three bumper wins from three starts for Elliott, and ended with a seventeen-length romp in what had promised to be a reasonably competitive bumper at Fairyhouse in April. The first time Don Cossack had really looked something out of the ordinary on a racecourse was on his previous start at Navan, however, when he managed to reel in long-time leader Rory O'Moore from a seemingly impossibly position, having had the best part of fifteen lengths to make up turning for home. Death Duty

251

won the same bumper four years on and, though he had the run of the race under a well-judged ride from Nina Carberry and won by just half a length, the form has certainly stood the test, given that subsequent Irish Grand National winner Our Duke was second. Death Duty met with defeat on his third bumper start for Elliott, but the form was again particularly strong given he had to concede weight to subsequent Champion INH Flat winner Blow By Blow, who is now also under Elliott's care but has not been seen since that Punchestown win for Willie Mullins.

With such strong bumper form and a big reputation to live up to, Death Duty was sent off at 3/1-on for his first start over hurdles, which came in a two and a half mile maiden at Roscommon in October. Death Duty proved a class apart from his rivals and quickly graduated to better things, taking the Grade 3 Monksfield Novices' Hurdle at Navan in November by seven and a half lengths before stepping up again to win the Grade 2 Navan Novices' Hurdle in mid-December by three and three quarter lengths from Monalee. Despite being downgraded from a Grade 1 after the 2013 running (the race has drawn consistently small fields), the Navan Novices' Hurdle has a strong history, its recent winners including the ill-fated No More Heroes who represented the same connections as Death Duty and went on to finish an unlucky third in the Spa at Cheltenham. Don Cossack, on the other hand, was a bitter disappointment in the Navan race (held in second when falling at the last) and missed Cheltenham altogether after further defeats on his two subsequent outings over hurdles. There were no such problems for Death Duty, though, as he took his record to four from four when winning the Grade 1 Lawlor's Hotel Novices' Hurdle (registered as the Slaney Novices' Hurdle) at Naas in January. Death Duty was sent off at odds on and, after looming up early in the straight, was produced to lead soon after two out. The only challenger to emerge from the chasing pack was the mare Augusta Kate, pitched in at the deep end on just her second start over hurdles. Augusta Kate—a listed bumper winner in the previous season—looked a big threat to Death Duty when drawing upsides coming to the last, only to fall. Although Augusta Kate looked likely to have thrown down a strong challenge to Death Duty, the winner found plenty himself, and it was impossible to say with confidence what would have happened.

Augusta Kate eventually got her Grade 1 win in the Mares' Novices' Hurdle Championship Final at Fairyhouse, but that was after another significant jumping error let her down in the Spa at Cheltenham. A jumping error at the last eventually put paid to Death Duty's Spa challenge, but he was already well beaten when unseating Bryan Cooper. Death Duty had seemed sure to be suited by the extra emphasis on stamina in the Spa, but he took a strong hold in a muddling race run on less testing ground than he had been winning on in Ireland. Death Duty could have taken on Spa winner Penhill over three miles at the Punchestown Festival, but connections opted to drop him back to two and a half miles for the Champion Novices' Hurdle—their representative in the longer race, Champagne Classic, sprung a 14/1 surprise when lowering the colours of Penhill. Death Duty got back on track to some extent in the Champion Novices', though he lacked the speed to go with Bacardys and Finian's Oscar approaching the last, eventually finishing a respectable third. Ground conditions were similar to those at Punchestown and Cheltenham, and Death Duty may well benefit from a return to racing on softer ground.

		Alleged	Hoist The Flag
	Shantou (USA)	(b 1974)	Princess Pout
	(b 1993)	Shaima	Shareef Dancer
Death Duty (IRE)		(b 1988)	Oh So Sharp
(b.g. 2011)		Presenting	Mtoto
	Midnight Gift (IRE)	(br 1992)	D'Azy
	(ch 2000)	Midnight Pond	Long Pond
		(ch 1994)	Midnight Oil

The well-made Death Duty was one of two new Grade 1 winners for his sire Shantou in 2016/17 (the other being the mare Airlie Beach), a season which also saw him sire another Cheltenham Festival winner in Tully East, who won the Close Brothers Novices' Handicap Chase. Death Duty's dam Midnight Gift won a bumper on her debut for Tom Hogan and went on to win twice over hurdles, including at three miles. Death Duty, who was bought for €145,000 as a three-year-old at the

Tattersalls Ireland Derby Sale, is the fourth foal out of Midnight Gift and the third to make the racecourse, the others being How About It (by Kayf Tara), a fairly useful handicap chaser at his best who stays three miles, and Lady Dromlac (by Beneficial), who was placed in bumpers for Tom Hogan. Death Duty is well worth another chance at three miles given his breeding and the fact that he finished strongly over two and a half. He acts on soft and heavy going and is a strong traveller who often races prominently. Despite the slightly disappointing end to his novice hurdling campaign, Death Duty remains an exciting chasing prospect. *Gordon Elliott, Ireland*

DEAUVILLE CRYSTAL (FR) 4 b.f. Raven's Pass (USA) – Top Crystal (IRE)   **h123**
(Sadler's Wells (USA)) [2016/17 h16.7s h15.8d² h16.8v* h16d² h18.8g* h16s* h20.3g⁵
Apr 20] good-topped filly: fairly useful on Flat, stays 1¼m: fairly useful hurdler: won maiden at Sedgefield in February, and juvenile handicap at Newbury and fillies' 4-y-o handicap at Warwick, both in March: stays 19f: acts on heavy going: wears tongue tie: usually races nearer last than first, often travels strongly. *Nigel Hawke*

DEAUVILLE DANCER (IRE) 6 b.g. Tamayuz – Mathool (IRE) (Alhaarth (IRE))   **h105**
[2016/17 h118: h16m⁴ h20.7g² h20d³ h16.3v* h16.3m h16.3g⁵ h20g⁴ h21g³ h17.1d²
h19.3m Oct 29] compact gelding: fair hurdler: won maiden at Stratford in June: stays 21f: acts on heavy going. *David Dennis*

DEBDEBDEB 7 b.m. Teofilo (IRE) – Windmill (Ezzoud (IRE)) [2016/17 h127: h19.5g   **h132**
h20.3s³ h19.9g h24.3d⁴ Apr 21] compact mare: useful handicap hurdler: fourth in mares event at Ayr (8 lengths behind Jennys Melody) in April: stays 3m: acts on soft going: has worn hood. *Dan Skelton*

DEBECE 6 b.g. Kayf Tara – Dalamine (FR) (Sillery (USA)) [2016/17 h101: h16g* h15.7g²   **h145**
h16.4g³ h20s³ h20.5s* h24.7g³ Apr 7] strong gelding: very much the type to make a chaser: bumper winner: smart form over hurdles: won novice at Kempton (by 8 lengths from Le Capricieux) in May and handicap at Newbury (by 19 lengths from Leaderofthedance) in March: third in Sefton Novices' Hurdle at Aintree (½ length behind The Worlds End) in April: stays 25f: acts on soft going: front runner/races prominently, often travels strongly. *Tim Vaughan*

DE BENE ESSE (IRE) 7 br.g. Scorpion (IRE) – Benedicta Rose (IRE) (Beneficial)   **c–**
[2016/17 c115, h–: c20.9dᵖᵘ h21.6vᶠ h16.7sᵖᵘ Feb 10] workmanlike gelding: little impact   **h–**
over hurdles: won 2-runner novice in 2015/16, only form in chases: has worn headgear, including last 2 starts: front runner/races prominently: has joined Chris Williams. *Alexandra Dunn*

DEBT TO SOCIETY (IRE) 10 ch.g. Moscow Society (USA) – Nobody's Darling (IRE)   **c–**
(Supreme Leader) [2016/17 c–§, h97§: c26.3sᵖᵘ h20g² h22.1g⁵ h25.4d⁵ h23.3g* h23.1g*   **h102 §**
h27g⁶ h20s³ h23.1d⁶ h23.8dᵖᵘ Jan 25] compact gelding: fair handicap hurdler: won at Uttoxeter in July and Market Rasen in August: modest chaser: stays 27f: acts on good to firm and heavy going: wears headgear/tongue tie: unreliable. *Richard Ford*

DEBUCHET (FR) 4 gr.g. Smadoun (FR) – Luzerne du Poitou (FR) (Royal Charter (FR))   **b114**
[2016/17 b16s² b16g* b16.4g² b16s* Apr 6] sturdy gelding: first foal: dam unraced: useful form in bumpers: won maiden at Leopardstown in January and listed event at Limerick (by 5 lengths from Cornelius Sulla) in April: second in Champion Bumper at Cheltenham (1¼ lengths behind Fayonagh) in March. *Ms Margaret Mullins, Ireland*

DECADE PLAYER (IRE) 9 b.g. Gamut (IRE) – Ballindante (IRE) (Phardante (FR))   **c113**
[2016/17 c87, h–: c19.4g* c17m* c19.9gᵖᵘ c21.1gᵖᵘ c20.3gᵖᵘ Apr 21] compact gelding: **h–**
won twice in points: winning hurdler: fair hunter chaser: won at Wetherby and Stratford in May: stays 19f: acts on soft and good to firm going: has worn headgear, including in 2016/17: usually wears tongue tie: front runner/races prominently. *Miss Kelly Morgan*

DECIDING MOMENT (IRE) 11 b.g. Zagreb (USA) – Fontaine Jewel (IRE)   **c108**
(Lafontaine (USA)) [2016/17 c120, h–: h24g* h23g* c22.6m⁴ h23m⁶ Aug 17] good-topped   **h112**
gelding: fair hurdler: won novices at Kempton and Worcester in May: fair handicap chaser: stays 3m: acts on soft and good to firm going: wears tongue tie. *Ben De Haan*

DECIMUS (IRE) 10 b.g. Bienamado (USA) – Catch Me Dreaming (IRE) (Safety Catch   **c– x**
(USA)) [2016/17 c–x, h117§: h23.1mᶠ h26.5m h26.5m² h23m h23.3g⁵ h26g³ h24.2g⁶   **h111 §**
h24.5s⁵ h23.9g² h24g Apr 19] lengthy, useful-looking gelding: fair handicap hurdler: winning chaser, often let down by jumping: stays 3¼m: acts on good to firm and heavy going: wears headgear: unreliable. *Jeremy Scott*

DECKERS DELIGHT 6 b.m. Tobougg (IRE) – Oleana (IRE) (Alzao (USA)) [2016/17   **h97**
b–: h15.8d h19.5v⁴ h15.8s h25.5s* h25.5vᵘʳ h25v³ h24v h20.5v⁶ Feb 27] modest handicap
hurdler: won mares event at Hereford in December: best effort at 3¼m: acts on heavy
going: in headgear last 4 starts. *Nigel Hawke*

DEDIGOUT (IRE) 11 b.g. Bob Back (USA) – Dainty Daisy (IRE) (Buckskin (FR))   **c–**
[2016/17 c–, h148: h20d⁴ h20d⁵ h24d⁵ h21s⁵ c26s⁴ c29dᵖᵘ Apr 17] big, deep-girthed   **h143**
gelding: high-class hurdler at best, well below that in 2016/17: winning chaser: bled final
start: stays 3m: acts on heavy going: wears tongue tie. *Gordon Elliott, Ireland*

DE DOLLAR MAN (IRE) 6 ch.g. Vinnie Roe (IRE) – Dollar Bay (IRE) (Beau Sher)   **h138**
[2016/17 b15.8v* h20.5v* h19.3s³ h21.1g Mar 15] €18,500 4-y-o, £75,000 5-y-o: tall,   **b103**
lengthy gelding: sixth foal: half-brother to bumper winner/fair hurdler Booley Bay (19f
winner, by Gulland): dam twice-raced half-sister to fairly useful hurdler/chaser (21f-3¼m
winner) Ballystone: won Irish point on debut: also won bumper at Uttoxeter (by 1¼ lengths
from Dead Right) in December: useful form over hurdles: won maiden at Ayr in January:
best effort when third in novice at Ascot (neck behind Beyond Conceit) in February: should
be suited by further than 2½m. *Evan Williams*

DEDUCE (FR) 4 b.f. Iffraaj – Count The Cost (USA) (Cozzene (USA)) [2016/17 h16vᵘʳ   **h–**
h15.8g³ Apr 3] fairly useful on Flat for Francois Rohaut, stays 13.5f: well held completed
start over hurdles. *James Eustace*

DEEBAJ (IRE) 5 br.g. Authorized (IRE) – Athreyaa (Singspiel (IRE)) [2016/17 h112:   **h103**
h16.3m² h20g⁶ h16m⁴ h19.3s⁶ h19.5v⁴ h20v⁴ h18.7g⁶ Apr 1] lengthy gelding: fair maiden
hurdler: stays 2½m: acts on soft going: has worn visor: in tongue tie last 2 starts:
temperament under suspicion. *Richard Price*

DEEP RESOLVE (IRE) 6 b.g. Intense Focus (USA) – I'll Be Waiting (Vettori (IRE))   **h–**
[2016/17 h91: h16.4sᵖᵘ Jan 7] fair hurdler at best, pulled up sole start in 2016/17: stays
2¼m: best form on heavy going. *Alan Swinbank*

DEEPSAND (IRE) 8 br.g. Footstepsinthesand – Sinamay (USA) (Saint Ballado (CAN))   **h114**
[2016/17 h–: h15.8s² h16.4s⁴ h15.7s⁸ h15.6gᶠ h16v⁴ Mar 10] fair handicap hurdler: won at
Haydock in January: raced around 2m: acts on heavy going: has worn headgear: usually
wears tongue tie. *Lucinda Russell*

DE FAOITHESDREAM (IRE) 11 br.g. Balakheri (IRE) – Cutteen Lass (IRE)   **c132**
(Tremblant) [2016/17 c131, h–: c15.9g⁴ c16.3dᶠ c15.5s⁵ c16s⁴ c15.5g⁵ Apr 22] useful-   **h–**
looking gelding: winning hurdler: useful handicap chaser: fourth at Cheltenham (4 lengths
behind Un Beau Roman) in November: stays 2½m: acts on good to firm and heavy going:
front runner/races prominently. *Evan Williams*

DEFI DU SEUIL (FR) 4 b.g. Voix du Nord (FR) – Quarvine du Seuil (FR) (Lavirco   **h151 p**
(GER)) [2016/17 b11.9s* h15.8d* h16.4s* h16.8d* h16s* h16.8s* h16.8g* h17g*   **b–**
Apr 6]

Here was the undisputed leader of the four-year-old generation in the British
Isles. It's not unusual for the top juvenile hurdler to go through the season unbeaten,
but Defi du Seuil's unblemished record was harder earned than most, established
over a full campaign of seven races stretching from October to April. In the last
dozen years or so, Penzance, Zaynar, Soldatino, Zarkandar, Our Conor and Peace
And Co all went unbeaten on the way to becoming the season's top juvenile, each
of them winning the Triumph Hurdle, but all were tested only three or four times.
Of those, only Zarkandar ran again after the Triumph when following up in the
Anniversary Hurdle at Aintree. Defi du Seuil ended his more extensive campaign
by completing the same Grade 1 double, a perfect ending to a season of dominance
in the major juvenile prizes the like of which had not been seen since Katchit ten
years earlier.

Katchit won seven races in his juvenile season, also winning both the Triumph
and Anniversary in the spring along with three other good prizes at Cheltenham,
which Defi du Seuil also ticked off along the way. Katchit did get beaten, though,
just once, when trying to concede 8 lb to the smart Flat performer Degas Art at
Wetherby on his third outing over hurdles, but that was a defeat he was to avenge
twice, later in the season at Cheltenham and Aintree. While their records may have
been similar, Katchit and Defi du Seuil were like chalk and cheese in other respects
and came to hurdling from very different backgrounds. Katchit was a Flat racer,
small in stature for a potential hurdler and already with lots of racing experience.

Defi du Seuil, on the other hand, is a purpose-bred jumper, a lengthy AQPS gelding who won the second of his two starts in 'French bumpers' for Emmanuel Clayeux in the spring as a three-year-old at Lyon Parilly.

On his first start for Philip Hobbs, Defi du Seuil was found the easiest of opportunities for his hurdling debut in a maiden event for juveniles at Ffos Las in October which he won with plenty in hand against four rivals who failed to win any of their races subsequently. There was stiffer opposition for Defi du Seuil on his next two starts at Cheltenham, but he came through both with ease as well. Both races were run as the JCB Triumph Trial Juvenile Hurdle; in the first of them, the first graded juvenile of the season (registered as the Prestbury) at the Open meeting, he was value for plenty more than the length and a quarter he had to spare over runner-up Diable de Sivola (the pair fifty-eight lengths clear), while the following month he was a ready winner by the same margin from Coeur de Lion of the less valuable class 2 contest. In theory, juvenile hurdlers have a mid-season highlight in the form of the Grade 1 Future Champions Finale Juvenile Hurdle at Chepstow on Welsh National day and, while some good three-year-olds have won it, in practice it is a race that struggles most seasons to attract anything like a championship-standard field, or even the best juvenile. Katchit hadn't contested the Finale, for example, and Defi du Seuil, who had just four rivals to beat, became the first winner of the race to go on to success in the Triumph Hurdle since the filly Mysilv back in 1993. Defi du Seuil had jumped fluently for his earlier wins, but he was rather scrappy in the closing stages at Chepstow, though that didn't stop him winning by his widest margin all season—thirteen lengths—and by then he had things sewn up anyway, impressing with the way he quickly settled matters once sent into the lead four out. The filly Evening Hush, who had won both her starts, including a listed contest at Aintree, followed him home after setting the early pace, while third was Dolos who had filled the same position behind France's unbeaten juvenile filly De Bon Coeur in the Prix Cambaceres at Auteuil on his last start.

On the same day that Defi du Seuil won at Chepstow, his owner J. P. McManus unveiled another exciting French import when Charli Parcs was an impressive winner of the juvenile hurdle at Kempton. Charli Parcs had the makings of Defi du Seuil's biggest threat thus far, though a first clash between the pair failed to materialise when Charli Parcs was announced a non-runner barely half an hour before the Finesse Juvenile Hurdle (another race run under the JCB Triumph Trial title) at Cheltenham's Trials meeting at the end of January. The late withdrawal of the Nicky Henderson-trained Charli Parcs prompted a stewards enquiry at which it was noted that the delay 'was due to difficulties with communications between the jockey, the trainer and the owner who was in Barbados.' The jockey in question was Barry Geraghty who had been declared to ride Charli Parcs but switched to Defi du Seuil instead, the intended mount of Richard Johnson. The owner's retained jockey had ridden Defi du Seuil in his two earlier wins at Cheltenham, while stable jockey Johnson had partnered him in his two other races. Charli Parcs' defection left a cakewalk for Defi du Seuil whose fifth win, by nine lengths from the dual Fontwell winner Rainbow Dreamer, revealed nothing new about him. Incidentally, anyone who had backed Defi du Seuil prior to the withdrawal of his main rival (who was actually a shade of odds-on at the time) would have benefited from a very advantageous Rule 4 deduction as the winner's adjusted odds were much longer than his SP of 5/1-on.

The meeting between the McManus-owned pair was only postponed as Defi du Seuil and Charli Parcs lined up as the first two in the betting, at 5/2 and 9/2 respectively, in a fifteen-runner field for the JCB Triumph Hurdle at the Festival. Charli Parcs had had another run in the meantime, falling with Geraghty when odds on for the Adonis Juvenile Hurdle at Kempton which resulted in the jockey sustaining injuries that caused him to miss Cheltenham. The Adonis winner Master Blueyes, an 8/1 chance, looked the main British-trained challenger to the first two in the betting, but the main question before the Triumph was how strong the Irish challenge—successful in three of the four previous Triumphs—would prove to be. McManus had an interest here too with Landofhopeandglory, a useful Flat recruit from Ballydoyle which had been the source of the owner's 2016 Triumph winner

JCB Triumph Hurdle, Cheltenham—champion jockey Richard Johnson doubles his 2017 Festival tally as Defi du Seuil proves far too strong for Irish raiders Mega Fortune (stripes), Bapaume (centre) and Ex Patriot (star on cap)

Ivanovich Gorbatov. The difference this time was that Landofhopeandglory's trainer Joseph O'Brien now had his own licence, unlike the year before when Ivanovich Gorbatov's success was officially credited to his father Aidan. McManus had also acquired the smart Flat performers Housesofparliament, second in the Great Voltigeur and third in the St Leger, and the Queen's Vase winner Sword Fighter, from the Coolmore partners to bolster his Irish juvenile team with O'Brien junior but neither of those made the grade over hurdles, unlike Landofhopeandglory who had won his first three starts, including a Grade 3 contest at Fairyhouse from a couple of the other leading Irish contenders in the Triumph, Bapaume and Mega Fortune, representing Willie Mullins and Gordon Elliott respectively. Mega Fortune had gone on to beat Bapaume in the Grade 1 Spring Juvenile at Leopardstown in February in which three O'Brien/McManus representatives, Housesofparliament and Sword Fighter included, were all soundly beaten. As a result, it was Mega Fortune at 7/1 who started at the shortest odds of six Irish-trained runners in the Triumph field.

Collectively, the Irish contingent performed well but none of them proved a match for Defi du Seuil who ran out a convincing winner, though his victory would have been more clear-cut still had the pace been stronger. As it was, he won by five lengths and a short head from Mega Fortune and Bapaume, with Ex Patriot and Landofhopeandglory the next two home for Ireland as well, and Charli Parcs completing the first six. Conditions weren't so soft as for Defi du Seuil's previous races but that made no difference to how well he travelled. Held up early on, Defi du Seuil made stealthy progress to be within striking distance of the leaders at the top of the hill and moved readily into the lead on the long run to the last which he jumped a couple of lengths clear before extending his lead on the run-in. Mega Fortune, who made most of the running, rallied to regain second from the more patiently-ridden Bapaume close home, while the two other McManus entries both proved one-paced when it mattered. Defi du Seuil was his trainer's third winner of the Triumph after Made In Japan in 2004 and Detroit City two years later, both of those also ridden by Johnson.

Both of the stable's previous Triumph winners had gone on to run in the Anniversary. Made In Japan just failed at Aintree under a penalty (when it was run for the final time as a Grade 2 contest) but Detroit City followed up his Cheltenham win, since when only Katchit and Zarkandar had completed the double. Only one of Defi du Seuil's seven rivals in the Doom Bar-sponsored Anniversary 4-Y-O Juvenile Hurdle had contested the Triumph (eighth-placed Landin) and, in a field lacking any Irish challengers, Defi du Seuil was sent off at 11/4-on. Flying Tiger and Divin Bere, who had fought out a close finish to the Fred Winter at Cheltenham, were the next two in the betting, Divin Bere now better off at the weights and the 7/2 second favourite. With a fit-again Geraghty back on board, Defi du Seuil accomplished his task in ready fashion, looming up before the second last and leading approaching the final flight. He didn't need to match his Triumph form but won with more in hand than the length and a quarter margin over Divin Bere. Bedrock, who had finished fifth in the Adonis on his only previous start over hurdles, finished four and a half lengths back in third, a long way clear of the rest who were headed by the Johnson-ridden Flying Tiger. It was decided after Aintree that Defi du Seuil had done enough for the season and would not run at Punchestown, making the trip to Ireland instead for a summer break at his owner's Martinstown Stud.

The 'du Seuil' name is no stranger to success at Cheltenham as Defi du Seuil's Triumph win came three years after Taquin du Seuil landed the Golden Miller Novices' Chase at the Festival. Defi du Seuil's first win at Cheltenham came on the same day that Taquin du Seuil (later second back over hurdles in the Coral Cup in March) won the BetVictor Gold Cup. Other than both being by the same sire, the now deceased Criterium de Saint-Cloud and Prix Lupin winner Voix du Nord, the pair are not related, though they are both products of the stud run by the family of champion French Flat jockey Pierre-Charles Boudot. A third horse to carry the stud's name, the fairly useful hurdler Catamaran du Seuil, contested the Martin Pipe at the latest Festival for Dr Richard Newland. He is a half-brother to Defi du Seuil's dam Quarvine du Seuil who died after developing colic just days after foaling him. The dam of only one other foal before Defi du Seuil, Quarvine du Seuil never ran over jumps though won twice, at a mile and a quarter and a mile and a half, in AQPS races on the Flat. Grandam Fleur du Tennis has now produced five winners, with Catamaran du Seuil being followed by four-year-old Diamant du Seuil (also by Voix du Nord) who made a winning debut, ridden by Boudot, in a bumper at Argentan in March. Fleur du Tennis won six times at up to fifteen furlongs on the Flat and finished second on her only start over hurdles. She was a sister to Jimmy Tennis, a

Doom Bar Anniversary 4-Y-O Juvenile Hurdle, Aintree—Barry Geraghty is back on board as Defi du Seuil rounds off a perfect campaign with a victory over Divin Bere (No.3); Royal runner Forth Bridge (right) drops back to fifth

useful chaser who won the Reynoldstown Novices' Chase on his first start in Britain for Venetia Williams. Another successful import to Britain from this family is useful hurdler Coo Star Sivola who won a listed event for novices at Cheltenham on New Year's Day. He made the frame at the Festival for the second year running when fourth in the Martin Pipe, having finished third in the previous season's Fred Winter.

		Valanour (b 1992)	Lomond / Vearia
	Voix du Nord (FR) (b 2001)	Dame Edith (b 1995)	Top Ville / Girl of France
Defi du Seuil (FR) (b.g. 2013)		Lavirco (bl or br 1993)	Konigsstuhl / La Virginia
	Quarvine du Seuil (FR) (b 2004)	Fleur du Tennis (b 1993)	Video Rock / Via Tennise

Life usually proves much harder for the leading juveniles once they have to tackle older opposition. Four of the unbeaten sextet mentioned at the start of the essay—Penzance, Soldatino, Our Conor and Peace And Co—failed to win the following season. It would be a major surprise, though, if Defi du Seuil followed suit. After all, a rigorous juvenile season did no harm to the future prospects of the tough Katchit who belied his lack of size to improve sufficiently to win the following year's Champion Hurdle, in the process becoming the only five-year-old to win the hurdling championship since 1985. The year before Katchit was successful, the five-year-old Detroit City was sent off 6/4 favourite for the Champion Hurdle after extending his winning run over hurdles to seven beforehand (he also won the Cesarewitch on the Flat) but he managed only sixth. Interestingly, Defi du Seuil has the same rating as Katchit achieved as a juvenile, 151. Katchit needed only to improve by 12 lb to win what was an ordinary Champion Hurdle in his year, but the chances are that Defi du Seuil will have to progress a lot more. That said, Defi du Seuil has a lot more scope to improve—hence the 'p' attached to his rating—than Katchit seemed to have. In fact, Defi du Seuil has the size for chasing if connections opt to go down that route with him sooner rather than later, given that his owner already has the reigning champion hurdler. A strong traveller who has raced only at around two miles over hurdles, Defi du Seuil acts on soft going. He wore a hood in the parade ring before the Triumph Hurdle but it was removed after he left the chute on the way to the start. *Philip Hobbs*

DEFINATELY VINNIE 7 ch.g. Vinnie Roe (IRE) – Sohapara (Arapahos (FR)) [2016/17 h56, b70: h23g⁵ h19.9g⁶ h23d h21.2m³ Oct 5] poor maiden hurdler: best effort at 23f. *Jane Mathias*   **h78**

DEFINING YEAR (IRE) 9 b.g. Hawk Wing (USA) – Tajaathub (USA) (Aljabr (USA)) [2016/17 h113: h15.7g h18.5g⁵ h16.3g Apr 23] maiden hurdler, fair at best: left Hugo Froud after first start: raced mainly around 2m: acts on good to soft going: often wears tongue tie: often races towards rear. *Dan Skelton*   **h89**

DEFINITE FUTURE (IRE) 8 b.g. Definite Article – Miss Marilyn (IRE) (Welsh Term) [2016/17 c109, h99: c23.8g³ c20d⁶ c20g* c19.4m⁴ c20g* c19.9m* c19.9m² c19.9m² c16.5g³ Nov 8] winning hurdler: fairly useful handicap chaser: won at Worcester in July, Uttoxeter in September and Huntingdon in October: stays 2½m: acts on soft and good to firm going: wears headgear: tried in tongue tie: often travels strongly. *Kerry Lee*   **c124** **h—**

DEFINITE JOKER 8 b.g. Definite Article – Sabi Sand (Minster Son) [2016/17 h19.5vᵖᵘ Feb 25] point winner in 2014: pulled up in maiden on hurdling debut. *Richard Woollacott*   **h—**

DEFINITELY GLAD (IRE) 10 b.m. Definite Article – Gladys May (IRE) (Moscow Society (USA)) [2016/17 c—, h90: h16.8s⁴ h16.2g² h16.2d⁵ h18.1m⁴ c16.4dᵖᵘ Dec 2] lengthy mare: modest maiden hurdler: hasn't taken to chasing: stays 2¼m: acts on soft and good to firm going: tried in hood: wears tongue tie: often races towards rear/travels strongly. *Susan Corbett*   **c—** **h86**

DEFINITE MEMORIES (IRE) 10 b.m. Definite Article – Memories (FR) (Darshaan) [2016/17 c24vᵖᵘ Feb 24] big mare: won Irish point on debut: winning hurdler: fairly useful chaser for David Bridgwater in 2013/14, pulled up sole start since in February: stays 3m: acts on soft going. *Venetia Williams*   **c—** **h—**

DEFINITE OUTCOME (IRE) 8 b.g. Definite Article – Magical Theatre (IRE) (King's **c126** Theatre (IRE)) [2016/17 h128: c23.6g* c25d^{ur} c23.6s^{pu} c23.6s^{pu} c20.1g^F Apr 28] big, **h–** strong gelding: fairly useful hurdler: similar form over fences: won novice at Chepstow in October: left Rebecca Curtis after fourth start: stays 3m: acts on heavy going: tried in cheekpieces: in tongue tie last 3 starts: front runner/races prominently. *Richard Hobson*

DEFINITE RIDGE (IRE) 10 ch.g. Definite Article – Do The Right Thing (Busted) **c86** [2016/17 c21.1d^{ur} c25.8d^4 h24d^{pu} c25.5g^4 c23.9g^5 c25.8g^4 h19g h20.5m^3 c25.1f^3 Apr 23] **h79** workmanlike gelding: poor handicap hurdler: modest handicap chaser: won at Cartmel in July: left P. York after first start: stays 3¼m: acts on soft and good to firm going: wears headgear: often travels strongly: hard to catch right. *Alexandra Dunn*

DEFINITE RUBY (IRE) 9 br.m. Definite Article – Sunset Queen (IRE) (King's Theatre **c131** (IRE)) [2016/17 c131, h–: c21s* c19.5d^2 h20v* c28.5g^4 c21d* Apr 28] angular mare: fairly **h124** useful handicap hurdler: won mares event at Punchestown in January: useful handicap chaser: won another mares race at same course in April (by 1¾ lengths from Slowmotion) for second successive year: best up to 25f: acts on good to firm and heavy going: wears headgear: often races prominently/travels strongly. *Gordon Elliott, Ireland*

DEFINITELY GREY (IRE) 6 gr.g. Daylami (IRE) – Caroline Fontenail (IRE) **h104** (Kaldounevees (FR)) [2016/17 h92: h22m^4 h20.3m* h23.4g^2 h20.3d Nov 15] good-topped gelding: Irish point winner: fair handicap hurdler: won at Southwell in September: stays 23f: acts on good to firm going: in tongue tie last 3 starts. *Charlie Longsdon*

DEFINITLY RED (IRE) 8 ch.g. Definite Article – The Red Wench (IRE) (Aahsaylad) **c160** [2016/17 c143, h141: h20d* c23.4s^3 c24.2s* c24.1s^{ur} c26s* c34.3d^{pu} Apr 8] sturdy gelding: **h141** useful form over hurdles: won handicap at Carlisle (by 3¼ lengths from Onefitzall) in October: high-class handicap chaser: won Rowland Meyrick Chase at Wetherby (by 7

Mr P. J. Martin's "Definitly Red"

lengths from Wakanda) in December and Grimthorpe Chase at Doncaster (by 14 lengths from The Last Samuri) in March: badly hampered sixth and saddle slipped when pulled up in Grand National at Aintree: should stay long distances: acts on heavy going. *Brian Ellison*

DEGOOCH (IRE) 8 ch.g. Gamut (IRE) – Blonde Ambition (IRE) (Old Vic) [2016/17 c–x, h108: h15.8g⁶ c20d⁴ c24.1g⁴ c21.1g* c20g³ c19.4m³ c19.4g⁴ Oct 28] fair handicap hurdler: fairly useful handicap chaser: won at Uttoxeter in July and Sedgefield in September: stays 21f: acts on soft and good to firm going: wears headgear: often races towards rear/travels strongly. *Johnny Farrelly* **c122 h81**

DEISE DIAMOND (IRE) 6 b.g. Scorpion (IRE) – Lakeshore Lodge (IRE) (Taipan (IRE)) [2016/17 b16g⁴ b18.3g² b17.7g* h15.8d³ h19.7g⁵ h20.6g h16g⁶ Apr 17] third foal: dam (h72), lightly raced in bumpers/over hurdles, half-sister to useful hurdler/fairly useful chaser (stayed 3m, became temperamental) Grey Report: fair form in bumpers: won at Fontwell in August: modest form over hurdles: left Miss Elizabeth Doyle after second start: should be suited by 2½m. *Neil King* **h94 b94**

DEISE VU (IRE) 9 b.g. Brian Boru – Deise Dreamer (IRE) (Beneficial) [2016/17 h20.3d³ c16.5g³ c17g³ c15.7g³ c16.5g² c15.7g⁵ c16.1v² c16v³ c16.1g³ c17g* c17g² Apr 23] winning pointer: modest form over hurdles: fair handicap chaser: won at Stratford in April: unproven beyond 17f: acts on heavy going: tried in cheekpieces/tongue tie: front runner, often races freely/jumps boldly. *Roy Brotherton* **c103 h93**

DEJA BOUGG 6 b.m. Tobougg (IRE) – La Riveraine (USA) (Riverman (USA)) [2016/17 h106: h20m³ h19g⁴ h20.5g⁴ h16sᵖᵘ h19.7v³ h24.5mᶠ Apr 4] fair maiden hurdler: stays 2½m: acts on good to firm and heavy going: in tongue tie last 4 starts: often let down by jumping. *Neil Mulholland* **h102 x**

DELATITE 5 b.g. Schiaparelli (GER) – Desiree (IRE) (Desert Story (IRE)) [2016/17 b15.8d⁶ b15.7m² Apr 13] third foal: dam, maiden on Flat (second at 1½m), ran once over hurdles: fair form in bumpers: wears cheekpieces. *John Berry* **b87**

DELGANY DEMON 9 b.g. Kayf Tara – Little Twig (IRE) (Good Thyne (USA)) [2016/17 c130, h124: c24gᵖᵘ c23.5v² c23.5g h26s⁴ c28s² c24s⁶ Mar 18] strong gelding: fair handicap hurdler: fairly useful maiden chaser: second in handicap at Lingfield in November: stays 3m: acts on heavy going: front runner/races prominently. *Neil King* **c122 h112**

DELIGHT MY FIRE (FR) 7 b.m. Way of Light (USA) – Darmagi (IRE) (Desert King (IRE)) [2016/17 c20.9g c27.3d² c20.9d* c24.9d² c25.8d* c25.8s* c30.2mᶠ Dec 9] compact mare: sixth foal: half-sister to ungenuine hurdler Fongoli (2m/17f winner, by Dr Fong): dam maiden on Flat (stayed 1½m): fair chaser: won minor event at Wroclaw in August, and cross-country events at Pardubice and Sluzewiec in October: in contention when fell twenty-seventh in cross-country handicap at Cheltenham final start: stays 3¼m: acts on soft going. *Radim Bodlak, Czech Republic* **c110**

DELIVERINGPROMISES (IRE) 5 b.g. Oscar (IRE) – Monanore Music (IRE) (Needle Gun (IRE)) [2016/17 b16m² b17d⁶ Aug 20] fell on point debut: poor form in bumpers: in tongue tie second start. *S. Curling, Ireland* **b65**

DELL'ARCA (IRE) 8 b.g. Sholokhov (IRE) – Daisy Belle (GER) (Acatenango (GER)) [2016/17 c141, h135: h22.8m⁴ h21g³ h19s h20.3g h23.5m* Apr 2] leggy gelding: useful handicap hurdler: won at Ascot (conditional, by 1¾ lengths from Pilansberg) in April: useful chaser: stays 3m: acts on good to firm and heavy going: wears headgear: tried in tongue tie. *David Pipe* **c– h138**

DELLA SUN (FR) 11 b.g. Della Francesca (USA) – Algarve Sunrise (IRE) (Highest Honor (FR)) [2016/17 c–, h–: h15.8m h20d⁶ Oct 15] workmanlike gelding: fair handicap hurdler at best in Britain: once-raced over fences: stays 2½m: acts on firm and soft going: has worn headgear. *Arthur Whitehead* **c– h89**

DELL ORO (FR) 4 b.g. Walk In The Park (IRE) – Kallistea (FR) (Sicyos (USA)) [2016/17 b13.6g* b16d Apr 26] sixth foal: half-brother to 3 winners on Flat in France, including Kyrnollia (6f-13f winner, by Timboroa): dam French 17f hurdle winner: fairly useful in bumpers: won at Fontwell in March. *Gary Moore* **b99**

DELL'S RAQUEL 4 ch.f. Sakhee's Secret – Ruthie (Pursuit of Love) [2016/17 b13.7d Nov 24] sixth foal: half-sister to 3 winners, including 1¼m bumper winner Rodneythetrotter (by Royal Applause): dam, 7f winner, half-sister to fairly useful hurdler/useful chaser (stayed 21f) Lease Lend: well beaten in junior bumper. *Pat Phelan* **b–**

DELPHYNE 5 ch.m. Mount Nelson – Darmiana (USA) (Lemon Drop Kid (USA)) [2016/17 b15.8v⁵ Dec 16] 3,000 3-y-o: first foal: dam, French 11f winner, half-sister to dam of top-class 1¼m performer Almanzor: tailed off in bumper: fair form in maidens on Flat. *Shaun Harris* **b**

DELTA BORGET (FR) 12 b.g. Kapgarde (FR) – L'Oceane (FR) (Epervier Bleu) **c114** [2016/17 c120, h–: c16.3g^{ur} c21g^4 c17m^5 c16.1g^2 c15.9s^2 c19.2g^3 Apr 11] multiple point **h–** winner: maiden hurdler: fair hunter chaser: placed 3 times in 2016/17: stays 21f: acts on good to firm and heavy going: wears cheekpieces: tried in tongue tie: front runner/races prominently. *L. Jefford*

DELUSIONOFGRANDEUR (IRE) 7 b.g. Mahler – Olivia Rose (IRE) (Mujadil **c136** (USA)) [2016/17 h132: c21.6v^4 c23.4s^4 c25.2d* c24.2s^4 c25.2s* c24.2d* c24.3g Apr 22] **h–** useful hurdler: useful chaser: won maiden in December and novice in February (by neck from The Bay Oak), both at Catterick, and novice at Wetherby in March: likely to stay long distances: acts on soft going: usually leads. *Sue Smith*

DEMOGRAPHIC (USA) 8 b.g. Aptitude (USA) – Private Line (USA) (Private Account **h105** (USA)) [2016/17 h100: h20.7g^2 h19.8d* h20.7d^F h19g h21.4m* Apr 5] fair handicap hurdler: won at Wincanton in November and April: stays 3m: acts on soft and good to firm going: wears visor: front runner/races prominently. *Emma Lavelle*

DENALI HIGHWAY (IRE) 10 ch.g. Governor Brown (USA) – Amaretto Flame (IRE) **c98** (First Trump) [2016/17 c114, h–: c20.3g^3 Jun 7] well-made gelding: maiden hurdler: fair **h–** handicap chaser: runner-up in point in January: stays 3¼m: acts on heavy going: has worn headgear, including last 3 starts. *Caroline Bailey*

DE NAME ESCAPES ME (IRE) 7 ch.g. Vinnie Roe (IRE) – Heartlight (IRE) **h116** (Accordion) [2016/17 h133p: h20d h16.3d h16.8g^{pu} Mar 17] sturdy gelding: well held on point debut: useful hurdler at best, little impact in 2016/17: stays 2½m: acts on heavy going: tried in hood. *Noel Meade, Ireland*

DENBOY (IRE) 7 b.g. King's Theatre (IRE) – Miss Denman (IRE) (Presenting) [2016/17 **c–** h99: h20.3s^{pu} c23.6g^{pu} Nov 8] poor form over hurdles: pulled up in novice handicap on **h–** chasing debut: unproven beyond 2m: usually wears tongue tie: often races prominently. *Jamie Snowden*

DENNIS OUR MENACE 7 b.g. Relief Pitcher – Pebble Dasher (Sula Bula) [2016/17 **h–** b15.8d h15.7d^{ur} h15.8d Dec 21] runner-up on point debut: no form in bumper/hurdles. **b–** *Tom Weston*

DENNY KERRELL 6 b.g. Midnight Legend – Tilla (Bin Ajwaad (IRE)) [2016/17 h83, **h77** b–: h24g h19.1d h20.5v h19.5v^4 h21.4d h21m^6 h16.8g^3 Apr 26] poor maiden hurdler: stays 19f: acts on heavy going: in cheekpieces/tongue tie last 4 starts: often travels strongly. *Seamus Mullins*

DENTLEY DE MEE (FR) 4 b.g. Lauro (GER) – Natty Twigy (FR) (Video Rock (FR)) **b88** [2016/17 b11.4g^6 b13.7m* b13.7d^5 b14s^6 Jan 1] half-brother to 3 winners, including bumper winner Baby Twig (by Network) and useful 2½m hurdle winner Twigline (by Martaline): dam French 17f chase winner: fair form in bumpers: won junior event at Huntingdon (dead-heated with Theydon Park) in October. *Nick Williams*

DE PLOTTING SHED (IRE) 7 b.g. Beneficial – Lady Willmurt (IRE) (Mandalus) **h147** [2016/17 h128p, b110: h20d h22s* h22.5g* h20g* h20d^2 h24d^6 h24d^4 h21s^2 h20d^2 h24d^4 Apr 27] useful-looking gelding: fell only start in points: smart hurdler: won minor events at Navan in September, Thurles in October and Naas (by 8 lengths from Jett) in November: most consistent: stays 3m: acts on heavy going. *Gordon Elliott, Ireland*

DEPUTY COMMANDER (IRE) 8 b.g. Shantou (USA) – Artic Native (IRE) (Be My **c119** Native (USA)) [2016/17 h117: c24d* c23.8v^3 c24d^3 c29.2v^{pu} c23.6g^6 Apr 8] fairly useful **h–** hurdler: similar form over fences: won novice handicap at Doncaster in November: stays 3m: acts on heavy going: has worn tongue tie. *Nigel Twiston-Davies*

DERINTOHER YANK (IRE) 6 b.g. Dubai Destination (USA) – Anns Present (IRE) **h120 §** (Presenting) [2016/17 b18s b16g^2 h20.9d^2 h17.1d* h20g* h19.9d^2 h19.7m^4 Apr 13] fourth **b94 §** foal: dam (b85), third in bumper, half-sister to fairly useful 3m hurdle winner The Phair Crier: fair form in bumpers: fairly useful form over hurdles: won novices at Carlisle in October and November: left Roger McGrath after second start: stays 2½m: acts on good to soft going: usually leads: has flashed tail/carried head awkwardly. *Donald McCain*

DERKSEN (IRE) 7 b.g. Robin des Champs (FR) – Anns Present (IRE) (Presenting) **h–** [2016/17 h95: h23.3s^{pu} Apr 30] pulled up on point debut: modest form over hurdles: has joined Francesca Nimmo. *Nicky Henderson*

DERRICK D'ANJOU (IRE) 6 b.g. Double Eclipse (IRE) – Belle d'Anjou (FR) (Saint **h99** Cyrien (FR)) [2016/17 b76: b16d h19.9d^6 h19.6d^4 h19.4g h19.7d^3 h24g^2 h26.4g^2 Apr 23] **b–** poor form in bumpers: modest form over hurdles: stays 3¼m: tried in blinkers: usually wears tongue tie. *Graeme McPherson*

DERRINTOGHER BLISS (IRE) 8 b.g. Arcadio (GER) – His Fair Lady (IRE) (In The Wings) [2016/17 c127p, h–: c24.1s² c23.4s⁴ c25.2v⁴ Feb 7] sturdy gelding: Irish maiden point winner: winning hurdler: fairly useful maiden chaser: second in handicap at Bangor in November: stays 27f: acts on soft and good to firm going: wears cheekpieces. *Kim Bailey* **c126 h–**

DERRYCHRIN (IRE) 11 ch.g. Flemensfirth (USA) – Queen Sophie (IRE) (Be My Native (USA)) [2016/17 c20s³ c25.8g⁵ h22v* Jun 28] fair form over hurdles: won handicap at Stratford in June: modest maiden chaser: stayed 2¾m: acted on heavy going: usually wore headgear: in tongue tie last 3 starts: dead. *Matt Sheppard* **c94 h108**

DERRYDOON 7 b.g. Multiplex – Wahiba Reason (IRE) (Robellino (USA)) [2016/17 b68: b15.8d h19.3dᵖᵘ h15.7s³ h19.3vᵖᵘ h16mᵈ Apr 28] poor form in bumpers/over hurdles: left Brian Rothwell after fourth start: sometimes in hood: in tongue tie last 3 starts. *Evan Williams* **h74 b–**

DERRYNANE (IRE) 6 b.g. Oscar (IRE) – Tessano Queen (IRE) (Jurado (USA)) [2016/17 b17.1g³ h16.7d⁴ h16.4v h16.7sꟳ h16.7d⁶ Apr 27] €7,800 3-y-o: sixth foal: closely related to fairly useful hurdler/useful chaser King High (2m-2¾m winner, by King's Theatre): dam (h92) bumper winner/maiden hurdler (stayed 3m): modest form in bumpers: poor form over hurdles: in tongue tie last 3 starts: tends to find little. *Donald McCain* **h70 b82**

DESARAY (IRE) 6 b.g. Milan – Shuil Mo Ghra (IRE) (Presenting) [2016/17 h16d² h20.8g⁴ Dec 9] €20,000 3-y-o, £40,000 5-y-o, resold £26,000 5-y-o: second foal: dam unraced half-sister to useful chaser (19f-3m winner) The Outlier out of half-sister to Scottish Grand National winner Baronet: won completed start in Irish maiden points: fair form over hurdles: better effort when second in novice at Warwick in November: should be suited by further than 2m. *Kim Bailey* **h106**

DESCARO (USA) 11 gr.g. Dr Fong (USA) – Miarixa (FR) (Linamix (FR)) [2016/17 c–§, h90§: h15.8m h18.7m h23gᵈ h16.3g⁵ h23.9g Sep 6] smallish gelding: poor handicap hurdler: little impact over fences: stays 2½m: acts on good to firm and heavy going: wears headgear/tongue tie: temperamental. *Giles Smyly* **c– § h75 §**

DESERT CROSS 4 b.g. Arcano (IRE) – Secret Happiness (Cape Cross (IRE)) [2016/17 h17.7g³ Sep 30] fair on Flat, stays 1½m: 11/4, some encouragement when third in juvenile maiden at Fontwell (3 lengths behind Sisania) on hurdling debut: open to improvement. *Jonjo O'Neill* **h93 p**

DESERT CRY (IRE) 11 b.g. Desert Prince (IRE) – Hataana (USA) (Robellino (USA)) [2016/17 c–, h114§: h20m³ h17.2m³ c21.2d⁶ h22.8v² h23.1s* h21.4s* h22.8d⁴ h20.5v* h24.7g h21.4g Apr 22] good-topped gelding: smart handicap hurdler: won at Bangor in December, and Ayr in January and March (by 27 lengths from One For Harry): smart chaser at best: stays 23f: acts on good to firm and heavy going: wears blinkers. *Donald McCain* **c– h145**

DESERTER (IRE) 6 ch.g. Tagula (IRE) – Lady Van Gogh (Dubai Destination (USA)) [2016/17 h16.3d⁵ h18.7m* h20g² h15.7g² h19.1g* h18.6g³ h19.8m* h19.7m⁵ Apr 13] fairly useful handicap hurdler: won at Stratford (conditional) in July, Fontwell in August and Wincanton (novice) in October: stays 2½m: acts on good to firm and heavy going: usually wears tongue tie: often races towards rear. *Warren Greatrex* **h117**

DESERT ISLAND DUSK 6 b.g. Superior Premium – Desert Island Disc (Turtle Island (IRE)) [2016/17 h93: h16.2d* h16.2m⁴ h16.2d* h17.1d⁴ h19.4d⁵ h16.2s h18.1d⁴ Apr 10] fair hurdler: won handicap in May and novice in June, both at Hexham: stays 2½m: acts on good to firm and good to soft going: has worn hood: wears tongue tie. *Maurice Barnes* **h105**

DESERT JOE (IRE) 11 b.g. Anshan – Wide Country (IRE) (Good Thyne (USA)) [2016/17 c121, h–: c24.2s c24.5d⁶ c23.5vᵖᵘ Jan 10] good-topped gelding: winning hurdler: fairly useful handicap chaser at best, below form in 2016/17: will stay long distances: acts on heavy going: has worn cheekpieces. *Alan King* **c95 h–**

DESERTMORE HILL (IRE) 7 b.g. Beneficial – Youngborogal (IRE) (Anshan) [2016/17 h107, b98: h20.3v⁴ h19.6dᵖᵘ h16m h18.7g⁴ h15.8d Apr 16] third in Irish maiden point: bumper winner: modest maiden hurdler: left Paul Morgan after fourth start: best effort at 17f: acts on soft going: has worn hood: usually finds little. *Kerry Lee* **h90**

DESERTMORE VIEW (IRE) 9 b.g. Fruits of Love (USA) – The Iron Lady (IRE) (Polish Patriot (USA)) [2016/17 c–, h–: c23.8sᵖᵘ Feb 19] prolific winning pointer: lightly-raced hurdler: fair hunter chaser at best, pulled up only start under Rules in 2016/17: stays 3m: best form on good going. *A. J. Rhead* **c– h–**

DESERT NOVA (IRE) 15 ch.g. Desert King (IRE) – Assafiyah (IRE) (Kris) [2016/17 c–, h–: h20.1d⁴ h21.2gᵖᵘ h20.8gᵖᵘ h24.1sᵖᵘ Jan 24] neat gelding: modest hurdler at best, of no account nowadays: fell only start over fences: tried in cheekpieces. *Mark Campion* **c– h–**

DESERT POINT (FR) 5 b.g. Le Havre (IRE) – Bonne Mere (FR) (Stepneyev (IRE)) **h78**
[2016/17 h15.6g⁴ h19.3d⁵ Jan 25] fairly useful on Flat, stays 1½m: poor form over hurdles:
in cheekpieces final start. *Keith Dalgleish*

DESERT QUEEN 9 b.m. Desert King (IRE) – Priscilla (Teenoso (USA)) [2016/17 h138: **c144**
c23.9g* c20s² c20.2sᶠ h19.8s⁴ c22.7g* c19.9s² Mar 5] good-topped mare: useful hurdler: **h126 +**
useful form over fences: won listed mares events at Market Rasen in November and
Leicester (by 10 lengths from Cresswell Breeze) in January: stays 3m: acts on soft going:
wears tongue tie: free-going front runner: has played up at start (sometimes led-in).
Harry Fry

DESERT RECLUSE (IRE) 10 ch.g. Redback – Desert Design (Desert King (IRE)) **h–**
[2016/17 h113: h16d h16g Sep 6] smallish gelding: fair handicap hurdler, well held in
2016/17: raced around 2m: acts on good to firm and good to soft going: often races lazily.
Henry Oliver

DESERT RETREAT (IRE) 6 b.g. Sandmason – Suny House (Carroll House) [2016/17 **c76**
b98: h20.6gʳᵒ h19.9d⁵ h20s⁵ h20.5g² h26v³ h26s² h24.2sᵖᵘ c23.6g⁴ Apr 8] fair maiden **h112 §**
hurdler: well beaten in novice handicap on chasing debut: stays 3¼m: acts on soft going:
in blinkers last 3 starts: temperamental. *Philip Hobbs*

DESERT SENSATION (IRE) 5 b.g. Authorized (IRE) – Awwal Malika (USA) **h120**
(Kingmambo (USA)) [2016/17 b90: h18.7g⁶ h16.7d⁵ h16m⁵ h23.3g⁵ h25.6s* h24.7g⁵
h23.1g³ h23.1s* h23.5d* h23.6s³ h23.4v⁵ h23.5s⁵ Feb 18] sturdy gelding: fairly useful
handicap hurdler: won at Fontwell in October, Exeter in November and Ascot (novice) in
December: stays 3¼m: acts on soft and good to firm going: wears headgear/tongue tie:
front runner/races prominently. *Dr Richard Newland*

DESERT STING 8 b.g. Scorpion (IRE) – Skipcarl (IRE) (Carlingford Castle) [2016/17 **h60**
h74: h19.6g⁶ May 14] multiple winning pointer: poor maiden hurdler: stays 2½m: acts on
heavy going: in blinkers/tongue tie last 2 starts. *Oliver Greenall*

DESERT TANGO 4 ch.f. Paco Boy (IRE) – Photographie (USA) (Trempolino (USA)) **h–**
[2016/17 h16.7sᵘʳ h15.7sᵖᵘ Feb 3] half-sister to fairly useful hurdler Downing Street
(2½m-3m winner, by Sadler's Wells) and fair hurdler Little Dutch Girl (17f winner, by
Dutch Art): modest on Flat, stays 1¼m: let down by jumping in juvenile hurdles.
Michael Mullineaux

DESHAN (GER) 6 b.g. Soldier Hollow – Desimona (GER) (Monsun (GER)) [2016/17 **b80**
b88p: b15.7s³ b16.3v³ Jun 28] modest form in bumpers. *Tim Vaughan*

DESILVANO 8 b.g. Desideratum – Cruz Santa (Lord Bud) [2016/17 h–: h22.8sᵖᵘ Jan 21] **h–**
workmanlike gelding: dual winning pointer: fairly useful hurdler at best, pulled up only
start in 2016/17: stays 25f: acts on heavy going. *James Evans*

DESOTO COUNTY 8 gr.g. Hernando (FR) – Kaldounya (Kaldoun (FR)) [2016/17 h133: **c129**
h20d c17.3m² c21.2m² h16.5v* h16.2g³ h16d Dec 27] lengthy gelding: Irish maiden point **h134**
winner: useful hurdler: won minor event at Sligo in August: fairly useful form over fences:
second in maidens at Cartmel in May/June: stays easy 21f: acts on good to firm and heavy
going: in headgear last 3 starts: wears tongue tie. *Gordon Elliott, Ireland*

DESSINATEUR (FR) 4 b.g. Alberto Giacometti (IRE) – Castagnette III (FR) (Tin **b97**
Soldier (FR)) [2016/17 b16v* Mar 23] €31,000 3-y-o: brother to useful hurdler/chaser Une
Artiste (2m-2½m winner) and half-brother to several winners in France, including bumper
winner Coup de Pinceau (by Buck's Boum): dam French 2½m-29f cross-country chase
winner: 8/1, won bumper at Chepstow (by 1¼ lengths from Warthog) in March: will be
suited by further than 2m. *Venetia Williams*

DESTINED TO SHINE (IRE) 5 b.g. Dubai Destination (USA) – Good Shine (IRE) **b96**
(Beneficial) [2016/17 b16s b15.7v* b17d³ Apr 5] €18,000 3-y-o: dam unraced
half-sister to fair hurdler/fairly useful chaser (2m-2½m winner) Court Leader and fairly
useful hurdler/useful chaser (stayed 2¾m) Mount Sandel: fairly useful form in bumpers:
won at Towcester in February. *Kerry Lee*

DESTINY AWAITS (IRE) 8 b.g. Dubai Destination (USA) – Mellow Jazz (Lycius **h80**
(USA)) [2016/17 h95: h23.9m³ h22.1g⁶ h23.9dᵖᵘ h20.2g h23.8g³ h19.4d⁶ Nov 14] poor
handicap hurdler: stays 3m: acts on good to firm going: tried in blinkers/tongue tie.
Keith Pollock

DESTINY'S GOLD (IRE) 7 b.g. Millenary – Knockhouse Rose (IRE) (Roselier (FR)) **c116**
[2016/17 h115x. h16s¹ h16m* h16g⁷ c20.g⁶ h20g h18.7g² h15.5g⁴ Dec 7] tall **h112**
gelding: fair hurdler: won maiden at Worcester in July: fairly useful form over fences:
unproven beyond 17f: acts on good to firm and good to soft going: wears headgear:
temperament under suspicion. *George Baker*

DESTINY'S SHADOW (IRE) 5 gr.g. Dark Angel (IRE) – Lunar Love (IRE) (In The **h83** Wings) [2016/17 h16.8g h16g⁴ h16.7g⁵ h15.8d³ h15.8d⁴ h15.7dᵖᵘ Nov 15] half-brother to fairly useful 2m hurdle winner Kabjoy (by Intikhab): poor maiden on Flat: similar form over hurdles: raced around 2m: acts on good to soft going: in cheekpieces last 3 starts: tried in tongue tie: often races prominently. *George Baker*

DESTINY'S STAR 5 br.g. Beneficial – Lady Cad (FR) (Cadoudal (FR)) [2016/17 h16d **h—** h20.5g⁶ h19.5sᵖᵘ Dec 27] little impact in novice/maiden hurdles. *Jonjo O'Neill*

DESTRIER (FR) 4 b.g. Voix du Nord (FR) – Razia (FR) (Robin des Champs (FR)) **b—** [2016/17 b16g Mar 18] lengthy gelding: tailed off in maiden bumper. *Dan Skelton*

DETANK (IRE) 10 b.g. Oscar (IRE) – Ou La La (IRE) (Be My Native (USA)) [2016/17 **c100** c20.9s² c25.8m³ c21.4gᵖᵘ Jul 16] won twice in points: maiden hurdler: fair form over **h—** fences: best effort when second in novice handicap at Stratford in June: stays 3¼m: acts on good to firm and heavy going. *Robert Stephens*

DETENTION 6 b.g. Kayf Tara – Late For Class (IRE) (Bob's Return (IRE)) [2016/17 **h—** b16g h21.4s h19.8d⁵ Mar 26] down field in bumper: well held both starts over hurdles: **b—** dead *Colin Tizzard*

DETOUR AHEAD 9 ch.m. Needwood Blade – My Tern (IRE) (Glacial Storm (USA)) **c85** [2016/17 c—, h84: c21.4g⁴ c20.3d* h19.9s c22.6mᵖᵘ c25.5g⁶ c19.8dᵖᵘ c20.3s⁶ c20.2gᵖᵘ **h—** c20d⁴ c21.1vᵖᵘ c23.6gᶠ c19.2g⁵ c23.6g⁵ Apr 28] leggy, close-coupled mare: fair hurdler at best: modest handicap chaser: won novice event at Bangor in May: stays 2¾m: acts on good to firm and heavy going: wears headgear: tried in tongue tie. *Clare Ellam*

DETROIT BLUES 7 ch.g. Tobougg (IRE) – Blue Missy (USA) (Swain (IRE)) [2016/17 **c—** h112: c23.8mᵖᵘ May 8] angular gelding: won Irish point on debut: fair hurdler: pulled up **h—** in novice handicap on chasing debut: stays 2½m: acts on any going: wears tongue tie. *Jamie Snowden*

DEVILS BRIDE (IRE) 10 b.g. Helissio (FR) – Rigorous (Generous (IRE)) [2016/17 **c157** c149, h139: c18g² c22.5g⁴ c18.2g* c20sᵘʳ c20d³ c15.9g c17s⁵ c20dᶠ Apr 26] useful hurdler: **h—** very smart handicap chaser: won at Galway (by 8 lengths from Draycott Place) in July: third in PWC Champion Chase at Gowran (12½ lengths behind Ballycasey) in October: left W. P. Mullins after fourth start: stays 2¾m: acts on soft going: tried in cheekpieces: usually wears tongue tie. *Henry de Bromhead, Ireland*

DEVILS WATER 6 b.g. Overbury (IRE) – Reel Charmer (Dancing High) [2016/17 b17m **h100** b16s h22.7sᵖᵘ h19.3d³ h17sᵖᵘ h19.4g³ h21.3d h23.1mᵖᵘ Apr 17] first foal: dam (c120/h131) **b—** 2½m-25f hurdle/chase winner: well held in bumpers: fair form over hurdles: best effort at 19f: sometimes in tongue tie. *George Charlton*

DEVIL TO PAY 11 b.g. Red Ransom (USA) – My Way (IRE) (Marju (IRE)) [2016/17 **c115** c116, h—: c17.4d³ c21gᵖᵘ c19.4d Jun 16] compact gelding: winning hurdler: fairly useful **h—** maiden chaser: stays 2¼m: acts on soft going. *Alan King*

DEVON DRUM 9 b.g. Beat Hollow – West Devon (USA) (Gone West (USA)) [2016/17 **h104** h16g³ h15.8m² h16m⁵ Jul 4] strong gelding: fair maiden hurdler: likely to prove best at 2m: acts on good to firm and good to soft going: in tongue tie last 2 starts. *David Brown*

DEVON GENERAL 9 b.g. Generous (IRE) – Lady Devondale (IRE) (Broken Hearted) **c104** [2016/17 c23d³ h23g⁶ c25.8g⁶ Aug 10] multiple winning pointer: sixth in maiden at **h72** Worcester on hurdling debut: fair form over fences: tried in cheekpieces/tongue tie. *Richard Woollacott*

DEVON RIVER (FR) 7 gr.g. Stormy River (FR) – Devon House (USA) (Chester House **c—** (USA)) [2016/17 c—, h81: h20.2d Jun 29] poor form over hurdles: well held both starts over **h—** fences: unproven beyond 2m: tried in cheekpieces. *Simon Waugh*

DE VOUS A MOI (FR) 9 b.g. Sinndar (IRE) – Dzinigane (FR) (Exit To Nowhere (USA)) **c125** [2016/17 c131, h—: c24.1v⁶ c22.9s c21.6v³ h22v* h19.9s Mar 18] fairly useful hurdler: won **h125** novice at Newcastle in February: fairly useful handicap chaser: third at Kelso in January: stays 2¾m: acts on heavy going: has worn headgear: front runner/races prominently. *Sue Smith*

DEWBERRY 6 br.m. Lucarno (USA) – Elderberry (Bin Ajwaad (IRE)) [2016/17 b—: b16d **h—** h15.8g h21vᵖᵘ h20.7g Apr 3] no form in bumpers/hurdles: in tongue tie last 2 starts. **b—** *Geoffrey Deacon*

DEXCITE (FR) 6 b.g. Authorized (IRE) – Belle Alicia (FR) (Smadoun (FR)) [2016/17 **h117** h123: h15.8s² h16.7g* h15.7g* h17.2m⁶ Jun 24] well-made gelding: fairly useful hurdler: won maiden at Bangor in May and novice at Southwell in June: stays 19f: acts on soft going: tried in hood: often races towards rear. *Tom George*

DEYRANN DE CARJAC (FR) 4 b.g. Balko (FR) – Queyrann (FR) (Sheyrann) **b78**
[2016/17 b16.3g Mar 25] rather unfurnished gelding: 14/1, shaped as if needed experience
when eleventh in Goffs UK Spring Sales Bumper at Newbury (18 lengths behind
Bullionaire) in March. *Alan King*

D'GENTLE REFLEXION (FR) 4 b.g. Gentlewave (IRE) – Reflexion (FR) (Discover **b75**
d'Auteuil (FR)) [2016/17 b16.7g⁶ Apr 22] second foal: half-brother to French 19f hurdle
winner Cote d'Azur (by Poliglote): dam (c124/h124), French 17f/2¼m hurdle/chase
winner, half-sister to useful hurdler/very smart chaser (stays 3½m) Vieux Lion Rouge:
well-backed 6/4, 21¾ lengths sixth to Juge Et Parti in conditionals/amateur bumper at
Bangor. *Warren Greatrex*

DIABLE DE SIVOLA (FR) 4 b.g. Noroit (GER) – Grande Route (IRE) (Lost World **h128**
(IRE)) [2016/17 h15.8g* h17.7d² h15.8g³ h16.4s² h16.6g³ h16.4g⁵ Mar 15] useful-looking
gelding: sixth foal: half-brother to French 17f/2¼m hurdle/chase winner Cougar de Sivola
(by Caballo Raptor) and French 17f hurdle winner Slick Chick (by Epalo): dam, French
15f/2m hurdle winner, half-sister to fairly useful hurdler/useful chaser (2m winner) Gringo:
fairly useful form over hurdles: won juvenile at Uttoxeter in July: second in Prestbury
Juvenile Hurdle at Cheltenham (1¾ lengths behind Defi du Seuil) in November: stays
2¼m: acts on soft going. *Nick Williams*

DIABLERETS (FR) 4 ch.g. Vendangeur (IRE) – Lavande (FR) (Iris Noir (FR)) [2016/17 **h—**
h16g⁴ Oct 9] tailed off in juvenile hurdle. *Richard Woollacott*

DIAKALI (FR) 8 gr.g. Sinndar (IRE) – Diasilixa (FR) (Linamix (FR)) [2016/17 h156: **h160**
h18.1v⁴ h16d* Apr 17] good-topped gelding: high-class hurdler: won minor event at
Fairyhouse (by 20 lengths from Stars Over The Sea) in April: stays 21f: acts on heavy
going: has worn headgear, including in 2016/17. *W. P. Mullins, Ireland*

DIAMANT BLEU (FR) 4 b.g. Montmartre (FR) – Cate Bleue (FR) (Katowice (FR)) **h119**
[2016/17 h16.8g⁵ h17.9s² Apr 21] half-brother to several winners, including very smart
chaser Alary (2¾m winner in France, by Dream Well), stays 3¾m, and winning French
hurdler/useful chaser Musica Bella (17f-21f winner, by Bateau Rouge): dam winning
chaser up to 25f in Italy (also French bumper winner): fairly useful form over hurdles:
better effort when second in juvenile at Auteuil in April. *Nick Williams*

DIAMANT DE L'OUEST (FR) 4 b.g. Epalo (GER) – Ortezia (FR) (Evening World **b—**
(FR)) [2016/17 b14d b16s Jan 6] no form in bumpers. *Brian Ellison*

DIAMOND BENNY (IRE) 5 b.g. Milan – Ben's Pride (Bollin Eric) [2016/17 b16g⁵ **h—**
h21.7s Dec 19] tailed off in bumper/novice hurdle. *Robert Stephens* **b—**

DIAMOND DUST 6 gr.m. Bandmaster (USA) – Absalom's Lady (Absalom) [2016/17 **b66**
b16.7g⁶ May 14] half-sister to several winners, including useful hurdler/smart chaser Bob
Bob Bobbin (2m-3¼m winner, by Bob Back) and fairly useful hurdler War General (2m
winner, by Classic Cliche): dam (c145/h158) 2m-2¼m hurdle/chase winner (stayed 3m):
3/1, sixth in mares bumper at Bangor. *Emma Lavelle*

DIAMOND FORT (IRE) 5 ch.g. Gamut (IRE) – Ellie Forte (Alflora (IRE)) [2016/17 **h116 p**
b15.7g⁴ b15.7d h19.7s³ h19.7v³ h19.5g* Apr 17] €7,000 3-y-o: second foal: dam unraced **b88**
half-sister to useful hurdler (stayed 2½m) Lucia Bay out of useful 2m-2¾m hurdle winner
Lucia Forte, herself sister to top-class staying chaser Teeton Mill: Irish maiden pointer: fair
form in bumpers: fairly useful form over hurdles: won handicap at Chepstow in April: will
stay beyond 19f: open to further improvement. *Fergal O'Brien*

DIAMOND GESTURE (IRE) 9 ch.m. Presenting – Rare Gesture (IRE) (Shalford **h—**
(IRE)) [2016/17 h54: h19.9gᶠ Aug 25] maiden hurdler: stays 2½m: acts on heavy and good
to firm going: has worn hood/tongue tie: often races in rear. *Gordon Elliott, Ireland*

DIAMOND GUY (FR) 4 b.g. Konig Turf (GER) – Unique Chance (FR) (Network (GER)) **b100**
[2016/17 b15.3m* Apr 5] first foal: dam unraced daughter of very smart French hurdler/
chaser (stayed 29f) Harmonie Tresor: 4/9, won maiden bumper at Wincanton (by 28
lengths from Rowley Park) in April. *Paul Nicholls*

DIAMOND KING (IRE) 9 b.g. King's Theatre (IRE) – Georgia On My Mind (FR) **c144**
(Belmez (USA)) [2016/17 h155: h24d⁴ c18.2d* c20d⁵ c19.5v⁴ c20.8gᵖᵘ c21dᵖᵘ Apr 28] **h—**
useful-looking gelding: smart hurdler: useful form over fences: won maiden at Galway (by
14 lengths from Lucky Pat) in October: stays 21f: acts on heavy going: wears tongue tie.
Gordon Elliott, Ireland

DIAMOND LIFE 11 b.g. Silver Patriarch (IRE) – Myrrh (Salse (USA)) [2016/17 c97, h–: **c74** c15.9f⁴ c15.9m⁵ c21.7g⁴ Mar 2] lengthy gelding: maiden hurdler/chaser: stays 19f: acts on **h–** heavy going: tried in cheekpieces: front runner/races prominently. *Mark Pitman*

DIAMOND LUCY (IRE) 6 b.m. Diamond Green (FR) – Hi Lyla (IRE) (Lahib (USA)) **h72** [2016/17 h16g⁵ h18.7g⁵ h19.2m⁴ h21d Nov 24] modest maiden on Flat: point winner: poor form over hurdles: best effort at 19f. *Tony Carroll*

DIAMOND REFLECTION (IRE) 5 b.g. Oasis Dream – Briolette (IRE) (Sadler's **h63** Wells (USA)) [2016/17 h–: h23.3v⁴ h16.6g h19.2vᵖᵘ Feb 15] poor maiden hurdler: in headgear last 4 starts: wears tongue tie. *Tom Weston*

DIAMOND REGGIE (IRE) 4 ch.g. Stowaway – Monilea Lady (IRE) (Accordion) **b75** [2016/17 b16.7s³ b15.8g Apr 9] workmanlike gelding: modest form in bumpers. *Peter Bowen*

DIAMOND ROCK 6 b.g. Kayf Tara – Crystal Princess (IRE) (Definite Article) [2016/17 **h102** h81, b70: h18.7m* h16.5h h16.8m⁶ h19m⁶ h16s⁵ h16d h18.7gᵖᵘ Apr 15] fair handicap hurdler: won at Stratford in October: will be suited by 2½m+: acts on soft and good to firm going: often races prominently. *Henry Oliver*

DIAMOND TAMMY (IRE) 11 b.g. Tamayaz (CAN) – Mary Dont Be Long (IRE) (The **c–** Bart (USA)) [2016/17 c16.5gᵖᵘ c16g h15.7d h15.5g h21sᶠ h15.7dᵖᵘ Feb 26] lengthy **h63** gelding: poor handicap hurdler: fair chaser at best: unproven beyond 2m: acts on good to firm and heavy going: wears headgear: tried in tongue tie. *Hannah James*

DIBBLE BRIDGE 6 ch.g. Spirit One (FR) – Willows World (Agnes World (USA)) **h–** [2016/17 h–: h22.1gᵖᵘ Jun 1] placed in points: maiden hurdler: tried in cheekpieces/tongue tie. *Mike Sowersby*

DICA (FR) 11 ch.g. Kapgarde (FR) – Easy World (FR) (Lost World (IRE)) [2016/17 c–, **c65** h–: c25.5g⁴ Jun 1] multiple winning pointer: winning hurdler: fair chaser at best: stays **h–** 3¼m: acts on firm and soft going: has worn tongue tie. *Paul Collins*

DICK DARSIE (IRE) 7 br.g. Darsi (FR) – Hurricane Jane (IRE) (Strong Gale) [2016/17 **c100** h21.2g⁵ h20g² h21.2d³ c24.2sᵖᵘ c21.5v⁵ c24.5s⁵ c20.9v³ Mar 9] €8,000 3-y-o: seventh foal: **h98** half-brother to fair/temperamental chaser Swing Hard (2½m-3m winner, by Zagreb): dam (h93) 2m hurdle winner: won Irish maiden point: modest form over hurdles: fair form over fences: should stay beyond 21f: acts on heavy going: front runner/races prominently: temperament under suspicion. *Sue Smith*

DICKY BOB 10 gr.g. Exit To Nowhere (USA) – She's A Gift (Bob's Return (IRE)) **c–** [2016/17 c110: c26.3gᵘʳ Apr 27] multiple point winner: fair form in hunter chases, let down by jumping sole start in 2016/17. *Miss V. J. Nicholls*

DIDNTITELLYA (IRE) 8 b.g. Presenting – Beauty Star (IRE) (Shalford (IRE)) [2016/17 **c–** c80, h–: c20sᵖᵘ May 11] maiden chaser: poor chaser: stays 2½m: acts on heavy going: in **h–** cheekpieces/tongue tie last 2 starts. *Kim Bailey*

DIDO 7 b.g. Killer Instinct – Bowdlane Barb (Commanche Run) [2016/17 c22.6m⁶ May **c66** 20] workmanlike gelding: multiple winning pointer: no form in bumper/hurdle in 2013/14: **h–** 33/1, 29½ lengths sixth of 14 to Our Chief in novice hunter at Stratford on chasing debut. *D. Peters*

DIEGO DU CHARMIL (FR) 5 b.g. Ballingarry (IRE) – Daramour (FR) (Anabaa Blue) **h146** [2016/17 h135: h16g* h15.7m h15.7d h15.6g* h16.8g Mar 17] good-topped gelding: useful handicap hurdler: won at Chepstow (by 1¼ lengths from Furiously Fast) in October and listed event at Musselburgh (by 5 lengths from Dominada) in February: raced around 2m: best form on good going: wears tongue tie. *Paul Nicholls*

DIEGO SUAREZ (FR) 7 b.g. Astarabad (USA) – Shabada (FR) (Cadoudal (FR)) **h82** [2016/17 h87: h19.2g h23.4g³ h20.3d⁵ h20.6s³ h23.1s⁶ h22sᵖᵘ h19.3s⁵ Feb 3] poor maiden hurdler: left Chris Bealby after first start: stays 21f: acts on soft going: wears headgear: often races towards rear: temperament under suspicion. *Laura Morgan*

DIESE DES BIEFFES (FR) 4 gr.g. Martaline – Chanel du Berlais (FR) (Saint Preuil **b76 p** (FR)) [2016/17 b16g⁵ Feb 25] €45,000 3-y-o: half-brother to 3 winners in France, including fairly useful 17f hurdle winner Caterina (by Maresca Sorrento) and hurdler/chaser Alto Mare (17f-2½m winner, by Bonnet Rouge): dam lightly-raced half-sister to dams of high-class French hurdler/useful chaser Bonito du Berlais (stayed 2¾m), smart hurdler/chaser Caid du Berlais (stays 25f) and smart hurdler/very smart chaser Mr Mole (best around 2m): 4/1, shaped as if needed experience when fifth in bumper at Kempton (12½ lengths behind Irish Prophecy) in February: should do better. *Dan Skelton*

DIFFERENT GRAVEY (IRE) 7 b.g. High Chaparral (IRE) – Newtown Dancer (IRE) (Danehill Dancer (IRE)) [2016/17 h156: c18.8d* c20.8d⁵ h19.1s⁵ h24.7gᵖᵘ Apr 8] tall gelding: smart hurdler: showed little interest when pulled up last 2 starts: similar form over fences: won maiden at Ascot (by 6 lengths from Brother Tedd) in November: stays 2½m: acts on heavy going: tried in cheekpieces: temperamental. *Nicky Henderson* **c144 §**
h– §

DIG A BIT DEEPER 4 b.g. Duke of Marmalade (IRE) – Dayia (IRE) (Act One) [2016/17 b14d⁴ b13g Nov 26] poor form in bumpers. *Tim Easterby* **b61**

DIG DEEPER 8 b.g. Overbury (IRE) – Tickle The Tiller (IRE) (Strong Gale) [2016/17 c120p: c20.9s² c25.2vᵖᵘ c24v³ c23.6s* c23.4dᵖᵘ Mar 24] maiden point winner: useful chaser: won novice at Huntingdon in March: best form on soft/heavy going: in cheekpieces last 2 starts: usually races close up. *Caroline Bailey* **c134**

DIG FOR VICTORY 6 gr.m. Nomadic Way (USA) – Grace Dieu (Commanche Run) [2016/17 b15.7v b16.3s b16.7g⁵ Mar 25] fourth foal: sister to fairly useful hurdler Cannon Fodder (2¾m-25f winner): dam temperamental maiden: modest form in bumpers: left Gary Hanmer after first start. *Michael Scudamore* **b78**

DIMPLE (FR) 6 gr.g. Montmartre (FR) – Dynella (FR) (Sillery (USA)) [2016/17 h105: h23.3d³ h20.2f c22.5vᵖᵘ c21.2g* c24.5dᵖᵘ Apr 28] unbeaten in 3 points: fair maiden hurdler: fair form over fences: won hunter at Tramore in April: left Pauline Robson after second start: stays 21f: acts on good to soft going: has worn hood: often races prominently. *A. Slattery, Ireland* **c116**
h95

DINARIA DES OBEAUX (FR) 4 b.f. Saddler Maker (IRE) – Indiana Jaune (FR) (Le Nain Jaune (FR)) [2016/17 h16s* h16s³ h16v* h16.8g h16d⁴ h16d⁵ Apr 29] rather unfurnished filly: fourth foal: dam French 2¾m-25f cross-country chase winner: useful form over hurdles: won juvenile maiden at Cork (by 29 lengths from Tout Est Permis) in December and Winning Fair Juvenile Hurdle at Fairyhouse (beaten head by Ex Patriot but awarded race after suffering interference run-in) in February: will stay 2½m: best form on soft/heavy going: in tongue tie last 2 starts: front runner/races prominently. *Gordon Elliott, Ireland* **h130**

DINEUR (FR) 11 ch.g. Discover d'Auteuil (FR) – Sky Rocket (FR) (Sky Lawyer (FR)) [2016/17 c127, h–: c25s⁶ c19.2g⁵ c23.8g² c20d* c20m³ c23.6gᵘʳ c25g c23.6v² c21.1g* Apr 6] workmanlike gelding: winning hurdler: useful chaser: won handicap at Worcester in June and Foxhunters' Chase at Aintree (by 1¾ lengths from Balnaslow) in April: barely stays 3m: acts on soft and good to firm going: has worn hood: wears tongue tie. *Mickey Bowen* **c131**
h–

Randox Health Foxhunters' Open Hunter Chase, Aintree—champion amateur Mr James King clears the fourth last aboard 16/1-shot Dineur (white face) as the pair go one place better than in 2016

DING DING 6 ch.m. Winker Watson – Five Bells (IRE) (Rock of Gibraltar (IRE))   **h107**
[2016/17 h73: h15.9g³ h17.7g h17.7d* h15.9g* h19.8s⁶ h20.5v³ h17.7v² h20.5s* h21.6s⁵
h20.5m³ Apr 17] short-backed mare: fair handicap hurdler: won at Plumpton in November
(twice) and February: stays 21f: acts on good to firm and heavy going. *Sheena West*

DINGO BAY 11 b.g. Karinga Bay – Do It On Dani (Weld) [2016/17 c20.5vᵖᵘ c20.1vᵖᵘ Feb   **c– §**
15] tall, good-topped gelding: lightly-raced hurdler: modest chaser at best, pulled up both   **h–**
starts in 2016/17 after long absence: stays 25f: acts on heavy going: wears headgear:
temperamental. *Rebecca Menzies*

DINGO DOLLAR (IRE) 5 ch.g. Golden Lariat (USA) – Social Society (IRE) (Moscow   **h126**
Society (USA)) [2016/17 h23.1v² h21s h23.1d* h24.4d h25.6g* Apr 12] €9,000 3-y-o,
£50,000 4-y-o: useful-looking gelding: first foal: dam (h105) 3m hurdle winner: Irish
maiden point winner: fairly useful form over hurdles: won maiden at Bangor in January
and novice at Fontwell in April: stays 3¼m: acts on good to soft going: front runner/races
prominently. *Alan King*

DINKY CHALLENGER 9 gr.g. Midnight Legend – Crusty Lily (Whittingham (IRE))   **h–**
[2016/17 h–: h15.3m h15.8g May 30] failed to complete all 3 starts in points: no form over
hurdles: tried in tongue tie. *Mark Gillard*

DINONS (FR) 4 b.g. Balko – Beni Abbes (FR) (Saint des Saints (FR)) [2016/17   **b106**
b16d² Apr 16] €55,000 3-y-o: second foal: half-brother to fairly useful French hurdler/
chaser Antoing (2m-21f winner, by Turgeon): dam, French hurdle/chase winner around
2¼m, half-sister to useful 2½m chase winner Bekkensfirth: 8/1, shaped with promise when
second in Tattersalls Ireland George Mernagh Memorial Sales Bumper at Fairyhouse (1¾
lengths behind Red Jack) in April: will prove suited by further than 2m. *Gordon Elliott,
Ireland*

DINO VELVET (FR) 4 b.g. Naaqoos – Matgil (FR) (Grape Tree Road) [2016/17 h16.4sᶠ   **h123**
h16s* h16s⁴ h16s² h15.8s² h16.4g Mar 15] sturdy gelding: fairly useful form over hurdles:
won juvenile at Sandown in December: raced only at 2m: acts on soft going. *Alan King*

DINSDALE 4 b.g. Cape Cross (IRE) – Emmy Award (IRE) (Sadler's Wells (USA))   **h116**
[2016/17 h17.7d⁴ h16s² h16.7s³ h16.3s* h18.8g⁴ h16g³ Apr 23] good-topped gelding:
fairly useful form over hurdles: won juvenile at Newbury in March: probably stays 19f:
acts on soft going: in cheekpieces last 3 starts. *Michael Scudamore*

DIRECT FLO (IRE) 10 b.m. Mr Combustible (IRE) – Direct Pursuit (IRE) (Hubbly   **c–**
Bubbly (USA)) [2016/17 c–, h66: h20g h23vᵖᵘ Jan 10] poor hurdler: maiden chaser: stayed   **h–**
27f: acted on good to firm and good to soft going: tried in headgear: dead. *Rob Summers*

DIRECTIONAL 5 b.g. Raven's Pass (USA) – Rose Street (USA) (Street Cry (IRE))   **h74**
[2016/17 h86: h16m h20s h18.2g Sep 23] staying gelding: poor maiden hurdler: left Tim
Vaughan after first start: unproven beyond 2m: acts on soft going: tried in visor/tongue tie.
Eoin Christopher McCarthy, Ireland

DIRTY DEXTER 6 b.g. Beat All (USA) – Redlands Charm (Classic Cliche (IRE)) [2016/17   **h–**
b15.7g b17.7g h15.8v h19.5s h19.5s h23.9gᵖᵘ Mar 30] of no account. *Grace Harris*   **b–**

DISCAY 8 b.g. Distant Music (USA) – Caysue (Cayman Kai (IRE)) [2016/17 c123, h92:   **c109**
c16.4d³ c16.5sᵖᵘ h19.9s³ h20.6gᵖᵘ h16g⁶ h23.3g² h19.9v⁵ Feb 11] modest handicap hurdler: **h97**
fair chaser: left Dr Richard Newland after second start: barely stays 23f: acts on good to
firm and heavy going: usually wears headgear: tried in tongue tie. *Philip Kirby*

DISCOURS D'UN ROI (FR) 5 ch.g. Vision d'Etat (FR) – Reine de Lestrade (FR)   **h–**
(Sahrehill (USA)) [2016/17 h16s h15.8g⁴ Apr 3] fair form on Flat: fairly useful hurdler in
France in 2015/16, well held in handicaps both starts in Britain: raced around 2m: acts on
good to firm and good to soft going: tried in tongue tie. *Nicky Henderson*

DISCOVERIE 9 b.g. Runyon (IRE) – Sri (IRE) (Sri Pekan (USA)) [2016/17 c91§, h81§:   **c112**
c16.4d* c16.4s* c17.3m h19.9g h16.8s* c15.7d* c19.2d h19.9s² Jan 29] lengthy gelding: **h102**
fair handicap hurdler: won at Sedgefield in November: fair handicap chaser: won at same
course (twice) very early in season and at Catterick in December: best around 2m
nowadays: acts on heavy going: wears headgear. *Kenneth Slack*

DISKO (FR) 6 gr.g. Martaline – Nikos Royale (FR) (Nikos) [2016/17 h126p, b115:   **c157**
h20s⁶ c20g* c22.5d³ c24d³ c21.3s* c19.9g³ c24.5d* Apr 25]   **h–**
    The Sir Henry Cecil-trained Baffin Bay was useful on the Flat in the late-
'nineties, but Disko, the Noel Meade-trained chaser who shares his name with an
island in the same stretch of water off the west coast of Greenland, has already made
a bigger splash, winning two top-level championship events in his novice season
and looking as if there are more good races to be won with him. Disko showed

Flogas Novices' Chase (Dr P. J. Moriarty), Leopardstown—
Disko gets first run and reverses Christmas form with Our Duke (centre)

fairly useful form over hurdles, including when finishing sixth in the Champion Novices' Hurdle at the 2016 Punchestown Festival (which took place shortly after the start of the 2016/17 British season), but connections wasted no time in switching him to chasing and, after a summer break, he began his latest campaign with an impressive debut win in a beginners chase at Punchestown in October. Gigginstown House Stud's retained number-one at the time, Bryan Cooper, had to watch from the sidelines because of injury, but he was impressed enough by Disko's ready eight-length win to plump for Disko ahead of A Toi Phil and Nambour in the Florida Pearl Novices' Chase back at Punchestown the following month. In a race run in dense fog, Disko started favourite but failed to give his running, managing only a distant third behind A Toi Phil. Disko showed that form to be all wrong when a close third to Our Duke and Coney Island next time in the Neville Hotels Novices' Chase (registered as the Fort Leney) at Leopardstown's Christmas meeting, faring much the best of Gigginstown's four runners despite being sent off at 20/1 and looking only the fourth string beforehand on jockey bookings.

Even better was to follow on Disko's next start when he reversed placings with Our Duke in the Flogas Novices' Chase (formerly the Dr P. J. Moriarty) at Leopardstown in February. In a steadily-run, and therefore somewhat unsatisfactory renewal, the 6/5 favourite Bellshill was already beaten when falling at the last, while Our Duke was seemingly undone by the emphasis being on speed back over a shorter trip. Disko's jockey Sean Flanagan (who also rode him for his debut win) controlled the pace, taking it up early and able to dictate things from the front, with Disko jumping well in the main and having all his rivals in trouble when really pressing on between the last two. The winning distance over Our Duke, who was outjumped at the last, was a length and three quarters, with a further six lengths between Our Duke and Balko des Flos in third. Disko's trainer, enjoying his first Grade 1 win since Apache Stronghold won the same race in 2015, and his jockey both highlighted the horse's fluent jumping after his Flogas win, with Meade saying: 'It's a great thrill to

Growise Champion Novices' Chase (Ellier), Punchestown—
Bryan Cooper and Disko have matters under control at the last

have one to jump as well as that and it never really looked a problem—it's lovely to be able to watch something like that.' Disko was duly cut to 8/1 for the Golden Miller Novices' Chase over the intermediate distance at the Cheltenham Festival— nominated by Meade as the horse's target—and he lined up there one month later as a 4/1 chance.

The Golden Miller (branded as the JLT Chase) was won by Yorkhill, but Disko was one of five in with a chance turning for home, and he actually moved into a narrow lead approaching two out before finishing a creditable third to Yorkhill and a rallying Top Notch, beaten a length and three lengths. Timeform's representative at the track felt Disko might have found the test on the sharp side, though that wasn't a view shared (initially at least) by Noel Meade who expressed some concerns about Disko's stamina after his Cheltenham effort ('I'm not sure he totally saw out the two and a half on this track'). Despite these reservations, Disko missed another meeting with Yorkhill in the Ryanair Gold Cup Novices' Chase at Fairyhouse in early-April (which was won by his stablemate Road To Respect after an errant display by Yorkhill) and was aimed instead at the Growise Champion Novices' Chase (registered as the Ellier) over three miles at Punchestown a fortnight later. As well as Road To Respect and Disko, Meade also trains A Genie In Abottle, who had been sent off the 4/1 favourite for the National Hunt Chase at the Cheltenham Festival where he ran a long way below form. A Genie In Abottle bounced back to his best when third to Disko in the Champion Novices' Chase, but it was the winner who really caught the eye, jumping and galloping with zest and showing in no uncertain terms that a lengthy campaign had not taken the edge off him in the slightest. Indeed, Disko looked to be thriving as he romped home under Cooper to win by five lengths from Anibale Fly, earning quotes of as low as 25/1 for the 2018 Cheltenham Gold Cup. Noel Meade changed his tune about the horse afterwards, saying 'We did think about running him in the Ryanair Gold Cup at Fairyhouse but he didn't come out of Cheltenham that well … in fact, I'd say if we made a mistake at Cheltenham it was running him in the wrong race. I wasn't worried about three miles on that ground today and I think we got it right this time.' It seems that Disko will now be aimed at the top staying chases in the next season, a course of action which certainly seems the best one to adopt. He has earned his chance in top open company.

Gigginstown House Stud's "Disko"

		Linamix (gr 1987)	Mendez
Disko (FR) (gr.g. 2011)	Martaline (gr 1999)		Lunadix
		Coraline (b 1994)	Sadler's Wells
			Bahamian
	Nikos Royale (FR) (b 1999)	Nikos (b or br 1981)	Nonoalco
			No No Nanette
		Rodara (b 1979)	D'Arras
			Rosenpappel

Disko's dam Nikos Royale, a daughter of a middle-distance winner in Rodara, was placed on both her starts over hurdles at Pau when trained by Phillipe Boisgontier but, after a short career at stud, died after giving birth to Disko. She is the dam of two other winners, Mylena du Luy (by Marathon) who won three times in the French Provinces, including in a two and a half mile chase, and Valse du Luy (by Valanour) who won seven times over jumps at up to the same distance. Disko is by one of the leading jumping sires in France, Martaline, one of three pattern-winning sons out of the Juddmonte mare Coraline. The two others, Martaline's brother Reefscape and his half-brother Coastal Path (the sire of Bacardys), have also sired at least one Grade 1 winner over jumps, Reefscape producing few foals due to fertility problems. Martaline stands at a fee of €15,000, but his first crop, bred off a fee of just €3,500, included the 2014 Ryanair winner Dynaste and the Spa Novices' Hurdle winner Very Wood (who ran for the same connections as Disko). Other noteworthy offspring currently in training include Relkeel Hurdle winner Agrapart and Thyestes Chase runner-up Ucello Conti. Martaline has also had two Grade 1-winning fillies in France in Kotkikova and Chimere du Berlais. Disko, who wears a hood, stays twenty-five furlongs and acts on soft going (the going was good to soft when he put up his best performance in the Champion Novices' Chase). *Noel Meade, Ireland*

DISPOUR (IRE) 7 ch.g. Monsun (GER) – Dalataya (IRE) (Sadler's Wells (USA)) **h130**
[2016/17 h–: h16d* h16.8g² h20g⁵ Jun 4] good-topped gelding: useful handicap hurdler:
won at Warwick in May: career-best second at Newton Abbot (conditional, neck behind
Bonobo) just 2 days later: stays 2½m: acts on soft going: has worn blinkers: wears tongue
tie: front runner/races prominently. *Dan Skelton*

DISPUTED (IRE) 7 b.g. Westerner – Pearly Princess (IRE) (Definite Article) [2016/17 **h122**
h124: h17.7d h16.3g² h19.1s⁴ h17.7s³ h20.5d³ h17.7s³ h19.1v³ h16.8s⁴ h19.5v² h16dᵖᵘ
Mar 11] short-backed gelding: fairly useful handicap hurdler: consistent in 2016/17 with
numerous placed efforts: stayed 21f: acted on good to firm and heavy going: usually wore
hood: raced in rear: dead. *Chris Gordon*

DISTANT HIGH 6 b.m. High Chaparral (IRE) – Distant Dreamer (USA) (Rahy (USA)) **h77**
[2016/17 h15.8g h16d h15.8s h16.2s Jan 4] fair on Flat, stays 1¼m: poor form over
hurdles: tried in cheekpieces. *Richard Price*

DISTANT RAIN (IRE) 7 b.g. Robin des Champs (FR) – Lala Nova (IRE) (Zaffaran **c106**
(USA)) [2016/17 h99: h15.8d² h15.3d c16.1d² c16.4d² Dec 2] modest maiden hurdler: fair **h97**
form over fences: unproven beyond 2m: acts on heavy going: tried in tongue tie: usually
races prominently. *Henry Oliver*

DISTANT SOUND (IRE) 10 b.g. Luso – Distant Dreams (IRE) (Saddlers' Hall (IRE)) **h86**
[2016/17 h82: h19.2g* h19.6g³ h25g² h18.7m⁶ h22gᶠ h21.6g⁵ h21.6m h21.6s³ h23.1s³
h23.9g² h23.9g⁴ h19gᶠ h19.2s³ h16.5m Apr 20] dual winning pointer: modest handicap
hurdler: won at Towcester (amateur) in May: left Grace Harris after thirteenth start: stays
3m: acts on heavy going: wears headgear. *Richard Hawker*

DISTIME (IRE) 11 b.g. Flemensfirth (USA) – Technohead (IRE) (Distinctly North **c96**
(USA)) [2016/17 c127, h–: c20s³ c21.1gᵘʳ Apr 6] workmanlike gelding: winning hurdler: **h–**
fairly useful chaser, below best completed start in 2016/17: stays 25f: acts on heavy going.
Mrs A. J. Loder

DISTRACTED (IRE) 9 b.m. Publisher (USA) – Richmond Usa (IRE) (Insan (USA)) **c105**
[2016/17 c106, h–: c26.1sᵖᵘ c24.1g⁶ c24.1d⁵ c23.6vᵖᵘ Mar 23] point winner: once-raced **h–**
hurdler: fair handicap chaser: left Robert Stephens after third start: stays 27f: acts on heavy
going: wears headgear. *R. Thomas*

DISTRICT ATTORNEY (IRE) 8 b.g. Lawman (FR) – Mood Indigo (IRE) (Indian **c–**
Ridge) [2016/17 c–, h83: h16.8g⁵ h23.3g May 24] maiden hurdler/chaser: stays 2½m: acts **h58**
on good to firm going. *Chris Fairhurst*

DISTURB 5 ch.g. Halling (USA) – Ataraxy (Zamindar (USA)) [2016/17 b82: b16.2d² **b73**
b16d Mar 21] poor form in bumpers. *Andrew Crook*

DITES RIEN (IRE) 5 b.m. Kalanisi (IRE) – Our Soiree (IRE) (Milan) [2016/17 b16.2s **h91**
h15.3s⁴ h18.5s⁵ h19g h20.6g³ h21.6g³ Apr 12] first foal: dam (h94), maiden hurdler (stayed **b–**
3m), half-sister to useful hurdler/smart chaser (best up to 2½m) Watson Lake: tailed off in
mares bumper: modest form over hurdles: best effort at 21f: best form on good going.
Neil Mulholland

DITTO PROSECCO 9 b.m. Grape Tree Road – Bobbie Dee (Blakeney) [2016/17 **h–**
h18.5m⁵ Apr 18] half-sister to 3 winners, including fair hurdler Voir Dire (2m winner, by
Vettori): dam maiden (stayed 1¼m on Flat, little form over hurdles): maiden pointer: 20/1,
fifth in maiden at Exeter on hurdling debut. *Polly Gundry*

DIVA RECONCE (FR) 4 b.f. Kap Rock (FR) – Kruscyna (FR) (Ultimately Lucky (IRE)) **b94**
[2016/17 b16v* Feb 24] £22,000 3-y-o: third foal: half-sister to fairly useful French 17f
hurdle winner Chacun Pour Soi (by Policy Maker): dam French 15f-2¼m hurdle/chase
winner: 11/4, won mares bumper at Warwick (by 7 lengths from Turn Turk) in February.
Kim Bailey

DIVIN BERE (FR) 4 b.g. Della Francesca (USA) – Mofa Bere (FR) (Saumarez) [2016/17 **h142**
h14.9s² h15.8s* h16.4g² h17g² Apr 6] good-topped gelding: brother to French 17f hurdle
winner Audacieux Bere: fair maiden on Flat, stays 9f: useful form over hurdles: won
juvenile at Huntingdon in January: second in Anniversary Hurdle at Aintree (1¼ lengths
behind Defi du Seuil) in April: left S. Culin after first start: raced around 2m: acts on soft
going. *Nicky Henderson*

DIVINE INTAVENTION (IRE) 13 b.g. Exit To Nowhere (USA) – Merrill Gaye (IRE) **c–**
(Roselier (FR)) [2016/17 c110: c26.3g Apr 27] tall gelding: prolific winning pointer: fairly
useful chaser at one time, well held in hunter very early in season: stays 25f: acts on good
to firm and heavy going. *Miss Francesca Moller*

DIVINE PORT (USA) 7 b.g. Arch (USA) – Out of Reach (Warning) [2016/17 h113: **h–**
h19.7g May 4] fair hurdler, well held only start in 2016/17: stays 2½m: best form on heavy
going: tried in tongue tie. *Alan Swinbank*

DIVINE SPEAR (IRE) 6 b.g. Oscar (IRE) – Testaway (IRE) (Commanche Run) [2016/17 **h127**
h119, b103: h17.7s* h16.8s³ h19.3s² h21g² h20.3g⁵ Apr 19] strong gelding: chasing type:
bumper winner: fairly useful handicap hurdler: won at Fontwell in December: stays 21f:
acts on heavy going: front runner/races prominently. *Nicky Henderson*

DIZZEY HEIGHTS (IRE) 5 b.m. Halling (USA) – Extreme Pleasure (IRE) (High **h86**
Chaparral (IRE)) [2016/17 h16s⁵ h16.8m⁴ Apr 15] fair maiden on Flat, stays 1¼m: modest
form over hurdles. *Stuart Kittow*

DJAKADAM (FR) 8 b.g. Saint des Saints (FR) – Rainbow Crest (FR) (Baryshnikov **c169**
(AUS)) [2016/17 c175, h–: c25d² c20d* c24d³ c26.3g⁴ c24.5d² Apr 26] **h–**

'If at first you don't succeed, try try again' was clearly the motto of The
Fellow's connections when it came to the Cheltenham Gold Cup—though,
admittedly, they might have pronounced it 'Si d'abord vous ne réussissez pas,
essayez à nouveau' instead! The Fellow was one of a trio of top-class chasers
known as the three musketeers (Ubu III and Ucello II were the two others) owned
by the Marquesa de Moratalla and trained by Francois Doumen who announced his
retirement in August 2017 after a fine career as a dual-purpose trainer, best known
in Britain and Ireland for his association with top jumpers such as The Fellow,
Baracouda, First Gold, Nupsala, Kasbah Bliss (a Group 1 winner on the Flat) and
others. The three musketeers dominated French jumping during the early-'nineties.
The Fellow became a familiar name to British racegoers due to his exploits in the
King George VI Chase (a race his trainer won five times) and Cheltenham Gold Cup.
Kempton quickly proved a happy hunting ground for him, with successive wins in
the Boxing Day showpiece in 1991 and 1992, but The Fellow's association with
Cheltenham's blue riband event was initially a frustrating one. A short head was the
margin of defeat when he finished runner-up in both 1991 (to Garrison Savannah)
and 1992 (to Cool Ground) before coming a disappointing fourth behind Jodami in
1993 when sent off 5/4 favourite in a field of sixteen. Punters had rather lost faith
in The Fellow by the time of the 1994 renewal, with his odds drifting to 7/1 on the
day, but he finally got his head in front with a length and a half victory over hot
favourite Jodami—in the process becoming only the second horse, after 1973 winner
The Dikler, to win the Cheltenham Gold Cup at the fourth attempt.

All of which must offer some solace to the connections of Djakadam, who
finds himself with an identical record to The Fellow at the same stage of his career.
Djakadam has also reached the age of eight with two Cheltenham Gold Cup second
places to his name, whilst he too was sent off favourite on his third tilt at the race
when he managed only fourth. In truth, Djakadam's three and a half lengths fourth
to Sizing John at Cheltenham in March was a more respectable showing than
The Fellow's display in the 1993 renewal, particularly as a blunder at the second
last (when in front) proved especially costly at the business end of a fairly muddling
race. Indeed, Djakadam's short-head defeat by Sizing John in the Punchestown
Gold Cup (his third successive second in that race!) on his only subsequent outing
is arguably a truer reflection of the two horses' merits, the fact that Djakadam might
even have edged the verdict but for another late mistake (this time at the last) further
emphasising that there is very little between the pair. Similar comments apply to
Djakadam and the Punchestown third Coneygree, who came out on top (by a length
and a half) when the pair met in the 2015 Cheltenham Gold Cup. Coneygree might
also have finished closer at Punchestown but for a late mistake of his own. With
the outstanding 2016 Cheltenham Gold Cup winner Don Cossack now retired due
to injury, it is fair to say things are pretty tight at the top among the established
staying chasers—a view also borne out by the bunched finish to the Lexus Chase at
Leopardstown in December, when Djakadam finished a close third behind Outlander
after being shuffled back at a vital stage. In common with The Fellow, Djakadam
may not be his connections' very best horse but he still appeals as probably their
most reliable option for the next Cheltenham Gold Cup—with the likes of Douvan
and Min, for example, having ended 2016/17 under an injury cloud (both have been

John Durkan Memorial Punchestown Chase, Punchestown—a second successive win in the race for Djakadam who holds off the Gigginstown-owned pair Outlander (No.4) and Sub Lieutenant

campaigned over much shorter trips to date in any case), and the tragic demise of Vautour having also robbed them of another top contender. Djakadam is a 16/1 chance, at the time of writing, in the ante-post betting for the Gold Cup, but only 10/1 (and as low as 7/1 in places) for the 2018 Ryanair Chase, which is clearly another option, particularly as Djakadam's only victories in the past two seasons have come in the John Durkan Memorial Punchestown Chase over two and a half miles. His second Punchestown Chase win in December came at the chief expense of the Gigginstown pair Outlander and Sub Lieutenant, with Djakadam beating the latter by further than Un de Sceaux did when winning the Ryanair Chase later in the season. Although Djakadam clearly has the speed for Grade 1 races at around two and a half miles, stamina doubts (mooted in some circles) should not influence any change to his Cheltenham Festival target. He saw the trip out really well at the end of strongly-run races in the Gold Cup both 2015 and 2016, and the fact that the strong-staying pair Minella Rocco and Native River relegated him to fourth late on in the latest renewal probably owed more to that aforementioned blunder at the second last than anything else.

Djakadam (FR) (b.g. 2009)	Saint des Saints (FR) (b 1998)	Cadoudal (br 1979)	Green Dancer
			Come To Sea
		Chamisene (b 1980)	Pharly
			Tuneria
	Rainbow Crest (FR) (b 1999)	Baryshnikov (gr 1991)	Kenmare
			Lady Giselle
		Rainbow Rainbow (b 1986)	Vision
			Ivory North

Djakadam's pedigree has been discussed thoroughly in previous editions of *Chasers & Hurdlers*. To recap, he is the fourth foal of maiden French hurdler Rainbow Crest and one of five winners she has produced to date, the latest being Djakadam's half-brother Nikodam (by Sholokhov), who won a seventeen-furlong juvenile hurdle at Toulouse for Arnaud Chaille-Chaille in April. Djakadam's half-sister Arkaline (by Martaline), who is also trained by Chaille-Chaille, is now a winner over fences as well as hurdles, showing fairly useful form when successful at Auteuil. Djakadam's year-younger brother Sambremont drew a blank for Mullins in what was a largely disappointing 2016/17 campaign—though it's worth noting that Sambremont's best recent effort came when runner-up over a testing three and a half miles, which lends some support to the strongly stated view about Djakadam's stamina. Rainbow Crest has since produced a 2014 sister (named Belladame) and a 2016 brother (Jalkadam) to Djakadam, and it would be no surprise to see either or both on Irish soil once their racing careers get under way.

Although a French-bred, Djakadam actually takes far more after The Dikler (a recruit from the Irish pointing ranks) than The Fellow in physical terms, being a strong, imposing individual who tends to travel very strongly. The Dikler also had clumsy tendencies early in his career (he fell when tackling the Gold Cup, as a novice, for the first time in 1970), but was essentially a good jumper, which certainly applies to Djakadam despite those late errors behind Sizing John on his last two starts and the fact that he has fallen twice at Cheltenham, in the 2014 Golden Miller Novices' and the 2016 Cotswold Chase. That said, Djakadam hasn't even reached halfway on his Gold Cup journey if he is to emulate The Dikler, who contested the race seven times, recording three placed efforts to go along with his win. Although he acts on heavy going, Djakadam doesn't need testing conditions (the going for his first Gold Cup appearance was good to soft and for his two subsequent ones it was good). He wore ear plugs on his latest Gold Cup appearance. *W. P. Mullins, Ireland*

DJARKALIN (FR) 5 b.g. Martaline – Djarissime (FR) (Dadarissime (FR)) [2016/17 **h107** b82p: h18.5g² h15.9g² h15.8v² h16s³ h15.8m² Apr 18] fair form over hurdles: unproven beyond 2m: acts on good to firm and heavy going: often races prominently/travels strongly: has joined Michael Roberts. *Dan Skelton*

DLTRIPLESEVEN (IRE) 4 gr.g. Dark Angel (IRE) – Namu (Mujahid (USA)) [2016/17 **h80** h19.8d Dec 13] fair on Flat, stays 17f: 66/1, seventh in maiden at Wincanton on hurdling debut. *Richard Hughes*

D'NAILOR (IRE) 7 b.g. Stowaway – Lanesboro Lights (IRE) (Millfontaine) [2016/17 **c97** h21m h20v h16d³ h16.5m h20g h19.9d c20v² c24.2vᵖᵘ c20.2sᵖᵘ c21.2g* c23.6g⁴ Apr 17] **h92** €22,000 3-y-o: half-brother to winning hurdler/fair chaser Wrapitup (winner up to 2¾m, by Aristocracy) and modest/unreliable 2½m hurdle winner Rushin' Russian (by Moscow Society): dam unraced: modest maiden hurdler: similar form over fences: won handicap at Fakenham in March: left L. J. Archdeacon after fifth start: stays 21f: acts on heavy going: has worn cheekpieces, including last 3 starts. *Jennie Candlish*

DOASUWOULDBEDONEBY (IRE) 6 b.g. Robin des Champs (FR) – Sarah Princess **h–** (IRE) (Presenting) [2016/17 h–, b–: h19.8dᵖᵘ Mar 26] no form in bumper/maiden hurdles. *David Arbuthnot*

DOCALI (IRE) 5 b.g. Dark Angel (IRE) – Housekeeping (Dansili) [2016/17 h16.2mᵘʳ **h–** h15.6g h15.6g⁶ h15.7g Jan 12] fair maiden on Flat, stays 1m: no form over hurdles. *Hugh Burns*

DOCTOR BRAVEHEART (IRE) 8 b.g. Dr Massini (IRE) – Letimavit (IRE) (Supreme **c98** Leader) [2016/17 c26g² c23.6m⁶ Apr 28] multiple point winner: modest form over fences: wears headgear. *David Brace*

DOCTOR HARPER (IRE) 9 b.g. Presenting – Supreme Dreamer (IRE) (Supreme **c140** Leader) [2016/17 c142p, h–: c21.3mᵖᵘ c27.3s c26.3s² c29.2sᵖᵘ c26g c34.3dᵖᵘ Apr 8] good- **h–** topped gelding: winning hurdler: useful handicap chaser: second at Cheltenham (short head behind Tour des Champs) in January: stays 3¼m: acts on heavy going: in headgear/ tongue tie last 2 starts: usually races towards rear. *David Pipe*

DOCTOR KEHOE 5 b.g. Cockney Rebel (IRE) – Ogre (USA) (Tale of The Cat (USA)) **h–** [2016/17 h15.8v Nov 21] modest on Flat, stays 1¾m: tailed off in maiden on hurdling debut (tongue tied). *Tim Vaughan*

DOCTOR LOOK HERE (IRE) 7 b.g. Dr Massini (IRE) – Eye Vision (IRE) (Taipan **h110** (IRE)) [2016/17 h114: h20d h21d⁶ h23.3v h21.4s⁴ h23.5s h26s* h24.3d Apr 21] good- topped gelding: fair handicap hurdler: won at Warwick in March: stays 3¼m: best form on soft/heavy going. *Susan Gardner*

DOCTOR PHOENIX (IRE) 9 br.g. Dr Massini (IRE) – Lowroad Cross (IRE) (Anshan) **c138** [2016/17 c137, h–: c15.2s² c15.7sᵖᵘ c15.2s² c19.4s⁴ c15.7d⁴ Feb 18] Irish maiden point **h–** winner: winning hurdler: useful handicap chaser: beaten at Wetherby in November (2¾ lengths behind Aye Well) and December (¾ length behind Yorkist): stays 21f: best form on soft/heavy going: tried in cheekpieces: often in tongue tie. *David Dennis*

DOCTOR THEA 4 b.f. Multiplex – Kallithea (IRE) (Dr Fong (USA)) [2016/17 b16d⁵ **b73** b16.7gᵖᵘ Mar 27] fifth foal: dam 10.7f-1½m winner: poor form in bumpers. *Jedd O'Keeffe*

DODDINGTON DI 5 b.g. Sulamani (IRE) – Maxilla (IRE) (Lahib (USA)) [2016/17 **b–**
b15.8d b16g Aug 21] no form in bumpers. *Tracey Barfoot-Saunt*

DODGING BULLETS 9 b.g. Dubawi (IRE) – Nova Cyngi (USA) (Kris S (USA)) **c155 d**
[2016/17 c157+, h–: c17.5m³ c21dᵖᵘ c19.9d⁴ c16.3s⁴ c16.4d³ c16.3gᵖᵘ Mar 17] lengthy, **h–**
useful-looking gelding: winning hurdler: top-class chaser at best (won 2015 Queen Mother
Champion Chase): third in Haldon Gold Cup at Exeter (11 lengths behind Sir Valentino) in
November: not in same form after: best around 2m: acted on good to firm and heavy going:
in cheekpieces last 2 starts: wore tongue tie: has been retired. *Paul Nicholls*

DODGYBINGO (IRE) 4 b.g. Roderic O'Connor (IRE) – Happy Flight (IRE) (Titus **h108**
Livius (FR)) [2016/17 h16d⁴ h16g* h16s² h16g⁴ h16.4g Mar 15] rather leggy gelding: fair
on Flat, stays 1¼m: fair over hurdles: won juvenile maiden at Down Royal in August:
raced only at 2m: acts on soft going: wears blinkers: front runner/races prominently, often
travels strongly. *Noel Meade, Ireland*

DOES IT IN STYLE (FR) 4 b.g. Balko (FR) – Malta de Ronceray (FR) (Dress Parade) **h–**
[2016/17 h15.7gᶠ h15.6g⁴ h15.8s h15.8d Feb 22] no form over hurdles. *Dan Skelton*

DOESLESSTHANME (IRE) 13 ch.g. Definite Article – Damemill (IRE) (Danehill **c91**
(USA)) [2016/17 c15.9s³ c21m⁴ Apr 2] sturdy gelding: winning hurdler: modest hunter **h–**
chaser nowadays: stays 2½m: acts on good to firm and heavy going: wears headgear/
tongue tie. *Mike Hammond*

DOESN'TBOTHERME (IRE) 6 b.m. Brian Boru – Nicky's Gun (IRE) (Needle Gun **h–**
(IRE)) [2016/17 h19.9m⁵ Apr 19] £6,500 5-y-o: fifth foal: half-brother to a winning pointer
by Publisher: dam once-raced half-sister to fairly useful hurdler/fair chaser (2½m-2¾m
winner) Ashgan: maiden pointer: well beaten in novice on hurdling debut. *Victor Thompson*

DOESYOURDOGBITE (IRE) 5 b.g. Notnowcato – Gilah (IRE) (Saddlers' Hall (IRE)) **h133**
[2016/17 h20.6g* h19.7s* h21g* h21d⁶ h19.3s h20.3g h24.7g Apr 8] compact gelding:
half-brother to useful hurdler/fairly useful chaser Ainama (2m-3m winner, by Desert
Prince) and fairly useful hurdler/fair chaser Dark And Dangerous (2m/17f winner, by
Cacique): fairly useful on Flat, stays 13.5f: useful hurdler: completed hat-trick in novices
at Market Rasen in October and Hereford in November, and handicap at Kempton (by 2
lengths from Spiritofthegames) in December: stays 21f: acts on soft going. *Jonjo O'Neill*

DOING FINE (IRE) 9 b.g. Presenting – Howaya Pet (IRE) (Montelimar (USA)) **c136**
[2016/17 c130, h–p: c25g⁵ h27g² c28.8d² c25.1d² c28.1g* c28.8g⁵ Apr 29] deep-girthed **h123**
gelding: fair useful form over hurdles: useful handicap chaser: won at Cheltenham in
April: left Rebecca Curtis after first start: stays 29f: acts on heavy going: wears headgear/
tongue tie: usually races in rear. *Neil Mulholland*

DOITFORJOE (IRE) 7 ch.g. Vinnie Roe (IRE) – Native Kin (IRE) (Be My Native **h116**
(USA)) [2016/17 h16g² h23g² h24g* h24m⁴ h19.8m² h25.5g⁴ h25g⁶ Apr 24] half-brother
to useful chaser Smiles For Miles (2¾m-3m winner, by Oscar) and fair but ungenuine
chaser The Big Boyo (2½m winner, by Luso), stayed 3m: dam (h101), 2m hurdle winner,
half-sister to fairly useful hurdler/chaser (stayed 2¾m) Kickham and fairly useful chaser
(stayed 2½m) Knocknagow Leader: Irish point winner: fairly useful hurdler: won maiden
at Southwell in August: stays 3m: acts on good to firm going: wears tongue tie. *David
Dennis*

DOITFORTHEVILLAGE (IRE) 8 b.g. Turtle Island (IRE) – Last Chance Lady (IRE) **c133**
(Mister Lord (USA)) [2016/17 c108, h105: c20d* c20sᵘʳ c16g* c16d⁵ c16v* c19.2s* c20v³ **h–**
c16.4g² c15.8gᶠ c16.2g* Apr 24] angular gelding: maiden hurdler: useful handicap chaser:
won at Warwick in May, Lingfield in December and January, Market Rasen in February
and again at Warwick (by length from Abidjan) in April: effective from 2m to 2½m on
heavy going: has worn hood, including in 2016/17: wears tongue tie. *Paul Henderson*

DOKTOR GLAZ (FR) 7 b.g. Mount Nelson – Deviolina (IRE) (Dr Devious (IRE)) **c103 p**
[2016/17 c98p, h96: h25d³ h19.7d* c20.9d³ h23.9g⁴ Apr 26] fair handicap hurdler: won **h103**
novice event at Wetherby in March: fair form over fences: stays 3m: acts on soft going:
should do better over fences. *Rose Dobbin*

DOLATULO (FR) 10 ch.g. Le Fou (IRE) – La Perspective (FR) (Beyssac (FR)) [2016/17 **c126**
c141, h–: c23.4v² c24s c23.8s* c26.3g Mar 17] close-coupled gelding: winning hurdler: **h–**
fairly useful hunter chaser: won at Ffos Las in February: stays 3¼m: acts on heavy going:
wears headgear: has worn tongue tie. *Ben Pauling*

DOLLNAMIX (FR) 6 b.g. Al Namix (FR) – Sleeping Doll (FR) (Sleeping Car (FR)) **b–**
[2016/17 b16s b16g Mar 18] sturdy gelding: no form in bumpers. *Harry Fry*

Fulke Walwyn Kim Muir Challenge Cup Amateur Riders' Handicap Chase, Cheltenham—outsider Domesday Book (left) rallies under a strong ride by Gina Andrews to overhaul top weight Pendra

DOLLY'S DOT (IRE) 6 b.m. Vertical Speed (FR) – Our Dot (IRE) (Supreme Leader) [2016/17 b16.2m h19.9g⁴ h19.3g Apr 15] £5,500 5-y-o: second foal: half-sister to a winning pointer by Craigsteel: dam, unraced, out of half-sister to dual Whitbread Gold Cup winner Topsham Bay: placed all 3 completed starts in points: tailed off in mares bumper: poor form over hurdles. *Victor Thompson* **h62 b—**

DOLORES DELIGHTFUL (FR) 7 b.m. Saint des Saints (FR) – Us Et Coutumes (FR) (Shining Steel) [2016/17 c117, h126: h23g³ h23.6g² h24.5g⁴ h21v⁴ Feb 11] strong mare: useful handicap hurdler: second at Chepstow (length behind Tobefair) in December: fairly useful form over fences: stays 3m: acts on heavy going: wears tongue tie: often races towards rear. *Nick Williams* **c— h130**

DOLOS (FR) 4 b.g. Kapgarde (FR) – Redowa (FR) (Trempolino (USA)) [2016/17 h14.9s³ h16g* h17.9s³ h16s³ h19g³ h16.4g h15.7m² h16g* h16g² Apr 29] good-topped gelding: second foal: half-brother to winning French hurdler/useful chaser Chahuteur (17f-2¾m winner, by Saint des Saints): dam, French hurdler/chaser (2m/21f winner), half-sister to useful chaser (2½m/21f winner) Casse Tete, out of half-sister to outstanding 2m chaser Azertyuiop: useful hurdler: won juvenile in October and novice in April, both at Chepstow: third in Prix Cambaceres at Auteuil (18 lengths behind De Bon Coeur) in November and second in juvenile handicap at Sandown (3¾ lengths behind Call Me Lord) in April: left Guillaume Macaire after first start: probably stays 19f: acts on soft going: wears tongue tie: often travels strongly. *Paul Nicholls* **h134**

DOMESDAY BOOK (USA) 7 br.g. Street Cry (IRE) – Film Script (Unfuwain (USA)) [2016/17 c136, h—: c21s⁴ c23g⁵ c24d⁶ c19.5v c20.2s³ c26g* Mar 16] workmanlike gelding: winning hurdler: useful handicap chaser: won Fulke Walwyn Kim Muir Chase at Cheltenham (by ¾ length from Pendra) in March: left Henry de Bromhead after fourth start: stays 3¼m: acts on heavy going: wears headgear: usually races close up. *Stuart Edmunds* **c139 h—**

DOMINADA (IRE) 5 b.g. Mastercraftsman (IRE) – Red Blossom (USA) (Silver Hawk (USA)) [2016/17 h104: h17.1d* h15.8m* h15.5g³ h19.4g* h15.6g² h16.8g h19.7m³ h21.4g⁵ Apr 22] useful handicap hurdler: won at Carlisle (conditional) and Ludlow in October, and Musselburgh in January: second in listed event at Musselburgh (5 lengths behind Diego du Charmil) in February: stays easy 21f: acts on good to firm and good to soft going: front runner/races prominently. *Brian Ellison* **h130**

DOMPERIGNON DU LYS (FR) 4 b.g. Great Pretender (IRE) – Milie (FR) (Ut*Useful **h129**
(FR)) [2016/17 b13.4g* h16.4s* h16.8d⁴ h16.7s* h16.4g h15.7m Apr 2] good-topped **b–**
gelding: sixth foal: half-brother to 2 winners in France by Saint des Saints, including
2¼m/19f chase winner Une Sainte du Lys: dam French bumper winner around 1½m: won
bumper at Les Sables-d'Olonne in August for J-L. Guillochon: fairly useful form over
hurdles: won juveniles at Newcastle in November and Market Rasen in February: raced
around 2m: acts on soft going: usually races towards rear. *Nicky Henderson*

DOMTALINE (FR) 10 gr.g. Martaline – Domna Noune (FR) (Dom Pasquini (FR)) **c119**
[2016/17 c122, h120: c19m³ h19.9g⁵ h16m c16g² c16.7g⁴ c17g* h16.7g⁴ c17.1m⁴ c15.2m³ **h100**
c17.1s³ c16.4d³ c19.1g² c20.2m⁵ c15.7g⁴ h16g⁵ Apr 23] good-topped gelding: fair handicap
hurdler: fairly useful handicap chaser: won at Stratford in September: stays 2½m: acts on
good to firm and heavy going. *Peter Winks*

DONAPOLLO 9 b.g. Kayf Tara – Star of Wonder (FR) (The Wonder (FR)) [2016/17 c98, **c94 §**
h–: c23.8d⁵ c23.9gᵖᵘ c23.8d³ c23.4sᵖᵘ c23.8g³ Dec 14] workmanlike gelding: maiden **h–**
hurdler: modest handicap chaser: stays 3m: acts on soft and good to firm going: has
worn cheekpieces: wears tongue tie: front runner/races prominently: temperamental.
Rose Dobbin

DON BERSY (FR) 4 b.g. Califet (FR) – Tropulka God (FR) (Tropular) [2016/17 h16.9s² **h133**
h16sᶠ h16s* h16s* h15.7d* h18.8g³ Mar 25] good-topped gelding: half-brother to several
winners, including fairly useful hurdler Prince de Bersy (19f-2¾m winner, by Useful): dam
French 17f hurdle winner on only start: useful form over hurdles: completed hat-trick with
wins in juveniles at Sandown, Warwick and Haydock in January/February: left G. Cherel
after first start. *Tom Symonds*

DONE A RUNNER (IRE) 11 b.g. Alderbrook – Last Wager (IRE) (Strong Gale) **c77**
[2016/17 c–: c21.2m⁵ May 30] multiple point winner: lightly-raced maiden hunter chaser:
in tongue tie last 2 starts. *D. Peters*

DON FRANCO (IRE) 7 b.g. Oratorio (IRE) – Handora (IRE) (Hernando (FR)) [2016/17 **c55**
c16.4g³ c15.6g Apr 25] winning hurdler: poor form over fences: stays 2½m: acts on heavy **h–**
going: has worn headgear: tried in tongue tie: usually races nearer last than first. *Stuart
Crawford, Ireland*

DONNACHIES GIRL (IRE) 4 b.f. Manduro (GER) – Russian Society (Darshaan) **b84**
[2016/17 b16d³ b16.8d³ b17g Apr 6] £7,000 3-y-o: sturdy filly: half-sister to 3 winners on
Flat, including useful 1m-1½m winner Petrovsky (by Daylami): dam, useful 1¼m winner,
half-sister to useful 2m hurdle winner Buckwheat (by Manduro): modest form in bumpers.
Alistair Whillans

DONNA'S DELIGHT (IRE) 6 b.g. Portrait Gallery (IRE) – Hot Lips (IRE) (Good **b96**
Thyne (USA)) [2016/17 b–: b16d² b16s* b16g Apr 22] fairly useful form in bumpers: won
at Ayr in January: will be suited by 2½m. *Sandy Thomson*

DONNA'S DIAMOND (IRE) 8 gr.g. Cloudings (IRE) – Inish Bofin (IRE) (Glacial **c–**
Storm (USA)) [2016/17 h129: c24.2gᵘʳ h22.8v⁴ Nov 19] fairly useful handicap hurdler: **h126**
fourth in Betfair Exchange "Fixed Brush" Handicap Hurdle at Haydock in November:
unseated rider third on chasing debut: stays 3¼m: acts on heavy going: front runner/races
prominently. *Chris Grant*

DONNA'S PRIDE 8 b.m. Beat All (USA) – Pennys Pride (IRE) (Pips Pride) [2016/17 **h94**
h100: h17.2d² h20.2g⁶ h15.8g² h15.8d² h19.9d⁴ h15.6g³ h16.4d² h19.3d⁵ Dec 13] modest
handicap hurdler: stays 2½m: acts on heavy going: usually races towards rear. *Keith Reveley*

DON PADEJA 7 br.g. Dansili – La Leuze (IRE) (Caerleon (USA)) [2016/17 h117: h16d* **h124**
h16.5d² h17dᵖᵘ Aug 19] fairly useful handicap hurdler: won at Warwick in May: unproven
beyond 2m: acts on good to firm and good to soft going: tried in cheekpieces: wears tongue
tie: often races towards rear/travels strongly. *Fergal O'Brien*

DON POLI (IRE) 8 b.g. Poliglote – Dalamine (FR) (Sillery (USA)) [2016/17 c170, h–: **c163**
c25d³ c24gᵖᵘ c24d² c24.3s³ Feb 12] strong gelding: winning hurdler: top-class chaser: **h–**
second in Lexus Chase in December (2¼ lengths behind Outlander) and third in Irish Gold
Cup in February (1½ lengths behind Sizing John), both at Leopardstown: left W. P. Mullins
after first start: will stay beyond 3¼m: acts on heavy going: has worn cheekpieces. *Gordon
Elliott, Ireland*

DON SEBASTIAN (IRE) 6 b.g. High Chaparral (IRE) – Quick Thinking (IRE) (Daylami **h89**
(IRE)) [2016/17 h20.3v h21.3s⁴ h19.9s⁵ h20.3g Mar 28] €29,000 3-y-o, £4,500 5-y-o: third
foal: half-brother to 2 winners on Flat in Italy by Holy Roman Emperor: dam unraced:
maiden Irish pointer: modest form over hurdles: tried in tongue tie. *David Thompson*

DON'T ACT UP 6 gr.g. Act One – Lucky Arrow (Indian Ridge) [2016/17 h16.3g Apr 1] **h–**
Irish maiden point winner: 8/1, seventh in novice at Stratford on hurdling debut.
Ian Williams

DON'T ASK (IRE) 4 b.g. Ask – Outback Ivy (IRE) (Bob Back (USA)) [2016/17 b15.8g⁵ **b69 p**
Apr 9] €35,000 3-y-o: fourth foal: half-brother to 1¾m bumper winner Glen Forsa (by
Mahler): dam (h85), maiden hurdler, half-sister to fairly useful staying chasers Native King
and Native Ivy: 3/1, needed experience when fifth in bumper at Ffos Las (18¼ lengths
behind Espoir de Teillee) in April: should improve. *Warren Greatrex*

DON'T BE HASTY (IRE) 6 b.g. Dubai Destination (USA) – Barrack Buster (Bigstone **h–**
(IRE)) [2016/17 h16g h16g h24s h20.5sᵖᵘ Jan 2] modest form on hurdling debut for David
Harry Kelly: disappointing all 4 starts in 2016/17: tried in tongue tie. *Miss Nicole
McKenna, Ireland*

DONT BE SHORT (IRE) 6 b.g. Darsi (FR) – Radcliff Star (IRE) (Alphabatim (USA)) **h–**
[2016/17 h19.5dᵖᵘ h23.1vᵖᵘ Dec 15] placed in Irish maiden points: pulled up both starts
over hurdles: tried in cheekpieces. *Jess Westwood*

DONT DO MONDAYS (IRE) 10 b.g. Rashar (USA) – Bit of A Chance (Lord Ha Ha) **c90**
[2016/17 c131, h–: c25.8g⁶ c20s³ Feb 20] winning hurdler: fairly useful chaser at best: won **h–**
point in April: left David Bridgwater after first start: stays 23f: acts on heavy going: wears
headgear: front runner/races prominently. *N. A. Pearce*

DON'TDROPMEIN (IRE) 7 b.g. Stowaway – Real Tempest (IRE) (Phardante (FR)) **c–**
[2016/17 c–, h103, b97: h20.3gᶠ May 24] workmanlike gelding: fair form over hurdles: **h–**
pulled up only start over fences: tried in cheekpieces: dead. *Neil Mulholland*

DONT EVEN GO THERE (IRE) 6 b.g. Brian Boru – Foreal (IRE) (Bigstone (IRE)) **h87**
[2016/17 b16.8s b15.3v⁵ h21.6m³ Apr 18] €6,700 3-y-o: fifth foal: dam 2m hurdle winner: **b–**
no form in bumpers: 12/1, third in novice at Exeter (8½ lengths behind Rouge Devils) on
hurdling debut: wears tongue tie. *Nicky Martin*

DON'T HANG ABOUT 12 ch.g. Alflora (IRE) – Althrey Flame (IRE) (Torus) [2016/17 **c92**
c101, h–: c26.1d² c24.1gᵖᵘ Apr 22] maiden hurdler: modest chaser nowadays: stays 3¼m: **h–**
acts on good to firm and good to soft going: tried in cheekpieces: often races towards rear/
travels strongly. *Gary Hanmer*

DONTMINDDBOYS (IRE) 8 gr.g. Portrait Gallery (IRE) – Native Ocean (IRE) (Be **c100**
My Native (USA)) [2016/17 h17.1d⁴ c16.1d c21.7d² c24v³ c24.2s³ c29.6sᵖᵘ c29.2vᵖᵘ Mar **h85**
22] tall gelding: modest maiden hurdler: fair form over fences: should stay long distances:
acts on heavy going: usually in tongue tie. *Robin Dickin*

DONT TELL CHRIS (FR) 5 b.g. Lawman (FR) – Enigma (GER) (Sharp Victor (USA)) **h–**
[2016/17 h18.6sᵖᵘ Dec 1] modest maiden on Flat, stays 9f: pulled up in novice on hurdling
debut. *Tim Easterby*

DONTTELLTHEMISSIS (IRE) 6 b.m. Flemensfirth (USA) – Blue Gale (IRE) (Be **b73**
My Native (USA)) [2016/17 b85p: b15.8d b16.7g² Jul 31] poor form in bumpers.
Gary Hanmer

DONT TELL VAL 5 b.m. Midnight Legend – Tentsmuir (Arctic Lord) [2016/17 b15.8d **h73 p**
b17.7d⁴ b15.7s⁴ h20.7g³ Apr 28] seventh foal: half-sister to useful hurdler/chaser Thomas **b92**
Brown (2¼m-3m winner, by Sir Harry Lewis) and a winning pointer by Alflora: dam,
bumper winner, sister to useful hurdler/fair chaser (stayed 3m) Tisrabraq: fair form in
bumpers: won mares event at Fontwell in October: 20/1, third in mares novice at
Huntingdon (39 lengths behind La Bague Au Roi) on hurdling debut: left Jennifer Mason
after first start: should stay at least 2½m: in tongue tie last 2 starts: should do better. *Fergal
O'Brien*

DON'T TOUCH IT (IRE) 7 b.g. Scorpion (IRE) – Shandora (IRE) (Supreme Leader) **c152**
[2016/17 h152, b96: h16d* c20d³ c19d³ c16.2s* c17s² c16.7d² c16d* Apr 27] bumper **h–**
winner: smart form over hurdles: similar form over fences: won maiden at Thurles (by 3
lengths from Dicosimo) in February and handicap at Punchestown (by ½ length from
Caolaneoin) in April: stays 19f: acts on heavy going: tried in cheekpieces: often races
prominently, usually travels strongly. *Mrs J. Harrington, Ireland*

DOODLE DANDY (IRE) 4 b.f. Starspangledbanner (AUS) – Grid Lock (IRE) (Van **b–**
Nistelrooy (USA)) [2016/17 b16v Feb 25] first foal: dam unraced half-sister to useful 2m
hurdle winner Altilhar: fair maiden on Flat, best effort at 1m: tailed off in maiden bumper.
Robin Mathew

DOOLIN 5 b.g. Rainbow High – Rabbit (Muhtarram (USA)) [2016/17 b15.7m³ h19.3d **h–** h21g Mar 18] £3,000 3-y-o, £20,000 4-y-o: compact gelding: third foal: dam (h95) **b85** temperamental 2½m-2¾m hurdle winner: runner-up in Irish maiden point: third in bumper at Ascot (3 lengths behind Coup de Pinceau) in October: well held both starts over hurdles: tried in tongue tie. *Charlie Mann*

DORMELLO MO (FR) 7 b.g. Conillon (GER) – Neogel (USA) (Theatrical) [2016/17 **c–** c144, h–: c20g h20dᵘʳ c21.4g Jul 16] useful-looking gelding: has had breathing operation: **h–** useful hurdler: useful handicap chaser, well below best in 2016/17: barely stays 21f: acts on good to firm and heavy going: wears tongue tie: often races prominently. *Paul Nicholls*

DORMOUSE 12 b.g. Medicean – Black Fighter (USA) (Secretariat (USA)) [2016/17 **h105** h113: h18.6g⁵ h15.5g h15.9v⁴ h15.5g h16.7sᵖᵘ Feb 10] compact gelding: fair handicap hurdler: stays 19f: acts on good to firm and heavy going: wears cheekpieces: tried in tongue tie: usually races towards rear. *Anabel K. Murphy*

DOTHRAKI RAIDER 6 b.g. Kayf Tara – French Spice (Cadeaux Genereux) [2016/17 **h96** b72: h16.3g h16g h16g h16.2g⁶ h20g* h20.3s³ h21.6m³ Apr 15] workmanlike gelding: modest hurdler: won handicap at Fakenham in October: stays 2¾m: acts on good to firm going: has worn hood: usually wears tongue tie: usually races towards rear: has awkward head carriage. *Sophie Leech*

DOUBLE ACCORD 7 ch.m. Double Trigger (IRE) – Got Tune (FR) (Green Tune **h98** (USA)) [2016/17 h99: h20.1g³ h21g³ h20m² Aug 30] fair handicap hurdler: stays 3m: acts on good to firm going: in tongue tie last 4 starts: often races prominently. *Anthony Honeyball*

DOUBLE BANK (IRE) 14 b.g. Double Trigger (IRE) – Misty Silks (Scottish Reel) **c113** [2016/17 c117, h–: c26.3gᵖᵘ c25.1m* Apr 5] strong gelding: multiple point winner: maiden **h–** hurdler: fair hunter chaser: won at Wincanton in April: stays 3¼m: acts on good to firm and heavy going. *Mrs Emma Oliver*

DOUBLE CHOCOLATE 14 b.g. Doubletour (USA) – Matching Green (Green Ruby **c98** (USA)) [2016/17 c92, h–: c24d* c25.5g c25.8dᵖᵘ c23.6gᵖᵘ Apr 3] maiden hurdler: modest **h–** handicap chaser: won at Warwick in May: stays 3½m: acts on soft and good to firm going: wears headgear: front runner/races prominently. *Martin Keighley*

DOUBLE COURT (IRE) 6 b.g. Court Cave (IRE) – Miss Top (IRE) (Tremblant) **h88** [2016/17 h64x: h21.4m⁶ h19.9m⁶ h15.8g h20g² h22g² h23m² h21.6m* h20.2s² h24g³ h19.9s⁶ h20.7sᵖᵘ h23.9g Apr 26] modest handicap hurdler: won at Newton Abbot in August: stays 3m: acts on good to firm and heavy going: has worn headgear, including in 2016/17. *Nigel Twiston-Davies*

DOUBLEDISDOUBLEDAT (IRE) 10 ch.g. Vinnie Roe (IRE) – Castle Graigue (IRE) **c99** (Aylesfield) [2016/17 c100, h–: c24.2d⁴ c20.1s⁵ c26.2s⁵ c23.9s³ c21.6dᵘʳ Apr 10] **h–** workmanlike gelding: maiden hurdler: modest handicap chaser: should be suited by 3m+: acts on good to soft going: usually races close up. *Stuart Coltherd*

DOUBLE MISS 6 b.m. Double Trigger (IRE) – Ladyalder (Alderbrook) [2016/17 b–: **h97** h23.3dᵖᵘ h21.6g³ May 25] modest form in novice hurdles: tried in visor. *Robert Stephens*

DOUBLE ROSS (IRE) 11 ch.g. Double Eclipse (IRE) – Kinross (Nearly A Hand) **c148** [2016/17 c150, h–: c23.6g* c25g⁵ c26g³ Nov 26] strong gelding: winning hurdler: smart **h–** handicap chaser: won at Chepstow (by ¾ length from Loose Chips) in October: third in Hennessy Gold Cup at Newbury (5½ lengths behind Native River) in November: stays 3¼m: acts on heavy going: tried in cheekpieces: has worn tongue tie: front runner/races prominently. *Nigel Twiston-Davies*

DOUBLE SHUFFLE (IRE) 7 b.g. Milan – Fiddlers Bar (IRE) (Un Desperado (FR)) **c152** [2016/17 c138, h–: c19.4g² c20.4sᵖᵘ c19.9g⁵ c24g* c24g² c34.3dᵖᵘ Apr 8] lengthy, useful- **h–** looking gelding: winning hurdler: smart handicap chaser: won at Kempton (by 3½ lengths from Go Conquer) in December: second in BetBright Chase there (½ length behind Pilgrims Bay) in February: stays 3m: acts on soft going: in hood last 3 starts: usually races prominently, often travels strongly. *Tom George*

DOUBLE SILVER 10 gr.m. Silver Patriarch (IRE) – Shadows of Silver (Carwhite) **c105** [2016/17 c116, h114: c23.9g³ c24m⁵ Jun 9] tall, lengthy, good-topped mare: fair hurdler: **h–** fair handicap chaser: stays 3m: acts on good to firm and good to soft going: usually races in rear. *Fergal O'Brien*

DOUBLE STORM 7 b.m. Double Trigger (IRE) – Storm Kitten (IRE) (Catrail (USA)) **h–** [2016/17 b–: b16.8g² b16g³ h20.5v⁵ Jan 16] lengthy mare: poor form in bumpers: tailed off **b67** in maiden on hurdling debut. *John Gallagher*

DOUBLETOILNTROUBLE (IRE) 11 b.g. Hubbly Bubbly (USA) – Boolindrum **c– §**
Lady (IRE) (Meneval (USA)) [2016/17 c19.2g^pu Apr 11] compact gelding: long-standing **h–**
maiden pointer: maiden hurdler: one-time modest chaser for Fergal O'Brien, pulled up in
hunter on sole start under Rules since 2014/15: stays 3½m: acts on heavy going: wears
headgear/tongue tie: temperamental. *Mrs D. J. Treneer*

DOUBLE TREASURE 6 b.g. King's Theatre (IRE) – Double Red (IRE) (Thatching) **c121**
[2016/17 h–, b–: h15.3m² h16.8m² h16.8s⁶ c16.5d² c20.3s c15.7s⁵ c19.4g* Apr 8] sturdy **h101**
gelding: fair form over hurdles: fairly useful form over fences: won handicap at Chepstow
in April: stays 19f: acts on good to firm and good to soft going: tried in hood: wears tongue
tie: often races in rear. *Jamie Snowden*

DOUBLE WHAMMY 11 b.g. Systematic – Honor Rouge (IRE) (Highest Honor (FR)) **c114**
[2016/17 c133, h–: c24.3v⁵ c26.2s⁶ c26.2d⁵ c30.6g Apr 28] leggy gelding: maiden hurdler: **h–**
useful handicap chaser, below best in 2016/17: stays 31f: acts on good to firm and heavy
going: wears headgear: races well off pace. *Iain Jardine*

DOUBLE W'S (IRE) 7 ch.g. Fruits of Love (USA) – Zaffre (IRE) (Mtoto) [2016/17 **c145**
h118: h20.1s² c15.9d* c15.2g* c16.4g c16.4d² c20.4g c15.8g* c15.5g^pu Apr 22] tall **h122**
gelding: fairly useful handicap hurdler: smart handicap chaser: won at Carlisle (by 5
lengths from The Herds Garden) and Wetherby (by 1¼ lengths from Fou Et Sage) in
October, and Red Rum Handicap Chase at Aintree (by length from Theinval) in April: best
around 2m: acts on soft going. *Malcolm Jefferson*

DOUBLY CLEVER (IRE) 5 ch.g. Iffraaj – Smartest (IRE) (Exceed And Excel (AUS)) **h119**
[2016/17 h130: h15.8g³ h16.7g h16.6g h16.8g h18.5s³ h17.7v⁵ h16.3v⁴ h19.9s⁴ Mar 18]
workmanlike gelding: fairly useful handicap hurdler: third at Uttoxeter in June: unproven
beyond 17f: acts on soft going: has worn hood: tried in tongue tie: often races towards rear.
Michael Blake

DOUNYA'S BOY 8 ch.g. Sakhee (USA) – Dounya (USA) (Caro) [2016/17 h–: h16.7g **h–**
Jul 3] maiden pointer: no form in hurdles: used to wear blinkers: dead. *Tim Vaughan*

Betway Red Rum Handicap Chase, Aintree—
novices dominate as Double W's (left) edges out Theinval (centre) and Bun Doran

DOUVAN (FR) 7 b.g. Walk In The Park (IRE) – Star Face (FR) (Saint des Saints **c182**
(FR)) [2016/17 c180p, h–: c16d* c17s* c17d* c16s* c15.9g Mar 15] **h–**

'Things don't always go your way, you've just got to accept it and move on.'
Good advice, of course, but it must have been hard for owner Rich Ricci to maintain
his equilibrium as the fates seemed to conspire against him in the latest season.
London-based couple Rich and Susannah Ricci (in whose name the horses run) said
they had more than sixty in training in the latest season (forty saw the racecourse).
'You're not going to make money at it, the best you can hope for is to cover training
costs out of prize money.' Like all the major owners, the Riccis need the big pay days
to sustain their operation, which involves vast expenditure on purchasing the horses
as well as footing the training bills. The patronage of the Riccis—former banker
Rich Ricci is now executive chairman of Dublin-based bookmakers BetBright—has
been very important in putting the County Carlow stable of Willie Mullins into a
dominant position over the past decade. The formidable owner/trainer combination
has picked up races at the Cheltenham Festival on a regular basis, particularly in
recent years, and the owners had a record-equalling five winners there in 2016,
Douvan in the Arkle, Annie Power in the Champion Hurdle (standing in for injured
Faugheen who had won the previous year's edition in the same colours), Vroum
Vroum Mag in the David Nicholson Mares' Hurdle, Vautour in the Ryanair Chase
and Limini in the Dawn Run Novices' Hurdle.

Douvan, Vautour and Faugheen had all won at the Festival at least once
before and, along with Annie Power, headed a formidable Ricci/Mullins team of
established stars at the start of the latest season. The first of them to fall by the
wayside was the estimable Vautour, a winner at the Cheltenham Festival three
years in a row, his victories in the Supreme Novices' Hurdle and the Golden Miller
Novices' Chase every bit as scintillating as his Ryanair triumph. Vautour seemed
to have earned a tilt at the 2017 Cheltenham Gold Cup (a race he had been widely
expected to contest until his late switch to the Ryanair) and Rich Ricci seemed to
have plans to chase the 'Classic Triple Crown' and its million-pound bonus, with
Vautour also tackling the Betfair Chase and the King George VI Chase. Such grand
plans were shattered, however, in early-November when Vautour had to be put down
after fracturing a foreleg in a freak accident in his paddock at Closutton.

After looking set fair to start their 2016/17 campaigns in November by
dividing up the Morgiana Hurdle at Punchestown and the Hatton's Grace at
Fairyhouse between them, Faugheen and Annie Power ended up not running at all
during the season. Faugheen was eventually billed to make a belated reappearance
in the Irish Champion Hurdle at Leopardstown at the end of January, a race he had
won the previous year by fifteen lengths and thirteen lengths from stablemates Arctic
Fire and Nichols Canyon (their latest Cheltenham Festival performances—winning
under top weight in the County Hurdle and taking the Stayers' Hurdle—highlighted
the loss to the Champion Hurdle field of Faugheen). A knee ligament injury sustained
by Annie Power at the end of January ruled her out of defending the Champion
Hurdle crown but Faugheen, who missed the Irish Champion after being found to
be 'wrong behind', was still expected to run (going straight to Cheltenham without
a preparatory race). Faugheen's season effectively came to an end, though, when
he suffered a stress fracture in early-February, around the same time as a cannon
bone injury ruled out the Ricci-owned Min, an exciting recruit to novice chasing
who was being aimed at the Arkle. Not long afterwards, the Ricci/Mullins ante-
post favourite for the Champion Bumper, Getabird, joined the injury list too with a
damaged sesamoid bone in a hind leg.

Although Annie Power didn't run at Cheltenham, she was expected to
recover in time for a swansong at the Punchestown Festival after she was tested
in foal to the dual Derby winner Camelot. Unfortunately, Annie Power was
eventually ruled out of Punchestown and a possible tilt at the Grande Course de
Haies at Auteuil and her retirement was confirmed. Annie Power had not raced since
following up her Champion Hurdle success (in record time) with a runaway victory
in the Aintree Hurdle, in which she recorded the best performance by a mare over
hurdles since the days of Dawn Run. Annie Power won fifteen of her seventeen
races, including some bloodless victories in races restricted to her own sex. Two of

her five Grade 1 wins were achieved in open company and her Champion Hurdle victory will be remembered as the defining moment of her career. However, the strength in depth in her own stable meant that Annie Power would never have run in that race but for Faugheen's being forced out through injury less than a month beforehand (Annie Power had to be supplemented). Her two other Cheltenham Festival appearances—also moulded to a large extent around plans for some of her illustrious stablemates—accounted for the only defeats on her record, when she went down in a memorable battle with More of That in the 2014 World (now Stayers') Hurdle and when she fell at the final flight with the 2015 David Nicholson Mares' Hurdle at her mercy, a fall that saved the bookmakers tens of millions of pounds in multiple bet liabilities after the Mullins stable had already won three races earlier on the card, with hot favourites Douvan, Un de Sceaux (not owned by the Riccis) and Faugheen. Annie Power never ran over fences but a switch to steeplechasing looked a possibility at one time and she was quoted in ante-post lists at the start of the 2014/15 season for no fewer than six Cheltenham Festival races, ranging from the Champion Hurdle to the Gold Cup (that was the year Annie Power contested the David Nicholson having not been seen since Punchestown the previous May after suffering a series of niggling training problems).

The Ricci horses won a staggering £771,779 at the 2016 Cheltenham Festival but the figure was down to £133,901 at the latest renewal when Let's Dance was their only winner, in the Dawn Run Mares' Novices' Hurdle. Seventy-one entries were initially made at the Festival for the big Ricci team and, even in the enforced absence of such as Faugheen, Annie Power, Min and Getabird, the Riccis still looked to have a good hand, with Djakadam a strong fancy for the Cheltenham Gold Cup, a race in which he had been second twice (he came fourth in the latest edition). Vroum Vroum Mag and Limini gave the Riccis two outstanding candidates for the David Nicholson—they finished second and third—and Let's Dance always looked like starting a short-priced favourite for the Dawn Run if connections chose that race for her; Bapaume had sound each-way prospects (finished third) in the Triumph Hurdle; Royal Caviar had place prospects (finished fourth) against Altior in the Arkle; and there were several carrying the pink, light green spots, pink sleeves and cap in the meeting's valuable handicaps, though none of them reached the frame.

The Ricci 'banker', though, was Douvan, the best chaser in training who was sent off at 9/2-on in the Queen Mother Champion Chase to extend his winning sequence to fourteen since joining the Mullins yard from France in the summer of 2014 (Douvan won the second of his two starts in France before moving to Mullins). In his first season at Closutton, Douvan won the Supreme Novices' Hurdle—his owners' third successive win in the race—and then followed in the hoof prints of Faugheen by winning the Champion Novices' Hurdle at Punchestown to make it four out of four in Britain and Ireland in his novice hurdling campaign. In three of those four races, incidentally, Sizing John was among Douvan's closest pursuers, Douvan having him twelve lengths back in second on his debut in a novice hurdle at Gowran (after which Sizing John won the Grade 1 Future Champions Novices' at Leopardstown's Christmas meeting); Sizing John was beaten seven lengths into third behind Douvan in the Supreme and seven and a half lengths when runner-up to him at Punchestown. The paths of Douvan and Sizing John crossed again when both were sent chasing in 2015/16 when Douvan started at odds on for all his races, including 4/1-on when winning the Arkle at Cheltenham, 13/2-on when taking the Maghull at Aintree and 9/2-on when completing a rarely-achieved spring festival treble in the Ryanair Novices' Chase at Punchestown (the last-named, for technical reasons, shown in the form figures for the 2016/17 season at the start of his essay). Douvan and Sizing John were meeting for the third time over fences in the Ryanair Novices', in which Sizing John was beaten twenty-two lengths into third (Douvan beat him eighteen lengths into second in the Racing Post Novices' Chase at Leopardstown's Christmas meeting and seven lengths into second in the Arkle at Cheltenham).

Connections spent the summer break mulling over whether to aim Douvan at the Queen Mother Champion Chase (which has been sponsored by Betway since 2015) or to step him up in trip with a view to going for the Cheltenham Gold Cup

Paddy Power Cashcard Chase, Leopardstown—
another imperious display from the best chaser in training ...

(Willie Mullins had won neither of those championship races before). The Mullins stable is renowned for taking its time before finalising its plans and the trainer himself would not be drawn, saying 'It makes no sense to talk about long-term targets so early in the season.' When Douvan eventually reappeared in December, it was over the shorter trip in the Kerry Group Hilly Way Chase at Cork, following uncertainty over whether Douvan might run in the Tingle Creek Chase the previous week (in the end, Un de Sceaux represented Closutton at Sandown but not before the usual guessing game had been played out, with Douvan's ante-post odds fluctuating from 4/1 at one time with some bookmakers to a general 7/4-on four days before the race when Un de Sceaux was available at around 11/4). With Ruby Walsh at Punchestown on the same day for Djakadam in the Grade 1 John Durkan Memorial Punchestown Chase, Paul Townend enjoyed an armchair ride on Douvan at Cork where he went on to ride a four-timer on the afternoon. Townend, who had ridden Douvan twice before, barely had to move a muscle as Douvan, travelling strongly all the way and jumping well, cruised clear from the fourth last to win by twenty-two lengths from the veteran Days Hotel, a regular in the race over the years and the only horse to win it in the last decade (back in 2012/13) that has not been trained by Willie Mullins.

Next on the agenda for Douvan was the traditional Grade 1 for the two-milers at Leopardstown's Christmas meeting, run nowadays as the Paddy Power Cashcard Chase. That race was also chosen for the reappearance of Sizing John, running for the first time for eight months, having changed stables in the interim, moving from Henry de Bromhead to Jessica Harrington. Sizing John filled the runner-up spot again behind the impeccable Douvan who won with plenty in hand by eight lengths, with British challenger Simply Ned (runner-up in 2015) finishing seven lengths behind Sizing John in third. Douvan's connections finally confirmed at Leopardstown—when Willie Mullins saddled five winners on the day (including four at Leopardstown)—that Douvan was 'unlikely' to be stepped up in trip over the rest of the season (Sizing John *was* campaigned over longer distances afterwards and went on to land a unique treble, the Irish Gold Cup, the Cheltenham Gold Cup and the Punchestown Gold Cup, presumably giving Douvan's connections plenty of food for thought). Douvan was warmed up for Cheltenham with another effortless domestic victory, sent off at 14/1-on against just three opponents in the Boylesports Tied Cottage Chase at Punchestown in February when he won hard held by six and a half lengths from Realt Mor. The bare form of the Tied Cottage Chase illustrates Ruby Walsh's style of riding on Closutton's top performers which is designed to preserve them for the bigger tasks ahead. The average distance by which Douvan has won the nine races in which he has been partnered by Walsh is just over eight lengths; the equivalent on the four outings on which Townend or Mr Patrick Mullins have deputised is sixteen and a half.

Douvan looked sure to add a third Cheltenham Festival victory to his collection and he started the shortest-priced favourite for the Queen Mother Champion Chase (or Two-Mile Champion Chase as it was then known) since Flyingbolt ran away with the race by fifteen lengths at 5/1-on in 1966, before finishing a creditable third, despite a bad mistake four out, in the following day's Champion Hurdle. Sprinter Sacre had started at 4/1-on when winning his first Queen Mother Champion Chase and he was second favourite to Douvan in the ante-post lists for the latest edition until a training injury forced his retirement in November before either he or Douvan had been seen out. Un de Sceaux, the third favourite in those early-season lists, was eventually switched to the Ryanair Chase at the Cheltenham Festival where he had been beaten at odds on by a resurgent Sprinter Sacre in the Champion Chase twelve months earlier. Opposition to Douvan at the latest Festival included the previous year's third and fourth, Special Tiara (also third in 2015) and God's Own, and Fox Norton, third to Douvan and Sizing John in the previous year's Arkle and last seen in the Game Spirit at Newbury chasing home the outstanding novice Altior, whose connections declined a showdown with Douvan and took the conventional Arkle option at the Festival.

The Queen Mother Champion Chase was generally expected to resemble more of a coronation than a horse race, firmly establishing Douvan as the undisputed king of the jumpers as he showcased his invincibility. However, it became clear

... takes the score to Douvan seven, Sizing John (noseband) nil

fairly early on in the race that something was wrong with him. His golden run was virtually over before the home straight, after he had added another jumping mistake at the third last to a totally out-of-character sketchy round, which included dragging his back legs through the third, ballooning the fourth, and then getting in too close to the fifth before going 'long' again at the open ditch that is the eighth of the thirteen fences. Ruby Walsh tried to get a response out of Douvan between the last two fences but he was already beaten and trailed home in seventh, nearly a dozen lengths behind the winner Special Tiara. Walsh said afterwards that 'He was beaten a long way out, he didn't jump and he felt shit!' It was clearly not the real Douvan and he was subsequently found to have suffered a hairline stress fracture to his pelvis. The prognosis is for a full recovery and an autumn return to action, all being well. Douvan is 3/1 second favourite for the next Queen Mother Champion Chase, for which Altior heads the market at 2/1 at the time of writing. Those looking forward to that clash might ultimately be disappointed, as it must be on the cards that Douvan will be stepped up in trip, particularly after the success in the staying division of Sizing John, to whom Douvan is manifestly superior (he has beaten him on all seven occasions that they have met).

The tall, good-topped Douvan is bred to stay a good deal further than two miles. He is from the second crop of the giant Derby runner-up Walk In The Park (a son of stoutly-bred Montjeu) who was raced by the Coolmore partners and then reacquired from France to stand at Grange Stud in County Cork after the successes of some of those from his first few crops, particularly Douvan and Min, the last-named from Walk In The Park's small third crop which numbered just over two dozen. Walk In The Park's fourth crop was even smaller but breeders have been falling over themselves to use him since he came under the Coolmore National Hunt umbrella and he covered two hundred and twenty-two mares in 2016, the majority of them 'black type' performers themselves or already dams of high-class jumpers, or sisters or half-sisters to them. The dam of Douvan, Star Face, ran only once over hurdles, finishing tailed-off last of five finishers, and she was exported to Tunisia after making only €2,000 at the sales in 2012; she has since been repatriated and was returned to Walk In The Park in both 2015 (produced a colt foal) and 2016. Full details of Douvan's pedigree have appeared in the last two Annuals but it is worth repeating that Star Face is by the leading French jumping sire Saint des Saints (the sire of Djakadam) who is a strong influence for stamina.

Douvan is a strong traveller who has plenty of speed and he usually leads, but his trainer has said that 'he would have no problem stretching out in distance' and there seems a good prospect—especially with Djakadam having had three tries in the Gold Cup and come up short—that Douvan might even be aimed at the greatest of the Cheltenham Festival races, the blue riband of steeplechasing, although connections will no doubt also consider the Ryanair Chase over the intermediate distance (a race they eventually chose for ill-fated Vautour in preference to the Gold Cup in 2016). Much is likely to depend on the soundness and the form of the Mullins stable stars at the time. The Riccis like Ruby Walsh to ride their best horses which is part of the reason they rarely run against each other in the big championship races. Douvan acts on heavy going but he doesn't need the mud. His Gold Cup chances—were he to run in the race—would probably be enhanced, in fact, under less testing conditions (both his Festival wins have come on good going). Nothing can be taken for granted in jumping, as Douvan's latest campaign illustrates, but let's hope Douvan comes back fully recovered from his injury in the Queen Mother Champion Chase. He is usually an excellent jumper of fences and a sight to behold in full flight, his best form fully entitling him to be regarded as the top steeplechaser in training in the latest season. *W. P. Mullins, Ireland*

DOUX PRETENDER (FR) 4 b.g. Great Pretender (IRE) – Lynnka (FR) (Passing Sale **b95 p**
(FR)) [2016/17 b11.9d* b15.8d⁴ Mar 15] sixth foal: half-brother to 3 winners in France,
including fairly useful hurdler/chaser Valligarro (2¼m-21f winner, by Ballingarry): dam,
French 1½m-14.5f bumper winner, half-sister to fairly useful hurdler/useful chaser (stayed
3m) Urcalin: fairly useful form in bumpers: won at Nantes in October for F. Foucher:
remains capable of better. *Nicky Henderson*

DOVE CRAG 6 b.m. Josr Algarhoud (IRE) – More Flair (Alflora (IRE)) [2016/17 b16.2d **b–**
Jun 4] fourth foal: half-sister to useful hurdler Central Flame (19f/2½m winner, by Central
Park) and fairly useful hurdler/winning pointer Catchamat (2½m/2¾m winner, by
Overbury): dam winning pointer: tailed off in bumper. *James Walton*

DOVE MOUNTAIN (IRE) 6 b.g. Danehill Dancer (IRE) – Virginia Waters (USA) **h109**
(Kingmambo (USA)) [2016/17 h16g* h16g² h16g³ h16.2s* h16g³ h16.2g³ Aug 20] fair on
Flat, stays 1½m: fair form over hurdles: won maiden at Down Royal (awarded race) in May
and novice at Perth in July: raced only at 2m: acts on soft going: in cheekpieces last 3 starts:
wears tongue tie. *Gordon Elliott, Ireland*

DOVILS DATE 8 gr.g. Clodovil (IRE) – Lucky Date (IRE) (Halling (USA)) [2016/17 h–: **h125**
h18.5g⁶ h20d³ h16g h20.3g* h19.9g* h20g⁴ h20.6g³ h19.4g⁵ Nov 3] sturdy gelding: fairly
useful handicap hurdler: won at Southwell in August and Uttoxeter in September: stays
21f: acts on soft going. *Tim Vaughan*

DO WE LIKE HIM (IRE) 7 b.g. Beneficial – Pattern Queen (IRE) (Alderbrook) **c–**
[2016/17 h106: h19.1gᵖᵘ h23g h21.6g⁶ c19.7mᵖᵘ Sep 18] workmanlike gelding: fair **h– §**
hurdler, no form in 2016/17: pulled up in novice handicap on chasing debut: often wears
hood: temperamental. *Chris Gordon*

DOWN TIME (USA) 7 b.g. Harlan's Holiday (USA) – Frappay (USA) (Deputy Minister **c–**
(CAN)) [2016/17 c103, h97: c19.3g⁶ h20.6d⁴ h27g⁴ h23.3d³ h19.6m⁴ h19.9g⁶ **h86**
h23.8g⁵ h21.3d³ h27g² h24.1m⁶ h27m⁶ Apr 19] leggy gelding: modest handicap hurdler:
fair chaser: stays 3m: acts on good to soft going: usually wears headgear: has worn tongue
tie. *Brian Ellison*

DOWNTON FOX 9 b.g. Oscar (IRE) – Leinthall Fox (Deep Run) [2016/17 h23.1s⁶ Dec **h–**
22] well beaten in novice hurdle on belated debut: wore tongue tie. *John Needham*

DOWNTOWN BOY (IRE) 9 br.g. Kheleyf (USA) – Uptown (IRE) (Be My Guest **c78 §**
(USA)) [2016/17 h95§: c16.4g c16.4s³ c15.6vᵗᵗ c16.4dᵖᵘ Dec 26] maiden hurdler: poor **h– §**
form over fences: stays 2½m: acts on soft going: wears headgear: often races in rear: one
to treat with caution (refused to race penultimate start). *Ray Craggs*

DOWN UNDER (IRE) 10 b.g. Milan – She's All That (IRE) (Bob Back (USA)) [2016/17 **c131**
c25g² c25g* c25sᵖᵘ c25g² c25d⁵ c24dᵖᵘ Nov 27] winning hurdler: useful handicap chaser: **h–**
won at Kilbeggan in June: stays 25f: acts on heavy going: has worn cheekpieces. *F. Flood,
Ireland*

DRAGON DE LA TOUR (FR) 6 b.g. Royal Dragon (USA) – Turga de La Tour (FR) **h98**
(Turgeon (USA)) [2016/17 h74p: h16d⁴ h20.3s³ h15.7s⁴ h21.2m² Apr 25] modest maiden
hurdler: stays 21f: acts on good to firm and good to soft going: tried in cheekpieces.
Dan Skelton

DRAGONFLI 5 b.g. Revoque (IRE) – Chiddingfold Chick (Zaffaran (USA)) [2016/17 **h–**
b15.7pᵖᵘ b16.7g b17.1d⁴ h16.4s h16.8d Dec 26] no form in bumpers/over hurdles. *Lucinda* **b–**
Egerton

DRAGON KHAN (IRE) 8 b.g. Dr Fong (USA) – Desert Magic (IRE) (Green Desert **h93**
(USA)) [2016/17 h16.5g h16.2s h15.7s h15.5v h15.9s⁶ h15.8s³ Apr 1] modest handicap
hurdler: left C. Roche after first start: raced only at 2m: best form on soft/heavy going:
sometimes wears headgear: often wears tongue tie: usually races nearer last than first. *John
O'Shea*

DRAGON'S DEN (IRE) 10 b.g. Antonius Pius (USA) – Tallassee (Indian Ridge) **c–**
[2016/17 c126, h122: h18.5g⁵ h19.9g⁵ h20g⁶ h24g h25g³ Apr 24] compact gelding: fair **h106**
handicap hurdler: winning chaser: left Chris Down after third start: has form at 3m,
probably best at shorter: acts on good to firm and heavy going: tried in hood: often races in
rear. *Jackie du Plessis*

DRAGOON GUARD (IRE) 6 b.g. Jeremy (USA) – Elougos (IRE) (Dalakhani (IRE)) **h96**
[2016/17 h90: h17.7g³ h20d² h19.9g³ h20m⁶ h15.9s² h15.9v⁴ h25gᵘʳ h23.1g Apr 11]
neat gelding: modest maiden hurdler: stays 2½m: acts on soft going: wears tongue tie:
temperament under suspicion. *Anthony Honeyball*

287

DRAYCOTT PLACE (IRE) 8 b.g. Oscar (IRE) – Power Again (GER) (Dashing Blade) **c136**
[2016/17 c20d c17d⁴ c16m² c23m⁴ c21.5d⁵ h16s c18.2g² c19.9g³ c20.5d⁴ h19.5g² h16s² **h127**
c20sᵘʳ c17.4v* c17d* h16g c20d⁶ c17v³ c24d h16s³ c17s³ h16s³ c16s³ c18vᶠ c18v h16d⁴
c20d⁶ Apr 26] lengthy, workmanlike gelding: fairly useful handicap hurdler: useful
handicap chaser: won at Sligo in September and Cork in October: stays 3m, effective at
much shorter: acts on good to firm and heavy going: wears tongue tie: usually races close
up. *John Patrick Ryan, Ireland*

DRAYTONIAN (IRE) 7 br.g. King's Theatre (IRE) – Full of Birds (FR) (Epervier Bleu) **c–**
[2016/17 h130: h15.7d³ h18.9s⁴ c20.2sᶠ Jan 7] rangy gelding: fairly useful handicap **h121**
hurdler: should have stayed beyond 2m: acted on soft going: often raced towards rear:
dead. *Philip Hobbs*

DR BEAUJOLAIS (IRE) 11 b.g. Dr Massini (IRE) – Satlin (IRE) (Satco (FR)) [2016/17 **c97**
c95, h–: c23.4d² c24.2g⁶ h23.3dᵘʳ h22.1d Jun 26] maiden hurdler: modest form over fences: **h–**
stayed 3m: acted on good to firm and heavy going: tried in cheekpieces: dead. *Richard Ford*

DR DUNRAVEN 6 b.g. Dr Massini (IRE) – Bajan Girl (FR) (Emperor Jones (USA)) **c68**
[2016/17 h20g⁴ h20s h15.3d h15.3s⁶ c16dᵖᵘ c19.4g⁴ Apr 1] fifth foal: half-brother to fair **h101**
hurdler/winning pointer Bajan Blu (2½m winner, by Generous): dam (h81), 17f hurdle
winner, half-sister to high-class hurdler/very smart chaser (2m-2½m winner) Wahiba
Sands: fell in Irish point: fair form over hurdles: well held sole completed start over fences:
tried in cheekpieces: front runner/races prominently: has joined Martin Keighley.
Philip Hobbs

DREAM BERRY (FR) 6 gr.g. Dream Well (FR) – Kalberry (FR) (Kaldounevees (FR)) **c– p**
[2016/17 h121p: c20sᵖᵘ h16.8s⁶ h16.7s* h21g³ h20g² h20.5d² Apr 29] rather leggy gelding: **h144**
useful handicap hurdler: won at Market Rasen in February: second in Ballymore Handicap
Hurdle at Punchestown (½ length behind Open Eagle) in April: pulled up in novice
handicap on chasing debut: stays 21f: acts on soft going: wears tongue tie: often races
towards rear. *Jonjo O'Neill*

DREAM BOLT (IRE) 9 ch.g. Urban Ocean (FR) – Riviera Dream (IRE) (Over The **c120**
River (FR)) [2016/17 c113, h106: c16s* c15.5v² c15.5s⁶ c16s⁵ Mar 11] fair hurdler: fairly **h–**
useful handicap chaser: won at Chepstow in January: stays 21f: acts on heavy going.
David Rees

DREAMCATCHING (FR) 4 b.g. Al Namix (FR) – New Zealand (FR) (Smadoun (FR)) **h117**
[2016/17 b11.9s* b11.9d h17.9s³ h16g⁶ h15.3d* h16.4g h16.7m* h19.8f* Apr 23] well- **b?**
made gelding: third foal: half-brother to French bumper winners Vingt Mars (12.5f winner,
by Califet) and Amantani (11.5f-2m winner, by Le Balafre): dam French 1½m-13.5f
bumper winner: won maiden bumper at Vittel in July: fairly useful form over hurdles: won
novices at Wincanton in February, and Market Rasen and again at Wincanton in April: left
G. Cherel after third start: stays 2½m: acts on firm and good to soft going: often races
prominently/travels strongly. *Paul Nicholls*

DREAM FLYER (IRE) 10 ch.g. Moscow Society (USA) – Bright Choice (IRE) (The **c105**
Parson) [2016/17 c84, h–: c26.2d⁶ c23.9d³ c23.8g* c24.2sᵖᵘ c20dᵖᵘ c21.6vᵖᵘ Mar 4] **h–**
winning hurdler: fair handicap chaser: won at Musselburgh in January: left Michael Smith
after second start: stays 25f: acts on soft going: tried in headgear in 2016/17: has worn
tongue tie: front runner/races prominently. *Keith Dalgleish*

DREAMINGOFREVELRY 6 b.m. Kalanisi (IRE) – Clandestine (Saddlers' Hall (IRE)) **h–**
[2016/17 b66: h16.3m h20.3gᵖᵘ Jun 7] poor form in bumpers: no form over hurdles.
David Dennis

DREAMING THE DREAM 6 b.g. Septieme Ciel (USA) – Red Typhoon (Belfort (FR)) **b–**
[2016/17 b16s b15.6g Jan 3] no form in bumpers. *Jean McGregor*

DREAM ON CAROLINE (IRE) 8 gr.m. Medaaly – Bonne Aventure (FR) (Kaldoun **h–**
(FR)) [2016/17 h19.9gᵖᵘ h19.9gᵖᵘ h24gᵖᵘ Aug 31] fourth foal: dam ran twice on Flat in
France: no form over hurdles. *Michael Appleby*

DREAMSOFTHEATRE (IRE) 9 gr.g. King's Theatre (IRE) – Caroline Fontenail **c123**
(IRE) (Kaldounevees (FR)) [2016/17 c128, h–: c24.1d* c24.1g³ c25.5d³ c24.2m c24.2sᵘʳ **h–**
c20g c19.2v⁵ c20vᵖᵘ c24.2dᵖᵘ c24g⁶ Mar 18] workmanlike gelding: winning hurdler: fairly
useful handicap chaser: won at Bangor in May: stays 27f: acts on soft and good to firm
going: has worn cheekpieces: wears tongue tie: not straightforward. *Jonjo O'Neill*

DRESDEN (IRE) 9 b.g. Diamond Green (FR) – So Precious (IRE) (Batshoof) [2016/17 c146, h119: c19.4g c17.5m c16.9d⁴ h16.8g c19.4s² c20v² c19.9s⁶ c20.8g⁴ Apr 19] good-topped gelding: winning hurdler: useful handicap chaser: second at Wetherby (2¼ lengths behind Oldgrangewood) and Warwick (neck behind No Buts) in February: stays 2½m: acts on good to firm and heavy going. *Henry Oliver* — **c141 h–**

DREWMAIN LEGEND 5 b.m. Midnight Legend – Ryders Hill (Zaffaran (USA)) [2016/17 b16s h16.8d⁴ h16v⁶ h15.8g⁵ Apr 3] second foal: dam winning pointer: well beaten in bumper: poor form over hurdles. *Ali Stronge* — **h79 b–**

DREYFUS (IRE) 6 ch.g. Notnowcato – Trauquebise (FR) (Kaldounevees (FR)) [2016/17 b15.8m⁵ May 8] 9/2, fifth in maiden bumper at Ludlow (6½ lengths behind Armaans Wish) in May. *Paul Webber* — **b84**

DR HOOVES (IRE) 4 b.g. Yeats (IRE) – Sejour (IRE) (Bob Back (USA)) [2016/17 b17d⁵ Apr 5] €130,000 3-y-o: seventh foal: brother to bumper winner/fairly useful hurdler Mossback (2½m winner) and half-brother to bumper winner/smart hurdler Staying Article (2m winner, by Definite Article): dam unraced: 5/1, fifth in bumper at Carlisle in April: likely to improve. *Lucinda Russell* — **b72 p**

DRIFTASHORE (IRE) 10 b.g. Jackson's Drift (USA) – Your Cheatin Heart (IRE) (Broken Hearted) [2016/17 h125: h25d⁶ h23.9d h23.3d⁶ h20m² Aug 17] won 3 times in points: fair handicap hurdler: stays 2½m: acts on good to firm and soft going: sometimes in blinkers: often leads. *Sally Randell* — **h111**

DRIFTWOOD HAZE 9 b.g. Nomadic Way (USA) – Kristal Haze (Krisinsky (USA)) [2016/17 c–, h125: h23.9g³ h21.9s³ h24g h23.6s h21.4d² h21.4s⁵ h23.9g² Apr 9] angular gelding: winning pointer: fairly useful handicap hurdler: placed 4 times in 2016/17: maiden chaser: stays 3m: acts on heavy going: tried in blinkers. *Phillip Dando* — **c– h125**

DRIFTWOOD PRIDE (IRE) 9 b.g. Balmont (USA) – Olivia's Pride (IRE) (Digamist (USA)) [2016/17 c23g³ c22.6g³ Apr 23] winning pointer: modest form in hunter chases: wears blinkers. *Miss Jane Western* — **c94**

DRINKS FOR LOSERS (IRE) 6 b.g. Mastercraftsman (IRE) – Heart's Desire (IRE) (Royal Applause) [2016/17 h16.2gᶠ Sep 6] modest maiden on Flat, stays 1m: behind when fell last in novice on hurdling debut. *R. Mike Smith* — **h–**

DRINKS INTERVAL 5 b.m. King's Theatre (IRE) – Dame Fonteyn (Suave Dancer (USA)) [2016/17 b15.3s⁵ b16g³ Apr 17] sixth foal: closely related to fairly useful chaser The Cider Maker (3¼m winner, by Kayf Tara) and half-sister to 2 winners, including fair chaser Rateable Value (2¾m-25f winner, by Classic Cliche): dam (h84), maiden hurdler (stayed 2¾m), 1¾m winner on Flat, sister to fairly useful hurdler (stayed 3m) Dubai Seven Stars: modest form in bumpers. *Colin Tizzard* — **b84**

DRIVE ON LOCKY (IRE) 10 b.g. Milan – Husyans Beauty (IRE) (Husyan (USA)) [2016/17 h82: h21.6dᵖᵘ h25g* h21.4m⁵ h25s* h23.1sᵖᵘ h19g Feb 21] modest handicap hurdler: won at Plumpton in May and December: stays 25f: acts on soft going: has worn headgear, including in 2016/17: wears tongue tie. *Johnny Farrelly* — **h94**

DR MIKEY (IRE) 8 b.g. Dr Massini (IRE) – Nicola Marie (IRE) (Cardinal Flower) [2016/17 b16m b16.6g b19s⁴ b16g* b16s* b16g⁵ h16v² h16s* h16v⁵ Jan 14] half-brother to useful hurdler/smart chaser The Knoxs (2m-3m winner, by Close Conflict): dam (h91) bumper/2½m hurdle winner: fairly useful bumper performer: won at Cork in August and Tipperary in October: useful form over hurdles: won maiden at former course in December: tried in hood: usually leads. *Ms M. Flynn, Ireland* — **h133 b101**

DR MOLONEY (IRE) 10 b.g. Dr Massini (IRE) – Solal Queen (Homo Sapien) [2016/17 c114, h–: c19.5d⁵ c23.8d³ c23.8s³ c23.8g³ Aug 20] winning hurdler: fair maiden chaser: stays 3m: acts on good to firm and heavy going: has worn headgear, including last 2 starts: in tongue tie last 4 starts: often travels strongly but finishes weakly. *Stuart Crawford, Ireland* — **c110 h–**

DROMNEA (IRE) 10 b.g. Presenting – Fifth Imp (IRE) (Commanche Run) [2016/17 c134, h–: c25g⁴ c22.5s² c20d⁴ c24.5d Dec 27] big, strong gelding: winning hurdler: useful chaser: stays 2¾m: acts on heavy going: tried in tongue tie. *M. F. Morris, Ireland* — **c133 h–**

DROP A GEAR (IRE) 7 b.g. Presenting – Indian Love (FR) (Indian Danehill (IRE)) [2016/17 c–p, h94: h23.9d⁴ h22.1dᵖᵘ h23.9g⁵ Sep 5] placed in Irish maiden points: modest maiden hurdler: fell on chase debut: stays 21f: acts on good to soft going: tried in cheekpieces. *Lucinda Russell* — **c– h82**

DRO

DROP OUT JOE 9 ch.g. Generous (IRE) – La Feuillarde (FR) (Nikos) [2016/17 c143, h–: c26.1g* c34.3dᴾᵘ Apr 8] angular gelding: winning hurdler: smart handicap chaser: won Summer Cup at Uttoxeter (by 2 lengths from Ballynagour) in June: stays 3¼m: acts on soft and good to firm going: wears cheekpieces: tried in tongue tie: front runner/races prominently. *Charlie Longsdon* **c149 h–**

DROPS OF JUPITOR (IRE) 5 gr.m. Dylan Thomas (IRE) – Fancy Intense (Peintre Celebre (USA)) [2016/17 b16d b16v⁴ b15.6g* b17g Apr 6] tall, good-topped mare: closely related/half-sister to several winners on Flat, including 11f/1½m winner Refractor (by Refuse To Bend): dam ran twice on Flat in France: pulled up in point: fair form in bumpers: won at Musselburgh in January: left J. G. Cosgrave after third start: tried in hood. *Anthony Honeyball* **b89**

DROPZONE (USA) 8 b.g. Smart Strike (CAN) – Dalisay (IRE) (Sadler's Wells (USA)) [2016/17 c–, h81§: h16m h21.6g² h20gᴾᵘ h19.6mᴾᵘ h21.4m h19.5d² h18.5m² h19.1s³ h23.9m* h23.9g c23g h21.6g³ h23.9m⁴ Apr 27] sturdy gelding: poor handicap hurdler: won at Taunton in December: maiden chaser: stays 3m: acts on good to firm and good to soft going: wears headgear: tried in tongue tie: usually races nearer last than first: temperamental. *Brian Forsey* **c– h78 §**

DR ROBIN (IRE) 7 b.g. Robin des Pres (FR) – Inter Alia (IRE) (Dr Massini (IRE)) [2016/17 h117: c25g⁴ c23.6d³ c23.8v² c23.6sᴾᵘ c21.1s* c16s² c22.6sᴾᵘ Mar 13] fair hurdler: fairly useful handicap chaser: won at Sedgefield in February: stays 3m: acts on soft going: wears headgear: usually races prominently. *Peter Bowen* **c116 h–**

DRUID'S FOLLY (IRE) 7 b.g. Beneficial – Sweet Vale (IRE) (Supreme Leader) [2016/17 b98: h20.6g³ h21d* h16v³ h19.8v⁵ h20.2g² Apr 27] tall gelding: bumper winner: fairly useful form over hurdles: won novice at Towcester in November: stays 21f: acts on good to soft going: in tongue tie last 4 starts. *Fergal O'Brien* **h121**

DRUIDS LODGE 6 b.g. Tiger Hill (IRE) – Mimiteh (USA) (Maria's Mon (USA)) [2016/17 b91: h19.9g³ h20m⁴ h20.5gᴾᵘ Oct 31] modest form over hurdles: tried in cheekpieces: often raced prominently: dead. *Neil Mulholland* **h90**

DRUMACOO (IRE) 8 b.g. Oscar (IRE) – My Native (IRE) (Be My Native (USA)) [2016/17 c140, h–: c23.4dᵘʳ Dec 14] tall gelding, lightly raced: winning hurdler: smart form over fences: unseated sole start in 2016/17: stays 3m: acts on heavy going: in hood last 3 starts. *Ben Pauling* **c– h–**

DRUMCLIFF (IRE) 6 b.g. Presenting – Dusty Too (Terimon) [2016/17 h–p, b101: h16.7v⁶ h16.7s² h16g² h15.6g⁵ h21dᵇᵈ Apr 26] well-made gelding: bumper winner: fairly useful form over hurdles: second in novice at Bangor in November: raced mainly around 2m: acts on soft going: tried in tongue tie: usually races towards rear. *Harry Fry* **h124**

DRUMHART (IRE) 8 ch.g. Beneficial – Nancylu (IRE) (Luso) [2016/17 c99, h98: c18.5d* c20g⁴ c21.5d* c23.8d⁶ h18.2g c18.5g⁶ c20sᴾᵘ Sep 24] maiden hurdler: fair handicap chaser: won at Downpatrick in May and June: stays 21f: acts on good to firm and good to soft going: wears tongue tie: often races towards rear. *Colin A. McBratney, Ireland* **c112 h–**

DRUMLANG (IRE) 11 b.g. Soviet Star (USA) – Sherekiya (IRE) (Lycius (USA)) [2016/17 c–, h112: c21.2gꟳ c20.3g h19.9gᴾᵘ h16.7g c22.6g c20.1g⁴ c20g⁵ Sep 20] rather leggy gelding: fair hurdler/fairly useful chaser at one time, has lost way: stays 21f: acts on good to firm and good to soft going: has worn headgear, including in 2016/17: tried in tongue tie. *Kevin Frost* **c78 h–**

DRUMLEE CITY (IRE) 5 b.g. City Honours (USA) – Alentio (IRE) (Luso) [2016/17 b15.7v² b16s⁵ Mar 13] first foal: dam pulled up in points: third in Irish maiden point on debut: modest form in bumpers: better effort when second at Towcester in February. *Nick Mitchell* **b84**

DRUMLEE LAD (IRE) 7 b.g. Millenary – Rockport Rosa (IRE) (Roselier (FR)) [2016/17 h112: c19.3d* c19.1g² c21.2gꟳ Dec 18] fair hurdler: fairly useful form over fences: won novice handicap at Sedgefield in November: stayed 2½m: acted on heavy going: tried in blinkers: sometimes wore tongue tie: often raced in rear/travelled strongly: dead. *Johnny Farrelly* **c125 h–**

DRUMLEE SUNSET (IRE) 7 br.g. Royal Anthem (USA) – Be My Sunset (IRE) (Bob Back (USA)) [2016/17 h127: h16.8g* c19.2g* c19.1d² c19.2d⁷ c19.2d⁷ c20.5dᴾᵘ Apr 21] compact gelding: fairly useful hurdler: won novice at Exeter in October: useful form over fences: won novice at same course in November: stays 2½m: acts on soft going: often leads. *Philip Hobbs* **c136 h116**

DRUMLISTER (IRE) 11 b.g. Luso – Murrurundi (IRE) (Old Vic) [2016/17 c102, h–: c21.3g May 4] point winner: winning hurdler: fair chaser: stays 3m: acts on soft and good to firm going: in cheekpieces last 2 starts: has worn tongue tie, including sole 2016/17 start. *Dianne Sayer* **c–**
h–

DRUMMULLAGH ROCKY (IRE) 8 b.g. Pasternak – Wind Scarlet (IRE) (Distinctly North (USA)) [2016/17 h20.2s* h16.2g⁵ h16d h22sᵖᵘ Mar 17] fair form over hurdles: won maiden at Perth in July: sometimes in tongue tie. *Sean McParlan, Ireland* **h101**

DRUMSHAMBO (USA) 11 b.g. Dynaformer (USA) – Gossamer (USA) (Seattle Slew (USA)) [2016/17 c107§, h–: c24.1g³ Apr 29] good-topped gelding: winning hurdler: fair handicap chaser: stays 3m: acts on heavy going: has worn headgear: often races prominently: temperamental. *Venetia Williams* **c98 §**
h–

DRUMS OF WAR (IRE) 5 b.g. Youmzain (IRE) – Min Asl Wafi (IRE) (Octagonal (NZ)) [2016/17 b15.6g³ b16.4g⁴ Mar 24] half-brother to several winners on Flat, including 9f/1¼m winner Flawless Filly (by Clodovil): dam ran once on Flat: fair form in bumpers: better effort when third in maiden at Musselburgh in November. *Chris Grant* **b87**

DRUMVIREDY (IRE) 8 b.m. Flemensfirth (USA) – Leitrim Bridge (IRE) (Earl of Barking (IRE)) [2016/17 h104: h19.5d² c21.7d⁴ c19.2v⁴ c24.1s* c22.7s⁵ c25.2s⁶ h25.5dᵖᵘ Mar 26] sturdy mare: fair handicap hurdler: similar form over fences: won handicap at Bangor (conditional) in January: stays 3m: acts on heavy going: unreliable. *Venetia Williams* **c108 §**
h105 §

DR WALLACE (IRE) 6 ch.g. Flemensfirth (USA) – Oscars Princess (IRE) (Oscar (IRE)) [2016/17 b16d* Dec 10] sixth foal: brother to bumper winner/useful 17f-21f hurdle winner Backspin and half-brother to fair chaser Dundrum Lad (2½m winner, by Westerner): dam unraced: 9/10, won maiden bumper at Navan (by 3¾ lengths from Minella Fair) in December: useful prospect. *Ms Margaret Mullins, Ireland* **b106 p**

DR WEST (IRE) 6 b.g. Westerner – Contessa Messina (IRE) (Dr Massini (IRE)) [2016/17 b87: b16.4d⁶ h22s⁵ h20.5s³ h22.7v⁴ Jan 15] poor form in bumpers: fair form over hurdles: should stay 2¾m+. *George Bewley* **h100**
b69

DRY OL'PARTY 7 ch.m. Tobougg (IRE) – Emergence (FR) (Poliglote) [2016/17 h110: h18.5g⁵ h16mᵖ h19.9g h16.8g³ h16g² h16.8m h19gᵖ Sep 20] fair handicap hurdler: stays 2¼m: acts on soft going: in blinkers last 2 starts. *Philip Hobbs* **h103**

DUBAI ANGEL (IRE) 6 b.g. Dubai Destination (USA) – Just Another Penny (IRE) (Terimon) [2016/17 b88: b15.7g² b17.1d* h16.4s² h16.8d* h22s² h22v* Mar 18] useful form in bumpers: won at Carlisle (by 22 lengths from Al Shahir) in October: fairly useful form over hurdles: won novice at Sedgefield in December and novice handicap at Newcastle in March: front runner/races prominently, strong traveller. *Malcolm Jefferson* **h129**
b112

DUBAI CELEBRITY 5 b.g. Sakhee (USA) – Aljana (IRE) (Exceed And Excel (AUS)) [2016/17 h82pᵘ h16.4g² h20.6m³ Apr 9] modest form over hurdles: likely to prove best at short of 2½m: tried in cheekpieces: often races prominently. *Chris Grant* **h99**

DUBAI DEVILS (IRE) 6 b.g. Dubai Destination (USA) – Saddlers Leader (IRE) (Saddlers' Hall (IRE)) [2016/17 h103, b75: h20v⁶ h24s² h20.1v³ Mar 28] maiden pointer: fair maiden hurdler: stays 3m: raced only on soft/heavy going: tried in cheekpieces. *Paul Stafford, Ireland* **h108**

DUBAI DIRHAM 4 ch.f. Dubai Destination (USA) – Rolline (IRE) (Revoque (IRE)) [2016/17 b12.6d⁵ Dec 14] £600 3-y-o: rather unfurnished filly: first foal: dam, (h89) maiden hurdler (stayed 2½m), half-sister to fairly useful hurdler (2½m winner) Flying Eagle: 14/1, fifth in fillies junior bumper at Newbury (14¼ lengths behind Cap Soleil) in December. *Chris Gordon* **b65**

DUBAI OR NOT DUBAI (IRE) 4 b.g. Dubai Destination (USA) – Silk Affair (IRE) (Barathea (IRE)) [2016/17 b14d* Oct 30] second foal: brother to 9.5f winner Wider World: dam (h133), 2m-2½m hurdle winner, also 1m winner on Flat, half-sister to useful hurdler/chaser (stayed 2¾m) Direct Bearing: 7/4, won junior bumper at Carlisle (by 2 lengths from Kelpies Myth) in October: open to improvement. *Keith Dalgleish* **b85 p**

DUBAI SHEN (IRE) 6 b.g. Dubai Destination (USA) – Graineuaile (IRE) (Orchestra) [2016/17 h77, b89: h16.2d⁴ h16.2f* h16.2dᵖᵘ h19.6g Jul 29] fair form over hurdles: won novice handicap at Perth in June: unproven beyond 2m: acts on firm going: in headgear last 2 starts. *Alistair Whillans* **h102**

DUBAWI ISLAND (FR) 8 b.g. Dubawi (IRE) – Housa Dancer (FR) (Fabulous Dancer (USA)) [2016/17 h130: c16.9dᵖᵘ Dec 16] round-barrelled gelding: fairly useful hurdler: pulled up in novice handicap on chasing debut: stays 21f: acts on heavy going. *Venetia Williams* **c–**
h–

DUBAWI LIGHT 6 b.g. Dubawi (IRE) – Shesadelight (Shirley Heights) [2016/17 **h–**
h16.3d^{pu} Jun 14] fair on Flat, stays 1¼m: pulled up in novice on hurdling debut. *Gary Moore*

DUBH DES CHAMPS (IRE) 5 br.g. Robin des Champs (FR) – Aneda Dubh (IRE) **h–**
(Presenting) [2016/17 h21.4s Jan 7] tailed off in novice hurdle on debut. *Harry Fry*

DUBH EILE (IRE) 9 br.m. Definite Article – Aine Dubh (IRE) (Bob Back (USA)) **h119**
[2016/17 h116: h20m^3 h24g^4 h25.4d^{pu} Aug 29] fairly useful handicap hurdler: won at
Southwell in August: stays easy 3m: acts on good to firm going: usually races towards rear.
Tim Vaughan

DUBLIN INDEMNITY 5 b.g. Presenting – Tazzarine (FR) (Astarabad (USA)) [2016/17 **b–**
b17d^5 Feb 20] tailed off in bumper. *Tom Symonds*

DUC DE BEAUCHENE (FR) 4 b.g. Saddler Maker (IRE) – Quatia d'Angron (FR) **b85**
(Verglas (IRE)) [2016/17 b15.8v^2 b16d Mar 31] €145,000 3-y-o: first foal: dam maiden
over fences in France: fair form in bumpers: better effort when second at Ffos Las in
March. *David Pipe*

DUC DE SEVILLE (IRE) 5 b.g. Duke of Marmalade (IRE) – Splendid (IRE) (Mujtahid **c – x**
(USA)) [2016/17 h–: h15.8g^4 h17.2m^5 h20.3g^4 c20g^4 c24.5m^F c21.2g^F h23.4g^5 h25d **h65**
h25.6s^{pu} h18.6m^6 Apr 17] little form over hurdles: well held sole completed start over
fences: has worn headgear. *Michael Chapman*

DUCKWEED (IRE) 9 b.m. Wolfe Tone (IRE) – Mertensia (IRE) (Musical Pursuit) **c124**
[2016/17 c20g* c19.9g^3 c24m* c25s^5 c25g^5 c24d^2 c25d^{ur} c24.4g^{pu} Oct 21] first foal: dam **h–**
unraced half-sister to fairly useful hurdler/winning chaser (stayed 25f) Uncle Arthur: fairly
useful hurdler: fairly useful chaser: won mares maiden at Down Royal in May and minor
event at Limerick in July: stays 25f: acts on good to firm and good to soft going: usually
races prominently. *Mrs J. Harrington, Ireland*

DUCLOYNE LADY (IRE) 8 b.m. Oscar (IRE) – Lizes Birthday (IRE) (Torus) [2016/17 **c–**
h16.2s h21.7v^5 Jan 11] sixth foal: sister to fairly useful hurdler/useful chaser Fabalu **h75**
(2¾m-3¼m winner): dam (h84), lightly raced in bumpers/over hurdles, half-sister to dam
of smart chaser (stays 23f) Hurricane Ben: point winner: well held both starts over hurdles:
modest form only outing over fences for David Harry Kelly in 2015/16. *Henry Oliver*

DUDETTE 5 ch.m. Apple Tree (FR) – Whatagale (Strong Gale) [2016/17 b15.7s Mar 8] **b–**
£3,500 4-y-o: half-sister to fairly useful chaser Ask The Weatherman (25f winner, by
Tamure) and useful hurdler/chaser Tot O'Whiskey (2m-3m winner, by Saddlers' Hall):
dam (c109) 21f-25f chase winner: tailed off in mares bumper. *Andrew Crook*

DUEL AT DAWN (IRE) 7 b.g. Presenting – Phillis Hill (Karinga Bay) [2016/17 h19.9s^5 **h132**
h24.4g* h24.4d^3 h23.1g* Mar 25] €100,000 3-y-o: half-brother to several winners,
including bumper winner/fairly useful hurdler Miles To Memphis (2m-2¼m winner, by
Old Vic) and fair hurdler Cove (2¾m winner, by Westerner), stays 25f: dam (b64) ran once
in bumper: runner-up on completed start in Irish maiden points: useful form over hurdles:
won novice at Doncaster in December and handicap at Bangor (by ½ length from Sam
Red) in March: will stay long distances: acts on soft going: usually races close up.
Alex Hales

DUELING BANJOS 7 gr.g. Proclamation (IRE) – Kayf Lady (Kayf Tara) [2016/17 **c130**
h135: c23.8d^F c24s^2 c25.2s^3 c22.7s^2 c19.4v* c23.4d^2 Mar 24] big, strong gelding: useful **h–**
hurdler: useful form over fences: won novice at Ffos Las in March: second in novice
handicap at Leicester (1¼ lengths behind Bells 'N' Banjos) in February: stays 3m: acts on
heavy going: in cheekpieces last 3 starts. *Kim Bailey*

DUE SOUTH (IRE) 6 b.g. City Honours (USA) – Lady Shackleton (IRE) (Zaffaran **c–**
(USA)) [2016/17 h–: c19.7d^3 Nov 14] well held in novice hurdle/chase. *Linda Jewell* **h–**

DUFFY ALLEN (FR) 4 b.g. Lucarno (USA) – Parade (FR) (Robin des Champs (FR)) **b81**
[2016/17 b16d^3 h16.7m Apr 17] €8,000 3-y-o: first foal: half-brother to fairly useful
hurdler Violoniste (2m-2½m winner, by Epalo) and French hurdler Cookie d'Allen (19f
winner, by Kotky Bleu): dam twice-raced half-sister to smart French hurdler/fairly useful
chaser (17f/2¼m winner) Vladimir: modest form in bumpers. *Nick Kent*

DUHALLOWCOUNTRY (IRE) 11 b.g. Beneficial – Milltown Lass (IRE) (Mister **c80 §**
Lord (USA)) [2016/17 c82§, h81§: c16.4s^5 c16m^4 c17.1m^2 c15.6d c17.2g^3 c16.4s^{pu} c15.5s^4 **h– §**
c16.4d^2 c16.4s^2 c16.4v^2 c16.4d* c15.7g c16.3g^6 Apr 8] winning pointer: maiden hurdler:
poor handicap chaser: won at Sedgefield in March: raced mainly at 2m: acts on heavy
going: wears headgear: races prominently: temperamental. *Victor Thompson*

DUKE ARCADIO (IRE) 8 b.g. Arcadio (GER) – Kildowney Duchess (IRE) (Jurado (USA)) [2016/17 h101: c24d² c21.7d^{pu} c24d^{pu} c24g⁴ Mar 28] won Irish maiden point on debut: fair form over hurdles/fences: stays 3m: acts on soft going: front runner/races prominently. *Oliver Sherwood* **c112 h–**

DUKE DEBARRY (IRE) 6 b.g. Presenting – Blue Dante (IRE) (Phardante (FR)) [2016/17 b15.8v⁴ b16s⁵ b16d⁵ Mar 31] €85,000 3-y-o: fourth foal: half-brother to bumper winner Dantes Firth (by Flemensfirth): dam (b115), won both starts in bumpers, out of sister to high-class staying chaser Marlborough: fair form in bumpers. *Nicky Henderson* **b88**

DUKE OF LUCCA (IRE) 12 b.g. Milan – Derravaragh Native (IRE) (Be My Native (USA)) [2016/17 c24.2s^{pu} c23.4d^{ur} c20.5m* Apr 18] lengthy gelding: winning hurdler: fairly useful hunter chaser: won at Kempton in April: stays 31f: acts on soft and good to firm going: wears headgear/tongue tie. *Francesca Nimmo* **c126 h–**

DUKE OF NAVAN (IRE) 9 b.g. Presenting – Greenfieldflyer (IRE) (Alphabatim (USA)) [2016/17 c137, h–: c16g² Apr 27] well-made gelding: winning hurdler: useful handicap chaser: second at Perth (4 lengths behind Pain Au Chocolat) in April after 18-month lay-off: stays 2¼m: acts on good to firm and heavy going. *Nicky Richards* **c139 h–**

DUKE OF SONNING 5 ch.g. Duke of Marmalade (IRE) – Moonshadow (Diesis) [2016/17 h124p: h15.8g^{pu} Apr 3] fairly useful form over hurdles for Alan King, pulled up sole start in 2016/17. *Shaun Harris* **h–**

DUKE STREET (IRE) 5 b.g. Duke of Marmalade (IRE) – Act of The Pace (IRE) (King's Theatre (IRE)) [2016/17 h129: h20g h21g² h20.6s² h21g⁴ h24.7g h24g³ h19.8g Apr 29] compact gelding: useful handicap hurdler: second at Kempton (2¾ lengths behind Younevercall) and Market Rasen (length behind Oscar Rock) in November: stays 21f: acts on soft and good to firm going: has worn cheekpieces, including last 2 starts: usually races prominently, often travels strongly. *Dr Richard Newland* **h133**

DUMBARTON (IRE) 9 br.g. Danehill Dancer (IRE) – Scottish Stage (IRE) (Selkirk (USA)) [2016/17 h105§: h20.1d³ h23.9s⁴ h20.2g² Aug 20] fair handicap hurdler: stays 2¾m: acts on soft going: has worn cheekpieces: tried in tongue tie: irresolute. *Donald Whillans* **h104 §**

DUN BAY CREEK 6 b.g. Dubai Destination (USA) – Over It (Overbury (IRE)) [2016/17 h89: h21.6d* h19.8s Feb 17] lengthy gelding: fair form over hurdles: won novice at Newton Abbot in June: should stay 3m. *Alan King* **h110**

DUNCOMPLAINING (IRE) 8 b.g. Milan – Notcomplainingbut (IRE) (Supreme Leader) [2016/17 h80p: h21.3d⁶ h20.8d⁵ c20.9s⁴ Mar 11] big, rangy gelding: fair form over hurdles: fourth in novice handicap at Hereford on chasing debut: should be suited by 2½m: in tongue tie last 3 starts: open to improvement. *William Kinsey* **c87 p h100 p**

DUNDEE BLUE (IRE) 9 gr.g. Cloudings (IRE) – Eurolucy (IRE) (Shardari) [2016/17 c83§, h–: c20.1g^{pu} May 24] little impact over hurdles: poor maiden chaser: best effort at 2m: acts on soft going: wears headgear/tongue tie: often races prominently: reluctant. *Henry Hogarth* **c– § h–**

DUN FAW GOOD 10 b.g. Grape Tree Road – Dun Rose (Roscoe Blake) [2016/17 c94: c26.2m^{pu} c15.6d³ c21.2d⁵ c23.8g⁶ c20.1d² c20.1s⁴ Sep 30] multiple point winner: modest maiden chaser: stays 25f: acts on good to soft going. *James Walton* **c91**

DUNLY (FR) 4 b.g. Gris de Gris (IRE) – Octavine du Meix (FR) (Le Tajer (FR)) [2016/17 b14.6s² b16s² b16v² b16.2v³ Mar 28] second foal: half-brother to French 1¾m winner Bill Mix (by Fragrant Mix): dam third in French 1½m bumper: fair form in bumpers, placed all 4 starts. *James Ewart* **b87**

DUNNICKS DELIA 8 b.m. Crosspeace (IRE) – Dunnicks Chance (Greensmith) [2016/17 b–: h21s^{pu} h23.1v^{pu} Dec 15] well held in bumper: pulled up both starts over hurdles. *Susan Gardner* **h–**

DUNRAVEN BLUE 4 b.f. Dr Massini (IRE) – Bajan Girl (FR) (Emperor Jones (USA)) [2016/17 h15.8g^{ro} Nov 10] sixth foal: half-sister to fair hurdler/winning pointer Bajan Blu (2½m winner, by Generous): dam (h81), 17f hurdle winner, half-sister to high-class hurdler/very smart chaser (2m-2½m winner) Wahiba Sands: behind when ran out 3 out in mares maiden hurdle on debut. *David Brace* **h–**

DUNRAVEN STORM (IRE) 12 br.g. Presenting – Foxfire (Lord Americo) [2016/17 c146x, h–: c18g* c17g⁴ c15.9g c20.4g⁵ Nov 11] sturdy gelding: winning hurdler: smart handicap chaser: won at Kempton (by 5 lengths from Turn Over Sivola) in May: stays 19f: acts on heavy going: often leads: often let down by jumping. *Philip Hobbs* **c143 x h–**

DUNROE BOY (IRE) 12 b.g. Catcher In The Rye (IRE) – Moon River (FR) (Groom **c– §**
Dancer (USA)) [2016/17 c20.1g^pu h23g^6 h23.7d c23g^5 h24d^pu Oct 4] point winner: poor **h67**
handicap hurdler: maiden chaser: stays 25f: acts on heavy going: usually wears headgear:
wears tongue tie: often races lazily: one to treat with caution. *Thomas Coyle, Ireland*

DUN SCAITH (IRE) 9 b.g. Vinnie Roe (IRE) – Scathach (IRE) (Nestor) [2016/17 c–, **c–**
h102: h16.7g^4 h21.4m h22.1g h21.6m* h26.5m^6 h19.6g^6 h24g^4 h21.6g* h24m^2 **h106 §**
h21.1g h23.6d^6 Nov 16] fair handicap hurdler: won selling race at Newton Abbot in July
and conditional event there in September: fell both starts over fences: stays 3m: acts on soft
and good to firm going: has worn hood: has worn tongue tie, including last 3 starts: often
races towards rear: temperamental. *Sophie Leech*

DURBAN GOLD 10 ch.m. Flemensfirth (USA) – Kohinor (Supreme Leader) [2016/17 **c–**
c103, h–: c25.3g^pu Apr 27] multiple winning pointer: once-raced hurdler: fair form at best **h–**
over fences: stays 3¼m: acts on heavy going: tried in cheekpieces. *Mrs D. Walton*

DURBANVILLE 5 b.g. Black Sam Bellamy (IRE) – Kealshore Lass (Alflora (IRE)) **h96**
[2016/17 h22s^4 h20.5s^4 Jan 2] first foal: dam (b86), bumper winner, out of half-sister to
Hennessy Gold Cup winner Couldnt Be Better: modest form over hurdles. *Keith Dalgleish*

DURHAM ROAD (IRE) 6 ch.g. Spadoun (FR) – Twilight Vic (Old Vic) [2016/17 **b–**
b15.8v Dec 12] well beaten in maiden bumper. *Rebecca Curtis*

DUROOB 15 b.g. Bahhare (USA) – Amaniy (USA) (Dayjur (USA)) [2016/17 c84, h82§: **c–**
h27g^pu Aug 25] lengthy gelding: poor handicap hurdler/chaser nowadays: stays 3½m: acts **h– §**
on good to firm and heavy going: wears headgear: has worn tongue tie: unreliable. *Anthony
McCann, Ireland*

DURSEY SOUND (IRE) 9 b.g. Milan – Glendante (IRE) (Phardante (FR)) [2016/17 **c119**
c126, h–: c20.3s^3 c23.8g^6 h20d^pu c21.1g^4 c24.2d* c25.2g^pu c19.3d^5 c22.4v^pu c20.3s^6 **h–**
c21.1m Apr 19] well-made gelding: winning hurdler: fairly useful handicap chaser: won at
Hexham in September: left Jonjo O'Neill after third start: stays 25f: acts on heavy going:
has worn headgear/tongue tie: races towards rear: not straightforward. *Ben Haslam*

DUSHYBEAG (IRE) 10 b.g. Dushyantor (USA) – Bula Beag (IRE) (Brush Aside **c–**
(USA)) [2016/17 c25g c26m c24m^pu c20g c25.6m^pu Oct 5] winning hurdler: useful chaser **h–**
at best, has lost his way: left M. Hourigan after third start: tried in headgear: often races
prominently. *Matt Sheppard*

DUSK TILL DAWN (IRE) 8 b.g. King's Theatre (IRE) – Savu Sea (IRE) (Slip Anchor) **c104**
[2016/17 h98, b90: c24s^ur c25.8g* c24.5g^3 c25.8m^pu c23g^6 c23g^5 Aug 11] modest hurdler: **h–**
fair form over fences: won novice handicap at Newton Abbot in May: stays 3¼m: acts on
heavy going: wears headgear: temperament under suspicion. *David Pipe*

DUSKY LARK 7 b.g. Nayef (USA) – Snow Goose (Polar Falcon (USA)) [2016/17 c135, **c140**
h–: c20.5s^2 c18.8d^2 c15.7s^2 c20.2v* c23.8s^4 Mar 2] good-topped gelding: winning hurdler: **h–**
useful handicap chaser: won at Wincanton (by 2 lengths from Vic de Touzaine) in February:
left Colin Tizzard after third start: stays 2½m: acts on heavy going: wears tongue tie: front
runner/races prominently. *Robert Walford*

DUSKY LEGEND 7 b.m. Midnight Legend – Tinagoodnight (FR) (Sleeping Car (FR)) **h138**
[2016/17 h131: h16d* h16.3g* h16.3d^2 h16.5g^2 h16.8g^3 h20.3g^2 Apr 20] sturdy mare:
useful hurdler: won maiden at Warwick in May and mares novice at Newbury in November:
third in Dawn Run Mares' Novices' Hurdle at Cheltenham (3 lengths behind Let's Dance)
in March and second in listed race there in April (neck behind Brillare Momento): stays
2½m: acts on heavy going: often travels strongly. *Alan King*

DUSKY RAIDER (IRE) 4 gr.g. Clodovil (IRE) – Rahila (IRE) (Kalanisi (IRE)) **h89**
[2016/17 h18.7g^3 Apr 15] fair on Flat, stays 1¾m: 8/1, third in novice at Stratford (10
lengths behind Little Chunk) on hurdling debut. *Tim Vaughan*

DU SOLEIL (FR) 5 ch.g. Zambezi Sun – Cykapri (FR) (Cyborg (FR)) [2016/17 b99: **h111 p**
h16s^3 Jan 8] bumper winner: 11/2, third in maiden at Chepstow (5¾ lengths behind Russian
Service) on hurdling debut: will stay further than 2m: sure to progress. *Venetia Williams*

DUSTY RAVEN 4 ch.g. Raven's Pass (USA) – Dust Dancer (Suave Dancer (USA)) **h96**
[2016/17 h17.7s^2 h16s^2 h15.5v^4 h18.8g h18.5g Apr 11] lengthy gelding: modest maiden on
Flat, probably stays 13.5f: modest form over hurdles: should stay 2¼m+: acts on soft
going: in headgear last 4 starts: often races towards rear. *Neil Mulholland*

DUTCH BARNEY 7 b.g. Dutch Art – Celeb Style (IRE) (Tagula (IRE)) [2016/17 **h–**
h15.8d^pu Jul 13] no form on Flat: pulled up in novice on hurdling debut. *Mark Brisbourne*

DUTCH CANYON (IRE) 7 b.g. Craigsteel – Chitabe (IRE) (Lord of Appeal) [2016/17   **c72 §**
h84§: c24.2s^pu c19.9d^pu h19s^3 h24.1s^pu h19.9s^3 c21.6d^4 Apr 10] poor maiden hurdler: **h76 §**
similar form over fences: stays 2¾m: acts on soft and good to firm going: wears headgear:
has worn tongue tie: usually races prominently, often travels strongly: ungenuine.
N. W. Alexander

DUTCHESOFRATHMOLYN (IRE) 8 b.m. Kutub (IRE) – Greenfieldflyer (IRE)   **h–**
(Alphabatim (USA)) [2016/17 h60: h21.6d^pu Apr 29] no form over hurdles: tried in tongue
tie. *Alison Batchelor*

DYLANSEOGHAN (IRE) 8 b.g. Pierre – Sabbatical (IRE) (Jurado (USA)) [2016/17   **c85**
h102, b–: c20v^pu c25.5d^3 Dec 6] winning pointer: fair form over hurdles: modest form over   **h–**
fences: best effort at 21f: acts on soft going: often races towards rear. *Zoe Davison*

DYLAN'S STORM (IRE) 5 b.g. Zebedee – Storm Lady (IRE) (Alhaarth (IRE))   **h54**
[2016/17 h83: h19g h18.7m h15.8g^6 h18.7g^6 h20g h16.8m^ur Apr 19] maiden pointer: poor
maiden hurdler: left David Dennis after fifth start: tried in cheekpieces: wears tongue tie.
Peter Niven

DYNAMIC DRIVE (IRE) 10 b.g. Motivator – Biriyani (IRE) (Danehill (USA))   **c–**
[2016/17 c80, h114: h16.2d^2 h16.2m^3 h16.2d^4 h17.2m^ur h17.2d^6 Jul 16] fairly useful   **h121**
handicap hurdler: won at Hexham in June: little impact over fences: stays 2¼m: acts on
good to firm and good to soft going: has worn headgear: wears tongue tie. *Maurice Barnes*

DYNAMITE DOLLARS (FR) 4 b.g. Buck's Boum (FR) – Macadoun (FR) (Cardoun   **b97**
(FR)) [2016/17 b16.5m^3 b14s^3 b16.3d^6 Feb 11] good-topped gelding: fifth foal: dam
second in 17f hurdle on only start in France: fairly useful form in bumpers: best effort when
third in listed 4-y-o event at Cheltenham (1¼ lengths behind Cap Soleil) in January.
Paul Nicholls

DYNAMO (IRE) 6 b.g. Galileo (IRE) – Trading Places (Dansili) [2016/17 c98, h102:   **c– x**
h19.9g^5 h18.7m^pu h16.8g Apr 26] fair maiden hurdler, well below best in 2016/17: modest   **h67 x**
form over fences: left Dan Skelton after second start: unproven beyond 17f: acts on soft
going: tried in cheekpieces: wears tongue tie: often let down by jumping. *Jamie Snowden*

DYNASTE (FR) 11 gr.g. Martaline – Bellissima de Mai (FR) (Pistolet Bleu (IRE))   **c131**
[2016/17 c160, h–: c24.2g^6 c22.3s c24.2s Jan 7] sturdy, lengthy gelding: has had breathing   **h–**
operation: winning hurdler: one-time top-class chaser, has deteriorated: stays 25f: acts on
soft going: wears headgear/tongue tie. *David Pipe*

DYSIOS (IRE) 9 b.g. Invincible Spirit (IRE) – Hataana (USA) (Robellino (USA))   **c132**
[2016/17 c131, h–: c17v^4 c17d^2 c17s c19.4s Feb 4] winning hurdler: useful handicap   **h–**
chaser: second at Leopardstown (1½ lengths behind Lake Takapuna) in December: raced
around 2m: acts on heavy going: wears tongue tie. *Denis W. Cullen, Ireland*

DYSTONIA'S REVENGE (IRE) 12 b.g. Woods of Windsor (USA) – Lady Isaac (IRE)   **c88 §**
(Le Bavard (FR)) [2016/17 c111§, h–: c24.2d^pu c20.1m^3 c21.2m c20.1d^pu c20g^3 c25.2g   **h–**
c25.2d^5 Jan 25] good-topped gelding: once-raced hurdler: modest handicap chaser
nowadays: stays 25f: acts on soft and good to firm going: in cheekpieces last 3 starts:
unreliable. *Sheena Walton*

E

EAGER TO KNOW (IRE) 7 b.g. Sayarshan (FR) – Drew (IRE) (Double Schwartz)   **h79**
[2016/17 h16s h19.9d^4 h17s h22s^5 h27s h16.8d^5 h27m^4 Apr 19] off mark in Irish maiden
points at fifth attempt: poor maiden hurdler: stays easy 27f: races towards rear.
Micky Hammond

EAMON AN CNOIC (IRE) 6 b.g. Westerner – Nutmeg Tune (IRE) (Accordion)   **h125**
[2016/17 h103p, b84: h16g* h15.7s* h23.1s Feb 12] second in Irish maiden point on debut:
fairly useful form over hurdles: won maiden at Fakenham in October and handicap at
Haydock (conditional) in December: should stay at least 2½m: often races towards rear.
David Pipe

EARCOMESTHEDREAM (IRE) 14 b.g. Marignan (USA) – Play It By Ear (IRE) (Be   **c– §**
My Native (USA)) [2016/17 c–§, h99§: h23.3d^6 h24g h24d^pu h23.3v^pu h25.5v^pu h23.6s^pu   **h70 §**
Mar 13] handicap hurdler, little form in 2016/17: maiden chaser: stays 3¼m: acts on good
to firm and heavy going: wears headgear: tried in tongue tie: ungenuine. *Peter Pritchard*

EARDISLAND 7 b.m. Kayf Tara – Aranga (IRE) (Supreme Leader) [2016/17 h110:   **h108**
h21.2m^6 h20m* h20g^6 h23.3d Oct 28] fair handicap hurdler: won mares event at Worcester
in August: stays 2½m: acts on good to firm and heavy going: wears tongue tie. *Philip Hobbs*

EARLS FORT (IRE) 7 b.g. Kalanisi (IRE) – Lillando (IRE) (Lando (GER)) [2016/17 h20.3v^pu h18.5d^3 h19.9g^4 h17.2g h19.1d^2 h19.5d* h19.9g* h20.5d* h19.5v^2 h19g^2 Apr 24] fairly useful handicap hurdler: won at Chepstow and Sedgefield in October, and at Plumpton (amateur) in November: stays 21f: acts on heavy going: wears cheekpieces/tongue tie: usually races close up, often travels strongly. *Neil Mulholland* **h115**

EARLSHILL (IRE) 6 b.g. Milan – Mrs Marples (IRE) [2016/17 h20.3v^2 h23.6s^pu h20.3v^4 h21s^2 Mar 30] €32,000 3-y-o: half-brother to useful hurdler/fairly useful chaser Golden Sunbird (2m-21f winner, by Bob Back): dam unraced half-sister to Festival Bumper winner/useful 2m hurdler Wither Or Which and to dam of top-class chaser Alexander Banquet: Irish point winner: fair form over hurdles: second in maidens at Southwell and Warwick: should stay beyond 21f: in tongue tie last 2 starts. *Dan Skelton* **h112**

EARL THE PEARL 7 b.g. Multiplex – Colorado Pearl (IRE) (Anshan) [2016/17 h19.9m^pu Jun 9] finally off mark in points shortly after end of season: maiden hurdler: lightly raced in chases: tried in blinkers. *Oliver Greenall* **c– h–**

EARLY BOY (FR) 6 b.g. Early March – Eclat de Rose (FR) (Scribe (IRE)) [2016/17 b–: h16s h16s h16.6d h16.6s^6 Mar 3] no form in bumpers/over hurdles. *Andrew Crook* **h–**

EARLY DU LEMO (FR) 4 gr.g. Early March – Kiswa (FR) (Top Waltz (FR)) [2016/17 h17.4s* h16.8s^3 h16v^3 Feb 24] good-topped gelding: half-brother to French chaser Ange du Lemo (2¾m winner, by Maille Pistol): once-raced on Flat: fairly useful form over hurdles: won newcomers race at Nantes in November: left P. J. Fertillet, shaped better than result both starts after: remains with potential. *Gary Moore* **h119 p**

EARLY RETIREMENT (IRE) 5 b.g. Daylami (IRE) – Deep Lilly (Glacial Storm (USA)) [2016/17 h82: h16d h19v^2 h19.2v h20.3s* Mar 20] fair form over hurdles: won handicap at Southwell in March: stays 2½m: acts on heavy going. *Caroline Bailey* **h105**

EARTH LADY 5 b.m. Presenting – Simply Divine (IRE) (Be My Native (USA)) [2016/17 b17.7d^4 h18.5s h18.5s h19g^5 h23.9g Mar 2] sister to bumper winner/fair hurdler Be My Present (2m winner) and half-sister to several winners, including fairly useful hurdler Will O'The West (2m-19f winner, by Westerner), stays 3m: dam winning pointer: fourth in mares bumper: modest form over hurdles: should be suited by 2½m+: remains capable of better. *Philip Hobbs* **h98 p b68**

EARTHMOVES (FR) 7 b.g. Antarctique (IRE) – Red Rym (FR) (Denham Red (FR)) [2016/17 h–: h19.8d^3 c23g^pu c23g^6 h23.5m c19.4g* Apr 9] lengthy gelding: fairly useful handicap hurdler: fair form over fences: won seller at Ffos Las in April: stays 19f: acts on soft going: tried in cheekpieces: wears tongue tie. *Paul Nicholls* **c110 h122**

EASILY PLEASED (IRE) 11 b.g. Beneficial – Bro Ella (IRE) (Cataldi) [2016/17 c121, h99: c19.2m^3 c20g^6 c21d h16.8g^5 c16.3g^2 c16.5m^5 Aug 30] maiden hurdler: fairly useful handicap chaser: stays 21f: acts on good to firm and heavy going: wears hood: often races in rear. *Martin Hill* **c119 h84**

EAST COKER (IRE) 4 b.g. Pour Moi (IRE) – Bounce (FR) (Trempolino (USA)) [2016/17 h16g^ur h16g^3 h16s^6 h16d^5 h15.3m^6 Oct 23] maiden on Flat: modest form over hurdles: left Mrs J. Harrington after fourth start: tried in headgear: dead. *David Dennis* **h95**

EASTER DAY (FR) 9 b.g. Malinas (GER) – Sainte Lea (FR) (Sirk) [2016/17 c142, h129: h26.4m^4 h21g^5 h26s^3 Mar 30] useful-looking gelding: fairly useful handicap hurdler: useful chaser: stays 3¼m: acts on heavy going: has worn headgear. *Henry Spiller* **c– h124**

EASTER HUNT (IRE) 8 br.g. Kalanisi (IRE) – Easter Day (IRE) (Simply Great (FR)) [2016/17 c111x, h100: h19.7s^ur Dec 26] maiden hurdler: fair chaser: stays 3¼m: acts on good to firm and heavy going: has worn headgear: usually wears tongue tie: often let down by jumping. *Sara Ender* **c– x h–**

EASTER IN PARIS (IRE) 8 b.m. Bienamado (USA) – Easter Saturday (IRE) (Grand Plaisir (IRE)) [2016/17 c21.2m c21.2g^F h21.6s^2 c17v^2 c19.9d^pu h20.5v^5 c20.9d* c19.2g^2 Apr 12] lengthy mare: second foal: half-sister to fair 3¼m chase winner Indiana Bay (by Indian River): dam (c82) winning pointer: winning pointer: modest form over hurdles: modest handicap chaser: won maiden event at Hereford in March: left W. J. Burke after first start: stays 2¾m: acts on heavy going: tried in hood. *Paul Henderson* **c94 h92**

EASTER MYTTON 5 b.m. Overbury (IRE) – Ma Dame Mytton (Hunting Lion (IRE)) [2016/17 b16.4v^5 Mar 7] first foal: dam unraced: tailed off in maiden bumper. *Hugh Burns* **b–**

EAST INDIA 5 ch.g. Galileo (IRE) – Field of Hope (IRE) (Selkirk (USA)) [2016/17 h17m^5 h20g^5 h15.9d h16.5m Apr 20] fairly useful on Flat, stays 1¼m: limited impact over hurdles, including in handicaps: left Rebecca Curtis after third start: has worn headgear. *George Baker* **h–**

EAST INDIES 4 b.g. Authorized (IRE) – Elan (Dansili) [2016/17 h15.9m* h16.4s^{pu} **h112**
h17.7d³ h16g h15.7m⁶ h15.9m² Apr 17] rather leggy gelding: fairly useful form on Flat,
stays 1¼m: fair form over hurdles: won juvenile at Plumpton in September: stays 2¼m:
acts on good to firm and good to soft going: wears hood: often leads/races freely.
Gary Moore

EASTLAKE (IRE) 11 b.g. Beneficial – Guigone (FR) (Esprit du Nord (USA)) [2016/17 **c150 §**
c145, h–: c25g^{pu} c20.4g^{pu} c16.3d* c16.3s^{pu} c16.3g c21.1g^{pu} Apr 7] rangy gelding: winning **h– §**
hurdler: smart handicap chaser: won at Cheltenham (by 1¾ lengths from Un Beau Roman)
in December: stays 21f: acts on good to firm and heavy going: has worn cheekpieces: wears
tongue tie: usually races nearer last than first: unreliable. *Jonjo O'Neill*

EASTVIEW BOY 6 ch.g. Iktibas – Eastview Princess (J B Quick) [2016/17 h112, b76: **c114**
h16.2d⁴ h20.6g⁴ h19.7g⁵ h19.7s⁵ c15.6v^{ur} c16.3s* c19.4d⁶ c16.3s² c16v^{pu} Feb 11] **h109**
workmanlike gelding: fair hurdler: fair form over fences: won novice handicap at
Newcastle in December: stays 21f: acts on heavy going: often races towards rear.
Philip Kirby

EASYONDEYE (IRE) 11 b.g. Beneficial – Lady of Appeal (IRE) (Lord of Appeal) **c–**
[2016/17 c20s^{ur} Feb 8] dual point winner: once-raced hurdler: fair chaser at best: left D. E. **h–**
Prendergast, folded quickly in hunter/point in 2016/17: stays 21f: acts on heavy going.
Patrick J. Hanly

EASYONTHEEYE (IRE) 6 br.m. Kalanisi (IRE) – Lady Bernie (IRE) (Supreme **h–**
Leader) [2016/17 b–: ab16g h19.1d Dec 6] no form in bumpers/novice hurdle: tried in **b–**
hood. *Linda Jewell*

EASY STREET (IRE) 7 b.g. High Chaparral (IRE) – Victorine (IRE) (Un Desperado **c127**
(FR)) [2016/17 h100p: h23s² c25.5d* c20m* c21.4g^{ur} c20g c24.2g² c24.2g⁵ c19.4s c20.5g⁵ **h104**
c21.1g* c19.9g^{pu} Apr 15] fair form over hurdles: fairly useful handicap chaser: won at
Fontwell and Uttoxeter (both novice events) in June and Fontwell again in March: stays
25f: acts on soft and good to firm going: held up. *Jonjo O'Neill*

EATON HILL (IRE) 5 b.g. Yeats (IRE) – Guilt Less (FR) (Useful (FR)) [2016/17 b89: **h120**
b16m² b16g² h19.7d* h19.7d³ h19.9s^{pu} h22g* Apr 23] fair form in bumpers: fairly useful **b89**
form over hurdles: won novices at Wetherby in January and Stratford in April: likely to stay
3m: usually races towards rear. *Kerry Lee*

EATON ROCK (IRE) 8 b.g. Rocamadour – Duchess of Kinsale (IRE) (Montelimar **c96**
(USA)) [2016/17 c100, h–: c23.6s² c16.1v³ c24v^{pu} Mar 6] winning hurdler: modest **h–**
handicap chaser: stays 3m: best form on soft/heavy going: in tongue tie last 5 starts: often
races towards rear. *Tom Symonds*

EAU DE NILE (IRE) 4 b.g. Robin des Champs (FR) – Rivervail (IRE) (River Falls) **b–**
[2016/17 b16.3g Mar 25] £58,000 3-y-o: useful-looking gelding: half-brother to fairly
useful hurdler/useful chaser Killer Crow (2½m winner, by Presenting): dam (h98) maiden
hurdler (raced at 2m), half-sister to fairly useful hurdler (stayed 3m) Aboriginal: 50/1, well
held in Goffs UK Spring Sales Bumper at Newbury. *Henry Daly*

EBADANI (IRE) 7 ch.g. Halling (USA) – Ebatana (IRE) (Rainbow Quest (USA)) **h114**
[2016/17 h110: h19.1d² h21.2g* h19.9g^{pu} May 29] fair hurdler: won maiden at Sedgefield
in May: stayed 21f: acted on good to soft going: often raced prominently: dead.
Jamie Snowden

EBAZAN (USA) 8 ch.g. Lemon Drop Kid (USA) – Ebaza (IRE) (Sinndar (IRE)) [2016/17 **h–**
h105: h17.1d^{pu} Oct 13] fair hurdler: shaped as if amiss only outing in 2016/17: stays easy
3m: acts on good to firm and heavy going: has worn headgear. *Brian Ellison*

EBONY ROSE 5 br.m. Kalanisi (IRE) – Cogolie (FR) (Cyborg (FR)) [2016/17 b16.2d **b73 §**
b16.2m⁴ b16.7d⁵ b15.6g⁶ Nov 3] fifth foal: half-brother to a winning pointer by Exit To
Nowhere: dam well held in bumper: poor form in bumpers: temperamental. *Susan Corbett*

ECHNATON (GER) 4 b.g. Lord of England (GER) – Easy Sunshine (IRE) (Sadler's **b–**
Wells (USA)) [2016/17 b16s Jan 14] tailed off in maiden bumper. *Lucy Wadham*

ECHO BEAT (IRE) 4 b.f. Beat Hollow – Calendula (Be My Guest (USA)) [2016/17 **b–**
b17d Apr 5] £4,000 3-y-o: half-sister to several winners, including bumper winner/smart
hurdler Son of Flicka (17f-21f winner, by Groom Dancer) and fairly useful hurdler The
Bear Trap (2½m winner, by Westerner): dam 1¼m-1½m winner: tailed off in bumper.
Tracy Waggott

ECHO BRAVA 7 gr.g. Proclamation (IRE) – Snake Skin (Golden Snake (USA)) [2016/17 **h105**
h88p: h15.7v² h16m² h18.7g⁵ h16.8g² Sep 16] fair form over hurdles: should stay beyond
17f. *Jim Best*

ECHO EXPRESS (IRE) 5 b.g. Echo of Light – If Dubai (USA) (Stephen Got Even (USA)) [2016/17 b16.6s* Mar 4] €35,000 3-y-o: fifth foal: half-brother to 3 winners on Flat, including useful 7f/1¼m winner Holy Warrior (by Holy Roman Emperor): dam ran twice on Flat: 11/2, won 4-runner conditionals/amateur bumper at Doncaster (by 2¼ lengths from Midnight Shadow) on debut. *Nicky Richards* **b92**

ECHO SPRINGS 7 b.g. Kayf Tara – Mrs Malt (IRE) (Presenting) [2016/17 h109: h24.7m⁵ May 13] bumper winner: fair maiden hurdler: stays 3m: acts on soft going: in tongue tie last 2 starts. *Christopher Kellett* **h98**

ECLECTICA GIRL 6 b.m. Multiplex – Evelith Abbey (IRE) (Presenting) [2016/17 b–: b16.7g May 14] no form in bumpers/point: tried in blinkers. *Henry Oliver* **b–**

EDDIEMAURICE (IRE) 6 ch.g. Captain Rio – Annals (Lujain (USA)) [2016/17 h106: h16s² h15.9g* h16d⁴ h16.4g⁴ h15.7d⁴ h16.8g h16g⁵ h16.3d h19g³ Apr 6] compact gelding: fairly useful hurdler: won novice at Ffos Las in May, and handicaps at Worcester in June and Ascot in November: unproven beyond 2m: acts on heavy going: tried in headgear: usually races nearer last than first. *John Flint* **h120**

EDDY 8 b.g. Exit To Nowhere (USA) – Sharway Lady (Shareef Dancer (USA)) [2016/17 h78: h21.4d h23.9gᵘʳ h19.8v⁵ h19.7d³ h21.6m⁶ Apr 15] poor maiden hurdler: stays 2¾m: acts on heavy going: tried in hood/tongue tie: often races prominently: joined Susan Gardner. *John Panvert* **h69**

EDEIFF'S LAD 10 ch.g. Loup Sauvage (USA) – Ede'iff (Tragic Role (USA)) [2016/17 c80, h68: c16.5m⁴ c20mᵖᵘ c21.1s⁴ c15.7d² c23g⁴ c19.4s³ c20.9vᵖᵘ c16v⁴ c24.2dᵘʳ c16.1g² c19.2m⁴ Apr 18] maiden hurdler: poor handicap chaser: stays 23f: acts on heavy going: wears hood. *Polly Gundry* **c75 h–**

EDE'S THE BUSINESS 6 ch.m. Halling (USA) – My Amalie (IRE) (Galileo (IRE)) [2016/17 h66: h15.8gᵖᵘ Jul 24] little form over hurdles: in blinkers last 3 starts. *Ken Wingrove* **h–**

EDGAR (GER) 7 b.g. Big Shuffle (USA) – Estella (GER) (Acatenango (GER)) [2016/17 c81, h–: c19.9g² c20.9s* c20d³ c16.3gᵖᵘ h19.7v⁶ c16.1v* c15.9s⁴ c17s⁴ c17.4d⁵ h18.7g² Apr 1] modest maiden hurdler: modest handicap chaser: won at Stratford (novice) in June and Towcester (conditional) in February: stays 21f: acts on heavy going: wears headgear: tried in tongue tie. *David Bridgwater* **c94 h97**

EDLOMOND (IRE) 11 gr.g. Great Palm (USA) – Samardana (IRE) (Hernando (FR)) [2016/17 c108§, h96: c16.3g⁴ c16.3s⁵ h16.7g⁵ c17.4g³ c16gʳᵒ c16.3gᵘʳ c16.5m⁵ Oct 30] tall gelding: winning hurdler: fair handicap chaser, largely out of form in 2016/17: stays 2½m: acts on soft going: wears headgear/tongue tie: temperamental. *Bill Turner* **c89 § h–**

EDMUND (IRE) 10 b.g. Indian River (FR) – Awomansdream (IRE) (Beneficial) [2016/17 c108, h–: c19.3d* c19.3g* c21.2m⁴ h21.2g⁶ c19.3d³ c20.1sᵖᵘ c21.1sᵖᵘ c19.2s⁵ Feb 28] lengthy, good-topped gelding: maiden hurdler: fairly useful handicap chaser: won twice at Sedgefield early in season: stays 21f: acts on good to firm and heavy going: wears blinkers: usually in tongue tie: often races prominently. *Ann Hamilton* **c118 h71**

EDUARD (IRE) 9 b.g. Morozov (USA) – Dinny Kenn (IRE) (Phardante (FR)) [2016/17 c21d⁴ c23.8dᵖᵘ Dec 17] strong gelding: winning hurdler: high-class chaser: fatally injured in Silver Cup at Ascot: stayed 2½m: acted on heavy and good to firm going. *Nicky Richards* **c148 h–**

EDWARD ELGAR 6 ch.g. Avonbridge – Scooby Dooby Do (Atraf) [2016/17 h107: h15.8g h23.4g⁶ h15.5d⁵ h19.7sᵖᵘ h16d* h15.7d³ h15.8s² h16g⁵ Apr 17] sturdy gelding: fair handicap hurdler: won selling event at Fakenham in February: unproven beyond 2m: acts on heavy going: has worn headgear, including last 4 starts: temperamental. *Caroline Bailey* **h100 §**

EDWULF 8 b.g. Kayf Tara – Valentines Lady (IRE) (Zaffaran (USA)) [2016/17 c134p, h111p, h–: c17d³ c20dᵘʳ c25.4s² c20v* c24sᶠ c20v* c31.8gᵖᵘ Mar 14] tall gelding: has stringhalt: winning hurdler: smart chaser: won maiden at Punchestown in January and novice handicap at Naas (by 8 lengths from Space Cadet) in February: second when went wrong after last in National Hunt Chase won by Tiger Roll at Cheltenham final start: stays 4m: acts on heavy going: wears tongue tie: often races towards rear/travels strongly. *Joseph Patrick O'Brien, Ireland* **c150 + h–**

EGRET (IRE) 7 b.g. Definite Article – Bright Sprite (IRE) (Beneficial) [2016/17 h101, b83: c21.5s⁵ Dec 5] runner-up in Irish maiden point: modest form over hurdles/on chasing debut: dead. *Lucinda Russell* **c98 h–**

EGYPT MILL REBEL 7 b.g. Cockney Rebel (IRE) – Beauchamp Jade (Kalaglow) [2016/17 b–: h16.8m⁵ h16.3g* h16.3dᵖᵘ Jun 14] fairly useful form over hurdles: won novice at Stratford in May: fatally injured there following month. *Tom George* **h121**

ELAV 7 b.g. Grape Tree Road – Raise A Gale (IRE) (Strong Gale) [2016/17 h15.8v h16s h19.5s^{pu} Jan 20] maiden pointer: no form over hurdles: wears tongue tie. *Peter Bowen* **h–**

EL BANDIT (IRE) 6 b.g. Milan – Bonnie Parker (IRE) (Un Desperado (FR)) [2016/17 h112p: h21d* h21.6d* h19.5g* h21.1g* h24.2d h26.1g* h24g Mar 16] tall, useful-looking gelding: useful hurdler: won handicap at Warwick in May, novice at Fontwell in June, Persian War Novices' Hurdle at Chepstow (by length from Coo Star Sivola) in October, novice at Cheltenham later in October and handicap at Musselburgh (by short head from Arthurs Secret) in February: stays 3¼m: acts on good to soft going: tried in hood. *Paul Nicholls* **h141**

EL BEAU (IRE) 6 ch.g. Camacho – River Beau (IRE) (Galileo (IRE)) [2016/17 h116: h16d h16.3d Mar 13] sturdy gelding: fairly useful hurdler at best, well held both starts in handicaps in 2016/17: raced around 2m: acts on heavy going. *John Quinn* **h–**

ELECTORAL (IRE) 4 b.g. Rip Van Winkle (IRE) – Sumingasefa (Danehill (USA)) [2016/17 b13.7m b14d Oct 30] poor form in bumpers. *David Loder* **b69**

ELECTRIC CONCORDE (IRE) 6 b.g. King's Theatre (IRE) – Cincuenta (IRE) (Bob Back (USA)) [2016/17 b16.6g* b17d² b20s* b21d³ b20.4s⁴ h24d* h22.7d^{pu} h24g⁶ h24d^{pu} Apr 18] €78,000 3-y-o: sturdy gelding: brother to useful hurdlers Sesenta and William Henry (both 2m-2½m winners), latter also bumper winner: dam, 1½m-2m winner, half-sister to smart hurdler (stayed 3m) Strangely Brown: useful form in bumpers: won maiden at Galway (by 3½ lengths from Robin des Foret) in July: useful hurdler: won maiden at Listowel in September and handicap at Leopardstown (by head from Isleofhopendreams) in December: stays 3m: acts on soft going: often races prominently. *J. Culloty, Ireland* **h135**
b105

ELEGANT ESCAPE (IRE) 5 b.g. Dubai Destination (USA) – Graineuaile (IRE) (Orchestra) [2016/17 h19.5d* h21.6d* h20.5d⁴ h20.3s⁵ h24g h24.7g Apr 7] €32,000 3-y-o, €150,000 4-y-o: well-made gelding: chasing type: sixth foal: brother to fair hurdler Dubai Shen (2m winner) and half-brother to fairly useful hurdler/chaser Fear Glic (2½m-2¾m winner, by Dr Massini) and fair hurdler Cailleach Annie (23f winner, by Blueprint): dam (c86) 2½m chase winner: runner-up in Irish maiden point on debut: useful form over hurdles: won maiden at Chepstow in October and novice at Ascot (by ¾ length from Laser Light) in November: stays 2¾m: acts on good to soft going. *Colin Tizzard* **h133**

ELEGANT (IRE) 6 b.m. Oscar (IRE) – Good Thought (IRE) (Mukaddamah (USA)) [2016/17 b16.7g³ ab16g³ Nov 8] sixth foal: half-sister to 2 winners on Flat, including winner up to 1½m Sir Boss (by Tagula): dam unraced: modest form in bumpers. *Don Cantillon* **b77**

ELEGANT STATESMAN (IRE) 10 b.g. Vinnie Roe (IRE) – Queen Astrid (IRE) (Revoque (IRE)) [2016/17 c130, h–: c20g² c20g* c24d^{pu} Oct 9] winning handicap chaser: won at Down Royal (by nose from Shantou Flyer) in June: stayed 2½m: acted on soft and good to firm going: sometimes wore cheekpieces: wore tongue tie: dead. *Henry de Bromhead, Ireland* **c132**
h–

ELENIKA (FR) 9 gr.g. Martaline – Nika Glitters (FR) (Nikos) [2016/17 c118§, h–: c20v^{pu} Nov 20] well-made gelding: maiden hurdler: useful chaser at best, no show only outing in 2016/17: stays 2½m: acts on good to firm and heavy going: tried in cheekpieces: has worn tongue tie. *Venetia Williams* **c–**
h–

ELGIN 5 b.g. Duke of Marmalade (IRE) – China Tea (USA) (High Chaparral (IRE)) [2016/17 b98: b17d² h16.4s* h16g* h15.7s² h16.2g² h16.4g Mar 14] lengthy, useful-looking gelding: bumper winner: useful form over hurdles: won maiden at Newcastle in November and novice at Kempton (by 1¾ lengths from Mohaayed) in December: second in Rossington Main Novices' Hurdle at Haydock (9 lengths behind Neon Wolf) in January and Dovecote Novices' Hurdle at Kempton (3½ lengths behind River Wylde) in February: likely to prove best at around 2m: acts on soft going. *Alan King* **h143**
b98

EL INDIO (IRE) 10 b.g. Flemensfirth (USA) – Final Bond (IRE) (Supreme Leader) [2016/17 c–, h69§: h25d⁶ h23.1s⁵ h23.3v h23v^{pu} Mar 6] poor maiden hurdler: pulled up only chase start: stays 27f: acts on heavy going: wears headgear/tongue tie: front runner/races prominently: temperamental. *Claire Dyson* **c–**
h65 §

ELKSTONE 6 b.g. Midnight Legend – Samandara (FR) (Kris) [2016/17 h100: c23.6g^F c16.1d⁶ c16.5d^F c15.7s³ c15.9s² c20.2s³ c17g² c15.7g² Apr 21] maiden hurdler: modest maiden chaser: unproven beyond 17f: acts on soft going: wears hood: has worn tongue tie: usually leads, often races freely: temperamental. *Caroline Bailey* **c97 §**
h–

ELLENS WAY 5 b.m. Black Sam Bellamy (IRE) – Function Dreamer (Overbury (IRE)) [2016/17 h21s⁵ h18.5s h21v* Dec 31] €11,000 3-y-o, £35,000 4-y-o: seventh foal: half-sister to modest chaser Digg Whitaker (3¼m winner, by Mounting Spendent) and bumper **h114**

winner McGowan's Pass (by Central Park): dam unraced half-sister to useful hurdler/top-class chaser (stayed 3m) Captain Chris: placed both starts in Irish maiden points: fair form over hurdles: won mares novice at Warwick in December: will stay 3m. *Jeremy Scott*

EL MASSIVO (IRE) 7 b.g. Authorized (IRE) – Umthoulah (IRE) (Unfuwain (USA))   **h110**
[2016/17 h116: h16g⁶ h16d h15.5g² h16s⁴ h16d* Jan 14] fair handicap hurdler: won at Wetherby in January: raced around 2m: acts on good to firm and heavy going. *Harriet Bethell*

ELOCUTION 4 b.f. Paco Boy (IRE) – Speech (Red Ransom (USA)) [2016/17 h15.9vᵖᵘ   **h–**
Feb 27] half-sister to fair hurdler Hatch Hall (2m winner, by Sleeping Indian), stays 2½m: modest on Flat, stays 1¾m: pulled up in maiden on hurdling debut. *Sheena West*

ELOPED 6 b.m. Midnight Legend – Southern Exit (Poliglote) [2016/17 b–: b15.8d³ h16.4s   **h73**
h15.7dᵘʳ h21.2d⁶ h20.7s Jan 13] sturdy mare: modest form in bumpers: poor form over   **b82**
hurdles: dead. *Ben Pauling*

EL TEL 5 ch.g. Sixties Icon – Chelsea (USA) (Miswaki (USA)) [2016/17 h15.8g⁶ h16.7g   **h–**
h15.7gᵖᵘ Aug 23] maiden on Flat: no form over hurdles. *Shaun Harris*

EL TERREMOTO (FR) 5 b.g. Spirit One (FR) – By Decree (USA) (With Approval   **c–**
(CAN)) [2016/17 h16g⁵ h22g* h18.9v* h18.9s³ h23.4v h21g Mar 18] lengthy gelding: **h124**
modest maiden on Flat: fairly useful hurdler: won maiden at Stratford in October and handicap at Haydock in November: runner-up in 3-y-o event at Cagnes, only chase outing: left Y. Fouin after final start in 2015/16: stays 2¾m: acts on heavy going. *Nigel Twiston-Davies*

EL TIBURON (IRE) 5 b.g. Court Cave (IRE) – Rongo's Last (IRE) (Little Bighorn)   **h–**
[2016/17 h74, b83: h16.8d h16d h19.1s h19.6s Jan 23] little form over hurdles: tried in cheekpieces. *Sam Thomas*

EL TOREROS (USA) 9 b.g. El Prado (IRE) – Soul Reason (USA) (Seeking The Gold   **c–**
(USA)) [2016/17 c–, h84: c17.4d⁴ h16.7g c17.4mᵖᵘ Sep 4] modest hurdler/maiden chaser   **h–**
at best, no form in 2016/17: stays 2½m: acts on good to firm and good to soft going: wears headgear/tongue tie. *Lawney Hill*

ELUSIVE CLASSIC (IRE) 9 b.g. Classic Cliche (IRE) – Zander Gander (IRE) (Oscar   **c–**
(IRE)) [2016/17 h16.2d h22.7s⁶ h22s⁵ c24.2sᵖᵘ Dec 26] Irish point winner: no form over   **h–**
hurdles/on chasing debut: tried in cheekpieces. *Gemma Anderson*

ELUSIVE COWBOY (USA) 4 ch.g. Elusive Quality (USA) – Sarmad (USA)   **h59**
(Dynaformer (USA)) [2016/17 h16s h15.8m⁴ Apr 18] close-coupled gelding: fair on Flat, stays 1½m: well held in juvenile hurdles. *Stuart Edmunds*

ELUSIVE THEATRE (IRE) 6 b.m. King's Theatre (IRE) – Miss Best (FR) (Grand   **h119**
Tresor (FR)) [2016/17 h20m³ h16d⁴ h16g⁴ h20.5s³ h19.7d³ h24.3vᶠ h16s* h16.4v² h24.3d³ Apr 21] €7,500 3-y-o, €47,000 4-y-o: sister to a winning pointer and half-sister to 3 winners, including bumper winner/useful hurdler Mister Nibbles (2m-2½m winner, by Kalanisi) and fairly useful chaser Iona Days (21f/2¾m winner, by Epistolaire): dam, French 2½m chase winner, sister to smart chaser (stayed 3m) Tresor de Mai: point/bumper winner: fairly useful hurdler: won mares maiden at Ayr in February: stays 3m: acts on good to firm and heavy going: has worn hood: front runner/races prominently. *Stuart Crawford, Ireland*

ELYSIAN PRINCE 6 b.g. Champs Elysees – Trinkila (USA) (Cat Thief (USA)) [2016/17   **h103**
h17m⁴ h15.8g⁴ h16.3d² h16.8g⁶ h18.6g h16.3g* h16.3g⁶ Apr 23] fairly useful on Flat, stays 1½m: fair handicap hurdler: won at Stratford in April: unproven beyond 17f: acts on good to firm going: has worn tongue tie. *Neil King*

EMERALD ROSE 10 b.m. Sir Harry Lewis (USA) – Swiss Rose (Michelozzo (USA))   **c116**
[2016/17 c116, h–: c29.1g⁶ c23g³ c23.9s* c20.8g c24.1g⁴ c24.1g⁴ Apr 22] angular mare: **h–**
winning hurdler: fairly useful handicap chaser: won at Market Rasen in November: should stay beyond 3m: acts on good to firm and heavy going: wears cheekpieces. *Julian Smith*

EMERALD THIEF (IRE) 6 b.g. Kalanisi (IRE) – Nevinch (IRE) (Needle Gun (IRE))   **c–**
[2016/17 b16.4s⁶ h22.7sᵖᵘ h19.7d h16d h19.3s⁵ c19.3dᶠ Mar 14] sixth in bumper at   **h–**
Newcastle: little impact over hurdles/on chasing debut: tried in tongue tie. *Chris Grant*   **b73**

EMERGING FORCE (IRE) 7 b.g. Milan – Danette (GER) (Exit To Nowhere (USA))   **c140 p**
[2016/17 h144p: h24dᵖᵘ c20.9g* c24.2m* c25.3g⁴ c25g⁵ Apr 8] tall gelding: useful hurdler: **h–**
useful form over fences: won maiden at Hereford (by 14 lengths from Rainy City) in October and novice at Exeter in November: should be suited by further than 3m: acts on soft and good to firm going: front runner/races prominently: remains with potential as a chaser. *Harry Whittington*

EMGEE (IRE) 8 b.g. Sandmason – Honey Rose (IRE) (Shahanndeh) [2016/17 c25.3g^pu   **c–**
Apr 27] point winner: pulled up in hunter on chasing debut. *A. Campbell*

EMINENT POET 6 b.g. Montjeu (IRE) – Contare (Shirley Heights) [2016/17 h120:   **h129**
h18.6g³ h20.6s⁴ h25v* h20.6s* h22.8d h19.5v* h25.8s³ Mar 25] compact gelding: fairly
useful handicap hurdler: won at Plumpton (conditional) in January, Market Rasen in
February and Lingfield in March: stays 3¼m: best form on soft/heavy going: often travels
strongly. *Venetia Williams*

EMIRATE ISLE 13 b.g. Cois Na Tine (IRE) – Emmajoun (Emarati (USA)) [2016/17   **c– x**
c20.1m^pu May 11] winning hurdler: poor chaser: best around 2m: acts on soft going: **h–**
usually wears headgear: often let down by jumping over fences. *Lisa Harrison*

EMMA SODA 12 b.m. Milan – Ms Trude (IRE) (Montelimar (USA)) [2016/17 c106, h–:   **c76**
c24.5d c23.6s c24d⁵ c29.2v^pu Mar 22] maiden hurdler: fair handicap chaser, well below   **h–**
form in 2016/17: stays 29f: best form on heavy going: wears headgear: front runner/races
prominently: inconsistent. *Paul Davies*

EMPEROR COMMODOS 10 b.g. Midnight Legend – Theme Arena (Tragic Role   **c100 §**
(USA)) [2016/17 h111: h19.3m h15.7v⁵ c16g² c16v^pu c16d⁵ c16d^F c18.2g⁵ c18.2g⁶ c16m⁴   **h– §**
Apr 18] sturdy gelding: maiden hurdler: fair maiden chaser: stays 2½m: acts on heavy
going: wears cheekpieces: has worn tongue tie, including final start: prone to mistakes, and
untrustworthy. *Robin Mathew*

EMPEROR SAKHEE 7 ch.g. Sakhee (USA) – Pochard (Inchinor) [2016/17 h–, b101:   **c–**
c20.1d^ur h21.2g^pu May 10] dual bumper winner: failed to complete in 3 starts over hurdles/   **h–**
fences: wears hood. *Karen McLintock*

EMPEROR'S CHOICE (IRE) 10 b.g. Flemensfirth (USA) – House-Of-Hearts (IRE)   **c127**
(Broken Hearted) [2016/17 c135, h–: c32.4s c29.5s^pu c29.2s^pu c32.6s⁵ c33.4s^pu Mar 18]   **h–**
good-topped gelding: winning hurdler: useful handicap chaser: largely out of sorts in
2016/17: stays 33f: acts on heavy going: has worn headgear, including last 2 starts.
Venetia Williams

EMPEROR'S HILL (IRE) 5 b.g. Scorpion (IRE) – Watermelon (IRE) (Beckett (IRE))   **h–**
[2016/17 b15.8v h23.1s^pu Jan 23] no show in bumper/novice hurdle. *Ben Pauling*   **b–**

EMPIRE OF DIRT (IRE) 10 b.g. Westerner – Rose of Inchiquin (IRE) (Roselier   **c163**
(FR)) [2016/17 c149, h–: c24d* c24.3s² c20.8g⁴ c25g^pu Apr 6]   **h–**
    The latest season was remarkable for Irish jumping, not least for the record
haul of nineteen races at the four-day Cheltenham Festival, the season's most
prestigious fixture. There were six winners apiece at that meeting for Ireland's
two top trainers Willie Mullins and Gordon Elliott whose battle for the Irish
trainers' championship wasn't finally decided until the last day of the Punchestown
Festival (Mullins secured the title for the tenth year in succession with the help of
five Grade 1 wins at the seasonal finale). The domination of the Irish jumping scene
by the Mullins and Elliott stables is illustrated by the fact that their individual win
totals—180 and a record-equalling 193 respectively—both exceeded the combined
number of races won by the third, fourth and fifth in the trainers' total prize money
table, Henry de Bromhead (68), Jessica Harrington (48) and Noel Meade (57). The
same applied to the win and place prize money totals in Ireland accrued by Mullins
and Elliott, both of whom won in excess of €4m; the pair each earned more than the
domestic tally of de Bromhead, Harrington and Meade put together. Ireland, though,
is still recovering from the effects of the global economic downturn, having been
the first European country officially to enter recession in 2008. The vibrant state
of the stables of Mullins, Elliott and those immediately below them in the table,
all of whom enjoy the support of one or more among the elite group of enormously
wealthy owners that dominate Irish racing nowadays, is in sharp contrast to those
further down the pecking order.
    The problems of Irish racing at the grassroots are reflected in the drop in
registered owners from 5,588 in 2007 to 3,663 in 2016 and in the associated number
of trainers who have handed in their licence (that total is down by nearly twenty
per cent compared to 2007). The widening gulf between the handful of top yards
and the rest has led to discontent among middle-market trainers who are finding it
increasingly hard to make a living. The generous spread of graded races in Ireland
have always been the preserve of the big owners and trainers, though the surfeit
of them tends to produce too many small fields, but the important handicaps now

seem increasingly to be out of reach of the average trainer too. The season's two most valuable handicaps, the Irish Grand National and the Galway Plate, were in their different ways typical: although the Irish Grand National finish featured horses owned by some 'smaller' owners, Gigginstown House Stud ran thirteen (it would have been fourteen but for a late non-runner) and Gordon Elliott saddled nine; the Galway Plate field was also top heavy with horses representing the big battalions of owners and trainers, the Elliott and Mullins stables filling the first six places between them. In addition, the very valuable Coral Handicap Hurdle at the 2016 Punchestown Festival had featured nine runners (including the winner Anibale Fly) owned by J.P. McManus in the twenty-five-runner field, albeit representing seven different trainers. One of the middle-ranking trainers who claims he is operating at a loss and 'being driven out of the game' is Cheltenham Festival-winning trainer Tony Mullins, brother of Willie. He made the headlines shortly after Ireland's magnificent Cheltenham when calling for a cap on the number of horses any owner can run in a major handicap chase or hurdle.

Horse Racing Ireland rejected any idea of limiting runners owned by the large owners, saying that if a horse is qualified for a race and is good enough to 'make the cut' it should be entitled to run 'no matter who owns it'. Most of the Gigginstown-owned runners in handicaps are there because they haven't made the grade in better races and, like all the owners' horses, they are campaigned openly and frequently run against one another. The financial commitment that big owners like Gigginstown make to Irish racing ought to be valued and appreciated, not criticised. Reducing entry fees for races worth €20,000 or less and extending prize money down to sixth in €40,000-plus races are among newly-introduced reforms designed to allay some of the concerns of trainers like Tony Mullins and Adrian Maguire, another who has spoken out, who can also now claim a grant of up to €1,000 to help with marketing and promotion. Changes to the racing programme include trialling a series of maiden hurdles for horses who cost less than €30,000 as stores, and introducing some higher-value handicaps with a ratings cap, as well as increasing the number of novice chases and novice hurdles with a rating restriction. A redistribution of some of the prize money from the plethora of graded races to the middle- and lower-tier events might also help those trainers struggling to make ends meet.

The Gigginstown-owned Empire of Dirt was transferred to Gordon Elliott for the latest season after Colm Murphy, for whom he won the Leopardstown Chase, before landing the Plate Handicap at the 2016 Cheltenham Festival, handed in his licence after claiming his operation was not economically viable (Murphy had a background in accountancy). Empire of Dirt made his first start for his new stable at Navan in late-November when he was one of eleven saddled by Elliott in a typically wide-open renewal of the Ladbrokes Troytown Handicap Chase, a race in which Empire of Dirt had looked the likely winner when departing late on twelve months earlier. Empire of Dirt gave Elliott his third successive victory in the Troytown, being patiently ridden by Gigginstown's number-one at the time Bryan Cooper (for whom another injury-hit season included a collapsed lung, liver lacerations, a broken arm and a broken pelvis—topped off when he learned after the end of the season that his retainer was not being renewed). Empire of Dirt took over in the lead in the Troytown between the last two fences and forged clear to win by four lengths and a length and a quarter from Abolitionist and Bonny Kate, with the Elliott-trained favourite Noble Endeavor fourth. Navan is Gordon Elliott's local course and he will remember November 27th 2016 as a red-letter day, Empire of Dirt being one of six winners from twenty-five runners for him on the card (the Willie Mullins odds-on shot Min in the beginners chase was the only winner not trained by Elliott). It was thought to be the first time a trainer had saddled six winners on the same card in Ireland; Paul Nicholls achieved the feat (running eight horses on a seven-race card) in Britain at Wincanton on January 21st 2006. Empire of Dirt's campaign continued with a very good second in the Irish Gold Cup on his first outing in Grade 1 company. With Jack Kennedy deputising for the injured Cooper, Empire of Dirt jumped well and travelled strongly at Leopardstown where he went down by three quarters of a length to Sizing John, recording a career best. Unfortunately, Empire of Dirt's season rather tapered off after that fine effort. He contested the Ryanair Chase at the Cheltenham Festival, in preference to the Gold Cup, but, starting second favourite, managed only fourth of eight behind Un de Sceaux, beaten nine lengths after not jumping so well as he can. An even more disconcerting performance followed in the Bowl at Aintree where Empire of Dirt was never travelling fluently and was eventually pulled up after losing touch, reportedly returning lame.

	Westerner	Danehill	Danzig
	(b 1999)	(b 1986)	Razyana
		Walensee	Troy
Empire of Dirt (IRE)		(b 1982)	Warsaw
(b.g. 2007)	Rose of Inchiquin (IRE)	Roselier	Misti Iv
	(ch 1993)	(gr 1973)	Peace Rose
		Boreen Belle	Boreen
		(b 1982)	Chestnut Belle

Empire of Dirt, a tall gelding, has a stamina-packed pedigree, being by the Gold Cup winner Westerner (who was himself from a stout family including the Grand Course de Haies winner World Citizen) out of a daughter of Roselier, a stallion whose offspring built up a particularly impressive record in the major Nationals (the general rule for Roselier's offspring was that the longer the distance and the softer the ground the better). Empire of Dirt's dam Rose of Inchiquin was a fairly useful hurdler/chaser who stayed three miles, though her most important victory, in the Lismullen Hurdle at Navan, came at two and a half miles when her four rivals gave her too much rope (runner-up Bannow Bay allowed front-running 33/1-shot Rose of Inchiquin the best part of a furlong start and his jockey, along with the three other beaten jockeys, received a one-day suspension for riding an injudicious race). Rose of Inchiquin is a daughter of the thoroughly useful staying hurdler Boreen Belle who won the second running of what is now the Sefton Novices' Hurdle at Aintree (she had an essay in *Chasers & Hurdlers 1988/89*). Boreen Belle went well in the mud, as did both Rose of Inchiquin and Rose of Inchiquin's half-sister Be My Belle, a

Gigginstown House Stud's "Empire of Dirt"

useful, front-running staying hurdler/chaser who won the Thyestes Chase. Rose of Inchiquin has had one other winner besides Empire of Dirt, the useful staying chaser Panther Claw (by Old Vic) who gained both his wins over fences on heavy going and finished fifth in Liberty Counsel's Irish Grand National on soft ground. Empire of Dirt is a strong traveller and has yet to race beyond three miles, but he may well appear in a Grand National one day (his trainer mentioned the latest National as a probable target for him after his victory in the Troytown but he was among the Gigginstown horses taken out of the race in a row over the weights they had been allotted). He acts on heavy going but seems not to need the mud, his 2016 Cheltenham Festival win coming on good going. Empire of Dirt has worn a tongue tie (including on his last three starts) and he is usually patiently ridden. *Gordon Elliott, Ireland*

EMPRESARIO (IRE) 8 ch.g. Hurricane Run (IRE) – La Stravaganza (USA) (Rainbow Quest (USA)) [2016/17 c124, h–: c17g6 c20s* c25g^{pu} c17d^{pu} Dec 3] winning hurdler: fairly useful handicap chaser: won at Navan in September: stays 2½m: acts on soft and good to firm going: has worn headgear: wears tongue tie: front runner/races prominently: inconsistent. *Matthew J. Smith, Ireland* **c124 h–**

EMPTY THE TANK (IRE) 7 b.g. Lawman (FR) – Asian Alliance (IRE) (Soviet Star (USA)) [2016/17 h104: h17.7g4 c19.7m^{ur} c17g^{pu} h16m Nov 8] useful-looking gelding: fair handicap hurdler, below form first/last starts in 2016/17: twice-raced over fences: third when unseated rider last in novice handicap won by Little Windmill at Plumpton: best effort at 2m: acts on good to firm and good to soft going: wears hood: often races prominently. *Jim Boyle* **c94 h70**

ENDEAVOR 12 ch.g. Selkirk (USA) – Midnight Mambo (USA) (Kingmambo (USA)) [2016/17 c99§, h97§: h16.8s* c17.3g h16.2d c17.3d* h17.2g6 c17.3d* c16g2 h16.2s c15.8g2 h16.2s c19.9g c17.1s^{pu} h15.6g5 h15.6g5 h15.8s^{pu} c15.2m4 h16.2g Apr 27] modest handicap hurdler: won at Sedgefield in May: fair handicap chaser: won at Cartmel in July and August: stays 2½m: acts on any going: has worn cheekpieces, including in 2016/17: often races towards rear: unreliable. *Dianne Sayer* **c102 § h90 §**

ENDLESS CREDIT (IRE) 7 b.g. High Chaparral (IRE) – Pay The Bank (High Top) [2016/17 h–: h16d h15.8d h16s2 h16.8s h15.6g6 c15.9d^{pu} c16g* Apr 27] fair handicap hurdler: fairly useful form over fences: won novice handicap at Perth in April: raced around 2m: acts on soft going: tried in tongue tie: usually races close up. *Micky Hammond* **c123 h110**

END OF LINE 6 b.g. Pastoral Pursuits – Just Devine (IRE) (Montjeu (IRE)) [2016/17 h16g h16.2f^{pu} Jun 5] useful at one time on Flat, stays 1m: poor maiden hurdler: usually wears tongue tie. *Gordon Elliott, Ireland* **h81**

ENGAGING SMILE 5 b.m. Exceed And Excel (AUS) – Bronze Star (Mark of Esteem (IRE)) [2016/17 h16.5s^{pu} Feb 5] fair at one time on Flat, has deteriorated: pulled up in novice on hurdling debut. *James Moon, Jersey* **h–**

EN JOULE 6 ch.m. Shirocco (GER) – Ancora (IRE) (Accordion) [2016/17 b16d4 b16.3m* h19.6g h17.7g3 h16g5 h21.3g^{pu} h21m^{F} Apr 4] fourth foal: dam unraced sister to very smart chaser (stayed 3¼m) The Tother One, closely related to top-class chaser (2m-25f winner) Carlingford Lough and half-sister to high-class chaser (stayed 21f) Thisthatandtother: fair form in bumpers: won mares event at Stratford in July: modest form over hurdles: front runner/races prominently: temperament under suspicion. *Neil Mulholland* **b89 h89**

ENJOY RESPONSIBLY (IRE) 8 b.g. Flemensfirth (USA) – Spice Patrol (IRE) (Mandalus) [2016/17 c133, h66: c16m4 c15.8d4 c16g4 c17.4g2 c17g2 c16.5g4 Sep 23] workmanlike gelding: maiden hurdler: fair handicap chaser: stays 19f: acts on good to firm and good to soft going: wears headgear: has worn tongue tie: front runner/races prominently. *Sam Thomas* **c113 h–**

ENMESHING 4 ch.g. Mastercraftsman (IRE) – Yacht Club (USA) (Sea Hero (USA)) [2016/17 h16.5g h16g5 Apr 8] fairly useful on Flat, stays 1½m: poor form over hurdles. *Alexandra Dunn* **h78**

ENNISCOFFEY OSCAR (IRE) 5 b.g. Oscar (IRE) – Enniscoffey (IRE) (Old Vic) [2016/17 ab16g* b17g2 Apr 7] €29,000 3-y-o, £45,000 4-y-o: tall gelding: has scope: second foal: dam, unraced, closely related to winning hurdler/high-class chaser (stayed 25f) Weird Al: second when fell last in Irish maiden point: useful form in bumpers: won at Lingfield (by short head from Take To Heart) in February: improved when second in Grade 2 at Aintree (2½ lengths behind Lalor) in April, staying on strongly: will stay at least 2½m. *Emma Lavelle* **b113**

ENNISTOWN 7 b.g. Authorized (IRE) – Saoirse Abu (USA) (Mr Greeley (USA)) **h136**
[2016/17 h132: h15.8g h21.6g³ h25.4d* h24.7dF Nov 5] good-topped gelding: useful
handicap hurdler: won at Cartmel in August: stays 25f: acts on soft going: has worn
headgear, including in 2016/17: in tongue tie last 4 starts. *David Pipe*

ENOLA GAY (FR) 4 b.g. Fuisse (FR) – Enolaland (FR) (Daliapour (IRE)) [2016/17 **h118**
h16.9s⁵ h16.9s² h16.3d⁶ Dec 31] useful-looking gelding: once-raced on Flat: fairly useful
form over hurdles: second in juvenile at Clairefontaine in July: left P. Peltier after.
Venetia Williams

ENZANI (IRE) 6 b.g. Cape Cross (IRE) – Eytarna (IRE) (Dubai Destination (USA)) **h102**
[2016/17 h20.2s² Jul 10] fairly useful on Flat, stays 1½m: fair form over hurdles: stays 19f:
tried in cheekpieces: wears tongue tie. *John McConnell, Ireland*

EPIC ETHEL 6 b.m. Midnight Legend – Violet Elizabeth (Overbury (IRE)) [2016/17 b93: **b81**
b15.8d⁴ Dec 4] fair form when won on first of 2 starts in bumpers: will be suited by further
than 2m. *Neil King*

EPISODE 6 br.g. Lucky Story (USA) – Epicurean (Pursuit of Love) [2016/17 h–, b86: **h92**
h19.7g h19.7d⁵ h16s h19.3g^ur h19.3s³ h16.6d* h19.4s^pu Mar 3] modest handicap
hurdler: won at Doncaster (conditional) in February: best effort at 17f: acted on good to
soft going: in cheekpieces last 3 starts: dead. *Philip Kirby*

EPSOM FLYER 7 ch.g. Haafhd – River Cara (USA) (Irish River (FR)) [2016/17 h92: **h–**
h17.7g May 29] modest hurdler, below form only outing in 2016/17: stays 21f: acts on
good to soft going. *Pat Phelan*

EQUITY SWAP (IRE) 8 ch.g. Strategic Prince – Medicean Star (IRE) (Galileo (IRE)) **c–**
[2016/17 c–, h109: h16g May 2] sturdy gelding: fair hurdler at best, well held in handicap **h–**
early in 2016/17: lightly-raced chaser/pointer: stays 2½m: acts on good to soft going: has
worn cheekpieces: tried in tongue tie. *Tim Vaughan*

EQULEUS 5 b.g. Equiano (FR) – Merle (Selkirk (USA)) [2016/17 h16.5g h15.3v h19g **h90**
h15.8d² Apr 16] half-brother to fair hurdler Consult (19f winner, by Dr Fong), stays 3m:
dam half-sister to useful hurdler (17f-21f winner) Solo Mio and fairly useful 2m hurdler/
chaser Kingham: fair on Flat, stays 9.5f: modest form over hurdles: tried in tongue tie.
Katie Stephens

EQUUS AMADEUS (IRE) 4 b.g. Beat Hollow – Charade (IRE) (Danehill (USA)) **b89**
[2016/17 b15.8v³ b16g³ Apr 24] third foal: dam ran twice on Flat: fair form in bumpers:
better effort when third at Warwick in April. *Tom Lacey*

EREYNA 8 gr.m. Erhaab (USA) – Tereyna (Terimon) [2016/17 h96: h23.3g⁵ h23.3m² **h107**
h23.3g* h24g³ h23.1s⁵ Mar 12] fair handicap hurdler: won at Uttoxeter in July: stayed 3m:
acted on good to soft and good to firm going: dead. *Stuart Edmunds*

ERICHT (IRE) 11 b.g. Alderbrook – Lady Orla (IRE) (Satco (FR)) [2016/17 c134§, h–: **c131 §**
c24g c19.4g^pu c19.9g² c20.4g² c20.5d⁴ c24g³ c19.9g^pu Mar 25] tall gelding: winning **h–**
hurdler: useful handicap chaser: second at Newbury (8 lengths behind Sandy Beach) and
Cheltenham (veterans, 1½ lengths behind Astracad) in November: stays 25f: acts on good
to firm and heavy going: wears cheekpieces: unreliable. *Nicky Henderson*

ERICUS ERICI 7 b.g. Include (USA) – Eze (USA) (Williamstown (USA)) [2016/17 **b–**
b16.2d Jun 4] point winner: tailed off in bumper. *Shane Crawley, Ireland*

ERMYN'S EDITH 6 b.m. Fair Mix (IRE) – Ivy Edith (Blakeney) [2016/17 b–: h15.9d^ur **h–**
h15.7d h15.9v h15.9v⁶ Jan 16] angular mare: no form over hurdles. *Pat Phelan*

ERMYN'S EMERALD 5 b.g. Alflora (IRE) – Emerald Project (IRE) (Project Manager) **h80**
[2016/17 b72: h15.9d⁴ h15.9g⁶ h15.9d h15.9v h21s h21m⁴ Apr 18] poor form over hurdles.
Pat Phelan

ESHTIAAL (USA) 7 b.g. Dynaformer (USA) – Enfiraaj (USA) (Kingmambo (USA)) **h129**
[2016/17 h127p: h25.4m* h22.1d* h23.9g^pu Oct 22] fairly useful handicap hurdler: won at
Cartmel in May and July: stays 25f: acts on firm and good to soft going: in cheekpieces last
4 starts: has worn tongue tie, including in 2016/17: often races prominently. *Gordon Elliott,
Ireland*

E SI SI MUOVE (IRE) 5 b.g. Galileo (IRE) – Queen of France (USA) (Danehill (USA)) **b65**
[2016/17 b16.4d Nov 11] 50/1, raced freely when seventh in maiden bumper at Newcastle.
Andrew Crook

ESKENDASH (USA) 4 ch.g. Eskendereya (USA) – Daffaash (USA) (Mr Greeley **b93**
(USA)) [2016/17 b16g² b13g² b16s² b16s² Feb 4] fifth foal: half-brother to 2 winners on
Flat, including useful 7f winner Ebn Arab (by Dixie Union): dam unraced: fair form in
bumpers: left Peter Niven after second start: won maiden on Flat debut in March. *Pam Sly*

ESPOIR DE TEILLEE (FR) 5 b.g. Martaline – Belle de Lyphard (FR) (Lyphard's Wish **b97**
(FR)) [2016/17 b16s⁶ b15.8g* Apr 9] €28,000 3-y-o, £220,000 4-y-o: third foal: brother to
French 2¼m hurdle winner Venus de Teillee and half-brother to French chaser Air de
Teillee (2½m-2¾m winner, by Air Eminem): dam French 2½m chase winner: in front when
fell last in Irish maiden point: fairly useful form in bumpers: won at Ffos Las in April: will
stay further than 2m. *Neil Mulholland*

ESSPRESSO (FR) 5 gr.g. Croco Rouge (IRE) – Kaldoubelle (FR) (Kaldounevees (FR)) **h–**
[2016/17 b15.8d³ h16s h15.8sᵖᵘ Feb 8] second foal: dam, French 19f hurdle winner, half- **b68**
sister to smart hurdler (2m-2½m winner) Le Rocher: third in maiden bumper at Ffos Las:
no show in maiden hurdles: tried in hood. *Evan Williams*

ETANIA 9 b.m. King's Theatre (IRE) – Linnet (GER) (Dr Fong (USA)) [2016/17 c93, h94: **c–**
h22m h23.3m h23.3g⁵ h23.3gᵖᵘ Jul 22] sturdy mare: modest handicap hurdler: below best **h84**
in 2016/17: winning chaser: stays 23f: acts on good to firm and heavy going: in cheekpieces
last 2 starts: often races prominently. *Ian Williams*

ETHELWYN 7 ch.m. Alflora (IRE) – Our Ethel (Be My Chief (USA)) [2016/17 h103p, **h105**
b75: h20.3g² h17.2d² h19.9g* h22.1g² h23.3d⁴ h16.2g² h19.9g Oct 27] fair hurdler: won
mares maiden at Uttoxeter in July: stays 2¾m: acts on good to soft going. *Malcolm Jefferson*

ETHERIDGE ANNIE 8 b.m. Leander – Lady Harriet (Sir Harry Lewis (USA)) [2016/17 **h77**
h–: h16.8d³ h19.2s⁴ Mar 16] runner-up in bumpers: poor form over hurdles. *Hugo Froud*

EVENING HUSH (IRE) 4 b.f. Excellent Art – Applause (IRE) (Danehill Dancer (IRE)) **h128**
[2016/17 h16.8s* h17s* h16s² h16g² h16.8g h16s⁵ Mar 30] angular filly: fairly useful on
Flat, stays 1¾m: fairly useful form over hurdles: won juvenile at Exeter in November and
listed fillies juvenile at Aintree (by 21 lengths from Castafiore) in December: second in
Finale Juvenile Hurdle at Chepstow (13 lengths behind Defi du Seuil) later in December
and Adonis Juvenile Hurdle at Kempton (11 lengths behind Master Blueyes) in February:
raced around 2m: acts on soft going: front runner/races prominently. *Evan Williams*

EVENING STANLEY (IRE) 7 b.g. Stowaway – Suzy Q (IRE) (King's Ride) [2016/17 **c–**
h–, b85: h20.6g⁶ c23gᵖᵘ Apr 6] failed to complete both starts in points: no form over **h–**
hurdles: pulled up in maiden hunter on chasing debut: left Oliver Sherwood after first start:
tried in hood. *G. B. Foot*

EVER SO MUCH (IRE) 8 b.g. Westerner – Beautiful World (IRE) (Saddlers' Hall **c104**
(IRE)) [2016/17 c108, h107: c19.3g³ c20.3g* h21g* h22.1m⁵ c20.1s h19.9gᵖᵘ c15.2d⁵ **h99**
c20.3gᵖᵘ Apr 21] modest handicap hurdler: won at Towcester in May: fair handicap chaser:
won at Southwell earlier in May: stays 21f: acts on good to soft going: wears headgear:
often races towards rear. *Ben Haslam*

EVERYBODYS HAPPY 7 b.g. Presenting – Graceful Dancer (Old Vic) [2016/17 **b88**
b17.7g² b17.7d² b16s Dec 8] strong gelding: second foal: dam (c101/h103) 2¾m-3¼m
hurdle/chase winner (stayed 29f): fair form when second in bumpers. *Chris Gordon*

EVERYLASTING (IRE) 10 b.g. Millenary – All French (IRE) (Lepanto (GER)) **c72**
[2016/17 c82, h–: c20.1g³ c21.2m⁶ c22.6g Jul 28] maiden hurdler: poor handicap chaser: **h–**
stays 25f: acts on soft and good to firm going: wears headgear: tried in tongue tie: front
runner/races prominently, tends to find little. *Rose Dobbin*

EVIAS 6 b.g. Tiger Hill (IRE) – Circadian Rhythm (Lujain (USA)) [2016/17 b17.7g May **b–**
8] well beaten in bumper. *Geoffrey Deacon*

EXACTORIS 6 b.g. Shantou (USA) – Klezmer (IRE) (Revoque (IRE)) [2016/17 **h130**
h20d* h20.7g³ h20d⁴ h20d* h24s⁶ Feb 5] €17,000 3-y-o: first foal: dam, unraced, out of
half-sister to useful 2m chaser Dines and Midlands Grand National winner G V A Ireland:
dual bumper winner: useful form over hurdles: won maiden at Tipperary in July and novice
handicap at Leopardstown (by 2 lengths from First To Boogie) in December: stays 3m: acts
on soft going: has worn tongue tie, including last 3 starts. *Joseph Patrick O'Brien, Ireland*

EXCELLENT RESULT (IRE) 7 b.g. Shamardal (USA) – Line Ahead (IRE) (Sadler's **h120**
Wells (USA)) [2016/17 h15.8m* h16.7g² h16.4g h16g* h15.8g² Apr 17] sturdy gelding:
useful on Flat, stays 1¾m: fairly useful form over hurdles: won novices at Huntingdon
in October and Kempton in March: raced around 2m: acts on good to firm going.
Richard Spencer

EXCELLENT TEAM 5 b.g. Teofilo (IRE) – Seradim (Elnadim (USA)) [2016/17 **h126**
h15.7g² h19.9d² h18.7g³ h16.8g³ h17.7g⁴ h16g² h1⁷./.⁄g⁴ h16.3g* h15.9m⁴ h15.8m² Apr
25] lightly-raced maiden on Flat: fairly useful hurdler: won handicap at Fontwell in August
and novice at Stratford in April: likely to prove best around 2m: acts on good to firm and
good to soft going: wears tongue tie: usually leads. *Dan Skelton*

EXCITABLE ISLAND (IRE) 10 b.g. Heron Island (IRE) – Miss Excitable (IRE) (Montelimar (USA)) [2016/17 c26g³ c27.5m^pu May 20] multiple winning pointer: modest form in chases: better effort when third in hunter at Cheltenham very early in season. *N. W. Padfield* **c97**

EXCLUSIVE RIGHTS 9 b.m. Fair Mix (IRE) – Rosie Ring (IRE) (Phardante (FR)) [2016/17 c22.6m² May 20] dual winning pointer: lightly-raced hurdler: 33/1, second in novice hunter at Stratford (½ length behind Our Chief) on chasing debut. *Mrs Pauline Harkin* **c87 h–**

EXCLUSIVE WATERS (IRE) 7 b.g. Elusive City (USA) – Pelican Waters (IRE) (Key of Luck (USA)) [2016/17 h16.2d^pu h16.2f⁵ Jun 5] modest on Flat, stays 12.5f, won in February for Garry Moss: maiden hurdler: best effort at 2m: in tongue tie last 2 starts. *George Charlton* **h68**

EXECUTIVE PRINCE (IRE) 7 bl.g. Presenting – Callanagh Pride (IRE) (Executive Perk) [2016/17 h60, b–: h16.8m³ h16m³ h16.8m^pu h15.9g⁶ Oct 17] Irish maiden pointer: modest form over hurdles: best effort at 2m: acts on good to firm going: free-going sort. *Jeremy Scott* **h99**

EXEMPLARY 10 b.g. Sulamani (IRE) – Epitome (IRE) (Nashwan (USA)) [2016/17 c–, h100: h22m⁴ h23.3s* c25.5m⁴ h26.5m⁴ h26.4g² h21.6g^pu h21.6d⁶ h25m^pu Oct 11] modest handicap hurdler: won at Uttoxeter in June: poor form over fences: stays 3¼m: acts on soft and good to firm going: has worn headgear: wears tongue tie: often races towards rear. *Johnny Farrelly* **c79 h96**

EXILES RETURN (IRE) 15 b.g. Needle Gun (IRE) – Moores Girl (IRE) (Mandalus) [2016/17 c–§, h57: h21.6g^pu h18.5m h16.8g⁴ Nov 9] lengthy gelding: bad handicap hurdler: pulled up only chase start: unproven beyond 17f: acts on good to firm going: tried in tongue tie: front runner/races prominently. *Jackie Retter* **c– h57**

EXITAS (IRE) 9 b.g. Exit To Nowhere (USA) – Suntas (IRE) (Riberetto) [2016/17 c121, h112: h15.8d⁶ h15.5d³ Dec 28] lengthy gelding: useful handicap hurdler at best, has deteriorated: maiden chaser: stays 19f: acts on heavy going: wears tongue tie. *Alex Hales* **c– h113**

EXIT TO FREEDOM 11 ch.g. Exit To Nowhere (USA) – Bobanvi (Timeless Times (USA)) [2016/17 c–, h57: h20.3s^pu h20.2f³ h20.6g³ h23.1g h24g⁵ h20.7d h19.9s^pu h20.6g⁵ h19.7m⁶ Apr 13] poor handicap hurdler: fell first only chase start: stays 2¾m: acts on firm and soft going: wears headgear: tried in tongue tie: unreliable. *John Wainwright* **c– h74 §**

EXMOOR CHALLENGE 8 b.g. Thank Heavens – Bullys Maid (Button Bright (USA)) [2016/17 c78x, h–: h27s⁵ h25g⁶ May 8] little form over hurdles/fences (poor jumper): in cheekpieces last 5 starts: tried in tongue tie: front runner/races prominently. *Neil King* **c– x h–**

EXMOOR MIST 9 gr.g. Kayf Tara – Chita's Flora (Aflora (IRE)) [2016/17 c120, h–: c19.4g c15.5s^pu Feb 17] rangy gelding: winning hurdler: fairly useful chaser at best, no form in 2016/17: stays 2¼m: acts on heavy going: wears tongue tie. *Victor Dartnall* **c– h–**

EXOTIC FRIEND (IRE) 9 ch.g. Croco Rouge (IRE) – Prima Nox (Sabrehill (USA)) [2016/17 h16.2g h19.6g^pu h19g h19.6g* Apr 22] workmanlike gelding: fair handicap hurdler: won at Bangor in April: left M. Palussiere/off nearly 3 years after final (2013/14) start: stays 2½m: acts on good to soft going. *Adrian Wintle* **h100**

EXPANDING UNIVERSE (IRE) 10 b.g. Galileo (IRE) – Uliana (USA) (Darshaan) [2016/17 c83, h–: c20s^pu Feb 8] sturdy gelding: maiden hurdler: modest chaser at best: won point in April: stays 27f: acts on heavy going: tried in blinkers: usually races prominently, often lazily. *Mrs S. Bowen* **c– h–**

EX PATRIOT (IRE) 4 b.g. Elusive Pimpernel (USA) – Carolobrian (IRE) (Mark of Esteem (IRE)) [2016/17 h16s* h16s⁵ h16v² h16.8g⁴ h16d³ Apr 17] sparely-made gelding: dam half-sister to useful hurdler (stayed 3m) Sweetheart: fairly useful maiden on Flat, stays 13f: useful form over hurdles: first past post in maiden at Fairyhouse in January and Winning Fair Juvenile Hurdle at same course (demoted after beating Dinaria des Obeaux a head) in February: third in Grade 2 juvenile at Fairyhouse (1½ lengths behind Project Bluebook) in April: likely to stay 2½m: acts on heavy going. *Ellmarie Holden, Ireland* **h137**

EXPEDITE (IRE) 6 b.g. Brian Boru – Angelica Garnett (Desert Story (IRE)) [2016/17 h108: h21.6g³ h23.1g* c23.8d^ur h20.5v⁵ h21g⁴ h23.5m³ Apr 2] compact gelding: fairly useful hurdler: won at Exeter in November: third at Ascot (conditional) final start: unseated rider first in novice handicap on chasing debut: stays 3m: acts on soft and good to firm going: in cheekpieces last 5 starts: front runner/races prominently: temperament under suspicion. *Ben Pauling* **c– h125**

EXPLAINED (IRE) 10 b.g. Exit To Nowhere (USA) – All Told (IRE) (Valanjou (FR))   c–
[2016/17 c112x, h–: c20g c19.2g^{su} c19.4d^{pu} Jun 16] winning hurdler: fairly useful chaser at   h–
best, no form in 2016/17: tried in cheekpieces: front runner/raced prominently: dead.
Tim Vaughan

EXTREME IMPACT 11 b.g. Rock of Gibraltar (IRE) – Soviet Moon (IRE) (Sadler's   h77 §
Wells (USA)) [2016/17 h109§: h24.2g h20.5d h23.9d^6 h26v Dec 31] small, close-coupled
gelding: fair handicap hurdler, below form in 2016/17: maiden chaser: stays 3¼m: acts on
heavy going: wears headgear: ungenuine. *Charlie Mann*

EYES OF A TIGER (IRE) 6 ch.g. Golan (IRE) – Backtothekingsnest (IRE) (King's   h115
Theatre (IRE)) [2016/17 h106, h87: h15.7g h16d* h16.6g^2 h15.6g^5 h15.6g^5 h15.7g Apr 15]
placed on completed start in Irish points: fairly useful handicap hurdler: won at Wetherby
in November: raced mainly at 2m: acts on heavy going: wears hood: usually forces pace.
Brian Ellison

F

FABRITIUS (IRE) 4 b.g. Dutch Art – Bay of Pearls (IRE) (Rock of Gibraltar (IRE))   b79
[2016/17 b13.7g^6 Nov 8] 4/1, sixth in junior bumper at Huntingdon. *Hugo Palmer*

FACE TO FACE 8 b.g. Kayf Tara – Monsignorita (IRE) (Classic Cliche (IRE)) [2016/17   h–
b83: h20.5g h16.3d Dec 14] strong gelding: point winner: no form in 2 starts over hurdles.
Mark Pitman

FACTION 4 b.g. Champs Elysees – Belladera (IRE) (Alzao (USA)) [2016/17 h16.8m^3 h98
h16.5m^4 Apr 27] fair maiden on Flat, stays 1¼m: modest form over hurdles. *Nigel Hawke*

FACT OF THE MATTER (IRE) 7 b.g. Brian Boru – Womanofthemountain (IRE)   c122
(Presenting) [2016/17 h105, b95: c20g* c19.9m^2 c24.2g* c24.2g^3 c25.3g* Apr 20] has had   h–
breathing operation: bumper winner: maiden hurdler: fairly useful form over fences: won
handicaps at Worcester (novice) in September, Exeter in October and Cheltenham (another
novice) in April: stays 25f: acts on good to firm going: in hood last 5 starts: wears tongue
tie: often races prominently. *Jamie Snowden*

FACTOR FIFTY (IRE) 8 b.g. Definite Article – Sun Screen (Caerleon (USA)) [2016/17   c–
c–, h106: h23.1g^5 h23.1g^3 h27g^4 Sep 1] fair handicap hurdler: well held only chase start: h98
stays 27f: acts on soft and good to firm going: in cheekpieces last 5 starts: tried in tongue
tie. *Philip Kirby*

FADAS (FR) 4 gr.f. Davidoff (GER) – Winkle (FR) (Turgeon (USA)) [2016/17 h16.9g   h116
h17.4s^{pu} h16.9s* h17.9d^4 h17.9d^5 h17.9s h15.3d^3 h16.4g h16s^{pu} h16.8m^3 Apr 19] seventh
foal: half-sister to 3 winners in France, including hurdlers Pafadas (useful 15f-2¼m
winner, by Martaline) and Prinkle (17f winner, by Priolo): dam French 10.5f/11f winner:
fairly useful hurdler: won fillies juvenile at Clairefontaine in August: left H. Billot, below
best after sixth start: stays 2¼m: acts on soft going: in cheekpieces/tongue tie last 3 starts.
Dan Skelton

FAFA 6 b.g. Westerner – Ifuseehersayhello (Kayf Tara) [2016/17 b13.6v^5 b16.3d^{ro} Mar 13]   b–
well held completed start in bumpers. *Tom Gretton*

FAGO (FR) 9 b.g. Balko (FR) – Merciki (FR) (Villez (USA)) [2016/17 c148§, h–: c18g   c– §
c16d^6 c30.2d^{pu} h20.5v^{pu} Feb 27] good-topped gelding: winning hurdler: smart chaser at   h–
best, no form in 2016/17: left Paul Nicholls after first start: has worn hood: in tongue tie last
5 starts: temperamental. *Patrick Griffin, Ireland*

FAHEEM 6 b.g. Halling (USA) – White Star (IRE) (Darshaan) [2016/17 b81: b17.7s^2 h83
b17.7d^4 h15.9d h17.7v^3 Jan 29] fair form in bumpers: poor form over hurdles: better effort   b88
when third in novice at Fontwell. *Lydia Richards*

FAINT HOPE 5 ch.g. Midnight Legend – Rhinestone Ruby (Kayf Tara) [2016/17 b15.8m^4 b80
Apr 18] 25/1, fourth of 6 in bumper (4½ lengths behind Dans Le Vent) at Ludlow.
Grace Harris

FAIR ASK 9 gr.m. Fair Mix (IRE) – Ask Me Not (IRE) (Shernazar) [2016/17 h19.2g^4 h62
h20.6g^{pu} h19.9g^5 h16.6g^{pu} Apr 22] second foal: half-sister to bumper winner/fair hurdler
Squeeze Me (2½m/2¾m winner, by Grape Tree Road): dam, winning pointer, half-sister to
useful hurdler/smart chaser (2½m-25f winner) According To John: off mark in points at
fifth attempt: poor form over hurdles: tried in cheekpieces. *Gary Hanmer*

FAL

FAIR DILEMMA (IRE) 12 b.g. Dr Massini (IRE) – Midnight Dilemma (IRE) (Eagle **c137**
Eyed (USA)) [2016/17 c133, h–: c17g* c17m⁵ Jul 10] winning hurdler: useful handicap **h–**
chaser: won at Stratford (by 2½ lengths* from Parsnip Pete) in May: stays 21f: acts on good
to firm and heavy going: has worn cheekpieces/tongue tie: front runner/races prominently.
Chris Gordon

FAIR FLORA 10 ch.m. Alflora (IRE) – Phildante (IRE) (Phardante (FR)) [2016/17 **h–**
h21mᵖᵘ h16d h21.6mᵖᵘ Jul 17] sixth foal: half-sister to a winning pointer by Classic Cliche:
dam winning pointer: no form over hurdles: wears hood. *Polly Gundry*

FAIR FOR ALL 6 b.g. Fair Mix (IRE) – Falcons Theatre (IRE) (King's Theatre (IRE)) **b–**
[2016/17 b17.1g Nov 7] tailed off in bumper. *Geoffrey Harker*

FAIR FRANK 6 gr.g. Fair Mix (IRE) – Firstflor (Alflora (IRE)) [2016/17 ab16g Feb 20] **b–**
well held in bumper. *David Bridgwater*

FAIRLEE GREY 8 gr.g. Fair Mix (IRE) – Halo Flora (Alflora (IRE)) [2016/17 h110: **h119**
h16.2s⁶ h16s² h16v* h18.1vᶠ h15.7v³ h16d⁴ Apr 21] fairly useful hurdler: won novice at
Ayr in January: should stay beyond 2m: acts on heavy going: front runner. *George Charlton*

FAIR LOCH 9 gr.g. Fair Mix (IRE) – Ardentinny (Ardross) [2016/17 c–p, h115§: c15.5d* **c129 §**
c15.8g⁴ c15.7g³ c15.8g⁴ c15.5d² Apr 21] good-topped gelding: fairly useful hurdler: fairly **h– §**
useful form over fences: won handicap at Ayr in October: unproven beyond 17f: acts on
heavy going: tried in headgear: has worn tongue tie: front runner/races prominently, often
finds little. *Brian Ellison*

FAIR TO MIDDLING 7 gr.g. Fair Mix (IRE) – Mtilly (Mtoto) [2016/17 h94: h19.6g* **h106**
h19.9gᵖᵘ h19.9g² h21.6g⁴ h21.6g⁶ h23.9g² Nov 24] fair handicap hurdler: won novice event
at Bangor in May: stays 3m: best form on good going: usually wears cheekpieces: has worn
tongue tie. *Peter Bowen*

FAIR TRADE 10 ch.g. Trade Fair – Ballet (Sharrood (USA)) [2016/17 h15.7g h23.9g Sep **c–**
6] useful-looking gelding: useful hurdler at best for Alan King, no form in 2016/17: let **h–**
down by jumping only chase start: unproven beyond 2m: acts on good to firm and heavy
going. *Wilf Storey*

FAIRY RATH (IRE) 11 ch.g. Accordion – Killoughey Fairy (IRE) (Torus) [2016/17 **c105**
c132, h–: c17g⁵ h19.1v⁶ c15.5s Feb 17] strong gelding: maiden hurdler: useful handicap **h89**
chaser, below form in 2016/17: stays 21f: acts on heavy going: has worn tongue tie,
including last 4 starts: usually races close up, often travels strongly. *Nick Gifford*

FAIRY THEATRE (IRE) 6 b.m. King's Theatre (IRE) – Fairy Native (IRE) (Be My **h106**
Native (USA)) [2016/17 h101, b75: h19.7g² h20.1g⁵ May 24] fair form over hurdles: tried
in hood: often travels strongly. *Iain Jardine*

FAITHFUL MOUNT 8 b.g. Shirocco (GER) – Lady Lindsay (IRE) (Danehill Dancer **h122**
(IRE)) [2016/17 h112: h19.4g² h16s⁶ Dec 3] sturdy gelding: fairly useful hurdler: fit from
Flat, second in handicap at Musselburgh in November: stays 19f: best form on good going:
in cheekpieces last 2 starts. *Ian Williams*

FAITH JICARO (IRE) 10 b.m. One Cool Cat (USA) – Wings To Soar (USA) (Woodman **c88**
(USA)) [2016/17 c97, h–: c16.3s³ c19.4mᵖᵘ c19.4gᵖᵘ h16.7g⁵ h16g³ h17.2g⁵ h15.8g **h83**
h19.2m⁵ h19.9d Oct 13] poor handicap hurdler: modest handicap chaser: left Mark
Brisbourne after sixth start: stays 2½m: acts on good to firm and good to soft going: has
worn cheekpieces, including last 5 starts: tried in tongue tie. *John Groucott*

FALCARRAGH (IRE) 10 ch.g. Alderbrook – Maghereareagh Lady (IRE) (Old Vic) **c– §**
[2016/17 c125§, h108: h21g* h20m⁵ Aug 17] lengthy gelding: fair hurdler: won handicap **h107 §**
at Kempton in May: fairly useful chaser: stays 21f: acts on soft going: tried in cheekpieces:
often races towards rear: temperamental. *Tim Vaughan*

FALCONS FALL (IRE) 6 ch.g. Vertical Speed (FR) – Ellie Park (IRE) (Presenting) **h118**
[2016/17 h–, b–: h19.5s⁴ h21v³ h23.6v* Mar 23] fairly useful form over hurdles: won
novice event on handicap debut at Chepstow in March, suited by longer trip: will stay
beyond 3m. *Tom Symonds*

FALCON'S REIGN (FR) 8 ch.g. Haafhd – Al Badeya (IRE) (Pivotal) [2016/17 h59: **h77**
h15.7v³ h15.8g³ h16s Jan 14] modest on Flat, stays 9f: poor form over hurdles: wears
cheekpieces. *Michael Appleby*

FALCOS (FR) 5 ch.g. Falco (USA) – Olvera (IRE) (Sadler's Wells (USA)) [2016/17 **h108**
h16.9s h16.9gᵖᵘ h17.9g³ h17d Apr 5] fair form on Flat and over hurdles: left L. Viel after
third start. *Rebecca Menzies*

FANTASY KING 11 b.g. Acclamation – Fantasy Ridge (Indian Ridge) [2016/17 c121, **c121** h104: c17.3m² c21.2d⁴ h17.2d c17.3g* h17.2g² c21.2d^F Aug 29] tall gelding: fair handicap **h102** hurdler: fairly useful handicap chaser: won at Cartmel in July: stays 21f: acts on good to firm and good to soft going: tried in cheekpieces/tongue tie. *James Moffatt*

FARADAY EFFECT (IRE) 4 b.g. Rip Van Winkle (IRE) – Faraday Light (IRE) **b–** (Rainbow Quest (USA)) [2016/17 b16.4g Mar 24] tailed off in bumper. *Gemma Anderson*

FARANG BER SONG 6 b.g. Selkirk (USA) – Dazzle (Gone West (USA)) [2016/17 b–: **h–** b15.7g b16.7g h21.2g^{pu} h20.6g^{pu} Nov 3] strong gelding: no form in bumpers/over hurdles: **b–** in tongue tie last 4 starts. *Sara Ender*

FARAWAY MOUNTAIN (IRE) 9 ch.g. Indian Haven – Muschana (Deploy) [2016/17 **h100** h–, b89: h21.5g³ h22d⁴ h21g^{pu} h20.2d⁴ h19.9g⁶ h21g Sep 29] fair hurdler: won maiden at Perth in June: left Gordon Elliott after fourth start: stays 2¾m: acts on good to soft going: in headgear last 4 starts. *Phil Middleton*

FARBREAGA (IRE) 11 b.g. Shernazar – Gleann Alainn (Teenoso (USA)) [2016/17 c72, **c–** h–: c23.6d c24s^{pu} Apr 1] good-bodied gelding: winning hurdler: fairly useful chaser at best, **h–** no form since 2014/15: stays 3¼m: acts on heavy going: wears headgear. *Harry Whittington*

FAREWELLTOCHEYENNE (IRE) 9 b.g. Zagreb (USA) – Valerie Ellen (IRE) **h–** (Accordion) [2016/17 h84: h19.7s^{pu} Jan 24] bumper winner: little impact over hurdles: tried in tongue tie: often races towards rear. *N. W. Alexander*

FAR FROM DEFEAT (IRE) 7 b.g. Robin des Pres (FR) – Clonsingle Native (IRE) (Be **c86** My Native (USA)) [2016/17 h95: c20.9s⁴ c20v^{pu} c20.2g^{pu} h23.9g h20.7s² Mar 5] good- **h92** topped gelding: modest maiden hurdler/chaser: stayed 2½m: acted on soft going: in headgear last 3 starts: usually raced in rear: dead. *Michael Scudamore*

FARM PIXIE (IRE) 11 b.g. Snurge – Blue Bobby (IRE) (Flemensfirth (USA)) [2016/17 **c59** c57, h–: c24.2d⁴ Apr 30] dual point winner: maiden hurdler/chaser: stays 3m: acts on heavy **h–** going: usually wears headgear. *Mrs K. Weir*

FARM THE ROCK (IRE) 6 b.g. Yeats (IRE) – Shades of Lavender (IRE) (Peintre **h109** Celebre (USA)) [2016/17 b16g⁵ h20g⁵ h21.6g² h19.7s⁴ h24.4g h21.2s⁴ Feb 22] fourth foal: **b78** closely related to a winner in Italy by High Chaparral and half-brother to Swiss/French 1m-1¼m winner Choix Celebre (by Choisir): dam, maiden on Flat (stayed 1¼m), half-sister to fairly useful hurdler (stayed 3m) Tritonville Lodge: off mark in Irish points at fourth attempt: mid-division in bumper: fair form over hurdles: stays 2¾m: usually races prominently. *Katy Price*

FARRAH'S CHOICE 5 b.m. Equiano (FR) – Esplanade (Danehill (USA)) [2016/17 **h–** h16d⁶ h16g h15.7g^{pu} h18.7m Aug 24] maiden on Flat: no form over hurdles: in tongue tie last 3 starts. *James Grassick*

FAR WEST (FR) 8 b.g. Poliglote – Far Away Girl (FR) (Cadoudal (FR)) [2016/17 h18.5s **c–** Jan 1] smallish, well-made gelding: smart hurdler at best, below form in handicap only **h–** outing in 2016/17: winning chaser: stays 21f: acts on heavy going: wears tongue tie nowadays. *Paul Nicholls*

FATHER EDWARD (IRE) 8 b.g. Flemensfirth (USA) – Native Side (IRE) (Be My **c132** Native (USA)) [2016/17 c123, h121: c25.5d* c21.4g^{pu} c20.2m⁴ c23g⁵ c26g c21.1g **h–** c31.8g^{pu} Apr 22] sturdy gelding: fairly useful hurdler: useful handicap chaser: won at Cartmel in August: below form after: stays 25f: acts on soft and good to firm going: has worn headgear, including last 5 starts: has worn tongue tie. *David Pipe*

FATHER OWEN 14 ch.g. Danzig Connection (USA) – Roisin Clover (Faustus (USA)) **c–** [2016/17 c32.5g^{pu} Apr 27] successful twice in points: no form in 2 hunter chases 7 years apart. *Mrs J. Branton*

FATHER PROBUS 11 ch.g. Fleetwood (IRE) – Nearly At Sea (Nearly A Hand) [2016/17 **c– §** c–, h86: h25d May 2] workmanlike gelding: fair hurdler/chaser at best, lightly raced and **h– §** largely out of form under Rules since 2012/13: stays 25f: acts on good to firm and heavy going: has worn headgear: temperamental. *Michael Appleby*

FATTSOTA 9 b.g. Oasis Dream – Gift of The Night (USA) (Slewpy (USA)) [2016/17 **h109** h15.7d² h15.6g* h16v² h15.7g* Mar 28] useful on Flat, stayed 12.5f: fair form over hurdles: won maiden at Musselburgh in January and novice at Southwell in March: raced at 2m: dead. *David O'Meara*

FAVORITE GIRL (GER) 9 b.m. Shirocco (GER) – Favorite (GER) (Montjeu (IRE)) **c–** [2016/17 c–, h118: h15.7d² h16.6g h15.5d h15.8s³ Mar 23] compact mare: fairly useful **h118** handicap hurdler: no promise in 2 runs over fences: probably best around 2m: acts on heavy going: usually leads. *Michael Appleby*

FAVORITO BUCK'S (FR) 5 b.g. Buck's Boum (FR) – Sangrilla (FR) (Sanglamore (USA)) [2016/17 h126: h20.5d c20.2spu c24m4 Apr 4] tall gelding: fairly useful hurdle winner on debut in France, disappointing in Britain including over fences: stays 2¼m: acts on soft going: tried in cheekpieces/tongue tie: tends to find little. *Paul Nicholls*   **c102 h–**

FAYETTE COUNTY (IRE) 10 b.g. Golden Lariat (USA) – Midsyn Lady (IRE) (Sharp Victor (USA)) [2016/17 c132, h–: c20g6 c19.4g4 c20g2 c23g* c25g3 c23.4s2 c25.2sF Feb 28] winning hurdler: useful handicap chaser: won novice event at Worcester (by head from Churchtown Champ) in October: stayed 25f: acted on heavy going: tried in hood: often raced towards rear, usually travelled strongly: dead. *Tim Vaughan*   **c135 h–**

FAYONAGH (IRE) 6 b.m. Kalanisi (IRE) – Fair Ina (IRE) (Taipan (IRE)) [2016/17 b16g b16d* b16v* b16.4g* b16d* Apr 26]   **b118**
    Fayonagh's wins in the season's two most important bumpers at the Cheltenham and Punchestown Festivals could not have been gained in more contrasting fashion. At Punchestown she made all the running, enjoying the run of things at the head of a field of just seven before settling the race in a matter of strides early in the straight. At Cheltenham, on the other hand, things were much less straightforward when she gained an unlikely-looking win from last position coming down the hill, not enjoying the clearest of runs and still having more of her twenty-one rivals in front of her than behind with less than two furlongs to run before storming home to lead in the last fifty yards. Both performances were impressive, but having made all for her first two wins in Ireland as well, it almost goes without saying that the very different manner of her win at Cheltenham was not by choice. Following a false start, the runners in the Weatherbys Champion Bumper were called back to be despatched by flag. Despite lining up in the front rank and being given every chance of getting away on terms from the standing start, Fayonagh remained rooted to the spot for a few seconds when the starter dropped his flag, leaving her last of all as the field came past the stands for the first time. The 2015 winner Moon Racer was another who suffered in the ragged restart and his jockey also had to adopt impromptu waiting tactics. Fayonagh was at the back until coming down the hill, her rider initially seeking to save ground up the inner but ultimately having to deliver her wide in the straight to get a clear run. Still with six ahead of her at the wings of where

Weatherbys Champion Bumper, Cheltenham—Fayonagh and Mr Jamie Codd overcome a disastrous start to beat the grey Debuchet and Claimantakinforgan (right)

Racing Post Champion INH Flat, Punchestown—far more straightforward this time as Fayonagh sees off Paloma Blue and stable-companion Poli Roi

the final flight of hurdles would normally be, Fayonagh burst through late to win by a length and a quarter from the four-year-old Debuchet, with Claimantakinforgan, a rare runner in the race for Nicky Henderson, another length and a half back in third, a neck in front of Next Destination, the longer-priced of Willie Mullins' two runners. Fayonagh was sent off at 7/1, only two in the field starting at shorter odds; the Dan Skelton-trained 9/2 favourite Cause Toujours managed only ninth and Mullins' other runner, the easy-to-back 11/2-shot Carter McKay, weakened to finish fifteenth.

One of only two mares in the field, Fayonagh became the third of her sex in twenty-five runnings to win the Champion Bumper. The two others had been Mucklemeg in 1994 and Total Enjoyment in 2004, each of whom had beaten other mares into second when successful, namely Aries Girl and Refinement. Aries Girl went on to turn the tables on Mucklemeg when having her back in sixth at Punchestown, while Refinement was successful in the Champion Bumper at Punchestown the year after finishing second at Cheltenham (she also came fourth in the 2005 Champion Bumper at Cheltenham). A son of Refinement, West Coast Time, was one of Fayonagh's rivals at Cheltenham (Total Enjoyment never had a stud career, put down after developing laminitis in her novice hurdling season). With just over three lengths covering the first five home in the latest Champion Bumper, it was not possible to take too high a view of the Cheltenham form, but there was a lot more daylight between the runners when Fayonagh followed up in the Racing Post Champion INH Flat Race at Punchestown. She was sent off the 11/8 favourite, with the Jessica Harrington-trained Leopardstown winner Someday (100/30) and stable-companion Poli Roi (9/2), an expensive Gigginstown purchase who had landed very short odds on his debut at Navan, her main market rivals. Carter McKay was the only one from Cheltenham to re-oppose Fayonagh, while the three others were all unbeaten, including British challenger Dell Oro, a winner at Fontwell for Gary Moore. Keeping on strongly having got away on terms this time, Fayonagh produced the sort of dominant display that she might well have done at Cheltenham but for her troubles at the start, winning by five and a half lengths from the Henry de Bromhead-trained Paloma Blue, a 12/1-shot who had made a winning debut at Fairyhouse, with a gap of seven back to Poli Roi, both placed horses appealing as fine jumping prospects. The hard-pulling Someday was only fifth ahead of Carter McKay who disappointed again in sixth. Fayonagh became the third to complete the double in the championship bumpers at Cheltenham and Punchestown after the Willie Mullins-trained pair Cousin Vinny in 2008 and Champagne Fever in 2012. Dunguib passed the post first in both races in 2009 but was later disqualified at Punchestown after testing positive for prohibited substances.

Punchestown was Fayonagh's fourth win in a row following a debut at Cork almost twelve months earlier which gave little clue that she would develop into one of the season's top bumper performers. She was beaten nearly twenty lengths into eighth in a big field on that occasion but proved a different proposition at Naas six months later when springing a 33/1 surprise in a mares event which turned out to be her final start for Wexford trainer Richard Rath. Like the aforementioned Moon

Racer, Fayonagh started life with a small yard but attracted the attention of a much bigger stable and, after being sold for £64,000 at the Cheltenham December Sales, she returned to Ireland to be trained by Gordon Elliott. On her first start for her new stable, Fayonagh gave notice that she was something out of the ordinary with a most impressive all-the-way success in a listed mares contest at Fairyhouse in February, winning by twenty lengths and fifteen. All three of Fayonagh's successes for Gordon Elliott came in the hands of top amateur Mr Jamie Codd, though he played a much bigger part in her success than that. It was Codd, who works for Tattersalls Ireland, who recommended her to her new owners, and it was he who suggested she should run at Cheltenham instead of going for the listed mares bumper at Sandown the weekend before, which had been the original plan.

	Kalanisi (IRE) (b 1996)	Doyoun (b 1985)	Mill Reef
Fayonagh (IRE) (b.m. 2011)			Dumka
		Kalamba (b 1991)	Green Dancer
			Kareena
	Fair Ina (IRE) (b 2002)	Taipan (b 1992)	Last Tycoon
			Alidiva
		Deep Peace (ch 1984)	Deep Run
			Bargy Music

Galloping rivals into the ground from the front was also how the popular mare Solerina won most of her twenty-two races, much like the Bowe family's even better hurdler and still more prolific winner, the top-class Limestone Lad. The very smart Solerina is a half-sister to Fayonagh's dam Fair Ina who shared the same style of running, if not quite the same ability, though she did manage to win a bumper at Punchestown and was placed on two of her three starts over hurdles. Solerina was

Mrs M. Gittins' "Fayonagh"

very smart at up to two and a half miles and emulated Limestone Lad by winning the Hatton's Grace Hurdle at Fairyhouse three times, her first win in 2003 gained when beating her useful half-brother Florida Coast (who, like Fair Ina, also ran in the Bowe colours) into second. Solerina has had three runners to reach the racecourse so far, none of whom has proved anything like so good as she was, though she did get her first winner early in the latest season when her four-year-old daughter Jaime Sommers won a maiden hurdle at Kilbeggan. Fair Ina, on the other hand, has come up trumps at the second attempt with Fayonagh, after her first foal Kallerina (also by Kalanisi) showed only a little ability in three bumpers for the Bowes. Fayonagh's grandam Deep Peace showed some ability over hurdles (she probably stayed two and three quarter miles) while great grandam Bargy Music was unraced. Solerina was not much to look at, being small and leggy, but the lengthy Fayonagh is an altogether more taking sort of mare. Aries Girl and Refinement, along with the two other mares to have won Punchestown's championship bumper, Liss A Paoraigh and Like-A-Butterfly, all went on to be useful over hurdles at the very least, the last-named winning the Supreme Novices', and there's every reason to think Fayonagh's prospects are just as bright. *Gordon Elliott, Ireland*

FEAR GLIC (IRE) 11 b.g. Dr Massini (IRE) – Graineuaile (IRE) (Orchestra) [2016/17 c101p, h–: c18m⁶ c22.6s* c21d* c25gᵖᵘ c21mᶠ Apr 15] winning hurdler: fairly useful handicap chaser: won at Stratford and Newton Abbot in June: stays 23f: acts on soft and good to firm going: usually races close up. *Jackie du Plessis* **c126 h–**

FEARLESS FANTASY (IRE) 6 b.m. Oscar (IRE) – Pharlen's Dream (IRE) (Phardante (FR)) [2016/17 b82: b17g² b20gᵖᵘ Jun 4] point/bumper winner: pulled up in maiden on hurdling debut: dead. *Katy Price* **h– b82**

FEARLESS TUNES (IRE) 9 b.g. Shantou (USA) – Miss Snapdragon (IRE) (Topanoora) [2016/17 h19.9s h23.3v² h20.5v² c24vᵖᵘ h20.6vᵖᵘ Mar 18] runner-up in Irish maiden point: fair maiden hurdler: pulled up in novice handicap on chasing debut: stays 23f: acts on heavy going: in cheekpieces last 2 starts. *Jennie Candlish* **c– h101**

FEARSOME FRED 8 b.g. Emperor Fountain – Ryewater Dream (Touching Wood (USA)) [2016/17 h87: h16.5g h19.5s h19.5g⁴ Apr 8] runner-up in point: modest form over hurdles. *Dr Jeremy Naylor* **h85**

FEARTHEDARK (IRE) 9 b.g. Flemensfirth (USA) – Pandalute (IRE) (Indian Danehill (IRE)) [2016/17 c24s* c23gᵖᵘ Jun 4] multiple winning pointer: fairly useful form when winning novice at Southwell in May on chasing debut: fatally injured next time. *Caroline Bailey* **c115**

FEAST OF FIRE (IRE) 10 ch.g. St Jovite (USA) – Bellagrana (Belmez (USA)) [2016/17 c98, h93: h27s⁴ c25.5m* May 28] tall gelding: winning hurdler: modest handicap chaser: won at Cartmel in May: stays 3¼m: acts on good to firm and heavy going: has worn headgear, including last 3 starts: tried in tongue tie. *Joanne Foster* **c95 h84**

FEATHERINTHEATTIC (IRE) 12 b.g. Bahri (USA) – Silk Feather (USA) (Silver Hawk (USA)) [2016/17 c–, h–: c25.5dᵖᵘ c25.5sᵖᵘ Feb 26] sturdy gelding: winning hurdler: maiden chaser, no longer of any account: has worn headgear, including in 2016/17: temperamental. *Miss K. Phillips-Hill* **c– § h–**

FEATHER LANE (IRE) 7 br.g. Court Cave (IRE) – Laffan's Bridge (IRE) (Mandalus) [2016/17 h74: h16.7g³ h19.6g May 30] failed to complete in 2 Irish points in 2014: poor form over hurdles: tried in tongue tie. *Donald McCain* **h80**

FEDERICI 8 b.g. Overbury (IRE) – Vado Via (Ardross) [2016/17 c131, h119: c26m⁵ h24s⁶ c24dᵖᵘ c25g³ c28g c21.1d⁶ c30g⁴ c25.2vʳ c28.5g⁵ c26g⁵ Apr 20] fairly useful handicap hurdler: useful handicap chaser: third in Grade 3 event at Punchestown (21½ lengths behind Sadler's Risk) in October and fourth at Catterick (7½ lengths behind Straidnahanna) in January: left Enda Bolger after fifth start: stays 3¾m: acts on heavy going: tried in cheekpieces. *Donald McCain* **c131 h111**

FEELING PECKISH (USA) 13 ch.g. Point Given (USA) – Sunday Bazaar (USA) (Nureyev (USA)) [2016/17 c–§, h–§: c21.7d c25.6vᵖᵘ c27.5gᵖᵘ Apr 23] sturdy, workmanlike gelding: maiden hurdler: winning chaser, no longer of any account: has worn blinkers: used to wear tongue tie: ungenuine. *Michael Chapman* **c– § h– §**

FEEL THE AIR (IRE) 7 br.m. Papal Bull – Zephyr Lilly (IRE) (Alhaarth (IRE)) **h99**
[2016/17 h106: h16d h24g⁵ h20.5s h23g⁵ h21gᵖᵘ h20.1s⁴ Sep 30] fair handicap hurdler:
largely below form in 2016/17: stays 3m: acts on soft going: tried in headgear/tongue tie:
tends to find little. *Mark McNiff, Ireland*

FEELTHERHYTHM (IRE) 6 b.m. Yeats (IRE) – Queen Althea (IRE) (Bach (IRE)) **h87**
[2016/17 h15.6g³ h20.6d⁶ h19.3g² h20.6d³ h19.7s h19.9v⁴ Feb 12] modest maiden on Flat,
stayed 16.5f: modest form over hurdles: in visor last 3 starts: dead. *Chris Grant*

FEISTY GIRL 7 ch.m. Erhaab (USA) – Dolly Duff (Alflora (IRE)) [2016/17 h–: h15.8sᵖᵘ **h–**
Dec 6] no form over hurdles: tried in hood. *Michael Mullineaux*

FENNANN 6 b.g. Dutch Art – Embraced (Pursuit of Love) [2016/17 h15.9v h15.7dᵖᵘ Feb **h–**
26] maiden hurdler, no form in 2016/17: best effort at 2¼m: wears blinkers. *Natalie Lloyd-Beavis*

FERGALL (IRE) 10 br.g. Norwich – Gaybrook Girl (IRE) (Alderbrook) [2016/17 c–, **c–**
h125: h15.7m⁴ h15.7d³ Dec 17] sturdy gelding: useful handicap hurdler: in frame in **h133**
listed event (¾ length behind Sternrubin) and Wessex Youth Trust Handicap Hurdle (in
cheekpieces, 5¼ lengths behind Brain Power) in 2016/17, both at Ascot: jumped poorly
only outing over fences: stays 2½m: acts on soft and good to firm going. *Seamus Mullins*

FERGAL MAEL DUIN 9 gr.g. Tikkanen (USA) – Fad Amach (IRE) (Flemensfirth **c123**
(USA)) [2016/17 c116, h–: c21.1d* c27.2s² c23.6g c20.2s⁵ c23dᵖᵘ c28.1g Apr 19] rangy **h–**
gelding: maiden hurdler: fairly useful handicap chaser: won at Fontwell in October: second
in Southern National there in November: stays 27f: acts on heavy going: has worn
headgear/tongue tie. *Colin Tizzard*

FERMAT (FR) 15 gr.g. Great Palm (USA) – Five Rivers (FR) (Cadoudal (FR)) [2016/17 **c–**
c26g Apr 27] good-topped gelding: multiple point winner: maiden hurdler/chaser: tried in **h–**
cheekpieces: used to wear tongue tie. *Mrs J. Smyth-Osbourne*

FERNAN (IRE) 5 br.g. Robin des Champs (FR) – Rosa Rugosa (IRE) (In The Wings) **b96**
[2016/17 b16s⁶ b15.7d² b16d⁵ Mar 21] £33,000 3-y-o: first foal: dam lightly raced on Flat:
fairly useful form in bumpers: best effort when second at Southwell in February.
Malcolm Jefferson

FESTIVE AFFAIR (IRE) 9 b.g. Presenting – Merry Batim (IRE) (Alphabatim (USA)) **c127**
[2016/17 c127: c16d² c16.5g³ c16.5g³ c16.9m³ c16.4d* c16d Dec 21] tall gelding: fairly
useful handicap chaser: won at Doncaster in November: unproven beyond 17f: acts on
good to firm and good to soft going: wears cheekpieces/tongue tie: front runner/races
prominently. *Jonjo O'Neill*

FFEEBEE 5 b.m. Phoenix Reach (IRE) – Honey's Gift (Terimon) [2016/17 b16g⁶ b16.7s **b62**
b16vᵖᵘ Feb 25] poor form in bumpers: tried in tongue tie: dead. *Peter Bowen*

FIASCO 8 b.g. Presenting – Deep Sunset (IRE) (Supreme Leader) [2016/17 c–, h–: c20.8g **c–**
Apr 27] poor winning pointer: no form under Rules: tried in tongue tie. *A. Campbell* **h–**

FIBRE OPTIC 5 b.g. Rip Van Winkle (IRE) – Wind Surf (USA) (Lil's Lad (USA)) **h65**
[2016/17 h98: h18.1mᵘʳ h20.2dᵘʳ h22.1gᵖᵘ Jul 18] maiden hurdler, little show in 2016/17.
Rose Dobbin

FIDDLER'S FLIGHT (IRE) 11 b.g. Convinced – Carole's Dove (Manhal) [2016/17 **h73**
h83: h16.8s³ h19.9vᵖᵘ h16.8s³ h16.8v⁵ h16.4v² h15.8s⁴ Apr 1] poor handicap hurdler:
probably stays 2½m: acts on heavy going: wears hood: usually races nearer last than first.
John Norton

FIDDLERS REEL 14 ch.g. Karinga Bay – Festival Fancy (Le Coq d'Or) [2016/17 c126, **c–**
h–: c26.2mᵖᵘ May 29] winning hurdler: fairly useful handicap chaser: pulled up sole outing **h–**
in 2016/17: stays 3¼m: acts on heavy going: tried in cheekpieces. *Jane Clark*

FIDELITY 5 b.g. Halling (USA) – Sir Kyffin's Folly (Dansili) [2016/17 h–: h21.6dᵖᵘ **h69**
h15.3m⁵ h20.5v h19.5v³ h21.4d³ h17.7g⁵ Mar 31] poor maiden hurdler: stays 19f: acts on
heavy going: often races towards rear. *Jonathan Geake*

FIDUX (FR) 4 b.g. Fine Grain (JPN) – Folle Tempete (FR) (Fabulous Dancer (USA)) **h128**
[2016/17 h15.7g* h16d* h15.6g⁴ h16g³ h16.4g h16g³ Apr 29] compact gelding: half-
brother to French 2m/19f hurdle winner Mykenirus (by Lear Fan): fairly useful on Flat
(stays 1½m) in France for K. Borgel: fairly useful form over hurdles: won juveniles at
Catterick in November and Kempton in January: will be suited by further than 2m: acts on
good to soft going: usually races close up. *Alan King*

FIELD MARSHALL (IRE) 7 b.g. Robin des Champs (FR) – Bridgequarter Lady (IRE) **h80**
(King's Ride) [2016/17 h19.9s h23.6g h23.1vᵖᵘ Dec 15] off mark in Irish points at third
attempt: poor form over hurdles: dead. *Jonjo O'Neill*

FIELDS OF GLORY (FR) 7 b.g. King's Best (USA) – Lavandou (Sadler's Wells (USA)) [2016/17 h105, b91: h15.8g c16.5m^pu c19.9g^3 c16d^2 c19.9g* c19.2s* c19.2s^4 c24m^F c23.8m^5 Apr 25] fair hurdler: fair handicap chaser: won at Musselburgh in January and Market Rasen in February: stays 2½m: acts on heavy going: wears tongue tie. *Tim Vaughan* **c105 h–**

FIELDSOFSILK (IRE) 5 b.g. Robin des Champs (FR) – Silk Style (Polish Precedent (USA)) [2016/17 h–, b–: h19.3m^5 h15.7g^4 h17.1d h20.3d c15.9s^3 c16s^4 c16d^3 c15.7s Feb 3] modest form over hurdles/fences: stays 19f: acts on good to firm going: in cheekpieces last 5 starts: often races prominently. *Jennie Candlish* **c88 h94**

FIFI L'AMOUR (IRE) 11 ch.m. Flemensfirth (USA) – Supreme Adventure (IRE) – (Supreme Leader) [2016/17 h73: h25g^pu May 8] good-topped mare: poor maiden hurdler: stays 25f: acts on soft going: tried in cheekpieces. *Linda Jewell* **h–**

FIFTY BOB (IRE) 6 b.g. Witness Box (USA) – Slogan (IRE) (Kris Kin (USA)) [2016/17 h15.8d h15.8v^6 h15.8v^5 h16.6d^2 h20.7s^ur h24g^5 Mar 28] £26,000 4-y-o: first foal: dam lightly raced on Flat: runner-up in Irish maiden point on debut: fair form over hurdles: should stay 3m: acts on soft going: tried in cheekpieces. *Kim Bailey* **h103**

FIGHT AWAY BOYS (IRE) 9 ch.g. Vertical Speed (FR) – Say Ya Love Me (IRE) (Presenting) [2016/17 c–, h–: c26.2d^ur Feb 10] multiple point winner: maiden hurdler: little show in hunter chases: tried in headgear/tongue tie. *Mrs Caroline Crow* **c– h–**

FIGHT COMMANDER (IRE) 8 b.g. Oscar (IRE) – Creidim (IRE) (Erins Isle) [2016/17 c116, h–: c23.9s^pu c24s c24.2s^pu c25.5d^2 Mar 18] lengthy gelding: maiden hurdler: fair handicap chaser: stays 25f: acts on good to firm and heavy going: tried in blinkers. *Oliver Sherwood* **c112 h–**

FIGHTER JET 9 b.g. Oasis Dream – Totality (Dancing Brave (USA)) [2016/17 c–, h115§: h23.1g^pu May 6] sturdy gelding: fairly useful hurdler at best, pulled up sole outing in 2016/17: showed nothing only start over fences: stays 25f: acts on good to firm and good to soft going: wears headgear: tried in tongue tie: ungenuine. *John Mackie* **c– h– §**

FIGHT FOR LOVE (FR) 4 b.g. Fuisse (FR) – Love Affair (FR) (Arctic Tern (USA)) [2016/17 b16s b13.6g^5 Mar 31] no form in bumpers. *Laura Mongan* **b–**

FILATORE (IRE) 8 ch.g. Teofilo (IRE) – Dragnet (IRE) (Rainbow Quest (USA)) [2016/17 h111§: h20s^2 h16d^4 h20g h23.9d h23.9g^6 h23.3v h25.5v^6 h21.9v^2 h23.6s^2 Mar 13] sturdy gelding: modest handicap hurdler: stays 3m: best form on soft/heavy going: wears headgear/tongue tie: temperamental. *Bernard Llewellyn* **h89 §**

FILBERT (IRE) 11 b.g. Oscar (IRE) – Coca's Well (IRE) (Religiously (USA)) [2016/17 c–, h–: c24g^4 c21.2m^6 c22.6m^pu h21.6g^5 h23.3d^pu h20d^5 Oct 15] rangy gelding: fairly useful hurdler/useful chaser at best: left Philip Hobbs after first start: stayed 2½m: acted on heavy going: usually wore headgear: often raced lazily: dead. *Sophie Leech* **c124 h104**

FILLE DES CHAMPS (IRE) 6 b.m. Robin des Champs (FR) – South Queen Lady (IRE) (King's Ride) [2016/17 h71, b–: h16d^4 h16.2s^5 h20v* h23.8s^4 h21.9v^3 h18.9g^4 Apr 15] modest handicap hurdler: won mares event at Ffos Las in December: stays 3m: acts on heavy going: in tongue tie last 2 starts. *Evan Williams* **h94**

FILL THE POWER (IRE) 11 b.g. Subtle Power (IRE) – Our Alma (IRE) (Be My Native (USA)) [2016/17 c132§, h–: c26.2d c28.4v^6 c22.3s^6 c26.2s^4 c27.6d c30g^pu c24.2d Feb 21] tall, lengthy, angular gelding: winning hurdler: useful handicap chaser at best, well below that in 2016/17 after long absence: well-held third in point in late-April: stays 3½m: acts on good to firm and heavy going: tried in cheekpieces: usually races close up: temperamental. *Sue Smith* **c108 § h–**

FILM DIRECTOR (IRE) 9 b.g. Tiger Hill (IRE) – Stage Manner (In The Wings) [2016/17 h106: h19.9s^2 h16.7g^3 h22.1m^4 May 28] fair maiden hurdler: stays 21f: acts on soft going: in cheekpieces last 2 starts. *Brian Ellison* **h105**

FINAGHY AYR (IRE) 9 ch.g. Lahib (USA) – Ali Ankah (IRE) (Insan (USA)) [2016/17 c–, h97: c24.5s* c26.9v^2 c31.9s^F c23.4s^pu Apr 3] winning hurdler: fair handicap chaser: won novice event at Carlisle in February after 15-month absence: stays 27f: best form on soft/heavy going: wears cheekpieces: has worn tongue tie, including final start: often races towards rear: often makes mistakes. *Ian Duncan* **c103 x h–**

FINAL ASSAULT (IRE) 8 b.g. Beneficial – Last Campaign (IRE) (Saddlers' Hall (IRE)) [2016/17 c136, h–: c20.5g^2 c22.4g^4 c20.1s^6 c21.6v^5 Jan 15] well-made gelding: winning hurdler: useful handicap chaser: in frame at Ayr (3¼ lengths behind Indian Temple) in October and Newbury (6½ lengths behind O Maonlai) in November: stays 3m: acts on heavy going: has worn hood: often races in rear, usually travels strongly. *Lucinda Russell* **c131 h–**

FINAL CHOICE 4 b.g. Makfi – Anasazi (IRE) (Sadler's Wells (USA)) [2016/17 h16s² **h117** h16.3d* h16.3s⁴ h15.7d⁴ h18.8g Mar 25] good-topped gelding: half-brother to fairly useful hurdler Zonergem (2m winner, by Zafonic): fair on Flat, stays 11.5f: fairly useful form over hurdles: won juvenile at Newbury in December: in cheekpieces last 2 starts: tried in tongue tie. *Warren Greatrex*

FINAL COUNTDOWN 6 ch.g. Selkirk (USA) – Culture Queen (King's Best (USA)) **h91** [2016/17 h78x: h16.2s h15.6g³ h15.6g h16.8m⁵ Apr 19] modest maiden hurdler: raced around 2m: acts on soft and good to firm going: tried in cheekpieces. *Rebecca Menzies*

FINAL FLING (IRE) 6 b.g. Milan – Supreme Singer (IRE) (Supreme Leader) [2016/17 **h83** h72, b82: h24.1m³ Apr 13] poor form over hurdles: stays 3m: acts on soft and good to firm going: often races towards rear. *Rose Dobbin*

FINAL NUDGE (IRE) 8 b.g. Kayf Tara – Another Shot (IRE) (Master Willie) [2016/17 **c139** h133: c24.2s* c23.4s³ c25.2d³ c20.9v* c23.4d* c33.4sᶠ c24.3g⁶ Apr 22] strong gelding: **h–** useful hurdler: useful chaser: won maiden at Fakenham in November, and novice handicaps at Hereford and Newbury (by 1¼ lengths from Lessons In Milan) in February: stays 33f: acts on heavy going: in cheekpieces last 4 starts. *David Dennis*

FINAL REMINDER (IRE) 5 b.m. Gold Well – Olde Kilcormac (IRE) (Supreme **h69** Leader) [2016/17 h16.2v h20.6sᵖᵘ h16.2g⁵ Apr 28] €5,200 3-y-o, £55,000 4-y-o: fifth foal: dam unraced half-sister to useful hurdler/fairly useful chaser (stayed 3¼m) Little Buck: won Irish maiden point on debut: poor form over hurdles. *N. W. Alexander*

FINANCIAL CLIMATE (IRE) 10 b.g. Exit To Nowhere (USA) – Claudia's Pearl **c106** (Deploy) [2016/17 c128, h–: c24gᵖᵘ c23.6d c25.5d c26d⁶ c25.5s³ c25.1dᵖᵘ c25.2s³ Mar 11] **h–** lengthy gelding: winning hurdler: fairly useful handicap chaser: well below best in 2016/17: stays 3¼m: acts on heavy going: wears headgear: has bled. *Oliver Sherwood*

FIN AND GAME (IRE) 5 b.g. Oscar (IRE) – Miss Cilla (IRE) (Shernazar) [2016/17 **b92** b16.7d² b17d⁴ Feb 20] €35,000 3-y-o: first foal: dam unraced half-sister to top-class hurdler/smart chaser (2m-2¾m winner) Peddlers Cross (by Oscar): fair form in bumpers: better effort when second at Bangor in January. *Donald McCain*

FINCH FLYER (IRE) 10 ch.g. Indian Ridge – Imelda (USA) (Manila (USA)) [2016/17 **c– §** c–, h–: c17.3g⁶ c15.7dᵖᵘ c19.4gᵖᵘ c21.2g c19.4g³ c15.7mᵖᵘ c16.1m⁴ c19.9m⁴ c16.1mᵇᵈ Apr **h–** 13] stocky gelding: winning hurdler: maiden chaser, no longer of any account: wears headgear: tried in tongue tie: usually races in rear: temperamental. *Aytach Sadik*

FIN D'ESPERE (IRE) 6 b.g. Zagreb (USA) – Rapsan (IRE) (Insan (USA)) [2016/17 **h–** h108, b77: h24.5sᵖᵘ h19.8dᵖᵘ Dec 13] rather unfurnished gelding: maiden hurdler, no form in 2016/17: stays 21f: acts on heavy going: wears tongue tie: usually races prominently. *Suzy Smith*

FINDUSATGORCOMBE 5 b.g. Tobougg (IRE) – Seemma (Romany Rye) [2016/17 **h–** h16.5gᵘʳ h15.3d h19g h18.5s Jan 1] off mark in points shortly after end of season: no form over hurdles. *Jimmy Frost*

FINEA (IRE) 10 b.g. Exit To Nowhere (USA) – Annies Carmen (IRE) (Zaffaran (USA)) **c– x** [2016/17 c111x, h–: h23.9d Jun 29] lightly-raced hurdler: fair chaser: stayed 3m: acted on **h–** heavy going: usually wore headgear: wore tongue tie: often let down by jumping: dead. *R. K. Watson, Ireland*

FINE JEWELLERY 8 b.g. Epalo (GER) – Lola Lolita (FR) (Dom Alco (FR)) [2016/17 **c73** h–: h15.8g² c18.2m⁴ Apr 20] poor maiden hurdler: 2/1, fourth in novice handicap at **h75** Taunton on chasing debut: left Tom Gretton after first start: stays 2¼m: acts on good to firm going: has worn hood: usually wears tongue tie: usually races towards rear/freely. *Jamie Snowden*

FINE PARCHMENT (IRE) 14 b.g. Presenting – Run For Cover (IRE) (Lafontaine **c– §** (USA)) [2016/17 c114§, h–: c23dᵖᵘ Jun 29] good-topped gelding: maiden hurdler: useful **h–** handicap chaser at best: tailed off in point in February: stays 3¼m: acts on good to firm and heavy going: wears cheekpieces/tongue tie: often leads: unreliable. *Charlie Mann*

FINE RESOLVE 8 b.g. Refuse To Bend (IRE) – Papillon de Bronze (IRE) (Marju (IRE)) **c77** [2016/17 c89, h–: c25.3gᵖᵘ h20m h20g² h19.9m* c20d⁴ h21.6m³ h23.3g h20g⁴ c17g **h95** c22.6mᵖᵘ h20g⁴ h20g³ c17.4g² c23g⁵ Nov 24] multiple point winner: modest handicap hurdler: won at Uttoxeter in June: maiden chaser: left A. B. Leyshon after first start, Grace Harris after eighth: stays 3m: acts on soft and good to firm going: has worn headgear/tongue tie, including last 3 starts. *Alexandra Dunn*

FINE RIGHTLY (IRE) 9 b.g. Alflora (IRE) – Bealtaine (IRE) (Zaffaran (USA)) **c142** [2016/17 c149, h–: h22.6d⁴ c17s³ c24d c21.6v⁴ c31.8g Apr 22] useful hurdler/chaser: stays **h135** 3¼m: acts on heavy going: wears hood: tried in tongue tie: usually races in rear. *Stuart Crawford, Ireland*

FINE THEATRE (IRE) 7 b.g. King's Theatre (IRE) – Finemar Lady (IRE) (Montelimar **c134** (USA)) [2016/17 c134p, h120: c18v³ c24.5d Apr 29] fairly useful hurdler: useful form over **h–** fences: third in handicap at Gowran (7½ lengths behind Kilcarry Bridge) in March after 11-month absence: stays 3m: acts on heavy going: in headgear last 5 starts: often in tongue tie. *Paul Nolan, Ireland*

FINGAL BAY (IRE) 11 b.g. King's Theatre (IRE) – Lady Marguerrite (Blakeney) **c–** [2016/17 c141, h–: h25.3s⁶ h23.4s⁶ h24s⁴ h23.1s⁶ h24g Mar 16] tall gelding: useful **h132** handicap hurdler: fourth at Cheltenham (10¾ lengths behind Cogry) in January: useful chaser: stays 3m: acts on heavy going: tried in headgear/tongue tie. *Philip Hobbs*

FINGERONTHESWITCH (IRE) 7 b.g. Beneficial – Houseoftherisinsun (IRE) **c131** (Fourstars Allstar (USA)) [2016/17 h134: c25.8g⁴ c21.2g² c25.1m³ c23.6g c24.2s* **h–** c24g c24.2g² c24.1g⁵ c20gᵖᵘ Apr 29] lengthy gelding: has reportedly had breathing operation: useful hurdler: useful handicap chaser: won at Wetherby in January: stays 3m: acts on soft going: usually wears cheekpieces: in tongue tie last 5 starts. *Neil Mulholland*

FINGERS CROSSED (IRE) 7 b.g. Bach (IRE) – Awesome Miracle (IRE) (Supreme **c97** Leader) [2016/17 h101: c19.9d c15.9g⁶ c16d² c18.2g c16.1m² Apr 13] good-topped **h–** gelding: fair hurdler: modest form over fences: unproven beyond 2m: acts on heavy going: tried in hood: usually leads. *Paul Webber*

FINIAN'S OSCAR (IRE) 5 b.g. Oscar (IRE) – Trinity Alley (IRE) (Taipan (IRE)) **h155** [2016/17 h21.7s* h16s* h16.8s* h20g* h20g³ Apr 28]
The market for Irish point-to-pointers is as buoyant as it has ever been judging from sale-ring records broken during the latest season. At the Cheltenham Festival Sales, for example, a five-year-old daughter of King's Theatre named Maire Banrigh was bought by owner John Hales for £320,000, making her the most expensive mare bought out of the pointing field. That followed the sale the previous month, at Cheltenham's rescheduled January Sales, of Flemenshill, a four-year-old son of Flemensfirth. He set a new auction record for a pointer when sold for £480,000 to become another expensive addition to the string of Ann and Alan Potts to go into training with Colin Tizzard whose stable earlier in the season had received fifteen of the couple's horses previously trained in Ireland. The new partnership was strengthened further by the private purchases of promising young chasers Fox Norton and Alary. That pair enjoyed contrasting fortunes for their new connections, with Fox Norton going on to Grade 1 success at Aintree and Punchestown in the spring, while Alary, one of France's top chasers bought as a Gold Cup prospect, fell well short of expectations. Potentially the most exciting addition, however, to the newly-forged association between Alan Potts and Tizzard is novice hurdler Finian's Oscar, at £250,000 another big-money purchase from Irish points, who has made an excellent fist so far of living up to his price tag. Not that recouping costs seems necessarily a priority for mining tycoon Alan Potts who described racing as 'how we spend the money, not how we earn it'. He went on to pay £300,000 for another winner of an Irish four-year-old point, Madison To Monroe, who was the top lot at the inaugural Aintree Sales.
Things moved quickly in the early months of Finian's Oscar's career, certainly at a faster rate than his trainer was accustomed to when it came to handling young horses. As Tizzard remarked after Finian's Oscar had become a Grade 1 winner within a couple of months of joining his yard, 'Always before, we've been buying store horses and waiting two or three years to find out if they're 0-90 horses.' Having made a winning debut in a four-year-old point at Portrush in Northern Ireland in October, Finian's Oscar was knocked down to his new connections at Cheltenham the following month and made his debut under Rules just before Christmas in a novice hurdle at Hereford. The corresponding meeting four years earlier had looked like being Hereford's final fixture (the track continued to stage points and Arab racing), but owners Arena Racing Company reversed their decision to close the track and it reopened in October in front of a crowd of 4,501, said to be the largest attendance for a midweek card there since at least the 'eighties.

32Red Tolworth Novices' Hurdle, Sandown—
Finian's Oscar makes further inroads into recovering his substantial purchase price

Finian's Oscar won easily by seven lengths from odds-on Acting Lass, putting up a really eye-catching performance, so much so that less than three weeks later he was pitched straight into Grade 1 company for the 32Red Tolworth Novices' Hurdle at Sandown. Despite dropping back the best part of six furlongs in trip, as well as stepping up in grade, there was no shortage of confidence in Finian's Oscar who started the 11/10 favourite in a field of six and again looked a horse with a big future in beating second favourite Capitaine by five lengths. Always going strongly, Finian's Oscar was untidy at the last but was well in control by then, after the runner-up had made a worse mistake two out. A very straightforward task in a listed novice hurdle at Exeter in February (when he started at 16/1-on!) should have put Finian's Oscar on course for Cheltenham where he held entries in both the Supreme and the Baring Bingham (he was expected to tackle the longer race for which he was ante-post favourite) but his preparation was held up by a bruised foot which meant that he made his next appearance at Aintree instead.

The Tizzard stable had a quiet spell at Cheltenham in any case, but it was a different story at Aintree where Finian's Oscar was ridden for the first time by Robbie Power in his new role as the Potts' retained rider (Tom O'Brien had ridden him previously under Rules). Finian's Oscar started the 3/1 favourite against a dozen rivals in the Betway Mersey Novices' Hurdle. Most of the field, in fact, had given Cheltenham a miss, the chief exception being 7/2 second favourite Messire des Obeaux, the Challow winner earlier in the season, who had finished third behind Willoughby Court and the ill-fated Neon Wolf in the Baring Bingham. The majority of the Mersey field were still closely grouped jumping the first flight in the home straight where Messire des Obeaux was the first to strike for home. Finian's Oscar had been pushed along to stay in touch with the leaders leaving the back straight but he was now among those in pursuit of the leader and took over in front approaching the last before staying on strongly to record a three-length win over Captain Forez, who had last been seen finishing second to the Tolworth runner-up Capitaine in the Kennel Gate Novices' Hurdle at Ascot in December. Messire des Obeaux was beaten a total of just over six lengths into third, though reportedly sustained a tendon injury in the race which will rule him out of 2017/18.

Finian's Oscar's connections enjoyed success at Punchestown too where wins in valuable handicaps for Sizing Granite and Sizing Codelco supplemented Fox Norton's Grade 1 win, but Finian's Oscar himself lost his unbeaten record, albeit

Betway Mersey Novices' Hurdle, Aintree—Finian's Oscar already has the measure of eventual third Messire des Obeaux (who sustained an injury) at the last

by the narrowest of margins in a thrilling finish to the two and a half mile Champion Novices' Hurdle. Sent off the 13/8 favourite against some of Ireland's top novices, including Let's Dance, winner of the Dawn Run Mares' Novices' at Cheltenham and Gigginstown's well-regarded Death Duty, Finian's Oscar quickened clear early in the straight but his lead was already being reduced by Bacardys approaching the final flight, the latter getting away from it the quicker and staying on to deny Finian's Oscar by a short head. Bacardys was already a Grade 1 winner himself and the loss of an unbeaten record did little to diminish Finian's Oscar's standing as one of the most exciting prospects among the latest crop of novice hurdlers.

Finian's Oscar (IRE) (b.g. 2012)	Oscar (IRE) (b 1994)	Sadler's Wells (b 1981)	Northern Dancer / Fairy Bridge
		Snow Day (b 1978)	Reliance II / Vindaria
	Trinity Alley (IRE) (b 2001)	Taipan (b 1992)	Last Tycoon / Alidiva
		Trinity Gale (b 1988)	Strong Gale / Trinity Air

A rangy, chasing type in appearance, Finian's Oscar had changed hands a few times already before his current connections snapped him up. He went through the sale-ring twice as a foal, bought back on the first occasion before being sold for €24,000 at Goffs December National Hunt Sale, and was then bought for €50,000 as a three-year-old at the Derby Sale. Finian's Oscar is out of a half-sister to Finian's Rainbow who denied Sizing Europe, arguably the best horse to carry the Potts's colours, a second win in the 2012 Queen Mother Champion Chase when the leaders came very close together bypassing the final fence. The top-class Finian's Rainbow went on to win the Melling Chase that season but most of his wins came at around two miles and he had been something of a tearaway as a novice, even though there was no shortage of stamina in his pedigree. Finian's Rainbow's dam Trinity Gale was a winning pointer who didn't produce any other winners; Trinity Alley, Finian's Oscar's dam, was lightly raced in Irish points and Finian's Oscar, her second foal, is her only runner to date. Further back in the pedigree, great grandam Trinity Air won five times over fences and was a half-sister to the dam of the useful chaser Lucky Town who was twice runner-up in the Galway Plate, as well as being placed twice in the Kerry National, and also finished second in the Heineken Gold Cup when it was the Punchestown Festival's most valuable race. Finian's Oscar travels strongly in his races but will stay three miles. He acts on soft ground and is one to look forward to in the next season, whether he's kept over hurdles or, more likely perhaps, is switched to fences. *Colin Tizzard*

320

FINISH THE STORY (IRE) 11 b.g. Court Cave (IRE) – Lady of Grange (IRE) **c105** (Phardante (FR)) [2016/17 c114, h96: c29.1g⁵ h23g c27.2s c25.3vᵖᵘ h25.6s* c28s⁴ c25.7s⁴ **h100** c25.5g³ Apr 12] compact gelding: fair handicap hurdler: won at Southwell in January: fair handicap chaser: out-and-out stayer: acts on heavy going: wears headgear/tongue tie: front runner/races prominently. *Johnny Farrelly*

FINNEGAN'S GARDEN (IRE) 8 b.g. Definite Article – Tri Folene (FR) (Nebos **c76** (GER)) [2016/17 c–p, h68: c25.2sᵖᵘ c19.7s⁶ c20.2s³ c20.2s* Mar 10] lightly-raced hurdler: **h–** poor form over fences: won handicap at Leicester in March: best effort at 2½m: acts on soft going: has worn hood. *Zoe Davison*

FINULA (IRE) 5 b.g. Robin des Champs (FR) – Glens Ruby (IRE) (Presenting) [2016/17 **h109** b16d⁶ b17m h15.8d* h19.6d⁶ h19.7s² h21m⁵ Apr 18] first foal: dam (c72/h82) maiden **b75** jumper who should have stayed beyond 2½m: modest form in bumpers: fair form over hurdles: won maiden at Huntingdon in November, standout effort: left E. U. Hales after second start. *Brendan Powell*

FIONN MAC CUL (IRE) 6 b.g. Oscar (IRE) – No Moore Bills (Nicholas Bill) [2016/17 **c–** h122p: c20.9sᵖᵘ Dec 11] third both starts in Irish points: fairly useful hurdler: shaped as if **h–** amiss on chasing debut: should be suited by 2½m+: acts on heavy going: usually races prominently. *Venetia Williams*

FIOSRACH (IRE) 7 b.g. Bachelor Duke (USA) – Saana (IRE) (Erins Isle) [2016/17 **h102** h16g⁴ h17m⁵ h16d h16d² h17.2g h16g⁴ h16d³ Mar 21] fair handicap hurdler: left Denis Hogan after sixth start: unproven beyond 2m: acts on soft going: has worn cheekpieces, including in 2016/17. *James Moffatt*

FIREBIRD FLYER (IRE) 10 b.g. Winged Love (IRE) – Kiora Lady (IRE) (King's **c134 d** Ride) [2016/17 c138x, h–: c24.1v² c29.5s c24.1sᵖᵘ c25.2vᵖᵘ c33.4sᵖᵘ h23.9g c31.8gᵖᵘ Apr **h–** 22] small, sturdy gelding: winning hurdler: useful handicap chaser: out of form after reappearance: stays 33f: acts on heavy going: in cheekpieces last 3 starts: in tongue tie last 2: often races in rear. *Evan Williams*

FIREING PIN 8 b.m. Needle Gun (IRE) – Coolvawn Lady (IRE) (Lancastrian) [2016/17 **h–** h16d Oct 25] no form, mainly in points: tried in tongue tie. *Anthony Honeyball*

FIRE IN HIS EYES (IRE) 6 br.g. Stowaway – Carrigeen Kohleria (IRE) (Luso) **c80** [2016/17 h96, b106: h16s⁵ h20g* h20g* h22.6dᵖᵘ c20g⁵ Apr 16] pulled up in point: useful **h129** bumper performer: fairly useful form over hurdles: won maiden at Punchestown in October and novice at Fairyhouse in November: jumped ponderously when well beaten in maiden on chasing debut: left A. J. Martin after first start: stays 2½m: best form on good going: has worn tongue tie, including in 2016/17. *Gordon Elliott, Ireland*

FIRE (IRE) 7 ch.g. Royal Anthem (USA) – Patsy's Choice (IRE) (Eurobus) [2016/17 c–, **c85** h–: c21.2gᶠ c24.2d c24d⁴ c20.1sᵖᵘ c24.2sᵖᵘ h15.8dᵖᵘ Mar 15] point winner: maiden hurdler: **h–** modest form in chases: stays 3m: acts on heavy going: usually in headgear: has worn tongue tie, including last 4 starts. *Laura Morgan*

FIRE ROCK (IRE) 6 b.g. Scorpion (IRE) – Cooline Jana (IRE) (Presenting) [2016/17 **h–** h–: h20.9d Sep 14] no form over hurdles. *Nicky Richards*

FIRESTORM (GER) 6 b.g. Dylan Thomas (IRE) – Fitness (IRE) (Monsun (GER)) **h–** [2016/17 h16dᵖᵘ Nov 6] sturdy gelding: useful at one time on Flat (stays 1½m), has lost his form completely: pulled up in maiden on hurdling debut. *Michael Attwater*

FIRM ORDER (IRE) 12 b.g. Winged Love (IRE) – Fairylodge Scarlet (IRE) (Mister **c–** Lord (USA)) [2016/17 c117, h–: c23gᵖᵘ Jul 21] good-topped gelding: winning hurdler: **h–** useful chaser at best, pulled up sole start in 2016/17: stays 3¼m: acts on good to firm and heavy going: wears headgear: has worn tongue tie. *Paul Webber*

FIRST AVENUE 12 b.g. Montjeu (IRE) – Marciala (IRE) (Machiavellian (USA)) **h100 §** [2016/17 h116§: h17.7d⁶ h20g⁴ h21.6g³ Aug 18] lengthy gelding: useful handicap hurdler at best, on downgrade: stays 2½m: acts on good to firm and heavy going: has worn headgear: usually races towards rear: temperamental. *Laura Morgan*

FIRST DRIFT 6 ch.g. Generous (IRE) – Supreme Cove (Supreme Leader) [2016/17 b95: **h–** b16m* h15.7m⁵ Oct 29] rather unfurnished gelding: won Irish maiden point on debut: **b96** fairly useful form in bumpers: won his second conditionals/amateur event at Worcester in May: tailed off in novice on hurdling debut. *Ben Case*

FIRST DU CHARMIL (FR) 5 ch.g. Ballingarry (IRE) – Famous Member (FR) (Peintre **h108 p** Celebre (USA)) [2016/17 b81: h15.7v³ h20.5s⁴ Mar 3] fourth in bumper: fair form over hurdles: better effort when third in novice at Towcester in February: remains with potential. *Tom Lacey*

FIRST FANDANGO 10 b.g. Hernando (FR) – First Fantasy (Be My Chief (USA))
[2016/17 c–, h120: h23.6m⁶ h19.8d h20.6s h18.6d h24.4gᵖᵘ h24.2d² h24g⁶ Apr 19] sturdy
gelding: fair handicap hurdler: winning chaser: stays 25f: acts on heavy going: has worn
headgear, including last 3 starts: usually wears tongue tie. *Tim Vaughan*
c–
h104

FIRST FLOW (IRE) 5 b.g. Primary (USA) – Clonroche Wells (IRE) (Pierre) [2016/17
b16.8s⁴ Feb 12] €4,500 3-y-o: seventh foal: dam unraced half-sister to useful hurdler/
chaser (stayed 25f) Ballinclay King: 20/1, some encouragement when fourth in bumper at
Exeter (7½ lengths behind Air Navigator) in February. *Kim Bailey*
b91

FIRST IN THE QUEUE (IRE) 10 b.g. Azamour (IRE) – Irina (IRE) (Polar Falcon
(USA)) [2016/17 h17.2d h18.5g⁶ h20g Sep 12] rather leggy gelding: useful hurdler at best,
lightly raced and no form since 2013/14. *Sheila Lewis*
h–

FIRST LIEUTENANT (IRE) 12 ch.g. Presenting – Fourstargale (IRE) (Fourstars
Allstar (USA)) [2016/17 c159, h–: c26m⁴ c22g³ c20g⁵ c25sᶠ c22.5g c20.5d⁵ c24v c24.1d³
c24s⁶ c30.2gᵘʳ c29d c33m³ Apr 27] big gelding: winning hurdler: top-class chaser in his
prime (won 2013 Aintree Bowl), though failed to win after 2012/13 and declined further in
final season: best form up to 3¼m: acted on good to firm and heavy going: usually wore
headgear: tried in tongue tie: reportedly retired. *M. F. Morris, Ireland*
c148 d
h–

FIRST OF NEVER (IRE) 11 b.g. Systematic – Never Promise (FR) (Cadeaux
Genereux) [2016/17 h64: h16g h19.9gᵖᵘ h15.8g h15.8gᵖᵘ h16.8d³ h16.6g³ h16.8s⁶ h15.8s⁶
Apr 1] poor maiden hurdler: stays 21f: acts on soft going: weak finisher. *Lynn Siddall*
h64 §

FIRST SUMMER 5 b.g. Cockney Rebel (IRE) – Silken Dalliance (Rambo Dancer
(CAN)) [2016/17 h16.7g⁴ Jul 16] modest on Flat, stays 11f: in cheekpieces, well held in
novice on hurdling debut. *Shaun Harris*
h73

FIRSTYMINI (FR) 6 gr.g. Slickly (FR) – Jolie Lola (FR) (Villez (USA)) [2016/17
h21.4sᵖᵘ h18.1s h19.3s h16v⁶ h16.2g Apr 27] fair hurdler for S. Foucher in France, no form
in handicaps in 2016/17: maiden chaser: stays 19f. *R. Mike Smith*
c–
h–

FIRTH OF BAVARD 10 b.g. Flemensfirth (USA) – Ice Bavard (Le Bavard (FR))
[2016/17 h20.5sᵖᵘ h20.5v⁵ h16v⁴ h19.3d Apr 5] no form over hurdles. *Robert Goldie*
h–

FIRTH OF THE CLYDE 12 b.g. Flemensfirth (USA) – Miss Nel (Denel (FR)) [2016/17
c144, h–: c23.4v² Feb 16] tall gelding: maiden hurdler: useful chaser: stays 3m: acts on
heavy going: in blinkers last 4 starts: usually races towards rear. *Malcolm Jefferson*
c140
h–

FISHERGATE 4 b.g. Pastoral Pursuits – Miss Meggy (Pivotal) [2016/17 h15.9v Jan 30]
fair at best on Flat (stays 1½m), has lost his form: well beaten in maiden on hurdling debut.
Richard Rowe
h–

FISHERMAN FRANK 6 b.g. Rail Link – Ribbons And Bows (IRE) (Dr Devious (IRE))
[2016/17 b84: b16.3g⁶ b16m* b16.4gᵖᵘ Mar 15] big gelding: fairly useful bumper
performer: won at Worcester in July: left Natalie Lloyd-Beavis after first start: has worn
tongue tie. *Michael Blake*
b98

FISHING BRIDGE (IRE) 12 ch.g. Definite Article – Rith Ar Aghaidh (IRE) (Phardante
(FR)) [2016/17 c–, h104§: c23.8m⁵ Apr 25] dual winning pointer: fair hurdler: lightly-
raced chaser: stays 3m: acts on good to firm and heavy going: wears headgear/tongue tie:
usually races towards rear: temperamental. *Miss E. Rodney*
c99 §
h– §

FIT AS A FIDDLE 8 b.g. With The Flow (USA) – Olly May (Silver Owl) [2016/17
h21.6mᵘʳ h21.6gᵖᵘ h16.5g h19gᵖᵘ Dec 30] workmanlike gelding: no form over hurdles.
Jimmy Frost
h–

FIT FOR FIFTY 5 ch.g. Lucarno (USA) – Just For Jean (IRE) (Presenting) [2016/17
b16.7g h20d³ h15.8s h17s⁵ h16.6s⁵ h20.6g⁶ Mar 27] €9,000 3-y-o, £14,000 4-y-o: first foal:
dam (h86), maiden hurdler (should have stayed beyond 17f), half-sister to fairly useful
hurdler/chaser (stayed 3m) World Wide Web: third on completed start in Irish points: tailed
off in bumper: poor form over hurdles: best effort at 21f: often races towards rear.
Donald McCain
h81
b–

FIT THE BRIEF 7 b.m. Kayf Tara – Tulipa (POL) (Jape (USA)) [2016/17 b93: h16sᶠ
h15.7s² h18.7dᵘʳ h16g⁵ h19.2g⁵ h20.5g⁵ h19.3s Feb 13] fair maiden hurdler: stays 2½m:
acts on soft going: wears hood: has worn tongue tie, including last 2 starts: races towards
rear/freely. *Tom George*
h106

FITZ VOLONTE 10 br.g. Passing Glance – Swordella (Broadsword (USA)) [2016/17
h16.8m c24.1gᵖᵘ c21.7g² c20.2s² c24.5s³ c21.1gᵖᵘ c22.6g* Apr 15] workmanlike gelding:
maiden hurdler: modest chaser: won novice handicap at Stratford in April: stays 3m: acts
on soft going: has worn headgear, including last 2 starts: often races in rear. *Andrew Martin*
c92
h–

FIVE FOR FIFTEEN (IRE) 8 b.g. Craigsteel – Gentle Eyre (IRE) (Aristocracy)   h–
[2016/17 b–: h19.3m⁶ h20.6g⁵ Jun 3] winning Irish pointer: well held both starts in novice
hurdles. *Donald McCain*

FIVE IN A ROW (IRE) 9 ch.g. Blueprint (IRE) – Ela Plaisir (IRE) (Grand Plaisir (IRE))   c132
[2016/17 c137, h114: c29.2g² c28.8dᵖᵘ c32.8gᵖᵘ Feb 4] good-topped gelding: fair hurdler: h–
useful handicap chaser: went as if amiss last 2 starts: stays 29f: acts on soft going: tried in
cheekpieces: usually races close up. *Brian Ellison*

FIVE PIERS (IRE) 9 ch.g. Presenting – Gales Return (IRE) (Bob's Return (IRE))   c72
[2016/17 c26.2d⁶ Apr 10] dual point winner: once-raced hurdler: 5/2, sixth in maiden   h–
hunter at Kelso (28 lengths behind Havana Jack) on chasing debut. *D. Holmes*

FIVE POINT PLAN (IRE) 11 b.g. Rashar (USA) – Grangeway (La Grange Music)   c77
[2016/17 h18.1s c15.6v³ c15.5s⁵ c20.1sᵘʳ h20.5v Jan 16] point/bumper winner: maiden   h–
hurdler: poor form over fences: unproven beyond 2m: raced mainly on soft/heavy going:
has worn hood: often races in rear. *Gemma Anderson*

FIXED RATE 4 b.g. Oasis Dream – Pretty Face (Rainbow Quest (USA)) [2016/17   h109
h16.3d² h16s h16v⁵ h16.2d² h16m* h16g⁶ Apr 29] close-coupled gelding: fairly useful on
Flat (stays 14.5f) for D. Smaga in France: fair form over hurdles: won handicap at
Kempton (conditional) in April: raced only at 2m: acts on good to firm and good to soft
going: in tongue tie last 4 starts. *Charlie Mann*

FIXE LE KAP (FR) 5 gr.g. Kapgarde (FR) – Lady Fix (FR) (Turgeon (USA)) [2016/17   h144
h139: h16d² Mar 11] good sort: useful handicap hurdler: second in Imperial Cup at
Sandown (length behind London Prize) in March after 12-month absence: will stay 2½m:
acts on heavy going: front runner/races prominently. *Nicky Henderson*

FIX UP LOOK SHARP 6 b.h. Sakhee (USA) – Featherlight (Fantastic Light (USA))   h–
[2016/17 h19.5g Dec 10] fair maiden on Flat, will stay beyond 1¾m: well held in novice
on hurdling debut. *Mark Hoad*

FIZZY DANCER 7 ch.m. Norse Dancer (IRE) – Mrs Fizziwig (Petoski) [2016/17 h103,   h101
b83: h20g⁵ May 3] workmanlike mare: fair form over hurdles: dead. *Kim Bailey*

FLAMING CHARMER (IRE) 9 ch.g. Flemensfirth (USA) – Kates Charm (IRE)   c116 §
(Glacial Storm (USA)) [2016/17 h23.6gᵖᵘ c19.2v* c19.2v² c20.2v⁴ c25.1v³ c25.1d³ Mar   h– §
26] tall gelding: winning hurdler: fairly useful handicap chaser: won at Exeter in December:
stays 25f: acts on heavy going: has worn tongue tie: temperamental. *Colin Tizzard*

FLAMING GORGE (IRE) 12 ch.g. Alderbrook – Solmus (IRE) (Sexton Blake)   c104
[2016/17 c117, h–: c21.4g³ c21.1dᵖᵘ Jun 1] tall gelding: winning hurdler: fair chaser   h–
nowadays: stays 25f: acts on good to firm and heavy going: has worn headgear, including
final start: in tongue tie last 5 starts: front runner/races prominently. *Lawney Hill*

FLAMINGO BEAT 7 ch.g. Beat Hollow – Flamingo Flower (USA) (Diesis) [2016/17   h62
h–: h23.3dᵖᵘ h15.8g⁵ h19.6g⁴ h15.8g³ h15.8d h15.9m h19.6m Oct 2] plain gelding: poor
maiden hurdler: best effort at 2m: often wears headgear. *Christine Dunnett*

FLAMING THISTLE (IRE) 13 b.g. Flemensfirth (USA) – Native Thistle (IRE) (Ovac   c–
(ITY)) [2016/17 c98x, h–: c24.3sᵖᵘ c24.3vᵖᵘ Jan 16] maiden hurdler: modest chaser at best,   h–
no form in 2016/17: stays 3¼m: acts on heavy going: has worn headgear, including last 3
starts. *John Hodge*

FLANAGANS FIELD (IRE) 9 b.g. Araafa (IRE) – Zvezda (USA) (Nureyev (USA))   h94
[2016/17 h15.8v* h17.7g² Mar 31] modest handicap hurdler: won at Ffos Las (conditional)
in March after 2-year absence: stays 19f: acts on good to firm and heavy going: has worn
headgear, including in 2016/17: tried in tongue tie. *Bernard Llewellyn*

FLANS O MAN (IRE) 7 b.g. Milan – Boro Supreme (IRE) (Supreme Leader) [2016/17   h–
h15.8d h15.8s Feb 8] maiden pointer: well held in maiden hurdles: wears tongue tie.
Sophie Leech

FLASH CRASH 8 b.g. Val Royal (FR) – Tessara (GER) (Big Shuffle (USA)) [2016/17   c85
c103, h96: h19.1d c16g⁴ c20.9vᵖᵘ Dec 12] leggy gelding: maiden hurdler: fair maiden   h–
chaser: below form in 2016/17: stays 3¼m: acts on good to firm and heavy going: has worn
headgear: wears tongue tie: often leads: temperament under suspicion. *Barry Brennan*

FLASH GARDEN (IRE) 9 b.g. Heron Island (IRE) – Latin Lady (IRE) (Dr Massini   c115
(IRE)) [2016/17 c108p: c25.2s² c21.1gᶠ Apr 6] compact gelding: unbeaten in 4 points: fair
form in chases: second in novice hunter at Catterick in March. *J. M. B. Cookson*

FLASHING GLANCE 4 b.g. Passing Glance – Don And Gerry (IRE) (Vestris Abu) **b89**
[2016/17 b13g³ b14s⁵ b16g⁵ Apr 22] smallish gelding: second foal: dam (h100) bumper/19f
hurdle winner: fair form in bumpers: best effort when third in junior event at Doncaster on
debut: left Richard Price after second start. *Tom Lacey*

FLASHJACK (IRE) 7 br.g. Soapy Danger – Open Miss (Dracula (AUS)) [2016/17 h128: **c118**
c24.2sᶠ c24.2s c25.2vᵖᵘ c21.7v⁵ c24.2sᵖᵘ Mar 7] well-made gelding: fairly useful hurdler: **h–**
shaping encouragingly when falling last in novice at Wetherby on chasing debut,
disappointing subsequently: probably stays 3m: acts on heavy going: in cheekpieces last 3
starts. *Henry Daly*

FLASHMAN 8 ch.g. Doyen (IRE) – Si Si Si (Lomitas) [2016/17 h107: h20.5g³ c16.5m⁵ **c107 §**
c17g² c20m⁵ c16.1d⁵ c15.9g³ c17g* c17mᵖᵘ Apr 16] workmanlike gelding: fair handicap **h82 §**
hurdler: fair handicap chaser: won at Plumpton in March: stays 2¼m: acts on soft going:
wears headgear: usually races close up: unreliable. *Gary Moore*

FLASH N SMART 4 b.f. Sakhee's Secret – Lady Trish (Red Ransom (USA)) [2016/17 **h–**
h15.8mᵖᵘ Oct 20] poor maiden on Flat: pulled up in juvenile on hurdling debut. *Nikki Evans*

FLASH TOMMIE (IRE) 9 b.g. City Honours (USA) – African Keys (IRE) (Quws) **c–**
[2016/17 c106, h–: c24.2dᵖᵘ Feb 17] maiden hurdler: fair chaser at best, has lost his form **h–**
(including in points): stays 2½m: acts on soft and good to firm going: usually wears
headgear: usually leads. *C. E. Ward*

FLATFOOT BOOGIE (FR) 12 b.g. King's Theatre (IRE) – Cure The Blues (IRE) **c82**
(Phardante (FR)) [2016/17 h24.4gᵖᵘ c22sᵖᵘ c20v c23.6d⁴ Mar 15] fairly useful hurdler at **h–**
best: little form in 2016/17 after long absence, mainly over fences: should stay 3m: acts on
soft and good to firm going: often races prominently. *Noel Glynn, Ireland*

FLAXEN FLARE (IRE) 8 ch.g. Windsor Knot (IRE) – Golden Angel (USA) (Slew O' **c133**
Gold (USA)) [2016/17 c124P, h–: h16v³ c21.2dᵘʳ Apr 9] sturdy gelding: smart hurdler at **h103 +**
best, some encouragement on return after long absence: useful form over fences: every
chance when unseated rider 2 out in minor event won by Akito at Tramore in April: stays
2½m: acts on soft going: usually wears headgear. *Gordon Elliott, Ireland*

FLED OR PLED (IRE) 5 b.g. Shantou (USA) – Desert Gail (IRE) (Desert Style (IRE)) **h88**
[2016/17 h–: h15.8g h21m* h23.1g³ h24g* h23.1s⁵ Dec 1] modest handicap hurdler: won
at Towcester in October (novice event) and November: stays 3m: acts on good to firm
going: wears hood: often races in rear. *David Dennis*

FLEMBRANDT (IRE) 7 b.m. Flemensfirth (USA) – Lady Rembrandt (IRE) (Blueprint **h–**
(IRE)) [2016/17 h21.7v h23.1s⁴ h21.2sᵖᵘ Feb 8] €5,000 3-y-o, £2,600 6-y-o: second foal:
half-sister to a winning pointer by Milan: dam unraced half-sister to fairly useful hurdler/
top-class chaser (stayed 29f) Sir Rembrandt: maiden pointer: no form over hurdles: in
cheekpieces last 2 starts. *Steve Flook*

FLEMCARA (IRE) 5 b.g. Flemensfirth (USA) – Cara Mara (IRE) (Saddlers' Hall (IRE)) **h103**
[2016/17 b16s⁵ h21.6v² h19.5v⁵ Mar 6] €62,000 4-y-o: first foal: dam (c117/h119) 2m-3m **b65**
hurdle/chase winner: runner-up in Irish maiden point on debut: fifth in bumper: fair form
over hurdles: better effort when second in novice at Fontwell in February. *Emma Lavelle*

FLEMENSBAY 9 b.m. Flemensfirth (USA) – Mandys Native (IRE) (Be My Native **c96 §**
(USA)) [2016/17 c–, h101: c24s³ c25.5dᵖᵘ c24dᶠ h23g h23.3gᵖᵘ Sep 18] fair hurdler at best, **h– §**
no form in 2016/17: modest form only completed start over fences: stays 3m: acts on soft
going: wears headgear: temperamental. *Richard Phillips*

FLEMENSKILL (IRE) 5 b.g. Flemensfirth (USA) – Nivalf (Gildoran) [2016/17 b17d³ **b97**
b15.8v² b18g Apr 28] €68,000 3-y-o: sixth foal: half-brother to fair chaser Mission To Mars
(2m winner, by Presenting) and bumper winner Ballyhooley Boy (by Oscar): dam unraced
half-sister to fairly useful hurdler/smart chaser Bosuns Mate, stayed 25f: fairly useful form
in bumpers: best effort when second at Ffos Las in March: will be suited by 2½m+.
Warren Greatrex

FLEMENTIME (IRE) 9 ch.m. Flemensfirth (USA) – Funny Times (Silver Patriarch **c116**
(IRE)) [2016/17 c–p, h119: c16.5s² May 11] good-topped mare: fairly useful hurdler: **h–**
similar form when second in handicap at Worcester, easily best effort over fences: stays
2½m: acts on heavy going: in headgear last 3 starts: tried in tongue tie. *Martin Keighley*

FLEMERINA (IRE) 8 b.m. Flemensfirth (USA) – Ballerina Laura (IRE) (Riot Helmet) **h94**
[2016/17 h87, b74: h20.6s⁴ h23.3v² h20.6s⁴ h23.1s* Mar 12] modest handicap hurdler:
won mares event at Market Rasen in March: thorough stayer: acts on heavy going.
Sue Smith

FLEMINATOR 5 b.m. Flemensfirth (USA) – Misleain (IRE) (Un Desperado (FR)) **b–**
[2016/17 b16.2s⁶ b16.8d⁴ Dec 26] fifth foal: half-sister to fair hurdler Vic's Last Stand
(17f-2½m winner, by Old Vic) and bumper winner Bedale Lane (by Kayf Tara): dam (h71),
ungenuine maiden hurdler, half-sister to fairly useful hurdler/chaser (stayed 27f) Schuh
Shine: no form in bumpers. *Micky Hammond*

FLEMI TWO TOES (IRE) 11 b.g. Flemensfirth (USA) – Silva Venture (IRE) **c– §**
(Mandalus) [2016/17 c–, h91§: h25m⁴ h24v* h25.5s³ h25.6sᵖᵘ Jan 31] workmanlike **h86 §**
gelding: modest handicap hurdler: won at Southwell (amateur) in December: winning
chaser: stays 3¼m: acts on heavy going: often in headgear: has worn tongue tie: ungenuine.
Laura Morgan

FLETCHERS FLYER (IRE) 9 b.g. Winged Love (IRE) – Crystal Chord (IRE) **c144**
(Accordion) [2016/17 c145, h–: c30d* c23.8d c23.8s³ c29dᵖᵘ Apr 17] good-topped gelding: **h–**
winning hurdler: useful handicap chaser: third in Reynoldstown Novices' Chase at Ascot
(2½ lengths behind Bigbadjohn) in February: stays 3¾m: acts on heavy going: wears
tongue tie: front runner/races prominently. *Harry Fry*

FLEUR DU POMMIER 4 br.f. Apple Tree (FR) – Jersey Countess (IRE) (Supreme **b–**
Leader) [2016/17 b16.7g Mar 25] third foal: dam (h79), maiden hurdler (form only at 2m),
half-sister to fairly useful hurdler/fair chaser (19f-21f winner) Carrick Oscar: well beaten
in maiden bumper. *G. C. Maundrell*

FLEUR DU WELD 9 ch.m. Weld – Midnight Walker (Exodal (USA)) [2016/17 h18.5g **h87**
h19.5gᵖᵘ h15.3sᵖᵘ h16.5g⁶ h18.5m³ Apr 15] fourth foal: half-sister to a winning pointer by
Opera Ghost: dam lightly raced on Flat: modest form over hurdles: should stay beyond
2¼m: acts on good to firm going: in tongue tie last 2 starts. *Gail Haywood*

FLICHITY (IRE) 12 br.g. Turtle Island (IRE) – Chancy Gal (Al Sirat) [2016/17 c56§, **c– §**
h–§: c24.2gᵖᵘ h16g c24dᵖᵘ c15.7g³ Apr 21] leggy gelding: winning hurdler/chaser, no form **h– §**
in 2016/17: has worn headgear: ungenuine. *John Cornwall*

FLIGHTS 6 b.m. King's Theatre (IRE) – Motcombe (IRE) (Carroll House) [2016/17 b–: **b–**
b17.7g May 8] winning pointer: no form in bumpers. *Robert Walford*

FLIGHT TO NOWHERE 5 ch.m. Aeroplane – River Beauty (Exit To Nowhere (USA)) **h84**
[2016/17 b15.8m h16g h16s h16v⁵ h15.8g⁶ Apr 17] first foal: dam (h98) winning hurdler/ **b–**
placed in bumpers: last in bumper: poor form over hurdles: in hood last 3 starts.
Richard Price

FLIGHTY FILIA (IRE) 5 gr.m. Raven's Pass (USA) – Coventina (IRE) (Daylami **h88**
(IRE)) [2016/17 h16.8m h18.5g² h18.5s h16.8s⁶ Jan 17] workmanlike mare: fair on Flat,
stays 2m: modest form over hurdles. *Jimmy Frost*

FLINDERS RIVER (IRE) ᵠ ch.g. Traditionally (USA) – Silver Tassie (FR) **h72**
(Kaldounevees (FR)) [2016/17 h22.2g⁵ h16d h25.8vᵖᵘ Jan 15] lightly-raced maiden
hurdler, little show in 2016/17: stays 2¾m: tried in blinkers. *Noel C. Kelly, Ireland*

FLINTHAM 8 b.g. Kayf Tara – Plaid Maid (IRE) (Executive Perk) [2016/17 c–, h142: **c139**
c23.6s⁴ c23.8s² c31.8gᵖᵘ Mar 14] sturdy gelding: useful hurdler: useful form over fences: **h–**
second in Reynoldstown Novices' Chase at Ascot (short head behind Bigbadjohn) in
February: stays 3¼m: acts on heavy going: wears headgear: front runner. *Mark Bradstock*

FLINTS LEGACY 5 gr.m. Sagamix (FR) – Luneray (FR) (Poplar Bluff) [2016/17 b89: **h92**
b15.8s³ h19.5vᵖᵘ h19.1d² h20.7s h19g Mar 30] placed in bumpers, better effort on debut in **b64**
2015/16: modest form over hurdles: front runner/races prominently. *Nigel Hawke*

FLOBURY 9 b.m. Overbury (IRE) – Miss Flora (Alflora (IRE)) [2016/17 h78: h16d **h90**
h19.9s² h23.3v³ h20.5g³ h19.2v² h23.3s* Mar 18] smallish mare: modest handicap hurdler:
won mares event at Uttoxeter in March: stays 23f: acts on soft going: usually races nearer
last than first. *Barry Leavy*

FLORA AURORA 9 ch.g. Alflora (IRE) – Dawn Spinner (Arctic Lord) [2016/17 h–: **h–**
h19.5dᵖᵘ h21.4dᵖᵘ Nov 17] no form in bumper/over hurdles: tried in tongue tie.
Jess Westwood

FLORAL BOUQUET 4 bl.f. Fair Mix (IRE) – Florarossa (Alflora (IRE)) [2016/17 **b83**
b16.6d b15.7s² b16.7g³ Mar 27] lengthy filly: second foal: dam (b85), second in bumper,
out of useful hurdler/chaser (winner up to 25f) Bayrouge: modest form in bumpers: best
effort when second in conditionals/amateur mares event at Catterick in March: will be
suited by further than 2m. *Gillian Boanas*

FLORAL QUEEN 4 b.f. Emperor Fountain – Florentino (Efisio) [2016/17 b16g Apr 17] **b–**
second foal: half-sister to useful hurdler/winning pointer Get On The Yager (21f winner, by
Tamure): dam (h97) 2m hurdle winner: 10/1, last in mares maiden bumper at Fakenham.
Neil Mulholland

FLORAMOSS 6 b.m. Alflora (IRE) – Brackenmoss (IRE) (Supreme Leader) [2016/17   **h101** b82: b16.8g³ h16.2v² h19.3d² h16.4v⁴ h20.1s² h22.7s² Apr 3] modest form in bumpers: fair   **b76** form over hurdles: stays 23f: acts on heavy going: often races towards rear. *Gillian Boanas*

FLORESCO (GER) 7 ch.g. Santiago (GER) – Fiori (GER) (Chief Singer) [2016/17   **h122** h116: h18.5g* h21g h16.8g⁴ h20.5d⁶ h15.3s⁴ h15.7g⁵ Apr 15] compact gelding: fairly useful handicap hurdler: won at Newton Abbot in May: stays 2¼m: acts on heavy going: in headgear last 2 starts: wears tongue tie. *Richard Woollacott*

FLORIDA CALLING (IRE) 8 ch.g. Presenting – Miami Nights (GER) (Tertullian   **c–** (USA)) [2016/17 c117, h104: c23.9gᵖᵘ c24dᵖᵘ Nov 25] lengthy gelding: winning Irish   **h–** pointer: maiden hurdler/chaser, no form in 2016/17: stays 3m: best form on good going: tried in cheekpieces: front runner/races prominently. *Tom George*

FLORRIE BOY (IRE) 6 b.g. Milan – Second Best (IRE) (Supreme Leader) [2016/17   **h131** h121, b86: h22.8m⁶ h21.1g h20s* h19.9s* Dec 6] sturdy gelding: useful handicap hurdler: won at Aintree and Uttoxeter (by 2½ lengths from Milord) in December: best around 2½m: acts on soft going. *Nigel Twiston-Davies*

FLO'SBOY SAM 4 b.g. Tobougg (IRE) – Madam Flora (Alflora (IRE)) [2016/17 b15.3v   **h–** h18.5d Feb 24] well beaten in bumper/novice hurdle. *Robert Walford*   **b–**

FLOWER BALL (FR) 5 b.g. Ballingarry (IRE) – Ma Flower (FR) (Mad Tax (USA))   **h–** [2016/17 b16.4g h19.5m⁶ h20g⁶ h21s h22g Apr 1] third on completed start in Irish points: **b–** no form in bumper/over hurdles: tried in blinkers. *Harry Whittington*

FLOWER POWER 7 ch.m. Bollin Eric – Floral Rhapsody (Alflora (IRE)) [2016/17   **h–** h107, b78: h20m h25.4dᵖᵘ h20.5g Nov 27] fair hurdler at best, no form in 2016/17 (though did win 1½m maiden on Flat in September). *Tony Coyle*

FLOW FROM DEVON 4 b.f. With The Flow (USA) – Sally Army (Silver Patriarch   **b–** (IRE)) [2016/17 b16.5gᵖᵘ Apr 6] second foal: dam (h67) maiden hurdler: 50/1, saddle slipped and soon pulled up in bumper. *Ron Hodges*

FLOW WITH EVE 8 b.m. With The Flow (USA) – Vercheny (Petoski) [2016/17 h16.8dᶠ   **h92** h21.7g⁶ h15.3s⁵ h17.7v h19s⁴ h19.8v h21.2m Apr 25] sturdy mare: modest maiden hurdler: left Polly Gundry after second start: stays 19f: acts on soft going: tried in hood: often races in rear. *Bill Turner*

FLUGZEUG 9 gr.g. Silver Patriarch (IRE) – Telmar Flyer (Neltino) [2016/17 c–, h91:   **c79** h26.5d c23g⁵ c25.5g³ c25.7gᵘʳ h25s⁵ h23v² c24.5v⁴ h23v³ h23.1g⁴ c25.7m² Apr 17] modest   **h85** handicap hurdler: poor handicap chaser: stays 3¼m: acts on good to firm and heavy going: usually wears cheekpieces nowadays. *Seamus Mullins*

FLYBALL 5 gr.g. Proclamation (IRE) – Bella Bertolini (Bertolini (USA)) [2016/17 h16sᵖᵘ   **h–** Nov 23] modest on Flat, stays 7f: jumped badly when pulled up in novice on hurdling debut: wore hood. *Dianne Sayer*

FLYBRIDGE 5 b.g. Avonbridge – Baytown Flyer (Whittingham (IRE)) [2016/17 b–:   **b–** b17.7d Jun 1] no form in bumpers: tried in visor. *Lydia Richards*

FLY CAMP (IRE) 7 gr.g. Westerner – Pearlsforthegirls (Cloudings (IRE)) [2016/17   **h126** h20g² h19.9g* h19.5s² h18.5s* h21.5sᵖᵘ Mar 10] second foal: dam twice-raced half-sister to fairly useful hurdler/smart chaser (probably stayed 3m) Hobbs Hill: twice-raced in Irish points, won completed start: fairly useful form over hurdles: won maiden at Uttoxeter in June and novice at Exeter in February: should be suited by further than 2½m: acts on soft going: front runner/races prominently. *Nicky Henderson*

FLY HOME HARRY 8 b.g. Sir Harry Lewis (USA) – Fly Home (Skyliner) [2016/17   **c100** c89, h–: c20.1g⁶ c24d* c24d* c22.7g c24g² c23.9m⁴ Apr 9] maiden hurdler: fair handicap   **h–** chaser: won at Southwell (twice) in November: stays 3m: acts on soft going: in cheekpieces last 3 starts: tried in tongue tie: often races towards rear. *Alan Swinbank*

FLYING ANGEL (IRE) 6 gr.g. Arcadio (GER) – Gypsy Kelly (IRE) (Roselier   **c154** (FR)) [2016/17 h143: c20.1s* c19.4gᶠ c20.4gᵖᵘ c16.2v* c19.9g⁶ c19.9g* c20.5gᵖᵘ   **h–** Apr 22]

    The Cheltenham Festival gods had smiled kindly on Nigel Twiston-Davies in 2016, Ballyandy eventually getting the gaps in the Champion Bumper and Blaklion capitalising on below-par performances from both the favourite More of That and ill-fated second favourite No More Heroes when landing the RSA Chase. Twiston-Davies may have used up his store of good fortune, though, as the 2017 Festival was not nearly so kind to him. Things started badly for the yard when Ballyandy, all the rage for the opening Supreme Novices' Hurdle after his win in the Betfair Hurdle at

Manifesto Novices' Chase, Aintree—Flying Angel (right) gets the better of the more fancied pair Cloudy Dream and Top Notch (largely hidden)

Newbury, was baulked at the second flight and never looked comfortable afterwards, eventually finishing over eleven lengths back in fourth. The first day of the Festival got worse for Twiston-Davies and his family when the Close Brothers Novices' Handicap Chase favourite Foxtail Hill—a game winner of the Trophy Chase at the course at the end of January—fell when in front at the eighth. Foxtail Hill was ridden by Nigel's youngest son Willy, who had only returned to riding over jumps in the latest season having ridden exclusively on the Flat since 2013. Willy initially got up from his fall and walked to the ambulance, but was later found to have fractured two vertebrae and cracked two ribs, necessitating a four-hour operation three days later.

Willy Twiston-Davies had been a promising young jockey over jumps when he began riding in 2011, though the most readily recalled moment of his early career was probably being dramatically unseated two out in the Foxhunter at Cheltenham on Baby Run, the horse that had provided older brother Sam with success in the same race the previous season. Willy went on to register a third win aboard Baby Run in the Aintree equivalent, but the horse missed 2011/12, a season in which Willy rode only two winners over jumps from seventy-six rides. A new partnership with champion trainer Richard Hannon helped him reach twenty winners on the Flat during 2012, and he passed the forty-winner mark in 2013, 2014 and 2015 before his most notable Flat win came at Royal Ascot in 2016 when riding the Alan King-trained Primitivo to victory in the King George V Stakes. Standing six feet, Willy's weight was always against him when it came to a career on the Flat, though, and disillusioned by the prospect of another winter riding on the all-weather he opted to return to jumping. He finished second in a bumper at Bangor in December on his first ride back and just two rides later had a Cheltenham winner—five seasons after being unseated on Baby Run—when winning a handicap hurdle on his father's Cogry on New Year's Day. More winners followed, notably on the Fergal O'Brien-trained Lord of The Island in a Grade 3 handicap hurdle at Sandown in February and then on Flying Angel for the Twiston-Davies stable in the Grade 2 Kingmaker Novices' Chase at Warwick. Flying Angel had been ridden by Ryan Hatch on nine of his eleven previous starts, but Hatch had also suffered a serious injury, also in a fall at Cheltenham, at the December meeting (ironically aboard Cogry).

With Hatch and Willy Twiston-Davies both side-lined and brother Sam— the only other jockey to have ridden Flying Angel—claimed for the Nicholls-trained Politologue, Noel Fehily came in the for the ride on Flying Angel in the Golden Miller (branded as the JLT Novices' Chase). The Twiston-Davies' Festival luck showed no signs of turning, however, as Flying Angel's chance was ended when he was badly hampered by the fall of Baily Cloud at the eleventh fence. This wasn't the first setback in Flying Angel's first season over fences. After making an impressive winning start in a novice event at Perth in September, Flying Angel failed to complete on his next two starts, already beaten when falling in a novice won by Rock The Kasbah at Chepstow next time and then looking laboured for a long way when tailed off at Cheltenham a month later. Given the consistency and the useful form that he had shown the previous season over hurdles (when he was placed in the Betfair Hurdle at Newbury and the Martin Pipe at the Cheltenham Festival, the last-named six days after winning the Imperial Cup at Sandown), Flying Angel's performance at Cheltenham in November was particularly disappointing. A pulled muscle was reportedly to blame, however, and after a three-month break he lined up in a field of six for the Kingmaker Novices' Chase at Warwick, attracting late support and eventually sent off the 7/2 third favourite behind Gino Trail and Overtown Express. Gino Trail already had some smart form at Warwick to his name, having finished two and a quarter lengths behind Buveur d'Air, who received 6 lb. Gino Trail set a strong pace in the Kingmaker on heavy ground and the emphasis on stamina suited Flying Angel—twice a winner already over two and a half miles— and, after jumping soundly, he challenged Gino Trail for the lead two out, and stayed on well to win by four and a half lengths.

Flying Angel's unlucky run in the Golden Miller on his next start came in a first-time tongue strap but that equipment was not fitted when he ran three weeks later in the Manifesto Novices' Chase at Aintree. Only six lined up but the field looked a strong one, with the second from both the Golden Miller (Top Notch) and the Arkle (Cloudy Dream) taking part along with Frodon who had won six of his eight starts over fences including the Pendil Novices' Chase at Kempton in February. The ground was much firmer than it had been for the Kingmaker and Flying Angel underlined not only his general improvement but also his versatility, landing his first Grade 1 success by a length from Cloudy Dream after a ding-dong battle in the straight, the pair pulling clear of a below-par Top Notch who finished four and a half lengths behind Cloudy Dream. Flying Angel was headed by Cloudy Dream coming to the last fence but regained the lead on the run-in. The pair clashed for a second time less than a month later on Ayr's Scottish Grand National card in the Future Champions Novices' Chase, but Flying Angel was unable to recover from a blunder five out in which Fehily did well to stay aboard. Flying Angel was pulled up as Cloudy Dream resumed winning ways after four successive second-place finishes.

		Monsun	Konigsstuhl
	Arcadio (GER)	(br 1990)	Mosella
	(b 2002)	Assia	Royal Academy
Flying Angel (IRE)		(b 1992)	Alys
(gr.g. 2011)		Roselier	Misti IV
	Gypsy Kelly (IRE)	(gr 1973)	Peace Rose
	(gr 1996)	Gallant Blade	Fine Blade
		(b 1981)	Arctic Tack

The good-topped Flying Angel is a first Grade 1 winner for his sire Arcadio, who stands at Arctic Tack Stud in County Wexford, Ireland at a fee of €3,000. Arcadio, runner-up in the 2005 Deutsches Derby and from the same family as the latest Supreme Novices' winner Labaik, is a son of Monsun, who has produced a number of other jumps sires, notably Getaway, Network (the sire of Sprinter Sacre), Ocovango and Shirocco (the sire of Minella Rocco and Annie Power). Though Flying Angel was Arcadio's first Grade 1 winner, his highest-rated performer to date is The Game Changer, who won three times at Grade 3 level before chasing home Douvan in both the Maghull Novices' Chase at Aintree and the Ryanair Novices' Chase at Punchestown in 2015/16. The Game Changer was well below his best during the most recent season, but Arcadio was also represented by Go Conquer, who was fifth in the Ultima Handicap Chase at the Cheltenham Festival. Flying Angel changed hands for €15,000 as a foal and is the seventh offspring out of the unraced Gypsy Kelly, a sister to the modest staying chaser Kung Hei Fat Choi and a half-sister to the Galway Plate runner-up Kelly's Pearl. Gypsy Kelly has produced two other winners, both by Great Palm, including the fair hurdler/chaser at up to two and a half miles Bhaltair. Flying Angel's brother Sizing Venezuela was bought for €44,000 by Willie Mullins and Harold Kirk at the Goffs Land Rover Sale in 2012 but failed to win in three starts. Flying Angel is usually reliable and responds well to pressure and he stays two and a half miles. He acts in the mud but does not need it. *Nigel Twiston-Davies*

FLYING GNU 11 b.m. Flying Legend (USA) – Not One Penny (IRE) (Pennekamp (USA)) [2016/17 c25.5d² c23g⁵ c23g c22.6m³ c23g⁶ c24d c20m^pu Oct 20] first foal: dam unraced: multiple winning pointer: poor maiden chaser: stays 25f: acts on good to firm and good to soft going: front runner/races prominently. *Mark Wall*   **c77**

FLYING JACK 7 b.g. Rob Roy (USA) – Milladella (FR) (Nureyev (USA)) [2016/17 h–, b–: h20.1g² h20.2d⁵ h20.1g⁴ h20.5d h22.7s Dec 4] long-backed gelding: modest maiden hurdler. *Maurice Barnes*   **h94**

FLYING SHADOW (GER) 5 b.g. Sholokhov (IRE) – Fitness (IRE) (Monsun (GER)) [2016/17 b16.3d* b15.7d³ h19g Mar 2] €55,000 3-y-o: third foal: half-brother to 2 winners in Germany, including useful 11f winner Firestorm (by Dylan Thomas): dam French/German 9f-11f winner: modest form in bumpers: won at Stratford in June: 14/1, eighth in novice at Taunton (34¼ lengths behind Spiritofthegames) on hurdling debut: left Warren Greatrex after second start: open to improvement over hurdles. *Emma Lavelle*   **h82 p**
b84

FLYING SOLO (IRE) 5 b.g. Getaway (GER) – Crimson Bow (GER) (Night Shift (USA)) [2016/17 b16.7g⁶ Oct 15] 9/1, sixth in bumper at Market Rasen: dead. *Jonjo O'Neill*   **b–**

FLYING TIGER (IRE) 4 bl.g. Soldier of Fortune (IRE) – Ma Preference (FR) (American Post) [2016/17 h117p: h16.9s² h17.9s^pu h16.8s⁶ h16.3s* h16g⁴ h16.4g* h17g⁴ Apr 6] useful hurdler: won juvenile at Newbury (by 11 lengths from Zalvados) in January and Fred Winter Juvenile Handicap Hurdle at Cheltenham (by neck from Divin Bere) in March: unproven beyond 17f: acts on soft going: usually races nearer last than first. *Nick Williams*   **h133**

FLY VINNIE (IRE) 8 b.g. Vinnie Roe (IRE) – Great Days (IRE) (Magical Strike (USA)) [2016/17 h20.2g Apr 28] maiden Irish pointer: useful hurdler at best: well held in handicap at Perth after 27-month absence: stays 3m: acts on soft going. *Sandy Thomson*   **h–**

FOCACCIA (IRE) 6 b.g. Milan – Dantes Term (IRE) (Phardante (FR)) [2016/17 b87: h16g^F h20d h16.6g² h16m² Apr 18] fair form over hurdles: should stay beyond 2m. *Dan Skelton*   **h108**

Fred Winter Juvenile Handicap Hurdle, Cheltenham—
trainer Nick Williams finally breaks his Cheltenham Festival duck as 33/1-shot Flying Tiger (right)
stays on late to beat Divin Bere (centre) and Nietzsche who makes a costly mistake

FOCAL POINT 7 ch.g. Pivotal – Centreofattention (AUS) (Danehill (USA)) [2016/17 b–: **b–**
b17m May 5] no form in bumpers. *Sue Smith*

FOIBLE 4 b.g. Fastnet Rock (AUS) – Nyarhini (Fantastic Light (USA)) [2016/17 h16s^pu **h–**
h16s h16s h24.1s^pu h19.9g^pu h24.1m^pu Apr 13] lightly raced on Flat: no form over hurdles:
tried in blinkers/tongue tie. *Mike Sowersby*

FOLLOWING MAMA (IRE) 6 b.m. Beneficial – Follow Mama (IRE) (Saddlers' Hall **h–**
(IRE)) [2016/17 b15.8s^6 h21.2d Dec 21] €14,000 3-y-o: fourth foal: sister to fairly useful **b61**
chaser Following Dreams (2½m winner): dam, unraced, closely related to fair hurdler/
high-class chaser (stayed 25f) Follow The Plan and useful hurdler/chaser (stays 3m)
Ballychorus: third in mares maiden point on debut: well beaten in mares bumper/novice
hurdle. *Alastair Ralph*

FOLLOWMYBUTTONS (IRE) 7 br.g. Kalanisi (IRE) – Clondalee (IRE) (Presenting) **c–**
[2016/17 h–: h20.3g h19.2g* h19.3m^pu c23g^F c23.6s^pu Jan 13] lengthy gelding: fair form **h101**
over hurdles: won maiden at Towcester in May: failed to complete both starts over fences:
stays 19f: in tongue tie last 4 starts. *David Arbuthnot*

FOLLOW THE BEAR (IRE) 5 b.g. King's Theatre (IRE) – Mrs Dempsey (IRE) **h115**
(Presenting) [2016/17 h19.6s^2 h23.1s^3 Dec 22] brother to bumper winner/smart hurdler
African Gold (19f-21f winner), stays 3m, a winning pointer: dam unraced half-sister to
fair hurdler/useful staying chaser Grattan Lodge: off mark in points at second attempt:
fairly useful form over hurdles: better effort when second in novice at Bangor in November:
should stay 3m. *Nicky Henderson*

FOLLOW THE MASTER 11 b.g. Alflora (IRE) – Daisy May (In The Wings) [2016/17 **h–**
h–: h16.8v^pu h23.1s h23.9g^pu Mar 2] maiden hurdler, no form in 2016/17. *Brian Forsey*

FOLLOW THE PALS (IRE) 11 ch.g. Accordion – Slaney Pal (IRE) (Supreme Leader) **h–**
[2016/17 h22.1d Jun 26] maiden pointer: well held over hurdles. *James Moffatt*

FOLLOW THE SWALLOW (IRE) 9 b.g. Dr Massini (IRE) – Old Chapel (IRE) **c116 x**
(Royal Fountain) [2016/17 c17d c19g^5 c22.7g^4 c24.2d^ur c24g^2 c25g^ur c19.2v^F c19.4d^5 **h54**
h20.3v^4 Mar 6] strong, close-coupled gelding: tailed off in novice handicap on hurdling
debut: fairly useful handicap chaser: left Miss Elizabeth Doyle after third start: stays 3m:
acts on soft going: often races in rear: often let down by jumping. *Graeme McPherson*

FOLLOW THE TRACKS (IRE) 9 b.g. Milan – Charming Mo (IRE) (Callernish) **c–**
[2016/17 c–, h86: h25g^3 h21.9v^pu h23.9g^2 Mar 30] winning pointer: poor handicap hurdler: **h83**
no form in chases: stays 3m: acts on heavy going. *Brian Barr*

FOLLY BERGERE (IRE) 4 ch.f. Champs Elysees – Rainbow Queen (FR) (Spectrum **h84 p**
(IRE)) [2016/17 h16.7s^3 Dec 1] fairly useful maiden on Flat, stays 2m: 13/2, third in
juvenile at Market Rasen (9½ lengths behind Linger) on hurdling debut: should do better.
James Eustace

FOLLY DAT (IRE) 6 b.m. Generous (IRE) – Maldagora (IRE) (Luso) [2016/17 h19.7d **h90**
h18s h16s^4 h16s^3 h16v Apr 1] second foal: sister to bumper winner Blue Empyrean: dam
unraced: modest form over hurdles: should stay further than 2m: acts on soft going: often
races towards rear. *Gordon Elliott, Ireland*

FOLSOM BLUE (IRE) 10 b.g. Old Vic – Spirit Leader (IRE) (Supreme Leader) **c139 §**
[2016/17 c138, h–: c30d^4 c24v^pu c24d^pu c24d c24.5d h20d c28s c24v* c24s^2 c28.5g **h95**
c24.7d Apr 17] winning chaser: useful handicap chaser: won veterans event at Navan in
March: second in Leinster National Handicap Chase at Naas week later: stays 29f: acts on
heavy going: wears headgear: tried in tongue tie: often races prominently: temperamental.
M. F. Morris, Ireland

FOND MEMORY (IRE) 9 b.g. Dr Massini (IRE) – Glacier Lilly (IRE) (Glacial Storm **c–**
(USA)) [2016/17 c117, h–: c24g May 2] sturdy gelding: winning hurdler: fairly useful **h–**
handicap chaser: well held sole start in 2016/17: stays 25f: acts on heavy going: wears
tongue tie: usually races towards rear. *Nigel Twiston-Davies*

FOOL TO CRY (IRE) 4 ch.f. Fast Company (IRE) – Islandagore (IRE) (Indian Ridge) **h107**
[2016/17 h15.8m* h16g* h16.8d^5 h15.8g^3 Apr 17] leggy filly: fairly useful on Flat, stays
1¼m: fair form over hurdles: won juvenile events at Ludlow (maiden) and Fakenham
(fillies) in October: likely to stay further than 2m. *Neil Mulholland*

FOOTPAD (FR) 5 b.g. Creachadoir (IRE) – Willamina (IRE) (Sadler's Wells (USA)) **h159**
[2016/17 h147: h19.4s* h19.4d* h19.4v^2 h16d^4 h16g^2 h16.4g^4 h24d^3 Apr 27] good-topped
gelding: very smart hurdler: second in Prix Renaud du Vivier at Auteuil (head behind
Capivari) in November and Irish Champion Hurdle at Leopardstown (length behind Petit

Mouchoir) in January: stamina seemed stretched when third in Champion Stayers' Hurdle at Punchestown (18 lengths behind Unowhatimeanharry) final start: barely stays 3m: acts on heavy going: tried in hood: usually races nearer last than first. *W. P. Mullins, Ireland*

FOOT THE BILL 12 b.g. Generous (IRE) – Proudfoot (IRE) (Shareef Dancer (USA)) **c–** [2016/17 c90, h62: c26.2d c23.8g⁶ c24d^pu h25.3d h25.3d⁵ c24.2s c25.2s⁶ h24d Feb 26] **h59** modest hurdler/chaser at best, very little form in 2016/17: stays 25f: acts on good to firm and heavy going: has worn headgear: tried in tongue tie. *Patrick Holmes*

FORBIDDING (USA) 4 ch.g. Kitten's Joy (USA) – La Coruna (USA) (Thunder Gulch **b81** (USA)) [2016/17 b16d⁴ b16.7m⁴ Apr 17] 10,000 3-y-o: fourth foal: brother to 2 winners on Flat abroad: dam US 9f winner: modest form in bumpers. *George Charlton*

FORCED FAMILY FUN 7 b.g. Refuse To Bend (IRE) – Juniper Girl (IRE) (Revoque **h–** (IRE)) [2016/17 h16.6g^pu Dec 10] leggy gelding: useful hurdler at best, has lost his form (including on Flat): raced around 2m: acts on heavy going. *George Baker*

FORCE OF FORCES (FR) 4 gr.g. Gris de Gris (IRE) – Rose Bombon (FR) (Cadoudal **h106** (FR)) [2016/17 h16s^F h16.7s Jan 23] €37,000 3-y-o: third foal: half-brother to French 2¼m hurdle winner Capvern (by Crossharbour): dam, French maiden (second in 17f chase), half-sister to fairly useful French hurdler/chaser (stayed 2¾m) Symphonie d'Anjou: fair form over hurdles: just headed when fell heavily last in juvenile won by Aislabie at Wetherby on debut: well beaten next time. *Venetia Williams*

FORECAST 5 ch.g. Observatory (USA) – New Orchid (USA) (Quest For Fame) [2016/17 **h120** h15.9g^bd h19.7g* h16v⁴ h23.9m² h19g^F h20.3g⁶ Apr 19] half-brother to fair hurdler Sand Blast (2½m winner, by Oasis Dream): fair maiden on Flat, stays 1½m: fairly useful form over hurdles: won novice at Hereford in October: stays easy 3m: acts on good to firm going: wears hood: in tongue tie last 5 starts: often races in rear/travels strongly. *Martin Keighley*

FORESEE (GER) 4 b.g. Sea The Stars (IRE) – Four Roses (IRE) (Darshaan) [2016/17 **h–** h16.7s Feb 7] neat gelding: fairly useful on Flat, stays 15f: well beaten in juvenile on hurdling debut. *Tony Carroll*

FOREST BIHAN (FR) 6 ch.g. Forestier (FR) – Katell Bihan (FR) (Funny Baby (FR)) **c151** [2016/17 h136: h20.6g^ur c16.1g* c16.3s² c16.3s* c16.4d* c15.9g⁵ c15.8g² Apr 8] good- **h124** topped gelding: useful handicap hurdler: smart form over fences: won novices at Towcester in November and Newcastle (by 19 lengths from Chidswell) in January, and Lightning

Sky Bet Lightning Novices' Chase, Doncaster—
Forest Bihan (striped cap) comes late to catch the grey Cloudy Dream and A Hare Breath

Mr P. J. Martin's "Forest Bihan"

Novices' Chase at Doncaster (by 1¾ lengths from Cloudy Dream) later in January: second in Maghull Novices' Chase at Aintree (head behind San Benedeto, outbattled) in April: stays 19f: acts on soft going: tried in hood: often travels strongly. *Brian Ellison*

FOREST DES AIGLES (FR) 6 b.g. Balko (FR) – Rose des Aigles (FR) (Le Nain Jaune (FR)) [2016/17 c20d c18s⁴ c17.1v³ c17.1s* c15.5d³ Apr 21] seventh foal: half-brother to fair chaser Orki des Aigles (25f-3½m winner, by Le Balafre): dam French 1¼m/1½m winner: winning hurdler: fairly useful form over fences: won handicap at Kelso in March: should stay 2½m: acts on good to firm and heavy going: wears tongue tie: often travels strongly. *Lucinda Russell*   c116 h–

FOREVER FIELD (IRE) 7 b.g. Beneficial – Sarahs Reprive (IRE) (Yashgan) [2016/17 h100: h16g² h18.6g* h20.6g² h20g* h19.5g³ h21g⁵ Nov 7] useful handicap hurdler: won at Market Rasen in June and Worcester in August: third in Silver Trophy at Chepstow (1¼ lengths behind Ballyoptic) in October: stays 21f: best form on good going. *Nicky Henderson*   h132

FOREVER GOLD (IRE) 10 b.g. Gold Well – Clonbrook Lass (IRE) (Lord Americo) [2016/17 c122, h130: c30d² h24d c28g² c29d* h22d c24.5d² Apr 29] fairly useful handicap hurdler: useful handicap chaser: won at Fairyhouse in December: second at Punchestown (3½ lengths behind Sizing Codelco) in April: stays 3¾m: acts on heavy going: wears headgear: usually races prominently. *Edward Cawley, Ireland*   c135 h126

FOREVER MY FRIEND (IRE) 10 b.g. King's Theatre (IRE) – Kazan Lady (IRE) (Petardia) [2016/17 c114, h–: c21d² c23d³ c23gᵖᵘ c21g⁶ c24.2m⁵ c20.9s* c23.8m* c19.9g⁴ Nov 3] smallish gelding: maiden hurdler: fairly useful handicap chaser: won at Ffos Las and Ludlow in October: stays 3m: acts on soft and good to firm going: wears headgear: tried in tongue tie: front runner/races prominently: unreliable. *Peter Bowen*   c119 § h–

332

FORGE MEADOW (IRE) 5 b.m. Beneficial – Ballys Baby (IRE) (Bob Back (USA)) **h134**
[2016/17 b104p: b16d² h16s* h16d⁵ h18v² h16v* h16.8g h16.5d⁴ Apr 25] bumper winner:
useful form over hurdles: won mares maiden at Wexford in November and Grade 2 novice
at Naas (by 8 lengths from Joey Sasa) in February: stays 2¼m: acts on heavy going. *Mrs J.
Harrington, Ireland*

FORGETTHESMALLTALK (IRE) 5 b.g. Flemensfirth (USA) – Mylane du Charmil **h106**
(FR) (Saint Cyrien (FR)) [2016/17 b16s⁴ h23.8s² h21s⁴ Mar 30] €27,000 3-y-o, £35,000 **b76**
4-y-o: first foal: dam unraced half-sister to useful hurdler/smart chaser (stayed 21f)
Mahogany Blaze and fairly useful hurdler/useful chaser (2m-2½m winner) Calusa Crystal:
Irish maiden point winner: fourth in bumper at Warwick: fair form over hurdles: better
effort when second in maiden at Ludlow in February. *Alan King*

FORGE VALLEY 13 b.g. Bollin William – Scalby Clipper (Sir Mago) [2016/17 c99: **c67**
c19.3s⁵ c25.5g⁶ c24.2s⁶ Feb 4] lengthy gelding: multiple point winner: maiden chaser:
stays 3¼m: acts on heavy going: wears cheekpieces. *Miss G. Walton*

FORGIVIENNE 10 b.m. Alflora (IRE) – Always Forgiving (Commanche Run) [2016/17 **c88 x**
c102, h–: c20.9g³ c23.8dᵖᵘ Jun 16] winning hurdler: maiden chaser: stays 3m: acts on **h–**
heavy going: in headgear last 2 starts: tried in tongue tie: front runner/races prominently:
often let down by jumping over fences. *Evan Williams*

FORGIVING GLANCE 5 gr.m. Passing Glance – Giving (Generous (IRE)) [2016/17 **h–**
h118: h16d⁵ May 7] fairly useful hurdler: well held on handicap debut in May, and not seen
out again: raced around 2m: acts on heavy going: often races towards rear. *Alan King*

FOR GOOD MEASURE (IRE) 6 b.g. King's Theatre (IRE) – Afdala (IRE) (Hernando **h135**
(FR)) [2016/17 h125: h23.1g² h23.9g² h21.1s⁵ h24g² h24g h24.7g Apr 8] sturdy gelding:
useful handicap hurdler: runner-up 3 times in 2016/17, including at Cheltenham (3¾
lengths behind Call To Order) in December: stays 25f: acts on heavy going: usually races
towards rear. *Philip Hobbs*

FOR GOODNESS SAKE (IRE) 5 b.m. Yeats (IRE) – Muschana (Deploy) [2016/17 **h107**
h104: h16.7g* h15.9g² h17.2d³ h16.8g² h16.7g² Sep 24] compact mare: fair hurdler: won
maiden at Market Rasen in May: raced around 2m: acts on heavy going: tried in
cheekpieces: front runner/races prominently: sent to USA. *Warren Greatrex*

FORGOTTEN GOLD (IRE) 11 b.g. Dr Massini (IRE) – Ardnataggle (IRE) **c139**
(Aristocracy) [2016/17 c141, h–: c25g c22.7f* c26g c23.8m³ Apr 2] stocky gelding: **h–**
winning hurdler: useful handicap chaser: won 3-runner veterans event at Leicester (by 5
lengths from Caulfields Venture) in November: stays 27f: acts on any going: in cheekpieces
last 3 starts: front runner/races prominently. *Tom George*

FORGOT TO ASK (IRE) 5 b.g. Ask – Lady Transcend (IRE) (Aristocracy) [2016/17 **b100 p**
b16g* Apr 8] €2,000 3-y-o, £35,000 5-y-o: second foal: dam, winning pointer, sister to
smart hurdler/chaser (stayed 3¼m) Lord Transcend: runner-up both completed starts in
Irish maiden points: 5/2, won bumper at Chepstow (by 11 lengths from Battle of Ideas) in
April: useful prospect. *Tom George*

FOR INSTANCE (IRE) 7 b.g. Milan – Justamemory (IRE) (Zaffaran (USA)) [2016/17 **h120**
h114p, h104: h24d² h24.1m* Apr 13] point/bumper winner: fairly useful form over
hurdles: won novice at Wetherby in April: stays 3m. *Jonjo O'Neill*

FORMAL BID (IRE) 10 b.g. Oratorio (IRE) – Sharamaine (IRE) (King Charlemagne **c–**
(USA)) [2016/17 c114§, h98: c17m May 20] compact gelding: winning hurdler: fairly **h–**
useful chaser at best, has lost his form (including in points): stays 2¼m: acts on soft and
good to firm going: wears headgear/tongue tie. *Miss Lydia Svensson*

FORMAL REQUEST 4 ch.g. Malinas (GER) – Rhetorique (FR) (Smadoun (FR)) **b–**
[2016/17 b16s b16.5g Feb 21] no form in bumpers: wears tongue tie. *Susan Gardner*

FORMATIVE 4 ch.g. Champs Elysees – Chasing Stars (Observatory (USA)) [2016/17 **b–**
b16.7m Apr 9] tailed off in bumper. *Noel Wilson*

FORMIDABLEOPPONENT (IRE) 10 b.g. Arakan (USA) – Sliding (Formidable **c111**
(USA)) [2016/17 c104, h–: c16.4d⁶ c20.1m² c17.3g c15.6dʳʳ c20.1d⁶ c17.3d c20.1s⁵ **h–**
c20.1g* c20.1d* c20.1s* c20.1g* c21.5g* c23.8g² c23.8d² c19.9sᵘʳ c19.9g² c23.8g⁶
c20.1gᵖᵘ Apr 27] winning hurdler: fair handicap chaser: completed 5-timer in September/
October, winning at Perth, Hexham (3 times) and Ayr: stays 3m: acts on soft and good to
firm going: wears blinkers: has worn tongue tie: has looked temperamental (even refusing
to race) but hard to fault for much of 2016/17. *William Young Jnr*

FOR 'N' AGAINST (IRE) 8 br.g. Presenting – Cut 'N' Run (IRE) (Mister Mat (FR)) **c120 §**
[2016/17 c109, h118: c25.5g² c23.9d* c23g⁵ c23g² c24.1d* h26g c24.2g⁴ c24.2mᵘʳ c25g⁶ **h– §**
Nov 11] lengthy gelding: fairly useful hurdler: fairly useful handicap chaser: won at

Market Rasen (novice) in June and Bangor in August: stays 25f: acts on good to soft going: usually wears headgear/tongue tie: often leads, held up last 2 starts: has finished weakly. *David Pipe*

FORREST BLUE (IRE) 8 b.g. Blueprint (IRE) – Margellen's Castle (IRE) (Castle Keep) [2016/17 c22.6m c21.1g⁴ c19.2d⁵ c25.7g³ c25.7g⁶ c25.7d³ c20v⁴ Jan 10] won twice in points: poor maiden chaser: left David Phelan after first start: in cheekpieces last 5 outings: in tongue tie last 2. *Diana Grissell*   **c71**

FORSMILES (IRE) 5 b.g. Mister Fotis (USA) – Smilingvalentine (IRE) (Supreme Leader) [2016/17 b16.8m⁵ ab16g Nov 22] poor form in bumpers. *Seamus Mullins*   **b62**

FORT CARSON (IRE) 11 b.g. Stowaway – The Red One (IRE) (Camden Town) [2016/17 h115: h16d² h18.5gᵖᵘ h16d h15.8s h18.6d h16.8s* h17.7d⁴ Mar 18] fair handicap hurdler: won at Exeter (conditional) in March: stays 2½m: acts on heavy going: has worn hood/tongue tie: usually races close up. *Neil King*   **h108**

FORT GABRIEL (FR) 6 ch.g. Ange Gabriel (FR) – Forge Neuve (FR) (Tel Quel (FR)) [2016/17 c86p, h81: c24.2g³ c22.6m⁶ c25.8g Aug 20] maiden hurdler: modest form over fences: stays 3m: acts on good to firm going: has worn headgear, including final start. *Fiona Kehoe*   **c86** **h–**

FORT GEORGE (IRE) 14 b.g. King's Theatre (IRE) – Barrack Village (IRE) (Montelimar (USA)) [2016/17 c101, h–: c21.3g c24.2g* c25.5m⁵ Jun 24] good-topped gelding: winning hurdler: modest handicap chaser nowadays: won at Fakenham in May: stays 3m: acts on good to firm and heavy going: wears cheekpieces: tried in tongue tie: usually races close up. *Sally Randell*   **c97** **h–**

FORTH BRIDGE 4 b.g. Bernardini (USA) – Sally Forth (Dubai Destination (USA)) [2016/17 h16s² h15.6g* h15.6g* h17g⁵ Apr 6] lengthy, useful-looking gelding: fairly useful on Flat, stays 1¾m: useful form over hurdles: won juveniles at Musselburgh in December and February (listed event, by ¾ length from Warp Factor): should stay beyond 2m. *Charlie Longsdon*   **h133**

FORTHEFUNOFIT (IRE) 8 b.g. Flemensfirth (USA) – Sommer Sonnet (IRE) (Taipan (IRE)) [2016/17 h125: c20d c23.8d⁶ c23.6g h23.6s h19.9vᵖᵘ h23.5s* h23.1s* h24.7g⁵ Apr 8] sturdy gelding: useful handicap hurdler: won at Ascot in February and Market Rasen (easily) in March: failed to take to chasing: stays 3m: acts on heavy going: in cheekpieces last 5 starts: usually races prominently. *Jonjo O'Neill*   **c89** **h131**

FORTIFIED BAY (IRE) 5 b.g. Makfi – Divergence (USA) (Red Ransom (USA)) [2016/17 b16.2d* b15.8v³ h16.7s h18.5s³ h21v² Mar 22] €11,000 3-y-o: third foal: half-brother to French 1½m winner Absent Minded (by Medicean): dam French 11f winner: fairly useful form in bumpers: won at Perth in June: fairly useful form over hurdles: best effort when second in maiden at Warwick in March: left S. Curling after first start: often races towards rear/travels strongly. *Alan King*   **h118** **b103**

FORT SMITH (IRE) 8 b.g. Presenting – Land of Honour (Supreme Leader) [2016/17 c134§, h114§: h19.7g⁶ h16.5d⁶ c19.4g⁴ c20sᵖᵘ c24d⁶ Feb 9] maiden hurdler: useful handicap chaser at best, has deteriorated markedly: stays 23f: acts on soft going: has worn headgear, including last 5 starts: wears tongue tie: one to leave alone. *Sam Thomas*   **c98 §** **h96 §**

FORTUNA GLAS (IRE) 5 gr.g. Verglas (IRE) – Fortuna Limit (Linamix (FR)) [2016/17 h56: h15.9g h16.7d⁴ Jun 17] poor maiden hurdler: raced around 2m: in hood last 4 starts: in tongue tie last 2: often races freely. *Dan Skelton*   **h55**

FORTUNATE GEORGE (IRE) 7 b.g. Oscar (IRE) – Fine Fortune (IRE) (Bob Back (USA)) [2016/17 h118p: h21.1s h21.6d⁴ h21.4s² h23.4v² h23.5s³ h19.9s* h22.8g⁵ Apr 15] good-topped gelding: useful handicap hurdler: won at Uttoxeter (by 2¼ lengths from Solstice Star) in March: stays 3m: acts on heavy going: wears visor: usually races close up/ travels strongly. *Emma Lavelle*   **h130**

FORTUNELLO 5 b.m. King's Theatre (IRE) – Wyldello (Supreme Leader) [2016/17 b15.7s b16.7g Mar 25] £20,000 3-y-o: fourth foal: sister to fairly useful hurdler/useful chaser Cogry (19f-3¼m winner), stays 33f, and half-sister to bumper winner/fairly useful hurdler The Caller (2m winner, by Yeats): dam (h122), bumper/17f hurdle winner, sister to high-class hurdler (2m-25f winner) Marello: well held in bumpers. *Tim Vaughan*   **b–**

FORT WORTH (IRE) 8 b.g. Presenting – Victorine (IRE) (Un Desperado (FR)) [2016/17 h125: c24.2g² c23g² c23g⁵ c21.4g³ c22.6gᵘʳ c25.2g² c24.2m³ c23gᵘʳ c26g² c24g* c23g² c24.1gᵖᵘ Apr 15] well-made gelding: fairly useful hurdler: useful handicap chaser: won at Doncaster (by ½ length from Behind The Wire) in January: stays 25f: acts on good to firm and good to soft going: tried in cheekpieces. *Jonjo O'Neill*   **c130** **h–**

FORTY CROWN (IRE) 11 b.g. Court Cave (IRE) – Forty Quid (IRE) (Exhibitioner) **c–**
[2016/17 c–, h–§: h23.3s³ h20.6s⁴ h22.7s* h25.3g² h25.3s⁴ h22.7v* h22.8v³ h22.7d Apr **h115 §**
10] fairly useful handicap hurdler: won at Kelso in December (amateur) and February:
maiden: stays 25f: acts on heavy going: has worn headgear: temperamental.
George Bewley

FOR YES (IRE) 8 b.g. Kutub (IRE) – Oscartan (IRE) (Oscar (IRE)) [2016/17 h22.1mᵖᵘ **h–**
Jun 24] winning pointer: pulled up in maiden on hurdling debut. *Stuart Coltherd*

FORZA MILAN (IRE) 5 b.g. Milan – Nonnetia (FR) (Trempolino (USA)) [2016/17 **h124 p**
b16g⁶ h20s² h19.6d² h19.5v* Feb 25] €68,000 3-y-o: fifth foal: brother to Grand National **b87**
winner One For Arthur and fairly useful hurdler Ritual of Senses (2m-19f winner), and
closely related to a winning pointer by Oscar: dam French 15f hurdle winner: sixth in
maiden bumper at Worcester: fairly useful form over hurdles: won maiden at Chepstow in
February: will stay beyond 2½m: remains open to improvement. *Jonjo O'Neill*

FOUBURG (FR) 5 b.g. Sageburg (IRE) – Folie Lointaine (FR) (Poliglote) [2016/17 h112: **c96**
h17.4s³ h15.8m⁵ c17g⁴ h16.5g h18.9d⁴ c20.4gᶠ Apr 16] fair maiden hurdler: modest form **h111**
on completed start over fences: beaten after second start, Harry Whittington after
fourth: unproven beyond 2m: acts on soft going: tried in cheekpieces: races freely. *S. Culin,
France*

FOU ET SAGE (FR) 6 b.g. Sageburg (IRE) – Folie Lointaine (FR) (Poliglote) [2016/17 **c135**
h137: c19.9s² c19.9gᵘʳ c21.4g² c21.9d⁴ c18.4g* c20.9g² c15.2g² c16.4g Nov 26] sturdy, **h–**
lengthy gelding: smart hurdler at best: useful chaser: won minor event at Craon in
September: second in novice handicap at Wetherby (1¾ lengths behind Double W's) in
October: left P. Peltier after sixth start: stays 21f: acts on heavy going: has worn tongue tie.
Harry Whittington

FOUNDATION MAN (IRE) 10 b.g. Presenting – Function Dream (IRE) (Strong Gale) **c127**
[2016/17 c119, h–: c20g³ c24g⁴ c20g⁵ c20g⁴ c22.6g² c23.9s⁴ c22.7f* c19.1g* c20.2m² Dec **h–**
28] very big gelding: lightly-raced hurdler: fairly useful handicap chaser: won at Warwick
in September, and at Leicester and Doncaster in November: stays 23f: acts on firm and
good to soft going: has worn headgear: tried in tongue tie: front runner/races prominently:
has reportedly suffered breathing problems. *Jonjo O'Neill*

FOUNDRY SQUARE (IRE) 11 br.g. Oscar (IRE) – Moon Approach (IRE) (Shernazar) **c–**
[2016/17 c121, h103: h26.4m⁵ c20m Jul 4] useful-looking gelding: fairly useful hurdler/ **h–**
useful chaser at best, well below that in early-2016/17 (also unplaced in 2 points in
December): stays 3½m: acts on soft and good to firm going: usually wears headgear.
David Evans

FOUNTAINS BLOSSOM 8 b.m. Passing Glance – Fountain Crumble (Dr Massini **h112**
(IRE) [2016/17 h103: h20s* h20m* h20m² h19.9g³ h20m* h17.7gᵖᵘ Aug 25] smallish
mare: fair hurdler: won seller at Worcester in May and claimer there in August: stayed 3m:
acted on good to firm and heavy going: wore tongue tie: dead. *Anthony Honeyball*

FOUNTAINS CIDER 9 b.g. Pasternak – Fountain Crumble (Dr Massini (IRE)) [2016/17 **c–**
h–: h25.6sᵖᵘ c25.7gᵘʳ c25.5sᵖᵘ Nov 16] winning pointer: maiden hurdler: failed to complete **h–**
both starts in chases: in tongue tie last 4 starts. *Anthony Honeyball*

FOUNTAINS FLYPAST 13 b.g. Broadway Flyer (USA) – Miss Flower Girl (Petoski) **c–**
[2016/17 c106, h108: c24.1gᶠ Apr 29] useful-looking gelding: fair hurdler nowadays: **h–**
lightly-raced maiden chaser: stays 2½m: acts on heavy going: wears tongue tie. *Anthony
Honeyball*

FOUNTAINS WINDFALL 7 b.g. Passing Glance – Fountain Crumble (Dr Massini **h144 +**
(IRE)) [2016/17 h121p, b101: h17.7g* h21d h23.4v³ h21.4s* h20.5s* h24.7g* Apr 8] well-
made gelding: useful hurdler: won maiden at Fontwell in May, novices at Wincanton and
Plumpton in March, and Grade 3 handicap at Aintree (by 8 lengths from No Comment) in
April: stays 25f: acts on heavy going: often travels strongly. *Anthony Honeyball*

FOUR MILE BEACH 4 gr.g. Dalakhani (IRE) – Rappel (Royal Applause) [2016/17 **h89 §**
h16.7g³ h16.7g² h17.2d⁶ h16.2d h15.7g² h17.1d⁶ h16.8s⁶ h16.8d h16.6g⁶ h16.8m³ Apr 19]
fair maiden on Flat, stays 1¼m: modest maiden hurdler: raced around 2m: acts on good to
firm going: often wears headgear: temperamental. *Malcolm Jefferson*

FOUROVAKIND 12 b.g. Sir Harry Lewis (USA) – Four M's (Majestic Maharaj) [2016/17 **c117**
c131, h–: c23.5g⁴ c24.2v³ Jan 1] winning hurdler: useful handicap chaser: stays 31f: **h–**
best form on heavy going: wears blinkers: often races towards rear. *Harry Whittington*

FOURTEEN RED 5 ch.g. Notnowcato – Choice (Azamour (IRE)) [2016/17 b16s Jan 6] **b–**
200/1, well held in bumper. *Nick Kent*

FOURTH ACT (IRE) 8 b.g. King's Theatre (IRE) – Erintante (IRE) (Denel (FR)) [2016/17 c133, h111: c23.8m⁴ c27.3s⁴ c23.8dᵖᵘ h26s⁶ c24.2d⁵ c28.1g³ Apr 19] angular gelding: fair handicap hurdler: useful handicap chaser: fourth in Grade 3 events at Ascot in October and Cheltenham (5½ lengths behind Viconte du Noyer) in November: stays 3½m: acts on good to firm and heavy going: has worn cheekpieces, including last 2 starts: usually wears tongue tie: usually races towards rear. *Colin Tizzard*   **c135 h108**

FOX APPEAL (IRE) 10 b.g. Brian Boru – Lady Appeal (IRE) (Phardante (FR)) [2016/17 c148x, h–: c21.4g⁴ c23.6g c21d⁴ c22.4g⁵ c23.8d* c20.2s⁶ c20.8s⁶ c23.8m⁶ c21m* Apr 15] smallish gelding: winning hurdler: useful handicap chaser: won at Ludlow in December and Newton Abbot (by 2½ lengths from Orbasa) in April: stays 3m: acts on good to firm and heavy going: tried in hood: wears tongue tie. *Emma Lavelle*   **c144 h–**

FOXCUB (IRE) 9 b.g. Bahri (USA) – Foxglove (Hernando (FR)) [2016/17 h138: c20.5g³ h19.6vᵖᵘ Nov 9] sturdy gelding: useful hurdler at best, has lost his form: well beaten in novice on chasing debut: stays 21f: acts on heavy going: tried in cheekpieces. *Tom Symonds*   **c86 h–**

FOX NORTON (FR) 7 b.g. Lando (GER) – Natt Musik (FR) (Kendor (FR)) [2016/17 c147, h–: c15.9g* c15.9s* c16.4d² c15.9g² c19.9g* c16d* Apr 25]   **c170 h–**

Fox Norton's fourth full season on the racecourse was a revelation. Just when it seemed that it might be safe to pigeon-hole him as a smart and thoroughly genuine chaser who had reached the limit of his ability, his career soared to new heights. His novice chasing campaign had yielded a creditable return of three wins from eight starts and third place in both the Arkle at the Cheltenham Festival and the Maghull at Aintree, both of which were won by the season's outstanding novice Douvan, who had Fox Norton ten and three quarter lengths away in the Arkle and thirty-two lengths back in the Maghull. Flat-bred Fox Norton, who was picked up for €20,000 as a yearling by the first of his three trainers Nick Williams, has never raced on the Flat and made a similar impression as a juvenile hurdler to the one he went on to make in his novice chasing campaign. He won first time out (at Fontainebleau) and progressed to win the Grade 2 Summit Juvenile narrowly at Doncaster on his fourth start before going on to finish sixth in the Anniversary Hurdle at Aintree and third in the Champion Four Year Old Hurdle at Punchestown (in which he wore a hood for the first time) on his last two starts. He was very lightly raced the following season but did win quite a valuable handicap at Taunton before being transferred from Nick Williams to Neil Mulholland. Fox Norton was still trained by Neil Mulholland when he reappeared in the latest season under 11-1 (off a BHA mark of 146) in the Randox Health Handicap Chase at Cheltenham's Showcase meeting in October. He put up a much improved performance on his first start over fences outside novice company and won by eleven lengths from the useful Sizing Platinum, in control from a long way out and looking—for the first time—a potentially high-class two-mile chaser.

The owners of Sizing Platinum, Ann and Alan Potts, were among those particularly taken by Fox Norton's performance, so much so that when Fox Norton lined up for the Shloer Chase at the same course in November he was in the colours of Ann and Alan Potts and trained by Colin Tizzard. 'He's only six and was brilliant when he beat us and that was good enough reason to buy him,' said Alan Potts who, with his wife, transferred fifteen horses from Ireland to the Tizzards at the start of the latest season. The acquisition and addition of Fox Norton to the team—one of a number during the season—proved inspired. Fox Norton won the Grade 2 Shloer Chase, a race marred by the fatal fall of Simonsig, to give his new owners an instant return. Fox Norton took over from front-running Special Tiara on the bridle two out and went on to win by nine lengths and the same from the very smart Simply Ned and Special Tiara. Fox Norton and Simply Ned were the only two in the line-up with a recent run under their belts but, even so, there was no denying that Fox Norton was already shaping as if he was going to develop into a Queen Mother Champion Chase contender (the retirement of reigning champion Sprinter Sacre had been announced on the same day and he was paraded at Cheltenham). Unfortunately, Fox Norton missed an intended outing in the Tingle Creek Chase at Sandown with a leg injury which necessitated a month's box rest and it was three months before he ran again.

Fox Norton reappeared in the Game Spirit Chase at Newbury's Betfair meeting in February but had plenty on his plate conceding 5 lb to the outstanding novice Altior and also ran as if in need of the race, keeping on but going down by

JLT Melling Chase, Aintree—
Fox Norton (noseband) clears two out before stretching further ahead of Sub Lieutenant

thirteen lengths. Fox Norton ran as well as he ever had, up to that point, in the Queen Mother Champion Chase at the Cheltenham Festival, staying on well, after finding himself tapped for toe at a vital stage, and narrowly failing to peg back Special Tiara on the run-in, beaten just a head in a race that made headlines as much for the eclipse of 9/2-on Douvan, the shortest-priced Cheltenham Festival favourite this century, as it did for the performances of the first two. In the end, the latest Queen Mother Champion Chase may not have been a vintage edition to match some of the recent runnings, but Fox Norton certainly did his bit to advertise the form, following up with victories in the JLT Melling Chase and the Boylesports Champion Chase at the two other major spring festivals, where he teamed up for the first time with the Potts's new retained rider Robbie Power.

The Melling at Aintree was Fox Norton's first start over two and a half miles and he relished the step up in trip, drawing clear of a good field from the second last and winning by six lengths from the Ryanair Chase runner-up Sub Lieutenant. Colin Tizzard had initially thought of Fox Norton as 'more of a Ryanair horse' than a 'flat-out two-miler' and there was talk after Aintree that he might be stepped up even further in distance in the next season with a view to tackling the King George VI Chase, though that race is said to be on the programme of Sizing John in the same ownership, while the Tizzard stable houses the last two King George winners, the veteran Cue Card and Thistlecrack who won the latest edition while still a novice.

Boylesports Champion Chase (Drogheda), Punchestown—win number four of an excellent campaign as Fox Norton gets the better of Un de Sceaux (centre) and God's Own (checks)

There is no open Grade 1 over two and a half miles at the Punchestown Festival and Fox Norton reverted to two miles for the Champion Chase (registered as the Drogheda), which also attracted the Ryanair Chase winner Un de Sceaux and the winner twelve months earlier God's Own (who had finished fifth behind Fox Norton in the Melling after filling the same position in the Queen Mother Champion Chase, in which he had been let down by late jumping errors). Those three filled the first three places in a strongly-run Champion Chase as Fox Norton—'flat to the boards the whole way' according to Power—lowered the colours of odds-on Un de Sceaux who led until after the last. Fox Norton won by a length and three quarters, staying on well, while God's Own ran as well as he had when winning the previous year's edition, finishing just a further half a length behind Un de Sceaux. Fox Norton didn't quite match his Melling form when winning at Punchestown and seems more likely to have the Ryanair Chase, rather than the Queen Mother Champion Chase, as his Cheltenham Festival target in the next season.

Fox Norton (FR) (b.g. 2010)	Lando (GER) (b 1990)	Acatenango (ch 1982)	Surumu Aggravate
		Laurea (b 1983)	Sharpman Licata
	Natt Musik (FR) (gr 2002)	Kendor (gr 1986)	Kenmare Belle Mecene
		Blue Mandolin (ch 1986)	The Minstrel Godetia

The well-made Fox Norton impressed in his juvenile days as having the physique of a horse with more of a long-term future in the game than some of his contemporaries. He wasn't a purpose-bred jumper, though, being by the now-deceased German sire Lando whose numerous wins in a fine career on the track included the 1995 Japan Cup. Fox Norton's dam Natt Musik raced on the Flat in France and was placed ten times in twenty-two starts, failing to get her head in front but showing that she stayed a mile and a quarter (second five times at around that trip). Natt Musik was a sister to the useful miler Blue King and a half-sister to another winner on the Flat in France, Bluedonix, who went on to show fairly useful form over hurdles at up to twenty-one furlongs for David Nicholson in the late-'nineties. Their dam Blue Mandolin was out of the Irish One Thousand Guineas and Irish Oaks winner Godetia. Fox Norton was the third foal produced by Natt Musik, who has now had six winners from six foals to reach the racecourse, including two others who have been successful over jumps in Britain, the five-year-old Pinkie Brown (by Gentlewave), who has shown useful form at two miles over fences for Neil Mulholland, and the four-year-old Night of Sin (by Sinndar) who won twice over hurdles, showing fairly useful form, for Nick Williams in the latest season. Both of those have been tried in a hood, equipment worn by Fox Norton since his early days. The reliable Fox Norton often travels strongly in his races, giving the impression that he is more about speed than stamina, and, although he stays two and a half miles, he is far from certain to prove as effective over much further. He acts on soft going. *Colin Tizzard*

FOXROCK (IRE) 9 b.g. Flemensfirth (USA) – Midnight Light (IRE) (Roselier (FR)) **c142**
[2016/17 c158, h121+: c25d⁵ c24s⁵ c22.6s* c24.1d* c24.3s* c25v* c29dᵖᵘ Apr 17] lengthy, **h–**
workmanlike gelding: fairly useful hurdler: useful chaser: completed 4-timer in hunters at Down Royal, Thurles (beating On His Own by 2 lengths), Leopardstown and Gowran between December and March: stays 25f: acts on heavy going: has worn headgear, including last 5 starts: wears tongue tie: usually races close up. *T. M. Walsh, Ireland*

FOXTAIL HILL (IRE) 8 b.g. Dr Massini (IRE) – Flynn's Girl (IRE) (Mandalus) **c141**
[2016/17 c104, h94: c20.1s⁶ c16.5g* c17g³ c15.7s⁵ c20.5d* c20.8s* c20.4gᶠ c15.8g **h–**
c20.8g² Apr 19] workmanlike gelding: winning hurdler: useful handicap chaser: won at Worcester in October, and at Kempton and Cheltenham (Trophy Chase, by length from Saphir du Rheu) in January: second in Silver Trophy Chase (Limited Handicap) at Cheltenham (4 lengths behind Henryville) in April: stays 21f: acts on soft going: usually leads. *Nigel Twiston-Davies*

FOXY ACT 6 ch.m. Act One – Brown Fox (FR) (Polar Falcon (USA)) [2016/17 b–: b16.8s **h74**
h18.5g³ Apr 26] no form in bumpers: 33/1, third in maiden at Exeter (19½ lengths behind **b–**
Stealing Mix) on hurdling debut. *Chris Down*

FOYNES ISLAND (IRE) 11 b.g. Presenting – Lucy Lodge (IRE) (Moscow Society **c109**
(USA)) [2016/17 c106, h–: c20.8g² c27.5m⁶ c23g Jan 11] rangy gelding: dual point winner: **h–**
maiden hurdler: fair hunter chaser: stays 25f: acts on good to firm going: wears headgear: tried in tongue tie. *Miss L. J. Cabble*

FRACTION MAN (IRE) 7 ch.g. Carlo Bank (IRE) – Lifinsa Barina (IRE) (Un **h–**
Desperado (FR)) [2016/17 h17.7g³ Aug 18] completed hat-trick in points in March/April: well held in novice on hurdling debut. *Pat Murphy*

FRAMLEY GARTH (IRE) 5 b.g. Clodovil (IRE) – Two Marks (USA) (Woodman **h88**
(USA)) [2016/17 h15.7g⁵ h15.7vᵖᵘ Mar 22] fair on Flat, stays 10.5f: modest form over hurdles: better effort when fifth in novice at Catterick in January. *Patrick Holmes*

FRAMPTON (IRE) 8 b.g. Presenting – Drumavish Lass (IRE) (Oscar (IRE)) [2016/17 **c–**
c122, h–: c25.1dᵖᵘ c24.2gᵖᵘ Apr 23] sturdy gelding: winning hurdler: maiden chaser, no **h–**
form in 2016/17 after long absence: stays 3m: best form on good going: wears cheekpieces: often leads. *Charlie Longsdon*

FRANCISCAN 9 b.g. Medicean – Frangy (Sadler's Wells (USA)) [2016/17 h–: h16.7gᵘʳ **h–**
Jul 29] compact gelding: useful hurdler at best, no form since 2013/14: unproven beyond 17f: usually wears headgear: tried in tongue tie: often races in rear. *Donald McCain*

FRANCOPHILE (FR) 5 ch.g. Sea The Stars (IRE) – Empress of France (USA) (Storm **b–**
Cat (USA)) [2016/17 b–: b16.3g⁵ Sep 3] no form in bumpers. *David Loder*

FRANKIE BALLOU (IRE) 8 br.g. Norwich – One Up (IRE) (Bob Back (USA)) **c87**
[2016/17 h16d h16.4s⁶ h20sᵖᵘ c15.7s³ c15.9sᵖᵘ c15.7s⁵ Mar 8] quite good-topped gelding: **h–**
maiden hurdler: modest form over fences: best effort when third in novice handicap at Catterick in February: left P. J. Rothwell after third start: stays 2½m: acts on soft/heavy going: wears headgear: tried in tongue tie: usually races close up. *Joanne Foster*

FRANKIE RAPPER (IRE) 5 b.g. Milan – Parkdota (IRE) (Good Thyne (USA)) **b85**
[2016/17 b16g³ b16g⁴ Apr 8] €54,000 3-y-o: fifth foal: half-brother to fair hurdler/chaser Jakros (2¾m-3m winner, by Beneficial): dam (b93), bumper winner, half-sister to fairly useful hurdler/useful chaser (stayed 3m) Jagoes Mills: fair form in bumpers. *Dan Skelton*

FRANK N FAIR 9 br.m. Trade Fair – Frankfurt (GER) (Celtic Swing) [2016/17 h85: **c85 ?** h25.6d^{pu} c21.1g^2 h23.4s^4 h25g^4 c21.3d^4 c19.7s^{ur} c25.7g^3 Mar 27] modest handicap hurdler, **h73** below best in 2016/17: no solid form over fences: stays 3¼m: acts on heavy going: tried in cheekpieces: often races in rear. *Zoe Davison*

FRANK THE SLINK 11 b.g. Central Park (IRE) – Kadari (Commanche Run) [2016/17 **c86** c98, h–: c26.3s^3 c24.2g^{pu} c25.5d^{pu} c24.2g c26g^3 c24.2s^{pu} c26.2g^6 c24.2g^2 Apr 25] strong **h–** gelding: maiden hurdler: fair handicap chaser at best, has deteriorated: stays 3¼m: acts on heavy going: tried in cheekpieces. *Micky Hammond*

FRANZ KLAMMER 5 b.g. Midnight Legend – Ski (Petoski) [2016/17 b16v b15.7s **h–** h21s^{pu} Mar 30] poor form in bumpers: pulled up in maiden on hurdling debut. *Charlie* **b69** *Longsdon*

FRASER CANYON 5 b.g. Halling (USA) – Valley of Gold (FR) (Shirley Heights) **h99** [2016/17 h–: h16.8g^6 h18.7m h16g h16.8m h19.1s^2 h19.7s^5 h20.6d^6 h23.9g^4 h23.6s^3 Mar 13] modest maiden hurdler: stays 21f: acts on soft going: in tongue tie last 5 starts. *Tim Vaughan*

FREDDIES PORTRAIT (IRE) 8 gr.g. Portrait Gallery (IRE) – Phara (IRE) (Lord **c113** Americo) [2016/17 h100: c15.9s^2 c20.5v^2 c15.9s* c20.9s^5 c20d^5 Apr 5] winning pointer: **h–** maiden hurdler: fair form over fences: won novice handicap at Carlisle in February: stays 2½m: acts on heavy going: usually leads. *Donald McCain*

FREDERIC 6 b.g. Zamindar (USA) – Frangy (Sadler's Wells (USA)) [2016/17 h96: **h119** h18.6g* h21.3g^5 h16g Oct 28] fairly useful handicap hurdler: won at Market Rasen in September: should stay beyond 19f: acts on good to soft going: has joined Keith Dalgleish. *Micky Hammond*

FREDERIC CHOPIN 6 ch.g. Tamayuz – Eliza Gilbert (Noverre (USA)) [2016/17 **h–** h106c h22.1m h17.2d Jul 16] fair hurdle winner, no form in handicaps in 2016/17: should stay 2½m. *James Moffatt*

FRED LE MACON (FR) 8 b.g. Passing Sale (FR) – Princess Leyla (Teenoso (USA)) **h99 §** [2016/17 h101§: h17.2m^5 h17.2g^4 h16.2d* h20.1s^4 h17.1d^5 h21.4d* h21.4s^{ur} h19.4d h19.3d^4 h20.1g Apr 25] smallish gelding: modest handicap hurdler: won at Hexham (conditional) in September and Ayr in October: stays 2¾m: acts on heavy going: tried in cheekpieces: moody. *Martin Todhunter*

FREDO (IRE) 13 ch.g. Lomitas – Felina (GER) (Acatenango (GER)) [2016/17 c117§, h–: **c85 §** c26.3g^6 c27.5g^{pu} c25.8m^{pu} Jul 1] workmanlike gelding: winning hurdler: fairly useful **h–** handicap chaser at best, out of form since 2015/16 reappearance: stays 29f: acts on heavy going: wears headgear: not straightforward. *Ian Williams*

FREE BOUNTY 4 b.c. Dick Turpin (IRE) – Native Ring (FR) (Bering) [2016/17 h16s^5 **h–** Dec 8] neat colt: fair on Flat, stays 2m: well beaten in juvenile on hurdling debut: wore tongue tie. *Philip McBride*

FREE FRIDAY (IRE) 5 gr.g. Oscar (IRE) – Help Yourself (IRE) (Roselier (FR)) **h–** [2016/17 b16s h16.5s^{pu} Feb 5] no show in bumper/novice hurdle. *Evan Williams* **b–**

FREE OF CHARGE (IRE) 8 ch.g. Stowaway – Sweetasanu (IRE) (Sri Pekan (USA)) **c94 §** [2016/17 c108, h–: c25.5d^3 c25.8m^2 c25.8g^{ur} c25.8g Aug 20] winning hurdler: modest **h–** maiden chaser: stays 3¼m: acts on firm and soft going: in blinkers last 3 starts: in tongue tie last 2: often jumps none too fluently/looks none too keen. *Philip Hobbs*

FREE ONE (IRE) 5 b.g. Fast Company (IRE) – Tatamagouche (IRE) (Sadler's Wells **h–** (USA)) [2016/17 h15.8g Apr 28] fair at one time on Flat, stays 8.5f, has lost his way (refused to race last 2 starts in 2016): well held in maiden on hurdling debut: wore hood. *Jo Davis*

FREE RETURN (IRE) 6 b.g. Mr Combustible (IRE) – Marisha (IRE) (Gulland) **c–** [2016/17 h19.7s h15.5g h19.6d h16s^{pu} h16.6g^5 c15.9s^6 Feb 16] runner-up on second of 2 **h67** starts in Irish points: poor form over hurdles: well held in novice handicap on chasing debut: in cheekpieces last 3 starts. *Tom Weston*

FREE STONE HILL (IRE) 7 b.g. Beneficial – Claramanda (IRE) (Mandalus) [2016/17 **h111** b91: h20g^3 h16.8d^3 h15.7s^{pu} h21s h16.8g* Apr 11] fair form over hurdles: won handicap at Exeter in April: should be suited by at least 2½m: in tongue tie last 5 starts: often races towards rear, has found little. *Dan Skelton*

FREEWHEEL (IRE) 7 br.g. Galileo (IRE) – La Chunga (USA) (More Than Ready **h88** (USA)) [2016/17 h16.8v^{pu} h16d^4 Mar 31] fairly useful on Flat, stays 1½m: modest form on completed start over hurdles. *Chris Grant*

FREE WORLD (FR) 13 b.g. Lost World (IRE) – Fautine (FR) (Fast Topaze (USA)) [2016/17 c89, h–: c20gᵖᵘ c16s² c17.4v³ c16vᵖᵘ c20s³ c20g c16m⁶ Apr 25] well-made gelding: winning hurdler: modest chaser nowadays: stays 2½m: acts on heavy going: tried in hood: has worn tongue tie. *Lady Susan Brooke* **c93** **h–**

FRENCH OPERA 14 b.g. Bering – On Fair Stage (IRE) (Sadler's Wells (USA)) [2016/17 c143, h–: c18g c19.4g⁶ c25.5gᵖᵘ May 29] compact gelding: winning hurdler: very smart chaser at best, no form in handicaps in early-2016/17: best efforts at up to 2½m: often races lazily nowadays. *Nicky Henderson* **c–** **h–**

FRENCH SEVENTYFIVE 10 b.g. Pursuit of Love – Miss Tun (Komaite (USA)) [2016/17 c80, h78: h24s* c23.9d* c24g³ c23.8d c23.9gᵖᵘ h24g³ h20.3s c26.3g⁴ h24.1m Apr 13] poor handicap hurdler/chaser: won at Southwell and Market Rasen in May: stays 3m: acts on soft going: has worn headgear. *Gillian Boanas* **c84** **h82**

FRENCH TICKET 6 b.g. Bollin Eric – Merry Tina (Tina's Pet) [2016/17 b16.2g² Apr 25] sixth foal: half-brother to a winning pointer by Minster Son: dam (c72), winning pointer, half-sister to useful staying chaser Merry Master: 16/1, second in bumper at Hexham (5 lengths behind Schiaparannie) in April. *James Walton* **b91**

FRESH BY NATURE (IRE) 10 b.m. Flemensfirth (USA) – Star Alert (IRE) (Darazari (IRE)) [2016/17 c–x, h110§: h23.1s⁶ h23.1s⁶ h27vᵖᵘ h24v⁵ h27gʳᵒ h23.3s* Apr 1] sturdy mare: modest handicap hurdler: won at Uttoxeter in April: winning chaser: stays 27f: acts on good to firm and heavy going: has worn headgear, including final start: often let down by jumping/attitude. *Harriet Bethell* **c– x** **h99 §**

FRIENDSHIP BAY 13 b.g. Midnight Legend – Friendly Fairy (Gunner B) [2016/17 h16.7d⁵ h16d⁴ Feb 17] workmanlike gelding: bumper winner: maiden hurdler, modest form in 2016/17: stays 21f. *James Evans* **h92**

FRIENDS OF AMA GI 8 b.g. Reel Buddy (USA) – Skovshoved (IRE) (Danetime (IRE)) [2016/17 h16.7s h15.8s h15.8vᵖᵘ h19.9vᵖᵘ Feb 11] no form over hurdles. *Barry Leavy* **h–**

FRIGHTENED RABBIT (USA) 5 b.g. Hard Spun (USA) – Champagne Ending (USA) (Precise End (USA)) [2016/17 h109: h20.1d h16.3g h16.8d h16.4s h15.6gᵖᵘ h16.4v* Mar 18] sparely-made gelding: modest handicap hurdler: in blinkers, won conditionals/amateur events at Newcastle in March: best effort at 2m: acts on heavy going: in tongue tie last 2 starts. *Susan Corbett* **h95**

FROBISHER BAY (IRE) 6 b.g. Touch of Land (FR) – Ballybeg Katie (IRE) (Roselier (FR)) [2016/17 b15.7g⁶ b16.3v² b17.1g b16.8s Nov 22] modest form in bumpers: dead. *Malcolm Jefferson* **b81**

FRODON (FR) 5 b.g. Nickname (FR) – Miss Country (FR) (Country Reel (USA)) [2016/17 c125p, h135: c16.3g* c21.1g* c20.2m* c20.4s c20.8s* c24gᶠ c19.9g* c20.5g* c19.9g⁵ Apr 6] **c148** **h–**

It is not unusual to see novice chasers with a sound jumping technique pitched into open handicap company before they are fully exposed. Even so, the BHA's handicappers are not renowned for taking chances with good novices from the top stables, though they can be caught out by a bright four-year-old chasing prospect in the autumn on account of the very generous official weight-for-age concession in that first part of the season. Paul Nicholls won Cheltenham's traditional big December handicap, run as the Caspian Caviar Gold Cup in the latest season, for the second time in five years with a four-year-old with previous jumping experience purchased out of Guillaume Macaire's stable. When the Nicholls-trained Unioniste won the equivalent event in 2012 on his third start in Britain he became the first four-year-old to win the race since it started life as the Massey-Ferguson Gold Cup in 1963. Unioniste had had plenty of experience over hurdles but had run only three times over fences (including a victory in France) and was among the bottom weights, scraping into the field as a reserve before going on to win by eleven lengths (ridden by the now-retired Harry Derham who claimed a handy 5 lb). Like Unioniste, Frodon was the only four-year-old in the line-up for the latest December Gold Cup but he too had had a lot of jumping experience for one of his age, including finishing a promising fourth in the graded Prix Congress for three-year-olds at Auteuil on his only start over fences for the Macaire stable, for whom he also won over hurdles as a three-year-old.

Frodon joined the Nicholls stable at the turn of the year in 2015/16 and won a juvenile hurdle, the Victor Ludorum at Haydock, and finished a respectable eighth in the Triumph Hurdle, as well as running creditably in defeat against his elders in a couple of handicap hurdles either side of his two runs in juvenile company. According to his trainer, Frodon had not properly acclimatised at that time and more was expected from him after a summer break. After showing promise over fences in France, Frodon was always going to make a chaser and he took exceptionally well to the larger obstacles, winning novice events at Newton Abbot and Fontwell in September (receiving weight from his older rivals in both races and starting at odds on). His first planned tilt at major handicap company was in the other big pre-Christmas handicap at Cheltenham, the BetVictor Gold Cup (in recent times run as the Paddy Power and originated in 1960 as the Mackeson). Unsure whether Frodon would get into the race, connections ran him again seven days beforehand in the Wincanton Rising Stars Novices' Chase, a Grade 2 event, with the aim of picking up a 5-lb penalty. Frodon completed his hat-trick in fine style, jumping well and brushing aside a useful rival in Shantou Village, before that horse departed at the last to leave Frodon to finish alone, his other opponent Virgilio having been pulled up after a bad mistake five from home. Frodon's performance was smart and he looked every inch a novice to keep on the right side. He was sent off second favourite for a good renewal of the BetVictor, in which half the field ran off a BHA handicap mark of 150 or above, with Frodon running off 151 with his penalty. Unfortunately, he was let down by his jumping, a bad blunder when in contention four out—the last open ditch—putting paid to his chance as he went on to trail in last of the ten finishers.

Frodon coped much better in an equally competitive field for the Caspian Caviar Gold Cup when the action switched to the New Course the following month. Stable jockey Sam Twiston-Davies was back in the saddle on Frodon on his return from damaging his ribs and spleen in an early-season fall (Frodon had been ridden by the season's leading conditional Harry Cobden on his two previous starts). A number of the runners in the BetVictor reappeared in the Caspian Caviar, headed by runner-up Village Vic who had won the Caspian Caviar twelve months earlier and started 6/1 joint favourite with the gambled-on Thomas Brown, just ahead of the BetVictor fourth and fifth Aso and Bouvreuil who were both sent off at 13/2. Front-running Village Vic made a bold bid to repeat his 2015 success, ensuring a stern test as the rain poured down but 14/1-shot Frodon, who was always travelling well in a handy position with stablemate Bouvreuil, took over after the last where

Caspian Caviar Gold Cup Handicap Chase, Cheltenham—Paul Nicholls wins this valuable prize with a four-year-old novice again as Frodon (left) stays on to beat Aso (right); the leaders Kylemore Lough and Bouvreuil (hoops) fade into fifth and sixth respectively

the new leader Kylemore Lough made a mistake. Aso stayed on for second, a length and a half behind Frodon, with the rallying Village Vic just a head further back in third; Kylemore Lough came a creditable fifth, a place ahead of Bouvreuil. Frodon's connections took the option of returning him to novice company after the Caspian Caviar and he added two further wins to his record, making it five wins from six completed starts over fences for the season when landing the odds in a quite valuable novice event at Musselburgh in February before following up in the BetBright-sponsored Pendil Novices' Chase at Kempton later the same month, jumping well and asserting between the last two to beat Gold Present by two lengths. Frodon bypassed the Cheltenham Festival and made his only subsequent appearance at Aintree, in the Manifesto Novices' Chase in which his long season finally seemed to catch up with him as he finished a well-beaten fifth of six behind Flying Angel.

Frodon (FR) (b.g. 2012)	Nickname (FR) (b 1999)	Lost World (b 1991)	Last Tycoon / Last Tango	
		Newness (b 1988)	Simply Great / Neomenie	
	Miss Country (FR) (b 2007)	Country Reel (b 2000)	Danzig / Country Belle	
		Miss d'Hermite (b 1987)	Solicitor / Surprise d'Hermite	

The rather unfurnished Frodon is by the now-deceased Nickname, the best of his generation as a juvenile hurdler in France and subsequently a high-class, mud-loving two-mile chaser when trained in Ireland (he had an essay in *Chasers & Hurdlers 2006/07* in which it was erroneously reported that, having raced as an entire in France, he had been gelded after joining Martin Brassil; he was, in fact, returned to France as a stallion after his racing days). Frodon's dam Miss Country, a half-sister to the top-class chaser Medermit (a close second in the 2011 December Gold Cup), won over hurdles in France at two and a quarter miles and was also represented on the racecourse in the latest season by the three-year-old Sao (by Great Pretender) who won at two miles over hurdles at Compiegne shortly after the end of the British season and has now joined his half-brother at Ditcheat. Miss Country is also the dam of Tidjy (by Slickly), a winner over fifteen furlongs over hurdles in France. Frodon's grandam Miss d'Hermite gained her only success from thirty-four outings in the French Provinces in a three-year-old maiden over nine furlongs. Her other winners include Miss Pistol, the dam of smart French chaser Saint Pistol, winner of the Prix du President de la Republique and third in a Grand Steeple-Chase de Paris.

Frodon stays twenty-one furlongs but he failed to stay three miles in the Kauto Star Novices' Chase at Kempton (he was left in a modest second by the fall of clear leader Might Bite at the last where he himself also came down). He acts on good to firm and heavy going. *Paul Nicholls*

FROGGY (IRE) 9 b.g. Kris Kin (USA) – Kate's Lass (IRE) (Montelimar (USA)) [2016/17 c19.5d⁴ c20g h20m c20.5m c22.6mᵖᵘ c22.5vᵖᵘ c24m Apr 25] winning pointer: maiden hurdler: maiden chaser, standout effort on return: best effort at 2½m: acts on good to soft going: in cheekpieces last 3 starts: usually races towards rear. *Brian Francis Cawley, Ireland* — **c100 ?** **h—**

FRONT AT THE LAST (IRE) 7 b.g. Golan (IRE) – Kilgefin Tina (IRE) (City Honours (USA)) [2016/17 h20d² h19.3s³ h24.3vᵖᵘ h19.3d² h23.1g⁵ Apr 22] second foal: half-brother to bumper winner/fair hurdler Black Jack Rover (21f winner, by Vinnie Roe), stayed 25f: dam unraced half-sister to fairly useful hurdler/useful chaser (2¼m-23f winner) Kilgefin Star: off mark in Irish points at fourth attempt: fair form over hurdles: easily best effort on debut: front runner/races prominently. *Donald McCain* — **h105**

FRONTIER VIC 10 b.g. Old Vic – Right On Target (IRE) (Presenting) [2016/17 c—, h104: h23.9g* h23.9d⁵ Sep 21] fair handicap hurdler: won at Ffos Las in June: let down by jumping over fences: stays 3m: acts on heavy going. *Nigel Twiston-Davies* — **c—** **h107**

FRONT LINE (IRE) 9 b.g. King's Theatre (IRE) – Thunder Road (IRE) (Mtoto) [2016/17 c111, h117: c20.5sᵘʳ c16.5d⁵ Dec 4] robust gelding: fairly useful hurdler: maiden chaser, well held completed start in 2016/17: stays 2¼m: acts on heavy going: has worn headgear. *Paul Cowley* — **c—** **h—**

FROZEN OVER 9 b.g. Iceman – Pearly River (Elegant Air) [2016/17 h104: h16g⁴ h16m² **h91** h16.8d⁶ h16.8m⁵ h18.5m³ h16.8g h16g h15.8m³ h15.8m h19g h16.5m* Apr 20] compact gelding: modest handicap hurdler: won at Taunton in April: unproven beyond 17f: acts on firm going: has worn headgear, including in 2016/17: wears tongue tie. *Chris Down*

FUHGEDDABOUDIT 10 ch.g. Generous (IRE) – Serraval (FR) (Sanglamore (USA)) **c91 x** [2016/17 h72: h18.5g² c24.1sᶠ c23g c23g⁵ c22.7s² c23.6gᵘʳ c20.3g⁵ Apr 21] modest maiden **h96** hurdler/chaser: stays 23f: acts on soft going: in cheekpieces last 4 starts: often let down by jumping over fences. *Seamus Mullins*

FULGUS (FR) 5 gr.g. Visionary (FR) – Rapsody In Love (FR) (Septieme Ciel (USA)) **h–** [2016/17 b16g⁵ b15.8d h17.7vᵘʳ h16.7s⁶ h15.8s h16vᵖᵘ Mar 22] rather unfurnished gelding: **b69** well held in bumpers: no form over hurdles: tried in cheekpieces. *Richard Hobson*

FULL BLAST (FR) 6 b.g. Khalkevi (IRE) – La Troussardiere (FR) (Maresca Sorrento **h–** (FR)) [2016/17 h102: h19.1g⁶ Aug 18] workmanlike gelding: maiden hurdler: stayed 2¼m: acted on good to firm and heavy going: wore head/tongue tie: dead. *Chris Gordon*

FULL CRY (IRE) 7 b.g. Milan – Gaye Melody (IRE) (Un Desperado (FR)) [2016/17 **c134** c20.2m³ c22sᶠ c19.9g* c22g* c20s³ c24.4g² c18s⁴ c25gᵖᵘ Apr 8] fifth foal: dam unraced **h–** half-sister to high-class chaser (stayed 3¼m) Kingsmark: winning hurdler: useful chaser: won maiden at Kilbeggan and minor event at Tramore in August: second in novice at Cheltenham (1¾ lengths behind Heron Heights) in October: stays 3m: acts on soft and good to firm going: wears tongue tie: often races towards rear. *Henry de Bromhead, Ireland*

FULL (FR) 5 b.g. Mr Sidney (USA) – Funny Feerie (FR) (Sillery (USA)) [2016/17 h16.9s² **h127** h17.4s² h16v⁵ h17.7g³ Apr 21] half-brother to 3 winning jumpers, including French hurdler/chaser Flagstaff (17f-3¼m winner, by Numerous) and fair hurdler/chaser First Feerie (2m-21f winner, by Turgeon): dam French 2¼m hurdle winner: fair maiden on Flat, stays 11f: fairly useful form over hurdles: second in 4-y-o event at Auteuil in May: left Y. Fouin, folded both starts in Britain, trained first one by David Pipe: has bled. *Neil Mulholland*

FULL IRISH (IRE) 6 b.g. Flemensfirth (USA) – Miss Kettlewell (IRE) (Saddlers' Hall **h126** (IRE)) [2016/17 h101: h19.7s⁴ h19.5s² h20.5v* h19.8d Mar 11] well-made gelding: bumper winner: fairly useful form over hurdles: won novice at Leicester in February: likely to stay beyond 2½m: often travels strongly. *Emma Lavelle*

FULL JACK (FR) 10 b.g. Kahyasi – Full Contact (FR) (Cadoudal (FR)) [2016/17 c129, **c118** h–: c20.8g⁴ c26.2m⁵ c26.2d h23.8g³ h23.8g⁴ c32.8g⁴ h24.3d⁴ Apr 21] fair handicap hurdler: **h106** fairly useful chaser: stays 31f, effective at much shorter: acts on good to firm and heavy going: often wears headgear. *Pauline Robson*

FULL OF MISCHIEF (IRE) 9 ch.m. Classic Cliche (IRE) – Drama Chick (Riverwise **h–** (USA)) [2016/17 h19.5vᵖᵘ Mar 6] fourth in bumper on debut: lightly raced and no form since. *Richard Rowe*

FULL SHIFT (FR) 8 b.g. Ballingarry (IRE) – Dansia (GER) (Lavirco (GER)) [2016/17 **c127** c137, h123: c21s c25gᵖᵘ c22.4g⁶ c20.8s c20.5g² c20.1g³ Apr 27] well-made gelding: **h–** winning hurdler: fairly useful handicap chaser: second at Kempton in February: stays 21f: acts on soft going: in cheekpieces last 3 starts: sometimes in tongue tie nowadays: often races towards rear: temperament under suspicion. *Nicky Henderson*

FULL TROTTLE (IRE) 8 ch.g. Vertical Speed (FR) – Keerou Lady (IRE) (Be My **c118** Native (USA)) [2016/17 c94: c20g* Apr 3] prolific winning pointer: fairly useful form in chases: maintained unbeaten record in hunters at Ludlow in April: stays 2¾m: in hood first start: wears tongue tie. *Miss L. Thomas*

FUNNY IRISH (FR) 6 b.g. Irish Wells (FR) – Funny Miss (FR) (Bering) [2016/17 h–: **c–** c20.5gᵖᵘ May 2] good-topped gelding: maiden pointer, failed to complete all 3 starts in **h–** 2016/17 (has refused to race): no show in maiden hurdle/novice chase. *Fiona Kehoe*

FUNNY OYSTER (IRE) 4 gr.f. Dark Angel (IRE) – Carpet Lover (IRE) (Fayruz) **h96** [2016/17 h17.7d⁶ h17.7sᶠ h15.9v² h15.9s⁴ h17.7s* Mar 13] angular filly: modest maiden on Flat, stays 1¼m: modest form over hurdles: won mares handicap at Plumpton in March: stays 2¼m: acts on heavy going. *Chris Gordon*

FURIOUSLY FAST (IRE) 5 b.g. Fast Company (IRE) – Agouti (Pennekamp (USA)) **h123** [2016/17 h16.8d⁵ h16.3g³ h16g² h16.2g* h16g² h15.8g* Nov 6] sturdy gelding: fair maiden on Flat, stays 13f: fairly useful form over hurdles: won handicap at Hereford in October and novice at Ffos Las in November: left Tom Lacey after first start: raced around 2m: best form on good going: front runner/races prominently, often travels strongly. *Dai Burchell*

GAI

FUSE WIRE 10 b.g. Tamayaz (CAN) – Zaffaranni (IRE) (Zaffaran (USA)) [2016/17 c–x, h85: h18.7m² h16.8s⁵ Jun 10] modest handicap hurdler: maiden chaser (often let down by jumping): stayed 3m: acted on soft and good to firm going: tried in headgear: dead. *Dai Burchell* — **c– x h88**

FUSIONFORCE (IRE) 10 b.g. Overbury (IRE) – Seviot (Seymour Hicks (FR)) [2016/17 h–: h19.9gᵖᵘ May 14] third in bumper in 2012/13: very lightly raced and no form in points/over hurdles: tried in tongue tie. *Gary Hanmer* — **h–**

FUTURE GILDED (FR) 8 b.g. Lost World (IRE) – Doree du Pin (FR) (April Night (FR)) [2016/17 c19.1gᶠ c19.2d* c19.4s² c24v² h23.1g⁵ Mar 27] winning hurdler: fairly useful handicap chaser: won at Catterick in January: second after at Wetherby and Warwick: stays 3m: acts on heavy going: races prominently. *Jamie Snowden* — **c127 h–**

FUZZY LOGIC (IRE) 8 b.g. Dylan Thomas (IRE) – Gates of Eden (USA) (Kingmambo (USA)) [2016/17 c111, h104: c21m⁵ h18.5m h21.6g³ Sep 16] modest handicap hurdler nowadays: maiden chaser: stays 21f: acts on soft and good to firm going: wears headgear. *Bernard Llewellyn* — **c89 h93**

FYRMYIN (FR) 6 b.g. Nickname (FR) – Fly To Sky (FR) (Loup Solitaire (USA)) [2016/17 h18.4s* c20.4g* h19.9g* h18.9v³ c20.9g⁶ Mar 18] fairly useful hurdler: won claimer at Vichy in September and handicap at Lyon Parilly in October: third in handicap at Haydock in November: fairly useful form over fences: won handicap at Lyon Parilly in September: stays 2½m: acts on good to firm and heavy going: has worn tongue tie. *Emmanuel Clayeux, France* — **c118 h122**

G

GABRIAL THE GREAT (IRE) 8 b.g. Montjeu (IRE) – Bayourida (USA) (Slew O' Gold (USA)) [2016/17 h112: c16.3d* c16.3m³ c15.7g³ h16.8g⁴ c20g* c19.4g⁵ c21m⁵ Apr 15] lengthy gelding: fairly useful handicap hurdler: useful chaser: won novice at Newton Abbot (by 5 lengths from Pass The Time) in June and handicap at Uttoxeter (by 3 lengths from Fayette County) in September: stays 2½m: acts on soft and good to firm going: has worn hood: tried in tongue tie. *David Pipe* — **c136 h118**

GABRIEL BRANDY (IRE) 9 ch.g. Urban Ocean (FR) – Right Style (IRE) (Right Win (IRE)) [2016/17 h76: h16.7g h18.2d h23g⁴ h20.2s⁵ h20mʳʳ h22.5d Oct 14] poor handicap hurdler: stayed 23f: best form on good going: wore tongue tie: dead. *Robert Hennessy, Ireland* — **h78**

GABRIEL OATS 8 ch.g. Grape Tree Road – Winnow (Oats) [2016/17 h–, b78: h21.2dᵖᵘ h18.7m h19.6g² h22g* h23.1g Sep 28] modest handicap hurdler: won novice event at Stratford in July: left Graeme McPherson after third start: stays 2¾m: acts on good to firm going: often travels strongly: remains with potential. *Tom Lacey* — **h88 p**

GAELIC FLOW 6 ch.g. With The Flow (USA) – Gaelic Lime (Lomitas) [2016/17 b16.8m b16.8g b16g h19.7sᶠ h15.3d h21.4s⁵ Jan 7] well held in bumpers: poor form in novice hurdles. *Chris Down* — **h66 b–**

GAELIC MAGNUM (IRE) 5 b.g. Lawman (FR) – Lapland (FR) (Linamix (FR)) [2016/17 b16.7s b16.3d Mar 13] tall gelding: well held both starts in bumpers. *Michael Scudamore* — **b–**

GAELIC MASTER (IRE) 4 b.g. Mastercraftsman (IRE) – Colomone Cross (IRE) (Xaar) [2016/17 h16sᵖᵘ Dec 8] lengthy gelding: showed little in maidens on Flat: pulled up in juvenile on hurdling debut. *Michael Scudamore* — **h–**

GAELIC MYTH 7 b.g. Midnight Legend – Shannon Native (IRE) (Be My Native (USA)) [2016/17 h–: h21.2m* h20.3gᵖᵘ Oct 3] fair handicap hurdler: won at Ludlow in May: likely to have stayed 3m: acted on soft and good to firm going: dead. *Kim Bailey* — **h114**

GAELIC SURPRISE 5 b.m. Arvico (FR) – Gaelic Lime (Lomitas) [2016/17 b15.8m⁵ b16m Nov 4] angular mare: fourth foal: half-sister to 1¼m-1½m winner Gaelic Ice (by Iceman): dam unraced: poor form in bumpers. *Stuart Kittow* — **b74**

GAITWAY 7 b.g. Medicean – Millicgait (Tobougg (IRE)) [2016/17 h16 8g⁶ h15 6g* h19.8d Mar 11] good sort: very lightly raced: smart winner of only start in bumpers: fairly useful form over hurdles: won maiden at Musselburgh (by 2½ lengths from Touch Kick) in February: reportedly bled final outing. *Nicky Henderson* — **h123**

345

GALA BALL (IRE) 7 b.g. Flemensfirth (USA) – Nuit des Chartreux (FR) (Villez (USA)) **c144**
[2016/17 h143: c17.4s² c16.2v³ c19.2s* c19.9s² c19.9g² Mar 25] rangy gelding: useful **h–**
hurdler: similar form in chases, and won novice at Exeter in February by 14 lengths from
Bivouac: in blinkers, good 1¼ lengths second to Warriors Tale in handicap at Newbury
final outing: stays 2½m: acts on heavy going: front runner/races prominently. *Philip Hobbs*

GALACTIC POWER (IRE) 7 ch.g. Gamut (IRE) – Celtic Peace (IRE) (Deploy) **c–**
[2016/17 h86: h15.8v³ c16s h16.5g³ h15.7d* h18.5d* h18.6m⁴ Apr 17] modest handicap **h90**
hurdler: won at Catterick in January and Exeter in March: well beaten in novice handicap
on chasing debut: stays 2½m: acts on good to firm and good to soft going: often races in
rear. *Robin Dickin*

GALARDO (IRE) 5 b.g. Presenting – Shuil Dearg (IRE) (Flemensfirth (USA)) [2016/17 **b–**
b16g b16s Dec 5] well held both starts in bumpers. *S. Wilson, Ireland*

GALE FORCE LUCEY (IRE) 10 b.m. Oscar (IRE) – Be My Soul Mate (IRE) (Be My **h70**
Native (USA)) [2016/17 h19.9s⁵ Jun 15] fifth foal: half-sister to bumper winner/smart
hurdler Alpha Ridge (2m-3m winner, by Glacial Storm): dam unraced: multiple point
winner: poor maiden hurdler: tried in blinkers. *Jan Mathias*

GALE FORCE OSCAR (IRE) 12 br.g. Oscar (IRE) – Distant Gale (IRE) (Strong Gale) **c84 §**
[2016/17 c83: c25.6v² c25.2sᵖᵘ h25.6sᵖᵘ c29.2vᵖᵘ Mar 22] smallish, angular gelding: **h– §**
prolific winning Irish pointer: pulled up in handicap on hurdling debut: poor handicap
chaser: stays 3¼m: acts on good to firm and heavy going: has worn headgear: wears tongue
tie: often races towards rear: temperamental. *Tom Symonds*

GALICE DU CIEL 6 br.g. Septieme Ciel (USA) – Galice du Soleil (FR) (Royal Charter **h–**
(FR)) [2016/17 h–, b–: h19dᵖᵘ h20.7gᵖᵘ May 17] good-topped gelding: no form in bumpers/
over hurdles: in cheekpieces final start. *Giles Smyly*

GALLANT OSCAR (IRE) 11 b.g. Oscar (IRE) – Park Wave (IRE) (Supreme Leader) **c–**
[2016/17 c154p, h106+: h20v⁴ c24.5d h24s Feb 5] lengthy gelding: fairly useful handicap **h129**
hurdler: smart chaser at best, well held only outing over fences in 2016/17: stays 25f: acts
on heavy going: tried in cheekpieces. *A. J. Martin, Ireland*

GALLEONS WAY 8 gr.g. Generous (IRE) – Yemaail (IRE) (Shaadi (USA)) [2016/17 **c81**
h87: c16mᵘʳ c17.1mᵖᵘ May 29] poor maiden hurdler/chaser: stays 2½m: in tongue tie last 2 **h–**
starts (bled final one). *Katie Scott*

GALLERY ARTIST (IRE) 7 gr.m. Portrait Gallery (IRE) – Distinctly Flo Jo (IRE) **c–**
(Distinctly North (USA)) [2016/17 h–: c25.3gᵖᵘ Apr 27] workmanlike mare: maiden **h–**
pointer: showed nothing in maiden hurdle and mares hunter chase, in cheekpieces in latter.
Miss Hannah Taylor

GALLERY EXHIBITION (IRE) 10 b.g. Portrait Gallery (IRE) – Good Hearted (IRE) **c131**
(Broken Hearted) [2016/17 c134, h–: c24gᵘʳ c24.2g³ c24.1v c23.8dᵖᵘ c23.8d c23.8s⁶ **h–**
c24m* Apr 18] rangy gelding: winning hurdler: useful handicap chaser: returned to form to
win at Kempton (by 9 lengths from Set List) on final start: stays 25f: acts on soft and good
to firm going: wears tongue tie: none too consistent. *Kim Bailey*

GALLIC DESTINY (IRE) 6 b.g. Champs Elysees – Cross Your Fingers (USA) **h–**
(Woodman (USA)) [2016/17 h118: h24.2g Nov 3] fairly useful form when winning 19f
novice in 2015/16, little impact over hurdles otherwise: tried in cheekpieces: wears tongue
tie: front runner/races prominently. *Jo Davis*

GALLO'S STAR (FR) 7 b.g. Gallo's Wells (IRE) – Krasota (FR) (Baryshnikov (AUS)) **c124**
[2016/17 c28.8g⁴ c24.9v³ c30.8dᶠ c22.9g* c29.8gᵈ c30.2m³ h18.9v⁴ Feb 25] angular **h106**
gelding: fair hurdler: fairly useful chaser: first past post in handicap at Waregem in August
and cross-country event at Merano (disqualified after taking wrong course) in September:
good effort when 9 lengths third of 7 to Cantlow in cross-country event at Cheltenham in
December (jockey mistook winning post 100 yds out, possibly costing second place): stays
3¾m: acts on soft and good to firm going: often in cheekpieces: has worn tongue tie.
Patrice Quinton, France

GALROS LADY (IRE) 7 b.m. Alhaarth (IRE) – Alleged Touch (USA) (Alleged (USA)) **c82**
[2016/17 c23.6g c20m* c21.1sᵖᵘ h25.5s⁶ c23g⁶ c27.5g⁴ Apr 23] half-sister to several **h71**
winners on Flat, including dam of useful hurdler (stayed 2½m) Ma du Fou: dam unraced:
multiple point winner: poor maiden hurdler: poor chaser: won handicap at Lingfield in
November: left A. Pennock after first start: stays 3¼m: acts on soft and good to firm going:
has worn cheekpieces, including last 3 starts: tried in tongue tie. *Tim Vaughan*

GALVESTON (IRE) 8 ch.g. Presenting – Rare Gesture (IRE) (Shalford (IRE)) [2016/17 **h99** h–p, b92: h19d^6 h19.6g h23.3s^2 h23g^F Aug 7] in frame both completed starts in Irish maiden points: modest maiden over hurdles: left Fergal O'Brien after third start: stays 23f: acts on soft going: tried in tongue tie. *Gordon Elliott, Ireland*

GALWAY JACK (IRE) 12 b.g. Witness Box (USA) – Cooldalus (IRE) (Mandalus) **c128** [2016/17 c135: c19.4g^F c24.2s* c22.7s* c23.8s^{pu} c20.3g^2 Apr 21] rangy gelding: fairly useful chaser: won hunters at Wetherby and Leicester in February, latter by 14 lengths from Toby Lerone: stays 3m: acts on heavy going: tried in tongue tie: front runner/races prominently. *Caroline Bailey*

GAMAIN (IRE) 8 b.g. Gamut (IRE) – Glass Curtain (IRE) (Old Vic) [2016/17 c109, h–: **c91** c24.5g^4 c19.9m^5 c21.2g^6 Oct 26] winning pointer/hurdler: handicap chaser, just modest **h–** form in 2016/17: stays 3m: best form on soft/heavy going: wears headgear: often races towards rear. *Ben Case*

GAMBLING GIRL (IRE) 8 ch.m. Hawk Wing (USA) – Gambling Spirit (Mister **c125** Baileys) [2016/17 h17.2s c17m* c16.6m* c16g^2 c16d c15.9g^{pu} Oct 21] lengthy mare: fairly **h–** useful hurdler at best: fairly useful chaser: won maiden at Killarney in May and novice at Roscommon in June: unproven beyond 17f: acts on good to firm and good to soft going: tried in hood: often travels strongly. *Mrs J. Harrington, Ireland*

GAMBOL (FR) 7 ch.g. New Approach (IRE) – Guardia (GER) (Monsun (GER)) [2016/17 **c97** c–, h103: c21.4g^F c21d^3 c19.9d^F h16.6d h16.3g* h18.5g* h20g^3 Apr 17] smallish gelding: **h102** fair hurdler: won conditionals selling handicap at Stratford in March and novice seller at Exeter in April: modest maiden chaser: should stay beyond 19f: acts on good to firm and good to soft going: often in headgear/tongue tie. *Ian Williams*

GAME ON (IRE) 5 b.g. Gamut (IRE) – Dar Dar Supreme (Overbury (IRE)) [2016/17 b–: **b92** b16v^4 Dec 31] much better effort in bumpers (8 months apart) when 7 lengths fourth of 17 to Marten at Warwick, making running. *Lucy Wadham*

GANBEI 11 ch.g. Lomitas – Native Ring (FR) (Bering) [2016/17 c–, h109: h26.4m^3 **c125** h26.4m* h26.5m^4 h23.1s^4 h23.8g c23.6d c26g c23.9m* c24.1g* Apr 22] sturdy gelding: **h119** multiple point winner: fairly useful handicap hurdler: won at Stratford in May: fairly useful handicap chaser: won at Market Rasen and Bangor in April: stays 3¼m: acts on soft and good to firm going: tried in cheekpieces/tongue tie: often races towards rear. *Michael Easterby*

GANGSTER (FR) 7 ch.g. Green Tune (USA) – Dahlia's Krissy (USA) (Kris S (USA)) **c137** [2016/17 h132: h24d^5 c16d^2 c19d^2 c19g^3 c20s^2 Mar 12] sturdy gelding: useful hurdler at **h129** best: also showed useful form when placed in maiden chases at Punchestown (1½ lengths second to American Tom) and Leopardstown (¾-length second to Bleu Et Rouge) in December, and Grade 3 novice chases at Leopardstown (7¾ lengths third to Yorkhill) in January and Naas (in cheekpieces, 15 lengths second to Ball d'Arc) on final outing: left W. P. Mullins after first start: stays 3m: acts on heavy going: usually races prominently. *Henry de Bromhead, Ireland*

GANNICUS 6 b.g. Phoenix Reach (IRE) – Rasmani (Medicean) [2016/17 h16g^3 h15.8v^6 **h104** h15.3d h16d^6 Jan 14] rather leggy gelding: brother to poor hurdler Razzle Dazzle 'Em (2m winner): fair on Flat, stays 1½m: fair form over hurdles: wears tongue tie. *Brendan Powell*

GANYMEDE 6 b.g. Oasis Dream – Gaze (Galileo (IRE)) [2016/17 h15.8g^6 h16.3m^6 **h89** h16.7g h16g^3 h15.8g* h15.8g h15.9g^5 Oct 17] fairly useful on Flat, stays 8.5f: modest handicap hurdler: won at Uttoxeter in September: raced around 2m: best form on good going: wears tongue tie. *Alex Hales*

GARDE FORESTIER (FR) 5 b.g. Forestier (FR) – Nette Rousse (FR) (Robin des Pres **h97** (FR)) [2016/17 h19.8d h15.3s^3 h15.3d h19.8d^5 Mar 26] first foal: dam unraced: modest form over hurdles: should be suited by further than 2m: wears tongue tie. *Charles Whittaker*

GARDEFORT (FR) 8 b.g. Agent Bleu (FR) – La Fresnaie (FR) (Exit To Nowhere **c145** (USA)) [2016/17 c139, h–: c15.7s^{ur} c16d^2 c16.4d^4 c15.7d* c16.3g^2 Mar 17] rangy gelding: **h–** winning hurdler: smart handicap chaser: won at Wincanton (by 1¼ lengths from Astre de La Cour) in February: 20/1, good 1¾ lengths second of 24 to Rock The World in Grand Annual at Cheltenham final outing, travelling strongly: stays 21f: acts on good to firm and heavy going: tried in cheekpieces. *Venetia Williams*

GARDE FOU (FR) 11 b.g. Kapgarde (FR) – Harpyes (FR) (Quart de Vin (FR)) [2016/17 **c–** c–, h95: h26.5d^3 Jun 21] tall, lengthy, angular gelding: modest handicap hurdler nowadays: **h99** maiden chaser: stays 3¼m: acts on heavy going: wears tongue tie. *Paul Henderson*

32Red Casino Handicap Chase, Sandown—
top-weight Garde La Victoire proves too strong for 2016 winner Bold Henry (hoops)

GARDE LA VICTOIRE (FR) 8 b.g. Kapgarde (FR) – Next Victory (FR) (Akarad (FR)) [2016/17 c147, h–: h15.8s* c17.5m² h19.3d³ c15.5s* c15.9g Mar 15] tall gelding: smart hurdler: won Welsh Champion Hurdle (Limited Handicap) at Ffos Las in October by 1¾ lengths from Welsh Shadow: very smart chaser: won handicap at Sandown in January by 2 lengths from Bold Henry: good short-head second to Sir Valentino in Haldon Gold Cup (Limited Handicap) at Exeter in November: ran poorly in Queen Mother Champion Chase at Cheltenham final start: stays 2½m: acts on good to firm and heavy going: front runner/races prominently. *Philip Hobbs* **c159 h151**

GARDE VILLE (FR) 7 ch.g. Kapgarde (FR) – Ville Eagle (FR) (Villez (USA)) [2016/17 h76: h23.3d c20.1g^pu h16d c17m^pu Jul 17] maiden hurdler, no form in 2016/17: showed nothing in 2 novice handicap chases: has worn headgear, including last 3 starts: tried in tongue tie. *Lisa Williamson* **c– h–**

GARDINERS HILL (IRE) 7 br.g. Stowaway – Mysterious Lass (IRE) (Satco (FR)) [2016/17 h–: c20.3d⁵ c23.8d³ c20g³ c20g⁵ c25.2s* c19.4s* c19.7s⁴ c20.9s³ Mar 11] maiden hurdler: fair handicap chaser: won at Hereford and Chepstow in January, and Hereford in February: stays 25f: acts on heavy going: usually races towards rear, often travels strongly. *David Rees* **c110 h–**

GARNOCK (IRE) 9 b.m. Craigsteel – Sister Stephanie (IRE) (Phardante (FR)) [2016/17 c98, h–: h24.7d⁴ h18.7m⁵ Jul 17] winning hurdler, fair at best: maiden chaser: stays 23f: acts on good to firm and good to soft going: sometimes wears cheekpieces. *David Bridgwater* **c– h91**

GARO DE JUILLEY (FR) 5 b.g. Ungaro (GER) – Lucy de Juilley (FR) (Goldneyev (USA)) [2016/17 h16.4g⁵ h16d⁶ h16.5g² h19g* h19m^pu Apr 20] useful on Flat, stays 1½m: fair form over hurdles: won novice at Taunton in April: stays 19f: best form on good going: tried in hood: in tongue tie last 3 starts: often races freely: temperament under suspicion. *Paul Nicholls* **h111**

GARRAHALISH (IRE) 9 b.g. Presenting – Savu Sea (IRE) (Slip Anchor) [2016/17 c119, h–: c24g⁵ c25.5g⁴ c25g c19.8m² Apr 13] good-bodied gelding: winning hurdler: handicap chaser, just fair form in 2016/17: stays 2½m: acts on good to firm and heavy going: tried in cheekpieces/tongue tie: front runner/races prominently. *Robin Dickin* **c111 h–**

GARRYDUFF CROSS (IRE) 7 b.g. Stowaway – Cooleycall (IRE) (Scribano) [2016/17 h–, b–: h18.5s^ur h21.6s^pu Jan 17] no sign of ability in bumpers/over hurdles: in hood/tongue tie last 2 starts. *Helen Nelmes* **h–**

GARY CHARM (FR) 9 gr.g. Ballingarry (IRE) – Charmelia (FR) (Crack Regiment (USA)) [2016/17 h25.4d h17.9s h17.9s c22.9g h18.9s c25g^ur c24.2m⁶ h23.1g⁶ h23.6d c25.1d⁴ c29.6s⁶ c24d^pu Feb 9] compact gelding: winning hurdler: fairly useful chaser in France: left Francois-Marie Cottin after fifth start, just fair form in handicaps in Britain: stays 25f: acts on soft going: has worn headgear, including last 4 starts: in tongue tie last 5 starts: usually races nearer last than first: signs of temperament. *David Pipe* **c113 h100**

GASK RIDGE (IRE) 7 b.g. High Chaparral (IRE) – Creative Approach (IRE) (Toulon) [2016/17 b16.7g³ h15.8v h15.8v h16.3s h20v³ h16g³ Apr 17] lengthy gelding: closely related to bumper winner Dynamic Approach and a winning pointer (both by Milan) and fair chaser Nautical Approach (21f winner, by Oscar), and half-brother to bumper winner **h91 b78**

Astute Approach (by Bob Back): dam unraced half-sister to smart hurdler/useful chaser (stayed 3m) Adamant Approach: fell both starts in Irish points: third only start in bumpers: modest form over hurdles: should stay further than 2m. *Christian Williams*

GAS LINE BOY (IRE) 11 b.g. Blueprint (IRE) – Jervia (Affirmed (USA)) [2016/17 c–, h–: c24s² c26.1g⁴ c24v³ c22.3s* c24.2s⁴ c28.4d⁴ c34.3d⁵ Apr 8] tall, useful-looking gelding: winning hurdler: smart handicap chaser: won veterans event at Kelso in December by 11 lengths from Cloudy Too: good fourth to Pete The Feat in Veterans' Handicap Chase Final at Sandown in January: 50/1, 16¾ lengths fifth of 40 to One For Arthur in Grand National at Aintree final outing: stays 4¼m: acts on heavy going: usually wears headgear: front runner/races prominently, often travels strongly. *Ian Williams* **c145 h–**

GASOLINE (IRE) 5 b.g. Mahler – Judelle de Thou (FR) (Trebrook (FR)) [2016/17 b–: b16.3m⁶ h16.7g h15.8g⁵ h16.6g⁵ h16.7s h16d h20.7g⁴ h25g Apr 28] poor form in bumpers/ over hurdles: best effort at 21f: wears tongue tie: usually races towards rear. *Ian Williams* **h78 b74**

GASSIN GOLF 8 b.g. Montjeu (IRE) – Miss Riviera Golf (Hernando (FR)) [2016/17 h–: h17.7s² h20.5d⁵ h16.3d⁶ h16d Mar 11] useful-looking gelding: handicap hurdler, fairly useful nowadays: best around 2m: acts on soft going: wears headgear: in tongue tie last 2 starts: usually races towards rear. *Kerry Lee* **h127**

GAUVAIN (GER) 15 b.g. Sternkoenig (IRE) – Gamina (GER) (Dominion) [2016/17 c–§, h–: c21.1d* May 12] good-topped gelding: multiple winning pointer: winning hurdler: fairly useful chaser nowadays: won lady riders' hunter at Fontwell in May: stays 3m: acts on soft and good to firm going: has worn headgear, including at Fontwell: wears tongue tie: unreliable. *Miss V. Collins* **c117 § h–**

GAYEBURY 7 b.g. Overbury (IRE) – Gaye Sophie (Environment Friend) [2016/17 b97: h20s* h21s² h19.7v² h23.6v* h24g h23.9g* Apr 26] sturdy gelding: bumper winner: useful form over hurdles: won maiden at Ffos Las in November, handicap at Chepstow in February and listed novice at Perth (by 3¾ lengths from Robbin'hannon) on final start: will stay beyond 3m: acts on heavy going: often races prominently. *Evan Williams* **h136**

GAYE FLIER (IRE) 6 b.m. Milan – Gaye Preskina (IRE) (Presenting) [2016/17 b16s h16v^F Feb 27] €14,000 3-y-o: second foal: dam unraced half-sister to useful hurdler/smart chaser (2¾m-3½m winner) Frantic Tan and fair hurdler/useful chaser (stayed 3¼m) Irish Raptor: tailed off in mares bumper: beaten when fell 2 out in novice at Ayr on hurdling debut. *Lucinda Russell* **h– b–**

G'DAY AUSSIE 4 b.g. Aussie Rules (USA) – Moi Aussi (USA) (Mt Livermore (USA)) [2016/17 h16.7d⁴ h16.2g² h16g³ h16.8g* h16g* h15.6g⁵ h16.3g³ h16d² h16d Apr 21] modest maiden on Flat, stays 1m: fair handicap hurdler: won at Sedgefield in October and Fakenham in December: raced around 2m: acts on good to soft going: in cheekpieces last 6 starts. *Brian Ellison* **h109**

GENERAL BROOK (IRE) 7 b.g. Westerner – Danse Grecque (IRE) (Sadler's Wells (USA)) [2016/17 h73: h16.8d³ Jun 21] poor maiden hurdler: tried in eyeshields. *John O'Shea* **h55**

GENERAL BUX 6 b.g. Lucarno (USA) – Cadoutene (FR) (Cadoudal (FR)) [2016/17 b86: h19.5s^pu Dec 27] big gelding: fair form only start in bumpers: off 14 months, no promise in maiden at Chepstow on hurdling debut. *Suzy Smith* **h–**

GENERAL GINGER 7 ch.g. Generous (IRE) – Nuzzle (Salse (USA)) [2016/17 h127: h20m May 13] fairly useful handicap hurdler, well below best only outing in 2016/17: stays 19f: acts on good to firm going: wears tongue tie: usually leads. *Harry Fry* **h–**

GENERAL GIRLING 10 b.g. General Gambul – Gold Charm (Imperial Fling (USA)) [2016/17 c–, h94: h19.5v h21.6v^pu h25v^pu c25.1v* c24.5s* c26.7d⁴ Mar 26] tall, angular gelding: modest handicap hurdler at best, no form in 2016/17: modest chaser: won novice handicap at Wincanton and handicap at Towcester in March: stays 3¼m: acts very well on heavy going: wears headgear. *Simon Hodgson* **c88 h–**

GENERAL MAHLER (IRE) 7 b.g. Mahler – High Dough (IRE) (High Roller (IRE)) [2016/17 h125, b64: h22.8m^pu h22.1m⁴ May 30] runner-up completed starts in Irish points: handicap hurdler: fairly useful nowadays, below best in 2015/16, not at best in 2 runs in 2016/17: should stay 3m: acts on heavy going: often races towards rear. *Brian Ellison* **h112**

GENERAL MALARKEY (IRE) 5 b.g. Scorpion (IRE) – Andreas Benefit (IRE) (Beneficial) [2016/17 b16s b16v⁵ b16g⁶ Apr 24] third foal: dam unraced half-sister to fairly useful hurdler (2m winner) Destiny's Gold: modest form on first of 3 starts in bumpers. *Nigel Twiston-Davies* **b81**

GENERAL PRINCIPLE (IRE) 8 b.g. Gold Well – How Provincial (IRE) (Be My Native (USA)) [2016/17 h129: c19d³ c18d² c20v² c16dᶠ c20v² c20v⁶ c20v* c24s* c29d⁵ Apr 17] well-made gelding: fairly useful hurdler: useful chaser: won maiden at Gowran and 6-runner Grade 3 novice at Limerick (by 6½ lengths from Twiss's Hill) in March: creditable 17¼ lengths fifth of 28 to Our Duke in Irish Grand National (Handicap) at Fairyhouse final outing: stays 29f: acts on heavy going. *Gordon Elliott, Ireland* **c140** **h–**

GENERAL ROSS (IRE) 10 b.g. Generous (IRE) – Rossmore Girl (IRE) (Scenic) [2016/17 c–, h–: h16.5g h15.8s⁶ Apr 1] maiden hurdler, no form in 2016/17: winning chaser: best effort at 2m: acts on good to firm and heavy going: usually in headgear: has worn tongue tie. *Adrian Wintle* **c–** **h–**

GENEROUS CHIEF (IRE) 9 br.g. Generous (IRE) – Yosna (FR) (Sicyos (USA)) [2016/17 c94§, h–§: c23.4d* c24.2g² c25.5m⁶ h22g* h24g* h22m⁴ h26.5g² h25.6g² c25.8g³ h25g² Apr 28] fair handicap hurdler: won at Stratford (novice event) in July and Southwell in August: fair handicap chaser: won selling event at Kelso in May: left Chris Grant after second start: stays 27f: acts on good and good to firm going: wears headgear: usually races prominently: lazy sort and is not one to rely on. *Graeme McPherson* **c101 §** **h107 §**

GENEROUS DAY (IRE) 5 b.g. Daylami (IRE) – Our Pride (Generous (IRE)) [2016/17 b16.7g h15.5g⁴ h16.7dᵘʳ h16.7dᶠ h15.7v⁶ h16.6s¹ Mar 3] £10,000 4-y-o: first foal: dam unraced half-sister to useful hurdler/very smart chaser (stayed 3m) Our Ben: well beaten in bumper: modest form in novice hurdles: bred to be suited by further than 2m: acts on good to soft going. *Henry Oliver* **h96** **b–**

GENEROUS HELPINGS (IRE) 8 ch.g. Generous (IRE) – Saffron Pride (IRE) (Be My Native (USA)) [2016/17 c88x, h89x: h19.2g³ h21.6g⁴ h25.6s⁶ h19.1d³ h25m* h20.5g⁵ h24gᵖᵘ Mar 28] fair handicap hurdler: won at Huntingdon in October: maiden chaser: stays 25f: acts on good to firm and good to soft going: wears headgear: front runner/races prominently: often let down by jumping. *Gary Moore* **c– x** **h101 x**

GENEROUS JACK (IRE) 8 ch.g. Generous (IRE) – Yosna (FR) (Sicyos (USA)) [2016/17 h104: h16m h19.9m³ h20.5g³ Oct 17] modest maiden hurdler: stays 21f: acts on good to firm and heavy going: tried in visor. *Jim Best* **h96**

GENEROUS JUNE (IRE) 9 ch.m. Generous (IRE) – Outo'theblue (IRE) (Grand Lodge (USA)) [2016/17 h–: h21mᵖᵘ May 16] little sign of ability in bumpers/over hurdles: tried in headgear. *Paddy Butler* **h–**

GENEROUS PET (IRE) 8 ch.g. Generous (IRE) – Sarahs Music (IRE) (Orchestra) [2016/17 c56, h113: h21.4s⁵ h19.7s Nov 23] unplaced in Irish maiden points: handicap hurdler, fair at best: well held only chase start: stays 21f: acts on heavy going: has worn hood: front runner/races prominently, often travels strongly. *Kenneth Slack* **c–** **h96**

GENEROUS RANSOM (IRE) 9 ch.g. Generous (IRE) – Penneyrose Bay (Karinga Bay) [2016/17 c123, h–: c19.9g³ c22.4gᵖᵘ Nov 26] tall, rather dipped-backed gelding: winning hurdler: fairly useful handicap chaser: stays 2¾m: acts on heavy going: wears cheekpieces: tried in tongue tie. *Philip Hobbs* **c118** **h–**

GENEVA TRUMPET 6 b.g. Virtual – Quotation (Medicean) [2016/17 b15.7d b15.7d b15.8d Mar 15] no form in bumpers. *Neville Bycroft* **b–**

GENTLE DUKE 10 b.g. Kayf Tara – Hopperdante (IRE) (Phardante (FR)) [2016/17 c95: c21.1d⁶ May 12] workmanlike gelding: winning pointer: maiden hunter chaser: stays 23f: acts on heavy going: sometimes in cheekpieces/tongue tie. *Miss L. Wallace* **c–**

GENTLEMAN FARMER 5 ch.g. Tobougg (IRE) – Sweet Shooter (Double Trigger (IRE)) [2016/17 b17.7s h21.6gᵖᵘ Nov 9] showed nothing in bumper/novice hurdle. *Richard Hawker* **h–** **b–**

GENTLEMAN JAMES 5 b.g. Sixties Icon – Cashback Rose (IRE) (Alflora (IRE)) [2016/17 h16.2dᵖᵘ h19.9g⁴ h20.9dᶠ h21.4vᵖᵘ h19.7dᵖᵘ Mar 21] no form over hurdles. *Dianne Sayer* **h–**

GENTLEMAN JON 9 b.g. Beat All (USA) – Sudden Spirit (FR) (Esprit du Nord (USA)) [2016/17 c122, h–: c21g* c21.4dᵖᵘ c20.2m³ c26.7m* c25.1m* c22.4g c23.8dᵖᵘ c26gᵖᵘ Apr 20] tall, well-made, attractive gelding: winning hurdler: useful handicap chaser: won at Newton Abbot in May, and at Wincanton in October and November (Badger Ales Trophy, by 25 lengths from Set List): stays 27f: acts on good to firm and heavy going: tried in blinkers: wears tongue tie: often races prominently: has bled. *Colin Tizzard* **c131** **h–**

GENTLEMAN MOORE (IRE) 7 b.g. Royal Anthem (USA) – Near Dunleer (IRE) **c106 §**
(Soviet Lad (USA)) [2016/17 h20.3g h20g* h19.9s⁴ c20g* c19.4gᵘʳ c19.2g c22.6gᵖᵘ **h102 §**
h18.7g⁴ h23g⁶ Sep 23] fifth foal: dam, (h90) 2m hurdle winner, also 1½m/13f winner on
Flat: fair form over hurdles: won seller at Ffos Las in June and conditionals selling
handicap at Stratford in September: also showed fair form when winning novice handicap
chase at Uttoxeter in July: stays 2½m: has worn headgear, including last 2 starts: tried in
tongue tie: often leads: one to treat with caution. *David Bridgwater*

GENTLEMAN'S DREAM (IRE) 5 b.g. Flemensfirth (USA) – Fair And Aisey (IRE) **h97**
(Mister Lord (USA)) [2016/17 h16.3dᵖᵘ h17.7sᵖᵘ h15.9v h15.9g⁴ Mar 27] €82,000 3-y-o:
rangy gelding: fourth foal: dam (h92), winning pointer, half-sister to smart hurdler (stays
3m) Meister Eckhart (by Flemensfirth) and useful hurdlers up to 25f Uncle Jimmy and
Sonnynelo: maiden hurdler: easily best effort (modest form) final start: bred to be suited
by much further than 2m. *Gary Moore*

GEORDIE DES CHAMPS (IRE) 6 br.g. Robin des Champs (FR) – Kilcoleman Lady **h137**
(IRE) (Presenting) [2016/17 b93: h16gᵈ h20d* h19.5d² h20.5d h21s⁶ h20g³ h20.5d
Apr 29] useful-looking gelding: bumper winner: useful hurdler: won novices at Aintree
in November and Chepstow in December: also first past post in novice at Chepstow on
reappearance, but tested positive for caffeine and subsequently disqualified: good length
third of 22 to Rather Be in Grade 3 handicap at Aintree in April: stays 21f: acts on good to
soft going. *Rebecca Curtis*

GEORGE FERNBECK 9 ch.g. Java Gold (USA) – Burmese Days (Montjeu (IRE)) **c– §**
[2016/17 c–§, h85§: h23.3d h23.3gᵖᵘ May 24] winning hurdler, no form in 2016/17: **h– §**
winning chaser: stays 27f: acts on good to soft going: has worn headgear, including last 4
starts: temperamental. *Micky Hammond*

GEORGE HERBERT 6 b.g. Yeats (IRE) – Colorado Dawn (Fantastic Light (USA)) **h88**
[2016/17 h18.5m³ Apr 18] maiden pointer: poor form in bumpers: in cheekpieces, third of
6 in maiden at Exeter (16 lengths behind Trevisani) on hurdling debut. *Fergal O'Brien*

GEORGE NYMPTON (IRE) 11 br.g. Alderbrook – Countess Camilla (Bob's Return **c– §**
(IRE)) [2016/17 c65§, h–§: c25.5dᵖᵘ h25g⁴ h21.6gᵖᵘ May 29] rangy gelding: maiden **h– §**
hurdler: winning chaser: usually in headgear: wears tongue tie: untrustworthy. *Zoe Davison*

GEORGIAN HERO 7 b.g. Arkadian Hero (USA) – Zulu Rose (Zulu (FR)) [2016/17 **h–**
h16.5s h15.3d h16.8dᵖᵘ h16.5g Apr 6] maiden pointer: no form in bumper/over hurdles:
tried in tongue tie. *Carroll Gray*

GEORGIE LAD (IRE) 9 b.g. Gold Well – Top Step (IRE) (Step Together (USA)) [2016/17 **c–**
c114, h117: c25.5dᵖᵘ Jun 26] strong gelding: winning Irish pointer: fairly useful hurdler: **h–**
maiden chaser, fair form at best: stays 23f: acts on good to firm going. *Barry Murtagh*

GEORGIESHORE (IRE) 9 b.g. Turtle Island (IRE) – Pride of St Gallen (IRE) **h78**
(Orchestra) [2016/17 h106: h19.5d⁶ h19.1vᵖᵘ h19.9v h16.8d⁵ h23vᵖᵘ Mar 2] well-made
gelding: maiden pointer: handicap hurdler, poor form in 2016/17: stays 2½m: best form on
heavy going: has worn headgear, including in 2016/17: front runner/races prominently.
Zoe Davison

GERALD 5 b.g. Bahri (USA) – Gerardina (Generous (IRE)) [2016/17 b16g⁶ Aug 21] well **b–**
held in bumper: dead. *Paul Webber*

GERMANY CALLING (IRE) 8 b.g. Germany (USA) – Markir (IRE) (Flemensfirth **c141**
(USA)) [2016/17 c138, h–: c20g³ c21.4g⁵ c20g c16.5g³ c20.3g* c16.9m c19.1d* c19.9g **h–**
c20.8gᶠ Mar 16] lengthy gelding: winning hurdler: useful handicap chaser: won at Bangor
in September and Doncaster (by 15 lengths from Drumlee Sunset) in November: stays
2½m: acts on soft and good to firm going: in cheekpieces last 4 starts: usually wears tongue
tie: front runner/races prominently. *Charlie Longsdon*

GERSJOEYCASEY (IRE) 8 b.m. Milan – Derrigra Sublime (IRE) (Flemensfirth **h–**
(USA)) [2016/17 h16.7g h17.7d h21mᶠ h20.5g⁵ h21.6sᵖᵘ Nov 13] €2,500 4-y-o, £1,800
6-y-o: second foal: closely related to modest hurdler Oscars Way (3¼m winner, by Oscar):
dam, well beaten in bumpers, half-sister to useful chaser (stayed 2½m) Gemini Lucy: dual
point winner: no form over hurdles. *Phil York*

GETABIRD (IRE) 5 b.g. Getaway (GER) – Fern Bird (IRE) (Revoque (IRE)) [2016/17 **b116**
b16d* b16d* Jan 26] €200,000 4-y-o: first foal: dam, ran once in point, half-sister to fairly
useful hurdler (stays 2½m) Charlie Stout and fairly useful hurdler/useful chaser (stays 3m)
Relentless Dreamer: won completed start in maiden points: smart form in bumpers: won
maiden at Fairyhouse in December (impressively by 12 lengths from Imperial Way) and
4-runner event at Gowran (making all and beating Hardline 1¼ lengths) in January.
W. P. Mullins, Ireland

GET

GETAWAY WHISKEY (IRE) 5 br.g. Getaway (GER) – Irish Whiskey (IRE) (Westerner) [2016/17 b16g⁴ b15.7g* Nov 30] £30,000 3-y-o: first foal: dam, unraced, out of sister to useful 2m hurdler Spirit Leader: fairly useful form in bumpers: 10/11, improved from debut when winning by 8 lengths from Helmsley Lad at Catterick: wears tongue tie. *Dan Skelton*   **b101**

GETBACK IN PARIS (IRE) 4 ch.g. Galileo (IRE) – Elusive Wave (IRE) (Elusive City (USA)) [2016/17 h16sᵘʳ h16.7s⁵ Feb 7] smallish, sturdy gelding: useful on Flat, stays 1¼m: poor form on completed start in juvenile hurdles. *Jamie Snowden*   **h79**

GET BACK TO ME (IRE) 10 br.g. Presenting – My Name's Not Bin (IRE) (Good Thyne (USA)) [2016/17 c22.5dᵖᵘ h20.7s³ c20.9d⁴ Mar 25] poor maiden hurdler/chaser: should stay at least 2½m: acts on soft going: tried in tongue tie. *Simon Earle*   **c74** **h79**

GET HOME NOW 9 b.g. Diktat – Swiftly (Cadeaux Genereux) [2016/17 h101: h20g⁶ h19.9g² h21.6d⁴ h20d h20g⁶ h21.2d⁴ Nov 28] fair handicap hurdler: stays 2¾m: acts on firm and soft going: usually wears headgear: wears tongue tie: usually leads. *Peter Bowen*   **h100**

GET IN PAT (IRE) 10 b.g. Flemensfirth (USA) – Clarin River (IRE) (Mandalus) [2016/17 h21.6s h19.9v³ c25.1s c24vᵖᵘ h20s⁴ h21.9v* h21.9v⁶ Mar 19] modest handicap hurdler: won at Ffos Las in March: showed nothing in 2 novice handicap chases: should stay beyond 2¾m: raced mainly on soft/heavy going: has worn headgear, including in 2016/17: often leads. *Tim Vaughan*   **c–** **h87**

GET INVOLVED (IRE) 8 b.g. Milan – Strong Red (Strong Gale) [2016/17 c116p, h113: h23.1m⁶ c23.9g³ c20sᵘʳ c23.4sᵘʳ c20.8sᵖᵘ c22.4s⁶ c24g³ c24m⁵ c23.6g² c25.3gᵘʳ c23.9d⁶ Apr 27] tall gelding: winning pointer: fair handicap hurdler: fair maiden chaser (sketchy jumper): stays 25f: acts on heavy going: wears headgear: has worn tongue tie, including last 5 starts: front runner/races prominently. *Robin Dickin*   **c113 x** **h101**

GET IT ON (IRE) 12 b.g. King's Theatre (IRE) – Keshia (Buckskin (FR)) [2016/17 c23g² May 27] winning pointer/hurdler: one-time useful handicap chaser: fair form when second in hunter at Worcester only outing in 2016/17: stays 23f: acts on good to firm and heavy going: has worn headgear. *Mrs A. Rucker*   **c109** **h–**

GETONSAM 5 ch.g. Black Sam Bellamy (IRE) – Pennepoint (Pennekamp (USA)) [2016/17 b16.2d⁶ b16.4v b16.2v Apr 26] sixth foal: dam unraced: no form in bumpers: 150/1, sixth in novice at Hexham (14½ lengths behind Applaus) on hurdling debut: tried in hood: in tongue tie last 2 starts. *Jonathan Haynes*   **h86** **b–**

GET ON THE YAGER 7 b.g. Tamure (IRE) – Florentino (Efisio) [2016/17 h20.6g* h22s² h21s⁴ h21s* h20.6s* h24.7g Apr 7] £3,800 3-y-o: good-topped gelding: first foal: dam (h97) 2m hurdle winner: won both starts in points: useful form over hurdles: won maiden at Market Rasen (by 13 lengths from Willoughby Court) in November, and novices at Kempton in February and Market Rasen in March: well held in Sefton Novices' at Aintree final start: stays 2¾m: acts on soft going: front runner/races prominently. *Dan Skelton*   **h131**

GETON XMOOR (IRE) 10 b.g. Heron Island (IRE) – Get On With It (IRE) (Old Vic) [2016/17 c–, h–: h21.6gᵖᵘ May 5] winning hurdler, lightly raced: fell second only chase start: stays 23f, effective at much shorter: acts on heavy going. *Richard Woollacott*   **c–** **h–**

GET READY FREDDY 7 b.g. Sixties Icon – Summer Shades (Green Desert (USA)) [2016/17 h93: h19.5dᵖᵘ h16.3g⁵ c19.2gᵖᵘ c16.1m* Apr 27] sparely-made gelding: maiden hurdler: poor form when winning handicap on chase debut at Taunton: unproven beyond 2m: acts on good to firm going: tried in cheekpieces. *Nick Mitchell*   **c80** **h60**

GET RHYTHM (IRE) 7 b.g. Kayf Tara – Ninna Nanna (FR) (Garde Royale) [2016/17 b89p: b16.2d⁵ h15.8d³ h16d³ h15.7sᶠ h19.4d h16.3v² h16g⁶ Apr 8] good-topped gelding: Irish point winner: fair form on first of 2 starts in bumpers: fair form over hurdles: should stay beyond 2m: acts on heavy going. *Tom George*   **h112** **b75**

GETTING BACK TO ME 6 b.g. Dr Massini (IRE) – Bahara (Barathea (IRE)) [2016/17 b16.7g Jul 31] pulled up both starts in points: tailed off in bumper. *Gary Hanmer*   **b–**

GET WISHING (IRE) 5 b.g. Getaway (GER) – Third Wish (IRE) (Second Empire (IRE)) [2016/17 b16.8s b16.2g Apr 28] well held both starts in bumpers. *Victor Dartnall*   **b–**

GEVREY CHAMBERTIN (FR) 9 gr.g. Dom Alco (FR) – Fee Magic (FR) (Phantom Breeze) [2016/17 c–§, h142§: h21.4sᵖᵘ h25s c24.1s⁶ c24s² c32.6sᵘʳ c33.4sᵖᵘ Mar 18] tall gelding: one-time smart hurdler: useful handicap chaser: second at Kempton (1¼ lengths behind Blameitalonmyroots) in February, only form in 2016/17: stays 25f: acts on heavy going: wears headgear: has worn tongue tie: temperamental. *David Pipe*   **c137 §** **h– §**

G FOR GINGER 7 ch.m. Lucarno (USA) – Kaream (Karinga Bay) [2016/17 b90:
b15.8d* b15.8m h21s h19.1d⁵ Dec 6] fair form in bumpers: won mares event at Uttoxeter
in May: poor form in mares novice hurdles: in hood last 2 starts: tried in tongue tie.
Anthony Honeyball **h57 b89**

GHAFAAN (IRE) 6 b.g. High Chaparral (IRE) – Nightdance Sun (GER) (Monsun
(GER)) [2016/17 b16s⁶ b16.4v³ Feb 25] £12,000 3-y-o: second foal: half-brother to useful
French 9.5f winner Day For Night (by Desert Style): dam unraced: fair form in bumpers:
better effort when third of 5 at Newcastle. *Chris Grant* **b85**

GHETTO BLASTER (IRE) 7 ch.g. Flemensfirth (USA) – Bachello (IRE) (Bach (IRE))
[2016/17 b16.8m⁴ b16.8g⁵ h20d⁶ h16.2s h19.9s Nov 22] modest form in bumpers: no form
over hurdles: left Seamus Mullins after third start: often leads. *Sam England* **h– b80**

GHOSTLY ARC (IRE) 5 b.g. Arcano (IRE) – Cheyenne's Spirit (IRE) (Sadler's Wells
(USA)) [2016/17 h16.7m⁴ Apr 9] fair on Flat, stays 1¾m: tailed off in novice on hurdling
debut. *Noel Wilson* **h–**

GHOST RIVER 7 ch.g. Flemensfirth (USA) – Cresswell Native (IRE) (Be My Native
(USA)) [2016/17 h116: h20g h24.4g⁶ h25v² h24.4gᵖᵘ h20v⁴ h19.5gᵖᵘ Apr 17] well-made
gelding: fair maiden hurdler: stays 25f: acts on heavy going: usually in headgear/tongue
tie: races prominently: often let down by jumping. *Peter Bowen* **h108 x**

GIANT REDWOOD (IRE) 5 b.g. Galileo (IRE) – Gwynn (IRE) (Darshaan) [2016/17
h16.8mᶠ Apr 19] fair on Flat, stays 2¼m: 33/1, fell 4 out (still to be asked for effort) in
novice won by Crackdelout at Sedgefield on hurdling debut. *Ben Haslam* **h–**

GIBBES BAY (FR) 5 gr.g. Al Namix (FR) – Nouvelle Donne (FR) (Sleeping Car (FR))
[2016/17 b92: b15.7v⁴ h21.7s⁶ h19.3m⁵ h21m³ Apr 18] tall gelding: fair form in bumpers
(won first of 2 starts) and in novice/maiden hurdles: front runner/races prominently.
Paul Nicholls **h106 b93**

GIBBSTOWN (IRE) 11 b.m. Bob Back (USA) – Kitty Maher (IRE) (Posen (USA))
[2016/17 c97§, h–: c24v² c24g c21sᵖᵘ c24.2v³ c24.8s⁶ c24.3v⁴ c24.5s² c24.2v² Mar 28]
maiden hurdler: modest handicap chaser: stays 25f: acts on heavy going: wears headgear:
has worn tongue tie, including in 2016/17: unpredictable. *Paul Stafford, Ireland* **c98 § h–**

GIBRALFARO (IRE) 5 b.g. Dalakhani (IRE) – Ronda (Bluebird (USA)) [2016/17 h138:
h16g³ h16.4g³ h20.5d² h19.6d⁶ h20.3gᶠ h21.4g Apr 22] compact gelding: useful handicap
hurdler: best efforts of 2016/17 when third at Chepstow (2½ lengths behind Diego du
Charmil) on reappearance and second at Newbury (length behind Onefitzall) in November:
stays 21f: acts on soft going: has worn headgear, including last 2 starts. *Alan King* **h141**

GIBSON PARK 4 b.g. Poet's Voice – Fifty (IRE) (Fasliyev (USA)) [2016/17 h16g
h17.7g* Apr 12] modest maiden on Flat, stays 12.5f: fairly useful form over hurdles: left
Andrew Oliver/off 6 months, much improved when winning maiden at Fontwell: should
continue to progress. *Dan Skelton* **h115 p**

GIFTED ISLAND (IRE) 7 b.g. Turtle Island (IRE) – Life Support (IRE) (High Estate)
[2016/17 h81: h15.3m h23m Aug 17] good-topped gelding: little sign of ability.
Tim Vaughan **h–**

GIFT FROM GOD 4 b.g. Teofilo (IRE) – Piffling (Pivotal) [2016/17 h15.8gᵖᵘ Apr 3]
modest maiden on Flat, stays 6f: in tongue tie, showed nothing in maiden on hurdling
debut. *Hugo Froud* **h–**

GILGAMBOA (IRE) 9 b.g. Westerner – Hi Native (IRE) (Be My Native (USA)) [2016/17
c163, h–: c16d² c17sᵇᵈ Dec 11] rangy gelding: winning hurdler: high-class chaser: not clear
run when short-head second of 6 to Arctic Skipper in Fortria Chase at Navan in November:
behind until brought down 3 out in Hilly Way Chase at Cork only other outing in 2016/17:
stays 4¼m, but effective at much shorter: acts on heavy going: tried in cheekpieces. *Enda
Bolger, Ireland* **c147 + h–**

GILLY GRACE 7 b.m. Morpeth – Miss Grace (Atticus (USA)) [2016/17 h16.8g h16.8d⁶
h18.5g h18.5g h15.3s h19g⁵ h19.5v⁵ Mar 23] third foal: sister to 17f hurdle winner North
London: dam (h72), lightly raced over hurdles, 1¼m winner on Flat, half-sister to useful
hurdler (stayed 3m) Simondiun: behind on completed start in points: poor maiden hurdler:
best effort at 19f. *Jimmy Frost* **h77**

GILT SHADOW (IRE) 9 b.g. Beneficial – Baile An Droichid (IRE) (King's Ride) [2016/17
h20.3vᵖᵘ h21.4g* Apr 22] rangy gelding: useful hurdler: pulled up on reappearance (first
start for 23 months), then won handicap at Ayr by 2½ lengths from Whatduhavtoget: ran in
2 maiden chases in 2014/15 (would have won but for falling last on chasing debut): will
stay 3m: acts on heavy and good to firm going: tried in hood. *Stuart Crawford, Ireland* **c– h141**

GIN AND TONIC 7 ch.g. Phoenix Reach (IRE) – Arctic Queen (Linamix (FR)) [2016/17 h106: h15.8g c20m⁶ h16g h16g⁶ h16g^pu h15.8g^pu Apr 28] handicap hurdler, only poor form in 2016/17: tailed off in novice handicap on chasing debut: raced mainly around 2m: acts on heavy going: tried in cheekpieces. *Michael Wigham* **c–h79**

GIN COBBLER 11 b.g. Beneficial – Cassia (Be My Native (USA)) [2016/17 c102§, h–: c16.4d⁴ c16.4g* c19.3g c15.6g c15.8g³ c15.5s^F c19.9g³ c17.2s* c16.3v^F c15.2d⁴ c19.2d⁵ Apr 27] maiden hurdler: modest handicap chaser: won at Sedgefield in May and Market Rasen in March: stays 2½m: acts on good to firm and heavy going: unreliable. *Victor Thompson* **c90 §h–**

GINGE DE SOPHIA (IRE) 4 b.f. Presenting – Me Grannys Endoors (IRE) (Tremblant) [2016/17 b16.3s² b16.3g Mar 25] £15,000 3-y-o: compact filly: half-sister to 3 winners, including useful hurdler Amber Brook (2¾m-25f winner, by Alderbrook) and fairly useful hurdler/chaser Medical Card (19f-3m winner, by Flemensfirth): dam raced out of half-sister to smart staying hurdler What A Question: poor form when runner-up on first of 2 starts in bumpers at Newbury. *Nigel Twiston-Davies* **b74**

GINGER FIZZ 10 ch.m. Haafhd – Valagalore (Generous (IRE)) [2016/17 h104: h16.7d⁶ h19.9g⁶ h16g³ h16g* h18.7g^pu h16.7d⁴ Apr 27] lengthy, angular mare: fair handicap hurdler: won mares event at Worcester in August: unproven beyond 17f: acts on good to firm and good to soft going: has worn headgear, including in 2016/17: wears tongue tie: front runner/races prominently. *Ben Case* **h101**

GINGILI 7 b.g. Beat All (USA) – Gentian (Generous (IRE)) [2016/17 h103: c20m^pu h23.9s^pu h19.9g⁴ h25m³ h23.1g* Oct 18] winning Irish pointer: fair handicap hurdler: won at Exeter on final start: pulled up in novice handicap on chasing debut: left Rose Dobbin after second start: stays 25f: acts on good to firm and good to soft going: often in headgear: in tongue tie last 3 starts: moody and not one to rely on. *Johnny Farrelly* **c–h110 §**

GINJO 7 b.m. Sakhee (USA) – Gulshan (Batshoof) [2016/17 h69: h16.8g³ h19.9m h18.5d⁴ h18.7m* h18.7m* Jul 17] poor handicap hurdler: won conditionals event and novice event at Stratford last 2 starts, both in July: stays 19f: acts on soft and good to firm going: wears cheekpieces: has worn tongue tie: often races towards rear: temperamental. *Bernard Llewellyn* **h78 §**

GINO TRAIL (IRE) 10 br.g. Perugino (USA) – Borough Trail (IRE) (Woodborough (USA)) [2016/17 c133, h–: c20s^pu c16g* c15.7s* c16.2v² c16s² c16.2v² c16s* c15.8g⁶ Apr 6] winning hurdler: smart chaser: won novice handicap at Ludlow in November, handicap at Haydock (by 6 lengths from Ut Majeur Aulmes) in December and novice at Ludlow (by 5 lengths from Beyeh) in March: also ran well when runner-up, in Kingmaker Novices' Chase at Warwick (4½ lengths behind Flying Angel) in February on last occasion: unproven beyond 2m: acts on heavy going: has worn hood: front runner. *Kerry Lee* **c146h–**

GIOIA DI VITA 7 b.g. Sakhee (USA) – Dhuyoof (IRE) (Sinndar (IRE)) [2016/17 h133: h21.6g⁴ h20g c20g⁵ Jul 24] handicap hurdler, useful at best: well beaten in novice on chasing debut: stays 2¾m: acts on good to firm and good to soft going: front runner/races prominently. *Dr Richard Newland* **c–h125**

GIOS LAST (GER) 7 gr.g. Paolini (GER) – Giovanella (IRE) (Common Grounds) [2016/17 h15.5g h16.5g Dec 20] fair on Flat, stays 1½m: little impact in novice/maiden over hurdles. *Sarah-Jayne Davies* **h–**

GIVEAGIRLACHANCE (IRE) 8 b.m. Iffraaj – Farewell To Love (IRE) (Darshaan) [2016/17 h103: h20m h17.7g⁵ May 29] winning hurdler: showed little in 2016/17: unproven beyond 2m: acts on soft going: often races towards rear. *Seamus Mullins* **h72**

GIVEAWAY GLANCE 4 br.f. Passing Glance – Giving (Generous (IRE)) [2016/17 h16g⁵ h16.6g* h15.7g* h18.5d^F h16s² Mar 30] sister to fairly useful 2m hurdle winner Forgiving Glance: fairly useful on Flat, stays 1m: also fairly useful over hurdles: won juvenile maiden at Doncaster in December and fillies juvenile at Catterick in January: good second in fillies' 4-y-o handicap at Warwick final start: raced mainly at 2m (closing when falling 3 out over 19f): acts on soft going: usually races towards rear, often travels strongly. *Alan King* **h117**

GIVE HIM TIME 6 b.g. Kalanisi (IRE) – Delayed (FR) (Fijar Tango (FR)) [2016/17 h–: h17.7g⁴ h15.9d^ur h16s⁴ h15.9d h19g^pu h16g^pu c17m³ Apr 16] placed in Irish maiden point: fair maiden hurdler: poor form when third in novice handicap at Plumpton on chasing debut: best effort at 2m: acts on soft going: in headgear last 2 starts: tried in tongue tie: front runner/races prominently. *Nick Gifford* **c72h103**

GIVEITACHANCE (IRE) 10 b.g. Clerkenwell (USA) – Native Lisa (IRE) (Be My h95 §
Native (USA)) [2016/17 h105: h25m³ h24d h21.4d³ h23.9g⁵ h26v² h25d⁴ h25dᵖᵘ h23.1s⁶
h26v⁴ h25gᵘʳ Apr 3] compact gelding: modest handicap hurdler: stays 3¼m: acts on heavy
going: wears tongue tie: unreliable. *Claire Dyson*

GIVE ME A COPPER (IRE) 7 ch.g. Presenting – Copper Supreme (IRE) (Supreme h136 p
Leader) [2016/17 b109p: h23.1v* h24.4d⁶ h20.5d* Apr 21] won maiden point on debut:
useful winner of only start in bumpers: useful form over hurdles: won maiden at Exeter in
December and novice at Ayr on final start: in tongue tie, well on top finish when beating
Burbank by 3½ lengths in latter: should stay at least 3m: open to further improvement over
hurdles, and exciting chasing prospect. *Paul Nicholls*

GLACIAL ROCK (IRE) 11 b.g. Sonus (IRE) – Glacial Princess (IRE) (Glacial Storm c–
(USA)) [2016/17 c97, h108: h23.9dᵖᵘ h20.2s h20.2g⁶ Aug 20] lightly-raced maiden h54
hurdler/chaser: stays 2¾m: best form on soft/heavy going: usually wears headgear.
Alistair Whillans

GLAMA 4 b.f. Shirocco (GER) – River of Silence (IRE) (Sadler's Wells (USA)) [2016/17 b–
b16.3s b16.7g Apr 22] second foal: dam, ran once on Flat, half-sister to useful hurdler
(stayed 21f) Loch Ard: no form in bumpers. *Nicky Henderson*

GLANCE BACK 6 b.g. Passing Glance – Roberta Back (IRE) (Bob Back (USA)) h87
[2016/17 b60: b16d h16.3d h16.5g⁶ h15.7d Feb 26] lengthy gelding: showed little in b–
bumpers: modest form at best over hurdles: in hood last 2 starts, in tongue tie last 3: front
runner. *Emma Baker*

GLANVILLES GUEST 5 ch.m. Sulamani (IRE) – Doubly Guest (Barathea Guest) b88
[2016/17 b16g* b16m⁵ b15.8d⁴ Feb 9] first foal: dam (h123), unreliable 2m hurdle winner
(stayed 19f), also 1m-17f winner on Flat: fair form in bumpers: won mares event at
Worcester in May. *Nick Mitchell*

GLARING 6 b.h. Champs Elysees – Brightest (Rainbow Quest (USA)) [2016/17 h15.8d* h121
h16g⁵ h16.4g h19.1g³ Mar 31] strong horse: useful on Flat, including winner: fairly useful form
when successful in novice at Huntingdon in December on hurdling debut: let down by
jumping next 2 starts, disappointing final one: should stay 19f. *Amanda Perrett*

GLEANN NA NDOCHAIS (IRE) 11 b.g. Zagreb (USA) – Nissereen (USA) (Septieme c113
Ciel (USA)) [2016/17 c119, h–: c20.1f³ c20.1d⁴ c20.1s⁴ c23.8g⁴ c20.1sᵖᵘ c21.5g³ c20g⁶ h–
Nov 7] winning hurdler: fair handicap chaser nowadays: stays 3¼m: acts on good to firm
and heavy going. *Alistair Whillans*

GLENARIFF 8 b.m. Kayf Tara – Lady Racquet (IRE) (Glacial Storm (USA)) [2016/17 h97
h99: h20m⁴ h21.6m³ h19.2mᵘʳ Oct 5] lengthy mare: modest maiden hurdler: should stay
beyond 2½m: acts on soft going: in cheekpieces last 5 starts. *Seamus Mullins*

GLENDERMOT (IRE) 8 b.g. Portrait Gallery (IRE) – Native Bandit (IRE) (Un c85 §
Desperado (FR)) [2016/17 c94, h94: c21.7dᵖᵘ c20vᵖᵘ h25.6sᵖᵘ c23.9s² c22.7s* c24s⁴ h–
c22.6gᵖᵘ Apr 15] maiden hurdler: modest handicap chaser: won at Leicester in March:
stays 3m: acts on soft going: has worn headgear, including in 2016/17: in tongue tie last 3
starts: front runner/races prominently: best treated with caution. *Paul Cowley*

GLENFORDE (IRE) 6 ch.g. Flemensfirth (USA) – Feel The Pride (IRE) (Persian Bold) h108
[2016/17 h21v⁴ h19.5v³ h23.6v⁵ Mar 23] €13,500 3-y-o, €42,000 5-y-o: fourth foal: half-
brother to fairly useful hurdler Old Pride (2m winner, by Old Vic), stays 21f: dam (c126/
h125), 2m/17f hurdle/chase winner, also 1½m winner on Flat: runner-up on second of 2
starts in Irish maiden points: fair form over hurdles: best effort when third in maiden at
Chepstow in February: should stay 3m. *Kim Bailey*

GLEN FORSA (IRE) 5 b.g. Mahler – Outback Ivy (IRE) (Bob Back (USA)) [2016/17 h100 p
b13.7d* h15.8s⁵ Jan 13] €33,000 3-y-o: third foal: dam (h85), maiden hurdler, half-sister to b91
fairly useful staying chasers Native King and Native Ivy: fair form when winning at
Huntingdon in November on only start in bumpers: 4/1, 21 lengths fifth of 11 to Burbank
in maiden there on hurdling debut, not unduly punished: open to improvement. *Mick
Channon*

GLENGRA (IRE) 8 gr.g. Beneficial – Zaraza (IRE) (Darshaan) [2016/17 h94: h21g² c108
h20.6d⁵ c19.1g² c21.2dᵖᵘ Feb 17] rather leggy gelding: placed in Irish points: modest h93
maiden hurdler: fair form over fences: better effort when second in novice handicap at
Doncaster in January: stays 21f: best form on good going. *Ian Williams*

GLENLYON 5 b.g. Thewayyouare (USA) – Helena (Helissio (FR)) [2016/17 b–: b15.7d b–
Nov 15] well held both starts in bumpers. *Paul Webber*

GLENMA (IRE) 6 br.g. Scorpion (IRE) – Scoop Thirty Nine (Petoski) [2016/17 h20.5d **h75**
h23.3v^{pu} h20.5s^F h20.5v⁵ h20.5s² Feb 14] poor maiden hurdler: stays 2½m: acts on soft
going. *R. Mike Smith*

GLENO (IRE) 5 ch.g. Ask – Lwitikila (Denel (FR)) [2016/17 b16d⁴ b16.2g⁵ Apr 28] **b93**
€8,000 3-y-o: seventh foal: half-brother to winning pointers by Mahler and Bach: dam
unraced: fair form in bumpers at Punchestown and Perth. *Stuart Crawford, Ireland*

GLENQUEST (IRE) 14 b.g. Turtle Island (IRE) – Solar Quest (IRE) (King's Ride) **c119**
[2016/17 c115, h–: c24.2d³ Apr 30] good-topped gelding: winning hurdler: fairly useful **h–**
handicap chaser: stays 29f: acts on heavy going: has worn headgear: tried in tongue tie.
Stuart Crawford, Ireland

GLENSTILE (IRE) 9 b.g. Alkaadhem – Entour (IRE) (Doubletour (USA)) [2016/17 **h–**
h16.8g^{pu} Aug 10] poor maiden hurdler: will be suited by 2½m+: acts on good to firm going:
in headgear last 2 starts. *Tim Vaughan*

GLENWOOD FOR EVER (IRE) 9 b.g. King's Theatre (IRE) – Decent Preacher **c105**
(Decent Fellow) [2016/17 c97, h–: c25g⁴ c20.5m³ c24m² c19.9g⁴ c22.7g⁵ c18.2g⁶ c18.2g **h–**
c19.4m^{pu} Aug 24] maiden hurdler: fair handicap chaser: won at Kilbeggan in May and
June: stays 25f: acts on soft and good to firm going: wears headgear/tongue tie. *Paul John
Gilligan, Ireland*

GLENWOOD PRINCE (IRE) 11 b.g. King's Theatre (IRE) – Moll Bawn (IRE) **c60 §**
(Presenting) [2016/17 c60§, h–: c26.3s⁴ c24.2g^{pu} c24.2d^{pu} c26g⁵ c24.2v^{pu} Dec 7] maiden **h–**
hurdler: poor handicap chaser: stays 3¼m: acts on heavy going: has worn cheekpieces/
tongue tie: usually races towards rear, often lazily: unreliable. *Kevin Hunter*

GLEVUM ACROBATIS 6 b.m. Kayf Tara – Top of The Dee (Rakaposhi King) [2016/17 **h–**
b–: h15.9s Feb 13] well held in bumper (tongue tied) and mares novice hurdle: dead.
Hugo Froud

GLIMPSE OF GOLD 6 b.g. Passing Glance – Tizzy Blue (IRE) (Oscar (IRE)) [2016/17 **h97**
h73, b72: h15.3m^{ro} h15.8g³ h16.8s h19.7s³ h15.8v^{pu} h16.6s³ h15.8s* h16.8g² Apr
26] modest handicap hurdler: won at Uttoxeter and Fakenham in April: best form around
2m: acts on soft going: wears tongue tie: often travels strongly. *Tim Vaughan*

GLINGERSIDE (IRE) 6 b.g. Milan – Kettle 'N Cran (IRE) (Zaffaran (USA)) [2016/17 **h115**
b16.2d h16v h16v* h20.5v² h24.3d Apr 21] €48,000 3-y-o: first foal: dam, unraced, out of **b–**
half-sister to useful chasers up to 25f Present Man and Caim Hill: tailed off in bumper:
fairly useful form over hurdles: won novice at Ayr in January: good second in novice there
in March: left Nicky Richards after first start: should stay beyond 2½m: acts on heavy
going: usually races towards rear. *R. Mike Smith*

GLITTERING LOVE (IRE) 5 b.g. Winged Love (IRE) – Glittering Image (IRE) **h–**
(Sadler's Wells (USA)) [2016/17 b16s h16.3d h16v h19.3g⁵ Apr 15] well beaten in bumper: **b–**
no form over hurdles: tried in tongue tie. *Nicky Richards*

GLOBAL DREAM 7 ch.g. Lucarno (USA) – Global Girl (Shambo) [2016/17 c106, h95: **c129**
c20v⁴ c20.3v³ h23.4s³ c22.7g⁴ c20.2s* c22.4d² c24.2m² c29.2g² Apr 24] modest handicap **h98**
hurdler: fairly useful handicap chaser: won at Leicester in January and March: stays 29f:
acts on good to firm and heavy going: tried in cheekpieces: usually responds generously to
pressure: consistent. *Caroline Bailey*

GLOBAL FERT (IRE) 7 b.g. Flemensfirth (USA) – Global Diamond (IRE) (Classic **h87**
Music (USA)) [2016/17 h16v⁴ h18.8g h16d Apr 16] seventh foal: dam, (c95/h109) 2m
hurdle winner, also 13f winner on Flat: second on completed start in Irish points: modest
form in maiden hurdles. *Noel C. Kelly, Ireland*

GLOBALISATION (IRE) 7 b.g. Tikkanen (USA) – On A Mission (IRE) (Dolphin **c116**
Street (FR)) [2016/17 c120§, h–: c27.5g⁴ h23g^{pu} h24.7g³ c23.8g* h24.2s⁵ c24m⁴ Apr 4] **h101**
fair maiden hurdler: fairly useful handicap chaser: won at Ffos Las (dead-heated) in
November: stays 3m: acts on heavy going: has worn headgear, including in 2016/17: wears
tongue tie. *Rebecca Curtis*

GLOBAL POWER (IRE) 11 b.g. Subtle Power (IRE) – Bartelko (IRE) (The Bart **c96**
(USA)) [2016/17 c24.1s⁶ c24.2v^{pu} c23.8v⁶ Mar 19] winning hurdler: one-time useful **h–**
handicap chaser: well below best in 2016/17 after long absence: stays 3¼m: acts on heavy
going: has worn cheekpieces, including in 2016/17. *Oliver Sherwood*

GLOBAL RULER 5 b.g. Kalanisi (IRE) – Queen's Leader (Supreme Leader) [2016/17 **h101**
b16v h21.3s h20.3s⁶ h15.7g² Mar 28] seventh foal: half-brother to fairly useful 2m hurdle **b–**
winner/winning pointer Queen Olivia (by King's Theatre) and fair 2m hurdle winner
Mobile Sizer (by Presenting): dam unraced: well beaten in bumper: fair form over hurdles:
easily best effort when second in novice at Southwell final start. *Dan Skelton*

GLOBAL STAGE 6 b.g. Multiplex – Tintera (IRE) (King's Theatre (IRE)) [2016/17 **h121** b15.7v² h16s⁴ h20.5g² h19vᶠ Feb 24] €27,000 3-y-o, £72,000 5-y-o: strong, good-topped **b107** gelding: chasing type: brother to 2 winners, including useful/unreliable hurdler/chaser Out Sam (19f-23f winner), and half-brother to 2 winners, including useful hurdler/fairly useful chaser Honest John (2½m-25f winner, by Alzao): dam unraced: Irish point winner: useful form when second at Haydock on only start in bumpers: fairly useful form over hurdles: best effort when 10 lengths fourth of 6 to Finian's Oscar in Tolworth Novices' at Sandown in January. *Fergal O'Brien*

GLOBAL THRILL 8 b.g. Big Shuffle (USA) – Goonda (Darshaan) [2016/17 h106: h16s **h94 §** h15.9g⁵ h16s⁴ h17.7d⁵ h16.5g⁶ h16.2s h16.6d³ h15.8v⁴ Mar 19] good-topped gelding: modest handicap hurdler: unproven beyond 17f: best form on soft/heavy going: wears headgear: has worn tongue tie, including in 2016/17: temperamental. *Bernard Llewellyn*

GLORIOUS DANCER 5 br.g. Royal Applause – Provence (Averti (IRE)) [2016/17 **h–** h19.3dᶠ h19.3dᵖᵘ Jan 25] modest on Flat, stays 1¼m: failed to complete both starts over hurdles. *Mike Sowersby*

GOAL (IRE) 9 b.g. Mujadil (USA) – Classic Lin (FR) (Linamix (FR)) [2016/17 c–, h102: **c–** h16.7g h15.9d⁵ h16g h16.7g h16m⁴ h15.8d³ h15.8d³ h15.8v⁴ h16.5g⁶ h15.8d* h16.5g* **h101** h16.7gᵖᵘ Mar 25] fair handicap hurdler: won at Ludlow (lady amateurs event) in December and Taunton in January: fell only outing over fences (in 2013/14): left Sally Randell after fourth start: stays 2¼m: acts on good to firm and good to soft going: wears headgear/tongue tie. *Tracey Watkins*

GO ANOTHER ONE (IRE) 5 b.g. Stowaway – Missusan (IRE) (King's Ride) [2016/17 **b112** b16.7g* b17d* b16d⁴ Apr 26] €15,000 3-y-o, £45,000 4-y-o: half-brother to 3 winners, including smart hurdler/chaser Sharp Rise (2m-2½m winner, by Croco Rouge) and fair hurdler Go Forty Go (2m winner, by Beneficial), stays 2¾m: dam unraced half-sister to useful hurdler/fairly useful chaser (winner up to 2½m) Treaty Flyer: runner-up in point: useful form in bumpers: won at Market Rasen in July and Killarney (by 6½ lengths from Electric Concorde) in August: 16¼ lengths fourth to Fayonagh in Champion INH Flat Race at Punchestown final start. *John McConnell, Ireland*

GO CONQUER (IRE) 8 b.g. Arcadio (GER) – Ballinamona Wish (IRE) (Kotashaan **c140** (FR)) [2016/17 c135p, h–: c21d² c23.8dᶠ c22g² c23.8s² c25g⁵ c21.1g Apr 7] strong **h–** gelding: winning hurdler: useful handicap chaser: good neck second to Present Man at Ascot on reappearance: better than result when 11¼ lengths fifth of 23 to Un Temps Pour Tout in Ultima Business Solutions Handicap at Cheltenham in March, jumping very well in front and still there 2 out but ultimately finding test too much: in tongue strap, run best excused in Topham Chase at Aintree final outing (badly hampered twelfth, also lost shoe): likely to prove best up to 3m: acts on soft going: often travels strongly. *Jonjo O'Neill*

GO DARSI GO (IRE) 8 b.g. Darsi (FR) – Nellie Heart (IRE) (Broken Hearted) [2016/17 **c133 p** h20d² c24.9g* May 9] second foal: dam unraced: third in point on debut: fairly useful **h127** handicap hurdler: good head second of 25 to Shamiran at Punchestown: 10/11, travelled well when winning 7-runner maiden at Roscommon on chasing debut by 14 lengths from Annamatopoeia: stays 25f: acts on heavy going: open to improvement over fences. *Conor O'Dwyer, Ireland*

GODSMEJUDGE (IRE) 11 b.g. Witness Box (USA) – Eliza Everett (IRE) (Meneval **c116 §** (USA)) [2016/17 c125, h–: c25g c22.7f³ c26g³ c27.6d³ h26s⁶ c29.6sᵖᵘ Feb 10] lengthy **h81** gelding: winning hurdler: fairly useful handicap chaser: stays 4m: acts on heavy going: has worn cheekpieces, including last 5 starts: wears tongue tie: temperamental. *David Dennis*

GOD'S OWN (IRE) 9 b.g. Oscar (IRE) – Dantes Term (IRE) (Phardante (FR)) [2016/17 **c165** c168, h–: c16d* c19.9g² c21d³ c15.5d³ c15.9g⁵ c19.9g⁵ c16d³ Apr 25] sturdy, good-topped **h–** gelding: winning hurdler: top-class chaser: second in Old Roan Handicap at Aintree (1¾ lengths behind Third Intention) in October, and third in 1965 Chase at Ascot (1¼ lengths behind Royal Regatta) in November, Tingle Creek Chase at Sandown (1¼ lengths behind Un de Sceaux) in December and Champion Chase at Punchestown (2¼ lengths behind Fox Norton) on final start: fifth in Queen Mother Champion Chase, let down by late jumping errors: effective at 2m to 21f: acts on good to soft going: tried in tongue tie. *Tom George*

GOGO BALOO 5 b.m. Schiaparelli (GER) – Tarabaloo (Kayf Tara) [2016/17 b15.7s **h87** h16.7s³ h16.8g⁴ Mar 29] second foal: half-sister to fair hurdler/chaser Milly Baloo (21f-25f **b–** winner, by Desideratum): dam (c115/h113) 19f-21f hurdle/chase winner: tailed off in maiden bumper: modest form over hurdles: better effort when fourth in mares novice at Sedgefield. *Tim Easterby*

GO GO LUCAS (IRE) 4 ch.g. Golan (IRE) – Bob Girl (IRE) (Bob Back (USA)) **b84**
[2016/17 b15.6g⁵ b16.4g³ Mar 24] fourth foal: half-brother to fair hurdler Bop Along
(2½m-3m winner, by Double Eclipse): dam unraced sister to useful hurdler/chaser (stayed
3m) Strongpoint: modest form in 2 bumpers at Musselburgh. *Simon West*

GOING CONCERN (IRE) 10 b.g. Overbury (IRE) – Scorpio Girl (Scorpio (FR)) **c125**
[2016/17 c133, h–: c19mᵇᵈ c15.8d⁶ c16vᶠ c16d³ c16.2s³ c19.3sᶠ Jan 29] lengthy gelding: **h–**
winning hurdler: handicap chaser, useful at best: unproven beyond 17f: acted on soft and
good to firm going: often raced prominently: dead. *Evan Williams*

GOINGFORAMOOCH 6 b.m. Primo Valentino (IRE) – Emmasflora (Alflora (IRE)) **h–**
[2016/17 b–: b15.3m h18.5mᵖᵘ Apr 15] showed nothing in bumpers/mares novice hurdle: **b–**
tried in hood. *Katie Stephens*

GOING FOR BROKE (IRE) 7 b.g. Gold Well – Kokopelli Star (Hernando (FR)) **h117**
[2016/17 h107: h15.8d* h16g* h16.7s⁴ h15.8s² h23.9g⁵ h21d Apr 26] fairly useful hurdler:
won conditionals maiden at Uttoxeter and novice at Worcester, both in May: stays 21f: acts
on soft going: wears cheekpieces. *Rebecca Curtis*

GOING GOLD (IRE) 5 b.g. Gold Well – Wednesday Girl (IRE) (Rudimentary (USA)) **b90**
[2016/17 b16g³ b15.7d Nov 19] £25,000 3-y-o, £80,000 4-y-o: rather unfurnished gelding:
first foal: dam third in point on only start: won Irish maiden point on debut in May: fair
form when third at Chepstow, much better effort in bumpers: has joined Richard Hobson.
Rebecca Curtis

GOING NOWHERE FAST (IRE) 12 b.g. Exit To Nowhere (USA) – Sister Gabrielle **c84**
(IRE) (Buckskin (FR)) [2016/17 c89, h65: c16.5s⁴ c15.7dᵖᵘ c16v⁶ c16s⁴ c16g⁴ Apr 9] **h–**
winning hurdler/chaser: stays 19f: acts on soft and good to firm going: has worn
cheekpieces, including last 3 starts: tried in tongue tie. *Bernard Llewellyn*

GOLAN DANCER (IRE) 9 b.g. Golan (IRE) – Seductive Dance (Groom Dancer **c98 §**
(USA)) [2016/17 c104, h–: c21.2gᵖᵘ h15.9g³ h19.6sᵖᵘ h15.5v² c19.7v³ c16v² h16.8d² **h99 §**
c19.2g³ Apr 11] good-topped gelding: modest maiden hurdler/chaser: left David
Bridgwater after seventh start: stays easy 19f: acts on heavy going: has worn headgear,
including in 2016/17: quirky sort, not one to trust. *Jimmy Frost*

GOLANOVA 9 b.g. Golan (IRE) – Larkbarrow (Kahyasi) [2016/17 c110§, h–: h25.6g⁴ **c109 §**
c25.7m² h25m⁶ c24m² c27.2sᵘʳ c25.7d⁶ c23.5vᵖᵘ c21.1g³ c23m² Apr 20] compact gelding: **h95 §**
modest handicap hurdler: fair handicap chaser: stays 3¼m: acts on good to firm and heavy
going: wears headgear: often races prominently: temperamental. *Gary Moore*

GOLAN SUN (IRE) 9 b.g. Golan (IRE) – Shandarr (IRE) (John French) [2016/17 **h91**
h23.3v² h23.9m² May 11] winning pointer: lightly-raced maiden over hurdles, modest
form: stays 3m. *Paul Stafford, Ireland*

GOLDANBLEU (IRE) 4 b.g. Gold Well – Lisa Bleu (IRE) (Pistolet Bleu (IRE)) **b56 p**
[2016/17 b15.8m³ Apr 25] €8,500 3-y-o: second foal: dam (h94) 2m hurdle winner: 7/1,
showed inexperience when 21 lengths third of 4 to Spider's Bite in bumper at Ludlow:
open to improvement. *Deborah Faulkner*

GOLDAN JESS (IRE) 13 b.g. Golan (IRE) – Bendis (GER) (Danehill (USA)) [2016/17 **h123**
h132: h23.1g³ h25.4d⁴ Aug 29] small, close-coupled gelding: handicap hurdler, fairly
useful nowadays: stays easy 3¼m: acts on good to firm and good to soft going: tried in
cheekpieces: front runner. *Philip Kirby*

GOLD BONNE RAINE (IRE) 6 b.m. Gold Well – Be My Bonne (Be My Native **h88**
(USA)) [2016/17 h–: h21.6d h16dᶠ h19.9v⁶ h16.8s⁴ h23.9g³ h23.3s⁴ Mar 18] modest
maiden hurdler: stays 3m: acts on good to soft going: in cheekpieces 2 of last 3 starts.
Evan Williams

GOLD CHAIN (IRE) 7 b.m. Authorized (IRE) – Mountain Chain (USA) (Royal **h106 §**
Academy (USA)) [2016/17 h94§: h20m⁶ h25.4m⁶ h20.2d* h20.2d* h17.2d h22.1g⁵
h20.2g⁴ h23.9d³ h19.9d⁵ h19.3g h19.3s h22.7vᵖᵘ h20.2g³ Apr 26] neat mare: fair handicap
hurdler: won twice at Perth (on consecutive days, conditionals event second time) in June:
stays 3m: acts on soft and good to firm going: often in headgear/tongue tie: untrustworthy.
Dianne Sayer

GOLD CLASS 6 ch.g. Firebreak – Silken Dalliance (Rambo Dancer (CAN)) [2016/17 **h94**
h95: h21.5gᵇᵈ h21g² h20g h20s h19.5g h16.2d h20m Oct 8] modest maiden hurdler: stays
21f: acts on good to soft going: wears headgear/tongue tie: usually races towards rear.
Robert Hennessy, Ireland

GOLDEN BANNER (IRE) 6 b.g. Gold Well – Banner Buzz (IRE) (King's Ride)   h–
[2016/17 b15.8d³ h16.8g⁶ h19.9g⁵ Sep 1] €10,000 3-y-o: fifth foal: half-brother to fair   **b88**
hurdler/winning pointer King Helissio (21f winner, by Helissio): dam of little account: fair
form when third in maiden bumper at Uttoxeter on debut: showed nothing in 2 starts over
hurdles: tried in cheekpieces. *Donald McCain*

GOLDEN BIRD (IRE) 6 b.g. Sinndar (IRE) – Khamsin (USA) (Mr Prospector (USA))   h–
[2016/17 h98: h25dᵖᵘ h16.2dᵖᵘ Jun 19] close-coupled gelding: maiden hurdler, no form in
2016/17: left Brendan Powell after first start: tried in headgear. *Andrew Hamilton*

GOLDEN BIRTHDAY (FR) 6 b.g. Poliglote – Gold Or Silver (FR) (Glint of Gold)   **h118**
[2016/17 b95: b15.3m* h15.3d² h16.3d⁶ h15.9v* h17.7v⁴ h16.3v³ h15.7g Apr 15] fairly   **b98**
useful form in bumpers: won at Wincanton in May: fairly useful hurdler: won novice at
Plumpton in January: stays 2¼m: acts on heavy going. *Harry Fry*

GOLDEN CANNON 6 b.m. Winker Watson – Kalmina (USA) (Rahy (USA)) [2016/17   b–
b17.7g b13.6v b13.6g Mar 31] second foal: dam, unraced, sister to fairly useful hurdler
(2m/17f winner) Kalmini: no form in bumpers/maiden on Flat. *Sheena West*

GOLDEN DOYEN (GER) 6 b.g. Doyen (IRE) – Goldsamt (GER) (Rienzi (EG))   **c134 x**
[2016/17 c136, h–: c19.2d² c21.4g⁴ h21.6g* h23.9g* h24g h24.7g h25gᶠ Apr 24]   **h138**
useful-looking gelding: useful handicap hurdler: won at Newton Abbot in August and
Cheltenham (by short head from For Good Measure) in October: useful maiden chaser:
better effort in 2016/17 when second in novice at Market Rasen in June: stays 3m: acts on
soft going: often let down by jumping over fences. *Philip Hobbs*

GOLDEN GATE BRIDGE (GER) 5 br.g. Kamsin (GER) – Galla Placidia (GER)   h–
(Kaldounevees (FR)) [2016/17 h96p, b91: h15.8d h18.8dᵖᵘ Dec 14] compact gelding:
dual bumper winner: modest form on first of 3 starts over hurdles: front runner/races
prominently. *Mark Pitman*

GOLDEN INVESTMENT (IRE) 8 b.g. Gold Well – Mangan Pet (IRE) (Over The   **c109**
River (FR)) [2016/17 h102, b90: h22.7d* c20.5dᵘʳ c24.2d³ c23.8g² c25.2s² c23.4g² c24.1g³   **h109**
Apr 22] angular gelding: winning Irish pointer: fair form over hurdles: won novice
handicap at Kelso in May: fair maiden chaser: stays 3m: acts on soft going: sometimes in
hood: in tongue tie last 4 starts: front runner/races prominently. *Donald McCain*

GOLDEN JEFFREY (SWI) 4 b.g. Soldier Hollow – Ange Doree (FR) (Sinyar (IRE))   **b97**
[2016/17 b15.7s³ b16v* Feb 27] first foal: dam Swiss 1m-1½m winner on Flat: fairly
useful form in bumpers: won conditionals/amateur event at Ayr in February, making all:
sold £28,000 in April and joined Iain Jardine. *Mark Johnston*

GOLDEN MILAN (IRE) 9 b.g. Milan – Belle Provence (FR) (Phantom Breeze)   c–
[2016/17 c115, h109: c24sᵖᵘ c23.6gᵘʳ c20.9dᵖᵘ Nov 30] useful-looking gelding: placed in   h–
points: fair handicap hurdler: maiden chaser, no form in 2016/17: wears tongue tie: has
worn tongue tie, including in 2016/17: usually races prominently. *Rebecca Curtis*

GOLDEN SPEAR 6 ch.g. Kyllachy – Penmayne (Inchinor) [2016/17 h15.7d⁴ h16g³   **h128**
h21gᵖᵘ h16d⁵ Apr 18] angular gelding: fairly useful handicap hurdler: good effort when
length third of 20 to Ice Cold Soul in Coral.ie Hurdle at Leopardstown in January: unproven
beyond 2m: acts on soft going: has worn cheekpieces: often in tongue tie. *A. J. Martin,
Ireland*

GOLDEN SUNRISE (IRE) 4 ch.g. Stowaway – Fairy Dawn (IRE) (Old Vic) [2016/17   **b87**
b17.7s⁴ Feb 26] £80,000 3-y-o: sixth foal: half-brother to fair hurdler/winning pointer
Queens Present (2½m winner, by Presenting): dam (b95), bumper winner on only start,
sister to Cheltenham Gold Cup winner Kicking King: 3/1, 6¾ lengths fourth of 6 to Larry
in maiden bumper at Fontwell, looking in need of experience. *Colin Tizzard*

GOLDEN THREAD 7 ch.g. Singspiel (IRE) – Alpenrot (IRE) (Barathea (IRE)) [2016/17   **h66**
b80: h20.7g³ May 30] fair maiden on Flat, stays 1¾m: modest form in bumpers: remote
third of 4 in maiden at Huntingdon on hurdling debut. *Neil King*

GOLDEN TOWN (IRE) 6 b.g. Invincible Spirit (IRE) – Princesse Dansante (IRE)   **h102**
(King's Best (USA)) [2016/17 h17.2g³ h17.2g³ h17.1d⁴ h15.6g² h15.6g² h15.7sᵖᵘ h16.2g²
Apr 27] smart on Flat, stays 1m: fair maiden hurdler: likely to prove best at sharp 2m: best
form on good going: tried in cheekpieces: in tongue tie last 4 starts. *James Moffatt*

GOLDEN VISION (FR) 5 bl.m. Vision d'Etat (FR) – My Gold du Fanil (FR) (Goldneyev   **h121**
(USA)) [2016/17 h16.9s² h17.9s* h17.9v² h16s* h15.7s³ Mar 8] tall mare: fifth foal: half-
sister to French hurdler/chaser Gold Bug (2¼m-2½m winner, by Malinas) and French

hurdler Dreamness (17f winner, by Dream Well): dam French hurdle/chase winner around 17f: fairly useful hurdler: won minor event at Compiegne in September and mares novice at Wetherby in February: left D. Sourdeau de Beauregard after third start: stays 2¼m: acts on soft going: has worn cheekpieces: in tongue tie last 2 starts. *Dan Skelton*

GOLD FUTURES (IRE) 8 b.g. Gold Well – Don't Discount Her (IRE) (Millfontaine) **c146**
[2016/17 c140, h–: c23.8f* Jun 5] winning hurdler: smart handicap chaser: won at Perth **h–**
(by 5 lengths from Menorah) on only start in 2016/17: stayed 3¼m: acted on firm and soft going: usually wore hood: dead. *Nicky Richards*

GOLD INGOT 10 ch.g. Best of The Bests (IRE) – Realms of Gold (USA) (Gulch (USA)) **c113**
[2016/17 c113, h–: c20g c19.2g* c21.4g³ c19.2g⁶ c19.3g⁴ c21.3d c24.2gᵘʳ Apr 17] good- **h–**
topped gelding: winning hurdler: fair handicap chaser: won at Market Rasen in June: stays 3m: acts on heavy going: in cheekpieces 2 of last 3 starts. *Caroline Bailey*

GOLD MOUNTAIN (IRE) 7 b.g. Gold Well – La Belle de Serk (IRE) (Shernazar) **c120 p**
[2016/17 h–: h16.5g h16.5g² c23g³ c19.4gᵘʳ c23m* Apr 20] runner-up in Irish point: **h98**
modest form over hurdles: fairly useful form when easily winning 3-runner handicap chase at Taunton final start: acts on good to firm going: usually in tongue tie: often races towards rear: open to further improvement over fences. *Alexandra Dunn*

GOLD OPERA (IRE) 8 b.g. Gold Well – Flute Opera (IRE) (Sharifabad (IRE)) [2016/17 **c125**
c114, h–: c20vᵖᵘ c18s⁴ c17.1sᵖᵘ c21.5v³ c20.1s* c20.5v* Mar 10] maiden hurdler: fairly **h–**
useful handicap chaser: won at Ayr in December, Newcastle in February and Ayr again (left alone 4 out) in March: stays 21f: best form on soft/heavy going: wears headgear: races prominently. *N. W. Alexander*

GOLD PRESENT (IRE) 7 br.g. Presenting – Ouro Preto (Definite Article) [2016/17 **c143**
h106: c19.1g* c20.5g⁵ c20.5g² c20.4g² c21.1gꟳ Apr 7] lengthy gelding: handicap hurdler, **h–**
fairly useful at best: useful form over fences: won novice handicap at Doncaster in November by 3¼ lengths from Drumlee Dad: good second in 4-runner Pendil Novices' Chase at Kempton (2 lengths behind Frodon) in February and 20-runner Close Brothers Novices' Handicap Chase at Cheltenham (1¼ lengths behind Tully East) in March: in touch when fell thirteenth in Topham Chase at Aintree final start: stays 2½m: acts on good to soft going: often travels strongly, though finishes weakly. *Nicky Henderson*

GOLDRAY 11 ch.m. Central Park (IRE) – Go Mary (Raga Navarro (ITY)) [2016/17 c–, **c–**
h101: h16s⁴ h19.9s² Jun 15] fair maiden hurdler: pulled up only chase start: stays 2½m: **h101**
acts on heavy going: usually races prominently. *Kerry Lee*

GOLDSLINGER (FR) 5 b.g. Gold Away (IRE) – Singaporette (FR) (Sagacity (FR)) **h96**
[2016/17 h94: h16.3d⁵ h15.9v⁵ Feb 27] neat gelding: modest maiden over hurdles: tried in hood. *Dean Ivory*

GOLIATH (IRE) 5 br.g. Golan (IRE) – Lady Shanakill (IRE) (Witness Box (USA)) **b–**
[2016/17 b16s⁶ Dec 19] tailed off in bumper. *Tristan Davidson*

GO LONG (IRE) 7 b.g. Hurricane Run (IRE) – Monumental Gesture (Head For Heights) **h–**
[2016/17 h134p: h16.5sᵖᵘ Feb 5] rangy gelding: chasing type: runner-up in Irish maiden point: useful winner of first of 2 starts over hurdles in 2015/16: pulled up in handicap only outing since. *Evan Williams*

GONALSTON CLOUD (IRE) 10 gr.g. Cloudings (IRE) – Roseoengus (IRE) (Roselier **c132**
(FR)) [2016/17 c124, h–: c28.4vᵖᵘ c24.1s⁵ c27.6d* c30g² c32.8g² c33.4s Mar 18] maiden **h–**
hurdler: useful handicap chaser: won at Market Rasen in December: good second at Catterick in January and Musselburgh in February: stays 33f: acts on heavy going: in cheekpieces last 4 starts. *Nick Kent*

GONEBEYONDRECALL (IRE) 14 b.g. Dr Massini (IRE) – Green Walk (Green **c97**
Shoon) [2016/17 c24g⁶ c24g³ c24m c20g c22.5s c24g⁴ c25sᵖᵘ Feb 5] lengthy gelding: **h–**
winning hurdler: modest handicap chaser nowadays: stays 3m: acts on soft going: usually wears headgear: tried in tongue tie. *Noel Glynn, Ireland*

GONE TOO FAR 9 b.g. Kayf Tara – Major Hoolihan (Soldier Rose) [2016/17 c128x, h–: **c133**
c19.2m* c20g c23m³ c23.8dᵖᵘ c23.8d⁴ c20sᵖᵘ c31.8gᵖᵘ Apr 22] well-made gelding: **h–**
winning hurdler: useful handicap chaser: won at Exeter in May: left Alan King and showed little after that start: stays 3m: acts on soft and good to firm going: has worn headgear, including last 4 starts. *David Pipe*

GONNABEGOOD (IRE) 6 b.g. Kutub (IRE) – Angels Flame (IRE) (Un Desperado **h78**
(FR)) [2016/17 h21.6g³ h19.5g h18.5s h23.8d h21.4dᵖᵘ Feb 18] poor form over hurdles: best effort at 2¾m: in cheekpieces last 2 starts. *Jeremy Scott*

GOODBYE DANCER (FR) 6 b.g. Dragon Dancer – Maribia Bella (FR) (Urban Ocean (FR)) [2016/17 h126: h24.7m² h25.4m⁵ h23.9d² h26.5g h24.7d² h25.3s c20vᵖᵘ c25.2vᵖᵘ h21.5s* Mar 10] rather leggy gelding: useful handicap hurdler: won at Sandown on final start by 2¼ lengths from Shaama Grise: showed no aptitude for chasing in 2 tries: stays 25f: acts on good to firm and heavy going: tried in hood: often races in rear. *Nigel Twiston-Davies* — c– h134

GO ODEE GO (IRE) 9 b.g. Alkaadhem – Go Franky (IRE) (Hollow Hand) [2016/17 h108: h18.5gᵖᵘ c20.1gᵖᵘ Jun 4] sturdy gelding: fairly useful hurdler at one time: didn't take to chasing in novice at Hexham: subsequently placed in points: stays 2½m: acts on good to firm and good to soft going: wears headgear: often races towards rear. *Dan Skelton* — c– h–

GOODGIRLTERESA (IRE) 7 b.m. Stowaway – Decheekymonkey (IRE) (Presenting) [2016/17 b16s² b15.8d⁵ h18.5s h23.3v³ h20.3g Mar 28] £15,000 6-y-o: third foal: dam second in a point: off mark in Irish points at fourth attempt: fair form in bumpers: poor form in novice hurdles: left Neil King after fourth start: often leads/races freely. *Neil Mulholland* — h84 b92

GOOD IDEA (IRE) 6 b.g. Arcadio (GER) – Aunt Annie (IRE) (Synefos (USA)) [2016/17 b75: b18.8g³ b16g⁵ Jun 4] modest form in bumpers: left Nicky Henderson after reappearance: in tongue tie final start. *Philip Hobbs* — b80

GOODKNIGHT PERCY (IRE) 4 ch.g. Sir Percy – Ekhraaj (USA) (El Prado (IRE)) [2016/17 h16.4sᵖᵘ h16s Dec 27] modest maiden on Flat, stays 7f: showed nothing in 2 starts over hurdles. *Donald Whillans* — h–

GOOD MAN HUGHIE (IRE) 8 ch.g. Flemensfirth (USA) – Good Dawn (IRE) (Good Thyne (USA)) [2016/17 h69, b66: h19.5dᵖᵘ h19.5v* Jan 31] winning Irish pointer: modest handicap hurdler: won at Lingfield in January: stays 19f: acts on heavy going: tried in cheekpieces/tongue tie. *Gary Moore* — h95

GOOD NEWS 5 b.g. Midnight Legend – Venetian Lass (First Trump) [2016/17 b17.7d¹ ab16g⁶ Feb 20] first foal: dam unraced: modest form both starts in bumpers. *Lydia Richards* — b84

GOODNIGHT CHARLIE 7 gr.m. Midnight Legend – Over To Charlie (Overbury (IRE)) [2016/17 h24d h24dᵖᵘ h21d h20.5d h23v h25.6sᵖᵘ h19.2v³ h19.2s* h22g Apr 1] £28,000 6-y-o: first foal: dam, winning pointer, half-sister to modest hurdler/fairly useful chaser (stayed 3¼m) Fox In The Box: won maiden point on debut: poor handicap hurdler: won at Towcester (conditionals event) in March: should stay beyond 19f: acts on soft going: in headgear last 3 starts: often races prominently. *Caroline Fryer* — h82

GOODNIGHT VIENNA (IRE) 11 b.g. High Roller (IRE) – Curragh Bridge (Pitpan) [2016/17 c89: c20.8g Apr 27] multiple winning pointer: lightly raced and modest form at best in hunter chases. *Mrs L. Redman* — c–

GOODNITESWEETHEART 6 b.m. Midnight Legend – Over To Charlie (Overbury (IRE)) [2016/17 b15.8d² h15.7v⁴ h15.3s h17.7v h21.6g* Apr 12] second foal: brother to 19f hurdle winner/winning pointer Goodnight Charlie: dam, winning pointer, half-sister to modest hurdler/fairly useful chaser (stayed 3¼m) Fox In The Box: maiden point winner: fair form when second in mares bumper at Uttoxeter: modest form over hurdles: much improved when winning mares handicap at Fontwell final start: stays 2¾m. *Harry Fry* — h98 b87

GOOD OF LUCK 8 b.g. Authorized (IRE) – Oops Pettie (Machiavellian (USA)) [2016/17 h124: h17.7d h16.3g⁶ h17.2mᶠ Jun 24] angular gelding: fairly useful handicap hurdler: based around 2m: acted on good to firm and good to soft going: usually wore cheekpieces: dead. *Warren Greatrex* — h117

GOOD THYNE TARA 7 b.m. Kayf Tara – Good Thyne Mary (IRE) (Good Thyne (USA)) [2016/17 b16g* b16s² h16.4v* h20d⁴ h16.3d³ Apr 27] seventh foal: half-sister to fair hurdler/fairly useful chaser Jacks Island (winner up to 33f, by Turtle Island) and 3m chase winner Thatildee (by Heron Island): dam, ran once in bumper, half-sister to fairly useful hurdler (stayed 3m) Thats Fine By Me: fairly useful bumper performer: won mares event at Cork in November: second in listed event at Navan (½ length behind Samcro) in December: useful form over hurdles: won mares maiden at Clonmel in February: best effort when third in mares novice at Punchestown (6½ lengths behind Asthuria) on final start: will stay beyond 2½m: usually travels strongly: open to further improvement. *W. P. Mullins, Ireland* — h130 p b104

GOODTOKNOW 9 b.g. Presenting – Atlantic Jane (Tamure (IRE)) [2016/17 c138, h–: c24.1v c23.6g⁵ c29.2s² c25.2v* c28.4dᵖᵘ c34.3d Apr 8] useful-looking gelding: winning hurdler: useful handicap chaser: won at Hereford (by 7 lengths from Mountainous) in February: 66/1, shaped better than distance beaten suggests when well-beaten thirteenth of — c142 h–

40 to One For Arthur in Grand National at Aintree final start, racing with enthusiasm and still close up when bumped twenty-fourth: stays 29f: acts on heavy going: wears headgear: races prominently. *Kerry Lee*

GOODTOSEEYABUDDY (IRE) 7 b.m. Robin des Pres (FR) – Ballymacoda Lady (IRE) (Lord Ha Ha) [2016/17 h16d h20.5d^pu Dec 12] half-sister to fairly useful chaser Freeze Up (3¼m winner) and 2 winning pointers, all by Presenting: dam (h101) 21f hurdle winner: showed nothing in Irish points and 2 novice hurdles. *Gary Moore* **h–**

GOOD TRADITION (IRE) 6 b.g. Pivotal – Token Gesture (IRE) (Alzao (USA)) [2016/17 h19.5g* h17s^5 h19.3d^3 h25.3d^4 h16.3g^2 Apr 15] half-brother to fair/unreliable hurdler Turn of Phrase (2m winner, by Cadeaux Genereux): useful on Flat, stays 1¾m: fair hurdler: won maiden at Kilbeggan in August: left D. K. Weld after first start: stays 19f: acts on good to soft going: front runner/races prominently. *Donald McCain* **h114**

GOOD VIBRATION (FR) 6 gr.g. Saddler Maker (IRE) – Queenhood (FR) (Linamix (FR)) [2016/17 h108: h19.7s Dec 26] winning Irish pointer: fair maiden hurdler, well held only outing in 2016/17: likely to stay beyond 2½m: acts on heavy going. *Sue Smith* **h–**

GOODWOOD MOONLIGHT 5 gr.g. Azamour (IRE) – Corrine (IRE) (Spectrum (IRE)) [2016/17 h16m h16.3g^5 h16g h15.8m^5 h15.9g^3 h16.8g^4 Oct 27] leggy gelding: half-brother to fair/unreliable hurdler Liszt (19f winner, by Galileo): dam half-sister to fairly useful hurdler around 2m Moon Shot: modest on Flat, stays 1¼m: poor form over hurdles: in tongue tie last 3 starts: usually races nearer last than first. *Ian Williams* **h83**

GOOHAR (IRE) 8 b.g. Street Cry (IRE) – Reem Three (Mark of Esteem (IRE)) [2016/17 c115, h–: c19.4m^6 c17g^ur c19.9d^2 c21.7d* c20.8s^5 c25.3g^3 Apr 20] rangy gelding: winning hurdler: fairly useful handicap chaser: won novice event at Towcester in December: stays 25f: acts on heavy going: usually wears cheekpieces: signs of temperament. *Henry Daly* **c119 h–**

GO ON HENRY (IRE) 9 b.g. Golan (IRE) – The Millers Tale (IRE) (Rashar (USA)) [2016/17 c100: c22.6m^ur h23.3d c20.9v^3 c16.5g^5 c19.4g^ur c22.6g^3 c20.3d^4 c16.5g^5 c20m^ur Oct 20] dual point winner: tailed off in handicap on hurdling debut: modest maiden chaser: left Mrs S. Case after first start: stays 3m: acts on heavy going: wears headgear/tongue tie. *Matt Sheppard* **c93 h–**

GOONJIM (IRE) 6 ch.g. Beneficial – Clogga Native (IRE) (Good Thyne (USA)) [2016/17 h–: h19.9s h16.6s^3 h16.8d^F c19.7s* c20.9d^3 c17g^2 c17g^4 Apr 15] poor maiden hurdler: poor form over fences: won novice handicap at Plumpton in March: best effort at 2½m: acts on soft going: wears hood/tongue tie: usually races towards rear. *Alexandra Dunn* **c80 h69**

GOONYELLA (IRE) 10 br.g. Presenting – Miss Fresher (FR) (Pampabird) [2016/17 c149, h116: c24s^6 c30.2m^4 Dec 9] well-made gelding: winning hurdler: handicap chaser, smart at best: 12¾ lengths fourth of 7 to Cantlow in cross-country event at Cheltenham final start, again not looking suited by type of contest: stays 33f: acts on good to firm and heavy going: has worn cheekpieces, including last 3 starts: usually in tongue tie. *J. T. R. Dreaper, Ireland* **c138 h–**

GOOSEN MAVERICK (IRE) 6 b.g. Morozov (USA) – Bonny River (IRE) (Exit To Nowhere (USA)) [2016/17 b18v h21.6g^4 h19.5g h16.5g h23.1s h23.9g^6 c24m^5 Apr 4] maiden pointer: tailed off in maiden bumper: poor maiden hurdler: well beaten in novice on chasing debut: left J. G. Cosgrave after first start. *Grant Cann* **c– h75 b–**

GORES ISLAND (IRE) 11 b.g. Beneficial – Just Leader (IRE) (Supreme Leader) [2016/17 c125, h124: h17.7d^4 h21.7d^2 c15.5s^2 c20g^2 c20s^3 c20.2v^5 c20.5g^F c20d^5 c17m^2 Apr 17] tall, lengthy gelding: fair handicap hurdler: fairly useful handicap chaser: stays 21f: acts on heavy going: tried in headgear in 2016/17: often races towards rear. *Gary Moore* **c121 h109**

GOREY LANE (IRE) 11 b.g. Oscar (IRE) – Supremely Deep (IRE) (Supreme Leader) [2016/17 c–x, h89: h23.3v^pu h23.3v^ur h25.8v^pu Jan 15] big gelding: handicap hurdler, no form in 2016/17: winning chaser (often let down by jumping): wears visor/tongue tie. *John Norton* **c– x h–**

GORING ONE (IRE) 12 b.g. Broadway Flyer (USA) – Brigette's Secret (Good Thyne (USA)) [2016/17 c–, h–: c21.1s^6 c21.7d^5 c21.1v* c23.5v^2 c25.5d^3 Mar 18] compact gelding: maiden hurdler: modest handicap chaser: won at Fontwell in February: stays 25f: acts on good to firm and heavy going: tried in visor. *Anna Newton-Smith* **c94 h–**

GORING TWO (IRE) 12 br.g. Needle Gun (IRE) – Kam Slave (Kambalda) [2016/17 c87§, h–: c21.1s^pu c19.7d^pu c17v^3 c16.1v^4 c20.2s^3 c25.1s^pu c19.1g^2 c19.7m^5 Apr 16] angular gelding: maiden hurdler: poor handicap chaser: stays 2½m: best form on soft/heavy going: has worn headgear, including last 3 starts: front runner/races prominently: unreliable. *Anna Newton-Smith* **c72 § h–**

GORRAN HAVEN (IRE) 7 ch.g. Stowaway – Diminished (IRE) (Alphabatim (USA)) **c93**
[2016/17 c23.5v^pu c24d² c15.9s⁴ c15.7g⁴ c20.3g² Apr 21] €60,000 3-y-o: seventh foal: half-
brother to fair hurdler The Ginger Man (2½m winner, by Carroll House) and poor hurdler
Powertakeoff (2m winner, by Court Cave): dam, well held over hurdles, half-sister to
useful hurdler/very smart chaser (2m-3m winner) Scotsirish: maiden pointer: modest form
over fences: stays 2½m: best form on good going: tried in cheekpieces/tongue tie.
Caroline Bailey

GORSKY ISLAND 9 b.g. Turtle Island (IRE) – Belle Magello (FR) (Exit To Nowhere **c–**
(USA)) [2016/17 c122, h106: c24s^pu Feb 10] maiden hurdler: useful chaser at best: off 14 **h–**
months, pulled up only outing in 2016/17: stays 25f: acts on soft going. *Tom George*

GORTROE JOE (IRE) 5 b.g. Beneficial – Rowlands Star (IRE) (Old Vic) [2016/17 **b85 p**
b16g³ Apr 24] fifth foal: half-brother to a winning pointer by Mountain High: dam well
beaten in bumper/points: placed on completed start in Irish maiden points: 7/2, shaped
promisingly when 12½ lengths third of 8 to World Premier in bumper at Warwick: should
improve. *Dan Skelton*

GO STEADY 5 b.g. Indian Danehill (IRE) – Pyleigh Lady (Zaffaran (USA)) [2016/17 **h108**
h19.5d⁴ h19.6s⁴ Nov 26] second foal: dam (h121) 19f/21f hurdle winner: runner-up in
maiden point on debut: fair form over hurdles: better effort when fourth in maiden at
Chepstow in October: should prove suited by at least 2½m. *Oliver Greenall*

GOT THE NAC (IRE) 8 br.g. Beneficial – Hey Jude (IRE) (Mandalus) [2016/17 c130, **c–**
h–: c17.5s^F Nov 20] winning hurdler: useful chaser at best: behind when fell last only **h–**
outing in 2016/17 (wore hood, raced too freely): raced around 2m: best form on soft/heavy
going. *Richard Woollacott*

GOULANES (IRE) 11 b.g. Mr Combustible (IRE) – Rebolgiane (IRE) (Red Sunset) **c–**
[2016/17 c29.5s^pu c26s^F c33.4s^pu Mar 18] lengthy gelding: has reportedly had wind **h–**
operation: winning hurdler: smart chaser at best: off 34 months, failed to complete in
2016/17: in blinkers last 5 starts, in tongue tie last 4. *Neil Mulholland*

GOWANAUTHAT (IRE) 9 ch.g. Golan (IRE) – Coolrua (IRE) (Commanche Run) **c131**
[2016/17 c94, h–: c21.2g* c20.5m* c21.1d* c21g* c22.6g* c20g² c21.1s³ c21.1g^ur c21.1g² **h–**
Apr 21] maiden hurdler: useful handicap chaser: much improved and won at Fakenham
and Kempton in May, Fontwell in June, Newton Abbot in August and Stratford in
September: creditable efforts when second at Worcester and Fontwell: stays 3m: acts on
good to firm and heavy going: has worn cheekpieces, including last 3 starts: wears tongue
tie: usually leads. *Charlie Mann*

GOWELL (IRE) 6 b.m. Gold Well – Glen Supreme (IRE) (Supreme Leader) [2016/17 **c–**
h99p: h19.1d^pu c17.5v⁵ c23.5v^ur h16.8s³ h20.3g^pu Apr 21] modest maiden hurdler: well **h90**
held completed start over fences. *Seamus Mullins*

GO WEST YOUNG MAN (IRE) 9 b.g. Westerner – Last of Her Line (Silver Patriarch **c119 §**
(IRE)) [2016/17 c–, h113§: h21g* h20m^ro h23.1s² c23.8d⁴ c22.7g² c23.6d⁴ c23.8m² Apr **h119 §**
18] rangy gelding: fairly useful handicap hurdler: won at Kempton in May: fairly useful
novice chaser: stays 3m: acts on good to firm and heavy going: often races in rear:
temperamental (normally hangs/refuses to go through with effort). *Henry Daly*

GRAASTEN (GER) 5 ch.g. Sholokhov (IRE) – Golden Time (GER) (Surumu (GER)) **h118**
[2016/17 h113p: h19.1s² h15.9g³ h15.9g* h16s h15.8s⁴ Mar 18] good-topped gelding:
fairly useful form over hurdles: won maiden at Plumpton in October: stays 19f: acts on soft
going. *Gary Moore*

GRACEFUL LADY 4 b.f. Sixties Icon – Leitzu (IRE) (Barathea (IRE)) [2016/17 h16.6g **h–**
Dec 29] fair form on Flat, stays 1¾m: 20/1, well held in juvenile maiden at Doncaster on
hurdling debut. *Robert Eddery*

GRACEFUL LEGEND 6 b.m. Midnight Legend – Clover Green (IRE) (Presenting) **h120**
[2016/17 h94, b89: h16g³ h19.2g* h15.8v² h19.8s⁴ h19.4g* h19.4d* h18.5d* Feb 24]
compact mare: fairly useful handicap hurdler: won mares events at Towcester in November,
Doncaster in December and January, and Exeter on final start: stays 19f: acts on heavy
going: front runner/races prominently. *Ben Case*

GRACE TARA 8 b.m. Kayf Tara – Fenney Spring (Polish Precedent (USA)) [2016/17 **h111**
h19.5v* h21v h21.4v² h15.8s² h24v³ h22.7s* Apr 3] won point in Ireland: successful on
only start in bumpers (in 2014/15): fair form over hurdles: won mares maiden at Lingfield
in November and mares novice at Kelso on final start: stays 3m: raced only on ground
softer than good: front runner/races prominently. *Michael Scudamore*

GRAMS AND OUNCES 10 b.g. Royal Applause – Ashdown Princess (IRE) (King's Theatre (IRE)) [2016/17 c–, h112: c16g3 c16.3g2 h16d5 h17.7g3 h19.1g5 h16m h19s3 h16.7s5 c16s3 h15.7s4 h16g3 h15.8m3 h16m4 Apr 28] sturdy gelding: modest handicap hurdler: fair maiden chaser: stays 2½m: acts on good to firm and heavy going: sometimes in cheekpieces: wears tongue tie: front runner/races prominently. *Grace Harris* **c110 h99**

GRANDADS HORSE 11 b.g. Bollin Eric – Solid Laund (FR) (Solid Illusion (USA)) [2016/17 c133, h–: c26.1gpu c25.5d3 h23.3g6 Jul 24] strong gelding: useful hurdler/chaser at best: only form in 2016/17 when third in handicap chase at Cartmel in July: stays 25f: acts on soft and good to firm going: wears headgear: in tongue tie last 2 starts. *Charlie Longsdon* **c129 h–**

GRAND COUREUR (FR) 5 b.g. Grand Couturier – Iris du Berlais (FR) (Bonnet Rouge (FR)) [2016/17 b77: h16.2gF h15.3d6 h19.5g h16.7d2 h16s Feb 10] rather unfurnished gelding: fair form over hurdles: best effort at 17f on good to soft going: usually races close up. *Nick Williams* **h102**

GRAND ENTERPRISE 7 b.g. Fair Mix (IRE) – Miss Chinchilla (Perpendicular) [2016/17 h99, b75: h15.8m4 h20.3g5 h18.7m4 h22m6 c20.1sF h16.8dpu h25.3d3 h24.4d* h24.1s4 h25d2 h23.8g5 h27g2 Apr 7] fair handicap hurdler: won at Doncaster in January: fell second in novice handicap on chasing debut: left Tom George after fourth start: stays 27f: acts on good and good to firm going: usually travels strongly. *Henry Hogarth* **c– h104**

GRAND GIGOLO (FR) 8 b.g. Enrique – Belle d'Ecajeul (FR) (Le Nain Jaune (FR)) [2016/17 c23g4 c23.9dF c23m5 c24dF h24g5 h25m3 h25mpu Oct 30] handicap hurdler, poor form in 2016/17: modest form over fences: left Ian Williams after fifth start: stays 3m: acts on soft and good to firm going: tried in cheekpieces. *Mike Sowersby* **c92 h79**

GRAND GOLD 8 b.g. Librettist (USA) – Night Symphonie (Cloudings (IRE)) [2016/17 h19.1v2 c19.2spu Jan 17] multiple winning pointer: fairly useful handicap hurdler: fair form on chasing debut, bled when pulled up only other chase start: stays 2½m: acts on good to firm and heavy going: wears tongue tie. *Jamie Snowden* **c– h118**

GRANDIOSO (IRE) 10 b.g. Westerner – Champagne Warrior (IRE) (Waajib) [2016/17 c120, h–: c20.8g3 c20.3v* c17.4d* c23g2 c20.9v4 c22.6s3 Mar 13] well-made gelding: winning hurdler: fairly useful chaser: won hunters at Southwell and Fontwell in May: effective at 17f to easy 23f: acts on good to firm and heavy going: tried in cheekpieces: wears tongue tie: often races towards rear. *Steve Flook* **c120 h–**

GRAND JESTURE (IRE) 9 b.g. Gold Well – Four Moons (IRE) (Cardinal Flower) [2016/17 c–§, h–: c22.6srr c26.3g Mar 17] workmanlike gelding: dual point winner: maiden chaser: one-time smart chaser: well held in Foxhunter Chase at Cheltenham final start: stays 25f: acts on heavy going: has worn headgear: very much one to avoid (has refused to race 3 times). *J. T. R. Dreaper, Ireland* **c– § h–**

GRAND MARCH 8 b.g. Beat All (USA) – Bora Bora (Bairn (USA)) [2016/17 c96, h–: c15.7g3 c16s3 c15.7dpu h15.5v6 h15.8s4 Apr 1] good-topped gelding: handicap hurdler, poor nowadays: modest maiden chaser: stays 2½m: acts on heavy going: wears cheekpieces: often races towards rear: ungenuine. *Kim Bailey* **c86 § h75 §**

GRANDMASTER GEORGE (IRE) 8 ch.g. Generous (IRE) – Merewood Lodge (IRE) (Grand Lodge (USA)) [2016/17 h98, b92: h21g4 h20m5 May 19] sturdy gelding: bumper winner: modest maiden hurdler: stays 21f: acts on soft going. *Seamus Mullins* **h95**

GRAND MEISTER 6 gr.g. Mastercraftsman (IRE) – Wait It Out (USA) (Swain (IRE)) [2016/17 h16.2f Jun 5] lightly-raced maiden over hurdles, in cheekpieces when well held only outing in 2016/17. *John Quinn* **h–**

GRAND PARTNER (IRE) 9 b.g. Millenary – Bens Partner (IRE) (Beneficial) [2016/17 h16g4 h17s2 h16g h16s* h16v3 h16v2 h16d h20.5d Apr 29] useful handicap hurdler: won at Leopardstown in February: stays 3m: acts on good to firm and heavy going: has worn headgear, including final start. *Thomas Mullins, Ireland* **h134**

GRAND TOUR 6 b.m. Rail Link – Cordoba (Oasis Dream) [2016/17 h16g h16g h16.2g Sep 6] first foal: dam 11f winner on only start: no form in maiden/handicap hurdles: wears tongue tie. *Patrick Griffin, Ireland* **h–**

GRAND TURINA 6 b.m. Kayf Tara – Cesana (IRE) (Desert Prince (IRE)) [2016/17 b88: h15.8sur h15.8s2 h16v* h20.5g Mar 25] sturdy mare: bumper winner: fair form over hurdles: won novice at Warwick in March: sweating, ran poorly final start: bred to stay beyond 2m: acts on heavy going: usually wore hood in 2016/17: takes strong hold. *Venetia Williams* **h113**

GRAND VISION (IRE) 11 gr.g. Old Vic – West Hill Rose (IRE) (Roselier (FR)) **c127**
[2016/17 c23.4v³ c24s* c20.3s² c26.3g Mar 17] tall gelding: winning hurdler: fairly useful **h–**
hunter chaser nowadays: won at Warwick (by 6 lengths from Pearlysteps) in January: 50/1,
shaped better than result when well held in 23-runner Foxhunter Chase at Cheltenham final
start, weakening straight: stays 25f: acts on heavy going: tried in cheekpieces. *Colin Tizzard*

GRANGE HALL (IRE) 10 b.m. Flemensfirth (USA) – Odeeka (IRE) (Posen (USA)) **c119**
[2016/17 c–, h102: c20.1v* c20d⁴ c22.4v² c20s⁵ h16v⁵ Jan 16] lengthy mare: fair hurdler **h–**
at best: fairly useful chaser: won maiden at Sligo in September: good second in handicap
at Hexham in December: stays 2¾m: acts on heavy going: has worn hood/tongue tie,
including in 2016/17. *Paul Stafford, Ireland*

GRANIA O'MALLEY (IRE) 4 ch.f. Beat Hollow – Oh Susannah (FR) (Turgeon **b90**
(USA)) [2016/17 b15.7s² b16.8g² Apr 20] €12,000 3-y-o: sixth foal: closely related to 3
winners by King's Theatre, including useful hurdler/fairly useful chaser Blacklough
(2m-19f winner) and fair hurdler Some Say (2¼m winner): dam (c104/h99), 15f/17f
hurdle/chase winner in France, half-sister to smart staying chaser Goonyella: fair form in
bumpers: better effort when second in conditionals/amateur event at Southwell in March.
Evan Williams

GRANIT (IRE) 7 b.g. Arcadio (GER) – Can't Stop (GER) (Lando (GER)) [2016/17 h–: **h–**
h21gᵖᵘ May 2] lengthy gelding: showed little in bumper and 2 novice hurdles: sold £2,000
in August, pulled up in point in December. *Nicky Henderson*

GRANIT MAN (FR) 11 b.g. Passing Sale (FR) – Red Flower (USA) (Trempolino **c– x**
(USA)) [2016/17 h18f⁵ h17gᵘʳ h17g c24.2m⁵ c25.2vᵘʳ c24vᵖᵘ h16f⁵ Apr 17] little sign of **h–**
ability in varied company: sketchy jumper. *James Moon, Jersey*

GRAN MAESTRO (USA) 8 ch.g. Medicean – Red Slippers (USA) (Nureyev (USA)) **c101**
[2016/17 h123: h20m⁶ h15.9g² h20dᵇᵈ c19.2g³ c19.2gᶠ h15.7g⁷ Aug 23] fairly useful **h120**
handicap hurdler: fair form on completed start in novice chases: stays 2½m: acts on good
to firm and good to soft going: wears headgear/tongue tie: often races lazily.
Dr Richard Newland

GRAN PARADISO (IRE) 5 ch.g. Galileo (IRE) – Looking Lovely (IRE) (Storm Cat **h109**
(USA)) [2016/17 h20.2s⁴ h20.6g³ h19.9g* h20.1d² h19.9g⁴ h22.7d³ Oct 22] fair maiden on
Flat, best effort at 13f: fair form over hurdles: won novice at Sedgefield in August: stays
21f: acts on good to soft going: wears cheekpieces: tried in tongue tie: often races lazily.
Micky Hammond

GRANVILLE ISLAND (IRE) 10 b.g. Flemensfirth (USA) – Fox Glen (Furry Glen) **c120**
[2016/17 h19.9v² h22.8s⁶ c16.3s⁵ c20s Feb 8] workmanlike gelding: handicap hurdler/ **h118**
chaser, fairly useful form in 2016/17 after long absence: stays 2½m: acts on heavy going.
Jennie Candlish

GRAPE TREE FLAME 9 ch.m. Grape Tree Road – Althrey Flame (IRE) (Torus) **h117**
[2016/17 h128: h24.7m⁴ h22.1m h23.8s h20.5vᵖᵘ Mar 4] sturdy mare: fairly useful
handicap hurdler: stays 27f: acts on heavy going: usually wears headgear. *Peter Bowen*

GRAPHICAL (IRE) 8 b.g. High Chaparral (IRE) – Woopi Gold (IRE) (Last Tycoon) **c–**
[2016/17 h25.6s h23.9g Dec 30] runner-up both starts in maiden points: no form over **h–**
hurdles: pulled up only chase start: in cheekpieces last 3 outings. *Johnny Farrelly*

GRAY DAY (IRE) 6 gr.g. Daylami (IRE) – Carrigeen Diamond (IRE) (Old Vic) [2016/17 **h116**
b16g h20.5g* h20.5d² h23.1s* h21.2v³ h22g³ Apr 23] €12,000 4-y-o: first foal: dam **b82**
unraced half-sister to useful 19f hurdle winner Benatar and fairly useful hurdler/chaser
(stayed 29f) Carrigeen Lechuga: modest form in bumper on debut: fairly useful form over
hurdles: won novices at Leicester (conditionals event) in December and Bangor in January:
stays 23f: acts on soft going (possibly not heavy): front runner/races prominently.
Donald McCain

GRAYHAWK (IRE) 7 gr.g. Kalanisi (IRE) – Saddler Regal (IRE) (Saddlers' Hall (IRE)) **c73 x**
[2016/17 h–: c17d³ c17sᵖᵘ h20.5vᵖᵘ c17vᶠ c19.7mᵘʳ c19.9g⁴ Apr 28] sturdy gelding: no **h–**
form in 2 runs over hurdles: poor maiden chaser, often let down by jumping: in cheekpieces
last 3 starts. *Diana Grissell*

GRAY HESSION (IRE) 10 b.g. Vinnie Roe (IRE) – Little Paddle (IRE) (Remainder **c83**
Man) [2016/17 c140, h–: c24gᵖᵘ h19.4g c25d⁵ c24.1gᵖᵘ Jul 29] sturdy gelding: winning **h–**
hurdler: useful handicap chaser at best: stayed 2¾m: acted on good to firm going: in
cheekpieces final start: sometimes wore tongue tie: dead. *Jonjo O'Neill*

GRAYS CHOICE (IRE) 6 b.g. Well Chosen – Pennyworth (IRE) (Zaffaran (USA))　**h86**
[2016/17 b104: h20.1g^{pu} h22.7s^{pu} h20g^4 h19.3d^5 h22s^5 h19.7d Feb 21] bumper winner:
modest form over hurdles: best effort at 2¾m: acts on soft going: in cheekpieces third/
fourth starts. *George Bewley*

GRAY WOLF RIVER 6 gr.m. Fair Mix (IRE) – Inkpen (Overbury (IRE)) [2016/17 h74:　**h–**
h19g^{pu} h15.8g^{pu} h22v^5 h20g^6 h15.8g h18.5d h15.8v^6 h15.9s h16g^5 h15.9v^6 h15.8d Mar 15]
plain mare: won completed start in points: maiden hurdler, no form in 2016/17: left Richard
Harper after second start, Ben Case after fourth: tried in hood. *Richard Harper*

GREAT DEMEANOR (USA) 7 b.g. Bernstein (USA) – Hangin Withmy Buds (USA)　**c–**
(Roar (USA)) [2016/17 c77, h66: c17.1m^{pu} May 29] poor maiden hurdler/chaser: unproven　**h–**
beyond 17f: acts on soft going: tried in headgear/tongue tie. *Dianne Sayer*

GREAT FIELD (FR) 6 b.g. Great Pretender (IRE) – Eaton Lass (IRE) (Definite　**c170 p**
Article) [2016/17 h140: c16d* c17s* c18s* c16d* Apr 27]　**h–**
　　　　There were some outstanding novice chasers in 2016/17, with no fewer
than five of them ending the campaign rated higher than 165—a ratings threshold
that has been breached in just eight seasons since the *Chasers & Hurdlers* series
began over forty years ago, the previous highest tally in a single season being three
in 2014/15 (Vautour, Coneygree and Un de Sceaux). In total, just fourteen novice
chasers had bettered a Timeform rating of 165 before 2016/17 and over half of them
had done so as a result of exploits outside novice company. For example, Strong
Promise and Danoli both won open Grade 1s against more experienced opposition
in 1996/7, whilst Gloria Victis and Beau were runaway winners of valuable staying
handicaps in 1999/00. Similarly bold campaigning was responsible for some of the
exalted ratings achieved by the 2016/17 crop too. Thistlecrack (174) and Our Duke
(167p) were most impressive winners of the King George VI Chase and Irish Grand
National respectively on just their fourth chase starts, and the flawless campaign by
Altior (175p) included comprehensive victories over the Queen Mother Champion
Chase first and second on his two starts outside novice company. Although Might
Bite (166) was kept to the novice ranks, much has been made of the fact that, before
he fell when clear at the last, in the Kauto Star Novices' Chase, he was set to record
a significantly faster time than Thistlecrack put up in the King George later on the
same card. Might Bite's remarkable win in the RSA Chase also showed him as being
out of the ordinary.
　　　　By far the least celebrated of the top-class quintet of 2016/17 has been Great
Field, no doubt because he was restricted to novice events on Irish soil, but he fully
deserves his place among those elite names already mentioned. Indeed, his rating
of 170p would have landed him the title of Timeform's leading novice chaser in
thirty-five of the forty-one previous editions of *Chasers & Hurdlers* and there is
even a chance that such a lofty figure does not do him full justice! Four pillar-to-
post wins from as many starts over fences doesn't tell the whole story, as in none
of those races did his opponents get anywhere near to extending Great Field, who
became increasingly impressive as he was stepped up in class each time. His final
start came in the Ryanair Novices' Chase at Punchestown, where he was sent off at
100/90-on in a field of eight. Great Field raced with typical zest at the head of affairs
and, although the field closed to be on his heels turning in, he stormed clear in the
straight under just hands and heels riding from Jody McGarvey, who was able to
start celebrating the biggest win of his career several strides from the post. It was
also the most fluent round of jumping so far from Great Field who pulled eleven
lengths clear of runner-up Ordinary World (fifteen lengths third behind Altior in
the Arkle at Cheltenham), with the prolific winners Ball d'Arc and Listen Dear the
next two home.
　　　　'At the start of the year I was only hoping to ride at the festivals—I never
dreamed I would be on an odds-on shot for Willie Mullins in a Grade 1,' was the
post-race reaction of McGarvey, whose surprising association with Great Field was
one of the most heart-warming stories of the Irish jumps season. The four wins
aboard Great Field were certainly the highlights of McGarvey's first full season
without a claim, though he also rode Western Boy to victory in a valuable handicap
hurdle earlier in Punchestown Festival week. Both of those Punchestown winners

were for powerful owner J.P. McManus who has been a loyal supporter of the young jockey—over half of McGarvey's career wins (which stood at seventy-five by the end of 2016/17) have been in the famous emerald green, yellow hoops, including his first one on Code of The West in a conditional jockeys handicap chase at Down Royal in February 2012. McManus' retained jockey Barry Geraghty endured an injury-ravaged season and was sidelined for Great Field's last three wins, but he was in action at Gowran on January 26th and even rode a winner for McManus and Mullins on Bon Papa in the opening maiden hurdle before partnering the well-fancied Rogue Trader (pulled up) in the Thyestes Chase. However, for some reason he was never jocked up to ride in the two-mile beginners chase that followed the Thyestes, despite the fact that McManus had two runners in the race. Geraghty's deputy Mark Walsh took the mount on second string Teacher's Pet as McGarvey (who has been based with Christy Roche for ten years) got the call for Great Field, even though he had never ridden for Mullins previously.

Great Field isn't a straightforward ride because of his headstrong tendencies—he ran away with Geraghty when joint favourite for the 2016 County Hurdle in which he was eventually pulled up—but such performers sometimes come into their own when sent chasing and that was certainly the case at Gowran, where Great Field ran out a very easy winner from the smart Mall Dini. Great Field's fast and low style of jumping can give his rider something of a white-knuckle experience at times—'he has his way of getting over his fences' is how Geraghty puts it!—though the closest Great Field and McGarvey came to parting company, ironically, was not as a result of a jumping error. Some above-average opponents were again unable to lay a glove on Great Field in a novice chase at Leopardstown in early-March, but he stumbled badly shortly after jumping the last and McGarvey performed miracles to maintain the partnership after losing his irons and coming very close to going out of the side door! Despite that impromptu piece of rodeo riding from McGarvey, Great Field still ran out an impressive eight-length winner from Don't Touch It (also owned by McManus), with a further length and three quarters back to Woodland Opera in third—the second and third both went on to land valuable handicaps under

big weights at the Punchestown Festival. A blunder at the second last was the only blemish on another scintillating performance by Great Field in the listed Pierce Molony Memorial Novices' Chase at Thurles later the same month, when he beat Hurricane Ben (winner of a valuable novice handicap at Fairyhouse's Easter meeting on his next start) by thirty-two lengths after opening up an unassailable lead early on the final circuit.

	Great Pretender (IRE) (b 1999)	King's Theatre (b 1991)	Sadler's Wells / Regal Beauty
		Settler (b 1992)	Darshaan / Aborigine
Great Field (FR) (b.g. 2011)			
	Eaton Lass (IRE) (br 2001)	Definite Article (b 1992)	Indian Ridge / Summer Fashion
		Cockney Lass (ch 1983)	Camden Town / Big Bugs Bomb

Great Field is the highest-rated representative to date by the 2002 Prix du Jockey Club fourth Great Pretender, who also showed useful form when winning both his starts over hurdles (including a listed event) before being sent to stud. A son of perennial champion jumps sire King's Theatre, Great Pretender sired a couple of notable performers before Great Field, the Paul Nicholls-trained pair Ptit Zig (a high-class hurdler/chaser at up to twenty-five furlongs) and Mr Mole (a quirky McManus-owned two-mile chaser who lost his way in 2016/17 after a stable switch). Great Field is the fourth foal out of the unraced Eaton Lass and her first winner (he was successful twice over hurdles as a juvenile in France for Emmanuel Clayeux), though his four-year-old half-brother Deadheat (by Buck's Boum) also won over both hurdles and fences at up to two and a quarter miles in the French Provinces in the spring. Eaton Lass has since produced a 2014 Anzillero gelding called Unexcepted, who has yet to race. This pedigree had something to recommend it even before Great Field arrived, though. His grandam Cockney Lass was a smart and thoroughly genuine mile and a quarter Flat performer, whose biggest win came in the 1987 Tattersalls Rogers Gold Cup (then a Group 2) for Dermot Weld. Her full brother was the 1997 Irish Champion Hurdle winner Cockney Lad (who was ridden by future Flat champion jockey Richard Hughes), who also showed useful form at up to twenty-five furlongs over fences later in his career. Great Field may well stay further given the chance (he is so far unraced beyond two and a quarter miles), but he looks sure to be kept at two miles at present given his exuberant style of racing.

History suggests that headstrong front-running two-mile chasers usually tend to come off second best when they bump into a true top-notcher. In the 'seventies, Tingle Creek, for example, was comprehensively beaten by both Pendil and Bula when he met them, and the Dickinsons' prolific trailblazer I'm A Driver was on the receiving end of a three-nil defeat in head to heads with Night Nurse later that decade. More recently, the top-class novice Sanctuaire was put firmly in his place by his contemporary Sprinter Sacre when they clashed the following season, with connections even desperately resorting (unsuccessfully) to waiting tactics on their final two meetings. All of which bodes well for the standard-setting Douvan and Altior should they encounter Great Field in the next season, though supporters of the last-named can point to several so-called 'tearaways' in the past who went on to prove themselves the best around—Dunkirk, Anaglogs Daughter and Desert Orchid are just three which spring to mind. As alluded to earlier, the very best of Great Field has almost certainly yet to be seen and he should warrant the utmost respect in top company in 2017/18, when he promises to be a particularly exhilarating ride, to say the least, for whoever gets the leg up. *W. P. Mullins, Ireland*

GREAT FIGHTER 7 b.g. Street Cry (IRE) – Evil Empire (GER) (Acatenango (GER)) **h130**
[2016/17 h122: h16d⁴ h18.9v⁶ h20s h19.4g⁵ h15.6g³ h15.6g⁴ h16d* h16.2g* Apr 26] useful handicap hurdler: improved and won at Ayr and Perth (by 4½ lengths from Mountain Kingdom) last 2 starts, both in April: stays 19f: acts on good to soft going: in headgear last 4 starts: usually races towards rear, often travels strongly. *Jim Goldie*

GREAT HALL 7 b.g. Halling (USA) – L'Affaire Monique (Machiavellian (USA)) **h116**
[2016/17 h116: h20m⁴ h16.5d³ h15.8g Jun 26] fairly useful handicap hurdler: stays 2½m: acts on good to firm and good to soft going: in cheekpieces last 2 starts: subsequently useful winner on Flat for Mick Quinn. *Kevin Frost*

GREAT LINK 8 b.g. Rail Link – The Strand (Gone West (USA)) [2016/17 c119, h107: **c–** c25.2gᵖᵘ h20.5d² h20s³ h20.5d⁵ h15.9v⁵ h16d³ Feb 17] leggy gelding: formerly fair hurdler/ **h89** fairly useful chaser, well below best in 2016/17: stays 2½m: acts on good to firm and heavy going: has worn blinkers, including last 5 starts: has worn tongue tie, including in 2016/17. *Lawney Hill*

GREAT ROAR (USA) 9 b.g. Thunder Gulch (USA) – Boasting (USA) (Kris S (USA)) **h–** [2016/17 h15.7gᵖᵘ h20.6mᵖᵘ Apr 9] well held in maidens on Flat: fair form in bumpers: no form over hurdles: usually in tongue tie. *Ronald Thompson*

GREAT TEMPO (FR) 4 b.g. Great Pretender (IRE) – Prima Note (FR) (Nononito (FR)) **h115** [2016/17 h16.9s⁵ h16.9s⁴ h17.4s² h16.2v* h18.9s h15.5d h16d h19.9s Apr 1] rather leggy gelding: third foal: half-brother to French hurdler Livingstone Devaig (2¼m winner, by Zambezi Sun): dam French hurdler (2m/19f winner): fairly useful hurdler: won juvenile maiden at Hexham in December: left P. Lenogue after third start: unproven beyond 17f: acts on heavy going: in cheekpieces last 2 starts. *David Pipe*

GREAT TRY (IRE) 8 b.g. Scorpion (IRE) – Cherry Pie (FR) (Dolpour) [2016/17 h20g **h–** Oct 23] tall, useful-looking gelding: bumper winner: fairly useful hurdler in 2014/15, behind in handicap only subsequent outing: would have stayed beyond 2½m: acted on soft going: dead. *Paul Nicholls*

GREEN FLAG (IRE) 10 b.g. Milan – Erin Go Brea (IRE) (Un Desperado (FR)) **c112** [2016/17 c23.4vᵖᵘ c23.4v⁵ c26.2d³ Apr 10] tall, workmanlike gelding: winning hurdler: fair **h–** chaser: stays 4m: acts on good to firm and heavy going. *Lucinda Russell*

GREENLAW 11 b.g. Helissio (FR) – Juris Prudence (IRE) (Law Society (USA)) [2016/17 **c118** c124, h–: c24g c26.2mᶠ May 29] lengthy gelding: winning hurdler: fairly useful handicap **h–** chaser: stayed 3¼m: acted on good to firm and heavy going: tried in cheekpieces: wore tongue tie: front runner/raced prominently: dead. *Charlie Longsdon*

GREEN LIGHT 6 b.g. Authorized (IRE) – May Light (Midyan (USA)) [2016/17 h15.6gᶠ **h94 p** Jan 3] useful on Flat, stays 1½m: held in third when fell last in maiden won by Fattsota at Musselburgh on hurdling debut: open to improvement. *Brian Ellison*

GREEN OR BLACK (IRE) 5 gr.m. Zebedee – Boucheron (Galileo (IRE)) [2016/17 **h89 p** h16.3g³ Apr 1] fairly useful maiden on Flat (stays 1¼m): showed aptitude when 15¾ lengths third of 11 to Excellent Team in novice at Stratford on hurdling debut: will prove best at sharp 2m: should do better. *Neil Mulholland*

GREEN TIKKANA 4 gr.f. Tikkanen (USA) – Think Green (Montjeu (IRE)) [2016/17 **b72** b12.4d⁶ b12.4d⁶ b16s⁴ b15.7s⁶ Mar 8] leggy filly: first foal: dam (h68) in frame in bumpers/ over hurdles: poor form in bumpers. *James Ewart*

GREEN WINTER (IRE) 9 ch.g. Well Made (GER) – Assistine (IRE) (Oscar (IRE)) **c–** [2016/17 c27.5mᵖᵘ May 20] multiple winning pointer: modest form only start in bumpers: pulled up in novice hunter on chasing debut. *J. R. Bryan*

GREENWORLDSOLUTION 5 b.g. Lucarno (USA) – Basford Lady (IRE) (Accordion) **h63** [2016/17 b62: h18.9v h19.3d⁶ Dec 13] behind in bumpers/novice hurdles. *Jennie Candlish*

GREEN ZONE (IRE) 6 b.g. Bushranger (IRE) – Incense (Unfuwain (USA)) [2016/17 **h97** h97: h16.2d h22.1m h16.2d⁶ h16.2s⁶ h20.2s* h20.2g³ h20.2g* h20.2sᵖᵘ h17.1d⁵ h24.7gᶠ h21.4d⁶ h21.4s³ h19.4dᵖᵘ h20.6s⁵ h19.4g h16d Jan 14] modest handicap hurdler: won at Perth in July (conditionals event) and September: stays 21f: acts on soft going. *Lisa Harrison*

GREGARIOUS (IRE) 4 gr.g. Big Bad Bob (IRE) – Sense of Greeting (IRE) (Key of **h111** Luck (USA)) [2016/17 h16s h15.9v³ h16s* h16d* h16g Apr 29] well-made gelding: fair maiden on Flat, stays 1m: fair form over hurdles: won at Sandown in February (novice) and March (juvenile handicap): will prove best at 2m: acts on soft going: in hood/tongue tie last 4 starts: front runner/races prominently. *Lucy Wadham*

GREXIT (IRE) 6 b.g. Oratorio (IRE) – Baboosh (IRE) (Marju (IRE)) [2016/17 h109: **h97** h16.2m³ h22.1m³ h20.9d³ h20.1g⁶ h16.4sᵖᵘ h15.6gᵖᵘ Mar 1] little impact in Irish points: modest maiden hurdler: stayed 2¾m: acted on soft and good to firm going: tried in cheekpieces: dead. *Lucinda Russell*

GREYBOUGG 8 gr.g. Tobougg (IRE) – Kildee Lass (Morpeth) [2016/17 c96, h–: **c130** c20.2dᵘʳ c19.2vᵘʳ c20.2sᵖᵘ c15.9s² c16.4s³ c16.4g³ c20a* Apr 1] lengthy gelding: winning **h–** hurdler: useful handicap chaser: won novice event at Uttoxeter on final start by 7 lengths from Buttercup: stays 3m, but at least as effective at shorter: acts on good to firm and heavy going: has worn hood: usually leads. *Nigel Hawke*

GREYED A (IRE) 6 gr.g. Daylami (IRE) – Broadcast (Broadsword (USA)) [2016/17 **h105** h20g⁶ h16.8s² h19.5d* h19.5s³ h23.8d⁶ h21.6sᵖᵘ Feb 26] €5,000 3-y-o: seventh foal: half-brother to fairly useful hurdler/chaser Kilronan High (19f-21f winner, by Mountain High), stays 3m, and a winning pointer by Turtle Island: dam (c65) temperamental maiden jumper: maiden pointer: fair handicap hurdler: won at Lingfield in November: stays 19f: acts on soft going: in cheekpieces final start: front runner/races prominently: temperament under suspicion. *Dr Richard Newland*

GREY GOLD (IRE) 12 gr.g. Strategic Choice (USA) – Grouse-N-Heather (Grey Desire) **c146** [2016/17 c152, h–: c19.4s⁵ c15.2d² c15.5v* c15.7dᵖᵘ c16v⁵ Feb 25] rather leggy gelding: **h–** winning hurdler: smart handicap chaser: won by 2 lengths from Dream Bolt at Sandown in February: ran poorly both subsequent starts: stays 2½m, races mainly at 2m: acts well on heavy going: often races prominently. *Kerry Lee*

GREY LIFE 11 gr.g. Terimon – More To Life (Northern Tempest (USA)) [2016/17 c121, **c58** h105: h18.6g⁴ h15.8d⁵ c16s h20.3s c15.2d c17.2s⁴ Mar 12] compact gelding: modest **h90** maiden hurdler: fairly useful handicap chaser at best, well below form in 2016/17: unproven beyond 2m: acts on soft and good to firm going: tried in cheekpieces/tongue tie in 2016/17. *Laura Morgan*

GREY MESSENGER (IRE) 8 gr.g. Heron Island (IRE) – Turlututu (FR) (Turgeon **c60** (USA)) [2016/17 h–: h23g³ h23d³ h22g h24g⁶ h20mᵖᵘ h20.3m h18.5m c20m⁴ c20.2fᵘʳ Nov **h69** 27] sturdy gelding: poor maiden hurdler/chaser: best effort at 23f: wears tongue tie. *Emma Baker*

GREY MONK (IRE) 9 gr.g. Alderbrook – Thats The Bother (IRE) (Roselier (FR)) **c–** [2016/17 c–, h112: h23.3d h23.1d* h23.1g h21.3sᵖᵘ h23.1s⁵ h21.2s⁴ h23.1g⁶ Mar 27] **h108 §** maiden point winner: fair handicap hurdler: won at Market Rasen in May: let down by jumping only start in chases: stays 23f: acts on good to firm and heavy going: usually in headgear: wears tongue tie: front runner/races prominently: hard to catch right. *Sara Ender*

GREY STORM (IRE) 6 gr.g. September Storm (GER) – Lady Blayney (IRE) (Mazaad) **h–** [2016/17 h–p: h20.5dᵖᵘ h22.7sᵖᵘ Nov 5] won Irish point on debut: no form over hurdles: in tongue tie final start. *Rose Dobbin*

GREY WARBLER 5 gr.m. Notnowcato – Cetti's Warbler (Sir Harry Lewis (USA)) **b87** [2016/17 b15.7s² b16v³ Feb 24] third foal: dam (c110/h94) 2m-21f hurdle/chase winner: fair form when placed in bumpers at Southwell and Warwick: will prove suited by 2½m. *Stuart Edmunds*

GREYWELL BOY 10 gr.g. Fair Mix (IRE) – Rakajack (Rakaposhi King) [2016/17 c–, **c–** h–: c15.5sᶠ Dec 2] good-topped gelding: maiden hurdler: fairly useful chaser at best: **h–** stayed 2½m: acted on heavy going: sometimes in headgear: dead. *Harry Fry*

GRIESENAU (IRE) 11 b.g. Luso – Persian Wonder (IRE) (Persian Mews) [2016/17 c–x, **c– x** h–: h15.3m⁶ h21.6g⁴ h20g Jul 12] winning hurdler: maiden chaser (often made mistakes), **h63** fair at best: stayed 21f: acted on soft going: wore hood: in tongue tie last 4 starts: usually raced nearer last than first: dead. *Paul Henderson*

GRIFFINGTON 8 b.g. Fantastic Spain (USA) – Sound Check (Formidable (USA)) **h–** [2016/17 h21.9dᵖᵘ Apr 16] in hood, showed nothing in novice hurdle on debut. *Grace Harris*

GRIMLEY GIRL 11 b.m. Sir Harry Lewis (USA) – Grimley Gale (IRE) (Strong Gale) **c–** [2016/17 c108, h112: h16.7d³ May 25] winning pointer: fair handicap hurdler/chaser: stays **h108** 21f: acts on heavy going: front runner/races prominently. *Henry Oliver*

GRIMTHORPE 6 ch.g. Alflora (IRE) – Sally Scally (Scallywag) [2016/17 b15.7g Jun 7] **b–** tailed off in bumper on debut. *Tina Jackson*

GRIS DE PRON (FR) 4 b.g. Gris de Gris (IRE) – Say Say (FR) (Garde Royale) [2016/17 **h116** h17.9d h16.9g⁴ h16s⁵ h16.2d* h16.7d⁵ Apr 27] fifth foal: dam (h117), French 17f/19f hurdle winner, also 11.5f/12.5f winner on Flat: fairly useful form over hurdles: won juvenile maiden at Hereford in March and novice at Market Rasen on final outing: left Francois Nicolle after second start: unproven beyond 17f: acts on soft going: in hood last 3 starts, in tongue tie last 2: often travels strongly. *Oliver Greenall*

GRISEDENUIT (FR) 5 b.m. Gris de Gris (IRE) – Ambacity (FR) (Sagacity (FR)) **h82** [2016/17 h57: h15.8g h15.9g⁴ h15.8g⁴ h15.8d h15.7g h15.8d Apr 16] poor maiden hurdler: raced around 2m: acts on soft going: in hood last 2 starts: often races towards rear. *Trevor Wall*

GRIVELIN (FR) 6 ch.g. Martaline – Griva (FR) (Discover d'Auteuil (FR)) [2016/17 **h–** h15.8d⁶ Jul 13] well held in novice hurdle on debut. *Jonjo O'Neill*

GROOMED (IRE) 9 b.g. Acclamation – Enamoured (Groom Dancer (USA)) [2016/17   **c107**
c107, h–: h19.9g h19.3g[6] c16.3s* c17.2d c20v[pu] c15.2d[6] c19.1s[pu] Mar 3] big gelding: **h58**
winning hurdler: fair handicap chaser: won at Newcastle in December: stayed 21f: acted on
good to firm and heavy going: sometimes wore headgear/tongue tie: dead. *Sue Smith*

GROOVEJET 6 b.m. Cockney Rebel (IRE) – Vino Veritas (USA) (Chief's Crown (USA))   **h108**
[2016/17 h15.8d[3] h16d[3] h16s h16.8g Mar 16] sparely-made mare: useful on Flat, stays
14.5f: fair form over hurdles. *Richard Spencer*

GROUNDUNDERREPAIR (IRE) 6 b.g. Milan – Discerning Air (Ezzoud (IRE))   **h110**
[2016/17 b100: ab16g[3] h19.1v[2] h20.5v[3] h16v* h20.5g[5] h21d Apr 26] placed 2 of 3 starts in   **b81**
bumpers: fair form over hurdles: won maiden at Lingfield in February: will stay further
than 2½m: acts on heavy going. *Warren Greatrex*

GROVE FIELD (IRE) 10 ch.g. Moscow Society (USA) – Wall-Nut Grove (IRE) (Satco   **c– x**
(FR)) [2016/17 h21.2g[6] Nov 10] poor handicap hurdler: maiden chaser, often let down by   **h61**
jumping: stays 3m: acts on good to firm going: often in cheekpieces. *David Brace*

GROVE PRIDE 12 b.g. Double Trigger (IRE) – Dara's Pride (IRE) (Darazari (IRE))   **c–**
[2016/17 c–, h–: c32.5g c27.5g[pu] h23.9d h23.1g[6] h23m h20g Sep 6] lengthy gelding: **h85**
modest handicap hurdler: useful chaser at best, no form since 2014/15: stays 29f: acts on
heavy going: sometimes in cheekpieces in 2016/17. *Alastair Ralph*

GROVE SILVER (IRE) 8 gr.g. Gamut (IRE) – Cobbler's Well (IRE) (Wood Chanter)   **c123**
[2016/17 c116, h–: c29.1g[2] c21.2g[3] c26.6g[3] c22.5v* c32.4s[F] c27.6d[5] c26.9v[pu] c28s[6] c20v*   **h–**
c20.6v[3] c23.8g[5] Apr 26] rather leggy gelding: winning hurdler: fairly useful handicap
chaser: won at Uttoxeter in November and Carlisle in March: stays 29f, effective at shorter
when conditions are testing: acts on heavy going: has worn headgear, including in 2016/17:
in tongue tie first 2 starts. *Jennie Candlish*

GROW NASA GROW (IRE) 6 ch.g. Mahler – Dereenavurrig (IRE) (Lancastrian)   **h–**
[2016/17 b86: h15.8s Apr 30] fair form in bumpers: 66/1, well held in maiden at Uttoxeter
on hurdling debut. *Peter Winks*

GUANCIALE 10 b.g. Exit To Nowhere (USA) – Thenford Lass (IRE) (Anshan) [2016/17   **c100 §**
c96§, h88§: c21.2g[3] c21g[3] c20g[6] h16.3m[pu] c16g* c15.7d* c16s[4] c19.4g c17g[4] Apr 23]   **h– §**
lengthy gelding: winning hurdler: fair handicap chaser: won at Ffos Las in November and
Wincanton in December: stays 3m: acts on good to firm and heavy going: wears
cheekpieces: has worn tongue tie: unreliable. *Dai Burchell*

GUANTOSHOL (IRE) 6 ch.g. Sholokhov (IRE) – Glicine (GER) (Tiger Hill (IRE))   **h91**
[2016/17 h101: h15.8g[6] h20.3v[4] h16.8g[5] h15.8d[2] Oct 28] modest maiden hurdler: left
Venetia Williams after second start: unproven beyond 2m: acts on heavy going: in tongue
tie last 2 starts. *Ian Williams*

GUARACHA 10 b.g. Halling (USA) – Pachanga (Inchinor) [2016/17 c104, h100: c15.7m[4]   **c89**
h17.7g[6] May 29] fair handicap hurdler/chaser in 2015/16, below best in 2016/17: stays   **h77**
2½m: acts on heavy going: has worn headgear, including last 4 starts. *Alexandra Dunn*

GUARDS CHAPEL 9 b.g. Motivator – Intaaj (IRE) (Machiavellian (USA)) [2016/17 c–,   **c–**
h106§: h21g h19.1g[3] h20.5g* h16m[4] Nov 8] rather leggy gelding: fair handicap hurdler: **h112 §**
won at Plumpton in October: well held only outing over fences: stays 21f: acts on good to
firm and good to soft going: wears headgear: often races towards rear: moody. *Gary Moore*

GUD DAY (IRE) 9 gr.g. Aussie Rules (USA) – Queen Al Andalous (IRE) (King's Best   **c–**
(USA)) [2016/17 c–, h79: h19g[3] h24s[5] May 18] close-coupled gelding: poor handicap   **h73**
hurdler: winning chaser: stays 2½m: acts on good to firm and heavy going: wears headgear:
has worn tongue tie. *Conor Dore*

GUIDING STARS (FR) 4 b.g. Bonbon Rose (FR) – Furika (FR) (Kadalko (FR))   **b–**
[2016/17 b13.7g Nov 8] 4/1, 11 lengths eleventh of 15 to White Valiant in junior bumper at
Huntingdon on debut, ridden when not clear run 2f out. *Harry Whittington*

GUITAR PETE (IRE) 7 gr.g. Dark Angel (IRE) – Innishmore (IRE) (Lear Fan (USA))   **c114 +**
[2016/17 c133, h–: c21s c17g h16d c17s[6] c25v[5] h19.7m[2] Apr 13] rather leggy gelding: **h138 +**
useful handicap hurdler: second of 5 at Wetherby (neck behind Applesandpierres) final
start: handicap chaser, just fair form in 2016/17: left Ms Sandra Hughes after fifth start:
stays 2½m: acts on good to firm and heavy going: wore headgear/tongue tie for former
yard. *Nicky Richards*

GUITING POWER 6 b.g. Lucarno (USA) – Sparkling Jewel (Bijou d'Inde) [2016/17   **h71**
h55: h21.6g h19.9d h25.6g[2] h23.8d[5] h24d[pu] h23.9g h21.9d[5] Apr 16] poor maiden hurdler:
stays 3¼m: acts on soft going: often in visor. *Nigel Twiston-Davies*

GULLY'S EDGE 7 b.g. Kayf Tara – Shuildante (IRE) (Phardante (FR)) [2016/17 h132p, **c118 x** b96: c20g⁴ c23.4s³ c25.2d⁵ c20g³ Apr 15] big gelding: useful hurdler: fairly useful maiden **h–** chaser, has been let down by jumping: stays 3m: acts on soft going: in headgear first 3 starts: wears tongue tie. *Malcolm Jefferson*

GULSHANIGANS 5 b.g. Sakhee (USA) – Gulshan (Batshoof) [2016/17 b–: b16.7g⁵ **h115** h16.4gᵘʳ h20g³ h20d⁴ h20.7d⁵ h23.8d² h21.2s² h21.4m³ h24.3d Apr 21] big gelding: poor **b67** form in bumpers: fairly useful maiden hurdler: stays 3m: acts on soft and good to firm going: in tongue tie last 4 starts. *Nigel Twiston-Davies*

GUNFLEET (IRE) 5 b.g. Oscar (IRE) – Lady Lincon (IRE) (Great Palm (USA)) **b96** [2016/17 b16.3g* Apr 1] fourth foal: half-brother to useful/ungenuine hurdler Silver Eagle (2¾m-3m winner, by Presenting): dam unraced half-sister to smart hurdler/useful chaser (stayed 3m) Kicks For Free: 16/1 and hooded, won 8-runner bumper at Stratford on debut by 2¼ lengths from Solomon Grey, despite racing freely. *Emma Lavelle*

GUNMONEY (IRE) 12 br.g. High Roller (IRE) – Tenpence Princess (IRE) (Prince Bee) **c119** [2016/17 c26.3g³ Apr 27] multiple point winner: fairly useful chaser: third in hunter at Cheltenham only outing in 2016/17: stays 3¼m: acts on heavy going: wears headgear. *G. T. H. Bailey*

GUNNER LINDLEY (IRE) 10 ch.g. Medicean – Lasso (Indian Ridge) [2016/17 h83: **h81** h16.8s h16.8s² h17.2g³ h16.2s² h16.2d² h18.1m h16.8d Dec 2] poor maiden handicap hurdler: unproven beyond 17f: acts on soft going: has worn headgear, including in 2016/17: usually races close up. *Stuart Coltherd*

GURKHA BRAVE (IRE) 9 b.g. Old Vic – Honeyed (IRE) (Persian Mews) [2016/17 **c132** c122, h122: c15.9m* c20.1g³ c20.1s⁴ c19.4g⁵ c17.1d³ c19.4mᶠ c20d* c19.9g Mar 25] **h–** rangy gelding: useful hurdler: useful handicap chaser: won novice events at Carlisle in May and October (by 2½ lengths from Ash Park): stays 2½m: acts on soft and good to firm going. *Karen McLintock*

GURTEEN (IRE) 7 b.g. Golan (IRE) – Aussieannie (IRE) (Arapahos (FR)) [2016/17 **c140 p** c17d³ h20s³ h16v⁶ h24d Apr 27] fifth foal: half-brother to smart hurdler/useful chaser Head **h121** of The Posse (2m-2½m winner, by Supreme Leader): dam, pulled up in points, sister to fairly useful chaser (stayed 25f) Call Me Dara: bumper winner: fairly useful hurdler: useful form when third in maiden at Navan (2¾ lengths behind Anibale Fly) on chasing debut: should prove suited by at least 2½m: acts on heavy going: should do better over fences. *Robert Tyner, Ireland*

GUSTAVE MAHLER (IRE) 7 ch.g. Mahler – Kloetta (IRE) (Grand Lodge (USA)) **h106** [2016/17 b17g* b16g* b16.4s h19.5g³ h19.4g³ h19.4g⁵ Jan 27] €13,000 3-y-o, £9,000 **b93** 5-y-o: sturdy gelding: second foal: dam Scandinavian 1m winner: maiden point winner: fair form in bumpers: won at Aintree (conditionals/amateur event) in May and Worcester in June: fair form in novice/maiden hurdles: front runner/races prominently. *Alastair Ralph*

GUSTAV (IRE) 7 b.g. Mahler – Pakaradyssa (FR) (Roakarad) [2016/17 h–, b–: h21g³ **c91** h21m⁶ h25.6gᵖᵘ h21.6s c23.6d⁶ c18.9s c20.2s² c19.2s³ c20.9d* Mar 25] compact gelding: **h91** modest maiden hurdler: modest form over fences: won novice handicap at Stratford in March: stays 21f: acts on good to soft going: in cheekpieces last 5 starts. *Zoe Davison*

GUSTY ROCKY (IRE) 8 b.g. King's Theatre (IRE) – Liss A Paoraigh (IRE) (Husyan **h137** (USA)) [2016/17 h20gᵖᵘ h24g* h20g³ h20g⁵ h24d⁴ h24d³ h19g Apr 16] fairly useful on Flat, stays 2¼m: useful handicap hurdler: won at Gowran in June: good efforts when fourth at Gowran in October and third at Clonmel in November: stays 3m: acts on good to soft going: races well off pace, often travels strongly. *Patrick J. Flynn, Ireland*

GVS IRPORTENSA (IRE) 5 ch.m. Trans Island – Greenfield Noora (IRE) (Topanoora) **b88** [2016/17 b15.7d² b16.8g² b16.7g⁵ Mar 27] eighth foal: half-sister to a winning pointer by Presenting: dam unraced sister to fairly useful hurdler (stayed 21f) No Where To Hyde: fair form in bumpers: in cheekpieces second start. *Warren Greatrex*

GWAFA (IRE) 6 gr.g. Tamayuz – Atalina (FR) (Linamix (FR)) [2016/17 h134p: h15.7m* **h141** h16.7g³ h16m⁵ Oct 16] sturdy gelding: useful hurdler: won Swinton Handicap at Haydock in May by 1¼ lengths from All Set To Go: creditable 2 lengths third to Red Tornado in Summer Hurdle (Handicap) at Market Rasen in July: reportedly lame final outing: raced around 2m: acts on soft and good to firm going: usually races prominently. *Paul Webber*

GWENCILY BERBAS (FR) 6 b.g. Nickname (FR) – Lesorial (FR) (Lesotho (USA)) **c132** [2016/17 h147: c18g⁴ c20d² c19d⁶ Dec 28] smart hurdler: useful form first 2 starts over **h–** fences, when fourth in Buck House Novices' Chase at Punchestown (5 lengths behind

Three Stars) and second in maiden at Navan (11 lengths behind Our Duke): visored, well below form final start: stays 2½m: acts on heavy going: usually in tongue tie: front runner/races prominently. *Alan Fleming, Ireland*

GWILI SPAR 9 ch.g. Generosity – Lady of Mine (Cruise Missile) [2016/17 c–, h58§: h20.3s⁴ h19.9g h24dᵖᵘ h23.3gᵘʳ h22g h24gᵖᵘ h20g c16g* c19.7gᵘʳ c15.7gᶠ Apr 21] poor maiden hurdler: poor form over fences: won handicap chase at Uttoxeter in September: stays 2½m: acts on good to soft going: has worn hood, including in 2016/17: wears tongue tie: not straightforward (no battler). *Laura Hurley* **c71 § h69 §**

GWORN 7 b.g. Aussie Rules (USA) – Crochet (IRE) (Mark of Esteem (IRE)) [2016/17 h16d⁵ h16.2sᶠ h16s⁵ h15.6g⁶ Jan 3] fair on Flat, stays 1¼m: lightly-raced maiden over hurdles, fair form: will prove best at 2m. *R. Mike Smith* **h105**

GYPSY GIRL 6 ch.m. Proclamation (IRE) – Argentine Rose (Bertolini (USA)) [2016/17 b16.2m May 29] first foal: dam unraced: tailed off in mares bumper. *Jim Goldie* **b–**

H

HAAFAPIECE 4 ch.g. Haafhd – Bonnet's Pieces (Alderbrook) [2016/17 b16s* b15.8s² b16.7d Apr 27] fifth foal: half-brother to 3 winners, including fairly useful hurdler/useful chaser Actinpieces (2m-25f winner, by Act One) and fair hurdler/chaser Bonnet's Vino (19f-21f winner, by Grape Tree Road): dam (c90/h90), maiden hurdler/chaser (stayed 2½m), half-sister to useful hurdler/smart chaser (stays 25f) Helpston: fairly useful form in bumpers: won maiden at Kempton in February. *Pam Sly* **b95**

HAAFFA SOVEREIGN 6 ch.g. Haafhd – Royal Nashkova (Mujahid (USA)) [2016/17 h15.7dᵖᵘ h16gᵖᵘ Mar 17] modest maiden on Flat, stays 1½m: pulled up both starts over hurdles. *Laura Morgan* **h–**

HAB SAB (IRE) 5 b.g. Papal Bull – Tamburello (IRE) (Roi Danzig (USA)) [2016/17 b–: b17.7g⁶ b13.6v⁴ b16.2g² Apr 21] good-topped gelding: little show in bumpers/novice hurdle. *Linda Jewell* **h– b–**

HADFIELD (IRE) 5 b.g. Sea The Stars (IRE) – Rezyana (AUS) (Redoute's Choice (AUS)) [2016/17 h121: h16g h20d³ h21.4sᵖᵘ h20.5s⁵ h19.9s³ Apr 1] fairly useful handicap hurdler: stays 2½m: acts on soft going: wears cheekpieces: in tongue tie last 4 starts: usually races towards rear. *Neil Mulholland* **h116**

HADLEY 4 b.g. Royal Applause – Brush Strokes (Cadeaux Genereux) [2016/17 h16gᵖᵘ h16sᵖᵘ Nov 23] modest maiden on Flat, raced mainly at 6f: pulled up both starts over hurdles. *Tracy Waggott* **h–**

HADRIAN'S APPROACH (IRE) 10 b.g. High Chaparral (IRE) – Gifted Approach (IRE) (Roselier (FR)) [2016/17 c141x, h–p: c23.8m c26g⁴ c26gᶠ Mar 16] lengthy gelding: winning hurdler: smart handicap chaser at best (won 2014 bet365 Gold Cup at Sandown): fourth in Hennessy Gold Cup at Newbury (6¾ lengths behind Native River) in November: stayed 29f: acted on soft going: sometimes wore cheekpieces: usually raced towards rear: prone to mistakes: dead. *Nicky Henderson* **c138 x h–**

HAGREE (IRE) 6 b.g. Haatef (USA) – Zuniga's Date (USA) (Diesis) [2016/17 h16gᵖᵘ May 3] modest on Flat, stays 8.5f: tongue tied when pulled up in seller on hurdling debut. *Neil King* **h–**

HAG STONE 6 b.g. Kayf Tara – Caoba (Hernando (FR)) [2016/17 b–: b17m² b16g³ h19.9g h16g³ h15.7g* h16s⁴ h19.9dᵖᵘ Dec 26] fair form in bumpers: similar level over hurdles: won novice at Southwell in October: dead. *Tom Lacey* **h110 b86**

HAHNENKAM (IRE) 7 b.g. Stowaway – Bahnasa (IRE) (Shardari) [2016/17 h83p: h16d⁴ h16d* h16.3m⁴ h16.7g⁶ h17.7d⁴ h19.9g⁴ h19.8m³ h16.8g² c18g² h19g c15.9s⁵ h19gᶠ Mar 30] well held in Irish maiden point: fair form in bumpers: won at Worcester in June: fair maiden hurdler: modest form in novice handicap chases: left Seamus Durack after ninth start, Ali Stronge after eleventh: may prove best at short of 2½m: acts on good to firm and good to soft going: tried in hood: often wears tongue tie: races towards rear. *Johnny Farrelly* **c98 h101 b87**

HAIGHALL (IRE) 5 b.g. Scorpion (IRE) – Longwhitejemmy (IRE) (Rashar (USA)) [2016/17 b16.8d⁵ Dec 2] 16/1, shaped as if needing run when fifth in bumper at Sedgefield. *Chris Grant* **b75**

HAIL THE BRAVE (IRE) 8 ch.g. Lahib (USA) – Parverb (IRE) (Parliament) [2016/17 h61: h17.2g Jun 1] winning hurdler, no form since 2014/15: often wears headgear: front runner/races prominently. *Michael Smith* **h–**

HAINAN (FR) 6 gr.g. Laveron – Honor Smytzer (Highest Honor (FR)) [2016/17 h119: c20d c20s c23.4s² c24.2s* c19.4s³ c24s⁵ Mar 18] fairly useful hurdler: useful form over fences: won novice handicap at Wetherby in January by 9 lengths from Crosspark: will stay long distances: acts on heavy going: usually leads. *Sue Smith* **c130 h–**

HALCYON DAYS 8 b.g. Generous (IRE) – Indian Empress (Emperor Jones (USA)) [2016/17 c84, h–: c16.4s² c15.6d³ c15.6g³ c15.5g* c16.9d² c15.6v* c15.9s* c16.3s³ c15.7s* c19.2s³ c16.3v* c15.9d* Apr 5] maiden hurdler: fair handicap chaser: much improved and enjoyed very successful season, winning at Ayr in October, Hexham and Carlisle in December, Catterick in February, Newcastle in March and Carlisle in April, half of them novice events: acts on heavy going: wears headgear: front runner/races prominently. *Rebecca Menzies* **c113 h–**

HALLINGHAM 7 b.g. Halling (USA) – In Luck (In The Wings) [2016/17 h–: h19g⁵ h15.9g* h18.7m³ h16.2f³ Jun 5] stocky, compact gelding: modest handicap hurdler: won at Plumpton in May: stays 19f: acts on good to firm going: in headgear last 4 starts: has joined Ken Cunningham-Brown. *Chris Gordon* **h87**

HALLINGS COMET 8 ch.g. Hallings (USA) – Landinium (ITY) (Lando (GER)) [2016/17 c–, h–: h16gᵘʳ h16.3g Apr 15] fair hurdler at best, no form in 2016/17: winning chaser: unproven beyond 2m: acts on good to firm going. *Shaun Lycett* **c– h–**

HALLO DOLLY 11 b.m. Turtle Island (IRE) – Monty's Lass (IRE) (Montelimar (USA)) [2016/17 c24.2m⁵ May 3] first foal: dam (c93) 3¼m chase winner: point winner: 28/1, fifth in hunter at Exeter on chasing debut. *Mrs S. Prouse* **c72**

HALLSTATT (IRE) 11 ch.g. Halling (USA) – Last Resort (Lahib (USA)) [2016/17 h90: h15.8d⁶ Oct 28] fair on Flat, stays 2¼m: lightly-raced maiden hurdler: raced around 2m: acts on soft going: in tongue tie last 3 starts. *John Mackie* **h70**

HALLY'S KITCHEN 5 b.m. Getaway (GER) – Crystal Ballerina (IRE) (Sadler's Wells (USA)) [2016/17 b16.8s Feb 12] £4,500 3-y-o: third foal: dam unraced sister to useful hurdler/fairly useful chaser (2½m/21f winner) Sizing Symphony: tailed off in bumper. *Fiona Shaw* **b–**

HAMMER GUN (USA) 4 b.g. Smart Strike (CAN) – Caraboss (Cape Cross (IRE)) [2016/17 h15.8m Oct 30] fairly useful on Flat, stays 1¼m: breathing problem when well held on hurdling debut. *Derek Shaw* **h–**

HAMMERSLY LAKE (FR) 9 b.g. Kapgarde (FR) – Loin de Moi (FR) (Loup Solitaire (USA)) [2016/17 c–p, h138: h20.6g³ c19.2g* c19.4g⁵ c15.9s² c21d³ c19.1d³ c20.4gᵖᵘ c16.5g* Apr 28] good-topped gelding: useful handicap hurdler: useful chaser: won novices at Market Rasen in August and Huntingdon in April: placed in Grade 2 novice at Cheltenham (4 lengths behind Le Prezien) in November and graduation event at Ascot (1¼ lengths behind Top Notch) in December: stays 21f: acts on good to firm and heavy going: often races towards rear. *Nicky Henderson* **c140 h139**

HANDPICKED 6 b.m. King's Theatre (IRE) – Hand Inn Glove (Alflora (IRE)) [2016/17 h93, b76: h15.8m⁵ h15.8g May 31] modest maiden hurdler: best effort at 21f. *Henry Daly* **h83**

HANDS OF STONE (IRE) 5 b.g. Shantou (USA) – Hayabusa (Sir Harry Lewis (USA)) [2016/17 b16s³ b16.7s⁴ b17v² Mar 9] €35,000 3-y-o: lengthy, rather unfurnished gelding: second foal: dam (b93), placed in bumpers, half-sister to useful chaser (21f-3¼m winner) Gunner Welburn: fair form in bumpers: bred to stay 2½m. *Evan Williams* **b89**

HANDSOME BUDDY (IRE) 10 br.g. Presenting – Moya's Magic (IRE) (Phardante (FR)) [2016/17 c97, h–: c24dᶠ May 7] maiden hurdler: modest chaser at best, has lost his form: stays 29f: acts on soft and good to firm going: often wears headgear: temperamental. *Michael Gates* **c– § h–**

HANDSOME DAN (IRE) 11 b.g. Busy Flight – Beautiful City (IRE) (Jurado (USA)) [2016/17 c–, h115: h18.6g² h20.6g⁴ h20.2g h18.6g⁴ h23.1mᵖᵘ Apr 17] fairly useful handicap hurdler: second at Market Rasen in June: winning chaser: stays 3m, effective at shorter: acts on good to firm and good to soft going: tried in blinkers/tongue tie: races well off pace. *Sarah Hollinshead* **c– h115**

HANDSOME SAM 6 ch.g. Black Sam Bellamy (IRE) – Rose Marine (Handsome Sailor) [2016/17 h110: h24.4g² h26v c19.2s² c23g⁴ c24gᵖᵘ c24m⁶ Apr 4] lengthy gelding: runner-up on second of 2 starts in Irish points: fair hurdler: similar form over fences: will prove best up to 3m: acts on heavy going: in headgear last 3 starts. *Alan King* **c106 h108**

HANDY ANDY (IRE) 11 b.g. Beneficial – Maslam (IRE) (Robellino (USA)) [2016/17 **c125 §**
c121§, h109§: c21g* h18.5g⁴ h26.5mᵖᵘ c25.5g⁶ c25g Oct 21] lengthy gelding: winning **h103 §**
pointer: fair handicap hurdler: fairly useful handicap chaser: won at Newton Abbot in May:
stays 3½m: acts on heavy going: wears headgear: usually wears tongue tie: usually races
prominently: unreliable. *Colin Tizzard*

HANG 'EM HIGH (IRE) 7 br.g. Westerner – Reticent Bride (IRE) (Shy Groom (USA)) **h–**
[2016/17 h16g Jul 26] tailed off in maiden hurdle (tongue tied). *Evan Williams*

HANG FIRE (IRE) 7 ch.m. Shirocco (GER) – Ambrosine (Nashwan (USA)) [2016/17 **h72**
h84, b–: h16g⁵ h16.3m² h15.8g⁶ h20g⁵ h22g Jul 28] poor maiden hurdler: unproven beyond
2m: tried in cheekpieces/tongue tie. *Tony Carroll*

HANIBAL LECTOR (IRE) 10 b.g. Dr Massini (IRE) – Pure Indulgence (IRE) **h–**
(Aristocracy) [2016/17 h21.4sᵖᵘ Jan 7] maiden Irish pointer: pulled up in novice on
hurdling debut. *Mark Gillard*

HANNAH JUST HANNAH 8 gr.m. Proclamation (IRE) – Evaporate (Insan (USA)) **h104**
[2016/17 h107: h16s³ h16.3g² h19.5s⁵ Dec 27] angular mare: fair maiden hurdler: unproven
beyond 2m: acts on heavy going (won bumper on good to firm): has worn hood, including
in 2016/17: wears tongue tie. *Matthew Salaman*

HANNAH'S PRINCESS (IRE) 8 b.m. Kalanisi (IRE) – Donna's Princess (IRE) **h119**
(Supreme Leader) [2016/17 h127: h19d³ h20.3s⁶ h19.8s⁶ Jan 7] good-topped mare: fairly
useful handicap hurdler: third at Warwick in May: stays 21f: acts on heavy going: often
races in rear. *Warren Greatrex*

HANNIBAL THE GREAT (IRE) 9 b.g. Milan – Town Gossip (IRE) (Indian Ridge) **c–**
[2016/17 h–: c19.4gᵖᵘ c21.1dᵖᵘ c23m² Dec 8] lengthy gelding: Irish maiden point winner: **h–**
winning hurdler: no form in chases: should stay beyond 2½m: acts on good to soft going:
wears tongue tie. *Charlie Longsdon*

HANNINGTON 6 ch.g. Firebreak – Manderina (Mind Games) [2016/17 h67: h16.2d **h–**
Jun 29] fair on Flat, stays 1¼m: no form over hurdles: in cheekpieces/tongue tie sole start
in 2016/17: has joined Michael Appleby. *Barry Brennan*

HANSUPFORDETROIT (IRE) 12 b.g. Zagreb (USA) – Golden Needle (IRE) (Prince **c105**
of Birds (USA)) [2016/17 c–, h113: h23.6d⁶ h23.9g⁶ c20.9d³ c20.3s⁴ c25.2sᶠ c19.4g⁴ **h74**
Apr 9] strong gelding: fair handicap hurdler/chaser: stays 3m: acts on heavy going: often
wears cheekpieces: has worn tongue tie, including in 2016/17: often races towards rear.
Bernard Llewellyn

HA'PENNY WOODS (IRE) 7 b.g. Wareed (IRE) – Muriel's Pride (IRE) (Mister Lord **h–**
(USA)) [2016/17 h105: h21.3g Oct 28] fair hurdler: best effort at 23f: dead. *Chris Grant*

HAPPY CHANCE 6 b.m. Indian Danehill (IRE) – Red Nose Lady (Teenoso (USA)) **b–**
[2016/17 b17.7d⁶ b16.8g Aug 10] third foal: half-sister to bumper winner/top-class hurdler
Unowhatimeanharry (21f-3m winner, by Sir Harry Lewis): dam (h89) 2m-2½m hurdle
winner (stayed 3m): well held in bumpers: unseated in point in March. *Philip Hide*

HAPPY DIVA (IRE) 6 b.m. King's Theatre (IRE) – Megans Joy (IRE) (Supreme Leader) **h131**
[2016/17 h111p: h15.7s³ h15.8g² h16.3d⁵ h21.6s* h24.1s* h24.4d⁴ h19.8s² h24.4s² h24.3d²
Apr 21] good-bodied mare: useful hurdler: won mares handicaps at Fontwell in December
and Wetherby in January: stays 3m: acts on soft going: wears tongue tie: usually travels
strongly. *Kerry Lee*

HAPPY HOLLOW 5 b.g. Beat Hollow – Dombeya (IRE) (Danehill (USA)) [2016/17 **b103**
b103p: b16.7g* May 6] fairly useful form in bumpers, completed hat-trick at Market Rasen
in May. *Alan Swinbank*

HAPPY JACK (IRE) 6 b.g. Elusive City (USA) – Miss Pelling (IRE) (Danehill Dancer **h–**
(IRE)) [2016/17 h–: h20gᵖᵘ h15.8v h15.7dᵖᵘ Feb 26] no form over hurdles: left Michael
Wigham after first start: in blinkers last 2 starts. *Dai Burchell*

HAPPY RING HOUSE (IRE) 8 b.g. Muhtathir – Pink Topaz (USA) (Tiznow (USA)) **c–**
[2016/17 c24.1gᵖᵘ Apr 29] winning pointer: pulled up in novice hunter on chasing debut.
Miss S. Whitehead

HARANGUE (IRE) 9 br.g. Street Cry (IRE) – Splendeur (FR) (Desert King (IRE)) **c–**
[2016/17 c120, h104: h20v h20g c22m c21.4gᵖᵘ c22.5g Jul 29] fair hurdler/fairly useful **h–**
chaser at best, well below that in 2016/17: stays 3¼m: acts on heavy going: usually wears
headgear: wears tongue tie: has joined Peter Fahey. *Paul John Gilligan, Ireland*

HARD AS A ROCK (FR) 6 b.g. Network (GER) – Fany Noune (FR) (Reste Tranquille **b–**
(FR)) [2016/17 b80p: b15.7m[6] Oct 29] tall, useful-looking gelding: modest form on first of
2 starts in bumpers. *Emma Lavelle*

HARDLINE (IRE) 5 b.g. Arcadio (GER) – Hidden Reserve (IRE) (Heron Island (IRE)) **h118 p**
[2016/17 b16d b16m[3] b16g* h16.2d[F] h16v[F] b16d[2] b16v[2] Mar 18] €155,000 3-y-o: third **b105**
foal: half-brother to fair hurdler Wolfslair (2¾m winner, by Yeats): dam (b103), bumper
winner, sister to fairly useful hurdler/chaser (stayed 2½m) Crocodiles Rock: won point on
debut: useful bumper performer: won maiden at Thurles in November: fell late both starts
in maiden hurdles, running to fairly useful level both times: bred to stay at least 2½m:
wears hood: usually travels strongly: remains with potential over hurdles. *Gordon Elliott,
Ireland*

HARDROCK DAVIS (FR) 6 b.g. Saint des Saints (FR) – Trumpet Davis (FR) (Rose **h66**
Laurel) [2016/17 b79: b15.8g[5] h19.5v h15.7g[5] Mar 28] signs of ability in bumpers/over **b71**
hurdles: tried in hood. *Tom George*

HARD TOFFEE (IRE) 6 b.g. Teofilo (IRE) – Speciale (USA) (War Chant (USA)) **b81**
[2016/17 b74: b15.7v[6] May 10] modest form in bumpers: fair on Flat, stays 1½m.
Conrad Allen

HARDTOROCK (IRE) 8 b.g. Mountain High (IRE) – Permissal (IRE) (Dr Massini **c–**
(IRE)) [2016/17 h56, b82: h21.6g h23g c23g[pu] c24.2m[ur] c25.1m[pu] Oct 14] sturdy gelding: **h64**
winning pointer: no form over hurdles/in chases: in cheekpieces last 2 starts: wears tongue
tie: has joined Seamus Mullins. *Liam Corcoran*

HAREFIELD (IRE) 4 b.g. Doyen (IRE) – Bobbi's Venture (IRE) (Bob Back (USA)) **b95**
[2016/17 b16.8s[2] b16.3g[4] Mar 25] £25,000 3-y-o: rangy, rather unfurnished gelding:
second foal: dam, ran twice in bumpers, half-sister to high-class hurdler/top-class chaser
(stays 25f) Menorah: fairly useful form in bumpers: fourth in Goffs UK Spring Sales
Bumper at Newbury in March. *Alan King*

HARGAM (FR) 6 gr.g. Sinndar (IRE) – Horasana (FR) (Galileo (IRE)) [2016/17 h156: **h139**
h16s[3] h16m* h16.4s h15.7d h16.3d h21.1g Mar 15] rather leggy gelding: useful hurdler
nowadays: won listed event at Kempton (by neck from Court Minstrel) in October: well
held in handicaps after: unproven beyond 17f: acts on soft and good to firm going: tried in
cheekpieces. *Nicky Henderson*

HARLEYS MAX 8 b.g. Winged Love (IRE) – Researcher (Cosmonaut) [2016/17 c84, **c96**
h72: c20.1m[3] c19.2d[4] c15.6g c20d[4] c21.5g[2] c19.9d[pu] c20.1s* c16.3s[2] Jan 23] maiden **h–**
hurdler: modest handicap chaser: won at Newcastle in January: stays 2¾m: acts on soft and
good to firm going: often races in rear. *Susan Corbett*

HARLY FOREST 4 b.g. Holy Roman Emperor (IRE) – Goslar (In The Wings) [2016/17 **h–**
h16.2d[pu] Jun 4] no form on Flat: pulled up in juvenile on hurdling debut. *Brian Ellison*

HARMONICAL 6 ch.m. Desideratum – First Harmony (First Trump) [2016/17 h22.1g[5] **h–**
h23.3d[pu] Jun 19] modest maiden on Flat, best effort at 2m: winning pointer: little impact in
2 starts over hurdles. *Mike Sowersby*

HARPS OF BRETAGNE 5 b.m. Monsieur Bond (IRE) – Lavernock Lady (Don't Forget **h–**
Me) [2016/17 h17.2m[pu] May 30] poor maiden on Flat: pulled up in novice on hurdling
debut. *Lisa Williamson*

HARRIET'S ARK 10 ch.m. Sir Harry Lewis (USA) – Brush The Ark (Brush Aside **h60**
(USA)) [2016/17 h62: h20.3s[5] h21.6d[3] Jun 1] little form over hurdles. *Julian Smith*

HARRIS (IRE) 10 b.g. Beneficial – Porter Tastes Nice (IRE) (Dry Dock) [2016/17 c–, h–: **c– §**
c26g[pu] Feb 22] multiple point winner: winning hurdler: one-time fair chaser, pulled up in **h–**
hunter sole start in 2016/17: stays 25f: acts on soft going: usually wears headgear:
temperamental. *Miss E. Smith-Chaston*

HARRISONS PROMISE 5 b.m. Westerner – Hello My Lovely (Presenting) [2016/17 **b86**
b16.4s[2] Jan 7] £8,500 3-y-o: first foal: dam (c85/h71), ungenuine 3m chase winner, sister
to useful chaser (winner up to 25f) Another Promise: 80/1, second in mares bumper at
Newcastle (1¼ lengths behind Illwalktheline) in January. *Susan Corbett*

HARRISTOWN 7 ch.g. Bering – New Abbey (Sadler's Wells (USA)) [2016/17 c105, **c–**
h121: h23.1g h23.1d[4] h24d* h23g[5] Jul 26] smallish gelding: fairly useful handicap hurdler: **h123**
won at Southwell in July: fair form over fences: stays 3m: acts on good to firm and heavy
going: wears cheekpieces. *Charlie Longsdon*

HARRY BOSCH 7 b.g. Kyllachy – Fen Guest (Woodborough (USA)) [2016/17 h15.7g[pu] **h–**
Aug 23] modest on Flat, stays 8.5f: pulled up in seller on hurdling debut. *Julia Feilden*

HARRY HUNT 10 b.g. Bertolini (USA) – Qasirah (IRE) (Machiavellian (USA)) [2016/17 **c109 §**
c–, h117: h26.4m⁶ h24.2g³ h24.4g⁵ h24.4g h21.2s c21.3d³ Mar 31] lengthy gelding: fair **h109 §**
handicap hurdler/chaser: stays 3¼m: acts on heavy going: has worn headgear: unreliable.
Graeme McPherson

HARRY HUSSAR 7 b.g. Primo Valentino (IRE) – Jessie May (IRE) (Supreme Leader) **h–**
[2016/17 b15.7d⁵ h21.3sᵘʳ Jan 6] poor form in bumpers: behind when unseated rider 2 out **b67**
in maiden on hurdling debut. *Peter Niven*

HARRY THE LEMMON (IRE) 11 br.g. Milan – Na Habair Tada (IRE) (Supreme **c–**
Leader) [2016/17 c25v⁶ c24.2g⁶ Apr 25] point winner: lightly-raced hurdler: fair chaser at **h–**
best: left Turlough O'Connor after first start: stays 25f: best form on soft/heavy going:
usually wears cheekpieces: tried in tongue tie. *Miss L. V. Horner*

HARRY THE VIKING 12 ch.g. Sir Harry Lewis (USA) – Viking Flame (Viking (USA)) **c124 §**
[2016/17 c127§, h–: c29.1g c26.2d² c32.4s* c30g c32.6s⁴ c26.2d⁴ c30.6g Apr 28] useful- **h–**
looking gelding: winning hurdler: fairly useful handicap chaser: won at Kelso in December:
stays 33f: acts very well on heavy going: wears headgear: front runner/races prominently:
temperamental. *Sandy Thomson*

HARRY TOPPER 10 b.g. Sir Harry Lewis (USA) – Indeed To Goodness (IRE) (Welsh **c141 x**
Term) [2016/17 c29.5sᵖᵘ c24.2s⁴ c26s⁴ Mar 4] useful-looking gelding: winning hurdler: **h–**
useful handicap chaser nowadays: should stay long distances: acts on heavy going: wears
cheekpieces: not a fluent jumper. *Kim Bailey*

HARRYTUR 6 b.g. Sula Blue – Millento (Lyphento (USA)) [2016/17 b16.8g b16g Sep **b–**
12] maiden pointer: well held in bumpers. *Debra Hamer*

HARTFORTH 9 ch.g. Haafhd – St Edith (IRE) (Desert King (IRE)) [2016/17 h114: **h115 §**
h24.3s* h24.3v⁶ h22.7v⁶ h22.7d⁶ Apr 10] smallish gelding: fairly useful handicap hurdler:
won at Ayr in December: stays 27f: acts on heavy going: tried in cheekpieces: often races
prominently: unreliable. *Donald Whillans*

HARTSIDE (GER) 8 b.g. Montjeu (IRE) – Helvellyn (USA) (Gone West (USA)) **h113**
[2016/17 h116: h16.7g² h16.2d h15.8g h16d⁶ h16.6g⁶ h16s³ h15.7s⁶ h16.8s³ h16.7s⁶ h17d²
h16.6s⁴ h16d Mar 21] sturdy gelding: fair handicap hurdler: unproven beyond 17f: acts on
heavy going: often wears headgear: often races in rear. *Peter Winks*

HARVEY (IRE) 6 br.m. Presenting – One Swoop (IRE) (Be My Native (USA)) [2016/17 **h74**
b–: b16g h21v h15.9s⁶ h16g Mar 18] sturdy mare: little form in bumpers/hurdles. **b–**
Laura Mongan

HASH BROWN (IRE) 8 ch.g. Vinnie Roe (IRE) – Keralba (USA) (Sheikh Albadou) **c130**
[2016/17 c126, h132: c21sᵖᵘ c26mᵖᵘ c20s³ c22.5s* c24dᵖᵘ c21g⁵ c24.5d⁴ Apr 29] useful **h–**
hurdler: useful handicap chaser: won at Galway in October: stays 25f: acts on heavy going:
in tongue tie last 2 starts: often races towards rear. *M. Hourigan, Ireland*

HASSLE (IRE) 8 b.g. Montjeu (IRE) – Canterbury Lace (USA) (Danehill (USA)) **h123**
[2016/17 h–: h16g* h15.8g* h16.7g h20.6g² h17.2g* h16.7g* h15.8s⁶ Oct 15] sturdy
gelding: fairly useful hurdler: won maiden at Fakenham in May, conditionals novice at
Uttoxeter in July, novice at Cartmel in August and listed handicap at Market Rasen (by 1½
lengths from Kapstadt) in September: stays 21f: acts on soft going: wears headgear: front
runner/races prominently. *Dr Richard Newland*

HASTEN WELL (IRE) 9 b.g. Indian Danehill (IRE) – Glentrasna Beauty (IRE) (Bob's **h–**
Return (IRE)) [2016/17 h23g Jul 12] awarded point in 2014: tailed off in maiden on
hurdling debut: wore cheekpieces. *Hannah James*

HASTRUBAL (FR) 7 br.g. Discover d'Auteuil (FR) – Miss Montrose (Tina's Pet) **h105**
[2016/17 h86, b81: h15.8s h15.8g⁴ h21.6d⁵ h15.7sᶠ Jan 21] useful-looking gelding: fair
form over hurdles: best effort at 2¾m. *Henry Daly*

HATCHER (IRE) 4 b.g. Doyen (IRE) – African Keys (IRE) (Quws) [2016/17 ab16g³ **b99**
b16.3d² b15.8g* Apr 17] fourth foal: half-brother to fair chaser Flash Tommie (2½m
winner, by City Honours): dam unraced half-sister to smart hurdler/top-class chaser (stayed
25f) China Rock and useful hurdler/chaser (stayed 21f) Barrakilla: fairly useful form in
bumpers: won at Huntingdon in April: keen-going sort, but bred to stay further than 2m: in
hood last 2 starts. *Dan Skelton*

HATEM (FR) 4 gr.g. Kendargent (FR) – Escolhida (IRE) (Montjeu (IRE)) [2016/17 h16g⁴ **h101**
h15.8g h15.8g⁴ Apr 28] fair form over hurdles. *Caroline Bailey*

HATTAAB 4 b.g. Intikhab (USA) – Sundus (USA) (Sadler's Wells (USA)) [2016/17 **b83**
b15.6g² Jan 3] £3,500 3-y-o: half-brother to several winners on Flat, including smart 7f/1m
winner Zawraq (by Shamardal): dam 1¼m winner: 3/1, second in bumper at Musselburgh
(12 lengths behind Beyond The Clouds) in January. *Kevin Morgan*

HATTERS RIVER (IRE) 10 b.g. Milan – Curzon Ridge (IRE) (Indian Ridge) [2016/17 c93x, h–: h22m⁴ h22g³ Aug 11] good-bodied gelding: fair handicap hurdler: maiden chaser: stays 2¾m: acts on soft and good to firm going: tried in cheekpieces: has worn tongue tie, including last 2 starts: often let down by jumping over fences. *Ali Stronge* **c– x h107**

HATTONS HILL (IRE) 8 b.g. Pierre – Cluain Chaoin (IRE) (Phardante (FR)) [2016/17 h–: c24.2spu c20.1s³ c25.2dpu c20.1v³ c24.2s* c24.2v* Mar 28] lightly-raced hurdler: modest form over fences: won handicaps at Hexham (twice) in March: stays 3m: best form on soft/heavy going: in cheekpieces last 2 starts. *Henry Hogarth* **c85 h–**

HAUGHTONS BRIDGE (IRE) 9 gr.g. Cloudings (IRE) – Miss Badsworth (IRE) (Gunner B) [2016/17 c79, h77: c16.3g c25.8g³ c22.6mpu Jul 10] point winner: maiden hurdler: poor maiden chaser: best efforts around 2½m: acts on good to firm and heavy going: sometimes wears tongue tie. *Martin Hill* **c66 h–**

HAUL US IN (IRE) 5 br.m. Kalanisi (IRE) – Shuilan (IRE) (Good Thyne (USA)) [2016/17 b16s⁵ b17s h20.5s h19.3s³ h20.1s³ Mar 16] fifth foal: sister to bumper winner Notre Ami and half-sister to fairly useful hurdler Shuilamach (2½m winner, by Presenting): dam (h113), bumper/19f hurdle winner, out of half-sister to Welsh National winner Jocks Cross: little impact in bumpers: modest form over hurdles: often races towards rear. *Lucinda Russell* **h95 b59**

HAUT BAGES (FR) 5 b.g. Archange d'Or (IRE) – Rotina (FR) (Crystal Glitters (USA)) [2016/17 h102p: h17m² May 13] fair form over hurdles: won point in April: raced around 2m: acts on good to firm and good to soft going: tried in tongue tie. *Oliver Sherwood* **h108**

HAVANA DANCER (IRE) 8 b.m. Flemensfirth (USA) – Senorita Rumbalita (Alflora (IRE)) [2016/17 h17.8g h16.4s* h16g³ h20.5s* h23.6d h20d³ h20s³ c20.1v³ c21m* c17.4s³ Nov 9] €11,000 4-y-o: second foal: dam (c115/h124) 2m-21f hurdle/chase winner: fair handicap hurdler: won at Roscommon in June and Sligo in July: similar form over fences: won maiden at Fairyhouse in October: best effort when third in listed mares novice at Bangor in November: stays 21f: acts on soft and good to firm going: tried in cheekpieces: wears tongue tie: usually races prominently. *Colin Bowe, Ireland* **c111 h101**

HAVANA JACK (IRE) 7 b.g. Westerner – Hackler Poitin (IRE) (Little Bighorn) [2016/17 c–, b–: c24.2d⁶ c23.8m³ c21.2m⁴ c19.9g⁵ c26.2d* Apr 10] winning pointer: modest hunter chaser: won maiden at Kelso in April: stays 3¼m: acts on good to firm and good to soft going: in headgear last 4 starts: usually races towards rear. *L. Kerr* **c96**

HAVE A GO HERO (IRE) 9 b.g. Flemensfirth (USA) – Blue Bank (IRE) (Burslem) [2016/17 c24s³ c23.5v³ c25.7v³ c21.7v⁴ c22.4spu c25.2d* c28.4g Apr 15] winning pointer: fair chaser: won novice at Hereford in March: stays 25f: acts on good to soft going: in visor last 2 starts. *Dai Williams* **c110**

HAVE ONE FOR ME (IRE) 10 b.g. Sonus (IRE) – Dunmanogue (IRE) (Supreme Leader) [2016/17 h88: h21.2g⁴ May 10] winning pointer: modest form at best over hurdles. *Victor Thompson* **h–**

HAVE THIS FOR NOW (IRE) 4 b.g. Daylami (IRE) – Annas Theatre (King's Theatre (IRE)) [2016/17 b13.7d⁴ b16s Feb 10] £19,000 3-y-o: first foal: dam, unraced, out of half-sister to high-class 2m chaser Nakir: modest form in bumpers. *Gary Moore* **b84**

HAVE YOU HAD YOURS (IRE) 11 br.g. Whitmore's Conn (USA) – Mandys Moynavely (IRE) (Semillon) [2016/17 c–, h–: c15.6d⁵ c19.9g⁴ c26.2mpu c20.1dpu c21.2d c18s⁵ c19.3d c16.3g⁴ c15.6g⁴ Apr 25] maiden hurdler: modest handicap chaser: stays 2½m: acts on heavy going: tried in cheekpieces. *Jane Walton* **c97 h–**

HAWAIAN ROSE 7 b.m. Helissio (FR) – Waimea Bay (Karinga Bay) [2016/17 h–§, b–§: h15.3m⁵ May 10] workmanlike mare: no form in bumpers/hurdles: in blinkers last 2 starts. *Colin Tizzard* **h–**

HAWAIIAN FREEZE 8 b.m. Avonbridge – Autumn Affair (Lugana Beach) [2016/17 h16g* h17g³ h17g⁵ h20g² h18m³ h16g⁶ h16vpu Feb 11] modest on Flat, stays 1½m: modest hurdler: won maiden at Les Landes in May: stays 2½m: best form on good going: tried in tongue tie. *James Moon, Jersey* **h88**

HAWDYERWHEESHT 9 b.g. Librettist (USA) – Rapsgate (IRE) (Mozart (IRE)) [2016/17 c63, h116: h16d May 2] fairly useful hurdler: let down by jumping on sole start over fences: stays 21f: acts on soft and good to firm going: wears headgear/tongue tie: front runner/races prominently. *David Dennis* **c– h–**

HAWK GOLD (IRE) 13 ch.g. Tendulkar (USA) – Heiress of Meath (IRE) (Imperial **h– §**
Frontier (USA)) [2016/17 h63§: h15.9g h17.7g May 29] poor hurdler: stays 21f: acts on
good to firm and good to soft going: wears headgear: unreliable. *Michelle Bryant*

HAWK HIGH (IRE) 7 b.g. High Chaparral (IRE) – Septembers Hawk (IRE) **h133**
(Machiavellian (USA)) [2016/17 h133: h16.6g³ h21.1g h20g h16g Apr 22] close-coupled
gelding: useful handicap hurdler: unproven beyond 17f: acts on good to firm and heavy
going: wears headgear. *Tim Easterby*

HAWKHURST (IRE) 7 b.g. Flemensfirth (USA) – Silaoce (FR) (Nikos) [2016/17 h116: **c112 §**
h21.6d³ h23.9s⁴ c20.9sF c25.2d⁴ c22.3v⁴ c21.6sᵘʳ c21.1g³ Apr 7] Irish maiden point winner: **h120 §**
fairly useful form over hurdles: third in handicap at Fontwell in October: fair form over
fences: left Paul Nicholls after second start: stays 2¾m: best form on soft/heavy going:
sometimes in headgear: often races towards rear: quirky and not one to trust. *Ben Haslam*

HAYMOUNT (IRE) 8 ch.g. Presenting – Ali's Dipper (IRE) (Orchestra) [2016/17 h130: **c148**
h24d⁵ c20s* c19.5v² c24s⁴ c24s³ c31.8g³ c29d Apr 17] workmanlike gelding: useful **h–**
handicap hurdler: smart form over fences: won maiden at Punchestown (by 3½ lengths
from Coney Island) in November: second in Grade 2 novice (3¼ lengths behind Bellshill)
at Limerick in December and third in National Hunt Chase at Cheltenham (3¾ lengths
behind Tiger Roll) in March: stays 4m: acts on heavy going. *W. P. Mullins, Ireland*

HAZAMAR (IRE) 4 gr.g. Manduro (GER) – Hazarafa (IRE) (Daylami (IRE)) [2016/17 **h108**
h16m⁵ h15.8m² h15.8m³ h16.4s⁴ h15.7m⁵ h15.8m* h16gᵖᵘ Apr 29] good-topped gelding:
fair hurdler: won juvenile at Ludlow in April: raced only at 2m: acts on good to firm going:
in cheekpieces last 3 starts: wears tongue tie. *Sophie Leech*

HAZY TOM (IRE) 11 b.g. Heron Island (IRE) – The Wounded Cook (IRE) (Muroto) **c108**
[2016/17 c117, h–: c23gᵖᵘ c21m² c20.5m³ Apr 18] lengthy gelding: winning pointer: **h–**
winning hurdler: fair chaser: barely stays 3m: acts on soft and good to firm going: has worn
headgear: often races towards rear. *Miss K. Phillips-Hill*

HEAD HIGH (IRE) 4 gr.g. Mastercraftsman (IRE) – Elisium (Proclamation (IRE)) **h107**
[2016/17 h15.8s⁶ h16.6g⁵ h15.8d⁶ h15.8g* Apr 1] fair maiden on Flat: similar form over
hurdles: won maiden at Huntingdon in April: will prove best at sharp 2m. *Sarah Hollinshead*

HEAD HUNTER (IRE) 4 b.g. Rip Van Winkle (IRE) – Superfonic (FR) (Zafonic (USA)) **b85**
[2016/17 b15.8s³ Mar 5] 6,000 3-y-o: half-brother to several winners on Flat, including
12.5f winner Unrequited (by Authorized): dam French 11.5f winner: 14/1, third in bumper
at Huntingdon (3¾ lengths behind I Know U Too Well) in March. *Michael Scudamore*

HEADLY'S BRIDGE (IRE) 11 b.g. Tillerman – Brockton Flame (Emarati (USA)) **c106**
[2016/17 c110, h–: c19.4g⁶ c19.2s⁴ c25.2s⁴ c19.4dᵖᵘ Apr 16] strong gelding: winning **h–**
hurdler: fair handicap chaser nowadays: stays 2½m: acts on heavy going: usually races
towards rear. *Simon Earle*

HEAD SPIN (IRE) 9 b.g. Beneficial – Who Tells Jan (Royal Fountain) [2016/17 c99§, **c– x**
h–: c25.5d⁴ Apr 29] lengthy gelding: maiden hurdler/pointer: modest handicap chaser: **h–**
stays 3¼m: acts on good to firm and heavy going: wears headgear: usually wears tongue
tie: often let down badly by jumping. *Seamus Mullins*

HEAD TO THE STARS 6 br.g. Kayf Tara – Sail By The Stars (Celtic Cone) [2016/17 **h118**
h–, b66: h18.9v h20.5d* h20.5v² h25.5s⁴ Mar 11] fairly useful form over hurdles: won
novice at Leicester in December: bred to stay at least 3m: acts on heavy going. *Henry Daly*

HEAR NO EVIL (IRE) 5 b.g. Getaway (GER) – Listening (IRE) (King's Theatre (IRE)) **b96**
[2016/17 b16s³ b15.8g² Apr 9] €150,000 3-y-o: first foal: dam (h93), second in 2½m
hurdle, half-sister to smart hurdler (2m/17f winner) Moorish and to grandam of top-class
hurdler/chaser around 2m Altior: fairly useful form in bumpers: better effort when second
at Ffos Las in April. *Dan Skelton*

HEARTASIA (IRE) 4 b.f. Danehill Dancer (IRE) – Big Heart (Mr Greeley (USA)) **b90**
[2016/17 b14d⁵ b16d⁴ b16g* Apr 23] second foal: dam unraced: fair form in bumpers: won
mares event at Wetherby in April: tried in hood: wears tongue tie. *Susan Corbett*

HEARTENING 9 b.m. Wace (USA) – Heartleys Quest (IRE) (Broken Hearted) [2016/17 **h–**
h62: h16.8s h16.8m h22g h23g Aug 11] little form over hurdles: in blinkers last 3 starts.
Paul Phillips

HEAR THE CHIMES 8 b.g. Midnight Legend – Severn Air (Alderbrook) [2016/17 **h106**
h111: h16g⁵ h17.2g⁴ h15.7s h15.8s³ h15.7s⁶ h15.7g³ Apr 21] sturdy gelding: fair handicap
hurdler: unproven beyond 2m: best form on soft/heavy going: often races towards rear.
Shaun Harris

HEART O ANNANDALE (IRE) 10 b.g. Winged Love (IRE) – She's All Heart (Broken **c89 x** Hearted) [2016/17 c–x, h89: c20m⁵ c23.8m² c24.2g* c24.2g⁵ c24.2d² h25.4d c23.8s³ **h83** c23.8s³ c26.6g³ c26.3g³ h23.9g³ Apr 26] poor handicap hurdler: modest handicap chaser: won novice event at Hexham in May: stays 27f: acts on soft and good to firm going: wears headgear/tongue tie: poor jumper of fences. *Iain Jardine*

HEART OF KERNOW (IRE) 5 b.g. Fruits of Love (USA) – Rathturtin Brief (IRE) **h83** (Saddlers' Hall (IRE)) [2016/17 h16d Nov 16] £5,000 3-y-o: second foal: dam unraced sister to useful hurdler (2½m/23f winner) Tailor's Hall: 150/1, seventh in novice hurdle at Chepstow (27¼ lengths behind Copain de Classe) on debut. *Nigel Hawke*

HEATED DEBATE (IRE) 7 b.g. Kayf Tara – Liss A Chroi (IRE) (Exit To Nowhere **h87** (USA)) [2016/17 h16g³ h19.7g⁴ Oct 31] useful-looking gelding: placed all 3 starts in bumpers: modest form over hurdles. *Charlie Longsdon*

HEATHER BURNING (IRE) 6 b.g. Mountain High (IRE) – Go To Blazes (IRE) **b78** (Aahsaylad) [2016/17 b16.4s⁵ Dec 8] 20/1, fifth in bumper at Newcastle (8½ lengths behind Mayo Star) in December. *Rose Dobbin*

HEATH HUNTER (IRE) 10 b.g. Shantou (USA) – Deep Supreme (IRE) (Supreme **c–** Leader) [2016/17 c91, h125: h17.7d h16d h16d h15.7s h21s Feb 10] useful-looking **h81** gelding: fairly useful handicap hurdler at best, out of sorts in 2016/17: let down by jumping only chase start: stays 2½m: acts on heavy going: wears headgear: has worn tongue tie, including last 2 starts. *David Pipe*

HEATH KING (IRE) 7 b.g. Fruits of Love (USA) – Shamaiyla (FR) (Sendawar (IRE)) **h–** [2016/17 h19.9g Sep 18] well held completed start in Irish points: modest form in bumpers: no form over hurdles. *Miss Imogen Pickard*

HEAT STORM (IRE) 6 b.g. Lawman (FR) – Coconut Show (Linamix (FR)) [2016/17 **h–** h16.7vᵖᵘ h20.5gᵖᵘ h16s⁵ Jan 1] poor maiden on Flat, stays 9f: no form over hurdles. *James Unett*

HEAVENLY GAIT 5 b.m. Revoque (IRE) – Still Runs Deep (Karinga Bay) [2016/17 **b–** b16s⁶ b16.7s Dec 22] third foal: half-sister to fairly useful hurdler Lieutenant Miller (19f/2½m winner, by Beat All), stayed 23f: dam, little sign of ability, sister to useful/temperamental hurdler/chaser (stayed 3m) General Miller: modest form on Flat: no form in bumpers: tried in hood. *Jason Ward*

HEAVENLY PROMISE (IRE) 6 ch.m. Presenting – Ambrosia's Promise (IRE) **c67** (Minster Son) [2016/17 b16g b20g b18g h19.9g h21.7g⁵ h16d h20.3d⁵ h15.8v³ h15.8v⁶ **h78** c20.2s⁵ c15.7g⁵ Mar 28] rather unfurnished mare: first foal: dam (c107/h106), 2m hurdle **b–** winner (stayed 3m)/winning pointer, half-sister to useful chaser (winner up to 25f) Another Promise (by Presenting): no form in bumpers: poor form over hurdles/fences: left James Joseph Mangan after third start: tried in hood: usually races towards rear. *John Groucott*

HEAVEN SCENT 4 ch.f. Phoenix Reach (IRE) – Hel's Angel (IRE) (Pyrus (USA)) **h101** [2016/17 h16.7g* h17.2d³ h17s⁵ h15.7d² h16.8s⁴ h19.9v² Feb 12] modest on Flat, stays 1¼m: fair form over hurdles: won juvenile at Market Rasen in July: left Ann Duffield after second start: stays 2½m: acts on heavy going: front runner/races prominently. *Donald McCain*

HECANSTING (IRE) 6 b.g. Scorpion (IRE) – Grandy Hall (IRE) (Saddlers' Hall (IRE)) **h–** [2016/17 h19.3dᵖᵘ Jan 1] placed in Irish maiden points: pulled up in novice on hurdling debut: dead. *Patrick Holmes*

HEDLEY LAMARR (IRE) 7 b.g. Gold Well – Donna's Tarquin (IRE) (Husyan (USA)) **c121** [2016/17 h122: c21.4s c24.1s⁴ c22.7g⁴ c25.2s⁵ c22.6g⁴ c23.8m³ Apr 25] fairly useful **h–** hurdler: similar form over fences: stays 23f: tried in cheekpieces. *Jonjo O'Neill*

HEIGHNOW 6 b.m. Indian Danehill (IRE) – Mooreheigh (Sir Harry Lewis (USA)) **h–** [2016/17 h–, b–: h17.7vᵖᵘ Jan 8] no form in bumpers/over hurdles: tried in hood. *Conrad Allen*

HEILAN REBEL (IRE) 7 b.g. Where Or When (IRE) – Nordice Equity (IRE) (Project **h57** Manager) [2016/17 h78, b70: h22.7d h22.7s h18.1s⁵ h19sᵖᵘ Dec 5] poor maiden hurdler: in headgear last 2 starts: tried in tongue tie: often races prominently. *N. W. Alexander*

HEIST (IRE) 7 b.g. Galileo (IRE) – Matikanehanafubuki (IRE) (Caerleon (USA)) [2016/17 **c127** c113, h102: c15.6d³ c20.3gᵘʳ h20d* c16s³ c19.9g* c25g* c23.8d³ c25.6m* h20.1g³ Apr 25] **h120** compact gelding: fairly useful handicap hurdler: won at Bellewstown in June: third at Hexham in April: fairly useful handicap chaser: won at Kilbeggan in August and September, and Ludlow in October: stays 3¼m: acts on soft and good to firm going: wears headgear/tongue tie: usually responds generously to pressure. *Patrick Griffin, Ireland*

HE KNOWS MY NAME (IRE) 8 b.m. Kayf Tara – Tigrera (IRE) (Helissio (FR)) **c–** [2016/17 h23.3v³ c19.9g Apr 21] first foal: dam, ran once on Flat in France, half-sister to useful hurdler/fairly useful chaser (2m winner) Topacio: placed in points: poor form over hurdles: tailed off in mares maiden on chasing debut: best effort at 23f: wears tongue tie. *R. K. Watson, Ireland* **h69**

HE LIKES TOBOUGGIE 6 ch.g. Tobougg (IRE) – Tamise (USA) (Time For A Change **h–** (USA)) [2016/17 b60: h16gᶠ May 22] poor form in bumpers: yet to be asked for effort when fell heavily 4 out in maiden at Fakenham on hurdling debut: tried in tongue tie. *Neil King*

HELIUM (FR) 12 b.g. Dream Well (FR) – Sure Harbour (SWI) (Surumu (GER)) [2016/17 **c118** c131, h–§: c18g⁵ c15.2m⁴ c15.8d⁴ c17.5sᵖᵘ h16g² h15.7d³ c15.5d³ c16mᵖᵘ Apr 18] strong **h102** gelding: fair handicap hurdler: fairly useful handicap chaser: stays 2½m: acts on any going: tried in cheekpieces: has worn tongue tie. *Alexandra Dunn*

HELLAVASHOCK 4 gr.g. Hellvelyn – Surprise Statement (Proclamation (IRE)) [2016/17 **h–** h15.8mᵖᵘ Oct 5] angular gelding: fair maiden on Flat, stays 1¼m: pulled up in juvenile maiden on hurdling debut: wore blinkers: has joined Alistair Whillans. *Giles Bravery*

HELLO BERTIE 5 b.g. Kayf Tara – I'm Delilah (Overbury (IRE)) [2016/17 b16.2g³ **b97** Apr 28] first foal: dam (c141/h121), 2m/17f hurdle/chase winner, half-sister to fair hurdler/ smart chaser up to 2½m Watch My Back: 4/1, third in bumper at Perth (3¾ lengths behind Planet Nine) in April. *Malcolm Jefferson*

HELLO FELLAS (IRE) 5 b.g. Gold Well – Archdale Ambush (IRE) (Heron Island **b96** (IRE)) [2016/17 b16s² b15.6g b16d⁶ Mar 21] €20,000 3-y-o: first foal: dam, once-raced in points, half-sister to fairly useful hurdlers/useful chasers Saints And Sinners (stays 2½m) and General Principle (stays 29f), both by Gold Well: fairly useful form in bumpers: best effort when second at Ayr in January. *Nicky Richards*

HELLO GEORGE (IRE) 8 b.g. Westerner – Top Ar Aghaidh (IRE) (Topanoora) **h131** [2016/17 h119: h18.5s⁵ h20.5v* Mar 4] lengthy gelding: useful handicap hurdler: won at Newbury (by 11 lengths from Spice Fair) in March: stays 21f: acts on good to firm and heavy going: in cheekpieces last 4 starts. *Philip Hobbs*

HELL'S KITCHEN 6 b.g. Robin des Champs (FR) – Mille Et Une (FR) (Trempolino **c132 P** (USA)) [2016/17 h127: c18.8d³ Nov 18] big, well-made gelding: useful hurdler: 3/1, **h–** shaped very well when third in maiden at Ascot (9 lengths behind Different Gravey) on chasing debut: should make considerable progress. *Harry Fry*

HELMSLEY FLYER (IRE) 7 b.g. Baltic King – Dorn Hill (Lujain (USA)) [2016/17 **h–** h15.7dᵖᵘ h15.8sᶠ h16vᶠ Mar 12] fair on Flat, stays 16.5f: no form over hurdles. *Trevor Wall*

HELMSLEY LAD 6 gr.g. Fair Mix (IRE) – Wuchowsen (IRE) (King's Ride) [2016/17 **h113** b89p: b16.8s² b15.7g² b16.8d⁴ h16.2v³ h19.9g² h23.3g⁴ Apr 25] fairly useful form **b97** in bumpers: won at Sedgefield in December: fair form over hurdles: usually leads. *Malcolm Jefferson*

HELPSTON 13 b.g. Sir Harry Lewis (USA) – Chichell's Hurst (Oats) [2016/17 c25.5g³ **c101** Apr 24] big, rangy gelding: placed in points: winning hurdler: one-time useful chaser for **h–** Pam Sly: stays 25f: acts on soft going: tried in cheekpieces/tongue tie. *S. R. Andrews*

HELUVAGOOD 5 b.g. Helissio (FR) – Cape Siren (Warning) [2016/17 b–: h21.6g h16s **h95** h16.8s h23.6v⁶ Mar 23] lengthy gelding: modest form over hurdles: likely to prove best up to 2½m: tried in tongue tie. *Victor Dartnall*

HENCHARD 6 b.g. Deltic (USA) – Kittenkat (Riverwise (USA)) [2016/17 h18.5d⁵ h21s **h85** Mar 30] second foal: dam (c108/h115), 2½m-25f hurdle/chase winner, stayed 4m: modest form on first of 2 starts over hurdles: should be suited by 2½m+. *Nick Mitchell*

HENLLAN HARRI (IRE) 9 br.g. King's Theatre (IRE) – Told You So (IRE) **c127** (Glacial Storm (USA)) [2016/17 c126, h124: c24gᵖᵘ c25dᵖᵘ h26.5m h23g⁵ h23.9g⁵ **h112** c22.4g³ c25.7v² c24g⁵ c20.9v* c23.8v² c23.8g³ c28.8g* Apr 29]

The affection that so many of jumping's followers hold for Sandown is not hard to understand. The layout of the steeplechasing course, in particular, may be eccentric but it provides some of the most spectacular sights in jumping. The seven obstacles that come thick and fast in the back straight, the last three plain fences known as the Railway fences, place the emphasis on quick and accurate jumping, and races can be won and lost there, particularly over two miles. The climb up the straight to the finish is severe until the ground levels out a hundred yards from the winning post, and Sandown's hill has become famous for producing dramatic finishes. The 1984 Whitbread Gold Cup will always be remembered as one of them, as the Queen Mother's Special Cargo, only fourth at the last fence and seemingly fighting a losing battle, came very late, sweeping past Plundering, Lettoch and his stablemate the top weight Diamond Edge (attempting his third win in the race) in the closing stages to snatch the race on the line where Special Cargo, Lettoch and Diamond Edge were separated by short heads. Diamond Edge's second victory in the race, three years earlier, had produced a similarly rousing climax as he staged a magnificent rally on the flat after looking beaten at the last, storming home between Father Delaney and lightweight Ottery News and hitting the front just fifty yards from home. That dramatic victory was an appropriate one to celebrate the twenty-fifth running of the Whitbread, a big handicap which, with the Hennessy Gold Cup, had ushered in the age of sponsored steeplechases and had created valuable opportunities for the staying steeplechasers at either end of the season.

Along with the King George VI Chase and the Cheltenham Gold Cup, the Hennessy and the Whitbread made up 'the big four', and both big handicaps became automatic targets in the late-'fifties and early-'sixties for the best of the staying chasers. Arkle and Mill House were the only ones to win all of 'the big four' but the winning roll in the Whitbread included other Cheltenham Gold Cup winners of that time, Pas Seul and What A Myth, while another, The Dikler, won the Whitbread in 1974 (on the disqualification of Proud Tarquin) and that great champion Desert Orchid won Sandown's feature in tremendous style in 1988, making nearly all and jumping superbly, before going on to add the Gold Cup to his string of successes the following year. Exactly when the quality of the fields for Sandown's end-of-season feature handicap began to fall from its heady heights is hard to pinpoint, but the development of other big races in Britain, including weight-for-age events, and the expansion of the Punchestown Festival in Ireland has provided plenty of alternatives which were not available to the likes of Diamond Edge, for example, a top-class chaser who won both his Whitbreads carrying top weight. The same went for a leading staying novice chaser like Lettoch for whom handicaps were still something of the norm after Cheltenham's Sun Alliance Chase had been run (Diamond Edge had been chased home by that season's Sun Alliance Chase winner Master Smudge when winning his first Whitbread in 1979). Lettoch came down when going well at the second last in the Sun Alliance won by A Kinsman who had his only other outing that season in the Golden Miller Handicap at Cheltenham's April fixture (the championship race at Aintree now known as the Mildmay Novices' Chase was still in its infancy).

Special Cargo's Whitbread coincided with a very dry spring in which firm or hard going was the order of the day for the jumpers—the going was hard at Sandown—and there were only thirteen runners. There were only thirteen in the latest running of Sandown's end-of-season feature too, an unusually small number for the bet365 Gold Cup, as the race is now known. As Special Cargo's Whitbread illustrated, however, a big field isn't a requirement for a spectacular race, and the bet365 Gold Cup turned into one of the most exciting of the latest season, producing a dramatic finish that will go down in the annals of the race. The Sandown Gold Cup may be no more than a shadow of the great event that it was in its very early days, but it is still a very valuable prize, with just the Grand National, the Scottish Grand National, the Hennessy (to be run as the Ladbrokes Trophy from 2017/18), the BetVictor Gold Cup and the Welsh Grand National worth more among the season's handicap chases. Top weight of 11-12 in the latest bet365 Gold Cup was carried by Theatre Guide who was running off a BHA handicap mark of 152, with Just A Par, the winner in 2015 and a close second in 2016, next on 11-9, ahead of the 2016 winner The Young Master (11-8) and two others who had run well in the race before, Le Reve (11-6) and The Druids Nephew (11-3). Doing Fine, a stablemate of The Young Master and The Druids Nephew and fresh from winning the race that used to be the Golden Miller at Cheltenham's April fixture (itself a shadow of the contest that regularly attracted Gold Cup winners and Sun Alliance Chase winners in the early-'eighties), started 9/2 favourite, ahead of 6/1-shots The Druids Nephew and Vyta du Roc, with Vyta du Roc's stablemate Sugar Baron, who had parted company

bet365 Gold Cup Handicap Chase, Sandown—a blanket finish to Sandown's end-of-season highlight, with 40/1-shot Henllan Harri edging out Vyta du Roc (far right) and Theatre Guide (noseband, left); the blundering Sugar Baron (No.11) drops back to seventh

with his rider at the first in the previous week's Scottish National, fellow novice Rock The Kasbah and The Young Master the only others at single-figure odds. The rank outsider at 40/1, racing from 4 lb out of the handicap, was Henllan Harri, a fairly useful chaser who had been plying his trade in class 3 and class 4 handicaps, ending a fairly long losing run when successful in a 0-120 handicap at Ffos Las in March. Ironically, Henllan Harri might not have been in the line-up at Sandown if he had run at Ludlow earlier in the week as intended (withdrawn with a vet's certificate with a minor foot problem).

Henllan Harri is best forcing the pace and, stepped up in trip at Sandown, he sprang the biggest surprise in Sandown Gold Cup history to give its Welsh stable its biggest win since Al Co (also at 40/1) in the 2014 Scottish Grand National. He had plenty of use made of him with trainer's son Sean Bowen giving him a well-judged ride after being allowed to control the tempo of the race. Pressing on in earnest from the Pond fence, Henllan Harri wasn't found wanting up the Sandown hill as challengers came at him from all sides. There were eight horses in with a chance jumping the last but Henllan Harri held on to win in a thrilling four-way photo with Vyta du Roc, Theatre Guide and the Scottish Grand National third Benbens, the distances between them a head and two necks, with the never-nearer Doing Fine, Rock The Kasbah, Sugar Baron and The Druids Nephew close behind, the first eight finishers covered by little more than two lengths. There were two-day bans for Sean Bowen and Vyta du Roc's jockey Daryl Jacob for using their whips above the permitted maximum, Jacob also hitting his mount after the finish as he seemed to mistake the line, riding out to the second winning post which is for use in races over hurdles. Jacob isn't the first professional to be caught out in such a way—the ITV cameraman got it wrong—while having two winning posts twenty-five yards apart regularly causes confusion with ordinary racegoers and those watching on television. The chase and hurdle courses do not run parallel and Sandown says that, if the chase course shared the same winning line, there would be a small difference in the distance to the line from the inside of the fence and the distance from the outside. The confusion has gone on far too long and Sandown needs to find an answer. There should just be one winning post, or the two posts should be much further apart.

Henllan Harri (IRE) (br.g. 2008)	King's Theatre (IRE) (b 1991)	Sadler's Wells (b 1981)	Northern Dancer, Fairy Bridge
		Regal Beauty (b 1981)	Princely Native, Dennis Belle
	Told You So (IRE) (br 1997)	Glacial Storm (b 1985)	Arctic Tern, Hortensia
		Bavards Girl (b 1991)	Le Bavard, All Gone

The lengthy Henllan Harri completed another fine season for the progeny of his now deceased sire King's Theatre, his last-day victory at Sandown's Finale meeting, coupled with that of Menorah in the Oaksey Chase, and Theatre Guide's place money, sealing the sires' championship (in Britain and Ireland combined) for the fifth time in the last six years. Cue Card, The New One, Carlingford Lough,

Bellshill, L'Ami Serge, Royal Regatta and Royal Vacation were others who contributed significantly to King's Theatre's prize money total as he headed the sires' table by a fairly narrow margin from Kayf Tara and the four-times champion Presenting. King's Theatre's final progeny earnings of £2,538,186 in the *Racing Post* table were below his earnings in the three previous seasons. Although his last crop are now five-year-olds, he should maintain his position among the leading sires for a few more years yet. Henllan Harri is from the family of the 2007 Grand National winner Silver Birch who is a half-brother to Henllan Harri's unraced grandam Bavards Girl. Henllan Harri's dam Told You So was also unraced but is a sister to the fairly useful Irish staying chaser Tell Me See and a half-sister to the useful chaser (third in a Scottish National) Mister Marker. Told You So is also the dam of Sun Tzu (by Definite Article) who was a fairly useful staying handicap chaser at his best for Henllan Harri's trainer. There are two other big names further back in Henllan Harri's family, his fourth dam Black Barret (Silver Birch's grandam) being a half-sister to Black-Crash, the dam of Wither Or Which and the grandam of Alexander Banquet, both winners of the Champion Bumper at Cheltenham for Willie Mullins in the late-'nineties. Alexander Banquet went on to make a name for himself over fences, winning the Hennessy Gold Cup at Leopardstown, though he failed to complete on both his attempts in the Grand National, a race that will be on the agenda for front-running Henllan Harri provided his trainer can get him high enough in the weights to make the cut. The Becher Chase might be a likely starting point in pursuit of that aim. Henllan Harri acts on heavy going but doesn't need the mud, and he wears headgear (blinkers in his most recent races, including at Sandown). He has also worn a tongue tie occasionally. *Peter Bowen*

HENPECKED 7 b.m. Footstepsinthesand – Poule de Luxe (IRE) (Cadeaux Genereux) [2016/17 h16.2v⁵ h17d⁴ h16.2g Apr 27] half-sister to fairly useful hurdler/chaser Calypso Bay (2¾m-27f winner, by Galileo): fair on Flat, stays 12.5f: poor form over hurdles: wears cheekpieces. *Alistair Whillans* — **h81**

HENRI PARRY MORGAN 9 b.g. Brian Boru – Queen of Thedaises (Over The River (FR)) [2016/17 c149p, h123: c26g c24.2sᵘʳ c20.8sᶠ h24s c24.2s² c25g c25g⁶ c31.8g Apr 22] sturdy gelding: fairly useful hurdler: smart handicap chaser, largely disappointing in 2016/17: stays 25f: acts on soft and good to firm going: usually wears headgear: wears tongue tie: often let down by jumping. *Peter Bowen* — **c134 x h–**

HENRY OLIVER (IRE) 9 b.g. Hasten To Add (USA) – Lisnabrin (IRE) (Witness Box (USA)) [2016/17 c–, h87§: h16.2g³ h17.2d h15.8g h16.7g⁶ c22.6mᵖᵘ c15.7mᶠ Sep 27] poor maiden hurdler: failed to complete all 3 starts over fences: stays 2½m: acts on good to firm going: wears headgear/tongue tie: temperamental. *Giles Smyly* — **c– § h77 §**

HENRYVILLE 9 b.g. Generous (IRE) – Aquavita (Kalaglow) [2016/17 c145, h–: c25d⁴ c20g c21.4gᵇᵈ c23.6g⁴ c25gᵖᵘ c21.1d³ c20.8g c21.1g c20.8g* Apr 19] sturdy gelding: winning hurdler: smart handicap chaser: won Silver Trophy Chase (Limited Handicap) at Cheltenham (by 4 lengths from Foxtail Hill) in April: stays 25f: acts on soft and good to firm going: often wears hood: wears tongue tie: held up. *Harry Fry* — **c147 h–**

HEPBURN 4 b.f. Sixties Icon – Mighty Splash (Cape Cross (IRE)) [2016/17 h16.7s⁴ h16.6gᶠ h19.5g⁶ Apr 17] half-sister to fairly useful hurdler Misterton (2m/2½m winner, by Sagamix) and fair hurdler Java Rose (21f winner, by Ishiguru): poor maiden on Flat: poor form over hurdles: wears tongue tie. *Ali Stronge* — **h80**

HEPIJEU (FR) 6 b.g. Palace Episode (USA) – Helenjeu (Montjeu (IRE)) [2016/17 c123, h116: c19mᵖᶠ c19.4g⁴ c15.8d⁶ c19.4v³ c24g⁵ c22.6g² h23.3g c23.6g⁴ c23.8m⁴ c19.9d⁵ Nov 19] good-topped gelding: winning hurdler: fair handicap chaser: likely to prove best at shorter than 3m: acts on soft and good to firm going: wears headgear/tongue tie: temperamental. *Charlie Longsdon* — **c106 § h–**

HEPPLEWHITE 4 b.g. Rail Link – Millistar (Galileo (IRE)) [2016/17 h15.8g⁶ Oct 2] fair on Flat, stays 1½m: well held in juvenile on hurdling debut: has joined William Muir. *Robert Eddery* — **h–**

HERBERT PARK (IRE) 7 b.g. Shantou (USA) – Traluide (FR) (Tropular) [2016/17 h–: h23.9g² h22.4g c20v c23.4s c24.2d² c23.8vᵖᵘ c29.2g⁴ Apr 24] tall gelding: useful handicap hurdler: won at Worcester in October: fairly useful form over fences: second in novice handicap at Exeter in February: stays 3m: acts on heavy going: wears headgear: temperament under suspicion. *David Pipe* — **c125 h130**

HER DREAM (IRE) 5 b.m. Yeats (IRE) – High Benefit (IRE) (Beneficial) [2016/17   **b–** b15.8d Feb 9] first foal: dam (h113), bumper/2m hurdle winner, half-sister to fairly useful hurdlers/chasers Larks Lad (stayed 3m) and Hersov (stayed 33f) out of half-sister to Champion Hurdle winners Granville Again and Morley Street: tailed off in mares bumper on debut. *Claire Dyson*

HERDSWICK HOLLOA (IRE) 6 ch.g. Marienbard (IRE) – Cash A Lawn (IRE)   **h79** (Executive Perk) [2016/17 b–: b17d⁵ ab16g⁴ h20.8g⁵ h23.3vᵖᵘ h20.8d h25g⁴ Apr 3] modest   **b75** form in bumpers: poor form over hurdles. *Neil King*

HERE ALL ALONG (IRE) 5 b.m. Getaway (GER) – Alongcameaspider (IRE) (High   **h92** Chaparral (IRE)) [2016/17 h16.8s² h15.8gᵖᵘ Apr 3] in frame completed start in points: modest form over hurdles: dead. *David Dennis*

HERE COMES ARTHUR (FR) 7 b.g. Smadoun (FR) – Toulouzette (IRE) (Frimaire)   **h–** [2016/17 h24d Nov 11] modest form over hurdles: tried in tongue tie: dead. *Mark Walford*

HERE COMES HOVIS 6 br.g. Fair Mix (IRE) – Granary House (Alflora (IRE)) [2016/17   **h–** b16.2d b16v h16.4vᵘʳ h18.1sᵖᵘ Apr 3] no form in bumpers/over hurdles. *Sandy Forster*   **b–**

HERE COMES LOVE (IRE) 7 b.g. Winged Love (IRE) – Heres McGoogan (IRE)   **c74** (Shaamit (IRE)) [2016/17 h65: c16s⁶ c20.1m h16v³ h19vᵖᵘ c15.6g Apr 25] poor form over   **h81** hurdles/fences: unproven beyond 17f: best form on heavy going: in cheekpieces last 3 starts: usually in tongue tie. *Patrick Griffin, Ireland*

HERE COMES MOLLY (IRE) 6 ch.m. Stowaway – Grange Melody (IRE) (Presenting)   **h72** [2016/17 h78: h20v h21g h24.6g h19d h16g⁶ h21.6d⁴ Mar 18] poor maiden hurdler: left John Joseph Hanlon after fifth start: tried in hood: often in tongue tie. *Tracey Barfoot-Saunt*

HERECOMESTROUBLE 10 b.g. Gentleman's Deal (IRE) – Owenreagh (IRE)   **c– x** (Glacial Storm (USA)) [2016/17 h20.3dᵖᵘ h16.8dᵘʳ h19.7s Jan 24] fair hurdler/chaser at   **h–** best, no form in 2016/17: tried in cheekpieces: dead. *Lucinda Egerton*

HEREFORDSHIRE 9 b.g. Beneficial – Handmemy Moneydown (IRE) (Saddlers' Hall   **c–** (IRE)) [2016/17 c23.8d⁵ Nov 30] off mark in points at second attempt: tongue tied when well beaten in maiden on chasing debut. *Kerry Lee*

HERE I AM (IRE) 10 br.g. Presenting – The Last Bank (IRE) (Phardante (FR)) [2016/17   **c–** c112, h–: c19.7g⁵ May 8] maiden hurdler: fair chaser: stays 2½m: acts on soft and good to   **h–** firm going: tried in cheekpieces: front runner. *Diana Grissell*

HERE'S HERBIE 9 b.g. Classic Cliche (IRE) – Tyre Hill Lilly (Jupiter Island) [2016/17   **c–** c–p, h133: h21.6g h20g³ h16.2s h18.5s² h19sᵘʳ h19.3s h20d⁵ Apr 16] workmanlike gelding: **h121** fairly useful handicap hurdler: fell both starts over fences: stays 2½m: acts on heavy going: usually wears tongue tie. *Susan Gardner*

HERESMYNUMBER (IRE) 7 b.g. Kalanisi (IRE) – Broken Rein (IRE) (Orchestra)   **h95** [2016/17 h86: h23.4gᶠ May 22] sturdy gelding: modest form over hurdles: in cheekpieces/ tongue tie last 2 starts. *Ali Stronge*

HERE'S TO HARRY 10 b.g. Helissio (FR) – Harrietfield (Nicholas Bill) [2016/17   **c–** h23.3vᵖᵘ c21.6sᵘʳ c20.1sᵖᵘ c20.1vᵖᵘ Feb 15] placed in points: no form over hurdles/fences: **h–** tried in tongue tie: dead. *N. W. Alexander*

HERMANUS (IRE) 5 ch.m. Golan (IRE) – Almost Trumps (Nearly A Hand) [2016/17   **b93** b16s* b17s³ b15.6g Jan 20] half-sister to fair hurdler/fairly useful chaser Mister Stickler (2m/17f winner, by Alflora) and bumper winner/fair hurdler Boris de Blae (3m winner, by Mahler): dam unraced sister to fairly useful hurdler/chaser (stayed 19f) Northern Saddler: fair form in bumpers: won mares event at Ayr in November. *Keith Dalgleish*

HERMARNA (IRE) 4 br.f. Heliostatic (IRE) – Louverissa (IRE) (Verglas (IRE))   **h92** [2016/17 h15.8d h15.9s³ h16.3s h15.8s⁴ h16.5m³ Apr 27] fair on Flat, stays 1½m: modest form over hurdles: raced only at 2m: acts on soft going: in headgear last 2 starts: often races prominently. *Neil King*

HERMOSA VAQUERA (IRE) 7 b.m. High Chaparral (IRE) – Sundown (Polish   **h97** Precedent (USA)) [2016/17 h90: h15.9g⁴ h20.5g² h17.7d² Dec 6] modest handicap hurdler: stays 21f: acts on good to soft going: has worn cheekpieces, including last 5 starts: has worn tongue tie, including last 2 starts. *Gary Moore*

HEROD THE GREAT 7 ch.g. Sakhee's Secret – Pella (Hector Protector (USA))   **c–** [2016/17 h–: c18ᴜᵢᶠ h19.9g Jul 22] rather leggy gelding: fairly useful hurdler at one time   **h–** for Alan King: struggling when fell heavily tenth in novice handicap won by Keppel Isle at Kempton on chasing debut: best around 2m: acts on soft going: in tongue tie last 2 starts. *Richard Phillips*

HER

HEROES OR GHOSTS (IRE) 8 br.g. Indian River (FR) – Awomansdream (IRE)   **c106**
(Beneficial) [2016/17 c103, h–: c22.5v² c23.5g² c23.5v⁴ c23gᵖᵘ Feb 21] Irish maiden   **h–**
point winner: maiden hurdler: fair maiden chaser: stays 3m: acts on heavy going: tried in
cheekpieces. *Jo Davis*

HERON HEIGHTS (IRE) 8 b.g. Heron Island (IRE) – Inter Alia (IRE) (Dr Massini   **c140**
(IRE)) [2016/17 c20g* c19.9g⁴ c19.5g* c19.9g c24d* c24.4g* c16s⁶ c24.4gᵖᵘ c24.5d³ Apr   **h–**
29] tall, close-coupled gelding: third foal: half-brother to fairly useful hurdler/useful chaser
Witness In Court (2m-21f winner, by Witness Box): dam unraced half-sister to Cheltenham
Gold Cup runner-up Take The Stand: maiden hurdler: useful chaser: won maiden at
Kilbeggan in May, and novices at Limerick in July, Clonmel in September and Cheltenham
in October: stays 25f: acts on heavy going: wears tongue tie. *Henry de Bromhead, Ireland*

HERONRY (IRE) 9 b.g. Heron Island (IRE) – In A Tizzy (Sizzling Melody) [2016/17   **c– §**
h20.5g⁶ Dec 7] rangy gelding: useful hurdler/chaser at best, well held sole start in 2016/17:   **h– §**
stays 3m: acts on good to firm and heavy going: usually in cheekpieces: unreliable.
Jamie Snowden

HERONS HEIR (IRE) 9 b.g. Heron Island (IRE) – Kyle Lamp (IRE) (Miner's Lamp)   **c128**
[2016/17 h111: c16g* c16.3gᶠ c15.8d⁵ h16.2g⁵ h16g* h16s³ h15.8d⁴ c15.9m³ c15.7d⁴   **h117**
Jan 25] good-topped gelding: fairly useful handicap hurdler: won at Kempton (conditional)
in November: similar form over fences: won handicaps at Warwick (novice) in May and
Catterick in January: unproven beyond 17f: acts on good to firm and heavy going: wears
tongue tie: often races towards rear, usually travels strongly. *Dan Skelton*

HERR LARRY HEWIS 9 b.g. Sir Harry Lewis (USA) – Avenches (GER) (Dashing   **c–**
Blade) [2016/17 h23.8dᵖᵘ c20.3s³ c24.1sᵖᵘ Jan 23] little form over hurdles/fences: tried in   **h–**
hood. *Sarah-Jayne Davies*

HE'S A BULLY (IRE) 8 b.g. Westerner – Kitty Maher (IRE) (Posen (USA)) [2016/17   **c112**
c108, h–: c23.8s² c23.6g³ Apr 8] well-made gelding: won completed start in points: maiden   **h–**
hurdler: fair handicap chaser: stays 25f: acts on soft and good to firm going: tried in hood.
Philip Hobbs

HE'S A CHARMER (IRE) 7 gr.g. Mahler – Sunny South East (IRE) (Gothland (FR))   **h–**
[2016/17 h110, b90: h23.3gᵖᵘ May 29] strong gelding: fair form over hurdles, reportedly
had breathing problem sole start in 2016/17: wears tongue tie. *Harry Fry*

HE'S MAGIC 6 b.g. Court Masterpiece – Lady Magician (Lord Bud) [2016/17 b16.7d⁴   **b74**
b16.7g⁶ Jul 31] poor form on Flat/in bumpers. *Tim Fitzgerald*

HES OUR ROBIN (IRE) 7 b.g. Robin des Pres (FR) – Poly Sandstorm (IRE) (Presenting)   **c109**
[2016/17 h20v h16d h21g² h17m³ h19s c16g⁵ c18.5g² h16.7g² h15.8m³ Apr 18] fair   **h104**
maiden hurdler: similar form over fences: left Thomas Mullins after seventh start: stays
21f: acts on good to firm going: in hood last 3 starts: has worn tongue tie. *Michael Mullineaux*

HESTER FLEMEN (IRE) 9 ch.m. Flemensfirth (USA) – Hester Hall (IRE) (Saddlers'   **c–**
Hall (IRE)) [2016/17 c134p, h–: c21.4s⁵ c26.2sᵖᵘ Feb 8] strong mare: very lightly raced: **h–**
useful hurdle/chase winner, no form over fences in 2016/17: stays 25f. *Nicky Richards*

HESTINA (FR) 4 b.f. Soldier of Fortune (IRE) – Diagora (FR) (Highest Honor (FR))   **h116 p**
[2016/17 h17s h16.6g² h16s⁵ h15.8g* h15.8g* Apr 17] dam half-sister to fairly useful
hurdler/useful chaser (stays 2¾m) De Vous A Moi: useful on Flat, stays 1½m: fairly useful
form over hurdles: won novices at Ludlow and Huntingdon in April: raced around 2m: best
form on good going: wears hood: in tongue tie last 4 starts: usually races nearer last than
first/freely: open to further improvement. *Dan Skelton*

HEURTEVENT (FR) 8 b.g. Hold That Tiger (USA) – Sybilia (GER) (Spectrum (IRE))   **c95**
[2016/17 c98, h–: c16.5s* c16.3g³ c20d c17.4g⁶ c17.4m⁶ h15.8d⁶ h19.5d⁶ Oct 25] winning   **h–**
hurdler: modest handicap chaser: won at Worcester (conditional) in May: unproven beyond
17f: acts on soft going: tried in headgear/tongue tie. *Tony Carroll*

HEY BILL (IRE) 7 b.g. Indian Danehill (IRE) – Grange More (IRE) (Ridgewood Ben)   **h112**
[2016/17 h86: h19d h20g* h24d* h22.3s Dec 17] maiden Irish pointer: fair form over
hurdles: won maiden at Worcester in October and handicap at Southwell in November:
stays 3m: acts on good to soft going. *Graeme McPherson*

HEY BOB (IRE) 5 br.g. Big Bad Bob (IRE) – Bounty Star (IRE) (Fasliyev (USA))   **h79 §**
[2016/17 h91: h16.8s⁵ h16gᶠ h16.2gᶠ h17.2g h17.2mᶠ h19.9g h16.8g³ h16.8d⁴ h16.4sᵖᵘ
h15.7d³ h16.4v³ h16.8mᶠ Apr 19] close-coupled gelding: poor maiden hurdler: unproven
beyond 17f: acts on heavy going: wears tongue tie: often races towards rear/travels
strongly: temperamental. *Chris Grant*

HEY LISTEN (IRE) 5 b.g. Kutub (IRE) – Crescendor (FR) (Lavirco (GER)) [2016/17 c–
c26.2d^F Apr 10] winning pointer: struggling when fell 5 out in maiden hunter at Kelso on
chasing debut. *Lucinda Russell*

HI BOB 9 b.g. Bollin Eric – Leading Line (Leading Man) [2016/17 c–, h–: c20.1d^pu c20.3v^r
c15.7g^pu h16.8d^2 h20.6s^2 c16.4d^5 Dec 26] poor maiden hurdler: poor handicap chaser:
left Lucinda Egerton after third start: stays 21f: acts on heavy going: wears headgear:
unreliable. *Kenneth Slack* — c62 § h75 §

HICKSON (IRE) 7 b.g. Catcher In The Rye (IRE) – Classic Motive (ITY) (Love The
Groom (USA)) [2016/17 h16.2g^pu Apr 27] placed in bumpers: pulled up in 2 points/novice
hurdle: tried in tongue tie. *Noel C. Kelly, Ireland* — h–

HI DANCER 14 b.g. Medicean – Sea Music (Inchinor) [2016/17 c–, h84: h16.8g* h17.2g^2
h16.8g^6 h16.8g c16.4s^4 c16.4g^2 c16.4m^4 Apr 19] small, leggy gelding: poor handicap
hurdler: won at Sedgefield in May: poor maiden chaser: stays 2¾m, effective at shorter:
acts on good to firm and heavy going: wears headgear: front runner/races prominently:
unreliable. *Ben Haslam* — c78 § h84 §

HIDDEN CARGO (IRE) 5 b.g. Stowaway – All Heart (Alhaarth (IRE)) [2016/17
b16.3g^3 h16.3d^5 h15.3d^2 h16.3s^4 h19g^3 Mar 30] €75,000 3-y-o: useful-looking gelding:
first foal: dam (c102/h113), 2m hurdle/chase winner (stayed 2½m), also 2m winner on Flat:
fair form when third at Newbury only start in bumpers: fair form over hurdles. *Alan King* — h115 b88

HIDDEN CYCLONE (IRE) 12 b.g. Stowaway – Hurricane Debbie (IRE) (Shahanndeh)
[2016/17 c157x, h133: h20m^4 h16.1g^2 h16s* h16g* h16.4s^3 h16g^5 h18.1v* h16d^3 Apr 17]
workmanlike gelding: smart hurdler: won minor events at Listowel (by 1½ lengths from
Draycott Place) in September, Punchestown (by 2¼ lengths from Rashaan) in October and
Leopardstown (by ¾ length from Bonbon Au Miel) in March: third in 'Fighting Fifth'
Hurdle at Newcastle (2½ lengths behind Irving) in November: very smart chaser: stays 23f:
acts on heavy going: wears headgear: usually leads: often let down by jumping over fences.
John Joseph Hanlon, Ireland — c– x h150 x

HIDDEN IDENTITY (IRE) 11 b.m. Beneficial – Swanbrook Leader (IRE) (Supreme
Leader) [2016/17 h19.5g^3 h19.5s^3 h19.9g^bd Mar 14] big, strong mare: fair handicap
hurdler: stays 2½m: acts on heavy going: wears tongue tie. *Tim Vaughan* — h114

HIDDEN IMPACT (IRE) 6 br.g. Oscar – Maiden Flight (Jurado (USA))
[2016/17 b16v^2 Feb 25] €25,000 3-y-o: fifth foal: half-brother to a winning pointer by
Vinnie Roe: dam (h76) maiden hurdler: runner-up in Irish point on debut: 10/3, second in
conditional/amateur maiden bumper at Chepstow (11 lengths behind Lad of Luck) in
February: wore tongue tie: has joined Richard Hobson. *Rebecca Curtis* — b87

HI GEORGE 9 b.g. Doyen (IRE) – Our Ethel (Be My Chief (USA)) [2016/17 h21.4s*
Nov 9] fairly useful handicap hurdler: won at Ayr in November on sole start since 2014/15:
winning chaser: stayed 21f: acted on soft going: sometimes wore tongue tie: dead.
Malcolm Jefferson — c– h117

HIGH ASPIRATIONS (IRE) 9 b.g. Dr Massini (IRE) – Divining (IRE) (Dowsing
(USA)) [2016/17 c105, h–: c20g^pu c22.5v^pu c20.3s c19.7s^5 c21.1v^pu c20.2s^ur c21m^4 Apr 15]
dipped-backed gelding: maiden hurdler: modest handicap chaser: stays 3¼m: acts on good
to firm and heavy going: usually wears headgear. *Michael Blake* — c94 h–

HIGH BRIDGE 6 b.g. Monsun (GER) – Ameerat (Mark of Esteem (IRE)) [2016/17 h118:
h16.3d* h15.7g* h16.3d* h16.4g Mar 14] workmanlike gelding: smart bumper performer:
useful form over hurdles: won maiden at Newbury in December, and novices at Catterick
in January and Newbury in February: front runner/races prominently, often travels strongly.
Ben Pauling — h140

HIGHBURY HIGH (IRE) 10 gr.g. Salford Express (IRE) – Betseale (IRE) (Step
Together (USA)) [2016/17 c68x, h95: h21.4m* h17.7g^3 h20d^6 c16.5g^2 c17.4g^2 c20g*
c21.1s^2 c20s^4 c21.4s* Jan 18] modest handicap hurdler: won at Wincanton in May: fair
handicap chaser: won at Warwick in September and Market Rasen in January: stays 2¾m:
acts on good to firm and heavy going: wears headgear/tongue tie: often let down by
jumping over fences. *Neil Mulholland* — c109 x h96

HIGH COUNSEL (IRE) 8 br.g. Presenting – The Bench (IRE) (Leading Counsel
(USA)) [2016/17 h–: h24.7m c21.7g^3 c20g c23.9g^4 c22.6m c23g^4 c22.6m^2 c24d^6 c26g^4
c20d^pu Dec 21] fair hurdler at best: modest maiden chaser: stays 3m: acts on good to firm
and good to soft going: has worn cheekpieces: usually races towards rear: temperament
under suspicion (has been reluctant at start). *Gary Hanmer* — c90 h–

HIGH FAIR 11 b.m. Grape Tree Road – Miss Tango (Batshoof) [2016/17 h88: h23.3g May
24] modest hurdler: stays 23f: acts on soft going: in cheekpieces last 3 starts. *Sandy Forster* — h–

HIGH HATTON 8 b.g. Silver Patriarch (IRE) – Leroy's Sister (FR) (Phantom Breeze) **c108**
[2016/17 c25.3g² c27.5m³ c26.6g³ c23g⁵ Apr 6] multiple point winner: fair form over
fences: tried in tongue tie. *J. W. Tudor*

HIGH KITE (IRE) 11 b.g. High-Rise (IRE) – Sister Rose (IRE) (Roselier (FR)) [2016/17 **c– x**
c107x, h–: c27.2d^pu May 12] sturdy gelding: maiden pointer: maiden hurdler: fair chaser: **h–**
stays 3m: acts on good to firm and heavy going: wears headgear: sketchy jumper of fences.
T. D. B. Underwood

HIGHLAND CASTLE 9 b.g. Halling (USA) – Reciprocal (IRE) (Night Shift (USA)) **h–**
[2016/17 h16g⁶ h15.7g Jan 12] fairly useful on Flat, stays 2m: no form over hurdles: left
David Elsworth after first start: wears tongue tie. *Lucinda Egerton*

HIGHLAND FLING (IRE) 5 br.g. Country Reel (USA) – High Fun (FR) (Kahyasi) **h118**
[2016/17 h18d h16d⁶ h16d h20s h16s h16.8d* h16g* h16.5g⁶ h16d h16.3d⁴ Apr 27] fairly
useful handicap hurdler: won at Sedgefield and Fakenham in March: acts on good to soft going: wears tongue tie. *Gavin Patrick Cromwell, Ireland*

HIGHLAND LIFE 7 b.m. Trans Island – High Life (Kayf Tara) [2016/17 h81: h19.6s **h89**
h19.6s* h20.7d h21.2g^pu Apr 3] has reportedly had breathing operation: placed once from
3 starts in points: modest handicap hurdler: won novice event at Bangor in January: stays
21f: acts on soft and good to firm going: tried in cheekpieces: usually wears tongue tie.
Steve Flook

HIGHLAND LODGE (IRE) 11 b.g. Flemensfirth (USA) – Supreme Von Pres (IRE) **c143 §**
(Presenting) [2016/17 c133§, h–: c25.5d² c34.3d^pu Apr 8] strong gelding: winning hurdler: **h–**
useful chaser: second in Becher Chase at Aintree in December: stays 27f: acts
on heavy going: usually wears headgear: usually leads, sometimes idles: temperamental.
James Moffatt

HIGHLAND PEAK 5 b.g. Distant Peak (IRE) – Flower Appeal (Diktat) [2016/17 **h–**
b16.2f³ b16.2s⁵ b16.2s⁶ h15.6g⁶ Nov 2] poor form in bumpers: well beaten in novice on **b68**
hurdling debut. *Jackie Stephen*

HIGHLAND REBEL (IRE) 6 b.g. Dandy Man (IRE) – Dancing Tempo (Vettori (IRE)) **h80**
[2016/17 h16.8d^pu h16g⁶ h16g h16g^F Aug 14] pulled up on point debut: poor maiden
hurdler: left Peter Croke after third start: in headgear last 3 starts: often in tongue tie:
usually races prominently. *Mrs Prunella Dobbs, Ireland*

HIGH NOON (IRE) 5 b.g. Westerner – Seymourswift (Seymour Hicks (FR)) [2016/17 **b99**
b16.3d³ Mar 13] £25,000 3-y-o: half-brother to 3 winners, including fairly useful hurdler/
useful chaser Operating (2½m/21f winner, by Milan) and fair hurdler/fairly useful chaser
Mercuric (2m-2½m winner, by Silver Patriarch), stayed 3m: dam (c112/h103) 2¼m-25f
hurdle/chase winner: 12/1, third in maiden bumper at Stratford (3¼ lengths behind
Clondaw Castle) in March. *Emma Lavelle*

HIGHPOWER (IRE) 8 b.g. Flemensfirth (USA) – Holly Grove Lass (Le Moss) [2016/17 **c82 §**
c111, h121: c24m⁶ h23g^pu h20.1g^R Apr 25] failed to complete in 3 points: fairly useful **h– §**
hurdler at best: lightly raced in chases: left Jonjo O'Neill after second start: stays 23f: acts
on soft going: wears headgear: temperamental. *Russell Ross*

HIGH RON 12 b.g. Rainbow High – Sunny Heights (Golden Heights) [2016/17 c129, h–: **c– §**
c20.3s⁵ c20d⁶ h24g⁶ c24d^pu Oct 2] maiden hurdler: fairly useful chaser, lost his way in **h–**
2016/17: tried in cheekpieces: usually wears tongue tie: temperamental. *Caroline Bailey*

HIGH SECRET (IRE) 6 b.g. High Chaparral (IRE) – Secret Question (USA) (Rahy **h130**
(USA)) [2016/17 h16.5g* h15.6g³ h16.5g* h16.5g⁴ Apr 7] good-topped gelding: useful on
Flat, stays 17f: useful form over hurdles: won novices at Taunton in January and March:
will be suited by 2½m. *Paul Nicholls*

HIGH TALK (IRE) 13 b.g. Craigsteel – Ponka (IRE) (Sir Mordred) [2016/17 c66, h–: **c–**
h23.3d h25.6d⁵ Jun 1] fair hurdler at best, no form in 2016/17: winning chaser: stays 27f: **h–**
acts on soft and good to firm going: wears headgear/tongue tie. *Barry Brennan*

HIGH TIDE (IRE) 4 b.g. Montjeu (IRE) – Moving Diamonds (Lomitas) [2016/17 b16v* **b106**
b16s⁵ Apr 6] fourth foal: half-brother to 3 winners on Flat, including smart 5f-7f winner
Dinkum Diamond (by Aussie Rules): dam 5f winner: useful form in bumpers: won maiden
at Leopardstown (by 7½ lengths from Us And Them) in March: wears tongue tie. *Joseph
Patrick O'Brien, Ireland*

HIGHWAY STAR (FR) 5 b.g. Vision d'Etat (FR) – Lyli Rose (FR) (Lyphard's Wish **b95**
(FR)) [2016/17 b15.8d⁵ b16.5g³ Apr 6] fifth foal: half-brother to 2
winners, including smart hurdler Rolling Star (2m-2¼m winner, by Smadoun): dam French
maiden (placed at 11.5f): fairly useful form in bumpers: better effort when third at Taunton
in April: likely to stay further than 2m: has joined Sarah Humphrey. *Nicky Henderson*

HIGHWAY STORM (IRE) 7 b.g. Stowaway – Snow In Summer (IRE) (Glacial Storm **c117** (USA)) [2016/17 h112, b–: c26.2d³ c20.9s* c23.8vᵖᵘ Dec 21] point winner: fair form over **h–** hurdles: fairly useful form over fences: won novice handicap at Ffos Las in November: stays 3m: acts on heavy going: in cheekpieces last 5 starts: usually leads/responds generously to pressure: has joined Richard Hobson. *Rebecca Curtis*

HIGH WHEELER (IRE) 6 b.g. Kalanisi (IRE) – Penny Farthing (Mind Games) **h–** [2016/17 b16.3g⁵ b16.7d³ h19.6m h21dᵖᵘ h20g h20.8d Jan 9] €9,000 3-y-o: sixth foal: **b88** half-brother to fair hurdler/winning handicap chaser Oscar Amy (2¾m winner, by Oscar): dam, 2¼m hurdle winner, half-sister to useful hurdler/chaser (third in Grand National) Simply Gifted: fair form in bumpers: no form over hurdles: left Lucy Wadham after first start. *Caroline Fryer*

HIJA 6 b.m. Avonbridge – Pantita (Polish Precedent (USA)) [2016/17 h83: h18.5gᶠ h16.8sᵖᵘ **h80** h18.5m h16.8g⁴ h21.6g³ h19g⁴ h16.5g h23.9g h23.9m* Apr 20] poor handicap hurdler: won mares event at Taunton in April: stays 3m: acts on good to firm and good to soft going: wears cheekpieces. *Gail Haywood*

HILLARY C 5 b.m. Kayf Tara – Dd's Glenalla (IRE) (Be My Native (USA)) [2016/17 **b62** b15.8m⁶ Jun 9] fifth foal: half-sister to 3 winners, including useful hurdler Colin's Sister (19f-21f winner, by Central Park) and fair hurdler/fairly useful chaser I Am Colin (19f-3m winner, by Zafeen): dam (h96) temperamental 25f hurdle winner: 11/4, sixth in mares bumper at Uttoxeter (15¼ lengths behind Queens Well) in June. *Nigel Twiston-Davies*

HILL FORT 7 ch.g. Pivotal – Cairns (UAE) (Cadeaux Genereux) [2016/17 h122: h17.7d⁵ **h104** h18.7m⁶ h15.8d⁶ h16.8g h19.5s h15.5g⁶ h15.8s⁴ h15.7s² h16g Apr 8] fair handicap hurdler: unproven beyond 17f: acts on good to firm and heavy going: wears tongue tie: usually races nearer last than first. *Matt Sheppard*

HILL OF GOLD (IRE) 9 ch.g. Beneficial – Cap The Waves (IRE) (Roselier (FR)) **c100** [2016/17 c83: c24.2g³ c23.6g* May 17] winning pointer: modest form over fences: won novice hunter at Huntingdon in May: stays 3m: wears headgear. *David Kemp*

HILLS OF DUBAI (IRE) 8 ch.g. Dubai Destination (USA) – Mowazana (IRE) (Galileo **h109** (IRE)) [2016/17 h19.6g⁶ h20d² h20.2d³ h19.5v³ Mar 23] Irish maiden point winner: fair form over hurdles. *Donald McCain*

HILLVIEW LAD (IRE) 9 b.g. Vinnie Roe (IRE) – Kabale (IRE) (Ikdam) [2016/17 h93: **h–** h19.6gᶜᵒ h19.9gᵖᵘ May 29] point winner: maiden hurdler: stays 2½m: acts on good to soft going. *Nick Kent*

HINDON ROAD (IRE) 10 b.g. Antonius Pius (USA) – Filoli Gardens (Sanglamore **c115 §** (USA)) [2016/17 c108, h–: c20.3g* c19.2g² c20d³ c20.3g³ c23.8gᵖᵘ Apr 28] rather leggy **h–** gelding: placed in points: winning hurdler: fairly useful handicap chaser: won at Bangor in May: left Alan King after third start: stays 3m: acts on soft going: has worn cheekpieces, including last 5 starts: travels strongly, but often flatters to deceive. *Mrs C. Drury*

HINT OF GREY (IRE) 4 gr.f. Mastercraftsman (IRE) – Anamarka (Mark of Esteem **h114** (IRE)) [2016/17 h16s⁵ h15.8s⁶ h15.8s² h16g* h16.8g* h15.8g² Apr 17] fair on Flat, stays 1½m: fair form over hurdles: won conditionals maiden at Fakenham and mares novice at Sedgefield in March: raced around 2m: acts on soft going. *Don Cantillon*

HINT OF MINT 8 b.g. Passing Glance – Juno Mint (Sula Bula) [2016/17 h15.7m h19.8d³ **h135** h19m² h16.5g* h16.5s* h16.5gᶠ h15.9mᵘʳ Apr 16] sturdy gelding: useful handicap hurdler: won at Taunton in December and February (by 1¼ lengths from Bertimont): stays 2½m: acts on good to firm and heavy going: tried in cheekpieces: often leads. *Harry Fry*

HINTON INDIANA 12 b.g. Kayf Tara – Hinton Grace (Vital Season) [2016/17 c103, h–: **c71** c25.2d⁶ Jan 25] lengthy, good-topped gelding: winning hurdler: fair handicap chaser, **h–** below form only start under Rules in 2016/17: stays 3¾m: acts on soft and good to firm going: tried in cheekpieces: wears tongue tie. *Dan Skelton*

HINXWORTH (IRE) 8 b.g. Milan – Open Cry (IRE) (Montelimar (USA)) [2016/17 h–: **h56** h21.6gᶠ h21.4m May 10] good-topped gelding: winning pointer: little form over hurdles: in cheekpieces/tongue tie last 3 starts. *Nick Mitchell*

HIPPIART 5 ch.g. Dutch Art – Hippogator (USA) (Dixieland Band (USA)) [2016/17 b–: **h–** b13.6d h15.7m³ Sep 27] no form in bumpers/novice hurdle: tried in cheekpieces/tongue tie. **b–** *David Bridgwater*

HIT AND RUN (IRE) 5 b.g. Getaway (GER) – Arrive In Style (IRE) (King's Theatre **h94** (IRE)) [2016/17 b15.7g h15.7sᶠ h16.7g⁶ h16.2g³ Apr 25] £14,000 3-y-o: second foal: dam, **b76** French maiden hurdler (placed at 17f), half-sister to useful hurdler (stays 23f) Theo's Charm out of smart hurdler/useful chaser (19f-3m winner) Kates Charm: modest form only start in bumper: similar form over hurdles: tried in hood. *Donald McCain*

HITHERJACQUES LADY (IRE) 5 br.m. Robin des Champs (FR) – Crackin' Liss (IRE) (Bob Back (USA)) [2016/17 b92: b16.4s h21.2d³ h20.7s² h21.4v* h19.5v* h20.5g Mar 25] sturdy mare: bumper winner: fairly useful form over hurdles: won mares novices at Wincanton and Lingfield in February: stays 21f: acts on heavy going: front runner/races prominently, usually travels strongly. *Oliver Sherwood* **h120 b–**

HI TIDE (IRE) 13 br.g. Idris (IRE) – High Glider (High Top) [2016/17 c–, h79: h20.3sᵖᵘ h16g⁴ h15.7g² h20.3m⁴ h16m⁶ h15.7dᵖᵘ Nov 15] sturdy gelding: poor handicap hurdler: winning chaser: stays 2½m: acts on good to firm and good to soft going: tried in cheekpieces/tongue tie: often races towards rear. *J. R. Jenkins* **c– h77**

HIT THE DIFF (IRE) 7 b.g. Indian River (FR) – Lucky Teeny (IRE) (Phardante (FR)) [2016/17 b17g May 13] winning pointer: well beaten in bumper. *Ms J. Johnston* **b–**

HIT THE HEADLINES (IRE) 11 b.g. Flemensfirth (USA) – Heather Breeze (IRE) (Lord Americo) [2016/17 c91, h–: c20.3g⁵ c19.7d⁵ Dec 12] tall gelding: winning hurdler: fairly useful chaser at best, lightly raced nowadays: stays 21f: acts on soft going: tried in cheekpieces: sometimes in tongue tie: weak finisher. *Luke Dace* **c75 h–**

HIT THE HIGHWAY (IRE) 8 b.g. Pierre – Highway Belle (IRE) (Germany (USA)) [2016/17 h130: h21.4sᵖᵘ c23.8s² c24vᵖᵘ Feb 24] useful-looking gelding: useful hurdler: fairly useful form over fences: better effort when second in novice at Ludlow in February: stays 3m: best form on soft/heavy going: tried in tongue tie. *Giles Smyly* **c119 h–**

HIT THE TOP (IRE) 10 b.g. Gold Well – Smooth Leader (IRE) (Supreme Leader) [2016/17 h20.1dᵖᵘ c15.6d⁵ c20dᵖᵘ Jul 13] placed all 3 completed starts in Irish maiden points: fairly useful hurdler/maiden chaser at best, no form in 2016/17. *Sue Smith* **c– h–**

HOGAN'S HEIGHT (IRE) 6 b.g. Indian River (FR) – Electre du Berlais (FR) (Royal Charter (FR)) [2016/17 b16s⁵ h19.5v² h21s⁶ Mar 30] £26,000 5-y-o: sixth foal: half-brother to French hurdler Couvre Chef (17f winner, by Bonnet Rouge): dam once-raced half-sister to dam of Hennessy Gold Cup winner Madison du Berlais: placed both starts in points: poor form in bumper: fair form over hurdles: better effort when second in maiden at Lingfield in March: tried in hood. *Jamie Snowden* **h106 b66**

HOIST THE COLOURS (IRE) 6 b.g. Sea The Stars (IRE) – Multicolour Wave (IRE) (Rainbow Quest (USA)) [2016/17 h–: h18.5g³ h19.9m⁶ Jun 9] good-topped gelding: modest maiden hurdler: stayed 2¼m: acted on good to soft going: often wore headgear: usually raced towards rear: dead. *Robert Walford* **h97**

HOKE COLBURN (IRE) 5 br.g. Beneficial – Ravaleen (IRE) (Executive Perk) [2016/17 b79p: b15.7v* h16.7g h19.7g³ h19.7s⁵ Nov 23] fairly useful form in bumpers: won conditionals/amateur event at Southwell in May: fair form over hurdles: front runner/races prominently. *Harry Whittington* **h106 b95**

HOLBROOK PARK 7 b.g. Midnight Legend – Viciana (Sir Harry Lewis (USA)) [2016/17 h110p, b87: h23.3d² h23.6g⁴ h23.3v² h20.5s⁴ h20.5g² Mar 27] fairly useful handicap hurdler: runner-up 3 times in 2016/17: stays 23f: acts on heavy going: tried in tongue tie: front runner/races prominently. *Neil King* **h119**

HOLDBACKTHERIVER (IRE) 5 b.g. Presenting – Fairy Lane (IRE) (Old Vic) [2016/17 b16.7d⁴ Jan 3] £25,000 3-y-o: fifth foal: half-brother to useful hurdler/chaser Kalane (2m-21f winner, by Kalanisi), stays 3m: dam unraced sister to Cheltenham Gold Cup winner Kicking King: 40/1, fourth in bumper at Bangor (8½ lengths behind Just A Sting) in January. *Evan Williams* **b85**

HOLD COURT (IRE) 10 br.g. Court Cave (IRE) – Tipsy Miss (IRE) (Orchestra) [2016/17 c–x, h104: h17m² h23s* h23.9g³ h23.9d⁴ h23g² h23g* c20g h23g Oct 19] good-topped gelding: fairly useful handicap hurdler: won at Worcester in May and July: winning chaser: stays 3m: acts on good to firm and heavy going: tried in cheekpieces: usually races towards rear: often let down by jumping over fences. *Evan Williams* **c– x h126**

HO LEE MOSES (IRE) 7 bl.g. Kalanisi (IRE) – Tipsy Miss (IRE) (Orchestra) [2016/17 h90: h23.3v⁴ Apr 30] maiden pointer/hurdler: should stay at least 2½m: acts on heavy going: usually races towards rear. *Evan Williams* **h67**

HOLEINTHEWALL BAR (IRE) 9 b.g. Westerner – Cockpit Lady (IRE) (Commanche Run) [2016/17 c17d c20g² c19g² h20v⁵ h21gᵖᵘ c17g⁴ c19.9g⁴ h16dᶠ h20d h20s² c20.5v³ c16.2s* c21.5vᶠ h16s Feb 19] fair handicap hurdler: fairly useful handicap chaser: won at Down Royal in January: left M. Hourigan after seventh start: stays 21f: acts on good to firm and heavy going: has worn headgear, including last 3 starts: tried in tongue tie. *Gordon Elliott, Ireland* **c125 h115**

HOLLIES PEARL 7 b.m. Black Sam Bellamy (IRE) – Posh Pearl (Rakaposhi King)   h–
[2016/17 h124: h21.4g Apr 22] fairly useful hurdler, below form sole start in 2016/17:
stays 3m: acts on soft going: in headgear last 4 starts: sometimes in tongue tie. *Peter Bowen*

HOLLINS HILL 7 b.g. Lucarno (USA) – Bonnie Buttons (Lord Bud) [2016/17 h–, b–:   h–
h16.4s h16s h19.7d⁶ Jan 14] little impact in novice/maiden hurdles. *Sam England*

HOLLOW BAY 7 ch.m. Beat Hollow – Cavernista (Lion Cavern (USA)) [2016/17 h99,   c95
b70: h20g⁴ h21m² h21.2m² c20s⁴ c20.8g⁵ h20.7gᵖᵘ Apr 17] angular mare: fair maiden   h103
hurdler: modest form over fences: stayed 21f: acted on good to firm and heavy going: often
wore tongue tie: dead. *Paul Webber*

HOLLOW BLUE SKY (FR) 10 gr.g. Turgeon (USA) – Run For Laborie (FR) (Lesotho   c103 §
(USA)) [2016/17 c113§, h–: c23.8g⁴ c25.3v⁶ c24.1s² c22.7s³ Feb 28] strong gelding: h–
maiden hurdler: fair handicap chaser: stays 3m: acts on heavy going: wears cheekpieces:
usually wears tongue tie: unreliable. *Nigel Twiston-Davies*

HOLLOW PARK (IRE) 5 b.m. Flemensfirth (USA) – Love And Beauty (IRE)   h90
(Presenting) [2016/17 b16.7g h19.5gᶠ Apr 17] €9,000 3-y-o: first foal: dam unraced half-   b–
sister to useful chaser (stays 3¼m) On The Fringe: runner-up in Irish mares maiden point
on debut: well beaten in maiden bumper: weakening when fell last in mares novice won by
Copper Kay at Chepstow on hurdling debut. *Katy Price*

HOLLY BUSH HENRY (IRE) 6 b.g. Yeats (IRE) – Maslam (IRE) (Robellino (USA))   c133
[2016/17 h135: c15.2g³ h16.3d⁶ c19.9g² c17.2s* c16g² c20.1g³ Apr 8] lengthy gelding: h–
useful hurdler: similar form over fences: won novice at Market Rasen in February: stays
2½m: acts on soft going: wears tongue tie. *Graeme McPherson*

HOLLYWOOD ALL STAR (IRE) 8 b.g. Kheleyf (USA) – Camassina (IRE) (Taufan   h96
(USA)) [2016/17 h106: h15.7s h15.5d⁶ h16.7s² h16vᵖᵘ h20.1vᵖᵘ Mar 28] compact gelding:
modest handicap hurdler: stays 2½m: acts on heavy going. *Graeme McPherson*

HOLLYWOODIEN (FR) 6 gr.g. Martaline – Incorrigible (FR) (Septieme Ciel (USA))   c140
[2016/17 c135p, h–: c16.3v⁴ c19.4s* c15.5s³ c19.9s³ Mar 4] winning hurdler: useful   h–
handicap chaser: won at Wetherby in December: stays 19f: acts on soft going: has worn
cheekpieces: usually races close up. *Tom Symonds*

HOLLYWOOD KEN (IRE) 4 b.g. Arcano (IRE) – Third Dimension (FR) (Suave   h100
Dancer (USA)) [2016/17 h17.7gᵖᵘ h16.8s h15.8s⁴ h16vᵖᵘ h16d⁶ h15.7m h16.5m³ h16.8g³
Apr 26] workmanlike gelding: half-brother to smart hurdler/very smart chaser Third
Intention (2m-2½m winner, by Azamour), stays 25f, and useful hurdler Orgilgo Bay
(2m-2¼m winner, by Lawman): fair maiden on Flat, stays 7f: modest maiden hurdler: will
prove best around 2m: acts on good to firm going: in headgear last 2 starts: wears tongue
tie: often races freely. *Richard Woollacott*

HOLLYWOOD ROAD (IRE) 4 b.g. Kodiac – Rinneen (IRE) (Bien Bien (USA))   h118
[2016/17 h15.8d² h15.8m* h15.8g* h16g Apr 29] fairly useful on Flat, stays 1¼m: similar
form over hurdles: won juvenile in October and novice in April, both at Huntingdon: tried
in blinkers. *Don Cantillon*

HOLY CROSS (IRE) 6 b.g. Yeats (IRE) – Bleu Ciel Et Blanc (FR) (Pistolet Bleu (IRE))   c–
[2016/17 b–: h16.3m³ h20g⁴ h18.7m⁵ h18.7g⁴ h16d⁵ h20.7g c23.8vᵘʳ Nov 21] fair form   h100
over hurdles: behind until unseated fourteenth in novice handicap at Ludlow on chasing
debut: left Rebecca Curtis after fourth start: stays 19f: acts on good to firm going: has worn
headgear: in tongue tie last 4 starts. *Claire Dyson*

HOLY STREET (IRE) 5 b.g. Presenting – Vigna Maggio (FR) (Starborough) [2016/17   b64 p
b16m⁴ Nov 2] €20,000 3-y-o: fifth foal: half-brother to fair hurdler Ballygrooby Bertie (19f
winner, by King's Theatre) and bumper winner Only Orvieto (by Kayf Tara): dam, French
1m winner, sister to fairly useful hurdler/chaser (stays 3¼m) Vincitore and half-sister to
moody but fairly useful hurdler/useful chaser (stayed 3m) Vodka Bleu: well beaten in
bumper: should do better. *Alan King*

HOLY WATER (IRE) 6 b.g. Holy Roman Emperor (IRE) – Gambling Spirit (Mister   h99
Baileys) [2016/17 h16.4s h17.5d⁶ h19.5g² h19.5d⁵ h20.2sᵖᵘ Sep 22] half-brother to fairly
useful hurdler/chaser Gambling Girl (2m/17f winner, by Hawk Wing): modest maiden
hurdler: stays 19f: acts on good to soft going: in cheekpieces last 4 starts: in tongue tie last
5 starts. *Mrs Lorna Fowler, Ireland*

HOLYWELL (IRE) 10 b.g. Gold Well – Hillcrest (IRE) (Thatching) [2016/17 c159, h–:   c–
h24.7d c26g c23.8dᵖᵘ c24d c25gᵖᵘ h24.7gᵖᵘ Apr 8] good-topped gelding: winning hurdler: h–
including of Pertemps Final at Cheltenham in 2012/13: very smart chaser at best, won 4

times in 2013/14, including Baylis & Harding Affordable Luxury Handicap at Cheltenham and Mildmay Novices' Chase at Aintree: could hardly have shown any less in 2016/17, and has reportedly been retired: stayed 3¼m: usually wore headgear. *Jonjo O'Neill*

HOLYWELL RYDE 14 b.g. Overbury (IRE) – Royal Ryde (Royal Vulcan) [2016/17 c24.1g⁴ Apr 29] point winner: 50/1, fourth in novice hunter at Bangor (28 lengths behind Stoleaway) on chasing debut: dead. *Miss B. Lewis* — **c78**

HOMERS ODYSSEY 7 b.g. Overbury (IRE) – Aikaterine (Kris) [2016/17 b–: b17.7s³ b15.7d⁶ h19.5g h17.7s h19.1v h25s³ h19.8v Mar 9] workmanlike gelding: modest form in bumpers/over hurdles: will prove best at short of 25f: acts on soft going. *Chris Gordon* — **h92 b83**

HONCHO (IRE) 5 gr.g. Dark Angel (IRE) – Disco Lights (Spectrum (IRE)) [2016/17 h16.2d³ h15.8m⁴ h16s³ Nov 15] fair on Flat, stays 7f: modest form over hurdles. *John Ryan* — **h97**

HONEST INTENT 6 b.g. Fair Mix (IRE) – Just Jenny (IRE) (King's Ride) [2016/17 b17.1g⁵ h16s³ h16s⁵ h16d⁶ h19.3s⁶ h20.3v³ h24g³ h20.3g Apr 21] €7,000 3-y-o, £4,000 5-y-o: sixth foal: half-brother to fairly useful chaser Castarnie (23f-25f winner, by Alflora): dam, placed twice in bumpers, half-sister to smart staying hurdler Celtic Native out of half-sister to Grand National winner Red Marauder: runner-up in point: well beaten in bumper: fair maiden hurdler: likely to prove best at short of 3m: acts on soft going: free-going front runner: has joined Ronald Thompson. *Ruth Carr* — **h100 b–**

HONEST VIC (IRE) 4 b.g. Kalanisi (IRE) – Miss Vic Lovin (IRE) (Old Vic) [2016/17 b15.8m⁵ Apr 18] 8/1, fifth in bumper at Ludlow (6¾ lengths behind Dans Le Vent) in April. *Henry Daly* — **b79**

HONEYCHILE RYDER 6 ch.m. Black Sam Bellamy (IRE) – Dusky Dante (IRE) (Phardante (FR)) [2016/17 h–: h22.7s⁴ Oct 22] poor form over hurdles. *Dianne Sayer* — **h61**

HONEYMOON COCKTAIL (FR) 6 gr.g. Martaline – Caipirinia (FR) (Hawk Wing (USA)) [2016/17 h16.3d⁶ Jun 14] fair on Flat, stays 1½m: in hood, tailed off in novice on hurdling debut. *David Pipe* — **h–**

HONEY ON TOAST 6 b.m. Victory Note (USA) – Honeyfantastic (Primitive Rising (USA)) [2016/17 b15.9g b16.3v⁶ Jun 28] second foal: dam pulled up in points: no form in bumpers. *Ron Hodges* — **b–**

HONEY POUND (IRE) 9 b.g. Big Bad Bob (IRE) – Moon Review (USA) (Irish River (FR)) [2016/17 c119x, h121: h16d³ h16.5d⁴ h16.3m h19.8dᶠ h20d⁶ h15.5d² h16v⁴ h16.6s⁵ h15.7m* Apr 13] workmanlike gelding: fair handicap hurdler: won at Towcester in April: maiden chaser: stays 2¼m: acts on soft and good to firm going: wears hood: races towards rear: often let down by jumping over fences. *Tim Vaughan* — **c– x h114**

HONGKONG ADVENTURE 4 b.g. Roderic O'Connor (IRE) – Queen Margrethe (Grand Lodge (USA)) [2016/17 h16s h16.3d h16.2v Jan 11] leggy gelding: fair maiden on Flat, stays 1½m: well held in juvenile hurdles. *Anabel K. Murphy* — **h–**

HONKYTONKTENNESSEE (IRE) 8 b.g. Scorpion (IRE) – Polly Platinum (IRE) (Phardante (FR)) [2016/17 h104: c17gᶠ c16.5mᵖᵘ c23.6g* h26.4g* Apr 23] fair handicap hurdler: won at Stratford in April: similar form over fences: won handicap at Huntingdon in April: left Hugo Froud after second start: stays 3¼m: acts on good to soft going: in hood last 2 starts: still unexposed as a chaser. *Dan Skelton* — **c106 p h109**

HONOURABLE EXIT (IRE) 10 b.g. Exit To Nowhere (USA) – Honor Love (FR) (Pursuit of Love) [2016/17 h–: h16.8g² h18.5g⁶ c16d⁵ c15.7d⁶ h21.6g Sep 16] winning pointer: poor maiden hurdler: no form over fences: best effort at 17f: sometimes in hood. *Alexandra Dunn* — **c– h84**

HONOURABLE GENT 9 b.g. Gentleman's Deal (IRE) – Gudasmum (Primitive Rising (USA)) [2016/17 c110, h100: c15.2m* c15.2g* Apr 23] fair hurdler: fairly useful form over fences: won handicaps at Wetherby (twice) in April: stays 2¼m: acts on soft and good to firm going: wears hood. *Rose Dobbin* — **c117 h–**

HONOURABLE HENRY 7 b.g. Kayf Tara – Kingara (Karinga Bay) [2016/17 h19.5mᵖᵘ h21.6vᵖᵘ Feb 14] off mark in maiden points at third attempt: no form over hurdles: tried in cheekpieces. *Michael Roberts* — **h–**

HONOUR PROMISE (IRE) 5 b.m. Jeremy (USA) – Karenaragon (Aragon) [2016/17 h16.8gᵘʳ h16g⁴ h16.8g³ h16.8d⁴ h19.5g h16d* h16.8d⁴ h15.5gᶠ Nov 27] modest hurdler: won seller at Chepstow in October: unproven beyond 17f: acts on good to soft going: usually wears cheekpieces. *Bernard Llewellyn* — **h91**

HOO BALLY DIVA (IRE) 6 b.m. Scorpion (IRE) – Dr Sandra (IRE) (Dr Massini (IRE)) [2016/17 b83: h21.6m³ h25.5s² h25.5s⁶ h23.9gᵖᵘ Jan 11] sturdy mare: modest form over hurdles: should be suited by 2½m+: usually races prominently. *Bob Buckler* — **h98**

HOOKS LANE 5 ch.g. Bertolini (USA) – Zaville (Zafonic (USA)) [2016/17 b–: h15.7s⁶ **h63** h19.4sᵘʳ h15.7g⁶ Mar 28] poor form over hurdles. *Shaun Harris*

HOOLA HULA 4 br.f. Yeats (IRE) – Dancing Dasi (IRE) (Supreme Leader) [2016/17 b14s⁴ **h90 p** b12.6d³ h16g³ Apr 8] rather unfurnished filly: fourth foal: closely related to a winning **b81** pointer by Kayf Tara: dam (h112) 2m-2½m hurdle winner: modest form in bumpers: 14/1, third in novice at Chepstow (6½ lengths behind Resolution Bay) on hurdling debut: open to improvement. *Susan Gardner*

HOOLEY TIME (IRE) 5 b.m. Rugby (USA) – Rahelly Lady (IRE) (Kheleyf (USA)) **h–** [2016/17 b–: b16.6g h16.7dᵖᵘ Dec 26] no form in bumpers: pulled up in novice on hurdling **b–** debut: in tongue tie last 2 starts. *Olly Williams*

HOOPER'S LEGEND 6 b.g. Midnight Legend – Norton Sapphire (Karinga Bay) **h100 p** [2016/17 b16.8g h16d⁴ h16s⁴ Dec 3] useful-looking gelding: second foal: brother to fair **b85** hurdler Midnight Sapphire (21f/2¼m winner): dam (c122/h117) 2m-23f hurdle/chase winner: fair form in bumper/hurdles: will be suited by further than 2m: remains capable of better. *Victor Dartnall*

HOORAY HEBE 10 b.m. Lahib (USA) – North End Lady (Faustus (USA)) [2016/17 h–: **h–** h23gᶠ h20gᵖᵘ Aug 11] pulled up in point: no form over hurdles: in cheekpieces/tongue tie both 2016/17 starts. *Emma Baker*

HOOVES THE DADDY (IRE) 4 b.g. Robin des Pres (FR) – Countessdee (IRE) (Arctic **b–** Lord) [2016/17 b15.3m³ Apr 5] well beaten in maiden bumper. *Seamus Mullins*

HOPE FOR GLORY 8 b.g. Proclamation (IRE) – Aissa (Dr Devious (IRE)) [2016/17 h–: **c–** c19.3g⁶ c17.1mᵖᵘ h17.2g⁶ h16.2g⁴ c16.4g⁴ c19.3g⁵ Sep 27] little form over hurdles/fences: **h63** has worn headgear, including last 3 starts: wears tongue tie: usually leads. *Maurice Barnes*

HOPEFULL 7 br.m. Overbury (IRE) – Maryscross (IRE) (Presenting) [2016/17 h64: **c–** h23.9mᵖᵘ c21.2mᵖᵘ Jun 24] no form over hurdles: pulled up in maiden on chasing debut. **h–** *R. Mike Smith*

HOPE'S WISHES 7 b.m. Kayf Tara – Otarie (FR) (Lute Antique (FR)) [2016/17 h118: **h112** h16.2s³ h16s⁴ h16.7s³ h16.4v³ h17.7s² h16.7g³ h20.3g Apr 20] fair handicap hurdler: stays 19f: acts on good to firm and heavy going: front runner/races prominently: quirky sort. *Barry Brennan*

HOPKINSTOWN BOY (IRE) 5 br.g. Court Cave (IRE) – Native Success (IRE) (Be **b–** My Native (USA)) [2016/17 b16gᵖᵘ b15.7dᵖᵘ Nov 15] no form in bumpers: wears tongue tie. *Sophie Leech*

HOP 'N POP (IRE) 10 b.m. Millenary – Rivita Princess (IRE) (Riverhead (USA)) **c–** [2016/17 c–, h–: h23.9m h23.3m Jun 9] maiden pointer: no form over hurdles/fences: tried **h56** in blinkers. *Hugh Burns*

HOPONANDSEE 6 b.m. Nomadic Way (USA) – Jago's Girl (Bob's Return (IRE)) **h79** [2016/17 h–, b86: h16g⁵ h18.7m⁴ Aug 24] rather unfurnished mare: poor form over hurdles. *George Baker*

HORACE HAZEL 8 b.g. Sir Harry Lewis (USA) – Kaream (Karinga Bay) [2016/17 h115: **c112** h23.3s⁴ h25.6g³ c23d* c23mᵖᵘ h25.6g⁶ Sep 30] good-topped gelding: fair handicap hurdler: **h110** similar form over fences: won novice handicap at Worcester in June: stays 3¼m: acts on soft going: has worn blinkers, including final start: tried in tongue tie. *Anthony Honeyball*

HORATIO HORNBLOWER (IRE) 9 b.g. Presenting – Countess Camilla (Bob's **c120** Return (IRE)) [2016/17 c130, h–: c23.8d⁶ c23.8g⁶ c26d c23.4s⁶ c23.8s³ c29.2v⁵ Mar 12] **h–** rangy gelding: winning hurdler: fairly useful handicap chaser: third at Ffos Las in February: stays 3m: acts on good to firm and heavy going: often races prominently. *Nick Williams*

HORIZONTAL SPEED (IRE) 9 b.g. Vertical Speed (FR) – Rockababy (IRE) (King's **c–** Ride) [2016/17 c71, h125: h23.1mᵘʳ May 3] tall, useful-looking gelding: winning pointer: **h–** useful hurdler/chaser at one time: stays 3m: acts on heavy going: in cheekpieces last 2 starts: usually races prominently. *David Dennis*

HORSEGUARDSPARADE 6 b.g. Montjeu (IRE) – Honorlina (FR) (Linamix (FR)) **c98** [2016/17 b–: h19.9d⁵ h20g² h20m² h19.9g⁵ h26g⁵ h15.7g h23.9d² h19.5s c19.4g³ Apr 9] **h109** sturdy gelding: fair maiden hurdler: 10/3, third in seller at Ffos Las (11¼ lengths behind Earthmoves) on chasing debut: stays 3m: acts on good to soft going: wears cheekpieces: often races towards rear. *Nigel Twiston-Davies*

HORSEHILL (IRE) 8 b.g. Flemensfirth (USA) – Maid For Adventure (IRE) (Strong **c–** Gale) [2016/17 c112, h–: c24g⁵ c26.2dᵖᵘ Oct 25] maiden hurdler: form over fences only on **h–** chasing debut in 2015/16: best effort at 23f: acts on heavy going: usually races towards rear. *Oliver Sherwood*

HORSTED VALLEY 7 gr.g. Fair Mix (IRE) – Kullu Valley (Turgeon (USA)) [2016/17 **h–**
h109: h24.7d h26.5m^{pu} Jul 17] workmanlike gelding: fair hurdler, no form in 2016/17:
stays 27f: acts on firm and good to soft going: in headgear last 5 starts. *Warren Greatrex*

HOSTILE FIRE (IRE) 6 b.g. Iffraaj – Royal Esteem (Mark of Esteem (IRE)) [2016/17 **c112**
c16f^2 c16s^F Jul 26] winning hurdler: fair form over fences: unproven beyond 2m: acted on **h–**
any going: sometimes wore hood: wore tongue tie: dead. *Gordon Elliott, Ireland*

HOT PEPPER 9 gr.g. Tikkanen (USA) – Copper Valley (Nearly A Hand) [2016/17 **c–**
h19.7s^{pu} c16s^F h16.5g h19s Feb 5] poor hurdler: fell first on chasing debut. *Chris Down* **h–**

HOUBLON DES OBEAUX (FR) 10 b.g. Panoramic – Harkosa (FR) (Nikos) [2016/17 **c142**
c155, h–: c29.5s^3 c29.2s^4 c28.4d c33.4s^4 c34.3d Apr 8] good-topped gelding: winning **h–**
hurdler: useful handicap chaser: in frame in Welsh Grand National at Chepstow in
December, Classic Chase at Warwick in January and Midlands Grand National at Uttoxeter
in March: stays 33f: acts on heavy going: wears cheekpieces. *Venetia Williams*

HOUNDSCOURT (IRE) 10 b.g. Court Cave (IRE) – Broken Rein (IRE) (Orchestra) **c86 §**
[2016/17 c107§, h–: c21.2m^{pu} c24v^4 c23g^F c20.3g^{pu} c24d^5 h25.3d^4 h24.1s^3 h24.1s* h27s^2 **h81 §**
h27g^5 h24.1m^4 c23.6g Apr 28] poor handicap hurdler: won at Wetherby in January: modest
handicap chaser: stays 27f: acts on heavy going: usually wears headgear: wears tongue tie:
front runner/races prominently: unreliable. *Joanne Foster*

HOUSEPARTY 9 b.g. Invincible Spirit (IRE) – Amusing Time (IRE) (Sadler's Wells **c– §**
(USA)) [2016/17 c77§, h–: c17.4g^{pu} May 29] compact gelding: maiden hurdler: poor **h–**
chaser: stays 2¼m: best form on good going: has worn headgear: often races in rear:
unreliable. *Diana Grissell*

HOUSESOFPARLIAMENT (IRE) 4 ch.g. Galileo (IRE) – Sharp Lisa (USA) **h127**
(Dixieland Band (USA)) [2016/17 h16d^2 h16s Feb 12] smart on Flat, stays 14.5f: fairly
useful form over hurdles: better effort when second in juvenile maiden at Leopardstown in
December: in hood then: wears tongue tie. *Joseph Patrick O'Brien, Ireland*

HOUSTON DYNIMO (IRE) 12 b.g. Rock of Gibraltar (IRE) – Quiet Mouse (USA) **c104**
(Quiet American (USA)) [2016/17 c119, h111: c21g^3 c20.9m^4 c21.1d^3 c23d^4 c25.8m^5 **h–**
c22.6g^6 c25.8m^2 c24.2m^4 h23.1g^6 h21.2g Nov 10] small, close-coupled gelding: winning
hurdler: fair handicap chaser: stays 3m: acts on soft and good to firm going: has worn
headgear/tongue tie: front runner/races prominently. *David Pipe*

HOW ABOUT IT (IRE) 8 b.g. Kayf Tara – Midnight Gift (IRE) (Presenting) [2016/17 **c108 §**
c127, h–: c25.6m^5 c28.4v^{pu} c23.8d^5 c23.6s^6 c21.7g^4 c23.8s^{pu} c20.9v* c23.6g Apr 28] **h–**
lengthy gelding: maiden hurdler: fair handicap chaser: won at Ffos Las in March: left
Rebecca Curtis after seventh start: stays 3m: acts on heavy going: wears headgear: tried in
tongue tie: hard to catch right. *Alexandra Dunn*

HOWABOUTNEVER (IRE) 9 b.g. Shantou (USA) – Sarah's Cottage (IRE) **h–**
(Topanoora) [2016/17 h119: h21.1s h24d^5 h20.5d^{pu} h24.2d^{pu} Mar 24] smallish gelding: fair
hurdler, no form in 2016/17: wears headgear. *Roger Teal*

HOWLONGISAFOOT (IRE) 8 b.g. Beneficial – Miss Vic (IRE) (Old Vic) [2016/17 **c121**
c138, h–: c24.1v c21.1d^F c24g c25.7v^5 c24.2s^6 c22.6s* c22.4d^4 Mar 24] strong gelding: **h–**
winning hurdler: fairly useful handicap chaser: won at Stratford in March: best at shorter
than 3m: acts on heavy going: wears headgear. *Chris Gordon*

HOW MUCH IS ENOUGH (IRE) 6 b.m. Moon Ballet (IRE) – Silankka (Slip Anchor) **c–**
[2016/17 c21.2m h22.7s^{pu} Apr 3] half-sister to several winners on Flat: dam, 1½m/13f **h–**
winner, half-sister to fairly useful hurdler (stayed 21f) Storm Dust: placed in Irish maiden
points: pulled up in mares novice on hurdling debut: tailed off in hunter on chasing debut:
left M. Hourigan after first start. *Richard Ford*

HOW'S MY FRIEND 12 b.g. Karinga Bay – Friendly Lady (New Member) [2016/17 **c91**
c25.5v^4 c23.6d^5 c26.7d^2 Mar 26] maiden hurdler: modest handicap chaser: stays 27f: acts **h–**
on soft and good to firm going: has worn tongue tie. *Grant Cann*

HOW'S VIENNA (IRE) 7 b.g. Westerner – Plant A Smacker (IRE) (Goldmark (USA)) **c87**
[2016/17 h–: h21s h19.5s h20.5v^3 h23.9g^5 c24v^3 c24.2d^3 c26.7d* c23.6g^6 Apr 17] sturdy **h77**
gelding: poor form over hurdles: modest form over fences: won handicap at Wincanton in
March: stays 27f: acts on good to soft going. *David Dennis*

HOWWOULDUNO (IRE) 9 b.g. Desert King (IRE) – Whadouno (IRE) (Abednego) **c114 §**
[2016/17 h16m h20g^5 c16g^4 h18.8g^6 h20.1g Apr 25] lengthy gelding: fair handicap hurdler: **h103 §**
useful handicap chaser at best: stays 2½m: acts on soft and good to firm going: tried in
hood: has worn tongue tie: one to treat with caution (has refused to race). *Liam Lennon,
Ireland*

HOWYA BUDDY (IRE) 12 b.g. Heron Island (IRE) – Boccachera (IRE) (Phardante (FR))   **h–**
[2016/17 h–: h22g^{pu} May 21] winning pointer: modest maiden hurdler in 2012/13: lightly
raced and no form since. *Adrian Wintle*

HUBAL (POL) 5 b.g. Safety Wire (IRE) – Hebra (POL) (Who Knows) [2016/17 h88:   **c91**
h16.2d^{pu} h20.2f^{ur} h23.1g h19.9g^{pu} c15.7g^6 c19.9d* c17.9v^2 c16.9v^3 c20.9g^5 Apr 25]   **h–**
slightly-built gelding: maiden hurdler, no form in 2016/17: modest form over fences: won
minor event at Milan in November: left George Charlton after sixth start: stays 2½m: wears
cheekpieces: tried in tongue tie. *G. Wroblewski, Czech Republic*

HUBERTAS 5 b.g. Lord of England (GER) – Western Eyes (IRE) (Rock of Gibraltar   **h90**
(IRE)) [2016/17 h16.7v^5 h18.6s^2 h20.8d Jan 9] useful on Flat, stays 14.5f: modest form
over hurdles: in headgear last 2 starts. *John Quinn*

HUEHUECOYTLE 7 br.g. Turgeon (USA) – Azturk (FR) (Baby Turk) [2016/17 h100§:   **h– §**
h19.9g Aug 25] modest form over hurdles: best effort at 21f: acts on heavy going: tried in
visor: front runner/races prominently: ungenuine. *Keith Dalgleish*

HUFF AND PUFF 10 b.g. Azamour (IRE) – Coyote (Indian Ridge) [2016/17 c–, h–:   **c121**
c19.4d^2 c20.2s^5 c23g* Mar 2] tall, workmanlike gelding: winning hurdler: fairly useful   **h–**
form over fences: won novice handicap at Taunton in March: stays 23f: acts on good to firm
and good to soft going. *Venetia Williams*

HUGHESIE (IRE) 8 b.g. Indian Danehill (IRE) – Collatrim Choice (IRE) (Saddlers' Hall   **c–**
(IRE)) [2016/17 c121, h–: h19.5v^5 h15.7s c24.2s^{pu} h16.7s^4 h16.7g^4 Mar 25] lengthy   **h96**
gelding: modest maiden hurdler: fairly useful form over fences: stays 19f: best form on
soft/heavy going: in headgear last 3 starts: in tongue tie last 2. *Evan Williams*

HUGH'S SECRET (IRE) 5 b.g. Yeats (IRE) – Walkyrie (FR) (Sleeping Car (FR))   **h65**
[2016/17 h–: h16.8d^6 h16d^5 h19.3s^5 h16.8v^5 Mar 5] neat gelding: little form over hurdles:
in headgear last 3 starts. *Philip Kirby*

HUGO'S REFLECTION (IRE) 5 b.g. Robin des Champs (FR) – Dawn Court   **b–**
(Rakaposhi King) [2016/17 b16g Mar 18] rangy gelding: tailed off in maiden bumper.
Ben Case

HUMBEL BEN (IRE) 14 br.g. Humbel (USA) – Donegans Daughter (Auction Ring   **c90 x**
(USA)) [2016/17 c90x, h–: h21.6g^3 h20g c17.4g* Oct 25] tall gelding: winning   **h76**
hurdler: modest handicap chaser: won at Fontwell in August and Bangor in October: left
John Flint after second start: stays 21f: acts on heavy going: usually wears cheekpieces:
sometimes wears tongue tie: sketchy jumper. *Alan Jones*

HUMBIE (IRE) 13 b.g. Karinga Bay – South Queen Lady (IRE) (King's Ride) [2016/17   **c110**
c120, h–: h23.3d^{pu} c25.5d c21.2d^2 Jul 16] lengthy gelding: winning hurdler: fair handicap   **h–**
chaser: stays 3m: acts on good to firm and heavy going: in cheekpieces last 2 starts.
Pauline Robson

HUNGER HILL 7 b.g. Desideratum – Madam Wurlitzer (Noble Patriarch) [2016/17   **h–**
h16.7g May 15] maiden pointer: tailed off in maiden on hurdling debut. *Mike Sowersby*

HUNTERS BELT (IRE) 13 b.g. Intikhab (USA) – Three Stars (Star Appeal) [2016/17   **c–**
c–, h100§: h16.2d Apr 30] workmanlike gelding: modest hurdler: no impact over fences: **h– §**
stays 25f: acts on good to firm and heavy going: wears headgear/tongue tie: often races in
rear: unreliable. *George Bewley*

HUNTERS HOOF (IRE) 8 b.g. Flemensfirth (USA) – Madgehil (IRE) (Anshan)   **c–**
[2016/17 h134: h22.8m c20.3g^3 h20s^2 Dec 3] good-topped gelding: fairly useful handicap   **h128**
hurdler: second at Aintree in December: tailed off in novice on chasing debut: stayed 2½m:
acted on soft going: dead. *Nicky Henderson*

HUNTERS LODGE (IRE) 11 ch.g. Subtle Power (IRE) – Native Orchid (IRE) (Be My   **c– §**
Native (USA)) [2016/17 c32.5g Apr 27] strong gelding: winning pointer: maiden hurdler: **h–**
fair handicap chaser at best for Nigel Twiston-Davies: stays 29f: acts on heavy going:
usually wears headgear: tried in tongue tie: hard ride and not one to rely on. *Alan Hill*

HUNTERS VISION (IRE) 8 ch.g. Hawk Wing (USA) – Stashedaway (IRE) (Treasure   **h90**
Hunter) [2016/17 h60: h15.8g^{pu} h19m h16d^6 h17.3g^{pu} h16d^4 h16g h16g^{pu} Sep 2] modest
maiden hurdler: stays 19f: acts on good to firm and good to soft going: has worn headgear,
including last 3 starts: wears tongue tie: front runner/races prominently. *Denis Hogan,
Ireland*

HUNTRESS (IRE) 5 b.m. Flemensfirth (USA) – Madgehil (IRE) (Anshan) [2016/17   **b91**
b17.7d ab16g^5 b17.7g* Mar 27] €21,000 3-y-o: third foal: sister to useful hurdler Hunters
Hoof (2m-2½m winner): dam, well held in bumpers, half-sister to smart 2m hurdler
Kilcash and useful hurdler/fairly useful chaser (2m-2¼m winner) Snow Dragon: fair form
in bumpers: won at Plumpton in March. *Suzy Smith*

HUNTSMANS LADY (IRE) 7 b.m. Shantou (USA) – Falika (FR) (Hero's Honor **h–**
(USA)) [2016/17 h18.5d Jun 21] little impact in points/hurdles: dead. *Jimmy Frost*

HUNTSMAN SON (IRE) 7 b.g. Millenary – Daly Lady (IRE) (Lord of Appeal) **h103 p**
[2016/17 h20g³ Jun 4] £36,000 6-y-o: third foal: half-brother to a winning pointer by King
Cheetah: dam unraced half-sister to fairly useful hurdler/useful staying chaser Willie John
Daly: won both completed starts in Irish points: 8/1, shaped with promise when third in
maiden at Worcester (2 lengths behind River of Intrigue) on hurdling debut: sure to
progress. *Alex Hales*

HURRABORU (IRE) 10 b.g. Brian Boru – Fastlass (Celtic Cone) [2016/17 c24.2dᵖᵘ **c– §**
c25.2sᵖᵘ Mar 8] dual winning pointer: winning hurdler: yet to complete in chases: stays **h– §**
25f: acts on good to firm and heavy going: wears headgear: temperamental. *M. V. Coglan*

HURRICANE BEN (IRE) 8 b.g. Beneficial – Atagirl (IRE) (Supreme Leader) [2016/17 **c148**
c21.2m* c23v* c17g* c17g⁴ c18.2g² c18.2d⁴ c18s² c16.7d* c16d⁴ Apr 27] second foal:
brother to fair 2¾m hurdle winner Masterleaderman: dam 19f bumper winner: winning
pointer: ran once in bumpers: smart chaser: won hunter at Tramore very early in season,
novice hunter at Tipperary and handicap at Ballinrobe (by 6 lengths from Rebel Cry) in
May, and novice handicap at Fairyhouse (by 8 lengths from Don't Touch It) in April: stays
23f, though effective at much shorter: acts on good to firm and heavy going: usually wears
tongue tie: often travels strongly. *James G. Sheehan, Ireland*

HURRICANE HUNTER (IRE) 5 br.g. Scorpion (IRE) – Broken Gale (IRE) (Broken **h–**
Hearted) [2016/17 h15.8d h19g h16vᵖᵘ h18.5g Apr 11] maiden pointer: no form over
hurdles. *Katy Price*

HURRICANE IVAN (IRE) 9 b.g. Golden Tornado (IRE) – Woodram Delight (Idiot's **c– §**
Delight) [2016/17 c90, h–: c24.2d h22.2g h23d c20.5sᵘʳ c24sʳʳ h20.2gᵖᵘ Apr 28] winning **h–**
hurdler/maiden chaser, no form in 2016/17: tried in cheekpieces: has worn tongue tie:
temperamental (has refused to race). *S. Wilson, Ireland*

HURRICANE RITA (FR) 7 gr.m. Sagamix (FR) – Madonna da Rossi (Mtoto) [2016/17 **h92**
h101: h24.3d h22.7s⁵ h20.6s h24.1s h25.8v⁶ h20.5v* h16.2s² Mar 16] has reportedly had
wind operation: modest handicap hurdler: won at Ayr in March: stays 2¾m: acts on heavy
going: tried in cheekpieces: in tongue tie last 3 starts: front runner/races prominently.
Stuart Coltherd

HURRICANE'S GIRL 8 b.m. Hurricane Run (IRE) – Wise Little Girl (Singspiel (IRE)) **c114**
[2016/17 c23.8d³ c24.2s⁵ Dec 27] maiden point winner: maiden hurdler: fair form over **h–**
fences: stays 3m: acts on good to soft going. *James Evans*

HURRICANE VOLTA (IRE) 6 ch.g. Hurricane Run (IRE) – Haute Volta (FR) (Grape **h–**
Tree Road) [2016/17 h–: h15.9g⁴ h19.1sᵖᵘ Nov 13] no form over hurdles: in cheekpieces
last 2 starts. *Peter Hedger*

HURRY HENRY (IRE) 8 b.g. Blueprint (IRE) – Tower Princess (IRE) (King's Ride) **c103**
[2016/17 h113: c16v³ c17.7s⁴ c20vᵖᵘ h16v⁴ c20.9v⁴ Mar 1] tall gelding: fair hurdler: fair **h–**
form over fences: left Henry de Bromhead after third start: stays 2¼m: raced only on soft/
heavy going: tried in cheekpieces: in tongue tie last 2 starts. *Brian Barr*

HUSTLE (IRE) 12 ch.g. Choisir (AUS) – Granny Kelly (USA) (Irish River (FR)) [2016/17 **h–**
h–: h16g⁶ h16m h15.8mᵖᵘ Jun 9] well-made gelding: maiden hurdler, no longer of any
account. *Clare Hobson*

HYDRANT 11 b.g. Haafhd – Spring (Sadler's Wells (USA)) [2016/17 h63: h15.7d Nov 15] **h–**
good-topped gelding: little form over hurdles. *Richard Guest*

HYGROVE PERCY 4 ch.g. Sir Percy – Hygrove Welshlady (IRE) (Langfuhr (CAN)) **h115**
[2016/17 h16.8m* h15.8g² h17.2d* h16.7g² h17.7g* h16d⁴ h18.8g⁶ Mar 25] sturdy
gelding: fairly useful hurdler: won juveniles at Newton Abbot in July and Cartmel in
August, and handicap at Fontwell in September: stays 2¼m: acts on good to firm and good
to soft going: usually leads. *Neil Mulholland*

I

I AM COLIN 8 b.g. Zafeen (FR) – Dd's Glenalla (IRE) (Be My Native (USA)) [2016/17 **c123**
c117, h–: c24.1s* c26dᵖᵘ c23.8dᵖᵘ c22.6g⁶ Apr 1] strong gelding: winning hurdler: fairly **h–**
useful handicap chaser: won at Bangor in November: stays 3m: acts on heavy going: in
cheekpieces on 4 of last 5 starts. *Nigel Twiston-Davies*

I BELIEVE 10 b.m. Exit To Nowhere (USA) – Musical Vocation (IRE) (Orchestra) **c56**
[2016/17 c22.6g⁵ Apr 23] fifth foal: half-sister to fair hurdlers Jackieandy (17f winner, by
Parthian Springs) and Boosha (2¾m winner, by Sir Harry Lewis): dam winning pointer:
dual point winner: in cheekpieces, tailed off in hunter on chasing debut. *Miss H. Brookshaw*

IBIS DU RHEU (FR) 6 b.g. Blue Bresil (FR) – Dona du Rheu (FR) (Dom Pasquini (FR)) **c145**
[2016/17 h145: c23.4g³ c23.6s² c20.8s³ c25gᵖᵘ Mar 14] well-made gelding: smart hurdler: **h–**
smart form over fences: placed in Worcester Novices' Chase at Newbury (14 lengths
behind Thistlecrack) in November and novice handicap at Chepstow (4½ lengths behind
Pobbles Bay) in December: stays 3m: acts on heavy going: wears hood/tongue tie.
Paul Nicholls

IBLEO (FR) 4 b.g. Dick Turpin (IRE) – Mahendra (GER) (Next Desert (IRE)) [2016/17 **h114**
h15.9s h16.9s* h16g Feb 25] fifth foal: half-brother to French hurdler/chaser Val de Saane
(17f-19f winner, by Rock of Gibraltar): well held in 3 starts on Flat: fair form over hurdles:
won juvenile at Compiegne early in season: left P. Leblanc after second start: tried in
cheekpieces. *Venetia Williams*

IBREEQ (IRE) 4 b.g. Intikhab (USA) – Cerulean Sky (IRE) (Darshaan) [2016/17 b14.6s **b–**
b16s Jan 6] modest maiden on Flat, stays 12.5f: no form in bumpers. *Roger Fell*

ICANMOTOR 10 b.m. Midnight Legend – Lochnagold (Lochnager) [2016/17 h76: **h82**
h19.6g³ h19.6g⁵ h19.9s h19.9g² h23.9m² Apr 20] poor maiden hurdler: tailed off from third
after third start: stays 3m: acts on good to firm and good to soft going: usually in
cheekpieces: wears tongue tie. *Fergal O'Brien*

ICARIO (FR) 4 ch.g. Soldier of Fortune (IRE) – Indianapolis (GER) (Tiger Hill (IRE)) **h118**
[2016/17 h16g⁵ h16bd h16d² h16d² h16s² h16v² h16.4gᶠ h18.8g³ h16g² Apr 21] rather
unfurnished gelding: fair on Flat for H-A. Pantall, stays 11.5f: fairly useful hurdler: second
in maiden at Navan in March: unproven beyond 2m: acts on heavy going: wears hood: tried
in tongue tie. *Gordon Elliott, Ireland*

ICE COLD SOUL (IRE) 7 b.g. Stowaway – Western Whisper (IRE) (Supreme Leader)) **h130**
[2016/17 h124: h16d h16g* h20g h16d Apr 18] well-made gelding: winning pointer: useful
handicap hurdler: won coral.ie Hurdle at Leopardstown (by ½ length from Tudor City)
in January: stays 2¼m: acts on heavy going: wears tongue tie: usually races prominently.
Noel Meade, Ireland

ICE COOL CHAMPS (IRE) 6 ch.g. Robin des Champs (FR) – Last of Many (IRE) **h116 p**
(Lahib (USA)) [2016/17 b16v² h19.7v* h21.7d³ Mar 26] third foal: dam unraced half- **b99**
sister to useful hurdler/high-class chaser (stayed 33f) Shotgun Willy and Welsh Grand
National winner Mini Sensation: promise when second in bumper at Warwick (2 lengths
behind Marten) in December: fairly useful form over hurdles: won maiden at Hereford in
February: will prove suited by 3m: remains capable of better. *Philip Hobbs*

ICE KONIG (FR) 8 gr.g. Epalo (GER) – Isarwelle (GER) (Sternkoenig (IRE)) [2016/17 **h94**
h94: h21.6g h16.8s² h16.8d² h16.8g³ h16d⁶ h19g h19g³ h21.6m⁵ h21.6g⁵ Apr 26] rather
leggy gelding: modest handicap hurdler: stays 2¾m: acts on soft and good to firm going:
tried in tongue tie. *Jimmy Frost*

coral.ie Hurdle (Extended Handicap), Leopardstown—Noel Meade saddles his first winner of the race since 1993 as Ice Cold Soul (right) holds off Tudor City (white face)

ICG

I C GOLD (IRE) 9 b.m. Gold Well – Longing For Cindy (USA) (Belong To Me (USA)) **c–**
[2016/17 h16g h20g h20g h23.3v^pu h23.8g^f h23.8g Mar 24] point winner: fairly useful **h85**
handicap hurdler at best, well below form in 2016/17: little impact in 3 starts over fences
in 2015/16: left Adrian McGuinness after third start: stays 3m: acts on good to firm and
good to soft going: often in headgear/tongue tie in 2016/17. *Paul Stafford, Ireland*

ICING ON THE CAKE (IRE) 7 b.g. Spadoun (FR) – Honeyed (IRE) (Persian Mews) **c128**
[2016/17 h112p: h17.7d^4 c16.4d* c20s^ur c15.5s^4 c19.9g^3 Mar 25] good-topped gelding: **h113 p**
won completed start in Irish maiden points: fair form over hurdles (open to improvement):
fairly useful form over fences: won novice handicap at Newbury in December: stays 2½m:
acts on soft going: usually races towards rear. *Oliver Sherwood*

ICONIC SKY 4 gr.f. Sixties Icon – Kentucky Sky (Cloudings (IRE)) [2016/17 h16g^2 **h106**
h16.7s^5 h16s* h15.8d^3 h16g h16s^3 Mar 30] half-sister to fairly useful hurdler Mystic Sky
(2m-19f winner, by Midnight Legend): fair form on Flat: fair form over hurdles: won
maiden at Fakenham in January: raced around 2m: acts on soft going: usually races in
cheekpieces: often races prominently. *Lucy Wadham*

IDAMAY (IRE) 6 br.m. Stowaway – Aguida (FR) (Kahyasi) [2016/17 h15.9g h18.7d^4 **h–**
h16g h22g^6 h23m h20g^6 h23.1g^pu Sep 28] no form: in tongue tie last 3 starts. *Katy Price*

IDDER (IRE) 6 br.g. Authorized (IRE) – Epiphany (Zafonic (USA)) [2016/17 h16m^5 **h110**
h16d^3 h15.6g* h19.3d^4 h16.4g^2 h16.2g^3 Apr 26] fairly useful on Flat for Roger Varian,
stays 10.5f: fair form over hurdles: won maiden at Musselburgh in January: left Paul
Webber after first start: unproven beyond 2m: acts on good to soft going: in cheekpieces
last 2 starts: often travels strongly. *James Moffatt*

IDENTITY THIEF (IRE) 7 b.g. Kayf Tara – Miss Arteea (IRE) (Flemensfirth (USA)) **c147**
[2016/17 h157: h16s^2 c16g* c16d* c17d^pu c17g^ur c17s^4 h20g^6 Apr 28] rather leggy **h–**
gelding: very smart hurdler at best, failed to beat a rival at Aintree and Punchestown
last 2 starts: smart form over fences: won maiden at latter course (by 14 lengths from
O Ceallaigh) in October and Craddockstown Novices' Chase there (by length from
Ordinary World) in November: stays 2½m, usually races at shorter: acts on heavy going.
Henry de Bromhead, Ireland

I'DLIKETHEOPTION (IRE) 6 b.g. Presenting – Supreme Dreamer (IRE) (Supreme **c127**
Leader) [2016/17 h120, b86: h15.8g h16.3m^3 c21m^2 c20m^ur c16m* c19.1g^4 c16.9d^3 c16g^2 **h112**
c16.2g^4 Apr 24] rather unfurnished gelding: fairly useful handicap hurdler: fairly useful
handicap chaser: won novice event at Ludlow in October: stays easy 21f: acts on good to
firm and good to soft going: wears tongue tie: often races towards rear/travels strongly.
Jonjo O'Neill

IFANDBUTWHYNOT (IRE) 11 b.g. Raise A Grand (IRE) – Cockney Ground (IRE) **c130**
(Common Grounds) [2016/17 c–, h131: h16.7g^pu h16.8g^4 h16g^3 h15.7v^pu h16d^5 h15.6g **h117**
c15.7s* c16g* c15.5g Apr 22] workmanlike gelding: fairly useful handicap hurdler
nowadays: third at Wetherby in October: useful handicap chaser: won at Southwell in
March and Ludlow (by 9 lengths from I'dliketheoption) in April: unproven beyond 2m: has
won on heavy going, but probably best under less testing conditions (acts on good to firm):
has worn hood: in tongue tie last 4 starts: often leads. *Tim Easterby*

IF IN DOUBT (IRE) 9 b.g. Heron Island (IRE) – Catchers Day (IRE) (Catcher In The **c– x**
Rye (IRE)) [2016/17 c–x, h151: h24d^5 h24.1g^5 Oct 29] strong gelding: smart hurdler: **h–**
below form at Wetherby in October, and not seen out again: winning chaser: stays 25f: acts
on heavy going: usually races towards rear: often let down by jumping over fences.
Philip Hobbs

IF THE CAP FITS (IRE) 5 b.g. Milan – Derravaragh Sayra (IRE) (Sayarshan (FR)) **b115**
[2016/17 b17.7g* b16.5g* b17g^4 Apr 7] £30,000 3-y-o: good-topped gelding: third foal:
dam unraced half-sister to useful hurdler/chaser (stays 31f) Duke of Lucca (by Milan):
smart form in bumpers: won at Plumpton (by 2¼ lengths from Puppet Warrior) in
November and Taunton (conditionals/amateur event, by 9 lengths from Or de Vassy) in
February: fourth in Grade 2 at Aintree (2¾ lengths behind Lalor) in April: will be suited
by 2½m+. *Harry Fry*

IFTIRAAQ (IRE) 6 b.g. Muhtathir – Alzaroof (USA) (Kingmambo (USA)) [2016/17 **c123**
h116: h16d^5 h16.7g^4 c16m^3 Oct 20] fairly useful form over hurdles: fourth in Summer **h119**
Hurdle (Handicap) at Market Rasen in July: 8/1, third in novice handicap at Ludlow (4½
lengths behind I'dliketheoption) on chasing debut: best at sharp 2m: acts on good to firm
and heavy going: wears headgear: tried in tongue tie: front runner/races prominently.
Seamus Durack

IF YOU SAY RUN (IRE) 5 b.m. Mahler – De Lissa (IRE) (Zaffaran (USA)) [2016/17 **b104 p**
b16g* Apr 17] €1,500 3-y-o, £80,000 4-y-o: fourth foal: dam, ran twice, out of half-sister
to Grand National winner Amberleigh House: won Irish maiden point on debut: in tongue
tie, 6/4, looked useful prospect when won mares bumper at Chepstow (by 13 lengths from
Rouergate) in April. *Paul Nicholls*

IGUACU 13 b.g. Desert Prince (IRE) – Gay Gallanta (USA) (Woodman (USA)) [2016/17 **h90**
h99: h19g⁵ h18.7m May 20] modest handicap hurdler nowadays: stays 19f: acts on good to
firm and good to soft going: tried in cheekpieces: often races towards rear. *Richard Price*

I JUST KNOW (IRE) 7 b.g. Robin des Pres (FR) – Desperado Queen (IRE) (Un **c133**
Desperado (FR)) [2016/17 h103: c24.3s* c23.9s² c24.2d² c24d* c25.2s* c25gᵖᵘ c24.3g³ **h–**
Apr 22] good-topped gelding: maiden hurdler: useful handicap chaser: won at Hexham
(novice event) in November, Doncaster (novice event) in January and Catterick in
February: stays 25f: acts on soft going: front runner. *Sue Smith*

I KNOW THE CODE (IRE) 12 b.g. Viking Ruler (AUS) – Gentle Papoose (Commanche **c71**
Run) [2016/17 h19.7dᵖᵘ h20.7sᵖᵘ c24.2d² c24.2gᵖᵘ Apr 25] angular gelding: modest hurdler **h–**
at best, pulled up first 2 starts in 2016/17: poor maiden chaser: stays 2½m: acts on heavy
going. *Lynn Siddall*

I KNOW U TOO WELL (IRE) 5 b.g. Stowaway – Kilbricken Leader (IRE) (Supreme **b104**
Leader) [2016/17 b15.8v* b15.8s* Mar 5] €55,000 3-y-o: fifth foal: half-brother to winning
pointers by Needle Gun and Great Palm: dam 2¼m bumper winner: fairly useful form in
bumpers: won at Ffos Las (maiden event) in December and Huntingdon in March: will stay
beyond 2m. *Jonjo O'Neill*

IKORODU ROAD 14 b.g. Double Trigger (IRE) – Cerisier (IRE) (Roselier (FR)) **c– §**
[2016/17 c129§, h–: c24gᵖᵘ May 14] good-topped gelding: winning hurdler: useful chaser **h–**
at best, pulled up sole outing in 2016/17: stays 3¼m: acts on soft and good to firm going:
wears headgear: temperamental. *Graeme McPherson*

IKRAAMM 4 b.g. Street Cry (IRE) – Red Dune (IRE) (Red Ransom (USA)) [2016/17 **b–**
b13.7d b16s Jan 26] well held in 2 bumpers. *Harry Whittington*

IKTIVIEW 9 ch.g. Iktibas – Eastview Princess (J B Quick) [2016/17 h93§: h23m h22m **h– §**
Aug 24] modest hurdler at best, no form in 2016/17: stayed 27f: acted on soft going: wore
headgear/tongue tie: temperamental: dead. *Matt Sheppard*

ILEWINDELILAH 9 b.m. Grape Tree Road – Bridepark Rose (IRE) (Kemal (FR)) **h–**
[2016/17 h17.7dᵖᵘ h19.1d h16.5g Dec 30] modest hurdler at best, no form in 2016/17: has
worn headgear, including in 2016/17. *Gary Moore*

ILEWIN FOR HANNAH 10 b.g. Generous (IRE) – Ilewin Janine (IRE) (Soughaan **c97**
(USA)) [2016/17 c–, h–: c25.5d* c25.5g² May 29] winning hurdler: modest form over **h–**
fences: won handicap at Fontwell early in season: stayed 3¼m: acted on soft going: dead.
Gary Moore

I'LL BE YOUR CLOWN (IRE) 6 b.g. Aqlaam – Lady Avenger (IRE) (Namid) [2016/17 **h113**
h16.3g* h15.8g³ Apr 17] fairly useful on Flat, stays 1½m: fair form over hurdles: won
novice at Stratford in April: raced only at 2m: acts on heavy going. *Dan Skelton*

I'LL HAVE A LOOK (IRE) 10 b.g. Milan – Kelly's Native (IRE) (Be My Native (USA)) **h95 §**
[2016/17 h98: h23g³ h21.6g² h21.6gᵖᵘ h21.6g² h23.1s h23.9g⁴ h23.9g⁶ h21.4d² h21.4d²
Mar 26] dual point winner: modest handicap hurdler: stays 3m: acts on heavy going: wears
headgear: usually races close up: temperamental. *Katie Stephens*

ILLWALKTHELINE (IRE) 5 b.m. Presenting – Jigs'n Reels (IRE) (Old Vic) [2016/17 **b95**
b16.2s⁴ b17s* b16.4s* b16d Mar 11] €16,000 3-y-o: useful-looking mare: fourth foal: dam
unraced half-sister to high-class hurdler/smart chaser (stayed 3m) Back In Front and fairly
useful hurdler/useful chaser (stays 3m) Another Hero: fairly useful form in bumpers: won
mares events at Carlisle in December and Newcastle in January: will stay 2½m+.
Nicky Richards

ILOVEMINTS 5 b.m. Kayf Tara – La Harde (FR) (Valanour (IRE)) [2016/17 b105p: **b88**
b17g⁶ b16.6d b16.5m³ Apr 27] fairly useful form at best in bumpers. *Warren Greatrex*

IL PRESIDENTE (GER) 10 ch.g. Royal Dragon (USA) – Independent Miss (GER) **h101**
(Polar Falcon (USA)) [2016/17 h92+: h19.2g² h16.7d* Jun 17] fair form over hurdles: won
novice handicap at Market Rasen in June: stays 2½m. *Ian Williams*

IL SASSICAIA 4 b.g. Dick Turpin (IRE) – Step Fast (USA) (Giant's Causeway (USA)) **h–**
[2016/17 h18.1dᵖᵘ h16.2gᵖᵘ Apr 27] modest maiden on Flat, stays 1¼m: no form over
hurdles: in tongue tie second start. *Jackie Stephen*

I'M A GAME CHANGER (IRE) 5 b.g. Arcadio (GER) – Drinadaly (IRE) (Oscar (IRE)) **h132**
[2016/17 b–: h16.7v h15.7d³ h16.7d* h15.8s* h16.3d⁴ Mar 24] useful-looking gelding:
useful form over hurdles: won novice at Bangor in January and handicap at Ludlow (by 11
lengths from Dino Velvet) in February: raced around 2m: acts on soft going: often races
towards rear/travels strongly. *Philip Hobbs*

IM ALL SET (IRE) 8 b.g. Darsi (FR) – Gathabawn Lass (IRE) (Norwich) [2016/17 c107: **c89**
c26.3g c25.1vᵘʳ c23g⁴ Apr 6] multiple point winner: modest maiden chaser: tried in
cheekpieces. *Mrs C. Hitch*

IMARI KID (IRE) 4 b.g. Pour Moi (IRE) – Breathe (FR) (Ocean of Wisdom (USA)) **h113 p**
[2016/17 h16s⁶ h16g³ Dec 27] compact gelding: fairly useful on Flat, stays 11f: fair form
when third in juvenile at Kempton on second of 2 starts over hurdles: capable of better.
Gary Moore

I'M BRITISH 4 b.g. Aqlaam – Libritish (Librettist (USA)) [2016/17 b13.7g Nov 8] 125/1, **b–**
ninth in junior bumper at Huntingdon. *Sarah Humphrey*

I'M IN CHARGE 11 b.g. Rakaposhi King – Cloudy Pearl (Cloudings (IRE)) [2016/17 **c118**
c105, h91: c25.1m* c25d^pu h21.6m* c20.2m² c26.7m² Oct 23] workmanlike gelding: fair **h103**
handicap hurdler: won novice event at Exeter in October: fairly useful handicap chaser:
won at Wincanton early in season: second there twice in October: stays 27f: acts on good
to firm going: wears tongue tie. *Grant Cann*

IMJOEKING (IRE) 10 b.g. Amilynx (FR) – Go Franky (IRE) (Hollow Hand) [2016/17 **c130**
c109, h–: c21.2d⁵ c20.1s⁵ c17.1d² c17.1s* c16.4g⁶ c15.2s⁴ c16.3s c15.5v* c21.1g^F Apr 7] **h–**
big gelding: winning hurdler: useful handicap chaser: won at Kelso (by 6 lengths from
Quick Decisson) in November and Ayr (by 8 lengths from Pistol Park) in March: stays
2½m: acts on good to firm and heavy going: wears tongue tie: usually leads. *Lucinda Russell*

IMPACT AREA (IRE) 11 gr.g. Portrait Gallery (IRE) – Walk On (IRE) (Welsh Term) **c–**
[2016/17 c121: c25.1m^pu Apr 5] multiple winning pointer: fairly useful hunter chaser,
pulled up sole outing in 2016/17: stays 3¼m: acts on heavy going: wears cheekpieces: front
runner/races prominently. *Mrs Harriet Waight*

IMPECCABILITY 7 b.m. Lucky Story (USA) – Impeccable Guest (IRE) (Orpen (USA)) **h89**
[2016/17 h94: h16.8s^pu h15.8g h15.8d* h15.8d Oct 28] modest handicap hurdler: won at
Uttoxeter in October: stays 2½m: acts on soft going: wears cheekpieces. *John Mackie*

IMPERIAL BAY (IRE) 5 br.g. Flemensfirth (USA) – Nun Better (IRE) (Presenting) **h118**
[2016/17 h21d⁴ h23.6s* h22v⁴ Feb 25] third foal: half-brother to fair hurdler Feenakilmeedy
(19f winner, by Alflora): dam, lightly raced in bumpers, half-sister to fairly useful hurdler/
chaser (stayed 2½m) Carmelite: fairly useful form over hurdles: won maiden at Chepstow
in January: will stay beyond 3m. *Ben Pauling*

IMPERIAL ELOQUENCE (IRE) 5 b.g. Kalanisi (IRE) – Babble On (IRE) (Anita's **b106**
Prince) [2016/17 b93: b16.4s³ b15.7d² b16.4g Mar 15] rangy gelding: useful bumper
performer: placed in listed events at Cheltenham (1¾ lengths behind Poetic Rhythm) in
November and Ascot (2 lengths behind Western Ryder) in December: sure to stay further
than 2m: often races towards rear. *Fergal O'Brien*

IMPERIAL GLANCE 7 br.g. Passing Glance – Juno Mint (Sula Bula) [2016/17 h56: **h77**
h16.8m³ h16.7g^F Oct 25] poor form over hurdles: likely to prove best at 2m: in hood/
tongue tie last 2 starts. *Harry Fry*

IMPERIAL JOEY (IRE) 12 b.g. Imperial Ballet (IRE) – Berkeley Bay (IRE) (Fit To **c–**
Fight (USA)) [2016/17 c17.3g c20g^pu Jul 21] winning hurdler: fair chaser at best, no **h–**
form in 2016/17: stays 2½m: acts on good to firm and heavy going: wears headgear.
Joanne Foster

IMPERIAL PRESENCE (IRE) 6 ch.g. Presenting – Penneyrose Bay (Karinga Bay) **c131**
[2016/17 h122: c17.5g² c16.4g⁵ c16.9d⁵ c16.4g* c16.9m² Apr 2] strong gelding: winning **h–**
hurdler: useful form over fences: won handicap at Newbury (by 3 lengths from
Doitforthevillage) in March: raced around 2m: acts on good to soft going: tried in hood:
front runner/races prominently. *Philip Hobbs*

IMPORTANT MOMENT (IRE) 8 b.g. Milan – Cuiloge Lady (IRE) (Beneficial) **h112**
[2016/17 h16.2s* h16s⁶ h19.4g⁴ h24.3d⁵ Apr 21] maiden point winner: fair form over
hurdles: won maiden at Perth in July: stays 3m: in tongue tie last 2 starts. *Stuart Crawford,
Ireland*

IMPROVED (IRE) 7 ch.g. Rainwatch – Show Potential (IRE) (Glacial Storm (USA)) **h95**
[2016/17 h105, b92: h24.1g⁵ h19.7g⁶ h21.3g h23.1sᵖᵘ h20.6d⁴ h24.4dᵖᵘ h23.4d* h23.8g⁶
Mar 1] bumper winner: modest handicap hurdler: won novice event at Fakenham in
February: stays 23f: acts on soft going: in cheekpieces last 2 starts: front runner/races
prominently. *Philip Kirby*

IMPULSIVE AMERICAN 5 b.g. American Post – Impulsive Decision (IRE) **c125**
(Nomination) [2016/17 h125: c19.2g* c16s* h16.2s² c20.1s⁴ c15.5g³ c15.9g c23g⁴ Nov 24] **h122**
rather leggy gelding: fairly useful handicap hurdler: second at Perth in July: fairly useful
form over fences: won novices at Market Rasen and Perth (finished alone) in July: stays
2½m: acts on soft going: wears headgear: tried in tongue tie. *David Pipe*

IMPULSIVE STAR (IRE) 7 b.g. Busy Flight – Impulsive Ita (IRE) (Supreme Leader) **h132 p**
[2016/17 h20s* h24s⁴ h25.3g* h23.1s* h24g Mar 16] €7,000 3-y-o: well-made gelding:
will make a chaser: first foal: dam, failed to complete in 3 points, sister to dam of smart
chaser (stays 23f) Hurricane Ben: point/bumper winner: useful form over hurdles: won
maiden at Ffos Las in November, novice at Catterick in January and handicap at Exeter (by
3½ lengths from Rocklander) in February: will stay long distances: acts on soft going:
usually races prominently: remains open to improvement. *Neil Mulholland*

I'M STILL WAITING (IRE) 5 ch.g. Stowaway – Prima Dona Sivola (FR) (Apple Tree **h96**
(FR)) [2016/17 b17.7d⁶ h19.8d h20.5d h18.6s⁵ Jan 18] £7,000 3-y-o: second foal: dam **b–**
French maiden jumper: needed experience in bumper: modest form on last of 3 starts over
hurdles. *Fergal O'Brien*

INCENTIVISE (IRE) 14 ch.g. Snurge – Festive Isle (IRE) (Erins Isle) [2016/17 c115, **c–**
h–: c25.5sᵖᵘ Jan 26] compact gelding: maiden hurdler: fairly useful chaser at best, pulled **h–**
up sole outing in 2016/17: stays 3¾m: acts on good to firm and heavy going. *Kerry Lee*

INCHCOLM (IRE) 7 br.g. Presenting – Rose of Inchiquin (IRE) (Roselier (FR)) [2016/17 **c83**
c82, h74: c24dᵖᵘ c24.2g⁵ c24.2s² c25.2s³ c26.3gᵖᵘ Mar 29] placed in Irish maiden points: **h–**
lightly-raced hurdler: poor maiden chaser: stays 25f: acts on soft going: in headgear last 3
starts. *Micky Hammond*

INCH LALA (IRE) 5 ch.m. Mahler – Aboo Lala (IRE) (Aboo Hom) [2016/17 b16.7g⁶ **b78**
Mar 27] second foal: dam winning pointer: second in Irish maiden point on debut: 7/1,
sixth in mares maiden bumper at Market Rasen. *Neil Mulholland*

INCH ROVER (IRE) 10 b.g. Dushyantor (USA) – Ban Gardai (IRE) (Mukaddamah **c–**
(USA)) [2016/17 h24gᵖᵘ h23.3g h19.9g³ h25m² h25m⁵ c23.8v³ c22.7fᵖᵘ Dec 1] maiden **h73**
pointer: poor maiden hurdler: little impact in 2 starts over fences: stayed 25f: acted on good
to firm going: wore headgear: tried in tongue tie: usually led: dead. *Jennie Candlish*

INCH WING (IRE) 9 b.m. Winged Love (IRE) – Incharder (IRE) (Slip Anchor) [2016/17 **h–**
h–: h15.9mᴿ Apr 16] no form. *Mark Hoad*

INDIANA BAY (IRE) 10 ch.g. Indian River (FR) – Easter Saturday (IRE) (Grand Plaisir **c107**
(IRE)) [2016/17 c110: c32.5g³ Apr 27] angular gelding: multiple winning pointer: fair
hunter chaser: stayed 33f: acted on heavy going: dead. *Mrs Jill Dennis*

INDIAN BRAVE (IRE) 6 b.g. Definite Article – Fridays Folly (IRE) (Flemensfirth **h121**
(USA)) [2016/17 h98p, b84: h19.4g² h22s⁶ h19.9s* Apr 1] fairly useful form over hurdles:
won conditionals maiden at Uttoxeter in April: second in novice handicap at Doncaster
in November: left Neil Mulholland after second start: stays 2½m: acts on soft going.
Anthony Honeyball

INDIAN CASTLE (IRE) 9 b.g. Dr Massini (IRE) – Indian Legend (IRE) (Phardante **c132**
(FR)) [2016/17 c128, h–: c25.8g² May 4] tall gelding: winning hurdler: useful handicap **h–**
chaser: second at Newton Abbot (8 lengths behind Shuil Royale) early in season: stays
3¼m: acts on heavy going: has worn cheekpieces, including last 2 starts. *Ian Williams*

INDIAN HARBOUR 4 b.g. Indian Haven – Hawait Al Barr (Green Desert (USA)) **b82**
[2016/17 b15.7s b16v² b15.7g⁶ Mar 28] half-brother to several winners, including
unreliable hurdler/chaser Excellent Vibes (2¾m-25f winner, by Doyoun): dam useful
1½m-2m winner: modest form in bumpers: best effort when second at Ayr in March.
Alan Swinbank

INDIAN HERCULES (IRE) 5 b.g. Whitmore's Conn (USA) – Carrawaystick (IRE) **b– p**
(Old Vic) [2016/17 b16v⁵ Mar 23] €6,000 3-y-o, £50,000 5-y-o: fifth foal: half-brother to
bumper winner/fair hurdler Crank Em Up (23f winner, by Royal Anthem): dam unraced
half-sister to useful hurdler/fairly useful chaser (17f-2½m winner) Indian Scout: won
second of 2 starts in Irish points: 7/4, fifth in bumper at Chepstow (18½ lengths behind
Dessinateur) in March: clearly thought capable of better. *Warren Greatrex*

401

INDIAN LEADER (IRE) 8 b.g. Indian Danehill (IRE) – Supreme Fivestar (IRE) **c–**
(Supreme Leader) [2016/17 b82: c23.6mᵖᵘ Apr 28] multiple point winner: in cheekpieces,
pulled up in novice hunter on chasing debut. *Mickey Bowen*

INDIAN NATIVE (IRE) 7 b.m. Oscar (IRE) – Roman Native (IRE) (Be My Native **h109**
(USA)) [2016/17 b18v⁴ h19.6d⁵ h24v³ h21s³ h19.7v* h19.5v³ Feb 20] sixth foal: closely **b80**
related to fairly useful 2m hurdle winner Prince of Lombardy (by Milan): dam (h104),
bumper/2m hurdle winner, half-sister to useful hurdler/chaser (stayed 3¼m) Basilea Star:
mares maiden point winner: some encouragement when fourth in mares maiden bumper:
fair form over hurdles: won mares handicap at Hereford in February: left James G. Sheehan
after first start: best effort at 2½m: acts on heavy going. *Alex Hales*

INDIAN REEL (IRE) 7 br.g. Indian River (FR) – Ceilidh Dancer (Scottish Reel) **h93**
[2016/17 h20g h23d h16.7d⁵ Apr 27] twelfth foal: dam ran twice on Flat: won completed
start in points: modest form on last of 3 starts over hurdles: left Ms Margaret Mullins after
second start: should stay at least 2½m. *Fergal O'Brien*

INDIAN RUPEE (IRE) 8 b.g. Indian Danehill (IRE) – Get A Few Bob Back (IRE) (Bob **c104 x**
Back (USA)) [2016/17 h20g⁵ h20d² c20g² c20.9gᵖᵘ c16.3g³ h25g³ c16g c20vᵖᵘ Jan 10] **h104**
sturdy gelding: fair handicap hurdler: fair form over fences: left Thomas Mullins after
second start: stays 2½m: acts on soft going: usually wears hood: often leads: sketchy
jumper of fences. *Dai Williams*

INDIAN SAHIB (IRE) 10 b.g. Indian Creek – Lady Ward (IRE) (Mujadil (USA)) **h–**
[2016/17 h16.2d h20.2sᵖᵘ Jul 10] little impact in 2 starts over hurdles. *Keith Pollock*

INDIAN STREAM 8 ch.m. Generous (IRE) – Zaffarimbi (IRE) (Zaffaran (USA)) **c143**
[2016/17 c134, h115: c24g² c21.4d* c23.6g c19.4g* h19.9g⁴ h20.3g³ Apr 20] lengthy, **h141**
workmanlike mare: useful hurdler: fourth in David Nicholson Mares' Hurdle at Cheltenham
in March: useful handicap chaser: won at Market Rasen early in season and Wetherby
(listed event) in October: stays 3m: acts on soft going: wears tongue tie: usually travels
strongly. *Neil Mulholland*

INDIAN TEMPLE (IRE) 8 b.g. Indian River (FR) – Ballycraggan (IRE) (Beneficial) **c131**
[2016/17 c128, h–: c20.5g* c22.4g c20.5d³ Apr 21] workmanlike gelding: maiden hurdler: **h–**
useful handicap chaser: won at Ayr (by 3¼ lengths from Final Assault) in October: third in
listed event there (5½ lengths behind Two Taffs) in April: stays 2¾m: acts on heavy going:
tried in cheekpieces: usually leads. *Tim Reed*

INDIAN VOYAGE (IRE) 9 b.g. Indian Haven – Voyage of Dreams (USA) (Riverman **c123**
(USA)) [2016/17 c137, h–: c17.1d⁶ c17.1d⁶ c15.2m⁵ c15.5g⁴ c19.4d³ c15.2d² c15.7s **h–**
c15.7g⁵ Jan 12] strong gelding: maiden hurdler: fairly useful handicap chaser nowadays:
second at Wetherby in December: stays 2½m: acts on good to firm and heavy going: wears
tongue tie. *Maurice Barnes*

INDIETIR (FR) 5 b.g. Muhtathir – Indietra (USA) (Vindication (USA)) [2016/17 h16s **h–**
Dec 3] lengthy gelding: fair maiden on Flat, stays 1¼m: useful hurdler for S. Culin in
2015/16 (second in Prix Cambaceres at Auteuil final start), well beaten sole outing in
2016/17: stays 2¼m: acts on soft going. *Dan Skelton*

INDIROCCO (GER) 4 ch.g. Shirocco (GER) – Indigo Girl (GER) (Sternkoenig (IRE)) **h105 P**
[2016/17 h16s³ Nov 23] sixth foal: half-brother to 2 winners, including very smart hurdler
Irving (15f-17f winner, by Singspiel): dam useful German 10.5f winner: 5/2, plenty of
promise when third in juvenile maiden hurdle at Wetherby (6¼ lengths behind Coeur de
Lion) on debut, finishing with running left: open to significant improvement. *Dan Skelton*

INDISPENSABELLE 8 b.m. Passing Glance – Belle Largesse (Largesse) [2016/17 **h–**
h15.9v⁵ h16g h20.5m⁴ Apr 16] sturdy mare: no form: in hood last 2 starts. *Linda Jewell*

INDOMITABLE SPIRIT 5 b.g. Zebedee – Gayala (IRE) (Iron Mask (USA)) [2016/17 **h–**
h16g⁶ h15.8d h16s⁴ h15.9s Mar 13] fair on Flat, stays 1m: no form over hurdles. *Martin
Smith*

INDULGENCE 5 b.m. Sir Percy – Kaloni (IRE) (Kalanisi (IRE)) [2016/17 b–: h20.6g **h–**
h19.4g⁵ Nov 26] failed to beat a rival in 2 starts over hurdles. *Pam Sly*

INDULGENT 4 b.g. Makfi – Santa Agata (FR) (Anabaa (USA)) [2016/17 h16.7g h16gᵖᵘ **h–**
h16.7sᵖᵘ h15.7d⁵ h15.7d h19.9s Feb 6] modest maiden on Flat, stays 1½m: no form over
hurdles: in hood last 3 starts. *Mike Sowersby*

INDY FIVE (IRE) 7 b.g. Vertical Speed (FR) – Beesplease (IRE) (Snurge) [2016/17 **h115**
b90p: h15.8d³ h19d* May 18] won maiden on completed start in Irish points: fairly useful
form over hurdles: won novice at Warwick early in season. *David Dennis*

INDY ISLAND (IRE) 8 gr.m. Indian Danehill (IRE) – Another Sparkle (Bustino) [2016/17 c20gpu h20.5s⁶ h19.7d⁴ h16s* h20v h19.9d² h19.9g⁶ h20.2gpu Apr 26] fifth foal: half-sister to a winning pointer by Pilsudski; dam (b64), ran twice in bumpers, half-sister to fair hurdler/useful chaser (stayed 25f) Sparkling Cone and useful hurdler (stayed 3m) Coworth Park: point winner: modest hurdler: won maiden at Down Royal in January: pulled up in mares maiden on chasing debut: stays 2½m: acts on soft going: tried in cheekpieces. *Stuart Crawford, Ireland*   c– h97

IN FAIRNESS (IRE) 8 b.g. Oscar (IRE) – Dix Huit Brumaire (FR) (General Assembly (USA)) [2016/17 c24.2g² c21.2g⁴ Apr 17] tall, useful-looking gelding: maiden pointer: winning hurdler: modest maiden chaser nowadays: stays 3m: acts on good going. *E. Turner*   c96 h–

INFINITE SUN 6 b.g. And Beyond (IRE) – Kingussie Flower (Scottish Reel) [2016/17 b16.7s* b16.3d b16.7d Apr 27] good-topped gelding: chasing type: fifth foal: dam, winning pointer, half-sister to useful chasers Kings Brook (stayed 2¾m) and Oakfield Legend (stayed 3¼m): fair form in bumpers: won at Market Rasen in November: will be suited by 2½m+: tried in tongue tie. *Fergal O'Brien*   b94

INFORMALITY (IRE) 6 b.m. Haafhd – Casual Glance (Sinndar (IRE)) [2016/17 h21gᴿ Sep 29] of no account on Flat: refused second on hurdling debut. *James Moon, Jersey*   h–

INICIAR (GER) 7 b.g. Galileo (IRE) – Iota (GER) (Tiger Hill (IRE)) [2016/17 h122: h21.2m⁴ h16g* Sep 6] fairly useful handicap hurdler: won at Worcester in September: should stay beyond 2m: acts on good to soft going: in headgear last 2 starts. *David Pipe*   h126

INISHRUSH (IRE) 16 br.g. Presenting – Ballyknock Lass (IRE) (Electric) [2016/17 c24dur Nov 15] dual winning pointer: lightly-raced hurdler: fair chaser at best: off 40 months, failed to complete sole outing in 2016/17: stays 3¼m: acts on good to firm and good to soft going: wears cheekpieces/tongue tie. *Bill Turner*   c– h–

INK MASTER (IRE) 7 b.g. Whitmore's Conn (USA) – Welsh Connection (IRE) (Welsh Term) [2016/17 c120, h120: c16m* c16d³ c16g⁶ c16.5g⁶ c16g* Apr 17] workmanlike gelding: winning hurdler: fairly useful handicap chaser: won at Ludlow early in season and Chepstow in April: raced around 2m: acts on good to firm and good to soft going: has finished weakly. *Philip Hobbs*   c129 h–

INNER DRIVE (IRE) 9 b.g. Heron Island (IRE) – Hingis (IRE) (Shernazar) [2016/17 c–p, h–: h16.3d² Mar 24] very lightly raced: easily won maiden point: useful hurdler: second in handicap at Newbury (1¼ lengths behind Maestro Royal) on sole outing in 2016/17: once-raced chaser: stays 21f. *Alan King*   c– h131

INNER LOOP 5 b.m. Rail Link – Sailing Days (Kris) [2016/17 b79: b16g⁶ b15.7d⁶ Jul 10] modest form in bumpers, well held both starts in 2016/17. *Robert Stephens*   b–

INNISFREE LAD (IRE) 5 b.g. Yeats (IRE) – Tasmani (FR) (Turgeon (USA)) [2016/17 b16s³ b16s h16g Apr 8] €23,000 3-y-o: second foal: closely related to fairly useful hurdler/chaser Cyclop (17f-3m winner, by King's Theatre), stays 3½m: dam unraced half-sister to fairly useful hurdler/smart chaser (2m-21f winner) Jim and useful French hurdler/fairly useful chaser (17f-19f winner) Mesange Royale: modest form on first of 2 starts in bumpers: well held on hurdling debut: left James Ewart after second start. *David Dennis*   h– b83

INNIS SHANNON (IRE) 7 br.m. Stowaway – Put On Hold (IRE) (Lord Americo) [2016/17 h98x: c20.1gF c23.4spu c24.2spu h23.3v³ Dec 7] modest handicap hurdler: failed to complete all 3 starts over fences: stays 2½m: acts on heavy going: tried in cheekpieces: often races in rear: often let down by jumping. *George Bewley*   c– x h69 x

INNOCENT GIRL (IRE) 8 b.m. King's Theatre (IRE) – Belle Innocence (FR) (Turgeon (USA)) [2016/17 c15.7g* h19.2m* c19.9mur h15.8d² c17.4g* c18.2g* h15.3m² c20.2f² Apr 23] sturdy mare: modest handicap hurdler: won mares event at Towcester in October: fair form over fences: won handicaps at Southwell (novice event) in October, Fontwell in November and Taunton (novice event) in March: stays 19f: acts on firm and good to soft going: wears hood/tongue tie: usually travels strongly. *Harry Fry*   c113 h88

INNOKO (FR) 7 gr.g. Carlotamix (FR) – Chalana (Ashkalani (IRE)) [2016/17 h96: h15.8g³ h15.5g h16g h16.5g² h15.5g Jan 24] good-topped gelding: fair handicap hurdler: raced only at 2m: acts on good to soft going: usually wears hood: tried in tongue tie: often races lazily. *Tony Carroll*   h100

INN THE BULL (GER) 4 ch.g. Lope de Vega (IRE) – Ile Rousse (Danehill (USA)) [2016/17 h15.8m* Oct 20] half-brother to fair/ungenuine hurdler Marc Aurele (2m winner, by Trempolino): dam half-sister to smart hurdler/chaser (2m-19f winner) Sporazene: fair on Flat, stays 7f: 3/1, won juvenile at Ludlow (by 1¼ lengths from Jazzy) on hurdling debut: open to improvement. *Alan King*   h100 p

IN ON THE ACT 7 b.g. Act One – Pequenita (Rudimentary (USA)) [2016/17 h119: **c82** h15.9g⁴ h16.8d³ h16g* h15.7g⁶ h20.5d³ h20d⁴ c23gᵖᵘ c18.2d⁴ c16d⁴ c19.4g⁶ Apr 1] fairly **h117** useful handicap hurdler: won at Worcester in July: third at Plumpton (amateur event) in November: poor form over fences: stays 21f: acts on good to soft going: usually races towards rear. *Evan Williams*

INSIGHT (IRE) 6 b.m. Bushranger (IRE) – Ribbon Glade (UAE) (Zafonic (USA)) **h82** [2016/17 h15.7d⁴ h16s h15.7v⁵ h15.6g⁶ h19.9sᵖᵘ Feb 6] modest maiden on Flat, stays 1½m: poor form over hurdles: unproven beyond 2m. *Lucinda Egerton*

INSPIRING (IRE) 6 br.m. Waky Nao – Newtown Dancer (IRE) (Danehill Dancer (IRE)) **h–** [2016/17 h–: h18.5gᵖᵘ May 5] no form. *Johnny Farrelly*

INSTAGRAM (FR) 5 b.g. Falco (USA) – Trumbaka (IRE) (In The Wings) [2016/17 **h–** h21.4sᵖᵘ h15.7sᵖᵘ Mar 16] well held in 2 maidens on Flat: fair form over hurdles for Francois Nicolle in 2015/16: in hood/tongue tie, pulled up both starts in 2016/17: best effort at 17f: acts on soft going. *David Pipe*

INSTANT KARMA (IRE) 6 b.g. Peintre Celebre (USA) – Kotdiji (Mtoto) [2016/17 **h129** h117: h16.7g² h16.3m* h18.5g* h15.7m² h21gᵖᵘ Dec 26] rather leggy gelding: fairly useful handicap hurdler: won at Stratford in July and Newton Abbot in August: second in listed event at Ascot in October: stays 2¼m: acts on soft and good to firm going. *Michael Bell*

INSTANT REPLAY (IRE) 5 ch.g. Fruits of Love (USA) – Ding Dong Belle (Minster **h–** Son) [2016/17 b16g² b15.7g⁶ h19.9d⁵ Dec 26] €10,000 3-y-o, £90,000 4-y-o: sixth foal: **b89** brother to 19f bumper winner/fair 2¼m chase winner Badgerfort and fair hurdler Coeur Tantre (2¼m winner): dam (h82), temperamental 2½m hurdle winner, half-sister to useful hurdler/chaser (2m-3m winner) Robbie: runner-up in Irish maiden point: fair form when second in conditionals/amateur event at Fakenham on first of 2 starts in bumpers: tailed off in novice on hurdling debut: should prove suited by further than 2m. *Brian Ellison*

INSTINGTIVE (IRE) 6 b.g. Scorpion (IRE) – Fully Focused (IRE) (Rudimentary (USA)) **c97** [2016/17 h–, b95: h21g⁵ h16.3d h20.5v c17v* c16v³ c20.9d⁵ c25.7m³ Apr 16] tall gelding: **h65** poor form over hurdles: modest form over fences: won novice handicap at Plumpton in January: left Harry Fry after first start: unproven beyond 17f: acts on heavy going: tried in blinkers: has worn tongue tie, including in 2016/17: front runner/races prominently. *Gary Moore*

INTENSE TANGO 6 b.m. Mastercraftsman (IRE) – Cover Look (SAF) (Fort Wood **h123** (USA)) [2016/17 h131: h16.6d⁴ h16g Apr 22] useful hurdler, below best in 2016/17: raced around 2m: acts on good to soft going: in tongue tie last 2 starts. *K. R. Burke*

INTERCOUNTY STAR (IRE) 8 b.g. Heron Island (IRE) – Lee Valley Native (IRE) **c– p** (Be My Native (USA)) [2016/17 h17s⁶ h16s⁴ h16g⁵ h16g⁴ c18.5g h16d⁶ h16v⁴ h19vᵖᵘ **h91** h19.5sᵘʳ h16s Apr 7] fourth foal: brother to a winning pointer: dam (h66) maiden hurdler: maiden pointer: modest maiden hurdler: well beaten in maiden on chasing debut: unproven beyond 2m: acts on good to soft going: wears hood: usually leads: open to improvement over fences. *Dermot Anthony McLoughlin, Ireland*

IN THE CROWD (IRE) 8 ch.g. Haafhd – Eliza Gilbert (Noverre (USA)) [2016/17 **h–** h98§: h19g h16.3mᵖᵘ h19g Nov 24] workmanlike gelding: fair hurdler at best, no form in 2016/17: wears headgear: has worn tongue tie. *Roy Brotherton*

INTHENICOFTIME 7 b.g. With The Flow (USA) – Rose Lir (Lir) [2016/17 h–, b–: **h–** h16mᵖᵘ h16.8sᵖᵘ Jan 17] no form. *Jess Westwood*

IN THE ROUGH (IRE) 8 b.g. Scorpion (IRE) – Sounds Charming (IRE) (Presenting) **c132** [2016/17 c109p, h–: c23d² c23g⁴ c24g* c26.2d³ c22.4g c18.8dᵖᵘ c20v c24.2d⁴ c24.2m **h–** Apr 13] workmanlike gelding: winning hurdler: useful chaser: won maiden at Uttoxeter in September: third in handicap at Carlisle (5 lengths behind Carrigdhoun) in October: stays 3¼m: acts on heavy going. *Jonjo O'Neill*

IN THE TUB (IRE) 8 b.g. Kutub (IRE) – County Classic (Noble Patriarch) [2016/17 c–: **c–** c19.2v⁶ c19.2s⁵ c25.1vᵖᵘ c24.5sᵖᵘ c20.2dᵖᵘ Mar 26] winning pointer: no form in chases: tried in blinkers: has worn tongue tie, including last 3 starts. *Carroll Gray*

INTIFADAH (IRE) 5 b.g. Intikhab (USA) – Cuilaphuca (IRE) (Danetime (IRE)) **h100** [2016/17 h15.8d³ h16.7g h16g* h16g h16.2g⁶ h16m h17.7g³ h15.8g² Apr 28] compact gelding: fair maiden on Flat, stays 1m: fair hurdler: won maiden at Tramore in August: left Patrick Griffin after third start: stays 2¼m: best form on good going: wears cheekpieces/tongue tie. *Tom Symonds*

INVICTUS (GER) 5 b.g. Exceed And Excel (AUS) – Ivowen (USA) (Theatrical) **h72**
[2016/17 h93p: h17s^pu h16.4v h16.8g^5 h16.8m^6 Apr 19] modest form in 2 starts over
hurdles in 2015/16, little impact in 2016/17: raced around 2m: acts on good to soft going:
tried in hood: usually races freely. *David Loughnane*

INVINCIBLE BOND 4 b.g. Monsieur Bond (IRE) – Royal Pardon (Royal Applause) **h–**
[2016/17 h16.2d^pu Sep 21] little form on Flat: pulled up in juvenile on hurdling debut.
Simon Waugh

INVINCIBLE WISH (IRE) 5 b.g. Vale of York (IRE) – Moonlight Wish (IRE) (Peintre **h103**
Celebre (USA)) [2016/17 h16.7g^5 h16.7v^3 Nov 9] fair on Flat, stays 1½m: fair form when
third in novice at Bangor on second of 2 starts over hurdles: wears hood. *Trevor Wall*

INVISIBLE MAN (FR) 12 ch.g. Mansonnien (FR) – J'y Reste (FR) (Freedom Cry) **c85**
[2016/17 c107, h–: c20s^4 c20s^5 Mar 2] lengthy gelding: winning pointer: maiden hurdler: **h–**
modest hunter chaser nowadays: stays 3m: acts on soft and good to firm going: tried in
cheekpieces: usually wears tongue tie. *Mrs D. J. Ralph*

INVITATION ONLY (IRE) 6 b.g. Flemensfirth (USA) – Norabelle (FR) (Alamo Bay **h135**
(USA)) [2016/17 h16p: b16d* h16d* h20s^3 h20s^6 Apr 2] won maiden on sole point **b–**
outing: smart bumper winner: useful form over hurdles: won maiden at Gowran in
November: best effort when third in Navan Novices' Hurdle (5¼ lengths behind Death
Duty) in December. *W. P. Mullins, Ireland*

INVOCATION (FR) 4 b.g. Intense Focus (USA) – Fabiola (GER) (Medicean) [2016/17 **h109**
h16.3m^3 h16.8m^2 h16.8g^2 h16m^2 h16.7g^5 Sep 24] dam half-sister to fairly useful hurdler/
useful chaser (stays 29f) Fredo: fairly useful maiden hurdler: raced around 2m: acts on good
to firm going: in headgear last 2 starts. *Alan King*

IONA DAYS (IRE) 12 br.g. Epistolaire (IRE) – Miss Best (FR) (Grand Tresor (FR)) **c99**
[2016/17 c109, h–: c20.3g^3 c21.1d^5 c20.9d^4 c19.8d^pu c19.4g^5 Apr 8] tall gelding: maiden **h–**
hurdler: modest handicap chaser nowadays: stays 3m: acts on good to firm and heavy
going: wears headgear: often races towards rear. *Julian Smith*

IORA GLAS (IRE) 8 gr.g. Court Cave (IRE) – Crossdrumrosie (IRE) (Roselier (FR)) **c111**
[2016/17 c72, h116: h23.9d^3 h26.5m c24g^5 c24g^3 c26.2d^2 c24.5g^3 c25.2g^4 h20.5g h24g* **h118**
Apr 19] fairly useful handicap hurdler: won at Cheltenham in April: fair maiden chaser:
stays 27f: acts on good to firm and heavy going: tried in cheekpieces: usually wears tongue
tie. *Fergal O'Brien*

IRISH CAVALIER (IRE) 8 gr.g. Aussie Rules (USA) – Tracker (Bustino) [2016/17 **c159**
c165, h–: c20d* c19.4g^5 c24.2g* c24.1v^pu c25s^3 c21s^5 c26.3g^pu c21.1g c20d^3 Apr 26] good- **h–**
topped gelding: winning hurdler: high-class chaser: won Charlie Hall Chase at Wetherby
(by ¾ length from Menorah) in October: largely below form after: stays 3m: acts on heavy
going: usually wears headgear: tried in tongue tie: usually races towards rear. *Rebecca Curtis*

*bet365 Charlie Hall Chase, Wetherby—the race-fit Irish Cavalier lowers the colours of previous
winners Menorah and Cue Card (noseband)*

IRISH FASHION 5 gr.m. Demetrius (IRE) – Flying Fashion (IRE) (Shaamit (IRE)) **b–**
[2016/17 b16d Feb 21] first foal: dam once-raced half-sister to useful/ungenuine staying
chaser Another Rum: well beaten in mares bumper. *Ian Duncan*

IRISH HAWKE (IRE) 5 b.g. Montjeu (IRE) – Ahdaab (USA) (Rahy (USA)) [2016/17 **h94**
h16.8s^pu h17.2g^4 h16.7g h16.7d^4 h16.7g^5 h15.7g^6 h16.8d^pu h15.7m^6 Apr 13] fairly useful
on Flat, stays 11.5f: modest handicap hurdler: won novice at Bangor in August: will stay
2½m: acts on good to soft going: wears tongue tie. *Donald McCain*

IRISH OCTAVE (IRE) 7 b.g. Gamut (IRE) – Fairytaleofnewyork (IRE) (Zaffaran **c–**
(USA)) [2016/17 h71§: h23.3v^3 h22g^6 h24d^3 c23g^5 c24d^6 Oct 13] poor maiden hurdler: no **h64 §**
form over fences: stays 23f: acts on heavy going: tried in headgear: not one to trust.
Rosemary Gasson

IRISH PROPHECY (IRE) 4 b.g. Azamour (IRE) – Prophets Honor (FR) (Highest **b101**
Honor (FR)) [2016/17 b13g* b16g* Feb 25] third foal: dam (b88), runner-up in bumper on
only start, half-sister to high-class hurdler/very smart chaser (2m-2½m winner) Wahiba
Sands: fairly useful form in bumpers: won at Doncaster (junior event) in November and
Kempton in February. *Emma Lavelle*

IRISH RANGER (IRE) 6 b.g. Gamut (IRE) – Erins Emblem (IRE) (Erins Isle) [2016/17 **h–**
b–: h16.3v h16.3m^5 h18.7g h18.7g h19.9d^pu Oct 13] no form. *Rosemary Gasson*

IRISH ROE (IRE) 6 b.m. Vinnie Roe (IRE) – Betty's The Best (IRE) (Oscar (IRE)) **b102**
[2016/17 b16.2g* b16.8g* b16.4s* b16.4g b17g Apr 6] €2,000 3-y-o: small, sparely-made
mare: third foal: sister to fairly useful hurdler Bobbie's Diamond (19f winner): dam,
unraced, closely related to fairly useful hurdler/useful chaser (stayed 3m) Dante Hall: fairly
useful bumper performer: won mares events at Perth in August, Sedgefield in September and
Cheltenham (listed event, dead-heated with My Khaleesi) in November: often travels
strongly. *Peter Atkinson*

IRISH SAINT (FR) 8 b.g. Saint des Saints (FR) – Minirose (FR) (Mansonnien (FR)) **c144**
[2016/17 h25.3s^5 c23.8d^6 c24.2v^3 c24g Feb 25] deep-girthed gelding: smart hurdler: off 19 **h128 +**
months, better than result on return: smart chaser, excuses on all 3 outings over fences in
2016/17: stays 2¾m: acts on good to firm and heavy going: wears tongue tie. *Paul Nicholls*

IRISH THISTLE (IRE) 10 b.g. Luso – Which Thistle (IRE) (Saddlers' Hall (IRE)) **c101 x**
[2016/17 c123, h–: c29.1g^F c16g^5 c16g^4 c16.4d^F c17.2d^4 c23.5v^pu c19.9d^3 c24.2s^F c18.2g^3 **h–**
c19.9d^2 c19.4g^3 c21m^2 Apr 15] workmanlike gelding: winning hurdler: fair handicap
chaser nowadays: stays 23f: acts on good to firm and heavy going: has worn headgear,
including final start: has worn tongue tie: sketchy jumper of fences. *Dai Williams*

IRIS'S PROMISE 5 gr.m. Black Sam Bellamy (IRE) – Cheeky Mare (Derrylin) [2016/17 **b–**
b15.8v b17s Dec 11] half-sister to fairly useful hurdler/useful chaser Lower Hope Dandy
(3m winner, by Karinga Bay) and a winning pointer by Alflora: dam unraced half-sister to
top-class hurdler/smart chaser (2½m-25f winner) Iris's Gift: well held in 2 bumpers.
Jennie Candlish

IRON CHANCELLOR (IRE) 12 b.g. Alderbrook – Masriyna (IRE) (Shahrastani **c109**
(USA)) [2016/17 c81, h–: c25.5g^2 Apr 24] lengthy gelding: maiden hurdler: fair hunter **h–**
chaser: stays 3¼m: acts on heavy going: has worn headgear. *Mrs Sue Popham*

IRONDALE EXPRESS 6 b.m. Myboycharlie (IRE) – Olindera (GER) (Lomitas) **h89**
[2016/17 h96: h15.8g^pu h15.8g^3 h16.2d^3 Jun 30] modest maiden hurdler: raced around 2m:
best form on good going: has worn cheekpieces, including final start. *Barry Brennan*

IRON HORSE 6 b.g. Kayf Tara – What A Vintage (IRE) (Un Desperado (FR)) [2016/17 **b65**
b15.8s^4 Mar 18] well beaten in bumper. *Richard Phillips*

IRVING 9 b.g. Singspiel (IRE) – Indigo Girl (GER) (Sternkoenig (IRE)) [2016/17 h155: **h153**
h16.4s* h15.7s^F h16v^3 h15.3d^6 Feb 18] sturdy gelding: smart hurdler: won 'Fighting Fifth'
Hurdle at Newcastle (by nose from Apple's Jade) in November for second time: raced
around 2m: acts on heavy going: tried in cheekpieces/tongue tie. *Paul Nicholls*

ISAAC BELL (IRE) 9 b.g. Fruits of Love (USA) – Oso Well (IRE) (Oscar (IRE)) **h113**
[2016/17 h114: h16d h18.6d^2 h18.6s^6 Jan 18] close-coupled gelding: fair handicap hurdler:
stays 19f: acts on soft going: in cheekpieces last 2 starts: wears tongue tie. *Alex Hales*

ISAACSTOWN LAD (IRE) 10 b.g. Milan – Fountains of Friends (IRE) (Phardante (FR)) **c–**
[2016/17 c–, h129: h23.1s^3 h21.4s^4 h20.5v^2 h25.8s^4 Mar 25] sturdy gelding: Irish maiden **h125**
point winner: fairly useful handicap hurdler: placed at Bangor in November and Ayr in
February: some promise only start over fences (in 2013/14): stays 27f: acts on heavy going:
tried in cheekpieces. *Nicky Richards*

ISAAC'S WARRIOR (IRE) 11 b.g. Pushkin (IRE) – Point The Finger (IRE) (Neshad (USA)) [2016/17 h23.3g^{pu} May 29] Irish maiden point winner: no form under Rules: tried in tongue tie. *Tracey Leeson*   **c–** **h–**

ISABELLESPRINCESS (IRE) 9 b.m. Westerner – Perkaway (IRE) (Oscar (IRE)) [2016/17 h96: h16.7s⁵ h15.7v^F Mar 6] rather sparely-made mare: winning pointer: fair maiden hurdler: stays 3m: acts on heavy going: has worn tongue tie. *Henry Oliver*   **h103**

I SEE YOU WELL (FR) 4 b.g. Air Chief Marshal (IRE) – Bonne Mere (FR) (Stepnevev (IRE)) [2016/17 b13.7d b16s⁶ h16s* h16.7s² h16.8g h15.8m² h16g⁴ Apr 29] compact gelding: fifth foal: half-brother to 3 winners on Flat, including smart 5f/6f winner Mister Hughie (by Elusive City): dam useful French 9f-1¾m winner: modest form in bumpers: fair form over hurdles: won maiden at Naas in January: left John Joseph Hanlon after fourth start: raced around 2m: acts on soft going: front runner/races prominently. *Seamus Mullins*   **h114** **b84**

I SHOT THE SHERIFF (IRE) 10 b.g. Westerner – Sherin (GER) (Surumu (GER)) [2016/17 h18.1v³ h20.3g^{pu} Mar 17] useful-looking gelding: lightly raced: useful hurdler: third in minor event at Leopardstown in March: stays 2¾m: acts on heavy going: wears tongue tie. *A. J. Martin, Ireland*   **h128**

ISKABEG LANE (IRE) 6 b.g. Westerner – Nosey Oscar (IRE) (Oscar (IRE)) [2016/17 h16.7g⁴ h18.6m⁴ Apr 17] £11,000 5-y-o: fifth foal: half-brother to a winning pointer by Golan: dam unraced sister to fair hurdler/fairly useful chaser (stayed 29f) Leon Og: placed in Irish maiden points: modest form on first of 2 starts over hurdles: will be suited by 2½m+. *Sue Smith*   **h88**

ISLA DI MILANO (IRE) 6 b.g. Milan – Monagee Island (IRE) (Fourstars Allstar (USA)) [2016/17 h–, b67: h19.5d h20.3d Nov 29] no form over hurdles. *Tim Vaughan*   **h–**

ISLA FERNANDOS (IRE) 7 ch.m. Flemensfirth (USA) – Kon Tiky (FR) (Perrault) [2016/17 h91p: h16d³ h15.9g⁴ h19.9s³ Jun 15] modest form over hurdles: tried in tongue tie. *Fergal O'Brien*   **h99**

ISLAND CONFUSION (IRE) 9 b.g. Heron Island (IRE) – Anshan Gail (IRE) (Anshan) [2016/17 c116, h–: h16.4s² Jan 7] fair maiden hurdler: lightly-raced chaser: raced only at 2m: best form on soft/heavy going: tried in hood/tongue tie. *Dan Skelton*   **c–** **h108**

ISLAND HEIGHTS (IRE) 8 b.g. Heron Island (IRE) – La Reina (IRE) (Executive Perk) [2016/17 c–, h126: h20d⁴ h22.8v⁶ h25s⁶ c26.2s⁶ Dec 29] compact gelding: fairly useful handicap hurdler: fairly useful chaser, below best sole outing over fences in 2016/17: stays 25f: acts on heavy going. *Lucinda Russell*   **c94** **h121**

stanjames.com 'Fighting Fifth' Hurdle, Newcastle—2014 winner Irving survives a blunder at the last to hold off Apple's Jade (left) and give the season's champion conditional Harry Cobden a Grade 1 win; Hidden Cyclone (second right) and Sceau Royal chase them home

ISLAND RENDEZVOUS (IRE) 7 b.g. Trans Island – Verlaya (FR) (Vertical Speed (FR)) [2016/17 b75: b16.3m h21.4d^{pu} h19.8d^{pu} h21.6m^2 Apr 18] modest form in bumpers/over hurdles: in hood/tongue tie last 2 starts. *Jeremy Scott* **h89** **b–**

ISLA PEARL FISHER 14 br.g. Supreme Sound – Salem Beach (Strong Gale) [2016/17 c110, h–: c23.8m^5 c23.8d^3 c23.8g^f Aug 20] rangy gelding: maiden hurdler: fairly useful chaser at best: stayed 3¼m: acted on soft going: wore headgear/tongue tie: dead. *N. W. Alexander* **c95** **h–**

ISLE OF EWE 6 b.m. Kayf Tara – Apple Town (Warning) [2016/17 b82: b15.8d^2 h20.3g* Aug 31] fair form in bumpers: 13/8, won novice at Southwell (by 28 lengths from Carrigkerry) on hurdling debut, soon clear: should improve. *Tom Lacey* **h117 p** **b85**

ISLEOFHOPENDREAMS 10 b.g. Flemensfirth (USA) – Cool Island (IRE) (Turtle Island (IRE)) [2016/17 c21v* h24d^2 h24s* h24g Mar 16] fairly useful handicap hurdler: won at Punchestown in February: 4/1, won maiden at Cork (by 5½ lengths from Annamatopoeia) on chasing debut: stays 3m: acts on heavy going: usually races nearer last than first: sure to progress over fences. *W. P. Mullins, Ireland* **c136 p** **h126**

ISLE VIEW (IRE) 9 b.g. Heron Island (IRE) – Mrs Cullen (Over The River (FR)) [2016/17 h19.9d^6 h23.6d c19d Aug 23] third in point: maiden hurdler, no form in 2016/17: tailed off in maiden on chasing debut: has worn headgear/tongue tie, including in 2016/17. *Jason Cairns, Ireland* **c–** **h–**

IS LOVE ALIVE 8 ch.g. Presenting – Lovely Origny (FR) (Robin des Champs (FR)) [2016/17 c20s^{ur} c24.1d^3 c24g^{pu} c21.6d^5 c22.5d^3 c22.6m^5 Oct 15] winning hurdler: fair maiden chaser: stays 3m: acts on soft going: has worn headgear, including final start: wears tongue tie. *Adrian Wintle* **c102** **h–**

ISTIMRAAR (IRE) 6 b.g. Dansili – Manayer (IRE) (Sadler's Wells (USA)) [2016/17 c100p, h117: h19d h19.6d^{pu} h19.9g^6 h16g^4 h15.7g h17.7g^2 h15.8m^2 h16d^2 c15.7d^6 h15.5g h21.4s h15.9v^4 h15.8d Apr 16] fair handicap hurdler: fair form on chasing debut in 2015/16, below that level sole outing over fences in 2016/17: left Nicky Henderson after fourth start: stays 2½m: best form on soft/heavy going: usually in headgear/tongue tie. *Alexandra Dunn* **c–** **h101**

ITALIAN RIVER 5 b.g. Milan – Over The Flow (Overbury (IRE)) [2016/17 b16.5g b16.8d Mar 21] well held in 2 bumpers. *Polly Gundry* **b–**

ITALIAN RIVIERA 8 b.g. Galileo (IRE) – Miss Corniche (Hernando (FR)) [2016/17 h24.6g^6 h23d h18g* h20d h18.1m* h19.3g* h19.4g^4 h19.3g* h19.3d^6 Jan 25] fair on Flat, stays 21f: fair handicap hurdler: won at Limerick in July, Kelso (novice event) in October, Catterick (conditional event) in November and Catterick again in January: left Eric McNamara after fourth start: stays 3m: acts on good to firm going: wears headgear: has worn tongue tie. *Kenneth Slack* **h114**

ITCHYMEI'MSCRATCH (IRE) 9 ch.g. Definite Article – Royal Molly (IRE) (Phardante (FR)) [2016/17 c22.6m^5 May 20] multiple point winner: maiden hurdler: 2/1, better than result when fifth in novice hunter at Stratford (10½ lengths behind Our Chief) on chasing debut: tried in tongue tie: open to improvement. *Gareth Moore* **c84 p** **h–**

ITOLDYOU (IRE) 11 ch.g. Salford Express (IRE) – Adisadel (IRE) (Petardia) [2016/17 c107§, h–: c19.7d c25.7g^2 c25.5s^2 c25.7v^3 h25s^6 c25.7s^3 c25.5g^2 Apr 12] sturdy gelding: lightly-raced hurdler: fair handicap chaser nowadays: stays 29f: acts on heavy going: wears headgear: has worn tongue tie, including in 2016/17: front runner/races prominently: one to treat with caution. *Linda Jewell* **c103 §** **h– §**

ITSABOUTIME (IRE) 7 gr.g. Whitmore's Conn (USA) – Blazing Love (IRE) (Fruits of Love (USA)) [2016/17 h95: h18.5g^5 May 25] angular gelding: modest maiden hurdler: should stay beyond 2½m: acts on heavy going: often races in rear. *Helen Nelmes* **h91**

ITS'AFREEBEE (IRE) 7 b.g. Danroad (AUS) – Aphra Benn (IRE) (In The Wings) [2016/17 h146, b97: c21.2g* c20.4g^5 c19.4d* c19.9s^3 c20.4g^{pu} h20.3g Apr 19] workmanlike gelding: smart hurdler at best, disappointed final outing in 2016/17: useful form over fences: won novices at Fakenham in October and Wetherby in December: third in Grade 2 novice at Haydock (21¼ lengths behind Waiting Patiently) in January: stays 21f: acts on heavy going: tried in cheekpieces: often in tongue tie: front runner/races prominently. *Dan Skelton* **c139** **h–**

IT'S A GIMME (IRE) 10 b.g. Beneficial – Sorcera (GER) (Zilzal (USA)) [2016/17 c140, h–: c16g c22.5g Jul 27] winning hurdler: useful chaser at best, no form in 2016/17: stays 2¾m, effective at shorter: acts on soft and good to firm going: has worn tongue tie, including in 2016/17: usually travels strongly. *Jonjo O'Neill* **c–** **h–**

IT'S ALL ABOUT ME (IRE) 5 b.m. King's Theatre (IRE) – Annie Spectrim (IRE) **b81**
(Spectrum (IRE)) [2016/17 b–: b15.7g³ b15.7s³ Mar 8] rather lightly-built mare: modest
form in bumpers: best effort when third at Catterick in November: will prove suited by at
least 2½m. *Micky Hammond*

IT'S ALL AN ACT (IRE) 9 br.g. Presenting – Royal Lucy (IRE) (King's Ride) [2016/17 **c– x**
c116x, h100: h16.5m h15.9v h15.9v h15.8g Apr 28] fair hurdler at best, no form in **h–**
2016/17: winning chaser: has worn headgear/tongue tie, including in 2016/17: tends to find
little: often let down by jumping over fences. *Daniel O'Brien*

ITS ALL GUESSWORK (IRE) 5 b.g. Mahler – La Lambertine (FR) (Glaieul (USA)) **h110 p**
[2016/17 h20.2d b16s⁶ b18g² Apr 28] €17,500 3-y-o: fourth foal: half-brother to a winning **b108**
pointer by Generous: dam (h113) ungenuine 2m/17f hurdle winner: useful form when
second in maiden at Punchestown (tongue tied, ¾ length behind Canardier) on second of 2
starts in bumpers: 25/1, shaped encouragingly when seventh in maiden at Leopardstown
(12¼ lengths behind Montalbano) on hurdling debut: will improve. *Gordon Elliott, Ireland*

ITS ALL OR NOTHING 8 gr.g. Terimon – Little Vera (Carlingford Castle) [2016/17 **c100**
c90: c26gᵖᵘ c24.2m² May 3] multiple point winner: fair form in hunter chases: best effort
when second at Exeter early in season. *Miss C. Rowe*

IT'S A LONG STORY (IRE) 6 b.g. Court Cave (IRE) – Rockholm Girl (IRE) (Eve's **h–**
Error) [2016/17 b16.2g⁴ h16.2s h17s⁶ h16.8d⁶ h16d h16.2g Apr 27] maiden Irish pointer: **b74**
fourth in conditionals/amateur bumper at Hexham (12½ lengths behind Vertigo) in
October: no form over hurdles. *Barbara Butterworth*

IT'S A MANS WORLD 11 b.g. Kyllachy – Exhibitor (USA) (Royal Academy (USA)) **c–**
[2016/17 c–, h99: h16.2d³ h19.9g h16.7g Jul 31] fair handicap hurdler, below form in **h81**
2016/17: maiden chaser: unproven beyond 17f: acts on soft and good to firm going: has
worn cheekpieces, including last 4 starts: has raced lazily. *Brian Ellison*

ITS A MISTAKE (IRE) 10 b.g. Aboo Hom – Creative Princess (IRE) (Creative Plan **c–**
(USA)) [2016/17 c19.4v⁵ Mar 1] winning pointer: modest form in bumpers: well held sole **h–**
start over hurdles/fences: tried in cheekpieces. *Sirrell Griffiths*

ITSAMYSTERYTOME 4 b.f. Shirocco (GER) – Mystery Lot (IRE) (Revoque (IRE)) **h89**
[2016/17 h16.7d² h16.3m⁴ h16.8m⁴ Jul 17] fifth foal: half-sister to 2m hurdle winners
Mystery Drama (fairly useful, by Hernando) and Mystery Code (fair, by Tobougg): dam
(h105), 17f hurdle winner, also 1¼m winner on Flat: modest form over hurdles: best effort
when second in juvenile at Market Rasen. *Philip Hobbs*

IT'S A STEAL (IRE) 10 b.g. Craigsteel – Mimosa Rose (IRE) (Be My Native (USA)) **c82**
[2016/17 c112, h95: h20g⁴ h20d³ c20g⁵ c20.3g⁵ Apr 21] useful-looking gelding: fair **h100**
maiden hurdler: fairly useful chaser at best, below that level in hunters in 2016/17: left
Evan Williams after second start: stays 2½m: acts on heavy going: wears tongue tie.
Alexandra Dunn

ITSHARD TO NO (IRE) 8 b.g. Helissio (FR) – Miniballist (IRE) (Tragic Role (USA)) **h104**
[2016/17 h123, b87: h19d⁴ May 7] fairly useful handicap hurdler, below form sole outing
in 2016/17: stays 2¼m: acts on heavy going: has worn hood: wears tongue tie. *Kerry Lee*

IT'S JENNIFER (FR) 5 b.m. Martaline – Shanxi Girl (Overbury (IRE)) [2016/17 **h116**
h17.9s² h17.9d⁵ h19.4v* h17.9s⁵ h17.9v h20.5g c17.9s² Apr 14] good-topped mare: third
foal: half-sister to fair hurdler Miss Mash (2½m winner) and a winning pointer (both by
Multiplex): dam (h93), 17f hurdle winner (stayed 2¾m), half-sister to smart chaser (stayed
29f) Ace High out of smart hurdler/fairly useful chaser (stayed 25f) Celtic Native: fairly
useful handicap hurdler: won at Auteuil in November: stays 21f: acts on heavy going. *Mlle
Louisa Carberry, France*

ITSNONOFURBUSINESS (IRE) 5 b.g. Flemensfirth (USA) – Moon Storm (IRE) **b69 p**
(Strong Gale) [2016/17 b16d Mar 31] €32,000 3-y-o: brother to fair 2m hurdle winner
The Boys Dont Know and half-brother to several winners, including useful hurdler/chaser
Warden Hill (21f-25f winner, by Presenting) and fairly useful hurdler/useful chaser
The Vicar (2½m/21f winner, by Bob Back), stayed 3m: dam unraced: won point on debut:
7/1, some encouragement when eighth in bumper at Wetherby (22¼ lengths behind
Kalashnikov) in March: should do better. *Dan Skelton*

ITSNOWCATO 6 b.g. Notnowcato – Blaenavon (Cadeaux Genereux) [2016/17 h111: **h97**
h21gᵖᵘ h17.7g² Aug 18] good-topped gelding: fair handicap hurdler: stays 2¼m: acts on
good to soft going: tried in tongue tie: front runner/races prominently. *Ben Pauling*

IT'S OSCAR (IRE) 10 b.g. Oscar (IRE) – Lady Bramble (IRE) (Be My Native (USA)) **c– §** [2016/17 c77§, h93§: h19.9g h19.6g h22v⁴ h24d* h23.8dᵖᵘ h24v⁵ h23.3vᵖᵘ h25.5v h20.7s⁴ **h87 §** h19.7d² h26.4g³ Apr 23] tall gelding: modest handicap hurdler: won at Southwell in July: maiden chaser: left James Evans after fourth start: best up to 3m: acts on good to firm and heavy going: wears headgear: has worn tongue tie, including last 4 starts: usually races prominently: ungenuine. *Alastair Ralph*

ITSTIMEFORAPINT (IRE) 9 b.g. Portrait Gallery (IRE) – Executive Pearl (IRE) **c120** (Executive Perk) [2016/17 c111, h71: c24d⁵ c32.4s³ c26.2s² c30g³ c32.8gᵖᵘ Feb 4] maiden **h–** hurdler: fairly useful handicap chaser: stays 4m: acts on heavy going: wears tongue tie. *Lucinda Russell*

ITSUPTOYOU (IRE) 13 b.g. Dr Massini (IRE) – I Blame Theparents (Celtic Cone) **c–** [2016/17 c110, h–: c17.2d⁶ c17.4g⁶ Jun 7] maiden hurdler: fairly useful chaser at best, no **h–** form in 2016/17: stays 19f: acts on good to firm and good to soft going: tried in hood: has worn tongue tie. *Arthur Whiting*

IT'S YOUR MOVE (IRE) 5 b.g. Flemensfirth (USA) – Jeruflo (IRE) (Glacial Storm **b82** (USA)) [2016/17 b16s³ b16.6s³ Mar 4] €52,000 3-y-o, £50,000 4-y-o: seventh foal: brother to bumper winner/fairly useful hurdler Winningtry (2½m/3m winner): dam (c80/h88) bumper/2m-2½m hurdle winner: third in maiden point on debut: modest form in bumpers: better effort when third at Wetherby in February: likely to stay further than 2m. *Brian Ellison*

IVAN GROZNY (FR) 7 b.g. Turtle Bowl (IRE) – Behnesa (IRE) (Suave Dancer (USA)) **h154** [2016/17 h152: h16d* h16s* h16s⁵ h16g⁶ Apr 28] angular gelding: smart hurdler: won Grimes Hurdle at Tipperary (by 11 lengths from Sempre Medici) in July and Istabraq Hurdle there (by 4¾ lengths from Bentelimar) in October: raced around 2m: acts on heavy going: wears hood: has worn tongue tie: often travels strongly. *W. P. Mullins, Ireland*

IVANHOE 7 b.g. Haafhd – Marysienka (Primo Dominie) [2016/17 h110: h16dᵘʳ h15.7sᵖᵘ **h–** Mar 16] angular gelding: fair hurdler at best, failed to complete both starts in 2016/17: stays 19f: best form on soft/heavy going. *Michael Blanshard*

IVANOVICH GORBATOV (IRE) 5 b.g. Montjeu (IRE) – Northern Gulch (USA) **h152** (Gulch (USA)) [2016/17 h156+: h16d³ h20g³ h16d³ h20d⁴ h16d³ h16g³ h16.8g⁶ Mar 17] round-barrelled gelding: smart hurdler: third in Morgiana Hurdle at Punchestown (17 lengths behind Nichols Canyon) in November and Ryanair Hurdle at Leopardstown (9¼ lengths behind Petit Mouchoir) in December: stays 2½m: acts on heavy going: has worn headgear, including final start: wears tongue tie. *Joseph Patrick O'Brien, Ireland*

IVOR'S QUEEN (IRE) 8 b.m. King's Theatre (IRE) – Sonnerschien (IRE) (Be My **c– p** Native (USA)) [2016/17 h78p: h16.8d* h15.8g² h17.7gᶠ h16.8d³ h19.5g³ h20.5g³ h21.4mᵖᵘ **h113** c17.5vᶠ Dec 15] sturdy mare: fair hurdler: won mares novice at Newton Abbot in June: weakening when fell heavily 2 out in mares novice won by Tagrita at Exeter on chasing debut: stays 21f: acts on good to soft going: tried in hood: wears tongue tie: should do better over fences. *Colin Tizzard*

I WONDER WHY (IRE) 10 br.g. Publisher (USA) – Wondering Lady (IRE) (Kemal **c89** (FR)) [2016/17 c21.2g² Apr 17] multiple winning pointer: 9/2, second in novice hunter at Fakenham (19 lengths behind Pride of Parish) on chasing debut. *G. T. H. Bailey*

IZBUSHKA (IRE) 6 b.g. Bushranger (IRE) – Zaynaba (IRE) (Traditionally (USA)) **h– §** [2016/17 h85§: h27sᵖᵘ May 3] modest hurdler at best, seemingly amiss sole outing in 2016/17: stays 25f: acts on soft and good to firm going: wears headgear: has worn tongue tie: untrustworthy. *David Thompson*

IZZY PICCOLINA (IRE) 9 b.m. Morozov (USA) – Chloara (IRE) (Flemensfirth **h–** (USA)) [2016/17 h90: h21.6g May 4] maiden hurdler, well held sole outing in 2016/17: stays 19f: acts on soft going: races towards rear. *Geoffrey Deacon*

J

JABBEA (IRE) 5 b.g. Robin des Pres (FR) – Welsh Bea (IRE) (Welsh Term) [2016/17 b–: **b–** b15.3m May 10] rather unfurnished gelding: no form in bumpers. *Mary Sanderson*

JABOLTISKI (SPA) 5 b.g. Delfos (IRE) – Sonic Sea (IRE) (Zafonic (USA)) [2016/17 **c112** h119: h16g⁶ c20s⁴ c19.2vᵖᵘ c18.2gᵖᵘ h21.6m⁴ Apr 15] good-topped gelding: fair hurdler: **h112** fair form on completed start over fences: stays 2¾m: acts on good to firm and heavy going: tried in cheekpieces. *Philip Hobbs*

JABULANI (FR) 4 gr.g. Martaline – Incorrigible (FR) (Septieme Ciel (USA)) [2016/17 **b96** b15.8v* b15.8g⁶ Apr 9] brother to 3 winners, including fair hurdler/useful chaser Hollywoodien (2m-19f winner) and fairly useful hurdler/chaser Carabinier (2m-2¾m winner): dam unraced: fairly useful form when won at Ffos Las in March on first of 2 starts in bumpers. *Nigel Twiston-Davies*

JACARNO 5 ch.g. Lucarno (USA) – Sparkling Jewel (Bijou d'Inde) [2016/17 b16.8g³ **b71** b15.8g b16d b16.2v⁵ Mar 28] poor form in bumpers. *Andrew Crook*

JACK BEAR 6 b.g. Joe Bear (IRE) – Colins Lady (FR) (Colonel Collins (USA)) [2016/17 **h90 p** h16.8gᵘʳ h15.9g³ h15.7d⁵ Nov 29] fairly useful on Flat, stays 1¼m: modest form on second of 3 starts over hurdles: remains open to improvement. *Harry Whittington*

JACKBLACK 5 b.g. Crosspeace (IRE) – Saharan Royal (Val Royal (FR)) [2016/17 b74: **h111** h15.9g³ h17.7g³ Apr 12] fair form over hurdles: better effort when third in maiden at Fontwell in April: in hood last 2 starts. *Brett Johnson*

JACKFIELD 7 b.g. Norse Dancer (IRE) – Small Amount (Sir Harry Lewis (USA)) **c63** [2016/17 h64: h22g* h25.6d⁴ c24d⁵ Jul 13] poor handicap hurdler: won novice event at **h67** Stratford early in season: 9/1, fifth in novice handicap at Uttoxeter on chasing debut: stays 2¾m: acts on good to firm and good to soft going: in headgear last 3 starts: often races prominently. *Robin Dickin*

JACK IN A BOX 7 b.g. Kayf Tara – La Dame Brune (FR) (Mansonnien (FR)) [2016/17 **c97** c20.3s² c19.3v² c19.1s³ c23.6v² Mar 23] £28,000 5-y-o: first foal: dam (h113), unreliable 2½m/21f hurdle winner, half-sister to fairly useful hurdler/useful chaser (2m-21f winner) Nikos Extra: maiden point winner: modest form over fences. *Nigel Hawke*

JACK LAMB 5 gr.g. Sulamani (IRE) – Charlotte Lamb (Pharly (FR)) [2016/17 b81: h16d **h85** h16g Apr 23] modest form on first of 2 starts over hurdles: left Sally Hall after that. *Jedd O'Keeffe*

JACKOFHEARTS 9 b.g. Beat Hollow – Boutique (Selkirk (USA)) [2016/17 h93: **c84** c23.8m² c20.1d c23.8s⁴ c20.1g² c23.8g c20.1s⁴ c20.5s⁵ c21.6d⁶ Apr 10] maiden hurdler: **h–** poor maiden chaser: stays 3m: acts on soft and good to firm going: tried in cheekpieces: often races towards rear. *Jean McGregor*

JACKS LAST HOPE 8 b.g. King's Theatre (IRE) – Ninna Nanna (FR) (Garde Royale) **h133** [2016/17 h87: h16.7g⁴ h19.6dᵖᵘ h16.2d* h16.3g² h16.2g² h16.8g³ h16g* h20g³ h16.5gᵖᵘ h20.2g* Apr 28] useful handicap hurdler: won at Perth in June, Wetherby in October and Perth again (by 2 lengths from Sky Khan) in April: stays 2½m: acts on heavy going: wears visor. *Chris Grant*

JACK SNIPE 8 b.g. Kirkwall – Sea Snipe (King Luthier) [2016/17 h78: h21.6g⁴ c20g **c85** h21.6g⁵ h21.4m² h25d² h21.4d c26.3g* c27.5g³ Apr 23] modest maiden hurdler: modest **h87** form over fences: won novice handicap at Taunton on chasing debut: stays 3¼m: acts on good to firm and good to soft going: wears headgear: often responds generously to pressure. *Jeremy Scott*

JACK STEEL (IRE) 7 b.g. Craigsteel – Wake Me Gently (IRE) (Be My Native (USA)) **c–** [2016/17 c121, h108: h20.1d⁴ h20d⁴ h17.1g³ c23.8d⁶ Nov 14] point winner: fair maiden **h92** hurdler at best, below form in 2016/17: fairly useful chaser at best, excuses sole outing over fences in 2016/17: stays 2½m: acts on soft going: in headgear last 2 starts. *Lucinda Russell*

JACK THE GENT (IRE) 13 b.g. Anshan – Asidewager (Brush Aside (USA)) **c– §** [2016/17 c111§, h–: c17.3dᵖᵘ Jun 26] big, well-made gelding: has reportedly had breathing **h–** operation: winning hurdler: fairly useful chaser at best, pulled up sole outing in 2016/17: stays 19f: acts on good to firm and heavy going: tried in visor/tongue tie: front runner/races prominently: unreliable. *Tim Easterby*

JACKTHEJOURNEYMAN (IRE) 8 b.g. Beneficial – Maslam (IRE) (Robellino **c100 §** (USA)) [2016/17 c105, h–: h16.7g⁶ c16.3sᵖᵘ h15.8g⁴ c16.5m* c15.7d³ c17.2m⁴ Apr 17] **h88** modest maiden hurdler: fair handicap chaser: won at Huntingdon in October: unproven beyond 2m: acts on good to firm and good to soft going: wears headgear: has worn tongue tie, including in 2016/17: front runner/races prominently: temperamental. *Tom Gretton*

JACK THE WIRE (IRE) 7 b.g. Scorpion (IRE) – Smiling Away (IRE) (Phardante (FR)) **c–** [2016/17 c90p, h86p, h105: h20d³ h16.7g* h16s* h16g h16.4s h23.1d³ h24d h24s Feb 5] **h120** workmanlike gelding: point/bumper winner: fairly useful hurdler: won maiden at Galway in July and handicap at Listowel in September: maiden chaser: stays 2½m: acts on soft going. *Denis Hogan, Ireland*

JAC THE LEGEND 8 b.g. Midnight Legend – Sky Burst (Gunner B) [2016/17 c117, **c116 §** h94: c29.2g³ c26gᵖᵘ c30g c25.2s³ h27v⁵ c26.3g h27g* h24.3d Apr 21] strong, compact **h106** gelding: fair handicap hurdler: won at Sedgefield in April: fairly useful handicap chaser: third at Sedgefield in October: stays 29f: acts on soft going: wears headgear: temperamental. *Brian Ellison*

JADE'S LEGEND 7 ch.m. Flying Legend (USA) – Ellina (Robellino (USA)) [2016/17 **c93** c22.9s⁴ c22.9g⁶ c19.9d⁵ c21.2g³ h20.3d⁶ h21.2d⁶ h16g³ h17.7vᵖᵘ c19.1gᵖᵘ Jan 27] modest **h97** form over hurdles: modest maiden chaser: left E. & G. Leenders after third start: stayed 2¾m: acted on soft going: tried in headgear: usually raced close up: dead. *Amy Murphy*

JAISALMER (IRE) 5 b.g. Jeremy (USA) – Shara (IRE) (Kahyasi) [2016/17 b86: h19.7s⁶ **h119 p** h20.5v² h21mᵘʳ Apr 4] fairly useful form over hurdles: still in front when stumbled and unseated last in novice at Kempton in April, would have won: open to further improvement. *Mark Bradstock*

JAKROS (IRE) 12 b.g. Beneficial – Parkdota (IRE) (Good Thyne (USA)) [2016/17 **c–** c32.5g c24.5sᵖᵘ Mar 16] winning pointer/hurdler: fair chaser at best, no form in 2016/17: **h–** left S. J. Gilmore after first start: stays 25f: acts on good to firm and heavy going: wears headgear. *Francesca Nimmo*

JALAMIE (IRE) 6 b.g. Mustameet (USA) – Caulfield Lady (IRE) (City Honours (USA)) **b75** [2016/17 b15.3s⁶ Dec 26] won Irish maiden point on debut: 16/1, promoted sixth in bumper at Wincanton (18¼ lengths behind disqualified Run To Milan) in December. *Giles Smyly*

JALEO (GER) 5 ch.g. New Approach (IRE) – Jambalaya (GER) (Samum (GER)) **h131** [2016/17 h130: h19.5g* h21dᶠ h19.3d³ h16.8gᶠ Mar 17] tall gelding: useful handicap hurdler: won at Lingfield (by ¾ length from Loves Destination) in December: stays 19f: acts on heavy going: tried in hood: usually races prominently. *Ben Pauling*

JAMBUL TREE 7 ch.m. Apple Tree (FR) – Jambles (Muhtarram (USA)) [2016/17 h–: **h–** h15.3mᵖᵘ May 5] in frame in bumpers in 2014/15: pulled up both starts over hurdles: often in hood. *Robert Walford*

JAMESGIFTKEYSANDAL (IRE) 6 b.g. Raintrap – Teanarco Lady (Averti (IRE)) **h–** [2016/17 h16.5s h15.3d h16s h16.3g h16.3g Apr 23] no form over hurdles: in hood last 3 starts. *Robert Stephens*

JAMESON 5 br.g. Midnight Legend – Shatabdi (IRE) (Mtoto) [2016/17 b16.7d* h15.8v² **h131** h19.7s³ h20g* h19.5m² Apr 28] second foal: half-brother to bumper winner/useful hurdler **b103** All The Answers (2m winner, by Kayf Tara): dam (c124/h136), 2m-2½m hurdle/chase winner, also 1½m winner on Flat, closely related to high-class chaser (stayed 21f) Rajdhani Express: won bumper at Bangor (by 10 lengths from Serpico) early in season: useful form over hurdles: won novice at Ffos Las (by 11 lengths from Ballyarthur) in April: left Paul Morgan after first start: in hood last 3 starts: often races prominently, usually travels strongly. *Nicky Henderson*

JAMHOORI 9 b.h. Tiger Hill (IRE) – Tanasie (Cadeaux Genereux) [2016/17 h94: h15.9g⁵ **h90** h16.8g² May 10] modest maiden hurdler: in visor, better effort in 2016/17 when second in maiden at Sedgefield. *Jim Best*

JAMMY MOMENT 6 ch.m. Duke of Marmalade (IRE) – Special Moment (IRE) **h–** (Sadler's Wells (USA)) [2016/17 h18.1d h16.2gᵖᵘ Apr 27] fair on Flat, stays 2m: no form over hurdles. *Sandy Thomson*

JAMRHAM (IRE) 10 b.g. Great Palm (USA) – Appleway (IRE) (Lord Americo) **c78** [2016/17 c75, h–: c19.2d* c19.8d² c20.9v⁴ c20.2s⁴ c19.2g³ c19.2d² Apr 27] maiden **h–** hurdler: poor handicap chaser: won at Fontwell in December: stays 21f: acts on heavy going: tried in cheekpieces: wears tongue tie: usually races towards rear. *Sam Thomas*

JAM SESSION (IRE) 5 ch.g. Duke of Marmalade (IRE) – Night Dhu (Montjeu (IRE)) **h111** [2016/17 b93: h15.9d² h16.8v⁴ h16.6s³ Mar 3] bumper winner: fair form over hurdles: best effort when second in novice at Plumpton in December: in tongue tie last 3 starts. *Ian Williams*

JANE LAMB 4 b.f. Haafhd – Lucinda Lamb (Kayf Tara) [2016/17 b16.7g² b16g³ Apr 23] **b83** third foal: half-sister to bumper winner Tom Lamb (by Central Park): dam (h69), placed 3 times in bumpers, half-sister to useful hurdler/fairly useful chaser (stayed 25f) Lord Lamb and useful 2m hurdler Mr Lamb: fair form when placed in 2 bumpers. *Jedd O'Keeffe*

JANES BOUTIQUE (IRE) 6 b.m. Presenting – Supreme Touch (IRE) (Supreme **b–** Leader) [2016/17 b15.7s Mar 20] £25,000 5-y-o: fifth foal: half-sister to bumper winner Glorious Feeling (by Old Vic): dam (c109/h115) 19f-2¾m hurdle/chase winner (stayed 3m): placed both starts in Irish points: tailed off in bumper. *Tom Symonds*

JANUARY DON 6 br.g. Overbury (IRE) – Little Bud (Lord Bud) [2016/17 h15.9g[5] h20.5d[5] Dec 12] fell in maiden point on debut: poor form over hurdles. *Gary Moore* — **h79**

JAPPELOUP (IRE) 8 b.g. Presenting – Crackin' Liss (IRE) (Bob Back (USA)) [2016/17 h16g h17m[6] h20g h20g[5] h17.7d[5] h25s[2] h23v c19.7s[F] Mar 13] poor maiden hurdler: no form over fences: left David Harry Kelly after fourth start: stays 25f: acts on soft and good to firm going. *Diana Grissell* — **c–** **h83**

JARDIN DES PLANTES (FR) 7 ch.g. High Rock (IRE) – Dear Marianne (FR) (Akarad (FR)) [2016/17 h18.1s[3] Apr 3] €5,500 3-y-o: half-brother to several winners in France, including 2¾m chase winner Dahyasi (by Kahyasi): dam French 1¼m/11f winner: runner-up completed start in Irish maiden points: in tongue tie, 16/1, some encouragement when third in maiden at Kelso (5¼ lengths behind Midnite Grace) on hurdling debut. *Donald McCain* — **h99**

JARLATH 6 b.g. Norse Dancer (IRE) – Blue Lullaby (IRE) (Fasliyev (USA)) [2016/17 h106: c16g[5] c21m[2] c16.3g[2] c16.5g* c20g[3] c16g[2] c18m[3] c19.7g[2] c20.2m[3] Nov 5] good-topped gelding: fair hurdler: fair handicap chaser: won novice event at Worcester in August: stays 21f: acts on good to firm going. *Seamus Mullins* — **c113** **h–**

JAROB 10 br.g. Beat All (USA) – Wishy (IRE) (Leading Counsel (USA)) [2016/17 c124, h136: h16g h24g h22.8g[5] h20g c19.5d[3] Oct 9] useful handicap hurdler: useful chaser: third in minor event at Limerick (13¼ lengths behind Sub Lieutenant) in October: stays 3m: acts on soft and good to firm going. *Andrew Lynch, Ireland* — **c130** **h131**

JARRY D'HONNEUR (FR) 8 b.g. Baroud d'Honneur (FR) – True Lovely (FR) (True Brave (USA)) [2016/17 c17d c17d c17d[5] c17s[F] Jan 15] winning hurdler: useful handicap chaser: stays 2½m: acts on heavy going. *W. P. Mullins, Ireland* — **c132** **h–**

JASLAMOUR (FR) 6 ch.g. Valanour (IRE) – Jasla (FR) (Highest Honor (FR)) [2016/17 h–, h81: h21g[6] May 2] rather unfurnished gelding: no form over hurdles: in hood last 3 starts. *Alexandra Dunn* — **h–**

JASPER JAY 4 b.g. Haafhd – Jenise (IRE) (Orpen (USA)) [2016/17 h15.7s[pu] Feb 3] modest maiden on Flat, stays 9f: in hood, pulled up in juvenile on hurdling debut. *Gemma Anderson* — **h–**

JASSUR 4 b.g. Canford Cliffs (IRE) – Child Bride (USA) (Coronado's Quest (USA)) [2016/17 h15.8g Apr 3] fair on Flat, stays 1¼m: 50/1, seventh in maiden at Huntingdon (27 lengths behind Head High) on hurdling debut. *Paul Webber* — **h–**

JAUNTY CLEMENTINE 5 b.m. Lucarno (USA) – Jaunty Spirit (Loup Sauvage (USA)) [2016/17 b15.8m[6] b15.8s h21.2d[pu] h15.8s[5] h20v[F] h21.2s[3] h19.5g Apr 8] second foal: dam unraced half-sister to useful hurdler/chaser (stayed 3m) Jaunty Flight and fairly useful hurdler/useful chaser (winner up to 3m) Jaunty Times: well held in bumpers: little form over hurdles: usually races nearer last than first. *Brian Eckley* — **h64** **b–**

JAUNTY FLYER 5 b.g. Sulamani (IRE) – Jaunty June (Primitive Rising (USA)) [2016/17 b15.8s[3] b16g[3] b16.8g* Apr 26] half-brother to 3 winners, including useful hurdler/chaser Jaunty Flight (2½m-3m winner, by Busy Flight) and fairly useful hurdler/useful chaser Jaunty Times (2f-3m winner, by Luso): dam (h94) 2½m hurdle winner (stayed 3¼m): fair form in bumpers: won maiden at Exeter in April: will be suited by 2½m+. *Brian Eckley* — **b87**

JAUNTY INFLIGHT 8 b.g. Busy Flight – Jaunty Walk (Overbury (IRE)) [2016/17 c102, h87: c16.5s[5] h16.8s[2] c16d[4] h16.7s[2] c15.7s[pu] c18.2m* Apr 20] sturdy gelding: modest handicap hurdler: fair handicap chaser: won at Lingfield in November and Taunton (novice) in April: left Brian Eckley after first start: best short of 3m: acts on good to firm and heavy going: front runner/races prominently. *Dr Richard Newland* — **c106** **h97**

JAUNTY SORIA 4 ch.f. Malinas (GER) – Jaunty Spirit (Loup Sauvage (USA)) [2016/17 b16g[4] b16.5m[2] Apr 27] third foal: dam unraced half-sister to useful hurdler/chaser (stayed 3m) Jaunty Flight and fairly useful hurdler/useful chaser (winner up to 3m) Jaunty Times: modest form when runner-up in mares event at Taunton on second of 2 starts in bumpers. *Brian Eckley* — **b82**

JAUNTY THOR 7 b.g. Norse Dancer (IRE) – Jaunty Walk (Overbury (IRE)) [2016/17 h92: h20m[2] h23.1d[5] h19.9d[5] h15.8v* h15.7d* h19.9s[5] h15.7s h18.6s[5] c20.9d[4] c20.3g Apr 21] fair handicap hurdler: won at Uttoxeter and Southwell in November: modest form on first of 2 starts over fences: left Brian Eckley after second start: stays 21f: acts on heavy going: in cheekpieces on 3 of last 4 starts: usually races towards rear. *Oliver Greenall* — **c97** **h105**

JAUNTY WARRIOR 5 b.g. Lucarno (USA) – Jaunty Walk (Overbury (IRE)) [2016/17 b16s b15.8v* Mar 1] fourth foal: half-brother to fair hurdler Jaunty Thor (2m winner, by Norse Dancer) and fair hurdler/chaser Jaunty Inflight (2m-2¼m winner, by Busy Flight): — **b89**

dam, ran once in bumper, half-sister to useful hurdler/chaser (stayed 3m) Jaunty Flight and fairly useful hurdler/useful chaser (winner up to 3m) Jaunty Times: fair form when won at Ffos Las on second of 2 starts in bumpers. *Brian Eckley*

JAVERT (IRE) 8 b.g. Kayf Tara – Royalrova (FR) (Garde Royale) [2016/17 c139, h–: c21.3m* May 7] strong gelding: lightly-raced gelding: smart form over fences: won handicap at Haydock (by 4½ lengths from Kalane) on sole outing in 2016/17: stays 2¾m, effective at much shorter: acts on soft and good to firm going: has worn hood: front runner/races prominently, often travels strongly. *Emma Lavelle*   **c149 h–**

JAWAHAL DU MATHAN (FR) 9 b.g. Smadoun (FR) – Stone's Glow (USA) (Arctic Tern (USA)) [2016/17 h–: h16d² h15.8d h19.7v Jan 11] poor maiden hurdler: unproven beyond 17f: acts on heavy going: tried in cheekpieces: has worn tongue tie. *Arthur Whitehead*   **h71**

JAYO TIME (IRE) 8 b.g. Morozov (USA) – Billythefilly (IRE) (Exit To Nowhere (USA)) [2016/17 c135, h107: c16mᶠ c16gᶠ Apr 3] smallish, angular gelding: winning hurdler: useful handicap chaser: fell both starts in 2016/17, likely to have finished second on first occasion: stays 2¾m, effective at shorter: acts on soft and good to firm going: wears headgear. *Kerry Lee*   **c128 h–**

JAZZ THYME (IRE) 8 b.m. Helissio (FR) – Thyne Square (IRE) (Good Thyne (USA)) [2016/17 h90, b87: h15.8gᵖᵘ h19.6g⁵ h16g h19g³ h19.9d⁵ h19.7g⁴ Oct 31] modest maiden hurdler: stays 19f: acts on good to firm going: often in tongue tie. *Robert Stephens*   **h88**

JAZZY (IRE) 4 b.g. Roderic O'Connor (IRE) – Lucayan Beauty (IRE) (Marju (IRE)) [2016/17 h16.2dᵖᵘ h16.3m* h15.8g⁴ h16g h15.8m² h16.4g h16.5m* h16s⁵ Feb 10] leggy gelding: fairly useful on Flat, stays 1½m: fair hurdler: won juvenile at Stratford in July and handicap at Taunton in December: raced only at 2m: acts on good to firm going: wears headgear: in tongue tie last 5 starts: usually leads. *Martin Keighley*   **h105**

JAZZY LADY (IRE) 6 b.m. Intikhab (USA) – Lock's Heath (CAN) (Topsider (USA)) [2016/17 h–: h16.8gᵖᵘ h20g* h16f* h18m* h19m⁵ Apr 27] fairly useful handicap hurdler: won at Les Landes in August (twice) and again in September: left Jim Best after first start: stays 2½m: acts on firm going: tried in headgear. *Susan Gardner*   **h117**

JEANNOT DE NONANT (FR) 5 ch.g. Full of Gold (FR) – Jolie Puce (FR) (General Assembly (USA)) [2016/17 h17.9s* h17.9s* c17.4d⁴ c17.9dᵖᵘ h16s h20v h16d³ h19g Apr 16] half-brother to French 17f hurdle winner Puce de Roches (by Agent Bleu): dam, French 15f-2¼m hurdle winner, half-sister to useful hurdler (2m-2¼m winner) Perle de Puce: useful handicap hurdler: won twice at Auteuil early in season: third at Limerick (1¾ lengths behind Adreamstillalive) in March: fair form on completed start over fences: left D. Bressou after fourth start: stays 2¼m: acts on soft going: in headgear on 4 of last 5 starts. *Gordon Elliott, Ireland*   **c106 + h140**

JEANS LADY 8 b.m. Milan – Indian Miss (Idiot's Delight) [2016/17 h90: h23mᵖᵘ h18.7g⁵ h22m Aug 24] poor maiden hurdler: best effort at 19f: acts on good to firm going: sometimes in headgear. *Martin Keighley*   **h68**

JEBS GAMBLE (IRE) 6 b.g. Dubai Destination (USA) – Gentle Caribou (IRE) (Dushyantor (USA)) [2016/17 b83: h19.1v⁶ h17.7v⁵ h15.7v³ h25s⁶ h21m Apr 4] modest form over hurdles: best effort at 2m: acts on heavy going: usually races towards rear. *Nick Gifford*   **h87**

JEBULANI 7 b.g. Jelani (IRE) – Susan's Dowry (Efisio) [2016/17 h75: h16.8s h16.8s⁵ May 3] poor hurdler, well held both starts in 2016/17: best effort at 17f: acts on soft going: tried in cheekpieces/tongue tie. *Barry Murtagh*   **h–**

JELLY MONGER (IRE) 5 b.m. Strategic Prince – Royal Jelly (King's Best (USA)) [2016/17 h17.7g* h16.7g³ h16.3m² h16m³ h19.8sᵖᵘ Dec 3] lengthy mare: fairly useful on Flat, stays 1¼m: fair form over hurdles: won mares novice at Fontwell in August: stays 2¼m: acts on good to firm going: often races towards rear. *Dominic Ffrench Davis*   **h111**

JENKINS (IRE) 5 b.g. Azamour (IRE) – Aladiyna (IRE) (Indian Danehill (IRE)) [2016/17 b120: b16d² h16.3d* h16g⁴ h16g⁴ h15.8d* Apr 16] good-topped gelding: useful bumper winner: similar form over hurdles: won maiden at Newbury (by 5 lengths from Bags Groove) in November and novice at Ffos Las in April: often travels strongly: remains with potential. *Nicky Henderson*   **h142 p b–**

JENNA PRIDE (IRE) 8 ch.m. Beneficial – Polly Native (IRE) (Be My Native (USA)) [2016/17 c25.5d⁴ May 12] third foal: sister to fairly useful chaser Never Complain (2½m winner): dam (h94), maiden hurdler (stayed 3m), sister to fairly useful staying chaser Sharp   **c65 h–**

Jack: dual winning pointer: modest form sole start over hurdles for Henry de Bromhead in 2014/15: in cheekpieces/tongue strap, 14/1, fourth in mares hunter at Fontwell (28 lengths behind Kimora) on chasing debut. *N. A. Pearce*

JENNIFER ANNE (IRE) 8 b.m. Darsi (FR) – Knockbawn (IRE) (Old Vic) [2016/17   **h–** h17.2d⁶ h22.1d h19.6g Jul 29] third foal: dam unraced: maiden pointer: no form over hurdles: in cheekpieces last 2 starts. *Julia Brooke*

JENNIFER CHIMES 9 b.m. Calcutta – Dream Seeker (IRE) (Kahyasi) [2016/17   **h–** h15.7m⁵ Apr 13] second foal: dam unraced: failed to complete either start in mares maiden points: pulled up in mares maiden on hurdling debut. *Barry Brennan*

JENNIFER ECCLES 7 b.m. Midnight Legend – Cherrygayle (IRE) (Strong Gale)   **h98 §** [2016/17 b86: h19.1d⁴ h21g^{pu} h19.3m⁶ h16.7d^{pu} Apr 27] rather leggy mare: bumper winner: modest form over hurdles: ungenuine. *Suzy Smith*

JENNYS DAY (IRE) 6 b.g. Daylami (IRE) – Jennys Oscar (IRE) (Oscar (IRE)) [2016/17   **h114** b18v³ h16v* h19.7g² h24.5s² h25s^{pu} h25.5v^{pu} h23.9s Feb 5] first foal: dam (h97) 2m hurdle   **b87** winner/winning pointer: runner-up on second start in maiden points: third in maiden bumper at Tipperary (4¾ lengths behind Westendorf): fair form over hurdles: won maiden at Listowel in September: left Michael Winters after second start: stays 3m: acts on heavy going: tried in hood. *Katy Price*

JENNYS MELODY (IRE) 8 b.m. Gamut (IRE) – Pharaway Stream (IRE) (Phardante   **h129** (FR)) [2016/17 h20d h18s⁴ h22.8s^{pu} h20v⁵ h20.9s^{pu} h24.3d* Apr 21] useful handicap hurdler: won mares event at Ayr in April: stays 3m: acts on heavy going: has worn hood: in tongue tie last 3 starts. *Benjamin Arthey, Ireland*

JENNYS SURPRISE (IRE) 9 b.m. Hawk Wing (USA) – Winning Jenny (IRE) (Leading   **c111** Counsel (USA)) [2016/17 c127, h121: c24s^{pu} c29.2g⁴ c27.2s^{ur} Nov 13] workmanlike mare: **h–** winning pointer: fairly useful handicap chaser, failed to stay on completed start in 2016/17: stays 25f: acts on heavy going. *Fergal O'Brien*

JEPECK (IRE) 8 b.g. Westerner – Jenny's Jewel (IRE) (Be My Native (USA)) [2016/17   **c118** c24.5s² Mar 16] prolific point winner: 13/8, second in hunter at Towcester (6 lengths behind Toby Lerone) on chasing debut. *Mrs Kayley Woollacott*

JERRYSBACK (IRE) 5 b.g. Jeremy (USA) – Get A Few Bob Back (IRE) (Bob Back   **h122 P** (USA)) [2016/17 h20.5v* h19.7d* Feb 21] fourth foal: half-brother to fair hurdler Indian Rupee (2m winner, by Indian Danehill), stays 2½m: dam (h93), maiden hurdler (stayed 2½m), out of half-sister to Champion Hurdle winner/top-class 3m chaser Celtic Shot: off mark in Irish maiden points at fourth attempt: fairly useful form over hurdles: won novices at Plumpton in January and Wetherby in February: capable of much better yet. *Philip Hobbs*

JER'S GIRL (IRE) 5 b.m. Jeremy (USA) – African Scene (IRE) (Scenic) [2016/17 h137:   **h140** h20s* h16d² h16d⁵ h19.9g^F Mar 14] angular mare: useful hurdler: second in Morgiana Hurdle at Punchestown (12 lengths behind Nichols Canyon) in November: stays 2½m: acts on heavy going. *Gavin Patrick Cromwell, Ireland*

JERUSALEM BELLS (IRE) 8 b.g. Kalanisi (IRE) – Quit The Noise (IRE) (Un   **c–** Desperado (FR)) [2016/17 c20.9s^{pu} Jun 14] point winner: modest maiden hurdler for Philip   **h–** Fenton in 2014/15: pulled up in novice handicap on chasing debut: likely to stay 3m: acts on soft and good to firm going: in tongue tie last 5 starts. *Alexandra Dunn*

JESSBER'S DREAM (IRE) 7 b.m. Milan – Maddy's Supreme (Supreme Leader)   **h132** [2016/17 h137, b76: h24.5s⁵ h20.3s⁴ h21v² h24.3d^{pu} Apr 21] winning Irish pointer: useful hurdler: second in listed mares event at Warwick (6 lengths behind Rons Dream) in February: stays 21f: best form on heavy going: tried in blinkers: wears tongue tie: usually races close up. *Paul Nicholls*

JESTER JET 7 br.m. Overbury (IRE) – Hendre Hotshot (Exit To Nowhere (USA))   **h106** [2016/17 h92: h19.9g² h20d³ h19.9s^F h19.7d* Apr 18] fair handicap hurdler: won novice event at Wetherby in March and mares event at Ludlow in April: left Tony Carroll after third start: stays 21f: acts on good to firm and good to soft going: often travels strongly. *Tom Lacey*

JETHRO (IRE) 6 b.g. Craigsteel – Wee Mo (IRE) (Zaffaran (USA)) [2016/17 h103, b71:   **c107** c17.3m⁶ c16.4g² c17g^{pu} c15.9d⁵ c16.3g^{pu} c15.2g² Apr 23] maiden hurdler: fair form over   **h–** fences: stays 19f: acts on good to soft going: has worn headgear, including in 2016/17: often races towards rear. *Brian Ellison*

JET MASTER (IRE) 11 b.g. Brian Boru – Whats The Reason (IRE) (Strong Gale)   **c127 x** [2016/17 c125, h120: h16.2m⁵ c20.1f⁶ h16.2s* h21.4d² c20.1d* c22.3s³ h18.1s c32.8g   **h114** h20.9s⁴ c23.8g³ Apr 26] neat gelding: fair handicap hurdler nowadays: won at Perth in

September: fairly useful handicap chaser: won veterans event at Newcastle in November: stays 3m: acts on good to firm and heavy going: wears hood/tongue tie: usually races in rear: often let down by jumping over fences. *N. W. Alexander*

JETSTREAM JACK (IRE) 7 b.g. Beneficial – Westgrove Berry (IRE) (Presenting) c137 [2016/17 h130: c23d* c22.5d² c24d c25d^F c24s⁵ c24v³ c20d^F Apr 26] rangy gelding: h– winning hurdler: useful chaser: won maiden at Tipperary in October: second in Grade 2 novice at Punchestown (7 lengths behind A Toi Phil) in November and third in novice handicap at Navan (12½ lengths behind Mick The Jiver) in March: stays 3m: acts on heavy going: tried in hood: in tongue tie last 3 starts: often races prominently. *Gordon Elliott, Ireland*

JETT (IRE) 6 b.g. Flemensfirth (USA) – La Noire (IRE) (Phardante (FR)) [2016/17 h126, c137 b100: h20s⁵ h20g² h22.6d⁶ c19d^{ur} c20v⁴ c19g² c20v⁴ Feb 18] useful form over hurdles: h132 second in minor event at Naas (8 lengths behind De Plotting Shed) in November: useful form over fences: second in Grade 3 novice at Leopardstown (1¼ lengths behind Yorkhill) in January: stays 2½m: acts on good to soft going. *Mrs J. Harrington, Ireland*

JEWELLED PRINCE 5 ch.g. Zamindar (USA) – Diamond Lass (IRE) (Rock of h85 Gibraltar (IRE)) [2016/17 h16g³ h15.8m h18.5d h15.8g h20m^{pu} Aug 30] dam half-sister to useful hurdler/chaser (stays 25f) Hash Brown: lightly raced on Flat: modest form over hurdles: left M. Hourigan/no show after first start: unproven beyond 2m: in headgear last 2 starts: tried in tongue tie. *Warren Greatrex*

JEWELLERY (IRE) 10 b.m. King's Best (USA) – Eilean Shona (Suave Dancer (USA)) c84 [2016/17 c–, h–: c20.1m² c21.2m h22.7s c23.8g^{pu} h19.3d c19.3d Dec 26] modest hurdler h– at best, no form in 2016/17: poor handicap chaser nowadays: stays 3m: acts on good to firm and good to soft going: has worn headgear: wears tongue tie. *Katie Scott*

JEZKI (IRE) 9 b.g. Milan – La Noire (IRE) (Phardante (FR)) [2016/17 h16s* h16v² h24g h147 h16d⁵ Apr 17] smallish, strong gelding: one-time top-class hurdler, smart nowadays: won minor event at Navan (by 1¾ lengths from Renneti) in January after long absence: second in Red Mills Trial Hurdle at Gowran (4 lengths behind Tombstone) in February: stays 3m, effective at shorter: acts on good to firm and heavy going: has worn headgear, including last 2 starts: usually travels strongly. *Mrs J. Harrington, Ireland*

JEZZEBELLE 5 ch.m. Schiaparelli (GER) – Megasue (Kayf Tara) [2016/17 b17.7g² h– b17.7d⁴ h16.8d⁵ h20.5g Oct 31] first foal: dam (h108), bumper/2m hurdle winner, sister to b81 useful hurdler (stayed 21f) Megastar and Champion Bumper/Betfair Hurdle winner Ballyandy: modest form when second at Fontwell on first of 2 starts in bumpers: well held both starts over hurdles. *Gary Moore*

JIGSAW FINANCIAL (IRE) 11 b.g. Brian Boru – Ardcolm Cailin (IRE) (Beneficial) h93 [2016/17 h97: h16s h24v³ h20g* h20g² h20g h20g h16.8s⁶ h18.5d Mar 21] leggy gelding: modest handicap hurdler: won at Worcester in August: stays 3m: acts on good to firm and heavy going: tried in cheekpieces. *Laura Young*

JIMBET 5 b.g. Bach (IRE) – Aphrodisias (FR) (Double Bed (FR)) [2016/17 b16.3d b– b16.7m Apr 17] well beaten in 2 bumpers. *Charles Pogson*

JIM DANDY 4 ch.g. Dandy Man (IRE) – Noctilucent (JPN) (Lammtarra (USA)) [2016/17 h97 h15.9m³ h15.8m³ h15.8m³ Oct 30] sturdy gelding: fairly useful on Flat, stays 1¼m: modest form when third on all 3 starts in juvenile hurdles: in cheekpieces last 2 starts. *Alan King*

JIMMIE BROWN (USA) 9 b.g. Street Cry (IRE) – Vid Kid (CAN) (Pleasant Colony c– (USA)) [2016/17 c–, h54: h15.7g c17.1s^{pu} Nov 5] rangy gelding: winning hurdler: maiden h– chaser: no longer of any account: has worn headgear/tongue tie: often races towards rear. *Andrew Crook*

JIMMY 4 ch.g. Norse Dancer (IRE) – Isintshelovely (IRE) (Broken Hearted) [2016/17 b– b13.6g⁴ Apr 21] 10/1, fourth in bumper at Fontwell (22½ lengths behind White Valiant) in April. *Chris Gordon*

JIMMY BELL 6 b.g. Tiger Hill (IRE) – Armada Grove (Fleetwood (IRE)) [2016/17 b83 b16.3d⁵ b16g⁵ Apr 8] seventh foal: half-brother to 3 winners on Flat, including 9.5f-1½m winner Covert Decree (by Proclamation): dam, 7f winner, half-sister to high-class hurdler/ smart chaser (stayed 3½m) Blazing Bailey: modest form in bumpers. *John O'Shea*

JIMMY BREEKIE (IRE) 7 b.g. Alkaadhem – Highland Breeze (IRE) (Kotashaan (FR)) h115 [2016/17 b91: b16g² b16g³ b16s* h20d h18d h19s h19s² h16v* h20.5d⁵ Apr 21] failed to b96 complete both starts in points: fairly useful bumper performer: won maiden at Punchestown in November: fairly useful form over hurdles: won maiden at Navan in April: stays 19f: best form on soft/heavy going: has worn hood, including in 2016/17. *Stuart Crawford, Ireland*

JIMMY SHAN (IRE) 9 b.g. Milan – Divine Prospect (IRE) (Namaqualand (USA))
[2016/17 c80, h106: c20.5m^{pu} May 16] winning pointer: fair maiden hurdler: maiden
chaser, bled sole outing in 2016/17: stays 3m: acts on good to firm and good to soft going:
wears hood: front runner/races prominently. *Tim Vaughan*

c–
h–

JIMMY THE JETPLANE (IRE) 9 b.g. Jimble (FR) – C'est Cool (IRE) (Roi Guillaume
(FR)) [2016/17 c20g^2 c23d^2 c24g^2 c22.5d^2 c26.3g* c21.7g^2 c28.8d c25.2d^5 c24m^3
Apr 4] well-made gelding: winning hurdler: useful handicap chaser: won novice event at
Sedgefield in October: stays 3¼m: acts on soft and good to firm going: in cheekpieces last
5 starts. *Kim Bailey*

c137
h–

JIMSNEVERRIGHT 9 b.g. Iktibas – Lady Lexie (Cape Cross (IRE)) [2016/17 h–:
h20.1g^{pu} May 24] leggy gelding: no form. *Ian Brown*

h–

JINSHA LAKE (IRE) 5 b.g. Galileo (IRE) – Al Ihsas (IRE) (Danehill (USA)) [2016/17
h87: h15.8g* h15.8g h16.7d^3 h16g h19.7s^{pu} h16.2v^{pu} h15.8d Apr 16] sturdy gelding:
modest handicap hurdler: won at Towcester early in season: raced mainly around 2m: tried
in cheekpieces: wears tongue tie. *Evan Williams*

h89

JOANS TART (IRE) 6 b.m. Scorpion (IRE) – Portorosa (USA) (Irish River (FR))
[2016/17 b16.5g^5 b16g b16d b16.2s^3 h15.8d Oct 28] closely related to 1m winner Mardi
(by Montjeu) and half-sister to several winners, including fairly useful hurdler Portrade
(2m-19f winner, by Trade Fair): dam French 9.5f winner: well held in maiden point:
modest form in bumpers: well beaten in mares maiden on hurdling debut: often in tongue
tie. *Gordon Elliott, Ireland*

h–
b78

JODIES JEM 7 br.g. Kheleyf (USA) – First Approval (Royal Applause) [2016/17 h16.3d
h15.8s^6 h15.8g^4 Apr 17] compact gelding: fairly useful on Flat, stays 8.5f: fair form over
hurdles: best effort when fourth in novice at Huntingdon in April: will prove best at sharp
2m. *Michael Banks*

h103

JOE FARRELL (IRE) 8 b.g. Presenting – Luck of The Deise (IRE) (Old Vic) [2016/17
b106: h20g* h20.5d h20.3s^6 h23.5s^2 h24.7g Apr 8] good-topped gelding: useful bumper
performer: fairly useful form over hurdles: won maiden at Ffos Las in November: second
in handicap at Ascot in February: stays 3m: acts on soft going. *Rebecca Curtis*

h129

JOE THE ROGUE (IRE) 10 gr.g. Amilynx (FR) – Roco-Bridge (IRE) (Lord Americo)
[2016/17 c–, h–: h21.6m h19.5d c23g^6 c23g^5 Dec 20] maiden pointer: maiden hurdler:
modest handicap chaser at best: stayed 3¼m: acted on soft going: dead. *Sarah Robinson*

c69
h–

JOEY SASA (IRE) 8 b.g. Winged Love (IRE) – Brescia (FR) (Monsun (GER)) [2016/17
b16.2d* b16g* h16d^2 h16s^2 h18d* h20g^3 h16v^2 h16.8g h16d Apr 18] third foal: half-
brother to bumper/modest 2¾m hurdle winner Degenerous (by Generous): dam unraced:
useful form in bumpers: won at Galway in October and Down Royal (by 3¼ lengths from
An Dearg Mor) in November: useful hurdler: won maiden at Leopardstown in December:
placed in Nathaniel Lacy & Partners Solicitors Novices' Hurdle at Leopardstown (17
lengths behind Let's Dance) in January and Grade 2 novice at Naas (8 lengths behind Forge
Meadow) in February: stays 2½m: acts on good to soft going. *Noel Meade, Ireland*

h133
b110

JOHANOS (FR) 6 ch.g. Limnos (JPN) – Madame Johann (FR) (Johann Quatz (FR))
[2016/17 b77: h15.3s^2 h19g^5 h15.8d^3 h19.3v* h18.9v* Mar 22] lengthy gelding: fairly
useful form in bumpers: similar form over hurdles: won novice at Carlisle and novice
handicap at Haydock in March: usually races prominently. *Nigel Hawke*

h122
b96

JOHN BISCUIT (IRE) 9 ch.g. Hawk Wing (USA) – Princess Magdalena (Pennekamp
(USA)) [2016/17 c–, h68: h15.3m^5 h15.8g h20.5g* h20.7g^5 h15.8d^3 h23.9m^5 Apr 27] poor
handicap hurdler: won at Plumpton (conditional) in October: fell on sole start over fences
in 2015/16: stays 21f: acts on good to soft going: tried in hood/tongue tie: often races
towards rear. *Jo Davis*

c–
h80

JOHN CONSTABLE (IRE) 6 b.g. Montjeu (IRE) – Dance Parade (USA) (Gone West
(USA)) [2016/17 h136: h15.7m^4 h15.7m h16.4s^6 h20.5d h16.8s h16.5g^F Apr 8] lengthy
gelding: useful handicap hurdler: fourth in Swinton Handicap Hurdle at Haydock (4½
lengths behind Gwafa) early in season: looked set to finish second when fell last at Aintree
in April: unproven beyond 2m: acts on soft going: tried in tongue tie. *Evan Williams*

h132

JOHN DANIELL 12 b.g. Overbury (IRE) – Hottentot (Sula Bula) [2016/17 c84: h21.4d^{pu}
c24.2d^5 Mar 21] multiple point winner: pulled up in handicap on hurdling debut: maiden
chaser: stays 3¼m: acts on heavy going. *Grant Cann*

c74
h–

JOHN MONASH 6 b.g. Kayf Tara – Miss Invincible (Invincible Spirit (IRE)) [2016/17 **h129**
h104, b88: h17.2s h16.2m* h22d² h20.2f² h16.2d² h20.2s* h23.9s* h22.1d* Aug 29]
lengthy, rather unfurnished gelding: fairly useful hurdler: won maiden at Perth early in
season, novices there (twice) in July and novice at Cartmel in August: stays 3m: acts on
firm and soft going: wears tongue tie: often races towards rear/travels strongly. *Gordon
Elliott, Ireland*

JOHNNY GO 7 b.g. Bollin Eric – Waverbeck (IRE) (Accordion) [2016/17 h98, b90: **h97**
h23.9m⁴ h22.1m h25.4dᵖᵘ h23.9s³ h23.9s* h23.9g h23.3g h24.7g h24.3s Nov 9] modest
handicap hurdler: won at Perth (amateur) in July: stays on soft going: has worn
cheekpieces, including in 2016/17: usually races prominently. *Lisa Harrison*

JOHNNY OG 8 b.g. Flemensfirth (USA) – Mrs Roberts (Bob Back (USA)) [2016/17 **c131**
c127, h101: c19.4g* c15.9g c18.8d c16.1gᵖᵘ c20vᵖᵘ h19.9sᵖᵘ c23.6g⁶ Apr 17] workmanlike **h–**
gelding: maiden hurdler: useful handicap chaser: won at Stratford (by 4 lengths from King
of The Wolds) in October: stays 2½m: acts on heavy going: wears headgear. *Martin Keighley*

JOHNNY PEDLAR 6 b.g. Revoque (IRE) – Festival Fancy (Le Coq d'Or) [2016/17 **b–**
b16.2s Sep 22] tailed off in bumper. *Sandy Thomson*

JOHNNYS LEGACY (IRE) 10 b.g. Ecton Park (USA) – Lexy May (USA) (Lear Fan **c–**
(USA)) [2016/17 c–, h63: h18.7m Jul 17] sturdy gelding: maiden hurdler, well beaten sole **h–**
outing in 2016/17: winning chaser: stays 2¾m: acts on good to firm and heavy going:
wears headgear: tried in tongue tie. *Ken Wingrove*

JOHN REEL (FR) 8 b.g. Country Reel (USA) – John Quatz (FR) (Johann Quatz (FR)) **h90**
[2016/17 h16s⁶ Jan 7] useful on Flat, stays 2¼m: fairly useful hurdler, below form sole
outing in 2016/17: should stay beyond 2m. *David Evans*

JOHNS LUCK (IRE) 8 b.g. Turtle Island (IRE) – Jemima Yorke (Be My Guest (USA)) **c111**
[2016/17 c103, h–: c20.9s⁵ c20.9d* c19.7s* c19.9d² c20.9v³ c20.3s² Mar 20] winning **h–**
hurdler: fair handicap chaser: won at Ffos Las in November and Plumpton in January: stays
3¼m, effective at much shorter: acts on heavy going: wears headgear: often races towards
rear. *Neil Mulholland*

JOHNS SPIRIT (IRE) 10 b.g. Gold Well – Gilt Ridden (IRE) (Heron Island (IRE)) **c130**
[2016/17 c138, h–: c19.2g⁴ c20.3g³ Sep 28] useful-looking gelding: winning hurdler: **h–**
useful handicap chaser nowadays: stays 3m: acts on heavy going: has worn headgear,
including in 2016/17. *Jonjo O'Neill*

JOHN WILLIAMS (IRE) 8 b.g. Presenting – Duhallow Park (IRE) (Flemensfirth **c99**
(USA)) [2016/17 h94: c17.1m⁵ c20.1d⁵ c15.6g² c19.9g* c19.9d³ c26.6g⁴ c21.6d² Apr 10] **h–**
maiden handicap chaser: modest handicap chaser: won novice event at Musselburgh in November:
stays 2¾m: acts on good to soft going: tried in cheekpieces: front runner/races prominently,
often travels strongly. *Sandy Thomson*

JOIN THE CLAN (IRE) 8 b.g. Milan – Millicent Bridge (IRE) (Over The River (FR)) **c134**
[2016/17 c128p, h135: c24.2s² c23.8d⁴ c18.8d c23.6s² c26.2s h23.6v c24.2gᶠ c24.2g* **h–**
Apr 17] workmanlike gelding: useful hurdler at best, below form sole outing in 2016/17:
useful handicap chaser: won at Fakenham in April: stays 3¼m: acts on heavy going: has
worn headgear, including last 4 starts. *Jonjo O'Neill*

JOIN TOGETHER (IRE) 12 b.g. Old Vic – Open Cry (IRE) (Montelimar (USA)) **c110 §**
[2016/17 c103, h–: c32.5g² c27.2d⁵ c25.8m⁴ Apr 15] multiple point winner: winning **h–**
hurdler: fair hunter chaser nowadays: stays 33f: acts on good to firm and heavy going: has
worn headgear: usually leads: temperamental. *Mrs Rose Loxton*

JOKE DANCER 4 ch.g. Authorized (IRE) – Missy Dancer (Shareef Dancer (USA)) **b65**
[2016/17 b14.6s⁶ Dec 17] 8/1, sixth in junior bumper at Newcastle (18½ lengths behind
Midnight Shadow) in December. *Sue Smith*

JOKER CHOKER (IRE) 12 b.g. Oscar (IRE) – Stormy Lady (IRE) (Glacial Storm **c100**
(USA)) [2016/17 c102, h–: c17.4d² May 12] workmanlike gelding: twice-raced maiden **h–**
pointer: winning hurdler: fair hunter chaser nowadays: stays 21f: acts on firm and good to
soft going. *Nicky Martin*

JOKERS AND ROGUES (IRE) 9 b.g. Beneficial – Ashfield Girl (IRE) (Beau Sher) **c–**
[2016/17 c61, h108: h16.8g² h16.2mᵖᵘ c17.1s⁶ h16.8g⁴ Apr 7] fair handicap hurdler: no **h105**
form over fences: stays 2½m: acts on heavy going: often in tongue tie nowadays: usually
leads. *Kenneth Slack*

JOLIE CRICKETTE (FR) 5 b.m. Laverock (IRE) – Crickette River (FR) (Cricket Ball **c114** (USA)) [2016/17 h17.4s h16.9s c18.9d² c17.4d* c18.4s* c18.4s⁴ c17.4s c17.9s³ **h97** h18.9vᵖᵘ h16.2s* h19.4g⁶ Mar 1] fourth foal: half-sister to 2 winners in France, including Tritone Crick (2¼m hurdle winner, by Le Triton): dam French 15f hurdle winner: modest hurdler: won mares novice at Kelso in December: fair chaser: won claimer at Dieppe and 4-y-o event at Clairefontaine in July: left G. Cherel after eighth start: stays 19f: acts on soft going: wears blinkers. *N. W. Alexander*

JOLI VISAGE 6 b.m. Dr Massini (IRE) – Focosa (ITY) (In The Wings) [2016/17 b16m⁶ **b–** b16.2s ab16g Feb 20] £1,500 4-y-o: seventh foal: half-sister to 2 winners, including fairly useful hurdler Spice Fair (19f winner, by Trade Fair): dam Italian 11f winner: no form in bumpers. *Henry Oliver*

JOLLY BOYS OUTING (IRE) 14 b.g. Glacial Storm (USA) – St Carol (IRE) **c– §** (Orchestra) [2016/17 c79§: c24.5gᵖᵘ May 9] sturdy gelding: fair chaser at best, pulled up sole outing in 2016/17: stays 3¾m: acts on good to firm and heavy going: temperamental. *Rosemary Gasson*

JOLLY ROGER (IRE) 10 b.g. Oratorio (IRE) – Chalice Wells (Sadler's Wells (USA)) **c–** [2016/17 c–, h–: h16.2s h15.8v³ h16gᵘʳ Apr 8] close-coupled gelding: modest handicap **h97** hurdler nowadays: winning chaser: stays 2½m: acts on any going: tried in cheekpieces. *Dai Burchell*

JOLLY'S CRACKED IT (FR) 8 b.g. Astarabad (USA) – Jolly Harbour (Rudimentary **h–** (USA)) [2016/17 h145: h15.7d Dec 17] well-made gelding: smart hurdler at best, well held sole outing in 2016/17: unproven beyond 2m: acts on heavy going. *Harry Fry*

JONAGOLD 6 b.g. Apple Tree (FR) – Single Handed (Cloudings (IRE)) [2016/17 h23g **c100** h18.7m³ h19.9g² h21.6d² h21.6g⁵ h19.9d⁶ h20s² c20.9v⁵ c18.2g⁴ c20.9v c23.8g⁵ Apr 3] **h108** £2,200 3-y-o, £5,000 5-y-o: third foal: dam (h86), placed in bumper/over hurdles at 17f, out of sister to very smart chaser up to 25f Hand Inn Hand: winning pointer: fair maiden hurdler: fair form over fences: stays 21f: acts on soft going: has worn headgear: wears tongue tie: usually races prominently. *Evan Williams*

JONNIE SKULL (IRE) 11 b.g. Pyrus (USA) – Sovereign Touch (IRE) (Pennine Walk) **c–** [2016/17 c106, h–: h16g⁴ h20gᵖᵘ Aug 14] fair hurdler at best, below form in 2016/17: fair **h68** form on sole start over fences in 2015/16: unproven beyond 2m: acts on good to firm going: wears tongue tie. *Phil McEntee*

JONNY DELTA (IRE) 10 ch.g. Sulamani (IRE) – Send Me An Angel (IRE) (Lycius (USA)) **h112** [2016/17 h104: h15.6g² h19.4d³ h19.4g* h15.6g⁴ h15.6g h15.6g³ h15.6g h20.5g Apr 22] fair handicap hurdler: won at Musselburgh in December: stays 19f: acts on heavy going. *Jim Goldie*

JONNY EAGER (IRE) 8 b.g. Craigsteel – Dishy (IRE) (Jurado (USA)) [2016/17 c113, **c110** h93: c24.2d⁶ c26.3s⁶ c26.2sᵖᵘ c26.9v* c26.9vᵖᵘ c31.9s⁴ Mar 16] winning hurdler: fair **h–** handicap chaser: won at Ayr in January: stays 4m: best form on soft/heavy going: has worn headgear: temperament under suspicion. *Alistair Whillans*

JONOFARK (IRE) 4 b.g. Arcano (IRE) – Dream Valley (IRE) (Sadler's Wells (USA)) **h73** [2016/17 h16sᵖᵘ h16s⁴ h16.6gᵖᵘ Feb 22] fair maiden on Flat, stays 1¼m: little form over hurdles. *Brian Rothwell*

JOPAAN (IRE) 10 ch.g. Pierre – No Precedent (IRE) (Be My Native (USA)) [2016/17 **h–** h71: h21.4m May 10] maiden pointer: maiden hurdler, well held sole outing in 2016/17: best effort at 2¾m: acts on heavy going: in tongue tie last 5 starts: front runner/races prominently. *Brian Barr*

JOSEPHINE K 4 b.f. Bahri (USA) – Montrachet Belle (Kadeed (IRE)) [2016/17 h16.2dᵖᵘ **h66** h15.6gᵖᵘ h16.4d⁴ h16.2v³ Dec 7] little sign of ability. *Susan Corbett*

JOSEPH MERCER (IRE) 10 b.g. Court Cave (IRE) – Vikki's Dream (IRE) (Kahyasi) **c94** [2016/17 c87§, h–: c20.1dᵖᵘ c24.2vᵖᵘ h24.1s² c24.2s² h24.1s³ h27s* h27v* h27v² c23.4v* **h101** Mar 18] fair handicap hurdler: won at Sedgefield (twice) in February: modest handicap chaser: won at Newcastle in March: stays 27f: acts on heavy going: wears headgear: usually leads. *Tina Jackson*

JOSH DARBY (IRE) 6 b.g. Scorpion (IRE) – Glory Queen (IRE) (Taipan (IRE)) **b–** [2016/17 b15.8s Dec 6] tailed off in bumper. *Dan Skelton*

Betfred Peterborough Chase, Huntingdon—
an all-the-way win for Josses Hill, who is chased home by Tea For Two (left) and More of That

JOSH PERRY 4 b.g. Hellvelyn – Emma Peel (Emarati (USA)) [2016/17 h16s Jan 26] **h—** modest maiden on Flat, stays 1m: in tongue tie, well beaten in juvenile on hurdling debut. *Chris Down*

JOSHUA LANE (IRE) 8 b.g. Gamut (IRE) – Teffia Native (IRE) (Kotashaan (FR)) **h131** [2016/17 h16d h17m^{pu} h16.5d* h20.4s^5 h22.6d^5 h16d^3 h16s^2 h16v^2 h16d Apr 18] close-coupled gelding: useful hurdler: won novice at Galway in October: second in handicap at Leopardstown (1¾ lengths behind Camlann) in March: stays 23f: acts on heavy going: tried in blinkers: has worn tongue tie. *Edward Harty, Ireland*

JOSSES HILL (IRE) 9 b.g. Winged Love (IRE) – Credora Storm (IRE) (Glacial Storm **c156** (USA)) [2016/17 c154x, h—: c20.5g* c19.9d* c24g^5 c20.8g^5 c19.9g c22.7g^3 Apr 29] strong, **h—** useful-looking gelding: winning hurdler: very smart chaser: won graduation event at Kempton (by 8 lengths from Camping Ground) in November and Peterborough Chase at Huntingdon (by 6 lengths from Tea For Two) in December: probably ideally suited by around 2½m: acts on good to firm and heavy going: has worn cheekpieces, including last 3 starts: front runner/races prominently. *Nicky Henderson*

JOUEUR BRESILIEN (FR) 5 b.g. Fuisse (FR) – Fille du Bresil (FR) (Smadoun (FR)) **h116** [2016/17 h15.8v^3 h19.5s^4 h16.3s^3 Jan 18] lengthy, useful-looking gelding: second foal: half-brother to French chaser Danceur Bresilien (17f winner, by Irish Wells): dam unraced: fairly useful form over hurdles: placed on second of 2 starts for Y. Fouin in 2015/16: third in novice at Ffos Las in December: stays 19f: raced on going softer than good (acts on heavy): often races prominently. *Rebecca Curtis*

JOVIAL JOEY (IRE) 6 b.g. St Jovite (USA) – Like A Bird (IRE) (Topanoora) [2016/17 **c130** h113p: h19.3m^2 h22.1m^2 h19.9g^5 h24.6d^6 c19.2g^3 c23.8g* c25.2d^2 c19.9g^3 c23.8g* **h101** Apr 26] fair maiden hurdler: useful form over fences: won novice handicaps at Musselburgh in December and Perth in April: stays 25f: acts on good to firm and good to soft going: wears tongue tie: front runner/races prominently, often travels strongly. *Maurice Barnes*

JOYRIDER (IRE) 5 b.g. Stowaway – Aileen Supreme (IRE) (Presenting) [2016/17 **b83** b15.8s^4 Dec 6] €70,000 3-y-o: first foal: dam, ran twice, out of half-sister to smart hurdler/ very smart chaser up to 3m Colonel Braxton: in hood, 12/1, fourth in bumper at Uttoxeter (19¼ lengths behind Neon Wolf) in December. *Emma Lavelle*

420

JOY'S SPIRIT 5 b.m. Milan – Molly's Spirit (IRE) (Anshan) [2016/17 h20.7g⁶ h23.1gᵖᵘ h–
Apr 22] first foal: dam (c83), winning pointer, sister to smart hurdler/chaser (2m/17f
winner) Dave's Dream and useful hurdler/chaser (stays 2¾m) Owen Glendower: little
promise in points/2 starts over hurdles. *Nicky Henderson*

J R HAWK (IRE) 9 b.g. Hawk Wing (USA) – Miss Shivvy (IRE) (Montjeu (IRE)) h–
[2016/17 h21.6m Jul 1] well held in bumper/maiden hurdle. *William Reed*

JUBILYMPICS 5 b.m. Kapgarde (FR) – Pepite de Soleil (FR) (Fly To The Stars) [2016/17 b87
b16.2s³ ab16g² b17.7g² Mar 27] first foal: dam (h129) 2m-19f hurdle winner: fair form
when placed in 3 bumpers. *Seamus Mullins*

JUDGE EARLE (IRE) 5 b.g. Court Cave (IRE) – Louis's Teffia (IRE) (Presenting) b83
[2016/17 b16.4v⁶ b16g Apr 22] €17,000 3-y-o: first foal: dam, winning pointer, half-sister
to fairly useful hurdler/useful chaser (stayed 3¾m) Night In Milan: modest form on second
of 2 starts in bumpers. *Richard Fahey*

JUGE ET PARTI (FR) 4 gr.g. Martaline – Nakota Rag (FR) (Nikos) [2016/17 b16.7g* b103 p
Apr 22] fourth foal: dam French maiden (placed around 2m over hurdles): 11/2, won
conditionals/amateur bumper at Bangor by 15 lengths from Asking Questions) in April,
impressively: open to improvement. *Christian Williams*

JULIE'S LAD 7 ch.g. Primo Valentino (IRE) – Sunny Parkes (Arkadian Hero (USA)) b–
[2016/17 b15.8v b16.8d Dec 26] tailed off in 2 bumpers. *Michael Mullineaux*

JULLY LES BUXY 7 b.m. Black Sam Bellamy (IRE) – Jadidh (Touching Wood (USA)) h–
[2016/17 h101: h23.3g May 14] sturdy mare: modest maiden hurdler, well held sole outing
in 2016/17: stays 3m: acts on heavy going. *Robert Walford*

JUMEIRAH LIBERTY 9 ch.g. Proclamation (IRE) – Gleam of Light (IRE) (Danehill c–
(USA)) [2016/17 c–, h63: c15.7mᵖᵘ May 5] small gelding: winning hurdler: little impact in h–
2 starts over fences: raced around 2m: acts on good to soft going: wears headgear/tongue
tie. *Zoe Davison*

JUMP AND JUMP (IRE) 7 br.m. Oscar (IRE) – My Twist (IRE) (Flemensfirth (USA)) c87
[2016/17 b–: h15.8d³ h20.5g⁴ h19.8d c17v³ Jan 30] failed to complete all 4 starts in points h92
(has refused to race): modest form over hurdles: in tongue tie, 9/1, some encouragement
when third in novice handicap at Plumpton (9 lengths behind Instingtive) on chasing debut.
Johnny Farrelly

JUMP UP 11 b.g. Carnival Dancer – Taylor Green (USA) (Green Dancer (USA)) [2016/17 c–
c23.6vᵖᵘ Mar 23] winning hurdler: maiden chaser: off 34 months, pulled up sole outing in h–
2016/17: stays 3m: acts on soft and good to firm going: tried in headgear/tongue tie.
Mark Robinson

JUNCTION FOURTEEN (IRE) 8 b.g. King's Theatre (IRE) – Chevet Girl (IRE) c144
(Roselier (FR)) [2016/17 c145, h–: c22.5g c19.4g⁶ c23.8m² c25gᵖᵘ Mar 14] sturdy gelding: h–
winning hurdler: useful handicap chaser: second in Grade 3 event at Ascot (4½ lengths
behind Antony) in October: stays 3m: acts on soft and good to firm going: wears tongue tie:
usually races close up. *Emma Lavelle*

JUNE CARTER (IRE) 5 b.m. Scorpion (IRE) – Evidence (Machiavellian (USA)) b71
[2016/17 b16.2d⁶ b18d b16v Dec 17] half-sister to several winners, including bumper
winners Rushvale (by Moss Vale) and Chestnut Kate (by Le Vie dei Colori): dam lightly
raced on Flat: poor form in bumpers. *Mark McNiff, Ireland*

JUNE FRENCH (FR) 9 b.m. Jimble (FR) – Sunbelt Broker (Lahib (USA)) [2016/17 c71 §
c80§, h–: c20.5m⁴ c20.9g³ c20g Jul 21] leggy mare: maiden hurdler: poor maiden chaser: h–
stays 21f: acts on soft and good to firm going: wears headgear: tried in tongue tie:
temperamental. *Neil Mulholland*

JUNIOR PACKAGE 6 gr.g. Kayf Tara – Shirley Cricket (Linamix (FR)) [2016/17 h–, h75
b88: h18.7m² h23.3g⁶ Jul 22] poor maiden hurdler: best effort at 19f: acts on good to firm
going: has worn blinkers, including last 3 starts: has worn tongue tie, including last 2 starts:
temperament under suspicion. *David Pipe*

JUPITER CUSTOS (FR) 5 b.g. Le Havre (IRE) – Angel Rose (IRE) (Definite Article) h105
[2016/17 h16d³ h16.7g³ Jul 16] fairly useful on Flat, stays 1½m: fair form when third in 2
novice hurdles. *Michael Scudamore*

JUPITER'S GIFT (IRE) 5 b.m. Scorpion (IRE) – Presenting Ally (IRE) (Presenting) h–
[2016/17 b15.8g b17.7d³ b15.7d h15.3s h16v⁵ h15.8g⁵ Apr 3] first foal: dam unraced half- b/4
sister to fairly useful hurdler (stayed 3m) Roadtoabbeyfeale: poor form in bumpers: no
form over hurdles. *Kim Bailey*

421

JURY DUTY (IRE) 6 b.g. Well Chosen – Swan Heart (IRE) (Broken Hearted) [2016/17 **h147** h24d² h22.6d* h23.6v² h24g³ h24d⁶ Apr 27] sturdy gelding: second foal: dam unraced: placed on second of 2 starts in points: smart handicap hurdler: won at Navan in 2015/16: also won there (by 1¾ lengths from Scoir Mear) in November: effective from 2½m to 3m: acts on heavy going: usually travels strongly. *Gordon Elliott, Ireland*

JUST ACTING (IRE) 7 b.g. Presenting – Azalea (IRE) (Marju (IRE)) [2016/17 h–p: **h–** h20gᵖᵘ Oct 19] second in Irish maiden point: pulled up both starts over hurdles: dead. *Paul Nicholls*

JUST A FEELING 7 ch.m. Flemensfirth (USA) – Precious Lady (Exit To Nowhere **h–** (USA)) [2016/17 h94, b84: h20.3g Mar 28] maiden hurdler: in tongue tie, well beaten sole outing in 2016/17: front runner/races prominently. *Paul Webber*

JUST A NORMAL DAY (IRE) 7 b.g. High Chaparral (IRE) – Thats Luck (IRE) (Posen **c–** (USA)) [2016/17 h118: h21.6g⁶ c23g³ May 27] fairly useful handicap hurdler: tailed off in **h112** novice on chasing debut: stays 3¼m: acts on soft and good to firm going: wears cheekpieces. *Dan Skelton*

JUST A PAR (IRE) 10 b.g. Island House (IRE) – Thebrownhen (IRE) (Henbit (USA)) **c146** [2016/17 c152, h–: c23.4d⁴ c32.8gᵖᵘ c26s* c34.3d c28.8g Apr 29] tall, lengthy, angular **h–** gelding: winning hurdler: smart handicap chaser: won veterans event at Newbury (by 2¼ lengths from No Duffer) in March: stays 29f: acts on heavy going, probably on good to firm: wears headgear: usually races nearer last than first. *Paul Nicholls*

JUST ARCHIE (USA) 9 b.g. Arch (USA) – Copper Rose (USA) (Unbridled (USA)) **c–** [2016/17 h21.4d h23.1sᵖᵘ Jan 17] maiden hurdler, no form in 2016/17: maiden chaser. **h–** *Dr Jeremy Naylor*

JUST A STING (IRE) 5 b.g. Scorpion (IRE) – Shanann Lady (IRE) (Anshan) [2016/17 **b99** b16.7d* b16.8d* Mar 21] fifth foal: half-brother to fair hurdler/chaser The Geegeez Geegee (17f-3m winner, by Beneficial): dam (c95/h82), 2½m chase winner, half-sister to useful hurdler (stays 21f) Gilt Shadow: fairly useful form in bumpers: won at Bangor in January and Exeter in March. *Harry Fry*

JUSTATENNER 6 b.g. Northern Legend – Shelayly (IRE) (Zaffaran (USA)) [2016/17 **c– p** h109, b76: h24.7g h24d³ c23.8gᵖᵘ h23.1d² h21.2s⁶ Feb 22] fair handicap hurdler: let down **h106** by jumping in novice handicap on chasing debut: left Colin Tizzard after first start: stays 3m: acts on soft going: should do better over fences. *Charlie Longsdon*

JUST A THOUGHT (IRE) 5 ch.m. Stowaway – Carrig Lucy (IRE) (Phardante (FR)) **b99** [2016/17 b15.8s* b16.2s* b16d³ Mar 11] €4,000 3-y-o: angular mare: seventh foal: half-sister to bumper winner/fair hurdler Cloudante (2m-19f winner, by Cloudings): dam unraced sister to useful hurdler/fairly useful chaser (stayed 3m) The Carrig Rua: runner-up in Irish maiden point on debut: fairly useful form in bumpers: won mares events at Ffos Las in November and Hereford in December: third in listed mares event at Sandown (6½ lengths behind Cap Soleil) in March: will be suited by further than 2m. *Rebecca Curtis*

JUST BEFORE DAWN (IRE) 8 b.g. Millenary – Knocka Beauty (IRE) (Allegoric **h123 p** (USA)) [2016/17 h21g² Mar 18] sturdy gelding: Irish point winner: won bumper in 2014/15: 12/1, promise when second in novice at Kempton (head behind Cultivator) on hurdling debut: should do better. *Tom George*

JUST BOBBY (IRE) 4 b.g. Black Sam Bellamy (IRE) – Blackwater Bay (IRE) (Supreme **b90** Leader) [2016/17 b16d³ Mar 31] £22,000 3-y-o: half-brother to useful hurdler/winning pointer Carrig Cathal (2¼m-2½m winner, by Fair Mix) and fairly useful hurdler/chaser Award Winner (19f-3m winner, by Aflora): dam (h97), 2m hurdle winner (stayed 2½m), half-sister to useful hurdler/smart chaser up to 3m Razor Royale: 25/1, third in bumper at Wetherby (7 lengths behind Kalashnikov) in March. *Micky Hammond*

JUST BROOKE 7 ch.m. Black Sam Bellamy (IRE) – Sports Express (Then Again) **h–** [2016/17 b–: h16s h16v h18.1sᵖᵘ Apr 3] no form. *N. W. Alexander*

JUST BRYAN 7 b.g. With The Flow (USA) – Straight Courage (Straight Knight) [2016/17 **b–** b15.3m b16.8g b16m Nov 2] no form in bumpers. *Colin Tizzard*

JUST CAMERON 10 b.g. Kayf Tara – Miss Fencote (Phardante (FR)) [2016/17 c152, **c150** h–: c15.9s⁶ c15.2s³ c15.2d* c16v⁴ Feb 26] tall gelding: winning hurdler: smart chaser: won **h–** handicap at Wetherby (by 2 lengths from Grey Gold) in January: stays 2½m: acts on heavy going: tried in cheekpieces: wears tongue tie: usually races prominently, often travels strongly. *Micky Hammond*

JUSTE POUR NOUS 4 b.g. Pour Moi (IRE) – Steam Cuisine (Mark of Esteem (IRE)) **h101 p**
[2016/17 h16m³ Apr 4] fairly useful on Flat, stays 12.5f: in blinkers/tongue tie, 33/1,
promise when third in novice at Kempton (5¼ lengths behind Man From Mars) on hurdling
debut: capable of better. *David Pipe*

JUSTFORJAMES (IRE) 8 b.g. Dr Massini (IRE) – Over The Road (IRE) (Executive **h117**
Perk) [2016/17 h21m⁴ h19.9d* h19.9d* h19.9s³ h19.9v² h22v³ Mar 18] winning pointer:
bumper winner: fairly useful hurdler: won novices at Sedgefield (twice, conditional/
amateur event on first occasion) in December: left Sean Aherne after first start: stays 3m:
acts on heavy going: has worn hood: front runner/races prominently, often travels strongly.
Micky Hammond

JUST FOR WILLIAM (IRE) 6 b.g. Dubai Destination (USA) – Buonissimo (IRE) **h–**
(Warcraft (USA)) [2016/17 b16v h15.7s⁵ h21gᵖᵘ Mar 18] workmanlike gelding: well **b–**
beaten in bumper: pulled up in 2 novice hurdles. *Dan Skelton*

JUST GEORGIE 7 b.g. Kayf Tara – Just Kate (Bob's Return (IRE)) [2016/17 h109: **c111**
c20.3g⁴ c20.1sᵇᵈ c22.4v³ c21.6s³ Dec 29] point winner: maiden hurdler: fair form over **h–**
fences: stays 2¾m: best form on soft/heavy going. *Sue Smith*

JUSTICE KNIGHT (IRE) 5 b.g. Raven's Pass (USA) – New Story (USA) (Dynaformer **b–**
(USA)) [2016/17 b15.8d b16s b16.5g Feb 21] no form in bumpers: wears hood. *Michael Scudamore*

JUSTICE SUPER (IRE) 4 b.g. Jeremy (USA) – Supercat (IRE) (Indian Rocket) **b78**
[2016/17 b16.5m⁵ b16g⁴ Mar 18] rather unfurnished gelding: modest form in bumpers.
Johnny Farrelly

JUSTIFICATION 9 b.g. Montjeu (IRE) – Colorspin (FR) (High Top) [2016/17 h15.9v⁴ **h115**
h19.8v³ h19.8s* h20.5v⁵ Mar 4] rather leggy gelding: fairly useful hurdler: won novice
handicap at Sandown in February: stays 2½m: acts on soft going. *Gary Moore*

JUST JOELLIOTT (IRE) 7 b.g. Great Exhibition (USA) – Solara (GER) (Danehill **h104**
(USA)) [2016/17 h19.5d h19.5m⁴ h16.3d h19.9v⁶ h23.8d* h25d³ h21v⁴ Mar 12] £18,000
5-y-o: angular gelding: fifth foal: brother to fairly useful hurdler Solaras Exhibition
(2m/17f winner): dam unraced: fell in Irish maiden point: fair handicap hurdler: won at
Ludlow (amateur event) in January: stays 3m: acts on good to soft going: tried in hood: in
tongue tie last 3 starts: often races towards rear. *Seamus Durack*

JUST LIKE DYLAN (IRE) 6 b.g. Brian Boru – Fainne Oir (IRE) (Montelimar (USA)) **h62**
[2016/17 h–, b75: h19.3m⁶ h23.3g³ h23.9d⁵ h23.3g h24gᵖᵘ h22.1dᵖᵘ Sep 16]
maiden pointer: poor maiden hurdler: stays 23f: tried in headgear/tongue tie. *Barry Murtagh*

JUST MILLY (IRE) 6 b.m. Milan – Out Performer (IRE) (Persian Bold) [2016/17 **h115**
b15.8d⁵ b15.8g² b16.2g³ b16.7g h15.8v⁵ h19.4g* h20.7g² h24.3d³ Apr 21] €6,000 4-y-o: **b76**
seventh foal: closely related to a winning pointer by King's Theatre and half-sister to fair
hurdler/useful chaser Loose Preformer (2½m-3m winner, by Luso): dam unraced half-
sister to high-class hurdler/top-class chaser Bacchanal: modest form in
bumpers: fairly useful form over hurdles: won novice at Doncaster in December: third in
novice handicap at Ayr in April: stays 3m: usually races nearer last than first. *John Mackie*

JUST MINDED (IRE) 6 b.g. Kayf Tara – Georgia On My Mind (FR) (Belmez (USA)) **h120**
[2016/17 b–: h17.1g* h16s³ h20.5v³ h16.7s* h20.6g² Apr 8] fair form in bumpers: won at **b93**
Carlisle in November: fairly useful form over hurdles: won novice at Market Rasen in
March: likely to stay beyond 2½m. *Sue Smith*

JUST SKITTLES 9 b.g. Storming Home – Miss Roberto (IRE) (Don Roberto (USA)) **c–**
[2016/17 c–, h54: h24g c21.7dᵖᵘ Nov 24] maiden pointer: little form over hurdles: pulled **h–**
up both starts in chases. *Richard Harper*

JUST SPOT 10 ch.m. Baryshnikov (AUS) – Just Jasmine (Nicholas Bill) [2016/17 **c–**
c19.8dᵖᵘ c20vᵖᵘ Dec 31] workmanlike mare: maiden hurdler: modest chaser at best: off 21 **h–**
months, pulled up both starts in 2016/17: stays 2½m: acts on heavy going: has worn tongue
tie. *Kevin Bishop*

JUST WHEN 8 b.g. Dalakhani (IRE) – Cape Grace (IRE) (Priolo (USA)) [2016/17 h94: **h–**
h15.9g h24dᵖᵘ h19g Feb 21] sturdy gelding: fair handicap hurdler at best, no form in
2016/17: unproven beyond 2m: acts on heavy going: wears headgear. *Patrick Chamings*

JUWIREYA 10 ch.m. Nayef (USA) – Katayeb (IRE) (Machiavellian (USA)) [2016/17 **h99**
h15.9g³ h16d² h16g⁶ h18.7m* h19.9g³ h21.6mᵖᵘ Oct 6] modest hurdler: won mares
handicap at Stratford in August: stays 19f: acts on good to firm and good to soft going.
Philip Hobbs

K

KABANGA BAY 6 b.g. Overbury (IRE) – Cresswell Zoey (IRE) (Zaffaran (USA)) [2016/17 b16.7g b17.7g³ h17.7dᶠ h17.7m³ h21m³ h19.6m³ h19.1s³ h19.8s⁶ Dec 2] third foal: dam unraced: placed in points: no form in bumpers: fair form over hurdles: stays 21f: acts on soft and good to firm going. *Phil York*   **h104 b–**

KACK HANDED 14 b.g. Terimon – Hand Inn Glove (Alflora (IRE)) [2016/17 c17m May 20] good-topped gelding: unseated in point: fair hurdler/chaser in 2012/13: well beaten in hunter chase on sole outing in 2016/17: stays 21f: acts on good to firm and heavy going. *P. S. Johnson*   **c– h–**

KADDYS DREAM 6 b.m. Kadastrof (FR) – Symbiosis (Bien Bien (USA)) [2016/17 h70p, b–: h16d² May 2] fair form over hurdles: second in maiden at Warwick on sole outing in 2016/17: bred to stay beyond 2m: tried in tongue tie: open to further improvement. *Robin Dickin*   **h100 p**

KADDYS GIRL 7 ch.m. Kadastrof (FR) – Dickies Girl (Saxon Farm) [2016/17 h71, b80, c15.7gᵖᵘ Oct 3] maiden hurdler: pulled up in novice handicap on chasing debut. *Robin Dickin*   **c– h–**

KAFELLA 5 gr.g. Kayf Tara – Sisella (IRE) (Bob Back (USA)) [2016/17 b88: h19.7gᶠ h15.8s² h21.3d² h20gᶠ Apr 9] tall gelding: fairly useful form over hurdles: second in novices at Uttoxeter in November and Wetherby in December: stayed 21f: in tongue tie last 4 starts: often travelled strongly: dead. *Dan Skelton*   **h120**

KAHALEESI 5 b.m. Shirocco (GER) – Maiden Voyage (Slip Anchor) [2016/17 b71: b16.7g⁵ h19.7sᵖᵘ h15.8g⁴ h18.7g Apr 15] useful-looking mare: poor form in bumpers: no form over hurdles: left Philip Hobbs after first start. *Anabel K. Murphy*   **h– b72**

KAHDIAN (IRE) 7 br.g. Rock of Gibraltar (IRE) – Katiykha (IRE) (Darshaan) [2016/17 h66: h21.4dᵖᵘ h23.9g h19s Feb 5] compact gelding: maiden hurdler, no form in 2016/17: has worn cheekpieces, including final start: tried in tongue tie. *Helen Rees*   **h–**

KAI BROON (IRE) 10 b.g. Marju (IRE) – Restiv Star (FR) (Soviet Star (USA)) [2016/17 c108, h–: c15.6d⁶ c20.1gᵖᵘ c20.1dᵖᵘ c16s⁵ c20.1g⁵ Sep 5] close-coupled gelding: winning hurdler: fair handicap chaser, below form in 2016/17: stays 2½m: acts on soft and good to firm going: wears headgear. *Lucinda Russell*   **c81 h–**

KAIDEN MICHAEL (IRE) 5 b.g. Westerner – Alfreeze (Alflora (IRE)) [2016/17 h20gᵖᵘ h21.2g h21.2dᵖᵘ h19.5s⁴ h19s h21.9v Mar 19] runner-up in maiden point: poor form over hurdles: best effort at 19f: acts on soft going: tried in visor. *Tim Vaughan*   **h77**

KAKI DE LA PREE (FR) 10 b.g. Kapgarde (FR) – Kica (FR) (Noir Et Or) [2016/17 c136p, h–: c23d* c24.1s² c29.2sᶠ c24v⁴ Feb 11] medium-sized, good-bodied gelding: winning hurdler: useful chaser: won novice at Worcester in June: second in handicap at Bangor (4½ lengths behind Ballyboker Breeze) in December: should stay further than 25f: acts on heavy going. *Tom Symonds*   **c138 h–**

KALA CASTLE 5 b.g. Kalanisi (IRE) – Dancing Hill (Piccolo) [2016/17 b16m⁴ May 19] 7/1, last of 4 in bumper at Worcester. *David Loder*   **b–**

KALAHARRY (IRE) 5 b.g. Kalanisi (IRE) – Full Imperatrice (FR) (Dernier Empereur (USA)) [2016/17 b–: h20.9dᶠ h16.2s³ h20.1g³ h20.1s² h18.1dᵖᵘ h20.1g⁶ Apr 25] modest form over hurdles: left Iain Jardine after fourth start: stays 2½m: best form on good going: usually races towards rear. *Alistair Whillans*   **h97**

KALA LORD (IRE) 6 b.g. Kalanisi (IRE) – Eimears Pet (IRE) (Lord Americo) [2016/17 b16v b15.7d h15.8d Mar 15] no form in bumpers: well held in maiden on hurdling debut. *Rosemary Gasson*   **h– b–**

KALANE (IRE) 8 b.m. Kalanisi (IRE) – Fairy Lane (IRE) (Old Vic) [2016/17 c134, h131: c21.3m² c23.9g⁴ c19.1g* c20.5g* Dec 29] good-topped mare: winning hurdler: useful chaser: won handicap and listed mares event (by 5 lengths from Colla Pier) at Doncaster in December: left Charlie Longsdon after first start: stays 3m: acts on soft and good to firm going. *Amy Murphy*   **c140 h–**

KALANGADOO 6 b.g. Grape Tree Road – Garota de Ipanema (FR) (Al Nasr (FR)) [2016/17 h15.7g h19.7gᵖᵘ Oct 28] well held in bumper: pulled up in novice on hurdling debut: wears tongue tie. *Ben Case*   **h– b–**

KALANISI CIRCLE (IRE) 5 b.g. Kalanisi (IRE) – Circle The Wagons (IRE) (Commanche Run) [2016/17 b89p: b16.4g Oct 22] fair form on first of 2 starts in bumpers. *Ben Pauling*   **b74**

KALANITI (IRE) 6 b.m. Kalanisi (IRE) – Miss Twinkletoes (IRE) (Zafonic (USA))   h109
[2016/17 b92: h16.2d* h16s* h18.9s⁶ h16.6s³ Mar 3] workmanlike mare: bumper winner:
fair form over hurdles: won maiden at Kelso in October and novice at Wetherby in
November: unproven beyond 17f. *Chris Grant*

KALARIKA (IRE) 4 br.f. Kalanisi (IRE) – Katariya (IRE) (Barathea (IRE)) [2016/17   b79
b16.3s⁴ b16g³ Apr 17] €10,000 3-y-o: seventh foal: half-sister to 6f winner Katehari (by
Noverre): dam ran twice on Flat: modest form in bumpers. *Colin Tizzard*

KALARIYA (IRE) 5 b.m. Kalanisi (IRE) – Katariya (IRE) (Barathea (IRE)) [2016/17   b–
b15.7g May 24] €14,000 3-y-o: sixth foal: half-sister to 6f winner Katehari (by Noverre):
dam ran twice on Flat: tailed off in mares bumper. *Nigel Twiston-Davies*

KALASHNIKOV (IRE) 4 br.g. Kalanisi (IRE) – Fairy Lane (IRE) (Old Vic) [2016/17   b101
b16d* Mar 31] sixth foal: brother to useful hurdler/chaser Kalane (2m-21f winner), stays
3m: dam unraced sister to Cheltenham Gold Cup winner Kicking King: 12/1, won bumper
at Wetherby (by 2 lengths from Minella Warrior) in March: will be suited by further than
2m. *Amy Murphy*

KALASKADESEMILLEY 6 b.g. Myboycharlie (IRE) – Congressional (IRE) (Grand   h101
Lodge (USA)) [2016/17 b79: h16m h16.7d³ h16m² h16.7g² h16.3m* h19.4g h16m⁶ Apr
18] fair hurdler: won maiden at Stratford in October: left Kevin Morgan after sixth start:
unproven beyond 17f: acts on good to firm going: often races prominently. *Martin Smith*

KALASTAR (IRE) 8 b.g. Kalanisi (IRE) – Katsura (Alflora (IRE)) [2016/17 c94:   c75 §
c24.2d^pu c23.8m⁴ May 12] multiple winning pointer: modest maiden chaser, below form in
2016/17: stays 3m: acts on good to soft going: often in blinkers: temperamental. *Katie Scott*

KALIFOURCHON (FR) 6 gr.g. Martaline – Kaly Flight (FR) (Great Palm (USA))   h113
[2016/17 h119: h23.1g* h20.6g h20g⁵ h27g⁴ h23.1g⁵ Nov 9] rather leggy gelding: fairly
useful handicap hurdler: won at Market Rasen in July: stays 27f: best form on good going:
tried in headgear: in tongue tie last 5 starts. *David Pipe*

KALOCI (IRE) 5 b.m. Stowaway – Eye And Ear (IRE) (Old Vic) [2016/17 b16g⁵ Sep 12]   b71
first foal: dam (h88), lightly raced in bumpers/over hurdles, closely related to fairly useful
hurdlers up to 3m Empire Theatre and Some Are Lucky: 33/1, fifth in bumper at Worcester
(10¾ lengths behind Red Square Revival) in September. *Kevin Bishop*

KALONDRA (IRE) 6 b.g. Spadoun (FR) – Mystic Vic (IRE) (Old Vic) [2016/17 h114,   h143
b74: h20.3g⁶ h20g³ h20m* h20g⁴ h19.7g² h19.4g³ h21.6d* h21d⁵ h19.6d* h21.1g h21.4g⁴
Apr 22] workmanlike gelding: third both starts in Irish points: useful hurdler: won novices
at Worcester (twice) in July, and handicaps at Ascot (conditional) in December and
Huntingdon (by 11 lengths from Allee Bleue) in February: stays 2¾m: acts on good to firm
and heavy going: wears tongue tie: usually races in rear, strong traveller. *Neil Mulholland*

KA MARESCO (FR) 5 b.g. Maresca Sorrento (FR) – Karlas World (FR) (Lost World   b–
(IRE)) [2016/17 b16d Oct 24] 25/1, ninth in bumper at Ayr (33 lengths behind Loud And
Clear) in October. *S. Curling, Ireland*

KAMOOL (GER) 7 ch.g. Mamool (IRE) – Kiss Me Lips (GER) (Dashing Blade)   h120
[2016/17 h105: h21g⁵ h19.9g³ h22m² h23.1g² h24g* h24m* h25gᶠ Oct 17] compact
gelding: fairly useful handicap hurdler: won at Southwell in August and September
(conditional): left Jonjo O'Neill after first start: stayed 3m: acted on good to firm and heavy
going: dead. *Graeme McPherson*

KANTURK BANK (IRE) 7 b.g. Carlo Bank (IRE) – Kanturk Belle (IRE) (King's Ride)   c101 p
[2016/17 h85, b–: h19.6m⁴ h25m⁶ h19.9v⁵ h17d c20.9v* c24.2s² Mar 16] Irish maiden   h81
point winner: poor maiden hurdler: fair form over fences: won novice handicap at Carlisle
in March: left Sarah Humphrey after third start: stays 3m: acts on good to firm and heavy
going: has worn headgear, including in 2016/17: tried in tongue tie: often leads: remains
with potential as a chaser. *Stuart Coltherd*

KAPGARDE KING (FR) 6 ch.g. Kapgarde (FR) – Cybertina (FR) (Cyborg (FR))   c99
[2016/17 h78: h19.9g c25.1m* c25.7g² c23.6d* c24.2d⁴ c23.6g³ Apr 17] poor maiden   h72
hurdler: modest form over fences: won handicaps at Wincanton (novice event) in October
and Huntingdon in December: stays 25f: acts on good to firm and good to soft going: wears
hood. *Jamie Snowden*

KAP JAZZ (FR) 7 b.g. Kapgarde (FR) – Jazz And Liquer (FR) (Kahyasi) [2016/17 c108,   c123
h106: c23.5vᶠ c20d* c20s* c24.2d³ Mar 21] sturdy gelding: winning hurdler: fairly useful   h–
form over fences: won handicap at Carlisle in February and novice handicap at Ludlow in
March: stays 21f: acts on soft going: often races prominently. *Venetia Williams*

KAPRICORNE (FR) 10 b.g. Kapgarde (FR) – Colombe Royale (FR) (Passing Sale (FR)) [2016/17 c89, h88: c23.6g^{ur} c23.8v⁴ c23.6d² c25.2s⁶ h25.5v³ h21.9v⁴ c24.5s⁴ c24.5m^{bd} c26.2m⁴ Apr 28] modest hurdler/maiden chaser, not at best in 2016/17: stays 3¼m: acts on heavy going: often wears headgear/tongue tie: sold to join Dan Skelton £2,000. *Sophie Leech*   **c75 h83**

KAPSTADT (FR) 7 b.g. Country Reel (USA) – King's Parody (IRE) (King's Best (USA)) [2016/17 h127: h16d^{pu} h16.3m⁶ h16.3m⁵ h16.7g² h16.8g* h16g⁴ h16.8g* h15.6g⁶ h16s⁵ h16.8g Mar 17] rather leggy gelding: useful on Flat, stays 10.5f: fairly useful handicap hurdler: won at Sedgefield in September and Cheltenham in December: raced around 2m: acts on soft and good to firm going: in tongue tie last 4 starts: usually races towards rear. *Ian Williams*   **h129**

KARALEE (FR) 6 gr.m. Martaline – Change Partner (FR) (Turtle Island (IRE)) [2016/17 h19d⁴ h20d³ Apr 29] fifth foal: half-sister to useful French hurdler/fairly useful chaser Jamal Malik (15f-2¼m winner, by Lavirco) and French chaser Almada (17f-19f winner, by Loup Solitaire): dam (c119/h127) French 2m-19f hurdle/chase winner: useful form over hurdles: won maiden at Killarney in 2015/16 and minor event at Limerick in March: third in Irish Stallion Farms EBF Mares Champion Hurdle at Punchestown (15¾ lengths behind Apple's Jade) in April. *W. P. Mullins, Ireland*   **h138**

KARA TARA 7 b.m. Kayf Tara – Matilda Too (IRE) (Definite Article) [2016/17 h100, b84: h19.7g^F h25g⁶ May 17] bumper winner: fair maiden hurdler, well below form completed start in 2016/17: stays 2½m: acts on soft going: tried in cheekpieces: often races towards rear. *Malcolm Jefferson*   **h79**

KARDINERO (GER) 4 ch.g. Adlerflug (GER) – Karsawina (GER) (Lando (GER)) [2016/17 h16.9g^F h17.6s⁶ h17.6s⁴ h17.6d³ h17.6v^{ur} h17.4d⁴ h21m² Apr 18] brother/half-brother to several winners on Flat abroad, including useful French/German 11f/1½m winner Karsabruni (by Speedmaster): dam useful French 1¼m-1½m winner: fairly useful maiden hurdler: second in novice at Kempton in April: left S. Foucher after sixth start: stays 21f: acts on soft and good to firm going: wears headgear: capable of better. *James Eustace*   **h119 p**

KARINGA DANCER 11 b.g. Karinga Bay – Miss Flora (Alflora (IRE)) [2016/17 c–, h137: h21.6g^{pu} May 5] lengthy gelding: smart hurdler at best, seemed amiss sole outing in 2016/17: winning chaser: stays 21f: acts on soft going: wears tongue tie. *Harry Fry*   **c– h–**

KARINGA DANDY (IRE) 11 b.g. Karinga Bay – Well Then Now Then (IRE) (Supreme Leader) [2016/17 c–, h–: c32.5g^{pu} c27.2d^{pu} May 12] rather leggy gelding: maiden hurdler: modest chaser at best, pulled up on both starts in 2016/17: stays 27f: acts on heavy going: tried in cheekpieces/tongue tie. *Miss R. D. Keeble*   **c– h–**

KARINGO 10 ch.g. Karinga Bay – Wild Happening (GER) (Mondrian (GER)) [2016/17 c–x, h–: h20.2s h20.5d⁶ h21.4s h22.7s h20.2g^{pu} Apr 28] modest maiden hurdler: let down by jumping on both starts over fences in 2015/16: stays 21f: acts on soft and good to firm going: in cheekpieces last 4 starts. *Lucy Normile*   **c– x h93**

KARISMA KING 8 br.g. Supreme Sound – Hollybush (IRE) (Ali-Royal (IRE)) [2016/17 h99: h19.7g h19.9d² h19.9v⁴ c16.3s³ c24v^{pu} c19.2s* c19.2g⁴ c21.1m* Apr 19] modest handicap hurdler: fair form over fences: won handicaps at Market Rasen in March and Sedgefield in April: should stay 3m: acts on good to firm and heavy going: often races prominently. *Sue Smith*   **c103 h98**

KARL MARX (IRE) 7 b.g. Red Clubs (IRE) – Brillano (FR) (Desert King (IRE)) [2016/17 h84: h21.6g h21.4m⁴ h26.5d⁵ h23m⁶ h21.6m² h21.6g⁴ h16.8m* h21.4m⁶ c20.2d^{pu} h23.1s h19g h15.3s³ h16v* c19.2m⁶ Apr 18] leggy gelding: poor handicap hurdler: won at Exeter (conditional) in October and Chepstow in March: no form over fences: stays 3¼m: acts on any going: wears headgear: tried in tongue tie: temperamental. *Mark Gillard*   **c– § h82 §**

KASHMIRI SUNSET 6 b.g. Tiger Hill (IRE) – Sagamartha (Rainbow Quest (USA)) [2016/17 h20g* h20.2g³ Sep 6] brother to fairly useful hurdler Darley Sun (2¾m winner) and half-brother to fairly useful/untrustworthy hurdler Mountain Hiker (2¾m winner, by Azamour): fairly useful on Flat, stays 2¼m: fair form over hurdles: won maiden at Limerick in July: stays 2½m: acts on heavy going: in tongue tie last 2 starts: front runner/races prominently. *Gordon Elliott, Ireland*   **h109**

KASHMIR PEAK (IRE) 8 b.g. Tiger Hill (IRE) – Elhareer (IRE) (Selkirk (USA)) [2016/17 h121: h20d² h17.2d⁴ c23g⁵ c22.6g³ c20g⁴ Sep 23] angular gelding: useful handicap hurdler: second at Worcester in June: fairly useful form over fences: best effort when third in novice at Stratford in August: stays 23f: acts on heavy going: tried in cheekpieces: in tongue tie last 5 starts. *Dan Skelton*   **c120 h127**

KASHSTAREE 6 b.m. Sakhee (USA) – Celestial Welcome (Most Welcome) [2016/17 h76§: h16.2d^pu h20.2d^pu Jun 29] fair hurdler at best, little form since 2014/15: unproven beyond 2m: best form on soft/heavy going: tried in cheekpieces: temperamental. *Lisa Harrison* — **h– §**

KASPIAN TERN 6 b.m. Kadastrof (FR) – Little Tern (IRE) (Terimon) [2016/17 b15.8g h16g h16.3g h15.7d^6 h19.6s^pu h19.7v^pu c18.2g^pu h21.6g h16.5m^4 Apr 27] fourth foal: sister to fair/temperamental chaser Tea Caddy (19f-25f winner): dam showed little both starts: mid-field in maiden bumper: modest maiden hurdler: pulled up in novice handicap on chasing debut: should be suited by further than 2m: acts on good to soft going: in headgear last 3 starts, in tongue tie last 4: tends to find little. *Jamie Snowden* — **c– h89 b59**

KASSIS 8 b.m. Kalanisi (IRE) – Gastina (FR) (Pistolet Bleu (IRE)) [2016/17 c109, h–: c19.9g^4 c20.9g^4 h20.5g* h19.4g^4 c22.7g^4 c19.9s^4 c24.1g^5 Mar 25] lengthy mare: fair handicap hurdler: won mares event at Leicester in November: fair handicap chaser: won at Huntingdon early in season: stays 23f: acts on heavy going: tried in tongue tie. *Jamie Snowden* — **c114 h104**

KASTANI BEACH (IRE) 11 br.g. Alderbrook – Atomic View (IRE) (Old Vic) [2016/17 c–, h99: h15.8g^4 h17.7g^5 h19.1s h15.9v^3 h16s^2 Mar 10] angular gelding: modest handicap hurdler: winning chaser: effective at 2m when conditions are testing, and stays 3m: acts on heavy going: often in headgear. *Seamus Mullins* — **c– h97**

KATACHENKO (IRE) 8 b.g. Kutub (IRE) – Karalee (IRE) (Arokar (FR)) [2016/17 c137, h–: c15.8d^5 c19.1d^3 c19.1g^5 c25.2s^2 c20.8g c21.1g^ur Apr 7] lengthy gelding: winning hurdler: useful handicap chaser: second at Catterick (6 lengths behind I Just Know) in February: effective at 2m to 25f: acts on heavy going: usually wears hood: front runner/races prominently: tends to hang/carry head awkwardly under pressure. *Donald McCain* — **c132 h–**

KATALYSTIC (IRE) 6 br.g. Kalanisi (IRE) – Beltane Queen (IRE) (Strong Gale) [2016/17 b16.2s^2 b16.2s^5 b16d h16.2s^3 h16.2v h19.4g^4 h19.4g Mar 1] €7,800 3-y-o: sixth foal: half-brother to poor chaser Shady Sadie (3m winner, by Dushyantor): dam lightly-raced sister to dam of smart staying chaser Idle Talk and useful hurdler (2m-2½m winner) Smart Talk: fair form on first of 3 starts in bumpers: modest form over hurdles. *Lucinda Russell* — **h90 b85**

KATARRHINI 8 b.m. Kayf Tara – Dedrunknmunky (IRE) (Rashar (USA)) [2016/17 h57: h16d^3 c19.7s^pu c23.6g^ur Apr 17] poor maiden hurdler: failed to complete on both starts over fences: left Harry Whittington after first start: should be suited by 2½m+: acts on heavy going: sometimes in tongue tie. *Jo Davis* — **c– h61**

KATE APPLEBY SHOES (IRE) 8 b.m. Flemensfirth (USA) – Gotta Goa (IRE) (Publisher (USA)) [2016/17 h16s^3 h18s^2 h18.5v* h22v* h24d^pu Apr 27] dual bumper winner: fairly useful form over hurdles: won mares maiden at Clonmel in February and Kerry Group EBF Shannon Spray Mares' Novices' Hurdle at Limerick (by 5 lengths from The Green Lady) in March: should stay 3m: best form on soft/heavy going: front runner/races prominently. *W. P. Mullins, Ireland* — **h128**

KATENKO (FR) 11 b.g. Laveron – Katiana (FR) (Villez (USA)) [2016/17 c–, h–: c24.1s^pu c24.2s c26s^6 Mar 4] big, well-made gelding: winning hurdler: very smart chaser at best, lightly raced and little form since 2013/14: stays 25f: acts on heavy going. *Venetia Williams* — **c– h–**

KATGARY (FR) 7 b.g. Ballingarry (IRE) – Kotkira (FR) (Subotica (FR)) [2016/17 c130, h–: c17.1d^5 c20.1f* c16.4s^2 c20.5d^4 Apr 21] good-topped gelding: winning hurdler: useful handicap chaser: won at Perth in June: second at Doncaster (length behind San Benedeto) in March: stays 21f: acts on any going: usually wears headgear: tried in tongue tie: often races prominently/travels strongly. *Pauline Robson* — **c138 h–**

KATIE GALE 7 b.m. Shirocco (GER) – Karla June (Unfuwain (USA)) [2016/17 h19.9g^6 h15.8g^3 h15.7g* h16m^3 h15.7m* h16.3m^6 h15.7d^2 Nov 15] dam closely related to useful hurdler (stayed 2½m) Moville: fairly useful on Flat, stays 16.5f: fair hurdler: won novices at Southwell in August (mares cvent) and September: unproven beyond 2m: acts on good to firm and good to soft going: front runner/races prominently. *Michael Appleby* — **h107**

KATIE KILMINSTER 5 b.m. Kayf Tara – Norma Hill (Polar Prince (IRE)) [2016/17 b15.7g^6 Aug 31] first foal: dam (c111/h130) 2m/17f hurdle/chase winner: 5/1, sixth in maiden bumper at Southwell (19¾ lengths behind Midas Gold) in August. *Tom Lacey* — **b58**

KATIE'S HEN (IRE) 7 b.m. Shantou (USA) – Borleagh Princess (IRE) (Presenting) [2016/17 b16.2d^3 h22.1g^3 h18.7d* h16.7g^4 h23g h16.8g^3 h15.8g h16.3m h19.7g^4 h19.6s^5 h20.5g^5 h19.4g^4 Mar 1] second foal: dam (h84) lightly raced in bumpers/over hurdles: — **h86 b79**

427

maiden Irish pointer: third in mares bumper at Hexham (1¼ lengths behind Book At Bedtime): modest hurdler: won mares novice at Stratford in June: stays 19f: acts on good to soft going: tried in cheekpieces: wears tongue tie. *Donald McCain*

KATIE'S MASSINI (IRE) 9 b.m. Dr Massini (IRE) – Our Lucky Supreme (IRE) **c–**
(Supreme Leader) [2016/17 c–, h–: c23g^{pu} Apr 6] point winner: maiden hurdler: no form in **h–**
chases. *Mrs E. Scott*

KATKEAU (FR) 10 b.g. Kotky Bleu (FR) – Levine (FR) (Luynes (USA)) [2016/17 c144, **c148**
h133: c24s* c26.1g^{pu} c23.4s^F c29.5s^{pu} c24.2s^6 Feb 12] small, angular gelding: winning **h–**
hurdler: smart handicap chaser: won at Uttoxeter (by ½ length from Gas Line Boy) early in
season: stays 25f: best form on soft/heavy going: wears hood/tongue tie. *David Pipe*

KATNAP (FR) 10 br.g. Sleeping Car (FR) – Kittygale (IRE) (Strong Gale) [2016/17 c25d **c135**
c21d c21g* c20s^4 c21.1g^2 Apr 7] rangy gelding: maiden hurdler: useful handicap **h–**
chaser: won at Leopardstown in January: second in Topham Chase at Aintree in April: left
Mrs S. A. Bramall after first start: stays 3m: acts on heavy going: tried in headgear: has
worn tongue tie, including last 4 starts: usually races close up, often travels strongly.
Joseph Patrick O'Brien, Ireland

KATY P 5 b.m. Ask – Kingara (Karinga Bay) [2016/17 b86p: b16d^3 b16.5m^5 b16m^2 h15.7d **h108**
h16.2s^3 h20.7g* Apr 3] leggy, unfurnished mare: fair form in bumpers: similar form over **b87**
hurdles: won mares novice at Huntingdon in April: left Mrs J. Harrington after second start:
should prove suited by further than 2½m. *Philip Hobbs*

KATY ROYAL 5 b.m. King's Theatre (IRE) – Water Stratford (IRE) (Jurado (USA)) **h–**
[2016/17 b17s b15.6g b15.7s h16.2g^{pu} Apr 28] quite good-topped mare: seventh foal: dam **b–**
(h115), bumper/2m/17f hurdle winner (stayed 21f), half-sister to fairly useful hurdler/
useful chaser (stayed 29f) Betty's Boy: no form in bumpers: pulled up in mares novice on
hurdling debut. *Bruce Mactaggart*

KAUTO LINGARRY (FR) 5 ch.g. Ballingarry (IRE) – Kauto Luisa (FR) (Jeune **b–**
Homme (USA)) [2016/17 b16s Mar 13] tailed off in bumper. *Samuel Drinkwater*

KAUTO RIKO (FR) 6 b.g. Ballingarry (IRE) – Kauto Relstar (FR) (Art Bleu) [2016/17 **h112**
h98: h18.6d* h19.3s* h19.9v^2 h20.6m^3 Apr 17] fair handicap hurdler: won at Market Rasen
in December and Catterick in February: stays 21f: acts on soft and good to firm going.
Tom Gretton

KAVANAGHS CORNER (IRE) 8 b.g. Coroner (IRE) – Annacarney (IRE) (Moscow **c81**
Society (USA)) [2016/17 h79: c20.3g^3 Apr 29] runner-up on second of 2 starts in Irish **h–**
points: maiden hurdler: 8/1, third in novice handicap at Bangor (10½ lengths behind
Ballycoe) on chasing debut: stays 2½m: acts on heavy going: has worn hood: often races
freely, tends to find little. *Simon Earle*

KAVEMAN 5 b.g. Kayf Tara – Megalex (Karinga Bay) [2016/17 b16s^6 Jan 14] brother to **b59 p**
several winners, notably smart bumper winner/useful but ungenuine hurdler Megastar (2m
winner), stayed 21f, and Champion Bumper/Betfair Hurdle winner Ballyandy, and half-
brother to a winner on Flat by Proclamation: dam (h92) 2½m hurdle winner: better than
result when well beaten in maiden bumper: should improve. *Gary Moore*

KAYF ADVENTURE 6 b.g. Kayf Tara – My Adventure (IRE) (Strong Gale) [2016/17 **h124**
h18.5s^3 h21.6v* h21.5s^3 h19.8d^2 Mar 26] fairly useful form over hurdles: won novice at
Fontwell in February: second in novice handicap at Wincanton in March. *Philip Hobbs*

KAYF BLANCO 8 b.g. Kayf Tara – Land of Glory (Supreme Leader) [2016/17 h134: **c129 p**
c16d^4 h16s^3 h18.5s^4 h16.3d^5 h16d Mar 11] tall gelding: useful handicap hurdler: third in **h130**
listed event at Sandown (4¾ lengths behind Brain Power) in December: 25/1, fourth in
maiden at Uttoxeter (13¾ lengths behind Charbel) on chasing debut: best around 2m: acts
on soft going: tried in hood/tongue tie: usually races towards rear: should improve over
fences. *Graeme McPherson*

KAYF CHARMER 7 b.m. Kayf Tara – Silver Charmer (Charmer) [2016/17 h89: h19g^4 **h92**
h16d^5 h20v* h15.8v h15.8d Apr 16] modest handicap hurdler: won at Ffos Las in
December: stays 2½m: acts on heavy going: tried in blinkers: often races prominently.
Linda Blackford

KAYF GRACE 7 b.m. Kayf Tara – Potter's Gale (IRE) (Strong Gale) [2016/17 b114: **h119 P**
h16.7s* Dec 9] useful-looking mare: useful bumper performer: 2/7, won novice at Bangor
(by 2½ lengths from Report To Base with plenty in hand) on hurdling debut: open to
significant improvement. *Nicky Henderson*

KAYFLEUR 8 b.m. Kayf Tara – Combe Florey (Alflora (IRE)) [2016/17 c123, h–: c21.1g^3 **c110**
c22.9s^3 c22.5v^F c20v^2 c28.4g^4 Apr 15] smallish, sturdy mare: winning hurdler: fair maiden **h–**
chaser: stays 21f: acts on heavy going: usually races towards rear. *Henry Daly*

KAYFLIN (FR) 9 b.m. Kayf Tara – Flinders (Henbit (USA)) [2016/17 c67, h81§: c25.7g^{pu} **c72** h19.1d h20.5v* h20.5g h20.5v^2 c19.7g^{ur} c19.2g^4 Apr 12] lengthy mare: modest handicap **h83 §** hurdler: won at Plumpton in January: poor form over fences: stays 21f: best form on soft/ heavy going: wears headgear: often races towards rear: unreliable. *Linda Jewell*

KAYF MARINER 5 b.g. Kayf Tara – Line Freedom (FR) (Freedom Cry) [2016/17 **b106** b16.7s* b16.3d^5 Feb 11] well-made gelding: useful form in bumpers: won at Bangor (by 3¼ lengths from Kildisart) in December: dead. *Alan King*

KAYF MOSS 9 b.g. Kayf Tara – Madam Mosso (Le Moss) [2016/17 c130, h–: h24.2d **c–** c24.1s^{pu} h23.6s h24.1s^5 c23.8s^{pu} Feb 19] sturdy gelding: useful hurdler/chaser at best, well **h97** below form in 2016/17: stays 3m: best form on heavy going: wears headgear/tongue tie: usually races prominently. *John Flint*

KAYFTON PETE 11 b.g. Kayf Tara – Jonchee (FR) (Le Thuit Signol (FR)) [2016/17 **c101** c105, h96: c21.3g^3 c20.5m^{ur} h20g Jul 12] workmanlike gelding: fair hurdler at best, well **h–** held sole outing in 2016/17: fair handicap chaser: stayed 21f: acted on soft and good to firm going: often used to wear headgear/tongue tie: front runner/raced prominently: dead. *Charles Pogson*

KAYF WILLOW 8 b.m. Kayf Tara – Mrs Philip (Puissance) [2016/17 h115: h21.6d^4 Sep **h100** 4] fair handicap hurdler: stays 2¾m: acts on soft and good to firm going. *Philip Hobbs*

KAYLA 7 b.m. Kayf Tara – Palila (Petoski) [2016/17 h101, b85: h23.3g^2 h24g* h23.3g* **h110** h23.1m^4 Apr 17] bumper winner: fair handicap hurdler: won at Towcester and Uttoxeter early in season: stays 3m: best form on good going: wears tongue tie. *Stuart Edmunds*

KAYSERSBERG (FR) 10 b.g. Khalkevi (IRE) – Alliance Royale (FR) (Turgeon (USA)) **c–** [2016/17 c–, h131: h23.1m h26.4m^5 May 20] lengthy gelding: useful hurdler at best, **h–** well held both starts in 2016/17: winning chaser: stays 25f: acts on good to firm and good to soft going: has worn cheekpieces, including both starts in 2016/17: usually leads. *Warren Greatrex*

KAZLIAN (FR) 9 b.g. Sinndar (IRE) – Quiet Splendor (USA) (Unbridled (USA)) [2016/17 **c93** c–p, h113: c16.3g^3 h16g^6 h20.6s^5 Feb 17] medium-sized gelding: modest handicap hurdler **h98** nowadays: modest form over fences: stays 19f: acts on heavy going: usually wears headgear nowadays: tried in tongue tie. *Johnny Farrelly*

KEATING (IRE) 5 b.g. King's Theatre (IRE) – Tus Nua (IRE) (Galileo (IRE)) [2016/17 **h102** h19.5d h16s^3 h16.8v h16s^6 h21.6g^2 Apr 11] €80,000 3-y-o: sturdy gelding: first foal: dam (b105) won both starts in bumpers: fell in Irish maiden point: fair form over hurdles: will prove best at shorter than 21f: acts on soft going: in hood last 2 starts: often races towards rear. *Philip Hobbs*

KEEL HAUL (IRE) 9 br.g. Classic Cliche (IRE) – Tara Hall (Saddlers' Hall (IRE)) **c125** [2016/17 c129, h–: h16g^5 c15.8d^2 c16.3d^6 h16.2s^5 c16.2s^4 c20s^5 c20.2s^5 h16.7g^6 Mar 25] **h102** leggy gelding: fair handicap hurdler nowadays: fairly useful handicap chaser: second at Aintree in November: unproven beyond 2m: acts on heavy going: usually wears headgear: often races prominently. *Henry Oliver*

KEEPER HILL (IRE) 6 b.g. Westerner – You Take Care (IRE) (Definite Article) **h139** [2016/17 h105: h20g^2 h19.6s* h19.7s* h19.6d* h21.1g h24.7g^6 Apr 7] tall gelding: chasing type: useful bumper winner: useful form over hurdles: won novices at Bangor in November, Hereford in January and Huntingdon (listed event, by neck from Messire des Obeaux) in February: stays 21f: acts on soft going. *Warren Greatrex*

KEEP IN LINE (GER) 5 b.g. Soldier Hollow – Kastila (GER) (Sternkoenig (IRE)) **h129** [2016/17 h20g^2 h19.6s* h19.4s^4 h15.7d^3 h20.3s h21g^F Mar 18] good-topped gelding: useful on Flat, stays 1½m: fairly useful form over hurdles: won maiden at Huntingdon and novice at Bangor in October: third in Kennel Gate Novices' Hurdle at Ascot (4½ lengths behind Capitaine) in December: unproven beyond 17f: acts on soft and good to firm going. *Alan King*

KEEPIN TIME 5 b.m. Fair Mix (IRE) – Pipsacre (Kayf Tara) [2016/17 b16s^5 h16.5g **h–** h19.4g h19.7s Jan 4] first foal: dam winning pointer: well beaten in mares bumper/over **b–** hurdles. *Dan Skelton*

KEEP MOVING (FR) 5 b.g. Linda's Lad – Keeping Gold (FR) (Goldneyev (USA)) **c103** [2016/17 c19.4d^5 c16.4d^5 c16s^4 c16d^{3d} c16.4s^5 Mar 3] good-topped gelding: first foal: dam **h–** fairly useful French 19f chase winner: well held in maiden on Flat: fair form on completed start over hurdles: fair maiden chaser: left G. Cherel after final (2015/16) start: stays 2¼m: acts on soft going: usually races towards rear. *Philip Hobbs*

KEEP ON TRACK (IRE) 10 ch.g. Rudimentary (USA) – Corries Rein (IRE) (Anshan)   **c–** [2016/17 c20.3v³ c17m May 20] lightly-raced hurdler: useful chaser at best, well held in 2   **h–** hunters in 2016/17: barely stays 33f: acts on soft and good to firm going: in tongue tie last 2 starts. *Richard Walker*

KEEP UP (GER) 5 b.g. Monsun (GER) – Katy Carr (Machiavellian (USA)) [2016/17   **h–** h97: h16.8s^{pu} h17.2m^{pu} h16.2d^{pu} h24d^{pu} Jul 10] maiden hurdler, no form in 2016/17: tried in cheekpieces/tongue tie. *Philip Kirby*

KEEP UP KEIRA (IRE) 6 b.m. Scorpion (IRE) – Perspex Queen (IRE) (Presenting)   **h75** [2016/17 h–, b80: h16m⁵ h19.5d h20.7g h21.4d^{pu} Dec 13] poor form over hurdles: should have been suited by 2½m+: acted on good to firm going: tried in cheekpieces: in tongue tie last 2 starts: dead. *Neil Mulholland*

KEEPYOURHEADUP 6 b.g. Sir Percy – Sweet Lemon (IRE) (Oratorio (IRE)) [2016/17   **h–** b–: h15.3d^{pu} h19g^{pu} Mar 20] no form. *Helen Nelmes*

KELKA 5 b.m. Exit To Nowhere (USA) – Scarvagh Diamond (IRE) (Zaffaran (USA))   **h125** [2016/17 b95: h16.2d² h16.2s* h20.9s* h19.9s² h19.8s⁵ h16.4v* h20.5d⁴ Apr 21] bumper winner: fairly useful hurdler: won maiden at Hexham in November, mares novice at Kelso in December and handicap at Newcastle in March: stays 21f: best form on soft/heavy going: usually races close up. *Malcolm Jefferson*

KELPIES MYTH 4 b.g. Dutch Art – Miss Respect (Mark of Esteem (IRE)) [2016/17   **b89** b13.7m³ b14d² b13g b16.4g* Mar 24] fifth foal: brother to useful/temperamental 6f winner Miss Azeza and half-brother to 1m/9f winner Taxiformissbyron (by Byron): dam unraced half-sister to fairly useful/untrustworthy hurdler (stayed 2¾m) Halifax: fair form in bumpers: won at Musselburgh in March. *Michael Herrington*

KELSEY (IRE) 7 ch.g. Robin des Champs (FR) – Lady Mariah (IRE) (Moonax (IRE))   **h92 §** [2016/17 h96: h23.3g³ h23.1g⁴ h23.9d³ h23.3v h25.6s^{pu} Jan 31] maiden pointer: modest handicap hurdler: stays 3m: acts on heavy going: has worn headgear, including last 4 starts: often in tongue tie: front runner/races prominently: temperamental. *Peter Bowen*

KELTUS (FR) 7 gr.g. Keltos (FR) – Regina d'Orthe (FR) (R B Chesne) [2016/17 c–,   **c139** h130: c20.1d* c20.3v² c20.1g* c16.3m² c21m³ c24.2g* c25g² c24.3g Apr 22] rather leggy   **h–** gelding: winning hurdler: useful chaser: won novices at Hexham (twice) early in season and handicap at Fakenham in October: stays 25f: acts on good to firm and heavy going: wears tongue tie. *Paul Nicholls*

KELVINGROVE (IRE) 7 b.g. Hurricane Run (IRE) – Silversword (FR) (Highest Honor   **h134** (FR)) [2016/17 h115: h23.1g* h23g⁴ h24.2d⁵ h24.4d³ h24d³ h22.8g* Apr 15] useful handicap hurdler: won at Market Rasen early in season and Haydock (by 3¼ lengths from Young Dillon) in April: stays 3m: acts on soft going: has worn cheekpieces, including last 5 starts. *Jonjo O'Neill*

KEMBOY (FR) 5 b.g. Voix du Nord (FR) – Vitora (FR) (Victory Note (USA)) [2016/17   **h140** h19d* h20g² h21.1g⁵ h20g Apr 28] sturdy gelding: dam half-sister to high-class hurdler (stayed 3m) Karabak: runner-up sole outing on Flat for F. Matzinger: useful form over hurdles: won maiden at Limerick in December: second in Nathaniel Lacy & Partners Solicitors Novices' Hurdle at Leopardstown (6 lengths behind Let's Dance) in January: will stay 3m. *W. P. Mullins, Ireland*

KEMICALLIE 5 b.m. Passing Glance – Jenny From Brean (Commanche Run) [2016/17   **b–** b–: b16.8g May 25] no form in bumpers: in tongue tie sole outing in 2016/17. *Carroll Gray*

KENDARI KING (IRE) 6 b.g. Misternando – Native Mistress (IRE) (Be My Native   **h– §** (USA)) [2016/17 h–, b80: h19d h23.4g^{pu} h25d^{pu} h23.3v^{pu} Dec 31] no form over hurdles: in headgear/tongue tie last 3 starts: temperamental. *Tim Vaughan*

KENOBE STAR (IRE) 5 b.g. Clodovil (IRE) – Maimana (IRE) (Desert King (IRE))   **h–** [2016/17 h88: h17.7g May 29] maiden hurdler, well held sole outing in 2016/17: tried in cheekpieces/tongue tie. *David Dennis*

KENSINGTON CASTLE 6 br.g. Grand Finale (IRE) – Gaelic Royale (IRE) (Welsh   **b–** Term) [2016/17 b15.9g May 28] tailed off in bumper. *Debra Hamer*

KENTFORD HEIRESS 7 b.m. Midnight Legend – Kentford Duchess (Jupiter Island)   **h110** [2016/17 h71.4m³ h21.4m³ h25.6d* h21.6g* h21.6d* h21.6d h24.1m³ h19.8s⁵ h21.6g³ h21.2m⁴ Apr 18] fair handicap hurdler: won at Fontwell in June, August and September (mares event): stays 3¼m: acts on soft and good to firm going. *Seamus Mullins*

KENTFORD MYTH 7 b.m. Midnight Legend – Quistaquay (El Conquistador) [2016/17 h103: h23s^{pu} h20d* h26.5m^5 h19.8s c20.2s* c20.2s^4 c22.7s^{ur} c20v^5 c25.7m^{pu} Apr 16] fair handicap hurdler: won at Worcester (conditional) in June: modest form over fences: won mares novice at Wincanton in December: barely stays 3¼m: acts on good to firm and heavy going: usually races towards rear. *Seamus Mullins* **c99 h103**

KENT RAGSTONE (USA) 8 ch.g. Stonesider (USA) – Sweet Charity (USA) (A P Indy (USA)) [2016/17 h–: h20.3s^6 May 18] lengthy gelding: no form over hurdles: in hood last 2 starts: tried in tongue tie. *Daniel Steele* **h–**

KENTUCKY STAR (FR) 8 ch.g. Kentucky Dynamite (USA) – La Gloria (Halling (USA)) [2016/17 h113: h19.8m^F h20.6g^6 h20g^6 h16g h22d^6 h23.8g* h23.8g^F h23.8g^{pu} c20s^3 Mar 17] angular gelding: fair handicap hurdler: won at Musselburgh (conditional) in December: 8/1, third in novice at Down Royal (33 lengths behind Bright Tomorrow) on chasing debut: left Dan Skelton after second start: stays 3m: acts on soft going: often in hood/tongue tie: usually races towards rear. *Shane Donohoe, Ireland* **c94 h112**

KEPPEL ISLE (IRE) 8 b.g. Heron Island (IRE) – Wadi Khaled (FR) (Bering) [2016/17 h89: c18m* c16.5g^5 c16.5m^6 h16m Apr 18] good-topped gelding: modest maiden hurdler, below form final outing in 2016/17: modest form over fences: won novice handicap at Kempton early in season: stays 2¼m: acts on good to firm and good to soft going: usually leads. *Laura Mongan* **c95 h–**

KEPPOLS QUEEN (IRE) 9 br.m. Indian River (FR) – Keppols Princess (IRE) (Soviet Lad (USA)) [2016/17 h135: h18d^3 c19d^4 c16s^2 c18s^2 c19.5s^{pu} c20d^F c16s^3 c20v^4 c20d^2 c21d^{ur} Apr 28] winning hurdler: useful maiden chaser, in frame all completed starts: third in listed mares event at Naas (6¼ lengths behind Slowmotion) in February and second in Grade 3 mares event at Fairyhouse (2¾ lengths behind Slowmotion) in April: stays 2½m: acts on heavy going: has worn hood, including in 2016/17: in tongue tie last 5 starts: front runner/races prominently. *Mrs J. Harrington, Ireland* **c130 h–**

KERISPER (FR) 8 b.g. Robin des Champs (FR) – Tina Rederie (FR) (Cadoudal (FR)) [2016/17 h123: c23g^3 Sep 23] Irish maiden point winner: fairly useful hurdler: 4/1, some encouragement when third in novice at Worcester (27½ lengths behind Southfield Vic) on chasing debut: stays 3m: acts on heavy going: should do better as a chaser. *Nigel Twiston-Davies* **c89 p h–**

KERROW (IRE) 7 b.g. Mahler – Olives Hall (IRE) (Saddlers' Hall (IRE)) [2016/17 h118: h24.1g^F h24.7g* c23.6g^6 c23g* c24g^2 c31.8g^6 Mar 14] smallish gelding: fairly useful form over hurdles: won handicap at Aintree (conditional) in October: useful form over fences: won handicap at Taunton in December: second in novice at Doncaster (neck behind Premier Bond) in January: should stay beyond 25f: acts on good to soft going. *Alan King* **c135 h126**

KERRY'S LORD (IRE) 8 br.g. Lend A Hand – Tesses Express (IRE) (Flemensfirth (USA)) [2016/17 h80, b–: h25g^{pu} h23.8d Nov 28] sturdy gelding: maiden pointer: little form over hurdles left Joanne Thomason-Murphy after first start: tried in tongue tie: usually races towards rear, often lazily. *Sarah Humphrey* **h–**

KEYBOARD GANGSTER (IRE) 6 b.g. Gamut (IRE) – Vic O'Tully (IRE) (Old Vic) [2016/17 b16.2d b16g^6 Apr 22] €4,600 3-y-o: fifth foal: dam unraced: modest form on second of 2 starts in bumpers: ungenuine. *Donald Whillans* **b83 §**

KEYCHAIN (IRE) 7 b.g. Key of Luck (USA) – Sarifa (IRE) (Kahyasi) [2016/17 c97§, h94: h21.6g c16.5g^6 h16.8m Oct 6] rather leggy gelding: modest hurdler/chaser at best, no form in 2016/17: best up to 2½m: acts on good to firm and heavy going: usually in headgear: has worn tongue tie, including last 3 starts: temperamental. *Brendan Powell* **c– § h–**

KEY PEOPLE (IRE) 10 b.g. Alderbrook – Diamond Forever (Teenoso (USA)) [2016/17 c98, h–: c22.6m^{pu} c23.8d^4 c23m^6 Jul 4] multiple point winner: maiden hurdler: poor maiden chaser: left J. Lean after first start: stays easy 3m: acts on good to firm going: in cheekpieces last 4 starts: tried in tongue tie. *Tim Vaughan* **c78 h–**

KEY TO MILAN 11 b.g. Milan – Key West (FR) (Highest Honor (FR)) [2016/17 c–, h104: h21.6g^2 h16d^6 h22m h21.6g Aug 20] modest handicap hurdler nowadays: pulled up sole outing over fences in 2013/14: stays 21f: acts on good to firm going: wears headgear/tongue tie: front runner/races prominently. *Chris Down* **c– h97**

KEY TO THE WEST (IRE) 10 b.g. Westerner – Monte Solaro (IRE) (Key of Luck (USA)) [2016/17 c123, h–: h13.8v^5 h16.2s^4 h15.3s^3 h19.9v^6 h21.2s Feb 22] good sort: fair handicap hurdler nowadays: winning chaser: stays 2½m: best form on soft/heavy going: has worn headgear, including final start: has worn tongue tie, including last 4 starts: usually races nearer last than first: one to treat with caution. *Matt Sheppard* **c– h105 §**

KHESKIANTO (IRE) 11 b.m. Kheleyf (USA) – Gently (IRE) (Darshaan) [2016/17 h59:   **h67**
h16.7g⁴ h19.2m h23.4sᵖᵘ Nov 15] poor maiden hurdler: has worn tongue tie. *Michael Chapman*

KHEZERABAD (FR) 5 ch.g. Dalakhani (IRE) – Khelwa (FR) (Traditionally (USA))   **h130**
[2016/17 h132: h16.4g² h16d* h15.7v³ h15.9d³ Dec 12] sturdy gelding: useful hurdler:
won maiden at Sandown (by 4½ lengths from Crystal Lad) in November: raced around 2m:
acts on good to soft going. *Nicky Henderson*

KHISMET 4 b.f. Kheleyf (USA) – Bisaat (USA) (Bahri (USA)) [2016/17 h16.3m⁵ h16.8g⁴   **h97**
h16m³ h16.8g* h16s⁵ Nov 15] half-sister to fair/unreliable hurdler At First Light (2m-2¾m
winner, by Echo of Light): dam sister to fairly useful hurdler/fair chaser (stayed 3m)
Maraafeq: fair on Flat, stays 1¼m: modest form over hurdles: won handicap at Newton
Abbot in October: tried in cheekpieces. *John Flint*

KIAMA BAY (IRE) 11 b.g. Fraam – La Panthere (USA) (Pine Bluff (USA)) [2016/17   **c–**
c105p, h–: h16g² May 3] good-bodied gelding: useful hurdler at best, went like best horse   **h100**
at weights in seller sole outing in 2016/17: maiden chaser: raced mainly around 2m: acts on
soft going: tried in visor. *Jim Best*

KICKING ELF (IRE) 9 b.g. Golan (IRE) – Broadfield Cruiser (IRE) (Shujan (USA))   **h–**
[2016/17 h15.3mᵖᵘ h24dᵖᵘ Nov 29] in frame in points: no form in bumpers/over hurdles.
Mark Shears

KICK ON DOTTIE (IRE) 4 ch.f. Getaway (GER) – Oddly Presented (IRE) (Presenting)   **b62 p**
[2016/17 b17d⁶ Apr 5] £6,000 3-y-o: fourth foal: half-sister to fair hurdler/chaser
Presenting Mahler (17f-2½m winner, by Mahler), stays 23f: dam (b73) winning pointer,
half-sister to fairly useful hurdler (stayed 3m) Really Unique: 16/1, sixth in bumper at
Carlisle (21¾ lengths behind Court Affairs) in April: should do better. *Malcolm Jefferson*

KID KALANISI (IRE) 6 b.g. Kalanisi (IRE) – Nut Touluze (IRE) (Toulon) [2016/17   **c105 p**
h98: h20.3g h19.1g² h21g⁵ h23.11m³ c23.6dᶠ c25.5s* h25v* h25d² Feb 9] well-made   **h107**
gelding: fair handicap hurdler: won at Plumpton in January: fair form when won handicap
at Fontwell in December on completed start over fences: left Dan Skelton after second
start: stays 25f: acts on good to firm and heavy going: wears headgear: tried in tongue tie:
often races towards rear: likely to progress further as a chaser. *Jeremy Scott*

KID VALENTINE (IRE) 7 b.g. Scorpion (IRE) – Supreme Nova (Supreme Leader)   **h119**
[2016/17 h113: h20.6g* Jun 3] Irish point winner: fairly useful form over hurdles: won
novice at Market Rasen in June: will stay 2¾m+. *Michael Smith*

KIE (IRE) 9 b.g. Old Vic – Asura (GER) (Surumu (GER)) [2016/17 c142, h106: h23.1m⁴   **c126**
c25g⁴ c20gᵖᵘ May 29] compact gelding: fairly useful handicap hurdler: fourth at Exeter in   **h118**
May: useful handicap chaser, below best in 2016/17: stays 23f: acts on soft and good to
firm going: tried in cheekpieces/tongue tie. *David Pipe*

KIESTOWN CHIEF (IRE) 14 b.g. Exit To Nowhere (USA) – Golden Native (IRE) (Be   **c80**
My Native (USA)) [2016/17 c24.1g⁶ c21.2m² c24.1dᵖᵘ Feb 18] poor maiden chaser
nowadays: stays 23f: acts on soft and good to firm going. *R. C. Garton*

KIKIMORA 4 gr.f. Malinas (GER) – Tikk Tokk (IRE) (Tikkanen (USA)) [2016/17 b16.7g   **b–**
Mar 25] £4,000 3-y-o: second foal: dam unraced half-sister to Prix Alain du Breil winner
Grand Souvenir and Prix Maurice Gillois winner Polivalente and to dam of useful hurdler/
smart chaser (stays 3¼m) Roi des Francs: well beaten in maiden bumper. *Oliver Greenall*

KILAS GIRL (IRE) 7 b.m. Millenary – Ballybeg Dusty (IRE) (Beneficial) [2016/17 h95:   **h–**
h23.3dᵖᵘ Jun 19] Irish point winner: modest maiden hurdler, pulled up sole outing in
2016/17: stays 25f: acts on soft going. *John Quinn*

KILBREE CHIEF (IRE) 9 b.g. Dr Massini (IRE) – Lame Excuse (IRE) (Presenting)   **c121**
[2016/17 c128, h–: c26.2d c32.4s⁶ c26.9v³ c26.9v* c28.4g Apr 15] good-topped gelding: **h–**
winning hurdler: fairly useful handicap chaser: won at Ayr in February: should stay long
distances: acts on heavy going: tried in cheekpieces. *Lucinda Russell*

KILBREE KID (IRE) 10 b.g. Cloudings (IRE) – Bustingoutallover (USA) (Trempolino   **c125**
(USA)) [2016/17 c133, h–: c25.1m² c26.1sᵖᵘ c23g³ c23.8g* c23.8d* c25.6m³ Oct 5] sturdy   **h–**
gelding: winning hurdler: fairly useful handicap chaser nowadays: won at Perth in August
and September: stays 3¼m: acts on soft and good to firm going: wears headgear/tongue tie.
Tom George

KILCARRY BRIDGE (IRE) 10 b.g. Balakheri (IRE) – Echo Queen (IRE) (Luso)   **c132 x**
[2016/17 c20.1v⁴ c20d³ c18.2d⁴ c22g⁴ c20d³ c16s⁴ h24g⁵ h24v c17.3v² c18v* c24v² c21d⁴   **h114**
Apr 28] fairly useful handicap hurdler: useful chaser: won maiden at Thurles in November

and handicap at Gowran in March: fourth in novice handicap at Punchestown (4½ lengths behind Woodland Opera) in April: stays 3m: acts on heavy going: wears tongue tie: usually leads: sketchy jumper of fences. *John Patrick Ryan, Ireland*

KILCASCAN 13 b.g. Alflora (IRE) – Peasedown Tofana (Teenoso (USA)) [2016/17 c87: c20.9v⁴ c23m³ c23g* c22.6g³ c24.5d c24v⁴ c27.5g⁵ Apr 23] modest handicap chaser: won at Worcester in July: stays 3¼m: acts on good to firm and heavy going: wears cheekpieces. *Rosemary Gasson* **c92**

KILCREA VALE (IRE) 7 b.g. Beneficial – Inflation (FR) (Port Etienne (FR)) [2016/17 h136: c20d* c21.4s² c17.4s* c19.9g⁵ c20g Apr 29] well-made gelding: useful hurdler: useful form over fences: won novices at Ludlow in December and Fontwell (by 2 lengths from As de Mee) in February: second in graduation event at Market Rasen (3 lengths behind Three Musketeers) in January: stays 21f: acts on soft going: often races prominently. *Nicky Henderson* **c143 h–**

KILCULLEN FLEM (IRE) 7 ch.g. Flemensfirth (USA) – Cansalrun (IRE) (Anshan) [2016/17 h113: c26.2d⁶ c23.6dᵘʳ c25.3v c29.6sᵖᵘ c24.1s* c22.4s⁴ c23.8g⁴ Apr 9] winning hurdler: fair handicap chaser: won novice event at Bangor in January: stays 3¼m: acts on heavy going: has worn headgear, including last 5 starts. *Rebecca Curtis* **c105 h–**

KILDISART (IRE) 5 br.g. Dubai Destination (USA) – Princess Mairead (IRE) (Blueprint (IRE)) [2016/17 b16.7s² Dec 9] third foal: half-brother to modest hurdler For Sinead (2¾m winner, by Presenting): dam (h82) ran 3 times over hurdles (best effort at 3m): runner-up in Irish maiden point: 10/11, second in bumper at Bangor (3¼ lengths behind Kayf Mariner) in December, clear of rest: likely to progress. *Ben Pauling* **b101 p**

KILFENORA (IRE) 5 b.g. Yeats (IRE) – Blazing Liss (IRE) (Supreme Leader) [2016/17 h20d h16d h16v h16.5v* h16d h22d⁴ Apr 17] sixth foal: dam (h125), bumper and 2m-2¼m hurdle winner, out of half-sister to very smart 2m-2½m hurdle winner Liss A Paoraigh: useful form over hurdles: won maiden at Punchestown (by 15 lengths from Mr Showtime) in February: fourth in handicap at Fairyhouse (5 lengths behind Showem Silver) in April: stays 2¾m: acts on heavy going. *Edward Harty, Ireland* **h131**

KILFINICHEN BAY (IRE) 9 b.g. Westerner – Cailin Deas (IRE) (Pistolet Bleu (IRE)) [2016/17 c138p, h132: c20dᵖᵘ c23g² c21.4gᵖᵘ c25.8g² c22.6g² c25.5g* c26.2d⁴ c25gᶠ c26g Mar 16] sturdy gelding: winning hurdler: useful handicap chaser: won at Warwick (by neck from Master Dee) in September: second at Stratford (7 lengths behind Gowanauthat) earlier in month: stays 3¼m: acts on good to firm and heavy going: has worn tongue tie, including last 4 starts: usually travels strongly. *Charlie Longsdon* **c133 h–**

KILGEEL HILL (IRE) 7 b.g. Oscar (IRE) – Park Jewel (IRE) (Executive Perk) [2016/17 h26sᵖᵘ Jan 14] lengthy gelding: runner-up in Irish maiden point: fairly useful hurdler: off 23 months, didn't last home on sole outing in 2016/17: stays 2¾m: acts on heavy going. *Harry Whittington* **h–**

KILGEFIN STAR (IRE) 9 b.g. Saddlers' Hall (IRE) – High Church Annie (IRE) (Bustomi) [2016/17 c132, h–: c21.3mᵖᵘ c20.1f h21.6s c22sᵖᵘ c29dᵖᵘ h20.3sᵖᵘ Mar 17] tall, angular gelding: fairly useful hurdler/useful chaser at best, no form in 2016/17: left Michael Smith after second start: tried in headgear: often leads. *R. P. McNamara, Ireland* **c– h–**

KILINAKIN (IRE) 7 ch.g. Definite Article – Topanberry (IRE) (Topanoora) [2016/17 h19.1sᵖᵘ h21s h18.5d h21m² Apr 4] £10,000 6-y-o: third foal: dam (h106), 2½m hurdle winner, half-sister to useful hurdler/smart chaser (stays 3¼m) Mendip Express: Irish point winner: modest form on last of 4 starts over hurdles. *Zoe Davison* **h86**

KILLABRAHER CROSS (IRE) 10 gr.g. Kasmayo – Enoughrose (IRE) (Roselier (FR)) [2016/17 c92, h67: c19.7g³ c17.4g⁴ c19.7g⁵ c19.7g⁶ c17.4g³ c19.2dᵖᵘ c19.7g³ c19.7m⁴ c17.4g² Apr 21] maiden hurdler: poor handicap chaser nowadays: stays 2½m: acts on good to soft going: in cheekpieces last 2 starts: front runner/races prominently. *Paddy Butler* **c84 h–**

KILLALA QUAY 10 b.g. Karinga Bay – Madam Bijou (Atraf) [2016/17 c139, h–: c23.6gᵖᵘ c23.8mᵖᵘ h23.4sᵖᵘ c24g* c26gᵖᵘ Mar 25] sturdy gelding: smart hurdler at best, pulled up sole outing in 2016/17: useful handicap chaser: won veterans event at Doncaster in February: stays 3m: acts on soft and good to firm going: wears cheekpieces: front runner/races prominently. *Charlie Longsdon* **c128 h–**

KILLARNEY LAKES (IRE) 6 b.g. Flemensfirth (USA) – Cecelia's Charm (IRE) (Mister Lord (USA)) [2016/17 h19.5g³ h16.5m⁶ h16d³ h23.4d h19.5s Mar 13] €42,000 3-y-o: sixth foal: brother to fairly useful 2¾m chase winner Clondaw Frisby and half-brother to 2 winners, including useful hurdler/fairly useful chaser Alderluck (21f-3¾m **h97**

winner, by Alderbrook): dam unraced half-sister to Irish Grand National winner The Bunny Boiler: modest form over hurdles: left Henry de Bromhead after third start: stays 19f: acts on good to soft going. *Tim Vaughan*

KILLARO BOY (IRE) 8 ch.g. Mr Dinos (IRE) – Auburn Roilelet (IRE) (Good Thyne (USA)) [2016/17 c18d³ c16.3s⁵ c20v* c20d* Apr 16] fifth foal: dam poor maiden jumper: winning pointer/hurdler: useful form over fences: won handicap at Gowran in February and novice at Fairyhouse in April: stays 2½m: acts on heavy going: usually in hood: usually races close up: open to further progress as a chaser. *Adrian Murray, Ireland* **c131 p / h–**

KILLIECRANKIE 9 b.g. Kayf Tara – Bella Macrae (Bustino) [2016/17 h63: h16.8g Oct 27] maiden hurdler, well held sole outing in 2016/17 (wore tongue tie): in hood last 3 starts. *Kenneth Slack* **h–**

KILLINEY COURT (IRE) 8 b.g. King's Theatre (IRE) – Thimble Royale (IRE) (Bob Back (USA)) [2016/17 c19.5dᶠ c17m⁵ h16d³ c19d* h20s⁴ c20d* c18.2d* c20.4gᶠ Mar 14] lengthy gelding: fair handicap hurdler: useful form over fences: won handicap at Ballinrobe in August and novices at Tipperary/Galway (by 9 lengths from Just Cause) in October: left Colm A. Murphy after fifth start: stays 2½m: acts on good to firm and heavy going: wears tongue tie. *Henry de Bromhead, Ireland* **c140 / h112**

KILLONE (IRE) 8 gr.g. Flemensfirth (USA) – Ceol Tire (IRE) (Roselier (FR)) [2016/17 c–, h–: h20.1gᶠ h22d⁵ h16.2sᵖᵘ h16.8dᵖᵘ h16.2g² Apr 25] maiden pointer: modest form on last of 5 starts over hurdles in 2016/17: pulled up sole outing in chases: left Stuart Colthred after fourth start: best effort at 2m: in tongue tie last 2 starts. *Alison Hamilton* **c– / h98**

KILMAINHAM (IRE) 9 b.g. Celtic Swing – Newhall (IRE) (Shernazar) [2016/17 c93, h86: c20.1g h20.9dᶠ Sep 14] fair hurdler/modest maiden chaser at best, no form in 2016/17: probably stayed 3m: best form on soft/heavy going: often wore cheekpieces: dead. *Martin Todhunter* **c– / h–**

KILMOGANNY (IRE) 5 b.g. Stowaway – Gowayourdat (IRE) (Saddlers' Hall (IRE)) [2016/17 h19.4g h16.7s⁴ h19.7s Mar 11] workmanlike gelding: unplaced completed start in Irish maiden points: poor form over hurdles. *Katy Price* **h68**

KILMURVY (IRE) 9 b.g. Shantou (USA) – Spagna (IRE) (Definite Article) [2016/17 c123, h–: c25.8g³ c27.5g² May 21] workmanlike gelding: winning hurdler: fairly useful handicap chaser: placed at Newton Abbot and Stratford early in season: stays 3½m: acts on good to firm and heavy going: wears headgear/tongue tie: usually races in rear. *Jeremy Scott* **c120 / h–**

KILRONAN CASTLE 6 ch.g. Indian River (FR) – Greatest Friend (IRE) (Mandalus) [2016/17 h115, b70: h19.9s⁴ h22.1m* c20.9d c20.3s³ c19.3d³ c24dᵖᵘ c19.2s² Feb 28] fair hurdler: won novice at Cartmel early in season: fair form over fences: stays 2¾m: acts on soft and good to firm going: often races prominently. *Donald McCain* **c108 / h101**

KILRONAN HIGH (IRE) 8 b.m. Mountain High (IRE) – Broadcast (Broadsword (USA)) [2016/17 c128, h–: c21.3m⁴ c23.8d² c20.9g* h20.3s c22.7gᵘʳ c19.9sᵘʳ c22.2gᵖᵘ Apr 15] sturdy mare: fairly useful hurdler at best, well held sole outing in 2016/17: fairly useful handicap chaser: won mares event at Hereford in October: stays 3m: acts on heavy going: wears tongue tie: inconsistent. *Nigel Twiston-Davies* **c128 / h–**

KILRUSH (IRE) 11 gr.g. Dilshaan – Pride of Passion (IRE) (Daylami (IRE)) [2016/17 c–, h77: h23g h19.8vᵖᵘ h25.6d⁴ h21.4d⁶ h23.1gᵖᵘ Apr 11] fairly useful hurdler at best, no longer of any account: maiden chaser: in cheekpieces last 3 starts: wears tongue tie nowadays. *John Berwick* **c– / h–**

KILTY CAUL (IRE) 8 b.m. Beneficial – Gale Johnston (IRE) (Strong Gale) [2016/17 h101, b–: h21g³ h16.7d⁴ c17m c22.6gᵖᵘ Aug 11] lengthy mare: Irish point winner: modest maiden hurdler, no form in 2016/17: little impact in 2 starts over fences: stays 2½m: acts on good to soft going: in cheekpieces last 3 starts, tongue tied last 5: often races towards rear. *Kim Bailey* **c– / h–**

KIMBERLITE CANDY (IRE) 5 b.g. Flemensfirth (USA) – Mandys Native (IRE) (Be My Native (USA)) [2016/17 h19.3d* h20.3sᵖᵘ Jan 28] €40,000 3-y-o: rather unfurnished gelding: brother to fair but temperamental hurdler (2½m-3m winner) Flemensbay and half-brother to 3 winners by Kayf Tara, including useful hurdlers/chasers Alfie Sherrin (2½m-3m winner), stayed 29f, and Hawkes Point (3m-29f winner): dam (h92) 21f hurdle winner (stayed 25f): won maiden point on debut: useful form over hurdles: won maiden at Ascot (by 7 lengths from Secret Investor) in November and novice at Newcastle in December: will stay 3m. *Tom Lacey* **h130**

KIMORA (IRE) 11 b.m. Bach (IRE) – Blue Gale (IRE) (Be My Native (USA)) [2016/17 c91§, h–§: c25.3g⁵ c25.5d* c25.5g May 29] multiple winning pointer: maiden hurdler: modest chaser: won mares hunter at Fontwell early in season: stays 3¼m: acts on good to firm and heavy going: tried in cheekpieces: wears tongue tie: untrustworthy. *Conrad Allen* **c88 § h– §**

KIMS OCEAN (IRE) 7 b.g. Urban Ocean (FR) – A Touch of Joy (IRE) (Tragic Role (USA)) [2016/17 h16mᵘʳ h15.8m⁵ h16.3v⁵ h16gꟳ Sep 6] modest form over hurdles. *Dai Burchell* **h86**

KINARI (IRE) 7 b.g. Captain Rio – Baraza (IRE) (Kalanisi (IRE)) [2016/17 c89, h94: c24.1g c25.7g² c20.9g* c23.8g* c23d* c23.8s² c20g⁶ c24g⁴ Oct 3] lightly-raced hurdler: fair handicap chaser: won at Ffos Las (twice, novice event on second occasion) and Worcester early in season: stays 3¼m: acts on good to soft going: wears headgear/tongue tie: front runner/races prominently. *Peter Bowen* **c110 h–**

KING ALFONSO 8 br.g. Desert King (IRE) – Satire (Terimon) [2016/17 c115, h115: h15.8g⁴ c19.4d⁶ Jun 16] compact gelding: fairly useful handicap hurdler/chaser at best, better than result both starts in 2016/17: stays 19f: acts on soft going: tried in tongue tie. *Neil Mulholland* **c81 h96**

KING BILLY BE 7 gr.g. Proclamation (IRE) – Flaming Cold (IRE) (Glacial Storm (USA)) [2016/17 h19gᵖᵘ Dec 30] pulled up in 3 points/novice hurdle. *Polly Gundry* **h–**

KING BORU (IRE) 9 b.g. Brian Boru – Final Instalment (IRE) (Insan (USA)) [2016/17 c–, h123: h23.1g h20m³ h23.3dᵖᵘ h25.4gᵖᵘ Jul 18] lengthy gelding: fair hurdler nowadays: failed to complete either start over fences: left Dan Skelton after second start: stays 3m: acts on soft and good to firm going: has worn headgear, including last 2 starts: wears tongue tie: often races towards rear. *Rebecca Menzies* **c– h105**

KING CHARLIE (IRE) 7 b.g. Chevalier (IRE) – Desert Treat (IRE) (Desert Prince (IRE)) [2016/17 h–, b–: h24d c25.5d² c25.5sᵖᵘ c23g² c24.2dᵖᵘ c25.5g⁵ Apr 12] runner-up on completed start in Irish points: maiden hurdler: poor form in chases: stays 25f: acts on good to soft going: in cheekpieces last 5 starts: wears tongue tie. *Suzy Smith* **c78 h–**

KING COOL 6 b.g. King's Theatre (IRE) – Cool Spice (Karinga Bay) [2016/17 h120: h19.5g⁵ h21d h21g h20.5vᵘʳ h20.5s h21.6g² h19.1g⁵ Apr 12] winning Irish pointer: fair handicap hurdler: stays 2¾m: acts on soft going. *Gary Moore* **h114**

KING GOLAN (IRE) 6 b.g. Golan (IRE) – Crimson Bow (GER) (Night Shift (USA)) [2016/17 b16.4d h20.3vᵖᵘ h16.2vᵖᵘ h16g Apr 23] unplaced on completed start in Irish maiden points: tailed off in maiden bumper: no form over hurdles. *Kenny Johnson* **h– b–**

KING JULIEN (IRE) 4 b.g. Canford Cliffs (IRE) – Western Sky (Barathea (IRE)) [2016/17 h16.2d² h15.8g² h15.6g³ h15.8s⁵ Jan 13] poor maiden on Flat, stays 1¾m: fair form over hurdles: tried in tongue tie. *John Ryan* **h100**

KING KILLER (IRE) 9 b.g. Classic Cliche (IRE) – River Puttens (IRE) (Over The River (FR)) [2016/17 h19.8v⁵ Mar 9] placed both starts in points: maiden hurdler, well held sole outing in 2016/17: dead. *Nicky Martin* **h–**

KING LEON (IRE) 8 b.g. Mountain High (IRE) – None The Wiser (IRE) (Dr Massini (IRE)) [2016/17 c23m* c22m² c20d* Jul 17] winning hurdler: useful handicap chaser: won at Ballinrobe and Tipperary (by 2¼ lengths from Coldstonesober) early in season: stays 25f: acts on good to firm and good to soft going: wears headgear: often leads: sometimes let down by jumping over fences. *Joseph Patrick O'Brien, Ireland* **c133 x h–**

KING MASSINI (IRE) 11 b.g. Dr Massini (IRE) – King's Linnet (IRE) (King's Ride) [2016/17 c122, h–: c29.1gᵖᵘ c23.8gᵖᵘ Jun 2] workmanlike gelding: maiden hurdler: fairly useful chaser at best, pulled up both starts in 2016/17: stays 3¼m: acts on heavy going: has worn headgear, including final start. *Evan Williams* **c– h–**

KING MURO 7 b.g. Halling (USA) – Ushindi (IRE) (Montjeu (IRE)) [2016/17 h116: h18.6g³ h16d⁴ h16.7g c16.3g³ Sep 16] rather leggy gelding: fairly useful handicap hurdler: 28/1, third in novice at Newton Abbot (8 lengths behind Frodon) on chasing debut: stays 19f: acts on good to firm and heavy going: wears hood/tongue tie: often races towards rear. *Fergal O'Brien* **c122 h114**

KING OF ALCATRAZ (IRE) 11 gr.g. Great Palm (USA) – Foxy Flame (IRE) (Tremblant) [2016/17 c104: c21.1d³ May 12] lengthy gelding: multiple winning pointer: fair chaser, below form sole outing in 2016/17: stays 3m: acts on firm and good to soft going. *R. C. Smith* **c90**

KING OF ARAGON (IRE) 5 b.g. Montjeu (IRE) – Crazy Volume (IRE) (Machiavellian (USA)) [2016/17 h17m⁵ h17d h17.1dᵖᵘ h15.6g h16.4s Jan 23] brother to useful hurdler Plinth (2m-2¾m winner) and half-brother to a winning jumper in Japan by Giant's **h99**

Causeway: fairly useful on Flat, stays 12.5f: modest maiden hurdler: left Joseph Patrick O'Brien after second start: raced around 2m: acts on heavy and good to firm going: usually wears hood/tongue tie. *Gemma Anderson*

KING OF FASHION (IRE) 7 ch.g. Desert King (IRE) – French Fashion (IRE) (Jamesmead) [2016/17 h80, b–: h20.5s² h20.5s* h20.5v³ h23.3v* h24.3d² h23.9g³ Apr 26] fairly useful hurdler: won maiden at Ayr in January and novice at Hexham in March: second in novice handicap at Ayr in April: stays 3m: acts on heavy going: wears tongue tie: usually races towards rear, often travels strongly. *Ian Duncan*   **h126**

KING OF GLORY 9 b.g. Kayf Tara – Glory Be (Gunner B) [2016/17 c114§, h–: c24.2s² c21.1s⁴ Feb 26] stocky gelding: maiden hurdler: fairly useful handicap chaser: second at Sandown in February: stays 3m: best form on soft/heavy going: one to treat with caution (regularly flatters to deceive). *Venetia Williams*   **c118 §**   **h–**

KING OF MILAN (IRE) 7 b.g. Milan – Opera Mask (IRE) (Moscow Society (USA)) [2016/17 h–: c16.5g³ c17.4d³ c19.2d c19.4mᵖᵘ c21.1s⁵ c18.9sᵖᵘ Dec 19] winning pointer: maiden hurdler: modest form over fences: best effort at 2m: tried in cheekpieces: temperamental. *Des Donovan, Ireland*   **c95 §**   **h–**

KING OF REALMS (IRE) 5 b.g. King's Theatre (IRE) – Sunny South East (IRE) (Gothland (FR)) [2016/17 b15.7d* b16s³ b17g Apr 7] tall, good-topped gelding: fifth foal: dam (c86), 25f chase winner, half-sister to fairly useful 2m hurdle winner Spirit of Park and fairly useful hurdler/chaser (winner up to 2½m) Dr Bones: fairly useful form in bumpers: won at Ascot in November. *Ian Williams*   **b101**

KING OF THE DARK (IRE) 10 b.g. Zagreb (USA) – Dark Bird (IRE) (Lashkari) [2016/17 c100, h64: c19.3d² c20.5sᵘʳ c20.5sᵖᵘ h22s⁶ h19.9s⁴ h19.9s⁴ c21.1v* c19.3v c19.3d⁵ c26.3g c20.9d⁶ h27m Apr 19] poor maiden hurdler: modest handicap chaser: won at Sedgefield in February: stays 2¾m: acts on heavy going: tried in cheekpieces. *Victor Thompson*   **c88**   **h74**

KING OF THE WOLDS (IRE) 10 b.g. Presenting – Azaban (IRE) (Be My Native (USA)) [2016/17 c126, h–: c19.4g² c16.4dᶠ c23.8dᵖᵘ c20sᵖᵘ c20.2sᵖᵘ Feb 1] tall, lengthy gelding: winning hurdler: fairly useful handicap chaser nowadays: stays 25f: acts on heavy going: in headgear last 2 starts: has worn tongue tie, including in 2016/17: front runner/races prominently. *Matt Sheppard*   **c121**   **h–**

KINGS BANDIT (IRE) 9 b.g. King's Theatre (IRE) – Gentle Lady (IRE) (Strong Gale) [2016/17 c113p, h–p: h20s⁶ h20.5d⁴ c15.5v³ Jan 17] well-made gelding: useful hurdler: fifth in handicap at Cork (1¼ lengths behind Emcon) in November: fairly useful form over fences: third in novice at Ayr in January: stays 2½m: acts on heavy going: tried in hood: in tongue tie last 3 starts. *Gordon Elliott, Ireland*   **c124**   **h133**

KING'S CHORISTER 11 ch.g. King's Best (USA) – Chorist (Pivotal) [2016/17 c78, h75: c20.1dᵘʳ h20.3sᵖᵘ h20.2dᵖᵘ h17.2g h17.2g h23.3s⁵ h22.7s⁵ h16.2s⁵ h16.4d⁶ h20.6s h20.5v⁶ h16.4v Feb 15] compact gelding: poor handicap hurdler nowadays: maiden chaser, no form in 2016/17: stays 2½m: acts on heavy going: tried in headgear: wears tongue tie. *Barry Murtagh*   **c–**   **h55**

KINGSCOURT NATIVE (IRE) 9 b.g. King's Theatre (IRE) – Freydis (IRE) (Supreme Leader) [2016/17 c125, h–: h23.1m⁵ h25.6g² h19.1g c21mᵖᵘ h23.3g⁴ c25.8g³ c24gᶠ Aug 31] tall, useful-looking gelding: winning pointer: fairly useful handicap hurdler: fair maiden chaser: stayed 3¼m: acted on soft and good to firm going: tried in cheekpieces: wore tongue tie: not a fluent jumper of fences: dead. *Colin Tizzard*   **c114 x**   **h121**

KINGS CROSS (FR) 7 b.g. King's Theatre (IRE) – Ladies Choice (FR) (Turgeon (USA)) [2016/17 c115, h–: c20.3sᵖᵘ c19.4g c19.2vᵖᵘ h16v c19.1s³ c20s³ c19.4d⁵ Apr 16] strong, compact gelding: maiden hurdler: fair handicap chaser, below best in 2016/17: stays 2¾m: acts on heavy going: has worn headgear, including in 2016/17: often races towards rear. *Tony Carroll*   **c97**   **h–**

KINGS ECLIPSE (IRE) 7 b.g. Double Eclipse (IRE) – Good Times Ahead (IRE) (King's Ride) [2016/17 h16.2s h18.6s⁵ h19.4g h25.8v³ h21.4v⁴ h20.6g Apr 8] off mark in Irish maiden points at fifth attempt: poor form over hurdles: seems to stay 3¼m: acts on heavy going: tried in hood. *Andrew Wilson*   **h76**

KINGS GREY (IRE) 13 gr.g. King's Theatre (IRE) – Grey Mo (IRE) (Roselier (FR)) [2016/17 c125§, h–: c17mᵖᵘ May 20] lengthy, good-topped gelding: maiden hurdler: useful chaser at best, pulled up sole outing in 2016/17: stays 2½m: acts on good to firm and heavy going: wears headgear: has worn tongue tie: front runner/races prominently: often finishes weakly. *Philip Kirby*   **c– §**   **h–**

KING SIMBA (IRE) 6 b.g. Let The Lion Roar – Anaaween (USA) (Diesis) [2016/17   **h–**
h107p, b–: h15.8m h15.8mᵖᵘ Oct 11] sturdy gelding: fair hurdler at best, no form in
2016/17: raced around 2m: acts on good to soft going. *Kim Bailey*

KINGSLEY (IRE) 4 b.g. Kalanisi (IRE) – Diva Antonia (IRE) (King's Theatre (IRE))   **b–**
[2016/17 b15.8g Apr 3] tailed off in bumper. *Stuart Edmunds*

KINGS LODGE 11 b.g. King's Theatre (IRE) – Mardello (Supreme Leader) [2016/17   **c– §**
c24.2gᵖᵘ Apr 25] good-topped gelding: winning pointer/hurdler: fairly useful chaser at   **h–**
best, pulled up sole outing in 2016/17: stays 2¾m: acts on soft going: tried in cheekpieces:
unpredictable. *W. H. Easterby*

KINGSMERE 12 b.g. King's Theatre (IRE) – Lady Emily (Alflora (IRE)) [2016/17 c–,   **c–**
h118: h23.1g³ h26.4m² May 20] angular gelding: fairly useful handicap hurdler: second at   **h116**
Stratford early in season: winning chaser: barely stays 3¼m: acts on soft and good to firm
going: often races in rear. *Henry Daly*

KING'S ODYSSEY (IRE) 8 b.g. King's Theatre (IRE) – Ma Furie (FR) (Balleroy   **c126**
(USA)) [2016/17 c147p, h–: c16.3v³ c20.8sᶠ c21.4s³ c20.8g Mar 16] winning hurdler: **h–**
smart chaser, below form in 2016/17: stays 21f: acts on heavy going. *Evan Williams*

KINGSPARK BOY (IRE) 10 b.g. Tillerman – Malacca (USA) (Danzig (USA))   **c–**
[2016/17 c20.9gᵖᵘ May 28] winning pointer: maiden hurdler/chaser: tried in cheekpieces: **h–**
dead. *David Rees*

KINGS RIVER (FR) 8 b.g. Lost World (IRE) – Si Parfaite (FR) (Solon (GER)) [2016/17   **c85**
c95, h87: c20.9g⁴ c25.8mᵖᵘ Aug 31] maiden hurdler: modest chaser: stays 2½m: best form   **h–**
on soft/heavy going: usually races prominently. *Venetia Williams*

KING'S SONG (FR) 7 b.g. King's Theatre (IRE) – Chanson Indienne (FR) (Indian River   **c96**
(FR)) [2016/17 c103, h93: c21.4gᵖᵘ c24gᵖᵘ h20d³ h24d² h23g c23.9g c23g² h23.3g⁴ c20g²   **h83**
c23.8mᶠ Oct 20] poor handicap hurdler: modest handicap chaser: stays 3m: acts on soft
going: wears headgear. *David Dennis*

KING'S TEMPEST 8 b.g. Act One – Queen of Spades (IRE) (Strong Gale) [2016/17   **h113**
h19.5s h23.1sᵖᵘ h16s² h16d³ Mar 31] big, well-made gelding: very much type to make a
chaser: fairly useful maiden hurdler at best: should be suited by further than 2m: acts on
soft going: tried in tongue tie. *Warren Greatrex*

KINGS TEMPTATION 5 b.g. King's Theatre (IRE) – Temptation (FR) (Lando (GER))   **h–**
[2016/17 b16d b16g⁴ h16.7d Apr 27] modest form on second of 2 starts in bumpers: 18/1,   **b78**
seventh in novice at Market Rasen on hurdling debut. *Ben Case*

KINGSTON (GER) 8 br.g. Dylan Thomas (IRE) – Katy Carr (Machiavellian (USA))   **c108**
[2016/17 h16s c20sᵖᵘ h20.5vᵖᵘ h16s⁵ h19.5s⁵ h19.9s⁶ c19.4d* Apr 16] sturdy gelding: **h86**
fairly useful handicap hurdler at best for D. Windriff: fair handicap chaser: won at Ffos Las
in April: stays 23f: acts on heavy going: has worn headgear, including in 2016/17.
Tony Carroll

KINGSTON MIMOSA 5 b.g. Kheleyf (USA) – Derartu (AUS) (Last Tycoon) [2016/17   **h93**
h–: h21.4m h17.7g* h18.5d² h20.5g³ h20.5dᵖᵘ h19.1d³ h19.1s⁴ Dec 26] angular gelding:
modest handicap hurdler: won novice event at Fontwell in June: stays 19f: acts on good to
soft going: wears headgear: tried in tongue tie: front runner/races prominently. *Mark Gillard*

KINGS WALK (IRE) 6 b.g. King's Theatre (IRE) – Shuil Sionnach (IRE) (Mandalus)   **h114**
[2016/17 b80: h21.6d h20.5v⁴ h20.5v* h20.5s⁶ h19.8g³ Apr 29] well-made gelding: fair
form over hurdles: won maiden at Plumpton in January: stays 21f: acts on heavy going.
Colin Tizzard

KINGSWELL THEATRE 8 b.g. King's Theatre (IRE) – Cresswell Native (IRE) (Be   **c133**
My Native (USA)) [2016/17 c135, h–: c23.6g³ c26.3sᵖᵘ c29.2s c30.7d* c30.2g c27.9d   **h–**
Apr 16] lengthy gelding: winning hurdler: useful handicap chaser: won at Exeter (by neck
from Millicent Silver) in February: stays 31f: acts on heavy going: has worn cheekpieces,
including last 3 starts: often races prominently. *Michael Scudamore*

KING'S WHARF (IRE) 8 gr.g. Clodovil (IRE) – Global Tour (USA) (Tour d'Or (USA))   **c134**
[2016/17 c20g c22gʳᵒ h16g⁶ h17d⁵ h17m* c20g* c17g* h20.2g² h24s⁴ c20d² c20d³ c20dᶠ   **h110**
c17g⁶ Jan 29] fair handicap hurdler: won at Killarney in July: useful handicap chaser: won
at Wexford in July and Killarney in August: barely stays 3m: acts on soft and good to firm
going: has worn hood, including in 2016/17: has worn tongue tie: often travels strongly.
W. P. Mullins, Ireland

KINGUSSIE 9 b.g. Diktat – Highland Gait (Most Welcome) [2016/17 h102: h16g[F] May 2] **h– §**
bumper winner: maiden hurdler: best effort at 2m: acts on heavy going: in headgear last 2
starts: often races prominently: temperamental (carries head awkwardly). *Ben Pauling*

KING UTHER 7 b.g. Master Blade – Cadbury Castle (Midyan (USA)) [2016/17 b94: **h108**
h21.6d[F] h20.5v[5] h21.6v[3] h19.5v* Mar 6] good-topped gelding: bumper winner: fair form
over hurdles: won maiden at Lingfield in March: will stay beyond 2½m: temperament
under suspicion. *Chris Gordon*

KING VINCE 4 gr.g. Mawatheeq (USA) – Tussah (Daylami (IRE)) [2016/17 b15.8v **b–**
Dec 12] well beaten in maiden bumper. *Stuart Kittow*

KINNITTY CASTLE (IRE) 7 b.g. Beneficial – Jendam (IRE) (Fourstars Allstar **h–**
(USA)) [2016/17 h20d[pu] h20g[pu] h16.3d h16v[pu] Apr 1] second in maiden point: bumper
winner in 2014/15: little form over hurdles: tried in headgear/tongue tie. *A. J. Martin,
Ireland*

KIPUKA 5 b.m. Authorized (IRE) – Rakata (USA) (Quiet American (USA)) [2016/17 h–: **h–**
h18.5g[F] May 4] little sign of ability: wore tongue tie: dead. *Nigel Hawke*

KISUMU 5 b.g. High Chaparral (IRE) – Arum Lily (USA) (Woodman (USA)) [2016/17 **h89 §**
h101: h17.1g[6] h19.3g[4] h19.3d[4] h19.7s[pu] Feb 3] modest maiden hurdler: stays 19f:
acts on heavy going: tried in cheekpieces: temperamental. *Micky Hammond*

KIT CASEY (IRE) 7 b.g. Robin des Pres (FR) – An Culainn Beag (IRE) (Supreme **h70**
Leader) [2016/17 h119p: h23.3d[5] May 5] winning pointer: fairly useful form when won
maiden hurdle in 2015/16: possibly amiss sole outing in 2016/17: in cheekpieces last 2
starts. *Rebecca Curtis*

KITCHAPOLY (FR) 7 b.g. Poliglote – Kotkicha (FR) (Mansonnien (FR)) [2016/17 **c117**
c112, h–: c16.5g[2] c20m[2] c20.3v[6] Dec 11] sturdy gelding: winning hurdler: fairly useful **h–**
handicap chaser: second at Warwick in November: stays 2½m: acts on good to firm and
good to soft going: tried in tongue tie: often travels strongly. *Dan Skelton*

KITEGEN (IRE) 11 b.g. Milan – Keen Gale (IRE) (Strong Gale) [2016/17 c106§, h–: **c– §**
c20.2m c21.7g[pu] h19.5g Apr 17] tall, lengthy gelding: fairly useful hurdler/chaser at best, **h–**
no form in 2016/17: unreliable. *Robin Dickin*

KITTEN ROCK (FR) 7 b.g. Laverock (IRE) – The Cat Eater (FR) (Tagel (USA)) **c152 +**
[2016/17 c20d[2] c20d[F] Dec 10] useful-looking gelding: winning hurdler: smart form over **h–**
fences: second in minor event at Gowran (1½ lengths behind Zabana) in November: stays
2½m: acts on heavy going: has worn hood. *E. J. O'Grady, Ireland*

KITTY FISHER (IRE) 7 b.m. Scorpion (IRE) – Luck of The Deise (IRE) (Old Vic) **h–**
[2016/17 b16.2d[5] b16.2m[6] h16.2d[5] h16.2d[6] h20.2g[4] h23.3s[pu] Sep 30] fourth foal: half-sister **b–**
to bumper winner/fairly useful hurdler Joe Farrell (2½m winner, by Presenting), stays 3m:
dam unraced half-sister to fairly useful hurdler up to 3m Bondi Storm: little sign of ability,
including in points. *Sandy Forster*

KITTY POWER (IRE) 8 b.m. Presenting – Hannigan's Lodger (IRE) (Be My Native **h73**
(USA)) [2016/17 b–: h18s h19s h16s h21.4v[3] Mar 11] poor form over hurdles: in hood last
4 starts: tried in tongue tie. *R. A. Curran, Ireland*

KIWAYU 8 b.g. Medicean – Kibara (Sadler's Wells (USA)) [2016/17 h19.9g[2] h19.9g* **h114**
h19.9g[3] Sep 27] fair hurdler: won maiden at Uttoxeter in September: stays 2½m: best form
on good going: tried in cheekpieces. *Mike Sowersby*

KIYANA 6 br.m. Authorized (IRE) – Karasta (IRE) (Lake Coniston (IRE)) [2016/17 b15.8d **b–**
b16v Feb 24] half-sister to several winners, including useful hurdler/fairly useful chaser
Karasenir (2m-21f winner, by Sendawar) and fairly useful hurdler/chaser Solstice Son
(3m-27f winner, by Haafhd): dam won May Hill Stakes, half-sister to useful hurdler/chaser
(stayed 2¾m) Kasthari: no form in bumpers: left Charlie Longsdon after first start: in
tongue tie second start. *Peter Bowen*

KK LEXION (IRE) 6 b.g. Flemensfirth (USA) – Kiloradante (IRE) (Phardante (FR)) **h131**
[2016/17 h98p: h22.7d[3] h20.3g* h16.4g[4] h19.9s[3] h21.4s* h23.4v[pu] h19.9s Mar 18]
small gelding: useful handicap hurdler: won at Southwell in October and Wincanton (by 10
lengths from Fortunate George) in January: stays 21f: acts on soft going: held up, often
travels strongly. *Tom George*

KLEITOMACHOS (IRE) 9 b.g. Barathea (IRE) – Theben (GER) (Monsun (GER)) **h109**
[2016/17 h104: h21.6g[3] h23.9g[2] Jun 2] fair hurdler: stays 3m: acts on soft going: wears
headgear: in tongue tie in 2016/17. *Stuart Kittow*

KLEPHT (IRE) 12 b.g. Great Palm (USA) – What A Mewsment (IRE) (Persian Mews) **c116**
[2016/17 c112, h126: c19.4g² May 4] strong gelding: dual point winner: winning hurdler: **h–**
fairly useful chaser nowadays: second in hunter at Wetherby early in season: stays 2¾m:
acts on good to firm and heavy going: wears tongue tie. *D. Holmes*

KNICK KNACK (IRE) 7 b.g. Kalanisi (IRE) – Full Imperatrice (FR) (Dernier Empereur **b–**
(USA)) [2016/17 b16.2d b16.2d b16.8d Dec 2] no form in bumpers. *Valerie Jackson*

KNIGHT BACHELOR 7 ch.g. Midnight Legend – Fenney Spring (Polish Precedent **h135**
(USA)) [2016/17 h115: h21d³ h22.1m* h19.9g* h20m² Sep 18] useful hurdler: won
maiden at Cartmel in June, handicap at Uttoxeter in July and novice at Worcester in
August: second in handicap at Plumpton (4½ lengths behind Listen And Learn) in
September: stays 25f: acts on good and good to firm going: wears headgear: has worn tongue
tie, including in 2016/17: front runner. *Warren Greatrex*

KNIGHT COMMANDER 4 br.g. Sir Percy – Jardin (Sinndar (IRE)) [2016/17 h16.8s **h74**
h16.7s h16.3d⁴ Dec 14] rather sparely-made gelding: fair maiden on Flat, stays 11.5f: poor
form over hurdles. *Anabel K. Murphy*

KNIGHT CRUSADER 5 b.g. Sir Percy – Lac Marmot (FR) (Marju (IRE)) [2016/17 **b54**
b16d³ Jun 22] in cheekpieces, 7/2, third in bumper at Worcester (21¾ lengths behind
Hahnenkam) in June. *David Pipe*

KNIGHTLY PLEASURE 6 b.m. Kayf Tara – Kim Fontenail (FR) (Kaldounevees (FR)) **h100**
[2016/17 b89: b13.6d⁴ h19.5v² h17.7s⁴ h16.3v⁵ h17.7s⁴ Mar 13] well-made mare: modest **b83**
form in bumpers: fair form on first of 4 starts over hurdles: in cheekpieces last 2 starts.
Gary Moore

KNIGHT OF NOIR (IRE) 8 b.g. Winged Love (IRE) – At Dawn (IRE) (Lashkari) **c117**
[2016/17 c23.6s c20.9v³ c24.2sᵖᵘ h21.5sᵖᵘ h23.9g³ Apr 9] point winner: useful handicap **h127**
hurdler, below best in 2016/17: fairly useful chaser on second of 3 starts over fences: stays
3m: acts on heavy going: usually in headgear: wears tongue tie: waited with.
Neil Mulholland

KNIGHT OFTHE REALM 8 b.g. Kayf Tara – Flow (Over The River (FR)) [2016/17 **c100**
h106: h23.6gᵖᵘ c21.7dᵖᵘ c23.6sᵖᵘ c20.9v² c24vᶠ c25.1vᶠ c24.2dᵖᵘ c25.5g* Apr 12] **h–**
workmanlike gelding: fair hurdler at best, pulled up on return: fair handicap chaser: won at
Fontwell in April: stays 25f: acts on heavy going: has worn cheekpieces, including last 5
starts. *Polly Gundry*

KNIGHT'S PARADE (IRE) 7 b.g. Dark Angel (IRE) – Toy Show (IRE) (Danehill **c–**
(USA)) [2016/17 c–, h119: c17.4d⁶ c20.5mᶠ h19.9g⁶ h19.9g⁶ h19s⁵ h20.7dᵖᵘ Dec 26] fair **h105**
handicap hurdler: little impact over fences: stays 2½m: acts on soft and good to firm going:
has worn headgear, including last 3 starts: wears tongue tie: front runner/races prominently.
Sarah Humphrey

KNIGHT'S REWARD 7 b.g. Sir Percy – Wardeh (Zafonic (USA)) [2016/17 h–: **c80**
h15.8gᵖᵘ h16.8g³ c16s* c16.5d⁵ c16.1gᶠ Mar 20] good-bodied gelding: poor maiden **h76**
hurdler: poor form over fences: won novice handicap at Hereford in November: unproven
beyond 17f: acts on soft going: in cheekpieces last 4 starts: has worn tongue tie, including
last 5 starts. *Tim Vaughan*

KNIGHT TO OPEN (IRE) 7 b.g. Oscar (IRE) – Sunset View (IRE) (Good Thyne **h–**
(USA)) [2016/17 b–: h24.5dᵖᵘ h21vᵖᵘ Feb 11] lengthy gelding: no form over hurdles: dead.
Ben Pauling

KNOCKALONGI 11 b.g. Fair Mix (IRE) – Understudy (In The Wings) [2016/17 c102, **c–**
h–: c24.5gᵖᵘ May 9] tall, lengthy gelding: maiden hurdler: fairly useful chaser at best, **h–**
pulled up sole outing in 2016/17: stays 23f: acts on soft going: tried in headgear. *Dominic
Ffrench Davis*

KNOCKANRAWLEY (IRE) 9 gr.g. Portrait Gallery (IRE) – Hot Lips (IRE) (Good **c133**
Thyne (USA)) [2016/17 c139, h–: c29.2s⁵ c32.6s² c27.9d⁶ Apr 16] workmanlike gelding: **h–**
winning hurdler: useful handicap chaser: second in Eider at Newcastle (4 lengths behind
Mysteree) in February: stays 33f: acts very well on heavy going: wears cheekpieces.
Kim Bailey

KNOCKARA BEAU (IRE) 14 b.g. Leading Counsel (USA) – Clairabell (IRE) **c–**
(Buckskin (FR)) [2016/17 c–, h135: h25s³ h24s h18.1v³ h25.8sᵖᵘ Mar 25] lengthy gelding: **h126**
smart hurdler/chaser at best, ran 7 times at Cheltenham Festival, making frame in RSA
Chase and Pertemps Final, and twice running with credit in Gold Cup: stayed 27f: acted on
heavy going: tried in tongue tie: usually made running: reportedly retired. *George Charlton*

KNOCKGRAFFON (IRE) 7 b.g. Flemensfirth (USA) – Gleaming Spire (Overbury **c147** (IRE)) [2016/17 h129: c20d³ c16.4g* c16.4d² c16.2v⁵ Feb 11] useful-looking gelding: **h–** winning hurdler: smart form over fences: won novice handicap at Newbury (by 10 lengths from Sirabad) in November: stays 2½m: acts on soft going: front runner/races prominently, usually travels strongly. *Dan Skelton*

KNOCKGRAFFON KING (IRE) 12 ch.g. Beneficial – Kilternan Gale (IRE) (Good **c–** Thyne (USA)) [2016/17 h21.4sᵖᵘ h25s c25.7vᵖᵘ c24.1gᵖᵘ Mar 25] big, strong gelding: fairly **h–** useful hurdler/chaser at best, no form in 2016/17: has worn headgear, including in 2016/17: has worn tongue tie, including last 2 starts. *Daniel Steele*

KNOCK HOUSE (IRE) 8 ch.g. Old Vic – Lady's Gesture (IRE) (Anshan) [2016/17 **c–** c143, h–: c24gᵖᵘ h22.8d⁶ c25gᵖᵘ Apr 8] sturdy gelding: useful hurdler, below form second **h115** outing in 2016/17: useful chaser at best, no form in 2016/17: stays 25f: acts on heavy going: tried in cheekpieces: in tongue tie last 2 starts. *Donald McCain*

KNOCKLAYDE (IRE) 5 b.g. Mountain High (IRE) – Foret Noire (IRE) (Barathea **h71** (IRE)) [2016/17 b86: h20.5s h16s h20.5s h17s h16vᵘʳ h21.4v² Mar 11] bumper winner: poor form over hurdles: stays 21f: best form on heavy going. *Katie Scott*

KNOCKLAYDE SNO CAT (IRE) 8 b.m. King's Theatre (IRE) – Sno-Cat Lady (IRE) **h93** (Executive Perk) [2016/17 h99: h22.1g² h20.2d² h20.2s³ h20.2s³ h23g h21.4v⁴ h17g h23.9g⁶ Apr 26] fell in Irish mares maiden point: modest maiden hurdler: stays 3m: acts on heavy going: has worn hood: wears tongue tie. *Stuart Crawford, Ireland*

KNOCKLONG (IRE) 9 b.g. Milan – Banningham Blaze (Averti (IRE)) [2016/17 c–x, **c122 x** h101: c25.2s* c20.3g* Apr 21] prolific in points: winning hurdler: fairly useful chaser: won **h–** hunters at Catterick (novice event) in March and Southwell in April: stays 25f: acts on heavy going: has worn headgear: often races towards rear: often makes mistakes over fences. *Justin Landy*

KNOCKNAMONA (IRE) 6 b.g. Trans Island – Faraday Lady (IRE) (Lord Americo) **h86** [2016/17 h20g⁵ h19.9s⁶ h16.2sᵇᵈ h19.3d h19.3gᵖᵘ h19.7s⁴ h19.9s⁶ h20.6v* h20.1s² h18.6m⁵ Apr 17] €7,700 3-y-o, £10,000 5-y-o: half-brother to bumper winner Cresswell Prince (by Bienamado): dam unraced sister to useful hurdler/top-class staying chaser Lord Noelie: maiden Irish pointer: modest handicap hurdler: won conditional event at Newcastle in March: stays 21f: best form on soft/heavy going. *Micky Hammond*

KNOCK OUT (IRE) 5 b.g. Flemensfirth (USA) – Saipan Storm (IRE) (Krayyan) **h–** [2016/17 h20sᵖᵘ h19.8d Dec 13] no form in 2 starts over hurdles. *Jonjo O'Neill*

KNOCKREA (IRE) 10 b.g. Pierre – Glynn Cross (IRE) (Mister Lord (USA)) [2016/17 **h–** h20gᵖᵘ h24g h16g Apr 23] maiden pointer: fair hurdler at best, no form in 2016/17: left Terence O'Brien after second start: tried in tongue tie. *Gemma Anderson*

KNOWHENTOFOLDEM (IRE) 10 b.g. Classic Cliche – Dear Empress (IRE) **c–** (Buckskin (FR)) [2016/17 c20.9sᵖᵘ h22.1g Jul 18] Irish point winner: poor form over **h–** hurdles for James Daniel Dullea in 2014/15: no form in 2016/17, including on chasing debut: often in headgear: tried in tongue tie. *Alexandra Dunn*

KNOW YOUR NAME 6 ch.g. Halling (USA) – Lady Agnes (Singspiel (IRE)) [2016/17 **h82** h16.7g⁴ h16.7v h15.8v h16.8d⁴ h16.5g⁵ h15.7d⁵ h16.4g⁵ Mar 24] dam half-sister to useful hurdler (stayed 21f) Halla San (by Halling): fair on Flat, stays 8.5f: poor maiden hurdler: raced around 2m: acts on good to soft going: in hood last 2 starts. *Donald McCain*

KNYSNA BAY 6 b.m. Millkom – Knysna Belle (Royal Fountain) [2016/17 h–, b–: **h–** h16.2dᵖᵘ Apr 30] no form. *Chris Grant*

KOALA KEEL (IRE) 5 ro.m. Kirkwall – Kayf Keel (Kayf Tara) [2016/17 b16.8g² **b79** Apr 26] third foal: dam (h105), 2m hurdle winner, sister to fair hurdler/useful chaser (stays 2¾m) Mystifiable and half-sister to useful hurdler/chaser (stayed 21f) Hidden Keel (by Kirkwall): runner-up on second of 2 starts in maiden points: 33/1, second in maiden bumper at Exeter (10 lengths behind Sword of Fate) in April. *D. M. G. Fitch-Peyton*

KODICIL (IRE) 9 b.g. Kodiac – Miss Caoimhe (IRE) (Barathea (IRE)) [2016/17 c127, **c–** h102: h19.9g⁶ h20.1dᵖᵘ h19.9g Jul 22] fair hurdler at best, no form in 2016/17: fairly useful **h–** chaser: wears headgear: tried in tongue tie: front runner/races prominently. *Mark Walford*

KOHUMA 7 ch.m. Halling (USA) – Kohiba (IRE) (Rock of Gibraltar (IRE)) [2016/17 **h97** h15.3s⁶ h16.3g⁴ h16m³ Apr 18] well held in maiden on Flat: modest form over hurdles. *Robert Walford*

K O KENNY 6 b.g. Apple Tree (FR) – Cool Island (IRE) (Turtle Island (IRE)) [2016/17 **h73** b75: h16.7g h17.2g⁶ h21.2d⁵ Dec 2] poor form over hurdles: should be suited by at least 2½m. *Andrew Crook*

KOKOMO 6 b.m. Shirocco (GER) – Kohiba (IRE) (Rock of Gibraltar (IRE)) [2016/17 b–: b13.6d h15.8d h15.8g⁶ h16.8g h18.7mᵖᵘ Aug 24] no form: tried in cheekpieces: dead. *Noel Williams* — h– b–

KOSHARI (FR) 5 br.g. Walk In The Park (IRE) – Honor May (FR) (Balleroy (USA)) [2016/17 h140p: h16s* h16d⁴ Nov 12] useful form over hurdles: reportedly struck into when last of 4 in Fishery Lane Hurdle at Naas (10¼ lengths behind Missy Tata) in November. *W. P. Mullins, Ireland* — h130 +

KOSTAQUARTA (IRE) 10 ch.g. Beneficial – Aclare Thyne (IRE) (Good Thyne (USA)) [2016/17 c23d⁵ h21.6m c23g⁶ c25.8g⁶ c23g Sep 12] multiple point winner: tailed off in maiden on hurdling debut: no form in chases: wears cheekpieces/tongue tie: front runner/races prominently. *Simon Hodgson* — c– h–

KOTKIKOVA (FR) 6 gr.m. Martaline – Kotkita (FR) (Subotica (FR)) [2016/17 h17.9s* h24d⁵ h24s Jan 28] rather leggy mare: fifth foal: half-sister to 3 winners, including useful hurdler/chaser Kotkidy (15f-21f winner, by Anabaa Blue): dam (c134/h137), French 15f-2¼m hurdle/chase winner (stayed 2¾m), out of sister/half-sister to Grand Steeple-Chase de Paris winners Kotkijet and Katko: useful hurdler: won minor event at Auteuil very early in season: top 4-y-o chaser in France in 2014/15 (smart form), unbeaten in 6 completed starts, including Prix Ferdinand Dufaure: left J-P. Gallorini after first start: stays 21f: acts on soft going. *Nicky Henderson* — c– h142

KOVERA (FR) 5 b.g. Antarctique (IRE) – Kesakao (FR) (Saint Estephe (FR)) [2016/17 h19dᵖᵘ h15.7v³ h16m h16g⁵ h23.3g Sep 18] poor form over hurdles. *Jonjo O'Neill* — h67

KRACKATOA KING 9 b.g. Kayf Tara – Firecracker Lady (IRE) (Supreme Leader) [2016/17 c123, h–: c29.6s⁴ c23.6s² c21.7v³ c28s³ c24v* Mar 22] well-made gelding: winning hurdler: fairly useful handicap chaser: won novice event at Warwick in March: thorough stayer: best form on soft/heavy going: wears headgear: front runner/races prominently: hard ride and one to be wary of. *Kerry Lee* — c125 § h–

KRAFTY ONE 5 ch.m. Mastercraftsman (IRE) – Wonderful Desert (Green Desert (USA)) [2016/17 h–: h16g Jul 12] no form over hurdles. *Michael Scudamore* — h–

KRIS CROSS (IRE) 10 ch.g. Kris Kin (USA) – Perfidia (Perpendicular) [2016/17 c–x, h115: h24.6dᶠ h25.8s⁶ Nov 5] workmanlike gelding: fairly useful hurdler at best, no form in 2016/17: winning chaser: stays 27f: acts on good to firm and heavy going: has worn cheekpieces, including in 2016/17: wears tongue tie: often races prominently: sketchy jumper of fences. *Lucinda Russell* — c– x h–

KRIS SPIN (IRE) 9 br.g. Kris Kin (USA) – Auditing Empress (IRE) (Accordion) [2016/17 c98P, h–: c20.9s³ c24v⁵ c24vᶠ Feb 24] workmanlike gelding: winning hurdler: modest maiden chaser: stays 25f: acts on heavy going. *Kerry Lee* — c86 h–

KRISTAL HART 8 b.m. Lucky Story (USA) – Moly (FR) (Anabaa (USA)) [2016/17 h15.3d⁵ h16d³ h15.3s² h15.3m⁴ Apr 5] half-sister to fair/temperamental chaser Basford Ben (25f/3¼m winner, by Trade Fair) and a winning pointer by Green Tune: fair on Flat, stays 11f: modest form over hurdles: wears cheekpieces. *Neil Mulholland* — h95

KRISTAL STAR 5 b.m. Midnight Legend – Royal Musical (Royal Abjar (USA)) [2016/17 b–: h16.7g b16.6d ab16g h16.7s⁴ h16.3g h16.7m³ Apr 9] modest form on last of 4 starts in bumpers: poor form over hurdles: in tongue tie last 5 starts. *Alex Hales* — h81 b76

KRISTIAN GRAY (IRE) 8 b.g. Heliostatic (IRE) – Missfortuna (Priolo (USA)) [2016/17 c20.2s* c20.9s³ Mar 13] multiple point winner: fair form in hunter chases: won maiden event at Leicester in February: third in novice event at Stratford in March. *F. A. Hutsby* — c100

KRISTJANO (GER) 5 b.g. Nayef (USA) – Kalahari Dancer (Dalakhani (IRE)) [2016/17 h16.8s h16.5g⁶ h19g Mar 2] fair maiden on Flat, stays 2m: modest form on second of 3 starts over hurdles. *Jimmy Frost* — h89

KRUGERMAC (IRE) 6 b.g. Kalanisi (IRE) – Vindonissa (IRE) (Definite Article) [2016/17 h122p, b97: h16s h19.3s Feb 18] tall, useful-looking gelding: will make a chaser: fairly useful form at best over hurdles, below that level both starts in 2016/17: tried in visor. *Gary Moore* — h99

KRUSEMAN 10 b.g. Doyen (IRE) – Polar Charge (Polar Falcon (USA)) [2016/17 h16.8gᵖᵘ Aug 10] rather leggy gelding: modest handicap hurdler at best: stayed 3m: acted on good to firm and heavy going: usually wore headgear: tried in tongue tie: dead. *Richard Woollacott* — h69

KRUZHLININ (GER) 10 ch.g. Sholokhov (IRE) – Karuma (GER) (Surumu (GER)) [2016/17 c150, h–§: c23.6gᵖᵘ h24.7d³ h22.8v* c24d² c28.4d⁶ c31.8gᵖᵘ Apr 22] lengthy, useful-looking gelding: useful handicap hurdler: won Betfair Exchange 'Fixed Brush' — c144 h140

Betfair Exchange 'Fixed Brush' Handicap Hurdle, Haydock—
Kruzhlinin exploits a lower hurdles mark as he runs out a game winner from Theo's Charm

Handicap Hurdle at Haydock (by 2½ lengths from Theo's Charm) in November: useful handicap chaser: second at Kempton (7 lengths behind Our Kaempfer) in January: stays 3¼m: acts on heavy going: in blinkers last 5 starts: front runner/races prominently. *Philip Hobbs*

KUBLAI (FR) 7 b.g. Laveron – Java Dawn (IRE) (Fleetwood (IRE)) [2016/17 h117: h21g² c21.4gᵖᵘ c21.1sᵖᵘ h23.1sᵖᵘ h19g h16v⁶ h19.9v h20v Mar 1] well-made gelding: fairly useful handicap hurdler: second at Kempton early in season: pulled up both starts over fences: left Philip Hobbs after second start: stays 2¾m: acts on soft going: in tongue tie last 4 starts. *Alexandra Dunn*
c–
h116

KUDA HURAA (IRE) 9 b.g. Montjeu (IRE) – Healing Music (FR) (Bering) [2016/17 c–, h111§: h20.3v h20.3g May 24] good-topped gelding: fair handicap hurdler, well below form both outings in 2016/17: fair form though failed to impress with jumping in 2 starts over fences in 2014/15: stays 21f: acts on soft going: tried in blinkers/tongue tie: temperamental. *Harriet Bethell*
c–
h– §

KUDU COUNTRY (IRE) 11 gr.g. Captain Rio – Nirvavita (FR) (Highest Honor (FR)) [2016/17 c–x, h–: h16g* h18.7m Jul 17] workmanlike gelding: fair hurdler nowadays: won seller at Fakenham early in season: winning chaser, though prone to mistakes: unproven beyond 2m: acts on heavy going: in headgear last 3 starts: wears tongue tie: usually races prominently. *Evan Williams*
c– x
h100

KUDU SHINE 11 b.g. Karinga Bay – Flora Bright (Alflora (IRE)) [2016/17 c–, h92: h21.4m May 10] sturdy gelding: winning pointer: maiden hurdler/chaser: stays 3m: acts on heavy going: tried in cheekpieces: has worn tongue tie, including last 3 starts: front runner/races prominently. *Richard Woollacott*
c–
h–

KUMBESHWAR 10 b.g. Doyen (IRE) – Camp Fire (IRE) (Lahib (USA)) [2016/17 c–, h109§: h16.2d⁴ h20.1d⁵ c17.3d* c17.3g³ c16gᵖᵘ c17.1s⁶ c16.3sᵖᵘ h18.1sᵖᵘ Dec 29] strong, lengthy gelding: one-time useful hurdler: fairly useful handicap chaser nowadays: won at Cartmel in June: stays 19f: acts on heavy going: usually wears headgear: wears tongue tie: often races towards rear: unenthusiastic these days. *Lucinda Russell*
c118
h93 §

KYLECRUE (IRE) 10 b.g. Gold Well – Sher's Adamant (IRE) (Shernazar) [2016/17 c20d c26m⁶ h19.5g² c22m³ c25s⁴ h20.5v* h22d² c20s* c20s* c24d³ c21g⁶ c25vᵖᵘ Feb 4] useful handicap hurdler: won at Sligo in August: useful chaser: won handicap and minor event at Listowel in September: third in Munster National Handicap Chase at Limerick (10¼ lengths behind Tiger Roll) in October: stays 3m: acts on good to firm and heavy going: wears headgear: tried in tongue tie: front runner/races prominently. *John Patrick Ryan, Ireland*
c134
h130

KYLEMORE LOUGH 8 b.g. Revoque (IRE) – One of The Last (Supreme Leader) [2016/17 c156p, h–: c21d² c20.8s⁵ c25.3s⁵ c19.9g⁴ Apr 7] tall gelding: winning hurdler: very smart chaser: second in 1965 Chase at Ascot (head behind Royal Regatta) in November and fifth in Caspian Caviar Gold Cup at Cheltenham (2½ lengths behind Frodon) in December: stays 2¾m: acts on heavy going: has joined Harry Fry. *Kerry Lee*
c159
h–

KYLLACHYKOV (IRE) 9 ch.g. Kyllachy – Dance On (Caerleon (USA)) [2016/17   **h78** h85: h24.1g⁴ h23.3g⁴ h23.3s⁵ h19.9g h24g⁴ Aug 14] poor maiden hurdler: stays 23f: acts on good to soft going: in tongue tie last 5 starts: often races towards rear. *Rebecca Bastiman*

L

LA BAGUE AU ROI (FR) 6 b.m. Doctor Dino (FR) – Alliance Royale (FR) (Turgeon   **h132** (USA)) [2016/17 b111: h15.8d* h16d* h16.3d* h16.8g h20g⁶ h20.7g* Apr 28] tall, useful-looking mare: useful bumper performer: useful form over hurdles: won mares maiden at Uttoxeter in October, and mares novices at Wetherby and Newbury (listed event, by 3¼ lengths from Dusky Legend) in November and Huntingdon (by 6 lengths from Treackle Tart) in April: stays 21f: acts on good to soft going: usually leads. *Warren Greatrex*

LABAIK (FR) 6 gr.g. Montmartre (FR) – Avanguardia (GER) (Choisir (AUS))   **h160 §** [2016/17 h16g* h16d* h16dʳʳ h20sʳʳ h16v⁶ h16.4g* h16.5d h16g⁴ Apr 28]

One way or another, Labaik is likely to have left a lasting impression in what looks to have been a brief but colourful career over jumps. After running at the Punchestown Festival he was found to have sustained a serious injury to the suspensory ligament in a hind leg which almost certainly means his racing days are over. That's bad luck on his connections who clearly had a talented hurdler on their hands, though whether Labaik will be missed more widely is less certain. His win in the Supreme Novices' Hurdle showed the form he was capable of when in the right frame of mind, and he certainly picked the right day to put his best foot forward, but the trouble was that, more often than not, he just dug his heels in and refused to race at all.

It certainly wasn't for a breath of sea air that Labaik made his Irish debut on the beach at Laytown in September, though his refusal to jump off from the tape start showed that his reluctance to race clearly ran deeper than an aversion to coming out of starting stalls. His Flat career for original owner Hamdan Al Maktoum had begun promisingly enough in France but Labaik failed to get his head in front and, on what proved to be his final start there as a four-year-old for John Hammond, he virtually refused to race. Labaik's owner gave him one more chance and he was well backed for a Lingfield handicap when making his British debut in May for Owen Burrows, but this time he simply refused to race at all. Not surprisingly then, his next public appearance came in the sale-ring, at Doncaster in August, where he was bought for £25,000, joining Gordon Elliott to race in the colours of bloodstock agent Aidan O'Ryan.

The Laytown experiment can't have given new connections much confidence about how Labaik would behave when he lined up at 16/1 for his first start over hurdles in a maiden contest at Punchestown in October. However, not only did he consent to jump off, he led on the bridle before the final flight and went on to win by five and a half lengths. Better still, he followed up a month later when beating his stable-companion Mick Jazz in the five-runner For Auction Novices' Hurdle, a Grade 3 contest at Navan. In between, Labaik also recorded an unofficial win on the Flat at Leopardstown in the final leg of the Corinthian Challenge Charity Race Series in aid of the charity Irish Injured Jockeys, ridden this time by Sheikh Fahad Al Thani. It finally looked as though the ability Labaik had been showing at home—he was said to work better than anything else in the yard—was starting to be reflected on the track.

But any hopes that hurdling might have helped Labaik turn over a new leaf were soon to be dashed. He refused to start again in the Royal Bond Novices' Hurdle at Fairyhouse at the beginning of December, and when he did the same in the Navan Novices' Hurdle a fortnight later it brought him a six-week suspension from racing. While such bans serve a purpose in punishing non-triers, it's hard to see what use they are in cases like Labaik's. If his absence from the racecourse was intended to protect punters, it was only a temporary reprieve because he was at it again when returned to action in a Grade 2 novice hurdle at Naas at the end of February. Admittedly, he did consent to set off this time but was hopelessly detached by the time he eventually did so and trailed round to pick up the few hundred euros for finishing last of the six who completed, officially seventy-one lengths behind the fifth horse. It was a very important sixth place as, technically, it did not count as another refusal to race—which would have triggered a ban that would have ruled out a run in the Supreme Novices'.

In the days before starting stalls, the problem of recalcitrant starters was more prevalent on the Flat and the Timeform Annuals warned readers of horses liable to give trouble at the start. Idle Rocks, for example, who had contested all three colts' classics the year before, had the following pithy comment in *Racehorses of 1957* (along with a double squiggle): 'a top-class colt when he consents to race but has not the least inclination to display his considerable ability: exported to some optimist.' The gelding Chalk Stream, who happened to be Robert Sangster's first horse, wasn't quite in the same league as Idle Rocks ('none too reliable at the gate'), but he was apt to jeopardise his chances by starting slowly when the tapes went up. As recounted in Patrick and Nick Robinson's book *Horsetrader*, Chalk Stream was strongly fancied by connections to win the 1961 Great Jubilee Handicap at Kempton, provided he got away on terms. In an era long before in-running betting on Betfair, Sangster and his trainer Eric Cousins hatched a plan to ensure that the owner would strike his bet only once he could be sure he was going to get a run for his money. Cousins took up a position high in the Kempton stands with his binoculars focussed on Chalk Stream at the start, with Sangster poised down at the rails ready to pounce once given the signal. Seeing Chalk Stream break on terms, Cousins raised his hat and Sangster swooped with £100 on at 8/1—Chalk Stream got up to win by a head.

Labaik's persistently mulish behaviour was making him unreliable as a betting proposition to most by now and he started at 25/1 for the Sky Bet Supreme Novices' Hurdle at Cheltenham, even though he boasted some of the best form in the line-up and would doubtless have been at much shorter odds had he been guaranteed to jump off. He had achieved more, for example, than 3/1 joint favourite Melon who had won just a maiden hurdle at Leopardstown, albeit by ten lengths, on his only previous start for Willie Mullins. The other joint favourite Ballyandy, the previous season's Champion Bumper winner, had more solid claims after winning the Betfair Hurdle. Mullins' second string Bunk Off Early, runner-up in the Deloitte Novices' Hurdle at Leopardstown, was a 6/1-shot, and the Nicky Henderson-trained River

Sky Bet Supreme Novices' Hurdle, Cheltenham—
the mercurial Labaik is very much on a going day as he sees off Min (right) and River Wylde

Herald Champion Novices' Hurdle, Punchestown—
a return to bad habits as Labaik virtually refuses to race

Wylde started at 8/1, having kept his unbeaten record over hurdles in the Dovecote Novices' Hurdle at Kempton. They were the leading contenders in a fourteen-runner field for what looked a more ordinary renewal of the Supreme than the recent editions won by Altior, Douvan and Vautour. Among the notable absentees were the Betfair runner-up Movewiththetimes, who had met with a setback, another former Champion Bumper winner Moon Racer, who had beaten Ballyandy in both his wins over hurdles, but made a late switch to contest the Champion Hurdle, and Neon Wolf who was aimed at the Baring Bingham instead.

With Elliott's assistant chasing him up with a long tom (something not permitted in Ireland) and the runners despatched smoothly, Labaik jumped off at the rear of the Supreme field. He took closer order coming down the hill and smoothly made further progress to join, and then pass, River Wylde and Melon approaching the final flight. Keeping on well up the hill, Labaik crossed the line with his seventeen-year-old rider Jack Kennedy standing in the stirrups in celebration of his first Festival win, with two and a quarter lengths to spare over Melon and another eight back to River Wylde in third, with Ballyandy completing the first four. Kennedy, who gained his first Grade 1 success on Outlander in the Lexus Chase earlier in the season, hadn't ridden a winner in Britain before, though he had finished second on the Venetia Williams-trained Tango de Juilley in the Plate at the previous year's Festival. Elliott's thoughts after the Supreme were also with Keith Donoghue who would have ridden Labaik but had recently decided to take a break from race riding after struggling with his weight. Donoghue had partnered Labaik on his successful debut over hurdles and was credited with doing a lot of work with him at home.

Labaik looked set to be the star lot at the inaugural Goffs UK Aintree Sales on the first day of the Grand National meeting but he was withdrawn following an apparent change of heart by his owners. In another twist to the story, there was, though, seemingly more to his withdrawal than met the eye. According to reports in the Irish media, Labaik's sale was blocked by Ireland's Criminal Assets Bureau, an agency which investigates organized crime and money laundering. It was reported that one of Labaik's part-owners, who had a criminal record that included drug dealing and theft, and who had been photographed celebrating in the Cheltenham winner's enclosure, was under investigation by the CAB for being a suspected leading member of a Dublin organised crime gang that laundered the profits from its criminal activities through the purchase of racehorses. The same reports stressed, however, that all this was without the knowledge of the rest of Labaik's connections.

It was also reported that any further prize money won by Labaik would have had to have been seized while, in a further development in June, the CAB went to the High Court in Dublin to take possession of Labaik himself.

At the Punchestown Festival, however, the more pressing concern, once again, was simply getting Labaik to start in the first place. He lined up for the Herald Champion Novices' Hurdle on the first day but was in no mood to take part and the rest of the field had gone nearly two furlongs before Labaik, who had demolished part of the running rail when backing into it, consented to give chase. It was a lost cause, however, and he finished a distant last of the seven runners behind the Supreme fifth Cilaos Emery who beat stable-companion Melon into second. To be fair to Labaik, his rivals' jockeys did him no favours by approaching the tape early, resulting in the runners being sent back to take a turn. A deliberate ploy or not, anything other than a smooth getaway was always liable to rattle Labaik. When he was turned out again three days later for the Punchestown Champion Hurdle, sent off the 11/2 third favourite behind Vroum Vroum Mag and Arctic Fire, Labaik was equipped with a visor for the first time and had a new jockey in Davy Russell. Labaik got away on terms this time, though with some unauthorised encouragement from his trainer down at the start who received a caution from the stewards for 'shaking a hand-held item'—reportedly a bottle full of stones—to keep him moving. Labaik ended up running well on his first start outside novice company to be beaten around two and a half lengths into fourth behind Wicklow Brave, My Tent Or Yours and Arctic Fire, and he might have finished a place or two closer but for a blunder three out.

Labaik (FR) (gr.g. 2011)	Montmartre (FR) (gr 2005)	Montjeu (b 1996)	Sadler's Wells / Floripedes
		Artistique (gr 1996)	Linamix / Armarama
	Avanguardia (GER) (b 2005)	Choisir (ch 1999)	Danehill Dancer / Great Selection
		Anthurium (b 1999)	Hector Protector / Assia

Mr A. J. O'Ryan's "Labaik"

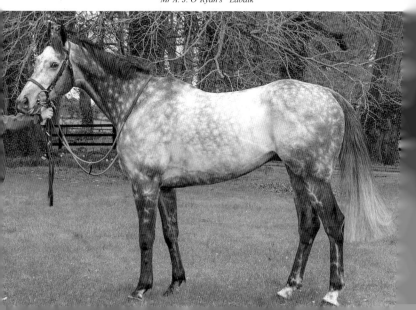

The sturdy Labaik, who was bought at Deauville as a yearling for €130,000, is the best jumper to date by his sire the Aga Khan's Grand Prix de Paris winner Montmartre. Labaik's dam Avanguardia showed useful form at best in France, gaining her only win over an extended five furlongs. She has since produced a second winner, Danza de La Barre (by Turtle Bowl), who won three times in claiming company in France as a two-year-old at up to nine and a half furlongs. Labaik's grandam Anthurium was also useful, with her four wins in Germany including a seven-furlong listed event; her four winners include A Southside Boy who gained one of his five wins over hurdles and is the only other winning jumper close up in Labaik's pedigree. However, Anthurium's half-brother Arcadio, a very smart performer on the Flat in Germany (successful at up to eleven furlongs), is now a successful Irish-based sire of jumpers whose runners include the smart novice chaser from the latest season Flying Angel. Labaik raced mainly at two miles and acted on good to soft ground. *Gordon Elliott, Ireland*

LABEL DES OBEAUX (FR) 6 b.g. Saddler Maker (IRE) – La Bessiere (FR) (Loup Solitaire (USA)) [2016/17 h132: c24.2s² c25.3g³ c23.5v² c23.8s* c24.2d* c25g c24.3g* Apr 22] compact gelding: useful hurdler: smart chaser: won novice at Ludlow in February, and novice handicaps at Exeter (by 4 lengths from Herbert Park) later in February and Ayr (by head from Calett Mad) in April: will be suited by 3¼m+: acts on heavy going: has worn cheekpieces. *Alan King* — **c151 h–**

LA CAVSA NOSTRA (IRE) 5 b.g. Flemensfirth (USA) – Pharenna (IRE) (Phardante (FR)) [2016/17 b16.4s b16.7d⁶ Jan 3] €68,000 3-y-o: sturdy gelding: sixth foal: half-brother to 3 winners, including fairly useful hurdler/smart chaser Changing Times (19f-2¾m winner, by Dr Massini) and fairly useful hurdler/chaser Phare Isle (2¾m-3¼m winner, by Turtle Island): dam (b80) lightly raced in bumpers: some promise on first of 2 starts in bumpers. *Rebecca Curtis* — **b83**

LAC FONTANA (FR) 8 b.g. Shirocco (GER) – Fontaine Riant (FR) (Josr Algarhoud (IRE)) [2016/17 h20.5d h24.2d⁵ h20.3g Mar 17] good-topped gelding: useful handicap hurdler: below best in 2016/17 after long absence: barely stays 3m: acts on heavy going: tried in cheekpieces. *Paul Nicholls* — **h124**

LACHARES (IRE) 4 ch.g. Manduro (GER) – Louve Imperiale (USA) (Giant's Causeway (USA)) [2016/17 h16s⁵ h16v³ h16d³ h16v² h16v* h16d* h19g³ Apr 16] lightly raced on Flat: fairly useful hurdler: won maiden at Gowran and novice at Limerick in March: third in handicap at Cork final start: stays 19f: acts on heavy going: front runner/races prominently. *Ellmarie Holden, Ireland* — **h124**

LACKAMON 12 b.g. Fleetwood (IRE) – Pearlossa (Teenoso (USA)) [2016/17 c128x, h80x: c26.2m⁶ c23.8s⁵ c24.5sᵖᵘ Mar 16] sturdy, medium-sized gelding: winning hurdler: fairly useful chaser: out of sorts in 2016/17, including in points: left Sue Smith after first start: stays 4m: acts on good to firm and heavy going: in headgear last 2 starts: lazy sort, and prone to mistakes. *Mrs Z. Hammond* — **c– x h– x**

LAC SACRE (FR) 8 b.g. Bering – Lady Glorieuse (FR) (Le Glorieux) [2016/17 c91, h103: h20g² h21.2v⁴ c20.9v⁴ h19.5s h23.9s³ h23v³ c23.6s² c23.6v* c23.6gᵖᵘ Apr 8] neat gelding: fair handicap hurdler: fair handicap chaser: won at Chepstow in March: stays 3m: acts on heavy going: wears headgear/tongue tie. *John Flint* — **c108 h101**

LA DAMA DE HIERRO 7 gr.m. Proclamation (IRE) – Altogether Now (IRE) (Step Together (USA)) [2016/17 h102: c23.4vᶠ c25.2sᵖᵘ c20.9v⁵ c20.9d c26.2g⁴ Apr 15] fair hurdler: modest form over fences: will prove best up to 3¼m: acts on heavy going: tried in cheekpieces. *Malcolm Jefferson* — **c94 h–**

LADFROMHIGHWORTH 12 b.g. Kier Park (IRE) – Cavisoir (Afzal) [2016/17 c120: c21d³ c23gᵖᵘ c21g⁴ c20g c22.6g⁶ Oct 27] fairly useful handicap chaser: lost form in 2016/17 after reappearance: stays 23f: acts on soft and good to firm going: usually races close up. *Jeremy Scott* — **c114**

LADIES DANCING 11 b.g. Royal Applause – Queen of Dance (IRE) (Sadler's Wells (USA)) [2016/17 c–, h104: h15.8m c16.3s² c17m h16.8m h18.5m³ h19.8dᵖᵘ h16.5g h16.8g⁴ Apr 26] angular gelding: fair handicap hurdler: below form in 2016/17: modest form over fences: best around 2m: acts on soft and good to firm going: usually wears headgear: tried in tongue tie. *Chris Down* — **c95 h75**

LAD OF LUCK (FR) 4 b.g. Soldier of Fortune (IRE) – Baraka du Berlais (FR) (Bonnet **b104 p** Rouge (FR)) [2016/17 b16v* Feb 25] third foal: half-brother to useful hurdler Let's Dance (2m-2½m winner, by Poliglote): dam useful French hurdler/fairly useful chaser (17f/2¼m winner): 5/2, won conditional/amateur maiden bumper at Chepstow (impressively by 11 lengths from Hidden Impact) on debut: exciting prospect. *Jonjo O'Neill*

LADY ARBELLA 6 b.m. Erhaab (USA) – Jersey Countess (IRE) (Supreme Leader) **b77** [2016/17 b16.7g³ May 14] first foal: dam (h79), maiden hurdler, half-sister to fairly useful hurdler/fair chaser (winner up to 21f) Carrick Oscar: 33/1, third in mares bumper at Bangor (15 lengths behind Tara View) in May. *Dominic Ffrench Davis*

LADY ASH (IRE) 7 gr.m. Scorpion (IRE) – La Fiamma (FR) (General Assembly (USA)) **h—** [2016/17 b65: h21.4vᵖᵘ h18.5s h21.4s h21.6g h23.9m⁶ Apr 20] no form over hurdles: tried in cheekpieces. *Robert Walford*

LADY AVERY (IRE) 5 b.m. Westerner – Bobs Article (IRE) (Definite Article) [2016/17 **b—** b15.8s Apr 1] £25,000 5-y-o: third foal: closely related to fairly useful/temperamental hurdler Towering (2½m-23f winner, by Catcher In The Rye): dam unraced sister to smart 2m hurdle winner Staying Article: off mark in Irish mares maiden points at second attempt: tailed off in mares bumper. *Alan Jones*

LADY BEAUFORT 6 ch.m. Shirocco (GER) – Kadassa (IRE) (Shardari) [2016/17 b91p: **h93** b15.8s h21vᵖᵘ h19.4s² h21v³ Mar 22] bumper winner: modest form over hurdles: **b—** should stay beyond 2½m: tried in tongue tie. *Kerry Lee*

LADY BROOME 6 ch.m. Erhaab (USA) – Minnesinger (Fraam) [2016/17 b—: b16.8s⁶ **h—** h19.7sᵘʳ h19.4gᵖᵘ Jan 27] rather unfurnished mare: no form in bumpers/over hurdles: left **b—** John David Riches after first start: has worn cheekpieces. *Mark Walford*

LADY BUTTONS 7 b.m. Beneficial – Lady Chapp (IRE) (High Chaparral (IRE)) **h129** [2016/17 h16sᵖᵘ h16.4s³ h16.4s* h20.3s* h16.6s* h20dᵖᵘ Apr 29] fairly useful handicap hurdler: won at Newcastle and Southwell in January, and mares event at Doncaster in March: stays 2½m: acts on soft going: often travels strongly. *Philip Kirby*

LADY CARDINAL (IRE) 6 ch.m. Papal Bull – St Finan's Bay (IRE) (Ashkalani (IRE)) **h—** [2016/17 b—: b16g⁶ b17.7d ab16g h15.3d h18.5s h16.8s h23.9g h25gᵖᵘ Apr 3] no form in **b—** bumpers/over hurdles: in cheekpieces last 2 starts. *Dr Jeremy Naylor*

LADY CLITICO (IRE) 6 b.m. Bushranger (IRE) – Villa Nova (IRE) (Petardia) [2016/17 **h91** h100: h16.7g³ h16.7g May 15] fair on Flat, stays 1½m: modest maiden hurdler: raced around 2m: acts on heavy going: tried in headgear. *Rebecca Menzies*

LADY FONTENAIL 4 gr.f. Compton Place – Nina Fontenail (FR) (Kaldounevees (FR)) **h—** [2016/17 h16.7dᵖᵘ Jun 17] half-sister to fairly useful hurdler Poetic Verse (17f-19f winner, by Byron): dam half-sister to fairly useful hurdler/chaser (stayed 25f) Dom Fontenail: poor maiden on Flat, stays 1½m: pulled up in juvenile on hurdling debut: wore hood. *Neil King*

LADY FROM GENEVA 10 ch.m. Generous (IRE) – Schizo-Phonic (Gildoran) [2016/17 **c—** c88, h90: h21.6gᵖᵘ c25.5gᵖᵘ Jun 7] modest hurdler (maiden)/chaser, no form in 2016/17: **h—** stays 3¼m: acts on good to firm and heavy going: wears tongue tie: usually races close up. *Brendan Powell*

LADY KARINA 6 b.m. Kayf Tara – Lady Rebecca (Rolfe (USA)) [2016/17 h19.7s⁶ **h109 p** h18.5s³ h21.7v* Jan 11] seventh foal: half-sister to bumper winner/useful hurdler Lord Generous (3m/25f winner, by Generous) and poor hurdler Lady Samantha (3m winner, by Fraam): dam (h165) bumper/2½m-3m hurdle winner: fair form over hurdles: won mares novice at Hereford in January: will stay 3m: open to further improvement. *Venetia Williams*

LADY LONDON (IRE) 6 b.m. Beneficial – Torduff Storm (IRE) (Glacial Storm (USA)) **h—** [2016/17 b16.2g⁵ h20.6dᵖᵘ h20.9sᵖᵘ h19.7d h15.7s⁴ h19.9gᵖᵘ Apr 7] €10,500 3-y-o, **b65** £36,000 5-y-o: quite good-topped mare: third foal: dam unraced half-sister to useful staying chaser Torduff Express: off mark in maiden points at second attempt: fifth in bumper: no form over hurdles: tried in hood/tongue tie. *Rose Dobbin*

LADY LONGSHOT 6 b.m. Needle Gun (IRE) – So Long (Nomadic Way (USA)) **h91** [2016/17 b—: b15.8d⁶ h18.5g⁶ h19.4g⁴ h16.2s h16.8s⁵ h15.3s² Mar 1] poor form in bumpers: **b65** modest form over hurdles: usually in hood: in tongue tie last 2 starts: often races towards rear/freely. *James Scott*

LADY MARKBY (IRE) 6 b.m. Oscar (IRE) – Leitrim Bridge (IRE) (Earl of Barking **h111** (IRE)) [2016/17 b93: h21s h15.8s³ h17.7v³ h18.6s* Feb 19] bumper winner: fair form over hurdles: won mares event on handicap debut at Market Rasen in February: should be suited by at least 2½m: has worn hood, including in 2016/17. *Emma Lavelle*

LADY MASTER 4 b.f. Native Ruler – Elmside Katie (Lord David S (USA)) [2016/17 **b65**
b15.7s⁵ b16g⁶ Apr 17] fifth foal: half-sister to useful chaser Noble Legend (2m-2¾m
winner, by Midnight Legend): dam of little account in points: poor form in bumpers.
Caroline Bailey

LADY MIX 4 gr.f. Fair Mix (IRE) – Et Voila (Alflora (IRE)) [2016/17 b16.3s* b17g² **b95**
Apr 15] £9,000 3-y-o: third foal: dam unraced half-sister to fair hurdler/fairly useful chaser
(stayed 3¼m) Take A Bow: fairly useful form in bumpers: won mares event at Newbury in
March. *Nigel Hawke*

LADY OF LONGSTONE (IRE) 7 ch.m. Beneficial – Christdalo (IRE) (Glacial Storm **c112**
(USA)) [2016/17 h124: h24g³ h20d c23g³ c25.8g⁵ c21m⁴ h23.6g⁵ h23.1sᵖᵘ h23.9gᵖᵘ **h113**
Mar 20] workmanlike mare: fairly useful handicap hurdler: lost her way in 2016/17,
including over fences: stays 3m: acts on soft and good to firm going: has worn headgear,
including usually in 2016/17: has worn tongue tie: often races prominently. *David Pipe*

LADY OF THE CLYDE 9 b.m. Lord Americo – Miss Nel (Denel (FR)) [2016/17 h20.5sᵘʳ **h– §**
h24.3vᵘʳ Jan 17] second foal: half-sister to useful chaser Firth of The Clyde (2m-3m
winner, by Flemensfirth): dam no sign of ability over hurdles: unseated both starts over
hurdles (at first on second occasion after trying to refuse). *Iain Jardine*

LADY OVERMOON 8 b.m. Overbury (IRE) – Lady Fleur (Alflora (IRE)) [2016/17 **h–**
h20.3gᵖᵘ May 24] limited impact in bumper/over hurdles. *Mark Bradstock*

LADY PERSEPHONE (FR) 6 br.m. Sir Percy – Acenanga (GER) (Acatenango (GER)) **h96**
[2016/17 h96p: h15.3m* h16.7d⁵ h18.7m⁴ Jul 10] smallish mare: modest hurdler: won
mares novice at Wincanton in May: may prove best at 2m: acts on soft and good to firm
going. *Alan King*

LADY RA (IRE) 8 br.m. Beneficial – Thethirstyscholars (IRE) (Be My Native (USA)) **h75**
[2016/17 h–: h16.2d* h16.2d h20gᵖᵘ h19.6d⁵ h22.1d h20.1s⁵ Sep 30] poor hurdler: won
seller at Hexham in June: stays 2½m: acts on good to firm and good to soft going: often
races towards rear. *Lucinda Egerton*

LADY ROBYN (IRE) 7 b.m. Robin des Champs (FR) – Iseefaith (IRE) (Perugino (USA)) **c–**
[2016/17 b16.8g³ b16g³ h24g² h24m² c23.6s c22.7s⁴ Feb 16] fifth foal: half-sister to a **h92**
winning pointer by Heron Island: dam (c89/h79), placed up to 2¾m over fences, half-sister **b86**
to fair hurdler/fairly useful chaser (stayed 27f) College Ace: runner-up all 4 completed
starts in Irish points: third in bumpers: modest form when second in maiden/novice
hurdles: well held both starts in handicap chases: wears cheekpieces: in tongue tie last 3
starts: often leads. *Peter Bowen*

LADY ROCKA 4 ch.f. Rock of Gibraltar (IRE) – Tap Dance Way (IRE) (Azamour (IRE)) **h–**
[2016/17 h18.7dᵖᵘ Mar 13] modest on Flat, stays 1¼m: pulled up in juvenile on hurdling
debut. *Anabel K. Murphy*

LADY SAMBACK 5 ch.m. Black Sam Bellamy (IRE) – Bob Back's Lady (IRE) (Bob **b–**
Back (USA)) [2016/17 b17s Dec 11] fifth foal: closely related to fairly useful hurdler
Bobs Lady Tamure (2m winner, by Tamure), stayed 21f, and bumper winner/fairly useful
hurdler Bobs Lord Tara (17f winner, by Kayf Tara): dam unraced: tailed off in mares
bumper: wore tongue tie. *Maurice Barnes*

LADY VALERIE 5 b.m. Darnay – Lackofcash (Makbul) [2016/17 b15.7d* b15.7s⁵ b16d **b90**
b16g Apr 23] tall, rather unfurnished mare: first foal: dam unraced: won mares bumper at
Southwell on debut in July: off 7 months and went wrong way subsequently. *Robert Stephens*

LADY VITESSE 4 b.f. Rail Link – Sainte Gig (FR) (Saint Cyrien (FR)) [2016/17 ab16g⁴ **b70**
b16.3d b16g⁵ Apr 17] half-sister to several winners, including French hurdler/cross-
country chaser Goldgig (17f-25f winner, by Goldneyev) and fairly useful hurdler Santera
(2m-2¾m winner, by Gold Away): dam unraced: poor form in bumpers. *Gary Moore*

LADY VIVONA 9 gr.m. Overbury (IRE) – Ladylliat (FR) (Simon du Desert (FR)) [2016/17 **h70**
h60: h23.9mᵖᵘ h23.3g⁵ h19.9g² h23.3g³ h23.9g h23.9g Sep 5] poor maiden hurdler: stays
23f: best form on good going: tried in cheekpieces: in tongue tie last 4 starts. *Lisa Harrison*

LADY WETHERED (IRE) 5 br.m. Westerner – Vics Miller (IRE) (Old Vic) [2016/17 **h73**
b16.8d h18.5m⁴ Apr 18] first foal: dam unraced half-sister to fair hurdler/useful chaser **b–**
(2¼m-3¾m winner) Maljimar: tailed off in bumper: 50/1, fourth of 6 in maiden at Exeter
(23 lengths behind Trevisani) on hurdling debut. *Linda Blackford*

LA FILLE FRANCAISE (FR) 4 b.f. Kapgarde (FR) – Pondimari (FR) (Marignan **b80**
(USA)) [2016/17 b14s⁶ b16.8d⁴ b16.8g⁴ Apr 20] £8,000 3-y-o: half-sister to 3 winners,
including fair hurdler/chaser Cranky Corner (2m-2½m winner, by Classic Cliche) and
bumper winner Ronnie Rhino (by Darsi): dam, French 9f-13f winner, half-sister to fairly
useful hurdler/smart chaser (stayed 25f) De Boitron: modest form in bumpers. *Robin Dickin*

Weatherbys Private Bank Standard Open National Hunt Flat, Aintree—33/1-shot Lalor provides trainer Richard Woollacott with the biggest win of his fledgling training career

LAFLAMMEDEGLORIE 11 b.g. Fair Mix (IRE) – Swazi Princess (IRE) (Brush Aside (USA)) [2016/17 h19.5d h21.6v c20v^pu c17.4v^pu Jan 29] big gelding: fair hurdler at best, well held in handicaps first 2 starts in 2016/17: no form over fences: stays 2¾m. *Jess Westwood*   c– h–

LAGANBANK (IRE) 11 b.g. Norwich – Listen Up (Good Thyne (USA)) [2016/17 c24.2g^pu Apr 17] winning hurdler: useful chaser at best, pulled up in hunter in April after long absence: stays 2¾m: acts on good to firm and heavy going: tried in tongue tie. *Mrs S. J. Stearn*   c– h–

LAGAVARA (IRE) 5 b.m. Exit To Nowhere (USA) – Knocklayde Rose (IRE) (Even Top (IRE)) [2016/17 b16g⁴ h15.8v³ h15.3s⁶ h16.8s³ h15.8v³ h18.9g h20.2g⁴ Apr 26] second foal: dam (h82), winning pointer, half-sister to dam of smart chaser (stays 3½m) Bishops Road: fourth in maiden bumper: fair form over hurdles: left Stuart Crawford after first start: stays 2½m: acts on heavy going. *Nigel Twiston-Davies*   h100 b77

L'AIGLE ROYAL (GER) 6 b.g. Sholokhov (IRE) – Laren (GER) (Monsun (GER)) [2016/17 h125: h20.6g* h21g³ h24g c16.3s³ Jan 7] compact gelding: fairly useful handicap hurdler: won at Market Rasen in October: well held in novice on chasing debut (should do better): best up to 21f: acts on soft going: has worn cheekpieces: often races towards rear. *Dan Skelton*   c89 p h115

LAIRD OF MONKSFORD (IRE) 8 b.g. Shantou (USA) – Back Log (IRE) (Bob Back (USA)) [2016/17 h–: h21.5g h22.1m⁴ h23.9g^pu Aug 20] poor maiden hurdler: stayed 2¾m: tried in headgear: in tongue tie last 4 starts: dead. *Gordon Elliott, Ireland*   h77

LAISSEZ DIRE (FR) 5 br.g. Konig Turf (GER) – Smaya (FR) (Smadoun (FR)) [2016/17 c19.2g* c17s^F Jan 2] once-raced on Flat: fairly useful form over hurdles: won twice at Pau in 2015/16 for G. Cherel: useful form over fences: won maiden at Catterick in November: yet to be asked for effort when fell fatally 4 out in novice won by Baron Alco at Plumpton: stayed 19f: acted on heavy going. *Alan King*   c139 h–

LAKE CHAPALA (IRE) 8 b.g. Shantou (USA) – Rathcolman Queen (IRE) (Radical) [2016/17 h87: h16.7g⁴ h18.7g³ c16d² c16g⁵ c16.5m^R c15.8g* c16g² c16s* h15.5v² h16d⁶ c17.2s⁵ c17m* Apr 16] sturdy gelding: modest maiden hurdler: fair handicap chaser: won at Musselburgh in November, Hereford in January and Plumpton (novice event) in April: left Tim Vaughan after eleventh start: stays 2¼m: acts on good to firm and heavy going: wears headgear: tried in tongue tie: has looked temperamental (refused early fifth outing). *Chris Gordon*   c105 § h86 §

LAKEFIELD REBEL (IRE) 11 b.g. Presenting – River Mousa (IRE) (Over The River (FR)) [2016/17 c24.2s^F c26g² c24.2s c25.2s⁵ c31.9s² c26.3g⁵ c26.2g⁵ Apr 15] Irish point winner: modest maiden chaser: stays 4m: acts on soft going. *Henry Hogarth*   c90 h–

LAKE MALAWI (IRE) 6 b.g. Westerner – Ariesanne (IRE) (Primo Dominie) [2016/17 h16d⁶ h20g² h18.5d* h20.2d⁵ h21d² h16.2s³ Sep 22] third foal: dam, 6f winner, half-sister to useful staying hurdler Paperprophet: fair form over hurdles: won maiden at Downpatrick in June: likely to stay 3m: acts on good to soft going. *Gordon Elliott, Ireland*   h109

LAKE PLACID 4 b.g. Champs Elysees – Phantom Wind (USA) (Storm Cat (USA)) [2016/17 h16g³ Oct 9] lightly raced on Flat: tailed off in juvenile on hurdling debut: wore tongue tie. *Nigel Hawke*   h–

LAKE SHORE DRIVE (IRE) 5 b.g. Thewayyouare (USA) – Labrusca (Grand Lodge (USA)) [2016/17 h24m⁵ h23.7m⁶ h15.8d⁵ h24.4d³ h19g Feb 21] maiden on Flat: modest maiden hurdler: left John Laurence Cullen after second start: stays 3m: acts on good to firm and good to soft going: often races in rear. *Johnny Farrelly*   h94

LAKESHORE LADY (IRE) 7 b.m. Lakeshore Road (USA) – Chiminee Chime (IRE) (Lord Americo) [2016/17 h102: c19.4m² c16.3g⁴ c20.9vᵖᵘ c23.9g c17.4g⁴ c19.7m⁴ c20.2s² c20.9d² c19.2g* c17.4g³ Apr 21] maiden hurdler: fair handicap chaser: won mares event at Fontwell in April: stays 21f: acts on good to firm and heavy going: has worn headgear, including in 2016/17: tried in tongue tie. *David Bridgwater* **c101 h–**

LAKESIDE CASTLE (IRE) 6 b.g. Stowaway – Beaver Run (IRE) (Be My Native (USA)) [2016/17 b20g² h21.3s* Jan 6] fair form in bumpers: left Ms M. M. Gannon/off 8 months, 7/4, won 9-runner maiden at Wetherby on hurdling debut by 23 lengths from Westend Story: dead. *Dan Skelton* **h125 b92**

LAKE VIEW LAD (IRE) 7 gr.g. Oscar (IRE) – Missy O'Brien (IRE) (Supreme Leader) [2016/17 h139, b95: c16.3d² c20.9s⁶ Dec 11] bumper winner: useful hurdler: useful form over fences: better effort when second in novice handicap at Newcastle (1½ lengths behind Pistol Park) in November, barely adequate test: stays 21f: acts on heavy going: front runner/races prominently. *N. W. Alexander* **c135 h–**

LALA'S SISTER (IRE) 8 b.g. Sandmason – Ballykeenan Trixie (IRE) (Safety Catch (USA)) [2016/17 c23g⁴ c23gᶠ c23dᵖᵘ c23.5v⁵ c23.5v⁶ Jan 31] winning Irish pointer: no form in chases. *Sarah Wall* **c–**

LALOR (GER) 5 b.g. It's Gino (GER) – Laviola (GER) (Waky Nao) [2016/17 b15.3s* b15.3v² b15.3v* b17g* Apr 7] €16,000 3-y-o: good-topped gelding: second foal: brother to German 1m winner Lilydale: dam German 1m winner: smart form in bumpers: won at Wincanton in December (awarded race) and March, and Grade 2 at Aintree (33/1, by 2½ lengths from Enniscoffey Oscar) in April: travels strongly. *Richard Woollacott* **b116**

Mr D. G. Staddon's "Lalor"

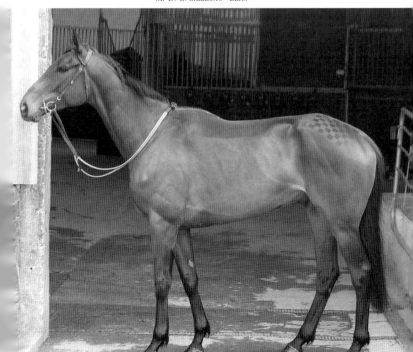

LA MADONNINA (IRE) 9 b.m. Milan – Supreme Nova (Supreme Leader) [2016/17 **c90** c/9, h–: c22.5g* c25.5g⁵ c20.9vᵖᵘ c23gᶠ c20.3dᵖᵘ Aug 19] maiden hurdler: modest **h–** handicap chaser: won at Uttoxeter in May: barely stays 25f: best form on good going: wears headgear. *Caroline Keevil*

LA MADRINA (IRE) 5 b.m. Milan – Edermine Blossom (IRE) (Bach (IRE)) [2016/17 **h–** b15.8d h16.2s h19g h15.3d h16.8s Mar 7] second foal: dam unraced half-sister to **b–** Champion Bumper winner/very smart hurdler (stayed 21f) Dunguib: well beaten in bumper/novice hurdles: left Henry Oliver after second start. *Katie Stephens*

LAMANVER ODYSSEY 5 b.m. Lucarno (USA) – Lamanver Homerun (Relief Pitcher) **h116** [2016/17 b90: h16g³ h21s h18.5s* h21.7v² h20.5g Mar 25] good-topped mare: bumper winner: fairly useful form over hurdles: won mares novice at Exeter in December: stays 2¼m: best form on soft/heavy going: front runner/races prominently. *Harry Fry*

LAMBEAU FIELD (USA) 4 b.g. Cape Blanco (IRE) – Xinji (IRE) (Xaar) [2016/17 **h107** h16d h16g⁴ h16.4s³ h15.8s h15.7m² h16g Apr 29] compact gelding: fair form on Flat, stays 12.5f: fair form over hurdles: left Charles O'Brien after second start: raced only at 2m: acts on good to firm going: usually races close up, often travels strongly. *Charlie Longsdon*

LAMBLORD (IRE) 10 b.g. Brian Boru – Princess Symphony (IRE) (Lashkari) [2016/17 **c–** h105: h20m³ c23gᵖᵘ Jun 4] fair handicap hurdler, below form on return: pulled up in novice **h74** on chasing debut: stays 23f, effective at shorter: acts on heavy going: has worn cheekpieces: usually races close up. *Robert Walford*

LAMB OR COD (IRE) 10 ch.g. Old Vic – Princess Lizzie (IRE) (Homo Sapien) [2016/17 **c135** c23.8d c23.6g* c26.3sᵖᵘ c26g c25gᵖᵘ c26g⁴ Apr 20] lengthy gelding: has reportedly had **h–** wind operation: winning hurdler: useful handicap chaser: won at Chepstow (by 2¾ lengths from Potters Cross) in December: not in same form after: stays 3¼m: has won on heavy going but seems best under less testing conditions (acts on good to firm): has worn blinkers: wears tongue tie. *Philip Hobbs*

LAMBORO LAD (IRE) 12 b.g. Milan – Orchard Spray (IRE) (Supreme Leader) **c91** [2016/17 c–, h–: c20.2m⁴ May 10] good-topped gelding: winning hurdler: useful chaser at **h–** best, not same force nowadays (maiden in points): stays 25f: acts on good to firm and heavy going: usually wears cheekpieces: wears tongue tie. *Mickey Bowen*

LAMB'S CROSS 11 b.g. Rainbow High – Angie Marinie (Sabrehill (USA)) [2016/17 **c56 x** c79x, h–: c25.7g³ c20dᵖᵘ c16.1gᵖᵘ c20.2sᵖᵘ Mar 1] good-topped gelding: winning hurdler: **h–** poor chaser: left Brian Barr after second start: stays 21f: acts on heavy going: has worn headgear, including final start: in tongue tie last 2 starts: often let down by jumping. *G. Hiscock*

L'AMI SERGE (IRE) 7 b.g. King's Theatre (IRE) – La Zingarella (IRE) (Phardante **c143 +** (FR)) [2016/17 c148, h–: c17.5v² h20.3s² h15.7s³ h19.1s³ h16.8g² h16g⁵ h21.5g* **h161** Apr 29]

First David Pipe, then Paul Nicholls, now Nicky Henderson. Three of Britain's top trainers have won the last three editions of France's most prestigious hurdle, the Grande Course de Haies d'Auteuil, having been shown the way by Willie Mullins, winner of four editions of the so-called 'French Champion Hurdle' earlier this century (Mullins' father Paddy also won the race with Dawn Run in 1984). Unlike Ireland's champion trainer, Henderson is not a regular visitor to Auteuil and L'Ami Serge was his first runner in the Grande Course de Haies, though he is one of the very few British trainers to have had a runner in the Grand Steeple-Chase de Paris in recent years when sending over former Gold Cup winner Long Run to contest the race in 2014. L'Ami Serge's owners, on the other hand, Simon Munir and Isaac Souede, with a large number of their string based across the Channel, are no strangers to success in France's top jumps races. Munir's French colours were carried into second place in the Grande Course de Haies for the second year running with Alex de Larredya, and were first past the post in two other races on the card, notably in the other Group 1, the Prix Alain du Breil for four-year-old hurdlers, in which Prince Ali followed the success of the Mullins-trained Footpad for the same owners the year before. Weeks earlier, Munir and Souede had five winners at Auteuil over Grand Steeple-Chase de Paris weekend, including the Group 1 chase for four-year-olds, the Prix Ferdinand Dufaure, won by Srelighonn in the absence through injury of their even better four-year-old chaser Edward d'Argent who has won all six of his starts over fences.

bet365 Select Hurdle, Sandown—a first hurdles win in over two years for L'Ami Serge as he beats 2016 winner Ptit Zig (hooped sleeves)

L'Ami Serge has always had considerable ability but he had become an enigmatic performer, to say the least, before making a nonsense of what nearly everyone thought they knew about him by winning at Auteuil. L'Ami Serge had been one of the best novice hurdlers around, winning the Tolworth Hurdle at Sandown in the manner of a potential top-notcher and running up an unbeaten record in Britain until the Supreme Novices' when he finished fourth, after a troubled passage, behind Douvan, Shaneshill and Sizing John. The following season, L'Ami Serge made a successful switch to fences and finished placed in the Golden Miller at Cheltenham and the Manifesto at Aintree. But L'Ami Serge's chasing career was quickly abandoned after he was beaten in a graduation chase at Exeter, jumping badly left, on his reappearance in the latest season, not his first defeat in a three-runner race, either. A return to hurdles only served to extend what was becoming a worrying sequence of placed efforts, which eventually reached eight in number. In most of those defeats, L'Ami Serge traded at long odds on in running, and it wasn't until the very last day of the British season that his diminishing band of followers were finally rewarded when he won the Select Hurdle at Sandown. By then, L'Ami Serge had acquired a 'squiggle' after too many unsatisfactory efforts. He was given the benefit of the doubt on the grounds of stamina when edged out by Agrapart in testing conditions for Cheltenham's Relkeel Hurdle over two and a half miles (his rider also lost an iron near the finish), but he looked half-hearted when third to The New One in the Champion Hurdle Trial at Haydock and was ultimately beaten a long way when filling the same position in the National Spirit Hurdle at Fontwell after his challenge petered out. But having run his worst race during this losing run, L'Ami Serge ran his best race in defeat next time when the switch to a strongly-run handicap with a big field over two miles seemed to suit him much better as he stayed on late to go down by a neck to top weight Arctic Fire in the County Hurdle at Cheltenham (L'Ami Serge was next in the weights, 6 lb below Arctic Fire, off a BHA mark of 152). The much more steadily run Scottish Champion Hurdle served L'Ami Serge less well and he was only able to stay on for a never-nearer fifth behind Chesterfield, nevertheless faring best of his owners' three runners in the race.

No sooner had L'Ami Serge looked as if he needed a well-run two miles to show his best than, just a week after Ayr, he finally consented to put his best foot forward in the bet365 Select Hurdle over twenty-one furlongs at Sandown, a race that hardly looked likely to suit him at the time. His trainer fielded four runners in the newly-promoted Grade 2 contest on Sandown's Finale card, though it was The New One who started favourite, the only runner in the field of eight not trained by either

Henderson or ten-times champion trainer Paul Nicholls with whom he was engaged in a battle for the title. After failing to settle, L'Ami Serge pulled his way to the front past The New One after three out, quickened clear after the next and was always holding on to beat the previous year's winner Ptit Zig by a length and a half in receipt of 8 lb. The Nicholls-trained Ptit Zig had gone on to win the Grande Course de Haies after a run beforehand in the main trial, the Prix La Barka, in 2016 and L'Ami Serge was sent to Auteuil for the same two races. L'Ami Serge ran another good race in the La Barka to be beaten three quarters of a length by Shaneshill who returned to form to give Willie Mullins a fourth win in the race. Never having raced over three miles or beyond raised serious doubts about whether L'Ami Serge would be anything like so well suited by the extra half mile of the Grande Course de Haies as the winner, a confirmed stayer. In a steadily-run contest for the La Barka, L'Ami Serge failed to settle and, after taking the lead after two out, he was outstayed by the rallying Shaneshill in the closing stages after jumping out to his left at the last. If stamina doubts could be set aside, L'Ami Serge was in theory entitled to turn the tables on Shaneshill in the Grande Course de Haies where they met at level weights. In the La Barka, L'Ami Serge was conceding 4 lb. The top French jumps races have been organised into a pattern-race structure since 1999—the Prix La Barka is classed as a Group 2 contest—but, oddly, unlike in Britain and Ireland, penalties in such races are still governed, as they were before the pattern classification was introduced, by the amount of prize money a horse has won in the current and previous year, rather than by the grade of race it has won. Although Shaneshill and L'Ami Serge were both Grade 2 winners earlier in the year, Shaneshill had not won enough prize money to incur any penalty in the La Barka. Given the high level of prize money on offer at Auteuil, compared to that for graded races in Britain and Ireland, the more successful French-trained jumpers are potentially badly treated under this system compared to their British or Irish-trained counterparts. Alex de Larredya, for example, who finished fifth in the La Barka, was lumbered with the maximum penalty, conceding 8 lb to Shaneshill, having won the €166,500 Grand Prix d'Automne the previous November. Shaneshill was the sixth British or Irish-trained winner of the La Barka in a row.

There was certainly a very different result when Shaneshill, L'Ami Serge and Alex de Larredya met again at level weights three weeks after the La Barka in the Grande Course de Haies. As well as the 2016 runner-up Alex de Larredya, the other principals from the year before were back again. Blue Dragon was sent off the short-priced favourite to atone for his dramatic capitulation in the closing stages twelve months earlier, when he had looked all over the winner for much of the straight only to weaken into third as Ptit Zig stayed on from off the pace. The front-running Blue Dragon had had competition for the lead on that occasion from Un de Sceaux who had himself won the Prix La Barka beforehand, before failing to see out the extended twenty-five furlongs of the Grande Course de Haies. Blue Dragon had twice finished third, conceding weight, to the same owner's Device before looking back to something like his top-class best when winning the Prix Leon Rambaud for the second year running later in the spring by twelve lengths. Device, incidentally, winner of all four of his completed starts since the previous summer before finishing third in the La Barka (another who would have been much better off at the weights in the Grande Course de Haies) was the main absentee due to a late setback.

Grande Course de Haies d'Auteuil Hurdle, Auteuil—a third successive British-trained winner of this race as Daryl Jacob drives home L'Ami Serge to win from Alex de Larredya (rail)

Passing the stands with a circuit to go, Blue Dragon was bowling along in an uncontested lead, with Ptit Zig, the other British challenger One Track Mind and Shaneshill prominent in the main body of the field. L'Ami Serge, on the other hand, was still in rear, Daryl Jacob (who is retained by Munir and Souede in Britain) having dropped him out in a detached last on the first circuit with a first-time hood clearly having the desired effect of helping him to settle much better than in the La Barka. But going down the back straight for the second time, Blue Dragon made two bad mistakes, the second one effectively ending his race as Alex de Larredya moved past him rounding the home turn. Blue Dragon was pulled up soon after the second last and was subsequently found to have suffered a pelvic injury. Meanwhile, L'Ami Serge was creeping into contention, saving ground round the inner and still on the bridle. While Alex de Larredya took the usual route on Auteuil's wide home straight, coming over to race right up against the stand rail, L'Ami Serge remained on the far side, the pair wide apart on the run-in. L'Ami Serge showed unexpected reserves of both resolution and stamina to edge ahead under strong driving, despite hanging to his right, and he won by a length and a half while, ten lengths behind the runner-up, Shaneshill narrowly won a private battle with Blue Dragon's stable-companion Bosseur to take third. Ptit Zig and the tailed-off One Track Mind were the last of the nine to finish.

			Sadler's Wells	Northern Dancer
L'Ami Serge (IRE)	King's Theatre (IRE)		(b 1981)	Fairy Bridge
(b.g. 2010)	(b 1991)		Regal Beauty	Princely Native
			(br 1981)	Dennis Belle
	La Zingarella (IRE)		Phardante	Pharly
	(b 1998)		(b 1982)	Pallante
			In Memoriam	Buckskin
			(b 1988)	Superdora

Like the two other recent British-trained winners of the Grande Course de Haies, L'Ami Serge began his career in France. He didn't win there, though, having six starts at Auteuil for Guillaume Macaire and finishing placed in all but one of them. He is the second Grande Course de Haies winner sired by the leading sire of jumpers in Britain and Ireland in recent seasons, King's Theatre, after Willie Mullins' first winner Nobody Told Me in 2003. Shaneshill is also by King's Theatre. L'Ami Serge is Irish bred and so was his dam, La Zingarella, a daughter of Phardante, though she raced exclusively at Auteuil and Enghien, showing fairly useful form at up to two and a half miles over both hurdles and fences. As well as breeding the dam of the latest Grande Course de Haies winner, Jameina Scarisbrick owned the 1997 winner of the same race, Bog Frog, he too by Phardante. La Zingarella was sold for €77,000 as a five-year-old at the end of her racing days, returning to her native Ireland, whereas, initially at least, L'Ami Serge, her fourth foal, made the opposite journey after being sold for €23,000 as a foal, his dam's racing record clearly making him of interest to French buyers. Further details of L'Ami Serge's family, which is also that of the Francois Doumen-trained Triumph Hurdle winner Snow Drop and Don't Touch It, a winner at the last two Punchestown Festivals, can be found in his earlier essays. Snow Drop, incidentally, is now the grandam of one of Ireland's top staying hurdlers, Snow Falcon. Like L'Ami Serge, his year-older half-brother Sizing Codelco (by Flemensfirth)—who also has an essay in this Annual—revealed untapped reserves of stamina when winning valuable staying handicap chases at Aintree and Punchestown in the spring, showing very smart form. La Zingarella's next foal after L'Ami Serge, Viens Chercher (by Milan, a son of Sadler's Wells like King's Theatre), showed useful form in novice chases in the latest season, while her latest foal to reach the track, Petit Oscar (by Oscar), hinted at ability in the first of two starts in Irish bumpers. A tall gelding, L'Ami Serge stays twenty-five furlongs and acts on heavy ground. He travels well in his races, sometimes too freely for his own good, though the application of the hood clearly helped him settle much better. L'Ami Serge did little wrong on his last few starts, in fact, seeming to turn over a new leaf and ridding himself of the 'squiggle' on his rating. *Nicky Henderson*

LAMOOL (GER) 10 b.g. Mamool (IRE) – Linara (GER) (Windwurf (GER)) [2016/17 **c–** c133, h133: h22.8m³ May 7] lengthy gelding: useful handicap hurdler: third at Haydock **h133** (5¼ lengths behind Whataknight) in May: useful chaser: stays 25f: acts on good to firm and heavy going: tried in cheekpieces: wears tongue tie: front runner/races prominently: reliable. *Tim Vaughan*

LANDECKER (IRE) 9 br.g. Craigsteel – Winsome Breeze (IRE) (Glacial Storm (USA))   **c–**
[2016/17 c–, h116§: h23.9d h24.6d h25.8s* h22.8v⁵ h23.8g h22.7v² h22.7d³ h26.6g⁵   **h118 §**
Apr 27] fairly useful handicap hurdler: won at Kelso in November: well beaten sole chase start: stays 27f: acts on heavy going: has worn headgear: tried in tongue tie: temperamental. *N. W. Alexander*

LANDIN (GER) 4 b.c. Sir Percy – Lupita (GER) (Niniski (USA)) [2016/17 h16s³ h16v²   **h128**
h16.8g h17g⁶ h16g Apr 29] smallish colt: useful on Flat, stays 11f: fairly useful form over hurdles: raced around 2m: acts on heavy going: usually races towards rear. *Seamus Mullins*

LAND LEAGUE (IRE) 6 b.g. Touch of Land (FR) – Be My Sunset (IRE) (Bob Back   **h113**
(USA)) [2016/17 h18.6s⁶ h15.7v² h15.8s³ h19.9s h17.7g^F Apr 21] third foal: half-brother to fairly useful hurdler/useful chaser Drumlee Sunset (2m-19f winner, by Royal Anthem): dam unraced sister to useful hurdler/chaser (2m-2½m winner) The Jigsaw Man: off mark in Irish maiden points at ninth attempt: fair form over hurdles: should prove suited by 2½m+ *Stuart Edmunds*

LANDMARQUE 8 b.g. Milan – M N L Lady (Polar Falcon (USA)) [2016/17 h20d³   **c99**
c20.5s⁴ h23.3vᵖᵘ h23.8g* c23.8g⁴ c23.8g⁶ c23.8g⁶ Mar 1] fair form over hurdles: won   **h100**
handicap at Musselburgh in January: similar form over fences: will stay beyond 3m: wears headgear. *James Ewart*

LANDMEAFORTUNE (IRE) 8 gr.g. Touch of Land (FR) – Mayrich (IRE) (Roselier   **c99**
(FR)) [2016/17 h89: c20.5s² c24.2v² c24.2sᵖᵘ c24.3v* c24.5s² c30.6g³ Apr 28] maiden   **h–**
hurdler: modest form over fences: won handicap at Ayr in January: stays 31f: acts on heavy going: has worn headgear, including in 2016/17. *Martin Todhunter*

LANDOFHOPEANDGLORY (IRE) 4 b.g. High Chaparral (IRE) – Wurfklinge (GER)   **h143**
(Acatenango (GER)) [2016/17 h16g* h16s* h16d* h16d² h16v³ h16.8g⁵ h16d² Apr 29] strong gelding: half-brother to fairly useful 2m hurdle winner Sir Fredlot (by Choisir), stayed 21f: useful on Flat, stays 2m: useful hurdler: won juveniles at Fairyhouse (maiden) and Punchestown in November, and Bar One Racing Juvenile 3-Y-O Hurdle at Fairyhouse (by length from Bapaume) in December: second behind same rival in Knight Frank Juvenile Hurdle at Leopardstown and AES Champion Four Year Old Hurdle at Punchestown: raced around 2m: acts on soft going: in tongue tie last 3 starts. *Joseph Patrick O'Brien, Ireland*

LAND OF VIC 9 b.m. Old Vic – Land of Glory (Supreme Leader) [2016/17 h20.3s c22.4d   **c103**
c20d* c24vᵖᵘ c24.1gᵖᵘ h24.3d⁶ Apr 21] sturdy mare: useful handicap hurdler at best, off 20   **h116**
months before return: fair form over fences: won mares novice at Ludlow in January: stays 3m: acts on heavy going: has worn cheekpieces, including in 2016/17. *Peter Bowen*

LANDSCAPE (FR) 9 b.g. Lando (GER) – Universelle (USA) (Miswaki (USA)) [2016/17   **h88 §**
h–: h19.9g h17.7g⁴ h21.6gᵖᵘ h19.5d h19.1sᵖᵘ h15.9s³ h25v² h21m⁴ Apr 4] rather leggy gelding: modest handicap hurdler nowadays: stays 25f: acts on good to firm and heavy going: has worn headgear/tongue tie, including usually in 2016/17: unreliable. *Daniel Steele*

LANSDOWNE ROAD (IRE) 9 b.g. Bienamado (USA) – Ballinamona Wish (IRE)   **h89**
(Kotashaan (FR)) [2016/17 h22.7s³ h24d⁵ Nov 29] won first of 3 starts in points in 2015: modest form over hurdles: better effort when third in novice at Kelso in November. *Joanne Foster*

LAOCH BEAG (IRE) 6 gr.g. King's Theatre (IRE) – Innocentines (FR) (Linamix (FR))   **h82**
[2016/17 b20g b20.5d⁵ b16g h19.1s³ h21.6g⁵ h19.7s h19g h21.4d⁴ h21.6m² Apr 15]   **b75**
unplaced in bumpers: poor form over hurdles: left Barry John Murphy after second start: best effort at 2¾m: acts on good to firm going. *Helen Nelmes*

LA PAIMPOLAISE (FR) 5 b.m. Linda's Lad – Medievale (FR) (Lost World (IRE))   **c–**
[2016/17 h122: h17.7s⁶ h19.5v⁶ h21.6sᵖᵘ c19.7sᵖᵘ Feb 13] good-topped mare: fairly useful   **h–**
hurdler at best, has gone the wrong way: pulled up in novice handicap on chasing debut. *Gary Moore*

LAPALALA (IRE) 6 b.m. Oscar (IRE) – Lala Nova (IRE) (Zaffaran (USA)) [2016/17   **h106**
h100, b–: h16s² h16.8s h19.8d⁴ h21.6s⁴ h21.4m^F Apr 5] fair maiden hurdler: should stay further than 2½m: acts on soft going. *Philip Hobbs*

L'APOGEE 4 ch.g. Rip Van Winkle (IRE) – Pappas Ruby (USA) (Red Ransom (USA))   **h–**
[2016/17 h16.2d Sep 21] fair on Flat, stays 1¼m: well held in juvenile on hurdling debut: sold 6,500 gns in February. *Richard Fahey*

LARGY BULL (IRE) 5 b.g. Beneficial – Any Other Way (IRE) (Musical Pursuit)   **h97**
[2016/17 b18d h20d⁴ h20.5s⁵ h22.7s³ h22sᵖᵘ h19.3v⁴ Mar 9] €7,000 3-y-o: second foal: **b–**
dam, unraced, out of half-sister to useful hurdler/smart chaser (2m-2½m winner) Ventana

Canyon: in frame in maiden points: well beaten in maiden bumper: modest form over hurdles: left Stuart Crawford after first start: should prove suited by 2¾m+: tried in cheekpieces: usually races prominently. *Benjamin Arthey, Ireland*

LARGY GIRL (IRE) 6 br.m. Kalanisi (IRE) – Sumability (IRE) (Oscar (IRE)) [2016/17   **h77** b80: b16.2f² h16g² Oct 29] modest form in bumpers: 18/1, sixth in novice at Wetherby   **b80** (21¼ lengths behind Ozzie The Oscar) on hurdling debut: left Stuart Crawford after first start. *Mark Walford*

LARKHALL 10 b.g. Saddlers' Hall (IRE) – Larkbarrow (Kahyasi) [2016/17 c76§, h–§:   **c77 §** c17.3g⁴ c21.2m³ c15.7d⁵ c19.4g⁴ c20.3g³ h19.9gᵖᵘ c16g² c15.7m⁵ c16.5m⁴ c20.2f³ c20.2g⁴   **h– §** Jan 12] good-topped gelding: maiden hurdler: poor handicap chaser: effective at 2m to 3m: acts on firm and good to soft going: tried in headgear: has worn tongue tie: usually races towards rear/travels strongly: weak finisher. *Mike Sowersby*

LARRY 4 b.g. Midnight Legend – Gaspaisie (FR) (Beyssac (FR)) [2016/17 b17.7s* b17g   **b96** Apr 7] £45,000 3-y-o: brother to bumper/fairly useful 2½m hurdle winner Chain Gang and half-brother to several winners, including smart 2m-2½m hurdle winners Mr Thriller (by Kapgarde) and Gaspara (by Astarabad): dam French 17f-2½m hurdle/chase winner: fairly useful form in bumpers: won maiden at Fontwell in February: well beaten in Grade 2 at Aintree. *Gary Moore*

LARTETA (FR) 8 b.g. Enrique – Ariel (IRE) (Caerleon (USA)) [2016/17 c95, h59: c21.2g⁵   **c74 §** c19.9g⁶ c19.4g³ h19.6m c19.9m⁴ h23.4g c19.7d² c23.6d³ c19.9d⁶ c23.6g⁴ c23.6g⁵ Apr 17]   **h63 §** poor hurdler/maiden chaser nowadays: barely stays 3m: acts on good to firm and heavy going: has worn headgear, including usually in 2016/17: front runner/races prominently: temperamental. *Sarah Humphrey*

LASER BLAZER 9 b.g. Zafeen (FR) – Sashay (Bishop of Cashel) [2016/17 h117: c20g³   **c109** c21.4g⁶ Jul 16] good-topped gelding: fairly useful hurdler: fair form over fences: stayed   **h–** 19f: acted on good to firm and good to soft going: tried in headgear: dead. *Alan King*

LASER HAWK (IRE) 10 b.g. Rashar (USA) – Alphablend (IRE) (Alphabatim (USA))   **c81** [2016/17 c121, h–: c19.4dᵖᵘ c19.4g⁵ c20.9vᵖᵘ Dec 12] rangy gelding: winning hurdler: **h–** fairly useful maiden chaser at best, has become disappointing: best effort at 2m: acts on heavy going: tried in visor: usually races close up. *Evan Williams*

LASER LIGHT (IRE) 6 b.g. Kutub (IRE) – Sioux Falls (IRE) (Monashee Mountain   **h130** (USA)) [2016/17 b101p: h19.5d* h21.6d² h24v² h20.5v³ h21m* Apr 4] well-made gelding: runner-up completed start in Irish maiden points: bumper winner: useful form over hurdles: won maiden at Chepstow in October and novice at Kempton in April: second in novice at Ascot (¾ length behind Elegant Escape) in November: stays 2¾m: acts on good to firm and good to soft going. *Alan King*

LASTBUTNOTLEAST (IRE) 7 ch.m. Flemensfirth (USA) – Lakil Princess (IRE)   **h127 p** (Bering) [2016/17 b93: h16.2v* h19.3s* h24.4s* Mar 4] sturdy mare: point/bumper winner: fairly useful form over hurdles: unbeaten in 3 starts, winning mares novices at Hexham in December, Carlisle in February and Doncaster (listed event, by 3¼ lengths from Happy Diva) in March: will stay further than 3m: front runner: will go on improving. *Donald McCain*

LAST ECHO (IRE) 6 b.m. Whipper (USA) – Priory Rock (IRE) (Rock of Gibraltar   **h64** (IRE)) [2016/17 h74: h19g h19.9s⁴ h22v⁶ Jun 28] angular mare: poor maiden hurdler: best effort at 2m: acts on heavy going: in cheekpieces last 4 starts: usually races prominently. *Tom Symonds*

LAST GOODBYE (IRE) 6 b.g. Millenary – Welsh Ana (IRE) (Welsh Term) [2016/17   **c140** h136p, b101: h20d c20g² c20s⁶ c20s* c20.4g⁵ c21d Apr 28] good-topped gelding: bumper   **h–** winner: useful hurdler: useful form over fences: won maiden at Down Royal in December: fifth in Close Brothers Novices' Handicap Chase at Cheltenham (8¼ lengths behind Tully East) in March: stays 2½m: acts on heavy going. *Miss Elizabeth Doyle, Ireland*

LASTIN' MEMORIES 5 b.g. Overbury (IRE) – Dusky Dante (IRE) (Phardante (FR))   **h95** [2016/17 b16.2v⁵ h16.2v³ h18.1d Apr 10] brother to several winners, including fairly   **b78** useful 2m hurdle winner Octagon, stays 21f, and half-brother to 3 winners by Karinga Bay, including bumper winner/fair hurdler Monogram (2½m winner): dam (c81/h72) maiden jumper: beat one in bumper at Kelso: modest form over hurdles: easily better effort when third in novice at same course in March. *Sandy Forster*

LAST OF THE BOYS (IRE) 10 b.g. Lacantun – No Chat (IRE) (Eurobus) [2016/17   **h–** h23dᵖᵘ h23gᵖᵘ Sep 6] maiden pointer: no show in novice hurdles: wears cheekpieces. *Lady Susan Brooke*

LAST OF THE OATS 9 b.g. Luso – Easter Oats (Oats) [2016/17 h20.5spu Nov 9] showed nothing in bumper/maiden hurdle 2½ years apart. *Robert Goldie*   h–

LAST PICK (IRE) 7 b.g. Gamut (IRE) – Polyzar (IRE) (Shernazar) [2016/17 b–: h16.2dpu h16.2spu Nov 4] maiden pointer: no form in bumper/maiden hurdles. *Barry Murtagh*   h–

LAST SHOT (FR) 10 b.g. Le Fou (IRE) – Lucky Shot (FR) (Corporate Report (USA)) [2016/17 c–, h–: c20.9m² c17.5s⁴ c20.3s⁵ c19.2s Jan 17] workmanlike gelding: maiden hurdler: fair handicap chaser nowadays: stays 21f: acts on good to firm and heavy going: has worn blinkers, including final start: front runner/races prominently. *Venetia Williams*   c106 h–

LAS TUNAS (FR) 5 br.g. Country Reel (USA) – Grey Winner (FR) (Take Risks (FR)) [2016/17 h17.4s⁶ h17.4s⁴ c20.5d⁵ c18s⁶ c16.3spu c17.1s⁶ c15.7s⁴ c15.5s* c18v³ c17.1spu c16g² Apr 27] maiden on Flat: fair hurdler: won claimer at Auteuil in June: fair handicap chaser: won at Ayr in February: left P. Chevillard after second start: unproven beyond 2¼m: acts on heavy going: often races prominently/travels strongly. *R. Mike Smith*   c105 h114

LATALANTA (FR) 14 b.g. Lost World (IRE) – Belle de Saigon (FR) (Deep Roots) [2016/17 c17.4dpu May 12] tall gelding: maiden pointer: winning hurdler: no form in hunter chases: stays 2¼m: tried in tongue tie. *Brian Tetley*   c– h–

LATE DATE (IRE) 6 b.g. Oscar (IRE) – Regents Ballerina (IRE) (Commanche Run) [2016/17 h16.2s⁴ h20d⁴ h16.2d⁵ h22.7s² h22.7s h20.5sur h22.7v² h20.6v³ h23.9g* Apr 26] £23,000 5-y-o: half-brother to fairly useful chaser Just For Men (2½m winner, by Glacial Storm), stayed 25f, and winning pointers by Glacial Storm and Flemensfirth: dam unraced: off mark in Irish maiden points at second attempt: fair handicap hurdler: won at Perth (amateur) in April: stays 3m: acts on heavy going. *Micky Hammond*   h102

LATE FOR SUPPER (IRE) 8 ch.g. Kahtan – Tillery (IRE) (Peintre Celebre (USA)) [2016/17 h57: h22.1d h23.3gᶠ Jul 22] pulled up sole start in points: maiden hurdler, no form in 2016/17: in tongue tie last 3 starts. *Richard Ford*   h–

LATE NIGHT LILY 6 b.m. Midnight Legend – Ready To Crown (USA) (More Than Ready (USA)) [2016/17 h110p, b95: h18.5gᵇᵈ h16.7g* h19.6m* h15.7v* h16.6d⁵ h16.3d³ h18.9g⁵ Apr 15] workmanlike mare: bumper winner: fairly useful hurdler: won mares novice at Market Rasen in September, novice at Huntingdon in October and mares handicap at Southwell in December: stays 2½m: acts on good to firm and heavy going: usually races towards rear. *Dan Skelton*   h122

LATE ROMANTIC (IRE) 7 b.g. Mahler – Mere Gaye (IRE) (Gildoran) [2016/17 h22.1m⁵ h19.9d⁴ h20d² Oct 20] £14,000 4-y-o: sixth foal: half-brother to dam of fairly useful hurdler/useful chaser (stays 2¾m) O Maonlai: dam unraced half-sister to fairly useful hurdler/smart staying chaser Simon: winning pointer: fair form over hurdles: second in novice at Carlisle in October: wears tongue tie. *Oliver Greenall*   h100

LATE SHIPMENT 6 b.g. Authorized (IRE) – Time Over (Mark of Esteem (IRE)) [2016/17 h88: h22m⁵ h23.3s³ h19.8d⁵ h23.6g⁶ h21.6v² h25.5s* h23.1s³ h25.5v* h25.5s* h26s² Mar 30] fairly useful handicap hurdler: won at Hereford in January (amateur), February (conditional) and March: progressed again when second at Warwick: stays 3¼m: best form on soft/heavy going: wears cheekpieces: usually races prominently. *Nikki Evans*   h119

LATEST FASHION (IRE) 11 ch.m. Ashkalani (IRE) – Musical Bramble (IRE) (Accordion) [2016/17 c–x, h59: h23.3d⁶ h23.3g² May 24] poor maiden hurdler: failed to complete both starts over fences: stays 23f: acts on soft going: has worn headgear, including in 2016/17: wears tongue tie. *Christopher Wilson*   c– x h74

LAUGHARNE 6 b.g. Authorized (IRE) – Corsican Sunset (USA) (Thunder Gulch (USA)) [2016/17 h105: h19.1d h19.5g² h23.9m* h24.5dpu h23.9g h25g Apr 28] rather leggy gelding: fair hurdler: won novice at Taunton in December: stays 3m: acts on good to firm and good to soft going: front runner/races prominently. *Luke Dace*   h107

LAUGHTON PARK 12 ch.g. Karinga Bay – Brass Castle (IRE) (Carlingford Castle) [2016/17 h119: h23.1g⁵ May 6] well-made gelding: fairly useful handicap hurdler: stays 23f: acts on soft going. *Suzy Smith*   h107

LAURIUM 7 ch.g. Gold Away (IRE) – Silver Peak (FR) (Sillery (USA)) [2016/17 h135: h22.8mpu c20.9g³ c24.2g* c25.3g⁵ c23.8s⁵ c24m* c24.3gpu Apr 22] sturdy gelding: useful hurdler: useful form over fences: won novice handicap at Exeter in November and novice at Kempton in April: stays 3m: acts on soft and good to firm going: often races towards rear. *Nicky Henderson*   c141 h–

LAUTARET (FR) 5 b.g. Al Namix (FR) – Lesoquera (FR) (Lesotho (USA)) [2016/17 c18.9g³ c17.9g³ c16m³ c16gᵖᵘ Dec 10] half-brother to useful French hurdler/chaser Protektion (15f-21f winner, by Protektor): dam (c114/h110), French 15f-17f hurdle/chase winner, half-sister to very smart hurdler/useful chaser (stayed 33f) Korelo: lightly raced on Flat/over hurdles: fair form over fences: left G. Cherel after second start: stays 19f: acts on soft going: usually wears headgear: signs of temperament. *Jamie Snowden*   **c104 h–**

LAVA LAMP (GER) 10 b.g. Shamardal (USA) – La Felicita (Shareef Dancer (USA)) [2016/17 c–, h110§: h23.1d⁴ h23.3s⁴ h20.3v³ h16.8gᵖᵘ h19g² h21.9v⁴ Mar 19] sturdy gelding: fair handicap hurdler nowadays: winning chaser: stays 3m: acts on good to firm and heavy going: has worn headgear, including last 5 starts: tried in tongue tie: unreliable. *Evan Williams*   **c– § h101 §**

LAVAL NOIR (FR) 6 b.g. Laveron – Vale of Honor (FR) (Singspiel (IRE)) [2016/17 b107: h21.6d⁵ Nov 19] lengthy, rather unfurnished gelding: useful winner only start in bumpers: 25/1, fifth in novice at Ascot (19½ lengths behind Elegant Escape) on hurdling debut: should improve. *Kim Bailey*   **h105 p**

LA VATICANE (FR) 8 gr.m. Turgeon (USA) – Taking Off (FR) (Kahyasi) [2016/17 c140, h–: c23.9g² c21.1d⁵ c24g* c22.7g⁵ c26gᵖᵘ c34.3d Apr 8] rather leggy mare: winning hurdler: useful handicap chaser: won at Doncaster (by 4 lengths from Wings Attract) in December: stays 3m: acts on heavy going: wears blinkers/tongue tie: often races towards rear. *David Pipe*   **c137 h–**

LAVELLA WELLS 9 b.m. Alflora (IRE) – Jazzy Refrain (IRE) (Jareer (USA)) [2016/17 h16.7s⁶ h16.7s⁶ h15.7s⁵ Mar 8] workmanlike mare: little form over hurdles. *Sue Smith*   **h–**

LA VOIX (FR) 5 b.m. Voix du Nord (FR) – Loupaline (FR) (Loup Solitaire (USA)) [2016/17 h60: h16.8s⁶ h18.5dᵖᵘ h16.8m Jul 17] little form over hurdles: tried in tongue tie. *Jimmy Frost*   **h54**

LAW GREEN (IRE) 7 b.g. Lawman (FR) – Green Lassy (FR) (Green Tune (USA)) [2016/17 b17.1g Nov 7] tailed off in bumper: wore tongue tie. *Miss Elizabeth Anne Lalor, Ireland*   **b–**

LAWLESS ISLAND (IRE) 8 b.g. Heron Island (IRE) – Nylon (GER) (Law Society (USA)) [2016/17 c91, h91: c24.2g² c23mᵖᵘ Jul 4] long-backed gelding: winning Irish pointer: maiden hurdler: modest form over fences: stays 3m: acts on soft going. *Tim Vaughan*   **c94 h–**

LAWTOP LEGEND (IRE) 5 b.g. Milan – Nolagh Supreme (IRE) (Supreme Leader) [2016/17 b15.7d⁶ Dec 13] tailed off in bumper. *George Bewley*   **b–**

LAYERTHORPE (IRE) 5 b.g. Vale of York (IRE) – Strobinia (IRE) (Soviet Star (USA)) [2016/17 h85: h15.9g⁶ h15.9g⁵ h16.9d h20g⁵ h20mᶠ h21.6m⁵ Oct 6] modest maiden hurdler: unproven beyond 2m: tried in headgear/tongue tie. *Debra Hamer*   **h89**

LEADEROFTHEDANCE 8 b.m. Norse Dancer (IRE) – Glenda Lough (IRE) (Supreme Leader) [2016/17 h112: h25.6gᵖᵘ h20.5s² h21.6d⁵ h21.2mᵖᵘ Apr 18] fair handicap hurdler: stays 21f: acts on soft going: flashes tail and isn't one to trust. *Nicky Henderson*   **h108 §**

LEADING SCORE (IRE) 7 b.g. Scorpion (IRE) – Leading Rank (IRE) (Supreme Leader) [2016/17 h103: h17.1g² h19.3g³ h15.7d⁶ h16.4g c16.4m² Apr 19] fair maiden hurdler: 2/1, second in novice handicap at Sedgefield (10 lengths behind Alys Rock) on chasing debut: should stay 2½m: best form on good going: has worn headgear, including last 5 starts. *James Ewart*   **c96 h102**

LEAGUE OF HIS OWN (IRE) 8 ch.g. Beneficial – Miss Eastwood (IRE) (Commanche Run) [2016/17 c–, h–: h22gᵖᵘ h15.9v⁵ h15.3sᵖᵘ Mar 1] lengthy gelding: winning pointer: little form under Rules, mainly over hurdles: left Claire Dyson after first start: has worn hood, including in 2016/17: usually races freely. *Nick Mitchell*   **c– h–**

LEAN BURN (USA) 11 b.g. Johannesburg (USA) – Anthelion (USA) (Stop The Music (USA)) [2016/17 h80: h19.9g³ h19.9m⁵ Jun 9] poor handicap hurdler: stays 2½m: acts on heavy going: has worn headgear, including in 2016/17: has worn tongue tie, including last 5 starts. *Barry Leavy*   **h76**

LEANNA BAN 10 b.g. Alflora (IRE) – Gurleigh (IRE) (Pivotal) [2016/17 c118, h98: h21.4s c20.1sᵖᵘ c19.2s² c21.3d² c21.3g³ Apr 23] strong gelding: maiden hurdler: fair handicap chaser: stays 25f: acts on heavy going: wears tongue tie. *Tristan Davidson*   **c111 h–**

LEAPING RIVER (IRE) 7 b.m. Touch of Land (FR) – Executive Dream (IRE) (Executive Perk) [2016/17 b15.8m Jun 9] half-sister to fair 25f chase winner/prolific winning pointer Executive Benefit (by Beneficial): dam ran once in bumper: well held only completed start in points in 2015: tailed off in mares bumper. *Oliver Greenall*   **b–**

LEATH ACRA MOR (IRE) 11 b.g. King's Theatre (IRE) – Happy Native (IRE) **c– §** (Be My Native (USA)) [2016/17 c–§, h100§: h23spu May 11] fairly useful hurdler at best, **h– §** pulled up only start in 2016/17: winning chaser: stays 25f: acts on soft going: wears headgear: unreliable. *Ian Williams*

LEAVING LAS VEGAS 6 b.g. Layman (USA) – Woven Silk (USA) (Danzig (USA)) **h84** [2016/17 h81, b86: h18.7m5 h16.7d5 h19.9g h23.3gpu Jul 22] poor maiden hurdler: stays 19f: has worn tongue tie, including in 2016/17: often races towards rear. *William Kinsey*

LE BACARDY (FR) 11 b.g. Bahhare (USA) – La Balagna (Kris) [2016/17 c138, h–: **c116 §** c17.2d2 c17.4g5 c19.4d5 c17.2g4 c17g4 h16g Sep 23] rangy gelding: winning hurdler: **h– §** useful chaser at best: not same force nowadays, but won twice in points in 2017: stays 2½m: acts on heavy going: has worn headgear, including most starts in 2016/17: tried in tongue tie: often races towards rear: temperamental. *Grace Harris*

LE BRAYE (IRE) 5 b.g. Court Cave (IRE) – Salsaparilla (FR) (Lost World (IRE)) **h97** [2016/17 h20s5 h19.5gur h16.3d h16.7s h15.8s5 h16.8d3 h22g h21.9dF Apr 16] €21,000 3-y-o: workmanlike gelding: second foal: dam, maiden on Flat/ran twice over hurdles, half-sister to dam of useful hurdler/chaser around 2m Romain de Senam: modest maiden hurdler: unproven beyond 2½m: acts on soft going. *Dan Skelton*

LE BREUIL (FR) 5 ch.g. Anzillero (GER) – Slew Dancer (Fabulous Dancer (USA)) **h136** [2016/17 b16d* b16.7g4 h19.9d* h20.5s* h20gpu Apr 8] useful-looking gelding: brother to **b101** French hurdler/chaser Belenien (17f-2½m winner) and half-brother to several winners there on Flat: dam, maiden on Flat, half-sister to fairly useful 2m hurdle winner Slew Man: fairly useful performer in bumpers: won at Warwick in May: useful form over hurdles: won novices at Sedgefield in November and Newbury (by 9 lengths from Benatar) in March: likely to stay 3m: front runner/races prominently. *Ben Pauling*

LE CAPRICIEUX (FR) 6 b.g. Alberto Giacometti (IRE) – Eria Flore (FR) (Hero's **h107** Honor (USA)) [2016/17 h101: h16g2 h15.8g2 h15.8s3 h16g5 Nov 7] close-coupled gelding: fair form over hurdles: raced around 2m: acts on soft going. *Gary Moore*

LE COEUR NET (FR) 5 ch.g. Network (GER) – Silverwood (FR) (Garde Royale) **h99** [2016/17 h16d6 h15.3d h15.8d h15.9g3 Mar 2] modest form over hurdles: best effort at 3m: tried in hood/tongue tie: often races towards rear. *Anthony Honeyball*

LE DAUPHIN (IRE) 6 b.g. Robin des Champs (FR) – Miss Denman (IRE) (Presenting) **h119** [2016/17 h79: h20.5df h16.3d2 h21.2spu h21m* Apr 18] good-topped gelding: fairly useful form over hurdles: won novice at Kempton in April: stays 21f: front runner/races prominently. *Nicky Henderson*

LE DELUGE (FR) 7 b.g. Oratorio (IRE) – Princess Sofia (UAE) (Pennekamp (USA)) **h–** [2016/17 h16.8vro Feb 12] fair on Flat, stays 1½m: clear when ran out third in maiden at Sedgefield on hurdling debut: wore tongue tie. *Micky Hammond*

LE DRAPEAU (FR) 5 ch.g. Satri (IRE) – La Bandera (Bahhare (USA)) [2016/17 b16.8v6 **b76** b15.3v3 Mar 9] modest form in bumpers. *Oliver Sherwood*

LEE SIDE LADY (IRE) 7 ch.m. Mountain High (IRE) – Vicante (IRE) (Old Vic) **h104** [2016/17 h94: h20g* h20g2 h20.5g4 h20.6s3 h21s Feb 10] winning pointer: fair handicap hurdler: won lady amateur event at Fakenham in May: stays 21f: acts on heavy going: front runner/races prominently. *Neil Mulholland*

LEESWOOD LILY 4 b.f. Alflora (IRE) – Showtime Annie (Wizard King) [2016/17 **b75** b14d3 b12.6d4 Dec 14] sparely-made filly: second foal: dam (h83), maiden jumper (form only around 2m over hurdles), 6f-1m winner who stayed 1½m on Flat: modest form in bumpers. *Jennie Candlish*

LE FRANK (IRE) 5 b.g. King's Theatre (IRE) – Dream Lass (IRE) (Bob Back (USA)) **b84** [2016/17 b16.4v3 Mar 7] fifth foal: dam unraced half-sister to high-class chaser (2m-3m winner) Function Dream, herself dam of top-class chaser up to 3m Captain Chris (by King's Theatre): 11/4, third in maiden bumper at Newcastle (13½ lengths behind Niceandeasy) on debut: wore tongue tie. *Lucinda Russell*

LEFT BACK (IRE) 5 b.g. Oscar (IRE) – Baldrica (FR) (Lost World (IRE)) [2016/17 **h–** h16v6 h20.2g Apr 26] down the field on completed start in Irish points: well held in maiden hurdles: tried in hood/tongue tie. *N. W. Alexander*

LEGAL EXIT (IRE) 10 ch.g. Exit To Nowhere (USA) – New Legislation (IRE) (Dominion **c111** Royale) [2016/17 c92, h–: c15.9m3 May 5] winning pointer/hurdler: maiden chaser, fairly **h–** useful form at best: stays 2½m: acts on heavy going: in tongue tie last 2 starts. *Tom Lacey*

LEGAL OK (IRE) 5 b.g. Echo of Light – Desert Trail (IRE) (Desert Style (IRE)) [2016/17 **h94 p** b16.6g h16s³ h19.3m Apr 2] tall gelding: seventh foal: half-brother to 2 winners, including **b–** unreliable hurdler/chaser Morning Time (2m winner, by Hawk Wing): dam useful 1m winner: off mark in Irish points at second attempt: tailed off in bumper: modest form over hurdles: tried in tongue tie: remains capable of better. *Stuart Edmunds*

LEGENDARA 5 b.m. Midnight Legend – Samandara (FR) (Kris) [2016/17 b–: b13.6d **h79 ?** h16g h15.8m⁵ h16.3g⁴ h19.5g Apr 8] unfurnished mare: no form in bumpers: little form **b–** over hurdles. *Charlie Longsdon*

LEGEND LADY 6 b.m. Midnight Legend – Aoninch (Inchinor) [2016/17 h111p: h16.2s² **h114** Nov 23] bumper winner: fair form over hurdles: second in mares handicap at Hereford on sole outing in 2016/17: likely to stay further than 2m. *Oliver Sherwood*

LEG IRON (IRE) 12 b.g. Snurge – Southern Skies (IRE) (Dr Massini (IRE)) [2016/17 **c– §** c118§, h–: c28.8dᵖᵘ c25.5dᵖᵘ c25.7vᵖᵘ c25.5dᵖᵘ c25.5gᵖᵘ Apr 12] stocky gelding: once- **h– §** raced over hurdles: fairly useful chaser at best, no form in 2016/17: wears headgear: temperamental. *Sheena West*

LEG LOCK LUKE (IRE) 7 b.g. Indian River (FR) – Delirious Tantrum (IRE) (Taufan **c98 §** (USA)) [2016/17 h88: c25.7gᵖᵘ c16d⁴ c19.2s² c21.7g² c21.1v³ c16.1gᵘʳ c18.2g⁶ Mar 30] **h–** Irish point winner: maiden hurdler: modest maiden chaser: stays 2¾m: acts on soft going: tried in headgear/tongue tie: usually races close up: temperamental. *Colin Tizzard*

LE GRAND CHENE (FR) 11 b.g. Turgeon (USA) – Faitiche d'Aubry (FR) (Le Nain **c115** Jaune (FR)) [2016/17 c103§, h94§: c18.5d⁵ c20.1d* c20.1s* c20d⁴ c19.9g Aug 6] medium- **h–** sized gelding: winning hurdler: fairly useful handicap chaser: won at Perth in June and July: stayed 25f: acted on heavy going: often wore headgear/tongue tie: dead. *Gordon Elliott, Ireland*

LEIGHTON LASS 8 b.m. Shirocco (GER) – Kokila (Indian Danehill (IRE)) [2016/17 **h73** h16d³ h23g⁵ h16g⁴ h23.1gᵖᵘ Sep 28] 2,500 5-y-o: second foal: dam maiden on Flat (stayed 8.6f): dual winning pointer: poor form over hurdles: wears tongue tie. *Dan Skelton*

LEITH HILL (IRE) 7 b.g. Mountain High (IRE) – Ballinacariga Rose (IRE) (Revoque **h79** (IRE)) [2016/17 h58, b–: h21.6d⁵ h23mᵖᵘ Jul 4] poor form over hurdles: in headgear last 4 starts. *Laura Mongan*

LEITH HILL LAD 7 b.g. Kayf Tara – Leith Hill Star (Comme L'Etoile) [2016/17 h102, **h115** b78: h21m* h21.1g⁶ h23.1s⁵ h22.8g⁶ h23.8m³ Apr 25] good-topped gelding: off mark in points at third attempt: fairly useful form over hurdles: won novice at Kempton in October: should stay 3m: acts on good to firm going: front runner/races prominently. *Charlie Longsdon*

LEITH HILL LEGASI 8 b.m. Kahyasi – Leith Hill Star (Comme L'Etoile) [2016/17 **c91** c93, h–: c25.5sᵖᵘ c25.7g⁴ c25.5s⁴ c24.5v² c24.5s⁶ Mar 16] maiden hurdler: modest **h–** handicap chaser: stays 3¼m: acts on good to firm and heavy going: usually wears headgear: wears tongue tie: front runner/races prominently. *Charlie Longsdon*

LE LEGRO (IRE) 7 b.g. Mountain High (IRE) – Good To Travel (IRE) (Night Shift **c–** (USA)) [2016/17 h101, b92: h23.3v⁵ h23d² h24dᵖᵘ h23.1g⁵ h20m² h20d h20s⁴ c16.4dᵖᵘ **h97 x** h20.6dᵖᵘ Dec 26] bumper winner: modest maiden hurdler: pulled up in novice handicap on chasing debut: left Charlie Mann after fourth start: stays 23f: acts on good to firm and good to soft going: wears tongue tie: often let down by jumping. *Alexandra Dunn*

LE MARTALIN (FR) 6 ch.g. Martaline – Hembra (FR) (Croco Rouge (IRE)) [2016/17 **h139** b16s* h16.5d* h16d³ h16d³ h16d⁶ h20sᵖᵘ Apr 2] £55,000 3-y-o: fourth foal: dam, ran 3 **b107** times over hurdles in France (second at 2m), 1¼m winner on Flat: once-raced in points: won maiden at Listowel (by 14 lengths from Perfect Leader) only start in bumpers: useful form over hurdles: won maiden at Galway in October: third in For Auction Novices' Hurdle at Navan (4 lengths behind Labaik) in November and Royal Bond Novices' Hurdle at Fairyhouse (9¼ lengths behind Airlie Beach) in December: should stay beyond 2m: acts on good to soft going: wears headgear: in tongue tie last 4 starts: front runner/races prominently. *Noel Meade, Ireland*

LE MERCUREY (FR) 7 b.g. Nickname (FR) – Feroe (FR) (Bulington (FR)) [2016/17 **c151** c148, h–: c19.5g³ c25s² c23.8d⁵ c23.4d² c23.4v³ c34.3d Apr 8] good-topped gelding: **h–** winning hurdler: smart chaser: second in listed event at Aintree (3½ lengths behind Many Clouds) in December and Betfair Denman Chase at Newbury (3¼ lengths behind Native River) in February: stays 25f: acts on soft going: wears headgear/tongue tie: often races prominently. *Paul Nicholls*

Racing Post Arkle Trophy Trial Novices' Chase (November), Cheltenham—
Some Plan crashes out at the second last, leaving the way clear for Le Prezien (hoops) to provide
Paul Nicholls with a tenth win in the race

L'EMIR D'ART (FR) 4 ch.g. Dubai Destination (USA) – Art Machine (USA) (Sky Mesa **h93** (USA)) [2016/17 h16.7s^F h16s^4 h16.2d^6 h16g Apr 8] lengthy gelding: lightly raced on Flat in France: modest form over hurdles: tried in cheekpieces. *Jennifer Mason*

LEMON'S GENT 10 br.g. Generous (IRE) – Lemon's Mill (USA) (Roberto (USA)) **c109** [2016/17 c110, h–: c18m^5 c20d^{pu} c20.3v* c20.5g^{pu} c19.2g^3 c19.7m^2 Apr 17] big gelding: **h–** maiden hurdler: fair handicap chaser: won at Southwell in December: stays 3m: acts on good to firm and heavy going: wears headgear/tongue tie: front runner/races prominently. *Paul Webber*

LENEY COTTAGE (IRE) 10 b.g. Witness Box (USA) – Fleur de Tal (Primitive Rising **c106** (USA)) [2016/17 c103, h94: c20m^3 May 5] maiden hurdler: fair form over fences: stays **h–** 27f: acts on good to firm and heavy going: in tongue tie last 3 starts: usually travels strongly, tends to find little. *Maurice Barnes*

LENTEN ROSE (IRE) 5 b.m. Milan – Our Song (Classic Cliche (IRE)) [2016/17 h19.7g **h–** Oct 12] €5,500 3-y-o, £18,000 4-y-o: third foal: closely related to fair hurdler Rooster Byron (2m winner, by Oscar): dam unraced half-sister to smart hurdler/useful chaser (stays 2½m) Value At Risk and useful hurdler/chaser (stayed 3½m) Battlecry: third on second of 2 starts in Irish maiden points: well beaten in novice on hurdling debut: wore tongue tie. *Henry Hogarth*

LEODIS (IRE) 5 ch.g. Shirocco (GER) – Leonica (Lion Cavern (USA)) [2016/17 b15.7g^5 **b88** Mar 28] sixth foal: half-brother to 3 winners, including fairly useful hurdler/chaser Rock of Leon (2¼m-3m winner, by Rock of Gibraltar): dam 1m winner: 7/1, fifth in bumper at Southwell (8½ lengths behind Royal Ruby) in March. *Tom Tate*

LEO LUNA 8 b.g. Galileo (IRE) – Eva Luna (USA) (Alleged (USA)) [2016/17 c134§, **c126 §** h–: c23.8d c25.5d^2 Dec 6] tall gelding: winning hurdler: fairly useful handicap chaser: **h–** stays 3¼m: acts on heavy going: wears headgear: often wears tongue tie: untrustworthy. *Gary Moore*

LEONCAVALLO (IRE) 5 br.g. Cape Cross (IRE) – Nafura (Dubawi (IRE)) [2016/17 **h134** h144: h16.4g^2 h16.4s h20s^{pu} h19.6d h21.1g h24.7g Apr 8] neat gelding: useful handicap hurdler: largely below form in 2016/17: unproven beyond 17f: acts on good to soft going: in cheekpieces last 3 starts. *Ben Pauling*

LE PREZIEN (FR) 6 br.g. Blue Bresil (FR) – Abu Dhabi (FR) (Saint Cyrien (FR)) [2016/17 h144: c16d^2 c15.9s* c17.5v* c20v^3 c16.3g c21d^{pu} Apr 28] useful-looking gelding: useful hurdler: smart form over fences: won Grade 2 novice at Cheltenham (by 4 lengths from Hammersly Lake) in November and graduation event at Exeter (by 2¾ lengths from L'Ami Serge) in December: third in Scilly Isles Novices' Chase at Sandown (6¼ lengths behind Top Notch) in February: stays 2½m: acts on heavy going: wears tongue tie. *Paul Nicholls*
   c145
   h–

LE REVE (IRE) 9 br.g. Milan – Open Cry (IRE) (Montelimar (USA)) [2016/17 c149, h–: c27.3s^{ur} h23.5m c28.8g^{pu} Apr 29] tall, good sort: winning hurdler: smart chaser: no form in 2016/17: stays 29f: wears headgear: front runner/races prominently. *Lucy Wadham*
   c–
   h–

LERICHI BELLE (IRE) 6 b.m. King's Theatre (IRE) – Lerichi (IRE) (Shardari) [2016/17 b15.8d^5 b16v^5 h16v^4 h16.3g^2 Apr 1] fifth foal: closely related to fairly useful hurdler/fair chaser Prince of Denial (19f/2½m winner, by Old Vic): dam maiden half-sister to very smart staying chaser Hey Big Spender: modest form in bumpers: fair form over hurdles: better effort when second in novice at Stratford: wears hood. *Martin Keighley*
   h106
   b84

LE ROCHER (FR) 7 b.g. Saint des Saints (FR) – Belle du Roi (FR) (Adieu Au Roi (IRE)) [2016/17 h15.7d^4 h18.9s^2 h19.9v* h19.1s^2 Feb 26] tall gelding: useful handicap hurdler: won at Uttoxeter (by length from Tintern Theatre) in January: second in National Spirit Hurdle at Fontwell (29 lengths behind Camping Ground) month later: stays 2½m: acts on heavy going. *Nick Williams*
   h145

L'ES FREMANTLE (FR) 6 b.g. Orpen (USA) – Grand Design (Danzero (AUS)) [2016/17 c–, h–: h20.3m h16.7d^{pu} Dec 26] poor maiden on Flat: no form over jumps. *Michael Chapman*
   c–
   h–

LESSONS IN MILAN (IRE) 9 b.g. Milan – Lessons Lass (IRE) (Doyoun) [2016/17 c130, h–: c23.4d^3 c22.4d^5 c23.4d^2 c26g c31.8g^5 Apr 22] big, rangy gelding: winning hurdler: useful maiden chaser: filled upsides fifth of 30 to Vicente in Scottish Grand National at Ayr final start: stays 4m: acts on heavy going: in cheekpieces last 3 starts: often races towards rear: temperament under suspicion. *Nicky Henderson*
   c136
   h–

LETBESO (IRE) 9 ch.g. Vinnie Roe (IRE) – Go Hunting (IRE) (Abednego) [2016/17 c–§, h109§: h23.9g^4 h22.1m* h23m^4 c24g* c25.5g h23g c25.6g^{pu} Nov 10] fair handicap hurdler: won at Cartmel in June: fairly useful handicap chaser: won at Southwell in August: stays 3¼m: acts on good to firm and heavy going: wears headgear/tongue tie: temperamental. *Peter Bowen*
   c123 §
   h113 §

LETEMGO (IRE) 9 b.g. Brian Boru – Leteminletemout (IRE) (Be My Native (USA)) [2016/17 c114, h–: c24d^{pu} h25.6g^5 h21.6d h20.5d^2 h25d^3 h25v^5 h21.6v* h21.6s^3 Feb 26] fair handicap hurdler: won at Fontwell in January: maiden chaser: left Giles Smyly after first start: stays 3m: acts on good to firm and heavy going: wears headgear: has worn tongue tie, including final start. *Chris Gordon*
   c–
   h102

LETHEGOODTIMESROLL (IRE) 6 ch.m. Mahler – Little Pearl (IRE) (Bigstone (IRE)) [2016/17 b–: b16.4s^4 Jan 7] won Irish maiden point on debut: no form in bumpers (ran out first start). *Brian Ellison*
   b– §

LET'S DANCE (FR) 5 b.m. Poliglote – Baraka du Berlais (FR) (Bonnet Rouge (FR)) [2016/17 h138p: h16d^2 h16d* h18s* h20d* h20g* h16.8g* h20d^2 h20g^4 Apr 28]
   h141

     There have been forty-eight-hour declarations for British Flat racing for over ten years (after trials with the all-weather, the system finally came in for all Flat races in the middle of 2006). On the jumping front, however, there has always been strong resistance to pushing back the declaration time. A piecemeal approach over the years has led to earlier declarations for Grade 1 non-novice events and the major handicaps (as well as for all racing on Sundays, for which runners are declared on Friday) but it really is time, particularly given the potential value of the global market for British racing, that forty-eight-hour declarations were extended to bring the whole of British racing more into line with the international standard for declarations. No other major racing country outside the British Isles operates a system of overnight declarations and none of the arguments against earlier declarations is particularly convincing. Most trainers know at least two days in advance which races their horses are going for, and the supposition that horses can develop heat in a leg or fail to eat up, or that sudden downpours can change the going, doesn't stand up to scrutiny. The well-being of horses can alter overnight—as shown by the number of self-certified withdrawals on the day of racing—and, given the vagaries of the British climate,

Nathaniel Lacy & Partners Solicitors '€50,000 Cheltenham Bonus For Stable Staff' Novices' Hurdle, Leopardstown—Let's Dance lands the odds in impressive fashion

the going can change in hours, let alone days. Both are poor reasons for objecting to forty-eight-hour declarations which are needed to enable the proper promotion of jumping in a crowded winter sporting calendar. Publicising the big meetings, in particular, could be more effective if all the runners were known earlier, and, with the prosperity of racing directly linked to the profits of the betting industry, anything that might help to stimulate higher turnover ought to be welcomed (so long as it does not affect the sport's integrity or its public appeal). To guard against any increase in the number of non-runners (which can never be eliminated entirely), it would probably be wise to come up with a disincentive for withdrawing horses, given that self-certification is open to abuse. Examples are not hard to find of horses being withdrawn on account of 'unsuitable going', only to start a couple of days afterwards in races for which the going description is virtually the same. Some steps have been announced to tackle abuses of the non-runner rule, including suspending a trainer's power to self-certify in certain circumstances, but perhaps horses that are withdrawn after the final declaration stage should be sidelined automatically for at least a further week before being allowed to run.

Forty-eight hour declarations already apply for the Grade 1 non-novice events at jumping's most prestigious meeting, the Cheltenham Festival, and it is nonsensical, given the importance of those four days, that the same is not done for the rest of the races at the fixture—irrespective of whether the system is ever universally adopted for jumping meetings. The final make-up of the fields at the Cheltenham Festival—a meeting anticipated by racegoers and punters all year—is too often shrouded in uncertainty and, apart from punters being frustrated through not knowing what is running, the sport is also missing out on valuable extra time created by forty-eight-hour declarations that could be given to promotion and the opportunity to bet at one of the year's most popular fixtures. The more publicity that can be generated around big meetings like Cheltenham, the more opportunity there is to widen interest in a branch of the sport that has much to offer at the moment.

The expansion of the Cheltenham Festival by the addition of a fourth day fulfilled a demand and enhanced the meeting's profitability, but it has also created more choice for the connections of good horses which, in turn, has made running plans hard for racegoers and punters to pin down.

No stable's running plans have become more difficult to guess in recent years than those of the 2016 Closutton juggernaut of Willie Mullins. In the ante-post betting for the 2016 Festival, for example, Annie Power, Bellshill, Black Hercules, Shaneshill, Vautour and Yorkhill were all favourite or joint favourite at one time for races in which, in the end, they did not run. Bellshill, Shaneshill and Yorkhill were back again at the latest Festival and Yorkhill, winner of the Baring Bingham Novices' Hurdle in 2016, had a range of options. A month before Cheltenham, he was prominent in the ante-post betting on the Arkle (second favourite behind Altior), the Champion Hurdle (favourite—in the enforced absence of Annie Power and Faugheen—with some bookmakers, though he needed supplementing) and the Golden Miller Novices' Chase (7/4 favourite generally in the race eventually chosen for him). Another Closutton inmate Vroum Vroum Mag held entries for no fewer than six races, while the novice hurdler Let's Dance, in the frame without winning on all starts in her 2015/16 campaign (including in the Triumph Hurdle and the Four Year Old Hurdle at Punchestown), had five entries.

Let's Dance had got off the mark in a maiden hurdle at Sligo in May (her second to Apple's Jade in the Four Year Old Hurdle technically being her first start in the latest season) and, after a summer break, she went on to complete a hat-trick by adding the listed Grabel Mares' Hurdle at Punchestown and the Grade 3 Mares' Hurdle at Leopardstown's Christmas fixture, jumping fluently and winning readily both times. A fourth successive win—again at short odds—was chalked up in January when Let's Dance beat male opposition in the Nathaniel Lacy & Partners Solicitors '€50,000 Cheltenham Bonus for Stable Staff' Novices' Hurdle over two and a half miles at Leopardstown, beating her stablemate Kemboy by six lengths. The two-mile Dawn Run Mares' Novices' Hurdle looked the most 'winnable' race for Let's Dance at Cheltenham but Mullins hinted after her Leopardstown victory at Christmas that the David Nicholson Mares' Hurdle over two and a half might be a more likely option. 'I'd say anyway that she may be going up in trip, rather than down,' he said after Leopardstown. The Dawn Run has Grade 2 status but, in addition to the David Nicholson, Let's Dance had three other Grade 1 entries in the novice races at Cheltenham, in the Supreme, the Baring Bingham and the Spa. Her ante-post odds a month before Cheltenham varied wildly for the Spa over three miles, ranging from 5/1 and 6/1 second favourite respectively with bet365 and Hills to 14/1 with Betfair, while her odds for the Baring Bingham over two miles five furlongs varied from 8/1 fourth favourite with Hills and Paddy Power to 16/1 with Betfair (Let's Dance was generally clear second favourite at 7/2 and 4/1 behind her unbeaten stablemate Airlie Beach in the Dawn Run and fifth best at 8/1 for the

Trull House Stud Mares' Novices' Hurdle (Dawn Run), Cheltenham—Let's Dance provides her connections with a second successive win in this new race; 2016 third Dusky Legend (second right) fills that position again, whilst Verdana Blue (centre) fades into fourth

David Nicholson, in which other stablemates Vroum Vroum Mag and Limini were more prominent in the betting). Not knowing until close to declaration time whether Let's Dance would run on Tuesday (in the Supreme or the David Nicholson), Wednesday (in the Baring Bingham), Thursday (in the Dawn Run) or Friday (in the Spa) was frustrating, not least because it was difficult to bet on any of the races in which she might be involved until a decision had been taken. The eventual choice of the Dawn Run (despite Let's Dance dropping back down in trip) was said to have been influenced by the stable-staff bonus on offer if she added a race at the Festival to her success in the Nathaniel Lacy & Partners Novices' Hurdle at Leopardstown.

The Dawn Run, branded as the Trull House Stud Mares' Novices' Hurdle, attracted a stronger field for its second running than the one beaten by Let's Dance's stablemate Limini twelve months earlier. Let's Dance, who was sweating profusely, was the choice of stable jockey Ruby Walsh and started 11/8 favourite in a field of sixteen, with 4/1-shot Airlie Beach, going for her eighth successive win, the only other runner at single-figure odds. The 14/1-shot Asthuria gave the Mullins stable a third string to its bow, while the Elliott-trained Darra added to Ireland's strong hand (Irish runners accounted for half the field). The home defence was headed by La Bague Au Roi, whose three wins in the current season included one at Newbury over the previous year's 50/1 runner-up Dusky Legend (a 20/1-shot this time), while Nicky Henderson saddled Verdana Blue, unbeaten on her completed starts over hurdles, and Paul Nicholls was represented by prolific winner Coillte Lass, who also had a victory in the current season over Dusky Legend to her name. The race was run at a strong gallop, which suited Let's Dance, who was produced at the last after being patiently ridden to win by two and three quarter lengths (giving her owners a belated visit to the winner's circle at the 2017 Festival) from Barra, who was also held up. Dusky Legend was just a neck behind in third, with Verdana Blue the same distance back in fourth. Fifth and sixth went to Irish-trained runners through Asthuria and 100/1-shot Awayinthewest, while the prominently-ridden La Bague Au Roi was below form in seventh. Fellow pace-setter Airlie Beach beat only one home.

Let's Dance, Barra and Airlie Beach met again in a good renewal of the Grade 1 novice event for mares over two and a half miles at Fairyhouse's Easter fixture and they finished in the same order as at Cheltenham, odds-on Let's Dance losing nothing in defeat when narrowly beaten by her stable-companion Augusta Kate, with Barra third and a below-form Airlie Beach only sixth of seven. Let's Dance again ran well when fourth behind another stablemate Bacardys, and two other Grade 1 winners in Finian's Oscar and Death Duty, in the Champion Novices' Hurdle over two and a half miles at Punchestown. Vroum Vroum Mag and Limini, both of whom also carry the pink, light green spots, pink sleeves and cap of Susannah and Rich Ricci, are clearly established at the top of the pecking order among the mares at Closutton, but there are undoubtedly more races to be won with the genuine Let's Dance who doesn't know how to run a bad race.

Let's Dance was bought by present connections after finishing second in a three-year-old hurdle for Guillaume Macaire and is by France's top sire of jumpers Poliglote, who is still plying his trade—though being carefully managed—at the Haras d'Etreham at the ripe old age of twenty-five. The dam of Let's Dance, Baraka du Berlais, was useful over hurdles and won in listed company as a juvenile when she was also second to Long Run in the Prix Georges de Talhouet-Roy, a Group 2 event; Baraka du Berlais, who went on to show fairly useful form over fences, was also represented on the racecourse in Britain in the latest season by her third foal Lad of Luck (by Soldier of Fortune), a year-younger half-brother to Let's Dance, who won a bumper at Chepstow for Jonjo O'Neill on his only start. Cindy Cad, the grandam of Let's Dance, was a sister to a leading French hurdler of the 'nineties

Mrs S. Ricci's "Let's Dance"

Tenerific and she won a fifteen-furlong hurdle at Auteuil as a three-year-old and was placed over fences. She has bred numerous winners in France, but one who didn't win was Boheme du Berlais who showed fair form when placed over hurdles and is the dam of probably the best known member of the family to British and Irish racegoers, the smart hurdler/chaser Gitane du Berlais who began her career in France before joining Willie Mullins, in whose care she became the first mare to win the Grade 1 Scilly Isles Novices' Chase. The well-made Let's Dance has the physique to make a chaser and, like the versatile pair Gitane du Berlais and Vroum Vroum Mag who have done particularly well for their stable, she might end up switching successfully between hurdling and chasing. Let's Dance travels strongly in her races but will almost certainly stay beyond two and a half miles (she is effective at shorter). She acts on heavy going but doesn't need testing conditions. She wore ear plugs at Cheltenham, as did a number of the other runners saddled by Willie Mullins. *W. P. Mullins, Ireland*

LETS DO THIS THING (IRE) 4 b.g. Thewayyouare (USA) – Margaux Dancer (IRE) **h–**
(Danehill Dancer (IRE)) [2016/17 h16.2d^{pu} Jun 4] pulled up in juvenile hurdle: wore cheekpieces. *Jamie Snowden*

LETS GET SERIOUS (IRE) 11 b.g. Overbury (IRE) – Vendimia (Dominion) [2016/17 **c– §**
c111§, h–: c26.3g^{pu} c24.2g^5 Apr 25] good-topped gelding: winning hurdler: useful chaser **h–**
at best, no form in hunters in 2016/17 after long absence: stays 3½m: acts on heavy going: has worn headgear: not one to trust. *C. J. Miller*

LETS GO DUTCHESS 7 h.m. Helissio (FR) – Lets Go Dutch (Nicholas Bill) [2016/17 **h98**
b82: b15.3m^3 h21.6g^{pu} h16g h16g^3 h16g^4 h16g^4 h19.9d^2 h19.8d^2 h19g^4 h19.8d^2 h21.6m* **b82**
Apr 15] sturdy mare: modest form in bumpers: modest handicap hurdler: won at Taunton in November and Newton Abbot in April: bred to stay 3m: acts on good to firm and good to soft going: often races in rear, usually travels strongly. *Kevin Bishop*

LETS HOPE SO 7 b.m. Generous (IRE) – Baily Mist (IRE) (Zaffaran (USA)) [2016/17   **h111**
h102p: h15.7s^F h16.8d^3 h16g* h19.5g^6 Oct 8] bumper winner: fair form over hurdles: won
mares maiden at Worcester in July: should stay beyond 2m: acts on heavy going: sometimes
in hood: usually travels strongly. *Emma Lavelle*

LET'S TANGO (IRE) 6 ch.g. Mahler – Miss Ogan (IRE) (Supreme Leader) [2016/17   **h96**
h–, b–: h20.5g^6 h19.4g^6 h19.7d^3 Mar 21] good-topped gelding: modest form over hurdles.
Ben Case

LETTER EXIT (IRE) 7 b.g. Exit To Nowhere (USA) – Letterwoman (IRE) (Fourstars   **c72**
Allstar (USA)) [2016/17 c–, h–: c19.9d^pu c23.5v^F Mar 6] placed in Irish maiden points: **h–**
twice-raced hurdler: failed to complete all 3 starts in chases (running to poor level when
falling 3 out in handicap at Lingfield in first-time hood). *Lucy Wadham*

LETTHERIVERRUNDRY (IRE) 7 br.g. Diamond Green (FR) – Dissitation (IRE)   **c91**
(Spectrum (IRE)) [2016/17 h116: h20.6g^2 h18.6d* c15.7d^4 c17.4s^pu h18.9s^pu Dec 17]   **h116**
big, strong gelding: fairly useful hurdler: won novice at Market Rasen in May: showed a
bit on first of 2 starts over fences: stays 21f: acts on good to soft going: tried in cheekpieces.
Brendan Powell

LEVELLING 5 ch.m. Pivotal – Lane County (USA) (Rahy (USA)) [2016/17 h96: h16d^3   **h94**
h16.2d^5 h15.7d^6 h15.5g Dec 1] modest maiden hurdler: left Dan Skelton after first start,
Marjorie Fife after third: raced around 2m: acts on good to soft going: sometimes in
cheekpieces. *Laura Morgan*

LEVIATHAN 10 b.g. Dubawi (IRE) – Gipsy Moth (Efisio) [2016/17 h116: h15.8v^4 h20.5s   **h94**
h15.8s^5 h19.2s^5 Mar 16] compact gelding: fairly useful handicap hurdler at best, on
downgrade: unproven beyond 2m: acts on heavy going. *Venetia Williams*

LEXINGTON LAW (IRE) 4 b.g. Lawman (FR) – Tus Nua (IRE) (Galileo (IRE))   **h92 p**
[2016/17 h15.8d^6 Feb 22] dam (b105) won both starts in bumpers: fairly useful maiden on
Flat, stays 1½m: 7/1, sixth in maiden at Ludlow (22¾ lengths behind Ridgeway Flyer) on
hurdling debut: should do better. *Alan King*

LEXI'S BOY (IRE) 9 gr.g. Verglas (IRE) – Jazan (IRE) (Danehill (USA)) [2016/17 h84:   **h65**
h16.4s^6 Jan 7] well-made gelding: fairly useful on Flat, stays 16.5f: useful hurdler at best,
has become disappointing: best form at 2m: acts on heavy going: in cheekpieces last 3
starts: in tongue tie last 4. *Donald McCain*

LEYLAND (IRE) 8 b.g. Peintre Celebre (USA) – Lasting Chance (USA) (American   **h–**
Chance (USA)) [2016/17 h21.2g^pu Nov 10] modest on Flat nowadays, stays 1½m: maiden
hurdler, no form since 2012/13: usually wears headgear. *Natalie Lloyd-Beavis*

L FRANK BAUM 10 b.g. Sinndar (IRE) – Rainbow City (IRE) (Rainbow Quest   **h80**
(USA)) [2016/17 h85: h18.5d^6 h19.5d^2 h23.8d^4 h23.3v^6 h25.5v^2 h20s^6 h23.6s Mar 13]
good-topped gelding: poor handicap hurdler: stays 3¼m: acts on heavy going: wears
headgear: often races prominently. *Bernard Llewellyn*

LIBBY T VALANCE (IRE) 6 b.m. Scorpion (IRE) – Dipp In The Dark (IRE)   **h95 p**
(Presenting) [2016/17 b16d* h19.5m^3 Nov 2] €12,500 3-y-o: first foal: dam (h84), lightly   **b83**
raced over hurdles, sister to useful hurdler (stayed 25f) Time Electric and fairly useful
hurdler/smart chaser (stays 4m) Haymount: won mares bumper at Worcester (by head from
Raveloe) in June: 11/4, third in maiden at Chepstow (2¼ lengths behind Burton Boru) on
hurdling debut: bred to stay 2¾m+: should improve. *Rebecca Curtis*

LIBECCIO (FR) 6 b.g. Shirocco (GER) – Francais (Mark of Esteem (IRE)) [2016/17   **h118**
h122: h20.5g^ur May 8] leggy gelding: fairly useful handicap hurdler: stayed 21f: acted on
heavy going: wore hood/tongue tie: dead. *Charlie Mann*

LICKPENNY LARRY 6 gr.g. Sagamix (FR) – Myriah (IRE) (Strong Gale) [2016/17   **h68**
b60: h18.6s^F h15.5d h15.8v^4 h16v Mar 12] lengthy, angular gelding: poor form over
hurdles: tried in tongue tie. *Tom Gretton*

LIEUTENANT COLONEL 8 b.g. Kayf Tara – Agnese (Abou Zouz (USA)) [2016/17   **c126**
c–, h148: h24d^6 c18d* c18g^pu c20d^pu h20d^5 h24d Apr 27] tall gelding: smart hurdler: fairly   **h148**
useful form over fences: won maiden at Gowran in October: pulled up in graded novices
next 2 starts: left Ms Sandra Hughes after first start: stays 3m: acts on good to firm and
heavy going: tried in cheekpieces: usually wears tongue tie nowadays: has carried head
awkwardly. *Gordon Elliott, Ireland*

LIEUTENANT GRUBER (IRE) 6 b.g. Scorpion (IRE) – Tanit Lady (IRE) (Presenting)   **h119**
[2016/17 b77: b17m* h18.6s^F h16.8g^3 Dec 9] strong, workmanlike gelding: fair form in   **b91**
bumpers: won at Carlisle in May: fairly useful form over hurdles: third to Pingshou in
novice at Cheltenham on completed start: left Henry Daly after first start: will stay 2½m.
Dan Skelton

LIFEBOAT MONA 7 b.m. Kayf Tara – Astar Love (FR) (Astarabad (USA)) [2016/17 **h134** h121: h21.6d* h19.8s* h19.9g Mar 14] tall, useful-looking mare: winning pointer: useful form over hurdles: won mares handicap at Ascot in November and listed mares event at Sandown (by 3 lengths from Midnight Jazz) in January: stays 2¾m: acts on heavy going: wears tongue tie: often travels strongly. *Paul Nicholls*

LIFE KNOWLEDGE (IRE) 5 ch.g. Thewayyouare (USA) – Rosa Bellini (IRE) **h95** (Rossini (USA)) [2016/17 h15.6g³ h15.7s² h16.4g⁴ Mar 24] fair on Flat, stays 12.5f: modest form over hurdles: best effort when fourth in novice handicap at Musselburgh. *Patrick Holmes*

LIFT THE LID (IRE) 7 b.g. Robin des Pres (FR) – Kindly Light (IRE) (Supreme **h112** Leader) [2016/17 h94p, b81: h22.1m⁶ h16s* h16s* Dec 26] fair handicap hurdler: won at Fakenham (novice) in November and Wetherby in December: best form at 2m: acted on soft going: in cheekpieces last 3 starts: in tongue tie last 2: usually raced close up: dead. *Neil Mulholland*

LIGHT BREAKS (IRE) 5 b.g. Dylan Thomas (IRE) – Anywaysmile (IRE) (Indian **h72** Ridge) [2016/17 h–: h16.8m⁵ h16.3gᵖᵘ Aug 18] poor form over hurdles: in cheekpieces last 2 starts. *Nigel Twiston-Davies*

LIGHTENING ROD 12 b.g. Storming Home – Bolero (Rainbow Quest (USA)) **c123 §** [2016/17 c124, h114: c17g³ c16.5g⁶ c17mᵖᵘ h16g⁶ h16d⁴ h16.8d⁵ c15.7d² c15.2d² c15.2m² **h105** Apr 13] workmanlike gelding: useful handicap hurdler at best, not same force nowadays: fairly useful handicap chaser (enthusiasm on wane): unproven beyond 17f: acts on good to firm and heavy going. *Michael Easterby*

LIGHTENTERTAINMENT (IRE) 9 b.g. King's Theatre (IRE) – Dochas Supreme **c–** (IRE) (Supreme Leader) [2016/17 h119: h19.8mᵖᵘ h20.5g² h20.3g⁵ h19.9v⁶ h19.5g **h112 d** h20.5sᵖᵘ c16vᵖᵘ h23.4gᵖᵘ Apr 17] workmanlike gelding: fair handicap hurdler: lost form after second start: pulled up in novice handicap on chasing debut: left Chris Gordon after third start: stays 21f: acts on heavy going: tried in cheekpieces. *Barry Brennan*

LIGHT FLICKER (IRE) 5 b.g. Royal Anthem (USA) – Five Cents More (IRE) **b–** (Flemensfirth (USA)) [2016/17 b16v⁶ Mar 12] well held in bumper. *Harry Chisman*

LIGHTNING STEPS 5 b.g. Champs Elysees – Fairy Steps (Rainbow Quest (USA)) **h84** [2016/17 h16.4d h20.8g⁴ h21.2d h24.1sᵖᵘ Dec 27] modest on Flat, stays 2m: little impact over hurdles: tried in blinkers. *Declan Carroll*

LIGHT OF AIR (FR) 4 b.g. Youmzain (IRE) – Height of Vanity (IRE) (Erhaab (USA)) **h93** [2016/17 h16s⁵ h16.3d h16s⁶ Jan 7] good-topped gelding: dam half-sister to useful hurdler (stayed 3m) Seventh Sign: fairly useful on Flat, stays 13f: best effort in juvenile hurdles when fifth at Sandown in December: tried in visor. *Gary Moore*

LIGHT OF THE MOON (IRE) 6 b.g. Echo of Light – Song of Sixpence (IRE) **h–** (Among Men (USA)) [2016/17 h17d h15.8m⁶ Oct 20] poor maiden on Flat: no form over hurdles: left Eugene M. O'Sullivan after first start: wears tongue tie. *David Evans*

LIGHTS OF BROADWAY (IRE) 11 b.m. Broadway Flyer (USA) – Supreme Call **c– x** (IRE) (Supreme Leader) [2016/17 c–x, h–: h20.5gᶠ h20.7dᵖᵘ Dec 26] angular mare: fair **h97** handicap hurdler: maiden chaser (let down by jumping): stays 2¾m: acts on heavy going: has worn tongue tie. *Mike Murphy*

LIGHT THAT (IRE) 5 b.g. Echo of Light – Tucum (IRE) (Diktat) [2016/17 h16.7d² **h131** h16d* h16g h16d* h16d h16g h16.5d² Apr 25] fair on Flat, stays 1¼m: useful hurdler: won maiden at Cork in October and novice at Gowran in November: second in handicap at Punchestown (1½ lengths behind Western Boy) in April: raced around 2m: acts on good to soft going: front runner/races prominently. *Mrs J. Harrington, Ireland*

LIGNY (FR) 4 ch.g. Fuisse (FR) – Light Wave (FR) (Marignan (USA)) [2016/17 b16.3g **b– p** Mar 25] £26,000 3-y-o: good-topped gelding: half-brother to several winners, including fair hurdler/useful chaser Lidar (2m/17f winner, by Take Risks) and French hurdler/chaser Afterlight (2m-3m winner, by Kahyasi): dam French 13f winner: 9/2, well beaten in Goffs UK Spring Sales Bumper at Newbury: should do better. *Nicky Henderson*

LIKE A DIAMOND (IRE) 7 b.g. Antonius Pius (USA) – Silk Law (IRE) (Barathea **h98** (IRE)) [2016/17 h16.2d³ h16.7g⁴ h17.1d h15.5g⁵ h15.6g Jan 3] fairly useful on Flat, stays 1½m: fair maiden hurdler: raced around 2m: acts on good to firm going: often in headgear: usually leads. *Brian Ellison*

LIKE SULLY (IRE) 9 b.g. Presenting – Swing Into Action (IRE) (Be My Native (USA)) **c108** [2016/17 c104, h89: c19.7g* c20d⁶ c19.7d⁴ c20g³ c19.7s² c25.7vᵖᵘ c24g⁵ Mar 18] **h–** good-topped gelding: winning hurdler: fair handicap chaser: won at Plumpton in May: stays 3¼m: acts on heavy going: has worn cheekpieces. *Richard Rowe*

LIKE THE SOUND (FR) 6 b.g. Soldier of Fortune (IRE) – Zalida (IRE) (Machiavellian (USA)) [2016/17 h19.1s h19.9v* h21s² h19.5v⁴ h22g* h21.9d² Apr 16] half-brother to fairly useful 2m hurdle winner Super Kenny (by Kendor): maiden on Flat in France: fairly useful hurdler: won conditional/amateur maiden at Uttoxeter in December and handicap at Stratford in March: stays 2¾m: acts on heavy going: front runner. *Charlie Mann* **h120**

LILAC TREE 7 b.g. Dubawi (IRE) – Kalidasa (USA) (Nureyev (USA)) [2016/17 h125: h16.3g h16.3mᵖᵘ h17.7g⁵ h15.8m³ h16m³ Nov 2] fairly useful handicap hurdler at best, below that level in 2016/17: stays easy 2½m: acts on soft and good to firm going: tried in hood: often races towards rear. *Richard Rowe* **h105**

LILBITLUSO (IRE) 9 b.g. Luso – Izntitgreat (IRE) (Montelimar (USA)) [2016/17 c26g* c27.5m² c23gᵖᵘ Jan 11] won all 4 completed starts in points: maiden hurdler: fair form in chases: won hunter at Cheltenham very early in season: stays 3½m: acts on soft and good to firm going: tried in hood: often races prominently. *J. J. O'Shea* **c112 h–**

LILLIAN (IRE) 6 b.m. Milan – Kay Tully (Kahyasi) [2016/17 b89: h21g* h21.2m⁴ h19.2g⁴ h20.7d⁵ h21.6v⁵ h23.1g³ h23.9m³ Jun 20] small mare: bumper winner: fair hurdler: won mares maiden at Towcester in May: stays 3m: acts on good to firm going. *Seamus Mullins* **h99**

LILLINGTON (IRE) 5 br.g. Westerner – Kind Word (IRE) (Yashgan) [2016/17 b75: h18.5g⁶ h16m⁴ h21s h15.3s² h16.2v³ h19.8d³ h19.5g³ Apr 17] fair maiden hurdler: stays 19f: acts on soft going: in tongue tie last 3 starts. *Colin Tizzard* **h111**

LILLY OF THE MOOR 9 b.m. Flemensfirth (USA) – Serenique (Good Thyne (USA)) [2016/17 h101: c20s* c24v⁵ c24v⁶ c22.5v² Jan 28] maiden hurdler: fair form over fences: won mares handicap at Warwick in November: stays 3¼m: acts on heavy going. *Ben Case* **c109 h–**

LILLY'S LEGEND 7 ch.m. Midnight Legend – Dalticia (FR) (Cadoudal (FR)) [2016/17 h76: h24v² h24.1s⁶ c24vᵖᵘ c20.9d c24.2g Apr 25] poor handicap hurdler: little show over fences: stays 25f: acts on good to firm and heavy going: wears cheekpieces. *Mark Walford* **c54 h78**

LIL ROCKERFELLER (USA) 6 ch.g. Hard Spun (USA) – Layounne (USA) (Mt Livermore (USA)) [2016/17 h155: h24.1g³ h19.3d² h24.4d² h20.3s⁴ h24g² h24d Apr 27] well-made gelding: high-class hurdler: placed in West Yorkshire Hurdle at Wetherby (3¼ lengths behind Silsol) in October, Coral Hurdle (¾ length behind Yanworth) in November and Long Walk Hurdle (4½ lengths behind Unowhatimeanharry) in December, last 2 at Ascot, and Stayers' Hurdle at Cheltenham (career-best effort, ¾ length behind Nichols Canyon) in March: stays 3m: acts on heavy going: wears cheekpieces. *Neil King* **h162**

LILY LITTLE LEGS (IRE) 8 gr.m. Westerner – Silvers Promise (IRE) (Presenting) [2016/17 c98, h94: c19.3dᵖᵘ c19.2gᵘʳ Jun 3] leggy mare: winning hurdler: modest handicap chaser: yet to be asked for effort when unseated 4 out at Market Rasen in June: stays 3m: acts on heavy going: tried in cheekpieces. *Mike Sowersby* **c? h–**

LILYWHITE GESTURE (IRE) 8 b.m. Presenting – Loyal Gesture (IRE) (Darazari (IRE)) [2016/17 h91: h20.3vᵖᵘ h20.1g h23.3mᵖᵘ h23.6d⁵ h27g* h22.1d⁴ h23.9g³ h23.9s⁴ h23.8m⁴ h23.3d⁴ h23.3v² h24sᵖᵘ Dec 11] rather leggy mare: fair handicap hurdler: won at Sedgefield in August: left Fergal O'Brien after third start: stays 27f: acts on good to firm and heavy going: wears tongue tie nowadays. *Gordon Elliott, Ireland* **h99**

LILY YEATS (IRE) 6 b.m. Yeats (IRE) – Opatja (Nashwan (USA)) [2016/17 h16.7d* h19.5g⁶ h16g* h20.2d² c18.5g² c16sᵘʳ Nov 22] first foal: dam (h105), 17f hurdle winner, also 9f-11f winner on Flat in Italy, half-sister to useful hurdler (2m/17f winner) Moving On Up: fair form over hurdles: won mares maiden at Bangor in May and mares handicap at Tramore in August: fair form over fences: second in mares maiden at Clonmel on completed start: stays 2½m: acts on good to soft going: in hood last 4 starts: wears tongue tie: front runner/races prominently: remains open to improvement over fences. *Shane Crawley, Ireland* **c106 p h112**

LIME STREET (IRE) 6 b.g. Presenting – Specifiedrisk (IRE) (Turtle Island (IRE)) [2016/17 h98, b79: h20.3d c23.6d⁴ c24.2s h25d⁴ h24sᵖᵘ h21.9d³ Apr 16] sturdy gelding: modest maiden hurdler: similar form on first of 2 starts over fences: stays 3m: acts on good to soft going: in headgear last 2 starts: often races prominently. *Tom Symonds* **c90 h94**

LIMINI (IRE) 6 ch.m. Peintre Celebre (USA) – Her Grace (IRE) (Spectrum (IRE)) [2016/17 h140: h16v* h20v* h19.9g³ Mar 14] angular mare: smart hurdler: won listed mares event at Punchestown (by 2 lengths from Apple's Jade) in February: third in David Nicholson Mares' Hurdle at Cheltenham (1½ lengths behind same rival) 3 weeks later: stays 2½m: acts on heavy going: usually travels strongly: wore ear plugs at Cheltenham. *W. P. Mullins, Ireland* **h150**

LIMITED RESERVE (IRE) 5 b.g. Court Cave (IRE) – Lady Blackie (IRE) (Definite **h118** Article) [2016/17 h17m⁶ b16.4m⁴ h16.7g⁵ h16.8g³ h21m⁵ h16m⁵ h16s* h15.8v* h15.7g² **b86** h19.8g⁵ Apr 29] €11,000 3-y-o: compact gelding: first foal: dam maiden pointer: fourth in maiden bumper: fairly useful handicap hurdler: won at Sandown (novice) and Ffos Las in December: second at Haydock in April: left P. M. J. Doyle after second start: best form at 2m: acts on good to firm and heavy going: usually races nearer last than first, often travels strongly. *Christian Williams*

LIMONCELLO (FR) 5 b.g. Maresca Sorrento (FR) – Isarella (GER) (Second Set (IRE)) **h98** [2016/17 h20g h20.5gᵖᵘ h23.1d⁵ h23.6s⁵ h21.9v³ Mar 19] fourth foal: dam, 2m/2¼m hurdle winner in Italy, also 7f/1m winner on Flat in Germany: runner-up in maiden on last of 3 starts in points: modest form over hurdles: may prove best short of 3m: acts on heavy going. *Nick Williams*

LIMPOPO TOM (IRE) 10 ch.g. Saffron Walden (FR) – Sharpe (FR) (Dr Devious **c–** (IRE)) [2016/17 c111, h103: h16.7g h20g c20.9sᵖᵘ Oct 15] fairly useful hurdler/chaser at **h–** best, has lost his form: stays 3m: usually wears headgear: has worn tongue tie. *David Rees*

LINED WITH SILVER (IRE) 8 gr.g. Cloudings (IRE) – Tinkers Lady (Sheer Grit) **c89** [2016/17 h83: c20.9s⁴ c20g c18.2m² c16.1m³ Apr 27] winning Irish pointer: maiden **h–** hurdler: modest form in chases: left Miss Hannah Taylor after second start: stays 2¼m: acts on soft and good to firm going. *Alan Phillips*

LINENHALL (IRE) 5 ch.g. Stowaway – Option (IRE) (Red Ransom (USA)) [2016/17 **b97** b15.7d² b15.8d⁴ b16.8s³ b15.8s⁵ Mar 18] half-brother to 3 winners, including fairly useful hurdler Right Option (21f/2¾m winner, by Daylami): dam maiden half-sister to useful hurdler/fairly useful chaser (2m/17f winner) Manorson: fairly useful form in bumpers: placed at Southwell in November and Exeter in February. *Ben Pauling*

LINGER (IRE) 4 b.g. Cape Cross (IRE) – Await So (Sadler's Wells (USA)) [2016/17 **h116** h16.2dᵘʳ h16g* h17.2d² h16s³ h16d⁴ h15.8g* h16.7s* h16.4gᵖᵘ Mar 15] neat gelding: fair maiden on Flat, stays 11f: fairly useful hurdler: won juveniles at Tipperary (maiden) in August, Ludlow in November and Market Rasen in December: raced around 2m: acts on soft going: usually races close up. *John Joseph Hanlon, Ireland*

LINGUINE (FR) 7 ch.g. Linngari (IRE) – Amerissage (USA) (Rahy (USA)) [2016/17 **h115** h109: h21m* h21.6d² h26.5mᵖᵘ h23.3g h19.1dᵘʳ h20g² h21.2m² h21.4m² h26m² h16s Dec 2] small gelding: fairly useful hurdler: won novice handicap at Kempton in May: stays 2¾m: acts on soft and good to firm going: wears headgear: front runner/races prominently. *Seamus Durack*

LINKENHOLT (IRE) 5 ch.g. Robin des Champs (FR) – Honest Chance (FR) (Trempolino **b–** (USA)) [2016/17 b16s b16g⁶ Feb 25] sturdy gelding: no form in bumpers. *Oliver Sherwood*

LION IN HIS HEART (IRE) 6 b.g. Westerner – Coolnasneachta (IRE) (Old Vic) **h134** [2016/17 b16g² h16d* h20d⁷ h16dʳᵒ h16d Dec 27] €30,000 3-y-o: first foal: dam unraced **b97** half-sister to dam of useful hurdler/smart chaser (stays 3¼m) The Romford Pele: fairly useful form in bumpers: second in maiden at Kilbeggan: useful form over hurdles: won maiden at Tipperary in October: in process of improving when falling 2 out in novice at Navan: hung off track next time: should prove suited by further than 2m: temperament under suspicion. *Henry de Bromhead, Ireland*

LIONS CHARGE (USA) 10 ch.g. Lion Heart (USA) – Fellwaati (USA) (Alydar (USA)) **h–** [2016/17 h85: h15.3s Dec 26] fair on Flat, stays 1½m: maiden hurdler: raced around 2m: often in cheekpieces: usually in tongue tie. *Seamus Mullins*

LIR FLOW 8 b.m. With The Flow (USA) – Rose Lir (Lir) [2016/17 h–: h21.4m⁵ h23.3mᵖᵘ **h–** h18.5dᵖᵘ Jun 21] no form over hurdles. *Jess Westwood*

LISDONAGH HOUSE (IRE) 15 b.g. Little Bighorn – Lifinsa Barina (IRE) (Un **h60 §** Desperado (FR)) [2016/17 h–§: h16.8s³ May 3] good-topped gelding: veteran handicap hurdler: stays 2½m: acts on heavy going: ungenuine. *Lynn Siddall*

LISHEEN PRINCE (IRE) 6 b.g. Oscar (IRE) – Dino's Monkey (IRE) (Mr Dinos (IRE)) **h119** [2016/17 b85p: h15.8g² h20d* h21g⁴ Dec 26] lengthy gelding: won Irish point on debut: fairly useful form over hurdles: won maiden at Ffos Las in November: stays 21f. *Philip Hobbs*

LISTEN AND LEARN (IRE) 9 b.g. Presenting – Loyal Gesture (IRE) (Darazari (IRE)) **c117** [2016/17 h120: c23.8mᶠ h23.1g⁴ h26.5m³ h23m² h25m* h26.5g⁵ h23.9g Oct 22] sturdy **h126** gelding: fairly useful handicap hurdler: won at Plumpton in September: third when fell 4 out in novice handicap only chase start: stayed 3¼m: acted on soft and good to firm going: usually wore headgear: often raced in rear: dead. *Jonjo O'Neill*

LISTEN BOY (IRE) 11 ch.g. Presenting – Buckalong (IRE) (Buckskin (FR)) [2016/17 **c99** c116, h–: c26.1d³ May 5] strong, close-coupled gelding: maiden hurdler: fairly useful **h–** handicap chaser at best: stayed 3m: acted on heavy going: dead. *Nigel Twiston-Davies*

LISTEN DEAR (IRE) 7 b.m. Robin des Champs (FR) – Crescendor (FR) (Lavirco **c136 p** (GER)) [2016/17 h130p, b101: h16g* c17s* c18g* c17s* c16s⁴ c16d⁴ Apr 27] useful form **h130 p** over hurdles: completed hat-trick in minor event at Down Royal (by 4½ lengths from The Nutcracker) in June: useful form over fences: won maiden at Ballinrobe in September, 2-runner mares event at Thurles in November and Grade 3 mares novice at Cork (by 8 lengths from Misty Lady) in December: stays 2¼m: acts on good to soft going: usually leads, strong traveller: remains open to improvement. *W. P. Mullins, Ireland*

LISTEN FOR ME 7 b.m. Rainbow High – Teeton Bubbley (Neltino) [2016/17 h20.7g **h– p** Apr 3] seventh foal: half-sister to fairly useful hurdler/winning pointer Teeton Babysham (3m winner, by Shambo) and winning pointers by Karinga Bay and Cloudings: dam winning pointer: runner-up completed start in mares maiden points: well beaten in mares novice on hurdling debut: should do better. *Paul Webber*

LISTEN TO THE MAN (IRE) 7 b.m. Court Cave (IRE) – Badia Dream (IRE) (Old **h117** Vic) [2016/17 b107: h20.6s² h15.7s³ h19.6s* h21v⁵ h15.3m* h16.5m² Apr 20] won Irish mares maiden point on debut: useful bumper performer: fairly useful form over hurdles: won maiden at Huntingdon in March and mares handicap at Wincanton in April: stays 2½m: acts on soft and good to firm going: usually races close up. *Dan Skelton*

LITHIC (IRE) 6 b.g. Westerner – Acoola (IRE) (Flemensfirth (USA)) [2016/17 b95: **h122 p** h15.9g⁶ h19.5m² h20.5d⁵ h18.5s⁶ h15.8s* h19.8d h16.8g² Apr 19] good-topped gelding: bumper winner: fairly useful handicap hurdler: won at Huntingdon in March: second in conditionals/amateur event at Cheltenham in April: stays 19f: acts on soft and good to firm going: often travels strongly: open to further improvement. *Jonjo O'Neill*

LITTERALE CI (FR) 4 b.f. Soldier of Fortune (IRE) – Cigalia (Red Ransom (USA)) **h113** [2016/17 h16.8s² h17s⁴ h16.7s² Jan 23] fairly useful form on Flat, stays 1¾m, won 2 of 3 starts in France: fair form over hurdles: second in juvenile at Exeter and mares handicap at Bangor. *Harry Fry*

LITTLE ACORN 6 b.m. Presenting – Whiteoak (IRE) (Oscar (IRE)) [2016/17 b–: **h100** b13.6d⁵ h15.5g⁵ h19g⁴ h20.7g⁴ Apr 3] unplaced in bumpers: fair form over hurdles: best **b–** effort when fourth in mares novice at Taunton in February. *Harry Fry*

LITTLE BOY BORU (IRE) 9 b.g. Brian Boru – How Is Things (IRE) (Norwich) **c–** [2016/17 c–, h116: h22.8s² Dec 17] lengthy gelding: fairly useful handicap hurdler: similar **h115** form only chase start: stays 3m: acts on heavy going: tried in headgear: usually races nearer last than first. *Suzy Smith*

LITTLE BRUCE (IRE) 5 b.g. Yeats (IRE) – Lady Rolfe (IRE) (Alzao (USA)) [2016/17 **h110** h95: h19.9s⁵ h17.1d h16gⁿ⁾ h17.1g⁴ h15.5g h19.7s* h20.5s* h19.3d³ h21.3d* Mar 31] fair handicap hurdler: won at Wetherby (novice) in December, Ayr in January and Wetherby again in March: will stay 2¾m: acts on heavy going: often races towards rear. *Philip Kirby*

LITTLE BUXTED (USA) 7 b.g. Mr Greeley (USA) – Mo Cheoil Thu (IRE) (In The **h89** Wings) [2016/17 h81: h16.8g³ h15.8g h15.9m h15.9g⁴ Oct 17] modest maiden hurdler: best effort at 17f: tried in headgear: front runner/races prominently. *Jim Best*

LITTLE CHIP (IRE) 10 b.g. Dushyantor (USA) – Aunt Chris (IRE) (Moscow Society **c106 §** (USA)) [2016/17 c27.2d³ May 12] multiple point winner: maiden hurdler: fairly useful **h–** chaser at best: third in hunter at Fontwell in May: stays 3¼m: acts on soft and good to firm going: tried in headgear: has worn tongue tie: temperamental. *Richard J. Bandey*

LITTLE CHUNK (IRE) 5 ch.g. Mr Dinos (IRE) – Daly Lady (IRE) (Lord of Appeal) **h118** [2016/17 b13.7d² b16v h15.8v³ h16.3d⁴ h15.9g* h18.7g* Apr 15] £14,000 3-y-o: sturdy **b81** gelding: fourth foal: half-brother to a winning pointer by King Cheetah: dam unraced half-sister to fairly useful hurdler/useful staying chaser Willie John Daly: modest form in bumpers: fairly useful form over hurdles: won maiden at Plumpton in March and novice at Stratford in April: should stay further than 19f: usually leads. *Warren Greatrex*

LITTLE CORNHAM (IRE) 10 b.g. Moscow Society (USA) – Benrue Supreme (IRE) **c89** (Supreme Leader) [2016/17 c21g³ c19.2g⁵ Apr 11] multiple point winner: modest maiden chaser: stays 3m: acts on good to firm and heavy going: in cheekpieces last 3 starts. *K. J. Cumings*

LITTLE DOTTY 8 br.m. Erhaab (USA) – Marsh Marigold (Tina's Pet) [2016/17 b–: **h93** h15.7d⁴ h15.7vⁿ⁾ Dec 11] bumper winner: modest form over hurdles: better effort when fourth in mares maiden at Towcester in November. *Giuseppe Fierro*

LITTLE DREAM (IRE) 10 b.m. Beneficial – Miss Franco (IRE) (Lanfranco) [2016/17 h85: h20g^{pu} h25m^{pu} c25.7g^{ur} Oct 31] winning Irish pointer: maiden hurdler, no form in 2016/17: unseated rider fifth on chasing debut: sometimes in hood. *Evan Williams* **c–** **h–**

LITTLE FRITZ (FR) 10 gr.g. Turgeon (USA) – Hunorisk (FR) (Mansonnien (FR)) [2016/17 c92x, h–: c21.6d^5 c26.2m^{pu} c26.6g^F Feb 4] maiden hurdler/chaser: stays 21f: acts on soft going: has worn tongue tie: often let down by jumping over fences. *L. Kerr* **c75 x** **h–**

LITTLE GLENSHEE (IRE) 11 gr.m. Terimon – Harrietfield (Nicholas Bill) [2016/17 c117, h–: c20d^6 c22.5v^{pu} c22.4v^{ur} h21.4s^5 h16v^3 Jan 16] fair handicap hurdler: fairly useful chaser at best, no form in 2016/17: stays 23f: acts on heavy going: tried in cheekpieces: has worn tongue tie. *N. W. Alexander* **c–** **h113**

LITTLE JIMMY 10 br.g. Passing Glance – Sementina (USA) (Silver Charm (USA)) [2016/17 c110, h–: c15.5s^4 c19.2d c19.2s^2 h16s^4 c20.3s^4 Mar 20] close-coupled gelding: modest form over hurdles: fair handicap chaser: stays 21f: acts on heavy going: usually wears headgear: wears tongue tie: races towards rear. *Tom Gretton* **c101** **h94**

LITTLE JON 9 b.g. Pasternak – Jowoody (Gunner B) [2016/17 c139x, h–: c23.6g c22.4g c22.9s^5 c23.4s^3 c23.8s^5 h19.8g^{pu} Apr 29] tall gelding: maiden hurdler: useful handicap chaser: third at Newbury (3¾ lengths behind Brandon Hill) in January: stays 23f: best form on soft/heavy going: wears cheekpieces nowadays: often let down by jumping over fences. *Nigel Twiston-Davies* **c130 x** **h–**

LITTLE LEGEND 13 b.g. Midnight Legend – Amber Bright (Little Wolf) [2016/17 c21.1d^4 May 12] smallish gelding: prolific winning pointer: fair hunter chaser at best: well held at Fontwell in May: stays 3¼m: acts on heavy going: wears cheekpieces. *Mrs Cynthia Woods* **c81**

LITTLE LOTTE (IRE) 4 b.f. Kodiac – Dancing Steps (Zafonic (USA)) [2016/17 h16.2d^{pu} h16.8m h17.7d^5 h16.8d h15.7d^6 h15.7v^3 h16.5g^3 h16f* Apr 17] sister to modest 2m hurdle winner Dance For Livvy and half-sister to 2 winning hurdlers, including fairly useful 17f winner Dance For Julie (by Redback): dam half-sister to fairly useful 2m hurdle winner Dilshaan's Prize: modest maiden at best on Flat, stays 8.5f: modest handicap hurdler: won at Les Landes in April: raced around 2m: acts on firm going: usually wears headgear: tried in tongue tie. *Tom Gretton* **h90**

LITTLE MISS FLOSSY 8 b.m. Kayf Tara – The Ginger Whinger (Sir Harry Lewis (USA)) [2016/17 h–, b–: h16.8g^5 h20.3g^{pu} Jun 7] no form over hurdles. *Andrew Crook* **h–**

LITTLE MISS POET 5 b.m. Yeats (IRE) – R de Rien Sivola (FR) (Robin des Champs (FR)) [2016/17 b102: h17.7v^2 h16.7s* h16.8d^2 h16.8g^2 h18.5m* Apr 15] rather unfurnished mare: bumper winner: fairly useful form over hurdles: won mares maiden at Market Rasen in February and mares novice at Newton Abbot in April: stays 2¼m: acts on good to firm and heavy going: often travels strongly. *Philip Hobbs* **h120**

LITTLE POP 9 b.g. Pasternak – Flagship Daisy May (IRE) (Kahyasi) [2016/17 c102, h101: h16g^5 h15.7g* h18.5m^3 c16g* c18g^{ur} c15.7d^5 c15.9m^4 Dec 28] angular gelding: fair handicap hurdler: won at Southwell in August: similar form over fences: won handicap at Hereford in October: unproven beyond 2m: acts on good to firm and good to soft going: in hood last 5 starts: has worn tongue tie: front runner/races prominently. *Nigel Twiston-Davies* **c110** **h112**

LITTLE ROCKY 9 b.g. Cadeaux Genereux – Tahirah (Green Desert (USA)) [2016/17 h16g^6 h19.9g^{pu} h16.2g h15.3m^5 h19.7s^{pu} h16.5g^5 h19.7v^5 Jan 11] smallish gelding: useful at one time on Flat, stays 1½m: fair maiden hurdler at best, has deteriorated considerably: left Alan Fleming after first start: stays 2½m: acts on heavy going: has worn headgear, including last 3 starts: usually in tongue tie nowadays. *Matt Sheppard* **h78**

LITTLE SALAMANCA 4 ch.g. Sakhee's Secret – Little Nymph (Emperor Fountain) [2016/17 h17.2d^{pu} Aug 29] modest form on Flat: pulled up in juvenile on hurdling debut: wore blinkers. *Fergal O'Brien* **h–**

LITTLE VIC 6 br.g. Overbury (IRE) – Vicky Bee (Alflora (IRE)) [2016/17 b–: h15.8d^{pu} Nov 19] no form in bumper/maiden hurdle: tried in hood. *Eugene Stanford* **h–**

LITTLE WELSHCAKE 4 ch.f. Generous (IRE) – Retro's Lady (IRE) (Zaffaran (USA)) [2016/17 b16g Apr 17] sister to temperamental but fairly useful hurdler/useful chaser And The Man (2½m-25f winner): dam (c115/h115) bumper/2½m-3m hurdle winner: well beaten in mares bumper. *Bernard Llewellyn* **b–**

LITTLE WINDMILL (IRE) 7 ch.g. Mahler – Ennismore Queen (IRE) (Glacial Storm (USA)) [2016/17 c90, h94: c21.2g^2 h23.4g^F h19.9m^{pu} h20.6d^6 h19.9g c19.7m* c22.6m* c24.2g^4 c25.7m* c19.7m^{ur} Apr 17] maiden hurdler, no form in 2016/17: fair handicap **c107** **h–**

473

chaser: won at Plumpton (novice events) in September and April, and at Stratford in October: stays 3¼m: acts on good to firm going: wears cheekpieces: has worn tongue tie: front runner. *Neil King*

LIVE FOR TODAY (IRE) 6 b.g. Alflora (IRE) – Uppermost (Montjeu (IRE)) [2016/17 b–: c23g^{pu} Apr 6] winning pointer: no form in bumper/maiden hunter: tried in tongue tie. *N. Williams* — c–

LIVELOVELAUGH (IRE) 7 b.g. Beneficial – Another Evening (IRE) (Saddlers' Hall (IRE)) [2016/17 h21s* h20d^4 h24s^3 h20s* h21.1g h20s^4 h20.5d^3 Apr 29] good-topped gelding: won Irish maiden point on debut: bumper winner: useful hurdler: won maiden at Ballinrobe in May and novice at Thurles in February: third in Ballymore Handicap Hurdle at Punchestown (½ length behind Open Eagle) final start: stays 21f: acts on soft going: front runner/races prominently. *W. P. Mullins, Ireland* — h135

LIVING LEADER 8 b.g. Oasis Dream – Royal Jade (Last Tycoon) [2016/17 h15.8v Dec 12] modest on Flat nowadays, won twice over 1m in 2017: tailed off in novice on hurdling debut: wore tongue tie. *Grace Harris* — h–

LIZZIE LANGTON 6 b.m. Kayf Tara – Madam Flora (Alflora (IRE)) [2016/17 h76: h18.5g h19.1d h15.3s h19.5g Apr 8] poor form over hurdles: in tongue tie last 2 starts. *Robert Walford* — h70

LLANTARA 6 b.m. Kayf Tara – Lady Llancillo (IRE) (Alflora (IRE)) [2016/17 h87: h19.7s^4 h15.5g h16.8d^3 h21v^{pu} Mar 22] placed once in bumpers: modest form over hurdles: usually races towards rear. *Tom Symonds* — h87

LOCAL SHOW (IRE) 9 b.g. Oscar (IRE) – Loughaderra Rose (IRE) (Roselier (FR)) [2016/17 c142, h–: c26g^{pu} h21d c26g^{pu} Mar 16] lengthy gelding: fairly useful hurdler: useful form over fences, pulled up both starts in handicaps in 2016/17: left Ben Pauling after second start: stays 3m: acts on heavy going. *Sarah Humphrey* — c– h129

LOCHALSH (IRE) 6 ch.g. Duke of Marmalade (IRE) – Kylemore (IRE) (Sadler's Wells (USA)) [2016/17 h112: h16.2d h17.2g h16.2d^{pu} h16.2s^4 h16.8s^5 h19s* h20.6s^5 h16.8d^2 h20.5s^5 h23.8g h19.9s^2 h19.9d^3 h19.9g^4 h24.1m^5 Apr 13] poor handicap hurdler: won at Ayr in December: stayed 3m: acted on firm and soft going: tried in cheekpieces: wore tongue tie: dead. *Katie Scott* — h81

LOCH BA (IRE) 11 b.g. Craigsteel – Lenmore Lisa (IRE) (Phardante (FR)) [2016/17 c115§, h–: c25.1v^{ur} c20.2s* c20.9v* c21.1g Apr 6] lengthy, good-topped gelding: maiden hurdler: fairly useful chaser: won hunters at Wincanton and Carlisle in March: stays 25f: acts on heavy going: has worn headgear: ungenuine. *Francesca Nimmo* — c120 § h– §

LOCH GARMAN ARIS (IRE) 7 b.g. Jammaal – See Em Aime (IRE) (Little Bighorn) [2016/17 h96: h19.3d Feb 20] runner-up once from 3 starts in Irish points: bumper winner: tailed off in novice on hurdling debut. *Gary Hanmer* — h–

LOCH LINNHE 5 b.g. Tobougg (IRE) – Quistaquay (El Conquistador) [2016/17 h81, b75: h19.7g^6 h16.2s^6 h20.6s* h20.1g^2 Apr 25] fair form over hurdles: won handicap at Newcastle in December: will prove best at 2½m+: acts on soft going: in cheekpieces last 2 starts. *Mark Walford* — h107

LOCHNELL (IRE) 8 br.m. Winged Love (IRE) – Nothing For Ever (IRE) (Tikkanen (USA)) [2016/17 h92: h21.4d h24.3s* h24.4g^2 h24.3s^2 h24.3v^3 c20.3s^2 h21.4v* h25.8s^2 h24.3d Apr 21] rather leggy mare: fair handicap hurdler: won at Ayr in November and March (mares event): remote second in mares novice on chasing debut: stays 3¼m: acts on heavy going: usually races in rear. *Ian Duncan* — c82 h109

LOCK TOWERS (IRE) 8 b.g. Classic Cliche (IRE) – Katieella (IRE) (King's Theatre (IRE)) [2016/17 c98, h–: c21.7d^4 c25.5s^{pu} c23.6d^{pu} Mar 15] winning pointer: maiden hurdler: maiden chaser, went wrong way in 2016/17 after comeback: stays 3m: acts on good to firm and heavy going: tried in cheekpieces/tongue tie: front runner/races prominently. *Ben Pauling* — c88 h–

LOFGREN 6 b.g. Multiplex – Sherry Darling (IRE) (Alflora (IRE)) [2016/17 h16g* h20.5d^2 h16s h20g^3 h16.2d^4 c16g^2 h22.8s c19.1d^5 c19.9d h18.8g^5 Mar 26] first foal: dam (b73) twice-raced half-sister to smart hurdler/chaser (stayed 25f) Tazbar: fairly useful hurdler: won novice at Cork in May: fair form over fences: left Enda Bolger after fifth start: stays 2½m: acts on soft going: tried in tongue tie: front runner/races prominently. *Donald McCain* — c105 h125

LOG ON (IRE) 6 b.g. Scorpion (IRE) – Go Girl (IRE) (Saddlers' Hall (IRE)) [2016/17 h16d h16.4v^4 h16v^3 h20.6v^4 h20.2g Apr 28] fourth foal: dam, lightly raced over hurdles, sister to fair hurdler/fairly useful chaser (stayed 31f) Rate of Knots: winning pointer: poor form over hurdles. *Rose Dobbin* — h82

Matchbook Imperial Cup Handicap Hurdle, Sandown—London Prize (stars on sleeves) comes through to beat the grey Fixe Le Kap and the visored leader Darebin

LOLLIPOP SHOES 6 b.m. Dr Massini (IRE) – Miss Muscat (Environment Friend) [2016/17 b16.3m b15.8m b16.7s Dec 22] first foal: dam (c81/h78) 2½m-27f hurdle/chase winner: no form in bumpers. *John O'Shea*   **b–**

LOMBARDY BOY (IRE) 12 b.g. Milan – Horner Water (IRE) (Over The River (FR)) [2016/17 h88: h19.2g² h25gᵖᵘ May 30] plain gelding: modest handicap hurdler: should have stayed beyond 21f: acted on soft and good to firm going: tried in cheekpieces: dead. *Michael Banks*   **h87**

LONDONIA 5 gr.g. Paco Boy (IRE) – Snowdrops (Gulch (USA)) [2016/17 h73: h15.9g⁵ h15.9g* h16d⁶ h16.8m³ h18.7g² h15.7g³ Nov 10] modest handicap hurdler: won at Ffos Las in June: stays 19f: acts on good to firm going: wears hood: in tongue tie last 5 starts. *Graeme McPherson*   **h90**

LONDON PRIZE 6 b.g. Teofilo (IRE) – Zibet (Kris) [2016/17 b101: h16g³ h15.5g* h16.7d² h15.6gᶠ h16d* h16g Apr 22] compact gelding: bumper winner: useful form over hurdles: won novice at Leicester in December and Imperial Cup at Sandown (by length from Fixe Le Kap) in March: raced around 2m: acts on good to soft going: often travels strongly. *Ian Williams*   **h133**

LONELY SOLDIER (IRE) 8 ch.g. Golan (IRE) – Crazy Bear (IRE) (King Charlemagne (USA)) [2016/17 h22.1dᵖᵘ Jul 16] maiden pointer: pulled up in novice on hurdling debut: wore tongue tie. *Adrian Wintle*   **h–**

LONG CALL 4 b.g. Authorized (IRE) – Gacequita (URU) (Ride The Rails (USA)) [2016/17 h16g⁶ h16d h16s h16.2v* h15.8s² h16.4g h16d Apr 17] lengthy gelding: fairly useful maiden on Flat, stays 1½m: fairly useful hurdler: won juvenile maiden at Hereford in January: raced only at 2m: acts on heavy going: has worn tongue tie, including last 4 starts: usually races towards rear. *A. J. Martin, Ireland*   **h117**

LONG HOUSE HALL (IRE) 9 b.g. Saddlers' Hall (IRE) – Brackenvale (IRE) (Strong Gale) [2016/17 c140p, h141: c20g⁴ c21.4g* Jul 16] useful-looking gelding: useful hurdler: smart form over fences: won Summer Plate at Market Rasen (by 8 lengths from Ballynagour) in July: should stay 3m: acts on good to firm and good to soft going: wears hood/tongue tie: often races towards rear, usually travels strongly. *Dan Skelton*   **c149 h–**

LONG JOHN 10 gr.g. Silver Patriarch (IRE) – Magic Valentine (Magic Ring (IRE)) [2016/17 c104, h–: c19.4d² c19.2vᵖᵘ c19.2vᵖᵘ c19.4s⁴ Jan 20] maiden hurdler: fair handicap chaser: stays 19f: acts on heavy going: tried in hood: has been reluctant to race, and one to treat with caution. *Jackie du Plessis*   **c99 § h–**

LONG LUNCH 8 b.g. Kayf Tara – Royal Keel (Long Leave) [2016/17 c119, h113: c20g* **c128** c21.2m² c22.5d³ c25g^F c24g² c24d c20.5g⁶ c21.1g^F Apr 7] good-bodied gelding: winning **h–** hurdler: fairly useful handicap chaser: won at Warwick in May: second to No Duffer at Doncaster in December: stays 3m: acts on good to firm and heavy going: wears cheekpieces/ tongue tie. *Charlie Longsdon*

LONG MILE ROAD (IRE) 5 br.g. Getaway (GER) – Andalusia (GER) (Pentire) **b88** [2016/17 b15.7d⁵ Feb 26] €60,000 3-y-o: first foal: dam unraced: 12/1, fifth in bumper at Southwell (9¼ lengths behind My Mate Mark) in February. *Jonjo O'Neill*

LONGMORE (GER) 6 br.g. Mamool (IRE) – Linara (GER) (Windwurf (GER)) [2016/17 **b–** b16.2v Mar 28] maiden Irish pointer: tailed off in maiden bumper. *Gemma Anderson*

LONGRIDGE 4 b.g. Aqlaam – Dea Caelestis (FR) (Dream Well (FR)) [2016/17 b13g **b62** Nov 26] 33/1, eighth in junior bumper at Doncaster. *Michael Dods*

LONG STRAND (IRE) 13 b.g. Saddlers' Hall (IRE) – Oh So Breezy (IRE) (Be My **c–** Native (USA)) [2016/17 c23.4d⁵ Mar 24] well-made gelding: multiple point winner: **h–** maiden hurdler: fairly useful chaser at best, well held in hunter in March: stays 3m: acts on heavy going: has worn headgear: wears tongue tie. *Miss Evanna McCutcheon, Ireland*

LONGTOWN (IRE) 6 b.g. Scorpion (IRE) – Desirable Asset (IRE) (Zagreb (USA)) **h118 p** [2016/17 b81p: h19.9v² h21.6s h21s* Mar 30] fairly useful form over hurdles: won maiden at Warwick in March: will stay at least 3m: open to further improvement. *Philip Hobbs*

LONGUEVILLE FLIER (IRE) 8 b.g. Definite Article – Talk The Talk (Terimon) **c–** [2016/17 c95: c24.2d^pu c24.2s h27v^pu h23.3s⁶ c26.3g c24.2g Apr 25] lightly raced over **h–** hurdles: modest chaser at best, no form in 2016/17: often wears headgear: has worn tongue tie. *Micky Hammond*

LOOE BAY 5 b.m. Kirkwall – Dragon Blue (Puget (USA)) [2016/17 b13.7d⁶ b15.8d⁵ **b80** ab16g Jan 31] first foal: dam lightly raced over hurdles: modest form in bumpers: tried in hood. *Dominic Ffrench Davis*

LOOKFORARAINBOW 4 b.g. Rainbow High – Look Here's May (Revoque (IRE)) **b79** [2016/17 b16v⁴ Mar 12] 25/1, fourth in bumper at Warwick (10¾ lengths behind Shivertimembers) in March. *Sarah Hollinshead*

LOOKING FOR MICK 8 ch.g. Milk It Mick – Seeker (Rainbow Quest (USA)) **h–** [2016/17 h86: h23g h16.8s^pu Jun 10] twice-raced pointer: maiden hurdler, no form in 2016/17: in headgear last 2 starts: tried in tongue tie. *Chris Down*

LOOKING WELL (IRE) 8 b.g. Gold Well – Different Level (IRE) (Topanoora) **c134** [2016/17 c126p, h–: c26.2m² c26.2m* c24d² c26s⁶ Mar 4] winning hurdler: useful **h–** handicap chaser: won at Kelso in May: second in Sky Bet Chase at Doncaster (3½ lengths behind Ziga Boy) in January: stays 3¼m: acts on soft and good to firm going: often travels strongly/races towards rear. *Nicky Richards*

LOOKSABITLIKEBRIAN (IRE) 5 b.g. Brian Boru – Sheebadiva (IRE) (Norwich) **h–** [2016/17 h19.9s^pu Mar 18] pulled up in novice hurdle. *Tim Vaughan*

LOOKS LIKE POWER (IRE) 7 ch.g. Spadoun (FR) – Martovic (IRE) (Old Vic) **c107** [2016/17 h100: h20m^pu h20v⁶ h15.8v* h15.3s⁴ c16v⁴ c16g* c19.4d³ Apr 16] modest **h99** handicap hurdler: fair form over fences: won handicap at Ffos Las in December: won handicap at same course in April: stays 21f, at least as effective at 2m: acts on heavy going: has worn headgear, including last 5 starts: wears tongue tie: often leads. *Debra Hamer*

LOOKSLIKERAINTED (IRE) 10 b.g. Milan – Kilcrea Gale (IRE) (Strong Gale) **c121 x** [2016/17 c–, h100: h23s³ h19.9m^pu h20g c23.4d³ Mar 24] rangy gelding: modest handicap **h92** hurdler: fairly useful chaser: should have won hunter at Newbury in March, well clear when rider mistook winning post: left Sophie Leech after third start: stays 3m: acts on heavy going: has worn headgear/tongue tie, including in 2016/17: usually races close up: often let down by jumping over fences. *Martin Wilesmith*

LOOKSNOWTLIKEBRIAN (IRE) 6 b.g. Brian Boru – Sheebadiva (IRE) (Norwich) **h111** [2016/17 h92, b81: h15.8g⁶ h19.1d* h19.5d* h21.1s⁶ h21.3s Dec 26] fair handicap hurdler: won at Fontwell (conditionals novice) and Chepstow in October: will stay 3m: acts on soft going: often races towards rear. *Tim Vaughan*

LOOK SURPRISED 4 ch.f. Kier Park (IRE) – Cloridja (Indian Ridge) [2016/17 b15.7s^pu **b–** Mar 20] sixth foal: sister to 6f winner One Big Surprise: dam unraced: pulled up in bumper. *Roger Teal*

LOOK WEST 8 b.g. Westerner – Uppermost (Montjeu (IRE)) [2016/17 h16.7g^pu h21.2g^pu **h–** Nov 10] no form over hurdles: in hood first start: dead. *Kerry Lee*

LOOSE CHIPS 11 b.g. Sir Harry Lewis (USA) – Worlaby Rose (Afif) [2016/17 c134, h–: c25g^{pu} c23.6g^2 c24.2d* c28.8d c24.2s^3 c24.2v^2 c26s^5 c23.8m* Apr 2] good-topped gelding: winning hurdler: useful handicap chaser: won veterans events at Sandown in November and Ascot (by head from Bob Tucker) in April: second in Masters Handicap Chase at Sandown (2¾ lengths behind Otago Trail) in February: stays 3½m: acts on good to firm and heavy going: wears headgear: bold-jumping front runner. *Charlie Longsdon* — **c140 h–**

LOOSE ENDS 4 b.f. Authorized (IRE) – Crooked Wood (USA) (Woodman (USA)) [2016/17 h16d^4 h16v^2 h16.4v Feb 2] dam half-sister to fairly useful hurdler/fair chaser (stayed 3m) Circus Maximus: modest maiden on Flat, stays 13.5f: modest form over hurdles: best effort when fourth in juvenile maiden at Punchestown: wears hood. *Gordon Elliott, Ireland* — **h96**

LORD ADARE (IRE) 9 b.g. Moscow Society (USA) – Gonearethedays (IRE) (Be My Native (USA)) [2016/17 c112, h–: h19.5s h23.9s^{pu} c16s^{pu} Mar 13] winning hurdler/maiden chaser, no form in 2016/17: tried in cheekpieces: often wears tongue tie. *Nikki Evans* — **c– h–**

LORD ALDERVALE (IRE) 10 br.g. Alderbrook – Monavale (IRE) (Strong Gale) [2016/17 h65: c25.7m^2 Apr 16] well-made gelding: point winner: maiden hurdler: second in novice handicap at Plumpton (7 lengths behind Little Windmill) on chasing debut: stays 3¼m: acts on soft and good to firm going: has worn headgear/tongue tie. *Steve Woodman* — **c76 h–**

LORD BALLIM (FR) 7 ch.g. Balko (FR) – Lady Pauline (FR) (Hamas (IRE)) [2016/17 c107, h98: h17.1d^3 h19.5d^6 h19.8d c25.1s h19.2v^2 h17d* h19.3d* c20g* c23.8g^{ur} c20.1g* Apr 28] fairly useful handicap hurdler: won at Carlisle in February and April (conditional event): fairly useful handicap chaser: won at Carlisle and Perth (novice event) later in April: stays 2½m: acts on heavy going: wears headgear/tongue tie: usually races in rear, strong traveller. *Nigel Hawke* — **c129 h117**

LORD BEN (IRE) 12 b.g. Beneficial – Lady Bluebell (IRE) (Mister Lord (USA)) [2016/17 c133, h119: h16d h17m h16m c18.2g h15.9m^3 c17.4g^4 h18.7m^4 c16.9m c23g^3 c23.9s^3 c16.4s^4 c16s^2 c16g^3 c19.2g^2 Apr 11] well-made gelding: fairly useful hurdler/ useful chaser at best, not quite same force nowadays: left Henry de Bromhead after fourth start: stays 3m: acts on good to firm and heavy going: front runner/races prominently. *Dai Williams* — **c120 h114**

LORD BRENDY 9 gr.g. Portrait Gallery (IRE) – Hervey Bay (Primitive Rising (USA)) [2016/17 c116, h–: c26.2d c25.2g Nov 30] winning hurdler: fairly useful chaser at best, no form in 2016/17: stays 3¼m: acts on heavy going. *Kenny Johnson* — **c– h–**

LORD BRYAN (IRE) 6 b.g. Brian Boru – Run Cat (IRE) (Lord Americo) [2016/17 b93: b17.7g^3 b15.8g^2 h23.1v^5 h19.5s^5 h23.6s^4 h25.5s^2 h23.3s^{pu} Apr 1] fair form in bumpers/over hurdles: stays 3¼m: acts on soft going. *Peter Bowen* — **h108 b87**

LORD BUNNACURRY 6 ch.g. Black Sam Bellamy (IRE) – Lunareva (USA) (Nureyev (USA)) [2016/17 b15.8v^6 b16.6g Feb 22] no form in bumpers. *Michael Mullineaux* — **b–**

LORD GRANTHAM (IRE) 10 b.g. Definite Article – Last of Her Line (Silver Patriarch (IRE)) [2016/17 c117, h–: c21m^4 Jul 1] strong gelding: winning hurdler: maiden chaser, fairly useful at best: stays 3m: acts on soft and good to firm going. *Henry Daly* — **c110 h–**

LORD HEATHFIELD (IRE) 11 br.g. Classic Cliche (IRE) – Garryduff Bridge (IRE) (Taipan (IRE)) [2016/17 c94, h74: c24v* c23.5v^3 c29.6s^2 c23.6s^F Mar 13] lengthy gelding: once-raced hurdler: fairly useful handicap chaser: won at Uttoxeter in December: stays 3¾m: best form on soft/heavy going: wears cheekpieces. *Graeme McPherson* — **c115 h–**

LORD HUNTINGDON 4 b.g. Lord of England (GER) – Marajuana (Robellino (USA)) [2016/17 h15.8g* h16m^{ur} h15.8g^2 h15.8m^F Apr 18] fair form on Flat, stays 1¼m: fair form over hurdles: won juvenile at Huntingdon in October. *Alan King* — **h110**

LORD JUSTICE (IRE) 4 b.g. Zoffany (IRE) – Roselita (IRE) (Sadler's Wells (USA)) [2016/17 h16s^4 h16.2s* h16d* h16g^3 h16.6g^2 h16d h16s Jan 25] fairly useful maiden on Flat, stays 1¼m: fairly useful hurdler: won juveniles at Ballinrobe (maiden) in September and Gowran in October: second in Summit Juvenile Hurdle at Doncaster (2¾ lengths behind Cliffs of Dover) in December: raced around 2m: acts on soft going: tried in cheekpieces: wears tongue tie. *Joseph Patrick O'Brien, Ireland* — **h122**

LORD LANDEN (IRE) 12 br.g. Beneficial – Agua Caliente (IRE) (Old Vic) [2016/17 c104§, h–: c20s^2 c21d^5 c18.9s^{pu} c20s^3 c20.2g^4 c25.2s h24d c19.4g^3 c19.4g^4 Apr 23] good-bodied gelding: maiden hurdler: modest handicap chaser: stays 2¾m: acts on good to firm and heavy going: usually in headgear: wears tongue tie: often races freely/finishes weakly. *Fergal O'Brien* — **c98 § h– §**

thetote.com Galway Plate (Handicap Chase), Galway—a sign of things to come as the stables of Elliott and Mullins dominate, with Lord Scoundrel (noseband) beating Alelchi Inois (left), the grey Ballycasey, Devils Bride and Clarcam (right)

LORD OF DRUMS (IRE) 11 b.g. Beat of Drums – Treat A Lady (IRE) (Lord Americo) [2016/17 c93, h–: h16.2g⁶ c17.3d³ c23.8sᵖᵘ c21.2g⁶ c16g Sep 18] maiden hurdler: fair handicap chaser at best, well below that in 2016/17: stays 2½m: acts on heavy going: has worn hood: in tongue tie last 4 starts: usually races close up. *Lucinda Russell* **c82 h73**

LORD OF THE ISLAND (IRE) 9 b.g. Heron Island (IRE) – Miss Morose (IRE) (Arctic Lord) [2016/17 h111: h23.3sᵖᵘ h21d* h18.5s³ h18.5sᶠ h21d³ h23.4v* Feb 4] sturdy gelding: close second when fell 2 out in Irish maiden point: useful handicap hurdler: won at Towcester in November and Sandown (by 6 lengths from Fortunate George) in February: left Sally Randell after first start: stays 23f: acts on heavy going: tracks pace. *Fergal O'Brien* **h131**

LORD SCOUNDREL (IRE) 8 b.g. Presenting – Noble Choice (Dahar (USA)) [2016/17 c144, h–: c21s⁵ c22.5g* c24vᶠ c25g² c24g³ c29d Apr 17] winning maiden: smart handicap chaser: won Galway Plate (by 1¼ lengths from Alelchi Inois) in July: placed in Grade 3 event at Punchestown (5½ lengths behind Sadler's Risk) in October and JNwine.com Champion Chase at Down Royal (15½ lengths behind Valseur Lido) in November: stays 3m: acts on good to firm and heavy going: has worn headgear. *Gordon Elliott, Ireland* **c154 h–**

LORDS PARK STAR (IRE) 8 b.g. Presenting – Mary's View (IRE) (Phardante (FR)) [2016/17 h85, b–: h19.9gᵖᵘ h15.7g³ h23g h23.3gᵖᵘ Jul 22] winning Irish pointer: modest maiden hurdler: best efforts at 2m: acts on good to soft going: in cheekpieces last 2 starts: in tongue tie last 3: often leads: unreliable. *Nicholas Pomfret* **h88 §**

LORD TOPPER 4 b.g. Sir Percy – Fugnina (Hurricane Run (IRE)) [2016/17 h15.8g⁴ h16m* Apr 13] fairly useful 13.5f winner on Flat: fair form over hurdles: won juvenile maiden at Wetherby in April: will stay beyond 2m. *Jamie Snowden* **h110**

LORD VALENTINE 9 b.g. Overbury (IRE) – Lady Fleur (Alflora (IRE)) [2016/17 h–: h21dᵖᵘ Dec 15] fair form in bumpers: no show both starts over hurdles. *Mark Bradstock* **h–**

LORD WINDERMERE (IRE) 11 b.g. Oscar (IRE) – Satellite Dancer (IRE) (Satco (FR)) [2016/17 c22d² c24d c25v⁵ c34.3d Apr 8] workmanlike gelding: winning hurdler: high-class chaser at one time: best effort in 2016/17 after long absence when second in listed event at Thurles (head behind Champagne Fever) in November: stays 3¼m: acts on heavy going: tried in headgear/tongue tie. *J. Culloty, Ireland* **c146 d h–**

LORD WISHES (IRE) 10 b.g. Milan – Strong Wishes (IRE) (Strong Gale) [2016/17 c124, h121: h20.1d* c21.2d* h22.1d⁵ h16.2s³ c19.4m* h21.1g c19.3d⁶ c24gᵖᵘ c20.1gᵘʳ h20.5g Apr 22] tall, good-bodied gelding: fairly useful handicap hurdler: won at Hexham in June: useful handicap chaser: won at Cartmel later in June and Wetherby in October: lost form after: stays 3m: acts on good to firm and heavy going: wears headgear: tried in tongue tie: often races lazily. *James Ewart* **c134 h124**

LOST FREQUENCY 5 b.g. Yeats (IRE) – Lauderdale (GER) (Nebos (GER)) [2016/17 h20.5d h19.6s⁶ Nov 26] off mark in Irish points at third attempt: down the field in maiden/novice hurdles. *Lucinda Russell* **h–**

LOST IN LECCE 5 ch.m. Midnight Legend – Ryde To Arms (Erhaab (USA)) [2016/17 h21.7g² h20.6g⁴ h23.9g³ h24.5gᵖᵘ h23.9g⁴ Mar 2] £5,000 3-y-o: sturdy mare: second foal: dam unraced half-sister to useful hurdler (2½m/21f winner) Ryde Back: in front when fell 4 out in mares maiden point on debut: fair form over hurdles: may prove best at around 2½m: raced only on good going. *Philip Hobbs* **h105**

LOST IN NEWYORK (IRE) 10 b.g. Arakan (USA) – Lace Flower (Old Vic) [2016/17 c74, h69: h19g² May 2] workmanlike gelding: poor handicap hurdler: maiden chaser: stays 2¾m: acts on soft and good to firm going: wears headgear: tried in tongue tie: usually races nearer last than first. *Nick Kent* **c– h70**

LOST LEGEND (IRE) 10 b.g. Winged Love (IRE) – Well Orchestrated (IRE) (King's Ride) [2016/17 c142, h–: c20m⁵ c20g c19.4g⁶ c20.5s⁴ c20.2m c20.2s c23.9m³ Apr 9] lengthy gelding: useful handicap chaser: lost his way in 2016/17: stays 25f: acts on good to firm and heavy going: usually wears headgear. *Jonjo O'Neill* **c89 § h–**

LOSTNFOUND 4 b.f. Midnight Legend – La Cerisaie (Old Vic) [2016/17 b16g⁴ Apr 23] second foal: dam, French 17f/2¼m hurdle/chase winner, half-sister to useful hurdler (stays 2½m) That's A Wrap: 7/1, held back by inexperience when fourth in mares bumper at Wetherby (9¾ lengths behind Heartasia) in April: should improve. *Jamie Snowden* **b77 p**

LOSTOCK HALL (IRE) 5 b.g. Lord Shanakill (USA) – Cannikin (IRE) (Lahib (USA)) [2016/17 h16.7g⁴ h16.8g³ h18.7m* h16g³ h16.8m* h18.7m Oct 15] half-brother to fair hurdler Canni Thinkaar (17f-2¾m winner, by Alhaarth): fair on Flat, stays 1¼m: fair form over hurdles: won maiden at Stratford in August and novice at Exeter in October: stays 19f: acts on good to firm going. *David Dennis* **h112**

LOTUS POND (IRE) 9 b.g. Beneficial – Capard Lady (IRE) (Supreme Leader) [2016/17 c20sᵖᵘ Feb 8] multiple winning pointer: maiden hurdler: pulled up in hunter on chasing debut: should stay 2½m+: tried in hood/tongue tie. *W. Bryan* **c– h–**

Gigginstown House Stud's "Lord Scoundrel"

LOUD AND CLEAR 6 b.g. Dalakhani (IRE) – Whispering Blues (IRE) (Sadler's Wells **b101** (USA)) [2016/17 b–: b16g* b16.7g³ b16d* b17g Apr 7] rather unfurnished gelding: fairly useful bumper performer: won at Worcester in August and Ayr in October. *Iain Jardine*

LOUGHALDER (IRE) 11 ch.g. Alderbrook – Lough Lein Leader (IRE) (Supreme **c114** Leader) [2016/17 c109, h–: c26.1d* c23.6dᵖᵘ c24s³ c24vᵖᵘ c23.6sᵖᵘ c24v⁴ c23.6vᵖᵘ c23.6gᵖᵘ **h–** Apr 8] workmanlike gelding: maiden hurdler: fair handicap chaser: won at Uttoxeter in May: largely ran poorly after: stays 29f: acts on heavy going: wears headgear/tongue tie: usually races close up: temperament under suspicion. *Matt Sheppard*

LOUGH DERG FARMER (IRE) 5 b.g. Presenting – Maryiver (IRE) (Runyon (IRE)) **h122 p** [2016/17 h21s⁵ h20.8d* h23.1s² h21.9d* Apr 16] £56,000 4-y-o: sturdy gelding: first foal: dam (c112/h114) 2m-21f hurdle/chase winner: Irish maiden point winner: fairly useful form over hurdles: won maiden at Doncaster in January and novice at Ffos Las in April: will stay beyond 23f: remains open to improvement. *Nicky Henderson*

LOUGH DERG ISLAND (IRE) 9 b.g. Court Cave (IRE) – Clondalee Fred (IRE) **c–** (Jurado (USA)) [2016/17 h92: h21.6s⁵ c25.5dᵖᵘ h15.3s² Dec 26] winning Irish pointer: **h98** modest maiden hurdler: pulled up in novice handicap on chasing debut: stays 2¾m: acts on heavy going: tried in tongue tie: often races in rear/travels strongly. *Alexandra Dunn*

LOUGH DERG JEWEL (IRE) 6 b.g. Oscar (IRE) – River Valley Lady (IRE) (Salt **h118** Dome (USA)) [2016/17 h20.5s⁶ h19.6s³ h22.7s* h22s⁴ h25.3s³ h19.6g³ h22.7d² Apr 10] £26,000 5-y-o: sixth foal: dam, fair 2m hurdle winner, also 1m winner on Flat: placed 3 of 5 starts in Irish maiden points: fairly useful hurdler: won maiden at Kelso in December: second in handicap at Kelso final start: stays 25f: acts on soft going: usually leads. *Donald McCain*

LOUGH DERG LEADER (IRE) 6 b.g. Craigsteel – Lady Elodie (IRE) (Supreme **h123** Leader) [2016/17 h21m² h23.1v* h24.4g* h26s* h21gᵖᵘ Feb 25] won Irish maiden point on debut: fairly useful form over hurdles: won maiden at Bangor in November and handicap at Doncaster in November: should have stayed 3¼m: acted on heavy going: dead. *Tom Lacey*

LOUGH DERG MYSTERY (IRE) 6 b.g. Oscar (IRE) – Have To Go (IRE) (Le Moss) **h91** [2016/17 b16.8g³ h20g h16v⁵ h18.8d h19.1v⁵ h18.5d⁶ Mar 21] £6,200 5-y-o: sturdy **b80** gelding: seventh foal: brother to bumper winner/useful hurdler Square Sphere (2½m-3m winner) and half-brother to a winning pointer by Fourstars Allstar: dam unraced half-sister to dam of smart hurdler/chaser (stayed 25f) Inchlady Rock: in frame both completed starts in Irish points: third in bumper at Newton Abbot: modest form over hurdles. *Nick Mitchell*

LOUGH DERG SPIRIT (IRE) 5 b.g. Westerner – Sno-Cat Lady (IRE) (Executive **h130** Perk) [2016/17 h16s* h15.7d⁴ h15.6g* h20gᵖᵘ Apr 8] €45,000 3-y-o, £190,000 4-y-o: well-made gelding: half-brother to fairly useful hurdler/chaser Sizing Machine (2m-2½m winner, by King's Theatre), fair hurdler Contradeal (3m winner, by Fourstars Allstar) and 2 winning pointers by Saddlers' Hall: dam unraced half-sister to high-class staying jumper Ten Plus: off mark in Irish maiden points at second attempt: useful form over hurdles: won novices at Kempton in November and Musselburgh by 2½ lengths from Peter The Mayo Man) in February: should stay beyond 2m. *Nicky Henderson*

LOUGH DERG WALK (IRE) 8 b.g. Turtle Island (IRE) – Whispers In Moscow (IRE) **h86** (Moscow Society (USA)) [2016/17 h21.4s⁴ Dec 19] good-topped gelding: point winner: fairly useful form over hurdles: well held in handicap at Ayr after long absence. *Donald McCain*

LOUGH KENT 8 b.g. Barathea (IRE) – King's Doll (IRE) (King's Best (USA)) [2016/17 **c–** c137, h116: h20mᵖᵘ h15.9g c15.5gᵖᵘ c19.3d h16.8d⁶ h15.7s⁶ h16.4s* h15.7s h18.1d⁵ **h109** Apr 10] good-topped gelding: fair handicap hurdler: won at Newcastle in January: useful chaser at best, ran poorly both starts over fences in 2016/17: left Nicky Henderson after second start: stays 19f: acts on soft going: has worn cheekpieces. *James Moffatt*

LOUGH SALT (IRE) 6 b.g. Brian Boru – Castlehill Lady (IRE) (Supreme Leader) **h110** [2016/17 h104, b63: h24.1d* h24.1d⁴ h21.3s³ h25.3s³ʳ h20.1g Apr 25] close-coupled gelding: fair handicap hurdler: won at Wetherby in November: stays 3m: acts on soft going: tried in cheekpieces: often races towards rear. *Mark Walford*

LOUGHSHORE (IRE) 5 b.m. Milan – Lough Coyne (IRE) (Bob Back (USA)) [2016/17 **b67 p** b16.2d⁵ Jun 11] first foal: dam (h79), placed in bumper/maiden hurdler, half-sister to useful hurdler/smart chaser (stays 3¼m) Mendip Express: maiden pointer, twice runner-up: 15/8, fifth in bumper at Hexham (18 lengths behind Black Ivory) in June: should do better. *Stuart Crawford, Ireland*

LOUGHVIEW LADDIE (IRE) 8 b.g. Shantou (USA) – Par Street (IRE) (Dolphin Street **h62** (FR)) [2016/17 b18s b19s h16.5v h20.1s^{pu} h16.2g Apr 27] tailed off in maiden bumper: **b–** poor form over hurdles: left Mrs John B. Ross after first start: in tongue tie last 4 starts. *Noel C. Kelly, Ireland*

LOUIE 5 b.g. Aeroplane – Over The Clouds (Cloudings (IRE)) [2016/17 b14d h19.5v^{pu} Feb **h–** 25] no show in bumper/maiden hurdle: tried in tongue tie. *Richard Price* **b–**

LOUIS LUDWIG (IRE) 12 b.g. Mull of Kintyre (USA) – Fantastic Bid (USA) (Auction **c– §** Ring (USA)) [2016/17 c–§, h–: h16.8m h16.3m⁶ h18.5m Nov 1] sturdy gelding: poor **h64 §** handicap hurdler: maiden chaser: barely stays 21f: acts on soft and good to firm going: has worn blinkers: has worn tongue tie, including last 3 starts: races towards rear: weak finisher. *Tim Vaughan*

LOUIS PHILLIPE (IRE) 10 ch.g. Croco Rouge (IRE) – Presenting's Wager (IRE) **c89** (Presenting) [2016/17 c83, h–: c20.9v³ c20.9g^{ur} c22.6m⁴ c22.6g⁶ c21g* c25.8m* c25.8g² **h–** Oct 7] maiden hurdler: modest handicap chaser: won at Newton Abbot (twice) in August: stays 3¼m: acts on good to firm and good to soft going: in cheekpieces last 4 starts: has worn tongue tie. *Linda Blackford*

LOUIS' VAC POUCH (IRE) 5 b.g. Oscar (IRE) – Coming Home (FR) (Exit To **h124** Nowhere (USA)) [2016/17 b84: b16.7g⁴ h20d⁶ h16.5g⁴ h15.7s* h16.8v^F h16.7g* h20.6m* **b87** Apr 17] useful-looking gelding: fair form in bumpers: fairly useful form over hurdles: won novices at Southwell in January and Market Rasen in March, and handicap at Market Rasen in April: stays 21f: acts on soft and good to firm going: in hood last 5 starts. *Philip Hobbs*

LOUKHAAR (IRE) 9 b.g. Westerner – Gold Air (Sri Pekan (USA)) [2016/17 c90, h–: **c55** c20.5m⁵ c19.4m Jul 10] well-made gelding: maiden hurdler/chaser: placed in points in **h–** 2017. *Jonathan Geake*

LOULOUMILLS 7 b.m. Rob Roy (USA) – Etching (USA) (Groom Dancer (USA)) **h91** [2016/17 h74: h16.8d⁴ h19.9g² h19.7g³ h22.7s h16.8d h20.6s⁴ h19.9g* h16.2g⁴ Apr 27] modest maiden hurdler: won mares novice at Sedgefield in April: stays 2½m: acts on heavy going: tried in cheekpieces: in tongue tie last 2 starts: often races prominently. *Maurice Barnes*

LOUP DE LOUVE (FR) 5 b.g. Turtle Bowl (IRE) – Signe de La Louve (FR) (Loup **h–** Solitaire (USA)) [2016/17 h19.3s h16.3v h17.7d^{pu} Mar 18] good-topped gelding: maiden on Flat: won juvenile at Fontainebleau on hurdling debut in 2015/16: no form in handicaps in Britain. *Gary Moore*

LOU VERT (FR) 5 b.g. Vertigineux (FR) – Lourinha (FR) (Loup Solitaire (USA)) **c116** [2016/17 h100: h16g³ h16.4g c16d² c18.2g² c20.2m^F c17m⁴ Apr 17] compact gelding: **h104** maiden hurdler: fairly useful form over fences: stays 2½m: acts on good to firm and good to soft going: tried in hood: wears tongue tie. *Paul Nicholls*

LOVEFROMABOVE (IRE) 6 b.m. Flemensfirth (USA) – Good Looking Woman (IRE) **h–** (Oscar (IRE)) [2016/17 h–, b55: h20g^{pu} May 28] maiden pointer: no form over hurdles. *Dan Skelton*

LOVELY BUBBLY 6 gr.g. Kayf Tara – Champagne Lil (Terimon) [2016/17 h98, b–: **c94** h16.7g⁴ h15.7g h20.5g⁶ h19.1d⁶ h16.8s³ c17m² Apr 16] modest maiden hurdler: 5/2, **h93** second in novice handicap at Plumpton (7 lengths behind Lake Chapala) on chasing debut: unproven beyond 17f: acts on soft and good to firm going: wears tongue tie. *Tim Vaughan*

LOVELY TOUCH (IRE) 8 b.g. Humbel (USA) – My Touch (IRE) (Supreme Leader) **h62** [2016/17 h16g* May 4] maiden Irish pointer: poor form over hurdles: left John David Riches, won novice handicap at Wetherby in May: should stay beyond 2m. *Sam Thomas*

LOVENORMONEY (IRE) 6 br.g. Winged Love (IRE) – Dixies Gem (IRE) (Anzillero **h119** (GER)) [2016/17 h21.6d⁴ h19.5s³ h23.3v* h25.5s³ Mar 11] €8,000 3-y-o, £47,000 5-y-o: good-topped gelding: first foal: dam (h86) lightly raced in points/over hurdles: won completed start in Irish maiden points: fairly useful form over hurdles: won novice at Uttoxeter in February. *Warren Greatrex*

LOVES DESTINATION 6 b.m. Dubai Destination (USA) – Bijou Love (IRE) (Winged **h111** Love (IRE)) [2016/17 h100: h19g² h21.6d³ h19.5g² h21.6s^{pu} h19.5s h21.6d* Mar 18] lengthy mare: fair handicap hurdler: won mares event at Fontwell in March: stays 2¾m: acts on heavy going. *Chris Gordon*

LOVE THE LEADER (IRE) 9 b.g. Fruits of Love (USA) – Suelena (IRE) (Supreme **c102** Leader) [2016/17 c105p, h108: h25g h24v² c23.9g⁵ c25.5g^{ur} h26.5g⁴ h24m⁵ Sep 27] fair **h109** handicap hurdler/chaser: stays 3¼m: acts on heavy going: has worn headgear, including in 2016/17. *Johnny Farrelly*

LOVETOHUNTGOLD 6 b.m. Rainbow High – Moorgate Gold (Presenting) [2016/17 **h–** b15.7d h19.9g⁶ Jul 22] first foal: dam unraced half-sister to fairly useful hurdlers Eight Is **b–** My Number (2½m winner) and Kayf Adventure (2¾m winner): tailed off in mares bumper/ maiden hurdle: wears tongue tie. *Chris Bealby*

LOWANBEHOLD (IRE) 10 gr.g. Cloudings (IRE) – Marble Quest (IRE) (Roselier **c96** (FR)) [2016/17 c121p, h93: c23.8sᵖᵘ c20.1g⁴ c20.1s³ c20.9d⁵ c21.5g⁴ c26.2s⁴ c20.5v³ **h–** c23.4v⁴ Mar 4] maiden hurdler: fairly useful handicap chaser at best, below that in 2016/17: stays 23f: acts on soft going: tried in cheekpieces: usually races prominently. *Sandy Forster*

LOWCARR MOTION 7 b.g. Rainbow High – Royalty (IRE) (Fairy King (USA)) **h103 §** [2016/17 h98: h24.7d² h23.9d⁴ h23.3g³ h23.1gᵖᵘ h23.3d⁶ h19.3d² Apr 5] fair handicap hurdler: stays 25f: acts on soft going: in cheekpieces last 4 starts: temperamental. *Micky Hammond*

LOWER HOPE DANDY 10 gr.g. Karinga Bay – Cheeky Mare (Derrylin) [2016/17 **c135** h117: h23.3v² h23.1s c24.1s² c24.2s* Mar 7] big, workmanlike gelding: fair handicap **h113** hurdler: useful form over fences: easily won novice handicap at Exeter in March: stays 3m: acts on heavy going: usually races prominently. *Venetia Williams*

LOW KEY (IRE) 10 b.g. Pentire – La Capilla (Machiavellian (USA)) [2016/17 h130: **h–** h23d⁵ Jun 22] useful hurdler at best, below that sole outing (tongue tied) in 2016/17: stays 21f: best form on good going. *David Pipe*

LOYAUTE (FR) 10 ch.m. Green Tune (USA) – Iles Marquises (IRE) (Unfuwain (USA)) **c–** [2016/17 c–, h111: h16.8g May 4] workmanlike mare: useful hurdler at best, on downgrade: **h–** maiden chaser: stays 21f: acts on heavy going: tried in cheekpieces: has worn tongue tie. *Chris Down*

L STIG 7 b.g. Striking Ambition – Look Here's May (Revoque (IRE)) [2016/17 h85: **h–** h15.8m Oct 5] maiden hurdler, has lost his form: unproven beyond 17f: acts on soft going: tried in cheekpieces/tongue tie. *John O'Shea*

LUBATIC (FR) 4 b.g. Sleeping Car (FR) – Luba (FR) (Mansonnien (FR)) [2016/17 **b92** b16.16g⁴ b15.3f* Apr 23] rather unfurnished gelding: seventh foal: half-brother to French 2½m chase winner Spad L'Amandour (by Spadoun): dam unraced: fair form in bumpers: won 3-runner event at Wincanton in April. *Neil Mulholland*

LUCA BRAZI (IRE) 5 b.g. Mahler – Carriacou (Mark of Esteem (IRE)) [2016/17 b–: **h–** h18.7g h15.8m³ Apr 25] unseated rider in point: no form in bumper/over hurdles: tried in hood. *Alastair Ralph*

LUCARNO DANCER 7 b.m. Lucarno (USA) – Sing And Dance (Rambo Dancer **h–** (CAN)) [2016/17 h–: h16.2s h16.8d⁵ h16.2g Apr 28] little form over hurdles: tried in hood: often in tongue tie. *Raymond Shiels*

LUCCOMBE DOWN 7 b.g. Primo Valentino (IRE) – Flaming Rose (IRE) (Roselier **c–** (FR)) [2016/17 h94: h19.9g* h23.1g* h22g* h27gᵇᵈ h26.5g⁴ h23.9g⁵ c23g⁶ h24g⁴ Apr 20] **h123** fairly useful handicap hurdler: won at Uttoxeter in June, Market Rasen in July and Stratford in August: tailed off in novice handicap on chasing debut: stays 3¼m: acts on good to firm and good to soft going: in blinkers last 3 starts: often races towards rear. *Fergal O'Brien*

LUCEMATIC 11 b.m. Systematic – Soldier's Song (Infantry) [2016/17 c113, h–: c26.2dᵖᵘ **c–** May 4] workmanlike mare: winning hurdler: maiden chaser, pulled up sole outing (in **h–** cheekpieces) in 2016/17: should stay at least 3m: acts on heavy going. *Chris Grant*

LUCKIME (IRE) 5 gr.g. Oscar (IRE) – Blossom Rose (IRE) (Roselier (FR)) [2016/17 **b90 p** b17d² Apr 5] €52,000 3-y-o: sixth foal: brother to bumper winner/fairly useful hurdler Oscar Blue (2½m/23f winner) and closely related to a winning pointer by Saddlers' Hall: dam twice-raced half-sister to dam of fairly useful hurdler/useful chaser (stayed 3m) Bideford Legend: 6/1, second in bumper at Carlisle (6 lengths behind Court Affairs) in April: will be suited by further than 2m: likely to improve. *Venetia Williams*

LUCKOFTHEDRAW (FR) 4 gr.g. Martaline – La Perspective (FR) (Beyssac (FR)) **b80** [2016/17 b15.8v³ Mar 1] fifth foal: half-brother to useful hurdler/chaser Dolatulo (15f-25f winner, by Le Fou): dam ran twice on Flat in France: 6/1, third in bumper at Ffos Las (7½ lengths behind Jaunty Warrior) in March: will stay further than 2m. *Paul Morgan*

LUCKY DIVA 10 ch.m. Lucky Story (USA) – Cosmic Countess (IRE) (Lahib (USA)) **h91** [2016/17 h16.8d h16.8m² h21.4mᵖᵘ Oct 14] modest on Flat, stays 17f: modest form over hurdles: standout effort when second in novice at Exeter in October: wears cheekpieces. *Bill Turner*

LUCKY GAL 7 b.m. Overbury (IRE) – Lucky Arrow (Indian Ridge) [2016/17 h–: h18.5g⁵ **h86** h19.5d h16d h19.8dᵖᵘ h16.2v⁶ Feb 1] modest form over hurdles: stays 2¼m: acts on good to soft going: tried in hood: often in tongue tie. *Martin Hill*

LUCKY JIM 6 b.g. Lucky Story (USA) – Lateralle (IRE) (Unfuwain (USA)) [2016/17 **c112**
c116, h116: c16g c18m² c20.3g⁵ c19.4g⁵ c21g⁵ c20g² c17s² Mar 13] compact gelding: **h–**
winning hurdler: fair maiden chaser: stays 2¾m: acts on good to firm and heavy going: in
cheekpieces last 4 starts: in tongue tie last 5. *David Dennis*

LUCKY THIRTEEN 9 b.g. Passing Glance – Lingua Franca (Formidable (USA)) **h85**
[2016/17 h15.8s⁵ h16.3v³ h20.3d h19g h24.4d² Jan 9] modest form over hurdles: stayed
3m: acted on heavy going: tried in cheekpieces: dead. *Richard Phillips*

LUCY MC (IRE) 6 gr.m. Tikkanen (USA) – Careless Abandon (IRE) (Mull of Kintyre **h95**
(USA)) [2016/17 b54: h20g⁵ h18.2d² h21g h16g⁵ h16.8g* h20.2d⁴ h15.5v³ h15.8v⁵ h16.3g⁴
Mar 25] maiden pointer: modest hurdler: won mares novice at Sedgefield in September:
left Gordon Elliott after sixth start: stays 2¼m: acts on good to soft going. *Barry Leavy*

LUKES HILL (IRE) 9 b.g. Bandari (IRE) – New Power (IRE) (Saddlers' Hall (IRE)) **h–**
[2016/17 h18.5g May 25] workmanlike gelding: maiden hurdler: won twice in points
shortly after end of season: stays 2½m: acts on soft and good to firm going: has worn
headgear: tried in tongue strap: quirky. *David Rees*

LUNAR FLOW 6 b.g. With The Flow (USA) – Misty Move (IRE) (Saddlers' Hall (IRE)) **c99**
[2016/17 h90, b–: h24g⁶ h21.6v c25.1s c24v* c24.5v⁴ c23.6s⁵ Mar 13] poor handicap **h79**
hurdler: modest form over fences: won handicap at Uttoxeter in February: stays 3m: acts
on heavy going: in blinkers last 3 starts: front runner/races prominently. *Jamie Snowden*

LUNAR LOGIC 5 b.g. Motivator – Moonmaiden (Selkirk (USA)) [2016/17 h16g h16dᵘʳ **h93**
h17.3g h16.8g⁵ Aug 25] modest form on Flat: modest maiden hurdler: raced only at 2m:
acts on good to soft going: tried in headgear last 3 starts. *Gordon Elliott, Ireland*

LURE DES PRES (IRE) 5 b.g. Robin des Pres (FR) – Pinkeen Lady (IRE) (Presenting) **h83**
[2016/17 b–: h16.8s⁶ h21.4m⁴ h18.5g⁴ Apr 26] poor form over hurdles: tried in tongue tie.
Linda Blackford

LUSIS NATUREA 6 b.g. Multiplex – Kenny's Dream (Karinga Bay) [2016/17 h15.6gᶠ **h78**
Jan 3] useful on Flat, stays 1½m: twice-raced pointer: fifth in bumper: held when fell last
in maiden won by Idder at Musselburgh on hurdling debut: has worn hood/tongue tie. *Noel
C. Kelly, Ireland*

LUTECE 5 b.m. Cape Cross (IRE) – Loutka (FR) (Trempolino (USA)) [2016/17 h118: **h–**
h16d⁶ h16d h19.9s h21.2sᵖᵘ Feb 8] useful-looking mare: maiden hurdler, no form in
2016/17: has worn headgear. *Venetia Williams*

LYCIDAS (GER) 8 b.g. Zamindar (USA) – La Felicita (Shareef Dancer (USA)) [2016/17 **h117**
h–: h16.7g² h16.2m* h16s³ h16.6g h16.2v² h16.6s⁴ h19.4g³ h16.4g² h16d⁵ Apr 21] fairly
useful hurdler: won novice at Kelso in May: probably stays 19f: acts on good to firm and
heavy going: usually wears hood: usually races prominently. *James Ewart*

LYDSTEP POINT 10 b.g. Beat All (USA) – Compton Chick (IRE) (Dolphin Street (FR)) **c–**
[2016/17 h20g h23.9dᵖᵘ h19.5sᵖᵘ Jan 8] lengthy gelding: winning pointer/chaser: maiden **h–**
hurdler, no form in 2016/17: tried in tongue tie. *Jan Mathias*

LYGON ROCK (IRE) 4 b.g. Robin des Champs (FR) – Cute Lass (IRE) (Flemensfirth **b–**
(USA)) [2016/17 b16s⁶ Mar 30] well beaten in maiden bumper. *Henry Daly*

LYME PARK 6 gr.m. Multiplex – So Cloudy (Cloudings (IRE)) [2016/17 b16d⁶ h19.6g⁴ **h96**
h20.3g⁴ h19.6g³ h17.1g h21d² h19.6s⁴ h24.1s⁴ h20.6s⁴ Jan 18] third foal: half-sister to fair **b–**
hurdler/chaser Nefyn Bay (2m-2½m winner, by Overbury): dam (h95), 2m-2½m hurdle
winner, out of half-sister to very smart chaser Cloudy Lane (stayed 3¼m): well beaten in
mares bumper: modest maiden hurdler: stays 21f: acts on good to soft going. *Donald McCain*

LYNDA'S BOY 6 b.g. Rainbow High – Braybrooke Lady (IRE) (Presenting) [2016/17 h–, **h–**
b–: h19.6m⁶ h15.8g h15.7dᵖᵘ Nov 29] no form in bumper/over hurdles. *Caroline Bailey*

LYRIC STREET (IRE) 9 b.g. Hurricane Run (IRE) – Elle Danzig (GER) (Roi Danzig **c–**
(USA)) [2016/17 c108, h–: h17m* h17.2g² h17.2d h19.6g* h16.2d³ h20.1sᵖᵘ Sep 30] good- **h115**
topped gelding: fairly useful handicap hurdler: won at Carlisle in May and Bangor in July:
maiden chaser: stayed 2½m: acted on heavy and good to firm going: tried in cheekpieces:
front runner/raced prominently: dead. *Donald McCain*

LYVIUS 9 b.g. Paolini (GER) – Lysuna (GER) (Monsun (GER)) [2016/17 c16.3s⁴ c19.4s⁶ **c104 §**
c16.4s⁴ h19.3d⁴ h18.1d Apr 10] close-coupled gelding: useful handicap hurdler at best, **h– §**
well held in handicaps last 2 starts in 2016/17: maiden chaser: stays 2½m: acts on heavy
going: has worn blinkers: temperamental. *Rose Dobbin*

M

MAB DAB (IRE) 6 b.g. Papal Bull – Pret A Porter (UAE) (Jade Robbery (USA)) [2016/17 **h106** b–: ab16g⁵ h17.7s h17.7v³ h21g h25m* Apr 17] good-topped gelding: poor form in **b65** bumpers: fair form over hurdles: upped again in trip, won handicap at Plumpton in April: stays 25f: acts on good to firm going. *Linda Jewell*

MACALLA (IRE) 5 b.g. Echo of Light – Rum Raisin (Invincible Spirit (IRE)) [2016/17 **h97** h16.2m² h17.2m⁴ h16.2d⁶ h16.2s³ h16.2g h16.2d Sep 21] poor maiden on Flat, stayed 11f: modest form over hurdles: best effort at 2m on good to firm going: usually in cheekpieces: tried in tongue tie: dead. *R. Mike Smith*

MACARTHUR 13 b.g. Montjeu (IRE) – Out West (USA) (Gone West (USA)) [2016/17 **c73 §** c100§, h102§: c23m Jul 4] winning pointer: fair hurdler: maiden chaser, fair form at best: **h– §** stays 21f: acts on good to firm and good to soft going: usually wears headgear: has worn tongue tie: usually races nearer last than first: temperamental. *David Rees*

MAC BELLA 5 ch.m. Black Sam Bellamy (IRE) – Macnance (IRE) (Mandalus) [2016/17 **h–** b15.8d h15.8g⁴ Apr 3] half-sister to several winners, including fair hurdlers Mac Beattie **b–** (19f winner) and Mac Bertie (2½m winner), both by Beat All: dam (c108/h105), 2m-2½m hurdle/chase winner (stayed 3m), sister to fair hurdler/very smart chaser (stayed 3¼m) Macgeorge and half-sister to smart hurdler/chaser (stayed 4m) Chief Dan George: tailed off in mares bumper: fell fourth in mares novice on hurdling debut. *Evan Williams*

MAC BERTIE 8 b.g. Beat All (USA) – Macnance (IRE) (Mandalus) [2016/17 c79, h104: **c96 §** c19.4g c16d² c17m⁴ c22.6g⁵ Aug 11] fair handicap hurdler: modest maiden chaser (has **h–** looked temperamental): stays 2¾m: acts on good to soft going: usually wears cheekpieces. *Evan Williams*

MACCA'S STOWAWAY (IRE) 4 b.f. Stowaway – Julies Vic (IRE) (Old Vic) [2016/17 **h84** b16s b16v h16s h16v⁴ h15.8g⁴ Apr 3] third foal: half-sister to a winning pointer by **b–** Mr Dinos: dam, won completed start in points, half-sister to useful hurdler (stays 2½m) Prince of Steal: no form in bumpers: poor form over hurdles. *Matt Sheppard*

MAC GREGORY 6 b.g. Multiplex – Macnance (IRE) (Mandalus) [2016/17 h104p, b91: **h108** h15.9g⁴ h15.8m² h16.4g h21.2d^pu Nov 28] sturdy gelding: bumper winner: fair form over hurdles: best effort at 2m on good to firm going: often raced towards rear: dead. *Evan Williams*

MACHIATO (IRE) 6 br.g. Milan – Wychnor Dawn (IRE) (Broken Hearted) [2016/17 **b95 p** b16.8g* Jul 25] seventh foal: closely related to smart hurdler Glingerburn (2m-2¼m winner, by King's Theatre) and half-brother to 2 winners, including bumper winner/useful hurdler Aegean Dawn (2m-21f winner, by Alflora): dam unraced half-sister to Cheltenham Gold Cup winner Cool Dawn: 2/1, won maiden bumper at Newton Abbot (by 2½ lengths from Our Merlin) on only start: seemed sure to progress. *Colin Tizzard*

MACHIAVELIAN STORM (IRE) 5 gr.m. Dark Angel (IRE) – Terri's Charmer (USA) **h–** (Silver Charm (USA)) [2016/17 h18.5g^pu h15.3d h15.3s^pu Dec 26] modest maiden on Flat, stays 1½m: no form over hurdles. *Richard Mitchell*

MACKEYS FORGE (IRE) 13 b.g. Mr Combustible (IRE) – Lucy Walters (IRE) **c–** (King's Ride) [2016/17 c69, h–: c21g^pu May 5] winning hurdler: one-time fairly useful **h–** chaser: has worn headgear: in tongue tie last 2 starts. *Hugo Froud*

MACKIE DEE (IRE) 5 b.g. Westerner – Whatdoyouthinkmac (IRE) (Supreme Leader) **h94** [2016/17 b15.8v b16s h24.1m³ h23.1g³ Apr 22] €34,000 3-y-o: fourth foal: half-brother to **b–** fairly useful hurdler/useful chaser No No Mac (19f-3m winner, by Oscar) and bumper winner/fairly useful hurdler Smiler (2m-2¼m winner, by Vinnie Roe): dam (h90), maiden hurdler (placed at 2m), half-sister to useful hurdler/high-class staying chaser Shotgun Willy and Welsh Grand National winner Mini Sensation: no form in bumpers: modest form over hurdles: better effort when third in maiden at Bangor: in hood last 2 starts. *John Mackie*

MADAM BE 7 b.m. Kayf Tara – Mrs Be (IRE) (Be My Native (USA)) [2016/17 c–, h–: **c–** h23m³ h23.3g² h21.6g c23g^pu h21.6m Oct 6] winning pointer: poor maiden handicap **h75** hurdler: little impact in 2 chase starts: stays 23f: acts on good to firm going: in cheekpieces/ tongue strap final start. *Brian Barr*

MADAME FIONA 5 gr.m. Overbury (IRE) – Roslin (Roscoe Blake) [2016/17 b16.8g² **h70** Apr 26] seventh foal: sister to fairly useful hurdler/fair chaser Georgian King (2¾m-3¼m winner) and half-sister to bumper winner/fair hurdler Madame Jasmine (25f winner, by Karinga Bay): dam unraced: 10/1/in hood, second in maiden bumper at Exeter (8 lengths behind Jaunty Flyer) on debut. *Martin Keighley*

MADAME LAFITE 5 b.m. Dutch Art – Poppo's Song (CAN) (Polish Navy (USA)) **h93**
[2016/17 h17.7d h21s h19.1d³ h20.5gᵇᵈ h21.4d h20.7d⁵ Mar 15] fair maiden on Flat, stays
2m: modest maiden over hurdles: stays 21f: acts on good to soft going: tried in cheekpieces.
Jonathan Portman

MAD BRIAN (IRE) 11 b.g. Brian Boru – Needle Doll (IRE) (Needle Gun (IRE)) **c110**
[2016/17 c–, h123: c17d⁵ c24vᵖᵘ h24g h23d⁵ c24d c28s⁴ h22.3s* c33.4sᵖᵘ c24.7dᵖᵘ Apr 17] **h127**
close-coupled gelding: fairly useful handicap hurdler: won at Navan in February: handicap
chaser, just fair form in 2016/17: stays 3m: acts on soft going: in hood first 2 starts: wears
tongue tie. *Mrs Gillian Callaghan, Ireland*

MADDOXTOWN (IRE) 11 b.g. Luso – Augusta Victoria (Callernish) [2016/17 c20d⁶ **c68**
c24d³ c23m⁶ Aug 17] maiden hurdler: maiden chaser, poor nowadays: stays 23f: acts on **h–**
good to soft and good to firm going: has worn headgear, including in 2016/17.
Richenda Ford

MADE IN MAY (IRE) 5 br.m. Dahjee (USA) – Black Dot Com (IRE) (Black Monday) **b–**
[2016/17 b16.8g⁴ Sep 16] third foal: half-sister to bumper winner Made In Germany (by
Germany): dam (h75) 3m hurdle winner/winning pointer: tailed off in bumper on debut.
Neil Mulholland

MAD JACK MYTTON (IRE) 7 b.g. Arcadio (GER) – Gilt Ridden (IRE) (Heron Island **c133**
(IRE)) [2016/17 h134: h16.4sᵖᵘ c19.9s² c16.1g² c20.2s⁵ c20.8gᶠ h20g Apr 7] lengthy **h–**
gelding: useful hurdler at best: useful form over fences: second in novice handicap at
Huntingdon and handicap at Taunton, both in January: stays 2½m, effective at shorter: acts
on soft and good to firm going: often races towards rear. *Jonjo O'Neill*

MAD MONEY (IRE) 11 b.g. Alderbrook – Merry Gladness (IRE) (King's Ride) **c101**
[2016/17 c86, h84: c16.3gᵘʳ c16.3g⁴ c23m³ c23g* c23.8d* h23.3sᵖᵘ h23.8gᶠ Nov 2] **h85**
multiple point winner: maiden hurdler: fair handicap chaser: won at Worcester and
Perth in September: left J. W. Tudor after first start: stays 3m: acts on good to soft going:
has worn headgear, including last 4 starts: has worn tongue tie: usually leads/travels
strongly. *Tim Vaughan*

MADNESS LIGHT (FR) 8 b.g. Satri (IRE) – Majestic Lady (FR) (Octagonal (NZ)) **c–**
[2016/17 h20.5d⁶ Nov 14] useful-looking gelding: one-time fairly useful hurdler: winning **h–**
chaser: stays 2½m: acts on good to firm and heavy going: often in cheekpieces. *Daniel Steele*

MA DU FOU (FR) 7 b.g. Le Fou (IRE) – Belle du Ma (FR) (Zamindar (USA)) [2016/17 **c127**
h139: c15.2d³ c20.3s³ c19.1d⁴ c24dᶠ Feb 9] sturdy gelding: useful hurdler: fairly useful **h–**
form in novice chases: stayed 2½m: acted on heavy going: in cheekpieces last 2 starts:
dead. *Warren Greatrex*

MAESTRO ROYAL 8 b.g. Doyen (IRE) – Close Harmony (Bustino) [2016/17 h126: **h130**
h17.7d² h20g h16.8g² h16s* h16.8s h16.3d* h20.2g Apr 28] useful-looking gelding: useful
handicap hurdler: won at Sandown in January and Newbury (by 1¼ lengths from Inner
Drive) in March: unproven beyond 17f: acts on soft going: tried in cheekpieces: usually
races towards rear. *Nicky Henderson*

MAFATE FORTIN (FR) 7 b.g. Enrique – Shining of Crystal (FR) (Shining Steel) **h–**
[2016/17 b16.2d² b16.2d⁵ h22.1d⁶ h16.7g Aug 13] €26,000 3-y-o, £1,500 4-y-o: third foal: **b85**
dam French 1½m/13f winner: maiden pointer: fair form on first of 2 starts in bumpers: well
held both starts over hurdles: wears tongue tie. *Keith Reveley*

MAGGIE BLUE (IRE) 9 b.m. Beneficial – Top Ar Aghaidh (IRE) (Topanoora) [2016/17 **c–**
c–, h105: h25.4m* h22.1d h25.8s⁴ h24.3s h22.7s³ h25.3g⁶ h22.7d⁴ Apr 10] fair handicap **h105**
hurdler: won mares event at Cartmel in May: maiden chaser: stays 3¼m: acts on good to
firm and heavy going: front runner. *Harriet Graham*

MAGGIE'S DAWN 5 b.m. Bach (IRE) – Maggie's Opera (Dr Massini (IRE)) [2016/17 **h69**
h16.7s⁵ h19.7s⁶ h15.8g⁶ h16.5m² Apr 27] third foal: dam unraced: poor form over hurdles.
David Brace

MAGGIO (FR) 12 b.g. Trempolino (USA) – La Musardiere (FR) (Cadoudal (FR)) **c132**
[2016/17 c147, h–: c20.5m⁴ h22.5g⁵ h24d c23.4v⁴ Feb 16] rather leggy gelding: fairly **h118**
useful hurdler/useful chaser: not at best in 2016/17: stays 25f: acts on good to firm and
heavy going: has worn headgear: wears tongue tie. *Patrick Griffin, Ireland*

MAGHERAL EXPRESS (IRE) 8 b.g. Gold Well – Patzanni (IRE) (Arzanni) [2016/17 **c73 §**
c85, h110: c24.1g⁵ Apr 29] won completed start in Irish points: fair maiden hurdler: poor **h– §**
form over fences: stays 3m: acts on soft going: tried in cheekpieces/tongue tie: tends to find
little. *Kerry Lee*

MAGICAL MAN 10 b.g. Lahib (USA) – Majestic Di (IRE) (Zaffaran (USA)) [2016/17 **c89 §** c88§, h–: c25.3v^{pu} c25.2s^4 c24.5v* c23.5v^4 c20.9v^5 Mar 19] maiden hurdler: modest **h–** handicap chaser: won at Towcester in February: stays 3m: acts on heavy going: wears headgear: temperamental (has run out). *Debra Hamer*

MAGICAL THOMAS 5 ch.g. Dylan Thomas (IRE) – Magical Cliche (USA) (Affirmed **h91** (USA)) [2016/17 h15.8g^6 h15.3d h16.8s h15.3v^3 h18.5d^{pu} h16g Apr 17] fairly useful on Flat, stays 1½m: modest form over hurdles: will prove best at 2m: acts on heavy going: tried in tongue tie. *Neil Mulholland*

MAGIC BULLET (IRE) 6 b.g. Flemensfirth (USA) – Some Bob Back (IRE) (Bob Back **h98** (USA)) [2016/17 b89: b15.7s^4 b16.3d^4 h15.8g^5 h15.8d h19.6d Dec 26] modest form in **b79** bumpers/over hurdles: should prove suited by further than 2m: in hood last 4 starts: often races towards rear. *Nicky Henderson*

MAGIC DANCER 5 b.g. Norse Dancer (IRE) – King's Siren (IRE) (King's Best (USA)) **h109** [2016/17 h110: h16s^3 h21.3d^2 h19.5g Apr 17] fair maiden hurdler: stays 21f: acts on soft going: wears cheekpieces/tongue tie: races prominently. *Charlie Longsdon*

MAGIC MONEY 9 b.m. Midnight Legend – Sticky Money (Relkino) [2016/17 h106: **c121** h23.3g^6 h25.4m^3 h23.3g^2 h21.6g^4 h23.3d^2 h24.5s^6 h24.4g^3 c20.5g^{ur} c22.7g^{pu} c22.7s^2 **h111** c25.5d* c22.2g* c20.8g^2 Apr 20] angular mare: fair handicap hurdler: fairly useful form over fences: won handicap at Fontwell in March and mares handicap at Haydock in April: left Kim Bailey after third start: stays 25f: acts on good to firm and good to soft going: wears cheekpieces. *Warren Greatrex*

MAGIC MUSIC MAN 6 b.g. Authorized (IRE) – Magic Music (IRE) (Magic Ring **h107** (IRE)) [2016/17 h114: h17m^3 h15.8g^2 h18.7g^4 h16.8g* h18.6g^6 Sep 24] fair hurdler: won maiden at Sedgefield in August: unproven beyond 17f: acts on soft and good to firm going: in headgear last 4 starts: usually leads. *Alan King*

MAGIC MUSTARD (IRE) 6 ch.g. Stowaway – Honey Mustard (IRE) (Roselier (FR)) **h100** [2016/17 h74, b–: h19.5d^4 h21.6s* h21s h23.1s* h23.1d^4 Jan 3] stocky gelding: fair handicap hurdler: won at Fontwell (novice event) in November and Bangor in December: will stay beyond 23f: acts on soft going: tried in cheekpieces, including in 2016/17: in tongue tie last 2 starts. *Kerry Lee*

MAGIC RIVER (IRE) 6 ch.g. Indian River (FR) – All Magic (IRE) (Ashkalani (IRE)) **h105** [2016/17 h16.5g^6 h16.5g^5 Jan 27] £25,000 5-y-o: first foal: dam unraced half-sister to fairly useful hurdler (19f-21f winner) Lord Ragnar: off mark in points at fourth attempt: fair form over hurdles: better effort when sixth in maiden at Taunton in December: will be suited by at least 2¼m. *Charles Whittaker*

MAGIE DU MA (FR) 4 b.f. Sageburg (IRE) – To Much Fun (Act One) [2016/17 h14.9s* **h130** h17.4s^5 h17.4s^2 h16.8g h16s* Mar 30] good-topped filly: first foal: dam, French 15f-17f hurdles winner, also 1½m winner on Flat: fair form on Flat: fairly useful hurdler: won fillies juvenile at Auteuil in May: second in Prix Sagan at Auteuil (2 lengths behind D'vina) in June: left P. Chevillard €210,000, below form in Triumph Hurdle at Cheltenham and fillies' 4-y-o handicap at Warwick: raced around 2m: acts on soft going: in hood last 2 starts, also in tongue tie final one. *David Pipe*

MAGISTRAL 7 b.g. Manduro (GER) – Tamalain (USA) (Royal Academy (USA)) **h88** [2016/17 h20.2g^6 Apr 26] fairly useful on Flat, stays 13f: modest form on second of 2 starts over hurdles. *Iain Jardine*

MAGNA CARTOR 7 b.g. Motivator – Hora (Hernando (FR)) [2016/17 h–, b93: h15.7g* **h118** h15.8g^2 h15.8d^f h18.7g^{ur} h18.7g^3 h16d^5 h16g* h16g* h16.4g h16d h16.4g h16d Apr 16] lengthy gelding: bumper winner: fairly useful hurdler: won novice at Southwell in May, and handicap at Punchestown and novice at Wexford in October: left Daniel Loughnane after fifth start: unproven beyond 2m: acts on good to soft going: has worn hood: usually races prominently. *John Joseph Hanlon, Ireland*

MAGNIFICENT MADIBA 4 b.g. Mount Nelson – Mrs Penny (AUS) (Planchet (AUS)) **h54** [2016/17 h16.3d^6 h15.8s Jan 13] angular gelding: fair on Flat, stays 1¼m: showed little in 2 juvenile hurdles. *George Baker*

MAGNOLIA RIDGE (IRE) 7 b.g. Galileo (IRE) – Treasure The Lady (IRE) (Indian **h90** Ridge) [2016/17 h66: h16.2g* h16.2d h16.7g* h16.3g^6 h19.9g^2 h16.2d^6 h19.9d h19.3d^{pu} h20.6g h16g^4 Apr 23] modest handicap hurdler: won at Hexham (amateurs novice event) in May and Market Rasen (lady amateurs event) in July: stays 2½m: best form on good going: wears cheekpieces. *Mark Walford*

MAGNUS ROMEO 6 b.g. Manduro (GER) – Chili Dip (Alhaarth (IRE)) [2016/17 h–:   **h93**
h19.6m h16.8g⁴ h16.8m³ h16.8s³ h15.9s⁶ h16.5g Jan 11] stocky gelding: modest maiden
hurdler: unproven beyond 17f: acts on soft and good to firm going: blinkered final start:
wears tongue tie. *Johnny Farrelly*

MAGUIRE'S GLEN (IRE) 9 b.g. Craigsteel – Next Venture (IRE) (Zaffaran (USA))   **c111**
[2016/17 c21vᵖᵘ c16v⁶ c19.5v⁵ c21.5d⁶ c17.5v³ c20v* c19.4d⁶ Apr 16] winning hurdler: **h–**
fair handicap chaser: won at Clonmel in March: left Miss Elizabeth Doyle after sixth start:
stays 2¾m: acts on heavy going: tried in cheekpieces in 2016/17. *Grace Harris*

MAHLER AND ME (IRE) 7 ch.g. Mahler – Tisindabreedin (IRE) (Zaffaran (USA))   **c–**
[2016/17 h108: h19.7g⁵ c21.2g⁶ c23.8sᵖᵘ Jul 10] won Irish maiden point on debut: fair   **h101**
handicap hurdler: some promise on first of 2 starts in chases: stays 2¾m: acts on heavy
going: in cheekpieces/tongue tie last 3 starts: often leads. *Alistair Whillans*

MAHLER BAY (IRE) 7 b.g. Mahler – Belalzao (IRE) (Alzao (USA)) [2016/17 h–, b–:   **h81**
h16.8g³ h18.1m³ h19.3dᵖᵘ h24.4d h24d h24gᵖᵘ h19.9m³ Apr 19] maiden pointer: poor
maiden hurdler: left Michael Smith after second start: should stay further than 17f: tried in
cheekpieces in 2016/17. *Kenny Johnson*

MAHLERDRAMATIC (IRE) 7 br.g. Mahler – Image of Vermont (IRE) (Accordion)   **h116**
[2016/17 b100: h16.6g* h16.8d³ h16.8s² Jan 29] maiden Irish pointer: bumper winner:
fairly useful form over hurdles: won novice at Doncaster in November, having run of race:
will stay further than 2m: front runner/races prominently. *Brian Ellison*

MAHLER LAD (IRE) 7 b.g. Mahler – Sister Merenda (IRE) (Dr Massini (IRE))   **c102**
[2016/17 h105: c23.9gᵖᵘ c24.1s³ c24.5s⁶ c26.3g* Apr 7] won Irish maiden point on   **h–**
debut: maiden hurdler: fair form over fences: won handicap at Sedgefield final outing:
stays 3¼m: acts on heavy going: in headgear last 3 starts: front runner/races prominently.
Donald McCain

MAHLERMADE (IRE) 4 ch.g. Mahler – Double Concerto (IRE) (Brahms (USA))   **b83**
[2016/17 b16.3g⁵ Apr 1] £36,000 3-y-o: second foal: dam poor maiden on Flat: 14/1,
showed a bit when 7¾ lengths fifth of 8 to Gunfleet in bumper at Stratford. *Alan King*

MAHLER'S FIRST (IRE) 5 b.g. Mahler – Fridays Folly (IRE) (Flemensfirth (USA))   **b–**
[2016/17 b16g Apr 8] tailed off in bumper on debut. *Victor Dartnall*

MAHLERS STAR (IRE) 7 ch.g. Mahler – Celestial Rose (IRE) (Roselier (FR))   **c112**
[2016/17 h114: h21g h18.7m³ h21.1s h21.2d² h23.3vᶠ h20.3s c20.3g² Apr 22] runner-up   **h105**
completed start in Irish points: fair maiden hurdler: fair form when second in novice
handicap at Bangor (nose behind Clondaw Draft) on chasing debut: likely to stay 3m: acts
on soft going: tried in tongue tie: often races/reins towards rear. *David Bridgwater*

MAHLERVOUS (IRE) 4 b.g. Mahler – Brook Style (IRE) (Alderbrook) [2016/17 b16g⁴   **b78**
Apr 24] 11/2, 16¼ lengths fourth of 8 to World Premier in bumper at Warwick.
Warren Greatrex

MAID OF MILAN (IRE) 6 br.m. Milan – Joes Lady (IRE) (Win Quick (IRE)) [2016/17   **h108**
h108, b–: h21m* h21.2m³ Oct 20] runner-up in Irish point: fair form over hurdles: won
mares maiden at Kempton in May: will stay 3m: front runner/races prominently.
Charlie Mann

MAID OF SILK (IRE) 11 b.m. Blueprint (IRE) – Silk Style (Polish Precedent (USA))   **c–**
[2016/17 c–, h–: c17mᶠ May 20] lengthy mare: maiden pointer: winning hurdler/chaser: no   **h–**
form in hunters: tried in cheekpieces: usually in tongue tie. *Mrs K. Lee*

MAID OF TUSCANY (IRE) 6 b.m. Manduro (GER) – Tuscania (USA) (Woodman   **h101**
(USA)) [2016/17 h101: h16g h17.7g* h15.7v³ h16g⁴ h16m⁵ h18.7g⁴ h15.8s Mar 2] fair
handicap hurdler: won at Fontwell in May: left Neil Mulholland after fifth start: stays 2¼m:
acts on good to soft going: has worn headgear, including in 2016/17. *Alexandra Dunn*

MAIFALKI (FR) 4 b.g. Falco (USA) – Makila (IRE) (Entrepreneur) [2016/17 b13.7m⁵   **b75**
Oct 2] fairly useful on Flat, stays 9.5f: 10/1, looked in need of experience when fifth in
junior bumper at Huntingdon (3 lengths behind dead-heaters Dentley de Mee and Theydon
Park). *Mark Walford*

MAIGH DARA (IRE) 8 br.g. Cacique (IRE) – Dara Diva (IRE) (Barathea (IRE))   **h80**
[2016/17 h–, b69: h21gᵖᵘ h21.6d⁴ Jun 1] workmanlike gelding: bumper winner: poor form
over hurdles. *Lydia Richards*

MA'IRE RUA (IRE) 10 ch.g. Presenting – Long Acre (Mark of Esteem (IRE)) [2016/17   **c68**
c54, h83: c19.7s⁵ c21mᵖᵘ Apr 15] lengthy, angular gelding: maiden hurdler: poor form over   **h–**
fences: unproven beyond 2m: acts on heavy going: in cheekpieces last 2 starts. *Alan Jones*

MAIZY MISSILE (IRE) 15 b.m. Executive Perk – Landsker Missile (Cruise Missile) **c85**
[2016/17 c83, h–: c16.3g³ c16.3s* c16.3g⁵ c17g⁴ c16g c17.4g Oct 25] winning hurdler: **h–**
modest handicap chaser: won at Newton Abbot in June: best around 2m: acts on good to
firm and heavy going: usually races close up. *Mary Evans*

MAJANALMA (IRE) 7 b.m. Robin des Pres (FR) – Evangelica (USA) (Dahar (USA)) **b–**
[2016/17 b17.7g May 8] half-sister to useful hurdler/smart chaser Call The Police
(2m-2½m winner) and a winning pointer (both by Accordion): dam (c122/h116) 2½m-3½m
hurdle/chase winner: tailed off in bumper on only start. *Steve Woodman*

MAJESTIC MOLL (IRE) 5 b.m. King's Theatre (IRE) – Artist's Muse (IRE) (Cape **b89**
Cross (IRE)) [2016/17 b16.6d⁶ b15.8d² b16g* Apr 17] €62,000 3-y-o: second foal: half-
sister to fairly useful hurdler Chase End Charlie (2½m/21f winner, by Scorpion): dam
(h123), 2m hurdle winner, also 7f/1m winner on Flat: fair form in bumpers: won mares
event at Chepstow on final start. *Emma Lavelle*

MAJESTIC TOUCH (IRE) 6 br.g. Kalanisi (IRE) – Alexander Divine (Halling (USA)) **h107 p**
[2016/17 b79: h16.6d⁶ h15.8s² Feb 8] modest form in bumpers: fair form over hurdles:
better effort when second in maiden at Ludlow: likely to progress further. *Philip Hobbs*

MAJINGILANE (IRE) 5 b.g. Winged Love (IRE) – Kiora Lady (IRE) (King's Ride) **h–**
[2016/17 h16.3dᵘʳ h19.1s h16s h19.5gᵘʳ Apr 8] rather unfurnished gelding: no form
over hurdles. *Warren Greatrex*

MAJOR DAVIS (FR) 5 b.g. Vision d'Etat (FR) – Majorica Sancta (FR) (Saint des Saints **h100 p**
(FR)) [2016/17 b–p: b15.7s³ b16v⁵ b17.7g⁴ h15.3f² Apr 23] angular gelding: fair form in **b86**
bumpers: 16/1, second of 4 in novice at Wincanton (9 lengths behind Capitaine) on
hurdling debut: open to improvement. *Warren Greatrex*

MAJOR FRANKO 5 ch.g. Major Cadeaux – Royal Future (IRE) (Royal Academy **h–**
(USA)) [2016/17 h15.8vᵖᵘ h16.5gᵖᵘ Dec 20] modest maiden on Flat, stays 13f: showed
nothing in 2 maiden hurdles. *Sarah-Jayne Davies*

MAJOR HINDRANCE (IRE) 7 ch.g. Kris Kin (USA) – Ten Dollar Bill (IRE) **h108 p**
(Accordion) [2016/17 h16g h15.8s⁴ h15.7d⁶ h19.5s⁶ h19.9v³ h21.7s* Mar 11] €15,000
3-y-o, £6,000 6-y-o: fifth foal: half-brother to smart chaser Monbeg Dude (3m-29f winner,
by Witness Box) and 19f chase winner Willies Girl (by Anshan): dam unraced: fair form
over hurdles: won handicap at Hereford final start: will stay at least 3m: acts on soft going:
open to further improvement. *Henry Oliver*

MAJOR IVAN (IRE) 8 b.g. Fruits of Love (USA) – Martinstown Queen (IRE) (Saddlers' **c125**
Hall (IRE)) [2016/17 c125, h125: c16.4g⁴ c20.9d² Oct 13] fairly useful handicap hurdler/ **h–**
maiden chaser: stayed 23f: acted on heavy going: tried in blinkers: front runner/raced
prominently: dead. *Malcolm Jefferson*

MAJOR MAC 5 ch.g. Shirocco (GER) – Spring Fashion (IRE) (Galileo (IRE)) [2016/17 **h121**
h104: h20.5g* h16s⁶ h20.5d⁵ h24.4d Jan 28] angular gelding: fairly useful form over
hurdles: won novice at Newbury in November: stays 21f: acts on soft going: tried in tongue
tie: usually leads, often travels strongly. *Hughie Morrison*

MAJOR MALARKEY (IRE) 14 b.g. Supreme Leader – Valley (IRE) (Flemensfirth **c91 §**
(USA)) [2016/17 c128§, h–: c32.5g⁶ Apr 27] sturdy gelding: winning hurdler: fairly useful **h–**
hunter chaser, well below best only outing in 2016/17: stays 33f: acts on soft and good to
firm going: wears headgear: unreliable. *Nigel Twiston-Davies*

MAJOR MARTIN (IRE) 8 b.g. Flemensfirth (USA) – Miss Emer (IRE) (Be My Native **c–**
(USA)) [2016/17 c77, h62: c25.7gᵖᵘ May 8] maiden hurdler/chaser, modest at best: stayed **h–**
21f: acted on soft going: sometimes in headgear: dead. *Gary Moore*

MAJOR MILBORNE 9 ch.g. Exit To Nowhere (USA) – Motown Melody (IRE) (Detroit **c–**
Sam (FR)) [2016/17 c93, h107: h25g h23.6d h21.6v Dec 15] strong gelding: maiden **h–**
hurdler, no form in 2016/17: winning chaser: often wore headgear: tried in tongue tie: dead.
Jamie Snowden

MAJOR RIDGE (IRE) 8 b.g. Indian Danehill (IRE) – Native Novel (IRE) (Be My **c82**
Native (USA)) [2016/17 c85, h–: c20.1d c26.3d³ c24.2s⁴ c25.2d* c24.5sF c23.8gᵖᵘ c24.2sᵖᵘ **h–**
c24.2gᵘʳ Apr 25] maiden hurdler: poor handicap chaser: won at Catterick in January: left
Robert Bewley after first start: stays 3¼m: acts on soft going: sometimes wore tongue tie
for previous yard: usually races close up. *Micky Hammond*

MAKE IT HAPPEN (IRE) 8 b.g. Saffron Walden (FR) – Kelpie (IRE) (Kahyasi) **c88**
[2016/17 h102: c16f⁴ c25.5dᵖᵘ h20.2sᵖᵘ h17.1d Oct 13] runner-up in Irish point: fair **h–**
handicap hurdler at best, no form in 2016/17: modest form on first of 2 starts in chases:
stays 2½m: acts on heavy going: in cheekpieces final outing. *Lucinda Russell*

MAKE ME A FORTUNE (IRE) 9 b.g. Heron Island (IRE) – Biora Queen (IRE) (Old Vic) [2016/17 h123: c20.1d³ c20.3vᵖᵘ c20g⁴ c20.9s c21.4dᵖᵘ c21.4s² c19.1gᵖᵘ c19.2s³ c24.2g³ c24gᶠ Mar 28] medium-sized gelding: fairly useful handicap hurdler: fair maiden chaser: stays 21f: acts on heavy going: wears cheekpieces. *Steve Gollings* — **c105 h–**

MAKE MY HEART FLY (IRE) 5 b.m. Stowaway – Poppy Maroon (Supreme Leader) [2016/17 b16.8g² b15.8m² b16.4s h16v h16v h15.8g² Apr 3] €3,200 3-y-o: sturdy mare: third foal: half-sister to bumper winner/fair hurdler Reves d'Amour (2½m winner, by Midnight Legend): dam (c103) 3m chase winner: modest form in bumpers: no form over hurdles: in hood last 2 starts: often races towards rear. *Ali Stronge* — **h– b79**

MAKETHEDIFFERENCE (IRE) 9 b.g. Shantou (USA) – La Panthere (USA) (Pine Bluff (USA)) [2016/17 c–, h114: h16.3g⁶ h15.7g h16g⁴ h16.2m* h15.8m³ h19.9d⁵ h16.3³ h15.8v⁴ c16.2s⁶ h15.8v h16v⁴ h16v³ h19.5s h19.9s Apr 1] well-made gelding: fair handicap hurdler: won at Kelso in October: lightly-raced maiden over fences: effective from 2m to 21f: acts on good to firm and heavy going: has worn headgear, including in 2016/17. *Tim Vaughan* — **c– h112**

MALANOS (IRE) 9 b.g. Lord of England (GER) – Majorata (GER) (Acatenango (GER)) [2016/17 c97, h95: c16d⁵ Nov 29] good-topped gelding: winning hurdler: maiden chaser: unproven beyond 2m: acts on heavy going. *Tony Carroll* — **c– h–**

MALAPIE (IRE) 9 b.g. Westerner – Victorian Lady (Old Vic) [2016/17 h–: h20.3s² h24v* h24.2dᵖᵘ Mar 24] maiden pointer: fair form over hurdles: won handicap at Southwell in March: stays 3m: acts on heavy going. *Caroline Bailey* — **h113**

MALIN BAY (IRE) 12 b.g. Milan – Mirror of Flowers (Artaius (USA)) [2016/17 h113: h23.9d³ h20.2g⁴ h23.3g⁴ h21.4dᶠ Oct 29] fair handicap hurdler: stayed 3m: had form on heavy going, best efforts on less testing ground (acted on good to firm): front runner/raced prominently: dead. *Nicky Richards* — **h113**

MALL DINI (IRE) 7 b.g. Milan – Winsome Breeze (IRE) (Glacial Storm (USA)) [2016/17 h142p: c20s³ c24v³ c20v³ c16d² c20v³ c26g⁵ Mar 16] good-topped gelding: point winner: useful hurdler: smart form over fences: placed in maidens first 5 starts, then 3 lengths fifth of 24 to Domesday Book in Fulke Walwyn Kim Muir Handicap Chase at Cheltenham: stays 3¼m: acts on heavy going: has worn tongue tie, including last 3 starts: often races prominently, usually travels strongly. *Patrick G. Kelly, Ireland* — **c145 h–**

MALLER TREE 10 b.g. Karinga Bay – Annaberg (IRE) (Tirol) [2016/17 c98§, h101§: c20.3d May 26] quite good-topped gelding: winning pointer: handicap hurdler, fairly useful at best: maiden chaser: stays 23f: acts on good to firm and heavy going: wears headgear: front runner/races prominently, often races lazily: unreliable. *David Dennis* — **c– § h– §**

MALPREEDY (IRE) 5 b.m. Mahler – Miles Apart (Roselier (FR)) [2016/17 b16.7d h16sᵖᵘ h19.6s⁴ h20.3s h19.9g Apr 7] fifth foal: half-sister to fair hurdlers Ocean Glandore (2½m-3m winner, by Whitmore's Conn) and Lillymile (2½m winner, by Revoque), latter also winning pointer: dam maiden: tailed off in bumper: poor form over hurdles. *David Loughnane* — **h68 b–**

MAMNOON (IRE) 4 b.g. Cape Cross (IRE) – Masaafat (Act One) [2016/17 b13.7m Oct 2] well held in junior bumper: fair form on Flat. *Roy Brotherton* — **b–**

MANBALLANDALL (IRE) 9 b.g. Flemensfirth (USA) – Omas Lady (IRE) (Be My Native (USA)) [2016/17 c106, h116: h23.3d⁴ May 7] workmanlike gelding: handicap hurdler, fairly useful at best: fair maiden chaser: stays 25f: best form on soft/heavy going: has worn headgear, including in 2016/17: wears tongue tie. *Susan Corbett* — **c– h88**

MANCE RAYDER (IRE) 4 b.g. Flemensfirth (USA) – J'y Viens (FR) (Smadoun (FR)) [2016/17 b16s* Mar 30] €155,000 3-y-o: second foal: dam (h104), lightly raced over hurdles in France (third at 2m), half-sister to fairly useful hurdler/very smart chaser (stayed 21f) J'y Vole and useful French hurdler/chaser (15f-23f winner) Si Tu Viens: 9/4, overcame inexperience when winning 9-runner maiden bumper at Warwick by neck from Bomber's Moon, travelling well and edging ahead final 100 yds: sure to progress. *Philip Hobbs* — **b93 p**

MANETTI (IRE) 5 b.g. Westerner – Mrs Wallensky (IRE) (Roselier (FR)) [2016/17 b16g Apr 22] off mark in Irish maiden points at second attempt: well held in bumper. *Ian Ferguson, Ireland* — **b–**

MAN FROM MARS 5 b.g. Schiaparelli (GER) – Diletia (Dilum (USA)) [2016/17 b82: h16d h15.8d⁵ h15.8s² h19.8d h16m* Apr 4] well-made gelding: fairly useful form over — **h119**

hurdles: won novice at Kempton final start, despite another sketchy round of jumping: should stay further than 2m: acts on soft and good to firm going. *Nick Williams*

MAN FROM SEVILLE 7 ch.g. Duke of Marmalade (IRE) – Basanti (USA) (Galileo (IRE)) [2016/17 h109: c21.4s^F h21.6d Dec 16] sturdy gelding: fair hurdler at best: fell fifth on chasing debut: unproven beyond 2m: acts on good to soft going: in tongue tie last 2 starts. *Fergal O'Brien*   c–
h–

MANGO CAP (FR) 6 gr.g. Zambezi Sun – Medjai (FR) (Kendor (FR)) [2016/17 h111: h18.5g^{pu} h23.9d* h21.4d³ h21.9s⁶ h24.3s c23g³ c20.5v⁵ c24g⁴ c20.5m⁴ Apr 18] sturdy gelding: fair handicap hurdler: won at Perth in September: fair form over fences: left David Pipe after eighth start: stays 3m: acts on heavy going: has worn headgear, including last 5 starts: wears tongue tie. *Matt Sheppard*   c113
h114

MANHATTAN MEAD 7 ch.g. Central Park (IRE) – Honey Nut (Entrepreneur) [2016/17 h104: h19.1d c23.6m⁴ Apr 28] workmanlike gelding: winning pointer: maiden hurdler, fair at best: 40/1, fourth in novice hunter at Chepstow (11½ lengths behind Repeat Business) on chasing debut: left Michael Madgwick after first start: stays 3m: acts on soft and good to firm going: has worn headgear, including on reappearance: temperamental. *Paul Hamer*   c102
h– §

MANHATTAN SWING (IRE) 7 b.g. Invincible Spirit (IRE) – Bluebell Park (USA) (Gulch (USA)) [2016/17 h137: h15.7m c21.4g² c19.2d^F h20.6g Jul 16] handicap hurdler, useful at best: fairly useful form when second in maiden at Market Rasen on chasing debut, and would have run to similar level but for falling 2 out in novice there next time: stays 21f: wears blinkers. *Brian Ellison*   c124
h115

MAN IN BLACK (FR) 8 gr.g. Turgeon (USA) – Mimosa de Wasa (FR) (Roakarad) [2016/17 h19.9s h19.9v³ c24.2s^{pu} c20.9d² Apr 5] winning Irish pointer: poor maiden hurdler/chaser: stays 21f: acts on good to soft going: sometimes in cheekpieces, including in 2016/17. *Philip Kirby*   c84
h78

MAN LOOK 5 b.g. Nayef (USA) – Charlecote (IRE) (Caerleon (USA)) [2016/17 h16.3d h16.6g h15.8v Feb 11] useful-looking gelding: useful on Flat, stays 12.5f: raced freely when well held all 3 starts over hurdles. *Donald McCain*   h–

MANNY OWENS (IRE) 5 b.g. Manduro (GER) – Arabian Coral (IRE) (Intikhab (USA)) [2016/17 h15.7d h16s h16.6g⁴ h16g⁴ Apr 23] fair on Flat, stays 1½m: modest form in maiden/novice hurdles: wears tongue tie: remains open to improvement. *Jonjo O'Neill*   h86 p

MAN OF LA MANCHA (IRE) 4 b.g. Zoffany (IRE) – Sarella Loren (USA) (Theatrical) [2016/17 h16g^{ur} Apr 23] modest maiden on Flat, stayed 6f: unseated rider second on hurdling debut: dead. *Ben Haslam*   h–

MAN OF PLENTY 8 ch.g. Manduro (GER) – Credit-A-Plenty (Generous (IRE)) [2016/17 h22.1m h22.1m⁶ h24d² h16.5g² h23.8g³ h16.8s² h19.3s Feb 18] good-topped gelding: fairly useful handicap hurdler: stays 3m: acts on soft going: in cheekpieces 3 of last 4 starts: wears tongue tie: often races towards rear. *Sophie Leech*   h118

MAN OF STEEL (IRE) 8 b.g. Craigsteel – Knappogue Honey (IRE) (Anshan) [2016/17 c108, h–: c26.3g c24.2g* c25.5g* c20s* c23.4d⁴ c24.2g³ Apr 17] multiple point winner: maiden hurdler: fair chaser: won hunters at Fakenham in May, Cartmel in June and Lingfield in February: stays 3¼m: acts on good to firm and heavy going: has worn headgear: in tongue tie last 4 starts. *Alan Hill*   c114
h– §

MAN O'WORDS (IRE) 6 b.g. Scorpion (IRE) – Mrs Malt (IRE) (Presenting) [2016/17 b87: b15.8g May 14] fair form at best in 3 bumpers. *Tom Lacey*   b68

MANSION (IRE) 5 b.g. Invincible Spirit (IRE) – Manoeuvre (IRE) (Galileo (IRE)) [2016/17 h16.3d⁶ h16.8s^{pu} h15.8s⁴ Mar 2] strong gelding: poor form over hurdles: lost shoe final start. *Venetia Williams*   h76

MANTON BOY 8 b.g. Revoque (IRE) – Got On A Lucky One (IRE) (Shernazar) [2016/17 h–, b66: h16.7s h16.7s h19.6s h15.7d^{pu} Feb 26] little sign of ability: in hood last 3 starts. *Michael Mullineaux*   h–

MANWELL (IRE) 7 b.g. Gold Well – Roborette (FR) (Robore (FR)) [2016/17 h15.8d h19.7g h18.6s⁶ h18.6s³ h15.8v* h15.8v⁵ h16.4v³ h16.8d² h16d Mar 31] £6,500 6-y-o: lengthy, workmanlike gelding: fourth foal: dam bumper winner/poor maiden hurdler: maiden Irish pointer: modest handicap hurdler: won at Uttoxeter in December: unproven beyond 17f: acts on heavy going: in hood last 2 starts, in tongue tie last 3: often races in rear, usually travels strongly. *Sam England*   h96

MAN WITH VAN (IRE) 11 b.g. Milan – Delibonne (IRE) (Erdelistan (FR)) [2016/17   **c–**
c126, h–: h22.3s c31.8g^{nu} Apr 22] useful hurdler/chaser at best, well below that in 2016/17:   **h91**
stays 3½m: acts on heavy going: usually wears headgear: has worn tongue tie. *Patrick*
Griffin, Ireland

MANY CLOUDS (IRE) 10 br.g. Cloudings (IRE) – Bobbing Back (IRE) (Bob Back   **c169**
(USA)) [2016/17 c166, h–: c25s* c25.3s* Jan 28]   **h–**

      'Stop this senseless cruelty to horses' … the sad death of Grand National
winner Many Clouds, minutes after he had crossed the line in front in the Cotswold
Chase on Cheltenham's Trials day in January, was seized on by Animal Aid which
campaigns to ban horse racing and can always rely on a sympathetic ear for its view
from some sections of the national media. Animal Aid was at its most opportunistic
in claiming that the death of Many Clouds was 'as predictable as it was tragic' and
was due to 'a life-threatening health condition' which had prompted the organisation
to warn the British Horseracing Authority in a letter in 2016 that Many Clouds
should be banned from racing. Without having a shred of hard medical evidence
to support such claims, Animal Aid called on the BHA, the horse's connections and
Cheltenham racecourse to be 'held to account'. The charges reached a vast audience
thanks to the sensationalist way the story was handled by some in the media and to
the lemming-like response of the keyboard warriors on social media. The link made
to the post-race ataxia exhibited by Many Clouds after his victory in the 2015 Grand
National, and after some other races, including his triumph in the 2014 Hennessy
Gold Cup at Newbury, turned out to be groundless. Needless to say, the results of the
post-mortem conducted on Many Clouds received a fraction of the coverage given to
the outrageous claims made by Animal Aid. Post-race ataxia is associated with a rise
in body temperature after exertion which can manifest itself in unsteadiness; Many
Clouds had been exhausted after his Grand National victory, his jockey dismounting
soon after the line, and he had been doused with buckets of water to help reduce his
body temperature as he was kept on the move before being taken to Aintree's newly-
introduced cooling down area, complete with spray mist and running water, where he
quickly recovered. Post-race ataxia is not normally associated with equine fatalities
and the post-mortem after the Betbright-sponsored Cotswold Chase showed, in any
case, that Many Clouds had not suffered a recurrence. Nor had he had a heart attack,

BetBright Trial Cotswold Chase, Cheltenham—
a grandstand finish followed by sadness as Many Clouds (noseband) is carried out on his shield
after lowering the colours of hot favourite Thistlecrack

as some had speculated. Many Clouds suffered a massive internal bleed, a 'severe pulmonary haemorrhage'. The BHA's chief veterinary officer stressed: 'Episodes such as this are rare and can occur in horses who have no underlying health issues [which the autopsy confirmed was the case with Many Clouds]'.

No victory in the latest season was gained at greater cost than that of Many Clouds when battling back to beat the King George VI Chase winner and Cheltenham Gold Cup favourite Thistlecrack by a head in the Cotswold Chase, a race Many Clouds had won in 2015 and in which he had been runner-up in 2016. Even by his standards, the most willing Many Clouds put up a tremendously gallant display to get the better of his rivals in an epic encounter after taking the lead some way out and then being headed briefly by Thistlecrack at the last. The first two recorded top-class performances and finished seventeen lengths in front of third-placed Smad Place, winner of the race the previous year. Many Clouds had been an outstanding winner of the Grand National—he carried more weight to victory in 2015 than any winner of the race since Red Rum in 1974—but, strictly on the form-book, his victory over Thistlecrack was even more meritorious and he could have had no better epitaph. Many Clouds collapsed on the racecourse while his jockey Leighton Aspell (who rode him in all his races) was about to give the now-familiar mounted post-race interview to a television reporter. Racegoers waiting to welcome Many Clouds into the winner's enclosure behind the stands were told of his demise over the racecourse public address system, an announcement met at first with stunned silence and then a spontaneous round of applause for a horse whose superb jumping, and the fact that he always tried his heart out, endeared him to the racing public ('He's the sort of horse who would go over a cliff for you,' his trainer had said after Many Clouds had won the Grand National). There may have been better steeplechasers among his contemporaries but none of them could give points to Many Clouds for gameness. It was a measure of the esteem in which he was held, and the sympathy felt for his connections, that he received sixty-five per cent of the votes in the *Racing Post*-backed Jumps Horse of the Year award which was presented to connections on the final afternoon of the season at Sandown.

The Cotswold Chase was the third win achieved by Many Clouds since his triumph at Aintree. Many National winners go backwards after their success, with 2014 winner Pineau de Re (over hurdles) and Many Clouds the first National winners since 2002 victor Bindaree to win another race. Many Clouds underwent a wind operation before reappearing in the latest season (he had suffered a breathing problem when well beaten in the 2016 National) and he returned to his best with an all-the-way victory, racing with zest and jumping superbly, in the Betfred Lotto '£100k Cash Giveaway' Chase over the Mildmay course at Aintree in early-December. All of the usual qualities of Many Clouds came into play and, with some thinking the keeping-on Minella Rocco might have got the better of him but for coming down at the last, it would have been a closely-run thing either way—which clearly reflected well on Many Clouds as he was conceding 5 lb to a rival who went on to finish second in the Cheltenham Gold Cup. As it was, Many Clouds stayed on strongly to beat Le Mercurey (also receiving 5 lb) by three and a half lengths. That race and the Cotswold were the only ones Many Clouds contested in his final season. He won twelve of his twenty-seven races in all and earned £928,000 in prize money.

Around one hundred and twenty-five jumpers died on Britain's racecourses in the latest season, among the best of them the 2013 Arkle Chase winner Simonsig, who fell and broke a leg in the Schloer Chase at Cheltenham, and the three-times Long Walk Hurdle winner Reve de Sivola who collapsed and died from a heart attack at Kelso in March. The high-class northern chaser Eduard broke a leg in the Silver Cup at Ascot, the smart pair Onenightinvienna and Arpege d'Alene were fatally injured (both on the flat) in the Welsh and Scottish Nationals respectively, and, although the Grand National meeting at Aintree passed without fatalities, Toe The Line, Consul du Thaix, Hadrian's Approach and Current Event died from injuries sustained at the Cheltenham Festival. Many of the others who died didn't make the news and the noteform comments on them in these pages will be the only lasting epitaph. They will not be remembered by the many, as Many Clouds will be, but just by the few who were closely associated with them or on whom they made a special impression. Their deaths, though, are a reminder of the price paid each year for the excitement and spectacle enjoyed by the followers of jumping. The sport can never be made perfectly safe and serious accidents will happen, as in every dangerous activity.

Many Clouds (IRE)
(br.g. 2007)
- Cloudings (IRE) (gr 1994)
  - Sadler's Wells (b 1981)
    - Northern Dancer
    - Fairy Bridge
  - Ispahan (gr 1981)
    - Rusticaro
    - Royal Danseuse
- Bobbing Back (IRE) (b 1997)
  - Bob Back (br 1981)
    - Roberto
    - Toter Back
  - Ballyvooney (br 1986)
    - Salluceva
    - Leveret

The tall, angular Many Clouds was the third Grand National winner owned by Trevor Hemmings, following Hedgehunter and Ballabriggs, both of whom are kept in retirement at the owner's home on the Isle of Man and regularly appear on Grand National day at Aintree in the pre-race parade of former winners. The sire of Many Clouds, the Sadler's Wells stallion Cloudings, who is still going strongly at the age of twenty-three at The Old Road Stud in Ireland, has been a favourite of Mr Hemmings who won the Fox Hunters' [Foxhunters'] over the National course with Cloudy Lane (sired when Cloudings stood in England) and also owns the smart novice chaser Cloudy Dream who gave his sire an Arkle runner-up in the latest season. The dam of Many Clouds, Bobbing Back, never won a race, showing her only sign of ability when fifth in a mares' bumper at Cork, but she is a sister to Back On Line who stayed four miles and finished third in the National Hunt Chase at the Cheltenham Festival. Many Clouds and his close relative the Grade 1-winning novice hurdler and useful chaser The Tullow Tank (by Oscar, another son of Sadler's Wells) were the third and fourth foals by Bobbing Back who could hardly have made a better start to her career as a broodmare. Many Clouds stayed thirty-five furlongs and showed his form on going ranging from good to heavy. He was a fine jumper and was usually ridden up with the pace. Thoroughly game and genuine, he was a most likeable individual and a great credit to his trainer and those who worked with him at Rhonehurst Stables in Lambourn where a memorial oak tree has been planted in his honour at the village's training ground. There will also be a lasting tribute to Many Clouds at Aintree too where the valuable staying chase in December over the Mildmay fences, which he won in the latest season, has been renamed the Many Clouds Chase and been upgraded to a Grade 2, after being run as a listed event for its first six renewals. *Oliver Sherwood*

MAOI CHINN TIRE (IRE) 10 b.g. Mull of Kintyre (USA) – Primrose And Rose (Primo Dominie) [2016/17 c–, h96: h20.2g⁵ h16.2g² h16.7g² h15.8m⁶ Oct 20] sturdy gelding: fair handicap hurdler: winning chaser: unproven beyond 17f: acts on good to firm going: has worn cheekpieces, including in 2016/17: tried in tongue tie: often races towards rear. *Jennie Candlish*   **c–** **h100**

MA PETIT LUMIER 7 b.g. Echo of Light – Alisdanza (Namaqualand (USA)) [2016/17 b16.8d⁵ h16g^pu Apr 23] showed nothing in bumper/novice hurdle. *Lee James*   **h–** **b–**

MAPLE STIRRUP (IRE) 5 b.m. Duke of Marmalade (IRE) – Street Shaana (FR) (Darshaan) [2016/17 h15.6g h19.4g⁵ Feb 5] half-sister to fairly useful French hurdler Sourabad (2¼m winner, by Halling): fair maiden on Flat, stays 16.5f: showed little in 2 novice hurdles. *Patrick Holmes*   **h–**

MARAWEH (IRE) 7 b.g. Muhtathir – Itqaan (USA) (Danzig (USA)) [2016/17 h112: h23.9m* h23.9d⁶ h23.9s³ h23.9d⁶ h24.6d h26.6g⁶ Apr 27] fair handicap hurdler: won at Perth in May: stays 27f: acts on good to firm and heavy going: wears headgear: front runner/races prominently: signs of temperament. *Lucinda Russell*   **h105**

MARBETH (IRE) 4 b.f. Frozen Power (IRE) – Suddenly (Puissance) [2016/17 h15.6g⁵ h16.4d³ h15.7g⁴ h15.7g³ h16.8s⁶ h16.4g h19.9g^pu Apr 7] modest maiden on Flat, stays 8.5f: poor maiden hurdler: unproven beyond 2m: best form on good going. *Hugh Burns*   **h80**

MARBLE MIST 5 gr.g. Martaline – Karolina (FR) (Pistolet Bleu (IRE)) [2016/17 b16s h15.7v h16.7s h16v h19g^pu h21.9d⁶ Apr 16] angular gelding: well beaten in bumper/over 6 hurdles: in blinkers/tongue tie final start. *Evan Williams*   **h–** **b–**

MARCILHAC (FR) 8 b.g. Smadoun (FR) – One Way (FR) (Exit To Nowhere (USA)) **c132**
[2016/17 c–, h–: c18.8d⁶ c20s⁴ c23d⁵ c23.8s* Mar 2] well-made gelding: useful hurdler in **h–**
2013/14: lightly raced over fences since, best effort (useful form) when winning handicap
at Ludlow on final start: stays 3m: acts on heavy going: often races prominently. *Venetia Williams*

MARCUS ANTONIUS 10 b.g. Mark of Esteem (IRE) – Star of The Course (USA) **c–**
(Theatrical) [2016/17 c–, h96: h16.8g⁶ h16.2s* h17.2g² h16.2s⁶ h16.2d⁴ h19.4d⁴ **h109**
h16.7s³ h18.1s* h16.2v⁶ Jan 15] good-topped gelding: fair handicap hurdler: won at Perth
(conditionals event) in July and Kelso in December: maiden chaser: stays 2¼m: acts on
heavy going: has worn hood: often races in rear. *Lucinda Russell*

MARDALE (IRE) 7 b.m. Robin des Champs (FR) – Lizzy Langtry (IRE) (King's Theatre **h121**
(IRE)) [2016/17 h118, b72: h17.2mᵘʳ h16.2s* h16.2g⁶ h16.2d⁵ h16dᵖᵘ Oct 29] fairly useful
handicap hurdler: won at Perth in July: stays 19f: acts on soft and good to firm going: wears
tongue tie. *Nicky Richards*

MARGARET'S ROSE (IRE) 7 b.m. Millenary – Alannah Rose (IRE) (Roselier (FR)) **h86**
[2016/17 h–: h19.5s h20.6s³ h23.9g⁵ h23v⁵ h23.3s² Mar 18] winning pointer: modest
maiden hurdler: best effort at 23f: acts on soft going: visored final start. *Nigel Twiston-Davies*

MARGOT FONTANE 7 b.m. Tobougg (IRE) – Quattro Fontane (Kayf Tara) [2016/17 **h99**
h19.5v⁶ h20.5d⁴ h20.5v³ h25vᵖᵘ h20.5s Feb 13] first foal: dam unraced: won both completed
starts in points: modest form over hurdles: stays 21f: acts on heavy going: usually races
close up. *Anna Newton-Smith*

MARGUERITE ST JUST 7 b.m. Sir Percy – Ships Watch (IRE) (Night Shift **h78**
(USA)) [2016/17 h16d⁴ h16g⁴ h17.7g⁵ Aug 25] modest maiden on Flat, stays 1¼m: won
2-runner mares maiden point in April 2017: poor form over hurdles: wears tongue tie.
Anthony Honeyball

MARIAH'S LEGEND 5 b.m. Flying Legend (USA) – Mariah Rollins (IRE) (Over The **h114**
River (FR)) [2016/17 b15.7v² b16m³ b15.8d h20.7s* h20.8d⁶ h20.3g³ h20.3g Apr 20] **b87**
fourth foal: half-sister to useful hurdler/smart chaser Pendra (2m-3m winner, by Old Vic)
and fair chaser Mercian King (2m winner, by Robin des Pres): dam (c137/h133) 2m-2½m
hurdle/chase winner (stayed 3m): fair form in bumpers: also fair form over hurdles, and
won mares maiden at Huntingdon in January: left Charlie Longsdon after first start: will
stay beyond 2½m: acts on soft going: tried in headgear. *Amy Murphy*

MARIA'S BENEFIT (IRE) 5 b.m. Beneficial – Youngborogal (IRE) (Anshan) [2016/17 **b96**
b16.6d² b15.8d* b17g Apr 6] rather unfurnished mare: third foal: sister to bumper winner
Desertmore Hill and half-sister to modest chaser Anti Cool (2m/17f winner, by Heron
Island): dam (h107), 19f hurdle winner, half-sister to fairly useful hurdler/chaser Glenwood
Knight and fairly useful chaser Glens Boy, both 3m winners: won mares maiden point in
Ireland on debut: fairly useful form in bumpers: won at Huntingdon in March: best effort
when second in mares event at Doncaster on debut. *Stuart Edmunds*

MARIET 8 ch.m. Dr Fong (USA) – Medway (IRE) (Shernazar) [2016/17 h94: h21.6dᵘʳ **h77**
h21.6g⁶ Jun 7] smallish mare: handicap hurdler, modest at best: stays 21f: acts on soft
going: wears hood. *Suzy Smith*

MARI ME OSCAR (IRE) 7 b.m. Oscar (IRE) – Nostra (FR) (Limnos (JPN)) [2016/17 **h–**
h71, b–: h20gᵖᵘ h20dᵖᵘ h19.6g⁴ h21d⁶ h25sᵖᵘ h21sᵖᵘ h16.5g Apr 6] maiden hurdler, no form
in 2016/17: tried in cheekpieces: sometimes in tongue tie. *Nikki Evans*

MARINERO (IRE) 8 b.g. Presenting – Peggy Maddock (IRE) (Oscar (IRE)) [2016/17 **c142**
c122, h136: c21s h24d* c22.5g² c20.5d² c23g* c22.5d² c24.4s² c24.4gᵘʳ c25g⁴ c24.5dᵖᵘ **h140**
Apr 29] rangy gelding: useful hurdler: won minor event at Tipperary in July: useful chaser:
won maiden at Downpatrick in September: good effort when second of 4 in novice at
Cheltenham (3¾ lengths behind Thistlecrack) in November: left A. J. Martin after first
start: stays 3m: acts on heavy going: has worn headgear, including on final outing: has
worn tongue tie, including on reappearance. *Henry de Bromhead, Ireland*

MARINERS MOON (IRE) 6 ch.g. Mount Nelson – Dusty Moon (Dr Fong (USA)) **h79**
[2016/17 h–: h16.7g⁵ h15.8g⁶ h16.7g⁴ h17.2m⁵ Jun 24] poor form over hurdles: in tongue
tie last 2 starts. *Patrick Holmes*

MARITO (GER) 11 b.g. Alkalde (GER) – Maratea (USA) (Fast Play (USA)) [2016/17 **c133**
c137, h–: c25s² c27.5m² May 20] good-topped gelding: smart hurdler/very smart chaser in **h–**
his prime: runner-up in Champion Hunters' Chase at Stratford in May, beaten 1¾ lengths
by Paint The Clouds: stays 3½m: acts on good to firm and heavy going: has worn headgear:
races towards rear. *Colin A. McBratney, Ireland*

MARJU'S QUEST (IRE) 7 b.g. Marju (IRE) – Queen's Quest (Rainbow Quest (USA)) **c–** [2016/17 c96, h114: h16.7g* h15.8g³ h18.6g⁶ h20.6g⁶ c16.3gᵖᵘ h16.3g³ h16m⁵ Apr 18] **h115 §** compact gelding: fairly useful handicap hurdler: won at Market Rasen in May: lightly-raced maiden over fences: left David Dennis after sixth start: stays 2½m: acts on firm and good to soft going: tried in hood/tongue tie: usually races close up: temperamental. *Adrian Wintle*

MARKET COURT (IRE) 6 b.g. Court Cave (IRE) – Piepowder (In The Wings) **b62** [2016/17 b17.7g⁶ May 8] 12/1, sixth in bumper at Plumpton on debut. *Nick Gifford*

MARKET ROAD (IRE) 7 gr.g. Tikkanen (USA) – Clydeside (IRE) (General Ironside) **c–** [2016/17 h15.7vᵖᵘ c19.2g⁵ h19.7v h17.7v⁵ c19.2s⁵ h15.8v² Mar 19] winning pointer: poor **h71** form over hurdles: well held both chase starts: should stay beyond 2m: acts on heavy going: often in headgear: in tongue tie last 4 starts. *Evan Williams*

MARKOV (IRE) 7 b.g. Morozov (USA) – Willoughby Sue (IRE) (Dabali (IRE)) **h120** [2016/17 h17.7d* h21dᵖᵘ h19.6d⁵ h19.4g³ h24.4s³ h23.5m⁴ h23.1g³ Apr 26] €16,000 4-y-o: **b88** close-coupled gelding: second foal: dam, well held on completed starts in bumpers, half-sister to very smart staying chaser Nil Desperandum: runner-up both starts in Irish maiden points: successful at Fontwell in November on only start in bumpers: fairly useful maiden hurdler: stays 3m: acts on soft and good to firm going. *Ben Pauling*

MARK'S FOLLY (IRE) 4 ch.f. Stowaway – Accordeon Royale (IRE) (Accordion) **b– p** [2016/17 b16.8g⁵ Apr 20] sixth foal: dam unraced sister to high-class hurdler/smart chaser Accordion Etoile and fair hurdler/useful chaser French Accordion, both 2m-2½m winners: 3/1, shaped as if needing experience when 7¾ lengths fifth of 6 to Melangerie in mares bumper at Cheltenham: should do better. *Philip Hobbs*

MARKY BOB (IRE) 12 b.g. Turtle Island (IRE) – Bobomy (IRE) (Bob Back (USA)) **c101 §** [2016/17 c99§, h–: c16.3g² c15.7g⁵ c16.3sᵖᵘ h21.6gʳʳ c16.3sᵖᵘ Nov 15] good-topped **h– §** gelding: winning hurdler: fair handicap chaser: stays 23f, effective at much shorter: acts on good to firm and heavy going: tried in headgear: unreliable (has refused to race, including on fourth outing). *Hugo Froud*

MARLAIS 5 b.g. Dylan Thomas (IRE) – Super Motiva (Motivator) [2016/17 h20g² **h101** h21.2g⁶ h16.7s Dec 22] modest form on Flat in France: fair form over hurdles: best effort when second in maiden at Worcester in October. *Arthur Whitehead*

MARLEE MASSIE (IRE) 8 b.g. Dr Massini (IRE) – Meadstown Miss (IRE) **c114** (Flemensfirth (USA)) [2016/17 h111: h24.3s² c21.5s* c21.6s⁵ c24.3v³ c20.5v* c23.4s² **h102** c30.6g Apr 28] sturdy gelding: fair handicap hurdler: fair form over fences: won novice handicaps at Ayr in December and March: stays 23f: acts on good to firm and heavy going: has worn cheekpieces. *N. W. Alexander*

MARLEY JOE (IRE) 6 b.g. Arcadio (GER) – Tuscarora (IRE) (Revoque (IRE)) [2016/17 **h108** h97, b67: h15.8g* h15.8g⁵ h16.3v² h18.7m² Jul 17] smallish gelding: fair handicap hurdler: won at Huntingdon in May: stayed 19f: acted on good to firm and heavy going: usually in hood: often raced towards rear/travelled strongly: dead. *Martin Keighley*

MARLPIT OAK 5 b.m. Midnight Legend – Lonicera (Sulaafah (USA)) [2016/17 c–, **c–** h85: h23m⁴ Jul 4] winning pointer: maiden hurdler, modest form at best: showed little in 2 **h78** hunter chases: stays 3¼m: acts on good to soft going: wears hood. *Seamus Mullins*

MARMONT 4 ch.g. Winker Watson – Five Bells (IRE) (Rock of Gibraltar (IRE)) [2016/17 **h94** h16.8m⁵ h17.7g² h16.3d⁵ Dec 14] £600 3-y-o: rather leggy gelding: third foal: brother to fair hurdler Ding Ding (2m-2½m winner) and half-brother to 7f-1½m winner Chilworth Bells (by Sixties Icon): dam ran twice on Flat: modest form in juvenile hurdles: in tongue tie last 2 starts. *Jo Davis*

MAROC 4 b.g. Rock of Gibraltar (IRE) – Zietory (Zieten (USA)) [2016/17 h15.8s⁵ h16v⁴ **h98** h16.2d³ Mar 26] fair maiden on Flat, stays 11.5f: modest form in juvenile hurdles. *Nikki Evans*

MAROCCHINO 4 gr.g. Tikkanen (USA) – Mocha (FR) (Mansonnien (FR)) [2016/17 **b–** b14.6s Dec 17] tailed off in junior bumper on only start. *James Ewart*

MARQUIS OF CARABAS (IRE) 7 b.g. Hurricane Run (IRE) – Miss Otis Regrets **h119** (IRE) (Bob Back (USA)) [2016/17 h111, b78: h19d* h16g² h21.3g² h21.1g h15.8s⁵ h19.4g³ h20s² h16.5s⁴ Feb 5] fairly useful hurdler: won novice at Warwick in May: stays 21f: acts on soft going. *David Dennis*

MARRACUDJA (FR) 6 b.g. Martaline – Memorial (FR) (Homme de Loi (IRE)) **c140** [2016/17 h137: c16.3g* c15.9g* c15.5d⁴ c16g² c16.4dᵖᵘ c16.3g² c16.5g² Apr 28] useful-**h–** looking gelding: useful hurdler: quickly reached similar level over fences and won novices at Newton Abbot in September and Cheltenham (by neck from Presenting Arms) in October: best subsequent effort when second in Wayward Lad Novices' Chase at Kempton (18 lengths behind Altior) on fourth start: raced around 2m: acts on soft going: wears hood/tongue tie: front runner. *Paul Nicholls*

MARTABOT (FR) 6 gr.g. Martaline – Reine de Sabot (FR) (Homme de Loi (IRE)) **h109**
[2016/17 h15.8v⁵ h16vˢᵘ h16.8s² h18.5d⁴ Mar 21] fourth foal: half-brother to French hurdler Mango Fil (2¼m winner, by Robin des Champs) and modest hurdler Zouti (19f winner, by Kayhasi): dam (h108), French 17f-2½m hurdle winner, also 5.5f-9.5f winner on Flat: fair maiden hurdler: unproven beyond 17f: acts on soft going. *David Pipe*

MARTELLO PARK (IRE) 5 b.m. Central Park (IRE) – Johnsalice (IRE) (Zaffaran **b102**
(USA)) [2016/17 b16d² b16v³ b16v³ b16.1v* b16d⁴ b17g⁶ Apr 6] sturdy mare: third foal: half-sister to smart hurdler/useful chaser Martello Tower (2½m winner, by Milan): dam unraced: fairly useful bumper performer: won mares maiden at Thurles in February: creditable sixth of 18 to Dame Rose in Nickel Coin Mares' National Hunt Flat Race at Aintree final start: will be suited by 2½m+: in cheekpieces last 3 starts. *Ms Margaret Mullins, Ireland*

MARTELLO TOWER (IRE) 9 b.g. Milan – Johnsalice (IRE) (Zaffaran (USA)) **c142**
[2016/17 h154: c17d² c21.5d* c24d⁴ c24s⁵ c31.8gᵖᵘ Mar 14] strong gelding: smart hurdler: **h–**
useful form over fences: won maiden at Fairyhouse (by neck from A Genie In Abottle) in December: pulled up lame in National Hunt Chase at Cheltenham final outing: stays 3m: acts on heavy going: in headgear last 2 starts: front runner/races prominently. *Ms Margaret Mullins, Ireland*

MARTEN (FR) 5 b.g. Martaline – Commande Blue (FR) (Commands (AUS)) [2016/17 **b102**
b16.6g⁵ b16v* b16.3d Feb 11] £70,000 3-y-o: sturdy gelding: third foal: dam placed at 15f over hurdles in France: fairly useful form in bumpers: easily best effort when winning at Warwick in December: will stay 2½m. *Ben Pauling*

MARTHA MCCANDLES 6 b.m. Tobougg (IRE) – Tabulate (Dansili) [2016/17 **h99**
h15.8m³ h19.5v³ h15.7vᵖᵘ h16.8s* h18.6s⁵ Feb 19] poor form in bumpers in 2014/15: fair maiden on Flat, stays 1¼m: fair form over hurdles: won mares handicap at Exeter in January: unproven beyond 17f: acts on soft and good to firm going: often races towards rear. *Alan King*

MARTHA'S BENEFIT (IRE) 8 b.m. Beneficial – Trajectus (Homo Sapien) [2016/17 **h70**
h–, b70: h24s⁴ May 18] successful in 2 points, second in April 2017: poor form in bumpers/completed start over hurdles. *Mike Sowersby*

MARTILA (FR) 5 b.m. Martaline – Paola Pierji (FR) (Cadoudal (FR)) [2016/17 h16.2d³ **h117**
h16.2m² h17.2d* h17.2d* h16.2d² h16.2m⁴ h16d² Oct 29] fifth foal: dam French 2m/17f hurdle/chase winner: fairly useful hurdler: won at Cartmel in June (mares novice) and July (mares handicap): will stay 2½m: acts on good to soft going: wears hood. *Pauline Robson*

MARTILOO (FR) 7 b.m. Martaline – Paola Pierji (FR) (Cadoudal (FR)) [2016/17 **c–**
c20.1vᵖᵘ Mar 7] third foal: dam French 2m/17f hurdle/chase winner: maiden hurdler/ **h–**
chaser, fair form in France for M. Rolland: off 17 months/in hood, pulled up in mares handicap chase at Newcastle (lost shoe): barely stays 21f: acts on soft going. *Pauline Robson*

MARTIN CASH (IRE) 11 b.g. Oscar (IRE) – Native Singer (IRE) (Be My Native **c84**
(USA)) [2016/17 c20.3g⁴ Apr 21] lengthy, workmanlike gelding: maiden pointer/hurdler: **h–**
fair chaser at best: stays 21f: acts on heavy going: has worn headgear/tongue tie. *Mrs Jo Messenger*

MARTIN CHUZZLEWIT (IRE) 8 ch.g. Galileo (IRE) – Alta Anna (FR) (Anabaa **h81**
(USA)) [2016/17 h17m h16.2g⁴ h19.9m³ h23.9d² h23.3g Jul 22] poor maiden hurdler: stays 2½m: acts on good to firm going: in cheekpieces 2 of last 3 starts: often races towards rear. *Martin Todhunter*

MART LANE (IRE) 12 br.g. Stowaway – Western Whisper (IRE) (Supreme Leader) **c–**
[2016/17 c98, h–: c21.2mᵖᵘ c20.9vᵖᵘ h24d⁴ Jul 10] leggy, light-framed gelding: one-time **h–**
useful hurdler/chaser: no form in 2016/17: usually wears headgear: tried in tongue tie: front runner/races prominently. *Sophie Leech*

MARVELLOUS MONTY (IRE) 7 br.m. Oscar (IRE) – Montys Miss (IRE) (Presenting) **h105**
[2016/17 h96, b–: h18.5g³ h19.9v² h19.6s³ h21.2d⁵ h20.7d² Mar 15] fair maiden hurdler: stays 21f: acts on heavy going: usually races prominently. *Johnny Farrelly*

MARY ELEANOR 5 b.m. Midnight Legend – Lady Rebecca (Rolfe (USA)) [2016/17 **b82** b15.8d³ b16.3s³ b16.7g⁶ Mar 25] half-sister to 3 winners, including bumper winner/useful hurdler Lord Generous (3m/25f winner, by Generous) and fair hurdler Lady Karina (2¾m winner, by Kayf Tara): dam (h165) bumper/2½m-3m hurdle winner: modest form in bumpers: will stay at least 2½m. *Tom Lacey*

MARY MY SECRET (IRE) 6 b.m. Court Cave (IRE) – Secret Can't Say (IRE) (Jurado **b66** (USA)) [2016/17 b16.7s ab16g ab16g Feb 20] seventh foal: sister to bumper winner/smart hurdler Clondaw Court (2¼m-2¾m winner) and fairly useful hurdler Just Cause (2½m-2¾m winner), and half-sister to bumper winner/fair hurdler Pro Pell (2½m winner, by Goldmark): dam (c82/h90) 3m chase winner: poor form in bumpers: in tongue tie last 2 starts. *Anthony Carson*

MASH POTATO (IRE) 7 b.g. Whipper (USA) – Salva (Grand Lodge (USA)) [2016/17 **h91** h16.2dᵘʳ h16m h20.5d h17.2g² h15.8g h20d h17.1g h16.4s h16.8v² h15.8s* h16.2g⁵ Apr 27] fair on Flat, stays 1¼m: modest handicap hurdler: won at Uttoxeter in April: stays 2½m: acts on soft going: in cheekpieces last 3 starts: wears tongue tie: usually races towards rear. *Noel C. Kelly, Ireland*

MASKED BANDIT 4 b.g. Dick Turpin (IRE) – Plaisterer (Best of The Bests (IRE)) **h–** [2016/17 h17.7s⁶ h16m Apr 4] showed nothing in 2 runs on Flat: refused to settle when well held both starts over hurdles. *Suzy Smith*

MASQUERADE (IRE) 8 b.g. Fruits of Love (USA) – Beechill Dancer (IRE) (Darnay) **c–** [2016/17 c–, h–: h19.9g² May 29] fair handicap hurdler: pulled up only start over fences: **h113** stays 2½m: acts on good to soft going (bumper form on soft). *Warren Greatrex*

MASSINI'S DREAM 6 b.m. Dr Massini (IRE) – Cathy's Dream (IRE) (Husyan (USA)) **b62** [2016/17 b15.8s b14d⁶ Dec 21] fifth foal: closely related to a winning pointer by Kayf Tara: dam, winning pointer, half-sister to fair hurdler/useful staying chaser American Jennie: poor form in bumpers. *Sophie Leech*

MASSINI'S LADY 6 b.m. Dr Massini (IRE) – Lady du Bost (FR) (Royal Charter (FR)) **c–** [2016/17 h65: h23.9mᵖᵘ h19s² h20.5s h19v³ c20.9v h20.1sᵖᵘ Mar 16] poor maiden hurdler: **h77 §** well beaten in novice handicap on chasing debut: stays 19f: raced mainly on soft/heavy going: tried in headgear: temperamental. *N. W. Alexander*

MASSINI'S TRAP (IRE) 8 b.g. Dr Massini (IRE) – Sparrow's Trap (IRE) (Magical **h131** Wonder (USA)) [2016/17 h20m h24g³ h22g h22.8g h24g⁴ h20s⁶ h20g* h18.9v² h20s h20.3g Mar 17] smallish gelding: useful handicap hurdler: won at Aintree (by 5 lengths from Born Survivor) in October: stays 3m: acts on good to firm and heavy going: wears headgear: tried in tongue tie: usually races towards rear. *James A. Nash, Ireland*

MASTER ALLY (IRE) 7 gr.g. Flemensfirth (USA) – Ally Rose (IRE) (Roselier (FR)) **h92** [2016/17 h88, b81: h23.3vᵖᵘ h23.1g² h20g Nov 6] winning pointer: modest maiden hurdler: stays 23f: acts on heavy going: in headgear last 4 starts: front runner/races prominently. *Rebecca Curtis*

MASTER APPEAL (IRE) 8 b.g. Brian Boru – Lady Appeal (IRE) (Phardante (FR)) **c110 p** [2016/17 c22gᵘʳ h22g⁴ h22.8g h22dᶠ h20g³ h20sᵘʳ h24d h20g* h20g⁵ h20v c20v c20v Jan **h133** 14] sixth foal: brother to smart hurdler/chaser Fox Appeal (19f-3m winner) and half-brother to 2 winners, including fairly useful hurdler/useful chaser Saved By John (2m-2¾m winner, by Revoque): dam unraced: useful handicap hurdler: won at Punchestown in October: maiden chaser, fair form: stays 3m: acts on heavy going: tried in hood: usually races towards rear: remains with potential as a chaser. *John E. Kiely, Ireland*

MASTER BLUEYES (IRE) 4 gr.g. Mastercraftsman (IRE) – Miss Blueyes (IRE) **h139** (Dushyantor (USA)) [2016/17 h16g⁴ h16g² h15.8s² h15.8s* h16g* h16.8g Mar 17] workmanlike gelding: half-brother to modest hurdler Bermeo (23f winner, by Definite Article): useful on Flat, stays 1¾m: useful form over hurdles: won juvenile at Ludlow and Adonis Juvenile Hurdle at Kempton (by 11 lengths from Evening Hush), both in February: 8/1, below expectations when 19½ lengths tenth of 15 to Defi du Seuil in Triumph Hurdle at Cheltenham final start (finished lame): raced around 2m: acts on soft going: often travels strongly. *Alan King*

MASTER BURBIDGE 6 b.g. Pasternak – Silver Sequel (Silver Patriarch (IRE)) **c115 p** [2016/17 h64: h24v h19.7s² h19g* h19g* c21.1g* Apr 7] strong gelding: fair handicap **h111** hurdler: won at Taunton in February and March. 11/8, also won novice handicap at Sedgefield on chasing debut by ½ length from Rolling Thunder: stays 21f: best form on good going: wears cheekpieces: often travels strongly: should progress over fences. *Neil Mulholland*

MASTER CYNK 10 ch.g. Diableneyev (USA) – Model View (USA) (Distant View **c66**
(USA)) [2016/17 c21.2g⁴ Jul 18] big, workmanlike gelding: bumper winner: maiden **h–**
hurdler: left Tom George/off 27 months, well beaten in maiden on chasing debut: stays 21f:
acts on good to soft going. *Tracey Barfoot-Saunt*

MASTER DANCER 6 gr.g. Mastercraftsman (IRE) – Isabella Glyn (IRE) (Sadler's **h113**
Wells (USA)) [2016/17 h16.8g* h15.7m² h21.1s Nov 13] fair form over hurdles: won
maiden at Newton Abbot in September: should stay 2½m: in cheekpieces last 3 starts.
Tim Vaughan

MASTER DEE (IRE) 8 b.g. King's Theatre (IRE) – Miss Lauren Dee (IRE) (Montelimar **c142**
(USA)) [2016/17 c90p, h–: c22.5s² c21.4g² c21m* c25.5g² c20m* c18.8m* c20.2m² **h–**
Dec 28] workmanlike gelding: useful chaser: winning hurdler: useful chaser: won novice handicaps at
Newton Abbot in August, and at Ludlow and Ascot (by ¾ length from San Benedeto) in
October: stays 25f: acts on soft and good to firm going: in cheekpieces last 3 starts: wears
tongue tie: front runner/races prominently. *Fergal O'Brien*

MASTER JAKE (IRE) 9 b.g. Pyrus (USA) – Whitegate Way (Greensmith) [2016/17 **c135**
h122: c16.4s³ c15.7s c21.4d² c20v² c16v² c17.1v² c24.2g* c24.2m* Apr 13] fairly useful **h–**
hurdler: useful handicap chaser: won at Fakenham (novice event) in March and at Wetherby
on final start: stays 3m: acts on good to firm and heavy going: has worn cheekpieces,
including in 2016/17: in tongue tie last 5 starts: often travels strongly. *Dan Skelton*

MASTER MAJIC (IRE) 6 b.g. Flemensfirth (USA) – Majic Times Ahead (Weld) **h94**
[2016/17 b65: h15.3v h15.3d Feb 18] workmanlike gelding: poor form in bumpers: modest
form in novice hurdles at Wincanton: bred to be suited by 2½m+. *Colin Tizzard*

MASTER MURPHY (IRE) 12 b.g. Flemensfirth (USA) – Awbeg Beauty (IRE) **c–**
(Supreme Leader) [2016/17 c–, h70: h27s³ h23.3g May 24] sturdy gelding: poor handicap **h71**
hurdler: maiden chaser: stays 27f: acts on heavy going: in cheekpieces last 5 starts, also in
tongue tie final one: often races towards rear. *Jane Walton*

MASTEROFDECEPTION (IRE) 9 b.g. Darsi (FR) – Sherberry (IRE) (Shernazar) **h112**
[2016/17 h120: h20g³ Sep 23] good-topped gelding: handicap hurdler, fairly useful at best:
stays 3m: acts on soft and good to firm going: has worn headgear, including last 3 starts: in
tongue tie last 2 starts. *Dr Richard Newland*

MASTER OF FINANCE (IRE) 6 ch.g. Mastercraftsman (IRE) – Cheal Rose (IRE) **h120 §**
(Dr Devious (IRE)) [2016/17 h16.2s² h16d* h16s⁴ h15.7s⁶ h16.5g² h16d² h16.5g Apr 8]
useful on Flat, stays 12.5f: fairly useful hurdler: won maiden at Ayr in October: raced
around 2m: acts on soft going: wears headgear: usually travels strongly: temperamental.
Malcolm Jefferson

MASTER OF IRONY (IRE) 5 b.g. Makfi – Mother of Pearl (IRE) (Sadler's Wells **h131**
(USA)) [2016/17 h19.3d* h19.3d² h18.6s* Jan 18] useful on Flat, stays 1¼m: useful form
over hurdles: won novices at Catterick in December and Market Rasen in January: good
second in novice at Catterick only other start: stays 19f. *John Quinn*

MASTER OF SPEED (IRE) 5 ch.g. Mastercraftsman (IRE) – Mango Groove (IRE) **h115 p**
(Unfuwain (USA)) [2016/17 h87p: h19.1d⁶ h16m* May 16] rather leggy gelding: fairly
useful form over hurdles: won maiden at Kempton on final start: capable of better still.
Gary Moore

MASTER OF THE GAME (IRE) 11 ch.g. Bob's Return (IRE) – Lady Monilousha **c–**
(IRE) (Montelimar (USA)) [2016/17 c109, h–: c20gᶠ May 2] rangy gelding: one-time **h–**
useful hurdler/chaser, has lost his way: stays 21f: acts on soft going: wears hood/tongue tie.
David Dennis

MASTER OF VERSE (IRE) 8 b.g. Milan – Bacchonthebottle (IRE) (Bob Back (USA)) **h130**
[2016/17 h21m² h18.2d² h16.5g² Jul 26] second foal: dam, unraced, out of half-sister to
high-class hurdler/top-class chaser (stayed 3m) Bacchanal: winning pointer: useful
hurdler: ½-length second to Penhill in novice at Galway on final start: should stay beyond
2¼m: wears hood: usually in tongue tie: front runner/races prominently. *W. P. Mullins,
Ireland*

MASTERPLAN (IRE) 7 b.g. Spadoun (FR) – Eurolucy (IRE) (Shardari) [2016/17 h120: **c116**
c20.9d⁶ c20s⁵ c21.4d⁶ c19.8m* Apr 13] useful-looking gelding: fairly useful hurdler/ **h–**
chaser: off the mark over fences in 3-runner handicap at Towcester on final start: stays
2¾m: acts on soft and good to firm going: tried in hood: has worn tongue tie, including in
2016/17: usually leads, tends to find little. *Charlie Longsdon*

MASTER RAJEEM (USA) 8 b.g. Street Cry (IRE) – Rajeem (Diktat) [2016/17 c110§, **c103 §**
h–§: c21.1s* c19.3g⁴ c24m c25.5gᵖᵘ c23.6g⁵ c24.2g⁶ c26.3s² h23.3v* c24.3v³ c20.1v⁶ Mar **h100 §**
28] well-made gelding: fair handicap hurdler/chaser: won over hurdles at Hexham in
December and over fences at Sedgefield in May: left Neil King after sixth start: stays 27f:
acts on heavy going: wears headgear: races prominently: temperamental. *Alison Hamilton*

MASTER RUFFIT (IRE) 9 ch.g. Blueprint (IRE) – Miss Ruffit (IRE) (Phardante (FR)) **c124**
[2016/17 h117: c19dᵖᵘ c17d c20d c20.5v* c20.5s² c20.5v³ Feb 27] fairly useful hurdler/ **h–**
chaser: won novice handicap chase at Ayr in January: stays 3m: best form on soft/heavy
going. *Neil McKnight, Ireland*

MASTER SERGEI 5 b.g. Mutamarkiz (IRE) – French Quartet (IRE) (Lycius (USA)) **b–**
[2016/17 b15.7g² b15.8s Oct 15] well held both starts in bumpers: tried in tongue tie.
Robert Stephens

MASTERS HILL (IRE) 11 gr.g. Tikkanen (USA) – Leitrim Bridge (IRE) (Earl of **c137**
Barking (IRE)) [2016/17 c140, h–: c25gᵖᵘ h21.4s⁶ h26sᶠ h19.8v² c24.2s³ c24.2d² c23.8m **h113**
Apr 2] strong gelding: handicap hurdler, fair nowadays: useful handicap chaser: stays
3½m: acts on heavy going: wears headgear: has worn tongue tie, including in 2016/17:
front runner/races prominently. *Colin Tizzard*

MASTERSON (IRE) 4 gr.g. Lawman (FR) – Indian Dumaani (Indian Ridge) [2016/17 **h77**
h16.3m⁶ h16mᵘʳ h17.7s⁴ h16d⁴ h15.9m⁴ Apr 17] leggy gelding: fairly useful on Flat, stays
16.5f: poor form in juvenile hurdles: should prove suited by further than 2m. *Mick Channon*

MASTER SQUIRREL 6 gr.g. Great Palm (USA) – Overthrow (Overbury (IRE)) **b–**
[2016/17 b16.7d b16.7dʳᵒ Jun 17] well held completed start in bumpers: in tongue strap, ran
out next time. *Christopher Kellett*

MASTER SUNRISE (IRE) 8 ch.g. Blueprint (IRE) – Aunty Dawn (IRE) (Strong Gale) **c87**
[2016/17 c24.1g³ c27.5mᵖᵘ May 20] dual point winner: better effort in novice hunter chases
when third at Bangor very early in season. *Mrs D. J. Ralph*

MASTER VINTAGE 9 b.g. Kayf Tara – What A Vintage (IRE) (Un Desperado (FR)) **h107**
[2016/17 h15.5g* h16s⁴ h18.6s⁶ Mar 12] fair handicap hurdler: won at Leicester in
January: unproven beyond 2m: acts on soft going: wears hood. *Richard Phillips*

MASTER WORKMAN (IRE) 11 b.g. Posidonas – Bobbie Magee (IRE) (Buckskin **c117**
(FR)) [2016/17 c109: c24.2dᵖᵘ c24.2g* Apr 17] multiple point winner: fairly useful chaser:
won hunter at Fakenham in April: stays 3m: acts on heavy going: wears cheekpieces.
David Kemp

MATCHAWAY (IRE) 8 b.g. Milan – Hatch Away (IRE) (Lord Americo) [2016/17 **h121**
h102p, b92: h15.8s* h19.9vᵖᵘ h16.2s⁴ h16.2s* h16.5s⁵ Feb 5] bumper winner: fairly useful
form over hurdles: won maiden at Uttoxeter very early in season and handicap at Hereford
in January: should stay 2½m: acts on soft going: in blinkers last 2 starts: usually races close
up. *Kerry Lee*

MATHAYUS (IRE) 4 b.g. Scorpion (IRE) – Prunelle (GER) (Waky Nao) [2016/17 **b–**
b16.4v⁵ Feb 15] shaped as if in need of experience when well held in maiden bumper: has
joined Sue Smith. *Jedd O'Keeffe*

MATORICO (IRE) 6 gr.g. Mastercraftsman (IRE) – Hashbrown (GER) (Big Shuffle **h–**
(USA)) [2016/17 h139: h22.8vᵘʳ Nov 19] rather leggy gelding: useful handicap hurdler:
unseated rider eighth only outing in 2016/17: stays 21f: acts on heavy going: in headgear
last 5 starts, in tongue tie last 3: often races towards rear. *Jonjo O'Neill*

MATROW'S LADY (IRE) 10 b.m. Cloudings (IRE) – I'm Maggy (NZ) (Danseur Etoile **c95**
(FR)) [2016/17 c92, h–: c23.5v* c20.9v³ c23.5v³ Mar 6] good-bodied mare: winning **h–**
hurdler: modest handicap chaser: won at Lingfield in January: stays 3m: acts on heavy
going: wears headgear/tongue tie. *Neil Mulholland*

MATTS LEGACY (IRE) 5 b.g. Arcadio (GER) – How Provincial (IRE) (Be My Native **h–**
(USA)) [2016/17 b15.8d⁵ h16.5g h15.3d h15.7d h19.5s Mar 13] behind in bumper/over **b67**
hurdles. *Tim Vaughan*

MAULESDEN MAY (IRE) 4 b.f. Dark Angel (IRE) – Jemima's Art (Fantastic Light **h64 p**
(USA)) [2016/17 h15.7g⁴ Jan 12] fair on Flat, stays 12.5f: 7/1, held back by inexperience
when fourth in fillies juvenile at Catterick (23¼ lengths behind Giveaway Glance) on
hurdling debut: capable of better. *Keith Dalgleish*

MAVROS 4 br.g. Authorized (IRE) – Barley Bree (IRE) (Danehill Dancer (IRE)) [2016/17 **b71**
b13g ab16g Dec 10] showed a bit on first of 2 starts in junior bumpers. *George Baker*

MAWAQEET (USA) 8 b.g. Dynaformer (USA) – Lady Ilsley (USA) (Trempolino **h95** (USA)) [2016/17 h108: h22m Jul 17] fair handicap hurdler: below form only outing in 2016/17: stays 3m: acts on good to firm and good to soft going: wears headgear. *Michael Appleby*

MAXANISI (IRE) 7 br.g. Kalanisi (IRE) – Maxis Girl (IRE) (Mister Mat (FR)) [2016/17 **c120** h119: c16.4g c23.6spu c25.2vF c20.9v² c20dF h20d⁶ Apr 16] workmanlike gelding: fairly **h–** useful hurdler in 2015/16, looked none too keen final outing in 2016/17: easily best effort (fairly useful form) over fences when second in handicap at Ffos Las in March: should stay further than 2½m: best form on soft/heavy going: in cheekpieces last 3 starts over fences: temperament under suspicion. *Evan Williams*

MAX DO BRAZIL (FR) 5 b.g. Blue Bresil (FR) – Lili Valley (FR) (Cadoudal (FR)) **h126** [2016/17 h19.4s h19.4s⁶ h17.9d⁴ h17.9d h18.9s³ h19.4v² h16.8spu h16dpu Mar 11] sturdy gelding: sixth foal: half-brother to 3 winners in France, including hurdler/chaser Good Man (17f-19f winner, by Al Namix): dam French hurdler/chaser (2m-2¾m winner): fairly useful handicap hurdler: second at Auteuil in November: left A. Chaille-Chaille £160,000, pulled up both outings in Britain: stays 19f: acts on heavy going: tried in cheekpieces: in tongue tie final start. *David Pipe*

MAX DYNAMO 7 b.g. Midnight Legend – Vivante (IRE) (Toulon) [2016/17 b71: b16d **h58** b16.3d b16m h15.8d h19v³ h19.7s⁴ Mar 11] poor form in bumpers/over hurdles: in hood **b–** last 4 starts. *Jim Wilson*

MAXED OUT KING (IRE) 9 ch.g. Desert King (IRE) – Lady Max (IRE) (Mandalus) **c111** [2016/17 h17.1d h20.3dpu c16.4d⁴ c20.1s* c16.3s³ Jan 23] maiden hurdler: fair form over **h62** fences: won novice handicaps at Sedgefield and Newcastle in December: stays 2½m: acts on soft going: front runner/races prominently. *Sue Smith*

MAX FORTE (IRE) 7 br.g. Indian River (FR) – Brook Forte (Alderbrook) [2016/17 **h120** h124: h21.1s h23.6gpu h23.5s⁴ h24g² Apr 19] rather leggy gelding: second in Irish point on debut: fairly useful handicap hurdler: back to form when second at Cheltenham final start: stays 3m: acts on good to soft going: front runner/races prominently. *Chris Down*

MAXI CHOP (FR) 9 b.g. Muhaymin (USA) – Scotch Mockery (FR) (Persifleur (USA)) **c119** [2016/17 c21g* c21.1d* c19.4g⁵ c21m⁶ Jul 1] sturdy gelding: point winner: maiden **h–** hurdler: fairly useful form over fences: won novice hunter at Newton Abbot and hunter at Fontwell, both in May: left Mrs Rose Loxton after second start: stays 21f: acts on heavy going: tried in cheekpieces: has worn tongue tie, including last 5 starts. *Paul Nicholls*

MAXIE T 6 b.g. Dalakhani (IRE) – Ballet Ballon (USA) (Rahy (USA)) [2016/17 h128: **h113** h20.6s h19.4g⁵ h21.3s⁶ h22.8s⁴ h22.7v³ h20.5v³ h25g⁶ h20.1g⁵ Apr 25] sturdy, close-coupled gelding: fair handicap hurdler: stays 2½m: acts on heavy going: in cheekpieces last 3 starts: often races prominently: temperament under suspicion. *Micky Hammond*

MAXIMISER (IRE) 9 gr.g. Helissio (FR) – Clydeside (IRE) (General Ironside) [2016/17 **c–** c139p, h144: h24.2dpu c19.9s⁵ Jan 21] lengthy, workmanlike gelding: smart hurdler/useful **h–** chaser at best: pulled up both starts in 2016/17: stays 21f: best form on soft/heavy going: tried in tongue tie, including on reappearance: front runner. *Simon West*

MAXIMUS MARIDIUS 6 br.g. Fair Mix (IRE) – Dutch Czarina (Prince Sabo) [2016/17 **h99** h15.5g⁶ h16g⁶ h19.7s⁵ h20.5vpu h19.4sur Mar 3] angular gelding: winning pointer: modest form over hurdles: stays 2½m: acts on soft going: sometimes in hood: tried in tongue tie. *Samuel Drinkwater*

MAX MILANO (IRE) 12 b.g. Milan – Stellissima (IRE) (Persian Bold) [2016/17 h–: **h81** h20.3s³ h19.6gpu h19.1g⁶ Apr 12] sturdy gelding: poor handicap hurdler nowadays: stays 2½m: acts on soft going: has worn hood, including in 2016/17: usually races towards rear. *Alan Jessop*

MAX THE MINISTER 7 bl.g. Pastoral Pursuits – Franciscaine (FR) (Legend of France **h84** (USA)) [2016/17 h100, b–: h19.2g h15.8m⁴ Jun 9] lengthy gelding: maiden hurdler, modest at best: stayed 19f: acted on good to soft going: blinkered final start: dead. *Hughie Morrison*

MAX WARD (IRE) 8 b.g. Milan – Made Easy (IRE) (Rudimentary (USA)) [2016/17 **c145** c16.5g* c15.5d³ c20.5gF c16.4s² c20.5g* c19.9g⁴ Apr 6] good-topped gelding: useful **h–** hurdler, missed 2015/16: smart form over fences: won novice handicap at Huntingdon in November and handicap at Kempton (by 5 lengths from Sir Note) in March: good 9½ lengths fourth of 6 to Flying Angel in Manifesto Novices' Chase at Aintree final outing: stays 2½m: acts on soft going: often travels strongly. *Tom George*

MAYBE FEESCARI 6 ch.m. Dreams End – Aristi (IRE) (Dr Fong (USA)) [2016/17   **h–**
b15.9g b16d h16g⁶ Jul 26] first foal: dam (h84), ungenuine 2¾m hurdle winner, also   **b–**
1¼m-2¼m winner on Flat: well held in bumpers and a maiden hurdle. *Bernard Llewellyn*

MAYBE I WONT 12 b.g. Kyllachy – Surprise Surprise (Robellino (USA)) [2016/17   **h90 §**
h100§: h22.1g h25.4d⁴ h22.1g³ h22.1d² Aug 29] close-coupled gelding: modest handicap
hurdler nowadays: stays 2¾m: acts on good to firm and heavy going: wears headgear:
usually races close up: temperamental. *James Moffatt*

MAYBELL 6 b.m. Black Sam Bellamy (IRE) – Chilly Squaw (IRE) (Commanche Run)   **h85**
[2016/17 h67: h16.9m h19.9g* May 29] modest form over hurdles: won novice handicap
at Uttoxeter in May: stays 2½m. *Alex Hales*

MAYBE PLENTY 8 b.m. Overbury (IRE) – Mays Delight (IRE) (Glacial Storm (USA))   **c–**
[2016/17 c103, h–: c24s^pu Apr 30] sturdy mare: winning hurdler/chaser, fair at best: stays   **h–**
3m: acts on heavy going: in cheekpieces last 2 starts: front runner/races prominently.
Giles Smyly

MAY COURT 10 b.g. Groomsbridge May I – Tudor Sunset (Sunyboy) [2016/17 h18.5g^pu   **h– §**
May 5] no sign of ability in 2 bumpers and a maiden hurdle: tried in tongue tie: refused to
line up and withdrawn, May 10. *Peter Purdy*

MAYDEN MASSINI 6 gr.g. Dr Massini (IRE) – Miss Tehente (FR) (Tehente (FR))   **b–**
[2016/17 b–: b13.6g⁵ Apr 21] little encouragement either start in bumpers. *Philip Hide*

MAY HAY 7 b.m. Dubai Destination (USA) – Trounce (Barathea (IRE)) [2016/17 h112:   **h116**
h20.3v h15.7v* h16.3v* h16.3g² h16.3m⁴ h16.2s^pu h15.7v² h16v⁵ Jan 10] angular mare:
fairly useful handicap hurdler: won at Southwell (mares event) and Stratford in June:
unproven beyond 2m: best form on soft/heavy going: front runner/races prominently.
Anthony Carson

MAY MIST 5 b.m. Nayef (USA) – Midnight Mist (IRE) (Green Desert (USA)) [2016/17   **b–**
b55: b15.8d May 5] well held both starts in bumpers: modest maiden on Flat (raced only
around 9f). *Trevor Wall*

MAYO STAR (IRE) 5 b.g. Stowaway – Western Whisper (IRE) (Supreme Leader)   **h106 p**
[2016/17 b80: b16.2d⁵ b16.4d² b16.4s* h18.1d³ Jan 10] fair form in bumpers: won at   **b91**
Newcastle in December: 11/4, 4 lengths third to Blue Hussar in novice at Kelso on hurdling
debut: left Kevin Ryan after first start: will stay 2½m: front runner/races prominently:
better to come. *Malcolm Jefferson*

MAYPOLE LASS 7 ch.m. Halling (USA) – Maigold Lass (Mark of Esteem (IRE))   **h80 §**
[2016/17 h94: h20g h21m⁴ h15.8g⁴ h15.8m⁶ h20.3g⁶ Aug 23] maiden hurdler, poor
nowadays: stays 3m: acts on good to soft going: usually wears headgear: has worn tongue
tie: temperamental. *Clare Hobson*

MAY'S BOY 9 gr.g. Proclamation (IRE) – Sweet Portia (IRE) (Pennekamp (USA))   **h–**
[2016/17 h99: h17.2m May 28] handicap hurdler, fair at best: well held only outing in
2016/17: best around 2m: acts on good to firm and good to soft going: in cheekpieces last
5 starts. *James Moffatt*

MAYZE BELL 8 br.m. And Beyond (IRE) – Eleanor May (Crofthall) [2016/17 h–, b–:   **h67**
h16.2d⁵ h16.2s⁵ h17.1d⁵ Oct 30] poor form over hurdles: will be suited by 2½m: usually
races nearer last than first. *Alistair Whillans*

MAZ MAJECC (IRE) 8 b.g. Robert Emmet (IRE) – Madam Elsa (IRE) (Lycius (USA))   **c87**
[2016/17 c79, h–: c20.1d^pu c24.2d* c24.2g⁴ c24.2g^pu Jun 4] winning pointer: maiden   **h–**
hurdler: modest handicap chaser: won at Hexham in May: stays 3m: acts on soft going:
wears headgear. *Jonathan Haynes*

MAZOVIAN (USA) 9 b.g. E Dubai (USA) – Polish Style (USA) (Danzig (USA))   **c–**
[2016/17 h95: h19.6g² h18.7m⁶ h23g^pu h20g c19.4g^pu c22.6g⁴ c16.5g Sep 12] modest   **h93**
handicap hurdler: no form over fences: stays 21f: acts on good to firm and good to soft
going: wears headgear/tongue tie: often races towards rear. *Matt Sheppard*

MCCABE CREEK (IRE) 7 b.g. Robin des Pres (FR) – Kick And Run (IRE) (Presenting)   **c124**
[2016/17 h117: h21g^ro h18.5g² h20.6g⁵ c16m⁵ c21.4s c20.2m^pu c19.4m⁴ Apr 28] sturdy   **h123**
gelding: fairly useful handicap hurdler/maiden chaser: stays 21f: acts on good to firm and
heavy going: has worn hood: often races towards rear/travels strongly, but finishes weakly.
Alan King

MCGINTY'S DREAM (IRE) 6 b.g. Flemensfirth (USA) – Laboc (Rymer) [2016/17   **h86**
h–, b–: h16.2s h17.1d h20d h19s⁴ h22s* h20.5s⁴ h22.7v⁵ Mar 4] modest handicap hurdler:
won at Newcastle in January: will stay 3m: acts on soft going: usually in hood: usually
races in rear. *N. W. Alexander*

MCGOWAN'S PASS 6 b.g. Central Park (IRE) – Function Dreamer (Overbury (IRE)) **b97**
[2016/17 b16v² b16.4v* Feb 25] £3,500 3-y-o: sixth foal: half-brother to modest chaser
Digg Whitaker (3¼m winner, by Mounting Spendent): dam unraced half-sister to useful
hurdler/top-class chaser (stayed 3m) Captain Chris: fairly useful form both starts in
bumpers, successful in 5-runner event at Newcastle: will stay 2½m. *Sandy Thomson*

MCKENZIE'S FRIEND (IRE) 6 b.g. Flemensfirth (USA) – Escrea (IRE) (Oscar **h99**
(IRE)) [2016/17 h124, b94: h19.8d⁶ h23.6s h19.8v³ h21.4d⁵ Feb 18] well-made gelding:
fairly useful hurdler, below form in handicaps in 2016/17: stays 21f: acts on soft going.
Oliver Sherwood

MCKINLEY 7 b.g. Kheleyf (USA) – Priera Menta (IRE) (Montjeu (IRE)) [2016/17 c132, **c–**
h139: h20g² Jul 8] strong gelding: useful hurdler: good effort when 1¾ lengths second of 6 **h140**
to Simenon in minor event at Cork, only outing in 2016/17: useful chaser: stays 2½m: acts
on good to firm and heavy going: has worn headgear, including last 4 starts. *W. P. Mullins,
Ireland*

MCLAREN VALE (IRE) 9 b.g. Darsi (FR) – Lunar Approach (IRE) (Mandalus) **c81**
[2016/17 c20,3g² c20.3dᶠ h20g c20.5g⁶ h19.9dᵖᵘ Oct 13] winning pointer: poor maiden **h–**
hurdler/chaser: stays 2¾m: best form on good going: tried in cheekpieces. *Thomas Coyle,
Ireland*

MCVICAR 8 b.g. Tobougg (IRE) – Aries (GER) (Big Shuffle (USA)) [2016/17 c–, h105: **c–**
h19.3s⁵ h19.4s* Mar 3] small gelding: fair handicap hurdler: returned to form to win at **h109**
Doncaster, making all: maiden chaser: stays 2½m: acts on heavy going: has worn
cheekpieces, including at Doncaster. *John Davies*

MEADOWCROFT BOY 8 b.g. Kayf Tara – Blackbriery Thyne (IRE) (Good Thyne **h–**
(USA)) [2016/17 h127: h16.2v⁵ h16.4v⁵ h16.2s⁵ h16.2gᵖᵘ Apr 26] angular gelding:
handicap hurdler, no form in 2016/17: has worn hood: tried in tongue tie: usually races
towards rear. *Alistair Whillans*

MEASUREOFMYDREAMS (IRE) 9 b.g. Shantou (USA) – Le Bavellen (Le Bavard **c131**
(FR)) [2016/17 c147, h–: c25dᵖᵘ c25g c34.3dᵘʳ c29d Apr 17] sturdy gelding: winning **h–**
hurdler: useful handicap chaser: 33/1, best effort of 2016/17 when 32¼ lengths ninth of 28
to Our Duke in Irish Grand National at Fairyhouse final start: stays 4m: acts on heavy
going: in cheekpieces penultimate start (unseated rider Chair in Grand National at Aintree).
Noel Meade, Ireland

MEDAL OF FREEDOM (IRE) 7 b.g. Mahler – Clashwilliam Girl (IRE) (Seymour **c82**
Hicks (FR)) [2016/17 h16.2d⁴ h20g³ h20.5s h18.1s h15.6g⁶ h16d c19.9gᵖᵘ c26.3g⁵ c24.2gᶠ **h77**
Apr 25] €42,000 3-y-o, £20,000 5-y-o: half-brother to fairly useful hurdler/smart chaser
Invictus (19f-3m winner, by Flemensfirth) and bumper winner/fair hurdler John's Eliza
(2½m winner, by Dr Massini): dam (h116) bumper/2½m-3m hurdle winner: placed all 3
completed starts in Irish points: poor maiden hurdler/chaser: likely to prove best up to 3m:
acts on good to soft going: often races towards rear. *Stuart Coltherd*

MEDINAH THEATRE (IRE) 6 b.m. King's Theatre (IRE) – Supreme Adventure **b75**
(IRE) (Supreme Leader) [2016/17 b16g⁵ b16.7d⁴ b16d⁵ Oct 24] €6,300 4-y-o: seventh foal:
dam twice-raced half-sister to dam of very smart hurdler/top-class chaser (stayed 25f)
Menorah (by King's Theatre): modest form in bumpers. *Peter Fahey, Ireland*

MEET THE LEGEND 6 b.g. Midnight Legend – Combe Florey (Alflora (IRE)) **h142**
[2016/17 h139p, b113: h15.7d h16dᶠ Jan 14] sturdy gelding: useful winner in bumpers/
over hurdles: still in front when falling last in handicap at Kempton final outing: stayed
2¼m: acted on heavy going (bumper win on good to firm): wore hood over hurdles, also in
tongue tie last 2 starts: dead. *Dan Skelton*

MEGABUCKS (IRE) 6 b.g. Well Chosen – Clonmayo (IRE) (Kasmayo) [2016/17 **h87 p**
b15.9g⁵ h20d⁴ Jun 16] €8,500 3-y-o, £35,000 4-y-o: third foal: dam unraced half-sister to **b81**
useful chaser (stayed 33f) Barryscourt Lad: won Irish maiden point on debut: modest form
only start in bumpers: 11/2, some encouragement when 22½ lengths fourth of 7 to West
Torr in novice at Ffos Las on hurdling debut (should do better): successful in another point
in April. *Evan Williams*

MEGA FORTUNE (FR) 4 b.g. Soldier of Fortune (IRE) – Far Across (Common **h145**
Grounds) [2016/17 h16gᶠ h16g* h16d³ h16d³ h16s* h16.8g² h16d⁴ Apr 29] well-made
gelding: fairly useful winner at 10.5f on Flat: smart hurdler: won juvenile at Down Royal
in November and Spring Juvenile Hurdle at Leopardstown (by 3½ lengths from Bapaume)
in February: creditable efforts when 5 lengths second of 15 to Defi du Seuil in Triumph
Hurdle at Cheltenham and 2¼ lengths fourth of 7 to Bapaume in AES Champion Four Year
Old Hurdle at Punchestown last 2 starts: will be suited by further than 2m: acts on soft
going: in cheekpieces last 3 starts: usually races close up. *Gordon Elliott, Ireland*

Mr C. Jones's "Mega Fortune"

MEISTER ECKHART (IRE) 11 b.g. Flemensfirth (USA) – Carrabawn (Buckskin (FR)) [2016/17 h20.5d[6] h24s[6] h22.8s[6] Jan 21] tall, angular gelding: one-time smart hurdler: off 32 months, fairly useful form in handicaps in 2016/17: pulled up only start over fences: stays 3m: acts on heavy going: in cheekpieces final outing. *John O'Shea* **c– h116**

MELANGERIE 5 b.m. Fair Mix (IRE) – Angie Marinie (Sabrehill (USA)) [2016/17 b15.8d b16.6d b16.7g* b16.8g* Apr 20] £15,000 3-y-o: half-sister to several winners, including useful hurdler/fairly useful chaser Scotsbrook Cloud (21f-25f winner, by Cloudings) and bumper winner/useful hurdler Cultivator (2m-21f winner, by Alflora): dam (h113), 2m/2¼m hurdle winner, also 1m winner on Flat: fairly useful form when winning mares bumpers at Market Rasen (maiden) and Cheltenham last 2 starts: in hood last 3 starts. *Nicky Henderson* **b98**

MELDRUM LAD (IRE) 8 b.g. Fruits of Love (USA) – Meldrum Hall (IRE) (Saddlers' Hall (IRE)) [2016/17 h16m c20.5m[5] c22d[3] c18.5g[5] c18.3d[F] c22g c18g c19.9d[5] c19.9g* c19.2g* c20.2f* Apr 23] sturdy gelding: winning hurdler: much improved over fences and won novice handicaps at Huntingdon and Exeter and handicap at Wincanton (useful form) on last 3 starts, all in April: left David Harry Kelly after seventh outing: best efforts around 2½m: acts on firm and soft going: sometimes in headgear for previous yard: in tongue tie last 4 starts: often races towards rear, usually travels strongly. *Seamus Durack* **c131 h–**

MELODIC RENDEZVOUS 11 ch.g. Where Or When (IRE) – Vic Melody (FR) (Old Vic) [2016/17 c–, h142: h16.2v[2] h16.8s[4] h19.9v[pu] h15.3d[4] h16.3v[5] Mar 4] lengthy, useful-looking gelding: useful hurdler nowadays, on downgrade: best effort of 2016/17 (seen to maximum effect) when 2¼ lengths second of 4 to Ch'tibello in minor event at Haydock on return: winning chaser: stays 19f: acts on heavy going: wears headgear: front runner/races prominently. *Jeremy Scott* **c– h138 d**

503

MELODYA (IRE) 4 b.f. Arcano (IRE) – Fall Habit (IRE) (Hamas (IRE)) [2016/17   **h– x**
h16.6g^{pu} h15.7g^{ur} h16s^{pu} h21.2s^{F} h15.7s^{pu} Mar 8] smallish, leggy filly: poor maiden on
Flat, stays 12.5f: no form over hurdles: poor jumper. *Mike Sowersby*

MELON 5 ch.g. Medicean – Night Teeny (Platini (GER)) [2016/17 h16g* h16.4g^{2} **h150**
h16.5d^{2} Apr 25]
      The Supreme Novices' Hurdle now firmly rivals the Champion Bumper as the
Festival race in which punters are most likely to latch on to a Willie Mullins-trained
runner. Tourist Attraction's 25/1 success in the 1995 Supreme was the first of the
trainer's fifty-four winners at the Cheltenham Festival and he has won the meeting's
opener on a further four occasions since. He had the winner three years running from
2013 to 2015 with Champagne Fever, Vautour and Douvan, but the stable's main
hope for the latest renewal, Melon, sent off the 3/1 joint favourite, met with the same
fate as his stable-companion Min, the 15/8 favourite twelve months earlier. Both
finished second, Melon going down by two and a quarter lengths to outsider Labaik
after holding every chance approaching the final flight. Like the stable's three most
recent winners he was bidding to emulate, Min had won at graded level in Ireland
beforehand, but Melon had no such form in the book, his place in the betting owing
more to his reputation than to anything he had actually achieved over hurdles. He
showed plenty of promise when making a winning debut over hurdles in a maiden
at Leopardstown at the end of January, but it was a race that lacked depth, Melon

Mrs J. Donnelly's "Melon"

winning by ten lengths and twelve from the only two rivals sent off at shorter than 25/1; Melon's own reputation had already preceded him and he started at 9/4-on. The bare form of Melon's debut win left him requiring about two stone improvement to win even a substandard Supreme. To be fair to him, he went a long way to living up to the highest expectations at Cheltenham, prominent throughout and finishing eight lengths clear of the third after racing freely in a steadily-run contest and still going strongly two out. Melon and Labaik re-opposed in the Herald Champion Novices' Hurdle at Punchestown. Melon's chances of going one better (he was a 5/4-shot) were improved greatly when 5/2-chance Labaik refused to jump off, but, after again racing keenly, in the lead this time, Melon was drawn into something of a private battle from halfway with the Top Novices' Hurdle winner Pingshou who had been a long way behind him at Cheltenham. Melon edged ahead again early in the straight, but his exertions left him vulnerable when the Supreme fifth Cilaos Emery, one of Mullins' two other runners in the race, joined him at the final flight before running out the winner by a length. Despite that reverse, Melon still rates as his stable's top two-mile novice hurdler.

Along with Vautour, Douvan and Min, Melon began his career in France but, unlike them, he was recruited from the Flat, having the physique of a jumper—he's a well-made gelding—if not the breeding of one. He made just four appearances for Nicolas Clement as a three-year-old, making his debut in the same newcomers race at Longchamp that was also contested by the now useful Paul Nicholls-trained hurdler Zubayr (as well as the the top French stayer Vazirabad). Melon won his third start, a mile and a half maiden at Moulins, showing fairly useful form. He was entered in Arqana's Deauville Autumn Sale later that year but didn't meet that engagement, having been sold privately in the interim. A €100,000 yearling, Melon comes from one of the most successful German classic families of recent years, his close family boasting two winners apiece of the German Derby and Oaks, as well as two more fillies who were runner-up in the latter contest, the Preis der Diana. Melon's dam Night Teeny, who won over a mile and a quarter in Germany, had already produced five winners, three of them useful, including Night of Magic (by Peintre Celebre) who was also a classic winner, not in Germany but in Italy where she won the Oaks d'Italia. Night of Magic's first foal Nightflower missed out on a classic win (second in the Preis der Diana) but won another German Group 1 contest, the Preis von Europa, for the second year running in 2016. Another of Melon's useful half-sisters Neele (also by Peintre Celebre) has produced the 2015 Deutsches Derby winner Nutan, her second Group 1 winner after the filly Nymphea (another Diana runner-up) who won the Grosser Preis von Berlin. Night Teeny is herself a half-sister to the Preis der Diana winner Night Petticoat (also second in the German St Leger) whose foals include Next Desert and Next Gina, winners of the German Derby and Oaks respectively. Night Petticoat, incidentally, was a contemporary of Annie Power's dam Anno Luce and they met on several occasions at three, with Anno Luce finishing third behind Night Petticoat in the Diana. Melon is the second smart hurdler by the Eclipse and Lockinge Stakes winner Medicean that the Mullins stable has sourced from the Flat in France, following Sempre Medici who contested the 2016 Champion Hurdle. Melon needs to improve further to be contesting Champion Hurdles but, with just three runs over hurdles, it is not out of the question that he will progress enough to do so, provided he learns to settle better (he wore ear plugs at Cheltenham). *W. P. Mullins, Ireland*

MELROSE BOY (FR) 5 b.g. Saint des Saints (FR) – Pollypink (FR) (Poliglote) [2016/17   **h117** b82: h19.9s³ h15.8d² h19.7d³ Jan 14] well-made gelding: fairly useful form in maiden/ novice hurdles: bred to stay further than 2½m. *Harry Fry*

MEME'S HORSE (IRE) 7 b.g. Scorpion (IRE) – Alittlebitofheaven (Cape Cross (IRE)) **h103**
[2016/17 h122p: h21.1s Nov 12] rangy gelding: fairly useful hurdle winner, behind in
handicap only outing in 2016/17: wore tongue tie: dead. *Harry Fry*

MEMORY OF LIGHT (IRE) 8 gr.g. Westerner – Be Thankfull (IRE) (Linamix (FR)) **c80**
[2016/17 h80: c15.7m^F May 5] poor handicap hurdler: in second when fell fatally 3 out in **h—**
novice handicap at Wincanton on chasing debut: in hood last 2 starts: wore tongue tie.
Sally Randell

MENACE 6 ch.g. Papal Bull – Wishfully Tropical (IRE) (Desert Prince (IRE)) [2016/17 **h79**
h88, b88: h19.9g h21g^4 h23.3g h22m h19.9g^4 Sep 27] maiden hurdler, poor form in
2016/17: will prove best up to 21f: best form on good going: in cheekpieces last 4 starts.
Noel Williams

MENAPIAN (IRE) 6 b.g. Touch of Land (FR) – Mannequin (IRE) (In The Wings) **b63**
[2016/17 b17.7d^3 b16.8v^pu Jan 1] poor form in bumpers. *Helen Nelmes*

MENDIP EXPRESS (IRE) 11 b.g. King's Theatre (IRE) – Mulberry (IRE) (Denel (FR)) **c133**
[2016/17 c133, h—: c25s^3 c23.8s^2 c26.3g c21.1g^5 c24.5d^2 Apr 28] tall, good-topped gelding: **h—**
prolific point winner: winning hurdler: useful chaser: best effort of 2016/17 when neck
second to Balnaslow in Champion Hunters' Chase at Punchestown on final start: stays
3¼m: acts on heavy going: wears tongue tie. *Philip Hobbs*

MENGLI KHAN (IRE) 4 b.g. Lope de Vega (IRE) – Danielli (IRE) (Danehill (USA)) **h136 p**
[2016/17 h16s^2 h16v^4 Feb 25] half-brother to fairly useful hurdler Akula (2m winner, by
Soviet Star): useful on Flat, stays 11f: also useful form over hurdles when 18 lengths fourth
of 9 to promoted Dinaria des Obeaux in Winning Fair Juvenile Hurdle at Fairyhouse,
pulling hard and not unduly punished: open to further improvement. *Gordon Elliott,
Ireland*

MENORAH (IRE) 12 b.g. King's Theatre (IRE) – Maid For Adventure (IRE) **c168**
(Strong Gale) [2016/17 c168x, h—: c23.8f^2 c26.1g^5 c24.2g^2 h24.2d^3 c22.7g* Apr 29] **h143**
    A bronze statue of Sir Anthony McCoy, who made a bonfire of jumping's
record books when he was a jockey, now graces Cheltenham racecourse, along with
those of Golden Miller, Arkle, Best Mate and Dawn Run (the last-named with her
jockey Jonjo O'Neill). McCoy won the last of his twenty jockeys' championships in
2014/15 and gave an interesting insight, in an interview with *The Mail on Sunday* in
March, into how retirement from the saddle has proven every bit as difficult for him
as he feared it was going to be. 'I woke up with a challenge every day and trying
to replace that, with that nervousness in the morning, is impossible … I get up now
and think "I might go to Jonjo's and ride, or I might go to Nicky Henderson's or I
might go racing somewhere if JP's got a runner" but it doesn't really matter if I go
or not. And that's difficult. I'm floating, I could go into something else but is it going
to make me happy? Am I going to get the same fulfilment I got from riding? I could
play more golf but I'm not going to win the US Open, am I? All the enjoyment I
got from riding was from being successful at it.' McCoy, who also now works as a
pundit for ITV Racing, says he would love to be riding again—'I'd give it all back,
even now, if I could just change my name and go back riding for another year or two
without anyone knowing it was me. There are a lot of moments when I think I retired
too early. But I'm too stubborn to admit I might have made a mistake.'
    McCoy said that Roger Federer's victory in the Australian Open early in 2017
had made a big impression on him. 'He is the best tennis player ever and you would
never lose respect for him, but for the last three years I had been wondering why he
is still playing. People were going to remember him ending up getting beat the last
three or four years he was playing, then he won the Australian Open [followed by a
record-breaking eighth Wimbledon since then] and you think he was right not to give
up. Do I think I could still do it? Well, it's all right thinking it. You have to go out
and do it, but you also have to be brave enough to think "I had my time". No matter
how good you are and how much you win, you can't stop getting old, so I don't
sit at home feeling sorry for myself and wishing I was still a jockey. I try to keep
busy and I'm fine if I don't have too much time to think about it.' McCoy says that
it was suggested that he might coach young jockeys but 'I thought "What happens
if they end up riding more winners than me?" There are a few lads I've helped but
I'd always be frightened they'd be the one.' McCoy takes genuine pleasure from the

fact that Richard Johnson, who finished runner-up to McCoy sixteen times in the jockeys' championship and sat next to him in the jockeys' changing room nearly all his career, has won the title in the two years since. Typical of McCoy, though, he says that 'Richard would have to ride to the age of forty-five or forty-six to catch my winners, and he is not going to win twenty championships, so the fact that he is champion again means I have got at least another twenty years before anyone could match that.'

Richard Johnson's second jockeys' championship, like his first, was in the bag well before the end of the season, though he couldn't match his total in the 2015/16 campaign of 235 wins. Johnson's total of 189 (from over a thousand rides) in the latest season was still the second best of his career, and the seventh time in the last eight years he has passed 150, and he finished forty-five ahead of the runner-up, northern-based Brian Hughes, who was the season's second-busiest jockey in Britain behind the tireless Johnson. Two of Johnson's biggest victories came on Native River in the Hennessy Gold Cup—a race he took delight in reminding McCoy afterwards that he never won—and in the Welsh Grand National. But Menorah's fourth successive win in the bet365 Oaksey Chase at Sandown's Finale meeting will probably take pride of place with Johnson himself as he has been associated with the horse since he was a four-year-old—partnering him on all bar two of his forty-one starts over jumps—and rode him to all fourteen of his victories in Britain (Menorah won a bumper in Ireland before joining Philip Hobbs). The Supreme Novices' Hurdle and the Manifesto Novices' Chase provided Menorah and Johnson with Grade 1 wins and they also numbered the International Hurdle, the Peterborough Chase and the Charlie Hall Chase among their other important victories together. This is the sixth and last essay in *Chasers & Hurdlers* on Menorah who will spend his retirement with Johnson who said of him 'There are good horses who might run at a Cheltenham Festival but only a few are like Menorah—good enough to run in and win a championship race there.'

Menorah's opportunities were more limited in his later years—'There are only two races for him, the Charlie Hall and the Oaksey Chase', his trainer had said—and, after running creditably under top weight in the Perth Gold Cup (second) and the Summer Cup (fifth) at Uttoxeter in June, he was given a break before being

bet365 Oaksey Chase, Sandown—
Menorah signs off with a fourth straight win in this race before his well-earned retirement

prepared for a third tilt at the Charlie Hall Chase at Wetherby in late-October. Menorah's good second, beaten three quarters of a length by Irish Cavalier, was much closer to his winning effort in 2014 than his dismal display in the race in between and he stuck to his task well, closing on the winner (to whom Menorah conceded 4 lb) as the line was reached. Menorah was seen out only once between the Charlie Hall and the Oaksey Chase, when appearing over hurdles for the first time in almost five years and showing smart form when third to Unowhatimeanharry in the Long Distance Hurdle at Newbury in November. As usual, Menorah was produced at the top of his game for the Oaksey Chase, a race he has made his own—literally— winning every renewal since it was added to Sandown's Finale meeting in 2014. Introduced with listed status, and surprisingly promoted to Grade 2 after just two runnings, the Oaksey Chase has only once attracted a field larger than seven and the latest six-runner edition was not a strong one by Grade 2 standards. Menorah made the most of the opportunity to bring a fitting end to a career that stretched over eight seasons. Waited with, Menorah jumped well—something he hasn't always done over fences—and took over in the lead at the fifteenth. Clear three from out, and holding a ten-length advantage at the last, Menorah had to be kept up to his work as the favourite Traffic Fluide closed the gap on the run-in. He won by four and a half lengths in the end, with another sixteen lengths back to third-placed Josses Hill. Menorah and Johnson received a well-deserved reception from the Sandown crowd of 10,903, the smallest for the fixture since it was last run as a mixed meeting and some way off the sell-out 18,621 for Tony McCoy's final farewell in 2015.

Menorah (IRE) (b.g. 2005)	King's Theatre (IRE) (b 1991)	Sadler's Wells (b 1981)	Northern Dancer Fairy Bridge
		Regal Beauty (b 1981)	Princely Native Dennis Belle
	Maid For Adventure (IRE) (br 1991)	Strong Gale (br 1975)	Lord Gayle Sterntau
		Fast Adventure (br 1982)	Deep Run First Adventure

Menorah, a tall gelding, is by the now-deceased King's Theatre whose season is covered in the essay on Henllan Harri who won the feature bet365 Gold Cup at the Sandown Finale. L'Ami Serge's win in the Select Hurdle gave King's Theatre a graded-race treble on the day. Menorah is still the only winner under Rules produced by his jumping-bred dam Maid For Adventure who won over both hurdles and fences and was successful at up to two and three quarter miles. More about the wider family has appeared in previous Annuals. Menorah stayed twenty-five furlongs and acted on any going. He ran well below form when tried once in cheekpieces. *Philip Hobbs*

MERCERS COURT (IRE) 9 b.g. Court Cave (IRE) – Vikki's Dream (IRE) (Kahyasi) [2016/17 c119, h118: c21.1d* c21.2g* c25d^{pu} c21.4g^5 h25m^4 c19.7g* c20.5s* c19.1g^F c24g^3 c19.9g^2 Apr 17] angular gelding: fairly useful handicap hurdler: useful handicap chaser: won at Fontwell in April, Fakenham in May, Plumpton (novice event) in October and Kempton in November: possibly best short of 3m: acts on soft and good to firm going: tried in tongue tie. *Neil King* **c135 h117**

MERCHANT IN MILAN (IRE) 5 b.g. Milan – Azaban (IRE) (Be My Native (USA)) [2016/17 h16.8v^{pu} h15.3v^F h16.5g^5 h16g^6 Apr 8] fourth on completed start in points: poor form over hurdles: in tongue tie last 3 starts. *Helen Nelmes* **h74**

MERCHANT OF DUBAI 12 b.g. Dubai Destination (USA) – Chameleon (Green Desert (USA)) [2016/17 h–: h19.4g h16.4d Nov 14] maiden hurdler, no form in 3 runs since 2014/15. *Jim Goldie* **h–**

MERCIAN KING (IRE) 6 b.g. Robin des Pres (FR) – Mariah Rollins (IRE) (Over The River (FR)) [2016/17 c110, h91: c21.1d^{pu} c16.3g^3 c16.3s* c20s^2 c17.4s^2 c16d^3 Feb 22] lengthy gelding: maiden hurdler: fair handicap chaser: won conditionals event at Fakenham in November: left Charlie Longsdon after first start: stays 2½m: acts on soft going: has worn cheekpieces, including final start. *Amy Murphy* **c110 h–**

MERCIAN PRINCE (IRE) 6 b.g. Midnight Legend – Bongo Fury (FR) (Sillery (USA)) [2016/17 h19.4s^{pu} c21.4v^3 c21.4s* c17.4d^F c20v^2 c20.3d* c20s* c20.8s^F c20.2s^4 c20.5g^3 Mar 18] sturdy gelding: third foal: dam (c124/h132), 2m hurdle/chase winner (stayed 19f), **c136 h–**

also 9f winner on Flat in France: maiden hurdler: useful chaser: won minor event at Auteuil in June (for E. & G. Leenders) and handicaps at Southwell in November and Sandown in January: stays 21f: acts on heavy going: tongue tied penultimate start. *Amy Murphy*

MERCIAN PRINCESS (IRE) 4 b.f. Saint des Saints (FR) – Bongo Fury (FR) (Sillery (USA)) [2016/17 b12.4d⁵ b16d Feb 17] lightly-made filly: fifth foal: half-sister to useful chaser Mercian Prince (2½m/21f winner, by Midnight Legend): dam, (c124/h132) 2m hurdle/chase winner (stayed 19f), also 9f winner on Flat in France: no form in bumpers. *Amy Murphy* **b–**

MERE ANARCHY (IRE) 6 b.g. Yeats (IRE) – Maracana (IRE) (Glacial Storm (USA)) [2016/17 h112: h16.7g⁵ h20.6g³ h20g³ h21.2g Apr 3] fair handicap hurdler: will prove best around 2m: acts on soft going: often races freely: signs of temperament. *Robert Stephens* **h99**

MERE DETAIL (IRE) 5 br.m. Definite Article – Grangeclare Dancer (IRE) (Top of The World) [2016/17 b16.3v⁵ b16.3m Jul 17] €30,000 3-y-o, £31,000 4-y-o: half-sister to 3 winners by Old Vic, including smart hurdler/chaser Real Steel (2m-19f winner) and useful hurdler Grangeclare Gold (2m-2½m winner): dam unraced: off mark in mares maiden points at second attempt: no form in bumpers. *Tony Carroll* **b–**

MERIBEL MILLIE 6 b.m. Kayf Tara – Ede'iff (Tragic Role (USA)) [2016/17 b93: b15.8d⁴ b19.5gᵖᵘ b18.5s h16.8s h21.2s h15.3d h19.9v* h18.6s² h20.7d⁶ Mar 15] modest form in bumpers: fair hurdler: won mares handicap at Sedgefield in March: left Harry Fry after second start: stays 2½m: best form on soft/heavy going: tried in hood: wears tongue tie: often races towards rear. *Neil Mulholland* **h108 b79**

MERI DEVIE (FR) 4 ch.f. Spirit One (FR) – Folle Biche (FR) (Take Risks (FR)) [2016/17 h16d* h16s⁴ h16d³ Apr 29] useful on Flat, stays 1¼m: useful form over hurdles: won juvenile maiden at Leopardstown in December by 5 lengths from Housesofparliament: best effort when 2¼ lengths third of 7 to Bapaume in AES Champion Four Year Old Hurdle at Punchestown final start. *W. P. Mullins, Ireland* **h135 +**

MERLIN'S WISH 12 gr.g. Terimon – Sendai (Le Moss) [2016/17 c107: c26.1dᵖᵘ May 5] strong gelding: fairly useful chaser at best, lightly raced and little form since 2013/14: in cheekpieces last 3 starts. *Martin Keighley* **c–**

MERRYDOWN VINTAGE (IRE) 10 ch.g. Ballingarry (IRE) – Cure The Blues (IRE) (Phardante (FR)) [2016/17 c–x, h–: c23.6g² May 17] prolific winner in points: maiden hurdler: modest maiden chaser: stays 3m: acts on soft going: wears headgear: tried in tongue tie: often let down by jumping. *Ray Fielder* **c94 x h–**

MESSERY (FR) 6 b.g. Poliglote – Iris du Berlais (FR) (Bonnet Rouge (FR)) [2016/17 h–: h18.8dᵖᵘ h19g Jan 27] short-backed gelding: no form over hurdles. *Tim Vaughan* **h–**

MESSIRE DES OBEAUX (FR) 5 b.g. Saddler Maker (IRE) – Madame Lys (FR) (Sheyrann) [2016/17 h124: h19.6v* h19.8s* h20.5d* h19.6d² h21.1g³ h20g³ Apr 8] good-topped gelding: smart hurdler: won handicap at Bangor in November, and Winter Novices' Hurdle at Sandown (by ½ length from Ballyandy) and Challow Hurdle at Newbury (by 2 lengths from Baltazar d'Allier) in December: continued to run well, on last 2 starts 3¼ lengths third of 15 to Willoughby Court in Baring Bingham Novices' Hurdle at Cheltenham and 6¼ lengths third of 13 to Finian's Oscar in Mersey Novices' Hurdle at Aintree (sustained tendon injury and will reportedly miss 2017/18): stays 21f: acts on heavy going: often travels strongly. *Alan King* **h147**

Betfred Challow Novices' Hurdle, Newbury—Messire des Obeaux survives an error at the last to hold off Irish raider Baltazar d'Allier (noseband)

MESSI'S MAGIC 7 br.m. Rock City – Yemaail (IRE) (Shaadi (USA)) [2016/17 b16.2d⁶ **b–**
Sep 14] sister to modest hurdler/chaser (2m-19f winner) Carters Rest and half-sister to
several winners, including fair hurdler/useful chaser Ross Comm (2½m-3¼m winner, by
Minster Son), stays 4m: dam unraced half-sister to useful hurdler/chaser up to 25f
Gallateen: 22/1, last of 6 in maiden bumper at Kelso. *Harriet Graham*

MESUT (FR) 6 bl.g. Early March – Alicesprings (FR) (Pelder (IRE)) [2016/17 c83, h–: **c–**
h19.1d h20.7d Dec 4] maiden hurdler/chaser, little form in Britain: in tongue tie final start. **h–**
Sarah Humphrey

METHAG (FR) 4 b.f. Pour Moi (IRE) – Kyria (Grand Lodge (USA)) [2016/17 h15.8d **h77**
h16.7s⁴ h16.3s⁶ h16g Apr 17] close-coupled filly: fair on Flat, stays 1½m: poor form over
hurdles. *Alex Hales*

ME VOILA (FR) 5 gr.g. Turgeon (USA) – Saintenitouche (FR) (Saint des Saints (FR)) **h79**
[2016/17 h94: h15.3d⁶ Nov 17] sturdy gelding: maiden hurdler, modest at best: dead.
Nick Williams

MEXICAN BORDER (GER) 8 b.g. Sholokhov (IRE) – Moricana (GER) (Konigsstuhl **h90**
(GER)) [2016/17 h88: h16.8g⁵ h16.8s h18.5d h18.7m⁶ h16.8m* h16.8g² Jul 25] modest
handicap hurdler: won novice event at Newton Abbot in July: unproven beyond 17f: acts
on good to firm going: has worn hood: has worn tongue tie, including last 3 starts: usually
travels strongly. *Martin Hill*

MEXICAN JIM 5 ch.g. Dubai Destination (USA) – Artic Bliss (Fraam) [2016/17 h15.7d **h58**
h15.9v h15.7v⁶ h16.6s h19.7d⁶ Mar 21] well held only start on Flat: little form over
hurdles. *Peter Hiatt*

MEXICAN MICK 8 ch.g. Atraf – Artic Bliss (Fraam) [2016/17 h20.5d Dec 28] well held **h–**
both starts over hurdles. *Peter Hiatt*

MEZENDORE (IRE) 8 ch.g. Bach (IRE) – Ballinard Lady (IRE) (Phardante (FR)) **c–**
[2016/17 c118: c19.9gᵖᵘ c19.4gᵖᵘ h16.8g³ h19.7g⁵ h19.7sᵖᵘ h23.1sᵖᵘ Dec 22] modest **h86**
maiden over hurdles: fairly useful chaser at best, no form in 2016/17: stays 2½m: acts on
heavy going: wears headgear: often races lazily. *Sheila Lewis*

MIAMI PRESENT (IRE) 7 b.g. Presenting – Miami Nights (GER) (Tertullian (USA)) **c103**
[2016/17 h111: h15.7g h20g² c19.2g⁴ c21.2g⁵ h19.3g c21.3dᵖᵘ Mar 21] good-topped **h107**
gelding: fair handicap hurdler/maiden chaser: stays 2½m: acts on soft going: wears hood:
waited with. *Harriet Bethell*

MIA'S ANTHEM (IRE) 9 ch.g. Royal Anthem (USA) – Windmill View (IRE) (Glacial **c127**
Storm (USA)) [2016/17 c127, h98: c20g⁶ h24m c25d* c25.5dᵖᵘ c25.5d⁶ c24g c32.4sᵖᵘ **h91**
Dec 4] angular gelding: modest handicap hurdler: fairly useful handicap chaser: won at
Aintree in June: stays 3¼m: acts on soft and good to firm going: tried in cheekpieces: wears
tongue tie: usually races nearer last than first. *Noel C. Kelly, Ireland*

MIA'S STORM (IRE) 7 b.m. September Storm (GER) – Letitia's Gain (USA) (Zaffaran **h121**
(USA)) [2016/17 h98p, b106: h19.7g* h21.6g* h21.6d⁵ h20.3s h19.4d* Jan 28] sturdy
mare: winning Irish pointer: fairly useful hurdler: won mares novices at Wetherby and
Newton Abbot in May, and handicap at Doncaster final start: stays 2¾m: acts on good to
soft going: strong traveller. *Alan King*

MICHAELA 5 ch.m. Sholokhov (IRE) – La Capilla (Machiavellian (USA)) [2016/17 **h–**
h16s⁵ h16.7dᵖᵘ May 26] half-sister to useful hurdler/chaser Lightning Strike (2m-23f
winner, by Danehill Dancer) and useful hurdler Low Key (19f winner, by Pentire): modest
maiden on Flat, stays 1½m: showed nothing in 2 starts over hurdles. *Paul Webber*

MICKIEBLUEEYES (IRE) 5 b.g. Dilshaan – Killerig Park (I'm Supposin (IRE)) **h– p**
[2016/17 b93: h19.5m Nov 8] fair form when successful on only start in bumpers: well
held in novice at Lingfield on hurdling debut, not unduly punished: should do better.
Diana Grissell

MICK JAZZ (FR) 6 b.g. Blue Bresil (FR) – Mick Maya (FR) (Siam (USA)) [2016/17 h–: **h148 +**
h16.5g* h16d² h16d³ h16s* Feb 5] well-made gelding: smart hurdler: won maiden at
Clonmel in October and listed novice at Punchestown by neck (from Cilaos Emery) on
final start: second in For Auction Novices' Hurdle at Navan (1¾ lengths behind Labaik) in
November: raced around 2m: acts on soft going: in hood last 5 starts: tried in tongue tie:
usually travels strongly. *Gordon Elliott, Ireland*

MICKLEGATE RUN 6 b.g. Tiger Hill (IRE) – Mamoura (IRE) (Lomond (USA)) **h–**
[2016/17 b103: b16m⁶ h16.8d⁴ Dec 26] fairly useful form at best in bumpers, won both **b87**
starts in 2015/16: well beaten in novice on hurdling debut. *Alan Swinbank*

MICK MAESTRO (FR) 4 b.g. Air Chief Marshal (IRE) – Mick Maya (FR) (Siam **b86** (USA)) [2016/17 b13.7d* Nov 24] fourth foal: half-brother to smart hurdler Mick Jazz (2m winner, by Blue Bresil): dam French 2m-19f hurdle/chase winner: 11/2, won junior bumper at Towcester by length from Scottsdale. *Tom George*

MICK THONIC (FR) 7 gr.g. Maresca Sorrento (FR) – Mick Madona (FR) (Dadarissime **c135** (FR)) [2016/17 c20g³ c17mᶠ c17dᵖᵘ c17s³ c19.8g² c15.9sᶠ c16.3g c16.3g* Apr 19] useful- **h–** looking gelding: fourth foal: closely related to French hurdler/chaser Mick Cleopatre (17f-19f winner, by Robin des Pres) and half-brother to French hurdler/chaser Mick Matis (17f-21f winner, by Mister Tullio): dam French 2m/17f hurdle/chase winner: winning hurdler: useful chaser: won 4-runner novice at Cheltenham on final start: best effort when second in novice at Cheltenham (4 lengths behind Shantou Village) in October: left Colm A. Murphy after fourth start: stays 2½m: acts on heavy going: wears tongue tie: jumps none too fluently. *Colin Tizzard*

MICQUUS (IRE) 8 b.g. High Chaparral (IRE) – My Potters (USA) (Irish River (FR)) **c75** [2016/17 h62: c17g⁴ c19.2d² c19.2g⁴ Mar 31] poor maiden hurdler/chaser: stays 2¾m: best **h–** form on good going: has worn visor, including final start: often races towards rear. *Jonathan Geake*

MIDAS GOLD (IRE) 5 b.g. Rip Van Winkle (IRE) – Hespera (Danehill (USA)) [2016/17 **b89** b15.7g* Aug 31] fourth foal: half-brother to 2 winners in France, including smart hurdler/ useful chaser Nando (17f-21f winner, by Hernando): dam ran twice in France (second at 1½m): 5/2, won 11-runner maiden bumper at Southwell on debut by 4½ lengths from Vancouver: sold £50,000 in November. *David Loder*

MIDDLEBROW (IRE) 6 b.g. Oscar (IRE) – O What A Girl (IRE) (Anshan) [2016/17 **h105** b17.2s* h16.2d³ h16.8d⁵ h15.6g³ h16d³ h18.9v² h16.3g⁵ Apr 23] £21,000 3-y-o: second **b90** foal: dam, well beaten over hurdles, out of sister to top-class hurdler (stayed 3m) Rhinestone Cowboy: runner-up completed start in points: won maiden bumper at Ballinrobe in May: fair form over hurdles: left Miss Elizabeth Doyle after first start: should stay beyond 2m: acts on good to soft going: in tongue tie last 4 starts. *Donald McCain*

MIDDLETON'S MINX (IRE) 8 b.m. Luso – River Moccasin (IRE) (Over The River **h98** (FR)) [2016/17 h18.5m³ h20.3gᶠ h19.9g⁴ Jul 22] fourth foal: dam unraced: in hood, modest form over hurdles: won a point in April. *Richard Phillips*

MIDNIGHT APPEAL 12 b.g. Midnight Legend – Lac Marmot (FR) (Marju (IRE)) **c94 x** [2016/17 c129x, h–: c21.2m⁶ c26.1sᵖᵘ h24dᵖᵘ Jul 10] good-topped gelding: winning **h–** hurdler/chaser, on the downgrade: stays 25f: acts on good to firm and heavy going: usually wears headgear/tongue tie: often let down by jumping over fences. *Sophie Leech*

MIDNIGHT BLISS 7 b.m. Midnight Legend – Violet Elizabeth (Overbury (IRE)) **h–** [2016/17 h16g h19.6dᵖᵘ h15.7vᵖᵘ h20.3vᵖᵘ Mar 6] £10,000 6-y-o: first foal: dam unraced half-sister to fairly useful hurdler/chaser around 2m Fair Loch and fairly useful hurdler (stays 3m) Total Submission: runner-up 3 of 6 starts in maiden points: no form over hurdles: tried in tongue tie. *Caroline Fryer*

MIDNIGHT CHARM 5 b.m. Midnight Legend – Cool Spice (Karinga Bay) [2016/17 **b82** b16.2s⁴ b16.6d b15.8s Apr 1] £15,000 3-y-o: fifth foal: half-sister to 3 winners, including useful hurdler Fahamore (2½m/21f winner) and fairly useful hurdler/chaser Brownville (2½m-3m winner) (both by Kayf Tara): dam (h119), 2m-19f hurdle winner, also 11.6f-13f winner on Flat: best effort (modest form) in bumpers when fourth in mares event at Hereford. *Tom Symonds*

MIDNIGHT CHILL 5 b.g. Midnight Legend – Chilla Cilla (Glacial Storm (USA)) **b90** [2016/17 b16.7g⁴ b15.7d⁶ b16.3g Mar 25] £31,000 3-y-o: good-topped gelding: first foal: dam (c80/h72), maiden jumper (placed up to 19f), half-sister to useful hurdler/chaser (stays 3m) Desert Queen: fair form in bumpers: tried in tongue tie. *Jamie Snowden*

MIDNIGHT CHORISTER 9 b.g. Midnight Legend – Royal Musical (Royal Abjar **c101** (USA)) [2016/17 c110, h–: c17.4d⁴ c16.5s⁴ c16gᵖᵘ c17.2m⁴ c16m⁵ Apr 25] compact **h–** gelding: maiden hurdler: fair handicap chaser: best around 2m: acts on soft going: has worn hood: wears tongue tie: often races towards rear. *Alex Hales*

MIDNIGHT COWBOY 6 gr.g. Midnight Legend – Kall (Linamix (FR)) [2016/17 h118, **h118** b87: h19d³ h23.3g⁴ h19.4g* h24.4g² h23.9g³ Mar 20] lengthy gelding: fairly useful handicap hurdler: won novice event at Doncaster in December: stays 3m: acts on heavy going: often travels strongly. *Alan King*

MIDNIGHT FOLIE 7 b.m. Midnight Legend – Lady Racquet (IRE) (Glacial Storm (USA)) [2016/17 h77, b74: h21.4m^{pu} c23.6g^2 c19.2d^F c23.6s^4 Jan 13] maiden hurdler: modest form over fences: looked set to go close when falling 2 out in handicap at Fontwell: likely to prove best at around 2½m: acts on heavy going. *Ben Pauling*　**c89 h–**

MIDNIGHT GEM 7 b.m. Midnight Legend – Barton Flower (Danzero (AUS)) [2016/17 h96, b76: h21.6d^2 h22m^6 h20.7g* h20.5g^3 h20.7d^3 h24.4g^F h24g^6 h21.2m^2 Apr 18] fair handicap hurdler: won at Huntingdon in November: may prove best at short of 3m: acts on good to firm and good to soft going: usually leads. *Charlie Longsdon*　**h108**

MIDNIGHT GLORY 5 b.m. Midnight Legend – Land of Glory (Supreme Leader) [2016/17 b91: b15.8s^5 h21.2d h20.5s* h19g^5 h24.2d^3 Mar 24] compact mare: fair form on first of 2 starts in bumpers: fair form over hurdles: won mares novice at Newbury in January: stays 3m: acts on soft going. *Philip Hobbs*　**h109 b74**

MIDNIGHT GYPSY 7 b.m. Midnight Legend – Romany Dream (Nomadic Way (USA)) [2016/17 h76, b90: h21.6m^5 h19.6m^{pu} h19.7g* h21.2g^4 Nov 10] sturdy mare: poor handicap hurdler: won at Hereford in October: best effort at 2½m: acts on good to firm going: wears hood: sometimes in tongue tie, including first 2 starts. *Stuart Kittow*　**h84**

MIDNIGHT JADE (IRE) 8 b.m. King's Theatre (IRE) – Hurricane Dawn (IRE) (Strong Gale) [2016/17 c82, h62, b–: c25.5s^4 c24d^2 c25.6v* c20.2g* c24v^3 c24.1g* Mar 25] workmanlike mare: maiden hurdler: maiden chaser: won at Southwell in December, Leicester in January and Bangor on final start: stays 3¼m: acts on heavy going: often races prominently/travels strongly. *John Groucott*　**c110 h–**

MIDNIGHT JAZZ 7 b.m. Midnight Legend – Ring Back (IRE) (Bob Back (USA)) [2016/17 h125: h20d h16.3m* h16g^2 h19.4g* h19.8s^2 h16.6d^2 h19.9g Mar 14] small mare: useful hurdler: won mares handicap at Stratford in October and handicap at Doncaster (by ½ length from Big Chief Benny) in December: good effort when head second of 5 to Vroum Vroum Mag in Doncaster Mares' Hurdle in January: stays 2½m: acts on good to firm and heavy going: often travels strongly: genuine and consistent. *Ben Case*　**h136**

MIDNIGHT JITTERBUG 5 b.g. Midnight Legend – Heebie Jeebie (Overbury (IRE)) [2016/17 b87: b15.7d^5 h18.8d h15.5d^6 h15.8s^4 h19g Apr 24] lengthy, rather unfurnished gelding: fair form at best in bumpers: modest form over hurdles: should stay 2½m. *Noel Williams*　**h89 b70**

MIDNIGHT KING 11 b.g. Midnight Legend – Phar Breeze (IRE) (Phardante (FR)) [2016/17 c–, h–: c25.3g^3 c27.5m c23m* c25.5g^4 Aug 25] prolific point winner: maiden hurdler: fair form over fences: won handicap at Worcester in August: left Mrs J. M. Mann after second start: stays 25f: acts on good to firm going: tried in cheekpieces: wears tongue tie. *Anthony Honeyball*　**c102 h–**

MIDNIGHT MAESTRO 5 b.g. Midnight Legend – Calamintha (Mtoto) [2016/17 b102: h16d* h16.8g h15.3v^2 h16.3d* h15.7g^{pu} Apr 15] useful-looking gelding: successful only start in bumpers: fairly useful form over hurdles: won novice at Warwick in November and handicap at Stratford in March: bad mistake fifth and pulled up shortly after on final start: raced around 2m: acts on heavy going. *Alan King*　**h120**

MIDNIGHT MAGIC 5 b.g. Midnight Legend – Arctic Magic (IRE) (Saddlers' Hall (IRE)) [2016/17 b16s b15.8s^6 Mar 18] well held both starts in bumpers. *David Pipe*　**b–**

MIDNIGHT MEMORIES 7 ch.m. Midnight Legend – Bajan Blue (Lycius (USA)) [2016/17 h67: h23m h20.3m Sep 27] little form over hurdles: usually wears headgear: usually leads. *Steph Hollinshead*　**h–**

MIDNIGHT MERLOT 5 b.g. Midnight Legend – Peel Me A Grape (Gunner B) [2016/17 b68: h15.8v^4 h20.5g^3 h20.5s h21g^4 Apr 24] poor form in bumpers: modest form over hurdles: stays 21f. *Noel Williams*　**h94 b68**

MIDNIGHTMISTRESS 5 b.m. Midnight Legend – Mistress Nell (Thethingaboutitis (USA)) [2016/17 b–: b15.8g b16g^5 May 27] well held all 3 starts in bumpers. *Jose Santos*　**b–**

MIDNIGHT MONARCH 6 b.m. Midnight Legend – Monarch's View (King's Ride) [2016/17 b15.8d^6 b16.3d^6 b15.7d^4 Jul 10] sixth foal: sister to a winning pointer and half-sister to a winning pointer by Anshan: dam second in point: poor form in bumpers. *Oliver Sherwood*　**b74**

MIDNIGHT MONTY 7 ch.g. Midnight Legend – Marello (Supreme Leader) [2016/17 c122, h–: c19.9g c15.6d^{pu} c22.4d^{pu} h25g* Apr 28] fair form over hurdles: blinkered first time, won handicap at Huntingdon final start: fairly useful chaser at best, no form in 2016/17: left Keith Reveley after second start: stays 25f: acts on soft going: tried in tongue tie. *Tom Lacey*　**c– h110**

MIDNIGHT MOSS 5 ch.g. Midnight Legend – Brackenmoss (IRE) (Supreme Leader) **h107 p**
[2016/17 b16.6g⁴ b15.7s³ h16.4v² Mar 7] second foal: dam (h114), bumper/2m hurdle **b92**
winner, sister to fairly useful hurdler (17f-2½m winner) Jeremy Cuddle Duck: fair form in
bumpers: 4/1, shaped well when ¾-length second of 6 to Reverant Cust in novice at
Newcastle on hurdling debut: open to improvement. *Gillian Boanas*

MIDNIGHT MUSTANG 10 b.g. Midnight Legend – Mustang Molly (Soldier Rose) **c82**
[2016/17 c–, h–: h21.6gᵖᵘ h23m c25.5s⁵ c25.6v³ c25.5s c20.2g³ c23.5v⁴ c23.9s* c20.2s* **h–**
Feb 28] stocky gelding: maiden hurdler, no form in 2016/17: poor handicap chaser: won at
Market Rasen and Leicester last 2 starts, both in February: stays 3¼m: acts on heavy going:
in cheekpieces last 2 starts. *Andrew Martin*

MIDNIGHT OWLE 7 ch.g. Midnight Legend – Owlesbury Dream (IRE) (Luso) **h–**
[2016/17 h54: h21s Dec 8] workmanlike gelding: lightly-raced hurdler, little form: wears
tongue tie. *Claire Dyson*

MIDNIGHT PRAYER 12 b.g. Midnight Legend – Onawing Andaprayer (Energist) **c129**
[2016/17 c139, h–: c27.3sᵇᵈ c24.1v³ c25.5d c29.2sᵖᵘ Jan 14] tall gelding: winning hurdler: **h–**
fairly useful handicap chaser nowadays: stays 4m: acts on good to firm and heavy going: in
cheekpieces final start. *Alan King*

MIDNIGHT QUEEN 7 b.m. Rainbow High – Questionit (Sovereign Water (FR)) **h–**
[2016/17 b16.3d⁵ b15.7d⁵ h18.7g h19.5s⁵ h20.5v h20s h21.9d Apr 16] first foal: dam, **b66**
winning pointer, sister to winning hurdler/useful chaser (3m/25f winner) Gypsy George:
off mark in points at fifth attempt: poor form in bumpers: no form over hurdles: left Tim
Vaughan after third start. *John Flint*

MIDNIGHT REQUEST 8 b.g. Midnight Legend – Friendly Request (Environment **c105 x**
Friend) [2016/17 c104x, h–: c24.5d³ c24.2vᵖᵘ h25.5v⁵ h25d* h23.1s³ h24s* h25g⁵ Apr 15] **h110**
fair handicap hurdler: won at Carlisle in February and Towcester in March: fair handicap
chaser: stays 25f: acts on heavy going: tried in visor: races prominently: often let down by
jumping over fences. *Nigel Hawke*

MIDNIGHT SAPPHIRE 7 ch.m. Midnight Legend – Norton Sapphire (Karinga Bay) **h114**
[2016/17 h101: h23.3sᵖᵘ h21.6s* h18.5m h22g⁶ h26.5g⁵ h21.6g* h21.6g* h21.6d² h19.8s²
h24.5g² h21.5sᵖᵘ Mar 10] angular mare: fair hurdler: won mares handicaps at Newton
Abbot in June and October, and handicap there later in October: stays 3¼m: acts on soft
going: wears tongue tie: usually races nearer last than first, responds generously to
pressure. *Victor Dartnall*

MIDNIGHT SEQUEL 8 b.m. Midnight Legend – Silver Sequel (Silver Patriarch (IRE)) **h100**
[2016/17 h100: h23g* h22.1g⁴ Aug 27] fair handicap hurdler: won mares event at
Worcester in August: stays 23f: acts on good to firm and good to soft going: usually wears
headgear/tongue tie. *Neil Mulholland*

MIDNIGHT SHADOW 4 b.g. Midnight Legend – Holy Smoke (Statoblest) [2016/17 **b95**
b14.6s* b16.6s² b16.3g Mar 25] £28,000 3-y-o: workmanlike gelding: brother to fair
chaser Unify (2m-21f winner) and half-brother to 3 winners on Flat: dam 1m-1¼m winner:
fairly useful form in bumpers: won junior event at Newcastle in December. *Sue Smith*

MIDNIGHT SHOT 7 b.g. Midnight Legend – Suave Shot (Suave Dancer (USA)) **h129**
[2016/17 h115: h20.6g² h19.1s* h21.1g* h21.1s h23.1s² h22.8gᵖᵘ Apr 15] sturdy gelding:
fairly useful handicap hurdler: won at Fontwell and Cheltenham in October: stays 23f: acts
on soft going: front runner. *Charlie Longsdon*

MIDNIGHT SILVER 7 gr.m. Midnight Legend – Ruggtah (Daylami (IRE)) [2016/17 **c108**
h110: h23.3v* h24.1s³ c22.5vᵘʳ h15.8s* h19.9v⁴ h20.3g⁵ Apr 20] fairly useful handicap **h116**
hurdler: won mares events at Uttoxeter in November and Ffos Las in February: 7/2, second
when tried to refuse and unseated rider 3 out in handicap at Uttoxeter on chasing debut:
stays 23f: best form on soft/heavy going: wears tongue tie: usually races close up.
Jamie Snowden

MIDNIGHT STROLL 5 b.g. Midnight Legend – Late For Class (IRE) (Bob's Return **b108**
(IRE)) [2016/17 b16.3g² b16d³ Apr 27] €30,000 3-y-o: good-topped gelding: second foal:
dam (b72) lightly-raced half-sister to fairly useful hurdler/useful chaser (stays 3½m) Tulsa
Jack: useful form in bumpers at Newbury (3½ lengths second of 20 to Bullionaire) and
Punchestown (4¾ lengths third of 7 to Dead Right in conditionals/amateur event). *Robert
Tyner, Ireland*

MIDNIGHT TARGET 7 b.m. Midnight Legend – Right On Target (IRE) (Presenting) **h107**
[2016/17 h92, b67: h21.2g* h21.2v³ h23.8s⁶ h21.2g² Apr 3] fair handicap hurdler: won at
Ludlow (amateur event) in November: should be suited by further than 21f: acts on heavy
going. *John Groucott*

MIDNIGHT TOUR 7 b.m. Midnight Legend – Uppermost (Montjeu (IRE)) [2016/17   **h138**
h114, b–: h21.2m* h19d² h16.2s* h20.3s⁵ h19g² h19.9g⁶ h20.3g* Apr 20] smallish mare:
bumper winner: useful hurdler: won novice at Ludlow in May, mares handicap at Hereford
(by 11 lengths from Legend Lady) in November and listed mares handicap at Cheltenham
(by 6 lengths from Carnspindle) on final outing: left David Loder after second start: stays
21f: acts on soft and good to firm going: often travels strongly. *Alan King*

MIDNIGHT TUNE 6 b.m. Midnight Legend – Harmonic Motion (IRE) (Bob Back   **h107**
(USA)) [2016/17 b90: h19.1s⁴ h20.7s³ h19.9v⁴ h25s² h21.6d² Mar 18] compact mare:
bumper winner: fair maiden hurdler: stays 25f: acts on soft going: wears tongue tie: often
travels strongly. *Anthony Honeyball*

MIDNIGHT WALK (IRE) 7 b.m. Oscar (IRE) – Lady Belvedere (IRE) (Lord Americo)   **h95**
[2016/17 b16.7s h15.5g h19.4s⁵ h19.9d⁴ h19.6g* Apr 22] £15,000 6-y-o: fifth foal: half-   **b–**
sister to a winning pointer by Beneficial: dam unraced: won Irish maiden point: unplaced
in mares maiden bumper: modest form over hurdles: won handicap at Bangor final outing:
should stay beyond 2½m: in tongue tie last 3 starts: front runner/races prominently, tends
to find little. *Donald McCain*

MIDNIGHT WHISPER 11 ch.g. Midnight Legend – Spread The Word (Deploy) [2016/17   **c–**
c–, h–: c22.6mᶠ Jul 10] point winner: winning hurdler: poor maiden chaser: stays 3m: acts   **h–**
on good to firm going: in cheekpieces last 4 starts: wears tongue tie. *Richard Woollacott*

MIDNITE GRACE 7 gr.m. Midnight Legend – Ardentinny (Ardross) [2016/17 h16.4v⁴   **h105 p**
h18.1s* Apr 3] £23,000 5-y-o: half-sister to several winners, including fairly useful
hurdler/chaser Fair Loch (winner around 2m, by Fair Mix) and bumper winner/fairly useful
hurdler Total Submission (2m-2¾m winner, by Kayf Tara): dam bumper winner: won
maiden point on debut: better effort (fair form) over hurdles when winning maiden at
Kelso: should continue to improve. *Pauline Robson*

MIDTECH STAR (IRE) 5 b.g. Kodiac – Royal Rival (IRE) (Marju (IRE)) [2016/17   **h–**
h76: h18.7mᶠ Jul 10] poor maiden hurdler: usually in headgear. *Ian Williams*

MIDTECH VALENTINE 6 b.m. Act One – Eveon (IRE) (Synefos (USA)) [2016/17   **c88**
h101, b89: h16.7d² h19.1g* h16s* h20.3s c16.4g⁴ c17.4v⁵ h15.8s² h18.9g³ Apr 15] lengthy   **h112**
mare: fair handicap hurdler: won mares event at Fontwell and conditionals event at
Kempton, both in November: failed to convince with jumping both starts over fences: stays
19f: acts on heavy going: in tongue tie final start: often races towards rear. *Ian Williams*

MIGHT BITE (IRE) 8 b.g. Scorpion (IRE) – Knotted Midge (IRE) (Presenting)   **c166**
[2016/17 c–p, h145: c19.4g² c19.1g* c24gᶠ c24d* c24.4g* c25g* Apr 7]   **h–**

No horse has ever won Britain's three most important races for staying
novice chasers, the Kauto Star (formerly the Feltham) at Kempton's Christmas
meeting, the RSA (known as the 'novices' Gold Cup') at the Cheltenham Festival
and the Mildmay Novices' Chase at Aintree's Grand National meeting. Might Bite
came within one fence of becoming the first to land this Grade 1 treble, crashing
out when in full control at the final obstacle in the Kauto Star, before going on to
win both the RSA and the Mildmay, in the process becoming only the third horse
to complete the double in the big staying novice chases at Cheltenham and Aintree
(following Monsieur Le Cure in 1994 and Star de Mohaison in 2006). Might Bite

*RSA Novices' Chase, Cheltenham—clear leader Might Bite (left) does his best to snatch defeat
from victory's jaws with a violent swerve right on the run-in ...*

... before, with the aid of the riderless Marinero, Nico de Boinville conjures a rally from his mount to pip stable-companion Whisper (right)

never met the season's leading staying novice Thistlecrack who contested the King George VI Chase instead of the Kauto Star at Kempton's Christmas meeting and would also have been in the Gold Cup field at the Cheltenham Festival had injury not intervened. If Thistlecrack's recovery progresses well, there is just a chance the pair could meet in the next edition of the King George VI Chase, a clash that would be worth going a long way to see. On only his fourth run over fences, the exuberant Thistlecrack became the first novice to win the King George VI Chase, beating his stablemate and 2015 winner Cue Card in the process. Although Might Bite was still sporting his L-plates at that time, he would have won the Kauto Star—had he stood up—in a faster time than Thistlecrack recorded in the King George over the same course and distance just over an hour later. It was the first time since 2003 that both races were completed in under six minutes. On that occasion, Strong Flow, the only horse to win the Hennessy Gold Cup at Newbury as a novice, won the Feltham and 25/1-shot Edredon Bleu—standing in for Best Mate—took the King George. As in that year, ground conditions for the latest editions of these steeplechases gave any horses for whom there might be stamina doubts as good a chance as they are likely to get to see out the three miles at Kempton.

Might Bite didn't see a racecourse until he was six and was brought along steadily, finishing third (to Thistlecrack's half-brother West Approach) in a bumper at Newbury on his debut before winning novice hurdles at Newbury and Cheltenham on his two other outings in his first season. He made his chasing debut in his second season (finishing fifth to More of That in a novice at Cheltenham) but reverted to hurdling for his two remaining outings, impressive when winning a handicap at Kempton on the first of them, showing smart form. That handicap victory was over twenty-one furlongs, the longest trip Might Bite had attempted before lining up for the 32Red Kauto Star Novices' Chase on his third outing in the latest season. Back over fences from the start, his jumping looked in need of some work when he was beaten by Binge Drinker in a three-runner novice chase at Ffos Las in early-November. Odds-on Might Bite was far from fluent at the seventh and eighth and then stumbled at the last after being headed between the last two. Might Bite got off the mark over fences the following month in a similar event at Doncaster, making all and being clear of his field from the tenth when winning by fourteen lengths from stablemate Premier Bond, despite jumping a little carefully at times.

It certainly looked as if Might Bite would have to produce a more polished display if he was going to hold his own in better company though, partly because of his home reputation, he still started joint third favourite behind Irish challenger Anibale Fly and the Nicholls-trained Frodon in the first double-figure line-up for the Kauto Star since Gloria Victis beat nine rivals in the 1999 running. The outstanding but ill-fated Gloria Victis won the Feltham, as it was known then, in spectacular style by eighteen lengths (in a faster time than seventeen-length-winner See More Business recorded in the King George) and Might Bite could well have won by even further than Gloria Victis had he not fallen heavily at the final fence. Coping really well on his first appearance in graded company, thrown straight in at the deep end in a Grade 1 championship event, Might Bite raced with tremendous zest and jumped well in the main, leading from the ninth and drawing clear, ridden along and stretching into an eighteen-length lead before coming to grief. Might Bite would have recorded a very smart performance, in all probability—in terms of form—up there with Coneygree's record-breaking forty-length victory in a depleted three-finisher field two years earlier and with three other noteworthy performances in the race of recent years, those of four-year-old Long Run who won by thirteen lengths on his British debut on Boxing Day 2009 and Grands Crus (who won from Silviniaco Conti and Bobs Worth, the trio over thirty lengths clear of the rest) and emphatic nine-length winner Dynaste, the two last-named in 2011 and 2012 respectively.

Dynaste went on to add the Mildmay at Aintree to his string of victories as a novice but, in between, after being a short-priced ante-post favourite for the RSA Chase since his stylish Kempton victory, he was a late defector to the Golden Miller Chase—then still a Grade 2—at the Festival where he lost his unbeaten record when second to Benefficient (Lord Windermere won the RSA Chase that year). Coneygree, of course, didn't run in any of the novice events at the Cheltenham Festival or at Aintree, connections taking the bold decision, after just three races over fences, to go for the Gold Cup in the face of 'so many emails' cautioning them against running, and reminding them of the fate of Gloria Victis who had been fatally injured tackling the Gold Cup as a novice. Coneygree became the first novice to win the Gold Cup for over forty years (he was an equally rare winner of the race to make all the running). Both Long Run and Grands Crus contested the RSA Chase, the former performing well below his Kempton form when third behind Weapon's Amnesty, and Grands Crus (also declared at the six-day stage for the Gold Cup) managing no better than a well-beaten fourth to Bobs Worth when starting 6/5 favourite for his RSA Chase. Reunited with stable jockey Nico de Boinville, after Daryl Jacob had deputised because of injury on his last two starts, Might Bite came through a confidence-boosting success at Doncaster between the Kauto Star and the RSA, starting at 7/1-on in a three-runner novice and winning by the best part of two fences from the only other finisher, 66/1-outsider Gorran Haven.

Starting 7/2 favourite for a good renewal of the RSA Chase, for which there were twelve runners after two editions with single-figure fields, Might Bite did his best to maintain the disappointing record of the principals in the Feltham/Kauto Star over the years in the RSA Chase—a race that places more emphasis on stamina—by nearly throwing the race away on the run-in. Giving another trailblazing performance, Might Bite led after the first and forced a strong pace which saw him twenty lengths clear by the third last. He came under pressure in the home straight but was still ten lengths to the good at the final fence, looking set to win decisively, when he made a mistake (having jumped well in the main) and then unexpectedly veered sharply right as he set off up the steep climb to the finish, at the same time seemingly trying to pull himself up and almost coming to a halt. Might Bite's stable-companion Whisper, second favourite on the strength of two wins over fences at Cheltenham (including the Dipper Novices' Chase) in the winter, looked set to become a fortunate winner as Might Bite's antics allowed him to draw level and then show just in front. But Nico de Boinville got Might

Bite going again just in time, helped by the loose Marinero coming through to join Might Bite, and, under strong pressure, Might Bite clawed his way back to win by a nose after a pulsating final hundred yards. Whisper, whose jockey received a four-day ban for excessive whip use, finished ten lengths clear of the Mullins-trained Bellshill in third, with another Irish challenger Alpha des Obeaux (who reportedly bled) completing the frame. The third Henderson-trained runner O O Seven and the runaway winner of the Ten Up Novices' Chase at Navan, Acapella Bourgeois, who was the main sufferer when caught sideways in a shambolic standing start, were the only others finishers. The RSA Chase was a notable triumph for Seven Barrows, with Nicky Henderson becoming the first trainer to saddle the first two in the race since Tom Dreaper achieved it with Arkloin and Doone Valley in 1965 when the race was known as the Totalisator Champion Chase.

Might Bite's zestful racing character, which some thought more suited to a flat track like Kempton, coupled with concerns about his jumping (he had made mistakes on most of his starts over fences), had not made him every pundit's idea of a potential RSA Chase winner. His evident quirkiness, though, had become more of a factor to be considered when he lined up with Whisper in the five-runner Betway Mildmay Novices' Chase at Aintree (it was the smallest field for the race since Silviniaco Conti beat four others in 2012). Might Bite hadn't shown his best side at Cheltenham in his hurdling days either, idling markedly on the run-in before rallying to regain the lead in the final strides when winning a novice event there in 2014/15. He is said to be a 'model citizen' at home, though, and gave no problems at all at Aintree where he jumped impeccably and kept straight for another all-the-way win, although de Boinville didn't send him clear from the start this time, riding a more conventional race than at Cheltenham. Whisper gave chase from the outset but

Betway Mildmay Novices' Chase, Aintree—
much more straightforward this time as Might Bite confirms Cheltenham placings with Whisper

didn't have enough to mount a winning challenge and Might Bite asserted in the last fifty yards, after seeming to idle approaching the last, to beat him by two lengths, with the three others (all starting at 14/1 or longer) well beaten off. Whisper's performances in both the RSA and the Mildmay would have won many an ordinary renewal of those races and Might Bite's clear superiority over him bodes well for his promotion to open company in the next season. His trainer has said 'The King George is the obvious place for him because we know you can roll around Kempton at that pace, whereas the Gold Cup will be a different ball game … although you never know!' First things first, of course, but, as his trainer was implying, it would be unwise to put a line through Might Bite's Gold Cup prospects just yet. He is a very exciting prospect.

Might Bite (IRE) (b.g. 2009)	Scorpion (IRE) (b 2002)	Montjeu (b 1996)	Sadler's Wells Floripedes
		Ardmelody (b 1987)	Law Society Thistlewood
	Knotted Midge (IRE) (b 2000)	Presenting (br 1992)	Mtoto D'Azy
		Bula Beag (b 1993)	Brush Aside Bulabos

Might Bite, a tall gelding, is by the 2005 St Leger winner Scorpion who now stands at Shade Oak Stud in Shropshire at a fee of £3,000, after starting his stud career under the Coolmore banner (Scorpion is a great grandson of Le Melody, the grandam of Alflora, a stalwart of the Shade Oak operation for so long). Might Bite, incidentally, isn't so called because he is by Scorpion (scorpions sting, they don't bite). Might Bite's dam Knotted Midge takes her name from a type of fishing fly (when the rod is cast, the fish 'might bite'). Might Bite is the second foal out

The Knot Again Partnership's "Might Bite"

of the winning pointer Knotted Midge, the first being the three-mile hurdler Beat That (by Milan) who won both the Sefton Novices' Hurdle at Aintree and the War of Attrition Novices' Hurdle at Punchestown for Might Bite's stable in 2013/14 but has been very lightly raced since. Knotted Midge is a sister to the useful chaser Drombeag who won the Foxhunter at Cheltenham and stayed four miles, so Might Bite's pedigree has plenty of stamina on both sides. Front-running Might Bite races with enthusiasm but he stays twenty-five furlongs. He has won on soft going but has shown his very best form under less testing conditions (the going was good for the RSA Chase and the Mildmay, as it was when he led the field a merry dance until his fall in the Kauto Star). *Nicky Henderson*

MIGHTY LEADER (IRE) 9 b.g. Milan – Madam Leader (IRE) (Supreme Leader) c–
[2016/17 c–, h107: h23.3s h20.3g⁶ h22g² h23.9g³ h25.5g³ h23.1m* c24.2gᶠ h24.2d⁶ h112
h21.4f⁴ Apr 23] angular gelding: winning Irish pointer: fair handicap hurdler: won at Exeter in November: fell first both chase starts: left Henry Oliver after second outing, Sally Randell after fourth: stays 3m: acts on soft and good to firm going: usually wears hood: wears tongue tie: often races towards rear. *Fergal O'Brien*

MIGHTY MISSILE (IRE) 6 ch.g. Majestic Missile (IRE) – Magdalene (FR) (College h114
Chapel) [2016/17 h118: h16.7g² h16.5d h16.3m⁵ h16.8gᵖᵘ h18.5m⁴ h15.8s h19g² h19g h23.9sᵖᵘ h16s³ h19g³ h18.7g² h19.8f* Apr 23] sturdy gelding: fair handicap hurdler: won amateur event at Wincanton on final outing: left Warren Greatrex after fifth start: stays 2½m: acts on firm and soft going: often in headgear/tongue tie. *Brian Barr*

MIGHTY MUSTANG 7 b.g. Passing Glance – Mustang Molly (Soldier Rose) [2016/17 h–
b–: h17.7sᵖᵘ h15.7v h15.9v⁴ h21sᵖᵘ Mar 30] sturdy gelding: no form in bumpers/over hurdles: tried in tongue tie. *Andrew Martin*

MIGHTY WHITEY (IRE) 11 b.g. Sesaro (USA) – Deeco Valley (IRE) (Satco (FR)) c–
[2016/17 c–, h110: h16.2dᵘʳ h16.4s⁵ h16.7g h16.2s Dec 4] handicap hurdler, modest h98
nowadays: winning chaser: stays 21f: acts on good to firm and heavy going: has worn headgear, including in 2016/17: wears tongue tie: often leads. *Noel C. Kelly, Ireland*

MILADY'S DILEMMA (IRE) 4 b.f. Doyen (IRE) – Mill Lady (IRE) (Jurado (USA)) b–
[2016/17 b16gᵖᵘ Apr 17] €5,500 3-y-o: closely related to 2 winners, including fair hurdler Millrock Lady (2¾m winner, by Court Cave), and half-sister to 2 winners, including fair hurdler/fairly useful chaser Askmeroe (2m/17f winner, by Rudimentary), stayed 25f: dam unraced: showed nothing in mares maiden bumper. *Seamus Mullins*

MILAN BOUND (IRE) 9 b.g. Milan – Bonnie And Bright (IRE) (Topanoora) [2016/17 c128
c–p, h124: c20g* h26.5g c23.8dᵖᵘ Dec 21] good-topped gelding: handicap hurdler, fairly h–
useful at best: easily best of 3 runs over fences when winning novice at Uttoxeter in July, showing fairly useful form: stayed 3¼m: acted on soft going: tried in blinkers: in tongue tie last 6 starts: dead. *Jonjo O'Neill*

MILAN DANCER (IRE) 6 b.m. Milan – Pawnee Trail (IRE) (Taipan (IRE)) [2016/17 c77
h93: h17.1g h22.7s⁶ h20.5s⁴ h20v⁵ c24.2s⁴ c26.3m⁵ Apr 19] placed in points: modest h95
maiden hurdler: poor form over fences: stays 2½m: best form on soft/heavy going: usually races nearer last than first. *Noel C. Kelly, Ireland*

MILAN EXPRESS (IRE) 7 b.m. Milan – Supreme Surprise (IRE) (Presenting) [2016/17 h102
h21.7g⁴ h15.8d⁶ h15.8s⁴ h19.7d² Apr 4] £24,000 6-y-o: rangy mare: first foal: dam well beaten in bumper: point winner: fair form over hurdles: should be suited by 2¾m+: acts on good to soft going: front runner/races prominently. *Kim Bailey*

MILAN HART (IRE) 7 b.m. Milan – Queen of Harts (IRE) (Phardante (FR)) [2016/17 h–
b80: b16s h21.4vᵖᵘ h18.5m⁵ Apr 15] modest at best in bumpers: showed little in 2 starts b–
over hurdles. *Martin Hill*

MILAN OF CRYSTAL (IRE) 8 b.m. Milan – Native Crystal (IRE) (Be My Native c66
(USA)) [2016/17 h83: h15.3m⁶ h20g³ h18.7m h23.1g⁴ c21.1g⁵ h16.8m⁵ h21.4m* c20.2f⁴ h82
h23.4g Dec 18] angular mare: winning pointer: poor handicap hurdler: won at Wincanton in October: poor form over fences: left Robert Stephens after seventh start: stays 21f: acts on good to firm going: usually in tongue tie. *Dave Roberts*

MILANSBAR (IRE) 10 b.g. Milan – Ardenbar (Ardross) [2016/17 c144, h–: c23.6g⁴ c133
c29.5sᵖᵘ c29.2sᵖᵘ c32.6sᵖᵘ Feb 25] big gelding: winning hurdler: useful handicap chaser: h–
pulled up last 3 starts (reportedly suffering from azoturia): stays 33f: acts on heavy going. *Neil King*

MILBOROUGH (IRE) 11 b.g. Milan – Fox Burrow (IRE) (Supreme Leader) [2016/17 **c124** c135, h–: c26.2d⁴ c25.5dᵘʳ h25s* h24.1s⁶ c32.6sᵖᵘ Feb 25] good-topped gelding: fairly **h124** useful handicap hurdler: won at Carlisle in December: useful handicap chaser, below form completed start in 2016/17: stays 33f: acts on good to firm and heavy going. *Ian Duncan*

MILBURN 11 ch.g. First Trump – Baroness Rose (Roselier (FR)) [2016/17 h–: c23g⁶ **c–** c24.2mᵖᵘ Oct 6] dual point winner: showed nothing over hurdles/in chases. *Gail Haywood* **h–**

MILES TO MEMPHIS (IRE) 8 b.g. Old Vic – Phillis Hill (Karinga Bay) [2016/17 h–: **h123** h21dᵖᵘ h16s* h19g² h16.5d Apr 25] fairly useful handicap hurdler: won at Navan in February: left Alan King after first start: should stay at least 2½m: acts on soft going: in tongue tie in 2016/17. *Mrs Denise Foster, Ireland*

MILES TO MILAN (IRE) 7 b.g. Milan – Princesse Rooney (FR) (Baby Turk) [2016/17 **h–** h118: h20g h20dᵖᵘ Nov 30] fairly useful hurdler at best, no form in 2016/17: best effort at 19f: acts on heavy going: usually races prominently. *Philip Hobbs*

MILESTONE (IRE) 7 b.g. Galileo (IRE) – Cassydora (Darshaan) [2016/17 h98: h21.6g **h80** h25g⁵ May 30] handicap hurdler, poor nowadays: stays 3m: acts on good to firm going: tried in headgear: wears tongue tie: usually races towards rear. *Evan Williams*

MILEVA ROLLER 5 b.m. Multiplex – Alikat (IRE) (Alhaarth (IRE)) [2016/17 b16.3m² **h–** b16.8g⁴ h16g h15.8d h15.8g⁶ Nov 10] fifth foal: half-sister to Grade 1 bumper winner/ **b86** useful hurdler The Liquidator (2m/17f winner, by Overbury) and bumper winner Allycat (by Beat All): dam (c96/h130) unguenine 19f-3¼m hurdle/chase winner: fair form in bumpers: down the field in mares novice/maiden hurdles. *Jonjo O'Neill*

MILGEN BAY 11 br.g. Generous (IRE) – Lemon's Mill (USA) (Roberto (USA)) [2016/17 **c113** c115, h–: c21.2g³ c25.5g³ c21.1d³ c21.7g⁴ c21.1dᵖᵘ c20.2m c20.3s⁵ c21.3g⁶ Apr 23] good- **h–** topped gelding: maiden hurdler: fair handicap chaser nowadays: won at Towcester in November: stays 21f: acts on firm and soft going: has worn headgear: front runner/races prominently. *Oliver Sherwood*

MILIAIR 7 ch.m. Muhtathir – Miliana (IRE) (Polar Falcon (USA)) [2016/17 h75: b16g² **h79** h18.7dᶠ h16m h18.7g⁴ h16v⁵ h20.3g⁴ Mar 28] fair form in bumpers: poor form over **b85** hurdles: left David Bridgwater after fourth start. *David Dennis*

MILITARIAN 7 b.g. Kayf Tara – Mille Et Une (FR) (Trempolino (USA)) [2016/17 b17g **h94 p** h16.3d h21s⁴ h15.8s⁴ Mar 5] £600 5-y-o: strong gelding: second foal: dam (c113/h113), **b–** French 2m/17f hurdle/chase winner, sister to useful French hurdler/chaser up to 25f Madox: off mark in maiden points at second attempt: behind in bumper: modest form in maiden hurdles: tried in tongue tie: remains open to improvement. *Andrew Martin*

MILLANISI BOY 8 b.g. Kalanisi (IRE) – Millennium Rose (IRE) (Roselier (FR)) **c125** [2016/17 h119: h21.1s³ h23.6sᶠ c20.9v⁴ c22.4s² h23.6s Mar 25] workmanlike gelding: **h120** fairly useful handicap hurdler: similar form over fences when 3¼ lengths second to Behind The Wire in novice handicap at Newbury in March: stays 23f: acts on heavy going: has worn tongue tie: often races prominently. *Richard Woollacott*

MILLE NAUTIQUE (FR) 6 b.g. Panis (USA) – Anoush (USA) (Giant's Causeway **c111** (USA)) [2016/17 c98p, h106: c19.9g* c21dᵖᵘ c23d c19.4g² c20g³ c19.9m⁴ c20.2m³ Oct 23] **h–** lengthy gelding: maiden hurdler: fair handicap chaser: won at Huntingdon in May: stays 2½m: best form on good going: front runner: inconsistent. *Alan King*

MILLER'S MAVERICK 9 b.g. Millkom – Gables Girl (Sousa) [2016/17 c–, h–: **c89 x** c24.1gᶠ c25.5g* h24g Nov 10] rather leggy gelding: maiden hurdler: modest form over **h–** fences (often let down by jumping): won handicap at Fontwell in May: stayed 25f: acted on soft going: in tongue tie last 4 starts: dead. *Grant Cann*

MILLFIRTH (IRE) 10 b.g. Flemensfirth (USA) – Northern Mill (IRE) (Distinctly North **c–** (USA)) [2016/17 c24.2dᵖᵘ Apr 30] maiden pointer: showed nothing in maiden hunter on chasing debut. *M. V. Coglan*

MILLICENT SILVER 8 gr.m. Overbury (IRE) – Common Girl (IRE) (Roselier (FR)) **c121 §** [2016/17 c117, h110: c32.4sᵇᵈ c29.6sᵖᵘ h23.8s³ c30.7d² c24.1g³ c28.1gᵖᵘ c30.6gᵖᵘ Apr 28] **h103 §** smallish, rather sparely-made mare: fair handicap hurdler: fairly useful handicap chaser: stays 31f: acts on heavy going: wears headgear: often races towards rear: moody (usually races very lazily). *Nigel Twiston-Davies*

MILLIE VANILLI 5 b.m. Midshipman – Canlastou (FR) (Tanlas (FR)) [2016/17 b16.8m **b–** b16.3m Jul 17] half-sister to several winners, including 17f hurdle winner Tiptronic (by Officiel) and French cross-country chaser Native Doctor (21f/2¾m winner, by Dear Doctor): dam French maiden chaser: showed nothing in 2 bumpers. *Bernard Llewellyn*

MILLY BALOO 6 b.m. Desideratum – Tarabaloo (Kayf Tara) [2016/17 h103: c23.9s[2] c21.4d[3] c23.4v[4] c25.2s* h23.1s[3] Mar 12] modest handicap hurdler: fair form over fences: won novice handicap at Catterick in February: stays 25f: best form on soft/heavy going. *Tim Easterby*   **c105 h99**

MILLY MALONE (IRE) 11 b.m. Milan – Sharp Single (IRE) (Supreme Leader) [2016/17 c96, h82: h23.3d[4] c24.5g[pu] c23m c23g[5] c24d[5] h23.1g[4] h25.6g[pu] h25d[pu] Nov 19] poor maiden hurdler: handicap chaser, poor nowadays: stays 3½m: acts on soft and good to firm going: tried in hood: wears tongue tie: usually races towards rear. *Adrian Wintle*   **c58 h68**

MILORD (GER) 8 br.g. Monsun (GER) – Montserrat (GER) (Zilzal (USA)) [2016/17 h119: h21d[4] c20m[4] h19.9s[2] h21.4s[5] h20.5v[4] h21.2s[3] h23.9g* h23.9g[5] Apr 6] compact gelding: fairly useful handicap hurdler: won at Taunton in March: fair form when fourth in novice handicap at Uttoxeter on chasing debut: stays 3m: acts on good to firm and heavy going: wears headgear: often leads. *Kim Bailey*   **c101 h118**

MILROW (IRE) 4 b.g. Tamayuz – Cannikin (IRE) (Lahib (USA)) [2016/17 h16.7d* h16.7g[2] h16.7g[6] h17.7d[3] h16.2d* h16g[2] h15.6g[3] Nov 3] half-brother to fair hurdler/chaser Canni Thinkaar (17f-2¾m winner, by Alhaarth) and fair hurdler Lostock Hall (17f/19f winner, by Lord Shanakill): fair maiden on Flat, stays 1½m: fairly useful juvenile hurdler: won at Market Rasen in June and Perth in September: raced around 2m: acts on good to soft going: in cheekpieces/tongue tie last 4 starts: strong traveller. *Dr Richard Newland*   **h116**

MILTON 5 br.g. Nomadic Way (USA) – Jesmund (Bishop of Cashel) [2016/17 h17.7s[5] Feb 26] well beaten in maiden bumper on debut. *Diana Grissell*   **b–**

MILZIPA (IRE) 5 b.g. Milan – Money For Buttons (IRE) (Alphabatim (USA)) [2016/17 b17.7d[5] h21s[5] h21g[6] h21m[6] Apr 18] €42,000 3-y-o: useful-looking gelding: seventh foal: half-brother to 3 winners, including fairly useful hurdler/smart chaser An Cathaoir Mor (2m/17f winner, by Turtle Island) and fair hurdler/fairly useful chaser Darby's Turn (2m winner, by Pistolet Bleu): dam unraced: fifth in bumper: best effort (fair form) in novice hurdles when fifth at Kempton in February. *Nicky Henderson*   **h100 b83**

MIN ALEMARAT (IRE) 6 ch.g. Galileo (IRE) – Baraka (IRE) (Danehill (USA)) [2016/17 h16.2s[3] h17.1d[3] h17.1d h19.9s[5] h16.8v[5] Feb 23] brother to useful hurdler Beyond Conceit (2m/19f winner, stays 3m: fairly useful on Flat, stays 2¼m: modest form over hurdles: should prove suited by further than 2m: acts on soft going: tried in blinkers. *Tim Easterby*   **h97**

MINELLA ARIS (IRE) 6 b.g. King's Theatre (IRE) – Liss Rua (IRE) (Bob Back (USA)) [2016/17 h122: h24d* h24.4d[5] h23.9g[6] Apr 9] ran twice in points, won maiden on completed start: fairly useful hurdler: won novice at Southwell in November: stays 3m: acts on heavy going: in tongue tie last 3 starts. *Tom George*   **h121**

MINELLA AWARDS (IRE) 6 b.g. Oscar (IRE) – Montys Miss (IRE) (Presenting) [2016/17 h125: h20.5v[2] h19.8d* h24d* Apr 27] good sort: second in Irish point on debut: useful form over hurdles: won EBF 'National Hunt' Novices' Handicap Hurdle Final at   **h142**

European Breeders' Fund Matchbook VIP 'National Hunt' Novices' Handicap Hurdle Final, Sandown—the first of two valuable spring prizes for Minella Awards who holds off outsider Prime Venture (far right)

Sandown in March by 1¼ lengths from Prime Venture: further improvement when following up in 25-runner handicap at Punchestown, beating No Comment a length: stays 3m: acts on good to soft going: in tongue tie last 3 starts. *Harry Fry*

MINELLACELEBRATION (IRE) 7 b.g. King's Theatre (IRE) – Knocktartan (IRE)   **c131** (King's Ride) [2016/17 h128: h21.2m⁵ c24.2m² c25g⁴ c24.2g⁴ c23g² c20.9sᶠ c23g³ c21m⁴   **h95** c23.6g* Apr 17] sturdy gelding: handicap hurdler, fairly useful at best: useful handicap chaser: won Aintree (novice event) in October and Chepstow final start: stays 25f: acts on heavy going. *Katy Price*

MINELLA CHARMER (IRE) 6 b.g. King's Theatre (IRE) – Kim Hong (IRE)   **c129 p** (Charnwood Forest (IRE)) [2016/17 h130, b82: c19.4dᶠ c19.2s³ h16.3dᶠ Mar 24] useful   **h–** hurdler in 2015/16: upsides when fell 2 out in handicap won by Maestro Royal at Newbury only outing over hurdles in 2016/17: fairly useful form over fences: every chance when fell 4 out in novice won by Its'afreebee at Wetherby in December: stays 21f: acts on heavy going: usually in tongue tie: remains with potential as a chaser. *Alan King*

MINELLA DADDY (IRE) 7 b.g. Flemensfirth (USA) – Moon Storm (Old Vic) [2016/17   **c143** h125p, b81: h22.8m² c23g² c23.8d* c23.8d* c23.8d² c24gᵖᵘ Dec 26] strong gelding: fairly   **h127** useful hurdler: useful form over fences: won maiden at Ffos Las in October and handicap at Ascot in November: more progress when 1¾ lengths second of 14 to Regal Encore in Silver Cup (Handicap) at Ascot in December: stays 25f: acts on good to firm and heavy going: wears headgear. *Peter Bowen*

MINELLA DEFINITELY (IRE) 10 br.g. Definite Article – West Along (Crash Course)   **c123 §** [2016/17 c120x, h–: c16d⁴ c17.3m* c20g⁵ c20.3g⁶ c16.5mᵖᵘ c15.9gᶠ Oct 22] lengthy   **h–** gelding: winning hurdler: fairly useful handicap chaser: won at Cartmel in May: stayed 2½m: acted on good to firm and heavy going: wore headgear: tried in tongue tie: often raced lazily: dead. *Neil Mulholland*

MINELLA FAIR (IRE) 6 b.g. Flemensfirth (USA) – Bell Walks Run (IRE) (Commanche   **b105** Run) [2016/17 b16d² b16d² b18s⁴ Dec 29] £72,000 4-y-o: brother to 2 winners, including top-class hurdler/very smart chaser Time For Rupert (19f-25f winner) and half-brother to bumper winner/useful hurdler Mahonia (17f winner, by Turtle Island): dam unraced: runner-up in point on debut: useful form in bumpers: won maiden at Limerick on final start by 10 lengths from Isodon, eased close home: wears tongue tie. *Noel Meade, Ireland*

MINELLA FIVEO (IRE) 9 b.g. Westerner – Autumn Sky (IRE) (Roselier (FR))   **c–** [2016/17 h19.6g⁶ h15.8v* c19.2sᶠ h19.3dᵖᵘ Feb 20] well-made gelding: maiden pointer: **h111** fair handicap hurdler: won at Uttoxeter in January: fell sixth in novice handicap on chasing debut: effective from 2m to 2½m: acts on heavy going: has worn cheekpieces. *Sue Smith*

MINELLAFORDOLLARS (IRE) 5 b.g. King's Theatre (IRE) – Another Dollar (IRE)   **b105** (Supreme Leader) [2016/17 b16v* Mar 19] sixth foal: dam (c108/h108), fair 2m-2½m hurdle/chase winner, half-sister to dam of smart staying chaser Monbeg Dude: won maiden point on debut: 6/4, useful form when winning 12-runner maiden bumper at Navan by 8½ lengths from Beyond The Law. *Gordon Elliott, Ireland*

MINELLA FORFITNESS (IRE) 10 b.g. Westerner – Ring of Water (USA) (Northern   **c121** Baby (CAN)) [2016/17 c126, h–: c19.9g² c21.4d⁴ c20m⁶ c24.1g c24g³ c21.4g⁵ c16.5g⁴   **h–** c20.3sᵖᵘ c15.7d⁵ c20.3g⁴ Apr 21] winning hurdler: fairly useful handicap chaser: stays 2¾m: acts on soft going: has worn headgear, including in 2016/17: front runner/races prominently, usually races freely. *Charles Pogson*

MINELLAFORLEISURE (IRE) 9 b.g. King's Theatre (IRE) – Dame Foraine (FR)   **c–** (Raintrap) [2016/17 c90, h128: h19dᶠ h15.8g⁵ h16.7g² h15.7m h19.6v⁴ h15.7d⁶ Nov 18]   **h128** lengthy gelding: fairly useful handicap hurdler: well held only completed start over fences: raced mainly around 2m: acts on good to soft going. *Alex Hales*

MINELLA FOR ME (IRE) 7 b.g. King's Theatre (IRE) – Irish Mystics (IRE) (Ali-   **h87** Royal (IRE)) [2016/17 b90: h16.8v⁵ h15.8d⁴ h18.5sᶠ Feb 12] good-topped gelding: won Irish maiden point on debut: modest form in maiden/novice hurdles: in hood final start: wears tongue tie. *Tom George*

MINELLA FOR PARTY (IRE) 10 b.g. Flemensfirth (USA) – Dame Foraine (FR)   **c95** (Raintrap) [2016/17 c–, h–: c25.5d³ c24sᵖᵘ Jan 26] good-topped gelding: prolific point   **h–** winner: maiden hurdler: modest maiden hunter chaser: stays 25f: acts on heavy going: sometimes in headgear, including on reappearance: tried in tongue tie. *Miss V. Collins*

MINELLA FORU (IRE) 8 b.g. King's Theatre (IRE) – Shannon Rose (IRE) (Topanoora) **c–**
[2016/17 c142p, h–: h16s⁴ c29d^F Apr 17] useful hurdler in 2013/14: fourth of 6 in **h117**
Limestone Lad Hurdle at Naas (21½ lengths behind Sutton Place) only outing over hurdles
since: useful handicap chaser: fell eighth in Irish Grand National at Fairyhouse only outing
over fences in 2016/17: stays 3m: acts on heavy going. *Edward Harty, Ireland*

MINELLA FOR VALUE (IRE) 11 br.g. Old Vic – Nightngale Express (IRE) (Strong **c128**
Gale) [2016/17 c26.3g⁶ c24.5d³ Apr 28] raw-boned gelding: multiple point winner: **h–**
winning hurdler: useful chaser: better effort in 2016/17 when 3½ lengths sixth of 23 to
Pacha du Polder in Foxhunter Chase at Cheltenham in March: stays 3¼m: acts on any
going. *Declan Queally, Ireland*

MINELLA GATHERING (IRE) 8 b.g. Old Vic – A Plus Ma Puce (FR) (Turgeon **h87 x**
(USA)) [2016/17 h21.4d² h19v³ h24v⁶ h25v* h25s⁵ Mar 13] compact gelding: in frame
once from 3 starts in points: modest handicap hurdler: won at Plumpton in February: stays
25f: best form on heavy going: often races in rear: often let down by jumping. *Paul
Henderson*

MINELLAHALFCENTURY (IRE) 9 b.g. Westerner – Shanakill River (IRE) **c73 §**
(Anshan) [2016/17 c124, h–: c25.1m⁴ May 10] strong gelding: has reportedly had breathing **h–**
operation: winning hurdler: handicap chaser, useful at best: let down by jumping/attitude
only outing in 2016/17: stays 3m: acts on heavy going: wears headgear/tongue tie: one to
be wary of. *Paul Nicholls*

MINELLA HERO (IRE) 9 b.g. Old Vic – Shannon Rose (IRE) (Topanoora) [2016/17 **c–**
c–, h103: h19.7g May 4] handicap hurdler, fair at best: pulled up only start over fences: **h76**
stayed 25f: acted on soft and good to firm going: tried in tongue tie: often raced in rear:
dead. *Micky Hammond*

MINELLA ON LINE (IRE) 8 b.g. King's Theatre (IRE) – Bally Bolshoi (IRE) (Bob **c133 x**
Back (USA)) [2016/17 c119, h116: c19.7d* c23.5v^ur c25.7s* c24.3g^pu Apr 22] well-made **h–**
gelding: fairly useful hurdler: useful handicap chaser: won at Plumpton in November and
February (novice event): stays 3¼m: acts on heavy going: has worn headgear: tried in
tongue tie: usually races close up: often let down by jumping over fences. *Oliver Sherwood*

MINELLA PRESENT (IRE) 8 b.g. Presenting – Dabaya (IRE) (In The Wings) **c139**
[2016/17 c135, h–: c20g* May 29] strong gelding: winning hurdler: useful handicap **h–**
chaser: won at Uttoxeter on only start in 2016/17: stays 2½m: acts on good to firm and
good to soft going: wears hood: tried in tongue tie: races towards rear. *Neil Mulholland*

MINELLA REBELLION (IRE) 5 b.g. King's Theatre (IRE) – Afdala (IRE) (Hernando **h102**
(FR)) [2016/17 h16.6g³ h21.2s⁵ h20d⁴ Feb 17] £90,000 4-y-o: brother to useful hurdler/
smart chaser Balthazar King (2½m-31f winner), stayed 35f, and useful hurdler For Good
Measure (2m-17f winner), stays 25f, and closely related to fairly useful hurdler/fair chaser
Wicked Spice (2½m-3m winner, by Old Vic): dam unraced: second in Irish maiden point
on debut: fair form over hurdles: best effort when third in novice at Doncaster in November:
bred to be suited by 2½m+: in tongue tie final start. *Nicky Henderson*

MINELLA ROCCO (IRE) 7 b.g. Shirocco (GER) – Petralona (USA) (Alleged **c167**
(USA)) [2016/17 c153p, h–: c27.3s³ c25s^F c24.3s^ur c26.3g² Mar 17] **h–**

Not many Cheltenham Gold Cup candidates go into the race with 'F' and
'ur' attached to the most recent form figures alongside their name—Mr Mulligan
(1997) was the last Gold Cup winner to fall on his final start before Cheltenham,
with Dawn Run (1986) the last to unseat. Although things hadn't gone his way since,
Minella Rocco's victory in a very good renewal of the National Hunt Chase at the
Festival twelve months earlier had been made to look even better by the exceptional
performances in the latest season of the runner-up Native River who was also in
the Cheltenham Gold Cup line-up. However, while Native River had won four
of his five races in the interim, including the Mildmay at Aintree, the Hennessy
at Newbury and the Welsh Grand National, Minella Rocco had been seen out just
three times, completing the course only when an encouraging third on his seasonal
reappearance in November in the BetVictor Handicap Chase at Cheltenham over
three miles three furlongs. That performance seemed to indicate that Minella Rocco
was heading in the right direction and that his best days were still very much ahead
of him. Those 'best days' seemed likely at the time to come—at least initially—in

one of the major Nationals, his essay in *Chasers & Hurdlers 2015/16* speculating that perhaps the near-doubling in value of the Irish Grand National would make that race a tempting target.

Minella Rocco had always looked a cracking chasing prospect in his novice hurdling days but his early experiences in novice chases had been anything but encouraging, his jumping no more than adequate on his debut and an early blunder on his second outing leading to his being pulled up. He trailed in well beaten on his third start, his first three runs leading to the BHA handicappers giving him a mark of 143 (on a par with the mark he had for his hurdling performances). A much improved performance had followed in the Reynoldstown Novices' Chase at Ascot where Minella Rocco finished second, ridden for the first time by Noel Fehily. Mr Derek O'Connor switched from Native River to ride Minella Rocco in the National Hunt Chase, in which Minella Rocco took plenty of time to warm up but stayed on strongly from some way back to beat the rallying Native River by a length and a quarter. Interestingly, Minella Rocco's trainer explained that the National Hunt Chase, rather than one of the Festival handicaps (his BHA mark had remained the same after the Reynoldstown), had been chosen because 'You need to be slick [referring to jumping technique] for those Festival handicaps and we hope he'll be in his comfort zone in the four-miler against novices.'

Jonjo O'Neill's words turned out to be prophetic. After his strong-finishing third to Viconte du Noyer at Cheltenham on his reappearance, Minella Rocco took on Many Clouds (who was conceding him 5 lb) and three others, including the Charlie Hall winner Irish Cavalier, in the Betfred Lotto-sponsored listed chase over the Mildmay course at Aintree's Becher Chase meeting. The challenge looked at first as if it might have ended disastrously, with Minella Rocco laying winded for a fair while after suffering a very heavy fall at the last, where he still looked to have a chance of pegging back the eventual winner Many Clouds (he would have finished second at worst). Minella Rocco was given plenty of time to get over this nasty experience and was next seen in mid-February when set a sizeable task in the Irish Gold Cup at Leopardstown, along with his stablemate More of That. Minella Rocco started at 7/1, half the odds of More of That, but made a very early exit, unseating his jockey Aidan Coleman at the fifth fence. More of That was running his best race over fences when departing at the last at Leopardstown and, when both lined up next in the Cheltenham Gold Cup, Minella Rocco started at longer odds than his stablemate (the mount of Coleman this time), an 18/1-shot in the field of thirteen, only four of whom went off at longer odds.

Equipped with cheekpieces for the first time and reunited with Noel Fehily (standing in for the injured Mark Walsh) for the first time since the Reynoldstown Chase, Minella Rocco ran the race of his life in the Gold Cup, jumping fluently and staying on very strongly after the race began in earnest three out. He was still only eighth turning for home and was disputing fifth at the last before finishing with a flourish to catch Native River in the dying strides, coming two and three quarter lengths behind the winner Sizing John, the first three all seven-year-olds. There was a sting in the tail for Fehily who picked up a two-day suspension for using his whip above the permitted level, the second time at the meeting that he was punished for a whip offence (he also got two days on the second day for hitting Neon Wolf in an incorrect place). Six different jockeys, three fewer than at the previous Festival, were given whip bans in the course of the four days, the longest suspension being the thirteen days imposed on amateur Gina Andrews after she had won the Kim Muir on 40/1-shot Domesday Book; she was fined £400, in addition to being suspended, after striking her mount 'above the permitted level and without giving her horse time to respond.' Miss Andrews said afterwards that 'I was doing everything I could to win. For an amateur, winning at the Festival is massive and to be honest you do try to win at all costs. When I pulled up I knew I'd used my whip too much. I ride enough to know better but, even so, I feel the number of days was harsh.' Charlie Longsdon, trainer of runner-up Pendra (beaten three quarters of a length), warmly congratulated the winning connections afterwards, but also shed light on the frustration felt by those who have a horse that is collared in such circumstances, when their own jockey has abided by the rules. Writing on his web site, Longsdon said: 'I do think the whip rules are a little strange sometimes. There should either be some discretion in the cauldron of the bigger meetings or there should be the potential to lose a race if you have whipped a horse well over the permitted level. Under the current rules, at the biggest Festivals, quite naturally jockeys are going to try and win at all costs if they know they will keep a race and only get a small ban.' The Kim Muir exposed the reality that the whip rules will go on being broken because they put jockeys in a dilemma, having to choose between incurring a suspension (and sometimes a fine) or possibly losing a race. It might be different if the stewards had the ultimate power—which they do not have at present—to disqualify horses in extreme cases of improper whip use. A first step might be to give the stewards the power to ban guilty jockeys from riding the horse in question on its next start. This could prove an effective deterrent in big races because it would inconvenience the winning connections, though admittedly it would have limited impact on amateurs.

Minella Rocco (IRE) (b.g. 2010)	Shirocco (GER) (b 2001)	Monsun (br 1990)	Konigsstuhl
			Mosella
		So Sedulous (b 1991)	The Minstrel
			Sedulous
	Petralona (USA) (b 1991)	Alleged (b 1974)	Hoist The Flag
			Princess Pout
		Media Luna (b 1981)	Star Appeal
			Sounion

Minella Rocco, a big gelding, held entries in both the Irish Grand National and the Grand National but, with an eye to the future and given that he is just seven, he was turned away for the summer and will no doubt be brought along steadily with another tilt at the Gold Cup in mind. He wasn't bred for jumping and is from a family on the distaff side that includes classic winners (his dam Petralona, a winner at twelve and a half furlongs in France, is a sister to Eva Luna, the dam of 2003 St Leger winner Brian Boru and grandam of 2010 Derby winner Workforce). Minella Rocco is a half-brother to several winners including the versatile Big Moment, successful on the Flat (twice placed in the Chester Cup), over hurdles and over fences. Minella Rocco, who wears a tongue tie, is a thorough stayer—he stays four miles—and acts on soft going, though he showed in the Gold Cup (which was barely enough of a test of stamina for him) that he doesn't need the mud. *Jonjo O'Neill*

MINELLA STYLE (IRE) 7 b.g. King's Theatre (IRE) – Rose of The Erne (IRE) (Presenting) [2016/17 ab16g³ h19g² h19.9s³ Mar 18] €46,000 3-y-o, £17,800 6-y-o: second foal: dam well held in bumpers: off mark in Irish maiden points at fourth attempt: third in bumper at Lingfield: better effort (fair form) over hurdles when second in novice at Taunton in March. *Neil King* **h110 b80**

MINELLA SUITE (IRE) 6 br.g. Oscar (IRE) – Ballymaguirelass (IRE) (Phardante (FR)) [2016/17 b16d h16.4s⁶ h22.7s⁶ h15.7g⁶ h16d² c15.7s² c21.6sᵘʳ Mar 25] £80,000 4-y-o: big, lengthy gelding: eighth foal: closely related to a winning pointer by Saddlers' Hall: dam, ran once in bumper/point, half-sister to dam of smart chaser up to 21f Go Roger Go: won Irish maiden point on debut: well beaten in bumper: modest form over hurdles: fair form over fences: second when unseated rider 2 out in novice handicap won by Ascot de Bruyere at Kelso final start: should stay beyond 2m: acts on soft going: should still do better over fences. *Rose Dobbin* **c100 p h97 b–**

MINELLA TILL DAWN (IRE) 5 br.g. Shantou (USA) – Have At It (IRE) (Supreme Leader) [2016/17 h20s² h20v* h16s³ h20sᶠ h20dᵖᵘ Apr 26] eighth foal: half-brother to a winning pointer by Topanoora: dam (h97) bumper winner: useful form over hurdles: won maiden at Fairyhouse (by length from Castlegrace Paddy) in December: upsides when fell last in Grade 2 novice won by Al Boum Photo at same course in April: reportedly lame when pulled up final outing: will stay further than 2½m. *Gordon Elliott, Ireland* **h139**

MINELLATILLMORNING (IRE) 5 gr.g. King's Theatre (IRE) – Line Kendie (FR) (Bonnet Rouge (FR)) [2016/17 b13.6g⁴ Mar 31] placed completed starts in Irish points: 4/1, 14¼ lengths fourth of 7 to Dell Oro in bumper at Fontwell, making running. *Neil Mulholland* **b80**

MINELLA TREASURE (IRE) 7 b.g. King's Theatre (IRE) – Ringzar (IRE) (Shernazar) [2016/17 h23d³ Jun 29] €26,000 3-y-o: fourth foal: half-brother to fairly useful hurdler/ useful chaser Rough Justice (2½m-23f winner) and a winning pointer (both by Beneficial): **h99 p**

dam (b73), ran twice in bumpers, sister to fairly useful hurdler/chaser (stayed 2¾m) Headford Flyer: runner-up both starts in Irish maiden points in 2015: 8/1, promise when third in novice at Worcester (2¾ lengths behind Sweetlittlekitty) on hurdling debut: should improve. *Alan King*

MINELLA WARRIOR (IRE) 5 b.g. King's Theatre (IRE) – Bobbi's Venture (IRE) **b100** (Bob Back (USA)) [2016/17 b15.7d b16d² Mar 31] £180,000 4-y-o: good sort: first foal: dam, well beaten both starts in bumpers, half-sister to very smart hurdler/top-class chaser (stayed 25f) Menorah (by King's Theatre): runner-up in Irish maiden point on debut: fairly useful form in bumpers: 2 lengths second of 13 to Kalashnikov at Wetherby. *Kim Bailey*

MINELLA WEB (IRE) 8 b.g. King's Theatre (IRE) – Azalea (IRE) (Marju (IRE)) **c98** [2016/17 c97, h–: c20.5m⁶ c21g³ Aug 10] maiden hurdler: modest handicap chaser: left **h–** Richard Woollacott after first start: probably stays 23f: acts on good to firm going: tried in cheekpieces: wears tongue tie: usually travels strongly. *Colin Tizzard*

MINE NOW (IRE) 9 b.g. Heron Island (IRE) – Aisjem (IRE) (Anshan) [2016/17 h20v² **h132** h24.8d h22.8g h20d² h20v* h20.5d Apr 29] winning pointer: useful handicap hurdler: won at Gowran (by 1¾ lengths from Rue Hill) in February: stays 3m: acts on heavy going: often races towards rear. *Peter Fahey, Ireland*

MIN (FR) 6 b.g. Walk In The Park (IRE) – Phemyka (FR) (Saint Estephe (FR)) **c160 P** [2016/17 h153+: c17d* c17d* Dec 26] **h–**

The late-'seventies and early-'eighties are rightly viewed as the golden era of hurdling, so it shouldn't be a surprise that a race from that period can lay claim to being the highest-quality contest in Cheltenham Festival history. That was the 1977 Champion Hurdle, which saw Night Nurse win the race for the second year running and end the season with a rating of 182 that remains the highest Timeform rating achieved by a hurdler in history (Night Nurse, of course, was also a top-class chaser later in his career, finishing a good second in the 1981 Cheltenham Gold Cup). Runner-up in the 1977 Champion Hurdle, Monksfield, went on to win the next two renewals, while fourth-placed Sea Pigeon became the era's third dual champion with wins in 1980 and 1981 (having come second in both 1978 and 1979). The strength in depth didn't end there, though, as the Champion Hurdle third Dramatist had won the Christmas Hurdle earlier in the season (he was later runner-up in the Queen Mother Champion Chase while still a novice) and the fifth home was the mercurial Bird's Nest (placed in 1976 and 1980), who was sent off a short-priced favourite in 1977 and is widely-regarded as the best horse never to win the Champion Hurdle (there is more about him in the essay on My Tent Or Yours). The top-class pair Beacon Light (third in 1979) and Master Monday (1977 Irish Champion Hurdle winner) managed only sixth and seventh—though perhaps the best illustration of the field's quality in depth is that True Lad, winner of that year's Schweppes Gold Trophy (now the Betfair) at Newbury, was pulled up having been sent off an unconsidered 50/1-shot. Out of interest, the 2012 Arkle Challenge Trophy Chase is probably the race that holds the most solid claims to dislodging the 1977 Champion Hurdle from its pedestal, at least in terms of quality. An imperious Sprinter Sacre came out on top that day by seven lengths from Cue Card, the duo pulling miles clear of a pair of top-class chasers in Menorah and Al Ferof. Fifth-placed Blackstairmountain also franked the form subsequently by winning the world's richest steeplechase, the Nakayama Grand Jump in Japan, just over twelve months later.

Al Ferof, Sprinter Sacre and Cue Card had filled three of the first four places in the 2011 Supreme Novices' and the legacy of another recent Festival novice race is also shaping up very well. The 2016 renewal of the Supreme Novices' Hurdle already looks one of the strongest (if not the strongest) in that race's long history, with a rich stream of big-race winners having emerged from it. The clear-cut winner Altior was the highest-rated of an outstanding crop of novice chasers in 2016/17 thanks to a flawless unbeaten campaign (which included three Grade 1 wins), while his stable-companion Buveur d'Air (third in the 2016 Supreme) won the Champion Hurdle and Aintree Hurdle after a promising novice chase campaign of his own was aborted. Eighth-placed Petit Mouchoir finished third behind Buveur d'Air in the Champion, having earlier won the Ryanair and Irish Champion Hurdles at Leopardstown. The seventh Supasundae (Coral Cup) and ninth North Hill Harvey (Greatwood Hurdle) both landed valuable handicaps back at Cheltenham in 2016/17,

Racing Post Novices' Chase, Leopardstown—a very impressive display by all-the-way winner Min

while fourth-placed Tombstone lowered the colours of former champion hurdler Jezki to win the Red Mills Trial Hurdle at Gowran Park. All of the aforementioned returned to compete at the 2017 Cheltenham Festival, but, unfortunately, they weren't joined at that meeting by Min, whose only defeat for current connections came when runner-up (beaten seven lengths) to Altior in the 2016 Supreme. Min was ruled out of a tilt at the Arkle Challenge Trophy (won by Altior) in early-February due to a 'little stress fracture' and, although it was initially hoped he would return in time for the festivals at Fairyhouse and Punchestown later in the spring, he ended up missing the rest of the season altogether.

Min, of course, had been trying to provide his connections—champion Irish trainer Willie Mullins and his big-spending owners Rich and Susannah Ricci—with their fourth successive Supreme win following Champagne Fever in 2013, Vautour in 2014 and Douvan in 2015, the latter accounting for Shaneshill, Sizing John and L'Ami Serge in another renewal in which the principals have all excelled since. Min also followed in the footsteps of Vautour and Douvan once sent chasing, tackling the same two races as them before the turn of the year. It was actually a fourth straight win (a run started by Ballycasey in 2013) for the Riccis and Mullins when Min landed the odds in the Irish Stallion Farms European Breeders Fund Beginners' Chase at Navan in late-November, his comfortable ten-length win from sixteen rivals every bit as impressive as either Vautour (eight-length winning margin) or Douvan (nine and a half lengths) had been. The opposition might have been stronger on his next start, but it was a similar story for Min as he emulated Douvan (who shares the same sire in Walk In The Park) with another dominant display to land the Racing Post Novices' Chase at Leopardstown on Boxing Day (Vautour had been a below-par second when tackling this race in 2014). It was a performance which fully demonstrated that Min had quickly developed into a better chaser than a hurdler, impressing with how fluently he travelled and jumped before storming clear to win by nine lengths with plenty in hand. Min looks open to significant further improvement on that bare form, a view backed up by the subsequent efforts of several horses he trounced at Leopardstown. Runner-up Ordinary World went on to be placed in both the Arkle (behind Altior) at Cheltenham and the Ryanair (behind Great Field) at Punchestown, while the third Road To Respect ended his campaign with two big-race wins, notably when lowering the colours of the wayward Yorkhill at Fairyhouse's Easter meeting. Even sixth-placed Tully East franked the form by winning the Close Brothers Novices' Handicap Chase at Cheltenham.

Mrs S. Ricci's "Min"

		Montjeu	Sadler's Wells
	Walk In The Park (IRE)	(b 1996)	Floripedes
	(b 2002)	Classic Park	Robellino
Min (FR)		(b 1994)	Wanton
(b.g. 2011)		Saint Estephe	Top Ville
	Phemyka (FR)	(b 1982)	Une Tornade
	(b 1996)	Stormyka	Akarad
		(b 1990)	Stormy Scene

The well-made Min's pedigree was discussed in *Chasers & Hurdlers 2015/16* and there is nothing new to add. To recap, he is the fifth foal of the French mile and a quarter winner Phemyka and her fourth winner, with his half-brother Gaone (by Sagacity) the only other one to have tasted success over jumps, in a nineteen-furlong hurdle in the French Provinces. Min also began his career on French soil, making the frame in two juvenile hurdles at Auteuil for Yannick Fouin before joining his current connections, with whom he has enjoyed a lofty home reputation virtually from the off. His speed means that he is likely to be kept at around the minimum trip for now, but, when the time comes, he should stay a fair bit further than two and a quarter miles (the longest trip he's tackled to date). The 2016 Supreme was run under the most resilient underfoot conditions (good ground) Min has faced so far and, although he handles heavy ground, he certainly doesn't appeal as a mudlark.

Min was just one of several star names from Closutton forced to miss the latest Cheltenham Festival. Considering that the group also included the Ricci-owned Champion Hurdle winners Faugheen and Annie Power, it was quite revealing to hear Willie Mullins say about the various setbacks: 'Min was probably the most disappointing one of them all, as he was a good, sound horse and doing everything right. He had improved hugely from last year and I thought he could close the gap on Altior, but we'll get another opportunity to see that one …' Jumping fans everywhere will hope so! *W. P. Mullins, Ireland*

MINMORE GREY (IRE) 8 gr.g. Primary (USA) – Hopeful Memory (IRE) (Roselier (FR)) [2016/17 h73, b–: c25.1m⁵ c23g c26.3g³ c25.1s⁶ c26.7d⁵ c24.5mᶠ Apr 13] maiden pointer: little form over hurdles/fences: tried to refuse and fell second final outing: often in headgear: best treated with caution. *Nick Lampard* c– §
h–

MINMORE OSCAR (IRE) 9 br.m. Oscar (IRE) – She's Our Daisy (IRE) (Supreme Leader) [2016/17 c22g⁵ c20d c21gᶠ c21v⁶ c25.2s c24.2s⁴ c21.3s Mar 5] first foal: dam (h105) bumper and 2m/17f hurdle winner: point winner: modest maiden chaser: best effort at 21f on heavy going: in cheekpieces last 2 starts: tried in tongue tie. *W. J. Martin, Ireland* c87

MINNIE MILAN (IRE) 8 b.m. Milan – Shiminnie (IRE) (Bob Back (USA)) [2016/17 h118: h25.4m³ h23.9d h23.3gᵖᵘ h25gᵖᵘ Apr 15] sturdy mare: fairly useful handicap hurdler: showed nothing after reappearance: left Neil King after third start: stays 3¼m: acts on good to firm and good to soft going. *Barbara Butterworth* h116

MINORITY INTEREST 8 ch.g. Galileo (IRE) – Minority (Generous (IRE)) [2016/17 h80: h21.6d c22.5d⁶ c21.1g² c23gᵖᵘ Jul 21] poor maiden hurdler/chaser: stays 2¾m: acts on heavy going: wears headgear: has worn tongue tie: temperamental (often races lazily). *Daniel O'Brien* c65 §
h–

MINOTAUR (IRE) 5 b.g. Azamour (IRE) – Mycenae (Inchinor) [2016/17 h17s² h20.3s Jan 1] useful on Flat, stays 2m: fair form over hurdles: much better effort when second of 6 in novice at Aintree in December: should prove suited by 2½m+. *Jonjo O'Neill* h109

MINSTREL ROYAL 7 b.g. Kayf Tara – Close Harmony (Bustino) [2016/17 h110, b82: h19.1d³ h20g³ h19.3m² h23.5d⁶ h24.4gᵖᵘ h19g* Apr 24] strong gelding: will make a chaser: fairly useful handicap hurdler: won at Warwick on final start: stays 2¾m: acts on good to firm and good to soft going: often races towards rear. *Nicky Henderson* h118

MINSTRELS GALLERY (IRE) 8 ch.g. Refuse To Bend (IRE) – Lilakiya (IRE) (Dr Fong (USA)) [2016/17 h124: h20.6s³ h19.4g⁴ h24d² Feb 26] workmanlike gelding: fairly useful handicap hurdler: stayed 3m: acted on heavy going: usually raced prominently: dead. *Lucy Wadham* h127

MIN TIKY (IRE) 5 b.m. King's Theatre (IRE) – Kon Tiky (FR) (Perrault) [2016/17 b15.8d b16.7g Apr 22] €32,000 3-y-o: seventh foal: half-sister to bumper winner Isla Fernandos (by Flemensfirth) and modest hurdler Baily Sunset (2m winner, by Presenting): dam unraced half-sister to outstanding 2m chaser Azertyuiop: well held both starts in bumpers. *Mark Bradstock* b–

MIRACLE CURE (IRE) 8 b.g. Whipper (USA) – Bring Back Matron (IRE) (Rock of Gibraltar (IRE)) [2016/17 h80: h15.3d* h16.5g² h19.8d⁵ h15.3s³ h16.2v⁴ h16v² c19.9gᵖᵘ Apr 3] close-coupled gelding: fair handicap hurdler: won conditionals/amateur event at Wincanton in November: no promise in novice handicap on chasing debut: stays 2½m: acts on heavy going: tried in headgear: often travels strongly/flatters to deceive. *Venetia Williams* c–
h105

MIRO (IRE) 5 b.g. Rock of Gibraltar (IRE) – Mission Secrete (IRE) (Galileo (IRE)) [2016/17 h18.2d⁵ h20g³ h16.4s h16s³ h18.2g* h19.9g³ h16.2g² h16g⁶ Oct 31] fair maiden on Flat, stays 9.5f: fair hurdler: won maiden at Downpatrick in August: stays 2½m: acts on soft going: tried in hood. *Gordon Elliott, Ireland* h111

MIRSAALE 7 ch.g. Sir Percy – String Quartet (IRE) (Sadler's Wells (USA)) [2016/17 h16.2g* h16.2g* h19.5g³ h16.4s² h16.4s⁵ h16.5g h21.3s⁴ Feb 4] smallish, angular gelding: useful on Flat, stays 2m: useful hurdler: won novices at Perth in August and September: ran well next 2 starts, when third in Persian War Novices' Hurdle at Chepstow (3 lengths behind El Bandit) and second in Sharp Novices' Hurdle at Cheltenham (2¼ lengths behind Moon Racer): will prove best up to 19f: acts on soft going: races prominently. *Keith Dalgleish* h130

MISFITS (IRE) 6 b.g. Beneficial – Park Rose (IRE) (Roselier (FR)) [2016/17 h106p, b80: h20.2s h23.9g⁴ h23.9g⁴ h23.9s⁵ c17.1s² c24dᵘʳ c23.9s³ c23.8g⁵ h19v⁴ h20.9s⁵ Mar 25] winning Irish pointer: fair maiden hurdler/chaser: stays 3m: acts on soft going: in tongue tie final start. *Lucinda Russell* c102
h100

MISS ATTYMON (IRE) 5 ch.m. Dubai Destination (USA) – Attymon Lill (IRE) (Marju (IRE)) [2016/17 h16v h16d h16v⁶ h16.5g h17.7g h21.6m Apr 15] seventh foal: half-sister to 3 winners, including modest 2¼m hurdle winner Ninfea (by Le Vie dei Colori): dam lightly raced on Flat: no form over hurdles: left Paul Cashman after third start: in hood final outing. *Dominic Ffrench Davis* h–

MISS BARBOSSA (IRE) 6 b.m. Gold Well – Queens Quay (Grand Lodge (USA)) **h81**
[2016/17 h66, b–: h17.1d³ h21.3g⁵ h16.4d³ h19.3g⁴ h23.8g² h19.4g³ h23.8g² Mar 24]
sturdy mare: poor maiden hurdler: stays 3m: acts on good to soft going: in cheekpieces last
2 starts: often races towards rear. *Martin Todhunter*

MISS BEATRICE (IRE) 5 b.m. Robin des Champs (FR) – Corries Rein (IRE) (Anshan) **h96 p**
[2016/17 b16.7g* b15.8m h16g³ Sep 6] €30,000 3-y-o: sixth foal: half-sister to fairly **b94**
useful chaser Keep On Track (2m-21f winner, by Rudimentary), stays 33f, and winning
pointers by High Roller and Heron Island: dam unraced: fair form in bumpers: won mares
event at Bangor in May: 7¼ lengths third to Solstalla in mares maiden at Worcester on
hurdling debut (reportedly finished lame): will stay 2½m: should improve. *Jonjo O'Neill*

MISS BENEFITZ (IRE) 6 ch.m. Beneficial – African Keys (IRE) (Quws) [2016/17 **h92**
h16m h16g³ h16.5g² h15.7g³ h15.5d h15.5g³ h19.1vᵖᵘ h15.7sᵖᵘ h16.5g h15.7m⁵ h20.3gᵖᵘ
Apr 21] small mare: second foal: half-sister to fair chaser Flash Tommie (2½m winner, by
City Honours): dam unraced half-sister to smart hurdler/top-class chaser (stayed 25f)
China Rock and useful hurdler/chaser (stayed 21f) Barrakilla: modest maiden hurdler: left
K. O'Sullivan after third start, Richard Fahey after fourth: unproven beyond 2m: best form
on good going: has worn hood, including last 2 starts: usually races freely. *Mike Hammond*

MISS BISCOTTI 9 ch.m. Emperor Fountain – Bellacaccia (IRE) (Beau Sher) [2016/17 **c96**
c86, h–: c21.6d⁴ c25.5g² c26.2s* Mar 25] winning hurdler: modest form over fences: won **h–**
3-runner hunter at Kelso final start: stays 3¼m: acts on soft going: sometimes in
cheekpieces: front runner/races prominently. *Gary Rutherford*

MISS BLANCHE 6 b.m. King's Theatre (IRE) – Keys Pride (IRE) (Bob Back (USA)) **h71**
[2016/17 h–: h16.2m⁴ h20.1g h16.2d Jun 30] poor maiden hurdler: wears hood: sold
€16,000 in December and joined Mark McNiff. *Lucinda Russell*

MISS BUTTERFLY (IRE) 5 b.m. Yeats (IRE) – Miss Opera (Alflora (IRE)) [2016/17 **b79**
b16g4 b16g b16v Jan 14] fourth foal: dam unraced half-sister to winner/small chaser
(2m-21f winner) Woodland Opera out of very smart chaser (2m-3m winner) Opera Hat:
modest form in bumpers. *P. J. Colville, Ireland*

MISS CONWAY 6 br.m. Midnight Legend – Miss Pross (Bob's Return (IRE)) [2016/17 **c83**
c62, h78: c20.1d⁴ c19.2d² c15.6d⁴ c15.7d² c17mᵖᵘ c15.6v⁴ c16.4dᵖᵘ c15.7g⁶ c15.6g* Apr **h–**
25] neat mare: maiden hurdler: poor handicap chaser: won at Hexham in June and on final
start: stays 2½m: acts on good to soft going: usually leads. *Mark Walford*

MISS CRICK 6 b.m. Midnight Legend – Kwaheri (Efisio) [2016/17 h107, b–: h16s* **h127**
h15.9g⁴ h15.8g² h18.5g* h20g* h16g³ h24.5sᵖᵘ h19.9gᵖᵘ h20.3g⁶ Apr 20] lengthy mare:
bumper winner: fairly useful hurdler: won mares maiden at Worcester in May, mares
novice at Ffos Las in June, and handicaps at Newton Abbot in July and Worcester in
September: third in listed Mares' Hurdle at Wetherby (½ length behind Stephanie Frances)
in October: stays 2½m: acts on soft going. *Alan King*

MISS DIMPLES (IRE) 8 gr.m. Tikkanen (USA) – Scolboa House (IRE) (Bob's Return **c– §**
(IRE)) [2016/17 c75, h–: c24dᵘʳ c20.9gᵖᵘ c21.2mᶠ c22.6mᵖᵘ c20g c22.6gᵖᵘ Jul 28] maiden **h–**
hurdler: poor chaser at best, no form in 2016/17: wears headgear: tried in tongue tie: often
races towards rear: temperamental. *Sarah-Jayne Davies*

MISSED APPROACH (IRE) 7 b.g. Golan (IRE) – Polly's Dream (IRE) (Beau Sher) **c146**
[2016/17 h146: c24.2s⁴ c23.5v* c24.2s³ c23.6vᵘʳ c31.8g² c31.8g Apr 22] smart hurdler/ **h–**
chaser: won novice chase at Lingfield in January by 6 lengths from Label des Obeaux:
good 3 lengths second of 18 to Tiger Roll in National Hunt Chase at Cheltenham in March
and respectable eighth of 30 to Vicente in Scottish Grand National at Ayr final outing: stays
4m: acts on heavy going: in cheekpieces last 2 starts: front runner/races prominently.
Warren Greatrex

MISSESGEEJAY 7 br.m. Beat All (USA) – Riverbank Rainbow (Overbury (IRE)) **h–**
[2016/17 b62: h61: h16.7d⁵ May 26] modest form in bumpers: well held in mares maiden at
Bangor on hurdling debut. *Richard Ford*

MISS ESTELA (IRE) 7 b.m. Tobougg (IRE) – Simply Divine (IRE) (Be My Native **h120**
(USA)) [2016/17 h111: h16d h16.7d* h16g⁴ h19.3m* h21.6d⁶ Nov 19] angular mare: fairly
useful handicap hurdler: won mares event at Market Rasen in May and novice event at
Ascot in October: left Warren Greatrex after third start: stays 19f: acts on good to firm and
heavy going: in cheekpieces second/third starts, in tongue tie last 2. *Johnny Farrelly*

MISS FEISTYPANTS 5 br.m. Virtual – Fu Wa (USA) (Distant View (USA)) [2016/17 **h71**
b62: b16.3m h15.7g⁵ h16g⁵ h16.8d Sep 26] poor form in bumpers/over hurdles: in hood **b–**
last 4 starts. *Seamus Mullins*

MISS FLEMING 5 b.m. Flemensfirth (USA) – Uppermost (Montjeu (IRE)) [2016/17 **h88** b83: h15.8d^F h15.8g^5 Nov 10] bumper winner: modest form on completed start in mares maiden hurdles: will be suited by 2½m: tried in visor: usually races towards rear. *David Loder*

MISS FORTYWINKS 8 gr.m. Act One – Andromache (Hector Protector (USA)) **c84** [2016/17 h97: c16.5m² c15.7g⁴ c19.7g⁴ Oct 31] winning hurdler: poor form over fences: **h–** unproven beyond 17f: acts on good to firm and good to soft going. *Seamus Mullins*

MISS GISELLE 8 b.m. Desideratum – Pride of The Oaks (Faustus (USA)) [2016/17 h–, **h63 §** b83: h18.5m⁶ h20g⁶ h21v^pu h20.5g^pu Jan 24] poor maiden hurdler: in cheekpieces final start: one to avoid. *Sam Thomas*

MISSILE MAN (IRE) 8 b.g. Winged Love (IRE) – Miss Ondee (FR) (Dress Parade) **h– x** [2016/17 h–: h20g h24g⁶ h25.6s h20.5g^pu Oct 17] bumper winner: no form over hurdles: blinkered final start: poor jumper. *Jim Best*

MISSION COMPLETE (IRE) 11 b.g. Milan – Kilmington Breeze (IRE) (Roselier **c– §** (FR)) [2016/17 c103§, h88§: c23m^ur Jul 4] sturdy gelding: fairly useful hurdler/chaser at **h– §** best: stayed 29f: acted on good to firm and heavy going: wore headgear/tongue tie: often raced prominently: not one to trust (looked a hard ride): dead. *Jonjo O'Neill*

MISSION TRIO (IRE) 5 b.g. Presenting – Miss Brandywell (IRE) (Sadler's Wells **b63** (USA)) [2016/17 b15.7d b17d Apr 5] showed little in 2 bumpers. *Patrick Holmes*

MISS JOANS 4 b.f. Midnight Legend – Tecktal (FR) (Pivotal) [2016/17 h15.9v^pu h15.9v^pu **h–** h16g h16m h16m^pu Apr 18] smallish filly: second foal: half-sister to 11.5f winner Reggie Perrin (by Storming Home): dam (c75/h71), 21f hurdle winner, also 11f winner on Flat: no form over hurdles. *Pat Phelan*

MISS JOEKING (IRE) 6 b.m. Alkaadhem – Go Franky (IRE) (Hollow Hand) [2016/17 **h74** h82, b–: h16.2d³ h20.2d h17.2d⁶ h19.6d⁶ h20.2g^pu h16.2s³ h19.9g⁴ Apr 7] poor handicap hurdler: stays 23f: acts on soft and good to firm going: often races towards rear. *Lucinda Russell*

MISS LILLIE 6 b.m. Exceed And Excel (AUS) – Never Lose (Diktat) [2016/17 h16g^pu **h–** Sep 12] fair on Flat, stays 1¼m: saddle slipped and pulled up before fourth in novice on hurdling debut. *Roger Teal*

MISS LIZZY LAMB 6 gr.m. Act One – Lizzy Lamb (Bustino) [2016/17 b16.8g⁶ b16s **h–** h19.3d h19.9d⁴ h21.2s^pu Feb 6] fifth foal: half-sister to fair hurdler/chaser Ballycoe **b–** (2½m-23f winner, by Norse Dancer) and temperamental chaser Hardwick Wood (21f winner, by Fleetwood): dam, ran twice (third in bumper), half-sister to useful hurdler/fairly useful chaser (stayed 25f) Lord Lamb and useful 2m hurdler Mr Lamb: no form in bumpers and novice hurdles. *Lucinda Egerton*

MISS MACARNO 6 b.m. Lucarno (USA) – Shady Minx (Gildoran) [2016/17 b15.8m **b–** b16d Jun 22] second foal: dam winning pointer: well held in bumpers, in hood first start: runner-up in point in January. *Pam Sly*

MISS MACKIE (IRE) 6 b.m. Mr Combustible (IRE) – Grannys Kitchen (IRE) **h73** (Flemensfirth (USA)) [2016/17 h75, b–: h16.2d⁴ h16.2g Apr 27] poor maiden hurdler: raced around 2m: acts on good to soft going: in cheekpieces final start. *R. Mike Smith*

MISS MAIDEN OVER (IRE) 5 br.m. Carlo Bank (IRE) – Rock Garden (IRE) **h115** (Bigstone (IRE)) [2016/17 b81: b15.8g h19.9g³ h19.5g⁵ h20.5s* h19.3g* h25.5s h20.2g* **b–** Apr 26] useful-looking mare: modest at best in bumpers: fairly useful form over hurdles: won maiden at Ayr and mares novice at Catterick in November, and mares handicap at Perth final start: stays 2½m: acts on soft going: often travels strongly. *Fergal O'Brien*

MISS MALARKY (IRE) 4 b.f. Presenting – The Shan Gang (IRE) (Anshan) [2016/17 **b–** b15.8s⁶ b17.7g Mar 27] €12,000 3-y-o: seventh foal: half-sister to a winning pointer by King's Theatre: dam unraced half-sister to useful hurdler/smart chaser (stayed 2½m) Watson Lake: no form in bumpers. *Diana Grissell*

MISS MASH 6 b.m. Multiplex – Shanxi Girl (Overbury (IRE)) [2016/17 h90, b–: h16m **h100** h19.9s³ h19.6s* h19.4g⁵ h20.5g⁴ h23.1s² Mar 12] compact mare: fair handicap hurdler: won mares event at Bangor in December: barely stays 23f: acts on soft going: often races towards rear. *Henry Daly*

MISSMEBUTLETMEGO 7 b.g. With The Flow (USA) – Bay Bianca (IRE) (Law **b–** Society (USA)) [2016/17 b–: b15.8g May 9] sturdy gelding: no form in 2 bumpers. *Alan Jones*

MISS MOBOT 7 b.m. Midnight Legend – Fleur de Nikos (FR) (Nikos) [2016/17 h–, b89:   **h120**
h19.9g^{pu} h21.6m^{bd} h19.9g^F h21.6g^{ur} h23g^3 h21.6m* h24m* h23.8m^3 Oct 5] lengthy mare:
bumper winner: fairly useful hurdler: won mares maiden at Newton Abbot in August and
mares novice at Southwell in September: stays 3m: acts on good to firm going: usually
travels strongly. *Philip Hobbs*

MISS NIGHT OWL 7 ch.m. Midnight Legend – Moyliscar (Terimon) [2016/17 b17g*   **h117**
b16.4s h15.7v^2 h16.2s^6 h15.8g* h16.2g* Apr 28] compact mare: third foal: sister to fair   **b93**
hurdler In By Midnight (2m winner) and half-sister to modest chaser Moonlight Maggie
(2m winner, by Pasternak): dam headstrong maiden chaser: placed 3 times in Irish mares
maiden points: fair form when winning mares bumper at Aintree in October: fairly useful
form over hurdles: won mares novice events at Ludlow and Perth last 2 starts, both in April:
raced only around 2m: best efforts on good ground: front runner/races prominently.
Tom George

MISS OSCAROSE (IRE) 10 b.m. Oscar (IRE) – Private Rose (IRE) (Roselier (FR))   **c79**
[2016/17 c84, h67: h19.5d c25.5s^{pu} c19.7d^4 c19.7s^3 c20.2s^2 c19.9d^4 c25.7m* Apr 17]   **h–**
lengthy, plain mare: maiden hurdler: poor handicap chaser: won at Plumpton in December
and April: stays 3¼m: acts on good to firm and heavy going: wears tongue tie: often races
prominently. *Paul Henderson*

MISS SASSYPANTS 8 ch.m. Hernando (FR) – Serraval (FR) (Sanglamore (USA))   **h105**
[2016/17 h111: h16.7d^4 h15.7v^2 h16g^5 h20m^4 Aug 30] small mare: fair handicap hurdler:
stays 2½m: acts on good to firm and heavy going: usually races towards rear. *Seamus Mullins*

MISS SERIOUS (IRE) 7 br.m. Kalanisi (IRE) – Burnt Out (IRE) (Anshan) [2016/17   **c123**
h120: c21m^3 c25.8m* c25.8g^2 c24.2g^F c26.7m^F c25.6g^4 Nov 10] lengthy mare: fairly   **h–**
useful handicap hurdler/chaser: won over fences at Newton Abbot in July: stays 3¼m: acts
on good to firm and good to soft going: wears tongue tie: often races in rear. *Jeremy Scott*

MISS SPENT (IRE) 7 b.m. Presenting – Cash And New (IRE) (Supreme Leader)   **h107**
[2016/17 b95: h16d h19.6d* h20.5s^5 h23.8s^{pu} h16.7d^5 Apr 27] good-topped mare: bumper
winner: fair form when winning mares novice at Huntingdon in November, easily best
effort over hurdles: should stay beyond 2½m: acts on good to soft going: in cheekpieces
penultimate start: usually races close up. *Lucy Wadham*

MISS TENACIOUS 10 b.m. Refuse To Bend (IRE) – Very Speed (USA) (Silver Hawk   **c131**
(USA)) [2016/17 c124, h–: c16d* c16.5g^2 c20d^3 c16.5g^5 c16.3g^3 c16.5m^4 c16.3g^4 c18m*   **h–**
c16.9m Oct 29] rather leggy mare: winning hurdler: useful handicap chaser: won at
Warwick in May and Kempton (by 1¾ lengths from Noche de Reyes) in October: stays
2¾m: acts on any going. *Ron Hodges*

MISS TIGER LILY 7 b.m. Tiger Hill (IRE) – Waitingonacloud (In The Wings) [2016/17   **h–**
h102: h23.3g h19.9g Jul 5] stocky mare: fair winner over hurdles, well held both outings in
2016/17: best effort at 2½m: in cheekpieces/tongue tie final start: front runner/races
prominently. *Jamie Snowden*

MISS TIGGY (IRE) 7 b.m. Milan – Rockwell College (IRE) (Supreme Leader) [2016/17   **h–**
h97: h20d Oct 20] lightly-raced maiden hurdler, modest form at best. *Lucinda Russell*

MISS TONGABEZI 8 b.m. Overbury (IRE) – Shiwa (Bustino) [2016/17 h93: h20.5g^2 **h116**
h20.7d* h23.8s* h20.5g h20.3g Apr 20] compact mare: fairly useful handicap hurdler: won
at Huntingdon in December and Ludlow (mares event) in March: stays 3m: acts on heavy
going: wears hood: usually in tongue tie. *Paul Webber*

MISS TYNTE (IRE) 5 b.m. Mahler – Top Quality (Simply Great (FR)) [2016/17 b16d^2 **b86**
b17s^4 Dec 11] half-sister to useful hurdler/chaser Special Catch (2m-2½m winner, by
Catcher In The Rye): dam (h82), lightly raced over hurdles, sister to useful hurdler/top-
class chaser (stayed 25f) Simply Dashing: fair form in bumpers: better effort when second
of 23 in maiden at Punchestown on debut, then left Peter Fahey/off 8 months. *David Pipe*

MISS WILLIAMS 6 b.m. Kayf Tara – Wee Dinns (IRE) (Marju (IRE)) [2016/17 h–:   **h86**
h16.3m^4 h15.8s^6 h15.8d h16.3g^6 h16.5m^6 Apr 20] modest form over hurdles: left David
Pipe after first start: best effort at 2m: acts on good to firm going: in hood last 3 starts: tried
in tongue tie: front runner/races freely. *Charlie Longsdon*

MISS YEATS (IRE) 6 b.m. Yeats (IRE) – Mrs Wallensky (IRE) (Roselier (FR)) [2016/17   **h102**
b72: h19.5g^3 h17.7v^5 h19.6s^2 h21.6g^6 Mar 31] fair form over hurdles: should stay beyond
2½m. *Laura Mongan*

MISSY MYRTLE 6 b.m. Indian Danehill (IRE) – She Likes To Boogy (IRE) (Luso)   **h–**
[2016/17 b–: h18.6s^{pu} h19.3d^{pu} Dec 13] no sign of ability in bumper/novice hurdles.
Peter Niven

MISSY TATA (FR) 5 b.m. Astarabad (USA) – Queen Running (FR) (Cadoudal (FR))   **h140**
[2016/17 h139: h16d* h17m* h18d* h16d* h16s* Dec 28] good-topped mare: useful
hurdler: unbeaten in 2016/17, winning mares event at Killarney in May, minor event at
Limerick in October, Fishery Lane Hurdle at Naas (by 4 lengths from Slowmotion) in
November and listed event at Limerick (by 6½ lengths from Cap d'Aubois) on final start:
raced around 2m: acts on soft and good to firm going: usually races close up, strong
traveller: has flashed tail. *Gordon Elliott, Ireland*

MISTER BIG (IRE) 6 b.g. Scorpion (IRE) – Back To Roost (IRE) (Presenting) [2016/17   **h107**
h16d^2 h16.3d h18.5s^F h16.8s^5 Mar 7] rangy gelding: fair form over hurdles: best effort
when second in novice at Chepstow: should stay beyond 2m. *Philip Hobbs*

MISTER BRICOLAGE (IRE) 10 b.g. Oscar (IRE) – Almost Trumps (Nearly A Hand)   **c– §**
[2016/17 c21.1d^6 May 12] well-made gelding: winning pointer: maiden hurdler/chaser: **h– §**
stays 27f: acts on soft going: sometimes in cheekpieces: has worn tongue tie: weak finisher
and can't be trusted. *C. J. Lawson*

MISTERCOBAR (FR) 5 b.g. Nicobar – Miss Decca (FR) (Smadoun (FR)) [2016/17   **b–**
b15.7s b18g Apr 28] runner-up on last of 3 starts in Irish maiden points: in tongue tie, well
held in 2 bumpers. *Graham McKeever, Ireland*

MISTER DICK (FR) 5 b.g. Great Journey (JPN) – Lyric Melody (FR) (Lyphard's Wish   **c91**
(FR)) [2016/17 h96: h20m^4 h20.3g^6 h23d^6 c22.6m* c19.9m^3 c24.2g^F c24.2g^5 c23.8v^2 **h94**
c27.5g Apr 23] modest maiden hurdler: modest form over fences: won novice handicap at
Stratford in August: stays 3m: acts on good to firm and heavy going: has worn blinkers/
tongue tie, including in 2016/17. *Jonjo O'Neill*

MISTER DON (IRE) 7 br.g. Presenting – Spring Flower (IRE) (Beneficial) [2016/17   **c107**
c60, h85: h22.7d^5 c23.4m* c23.4s^{pu} c24.2g^2 c23.8d^4 c26g* c24.2d^4 c23.8g^3 c23.8g^2 **h82**
c25.2d^3 c30.6g^2 Apr 28] medium-sized, good-topped gelding: poor maiden hurdler: fair
handicap chaser: won at Kelso (novice event) in October and Doncaster (conditionals
event) in November: stays 31f: acts on good to firm and heavy going: wears cheekpieces:
tried in tongue tie. *Rose Dobbin*

MISTER DOUBLE DUCE (IRE) 6 ch.g. Vertical Speed (FR) – Here Comes Sally   **b–**
(IRE) (Rashar (USA)) [2016/17 b16.7g Jul 31] tailed off in bumper on debut. *Peter Bowen*

MISTER DRIFTER (IRE) 5 b.g. Stowaway – Graces Choice (IRE) (Luso) [2016/17   **b82**
b15.8s^6 b16s Jan 26] second foal: dam (h88), bumper winner, half-sister to fairly useful
hurdler/useful chaser (stays 3¼m) Bally Longford: modest form in bumpers: in cheekpieces
second start. *David Pipe*

MISTER FIRST (IRE) 11 b.g. Trempolino (USA) – Queen Running (FR) (Cadoudal   **c128**
(FR)) [2016/17 c123, h–: c23.8m* c20.1m* c20.1f^4 c20.5g^6 c24.1s c22.5s h20d^6 c24s   **h110**
h18.8g^2 Mar 26] fair handicap hurdler: fairly useful handicap chaser: won twice at Perth in
May: stays easy 25f, at least as effective at shorter: acts on good to firm and heavy going:
tried in headgear: has worn tongue tie, including in 2016/17. *Robert Hennessy, Ireland*

MISTER FIZZ 9 b.g. Sulamani (IRE) – Court Champagne (Batshoof) [2016/17 h138:   **h–**
h19.3s h21g Mar 18] leggy gelding: useful hurdler at best, no form in 2016/17: stays 2¾m:
acts on good to firm and good to soft going: in cheekpieces final start. *Miss Imogen Pickard*

MISTER FLIP FLOP (IRE) 4 b.g. Danehill Dancer (IRE) – Heavenly Bay (USA)   **b–**
(Rahy (USA)) [2016/17 b14.6s Dec 17] tailed-off last in bumper, and in maiden and seller
on Flat. *Adam West*

MISTER GREZ (FR) 11 gr.g. Turgeon (USA) – Yoruba (FR) (Cyborg (FR)) [2016/17   **c120**
h22.8v^{pu} h19.5g h21g^{pu} c20.2s^2 Feb 1] good-topped gelding: fairly useful hurdler at best,   **h–**
no form in 2016/17 after long absence: handicap chaser: tongue tied, fairly useful form
when second at Leicester final outing: stays 21f: acts on heavy going: often in blinkers.
Dan Skelton

MISTER KIT 9 gr.g. Tikkanen (USA) – Rosie Mist (Missed Flight) [2016/17 h125p: **c119**
h17.1d^2 h16g^4 h15.6g^2 c19.9g^4 c20g^2 Apr 15] placed in points: lightly-raced hurdler, useful   **h133**
form: useful form over fences: better effort when second in novice at Carlisle: stays
2½m: acts on good to soft going: usually leads. *Chris Grant*

MISTER MALARKY 4 ch.g. Malinas (GER) – Priscilla (Teenoso (USA)) [2016/17   **b78**
b16.8v^3 b16s^6 b16.3g Mar 25] lengthy gelding: modest form in bumpers: will be suited by
2½m+. *Colin Tizzard*

MISTER MARKER (IRE) 13 ch.g. Beneficial – Bavards Girl (IRE) (Le Bavard (FR)) **c99 §**
[2016/17 c110§, h–: c23.8m* c23.4v⁴ c23.4v⁴ c26.2s³ Mar 25] winning hurdler: modest **h–**
chaser nowadays: won hunter at Perth in May: stays 4m: acts on good to firm and heavy
going: front runner/races prominently: temperamental. *Nicky Richards*

MISTER MIYAGI (IRE) 8 b.g. Zagreb (USA) – Muckle Flugga (IRE) (Karinga Bay) **h147**
[2016/17 h143: h16m³ h20d² h16.8s⁶ h21.1g Mar 15] lengthy gelding: third only completed
start in points: smart hurdler: best effort of 2016/17 when 2 lengths second of 4 to Un
Temps Pour Tout in minor event at Aintree in November: stays 2½m: acts on good to firm
and good to soft going: usually races towards rear/travels strongly. *Dan Skelton*

MISTER PHILSON (IRE) 12 b.g. Saddlers' Hall (IRE) – Molo River (IRE) (Fourstars **c–**
Allstar (USA)) [2016/17 c–, h–: c32.5g c24sᵖᵘ Jan 26] winning pointer: maiden hurdler: **h–**
fair chaser at best, no form in 3 runs since 2014/15: wears headgear. *Mrs L. Pomfret*

MISTER RAINMAN (IRE) 5 b.g. Westerner – Khimki (IRE) (Moscow Society (USA)) **b–**
[2016/17 b16.3d Mar 13] tailed off in maiden bumper on debut. *Adrian Wintle*

MISTER SERIOUS (IRE) 8 b.g. Kalanisi (IRE) – Mack Tack (IRE) (Shardari) [2016/17 **h107**
h19.1g² Mar 31] €14,000 4-y-o, £2,000 7-y-o: fifth foal: half-brother to fairly useful
hurdler/chaser Cruchain (2m-2¾m winner, by Shernazar) and modest chaser Son of Moyne
(3m winner, by Sonus): dam of no account: dual winning pointer: 33/1, 9 lengths second of
3 to Brave Eagle in novice at Fontwell on hurdling debut. *Hugo Froud*

MISTER SPINGSPRONG (IRE) 10 b.g. Flemensfirth (USA) – Watts Hill (IRE) (Old **c125**
Vic) [2016/17 c20.1d² c20.1g² c21.4dᵖᵘ c16.9d⁴ c15.7d³ c20.1s⁶ h19.7m⁴ Apr 13] **h–**
workmanlike gelding: winning Irish pointer: useful hurdler at best, bled when well held
in seller final start: fairly useful maiden chaser: left Michael Smith after third start: stays
2½m: acts on heavy going: often leads. *Brian Ellison*

MISTERTON 6 gr.g. Sagamix (FR) – Mighty Splash (Cape Cross (IRE)) [2016/17 h98: **h126**
b16.8g* h16.5g* h16.8gᵖᵘ h18.5s² h19.8d* Mar 26] lengthy gelding: fairly useful form in **b99**
bumpers: won at Newton Abbot in October: also fairly useful over hurdles: won novice at
Taunton in November and novice handicap at Wincanton final start: stays 2½m: acts on soft
going: usually races prominently. *Harry Fry*

MISTER UNIVERSUM (GER) 5 b.g. Cape Cross (IRE) – Miss Europa (IRE) (Monsun **h99**
(GER)) [2016/17 h16.3d⁴ h16g Feb 25] rather leggy gelding: useful on Flat, stays 1½m:
modest form over hurdles: better effort when fourth in introductory event at Newbury in
December. *Dan Skelton*

MISTER WHITAKER (IRE) 5 b.g. Court Cave (IRE) – Benbradagh Vard (IRE) (Le **h111**
Bavard (FR)) [2016/17 b16.7g² b16.7g⁶ h16.6d³ h16.6g⁴ h20.6m³ Apr 9] half-brother to **b85**
several winners, including smart hurdler/chaser Broadway Buffalo (2m-3m winner, by
Broadway Flyer), stayed 4m, and bumper winner/useful hurdler Christdalo (2¾m-3m
winner, by Glacial Storm): dam in frame both starts in bumpers: fair form when placed in
bumper and in novice/maiden hurdles: bred to stay 2½m+: usually races prominently.
Mick Channon

MISTRESS MASSINI 6 b.m. Dr Massini (IRE) – Mistress Willie (Master Willie) **b86**
[2016/17 b15.8m* b17g⁴ Oct 23] sturdy mare: first foal: dam unraced: pulled up in maiden
point on debut: fair form in bumpers: won mares event at Ludlow in October.
Anthony Honeyball

MIST THE BOAT 9 b.g. Generous (IRE) – Baily Mist (IRE) (Zaffaran (USA)) [2016/17 **c–**
c96, h92: h23g⁶ May 19] maiden hurdler/chaser, fair at best: stays 3m: acts on good to **h–**
firm and good to soft going: in headgear last 5 starts: front runner/races prominently.
Tim Vaughan

MISTY MAI (IRE) 7 b.m. Westerner – Arcanum (IRE) (Presenting) [2016/17 h20g* **c–**
h20d⁵ h19.9gᵖᵘ h25g⁵ h19.5s⁶ h25s⁵ h25.5s⁶ Mar 11] fifth foal: sister to fairly useful **h102**
chaser Mr Mercurial and fair hurdler/chaser Black Narcissus (both 2½m-25f winners): dam
unraced: winning pointer: fair hurdler: won novice at Ffos Las in May: well held only start
in chases in 2015/16 for John F. Gleeson): stays 2½m: acts on heavy going. *David Rees*

MITCD (IRE) 6 gr.m. Mastercraftsman (IRE) – Halicardia (Halling (USA)) [2016/17 h62: **h86**
h18.1m² h16.4d* h16.8s² h16.4s⁵ h16.4g⁴ h19.9g* h16.8mᶠ Apr 19] modest handicap
hurdler: won at Musselburgh in November and mares event at Sedgefield in April: stays
2½m: acts on good to soft going: often travels strongly. *George Bewley*

MIXBOY (FR) 7 gr.g. Fragrant Mix (IRE) – Leston Girl (FR) (Lesotho (USA)) [2016/17   **c138** h119: c21.2g* c16.4g* c15.8g* c20.4g^{pu} c15.5g^F Apr 22] angular gelding: fairly useful   **h–** hurdler: useful form over fences: won maiden at Cartmel in July, novice at Sedgefield in September and handicap at Musselburgh in January: stays 21f: acts on heavy going: has worn hood: front runner/races prominently. *Keith Dalgleish*

MIXCHIEVOUS 6 gr.g. Fair Mix (IRE) – Cheeky Mare (Derrylin) [2016/17 h86: h15.8d^6 **h105** h15.8d^5 h15.5d^6 h19.8v^2 h19.8s^3 h21.2s^3 Mar 2] good-topped gelding: fair maiden hurdler: stays 2½m: acts on heavy going: not straightforward. *Venetia Williams*

MIZEN MASTER (IRE) 4 b.g. Captain Rio – Nilassiba (Daylami (IRE)) [2016/17   **h97** h16d^3 h16.5g h16.3d Dec 31] angular gelding: modest maiden on Flat (stays 8.5f) and over hurdles: left John Joseph Murphy after first start. *Anabel K. Murphy*

MOABIT (GER) 5 b.g. Azamour (IRE) – Moonlight Danceuse (IRE) (Bering) [2016/17   **h132** h114p: h16.8m* h15.3m* h16.3g* h16.8d* h16.7g^5 h16.2g^{pu} Aug 20] useful hurdler: won maiden at Exeter, novice at Wincanton and handicap at Stratford, all in May, and novice at Newton Abbot in June: strong-travelling sort, will prove best at 2m with emphasis on speed: acts on good to firm and good to soft going: wears tongue tie. *Paul Nicholls*

MOCCASIN (FR) 8 b.g. Green Tune (USA) – Museum Piece (Rainbow Quest (USA))   **h–** [2016/17 h19.9d^{pu} h18.6s^{pu} Dec 1] modest on Flat, stays 1½m: showed nothing in 2 novice hurdles, visored in second. *Geoffrey Harker*

MO CHAILIN (IRE) 6 b.m. Milan – Consultation (IRE) (Camden Town) [2016/17 h103,   **h106** b78: h20g^2 h16.7d h16.8d^2 h19.4d^3 h18.6s^3 h23.1s^6 h18.9g^{pu} Apr 15] fair handicap hurdler: stays 2½m: acts on heavy going: blinkered final start. *Donald McCain*

MODELIGO (IRE) 8 b.g. Indian Danehill (IRE) – Glens Lady (IRE) (Mister Lord   **c112** (USA)) [2016/17 c98, h97: c16.5s* c17g^5 c16.5g^2 c16.5g c19.4d^4 c20s^{pu} c16v* c19.4g*   **h–** Apr 1] angular gelding: winning hurdler: fair handicap chaser: won at Worcester in May, Chepstow in February and Stratford on final start: stays 2½m: acts on heavy going: wears cheekpieces/tongue tie. *Matt Sheppard*

MODEM 7 b.g. Motivator – Alashaan (Darshaan) [2016/17 h139: h16d h16.1g^4 h16d^4 **h139** h20.5d Apr 29] useful handicap hurdler: creditable fourth of 20 in Galway Hurdle (3¼ lengths behind Clondaw Warrior) in July: unproven beyond 17f: acts on heavy going: usually wears headgear. *Mrs J. Harrington, Ireland*

MODERATOR (CZE) 7 b.g. Security Risk (USA) – Modrenka (CZE) (Laban (CZE))   **c?** [2016/17 c17.4d^2 c19.9d^2 c22.4g^6 h15.9d^5 h15.9g h18.7g^2 Apr 15] third foal: dam Czech   **h90** 19f/2¾m chase winner: modest form over hurdles: winning cross-country chaser in Czech Republic in 2014/15: left Dennis Persson in Sweden after fifth start: stays 2½m: has worn blinkers. *Arthur Whitehead*

MODULE (FR) 10 b.g. Panoramic – Before Royale (FR) (Dauphin du Bourg (FR))   **c131** [2016/17 c15.9s^4 c20.8s^{pu} c16v^{pu} Feb 25] useful-looking gelding: winning hurdler: very   **h–** smart chaser in 2013/14, lightly raced and mainly disappointing since: stays 2½m: acts on good to firm and heavy going: tried in cheekpieces/tongue tie. *Tom George*

MODULUS 8 b.g. Motivator – Wild Academy (IRE) (Royal Academy (USA)) [2016/17   **c–** h19.9g^2 h23g^4 h20.7d h23.4g^4 c24.2s^{pu} h16.6g^4 h19.9v* h19.7d^6 h16.4v* h16.8d* h20.1v*   **h108** Mar 28] part winner: fair handicap hurdler: won at Uttoxeter (novice event) in February and at Newcastle, Sedgefield (novice event) and Hexham in March: pulled up only chase start: stays 2½m: acts on heavy going: wears headgear: races prominently: often races lazily, but usually responds generously to pressure. *Peter Winks*

MODUS 7 ch.g. Motivator – Alessandra (Generous (IRE)) [2016/17 h131, b120: h15.7m^3 **h155** h16.4s^2 h15.7d h21d* h21.1g^6 h21.5g^5 Apr 29] lengthy gelding: very smart hurdler: won Lanzarote Handicap Hurdle at Kempton in January by 2¾ lengths from Templeross: good effort when 6¼ lengths sixth of 25 to Supasundae in Coral Cup (Handicap) at Cheltenham in March: stays 21f: acts on soft and good to firm going: usually wears hood: has looked tricky ride at times. *Paul Nicholls*

MOGESTIC (IRE) 8 b.g. Morozov (USA) – Crosschild (IRE) (Buckskin (FR)) [2016/17   **h102** h98: h25d* h26.4m h21.6g h21.1s h26v^4 h25s h23.1s^5 Mar 7] fair handicap hurdler: won at Warwick in May: stays 3¼m: acts on heavy going: often races towards rear. *Seamus Mullins*

MOHAAYED 5 b.g. Intikhab (USA) – Reyaada (Daylami (IRE)) [2016/17 h16g^2 h15.7s^4 **h135 p** h16.5s* h16.8g h16g^3 Apr 22] sturdy gelding: useful on Flat, stays 9.5f: useful form over hurdles: won novice at Taunton (by 14 lengths from Volpone Jelois) in February: shaped well when 2¼ lengths third of 16 to Chesterfield in Scottish Champion Hurdle (Handicap) at Ayr final start: likely to prove best at 2m: acts on soft going: wears tongue tie: usually races towards rear: open to further improvement. *Dan Skelton*

MOHAWK WARRIOR (IRE) 9 b.g. Milan – Super Aisling (IRE) (The Bart (USA)) c–
[2016/17 c20d^{pu} Jun 22] pulled up both starts in points, and in novice on chasing debut. *Seamus Mullins*

MOIDORE 8 b.g. Galileo (IRE) – Flash of Gold (Darshaan) [2016/17 h128: h24g^4 h23.3v^4 **h114**
h26s^{pu} h24.4d^6 h24.4g h15.7s^6 h23.1g^3 h24g Apr 19] good-topped gelding: handicap hurdler, fair form at best in 2016/17: stays 23f: acts on heavy going: tried in cheekpieces/tongue tie in 2016/17. *Charles Pogson*

MOLE TRAP 6 b.m. Kayf Tara – Fairly High (IRE) (Sri Pekan (USA)) [2016/17 b15.8d **h–**
b17.7d^6 h19.6d^6 Nov 19] first foal: dam (c61/h76), 2m hurdle winner, also 6f winner on Flat: **b63**
poor form in bumpers: well beaten in mares novice on hurdling debut. *Charlie Longsdon*

MOLINEAUX (IRE) 6 b.g. King's Theatre (IRE) – Steel Grey Lady (IRE) (Roselier **h105**
(FR)) [2016/17 b–: h15.3d^2 h19g^3 Mar 20] well held in bumpers: fair form when second in novice at Wincanton, much better effort over hurdles: bred to be suited by further than 2m. *Colin Tizzard*

MOLLASSES 6 b.m. Authorized (IRE) – Muscovado (USA) (Mr Greeley (USA)) **h–**
[2016/17 h–: h16.3g h16.5d Jun 10] sturdy mare: fair hurdler at best, no form in 2016/17: raced only at 2m: acts on soft going: tried in tongue tie. *Harry Whittington*

MOLLIES GENT (IRE) 9 b.g. Court Cave (IRE) – Zaffalong (IRE) (Zaffaran (USA)) **c101**
[2016/17 c24d^4 c23.8s^F c20.5g c23.8g* c23.8d^6 c24d^4 c23.8g^3 c23.8g c26.6g^5 Mar 24] **h–**
winning pointer: maiden hurdler: fair handicap chaser: won novice event at Perth in September: stays 3m: acts on soft going: tried in visor: wears tongue tie. *Paul Stafford, Ireland*

MOLLYANNA (IRE) 8 b.m. Oscar (IRE) – Baywatch Star (IRE) (Supreme Leader) **c92**
[2016/17 h93: c20.2s^2 c21.3d^5 Feb 21] mares maiden point winner: winning hurdler: better **h–**
effort (modest form) in chases when second in mares novice at Wincanton in December: stays 2¾m: acts on soft going: has worn cheekpieces, including on final start when also tongue tied. *Jamie Snowden*

MOLLY CAREW 5 b.m. Midnight Legend – Moyliscar (Terimon) [2016/17 ab16g **h108**
b16.2s h17.7v^6 h16v* h19.9d* Mar 14] fourth foal: sister to fair 2m hurdle winners In By **b–**
Midnight and Miss Night Owl (latter also bumper winner) and half-sister to modest chaser Moonlight Maggie (2m winner, by Pasternak): dam headstrong maiden chaser: no form in bumpers: fair form over hurdles: won mares novice events at Lingfield in January and Sedgefield in March: should stay further than 2½m. *Neil Mulholland*

MOLLY CHILDERS (IRE) 5 b.m. Stowaway – Hushaby (IRE) (Eurobus) [2016/17 **b96**
b16.6g^2 b15.7d^2 b16d^2 b16d^5 Mar 11] £22,000 4-y-o: sturdy mare: half-sister to several winners, including useful hurdler Gusda (2½m winner, by Lend A Hand), stayed 3m, and fairly useful hurdler/chaser Days Ahead (2m-23f winner, by Kheleyf): dam unraced: runner-up completed start in maiden points: fairly useful form when second in bumpers: in cheekpieces final start. *Stuart Edmunds*

MOLLYLIKESTOBOOGIE 7 b.m. Tobougg (IRE) – Two Aye Em (Double Trigger **h82**
(IRE)) [2016/17 b–: b16.8g h18.7d^2 h21.6g^{pu} h18.7g^3 h18.7m h15.9s^{pu} Feb 13] no form in **b–**
bumpers: poor form over hurdles: left Linda Blackford after fifth start: best effort at 19f on good to soft going: in hood/tongue tie final outing. *Nigel Twiston-Davies*

MOLLY OSCAR (IRE) 11 b.m. Oscar (IRE) – Bishop's Folly (Weld) [2016/17 c78, h–: **c84 §**
c25.5d^3 c25.7g* c25.8g^6 c25.8d^3 Jun 21] winning pointer: maiden hurdler: poor handicap **h–**
chaser: won at Plumpton in May: stays 3¼m: acts on heavy going: wears headgear: tried in tongue tie: front runner/races prominently: temperamental. *Johnny Farrelly*

MOLLYOW (IRE) 9 ch.m. Iceman – Corryvreckan (IRE) (Night Shift (USA)) [2016/17 **h85**
h19.9g* h15.9g^3 h19.9g^5 h18.7m^3 Jul 10] small, plain mare: modest handicap hurdler: won at Uttoxeter in May: stays 21f: acts on good to firm and good to soft going. *Dai Burchell*

MOLLY THE DOLLY (IRE) 6 b.m. Flemensfirth (USA) – Pistol Flash (IRE) (Pistolet **b89**
Bleu (IRE)) [2016/17 b15.8d^3 b16.8v^2 Mar 5] €24,000 3-y-o, £82,000 5-y-o: first foal: dam (h116), bumper winner/maiden hurdler (best at 2m), also 1¼m winner on Flat: winning pointer: fair form when placed in bumpers at Huntingdon (mares event) and Sedgefield. *Ian Williams*

MOLTEN BROWN 12 b.g. Needle Gun (IRE) – Molten (Ore) [2016/17 c100: c23.8m^2 **c98**
c26.2m^{pu} c25.5g^5 c23.4v^{pu} c23.8g^4 Apr 28] multiple winning pointer: modest chaser: stays 3m: acts on soft and good to firm going: wears cheekpieces. *Tony Hogarth*

MOMKINZAIN (USA) 10 b.g. Rahy (USA) – Fait Accompli (USA) (Louis Quatorze (USA)) [2016/17 h69§: h16.8g⁶ h17.2g⁶ h20.2d h20.2s⁶ h20.9d* h23.3s⁶ h22.7s c16.9d³ h19s⁶ h16.2g Apr 27] maiden pointer: poor handicap hurdler: won at Kelso in September: third in novice handicap at Musselburgh on chasing debut: stays 21f: acts on soft and good to firm going: wears headgear/tongue tie: often races towards rear: unreliable. *Lucinda Russell* — **c70 h79 §**

MONALEE (IRE) 6 b.g. Milan – Tempest Belle (IRE) (Glacial Storm (USA)) [2016/17 b18s² h22d⁴ h20s² h24v* h24g² h24d⁴ Apr 26] tall gelding: fifth foal: closely related to fair hurdler/fairly useful chaser Many Stars (3m/3¼m winner, by Oscar) and bumper winner/fair hurdler Brijomi Queen (2m winner, by King's Theatre), stayed 2½m: dam unraced half-sister to useful hurdler/chaser up to 25f Be My Belle: winning pointer: useful form in bumpers: second in maidens at Gowran and Punchestown: smart form over hurdles: won maiden at Punchestown (by 1¾ lengths from The Storyteller) in November and Surehaul Mercedes-Benz Novices' Hurdle at Clonmel (by 4¾ lengths from Battleford) in February: second in Navan Novices' Hurdle (3¾ lengths behind Death Duty) in December, and further improvement when 3½ lengths second of 15 to Penhill in Albert Bartlett Novices' Hurdle (Spa) at Cheltenham in March: below form final start: stays 3m: acts on heavy going: front runner/races prominently, often travels strongly. *Henry de Bromhead, Ireland* — **h149 b109**

MON AMI BOB 4 ch.g. Schiaparelli (GER) – Maid of Perth (Mark of Esteem (IRE)) [2016/17 b16.6g Feb 22] tailed off in bumper. *James Bethell* — **b–**

MONAR LAD (IRE) 5 b.g. Mountain High (IRE) – Cottage Lady (IRE) (Moscow Society (USA)) [2016/17 b16d⁵ b16s Mar 13] £19,000 3-y-o: good-topped gelding: first foal: dam (h108), 2m hurdle winner, half-sister to useful hurdler/smart chaser (stayed 3¼m) Bold Chief: signs of ability in bumpers: left Paul Webber after first start. *Dai Burchell* — **b–**

MONAR ROSE 5 b.m. Yeats (IRE) – Rhapsody Rose (Unfuwain (USA)) [2016/17 b15.8d b16d³ b16.7g² b17g Apr 6] lengthy, rather unfurnished mare: third foal: half-sister to useful chaser Rhapando (2½m winner, by Hernando): dam (h101), 2m/17f hurdle winner, also 9.5f winner on Flat: fair form in bumpers: wears hood: in tongue tie last 3 starts. *Ben Case* — **b92**

MONBEG AQUADUDE (IRE) 6 b.g. Flemensfirth (USA) – Mite Dash (IRE) (Anshan) [2016/17 b16s h19.5s⁵ h19.5v⁴ h20v* h20.9s⁵ Apr 3] €23,000 3-y-o, £80,000 4-y-o: fourth foal: half-brother to a winning pointer by Milan: dam unraced half-sister to fairly useful hurdler/fair chaser (19f-21f winner) She's Our Native: won Irish maiden point on debut in 2015: tailed off in bumper: fair form over hurdles: won maiden at Ffos Las in March: should stay further than 2½m. *Michael Scudamore* — **h112 b–**

MONBEG CAVE (IRE) 5 b.g. Court Cave (IRE) – Reynella Cross (IRE) (Torus) [2016/17 h16.2s⁵ h17.1d h16d h17.1g h19.3d h16.2g Apr 27] fourth on completed start in Irish points: no form over hurdles. *Martin Todhunter* — **h–**

MONBEG CHARMER (IRE) 6 br.g. Daylami (IRE) – Charming Present (IRE) (Presenting) [2016/17 b100: h20g* h19.7d² h23.8g* h24.7gᵖᵘ Apr 7] lengthy, angular gelding: type to make a chaser: won Irish point on debut: bumper winner: fairly useful form over hurdles: won maiden at Worcester in October and novice at Musselburgh in February: ran no sort of race in Grade 1 event at Aintree final outing: stays 3m: usually leads/races freely. *Charlie Longsdon* — **h127**

MONBEG DOLLY (IRE) 7 ch.m. Flemensfirth (USA) – Laughing Lesa (IRE) (Bob Back (USA)) [2016/17 h100: h20.1g May 24] placed in Irish mares maiden points: winning hurdler, lightly raced and fair form at best: will be suited by further than 2½m. *Alistair Whillans* — **h–**

MONBEG FARMER (IRE) 6 b.g. Arcadio (GER) – Family Affair (IRE) (Moscow Society (USA)) [2016/17 b16.7d h16.7g⁶ h20.6g⁵ h24g² h25m⁴ h25mᵖᵘ Oct 30] €13,000 3-y-o, £8,000 5-y-o: third foal: dam (c95/h83) 2¼m hurdle winner: fourth on last 2 of 3 starts in Irish maiden points: tailed off in bumper: modest form over hurdles: stays 25f: acts on good to firm going. *Olly Williams* — **h98 b–**

MONBEG GOLD (IRE) 7 b.g. Gold Well – Little Hand (IRE) (Carroll House) [2016/17 h126: c21.1s² c23.4d c23.4s⁵ c20.5g⁵ c24.1g⁴ Apr 15] rangy gelding: point winner: fairly useful hurdler: fairly useful form in handicap chases, second in novice event at Fontwell: stays 23f: acts on heavy going: in headgear last 4 starts. *Jonjo O'Neill* — **c126 h–**

MONBEG NOTORIOUS (IRE) 6 b.g. Milan – Borleagh Princess (IRE) (Presenting) [2016/17 b18s³ b20d* h22.2g* h24s² h22.5v* Mar 19] €30,000 3-y-o, £155,000 4-y-o: third foal: half-brother to modest 19f hurdle winner Katie's Hen (by Shantou): dam (h84) — **h131 b108**

lightly raced in bumpers/over hurdles: won completed start in points: useful form in bumpers: won maiden at Tipperary (by 15 lengths from Indrik) in October: also useful over hurdles, and won maiden at Down Royal in November and novice at Navan (by 5½ lengths from Augustin) on final start: stays 3m: wore blinkers at Navan: front runner/races prominently. *Gordon Elliott, Ireland*

MONBEG OSCAR (IRE) 5 b.g. Oscar (IRE) – Simply Joyful (Idiot's Delight) [2016/17 **h111 p** b15.8v⁴ h15.8d³ h18.6s² Jan 18] €17,000 3-y-o, £90,000 4-y-o: half-brother to fairly useful **b89** hurdler/chaser Hoopy (2½m-25f winner, by Presenting) and bumper winner The Unsub (by Flemensfirth): dam, placed in points, half-sister to useful hurdler/chaser (stayed 3¾m) Papo Kharisma: won Irish maiden point on debut: fourth only start in bumpers: fair form when placed in maiden and novice over hurdles: will be suited by at least 2½m: remains capable of better. *Evan Williams*

MONBEG RIVER (IRE) 8 b.g. Indian River (FR) – So Pretty (IRE) (Presenting) **c129** [2016/17 c132, h–: c15.2m² c15.9g⁵ c19.9sᵇᵈ c19.4s³ Jan 24] workmanlike gelding: maiden **h–** hurdler: fairly useful handicap chaser: best around 2m: acts on good to firm and heavy going: in tongue tie last 2 starts: usually travels strongly. *Martin Todhunter*

MONBEG WORLDWIDE (IRE) 5 b.g. Lucarno (USA) – Molly Duffy (IRE) (Oscar **b113** (IRE)) [2016/17 b16v* b16v* b16v* Feb 26] €40,000 3-y-o: first foal: dam, unraced, out of half-sister to Champion Hurdle winners Granville Again and Morley Street: won Irish maiden point on debut: useful form in bumpers: won at Roscommon (maiden) in October and Cork in November: off 3 months, 4/11, completed hat-trick in 5-runner event at Naas by neck from Scheu Time: will be suited by at least 2½m. *Gordon Elliott, Ireland*

MONDA'S LEGACY 4 b.f. Tamure (IRE) – Monda (Danzig Connection (USA)) **b–** [2016/17 b16.8d b16.5m⁶ Apr 27] third foal: dam 7f winner: showed nothing in bumpers. *Martin Hill*

MONDAY CLUB 4 ch.g. Strategic Prince – Support Fund (IRE) (Intikhab (USA)) **h97** [2016/17 h16s³ h15.8v³ h16s⁵ h15.5g Jan 24] neat gelding: fair on Flat, stays 1¼m: modest form over hurdles: in cheekpieces final start. *Dominic Ffrench Davis*

MONDELLO (GER) 6 b.g. Soldier Hollow – Mandrella (GER) (Surumu (GER)) **h97** [2016/17 h85: h16.8gᵖᵘ h19.9g² h19.6m h16.8gᵖᵘ h23.9g⁴ h21.4s² h21.44d⁶ h20v⁶ Mar 19] modest maiden hurdler: stays 3m: acts on soft going: in headgear last 5 starts: wears tongue tie: usually races nearer last than first, often travels strongly. *Richard Woollacott*

MONDERON (FR) 10 b.g. Laveron – Lomonde (FR) (Great Lakes) [2016/17 c102p, h–: **c94** c26.3gᵇᵈ c25.2sᵖᵘ c22.7g³ c23.9sᵖᵘ h19.8f⁴ h21.6g³ Apr 26] close-coupled gelding: modest **h94** handicap hurdler: modest maiden chaser: stays 23f: acts on heavy going: has worn headgear, including in 2016/17: in tongue tie fourth start. *Fergal O'Brien*

MONDLICHT (USA) 7 b.g. Malibu Moon (USA) – Moonlight Cruise (USA) (Silver **h104 §** Deputy (CAN)) [2016/17 h103§: h22.1m⁶ h17.2m³ h25.4g³ h22.1d² h20.1g² h19.9d³ h22.7dᵖᵘ Apr 10] fair hurdler: won novice at Musselburgh in November: stays 2¾m: acts on heavy going: wears headgear: temperamental. *James Moffatt*

MONDO CANE (IRE) 10 b.g. Beneficial – La Vita E Bella (FR) (Le Nain Jaune (FR)) **c–** [2016/17 c105, h105: c20.3gᵖᵘ h20.3gᵖᵘ Jun 7] fair handicap hurdler/chaser in 2015/16, **h–** pulled up both starts in 2016/17: stays 27f: acts on heavy going: wears headgear: often races prominently. *Charles Pogson*

MON ELDORADO (FR) 5 b.g. Gentlewave (IRE) – Miryea (FR) (Shining Steel) **b90 p** [2016/17 b16d⁶ b16v³ Mar 21] €80,000 3-y-o: seventh foal: half-brother to 2 winners on Flat in France, including 9f/1¼m winner Magany (by American Post): dam, French 5.5f-1m winner, half-sister to dam of smart hurdler/fairly useful chaser (2m-2½m winner) Rodock: fair form in bumpers: in hood, better effort when third in maiden at Clonmel: left Paul Morgan after first start: open to further improvement. *Gordon Elliott, Ireland*

MONETAIRE (FR) 11 b.g. Anabaa (USA) – Monitrice (FR) (Groom Dancer (USA)) **c126** [2016/17 c123, h122: c22.6g³ c19.9g⁵ Apr 15] compact gelding: winning hurdler: handicap **h–** chaser, fairly useful nowadays: best form up to 21f: acts on good to firm and heavy going: has worn headgear/tongue tie. *David Pipe*

MONET MOOR 8 b.m. Morpeth – Miracle Monarch (Elegant Monarch) [2016/17 h–: **c–** h18.5m h23.9gᵖᵘ c24.2d Mar 21] sturdy mare: winning pointer: no show over hurdles: well **h–** held in novice handicap on chasing debut. *Jimmy Frost*

MONEY FOR NOTHING 8 b.g. Kayf Tara – Top of The Dee (Rakaposhi King) **c94 §** [2016/17 c99§, h–: c20.3v³ c15.7d² c16.4dᵖᵘ h15.7s⁴ Mar 8] lengthy gelding: modest **h88 §** maiden hurdler/chaser: left Harriet Bethell after first start: stays 2½m: acts on heavy going: usually wears hood: wears tongue tie: temperamental (has found little). *Tristan Davidson*

MONEY MAID (IRE) 9 ch.m. Blueprint (IRE) – Maid of Music (IRE) (Orchestra) **c109**
[2016/17 h99: h21d⁴ c20.1s² c24.2s² c25.2sᵖᵘ c21.3d* Feb 21] small, plain mare: modest **h90**
maiden hurdler: fair form over fences: won novice handicap at Wetherby final start: stays
3m: acts on heavy going. *Graeme McPherson*

MONEYSTOWN (IRE) 7 b.m. Touch of Land (FR) – Karinga Duff (Karinga Bay) **c55**
[2016/17 h17.7v h15.9s h20.5s³ c21.1g⁴ Apr 12] fifth foal: half-sister to a winning pointer **h61**
by Subtle Power: dam unraced: off mark in Irish maiden points at third attempt: little
impact over hurdles/in novice chase. *Linda Jewell*

MONEY TALKS 7 br.g. Motivator – Mone Mogul (Sakhee (USA)) [2016/17 c102, h–: **c91**
c17.4d⁵ c19.7g⁴ h19.1gᵖᵘ h16g h20.5m² Apr 17] workmanlike gelding: fair handicap **h103**
hurdler: modest maiden chaser: stays 21f: acts on soft and good to firm going: tried in
headgear: has worn tongue tie, including in 2016/17. *Michael Madgwick*

MONFALCONE (GER) 12 b.g. Big Shuffle (USA) – Molto In Forma (GER) (Surumu **c78**
(GER)) [2016/17 h17.1g⁴ c22.4g⁵ h23.9m* h17.1g² c20.9g⁴ c22.4g³ h16g⁴ Mar 17] 11f **h104**
winner on Flat: winning hurdler/chaser in Scandinavia, fair form when winning minor
event over hurdles at Gothenburg in July: left T. Ellefsen after sixth start: stays 3m: acts on
good to firm and good to soft going: wears headgear: tried in tongue tie. *Rune Haugen*

MONFASS (IRE) 6 b.g. Trans Island – Ajo Green (IRE) (Moscow Society (USA)) **h107**
[2016/17 h82: h16.2m⁶ h15.6g⁴ h15.6g⁵ h16.6s* h16d h16g Apr 23] fair form over hurdles:
won novice handicap at Doncaster in March: raced at 2m: acts on soft going: has worn
hood, including in 2016/17: often races towards rear. *Rose Dobbin*

MONKEY KINGDOM 9 b.g. King's Theatre (IRE) – Blast Freeze (IRE) (Lafontaine **c119 §**
(USA)) [2016/17 c131, h–: c19.9g³ c25dᵖᵘ c19.4v⁴ Jun 28] tall, angular gelding: winning **h–**
hurdler: fairly useful handicap chaser: seemingly stays 3m: acts on heavy going: wears
headgear/tongue tie: temperamental. *Rebecca Curtis*

MONKEY PUZZLE 5 ch.g. Sulamani (IRE) – Hunca Munca (IRE) (Presenting) **h115**
[2016/17 h19.4g² Dec 29] £42,000 4-y-o: fifth foal: half-brother to bumper winner/smart
hurdler Presenting Percy (2m-3m winner, by Sir Percy): dam, winning pointer, half-sister
to useful hurdler/chaser (stayed 29f) Western Charmer: runner-up in Irish maiden point:
3/1, fairly useful form when 1½ lengths second to Just Milly in novice at Doncaster on
hurdling debut. *Oliver Sherwood*

MONKHOUSE (IRE) 7 b.g. Scorpion (IRE) – Gold Shot (Polish Precedent (USA)) **c–**
[2016/17 h110: h21g⁴ h23.1d² c24gᵖᵘ h23.1m⁶ h21.2v⁵ h25d⁶ h20.6gᵖᵘ Mar 27] rangy **h94**
gelding: modest maiden hurdler: pulled up only outing over fences: should have proved
suited by 2¾m+: acted on soft going: in headgear last 5 starts: dead. *Kim Bailey*

MONKSHOOD (IRE) 5 br.g. Stowaway – Flirthing Around (IRE) (Flemensfirth (USA)) **h115 p**
[2016/17 h19v⁴ h20s³ b16.2v* Feb 16] €78,000 3-y-o: first foal: dam (c100/h108), **b106**
bumper/2m hurdle winner, sister to fairly useful hurdler/chaser (2½m-3m winner) Ernst
Blofeld: won maiden bumper at Clonmel (by 12 lengths from Arvico Bleu) on final start:
fairly useful form when in frame in maiden hurdles at Limerick and Navan: will stay
2¾m+: should do better over hurdles. *Gordon Elliott, Ireland*

MONKSLAND (IRE) 10 b.g. Beneficial – Cush Novel (IRE) (Executive Perk) [2016/17 **c143**
c150, h147: c22.5d* c24gᶠ c20d³ h20d⁶ h20d² h21.1g⁴ Mar 15] useful-looking gelding: **h147**
smart hurdler: 66/1, best effort of 2016/17 when 5½ lengths fourth of 25 to Supasundae in
Coral Cup (Handicap) at Cheltenham final outing: smart chaser: won minor event at
Galway in October by head from Marinero: stays 3m: acts on heavy going: wore hood in
2016/17. *Noel Meade, Ireland*

MON PALOIS (FR) 5 b.g. Muhaymin (USA) – Gastinaise (FR) (Cadoudal (FR)) **b98**
[2016/17 b16s* b15.7d⁴ Feb 26] sixth foal: dam, French 2m hurdle winner, half-sister to
very smart hurdler (winner up to 2½m) Mr Thriller and smart hurdler up to 3m Gaspara: off
the mark in Irish points at second attempt: fairly useful form in bumpers: won at Wetherby
in February: will stay 2½m. *Kim Bailey*

MON PARRAIN (FR) 11 b.g. Trempolino (USA) – Kadaina (FR) (Kadalko (FR)) **c122 §**
[2016/17 c141§, h–: c23g⁵ c25.5s* c20v² c25.8m⁵ Apr 15] lengthy, useful-looking gelding: **h–**
has had breathing operation: maiden hurdler: fairly useful chaser nowadays: won hunter
at Fontwell in February: stays 3¼m: acts on heavy going: wears headgear/tongue tie:
unreliable. *Paul Nicholls*

MON PORT (IRE) 5 b.g. Scorpion (IRE) – Sounds Charming (IRE) (Presenting) **b86**
[2016/17 b16.3g⁴ b15.8s b15.8m² Apr 18] €32,000 3-y-o: fourth foal: brother to useful
hurdler/chaser In The Rough (2½m-25f winner): dam unraced half-sister to fairly useful
chaser (stayed 25f) The Reverend: fair form in bumpers. *Ben De Haan*

MONROCCO 4 b.f. Shirocco (GER) – Molly Flight (FR) (Saint Cyrien (FR)) [2016/17 **b—**
b16g⁶ Apr 17] second foal: half-sister to fair hurdler/fairly useful chaser Return Flight
(2m-21f winner, by Kayf Tara): dam unraced sister to Prix La Haye Jousselin winners
Sunny Flight and Golden Flight: tailed off in mares bumper. *Kim Bailey*

MONSART (IRE) 5 gr.g. Echo of Light – Monet's Lady (IRE) (Daylami (IRE)) [2016/17 **h91**
h79: h16.3m⁴ h20.7g Nov 8] lightly-raced maiden over hurdles, modest form at best.
Shaun Lycett

MONSIEUR ARKADIN (FR) 6 b.g. Dream Well (FR) – Quenta des Bordes (FR) **h104**
(Bateau Rouge) [2016/17 b15.8g* h19.9d⁴ h21.3d⁴ h25.3s³ h26.4g² Apr 15] €40,000 3-y-o, **b92**
£27,000 4-y-o: angular, rather lightly-made gelding: first foal: dam (c138/h134), French
2¼m/19f hurdle/chase winner, half-sister to winning hurdle/chaser Utopie des Bordes
(stayed 3m): winning pointer: won bumper at Huntingdon in May: fair form over hurdles:
stays 3¼m: often races prominently. *Tim Vaughan*

MONSIEUR CO (FR) 4 b.g. Turgeon (USA) – Cayras Style (FR) (Trempolino (USA)) **c121 p**
[2016/17 h16.9s² h16.9d* h17.4d⁴ h17.9s h17.9s⁶ c18.9g² c17.4v* h15.3s* h19v⁴ Feb 24] **h128**
fourth foal: brother to useful hurdler/fair chaser Pur Style (17f winner) and half-brother
to 2 winners, including fair French hurdler/fairly useful chaser Styline (17f-2½m winner,
by Martaline): dam French 17f-19f chase winner: fairly useful hurdler: won juvenile at
Nancy in May and novice at Wincanton in January: fourth in Prix Aguado at Auteuil
(7¼ lengths behind Kalifko) in June: fairly useful form over fences: won 3-y-o event at
Enghien in November (left Guillaume Macaire after): stays 19f: acts on heavy going: in
tongue tie last 2 starts: open to further improvement over fences. *Paul Nicholls*

MONSIEUR DARSI (IRE) 7 b.g. Darsi (FR) – Durgams Delight (IRE) (Durgam **h—**
(USA)) [2016/17 b75: h21.7sᵖᵘ Dec 19] showed little in 2 bumpers and a novice hurdle.
Philip Hobbs

MONSIEUR GIBRALTAR (FR) 6 ch.g. Spirit One (FR) – Palabras de Amor (FR) **c131**
(Rock of Gibraltar (IRE)) [2016/17 h120: c20.5g² c17.4g² c16.3d⁴ c19.2g² c21.4gᶠ c22.6g² **h—**
c16.5g⁴ c16.1g* c21m* c24.5d⁶ Apr 28] good-topped gelding: easy winner of both point
starts: winning hurdler: useful chaser: won hunters at Taunton in February and Ascot in
April: left Paul Nicholls after seventh start: stays 21f: acts on good to firm and heavy going:
blinkered fourth to seventh starts: has worn tongue tie, including in 2016/17: often travels
strongly. *Mrs Rose Loxton*

MONSIEUR JOURDAIN (IRE) 11 b.g. Royal Applause – Palwina (FR) (Unfuwain **c106**
(USA)) [2016/17 c108, h—: c23.8g² Apr 28] sturdy gelding: multiple winning pointer: **h—**
winning hurdler: fair hunter chaser: stays 27f: acts on good to firm and heavy going: wears
cheekpieces. *W. H. Easterby*

MONTALBANO 5 ch.g. Monsieur Bond (IRE) – Alpen Glen (Halling (USA)) [2016/17 **h138**
h20.2d* h20g⁵ h16s³ h16g* Apr 28] useful on Flat, stays 15f: useful form over hurdles: won
C. Ferland, won maiden at Leopardstown in December and novice at Punchestown final
start, latter by neck from Riven Light: also ran well when 4¼ lengths third to Bleu Berry in
Rathbarry & Glenview Studs Novices' Hurdle at Fairyhouse: stays 2½m: acts on soft
going: wears hood. *W. P. Mullins, Ireland*

MONTANA BELLE (IRE) 7 b.m. High Chaparral (IRE) – Stiletta (Dancing Brave **h119**
(USA)) [2016/17 h16.2d⁴ h16.2d² h16v* h16s⁶ h16.8g Mar 16] good-topped mare: bumper
winner: fairly useful form over hurdles: won mares maiden at Fairyhouse in January: raced
around 2m: acts on heavy going: wears tongue tie: front runner/races prominently. *Henry
de Bromhead, Ireland*

MONTBAZON (FR) 10 b.g. Alberto Giacometti (IRE) – Duchesse Pierji (FR) (Cadoudal **h—**
(FR)) [2016/17 h121: h16.3v Mar 4] lengthy gelding: one-time smart hurdler, deteriorated
considerably: unproven beyond 17f: tried in blinkers: reportedly retired. *Alan King*

MONT CHOISY (FR) 7 b.g. Vic Toto (FR) – Rhapsodie St Eloi (FR) (Ragmar (FR)) **h116 x**
[2016/17 h129, b91: h23.3d h23g⁵ h23.6g h26sᵖᵘ Jan 26] sturdy gelding: winning pointer:
fairly useful handicap hurdler: stays 23f: acts on good to soft going: often leads: often let
down by jumping. *Nigel Twiston-Davies*

MONT DES AVALOIRS (FR) 4 b.g. Blue Bresil (FR) – Abu Dhabi (FR) (Saint Cyrien **b90 p**
(FR)) [2016/17 b16g² Apr 8] second foal: brother to useful hurdler/smart chaser Le Prezien
(2m-2¼m winner): dam French maiden (placed around 2m over hurdles): 2/1, shaped with

promise when 9 lengths second of 9 to Truckers Lodge in bumper at Chepstow on debut: sure to progress. *Paul Nicholls*

MONTE WILDHORN (IRE) 9 b.g. Old Vic – Miss Lloyds (IRE) (Take Risks (FR)) **c88** [2016/17 h113: c18.2dᵖᵘ c15.9s⁴ c18.2g⁶ h16v⁴ h17.7g⁴ h20.5m⁴ Apr 16] handicap hurdler, **h83** poor nowadays: modest maiden chaser: stays 21f: acts on good to firm and heavy going: has worn cheekpieces/tongue tie, including in 2016/17. *David Bridgwater*

MONTRACHET MIX (FR) 4 gr.g. Al Namix (FR) – La Collancelle (FR) (Sassanian **h–** (USA)) [2016/17 h16s h16g Dec 27] good-topped gelding: showed little in 2 juvenile hurdles. *Dan Skelton*

MONT ROYALE 9 b.g. Hurricane Run (IRE) – Wild Academy (IRE) (Royal Academy **c125** (USA)) [2016/17 c126, h121: c19.4g³ c20g* c20.9m⁵ c23.8dᵘʳ Dec 21] good-topped **h–** gelding: fairly useful hurdler: fairly useful handicap chaser: won at Worcester in September: barely stays 23f: acts on soft and good to firm going: has worn headgear. *Jonjo O'Neill*

MONTY'S AWARD (IRE) 5 b.g. Oscar (IRE) – Montys Miss (IRE) (Presenting) **b103** [2016/17 b16g* b16.6g⁴ Feb 22] €55,000 3-y-o: fifth foal: brother to hurdler/chaser Montys Meadow (2m/2½m winner) and hurdler Minella Awards (2½m/3m winner), both useful: dam, unraced, out of half-sister to dams of top-class staying chaser Harbour Pilot and Grand National winner Monty's Pass: fairly useful form when winning maiden at Worcester in October, easily better effort in bumpers: will stay at least 2½m. *Charlie Longsdon*

MONTYS MEADOW (IRE) 9 b.g. Oscar (IRE) – Montys Miss (IRE) (Presenting) **c144** [2016/17 c141p, h–: h24sᵘʳ c19.5v² c25d c20v⁴ Feb 18] useful hurdler at best: useful **h–** handicap chaser: ½-length second of 16 to Westerner Point at Limerick in December: stays 25f: best form on heavy going. *James Joseph Mangan, Ireland*

MONTY'S REVENGE (IRE) 12 b.g. Bob's Return (IRE) – Native Bavard (IRE) (Be **c– §** My Native (USA)) [2016/17 c78§, h–: c24.2gᵖᵘ c24vᵖᵘ Jun 20] lengthy gelding: winning **h–** hurdler: poor handicap chaser: stays 3¼m: acts on good to firm and heavy going: wears headgear: usually leads: unreliable. *Martin Keighley*

MONYJEAN (FR) 6 b.g. Califet (FR) – Rose Beryl (FR) (Lost World (IRE)) [2016/17 **c–** c–, h–: h20.6sᵖᵘ Feb 7] strong gelding: winning hurdler: no form since 2014/15, including **h–** over fences: in tongue tie last 2 starts. *Fergal O'Brien*

MONZINO (USA) 9 b.g. More Than Ready (USA) – Tasso's Magic Roo (USA) (Tasso **c64 x** (USA)) [2016/17 c–, h65: h16.7d⁶ h24gᵖᵘ h15.7g c21.2g⁴ c16.3g⁴ h20s⁵ Nov 15] **h– §** workmanlike gelding: little form over hurdles and fences (sketchy jumper). *Michael Chapman*

MOOJANED (IRE) 6 b.g. Raven's Pass (USA) – Mufradat (IRE) (Desert Prince (IRE)) **h95** [2016/17 h–: h16.3m³ May 15] modest maiden hurdler: likely to prove best around 2m: acts on good to firm going. *David Evans*

MOON ARROW (IRE) 4 b.g. Authorized (IRE) – Moon Sister (IRE) (Cadeaux **h100** Genereux) [2016/17 h15.7s² h16.2d⁵ h16m⁶ Apr 13] dam half-sister to useful hurdler/smart chaser (stayed 3m) Tarxien: modest maiden on firm, stays 11f: fair form over hurdles: best effort when second in juvenile at Catterick in February: wore hood final start. *Michael Blake*

MOONDAY SUN (USA) 8 gr.g. Mizzen Mast (USA) – Storm Dove (USA) (Storm Bird **h126** (CAN)) [2016/17 h16.3m⁴ h16.7g³ h16.7d* h16m* h16.2s³ h15.7m* h15.3m² Oct 14] fairly useful on Flat, stays 1¼m: fairly useful form over hurdles: won maiden at Bangor and handicap at Worcester in August, and handicap at Towcester in October: raced around 2m: acts on soft and good to firm going: sometimes in hood: has worn tongue tie: races towards rear: has joined Gordon Elliott. *Nigel Twiston-Davies*

MOON INDIGO 11 b.g. Sadler's Wells (USA) – Solo de Lune (IRE) (Law Society **c77** (USA)) [2016/17 h24.3s h24.3v c21.6vᵖᵘ c21.6d Apr 10] winning hurdler/chaser: very **h–** lightly raced and little impact since 2011/12: stays 2¾m: acts on soft going: in headgear last 2 starts, in tongue tie last 4. *Rebecca Menzies*

MOONLIGHT FLYER (IRE) 5 b.g. Broadway Flyer (USA) – Monteleena (IRE) **h65** (Montelimar (USA)) [2016/17 b16g h15.8v⁶ h16s h15.3d Feb 18] tailed off in maiden **b–** bumper: poor form over hurdles: will stay at least 2½m. *Jeremy Scott*

Professor Caroline Tisdall & Bryan Drew's "Moon Racer"

MOONLIGHT HAZE 6 b.g. Helissio (FR) – Bella Haze (Midnight Legend) [2016/17 **b—**
b15.8v Dec 12] tailed off in maiden bumper (wore hood). *Phillip Dando*

MOONLONE LANE (IRE) 10 b.g. Oscar (IRE) – Shandarr (IRE) (John French) **c108**
[2016/17 c94, h103: h20g h20g c20.3s^{ur} c20s* Dec 26] fair hurdler at best, well held first 2 **h—**
starts in 2016/17: fair handicap chaser: won at Down Royal in December: stays 21f: acts on
heavy going: usually wears headgear: has worn tongue tie. *Paul Stafford, Ireland*

MOON OVER RIO (IRE) 6 b.m. Captain Rio – Moonchild (GER) (Acatenango **h80**
(GER)) [2016/17 h—: h15.8g^2 h15.7g h16.8s^F h15.7d^6 Jan 25] poor maiden hurdler: raced
around 2m: front runner/races prominently. *Ben Haslam*

MOON RACER (IRE) 8 b.g. Saffron Walden (FR) – Angel's Folly (Wesaam (USA)) **h133**
[2016/17 b122+: b16d^2 h16.2s* h16.4s* h16.4g^{pu} h16.5g^6 Apr 7] good-topped gelding:
smart form in bumpers: useful form over hurdles: won novice at Perth in September and
Sharp Novices' Hurdle at Cheltenham (by 2¼ lengths from Mirsaale) in November: ran as
though all wasn't well in Champion Hurdle at Cheltenham and Top Novices' Hurdle at
Aintree last 2 starts: raced at 2m: acts on soft going: usually races prominently. *David Pipe*

MOONSHINE LAD (IRE) 9 b.g. Milan – Parsons Term (IRE) (The Parson) [2016/17 **c131**
c20s^{ur} h20s^2 c21.5d^4 c20s^{ur} c20s^3 Jan 21] tall gelding: maiden point winner: fairly useful **h125**
hurdler: useful form over fences: best effort when fourth in maiden at Fairyhouse (9½
lengths behind Martello Tower) in December: stays 21f: acts on soft going: often races
towards rear. *Gordon Elliott, Ireland*

MOON TRIP 8 b.g. Cape Cross (IRE) – Fading Light (King's Best (USA)) [2016/17 h94: **h64** h20.5v⁶ Jan 2] handicap hurdler, modest at best: stays 3m: acts on heavy going: tried in cheekpieces/tongue tie: usually races towards rear. *Geoffrey Deacon*

MOONTRIPPER 8 b.m. Doyen (IRE) – Moon Spinner (Elmaamul (USA)) [2016/17 **h–** h78, b71: h20g⁰ᵖᵘ May 28] winning pointer: poor maiden hurdler. *Phillip Dando*

MOORLANDS GEORGE 9 b.g. Grape Tree Road – Sandford Springs (USA) **c106** (Robellino (USA)) [2016/17 c99, h–: c24.1g* c26.1s² c23g c25.8m³ c25.8g* c24.2g⁶ Nov **h–** 9] maiden chaser: fair handicap chaser: won at Bangor in May and Newton Abbot in October: stays 3¼m: acts on soft and good to firm going: wears tongue tie. *Jeremy Scott*

MOORLANDS JACK 12 b.g. Cloudings (IRE) – Sandford Springs (USA) (Robellino **c108 §** (USA)) [2016/17 c119, h–: c19.9g⁶ c19.4g c20g⁰ᵖᵘ c20.9s³ c19.9d⁶ c20s⁵ c20vᵖᵘ c21m* Apr **h– §** 15] strong gelding: winning hurdler: fair handicap chaser: won at Newton Abbot final start: stays 2¾m: acts on soft and good to firm going: wears headgear: tried in tongue tie: often races towards rear: unreliable. *Jeremy Scott*

MOORLANDS MIST 10 gr.g. Fair Mix (IRE) – Sandford Springs (USA) (Robellino **c106 §** (USA)) [2016/17 c90, h123: c24sᵖᵘ c20.9s⁴ c25.3v⁵ c24.1s³ c25.1v⁴ Mar 9] good-topped **h–** gelding: fairly useful hurdler: fair maiden chaser: stays 3m: acts on heavy going: has worn headgear, including in 2016/17: tried in tongue tie: temperamental. *Evan Williams*

MOORSTONE 5 b.m. Manduro (GER) – Pan Galactic (USA) (Lear Fan (USA)) [2016/17 **b87** b–: b17.7d³ b17.7d⁶ b16.4s Nov 12] compact mare: fair form in bumpers: won mares event at Fontwell in September: out of depth final start. *Giles Bravery*

MOORSTOWN (IRE) 7 b.g. Oscar (IRE) – Glacial Princess (IRE) (Glacial Storm **c88** (USA)) [2016/17 h79: h20d c24.1s* c24.2s⁶ Dec 26] winning Irish pointer: lightly-raced **h–** maiden over hurdles: modest form over fences: won novice handicap at Bangor in November: bled next time: stays 3m: acts on soft going. *Lucinda Russell*

MOOTABAR (IRE) 10 gr.g. Verglas (IRE) – Melanzane (Arazi (USA)) [2016/17 h57: **h–** h16.4vᵖᵘ h20.6vᵖᵘ h19.9gᵖᵘ Mar 29] good-topped gelding: handicap hurdler, modest at best: no form in 2016/17: has worn visor. *Chris Fairhurst*

MORAL HAZARD (IRE) 8 br.g. Milan – Maria Thai (FR) (Siam (USA)) [2016/17 **c107** c23g² c23.6mᵖᵘ Apr 28] multiple point winner: once-raced hurdler: fair form when second **h–** in maiden hunter at Taunton on chasing debut: disappointing next time. *Miss Beverley Thomas*

MORE BUCK'S (IRE) 7 ch.g. Presenting – Buck's Blue (FR) (Epervier Bleu) [2016/17 **c131** c114, h112: c19.2s* c20d² c21.1s* c24.2s* c24g⁴ c20.8sꟳ c19.9sᵖᵘ c21.4m³ Apr 9] well- **h–** made gelding: fair hurdler: useful chaser: won novice handicaps at Fontwell in October and November, and amateurs handicap at Sandown in December: reportedly lame final outing: stays 3m: acts on heavy going: has worn hood: wears tongue tie: usually leads. *Paul Nicholls*

MOREECE (IRE) 8 b.g. Chevalier (IRE) – Jumbo Romance (IRE) (Tagula (IRE)) **c101** [2016/17 h82: h19.6g³ h20.5g c23.6m⁵ Apr 28] winning pointer: modest maiden hurdler: **h85** fair form when fifth in novice hunter at Chepstow on chasing debut: left Tim Vaughan after second start: stays 3m: acts on soft and good to firm going: in headgear in 2016/17. *J. Lean*

MORELLO ROYALE (IRE) 7 b.m. King's Theatre (IRE) – Mystic Cherry (IRE) **c–** (Alderbrook) [2016/17 h134: h24.5s⁴ c20sꟳ h24.5g³ h19.8s h24.2d² h21.1g h24.7g Apr 8] **h136** compact mare: useful handicap hurdler: second at Newbury (1½ lengths behind Tobefair) in February: fell first in listed mares event at Warwick on chasing debut: stays 3m: acts on good to firm and heavy going: wears tongue tie: often races towards rear. *Colin Tizzard*

MORE MADNESS (IRE) 10 b.g. Dr Massini (IRE) – Angelic Angel (IRE) (Phardante **c85** (FR)) [2016/17 c97, h86: c26.2d⁴ c24.2d⁴ c25.5g³ h23.1gꟳ h24g⁴ h23.3s³ h24.3d⁶ h24.1s⁵ **h81** h25.3d⁶ Jan 1] poor maiden hurdler: modest handicap chaser: left N. W. Alexander after first start: stays 3m: acts on heavy going: wears headgear. *Julia Brooke*

MORE OF THAT (IRE) 9 b.g. Beneficial – Guigone (FR) (Esprit du Nord (USA)) **c159** [2016/17 c150+, h–: c20.4sᵖᵘ c19.9d³ c24d⁶ c24.3sᵘʳ c26.3g⁶ c34.3dᵖᵘ Apr 8] strong, **h–** lengthy gelding: winning hurdler: very smart chaser: yet to be asked for full effort when unseated rider last in Irish Gold Cup won by Sizing John at Leopardstown in February: respectable never-nearer sixth of 13 to Sizing John in Cheltenham Gold Cup following month: not persevered with once held (pulled up before last) in Grand National at Aintree final outing: stays 3¼m: acts on heavy going: in cheekpieces last 4 starts: tried in tongue tie. *Jonjo O'Neill*

MORESTEAD (IRE) 12 ch.g. Traditionally (USA) – Itsy Bitsy Betsy (USA) (Beau **c–** §
Genius (CAN)) [2016/17 c17.4d May 12] good-topped gelding: winning hurdler: poor **h–** §
chaser nowadays: stays 2¾m: acts on good to firm and heavy going: usually wears
headgear: has worn tongue tie: ungenuine. *Brendan Powell*

MORE THAN LUCK (IRE) 6 br.g. Gothland (FR) – Pretty Impressive (IRE) **h97**
(Presenting) [2016/17 h24d⁵ h21d h19.7s h25.5v⁴ h27vᵖᵘ Mar 5] €7,500 3-y-o: first foal:
dam second in point: third completed start in points: modest form over hurdles: will stay
long distances: acts on heavy going: in cheekpieces last 2 starts. *Sam Thomas*

MORGA (IRE) 7 b.m. Whipper (USA) – Langfuhrina (USA) (Langfuhr (CAN)) [2016/17 **h135**
h16d h16.1g⁴ h16.2d² h16d³ h16d² h16d Dec 27] useful handicap hurdler: good effort
when ¾-length second of 17 to Waxies Dargle at Fairyhouse in December: raced around
2m: acts on soft going: has worn hood, including in 2016/17: often races prominently.
Desmond McDonogh, Ireland

MORGAN (IRE) 5 br.g. Big Bad Bob (IRE) – Gilt Ridden (IRE) (Heron Island (IRE)) **h131**
[2016/17 b19d⁹* b16g³ h16.8s⁵ h16v* h16d² h16g⁴ Apr 28] €170,000 3-y-o: sixth foal: half- **b104**
brother to useful hurdler/very smart chaser Johns Spirit (2m-2½m winner, by Gold Well),
useful hurdler/very smart chaser The Game Changer (2m-2½m winner) and useful 2m
hurdle winner Mad Jack Mytton (latter pair by Arcadio): dam unraced: fairly useful form
in bumpers: won at Cork in October: also useful over hurdles: won maiden at Naas in
February: good second in novice at Limerick (6½ lengths behind Lachares) in March: will
prove suited by 2½m: in hood last 4 starts. *Gordon Elliott, Ireland*

MORGAN'S BAY 12 b.g. Karinga Bay – Dubai Dolly (IRE) (Law Society (USA)) **c57 x**
[2016/17 c97x, h–: h15.8m⁴ c20g⁵ Dec 10] strong gelding: lightly-raced hurdler: handicap **h54**
chaser nowadays: stays 2½m: acts on soft going: often let down by jumping over
fences. *Laura Mongan*

MORIANOUR (FR) 6 b.g. Valanour (IRE) – Moriane (FR) (Manninamix) [2016/17 **h113 p**
b16.3m² h19.9d* h19.6d² Aug 19] £3,200 3-y-o: fifth foal: dam French maiden: fell in **b82**
maiden point on debut: modest form only start in bumpers (for Tim Fitzgerald): fair form
over hurdles: won conditionals maiden at Uttoxeter in July: remains with potential.
Evan Williams

MORITO DU BERLAIS (FR) 8 b.g. Turgeon (USA) – Chica du Berlais (FR) **c110**
(Cadoudal (FR)) [2016/17 h137: c25.2s⁴ c23.6sᵖᵘ h26.1g Feb 5] has reportedly had **h–**
breathing operation: useful handicap hurdler at best: left Paul Nicholls, well held final start:
fair form on first of 2 outings over fences: stays 3¼m: acts on heavy going: has worn
headgear: wears tongue tie. *Lucinda Russell*

MORNEY WING (IRE) 8 b.g. Antonius Pius (USA) – Tillan Fuwain (FR) (Unfuwain **c124 §**
(USA)) [2016/17 c119§, h–: c29.1g³ c26.2d⁵ c27.2s⁴ c28.8d³ c28.5s* c26.7sᵖᵘ c32.6sᵖᵘ **h–**
c24.2d⁴ c26.2s⁵ c29.2g³ Apr 24] workmanlike gelding: maiden hurdler: fairly useful handicap
chaser: won at Plumpton in January: stays 29f: acts on heavy going: wears headgear/tongue
tie: often races prominently: unreliable. *Charlie Mann*

MORNING HERALD 6 br.m. Lucky Story (USA) – Wakeful (Kayf Tara) [2016/17 **h121**
h119p, b–: h18.5m* h23.8m² h21.6d Dec 16] angular mare: fairly useful form over hurdles:
won novice at Exeter in May: stays 3m: acts on good to firm going: often races prominently.
Martin Keighley

MORNING REGGIE 8 gr.g. Turgeon (USA) – Nile Cristale (FR) (Northern Crystal) **c120**
[2016/17 c122, h–: c19.9g⁵ c20.5s³ c20s c20d* c19.9g Apr 15] well-made gelding: winning **h–**
hurdler: fairly useful handicap chaser: won at Sandown in March: stays 3m: acts on heavy
going: usually in headgear. *Oliver Sherwood*

MORNING ROYALTY (IRE) 10 b.g. King's Theatre (IRE) – Portryan Native (IRE) **c136**
(Be My Native (USA)) [2016/17 c125, h–: c21.2m* c21.2d³ h22.1d⁶ h20s⁶ c15.7s³ h21.4s³ **h114**
h19.3v² c17.1s* Apr 3] small, sturdy gelding: fair handicap hurdler: useful handicap
chaser: won at Cartmel in May and Kelso (by 3 lengths from Vengeur de Guye) on final
start: stays 25f: acts on good to firm and heavy going: often races towards rear.
James Moffatt

MORNING TIME (IRE) 11 b.g. Hawk Wing (USA) – Desert Trail (IRE) (Desert Style **c65 §**
(IRE)) [2016/17 c54, h80: h16.2d⁵ h16.2d h16.2d c15.6g⁵ c20.1s⁴ c15.6g Apr 25] **h64 §**
tall, good-topped gelding: poor handicap hurdler/chaser: unproven beyond 2m: acts on
good to firm and heavy going: wears headgear/tongue tie: usually races towards rear:
temperamental. *Lucinda Russell*

MORNING WITH IVAN (IRE) 7 b.m. Ivan Denisovich (IRE) – Grinneas (IRE) (Barathea (IRE)) [2016/17 c92, h94: h15.8m h20.2d² h17.2g* Jul 18] poor handicap hurdler: won at Cartmel in July: maiden chaser: stays 2½m: acts on soft going: has worn headgear: tried in tongue tie. *Martin Todhunter* **c–** **h77**

MO ROUGE (IRE) 9 b.g. Croco Rouge (IRE) – Just A Mo (IRE) (Supreme Leader) [2016/17 c99, h–: c23.8m² c23.8d⁶ c23.8g c23.4m⁵ c23.8g³ c26.2g² Apr 15] winning hurdler: modest maiden chaser: stays 3¼m: acts on good to firm and good to soft going: wears headgear: temperamental. *Jackie Stephen* **c95 §** **h–**

MORRIS THE MINER 7 b.g. Apple Tree (FR) – Miner Yours (Miner's Lamp) [2016/17 h–, b–: h21.4m² May 5] stocky gelding: very lightly raced and only poor form over hurdles. *Neil Mulholland* **h80**

MORTENS LEAM 5 b.g. Sulamani (IRE) – Bonnet's Pieces (Alderbrook) [2016/17 b–: b15.7v b16.7d² h15.8s h20.5g⁴ h19.4g h19.7d h16d³ h16g² Apr 23] poor form in bumpers: fair maiden hurdler: suited by sharp 2m: acts on good to soft going: front runner/races prominently. *Pam Sly* **h105** **b72**

MORTHANALEGEND 8 b.g. Midnight Legend – Morwenna (IRE) (Zaffaran (USA)) [2016/17 h106, b91: c16.3gᵖᵘ May 4] lengthy gelding: bumper winner: maiden hurdler: bled on chasing debut: best effort at 17f: acts on heavy going: in tongue tie last 5 starts. *Brendan Powell* **c–** **h–**

MORTLESTOWN (IRE) 9 b.g. Milan – Pima (IRE) (Commanche Run) [2016/17 c118, h–: c20gᵖᵘ h16sᵖᵘ c22.6sᵖᵘ Jun 14] point winner: fair maiden hurdler/fairly useful handicap chaser at best, no form in 2016/17: wears headgear: one to treat with caution. *Martin Keighley* **c– §** **h–**

MOSCANISI (IRE) 6 b.m. Kalanisi (IRE) – Renvyle Society (IRE) (Moscow Society (USA)) [2016/17 h20.9s³ h19.7s* Dec 26] €6,000 3-y-o: fifth foal: half-sister to fairly useful hurdler/useful chaser Horendus Hulabaloo (19f-2¾m winner, by Beneficial); dam, maiden hurdler (stayed 3m), half-sister to useful hurdler/chaser (stayed 21f) Chasing Cars: winning Irish pointer: fair form over hurdles: won mares novice at Wetherby in December, suited by emphasis on stamina: will stay 2¾m+: open to further improvement. *Rebecca Menzies* **h108 p**

MOSCATO 6 gr.g. Hernando (FR) – Alba Stella (Nashwan (USA)) [2016/17 h15.7m³ h21.2g² h15.5g² h21g h18g² h17g* Apr 29] well-made gelding: half-brother to a winning jumper in USA by Galileo: useful on Flat, stays 2½m: fairly useful hurdler: left Oliver Sherwood after fourth start: won maiden at Charlotte in April: should prove suited by 2½m+: blinkered last 3 starts. *Jack O. Fisher, USA* **h117**

MOSCOW CALLING (IRE) 6 b.g. Morozov (USA) – Bubble Bann (IRE) (Hubbly Bubbly (USA)) [2016/17 h–: h16.2m h16.2m h16.2d h16d h23.8g² h23.8g Jan 20] poor form over hurdles: best effort at 3m: in blinkers last 2 starts. *Nicky Richards* **h76**

MOSCOW CHANCER (IRE) 11 b.g. Moscow Society (USA) – I'll See You Again (IRE) (Presenting) [2016/17 c20s Feb 8] sturdy gelding: lightly-raced hurdler: fair hunter chaser: well below best only outing in 2016/17: stays 2½m: acts on soft and good to firm going: wears headgear: irresolute. *A. Campbell* **c72 §** **h– §**

MOSCOW ME (IRE) 10 b.g. Moscow Society (USA) – Just Trust Me (IRE) (Warcraft (USA)) [2016/17 c110, h–: c16.5g⁶ h16.8s⁴ c17.2d⁶ h15.5v⁴ c15.9s³ c18.2g⁴ h15.7m³ Apr 13] handicap hurdler/chaser, modest nowadays: unproven beyond 2m: acts on soft and good to firm going: in cheekpieces final start. *Henry Oliver* **c87** **h97**

MOSCOW MENACE (IRE) 10 b.g. Moscow Society (USA) – Sky Flagship (FR) (Sky Lawyer (FR)) [2016/17 c–, h–: c23.4d c23.4sᵖᵘ c20.1sᵖᵘ c24d c21.6d³ Apr 10] winning pointer: maiden handicap chaser: poor handicap chaser: stays 3¼m: acts on good to soft going: in blinkers last 3 starts: has worn tongue tie, including last 4 starts: usually races close up. *Katie Scott* **c74** **h–**

MOSCOW PRESENTS (IRE) 9 b.g. Presenting – Moscow Madame (IRE) (Moscow Society (USA)) [2016/17 c–, h105: h23.3sᵖᵘ Apr 30] handicap hurdler, fair at best: pulled up in novice handicap only outing over fences: stays 27f: best form on soft/heavy going: usually in headgear. *Philip Kirby* **c–** **h–**

MOSSIES WELL (IRE) 8 b.g. Morozov (USA) – Kidora (IRE) (Broadsword (USA)) [2016/17 c118, h–: h20.1sᵖᵘ c26.9v⁴ c23.4vᵘʳ c20v⁵ c23.4gᶠ Apr 8] winning hurdler, fair at best: fairly useful chaser, not at best in 2016/17: stays 3m: acts on heavy going: usually tongue tied. *Sandy Thomson* **c104** **h–**

MOSS ON THE MILL 9 br.g. Overbury (IRE) – Mimis Bonnet (FR) (Bonnet Rouge **c127**
(FR)) [2016/17 c–, h106: h21.2m² h23.1g* h23d² h23g⁶ c25.6g* c23g⁵ c23g h24.4g **h117**
c25.1d* c24.1g⁶ Apr 15] fairly useful handicap hurdler/chaser: won over hurdles at Market
Rasen in June, and over fences at Ludlow in November and Wincanton in March: stays
3¼m: acts on good to firm and heavy going: wears headgear. *Tom George*

MOSSPARK (IRE) 9 b.g. Flemensfirth (USA) – Patio Rose (Petoski) [2016/17 c134, h–: **c119**
c24s c27.2s⁶ h21gᵖᵘ Dec 26] tall gelding: lightly-raced hurdler/chaser, useful at best: **h–**
disappointing in 2016/17: stays 3m: acts on heavy going: has worn headgear. *Emma Lavelle*

MOSS STREET 7 b.g. Moss Vale (IRE) – Street Style (IRE) (Rock of Gibraltar (IRE)) **c–**
[2016/17 c–, h–: h15.9d³ h15.8d² h16.7g* h20g² h15.8m* h20.5g⁴ h15.5g⁵ h15.7s h15.5g **h106**
h20.6sᵖᵘ h15.7dᵖᵘ Feb 26] small gelding: fair hurdler: won handicap at Bangor in July and
claimer at Huntingdon in October: winning chaser: left John Flint after fifth start: stays
2½m: acts on soft and good to firm going: wears blinkers: has worn tongue tie, including
last 4 starts: often races in rear. *Conor Dore*

MOST CELEBRATED (IRE) 4 b.g. New Approach (IRE) – Pietra Santa (FR) **h121**
(Acclamation) [2016/17 h16s* h15.7d³ h16.3s² h16.3g² h15.9m* Apr 17] good-topped
gelding: fairly useful on Flat, stays 1½m: fairly useful form over hurdles: won juvenile
maiden at Wetherby in January and juvenile at Plumpton in April: raced only at 2m: acts on
soft and good to firm going: in hood last 3 starts: often travels strongly. *Neil Mulholland*

MOTCOMB STREET (USA) 4 b.g. Street Cry (IRE) – Zaeema (Zafonic (USA)) **b82**
[2016/17 b13g⁴ Nov 26] £10,000 3-y-o: half-brother to several winners on Flat, including
smart 7f/1m winner Zibelina (by Dansili): dam 7f winner on only start: 11/4, 4½ lengths
fourth of 13 to Irish Prophecy in junior bumper at Doncaster on debut, fading after looking
in control 2f out. *John Joseph Hanlon, Ireland*

MOTHER MELDRUM (IRE) 8 b.m. Milan – Europet (IRE) (Fourstars Allstar (USA)) **c100**
[2016/17 c–, h105: h18.5g⁴ h20d⁴ h23.1m² c24.2g⁴ c25.5dᵖᵘ Dec 6] workmanlike mare: **h106**
fair handicap hurdler: fair form when fourth in handicap at Exeter on completed start over
fences: stays 3m: acts on good to firm and heavy going: wears cheekpieces/tongue tie:
often races towards rear. *Victor Dartnall*

MOTION TO STRIKE (IRE) 7 b.g. Beneficial – Comeragh Girl (IRE) (Imperial Ballet **h86**
(IRE)) [2016/17 h101, b–: h22.1m h16.2s⁵ h16.2s h16.4sᵖᵘ h18.1d h20.2g Apr 28]
winning Irish pointer: modest maiden hurdler: left Rebecca Menzies after first start: best
around 2m: acts on soft going: has worn headgear, including in 2016/17: wears tongue tie.
Jackie Stephen

MOTLEY CREW 4 b.g. Mount Nelson – Greensand (Green Desert (USA)) [2016/17 **b72**
b16.6s⁴ b16d Mar 31] poor form on first of 2 starts in bumpers. *Michael Easterby*

MOTTS CROSS (IRE) 6 b.g. Scorpion (IRE) – Rainy Season (IRE) (Sulamani (IRE)) **h99**
[2016/17 h97, b93: h25d⁶ h24g² h26.5d h21.6m³ Oct 6] lengthy gelding: maiden pointer:
modest handicap hurdler: stays 3m: acts on good to firm and heavy going: wears
cheekpieces: often races prominently. *Chris Down*

MOTUEKA (IRE) 5 b.g. King's Theatre (IRE) – Tchouina (FR) (Broadway Flyer (USA)) **b84**
[2016/17 b16g⁴ b16v⁴ b16.8d³ Mar 21] fourth foal: half-brother to French 2¼m hurdle
winner Miss Chief (by Shirocco): dam (h96), placed over hurdles in France (10.5f winner
on Flat), half-sister to useful French 2¼m/19f hurdle winner Magic Fabien: modest form in
bumpers. *Philip Hobbs*

MOULIN A VENT 5 gr.g. Sagamix (FR) – Bahia Blanca (FR) (Astarabad (USA)) **h131**
[2016/17 b16d³ b16.5d* h22.2g² h20s* h20s⁴ h20.3v² h24d Apr 26] €55,000 3-y-o: second **b109**
foal: dam (h91), runner-up in bumpers, sister to fair French hurdler/fairly useful chaser
(winner up to 2½m) Aviador: useful form in bumpers: won maiden at Galway in October:
also useful over hurdles: won maiden at Punchestown in November: best effort when
length second to Tin Soldier in Michael Purcell Memorial Novices' Hurdle at Thurles in
February: should stay 3m: acts on heavy going. *Noel Meade, Ireland*

MOULIN ROUGE (DEN) 6 ch.m. Zambezi Sun – Embattle (FR) (Dernier Empereur **h96**
(USA)) [2016/17 h76: h15.8gᵖᵘ h19.6d⁴ h15.7g³ h18.5d² h16.8g² h18.7g* h19.7g⁶ h19g⁵
Nov 24] modest hurdler: won seller at Stratford in October: left Kevin Frost after third
start: stays 19f: acts on good to soft going: in cheekpieces last 3 starts: in tongue tie last 5
starts. *Brian Barr*

MOUNTAIN CHIMES 5 b.g. Winged Love (IRE) – Threerockmountain (IRE) (Lahib **b–**
(USA)) [2016/17 b14d b15.7g Mar 28] well held both starts in bumpers. *Evan Williams*

MOUNTAIN EAGLE (IRE) 8 b.g. Mountain High (IRE) – Ceart Go Leor (IRE) **c111 p**
(Montelimar (USA)) [2016/17 h115, b87: c19.4m³ May 15] winning pointer: fairly useful **h–**
maiden hurdler: fair form when third in novice handicap at Stratford on chasing debut, let
down by jumping latter stages: stays 21f: acts on good to firm and heavy going: wears
hood/tongue tie: often travels strongly: should improve over fences. *Harry Fry*

MOUNTAIN HAWK (IRE) 5 b.g. Mountain High (IRE) – Septembers Hawk (IRE) **b92 p**
(Machiavellian (USA)) [2016/17 b15.7s⁴ Feb 13] fifth foal: half-brother to smart hurdler
Hawk High (2m/17f winner, by High Chaparral) and fair hurdler Dactik (2½m winner, by
Diktat): dam unraced: 5/1, promise when 9¼ lengths fourth of 12 to Brecon Hill in
conditional/amateur maiden bumper at Catterick on debut: should improve. *Malcolm
Jefferson*

MOUNTAIN KING 8 b.g. Definite Article – Belle Magello (FR) (Exit To Nowhere **c134**
(USA)) [2016/17 c132, h–: c18.2g c20.1g* c20.9m² c24d c19.4s⁵ c20.5s⁴ Feb 14] rangy **h–**
gelding: winning hurdler: useful handicap chaser: won at Perth in September: stays 2½m:
acts on heavy going: tried in cheekpieces: in tongue tie last 5 outings: usually races towards
rear. *Gordon Elliott, Ireland*

MOUNTAIN KINGDOM (IRE) 6 b.g. Montjeu (IRE) – Althea Rose (IRE) (Green **h112**
Desert (USA)) [2016/17 h17.2s h16g h18.5d⁴ h16.2s² h16.2g² h18.5g* h18.8g h16d⁶
h16.2g² Apr 26] modest maiden on Flat, stays 2m: fair hurdler: won maiden at Downpatrick
in August: left John Larkin after third start: stays 2¼m: acts on soft going: has worn hood,
including last 2 starts: wears tongue tie: often races in rear. *Colin A. McBratney, Ireland*

MOUNTAIN OF MOURNE (IRE) 8 ch.g. Mountain High (IRE) – Katies Native **c– §**
(IRE) (Be My Native (USA)) [2016/17 c111, h110: c23.6dᵖᵘ c20.9vᵖᵘ h19.5s² h16v⁶ h23.1d **h104 §**
c23.6vᵖᵘ Mar 23] compact gelding: fair handicap hurdler: maiden chaser, no form in
2016/17: stays 19f: best form on soft/heavy going: has worn headgear, including last 4
starts: temperamental (often races lazily). *Linda Blackford*

MOUNTAINOUS (IRE) 12 b.g. Milan – Mullaghcloga (IRE) (Glacial Storm (USA)) **c132**
[2016/17 c139, h–: c28.8dᵖᵘ c29.5sᵖᵘ c29.2s c25.2v² c32.6s Feb 25] well-made gelding: **h–**
winning hurdler: useful handicap chaser: won Welsh Grand National on 2 occasions: easily
best effort of 2016/17 when second at Hereford in February: stayed very well: best on
heavy going: wore cheekpieces: has been retired. *Kerry Lee*

MOUNTAIN PATH 4 b.f. Mount Nelson – Vino (Efisio) [2016/17 b12.4d* b17g Apr 6] **b89**
leggy filly: third foal: half-sister to 2 winners, including 1½m bumper winner Sherry (by
Tobougg): dam 7f winner: fair form when winning mares bumper at Wetherby in January
by neck from Shearling: left Micky Hammond/off 12 weeks, well held in Nickel Coin
Mares' National Hunt Flat Race at Aintree. *Jonjo O'Neill*

MOUNTAIN ROCK (IRE) 5 b.g. Mountain High (IRE) – Ajo Green (IRE) (Moscow **b104**
Society (USA)) [2016/17 b17m* b16m* b16s³ b16.4s⁵ b16.4g Mar 15] rather unfurnished
gelding: sixth foal: half-brother to fairly useful hurdler/chaser Green Wizard (2½m-25f
winner, by Wizard King) and fair 2m hurdle winner Monfass (by Trans Island): dam
unraced sister to useful hurdler/smart chaser (stayed 2¾m) Mossy Green: ran 3 times in
points: fairly useful bumper performer: won at Killarney (maiden) and Galway in July:
eighth of 22 to Fayonagh in Champion Bumper at Cheltenham: fourth in minor event on
Flat debut. *A. P. Keatley, Ireland*

MOUNTAINSIDE 5 ch.g. Dubawi (IRE) – Maids Causeway (IRE) (Giant's Causeway **h125**
(USA)) [2016/17 h123: h16.2d⁶ h15.7g⁵ h15.8g* h16.7g h20.2g* h20.1s⁵ Sep 30] fairly
useful handicap hurdler: won at Uttoxeter in June and Perth in August: left Lucinda
Egerton after first start: stays 2½m: acts on good to soft going: has worn cheekpieces/
tongue tie: often races prominently. *Mark Walford*

MOUNTAIN TUNES (IRE) 8 b.g. Mountain High (IRE) – Art Lover (IRE) (Over The **c115**
River (FR)) [2016/17 c90, h115: h23.9d⁷ h24d⁶ c25.5g* Aug 27] useful-looking gelding: **h114**
winning pointer: fair handicap hurdler: fairly useful form over fences: won handicap at
Cartmel in August: stays 25f: acts on heavy going: sometimes in headgear, including at
Cartmel: tried in tongue tie. *Jonjo O'Neill*

MOUNT HAVEN (IRE) 7 b.g. Mountain High (IRE) – Castlehaven (IRE) (Erins Isle) **c105 p**
[2016/17 h112: c19.4m⁴ May 15] sturdy gelding: runner-up in Irish maiden point: fair **h–**
hurdler: in cheekpieces, fair form when fourth in novice handicap at Stratford on chasing
debut: stays 2¾m: acts on heavy going: tried in blinkers: should improve over fences.
David Pipe

MOUNT MEWS (IRE) 6 b.g. Presenting – Kneeland Lass (IRE) (Bob Back (USA)) **h140 p**
[2016/17 b104p: b16.2d* h16.2s* h19.7d² h16.6g* h18.1v* h16.5g² Apr 7] well-made **b115**
gelding: useful form in bumpers: second win in 2 starts at Kelso in May: similar form over
hurdles: won novices at Kelso in December, Doncaster in January and Kelso again
(Premier Kelso Novices' Hurdle, by 49 lengths from Chalonnial) in March: shaped well
when 4½ lengths second of 9 to Pingshou in Top Novices' Hurdle at Aintree final outing,
leaving firm impression should have finished even closer: stays 2¼m: acts on heavy going:
usually travels strongly: remains likely to go on to even better things. *Malcolm Jefferson*

MOUNT PROSPEX (IRE) 8 ch.g. Golan (IRE) – No Blues (IRE) (Orchestra) [2016/17 **c88**
c89, h86: c25.8g² c25.8dᵖᵘ c23m c25.8g⁵ Oct 20] maiden hurdler: modest maiden chaser: **h–**
stays 3¼m: acts on good to soft going: in headgear last 4 starts: often races in rear.
Tim Dennis

MOUNT RUSSELL (IRE) 7 b.g. Indian River (FR) – Norwich Breeze (IRE) (Norwich) **c– p**
[2016/17 h24g⁵ b16g h20g h16g⁴ h19.8d⁴ c16s h19.7d Mar 21] sixth foal: dam (b74) ran **h95**
twice in bumpers: maiden pointer: tailed off in maiden bumper: modest form over hurdles: **b–**
well beaten in novice handicap on chasing debut: left Daniel William O'Sullivan after third
start: best effort at 3m: often races prominently: should do better over fences. *Henry Oliver*

MOUNT SHAMSAN (IRE) 7 b.g. Danehill Dancer (IRE) – Shamaiel (IRE) (Lycius (USA)) **h82**
[2016/17 h81: h18.5dᵘʳ h15.5g h15.9s h15.9vᵖᵘ h16.3g² h16.5g² h17.7m⁴ Apr 17] poor
maiden hurdler: raced mainly at 2m: in visor last 3 starts: front runner/races prominently.
Gary Moore

MOUNT VESUVIUS (IRE) 9 b.g. Spartacus (IRE) – Parker's Cove (USA) (Woodman **c71**
(USA)) [2016/17 c76, h84: c19.4m⁵ c16.3g⁶ h16.8g* h21.6g⁶ h17.7g² h16.8m² h15.9m³ **h86**
c19.3g⁶ h20.5g³ h20.7g h19.8dᵖᵘ h17.7d⁶ h21.6g* Apr 26] compact gelding: modest
handicap hurdler: won at Newton Abbot in August and Exeter on final start: poor maiden
chaser: stays 2¾m: acts on good to firm and heavy going: has worn cheekpieces: wears
tongue tie: usually races in rear. *Paul Henderson*

MOUSKERSIZE (IRE) 6 b.m. Lawman (FR) – Sesenta (IRE) (King's Theatre (IRE)) **h–**
[2016/17 h16s⁶ h16.7gᵖᵘ Jul 31] dam (h139) 2m-2½m hurdle winner: fair maiden on Flat,
stays 11f: maiden hurdler, no form in 2016/17: raced around 2m: acts on good to firm
going: in tongue tie last 2 starts. *John McConnell, Ireland*

MOVEABLE ASSET (IRE) 9 b.g. Trans Island – Mica Male (ITY) (Law Society **c–**
(USA)) [2016/17 c94, h83: h18.7mᵖᵘ h23gᵖᵘ h18.5dᵖᵘ Sep 26] sturdy gelding: fairly useful **h– §**
hurdler at best, no form in 2016/17: maiden chaser: has worn headgear/tongue tie:
ungenuine. *Henry Tett*

MOVE TO THE GROOVE (IRE) 7 b.g. Catcher In The Rye (IRE) – Valley of Love **c–**
(IRE) (Lure (USA)) [2016/17 h84, b75: h16.2d* h18.1m* h19.6d* c20gᶠ c15.9d⁶ Oct 13] **h129**
won only completed start in points: fairly useful form over hurdles: won novice at Hexham
and novice handicap at Kelso in May, and novice at Bangor in August: well held on
completed start in 2 chases: stays 2½m: acts on good to firm and good to soft going: front
runner/races prominently. *Donald McCain*

MOVEWITHTHETIMES (IRE) 6 ch.g. Presenting – Dare To Venture (IRE) (Darazari **h145**
(IRE)) [2016/17 b101: h17.7d* h16.4s⁵ h15.3d* h16.3d² Feb 11] well-made gelding:
successful on only start in bumpers: smart form over hurdles: won novices at Fontwell in
October and Wincanton in December: much improved on handicap debut when ¾-length
second of 16 to Ballyandy in Betfair Hurdle at Newbury final outing: will stay 2½m.
Paul Nicholls

MOVIE LEGEND 7 b.g. Midnight Legend – Cyd Charisse (Kayf Tara) [2016/17 h102, **c120**
b–: h21d² h19.4g³ c19.9d² h18.6s³ h23.4d³ c19.2sᵖᵘ c17.2g² c17.2m* Apr 17] workmanlike **h109**
gelding: fair maiden hurdler: fairly useful form over fences: won novice handicap at
Market Rasen final start: stays 23f: acts on soft and good to firm going: in cheekpieces last
2 starts: has worn tongue tie, including in 2016/17: usually travels strongly. *Lucy Wadham*

MOVIE MAGIC 6 b.m. Multiplex – Alucica (Celtic Swing) [2016/17 h16d h20.5vᵖᵘ **h–**
h15.9s h15.9vᵖᵘ Feb 27] plain mare: modest maiden on Flat, stays 2m: no form over
hurdles: tried in headgear/tongue tie. *Mark Hoad*

MOVING WAVES (IRE) 6 b.m. Intense Focus (USA) – Kimola (IRE) (King's Theatre **h–**
(IRE)) [2016/17 h–: h15.9g May 8] maiden hurdler, no form since 2014/15: has worn
headgear: tried in tongue tie. *Johnny Farrelly*

MOZO 6 b.m. Milan – Haudello (FR) (Marignan (USA)) [2016/17 h93, b97: h16d⁴ h19.6g⁵ **h90**
h16d h15.8v⁵ h15.8v Dec 31] bumper winner: modest maiden hurdler: left David Pipe after
first start: best effort at 2m: acts on good to soft going: in hood third start. *Barry Brennan*

MR BACHSTER (IRE) 12 b.g. Bach (IRE) – Warrior Princess (IRE) (Mister Lord **c95**
(USA)) [2016/17 c99, h–: c19.4s³ c18.9s⁶ c17.4v* c17.4d³ Mar 18] compact gelding: **h–**
maiden hurdler: modest handicap chaser: won at Fontwell in January: stays 23f: acts on
heavy going: wears cheekpieces: usually races prominently. *Kerry Lee*

MR BIEN (IRE) 8 b.g. Bienamado (USA) – Aboulia (IRE) (Presenting) [2016/17 h93: **c–**
h23gᵖᵘ h22g c19.7m⁵ h20mᵖᵘ Oct 8] maiden hurdler, no form in 2016/17: tailed off in **h–**
novice handicap on chasing debut: has worn headgear, including in 2016/17. *David Peter
Dunne, Ireland*

MR BIG SHOT (IRE) 6 br.g. Flemensfirth (USA) – Une Etoile (IRE) (Un Desperado **h125 p**
(FR)) [2016/17 b111p: h16d⁴ h17d* Apr 5] useful form when successful only start in
bumpers: fairly useful form over hurdles: won novice at Wetherby in January by 8 lengths
from Cousin Oscar: simple task when easily following up in similar event at Carlisle: will
stay 2½m: should go on to better things. *David Pipe*

MR BLUE NOSE 7 b.g. Tobougg (IRE) – Cape Siren (Warning) [2016/17 h–: h16.2d⁵ **h90**
h20.2m⁴ h22.1m⁵ h23.9d Jun 29] modest maiden hurdler: stays 21f: acts on soft and good
to firm going: often races prominently. *Simon Waugh*

MR BRINKLEY (IRE) 6 b.g. Scorpion (IRE) – Mandysway (IRE) (Mandalus) [2016/17 **h–**
h24dᵖᵘ h18.5sᵖᵘ Feb 12] won Irish maiden point on debut: pulled up both starts over hurdles
(bled second occasion). *Kim Bailey*

MR BURGEES (IRE) 8 b.g. Westerner – My Kinda Girl (IRE) (Supreme Leader) **c127**
[2016/17 c111, h94: c25.7m⁴ c20d* c23.9g⁴ Nov 3] winning hurdler: fairly useful handicap **h–**
chaser: won at Uttoxeter in October: stays 21f: acts on soft and good to firm going: in
blinkers last 2 starts: in tongue tie last 3: usually races close up. *David Pipe*

MR CAFFREY 5 b.g. Duke of Marmalade (IRE) – Quest For Eternity (IRE) (Sadler's **h92**
Wells (USA)) [2016/17 h104: h20m h21g² h19.9g h16m h19.7sᵖᵘ h23.1sᵖᵘ h20s h23.6s
h21.9d³ h23.9m Apr 27] modest maiden hurdler: stays 2¾m: acts on soft going: usually
wears headgear. *John Flint*

MR CARDLE (IRE) 8 b.g. Golan (IRE) – Leave Me Be (IRE) (Be My Native (USA)) **c95 §**
[2016/17 h98§: h23.8d c22.7s³ c17sᵘʳ c16s³ c18.2g³ c21.2g³ c16.2g⁵ Apr 24] modest **h– §**
maiden hurdler/chaser: stays 23f: acts on firm and soft going: wears headgear: often races
towards rear: temperamental. *Steve Flook*

MR CLARKSON (IRE) 5 b.g. Jeremy (USA) – Wynsleydale (USA) (Theatrical) **h128**
[2016/17 b18d⁶ b16.8v* h16.8s* h18.5sᵖᵘ h16.8v* h19.8s² h19.9g* h24g Apr 20] €17,000 **b102**
3-y-o: half-brother to several winners abroad, including a couple over jumps in Italy by
Thunder Gulch and Dubawi: dam unraced: runner-up in point on debut: fairly useful form
in bumpers: won maiden at Exeter in January: also fairly useful form over hurdles: won maiden
at Exeter in January, conditionals novice at Sedgefield in February and handicap at
Sedgefield in March: left Stuart Crawford after first start: stays 2½m: acts on heavy going:
usually races close up. *David Pipe*

MR CONDUCTOR (IRE) 8 b.g. Brian Boru – Crafty Classy (IRE) (Warcraft (USA)) **h–**
[2016/17 h23.3dᵖᵘ Jun 11] modest pointer, finally off mark in April 2017: pulled up in
novice on hurdling debut. *Mark Walford*

MR DIABLO (IRE) 8 br.g. Presenting – Aremebooksready (IRE) (Good Thyne (USA)) **c138**
[2016/17 c132, h–: c21s² c24.6m³ c17d c21.3s* c21.1g c20dᵇᵈ Apr 26] workmanlike **h–**
gelding: winning hurdler: useful handicap chaser: won by 1¾ lengths from Emcon at
Leopardstown in March: stays 25f: acts on good to firm and heavy going: has worn hood:
in tongue tie last 3 starts. *J. P. Dempsey, Ireland*

MR DORRELL SAGE (FR) 4 b.g. Sageburg (IRE) – Miss Breezy (FR) (Sicyos (USA)) **b–**
[2016/17 b16.7m Apr 17] well beaten in maiden bumper. *Charlie Longsdon*

MR ELEVATOR (IRE) 7 br.g. Sandmason – Greenwood Lady (IRE) (Roselier (FR)) **c–**
[2016/17 h–: c24.2gᵖᵘ c15.7d³ Jul 10] maiden pointer: no form over hurdles/fences: in **h–**
tongue tie last 2 starts. *Charles Pogson*

MR FENTON (IRE) 6 b.g. Trans Island – Carnagh Girl (IRE) (Saddlers' Hall (IRE)) **h112**
[2016/17 b93: h21s h21g⁵ h21m² Apr 4] chunky gelding: fair form over hurdles: best effort
when second in novice at Kempton, though was reluctant to set off: stays 21f: tried in hood.
Emma Lavelle

MR FICKLE (IRE) 8 b.g. Jeremy (USA) – Mamara Reef (Salse (USA)) [2016/17 h117: h19.8d⁶ h21d h19.1v⁵ h20.6sᵖᵘ h20.5g* h21.4m² Apr 5] smallish gelding: fair handicap hurdler: won at Plumpton in March: stays 21f: acts on good to firm and heavy going: has worn headgear, including last 4 starts: temperamental. *Gary Moore* **h114 §**

MR FIFTYONE (IRE) 8 b.g. Jeremy (USA) – Maka (USA) (Diesis) [2016/17 c137, h–: c16d⁴ c16m* c18g* c17g⁵ c18.2g c20d⁶ c15.9g⁴ c16.3g c16d⁶ Apr 27] winning gelding: winning hurdler: useful chaser: won at Punchestown in May (handicap) and June (minor event, by 1¼ lengths from Devils Bride): stays 21f: acts on good to firm and heavy going: has worn cheekpieces. *Mrs J. Harrington, Ireland* **c140 h–**

MR FITZROY (IRE) 7 ch.g. Kyllachy – Reputable (Medicean) [2016/17 h112: h17.7v* c19.7v² c17.1sᵖᵘ Apr 3] small gelding: fairly useful handicap hurdler: won at Fontwell in January: similar form when second in novice handicap at Plumpton on chasing debut: badly let down by jumping next time: may prove best short of 2½m: best form on soft/heavy going: tried in cheekpieces: sometimes in tongue tie: usually leads. *Jo Davis* **c120 h118**

MR GLOBETROTTER (USA) 4 b.g. Henrythenavigator (USA) – Sunshine For Life (USA) (Giant's Causeway (USA)) [2016/17 h16s⁵ h16s³ h15.7s³ h20.3vᵖᵘ h20.2g⁶ Apr 27] fairly useful on Flat, stays 16.5f: modest maiden over hurdles: should stay beyond 2m: acts on soft going. *Iain Jardine* **h97**

MR GREY (IRE) 9 gr.g. Great Palm (USA) – Presenting Shares (IRE) (Presenting) [2016/17 c20sᵘʳ c20.3d² Nov 29] strong, lengthy gelding: winning pointer: fairly useful hurdler: similar form when second in handicap at Southwell on completed start in chases: likely to stay 3m: acts on soft going: wears tongue tie. *Ben Case* **c122 h–**

MR GRUMPY 4 b.g. Sir Percy – Panna (Polish Precedent (USA)) [2016/17 h15.6g⁵ h16.2g⁵ Apr 27] half-brother to fairly useful hurdler Hot Diamond (2m winner, by Desert Prince): fairly useful on Flat, stays 1¼m: better effort over hurdles when fifth in novice at Perth: in hood first start: open to further improvement. *Lucinda Russell* **h81 p**

MR JIM 8 b.g. Fraam – Coddington Susie (Green Adventure (USA)) [2016/17 c16sᶠ c17.2s³ c15.9s⁵ c19.7g* Mar 27] maiden pointer: modest form over fences: won handicap at Plumpton (conditionals event) in March: stays 2½m: best effort on good ground. *Tony Carroll* **c94**

MR K (IRE) 6 b.g. Kheleyf (USA) – Undertone (IRE) (Noverre (USA)) [2016/17 h–: h16g⁶ h20.7g⁴ May 17] workmanlike gelding: modest form over hurdles: likely to prove best at around 2m: in cheekpieces last 2 starts. *Paul Webber* **h93**

MR KIT CAT 7 ch.g. Lucarno (USA) – Makeabreak (IRE) (Anshan) [2016/17 h113: h16.8g* h16d* h18.5g² h16.5g h16.5gᶠ Mar 30] good-topped gelding: fairly useful hurdler: won maiden at Sedgefield in May and novice at Worcester in June: will stay 2½m: acts on good to soft going: in hood first 3 starts: usually leads. *Evan Williams* **h117**

MR KITE 6 b.g. Sixties Icon – Mar Blue (FR) (Marju (IRE)) [2016/17 h99p, b91: h16g³ h15.8g⁹ h18.7m⁶ h16.2g³ h15.6g³ h16.4g* Mar 24] well-made gelding: bumper winner: fair hurdler: won novice handicap at Musselburgh final outing: left Harry Fry after third start: unproven beyond 2m: best form on good going: in tongue tie last 4 starts: usually races nearer last than first. *Susan Corbett* **h107**

MR LANDO 8 b.g. Shirocco (GER) – Capitana (GER) (Lando (GER)) [2016/17 c–, h107: h16g³ h15.9g² h16m³ h15.7g³ h19.1g⁴ h18.5m⁴ Jul 17] close-coupled gelding: fair handicap hurdler: well held only outing over fences: left Alison Batchelor after fifth start: stays 2¼m: acts on good to firm and heavy going: has worn hood: tried in tongue tie: front runner. *Johnny Farrelly* **c– h102**

MR LOVE (IRE) 5 b.g. Winged Love (IRE) – Bonny Rathlin (IRE) (Beauchamp King) [2016/17 h24.5d⁴ h23.3v² h21s⁵ Mar 30] €6,500 3-y-o, £72,000 4-y-o: sturdy gelding: fourth foal: dam unraced half-sister to useful hurdler/winning chaser (stayed 3m) Santableus: runner-up in Irish maiden point on debut: fair form in novice events on first 2 starts over hurdles. *Lucy Wadham* **h104**

MR MADEIT (IRE) 11 b.g. Brian Boru – Henrietta Howard (IRE) (King's Ride) [2016/17 c115, h–: c24.2dᶠ c20v³ Mar 12] workmanlike gelding: prolific point winner: maiden hurdler: fairly useful hunter chaser: stays 25f: acts on heavy going. *G. T. H. Bailey* **c116 h–**

MR MAFIA (IRE) 8 b.g. Zerpour (IRE) – Wizzy (IRE) (Presenting) [2016/17 c104, h98: h19g h23g² c23gᵗ h22m⁵ c23.6g² h23.6d⁵ c23.8gᵖᵘ Nov 28] modest maiden hurdler: fair handicap chaser: stays 3m: acts on good to firm and good to soft going: wears tongue tie: often races towards rear. *Tony Carroll* **c102 h93**

MR MARCHWOOD 4 gr.g. Medicean – Crocus Rose (Royal Applause) [2016/17 h16.6g Feb 22] modest on Flat, stays 1½m: tailed off in juvenile on hurdling debut. *Dominic Ffrench Davis* **h–**

MR MCGO (IRE) 6 b.g. Touch of Land (FR) – La Principal (IRE) (Saddlers' Hall (IRE)) [2016/17 h19.9s h16.7s* h19.5s* h20.3s h24.7g Apr 8] £24,000 5-y-o: sturdy gelding: fourth foal: half-brother to a winning pointer by Exit To Nowhere: dam unraced: won completed start in points: fairly useful form over hurdles: won novices at Bangor in November and Chepstow in January: stays 19f: acts on soft going: front runner/races prominently. *Donald McCain* **h128**

MR MCGUINESS (IRE) 7 b.g. Kalanisi (IRE) – Maig Mandy (IRE) (Mandalus) [2016/17 h98: h15.8m³ h15.8g² h20.3g^F h20.3d* h20g h19.8m^su Oct 14] fair handicap hurdler: won at Southwell in July: stays 2½m: acts on good to firm and good to soft going: usually races towards rear. *Rosemary Gasson* **h108**

MR MEDIC 6 b.g. Dr Massini (IRE) – Danse Slave (FR) (Broadway Flyer (USA)) [2016/17 h87, b–: c17g* c20m* c18.2g^ur Mar 20] sturdy gelding: modest form over hurdles: fairly useful form over fences: won novice handicaps at Plumpton in October and Lingfield in November: closing when unseated 3 out in handicap at Taunton final outing (looked sure to be involved in the finish): stays 2½m: acts on good to firm going: often races prominently: remains with potential over fences. *Robert Walford* **c117 p** **h–**

MR MERCURIAL (IRE) 9 b.g. Westerner – Arcanum (IRE) (Presenting) [2016/17 c113: c27.5m⁴ c23.8s* c21.1g c25.5g^ur Apr 24] good-topped gelding: multiple point winner: fairly useful chaser: won hunter at Ludlow in February: stays 3½m: acts on soft and good to firm going: tried in headgear: wears tongue tie. *Mrs Sheila Crow* **c125**

MR MIX (FR) 6 gr.g. Al Namix (FR) – Royale Surabaya (FR) (Turgeon (USA)) [2016/17 h136: h19.5g⁵ h21.4s* h23.4v^pu c21.2d^ur h24g Mar 16] angular gelding: useful hurdler: won handicap at Wincanton in December by ¾ length from Ruacana: evens, still to be asked for effort when unseated rider 2 out in novice won by Bonnet's Vino at Fakenham on chasing debut: stays 21f: acts on heavy going: in cheekpieces third start: front runner/races prominently: open to improvement over fences. *Paul Nicholls* **c120 p** **h138**

MR MOLE (IRE) 9 br.g. Great Pretender (IRE) – Emmylou du Berlais (FR) (Kadalko (FR)) [2016/17 c–, h–: c19.9d^pu c16.4g c15.2s^pu c19.3s^F c16g⁵ Apr 27] tall, useful-looking gelding: winning hurdler: high-class chaser in 2014/15, has shown little since: in blinkers last 2 starts: usually wears tongue tie: temperamental. *Ben Haslam* **c– §** **h–**

MR MONOCHROME 6 br.g. Indian Danehill (IRE) – Our Ethel (Be My Chief (USA)) [2016/17 b87p: b16.2d* b16.7d² b16.2g³ h16d* h18.6s² h19.3s³ Feb 3] leggy, useful-looking gelding: fairly useful form in bumpers: won at Hexham in June: also fairly useful over hurdles: won novice at Ayr in October: best effort when second in similar event at Market Rasen: stays 19f: acts on soft going. *Malcolm Jefferson* **h127** **b96**

MR MOONDANCE 6 ch.g. Windsor Knot (IRE) – Miss Sundance (IRE) (Desert Sun) [2016/17 h16g h16d³ h16.4s² h16.4s³ h16.5v³ h16.7d^F h16d h16s h16s Apr 7] modest on Flat, stays 1m: modest maiden hurdler: raced around 2m: acts on heavy going: tried in hood: races well off pace. *Mark McNiff, Ireland* **h93**

MR MOONSHINE (IRE) 13 b.g. Double Eclipse (IRE) – Kinross (Nearly A Hand) [2016/17 c135, h139: c25g^pu h21.3g Oct 12] lengthy gelding: useful hurdler/chaser, showed nothing in 2 starts in 2016/17: stays 3¼m: acts on good to firm and heavy going: front runner/races prominently. *Sue Smith* **c–** **h–**

MR MOSS (IRE) 12 b.g. Moscow Society (USA) – Yesterdays Gorby (IRE) (Strong Gale) [2016/17 c121x, h–: c22.5d³ h23g⁴ c20.3g* c24g² c20s c21.1g^pu c23.8m Apr 25] good-topped gelding: winning pointer: maiden hurdler: fair chaser: won handicap at Southwell in August: left S. Rea after first start, Dan Skelton after fourth: stays 3¼m: acts on good to firm and heavy going: has worn cheekpiece/tongue tie, including in 2016/17. *S. Rea* **c105** **h80**

MR MOUNTAIN (IRE) 7 b.g. Mountain High (IRE) – Not Mine (IRE) (Oscar (IRE)) [2016/17 b86. h16g h21.6m⁶ h21.6g* h21.6g² h23.3g^pu c20.5m^ur Apr 18] lengthy gelding: won both starts in Irish points in 2014: fair form over hurdles: won maiden at Newton Abbot in July: struggling when reluctant and unseated 3 out in novice handicap at Kempton on chasing debut: stays 2¾m: best form on good going: has worn hood. *Emma Lavelle* **c–** **h113**

MR MUDDLE 10 gr.g. Imperial Dancer – Spatham Rose (Environment Friend) [2016/17 **c112** c115, h–: c20g^{ur} c19.2v^3 c16v^4 c15.5s^2 c16v^5 c17.4g^3 Mar 31] compact gelding: winning **h–** hurdler: fair handicap chaser: left Sheena West after first start: stays 2¾m: acts on heavy going: often in cheekpieces nowadays. *Gary Moore*

MR MULLINER (IRE) 8 br.g. Millenary – Mrs Battle (IRE) (Be My Native (USA)) **c–** [2016/17 h23.3d^3 h24.8d^{pu} h24.8d^{pu} h27g^5 h20.1s^3 c18.5d c22g^5 Nov 3] fair handicap **h108** hurdler: won at Downpatrick in June: lightly-raced maiden chaser: stays 23f: acts on good to soft going: has worn headgear, including in 2016/17: wears tongue tie. *Mark McNiff, Ireland*

MR ONE MORE (IRE) 5 b.g. Asian Heights – Norah's Quay (IRE) (Witness Box **b102** (USA)) [2016/17 b16.7g* Oct 25] second foal: dam unraced sister to dam of useful hurdler/ smart chaser (stayed 25f) Kings Palace: 10/1, won bumper at Bangor on debut by 3¾ lengths from Robin The Raven. *Harry Fry*

MR PIPPIN 6 gr.g. Daylami (IRE) – Fionnula's Rainbow (IRE) (Rainbows For Life **h–** (CAN)) [2016/17 b16v h19.7v h15.8s h15.7v Feb 15] failed to complete both starts in **b–** points: tailed off in bumper/over hurdles: in blinkers last 2 starts. *Alan Phillips*

MR RAJ (IRE) 9 b.g. Oscar (IRE) – Chapel Wood Lady (IRE) (Zaffaran (USA)) [2016/17 **c110** c21.1d^3 c23g* Apr 6] multiple point winner: fair form over fences: in tongue tie, won maiden hunter at Taunton: stays 23f. *T. Gallagher*

MR ROBINSON (FR) 10 b.g. Robin des Pres (FR) – Alberade (FR) (Un Desperado **c62** (FR)) [2016/17 c80§, h–: c22.6m^{pu} c22.6g^{pu} h23m c22.5d^4 c22.6m^4 c19.7g^3 c20.2f^6 **h–** c19.8d^{pu} Dec 15] maiden hurdler: poor handicap chaser: stays 2¾m: acts on good to soft going: has worn headgear: often races towards rear. *Rob Summers*

MR SANDGATE (IRE) 4 b.g. Sandmason – Ballybeg Princess (IRE) (The Bart (USA)) **b–** [2016/17 b16v^6 Feb 27] tailed off in bumper. *R. Mike Smith*

MR SATCO (IRE) 9 b.g. Mr Combustible (IRE) – Satlin (IRE) (Satco (FR)) [2016/17 **c116 §** c109§, h–: c20.2m* c21g^6 c19.2g* Apr 11] workmanlike gelding: winning hurdler: fairly **h–** useful chaser: won hunters at Wincanton in May and Exeter on final outing: trained on second start by Chris Down: stays 3m: acts on good to firm going: wears headgear: front runner/races prominently: moody and not one to trust. *Mrs Emma Oliver*

MR SAWYER 8 b.g. Striking Ambition – Willows World (Agnes World (USA)) [2016/17 **c94** c17m^2 c20s^{pu} Feb 8] winner of 3 points: better effort in hunter chases when second at Stratford in May. *K. Jacka*

MRS BURBIDGE 7 b.m. Pasternak – Twin Time (Syrtos) [2016/17 c–, h62: h15.8g* **c–** h23.3m^6 h15.8g^4 h15.8g^4 c17.4m^5 h15.8g^4 h20.3d* h19.9s* h19.1s^3 Dec 26] modest **h96** handicap hurdler: won at Towcester (conditionals mares event) in May, Southwell in November and Uttoxeter (novice event) in December: little impact in 2 starts over fences: stays 2½m: acts on heavy going: wears cheekpieces/tongue tie: often travels strongly. *Neil Mulholland*

MR SELBY 8 b.g. Terimon – Bee-A-Scally (Scallywag) [2016/17 h104: h17s^{pu} h15.7s^{pu} **h–** h16.8m Apr 19] maiden pointer: fair hurdler at best, no form in 2016/17: in hood second start. *Martin Todhunter*

MRS GRASS 10 ch.m. And Beyond (IRE) – Tempted (IRE) (Invited (USA)) [2016/17 **h77 §** h59: h16.8s^2 h16.8g^2 h19.9m h16.2d* h16.2s^{pu} h17.2g h16.2d h16.8g^{pu} h16.2s h16.8s^5 h16.4s^{pu} h16.4s^2 h16.8d^5 h15.8v^3 h20.5v h16.8s h16.8v^6 h16.2s^4 h17g^2 Apr 15] small mare: poor handicap hurdler: won at Hexham in June: races mainly around 2m: acts on heavy going: wears headgear: has worn tongue tie, including in 2016/17: unreliable. *Jonathan Haynes*

MR SHAHADY (IRE) 12 b.g. Xaar – Shunaire (USA) (Woodman (USA)) [2016/17 c–, **c–** h–: c21.6d^{pu} c16m^6 c20.1g May 24] winning pointer: maiden hurdler/chaser: has worn **h–** headgear: usually leads. *Victor Thompson*

MR SHANTU (IRE) 8 b.g. Shantou (USA) – Close To Shore (IRE) (Bob Back (USA)) **c128** [2016/17 h139: h25d^4 h24g^2 h23d^3 h23.1g^4 c23g* h25.4d^5 c25.3g^{ur} Apr 20] good-topped **h126 x** gelding: fairly useful handicap hurdler: similar form when winning maiden at Worcester in July on chasing debut: hampered and unseated 5 out (still to be asked for effort) in novice handicap at Cheltenham final outing: stays 3¼m: acts on good to soft going: has worn headgear, including last 4 starts: wears tongue tie: usually races towards rear: often let down by jumping over hurdles. *Jonjo O'Neill*

MR SNOOZY 8 b.g. Pursuit of Love – Hard To Follow (Dilum (USA)) [2016/17 h101: **c–** h20.6d* h20.6g² c21.4g^pu h19.9d h20.6s⁴ h19.9d² h19.3g h19.9s* h21.3d² h19.7m* **h108** Apr 13] sturdy gelding: fair hurdler: won handicap at Market Rasen in June, and sellers at Sedgefield in January and Wetherby final start: pulled up in novice handicap on chasing debut: stays 2¾m: acts on soft and good to firm going: wears headgear. *Mark Walford*

MRSROBIN (IRE) 7 b.m. Robin des Pres (FR) – Regents Dancer (IRE) (Flemensfirth **c101** (USA)) [2016/17 c96, h89: c25.5g^pu c23m⁴ c23g³ c25.8g* c25.8g⁴ c23g⁴ c23.6d⁵ c21.2g⁵ **h–** c16g⁴ c20.2s³ c20.9d⁴ Mar 26] lengthy mare: maiden hurdler: fair handicap chaser: won novice event at Newton Abbot in August: left Emma Lavelle after sixth start: stays 3¼m: acts on good to firm and heavy going: wears headgear: usually races close up. *Barry Brennan*

MR STANDFAST 4 b.g. Mullionmileanhour (IRE) – Phantom Ridge (IRE) (Indian **h–** Ridge) [2016/17 h16v^pu Mar 12] modest maiden on Flat: showed nothing in novice on hurdling debut. *Alan Phillips*

MR STEADFAST (IRE) 7 b.g. Kalanisi (IRE) – Lady of The Mill (IRE) (Woods of **c101** Windsor (USA)) [2016/17 c–p, h112: c20g c21.2g⁴ h19.9g⁵ h20g h20s⁵ Jan 1] fair hurdler **h–** at best, no form in 2016/17: fair maiden chaser: left Gordon Elliott after second start: stays 2½m: acts on soft and good to firm going: tried in cheekpieces: wears tongue tie: often races towards rear. *Sarah Humphrey*

MR STORYTELLER 5 b.g. Rocamadour – Flying Iris (IRE) (Un Desperado (FR)) **b–** [2016/17 b16.8d Mar 21] green when well held in bumper. *Chris Down*

MRS WINCHESTER (IRE) 8 b.m. Scorpion (IRE) – Supreme Nova (Supreme Leader) **c–** [2016/17 h–: h21.6d^pu c24v^pu c20g^pu h22g Jul 28] of no account. *Caroline Keevil* **h–**

MR SYNTAX (IRE) 13 b.g. King's Theatre (IRE) – Smile Awhile (USA) (Woodman **c107 §** (USA)) [2016/17 c95§, h–: c19.3d⁵ c21.2m² c17.3d^pu c20s Mar 2] tall, lengthy gelding: **h–** maiden hurdler: fair chaser: left Chris Grant after third start: won point in April: stays 3m: acts on good to firm and heavy going: in cheekpieces second/third starts: has worn tongue tie: no battler. *Miss Michelle Bentham*

MR UTAH 10 b.g. Presenting – Raphuca (IRE) (Be My Native (USA)) [2016/17 h23.1s^F **h–** Jan 18] fairly useful hurdler in 2013/14, has shown nothing in 2 runs since: tried in tongue tie. *Henry Hogarth*

MR WITMORE (IRE) 7 b.g. Whitmore's Conn (USA) – Bright Future (IRE) (Satco **c–** (FR)) [2016/17 h83, b81: h21.2g³ h20.1g³ h23.3d⁶ h20.6s h23.8g c25.6d⁵ c21.1g⁵ Apr 7] **h87** modest maiden hurdler: showed little in 2 starts over fences: left Michael Smith after third outing: stays 2½m: acts on good to soft going: often races towards rear. *Kenny Johnson*

MS ARSENAL 5 b.m. Mount Nelson – Magical Dancer (IRE) (Magical Wonder (USA)) **b–** [2016/17 b86: b15.7g^pu May 24] fair form in mares bumper on debut, saddle slipped in similar event on reappearance (again looked headstrong): little impact on Flat subsequently. *Giles Bravery*

M SEVEN SEVEN GUS (IRE) 5 gr.m. Ask – Anns Island (IRE) (Turtle Island (IRE)) **b89** [2016/17 b16s⁴ b15.7s b16.8d² Mar 14] €2,200 3-y-o: third foal: half-sister to bumper winner/fairly useful hurdler Baby Bach (2m-19f winner, by Bach): dam (h87) lightly raced in bumpers/over hurdles, half-sister to fairly useful chaser (stayed 25f) Just For Men: fair form in bumpers: in hood, best effort when second in mares event at Sedgefield final start. *Stuart Crawford, Ireland*

MS PARFOIS (IRE) 6 ch.m. Mahler – Dolly Lewis (Sir Harry Lewis (USA)) [2016/17 **h118** b94: b16.4s h16.3d⁴ h18.9s³ h21s* h19.8s³ h21.6d* Mar 18] lengthy mare: won Irish mares **b87** maiden point on debut: fair bumper winner: fairly useful form over hurdles: won mares novices at Warwick in January and Fontwell final start: good effort when 10 lengths third of 5 to Colin's Sister in Jane Seymour Mares' Novices' Hurdle at Sandown: stays 2¾m: acts on soft going: tried in hood: in tongue tie last 5 starts: front runner/races prominently: excitable sort. *Anthony Honeyball*

MUBROOK (USA) 12 b.g. Alhaarth (IRE) – Zomaradah (Deploy) [2016/17 h–: h19.9m **h80** h25.4g² h24.3d^F h25.3d Dec 13] poor handicap hurdler: stays 25f: acts on heavy going: wears headgear: usually leads. *Tristan Davidson*

MUCKLE ROE (IRE) 8 b.g. Westerner – Island Crest (Jupiter Island) [2016/17 c115, **c117** h–: c21.4g³ c20d⁴ c23.8g² c24v* c24v³ c24s² c24.1g³ Apr 15] tall gelding: maiden hurdler: **h–** fairly useful handicap chaser: won at Warwick in December: stays 3m: acts on heavy going: waited with. *Nigel Twiston-Davies*

MUFFINS FOR TEA 7 ch.g. With The Flow (USA) – Countess Point (Karinga Bay) **h110**
[2016/17 h114, b66: h23.1s h19.7v⁴ h23.1d⁵ h21.7s⁶ h16g² Apr 8] fair maiden hurdler:
should stay 23f: acts on soft going: in tongue tie last 2 starts: often races prominently.
Colin Tizzard

MUHTARIS (IRE) 7 b.g. Teofilo (IRE) – Fann (USA) (Diesis) [2016/17 h120: h20.5d^pu **h–**
Dec 31] sturdy gelding: fairly useful handicap hurdler: ran no sort of race only outing in
2016/17: stays 21f: acts on heavy going: has worn cheekpieces: often races in rear.
James Evans

MUILEAN NA MADOG (IRE) 6 b.g. Papal Bull – Truly Precious (IRE) (Pennekamp **h–**
(USA)) [2016/17 b16d⁴ b16g⁵ h15.8d^pu h15.9v^pu Feb 27] fifth foal: half-brother to fair 2m **b91**
hurdle winner Spot The Pro (by Barathea): dam unraced half-sister to useful hurdler/
winning chaser (2m/2¼m winner) Nawamees: fair form in bumpers: pulled up both starts
over hurdles: left Sean P. Hennessy after debut. *David Bridgwater*

MULCAHYS HILL (IRE) 5 b.g. Brian Boru – Belsalsa (FR) (Kingsalsa (USA)) **b93**
[2016/17 b15 8d² b16g Dec 27] €5,000 3-y-o, £61,000 4-y-o. third foal: half-brother to
bumper winner/fairly useful hurdler Penn Lane (21f winner, by Scorpion): dam French 15f
hurdle winner: won point on debut: much better effort (fair form) in bumpers when second
in maiden at Ffos Las in November. *Warren Greatrex*

MULLAGHBOY (IRE) 6 b.g. Beneficial – Mellowthemoonlight (IRE) (Un Desperado **h102**
(FR)) [2016/17 b16d h21.4v³ h16d h20.2g Apr 26] €32,000 3-y-o: fifth foal: half-brother to **b–**
modest 2¾m hurdle winner Hello Louie (by Luso): dam (h85) 2m hurdle winner: fourth
when fell last in Irish point: tailed off in bumper: fair maiden over hurdles: may prove best
at around 2m: tried in hood: in tongue tie last 2 starts. *Stuart Crawford, Ireland*

MULLIGAN'S MAN (IRE) 10 b.g. Morozov (USA) – Rashmulligan (IRE) (Rashar **c–**
(USA)) [2016/17 c–, h99: h19.9g h15.8d Jul 13] angular gelding: modest handicap hurdler: **h86**
maiden chaser: stays 2½m: acts on good to firm and heavy going: has worn headgear,
including last 5 starts: front runner/races prominently. *Clare Ellam*

MULTICULTURE (IRE) 5 b.g. Mount Nelson – Gracious Melange (Medicean) **h129**
[2016/17 h15.8v* h16.3d³ h15.3v* h16v* Mar 22] good-topped gelding: fairly useful on
Flat, stays 11.5f: fairly useful form over hurdles: won conditionals maiden at Uttoxeter in
January, and novices at Wincanton and Warwick in March: raced only at 2m: acts on heavy
going. *Philip Hobbs*

MULTIGIFTED 4 b.f. Multiplex – Attlongglast (Groom Dancer (USA)) [2016/17 **h98**
h16.3s⁵ h16v² Mar 23] dam half-sister to fairly useful hurdler (stayed 2¼m) Devil To Pay:
fair on Flat, stays 2m: modest form over hurdles: better effort when second in mares novice
at Chepstow (wore tongue tie). *Michael Madgwick*

MULTI GRAIN 5 b.m. Sir Percy – Grain Only (Machiavellian (USA)) [2016/17 h91: **h–**
h16.7d⁵ h17.2g^ur Aug 27] small mare: maiden hurdler, modest form at best: raced around
2m: acts on heavy going: in cheekpieces last 2 starts, also tongue tied final one.
Micky Hammond

MULTIPEDE 5 b.g. Multiplex – Playful Lady (Theatrical Charmer) [2016/17 b79: **h84**
b16.4d⁵ h22.7s^pu h16.2v h15.6g h16.2v⁴ h19.9g⁶ h27m³ Apr 19] poor form in bumpers/over **b72**
hurdles: stays easy 27f: acts on good to firm going: usually races towards rear. *James Ewart*

MUMGOS DEBUT (IRE) 9 b.g. Royal Anthem (USA) – Black Queen (IRE) (Bob Back **c115**
(USA)) [2016/17 c97, h–: c15.5g^F c20.1s* c20.3s* c22.5v² c16v^F c15.5s³ c20.5v^ur c20d* **h–**
c19.9g^pu Apr 15] has reportedly had wind operation: maiden hurdler: fairly useful handicap
chaser: won at Hexham (conditionals event) and Bangor in November, and Carlisle in
April: stays 2½m: acts on heavy going: wears tongue tie. *Lucinda Russell*

MUNSAAB (IRE) 11 b.g. Alhaarth (IRE) – Claustra (FR) (Green Desert (USA)) [2016/17 **c119**
c25.5d* c25.5d c25.5d⁴ c20.9d³ c22.4v* h20.6s Jan 23] winning hurdler: fairly useful **h–**
handicap chaser: won at Cartmel in June and Hexham in December: stays 25f: acts on
heavy going: has worn cheekpieces/tongue tie. *James Moffatt*

MURIFIELD 7 b.g. Tobougg (IRE) – Kiwi Katie (Kayf Tara) [2016/17 b–: h21.6m⁴ Nov **h–**
1] good-topped gelding: off mark in points at fifth attempt: well held in bumper (tongue
tied) and a novice hurdle. *Harry Fry*

MURPHY'S NAILS 5 b.g. Milan – Definite Artist (IRE) (Definite Article) [2016/17 **h62**
b16.2v h20g⁵ Apr 9] tailed off in bumper and a novice hurdle: in cheekpieces in latter. **b–**
Tom Symonds

MURRAYANA (IRE) 7 b.g. King's Theatre (IRE) – Royalrova (FR) (Garde Royale) c–
[2016/17 c120, h129: c20.2s^pu Mar 1] handicap hurdler/maiden chaser, fairly useful at best: h–
won a point in February but pulled up in hunter on return to chasing: stays 25f: acts on
heavy going: wears tongue tie. *N. A. Pearce*

MURRAY MOUNT (IRE) 7 b.g. Trans Island – Ash (Salse (USA)) [2016/17 h104: c83
h19.6d^4 h16d^3 h15.7g^6 h16.5g^4 h16.8s^5 c22.6g^2 Apr 15] good-topped gelding: modest h97
handicap hurdler: remote second in novice handicap at Stratford on chasing debut: stays
2½m: acts on good to soft going: in blinkers penultimate start. *Henry Oliver*

MURTYS DELIGHT (IRE) 10 b.g. Bach (IRE) – Valley Supreme (IRE) (Supreme c–
Leader) [2016/17 c–, h–: h20.2m^pu c20.1d^pu h16.2s^pu c17.3d h22.1d^pu Aug 29] winning h–
hurdler/maiden chaser, no form since 2014/15: has worn headgear/tongue tie, including in
2016/17. *Lisa Harrison*

MUSICAL MOON 7 b.g. Piccolo – Lunasa (IRE) (Don't Forget Me) [2016/17 h16.7s h–
h15.5d h19.7v^6 h16.3g^6 h16g Apr 17] fair maiden on Flat, stays 1¾m: failed to complete in
points: no form over hurdles: in cheekpieces last 4 starts. *Steve Flook*

MUSICAL WEDGE 13 ch.g. Sir Harry Lewis (USA) – Wedge Musical (What A Guest) c57 §
[2016/17 c77§, h–: c25.6v^4 c25.2s^pu c24.5v^pu c22.7s^4 c29.2v^pu Mar 22] tall, sparely-made h–
gelding: winning hurdler: poor handicap chaser: stays 3¾m: acts on heavy going: front
runner/races prominently: temperamental. *Claire Dyson*

MUSIC HALL (FR) 7 gr.g. Stormy River (FR) – Aaliyah (GER) (Anabaa (USA)) h–
[2016/17 h–: h15.7g May 24] modest on Flat nowadays: no form in 3 starts over hurdles.
Shaun Harris

MUSKETEER 5 ch.g. Schiaparelli (GER) – Suave Shot (Suave Dancer (USA)) [2016/17 b60
b15.3m^5 b16m^6 Nov 2] poor form in bumpers: in hood second start. *Robert Stephens*

MUSTANG ON 7 b.g. Croco Rouge (IRE) – More To Life (Northern Tempest (USA)) h102
[2016/17 b71: h16.4d^pu h16.7d h16.6d^5 h16.6d^6 h16.6s^2 h16.7g^3 Mar 27] workmanlike
gelding: fair form in novice events and a handicap over hurdles: raced around 2m: acts on
soft going: has worn hood, including in 2016/17. *Nick Kent*

MUSTMEETALADY (IRE) 7 b.g. Mustameet (USA) – Ladymcgrath (IRE) c129
(Jamesmead) [2016/17 h127: c24s^2 c23.8d^4 c24.2s^3 c23.4d^5 c24s^4 c28.4g* Apr 15] good- h–
topped gelding: fairly useful hurdler: showed himself just as good over fences in 2016/17,
and won handicap at Haydock on final start: stays 3½m: acts on soft going: in cheekpieces
last 2 starts: usually races towards rear. *Jonjo O'Neill*

MUTDULA (IRE) 7 b.g. Gamut (IRE) – Calendula (Be My Guest (USA)) [2016/17 b85: b–
b17m^5 May 5] modest form at best in bumpers: failed to complete in 3 points. *Alan Swinbank*

MUTHABIR (IRE) 7 b.g. Nayef (USA) – Northern Melody (IRE) (Singspiel (IRE)) h112
[2016/17 h119, b87: h19d h19.1g^5 h16m^4 h20.7d* h21g^6 h19.4d^4 h24.4g^5 h23.9g* h23.1d^4
Apr 27] sturdy gelding: handicap hurdler, fair nowadays: won at Huntingdon in December
and Taunton in April: stays 3m: acts on heavy going: in cheekpieces second start: often
races towards rear. *Richard Phillips*

MUWALLA 10 b.g. Bahri (USA) – Easy Sunshine (IRE) (Sadler's Wells (USA)) [2016/17 c95 §
c107, h92: c17.3g^5 c19.3g^2 c16g^4 c16g^6 Sep 18] sturdy, good-bodied gelding: winning h–
hurdler: modest handicap chaser: stays 19f: acts on soft and good to firm going: has worn
cheekpieces: wears tongue tie: often races towards rear: one to be wary of (weak finisher).
Lisa Harrison

MWALESHI 12 b.g. Oscar (IRE) – Roxy River (Ardross) [2016/17 c116, h116: h22.1m c–
h16.2s^4 h18.6d^3 h23.1s^2 h20.6s^2 Feb 7] compact gelding: fairly useful handicap hurdler/ h112
chaser in 2015/16, raced only over hurdles and showed just fair form in 2016/17: stays 23f:
acts on heavy going: has worn hood: tried in tongue tie: front runner/races prominently.
Sue Smith

MY ANCHOR 6 b.g. Mount Nelson – War Shanty (Warrshan (USA)) [2016/17 h104: c–
h21.6d^F c20m^pu h23d^pu h20.3m h20.6d^2 Dec 26] sturdy gelding: maiden hurdler, poor form h83
in 2016/17: pulled up in novice handicap on chasing debut: left Charlie Mann after third
start: stays 21f: acts on good to soft going: usually in tongue tie: usually races towards rear.
Anthony Day

MY BOY GEOFFREY (IRE) 6 b.m. Craigsteel – Nikikita (IRE) (Nikos) [2016/17 b–
b15.7d b15.8d^6 Feb 9] fifth foal: sister to fairly useful hurdler/winning pointer Nikki Steel
(2m/21f winner): dam, ran once over hurdles, half-sister to useful hurdler (2m-2½m
winner) Slim Pickens (by Craigsteel): well held both starts in bumpers. *John Butler*

MY BOY JAMES (IRE) 5 br.g. Getaway (GER) – Parkality (IRE) (Good Thyne (USA)) **h111** [2016/17 b13.6d³ b17.7s⁵ b16.3g⁵ b16v² h16s² h16g⁵ Apr 8] €25,000 3-y-o: half-brother to **b84** fairly useful hurdler/useful chaser Macs Flamingo (2m-2¾m winner, by Rashar) and fairly useful hurdler Parish Business (2½m-3m winner, by Fruits of Love): dam unraced half-sister to useful hurdler/maiden chaser (stayed 4m) Prudent Honour: modest form in bumpers: fair form over hurdles: bred to be suited by further than 2m: usually races prominently. *Laura Mongan*

MY BROTHER SYLVEST 11 b.g. Bach (IRE) – Senna da Silva (Prince of Birds **c– §** (USA)) [2016/17 c139, h–: c19.2g h19.1g⁶ h15.7g* h18.5m² h15.9mᶠ h15.3m³ h15.8m² **h109 §** h16.5g Nov 24] sturdy gelding: fair hurdler: won seller at Southwell in August: useful chaser at best, well held only outing over fences in 2016/17: left David Pipe after second start: stays 2¾m: acts on firm and soft going: has worn headgear, including in 2016/17: has worn tongue tie: front runner, often races freely: temperamental. *Brian Barr*

MY BROWN EYED GIRL 4 b.f. Ferrule (IRE) – Chalosse (Doyoun) [2016/17 h15.7d **h–** h16s⁶ h15.6g h17s h21.4v⁵ h19.9gᵘʳ h23.9g Apr 26] little form on Flat/over hurdles: sometimes in hood. *Susan Corbett*

MY CHARITY (IRE) 6 b.g. King's Theatre (IRE) – Benefit Ball (IRE) (Beneficial) **b–** [2016/17 b15.8v⁵ Mar 19] well beaten in bumper on debut. *Oliver Sherwood*

MY COUSIN RACHEL (IRE) 6 br.m. Presenting – Countess Camilla (Bob's Return **h96** (IRE)) [2016/17 b65: b15.8d h15.7d³ h15.7d h15.8s h20.7d h15.8d* Apr 16] well-made **b–** mare: poor at best in bumpers: modest form over hurdles: in cheekpieces, won handicap at Ffos Las final start: unproven beyond 2m: acts on good to soft going: wears tongue tie: temperament under suspicion. *Kim Bailey*

MY DIAMOND (IRE) 6 b.g. Brian Boru – Our Idol (IRE) (Mandalus) [2016/17 h65, **h–** b63§: h22m h23.3gᶠ h21.6gᵖᵘ Aug 20] maiden hurdler, no form in 2016/17: has worn headgear, including last 4 starts. *Laura Young*

MYDOR (FR) 7 ch.g. Stormy River (FR) – Fabulousday (USA) (Diesis) [2016/17 c117p, **c108** h133: c18d h22.6d c20d⁴ h24d h24g² h23.8d c20s⁵ h22d Apr 17] lengthy gelding: fairly **h129** useful handicap hurdler: good second at Leopardstown in January: fair maiden chaser: stays 3m: acts on heavy going: wears headgear: in tongue tie last 4 starts: often races towards rear. *A. J. Martin, Ireland*

MY ESCAPADE (IRE) 6 ch.m. Tamayuz – Highly Respected (IRE) (High Estate) **c–** [2016/17 h96: h16.2d h17.2g h16.2d² h16.2d⁵ h19.3g c15.9s Dec 11] modest maiden **h90** hurdler: well held in novice handicap on chasing debut: unproven beyond 17f: acts on good to firm and good to soft going. *Simon Waugh*

MY FRIEND GEORGE 11 ch.g. Alflora (IRE) – Snowgirl (IRE) (Mazaad) [2016/17 **c101** c107, h–: c21.1s² May 3] maiden hurdler: fair handicap chaser: stays 3¼m: acts on good to **h–** firm and heavy going: wears headgear: usually races prominently. *Kenneth Slack*

MY IDEA 11 b.g. Golan (IRE) – Ghana (GER) (Bigstone (IRE)) [2016/17 c–, h–: c20.1d² **c100** c20.1m⁵ c21.2m³ c20.1g³ c23.4sᵘʳ c20.1s⁵ c19.9g⁶ c23.8g⁵ c16.3g² c15.6g⁵ Apr 25] rather **h–** leggy gelding: winning hurdler: fair handicap chaser: stays 25f, still effective at 2m: acts on heavy going: has worn cheekpieces, including last 5 starts: wears tongue tie. *Maurice Barnes*

MY JUDGE 5 b.g. Nayef (USA) – Full Steam (Oasis Dream) [2016/17 b16m⁶ Aug 17] **b–** well beaten in bumper on debut. *Paul Webber*

MY KHALEESI 6 b.m. Kayf Tara – Katess (IRE) (Spectrum (IRE)) [2016/17 b94: **h120 p** b16.4s* h19.1dᵘʳ h18.9s² h17.7v* h19.3s⁵ Feb 18] rather unfurnished mare: fairly useful **b102** form in bumpers: won listed mares event at Cheltenham (dead-heated with Irish Roe) in November: also fairly useful form over hurdles, and won mares maiden at Fontwell in January by nose from Little Miss Poet: second in listed mares novice at Haydock (6 lengths behind Colin's Sister) in December: stays 19f: remains with potential. *Alan King*

MY KING (FR) 5 b.g. Kingsalsa (USA) – My Belle (FR) (Smadoun (FR)) [2016/17 h59p: **h90** h15.9g⁵ h16m h16.8s h19g h23.8d h23.9g⁵ h23.9m⁶ Apr 27] modest maiden hurdler: in headgear last 2 starts: often races lazily. *Nigel Hawke*

MY LITTLE CRACKER (IRE) 7 b.m. Scorpion (IRE) – Cailin Gruaig Dubh (IRE) **c80** (Danehill Dancer (IRE)) [2016/17 h111, b99: h19.9g c15.6v³ c22.5vᵖᵘ h19.9v³ h19.4g² **h115** h16.2s* h16.7g* h16.7d² Apr 27] bumper winner: fairly useful handicap hurdler: won

556

conditionals mares event at Hexham and mares event at Market Rasen, both in March: poor form on completed start over fences: stays 19f: acts on heavy going: wears cheekpieces: front runner/races prominently. *Iain Jardine*

MY LITTLE HOPE (IRE) 6 ch.g. Daylami (IRE) – Key of Fortune (IRE) (Key of Luck (USA)) [2016/17 h17.1d⁶ Oct 13] showed nothing in novice hurdle: dead. *Martin Todhunter* **h–**

MYLITTLEMOUSE (IRE) 9 b.m. Turtle Island (IRE) – Ballybeg Rose (IRE) (Roselier (FR)) [2016/17 h79: h19.7sᵖᵘ h16.8sᵖᵘ Jan 17] lightly raced and little form over hurdles. *Helen Nelmes* **h–**

MYLYNY 4 b.f. Tobougg (IRE) – Water Flower (Environment Friend) [2016/17 b14s b16.7s b16.8v h15.8s h19gᵖᵘ Feb 21] sixth foal: sister to 1¾m bumper winner Water Willow and half-sister to 2 winners, including fair/unreliable hurdler Lucy's Perfect (17f/19f winner, by Systematic): dam (h95), 17f hurdle winner, also 1½m winner on Flat: no form in bumpers/over hurdles: left Alexandra Dunn after first start: in headgear last 4 starts: tried in tongue tie: often races lazily. *Bill Turner* **h– b–**

MY MANEKINEKO 8 b.g. Authorized (IRE) – Echo River (USA) (Irish River (FR)) [2016/17 h121: h16g h17m⁴ h16g² h20g⁴ h16g² h15.7m⁶ h16g⁴ h15.6g² h16d Apr 18] good-topped gelding: fairly useful handicap hurdler: stays 2½m: acts on good to firm going: usually races in rear. *James A. Nash, Ireland* **h125**

MY MAN FRANKIE (IRE) 5 b.g. Gamut (IRE) – Miss Emer (IRE) (Be My Native (USA)) [2016/17 b16d b15.7s Feb 13] well held both starts in bumpers. *Benjamin Arthey, Ireland* **b–**

MY MATADOR (IRE) 6 b.g. Kandahar Run – My Special (IRE) (Peintre Celebre (USA)) [2016/17 h19.5g h24.6g⁶ h24s h19g h18.5g⁴ h20.2g⁴ Apr 28] fair on Flat, stays 12.5f: modest maiden hurdler: left E. J. O'Grady after third start: stays 19f: acts on good to soft going: in headgear last 5 starts, also in tongue tie fourth outing: front runner/races prominently: has looked awkward. *Victor Dartnall* **h98**

MY MATE MARK 4 b.g. Sakhee (USA) – Florie (Alflora (IRE)) [2016/17 b16.3s² b15.7d* b16.4g Mar 15] rather unfurnished gelding: fifth foal: half-brother to bumper winner/fair hurdler Rafafie (2m/19f winner, by Kayf Tara): dam unraced: fairly useful form in bumpers: won at Southwell in February: stiff task and did too much too soon when well held in Champion Bumper at Cheltenham final start. *Martin Smith* **b97**

MY MISS LUCY 11 b.m. Alflora (IRE) – Corn Lily (Aragon) [2016/17 c–, h–: h19g⁴ May 2] lengthy mare: fair winner over hurdles in 2013/14: very lightly raced since, and just poor form only outing in 2016/17: pulled up both starts over fences: stays 2½m: acts on soft going. *Richard Phillips* **c– h77**

MY MISTRESS (IRE) 5 ch.m. Mastercraftsman (IRE) – Majestic Eviction (IRE) (King's Theatre (IRE)) [2016/17 h82: h16.3mᶠ h15.9m c15.7gᵖᵘ Oct 3] maiden hurdler, no form in 2016/17: showed nothing in novice handicap on chasing debut. *Phil McEntee* **c– h–**

MY MO (FR) 5 b.g. Silver Frost (IRE) – Anna Ivanovna (FR) (Fasliyev (USA)) [2016/17 h16.3d h16m³ h18.7g* h16m² h18.6g² h19.6m² h19.6m⁶ h16g³ Apr 23] fair on Flat, stays 1¼m: fair hurdler: won maiden at Stratford in July: stays 2½m: acts on good to firm going: wears cheekpieces: front runner/races prominently. *David Dennis* **h112**

MYPLACEATMIDNIGHT 5 b.g. Midnight Legend – Zahra's Place (Zaha (CAN)) [2016/17 b16.7m* Apr 17] first foal: dam (h116) bumper/2m hurdle winner: 10/3, won maiden bumper at Market Rasen on debut by 3¾ lengths from Potters Hedger. *Neil King* **b99**

MY RENAISSANCE 7 b.g. Medicean – Lebenstanz (Singspiel (IRE)) [2016/17 h69: h15.8g h15.7d⁴ Nov 15] maiden hurdler, poor form: left Ben Case after first start: unproven beyond 2m: acts on good to soft going: usually in tongue tie for previous yard (also in blinkers on reappearance): usually races prominently: won 3 1½m handicaps on Flat between December and February: capable of better over hurdles. *Sam England* **h68 p**

MYROUNDORURS (IRE) 7 b.g. Arakan (USA) – Six Bob (IRE) (Anshan) [2016/17 h77: c16.5m* c16.5g* c16.5g² c16.3g³ Jul 25] maiden hurdler: fair form over fences: won novice handicaps at Worcester in May and June: unproven beyond 2m: acts on good to firm going: wears hood: usually leads. *Robin Dickin* **c109 h–**

Betfred Eider Handicap Chase, Newcastle—
long-distance chase specialist Robbie Dunne adds another valuable prize to his collection as
Mysteree holds off the grey Knockanrawley and 2016 runner-up Shotgun Paddy (left)

MYSTEREE (IRE) 9 b.g. Gold Well – Hillside Native (IRE) (Be My Native (USA)) **c136**
[2016/17 c120, h–: c28.4v* c28.5s^{pu} c32.6s* c33.4s² Mar 18] angular gelding: winning **h–**
hurdler: useful handicap chaser: won at Haydock in November and Betfred Eider Chase at
Newcastle (by 4 lengths from Knockanrawley) in February: good 1½ lengths second of 20
to Chase The Spud in Midlands Grand National at Uttoxeter final start: stays 33f: acts on
heavy going. *Michael Scudamore*

MYSTERIOUS MAN (IRE) 8 b.g. Manduro (GER) – Edabiya (IRE) (Rainbow Quest **h111**
(USA)) [2016/17 h20g* h17.7d³ Sep 4] half-brother to 2 winning hurdlers, including
useful 2m winner Edeymi (by Barathea): useful on Flat (stays 2½m) in 2013 for Andrew
Balding: fair form both starts over hurdles, winning maiden at Worcester in August: will
stay beyond 2½m. *Brendan Powell*

MYSTERY DRAMA 7 b.m. Hernando (FR) – Mystery Lot (IRE) (Revoque (IRE)) **h78**
[2016/17 h–: h15.8g h15.9g h19g h16.8s⁶ h16v³ Mar 23] compact mare: poor handicap
hurdler: unproven beyond 17f: acts on heavy going: in tongue tie third start: often races
towards rear. *Alexandra Dunn*

MYSTICAL KNIGHT 8 b.g. Kayf Tara – Dark Diva (Royal Fountain) [2016/17 h125, **c135**
b114: c25.2s* c24s^{pu} c23.6v³ c21d⁶ Apr 28] well-made gelding: fairly useful hurdler: **h–**
useful form over fences: won novice at Hereford in December by 5 lengths from Chef
d'Oeuvre: not disgraced in novice handicap at Punchestown final start: stays 25f: acts on
heavy going: in tongue tie last 4 starts. *Rebecca Curtis*

MYSTIC SKY 6 b.m. Midnight Legend – Kentucky Sky (Cloudings (IRE)) [2016/17 **h117**
h122, b92: h18.6g* h19.1g² h15.8g³ h16.6g⁵ h24.5g⁵ Dec 27] lengthy mare: bumper
winner: fairly useful hurdler: won minor event at Market Rasen in May: stays 19f: acts on
good to soft going: wears blinkers: usually races towards rear. *Lucy Wadham*

MYSTIFIABLE 9 gr.g. Kayf Tara – Royal Keel (Long Leave) [2016/17 c135p, h107: **c132**
c22.4g c20s c20.1g* Apr 27] sturdy gelding: fair hurdler: useful handicap chaser: won by **h–**
2½ lengths from Special Catch at Perth final start: stays 2¾m: acts on soft going: tried in
hood: wears tongue tie: usually travels strongly. *Fergal O'Brien*

MY STORY (IRE) 5 b.g. Court Cave (IRE) – Holloden (IRE) (Shantou (USA)) [2016/17 **b77 p** b16.5g⁴ Feb 21] €17,000 3-y-o, €90,000 4-y-o: first foal: dam unraced half-sister to useful hurdler (2m-2¼m winner) Bywell Beau and useful staying chaser Rugged River: won Irish maiden point on debut: 3/1, fourth of 10 in conditionals/amateur bumper at Taunton (24 lengths behind If The Cap Fits) on debut: capable of better. *Neil Mulholland*

MY STROPPY POPPY 8 b.m. Multiplex – Aspen Ridge (IRE) (Namid) [2016/17 **h–** h15.8g May 14] no form over hurdles: wears hood: tried in tongue tie. *Grace Harris*

MY TENT OR YOURS (IRE) 10 b.g. Desert Prince (IRE) – Spartan Girl (IRE) **h163** (Ela-Mana-Mou) [2016/17 h164: h16s³ h16.2v³ h16.8s² h16g⁴ h16.4g² h20g² h16g² Apr 28]

Despite winning six of his first eight starts over hurdles, including the Betfair Hurdle as a novice and the following season's 'Fighting Fifth' and Christmas Hurdles, it looks as though My Tent Or Yours will be best remembered now for the races he didn't win, and specifically for his record of having finished runner-up in three Champion Hurdles. Things might have been different had his connections not decided to abandon a novice chasing campaign with stable-companion Buveur d'Air and aim him at the Champion Hurdle instead. Without Buveur d'Air in the field, the ten-year-old My Tent Or Yours would have emulated Sea Pigeon, who in 1980 became the last horse of that age to win the hurdling championship, after twice finishing runner-up. As it was, My Tent Or Yours was beaten four and a half lengths into second by Buveur d'Air, exactly the same margin which had separated him from the winner Annie Power twelve months earlier when he was returning from the best part of two years off the course. As in his latest attempt, My Tent Or Yours was denied by another of his owner's hurdlers in his first bid for a Champion Hurdle when Jezki held him off by a neck in the 2014 renewal. That had been the second time that My Tent Or Yours had been led back to the runner-up spot at the Cheltenham Festival, following his half-length second to Champagne Fever in the Supreme Novices' the year before. 'You have to feel sorry for him,' said Nicky Henderson after the latest Champion Hurdle. 'It's been a remarkable story and he has just been a legend and he did so deserve to win one, you have to sympathise with him.' J. P. McManus, owner of My Tent Or Yours, had only recently had another hurdler who had finished runner-up at four Festivals. The Jonjo O'Neill-trained Get Me Out of Here, like My Tent Or Yours, finished second in the Supreme (beaten a head by Menorah) and on subsequent visits went down by a nose in the County Hurdle and was twice runner-up in the Coral Cup, on the second occasion beaten a short head.

The Champion Hurdle was one of four occasions in the latest season when My Tent Or Yours had to settle for second. In December, also at Cheltenham, he went down to old rival The New One in the International Hurdle when in receipt of 8 lb from the winner, who was winning that race for the third time. It was the first time that The New One had got the better of My Tent Or Yours (which he also did at Kempton on their next start), but the balance was redressed and their head-to-head record stood at six-two in My Tent Or Yours's favour by the end of the season. The New One himself contested his fourth Champion Hurdle in March, finishing fifth for the second time (as in 2015), to go with his third place in 2014 and fourth in 2016. Like the year before, My Tent Or Yours went on to Aintree and Punchestown after the Champion Hurdle. In less testing conditions than the year before, and ridden with an eye to seeing out the longer trip, My Tent Or Yours was beaten five lengths when splitting Buveur d'Air and The New One in the Aintree Hurdle, running a better race than when chasing home Annie Power in 2016. At Punchestown (where he'd finished only third behind Vroum Vroum Mag in 2016), My Tent Or Yours came closest to getting his head in front for the first time since his narrow defeat in the 2014 Champion Hurdle, beaten a length and a half by the enterprisingly ridden Wicklow Brave who had finished only eighth behind him at Cheltenham. My Tent Or Yours' three runs in the spring were the pick of his efforts in the latest season. He finished only third of four in heavy ground on his return in a muddling Betfair Price

Rush Hurdle at Haydock and, after his next run in the International, wasn't seen to best effect when fourth of five in the Christmas Hurdle at Kempton behind his owner's other Champion Hurdle horse Yanworth.

The only other horse to have finished runner-up in three Champion Hurdles was the Aidan O'Brien-trained Theatreworld who was second to Make A Stand in 1997 and then chased home his outstanding stable-companion Istabraq in the next two years before finishing well beaten when the latter completed his hat-trick in 2000. Theatreworld ended his career with a Timeform 'squiggle', proving moody in his latter years, and it looked at one time as though My Tent Or Yours' temperament—he was a hard-puller in his younger days—might also get the better of him. My Tent Or Yours can still take a strong hold, though he settled better at Aintree, for example, and is fitted with a hood nowadays. Temperament got in the way of probably the best hurdler never to have won the Champion Hurdle. Bird's Nest was a magnificent servant to his stable, winning sixteen races over hurdles and racing until the age of twelve. While his record away from the Festival included three 'Fighting Fifth' Hurdles, three Bula [International] Hurdles, two Scottish Champion Hurdles and a Christmas Hurdle, he was placed twice from six consecutive unsuccessful attempts at the Champion Hurdle between 1976 and 1981, finishing runner-up to Night Nurse that first year and third behind Sea Pigeon and Monksfield when a ten-year-old in 1980. Bird's Nest was unfortunate to be a contemporary of some exceptional hurdlers, but he was better than many Champion Hurdle winners himself and blessed with a fine turn of foot, though his waywardness manifested itself by a marked tendency to hang left off the bridle. In fact, it cost him a fourth 'Fighting Fifth' when he was demoted to second for hampering Sea Pigeon. As well as his two placed efforts in the Champion Hurdle, Bird's Nest was also fifth twice (including when sent off the 6/4 favourite when Night Nurse won again in 1977) and seventh twice as well.

My Tent Or Yours (IRE) (b.g. 2007)	Desert Prince (IRE) (b 1995)	Green Desert (b 1983)	Danzig
			Foreign Courier
		Flying Fairy (ch 1983)	Bustino
			Fairy Footsteps
	Spartan Girl (IRE) (ch 1994)	Ela-Mana-Mou (b 1976)	Pitcairn
			Rose Bertin
		Well Head (b 1989)	Sadler's Wells
			River Dancer

My Tent Or Yours has had three different jockeys in his Champion Hurdles, Tony McCoy, Barry Geraghty and Aidan Coleman. Coleman rode him for the first time at Cheltenham in the latest season and kept the ride on his two subsequent starts. If My Tent Or Yours had something of a frustrating Festival record, spare a thought for his jockey who was runner-up to Richard Johnson in the jockeys' championship in 2015/16. Coleman broke his duck at the Festival in 2009 on Kayf Aramis in the Pertemps Final but, by the end of the latest Festival, had failed to add to his score from a further ninety-nine rides. His luck finally seemed to have changed when riding Any Currency to victory in the 2016 Glenfarclas Chase only for that win to be expunged from the records when his mount subsequently tested positive for a banned substance. As well as in the Champion Hurdle, Coleman also finished second at the latest Festival on Taquin du Seuil in the Coral Cup and on Fox Norton, who was beaten a head in the Queen Mother Champion Chase. He was also on board for both of Buveur d'Air's wins over fences earlier in the season. There are no further details to add to the pedigree notes which have appeared in My Tent Or Yours' previous essays in *Chasers & Hurdlers*. A strong, rangy gelding, he is best at around two miles and acts on soft and good to firm ground. *Nicky Henderson*

MYTHICAL LEGEND 6 ch.m. Midnight Legend – Materiality (Karinga Bay) [2016/17 **b91** b78: b16.7g² May 14] fair form in bumpers: much improved from debut when 2¾ lengths second of 7 to Miss Beatrice in mares event at Bangor. *Emma Lavelle*

MY VALENTINO (IRE) 4 ch.g. Duke of Marmalade (IRE) – Nadwah (USA) (Shadeed **h—** (USA)) [2016/17 h16g h16s h15.7g⁶ h15.6g⁴ h16.2g Apr 27] modest maiden on Flat, stays 11f: no form over hurdles: tried in cheekpieces. *Dianne Sayer*

MY WIGWAM OR YOURS (IRE) 8 b.g. Beneficial – Midnight Pond (IRE) (Long **c108**
Pond) [2016/17 h21.1g h21.1s c22.4d c24.2dʳᵒ c19.9g⁴ c23.8m³ Apr 18] sturdy gelding: **h–**
one-time useful hurdler: off 22 months, no form in 2016/17: maiden chaser, just fair form
at best in 2016/17: stays 21f: acts on soft and good to firm going: in cheekpieces last 2
starts. *Nicky Henderson*

N

NAASIK 4 b.g. Poet's Voice – Shemriyna (IRE) (King of Kings (IRE)) [2016/17 b15.7s **b66**
b16.7m⁴ Apr 9] poor form in bumpers. *John Norton*

NABHAN 5 b.g. Youmzain (IRE) – Danidh Dubai (IRE) (Noverre (USA)) [2016/17 h116: **h–**
h16.8g⁶ Apr 19] angular gelding: fairly useful on Flat, stays 13.5f: fairly useful hurdler at
best, probably needed run only outing in 2016/17: raced around 2m: acts on heavy going:
front runner/races prominently. *Bernard Llewellyn*

NABURN 9 b.g. Cape Cross (USA) – Allespagne (USA) (Trempolino (USA)) [2016/17 **h73 x**
h96x: h23.9m⁶ May 11] maiden hurdler, modest at best: stays 21f: acts on good to firm and
heavy going: usually races nearer last than first: often let down by jumping. *Andrew Wilson*

NACHI FALLS 4 ch.g. New Approach (IRE) – Lakuta (IRE) (Pivotal) [2016/17 h15.8g³ **h117**
h16.8g* h17.7d* h16.7g* h16.8g⁴ h16.8d³ h15.5dᵖᵘ h15.6g⁶ h15.8s Feb 22] compact
gelding: fair form on Flat: fairly useful hurdler: won juveniles at Newton Abbot in August,
and Fontwell and Market Rasen in September: stays 2¼m: acts on good to soft going:
wears tongue tie. *Nigel Hawke*

NAFAATH (IRE) 11 ch.g. Nayef (USA) – Alshakr (Bahri (USA)) [2016/17 c–, h101: **c–**
h16.8d⁴ h15.8d* h15.6g⁴ h15.8d⁴ h16.4s⁴ h19.3s⁴ Feb 28] deep-girthed gelding: modest **h97**
handicap hurdler: won at Uttoxeter in October: maiden chaser: stays 2½m: acts on good
to firm and heavy going: wears headgear: tried in tongue tie: usually races prominently.
Donald McCain

NAILER (IRE) 7 b.g. Coroner (IRE) – Celtic Serenade (IRE) (Yashgan) [2016/17 b–: **h–**
b16.4d h22sᵖᵘ Jan 23] no form in bumpers/novice hurdle: has worn tongue tie. *Tristan* **b–**
Davidson

NAIL 'M (IRE) 9 b.g. Milan – Honor Kicks (FR) (Highest Honor (FR)) [2016/17 c107, **c102 §**
h–: c29.1gᵘʳ c24.2s⁶ c29.6s³ c28.5sᵖᵘ c24.1sᵖᵘ h27v³ Mar 5] strong gelding: modest maiden **h92 §**
hurdler: fair handicap chaser: stays 31f: acts on heavy going: usually wears headgear: has
worn tongue tie, including in 2016/17: ungenuine. *Nigel Hawke*

NAKADAM (FR) 7 b.g. Nickname (FR) – Cadoudame (FR) (Cadoudal (FR)) [2016/17 **c108**
c112, h88: c26.2dᵖᵘ c26.3s c20.5v² c26.9v³ c26.2d² c30.6g⁴ Apr 28] maiden hurdler: fair **h–**
handicap chaser: barely stays 31f: acts on heavy going: has worn cheekpieces, including
last 5 starts: wears tongue tie: often races towards rear, usually travels strongly.
R. Mike Smith

NAMBOUR (GER) 7 b.g. Sholokhov (IRE) – Nanouska (GER) (Dashing Blade) **c134**
[2016/17 h134, b106: c22.5s* c22.5d⁴ Nov 20] useful hurdler: useful form over fences: **h–**
won maiden at Galway in October: fourth in Grade 2 novice at Punchestown 3 weeks later:
stays 3m: acts on heavy going: in tongue tie last 5 starts: often travels strongly. *M. F. Morris,*
Ireland

NANCY'S TRIX (IRE) 8 br.m. Presenting – Murrurundi (IRE) (Old Vic) [2016/17 h94, **c78**
b68: h21m⁴ h24v³ c19.2g⁵ Apr 11] won completed start in Irish points: modest form over **h99**
hurdles: 5/2, fifth in novice handicap at Exeter (28¼ lengths behind Meldrum Lad) on
chasing debut: left David Loder after second start: stays 25f: acts on good to firm and heavy
going. *Tom George*

NANDO (GER) 5 b.g. Dai Jin – Natalis (GER) (Law Society (USA)) [2016/17 b16.4d⁴ **b79 p**
Nov 1] €50,000 3-y-o: third foal: half-brother to a winning pointer by Sholokhov: dam
German maiden (second at 11f): 2/1, fourth in maiden bumper at Newcastle (11½ lengths
behind Solighoster) on debut: should do better. *Nicky Richards*

NANSAROY 7 br.g. Indian River (FR) – Jurado Park (IRE) (Jurado (USA)) [2016/17 **c123**
h119: c16.4s⁴ c20v⁵ c20.9v² c23.8s² c23.8v⁴ Mar 19] angular gelding: winning hurdler: **h–**
fairly useful form over fences: second in handicaps at Hereford (novice) and Ludlow: stays
3m: acts on heavy going: in cheekpieces last 3 starts. *Evan Williams*

NARANJA 5 ch.m. Black Sam Bellamy (IRE) – Full of Fruit (FR) (Apple Tree (FR)) **h102**
[2016/17 b96: b16.4s³ b17s² h16v³ h24.4s⁴ h20.3g⁶ Apr 20] lengthy mare: fairly useful **b95**
form in bumpers: third in listed mares event at Cheltenham (6 lengths behind dead-heaters

My Khaleesi and Irish Roe) in November: fair form over hurdles: best effort when third in mares novice at Lingfield in January: should prove suited by 2½m+: tried in tongue tie: front runner/races prominently. *Jamie Snowden*

NATHANS PRIDE (IRE) 9 ch.g. Definite Article – Tricias Pride (IRE) (Broken Hearted) [2016/17 c–, h123: h20m* h21g h21g Mar 18] workmanlike gelding: fairly useful handicap hurdler: won at Aintree in May: well beaten only chase start: stays 2½m: acts on good to firm going. *Tim Vaughan* **c– h125**

NATIVE DISPLAY (IRE) 7 b.g. Presenting – Native Shore (IRE) (Be My Native (USA)) [2016/17 h97: h20m² h20.3gᵖᵘ h19.9g² c20gᶠ h20.3d Nov 15] good-topped gelding: fair handicap hurdler: fourth when fell heavily 3 out in maiden won by Roadie Joe at Worcester on chasing debut: left Nicky Henderson after third start: stays 2½m: acts on good to firm and good to soft going: wears hood: tried in tongue tie: often races towards rear/travels strongly: has finished weakly. *Caroline Bailey* **c– h105**

NATIVE OPTIMIST (IRE) 10 b.g. Broadway Flyer (USA) – Native Orchid (IRE) (Be My Native (USA)) [2016/17 h116: h23.3gᵖᵘ h24.1dᵖᵘ h22.7sᵖᵘ h20.6s h24.3s⁶ Feb 14] angular gelding: fair hurdler at best, no form in 2016/17: tried in tongue tie. *Sheena Walton* **h–**

NATIVE RIVER (IRE) 7 ch.g. Indian River (FR) – Native Mo (IRE) (Be My Native (USA)) [2016/17 c152f, h–: h24.1g² c26g* c29.5s* c23.4d* c26.3g³ Mar 17] **c166 h153**
    There was uproar among jumping fans at the turn of the century when the sponsors of the iconic Whitbread Gold Cup, the first instance of commercial sponsorship in British sport when it was founded in 1957, announced they were ending their involvement. The Queen Mother was among those who lobbied the management of the umbrella company of the brewing giant to change its mind, but there was only a short-lived reprieve. The last Whitbread Gold Cup was run in 2001 (the conglomerate sold its breweries and other brewing interests the same year) and, after short spells under the banners of attheraces and Betfred, the race seems to have found an on-going sponsor with bet365 which has supported the last big handicap of the season since 2008. The Hennessy Gold Cup, which was inaugurated six months after the Whitbread, took over the mantle as jump racing's longest-running sponsorship, but that race too is now to undergo a name change—to the Ladbrokes Trophy. The sixtieth and final Hennessy Gold Cup was run in November and the race

1966 Hennessy Gold Cup, Newbury—
Stan Mellor pounces late on the grey Stalbridge Colonist (receiving 35 lb) to inflict a rare defeat on Arkle, making the last of his four appearances in a race which he won twice under 12-7

*Hennessy Gold Cup Chase (Handicap), Newbury—heavily-backed favourite
Native River (left) clears the second last alongside eventual third Double Ross, with runner-up
Carole's Destrier (right, noseband) still having ground to make up*

had a fitting send-off with a fiercely competitive field for its £113,900 first prize, the third biggest prize for a handicap in Britain after those for the Grand National and the Scottish Grand National.

With the Grand National no longer an automatic target for the top chasers by the middle of the twentieth century, the Hennessy and the Whitbread combined in their early days with the King George VI Chase and the Cheltenham Gold Cup to make 'the big four' over jumps. Arkle and Mill House remain the only ones to have won all four. The first two Hennessys were won by six-year-olds, Mandarin (who was owned by a member of the Hennessy family and won the race again as a ten-year-old) and Taxidermist (the first horse to win both the Whitbread and the Hennessy), with both of them winning the race from that year's Cheltenham Gold Cup winner (Linwell and the mare Kerstin, the latter going on to win the third running of the Hennessy). The Hennessy moved from Cheltenham to Newbury after its first three runnings and Mill House was the next six-year-old to win, in 1963 when, under 12-0, he became the first reigning Cheltenham Gold Cup winner to win the Hennessy. That was the year that Arkle came third (under 11-9) after slipping on landing at the last open ditch. Arkle ran in four successive Hennessys, winning the race twice as the reigning Cheltenham Gold Cup winner (under 12-7 both times, with Mill House fourth carrying 12-4 on the first occasion). A third successive victory for Arkle in 1966, when he didn't have a preparatory race, was foiled by 25/1-shot Stalbridge Colonist who, in receipt of 35 lb, got the better of Arkle by half a length after being brought with a well-timed challenge after the last. Two years of 'magnificent processions'—including a Whitbread also under 12-7 incidentally— came to an end. Arkle hadn't been beaten since the Massey-Ferguson Gold Cup in 1964, a week after he had won his first Hennessy, a penalty for which took his weight at Cheltenham to 12-10.

Weight was Arkle's conqueror in the Hennessy (he had 12-7 again), as it had been in the Massey-Ferguson, and the magnitude of his performance at Newbury was emphasised when Stalbridge Colonist went on to be placed in the next two Cheltenham Gold Cups, beaten three quarters of a length on the first occasion and a length and a neck on the second (What A Myth, third to Stalbridge Colonist and Arkle at Newbury, ran third in that season's Cheltenham Gold Cup and won the race in 1969). Cheltenham Gold Cup winners regularly contested the Hennessy under big weights until the mid-'seventies, with Mandarin, Kerstin, Mill House and Arkle the first winners of both races. Bregawn and Burrough Hill Lad added their names to that particular roll of honour in the 'eighties, the last-named in 1984 when he was the reigning Gold Cup winner and became the first horse since Mill House and Arkle to carry 12-0 or more to victory in the Newbury race. This century has seen dual Hennessy winner Denman (who won under 11-12 both times) and Bobs Worth join the list of horses who have won both the Hennessy and the Cheltenham Gold Cup, despite the Hennessy facing increasing competition for runners from Grade 1

Coral Welsh Grand National Handicap Chase, Chepstow—Native River and Richard Johnson (nearest camera) take over from 2014 winner Emperor's Choice at halfway

races such as the JNWine Champion Chase at Down Royal, created in 1999, and particularly the Betfair Chase at Haydock, first run in 2005 when it succeeded the Hennessy as the most valuable event over fences in Britain before Christmas.

The weights for the sixtieth Hennessy Gold Cup were headed by the previous year's winner Smad Place, who had gone on to finish fourth in the King George VI Chase and sixth in the Cheltenham Gold Cup. The betting market was dominated, though, by up-and-coming types headed by Native River, who started 7/2 favourite after coming through a preparatory outing with flying colours when second in the West Yorkshire Hurdle at Wetherby. The Hennessy looked tailor-made for Native River who had finished second in a very strong edition of the National Hunt Chase at Cheltenham before winning the Mildmay Novices' Chase at Aintree in fine style from Henri Parry Morgan, the RSA Chase winner Blaklion and Un Temps Pour Tout, all of whom were also among the leading fancies for the Hennessy, as were two other second-season chasers, Vyta du Roc, who had won the previous season's Reynoldstown Chase, and Vicente, who had won the Scottish Grand National after finishing fifth in the National Hunt Chase. Among the more seasoned performers in the nineteen-runner line-up were Saphir du Rheu, winner of the Mildmay in 2015 who looked on a generous mark (10 lb lower than when starting favourite and coming fifth in 2015). Saphir du Rheu started joint third favourite with Vyta du Roc behind Native River and Blaklion (13/2). The field also included Hennessy regulars such as 2013 winner Triolo d'Alene (the last of eleven six-year-olds to win before Native River) and Native River's stablemate Theatre Guide who had already been placed in two Hennessys, including when second to Smad Place. The Hennessy was Native River's first race over fences outside novice company and, as in the Mildmay at Aintree, the forcing tactics adopted on him by Richard Johnson, allied to a fluent round of jumping, paid off. Native River and the 50/1-shot Double Ross made it a thorough test and, after coming under pressure on the home turn, Native River looked to have the race won when three lengths clear after jumping the last. In the end, he had to be driven out, after idling, to hold off the staying-on 25/1-shot Carole's Destrier by half a length. Double Ross finished five lengths further behind Carole's Destrier in third, with the 2014 bet365 Gold Cup winner Hadrian's Approach completing the frame; Blaklion, Vyta du Roc, Smad Place and Theatre Guide came next (Saphir du Rheu got only as far as the fourth and Vicente was also a faller late on, although he was well held at the time).

Native River's Hennessy win, and the victory earlier on the same card of the star novice Thistlecrack, led to talk about the Tizzard stable's having three potential Cheltenham Gold Cup candidates (stable stalwart Cue Card had won the Betfair Chase seven days earlier). Colin Tizzard's post-race remark that he had 'got all the toys at the moment' looked even more applicable a month later, when Thistlecrack and Cue Card finished first and second in the King George VI Chase at Kempton and, twenty-four hours later, Native River won the Coral Welsh Grand National under top weight of 11-12 to keep up the stable's fine run (stablemate Royal Vacation also won the Grade 1 Kauto Star Novices' Chase at Kempton, albeit fortuitously). Chepstow on Welsh Grand National day has become associated with stamina-sapping very soft or heavy ground, with the big-race itself a gruelling slog, but, although the going was soft, conditions were nowhere near so extreme as they can be. The prevailing conditions were clearly a factor in the decision to run Native River—no top weight had won the Welsh National since the outstanding Carvill's Hill, who also had 11-12, in 1991—but the weights for the Welsh National come out before the Hennessy and Native River avoided a penalty for his Newbury success because the conditions for the Welsh National do not allow a horse's weight to go above 11-12. Native River was reopposed on the same terms by Carole's Destrier who started second favourite to him, with the ill-fated Onenightinvienna the only other runner in the twenty-strong line-up to start at single-figure odds. It wasn't a vintage Welsh National field, although it contained a number who had run well in the race previously, including dual winner Mountainous, the 2014 winner Emperor's Choice, and Midlands National winner Firebird Flyer (also runner-up to Mountainous twelve months before).

Native River started 11/4 favourite and won the Welsh National in similar fashion to the Hennessy, jumping boldly and well in the main and giving another magnificent display of resolute galloping before drawing clear from the fourth last. The 33/1-shot Raz de Maree, faring best of those held up, closed the gap late on but Native River kept on to win by a length and three quarters, with a fifteen-length gap back to two more 33/1-shots Houblon des Obeaux and Beg To Differ who completed the frame. Native River didn't need to better the form he had shown in the Hennessy but his Chepstow performance put him among the very best winners of the Welsh Grand National in the last quarter of a century. He was also, incidentally, the first horse to win the Hennessy and the Welsh Grand National since Playschool won both races in 1987, ridden by Paul Nicholls. Playschool went on to win the Irish Gold Cup

Betfair Denman Chase, Newbury—late stand-in Aidan Coleman steers Native River to victory over Le Mercurey (left) and the grey Bristol de Mai in a muddling three-runner affair

Brocade Racing's "Native River"

before starting favourite for the Cheltenham Gold Cup, in which he was pulled up after never jumping or moving with his usual fluency (Nicholls reported 'something seriously wrong' and the horse's trainer David Barons was convinced the horse had been got at, though subsequent investigations by the Jockey Club's security services found no evidence to support the claim).

The Grand National looked the best end-of-season target for Native River but, because of his young age, his owners decided not to risk him at Aintree (he was never entered). He was in the Cheltenham Gold Cup line-up, though, after completing his preparation when adding the three-runner Betfair Denman Chase at Newbury in February, showing unexpectedly good acceleration to see off Le Mercurey and odds-on Bristol de Mai after being ridden with more restraint in front by Aidan Coleman, a late replacement for Richard Johnson who was suffering from flu. With Johnson back on board at Cheltenham, Native River started second favourite behind Irish challenger Djakadam in the Gold Cup, just preferred to stablemate Cue Card (Thistlecrack missed the race through injury). Native River put up another battling, front-running performance, keeping on well to finish third, beaten two and three quarter lengths and a short head by another Irish challenger Sizing John and by Minella Rocco, who had also beaten Native River in the previous season's National Hunt Chase (Cue Card fell in the Gold Cup when still in touch at the third last, while Djakadam faded into fourth after blundering at the next). Three Hennessy winners, Triolo d'Alene, Many Clouds and Smad Place, had attempted to add the Gold Cup in the same season since Bobs Worth achieved the double in 2012/13, the best effort being the sixth (not beaten so far as Smad Place in 2016)

566

achieved by Many Clouds who famously went on four weeks later to become the only horse to win the Hennessy and the Grand National (Red Rum was beaten a short head in the Hennessy in the 1973/4 season before going on to win his second Grand National, carrying 12-0 at Aintree; the 2001 Hennessy winner What's Up Boys passed the elbow in the same season's Grand National with a three-length lead only to be collared fifty yards from the line by Bindaree, who had finished fifth in the Hennessy).

		Cadoudal	Green Dancer
		(br 1979)	Come To Sea
	Indian River (FR)		
	(b 1994)	The Fun	Funny Hobby
Native River (IRE)		(b 1979)	The Lark
(ch.g. 2010)			
		Be My Native	Our Native
	Native Mo (IRE)	(br 1979)	Witchy Woman
	(b 1996)		
		Milford Run	Deep Run
		(b 1985)	Belle of The West

The well-made Native River is by the Cadoudal stallion Indian River who was one of the first of the influx of ex-French jumps stallions that have been imported into Ireland in the last decade or so. Native River's dam Native Mo, bred on traditional Irish jumping lines by Be My Native out of a Deep Run mare, never reached the racecourse but has now bred three winners. Native River's five-year-old half-brother Mahler Ten (by Mahler) won a maiden hurdle at Downpatrick in October and went on to show useful form in handicaps at up to three miles. Native Mo had already produced a notable winner before Native River in Orpheus Valley (by Beneficial), a winning hurdler/useful chaser who won the Guinness Handicap Chase at Punchestown in 2014. Further background to Native River's pedigree can be found in the essay on him in last year's Annual. Native River stays four miles and will get the Grand National trip, and he acts on heavy going, though he doesn't require testing conditions to show his best (the ground was good for both the Hennessy and the Gold Cup). He wears cheekpieces but is game and reliable. He gets on well with Richard Johnson and is a bold jumper who is a fine sight out in front forcing the pace. Native River looks a natural for Aintree and could be the one to break Johnson's duck in the National, a race in which he has troubled the judge only once (when runner-up on Balthazar King in 2014) since that agonising defeat on What's Up Boys in 2002. *Colin Tizzard*

NATIVE ROBIN (IRE) 7 br.g. Robin des Pres (FR) – Homebird (IRE) (Be My Native (USA)) [2016/17 c118p, h98, b–: c21g[pu] May 25] maiden pointer: maiden hurdler: fairly useful form in chases, pulled up only outing in 2016/17: stays 2½m: acts on soft going: often travels strongly. *Jeremy Scott*   **c–** **h–**

NATTER JACK CROAK (IRE) 5 b.g. Gold Well – Native Euro (IRE) (Be My Native (USA)) [2016/17 b16.7g Oct 25] won Irish maiden point on debut: 8/1, eighth in bumper at Bangor (21½ lengths behind One More) in October. *Rebecca Curtis*   **b75**

NAUTICAL NITWIT (IRE) 8 b.g. Let The Lion Roar – Mrs Pugwash (IRE) (Un Desperado (FR)) [2016/17 h116: h20.3g[pu] h23.1g³ h20.1d² h19.9g* h20g³ h21.3g* h21.1s[bd] h24.2d h21.3s[F] h19.7d² h26.1g h24d* h20g Apr 7] compact gelding: maiden pointer: fairly useful handicap hurdler: won at Sedgefield in August, Wetherby in October and Southwell in February: stays 25f: acts on soft and good to firm going: races towards rear. *Philip Kirby*   **h129**

NAUTICAL TWILIGHT (IRE) 7 gr.m. Proclamation (IRE) – Anabranch (Kind of Hush) [2016/17 c126, h–: c17.1d⁵ c15.2d⁵ c19.2d³ h16.7g⁴ Mar 27] lengthy mare: fair handicap hurdler/chaser: unproven beyond 17f: acts on heavy going: wears headgear. *Malcolm Jefferson*   **c104** **h107**

NEAREST THE PIN (IRE) 12 b.g. Court Cave (IRE) – Carnbelle (IRE) (Electric) [2016/17 c127, h91: c20.5m² c17.2d⁵ c17.4g² c17.2g⁶ h20.4g⁶ Aug 14] lengthy gelding: winning hurdler: fair handicap chaser nowadays: stays 2½m: acts on soft and good to firm going: usually wears headgear/tongue tie: unreliable. *Dai Williams*   **c100 §** **h–**

NEARLY NAMA'D (IRE) 9 b.g. Millenary – Coca's Well (IRE) (Religiously (USA)) [2016/17 c141, h–: c20v² c17s⁶ Apr 2] winning hurdler: useful chaser: second in Webster Cup Chase at Navan (8 lengths behind A Toi Phil) in March after long absence: stays 2½m: acts on good to firm and heavy going: has worn hood: usually races close up. *Ms Sandra Hughes, Ireland*   **c134** **h–**

NEAR TO TEARS (IRE) 7 br.m. Robin des Pres (FR) – Tears of Jade (IRE) (Presenting) **h82**
[2016/17 h80: h15.6g² h20.9s⁴ h15.6g Jan 3] poor maiden hurdler: should prove suited by
2½m+: acts on soft going. *Lucinda Russell*

NEBULA STORM (IRE) 10 b.g. Galileo (IRE) – Epping (Charnwood Forest (IRE)) **h– §**
[2016/17 h105§: h16g h15.9vᶠ h15.5g h16d Feb 17] fair hurdler at best, no form in
2016/17: wears headgear: has worn tongue tie: quirky. *Michael Blake*

NECK OR NOTHING (GER) 8 b.g. Intikhab (USA) – Nova (GER) (Winged Love **c–**
(IRE)) [2016/17 c–, h94: c16.5gᵖᵘ h16d⁵ h16g⁶ Jul 12] heavy-topped, rather plain gelding: **h95**
maiden hurdler, fair at best: pulled up both starts over fences: raced around 2m: acts on
good to soft going: in cheekpieces last 2 starts: has worn tongue tie, including in 2016/17:
often races towards rear/travels strongly. *Neil Mulholland*

NEEDLESS SHOUTING (IRE) 6 b.g. Footstepsinthesand – Ring The Relatives **c–**
(Bering) [2016/17 h103: h15.7g⁶ h19.3gᶠ c25.2d⁶ c17.2d⁵ Apr 27] rather leggy gelding: **h82**
fair hurdler at best, has deteriorated: no form over fences: unproven beyond 2m: acts on
good to soft going: tried in visor. *Joanne Foster*

NEFYN BAY 8 b.g. Overbury (IRE) – So Cloudy (Cloudings (IRE)) [2016/17 c82, h–: **c112**
c15.7m* c17.1m c17m² c20.1s* c20.1g³ c20.1s² c16.4g c15.9f² c19.2d² c16d² Jan 25] **h–**
smallish gelding: winning hurdler: fair handicap chaser: won at Wincanton (novice) in May
and Perth in July: stays 21f: acts on soft and good to firm going: wears cheekpieces/tongue
tie: front runner/races prominently. *Donald McCain*

NELLY LA RUE (IRE) 10 b.m. Flemensfirth (USA) – Desperately Hoping (IRE) (Un **c73**
Desperado (FR)) [2016/17 h–: c16.4g⁴ c26.2d⁴ c26.3m³ Apr 19] winning pointer: no form **h–**
over hurdles: poor form in chases: stays 3¼m: in cheekpieces last 5 starts. *Victor Thompson*

NELSON'S TOUCH 4 gr.g. Mount Nelson – Lady Friend (Environment Friend) **b99**
[2016/17 b13.2g³ b13.7d³ h16.8v² b16.4d⁴ h16.4g Mar 15] angular gelding: first foal: dam
(h72), lightly raced over hurdles, 1¼m winner on Flat: fairly useful bumper performer:
fourth in listed event at Newbury (7¾ lengths behind Daphne du Clos) in February.
Denis Coakley

NELSON'S VICTORY 7 b.g. Green Horizon – First Class Girl (Charmer) [2016/17 b–: **b–**
b17.7g May 8] no form in bumpers/Flat maiden. *Diana Grissell*

NENERGY'S QUEST 6 b.m. Pasternak – Coolers Quest (Saddlers' Hall (IRE)) [2016/17 **b–**
b13.7m b15.3f³ Apr 23] rather unfurnished mare: second foal: dam (c83/h76) 3¼m chase
winner: no form in bumpers. *Richenda Ford*

NEON WOLF (IRE) 6 b.g. Vinnie Roe (IRE) – Missy O'Brien (IRE) (Supreme **h152**
Leader) [2016/17 b15.8s* h18.5s* h15.7s* h21.1g² Mar 15] **b110**
    The extended entry on Many Clouds recounts the fate of some of the jumpers
who have died on Britain's racecourses in the last twelve months. The deaths
illustrate that horse racing can never be made perfectly safe, but the demise of the
highly promising Neon Wolf is a reminder that serious injury can strike at home as
well as on the racecourse. Neon Wolf had to be put down in August after a freak
accident in his stable in which he lacerated his off-hind deep digital flexor tendon,
an injury from which he could not be saved. He looked a very exciting prospect
and his loss must have been a grievous blow to his connections and all who worked
with him at Manor Farm, Seaborough. Although Neon Wolf was beaten when a hot
favourite for the latest renewal of the Baring Bingham at the Cheltenham Festival
(sent off at 2/1) he was arguably an unlucky loser, a peck at the last proving costly
as he went down by a head to the very game front runner Willoughby Court. Neon
Wolf's jumping had been fine until then and there was plenty to admire about his
performance, as he travelled easily through the race before knuckling down well
under pressure on the run-in.
    Connections ruled out Neon Wolf from the Supreme Novices' Hurdle only
two days before the Festival and some felt he had contested the wrong race, though
it would be quite wrong to suggest that he was found wanting for stamina over the
longer trip. That said, Neon Wolf certainly wasn't short of speed. The fine turn of
foot he showed in the Grade 2 Sky Bet Supreme Trial Rossington Main Novices'
Hurdle over just short of two miles at Haydock on his previous outing had marked
him out as a novice right out of the top drawer. Sent off at 5/4-on, Neon Wolf pulled
clear to win by nine lengths (winning with plenty to spare) and the form worked
out pretty well during the remainder of the season—runner-up Elgin filled the same

Sky Bet Supreme Trial Rossington Main Novices' Hurdle, Haydock—
Neon Wolf warms up for Cheltenham with a scintillating victory over Elgin

spot in the Dovecote at Kempton next time and fourth-placed Mohaayed went on to finish a good third in the Scottish Champion Hurdle at Ayr. That Haydock win in late-January stretched Neon Wolf's unbeaten start to his career to four wins, having also landed a bumper at Uttoxeter in December and a two and a quarter mile novice hurdle at Exeter earlier in January for present connections, scoring most impressively both times. His debut had come in the Irish pointing ranks, in which he won a maiden event for five-year-olds in March 2016, the larger obstacles being very much where his future was going to lie.

Neon Wolf (IRE) (b.g. 2011)	Vinnie Roe (IRE) (b 1998)	Definite Article (b 1992)	Indian Ridge
			Summer Fashion
		Kayu (ch 1985)	Tap On Wood
			Ladytown
	Missy O'Brien (IRE) (gr 2002)	Supreme Leader (b 1982)	Bustino
			Princess Zena
		Rongai (gr 1993)	Commanche Run
			Dame Blakeney

A son of four-times Irish St Leger winner Vinnie Roe, Neon Wolf was the second foal of Irish mare Missy O'Brien, who made the frame on all three starts in bumpers (showing fair form) for Mags Mullins prior to flopping when a short-priced favourite for a Clonmel maiden on her only outing over hurdles. Her only other runner to date has been the bumper winner and useful hurdler Lake View Lad (by Oscar), who stays twenty-one furlongs. Missy O'Brien has since produced a 2013 brother to Neon Wolf (the as yet unraced Young Wolf) and a 2015 colt by Scorpion. Missy O'Brien is a half-sister to three winners, notably the fairly useful staying hurdler Young Dillon (also by Neon Wolf's sire Vinnie Roe), who scored twice during the latest campaign. However, the most high profile name in this pedigree is Baron Blakeney, who was a brother to Neon Wolf's third dam, the unraced Dame Blakeney. Baron Blakeney lowered the colours of Broadsword to win the 1981 Triumph Hurdle (at 66/1), in the process providing Martin Pipe with the first big-race win of his record-breaking training career. Baron Blakeney proved his shock Cheltenham win to be no fluke, developing into a useful staying chaser who won the 1984 renewal of what is now the Mildmay Novices' Chase at Aintree before being retired to stud. Ironically for such a stout stayer (he also made the frame in a Midlands National), Baron Blakeney's best representative from his largely undistinguished spell as a stallion was the smart hurdler/chaser High Baron, who was raced mainly at around two miles (though he was also a winner at two and a half miles).

Underfoot conditions, rather than concerns about the trip, were reportedly the main factor behind the choice of Cheltenham Festival target for Neon Wolf. 'We've made no secret of the fact he's a big heavy unit, a tank of a horse really, so it would have to be slow ground for him to run in the Supreme,' explained trainer Harry Fry, who sidestepped the Festival altogether with his exciting chaser American because of the drying ground. Neon Wolf clearly handled soft ground very well, as was demonstrated by his three wins before Cheltenham, but he certainly didn't seem inconvenienced by the more resilient surface in the Baring Bingham. *Harry Fry*

NESTERENKO (GER) 8 b.g. Doyen (IRE) – Nordwahl (GER) (Waajib) [2016/17 h127: h19d* c20.9s⁴ c23.6v⁴ c23.6sᵖᵘ Mar 5] sturdy gelding: fairly useful handicap hurdler: won at Warwick in May: failed to take to chasing: left Nicky Henderson after first start: should stay further than 19f: acts on soft going: usually wears hood. *Venetia Williams*
c–
h122

NET WORK ROUGE (FR) 8 b.g. Network (GER) – Lychee de La Roque (FR) (Officiel (FR)) [2016/17 c–, h128: h24dᵖᵘ c23.9g² c21.4g³ c23g² c22.6g* c24.1g³ c23.6g* Apr 17] useful-looking gelding: fairly useful hurdler: similar form over fences: won novices at Stratford in August and Huntingdon in April: will stay beyond 3¼m: acts on heavy going: wears headgear/tongue tie: front runner: temperamental. *Kim Bailey*
c128 §
h–

NEUMOND (GER) 6 b.g. Sholokhov (IRE) – Natalis (GER) (Law Society (USA)) [2016/17 h95: h20mᵖᵘ May 19] sturdy gelding: multiple point winner: maiden hurdler, modest form at best. *Nicky Henderson*
h–

NEVADA 4 gr.g. Proclamation (IRE) – La Columbina (Carnival Dancer) [2016/17 b14.6s⁴ b16s⁵ b15.7s⁵ Jan 31] poor form in bumpers. *Steve Gollings*
b74

NEVER BEEN WRONG (IRE) 6 b.m. Robin des Champs (FR) – Main Dans La Main (FR) (Pistolet Bleu (IRE)) [2016/17 b15.8v Dec 31] €45,000 3-y-o: sixth foal: half-sister to fair chaser Handtheprizeover (2m-3m winner, by Exit To Nowhere): dam unraced half-sister to fairly useful hurdler/useful chaser (stayed 3m) Exit To Wave: tailed off in bumper. *Tom Symonds*
b–

NEVER COMPLAIN (IRE) 9 ch.g. Beneficial – Polly Native (IRE) (Be My Native (USA)) [2016/17 c125, h–: c20.2m² c21.1gᵘʳ Apr 6] workmanlike gelding: winning pointer: maiden hurdler: fairly useful chaser: best form at 2½m: acts on good to firm and heavy going: tried in cheekpieces. *Mrs F. Marshall*
c109
h–

NEVER EQUALLED (IRE) 8 br.g. Brian Boru – Broken Thought (IRE) (Broken Hearted) [2016/17 h122: c19.4g³ c20.3s² c20.8s⁴ c19.4d⁴ c19.4v³ h20v* Mar 19] lengthy gelding: fairly useful hurdler: won handicap at Ffos Las in March: similar form over fences: second in novice at Bangor in November: stays 21f: best form on soft/heavy going: in cheekpieces last 2 starts. *Bernard Llewellyn*
c126
h122

NEVER LEARN (IRE) 6 b.g. King's Theatre (IRE) – Hamari Gold (IRE) (Priolo (USA)) [2016/17 h83, h–: h19.5d h16d³ h19.8d h19.5s⁴ h25.5s³ Mar 11] workmanlike gelding: fair maiden hurdler: likely to prove best up to 3m: acts on soft going. *Colin Tizzard*
h105

NEVEROWNUP (IRE) 12 b.g. Quws – Cobble (IRE) (Bigstone (IRE)) [2016/17 c109, h–: c20sᵖᵘ h20dᵖᵘ Jun 29] winning hurdler/chaser, no form in 2016/17: stays 3m: acts on soft and good to firm going: has worn cheekpieces/tongue tie, including final start: usually races close up. *Linda Blackford*
c–
h–

NEVER UP (GER) 6 b.g. Danehill Dancer (IRE) – Never Green (IRE) (Halling (USA)) [2016/17 c86p, h109: c16s⁵ c17.3m⁴ c15.7v³ h15.7s⁴ c15.7d* c15.7v* c17.2g⁴ c21.1m³ Apr 19] winning hurdler: fair handicap chaser: won at Southwell in February and March (novice event): stays 21f: acts on good to firm and heavy going: usually races close up. *Sue Smith*
c114
h96

NEVERUSHACON (IRE) 6 b.g. Echo of Light – Lily Beth (IRE) (Desert King (IRE)) [2016/17 c17m⁵ c17.4m⁴ c18.2g³ c20.5gᵘʳ c18.2d⁵ c16d² c15.9g⁴ c16.7d⁴ c16d³ Apr 27] winning hurdler: useful chaser: won maiden at Limerick in July: second in Grade 3 novice
c138
h–

at Gowran (nose behind Ridestan) in October and third in handicap at Punchestown (length behind Don't Touch It) in April: stays 2¼m: acts on soft and good to firm going. *Mrs J. Harrington, Ireland*

NEVILLE 9 b.g. Revoque (IRE) – Dudeen (IRE) (Anshan) [2016/17 c–, h–: h23gpu Jun 4] winning pointer: maiden hurdler: failed to beat a rival in 2 chases: has finished weakly. *Bob Buckler*   **c–** **h–**

NEVILLE WOODS 10 b.g. Alflora (IRE) – Angie Marinie (Sabrehill (USA)) [2016/17 c96, h92: h16.2d³ c17.1m⁴ h16.2dpu c20.1d⁶ c23.9g h16.8gpu Sep 1] modest handicap hurdler/maiden chaser: won twice in points in 2017: unproven beyond 2¼m: acts on good to firm and heavy going: has worn cheekpieces: tried in tongue tie. *George Charlton*   **c89** **h90**

NEW AGENDA 5 b.g. New Approach (IRE) – Prove (Danehill (USA)) [2016/17 h16m² h16g⁴ Nov 7] fairly useful on Flat, stays 9.5f: fair form over hurdles: better effort when second in listed novice at Kempton: will prove best at sharp 2m: tried in hood. *Paul Webber*   **h108**

NEWBERRY NEW (IRE) 5 b.g. Kodiac – Sunblush (UAE) (Timber Country (USA)) [2016/17 h123: h16dpu h19.9vpu c19.4d³ c19.4s⁴ c19.4d c19.2d³ c20d⁶ Feb 20] good-topped gelding: fairly useful hurdler at best for Mrs J. Harrington, pulled up in handicaps first 2 starts in 2016/17: fair form over fences: stays 19f: acts on heavy going. *Harriet Bethell*   **c112** **h–**

NEW DIRREEN (IRE) 6 ch.g. Trans Island – Strong Irish (IRE) (Corrouge (USA)) [2016/17 b16m⁵ h19.9g Sep 7] maiden pointer: well beaten in bumper/maiden hurdle: tried in tongue tie. *Henry Oliver*   **h–** **b–**

NEWERA 5 ch.g. Makfi – Coming Home (Vettori (IRE)) [2016/17 h15.5g h16.7s⁵ h15.8s⁶ Jan 19] fairly useful on Flat, stays 12.5f: fair form over hurdles: best effort when fifth in novice at Bangor in December. *John Groucott*   **h110**

NEW GRANADA 4 b.g. Zamindar (USA) – Costa Rica (IRE) (Sadler's Wells (USA)) [2016/17 b15.6g⁵ b16.7m Apr 9] modest form on first of 2 starts in bumpers. *Chris Grant*   **b76**

NEW HORIZONS (IRE) 7 b.g. Presenting – Namloc (IRE) (Phardante (FR)) [2016/17 h112: c23.6spu c24g Mar 18] lengthy gelding: fair hurdler: no form in 2 chases after long absence: stays 3m: acts on good to firm and good to soft going. *Caroline Fryer*   **c–** **h–**

NEW LIST 4 ch.g. Pivotal – Angel's Tears (Seeking The Gold (USA)) [2016/17 b16d h16m³ Apr 13] £10,000 3-y-o: first foal: dam unraced half-sister to useful hurdler (stayed 3m) Aalim: won point bumper in January before seventh in bumper at Wetherby: 8/1, third in juvenile maiden at same course (6½ lengths behind Lord Topper) on hurdling debut: should be suited by further than 2m. *Brian Ellison*   **h102** **b76**

NEW MEMBER (IRE) 6 b.g. Alhaarth (IRE) – Sincere (IRE) (Bahhare (USA)) [2016/17 b86p: b15.7g h16.7g h15.8m* h16.2g³ h19.7s³ h15.8d* h16g⁴ h16dpu Jan 14] useful-looking gelding: placed on first of 2 starts in bumpers: fairly useful hurdler: won novice at Ludlow in October and handicap at Huntingdon in December: stays 2½m: acts on soft and good to firm going: sent to race in USA. *Tom Lacey*   **h126** **b–**

NEW MILLENNIUM (IRE) 4 b.c. Galileo (IRE) – Banquise (IRE) (Last Tycoon) [2016/17 h16s³ h15.8s⁶ h16m⁴ Apr 4] half-brother to fair hurdler Diamondgeezer Luke (19f/2½m winner, by War Chant): mid-field at best in maidens on Flat: fair form over hurdles: best effort when fourth in novice at Kempton in April: left John Halley after first start: will prove best at 2m: open to further improvement. *Philip Hobbs*   **h101 p**

NEWORLD (FR) 8 gr.g. Lost World (IRE) – Crusch Alva (FR) (Unfuwain (USA)) [2016/17 c–, h96: h16g³ h15.8g⁵ h15.8m³ h15.8g⁵ c21.5mF Jul 13] modest handicap hurdler: failed to complete both starts over fences: left Richard Hobson after fourth start: raced mainly at 2m: acted on soft and good to firm going: usually wore headgear: often tongue tied: dead. *Dai Williams*   **c–** **h96**

NEWQUAY CARDS (IRE) 5 gr.g. Tikkanen (USA) – Sanadja (IRE) (Slip Anchor) [2016/17 b16.3s b15.8v Mar 1] big, workmanlike gelding: no form in bumpers. *Evan Williams*   **b–**

NEW REACTION 6 b.g. New Approach (IRE) – Intaaj (IRE) (Machiavellian (USA)) [2016/17 h–: h15.3d h16.3d h19.7sF h19spu h19.9v² h19gpu h21.6m Apr 15] close-coupled gelding: modest maiden hurdler: best effort at 2½m: acts on heavy going: in headgear last 3 starts. *Alexandra Dunn*   **h87**

NEW REPUBLIC (IRE) 6 b.g. Morozov (USA) – Saltee Great (IRE) (Fourstars Allstar (USA)) [2016/17 h–: h15.8v h15.3s* h19.7vpu Jan 11] smallish, workmanlike gelding: modest form over hurdles: standout effort when won novice handicap at Wincanton in January: should stay beyond 2m: acts on soft going: in cheekpieces/tongue tie last 2 starts. *Evan Williams*   **h87**

NEWSPAGE (IRE) 11 b.g. Blueprint (IRE) – Newlineview (IRE) (Saddlers' Hall (IRE)) c– §
[2016/17 c85§, h–: c23.4s^{pu} Oct 22] won 4 times in points: maiden hurdler: maiden chaser, h–
pulled up in handicap only outing (tongue tied) in 2016/17: stays 21f: acts on soft going:
wears blinkers nowadays: front runner/races prominently: weak finisher. *Rebecca Menzies*

NEWSTART (IRE) 6 br.g. Stowaway – Joes Annie (IRE) (Norwich) [2016/17 b16g⁶ h99
h20g b19.8s⁵ h16g⁶ h19.5d⁴ h22.1d^{pu} h19.9d h21.3d* h20.6m⁵ h19.7m³ Apr 13] €32,000 b81
3-y-o: first foal: dam unraced half-sister to fairly useful hurdler/useful chaser (stayed 2½m)
Rinroe: modest form in bumpers: modest hurdler: won seller at Wetherby in March: left
John Joseph Hanlon after seventh start: stays 21f: acts on good to firm and good to soft
going: tried in cheekpieces. *Brian Ellison*

NEWSWORTHY (IRE) 7 br.g. Presenting – Cousin Jen (IRE) (Oscar (IRE)) [2016/17 c108
h122p, b92: h19.6g* h20g⁴ h21.2g³ h21.1s^{pu} h19m h25v⁶ h18.8g^{ur} c20v⁵ h16g³ Apr 21] h115
lengthy, angular gelding: bumper winner: fairly useful hurdler: won novice at Bangor very
early in season: 28/1, fifth in maiden at Navan (25¼ lengths behind Champagne Harmony)
on chasing debut: left Nicky Henderson after first start, Tom Symonds after fourth, Neil
Mulholland after sixth: stays 21f: acts on good to soft going: has worn headgear. *Mrs D. A.
Love, Ireland*

NEW TARABELA 6 ch.g. New Approach (IRE) – Tarabela (CHI) (Hussonet (USA)) h78 §
[2016/17 h–: h16.3g³ h24.1m Apr 13] compact gelding: poor maiden hurdler: should stay
further than 2m: acts on heavy going: tried in blinkers: often races prominently: ungenuine.
Tony Carroll

NEWTON GERONIMO 8 b.g. Brian Boru – Newton Commanche (IRE) (Commanche c–
Run) [2016/17 c105, h111§: h16.7g³ h19.1g* h20d* h20.6g⁶ h20.3g⁵ Aug 31] fairly useful h129 §
handicap hurdler: won at Fontwell and Worcester in June: lightly-raced maiden chaser:
stays 2½m: acts on good to firm and good to soft going: has worn hood: one to treat with
caution (has twice refused to race). *Ben Pauling*

NEWTON THISTLE 10 b.g. Erhaab (USA) – Newton Venture (Petoski) [2016/17 c120, c–
h–: h24v^{pu} c30g^F Jan 12] winning hurdler: fairly useful chaser at best: stayed 3m: acted on h–
heavy going: tried in cheekpieces: wore tongue tie: dead. *Ben Pauling*

NEWTOWN LAD (IRE) 7 b.g. Craigsteel – Rocher Lady (IRE) (Phardante (FR)) c124
[2016/17 h109p, b76: h23.3d⁴ c20.5d³ c22.5v* c23.6g c24.3s³ c24.3v* c24s^F Mar 18] fair h109
form over hurdles: fairly useful form over fences: won handicaps at Uttoxeter in November
and Ayr (novice) in January: stays 3m: acts on heavy going: in blinkers last 2 starts: wears
tongue tie: front runner/races prominently. *Lucinda Russell*

NEW VENNTURE (FR) 5 b.m. Kapgarde (FR) – Polyandry (IRE) (Pennekamp (USA)) h–
[2016/17 h90: h19g^{pu} h16.8s^{pu} h19s^{ur} Feb 21] close-coupled, sparely-made mare:
maiden hurdler, no form in 2016/17: in cheekpieces last 2 starts: dead. *Harry Fry*

NEW VIC (IRE) 11 ch.g. Old Vic – Innovate (IRE) (Posen (USA)) [2016/17 c103, h–: c95
c21.6d³ c26.2m^{pu} c21.5s Dec 19] no form over hurdles: fair hunter chaser: stays 3¼m: acts h–
on good to soft going: tried in hood: in tongue tie last 4 starts. *Sandy Thomson*

NEW WORLD 8 b.g. Presenting – Nova Rose (Ra Nova) [2016/17 c20.5g^{pu} May 2] c–
lengthy gelding: fair winning hurdler in Ireland: pulled up in novice on chasing debut h–
(tongue tied): bred to stay 2½m. *Ben Pauling*

NEWYEARSRESOLUTION (IRE) 13 b.g. Mr Combustible (IRE) – That's Magic c–
(IRE) (Lord Americo) [2016/17 c–, h76: c24.2d May 7] point winner: poor hurdler: maiden h–
chaser: stays 25f: acts on heavy going: usually races nearer last than first. *Simon Waugh*

NEXIUS (IRE) 8 b.g. Catcher In The Rye (IRE) – Nicolaia (GER) (Alkalde (GER)) c–
[2016/17 c132, h–: h21.6g h23g⁶ h21g⁶ h20.5d Dec 31] strong gelding: useful hurdler at h–
best, little impact in handicaps in 2016/17: winning chaser: stays 2½m: in headgear last 4
starts: tried in tongue tie. *Paul Nicholls*

NEXT DESTINATION (IRE) 5 b.g. Dubai Destination (USA) – Liss Alainn (IRE) b115
(Flemensfirth (USA)) [2016/17 b16v* b16.4g⁴ b16d² Apr 27] rather unfurnished gelding:
second foal: dam unraced half-sister to useful hurdler (stays 2¾m) Kilfenora: winning
pointer: smart form in bumpers: won maiden at Fairyhouse (by ¾ length from Derrinross)
in January: fourth in Champion Bumper at Cheltenham (3 lengths behind Fayonagh) in
March. *W. P. Mullins, Ireland*

NEXT EDITION (IRE) 9 b.g. Antonius Pius (USA) – Starfish (IRE) (Galileo (IRE)) h96
[2016/17 h18.6g² h20.6s³ h18.6d h15.6g⁴ h19.7d Feb 21] fair on Flat, stays 16.5f: modest
handicap hurdler: stays 21f: acts on soft and good to firm going: sometimes in cheekpieces
nowadays: usually races towards rear/freely. *Philip Kirby*

NEXT EXIT (IRE) 12 b.g. Exit To Nowhere (USA) – Pilgrim Star (IRE) (Marju (IRE)) **c73 x**
[2016/17 c65x, h–: c24s^{pu} c15.7g^{pu} h15.8g c15.7m^6 c17.2g^3 c17.2g^4 c20.2f* c15.9f^3 **h–**
c20.2m^3 c20.2g^5 c23.6d c23.6g^3 c16.5g^3 Apr 28] winning hurdler: poor handicap chaser:
won at Leicester in November: stays 21f: acts on any going: wears tongue tie: often let
down by jumping. *John Cornwall*

NEXT HIGHT (IRE) 10 b.g. High Chaparral (IRE) – Night Petticoat (GER) (Petoski) **c– §**
[2016/17 h16.2d^4 h23.3g^6 h19.9m c24.2d^{pu} c16.4s^{pu} h23.3v^{pu} h16d h20.6v^{pu} h20.6g^4 **h65 §**
h27m^5 Apr 19] leggy gelding: poor handicap hurdler nowadays: maiden chaser: stays 3m:
acts on heavy going: tried in headgear: front runner/races prominently: untrustworthy.
Jonathan Haynes

NEXT LEVEL (IRE) 6 b.g. Mahler – Molly Be (First Trump) [2016/17 h21d^{pu} h24x^4 **h83**
h23.6s^{pu} h19.1s^{pu} Feb 26] off mark in points at sixth attempt: poor form over hurdles.
Paul Cowley

NEXT LOT 7 b.g. Mountain High (IRE) – Martha Reilly (IRE) (Rainbows For Life **h84**
(CAN)) [2016/17 b–: h19d h19.9g^4 h19.9s^{pu} h23.8d^{ur} h23.9g h24.4d h25d^5 h25g^2 Apr 3]
winning pointer: poor maiden hurdler: stays 25f: acts on good to soft going: in hood last 2
starts. *Richard Phillips*

NEXT SENSATION (IRE) 10 b.g. Brian Boru – Road Trip (IRE) (Anshan) [2016/17 **c131 §**
c123, h–: c20g^{pu} c16g^4 c17.3g^F c16.3g^4 c18m^{pu} c17.1s^{pu} Apr 3] big, rangy gelding: maiden **h–**
hurdler: useful handicap chaser: won at Newton Abbot in September: best around 2m: acts
on heavy going: has worn hood: wears tongue tie: front runner, tends to find little and is one
to be wary of. *Michael Scudamore*

NICEANDEASY (IRE) 4 b.g. Kalanisi (IRE) – High Priestess (IRE) (Priolo (USA)) **b99**
[2016/17 b16.4v* Mar 7] €14,000 3-y-o: fifth foal: half-brother to bumper winner/useful
hurdler Princely Conn (2m winner, by Whitmore's Conn): dam (h112), 2m hurdle winner,
also useful 1½m-1¾m winner on Flat: 7/2, overcame greenness when won maiden bumper
at Newcastle (by 10 lengths from Sultans Pride) on debut. *Keith Dalgleish*

NICELY INDEED (IRE) 7 b.g. Marienbard (IRE) – Rare Dollar (IRE) (Bob's Return **h103 +**
(IRE)) [2016/17 h114p, b104: h16g^6 Mar 18] good-topped gelding: unseated in Irish point:
dual bumper winner: fair form over hurdles: encouragement when sixth in novice at
Kempton on sole outing in 2016/17: will be suited by further than 2m: may yet do better.
Kim Bailey

NICE THOUGHTS (IRE) 5 b.g. Shamardal (USA) – Zacheta (Polish Precedent (USA)) **h101**
[2016/17 h101: h15.9g^2 h16m^4 h16g h16m^4 h16.7s^{pu} Apr 3] angular gelding: fair maiden
hurdler: best effort at 2m: acts on heavy going: wears cheekpieces: tried in tongue tie.
David Pipe

NICHOLASCOPERNICUS (IRE) 8 ch.g. Medicean – Ascendancy (Sadler's Wells **h–**
(USA)) [2016/17 h102: h20m^{pu} May 19] maiden hurdler, pulled up in handicap sole outing
in 2016/17: unproven beyond 2m: best form on soft/heavy going: in cheekpieces last 2
starts: in tongue tie last 4. *Kerry Lee*

NICHOLAS T 5 b.g. Rail Link – Thorntoun Piccolo (Groom Dancer (USA)) [2016/17 **b92**
b85: b16.2d^2 May 4] fair form in bumpers: second at Kelso in May: fairly useful on Flat,
stays 1¼m. *Jim Goldie*

NICHOLS CANYON 7 b.g. Authorized (IRE) – Zam Zoom (IRE) (Dalakhani **h165**
(IRE)) [2016/17 h164: h24g^3 h16d* h16d^2 h16g^F h24g* h24d^2 Apr 27]
Still only seven, Nichols Canyon has already achieved plenty in a varied
career. He started out as a smart performer on the Flat with John Gosden, winning
two listed races and finishing second in the St Simon Stakes at Newbury. In his
first campaign over hurdles with Willie Mullins he won four Grade 1 novices, in
his second season he became the only horse to date to have lowered the colours of
his Champion Hurdle-winning stable-companion Faugheen and he finished third in
the Champion Hurdle himself, while in the latest season he successfully stepped
up in trip to give his trainer a first success in the Stayers' Hurdle. Until the latest
Festival, Nichols Canyon had done most of his racing at two miles but his last
couple of wins as a novice at Aintree and Punchestown had been over two and a
half, following a third in the Baring Bingham at Cheltenham. His only previous try
at three miles had seen him well below his best, though that performance had come
in the unfamiliar surroundings of Percy Warner Park in Tennessee in the Iroquois
Hurdle in May 2016. Nichols Canyon was beaten just over three lengths behind the
useful ex-Irish winner Rawnaq but appeared not to see the trip out quite so well as

stanjames.com Morgiana Hurdle, Punchestown—thick fog mars the spectacle as Nichols Canyon repeats his victory of the previous season, though without the surprise element this time; he gives trainer Willie Mullins a sixth straight win in the race

stable-companion Shaneshill who stayed on to go down by a neck. Nichols Canyon had actually put up his most encouraging staying performance on his final start on the Flat when winning a listed race in heavy ground at Saint-Cloud over just short of two miles, with the field strung out behind him at intervals more reminiscent of a jumps race.

Before Cheltenham, though, Nichols Canyon was his stable's chief representative in Ireland's top two-mile hurdles during what was expected to be only the temporary absence of Faugheen and Annie Power. Six months after his trip across the Atlantic, Nichols Canyon made his reappearance again in the stanjames. com Morgiana Hurdle at Punchestown in November, the race in which he had upset Faugheen twelve months earlier. In a field of five that included stable-companions Sempre Medici and Simenon, 13/8-on shot Nichols Canyon stood out as the one to beat and won accordingly from the four-year-olds Jer's Girl and Ivanovich Gorbatov. Nichols Canyon made all the running, as he had done against Faugheen, tracked by Jer's Girl before easily drawing twelve lengths clear of that filly at the line, with the Triumph Hurdle winner another five lengths back in third. The first three met again in the following month's Ryanair Hurdle at Leopardstown which Nichols Canyon was also bidding to win for the second year. Another four-year-old, stable-companion Footpad, joined him in the line-up with the field completed by former stablemate Petit Mouchoir, last seen taking a fall when looking sure to play a part in the finish of the 'Fighting Fifth' at Newcastle. Nichols Canyon was sent off at 5/2-on but it was Petit Mouchoir who made all the running this time, Nichols Canyon not for the first time compromising his chance by jumping out to his right, notably at the last couple of hurdles, and running below form as a result, seven lengths behind the winner. In a rematch with Petit Mouchoir in the Irish Champion Hurdle back at Leopardstown a month later (a race that had been scheduled for the return of the previous year's winner Faugheen), Nichols Canyon's jumping ultimately let him down again and he fell at the last, giving the overriding impression that he was again wanting for pace, looking booked for a close third behind Petit Mouchoir and Footpad when departing, the latter closing on him at the time.

Among Nichols Canyon's opponents in the Stayers' Hurdle at Cheltenham was the 2014 Champion Hurdle winner Jezki, bidding to become the first horse to win both races since the Stayers' took its current form. In the *Chasers & Hurdlers* era, Gaye Brief fared best of the four Champion Hurdle winners before Jezki, coming fourth in 1988 and 1989, the three others being Comedy of Errors, Hardy Eustace and Katchit. Former top two milers have won the Stayers' Hurdle, most recently Solwhit in 2013, himself a dual winner of the Morgiana like Nichols Canyon and, before him, the 1992 winner Nomadic Way who had twice finished runner-up in the Champion Hurdle. Nichols Canyon might have had minimal experience over three miles, but a number of Stayers' Hurdle winners have been successful on their first try at the trip. Nomadic Way was one (the Stayers' Hurdle was even more of a test then, run over twenty-five furlongs on the Old Course) and, more recently, More of That in 2014 when he beat Annie Power the only time she was tried over three miles. Inglis Drever was also trying three miles for the first time when he won the first of what became three staying championships for Nichols Canyon's owners, Andrea and Graham Wylie, in 2005. Inglis Drever had been campaigned exclusively over two miles earlier that season, finishing second in the 'Fighting Fifth' and the Bula and winning the Champion Hurdle Trial at Haydock and the Kingwell, and he took his chance in the Stayers' Hurdle when the same owners' Royal Rosa went lame.

Inglis Drever's first win in the 'Stayers' Hurdle' coincided with the rebranding of the race under Ladbrokes sponsorship when it took on the spurious title of the World Hurdle, the year also that the stayers' championship was given top billing for the first time on the third day of the newly-expanded Festival. The World Hurdle title was retained when Ryanair stepped in to sponsor the 2016 renewal after Ladbrokes were barred from sponsoring when they refused to sign up to the BHA's authorised betting partner scheme, but the race reverted to its old name in the latest season when sponsored for the first time by Sun Bets (bizarrely the race day edition of *The Sun* featured a front page reader offer for a free bet with Ladbrokes!). There was a hot favourite for the second year running, with the previous year's Spa winner Unowhatimeanharry, a 6/5-on shot after being successful in his last eight races. He had taken an identical path to Thistlecrack the year before, arriving at Cheltenham after contesting the Long Distance Hurdle at Newbury, the Long Walk at Ascot and the Cleeve at Cheltenham. Jezki, winner of the World Series Hurdle over three miles at the 2015 Punchestown Festival and successful in the first of his only two starts since over two miles early in the year, was next in the betting on 15/2, ahead of 9/1-shot the 2015 winner Cole Harden, runner-up to Unowhatimeanharry in the Cleeve when receiving weight, and Nichols Canyon on 10/1. Among those at longer odds were Shaneshill, winner of the Galmoy Hurdle at Gowran from Snow Falcon (also in the line-up), Mullins' other runner Clondaw Warrior who had come third in the same race, Thistlecrack's half-brother West Approach (third in the Cleeve) and, at 33/1, Lil Rockerfeller who had chased home Unowhatimeanharry in the Long Walk.

In truth, the Stayers' Hurdle field was closely matched with the exception of the favourite and, with Unowhatimeanharry having something of an off-day, it took less winning than might have been expected. After Cole Harden had made much of the running as usual, Lil Rockerfeller was the first to go for home after the final

Sun Bets Stayers' Hurdle, Cheltenham—Nichols Canyon (left) is produced late to beat outsider Lil Rockerfeller (checked sleeves) and hot favourite Unowhatimeanharry (right)

Andrea & Graham Wylie's "Nichols Canyon"

turn and was still narrowly in front jumping the last, where Unowhatimeanharry was making heavy weather of trying to reel him in. Ruby Walsh had settled Nichols Canyon towards the rear for much of the race and brought his mount with a sustained run up the stand rail. Nichols Canyon skipped over the last but Lil Rockerfeller had gamely seen off the favourite halfway up the run-in and stuck to his task, Nichols Canyon only overhauling him close home to win by three quarters of a length. There was a three and a half length gap to Unowthatimeanharry and the same distance back to Cole Harden who came fourth for the second year running, though finishing a lot closer than he had to Thistlecrack. Cole Harden's trainer was critical of the decision to water the track (though the going was no softer than good), feeling it was prejudicial to the horse whose win two years earlier had come on good to firm ground (although the official description on that occasion was 'good'). Conditions were said to be firmer on the New Course, which hadn't been raced on since the autumn, and the watering looked justified on safety grounds, considering that the combination of firmish going and big fields at championship meetings tends to increase the risk of injuries. Whilst Nichols Canyon filled in one of the few remaining blanks in his trainer's record in Grade 1 contests at the Festival, it was a fifth win in the race for Walsh who partnered Big Buck's to all four of his victories. Graham Wylie, whose Yorkhill won the Golden Miller earlier on the card and initiated a four-timer for Mullins and Walsh on the day, was even more pleased with Nichols Canyon's success in his favourite race at the Festival, thanks to Inglis Drever's exploits. Connections revealed afterwards that Nichols Canyon had been bought with the race in mind. 'Willie rang me one day to say he had a horse for me and he could be the next Inglis Drever,' Wylie said. 'Nichols Canyon reminds me of him—he's not big, but he's a terrier.'

Most of the Stayers' Hurdle principals went on to contest the Champion Stayers' Hurdle at Punchestown where Nichols Canyon found a back-to-form Unowhatimeanharry a more formidable opponent. Nichols Canyon went down by a head in a thrilling finish, the pair pulling a long way clear of the rest, but only after Nichols Canyon conceded first run, the winner leading entering the straight and Nichols Canyon staying on well but just failing (he was in front a stride past the line). Another crack at the Iroquois Hurdle was pencilled in for Nichols Canyon weeks later, as he was eligible for the 500,000-dollar bonus for any horse winning the Iroquois and the Stayers' Hurdle within the same twelve months. However, Nichols Canyon sustained an injury travelling to the States and was unable to take part. Injury had also ruled Rawnaq out of his own bid for the bonus in the Stayers' Hurdle, for which he had been entered earlier in the year after Ruby Walsh had ridden him to victory in the Grade 1 Grand National Hurdle at Far Hills in October. Runner-up in that contest was the easy winner of the latest Iroquois Hurdle, Scorpiancer, a fairly useful hurdler for Rebecca Curtis earlier in his career, who had finished more than a dozen lengths behind Nichols Canyon when fourth in the 2016 Iroquois.

Nichols Canyon (b.g. 2010)	Authorized (IRE) (b 2004)	Montjeu (b 1996)	Sadler's Wells Floripedes
		Funsie (b 1999)	Saumarez Vallee Dansante
	Zam Zoom (IRE) (gr 2005)	Dalakhani (gr 2000)	Darshaan Daltawa
		Mantesera (ch 2000)	In The Wings Lucayan Princess

Nichols Canyon's essentially Flat pedigree has been covered in the last two editions of *Chasers & Hurdlers*. He was one of two Cheltenham Festival winners for his sire the 2007 Derby winner Authorized, along with the National Hunt Chase winner Tiger Roll. Nichols Canyon is therefore a grandson of Montjeu, as is stable-companion Douvan (by Derby runner-up Walk In The Park)—no coincidence, perhaps, given that Montjeu sired Mullins' 'horse of a lifetime' Hurricane Fly. The compact Nichols Canyon, ridden much more patiently on his last two starts than he used to be over shorter trips (he also wears ear plugs nowadays), clearly stays three miles well now. He acts on heavy ground but doesn't need the mud. He'll no doubt be aimed at giving his owners a fifth win in the Stayers' Hurdle. *W. P. Mullins, Ireland*

NICKI'S NIPPER 9 b.m. Denounce – Mistress Star (Soldier Rose) [2016/17 h72: h16.8s⁴ h19.6g h17.2g⁴ h16.7d² h15.8g⁴ h17.2g⁴ c16.4d⁴ h16.8s² h16.8sᵖᵘ h15.7d h15.7v² h19.9g² h19.9g³ h27mᵘ Apr 19] modest handicap hurdler: won at Sedgefield very early in season, Cartmel in June and Sedgefield again in April: fourth in novice handicap at Sedgefield (23¼ lengths behind Maxed Out King) on chasing debut: stays easy 27f: acts on soft and good to firm going: wears headgear: front runner/races prominently. *Sam England* **c80 h88**

NICKNAME EXIT (FR) 7 b.g. Nickname (FR) – Exit To Fire (FR) (Exit To Nowhere (USA)) [2016/17 c30dᵖᵘ c22g³ c25sᵖᵘ c22d c20.9vᵖᵘ c20s⁶ Mar 2] winning hurdler: useful chaser at best, disappointing in 2016/17: left Gordon Elliott after fourth start: stays 3m: acts on heavy going: usually wears headgear nowadays: temperamental. *J. M. Ridley* **c– § h–**

NICOLAS CHAUVIN (IRE) 9 b.g. Saffron Walden (FR) – Kenzie (IRE) (Presenting) [2016/17 c121, h–: c16.5g⁸ c16g c20g⁴ c16.5g³ c16m² c16.4g² Dec 29] winning hurdler: fairly useful chaser: won novice at Huntingdon in May: unproven beyond 2m: acts on good to firm and good to soft going: usually in hood in 2016/17: often races freely. *Nicky Henderson* **c125 h–**

NICOLOSIO (IRE) 7 b.g. Peintre Celebre (USA) – Nicolaia (GER) (Alkalde (GER)) [2016/17 h16v h15.8s Mar 5] sturdy gelding: useful on Flat (stays 11f) when trained in Germany: well beaten over hurdles. *Paul Cowley* **h–**

NIETZSCHE 4 ch.g. Poet's Voice – Ganga (IRE) (Generous (IRE)) [2016/17 h16g² h16.4s² h15.7d* h15.6g³ h18.6s* h19.3d* h16.4g³ Mar 15] angular gelding: half-brother to several winning jumpers, including useful hurdler Arrayan (2m/17f winner, by Catcher In The Rye): useful on Flat, stays 13f: fairly useful hurdler: won juvenile at Catterick in December, and handicaps at Market Rasen (conditional) and Catterick in January: third in Fred Winter Hurdle at Cheltenham in March: stays 19f: acts on soft going: in hood last 3 starts. *Brian Ellison* **h129**

NIGHT ALLIANCE (IRE) 12 ch.g. Pierre – Next Venture (IRE) (Zaffaran (USA)) **c111 §**
[2016/17 c114§, h–: c32.5g c24s c20.9v^{pu} c23.8s^2 c22.7s^5 c23.6v^{pu} Mar 23] workmanlike **h–**
gelding: winning hurdler: fair hunter chaser nowadays: stays 3m: acts on heavy going:
wears headgear/tongue tie: usually races prominently: unreliable. *P. R. M. Philips*

NIGHTCAP JACK (IRE) 10 b.g. Gamut (IRE) – Delgany Rose (IRE) (Roselier (FR)) **c–**
[2016/17 c21.2m^{pu} May 30] multiple point winner: pulled up in maiden hunter on chasing
debut. *J. T. B. Hunt*

NIGHT COMES IN (IRE) 5 b.g. Definite Article – Couture Daisy (IRE) (Desse Zenny **h89**
(USA)) [2016/17 b16s^6 h20.2g^5 Apr 26] €17,500 3-y-o: fourth foal: half-brother to bumper **b–**
winner/useful hurdler Tullyesker Hill (3m/25f winner, by Shantou): dam (h89) 17f hurdle
winner: needed experience in bumper: 80/1, fifth in maiden at Perth (25½ lengths behind
Royal Village) on hurdling debut. *Donald Whillans*

NIGHTFLY 6 br.m. Midnight Legend – Whichway Girl (Jupiter Island) [2016/17 b91: **h100**
h15.8d^5 h19.6d^4 h16.2s^4 h20.7d^4 Mar 15] runner-up in bumpers: fair form over hurdles:
bred to stay 3m: tried in tongue tie. *Charlie Longsdon*

NIGHTLINE 7 b.g. Midnight Legend – Whichway Girl (Jupiter Island) [2016/17 h117: **c118**
c21.4s^{pu} c21.7d^{ur} c21.3d^3 c24.1g^2 Apr 22] tall gelding: fairly useful hurdler: similar form **h–**
over fences: stays 3m: acts on heavy going: tried in hood: has worn tongue tie, including in
2016/17. *Charlie Longsdon*

NIGHT OF SIN (FR) 4 gr.g. Sinndar (IRE) – Natt Musik (FR) (Kendor (FR)) [2016/17 **h125**
h16.7g^4 h16g h16.7s* h16v* h18.8g Mar 25] lengthy gelding: sixth foal: half-brother to 3
winners, notably smart hurdler/top-class chaser Fox Norton (2m-2½m winner, by Lando)
and fairly useful hurdler/useful chaser Pinkie Brown (2m winner, by Gentlewave): dam
French maiden (stayed 10.5f): fairly useful form over hurdles: won juveniles at Bangor in
January and Warwick in February, making all both times: unproven beyond 17f: best form
on soft/heavy going: tried in hood. *Nick Williams*

NIKKI STEEL (IRE) 7 b.g. Craigsteel – Nikikita (IRE) (Nikos) [2016/17 h16g^2 h15.8s* **h117**
h15.8g^3 h16g^2 h21.6g* h20.3g^2 Aug 31] fourth foal: dam, ran once over hurdles, half-sister
to useful hurdler (2m-2½m winner) Slim Pickens (by Craigsteel): winning pointer: fairly
useful hurdler: won maiden at Uttoxeter in June and novice handicap at Newton Abbot
in August: left Paul Power after first start: stays 2¾m: acts on soft going: often races
prominently/travels strongly. *Dr Richard Newland*

NINE ALTARS (IRE) 8 b.g. Heron Island (IRE) – Tawny Owl (IRE) (Be My Native **c115**
(USA)) [2016/17 h116, b–: c17.3m^3 h16.2m^3 c16.4g^6 c15.7g^2 c15.9s^4 c19.2s^3 c17.1s^2 **h97**
c15.2m^3 Apr 13] strong gelding: fair hurdler: fairly useful maiden chaser: second in
handicaps at Catterick in January and Kelso in March: unproven beyond 17f: acts on heavy
going. *Ann Hamilton*

NINEPOINTSIXTHREE 7 b.g. Bertolini (USA) – Armada Grove (Fleetwood (IRE)) **h107 §**
[2016/17 h105: h16.8m^2 h20.7g^2 h15.9g^4 h20v^{rr} Mar 19] lengthy gelding: fair maiden
hurdler: stays 21f: has worn headgear, including final start (refused to race): one to leave
alone. *John O'Shea*

NI SIN E MO AINM (IRE) 9 b.g. Balakheri (IRE) – Bramslam (IRE) (Glacial Storm **c104**
(USA)) [2016/17 c25.8m^3 Apr 15] won 3 times in points: winning hurdler: 11/2, third in **h–**
hunter at Newton Abbot (15 lengths behind Pantxoa) on chasing debut: stays 3¼m: acts on
good to firm going: often in cheekpieces. *Miss Alexandra Bell*

NJORLS SAGA 6 b.m. Sagamix (FR) – Programme Girl (IRE) (Definite Article) [2016/17 **h–**
b16s h19.3g Apr 15] second foal: dam (h115) bumper and 2m/17f hurdle winner: well held **b–**
in bumper/novice hurdle. *Nigel Hawke*

NO ALTERATIONS (IRE) 9 ch.g. Lahib (USA) – Simmer (IRE) (Zaffaran (USA)) **h–**
[2016/17 h24d Nov 15] point winner: tailed off in novice on hurdling debut. *Nick Kent*

NOBBY KIVAMBO 12 b.g. Anabaa (USA) – Kivavite (USA) (Kingmambo **c–**
(USA)) [2016/17 c20.9v^{pu} Feb 1] medium-sized gelding: multiple winning pointer: maiden **h–**
hurdler/chaser: stays 25f: acts on good to firm and heavy going: often wears headgear. *J. S.
Warner*

NOBEL LEADER (IRE) 7 b.g. Alflora (IRE) – Ben Roseler (IRE) (Beneficial) [2016/17 **c106**
h98, b84: h20d^5 h19.9s^{pu} c21.4d^4 c19.2s^3 c15.7g* Mar 28] modest maiden hurdler: fair **h95**
form over fences: won handicap at Southwell in March: stays 21f: acts on good to soft
going: has worn headgear. *James Evans*

NOBLE CALL (IRE) 9 b.g. King's Best (USA) – Really (IRE) (Entrepreneur) [2016/17   **c90**
h16g[6] h16g h19.6d* h17.2g[3] h20.9d h15.8d c17.1s[5] c19.9g[2] Apr 28] modest handicap   **h91**
hurdler: won at Bangor in August: similar form over fences: left P. J. Rothwell after
second start: stays 2½m: acts on soft going: usually wears headgear: wears tongue tie.
Joanne Foster

NOBLE ENDEAVOR (IRE) 8 b.g. Flemensfirth (USA) – Old Moon (IRE) (Old   **c158**
Vic) [2016/17 c146, h–: c25d[pu] h20d[5] c24d[4] c24.5d* c25g[3] c29d[6] Apr 17]   **h137 +**

    Gordon Elliott's nine-horse assault on the Irish Grand National, Ireland's
richest race, was foiled by Our Duke but he was otherwise virtually unstoppable in
the most valuable domestic handicap chases. Horses trained by him won the Galway
Plate (Lord Scoundrel), the Paddy Power (Noble Endeavor), the Kerry National
(Wrath of Titans), the Dan Moore Memorial (Ball d'Arc), the Leopardstown Chase
(A Toi Phil), the Munster National (Tiger Roll) and the Troytown Chase (Empire
of Dirt), among others. Elliott marshalled his forces most effectively all season to
give perennial champion trainer Willie Mullins a real run for his money for the
title, the destiny of which was in the balance right down to the final day of the Irish
season when the superior strength of the Mullins string in the major graded races
finally tilted the balance. Elliott's big handicap successes usually involved a multiple
challenge—he threw the kitchen sink at the Troytown with eleven runners—but,
except for his winners, a surprisingly large number of the challengers made little
impact, leading to speculation that perhaps the stable often ran badly handicapped or
out of form horses simply to keep out lowly-weighted entries from other stables that
might pose a more serious threat to its leading contenders (Willie Mullins entered
three in the Thyestes Chase, for example, but two of them missed out, making the
final list only as reserves, while Elliott fielded seven, including runner-up Ucello
Conti). The Elliott juggernaut fared particularly well in the Galway Plate in which
two others from a team of five reached the first six, and Noble Endeavor made the
frame behind Empire of Dirt in the Troytown, but they were exceptions.

    Noble Endeavor started the season on a handy mark (Irish Turf Club 141),
looking a possible type for one of the big staying handicap chases. He had shown
smart form as a novice and was staying on in sixth, and by no means a forlorn
hope to make the frame (alongside eventual runner-up Native River at the time),
when falling at the second last in a very strong National Hunt Chase at Cheltenham
(the form of which was advertised in no uncertain terms when Native River won

*Paddy Power Chase (Extended Handicap), Leopardstown—Noble Endeavor (stripes) challenges
between the third Oscar Knight (hoops) and fourth Stellar Notion (right) at the last*

Mr C. Jones's "Noble Endeavor"

the Hennessy Gold Cup the day before the Troytown). Noble Endeavor had clearly not been himself when pulled up in the Champion Novices' Chase at Punchestown shortly after the end of the British season and, following a summer break and a pipe-opener over hurdles behind Snow Falcon in the Lismullen Hurdle at Navan, he started 7/2 favourite for the Troytown Handicap Chase at the same track on the last Sunday in November. Noble Endeavor failed to justify the strong market support on this occasion, finishing five and three quarter lengths fourth in the big field behind his stablemate Empire of Dirt (in different ownership) after having every chance from the second last. The Paddy Power Chase at Leopardstown's Christmas meeting was the next port of call for Noble Endeavor. He didn't start favourite this time, in the face of very strong support for the Willie Mullins-trained The Crafty Butcher who was backed down from 7/1 to 11/4 favourite in an extremely competitive renewal. Noble Endeavor was well backed too, sent off at 6/1, the shortest-priced of the six Elliott runners (four of which started at odds ranging from 33/1 to 66/1). Noble Endeavor thwarted the gamble on The Crafty Butcher to maintain his stable's splendid run in the big handicaps, which had already included the Galway Plate, the Kerry National and the Munster National, as well as the Troytown. Noble Endeavor showed improved form as he led at the last and held The Crafty Butcher readily by three and a half lengths, with Oscar Knight and Stellar Notion completing the frame. Ucello Conti, runner-up in the race twelve months earlier and a 10/1-shot this time, was the only other Elliott-trained runner to make any impression, in contention briefly at the second last before coming seventh (his three other finishers Bless The Wings, Cause of Causes and Captain Von Trappe ended up in eleventh, fourteenth and eighteenth, none of them ever on terms, while Shadow Catcher had already lost his place when unseating his rider at the twelfth). Noble Endeavor made just two other appearances, finishing a good third to Un Temps Pour Tout when second favourite for the Ultima Handicap Chase at the Cheltenham Festival (when he suffered from post-race ataxia) and then running respectably when stepped back up in trip and finishing sixth in the Irish Grand National at Fairyhouse, where Bless The Wings started shortest of the big Elliott contingent and finished runner-up for the second successive year. Noble Endeavor lost his place when not fluent at the nineteenth and was untidy again at the fourth last, but he plugged on well enough in the closing stages to suggest he will be worth persevering with over marathon trips in the next season.

Noble Endeavor (IRE) (b.g. 2009)

Flemensfirth (USA) (b 1992) — Alleged (b 1974) — Hoist The Flag / Princess Pout
Etheldreda (ch 1985) — Diesis / Royal Bund
Old Moon (IRE) (b 2001) — Old Vic (b 1986) — Sadler's Wells / Cockade
Moon Storm (br 1994) — Strong Gale / Luminous Run

Noble Endeavor, a strong gelding, is by the veteran Beeches Stud stallion Flemensfirth who is still going strongly on the Coolmore jumping roster at the age of twenty-five and ended the latest season in sixth in the combined table of leading sires in Britain and Ireland (Sizing Codelco, who also has an essay in this Annual, and the Leinster National winner Abolitionist were among the other sizeable contributors to Flemensfirth's total). Noble Endeavor's unraced dam Old Moon, a half-sister to the useful staying hurdler/chaser Warden Hill, has bred five winners, all of them by Flemensfirth. Valley Lad and Benign Dictator were bumper winners for Tim Vaughan and Emma Lavelle respectively, while Old Moon was also represented on the racecourse in the latest season by her two other winners, the useful Minella Daddy, who won over fences at Ffos Las and Ascot before finishing second in the Silver Cup at Ascot, and Planet Nine who won bumpers at Thurles and Perth and looks the type to progress when he gets the chance to race over further than two miles. The great grandam of Noble Endeavor, Luminous Run, was a sister to that notable character the high-class hurdler Mole Board who made the last of four appearances (he came fourth twice) in the Champion Hurdle at the ripe old age of thirteen and won a quite valuable event at Ascot as a fourteen-year-old. Luminous Run is also the grandam of the latest Close Brothers Novices' Handicap Chase winner at the Festival, Tully East. Noble Endeavor has done his winning so far at up to three miles but he probably stays much longer distances and will be an interesting Grand National contender one day. He acts on heavy going. He has worn cheekpieces but didn't do so when winning the Paddy Power, or on his subsequent appearances. *Gordon Elliott, Ireland*

NOBLE FRIEND (IRE) 9 b.g. Presenting – Laragh (IRE) (Oscar (IRE)) [2016/17 c121, h101: h20m^4 May 19] workmanlike gelding: modest maiden hurdler: fairly useful chaser at best: pulled up all 3 starts in points in 2017: stays 2¾m: acts on soft and good to firm going: wears headgear: tried in tongue tie: usually races nearer last than first. *Chris Gordon* — c– h97

NOBLE GALILEO (GER) 7 b.g. Galileo (IRE) – Nordtanzerin (GER) (Danehill Dancer (IRE)) [2016/17 h76: h20m^5 h18.6g^4 h16d h19.9d^5 Mar 14] modest maiden hurdler: stays 19f: acts on soft going: has worn headgear, including last 3 starts: tried in tongue tie: often races towards rear. *Tim Vaughan* — h90

NOBLE GLANCE 4 b.f. Schiaparelli (GER) – Ragdollianna (Kayf Tara) [2016/17 b13.6g Apr 21] first foal: dam (h100), bumper winner/maiden hurdler around 2m, also winner around 1½m on Flat: tailed off in bumper. *Mark Hoad* — b–

NOBLE LEGEND 10 b.g. Midnight Legend – Elmside Katie (Lord David S (USA)) [2016/17 c124§: c24.2g^{pu} c20d^6 c22.5v^3 c21.2g^6 c21.4s^{pu} Jan 18] lengthy, angular gelding: fairly useful handicap chaser, out of form in 2016/17: stays 25f: acts on heavy going: usually wears headgear: usually leads: often shapes as if amiss. *Caroline Bailey* — c– §

NOBLE QUEST 5 b.g. Kalanisi (IRE) – Katalina (Hernando (FR)) [2016/17 b16.3g May 21] well beaten in maiden bumper. *Warren Greatrex* — b–

NOBLE ROBIN (IRE) 6 b.g. Robin des Champs (FR) – Which Thistle (IRE) (Saddlers' **h98 p**
Hall (IRE)) [2016/17 h21.9v⁴ Dec 21] £35,000 3-y-o: fifth foal: brother to bumper winner/
fairly useful hurdler Aengus (19f-25f winner) and half-brother to 2 winners, including
fairly useful hurdler/useful chaser Irish Thistle (2m-2½m winner, by Luso): dam unraced:
won Irish maiden point on debut: 9/4, shaped better than result when fourth in novice at
Ffos Las (19 lengths behind Ballymalin) on hurdling debut, all but coming down 4 out: will
improve. *Jonjo O'Neill*

NO BUTS 9 b.g. Kayf Tara – Wontcostalotabut (Nicholas Bill) [2016/17 c115, h–: c24g⁴ **c126**
c20.9m⁴ c23.8d c20v³ c20v* c19.9g c23.6g⁴ c28.4m* Apr 27] leggy, lengthy gelding: **h–**
maiden hurdler: fairly useful handicap chaser: won at Warwick in February and Taunton in
April: stays 3½m: acts on good to firm and heavy going: has worn cheekpieces: tried in
tongue tie: often races prominently. *David Bridgwater*

NOBUTTABOY (IRE) 6 b.g. Darsi (FR) – Buckalong (IRE) (Buckskin (FR)) [2016/17 **h116 §**
h24d² h24v* h25.3g³ h24d⁶ h21.7dᵖᵘ Mar 26] €5,000 3-y-o, £12,000 5-y-o: half-brother to
fairly useful chaser Listen Boy (2½m/23f winner, by Presenting) and 3 winning pointers:
dam unraced: point winner: fairly useful form over hurdles: won novice at Southwell in
December: looks a thorough stayer: acts on heavy going: tried in cheekpieces: front runner/
races prominently: temperamental. *Ben Pauling*

NO CEILING (IRE) 7 b.g. Turtle Island (IRE) – Pyrexie (FR) (Pistolet Bleu (IRE)) **c107**
[2016/17 h105: h16.3d³ h16g³ h15.7g* c16.4g* c16g³ c16.5g³ c17.2d² Dec 26] rather **h115**
leggy gelding: fairly useful handicap hurdler: won at Southwell in August: won novice over
fences: won novice handicap at Sedgefield later in August: likely to prove best at 2m: acts
on good to soft going: wears hood: often races towards rear/travels strongly. *Ian Williams*

NOCHE DE REYES (FR) 8 b.g. Early March – Cochinchine (IRE) (Namaqualand **c129**
(USA)) [2016/17 c128, h–: c16m² c18m² c16.9m² c16v³ c16d⁶ c16m² Apr 25] lengthy **h–**
gelding: winning hurdler: fairly useful handicap chaser: runner-up 4 times in 2016/17,
including in listed event at Ascot (6 lengths behind Quite By Chance) in October: stays
2¼m: acts on good to firm and heavy going: tried in tongue tie. *Tom George*

NO COMMENT 6 br.g. Kayf Tara – Dizzy Frizzy (Loup Sauvage (USA)) [2016/17 **h143**
h123p, b106+: b18s* h19.5gᵘʳ h20g² h18.6s* h20.5d* h20.5v* h20.3g h24.7g² h24d² Apr **b–**
27] well-made gelding: bumper winner: useful hurdler: won novices at Market Rasen in
November, and at Plumpton in December and January: second in handicaps at Aintree and
Punchestown (length behind Minella Awards) in April: stays 25f: acts on heavy going: in
hood last 5 starts: strong traveller. *Philip Hobbs*

NO DUFFER 10 ch.g. Karinga Bay – Dolly Duff (Alflora (IRE)) [2016/17 c136, h–: **c142**
h23.9g⁶ c24g* c24dᵖᵘ c26s² c23.8m⁵ Apr 2] deep-girthed gelding: maiden hurdler: useful **h–**
handicap chaser: won at Doncaster in December: second in veterans event at Newbury
(2¼ lengths behind Just A Par) in March: stays 3¼m: acts on heavy going: wears tongue
tie: often races prominently. *Tom George*

NO HASSLE HOFF (IRE) 5 b.g. Craigsteel – Endless Patience (IRE) (Miner's Lamp) **h133**
[2016/17 h19.1dᶠ h25.5s* h24s³ h24.4d² h22.8d² h24.7g⁴ Apr 8] good-topped gelding:
half-brother to 3 winners, including fairly useful hurdler/chaser Arkose (2½m-3¼m
winner, by Luso) and fairly useful hurdler/winning pointer Iwillrememberyou (21f-25f
winner, by Lord Americo), stayed 3½m: dam unraced: runner-up in Irish maiden point on
debut: useful form over hurdles: won maiden at Hereford in November: placed in Albert
Bartlett Novices' Hurdle (Bristol) at Cheltenham (4¼ lengths behind Wholestone) in
December, River Don Novices' Hurdle at Doncaster (head behind Constantine Bay)
in January and Prestige Novices' Hurdle at Haydock (9 lengths behind The Worlds End) in
February: stays 3¼m: acts on soft going: often travels strongly. *Dan Skelton*

NO HIDING PLACE (IRE) 4 b.g. Stowaway – Subtle Gem (IRE) (Subtle Power (IRE)) **b86**
[2016/17 b15.8g³ Apr 17] €25,000 3-y-o: second foal: dam, unraced, closely related to very
smart hurdler/winning chaser (17f-2¾m winner) Oscar Dan Dan: 7/2, raced freely when
third in bumper at Huntingdon (7 lengths behind Hatcher) in April. *Nicky Henderson*

NOLECCE 10 ch.g. Reset (AUS) – Ghassanah (Pas de Seul) [2016/17 h71: h15.8dᶠ Oct 2] **h–**
poor hurdler: raced around 2m: acted on heavy going: sometimes wore cheekpieces: dead.
Tony Forbes

NO LIKEY (IRE) 10 b.g. Helissio (FR) – Money Galore (IRE) (Monksfield) [2016/17 **c126**
c124, h99: c19.4g* c20m⁴ c20g c19.4m⁵ c20g⁴ c20.9mᵘʳ c19.4g³ Oct 27] winning hurdler: **h–**
fairly useful handicap chaser: won at Stratford in May: stays 2½m: acts on good to firm and
heavy going: wears cheekpieces/tongue tie. *Philip Hobbs*

NOMADIC STORM 11 b.g. Nomadic Way (USA) – Cateel Bay (Most Welcome) [2016/17 h16.3m* h16.7g⁶ h20.3dᵖᵘ Jul 10] fair hurdler: won novice at Stratford in May after long absence: winning chaser: stays 2½m: acts on good to firm and heavy going: wears cheekpieces: has worn tongue tie, including in 2016/17. *David Bridgwater* **c–** **h110**

NOMOREBLACKJACK (IRE) 6 b.g. Robin des Pres (FR) – Hardabout (IRE) (Alderbrook) [2016/17 h22.7d⁶ h19.7d⁴ h16.4s⁴ c21.4d⁵ c16.3sᵖᵘ c15.7s² c19.2s* c19.2s* c15.5dᵘʳ Apr 21] €10,000 3-y-o, £31,000 5-y-o: angular gelding: third foal: dam unraced: modest form over hurdles: useful form over fences: won handicaps at Catterick in February and March: stays 19f: acts on soft going: front runner/races prominently: remains open to improvement. *Sue Smith* **c130 p** **h87 p**

NONCHALANT 6 gr.g. Oasis Dream – Comeback Queen (Nayef (USA)) [2016/17 h16.2d⁵ Sep 16] fair on Flat, stayed 12.5f: well beaten in maiden hurdle: dead. *David O'Meara* **h–**

NO NO CARDINAL (IRE) 8 ch.g. Touch of Land (FR) – Four Moons (IRE) (Cardinal Flower) [2016/17 c82, h–: c15.7m³ c16.3g² c16.5m c15.7d⁵ c15.7d⁴ h16.5g c16.1g⁴ c17g³ c18.2g² c16.1m² Apr 27] maiden hurdler: modest handicap chaser: unproven beyond 17f: acts on good to firm going: usually wears headgear: has worn tongue tie: weak finisher. *Mark Gillard* **c86 §** **h– §**

NO NO JOLIE (FR) 5 gr.m. Martaline – Virgata (FR) (Turgeon (USA)) [2016/17 b17.7d b16.7g Mar 27] second foal: dam French 1½m winner: no form in bumpers: left Charlie Longsdon after first start. *Oliver Sherwood* **b–**

NO NO LEGEND 4 b.f. Midnight Legend – Karinga Madame (Karinga Bay) [2016/17 b15.7s Mar 20] first foal: dam, ran once in bumper, half-sister to useful hurdler/chaser (stays 19f) Overtown Express: well held in bumper. *Charlie Longsdon* **b–**

NO NO MAC (IRE) 8 b.g. Oscar (IRE) – Whatdoyouthinkmac (IRE) (Supreme Leader) [2016/17 c–, h–: c23.9g* c21.7g* c25.2g³ c21.6s⁵ c20.5s* c24.3v³ c24.3g c20.1g³ Apr 28] sturdy gelding: winning hurdler: useful chaser: won handicap at Market Rasen and novice at Towcester in May, and handicap at Ayr (by 3½ lengths from Master Ruffit) in February: left Charlie Longsdon after fourth start: stays 25f: acts on heavy going: has worn headgear: has worn tongue tie, including last 4 starts. *Ian Duncan* **c132** **h–**

NO NO TUBS (IRE) 5 b.g. Let The Lion Roar – Line Grey (FR) (Le Nain Jaune (FR)) [2016/17 b16d May 7] well beaten in bumper. *Charlie Longsdon* **b–**

NOOJISTHAUDON 8 b.g. Beat Hollow – Boutique (Selkirk (USA)) [2016/17 h20.2dᵖᵘ h20.2sᵖᵘ Jul 10] no form over hurdles. *Jean McGregor* **h–**

NOOR AL HAYA (IRE) 7 b.m. Tamayuz – Hariya (IRE) (Shernazar) [2016/17 h16m h17.7gᵖᵘ Jun 7] poor maiden hurdler: in hood last 4 starts. *Laura Mongan* **h62**

NO PLANNING 10 b.g. Kayf Tara – Poor Celt (Impecunious) [2016/17 c135, h140: c24s⁴ c26.2d⁶ c23.4s⁶ c20.1s³ c23.4s⁴ c20.1g* c19.9g⁶ Apr 15] big gelding: useful hurdler: useful handicap chaser: won at Newcastle (by ¾ length from Special Catch) in April: stays 25f: acts on heavy going: front runner/races prominently. *Sue Smith* **c130** **h–**

NORAB (GER) 6 b.g. Galileo (IRE) – Night Woman (GER) (Monsun (GER)) [2016/17 h15.8d⁴ h22g³ h23.6g Dec 3] fairly useful on Flat, stays 2m: fair form over hurdles: best effort when third in maiden at Stratford in October: wears cheekpieces. *Bernard Llewellyn* **h103**

NORDICAL (IRE) 7 b.g. Beneficial – Nordic Abu (IRE) (Nordico (USA)) [2016/17 h83: h16.8gᵖᵘ May 10] sturdy gelding: maiden hurdler: wears tongue tie: usually races in rear. *Evan Williams* **h–**

NORDIC NYMPH 8 b.m. Norse Dancer (IRE) – Silken Pearls (Leading Counsel (USA)) [2016/17 h23.8m* h23.1s* h24.5g* h22.8d⁴ h24.3dᵖᵘ Apr 21] lengthy mare: fairly useful handicap hurdler: won at Ludlow in November, Bangor in November and Kempton in December, 2 of them mares events: stays 3¼m: acts on good to firm and heavy going: front runner/races prominently. *Henry Daly* **h115**

NORMAN CROW (IRE) 5 b.g. Lawman (FR) – Viola d'Amore (IRE) (Celtic Swing) [2016/17 b17g May 13] runner-up in maiden point on debut: 20/1, eighth in conditionals/amateur bumper at Aintree (14½ lengths behind Gustave Mahler) 2 weeks later. *Miss H. Brookshaw* **b68**

NORMANDY KING (IRE) 6 b.g. King's Theatre (IRE) – Clairefontaine (Alflora (IRE)) [2016/17 h95, b91: h19.3g h23.4s⁴ c19.1g⁵ Jan 27] modest handicap hurdler: well beaten in novice handicap on chasing debut: should stay beyond 2½m: acts on heavy going: tried in tongue tie: should do better over fences. *Tim Vaughan* **c73 p** **h85**

stanjames.com Greatwood Handicap Hurdle, Cheltenham—North Hill Harvey comes out on top in a four-way finish from Modus (right), Song Light (left) and A Hare Breath (second right)

NORMAN THE RED 7 ch.g. Tobougg (IRE) – Linden Lime (Double Trigger (IRE)) h98 [2016/17 h103, b–: h21.6s² h24.2d⁴ Mar 24] lengthy, angular gelding: fair maiden hurdler: stays 2¾m: acts on heavy going: tried in hood. *Paddy Butler*

NORMANTON (IRE) 7 b.g. Norwich – Fly Like A Bird (Keen) [2016/17 h16g h15.3mᵖᵘ h– h15.7vᵖᵘ Jun 20] lengthy gelding: no form in bumper/over hurdles: tried in hood/tongue tie. *Seamus Mullins*

NORPHIN 7 b.g. Norse Dancer (IRE) – Orphina (IRE) (Orpen (USA)) [2016/17 h–: c– c17mᵘʳ h16.3g h16.8m h21.4m³ h15.3d² h15.3s⁶ h16.6g h15.3s⁵ Mar 1] poor maiden h69 hurdler: unseated fifth in novice handicap on chasing debut: unproven beyond 2m: acts on good to soft going: has worn hood: tried in tongue tie. *Simon Hodgson*

NORSE CASTLE 4 b.g. Norse Dancer (IRE) – Hursley Hope (IRE) (Barathea (IRE)) h– [2016/17 h16.3g h15.9m⁵ h15.8g Apr 28] modest maiden on Flat, stays 1½m: no form over hurdles. *Martin Bosley*

NORSE DA 7 b.g. Norse Dancer (IRE) – End of An Error (Charmer) [2016/17 b–: h16.5g h– h19g h19.1vᵖᵘ h19.2sᵘʳ Mar 16] of little account. *Helen Nelmes*

NORSE LIGHT 6 ch.g. Norse Dancer (IRE) – Dimelight (Fantastic Light (USA)) c98 [2016/17 h101: c15.7m² c16.3g⁶ c17g⁵ c16.5m² c16gᶠ h21s⁶ h19g⁵ h18.6s² h20.5v⁶ h95 c18.2g⁵ h20.6g² h21m⁵ Apr 4] strong gelding: modest handicap hurdler: similar form over fences: stays 21f: acts on good to firm and heavy going: usually wears headgear: wears tongue tie: often races towards rear. *David Dennis*

NORSE MAGIC 4 b.f. Norse Dancer (IRE) – Gift of Love (IRE) (Azamour (IRE)) h– [2016/17 h16s h15.7g⁵ Jan 12] dam half-sister to useful hurdler/chaser (stayed 3m) Gold Medallist: fairly useful maiden on Flat, stays 8.5f: well held in juvenile hurdles. *Warren Greatrex*

NORTHANDSOUTH (IRE) 7 ch.g. Spadoun (FR) – Ennel Lady (IRE) (Erin's Hope) c101 [2016/17 h93: h15.8g* c16d⁵ c21.2g⁵ c18.9s² c21.2g³ c23.6s⁶ c20.2sᴿ h18.7g⁵ Apr 15] h97 modest handicap hurdler: won at Uttoxeter in May: fair form over fences: stays 21f: acts on soft going: tried in hood. *Nigel Twiston-Davies*

NORTH COUNTRY BOY 8 b.g. Revoque (IRE) – She Likes To Boogy (Luso) c– [2016/17 h20.6sᵖᵘ h20.6s c25.2sᵖᵘ Feb 13] maiden hurdler: no form in 2016/17, including h– on chasing debut. *Peter Niven*

NORTHERN BAY (GER) 7 b.g. Desert Prince (IRE) – Nova Scotia (GER) (Sholokhov h– (IRE)) [2016/17 h15.7g Aug 31] maiden hurdler, fair at best: not knocked about only outing in 2016/17: stays 19f: acts on soft going: wears headgear/tongue tie. *Keith Reveley*

584

NORTHERN GIRL (IRE) 4 b.f. Westerner – Janebailey (Silver Patriarch (IRE)) **b67**
[2016/17 b12.4d b15.7s⁶ b16v³ b16.7g⁶ Mar 27] €9,000 3-y-o: leggy filly: third foal: half-
sister to useful hurdler/winning pointer Scorpiancer (2m-21f winner, by Scorpion) and a
winning pointer by Mahler: dam unraced: poor form in bumpers. *Philip Kirby*

NORTHERN MEETING (IRE) 7 b.m. Dylan Thomas (IRE) – Scottish Stage (IRE) **h109 §**
(Selkirk (USA)) [2016/17 h105: h16s³ h15.7v⁴ h16g* h16g⁵ Sep 29] fair handicap hurdler:
won mares event at Worcester in July: stays 2¼m: acts on soft going: wears headgear:
usually races close up: temperamental. *Robert Stephens*

NORTHERN OSCAR (IRE) 9 b.g. Oscar (IRE) – Cailin's Princess (IRE) (Luso) **c–**
[2016/17 h–: c17.4g⁴ May 14] maiden hurdler: tailed off in novice on chasing debut: stays **h–**
19f: acts on heavy going: has worn headgear: tried in tongue tie. *Charles Pogson*

NORTHGEORGE 9 b.g. Overbury (IRE) – River Treasure (IRE) (Over The River (FR)) **c85**
[2016/17 c80: c22.6m³ May 20] multiple winning pointer: modest form in hunter chases.
J. W. Tudor

NORTH HILL HARVEY 6 b.g. Kayf Tara – Ellina (Robellino (USA)) [2016/17 h142: **h144**
h16.4s* h16.8g h20g Apr 7] useful-looking gelding: point winner: useful handicap hurdler:
won Greatwood Hurdle at Cheltenham (by ½ length from Modus) in November: stays
2½m: acts on soft going. *Dan Skelton*

NORTH HILL (IRE) 6 b.g. Westerner – Hill Fairy (Monsun (GER)) [2016/17 h103, b79: **h104**
h21d⁶ h16s h20.3g⁶ h22g* Apr 1] sturdy gelding: fair handicap hurdler: won at Stratford
in April: stays 2¾m: best form on good going: wears hood: often races towards rear.
Ian Williams

NORTH ISLAND (FR) 4 b.g. Sholokhov (IRE) – Jade (PER) (Combsway (USA)) **b–**
[2016/17 b15.6g⁶ Jan 3] fatally injured in bumper. *Philip Kirby*

NORTONTHORPELEGEND (IRE) 7 b.g. Midnight Legend – Tanit (Xaar) [2016/17 **c119**
c103, h–: c20m⁶ c24.2g⁶ c23.4m² c24.2d³ c26.3s* c25.2g* c24.3s* c26.9vᶠ c25.2s⁴ **h–**
c23.4gᵖᵘ Apr 8] maiden hurdler: fairly useful handicap chaser: won at Sedgefield and
Catterick in November, and at Ayr in January: left John Wade after third start: stays 3¼m:
acts on soft and good to firm going. *Rebecca Menzies*

NOSEY BOX (IRE) 11 b.m. Witness Box (USA) – Cautious Leader (Supreme Leader) **c96**
[2016/17 c115, h–: c24.2d⁵ c20.1g⁴ c24.2g⁴ Jun 4] point winner: winning hurdler: maiden **h–**
chaser, modest form in 2016/17: stays 3m: acts on heavy going: wears headgear/tongue tie:
often races towards rear. *Noel C. Kelly, Ireland*

NOSPER (FR) 5 b.g. Whipper (USA) – Nostaltir (FR) (Muhtathir) [2016/17 h–: h21.6d⁴ **h101**
Jun 10] 1m winner on Flat in France: fair form over hurdles: easily best effort when fourth
in novice at Newton Abbot. *Martin Hill*

NO SUCH NUMBER 9 b.g. King's Best (USA) – Return (USA) (Sadler's Wells (USA)) **c76**
[2016/17 c–, h81: c16m⁵ c17.1m c20.1d⁴ c20.1g² c23.8d⁴ c23.8gᵖᵘ c24.2gᵖᵘ Apr 25] **h–**
winning hurdler: poor maiden chaser: left Sandy Forster after sixth start: stays 2½m: acts
on good to soft going: wears cheekpieces. *Maurice Barnes*

NOT A BOTHER BOY (IRE) 9 b.g. Flemensfirth (USA) – Cab In The Storm (IRE) **c109**
(Glacial Storm (USA)) [2016/17 c117, h102: h23.3gᵖᵘ c29.2gᵖᵘ c24.1s³ c24sᴿ Apr 1] **h–**
lengthy, workmanlike gelding: fair handicap hurdler/chaser: largely below form in 2016/17:
stays 3½m: acts on heavy going: front runner/races prominently. *Sue Smith*

NOT ANOTHER MUDDLE 6 b.g. Kayf Tara – Spatham Rose (Environment Friend) **h118**
[2016/17 b94: h20.5v² h19.1v* h17.7v² h16d⁵ Mar 11] good-topped gelding: fairly useful
form over hurdles: won novice at Fontwell in January: often races freely. *Gary Moore*

NOTARFBAD (IRE) 11 b.g. Alderbrook – Angels Flame (IRE) (Un Desperado (FR)) **c131**
[2016/17 c19.4vᵖᵘ c16g* c16.3g* c16.5g⁴ c17.4g³ c18mᵇᵈ c20.4g⁶ c18.2m² c15.7s³ Dec 26] **h–**
lengthy gelding: winning hurdler: useful handicap chaser: won at Uttoxeter in July and
Newton Abbot (by 21 lengths from Easily Pleased) in August: stays 21f: acts on good to
firm and heavy going: wears hood: front runner/races prominently. *Jeremy Scott*

NOT A ROLE MODEL (IRE) 5 b.g. Helissio (FR) – Mille Et Une Nuits (FR) (Ecologist) **b63**
[2016/17 b16g⁶ Apr 8] in frame both starts in Irish maiden points: well beaten in bumper.
Sam Thomas

NOT AT ALL (FR) 4 b.g. Martaline – Not Lost (FR) (Lost World (IRE)) [2016/17 **b72**
b15.7g² Apr 21] first foal: dam unraced sister to useful hurdler/high-class chaser (15f-21f
winner) Nickname: 5/6, remote second of 4 in bumper at Southwell. *Jonjo O'Neill*

NOTEBOOK 6 b.g. Invincible Spirit (IRE) – Love Everlasting (Pursuit of Love) [2016/17 **h– §** h98§: h16.8g h16.4s⁶ h16.4sʳʳ Dec 17] smallish gelding: modest hurdler at best, no form in 2016/17: often wears cheekpieces: has twice refused to race. *Simon Waugh*

NOT FAR WRONG (IRE) 5 b.g. Court Cave (IRE) – Aqua Breezer (IRE) (Namaqualand **b–** (USA)) [2016/17 b16.2d⁵ b16.7g Sep 24] behind in bumpers. *John Wainwright*

NO THROUGH ROAD 10 b.g. Grape Tree Road – Pendil's Delight (Scorpio (FR)) **c92 §** [2016/17 c111, h–: c20gᵖᵘ c24d³ c23d Jun 29] maiden hurdler: fair handicap chaser, below **h–** form in 2016/17: stays 25f: acts on heavy going: has worn tongue tie: unreliable. *Michael Scudamore*

NOT NEVER 5 ch.g. Notnowcato – Watchoverme (Haafhd) [2016/17 h15.9v⁴ h15.3v⁴ **h108 p** h16.3d h16v⁶ h15.8g* Apr 28] neat gelding: useful on Flat, stays 1¼m: fair form over hurdles: won handicap at Huntingdon in April: raced only around 2m: often races towards rear: open to further improvement. *Gary Moore*

NOTNOWSAM 6 ch.g. Notnowcato – First Fantasy (Be My Chief (USA)) [2016/17 **c–** c124, h101: c19.4d c19.1g c19.4s c21.1sᵖᵘ c21.3dᵖᵘ c19.2d⁶ Apr 27] winning hurdler: fairly **h–** useful chaser at best, out of form in 2016/17: stays 2½m: often wears headgear: races towards rear, often lazily. *Micky Hammond*

NOTNOW SEAMUS 6 b.g. Notnowcato – Special Beat (Bustino) [2016/17 b16.4s² **h91** b16s⁴ b16v⁵ h21.4v² h24.1m⁴ Apr 13] closely related to fairly useful/ungenuine hurdler/ **b86** winning pointer Special Occasion (2m-19f winner, by Inchinor) and half-brother to several winners, including fairly useful/unreliable hurdler/chaser Gee Dee Nen (21f-3m winner, by Mister Baileys): dam (h119), 19f/2½m hurdle winner, also 17f winner on Flat: in frame in bumpers: modest form over hurdles: better effort when second in maiden at Ayr in March: has worn cheekpieces. *Marjorie Fife*

NOTONEBUTTWO (IRE) 10 b.g. Dushyantor (USA) – Daiquiri (IRE) (Houmayoun **c–** (FR)) [2016/17 c87, h70: c26.3sᵖᵘ h24dᵖᵘ h24vᵖᵘ h22.7s⁴ c24.2s⁵ h25.8v⁵ h27s⁶ h24.3v⁴ **h–** c24.2vᵖᵘ h23.9g Apr 26] compact gelding: modest handicap hurdler/chaser at best, no form in 2016/17: left Chris Grant after first start: stays 3¼m: acts on heavy going: usually wears headgear/tongue tie. *Kenny Johnson*

NOTORIOUS ONE (IRE) 6 b.g. Papal Bull – Sit And Settle (IRE) (Lake Coniston **h99** (IRE)) [2016/17 h18.8g h16d h16.2g⁴ Apr 25] fourth foal: dam, 7f winner, half-sister to useful hurdler/smart chaser (stayed 2½m) Dan Breen: modest form in maiden/novice hurdles: will prove suited by 2¼m+. *Liam Lennon, Ireland*

NOTRE AMI (IRE) 6 br.g. Kalanisi (IRE) – Shuilan (IRE) (Good Thyne (USA)) [2016/17 **b96** b85: b17.7d* ab16g² Nov 22] good-topped gelding: fairly useful form in bumpers: won at Fontwell in June: bred to stay 2½m: wears hood. *Nick Gifford*

NOT THAT FUISSE (FR) 4 b.g. Fuisse (FR) – Edelmira (FR) (Kahyasi) [2016/17 **b103** b16g* Apr 24] €20,000 3-y-o: second foal: brother to fairly useful hurdler Peruvien Bleu (2m winner): dam (h110) French 2m hurdle winner: 9/2, won bumper at Warwick (by 4 lengths from Quick Pick) on debut. *Dan Skelton*

NOTTS SO BLUE 6 b.m. Pastoral Pursuits – Blue Nile (IRE) (Bluebird (USA)) [2016/17 **h–** h77: h16.3mᵖᵘ May 15] maiden hurdler: tried in blinkers. *Shaun Harris*

NOUAILHAS 11 b.g. Mark of Esteem (IRE) – Barachois Princess (USA) (Barachois **c71 §** (CAN)) [2016/17 c73§, h–§: c16.3g⁴ h21.6gᵖᵘ c20gᵖᵘ h15.9s h19.5v⁶ c17vᵖᵘ h15.9sᵖᵘ **h– §** Mar 13] leggy gelding: modest hurdler at best, no form in 2016/17: poor maiden chaser: stays 2½m: acts on soft going: usually wears headgear: tried in tongue tie: front runner/ races prominently: temperamental. *Daniel O'Brien*

NOVALIS (GER) 5 b.g. Soldier Hollow – Naomia (GER) (Monsun (GER)) [2016/17 **h120** h17.4v* h19.8g Apr 29] won at 10.5f/11.5f on Flat in Belgium early in 2017: fairly useful form over hurdles: won for second time in 2 starts at Strasbourg in March: well held in handicap at Sandown following month. *C. von der Recke, Germany*

NOVEMBERSTORM (IRE) 5 br.g. September Storm (GER) – Glacial Shoon (IRE) **h91** (Glacial Storm (USA)) [2016/17 b16g² b16d⁶ h25.5s h19.4g⁵ h20.8dᵖᵘ Feb 9] placed in **b81** Irish maiden points: modest form in bumpers/over hurdles: dead. *Nigel Twiston-Davies*

NOVO DAWN (IRE) 8 b.g. Gamut (IRE) – Curious Kate (IRE) (Phardante (FR)) **h80** [2016/17 h16.2d⁵ h16.2d⁴ h20.2s⁶ Jul 10] point winner: poor form over hurdles: in tongue tie last 2 starts. *Stuart Crawford, Ireland*

NOW BEN 9 b.g. Beneficial – Bannow Beach (IRE) (Saddlers' Hall (IRE)) **c115** [2016/17 c23.8sᵖᵘ c23.8m* Apr 25] prolific point winner: once-raced hurdler: fairly useful **h–** form when easily won hunter chase at Ludlow in April. *Philip Rowley*

NO WIN NO FEE 7 b.g. Firebreak – Milliscent (Primo Dominie) [2016/17 h93: h15.9g h15.8g[4] h15.8m[3] h16.3m* h16.3g[4] h15.7g[3] h16g[6] h16.2d[6] h16.7s[pu] h16g[3] Mar 17] fair hurdler: won maiden at Huntingdon in May and novice at Stratford in July: left Dr Richard Newland after eighth start: raced around 2m: acts on good to firm going: wears headgear. *Barry Leavy* **h112**

NOW THIS IS IT (IRE) 13 ch.g. Accordion – Leitrim Bridge (IRE) (Earl of Barking (IRE)) [2016/17 c–, h113: h20m[pu] h16.2s[4] h20.2g Aug 20] useful handicap hurdler at one time, has deteriorated markedly: winning chaser: stays 2¾m: acts on good to firm and good to soft going: in cheekpieces last 2 starts. *Stuart Crawford, Ireland* **c–** **h92**

NOWURHURLIN (IRE) 10 b.g. Saddlers' Hall (IRE) – Pint Taken (IRE) (Needle Gun (IRE)) [2016/17 c114, h–: c20.3v[2] c26.2m[2] c23.4v[pu] c24.2s[5] Feb 4] strong gelding: winning hurdler: fair hunter chaser: stays 3¼m: acts on good and heavy going: has worn headgear. *Mrs S. J. Stilgoe* **c114** **h–**

NUCKY THOMPSON 4 b.g. Cockney Rebel (IRE) – Vino Veritas (USA) (Chief's Crown (USA)) [2016/17 h16g[4] h16m* h16.4s[pu] h17g[pu] Mar 18] compact gelding: fairly useful on Flat, stays 1½m: fairly useful form over hurdles: won juvenile maiden at Warwick in November: will prove best at sharp 2m: wears hood: tried in tongue tie. *Richard Spencer* **h119**

NUMBER ONE LONDON (IRE) 7 b.g. Invincible Spirit (IRE) – Vadorga (Grand Lodge (USA)) [2016/17 h112: h16s h19.6d[pu] h23.3s Jun 15] fair hurdler at best, no form in 2016/17: tried in cheekpieces. *Tim Vaughan* **h–**

NUTS WELL 6 b.g. Dylan Thomas (IRE) – Renada (Sinndar (IRE)) [2016/17 h134, b90: h15.7m h16g[2] h16d[5] h15.6g h16.2v[3] h16.4v[2] h16.4v[2] h16.4g* h20.2g[5] Apr 28] useful handicap hurdler: won at Newcastle (by 3½ lengths from Lycidas) in April: best around 2m: acts on heavy going: usually races prominently. *Ann Hamilton* **h130**

O

OAKIDOAKI 5 b.g. Sulamani (IRE) – Sweet Robinia (IRE) (Bob Back (USA)) [2016/17 b17.7g[4] b13.7d[3] h19.5g[5] h19.1v[3] h20d[6] Feb 17] second foal: dam (h95), placed in bumpers/ maiden hurdler, sister to fairly useful/ungenuine chaser (stayed 3m) Big Rob: modest form in bumpers: fair form in novice/maiden hurdles: will be suited by 2¾m+: usually races close up. *Brendan Powell* **h101** **b79**

OAKLANDS BOBBY 15 b.g. Busy Flight – Bonnie Buttons (Lord Bud) [2016/17 c19.3s[2] Apr 28] prolific winning pointer: poor maiden chaser: stays 25f: acts on soft going. *R. G. Russ* **c83**

OAK VINTAGE (IRE) 7 b.g. Fruits of Love (USA) – Brandam Supreme (IRE) (Supreme Leader) [2016/17 h98, b–: h20.9m[2] h16.2d[4] h19.9d c21.6s[ur] c16.3s[4] c16.4s[pu] c16.4v[5] c20.1v c16.3g[5] Apr 8] fair hurdler: poor form over fences: stays 21f: acts on good to firm and heavy going. *Ann Hamilton* **c82** **h103**

OATHKEEPER (IRE) 7 b.g. Oscar (IRE) – Lady Lamb (IRE) (Executive Perk) [2016/17 b113: b20g* b20g* h16.5g[3] h20v[F] h24d[2] h20.4s[2] h24d Apr 27] smart form in bumpers, second win at Listowel in June: useful form over hurdles: won maiden at Killarney in July: third in novice at Galway (length behind Penhill) in July: stays easy 3m: acts on soft going: tried in tongue tie. *Joseph Patrick O'Brien, Ireland* **h130** **b115**

OBISTAR (FR) 7 b.g. Astarabad (USA) – Vallee du Luy (FR) (Oblat (FR)) [2016/17 h110: h23.9d[5] c24.2s[F] h26v[4] h23.1d[4] Feb 24] fair handicap hurdler: fell second in novice handicap on chasing debut: stays 25f: best form on heavy going: wears headgear. *David Pipe* **c–** **h104**

OCCASIONALLY YOURS (IRE) 13 b.g. Moscow Society (USA) – Kristina's Lady (IRE) (Lafontaine (USA)) [2016/17 c–, h103: h20.3v[6] h19.6g* h17.7g[4] h25m[4] Oct 2] tall gelding: fair handicap hurdler: won at Huntingdon in May: maiden chaser: stays 23f: acts on good to firm and heavy going: has worn headgear: often races prominently. *Alan Blackmore* **c–** **h103**

OCEAN BENTLEY (IRE) 5 b.g. Amadeus Wolf – Bentley's Bush (IRE) (Barathea (IRE)) [2016/17 h16g[5] h15.8d[6] h16.3m[4] h16d Oct 25] poor maiden on Flat, stays 1¾m: seemingly best effort over hurdles when last of 4 in seller at Stratford: in tongue tie last 2 starts. *Tony Carroll* **h91**

OCEAN KAVE 7 b.g. Silca Blanka (IRE) – Fiery Angel (IRE) (Machiavellian (USA)) [2016/17 b16.8m[pu] b16.8g[pu] Jul 25] no form in bumpers/Flat maiden: tried in tongue tie. *Tony Newcombe* **b–**

OCHOS RIOS 4 b.g. Shirocco (GER) – Society Rose (Saddlers' Hall (IRE)) [2016/17   **h92** h17.7g⁵ h15.8d² h16.7s h20s³ Feb 19] modest maiden on Flat (stays 11.5f) and over hurdles. *Neil Mulholland*

OCKEY DE NEULLIAC (FR) 15 ch.g. Cyborg (FR) – Graine de Neulliac (FR) (Le   **c–** Nain Jaune (FR)) [2016/17 c122, h–: c20.3gᵖᵘ c22.6sᵖᵘ Jun 14] tall gelding: multiple   **h–** winning pointer: winning hurdler: fairly useful chaser at best, pulled up both starts in 2016/17: stays 25f: acts on heavy going: front runner/races prominently. *Neil Mechie*

OCTAGON 7 b.g. Overbury (IRE) – Dusky Dante (IRE) (Phardante (FR)) [2016/17 h118:   **h123** h16.2g² Oct 6] fairly useful handicap hurdler: stays 21f: acts on heavy going: usually races in rear: often travels strongly, but tends to find little. *Harry Whittington*

ODDS ON DAN (IRE) 11 b.g. Oscar (IRE) – Grange Classic (IRE) (Jurado (USA))   **c84** [2016/17 c76§: c16.4g² c19.2d* c20.1g² c20.1d² c21.2m Jun 24] poor handicap chaser: won at Market Rasen in May: stays 2¾m: acts on soft going: wears cheekpieces/tongue tie: usually races nearer last than first. *Lucinda Egerton*

ODDS ON OSCAR (IRE) 7 b.g. Oscar (IRE) – No Odd's (IRE) (Muroto) [2016/17   **b–** b15.8gᵖᵘ Jul 22] off mark in points at fourth attempt: shaped as if amiss when pulled up in bumper. *Oliver Greenall*

ODELLO 6 b.m. King's Theatre (IRE) – Isabello (IRE) (Presenting) [2016/17 b16m*   **h87** h19.5v⁵ Nov 22] first foal: dam unraced half-sister to useful hurdler/chaser (stayed 3m)   **b92** Banjaxed Girl (by King's Theatre): fairly useful form when winning at Warwick in November on only start in bumpers: 11/8, disappointing fifth of 9 in mares maiden at Lingfield on hurdling debut: should be suited by further than 2m. *Warren Greatrex*

O'FAOLAINS BOY (IRE) 10 b.g. Oscar (IRE) – Lisa's Storm (IRE) (Glacial Storm   **c134** (USA)) [2016/17 c162, h119+: c23.8sᵖᵘ c26sᵖᵘ c34.3dᵖᵘ c24.5d⁶ Apr 29] well-made   **h–** gelding: winning hurdler: high-class chaser at best: just useful form on only completed start in 2016/17, when 13½ lengths sixth of 13 to Sizing Codelco in handicap at Punchestown: should stay beyond 3m: acts on good to firm and heavy going: tried in cheekpieces/tongue tie, including in 2016/17. *Rebecca Curtis*

OFFICER CADET 8 b.g. Kayf Tara – Miss Invincible (Invincible Spirit (IRE)) [2016/17   **c71** c107, h105: c17.3m⁴ c22.6gᵖᵘ c24.2dᵖᵘ Sep 16] maiden hurdler/chaser, fair at best: out of   **h–** sorts in 2016/17: stays 3¼m: acts on soft and good to firm going: wears hood: has worn tongue tie: has hinted at temperament. *Karen McLintock*

OFFICER HOOLIHAN 7 b.g. Kayf Tara – Major Hoolihan (Soldier Rose) [2016/17   **h117** h106, b77: h19.3m* h19.9g³ h15.8d² h19.3g* Apr 15] fairly useful hurdler: won novice at Carlisle in May: off 6 months, made all when landing odds in similar event three final start despite jumping left then hanging left under pressure: should prove suited by further than 2½m: acts on soft and good to firm going: in hood last 4 starts: wears tongue tie. *Tim Vaughan*

OFFSHORE OSCAR (IRE) 6 gr.g. Oscar (IRE) – La Fiamma (FR) (General Assembly   **b– p** (USA)) [2016/17 b16.4s Dec 8] €26,000 3-y-o: closely related to bumper winner Accordingtojodie (by Accordion) and half-brother to 3 winners in France, including chaser Le Famioso (2½m/21f winner, by Sleeping Car): dam French 15f-17f hurdle winner: well-backed 7/2, weakened when 26 lengths ninth of 13 to Mayo Star in bumper at Newcastle on debut: clearly thought capable of better. *Eric McNamara, Ireland*

OFF THE GROUND (IRE) 11 b.g. Oscar (IRE) – Kaysel (IRE) (Torus) [2016/17 c136,   **c128** h–: c20gᵖᵘ c19.4m⁵ Oct 12] good-topped gelding: winning hurdler: handicap chaser, useful   **h–** at best: shaped better than position suggests when fifth of 10 at Wetherby on completed start in 2016/17: stays 2½m: acts on good to firm and heavy going: has worn headgear: has worn tongue tie, including on reappearance. *Charlie Longsdon*

OFF THE HOOK (IRE) 5 b.m. Getaway (GER) – Call Her Again (IRE) (Old Vic)   **h86** [2016/17 b16.2s b16s b16s b16.4s⁶ Feb 14] €6,000 3-y-o: second foal: dam unraced half-   **b–** sister to useful chaser (stays 3¾m) Sizing Coal: no form in bumpers: 80/1, fourth in mares maiden at Ayr (13½ lengths behind Elusive Theatre) on hurdling debut: will be suited by further than 2m. *N. W. Alexander*

OFICIAL BEN (IRE) 8 b.g. Beneficial – Up A Dee (IRE) (Executive Perk) [2016/17   **c99** c108, h–: c16gᵖᵘ c15.7v⁴ c16.5g³ c19.2g Jul 31] winning pointer: maiden hurdler: modest   **h–** maiden chaser: may prove best around 2m: acts on heavy going: has worn hood, including in 2016/17: wears tongue tie. *Jonjo O'Neill*

OGARITMO 8 ch.m. Manduro (GER) – Querida (Rainbow Quest (USA)) [2016/17 h92: h15.8g May 9] modest handicap hurdler: blinkered when well held only outing in 2016/17: unproven beyond 2m: acts on soft going: wears tongue tie: often races in rear: temperamental. *Alex Hales*   h– §

OH LAND ABLOOM (IRE) 7 b.g. King's Theatre (IRE) – Talinas Rose (IRE) (Definite Article) [2016/17 h124: h20.5g⁵ h24g² h21.6g² h19.9g³ h24.4g² h20.6m² Apr 17] close-coupled gelding: fairly useful handicap hurdler: stays 3m: acts on good to firm and good to soft going: in cheekpieces on reappearance: has worn tongue tie. *Neil King*   h126

OH MICHELLE 6 br.m. Kayf Tara – Grenfell (IRE) (Presenting) [2016/17 b15.8s² b15.8d⁶ b16.7s² b16.6d³ Jan 28] first foal: dam, (c102/h87), bumper winner/winning pointer, half-sister to fairly useful/untrustworthy chaser (stayed 3m) Shining Light: fairly useful form in bumpers: will be suited by 2½m+. *Nigel Twiston-Davies*   b95

OHMS LAW 12 b.g. Overbury (IRE) – Polly Live Wire (El Conquistador) [2016/17 c–, h–: h20.6g c19.2d* Apr 27] no form over hurdles: poor form over fences: won handicap at Market Rasen in April: stays 2½m: acts on soft going. *Anthony Day*   c82 h–

OH SO FRUITY 7 b.g. Midnight Legend – Recipe (Bustino) [2016/17 h–: h20.7gᵖᵘ Nov 8] lightly-raced maiden hurdler: breathing problem only outing in 2016/17: should prove suited by 3m: acts on heavy going. *Gary Moore*   h–

OH SO GIGOLO (IRE) 7 b.g. Milan – Oh So Breezy (IRE) (Be My Native (USA)) [2016/17 h–, b84: h19.9g⁶ h19.9d h19.9g h18.1s h16.4s⁴ h19.7d h16.8m² Apr 19] lengthy gelding: poor maiden hurdler: left Nicky Henderson after second start, Kenneth Slack after fifth, Dianne Sayer after sixth: bred to stay at least 2½m: acts on good to firm going: in blinkers last 3 starts. *Kenneth Slack*   h74

OH TOODLES (IRE) 10 b.g. Milan – Be My Granny (Needle Gun (IRE)) [2016/17 c23gᵘʳ c23.8mᵘʳ Apr 25] prolific winner in points: modest form in hunter chases: tongue tied final outing, *Mrs C. J. Robinson*   c96

OISHIN 5 b.g. Paco Boy (IRE) – Roshina (IRE) (Chevalier (IRE)) [2016/17 b60: b16.8s³ b16.8g⁴ h16.2d h16.2s h16.4s h16.4s* h17s⁵ h17d⁴ h16.4v⁴ h23.8g³ h20.6g h20.2g⁶ Apr 28] poor form in bumpers: modest handicap hurdler: won at Newcastle in December: probably stays 3m: acts on soft going: in tongue tie last 5 starts. *Maurice Barnes*   h95 b70

OKMYWAY 4 br.f. Passing Glance – Highlight Girl (Forzando) [2016/17 b14s b12.6d Dec 14] sturdy filly: second foal: dam little form: well held both starts in bumpers: in hood on debut. *Robin Dickin*   b–

OLD FASHION 5 b.m. Shirocco (GER) – Oriental Dance (Fantastic Light (USA)) [2016/17 h66: h16.3m⁵ May 15] fair on Flat, stays 1½m: little form over hurdles: tried in blinkers/tongue tie. *Neil King*   h–

OLDGRANGEWOOD 6 b.g. Central Park (IRE) – Top of The Class (IRE) (Rudimentary (USA)) [2016/17 h118p: h17.1d³ c18g⁴ c19.9sᵇᵈ c19.4s* c19.4s* c19.9sᵖᵘ c20.5g³ Apr 22] rangy gelding: fairly useful at best over hurdles: smart form over fences: won novice handicaps at Kempton in November and Wetherby in December, and handicap at Wetherby (by 2¼ lengths from Dresden) in February: 14/1, best effort when 5¾ lengths third of 5 to Cloudy Dream in Future Champions Novices' Chase at Ayr final outing: will probably stay 3m: acts on heavy going: often races towards rear/travels strongly. *Dan Skelton*   c147 h108 +

OLD GUARD 6 b.g. Notnowcato – Dolma (FR) (Marchand de Sable (USA)) [2016/17 h154: c16.3gᵖᵘ c17.5g* h16.2v⁴ h16.8s³ h21d⁴ h24s h21.1g h20g⁴ h21.5g Apr 29] useful-looking gelding: smart hurdler: one of best efforts in 2016/17 when seventh of 25 to Supasundae in Coral Cup (Handicap) at Cheltenham in March: not fluent but useful form when winning maiden chase at Exeter in October by neck from Imperial Presence: stays 21f: acts on heavy going: in cheekpieces third start: remains capable of better over fences. *Paul Nicholls*   c136 p h149

OLD HARRY ROCKS (IRE) 5 b.g. Milan – Miss Baden (IRE) (Supreme Leader) [2016/17 b16g³ b15.8v² b16.3s⁶ b16.3g⁶ h17.7g² Apr 12] £22,000 3-y-o: smallish gelding: third foal: brother to fair 23f hurdle winner Classical Milano and closely related to a winning pointer by Kayf Tara: dam, unraced, out of sister to high-class chaser (stayed 21f) Thisthatandtother and half-sister to top-class staying chaser Carlingford Lough: fairly useful form in bumpers: fair form over hurdles: better effort when second in maiden at Fontwell: will be suited by 2½m+, *Harry Fry*   h112 b98

OLD MAGIC (IRE) 12 b.g. Old Vic – Maeve's Magic (IRE) (Mandalus) [2016/17 h86: h16.8dᵖᵘ h15.5v h16.8dᵖᵘ h16v⁵ h19.5m Apr 28] poor handicap hurdler: stays 23f: acts on heavy going: has worn headgear: usually in tongue tie. *Sophie Leech*   h75

OLD

OLD PRIDE (IRE) 9 ch.g. Old Vic – Feel The Pride (IRE) (Persian Bold) [2016/17 c–, h117: c16g⁶ c20dᵖᵘ h20m³ c20sᶠ Feb 8] fairly useful hurdler at best: fair maiden chaser: left David Loder after third start: stays 21f: acts on soft and good to firm going: has worn hood, including on final start: front runner/races prominently: won points in March/April. *Mrs D. J. Ralph* **c101 h112**

OLD SALT (IRE) 5 b.g. Craigsteel – Andrea Gale (IRE) (Presenting) [2016/17 h15.8v* h15.8v⁵ h19.9s⁴ h19.5v³ h23.3s⁵ Apr 1] fifth foal: dam (h81), 2½m hurdle winner, half-sister to useful hurdler (stayed 2¾m) Trucking Along: third on second of 2 completed starts in Irish points: fair form over hurdles: won maiden at Ludlow in November: should be suited by further than 2m. *Evan Williams* **h113**

OLD STORM (IRE) 8 b.g. Old Vic – Sissinghurst Storm (IRE) (Good Thyne (USA)) [2016/17 c99, h–: c20.1gᵖᵘ c20.1gᶠ Oct 8] winning pointer: maiden hurdler/chaser, modest form at best: stayed 2¾m: best form on good going: sometimes wore headgear/tongue tie: front runner: dead. *Brian Ellison* **c– h–**

OLIVER'S GOLD 9 b.g. Danehill Dancer (IRE) – Gemini Gold (IRE) (King's Best (USA)) [2016/17 c134, h114: h16.2d² h16.2d⁵ c16g c19.4g⁶ c17.1s⁴ c16.4d² c15.8g³ c16.3s³ h19.9vᵖᵘ c17.2m* Apr 17] sturdy gelding: fairly useful handicap hurdler/chaser: won over fences at Market Rasen final start: best around 2m: acts on soft and good to firm going: has worn cheekpieces, including in 2016/17: often races towards rear. *Mark Walford* **c124 h117**

OLIVER'S HILL (IRE) 8 b.g. Shantou (USA) – River Rouge (IRE) (Croco Rouge (IRE)) [2016/17 c104, h–: h26.5g c20.3m⁵ c19.7g* c25.7gᶠ c20m³ c22.7f³ c20.2f* c20.2m* c22.7g⁶ c25.7g² c20.5mᵖᵘ Apr 18] lengthy gelding: winning hurdler: fair handicap chaser: won at Plumpton in October and twice at Leicester (novice event on first occasion) in December: stays 3¼m: acts on any going: wears headgear/tongue tie. *Lawney Hill* **c111 h–**

OLIVER'S ISLAND (IRE) 5 b.g. Milan – Leading Rank (IRE) (Supreme Leader) [2016/17 h15.7v⁴ b16s h16g⁴ h15.8m⁴ h16.5m⁵ Apr 27] £1,800 3-y-o: fourth foal: dam unraced half-sister to useful hurdler/chaser (stayed 29f) There's No Panic: runner-up in point bumper: modest form in bumpers/over hurdles: will prove suited by at least 2½m: usually races nearer last than first. *Jamie Snowden* **h85 b77**

OLIVIA JOAN 6 ch.m. Grape Tree Road – Thorterdykes Lass (IRE) (Zaffaran (USA)) [2016/17 b–: b12.6v⁶ Feb 16] showed little in 2 bumpers. *Alistair Whillans* **b–**

OLLIE G 9 b.g. Denounce – Silver Rosa (Silver Patriarch (IRE)) [2016/17 h16.4v⁶ Mar 18] fair form in bumpers/novice hurdle in 2013/14: well held in novice hurdle on return. *Chris Grant* **h–**

OLOFI (FR) 11 gr.g. Slickly (FR) – Dona Bella (FR) (Highest Honor (FR)) [2016/17 c–, h119: c22.7s* c20.9s² c21mᵖᵘ Apr 2] well-made gelding: fairly useful hurdler: similar form over fences: won novice hunter at Leicester in February: stays 23f: acts on soft going: wears headgear/tongue tie. *Tom George* **c125 h–**

OLYMPIAN BOY (IRE) 13 b.g. Flemensfirth (USA) – Notanissue (IRE) (Buckskin (FR)) [2016/17 c88, h101: c17.3g h21.6m⁶ Jul 1] workmanlike gelding: winning hurdler/chaser, showed little in 2016/17: effective at testing 2m to 3m: acts on good to firm and heavy going: tried in visor: wears tongue tie: usually races towards rear. *Sophie Leech* **c– h79**

O MAONLAI (IRE) 9 b.g. Oscar (IRE) – Another Gaye (IRE) (Classic Cliche (IRE)) [2016/17 c134§, h–: c25gᵖᵘ c22.4g* c24.1sᵖᵘ c19.9s⁴ c19.9g⁵ Mar 25] workmanlike gelding: winning hurdler: useful handicap chaser: won at Newbury (by 5 lengths from Warriors Tale) in November: stays 2¾m: acts on heavy going: usually wears tongue tie: patiently ridden, strong traveller. *Tom George* **c140 h–**

OMESSA HAS (FR) 5 gr.m. Martaline – Ombre Folle (Celtic Swing) [2016/17 c111, h129: h16.3d⁵ h21g⁵ c21.2d² Feb 17] sturdy mare: fairly useful handicap hurdler: lightly-raced maiden chaser, modest form only outing over fences in 2016/17: stays 21f: acts on soft going: in tongue tie last 2 starts. *Nicky Henderson* **c98 h126**

OMID 9 b.g. Dubawi (IRE) – Mille Couleurs (FR) (Spectrum (IRE)) [2016/17 h100§: h22.1m⁶ h25.4d* h27gᶠ Sep 1] strong, close-coupled gelding: fair handicap hurdler: won at Cartmel in June: stays 27f: acts on soft and good to firm going: wears headgear/tongue tie: front runner/races prominently: unreliable. *Kenneth Slack* **h111 §**

ON ALBERTS HEAD (IRE) 7 b.g. Mountain High (IRE) – Dear Money (IRE) (Buckskin (FR)) [2016/17 h–: c24.2m³ h19.6g* h21.6g⁵ c19.4mᵘʳ c20gᵖᵘ h20g h20m⁴ h15.8d Apr 16] winning pointer: modest handicap hurdler: won conditionals event at Huntingdon in May: modest maiden chaser: stays 2½m: acts on good to firm and good to soft going: wears headgear/tongue tie. *Richard Woollacott* **c87 h97**

ON A PROMISE (IRE) 5 gr.g. Definite Article – Silvers Promise (IRE) (Presenting) **h58**
[2016/17 h20.5s h16.2s h16.6d h16.4v⁵ Feb 15] has shown little over hurdles, including in
a handicap. *Nicky Richards*

ON BUDGET (IRE) 4 b.g. Duke of Marmalade (IRE) – Henties Bay (IRE) (Cape Cross **h–**
(IRE)) [2016/17 h16.7gᵖᵘ Jul 31] no sign of ability on Flat and in a juvenile hurdle.
Anthony Carson

ON DEMAND 6 ch.m. Teofilo (IRE) – Mimisel (Selkirk (USA)) [2016/17 h82: h21.6g² **h117**
h21.4m³ h21.4m* h19.7g² h21.4m* h19.8d⁴ h20.3s² h15.3s⁴ h21.2s² h16.8g h20.3g Apr
20] rather leggy mare: fairly useful handicap hurdler: won at Wincanton in October and
November (mares event): stays 2¾m: acts on soft and good to firm going: tried in hood:
wears tongue tie: usually leads. *Colin Tizzard*

ONDERUN (IRE) 8 b.g. Flemensfirth (USA) – Warts And All (IRE) (Commanche Run) **c113**
[2016/17 c111, h–: c23.5g⁴ c28.5s⁴ c26.7sᵖᵘ c28s⁵ c24.1gᵖᵘ Apr 15] well-made gelding: **h–**
maiden hurdler: fair handicap chaser: won at Lingfield in December: stays 23f: acts on soft
going: tried in cheekpieces, including in 2016/17. *Emma Lavelle*

ONE BIG LOVE 9 b.m. Tamure (IRE) – Sound Appeal (Robellino (USA)) [2016/17 **h107**
h113: h15.7v³ h24.5gᵖᵘ h18.6s⁴ h21v⁴ Mar 22] workmanlike mare: fair maiden hurdler:
stays 2¾m: acts on good to soft going. *Harry Fry*

ONE BRILLIANT DAY (IRE) 5 gr.g. Tikkanen (USA) – Kay Theatre (IRE) (King's **h–**
Theatre (IRE)) [2016/17 b17.7d h20.5dᵘʳ h21.7s h20.5v h21.2sᵖᵘ h23.9gᵖᵘ h16.3gᵖᵘ Mar **b–**
25] has been in bumper/over hurdles: tried in headgear last 2 starts. *Neil Mulholland*

ONE CONEMARA (IRE) 9 b.g. Milan – Rose of Kerry (IRE) (Roselier (FR)) [2016/17 **c95**
c32.5g⁵ c24.2s⁴ Feb 4] useful-looking gelding: multiple winning pointer: winning hurdler: **h–**
modest form in chases: should stay beyond 3m: acts on heavy going: blinkered on
reappearance. *Mrs C. A. Coward*

ONE COOL BOY (IRE) 8 b.g. One Cool Cat (USA) – Pipewell (IRE) (Lake Coniston **h96**
(IRE)) [2016/17 h93: h15.8g² h15.8gᵘʳ h16.7s h15.8d⁵ Mar 15] lengthy gelding: modest
handicap hurdler: best form at 2m: acts on soft going: has worn headgear: often races
towards rear. *Tracey Watkins*

ONE COOL CLARKSON 10 b.g. Clerkenwell (USA) – Decent Dime (IRE) (Insan **c78**
(USA)) [2016/17 c90: c23gᵖᵘ c20s⁵ h24.3v³ c20.9v⁴ Mar 9] winning Irish pointer: showed **h66**
little on hurdling debut: maiden chaser, poor nowadays: stays 3m: acts on heavy going:
tried in cheekpieces. *Neil McKnight, Ireland*

ONE COOL SCORPION (IRE) 6 b.g. Scorpion (IRE) – One Cool Kate (IRE) (Definite **h91**
Article) [2016/17 h110p, b91: h24.7g h23.6d h21.6d Dec 16] lengthy, workmanlike
gelding: bumper winner: handicap hurdler, just modest form in 2016/17: stays 3m: acts on
good to soft going. *Philip Hobbs*

ONE DAY LIKE THIS (IRE) 7 ch.g. Robin des Champs (FR) – Glebe Dream (IRE) **c–**
(Be My Native (USA)) [2016/17 h–: h21.4dᵖᵘ c25.2s⁶ c24.5vᵖᵘ Feb 15] no form over **h–**
hurdles/fences: in tongue tie last 3 starts, also in cheekpieces final outing. *Tim Vaughan*

ONEFITZALL (IRE) 7 b.g. Indian Danehill (IRE) – Company Credit (IRE) (Anshan) **h134**
[2016/17 h122: h20d² h20.5d* h21.4s⁵ Dec 26] well-made gelding: useful form over
hurdles: won handicap at Newbury in November by length from Gibralfaro: stays 21f: acts
on soft going: often races prominently. *Philip Hobbs*

ONE FOR ALL 4 b.g. Pivotal – Midpoint (USA) (Point Given (USA)) [2016/17 ab16g **b–**
Dec 10] tailed off in junior bumper. *Christine Dunnett*

ONE FOR ARTHUR (IRE) 8 b.g. Milan – Nonnetia (FR) (Trempolino (USA)) **c157 p**
[2016/17 c131, h–: c26.2d* c25.5d⁵ c29.2s* c34.3d* Apr 8] **h–**

On a run-of-the-mill Thursday in mid-October, at Carlisle's first jumps
meeting of the autumn, the opportunity was taken to celebrate what might have
seemed a rather nondescript anniversary. It was forty years since Red Rum's last
win at the Cumbrian course and the course executive revived the Windermere
Chase especially for the occasion. It was the race Red Rum won in 1972, 1973 and
1976 and, after each of those victories, he went on to win the Grand National the
following spring, achieving legendary status as the only horse to win three Grand
Nationals, having come second in both Nationals between his second and third
victories. 'Red Rum Day' at Carlisle had some fitting winners, among them two
saddled by Donald McCain, son of Red Rum's trainer Ginger (whose widow Beryl

was present). The Windermere Chase itself was won by Carrigdhoun, owned and trained in Cumbria by Maurice Barnes, now in his mid-sixties, who won the Grand National on Rubstic in 1979, two years after Red Rum's third win.

Rubstic himself made history by becoming the first Scottish-trained winner of the Grand National, in which he was among nineteen (although several carried overweight) of the thirty-four runners lumped on the 10-0 mark and was sent off at 25/1. His was a triumph for a small stable, his trainer John Leadbetter chalking up just six wins that season, and he was a first Grand National mount for Maurice Barnes, for whom he was one of sixteen winning rides that season. Barnes had ridden Rubstic in fourteen consecutive races before the National, winning the Durham National at Sedgefield on him twice (including on his most recent outing before Aintree) and also winning on him at Haydock the previous season when he lowered the course record for three and a half miles. Rubstic had also twice been runner-up in the Scottish National, in 1975 when trained by Harry Bell, and in the season before he won at Aintree, when he had also won the race at Haydock (the St Helens Handicap), as well as the first of his Durham Nationals.

1979 Grand National—Rubstic (noseband) defeats Zongalero (centre) and Rough and Tumble to become Scotland's first Grand National winner, before receiving a hero's welcome twenty-four hours later (below)

1940 Grand National—Scottish hope MacMoffat (centre) goes close in the final Grand National before the World War II shutdown, chasing home Bogskar whose jockey Mervyn Jones, who joined the RAF, became one of four Grand National-winning jockeys to die in service during the war

In the front rank all the way at Aintree, Rubstic came to the last neck and neck with Zongalero and Rough and Tumble, and he wore down his rivals to win by a length and a half from Zongalero. Rubstic ran in the next two Nationals as well, starting favourite (after winning his third Durham National) and falling, for the only time in his career, at the Chair in the year that Ben Nevis won from Rough and Tumble, before then finishing seventh in Aldaniti's year. 'My three Aintree rides all came on Rubstic,' says Maurice Barnes, 'and the worst part about winning was being interviewed afterwards on *Grandstand* by David Coleman, that's never been my scene.' John Leadbetter has recounted his own memory of watching Rubstic's win near the weighing room 'on Judith Chalmers' monitor and she wasn't too pleased with my language on the run-in! She soon changed when she realised she had an exclusive interview with the winning trainer, and she never forgot that afternoon and sends me a Christmas card every year.' Leadbetter added that 'it seemed that the whole of Scotland turned up in Denholm the next day to see Rubstic, the scenes were amazing and people came to visit for months.' Rubstic spent his retirement with Leadbetter until he died at the age of twenty-six and is buried at the top of the drive at the stables at Ladykirk in the Scottish Borders to which the trainer eventually moved to concentrate on point-to-pointers.

Although Rubstic was the first Scottish-trained winner, the record in the Grand National of horses trained north of the border had included some near-misses and some remarkable stories of courage and perseverance. In the forty years before Rubstic's victory, the Grand National runner-up was Scottish-trained on no fewer than nine occasions (the winner of the first televised Grand National, Merryman II in 1960, was trained by Neville Crump but had been bred in Scotland by the Marquess of Linlithgow and bought by Miss Winifred Wallace of Edinburgh who rode him in points and trained him to win a hunter chase at Kelso before sending him to Crump in Middleham). Wyndburgh was second three times in the National in the late-'fifties and early-'sixties when he was a fixture in races over the big National fences, running over them ten times in all, winning the 1957 Grand Sefton and contesting six Grand Nationals (he also won the Christmas Cracker Handicap over the Mildmay fences). Maurice Barnes's father Tommy rode Wyndburgh when he chased home fellow twelve-year-old Kilmore in the 1962 National, his final appearance in the race, but the most celebrated of Wyndburgh's three seconds had come three years earlier when Tim Brookshaw, in one of the National's great feats of horsemanship, rode Wyndburgh without stirrups from second Becher's after one of his irons snapped. Wyndburgh went down by a length and a half to Oxo and was one of the unluckiest losers in the long history of the Grand National. Brookshaw broke his back in a fall at Aintree over hurdles in December 1963 and, when Paddy Farrell was also paralysed three months later in a fall at the Chair in the Grand National, it provided the impetus which led to a group including Clifford Nicholson, Edward Courage and John Lawrence (later Lord Oaksey) establishing the Injured Jockeys Fund which has helped so many jockeys and their families over the years.

If Wyndburgh's Aintree record was remarkable, then so too was that of MacMoffat who was second in the race in both 1939 and 1940 for his owner-trainer Captain Scott Briggs before, like others on the threshold of their careers, he lost his best years with the outbreak of war. MacMoffat, who had also finished second in the Grand Sefton in 1938, was returned to Aintree in 1946 when he finished second (after falling and being remounted) to Prince Regent in the three-runner Champion Chase in the autumn between appearances in the 1946 and 1947 Grand Nationals, falling both times and, on the second occasion at the age of fifteen, becoming one of the oldest ever National runners. MacMoffat's second Grand National appearance came almost seven months after World War II had been declared, and when, at first, the Government was in favour of maintaining some public entertainment as good for morale. Snow and frost were more of an impediment to the sport at first than any threat from the enemy, and no racing took place in Britain between December 28th and February 21st. With a news blackout on announcing cancellations or postponements of sporting fixtures, the period was a difficult one. However, once racing resumed, it continued uninterrupted up to the Grand National which, with the city of Liverpool being turned into a garrison, was won by Bogskar on whom Mervyn Jones, who had joined the RAF just before war broke out, took the mount, with his brother Hywel also joining him on leave for the day from the RAF to ride

1959 Grand National—the one that got away for three-times Scottish-trained runner-up Wyndburgh (white bandages), with jockey Tim Brookshaw forced to ride without irons after a stirrup leather broke at second Becher's

1965 Grand National—popular Scottish chaser Freddie (right) has to give best to one who's come from even further afield, US raider Jay Trump; Freddie was runner-up again in 1966

National Night. National Night fell at the fourteenth but, continuing riderless, was to play some part in Bogskar's victory, his unwelcome attentions causing problems for front-running MacMoffat and his rider 'Ben' Alder who couldn't shake him off in the closing stages. The riderless National Night was actually the first to pass the post after Bogskar drew level with MacMoffat at the last and pulled away from him to win by four lengths.

There had been mixed feelings in Government circles about staging the Grand National at Aintree so close to industry and to the docks (at one point it seemed a substitute race might be held at Newbury or Gatwick) but the three-day meeting took place in the end and the National was run in front of a crowd of around 70,000, 5,000 of whom were members of the armed forces admitted at half price. The race card and the newspapers on the day included instructions on what to do in the event of an air raid—fighter planes flew overhead during the meeting—and extra ambulances and fire tenders were drafted in, along with three hundred air raid wardens. When the 1997 Grand National was swiftly rearranged after an IRA bomb threat disrupted the original running, restaging the race was seen as sending a message of defiance. It had been the same in 1940 as the opening words of the Pathé newsreel of the event illustrate—'War has changed many things, but not the Grand National … the spirit behind it is the same: the British love of sport and fair play, the admiration of fine horses, the thrill of a gamble. The Grand National is a symbol of our national life, the freedom to enjoy ourselves in the way we love best, the freedom we are fighting for.' Only two months later, the evacuation of Dunkirk, which brought back 330,000 troops to Britain, accelerated the requisitioning of racecourses for use as temporary

Randox Health Grand National Handicap Chase, Aintree—it takes three attempts to get the field away some seven minutes after the scheduled start time of 5.15

camps and the military occupied Aintree for the rest of the war (it was taken over by the Americans from 1942). Aintree made enquiries about staging the Grand National again in 1941 but the authorities turned down the request on the grounds of public safety as 'Liverpool is the most frequently attacked city in the region and it is not advisable to have a large concourse of people on the edge of Liverpool in the spring of 1941 [the racecourse was hit several times during a blitz of bombing in May 1941].' There was a sad postscript to the 1940 Grand National when Bogskar's jockey, by then a pilot sergeant, was killed in action on reconnaissance over Norway two years into the war; four Grand National-winning jockeys died on service in World War II, the others being Frank Furlong of the Fleet Air Arm, who won the 1935 National on Reynoldstown, Bobby Everett of the Navy who had won on Gregalach in 1929 and Tommy Cullinan who won on Shaun Goilin in 1930 and died when based at an RAF station in Oxfordshire.

The performances of MacMoffat and Wyndburgh at Aintree were marked by plaques in the runner's up spot in the original unsaddling enclosure (now a hospitality area), but there was another Scottish-trained chaser who equalled MacMoffat's achievement of finishing second in the race in successive years. That was the 'Pride of Scotland', the leading hunter chaser Freddie, owned and trained by Borders farmer Reg Tweedie. He started a short-priced favourite for the Grand National in both 1965 (under top weight of 11-10) and 1966 (under 11-7), starting at 11/4 in a field of forty-seven on the second occasion, the shortest-priced Grand National runner since Golden Miller was sent off at 2/1 in 1935. Freddie found the multiple Maryland Hunt Cup winner Jay Trump just too good in 1965 (beaten three quarters of a length, with the pair twenty lengths clear of the third). It wasn't so close twelve months later with 50/1-shot Anglo (trained like Jay Trump by Fred Winter who had only just begun his new career) stretching right away from Freddie to beat him by twenty lengths.

In both years, incidentally, there was a serious question over whether the Grand National would continue at its traditional home. Mrs Mirabel Topham had announced in July 1964 that she was selling the course to Capital and Counties for development. Two other major racecourses in large urban areas had recently closed, Hurst Park in 1962 and Manchester in 1963 (Birmingham was to follow in 1965), but the announcement about Aintree came as a major surprise to almost everyone in racing. It transpired that Mrs Topham had vested all the rights associated with the Grand National itself in a separate company and wanted to licence another course—'modernly equipped' Ascot her preferred choice—to stage the race after the sale of Aintree. With many in racing seemingly resigned to the closure of Aintree, the former owner of the course Lord Sefton applied for, and won, an injunction in the High Court to prevent the sale on the grounds that it breached a covenant in his sale agreement with Tophams in 1949 that Aintree could not be used during his lifetime, or that of his wife, for purposes other than horse racing and agriculture. The High Court found for Lord Sefton but Mrs Topham went to the Appeal Court, which also found for Lord Sefton in April 1965 (after the running of the National). After agreeing to run the National in 1966, Mrs Topham then took the matter to the House of Lords, having lodged her own planning application after Capital and Counties withdrew their scheme. The Law Lords found in Mrs Topham's favour by a margin of 3-2, which ended Lord Sefton's involvement in trying to save Aintree ('I cannot believe that the British public will stand by and see the greatest race die through lack of initiative'). How racing at Aintree was eventually secured, and the long tortuous route that led to that eventual conclusion in May 1983, is touched on in the essay on Thistlecrack, in which the plans of Jockey Club Racecourses to sell Kempton Park for development are discussed.

Wyndburgh was trained for much of his career by the most successful Scottish-based trainer of the twentieth century, Ken Oliver, who also trained Moidore's Token, whose Grand National second to Red Alligator followed closely after Freddie's fine efforts. The 1977 Scottish Grand National winner Sebastian V was a most gallant runner-up at Aintree for Harry Bell's stable twelve months before Rubstic's victory, jumping superbly and leading from the Chair until collared on the run-in by Lucius who beat him by half a length in a thrilling finish also involving Drumroan, Coolishall and The Pilgarlic. Harry Bell and Ken Oliver, by the way, saddled eight winners of the Scottish Grand National between them, with Cockle Strand, who became the joint-record fifth of Oliver's winners when he beat his stablemate Three To One in 1982, being the last home-trained winner of that race until Merigo won in 2010 and again in 2012 for Andrew Parker. Since Rubstic's victory, there have been two other Scottish-trained runners-up in the Grand National at Aintree, 66/1-shot Young Driver (trained by John Wilson) who was in front at the last in 1986 before West Tip headed him approaching the elbow to win by two lengths, and the ill-fated Blue Charm who led the field a merry dance in 1999 before Bobbyjo drew away on the run-in to beat him by ten lengths.

Blue Charm was trained by Sue Bradburne and it was a female trainer, Lucinda Russell, who gave Scotland its second winner of the Grand National when the latest running was won by the progressive One For Arthur, a horse originally bought out of Irish point-to-points and named after Ireland's most famous brewer Arthur Guinness ('Let's have one for Arthur, and one more for the road'). Lucinda Russell's Arlary House Stables in Kinross set a new record for the number of wins achieved in a jumps season by a Scottish-based trainer when chalking up sixty-six successes in 2013/14 (Len Lungo held the record of sixty-three, which he set in 2002/3). Former event rider Russell and eight-times champion jockey Peter Scudamore, whose father Michael was Oxo's jockey in the 1959 National, are very much a double act and run a successful yard. Scudamore had been involved in the training of two previous Grand National winners, Earth Summit and Bindaree, when assistant trainer to Nigel Twiston-Davies, but no-one knows more than him how difficult it is to win a Grand National (he rode in the race twelve times without success, third on Corbiere in 1985 his best finish, and he also completed a circuit on the strongly-fancied Captain Dibble in the shambolic void race of 1993, his last National as he retired four days later). Lucinda Russell had saddled three Grand National runners before One For Arthur—100/1-shot Greenhill Raffles in 1996,

First Becher's—Aintree specialist Mr Sam Waley-Cohen crashes out on The Young Master (No.13), whose fall also effectively ends the race for second favourite Definitly Red (striped cap) who is very badly hampered

First Canal Turn—the Gigginstown trio of Roi des Francs (left), Rogue Angel (second left) and Thunder And Roses (No.36) lead the way with 2016 runner-up The Last Samuri (noseband)

Strong Resolve in 2005 and Silver By Nature in 2011—and all three had completed the course, Silver By Nature finishing a best-placed twelfth when sent off joint favourite after winning Haydock's Grand National trial for the second year.

There was no shortage of stable confidence behind One For Arthur, said by his trainer to be 'more versatile than my previous runners [regarding going requirements] and just the right type for the race', and he started at 14/1 to end the thirty-eight-year wait for another Scottish-trained winner and to give his trainer the distinction of becoming the fourth woman to saddle a Grand National winner, following Jenny Pitman (successful with Corbiere and Royal Athlete), Venetia Williams (Mon Mome) and, most recently, Sue Smith (Auroras Encore whose rider Ryan Mania was the first winning Scottish jockey for 117 years). Peter Scudamore revealed that, when he was assistant to Nigel Twiston-Davies, the stable had a poor run of form up to the Christmas before Earth Summit won, until a change in the feed appeared to improve things. 'Exactly the same has happened at Arlary House and it is a plus for One For Arthur that our string's form in the last month has been the best for the entire season … the work we have been seeing on the gallops suggests One For Arthur has improved significantly since he won at Warwick in January.'

One For Arthur's progress through the chasing ranks had been eye-catching as he improved for being stepped up in trip and really impressed with the accuracy of his jumping. He won only once from seven starts in varied company in his novice season over fences but showed improved form when winning a handicap at Kelso in good style on his reappearance in October, seeming to appreciate the step up in trip to three and a quarter miles, and then shaped very well—having been raised 10 lb by the BHA handicapper for his Kelso win—when a keeping-on fifth (beaten less than three lengths) behind Vieux Lion Rouge in the Becher Chase over the Grand National fences at Aintree in December. One For Arthur continued his progress and put himself firmly in the Grand National picture when winning the twenty-runner Betfred Classic Handicap at Warwick in January, relishing tackling an extreme distance (three miles five furlongs) for the first time and cutting down the opposition on the bridle in the home straight after falling behind early on when badly hampered by a faller at the second. He stayed on strongly to lead two out and another bold leap at the last settled things as he romped home by six lengths and four and a half from Goodtoknow and 2014 winner Shotgun Paddy, who had also come third in 2015.

One For Arthur's performance at Warwick virtually assured him of a place in the Grand National line-up, in which he looked the runner with clearly the most improvement in him. Given the standard required nowadays to get into the National field—a BHA mark of 143 was the cut-off in the latest edition—it is very rare to see a Grand National runner still with the Timeform 'p' against his rating, indicating that he is likely to improve. There were some concerns over whether young stable-jockey Derek Fox (who took over when long-serving Peter Buchanan retired at the end of 2015/16) would be fit to ride One For Arthur. With champion jockey Richard Johnson on stand-by, Fox eventually won his personal race against time, to take the biggest ride of his career, after he had broken his left wrist and dislocated a collar bone in a fall at Carlisle on March 9th (he spent three weeks undergoing intensive rehabilitation at Jack Berry House, the Injured Jockeys Fund centre at Malton in

The water—Roi des Francs (left) and Rogue Angel still lead the way, with the well-fancied trio of Vieux Lion Rouge (striped sleeves), Pleasant Company (hood) and Blaklion (star on cap) just jumping the obstacle ...

North Yorkshire). Fox got medical clearance to ride on the Monday before the National and rode in only a handful of races before partnering One For Arthur, his ride on the outsider Imjoeking over the National fences in the Topham at Aintree on Friday ending with a fall at the fifth last.

The Grand National fences may not be so fearsome as they once were but they are still big, and plenty of attention was focussed as usual on runners with previous form over them. Irish-trained entries dominated the weights when they came out in February but, after a war of words between Michael O'Leary, the owner of Gigginstown House Stud, and BHA Head of Handicapping Phil Smith over the treatment of three of his horses, Outlander, Empire of Dirt and Don Poli, three of the original four top weights, a series of Irish withdrawals at the first scratching deadline left the previous year's runner-up The Last Samuri at the head of the weights—raised 10 lb for his sterling National effort and then a further 2 lb for his good third in the Becher. Mr Smith's practice of favouring the top horses when framing the Grand National handicap seems, thankfully, to be a thing of the past but putting original top weight Outlander on a BHA mark of 166, 2 lb higher than his Irish Turf Club assessment, with Empire of Dirt, Don Poli (and Carlingford Lough) also given elevated marks, caused a much bigger row at the event held to launch the weights, where Smith had to defend charges of 'penalising high-class Irish entries' (the BHA says it maintains its own handicap for Irish racing which sometimes differs from that of the Irish Turf Club handicappers).

The next four in the weights below The Last Samuri were British-trained, including the Gold Cup fifth and sixth Saphir du Rheu and More of That, both 16/1-shots at Aintree, but none of that group had previous form over the National fences, and nor did the highest-weighted Irish runners, Roi des Francs and Wounded Warrior, who were among five owned by Gigginstown House Stud in the line-up (Gigginstown had had the previous year's winner Rule The World who had become the first Irish-trained horse to win the National for nine years). The Gigginstown batch included two winners of the Irish Grand National, Rogue Angel and Thunder And Roses, both of whom had experienced the Aintree fences, without notable success, in runnings of the Becher Chase, behind the latest winner Vieux Lion Rouge (the mount of Peter Scudamore's son Tom) and Highland Lodge respectively, both of whom also had other good efforts to their name over the big fences and were among those who featured in many National previews. Highland Lodge had 'missed the cut' for the previous year's National but his official handicap mark had been artificially inflated by no less than 8 lb to guarantee him a start this time, ridden by Henry Brooke whose remarkable recovery from a horror fall at Hexham in October, that had put him in a coma, had seen him back in action to partner Highland Lodge to a much publicised second to Vieux Lion Rouge in the Becher Chase. Cashing in on their good fortune with Highland Lodge's mark and the publicity surrounding the horse, the connections of Highland Lodge sold him to Patricia Thompson of Cheveley Park Stud a week before the National (Party Politics had been bought from owner-breeder David Stoddart, who died in March 2017, as a gift for Mrs Thompson just forty-eight hours before his 1992 National win). Mrs Thompson also purchased two of the Paul Nicholls-trained runners in the National, Le Mercurey and Just A Par, the last-named a £100,000 purchase at the Aintree Sales two days before the race in which he carried the colours of Mrs Thompson's son Richard. Nicholls saddled five in all, with Saphir du Rheu his main hope, although there was support for the stable's reigning Scottish Grand National winner Vicente who had been purchased by 'Mr Grand National' Trevor Hemmings as a replacement Grand National runner for his ill-fated Many Clouds. Around half the field had previous experience of the fences, also among them the runner-up to Many Clouds in the 2015 Grand National, Saint Are, the three-times Cheltenham Festival winner Cause of Causes who had also completed behind Many Clouds, and the previous year's Grand National sixth Ucello Conti who had finished fourth in the latest edition of the Becher Chase.

The betting market on Grand National day, however, was headed by three horses who had never run over the Grand National fences, the 8/1 favourite being the previous year's RSA Chase winner Blaklion (second to Vieux Lion Rouge—a 12/1-shot in the National—in Haydock's Grand National Trial last time). Second favourite at 10/1 was the only entrant from a Yorkshire stable, the in-form Definitly Red (who had beaten The Last Samuri in clear-cut fashion in the Grimthorpe Chase at Doncaster). Definitly Red started a point longer than the Willie Mullins-trained Pleasant Company, winner of the Bobbyjo Chase at Fairyhouse and the mount of Ruby Walsh. The SP over-round (the theoretical mark-up in favour of the bookmakers) on the Grand National was 154%, once again underlining that punters should always take a morning price on the big race (the over-round in the *Pricewise* table in the *Racing Post* on the morning was 110%).

The vexing issue of starting procedures and false starts reared its head again in the latest Grand National, the first sponsored by Randox Health, with the field recalled twice before the starter let them go at the third attempt from a standing start (as in 2014, transgressions by the jockeys were eventually dealt with at a BHA hearing some time after the race, with twenty-six of the thirty-one riders reported by the Aintree stewards, including winning rider Derek Fox, stood down for a day for not obeying the starter). The start for the Grand National was moved ninety yards further away from the stands in 2013 to create a quieter atmosphere for the horses, but the latest shenanigans resulted in the race being off seven minutes late, with the chances of some of the runners on a day of Mediterranean temperatures, most notably The Last Samuri and Raz de Maree who both became very edgy, being needlessly affected before the race had even begun (nineteen amateurs in the Foxhunters' two days earlier had received one-day suspensions for cantering in at the start).

With the forty Grand National runners setting off spread right across the course, Vicente and 33/1-shot Cocktails At Dawn, both towards the outside, got no further than the first. However, there were no more casualties until Becher's as Highland Lodge, Roi des Francs, The Last Samuri, Rogue Angel and The Young

... whilst One For Arthur (white face) is still among the backmarkers, which also include the Katie Walsh-ridden Wonderful Charm (No.8)

Master all showed among the leaders. The Young Master fell heavily at Becher's where he effectively put Definitly Red out of the race, hampering him so severely that Definitly Red's saddle slipped round when he was jolted. Jockey Danny Cook did very well to remain with his mount but, after jumping two more fences without stirrups, he had no alternative but to pull up Definitly Red. The luckless Raz de Maree had also gone at Becher's where he unseated his rider after being hampered in the melee caused by The Young Master's fall. The Gigginstown pair Roi des Francs and Rogue Angel led from Highland Lodge at the Canal Turn, with Double Shuffle, Goodtoknow and Saint Are close behind. Thunder And Roses became another of the race's hard-luck stories when unseating his jockey after being badly hampered by a loose horse at Valentine's while Saphir du Rheu went two fences later.

However, after an otherwise largely incident-free first circuit, thirty-one of the field (the same number as the previous year) set off into the country for a second time. Rogue Angel and Roi des Francs, who was carried very wide by a loose horse, were still at the head of affairs, followed by Goodtoknow, Highland Lodge, Double Shuffle, Pleasant Company, Vieux Lion Rouge, Saint Are, Blaklion, Perfect Candidate and The Last Samuri. One For Arthur was among the backmarkers where he had been from the start, his jockey riding the sort of patient race seldom seen on a National winner nowadays (jockeys used to be advised to 'hunt round' on the first circuit and not to think about riding a race until second time round).

As on the first circuit, the run down to Becher's was fairly uneventful by traditional Grand National standards—the modified fences again caused relatively few problems—and the next casualty was Ucello Conti, in touch and travelling well on the inside when making a mistake at Becher's and unseating his jockey, possibly distracted by Saint Are jumping across him at the fence. No other horses parted company with their riders after Ucello Conti's departure, though eleven were pulled up in the latter stages once their chance had gone. Blaklion and Vieux Lion Rouge had moved into contention, on the heels of Roi des Francs and Rogue Angel, at second Becher's and, after Pleasant Company ruined his chance with a blunder at Valentine's which saw him on his nose, the race began to take its final shape.

Blaklion was sent up to dispute the lead with Rogue Angel at the last open ditch, four from home, and was three lengths clear of the rest crossing the Melling Road with just the two fences on the main racecourse still to jump. Rogue Angel, Vieux Lion Rouge and the improving Cause of Causes were Blaklion's closest pursuers but One For Arthur, who hadn't been in the first twenty at the second Canal Turn and still had ten in front of him at the third last, was now making significant progress on the outside (his jockey had kept him towards the outer most of the way). The 50/1-shot Gas Line Boy also joined the fray coming back on to the racecourse proper and was also among the four right in contention at the second last where Blaklion's lead had been whittled away. One For Arthur jumped into the back of

602

Blaklion at that fence where Cause of Causes and Gas Line Boy also bumped each other. One For Arthur was in full flow, though, and stayed on very strongly, ridden right out after leading at the last, to win by four and a half lengths from the keeping-on Cause of Causes who had every chance. Third place, a further three and three quarter lengths back, went to the rallying Saint Are who posted another notable effort at Aintree (he also won the Sefton Novices' Hurdle and was then successful over the Mildmay fences at the meeting earlier in his career). The tiring Blaklion, who might have finished closer had he not been sent for home from so far out, completed the frame, half a length behind Saint Are. Next came Gas Line Boy and Vieux Lion Rouge, who ran well but again seemed not to see out the trip fully (as when seventh the previous season while still a novice).

There were nineteen finishers and the 2014 Cheltenham Gold Cup winner Lord Windermere led home the rest, taking to the course better than when pulled up in the 2015 National and the only runner apart from the winner to land any sort of blow after being dropped out on the first circuit. Pleasant Company did well after his bad mistake to finish ninth, remaining one to be interested in another year, and The Last Samuri finished sixteenth after losing touch second time around. Roi des Francs paid for the dashing ride given to him, weakening from the home turn and beating only one home, while Rogue Angel was eventually pulled up after he had folded tamely from early in the home straight. The numerous jockeys who pulled up their mounts—perhaps briefed beforehand given how warm it was—deserve credit for putting horse welfare first. There have been too many instances in the race's history when riders have continued on exhausted horses just for the satisfaction of completing.

The winner's time of 9m 2.00sec was a record for the Grand National over its shorter, modified course but the gallop was by no means end-to-end, with the field bunching up at around halfway when the tempo set by Rogue Angel and Roi des Francs dipped for a brief period. The first three, who had previous experience of the course, were all keeping on strongly at the line and One For Arthur arguably deserved extra credit for coming from so far back in a race which didn't favour the patient tactics that were adopted on him. 'As much as I would have liked to be handy,' said the winning jockey afterwards, 'One For Arthur is a bit one-paced and has his own way of running and I was worried that if I got him out of his "comfort zone" I would have put him on his head and made him make mistakes [he made only one discernible error, at the nineteenth]. In the end, I probably finished up in front sooner than I wanted, it is a long run-in and the roar of the crowd is a distraction so I kept him up to his work [Fox used his whip on the run-in the maximum eight times permitted under the rules without triggering a possible inquiry].'

The second last—the favourite Blaklion leads the way from the rapidly-improving One For Arthur, whilst Cause of Causes (hoops) and Gas Line Boy bump on landing

The last—One For Arthur has hit the front, with Cause of Causes emerging as his main danger with Blaklion and Gas Line Boy (right) having no more to give

Derek Fox had to forgo the Grand National custom of being led back on his mount to the winner's enclosure flanked by police horses. All the jockeys had been told beforehand that, because of the unseasonable twenty-degree heat, they were to dismount after crossing the line and lead their horses to the special covered wash-down area that has been in place for the last few years (modelled on similar facilities developed for equine events at recent Olympics). Veterinary and ancillary support is also more extensive on Grand National day nowadays than it used to be, with a large team—including ten vets—employed for the latest running. Riders in the 2011 Grand National had received a similar instruction to dismount straight after the line for the welfare of the horses (it was a similarly hot day) but, on that occasion, the media had not been notified, which led to confusion over whether the winner Ballabriggs was either injured or close to collapse through exhaustion (neither of which was true) but generated needless bad publicity.

Racegoers at Aintree for the latest National could hardly miss the many references around the course to horse welfare and the number of mentions during the terrestrial television coverage of the equine welfare arrangements for the National runners left the impression that new broadcaster ITV was particularly keen to support the public relations exercise on welfare that was seemingly being promoted by Aintree. The broadcaster would have put itself in a difficult position if there had been awkward questions to ask after the race. This was the fifth 'plastic' National since the fence construction was changed to make the obstacles 'more forgiving' and, although the National had had a couple of tough years before the changes, there was an air of unseemly desperation about Aintree's 'charm offensive' at the latest running portraying the modern Nationals as much better regulated and safer than their predecessors. Also displayed around the course were reminders marking some memorable anniversaries, including the drama of Foinavon's National fifty years ago, Red Rum's third Grand National victory forty years ago and even the IRA bomb evacuation of twenty years ago (there was an armed police presence for the first time, and very tight security, for the latest National after a series of Islamist terrorist outrages around the world, including a very recent one outside Parliament in London). Horse welfare wasn't a particularly hot topic in the days of Foinavon and Red Rum (two horses were killed in the 1977 National but their deaths merited little more than a footnote).

The fatal fall of the Cheltenham Gold Cup winner Alverton in Rubstic's Grand National did, however, prompt a furore, reviving criticism of the race that had reared its head periodically down the years. *Chasers & Hurdlers 1978/79* raised the question of the unfairness of Becher's in the essay on Alverton who caught the top of the fence and fell awkwardly. Alverton's fall was not typical of those at Becher's, the majority of which were caused by the sloping drop on the landing side, but *Chasers & Hurdlers* warned: 'The big drop onto the brook's sloping bank perhaps asks too much of any horse, not least for a horse who has thirty fences in all to negotiate and a distance of four and a half miles to cover.' *Chasers & Hurdlers* continued to be critical of Becher's, the fence that, more than any other, presented opponents of the National with their best ammunition, but the issue didn't reach a head until two more fatalities at the fence marred the 1989 running. Influential commentators Peter O'Sullevan and John Oaksey had joined in the criticism of Becher's after the much publicised death of Dark Ivy at the fence two years earlier ('It has, I admit, taken me a long time to recognise the fact but I am now convinced that those few sloping yards on the landing side of Becher's are the only unfair part of the Grand National course [causing undeserved falls by trapping good jumpers and increasing the chance of serious injury] and a part which could be altered without damaging the race in any way,' Oaksey wrote in *Horse and Hound* on April 30th 1987.

A Jockey Club review after the two deaths in 1989 finally led to the brook at Becher's being partly filled in and the landing side of the fence being regraded to remove the tricky camber. There have been only three further fatalities at the fence in the Grand National since this work was completed in time for the 1990 running and that modification alone seemed sufficient to strike a fair balance between the need

Across the line—Derek Fox starts the celebrations;
further back, 2015 runner-up Saint Are (diamonds on sleeves) stays on well to claim third

Lucinda Russell runs to greet the winning jockey, who (in common with all the riders in the National) was ordered to dismount on the course by the stewards on safety/welfare grounds because of the unseasonably hot weather

to make Becher's less hazardous without detracting from the spectacle. Subsequent changes, the first of them before the 2005 race and the most recent in 2013, have gone much further and, close up, Becher's is unrecognisable today as the daunting obstacle it used to be, and really not greatly different from a number of the other 'drop' fences, such as Valentine's.

The changes to the Grand National course and its fences have been designed to make the race less open to ill-informed criticism in a modern society in which unchecked stories on social media, quickly passed on to other users, can go viral within hours and cause untold damage to reputations. Everyone in racing will be pleased that, for the fifth year in succession, all the Grand National runners returned safely. The race, though, seems to be going through some sort of transitional identity crisis, with Aintree still seeking to have it both ways—celebrating all the old anniversaries with gusto, while at the same time being at pains to insist that the new race is, in so many ways, much better than the old ones. Is the course proud of the Grand National's heritage or ashamed of it?

The Grand National viewing figures for ITV's first showing of the race, since the contract moved from Channel 4, showed an abrupt decline from 10.1m (measured by a five-minute peak) in 2016 to 8.2m for the latest running. Although the figures must, at least partly, reflect a slide in the Grand National's popularity, the fine and warm weather across the country was the likeliest reason for an overall fall in the numbers watching TV on the afternoon, and the fact that the Grand National's share of the terrestrial audience at the time of the race was up from 58% to 62% was a little more encouraging for racing's new broadcasting partner. ITV reportedly paid around £30m for the four-year deal for exclusive terrestrial coverage of the sport, aiming to more than recoup its outlay from additional betting-related advertisements and programme sponsorship (William Hill are said to be paying £12m to sponsor the ITV Sport racing output). The Grand National was again run at 5.15, the late-afternoon slot introduced the previous year in the hope of increasing viewing figures (Aintree's management had hoped for at least 12m viewers, given ITV1's much bigger audience base, with the first tea-time National having seen a year-on-year jump on Channel 4 of 1.3m). Among the various Grand National anniversaries being celebrated with the running of the latest edition, by the way, was one that went virtually unsung. The Grand National's history remains inextricably linked to the BBC, which lost its television contract in 2012, but the corporation celebrated its ninetieth year of broadcasting the race from Aintree when covering the race on Radio 5 Live and on its World Service which reached an estimated global audience of 500m.

The fact that the latest winner would not be coming into the winner's circle, the traditional focal point after any Grand National, left the ITV commentary team to concentrate on the winning connections. The winning jockey took several minutes to carry his saddle back through the crowd to reach the scales and weigh in, thankfully arriving with all his tack and saddle lead still in place! One For Arthur's owners 'Two Golf Widows' were revealed as Belinda McClung and Deborah Thomson, friends since their schooldays who had bought One For Arthur, after he had won a maiden point in Ireland at the fifth attempt, for £60,000 as a four-year-old at the Cheltenham Sales in December 2013. 'My husband Fraser and Deb's partner Colin are off playing golf every weekend and we wanted an activity that we could both enjoy,' said Mrs McClung, 'but we never thought we'd ever have a horse to run in the National, let alone win it!' The only other time One For Arthur had run at Aintree before the latest season he had started at 40/1 and come off the bridle a long way out before being pulled up behind Thistlecrack in the 2015 Sefton Novices' Hurdle.

After the National, it was at least forty minutes before One For Arthur emerged from the wash-down area, and an hour before he was paraded on the course. Already under pressure from the 5.15 start time, the Sunday newspaper reports had no post-race pictures of the winner. Only five of the national Sundays carried the story on their front page. *The Observer* used a shot of One For Arthur crossing the line, with the headline 'Arthur's feat—Scottish chaser wins thrilling Grand National'; *The Sunday Telegraph* used a picture of the owners with 'Grand National victory for the golf widows'; *The Sunday Times* chose a picture of racegoers cheering on the runners under 'A winning day for the ladies at Aintree'; the *Sunday People* carried the headline 'Bradley's Champion' with a shot of the winning jockey carrying five-year-old cancer victim Bradley Lowery on his shoulders (the youngster, who died in July, had been a VIP guest at Aintree and had been listed as number 41 after the Grand National runners on the official race card); the *Sunday People*'s sister paper the *Sunday Mirror* used the same picture but more prominently. There was no mention of the Grand National on the front pages of *The Mail*, the *Express* or *The Sun On Sunday* (which carried a picture of trendy young adult racegoers on one of its inside pages under the headline 'National stunners and riders').

One For Arthur, a tall gelding, didn't see a racecourse until he was four, at which age he achieved his point-to-point win in a maiden at Lingstown in County Wexford for Liam Kenny. In hindsight, it turned out to be a particularly noteworthy event as none other than Blaklion finished third (the runner-up The Wexfordian is a winning pointer but was still a maiden after fifteen outings under Rules at the end of the latest season, finishing third on his final start off a BHA mark of 102 in a five-runner novice handicap chase at Stratford). One For Arthur is by one of the top Coolmore National Hunt stallions the 2001 St Leger winner Milan who stands at a fee of €7,500. One For Arthur's Grand National victory makes him the second biggest earner for his sire behind Champion Hurdle winner Jezki. One For Arthur's dam Nonnetia, winner of a three-year-old hurdle over fifteen furlongs in France, was bought privately by One For Arthur's breeder John Dwan after she had gone through the sale-ring unsold at the Goffs France Sales in July 2006.

Two Golf Widows' "One For Arthur"

One For Arthur (IRE) (b.g. 2009)	Milan (b 1998)	Sadler's Wells (b 1981)	Northern Dancer
			Fairy Bridge
		Kithanga (b 1990)	Darshaan
			Kalata
	Nonnetia (FR) (ch 2003)	Trempolino (ch 1984)	Sharpen Up
			Trephine
		Wavy Kris (b 1993)	Persian Bold
			Wavy Reef

All four of Nonnetia's foals to reach the racecourse so far have won, albeit her first foal Camille Montes (by Oscar) managed just a point-to-point. One For Arthur is Nonnetia's second foal and his fairly useful younger brothers Ritual of Senses and Forza Milan were both successful in the latest season, the former in a maiden hurdle at Plumpton and a novice event at Fontwell (over two miles three furlongs) for Warren Greatrex, and the latter in a maiden hurdle at Chepstow (two miles three and a half furlongs) for Jonjo O'Neill. Nonnetia has subsequently produced foals to Getaway, Arakan and Yeats and was scanned in foal to Kayf Tara in the latest season. One For Arthur's family on the distaff side is Flat-oriented and his grandam Wavy Kris won in Spain as a two-year-old and is a half-sister to the smart miler Wavy Run who won thirteen races in Spain (where he was the champion three-year-old colt), France and North America (where he won the Grade 2 San Francisco Mile Handicap). Another half-sister to Wavy Kris is the miler Agnus who won twice in Belgium and is the dam of the smart miler Dolores (in the frame in the One Thousand Guineas and Coronation Stakes). There is stamina further back in the family and Dolores herself is the dam of those two smart stayers on the Flat, Duncan

608

and Samuel. Samuel won the Doncaster Cup and Duncan the Yorkshire Cup (he also dead-heated in the Irish St Leger). A half-sister to Duncan and Samuel, Gretchen, earned further kudos for the family when successful in the 2015 Park Hill Stakes. One For Arthur, who wore a tongue tie on his last two starts, is suited by extreme distances and acts on heavy going, though he doesn't need testing conditions (he has won on good and the going on Grand National day was good to soft, and drying out all the time). He takes time to warm up in his races and is often towards the rear early on. A fine jumper, he is probably still open to further improvement. *Lucinda Russell Postscript*: As befitted his historic achievement, One For Arthur was feted when he returned to Scotland, putting in appearances at several of the country's race meetings in the weeks following the National and being given an enthusiastic reception. His groom Jaimie Duff, who missed the presentations at Aintree when One For Arthur did not return to the winner's circle, received her award at Musselburgh a week after the Grand National, along with work rider Ailsa McClung. One For Arthur was also on view at Ayr on Scottish Grand National day (he had been entered for the race but, after winning at Aintree, did not run again). By joining the ranks of Grand National winners, One For Arthur immediately became a racing 'celebrity'. Not many other big-race winners enjoy the same fame as a winner of Britain's most valuable steeplechase, and, still only eight, One For Arthur has plenty of time to attain an even more elevated place in Grand National history—perhaps by becoming the first since Red Rum to win the race more than once. Hopefully, he will eventually retire in one piece and join the annual parade of former winners that is a highlight of Grand National day. Alas, that parade won't be quite so long in the next season, after the unprecedented death toll among former winners. No fewer than six died in 2016/17, including the oldest surviving winner Rough Quest who was thirty when he passed away in October and had not been at Aintree for a few years. The others to succumb were Lord Gyllene (winner of the bomb scare Grand National), Papillon, Red Marauder, Amberleigh House and Comply Or Die who had all been regulars in the parade in recent times. Leading the Aintree pageant at the next Grand National is likely to be the 2002 winner Bindaree who will be twenty-four.

ONE FOR BILLY 5 b.g. Midnight Legend – Saxona (IRE) (Jade Robbery (USA)) **h93 p** [2016/17 b17d⁶ b15.7d³ h19.8d³ Mar 26] £50,000 3-y-o: second foal: half-brother to **b90** bumper winner (including at 19f)/winning pointer Carter McKay (by Martaline): dam (b87), bumper winner, also 17f winner on Flat: fair form in bumpers: 4/1, shaped much better than result when third in maiden at Wincanton (22½ lengths behind Winningtry) on hurdling debut: in tongue tie last 2 starts: will improve. *Dan Skelton*

ONE FOR HARRY (IRE) 9 b.g. Generous (IRE) – Strawberry Fool (FR) (Tel Quel **h134** (FR)) [2016/17 h135x: h25sᵖᵘ h19.7d* h18.1v² h20.5v² h20.2g⁴ Apr 28] sturdy gelding: useful handicap hurdler: won at Wetherby (by length from Nautical Nitwit) in January: stays 3m, effective at shorter: acts on heavy going: tried in cheekpieces: usually races prominently. *Nicky Richards*

ONE FOR HOCKY (IRE) 9 b.g. Brian Boru – Wire Lady (IRE) (Second Set (IRE)) **c–** [2016/17 c107, h118: h20.2d² h19.6g h16.2s* h23.8gᶠ Dec 14] fairly useful handicap **h124** hurdler: won at Kelso in December: maiden chaser: stayed 3m: acted on good to firm and heavy going: tried in hood: dead. *Nicky Richards*

ONE FOR THE BOSS (IRE) 10 b.g. Garuda (IRE) – Tell Nothing (IRE) (Classic **c124** Secret (USA)) [2016/17 c81, h–: c20g⁶ c21d* c19.4v* c20g² c23.6gᵖᵘ c19.4sᵖᵘ c23.4s **h–** c22.6g⁵ Apr 1] workmanlike gelding: maiden hurdler: fairly useful handicap chaser: won at Newton Abbot and Stratford in June: stays 3m: acts on heavy going: wears cheekpieces: has worn tongue tie. *Dai Burchell*

ONE FOR THE GUV'NR (IRE) 8 b.g. Oscar (IRE) – Wintry Day (IRE) (Presenting) **c116 p** [2016/17 h122: h15.8g⁶ c20gᵘʳ c19.2g³ Aug 13] lengthy gelding: lightly-raced handicap **h113** hurdler, just fair form on reappearance: better effort (fairly useful form) over fences when third in novice at Market Rasen: may prove best around 2m: acts on soft going: capable of better over fences. *Nicky Henderson*

ONEFORTHENURE (IRE) 8 b.m. Court Cave (IRE) – Shining Willow (Strong Gale) **h–** [2016/17 h78, b64: h23.3sᵖᵘ h23.3g h23g Aug 11] sturdy, compact mare: off mark in Irish points at eighth attempt: poor maiden hurdler: in cheekpieces final start: has worn tongue tie, including in 2016/17. *Richard Woollacott*

ONE FORTY SEVEN (IRE) 5 b.g. Beneficial – Still Bubbly (IRE) (Hubbly Bubbly **h119 p**
(USA)) [2016/17 h20.6g^{ur} h19.9d^2 h18.9v^{pu} h20.5g^3 Nov 27] £70,000 4-y-o: fourth foal:
half-brother to modest hurdler/winning pointer Celtic Passion (23f winner, by
Flemensfirth): dam (h72), winning pointer/lightly raced over hurdles, half-sister to useful
hurdler/very smart staying chaser Nil Desperandum and to dam of smart hurdler (stays
21f) Willoughby Court: won Irish maiden point on debut: fairly useful form in novice
hurdles: dead-heated with Cracking Final at Uttoxeter in October, but demoted after
causing interference: will stay further than 2½m: remains open to improvement. *Nigel
Twiston-Davies*

ONEIDA TRIBE (IRE) 8 b.g. Turtle Island (IRE) – Glory Queen (IRE) (Taipan (IRE)) **c98 p**
[2016/17 h94: c21.7d^{ur} c25.1s^4 Jan 7] off mark in Irish points at fifth attempt: maiden **h–**
hurdler: modest form on completed start in novice handicap chases (stamina seemingly
stretched over testing 25f): front runner/races prominently: remains with potential over
fences. *Robin Dickin*

ONE MORE GO (IRE) 6 b.g. Papal Bull – Enchanted Wood (IRE) (Hawk Wing (USA)) **h127**
[2016/17 h92p: h20g* h20.6g* h20.6g h16.7g^2 h16g^F Oct 9] fairly useful form over
hurdles: won maiden at Worcester in June and novice at Market Rasen in July: stayed 2½m:
front runner/raced prominently: dead. *Dr Richard Newland*

ONE MORE HERO (IRE) 6 b.g. Milan – Classy Society (IRE) (Moscow Society **h– p**
(USA)) [2016/17 h23.8s^4 Feb 22] £100,000 5-y-o: fourth foal: closely related to fair chaser
Thegreendalerocket (3¼m winner, by Oscar): dam (b78) ran once in bumper, half-sister to
fairly useful hurdler/chaser (21f-23f winner) Topsham Belle: off mark in Irish maiden
points at second attempt: breathing problem when well held in maiden on hurdling debut:
should do better. *Paul Nicholls*

ONE MORE TUNE (IRE) 9 b.g. Luso – Strong Gale Pigeon (IRE) (Strong Gale) **c79**
[2016/17 c106, h–: c26g^3 Feb 22] strong gelding: multiple winning pointer: winning **h–**
hurdler: maiden hunter chaser: stays 3¼m: acts on good to firm going: in cheekpieces last
2 starts, also in tongue tie final one. *Philip Rowley*

ONENIGHTINVIENNA (IRE) 8 b.g. Oscar (IRE) – Be My Granny (Needle Gun (IRE)) **c148**
[2016/17 c142, h–: c24.5g* c29.5s^{pu} Dec 27] workmanlike gelding: winning hurdler: smart **h–**
chaser: won 2-runner graduation event at Carlisle in November by 1¾ lengths from Seldom
Inn: pulled up in Welsh Grand National final start: stayed 25f: acted on heavy going: in
cheekpieces 3 of last 4 starts: usually raced close up: dead. *Philip Hobbs*

ONE OF US 5 b.g. Presenting – One Gulp (Hernando (FR)) [2016/17 b89: h16.3g^3 h19.3d^3 **h99**
h21s^4 h23.3s^3 Apr 1] well-made gelding: modest form over hurdles, including in handicaps.
Nick Williams

ONE TERM (IRE) 10 b.g. Beneficial – One Edge (IRE) (Welsh Term) [2016/17 c118, h–: **c–**
c23.8s^{pu} Feb 19] well-made gelding: winning hurdler: useful chaser at best: pulled up in **h–**
hunter only outing in 2016/17: stays 2½m: acts on soft and good to firm going: wears
headgear. *Rebecca Curtis*

ONE TRACK MIND (IRE) 7 b.g. Flemensfirth (USA) – Lady Petit (IRE) (Beneficial) **c125**
[2016/17 h160: h24d* c19.9g^5 c25.2d^3 h24d^5 Apr 27] workmanlike gelding: very smart **h148**
hurdler: in cheekpieces, below best when fifth of 12 to Unowhatimeanharry in Champion
Stayers' Hurdle at Punchestown (won race 12 months earlier) final start: better effort over
fences, though went in snatches, when 10½ lengths third of 7 to Delusionofgrandeur in
maiden at Catterick: stays 25f: acts on heavy going: often races prominently.
Warren Greatrex

ONGENSTOWN LAD (IRE) 13 b.g. Bach (IRE) – Lantern Logic (IRE) (Royal **c–**
Fountain) [2016/17 c–, h124: h24d h25.4m^4 h24.8d^{pu} Jul 5] smallish gelding: fairly useful **h112**
handicap hurdler in 2015/16, not at best in 2016/17: maiden chaser: stays 25f: acts on soft
and good to firm going: has worn headgear: wears tongue tie: usually races in rear. *Mrs
Gillian Callaghan, Ireland*

ON HIS OWN (IRE) 13 b.g. Presenting – Shuil Na Mhuire (IRE) (Roselier (FR)) **c137**
[2016/17 c156§, h–: c24.1d^2 Jan 19] rangy gelding: winning hurdler: high-class chaser in **h–**
his prime: won Thyestes Handicap Chase at Gowran for second time in 2013/14, when also
runner-up to Lord Windermere in Cheltenham Gold Cup: 2 lengths second to Foxrock in
hunter at Thurles, only chase outing in 2016/17 (won point earlier in January): stayed 3¼m:
acted on heavy going: usually wore headgear: front runner/raced prominently: inconsistent
(tended to jump right): has been retired. *W. P. Mullins, Ireland*

ONLY A TIPPLE 6 b.g. Multiplex – Heathyards Tipple (IRE) (Marju (IRE)) [2016/17 **h74**
b71: h19.2g^5 h19.9g^5 h16g^5 h19.9g^5 h19.6s^2 h19.3s^4 h16.8g^6 Apr 26] maiden pointer: poor
maiden hurdler: stays 2½m: acts on soft going: in cheekpieces last 2 starts. *Donald McCain*

ONLYFOOLSOWNHORSES (IRE) 6 br.g. Presenting – Lizzy Langtry (IRE) (King's **h88**
Theatre (IRE)) [2016/17 h–: h21.3s⁶ h22sᵖᵘ h19.3d³ Feb 20] modest form in maiden/novice
hurdles: should stay beyond 19f: in tongue tie final start: usually races nearer last than first.
Micky Hammond

ONLY FOR LOVE 6 br.m. Kalanisi (IRE) – Sardagna (FR) (Medaaly) [2016/17 b90: **h117**
b15.8d* h19.9g* h16d* h20.6g² h23g² Aug 11] rather unfurnished mare: fair form in **b89**
bumpers: won mares event at Uttoxeter in May: fairly useful form over hurdles: won mares
maiden at Uttoxeter in May and conditionals novice at Worcester in June: stays 23f: usually
races close up/responds generously to pressure. *Nicky Henderson*

ONLY GORGEOUS (IRE) 8 b.g. Vertical Speed (FR) – Pure Beautiful (IRE) (Un **c110**
Desperado (FR)) [2016/17 c78, h98, b69: h19.8m⁴ c16.1d c19.2v* c19.2s c20.2s² c17.4v⁴ **h80**
c19.2s² c21.1g⁵ c24.2g* c30.7m* c28.4m³ Apr 27] point winner: maiden hurdler: fair
handicap chaser: won at Exeter in January and April (twice): stays 31f: acts on good to firm
and heavy going. *Susan Gardner*

ONLY ORSENFOOLSIES 8 b.g. Trade Fair – Desert Gold (IRE) (Desert Prince (IRE)) **c–**
[2016/17 c120, h–: h19.4g² h21.3s⁵ h21.4s² h24.1s⁴ Feb 4] fairly useful handicap hurdler/ **h121**
maiden chaser: stays 21f: acts on heavy going: held up. *Micky Hammond*

ONLY ORVIETO (IRE) 6 b.m. Kayf Tara – Vigna Maggio (FR) (Starborough) [2016/17 **h–**
b96: h20.2d⁵ Sep 21] fairly useful form when successful on only start in bumpers: off 6
months, 11/4, well-beaten last of 5 in mares novice at Perth on hurdling debut. *Malcolm
Jefferson*

ONLY TIME'LL TELL (IRE) 9 b.g. Gamut (IRE) – Rock Abbey (IRE) (College **c84**
Chapel) [2016/17 c21.1d² c20s⁵ c25.5sᵖᵘ Feb 26] winning pointer: poor form over fences:
best effort when second in hunter at Fontwell in May. *D. M. Carden*

ON THE BRIDGE (IRE) 12 b.g. Milan – Bay Dove (Alderbrook) [2016/17 c128, **c115 §**
h126§: c27.5mᶠ c26.1gᵖᵘ h23.3g⁵ c23m c25.8g⁴ c24.2m⁶ c25.6gᵘʳ Nov 10] tall gelding: **h– §**
useful hurdler at best, well held only outing in 2016/17: fairly useful handicap chaser: stays
27f: acts on soft and good to firm going: wears cheekpieces/tongue tie: usually races nearer
last than first: quirky. *Jeremy Scott*

ON THE FRINGE (IRE) 12 b.g. Exit To Nowhere (USA) – Love And Porter (IRE) **c129**
(Sheer Grit) [2016/17 c138: c25s* c24.3s² c26.3g⁴ c21.1gᵖᵘ c24.5d⁵ Apr 28] rangy gelding:
useful chaser: dominant in hunters in his prime, winning main events at all 3 major
Festivals (Cheltenham, Aintree and Punchestown) in 2015 and 2016: looked on wane
since, even when 2½ lengths fourth of 23 to Pacha du Polder in Foxhunter Chase at
Cheltenham in March: stays 3¼m: acts on soft going: wore cheekpieces final start: sound
jumper. *Enda Bolger, Ireland*

ON THE PROWL (IRE) 5 b.g. Kalanisi (IRE) – Prowler (IRE) (Old Vic) [2016/17 **b–**
b15.7d b15.8d Dec 26] strong gelding: well held both starts in bumpers. *Ben Case*

ON THE ROAD (IRE) 7 b.g. Stowaway – B Greenhill (Gunner B) [2016/17 h86p: **c130**
h19.1s* h21.6s* c26.3d² c20.3d² c20v* c21.1v* c21.1v* Mar 5] fair handicap hurdler: won **h104**
at Fontwell and Exeter in November: useful form over fences: won novice handicaps at
Lingfield in January and Sedgefield in February and handicap at Sedgefield (by 3½ lengths
from Wolf Sword) on final start: stays 3¼m, effective at shorter: acts on heavy going: in
cheekpieces last 3 starts. *Evan Williams*

ON TOUR (IRE) 9 b.g. Croco Rouge (IRE) – Galant Tour (IRE) (Riberetto) [2016/17 **c137**
c140, h–: c19.9d² c22.4g c19.4s³ c20.8s⁵ c20v⁴ Feb 11] workmanlike gelding: winning **h–**
hurdler: useful handicap chaser: best effort of season when second at Aintree (length
behind Thomas Brown) in November: stays 2½m: acts on heavy going: usually races
towards rear. *Evan Williams*

ONURBIKE 9 b.g. Exit To Nowhere (USA) – Lay It Off (IRE) (Strong Gale) [2016/17 h–: **c–**
c22.5dᵖᵘ c25.5sᵖᵘ c21.7dᵘʳ Nov 24] no form over hurdles/fences: blinkered final start. *John* **h–**
O'Neill

ONWITHTHEPARTY 8 b.g. Sir Harry Lewis (USA) – Kentford Fern (El Conquistador) **c–**
[2016/17 c–, h97§: h25g⁵ h24.3d⁴ h24d² h25.3d³ h27s⁴ h25d h27g* Mar 29] modest **h96 §**
handicap hurdler: won at Sedgefield in March: well held only chase start: left Chris Gordon
after first start: stays 27f: acts on heavy going: has worn headgear, including last 3 starts:
usually races prominently: ungenuine. *Kenneth Slack*

ON YOUR MAX 9 b.g. Tobougg (IRE) – Maxilla (IRE) (Lahib (USA)) [2016/17 h87: **c90**
h16.7gᵖᵘ c21.1g⁴ c17.4m² c19.7m² Sep 18] dual winning pointer: maiden hurdler: modest **h–**
form over fences: stays 2½m: acts on good to firm and good to soft going. *Phil York*

OOLOGIST 6 gr.g. Proclamation (IRE) – Orchid's Silver (Silver Patriarch (IRE)) **b82**
[2016/17 b16d⁶ b15.8s² b15.7g Nov 10] first foal: dam (h63), maiden hurdler, half-sister to
fair hurdler/fairly useful chaser (stayed 3m) Bobby Gee: modest form in bumpers.
John Gallagher

OORAYVIC (IRE) 10 ch.g. Snurge – Miss Murtle (IRE) (Old Vic) [2016/17 h15.8dᵖᵘ Oct **c–**
28] tall gelding: maiden hurdler: winning chaser: stayed 19f: acted on soft going: dead. **h–**
Sue Smith

O O SEVEN (IRE) 7 b.g. Flemensfirth (USA) – Kestral Heights (IRE) (Eagle Eyed **c150**
(USA)) [2016/17 h145: h20s² c20.4g* c24g³ c19.9s* c24.4g⁵ c21.1g⁴ Apr 7] good sort: **h–**
smart hurdler: similar form over fences: won novice at Cheltenham (by 10 lengths from
Sizing Tennessee) in November and novice handicap at Huntingdon (by ½ length from
Mad Jack Mytton) in January: creditable 7¼ lengths fourth of 29 to Ultragold in Topham
Chase (Handicap) at Aintree final start: stays 3m, effective at shorter: acts on heavy going.
Nicky Henderson

OPECHEE (IRE) 6 b.g. Robin des Champs (FR) – Falcons Gift (IRE) (Zaffaran (USA)) **c99**
[2016/17 h91p, b–: h15.7g³ h20g⁵ c15.9f² c20v⁶ c19.1g Jan 27] modest maiden hurdler/ **h89**
chaser: unproven beyond 2m: acts on firm going: in hood on chasing debut. *David
Bridgwater*

OPEN EAGLE (IRE) 8 b.g. Montjeu (IRE) – Princesse de Viane (FR) (Kaldoun (FR)) **h149**
[2016/17 h140: h24s* h20.5d* Apr 29] lengthy gelding: smart hurdler: won minor event at
Thurles (by 3¼ lengths from Woods Well) in March and Ballymore Handicap Hurdle at
Punchestown (by ½ length from Dream Berry) in April: barely stays 3m: acts on heavy
going: usually travels strongly. *W. P. Mullins, Ireland*

OPEN HEARTED 10 b.g. Generous (IRE) – Romantic Dream (Bustino) [2016/17 c142, **c123**
h–: c24sᵖᵘ c24.2s³ c20v⁵ c21.3d* c24.2g² Apr 17] tall gelding: winning hurdler: fairly **h–**
useful chaser: won handicap at Wetherby in March: stays 3m: acts on soft going: in
cheekpieces last 2 starts: wears tongue tie. *Dan Skelton*

OPENING BATSMAN (IRE) 11 b.g. Morozov (USA) – Jolly Signal (IRE) (Torus) **c136**
[2016/17 c140, h–: c24g³ c24.2d⁵ c24g⁵ c24g c23.8g* c21.1g* Apr 21] workmanlike **h–**
gelding: winning hurdler: useful handicap chaser: won at Ludlow and Fontwell (by neck
from Gowanauthat) in April: stays 3m: acts on heavy going: wears headgear/tongue tie:
often races freely. *Harry Fry*

OPERA BUFFA (IRE) 4 b.f. Exceed And Excel (AUS) – Dubai Opera (USA) (Dubai **h–**
Millennium) [2016/17 h15.8mᵖᵘ h15.8dᵖᵘ Oct 13] modest maiden on Flat, stays 1¼m:
tongue tied, showed nothing in 2 outings over hurdles: also in cheekpieces second start
(bled). *Steve Flook*

OPERA OG (IRE) 11 b.g. Oscar (IRE) – Maspaloma (IRE) (Camden Town) [2016/17 **c–**
c106, h–: c19.4g⁴ May 4] good-topped gelding: prolific point winner: maiden hurdler: **h–**
fairly useful chaser in his prime, well held in hunter only outing in 2016/17: stays 21f: acts
on good to firm and heavy going: often travels strongly/has finished weakly. *Sean Murray*

OPERA ROCK (FR) 6 b.g. Kap Rock (FR) – Open Up (FR) (Fabulous Don (SPA)) **h–**
[2016/17 b87p: h19.7sᵖᵘ Nov 23] rather unfurnished gelding: modest form only start in
bumpers: pulled up in novice on hurdling debut. *Venetia Williams*

OPTICAL HIGH 8 b.g. Rainbow High – Forsweets (Forzando) [2016/17 c–, h88: **c–**
h19.3gᵘʳ h25.3d h24dᵖᵘ h20.3g Mar 28] modest hurdler at best, no form in 2016/17: maiden **h–**
chaser: left Sue Smith after second start: in cheekpieces last 2 starts: usually races close up.
Tony Forbes

OPTIMA PETAMUS 5 gr.g. Mastercraftsman (IRE) – In A Silent Way (IRE) (Desert **h73**
Prince (IRE)) [2016/17 h15.6g³ h15.6g⁵ Feb 5] fair on Flat, stays 10.5f: poor form in
maiden/novice hurdles at Musselburgh. *Patrick Holmes*

OPTIMISTIC BIAS (IRE) 8 b.g. Sayarshan (FR) – Dashers Folly (IRE) (Dr Massini **c120**
(IRE)) [2016/17 h120: c21.4g⁴ c23m⁵ h27g* h23.3d⁵ c23.9g⁴ c23.8s³ c30.7s³ c24s* Apr 1] **h119**
fairly useful handicap hurdler/chaser: won over hurdles at Sedgefield in September and
over fences at Uttoxeter final start: left Jonjo O'Neill after fifth start (when tried in tongue
tie): stays 27f: acts on soft going. *James Evans*

OPTIMUS PRIME (FR) 5 b.g. Deportivo – Diluvienne (FR) (Kaldoun (FR)) [2016/17 **c119 +**
c17.4s h15.8g² h15.6gᵖᵘ h16.3d⁶ Mar 24] 1¼m winner on Flat: useful handicap hurdler: **h138**
good second at Huntingdon (1½ lengths behind Robinshill) in November: fairly useful

maiden over fences: in cheekpieces, eighth of 13 in handicap at Enghien on first outing in 2016/17, left Francois Nicolle after: unproven beyond 17f: acts on soft going: in tongue tie final start. *Dan Skelton*

ORANGE NASSAU (FR) 11 gr.g. Martaline – Vilaya (FR) (Cadoudal (FR)) [2016/17 c117, h–: c26.1d^{pu} May 5] winning hurdler: fairly useful chaser at best, very much on the downgrade: stays 29f: acts on heavy going: has worn headgear, including in 2016/17: tried in tongue tie: usually leads. *Charlie Longsdon*   c– h–

ORBASA (FR) 6 b.g. Full of Gold (FR) – Ierbasa de Kerpaul (FR) (Cadoubel (FR)) [2016/17 c137, h–: c19.9d^{pu} c18.8d c20.2s^2 c20.2s^3 c21m^2 c20.2f^3 c19.4m^3 Apr 28] good-topped gelding: winning hurdler: fairly useful handicap chaser: stays 21f: acts on soft and good to firm going: has worn headgear, including in 2016/17: wears tongue tie: usually races close up. *Paul Nicholls*   c129 h–

ORBY'S MAN (IRE) 8 b.g. Arcadio (GER) – Gleann Oisin (IRE) (Le Bavard (FR)) [2016/17 c113, h115: c24.5g* c23.4m^3 May 29] winning hurdler: fair handicap chaser: won at Towcester in May: stays 3m: acts on good to firm and good to soft going: wears headgear: has worn tongue tie: usually races prominently. *Charlie Longsdon*   c113 h–

ORCHARD BOY (IRE) 9 b.g. Oscar (IRE) – Beech Lodge (IRE) (Supreme Leader) [2016/17 h120: c20d^{pu} h20.5g^2 h19.5g^6 h20.5v h23.9g^{pu} Mar 20] rangy gelding: maiden hurdler, fairly useful at best: pulled up only outing over fences: stayed 2½m: acted on soft going: in headgear last 5 starts: front runner/raced prominently: dead. *Paul Webber*   c– h113

ORCHARD PARK (IRE) 6 b.g. Milan – Tough As Leather (IRE) (Flemensfirth (USA)) [2016/17 b86: h19.9s^3 h16.8g^2 h16m^2 h16.2s^2 h19.4m^F Jan 28] bumper winner: fair maiden over hurdles: unproven beyond 17f: acted on soft and good to firm going: front runner/raced prominently: dead. *Jamie Snowden*   h113

ORCHARDSTOWN CROSS (IRE) 6 b.g. Westerner – Shang A Lang (IRE) (Commander Collins (IRE)) [2016/17 h21v^5 c25.2d^4 Mar 26] €18,000 3-y-o: second foal: dam (b72), ran twice in bumpers, closely related to fairly useful hurdler/smart chaser (stayed 2½m) Down In Neworleans and half-sister to smart hurdler (stayed 21f) Chomba Womba: placed in Irish maiden point on debut: modest form when fifth in novice at Warwick on hurdling debut: showed nothing in novice on chasing debut. *Tim Vaughan*   c– h89

ORCHESTRATED (IRE) 6 b.g. Mahler – Rose Island (Jupiter Island) [2016/17 b16.8g h22g^{pu} h19.7s h16.3s h15.8v^{pu} Jan 28] compact gelding: showed nothing in bumper/over hurdles. *David Bridgwater*   h– b–

ORDER OF SERVICE 7 ch.g. Medicean – Choir Gallery (Pivotal) [2016/17 h15.5v^5 Feb 1] fairly useful on Flat, stays 8.5f: well beaten in novice claimer on hurdling debut. *Shaun Harris*   h–

OR DE VASSY (FR) 5 b.g. Assessor (IRE) – Mona Vassy (FR) (Sleeping Car (FR)) [2016/17 b15.7g^3 b15.7g^2 b16.5g^2 b15.8s^2 Mar 23] second foal: dam, placed up to 19f over hurdles/fences in France, half-sister to smart hurdler (2m-21f winner) James de Vassy: fairly useful form in bumpers: bred to stay at least 2½m. *Dan Skelton*   b96

ORDINARY WORLD (IRE) 7 br.g. Milan – Saucy Present (IRE) (Presenting) [2016/17 h16d c16m* c16d^2 c17d^2 c15.9g^3 c16d^2 Apr 27] €68,000 3-y-o: good-topped gelding: third foal: closely related to fair hurdler May Dullea (2½m winner, by King's Theatre): dam unraced half-sister to dam of useful hurdler/chaser (stays 25f) Peckhamecho: fairly useful hurdler at best: smart form over fences: won maiden at Fairyhouse (by 4 lengths from Attribution) in October: placed in Craddockstown Novices' Chase at Punchestown (length second to Identity Thief), Racing Post Novices' Chase at Leopardstown (9 lengths second to Min), Arkle Chase at Cheltenham (15 lengths third to Altior) and Ryanair Novices' Chase at Punchestown (11 lengths second to Great Field, best effort): raced around 2m: acts on good to firm and heavy going: wore hood and tongue tie last 3 starts over hurdles: front runner/races prominently. *Henry de Bromhead, Ireland*   c152 h–

ORDO AB CHAO (IRE) 8 b.g. Heron Island (IRE) – Houldyurwhist (IRE) (Supreme Leader) [2016/17 h19.3s h19.9s Mar 18] useful-looking gelding: fell last both starts in Irish maiden points: smart hurdler in 2014/15: off 23 months, well below that level in 2 starts in 2016/17: should stay 3m: acts on soft going. *Alan King*   h110

OREGON GOLD (FR) 4 b.g. Confuchias (IRE) – Gold Wine (FR) (Holst (USA)) [2016/17 b15.8d b16.7d^6 Apr 27] £3,000 3-y-o: half-brother to fair chaser Indiana Gold (2m-19f winner, by Sleeping Car): dam lightly-raced half-sister to useful French hurdler/chaser (stayed 21f) Nono des Ongrais: fair form in bumpers. *Nick Kent*   b86

ORFEO CONTI (FR) 15 ch.g. Bulington (FR) – Gazelle Lulu (FR) (Altayan) [2016/17   **c–** §
c77§, h–§: c27.2d^{pu} May 12] sturdy gelding: point winner: maiden hurdler: winning   **h–** §
chaser: stays 3½m: acts on good to firm and good to soft going: has worn blinkers: tried in
tongue tie: ungenuine. *Miss Rose Grissell*

ORIENTAL CROSS (IRE) 4 b.f. Cape Cross (IRE) – Orion Girl (GER) (Law Society   **b93**
(USA)) [2016/17 b16.7d^3 Apr 27] 7,000 3-y-o: fourth foal: half-sister to 3 winners on Flat
in France, including useful 1¼m/1½m winner Oriental Wind (by Zamindar): dam useful
French 11.5f winner: 16/1, 9¼ lengths third of 10 to Settie Hill in bumper at Market Rasen.
Patrick Chamings

ORIENTAL FIXER (IRE) 8 b.g. Vertical Speed (FR) – Hannah Rose (IRE) (Un   **h93**
Desperado (FR)) [2016/17 h16g^5 h16.7v h15.8v^4 h16.6g h20.3v^{pu} h26.4g^5 Apr 23] modest
maiden hurdler: should stay beyond 2m: acts on heavy going: tried in hood. *Michael
Scudamore*

ORIONINVERNESS (IRE) 6 b.g. Brian Boru – Woodville Leader (IRE) (Supreme   **c100**
Leader) [2016/17 h92, b62: c20.1s^{pu} c22.4v c24.5s^F h24.3v^4 c24.5s h25d^6 c20.1v* c24.2g^4 **h65**
Apr 25] poor maiden hurdler: fair form over fences: won handicap at Hexham in March:
may prove best around 2½m: acts on heavy going: in cheekpieces last 4 starts: wears
tongue tie. *Lucinda Russell*

ORIONS GOLD 6 b.g. Proclamation (IRE) – Charm of Gold (Gildoran) [2016/17 b15.7g^6 **h–**
b16g^6 h20.5g^{pu} h15.7d h15.8s^{pu} h15.8d h20.5m^5 Apr 16] first foal: dam (c84), winning   **b82**
pointer, out of half-sister to Whitbread Gold Cup winner Plundering: modest form in
bumpers: no form over hurdles: left David Bridgwater after sixth start: tried in hood.
Samuel Drinkwater

ORION'S MIGHT (IRE) 7 b.g. Antonius Pius (USA) – Imperial Conquest (IRE)   **h89** §
(Imperial Ballet (IRE)) [2016/17 h105: h16.7g h20m h16d h16.3v^3 h18.7m^3 h22g h15.8g^5
h15.8m^2 h21.4m^5 h18.5d^{pu} h16.5g^5 Apr 18] sturdy gelding: modest maiden
hurdler: stays 19f: acts on good to firm and good to soft going: has worn headgear,
including last 2 starts: in tongue tie third outing: often races towards rear: temperamental.
Matt Sheppard

ORO REBELDE 4 b.g. Cockney Rebel (IRE) – Corsa All Oro (USA) (Medaglia d'Oro   **b–**
(USA)) [2016/17 b13g b15.7s Jan 31] well held both starts in bumpers. *Gary Hanmer*

ORSM 10 b.g. Erhaab (USA) – Royal Roulette (Risk Me (FR)) [2016/17 h77: h21.6d^6 **h73**
h26.4g^{pu} Aug 11] rather sparely-made gelding: poor handicap hurdler: stays 27f: acts on
good to soft going: has worn cheekpieces, including last 2 starts: wears tongue tie. *Laura
Mongan*

ORTHODOX LAD 9 ch.g. Monsieur Bond (IRE) – Ashantiana (Ashkalani (IRE))   **c96**
[2016/17 h104: c16d^3 c17m^{pu} h15.8m h16.8g^6 h20g^4 h19.8d^6 h15.9g^6 h15.8v^3 h15.9v^3 **h83**
h15.5d^3 h15.5g^5 h16v^F h15.8s h15.8d^5 h16m Apr 28] angular gelding: poor handicap
hurdler: modest form on completed start over fences: stays 2½m: acts on soft and good to
firm going: wears cheekpieces. *Grace Harris*

OSCAR BLUE (IRE) 7 gr.g. Oscar (IRE) – Blossom Rose (IRE) (Roselier (FR))   **c104 p**
[2016/17 h122: c20.9d^4 Oct 13] runner-up on completed start in Irish points: fairly useful   **h–**
hurdler: 26¼ lengths fourth of 9 to Amilliontimes in novice handicap at Carlisle on chasing
debut: stays 23f: acts on heavy going: tried in blinkers: should do better over fences.
Brian Ellison

OSCAR BRAVO (IRE) 6 br.g. Oscar (IRE) – Brave Commitment (IRE) (Henbit (USA))   **b77**
[2016/17 b67: b16.3m^3 b16d Jun 22] modest form in bumpers: in hood/tongue tie last 2
starts. *Heather Dalton*

OSCAR DAY (IRE) 9 b.m. Oscar (IRE) – Secret Mint (IRE) (Victory Note (USA))   **c87**
[2016/17 c24g^6 c24g^4 c20g^5 c23.8s^2 c25g c20.1g^{pu} c22d c24m^6 c20d^{pu} Apr 28] second foal:
dam (h73) maiden half-sister to dam of Grand National winner Hedgehunter: winning
pointer: modest maiden chaser: may prove best at shorter than 3m: acts on soft and good to
firm going: usually in cheekpieces. *Peter Maher, Ireland*

OSCAR DELTA (IRE) 14 b.g. Oscar (IRE) – Timerry (IRE) (Alphabatim (USA))   **c86**
[2016/17 c91: c25.3g c24.5g^2 May 9] strong gelding: multiple point winner: hunter chaser:
modest nowadays: stays 3¼m: acts on soft going: tried in blinkers/tongue tie. *C. Price*

OSCAR DU BERLAIS (IRE) 8 b.g. Oscar (IRE) – Marina du Berlais (FR) (Mister Sicy   **h–**
(FR)) [2016/17 h23d Jun 29] unplaced completed starts in maiden points in 2014: tailed off
in novice on hurdling debut (wore tongue tie). *Oliver Greenall*

OSCAR FIAIN (IRE) 9 b.g. Oscar (IRE) – Produzione (FR) (Baby Turk) [2016/17 c–,   **c–** h–: h23s^{pu} h23.1g^2 h23g^6 h21.6g^3 c25.8g^5 c25.7g^{pu} Oct 31] fair maiden hurdler: maiden   **h100** chaser, no form in 2016/17: stays 3m: acts on heavy going: in headgear last 3 starts: won point in April. *Tim Vaughan*

OSCAR HOOF (IRE) 9 b.g. Oscar (IRE) – New Legislation (IRE) (Dominion Royale)   **h126** [2016/17 h19.3s^{pu} h21m^2 h19.8g^{pu} Apr 29] fairly useful handicap hurdler, very lightly raced (off 35 months prior to reappearance): stays 21f: acts on good to firm and good to soft going. *Nicky Henderson*

OSCAR JANE (IRE) 10 b.m. Oscar (IRE) – Turrill House (Charmer) [2016/17 h97:   **h76** h25du h20.5g^5 h23.9g h25s h23.1g^5 Apr 11] handicap hurdler, only poor form in 2016/17: stays 3m: acts on heavy going: wears headgear/tongue tie: usually races close up. *Johnny Farrelly*

OSCAR KNIGHT (IRE) 8 b.g. Oscar (IRE) – Cool Supreme (IRE) (Supreme Leader)   **c138** [2016/17 c18.2d* c22s c20d* c24.5d^3 c24v^6 h22.3v^3 c29d^{ur} Apr 17] fair handicap hurdler: **h114** useful handicap chaser: won at Galway in October and Navan in December: good third of 28 in Paddy Power Chase at Leopardstown (5 lengths behind Noble Endeavor) on fourth outing: stays 3m: acts on heavy going: often races towards rear. *Thomas Mullins, Ireland*

OSCAR LATEEN (IRE) 9 b.g. Oscar (IRE) – Storm Call (Celestial Storm (USA))   **c79 x** [2016/17 c97, h–: c20.1d c20.1m^{ur} c21.5s^{ur} c20.1s^F c23.8g^{pu} c20.1v c23.8g^4 c26.6g*   **h–** c26.3g c26.2g Apr 15] maiden hurdler: handicap chaser, poor nowadays: won at Musselburgh (conditionals event) in March: stays 27f: acts on heavy going: has worn headgear: often let down by jumping. *Victor Thompson*

OSCAR MAGIC (IRE) 10 b.g. Oscar (IRE) – Just An Illusion (IRE) (Shernazar)   **c88** [2016/17 c108, h–: c20d^4 May 18] sturdy gelding: fairly useful hurdler: maiden chaser, fair   **h–** at best: stayed 2½m: acted on heavy going: sometimes wore tongue tie: dead. *Nigel Twiston-Davies*

OSCAR MOR (IRE) 5 b.g. Oscar (IRE) – Gran Chis (IRE) (Moscow Society (USA))   **b81** [2016/17 b16s^5 b16.4v^4 b16g Apr 8] £50,000 4-y-o: second foal: dam winning pointer: won Irish maiden point on debut: modest form in bumpers: will be suited by 2½m+. *Warren Greatrex*

OSCAR O'SCAR (IRE) 9 b.g. Oscar (IRE) – Shining Lights (IRE) (Moscow Society   **c114 §** (USA)) [2016/17 c117, h103§: c21.6s^{ur} c25.2g^6 c24.2s^4 c24.2d c26.2d c21.1m^2 Apr 19]   **h– §** maiden hurdler: fair handicap chaser: stays 3m: acts on good to firm and heavy going: has worn cheekpieces, including last 2 starts: not one to trust. *Micky Hammond*

OSCAR ROCK (IRE) 9 b.g. Oscar (IRE) – Cash And New (USA) (Supreme Leader)   **c–** [2016/17 c149, h–: h20.6s* Nov 17] good-topped gelding: useful handicap hurdler: won at   **h144 +** Market Rasen (by length from Duke Street) on only outing in 2016/17: smart handicap chaser: seems to stay 29f: acts on soft and good to firm going: wears headgear: usually races towards rear. *Malcolm Jefferson*

OSCAR ROSE (IRE) 5 b.m. Oscar (IRE) – Ben Roseler (IRE) (Beneficial) [2016/17   **b107** b16d^3 b16.3m^4 b16.4s^4 b15.8d* b16d b17g^2 Apr 6] £14,000 3-y-o: lengthy mare: closely related to smart hurdler/chaser Lie Forrit (2½m-29f winner, by Subtle Power) and half-sister to 3 winners, including fair chaser Nobel Leader (2m winner, by Alflora): dam unraced: useful bumper performer: won listed mares event at Huntingdon (by neck from Peggies Venture) in December: best effort when ½-length second of 18 to Dame Rose in Nickel Coin Mares' National Hunt Flat Race at Aintree final start: will prove suited by at least 2½m. *Fergal O'Brien*

OSCAR SAM (IRE) 8 b.g. Oscar (IRE) – Good Thyne Jenny (IRE) (Good Thyne (USA))   **h140** [2016/17 h134: h22.6d h24d h24g* h24s^3 h24d^{bd} h20.5d Apr 29] lengthy, rather sparely-made gelding: useful handicap hurdler: won at Leopardstown in January: good third of 20 at Punchestown (4 lengths behind Isleofhopendreams) in February: stays 3m: acts on heavy going: has worn cheekpieces. *Mrs J. Harrington, Ireland*

OSCARS BOSS 7 b.g. Norse Dancer (IRE) – Kimmeridge Bay (Karinga Bay) [2016/17   **h104** b16d* b16s^3 h15.9v^2 h21v^5 Mar 22] €30,000 3-y-o: third foal: dam lightly-raced half-sister   **b106** to useful hurdler/fair chaser (stayed 25f) Country Beau: useful form in bumpers: won at Tipperary in July: fair form over hurdles: better effort when second in maiden at Plumpton in January: left Adrian Maguire after second start: bred to stay at least 2½m: often races towards rear. *Neil Mulholland*

OSCARS CROSS 5 b.g. Oscar (IRE) – Mystockings (Idiot's Delight) [2016/17 b16v⁴ **b83**
Mar 23] sixth foal: closely related to fairly useful hurdler/smart chaser Giles Cross
(23f-3½m winner, by Saddlers' Hall): dam ran twice: 16/1, 11½ lengths fourth of 5 to
Dessinateur in bumper at Chepstow on debut. *Victor Dartnall*

OSCAR'S PROSPECT (IRE) 5 b.m. Oscar (IRE) – Divine Prospect (IRE) **h100**
(Namaqualand (USA)) [2016/17 b72: h20.6d⁴ h20.9s² h22s² h24.3s² h23.1s⁴ Mar 12] fair
form over hurdles, including in handicaps: stays 3m: acts on soft going: usually races
towards rear. *Jedd O'Keeffe*

OSCAR'S SONG (IRE) 6 b.m. Oscar (IRE) – Bint Bladi (FR) (Garde Royale) [2016/17 **h86 p**
b15.8d³ b16.6d h19.9d³ Mar 14] €20,000 4-y-o: closely related to fairly useful French **b80**
hurdler/chaser King's Daughter (2¼m/19f winner, by King's Theatre) and half-sister to
several winners, including useful hurdler/very smart chaser Lyreen Legend (2m-2¾m
winner, by Saint des Saints): dam, French 15f hurdle winner, also 1¼m winner on Flat:
modest form in bumpers: 5/2, third of 5 in mares novice at Sedgefield (4 lengths behind
Molly Carew) on hurdling debut: open to improvement. *Charlie Longsdon*

OSCAR STAR (IRE) 4 b f. Oscar (IRE) – Tucacas (FR) (Highest Honor (FR)) [2016/17 **b83**
b16.7g⁴ b16g² Apr 17] €15,000 3-y-o: fourth foal: closely related to useful hurdler/fairly
useful chaser Ixora (2m-21f winner, by Milan): dam (c122/h137), 2m-21f hurdle/chase
winner, also 7.5f-11.5f winner on Flat, half-sister to useful French hurdler/chaser (stays
23f) Djagble: modest form in mares bumpers at Market Rasen and Chepstow.
Jamie Snowden

OSCAR SUNSET (IRE) 10 b.g. Oscar (IRE) – Derravarra Sunset (IRE) (Supreme **c103**
Leader) [2016/17 c138, h–: h20.5d c17.5v³ c20.2vᵖᵘ h15.3v² Mar 9] lengthy gelding: **h124**
useful hurdler/chaser at best: disappointing over hurdles final outing but disappointing
otherwise in 2016/17: stays 2¾m: acts on heavy going. *Evan Williams*

OSCARS WAY (IRE) 9 b.g. Oscar (IRE) – Derrigra Sublime (IRE) (Flemensfirth (USA)) **c103 §**
[2016/17 c–, h–: c25.8gᵖᵘ c21.1g³ c24g⁶ c16.3g³ c24.2m⁴ c17.5g⁴ c24.2m³ c23g c26.3g⁴ **h–**
c19.2d³ c20.2d³ Mar 26] workmanlike gelding: winning hurdler: fair maiden chaser: stays
3¼m: acts on soft and good to firm going: wears headgear/tongue tie: usually races nearer
last than first: temperamental. *Mark Gillard*

OSCARTEEA (IRE) 8 b.g. Oscar (IRE) – Miss Arteea (IRE) (Flemensfirth (USA)) **h122 §**
[2016/17 h130: h16.2s⁵ h19s⁵ h20.5vᵖᵘ h23.9g Apr 9] well-made gelding: handicap
hurdler, useful in 2015/16 but generally disappointing in 2016/17: stays 21f: acts on heavy going:
has worn tongue tie, including last 5 starts: temperamental. *Neil Mulholland*

OSCATARA (IRE) 10 b.g. Oscar (IRE) – Nethertara (Netherkelly) [2016/17 c–, h–: **c117 §**
c16g² c17.4gᵖᵘ c15.5d⁶ c15.7d³ c15.2d⁵ c19.8m³ Apr 13] winning hurdler: fairly useful **h–**
handicap chaser: stays 19f: acts on heavy going: in cheekpieces last 3 starts: often races
towards rear: unreliable. *Donald McCain*

OSGOOD 10 b.g. Danehill Dancer (IRE) – Sabreon (Caerleon (USA)) [2016/17 h101: **c–**
h17.7g h16m h17.7g³ h15.9m* h15.8m³ c16g⁶ h16.5m Apr 20] rather leggy gelding: **h98 §**
modest handicap hurdler: won at Plumpton in September: well beaten in novice handicap
on chasing debut: stays 19f: acts on soft and good to firm going: usually wears headgear:
often races towards rear: inconsistent. *Gary Moore*

OSKAR DENARIUS (IRE) 6 b.g. Authorized (IRE) – Elizabethan Age (FR) (King's **h78**
Best (USA)) [2016/17 h16.7s h15.7s⁵ h16s⁴ h15.7s h19.5g⁶ Apr 8] fairly useful on Flat,
stays 11.5f: poor form over hurdles: wears hood: tried in tongue tie. *Jennifer Mason*

OSKAR'S EVA (IRE) 7 gr.m. Black Sam Bellamy (IRE) – Sardagna (FR) (Medaaly) **h106**
[2016/17 h89, b–: h19g h19.9d* h20.5g² h19.8s Dec 3] workmanlike mare: fair handicap
hurdler: won at Uttoxeter in October: stays 21f: acts on good to soft going: often travels
strongly. *Tim Vaughan*

OSKI (IRE) 5 b.g. Oscar (IRE) – Mossville (FR) (Villez (USA)) [2016/17 b15.7s* b15.8s⁵ **b95**
b16s⁴ b15.8g³ Apr 3] €70,000 3-y-o: first foal: dam (h117), 2¾m-3m hurdle winner/
winning pointer, half-sister to very smart hurdler (stayed 3m) Karabak: fairly useful form
in bumpers: won at Southwell in May: will prove suited by 2½m: in hood first 2 starts.
Ben Case

OSSIE'S DANCER 8 ch.g. Osorio (GER) – Nina Ballerina (Kahyasi) [2016/17 h120: **h98**
h21.4sᵖᵘ h19.6d h21.5s⁵ h21.6g⁴ Mar 31] handicap hurdler, just modest form in 2016/17:
stays 21f: acts on heavy going: tried in tongue tie: often races towards rear. *Martin Smith*

OSWALD COBBLEPOT (IRE) 5 b.g. Darsi (FR) – Miracle Millie (IRE) (Accordion) **h–**
[2016/17 b16s h16s Jan 8] tailed off in bumper/maiden hurdle. *Nigel Slevin, Ireland* **b–**

OTAGO TRAIL (IRE) 9 b.g. Heron Island (IRE) – Cool Chic (IRE) (Roselier (FR)) **c158**
[2016/17 c142, h–: c23.4s* c24.5d^{pu} c24.1s^2 c24.2v* Feb 4] medium-sized gelding: **h–**
winning hurdler: very smart handicap chaser: further progress in 2016/17 and won at
Newcastle (Rehearsal Chase, by 3¼ lengths from Bristol de Mai) in November and
Sandown (beat Loose Chips 2¾ lengths) on final start: stays 3m well (still relatively
unexposed as a stayer): best form on soft/heavy going. *Venetia Williams*

OTTER MOON 5 b.g. Midnight Legend – Highland Dawn (Primitive Rising) (USA)) **h82 p**
[2016/17 b13.7m^4 b15.7g^4 h15.8d h19.7s h15.8d^6 Jan 25] second foal: dam unraced half- **b86**
sister to fair hurdler/fairly useful chaser Allumee (2m/17f winner) in bumpers:
some promise in maiden/novice hurdles: sure to improve. *Tom George*

OULAMAYO (FR) 6 b.g. Solon (GER) – La Titie du Perche (FR) (Rochesson (FR)) **h85**
[2016/17 h98, b72: h16g^3 May 27] sturdy gelding: in frame both starts in bumpers: lightly-
raced maiden hurdler, modest form: raced around 2m. *Dan Skelton*

OUR BELLE AMIE 5 b.m. Black Sam Bellamy (IRE) – Very Special One (IRE) **b88**
(Supreme Leader) [2016/17 b16.2s^5 b16.6d^5 b16d^2 Feb 21] £10,000 3-y-o: first foal: dam
(c98/h122), 3¼m hurdle winner, half-sister to useful hurdler/chaser (stayed 3¾m) The
Bishop Looney: fair form in bumpers: will be suited by 2½m+: wears tongue tie. *Kim Bailey*

OUR CAT (IRE) 9 b.m. Royal Anthem (USA) – Run Cat (IRE) (Lord Americo) [2016/17 **c123**
c–, h–: c21.4g* c23.9d^{pu} c19.2g^4 c20.1d^3 c19.2g* c19.4g^2 h20.2g* h20.2d* Sep 21] **h113**
workmanlike mare: fair form over hurdles: won novices at Perth in September on last 2
starts, second a mares event: fairly useful handicap chaser: won at Market Rasen in May
and July: stays 21f: acts on soft going: has worn hood/tongue tie: usually races nearer last
than first: sometimes finishes weakly. *Fergal O'Brien*

OUR CHIEF (IRE) 8 b.g. Old Vic – Torsha (IRE) (Torus) [2016/17 h89: c22.6m* c23g^{pu} **c94**
c19.2g^F Apr 11] dual winning pointer: maiden hurdler: modest form over fences: won **h–**
novice hunter at Stratford in May: stays 23f: acts on good to firm and good to soft going:
sometimes in headgear: in tongue tie last 5 starts. *Mrs Teresa Clark*

OURCRAZYANNE 8 b.m. Lahib (USA) – Shareef Walk (Shareef Dancer (USA)) **h–**
[2016/17 h15.9g^6 h23g^{pu} h19.9g^{pu} h20.5v^{pu} Jan 16] angular mare: half-sister to bumper
winner Rojo Vivo (by Deploy) and a winning pointer by Pasternak: dam, of little account,
daughter of Imperial Cup winner Travel Mystery: no form over hurdles: tried in hood.
Roger Ingram

OUR DANCING DANDY (IRE) 7 b.g. Scorpion (IRE) – Woodsia (Woodman (USA)) **h105 p**
[2016/17 b111: h18.9v^6 h22s^2 Dec 8] runner-up completed start in Irish maiden points:
useful form when successful on only start in bumpers: fair form in novice hurdles at
Haydock and Newcastle: remains open to improvement. *Donald McCain*

OUR DELBOY 5 gr.g. Multiplex – Dawn's Della (Scottish Reel) [2016/17 h15.8d h15.8d^5 **h102**
h15.8d h16.4v^3 h16d^6 h21.2m^4 Apr 25] half-brother to 3 winners, including fairly useful **b–**
hurdler/smart chaser Our Mick (17f-2½m winner, by Karinga Bay) and fairly useful
hurdler/chaser Our Jasper (2m-2½m winner, by Tina's Pet), both ungenuine/stayed 3m:
dam (h63) lightly raced in bumpers/over hurdles: well beaten in bumper: fair form over
hurdles: should stay beyond 2m: acts on heavy going: front runner/races prominently.
Donald McCain

OUR DUKE (IRE) 7 b.g. Oscar (IRE) – Good Thyne Jenny (IRE) (Good Thyne **c167 p**
(USA)) [2016/17 h132p, b114: c20d* c24d* c21.3s^2 c29d* Apr 17] **h–**

It seemed odd to see Cheltenham Gold Cup-winning trainer Jessica
Harrington among those cast in the role of a Dot Love, Tom Gibney or James
Motherway when Our Duke contested Ireland's richest jumps race, the Irish Grand
National at Fairyhouse on Easter Monday. A massive boost in prize money for the
Boylesports-sponsored event—the total prize was €500,000—led to the 2017 Irish
National attracting a modern-day record initial entry of one hundred and twenty-
four, headed by Outlander, Don Poli, Empire of Dirt and Carlingford Lough who
had also topped the original weights for the Grand National at Aintree. Reporting
of the official launch of the Grand National weights focussed on a row between
Michael O'Leary, owner of Gigginstown House Stud, and the BHA's Head of
Handicapping Phil Smith over the 'harsh' weights allotted to Outlander, Don Poli
and Empire of Dirt (all three were taken out of the Aintree race at the first forfeit).
Gigginstown also found itself the centre of attention, and the butt of some criticism,
over the composition of the Irish Grand National field. While Outlander, Don Poli

and Empire of Dirt missed the race in the end, the quality of the eventual line-up was still noticeably higher than for some recent renewals, with Gigginstown, seeking a third successive win in the race, fielding no fewer than thirteen of the twenty-eight runners.

The Gigginstown complement came from three different stables, with Gigginstown's main trainer Gordon Elliott saddling a third of the field. The criticism of an unfair monopoly—nearly forty horses had to be eliminated from the race at the final declaration stage—received backing of sorts from the Irish Turf Club's official handicapper who commented: 'What you have when the weights go up like this [to reflect the better quality entry] is a race where the Thomas Gibneys, Dot Loves and James Motherways can't even get in. You risk losing those fairytale results.' Motherway, Gibney and Mrs Love were the trainers of Bluesea Cracker, Lion Na Bearnai and Liberty Counsel, the Irish Grand National winners of 2010, 2012 and 2013 at respective odds of 25/1, 33/1 and 50/1. Bluesea Cracker, the first mare to win the Irish National for seventeen years, was one of only six jumpers sent out by James Motherway's yard in 2009/10 when the trainer won just three races; Lion Na Bearnai was one of just three horses who represented his trainer Thomas Gibney in 2011/12; Liberty Counsel, the longest-priced winner in the history of the race, was an obscurely-bred mare from the stable of Danish-born Dot Love which was being used principally as a pre-training yard for horses owned by Gigginstown House Stud. Small-scale owners and trainers always make good stories when they are successful in big races, but just eight of the runners in the latest Irish Grand National belonged to owners who could be termed 'smaller' owners. Ironically, the owners of the exciting novice Our Duke, who started 9/2 favourite, were among that 'under privileged' octet, carrying the colours of the Cooper Family Syndicate from Coolrain in County Laois which has owned horses for twenty years and had three in training with Jessica Harrington in the latest season, also including Our Duke's year-older brother the useful handicap hurdler Oscar Sam who won at Leopardstown in January.

Jessica Harrington had a season she will never forget, with Our Duke's Irish Grand National win putting the icing on the cake after she had sent out new recruit Sizing John to win the Irish Gold Cup and the Cheltenham Gold Cup (he went on to complete a unique treble by adding the Punchestown Gold Cup). Sizing John's Cheltenham victory was one of three at the Festival for the stable which also won the Coral Cup with Supasundae and the Grand Annual with Rock The World, those wins making Mrs Harrington the most successful female trainer in Cheltenham Festival history (she has now had eleven wins, including those of Moscow Flyer in the Arkle and the Queen Mother Champion Chase, a race he won twice, and of Jezki in the Champion Hurdle). All the stable's major winners in the latest season were ridden by Robbie Power, who also had the Midas touch, chalking up a string of big wins at the three major spring festivals at Cheltenham, Aintree and Punchestown, mostly in the colours of Alan and Ann Potts with whom Mrs Harrington shared the services of Power in the latter stages of the season. Robbie Power might have a difficult choice to make at some point in the next season between the Potts-owned Sizing John and the Cooper-owned Our Duke if they both end up in the Cheltenham Gold Cup line-up (they will presumably be kept apart before then). Make no mistake, Our Duke is a young chaser going places and he put up the best performance seen in Ireland's most prestigious handicap chase for over twenty years, in fact since Flashing Steel won under 12-0 in the 1995 edition, a performance that *Chasers & Hurdlers* described as one 'that some Gold Cup winners would have been hard pressed to equal' (Flashing Steel's best effort before that had come when fourth in The Fellow's Cheltenham Gold Cup the previous season). Desert Orchid had also won the Irish National five years earlier carrying 12-0 (conceding lumps of weight all round and winning by twelve lengths) but, apart from him, no horse has had his name engraved on the roll of honour in both the Irish National and the Cheltenham Gold Cup since Arkle, although Tied Cottage was briefly a member of this select group too, claiming an emotional win in the 1979 Irish Grand National (ridden by his owner) before running away with the 1980 Cheltenham Gold Cup, which he lost later when among those involved in a spate of failed dope tests traced to contaminated feed. Arkle, by the

Neville Hotels Novices' Chase (Fort Leney), Leopardstown—
Our Duke (No.9) rallies strongly to overhaul Coney Island (noseband) and the grey Disko

way, was the fifth successive Irish National winner saddled by Tom Dreaper who went on to win the race seven years in a row with seven different horses in the 'sixties without, so far as anyone can recall, facing criticism for 'monopolising' the race, although there were single-figure fields for three of the renewals (the race was run over three and a quarter miles in this period). Arkle also won the Irish National under 12-0, as did the dual Two-Mile Champion Chase winner Fortria when he became the second in Dreaper's Irish National sequence, while the last of the seven, Flyingbolt, carried 12-7 to victory weeks after winning the Two-Mile Champion Chase in a canter; Tom Dreaper won the Irish National a record-breaking ten times and his son Jim won the race four times in five years in the 'seventies, three of them with Brown Lad who gained his last two victories under 12-0 and 12-2 in 1976 and 1978 respectively, also finishing runner-up in the Cheltenham Gold Cup in both years. 'The likes of Arkle and Flyingbolt ran in the Irish National under top weight because there was nowhere else to go,' says Jim Dreaper. 'We're talking about the 'sixties here and the races that the Gold Cup and Two-Mile Champion Chase winners run in now weren't there. Good horses had to carry weight in those days out of necessity, but times change and there's a phobia about running Grade 1 horses in handicaps nowadays.'

The Irish Grand National marked the handicap debut of Our Duke, who had run only three times before over fences, but whether he will ever contest another handicap, while in his prime, must be doubtful. An impressive winner of a bumper (beating the now smart hurdler De Plotting Shed by twenty-one lengths) on his racecourse debut as a five-year-old, he also got hurdling out of the way in his first season when showing himself a useful performer in that sphere, winning a maiden at Leopardstown and finishing a good third in the Grade 2 Festival Novices' Hurdle at the Fairyhouse Easter meeting (the day before the Irish National) on his final start. Our Duke made a winning start to his career over fences in a beginners chase at Navan in December, scarely putting a foot wrong and drawing eleven lengths clear of Gwencily Berbas after Edwulf had unseated his jockey at the last when looking booked for second.

Our Duke was stepped up to Grade 1 company for just his second steeplechase, the Fort Leney Novices' Chase (branded as the Neville Hotels) at Leopardstown's Christmas meeting. He started second favourite to the Drinmore Novices' Chase winner Coney Island in a smart renewal in which Our Duke's lack of steeplechasing experience looked likely, at one stage, to catch him out. He made a series of jumping errors, admittedly nearly all of them minor ones, but he looked in trouble when dropping back to fourth on the home turn after a slow jump at

619

Boylesports Irish Grand National Chase (Extended Handicap), Fairyhouse—a stunning performance from the novice Our Duke ...

the second last. Robbie Power stoked up Our Duke again on the long run to the last and he found plenty to get up close home to beat Coney Island by half a length, with 20/1-shot Disko the same distance further behind in third, that trio pulling over twenty lengths clear of the remainder. 'He must be some horse ... if he'd jumped well, he'd have won by ten lengths,' the winning jockey said afterwards. The winning trainer won the race with Bostons Angel in 2010 before that horse went on to Cheltenham Festival success in the RSA Chase (Don Poli did the same double in 2014/15) and, immediately afterwards, Mrs Harrington said that the RSA Chase could suit Our Duke well. But Our Duke wasn't sent to Cheltenham in the end, after losing his unbeaten record over fences to Disko in the two mile five furlong Flogas Novices' Chase (for so long known as the Dr P. J. Moriarty) on Irish Gold Cup day at Leopardstown. It wasn't Our Duke's jumping that was to blame for his defeat, but rather the muddling nature of the race, which was steadily run and put too much emphasis on speed for Our Duke, who had been doing all his best work at the finish over three miles in the Fort Leney. Disko's jockey controlled the race well from the front and had everything in trouble when pressing on between the last two. Our Duke was outpaced at first but rallied well in the closing stages to go down by a length and three quarters.

If Our Duke's connections had followed a more orthodox route, he would have lined up against fellow novices for the Ryanair Gold Cup at the Fairyhouse Easter meeting, rather than the Irish Grand National. The Ryanair, though, is two and a half miles and Our Duke was shaping very much like a horse whose strong suit would prove to be stamina. He carried 11-4 (equivalent to a Turf Club mark of 153) in the National and was joint third top weight behind the Galway Plate winner Lord Scoundrel (11-7)—seeking to become the first top weight to win since Flashing Steel—and the Paddy Power Chase winner Noble Endeavor (11-5), the

... as he routs a competitive field, with 2016 runner-up Bless The Wings (left) second again; Abolitionist (star on cap) and 2015 winner Thunder And Roses (right) are the next two home

pair heading the nine-strong challenge of the Gordon Elliott stable, which also included the 2016 runner-up Bless The Wings. Lord Scoundrel was also part of the Gigginstown contingent, which included the last two winners Thunder And Roses (who won the race as a novice) and Rogue Angel, although it was the Elliott-trained novice General Principle, fresh from easy wins at Gowran and Limerick, who was the pick of Gigginstown's then number-one rider Bryan Cooper from the baker's dozen he had to choose from—finding enough distinguishing caps for the twelve other jockeys must have been a logistical nightmare! Ireland's other dominant owner J. P. McManus had three in the race and had also had the three reserves, among them the Paddy Power Chase third Oscar Knight, who had been first reserve until another McManus runner Double Seven became a non-runner (the Elliott-trained Tell Us More was also a late non-runner, reducing by one Gigginstown's original fourteen representatives!). The two other McManus runners were the previous year's Paddy Power winner Minella Foru and Shutthefrontdoor, who had won the 2014 Irish National as a novice. Joining Shutthefrontdoor from Britain was Fletchers Flyer, running at Fairyhouse in preference to the Scottish National at Ayr later in the week.

Once the Irish National got under way, Our Duke was soon prominent, kept wide to give him a good sight of his fences, but the field was led for a long way by Rogue Angel and Stellar Notion, both of whom were among the seven runners who had contested the Grand National at Aintree nine days earlier. Fletchers Flyer joined the front rank and, racing with Stellar Notion, was ahead at the top of the hill with nine fences to jump, with Our Duke a close third. Our Duke went on four from home and stayed on strongly to slam his field by fourteen lengths

Cooper Family Syndicate's "Our Duke"

with the keeping-on Bless The Wings getting the better of a fairly close race for the minor honours with the Leinster National winner Abolitionist, who chased Our Duke into the home straight, and the staying-on Thunder And Roses. Thunder And Roses and ninth-placed Measureofmydreams (also Gigginstown-owned) were the only ones to complete from the seven who had run in the Grand National. General Principle produced his best effort over fences to finish fifth, with Noble Endeavor a respectable sixth. Of the two British-trained challengers, Shutthefrontdoor looked a light of other days and Fletchers Flyer was pulled up after paying the price for helping to force the pace on the final circuit. Minella Foru fell at the eighth, inflicting a broken arm on his rider Barry Geraghty, who had also missed the Cheltenham Festival through injury (before enjoying a Grade 1 treble at Aintree). Geraghty also had to sit out the Punchestown Festival. Ironically, in view of all the fuss made about Gigginstown's assault on the race, the first three all belonged to members of the group of eight 'smaller owners' who took on 'the big boys'. Bless The Wings is owned by Adrian Butler/S. P. O'Connor and Abolitionist by Mrs Catherine Holden.

		Oscar (IRE) (b 1994)	Sadler's Wells (b 1981)	Northern Dancer / Fairy Bridge
Our Duke (IRE) (b.g. 2010)			Snow Day (b 1978)	Reliance II / Vindaria
		Good Thyne Jenny (IRE) (b 1994)	Good Thyne (br 1977)	Herbager / Foreseer
			Cant Be Done (gr 1983)	Decent Fellow / Two Stars

Our Duke is the latest in a long line of successes over jumps for the Sadler's Wells stallion Oscar who was retired at the age of twenty-one in 2015. He has never been champion sire but has regularly appeared towards the top of the end-of-the-season rankings (he was fifth in the combined table produced by the *Racing Post* for Britain and Ireland in 2016/17). Our Duke's dam Good Thyne Jenny was a poor maiden hurdler and, as her name suggests, is a daughter of Good Thyne, runner-up in the 1980 Irish St Leger, who is probably best known for siring the top-class hurdlers Brave Inca, Bannow Bay and Mighty Mogul, as well as the dams of Cheltenham Gold Cup winners Kicking King and War of Attrition. Good Thyne Jenny has now bred four winners who have carried the colours of the Cooper Family Syndicate. As well as Our Duke and Oscar Sam, their close relative Billy To Jack (by another Sadler's Wells stallion Old Vic) won over hurdles at two miles and Flying Windsor (by Flying Legend) won a point for the Coopers before going on to win over fences at two miles four furlongs for another owner. The genuine Our Duke stays twenty-nine furlongs and acts on heavy going (yet to race on good ground or firmer). He usually races prominently or makes the running and, still fairly lightly raced, is likely to continue progressing as a chaser. *Mrs J. Harrington, Ireland*

OUR FOLLY 9 b.g. Sakhee (USA) – Regent's Folly (IRE) (Touching Wood (USA)) [2016/17 h101: h23.3s³ h22m³ h23.3g* h23.1g⁴ Oct 18] rather leggy gelding: fair handicap hurdler: won at Uttoxeter in September: stays 23f: acts on soft and good to firm going: tried in cheekpieces: wears tongue tie: often travels strongly. *Stuart Kittow* **h105**

OUR GEORGIE GIRL 10 ch.m. Zafeen (FR) – Rosina May (IRE) (Danehill Dancer (IRE)) [2016/17 c–, h–: c25.5d^pu c16.5m⁶ c17.4g^pu h21.6s⁴ c20d c16.3m⁵ c22.6g^pu h23g⁴ Aug 11] little form over hurdles/fences: usually wears headgear. *Paul Phillips* **c–** **h–**

OUR ISLAND (IRE) 12 b.g. Turtle Island (IRE) – Linda's Leader (IRE) (Supreme Leader) [2016/17 c–§, h–: c27.2d² May 12] good-topped gelding: winning hurdler: fair chaser: stays 4m: acts on heavy going: has worn headgear: ungenuine. *Hugo Froud* **c106 §** **h–**

OUR KAEMPFER (IRE) 8 b.g. Oscar (IRE) – Gra-Bri (IRE) (Rashar (USA)) [2016/17 h140p: c19.4g² c22.4g² c19.9g³ c24.2s^ur c24.4g^pu c25g^pu Apr 8] tall gelding: useful hurdler: smart chaser: won handicap at Kempton in January by 7 lengths from Kruzhlinin: stays 3m: acts on good to soft going: in tongue tie last 5 starts. *Charlie Longsdon* **c145** **h–**

OUR KYLIE (IRE) 5 b.m. Jeremy (USA) – Prakara (IRE) (Indian Ridge) [2016/17 h101b: h16.7g* h16.5g* Jul 27] sturdy mare: fair handicap hurdler: won at Market Rasen in May and mares event at Galway in July: raced around 2m: acts on heavy going: tried in cheekpieces: often races prominently: open to further improvement. *Brian Ellison* **h114 p**

OURLITTLE MYRTLE 5 gr.m. Fair Mix (IRE) – Garota de Ipanema (FR) (Al Nasr **b–**
(FR)) [2016/17 b16.8g b16g b16.3g⁴ Sep 3] eighth foal: dam (h83), maiden hurdler, French
10.5f winner on Flat: no form in bumpers: in blinkers last 2 starts, also in tongue tie final
one. *Miss Imogen Pickard*

OUR LUCAS (IRE) 5 b.g. Jeremy (USA) – Alassio (USA) (Gulch (USA)) [2016/17 **h–**
h16g h16d h16g h16.4s Dec 17] maiden hurdler, no form in 2016/17: left P. M. Cloke after
third start. *R. Mike Smith*

OURMANMASSINI (IRE) 9 b.g. Dr Massini (IRE) – Aunty Dawn (IRE) (Strong Gale) **c– §**
[2016/17 c–, h106§: h16.7g⁵ h17.7g⁶ h17.7g⁵ h20.6d³ Jun 17] sturdy gelding: maiden **h93 §**
hurdler, just modest form in 2016/17: well held only outing in chase: should stay 2½m: acts
on soft going: has worn headgear, including in 2016/17: wears tongue tie: usually races
close up: temperamental. *Suzy Smith*

OUR MERLIN 5 b.g. Pasternak – Lorgnette (Emperor Fountain) [2016/17 b16.8g² **h– p**
h19.3d h19.8d h19g Jan 11] sturdy gelding: fourth foal: dam (c95/h111) bumper/21f-3m **b88**
hurdle winner: second in maiden bumper at Newton Abbot: well held in maiden/novice
hurdles: type to do better in handicaps. *Robert Walford*

OUR MORRIS (IRE) 6 b.g. Milan – Broken Gale (IRE) (Broken Hearted) [2016/17 b81: **h79**
b16.8s⁶ h22.7sᵘʳ h21.3s h22s⁶ h19.3s⁴ h16.2g Apr 25] modest form at best in bumpers: poor **b71**
maiden over hurdles. *George Bewley*

OURNIAMHEEN (IRE) 7 b.m. Papal Bull – Still As Sweet (IRE) (Fairy King (USA)) **h– §**
[2016/17 b–: b16g b16.3d b16d h16gʳʳ Jul 21] no form in bumpers: refused to race in **b–**
novice on hurdling debut: usually in headgear/tongue tie: one to treat with caution.
Hannah James

OURO BRANCO (FR) 4 b.g. Kapgarde (FR) – Dolce Vita Yug (Emperor Jones (USA)) **b95**
[2016/17 b16.5g³ b17v* b17d⁴ Apr 5] sixth foal: dam 5f-1m winner in Europe: fairly
useful winner in bumpers: won 3-runner event at Carlisle in March. *Nigel Hawke*

OUR PHILLIE LILY 5 b.m. Sulamani (IRE) – Tyre Hill Lilly (Jupiter Island) [2016/17 **h–**
b15.8s b16.8vᶠ h15.3d h20g Apr 9] fourth foal: half-sister to fairly useful hurdler Here's **b–**
Herbie (19f winner, by Classic Cliche): dam (h82) winning pointer: no show in bumpers/
novice hurdles. *Susan Gardner*

OUR PHYLLI VERA (IRE) 8 b.m. Motivator – With Colour (Rainbow Quest (USA)) **c–**
[2016/17 c–, h80: h21.2d c20.1gᵇᵈ h16.2dᵖᵘ Jun 19] one-time fair hurdler, has lost her form: **h–**
no promise over fences: wears headgear. *Joanne Foster*

OUR REWARD (IRE) 7 b.g. Morozov (USA) – Paddyeoin (IRE) (Insan (USA)) **h115**
[2016/17 b89: h19.9s* h23g⁴ h19.9g* h19.9g² h20.8g³ h20.5m² Apr 16]
winning Irish pointer: fairly useful hurdler: won novices at Sedgefield in May and
September (conditionals event): should be suited by further than 21f: acts on soft and good
to firm going: front runner/races prominently. *Jamie Snowden*

OUR SOX (IRE) 8 b.g. September Storm (GER) – Winning Sally (IRE) (Lancastrian) **c112**
[2016/17 c115, h104: h20d c22.5g h24g² c26.6g² c25g Nov 11] angular gelding: fair **h101**
handicap hurdler/maiden chaser: stays 27f: best form on good going: wears tongue tie:
usually races nearer last than first. *A. J. Martin, Ireland*

OUR THOMAS (IRE) 5 b.g. Dylan Thomas (IRE) – Sinamay (USA) (Saint Ballado **h113**
(CAN)) [2016/17 h121: h16d⁵ h16.6g⁴ h18.6d h16.8s⁵ h15.7s⁵ h16d² h16.8g² h15.7g
Apr 15] sturdy gelding: fair handicap hurdler: stays 2¼m: acts on good to soft going: in
cheekpieces/tongue tie last 3 starts. *Tim Easterby*

OUR THREE SONS (IRE) 6 b.g. Shantou (USA) – Ballyquinn (IRE) (Anshan) **h115**
[2016/17 h98, b86: h17.7g² h20.6d h16.7g³ h16.7d² h19.9g⁴ h16.3g* Apr 23] fairly useful
handicap hurdler: won novice event at Stratford final start: stays 2¼m: acts on good to soft
going: in cheekpieces fourth/fifth starts: usually leads. *Jamie Snowden*

OUR VALENTINA (IRE) 6 b.m. Shantou (USA) – Par Street (IRE) (Dolphin Street **h98**
(FR)) [2016/17 b16gˢᵘ b16d b16vˣ b16s h16s² h16v³ h16v* h20.2g⁵ Apr 26] €6,000 4-y-o: **b84**
sixth foal: sister to bumper winner/fairly useful hurdler Earls Quarter (2m/2¼m winner)
and a winning pointer, and half-sister to bumper winner up to 2½m Not For Converting (by
Bob Back): dam untraced: modest form in bumpers: won mares maiden at
Navan in April: stays 2½m: front runner/races prominently. *Stuart Crawford, Ireland*

OUR YOUNG UN 4 b.g. Native Ruler – Dani (IRE) (Modigliani (USA)) [2016/17 b16s **b–**
Jan 14] tailed off in maiden bumper. *John Gallagher*

OUTLANDER (IRE) 9 b.g. Stowaway – Western Whisper (IRE) (Supreme Leader)   **c165**
[2016/17 c153, h–: c25d² c19.5g² c20dᶠ c20d² c24d* c26.3g c24.5dᵖᵘ Apr 26]   **h–**

    The number of licenced professional jump jockeys in Ireland is at its lowest (around a hundred) for fifteen years which is thought by some to be another consequence of the 'polarisation' of Irish jump racing around a small number of top owners and a handful of top stables (a topic discussed in the essay on Empire of Dirt). The domination of the 'big battalions' certainly makes it harder for jockeys to break through, though any aspiring young rider should take heart from the story of precocious teenager Jack Kennedy who, in just two seasons, has forced his way into the thick of the action and was leading the Irish jockeys' table in the latest season until fracturing the fibula in his left leg twice, at Downpatrick in September and on his first ride back in October. Ironically, it was the injuries suffered by Bryan Cooper, who missed all of June (due to leg surgery) and August (after lacerating his liver and having a collapsed lung at the Galway Festival), that helped Kennedy build up that early championship lead. The opportunities with Gigginstown House Stud (the main owner at the stables of Kennedy's boss Gordon Elliott) provided a link-up that helped Kennedy to reach another notable landmark by notching his first Grade 1 winner—and becoming the youngest jockey to win a Grade 1—when the Gigginstown-owned Outlander won the Lexus Chase at Leopardstown's Christmas meeting to give him his hundredth win. He rode his second Grade 1 winner soon afterwards on novice hurdler Death Duty, also for Gigginstown and Elliott.

    Kennedy started pony racing in Ireland when he was just nine and was pony champion three times, recording over two hundred wins, including the coveted Dingle Derby in 2014 on a horse trained by his father. As soon as he was sixteen and permitted to ride thoroughbreds, Kennedy made a successful transition and was champion conditional in Ireland in his first season, 2015/16. The ball has certainly carried on rolling since he lost his claim and became a fully-fledged professional. So much in life depends on being in the right place at the right time and, although he has had to take a back seat at Gigginstown House Stud when Bryan Cooper has been fit, Kennedy's connection with the Elliott stable—for which he rode a first Cheltenham

Lexus Chase, Leopardstown—a first Grade 1 win for teenage sensation Jack Kennedy as Outlander (No.8) gets the better of stable-companion Don Poli (white face); favourite Djakadam (left) rallies, whilst Gigginstown 'first string' Valseur Lido fades into fourth

Festival winner on Labaik—gives him plenty of opportunities and he was runner-up to Ruby Walsh in the jockeys' table in the latest season with sixty-eight wins. Some of the sages of Irish jumping are already comparing Jack Kennedy's horsemanship to that of the likes of Paul Carberry and Walsh himself and his future seems assured.

Jack Kennedy was still just seventeen when the chance came to ride Outlander in the Lexus. After showing smart form over hurdles, Outlander made a name for himself in his first season over fences when winning the Flogas Novices' Chase (Dr P.J. Moriarty) at Leopardstown and finishing second in the Ryanair Gold Cup at Fairyhouse and the Champion Novices' Chase at Punchestown (which was, technically, his first start in the latest season). By the time Outlander returned to training after his summer break, he had been transferred from Willie Mullins to Gordon Elliott, one of sixty horses dispersed around a number of yards, also including those of Henry de Bromhead, Noel Meade, Mouse Morris and Joseph O'Brien, after Gigginstown House Stud's owner Michael O'Leary fell out with Mullins over an increase in the training fees at Closutton. The public fascination over the split between Ireland's champion owner and champion trainer seemed to last nearly all season and was still a topic at the trainer's County Carlow pre-Cheltenham open day in February when Mullins deftly dodged a question about whether he would be flying over by Ryanair (where O'Leary is the supremo) or Aer Lingus, by joking that he might take the ferry!

The latest renewal of the Lexus Chase was a strong one, with plenty of depth to the thirteen-runner field, and the finish proved quite a spectacle with four horses that had all been in the care of Willie Mullins twelve months earlier in the air together at the last. Outlander, Don Poli, Djakadam and Valseur Lido, the last-named seemingly the pick of a Gigginstown quintet and ridden by Bryan Cooper. Valseur Lido had won the JNwine.com Champion Chase at Down Royal on his first start for Henry de Bromhead and started second favourite in the Lexus behind Djakadam who had finished runner-up in the last two Cheltenham Gold Cups. Outlander had had three runs for the Gordon Elliott stable by this stage, finishing second to fellow Gigginstown representative Sub Lieutenant in the Grade 2 Titanic Belfast Chase at Down Royal on the same day as the Champion Chase, falling at the last in the Clonmel Oil Chase with the race at his mercy and finishing a good second to Djakadam in the Punchestown Chase (turning the tables on Sub Lieutenant in third and recording a career-best effort, jumping better than he sometimes has). Don Poli, who had won the Lexus twelve months earlier, had been pulled up in the Champion Chase at Down Royal on his seasonal return for Gordon Elliott.

In the race itself, the patiently-ridden Outlander crept closer before the third last and found extra, after edging ahead at the last, to win by two and a quarter lengths and a head from a back-to-form Don Poli and Djakadam, with Valseur Lido fading into fourth after being produced to lead at the last. The step back up to three miles in the Lexus seemed to suit Outlander, and the Irish Gold Cup at Leopardstown was mooted as the next port of call for him. However, he wasn't seen out again until the Cheltenham Gold Cup in which Cooper took over. Outlander was among the first in trouble and trailed home last of ten finishers. He ran just as badly in the Punchestown Gold Cup, pulled up when behind at the tenth, and clearly has questions to answer in the next season.

A lengthy gelding, Outlander is by the now deceased Stowaway (a son of stamina influence Slip Anchor) who finished tenth in the sires' list compiled by the *Racing Post* for Britain and Ireland combined. Champagne Classic and The Worlds End were others who boosted his progeny earnings in the latest season. Outlander's dam Western Whisper ran twice without success in bumpers but has done well at stud, breeding six winners so far, all of them by Stowaway, the pick after Outlander

Gigginstown House Stud's "Outlander"

being the useful hurdler/chaser Western Leader, who stayed three miles, and Mart Lane, who was fairly useful over hurdles and useful over fences at his best and also stays three miles. A couple of Outlander's younger brothers were also successful in the latest season. Ice Cold Soul won the valuable coral.ie Hurdle at Leopardstown in January, while the previous month had seen Mayo Star get off the mark in a bumper at Newcastle. There are a couple of notable winners further back, Outlander's great grandam Kirin being one of ten winners bred by Mag, the best of them being the useful juvenile (winner of the Aurelius Hurdle) Lir, though, more significantly, it was another of Mag's winners, the winning hurdler Mazuma, who boosted the family's reputation by becoming the dam of Aintree Hurdle winner Asian Maze—who won four Grade 1s in all—and of her brother Quantitativeeasing who won the December Gold Cup at Cheltenham. Outlander stays twenty-five furlongs but is effective over shorter, and he acts on heavy going. *Gordon Elliott, Ireland*

Postscript: The Lexus is the only race in which Jack Kennedy has partnered Outlander on the racecourse but, when he returns from injury in the autumn (after breaking a leg in a fall at Punchestown just after the end of the season), he should find that he gets more opportunities for Gigginstown who will not be retaining a first-jockey in the next season. Bryan Cooper, whose demotion was announced in July, will still ride for Gigginstown but he will no longer have first call, with Gigginstown adopting a policy of using the best available on a race-by-race basis.

OUTLAW JOSEY WALES (IRE) 6 b.g. Jeremy (USA) – Trinity Scholar (IRE) **h71**
(Invincible Spirit (IRE)) [2016/17 h111, b86: h16.2m⁶ h16.2d h16.2sᶠ h19.4dᵖᵘ h16.2g
Apr 25] maiden hurdler, poor on balance of form: unproven beyond 2m. *R. Mike Smith*

OUT NOW (IRE) 13 br.g. Muroto – Raven Night (IRE) (Mandalus) [2016/17 c96, h–: **c109 §**
c23.9s² c22.7sᶠ Feb 28] well-made gelding: winning pointer: maiden hurdler: fair hunter **h–**
chaser: stays 29f: acts on heavy going: temperamental. *Mrs Kim Smyly*

OUT OF REACH 6 ch.m. Phoenix Reach (IRE) – Dand Nee (USA) (Kabool) [2016/17 **b–**
b16.8d⁶ Dec 26] first foal: dam (b94), 13f bumper winner, also 9f-1½m winner on Flat:
tailed off in bumper on debut. *Tracy Waggott*

OUT OF STYLE (IRE) 6 b.g. Court Cave (IRE) – Portanob (IRE) (Be My Native **b88 p**
(USA)) [2016/17 b16.3d⁴ Mar 13] €21,000 3-y-o, €80,000 4-y-o: closely related to fairly
useful hurdler/useful chaser Risk A Fine (17f-21f winner, by Saffron Walden) and a
winning pointer by Accordion: dam unraced: won Irish maiden point on debut: 11/8, 10¼
lengths fourth of 11 to Clondaw Castle in maiden bumper at Stratford, needing stiffer test:
likely to improve. *Fergal O'Brien*

OUTOFTHISWORLD (IRE) 4 b.f. Shantou (USA) – Mystic Masie (IRE) (Turgeon **b97 P**
(USA)) [2016/17 b16.7g* Mar 27] second foal: dam unraced half-sister to useful hurdler/
smart chaser around 2m Toubab: strong 5/2, won 9-runner mares maiden bumper at Market
Rasen impressively by 11 lengths from Jane Lamb, leading on bridle around 2f out and
quickly drawing clear: useful prospect. *Harry Fry*

OUTRAGEOUS ROMANA (IRE) 6 b.m. Mahler – South West Nine (IRE) (Oscar **h–**
(IRE)) [2016/17 b71: h16.8d h16.2g h15.8g h15.7d h21.2dᵖᵘ h20.7sᵖᵘ Mar 5] unseated
rider in point on debut: no form in bumper/over hurdles. *John O'Shea*

OUT SAM 8 b.g. Multiplex – Tintera (IRE) (King's Theatre (IRE)) [2016/17 c141p, h124: **c134 §**
h25.3s c26gᶠ c24g³ c24d⁴ c32.6sᵖᵘ c33.4sᵖᵘ h23.9g Apr 9] lengthy gelding: fair handicap **h111 §**
chaser nowadays: useful handicap chaser: largely out of sorts in 2016/17: stays 3m: acts on heavy
going: often in cheekpieces in 2016/17: unreliable. *Warren Greatrex*

OUTSMARTIN (IRE) 5 b.g. Marienbard (IRE) – Fair Gina (IRE) (Long Pond) [2016/17 **b74**
b16m³ b16g⁴ Oct 9] showed a bit on first of 2 starts in bumpers. *Deborah Faulkner*

OUTSPOKEN (IRE) 5 b.g. Galileo (IRE) – Riskaverse (USA) (Dynaformer (USA)) **h140**
[2016/17 h16d² h16s* h16s² h16s² h20gᵖᵘ Apr 28] closely related to smart but moody
hurdler/chaser Sadler's Risk (2m-25f winner, by Sadler's Wells): smart on Flat, stays 1¾m:
useful form over hurdles: won maiden at Naas in February: runner-up to Bleu Berry in
listed novice at Naas (beaten short head) in March and Rathbarry & Glenview Studs
Novices' Hurdle at Fairyhouse (beaten 2¼ lengths) in April: should stay beyond 2m: acts
on soft going: wears tongue tie: front runner/races prominently, often travels strongly.
Joseph Patrick O'Brien, Ireland

OVER AND ABOVE (IRE) 11 b.g. Overbury (IRE) – Rose Gold (IRE) (Nucleon **c– §**
(USA)) [2016/17 c85§, h80: c23.8m⁶ c25.5mᵖᵘ Jun 24] maiden hurdler: modest chaser at **h–**
best, no form in 2016/17: stays 27f: acts on soft and good to firm going: wears headgear/
tongue tie: temperamental. *Henry Hogarth*

OVERAWED 6 b.m. Overbury (IRE) – Alleged To Rhyme (IRE) (Leading Counsel **h102**
(USA)) [2016/17 b–: h15.8g³ h15.8s h15.6g⁵ h15.7v* Mar 6] fair form over hurdles:
fortunate winner of mares handicap at Southwell final start, joined when left clear 2 out:
bred to be suited by 2½m: acts on heavy going. *Tom George*

OVERLAND FLYER (IRE) 6 b.g. Westerner – Love Train (IRE) (Sadler's Wells **h120**
(USA)) [2016/17 h23.9g* h23.8g⁴ Feb 5] €40,000 3-y-o: second foal: dam (b71), ran twice
in bumpers, sister to useful hurdler/fairly useful chaser (2½m/21f winner) Sizing
Symphony and closely related to fairly useful hurdler (stayed 2½m) Monbeg Theatre: dual
winning pointer: fairly useful form when winning maiden at Taunton (by 22 lengths from
Stay Out of Court) in January on hurdling debut: disappointing only subsequent start:
wears tongue tie. *Paul Nicholls*

OVER MY HEAD 9 gr.g. Overbury (IRE) – Altesse de Sou (FR) (Saint Preuil (FR)) **c65**
[2016/17 c–, h79: h25d⁴ h26v⁵ h23v² h23.6s⁶ c24.1g³ Mar 25] tall gelding: poor handicap **h65**
hurdler/maiden chaser: stays 3m: best form on soft/heavy going: wears tongue tie: front
runner/races prominently. *Claire Dyson*

OVERRIDER 7 b.g. Cockney Rebel (IRE) – Fustaan (IRE) (Royal Applause) [2016/17 **h78**
h15.8g⁵ h16d h16.3v Jun 28] modest on Flat, stays 9.5f: poor form over hurdles: wears
tongue tie. *Shaun Lycett*

OVER THE AIR 9 br.m. Overbury (IRE) – Moonlight Air (Bold Owl) [2016/17 h107: h20.3gF May 24] fair handicap hurdler: fell 3 out (making headway) at Southwell only start in 2016/17: stays 3m: acts on soft going. *John Spearing* h–

OVER THE BRIDGE 7 b.g. Multiplex – Do It On Dani (Weld) [2016/17 h–, b–: h23.3d6 h21.2mpu May 8] no sign of ability in bumpers/over hurdles: wears hood: also in tongue tie final start. *Steve Flook* h–

OVERTHEEDGE (IRE) 8 b.g. Morozov (USA) – Ballyroe Hill (IRE) (Over The River (FR)) [2016/17 c–, h110: h16.8s3 h20.2f2 h20.6d2 h23.1d2 Apr 27] won once from 6 starts in Irish points: fair handicap hurdler: failed to complete both chase starts: stays 23f: acts on soft going. *Simon West* c– h108

OVER TO MIDNIGHT 7 b.m. Midnight Legend – Makeover (Priolo (USA)) [2016/17 h82, b–: h23.1g6 h20m6 h15.8d h15.8s5 h21.2g5 h21.2m6 Apr 18] maiden hurdler, no form in 2016/17: often races freely. *Lady Susan Brooke* h–

OVER TO SAM 6 b.g. Black Sam Bellamy (IRE) – Lady Brig (Overbury (IRE)) [2016/17 h21.6s* h23.1s3 Feb 10] well-made gelding: chasing type: first foal: dam, winning pointer, half-sister to fair hurdler/fairly useful chaser (2¾m-3¼m winner) Taramoss: winning pointer: fairly useful form over hurdles: won maiden at Exeter in January by 6 lengths from Coole Cody: may prove best at shorter than 2¾m. *Harry Fry* h120

OVERTOUJAY 7 b.g. Overbury (IRE) – Ouh Jay (Karinga Bay) [2016/17 b16.8m4 b16.8g5 b16.7g4 h22g h24d h15.5g4 h20.6d5 h24.4d5 h20.3gur Apr 21] first foal: dam (c76/h119) 2½m-3m hurdle winner: maiden pointer: modest form in bumpers/over hurdles: left Debra Hamer after second start: stays 3m: acts on good to soft going. *Charles Pogson* h89 b80

OVERTOWN EXPRESS (IRE) 9 b.g. Overbury (IRE) – Black Secret (Gildoran) [2016/17 h126: c17g3 c18.8d4 c16.2s* c16.2v6 Feb 11] workmanlike gelding: fairly useful hurdler: useful form over fences: won handicap at Warwick in January by 7 lengths from Artifice Sivola: disappointing in Kingmaker Novices' Chase there only subsequent start: stays 19f: best form on soft/heavy going: usually races nearer last than first. *Harry Fry* c142 h–

OVERTURES 5 b.g. New Approach (IRE) – Most Charming (FR) (Darshaan) [2016/17 h21.5g2 h20.5d3 h22d2 c20g3 c22g4 c20.1g5 Aug 20] fair maiden on Flat, gained 1¼m: fair maiden hurdler: modest form over fences: stayed 2¾m: acted on good to firm and good to soft going: often wore hood: dead. *Gordon Elliott, Ireland* c96 h106

OWEN GLENDOWER (IRE) 12 br.g. Anshan – Native Success (IRE) (Be My Native (USA)) [2016/17 c121x, h103: h20d c29.4m4 May 30] winning hurdler: handicap chaser, just fair nowadays: stays 2¾m: acts on good to firm and heavy going: has worn cheekpieces, including in 2016/17: wears tongue tie: races towards rear: often let down by jumping over fences. *Sophie Leech* c100 x h80

OWEN NA VIEW (IRE) 9 b.g. Presenting – Lady Zephyr (IRE) (Toulon) [2016/17 c131, h120: c16d5 c15.8dpu c16g c17.4g3 c17g2 c16.5m* c16.3g5 c15.2m* c15.9g5 c16v2 c16.3dpu Dec 10] angular gelding: winning hurdler: fairly useful handicap chaser: won at Worcester in August and Wetherby in October: stays 21f: acts on good to firm and good to soft going: has worn headgear, including last 4 starts: has worn tongue tie, including in 2016/17: often leads: sometimes finishes weakly. *Fergal O'Brien* c124 h–

OWL 6 b.m. Overbury (IRE) – Lady Howe (Lord Americo) [2016/17 b17g6 Apr 15] third foal: dam, no form in bumpers/over hurdles, half-sister to useful hurdler/smart chaser (stayed 4m) Rambling Minster: tailed off in mares bumper. *Sandy Forster* b–

OWNERS DAY 7 gr.m. Fair Mix (IRE) – Charmeille (FR) (Exit To Nowhere (USA)) [2016/17 b60: h15.3d* h16g* h16.7s4 Jan 23] rather leggy mare: fair handicapper on Flat, stays 1¼m: fair form over hurdles: won maiden at Wincanton in November and mares novice at Fakenham in December: will prove best around 2m. *Neil Mulholland* h112

OXWICH BAY (IRE) 5 b.g. Westerner – Rose de Beaufai (FR) (Solon (GER)) [2016/17 b–p: b16.8s* h15.8v3 h15.8d2 Jan 25] unfurnished gelding: fair form on second start in bumpers when winning at Sedgefield in November: fairly useful form over hurdles: better effort when second in maiden at Ludlow: will be suited by 2¼m+: remains with potential. *Evan Williams* h116 p b93

OYSTER SHELL 10 br.g. Bollin Eric – Pearly-B (IRE) (Gunner B) [2016/17 c–, h–§: c17mpu May 20] one-time useful hurdler/fairly useful chaser, no form since 2014/15: in cheekpieces only outing in 2016/17: in tongue tie last 3 starts: temperamental. *Edward Glassonbury* c– § h– §

OZZIE THE OSCAR (IRE) 6 b.g. Oscar (IRE) – Private Official (IRE) (Beneficial) [2016/17 h136, b88: h16.8g2 h16g* h16.3dpu h16d4 h16.8g3 h16g Apr 22] useful-looking gelding: useful hurdler: won novice at Wetherby (by 6 lengths from Zipple Back) in h136

October: good effort when ½-length third of 25 to Arctic Fire in County Hurdle (Handicap) at Cheltenham in March: 6¾ lengths eleventh of 16 to Chesterfield in Scottish Champion Hurdle (Handicap) at Ayr final start: raced around 2m: winner on soft going, best efforts on good: usually races prominently. *Philip Hobbs*

OZZY THOMAS (IRE) 7 b.g. Gold Well – Bramble Leader (IRE) (Supreme Leader) **c125** [2016/17 c127, h118: c16m⁵ c16gᶠ h15.5d² h20.6s⁴ h19.5g² Apr 17] rather leggy gelding: **h115** fairly useful handicap hurdler/maiden chaser: stays 2½m: acts on soft going: in cheekpieces final start: tried in tongue tie. *Henry Oliver*

P

PACHA DU POLDER (FR) 10 b.g. Muthathir – Ambri Piotta (FR) (Caerwent) **c137** [2016/17 c136, h–: c27.5m³ c26.1g³ c23m⁴ c20.3s* c26.3g* c21.1g⁴ Apr 6] **h–**
Less is more. That would appear to be the thinking behind the BHA's major overhaul of its licencing and training procedures for aspiring jockeys, which came into force in April. Under the new stricter measures, there will be fewer training places available for the BHA's apprentice/conditional jockeys courses, and all applicants must now undergo a pre-licence assessment. The length of the courses has been extended from five days to ten days and the cost of them has more than doubled (from £700 to £1,650 per attendee). The aim is to ensure that better-prepared jockeys enter the profession, which currently experiences a high turnover. The hope is also to reduce the number of those retiring from the saddle prematurely because they cannot make it pay. 'Too many jockeys mean reduced opportunities for riders who might make the grade. Currently 30% of licencing course attendees do not ride a winner, and 88% do not ride out their claim,' the BHA stated at the launch, which came after a three-year review that also included input from the Professional Jockeys' Association (PJA), the National Trainers' Federation (NTF) and the Jockeys Employment and Training Scheme (JETS). Whether or not these changes have the desired effect, the BHA should be applauded for trying to raise the standards among prospective jockeys, with the introduction in recent years of services such as jockey coaches and nutritionists also being welcome, particularly when it is considered that this sort of professional support has been common in many other sports for decades.
Similarly proactive action was also taken by the BHA in June, when it barred 7-lb claiming apprentice Gina Mangan from taking the ride on controversial no-hoper Diore Lia in the Derby—albeit only after taking a jeweller's eyepiece to the rule book in order to exercise the little-used Rule (F) 83, which states that the BHA can refuse the declaration of a rider for a horse. At the time, Mangan had ridden just one winner (in 2009) from sixty-nine rides during a nine-year career and was deemed too inexperienced to partner the twice-raced maiden filly, who was a general 1000/1-shot (in another change, horses will need to have a minimum BHA mark of 80 to contest a Group 1 on the Flat in future, with similar restrictions being introduced over the jumps). 'Everyone in horse racing has a responsibility to place the welfare of our participants, both equine and human, first. It is in this context that the decision has been made,' explained BHA chief regulatory officer Jamie Stier. 'Miss Mangan has never ridden at Epsom and certainly never ridden in a race on the scale and stage of the Derby, with all the unique challenges it presents.' There was widespread support for this decision, including from dual Derby winner Ryan Moore in his Betfair column, particularly as the media circus surrounding Diore Lia (who was eventually withdrawn on the morning of the race due to a pulled muscle) had angered many in the sport. By contrast, the filly's owner-breeder Richard Aylwood was outspoken: 'I am disgusted with the BHA for what they have done. It was okay for Victoria Pendleton to go round Cheltenham after riding a bike all her life.' Aylwood's behaviour around Diore Lia's Derby bid was, at times, rather eccentric, but there was some substance to his point about Victoria Pendleton. The dual Olympic-winning cyclist attracted a blaze of publicity when partnering Pacha du Polder to fifth in the St James's Place Foxhunter Chase at Cheltenham in 2016. It produced a good story for horse racing in the end, with Pendleton's professional approach shining through from her background in elite sport. However, as a general

rule, it would seem inconsistent for the BHA to allow someone to compete at the Cheltenham Festival with so little race-riding experience. The Foxhunter usually attracts a maximum field of twenty-four and is run over the same course and distance at the Gold Cup, and over twenty-two of the stiffest fences in the country. Pendleton had completed a two-day BHA amateur course and had ridden in just two chases under Rules—producing one unseat and one win—before the 2016 Foxhunter (she had also ridden five times on the Flat). With due respect to the Corinthian spirit, perhaps it is time for more stringent riding guidelines in the amateur ranks too? Hunter chases still regularly feature riders of limited ability and/or experience and it could be argued that plenty of these amateurs would be barred if the BHA were to adopt a similarly hard-line stance with them as it adopted with Gina Mangan.

Stewards did intervene at the eleventh hour before the latest renewal of the Foxhunter in March, though their actions weren't focussed on a jockey on this occasion. Irish raider Anseanachai Cliste (generally available at 33/1) was ordered to be withdrawn because stewards were not satisfied the nine-year-old had been administered normal feed and water—a bloody syringe was discovered at the racecourse stables and the gelding subsequently failed the resulting routine drug test (this case is ongoing and will no doubt be covered again in a future *Chasers & Hurdlers*). The season's leading hunter chaser Foxrock was also prevented from running, as he was ineligible under the conditions of the Cheltenham race (he had been placed in a Grade 1 chase, the Lexus, the previous season). It still looked an up-to-scratch renewal, however, with twelve-year-old On The Fringe a hot favourite to become the first horse to win three times in the race's long history. On The Fringe had been the dominant hunter chaser of recent years (he also won at Aintree and Punchestown in both 2015 and 2016), but 11/8 did seem short odds considering that just over three lengths had covered the first six home in 2016—third Paint The Clouds (11/1), fourth Current Event (66/1), fifth Pacha du Polder (16/1) and sixth Aupcharlie (33/1) were again in opposition (Wonderful Charm at 7/2 and prolific winning pointer Ask The Weatherman at 13/2 were the only others at single-figure odds, though). A similarly bunched finish materialised in the latest running (just over three lengths again covered the first six home) though there were different reasons,

St James's Place Foxhunter Challenge Cup Open Hunters' Chase, Cheltenham— reigning champion trainer Paul Nicholls breaks his 2017 Festival duck as Pacha du Polder in the end has to hold off stable-companion Wonderful Charm (left) in a bunched finish; outsider Barel of Laughs (cheekpieces) eventually takes third as long-time leader Balnaslow (No.4) fades into fifth

with the gallop being much stronger than for the muddling 2016 renewal—the winning time corresponded to a performance only 15 lb inferior to that recorded by Sizing John when winning the Cheltenham Gold Cup forty minutes earlier. Irish raider Balnaslow and Paint The Clouds were largely responsible for this, forcing the issue from some way out on the final circuit until their exertions told in the straight. Pacha du Polder, with Bryony Frost in the saddle this time around, was ridden with a good deal more dash than in the 2016 renewal and always had the front runners in his sights—as opposed to On The Fringe and Wonderful Charm, who were still only eleventh and twelfth jumping five out. Produced to lead at the last, Pacha du Polder was all out to hold on by a neck from his fast-finishing stable-companion Wonderful Charm, with a further neck back to 100/1-shot Barel of Laughs in third. On The Fringe had to settle for fourth this time, whilst Balnaslow faded into fifth after fluffing the last (Ask The Weatherman and Paint The Clouds were seventh and eighth respectively).

It was a third win in the Foxhunter for Paul Nicholls, following on from the popular veteran Earthmover in 2004 and Sleeping Night in 2005. More importantly, however, Pacha du Polder's success ensured the champion trainer didn't have to endure his first blank Festival since 2002—it also meant Nicholls moved past the legendary Fulke Walwyn in the all-time list of the most successful Festival trainers, his tally of forty-one placing him third behind Nicky Henderson (fifty-eight) and Willie Mullins (fifty-four). By contrast, it was a first Cheltenham Festival success for twenty-one-year-old Frost, daughter of former jockey Jimmy Frost, whose three Festival wins included the 1991 Champion Hurdle on Morley Street. Older brother Hadden also tasted Festival success when winning the 2010 Pertemps Final aboard Buena Vista, though he retired in his mid-twenties to set up a saddlery business (he did, however, finish runner-up in the Maryland Hunt Cup during a busman's holiday in the States, qualifying to ride as an amateur as he hadn't ridden as a professional in over two years). Bryony Frost is a pupil assistant trainer at Nicholls' Manor Farm Stables and reportedly has ambitions to follow in the footsteps of predecessors such as Dan Skelton and Harry Fry by training in her own right at some stage. In the meantime, she is enjoying increased opportunities in the saddle which included a tilt at the Foxhunters' Chase at Aintree in April, where Pacha du Polder was sent off 11/2 second favourite (behind disappointing 7/4-shot On The Fringe) to go one better than when runner-up in 2015 (he finished a below-par sixth in 2016). Pacha du Polder ran respectably without fully reproducing his Cheltenham form, finishing a close fourth behind 2016 runner-up Dineur, Balnaslow and the veteran Big Fella Thanks.

Pacha du Polder (FR) (b.g. 2007)	Muhtathir (ch 1995)	Elmaamul (ch 1987)	Diesis
			Modena
		Majmu (b 1988)	Al Nasr
			Affirmative Fable
	Ambri Piotta (FR) (b 1991)	Caerwent (b 1985)	Caerleon
			Marwell
		Alkmene (b 1980)	Matahawk
			Astrale

A well-made gelding, Pacha du Polder is the final foal of useful Flat performer Ambri Piotta, who was a prolific winner in the French Provinces at trips of around ten and eleven furlongs, her wins including a listed race at Toulouse. All seven of her other foals to reach the racecourse are also winners, notably the smart mile/nine-furlong winner Agata (by Poliglote). Her winning jumpers include the fair Irish two-mile hurdler Airolo (by Exit To Nowhere) and the modest hurdler at up to two and three quarter miles Aspra (by Green Tune). This is a Flat-oriented pedigree looking further back and, although largely devoid of significant performers, the mares on the bottom line have proved a plentiful source of success on French soil—nine of grandam Alkmene's thirteen foals were winners, while Pacha du Polder's great grandam Astrale had four of her five runners turn out victorious.

Pacha du Polder also began life in France, winning a juvenile hurdle at Enghien before joining present connections. Although he won the Future Champions Novices' Chase at Ayr in 2012 and the Greatwood Gold Cup at Newbury in 2013, it is fair to say Pacha du Polder never fully lived up to the high hopes held for him after that switch from France, even earning a Timeform 'squiggle' in 2013/14 because of his unreliability. The switch to hunter chasing in 2015 rejuvenated him, however, so much so that he performed well when dipping his toe back into handicap company early in the latest campaign, his good third to Drop Out Joe in the valuable John Smith's Summer Cup at Uttoxeter in June being arguably his best effort of the season. A notably sound jumper, Pacha du Polder is fully effective at around two and a half miles to three and a quarter miles and is also versatile with regards to ground, having won on good to firm and heavy (plus all going descriptions in between). In fact, he now very much fits that oft-used Timeform description from yesteryear of being an 'ideal mount for an amateur'. *Paul Nicholls*

PACIFIC PEARL (IRE) 6 b.m. Westerner – Claudia's Pearl (Deploy) [2016/17 b–§: b16.7g May 14] sturdy mare: no form in 2 bumpers, looking very hard ride on debut. *Sam Thomas* — **b– §**

PADAWAN (IRE) 8 br.g. Stowaway – Afsana (IRE) (Bluebird (USA)) [2016/17 h21s h15.7s h21.6v^{pu} Feb 14] lengthy gelding: off mark in Irish points at fifth attempt: poor form over hurdles. *David Dennis* — **h60**

PADDLING (FR) 6 b.g. Walk In The Park (IRE) – Sea Mamaille (FR) (Sea Full (FR)) [2016/17 b64: b16s h19.3d^5 h19.9s^{pu} h16.4v c15.7s^4 Mar 8] close-coupled gelding: poor form in bumpers/novice hurdles, and when fourth in novice handicap at Catterick on chasing debut. *Micky Hammond* — **c84 h80 b–**

PADDOCKS LOUNGE (IRE) 10 b.g. Oscar (IRE) – Sister Rosza (IRE) (Roselier (FR)) [2016/17 h100: h19.5d^2 c21.7d^F h16.7d^2 h20.5d* h15.5v* h19.8s^4 c16v^4 h16.8d* h18.5g^3 Apr 11] lengthy gelding: Irish point winner: fair hurdler: won at Leicester in January (seller) and February (novice claimer) and at Exeter (novice seller) in March: modest form on completed start in chases: left Sophie Leech after eighth start: stays 2½m: acts on good to firm and heavy going: usually wears hood/tongue tie: front runner. *Aytach Sadik* — **c93 h110**

PADDYPLEX 4 b.g. Multiplex – Turtle Bay (Dr Fong (USA)) [2016/17 b13g^6 b15.6g b16.4g^6 Mar 24] fourth foal: brother to bumper winner/fair 2½m hurdle winner Starplex: dam (h77), maiden hurdler (best around 2m), half-sister to fairly useful hurdler (2m-21f winner) Valento: modest form in bumpers. *Keith Dalgleish* — **b75**

PADDY'S FIELD (IRE) 7 b.g. Flemensfirth (USA) – Kittys Oscar (IRE) (Oscar (IRE)) [2016/17 h115, b91: c19.3d^5 c24s c24g^6 Jan 27] useful-looking gelding: fairly useful hurdler: best effort over fences (fairly useful form) when fifth in novice handicap at Sedgefield in November: should stay beyond 19f: acts on heavy going: in cheekpieces second start: front runner/races prominently. *Ben Pauling* — **c117 h–**

PADDYS MOTORBIKE (IRE) 5 ch.g. Fast Company (IRE) – Saffa Garden (IRE) (King's Best (USA)) [2016/17 h19.5m^5 h20d^3 h21.9v^5 h20v^2 h21.9d^3 Apr 16] fairly useful on Flat, stays 1½m: fair form over hurdles: likely to stay 3m: acts on heavy going. *Christian Williams* — **h111**

PADDY'S POEM 6 b.g. Proclamation (IRE) – Ashleys Petale (IRE) (Ashley Park (IRE)) [2016/17 b16s b16s^3 Mar 30] first foal: dam 1¾m bumper winner/maiden hurdler (stayed 21f): better effort (fair form) in maiden bumpers when third at Warwick. *Nick Gifford* — **b92**

PADDYS RUNNER 5 gr.g. Sir Percy – Frosty Welcome (USA) (With Approval (CAN)) [2016/17 h122: h20.6g^4 h16d^3 h19.4g h18.5s h15.3s* h16.5g^2 h15.7g Apr 15] close-coupled gelding: fairly useful handicap hurdler: won at Wincanton in January: should be suited by further than 2m: acts on soft going: visored final start. *Alan King* — **h118**

PADDY'S YARN (IRE) 7 ch.g. Houmayoun (FR) – Deidamia (USA) (Dayjur (USA)) [2016/17 h87, b66: h22.7d h22.7s^3 h22s^{pu} h23.8g^6 h23.8g^F Mar 24] poor maiden hurdler: stays 3m: acts on soft going: has worn tongue tie: often races towards rear/freely. *Valerie Jackson* — **h78**

PADDY THE DEEJAY (IRE) 8 b.g. Fruits of Love (USA) – Sue Pickering (IRE) (Tremblant) [2016/17 c108, h115: c20g^{ur} c21.1d^4 c23.6d^5 c21.7d c15.9m^{pu} Dec 28] tall gelding: dual point winner: fairly useful maiden hurdler: fair maiden chaser: stays 21f: acts on soft going: in cheekpieces final start. *Stuart Edmunds* — **c110 h–**

PADDY THE OSCAR (IRE) 14 b.g. Oscar (IRE) Parsonage (The Parson) [2016/17 c118, h–: c24v^{pu} c24v^2 c23.6s c25.1d^2 c22.7s^4 c23.6v^4 c23.6g^4 Apr 8] maiden hurdler: fair handicap chaser: stays 3¼m: acts on heavy going: tried in cheekpieces/tongue tie: front runner/races prominently. *Grace Harris* — **c110 h–**

PADDY THE STOUT (IRE) 12 b.g. Oscar Schindler (IRE) – Misty Silks (Scottish **c91 §**
Reel) [2016/17 c82, h–: c17.4g³ c21.1g* c23.8d^pu Jun 16] strong gelding: maiden hurdler: **h–**
modest handicap chaser: won at Fontwell in June: stays 21f: acts on heavy going: wears
tongue tie: usually races nearer last than first: unreliable. *Paul Henderson*

PADRE TITO (IRE) 9 b.g. Milan – Augusta Brook (IRE) (Over The River (FR)) **c–**
[2016/17 c–, h103: h17.2s h24m h16.2f² h16.2d³ h23.9s⁶ Jul 10] tall gelding: in frame **h103**
in points: fair maiden hurdler: pulled up only chase start: stays 2¾m: acts on any going: has
worn headgear, including last 3 starts: in tongue tie last 4 starts. *Gordon Elliott, Ireland*

PADS (IRE) 7 b.g. Luso – Augusta Victoria (Callernish) [2016/17 b16.2d⁴ b16.2s⁵ h16.2g^ur **h109**
h20.9d⁴ h16d h20.5s² h19.3s⁵ h16.7d³ h18.6s⁴ h23.8g⁵ h20.5v^pu h24.3v³ h16g⁶ Apr 23] **b67**
half-brother to fair hurdler/chaser The Screamer (2m winner, by Insan) and winning
pointers by Over The River and Scribano: dam unraced sister to useful staying chaser On
The Twist: poor form in bumpers: fair maiden hurdler: stays 2½m: acts on soft going: often
wears hood: often races towards rear. *Iain Jardine*

PAIN AU CHOCOLAT (FR) 6 b.g. Enrique – Clair Chene (FR) (Solido (FR)) [2016/17 **c139**
c143p, h134: h18.9s c17.5m⁶ c16.3v² c19.9g^pu c20.5s² c15.7d⁵ h20.3g c16g⁴ Apr 27] **h84**
good-topped gelding: useful hurdler at best, showed little in 2016/17: useful handicap
chaser: won at Perth (by 4 lengths from Duke of Navan) on final outing: left Dan Skelton
after seventh start: stays 2½m: acts on heavy going: usually wore hood/tongue tie for
previous yard: often races prominently. *Rebecca Menzies*

PAINTERS LAD (IRE) 6 b.g. Fruits of Love (USA) – Great Cullen (IRE) (Simply Great **h–**
(FR)) [2016/17 b–: h15.6g⁵ Jan 3] well held in bumper/maiden hurdle, tongue tied in latter.
Alison Hamilton

PAINT THE CLOUDS 12 b.g. Muhtarram (USA) – Preening (Persian Bold) [2016/17 **c134**
c135, h–: c25s⁵ c27.5m* c26g* c26.3g Mar 17] lengthy gelding: winning hurdler: useful **h–**
hunter chaser: won at Stratford (Champion Hunters' Chase, by 1¾ lengths from Marito) in
May and Doncaster (by 2¾ lengths from Ardea) in February: creditable 5¾ lengths eighth
of 23 to Pacha du Polder in Foxhunter Chase at Cheltenham final start, weakening run-in:
stays 29f: acts on soft and good to firm going: front runner/races prominently, often travels
strongly: usually sound jumper. *Warren Greatrex*

PAIROFBROWNEYES (IRE) 8 b.g. Luso – Frankly Native (IRE) (Be My Native **c141**
(USA)) [2016/17 c137, h–: c20d³ c21s³ c20d⁵ c19.5d² c15.9g² c19.5v³ c17s² c16v² c16.3g **h116**
h19g⁶ Apr 16] workmanlike gelding: fairly useful handicap hurdler: useful handicap
chaser: held his form well and placed on most starts in 2016/17: stays 21f, effective at
shorter: acts on heavy going: wears cheekpieces. *Barry John Murphy, Ireland*

PAIR OF JACKS (IRE) 9 ch.g. Presenting – Halona (Pollerton) [2016/17 c136, h–: c20g **c134**
c24.2d² c25.5d* c25.5d c25.5g⁵ c19.4m² c19.4g⁶ Oct 28] winning hurdler: useful handicap **h–**
chaser: won by length from Alderbrook Lad at Cartmel in July: stays 25f: acts on good to
firm and good to soft going. *Malcolm Jefferson*

PAISLEY PARK (IRE) 5 b.g. Oscar (IRE) – Presenting Shares (IRE) (Presenting) **b97**
[2016/17 b16s² Jan 14] €60,000 3-y-o: half-brother to several winners, including fairly
useful hurdlers Henry King (17f-19f winner) and Mr Grey (2½m winner) (both by Great
Palm), latter also winning pointer: dam unraced half-sister to useful chaser (stayed 3m)
Preists Leap: 6/1, staying-on length second of 14 to Point of Principle in maiden bumper at
Warwick on debut. *Emma Lavelle*

PALADIN (IRE) 8 b.g. Dubawi (IRE) – Palwina (FR) (Unfuwain (USA)) [2016/17 h–: **h–**
h21s Feb 10] fair on Flat, stays 1½m: very lightly-raced maiden over hurdles: in hood only
outing in 2016/17: tried in tongue tie. *Michael Blake*

PALM GREY (IRE) 9 gr.g. Great Palm (USA) – Lucy Cooper (IRE) (Roselier (FR)) **c128**
[2016/17 c90, h117: h23.3s c20.9d^pu c20g* c21.4s² c20.9s* c19.4s^ur c19.9d⁴ c20s⁴ c24.2g* **h70**
Apr 23] workmanlike gelding: handicap hurdler, fairly useful at best: fairly useful handicap
chaser: won at Carlisle in November and December (novice event), and at Wetherby on
final start: will stay beyond 3m: acts on heavy going: usually races close up. *Sue Smith*

PALOMA BLUE (IRE) 5 br.g. Stowaway – Court Leader (IRE) (Supreme Leader) **b118**
[2016/17 b16s* b16g² Apr 26] €160,000 3-y-o: fifth foal: dam (c123/h110) hurdle/chase
winner up to 2½m (stayed 3m), sister to fairly useful hurdler/useful chaser (stayed 2¾m)
Mount Sandel: smart form in bumpers: won maiden at Fairyhouse (by 1¼ lengths from
Oakley Hall) on debut in January: 12/1, improved when 5½ lengths second of 7 to
Fayonagh in Champion INH Flat Race at Punchestown. *Henry de Bromhead, Ireland*

PALOMA'S PRINCE (IRE) 8 ch.g. Nayef (USA) – Ma Paloma (FR) (Highest Honor **h85**
(FR)) [2016/17 h90: h24.7d h24d⁵ h23.3g h20.5g⁵ h19.1d Dec 6] modest handicap hurdler:
stays 21f: acts on good to firm and good to soft going: usually in tongue tie in 2016/17, also
in blinkers last 2 starts: usually races close up. *Richard Phillips*

PAMAK D'AIRY (FR) 14 b.g. Cadoubel (FR) – Gamaska d'Airy (FR) (Marasali) **c79 §**
[2016/17 c98, h–: c16.4s² c16.4d⁶ᵘ c16.3sᵖᵘ Jan 23] tall, useful-looking gelding: winning **h–**
hurdler: poor handicap chaser nowadays: stays 2¾m: acts on good to firm and heavy going:
wears headgear: temperamental. *Henry Hogarth*

PAMPANINI 6 b.m. Milan – Loxhill Lady (Supreme Leader) [2016/17 b89: b15.7g⁵ **h95**
ab16g² h16.7s³ Feb 7] small mare: modest form in bumpers, and when third in mares **b80**
maiden hurdle at Market Rasen: in tongue tie last 4 starts: dead. *Harry Fry*

PANDY WELLS 8 b.m. Kayf Tara – Alina Rheinberg (GER) (Waky Nao) [2016/17 c91, **c69**
h72: c22.5g⁵ May 14] maiden hurdler: modest handicap chaser at best: stays 3m: acts on **h–**
soft going. *Graeme McPherson*

PANIS ANGELICUS (FR) 8 b.g. Panis (USA) – Pyu (GER) (Surumu (GER)) [2016/17 **h92**
h113: h23.1d⁶ h19.9g h20g h20.3g⁵ h20d h23.1m Nov 1] workmanlike gelding: handicap
hurdler, modest nowadays: stays 2¾m: acts on good to firm going: has worn visor,
including in 2016/17: often races lazily. *Tim Vaughan*

PANTXOA (FR) 10 b.g. Daliapour (IRE) – Palmeria (FR) (Great Palm (USA)) [2016/17 **c120**
c–, h–: c25d⁶ c22.6mᵖᵘ c25.8m* Apr 15] sturdy gelding: winning hurdler: fairly useful **h–**
hunter chaser nowadays: won at Newton Abbot in April: left Richard Phillips after second
start: stays 27f: acts on soft and good to firm going: usually races close up: none too
reliable. *Fergal O'Brien*

PAO DE ACUCA (IRE) 5 b.g. Rip Van Winkle (IRE) – Splendeur (FR) (Desert King **h–**
(IRE)) [2016/17 h–: h21.6dᵖᵘ Jun 1] no promise in 2 novice hurdles: in hood first start:
wears tongue tie. *Jose Santos*

PAPAL EDICT (IRE) 5 b.g. Papal Bull – Tarayib (Hamas (IRE)) [2016/17 ab16g **b–**
Nov 29] tailed off in bumper. *Paddy Butler*

PAPER ROSES (IRE) 6 b.m. Gamut (IRE) – Rose Vic (IRE) (Old Vic) [2016/17 b89: **h109**
b16.2s³ h16.2sᵘʳ h15.6g h16.2v³ h19.4g h20.2g² Apr 26] modest form in bumpers: fair form **b76**
over hurdles: stays 2½m: acts on heavy going. *Donald Whillans*

PARC DES PRINCES (USA) 11 b.g. Ten Most Wanted (USA) – Miss Orah (Unfuwain **h69 §**
(USA)) [2016/17 h97§: h23.9m⁶ h20.2d⁶ h23.1g h19s h16.7d h19.4g⁵ h23.8g⁶ Mar 24]
poor handicap hurdler: stays 3m: acts on soft and good to firm going: tried in blinkers:
temperamental. *Nicky Richards*

PARIS BOUND 4 b.g. Champs Elysees – Averami (Averti (IRE)) [2016/17 b16.5m⁴ **b81**
b16.3s Jan 18] useful-looking gelding: half-brother to several winners, including smart
hurdler Taglietelle (2m-3m winner, by Tagula) and fair hurdler Spectator (2m winner, by
Passing Glance): dam 7f winner on Flat: modest form on first of 2 starts in bumpers: fair
form when placed at up to 1¾m on Flat. *Andrew Balding*

PARISH BOY 5 gr.g. New Approach (IRE) – Requesting (Rainbow Quest (USA)) **h–**
[2016/17 h16vᵖᵘ h16d⁵ h18.7g Apr 15] useful on Flat, stays 9f: no form over hurdles. *David
Loughnane*

PARISH BUSINESS (IRE) 9 b.g. Fruits of Love (USA) – Parkality (IRE) (Good Thyne **c–**
(USA)) [2016/17 c121, h–: h25d h26.5m h21.6d* h21g⁴ h24.4g* Dec 29] useful-looking **h128**
gelding: fairly useful handicap hurdler: won at Fontwell in October and Doncaster final
start: fairly useful maiden chaser: stays 3m: acts on soft going: in cheekpieces second start:
wears tongue tie: front runner/races prominently. *Emma Lavelle*

PARISIAN CHARMER 10 gr.g. Paris House – Tea For Texas (Weldnaas (USA)) **h–**
[2016/17 h19.3d h15.7g h15.8vᵖᵘ Jan 28] close-coupled gelding: no form over hurdles: in
cheekpieces final start. *Mark Weatherer*

PARISIAN STAR 5 ch.m. Champs Elysees – Cavallo da Corsa (Galileo (IRE)) [2016/17 **b–**
b–: ab16g Nov 8] leggy mare: no form in bumpers. *J. R. Jenkins*

PARKAM JACK 11 b.g. Grape Tree Road – Rakajack (Rakaposhi King) [2016/17 c108, **c–**
h–: c16.1g⁵ Feb 21] multiple point winner: winning hurdler: hunter chaser, fair at best: **h–**
stays 23f: acts on good to firm and good to soft going: tried in headgear/tongue tie.
Mrs Kayley Woollacott

PARK HOUSE 8 b.g. Tillerman – Rasin Luck (Primitive Rising (USA)) [2016/17 h89: **h88**
h18.1s³ h20.6s⁶ h24g* Apr 8] modest handicap hurdler: won conditionals novice event at
Newcastle final start: stays 3m: acts on good to firm going. *Ray Craggs*

PARKIE BOY 6 b.g. Central Park (IRE) – Parlour Game (Petoski) [2016/17 h–: h16.2d **h75** h16spu h16v[3] h16.4vpu h16.4g h16.2gpu Apr 27] poor maiden hurdler: raced only at 2m: acts on heavy going: in tongue tie last 4 starts: races close up /freely. *Alison Hamilton*

PARK STEEL (IRE) 7 b.g. Craigsteel – Orient Star (IRE) (Mandalus) [2016/17 b16.3m[5] **b75** May 15] off mark in Irish maiden points at second attempt: 15/2, 7½ lengths fifth of 11 to Burlington Bert in bumper at Stratford: bred to be suited by 2½m+. *Sarah Humphrey*

PARLOUR MAID 6 gr.m. Dr Massini (IRE) – Charliebob (Nomadic Way (USA)) **h–** [2016/17 h18.5g h15.7d h15.8s Dec 6] third foal: half-sister to poor chaser Beaujolais Bob (2½m winner, by Grape Tree Road): dam winning pointer: off mark in maiden points at third attempt: no form in mares maiden hurdles: wears tongue tie. *Richard Hawker*

PARSNIP PETE 11 b.g. Pasternak – Bella Coola (Northern State (USA)) [2016/17 c–, h–: **c138** c18g[4] c17g[2] c15.8d* c16g[3] c17m[3] c15.8d[3] c16.4g[2] c16.3d c15.8gpu Apr 6] sturdy gelding: **h–** winning hurdler: useful handicap chaser: won by length from Walden Prince at Aintree in June: unproven beyond 17f: acts on soft and good to firm going: wears tongue tie: strong-travelling sort, has found less than seemed likely. *Tom George*

PART AND PARCEL (IRE) 9 b.g. Zerpour (IRE) – Carriacou (Mark of Esteem (IRE)) **h85** [2016/17 h100: h20.3dpu h20s h24dpu h19.5g[3] h18.7gpu Apr 15] dual point winner: modest maiden hurdler: stays 23f: acts on good to firm going: in tongue tie third start. *Hannah James*

PARTHIAN EMPIRE 11 b.g. Parthian Springs – Dudeen (IRE) (Anshan) [2016/17 c–, **c–** h–: c22.5dpu May 5] big, well-made gelding: winning hurdler: maiden pointer/hunter **h–** chaser: in cheekpieces/tongue tie only outing in 2016/17. *W. M. Wanless*

PARTING WAY (IRE) 9 b.g. Golan (IRE) – Best Mother (IRE) (King's Theatre (IRE)) **c–** [2016/17 c93, h–: c16dpu Jun 16] good-topped gelding: winning pointer: maiden hurdler/ **h–** chaser, modest at best: stays 21f: acts on heavy going. *Tim Vaughan*

PARTY ROCK (IRE) 10 b.g. Vinnie Roe (IRE) – Garryduff Eile (IRE) (Oscar (IRE)) **c134** [2016/17 h135: h20m[2] c19.2d* c19.2gpu Jul 3] lengthy gelding: useful handicap hurdler: **h137** useful form on chasing debut when winning novice at Market Rasen in June by 2 lengths from Golden Doyen: possibly amiss only subsequent start: stays 2½m: acts on good to firm and heavy going: usually races close up. *Jennie Candlish*

PARWICH LEES 5 ch.g. Pasternak – Barton Dante (Phardante (FR)) [2016/17 b15.7s[4] **b80** Jan 31] 10/1, 15½ lengths fourth of 10 to Champ in maiden bumper at Southwell on debut. *Neil Mulholland*

PASHTUNWALI (IRE) 6 b.g. Golan (IRE) – Crazy Bear (IRE) (King Charlemagne **c–** (USA)) [2016/17 h21gpu h20d h24g h20m[4] h23.6d h20d h16v[2] h16d[3] h17.1d[2] h20g h16d[5] **h99** c21s c17.5vpu Feb 16] second foal: dam, ran twice over hurdles, 1½m winner on Flat, half-sister to smart hurdler/very smart chaser (stayed 3m) Glencove Marina: bumper winner: modest maiden hurdler: no form over fences: stays 2½m: acts on good to firm and heavy going: blinkered last 5 starts over hurdles. *Eoin Griffin, Ireland*

PASSAM 5 b.g. Black Sam Bellamy (IRE) – One Wild Night (Rakaposhi King) [2016/17 **b75** b16s Feb 10] in tongue strap, 100/1, 17¼ lengths seventh in maiden bumper at Kempton. *Claire Dyson*

PASSING CALL 4 b.f. Passing Glance – Call Me A Legend (Midnight Legend) [2016/17 **b90** b14s[3] b12.4d[4] b15.8d[2] Feb 9] lengthy filly: second foal: dam (c139/h118), 2m-2¼m hurdle/ chase winner (stayed 21f), sister to useful hurdler (stayed 21f) Call Me A Star: fair form in bumpers. *Alan King*

PASSING DU MOULIN (FR) 6 gr.g. Passing Sale (FR) – Ruaha River (FR) (Villez **b69** (USA)) [2016/17 b–: b16m[3] b15.8d Nov 30] poor form in bumpers. *Harry Whittington*

PASSING FIESTA 8 b.m. Passing Glance – Clarice Starling (Saddlers' Hall (IRE)) **c–** § [2016/17 c82§, h–: c16.3gpu c16.5s[F] h16.7d May 25] winning hurdler/maiden chaser, **h–** no form in 2016/17: has worn headgear, including last 2 starts: has worn tongue tie: temperamental. *Sarah-Jayne Davies*

PASSMORE 5 b.m. Passing Glance – Call Me A Legend (Midnight Legend) [2016/17 **h107** b78: h16g[2] h18.5g[3] h16.6g[6] h16m[3] Apr 18] fair maiden hurdler: best effort at 2m on good ground. *Alan King*

PASS ON THE MANTLE 9 b.g. Bollin Eric – Swiss Rose (Michelozzo (USA)) **h–** § [2016/17 h78§: h22g h16.5g h21mpu Apr 4] workmanlike gelding: poor handicap hurdler, no form in 2016/17: tried in cheekpieces: usually races nearer last than first: temperamental. *Julian Smith*

PASS THE TIME 8 b.m. Passing Glance – Twin Time (Syrtos) [2016/17 c104, h135: h18d⁶ c17.4d* c16.3d² c19.4g* c16.3g⁴ h16g⁴ h19.9gᵇᵈ Mar 14] small mare: useful hurdler at best, below that in 2016/17: useful form in novice chases, winning at Fontwell in June and Stratford in September: stays 2½m: acts on soft and good to firm going: wears cheekpieces: front runner/races prominently. *Neil Mulholland*   **c131 h121**

PATIENCE TONY (IRE) 6 b.g. Windsor Knot (IRE) – Johar Jamal (IRE) (Chevalier (IRE)) [2016/17 b89: b16.8g* b16.7g⁵ Jul 31] modest form in bumpers: won maiden at Sedgefield in May. *Alan Swinbank*   **b79**

PATRICKTOM BORU (IRE) 10 b.g. Brian Boru – Brehon Law (IRE) (Alphabatim (USA)) [2016/17 c100, h94: c22.6m⁴ May 20] multiple winning pointer: winning hurdler: fair chaser: stays 3m: acts on soft and good to firm going: often races prominently. *R. W. J. Willcox*   **c111 h–**

PATRONNE (FR) 5 b.m. Solon (GER) – Parla (GER) (Lagunas) [2016/17 h–: h15.3m² h16.7dᵖᵘ Jun 17] poor maiden over hurdles: has raced freely/carried head high. *Harry Whittington*   **h80**

PATSY MILAN (IRE) 6 b.m. Milan – Cousin Kizzy (IRE) (Toulon) [2016/17 b16d h16.2s⁴ Dec 29] third foal: dam (h92) 2m hurdle winner (stayed 2½m): maiden pointer: well held in listed mares bumper and a mares novice hurdle: left Colin Bowe after first start. *Donald McCain*   **h– b–**

PATSYS CASTLE (IRE) 10 ch.g. Windsor Castle – Annienoora (IRE) (Topanoora) [2016/17 c24s³ c22.5sᵖᵘ c25.8g⁴ c25.8gᵖᵘ h26g* h24.2g* h24.1d⁵ h24g⁴ h21.4m h23.1g³ Apr 22] good-bodied gelding: successful twice in Irish points: fair handicap hurdler: won at Warwick in September and Newbury in November: only form in chases when third of 5 in novice on reappearance (first start for 20 months): stays 3¼m: acts on good to firm and good to soft going: wears headgear: front runner/races prominently. *Kim Bailey*   **c96 h114**

PATTARA 8 b.m. Kayf Tara – Fortunes Course (IRE) (Crash Course) [2016/17 h90: h20g⁶ h21.6m h20.7d² h20.7d h21.6g Apr 12] modest handicap hurdler: stays 21f: acts on good to soft going: wears hood/tongue tie: usually races prominently, tends to find little: unreliable. *Noel Williams*   **h88 §**

PAUL (FR) 6 b.g. Boris de Deauville (IRE) – Bartjack (FR) (Lost World (IRE)) [2016/17 b–: h19.9d Oct 2] Irish maiden point winner: tailed off in bumper/maiden hurdle. *Rebecca Curtis*   **h–**

PAWN STAR (IRE) 7 b.g. Beneficial – Missindependence (IRE) (Executive Perk) [2016/17 h102: h22m* c23m* c25m* c25g³ c24.2m* c25g³ c23.6g² Apr 17] smallish gelding: fair hurdler: won handicap at Stratford in May: fairly useful form over fences: won novice handicap at Worcester in August and handicap at Exeter in October: good second in handicap at Chepstow final start: stays 3¼m: acts on soft and good to firm going. *Emma Lavelle*   **c127 h100**

PAY THE KING (IRE) 10 b.g. King's Theatre (IRE) – Knocktartan (IRE) (King's Ride) [2016/17 c93, h–: c21.3g⁵ c24.2gᶠ c25.5gᵖᵘ Jul 18] well-made gelding: winning hurdler: poor maiden chaser: stays 21f: acts on soft going: has worn cheekpieces, including final start: often races towards rear. *Micky Hammond*   **c72 h–**

PAY YOUR WAY (IRE) 9 gr.g. Cloudings (IRE) – Supreme Bond (IRE) (Supreme Leader) [2016/17 h91: c16d* h15.8g⁵ h15.8gᵖᵘ h15.8g⁵ c20.9vᶠ c20s Feb 8] poor handicap hurdler: modest form over fences: won novice handicap at Ffos Las in June: left David Rees after fourth start: stays 2½m: acts on soft and good to firm going: often in hood: has worn tongue tie: usually races nearer last than first. *A. J. Rhead*   **c96 h78**

PEACE AND CO (FR) 6 b.g. Falco (USA) – Peace Lina (FR) (Linamix (FR)) [2016/17 h140: h16g Apr 22] good-topped gelding: high-class hurdler as a juvenile, very lightly raced and disappointing since: in hood, 6¾ lengths tenth of 16 to Chesterfield in Scottish Champion Hurdle (Handicap) at Ayr only outing in 2016/17: raced around 2m: has won on soft going, but keen-going and best efforts under less testing conditions: temperament under suspicion. *Nicky Henderson*   **h–**

PEACE NEWS (GER) 5 b.g. Sholokhov (IRE) – Peaceful Love (GER) (Dashing Blade) [2016/17 h16v* h16dᶠ h16d⁵ h20g⁴ h16v⁴ Feb 26] fairly useful on Flat in France for Francois Rohaut, stays 14.5f: fairly useful form over hurdles: won maiden at Cork in November: should stay beyond 2m: acts on heavy going: in tongue tie last 2 starts, also in cheekpieces final one. *Henry de Bromhead, Ireland*   **h132**

PEADAR MIGUEL 10 b.g. Danroad (AUS) – La Corujera (Case Law) [2016/17 h16d h15.8d⁴ h15.8g² h16.7g* Jul 31] modest handicap hurdler: won at Market Rasen final start: best at sharp 2m: acts on good to firm going: in hood last 5 starts. *Michael Mullineaux*   **h95**

PEAK SEASONS (IRE) 14 ch.g. Raise A Grand (IRE) – Teresian Girl (IRE) (Glenstal (USA)) [2016/17 c–x, h–x: c21.4g^pu c20.2f^5 h25.6s^pu c21.2g^pu c20.3g Apr 21] leggy, close-coupled gelding: winning hurdler/chaser, no longer of any account: has worn blinkers: often let down by jumping. *Michael Chapman*   c– x
h– x

PEAK TO PEAK (IRE) 5 br.g. Authorized (IRE) – Bayourida (USA) (Slew O' Gold (USA)) [2016/17 h19.1s* h20.5d h21s^3 h19.1s^5 h20.5m* h19.5m* Apr 28] well-made gelding: closely related to useful hurdler/chaser Gabriel The Great (2m-2½m winner, by Montjeu): 11f winner on only start on Flat (in France for M. Delzangles): useful form over hurdles: won maiden at Fontwell in November and novices at Plumpton and Chepstow (by ¾ length from Jameson) in April: stays 21f: acts on soft and good to firm going. *Paul Nicholls*   h130

PEAL OF BELLS 6 b.m. Martaline – Tambourine Ridge (IRE) (Tamure (IRE)) [2016/17 h91, b–: h21g^2 h19.9g h23.3g^4 h21m^pu h25m^pu h23.9g* h25g* Apr 3] stocky mare: modest handicap hurdler: won at Taunton in December and Huntingdon in April: left Henry Daly after second start, Mike Sowersby after fifth: stays 25f: best form on good going. *Harry Whittington*   h98

PEARLESQUE (FR) 5 gr.m. Martaline – Anazeem (IRE) (Irish River (FR)) [2016/17 b16.3s b16.3s^6 Mar 3] €65,000 3-y-o: compact mare: seventh foal: sister to fair French hurdler/fairly useful chaser Eudemis (15f-17f winner) and half-sister to 2 winners, including fair hurdler Andijan (17f-2¾m winner, by Marju): dam, ran twice on Flat, half-sister to smart hurdler/chaser (stayed 2¾m) Ansar: poor form in 2 bumpers at Newbury. *Nicky Henderson*   b71

PEARLITA 5 b.m. Milan – Pearl Buttons (Alflora (IRE)) [2016/17 b–: h16.7s h16s^pu h21.7v^5 h23.1s^pu h22g^5 Apr 1] angular mare: poor form over hurdles: best effort at 2¾m: in headgear last 2 starts. *Henry Daly*   h83

PEARL ROYALE (IRE) 5 b.m. Robin des Champs (FR) – Dartmeet (IRE) (Presenting) [2016/17 b15.8g^3 b16.4s^5 b15.8v^2 h20.5s^2 h19.2v^2 h20.3v* Mar 6] £16,000 3-y-o: workmanlike mare: fourth foal: closely related to fair hurdler Postbridge (2m/19f winner, by Robin des Pres) and half-sister to modest chaser Brave Encounter (25f/3¼m winner, by Indian Danehill): dam, winning pointer, sister to smart hurdler/chaser (stays 3¼m) Bear's Affair: fair form in bumpers: fairly useful form over hurdles: much improved when winning novice handicap at Southwell final start: will stay beyond 2½m: front runner/races prominently. *Nigel Hawke*   h118
b90

PEARLS LEGEND 10 b.g. Midnight Legend – Pearl's Choice (IRE) (Deep Run) [2016/17 c138, h–: c15.8d c15.5v^6 c16v^3 c16s^4 c16.4g c17m* Apr 17] rather leggy gelding: winning hurdler: handicap chaser, fairly useful nowadays: won at Plumpton final start: stays 2½m: acts on good to firm and heavy going: in cheekpieces third to fifth starts: front runner/races prominently. *John Spearing*   c128
h–

PEARL SWAN (FR) 9 b.g. Gentlewave (IRE) – Swanson (USA) (Diesis) [2016/17 c–, h131: c24d^2 c23.8d* c23.6s^4 c20.3s* c23.8s* Feb 19] good-topped gelding: useful handicap hurdler: useful chaser: won maiden at Ffos Las in November, novice at Southwell in January and handicap at Ffos Las on final start (reportedly finished lame): stays 3m: acts on soft going: usually in headgear/tongue tie: usually leads. *Peter Bowen*   c137
h–

PEARLY HEIGHTS (IRE) 7 gr.m. Definite Article – Fille d'Argent (IRE) (Desert Style (IRE)) [2016/17 b16d b15.7d Jul 10] €4,000 3-y-o: sixth foal: half-sister to bumper winner/fairly useful hurdler Flying Eagle (2½m winner, by Oscar): dam maiden half-sister to fairly useful 2m hurdler Talina's Law, herself dam of useful hurdler/smart chaser (stayed 3m) Majestic Concorde (by Definite Article): no form in points/bumpers. *Alan Phillips*   b–

PEARLYSTEPS 14 ch.g. Alflora (IRE) – Pearly-B (IRE) (Gunner B) [2016/17 c127, h–: c26.3g* c24s^2 c24.1d^4 c23.8s* Mar 23] sturdy gelding: winning hurdler: fairly useful chaser: won hunters at Cheltenham very early in season and at Ludlow final start: stays 3¼m: acts on good to firm and heavy going: tried in cheekpieces: front runner/races prominently. *Henry Daly*   c127
h–

PECKHAMECHO (IRE) 11 b.g. Beneficial – Nolans Pride (IRE) (Good Thyne (USA)) [2016/17 c–, h–: h15.3m^ur h19.8d c25.5s* Jan 26] useful-looking gelding: useful hurdler at best, no form in 2016/17: handicap chaser: in tongue tie, fair form when winning at Warwick in January, only outing over fences in 2016/17: stays 25f: acts on heavy going. *Sophie Leech*   c109
h

PECULIAR PLACES (IRE) 5 b.g. Presenting – Blu Louisiana (IRE) (Milan) [2016/17 **b112**
b16.7d² Apr 27] €35,000 3-y-o: second foal: dam, maiden on Flat in Italy, half-sister to
Champion Bumper winner/very smart hurdler (stayed 21f) Dunguib (by Presenting): well-
backed 9/4, showed plenty when neck second of 10 to Settie Hill in bumper at Market
Rasen on debut, collared only late on: sold £100,000 in June. *Ronald O'Leary, Ireland*

PEGGIES VENTURE 6 b.m. Presenting – Peggies Run (Kayf Tara) [2016/17 b87: **h97**
b17.7d² ab16g* b15.8d² h20.7s⁴ h16g h17.7g⁴ Apr 12] smallish, sturdy mare: fairly useful **b99**
form in bumpers: won mares event at Lingfield in November: neck second to Oscar Rose
in listed mares event at Huntingdon following month: modest form in maiden/novice
hurdles: bred to stay at least 2½m: usually races prominently. *Alan King*

PEKANHEIM (IRE) 9 b.g. Putra Pekan – Delheim (IRE) (Un Desperado (FR)) [2016/17 **c92**
c113, h88: h19.3mᵘʳ h16.2d c17.3g² c15.6d c17.3d³ c17.3d⁴ c21.2g² c20.1d³ c20.1s⁶ **h65**
c15.5g³ c19.9g⁴ c19.9g* h16.4g⁶ c15.6g² Apr 25] poor handicap hurdler: modest handicap
chaser: won at Musselburgh in March: stays 2½m: acts on heavy going: has worn
cheekpieces, including in 2016/17: often races towards rear. *Martin Todhunter*

PEMBA (FR) 5 ch.m. Zanzibari (USA) – Ayaam (IRE) (Danehill (USA)) [2016/17 h113: **c107**
h16d² h20.6g⁵ c16.2s² c16.3s* c20d³ Jan 19] tall mare: fair handicap hurdler: fair form over **h113**
fences: best effort when second in novice at Warwick in November: left Alan King after
first start: unproven beyond 17f: acts on heavy going: usually in cheekpieces in 2016/17.
Fergal O'Brien

PEMBRIDGE 8 b.m. Kayf Tara – Supreme Gem (IRE) (Supreme Leader) [2016/17 h66: **h73**
h15.8g⁴ h19.9g h15.8g h22m* h21.6m³ h20.3m⁶ Sep 27] poor handicap hurdler: won at
Stratford in August: best effort at 2¾m: acts on good to firm going: wears tongue tie:
usually races towards rear. *Adrian Wintle*

PEMBROKE HOUSE 10 gr.g. Terimon – Bon Coeur (Gunner B) [2016/17 c104, h86: **c100**
c20g² c16.3g² c20.9v⁴ c18.9s² c16v³ c15.7d³ c21.2g³ c16m² c16m³ Apr 25] winning **h–**
hurdler: fair handicap chaser: stays 2½m: acts on good to firm and heavy going: wears
cheekpieces. *Sarah-Jayne Davies*

PENA DORADA (IRE) 10 b.g. Key of Luck (USA) – Uluwatu (IRE) (Unfuwain (USA)) **c105**
[2016/17 c115, h–: c26.2m² c25.5d³ c24g³ c25.5g³ c24.2d³ c24.5d⁴ c26.2d³ c26.6g⁴ Feb 4] **h–**
stocky gelding: winning hurdler: fair handicap chaser nowadays: left Alistair Whillans
after seventh start: stays 27f: acts on soft and good to firm going: has worn cheekpieces,
including in 2016/17: front runner/races prominently. *Alan J. Brown*

PENDRA (IRE) 9 ch.g. Old Vic – Mariah Rollins (IRE) (Over The River (FR)) [2016/17 **c148**
c145, h–: c26g² Mar 16] rather plain gelding: winning hurdler: smart handicap chaser: off **h–**
11 months, at least as good as ever when ¾-length second of 24 to Domesday Book in
Fulke Walwyn Kim Muir Chase at Cheltenham, only outing in 2016/17: stays 3¼m: acts on
good to firm and heavy going: blinkered at Cheltenham, in cheekpieces previous 4 starts.
Charlie Longsdon

PEN HER IN 7 b.m. Lucarno (USA) – Two A Penny (Classic Cliche (IRE)) [2016/17 **h–**
h16.8g⁶ h22.1mᵘʳ h22.1gᵖᵘ h16.8dᵖᵘ h15.7gᵖᵘ Jan 12] first foal: dam winning pointer: no
form over hurdles: wears headgear. *Kenneth Slack*

PENHILL 6 b.g. Mount Nelson – Serrenia (IRE) (High Chaparral (IRE)) [2016/17 **h152**
h16g* h17m⁶ h16.5g* h16s* h16s* h16d⁴ h24s* h24g* h24d² Apr 26]

Racehorse ownership is an expensive pastime but it isn't quite on the same
level as owning a football club just yet. It has been reported that £250m has been
spent by Brighton & Hove Albion owner Tony Bloom since 2009 when he took
control of the club, which gained promotion to the Premier League in the latest
season. At the time of the purchase, Bloom was described in one newspaper as a
'multi-millionaire property developer', but his story is perhaps a great deal more
interesting than that. His love of sports betting developed from a young age—fake
IDs allowed him to place bets in bookmakers from the age of fifteen while still a
student at £23,000-a-year Lancing College—and by the time he left his first full-
time job (after studying mathematics at Manchester University) with accountancy
firm Ernst & Young, he was reportedly earning a tidy sum from gambling. Bloom
gambled professionally in the mid-'nineties before starting work for bookmaker
Victor Chandler, using his mathematical background to develop the company's
international betting operation, specifically focusing on Asian handicap football
betting. Bloom's crowning moment at Victor Chandler came in the World Cup Final
at France '98, when the bookmaker reportedly risked all of its profits for the whole

tournament on a French 'home' win in the final—France won 3-0. Sports betting was not the only form of gambling which Bloom mastered. Tony 'The Lizard' Bloom is believed to have netted over three million dollars playing live poker, a venture which he treats as a hobby, although he competes at the highest level against professional poker players. Bloom's poker nickname stuck and was the inspiration behind the name Starlizard which was given to his next venture, a betting consultancy employing over a hundred and fifty which predicts the outcome of football matches using complex mathematical calculations.

On top of his football, poker and business interests, Bloom has also made his mark in the racing world, and enjoyed success in the 2009 Wokingham Stakes with High Standing, a horse owned in partnership with Harry Findlay, a larger-than-life professional gambler who is perhaps best known for his connection with Gold Cup winner Denman. High Standing went on to win the Hackwood Stakes at Newbury and was placed in the Sprint Cup at Haydock in the purple and white colours of Findlay & Bloom during the 2009 season, but the partnership between the pair came to an end shortly after. 'It's not a question of us falling out,' Findlay said at the time, 'What it comes down to is that we're looking for completely different types of horses, he's more interested in having a horse or two for big meetings like Royal Ascot. For me, it's a full-time thing, and the big enjoyment is having horses that will be running all the time, and going to see them work in the morning and all the rest of it.' The pair's forty-strong string was dissolved, with Bloom taking over ownership of High Standing as well as some of the other better horses, including listed-winning three-year-old Triple Aspect. Bloom has continued his interest in horses on both the Flat and over jumps, Librisa Breeze winning two big handicaps, the International Stakes and the Challenge Cup, at Ascot in 2016, while the ill-fated Little Josh won the 2010 Paddy Power Gold Cup and 2012 Grand Sefton Chase at Aintree. The useful handicap hurdlers Sleep Easy and Templeross also carried his royal blue, white seams with distinction during the most recent jumps season. However, arguably Bloom's finest moment as an owner—while he has been on his own at least—came when Penhill won the Spa Novices' Hurdle at the latest Cheltenham Festival.

Penhill was purchased out of James Bethell's yard for 230,000 guineas after the 2014 season, and made his first start in Bloom's colours a winning one when taking a mile and a half handicap at Ascot from a mark of 86 for his new trainer Luca Cumani. Penhill had won three times for Bethell as a three-year-old and, a strong-travelling enthusiastic sort during his earlier days, had shaped like a non-stayer in

Albert Bartlett Novices' Hurdle (Spa), Cheltenham—
the sixth and biggest win of a tremendous campaign for Penhill (right) who pulls away from
fellow Irish raider Monalee (stars) and Wholestone

the 2014 Melrose Handicap at York on his only start beyond a mile and a half, though he had looked comfortable running in what is often one of the most hotly contested three-year-old handicaps of the season. Penhill was kept to a mile and a half during his time with Cumani, winning a second race for that yard at Haydock and running creditably in both the Old Newton Cup (fourth) and the November Handicap (sixth). Penhill joined Willie Mullins after the 2015 season and began life for Ireland's champion jumps trainer in a modest maiden hurdle at Tramore in early-May, when he justified odds of 11/4-on with the minimum of fuss. Penhill's progress for Mullins continued throughout the summer of 2016, with the only blip coming on his second start at Killarney, though he was found to have bled after dropping away tamely that day. He did plenty wrong on his next start in a novice hurdle at the Galway Festival, taking a keen hold and making early jumping errors before eventually surging home in remarkable fashion to win by half a length having been only sixth (and matched at 1000/1 in running on the Betfair Exchange) when putting in another untidy leap at the last.

Early jumping errors were also a feature on Penhill's next couple of starts, though he still won both times, in a novice hurdle at Listowel and the Grade 3 Joe Mac Novices' Hurdle at Tipperary in October. Penhill couldn't land the four-timer on his first start at Grade 1 level in the Royal Bond at Fairyhouse in December (incidentally a race in which subsequent Supreme Novices' Hurdle winner Labaik refused to race), but he was hampered by the fall of Peace News at the second last flight and just kept on at one pace for fourth behind stablemate Airlie Beach (Penhill was the first string of the three Mullins runners). Up until that point Penhill had been kept to around two miles, but he resumed winning ways in the three-mile Guinness Novices' Hurdle at Limerick later in December, winning easily from Call The Taxie. The race had provided two future Cheltenham Festival winners in its last

Mr Tony Bloom's "Penhill"

three renewals, having been Faugheen's last port of call before he won the Baring Bingham in 2014, and Martello Tower's penultimate pre-Festival run when he won the Spa in 2015. The race, which has had various sponsors, was upgraded from a Grade 3 to a Grade 2 in 2015 and Penhill provided further justification for that change when following up his seven-length win in the race by becoming its latest winner to go on to success at Cheltenham. The Spa—branded as the Albert Bartlett Novices' Hurdle—can often be a searching test of stamina but, despite attracting the usual big field, the latest renewal was run at a muddling pace and several of the main protagonists, including 13/8 favourite Death Duty, who was held when unseating his rider at the last, failed to run up to expectations. Penhill's Flat background equipped him well to cope with a fairly tactical affair on good ground (only two flights are jumped in the final seven furlongs on Cheltenham's New Course), but he still had to overcome some trouble in running, being hampered and forced wide as a result of the fall of The Worlds End at the second last, which also badly impeded the eventual fourth Constantine Bay. Despite meeting trouble, Penhill loomed up alongside the hard-ridden Monalee (who had been up with the pace throughout) before the last, where he sealed the race with a good jump, eventually winning by three and a half lengths from Monalee, with Wholestone a further four lengths back in third.

Hold-up tactics didn't serve Penhill quite so well on his final start in the War of Attrition (branded as the Irish Daily Mirror Novices' Hurdle') at Punchestown, and he would undoubtedly have made more of a race of it with the Martin Pipe Conditional Jockeys' Handicap Hurdle winner Champagne Classic had he not given the strong-staying winner such a head start (he finished second, beaten two and a quarter lengths). Mullins is no stranger to bringing ex-Flat horses back to their original sphere and this was a possible avenue mentioned by connections after Penhill's Cheltenham Festival win, though he wasn't seen out during the summer. Nichols Canyon finally broke his trainer's duck in the Stayers' Hurdle at the latest Cheltenham Festival and that race appeals as a possible target for Penhill in the next season. He has a similar profile to the reigning title-holder and it could turn out to be a tricky decision for Ruby Walsh choosing between the pair. If Walsh were to opt for Nichols Canyon, it is worth bearing in mind that his understudy Paul Townend is unbeaten on three rides on Penhill, including in the Spa.

Penhill is the second foal out of the unraced Serrenia, a daughter of High Chaparral who is a close relative or half-sister to no fewer than ten winners on the Flat, notably the Hollywood Derby runner-up Fast And Furious and Herboriste, a Grade 2 winner over a mile and a half in the States. Another of her half-sisters produced the 2010 Derby runner-up At First Sight. A couple of Serrenia's siblings, Hartside and Western Ridge, have also been fair winners over hurdles. Penhill's sire Mount Nelson is also the sire of the same owner's very smart six- and seven-furlong performer Librisa Breeze, his best Flat horse from eight seasons at Newsells Park Stud, but Mount Nelson was switched to dual purpose production at Boardsmill Stud in County Meath for the latest covering season. Penhill travels strongly in his races and is often held up off the pace. He acts on soft going and stays three miles. He wore ear plugs at Cheltenham. *W. P. Mullins, Ireland*

PENMORE MILL (IRE) 12 b.g. Shernazar – Stephens Street (IRE) (Kahyasi) [2016/17 c122: c22.5d* c22.6m* c22.7s³ c23.8sᵖᵘ Mar 23] multiple winning pointer: fairly useful chaser: won hunters at Uttoxeter and Stratford (lady riders) in May: stays 27f: acts on good to firm and heavy going. *T. A. Hutsby*   **c120**

PENNIES AND POUNDS 10 b.m. Sir Harry Lewis (USA) – Sense of Value (Trojan Fen) [2016/17 c–, h–: h19.9g h19g h19.6g² Apr 22] poor handicap hurdler: no promise only outing over fences: stays 2½m: best form on good going. *Julian Smith*   **c–**
  h68

PENN LANE (IRE) 6 b.g. Scorpion (IRE) – Belsalsa (FR) (Kingsalsa (USA)) [2016/17 **h118 p** h112p, b104: h20.6g* May 6] lightly-raced gelding: bumper winner: fairly useful form over hurdles: won novice at Market Rasen on sole outing in 2016/17: will stay beyond 2½m: likely to progress further. *Warren Greatrex*

PENNYS DOUBLE 7 ch.m. Double Trigger (IRE) – Pennys Pride (IRE) (Pips Pride) **h68** [2016/17 h23.3dpu h23.3dpu h16.2d⁴ Sep 16] poor form over hurdles: should stay beyond 2m. *Keith Reveley*

PENNYWELL (IRE) 7 b.m. Gold Well – Boyne Bridge (IRE) (Lord Americo) [2016/17 **h102** h99: h23.3g³ May 14] compact mare: winning Irish pointer: fair maiden hurdler: stays 23f: acts on heavy going: in cheekpieces sole outing in 2016/17. *Warren Greatrex*

PENSION MADNESS (IRE) 4 b.g. Vocalised (USA) – Grinneas (IRE) (Barathea **h95** (IRE)) [2016/17 h16.8s h17.7d h16.3d³ h16.7s⁶ h19.9vpu h16d⁵ h18.5g⁶ Apr 11] compact gelding: half-brother to fair hurdler Morning With Ivan (2m/17f winner, by Ivan Denisovich), stays 2½m: modest maiden on Flat, stays 13f: modest maiden hurdler: unproven beyond 2m: acts on good to soft going: in headgear last 3 starts. *Mark Usher*

PENTIFFIC (NZ) 14 br.g. Pentire – Sailing High (NZ) (Yachtie (AUS)) [2016/17 c121§: **c120 §** c32.5g⁴ c24s³ c24.1d² c26.3g Mar 17] sturdy gelding: fairly useful chaser: placed in hunters at Warwick and Haydock, easily best efforts in 2016/17: stays 33f: acts on soft going: has worn headgear: unreliable. *P. P. C. Turner*

PENZFLO (IRE) 11 b.m. Luso – Penzita (IRE) (The Bart (USA)) [2016/17 h88: h21.6s⁵ **c–** c24vur Jun 20] lightly-raced maiden pointer/hurdler: blinkered/tongue tied, unseated rider **h–** first only chase start: dead. *Johnny Farrelly*

PEPPAY LE PUGH (IRE) 6 b.g. Arakan (USA) – Pinaflore (FR) (Formidable (USA)) **h96 §** [2016/17 h94: h16.2dpu h16.5g⁶ h16.7d⁵ h19.4g⁵ h16s h15.3s⁶ h19.7d⁴ h15.8s² h15.7g Apr 21] modest maiden hurdler: best around 2m: acts on soft going: often in headgear: tried in tongue tie: usually races freely: temperamental. *David Dennis*

PEPPERELLO 6 b.g. Lucky Story (USA) – Rhuby River (IRE) (Bahhare (USA)) **h–** [2016/17 h15.7v⁶ h15.8g h16.3dpu h15.8g h19.7spu h15.8vpu Dec 16] poor maiden on Flat: no form over hurdles: tried in hood/tongue tie. *Laura Hurley*

PERCEUS 5 b.g. Sir Percy – Lady Hestia (USA) (Belong To Me (USA)) [2016/17 h112: **h–** h20gpu Oct 14] fair hurdler: stayed 2½m: acted on heavy going: dead. *James Eustace*

PERCY'S ENDEAVOUR 4 b.f. Sir Percy – Bruma (IRE) (Footstepsinthesand) [2016/17 **h–** h17.2dpu Aug 29] well held 4 starts on Flat: pulled up in juvenile on hurdling debut. *Mark Walford*

PERCYS PRINCESS 6 b.m. Sir Percy – Enford Princess (Pivotal) [2016/17 h15.7gpu **h–** Aug 14] fair on Flat, stays 1¾m: no promise in mares novice on hurdling debut. *Michael Appleby*

PERCY STREET 4 br.c. Sir Percy – Star of Gibraltar (Rock of Gibraltar (IRE)) [2016/17 **h117** h16.3d⁴ h16.5g* h16s² h16g⁶ h16.4g⁶ h15.7m³ Apr 2] compact colt: useful on Flat, stays 1½m: fairly useful form over hurdles: won novice at Taunton in January: best effort when third in juvenile handicap at Ascot final start: likely to stay further than 2m: acts on good to firm going: often races prominently. *Nicky Henderson*

PEREGRINE RUN (IRE) 7 b.g. King's Theatre (IRE) – Masriyna's Article (IRE) **h141** (Definite Article) [2016/17 h16d h20d h20g* h20g* h21d* h21.1g* h21s³ h21.1g Mar 15] good-topped gelding: fourth foal: brother to useful hurdler Takeyourcapoff (2m-2½m winner): dam (b96) bumper winner: bumper winner: useful hurdler: won maiden at Down Royal in August, handicap at Gowran in September, listed novice at Limerick in October and Hyde Novices' Hurdle at Cheltenham (by length from Wholestone) in November: third in Leamington Novices' Hurdle at Warwick (9¼ lengths behind Willoughby Court) in January: stays 21f: acts on soft going: strong traveller. *Peter Fahey, Ireland*

PERENNIAL 8 ch.g. Motivator – Arum Lily (USA) (Woodman (USA)) [2016/17 h94§: **h– §** h20gpu Jul 21] maiden hurdler: modest form at best: stays 3m: acts on soft and good to firm going: in headgear last 5 starts: not straightforward and one to be wary of. *Philip Kirby*

PERFECT CANDIDATE (IRE) 10 b.g. Winged Love (IRE) – Dansana (IRE) (Insan **c152** (USA)) [2016/17 c145, h–: c24.1v c26g² c25.3spu c24.2s* c34.3dpu Apr 8] strong gelding: **h–** winning hurdler: smart handicap chaser: won veterans event at Exeter (by 5 lengths from Whats Happening) in February: possibly amiss in Grand National at Aintree final start, stumbling 5 out and pulled up quickly: stays 27f: acts on heavy going: in cheekpieces last 4 starts: has worn tongue tie. *Fergal O'Brien*

PERFECT HARMONY (IRE) 5 b.g. Definite Article – Brandam Supreme (IRE) **b102**
(Supreme Leader) [2016/17 b16.3s* b16.4g Mar 15] £65,000 4-y-o: tall gelding: second
foal: half-brother to fair hurdler Oak Vintage (2½m winner, by Fruits of Love): dam, ran
once in bumper, also placed in points: fell in Irish maiden point on debut: fairly useful form
in bumpers: won at Newbury (by ½ length from My Mate Mark) in January: 33/1, still
looked in need of experience when 13 lengths eleventh of 22 to Fayonagh in Champion
Bumper at Cheltenham. *Alan King*

PERFECT MOMENT (IRE) 4 b.f. Milan – Faucon (Polar Falcon (USA)) [2016/17 **b74**
b12.4d⁴ ab16g⁶ Mar 6] leggy, lightly-built filly: closely related to 2 winners, including
bumper winner/useful hurdler As I Am (2m-2½m winner, by Old Vic), and half-sister to 2
winners, including bumper winner/fairly useful hurdler Western Way (19f-3m winner, by
Westerner): dam 11f winner: showed a little ability both starts in bumpers. *Don Cantillon*

PERFECT PIRATE 5 b.g. Black Sam Bellamy (IRE) – Supreme Gem (IRE) (Supreme **h123**
Leader) [2016/17 b16g h21d* h22.7v² h19.9s⁴ Mar 18] £6,000 3-y-o: fourth foal: closely **b–**
related to fairly useful hurdler River Arrow (2½m winner) and poor hurdler Pembridge
(2¾m winner), both by Kayf Tara: dam (h81) lightly-raced half-sister to winning hurdler/
fairly useful chaser (stayed 27f) He's The Gaffer: behind in maiden bumper on debut:
fairly useful form over hurdles: won novice at Towcester in December: best effort when
second in similar event at Kelso, suited by emphasis on stamina: will stay at least 3m.
Ben Pauling

PERFECT POISON (IRE) 9 b.g. Vinnie Roe (IRE) – Noddys Confusion (IRE) **c– x**
(Supreme Leader) [2016/17 h98: c19.4m⁵ c21.2mᵘʳ c20gᵖᵘ h23.1g² h22.1d* h25m* Oct 11] **h110**
fair handicap hurdler: won at Cartmel in August and Huntingdon final start: no form over
fences (let down by jumping last 2 starts): stays 25f: acts on good to firm and good to soft
going: has worn cheekpieces, including in 2016/17. *Donald McCain*

PERFECT SUMMER (IRE) 7 b.m. High Chaparral (IRE) – Power of Future (GER) **h108**
(Definite Article) [2016/17 h97: h16.3m* h20d* h20.3v* h20.3g³ h24m³ Sep 27] fair
hurdler: won mares novice seller at Stratford in May, and mares handicap at Aintree and
conditionals handicap at Southwell in June: stays 2½m: acts on good to firm and heavy
going: wears headgear: front runner/races prominently. *Ian Williams*

PERFECT TIMING 9 b.g. Shantou (USA) – Winnetka Gal (IRE) (Phardante (FR)) **c118**
[2016/17 c123, h–: c21gᵖᵘ c19.4d c19.2g c22.6g⁴ c20.1s² c19.9m* c19.7m* Apr 11] strong **h–**
gelding: maiden hurdler: fairly useful handicap chaser: won at Huntingdon in October and
Plumpton in April: stays 3m: acts on good to firm and heavy going: wears headgear: tried
in tongue tie. *Neil Mulholland*

PERFECT TIMING (FR) 7 b.m. Sassanian (USA) – Royale Sulawesie (FR) (Jimble **h–**
(FR)) [2016/17 h71: h22gᵖᵘ h23.9g h20.7s⁵ h18.7g⁵ Apr 1] maiden hurdler, no form in
2016/17: left Paul Webber after first start: tried in cheekpieces/tongue tie. *Andrew Martin*

PERFORM (IRE) 8 b.g. King's Theatre (IRE) – Famous Lady (IRE) (Presenting) **h126**
[2016/17 h130p: h20g⁶ h23.9g⁴ Apr 9] strong gelding: handicap hurdler, very lightly raced:
better effort (fairly useful form) in 2016/17 when sixth of 15 at Aintree in October: stays
3m. *Philip Hobbs*

PERIQUEST 8 b.g. Overbury (IRE) – Rippling Brook (Phardante (FR)) [2016/17 h100: **h79**
h19.9v h21.4d⁵ Feb 18] lightly-raced handicap hurdler, fair at best: stays 21f: acts on soft
going: wears tongue tie. *Alex Hales*

PERMISSION GRANTED (IRE) 5 b.g. Oscar (IRE) – Ask The Misses (IRE) **b–**
(Supreme Leader) [2016/17 b17d Apr 5] tailed off in bumper on debut. *Rose Dobbin*

PERSAVERANCE 4 b.g. Sir Percy – Marliana (IRE) (Mtoto) [2016/17 h16s h16.3d **h–**
h16.3s Mar 3] lengthy gelding: fair maiden on Flat, stays 1½m: well held in juvenile
hurdles. *Gary Moore*

PERSEID (IRE) 7 br.g. Robin des Pres (FR) – Cowanstown Miss (IRE) (Presenting) **h108**
[2016/17 h97: h19.3m⁵ h23.1d* h23.3d⁵ h16.8d* h20.6s⁶ h19.9s Apr 1] fair handicap
hurdler: won at Bangor in May and Sedgefield in December: stays 3m: acts on soft and
good to firm going: front runner/races prominently. *Sue Smith*

PERSHING 6 gr.g. Mount Nelson – La Gandilie (FR) (Highest Honor (FR)) [2016/17 **c–**
h100: h16.2s⁴ h16.2s⁵ c16d Oct 6] maiden hurdler, fair at best: well held in novice at **h77**
Tramore on chasing debut: raced around 2m: acts on soft going: usually wears headgear:
wears tongue tie: front runner/races prominently, usually finds little. *Robert Hennessy,
Ireland*

PERSIAN BREEZE 5 b.m. Pivotal – Persian Jasmine (Dynaformer (USA)) [2016/17 **h72**
h95: h20g⁶ h16g⁵ h19.5g⁴ h16d h20d Oct 30] close-coupled mare: poor maiden hurdler:
left Lucy Wadham after first start: unproven beyond 2m: acts on soft going: in cheekpieces
final start. *Donald Cashman, Ireland*

PERSIAN DELIGHT 7 b.g. Lucarno (USA) – Persian Walk (FR) (Persian Bold) **h123**
[2016/17 h19.5d² h19.5s³ h21.4d* Feb 18] useful bumper winner, missed 2015/16: fairly
useful form over hurdles: won handicap at Wincanton final start by neck from Driftwood
Haze: stays 21f: wears tongue tie. *Paul Nicholls*

PERSIAN FASHION (IRE) 8 b.m. Lahib (USA) – Kiera's Gale (IRE) (Strong Gale) **h–**
[2016/17 h–: h16sᵖᵘ Feb 14] no sign of ability in bumper/over hurdles: sometimes in
tongue tie. *Ian Duncan*

PERSIAN SNOW (IRE) 11 b.g. Anshan – Alpine Message (Tirol) [2016/17 c20s* c20s* **c128**
Mar 2] good-topped gelding: winning hurdler: hunter chaser nowadays: off 22 months, **h–**
fairly useful form when winning at Ludlow in February and March on only starts in
2016/17: best around 2½m: acts on good to firm and heavy going: wears tongue tie.
Philip Hobbs

PERSIAN STEEL (IRE) 5 ch.g. Lucarno (USA) – Persian Walk (FR) (Persian Bold) **b70**
[2016/17 b–: b15.7d⁴ Nov 29] poor form in bumpers: fairly useful winner at 1½m on Flat
in January. *Brian Ellison*

PERSONAL SHOPPER 10 b.m. King's Theatre (IRE) – Island Hopper (Be My Native **c82**
(USA)) [2016/17 c78, h83: h17.8g⁶ c18.5d² c20g³ c18.5d³ h18.2d c20g h23g⁶ h18.5g⁵ h20s **h74**
c21.5d⁵ c20.5sᵖᵘ c20sᵖᵘ Dec 26] poor handicap hurdler: poor maiden chaser: stays 23f: acts
on good to firm and heavy going: has worn headgear, including in 2016/17. *Harry Smyth,
Ireland*

PERSPICACE 6 b.g. Sir Percy – Cassique Lady (IRE) (Langfuhr (CAN)) [2016/17 h111: **h118**
h15.8g² h20m* h15.8g* h16.3m h18.5g⁴ h23m³ h20g h24.7g h19s⁶ h19g* Mar 2] fairly
useful hurdler: won handicaps at Worcester and Uttoxeter in May, and seller at Taunton
final start: stays 23f: acts on good to firm and good to soft going: wears headgear: has worn
tongue tie, including in 2016/17. *David Pipe*

PERTUIS (IRE) 11 gr.g. Verglas (IRE) – Lady Killeen (IRE) (Marju (IRE)) [2016/17 **h–**
h16dᵘʳ h19.3s h16.4v⁶ Mar 18] leggy gelding: maiden hurdler, no form in 2016/17: has
worn headgear. *Micky Hammond*

PERUVIEN BLEU (FR) 5 b.g. Fuisse (FR) – Edelmira (FR) (Kahyasi) [2016/17 h16g **h123**
h15.3m³ h15.9g⁵ h16.8s³ h16.8m³ h16.8g³ h15.7g* h15.5g² h15.8s⁴ h16.2s h15.8d³
h15.8m* Apr 25] rather unfurnished gelding: first foal: dam (h110) French 2m hurdle
winner: once-raced maiden on Flat: fairly useful hurdler: won handicap at Towcester in
November and novice at Ludlow final start: raced around 2m: acts on soft and good to firm
going: has worn tongue tie. *Nick Williams*

PETAPENKO 6 b.g. Archipenko (USA) – Tricoteuse (Kris) [2016/17 h102, b88: h16.2d⁴ **h92**
h22.1m⁴ Jun 24] bumper winner: modest maiden hurdler: unproven beyond 17f: sometimes
in blinkers. *Donald McCain*

PETERBROWN (IRE) 9 b.g. Shantou (USA) – Grove Juliet (IRE) (Moscow Society **c106**
(USA)) [2016/17 c101, h–: c24.2m⁶ c23.8d* c23m* h26.5m³ c25.8m⁵ Aug 31] dual **h98**
winning pointer: modest maiden hurdler: fair form over fences: won handicaps at Ffos Las
in June and Worcester in July: left Mrs K. Heard after first start: stays 3¼m: acts on good
to firm and heavy going: tried in cheekpieces. *Philip Hobbs*

PETER FROM PARIS (IRE) 11 b.g. Pierre – Queensfold Flame (IRE) (Royal **c100**
Fountain) [2016/17 c30dᵖᵘ c25.2s³ Mar 8] maiden pointer: winning hurdler: fair form over **h–**
fences: left D. E. Prendergast after first start: stays 25f: acts on heavy going: in cheekpieces
final outing: usually leads. *Miss J. E. Gillam*

PETERGATE 6 b.g. Alhaarth (USA) – Shamayel (Pivotal) [2016/17 h58: h16.8gᵖᵘ h18.7m **h78**
h20g* h22g³ h21.6gᵖᵘ Apr 21] poor handicap hurdler: won selling event at Worcester in
July: reportedly lame when pulled up final outing: stays 2½m: acts on good to soft going:
wears headgear: in tongue tie last 3 starts. *Nigel Hawke*

PETERPANOPIRATEMAN (IRE) 8 b.g. Kalanisi (IRE) – Year'fthehorse (IRE) **h–**
(Zaffaran (USA)) [2016/17 h67: h16sᵖᵘ h19.5v h23.6s Mar 13] third in Irish maiden point:
maiden hurdler, no form in 2016/17: tried in hood. *Ben Case*

PETERS GREY (IRE) 7 gr.g. Aussie Rules (USA) – Aliyshan (IRE) (Darshaan) **h–**
[2016/17 h106: h16v⁴¹ Jan 30] maiden hurdler, fair at best: off 20 months, well held only
outing in 2016/17: raced around 2m: acts on good to firm and heavy going. *R. Mike Smith*

32RedSport.com Veterans' Handicap Chase (Final), Sandown—
a typically game display out in front by Pete The Feat (centre), who holds off Theatrical Star (right)
and stable-companion Loose Chips (blinkers)

PETER SILVER (FR) 6 b.g. Silver Cross (FR) – Sainte Mante (FR) (Saint des Saints (FR)) [2016/17 c–, h106: h19d³ h24v⁵ h23.1g Jul 31] maiden hurdler, modest form at best in Britain: twice-raced maiden over fences: stays 2¼m: best form on soft/heavy going: has worn headgear, including in 2016/17: in tongue tie final start: usually races close up: has joined Gordon Elliott. *Giles Smyly* **c–** **h98**

PETER THE HORSE 10 b.g. Groom Dancer (USA) – Broughton Melody (Alhijaz) [2016/17 h–: h20g h23gᵖᵘ Aug 21] bumper winner: no form over hurdles. *Joanne Thomason-Murphy* **h–**

PETER THE MAYO MAN (IRE) 7 ch.g. Dylan Thomas (IRE) – Mommkin (Royal Academy (USA)) [2016/17 h108p: h16g* h16g* h16.3g* h15.6g² h16g³ h16.5d⁶ Apr 25] useful hurdler: won novices at Worcester and Warwick in September, and handicap at Newbury (by 11 lengths from Clayton) in November: third in Dovecote Novices' Hurdle at Kempton (6½ lengths behind River Wylde) in February: raced around 2m: best form on good going. *Neil Mulholland* **h132**

PETE THE FEAT (IRE) 13 b.g. King's Theatre (IRE) – Tourist Attraction (IRE) (Pollerton) [2016/17 c131, h–: c27.2s c25.5d³ c24.2s* c24.2s⁵ c26g⁵ Mar 25] angular gelding: winning hurdler: fairly useful handicap chaser nowadays: won Veterans' Handicap Chase Final at Sandown in January by 2 lengths from Theatrical Star: stays 29f: acts on heavy going: wears tongue tie: front runner/races prominently. *Charlie Longsdon* **c128** **h–**

PETETHEPEAR (IRE) 7 br.g. Pierre – Rockababy (IRE) (King's Ride) [2016/17 h125, b88: h23.9g c24.2dᵖᵘ Mar 21] fairly useful hurdler at best: pulled up only outing over fences: stayed 3m: acted on soft going: tried in cheekpieces: front runner/raced prominently: dead. *Stuart Edmunds* **c–** **h–**

PETIT ECUYER (FR) 11 b.g. Equerry (USA) – Petite Majeste (FR) (Riverquest (FR)) [2016/17 c74§, h–: c21.2g⁴ h16.7g Jul 3] sturdy gelding: winning hurdler: poor handicap chaser: stays 29f: acts on heavy going: has worn headgear, including last 4 starts: often races in rear: unreliable. *Dai Williams* **c– §** **h–**

PETITE GANACHE (IRE) 5 ch.g. Presenting – Ain't Misbehavin (IRE) (Trempolino (USA)) [2016/17 h16.7d h16v h20.6sᵖᵘ h16.2g Apr 25] good-topped gelding: no form in novice hurdles. *Nicky Richards* **h–**

PETITE JACK 4 ch.g. Champs Elysees – Pilcomayo (IRE) (Rahy (USA)) [2016/17 h16.8g⁶ Aug 10] useful on Flat, stays 1½m: 20/1, last of 6 in juvenile at Newton Abbot on hurdling debut: should do better. *Neil King* **h– p**

PETITE POWER (IRE) 8 b.g. Subtle Power (IRE) – Little Serena (Primitive Rising (USA)) [2016/17 h108, b80: h26.4m⁴ h23.9d h23.1d* c20v² c23.6d* h23.4d⁶ c23.6gᶠ c23.8g⁴ h26.6g⁴ Apr 27] winning pointer: fair handicap hurdler: won at Bangor in January: fairly useful form over fences: won novice handicap at Huntingdon in February: left Ali Stronge after second start: stays 3m: acts on good to soft going: has worn cheekpieces, including in 2016/17: wears tongue tie. *Fergal O'Brien* **c125** **h113**

PETIT MOUCHOIR (FR) 6 gr.g. Al Namix (FR) – Arnette (FR) (Denham Red **h162**
(FR)) [2016/17 h151, b108: h16d² h16g³ h16.4sᶠ h16d* h16g* h16.4g³ Mar 14]

With the various to-ings and fro-ings that took place in the autumn when
owners Gigginstown House Stud and Ann and Alan Potts moved members of their
powerful strings, trainer Henry de Bromhead was one of the biggest losers. Not
much could make up for the loss of the Potts-owned future Gold Cup winner Sizing
John whom he had previously trained, but de Bromhead still had plenty of big-race
success with transfers from other yards, including the leading chasers Champagne
West (ex-Philip Hobbs), Sub Lieutenant (ex-Sandra Hughes) and Valseur Lido
(ex-Willie Mullins). The last-named was switched after Gigginstown's split with
Mullins which was also the source for Petit Mouchoir. Ironically, Petit Mouchoir had
begun his career with Gordon Elliott who ended up receiving most of the Gigginstown
horses transferred from Mullins. Elliott used to have the job of educating some of
the younger Gigginstown horses before their dispersal to other yards and, after
Petit Mouchoir had won his only start in points and then made a winning debut
under Rules in the Goffs Land Rover Bumper at the 2015 Punchestown Festival, he
was sent to Closutton. Mullins and his agent Harold Kirk had been responsible for
buying him on Gigginstown's behalf for €100,000 at the Goffs Land Rover Sale as
an unbroken three-year-old. His only win for Mullins came in a maiden at Thurles
on his hurdling debut but he still developed into one of the leading novice hurdlers of
2015/16, coming within a neck of causing a 40/1 shock in the Top Novices' Hurdle
at Aintree. Petit Mouchoir went on to also finish a close second to Don't Touch It in
the Herald Champion Novices' Hurdle at Punchestown as well (that race technically
took place shortly after the start of the 2016/17 season), but in hindsight it was his
Aintree effort, where he had run Buveur d'Air so close, which was to prove even
better form than it had looked at the time. That didn't really become apparent until
the pair met again in the Champion Hurdle, though by then Petit Mouchoir had won
a couple of Grade 1 contests himself.

Petit Mouchoir made an encouraging first start for de Bromhead in the WKD
Hurdle at Down Royal in November, catching the eye when finishing a close third
of the four runners behind Rashaan and Apple's Jade in a muddling contest in which
he had to be switched between the last two flights and conceded first run. He didn't
get the chance to confirm that promise in the 'Fighting Fifth' Hurdle at Newcastle
later in the month (stable-companion Identity Thief had won both races for the same
connections the previous season) but was in the process of running well when falling
three out, in the process hampering favourite (and fellow Gigginstown performer)

*Ryanair Hurdle, Leopardstown—Petit Mouchoir gains ample compensation for his Newcastle spill
with an impressive all-the-way win*

BHP Insurance Irish Champion Hurdle, Leopardstown—a bit closer this time, as Petit Mouchoir is pressed late by Footpad after Nichols Canyon had crashed out at the last

Apple's Jade who went on to finish a close second (Petit Mouchoir was a 4/1-shot but seemed to be the Gigginstown first string on jockey bookings and looked to be going the better of the pair when he fell). Identity Thief had gone on to finish second to Nichols Canyon in the Ryanair Hurdle (better known as the December Festival Hurdle) at Leopardstown just after Christmas the year before, and Petit Mouchoir took the same route, also coming up against his former stable-companion Nichols Canyon who had again won the Morgiana Hurdle at Punchestown beforehand. Nichols Canyon was sent off at 5/2-on to win the Ryanair again with Petit Mouchoir at 6/1 in a field of five completed by the four-year-olds Jer's Girl, Ivanovich Gorbatov and Footpad, the first two of whom had been placed behind Nichols Canyon in the Morgiana. However, in a race in which the emphasis was on speed, Petit Mouchoir, going with zest in front and jumping fluently, had too much pace for the favourite who did himself no favours by jumping out to his right, particularly at the last couple of flights. Petit Mouchoir was impressive in winning by seven lengths, with Ivanovich Gorbatov faring best of the rest in third. The following month's BHP Insurance Irish Champion Hurdle over the same course and distance looked like taking more winning, at least until the previous year's winner Faugheen, declared to make his return after exactly twelve months off, was announced as being a non-runner the day before. That left a virtual re-run of the previous month's race, with Jer's Girl, last in the Ryanair Hurdle, the only one not to take her chance again. Although pressed harder for the lead this time, once again Petit Mouchoir made all and had too much speed for Nichols Canyon who would probably have finished third but for falling heavily at the last. Mullins' other runner Footpad was closing at the time and went on to reduce Petit Mouchoir's advantage to a length at the line after the winner was untidy at the last, while Ivanovich Gorbatov trailed throughout, finishing a remote last of the three finishers.

Petit Mouchoir ended Mullins' domination of the Irish Champion Hurdle which Hurricane Fly had won five times in a row before the success of Faugheen. On three of those occasions Hurricane Fly won the December Festival Hurdle beforehand, while Istabraq, Macs Joy, Brave Inca and Solwhit were the others to win both races in the same season this century. Henry de Bromhead had previously won the 2008 Irish Champion Hurdle with Sizing Europe (owned by Ann and Alan Potts). Sizing Europe's impressive win at Leopardstown over the previous year's winner Hardy Eustace meant he started the 2/1 favourite for the Champion Hurdle but, after being poised full of running going to two out at Cheltenham, he capitulated so badly that he finished a tailed-off last. Petit Mouchoir's claims at Cheltenham weren't so strong as Sizing Europe's had been, but in an open year he was sent off the 6/1 third favourite and ran creditably, leading until approaching the last and finishing third, seven and a half lengths behind the winner Buveur d'Air.

Petit Mouchoir (FR) (gr.g. 2011)	Al Namix (FR) (gr 1997)	Linamix (gr 1987)	Mendez
			Lunadix
		Dirigeante (b 1991)	Lead On Time
			Daytona
	Arnette (FR) (b 2000)	Denham Red (b 1992)	Pampabird
			Nativelee
		Gashaka (b 1989)	Cariellor
			Ironique

A strong-travelling front runner, the good-topped Petit Mouchoir looks very much at home over two miles for all that he has won a point. His sire Al Namix got another high-class two-mile hurdler in Grandouet, whose wins included the

Gigginstown House Stud's "Petit Mouchoir"

Champion Four Year Old Hurdle at Punchestown and the International Hurdle at Cheltenham, though he is also the sire of Saphir du Rheu who is clearly more of a stayer. Petit Mouchoir's dam is by Un de Sceaux's sire Denham Red, again suggesting speed, though the 2016 Grande Course de Haies winner Ptit Zig is also out of a mare by the same sire. Although Mullins ended up losing Petit Mouchoir, he still has his year-younger half-sister Pravalaguna (by Great Pretender) who made a successful debut over hurdles at Navan in December after winning her sole start on the Flat in France. Their dam Arnette showed just fair form over hurdles in France, mainly competing in claiming company, and she won three times at up to nineteen furlongs, twice at Dieppe and once at Auteuil. Petit Mouchoir's grandam Gashaka produced a Flat winner besides Arnette and won under both codes herself, her wins over jumps coming over hurdles at Auteuil as a three-year-old, though she went on to be placed over fences there at around two and a half miles. Petit Mouchoir acts on heavy going and should make a good novice chaser at around two miles. He wore ear plugs (which were removed at the start) before the Champion Hurdle and he also wore a hood in his early races though he has not done so since finishing eighth in the Supreme at Cheltenham as a novice. *Henry de Bromhead, Ireland*

PETIVILLE (FR) 5 gr.g. Montmartre (FR) – Aegle (IRE) (Night Shift (USA)) [2016/17 b15.8d⁵ b16.2v⁴ h16.3g² h20.2g³ Apr 26] €28,000 3-y-o: fourth foal: half-brother to French 1½m winner Apollon (by Green Tune): dam French 1m/9f winner: poor form in bumpers: fair form over hurdles: better effort when third in maiden at Perth: left Rebecca Curtis after second start: stays 2½m: tried in tongue tie. *Richard Hobson* — **h113 b71**

PETRIFY 7 b.g. Rock of Gibraltar (IRE) – Frigid (Indian Ridge) [2016/17 h–: h15.8d h15.3d³ h15.3s Dec 26] poor form over hurdles: in cheekpieces last 3 starts, in tongue tie last 4. *Bernard Llewellyn* — **h62**

PETROU (IRE) 7 b.g. Mountain High (IRE) – Evnelu (IRE) (Old Vic) [2016/17 h104: h23s h20.3v² Jun 20] fair maiden hurdler: stays 2½m: acts on heavy going: tried in cheekpieces, blinkered in 2016/17: sold £5,000 in August and joined Dan Skelton. *Ben Case* — **h104**

PETRUCCI (IRE) 5 b.g. Azamour (IRE) – Spring Symphony (IRE) (Darshaan) [2016/17 h20.8d h15.7d⁵ h15.8s h15.7s⁵ Mar 20] fairly useful on Flat, stays 11f: poor form over hurdles. *Derek Shaw* — **h84**

PETTAL 6 b.m. Indian Danehill (IRE) – Fields of Home (IRE) (Synefos (USA)) [2016/17 h–, b–: h16.2v h16g⁴ h20.6s⁵ c19.1g c21.1gᴿ Apr 7] no form in various events: in tongue tie last 5 starts. *Sam England* — **c– h– b–**

PETTICOAT TAILS 5 b.m. Presenting – Theatre Girl (King's Theatre (IRE)) [2016/17 b16s* b15.8d* b16d² b17g³ Apr 6] good-topped mare: third foal: sister to fairly useful 3m hurdle winner Call To Order: dam (h135), bumper/2m-2¼m hurdle winner, half-sister to smart hurdler/useful chaser (2m-2½m winner) Ring The Boss: useful form in bumpers: won mares events at Wetherby in November and Huntingdon in February: second in listed mares event at Sandown (½ length behind Cap Soleil) in March and third in Nickel Coin Mares' National Hunt Flat Race at Aintree (in cheekpieces, hung badly left final 1f when beaten 4¼ lengths by Dame Rose) final start. *Warren Greatrex* — **b107**

PHANGIO (USA) 8 ch.g. Invasor (ARG) – Muneera (USA) (Green Dancer (USA)) [2016/17 h24g c22s² c22.5g c25d c16g c23.6m* c23.8vᵖᵘ c22.7f³ c23.6s³ c19.4s c24v⁵ c23.6g² c26.2m* Apr 28] sturdy gelding: fair maiden on Flat, stays 1½m: winning hurdler: fair handicap chaser: won at Chepstow in November and April: left Colin Bowe after fourth start: stays 3¼m: acts on good to firm and heavy going: wears headgear: usually races prominently: sometimes let down by attitude. *Matt Sheppard* — **c104 § h–**

PHANTOMINE (IRE) 5 br.m. Jeremy (USA) – Phantom Waters (Pharly (FR)) [2016/17 b16g Aug 11] sister to useful hurdler Goodwood Mirage (2m winner) and fairly useful hurdler/fair chaser Phantom Prince (17f-2½m winner) and half-sister to several winners: dam 1½m winner: tailed off in mares bumper, in maiden on Flat. *Brendan Powell* — **b–**

PHANTOM ISLE 4 b.g. Teofilo (IRE) – Antillia (Red Ransom (USA)) [2016/17 b16d Mar 31] green when tenth in bumper at Wetherby. *Chris Grant* — **b–**

PHANTOM PRINCE (IRE) 8 b.g. Jeremy (USA) – Phantom Waters (Pharly (FR)) [2016/17 c103, h121: h23.3g h16.8g* h18.2g³ Aug 10] leggy gelding: handicap hurdler, fair nowadays: won at Newton Abbot in July: fair winner only start over fences (in 2015/16): stays 2½m: acts on heavy going: has worn cheekpieces: in tongue tie last 3 starts: often races prominently. *Jimmy Frost* — **c– h112**

PHARAWAYDANTE (IRE) 9 gr.g. Cloudings (IRE) – Waydante (IRE) (Phardante (FR)) [2016/17 c–: c24.2d c21.2m^{pu} May 30] dual winning pointer: no form in 3 hunter chases: in cheekpieces last 2 starts. *Norman Sanderson*   **c–**

PHAR AWAY ISLAND (IRE) 9 br.g. Heron Island (IRE) – Phar From Men (IRE) (Phardante (FR)) [2016/17 h–: h21.4m^3 h21.6g^{pu} h21.6m h26v^{pu} h23v^4 h23.6s* h23.9g h21m h23.1g^6 Apr 11] winning pointer: poor handicap hurdler: won at Chepstow in March: stays 27f: acts on soft going: wears cheekpieces. *John Berwick*   **h79**

PHARE ISLE (IRE) 12 b.g. Turtle Island (IRE) – Pharenna (IRE) (Phardante (FR)) [2016/17 c–x, h108: h25g^3 h24g^4 h25m^5 h23.1m^5 h24.5s^6 h24v^4 h24.4d^4 h21.4d h24s^4 h25g^3 h23.4g* Apr 17] sturdy gelding: fair handicap hurdler: won at Fakenham final start: winning chaser: stays 3¼m: acts on soft and good to firm going: wears cheekpieces/tongue tie: often let down by jumping over fences. *Ben Case*   **c– x** **h100**

PHOBIAPHILIAC (IRE) 6 b.g. Beneficial – Denys Eyre (IRE) (Eurobus) [2016/17 b83: h15.8d^2 h20.3g* h19.5m* h20.5d^{pu} h19g^2 h19.8d^{pu} h20d^{pu} Apr 16] sturdy gelding: fairly useful hurdler: won maiden at Southwell in May and novice at Lingfield in November: stays 2½m: acts on good to firm going: in hood last 3 starts: front runner, tends to find little. *Nicky Henderson*   **h127**

PHOEBUS LESCRIBAA (FR) 5 b.g. Policy Maker (IRE) – Mia Lescribaa (FR) (Saint des Saints (FR)) [2016/17 b16s^3 b15.8g Apr 9] third foal: dam unraced close relative to fair hurdler/fairly useful chaser (stayed 27f) Milord Lescribaa: won Irish maiden point on debut: much better effort (fair form) in bumpers when third at Chepstow in March. *Rebecca Curtis*   **b85**

PHOENICIANA 6 b.m. Phoenix Reach (IRE) – Viciana (Sir Harry Lewis (USA)) [2016/17 b76: b16d^3 b16m^5 h15.7d^3 h15.7d^2 h16v^2 h15.9s^4 Feb 13] modest form in bumpers: fair form in maiden/novice hurdles: will stay 2½m: usually races prominently. *Lucy Wadham*   **h106** **b75**

PHOENIX FIREBIRD 4 b.f. Flying Legend (USA) – Flamebird (IRE) (Mukaddamah (USA)) [2016/17 b16.8s h16.8s^6 h16v Mar 23] £2,000 3-y-o: half-sister to modest hurdler Silver Phoenix (3m winner, by Silver Patriarch): dam (h80), maiden, third on completed start over hurdles: showed little in bumper/mares novice hurdles. *Nigel Hawke*   **h–** **b–**

PICCOMORE 7 b.m. Morpeth – Ivorsagoodun (Piccolo) [2016/17 h–, b–: h21.6g^{pu} Jul 25] no sign of ability in bumpers/over hurdles: sometimes in tongue tie. *Polly Gundry*   **h–**

PICKAMIX 6 gr.g. Sagamix (FR) – Star of Wonder (FR) (The Wonder (FR)) [2016/17 b88: b16.7d* h19.9d* h21.1g^3 h21g^2 h18.6m* Apr 17] fairly useful form in bumpers: won at Market Rasen in June: fairly useful form over hurdles: won conditionals maiden at Uttoxeter in October and novice at Market Rasen final start: will stay beyond 21f: acts on good to firm and good to soft going: in tongue tie last 3 starts. *Charlie Mann*   **h118** **b99**

PICKNICK PARK 5 b.g. Sulamani (IRE) – Eva's Edge (IRE) (Good Thyne (USA)) [2016/17 b63: b16.7d^5 h20.6g^6 h16.7d^6 h18.6s^3 h21.2v^2 h20.6m^6 Apr 9] showed little in bumpers: 100/1, standout effort (probably flattered) over hurdles when third in novice at Market Rasen in January: often races towards rear. *Nick Kent*   **h105?** **b–**

PICTURE PAINTER (IRE) 4 gr.g. Zoffany (IRE) – Sisceal (Dalakhani (IRE)) [2016/17 h19.4g h18.1d Apr 10] fair maiden on Flat, stays 1m: poor form in 2 novice hurdles (wore hood). *Jim Goldie*   **h80**

PIED DU ROI (IRE) 7 b.g. Robin des Pres (FR) – Long Acre (Mark of Esteem (IRE)) [2016/17 h101: c20.3g c20g^2 c21.1g* Aug 18] fair handicap hurdler: similar form over fences: won novice handicap at Fontwell final start: stays 21f: acts on heavy going: wears cheekpieces: often races prominently. *Charlie Longsdon*   **c102** **h–**

PIKARNIA 7 b.g. Authorized (IRE) – Kartuzy (JPN) (Polish Precedent (USA)) [2016/17 b73: b16.2d^6 h16s^4 h17s^3 h16v^{pu} h16.8d^4 h19.9g* h24.1m^2 Apr 13] poor form at best in bumpers: fair form over hurdles: won handicap at Sedgefield in March: stays 3m: acts on soft and good to firm going: in tongue tie last 4 starts. *Rebecca Menzies*   **h105** **b–**

PIKES PEAK (IRE) 8 br.g. Kutub (IRE) – Accordionline (IRE) (Accordion) [2016/17 h77: h23.3d^4 May 7] workmanlike gelding: runner-up on last of 3 starts in Irish maiden points: very lightly-raced maiden over hurdles, modest form. *Chris Grant*   **h88**

PILANSBERG 5 b.g. Rail Link – Posteritas (USA) (Lear Fan (USA)) [2016/17 h–p: h20g* h21.1g h21g^3 h23.5m^2 h21.6g* h19.8g Apr 29] compact gelding: useful hurdler: won novices at Fakenham in October and Fontwell in April: good effort when 1¾ lengths second to Dell' Arca in conditionals handicap at Ascot: stays 3m: acts on good to firm going: in headgear last 5 starts, also tongue tied final outing. *Paul Nicholls*   **h131**

BetBright Handicap Chase, Kempton—James Best excels on the far-from-straightforward Pilgrims Bay (centre) who defeats Double Shuffle (right) and 2016 winner Theatre Guide (stars)

PILGRIMS BAY (IRE) 7 b.g. Turtle Island (IRE) – Lady Ariadna (IRE) (Supreme Leader) [2016/17 h119§, b84§: c20s* c19.4s^F c20.2s² c20.2v³ c24g* c25g Mar 14] workmanlike gelding: fairly useful hurdler: useful form over fences: won novice handicap at Sandown in December and BetBright Chase (Handicap) at Kempton in February, latter by ½ length from Double Shuffle: stays 3m: acts on heavy going: wears headgear: races well off pace: irresolute. *Neil Mulholland* **c135 §**
h–

PILLARD (FR) 5 b.g. Muhaymin (USA) – Ultime Moment (IRE) (Anabaa (USA)) [2016/17 h117: h20.5g³ h19.3d⁵ h15.8g³ h24g⁴ Apr 19] lengthy, sparely-made gelding: fairly useful handicap hurdler: will prove best at short of 3m: acts on heavy going: has worn headgear, including in 2016/17: in tongue tie last 4 starts: often travels strongly. *Jonjo O'Neill* **h119**

PINCH OF GINGER (IRE) 6 ch.g. Golden Lariat (USA) – Espiritu Santo (IRE) (Trans Island) [2016/17 b16.7s⁴ h16.9v³ h23.3v² Mar 28] €1,300 4-y-o: third foal: dam ran once on Flat: off mark in Irish maiden points at second attempt: showed little in bumper: modest form in maiden/novice hurdles. *Donald McCain* **h87**
b69

PINEAPPLE CRUSH (IRE) 5 b.m. Milan – Katie Snurge (IRE) (Snurge) [2016/17 h19.3d⁶ h16.2s³ h19.4g h19.9g⁶ Apr 7] second foal: dam unraced half-sister to fairly useful hurdler/chaser (2m/17f winner) Dominican Monk out of sister to top-class staying chaser The Grey Monk: in frame all 3 starts in Irish mares maiden points: no form over hurdles. *Martin Todhunter* **h–**

PINEAU DE RE (FR) 14 b.g. Maresca Sorrento (FR) – Elfe du Perche (FR) (Abdonski (FR)) [2016/17 c137, h137: c24s^{pu} Apr 30] rather leggy gelding: useful handicap hurdler: smart handicap chaser: won Grand National at Aintree in 2013/14: reportedly retired after pulled up last outing in 2016/17: stayed 35f: acted on heavy going: in cheekpieces last 3 starts: often travelled strongly. *Dr Richard Newland* **c–**
h–

PINEROLO 11 b.g. Milan – Hollybush (IRE) (Ali-Royal (IRE)) [2016/17 c120§, h–§: c24.2d^{pu} c20.3g⁶ c24v* Jun 20] workmanlike gelding: winning hurdler: handicap chaser, fair nowadays: won at Southwell final start: stays 25f: acts on heavy going: has worn headgear, including in 2016/17: in tongue tie last 4 starts: ungenuine. *Joanne Foster* **c104 §**
h– §

PINE WARBLER 8 b.g. Pilsudski (IRE) – Cetti's Warbler (Sir Harry Lewis (USA)) [2016/17 h112: h21d⁶ h23.3v⁵ h23.6s^{pu} h23.3s² Apr 1] fairly useful maiden hurdler: stays 23f: acts on soft going: in cheekpieces second outing: tongue tied last 2 starts. *Stuart Edmunds* **h116**

PING (IRE) 6 b.g. Mahler – Cottavilla (IRE) (Yashgan) [2016/17 h ; h18.6g⁵ h23.9d³ h23.9g⁵ h24.3d h18.1s* h20.6d^{pu} Dec 26] strong gelding: poor handicap hurdler: won novice event at Kelso in November: best effort at 2¼m: acted on soft going: sometimes in headgear: dead. *Nicky Richards* **h67**

PINGSHOU (IRE) 7 b.g. Definite Article – Quest of Passion (FR) (Saumarez) **h141**
[2016/17 h16.3d⁴ h16.8g* h20.3s⁴ h16.4g h16.5g* h16.5d³ Apr 25]

The oft-quoted Robert Burns line 'The best laid schemes o' mice an' men / Gang aft a-gley' often has rueful connotations, but, judging by comments before Pingshou's 16/1 win in the Top Novices' Hurdle at the Aintree Festival, and the way things turned out, connections will have been only too happy with their decision to persevere with the horse's ambitious campaign in the top novice races after he finished well held at the Cheltenham Festival. Joe Tizzard, assistant trainer to his father Colin, wrote in the build up to the Aintree race: 'I'm not getting carried away and saying he'll be very competitive in this, but we'd be delighted if he finished close to the placings.' The Crabbie's Top Novices' Hurdle, which was being run as a Grade 1 for just the second time, featured an all domestic field, as it had in five of the ten previous seasons. Of the forty Grade 1s in Britain in the most recent season, thirteen failed to attract a single Irish challenger and, of those, five were won by Colin Tizzard-trained horses who won eight Grade 1s in all in Britain. The Top Novices' was one of a number of Grade 1s in which the winning performance was significantly lower than the five-year-average for the race, and the Top Novices' was undoubtedly one of the races which suffered most from the absence of any runners from Willie Mullins, Gordon Elliott, Henry de Bromhead and the like. As an example, the 2016 renewal was fought out between Buveur d'Air and Petit Mouchoir, who went on to finish first and third in the Champion Hurdle in the latest season. Several of those further back won good prizes on both sides of the Irish Sea in 2016/17. The early signs are that the latest Top Novices' won't prove such strong form, particularly as the race itself was a muddling one, as it wasn't run at a true gallop and positioning proved all important. Pingshou was always handy and given what appeared to be a more prudent ride than the runner-up, while the contest was further weakened by the failure of Supreme Novices' Hurdle third River Wylde and Sharp Novices' Hurdle winner Moon Racer, who had the best form coming into the race, to give their running. In the hands of Robbie Power, Pingshou tracked the leisurely early pace set by outsider Chti Balko, and, after travelling with zest, jumped on three out, getting first run and keeping the gallop up to win by four and a half lengths from Mount Mews, with a further two and a half back to recent Taunton handicap winner The Unit.

Pingshou ran once in 2014/15 for Henry de Bromhead, beating only one home in a heavy-ground Leopardstown bumper, and it was nearly two years before Pingshou was seen on the racecourse again, shaping well when finishing fourth to Jenkins in a maiden hurdle at Newbury in November on his first start for Colin Tizzard. 'He came to us with a health warning,' said Tizzard. 'He was a bleeder and had been turned out in a field. We put him in our stable and carried on like we do with each of them.' The Newbury race was strong form, with three of the first four ending the season with ratings higher than 140. Jenkins was made favourite for the Supreme Novices' after his five-length win, but suffered an injury on his next

Crabbie's Top Novices' Hurdle, Aintree—the first win of a memorable meeting for the Colin Tizzard stable as 14/1-shot Pingshou (right) defeats Mount Mews (white sleeves) in a falsely-run race

outing, forcing him to miss the Cheltenham Festival, while runner-up Bags Groove went on to win two novices at Taunton and the third Captain Forez was runner-up to Pingshou's stable-companion Finian's Oscar in the Mersey Novices' Hurdle at Aintree. Pingshou was turned out at Cheltenham's International meeting two weeks after his Newbury effort and got off the mark in good style, beating a field which included the subsequent dual winner William Henry, as well as Brio Conti, who also won two races before finishing fifth in the Mersey. Pingshou was a creditable fourth when stepped up in trip for his next start in a listed novice hurdle at Cheltenham on New Year's Day, but faced a stiff task when only beating four rivals as a 25/1-shot in the Supreme Novices', again at Cheltenham, in March. After bouncing back in style to win the Top Novices', plans for Pingshou to be put out to grass were changed and he went on to finish a good third (beaten four and a quarter lengths) to Cilaos Emery in the Champion Novices' Hurdle at the Punchestown Festival in late-April, when he paid the price for getting into a duel for the lead with the runner-up Melon from halfway.

Pingshou (IRE) (b.g. 2010)	Definite Article (b 1992)	Indian Ridge (ch 1985)	Ahonoora / Hillbrow
		Summer Fashion (b 1985)	Moorestyle / My Candy
	Quest of Passion (FR) (b 1994)	Saumarez (b or br 1987)	Rainbow Quest / Fiesta Fun
		Autocratic (b 1974)	Tyrant / Flight Table

Pingshou is by the 1995 Irish Derby runner-up Definite Article, sire of four-times Irish St Leger Vinnie Roe (himself sire of the ill-fated Neon Wolf) on the Flat and also of the Rowland Meyrick and Grimthorpe winner Definitly Red in the latest jumps season. Pingshou's dam Quest of Passion, placed up to fifteen

Ann & Alan Potts's "Pingshou"

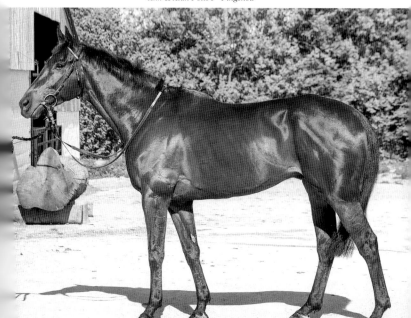

furlongs in France, is a sister to the smart French middle-distance colt Supreme Commander and a half-sister to the dam of high-class mile and a half performer White Muzzle/grandam of Dubai World Cup winner Almutawakel, and has been a fine broodmare. Pingshou's two-years-older brother Sizing Platinum is a useful chaser who won three times at up to two and a quarter miles when trained by Henry de Bromhead, while Pingshou's half-brother Mughas (by Sadler's Wells—the dam visited top Flat sires earlier in her career), who was trained by Alan King, was a five-time winner over hurdles who showed smart form at up to three miles. The pick of Pingshou's siblings to run on the Flat was his useful half-sister Piety (by Danehill) who won twice for Mark Johnston (and was later successful in Australia), while the offspring of Mughas' full sister Prairie Bell include Cailin Annamh (a daughter of Definite Article), winner of ten races including the Grade 2 PWC Champion Chase at Gowran in 2015. The youngest of Pingshou's siblings, his half-sister Magic of Light (by Flemensfirth), won a twenty-five-runner handicap hurdle at the most recent Punchestown Festival. Despite running below form on his sole attempt at two and a half miles and being a strong traveller, Pingshou should eventually stay beyond seventeen furlongs. He acts on soft going and has the build of a chaser. *Colin Tizzard*

PINK COAT 10 gr.g. Alhaarth (IRE) – In The Pink (IRE) (Indian Ridge) [2016/17 c17vᵖᵘ h17.2m h24d⁴ Jul 10] fair handicap hurdler: maiden chaser, fair form at best: left Ms Sandra Hughes after first start: stays 2½m: acts on heavy going: has worn headgear/tongue tie, including in 2016/17. *Sam England* **c–** **h101**

PINK EYED PEDRO 6 b.g. Dr Massini (IRE) – Poacher's Paddy (IRE) (Jurado (USA)) [2016/17 c23.6m Apr 28] multiple winner in points: in hood and tongue strap, 20/1, folded after clouting 3 out in novice hunter at Chepstow on chasing debut. *David Brace* **c72**

PINK GIN 9 ch.g. Alflora (IRE) – Miss Mailmit (Rakaposhi King) [2016/17 h71: h19.9v⁴ h23.1s* h24v² c22.4s³ c23.6v⁵ Mar 23] workmanlike gelding: fair handicap hurdler: won at Exeter in January: fair form over fences: better effort when third in novice handicap at Newbury in March: stays 3m: raced only on going softer than good (acts on heavy): has worn tongue tie. *Nigel Twiston-Davies* **c110** **h109**

PINKIE BROWN (FR) 5 gr.g. Gentlewave (IRE) – Natt Musik (FR) (Kendor (FR)) [2016/17 h119: h16d⁵ h18.5g c16.1m* c15.9gᶠ c16.2m* c16.1g² c20.8gᵖᵘ h16.3d³ Apr 27] largeish leggy gelding: fairly useful hurdler: good effort when 1¾ lengths third of 25 to Bobabout at Punchestown final start: useful form over fences: won novices at Towcester in October and Warwick (finished alone) in November: unproven beyond 17f: acts on good to firm and heavy going: wears hood: has joined Johnny Farrelly. *Neil Mulholland* **c134** **h125**

PINK PLAY (IRE) 6 b.m. King's Theatre (IRE) – Strawberry Fool (FR) (Tel Quel (FR)) [2016/17 h119p, b91: h20.6gᵖᵘ Oct 15] smallish mare: fairly useful hurdler, lightly raced: reportedly bled when pulled up only outing in 2016/17: should stay beyond 2m: acts on heavy going. *Harry Whittington* **h–**

PINNACLE PANDA (IRE) 6 b.g. Scorpion (IRE) – Scartara (FR) (Linamix (FR)) [2016/17 h129, b88: c20dᵇᵈ c21.4s⁵ c23.4g⁴ Nov 2] lengthy gelding: winning pointer: fairly useful handicap hurdler/maiden chaser: stayed 3m: acted on heavy going: tried in headgear: often raced in rear: dead. *Tom Lacey* **c124** **h–**

PINNACLE PETER (IRE) 6 gr.g. Flemensfirth (USA) – The Blushing Rose (FR) (Blushing Flame (USA)) [2016/17 h19.6s⁵ h21d h19.5s h24v c24.2dᵖᵘ Mar 21] off mark in points at fifth attempt: no solid form over hurdles: in cheekpieces, pulled up in novice handicap on chasing debut. *Tom Lacey* **c–** **h–**

PINSANDNEEDLES 12 b.g. Needle Gun (IRE) – Ripple (IRE) (Bob Back (USA)) [2016/17 c17.4d⁶ May 12] winning pointer: maiden hunter chaser: tried in cheekpieces. *Mrs G. Drury* **c–**

PINWOOD (IRE) 4 b.g. Bushranger (IRE) – Anne Bonney (Jade Robbery (USA)) [2016/17 h16mᵖᵘ Apr 13] fairly useful on Flat, stays 2m: in tongue tie, no promise in juvenile maiden on hurdling debut. *Adam West* **h–**

PIPER BILL 6 b.g. Halling (USA) – Murielle (Diktat) [2016/17 h16d Oct 29] poor maiden on Flat: well beaten in maiden on only outing over hurdles: dead. *Jim Goldie* **h–**

PIPPA THE DANCER (IRE) 5 b.m. Papal Bull – Pret A Porter (UAE) (Jade Robbery **h–**
(USA)) [2016/17 h17.7v h15.9s h20.5s⁴ h20.5m⁶ Apr 16] second foal: sister to fair 25f
hurdle winner Mab Dab: dam (h95), lightly raced over hurdles, 9.5f-12.6f winner on Flat,
half-sister to useful hurdler (stays 21f) Silk Hall: no form over hurdles: tried in hood.
Linda Jewell

PIQUERO 5 ch.g. Pasternak – Daurica (Dolpour) [2016/17 b16g ab16g Feb 20] no form **b–**
in bumpers: dead. *Stuart Edmunds*

PIQUE ROCK 5 b.m. King's Theatre (IRE) – Flutter Bye (IRE) (Alflora (IRE)) [2016/17 **b82**
b16.4s b16.7s⁵ b16.8g⁶ Apr 20] close-coupled mare: first foal: dam (h87), maiden hurdler
(stayed 21f), half-sister to useful hurdler/smart chaser (2m/17f winner) I'msingingtheblues:
modest form in bumpers: in hood final start. *Alan King*

PIQUE SOUS (FR) 10 gr.g. Martaline – Six Fois Sept (FR) (Epervier Bleu) [2016/17 **h135**
h19g h16.5d⁴ h20.5dF Apr 29] good-topped gelding: useful on Flat, stays 21.5f: useful
hurdler: easily best effort in 2016/17 when 2½ lengths fourth of 11 to Western Boy in
handicap at Punchestown in April: should be suited by 19f+: acts on soft going: wears
tongue tie. *W. P. Mullins, Ireland*

PISTOL (IRE) 8 b.g. High Chaparral (IRE) – Alinea (USA) (Kingmambo (USA)) **c–**
[2016/17 c–, h119§: h21.4s³ h21.4s⁵ h19.3v⁴ h25g⁴ Apr 15] useful-looking gelding: fair **h111 §**
handicap hurdler: maiden chaser: probably stays 25f: acts on heavy going: has worn
headgear: ungenuine. *John Dixon*

PISTOL PARK (FR) 6 b.g. Poliglote – Pistolera (GER) (Monsun (GER)) [2016/17 c17d³ **c137**
c15.6d* c20d⁴ c16.3d* c20v² c16.3s² c16.3v* c15.5v² Mar 11] fairly useful hurdler: useful **h–**
chaser: won novice at Hexham in June, novice handicap at Newcastle in November and
handicap at latter course (by 8 lengths from Vengeur de Guye) in February: left Alan
Fleming after first start: stays 2½m: acts on heavy going: has worn cheekpieces, including
on reappearance: usually races prominently, often travels strongly. *Brian Ellison*

PITHIVIER (FR) 7 b.g. Poliglote – Kelbelange (FR) (Ganges (USA)) [2016/17 h121: **c118**
c24.2s³ c24.1d² c24dᵖᵘ c24.2dF Mar 21] sturdy gelding: fairly useful handicap hurdler: **h–**
similar form when placed over fences: stays 3m: acts on soft going: often races prominently.
Ben Pauling

PITON PETE (IRE) 6 b.g. Westerner – Glenair Lucy (IRE) (Luso) [2016/17 b91: **h101 p**
h15.9g³ May 8] fair form in bumpers: 8 lengths third of 9 to Ritual of Senses in maiden at
Plumpton on hurdling debut, rallying after mistake 2 out: will prove suited by 2½m: open
to improvement. *Oliver Sherwood*

PIVOTAL FLAME (IRE) 4 b.f. Pivotal – Saadiah (IRE) (Dubai Destination (USA)) **h95**
[2016/17 h16g h16mᵘʳ Apr 4] sparely-made filly: fair on Flat, stays 1½m: 200/1, third when
unseated last in novice hurdle at Kempton. *Pat Phelan*

PIXEL (IRE) 4 b.f. Rip Van Winkle (IRE) – Hadarama (IRE) (Sinndar (IRE)) [2016/17 **h–**
h20sᵖᵘ Jan 1] modest maiden on Flat, stays 1¼m: showed nothing in seller on hurdling
debut. *Denis Quinn*

PIXIEPOT 7 b.m. Alflora (IRE) – Folly Foster (Relkino) [2016/17 h91, b–: h19.9g h18.6g² **h95**
h16.8g² Sep 1] bumper winner: modest maiden hurdler: stays 21f: acts on good to firm and
heavy going: in cheekpieces on reappearance: usually travels strongly. *Peter Niven*

PLACEDELA CONCORDE 4 b.g. Champs Elysees – Kasakiya (IRE) (Zafonic **h–**
(USA)) [2016/17 h16.8gᵖᵘ Apr 7] showed little on Flat, and no promise in novice on
hurdling debut (wore tongue tie). *Maurice Barnes*

PLAISIR D'AMOUR (FR) 5 b.m. Linngari (IRE) – Analfabeta (FR) (Anabaa (USA)) **c137**
[2016/17 c22.5vᵖᵘ c15.2d* c16.4s* c16s³ c20.8g* c20g⁵ Apr 29] fairly useful hurdler: **h–**
useful chaser: won handicaps at Wetherby in February and Newbury in March, and listed
mares novice handicap at Cheltenham (by 6 lengths from Magic Money) in April: good 3¾
lengths fifth to Shantou Village in novice handicap at Sandown final start: will stay 3m:
acts on heavy going. *Venetia Williams*

PLAN AGAIN (IRE) 10 b.g. Gamut (IRE) – Niamh's Leader (IRE) (Supreme Leader) **c–**
[2016/17 c–, h–: h23.9g² h21.6mF Apr 15] lightly-raced handicap hurdler, fair nowadays: **h110**
fairly useful form on first of 2 starts in chases: stays 3m: acts on soft and good to firm
going: in tongue tie last 2 starts. *Johnny Farrelly*

PLANET NINE (IRE) 5 b.g. Flemensfirth (USA) – Moon Storm (Old Vic) [2016/17 **b108**
b16s* b16.2g* Apr 28] €68,000 3-y-o: brother to several winners, including smart hurdler/
very smart chaser Noble Endeavor (2½m-3m winner) and fairly useful hurdler/useful
chaser Minella Daddy (23f/3m winner): dam unraced: useful form in bumpers: won

maiden at Thurles on debut in February: left T. E. Hyde £135,000, improved when following up in 8-runner event at Perth by 3¾ lengths from Whatswrongwithyou: will be suited by further than 2m. *Rose Dobbin*

PLANETOID (IRE) 9 b.g. Galileo (IRE) – Palmeraie (USA) (Lear Fan (USA)) [2016/17 **h109 x** h117x: h21g³ May 2] sturdy gelding: handicap hurdler, fairly useful at best: stays 21f: acts on soft and good to firm going: in headgear last 4 starts: often let down by jumping. *Jim Best*

PLANTAGENET 5 b.g. Midnight Legend – Marsh Court (Overbury (IRE)) [2016/17 **h77** b16.8m h21.6m⁵ h21d h23.1vᵖᵘ h19.7vᵖᵘ h21m² h21.6g⁴ Apr 21] rangy, rather unfurnished **b—** gelding: well beaten in bumper: poor form over hurdles: best effort at 21f: acts on good to firm going: in hood last 2 starts. *Mark Bradstock*

PLAYINGWITHNUMBERS (IRE) 6 b.g. Tikkanen (USA) – Marhab Dancer (IRE) **h102** (Oscar (IRE)) [2016/17 h23d h20g² h18.7g h23g⁵ Aug 11] placed twice in Irish maiden points: fair maiden hurdler: tried in hood: in tongue tie last 3 starts: dead. *Katy Price*

PLAY THE ACE (IRE) 8 b.g. Scorpion (IRE) – Henris Blaze (IRE) (Be My Native **c113** (USA)) [2016/17 b55: c19.3s* c17.4d³ c20.9vᵘ c19.2g³ c22.6g* c23m⁴ c19.2sᵘʳ c21.2g³ c23g⁵ c24.1sᵖᵘ Jan 23] fair chaser: won hunter at Sedgefield very early in season and handicap at Stratford in August: left A. Pennock after second start: should stay 3m: acts on heavy going: wears cheekpieces/tongue tie: front runner/races prominently. *Peter Bowen*

PLEASANT COMPANY (IRE) 9 b.g. Presenting – Katie Flame (IRE) (Alderbrook) **c151** [2016/17 c147, h131: c25d* c25d⁴ c25v* c34.3d Apr 8] tall gelding: useful maiden over **h—** hurdles: smart chaser: won Bobbyjo Chase at Fairyhouse (by ½ length from Thunder And Roses) in February: 11/1, better than result when 28 lengths ninth of 40 to One For Arthur in Grand National at Aintree final outing, typically travelling strongly and every chance when bad mistake twenty-fifth: stays 25f: acts on heavy going: in hood last 4 starts: tried in tongue tie. *W. P. Mullins, Ireland*

PLEASURE DOME 4 b.f. Makfi – Nouvelle Lune (Fantastic Light (USA)) [2016/17 **h91 p** h17s³ h16g⁵ Dec 27] good-topped filly: dam half-sister to useful hurdler (2m-3m winner) Lord Jim: fairly useful on Flat, stays 1¾m: modest form in 2 juvenile hurdles: open to improvement. *Jonjo O'Neill*

PLINTH (IRE) 7 b.g. Montjeu (IRE) – Crazy Volume (IRE) (Machiavellian (USA)) **c– p** [2016/17 h144: h17m h19.5g⁴ h16d⁴ h16.1g c16g h19.5d* h16s⁴ h16g⁵ Oct 12] rather **h137** leggy gelding: useful hurdler: won minor event at Kilbeggan (by head from Killer Crow) in August: 6/1, considerably handled when eighth of 11 in maiden at Tramore on chasing debut: stays 2¾m, effective at shorter: acts on soft and good to firm going: wears headgear/tongue tie: usually races nearer last than first: should do better over fences. *Joseph Patrick O'Brien, Ireland*

PLUS JAMAIS (FR) 10 b.g. Caballo Raptor (CAN) – Branceilles (FR) (Satin Wood) **c117** [2016/17 c114, h–: c20.1s² h24.3s³ h24.3s³ c21.5v² h24.3s* c23.4v* Mar 7] sturdy gelding: **h113** fair handicap hurdler: won at Ayr in February: fairly useful handicap chaser: won at Newcastle final start: stays 3m: acts on heavy going: has worn headgear, including last 4 starts: front runner/races prominently. *Iain Jardine*

PLUS ONE (IRE) 5 b.g. Winged Love (IRE) – Balwaney (FR) (Exit To Nowhere (USA)) **h114 p** [2016/17 h19.7d² Feb 21] €16,500 3-y-o, £90,000 4-y-o: second foal: dam unraced half-sister to useful hurdler/fair chaser (stayed 2½m) Balapour: off mark in Irish maiden points at second attempt: 6/1, encouragement when 1½ lengths second of 10 to Jerrysback in novice at Wetherby on hurdling debut: should improve. *Jonjo O'Neill*

POBBLES BAY (IRE) 7 b.g. Oscar (IRE) – Rose de Beaufai (FR) (Solon (GER)) **c144** [2016/17 c123: c20s* c23.6s* c24s⁵ Jan 14] good-topped gelding: fairly useful handicap **h—** hurdler: useful form over fences: won novice handicaps at Uttoxeter in November and Chepstow in December, by 4½ lengths from Ibis du Rheu at latter: not at best final start: will stay beyond 3¼m: raced only on soft/heavy going: often races towards rear. *Evan Williams*

POCAS PLUMAS 6 b.m. Kayf Tara – Gentle Thoughts (Darshaan) [2016/17 b15.8d **b—** b15.7g May 24] closely related to smart hurdler Blue Bajan (2m winner, by Montjeu) and half-sister to several winners, including fairly useful hurdler Aine's Delight (2m winner, by King's Best), stayed 19f: dam maiden (stayed 9f): no encouragement in 2 bumpers. *Anabel K. Murphy*

POETIC LICENSE (IRE) 5 b.g. Dylan Thomas (IRE) – Bright Bank (IRE) (Sadler's **h58** Wells (USA)) [2016/17 h16d h16m⁶ h16g⁵ h15.7dᵖᵘ h19.9sᵖᵘ h15.8vᵖᵘ Dec 31] poor maiden on Flat and over hurdles: in tongue tie last 5 starts: often races prominently. *James Grassick*

POETIC LORD 8 b.g. Byron – Jumairah Sun (IRE) (Scenic) [2016/17 c–, h79: h16.7g⁶ **c81** h17.2g⁵ c17.3d⁴ c17m⁵ c20.1d⁶ h16d Oct 6] poor handicap hurdler/maiden chaser: left **h83** Rebecca Menzies after fifth start: stays 2¼m: acts on good to soft going: has worn headgear/tongue tie, including in 2016/17: often races in rear. *Patrick Griffin, Ireland*

POETIC RHYTHM (IRE) 6 ch.g. Flemensfirth (USA) – Sommer Sonnet (IRE) (Taipan **h131** (IRE)) [2016/17 b17g⁵ b16g* b16.4s* h16.8g⁵ h20.3s³ h20.3s³ h21.1g Mar 15] €27,000 **b107** 3-y-o, £35,000 4-y-o: strong gelding: fourth foal: brother to useful hurdler Forthefunofit (2½m-23f winner): dam unraced half-sister to high-class French hurdler/smart chaser (stayed 25f) Bog Frog: winning pointer: useful form in bumpers: won at Chepstow in October and listed event at Cheltenham in November: useful form over hurdles: best effort when 8 lengths third of 10 to Wholestone in Classic Novices' Hurdle at Cheltenham: well held in Baring Bingham Novices' Hurdle there final start, not recovering after badly hampered fifth: should stay beyond 2½m. *Fergal O'Brien*

POETRY EMOTION (IRE) 6 b.g. Gamut (IRE) – Vivre Aimer Rire (FR) (Cyborg **h–** (FR)) [2016/17 b58: h21.2m⁶ May 8] well held in bumpers, and in novice on hurdling debut. *Nicky Henderson*

POGGY'S STAR (IRE) 5 b.m. Stowaway – Pamsy Wamsy (IRE) (Taipan (IRE)) **b61** [2016/17 b16.7g⁴ b16.3s b15.8s Apr 1] £11,500 3-y-o: sixth foal: dam unraced half-sister to fairly useful hurdler (stayed 2¾m) Tuesday: poor form in bumpers. *Warren Greatrex*

POINTED AND SHARP (IRE) 5 b.g. Scorpion (IRE) – Leamybe (IRE) (Religiously **b70** (USA)) [2016/17 b16g⁵ Mar 18] has scope: 20/1, green under pressure when 25 lengths fifth of 14 to Captain McGarry in maiden bumper at Kempton on debut. *Philip Hobbs*

POINT N SHOOT (IRE) 6 b.g. Broadway Flyer (USA) – Ali's Dipper (IRE) (Orchestra) **h95** [2016/17 h16.8g⁴ h16d h19.5g⁵ h19.5s⁶ h23v⁴ h25.6s^pu h23v* h23.6s³ Mar 13] £13,000 **b63** 3-y-o: half-brother to useful hurdler Time Electric (2½m winner) and useful hurdler/smart chaser (2m/2½m winner) Haymount (both by Presenting), latter stays 4m: dam failed to complete in points: fourth in bumper: modest handicap hurdler: won at Lingfield in March: stays 23f: acts on heavy going: tried in cheekpieces: races towards rear. *Nigel Hawke*

POINT OF DEPARTURE (IRE) 6 b.g. Mahler – Miranda's Lace (IRE) (Bach (IRE)) **h91** [2016/17 b15.8g⁶ b15.8d h23.1g⁴ Apr 22] €5,000 3-y-o: fourth foal: half-brother to fairly **b77** useful hurdler Ivan Boru (17f-2½m winner, by Brian Boru): dam unraced half-sister to useful hurdler/fairly useful chaser (2m-2½m winner) Mounthenry: won Irish maiden point on debut: modest form in bumpers: 20/1, 23½ lengths fourth of 6 to Work du Breteau in maiden at Bangor on hurdling debut. *Gary Hanmer*

POINT OF PRINCIPLE (IRE) 4 b.g. Rip Van Winkle (IRE) – L'Ancresse (IRE) **b107** (Darshaan) [2016/17 b16s* b17d² b13.9g Apr 7] £8,500 3-y-o: brother/closely related to winners on Flat and half-brother to fair hurdler Light Well (2m winner, by Sadler's Wells): dam, very smart winner up to 1½m, half-sister to fairly useful hurdler/useful chaser (stays 2¾m) Moon Indigo: useful form in bumpers: won maiden at Warwick in January: 66/1, 5¼ lengths seventh of 19 to Lalor in Grade 2 event at Aintree final outing. *Tim Vaughan*

POINT OF RESCUE (IRE) 8 ch.g. Vinnie Roe (IRE) – Pisa (IRE) (Carlingford Castle) **c84** [2016/17 c23d^pu h24.2s³ c25g⁴ h24g^pu Aug 14] modest handicap hurdler: poor form over **h90** fences: stays 25f: acts on good to firm and heavy going: wears headgear. *James A. Nash, Ireland*

POINT THE WAY (IRE) 6 br.g. Brian Boru – Caslain Og (IRE) (Supreme Leader) **h125** [2016/17 h128, b93: h27g³ h22.8v⁶ h24.1s³ h24.4s⁵ Mar 4] good-topped gelding: runner-up in Irish maiden point: bumper winner: fairly useful handicap hurdler: stays 27f: acts on heavy going: in cheekpieces final start: usually races close up. *Brian Ellison*

POINTVIEW GALE (IRE) 8 b.g. Exit To Nowhere (USA) – Deerpark Gale (IRE) **c98** (Strong Gale) [2016/17 c20m⁴ c23d^pu c24.3s⁶ Feb 12] maiden pointer: modest maiden chaser: stays 2½m: acts on soft and good to firm going. *Liam Lennon, Ireland*

POISONED BERRY (IRE) 5 b.m. Scorpion (IRE) – Prunelle (GER) (Waky Nao) **h99** [2016/17 b92: b16g* h21.6m⁴ h16.8m⁶ h18.5g* h16d⁵ h19.1d⁴ h18.7g⁴ h23.1g Apr **b89** 11] leggy mare: fair form in bumpers: won mares event at Worcester in August: modest hurdler: won mares novice at Exeter in November: stays 19f: tried in blinkers: often races prominently: temperament under suspicion. *David Pipe*

POKARI (FR) 5 ch.g. Bonbon Rose (FR) – Pokara (FR) (Kutub (IRE)) [2016/17 b–: **b94** b16.8m² b16.8g* Sep 16] fair form in bumpers: won 4-runner event at Newton Abbot in September. *Alan Jones*

POKER PLAY (FR) 4 ch.g. Martaline – Becquarette (FR) (Nombre Premier) [2016/17 **h126**
h17.4s² h17.4v* h16d² h16.4g Mar 15] good-topped, attractive gelding: sixth foal: brother
to fairly useful French hurdler/useful chaser Pokerdor (17f winner) and half-brother to 2
winners, including smart French hurdler/useful chaser Storminator (17f-19f winner, by
Stormy River): dam French 9.5f-10.5f winner: fairly useful form over hurdles: won
juvenile at Enghien in November, then left Y. Fouin £280,000: in tongue strap, 16/1, not
seen to best effect when 18¾ lengths fourteenth of 22 to Flying Tiger in Fred Winter
Handicap Hurdle at Cheltenham final start, shuffled back home turn. *David Pipe*

POKER SCHOOL (IRE) 7 b.g. Gold Well – Broken Pockets (IRE) (Broken Hearted) **c136**
[2016/17 c–, h121: h20d h20g⁶ h16d* c20s⁴ c18.8d* c20.5g* h16.8g⁴ c20g⁶ Apr 29] **h122**
lengthy gelding: fairly useful handicap hurdler: won at Sandown in November: useful form
over fences: won handicap at Ascot and novice handicap at Kempton, both in December:
stays 21f: acts on soft going: often races in rear. *Ian Williams*

POKORA DU LYS (FR) 6 b.g. Saint des Saints (FR) – Shailann (FR) (Gaspard de La **h111**
Nuit (FR)) [2016/17 h15.7d⁴ h15.7s Dec 17] half-brother to several winners in France,
including winning hurdler/useful chaser Northwest du Lys (2¼m-21f winner, by Medaaly):
twice-raced maiden on Flat: fair form over hurdles: left J-L. Guillochon after only 2015/16
start: raced around 2m. *Dan Skelton*

POLARBROOK (IRE) 10 br.g. Alderbrook – Frozen Cello (IRE) (Arctic Lord) **c57**
[2016/17 c–x, h94: h16.8g h15.7d h20.3d⁴ h21s h16g⁵ c15.7s⁴ Jan 31] angular gelding: **h77**
handicap hurdler/chaser, out of sorts in 2016/17: stays 23f, races over shorter nowadays:
acts on good to firm and heavy going: has worn tongue tie. *Derek Shaw*

POLICY BREACH (IRE) 6 b.g. Kayf Tara – Just Stunning (IRE) (Presenting) [2016/17 **h120**
h114, h98: h21.6d² h22m* h23.3g h20gᵘʳ h23.1g² Apr 22] fairly useful handicap hurdler:
won at Stratford in July: will stay beyond 23f: acts on good to firm going: wears tongue tie.
Kim Bailey

POLIDAM (FR) 8 b.g. Trempolino (USA) – Eladame (FR) (Snurge) [2016/17 h17.9s⁶ **c134**
h19.4g c18.4s* c21.4v³ c20d Apr 26] fairly useful hurdler: useful chaser: in cheekpieces, **h116**
won amateurs event at Auteuil in October: third in listed event there following month, then
left A. Chaille-Chaille £145,000: in hood, 7/4, shaped much better than position suggests
when seventh of 14 in handicap at Punchestown final start (badly hampered fifth and not
persevered with after mistake 2 out): stays 23f: acts on heavy going. *W. P. Mullins, Ireland*

POLI ROI (FR) 5 b.g. Poliglote – Belle du Roi (FR) (Adieu Au Roi (IRE)) [2016/17 **b113**
b16s* b16d³ Apr 26] £46,000 3-y-o, £300,000 4-y-o: closely related to French chaser Roi
Garry (19f-23f winner, by Ballingarry) and half-brother to several winners, including smart
hurdler Le Rocher (2m-2½m winner, by Saint des Saints): dam (h118), placed over hurdles
in France, 6f-10.5f winner on Flat: won maiden point on debut: useful form in bumpers:
won maiden at Navan in February by 2 lengths from Impact Factor: 12½ lengths third of 7
to Fayonagh in Champion INH Flat Race at Punchestown. *Gordon Elliott, Ireland*

POLISKY (FR) 10 b.g. Poliglote – Dusky Royale (FR) (Double Bed (FR)) [2016/17 **c110 §**
c117§, h–§: c21.1d² May 12] good-topped gelding: winning hurdler: fair hunter chaser **h– §**
nowadays: stays 3m: acts on soft and good to firm going: wears headgear/tongue tie:
temperamental. *Paul Nicholls*

POLITBUREAU 10 b.g. Red Ransom (USA) – Tereshkova (USA) (Mr Prospector **h70**
(USA)) [2016/17 h19.7s⁶ h25.3dᵖᵘ h19.9d h21.2s h19.9s h19.7d h16.4v h16.4v⁵ Mar 18]
poor handicap hurdler: stays 2½m: acts on heavy going: wears headgear: in tongue tie last
2 starts: often races towards rear. *Micky Hammond*

POLITENESS (FR) 8 b.g. Poliglote – Martininquaise (FR) (Anabaa (USA)) [2016/17 h111: **h–**
h17d Feb 20] fair hurdler at best, well held only outing in 2016/17: barely stays 2½m: acts
on good to firm and good to soft going: usually wears hood. *Rose Dobbin*

POLITICAL QUIZ 7 b.g. Lucarno (USA) – Quiz Night (Kayf Tara) [2016/17 h112: **h120**
h17.7d⁴ h15.5d* h19.4d h19.3d* h15.8g² h20.3g* Apr 19] good-topped gelding: fairly
useful handicap hurdler: won at Leicester in January, Carlisle in February and Cheltenham
on final start: stays 2½m: acts on good to soft going. *Tom Symonds*

POLITOLOGUE (FR) 6 gr.g. Poliglote – Scarlet Row (FR) (Turgeon (USA)) [2016/17 **c153**
h138: c21.6v* c21d* c19.9s² c20.5s* c19.9g⁴ c15.8gᶠ Apr 8] good-bodied gelding: useful **h–**
hurdler: smart form over fences: won novice at Haydock (by 10 lengths from Vintage
Clouds) in November, Noel Novices' Chase at Ascot (by 4 lengths from Rock The Kasbah)
in December and graduation event at Kempton (by 11 lengths from Pain Au Chocolat) in
February: would also have been successful in Maghull Novices' Chase at Aintree but for

Mr J. Hales's "Politologue"

tripping and falling soon after last, holding narrow lead at the time: effective at 2m and stays 2¾m: acts on heavy going: in hood last 3 starts: usually races close up, often travels strongly. *Paul Nicholls*

POLKARENIX (FR) 5 b.g. Policy Maker (IRE) – Arenix (FR) (Fragrant Mix (IRE)) [2016/17 c20.4g⁴ c17g⁴ c15.7s c19.9s⁵ c19.4s c19.7vᵖᵘ Feb 27] fairly useful on Flat, stays 1¼m: winning hurdler: modest form over fences: left Emmanuel Clayeux after first start: stays 2¼m: acts on soft going: in hood last 4 starts. *Brendan Powell* — **c89 h–**

POLLY'S PURSUIT (IRE) 5 br.m. Westerner – Miss Denman (IRE) (Presenting) [2016/17 b83p: b16.7s⁴ ab16g* ab16g² b17g Apr 6] sturdy mare: fairly useful bumper performer: won mares event at Lingfield in January: bred to stay at least 2½m. *Nicky Henderson* — **b96**

POLO SPRINGS 10 gr.m. Baryshnikov (AUS) – Cristal Springs (Dance of Life (USA)) [2016/17 h–: h18.7m³ h23.1g³ Jul 29] point winner: modest handicap hurdler: barely stays 23f: acts on good to firm and good to soft going: wears tongue tie. *Graeme McPherson* — **h95**

POLO THE MUMM (FR) 7 b.g. Great Journey (JPN) – Maido (FR) (French Glory) [2016/17 c–, h84: h18.5d⁶ h20g* h21.6g* h21.6d⁵ h19.8d c21.7g³ c18.2m³ Apr 20] point winner: fair handicap hurdler: won at Worcester in July and Newton Abbot in August: modest maiden chaser: stays 2¾m: best form on good going: wears tongue tie. *Jackie du Plessis* — **c95 h102**

POLSTAR (FR) 8 b.g. Poliglote – Star Dancing (Danehill Dancer (IRE)) [2016/17 c–, h115: h16.2m⁶ h15.7g h16d h18.5m⁶ h23.1g³ Aug 13] neat gelding: handicap hurdler, just modest form in 2016/17: well held only outing in chase: probably best around 2m: acts on heavy going: often races towards rear: temperamental. *Harry Whittington* — **c– h98 §**

659

POLVERE D'ORO 7 b.g. Revoque (IRE) – Dusty Anne (IRE) (Dushyantor (USA)) **h–**
[2016/17 h15.8d⁵ h15.8dᵖᵘ Oct 13] poor maiden hurdler: best efforts at 2m on soft going.
Daniel Loughnane

POLYDORA (IRE) 5 b.g. Milan – Mandysway (IRE) (Mandalus) [2016/17 b16.7g⁵ **b78**
b16.3g Nov 3] close up when unseated 2 out in maiden point: modest form in bumpers:
bred to be suited by 2½m+. *Tom Lacey*

POMME 6 b.m. Observatory (USA) – Mirthful (USA) (Miswaki (USA)) [2016/17 h100p: **h110**
h19.4g⁴ h19.3s⁵ Feb 8] bumper winner: lightly-raced maiden over hurdles, fair form at
best: will stay 2½m. *Nigel Hawke*

PONGO TWISTLETON 4 b.g. Champs Elysees – Pretty Girl (IRE) (Polish Precedent **h104 p**
(USA)) [2016/17 h16m⁴ h16s⁴ h16s⁵ h20.3g⁴ Apr 21] fair maiden on Flat, stays 1½m: fair
form over hurdles: off 4 months, shaped encouragingly when staying-on fourth in 2½m
novice handicap at Southwell final start: remains with potential. *Jonjo O'Neill*

POOLE MASTER 12 ch.g. Fleetwood (IRE) – Juste Belle (FR) (Mansonnien (FR)) **c121**
[2016/17 c106, h–: c24s⁵ c20.3s⁴ c20v* c21.1g Apr 6] tall gelding: winning hunter: fairly **h–**
useful hunter chaser nowadays: won at Warwick (by 2¾ lengths from Mon Parrain) in
March: stays 3m: acts on heavy going: has worn headgear: has worn tongue tie, including
in 2016/17: usually races prominently. *Chris Honour*

POPAWAY 12 b.m. Nomadic Way (USA) – Sea Poppy (Baron Blakeney) [2016/17 c95: **c109**
c25.3g* c22.6m² c23gᵘʳ c24.2dᵘʳ Feb 17] multiple point winner: fair chaser: won mares
hunter at Cheltenham very early in season: stays 25f: acts on soft and good to firm going:
wears tongue tie. *Mrs Pauline Harkin*

POPELYS GULL (IRE) 5 ch.g. Recharge (IRE) – Circus Rose (Most Welcome) **h113**
[2016/17 b–: b16.7g⁴ h19.6m⁵ h21d⁴ h21d h19.3g⁴ h23.4d² h24v² h23.1g² Mar 27] poor **b72**
form in bumpers: fair handicap hurdler: stays 3m: acts on heavy going. *Pam Sly*

POPPING ALONG 8 ch.m. Volochine (IRE) – So Long (Nomadic Way (USA)) [2016/17 **h104**
h109: h20m* h20d⁶ h21.6g h21.4m⁴ h19m h21.2m⁵ Apr 18] sturdy mare: fair handicap
hurdler: won mares event at Aintree in May: stays 2¾m: acts on soft and good to firm
going: wears cheekpieces/tongue tie: often races towards rear. *Jeremy Scott*

POPPYINTHEPARK 4 b.f. Bahri (USA) – Lark In The Park (IRE) (Grand Lodge **b67**
(USA)) [2016/17 b13.7m⁶ b14s Nov 16] fifth foal: half-sister to 3 winners on Flat,
including useful 5f-7f winner Secretinthepark (by Sakhee's Secret): dam 1m winner: poor
form in bumpers. *Richard Ford*

POPPY KAY 7 b.m. Kayf Tara – Double Red (IRE) (Thatching) [2016/17 b100p: h15.8d⁴ **h126**
h15.8v* h16sᵖᵘ h15.8v* h18.9g² Apr 15] successful on only start in bumpers: fairly useful
form over hurdles: won novice at Uttoxeter in November and mares handicap there in
February: good neck second to Secret Door in mares handicap at Haydock final start: stays
19f: acts on heavy going. *Philip Hobbs*

POP ROCKSTAR (IRE) 5 b.g. Flemensfirth (USA) – Special Ballot (IRE) (Perugino **h108 p**
(USA)) [2016/17 b16.4m⁶ h19.1sᵖᵘ h15.9d⁵ h15.8v⁴ h19.5s⁴ h20.5v² Feb 1] €40,000 3-y-o: **b78**
fourth foal: half-brother to chaser Uncle Pettit (23f winner, by Heron Island): dam maiden
sister to useful hurdler/chaser (stayed 3m) First Ballot: showed a bit only start in bumpers,
subsequently left Adrian Maguire: fair form over hurdles: likely to stay 3m: remains with
potential. *Jonjo O'Neill*

PORLOCK BAY (IRE) 10 b.g. Dr Massini (IRE) – Fortlawn Bay (IRE) (Tidaro (USA)) **c–**
[2016/17 c22.6mᵖᵘ May 20] prolific winner in points: lightly-raced maiden over hurdles: **h–**
showed nothing in novice hunter on chasing debut: in headgear last 2 starts: tried in tongue
tie. *Luke Harvey*

PORT 5 b.g. Hurricane Run (IRE) – Captain's Paradise (IRE) (Rock of Gibraltar (IRE)) **h–**
[2016/17 h16m⁵ h15.7d h16gᵖᵘ Dec 26] lengthy, sparely-made gelding: fair maiden on Flat,
stays 1¼m: little impact in 3 runs over hurdles. *Jimmy Fox*

PORTERS LANE 6 ch.g. Generous (IRE) – Private Company (IRE) (Great Marquess) **c–**
[2016/17 b16d h20.3d⁴ c15.7g⁶ c16.5g⁵ c24gᵖᵘ c20g c24.5mᶠ c22.6mᵖᵘ c16.1gᵖᵘ c16.2s⁴ **h–**
Nov 16] placed in points: no sign of ability otherwise: usually wears cheekpieces. **b–**
Aytach Sadik

PORT LAIRGE 7 b.g. Pastoral Pursuits – Stylish Clare (IRE) (Desert Style (IRE)) **h83**
[2016/17 h15.7v⁴ h15.7sᵘʳ h20.6sᵖᵘ h16g⁵ h20.6g⁴ Mar 27] fair on Flat, stays 11f: poor
form over hurdles: best effort at 21f on good ground. *Michael Chapman*

PORT MELON (IRE) 9 br.g. Presenting – Omyn Supreme (IRE) (Supreme Leader) **c130**
[2016/17 c139, h–: c25.8g⁵ c23.8d⁵ c28.4g⁴ c28.1g⁶ Apr 19] tall, good sort: has reportedly **h–**
had breathing operation: winning hurdler: useful handicap chaser, not at best in 2016/17:
stays 3m: acts on soft going: has worn headgear, including on last 2 starts: tried in tongue
tie. *Paul Nicholls*

PORT NAVAS (IRE) 6 b.g. Court Cave (IRE) – Mrs Quigley (IRE) (Mandalus) [2016/17 **c60**
h79p, b–: h17.2g h25m² h21.6s² h23.9m⁴ h23.9g c25.1s Jan 7] modest maiden hurdler: **h86**
little encouragement on chasing debut: stays 3m: acts on soft going: wears headgear:
usually races close up. *David Pipe*

PORTO DU SUD (FR) 4 gr.g. Lord du Sud (FR) – Queen du Vallon (FR) (Jeune Homme **b–**
(USA)) [2016/17 b16.4g Mar 24] well beaten in bumper. *James Ewart*

PORT PARADISE 4 gr.g. Paco Boy (IRE) – Yacht Woman (USA) (Mizzen Mast (USA)) **h–**
[2016/17 h16sᵖᵘ h16.7sᵖᵘ Feb 7] sparely-made gelding: fair on Flat, stays 1¼m: in hood,
pulled up both starts over hurdles (saddle slipped first time). *William Jarvis*

PORTRAIT KING (IRE) 12 gr.g. Portrait Gallery (IRE) – Storm Queen (IRE) (Le Bavard **c126**
(FR)) [2016/17 c129, h–: h24.7g h23d c25.5d⁶ h24.3v⁴ c32.6sᵇᵈ c33.4s c21.1g³ c31.8g Apr **h111**
22] sturdy gelding: fair maiden hurdler: fairly useful handicap chaser: best effort in
2016/17 when 7 lengths third of 29 to Ultragold in Topham Chase at Aintree penultimate
start, staying on strongly: stays 33f: acts on heavy going: usually wears headgear. *Patrick
Griffin, Ireland*

PORTRUSH TED (IRE) 5 b.g. Shantou (USA) – Village Queen (IRE) (King's Theatre **b103**
(IRE)) [2016/17 b15.8s* Mar 18] €53,000 3-y-o: third foal: brother to useful hurdler/smart
chaser Shantou Village (2½m/21f winner) and fairly useful hurdler/useful chaser Bun
Doran (19f/2½m winner): dam unraced half-sister to useful hurdler (2m winner) In The
Forge: 11/4, overcame inexperience when winning 6-runner bumper at Uttoxeter on debut
by 2¾ lengths from Victarion: will stay 2½m: promising. *Warren Greatrex*

PORTWAY FLYER (IRE) 9 br.g. King's Theatre (IRE) – Next Best Thing (IRE) **c130**
(Taipan (IRE)) [2016/17 c124, h–: c21g² May 4] good-topped gelding: winning hurdler: **h–**
useful handicap chaser: good second at Newton Abbot (head behind Art Mauresque) only
outing in 2016/17: stays 21f: acts on soft going: wears tongue tie. *Ian Williams*

POSITIVELY DYLAN 6 b.g. Multiplex – Wou Oodd (Barathea (IRE)) [2016/17 h105: **h106**
h15.8v h23.3v⁴ h21.2s⁴ h19.5v³ Mar 6] second in Irish point on debut: useful bumper
performer: just fair form in novice/maiden hurdles (rider lost irons final start): should stay
at least 2½m. *Evan Williams*

POSITIVE TOUCH (IRE) 6 b.g. Misternando – Independant Flora (Alflora (IRE)) **h–**
[2016/17 h17.4g h16m h23gᵖᵘ Sep 23] failed to complete all 5 starts in points: no form over
hurdles. *Dai Williams*

POSSIBLY FLORA 12 b.m. Rakaposhi King – Calling Flora (Alflora (IRE)) [2016/17 **c–**
c22.5dᵖᵘ May 5] angular mare: maiden pointer/hurdler: winning chaser, pulled up in hunter **h–**
only outing in 2016/17: stays 23f: acts on heavy going: wears tongue tie. *R. Mitford-Slade*

POSTBRIDGE (IRE) 6 br.m. Robin des Pres (FR) – Dartmeet (IRE) (Presenting) **h110**
[2016/17 h91: h17.7v h16v³ h15.9s* h21.6d² h19.2m* Apr 13] fair form over hurdles: won
mares novice at Plumpton in February and novice at Towcester final start: stays 2¾m: acts
on soft and good to firm going: tried in hood: usually leads. *Warren Greatrex*

POST WAR 6 b.g. Nayef (USA) – Antebellum (FR) (Anabaa (USA)) [2016/17 b89: **h122**
h20.8g* h21s³ Feb 10] maiden Irish pointer: fair form in bumpers: fairly useful form over
hurdles: won maiden at Doncaster in December: 1½ lengths third to Captain Buck's in
novice at Kempton: will stay beyond 21f. *Nicky Henderson*

POT COMMITTED (IRE) 6 b.g. Presenting – Keats Dream (Turtle Island (IRE)) **h116**
[2016/17 b16.2d⁶ b16d³ h20.5s h15.6g* h19.4g* Mar 24] €28,000 3-y-o: first foal: dam **b78**
(h105) bumper/2m hurdle winner: modest form in bumpers: fairly useful form over
hurdles: won maiden at Musselburgh in December and novice there on final outing: left
Stuart Crawford after first start: stays 19f. *Iain Jardine*

POT DE FLEUR 5 b.m. Revoque (IRE) – Glen Clova (Elmaamul (USA)) [2016/17 **b–**
b16.8gᵖᵘ Sep 27] third foal: dam, lightly raced in points, half-sister to fairly useful hurdler/
chaser (stays 3m) Thedrinkymeister: pulled up in mares bumper on debut. *Chris Grant*

POTTERS ANGELIQUE 5 b.m. Midnight Legend – Craughwell Suas (IRE) (Turtle **b71**
Island (IRE)) [2016/17 b16v⁶ b15.7s³ Mar 20] second foal: sister to bumper winner Potters
Midnight: dam (h92) 2m hurdle winner (stayed 2½m): poor form in bumpers. *Giles Bravery*

POTTERS APPROACH (IRE) 6 b.g. Scorpion (IRE) – Moon Approach (IRE) **h114** (Shernazar) [2016/17 b16d² h20.5d³ h19.1v⁵ h20.3s⁴ h26.4g* Apr 15] €20,000 3-y-o, **b90** £30,000 5-y-o: sturdy gelding: sixth foal: half-brother to fairly useful/useful chaser Foundry Square (2½m-23f winner, by Oscar), stays 3½m: dam unraced: off mark in maiden points at third attempt: second in bumper at Sandown: fair form over hurdles: won handicap at Stratford final start: stays 3¼m: front runner/races prominently. *Warren Greatrex*

POTTERS CORNER (IRE) 7 b.g. Indian Danehill (IRE) – Woodford Beauty (IRE) **c134** (Phardante (FR)) [2016/17 h129: h17.9s² c23.6g³ c23.8d⁴ c23.4s² Jan 18] sturdy gelding: **h129** fairly useful hurdler: useful form over fences: again shaped well when neck second of 13 to Brandon Hill in handicap at Newbury final start: stays 3m: acts on good to firm and heavy going. *Paul Morgan*

POTTERS CROSS 10 b.g. Alflora (IRE) – Teeno Nell (Teenoso (USA)) [2016/17 c123+, **c135 §** h–: c25d⁶ c23.6g* c20.4sᵖᵘ c23.6g² c26d* c24dᵖᵘ c26gᵖᵘ c27.9dᵖᵘ Apr 16] big **h–** gelding: winning hurdler: useful handicap chaser: won at Chepstow in October and Newbury (by 2 lengths from Treaty Girl) in December: stays 3¼m: acts on heavy going: in cheekpieces final start: has worn tongue tie: front runner/races prominently. untrustworthy. *Rebecca Curtis*

POTTERS GRENADIER 7 b.g. Notnowcato – Mountain Stream (FR) (Vettori (IRE)) **h–** [2016/17 b16v h20.3sᵖᵘ h15.8gᵖᵘ Apr 17] no sign of ability in bumper/over hurdles. **b–** *Giles Bravery*

POTTERS HEDGER 5 b.g. Midnight Legend – Loose Morals (IRE) (Luso) [2016/17 **b91** b15.8d b16s⁶ ab16g⁵ b16.7m² Apr 17] second foal: brother to useful hurdler/chaser Potters Legend (2m-3m winner): dam (c81/h76) maiden jumper (stayed 25f): fair form in bumpers: will stay at least 2½m. *Lucy Wadham*

POTTERS LEGEND 7 b.g. Midnight Legend – Loose Morals (IRE) (Luso) [2016/17 **c141 p** h136, b114: c24g* c20.3s* c24g² c22.4d⁴ c20.8s² c26g⁴ c25g⁴ Apr 8] well-made gelding: **h–** useful hurdler: quickly reached similar standard over fences, and won novices at Kempton and Bangor in November: best subsequent efforts when second in Grade 2 novice at Doncaster (1¾ lengths behind Present Man) and fourth of 24 in Fulke Walwyn Kim Muir Chase (Handicap) at Cheltenham: stays 3¼m: acts on heavy going: in cheekpieces final start (ran creditably despite reportedly losing a shoe): remains with potential. *Lucy Wadham*

POTTERS POINT (IRE) 7 b.g. Robin des Champs (FR) – Tango Lady (IRE) (King's **c131 p** Theatre (IRE)) [2016/17 h16.2d* c16.5d* c16d⁵ Apr 27] £260,000 4-y-o: first foal: dam **h118 p** unraced: second in point: bumper winner: fairly useful form over hurdles: won maiden at Galway in October: useful form over fences: won maiden at Fairyhouse in April by ½ length from Flaviana: ran well when fifth in handicap at Punchestown (4¾ lengths behind Don't Touch It) later in month: should stay 2½m: acts on soft going: in tongue tie last 3 starts: often leads: remains with potential. *Gordon Elliott, Ireland*

POTTERS SAPPHIRE 4 b.f. Aussie Rules (USA) – Arabescato (UAE) (Gone West **b83** (USA)) [2016/17 b12.4d⁵ b16d b16.7g³ b16g³ Apr 17] compact filly: half-sister to 3 winners, including bumper winner Potters Lady Jane (by Sir Percy): dam unraced: modest form in bumpers: in headgear last 3 starts. *Lucy Wadham*

POTTERS STORY 5 b.g. Kayf Tara – Lily Potter (Karinga Bay) [2016/17 b16m* b16s **h114** b16s⁴ h15.8s* h15.7v² Mar 22] fourth foal: dam unraced half-sister to useful hurdler/ **b98** winning chaser (2m-19f winner) Missis Potts and fair hurdler/useful chaser (2m winner) Woodbank out of half-sister to Cheltenham Gold Cup winner Denman: fairly useful form in bumpers: won at Worcester in August: fair form over hurdles: won novice at Ffos Las in February: will be suited by at least 2½m: front runner/races prominently. *Peter Bowen*

POUGNE BOBBI (FR) 6 b.g. Protektor (GER) – Amicus (Xaar) [2016/17 h127p, b97: **c140** c17.4s⁵ c20s* c15.5s⁵ c24s Mar 18] fairly useful hurdler: useful form over fences: won **h–** handicap at Ludlow (by 9 lengths from Pull The Chord) in February, easily best effort: stays 2½m: acts on heavy going: often races prominently. *Nicky Henderson*

POUR L'AMOUR (IRE) 4 b.f. Aqlaam – Passion Fruit (Pursuit of Love) [2016/17 **h–** h15.8gᵖᵘ Nov 10] fair form on Flat, stays 12.5f: no promise only outing over hurdles. *David Loder*

POURQUOI MOI 4 b.f. Multiplex – Sweet Applause (IRE) (Acclamation) [2016/17 **b** b15.8d Feb 9] second foal: half-sister to 1m-1¼m winner Captain Felix (by Captain Gerrard): dam 6f winner: tailed off in mares bumper: showed little in maiden on Flat. *George Scott*

POWDERONTHEBONNET (IRE) 9 b.g. Definite Article – Zuhal (Busted) [2016/17   **c–** c–, h92: h21.6g² h23g² h26.5dᵖᵘ h23m h19.9g Sep 18] sturdy gelding: modest handicap   **h90** hurdler: pulled up only start in chases: stays 3m: acts on good to firm and heavy going. *Richard Phillips*

POWERFUL SYMBOL (IRE) 7 b.g. Robin des Champs (FR) – Be My Rainbow (IRE)   **c114** (Be My Native (USA)) [2016/17 h94ᵖ, b92: h24d³ h23.1v c25.2sᵘʳ c22.7s² c21.3d⁶   **h98** Mar 21] winning pointer: modest maiden over hurdles: fair form over fences: would have won novice handicap at Catterick in February but for unseating rider 3 out: not fluent both subsequent starts: raced mainly around 3m: acts on heavy going: in cheekpieces over fences, also in tongue tie final start. *Jonjo O'Neill*

POWERSBOMB (IRE) 7 ch.g. Trans Island – Black Ouzel (IRE) (Taipan (IRE)) [2016/17   **c138** h20m³ h20v h21g³ h18.2g² h20g h21.1g c18dᵘʳ c16.3s* c17dꟳ c17g² c20.4g⁴ c16d⁵ Apr 27]   **h120** €8,800 3-y-o: rangy gelding: fourth foal: half-brother to bumper/point winner In The Binyanis (by Waky Nao): dam (h85) 2¾m hurdle winner: fairly useful handicap hurdler: useful form over fences: won maiden at Clonmel (by length from Laid Back Luke) in December: best effort when 7½ lengths fourth of 20 to Tully East in Close Brothers Novices' Handicap at Cheltenham in March: stays 2¾m, at least as effective around 2m: acts on good to firm and heavy going: wears hood: front runner/races prominently. *Brian M. McMahon, Ireland*

PRAIRIE IMPULSE 4 b.f. Major Cadeaux – Prairie Sun (GER) (Law Society (USA))   **h70 p** [2016/17 h16.2dꟳ h15.7d⁶ h16.8s⁵ Jan 29] dam 2m/17f hurdle winner: modest maiden on Flat: poor form over hurdles, though did shape with some promise on handicap debut final start: left Ann Duffield after second outing: should do better. *Rebecca Menzies*

PRAIRIE TOWN (IRE) 6 b.g. High Chaparral (IRE) – Lake Baino (Highest Honor   **c125** (FR)) [2016/17 h124: h16.4g h16d² h19.4g h16s c16.4s² c17.2s² h16dꟳ h16.3d³ h16d³ Apr   **h121** 21] rather leggy gelding: fairly useful handicap hurdler: similar form when runner-up in 2 novice chases, first of them a handicap: unproven beyond 17f: acts on heavy going: in cheekpieces last 3 starts. *Tony Carroll*

PRAVALAGUNA (FR) 5 b.m. Great Pretender (IRE) – Arnette (FR) (Denham Red (FR))   **h133** [2016/17 h20d* h18v⁴ h16vꟳ h16.3d² Apr 27] half-sister to high-class 2m hurdler Petit Mouchoir (by Al Namix): successful over 14.7f only start on Flat (in France for Alain Couetil): useful form over hurdles: won mares maiden at Navan in December: in lead and still to be asked for effort when fell 2 out in Paddy Power Shops Better Value Novices' Hurdle won by Forge Meadow at Naas in February: stays 2½m: acts on heavy going: in hood last 2 starts. *W. P. Mullins, Ireland*

PRAYER TIME 5 ch.g. Pastoral Pursuits – Nice Time (IRE) (Tagula (IRE)) [2016/17   **h–** h16.7gᵘʳ h16g⁵ h16.7g⁵ Jun 3] fair on Flat, stays 1½m: showed little in 3 starts over hurdles. *Mark H. Tompkins*

PRAY FOR A RAINBOW 6 b.g. Rainbow High – Blackchurch Lass (IRE) (Taum Go   **c–** Leor (IRE)) [2016/17 h90, b–: h23.3g³ c24vᵖᵘ Jun 20] winning pointer: lightly-raced   **h74** maiden over hurdles, modest form at best: no promise in novice handicap on chasing debut: in cheekpieces last 2 starts. *Evan Williams*

PRECIOUS GROUND 7 b.g. Helissio (FR) – Wild Ground (IRE) (Simply Great (FR))   **c97** [2016/17 h97: h25d³ h23.1s³ c21.7d³ c23g⁴ Dec 30] workmanlike gelding: modest   **h95** handicap hurdler: similar form both starts over fences, in novice handicaps: stays 23f: acts on heavy going. *Kevin Bishop*

PRECISION FIVE 8 b.m. Proclamation (IRE) – Sashay (Bishop of Cashel) [2016/17   **h110** h104: h16g² h19.6g* h20.3g* h20g³ Sep 23] fair form over hurdles: won mares maiden at Bangor in July and mares novice at Southwell in August: stays 2½m: raced only on good going: wears cheekpieces. *Alan King*

PREDICT A RIOT (IRE) 6 ch.g. Flemensfirth (USA) – Ballerina Laura (IRE) (Riot   **h101** Helmet) [2016/17 h26m³ h24d⁴ h23.1s⁴ h26v h21vᵖᵘ Mar 12] €23,000 3-y-o, £50,000 5-y-o: brother to modest hurdler Flemerina (17f/23f winner) and a winning pointer, and half-brother to bumper winner/fairly useful 2½m hurdle winner Werenearlyoutofit (by Asian Heights): dam unraced half-sister to top-class chaser (stayed 29f) Joe Lively (by Flemensfirth): won completed start in Irish maiden points: fair form over hurdles: best effort at 23f on soft going: tried in cheekpieces: front runner/races prominently. *Dan Skelton*

PREMIER BOND 7 b.g. Kayf Tara – Celtic Native (IRE) (Be My Native (USA))   **c138** [2016/17 h130: c19.1g² c25.2d* c24g* c26g³ c31.8gᵖᵘ Apr 22] rangy gelding: useful   **h–** hurdler: useful form over fences: won novices at Catterick and Doncaster (by neck from Kerrow) in January: best effort when 1½ lengths third of 24 to Domesday Book in Fulke

Walwyn Kim Muir Chase (Handicap) at Cheltenham in March: stays 3¼m: acts on soft going: in cheekpieces last 4 starts: tried in tongue tie, including on final outing (ran badly): often races prominently. *Nicky Henderson*

PREMIER CURRENCY (IRE) 4 b.g. Elusive Pimpernel (USA) – Zeena (Unfuwain (USA)) [2016/17 h16d⁵ h15.8s h15.8d Mar 15] workmanlike gelding: modest on Flat, stays 8.5f: showed little in 3 runs over hurdles: wears tongue tie. *Mike Murphy* **h–**

PREMIER GRAND CRU (FR) 11 b.g. Kaldounevees (FR) – Last Harvest (FR) (Kahyasi) [2016/17 c15.5d³ c18s³ c21.1s³ c19.1sᵖᵘ Mar 3] strong gelding: winning hurdler: handicap chaser: off 21 months, just fair form in 2016/17: stays 2¾m: acts on soft going: often in cheekpieces: has worn tongue tie, including last 2 starts. *James Ewart* **c103** **h–**

PREMIER PORTRAIT (IRE) 10 b.g. Portrait Gallery (IRE) – Shesnotthelast (IRE) (Mandalus) [2016/17 c23.4v* c26.3g c21.1gᵘʳ Apr 6] useful-looking gelding: prolific winning pointer: fair chaser: won hunter at Kelso in February: should stay further than 3m: acts on heavy going: wears headgear: temperamental. *Dr Charles Levinson* **c111 §** **h– §**

PREMIER ROSE (IRE) 8 b.m. Westerner – Alltoplayfor (IRE) (Broken Hearted) [2016/17 h–, b–: h16m h20g⁵ h18.7mᶠ h15.8g⁵ h21.6g⁵ h19.7gᵖᵘ h19.6s² h23v⁵ h20.5gᵖᵘ h20.5v⁴ Feb 27] winning Irish pointer: poor maiden hurdler: in cheekpieces last 2 starts. *Katy Price* **h80**

PRESELI ROCK (IRE) 7 ch.g. Flemensfirth (USA) – Chantoue Royale (FR) (Cadoudal (FR)) [2016/17 h117, b95: h23.3g* h23d⁴ c21.4s c25.2vᵖᵘ Feb 7] fairly useful form over hurdles: won maiden at Uttoxeter in May: no form over fences: stays 23f: acts on heavy going: tried in cheekpieces. *Oliver Sherwood* **c–** **h119**

PRESELI STAR (IRE) 7 b.g. Scorpion (IRE) – Horner Hill (IRE) (Oscar (IRE)) [2016/17 h75, b85: h16g⁶ h19.9dᵖᵘ h19.1dᵖᵘ Oct 19] bumper winner: has shown little over hurdles: in headgear last 3 starts. *George Baker* **h–**

PRESENCE FELT (IRE) 9 br.g. Heron Island (IRE) – Faeroe Isle (IRE) (Erins Isle) [2016/17 c–, h116: h23.9g⁵ h23d⁶ h23.3d³ h23.1gᵖᵘ h24g² h23.3g³ h26g⁴ c23.8m⁶ h24.1d* h24.3s⁴ Dec 19] good-topped gelding: fair handicap hurdler: won at Wetherby in December: handicap chaser, fair at best (generally let down by jumping/attitude): left Jonjo O'Neill after eighth start: stays 25f: acts on good to firm and heavy going: has worn headgear: front runner/races prominently. *John Dixon* **c89 §** **h114**

PRESENT ACCEPTED 10 b.g. Presenting – Kwaheri (Efisio) [2016/17 c20.3g⁴ c20.5mᶠ c20.9g* c22.6m* c25.8g* c22.6gᵖᵘ Aug 18] maiden hurdler: modest form over fences: won handicaps at Ffos Las in June, and Stratford and Newton Abbot in July: stays 3¼m: acts on firm going: often travels strongly. *Rod Millman* **c96** **h–**

PRESENTANDCORRECT (IRE) 16 ch.g. Presenting – Friston (IRE) (Roselier (FR)) [2016/17 c22.6gᶠ Apr 23] tall gelding: multiple point winner: winning hurdler: one-time fairly useful chaser: stays 25f: acts on good to firm and good to soft going: has worn headgear: temperamental. *T. F. Sage* **c– §** **h–**

PRESENT DESTINY (IRE) 5 b.g. Dubai Destination (USA) – Anns Present (IRE) (Presenting) [2016/17 b79: b15.7m² b15.7d b15.3v⁶ Mar 9] lengthy gelding: fair form in bumpers. *Seamus Mullins* **b86**

PRESENTED (IRE) 10 ch.g. Presenting – Rustic Court (IRE) (Quayside) [2016/17 c117, h89: c26.2m⁵ c25dᵖᵘ c23.8d⁵ c25.5d⁴ c23.8s* c23.8gᵖᵘ c25.5d c23.8d c24.5d² c26.2dᵖᵘ c26.2dᵖᵘ c23.8d⁵ Nov 14] rather leggy gelding: maiden hurdler: fair handicap chaser: won at Perth in July: stays 33f: acts on good to firm and heavy going: has worn headgear: tried in tongue tie: often races prominently: temperamental. *Lisa Harrison* **c111 §** **h– §**

PRESENTING ARMS (IRE) 10 b.g. Presenting – Banningham Blaze (Averti (IRE)) [2016/17 c131, h131: c20g² c20d² c20gᶜᵒ c20.3g³ c21.4g² c15.9g² c17.5m⁴ Nov 1] compact gelding: useful hurdler: useful handicap chaser: second in listed event at Market Rasen (2 lengths behind Vintage Vinnie) in September and novice at Cheltenham (neck behind Marracudja) in October: reportedly finished lame final outing: stays 21f: acts on good to firm and heavy going: in cheekpieces last 3 starts: wears tongue tie. *Harry Fry* **c140** **h–**

PRESENTING BERKLEY (IRE) 7 br.g. Presenting – Tynelucy (IRE) (Good Thyne (USA)) [2016/17 h16.8g h15.8d h21.2g² h20vᵖᵘ h23.8g⁴ h21m³ Apr 4] poor maiden hurdler: stays 3m: in headgear last 2 starts: often races towards rear. *Tim Vaughan* **h84**

PRESENTING JULIO (IRE) 9 b.g. Presenting – Ouro Preto (Definite Article) [2016/17 h18.5g⁶ h16.3m* h22.2g h20d c17s c19.2g³ c21.2g* c22d⁴ Apr 18] fair on Flat, stays 2m: fair handicap hurdler: won amateurs event at Stratford in October: fair form over fences: won handicap at Tramore in April: left Liam Lennon after fifth start: stays 21f: acts on good to firm going: has worn headgear: wears tongue tie. *Gordon Elliott, Ireland* **c100** **h101**

PRESENTING JUNIOR (IRE) 10 b.g. Presenting – Dr Alice (IRE) (Dr Massini (IRE)) **c123**
[2016/17 c135, h89: c25g³ c21.2m³ c19.4m⁶ c20.5g⁵ c24.3s⁴ c21.5v c25.2s^pu c20g³ Apr 15] **h–**
maiden hurdler: handicap chaser, just fairly useful form in 2016/17: stays 3¼m: acts on soft
and good to firm going: has worn headgear, including in 2016/17. *Martin Todhunter*

PRESENTING LISA (IRE) 8 b.m. Presenting – Miss Esther (GER) (Alkalde (GER)) **c125**
[2016/17 h102: c20d^pu c17.4g⁴ c16.3g⁴ c16.5m* c17.4s² Nov 9] useful-looking mare: fair **h–**
hurdler: fairly useful form over fences: won handicap at Bangor in July and novice
handicap at Huntingdon in October: stays 21f: acts on soft and good to firm going: front
runner/races prominently. *Alan King*

PRESENTING LUCINA (IRE) 5 b.m. Presenting – Lucina (GER) (Groom Dancer **h71**
(USA)) [2016/17 h17.7g⁴ h16g⁶ Sep 6] £7,000 4-y-o: fifth foal: sister to a winning pointer
and half-sister to a winning jumper in Czech Republic by Tobougg: dam French 11.5f/1½m
winner: poor form in mares novice/maiden hurdles. *Neil Mulholland*

PRESENTING PEARL (IRE) 4 b.f. Presenting – Asigh Pearl (IRE) (Lord of Appeal) **b87**
[2016/17 b16.7g² b16g⁴ Apr 17] second foal: dam (h128) bumper and 2m/17f hurdle
winner: fair form in mares maiden bumpers. *Jamie Snowden*

PRESENTING PERCY 6 b.g. Sir Percy – Hunca Munca (IRE) (Presenting) **h152**
[2016/17 b16d h16.5d⁴ h16.2d* h16s* h24d⁵ h24s⁴ h20v* h24g* h24d⁶ Apr 26] **b–**
    Albert Reynolds was Taoiseach when securing the Downing Street
Declaration in 1993, an Anglo-Irish pact which paved the way for an end to the
troubles in Northern Ireland, so it was ironic that one of the horses owned by his son
Philip, Presenting Percy, should be involved in an Anglo-Irish disagreement over
handicapping twenty-four years later, specifically over the treatment of Irish runners
in British jumps handicaps. The issue, which is touched on in the essay on One For
Arthur, is a recurring one—see the essay on Sky's The Limit in *Chasers & Hurdlers
2005/06*—but it reared its head for the first time in the latest season with the release
of the Grand National weights in mid-February, when both Eddie and Michael
O'Leary vociferously complained about the BHA handicapper's assessment of some
of the more highly weighted Gigginstown-owned horses in the Aintree showpiece.
So heated was the exchange between the O'Learys and BHA Head of Handicapping
Phil Smith over the following days that the latter included a statement alongside the
publication of the weights for the handicaps at the Cheltenham Festival, released
on March 1st. Smith's statement said that the BHA's handicapping approach with
Irish horses had provided 'greater equality and fairness' after years of what he felt
was a 'disproportionately high success rate of Irish runners in British handicaps'. It
continued: 'The jump handicappers are confident that there is no semblance of any
anti-Irish bias and that keeping our own Irish performance figures has given our
handicaps greater equality and fairness.'
    The team of BHA handicappers gave Presenting Percy a mark of 146 in
the Pertemps Network Final—6 lb above his Irish Turf Club mark at the time—
immediately picked up by Presenting Percy's connections and described by his
jockey Davy Russell as 'confusing' and 'frustrating'. Russell said: 'I just think there
are talented horses in Ireland, races are more competitive and it's less competitive
in England, you've more meetings. It's unfortunate we have to suffer at a Festival, it

Pertemps Network Final Handicap Hurdle (Listed), Cheltenham—
Presenting Percy provides his connections with a second successive win in the race;
Barney Dwan (right) and Jury Duty (left, diamonds) fill the places

doesn't happen on the Flat and English horses don't get penalised in Ireland.' As it turned out, given the ease with which Presenting Percy won the Pertemps, *another* 6 lb wouldn't have stopped him. In fact, Presenting Percy was one of seven Irish-trained winners of the ten handicaps run at the Cheltenham Festival—Tully East, Supasundae, Road To Respect, Arctic Fire, Champagne Classic and Rock The World were the six others—and there were a further six Irish-trained runners placed in them too. Both Presenting Percy's owner and jockey publicly apologised to Smith after the race, though not in such emphatic fashion as they had voiced their displeasure before it. However, as they had done following the win of Mall Dini for them in the same race twelve months earlier, the owner and jockey directed their praise on to Presenting Percy's trainer Patrick Kelly.

Bar his final run of the season, Presenting Percy progressed on each of his starts, winning a maiden at Galway and a novice handicap at Punchestown in the autumn before shaping well on his first two attempts at three miles, including when fourth in a Pertemps qualifier at the latter track in February. He was well backed and, in a first-time tongue strap, showed further improvement when resuming winning ways in good style at Fairyhouse in February, a performance which earned him a 10-lb rise to an Irish Turf Club mark of 140. As a result of the BHA's additional 6-lb levy, Presenting Percy carried just a pound less than top weight Gayebury in the Pertemps Final in which the twenty-four runners were covered by just 10 lb in the handicap. Presenting Percy looked a graded performer in waiting as he came from the back of the field to the front with an irresistible, sweeping run down the outside in the straight, all without being anything like hard ridden. Merely kept up to his work once there, Presenting Percy recorded a performance good enough to have won every running bar one (Bobs Worth's) of the Spa Novices' Hurdle (Albert Bartlett) since its introduction in 2005, and more than a stone better than Mall Dini had achieved in the Pertemps a year earlier. Barney Dwan was three and three quarter lengths second, Jury Duty a further two lengths away in third, with The Tourard Man a further four and a half lengths back in fourth. Four of the first six were trained in Ireland, though Kadoun (2006) had been the most recent Irish winner of the race before the two most recent renewals. Presenting Percy was stepped up in class for the Grade 1 War of Attrition Novices' Hurdle (Irish Daily Mirror) at the Punchestown Festival for his final start of the season, but ran well below form in a disappointing sixth of eight behind Champagne Classic.

Presenting Percy was a first Cheltenham Festival winner for his sire Sir Percy, one of four Derby-winning stallions—along with Authorized, Galileo and High Chaparral—whose progeny won races at the latest renewal. He is much the best jumper to date for Sir Percy who stands at £7,000 at Lanwades Stud in Newmarket and has been represented by several smart performers on the Flat. Presenting Percy's dam Hunca Munca, a winning pointer who is named after one of the protagonists in Beatrix Potter's *The Tale of Two Bad Mice*, is a half-sister to the useful hurdler/chaser Western Charmer who finished second in the 2011 Irish Grand National. Further back, this is also the family of the 2006 Cheltenham Gold Cup winner War of Attrition with whom Presenting Percy shares his great grandam Tullow Performance. She is also the grandam of another Festival winner King Harald who was successful in the first running of the novices' handicap chase. Presenting Percy's five-year-old half-brother Monkey Puzzle (by Sulamani) showed fair form when second at Doncaster on his hurdling bow for Oliver Sherwood in December. Other siblings include the dual winning pointer Chipmunk (by Kayf Tara) and her brother Just Imagine It, another winner 'between the flags'. The latter was sold to Jack Barber for only £2,000 at Goffs' January Sales, as part of the dispersal of the bloodstock of owner Graham Roach who died in September at the age of sixty-nine. Viking

Mr Philip J. Reynolds' "Presenting Percy"

Flagship won the Queen Mother Champion Chase in 1994 and 1995 in the Roach colours, which were also carried with distinction by such as Thisthatandtother, The Tother One, Cornish Rebel, Prideaux Boy, Shotgun Willy, Just A Par and others. The good-topped Presenting Percy, described by his owner as 'a horse who could make a lovely chaser', looks set to follow the example of the same connections' Mall Dini and switch to chasing with a view to a campaign geared around one of the staying handicaps at the Cheltenham Festival; Mall Dini caught the eye on several occasions during his first season over fences and finished a never-nearer fifth in the Fulke Walwyn Kim Muir on his final start. Presenting Percy, who stays three miles and acts on heavy going, often races towards the rear. He has worn a tongue strap on his last three starts. *Patrick G. Kelly, Ireland*

PRESENTING RED (IRE) 7 b.g. Presenting – Bolly (IRE) (Jolly Jake (NZ)) [2016/17 **h80** h24g⁴ h22.7d⁴ Oct 22] poor form in maiden/novice hurdle, only outings. *Tim Vaughan*

PRESENTING ROSE (IRE) 7 b.m. Presenting – Berkeley House (IRE) (Beneficial) **h100** [2016/17 h108, b81: h21.4d⁴ Oct 29] fair handicap hurdler: stays 21f: acts on heavy going: front runner/races prominently. *N. W. Alexander*

PRESENTING STREAK (IRE) 8 b.g. Presenting – Kuwalla (IRE) (New Frontier **c113** (IRE)) [2016/17 h103, h79: h22m² c20.3d³ h16m³ c17m* c19.4g* c24g² c20.9dᵖᵘ Oct 13] **h103** runner-up once from 6 starts in Irish maiden points: fair maiden hurdler: fair form over fences: won 2 novice handicaps at Stratford in July: stays 3m, effective at much shorter: acts on soft and good to firm going: tried in hood: wears tongue tie. *Peter Winks*

PRESENT LODGER (IRE) 9 b.g. Presenting – Hannigan's Lodger (IRE) (Be My **c117**
Native (USA)) [2016/17 c114, h–: c23.8g² c24.2d⁴ c21.6s⁴ c21.5v⁴ c32.8g^pu Feb 4] useful- **h–**
looking gelding: fairly useful handicap chaser: stays 3m: acts on heavy
going: wears tongue tie. *Lucinda Russell*

PRESENT MAN (IRE) 7 b.g. Presenting – Glen's Gale (IRE) (Strong Gale) [2016/17 **c142**
c125, h116: c25.1m² c20.2m* c25.1m^ur c21d* c24g* c24g⁴ c21m* c28.8g^pu Apr 29] rangy **h–**
gelding: fairly useful form over hurdles: useful chaser: won handicaps at Wincanton in
October and Ascot in November, Grade 2 novice at Doncaster (by 1¾ lengths from Potters
Legend) in December and novice at Ascot (by 1¾ lengths from Dark Flame) in April: stays
25f: acts on good to firm and heavy going: tried in headgear: wears tongue tie: front runner/
races prominently. *Paul Nicholls*

PRESENT TIMES (IRE) 6 b.g. Kalanisi (IRE) – Beguiling (IRE) (Dr Massini (IRE)) **h110**
[2016/17 h98: h16.8s⁵ h15.8v² h19.2v* h17v* Mar 9] sturdy gelding: fair handicap
hurdler: won at Towcester in February and Carlisle (novice event) on final start: stays 19f:
acts on heavy going. *Evan Williams*

PRESENT TREND (IRE) 8 br.m. Presenting – Trendy Attire (IRE) (Luso) [2016/17 h–: **h81**
h15.8g h20g* h22.7s³ h16d⁶ Nov 16] poor handicap hurdler: won conditionals/amateur
event at Worcester in September: stays 2½m: acts on good to firm going: tried in tongue tie.
Richard Ford

PRESIDING (IRE) 8 b.g. Flemensfirth (USA) – Magherareagh Lady (IRE) (Old Vic) **h–**
[2016/17 h19g h19.5s⁶ Jan 20] winning pointer: well held in bumper, and when tongue tied
in 2 novice hurdles. *Nick Mitchell*

PRESSURIZE (IRE) 11 b.g. Witness Box (USA) – Cockpit Rose (IRE) (Be My Native **c100**
(USA)) [2016/17 c131, h–: c20v⁴ c25.1d^pu Mar 26] maiden hurdler: useful handicap **h–**
chaser, well below best in 2016/17: stays 21f: acts on heavy going. *Venetia Williams*

PRET A THOU (FR) 14 ch.g. Funny Baby (FR) – Va Thou Line (FR) (El Badr) [2016/17 **c–**
c113, h99: h19.9v^pu h16.7s³ c16v⁴ c16v⁵ Feb 11] workmanlike gelding: modest handicap **h85**
hurdler: fair handicap chaser in 2015/16, well held both outings over fences in 2016/17:
stays 2½m: acts on good to firm and heavy going: has worn cheekpieces: usually races
close up. *John Groucott*

PRETTY LITTLE LIAR (IRE) 4 br.f. Excellent Art – Pont Allaire (IRE) (Rahy **h76**
(USA)) [2016/17 h16.6g⁵ h16s h16s Jan 28] poor maiden on Flat and over hurdles. *David
Peter Dunne, Ireland*

PRETTYLITTLETHING (IRE) 7 b.m. Tajraasi (USA) – Cloncunny Girl (IRE) **c99 p**
(Roselier (FR)) [2016/17 h16.3m⁵ c16.3m⁴ h15.8g h16.8g c17.4g³ c23g² c24.5m* c25.1m² **h90 p**
c23.6g* h23.4s* Nov 15] fourth foal: dam winning pointer: maiden Irish pointer: modest
form over hurdles: won mares handicap at Fakenham final start: modest form over fences:
won handicap at Towcester in October and novice handicap at Huntingdon in November:
stays 25f: acts on soft and good to firm going: usually travels strongly: open to further
improvement. *Neil Mulholland*

PRETTY MISS MAHLER (IRE) 6 b.m. Mahler – So Pretty (IRE) (Presenting) **h99**
[2016/17 h90: h20d^f h16.2s² h20.5g h19s² h20.6s⁶ h23.8g h19.7d⁵ h20.2g* Apr 28] runner-
up on completed start in Irish points: modest handicap hurdler: won at Perth final start:
stays 2½m: acts on soft going: in cheekpieces 4 of last 5 starts. *Martin Todhunter*

PRETTY MOBILE (FR) 6 gr.m. Al Namix (FR) – Gobeline (FR) (Robin des Champs **c–**
(FR)) [2016/17 h–: h19.6g c20.3d^ur c15.7g^pu h19.1d^ur Oct 19] poor maiden hurdler: no **h–**
encouragement in 2 runs over fences: in cheekpieces last 2 starts, in tongue tie 3 of last 4.
Paul Webber

PRETTY RECKLESS (IRE) 4 b.f. Scorpion (IRE) – Deep Supreme (IRE) (Supreme **h97**
Leader) [2016/17 b13.7m b16.7s⁶ h15.8d⁶ h15.8s h16.8v⁴ h20.3g⁶ Apr 21] seventh foal: **b64**
half-sister to bumper winner/useful hurdler Heath Hunter (17f-2½m winner, by Shantou):
dam unraced sister to high-class chaser (stayed 3m) Nick Dundee and half-sister to high-
class hurdler/smart chaser (stayed 3¼m) Ned Kelly: poor form in bumpers: modest form
over hurdles: races towards rear. *Dan Skelton*

PRETTY ROSE (IRE) 7 b.m. King's Theatre (IRE) – Rosies All The Way (Robellino **h98**
(USA)) [2016/17 h86, b78: h15.8g⁵ h19.9s* h24d^nu h23g⁵ h26.4g⁴ h22m h19.2m² h19.7g⁵
h21d³ h20.7d* h21.6g⁶ Apr 12] modest handicap hurdler: won mares events at Uttoxeter in
June and Huntingdon in March: should stay beyond 2½m: acts on soft and good to firm
going: often wears cheekpieces: inconsistent. *Ben Case*

PRIDE OF PARISH (IRE) 7 br.g. Indian Danehill (IRE) – Inchneedlequinn (IRE) **c107**
(Needle Gun (IRE)) [2016/17 c21.2g* Apr 17] £11,500 5-y-o: seventh foal: dam unraced
daughter of useful hurdler/fair chaser (stayed 2½m) Lucky Baloo: won 3 times in points,
including in April: 7/4, successful on chasing debut later in month in novice hunter at
Fakenham, left in front when clear leader Are They Your Own fell at the last. *Alan Hill*

PRIDE OF PEMBERLEY (IRE) 5 ch.g. Flemensfirth (USA) – On Galley Head (IRE) **b85**
(Zaffaran (USA)) [2016/17 b15.8v⁵ b16s⁴ Feb 4] £12,000 3-y-o: first foal: dam (b91), 2¼m
bumper winner, half-sister to useful hurdler/smart chaser (stays 21f) Dare Me: fair form in
bumpers: bred to be suited by further than 2m. *Jamie Snowden*

PRIDEOFTHECASTLE (IRE) 10 b.g. Waky Nao – Park's Pet (IRE) (Bob Back **c118**
(USA)) [2016/17 c128, h–: c29.1g⁴ May 3] winning hurdler: fairly useful handicap chaser: **h–**
stays 29f: acts on heavy going: in cheekpieces only start in 2016/17: usually races towards
rear, often travels strongly. *David Pipe*

PRIMA VISTA 12 b.g. Singspiel (IRE) – Papering (IRE) (Shaadi (USA)) [2016/17 **c84**
c16.3gᵖᵘ c17.3d⁵ c16g⁵ Sep 18] tall, close-coupled gelding: winning hurdler: maiden **h–**
chaser, failed to complete last one time for Noel Meade: stays 2¾m: acts on heavy going: has worn
headgear/tongue tie, including last 3 starts. *Gary Hanmer*

PRIME VENTURE (IRE) 6 br.g. Primary (USA) – Next Venture (IRE) (Zaffaran **h127**
(USA)) [2016/17 b98: h16.8d* h16v² h19.5s² h17.7v³ h19.3s⁴ h19.8d² Mar 11] useful-
looking gelding: bumper winner: fairly useful form over hurdles: won novice at Sedgefield
in November: second to Minella Awards in EBF 'National Hunt' Novices' Handicap
Hurdle Final at Sandown in March: will be suited by further than 2½m: acts on heavy
going. *Evan Williams*

PRIMO BLUE 7 b.g. Primo Valentino (IRE) – Flintwood (Gunner B) [2016/17 h–: **c–**
c19.1gᶠ h21.9v⁶ h19g⁶ Jan 11] fair form over hurdles: fell heavily first on chasing debut. **h104**
Noel Williams

PRIMO ROSSI 8 b.g. Primo Valentino (IRE) – Flaming Rose (IRE) (Roselier (FR)) **h75**
[2016/17 h65: h19g h18.6g* h20gᶠ h18.7gᶠ h21.4m⁵ h18.5m h19.6g⁵ Apr 22] smallish
gelding: poor handicap hurdler: won novice at Market Rasen in June: stays 19f: best form
on good going: wears cheekpieces/tongue tie: often races freely. *Tom Gretton*

PRIMO TIME 6 b.g. Primo Valentino (IRE) – Eva's Edge (IRE) (Good Thyne (USA)) **b97**
[2016/17 b–: b16.3m⁴ b15.8g* Jul 22] fairly useful form in bumpers: won at Uttoxeter in
July: has joined Sam England. *Michael Appleby*

PRIMROSE BROWN 6 b.m. Indian Danehill (IRE) – Royal Tango (Petoski) [2016/17 **h–**
b78: h15.7g Aug 14] fair form on Flat: in hood, tailed off in mares novice on hurdling
debut: won 2-runner point in April. *Conrad Allen*

PRIMROSE COURT (IRE) 7 ch.m. Golan (IRE) – Sugar Kane Kowa (IRE) **h–**
(Flemensfirth (USA)) [2016/17 b87: b15.7g h18.5sᵖᵘ Dec 15] fair form in bumpers: pulled **b–**
up in mares novice on hurdling debut. *Laura Young*

PRINCE BLACKTHORN (IRE) 11 b.g. Desert Prince (IRE) – Notable Dear (ITY) **c–**
(Last Tycoon) [2016/17 c65, h–: h16.8sᵖᵘ h23.3vᵖᵘ Dec 7] lengthy gelding: maiden hurdler, **h–**
pulled up both starts in 2016/17: poor handicap chaser: stays 2½m: best form on soft/heavy
going: tried in cheekpieces: has worn tongue tie: usually races nearer last than first.
Barry Murtagh

PRINCE FLORBURY 4 b.g. Prince Flori (GER) – Lady Sambury (Overbury (IRE)) **b–**
[2016/17 b14.6s b16v Jan 30] no form in bumpers. *Maurice Barnes*

PRINCE KHURRAM 7 b.g. Nayef (USA) – Saree (Barathea (IRE)) [2016/17 h110: **c119**
c15.9m² c16f* c17.3d² c17.2g³ c16.4g³ c16.4g² c18m² c19.9g³ c20.2f² h16.8s h15.8s⁶ **h98**
h16.7g⁵ h19.6g⁴ Apr 22] useful-looking gelding: fair handicap hurdler: fairly useful chaser:
won novice at Perth in June: stays 2½m: acts on any going: has worn cheekpieces: wears
tongue tie. *Donald McCain*

PRINCELY CONN (IRE) 8 b.g. Whitmore's Conn (USA) – High Priestess (IRE) **h137**
(Priolo (USA)) [2016/17 h20d h16.5g* h16g² h19.5g⁶ h16.1g³ Jul 28] useful hurdler: won
minor event at Clonmel in May: second in handicap at Punchestown in June and third in
Galway Hurdle in July (1¼ lengths behind Clondaw Warrior): unproven beyond 2m: acts
on soft and good to firm going: tried in cheekpieces. *Thomas Mullins, Ireland*

PRINCE MAHLER (IRE) 7 b.g. Mahler – Strokestown Queen (IRE) (Presenting) **c–**
[2016/17 h96: h19.1d h21.6s h21.6v⁶ c23gᶠ c21.7g⁵ h21.4d h19g⁴ h21.9d* h23.9m* **h95**
Apr 27] modest handicap hurdler: won at Ffos Las and Taunton in April: no form over
fences: left Caroline Keevil after first start: stays 3m: acts on soft and good to firm going:
wears tongue tie. *Richard Woollacott*

PRINCE OF CARDAMOM (IRE) 5 b.g. Nayef (USA) – Tiger Spice (Royal Applause) **h–**
[2016/17 h–: h19dᵖᵘ May 2] no form over hurdles: tried in visor/tongue tie. *Jonathan Geake*

PRINCE OF SCARS (IRE) 7 b.g. Flemensfirth (USA) – Spirit Leader (IRE) (Supreme **c134**
Leader) [2016/17 h163: c19d² c20d³ c24d⁶ c25dᵖᵘ c20s³ Mar 12] sturdy gelding: high-class **h–**
hurdler: useful form over fences: second in maiden at Naas in November: stays 3m: acts on
heavy going. *Gordon Elliott, Ireland*

PRINCE OF SILVER 11 gr.g. Helissio (FR) – Fittleworth (IRE) (Bijou d'Inde) [2016/17 **c–**
c–, h60: c19.4g⁶ May 4] poor form over hurdles: no form over fences: wears tongue tie: **h–**
often races prominently. *M. V. Coglan*

PRINCE OF STEAL (IRE) 7 b.g. Craigsteel – Princess Gloria (IRE) (Prince Rupert (FR)) **c121**
[2016/17 h132, b73: c24.2sᶠ h23.4sᵖᵘ c21.2dᵘᶠ h23.1sᵖᵘ Mar 12] good-topped gelding: Irish **h–**
point winner: useful hurdler: failed to complete all starts in 2016/17, including twice over
fences (short of room in third when fell last in maiden at Fakenham on return): should stay
3m: acts on good going: tried in blinkers: often races freely. *James Evans*

PRINCE OF THIEVES (IRE) 7 b.g. Robin des Pres (FR) – Sly Empress (IRE) (Supreme **h60**
Leader) [2016/17 h82: h15.8g⁶ May 14] good-topped gelding: poor maiden hurdler: best
effort at 2¼m: acts on good to soft going: tried in blinkers: wears tongue tie: second in
point in January. *Anthony Honeyball*

PRINCESSE FLEUR 9 b.m. Grape Tree Road – Princesse Grec (FR) (Grand Tresor **c89**
(FR)) [2016/17 c79, h–: c20s* h23gᵖᵘ c20dᶠ c20d c23g⁵ Jul 21] modest handicap chaser: won at Worcester in May: stays 23f: acts on soft and good to firm **h–**
going: tried in cheekpieces: often races towards rear. *Michael Scudamore*

PRINCESS MONONOKE (IRE) 6 b.m. Oscar (IRE) – Grande Solitaire (FR) (Loup **h97**
Solitaire (USA)) [2016/17 b16.4s³ h15.6g h16s⁵ h16.2s* h17g³ Apr 15] £15,000 5-y-o: **b77**
closely related to fair 3m hurdle winner Medinah Gold (by Gold Well), and half-sister to
smart bumper winner Killyglass (by Heron Island) and fair/temperamental hurdler/chaser
Solitary Palm (2m-23f winner, by Great Palm): dam unraced half-sister to Prix Alain du
Breil winner Grand Souvenir and Prix Maurice Gillois winner Polivalente: Irish maiden
point winner: modest form when third in mares bumper at Newcastle (7¾ lengths behind
Illwalktheline) in January: modest form over hurdles: won mares novice at Hexham in
March: will stay beyond 2m. *Donald McCain*

PRINCESS ROANIA (IRE) 6 b.m. Dubai Destination (USA) – Lady Roania (IRE) **h105**
(Saddlers' IRE)) [2016/17 h103p, b96: h18.5g² h16g² h19.9g² h21.6g² h26.4gᵖᵘ Aug
11] bumper/Flat winner: fair maiden over hurdles: should stay 3m: best form on good
going: tried in cheekpieces: in tongue tie last 2 starts. *Peter Bowen*

PRINCESS SONOMA 7 ch.m. Apple Tree (FR) – Sonoma (IRE) (Dr Devious (IRE)) **h–**
[2016/17 h16.5sᵖᵘ Feb 5] first foal: dam (h102), 19f-2¾m hurdle winner, also 1¾m-2m
winner on Flat: pulled up in novice hurdle. *Jeremy Scott*

PRINCESS TIANA (IRE) 6 b.m. Yeats (IRE) – Ar Muin Na Muice (IRE) (Executive **h99**
Perk) [2016/17 h–: h23.3vᵖᵘ h25g³ h23.3s* h24d* h23g² h26.5g h25m⁶ Oct 11] modest
handicap hurdler: won at Uttoxeter (novice) in June and Southwell in July: stays 3m: acts
on soft going: wears tongue tie: often travels strongly. *Jonjo O'Neill*

PRINCETON ROYALE (IRE) 8 br.g. Royal Anthem (USA) – Shelikesitstraight (IRE) **c131**
(Rising) [2016/17 h137: h22.8m h25dᵖᵘ c21.2m* c20g³ c21.2g* c21.4g⁵ c24.2g² c19.9d³ **h–**
Nov 5] lengthy gelding: useful hurdler: useful form over fences: won maiden in June and
2-runner novice (by 8 lengths from Fingerontheswitch) in August, both at Cartmel: stays
25f: acts on good to firm and heavy going: wears headgear: front runner. *Neil King*

PRIORY LAD (IRE) 6 b.g. Arcadio (GER) – Auction Hall (Saddlers' Hall (IRE)) **h86**
[2016/17 h16.2s h19.9s⁴ h19.9d⁵ Dec 2] modest form over hurdles: dead. *Sue Smith*

PRIVATE JONES 8 br.g. Trade Fair – Dafne (Nashwan (USA)) [2016/17 c–, h79: h16g **c60**
c16.5m³ c15.7gᵖᵘ h19.9m h16d c20g Jul 21] sturdy gelding: little form over hurdles/ **h–**
fences: tried in cheekpieces/tongue tie: failed to complete in points in 2017. *Miss
Imogen Pickard*

PRIVATE MALONE (IRE) 8 b.g. Darsi (FR) – Native Artist (IRE) (Be My Native **c122**
(USA)) [2016/17 c135, h–: c24.2s⁵ c23.4d c24.2sᵖᵘ c22.4d³ Mar 24] useful-looking **h–**
gelding: winning hurdler: fairly useful maiden chaser: third in handicap at Newbury in
March: stays 2¾m: acts on heavy going: tried in cheekpieces. *Emma Lavelle*

PROBABLY GEORGE 10 gr.g. Silver Patriarch (IRE) – Java Dawn (IRE) (Fleetwood **c98**
(IRE)) [2016/17 c87, h–: c25.5g³ Jun 1] point winner: well held sole start over hurdles: **h–**
modest form in hunter chases: stays 25f: acts on good to soft going. *Mrs K. Lynn*

PROBLEMA TIC (FR) 11 b.g. Kapgarde (FR) – Atreide (FR) (Son of Silver) [2016/17   **c–** **§** c103§, h–: h23.8g Dec 14] good-topped gelding: fairly useful hurdler at best, well held sole   **h–** start in 2016/17: fairly useful chaser: stays 25f: acts on good to firm and heavy going: has worn headgear: wears tongue tie: usually races in rear: unreliable. *Jackie Stephen*

PRODUCT OF LOVE (IRE) 6 b.g. Fruits of Love (USA) – Annshoon (IRE) (Jurado   **b107** (USA)) [2016/17 b17m* b16d³ Apr 17] €25,000 3-y-o: fifth foal: dam (c104) 2m-2½m hurdle/chase winner: off mark in points on second attempt: useful form in bumpers: won maiden at Killarney (by 16 lengths from Winsor Vixen) in May. *Alan Fleming, Ireland*

PROFESSOR PLUM (IRE) 7 b.g. Kalanisi (IRE) – Miss Plum (Ardross) [2016/17 h88:   **h101** h25.3g⁵ h25d^pu Feb 20] dual bumper winner: fair form over hurdles, lightly raced. *Rose Dobbin*

PROFIT COMMISSION (IRE) 7 b.g. Presenting – Silver Pursuit (Rainbow Quest   **h–** (USA)) [2016/17 h92: h20d⁶ h16.7d h22.1d⁶ Aug 29] maiden hurdler, failed to beat a rival in 2016/17: tried in cheekpieces: in tongue tie last 4 starts. *Gary Hanmer*

PROFOUNDLY (IRE) 9 b.m. Motivator – Deeply (IRE) (Darshaan) [2016/17 h17.3g   **c–** h20g³ h16v^F c18.5g c22d h19.7g h15.7d² h20.3d Nov 29] sixth foal: half-sister to a   **h86** winning pointer by Lomitas and a winner on Flat in Japan by Singspiel: dam useful 1¼m-1¾m winner: modest maiden hurdler: in rear in maiden chases: stays 2¼m: acts on good to firm and good to soft going: wears hood: usually races nearer last than first. *D. McNamara, Ireland*

PROGRESS DRIVE (IRE) 6 b.g. Stowaway – Dolphins View (IRE) (Dolphin Street   **h123** (FR)) [2016/17 b92: h20.5d² h20.5s* h22.7v* h22.8d⁴ h20.5v* h23.9g⁵ Apr 26] bumper winner: fairly useful form over hurdles: won novices at Ayr in December, Kelso in January and again at Ayr in March: stays 23f: best form on soft/heavy going: tried in cheekpieces. *Nicky Richards*

PROJECT BLUEBOOK (FR) 4 bl.g. Sinndar (IRE) – Apperella (Rainbow Quest   **h136** (USA)) [2016/17 h15.7d² h15.6g* h15.6g* h15.6g³ h16.4g⁴ h16d* Apr 17] workmanlike gelding: fairly useful on Flat, stays 14.5f: useful form over hurdles: won juvenile and handicap at Musselburgh in January, and Grade 2 juvenile at Fairyhouse (by ½ length from Dandy Mag) in April: likely to stay further than 2m: acts on good to soft going. *John Quinn*

PROJECT MARS (IRE) 5 b.g. Presenting – Molly Massini (IRE) (Dr Massini (IRE))   **h109 p** [2016/17 b16s⁵ b15.7v³ h19.2m² Apr 13] second foal: dam (c90/h113), 2½m hurdle   **b83** winner, sister to smart hurdler/chaser (2m-3m winner) Massini's Maguire and closely related to fairly useful hurdler/useful chaser (stays 25f) Twirling Magnet: modest form in bumpers: 5/1, some encouragement when second in novice at Towcester (1¼ lengths behind Postbridge) on hurdling debut. *Nick Gifford*

PROMANCO 8 b.m. Kayf Tara – Shelayly (IRE) (Zaffaran (USA)) [2016/17 h117:   **c117** h20.3d c20g² c22.6g⁴ c20g Sep 6] sturdy mare: point winner: fair hurdler: fairly useful   **h–** form over fences: best effort when second in novice at Uttoxeter in July: stays 21f: acts on good to firm going: often in cheekpieces: wears tongue tie: usually races towards rear. *Charlie Longsdon*

PROOFREADER 8 b.g. Authorized (IRE) – Blixen (USA) (Gone West (USA)) [2016/17   **h103** h117: h16d h15.7g⁶ May 24] fair handicap hurdler: raced only at 2m: acted on good to soft going: wore hood: usually raced in rear: dead. *Neil Mulholland*

PROSPECTUS 4 b.g. Sakhee (USA) – Some Sunny Day (Where Or When (IRE))   **h126** [2016/17 h16v* h16d h16s* h16.4g^pu Mar 15] angular gelding: fair on Flat, stays 1½m: fairly useful form over hurdles: won juvenile maiden in December and juvenile in January, both at Fairyhouse: should prove suited by further than 2m. *Gavin Patrick Cromwell, Ireland*

PROSPERA PASCHA 4 br.f. Robin des Champs (FR) – Easter Legend (Midnight Legend)   **b66** [2016/17 b15.8d⁵ b16g⁵ Apr 17] first foal: dam (c140/h137), 19f-2¾m hurdle/chase winner, sister to smart chaser (stayed 21f) Easter Meteor: poor form in bumpers: wears hood/tongue tie. *David Pipe*

PROTEK DES FLOS (FR) 5 b.g. Protektor (GER) – Flore de Chantenay (FR) (Smadoun   **c– p** (FR)) [2016/17 h16.4d⁴ h19.6d⁴ h20.5d Apr 29] useful-looking gelding: useful   **h129** hurdler: well beaten in Fuller's London Pride Novices' Chase (Berkshire) at Newbury on chasing debut: stays 2¼m: best form on soft/heavy going: often races towards rear: should do better over fences. *Nicky Henderson*

PROUD GAMBLE (IRE) 8 b.g. Brian Boru – Sister Anna (Gildoran) [2016/17 c79, h–: **c100** c24.2g c23.8d² c23.9g* c23.4s² c23.8g* c23.8d³ c23.8g* c23.8g³ c25.2s⁴ Feb 3] maiden **h–** hurdler: fair handicap chaser: won at Market Rasen in August, and Musselburgh in November and December: stays 3m: acts on soft going: wears tongue tie. *Rose Dobbin*

PROUD TIMES (USA) 11 b.g. Proud Citizen (USA) – Laura's Pistolette (USA) (Big **c–** Pistol (USA)) [2016/17 c–, h91: c17.4vᵖᵘ c20.2sᶠ c20.9v⁶ Mar 19] rather leggy gelding: **h–** winning hurdler: fair chaser at best, no form in 2016/17: usually wears headgear: has worn tongue tie, including last 3 starts. *Ali Stronge*

PROUTS PUB (IRE) 8 b.g. Catcher In The Rye (IRE) – A Woman In Love (Muhtarram **c–** (USA)) [2016/17 c–, h124: h17.7s⁵ h24.4d h21.6g h19.1g² Apr 12] angular gelding: fairly **h117** useful hurdler: second at Fontwell (conditional) in April: no form over fences: stays 2½m: acts on heavy going: tried in blinkers. *Nick Gifford*

PROVINCIAL PRIDE (IRE) 10 b.g. Whitmore's Conn (USA) – Soraleda (IRE) **c71** (Toulon) [2016/17 c99, h83: c22.6mᵖᵘ c23g⁴ c24.5m⁵ Oct 5] winning hurdler: modest **h–** maiden chaser at best: stays 23f: acts on soft and good to firm going: has worn headgear, including in 2016/17: wears tongue tie. *Mike Hammond*

PRUSSIAN EAGLE (IRE) 6 br.g. Jeremy (USA) – Absolutely Cool (IRE) (Indian **c75** Ridge) [2016/17 h15.8g h15.8v⁶ c16dᵖᵘ c16s⁴ Feb 19] fairly useful hurdler at best, no form **h–** in 2016/17: poor form over fences: unproven beyond 2m: acts on heavy going: tried in cheekpieces: often races towards rear. *Evan Williams*

PSYCHOCANDY (IRE) 5 b.m. Oscar (IRE) – Derrigra Sublime (IRE) (Flemensfirth **h84** (USA)) [2016/17 b15.7d⁵ b16s h16.6d h16.6g h19.7sᵘʳ h16v² Mar 22] €22,000 3-y-o: **b–** fourth foal: sister to modest hurdler Oscars Way (3¼m winner) and closely related to a winning pointer by Milan: dam, tailed off in bumpers, half-sister to fairly useful hurdler/ useful chaser (stayed 2½m) Gemini Lucy, herself dam of useful hurdler (stays 25f) Dadsintrouble: no form in bumpers: poor form over hurdles: should be suited by further than 2m: tried in cheekpieces: usually races towards rear. *Ian Williams*

PSYCHOLOGY 4 b.g. Shamardal (USA) – Emotion Parade (ARG) (Parade Marshal **b–** (USA)) [2016/17 b14d b13g Nov 26] modest maiden on Flat, stays 16.5f: no form in bumpers: in tongue tie second start. *Kenny Johnson*

PTIT ZIG (FR) 8 b.g. Great Pretender (IRE) – Red Rym (FR) (Denham Red (FR)) **c–** [2016/17 c164, h162: h21.4s⁴ h25.4d⁴ h23.9s³ h24.4d⁴ h24s h24.7g⁶ h21.5g² Apr 29] strong **h161** gelding: high-class hurdler: third in Grand Prix d'Automne at Auteuil (9 lengths behind Alex de Larredya) in November and second in Select Hurdle at Sandown (1½ lengths behind L'Ami Serge) in April: high-class chaser when last seen over fences in 2015/16 season: stays 25f: acts on good to firm and heavy going: wears blinkers. *Paul Nicholls*

PUDSEY HOUSE 10 b.g. Double Trigger (IRE) – Dara's Pride (Darazari (IRE)) **h–** [2016/17 h19.3gᵖᵘ h25.3dᵖᵘ Dec 13] fair hurdler at best, no form in 2016/17: stays 25f: acts on soft going: wears headgear. *Chris Grant*

PUFFIN BILLY (IRE) 9 b.g. Heron Island (IRE) – Downtown Train (IRE) (Glacial **c–** Storm (USA)) [2016/17 h24.7gᵖᵘ Apr 8] workmanlike gelding: useful hurdler at best, **h–** pulled up sole start in 2016/17: smart chaser: stays 25f: acts on good to firm and heavy going. *Oliver Sherwood*

PULLED ANOTHER 6 b.m. Tobougg (IRE) – Mini Mandy (Petoski) [2016/17 b15.7gᵖᵘ **b–** May 24] no form in bumpers. *David Bridgwater*

PULLING POWER 7 br.m. Erhaab (USA) – Pulling Strings (IRE) (Accordion) [2016/17 **h112** h113, b89: h21.6d⁴ h20.5gᵘʳ h24vᵖᵘ h21.2g³ Apr 3] good-bodied mare: fair handicap hurdler: should stay 3m: acts on heavy going: wears tongue tie: usually races close up. *Kim Bailey*

PULL THE CHORD 7 b.g. St Jovite (USA) – Gold Chord (IRE) (Accordion) **c133** [2016/17 h129: c20m² c18.8dᶠ c19.2v³ c20s² c23g⁴ c22.6g² Apr 1] useful-looking gelding: **h–** fairly useful hurdler: useful form over fences: second in handicap at Ludlow (9 lengths behind Pougne Bobbi) in February: stays 2¾m: acts on good to firm and heavy going. *Philip Hobbs*

PULL THE TRIGGER 6 b.g. Double Trigger (IRE) – Soloism (Sulaafah (USA)) [2016/17 **h–** b17.7g⁴ h20v⁵ Mar 1] runner-up in maiden point on debut: tailed off in bumper/novice **b–** hurdle. *Tim Vaughan*

PULP FICTION (IRE) 5 b.g. Robin des Champs (FR) – Bean Ki Moon (IRE) (King's **b94**
Theatre (IRE)) [2016/17 b16.4g³ Oct 22] €36,000 3-y-o, £55,000 4-y-o: second foal: dam
unraced out of useful 2m hurdle winner Titled Dancer: third in Irish maiden point on debut:
in hood, 25/1, third in bumper at Cheltenham (6¼ lengths behind Brahms de Clermont) in
October. *Ben Case*

PULPITARIAN (USA) 9 b.g. Pulpit (USA) – Bedanken (USA) (Geri (USA)) [2016/17 **h95**
h87: h18.1s² h16.2s h19.4g³ h23.8g* h23.8gᵖᵘ Mar 1] small gelding: modest handicap
hurdler: won at Musselburgh in January: stays 3m: acts on soft going: wears headgear:
races prominently. *Lucinda Russell*

PUPPET WARRIOR 5 ch.g. Black Sam Bellamy (IRE) – Rakajack (Rakaposhi King) **b95**
[2016/17 b17.7g² b16s² b17.7s³ Mar 30] €20,000 3-y-o, resold £14,000 3-y-o:
closely related to fair 2½m hurdle winner Dundock (by Cloudings) and half-brother to
several winners, including fairly useful chaser Greywell Boy (2m winner, by Fair Mix),
stayed 2½m: dam unraced half-sister to dams of useful staying chasers Ballyfitz and You're
Agoodun: fairly useful form when placed all 4 starts in bumpers: will be suited by 2½m+.
Nick Gifford

PURCELL'S BRIDGE (FR) 10 b.g. Trempolino (USA) – Theatrical Lady (USA) **c115**
(Theatrical) [2016/17 c112, h–: c20d c22.9v* c24.2m⁴ Apr 13] winning hurdler: fairly **h–**
useful handicap chaser: won veterans event at Haydock in March: stays 3¼m: acts on good
to firm and heavy going: wears hood. *Rose Dobbin*

PURE POTEEN (IRE) 9 ch.g. Flemensfirth (USA) – Taking My Time (IRE) (High Roller **c96 x**
(IRE)) [2016/17 c111, h–: c23g c23.9g⁶ c25.8m⁶ h23.1g⁴ c23.6gᵖᵘ Oct 8] sturdy gelding: **h82**
poor hurdler: fair handicap chaser: stayed 25f: acted on heavy going: tried in hood:
often wore tongue tie: usually raced towards rear: often let down by jumping: dead.
Neil Mulholland

PURE VISION (IRE) 6 b.g. Milan – Distillery Lane (IRE) (Exit To Nowhere (USA)) **h117**
[2016/17 h85+, b107: h16s⁶ h16d h16g* h19.9v² h21.4s⁴ h23.1d* Mar 21] useful-looking
gelding: useful bumper performer: fairly useful handicap hurdler: won at Lingfield in
December and Exeter (novice) in March: stays 23f: acts on heavy going: has worn tongue
tie, including last 4 starts: usually races towards rear. *Anthony Honeyball*

PURPLE GENIE (GR) 5 ch.m. Tiantai (USA) – Purple Way (GR) (Apotheosis (USA)) **h–**
[2016/17 h–, b76: h16.3m May 15] close-coupled mare: no form over hurdles. *Patrick
Chamings*

PURPLE HARRY 9 gr.g. Sir Harry Lewis (USA) – Ellfiedick (Alfie Dickins) [2016/17 **c97**
h23.3sᵖᵘ c23.4s* Apr 3] fair hurdler in 2014/15, pulled up on return: 9/1, won novice **h–**
handicap at Kelso (by 2¼ lengths from Marlee Massie) on chasing debut: stays 25f: acts on
heavy going. *Tina Jackson*

PURPLE 'N GOLD (IRE) 8 b.g. Strategic Prince – Golden Dew (IRE) (Montjeu (IRE)) **c134**
[2016/17 c134, h120: c18g c19m* c20g⁴ c16.5g⁴ h20d³ c17m⁴ c20g³ c20.3g⁴ c19.4m⁶ **h118**
c22.6g³ c17.4g² c25.2g⁶ h16.4g c17.5m c16g⁴ Apr 17] compact gelding: fairly useful
handicap hurdler: third at Worcester in June: useful handicap chaser: won at Haydock in
May: stays 2½m: acts on good to firm and good to soft going: wears headgear. *David Pipe*

PURSUITOFHAPPINESS (IRE) 9 b.g. Classic Cliche (IRE) – Lake Tour (IRE) **c–**
(Aristocracy) [2016/17 c81, h–: c21.2gᴿ h19.7vᵖᵘ Jan 11] strong gelding: little form over **h–**
hurdles/fences: in headgear last 4 starts: in tongue tie last 3. *Neil Mulholland*

PUT THE BOOT IN (IRE) 5 ch.g. Duke of Marmalade (IRE) – Mubkera (IRE) (Nashwan **h–**
(USA)) [2016/17 h91: h16g h15.8g h18.6g⁶ h15.3sᵖᵘ h16.8dᵖᵘ h16.8g Apr 26] sturdy
gelding: maiden on Flat: little form over hurdles: tried in cheekpieces: has joined Nikki
Evans. *Barry Brennan*

PUTTING GREEN 5 ch.g. Selkirk (USA) – Ryella (USA) (Cozzene (USA)) [2016/17 **h108**
h16g h16.3g⁴ h15.7d⁴ h16.8s h15.8v² h15.8d⁴ Mar 15] strong, compact gelding: useful on
Flat, stays 1¾m: fair form over hurdles: should prove suited by 2¼m+: acts on good to soft
going. *Venetia Williams*

PUYOL (IRE) 15 b.g. Zaffaran (USA) – Star Mover (Move Off) [2016/17 c87, h–: c24.1g **c– §**
Apr 29] tall gelding: winning pointer/hurdler: poor hunter chaser nowadays: stays 2½m: **h–**
acts on heavy going: tried in cheekpieces: temperamental. *Patricia Rigby*

PYJ

PYJAMA GAME (IRE) 11 b.g. Hernando (FR) – Princess Claudia (IRE) (Kahyasi) **c63 §**
[2016/17 c93§, h–§: c26.2m⁶ May 29] winning pointer: maiden hurdler: poor chaser: stays **h– §**
27f: acts on good to firm and heavy going: has worn headgear: temperamental. *Captain W. B. Ramsay*

PYM (IRE) 4 b.g. Stowaway – Liss Rua (IRE) (Bob Back (USA)) [2016/17 b16g* Apr 22] **b106**
€35,000 3-y-o: half-brother to 3 winners, including fairly useful hurdlers Beneagles (25f winner, by Milan) and Minella Aris (3m winner, by King's Theatre): dam (h97), bumper winner (placed up to 3m over hurdles), half-sister to very smart hurdler (winner up to 2½m) Liss A Paoraigh: 12/5, won bumper at Ayr (by 4 lengths from Cool Mix) on debut. *Nicky Henderson*

PYRIOS (FR) 4 b.g. Heliostatic (IRE) – Nuance Tartare (FR) (Nononito (FR)) [2016/17 **b–**
b16.3g⁶ Apr 1] well beaten in bumper. *Philip Hobbs*

PYROMANIAC (IRE) 7 b.g. Invincible Spirit (IRE) – Silly Goose (IRE) (Sadler's Wells **c104**
(USA)) [2016/17 h134: h17m³ h16.1g h15.7d⁶ c17v³ c17s³ c16.5d Apr 18] sturdy gelding: **h134**
useful handicap hurdler: third at Killarney (4¼ lengths behind Ancient Sands) in May: fair form over fences: unproven beyond 17f: acts on good to firm and heavy going: has worn cheekpieces, including last 3 starts: wears tongue tie. *A. J. Martin, Ireland*

PYRSHAN (IRE) 8 b.g. Pyrus (USA) – Runshangale (IRE) (Anshan) [2016/17 h106: **c108**
h23.6d⁴ c24d³ c19.9d³ Dec 26] good-topped gelding: placed both completed starts in Irish **h96**
points: fair maiden hurdler: similar form over fences: stays 3m: acts on soft going: wears tongue tie: often races in rear. *Graeme McPherson*

PYTHON 5 b.g. Dansili – Imbabala (Zafonic (USA)) [2016/17 b16.2d Jun 30] tailed off in **b–**
bumper/Flat maidens. *Andrew Crook*

Q

QATEA (IRE) 5 ch.g. Duke of Marmalade (IRE) – Taking Liberties (IRE) (Royal Academy **h–**
(USA)) [2016/17 h76: h17.2g h16.8m Apr 19] little form over hurdles: tried in blinkers/tongue tie. *Donald McCain*

QIBTEE (FR) 7 b.g. Antonius Pius (USA) – Embers of Fame (IRE) (Sadler's Wells **h–**
(USA)) [2016/17 h19.7d⁶ h15.7d Feb 26] modest/quirky on Flat, stays 1½m: little impact over hurdles. *Les Eyre*

QODIAQ (IRE) 4 b.g. Kodiac – Queen Althea (IRE) (Bach (IRE)) [2016/17 b13.7g **h77**
ab16g⁵ h15.7v⁵ Feb 2] modest form in bumpers: 25/1, fifth in novice at Towcester on **b77**
hurdling debut. *Caroline Bailey*

QORTAAJ 4 b.g. Kyllachy – Cardrona (Selkirk (USA)) [2016/17 h15.7sᵖᵘ Jan 31] modest **h–**
maiden on Flat, stays 9.5f: pulled up in novice on hurdling debut. *David Loughnane*

QRACKERS (FR) 13 b.g. Lahint (USA) – Babolna (FR) (Tropular) [2016/17 c–, h–: **c112**
c20g³ Apr 3] tall, angular gelding: point winner: winning hurdler: fair hunter chaser: stays **h–**
3m: acts on good to firm and heavy going: usually wears tongue tie. *Miss V. Collins*

QUADRILLER (FR) 10 b.g. Lando (GER) – Tabachines (FR) (Art Francais (USA)) **c117**
[2016/17 c109, h99: c17.4d* c17.4g* Jun 7] winning hurdler: fairly useful form over **h–**
fences: won handicaps at Fontwell early in season: stays 2¼m: acts on soft and good to firm going: wears tongue tie. *Philip Hobbs*

QUALANDO (FR) 6 b.g. Lando (GER) – Qualite Controlee (FR) (Poliglote) [2016/17 **c130**
h144: c19.8g³ c18.8d⁴ c23g⁵ h19g² h20.3g² Apr 19] good-topped gelding: useful handicap **h136**
hurdler: second at Cheltenham (½ length behind Political Quiz) in April: similar form over fences: won handicap after third start: stays 2½m: acts on heavy going: wears headgear: often races towards rear. *Alan Jones*

QUANTITATIVE EASING (IRE) 12 ch.g. Anshan – Mazuma (IRE) (Mazaad) [2016/17 **c–**
c140, h–: c33g* c24g² h21.6s c30.2gᵖᵘ Mar 15] workmanlike gelding: useful hurdler/ **h–**
chaser at best (has run at 8 Cheltenham Festivals, last 4 appearances in Cross Country Chase): stays 33f: acts on heavy going: often wears headgear. *Enda Bolger, Ireland*

QUANTUM OF SOLACE 7 b.m. Kayf Tara – Fashion House (Homo Sapien) [2016/17 **c87**
h98: h16m⁶ h23g⁶ h18.7m³ h15.8g* c16.5m⁴ c16gᵖᵘ Nov 10] modest handicap hurdler: **h91**
won mares event at Uttoxeter in September: similar form over fences: left Noel Williams after first start: unproven beyond 2m: acts on good to firm and good to soft going: wears hood: tried in tongue tie: often races freely. *Martin Keighley*

QUARENTA (FR) 5 b.g. Voix du Nord (FR) – Negresse de Cuta (FR) (Baroud d'Honneur (FR)) [2016/17 b97: h18.5g h15.8s h19g⁴ h20.5sᵖᵘ Mar 3] bumper winner: fair form over hurdles: often races prominently. *Jonjo O'Neill* **h110**

QUARRY LAMI (IRE) 6 gr.g. Daylami (IRE) – Lady Leila (IRE) (Taipan (IRE)) [2016/17 h16.7g h16d h19.5g h16.7d Dec 26] runner-up on second of 2 starts in Irish maiden points: no form in bumper/over hurdles. *Sophie Leech* **h–** **b–**

QUARRYMAN 6 ch.g. Act One – Bluebell Path (Classic Cliche (IRE)) [2016/17 h101, b–: h18.5g² h20m⁶ h15.3dᵖᵘ h23.9g⁵ h15.9s³ h15.3s c19.7sᵖᵘ h19.5g⁵ h21.6m Apr 15] modest maiden hurdler: pulled up in novice handicap on chasing debut: stays 2¼m: best form on soft/heavy going: usually wears headgear: temperament under suspicion. *Ron Hodges* **c–** **h90**

QUARRY WIZARD (IRE) 7 b.g. Trans Island – Hazel Green (IRE) (Teamster) [2016/17 h16g⁶ h16.3m h16s h19.5v³ h24v⁵ h19.7d h19.8v Mar 9] €7,000 3-y-o: strong gelding: first foal: dam unraced half-sister to useful hurdler/smart chaser (stayed 2¾m) Mossy Green: Irish point winner: modest maiden hurdler: should stay 2½m+: acts on heavy going: wears hood. *Sophie Leech* **h87**

QUEBEC 6 b.g. Dansili – Milford Sound (Barathea (IRE)) [2016/17 h114: c21.4g⁵ h19.9g² h21g⁶ h21d h23.6gᵖᵘ h21.4s h19.9v Feb 11] good-topped hurdler: well held in novice handicap on chasing debut: left Charlie Mann after third start: stays 2½m: acts on soft going: has worn cheekpieces: tried in tongue tie: usually races nearer last than first. *Matt Sheppard* **c–** **h104**

QUEEN ODESSA (IRE) 6 b.m. King's Theatre (IRE) – Ma Furie (FR) (Balleroy (USA)) [2016/17 b105: b16.4s h16.7s³ Feb 19] good-topped mare: fair form in bumpers: 11/10, third in mares novice at Market Rasen (9¾ lengths behind All My Love) on hurdling debut: likely to stay 2½m: should do better. *Harry Fry* **h102 p** **b–**

QUEEN OF AVALON (IRE) 6 b.m. Westerner – Courtain (USA) (Diesis) [2016/17 b16s b17s h16.2s³ Dec 29] half-sister to several winners, including fairly useful hurdlers Dreadnot (2m-3m winner, by Dr Fong) and Upsanddowns (17f-21f winner, by Definite Article) and a winning pointer by Beneficial: dam unraced: no form in bumpers: 25/1, third in mares novice at Kelso (13 lengths behind Jolie Crickette) on hurdling debut. *N. W. Alexander* **h83** **b–**

QUEEN OF DRAGONS 5 b.m. Recharge (IRE) – Primitive Princess (Primitive Rising (USA)) [2016/17 b16.2s b16s Jan 26] first foal: dam unraced: poor form in bumpers. *Alastair Ralph* **b72**

QUEEN OF EPIRUS 9 ch.m. Kirkwall – Andromache (Hector Protector (USA)) [2016/17 h16.5g⁶ h19s² Feb 5] poor maiden hurdler: best at 2m: acts on soft going: tried in tongue tie. *Nigel Hawke* **h81**

QUEEN OF NORWAY (IRE) 6 b.m. Papal Bull – Fanacanta (IRE) (Olden Times) [2016/17 h17.7dᵖᵘ Sep 4] fair maiden at best on Flat, has regressed: in cheekpieces, pulled up in novice on hurdling debut. *Paddy Butler* **h–**

QUEEN OLIVIA 9 b.m. King's Theatre (IRE) – Queen's Leader (Supreme Leader) [2016/17 c95, h–: c16.3gᶠ May 9] winning hurdler: modest form over fences: unproven beyond 2m: acts on heavy going: usually wears hood: tried in tongue tie: won twice in points in April 2017. *Oliver Sherwood* **c–** **h–**

QUEENS BAY 11 b.m. Karinga Bay – Minibelle (Macmillion) [2016/17 c22.6m³ c23gᵖᵘ c23.8d² c25.8gᶠ c24.2gᵖᵘ Oct 28] tall mare: won all 4 starts in points: winning hurdler: fair maiden chaser: left Jack R. Barber after first start: stays 25f: acts on soft going: tried in cheekpieces: has worn tongue tie: often let down by jumping. *Neil Mulholland* **c102 x** **h–**

QUEENS CLOAK (IRE) 4 b.f. Definite Article – Love Divided (IRE) (King's Ride) [2016/17 b16.5m⁵ Apr 27] seventh foal: half-sister to bumper winner/modest hurdler Belcanto (2¼m winner, by Bach) and a winning pointer by Milan: dam (h89), placed in point/over hurdles from 2 starts, half-sister to fair hurdler/fairly useful chaser (winner up to 2¾m) Contempo Suite: well beaten in mares bumper. *Jamie Snowden* **b–**

QUEENS PRESENT (IRE) 6 ch.m. Presenting – Fairy Dawn (IRE) (Old Vic) [2016/17 h20.5g* h21s h21v³ h24.4g³ h24v⁴ h21.6d³ h25.6g² Apr 12] £55,000 5-y-o: fifth foal: dam (b95), bumper winner on only start, sister to Cheltenham Gold Cup winner Kicking King: winning pointer: fair hurdler: won mares novice at Plumpton in October: stays 3¼m: acts on heavy going: tried in cheekpieces. *David Arbuthnot* **h112**

QUEEN SPUD 8 b.m. Multiplex – Hurtebise (FR) (Groom Dancer (USA)) [2016/17 c82, h103: c20g⁵ c20d² c20.3gꟳ c24g³ c23gꟳ c20g⁶ c21.2g* c24.2s* c20.8g³ c24.1g⁶ c22.2g⁵ Apr 15] compact mare: fair hurdler: fair handicap chaser: won at Fakenham in October and November (mares event): stays 3m: acts on soft going: usually wears cheekpieces: front runner/races prominently: often let down by jumping. *Henry Daly* **c112 x h—**

QUEENS WELL (IRE) 6 b.m. King's Theatre (IRE) – Kaniskina (IRE) (Bob Back (USA)) [2016/17 b15.8m* h19.5g² h20.5g² Oct 31] €13,500 3-y-o: second foal: sister to a winning pointer: dam unraced sister to St Leger winner Bob's Return: in frame all 4 starts in Irish points: won mares bumper at Uttoxeter (by 2¾ lengths from Betterlatethanneva) in June: fair form over hurdles, runner-up both starts in mares novices: left Fergal O'Brien after first start: will be suited by further than 2½m: in tongue tie last 2 starts. *Jamie Snowden* **h114 b83**

QUEER TIMES (IRE) 8 b.g. Zagreb (USA) – Lucy Walters (IRE) (King's Ride) [2016/17 h20d h21d Dec 15] Irish maiden point winner: well held both starts over hurdles: dead. *Kim Bailey* **h—**

QUEL ELITE (FR) 13 b.g. Subotica (FR) – Jeenly (FR) (Kadalko (FR)) [2016/17 h112§: c23.8g⁵ Apr 28] lengthy, angular gelding: dual winning pointer: fair hurdler: well beaten in hunter on chasing debut: stays 25f: acts on heavy going: has worn headgear: irresolute. *Miss G. Walton* **c63 § h— §**

QUENCH TARA 10 b.m. Kayf Tara – Madam Min (Overbury (IRE)) [2016/17 h87: h19.9g h19.9g⁶ h19.1g⁵ h20mᵖᵘ Aug 30] poor maiden hurdler: usually in hood: often races in rear. *Michael Scudamore* **h81**

QUERRY HORSE (FR) 5 b.g. Equerry (USA) – La Richelandiere (FR) (Garde Royale) [2016/17 h120: c16.5g² c17.4s⁴ c19.1d* c23.8sᵘʳ c22.6gᵖᵘ Apr 1] fairly useful hurdler: similar form over fences: won novice at Doncaster in January: should stay beyond 19f: acts on soft going: tried in blinkers. *Oliver Sherwood* **c125 h—**

QUE SERA (IRE) 7 b.g. Rakti – Mitsina (Fantastic Light (USA)) [2016/17 h114: h19.9vᵖᵘ h15.8s⁵ Dec 6] fair hurdler: unproven beyond 2m: acts on heavy going: in headgear last 3 starts: tried in tongue tie. *Philip Hobbs* **h99**

QUESTIONATION (IRE) 6 b.m. Dubai Destination (USA) – How Is Things (IRE) (Norwich) [2016/17 b16d⁴ b16d⁴ b16.2g Apr 25] fourth foal: half-sister to fairly useful hurdler Little Boy Boru (2½m/21f winner, by Brian Boru), stays 3m, and bumper/fair hurdler King of Firth (2m winner, by Flemensfirth): dam (c96/h91) 2¼m/2½m hurdle/chase winner: modest form in bumpers. *Stuart Crawford, Ireland* **b81**

QUEST MAGIC (IRE) 11 ch.g. Fantastic Quest (IRE) – Magic Sign (IRE) (The Parson) [2016/17 h100: h16.2s³ h22.7sᵘʳ h16.4sᵖᵘ h23.8g h19.3gᵖᵘ c20.9vᵖᵘ Mar 9] fair maiden hurdler at best: pulled up in novice handicap on chasing debut: left George Bewley after fifth start: stays 2½m: acts on good to firm and good to soft going: usually wears headgear: tried in tongue tie: front runner/races prominently. *Tristan Davidson* **c— h81**

QUICKASYOUCAN (IRE) 9 b.g. Beneficial – Nativebaltic (IRE) (Be My Native (USA)) [2016/17 h23.9s⁶ Jul 26] tall gelding: fairly useful hurdler at best: maiden chaser: stays 3m: acts on soft going: tried in headgear/tongue tie. *Colin A. McBratney, Ireland* **c— h107 ?**

QUICK BREW 9 b.g. Denounce – Darjeeling (IRE) (Presenting) [2016/17 c110, h112: c20.1g⁴ c15.6d² c16d³ c20.3g⁴ c16.4gꟳ c16.4g⁵ c20.1g* c19.9d⁵ h20.1g Apr 25] winning hurdler: fair handicap chaser: won novice event at Hexham in October: stays 2½m: acts on soft going: has worn headgear, including in 2016/17: wears tongue tie: races towards rear. *Maurice Barnes* **c103 h103**

QUICK DECISSON (IRE) 9 b.g. Azamour (IRE) – Fleet River (USA) (Riverman (USA)) [2016/17 c112, h108: c15.6d c15.5d² c17.1s² c19.9d* Nov 14] lengthy gelding: winning hurdler: fair handicap chaser: won at Musselburgh in November: stays 2½m: acts on heavy going: has worn headgear. *Stuart Coltherd* **c107 h—**

QUICK GRABIM (IRE) 5 b.g. Oscar (IRE) – Top Her Up (IRE) (Beneficial) [2016/17 b16v² b16d* b16.8s b16.4g Mar 15] €30,000 3-y-o: smallish gelding: brother to bumper winner Cougar's Gold, closely related to fairly useful hurdler/chaser Acordeon (2m winner, by Accordion) and half-brother to 2 winners, including fairly useful chaser Having A Cut (2½m/21f winner, by Supreme Leader): dam unraced: useful form in bumpers: won at Leopardstown in December. *R. P. McNamara, Ireland* **b105**

QUICK JACK (IRE) 8 ch.g. Footstepsinthesand – Miss Polaris (Polar Falcon (USA)) [2016/17 h143: h16.1g h15.7d⁵ Dec 17] smallish, lengthy gelding: useful handicap hurdler: likely to stay further than 2m: acts on good to soft going. *A. J. Martin, Ireland* **h145**

QUICK PICK (IRE) 6 b.g. Vinnie Roe (IRE) – Oscars Arrow (IRE) (Oscar (IRE)) **b91**
[2016/17 b16g² Apr 24] €1,200 4-y-o: third foal: dam, placed in points, out of sister to
outstanding chaser Captain Christy: won maiden on third start in Irish points: 10/1, second
in bumper at Warwick (4 lengths behind Not That Fuisse) in April. *Jennie Candlish*

QUIDS IN (IRE) 4 b.g. Pour Moi (IRE) – Quixotic (Pivotal) [2016/17 h16s⁴ h16.2v² **h115**
h15.8v* h16.3s³ h16.3g³ h16g⁵ Apr 29] fairly useful form over hurdles: won maiden at
Uttoxeter in February: raced around 2m: acts on heavy going. *Oliver Greenall*

QUIET ACCOUNT (IRE) 9 b.g. Jimble (FR) – Celia's Pet (IRE) (Kemal (FR)) **c117**
[2016/17 c27.5m* c22.6s⁵ c24.3sᵘʳ c20s² Mar 17] multiple point winner: maiden hurdler: **h–**
fairly useful hunter chaser: won novice at Stratford in May: stays 3½m: acts on soft and
good to firm going. *Colin A. McBratney, Ireland*

QUIET CANDID (IRE) 8 b.m. Beneficial – Lady of Appeal (IRE) (Lord of Appeal) **c105**
[2016/17 h105: c19.4g c15.7v² Jun 02] lengthy mare: won Irish mares maiden point on **h–**
debut: fair hurdler: similar form over fences: unproven beyond 17f: acts on heavy going:
wears hood: usually travels strongly. *Nicky Henderson*

QUIETLY (IRE) 6 b.g. Oscar (IRE) – Gimme Peace (IRE) (Aristocracy) [2016/17 b–: **h115**
h16.2s² h21.3d³ h22.7vᵘʳ h22s³ h24.1m² Apr 13] sturdy gelding: fairly useful form over
hurdles: placed 4 times in 2016/17: should stay 3m: acts on soft going: usually leads.
Sue Smith

QUIETO SOL (FR) 6 ch.g. Loup Solitaire (USA) – First Wonder (FR) (Mansonnien **h112**
(FR)) [2016/17 h112p, b87: h20.3g² h19.3m³ h19m⁵ h23.8g⁴ Feb 4] angular gelding: fair
handicap hurdler: likely to prove best at shorter than 3m: acts on good to firm and good to
soft going: tried in cheekpieces: often travels strongly. *Charlie Longsdon*

QUIGLEY COURT (IRE) 5 b.g. Court Cave (IRE) – Mrs Quigley (IRE) (Mandalus) **h–**
[2016/17 b16.7d h15.8s h15.8d h19.7s h20.3s Mar 20] no form in bumper/over hurdles. **b–**
Evan Williams

QUILL ART 5 b.g. Excellent Art – Featherweight (IRE) (Fantastic Light (USA)) [2016/17 **h96**
h102: h16.7gᵖᵘ h19.3g h19.4d h15.7s³ h15.8dᵘʳ h16d h15.7g Apr 21] modest handicap
hurdler: unproven beyond 17f: acts on soft going: in headgear last 3 starts. *Richard Fahey*

QUILL STREET (IRE) 7 b.m. Kalanisi (IRE) – Anshabella (IRE) (Anshan) [2016/17 **h–**
h19.2vᵖᵘ Feb 2] €16,000 3-y-o, £16,000 5-y-o: second foal: dam unraced half-sister to
useful hurdler/smart chaser (stayed 3½m) Strath Royal and to dam of Irish Grand National
winner Niche Market: runner-up in Irish maiden point: pulled up in mares novice on
hurdling debut. *Henry Daly*

QUINCY MAGOO (IRE) 8 ch.g. Mountain High (IRE) – Vicky's Lodge (IRE) **h95**
(Daggers Drawn (USA)) [2016/17 h92: h19.9vᵘʳ h15.9v⁶ h23.4d⁴ Feb 17] sturdy gelding:
modest form over hurdles: best effort at 23f: acts on good to soft going: usually races nearer
last than first. *Neil King*

QUINE DES CHAMPS 5 b.m. Midnight Legend – Quine de Sivola (FR) (Robin des **b61**
Champs (FR)) [2016/17 b15.8v⁴ b15.7s Feb 18] £9,500 4-y-o: first foal: dam unraced half-
sister to fairly useful hurdler/useful maiden chaser (stayed 33f) Nine de Sivola: poor form
in bumpers. *David Loder*

QUINSMAN 11 b.g. Singspiel (IRE) – Penny Cross (Efisio) [2016/17 c24.2g⁵ May 3] **c–**
rather leggy gelding: multiple winning pointer: winning hurdler: fair chaser at best: stays **h–**
23f: acts on good to soft and good to firm going: usually wears cheekpieces. *Miss
Louise Allan*

QUINTO 7 ch.g. Desideratum – Cruz Santa (Lord Bud) [2016/17 h114, b78: h21.6d h23.1g **c101**
h23.1s⁵ h26v c24.2s² c21.1v² c24.2s³ c24.2g² Apr 11] medium-sized gelding: winning **h101**
pointer: fair handicap hurdler: similar form over fences: stays 25f: acts on heavy going:
often races in rear. *Jimmy Frost*

QUITE BY CHANCE 8 b.g. Midnight Legend – Hop Fair (Gildoran) [2016/17 c131, h–: **c148**
c21g⁶ c16.9m* c16.9d² c20.8s⁴ c20.8s⁶ c20.5d⁴ c16.3g c21.1gᵖᵘ Apr 7] sturdy gelding: **h–**
maiden hurdler: smart handicap chaser: won listed event at Ascot (by 6 lengths from Noche
de Reyes) in October: fourth in Caspian Caviar Gold Cup at Cheltenham (2 lengths behind
Frodon) in December: stays 23f: acts on good to firm and heavy going. *Colin Tizzard*

QUITE SPARKY 10 b.g. Lucky Story (USA) – Imperialistic (IRE) (Imperial Ballet **h–**
(IRE)) [2016/17 h–: h16.2d Apr 30] plain, rather sparely-made gelding: poor maiden
hurdler: stays 19f: acts on soft going: often wears headgear: has worn tongue tie.
Lucinda Egerton

QUITO DU TRESOR (FR) 13 b.g. Jeune Homme (USA) – Itiga (FR) (Djarvis (FR)) [2016/17 c112§, h–: c20.1d⁵ c20.1s⁴ c19.9g⁴ c19.9g³ c19.9g Jan 20] neat gelding: winning hurdler: modest handicap chaser nowadays: stays 3m: acts on soft and good to firm going: wears cheekpieces: unreliable. *Lucinda Russell* **c99 §** **h–**

QUIZ MASTER (IRE) 5 b.g. Ask – Good Bye Dolly (IRE) (Buckskin (FR)) [2016/17 b16g⁶ h19.1sᵖᵘ h15.3v³ h15.3d³ Mar 26] £40,000 3-y-o: sixth foal: dam (h90), 2¼m hurdle winner, half-sister to fairly useful staying chaser Radiation: sixth in bumper: poor form over hurdles: bred to be suited by 2½m+: in tongue tie last 2 starts: still unexposed. *Colin Tizzard* **h84 p** **b73**

QULINTON (FR) 13 b.g. Bulington (FR) – Klef du Bonheur (FR) (Lights Out (FR)) [2016/17 c94, h–§: c25.5gᵖᵘ May 29] useful-looking gelding: winning hurdler: useful chaser at best for David Pipe: stays 3¾m: acts on good to firm and heavy going: has worn headgear/tongue tie: front runner/races prominently: has looked less than keen, and not one to rely on. *Johnny Farrelly* **c–** **h– §**

R

RAAJIH 9 gr.g. Dalakhani (IRE) – Thakafaat (IRE) (Unfuwain (USA)) [2016/17 c–, h–: c20.2dᵖᵘ c20.2s⁴ c25.1df⁷ c23.6gᵖᵘ Apr 17] leggy gelding: winning hurdler: useful chaser at best, little form in 2016/17: stays 25f: acts on good to firm and heavy going: has worn headgear/tongue tie. *Ron Hodges* **c103** **h–**

RABUNDA (IRE) 7 b.g. Milan – Cush Ramani (IRE) (Pistolet Bleu (IRE)) [2016/17 h19.7s h16.3g⁵ Apr 1] useful-looking gelding: runner-up in Irish maiden point: lightly raced over hurdles: best effort at 2½m: tried in tongue tie. *Tom George* **h83**

RACHAEL'S RUBY 10 b.m. Joe Bear (IRE) – Fajjoura (IRE) (Fairy King (USA)) [2016/17 h–: h15.8gᵖᵘ h16m h16g Sep 6] angular mare: maiden hurdler: usually wears headgear. *Roger Teal* **h–**

RACING PULSE (IRE) 8 b.g. Garuda (IRE) – Jacks Sister (IRE) (Entitled) [2016/17 c134, h–: c25gᵘʳ c27.3sᵇᵈ c26.3s⁶ c25.2vᵖᵘ h23.6v Feb 25] sturdy gelding: winning hurdler: useful chaser at best, little form in 2016/17: stays 3m: acts on heavy going: tried in cheekpieces: has worn tongue tie: has joined Richard Hobson. *Rebecca Curtis* **c113** **h–**

RACING SPIRIT 5 ch.g. Sir Percy – Suertuda (Domedriver (IRE)) [2016/17 h82: h15.8m³ h15.5g⁶ h16g⁴ h19v⁶ h21.2m³ Apr 25] modest form over hurdles: left Kevin Frost after first start: stays 21f: acts on good to firm going: tried in cheekpieces. *Dave Roberts* **h87**

RADICAL ARCHIE 6 ch.g. Prince Arch (USA) – Radical Gunner (Gunner B) [2016/17 b16d⁴ ab16g⁶ h16s⁶ Jan 8] first foal: dam, third in point, half-sister to useful/staying chaser Tyneandthyneagain: fair form in bumpers: 20/1, sixth in maiden at Chepstow (13¼ lengths behind Russian Service) on hurdling debut: left Shane Donohoe after first start: will stay beyond 2m: should do better. *Evan Williams* **h101 p** **b90**

RADMORES REVENGE 14 b.g. Overbury (IRE) – Harvey's Sister (Le Moss) [2016/17 h19.9v Feb 11] sturdy gelding: fairly useful hurdler at best, well held sole start in 2016/17 after 2-year absence: stays 3m: best form on ground softer than good (acts on heavy): has worn cheekpieces. *Sophie Leech* **h–**

RADSOC DE SIVOLA (FR) 12 bl.g. Video Rock (FR) – Kerrana (FR) (Cadoudal (FR)) [2016/17 c–§, h–: c15.7vʳʳ Mar 6] sturdy gelding: winning hurdler: maiden chaser, no longer of any account: has worn blinkers: refused to race last 2 starts. *John Cornwall* **h–**

RADUIS BLEU (FR) 12 gr.g. Dadarissime (FR) – Regence Bleue (FR) (Porto Rafti (FR)) [2016/17 c66, h59: c24.1g⁶ h25.5s c20.9vᵖᵘ Feb 7] leggy gelding: maiden hurdler: fair chaser at best, retains little ability: has worn cheekpieces. *Lady Susan Brooke* **c–** **h–**

RAENNAVICH 5 b.m. Black Sam Bellamy (IRE) – Lady Wright (IRE) (King's Theatre (IRE)) [2016/17 b16d b16.8d⁶ h16.8g h16.8g⁶ Apr 7] first foal: dam (h99), 2½m hurdle winner, out of sister to high-class hurdler (2m/2¼m winner) Colonel Yeager: limited impact in bumpers/over hurdles. *Michael Easterby* **h–** **b–**

RAE'S CREEK 7 ch.g. New Approach (IRE) – All's Forgotten (USA) (Darshaan) [2016/17 c15.7sᵖᵘ Dec 17] fairly useful form over hurdles for Mrs J. Harrington: failed to complete in 2 starts in chases: stays 2¼m: acts on good to soft going: wears hood: should do better over fences. *Jonjo O'Neill* **c– p** **h–**

RAFAFIE 9 b.g. Kayf Tara – Florie (Alflora (IRE)) [2016/17 h104: h26.4m^{pu} h16.2s h15.7s^5 h19.1v^2 h19.5s* Mar 13] fair handicap hurdler: won at Chepstow in March: stays 19f: best form on soft/heavy going. *Susan Gardner* **h102**

RAGDOLLIANNA 13 b.m. Kayf Tara – Jupiters Princess (Jupiter Island) [2016/17 h92: h16d^4 Jun 19] sturdy mare: modest maiden hurdler: unproven beyond 17f: acts on good to firm and good to soft going. *Mark Hoad* **h83**

RAGGED WOOD (IRE) 5 b.g. Yeats (IRE) – She's All That (IRE) (Bob Back (USA)) [2016/17 b16.2g^4 Apr 28] €45,000 3-y-o: closely related to fair hurdler/useful chaser Down Under (2½m-25f winner, by Milan): dam unraced: maiden pointer: 12/1, fourth in bumper at Perth (5¼ lengths behind Planet Nine) in April. *Nigel Twiston-Davies* **b95**

RAID STANE (IRE) 11 b.g. Morozov (USA) – Rashhattan (IRE) (Rashar (USA)) [2016/17 c–, h87: h23.9m* h22.1d* Jun 26] winning pointer: fair handicap hurdler: won novice events at Perth in May and Cartmel in June: maiden chaser: stays 3¼m: acts on good to firm and heavy going: wears headgear: has worn tongue tie. *Julia Brooke* **c–** **h103**

RAIFTEIRI (IRE) 10 b.g. Galileo (IRE) – Naziriya (FR) (Darshaan) [2016/17 c–x, h66: c17.3m c20.1g c20.1d c20.1d c25.5g^{pu} Jul 18] rather leggy gelding: winning pointer: winning hurdler: maiden chaser, little form nowadays: wears headgear, including in 2016/17: has worn tongue tie: often let down by jumping over fences. *William Young Jnr* **c– x** **h–**

RAILWAY DILLON (IRE) 12 b.g. Witness Box (USA) – Laura's Native (IRE) (Be My Native (USA)) [2016/17 c108, h–: c23.8m^4 c26.6g^{pu} Feb 4] strong, lengthy gelding: winning pointer: winning hurdler: fair chaser: dual winner on heavy going: has worn headgear, including last 2 starts: has worn tongue tie. *Mrs C. Drury* **c100** **h–**

RAILWAY STORM (IRE) 12 ch.g. Snurge – Stormy Bee (IRE) (Glacial Storm (USA)) [2016/17 c105, h–: c25.8g^4 c25.8m^{pu} c30.7m^3 Apr 18] tall gelding: winning pointer: maiden hurdler: modest handicap chaser: stays 31f: acts on good to firm and heavy going: tried in cheekpieces: has worn tongue tie. *Jimmy Frost* **c95** **h–**

RAILWAY VIC (IRE) 10 b.g. Old Vic – Penny Apples (IRE) (Jolly Jake (NZ)) [2016/17 c–, h66: h19.9g h21.6g^4 h20g^3 h19.5d^6 h23.9g Dec 20] winning pointer: poor maiden hurdler: well held only outing over fences: stays 2½m: acts on soft going: tried in blinkers/tongue tie. *Jimmy Frost* **c–** **h62**

RAINBOW BLUES 6 b.g. Rainbow High – Royal Fontaine (IRE) (Royal Academy (USA)) [2016/17 b16.8g^5 b16g h21.4m^3 h22g^{pu} Oct 27] no form in bumpers/hurdles. *Brian Barr* **h–** **b–**

RAINBOW DREAMER 4 b.g. Aqlaam – Zamhrear (Singspiel (IRE)) [2016/17 h16g^2 h16g^3 h17.7d* h17.7s* h16.8s^2 h16.4g Mar 15] lengthy gelding: dam half-sister to fairly useful hurdler (2m winner) Dalaki: useful on Flat, stays 2¼m: fairly useful form over hurdles: won juveniles at Fontwell (twice) in December: second in Triumph Hurdle Trial (Finesse) at Cheltenham (9 lengths behind Defi du Seuil) in January: stays 2¼m: acts on soft going: in headgear last 4 starts: usually races close up. *Alan King* **h125**

RAINBOW HAZE 11 b.g. Rainbow High – Kristal Haze (Krisinsky (USA)) [2016/17 c–, h99: h23g^2 h20g h20v^5 h25.5s^{pu} h21.4d^{pu} Feb 18] point winner: modest handicap hurdler: pulled up only outing over fences: stays 3m: acts on heavy going: tried in blinkers/tongue tie: front runner. *Phillip Dando* **c–** **h90**

RAINBOW RISE 7 b.g. Rainbow High – Inglerise (Primitive Rising (USA)) [2016/17 b16d Jun 22] tailed off in bumper. *Michael Mullineaux* **b–**

RAIN IN THE FACE 4 b.g. Naaqoos – Makaaseb (USA) (Pulpit (USA)) [2016/17 h15.7s h16.8v^5 h15.7d h16g^6 h16.2v^4 h15.7g^{pu} Apr 21] fair maiden on Flat, stays 1m: no form over hurdles. *Sam England* **h–**

RAINY CITY (IRE) 7 b.g. Kalanisi (IRE) – Erirante (IRE) (Denel (FR)) [2016/17 h122: h21.4m* h20.2f* h21.6d^2 c20.9g^2 h23.4s^3 h21g Feb 25] lengthy, useful-looking gelding: useful hurdler: won novices at Wincanton in May and Perth in June: 5/2, second in maiden at Hereford (14 lengths behind Emerging Force) on chasing debut: stays 23f: acts on firm and soft going: wears tongue tie: usually races close up, often travels strongly: should do better over fences. *Paul Nicholls* **c126 p** **h133**

RAINY DAY DYLAN (IRE) 6 br.g. Spadoun (FR) – Honeyed (IRE) (Persian Mews) [2016/17 b19s* b17d^{pu} h19.7v^5 h19.5v^5 h19.8v^2 Mar 9] €12,000 3-y-o: brother to fairly useful 2m chase winner Icing On The Cake (stays 2½m) and half-brother to 2 winners by Old Vic, including fairly useful hurdler/useful chaser Gurkha Brave (2m-2½m winner): **h95** **b96**

dam unraced half-sister to smart 2m hurdler Carobee: pulled up both starts in points: fairly useful form in bumpers: won maiden at Cork in August: modest form over hurdles: left Shane Donohoe after second start: usually leads. *Neil Mulholland*

RAISE A SPARK 7 b.g. Multiplex – Reem Two (Mtoto) [2016/17 h109§: h19.7s² h16.7s* h18.1s h15.7s³ h15.7s* h16.4v³ h19.3v* h16.8d³ h16.5g⁴ Apr 8] fairly useful handicap hurdler: won at Bangor (conditional) in December, Catterick in February and conditionals/ amateur event at Carlisle in March: stays 2½m: acts on heavy going: wears hood. *Donald McCain* **h120**

RAISED ON GRAZEON 6 ch.m. Lucky Story (USA) – Graze On And On (Elmaamul (USA)) [2016/17 b93: b16.3g² Sep 3] fair form at best in bumpers. *John Quinn* **b75**

RAISING HOPE (IRE) 8 b.m. Turtle Island (IRE) – Jurado It Is (IRE) (Jurado (USA)) [2016/17 h20g h20d h20g⁵ h20.6s⁵ h25s⁴ c20.2spu Feb 28] point winner: poor maiden hurdler: pulled up in novice handicap on chasing debut: left John J. Walsh after second start: tried in tongue tie. *Paul Henderson* **c–** **h71**

RAISING THE BAR (IRE) 5 b.g. Kalanisi (IRE) – Cool Quest (IRE) (Turtle Island (IRE)) [2016/17 b16s⁶ b15.8g⁵ Apr 3] rather unfurnished gelding: modest form in bumpers: will be suited by 2½m. *Nicky Henderson* **b79**

RAJAPUR 4 gr.g. Dalakhani (IRE) – A Beautiful Mind (GER) (Winged Love (IRE)) [2016/17 h16.2d² Jun 4] modest maiden on Flat: in cheekpieces, 25/1, second in juvenile at Hexham (neck behind Skylark Lady) on hurdling debut. *Philip Kirby* **h93**

RAKTIMAN (IRE) 10 ch.g. Rakti – Wish List (IRE) (Mujadil (USA)) [2016/17 c129, h102: h21.3g c19.3d⁴ c21.2g² c30g c19.3s² c21.2d³ c26.3v* c22.6g Apr 1] quite good-topped gelding: fairly useful hurdler at best: fairly useful handicap chaser: won at Sedgefield in March: stays 3¼m: acts on good to firm and heavy going: has worn cheekpieces: wears tongue tie. *Sam England* **c124** **h–**

RALEAGH MOUNTAIN (IRE) 6 b.g. Mountain High (IRE) – Culmore Lady (IRE) (Insan (USA)) [2016/17 h16m h16.2d³ h20.2s⁴ Jul 26] €35,000 3-y-o: third foal: dam (h80) bumper winner/maiden hurdler (stayed 2½m): modest form over hurdles: in tongue tie last 2 starts: has joined Dan Skelton. *Colin A. McBratney, Ireland* **h87**

RAMBLE ON (IRE) 7 br.g. Arcadio (GER) – Soviet Princess (IRE) (Soviet Lad (USA)) [2016/17 c23.6mpu Apr 28] won all 3 completed starts in points: poor form over hurdles: pulled up in novice hunter on chasing debut: in cheekpieces last 2 starts. *Kieran Price* **c–** **h–**

RAMBLING QUEEN (IRE) 4 gr.f. Mastercraftsman (IRE) – Dos Lunas (IRE) (Galileo (IRE)) [2016/17 b16.7g Mar 27] first foal: dam ran twice on Flat in France: tailed off in mares maiden bumper on debut. *Brian Rothwell* **b–**

RAMBLING RECTOR (FR) 5 ch.g. Bonbon Rose (FR) – Califea (FR) (Nikos) [2016/17 b16s⁵ Mar 30] won Irish point on debut: 5/2, fifth in maiden bumper at Warwick in March. *Warren Greatrex* **b–**

RAMONEX (GER) 6 b.g. Saddex – Ramondia (GER) (Monsun (GER)) [2016/17 b15.8m³ b16.3g⁶ h20sF h16.5g⁵ h16.2g* Apr 27] third foal: dam German 6f/7f winner: fair form in bumpers: similar standard over hurdles: won novice at Perth in April: left Rebecca Curtis after fourth start: likely to prove best at easy 2m: tried in tongue tie: front runner/ races prominently. *Richard Hobson* **h107** **b88**

RAMORE WILL (IRE) 6 gr.g. Tikkanen (USA) – Gill Hall Lady (Silver Patriarch (IRE)) [2016/17 b16g⁵ h18s h18d h16d h20s⁴ h19.4g⁴ h20.2g Apr 26] first foal: dam, unraced, out of half-sister to smart staying chaser Frenchman's Creek: point winner: little impact in bumpers: modest maiden hurdler: stays 2½m: acts on soft going: has joined Chris Gordon. *Ian Ferguson, Ireland* **h96** **b–**

RAMSES DE TEILLEE (FR) 5 gr.g. Martaline – Princesse d'Orton (FR) (Saint Cyrien (FR)) [2016/17 h16.5g⁴ h16.5g³ h16.6d² h19.8d⁶ Mar 11] £27,000 3-y-o, £55,000 4-y-o: leggy gelding: brother to French 19f chase winner Sissi de Teille and half-brother to 3 winners in France, including cross-country chaser Diva de Teille (2½m-25f winner, by Great Journey): dam ran once in France: off mark in Irish maiden points at second attempt: fair form over hurdles: in tongue tie last 2 starts. *David Pipe* **h112**

RANJAAN (FR) 9 b.g. Dubai Destination (USA) – Ridafa (IRE) (Darshaan) [2016/17 h20g h16d h16v⁴ h16d⁶ Apr 21] rangy gelding: fair handicap hurdler: unproven beyond 17f: acts on heavy going: has worn headgear/tongue tie. *S. Wilson, Ireland* **h106**

RAPANUI (IRE) 5 ch.g. Flemensfirth (USA) – Beautiful Night (FR) (Sleeping Car (FR)) [2016/17 h19.5dpu h21g³ h19.5s⁶ h21s⁶ Feb 10] poor form over hurdles: tried in cheekpieces. *Jonjo O'Neill* **h63**

RASASEE (IRE) 4 gr.g. Rip Van Winkle (IRE) – Gleaming Silver (IRE) (Dalakhani **h64**
(IRE)) [2016/17 h15.8m³ Apr 18] fairly useful maiden on Flat, stays 1¾m: 12/1, third in
juvenile at Ludlow on hurdling debut: wore hood. *Tim Vaughan*

RASCO (IRE) 8 b.g. Oscar (IRE) – Birdless Bush (IRE) (Be My Native (USA)) [2016/17 **h76**
h20sᵖᵘ h16d h21vᵖᵘ h23.8g⁶ Jan 3] fair hurdler at best, has deteriorated considerably: stays
2¼m. *L. Young, Ireland*

RASHAAN (IRE) 5 ch.g. Manduro (GER) – Rayyana (IRE) (Rainbow Quest (USA)) **h146**
[2016/17 h136: h16d h16.1g h16v⁵ h16g² h16g* h16v³ h20g⁵ h16g Apr 28] smart hurdler:
won WKD Hurdle at Down Royal (by 1½ lengths from Apple's Jade) in November: third
in Red Mills Trial Hurdle at Gowran (5¼ lengths behind Tombstone) in February: raced
mainly around 2m: acts on heavy going. *Colin Thomas Kidd, Ireland*

RAT A TAT TAT 5 b.g. Getaway (GER) – Knock Down (IRE) (Oscar (IRE)) [2016/17 **b–**
b16.7g⁵ May 15] tailed off in bumper on debut. *Tim Vaughan*

RATHEALY (IRE) 6 b.g. Baltic King – Baltic Belle (IRE) (Redback) [2016/17 h–: h20g⁵ **h106**
h18.5m⁵ h21.6gᵖᵘ h20g h19.5d⁵ h15.5g* h20.5d* h20s² h19.4d h15.9v⁶ h16dᵖᵘ Mar 31]
rather leggy gelding: fair hurdler: won sellers at Leicester (twice) in December: left David
Pipe after eighth start: stays 2½m: acts on heavy going: wears headgear/tongue tie: front
runner. *Christine Dunnett*

RATHER BE (IRE) 6 b.g. Oscar (IRE) – Irish Wedding (IRE) (Bob Back (USA)) [2016/17 **h143**
b113: h16.2g* h19.6d* h16v² h20.3gᵘʳ h20g* h21.5g Apr 29] good-topped gelding: useful
bumper performer: useful form over hurdles: won novices at Hereford in October and
Huntingdon in December, and Grade 3 handicap at Aintree (by ½ length from Dream
Berry) in April: stays 2½m: acts on heavy going: tried in hood: often travels strongly.
Nicky Henderson

RATHLIN 12 b.g. Kayf Tara – Princess Timon (Terimon) [2016/17 c142, h–: c15.2s **c111**
c15.2d⁴ c19.4s⁴ c15.2d⁵ c16.3v⁴ Feb 15] strong, deep-girthed gelding: has reportedly had **h–**
breathing operation: winning hurdler: useful handicap chaser, below best in 2016/17: stays
2¾m: acts on good to firm and heavy going: often wears cheekpieces: wears tongue tie:
often races freely. *Micky Hammond*

RATHLIN ROSE (IRE) 9 b.g. Bonbon Rose (FR) – A Plus Ma Puce (FR) (Turgeon **c136**
(USA)) [2016/17 c127, h–: c23.4s⁴ c24.2s* c24.2d* c24.1gᵖᵘ Apr 15] good-topped **h–**
gelding: winning pointer/hurdler: useful form over fences: won Royal Artillery Gold Cup
(Amateur Riders) in February and Grand Military Gold Cup (Amateur Riders) in March,
both at Sandown: stays 25f: acts on soft and good to firm going: usually wears headgear.
David Pipe

Alder Hey Children's Charity Handicap Hurdle, Aintree—Rather Be (No.7) outbattles the grey
Dream Berry after Clondaw Kaempfer's final-flight blunder leaves them clear

RATHNURE REBEL (IRE) 7 b.g. Beneficial – Euro Magic (IRE) (Eurobus) [2016/17 **h132** b16d⁶ h20.5d h19.3d* h24s* h24s⁴ h24v⁵ Feb 2] third foal: brother to fair 2m hurdle **b69** winner Corbally: dam unraced half-sister to smart hurdlers up to 3m Earth Magic and Sweet Kiln (latter by Beneficial): winning pointer: well beaten in maiden bumper: useful form over hurdles: won maiden at Clonmel in November and Kerry Group Stayers Novices' Hurdle at Cork (by 11 lengths from Monbeg Notorious) in December: stays 3m: acts on soft going: sometimes in hood: front runner/races prominently. *Noel Meade, Ireland*

RATHPATRICK (IRE) 9 b.g. Oscar (IRE) – Rua Lass (IRE) (Beau Sher) [2016/17 c–, **c–** h136: h24dᵖᵘ h22.8vᵘʳ h24d h20v⁵ h19s* h24dᵇᵈ Apr 27] angular gelding: useful handicap **h135** hurdler: won at Naas (by 1½ lengths from Carrig Cathal) in March: no form over fences: stays 3m: acts on heavy going. *Eoin Griffin, Ireland*

RATIFY 13 br.g. Rakaposhi King – Sea Sky (Oats) [2016/17 c114, h90: c19.4d c19.2v³ **c99** h19.5s Mar 13] sturdy, good-bodied gelding: maiden hurdler: fair handicap chaser: stays **h–** 25f: acts in visor: has worn tongue tie: front runner. *Dai Burchell*

RAVELOE 5 b.m. Midnight Legend – Over Sixty (Overbury (IRE)) [2016/17 b16d² **h–** b16.3m³ b15.8m⁴ b17.7d⁴ h20s b17v⁶ Feb 18] close-coupled mare: second foal: half-sister **b82** to bumper winner/useful hurdler Spirit of Kayf (2m/2¾m winner, by Kayf Tara): dam (c128/h135), 2m-2¾m hurdle/chase winner, half-sister to useful hurdler (stayed 3m) Diamant Noir: modest bumper performer: tailed off in mares maiden on hurdling debut: left Harry Fry after fourth start. *P. A. Fahy, Ireland*

RAVENHILL ROAD (IRE) 6 ch.g. Exit To Nowhere (USA) – Zaffarella (IRE) **b110** (Zaffaran (USA)) [2016/17 b16.7g* b16.6g* Nov 25] £100,000 5-y-o: first foal: dam (h112), 2m-3m hurdle winner, half-sister to fair hurdler/fairly useful chaser (stayed 2½m) Prosecco: won Irish maiden point on debut: useful form in bumpers: won at Market Rasen (by 14 lengths from Temple Man) in October and Doncaster (by 4½ lengths from Molly Childers) in November. *Brian Ellison*

RAVENOUS 6 b.g. Raven's Pass (USA) – Supereva (IRE) (Sadler's Wells (USA)) **h89** [2016/17 h15.9g⁴ Oct 17] angular gelding: fair maiden hurdler at best: will prove best around 2m: acts on soft going: sometimes in cheekpieces. *Luke Dace*

RAVENS HILL (IRE) 4 ch.g. Raven's Pass (USA) – Sister Red (IRE) (Diamond Green **h108 p** (FR)) [2016/17 h16d⁶ h16g³ h16.2s⁴ h16m² Apr 13] modest maiden on Flat, stays 1¼m: fair form over hurdles: left P. J. Prendergast after third start: likely to progress further. *Dan Skelton*

RAVEN'S TOWER (USA) 7 b.g. Raven's Pass (USA) – Tizdubai (USA) (Cee's Tizzy **c130** (USA)) [2016/17 c137, h–: c17gᵖᵘ h20d⁵ c17.4g⁵ c18m³ c15.8d* c16.4g³ c18.8d c15.2d³ **h119** c15.5s c15.8gᵖᵘ Apr 6] compact gelding: fairly useful handicap hurdler: useful handicap chaser: won at Aintree (by 2¼ lengths from Keel Haul) in November: best form at 2m: acts on good to firm and heavy going: tried in blinkers/tongue tie. *Ben Pauling*

RAY DIAMOND 12 ch.g. Medicean – Musical Twist (USA) (Woodman (USA)) [2016/17 **c101 §** c94, h–: c20v² c19.7s³ c19.2s⁶ h25g² c21mᵖᵘ Apr 15] close-coupled gelding: winning **h87** hurdler: fair handicap chaser: best at short of 3m: acts on good to firm and heavy going: usually wears headgear: temperamental. *Jackie du Plessis*

RAYMOND REDDINGTON (IRE) 6 b.g. Spadoun (FR) – Martovic (IRE) (Old Vic) **h–** [2016/17 h80, b79: h19.9sᵖᵘ May 3] poor form over hurdles: front runner/races prominently: won point in April 2017. *Chris Grant*

RAYVIN BLACK 8 b.g. Halling (USA) – Optimistic (Reprimand) [2016/17 h144: h16m⁴ **c86 p** h15.3m² h15.7d c16s³ h16v² h15.3d⁵ h17.9v Mar 5] good-topped gelding: useful hurdler: **h143** second in listed event at Sandown (1½ lengths behind Buveur d'Air) in February: well held in novice on chasing debut: best around 2m: acts on good to firm and heavy going: often wears cheekpieces: usually leads: should do better over fences. *Oliver Sherwood*

RAZ DE MAREE (FR) 12 ch.g. Shaanmer (IRE) – Diyala III (FR) (Quart de Vin (FR)) **c141 x** [2016/17 c30dᵘʳ c25d² c28g* c24d c29.5s² h23.1s² c34.3dᵘʳ c29dᵖᵘ c30d Apr 29] sturdy **h118** gelding: fairly useful handicap hurdler: useful handicap chaser: won Cork National (by ½ length from Forever Gold) in November: second in Welsh Grand National at Chepstow (1¾ lengths behind Native River) in December: stays 33f: acts on heavy going: has worn headgear: often let down by jumping. *Gavin Patrick Cromwell, Ireland*

RAZZLE DAZZLE 'EM 8 b.g. Phoenix Reach (IRE) – Rasmani (Medicean) [2016/17 **c76** h78: c17.3m⁵ c15.6d⁵ c21.2m h18.7m c20gᵘʳ h16g³ h16.8g Oct 27] poor handicap hurdler: **h66** similar form over fences: unproven beyond 2m: acts on soft going: has worn tongue tie. *Shaun Harris*

READY TOKEN (IRE) 9 gr.g. Flemensfirth (USA) – Ceol Tire (IRE) (Roselier (FR)) **c125** [2016/17 c112, h–: c24d* c24g* c29.2gᵖᵘ c23.8d c24g⁴ Dec 29] workmanlike gelding: **h–** maiden hurdler: fairly useful handicap chaser: won at Warwick in May and September: stays 25f: acts on soft and good to firm going: has worn headgear: wears tongue tie: usually leads. *Charlie Longsdon*

REAL ACROBAT (IRE) 6 b.g. Acrobat (IRE) – Snurges Pie (IRE) (Snurge) [2016/17 **h–** h20.5dᵖᵘ h20.5sᵖᵘ h20.5sᵖᵘ Dec 5] failed to complete both starts in Irish maiden points: pulled up all starts over hurdles: tried in tongue tie. *R. Mike Smith*

REALITY BITES (IRE) 6 b.g. Mahler – Seeds of Doubt (IRE) (Night Shift (USA)) **h–** [2016/17 h19.3dᵖᵘ Nov 18] won Irish maiden point on debut: pulled up in maiden on hurdling debut. *Alan King*

REAL KING 5 b.g. Multiplex – Gertrude Webb (Central Park (IRE)) [2016/17 b15.7g³ **b75** Aug 31] 66/1, third in maiden bumper at Southwell (11½ lengths behind Midas Gold) on debut. *Charles Pogson*

REAL MILAN (IRE) 12 b.g. Milan – The Real Athlete (IRE) (Presenting) [2016/17 c–, **c112** h–: c23gᵘʳ c23.8s² Mar 23] useful-looking gelding: multiple point winner: winning hurdler: **h–** fair chaser: stays 25f: acts on heavy going: has worn headgear, including last 5 starts: has worn tongue tie. *Nick J. Jones*

REALT MOR (IRE) 12 b.g. Beneficial – Suez Canal (FR) (Exit To Nowhere (USA)) **c137 x** [2016/17 c132, h–: c23.8f⁴ c20g c20.1s³ c17d* c24vᶠ c20sᵖᵘ c16g* c20.4g³ c24d h20d⁴ **h136** h20d* c16s² c18v³ c20sᵖᵘ c17s⁴ c24g⁶ c16dᶠ Apr 25] tall gelding: useful form over hurdles: won handicap at Thurles (by 4¾ lengths from Inch Rise) in January: useful chaser: won minor event at Ballinrobe in August and handicap at Down Royal in November: second in Tied Cottage Chase at Punchestown (6½ lengths behind Douvan) in February: stays 2½m: acts on heavy going: tried in hood/tongue tie: often races in rear: often let down by jumping. *Gordon Elliott, Ireland*

REAR ADMIRAL (IRE) 11 b.g. Dushyantor (USA) – Ciaras Charm (IRE) (Phardante **c118 §** (FR) [2016/17 c118§, h–: c20.1d³ c19.1g⁴ c21.2d* c24.2g⁴ Mar 17] big, lengthy gelding: **h–** winning hurdler: fairly useful handicap chaser: won at Fakenham in February: stays 21f: acts on soft going: wears tongue tie: usually races towards rear: consistent, but irresolute. *Michael Easterby*

REBECCAS CHOICE (IRE) 14 b.g. Religiously (USA) – Carolin Lass (IRE) **c115** (Carlingford Castle) [2016/17 c112, h94: c29.1g* c29.4m² c25.5d⁶ h23.6d c24.1sᵖᵘ **h–** c23.6sᵖᵘ Mar 13] sturdy gelding: winning hurdler: fairly useful handicap chaser: won at Fakenham in May: stays 33f: acts on good to firm and heavy going: wears headgear: usually races nearer last than first. *Dai Burchell*

REBEL BEAT 6 b.g. Lucarno (USA) – Callitwhatyalike (Tamure (IRE)) [2016/17 b89: **h94** h20d h20.5gᶠ h19g⁵ h16.8s⁵ h16.2v⁵ h18.5d³ Mar 21] modest form over hurdles: best effort at 2¼m: acts on good to soft going. *David Dennis*

REBEL BENEFIT (IRE) 9 b.g. Craigsteel – Tourmaline Girl (IRE) (Toulon) [2016/17 **c83 §** c99, h96: c24.1g⁴ c25.8gᵖᵘ h25g* c24.5gᵖᵘ h22gᵖᵘ h23m Aug 17] winning pointer: modest **h90 §** hurdler: won handicap at Huntingdon in May: poor maiden chaser: stays 25f: acts on good to soft going: wears headgear/tongue tie: unreliable. *David Dennis*

REBEL COMMANDER (IRE) 5 b.g. Flemensfirth (USA) – Pharney Fox (IRE) **b–** (Phardante (FR)) [2016/17 b16g Mar 18] useful-looking gelding: well beaten in maiden bumper. *Nicky Henderson*

REBEL HIGH (IRE) 13 ch.g. Hymns On High – Celia's Fountain (IRE) (Royal Fountain) **c– §** [2016/17 c59§, h–: c19.7gᵖᵘ May 8] tall gelding: winning pointer: maiden hurdler: poor **h–** maiden chaser: stays 21f: acts on soft and good to firm going: wears headgear: temperamental. *Derek Frankland*

REBEL REBELLION (IRE) 12 b.g. Lord Americo – Tourmaline Girl (IRE) (Toulon) **c122** [2016/17 c25.1v² c22.7s⁶ c21.1g Apr 6] big, strong gelding: winning hurdler: fairly useful **h–** hunter chaser nowadays: second at Wincanton in February: stays 3m: acts on heavy going: usually wears headgear: wears tongue tie. *Paul Nicholls*

REBEL ROGER 8 b.g. Revoque (IRE) – Sally Scally (Scallywag) [2016/17 h–: h22.7s^pu h19.7d^pu h20.6g^pu Apr 8] no form in bumpers/over hurdles: tried in headgear: in tongue tie last 2 starts. *Tina Jackson*　**h–**

REBLIS (FR) 12 b.g. Assessor (IRE) – Silbere (FR) (Silver Rainbow) [2016/17 c104§, h108§: c24.5g^3 c24.5g^2 h19.5d c25.5s^pu h23v^pu Jan 10] leggy gelding: maiden hurdler: modest handicap chaser: stays 29f: acts on good to firm and heavy going: usually wears headgear: tried in tongue tie: unreliable. *Gary Moore*　**c99 §** **h– §**

REBOUND (IRE) 4 b.g. Big Bad Bob (IRE) – Shine Silently (IRE) (Bering) [2016/17 b13.6g^2 Mar 31] brother to 2 winners, including useful hurdler Bob Le Beau (2m-2½m winner), and half-brother to 2 winners on Flat abroad: dam unraced: 13/8, second in bumper at Fontwell (3¼ lengths behind Dell Oro) on debut. *Anthony Honeyball*　**b94**

RECENTLY ACQUIRED 5 b.g. Beat Hollow – Acquisition (Dansili) [2016/17 h–: h16m^6 h17.9m^5 h17.4m^4 c17.4m* c17.4d* c17.4s^2 c17.4m^2 c19.9f* Apr 22] modest form over hurdles in Britain: left David Loder 7,000 gns after second start: did well in Italy after, winning over fences at Pisa (2) and Milan: stays 2½m: acts on firm and good to soft going: trained by P. Favero third and fourth outings. *Arnaldo Bianco, Italy*　**c?** **h?**

RECOGNITION (IRE) 4 gr.g. Rip Van Winkle (IRE) – Bali Breeze (IRE) (Common Grounds) [2016/17 h16.7g* h16.8g^3 h19.3g h15.7d^4 h15.6g^F h16.6s^pu Mar 3] dam (h99) 2m hurdle winner: fair on Flat, stays 1½m: fair form over hurdles: won juvenile at Market Rasen in July: left Nicky Henderson after second start: unproven beyond 17f: best form on good going: in cheekpieces last 2 starts. *Barry Murtagh*　**h100**

RED ADMIRABLE (IRE) 11 b.g. Shantou (USA) – Eimears Pet (IRE) (Lord Americo) [2016/17 c120x, h–: c26.1d^pu c23.8m^F h23.1g^4 h20.7d^4 h20.7d^4 h25.6s^pu h24d^4 h19.7d^4 h15.8m^5 Apr 18] modest handicap hurdler: fairly useful chaser at best: stays 3m: acts on heavy going: usually wears cheekpieces: wears tongue tie: often let down by jumping. *Graeme McPherson*　**c– x** **h94**

RED ANCHOR (IRE) 13 ch.g. Snurge – Clonartic (IRE) (Be My Native (USA)) [2016/17 c79§, h–: c25.5d^6 Apr 29] light-framed gelding: maiden hurdler: modest chaser at best: stays 3¼m: acts on heavy going: often wears headgear: moody. *Linda Jewell*　**c– §** **h–**

REDBRIDGE MILLER (IRE) 5 b.g. Milan – Definite Miller (IRE) (Definite Article) [2016/17 h19.5d h16m h21.4d^4 h23.1g^pu h19.5m* Apr 28] £11,500 4-y-o: third foal: half-brother to fairly useful hurdler Western Miller (winner around 2½m, by Westerner): dam unraced half-sister to fair hurdler/useful chaser (2¼m-3¾m winner) Maljimar: placed on first of 3 starts in Irish maiden points: modest form over hurdles: won handicap at Chepstow in April: stays 19f: acts on good to firm going: tried in tongue tie. *Chris Down*　**h100**

RED DEVIL LADS (IRE) 8 b.g. Beneficial – Welsh Sitara (IRE) (Welsh Term) [2016/17 c136, h121: h24.7m h21.9s^2 h23.6s c23g^pu Jan 11] fairly useful handicap hurdler: second at Ffos Las in November: useful chaser at best: stays 25f: acts on heavy going: has worn hood, including last 4 starts: usually leads. *Rebecca Curtis*　**c–** **h121**

RED DEVIL STAR (IRE) 7 b.g. Beneficial – Gortbofearna (IRE) (Accordion) [2016/17 h123: c19.2d^3 c15.7d^2 c15.5s^3 c16.9d* c16.4s^ur c16.4s^2 c16.4g^5 c16.9m^4 Apr 2] lengthy gelding: fairly useful handicap hurdler/chaser: won novice over fences at Ascot in December: stays 19f: acts on heavy going: wears tongue tie. *Suzy Smith*　**c121** **h–**

REDDINGTON (IRE) 5 b.g. Getaway (GER) – Nikkis Alstar (IRE) (Fourstars Allstar (USA)) [2016/17 b17.7s h19.5d h20s h15.9g h19.5v Jan 31] tailed off in maiden bumper: little impact over hurdles. *Tim Vaughan*　**h57** **b–**

REDEMPTION SONG (IRE) 5 gr.m. Mastercraftsman (IRE) – Humilis (IRE) (Sadler's Wells (USA)) [2016/17 b16.6d^4 b16d* b17g^5 Apr 6] £65,000 4-y-o: workmanlike mare: sixth foal: half-sister to smart hurdler/useful chaser Starchitect (2m-2¾m winner, by Sea The Stars): dam useful 1¼m winner: off mark in Irish maiden points at second attempt: fairly useful form in bumpers: won mares event at Wetherby in February: will be suited by 2½m+. *Kevin Frost*　**b100**

RED HAMMER 5 b.g. Falco (USA) – Voie de Printemps (FR) (Della Francesca (USA)) [2016/17 h109: h16d^4 h16.3g^6 h17f^4 h17g^5 Apr 29] fair hurdler: left Nicky Henderson after second start: likely to prove best at 2m: acts on heavy going: tried in hood: often races freely, tends to find little. *Richard J. Hendriks, USA*　**h108**

RED HANRAHAN (IRE) 6 b.g. Yeats (IRE) – Monty's Sister (IRE) (Montelimar (USA)) [2016/17 h125: h24.2d^6 h23.6v^pu c21.1g^2 Apr 12] sturdy gelding: won on second start in Irish points: fairly useful hurdler, below best in 2016/17 (one to treat with caution): 4/1, second in novice at Fontwell (12 lengths behind Shantou Village) on chasing debut (open to improvement): stays 2¾m: acts on soft going: wears tongue tie. *Paul Nicholls*　**c114 p** **h– §**

RED HOT CHILLY (IRE) 4 ch.g. Frozen Power (IRE) – She's Got The Look (Sulamani (IRE)) [2016/17 h15.8g h15.8d^{ur} h16.4s^5 Nov 12] rather leggy gelding: fair maiden on Flat, stays 1½m: modest form over hurdles. *Dai Burchell*   **h98**

REDHOTFILLYPEPPERS (IRE) 5 ch.m. Robin des Champs (FR) – Mhuire Na Gale (IRE) (Norwich) [2016/17 b18d* b16d^6 b16v^4 Apr 1] €29,000 3-y-o, £200,000 4-y-o: rangy mare: third foal: half-sister to fairly useful hurdler/useful chaser Wild West Wind (2½m-25f winner, by Westerner): dam unraced half-sister to dam of high-class staying chaser On His Own: won on sole point start: fair form in bumpers: won mares maiden at Punchestown in December: tried in hood. *W. P. Mullins, Ireland*   **b92**

RED INDIAN 5 b.g. Sulamani (IRE) – Rafiya (Halling (USA)) [2016/17 b95: b16.7g^3 h15.8v* h16.2v^2 Jan 15] fair form in bumpers: fairly useful form over hurdles: won novice at Ffos Las in December: will stay beyond 2m. *Ben Pauling*   **h126 b86**

RED INFANTRY (IRE) 7 ch.g. Indian River (FR) – Red Rover (Infantry) [2016/17 h109, b78: h23.3s^3 h24s^2 h19.8d* h21.1s^4 h23.5d^5 h21.3s^4 h20.5g^3 Apr 22] stocky gelding: fair handicap hurdler: won at Sandown (conditional) in November: stays 3m: acts on soft going: tried in cheekpieces: usually races prominently. *Ian Williams*   **h114**

RED JACK (IRE) 4 b.g. Mahler – Hollygrove Bonnie (IRE) (Lord Americo) [2016/17 b16s* b16d* Apr 16] €23,000 3-y-o: first foal: dam, unraced, out of half-sister to dam of Grand National winner Numbersixvalverde: smart form in bumpers: won maiden at Naas (by 2¾ lengths from Debuchet) in January and Tattersalls Ireland George Mernagh Memorial Sales Bumper at Fairyhouse (cosily, by 1¾ lengths from Dinons) in April. *Noel Meade, Ireland*   **b115**

REDKALANI (IRE) 9 b.g. Ashkalani (IRE) – La Femme En Rouge (Slip Anchor) [2016/17 c–, h100: h23.3d^{pu} h23.3d^6 h22s^3 h25.6s^{pu} h25.3s* h23.3s^5 h27g^4 Apr 7] tall gelding: fair handicap hurdler: won at Catterick in March: pulled up both starts over fences in 2015/16: stays 25f: best form on soft/heavy going: often wears blinkers: front runner/races prominently. *Gillian Boanas*   **c– h102**

RED LECTRA 7 b.g. Beat All (USA) – Coronation Queen (Pivotal) [2016/17 b–: b16d^{pu} May 7] no form in bumpers. *Peter Bowen*   **b–**

REDMOND (IRE) 7 b.g. Tikkanen (USA) – Medal Quest (FR) (Medaaly) [2016/17 h–: h21.2m h16.7s^4 c16s^{pu} c20.2g^3 Jan 12] rangy gelding: won 2 of 5 starts in Irish points: poor form over hurdles: modest form over fences: tried in blinkers: front runner/races prominently: should improve over fences *Venetia Williams*   **c89 p h84**

RED OCHRE 4 b.g. Virtual – Red Hibiscus (Manduro (GER)) [2016/17 b15.7s^5 b16d Mar 21] first foal: dam unraced half-sister to fairly useful hurdler/useful chaser (stayed 27f) Samstown: promise on first of 2 starts in bumpers. *John Quinn*   **b87**

RED ORATOR 8 ch.g. Osorio (GER) – Red Roses Story (FR) (Pink (FR)) [2016/17 h83p: h15.3m h22v^2 h19.1g* h17.7g* h20.5g Oct 31] workmanlike gelding: fair handicap hurdler: won at Fontwell (twice) in August: stays 2¾m: acts on heavy going. *Jim Best*   **h102**

RED PENNY (IRE) 10 b.m. Definite Article – Hurricane Dawn (IRE) (Strong Gale) [2016/17 c84p, h–: c22.5g^4 c23.8g^2 c25.8d^2 c25.8g^3 c24.5m^2 Oct 5] winning pointer: maiden hurdler: fair maiden chaser: stays 3¼m: acts on good to firm and heavy going: in tongue tie last 2 starts. *Jimmy Frost*   **c103 h–**

RED RED ROVER (IRE) 7 ch.g. Royal Anthem (USA) – Ithastobedone (IRE) (Be My Native (USA)) [2016/17 h98: h22m^2 h16g h15.8m Oct 5] lengthy gelding: fourth on completed start in points: modest maiden hurdler: left Nigel Hawke after first start: stays 2¾m: acts on good to firm and heavy going: tried in cheekpieces. *Grace Harris*   **h98**

RED RISING (IRE) 6 ch.g. Flemensfirth (USA) – Fugal Maid (IRE) (Winged Love (IRE)) [2016/17 h25.3s* Feb 28] third foal: brother to bumper winner/fairly useful 19f hurdle winner Sizinguptheamazon: dam unraced half-sister to fair hurdler/useful chaser (stayed 29f) Manus The Man: off mark in Irish maiden points at second attempt: 4/6, won novice at Catterick (by 15 lengths from Ronn The Conn) on hurdling debut: looks thorough stayer: open to improvement. *Dan Skelton*   **h125 p**

RED ROSSO 12 ch.g. Executive Perk – Secret Whisper (Infantry) [2016/17 c71x, h–: c16.5g^{pu} c16.5g Sep 12] maiden hurdler: poor chaser: unproven beyond 2m: acts on good to firm and good to soft going: tried in cheekpieces: usually in tongue tie: often let down by jumping. *Rob Summers*   **c– x h–**

RED SHERLOCK 8 ch.g. Shirocco (GER) – Lady Cricket (FR) (Cricket Ball (USA)) [2016/17 h23.1s^{pu} Feb 12] tall gelding: smart hurdler in 2013/14, pulled up on return from long absence: should stay beyond 2½m: acts on heavy and good to firm ground: tried in tongue tie: flashes tail. *David Pipe*   **h–**

RED SIX (IRE) 6 ch.g. Flemensfirth (USA) – Glacial Missile (IRE) (Glacial Storm (USA)) [2016/17 b75: h20g May 28] sturdy gelding: bumper winner: well beaten in novice on hurdling debut: dead. *Peter Bowen* **h–**

RED SKIPPER (IRE) 12 ch.g. Captain Rio – Speed To Lead (IRE) (Darshaan) [2016/17 c108, h65: h16.8d Jun 21] compact gelding: fair hurdler/chaser at best: stays 2½m: acts on good to firm and good to soft going. *John O'Shea* **c–** **h–**

RED SPINNER (IRE) 7 b.g. Redback – Massalia (IRE) (Montjeu (IRE)) [2016/17 c141, h–: c19.4gpu c19.9g² c19.4s⁵ c16s³ c16g² Apr 17] sturdy gelding: winning handicap chaser: second at Chepstow (3 lengths behind Ink Master) in April: stays 2½m: acts on good to firm and heavy going: tried in cheekpieces. *Kim Bailey* **c140** **h–**

RED SQUARE REVIVAL (IRE) 6 b.g. Presenting – Alder Flower (IRE) (Alderbrook) [2016/17 b16g* h20.5s h16.7d⁶ h16.8s h16.5g Jan 27] first foal: dam unraced sister to fair hurdler/useful chaser (stayed 25f) Flaming Gorge: fair form when winning bumper at Worcester (by 6 lengths from Tell The Tale) in September: poor form over hurdles: often in hood: in tongue tie last 2 starts. *David Pipe* **h83** **b96**

RED STORY 6 b.g. Kayf Tara – Marabunta (SPA) (Exit To Nowhere (USA)) [2016/17 h69, b–: h22.7d⁶ c20.1d c15.9s⁶ c20.1sᶠ c24.5sᵖᵘ c24.2gᵖᵘ Apr 25] poor form over hurdles: little show over fences. *Alistair Whillans* **c–** **h–**

RED TANBER (IRE) 14 ch.g. Karinga Bay – Dreamy Desire (Palm Track) [2016/17 c20.1m⁶ c20.1f c21.2mᵘʳ c16dᵖᵘ Jun 30] leggy, rather sparely-made gelding: maiden hurdler: fairly useful chaser at best, retains little ability: stays 2½m: acts on firm and good to soft going: has worn tongue tie. *Bruce Mactaggart* **c64** **h–**

RED TORNADO (FR) 5 ch.g. Dr Fong (USA) – Encircle (USA) (Spinning World (USA)) [2016/17 h123p: h15.8m* h15.8m* h16.7g* h16.7g h16.5g³ h16.8g³ Apr 19] fairly useful hurdler: won novices at Ludlow in May and Uttoxeter in June, and Summer Hurdle (Handicap) at Market Rasen (by 1¼ lengths from Minellaforleisure) in July: raced around 2m: acts on soft and good to firm going: usually races towards rear. *Dan Skelton* **h133**

RED TORTUE (IRE) 8 b.g. Turtle Island (IRE) – Howrwedoin (IRE) (Flemensfirth (USA)) [2016/17 c82, h–: c24d⁶ May 18] sturdy gelding: maiden point winner: winning hurdler: well held both starts in chases: should stay beyond 2½m: acts on heavy going: tried in tongue tie. *Mark Wall* **c–** **h–**

RED TURTLE (FR) 6 ch.g. Turtle Bowl (IRE) – Morlane (IRE) (Entrepreneur) [2016/17 h20gpu Apr 17] fairly useful on Flat, stays 1½m: in cheekpieces, pulled up in seller on hurdling debut: dead. *Rune Haugen* **h–**

RED TYPE 6 ch.g. Blueprint (IRE) – Miss Fahrenheit (IRE) (Oscar (IRE)) [2016/17 b16.7d b16g Dec 3] no form in bumpers: dead. *John O'Shea* **b–**

RED WHISPER 13 ch.g. Midnight Legend – Secret Whisper (Infantry) [2016/17 c86, h–: h19.9m c16gpu h16.3mpu c18.9spu Dec 19] modest hurdler/chaser at best, no form for long while: tried in cheekpieces: wears tongue tie: temperamental. *Rob Summers* **c– §** **h–**

REEL LEISURE (GR) 4 ch.f. Reel Buddy (USA) – Leisurely Way (Kris) [2016/17 b14s⁵ b12.6d² b13.6v⁶ Feb 14] compact filly: second foal: dam, 1m winner, half-sister to fairly useful hurdler (stayed 27f) Midas Way out of sister to very smart staying hurdler Rubhahunish: fair form in bumpers: best effort when second in fillies junior event at Newbury in December: wears hood. *Amanda Perrett* **b85**

REFUSED A NAME 10 b.g. Montjeu (IRE) – Dixielake (IRE) (Lake Coniston (IRE)) [2016/17 c18.2d c19.2s² c20s³ c21v² c20v c17.5v Feb 16] maiden hurdler: modest handicap chaser: stays 2½m: best form on soft/heavy going: wears headgear/tongue tie. *John Joseph Hanlon, Ireland* **c99** **h–**

REGAL ENCORE (IRE) 9 b.g. King's Theatre (IRE) – Go On Eileen (IRE) (Bob Back (USA)) [2016/17 c144, h–: c25d² c26gpu c26gpu c23.8d* c20.8spu c34.3d Apr 8] compact gelding: winning hurdler: smart handicap chaser: won Silver Cup at Ascot (by 1¾ lengths from Minella Daddy) in December: stays 25f: acts on soft going: has worn hood: wears tongue tie: often races towards rear. *Anthony Honeyball* **c147** **h–**

REGAL FLOW 10 b.g. Erhaab (USA) – Flow (Over The River (FR)) [2016/17 c125, h89: c25g c23.6d c24.2s⁴ c25.1vᵘʳ c24s* c24.1g² Apr 15] sturdy gelding: winning hurdler: fairly useful handicap chaser: won at Warwick in March: stays 3¼m: acts on any going: tried in cheekpieces. *Bob Buckler* **c123** **h–**

REGAL GAIT (IRE) 4 b.g. Tagula (IRE) – Babylonian (Shamardal (USA)) [2016/17 h16.7s² h16.3d⁵ h16s² h18.7d² Mar 13] neat gelding: dam half-sister to fairly useful 2m hurdle winner Great Fighter: fair form on Flat, stays 1¾m: fair form over hurdles: runner-up in 3 juvenile events. *Harry Whittington* **h101**

REGAL GALAXY 4 b.f. Royal Applause – Astromancer (USA) (Silver Hawk (USA)) **h61**
[2016/17 h16.6g⁶ Dec 29] modest maiden on Flat, stays 1¾m: 25/1, sixth in juvenile
maiden at Doncaster on hurdling debut. *Mark H. Tompkins*

REGISTAN (IRE) 5 b.g. Darsi (FR) – Hannabelle (IRE) (Rudimentary (USA)) [2016/17 **b–**
b17d Feb 20] in tongue tie, tailed off in bumper on debut. *George Charlton*

REGULATION (IRE) 8 br.g. Danehill Dancer (IRE) – Source of Life (IRE) (Fasliyev **h124**
(USA)) [2016/17 h129: h15.7m h15.8g² h16.7gᶠ h15.9m⁴ h16g h16.5g h16g⁴ h15.9m³ Apr
16] fairly useful handicap hurdler: best with emphasis on speed around 2m: acts on good to
firm and good to soft going: has worn headgear, including in 2016/17: usually races
towards rear. *Neil King*

REIGNING SUPREME (IRE) 6 b.g. Presenting – Gli Gli (IRE) (Supreme Leader) **h128 p**
[2016/17 h20.5d* h20.5v⁴ h20.5d* Mar 24] €28,000 3-y-o, £130,000 4-y-o: useful-looking
gelding: fourth foal: dam (c95/h103), 2½m bumper/3m hurdle winner, out of half-sister to
Cheltenham Gold Cup winner Garrison Savannah: second on completed start in Irish
maiden points: fairly useful form over hurdles: won novices at Newbury in November and
March: will stay beyond 2½m: remains open to improvement. *Nicky Henderson*

REILLY'S MINOR (IRE) 6 b.g. Westerner – Ringzar (IRE) (Shernazar) [2016/17 b86: **h114**
h19d³ h20g⁴ h19s² h19g* h25.3g⁴ h21s* h20.5sᵖᵘ Mar 3] sturdy gelding: late faller (looked
likely winner) in Irish maiden point on debut: fair handicap hurdler: won at Taunton
(conditional) in December and Kempton in February: stays 21f: acts on soft going: in
cheekpieces last 4 starts: front runner/races prominently. *Warren Greatrex*

REINE DES MIRACLES 4 br.f. Poet's Voice – Cheerleader (Singspiel (IRE)) [2016/17 **b81**
b12.4d² b16.7g Mar 27] 3,000 3-y-o: smallish filly: sixth foal: closely related to 1¼m
winner Joyful Friend (by Dubawi) and half-sister to 2 winners, including 17f hurdle winner
Leader of The Land (by Halling): dam 9f winner: modest form in bumpers: better effort
when second in mares event at Wetherby: left Micky Hammond after that. *Jonjo O'Neill*

REIVERS LAD 6 b.g. Alflora (IRE) – Reivers Moon (Midnight Legend) [2016/17 h96: **h120**
h21.4v⁴ h16.2v* h16.2v* h16.4v* h20gᵖᵘ Apr 8] strong gelding: will make a chaser:
bumper winner: fairly useful form over hurdles: won novices at Kelso (2) and Newcastle
in February/March: should stay beyond 2m: best form on heavy going: front runner/races
prominently. *Nicky Richards*

*Lavazza Jolie Silver Cup Handicap Chase (Listed), Ascot—Regal Encore (right) swoops late in the
gloom to overhaul Minella Daddy (blinkers) and Tenor Nivernais (left)*

REIVERS LODGE 5 b.m. Black Sam Bellamy (IRE) – Crystal Princess (IRE) (Definite **b–**
Article) [2016/17 b16.4g b16.2g⁶ Apr 25] £800 5-y-o: second foal: closely related to fair
hurdler Diamond Rock (19f winner, by Kayf Tara): dam unraced half-sister to useful
hurdler (19f winner) Bags Groove and fairly useful hurdler/chaser (stayed 3m) My
Moment: no form in bumpers: in hood second start. *Susan Corbett*

REJAAH 5 b.m. Authorized (IRE) – Dhan Dhana (IRE) (Dubawi (IRE)) [2016/17 h124p: **c114**
h16d* h16.7g* h16.7g c19.2g² c16.5g* c20.1s² Sep 22] fairly useful form over hurdles: **h128**
won fillies' 4-y-o handicap at Warwick in May and novice at Market Rasen in June: fair
form over fences: won novice at Worcester in September: stays 19f: acts on good to firm
and good to soft going: wears tongue tie: often travels strongly. *Nigel Hawke*

RELENTLESS DREAMER (IRE) 8 br.g. Kayf Tara – Full of Elegance (FR) **c133**
(Cadoudal (FR)) [2016/17 c121, h–: c24.1dᵖᵘ c19.4g³ c19.4d* c21m* c22.6m² **h–**
c23g* c25.3g⁶ c20.4g c25gᵖᵘ c21d Apr 28] tall gelding: winning hurdler: useful handicap
chaser: won at Ffos Las in June, Newton Abbot in July and Taunton (by 11 lengths from
Minellacelebration) in November: stays 3m: acts on good to firm and heavy going: wears
headgear/tongue tie. *Rebecca Curtis*

RELENTLESS (IRE) 7 b.g. Dylan Thomas (IRE) – Karamiyna (IRE) (Shernazar) **h–**
[2016/17 h16.8g h16.8g⁵ h16d h23.9m h23.1s Jan 17] no form over hurdles: left Jimmy
Frost after third start: tried in tongue tie. *Susan Gardner*

RELIGHT THE FIRE 6 ch.g. Firebreak – Alula (In The Wings) [2016/17 b88: h20gᵖᵘ **h–**
h20gᵖᵘ Aug 11] placed in bumpers: no form over hurdles: tried in cheekpieces/tongue tie.
Denis Quinn

RELKWOOD (IRE) 7 gr.g. Beneficial – Rose Wood (Derring Rose) [2016/17 h–: h20g⁴ **c91 §**
c20d⁴ h23.1dᵖᵘ c25.8d* c24g c25.8g⁵ c24.5m⁴ Oct 5] poor form over hurdles: modest form **h83**
over fences: won handicap at Newton Abbot in June: likely to stay long distances: acts on
good to soft going: has worn tongue tie, including last 4 starts: races towards rear:
temperamental. *Paul Morgan*

REMEDIO (IRE) 7 b.g. Ramonti (FR) – Cant Hurry Love (Desert Prince (IRE)) [2016/17 **h–**
h16.7g Jun 3] no form in varied events. *Andrew Crook*

REMEMBER FOREVER (IRE) 7 b.g. Indian River (FR) – Running Wild (IRE) **c93**
(Anshan) [2016/17 h80, b–: h21g⁴ h25g h21.6g c17g⁶ c20m² c20v* c25.5d⁴ c20vᵖᵘ c19.7sᵘʳ **h73**
c19.2g* c19.7m* Apr 16] lengthy gelding: poor form over hurdles: modest handicap
chaser: won at Lingfield in November, Fontwell in March and Plumpton in April: stays
2½m: acts on good to firm and heavy going: usually leads. *Richard Rowe*

REMILUC (FR) 8 b.g. Mister Sacha (FR) – Markene de Durtal (FR) (Sharken (FR)) **c120 +**
[2016/17 h19.1s³ h17.7s* c16.4g³ c20.5gᵖᵘ h17.7v² h19s⁶ h16.3v* h20.3g h16.5g Apr 8] **h135**
strong gelding: useful handicap hurdler: won at Fontwell in November and Newbury
(by 2¾ lengths from Chesterfield) in March: fairly useful form over fences: stays 19f: acts
on heavy going: has worn tongue tie, including last 5 starts: often races prominently.
Chris Gordon

REMINDING 4 b.g. Passing Glance – Matilda's Folly (IRE) (Exit To Nowhere (USA)) **b–**
[2016/17 b16s b16d Mar 21] no form in bumpers. *Julia Brooke*

REMIND ME LATER (IRE) 8 b.g. Zerpour (IRE) – Two T'three Weeks (Silver **c118**
Patriarch (IRE)) [2016/17 c122p, h122p: c19.7g³ c18.8m³ Oct 29] sturdy gelding: won **h–**
both starts in points: fairly useful hurdler: similar form over fences: should stay 2½m: acts
on firm going, probably good to soft. *Gary Moore*

RENARD (FR) 12 b.g. Discover d'Auteuil (FR) – Kirmelia (FR) (Chamberlin (FR)) **c117**
[2016/17 c123, h–: c20v c24.2s³ c24.2d² c22.6d² Mar 25] good-topped gelding: winning **h–**
hurdler: fairly useful chaser: second in handicap at Stratford in March: acts on
good to firm and heavy going: usually wears headgear: usually leads. *Venetia Williams*

RENDL BEACH (IRE) 10 b.g. Milan – Erins Emblem (IRE) (Erins Isle) [2016/17 c–, **c–**
h114: h20v⁶ h26.4gᵖᵘ Apr 15] workmanlike gelding: fairly useful hurdler at best: maiden **h–**
chaser: stays 2¾m: best form on soft/heavy going: has worn headgear, including last 4
starts: wears tongue tie: tends to find little. *Robert Stephens*

RENE'S GIRL (IRE) 7 b.m. Presenting – Brogella (IRE) (King's Theatre (IRE)) **h127**
[2016/17 h120: h19.6vᵖᵘ h22g² h23.8m* Apr 25] tall mare: fairly useful handicap hurdler:
won at Ludlow in April: stays 3m: acts on soft and good to firm going: usually races
towards rear. *Dan Skelton*

RENEWING 6 b.g. Halling (USA) – Electric Society (IRE) (Law Society (USA))   **h97**
[2016/17 h19.9g³ h19.9d³ h23g⁴ h23.9g h20.7g h21sᵖᵘ Dec 8] sturdy gelding: poor maiden
on Flat, stays 1½m: modest form over hurdles: in cheekpieces last 4 starts. *Roy Brotherton*

RENNETI (FR) 8 b.g. Irish Wells (FR) – Caprice Meill (FR) (French Glory) [2016/17 **h154 §**
h148: h16s² h21s³ h16.8g h20d* h20.5d⁶ Apr 29] sturdy gelding: smart hurdler: won
Keelings Irish Strawberry Hurdle at Fairyhouse (by 9 lengths from De Plotting Shed) in
April: third in Boyne Hurdle at Navan (6¼ lengths behind Sutton Place) in February: stays
2½m: acts on heavy going: often in blinkers: usually races in rear/travels strongly: not one
to trust (has refused to race/looked half-hearted under pressure). *W. P. Mullins, Ireland*

RENTA GALLERY (IRE) 11 ch.m. Portrait Gallery (IRE) – Renty (IRE) (Carlingford   **c–**
Castle) [2016/17 c23.8sᵖᵘ Feb 19] winning pointer: pulled up both starts in hunter chases.
R. Thomas

REPEAL 7 b.g. Revoque (IRE) – Capania (IRE) (Cape Cross (IRE)) [2016/17 b–: c17m **c–**
May 20] point winner: in hood, tailed off in hunter on chasing debut. *S. Allwood*

REPEAT BUSINESS (IRE) 9 b.g. Croco Rouge (IRE) – Bay Pearl (FR) (Broadway **c114**
Flyer (USA)) [2016/17 c106, h–: c23.6m* Apr 28] multiple point winner: maiden hurdler: **h–**
fair form over fences: won novice hunter at Chepstow in April: stays 25f: acts on good to
firm going: tried in cheekpieces. *J. W. Tudor*

REPEAT THE FEAT (FR) 6 br.g. Kingsalsa (USA) – Sharon du Berlais (FR) (Lute **h59**
Antique (FR)) [2016/17 h56, b–: h19.9g⁶ h20.5g h25d h21sᵖᵘ Dec 8] good-topped gelding:
little form over hurdles: tried in cheekpieces. *Charlie Longsdon*

REPLACEMENT PLAN (IRE) 8 b.g. Flemensfirth (USA) – Shannon Pearl (IRE) **c84 §**
(Oscar (IRE)) [2016/17 c92§, h84§: h21.6g⁶ h18.5g h21.6g* h23m c23g³ c22.6gᵇᵈ c22.6m⁶ **h84 §**
h21.6m c25.1m³ c24.2g² c23g c25.3v² c25.1s c24vᵖᵘ c25.7vᵖᵘ Feb 27] poor handicap
hurdler: won at Fontwell in June: poor maiden chaser: stays 25f: acts on heavy going: often
wears headgear: wears tongue tie: usually races close up: temperamental. *Richard Woollacott*

REPORT TO BASE (IRE) 5 b.g. Westerner – Marina du Berlais (FR) (Mister Sicy **h132**
(FR)) [2016/17 h15.8s* h16.7s² h20.3s² h22.8d⁵ Feb 18] €32,000 3-y-o, £85,000 4-y-o:
seventh foal: half-brother to useful hurdler Surtee du Berlais (2m-3m winner, by High
Chaparral) and fair chaser Rosie du Berlais (25f winner, by Beneficial): dam, French 1¾m
winner, half-sister to useful hurdler/smart chaser (stayed 3¼m) Michel Le Bon: won Irish
maiden point on debut: useful form over hurdles: won novice at Uttoxeter in November:
second in listed novice at Cheltenham (4½ lengths behind Coo Star Sivola) in January: best
effort at 2½m. *Evan Williams*

REPRESENTINGCELTIC (IRE) 12 ch.g. Presenting – Nobull (IRE) (Torus) [2016/17 **c92**
c–, h–: c24gᵖᵘ c25.5g⁴ May 29] lengthy gelding: maiden hurdler: modest handicap chaser: **h–**
stays 3m: acts on soft and good to firm going. *Pat Phelan*

RESCUED GLORY (IRE) 8 b.g. Milan – Stand Girl (IRE) (Standiford (USA)) **h104**
[2016/17 h25.5s⁵ h23.1vᶠ h18.5s h23.1s² Jan 17] dual winning pointer: fair form over
hurdles. *Jeremy Scott*

RESOLUTE REFORMER (IRE) 8 b.g. Arcadio (GER) – Booking Note (IRE) (Brush **c95**
Aside (USA)) [2016/17 c78, h–: c20.1d c23.8m* May 12] maiden hurdler: modest **h–**
handicap chaser: won at Perth in May: stays 25f: acts on good to firm and good to soft
going: often races lazily. *Stuart Coltherd*

RESOLUTION BAY 5 b.g. Presenting – Parthenia (IRE) (Night Shift (USA)) [2016/17 **h121**
b–: h16.8m* h15.7d³ h19g⁵ h16.5gᶠ h16g* Apr 8] well-made gelding: fairly useful form
over hurdles: won novices at Exeter in November and Chepstow in April: best effort when
third in introductory event at Ascot in November: should be suited by further than 2m: acts
on good to firm and good to soft going: races prominently. *Philip Hobbs*

REST EASY 5 b.m. Rip Van Winkle (IRE) – Early Evening (Daylami (IRE)) [2016/17   **h–**
h85: h16.8m h15.9gᵖᵘ Oct 17] angular mare: poor form over hurdles: won 2-runner point
in April 2017. *Seamus Mullins*

RESTRAINT 6 b.g. Kheleyf (USA) – Inhibition (Nayef (USA)) [2016/17 b15.7v b15.9g   **h–**
h16s Jan 8] fair at best in bumpers, well held in 2016/17: tailed off on hurdling debut: tried   **b–**
in tongue tie. *Adrian Wintle*

RESTRAINT OF TRADE (IRE) 7 br.g. Authorized (IRE) – Zivania (IRE) (Shernazar) **c107**
[2016/17 h119: h18.7m⁵ c16.4g⁴ c19.3d⁴ c20v⁶ h16.2s⁶ h15.5d h15.8v² Jan 28] sturdy **h106**
gelding: fair handicap hurdler: similar form over fences: stays 19f: acts on heavy going: has
worn headgear/tongue tie: often races in rear. *Jennie Candlish*

RETOUR EN FRANCE (IRE) 7 b.m. Robin des Champs (FR) – Rayane (FR)   **c123**
(Kaldounevees (FR)) [2016/17 h21.3d^2 c17.4v^2 c21.5v* c24v^5 c21d^4 Apr 28] first living   **h128**
foal: dam unraced half-sister to useful hurdler/smart chaser (stayed 25f) Tamarindo and to
dam of top-class chaser (stays 3¼m) Djakadam: useful form over hurdles: second in minor
event at Galway in September: fairly useful chaser: won mares maiden at Fairyhouse in
February: stays 3m: acts on heavy going: has worn cheekpieces. *W. P. Mullins, Ireland*

RETURN FLIGHT 6 b.g. Kayf Tara – Molly Flight (FR) (Saint Cyrien (FR)) [2016/17   **c129 p**
h95, b87: h15.7g* h16g^4 c20.9s^2 c20.9s* c20.5d^F Jan 14] lengthy gelding: fair handicap   **h102**
hurdler: won at Southwell in October: fairly useful form over fences: won novice handicap
at Uttoxeter in December: stays 21f: acts on heavy going: has worn hood: usually races
close up: should do better over fences. *Dan Skelton*

RETURN SPRING (IRE) 10 b.g. Vinnie Roe (IRE) – Bettys Daughter (IRE) (Supreme   **c– §**
Leader) [2016/17 c129§, h122§: c25.1v^{pu} c23.8m^{pu} Apr 25] sturdy, workmanlike gelding: **h– §**
fairly useful hurdler: useful chaser at best, pulled up in 2 hunters in 2016/17: stays 25f: acts
on heavy going: often wears headgear: one to treat with caution. *Ian Prichard*

REVAADER 9 b.m. Revoque (IRE) – Wave Rider (Zaffaran (USA)) [2016/17 c–, h–:   **c–**
c16.3g^{pu} May 4] good-topped mare: winning hurdler: well held completed start over   **h–**
fences: stays 19f: acts on heavy going. *Mark Gillard*

REVE DE SIVOLA (FR) 12 b.g. Assessor (IRE) – Eva de Chalamont (FR) (Iron Duke   **c– x**
(FR)) [2016/17 c108x, h161: h23.9s h24.2d^5 h24.4d^6 h24s h23.1s h25.8s^{pu} Mar 25] rangy   **h135**
gelding: high-class hurdler, won Long Walk Hurdle at Ascot in 2014/15 for third successive
season (second in 2015/16): well below best in 2016/17, and collapsed and died from a
heart attack at Kelso: useful chaser, though often let down by jumping: stayed 25f: acted on
heavy going: tried in cheekpieces: front runner/raced prominently. *Nick Williams*

REVERANT CUST (IRE) 6 gr.g. Daylami (IRE) – Flame Supreme (IRE) (Saddlers'   **h108**
Hall (IRE)) [2016/17 b56: h16.8s h16d^5 h19.3s^2 h16.8v^3 h16.4v* h16.4v^3 h19.9g^3 Mar 29]   **b–**
no form in bumpers: fair form over hurdles: won novice at Newcastle in March: stays
2½m: acts on heavy going: wears tongue tie. *Peter Atkinson*

REVERSE THE CHARGE (IRE) 10 b.g. Bishop of Cashel – Academy Jane (IRE)   **c80**
(Satco (FR)) [2016/17 c69, h–: c19.3g^3 c20.1g^2 c15.6d^2 c20.1d^3 c17.3d^2 c16.4g^5 c20.1g^3 **h–**
c20.1s^{pu} c21.6d^{pu} Apr 10] winning pointer: maiden hurdler: poor maiden chaser: stays
2½m: acts on good to soft going: usually wears cheekpieces: tried in tongue tie: often races
freely. *Jane Walton*

REVOCATION 9 b.g. Revoque (IRE) – Fenella (Phardante (FR)) [2016/17 c107, h–:   **c122**
c20d^2 c20.1s* c20.9s^2 c23.4s^3 Jan 7] winning hurdler: fairly useful form over fences: won   **h–**
handicap at Newcastle in November: stays 21f: acts on soft going: usually races close up,
often travels strongly. *Lucinda Russell*

REV UP RUBY 8 b.m. Revoque (IRE) – Kingennie (Dunbeath (USA)) [2016/17 c102,   **c96**
h114: h23.3g^6 h23.8g* h23.8g^5 c23.8g^4 c26.6g^6 h25g Apr 15] fair handicap hurdler: won at   **h111**
Musselburgh in November: modest maiden chaser: stays 25f: acts on soft and good to firm
going: has worn hood: tried in tongue tie. *George Bewley*

REYNO 9 b.g. Sleeping Indian – Tereyna (Terimon) [2016/17 c81, h102: h19.6g^4 May 17]   **c–**
modest maiden hurdler: didn't take to chasing only try: stays 21f: acts on heavy going: **h91**
usually wears headgear/tongue tie. *Stuart Edmunds*

RGB THE ARCHITECT 4 b.g. Mount Nelson – Dialma (USA) (Songandaprayer   **b–**
(USA)) [2016/17 b16.5g^{pu} Apr 6] pulled up in bumper. *Nigel Hawke*

RHAPANDO 8 b.g. Hernando (FR) – Rhapsody Rose (Unfuwain (USA)) [2016/17   **c–**
c20.5d^{bd} c24s^{pu} Feb 10] well-made gelding: maiden hurdler: useful chaser in 2014/15:   **h–**
stayed 2½m: acted on good to soft going: wore cheekpieces: dead. *Paul Webber*

RHIANNA 6 b.m. Robin des Champs (FR) – La Harde (FR) (Valanour (IRE)) [2016/17   **h63**
b62: h15.7s^5 h19.9g^4 h16.8d^6 h23.3g^{pu} Jul 22] maiden pointer: poor form in bumpers/
hurdles: often in tongue tie. *Kim Bailey*

RHYMERS STONE 9 b.g. Desideratum – Salu (Ardross) [2016/17 h89: h18.1s^3 h19.3g^3 **h111**
h20.6s* h22.7v^4 h20.6v^2 h20.9s* h20.9s^2 Apr 3] fair handicap hurdler: won at Newcastle
in January and Kelso in March: stays 21f: acts on heavy going: often wears cheekpieces:
often races prominently, strong traveller. *Harriet Graham*

RHYTHM OF SOUND (IRE) 7 ch.g. Mahler – Oscarvail (IRE) (Oscar (IRE)) [2016/17   **c–**
h85: h24.1s^F h19.3s c20.9v Mar 9] poor maiden hurdler: well beaten in novice handicap on   **h–**
chasing debut. *Micky Hammond*

RHYTHM STAR 7 b.m. Beat All (USA) – Star Award (IRE) (Oscar (IRE)) [2016/17 c85, h–: c20.9v^pu Apr 30] winning hurdler: modest form over fences: stays 2¾m: best form on heavy going: often in headgear. *Jamie Snowden* — c– h–

RICHARDOFDOCCOMBE (IRE) 11 b.g. Heron Island (IRE) – Strike Again (IRE) (Phardante (FR)) [2016/17 c76, h95: h16.8d c23.6v^pu Mar 23] modest hurdler: poor form over fences: best effort at 19f: acts on soft going: has worn tongue tie. *Gail Haywood* — c– h–

RICH MAN POOR MAN (IRE) 4 br.g. Robin des Champs (FR) – Mistaken Identity (IRE) (Jimble (FR)) [2016/17 h16s^pu h19.3s^pu h19.7d h19.4s^pu h20.1s^pu Mar 16] no form over hurdles. *Philip Kirby* — h–

RICHMOND (FR) 12 b.g. Assessor (IRE) – Hirondel de Serley (FR) (Royal Charter (FR)) [2016/17 c119, h–: c26.3g c23g^4 c20.9v^3 c23.8s^3 c23.6v^3 c21.1g Apr 6] sturdy gelding: maiden hurdler: fair chaser nowadays: won point in March: stays 3m: acts on good to firm and heavy going: in cheekpieces last 4 starts. *P. P. C. Turner* — c101 h–

RIDDLESTOWN (IRE) 10 b.g. Cloudings (IRE) – Gandi's Dream (IRE) (Commanche Run) [2016/17 c98, h107: c20.3v^2 c21.1g^5 c24v^2 h20.3d c19.8d^3 c23.6d^4 c20.2g^6 h20.3s^5 h24d^3 c24v* c23.6d^6 c24.5s^3 h20.3g* c20.3g* Apr 21] strong gelding: fair handicap hurdler: won conditionals/amateur event at Southwell in March: fair handicap chaser: won at same course in March and April: stays 3¼m: acts on heavy going: wears headgear: often travels strongly: not one to rely on. *Caroline Fryer* — c111 § h107 §

RIDESTAN (IRE) 7 b.g. Linngari (IRE) – Ridakiya (IRE) (Desert King (IRE)) [2016/17 c17m c18.2g^5 c17d* c16d* c15.9g^pu Oct 21] winning hurdler: useful form over fences: won maiden at Killarney in August and Grade 3 novice at Gowran (by nose from Neverushacon) in October: stayed 2¼m: acted on good to firm and heavy going: tried in cheekpieces: dead. *Henry de Bromhead, Ireland* — c130 h–

RIDE THE RANGE (IRE) 8 br.g. High Chaparral (IRE) – Jade River (FR) (Indian River (FR)) [2016/17 h20.1g Apr 25] fair hurdler at best: stays 2½m: acts on soft going. *Chris Grant* — h–

RIDGEWAY FLYER 6 b.g. Tobougg (IRE) – Running For Annie (Gunner B) [2016/17 b100: h19.3d^4 h15.3d^5 h16.8s^2 h15.8d* h19m* Apr 20] good-topped gelding: bumper winner: fairly useful form over hurdles: won maiden at Ludlow in February and novice at Taunton in April: stays 19f: acts on soft and good to firm going: in tongue tie last 4 starts: usually races towards rear: remains open to improvement. *Harry Fry* — h124 p

RIEN DU TOUT (IRE) 5 b.g. Curtain Time (IRE) – Back In Debt (IRE) (Bob Back (USA)) [2016/17 b–: b15.7v^5 May 10] maiden pointer: modest form in bumpers. *Mark Wall* — b83

RIGADIN DE BEAUCHENE (FR) 12 b.g. Visionary (FR) – Chipie d'Angron (FR) (Grand Tresor (FR)) [2016/17 c131, h–: c28.4v^4 c29.2s^6 c26.2s c29.2v^6 Mar 12] useful-looking gelding: maiden hurdler: fairly useful handicap chaser: stays 33f: acts on heavy going: wears headgear: front runner/races prominently. *Venetia Williams* — c121 h–

RIGHTDOWNTHEMIDDLE (IRE) 9 b.g. Oscar (IRE) – Alternative Route (IRE) (Needle Gun (IRE)) [2016/17 c20g^6 h21g c18.2g c20s^2 c20d c21g h22.3s^2 c24s^pu c25g^2 c20d^F Apr 26] fairly useful handicap hurdler: second at Navan in February: useful handicap chaser: second in listed event at Aintree (13 lengths behind Sizing Codelco) in April: left Michael Mulvany after fifth start: stays 25f: acts on good to firm and heavy going. *Gordon Elliott, Ireland* — c138 h115

RIGHT ENOUGH 12 gr.g. Bollin William – Miss Accounts (IRE) (Roselier (FR)) [2016/17 c24d^4 h23.3g^4 c23m^2 Aug 17] tall, quite good-topped gelding: multiple point winner: poor maiden hurdler: modest form over fences: won novice handicap at Uttoxeter in July: stays 3m: acts on good to firm and heavy going: in blinkers last 4 starts: in tongue tie last 3. *Jamie Snowden* — c95 h73

RIGHT MADAM (IRE) 5 b.m. Jeremy (USA) – Mawaared (Machiavellian (USA)) [2016/17 h56: h15.8m^2 h19.9g^5 h15.8g h15.8g^6 h18.7m^3 h16.3g^6 h15.5g^3 h15.5g^6 Dec 7] modest maiden hurdler: unproven beyond 2m: acts on good to firm going: wears headgear. *Sarah Hollinshead* — h85

RIGHT OF REPLY (IRE) 6 b.g. Presenting – Baliya (IRE) (Robellino (USA)) [2016/17 h23.3g^3 Apr 25] €60,000 3-y-o: sixth foal: half-brother to 3 winners, including useful hurdler/chaser Edmund Kean (17f-3m winner) and useful hurdler Brave Vic (2½m winner) (both by Old Vic): dam (b78), second in bumper, half-sister to useful hurdler/fair chaser (stayed 2½m) Balapour: unplaced on completed starts in Irish maiden points: 25/1, third in maiden at Hexham (15¼ lengths behind Classical Milano) on hurdling debut. *Alistair Whillans* — h91

RIGHT OLD TOUCH (IRE) 4 b.g. Stowaway – No Easy Way (IRE) (Mandalus) [2016/17 **b– p**
b16.3g Mar 25] £32,000 3-y-o: useful-looking gelding: has scope: half-brother to smart
hurdler/chaser Made In Taipan (2m-2½m winner, by Taipan) and fairly useful hurdler/
chaser Made In Time (19f-23f winner, by Zagreb): dam unraced half-sister to fairly useful
staying chaser On The Other Hand: 16/1, showed signs of inexperience when thirteenth in
Goffs UK Spring Sales Bumper at Newbury (25 lengths behind Bullionaire) in March:
should do better. *Gary Moore*

RIGHT ROYALS DAY 8 b.m. Beneficial – Just For A Laugh (Idiot's Delight) [2016/17 **h–**
b–: h16.7s Dec 22] no form in bumpers/novice hurdle: tried in tongue tie. *John Needham*

RIGHT STEP 10 b.g. Xaar – Maid To Dance (Pyramus (USA)) [2016/17 c–, h102: h16g **c–**
May 2] strong gelding: fair handicap hurdler at best: pulled up sole start over fences: stays **h76**
2¼m: acts on heavy going: wears tongue tie: usually races close up. *Pat Phelan*

RINNAGREE ROSIE 11 gr.m. Silver Patriarch (IRE) – Gretton (Terimon) [2016/17 **h83**
h90: h19s h20.5s h20.6v² h20.1v⁶ Mar 28] poor handicap hurdler: stays 21f: best form on
soft/heavy going: wears cheekpieces. *Lucy Normile*

RIO BRAVO (IRE) 6 b.g. Westerner – Diaconate (IRE) (Cape Cross (IRE)) [2016/17 **h92**
b73: b16.7s³ h19.4g h16.6g³ Jan 27] maiden pointer: poor form in bumpers: modest form **b70**
over hurdles: wears tongue tie. *Graeme McPherson*

RIOJA DAY (IRE) 7 b.g. Red Clubs (IRE) – Dai E Dai (USA) (Seattle Dancer (USA)) **h74**
[2016/17 h83: h15.6g² h16.4d⁴ h19s⁴ h15.6g⁶ h16vᵘʳ h19v⁵ h16v⁵ Feb 27] poor maiden
hurdler: unproven beyond 2m: acts on heavy going: usually wears blinkers. *Jim Goldie*

RIOR (IRE) 10 b.g. King's Theatre (IRE) – Sara's Gold (IRE) (Ashkalani (IRE)) [2016/17 **c91**
c–, h101: h16g h18.5g⁴ h21.6g² h21.6m c25.8g³ Jul 25] leggy gelding: modest handicap **h95**
hurdler: similar form over fences: stays 27f: acts on good to firm and heavy going: tried in
blinkers. *Paul Henderson*

RIOT ACT (IRE) 5 b.g. Milan – Beautiful Tune (FR) (Green Tune (USA)) [2016/17 **h108**
h20s² h19.5g Dec 10] €92,000 3-y-o: seventh foal: brother to useful hurdler/chaser Lambro
(2¼m-3m winner) and closely related to bumper winner Captain Bocelli (by Kayf Tara):
dam French 17f hurdle winner: fair form over hurdles: better effort when second in maiden
at Ffos Las in November: wears tongue tie. *Jonjo O'Neill*

RISING MARIENBARD (IRE) 5 b.g. Marienbard (IRE) – Dromkeen Wood (Primitive **h74**
Rising (USA)) [2016/17 b16d h17d⁶ Apr 5] won Irish maiden point on debut: well beaten **b–**
in bumper/novice hurdle: wears tongue tie. *Lucinda Russell*

RISING TIDE (IRE) 6 b.g. Dubai Destination (USA) – Erins Love (IRE) (Double Bed **h73**
(FR)) [2016/17 h16d⁴ h16.2s⁵ Dec 4] poor form over hurdles: in tongue tie last 2 starts.
Lucinda Russell

RITUAL OF SENSES (IRE) 7 b.g. Milan – Nonnetia (FR) (Trempolino (USA)) **h123**
[2016/17 b72: h15.9g* h19.1g* h15.8g³ h16.3d⁴ h21.6d⁶ Dec 16] good-topped gelding:
fairly useful form over hurdles: won maiden at Plumpton in May and novice at Fontwell
in June: stays 19f: best form on good going: often races prominently/travels strongly.
Warren Greatrex

RIVABODIVA (IRE) 7 ch.m. Flemensfirth (USA) – Sheebadiva (IRE) (Norwich) **c100**
[2016/17 h100: c23.8g⁴ c20.1g⁵ c23.8gᵖᵘ h20.6d³ h20.6sᵖᵘ h19v² h20.5s³ h20.9s³ Mar 25] **h97**
winning Irish pointer: modest maiden hurdler: fair form over fences: stays easy 3m: acts on
heavy going: tried in cheekpieces: in tongue tie last 4 starts: usually races towards rear,
often travels strongly. *Lucinda Russell*

RIVEN LIGHT (IRE) 5 b.g. Raven's Pass (USA) – Vivacity (Trempolino (USA)) **h138**
[2016/17 h16.2d* h16d⁴ h18s h16s⁴ h16s⁴ h16g² Apr 28] half-brother to French hurdler
Grypas (2¼m/19f winner, by Medicean): useful on Flat, stays 1¼m: useful form over
hurdles: won maiden at Thurles in December: second in novice at Punchestown (neck
behind Montalbano) in April: should prove suited by 2¼m+: acts on soft going: usually
races nearer last than first. *W. P. Mullins, Ireland*

RIVER ARROW 6 b.m. Kayf Tara – Supreme Gem (IRE) (Supreme Leader) [2016/17 **h118**
b75: h21.7v⁴ h21sᵖᵘ h20.3v* h20.5g³ Mar 25] sturdy mare: fairly useful form over hurdles:
won novice at Southwell in March: third in Mares 'National Hunt' Novices' Hurdle Finale
at Newbury next time: often races freely: signs of temperament. *Tom Symonds*

RIVER BRAY (IRE) 4 ch.g. Arakan (USA) – Cill Fhearga (IRE) (Lahib (USA)) [2016/17 **b89**
b16s⁴ Feb 10] first foal: dam, well held in bumpers/fell in point, out of half-sister to useful
2m hurdler Crowded House: 11/1, fourth in maiden bumper at Kempton (4¼ lengths
behind Haafapiece) on debut. *Victor Dartnall*

RIVER DUN 7 br.m. Indian River (FR) – Sight'n Sound (Chief Singer) [2016/17 b86: b17.8g³ h15.8d h18.5g h16.5g⁵ h19g h15.3s⁵ h23.9gᵇᵈ h23.9gᵖᵘ Mar 30] modest form in bumpers: modest maiden hurdler: left Stuart Crawford after first start: unproven beyond 2m: acts on soft going: tried in hood: often races towards rear. *Gordon Edwards*   **h91 b75**

RIVER FROST 5 b.g. Silver Frost (IRE) – River Test (Beat Hollow) [2016/17 h15.8g³ h15.9g* h16d* h19.8vᶠ h21g* h21.1g Mar 15] good-topped gelding: fairly useful on Flat, stays 13f: useful form over hurdles: won novice at Plumpton in November, and handicaps at Kempton in January and February: stays 21f: acts on good to soft going. *Alan King*   **h140**

RIVER ICON 5 b.m. Sixties Icon – River Alder (Alderbrook) [2016/17 b16.2d³ b15.7d³ b16.6d h19.4g⁵ h16.8g⁵ h16.2g³ Apr 28] first foal: dam (c113/h118) 2m-2¾m hurdle winner/winning pointer (stayed 25f): modest form in bumpers/over hurdles: should be suited by 2½m+: usually races nearer last than first: will improve over hurdles. *Iain Jardine*   **h87 p b81**

RIVER MYTH 6 b.m. Midnight Legend – Zolotaya (Kayf Tara) [2016/17 b16g Jun 4] second foal: dam (b73), ran once in bumper, half-sister to Mr Cool and Very Cool (both useful hurdlers/fairly useful chasers up to around 3m): winning pointer: tailed off in bumper. *Jennifer Mason*   **b–**

RIVER OF INTRIGUE (IRE) 7 b.g. Indian River (FR) – Molly Hussey (IRE) (Flemensfirth (USA)) [2016/17 b88: h21.2m⁴ h20g* h24d³ h19.6g⁴ h24.5s³ h25d⁴ h21.2g Apr 3] fair hurdler: won maiden at Worcester in June: stays 21f: best form on good going. *Nicky Henderson*   **h105**

RIVER OF TIME (IRE) 9 br.g. Oscar (IRE) – Murrosie (IRE) (Anshan) [2016/17 c113, h–: c27.5mᵖᵘ May 20] won 3 times in points: maiden hurdler: fair form over fences: in tongue tie last 5 starts. *K. M. Hanmer*   **c– h–**

RIVER PURPLE 10 b.g. Bollin Eric – Cerise Bleue (FR) (Port Lyautey (FR)) [2016/17 c115§, h–: c19.3dᵖᵘ c20d⁵ c19.2g c20sᵖᵘ c19.1sᵖᵘ c16m³ c16m* Apr 25] maiden hurdler: fair handicap chaser: won at Ludlow in April: left John Mackie after third start: stays 2¾m: acts on soft and good to firm going: usually wears tongue tie: unreliable. *Lady Susan Brooke*   **c103 § h–**

RIVERSBRIDGE 8 b.g. Desert King (IRE) – Kinsford Water (Then Again)) [2016/17 c–, h–: c20.9vᵖᵘ Apr 30] no form over hurdles/fences: wears headgear: in tongue tie last 3 starts. *Johnny Farrelly*   **c– x h–**

RIVER WYLDE (IRE) 6 b.g. Oscar (IRE) – Clarin River (IRE) (Mandalus) [2016/17 b95p: b16d* b16.4g h15.8d* h15.8s* h16g* h16.4g³ h16.5g⁵ Apr 7] strong, compact gelding: runner-up in Irish point: fairly useful form in bumpers: won at Warwick in May: smart form over hurdles: won maiden in December and novice in January, both at Ludlow,   **h149 b96**

Sky Bet Dovecote Novices' Hurdle, Kempton—
River Wylde already has the measure of runner-up Elgin as that one fluffs the last

and Dovecote Novices' Hurdle at Kempton (by 3½ lengths from Elgin) in February: third in Supreme Novices' Hurdle at Cheltenham (10¼ lengths behind Labaik) in March: likely to prove best around 2m: acts on soft going: often travels strongly. *Nicky Henderson*

RIZAL PARK (IRE) 6 b.g. Amadeus Wolf – Imelda (USA) (Manila (USA)) [2016/17 h16.3d h16.3v⁶ h15.8d³ h15.8g h19.6m Oct 2] modest on Flat, stays 1½m: poor form over hurdles: often in hood: often races towards rear. *James Evans*   **h70**

ROADIE JOE (IRE) 8 b.g. Golan (IRE) – Granny Clampett (IRE) (Be My Native (USA)) [2016/17 h133, b90: h21.6g⁵ c20g* c17.4sᵖᵘ h21.4s h19sᶠ h19g⁵ Mar 2] sturdy gelding: winning Irish pointer: bumper winner: fairly useful handicap hurdler: fair form over fences: won maiden at Worcester in September: stays 2½m: acts on soft going: in cheekpieces last 2 starts. *Evan Williams*   **c107 h121**

ROAD TO GOLD (IRE) 8 b.g. Gold Well – Haut de Gamme (IRE) (Carmelite House (USA)) [2016/17 h122: c15.9d³ c23.4s⁵ Dec 4] winning Irish pointer: fairly useful form over hurdles: last in maiden/novice chases: stays 2½m: best form on heavy going: usually races close up. *N. W. Alexander*   **c– h–**

ROAD TO RESPECT (IRE) 6 ch.g. Gamut (IRE) – Lora Lady (IRE) (Lord America) [2016/17 h24d c19d* c20d⁴ c17d³ c16s² c24s² c20.8g* c20d* Apr 16]   **c156 + h–**

    'We have seldom seen such an example of monumental stupidity on the part of experienced jockeys as was provided by the Scottish National—it would not have been inappropriate had the stewards called in all the jockeys and reprimanded each of them for having ridden an injudicious race,' thundered *Chasers & Hurdlers 1980/81* in its essay on Astral Charmer, the rank outsider who landed that season's renewal of the Ayr showpiece from 21 lb out of the weights. Ridden by 4-lb claimer John Goulding, Astral Charmer built up an enormous early lead (despite trying to run out at the racecourse stables at one stage!) and was nearly a fence clear going out on to the final circuit as the main field pottered around at a steady pace. Although Astral Charmer tired late on, he managed to hold on by a rapidly-diminishing three lengths from the well-fancied trio of Current Gold, Jer and Father Delaney, who all finished full of running having been asked for their efforts too late. Social media, of course, wasn't a factor in 1981 but it is safe to assume that, had it been, the level of criticism directed at jockeys would have been far more vitriolic than even that Timeform view!

Brown Advisory & Merriebelle Stable Plate Handicap Chase, Cheltenham—
a second successive win in the race for Gigginstown House Stud and Bryan Cooper
as Road To Respect pulls clear of fellow novice Baron Alco

Ryanair Gold Cup Novices' Chase, Punchestown—
a sweet win for connections as Road To Respect reels in the very wayward Yorkhill

An example of the type of reaction expected nowadays could be found after the latest renewal of the Grade 2 Ten Up Novices' Chase over three miles at Navan in February, which saw the well-backed second favourite Acapella Bourgeois run out a wide-margin winner after being gifted a clear lead early on by his seven rivals. 'Shambles', 'laughable' and 'a disgrace' were just some of the post-race reactions on the internet to the efforts of the losing jockeys, with tempers further inflamed by the subsequent stance taken by officials. 'We didn't feel any need to call an inquiry. We felt that the winner jumped and stayed, that the remaining runners could make no headway on him at all and that a lot of them were at it from a mile out. The winner just went further clear and we didn't feel any riding offence was committed,' was the explanation by stewards' secretary Hugh Hynes. While it is true that Acapella Bourgeois increased his lead throughout the final circuit, and might simply have been by far the best horse on the day, the criticism of the other riders surely couldn't just be dismissed as the ranting of out-of-pocket punters? After all, Acapella Bourgeois was a dual Grade 2 winning hurdler in 2015/16 (not a supposed no-hoper as Astral Charmer had been), so it would surely have been reasonable for the stewards to ask why he was allowed to open up such a big advantage (he was already some twenty lengths clear going out on to the final circuit). Hopefully, in any similar case in the future, the stewards will at least hold an inquiry and ask the relevant questions. Subsequent events suggested that the Navan result was indeed too good to be true, with Acapella Bourgeois flopping at both the Cheltenham and Punchestown Festivals, though he will still warrant plenty of respect granted similar ground conditions and circumstances again—particularly with the news that he has been switched to champion trainer Willie Mullins for 2017/18 after the decision of Sandra Hughes to hand in her training licence.

Whatever the merits of the arguments about whether the Navan jockeys were guilty or not of ignoring Acapella Bourgeois, form students and punters would have been well served to disregard him when assessing the result. With the benefit of hindsight, runner-up Road To Respect—thirty-two lengths behind the winner—did very well to beat the five other finishers so comprehensively, in what had looked a decent field beforehand, especially as waiting tactics weren't the best option on the day, and because he was also hampered by a faller at halfway. Indeed, an eleventh-length advantage over third-placed Haymount at level weights reads very well in isolation though, understandably, not many seemed to take that form literally when Road To Respect lined up for the Brown Advisory & Merriebelle Stable Plate Handicap Chase at Cheltenham just under four weeks later, when he was sent off a largely unconsidered 14/1-shot. Bar a bump at the first, however, there was barely a moment's worry for backers of Road To Respect, who travelled strongly in touch towards the outer and could be named the winner some way out. He took over from fellow novice Baron Alco (bidding to win a £60,000 bonus offered by SIS and Plumpton racecourse) approaching two out and wasn't fully extended to pull six lengths clear of that rival, with the fancied pair Bouvreuil and Thomas Crapper completing the frame. It was a fifth Cheltenham Festival win (and a first over fences) for trainer Noel Meade, whose long association with the meeting has also been interspersed with some agonising reverses. Batista (1980 Triumph Hurdle) and Native Dara (2000 Coral Cup) were both collared on the line after looking certain winners, while Hill Society came off worse in a photo-finish to the 1998 Arkle Chase that took several minutes to decipher. Perhaps most notorious of all, however, was the 2005 Champion Hurdle, in which the mercurial Harchibald finished runner-up under a controversial ride from Meade's long-standing virtuoso stable jockey Paul Carberry, who was forced to retire (aged forty-two) during the latest season due to injury.

Injury was also a recurring theme for Gigginstown House Stud's then retained jockey Bryan Cooper. He had a horror fall in the 2014 Fred Winter Juvenile Handicap Hurdle, but he has enjoyed a brace of wins (all for Gigginstown) at each of the last two Cheltenham Festivals, with Road To Respect providing him with a second successive triumph in the Plate after Empire of Dirt in 2016. Road To Respect had been highly tried since making a winning debut over fences in a beginners chase at Naas in November (when Meade's new stable jockey Sean Flanagan deputised for the sidelined Cooper), making the frame twice in Grade 1 company before his distant second behind Acapella Bourgeois. In truth, he would have had to settle for minor honours at that level again on his final outing had Yorkhill not thrown away certain victory in the Ryanair Gold Cup Novices' Chase at Fairyhouse by jumping repeatedly left, so much so that he nearly ran out at the last. Although clearly a fortunate winner on the day, Road To Respect nevertheless confirmed himself a much improved performer and kept on well to hold on by a neck after heading the errant favourite early on the run-in.

	Gamut (IRE) (b 1999)	Spectrum (b 1992)	Rainbow Quest
			River Dancer
		Greektown (ch 1985)	Ela-Mana-Mou
Road To Respect (IRE) (ch.g. 2011)			Edinburgh
	Lora Lady (IRE) (b 2001)	Lord Americo (b 1984)	Lord Gayle
			Hynictus
		Bellora (br 1991)	Over The River
			Chorabelle

A son of the very smart middle-distance stayer Gamut, Road To Respect hails from a family which has already served his connections very well. His dam Lora Lady is a half-sister to their top-class chaser Road To Riches (also by Gamut), who landed several big wins before finishing a close third in the 2015 Cheltenham Gold Cup (he has struggled to recapture his best following a heavy fall at the 2016 Punchestown Festival). Road To Respect is Lora Lady's seventh foal and her only winner to date.

Gigginstown House Stud's "Road To Respect"

She has since produced a 2015 brother and 2016 half-sister (by Leading Light) to Road To Respect, both as yet unnamed. There are, however, other notable names to be found further back in this family tree, as Road To Respect's grandam Bellora (also unraced) was a sister to useful staying chaser Sullane River and a half-sister to the dam of the smart hurdler at up to two and a half miles Davenport Milenium.

'He's only six and we think there is plenty of improvement to come. He'll appreciate longer distances too,' was Meade's verdict after Road To Respect's Fairyhouse win, which explains why the Irish Grand National was considered an alternative option at that track's three-day Easter meeting. Road To Respect has tackled a variety of trips already and, although two miles has looked too sharp for him at the highest level, he seems equally effective at around two and a half miles or three miles. He clearly handles soft/heavy ground well, though it is worth noting that his Cheltenham and Fairyhouse wins came under the most resilient conditions he has faced to date. Such versatility should stand him in good stead in 2017/18, when there is likely to be a fair bit of juggling again in the Gigginstown ranks as their leading performers tackle the same sort of races—Road To Respect ended 2016/17 with seven Gigginstown performers rated above him, although stable-companion Disko is the only one of the septet whose form is on a similarly upward curve. *Noel Meade, Ireland*

ROAD TO RICHES (IRE) 10 b.g. Gamut (IRE) – Bellora (IRE) (Over The River (FR)) [2016/17 c168, h–: c25d^F c22.5g^{pu} c20d^2 c24d c24.3s^5 Feb 12] rangy gelding: winning hurdler: high-class chaser at best: lost his way in 2016/17, though left plenty to do when second in PWC Champion Chase at Gowran (11 lengths behind Ballycasey) in October: stays 3¼m: acts on heavy going: tried in cheekpieces. *Noel Meade, Ireland*

c152
h–

697

ROAD* TO ROME (IRE) 7 b.g. Choisir (AUS) – Tibbie (Slip Anchor) [2016/17 h109, **h112** b–: h19.6g⁴ h16.8sᵖᵘ h16.7g² Mar 25] fair form over hurdles: may prove best around 2m: tried in hood: often races towards rear. *William Kinsey*

ROAD WEST (IRE) 8 b.g. Westerner – Gentian Blue (IRE) (Tirol) [2016/17 c–: c24.2d⁴ **c78** Mar 31] dual point winner: poor form over fences: stays 3m: tried in cheekpieces. *Mrs C. J. Robinson*

ROALCO DE FARGES (FR) 12 gr.g. Dom Alco (FR) – Vonaria (FR) (Vorias (USA)) **c–** [2016/17 c–, h–: c24.2d⁴ c23.4dᵖᵘ Mar 24] useful-looking gelding: winning hurdler: useful **h–** chaser at best for Philip Hobbs, pulled up in hunters in 2016/17: stays 29f: acts on heavy going: tried in cheekpieces. *Miss P. C. Lownds*

ROBBEN 5 b.g. Dutch Art – Little Greenbird (Ardkinglass) [2016/17 h92: h20.3v⁵ h18.6g **h91** h16.8g h19.1s h16.8d* h16.7s⁴ Dec 9] modest handicap hurdler: won novice event at Sedgefield in December: left John Mackie after second start: unproven beyond 17f: acts on good to firm and good to soft going: has worn headgear: front runner/races prominently. *Alexandra Dunn*

ROBBING THE PREY (IRE) 6 b.g. Robin des Pres (FR) – Derravarra Lady (IRE) **h115** (Flemensfirth (USA)) [2016/17 b94: h20.6g h19.7g⁴ h16s² h16s³ h16d⁷ Jan 24] fairly useful form over hurdles: left Nick Kent after first start: unproven beyond 2m: acts on soft going: tried in hood: often races prominently. *Malcolm Jefferson*

ROBBIN'HANNON (IRE) 6 ch.g. Robin des Champs (FR) – Culleen Lady (IRE) **h131 p** (Presenting) [2016/17 h21v* h23.9g² Apr 26] €55,000 3-y-o: second foal: dam unraced: won Irish maiden point on debut: useful form over hurdles: won maiden at Warwick in March: second in listed novice at Perth (3¾ lengths behind Gayebury) month later: open to further improvement. *Philip Hobbs*

ROBERT DE BRUCE (IRE) 6 b.g. Brian Boru – Have At It (IRE) (Supreme Leader) **h–** [2016/17 b16v⁴ h19.9s h23.3g⁶ Apr 25] little impact in Irish maiden points: well beaten in **b67** bumper/maiden hurdles: will be suited by further than 2m. *Donald McCain*

ROBERTO PEGASUS (USA) 11 b.g. Fusaichi Pegasus (USA) – Louju (USA) (Silver **c–** Hawk (USA)) [2016/17 c109, h–: c21.1dᵖᵘ Apr 29] useful-looking gelding: winning hurdler/ **h–** chaser: successful in point in February: stays 2½m: acts on soft going: in cheekpieces last 2 starts. *Alan King*

ROBERTSON (IRE) 7 b.g. Duke of Marmalade (IRE) – Mythologie (FR) (Bering) **h81** [2016/17 h19.3dᵘʳ h19.7d⁴ Feb 21] fairly useful maiden on Flat, stays 1½m: poor form over hurdles: likely to prove best around 2m. *Laura Morgan*

ROBERT'S STAR (IRE) 7 b.g. Oscar (IRE) – Halona (Pollerton) [2016/17 h95: h23.3d³ **c109 p** h23g* h23g² c24g² c18g³ h21.4sᵖᵘ Dec 26] fair form over hurdles: won novice handicap at **h110** Worcester in June: similar form over fences: stays 3m: acts on good to soft going: tried in hood: front runner: should do better over fences. *Mark Bradstock*

ROBIN DE BOSS (IRE) 7 b.g. Robin des Pres (FR) – Gevity (Kris) [2016/17 b17g⁶ **b83** May 13] seventh foal: half-brother to 7f winner Longevity (by Olden Times): dam 1m/8.5f winner: point winner: 14/1, sixth in conditionals/amateur bumper at Aintree (3¼ lengths behind Gustave Mahler) in May. *Tommy Morgan*

ROBINDENEST (IRE) 5 br.g. Robin des Pres (FR) – Baby Harriet (IRE) (Cape Cross **h80** (IRE)) [2016/17 b16d⁵ h19.5g h21.4sᵖᵘ h17.7v⁶ h19.8v³ Mar 9] well beaten in bumper: **b–** poor form over hurdles. *Seamus Mullins*

ROBIN DEUZ POIS (IRE) 5 ch.m. Robin des Champs (FR) – Native Wood (IRE) **h80** (Be My Native (USA)) [2016/17 h21vᵖᵘ h19.4s⁴ Mar 3] €20,000 3-y-o, £47,000 4-y-o: half-sister to fairly useful hurdler/useful chaser Hangover (2m-2¾m winner) and fairly useful hurdler Paradise Valley (2m winner) (both by Presenting) and a winning pointer by Good Thyne: dam, unraced, out of sister to top-class chaser up to 3¼m Strong Promise: runner-up in Irish mares maiden point on debut: poor form over hurdles. *Paul Webber*

ROBINESSE (IRE) 6 ch.m. Robin des Champs (FR) – Jennifers Diary (IRE) (Supreme **h106** Leader) [2016/17 h112, b89: h19.6d³ h19.1s⁵ Feb 26] good-topped mare: bumper winner: fair form over hurdles: should stay 2½m: acts on heavy going: usually races prominently. *Oliver Sherwood*

ROBINETTA (IRE) 4 b.f. Robin des Champs (FR) – Seekayclaire (IRE) (Westerner) **h–** [2016/17 h15.8d h16.8dᵖᵘ Feb 24] first foal: dam unraced half-sister to useful hurdler/fairly useful chaser (stayed 2½m) Kalderon: no form over hurdles. *Jeremy Scott*

ROBIN OF LOCKSLEY (IRE) 7 b.g. Robin des Pres (FR) – Duggary Dancer (IRE) **h130** (Saddlers' Hall (IRE)) [2016/17 h119: h21.1g³ h21.1s h19.9v⁵ h16.8s⁶ h21v* h22.8vᶠ h25g⁵ Apr 24] tall gelding: point winner: useful handicap hurdler: won at Warwick (by 35 lengths from Chateau Robin) in March: left Dan Skelton after fourth start: stays 21f: acts on heavy going: usually in hood: tried in tongue tie: front runner/races prominently. *Caroline Bailey*

ROBIN ROE (IRE) 6 b.g. Robin des Champs (FR) – Talktothetail (IRE) (Flemensfirth **h140 p** (USA)) [2016/17 b98p: h20g* h20.5dᶠ Dec 31] strong gelding: off mark in Irish points at second attempt: bumper winner: useful form over hurdles: won maiden at Aintree (by 12 lengths from No Comment) in October: reportedly injured knee when fell next time: likely to stay beyond 2½m: should still do better. *Dan Skelton*

ROBINROYALE (IRE) 6 b.g. Robin des Champs (FR) – Rosafi (IRE) (Roselier (FR)) **c–** [2016/17 c25.2gᵘʳ h23.6g* h24.5d⁵ h23.1s⁴ h21.6v⁵ h24.3d³ Apr 21] €55,000 3-y-o, **h114** £18,000 5-y-o: strong gelding: fourth foal: half-brother to modest hurdler/poor chaser Snowball (3m/25f winner, by Alderbrook): dam, winning pointer, half-sister to useful hurdler/smart chaser (stayed 25f) Alexander Taipan: won once from 5 starts in Irish points: fair form over hurdles: won conditionals novice at Chepstow in December: unseated rider fifth on chasing debut: stays 3m: acts on good to soft going: in cheekpieces last 2 starts. *Seamus Mullins*

ROBINSFIRTH (IRE) 8 b.g. Flemensfirth (USA) – Phardester (IRE) (Phardante (FR)) **c144 p** [2016/17 c20.2d² c19.2v* c23.6sᵘʳ Jan 20] rangy gelding: winning hurdler: useful form **h–** over fences: won maiden at Exeter in January: likely to stay 3m: acts on heavy going: remains capable of better over fences. *Colin Tizzard*

ROBINSHILL (IRE) 6 ch.g. Robin des Champs (FR) – I Remember It Well (IRE) (Don't **h132** Forget Me) [2016/17 h109: h15.8m⁶ h15.9d* h17.2m² h16.7g h16g* h15.8g* h20.5d h15.8v* h16s² h16.8s h21.1g h16.5g Apr 8] sturdy gelding: useful handicap hurdler: won at Ffos Las in June, Wetherby in October, Huntingdon in November and novice at Ffos Las (by ¾ length from Stay Out of Court) in December: unproven beyond 2m: acts on heavy going: has worn tongue tie. *Nigel Twiston-Davies*

ROBINS LEGEND (IRE) 5 b.g. Robin des Pres (FR) – Lemons Legend (Midnight **h85** Legend) [2016/17 b16.2d h22.7d⁵ h22.7s⁵ h19.9s h23.8g³ h23.8g⁵ h25.3sᵖᵘ h27gᶠ Mar 29] **b–** sturdy gelding: tailed off in bumper: poor maiden hurdler: in visor last 4 starts. *Chris Grant*

ROBIN'S WAGER (IRE) 7 b.g. Robin des Champs (FR) – Good Side Wager (IRE) **c99** (Good Thyne (USA)) [2016/17 c23d⁴ c21.2mᵖᵘ h18.7m⁶ Jul 17] £3,000 5-y-o, £800 6-y-o: **h–** third foal: dam unraced half-sister to fairly useful/unreliable hurdler/chaser (stayed 19f) Jack The Gent: point winner: tailed off in seller on hurdling debut: modest form over fences: tried in tongue tie. *Sarah-Jayne Davies*

ROBINTHEAULAD (IRE) 6 b.g. Robin des Champs (FR) – Brotenstown (IRE) **h98** (Presenting) [2016/17 b97: h16d⁴ h19.7d³ h21.3d⁴ h24.3d⁴ Apr 21] third completed start in Irish maiden points: bumper winner: modest form over hurdles: should stay at least 2½m: wears tongue tie: front runner/races prominently. *Sandy Thomson*

ROBIN THE RAVEN (IRE) 5 b.g. Robin des Pres (FR) – Omyn Supreme (IRE) **b99** (Supreme Leader) [2016/17 b15.8m² b16.7g² b15.7g* b16.4g Mar 15] €12,000 3-y-o: good-topped gelding: fourth foal: brother to 19f bumper winner/fairly useful 2m hurdle winner Robin des Foret and half-brother to fairly useful hurdler/useful chaser Port Melon (19f-3m winner, by Presenting): dam unraced: fairly useful form in bumpers: won maiden at Towcester in November: left Roy Brotherton after first start: bred to stay at least 2½m: tried in cheekpieces. *Kim Bailey*

ROBIN WHY NOT (IRE) 5 b.g. Robin des Pres (FR) – Lady Mariah (IRE) (Moonax **h77** (IRE)) [2016/17 h16.5g h16.5s⁴ h18.5d⁶ h18.6sᵖᵘ h19.5gᵖᵘ Apr 8] poor form over hurdles: tried in cheekpieces. *Nigel Hawke*

ROBIN WILL (FR) 12 bl.g. Dark Moondancer – Gleep Will (FR) (Cadoudal (FR)) **c–** [2016/17 c88, h–: c24.2gᵖᵘ Apr 25] tall, useful-looking gelding: maiden hurdler: fairly **h–** useful chaser at best, retains little ability: stays 3m: acts on good to firm and heavy going: wears headgear. *Gemma Anderson*

ROB ROYAL (IRE) 9 b.g. Royal Anthem (USA) – Shamble Street (IRE) (Bob Back **h–** (USA)) [2016/17 h16.7g Jul 29] well held in novice hurdle. *Richard Ford*

ROCCO'S DELIGHT 3 b.g. Multiplex – No Page (IRE) (Statue of Liberty (USA)) **h–** [2016/17 h17.2m May 30] fairly useful on Flat, stays 1m: 5/2, well held in novice at Cartmel on hurdling debut: has joined Shane Kieran Ryder. *Brian Ellison*

ROC D'APSIS (FR) 8 gr.g. Apsis – Rocapina (FR) (Solon (GER)) [2016/17 c135x, h–: **c129 x** c25.2g⁴ c25.1m⁵ c23g² c23.8s³ c23.8g⁴ Apr 3] well-made gelding: maiden hurdler: useful **h–** handicap chaser: second at Taunton in January: stays 3m: acts on soft going: wears cheekpieces: often let down by jumping. *Tom George*

ROC DE GUYE (FR) 12 b.g. Video Rock (FR) – Kasibelle de Guye (FR) (Scooter Bleu **c73** (IRE)) [2016/17 c–, h–: c22.5gᵖᵘ c19.2d⁶ c15.7d c22.5d⁵ Oct 2] lightly-raced hurdler: **h–** fair chaser, on downgrade nowadays: stays 25f: acts on heavy going: wears headgear. *James Evans*

ROCKABILLY RIOT (IRE) 7 br.g. Footstepsinthesand – Zawariq (IRE) (Marju (IRE)) **h84** [2016/17 h96: h16.2d³ h16.2d h19s⁵ h16.4s² h16.4s⁶ Dec 17] poor handicap hurdler: raced mainly around 2m: acts on soft going: in hood last 3 starts: often races towards rear. *Martin Todhunter*

ROCK A DOODLE DOO (IRE) 10 b.g. Oratorio (IRE) – Nousaiyra (IRE) (Be My **h–** Guest (USA)) [2016/17 h–: h19.7g May 4] fair hurdler at best: unproven beyond 2m: acts on heavy going: has worn cheekpieces, including sole start (well held) in 2016/17: has joined Sean Regan. *Sally Hall*

ROCKALZARO (FR) 5 gr.g. Balko (FR) – Royale Wheeler (FR) (Rusticaro (FR)) **b83** [2016/17 b16.2v⁶ b16.7g³ Apr 22] €22,000 3-y-o: fifth foal: half-brother to French 17f hurdle winner Rock Avel (by Ultimately Lucky) and a winning pointer by Laveron: dam French maiden: modest form in bumpers. *Donald McCain*

ROCK AND ROLL KING (IRE) 5 b.g. King's Theatre (IRE) – Lunar Path (IRE) **h102** (Night Shift (USA)) [2016/17 b16s h15.8s⁴ h19.9s⁵ h20g³ Apr 9] €18,000 3-y-o: second **b–** foal: dam, French 2¼m hurdle winner (also 9f winner on Flat), half-sister to useful hurdler/ chaser (21f-25f winner) Celtic Son and to dam of useful hurdler/very smart staying chaser Junior: well beaten in maiden bumper: fair form over hurdles. *Evan Williams*

ROCKCHASEBULLETT (IRE) 9 b.g. Catcher In The Rye (IRE) – Last Chance Lady **c103** (IRE) (Mister Lord (USA)) [2016/17 h16.8s c22.4d⁵ c24.1gᵖᵘ Apr 22] lightly-raced **h–** hurdler: fair handicap chaser: stays 21f: acts on good to firm and good to soft going: has worn tongue tie, including last 3 starts. *Fergal O'Brien*

ROCK CHICK SUPREMO (IRE) 6 b.m. Scorpion (IRE) – Ballerina Queen (IRE) **h86 p** (Be My Native (USA)) [2016/17 h71, b69: h25dᶠ May 2] poor form over hurdles: should do better. *Dan Skelton*

ROCK GONE (IRE) 9 b.g. Winged Love (IRE) – Guillem (USA) (Nijinsky (CAN)) **c138** [2016/17 h130: c20v⁶ c19.4d* c17.4s³ c20.8g Mar 16] tall gelding: useful hurdler: similar **h–** form over fences: won novice at Wetherby in January: stays 3m: acts on heavy going. *Dr Richard Newland*

ROCKLANDER (IRE) 8 b.g. Oscar (IRE) – Rua Lass (IRE) (Beau Sher) [2016/17 **h135** h20.3g² h15.8s² h16m* h15.5g² h18.5s² h24s² h23.1s² h24g Mar 16] sturdy gelding: brother to bumper winner/useful hurdler Rathpatrick (2m-3m winner) and half-brother to fair hurdler Realt Den Chathair (2m-3m winner, by Soviet Star): dam (h128) bumper/17f-2¾m hurdle winner: useful handicap hurdler: won at Chepstow and Leicester in November: also second on 5 occasions in 2016/17: stays 3m: acts on soft and good to firm going: usually travels strongly. *Tom George*

ROCKLIFFE 4 b.g. Notnowcato – Hope Island (IRE) (Titus Livius (FR)) [2016/17 h15.8m⁴ **h84** h15.6g⁴ Nov 3] modest on Flat, stays 11.5f: poor form over hurdles. *Micky Hammond*

ROCKLIM (FR) 7 b.g. Laverock (IRE) – Stille Baroque (FR) (Cyborg (FR)) [2016/17 **h105** h104: h24.1dᶠ h24.1d³ h24.3s⁴ h23.8gᶠ Feb 4] fair handicap hurdler: stayed 3m: acted on soft going: wore cheekpieces last 3 starts: dead. *James Ewart*

ROCK ME ZIPPO (IRE) 9 b.g. Millenary – Babylonia (IRE) (Be My Guest (USA)) **c–** [2016/17 h15.9g c23.5vᵘʳ Jan 10] runner-up on completed start in Irish maiden points: **h–** well held over hurdles: beaten when unseated 4 out in novice won by Missed Approach at Lingfield on chasing debut. *Gary Moore*

ROCK MY STYLE (IRE) 5 b.g. Marienbard (IRE) – Meara Trasna (IRE) (Rock **h118** Hopper) [2016/17 b15.8v³ h21.3s² h19.5v² h19.9sᵖᵘ Mar 18] €14,000 3-y-o, £28,000 4-y-o: **b80** second foal: dam, maiden pointer, sister to fairly useful hurdler/chaser (stayed 21f) Mhilu: runner-up in Irish maiden point on debut: third in bumper at Uttoxeter: fairly useful form over hurdles, runner-up both completed starts. *Warren Greatrex*

ROCK N RHYTHM (IRE) 7 b.g. Rock of Gibraltar (IRE) – Dark Rosaleen (IRE)   **c–**
(Darshaan) [2016/17 c105, h122: h17.7d³ h16d h16m⁴ h17.2g Aug 27] compact gelding: **h109**
fair handicap hurdler: fair form over fences: left Jonjo O'Neill after third start: stays 19f:
acts on good to firm and heavy going: in cheekpieces last 2 starts: has worn tongue tie:
usually races prominently. *David Thompson*

ROCKNROBIN (IRE) 6 br.g. Robin des Pres (FR) – Our Presenting (IRE) (Presenting)   **c96**
[2016/17 c97, h–: c21.1d⁵ h19.2g⁴ h21.6g* c25.5d² c21.2m⁵ h25.4dᵖᵘ Jun 26] modest   **h88**
handicap hurdler: won at Fontwell in May: modest chaser: probably stays 25f: acts on soft
going: in cheekpieces last 4 starts: front runner/races prominently. *Chris Gordon*

ROCKNROLLRAMBO (IRE) 10 b.g. Winged Love (IRE) – Lady Padivor (IRE)   **c112**
(Zaffaran (USA)) [2016/17 h–: h23.6dᵖᵘ c23.6dᵘʳ h24dᵖᵘ h20.7d⁶ c23.6d* c23.8g* c23.6g*   **h79**
Apr 17] maiden pointer: fair hurdler at best: similar form over fences: completed hat-trick
in handicaps at Huntingdon in March, and Ffos Las and Chepstow (novice) in April: stays
3m: acts on heavy going: in cheekpieces last 3 starts: sometimes in tongue tie. *Ian Williams*

ROCK OF AGES 8 ch.g. Pivotal – Magic Peak (IRE) (Danehill (USA)) [2016/17 c78,   **c–**
h62: c22.5dᵖᵘ c20.9vᵖᵘ Feb 1] good-quartered gelding: maiden hurdler: poor form over   **h–**
fences: left Steve Flook after first start: should stay beyond 2½m: acts on heavy going:
usually in headgear/tongue tie. *Ann Price*

ROCK OF LEON 6 b.g. Rock of Gibraltar (IRE) – Leonica (Lion Cavern (USA))   **c121 x**
[2016/17 h121: c19.3g² c24sᵘʳ c20.1gᵘʳ c21.2mᵘʳ h18.7g⁵ h23g* c24.2m* c24.2gᵘʳ c22.4dᵘʳ   **h108**
h20.5dᵖᵘ Jan 12] sturdy gelding: fair hurdler: won seller at Worcester in September on
second start for Nigel Twiston-Davies: fairly useful chaser: won maiden at Exeter in
October: left Dan Skelton after second start, trained by N. W. Alexander third/fourth starts
only: stays 3m: acts on good to firm and heavy going: has worn headgear, including last 5
starts: has worn tongue tie: often let down by jumping over fences. *Nigel Hawke*

ROCK ON OSCAR (IRE) 7 b.g. Oscar (IRE) – Brogeen Lady (IRE) (Phardante (FR))   **c125**
[2016/17 h134: c20d² May 7] rangy gelding: won sole start in points: useful hurdler: 3/1,   **h–**
second in novice at Warwick (13 lengths behind Virgilio) on chasing debut: stays 21f: acts
on good to soft going: in hood last 5 starts: wears tongue tie: often travels strongly: carries
head awkwardly. *Paul Nicholls*

ROCK ON ROCKY 9 b.g. Overbury (IRE) – Tachometer (IRE) (Jurado (USA)) [2016/17   **c126**
c–, h121: h19.6g⁵ h23.9g c19.4d³ c16v² c16v² c16v⁵ c16v* c16s* c15.5d* c15.8gᵖᵘ   **h92**
Apr 6] lengthy gelding: fairly useful handicap hurdler: fairly useful handicap chaser:
completed hat-trick at Uttoxeter and Ffos Las (novice) in February, and Sandown in
March: stays 2½m: acts on heavy going: wears cheekpieces/tongue tie: usually races close
up. *Matt Sheppard*

ROCK ON THE MOOR (IRE) 9 b.m. Flemensfirth (USA) – Home At Last (IRE)   **c134**
(Mandalus) [2016/17 h137: h18d⁴ c20d³ c20s⁴ h20v³ h19.9g c21d⁵ Apr 28] rather leggy   **h132**
mare: useful hurdler: third in listed mares event at Punchestown (16 lengths behind Limini)
in February: useful form over fences: fifth in mares handicap there (8½ lengths behind
Definite Ruby) in April: stays 21f: acts on heavy going. *Mrs J. Harrington, Ireland*

ROCKPOINT 4 b.g. Shirocco (GER) – Tinagoodnight (FR) (Sleeping Car (FR)) [2016/17   **b72**
b16.5g⁵ Feb 21] well beaten in bumper. *Colin Tizzard*

ROCKPORTIAN (IRE) 7 b.g. Definite Article – Wilmott's Fancy (Buckley) [2016/17   **h108**
b15.8g* h20.5d⁶ h16d³ h20.8d⁴ h24.3d Apr 21] €10,000 3-y-o: fifth foal: half-brother to   **b97**
bumper winner Alexander Seaview (by Bob Back) and fairly useful hurdler Lough Cuan
(2m winner, by Zaffaran), stayed 3m: dam (h118), bumper/17f-19f hurdle winner, half-
sister to smart chaser (stayed 25f) Percy Smollett: won Irish maiden point on debut: also
won bumper at Uttoxeter (by 3¼ lengths from Senatus) in May: fair form over hurdles:
should stay 3m: often races freely. *Warren Greatrex*

ROCK SOLID (IRE) 8 b.m. Beneficial – Gaelic (IRE) (Strong Gale) [2016/17 h20.1sᵖᵘ   **h89**
h19.4g⁶ h19s⁵ Apr 6] sixth foal: sister to 2 winning pointers: dam (h73) 17f/2½m hurdle
winner: point winner: modest form over hurdles. *Paul Stafford, Ireland*

ROCK THE KASBAH (IRE) 7 ch.g. Shirocco (GER) – Impudent (IRE) (In The   **c144**
Wings) [2016/17 l₁147. c19.4g* c20.4g³ c21d² c24.2v⁴ c23.6v* c24s² c28.8g⁶ Apr 29]   **h–**
useful-looking gelding: smart hurdler: smart chaser: won novices at Chepstow in October
and February: sixth in bet365 Gold Cup (2 lengths behind Henllan Harri) at Sandown in
April: stays 29f: acts on heavy going. *Philip Hobbs*

Johnny Henderson Grand Annual Challenge Cup Handicap Chase, Cheltenham—
Rock The World (left) goes two places better than in 2016 to round off a memorable Gold Cup day
for Jessica Harrington and Robbie Power; Gardefort (armlets) and Theinval (centre) fill the places

ROCK THE WORLD (IRE) 9 b.g. Orpen (USA) – Sue N Win (IRE) (Beneficial) **c157**
[2016/17 c154, h138: c16d² h16.1g c20d c15.9g c16.3g* c16d⁴ Apr 25] sturdy gelding: **h–**
winning hurdler: very smart handicap chaser: won Grand Annual at Cheltenham (by 1¾
lengths from Gardefort) in March: stays 2½m: acts on heavy going: tried in cheekpieces:
wears tongue tie. *Mrs J. Harrington, Ireland*

ROCKU 7 b.g. Great Palm (USA) – Suetsu (IRE) (Toulon) [2016/17 b–: h23.3d^pu h22.7s⁴ **h81**
h22.7v^pu h22s h20.1s³ h27g⁶ Mar 29] third in maiden point on debut: poor form over
hurdles: in hood last 5 starts: usually races nearer last than first: has joined Dan Skelton.
Russell Ross

ROCKWEILLER 10 b.g. Rock of Gibraltar (IRE) – Ballerina Suprema (IRE) (Sadler's **h–**
Wells (USA)) [2016/17 h–: h15.8g May 17] no form over hurdles. *Shaun Harris*

ROCKY BENDER (IRE) 12 b.g. Saddlers' Hall (IRE) – Silver Spirit (IRE) (Parliament) **c106 §**
[2016/17 c115§, h–: c26.1d^pu c20d^pu c29.6s⁵ Dec 22] sturdy gelding: maiden chaser: fair **h–**
handicap chaser: stays 31f: acts on heavy going: has worn headgear: often races towards
rear: temperamental. *Venetia Williams*

ROCKY CREEK (IRE) 11 b.g. Dr Massini (IRE) – Kissantell (IRE) (Broken Hearted) **c146 §**
[2016/17 c153§, h–: c23.6g⁶ c24.2d⁴ c28.8d* c24.2s c30.2d⁶ c26s^pu Mar 4] lengthy, well- **h–**
made gelding: winning hurdler: smart handicap chaser: won Betfair London National at
Sandown (by neck from Doing Fine) in December: stays 29f: acts on heavy going: tried in
headgear: has worn tongue tie: unreliable. *Paul Nicholls*

ROCKY ELSOM (USA) 10 b.g. Rock of Gibraltar (IRE) – Bowstring (IRE) (Sadler's **c–**
Wells (USA)) [2016/17 h16v h21.2s^pu h19.7d⁶ h19.6g⁶ Apr 22] rather leggy gelding: fair **h–**
hurdler at best, no form in 2016/17: maiden chaser: tried in cheekpieces: has worn tongue
tie, including last 5 starts. *Sophie Leech*

ROCKY ISLAND (IRE) 9 b.g. Heron Island (IRE) – Loury The Louse (IRE) (Hollow **c–**
Hand) [2016/17 c–, h–: c24.1g^pu Apr 29] winning pointer: maiden hurdler/chaser: should **h–**
stay 3m: tried in cheekpieces. *T. H. Messenger*

ROCKY REBEL 9 b.g. Norse Dancer (IRE) – Gulchina (USA) (Gulch (USA)) [2016/17 **c97**
c–, h107: c20.3v^F May 10] fair hurdler: modest form over fences: barely stayed 2½m: acted **h–**
on soft going: often wore headgear: dead. *Michael Blake*

ROCKY STONE (IRE) 9 b.g. Cloudings (IRE) – Crandon Park (Sir Harry Lewis (USA)) **c–**
[2016/17 c89, h86: c24.1g^pu May 14] tall, rather leggy gelding: winning Irish pointer: **h–**
winning hurdler: modest form over fences: stays 27f: acts on soft going: in cheekpieces
last 2 starts: often in tongue tie. *Donald McCain*

702

ROCKY'S TREASURE (IRE) 6 b.g. Westerner – Fiddlers Bar (IRE) (Un Desperado (FR)) [2016/17 h19.7s³ h20.3v⁴ h24.4g* h23.9g* Apr 9] €15,000 4-y-o, £60,000 5-y-o: fifth foal: half-brother to useful hurdler/smart chaser Double Shuffle (2m-3m winner) and a winning pointer (both by Milan): dam (c96/h96) 2½m bumper/hurdle winner: won Irish maiden point on debut: fairly useful form over hurdles: won handicaps at Doncaster in February and Ffos Las in April: stays 3m: likely to progress further. *Kim Bailey* **h126 p**

ROCKY TWO (IRE) 7 ch.g. Rock of Gibraltar (IRE) – Toorah Laura La (USA) (Black Minnaloushe (USA)) [2016/17 h98: h16.8s⁴ h20.3d² h15.7gᶠ h18.6g⁵ h19.3g⁶ h19.3d⁶ h16d² h19.7s⁵ h15.7d⁴ h19.7d⁵ Mar 21] modest maiden hurdler: stays 2½m: acts on good to firm and good to soft going: wears cheekpieces. *Philip Kirby* **h89**

RODEO DODO (IRE) 7 b.g. Milan – Laney Mary (IRE) (Mister Lord (USA)) [2016/17 h16g Apr 8] winning pointer: 13/2, seventh in novice at Chepstow on hurdling debut. *Dan Skelton* **h63**

RODERICK RANDOM 7 b.g. Kayf Tara – Clotted Cream (USA) (Eagle Eyed (USA)) [2016/17 h72: c20.9s³ c17.2gᵖᵘ c19.9gᵖᵘ Nov 2] maiden point winner: poor form over hurdles/fences: left Dan Skelton after second start: may prove best short of 21f: acts on soft going: in cheekpieces last 4 starts: in tongue tie last 3. *David Thompson* **c82 h–**

RODY (FR) 12 ch.g. Colonel Collins (USA) – Hamelie II (FR) (Dress Parade) [2016/17 c15.9ᵘʳ c19.2gᵖᵘ Apr 11] compact gelding: maiden hurdler: useful chaser at best for Tom George, failed to complete in 2016/17, including in point: stays 19f: acts on heavy going: has worn headgear: wears tongue tie. *C. M. Casey* **c– h–**

ROGUE ANGEL (IRE) 9 b.g. Presenting – Carrigeen Kohleria (IRE) (Luso) [2016/17 c145, h–: c25d c24d c28g c25.5d c24.5d c25d⁵ c34.3dᵖᵘ c29dᵖᵘ Apr 17] workmanlike gelding: winning hurdler: useful handicap chaser: stays 4m: acts on good to firm and heavy going: wears blinkers/tongue tie. *M. F. Morris, Ireland* **c132 h–**

Michael Buckley/J. Carthy's "Rock The World"

ROGUE DANCER (FR) 12 b.g. Dark Moondancer – Esperanza IV (FR) (Quart de Vin (FR)) [2016/17 c–, h–: c23.6g^{ur} c23.6g^3 Apr 28] tall gelding: maiden hurdler: poor handicap chaser: stays 3¼m: acts on good to firm going: has worn tongue tie. *Michael Banks* · c78 h–

ROGUE TRADER (IRE) 8 b.g. Milan – Bonnie Parker (IRE) (Un Desperado (FR)) [2016/17 c134, h131: c20d^5 c22s* c24.5d^5 c25d^{pu} c25v^{pu} c24.5d^{pu} Apr 29] useful hurdler: useful handicap chaser: won at Punchestown in November: stays 3m: acts on heavy going: usually races towards rear. *Tom J. Taaffe, Ireland* · c139 h–

ROI DES FRANCS (FR) 8 b.g. Poliglote – Grande Souveraine (FR) (Sillery (USA)) [2016/17 c144, h104: c22d^3 c21v^2 c25d c28s^5 c25v^4 c26s* c34.3d c29d^{pu} Apr 17] big gelding: fair hurdler: smart chaser: won minor event at Down Royal (by 7 lengths from Sizing Coal) in March: stays 3¼m: acts on heavy going: has worn headgear, including in 2016/17. *Gordon Elliott, Ireland* · c153 h–

ROJA DOVE (IRE) 8 b.m. Jeremy (USA) – Knight's Place (IRE) (Hamas (IRE)) [2016/17 h112: h16.2d^4 h17.2d h17.2d^3 h15.8g^5 h18.7m^5 h20.2g^3 h20.2s h17g^6 Apr 15] angular mare: modest handicap hurdler nowadays: stays easy 2½m: acts on heavy going: often wears headgear. *David Thompson* · h84

ROKSANA (IRE) 5 b.m. Dubai Destination (USA) – Talktothetail (IRE) (Flemensfirth (USA)) [2016/17 b16g^4 Apr 8] fourth foal: half-sister to bumper/useful 2½m hurdle winner Robin Roe (by Robin des Champs): dam (c104/h104) bumper/3m chase winner: in hood, 5/1, fourth in bumper at Chepstow (12½ lengths behind Forgot To Ask) on debut: entitled to progress. *Dan Skelton* · b75 p

ROLLING DOUGH (IRE) 9 b.m. Indian Danehill (USA) – High Dough (IRE) (High Roller (IRE)) [2016/17 h83: h21.6d* h19.6g^2 h21.6g^{pu} h18.7m h20.5g^6 h19.1s h19.1d^{pu} h20.5v Jan 2] poor handicap hurdler: won at Fontwell early in season: stays 2¾m: acts on soft going: has worn cheekpieces, including last 2 starts: often races towards rear. *Diana Grissell* · h79

ROLLING DYLAN (IRE) 6 ch.g. Indian River (FR) – Easter Saturday (IRE) (Grand Plaisir (IRE)) [2016/17 h122, b99: h19.5d^2 h19.9s* h23.6s^2 h23.4v^{pu} h25.5s^2 Mar 11] sturdy gelding: second in Irish maiden point on debut: bumper winner: fairly useful hurdler: won maiden at Uttoxeter in November: stays 3m: acts on heavy going: tried in cheekpieces. *Philip Hobbs* · h128

ROLLING MAUL (IRE) 9 b.g. Oscar (IRE) – Water Sports (IRE) (Marju (IRE)) [2016/17 c73§, h126§: h23.1m^2 h26.4m^3 h25.4m h23d* h23.1g^2 h22.1d^4 h25.4d^{pu} c24.1g* c21.2g^2 h24g h24s^5 h24.2d^3 h23.6v^6 h23.1g^5 h24g^2 Apr 20] good-topped gelding: fairly useful handicap hurdler: won at Worcester in June: useful form over fences: won novice chase at Bangor (by 15 lengths from Aqalim) in September: stays 25f: acts on good to firm and heavy going: wears headgear: has worn tongue tie: temperamental. *Peter Bowen* · c133 § h128 §

ROLLING THUNDER (IRE) 7 gr.g. Cloudings (IRE) – Peazar (IRE) (Inzar (USA)) [2016/17 h98, b82: c20.5s^{pu} c23.8g* c24.1s^5 c25.2s^4 c21.1g^2 Apr 7] fair maiden hurdler: fairly useful form over fences: won novice handicap at Musselburgh in January: should stay further than 3m: acts on heavy going: in headgear last 4 starts: tried in tongue tie: front runner/races prominently. *Donald McCain* · c116 h–

ROLL OF THUNDER 8 b.g. Antonius Pius (USA) – Ischia (Lion Cavern (USA)) [2016/17 h88: h20.3s^{pu} h16.2d^2 h16.2d^6 h16.2s^6 h16.8g^4 h16.2m h16.2s^6 Nov 4] modest handicap hurdler: stays 21f: acts on good to firm and good to soft going. *James Walton* · h90

ROLLO'S REFLECTION (IRE) 7 b.g. Shantou (USA) – Lola's Reflection (Presenting) [2016/17 b91: h19.4g^{pu} Jan 27] runner-up in maiden point/bumper: pulled up in maiden on hurdling debut. *Ben Case* · h–

ROLL THE DICE (IRE) 11 b.g. Oscar (IRE) – Sallowglen Gale (IRE) (Strong Gale) [2016/17 c–x, h–: c26.2m^{pu} May 29] leggy gelding: winning pointer/hurdler: fair chaser at best, pulled up in hunter sole start in 2016/17: stays 25f: acts on good to firm going: has worn headgear: often let down by jumping/attitude. *Jacqueline Coward* · c– x h–

ROLL THE DOUGH (IRE) 8 b.g. Definite Article – High Dough (IRE) (High Roller (IRE)) [2016/17 h114p: c23g^4 c20s^5 Nov 12] won last of 4 starts in points: fairly useful form over hurdles, won both starts in 2015/16: promise on first of 2 starts in chases. *Philip Hobbs* · c117 h–

ROLLY BABY (FR) 12 b.g. Funny Baby (FR) – Vancia (FR) (Top Dancer (FR)) [2016/17 c139p, h–: c24.5d c21g^3 Jan 22] winning hurdler: useful chaser: third in Leopardstown Handicap Chase in January (1¾ lengths behind A Toi Phil): stays 3m: acts on good to firm and heavy going: usually races prominently. *W. P. Mullins, Ireland* · c134 h–

ROMAIN DE SENAM (FR) 5 b.g. Saint des Saints (FR) – Salvatrixe (FR) (Housamix **c133** (FR)) [2016/17 h138: c17g² c16.4d³ c15.9g* c16.4d⁵ c20.5g c15.8g⁵ c15.5g² Apr 22] well- **h–** made gelding: useful hurdler: useful chaser: won novice at Leicester in January: second in listed handicap at Ayr in April: should stay 2½m: acts on soft going: usually wears hood: wears tongue tie: often races towards rear. *Paul Nicholls*

ROMAN COIN 6 b.g. I Was Framed (USA) – Classic Quartet (Classic Cliche (IRE)) **b–** [2016/17 b15.7g Aug 31] well beaten in maiden bumper. *David Thompson*

ROMANEE VIVANT 7 b.m. Multiplex – Mrs Oh (IRE) (Arctic Lord) [2016/17 h–, b77: **h–** h19.9gᵖᵘ h20.3gᵖᵘ h21.6mᵘʳ h19.9g h25.6sᵖᵘ Oct 1] no form over hurdles. *Neil King*

ROMAN FLIGHT (IRE) 9 b.g. Antonius Pius (USA) – Flight Sequence (Polar Falcon **c142** (USA)) [2016/17 c118p, h140: h15.7m h16.3g c16g² c17m* c16.5g⁴ c19.4m² c16.5m² **h–** c17.1d⁴ c21.4g c20.9m* c16.9m⁴ c19.9g* c20.8s Dec 10] smallish gelding: useful at best over hurdles: useful handicap chaser: won at Stratford in July and October (by 16 lengths from Mountain King), and Newbury in November: stays 21f: acts on good to firm and heavy going: wears headgear. *David Dennis*

ROMANN ANGEL 8 b.m. Sir Harry Lewis (USA) – Roman Gospel (Roi de Rome **h80** (USA)) [2016/17 b–: h19d⁵ h20.7g⁴ h16d⁵ h19.6g² h19.7gᵖᵘ h19.6sᵖᵘ Dec 22] poor form over hurdles: usually leads. *Michael Mullineaux*

ROMAN NUMERAL (IRE) 9 b.g. King's Best (USA) – Trespass (Entrepreneur) **c–** [2016/17 c105, h107: h19.7gᵇᵈ h20.3g² h20.3g⁴ h22.1m⁴ h23.3sᵖᵘ h16.8s⁴ h20.6s c19.3dᶠ **h91** Dec 26] fair handicap hurdler: similar form over fences, fell final outing in 2016/17: stays easy 2¾m: acts on good to firm and heavy going: has worn headgear: usually wears tongue tie. *David Thompson*

ROMANY RYME 11 ch.g. Nomadic Way (USA) – Rakaposhi Ryme (IRE) (Rakaposhi **c–** King) [2016/17 c108, h112: c21gᵖᵘ h26.5mᵖᵘ c25.8gᵖᵘ h20g h21.6mᵖᵘ Aug 31] stocky **h–** gelding: winning pointer: fair hurdler/chaser, no form in early-2016/17: has worn headgear, including last 4 starts: in tongue tie last 2 starts. *Katie Stephens*

ROMEO AMERICO (IRE) 10 b.g. Lord Americo – Crazy Falcon (Polar Falcon **c–** (USA)) [2016/17 c109, h93: h19.1s⁵ h15.9s h23.9g⁵ h23v⁶ h26v² h25.6d² h20.5m* Apr 16] **h92** modest handicap hurdler: won at Plumpton (conditional) in April: maiden chaser: barely stays 3¼m: acts on soft and good to firm going: has worn hood: often travels strongly. *Seamus Mullins*

ROMEO IS BLEEDING (IRE) 11 b.g. Carroll House – Ean Eile (IRE) (Callernish) **c–** [2016/17 h101: h20m c23.6m Apr 28] multiple winning pointer: maiden hurdler: well **h–** beaten in novice hunter on chasing debut: left David Rees after first start: stays 2¾m: acts on good to firm and good to soft going: tried in cheekpieces: in tongue tie last 2 starts: usually races nearer last than first: has joined Ronald Harris. *Carl Price*

ROMULUS DU DONJON (IRE) 6 gr.g. Stormy River (FR) – Spring Stroll (USA) **h–** (Skywalker (USA)) [2016/17 h116: h18.6g Aug 13] lengthy gelding: fair hurdler for Oliver Sherwood, down the field only outing in 2016/17: stays 2½m: acts on good to soft going: usually wears headgear. *Rose Dobbin*

RONALDINHO (IRE) 7 b.g. Jeremy (USA) – Spring Glory (Dr Fong (USA)) [2016/17 **h88** h105: h18.1m⁴ h16.2d² h25.4gᵖᵘ h22.7sᵖᵘ h19.4g h19.4g³ h22.7vᵖᵘ h20.2g³ Apr 28] rather leggy gelding: modest maiden hurdler: stays 2½m: acts on heavy going: wears headgear/ tongue tie: often races towards rear. *Dianne Sayer*

RONALDJAMESSACH (IRE) 4 ch.g. Lord Shanakill (USA) – Boschendal (IRE) **h–** (Zamindar (USA)) [2016/17 h17.2dᵖᵘ h16.7sᵖᵘ h19.5v h19.8v⁶ Mar 9] poor maiden on Flat: no form over hurdles: left James Bethell after first start: tried in hood. *Johnny Farrelly*

RON HEGARTY (IRE) 6 b.g. Gamut (IRE) – Financial Heiress (IRE) (Oscar (IRE)) **b–** [2016/17 b61: b15.8g Apr 9] no form in bumpers: in tongue tie last 2 starts. *Seamus Durack*

RONNIE BAIRD 4 ch.g. Poet's Voice – Fleur de Lis (Nayef (USA)) [2016/17 h16.3d **h109** h16.8s⁴ h16g⁶ h16.3g² h17g Apr 6] leggy gelding: dam half-sister to fairly useful hurdler/ useful chaser (stayed 25f) Song of The Sword: fair on Flat, stays 10.5f: similar standard over hurdles: in hood last 4 starts. *Laura Young*

RONN THE CONN (IRE) 5 ch.g. Whitmore's Conn (USA) – Speedy Fairy (IRE) **h109** (Speedmaster (GER)) [2016/17 h19.7d⁵ h21.2s² h25.3s² Feb 28] second foal: dam unraced half-sister to very smart hurdler/smart chaser (stayed 3¼m) Fair Along: fair form over hurdles. *Chris Grant*

RONS DREAM 7 b.m. Kayf Tara – Empress of Light (Emperor Jones (USA)) [2016/17 **c– p** h139: h24.5s² c20sᵖᵘ h21v* h19.9g h24.7g h24.3d⁵ Apr 21] workmanlike mare: useful **h137** hurdler: won listed mares event at Warwick (by 6 lengths from Jessber's Dream) in February: pulled up in similar event on chasing debut: stays 25f: acts on heavy going: tried in tongue tie: usually races prominently: tough and reliable: should do better over fences. *Peter Bowen*

RON WAVERLY (IRE) 7 ch.g. Haatef (USA) – Mermaid Beach (Slew O' Gold (USA)) **h–** [2016/17 h15.9g h20.5g Oct 31] little form over hurdles: tried in cheekpieces: in tongue tie last 2 starts. *Michelle Bryant*

ROOSTER COGBURN (IRE) 4 b.g. Westerner – Hollygrove (IRE) (Commander **b–** Collins (IRE)) [2016/17 b16g⁶ Mar 18] €65,000 3-y-o: tall gelding: third foal: half-brother to a winning pointer by Spadoun: dam, ran twice, closely related to fairly useful hurdler/ very smart chaser (stayed 3½m) Cane Brake and fairly useful hurdler/useful chaser (stayed 3m) Bob Hall: well beaten in maiden bumper. *Emma Lavelle*

ROOSTER SPIRIT (IRE) 4 gr.g. Craigsteel – Turlututu (FR) (Turgeon (USA)) **b85 §** [2016/17 b16s³ b16v⁴ b16gʳʳ Apr 22] €5,800 3-y-o: fifth foal: dam, placed up to 2m on Flat in France, sister to fairly useful French hurdler/chaser (stayed 2½m) Turlyr: fair form in bumpers: temperamental. *R. Mike Smith*

ROPARTA AVENUE 10 b.g. Nomadic Way (USA) – Miss Fizz (Charmer) [2016/17 c82, **c72 §** h–: c25.5d⁴ c25.5vᶠ c23.5vᵖᵘ h25vᵖᵘ c23.6g⁶ Apr 28] no form over hurdles: poor handicap **h–** chaser: stays 3¼m: acts on heavy going: tried in cheekpieces: temperamental. *Diana Grissell*

RORY'S VALENTINE (IRE) 6 br.m. Windsor Knot (IRE) – Housekeeping (Dansili) **c–** [2016/17 h18.2g⁶ h20g⁶ h20s h18.2d c20.9dᵖᵘ c26.2gᵖᵘ Apr 15] €7,500 3-y-o: fourth foal: **h77** half-sister to fairly useful hurdler/chaser Gentleman Duke (2m/17f winner, by Bachelor Duke) and fair hurdler/useful chaser Johannisberger (2m-2½m winner, by Arakan): dam ran once on Flat in France: poor form over hurdles: pulled up both starts over fences: left John Larkin after fourth start: best effort at 2½m: usually in tongue tie. *Katie Scott*

ROSA DAMASCENA (FR) 4 b.f. Kalanisi (IRE) – Rosewater (GER) (Winged Love **h–** (IRE)) [2016/17 h15sᵖᵘ Dec 3] fairly useful on Flat, best effort at 1¼m: pulled up in listed juvenile fillies event on hurdling debut. *Alan King*

ROSA FLEET (IRE) 9 b.m. Alflora (IRE) – Crimond (IRE) (Zaffaran (USA)) [2016/17 **c98** c111, h–: c24.1g⁴ Apr 29] winning hurdler: fair handicap chaser: stays 3m: acts on heavy **h–** going: tried in hood: often races prominently. *Venetia Williams*

ROSARIOS (FR) 4 b.g. Alexandros – Rose of Logis (FR) (Slickly (FR)) [2016/17 **h73** h16.4s⁴ h15.6g⁶ Dec 14] fair maiden on Flat, stayed 17f: poor form over hurdles: dead. *Rebecca Menzies*

ROSEMARY RUSSET 5 b.m. Midnight Legend – Apple Days (Sovereign Water (FR)) **b93** [2016/17 b15.3vᵘʳ b16.8s⁶ b15.7s* Mar 20] first foal: dam, winning pointer, half-sister to useful chaser (stayed 29f) Strongbows Legend (by Midnight Legend): fair form in bumpers: won conditionals/amateur event at Southwell in March. *Harry Fry*

ROSE RED 10 ch.m. Weld – Secret Whisper (Infantry) [2016/17 h78: h15.8m* h15.8g⁶ **h81 §** h15.8d h18.7g h18.7m² h15.8g⁶ h19.2m⁶ h15.5g⁵ h19.6s⁶ Dec 22] poor handicap hurdler: won at Uttoxeter in June: stays 19f: acts on good to firm and good to soft going: tried in cheekpieces: wears tongue tie: often races towards rear: temperamental. *Rob Summers*

ROSE REVIVED 6 b.m. Midnight Legend – Miniature Rose (Anshan) [2016/17 h82p: **h102** h20.3v² h20g* h19.9g² Jul 5] lengthy, unfurnished mare: fair handicap hurdler: won mares event at Ffos Las in May: stays 2½m: best form on good going: tried in tongue tie. *Jonjo O'Neill*

ROSE TREE (IRE) 4 b.f. Yeats (IRE) – Isabellareine (GER) (Goofalik (USA)) [2016/17 **b85** b16g² Apr 17] first foal: dam (h127), 2m hurdle winner, also 1m-2m winner on Flat: 2/1, second in mares maiden bumper at Fakenham (6 lengths behind Sunshade) in April. *Pam Sly*

ROSIE FIFTY ONE (IRE) 5 b.m. Milan – Prima Belle (FR) (Villez (USA)) [2016/17 **b75** b16.2d b16.2s⁴ b16.2g⁴ Aug 20] €6,000 3-y-o: second foal: dam unraced: modest form in bumpers. *Stuart Crawford, Ireland*

ROSIE LEA 4 b.f. Manduro (GER) – Saralea (FR) (Sillery (USA)) [2016/17 **b55 p** b12.6d⁶ Dec 14] compact filly: half-sister to bumper winner around 1½m Woolstone One (by Authorized) and several winners on Flat abroad: dam useful French/US 5.5f-9f winner: 3/1, sixth in fillies junior bumper at Newbury: should do better. *Stuart Kittow*

ROSIE MCQUEEN (IRE) 5 b.m. Milan – Royal Rosy (IRE) (Dominion Royale) **h112 p**
[2016/17 h16.7s² h19.6sᶠ Mar 5] €28,000 3-y-o, £95,000 4-y-o: good-topped mare: closely
related to fair hurdler/high-class chaser Follow The Plan (2m-25f winner, by Accordion)
and useful hurdler/chaser Ballychorus (2m-3m winner, by King's Theatre): dam (c114/
h119) 2m-2¾m hurdle/chase winner: off mark in Irish mares maiden points at second
attempt: fair form over hurdles: should prove suited by 2½m+: open to further improvement.
Jonjo O'Neill

ROSQUERO (FR) 12 ch.g. Blushing Flame (USA) – Kingsgirl (FR) (Dom Alco (FR)) **c105 §**
[2016/17 c88§, h–: c21.3g* c24.2g⁴ c20.1gᵖᵘ c23.4s³ c20.1d² c20.1sᵇᵈ c16.3s² c17.1s* **h– §**
c19.4d c16.3sᵖᵘ h16.4v³ c21.6v² c23.4v² c21.6dᵘʳ c21.3g² Apr 23] tall gelding: winning
hurdler: fair handicap chaser: won at Wetherby in May and Kelso in December: barely
stays 23f: acts on heavy going: wears headgear: often races towards rear: unreliable.
Kenny Johnson

ROSSETTI 9 gr.g. Dansili – Snowdrops (Gulch (USA)) [2016/17 h15.7g² h16.3d* h17g* **h130**
h16.3g* h16.3m* h16.3g³ h16.4sᵖᵘ h15.9mᵖᵘ Apr 16] compact gelding: useful handicap
hurdler: completed 4-timer with wins at Stratford (3) and Les Landes (minor event) in
summer: unproven beyond 17f: acts on good to firm and good to soft going: wears hood:
front runner/races prominently. *Neil Mulholland*

ROSSINGTON 8 b.g. Gentleman's Deal (IRE) – Ettrbee (IRE) (Lujain (USA)) [2016/17 **h98**
h–: h16.7g⁶ h16.8g⁴ h16.7g³ h15.7dᵖᵘ Nov 15] modest maiden hurdler: best effort at 17f:
wears hood: often leads. *John Wainwright*

ROSS KITTY (IRE) 8 b.m. Scorpion (IRE) – Kitty True (IRE) (Pasternak) [2016/17 **h79**
h16.3v² h18.7mᵖᵘ Jul 17] €6,500 3-y-o: second foal: dam unraced half-sister to smart 2m
hurdler Kimanicky: poor form over hurdles: tried in hood. *Henry Oliver*

ROTHMAN (FR) 7 b.g. Michel Georges – Bravecentadj (FR) (True Brave (USA)) **c115**
[2016/17 c120, h–: c21g² c21.1d² c21d³ h21g c20.5d² c20.2v⁶ c21.1s³ Feb 26] rather leggy **h109**
gelding: fair handicap hurdler: fairly useful handicap chaser: placed 5 times in 2016/17:
left Paul Nicholls after first start: stays 21f: acts on heavy going: wears hood/tongue tie.
Chris Gordon

ROUERGATE (FR) 4 b.f. Sageburg (IRE) – Rouge des Champs (FR) (Robin des **b87**
Champs (FR)) [2016/17 b16g² Apr 17] first foal: dam, fell only start over fences in France,
sister to fairly useful hurdler/useful chaser (17f-19f winner in France) Ruthenoise and half-
sister to fairly useful French hurdler/chaser (2¼m/19f winner) Rouge Et Sage (by
Sageburg): 7/1, shaped as if needed experience when second in mares bumper at Chepstow
(13 lengths behind If You Say Run) on debut. *Venetia Williams*

ROUGE DEVILS (IRE) 6 b.g. Scorpion (IRE) – Penny's Dream (IRE) (Saddlers' Hall **h115**
(IRE)) [2016/17 b–: h25.5g³ h21.4m* h21.4m* h23.6g h21.6m* h23.1g² Apr 26] won last
2 of 3 point starts: fairly useful form over hurdles: won maiden and novice at Wincanton in
October, and novice at Exeter in April: stays 23f: acts on good to firm going: in headgear
last 5 starts: front runner/races prominently. *Paul Nicholls*

ROUGE ET BLANC (FR) 12 ch.g. Mansonnien (FR) – Fidelety (FR) (Villez (USA)) **c–**
[2016/17 c128, h–: c21.1dᵘʳ c20.2vᵖᵘ Feb 2] good-topped gelding: maiden hurdler: fairly **h–**
useful chaser at best, failed to complete both starts in 2016/17: stays 21f: acts on heavy
going: wears cheekpieces: tried in tongue tie. *Oliver Sherwood*

ROUGE ET SAGE (IRE) 9 b.g. Sageburg (IRE) – Rouge Amour (FR) (Cadoudal (FR)) **c99**
[2016/17 c20.9g⁵ c22.4gᶠ c22.4g h17.9s* h19.4s² h19.4sᵖᵘ h19.4dᵖᵘ h20.5v⁴ Mar 11] **h124**
sixth foal: half-brother to fairly useful hurdler/useful chaser Ruthenoise (17f-19f winner in
France) and fairly useful hurdler Robin du Bois (15f/2m winner) (both by Robin des
Champs): dam lightly raced in France (third in 15f hurdle): fairly useful hurdler: won
claimer at Auteuil in September for P. Peltier: second in handicap there in October: fairly
useful chaser at best: left Richard Chotard after seventh start: stays 2¾m: acts on soft
going: tried in headgear. *Susan Corbett*

ROUGH JUSTICE (IRE) 9 b.g. Beneficial – Ringzar (IRE) (Shernazar) [2016/17 c131, **c101 §**
h–: h20.6g h23.3gᵖᵘ c24.1dᵖᵘ c21.1g² c21.6d⁴ c24dᵖᵘ c24.2g³ c23.9d⁴ Apr 27] fairly useful **h–**
hurdler at best: fair handicap chaser: stays 3m: acts on good to firm and good to soft going:
wears headgear: has worn tongue tie, including last 5 starts: front runner/races prominently:
temperamental. *Alan Brown*

ROUND TOWER (IRE) 8 br.g. Presenting – Cash Customer (IRE) (Bob Back (USA)) **c122**
[2016/17 h111: h22gᶠ h16g h21d² h19d² h21g* h20.2g² h23.9s³ c16m⁴ c22g² c19.5g³ **h114**
Nov 4] fair hurdler: won maiden at Ballinrobe in August: fairly useful form over fences:
best effort when third in maiden at Down Royal in November: should stay 3m: acts on soft
going: wears hood: in tongue tie last 3 starts: usually leads. *Karl Thornton, Ireland*

ROUQUINE SAUVAGE 9 ch.m. Loup Sauvage (USA) – No Need For Alarm (Romany Rye) [2016/17 c111, h–: c20.9s³ Nov 18] winning hurdler: fair maiden chaser: stays 21f: best form on soft/heavy going: in hood last 5 starts: wears tongue tie: often races freely. *Anthony Honeyball* **c102 h–**

ROUTINE PROCEDURE (IRE) 7 b.g. Arcadio (GER) – Wayward Bride (IRE) (Shernazar) [2016/17 c–, h–: h15.7d h19.9s⁵ h19v⁴ c15.9g⁴ c19.1g⁶ Jan 27] lengthy gelding: maiden Irish pointer: poor maiden hurdler: poor form over fences: unproven beyond 2m: acts on heavy going: tried in headgear: wears tongue tie. *Robin Dickin* **c69 h81**

ROWDY ROCHER (IRE) 11 br.g. Winged Love (IRE) – Madam Rocher (IRE) (Roselier (FR)) [2016/17 c–, h116: h24.1d⁵ h24.3s* c21.5v* h22.7v⁵ c20d⁶ Apr 5] rather lightly-built gelding: fairly useful hurdler/chaser: won handicap in each sphere at Ayr in January: stays 3m: acts on heavy going: has worn cheekpieces: often races towards rear. *Sandy Thomson* **c119 h117**

ROWLEY PARK (IRE) 4 b.g. Golan (IRE) – Atomic Winner (IRE) (Poliglote) [2016/17 b15.3m² Apr 5] well-beaten second of 4 in maiden bumper. *Linda Blackford* **b58**

ROWNAK (IRE) 4 ch.g. Rip Van Winkle (IRE) – Apache Dream (IRE) (Indian Ridge) [2016/17 b15.6g⁴ b15.7s Feb 13] modest form in bumpers. *Brian Ellison* **b78**

ROXY BELLE 7 b.m. Black Sam Bellamy (IRE) – Royal Roxy (IRE) (Exit To Nowhere (USA)) [2016/17 b–: b15.8g b15.8d Dec 4] compact mare: no form in bumpers: has joined Jack R. Barber. *Mark Rimell* **b–**

ROXYFET (FR) 7 b.g. Califet (FR) – Roxalamour (FR) (Valanour (IRE)) [2016/17 c112, h105: c16.4d c19.3d c15.2s c19.2d c15.7g⁶ c15.7d c16.4s⁴ c16.4v³ c16.4d² c16.3v³ c15.2d² c17.1d⁶ c15.6g Apr 25] fair hurdler: modest handicap chaser: stays 19f: acts on heavy going: has worn headgear, including last 4 starts: has worn tongue tie: usually races towards rear: temperamental. *Micky Hammond* **c92 § h–**

ROXY MADAM 8 br.m. Generous (IRE) – Masouri Sana (IRE) (Broken Hearted) [2016/17 h16.3m^pu May 15] poor form in bumpers/on Flat: pulled up in mares novice seller on hurdling debut: in hood last 3 starts: tried in tongue tie. *Mandy Rowland* **h–**

ROXY THE REBEL 7 b.m. Bollin Eric – Petrea (St Ninian) [2016/17 h63: h21.3g Oct 28] little form over hurdles. *Simon Waugh* **h–**

ROYAL ACT 5 b.g. Royal Anthem (USA) – Native's Return (IRE) (Presenting) [2016/17 b17d⁶ b16.7m⁶ Apr 17] poor form in bumpers. *Sam England* **b74**

ROYAL BATTALION 6 b.g. Sea The Stars (IRE) – Yummy Mummy (Montjeu (IRE)) [2016/17 h108: h20m² h24g^pu h21.6g* h26g h25g² h19.8d h20.5m⁴ Apr 17] sturdy gelding: fair handicap hurdler: won at Fontwell in August: stays 2¾m: acts on soft and good to firm going: wears headgear. *Gary Moore* **h105**

ROYAL BENIFET (IRE) 9 ch.g. Royal Anthem (USA) – Beneficial Lady (IRE) (Beneficial) [2016/17 c21.4g⁶ c19.2d⁶ c21.2m⁵ c24d⁵ c23.9g h24g³ h22.1d Aug 29] dual winning pointer: poor form over hurdles/fences: tried in blinkers. *Mike Sowersby* **c65 h67**

ROYAL CAPTAIN (IRE) 8 br.g. Presenting – Dunahall Queen (IRE) (Saddlers' Hall (IRE)) [2016/17 c–, h–: c23.6g^pu c19.2s⁵ Dec 1] dual winning pointer: maiden hurdler: no form over fences: best effort at 2¼m: tried in tongue tie. *Ben Case* **c– h–**

ROYAL CAVIAR (IRE) 9 b.g. Vinnie Roe (IRE) – Blackwater Babe (IRE) (Arctic Lord) [2016/17 h136: c18s* c17gᶠ c15.9g⁴ Mar 14] well-made gelding: useful hurdler: smart form over fences: won maiden at Thurles in December: stays 2¼m: acts on heavy going: wears hood: tried in tongue tie: often travels strongly: has joined Cyril Murphy, USA. *W. P. Mullins, Ireland* **c145 h–**

ROYAL CHATELIER (FR) 12 b.g. Video Rock (FR) – Attualita (FR) (Master Thatch) [2016/17 c97, h–: c23.8m^pu May 11] winning pointer: winning hurdler: fair chaser: stays 25f: acts on good to firm and heavy going: tried in cheekpieces. *N. W. Alexander* **c– h–**

ROYAL CHIEF (IRE) 8 gr.g. Royal Anthem (USA) – Help Yourself (IRE) (Roselier (FR)) [2016/17 c105, h102: c21g⁴ h22m³ h23g⁴ h21.6g³ h16.7g³ Jul 3] winning pointer: modest hurdler/chaser: stays 3m: acts on good to firm and heavy going: wears headgear. *Alexandra Dunn* **c67 h95**

ROYAL CLARET 5 b.m. Yeats (IRE) – Kerada (FR) (Astarabad (USA)) [2016/17 b15.8s⁴ b16.7s³ b16v⁴ b15.8s¹ Apr 1] £14,000 3-y-o: first foal: dam (c137/h127) 2m-3m hurdle/chase winner: fair form in bumpers: will prove suited by 2½m: wears tongue tie. *Tom Symonds* **b86**

ROYAL CLASSIC (FR) 7 b.g. Anabaa Blue – Rapid Lomita (GER) (Lomitas) [2016/17 c19.2s^pu c18.2g^pu Mar 30] tall gelding: maiden hurdler: no form over fences. *Gary Moore* **c– h–**

708

ROYAL CONCORDE (IRE) 6 br.g. Kalanisi (IRE) – Talinas Rose (IRE) (Definite **b72**
Article) [2016/17 b17.7g⁵ Nov 28] 33/1, fifth in bumper at Plumpton (19¼ lengths behind
If The Cap Fits) on debut. *Linda Jewell*

ROYAL CRAFTSMAN (IRE) 7 b.g. Robin des Pres (FR) – Crafty Women (IRE) **h– x**
(Warcraft (USA)) [2016/17 h85x: h19.9gᵖᵘ May 29] poor maiden hurdler: in headgear last
2 starts: tried in tongue tie: often let down by jumping. *Peter Bowen*

ROYAL DEBUTANTE (IRE) 6 b.m. Presenting – Chinatownqueen (IRE) (Westerner) **h114**
[2016/17 b97: h15.8m³ h19.6d² h19.8s h20.7g³ h16.7d* Apr 27] rather unfurnished mare:
bumper winner: fair form over hurdles: won mares handicap at Market Rasen in April:
stays 2½m: acts on good to soft going: tried in tongue tie. *Paul Webber*

ROYALE CHAMP (IRE) 5 b.m. Robin des Champs (FR) – Rosafi (IRE) (Roselier **h73**
(FR)) [2016/17 b17.7d⁵ h19.5v h16.8d⁵ h21.6d³ Mar 18] €12,500 3-y-o, £7,000 4-y-o: fifth **b65**
foal: half-sister to fair 3m hurdle winner/winning pointer Robinroyale (by Robin des
Champs) and modest hurdler/poor chaser Snowball (3m/25f winner, by Alderbrook): dam,
winning pointer, half-sister to useful hurdler/smart chaser (stayed 25f) Alexander Taipan:
third in Irish mares maiden point on debut: fifth in mares bumper: poor form over hurdles.
Nick Mitchell

ROYALE DJANGO (IRE) 8 b.g. Kayf Tara – Royale Boja (FR) (Kadalko (FR)) **c–**
[2016/17 c133, h–: c21.3m⁵ h23.1gᶠ Jul 3] fairly useful hurdler at best: useful chaser: stays **h–**
3m: acts on good to firm and heavy going: tried in cheekpieces: often races prominently.
Tim Vaughan

ROYALE KNIGHT 11 b.g. King's Theatre (IRE) – Gardana (FR) (Garde Royale) **c128**
[2016/17 c145, h118: h23.3g⁵ c29.2g⁶ c32.4s⁴ c29.5s Dec 27] fair handicap hurdler: useful **h110**
handicap chaser: stays 35f: acts on good to firm and heavy going: has worn headgear,
including last 2 starts. *Dr Richard Newland*

ROYAL ESCAPE (IRE) 5 b.g. Getaway (GER) – Echo Queen (IRE) (Luso) [2016/17 **b88**
b16g⁵ Apr 24] €40,000 3-y-o: fourth foal: half-brother to fair hurdler/fairly useful chaser
New Kid In Town (2½m-3m winner, by Gamut) and fairly useful hurdler/useful chaser
Kilcarry Bridge (2m-2¾m winner, by Balakheri): dam unraced sister to Irish Grand
National winner Hear The Echo: 9/1, fifth in bumper at Warwick (6¼ lengths behind Not
That Fuisse) on debut. *Jonjo O'Neill*

ROYAL ETIQUETTE (IRE) 10 b.g. Royal Applause – Alpine Gold (IRE) (Montjeu **h88**
(IRE)) [2016/17 h–: h20.5g² h15.9v² h15.9v² h15.9s⁵ Mar 13] angular gelding: modest
maiden hurdler: stays 2½m: acts on good to firm and heavy going: wears headgear/tongue
tie: often races towards rear. *Lawney Hill*

ROYAL FLUSH 6 b.g. Multiplex – Mystical Feelings (BEL) (Feelings (FR)) [2016/17 **h–**
h20.2dᵖᵘ Jun 30] well held in maiden on Flat: pulled up in similar event on hurdling debut.
Simon Waugh

ROYAL GUARDSMAN (IRE) 10 b.g. King's Theatre (IRE) – Lisa du Chenet (FR) **c–**
(Garde Royale) [2016/17 c–, h128: h20.5d h20.5v³ Mar 4] tall gelding: fairly useful **h114**
handicap hurdler at best: maiden chaser: stays 2¾m: acts on heavy going: tried in
cheekpieces: in tongue tie last 2 starts. *Ali Stronge*

ROYAL HALL (FR) 5 b.g. Halling (USA) – Royal Fantasy (IRE) (King's Best (USA)) **h109**
[2016/17 h17.9g² h16.3s⁵ h15.9v⁵ h16s h15.9v Feb 27] sturdy gelding: runner-up in 11.5f
maiden on Flat and on hurdling debut for L. Viel: no form in Britain. *Gary Moore*

ROYAL IRISH HUSSAR (IRE) 7 b.g. Galileo (IRE) – Adjalisa (IRE) (Darshaan) **h124**
[2016/17 h132: h18.5g⁴ h15.9m² h16d⁴ h16.5g⁴ Dec 20] close-coupled gelding: fairly
useful handicap hurdler: second at Plumpton in September: should stay 2½m: acts on soft
and good to firm going: often wears cheekpieces: usually races close up. *Nicky Henderson*

ROYAL MACNAB (IRE) 9 b.g. Beneficial – Tina McBride (IRE) (Oscar (IRE)) **c118**
[2016/17 c120, h–: c21.4g⁴ c19.2g³ c20.1d² c20.1s² c20.1s² c19.9g⁵ c19.1g³ c19.9g* **h–**
c19.9g⁶ c19.4d³ Jan 14] maiden hurdler: fairly useful handicap chaser: won at Musselburgh
in December: stays 2½m: acts on heavy going: tried in hood: front
runner/races prominently, often travels strongly. *Rebecca Menzies*

ROYAL MANDATE (IRE) 5 ch.g. Manduro (GER) – Hesperia (Slip Anchor) [2016/17 **h–**
h16gᶠ Sep 29] fell first in novice hurdle on debut. *Dan Skelton*

ROYAL MILAN (IRE) 7 b.g. Milan – Aimees Princess (IRE) (Good Thyne (USA)) **c63**
[2016/17 h112: h24.1g³ c23.8dᵇᵈ c23.4d c24d⁶ c23.6dᵖᵘ Feb 9] workmanlike gelding: fairly **h118**
useful form over hurdles: poor form over fences: stays 25f: acts on good to soft going: tried
in cheekpieces: wears tongue tie. *Philip Hobbs*

Stella Artois 1965 Chase, Ascot—course specialist Royal Regatta springs a surprise from Kylemore Lough (striped sleeves) and God's Own (No.1)

ROYAL NATIVE (IRE) 9 b.g. King's Theatre (IRE) – Hollygrove Native (IRE) (Be My Native (USA)) [2016/17 c94, h99: c25.5d^{ur} c24.5d^5 Dec 15] sturdy gelding: fair hurdler/chaser: stayed 27f: acted on good to soft going: wore tongue tie: dead. *Anthony Honeyball* — **c98** **h–**

ROYAL PALLADIUM (FR) 9 gr.g. King's Theatre (IRE) – Dent Sucree (FR) (Turgeon (USA)) [2016/17 c123, h–: c24.2s* c26d^{pu} c23.8d^6 Jan 19] useful-looking gelding: maiden hurdler: fairly useful handicap chaser: won at Exeter in November: stays 3¼m: acts on heavy going: front runner/races prominently: unreliable. *Venetia Williams* — **c123 §** **h–**

ROYAL PEARL 4 gr.f. Aussie Rules (USA) – Gower Diva (Sakhee (USA)) [2016/17 h15.8g^{pu} h15.8d^5 h16.4d^2 h16.6g h15.8g^{pu} Apr 17] fair on Flat, stays 1m: poor form over hurdles: in tongue tie last 2 starts. *Tom Gretton* — **h81**

ROYAL PLAZA 6 b.g. King's Theatre (IRE) – Friendly Craic (IRE) (Mister Lord (USA)) [2016/17 b93: h15.9g^4 h20.3g^3 h16m^3 h16g^3 h19.9g^4 h19.9d^2 h19.6g^2 h19s* h19.7s^{ur} h19.1v h21.2s^F Mar 2] fairly useful handicap hurdler: won at Warwick (conditional) in November: stays 2½m: acts on soft and good to firm going: wears hood/tongue tie: often races in rear. *Alan King* — **h119**

ROYALRAISE (IRE) 8 b.g. Royal Anthem (USA) – Raise The Issue (IRE) (Galileo (IRE)) [2016/17 c123, h119: c23.8m* c21.4g* c22.6m^{pu} Jul 17] lengthy gelding: fairly useful hurdler: fairly useful form over fences: won novice handicap at Ludlow (awarded race) in May and maiden at Market Rasen in June: stays 3m: acts on soft and good to firm going: in blinkers last 3 starts: front runner/races prominently. *Oliver Sherwood* — **c125** **h–**

ROYAL REDEMPTION (IRE) 8 b.g. Milan – Royale Laguna (FR) (Cadoudal (FR)) [2016/17 c20d^{pu} c25.1d^{pu} Feb 18] runner-up in Irish maiden point: maiden hurdler: pulled up both starts over fences: should stay 3m: acts on heavy going: in tongue tie last 4 starts. *Charlie Mann* — **c–** **h–**

ROYAL REGATTA (IRE) 9 b.g. King's Theatre (IRE) – Friendly Craic (IRE) (Mister Lord (USA)) [2016/17 c152, h–: c19.9g^5 c21d* c16.3s^{pu} c21s^3 c19.9g^{pu} Apr 7] useful-looking gelding: winning hurdler: very smart chaser: won 1965 Chase at Ascot (by head from Kylemore Lough) in November: third in Betfair Ascot Chase in February: stays 21f: acts on soft going: wears headgear/tongue tie: usually leads. *Philip Hobbs* — **c157** **h–**

ROYAL RESERVE 4 b.g. Duke of Marmalade (IRE) – Lady Hawkfield (IRE) (Hawk Wing (USA)) [2016/17 h15.6g^4 h16g^4 h16s^4 h15.8d^4 Feb 22] lengthy gelding: fairly useful on Flat, stays 1¼m: fair form over hurdles: has joined David O'Meara. *Ian Williams* — **h111**

ROYAL RIVIERA 11 b.g. Nayef (USA) – Miss Cap Ferrat (Darshaan) [2016/17 c23g^6 May 27] sturdy gelding: winning pointer: winning hurdler: fair chaser at best: stays 3m: acts on good to firm and heavy going: in headgear last 3 starts: wears tongue tie. *Mrs N. Sheppard* — **c–** **h–**

ROYAL ROO 8 b.m. Overbury (IRE) – Royal Roxy (IRE) (Exit To Nowhere (USA)) [2016/17 h57: h21.4m^{pu} c20.3d^{pu} May 26] little form over hurdles: pulled up in novice handicap on chasing debut: in tongue tie last 4 starts. *Mark Rimell* — **c–** **h–**

ROYAL RUBY 5 b.g. Yeats (IRE) – Close Harmony (Bustino) [2016/17 b15.7g* Mar 28] **b98**
closely related to 3 winners, including useful hurdler/very smart chaser Barbers Shop
(17f-3¼m winner, by Saddlers' Hall), and half-brother to 2 winners, including bumper
winner/useful hurdler Heather Royal (17f winner, by Medicean), stayed 21f: dam (h89),
maiden hurdler (stayed 2½m), sister to fairly useful 2m hurdler Bella Macrae: in hood, 5/2,
won bumper at Southwell (by 1½ lengths from Chesterman) in March. *Nicky Henderson*

ROYAL SALUTE 7 br.g. Flemensfirth (USA) – Loxhill Lady (Supreme Leader) [2016/17 **c116**
h101: c20.3g⁶ c21.1s* c19.4s² c25.1d³ c25.7v* c25.7v* c25.7s³ c24sᶠ Apr 1] well-made **h–**
gelding: fair hurdler: fairly useful handicap chaser: won at Fontwell in November and
Plumpton (twice) in January: stays 3¼m: acts on heavy going: in blinkers last 4 starts:
wears tongue tie. *Anthony Honeyball*

ROYALS AND REBELS (IRE) 7 b.g. Robin des Pres (FR) – Native Deal (IRE) (Be **c99**
My Native (USA)) [2016/17 h21.2g⁵ h25.5s⁴ h23.1v h23.1d⁴ c25.7s² c24v⁴ c25.7s* **h103**
c29.2vᵖᵘ Mar 22] £13,000 6-y-o: sixth foal: half-brother to fair hurdler/fairly useful chaser
Who's Deal (2m-19f winner, by Pistolet Bleu) and fair chaser Saddlers Deal (2m-2½m
winner, by Saddlers' Hall): dam unraced: Irish maiden point winner: fair form over hurdles:
modest form over fences: won handicap at Plumpton in March: stays 3¼m: acts on soft
going: in headgear last 3 starts: wears tongue tie. *Charlie Mann*

ROYAL SUPREMO (IRE) 6 b.g. Beneficial – Slaney Athlete (IRE) (Warcraft (USA)) **h111**
[2016/17 b92: b16.8s* h19.9g* h19.9d³ h19g h25g³ Apr 28] runner-up in Irish maiden **b92**
point: fair form in bumpers: won at Sedgefield early in season: fair form over hurdles: won
novice at Uttoxeter in May. *Kim Bailey*

ROYAL TROOPER (IRE) 11 b.g. Hawk Wing (USA) – Strawberry Roan (IRE) **h§§**
(Sadler's Wells (USA)) [2016/17 h19.9vᵗᵗ Dec 16] maiden hurdler: refused to race sole
start in 2016/17, as he had on last 4 outings on Flat: has worn visor/tongue tie: one to avoid.
Mark Brisbourne

ROYAL VACATION (IRE) 7 b.g. King's Theatre (IRE) – Summer Break (IRE) **c146**
(Foxhound (USA)) [2016/17 h128: c19.2d² c24.2g² c23.5v* c21d³ c24g* c20.8s* c24.4gᵖᵘ **h–**
c20gᵖᵘ Apr 29] useful-looking gelding: fairly useful hurdler: smart chaser: won handicap
at Lingfield in November, Kauto Star Novices' Chase at Kempton (by 12 lengths from

32Red Kauto Star Novices' Chase, Kempton—
33/1-shot Royal Vacation takes advantage of clear leader Might Bite's final-fence departure

Timeform Novices' Handicap Chase, Cheltenham—no such good fortune needed this time as Royal Vacation puts up a smart performance under top weight

Virgilio) in December and Timeform Novices' Handicap Chase at Cheltenham (by 8 lengths from Potters Legend) in January: stays 3m: acts on heavy going: has worn headgear, including last 5 starts: wears tongue tie: often races prominently. *Colin Tizzard*

ROYAL VILLAGE (IRE) 5 b.g. Scorpion (IRE) – Etoile Margot (FR) (Garde Royale) [2016/17 b15.7d* h20.5d³ h20.3v² h20.6m² h20.2g* Apr 26] €28,000 3-y-o: sixth foal: brother to fairly useful 2m hurdle winner Yorgonnahearmeroar and half-brother to 2 winners, including fairly useful hurdler/very smart chaser Village Vic (17f-21f winner, by Old Vic): dam, French 17f chase winner, also 11f winner on Flat: fell in Irish maiden point: won bumper at Southwell (by 2 lengths from Al Shahir) in November: fairly useful form over hurdles: won maiden at Perth in April. *Philip Hobbs* **h116 b106**

ROYALZARO (FR) 7 gr.g. Laveron – Royale Wheeler (FR) (Rusticaro (FR)) [2016/17 b96: h19g⁵ Mar 30] dual winning pointer: off 16 months, fatally injured when fifth in maiden at Taunton on hurdling debut. *Harry Fry* **h80**

ROYSTA'S SPIRIT 6 b.m. Helissio (FR) – Seviot (Seymour Hicks (FR)) [2016/17 b17g May 13] third foal: dam third only completed start in points: won point in April 2016: 9/1, better than result when tenth in conditionals/amateur bumper at Aintree (15½ lengths behind Gustave Mahler) in May: open to improvement. *Philip Rowley* **b– p**

R THEVERYMAN 8 b.g. Overbury (IRE) – Dame Maggie (Karinga Bay) [2016/17 h20.3d^pu c21.2g³ Jul 18] dual winning pointer: pulled up in novice seller on hurdling debut: well beaten in maiden on chasing debut. *Jacqueline Coward* **c68 h–**

RUACANA 8 b.g. Cape Cross (IRE) – Farrfesheena (USA) (Rahy (USA)) [2016/17 c–, h140: h16.2d⁴ h21.1g⁶ h15.8g⁵ h21.4s² h23.4v^pu h24.4s h21m⁵ Apr 18] smallish, sturdy gelding: fairly useful handicap hurdler: second at Wincanton in December: jumped sketchily only chase start: stays 21f: acts on heavy going: has worn headgear, including last 2 starts. *Tim Vaughan* **c– h129**

RUAPEHU (IRE) 11 b.g. Presenting – Silver Prayer (IRE) (Roselier (FR)) [2016/17 c116: c25.1m³ May 10] workmanlike gelding: has reportedly had breathing operation: fairly useful chaser at best: stays 3¼m: acts on good to firm going: tried in headgear: has worn tongue tie, including last 5 starts. *Charles Whittaker* **c93**

RUARAIDH HUGH (IRE) 8 b.g. Craigsteel – Decent Shower (Decent Fellow) [2016/17 h112: h20.3g h23.3d h20.3d⁶ h23.1g* h20.2g h18.6g⁵ h20g⁶ Oct 14] fair handicap hurdler: left Chris Bealby after winning at Market Rasen in July: stays 23f: acts on good to firm and good to soft going: wears headgear. *Laura Morgan* **h111**

RUBEN COTTER (IRE) 11 b.g. Beneficial – Bonnie Thynes (IRE) (Good Thyne (USA)) [2016/17 c141, h–: c20g⁵ c23.6g^pu c25g^pu c33m⁵ Apr 27] strong gelding: winning hurdler: useful handicap chaser: fifth at Uttoxeter (3¼ lengths behind Minella Present) in May: left Paul Nicholls after second start, Mark McNiff after third: stays 3¼m: acts on heavy going: tried in cheekpieces/tongue tie: often races prominently. *Peter Maher, Ireland* **c140 h–**

RUBY REDHEAD 7 b.m. Distant Peak (IRE) – Redhead (IRE) (Redback) [2016/17 b–: b16.8m Jul 1] no form in bumpers. *Alexandra Dunn* — b–

RUBY RUSSET 5 b.m. Apple Tree (FR) – Fair Coppelia (Saddlers' Hall (IRE)) [2016/17 b17.7d² b16.2s h17.7vᵖᵘ h15.3s³ h15.3d⁴ Mar 26] second foal: dam (h74) lightly raced in bumpers/over hurdles: modest form in bumpers/over hurdles: tried in tongue tie. *Colin Tizzard* — h92 b75

RUBYS CUBE 4 b.f. Multiplex – Cresswell Ruby (IRE) (Rashar (USA)) [2016/17 b14s Nov 16] second foal: dam (h101) 19f-3¼m hurdle winner: well beaten in fillies junior bumper. *Debra Hamer* — b–

RUBY VODKA 6 b.m. Oscar (IRE) – Auntie Kathleen (Terimon) [2016/17 b–: h20d h20.6gᵖᵘ h19.3gᵖᵘ h15.7s⁵ h20.1sᵖᵘ h17g Apr 15] no form over hurdles: tried in hood. *Sharon Watt* — h–

RUBY WHO (IRE) 5 gr.g. Daylami (IRE) – Lelepa (IRE) (Inchinor) [2016/17 b16.4s h16.2v h16.6sᵖᵘ h19.4g h18.1s Apr 3] well beaten in bumper: no form over hurdles. *Rose Dobbin* — h– b–

RUBY WILDE (IRE) 6 b.m. Oscar (IRE) – Hazel Grove (IRE) (Definite Article) [2016/17 b–: b16.2d² h19.5d⁶ h18.5s⁵ h21v Dec 31] modest form in bumpers: modest form over hurdles: remains with potential. *Graeme McPherson* — h96 p b80

RUBY YEATS 6 b.m. Yeats (IRE) – Newby Lady (Terimon) [2016/17 h–: h15.7v* h16.2s² h20.5g Mar 25] workmanlike mare: maiden pointer: fair form over hurdles: won mares maiden at Southwell in December. *Harry Whittington* — h114

RUDDY ARTICLE (IRE) 9 ch.g. Definite Article – Cherry Tart (IRE) (Persian Mews) [2016/17 c–p, h118: c23g² c23dᵖᵘ c25.8m⁴ c23g⁶ h21.6d c24.2m⁴ h23.6dᵖᵘ Nov 16] lengthy gelding: multiple point winner: fairly useful hurdler/chaser, mostly out of form in 2016/17 after reappearance: left Paul Nicholls after fifth start: stayed 23f: best form on good going: tried in cheekpieces: wore tongue tie: dead. *Katie Stephens* — c124 h–

RUDE AND CRUDE (IRE) 8 b.g. Rudimentary (USA) – Sorry Sarah (IRE) (Good Thyne (USA)) [2016/17 h98: c20.2s⁴ c17s³ c19.7m³ Apr 16] tall gelding: point winner: modest maiden hurdler: similar form over fences: stays 2½m: acts on good to firm and heavy going: has worn tongue tie. *Gary Moore* — c95 h–

RUE BALZAC (IRE) 4 b.g. Champs Elysees – Rondo Alla Turca (IRE) (Noverre (USA)) [2016/17 h17.7g⁴ h16g⁵ Oct 12] dam half-sister to smart hurdler/useful chaser (stayed 3m) Kadoun: modest form on Flat/over hurdles: wears cheekpieces. *Neil King* — h93

RULER OF THE NILE 5 b.g. Exceed And Excel (AUS) – Dinka Raja (USA) (Woodman (USA)) [2016/17 h15.7d h15.8v h19g⁶ h16.2vᵖᵘ h16.6s h19.5m³ Apr 28] fairly useful on Flat, stays 16.5f: modest form over hurdles. *Robert Stephens* — h90

RUMBURY GREY 14 gr.g. Overbury (IRE) – Polly Buckrum (Buckley) [2016/17 c–: c25.3gᵖᵘ c27.2dᵖᵘ May 12] workmanlike gelding: 3-time winning pointer: fairly useful chaser at best, no form since 2013/14: stays 3½m: acts on good to soft going. *Steve Flook* — c–

RUNASIMI RIVER 4 ch.f. Generous (IRE) – Zaffaranni (IRE) (Zaffaran (USA)) [2016/17 b16.2v* Feb 1] fifth foal: half-sister to modest hurdler Fuse Wire (2¼m winner, by Tamayaz), stayed 3m: dam (c103/h96), 2½m-3m hurdle/chase winner, sister to useful hurdler/winning chaser (stayed 3m) Santablesz: 7/1, won bumper at Hereford (by 4½ lengths from Well Smitten) on debut: will be suited by 2½m+. *Neil Mulholland* — b83

RUN BOB RUN 6 b.g. Beat All (USA) – Rash-Gale (IRE) (Rashar (USA)) [2016/17 h–, b76: h23.1g³ h23.4g² h23.1g⁶ h25.6g Nov 4] poor maiden hurdler: best effort at 23f: in cheekpieces last 4 starts. *John Flint* — h73

RUNFORDAVE (IRE) 5 b.g. Stowaway – Poetics Girl (IRE) (Saddlers' Hall (IRE)) [2016/17 b16d⁴ b17m² b16g* h20s³ h18d* h20vᶠ h16v³ h18.5v* h20.3g³ h20s³ h20gᶠ Apr 28] fairly useful form in bumpers: won maiden at Down Royal in November: useful hurdler: won maiden at Fairyhouse in December and minor event at Clonmel in February: third in Martin Pipe Conditional Jockeys' Handicap Hurdle at Cheltenham (3½ lengths behind Champagne Classic) in March: fell fatally at Punchestown: stayed 2½m: acted on heavy going. *Gordon Elliott, Ireland* — h141 b95

RUN FOR EVA 4 b.f. Westerner – Glorybe (GER) (Monsun (GER)) [2016/17 b13g b12.6d b15.7v Feb 15] leggy filly: first foal: dam (h103), 2m hurdle winner, also 11f winner on Flat in Germany, half-sister to useful hurdler/high-class chaser (stayed 21f) Ghizao: no form in bumpers. *Olly Williams* — b–

RUN FOR GER (IRE) 9 b.g. High Roller (IRE) – Medieval Banquet (IRE) (Mister Lord (USA)) [2016/17 h19.8m⁴ h21m c16.5g^pu h18.5d^pu Sep 26] maiden pointer: modest maiden hurdler: let down by jumping both starts over fences: left David Edward Finn after second start: stays 21f: acts on good to firm and good to soft going: tried in headgear: usually wears tongue tie: front runner/races prominently. *Evan Williams* **c–** **h90**

RUNITAGAINSAM 6 b.m. Samraan (USA) – Hollywood (Bin Ajwaad (IRE)) [2016/17 b15.7g b16g h15.5g^bd h15.5g Dec 7] first foal: dam (h94) 2½m/2¾m hurdle winner: no form in bumpers/over hurdles: in tongue tie last 2 starts: has rejoined Carole Ikin (left yard after debut). *Fergal O'Brien* **h–** **b–**

RUNNING IN HEELS (IRE) 8 br.m. September Storm (GER) – Ceo Draiochta (IRE) (Erins Isle) [2016/17 c55: c25.5d³ May 12] won 3 times in points: poor form in hunter chases: wears cheekpieces. *David Phelan* **c71**

RUNNING SQUAW 9 ch.m. Denounce – Georgie McTaggart (Minster Son) [2016/17 h15.7m⁶ h16m^pu Apr 28] second foal: dam unraced daughter of useful staying chaser Cheeny's Brig: no form over hurdles. *Pam Ford* **h–**

RUNNING WOLF (IRE) 6 b.g. Amadeus Wolf – Monet's Lady (IRE) (Daylami (IRE)) [2016/17 h93: h21g⁶ h20.7g⁴ c21.2g⁴ c19.9d⁴ c22.7g² c19.9d⁴ c23.6d³ Mar 15] lengthy, workmanlike chaser: modest handicap hurdler: similar form over fences: stays 23f: acts on soft going: wears tongue tie: unreliable. *Alex Hales* **c94 §** **h82 §**

RUN RUCTIONS RUN (IRE) 8 b.m. Westerner – Perfect Prospect (IRE) (Golan (IRE)) [2016/17 c131, h127: c23.9g³ h24.5s³ h20.3s h19.9v^F Dec 31] workmanlike mare: useful handicap hurdler: third in listed mares event at Kempton (11¼ lengths behind Surtee du Berlais) in November: useful chaser: third in similar event at Market Rasen (6¾ lengths behind Desert Queen) same month: stays 3m: acts on heavy going: wears headgear: often races prominently. *Dr Richard Newland* **c131** **h119**

RUNSWICK DAYS (IRE) 10 b.g. Presenting – Miss Lauren Dee (IRE) (Montelimar (USA)) [2016/17 c77, h–: c16.4g^pu c24.2g^pu c23.4s* c24.2d⁶ c24.2v⁵ c23.8g^pu Feb 4] maiden hurdler: modest handicap chaser: won at Kelso in October: left John Wade after second start: stayed 23f: acted on heavy going: tried in headgear/tongue tie: dead. *George Bewley* **c88** **h–**

RUNSWICK RELAX 11 ch.g. Generous (IRE) – Zany Lady (Arzanni) [2016/17 c98, h82: c19.3d³ Apr 28] lengthy gelding: winning hurdler: modest handicap chaser: stays 25f: acts on heavy going: wears cheekpieces/tongue tie: front runner/races prominently: often let down by jumping over fences. *Kenneth Slack* **c94 x** **h–**

RUNSWICK ROYAL (IRE) 8 ch.g. Excellent Art – Renada (Sinndar (IRE)) [2016/17 c146, h–: c19.9g^pu h20.5v* h16.2s* h20g Apr 7] good-topped gelding: useful handicap hurdler: won at Ayr in February and Kelso (by 7 lengths from Sleepy Haven) in March: smart chaser at best: probably stays 25f, effective at much shorter: acts on good to firm and heavy going. *Ann Hamilton* **c–** **h136**

RUN TO MILAN (IRE) 5 b.g. Milan – Run Supreme (IRE) (Supreme Leader) [2016/17 b15.3s^d b17g Apr 7] rather unfurnished gelding: brother to fairly useful hurdler/chaser City Supreme (2½m/3m winner) and closely related to fair hurdler Boyoboy (3m winner, by Saddlers' Hall): dam unraced half-sister to useful hurdler/fair chaser (stayed 25f) No Discount and fairly useful hurdler/useful chaser (stayed 2½m) Old Flame: useful form in bumpers: first past post at Wincanton in December, 3½ lengths ahead of Lalor, but subsequently disqualified due to positive sample. *Victor Dartnall* **b105**

RUN WITH THE WIND (IRE) 11 b.g. Sadler's Wells (USA) – Race The Wild Wind (USA) (Sunny's Halo (CAN)) [2016/17 c127, h–: h20g² c20.1s^F c19.9g^pu h16g Aug 26] workmanlike gelding: fairly useful hurdler/chaser: stays 2½m: acts on good to firm and heavy going: sometimes in cheekpieces: wears tongue tie: usually races prominently. *Stuart Crawford, Ireland* **c–** **h115**

RUNYON RATTLER (IRE) 7 b.g. Runyon (IRE) – Lake Majestic (IRE) (Mister Majestic) [2016/17 h16g* h17d² h16.2s² h16.4g h20d⁶ h16d h16s⁵ h16v h16.3d² Apr 27] sturdy gelding: bumper winner: fairly useful hurdler: won maiden at Wexford in July: unproven beyond 17f: acts on soft going: tried in hood. *P. J. Rothwell, Ireland* **h117**

RUPERRA TOM 9 b.g. Kayf Tara – Cathy's Dream (IRE) (Husyan (USA)) [2016/17 h77: c20.3g^pu Apr 29] point winner: maiden hurdler: pulled up in novice handicap on chasing debut: best effort at 2½m: acts on good to soft going: wears hood: tried in tongue tie: has joined N. Williams: should do better over fences. *Sophie Leech* **c– p** **h–**

RUPERT BEAR 11 b.g. Rambling Bear – Glittering Stone (Dancing High) [2016/17 c94, h–: c16.4s⁵ c15.6vᵖᵘ Dec 7] winning hurdler: poor maiden chaser: unproven beyond 17f: acts on heavy going: wears cheekpieces: tried in tongue tie. *James Walton* **c75 h–**

RUSHVALE (IRE) 8 b.g. Moss Vale (IRE) – Evidence (Machiavellian (USA)) [2016/17 h109x: h20.6g⁵ May 6] compact gelding: fair maiden hurdler: stayed 21f: best form on soft/heavy going: tried in hood: usually raced close up: often let down by jumping: dead. *Ben Case* **h– x**

RUSSBOROUGH (FR) 8 b.g. Turgeon (USA) – Heritage River (FR) (Kaldounevees (FR)) [2016/17 c120§, h–: c23.9g⁴ May 6] maiden hurdler: fair handicap chaser: stays 2½m: acts on soft going: tried in cheekpieces: often races prominently: unreliable. *Venetia Williams* **c110 § h–**

RUSSE BLANC (FR) 10 wh.g. Machiavellian Tsar (FR) – Fleur de Mad (FR) (Maiymad) [2016/17 c132, h–: c27.2sᵖᵘ c22.9s⁶ c29.2s c26.2s² c32.6sᵖᵘ c24s⁵ Mar 30] angular gelding: maiden hurdler: fairly useful handicap chaser: second at Carlisle in February: stays 29f: acts on heavy going: wears headgear: often races towards rear. *Kerry Lee* **c129 h–**

RUSSIAN APPROVAL 5 b.m. Authorized (IRE) – Russian Rhapsody (Cosmonaut) [2016/17 b72: ab16g b17.7g⁶ h16mᵖᵘ Apr 18] poor in bumpers: pulled up in mares novice on hurdling debut. *Gary Moore* **h– b–**

RUSSIAN BOLERO (GER) 6 ch.g. Tertullian (USA) – Russian Samba (IRE) (Laroche (GER)) [2016/17 c98, h–: h16m h17.7g Aug 18] fair hurdler at best for David Bridgwater in 2014/15: modest form in chases: unproven beyond 2m: acts on good to firm and good to soft going: sometimes in headgear: tried in tongue tie: has joined Dan Skelton. *David Dennis* **c– h–**

RUSSIAN EMPIRE (IRE) 9 ch.g. Moscow Society (USA) – Cashla (IRE) (Duky) [2016/17 h23m Jul 4] winning pointer: no form over fences: pulled up sole start over fences: unproven beyond 2m: tried in cheekpieces/tongue tie: dead. *Katy Price* **c– h–**

RUSSIAN RASCAL 4 b.g. Kyllachy – Russian Ruby (FR) (Vettori (IRE)) [2016/17 h16m Apr 13] poor maiden on Flat: well beaten in juvenile maiden on hurdling debut. *Maurice Barnes* **h–**

RUSSIAN REGENT (IRE) 13 b.g. Moscow Society (USA) – Micro Villa (IRE) (Electric) [2016/17 c128, h87: h24.6g⁴ c21.5d³ c23.8d* c23.8s² h23.9s² c25.5d⁵ c25g⁶ Oct 23] tall gelding: modest maiden hurdler: useful handicap chaser: won at Perth in June: stays 25f: acts on good to firm and heavy going: has worn cheekpieces. *Gordon Elliott, Ireland* **c133 h92**

RUSSIAN ROYALE 7 b.m. Royal Applause – Russian Ruby (FR) (Vettori (IRE)) [2016/17 h110: h17.2d h16.8g⁵ h16g⁵ h19.9g Oct 27] smallish mare: fair hurdler, below form in 2016/17: stays easy 2½m. *Micky Hammond* **h95**

RUSSIAN SERVICE 5 b.g. Robin des Champs (FR) – Just Kate (Bob's Return (IRE)) [2016/17 b16g³ h24d⁴ h21.7s h16s* h19.8v⁶ h20v⁵ Mar 19] €38,000 3-y-o: rather unfurnished gelding: sixth foal: half-brother to bumper winner/useful hurdler The Govaness (19f-21f winner) and a winning pointer (both by Kayf Tara): dam (h110) 21f/2¾m hurdle winner: won only start in maiden points: third in bumper at Chepstow: fairly useful form over hurdles: won maiden at same course in January: should stay beyond 2m: acts on soft going: often races prominently. *Tom Lacey* **h119 b76**

RUSSIAN'S LEGACY 7 b.m. Kayf Tara – Ruby Star (IRE) (Grand Plaisir (IRE)) [2016/17 b–: b16d⁴ Jun 22] no form in bumpers. *Gail Haywood* **b–**

RUSTAMABAD (FR) 7 ch.g. Dylan Thomas (IRE) – Rosawa (FR) (Linamix (FR)) [2016/17 h103, b–: h21m⁵ May 16] fair maiden hurdler, well held sole start in 2016/17: should stay beyond 2m: in tongue tie last 3 starts. *Tim Vaughan* **h–**

RUSTY 4 ch.g. Dream Ahead (USA) – Fondant Fancy (Falbrav (IRE)) [2016/17 b16.4v⁶ Mar 7] in blinkers, tailed off in maiden bumper. *Donald McCain* **b–**

RUWASI 6 b.g. Authorized (IRE) – Circle of Love (Sakhee (USA)) [2016/17 h16g³ h15.9g² Mar 7] sturdy gelding: brother to fair 17f hurdle winner Countersign: useful on Flat, stays 1½m: fair form over hurdles: better effort when second in maiden at Plumpton in March. *Gary Moore* **h109**

RUZEIZ (USA) 8 b.g. Muhtathir – Saraama (USA) (Bahri (USA)) [2016/17 h–: h16.8m h19d h21.4sᵘʳ h15.3vᵖᵘ Mar 9] no form over hurdles: tried in headgear. *Peter Hedger* **h–**

RYALEX (IRE) 6 b.g. Arcadio (GER) – Lady Ramona (IRE) (Lord Americo) [2016/17   **c102** h102, b–: h20.2m² h22d⁴ c15.9s³ c20.9vF c15.9d³ Apr 5] winning pointer: fair form over   **h102** hurdles/fences: stays 2½m: acts on soft and good to firm going: usually wears hood: usually leads. *Lucinda Russell*

RYEDALE RACER 6 b.g. Indian Danehill (IRE) – Jontys'lass (Tamure (IRE)) [2016/17   **h118** h108, b97: h20d* h20.1s* h22.8s⁵ h22.7v³ h20.5v⁴ h20.1v⁴ Mar 28] bumper winner: fairly useful hurdler: won novices at Carlisle in October and Hexham in November: stays 23f: acts on heavy going: usually leads. *Malcolm Jefferson*

RYE HOUSE (IRE) 8 b.g. Dansili – Threefold (USA) (Gulch (USA)) [2016/17 h95:   **h–** h16.8g May 5] modest maiden hurdler: stays 2¼m: acts on good to firm going: in headgear last 2 starts: has worn tongue tie, including last 5 starts. *Tim Vaughan*

RYEOLLIEAN 6 ch.g. Haafhd – Brave Mave (Daylami (IRE)) [2016/17 h117: h16d³   **h111** h17.7v⁶ h15.8g* h20.5m* Apr 17] smallish gelding: fair handicap hurdler: won at Huntingdon and Plumpton in April: stays 21f: acts on soft and good to firm going: wears headgear: front runner/races prominently. *Gary Moore*

<h1 style="text-align:center">S</h1>

SABRAGE (IRE) 5 b.g. Fastnet Rock (AUS) – Champagne Toni (IRE) (Second Empire   **b78** (IRE)) [2016/17 b15.3m⁴ ab16g⁴ Nov 29] sturdy gelding: modest form in bumpers: tried in blinkers. *Seamus Durack*

SABROCLAIR (FR) 8 b.g. Robin des Champs (FR) – Malicka Madrik (FR) (Volochine   **c70** (IRE)) [2016/17 c91, h70: c16.3g⁶ c25.8gᵖᵘ c20d³ c20g² Jul 5] maiden hurdler: poor   **h–** maiden chaser: likely to prove best around 2½m: wears headgear/tongue tie: usually races towards rear. *Richard Woollacott*

SACRAMENTO KING (IRE) 8 gr.g. Desert King (IRE) – Kindle Ball (FR)   **h87** (Kaldounevees (FR)) [2016/17 h19.8v h23.9g⁴ Mar 30] workmanlike gelding: third in Irish maiden point on debut: modest form over hurdles: stays 3m: best form on good going: tried in tongue tie. *Jonathan Geake*

SACRED SUMMIT (IRE) 6 ch.g. Mountain High (IRE) – D'ygrande (IRE) (Good   **h–** Thyne (USA)) [2016/17 b–: b13.7d h16.7dᵖᵘ h16.5s h19vᵘʳ Feb 24] no form in bumpers/   **b–** over hurdles: in tongue tie last 3 starts. *Tim Vaughan*

SACRE MALTA (FR) 11 ch.g. Discover d'Auteuil (FR) – Neira Malta (FR) (Cardoun   **c68** (FR)) [2016/17 c92, h95: c22.5d c21.2m c17.3d⁶ Jul 16] winning hurdler: maiden chaser,   **h–** below form in 2016/17: left Dominic Ffrench Davis after first start: stays 25f: acts on heavy going: has worn headgear, including last 4 starts: has worn tongue tie. *Julia Brooke*

SACRE TOI (FR) 11 b.g. Network (GER) – Magicielle (FR) (Video Rock (FR)) [2016/17   **c98** c25.1v³ Feb 2] point winner: fairly useful hurdler: won 3 times in 2015/16 for Francois   **h–** Nicolle: similar standard at best over fences: well-held third in hunter in February: stays 19f: acts on heavy going: often wears headgear. *Mrs Fiona Read*

SADDLERS ENCORE (IRE) 8 br.g. Presenting – Saddlers Leader (IRE) (Saddlers'   **c109 p** Hall (IRE)) [2016/17 h129: c23.6d³ Oct 25] big gelding: fairly useful hurdler: 11/2, third in   **h–** novice at Chepstow (33 lengths behind Thistlecrack) on chasing debut: stays 23f: acts on soft going: usually races prominently: should do better over fences. *Philip Hobbs*

SADDLERS' SECRET (IRE) 12 b.m. Saddlers' Hall (IRE) – Birdless Bush (IRE) (Be   **h–** My Native (USA)) [2016/17 h–: h19.2g⁶ h23.3mᵖᵘ Jun 9] little form over hurdles. *Mark Campion*

SADLER'S GOLD (IRE) 7 b.g. Gold Well – Mrs Quigley (IRE) (Mandalus) [2016/17   **h–** h18.5s Jan 1] fair hurdle winner, well held in handicap sole outing in 2016/17: in tongue tie last 2 starts. *David Pipe*

SADLER'S RISK (IRE) 9 b.g. Sadler's Wells (USA) – Riskaverse (USA) (Dynaformer   **c150 §** (USA)) [2016/17 c152§, h–§: c22g² h24.4g² c25g* c24g⁴ h24s⁴ Mar 25] strong, sturdy   **h129 §** gelding: useful hurdler: smart chaser: won Grade 3 event at Punchestown (by 5½ lengths from Lord Scoundrel) in October: stays 25f: acts on heavy going: tried in blinkers: has worn tongue tie: usually races prominently: moody. *Henry de Bromhead, Ireland*

SADMA 8 gr.g. Street Cry (IRE) – Blue Dress (USA) (Danzig (USA)) [2016/17 c–, h106:   **c–** h16.5m⁴ Dec 8] fair handicap hurdler, well held only outing in 2016/17: pulled up sole start   **h75** over fences: raced around 2m: acts on soft and good to firm going. *Nick Lampard*

SAFARI JOURNEY (USA) 13 ch.g. Johannesburg (USA) – Alvernia (USA) (Alydar (USA)) [2016/17 c97§, h–: c17.2g² c20.3d³ c17.3d² c19.3g* c20.1g⁵ c20.1sᵖᵘ c20.3d⁶ c20.3v⁴ c19.3d⁶ c19.9g Jan 20] tall, good-topped gelding: winning hurdler: fair handicap chaser: won at Sedgefield in September: stays 2½m: acts on soft and good to firm going: wears headgear: often races in rear: unreliable. *Lucinda Egerton*   **c103 §** **h–**

SAFE HARBOUR (IRE) 5 b.g. Stowaway – Beharista (FR) (Sendawar (IRE)) [2016/17 b70: h19.1s⁶ h19.9v h19.1v³ Jan 29] modest form over hurdles: best effort when third in novice at Fontwell in January. *Oliver Sherwood*   **h92**

SAFFRON PRINCE 9 b.g. Kayf Tara – Jan's Dream (IRE) (Executive Perk) [2016/17 c112, h–: c16.1mᶠ Apr 13] winning hurdler: maiden chaser, fair at best: should stay 2½m: acts on heavy going. *David Bridgwater*   **c–** **h–**

SAFFRON WELLS (IRE) 9 b.g. Saffron Walden (FR) – Angel's Folly (Wesaam (USA)) [2016/17 c123, h124: h19.5g⁵ c21.2d² c24.2gᵘʳ h23.1m* Apr 17] good-topped gelding: fairly useful handicap hurdler: won at Market Rasen in April: similar form over fences: stays 23f: acts on good to firm and heavy going: in cheekpieces last 2 starts: often races lazily. *Neil King*   **c120** **h125**

SAGE MONKEY (IRE) 8 br.g. Craigsteel – Braw Lass (Alflora (IRE)) [2016/17 c25.2g² c20.3s⁵ c16s⁴ c25.2vᵖᵘ Feb 1] placed in Irish maiden points: no form in bumper/chases: tried in cheekpieces/tongue tie. *Kerry Lee*   **c–**

SAHALIN 4 b.f. Red Rocks (IRE) – Tamathea (IRE) (Barathea (IRE)) [2016/17 h19.5m³ Apr 28] fair on Flat, stays 8.5f: well beaten in novice on hurdling debut. *John Flint*   **h–**

SAHARA HAZE 8 b.m. Rainbow High – Gypsy Haze (Romany Rye) [2016/17 h97, b–: h20g h20g h20s⁵ h25.5s² h25.5v h23.8s⁴ h25.5d³ Mar 26] placed twice from 3 starts in points: modest maiden hurdler: stays 3¼m: acts on soft going. *Phillip Dando*   **h93**

SAILOR SAM 4 b.g. Sulamani (IRE) – Lago d'Oro (Slip Anchor) [2016/17 b16g Apr 24] tailed off in bumper. *Tim Vaughan*   **b–**

SAILORS WARN (IRE) 10 b.g. Redback – Coral Dawn (IRE) (Trempolino (USA)) [2016/17 h111: h16g² h16.3g* h15.7g⁴ h16.6g³ h17d⁵ h16g² h18.7g³ Apr 1] small, stocky gelding: fair handicap hurdler: won at Stratford in August: stays 2¼m: acts on heavy going: tried in cheekpieces: has worn tongue tie: usually races towards rear. *Daniel Loughnane*   **h111**

SAIL WITH SULTANA 6 ch.m. Black Sam Bellamy (IRE) – Strathtay (Pivotal) [2016/17 h–: h21s Mar 30] modest on Flat, stays 16.5f: no form in maiden hurdles. *Mark Rimell*   **h–**

SAINLOUIS DES PRES (FR) 4 b.g. Saint des Saints (FR) – Miss Courteillaise (FR) (Lavirco (GER)) [2016/17 b15.8g⁴ Apr 9] third foal: dam, lightly raced on Flat in France, half-sister to fairly useful French 2¼m hurdle winner Gris Courteillais: 11/4, fourth in bumper at Ffos Las (15¾ lengths behind Espoir de Teillee) on debut: should do better. *Paul Nicholls*   **b72 p**

SAINT ARE (FR) 11 b.g. Network (GER) – Fortanea (FR) (Video Rock (FR)) [2016/17 c146, h–: c23.6g⁵ c24.2d³ c25.5dᶠ c24g² c34.3d³ Apr 8] workmanlike gelding: winning hurdler: smart handicap chaser: placed in Grand National at Aintree (8¼ lengths behind One For Arthur) for second time in 3 years: stays 35f: acts on heavy going: usually wears headgear: wears tongue tie: front runner/races prominently. *Tom George*   **c148** **h–**

SAINT BREIZ (FR) 11 b.g. Saint des Saints (FR) – Balladina (FR) (Saint Cyrien (FR)) [2016/17 c102, h–: c20.5mᵖᵘ h23.6d c19.2vᵖᵘ h21.4d⁴ c21.7gᶠ Mar 2] lengthy gelding: Irish point winner: fair hurdler/maiden chaser at best, well below that in 2016/17: stays 23f: acts on heavy going: has worn headgear, including in 2016/17: wears tongue tie. *Carroll Gray*   **c85** **h84**

SAINT CAJETAN (FR) 5 b.g. Saint des Saints (FR) – Erivieve (FR) (Marchand de Sable (USA)) [2016/17 b16.7g⁵ h15.7g³ h19.7g² h20.5g⁴ h19.4d⁶ h19.4s² h19.9s⁵ h19g⁵ Apr 24] €37,000 3-y-o: fourth foal: half-brother to French 1¼m winner Rock des Clos (by High Rock): dam, French 1½m/12.5f winner, half-sister to smart French hurdler (stayed 25f) Grande Haya: fifth in bumper: fair maiden hurdler: stays 2½m: acts on soft going. *Charlie Longsdon*   **h106** **b–**

SAINT CHARLES (FR) 7 b.g. Manduro (GER) – Tropical Barth (IRE) (Peintre Celebre (USA)) [2016/17 h100: h20m⁵ c20d⁴ c15.7d* c15.7g⁴ c20g³ c16.1m³ Oct 5] angular gelding: winning hurdler: fairly useful form over fences: won novice at Southwell in July: left Nicky Henderson after second start: stayed 2½m: acted on soft going: usually wore hood: dead. *Ben Haslam*   **c129** **h103**

SAINT CONTEST (FR) 4 b.g. Air Chief Marshal (IRE) – Sainte Adresse (Elusive City   **h106**
(USA)) [2016/17 h15.3d³ h16.3d³ Dec 31] good-topped gelding: fairly useful on Flat, stays
12.5f: fair form over hurdles: third in maiden at Wincanton and juvenile at Newbury,
finding little both times. *Alan King*

SAINT DE VASSY (FR) 4 br.g. Saint des Saints (FR) – Mona Vassy (FR) (Sleeping Car   **b91**
(FR)) [2016/17 b16s⁴ Mar 30] third foal: half-brother to French 19f chase winner Grassland
Sulpice (by Epalo): dam, placed up to 19f over hurdles/fences in France, half-sister to
smart hurdler (2m-21f winner) James de Vassy: 22/1, fourth in maiden bumper at Warwick
(9½ lengths behind Whiskey In The Jar) on debut. *Tom Symonds*

SAINTE LADYLIME (FR) 6 b.m. Saint des Saints (FR) – Lady Pauline (FR) (Hamas   **c133**
(IRE)) [2016/17 h125, b89: c19.9d⁵ᵘʳ c17.5v² c20.3sꟳ h18.5d⁵ᵘʳh21.6d⁴ Mar 18] workmanlike   **h125**
mare: fairly useful form over hurdles: useful form over fences: every chance when fell last
in mares novice won by Antartica de Thaix at Bangor: stays 23f: acts on heavy going: front
runner/races prominently. *Kim Bailey*

SAINT ELM (FR) 7 b.g. Poliglote – Place d'Armes (IRE) (Spinning World (USA))   **c99**
[2016/17 c92, h76: c15.7mᵘʳ c16.5mꟳ May 19] maiden hurdler: modest form over fences: **h–**
stayed 2¼m: acted on good to firm and good to soft going: tried in hood/tongue tie: dead.
Richard Woollacott

SAINTEMILION (FR) 4 b.g. Diamond Green (FR) – Matakana (FR) (Green Tune   **h125**
(USA)) [2016/17 h16.9d² h16.9s⁴ h16.9g* h16.9sꟳ h17.9s⁴ h17.7s³ Dec 26] lightly raced
on Flat: fairly useful form over hurdles: won juvenile at Nancy in July: left W. Himmel,
well below best final start: stays 2¼m: acts on soft going: has worn tongue tie. *Paul Nicholls*

SAINT HELENA (IRE) 9 b.m. Holy Roman Emperor (IRE) – Tafseer (IRE) (Grand   **h–**
Lodge (USA)) [2016/17 h16.5gᵖᵘ Dec 30] fair on Flat, won twice over 1m in 2016: modest
hurdler at best: raced mainly around 2m: acts on good to soft going: wears headgear.
Mark Gillard

SAINT JOHN HENRY (FR) 7 b.g. Saint des Saints (FR) – Noceane (FR) (Pistolet Bleu   **h118 x**
(IRE)) [2016/17 h117x: h23.3v⁶ h26v* h26s h24d⁵ h26sᵖᵘ Mar 30] angular gelding: fairly
useful handicap hurdler: won at Warwick (conditional) in December: stays 3¼m: acts on
heavy going: wears headgear: in tongue tie last 2 starts: front runner/races prominently:
often let down by jumping. *David Pipe*

SAINT RAPH (FR) 9 gr.g. Saint des Saints (FR) – Speed Padoline (FR) (Saint Preuil   **c–**
(FR)) [2016/17 c123, h–: c25gᵖᵘ c23.5gᵘʳ Dec 10] well-made gelding: maiden hurdler: **h–**
fairly useful chaser at best, failed to complete both starts in 2016/17: stayed 25f: acted on
good to firm and heavy going: tried in cheekpieces: wore tongue tie: dead. *Robert Walford*

SAINT ROQUE (FR) 11 b.g. Lavirco (GER) – Moody Cloud (FR) (Cyborg (FR))   **c138**
[2016/17 c141, h–: c25.5g² c26.1gᵖᵘ Jun 26] good-topped gelding: winning hurdler: useful   **h–**
handicap chaser: stays 25f: acts on soft and good to firm going: tried in cheekpieces: wears
tongue tie: usually travels strongly. *Paul Nicholls*

SAKHEE'S CITY (FR) 6 b.g. Sakhee (USA) – A Lulu Ofa Menifee (USA) (Menifee   **h126 §**
(USA)) [2016/17 h119: h16.2d² h16d² h16dꟳ h15.7s² h19.9v h16.7s³ h16.4v⁴ Mar 18]
rangy gelding: fairly useful handicap hurdler: unproven beyond 17f: acts on heavy going:
in cheekpieces last 5 starts: temperamental. *Philip Kirby*

SALLY SPARROW (IRE) 4 b.f. Scorpion (IRE) – Bargante (IRE) (Phardante (FR))   **b–**
[2016/17 b15.7s b16g Apr 17] half-sister to useful hurdler/smart chaser Double Seven
(2m-25f winner, by Milan), stays 35f, and fair chaser Lugante (17f winner, by Luso),
stayed 2½m: dam unraced: no form in bumpers. *David Dennis*

SALOMO (GER) 11 b.g. Monsun (GER) – Salka (GER) (Doyoun) [2016/17 h15.8d   **h78**
h15.8g⁵ Jul 24] very lightly raced: winning hurdler: signs of retaining ability on last of 3
starts (including point) in early-2016/17 following 4-year absence: raced only at 2m: best
form on soft/heavy going: usually in tongue tie. *Adrian Wintle*

SALOPIEN (IRE) 5 b.g. Gold Well – Musicienne (IRE) (Selkirk (USA)) [2016/17 b16g   **h–**
h16d h15.8s Mar 5] no form in bumper/over hurdles. *Jonjo O'Neill*   **b–**

SALSIFY (IRE) 12 b.g. Beneficial – Our Deadly (IRE) (Phardante (FR)) [2016/17 c128,   **c123**
h–: c25s⁴ c24.1dꟳ c24.3s⁴ c26.3g Mar 2] good-topped gelding: maiden hurdler: fairly   **h–**
useful hunter chaser nowadays: stays 3½m: acts on heavy going: usually races nearer last
than first. *Rodger Sweeney, Ireland*

SALTO CHISCO (IRE) 9 b.g. Presenting – Dato Fairy (IRE) (Accordion) [2016/17 h–: c16g² c16.3g* c16.5g⁶ c16.5m³ c16.3g* c20.3d⁴ c19.2sᵖᵘ h18.7g⁴ Apr 15] maiden hurdler: fair handicap chaser: won at Fakenham in May (novice event) and October: left Oliver Sherwood after third start: probably best around 2m: acts on soft and good to firm going: usually races close up. *Harry Whittington*   **c111 h97**

SALUT HONORE (FR) 11 b.g. Lost World (IRE) – Kadalkote (FR) (Kadalko (FR)) [2016/17 c81, h–: c20.9vᵖᵘ c25.6vᵖᵘ Dec 11] tall gelding: maiden hurdler: modest chaser at best, no form in 2016/17: stays 3¼m: acts on heavy going: wears tongue tie: often let down by jumping. *Alex Hales*   **c– x h–**

SAMARNNI 9 ch.g. Samraan (USA) – Miss Zarnni (Arzanni) [2016/17 c22.7sᵖᵘ Feb 16] multiple point winner: pulled up in novice hunter on chasing debut: wore tongue tie. *T. Ellis*   **c–**

SAMBA TIME 5 gr.m. Black Sam Bellamy (IRE) – Tikk Tokk (IRE) (Tikkanen (USA)) [2016/17 b16d Feb 21] £7,500 3-y-o: first foal: dam unraced half-sister to Prix Alain du Breil winner Grand Souvenir and Prix Maurice Gillois winner Polivalente and to dam of useful hurdler/smart chaser (stays 3¼m) Roi des Francs: behind in mares bumper. *George Bewley*   **b–**

SAMBREMONT (FR) 7 b.g. Saint des Saints (FR) – Rainbow Crest (FR) (Baryshnikov (AUS)) [2016/17 c137, h–: c21s c24dᵇᵈ c24.5dᵖᵘ c28s² c24sᵖᵘ c29dᵖᵘ c30dᵖᵘ Apr 29] winning hurdler: useful handicap chaser: second at Punchestown (4¾ lengths behind Baie des Iles) in February, standout effort in 2016/17: stays 3½m: best form on soft/heavy going: tried in cheekpieces. *W. P. Mullins, Ireland*   **c134 h–**

SAM BROWN 5 b.g. Black Sam Bellamy (IRE) – Cream Cracker (Sir Harry Lewis (USA)) [2016/17 b15.3v* b16.3v* Mar 4] fourth foal: half-brother unfurnished gelding: third foal: dam (c113/h123) 2m hurdle/chase winner (stayed 2¾m): useful form in bumpers: won at Wincanton in February and Newbury (by ¾ length from Chef des Obeaux) in March: will be suited by further than 2m. *Anthony Honeyball*   **b113**

SAMBURU SHUJAA (FR) 4 b.g. Poliglote – Girelle (FR) (Le Nain Jaune (FR)) [2016/17 b13.7g b16s² Mar 30] fourth foal: half-brother to French hurdler Blinis (17f winner, by Baroud d'Honneur) and French hurdler/chaser Safre (17f-3m winner, by Sassanian): dam French maiden (third in 17f hurdle): fairly useful form in bumpers: easily better effort when second to Whiskey In The Jar in maiden at Warwick: will be suited by 2½m+. *Philip Hobbs*   **b95**

SAM CAVALLARO (IRE) 11 b.g. Oscar Schindler (IRE) – Gaelic Holly (IRE) (Scenic) [2016/17 c113: c16.3g* c17m³ c20s⁵ c20s⁴ c21.1gᶠ Apr 6] good-topped gelding: multiple winning pointer: fair chaser: won hunter at Cheltenham very early in season: stays 21f: acts on good to soft going: tried in hood: has worn tongue tie: often races towards rear. *Miss H. Brookshaw*   **c112**

SAMCRO (IRE) 5 ch.g. Germany (USA) – Dun Dun (IRE) (Saddlers' Hall (IRE)) [2016/17 b16d* b16s* b16d* b16d* Apr 17] €95,000 3-y-o, £335,000 4-y-o: fourth foal: half-brother to fairly useful hurdler/winning pointer Cocacobana (2½m-3m winner, by Snurge): dam unraced sister to fairly useful hurdler/very smart chaser (stayed 25f) Master of The Hall and smart hurdler (stayed 21f) Featherbed Lane: won maiden bumper on debut: smart form in bumpers, unbeaten in 3 starts: won at Punchestown in November, Navan (listed event, by ½ length from Good Thyne Tara) in December and Fairyhouse (impressively by 17 lengths from Cluan Dara) in April: exciting prospect. *Gordon Elliott, Ireland*   **b115 p**

SAMDIBIEN (FR) 5 b.g. Day Flight – Sambirane (FR) (Apeldoorn (FR)) [2016/17 h–, b86: h17.7g³ h19g⁴ h21.6vᶠ h19.9vᵖᵘ h19.5v⁴ h20.3g² Apr 21] fair maiden hurdler: stays 2½m: acts on heavy going: in tongue tie last 5 starts. *Sam Thomas*   **h107**

SAME CIRCUS (IRE) 6 b.m. Brian Boru – Curragh Orpen (IRE) (Orpen (USA)) [2016/17 h16.2g* h16.3g h19.4g² h19.7s² h25.3g² h25.3s* h20.5g h24.3d Apr 21] £10,000 5-y-o: smallish mare: third foal: sister to a winning pointer: dam unraced: won Irish maiden point on debut: fairly useful hurdler: won mares novices at Hexham in October and Catterick in February: stays 25f: acts on soft going: front runner/races prominently. *Donald McCain*   **h115**

SAME DIFFERENCE (IRE) 11 b.g. Mr Combustible (IRE) – Sarahs Reprive (IRE) (Yashgan) [2016/17 c–, h–: c25.1mᵖᵘ May 5] tall gelding: winning hurdler: smart chaser at best, very lightly raced and no form under Rules since 2013/14: placed in points in 2017: stays 29f: acts on heavy going: wears headgear. *Warren Greatrex*   **c– h–**

SAM

SAME OLE TRIX (IRE) 7 gr.g. King's Theatre (IRE) – Reklame's Gorl (GER) (Neshad **h–**
(USA)) [2016/17 h–: h19g May 2] no form over hurdles: tried in cheekpieces: wears
tongue tie. *Kim Bailey*

SAM FAIRYANN 6 b.g. Black Sam Bellamy (IRE) – Folly Foster (Relkino) [2016/17 **b–**
b60: b16.7d Jun 17] little show in bumpers: dead. *Peter Niven*

SAMINGARRY (FR) 10 ch.g. Ballingarry (IRE) – Samansonnienne (FR) (Mansonnien **c–**
(FR)) [2016/17 c142, h–: c24g c26.3s^{pu} c24g^{pu} h22.8v^2 h26s^6 Mar 30] sturdy gelding: **h117**
fairly useful handicap hurdler: second at Haydock in March: useful chaser at best, little
form in 2016/17 after long absence: stays 3¼m: acts on heavy going: has worn headgear/
tongue tie, including in 2016/17. *Nigel Hawke*

SAMIZDAT (FR) 14 b.g. Soviet Star (USA) – Secret Account (FR) (Bering) [2016/17 c–, **c–**
h–: h19.2g h20g^6 May 22] winning hurdler, no longer of any account: once-raced chaser: **h–**
has worn headgear/tongue tie. *John O'Neill*

SAMMY B 7 br.g. Overbury (IRE) – This Thyne (Good Thyne (USA)) [2016/17 b95: **h119**
h20.2m^6 h16.2d^2 h20.5s^4 h19.4g h23.8g* h22.7v* h22.8v* h24.3d^6 Apr 21] bumper
winner: fairly useful handicap hurdler: won at Musselburgh in February, and at Kelso and
Haydock in March: stays 3m: acts on heavy going. *Lucinda Russell*

SAM NOIR 5 ch.g. Black Sam Bellamy (IRE) – United (GER) (Desert King (IRE)) **h91 p**
[2016/17 b16.3v* b15.8g^4 b16.8g h20g^6 h21s h21.2s Jan 19] €23,000 3-y-o: second foal: **b89**
dam (h150), 2m-3m hurdle winner, also 1¼m/11f winner on Flat in Germany: fair form in
bumpers: won conditionals/amateur event at Stratford in June: modest form over hurdles:
should stay beyond 2m: tried in tongue tie: type to do better in handicaps. *Peter Bowen*

SAMOSET 7 b.g. Sir Percy – Great Quest (IRE) (Montjeu (IRE)) [2016/17 h108: h15.8g **h105**
h17.2m* h18.5m h16.3g^5 h16m^6 Aug 30] sturdy gelding: fair handicap hurdler: won novice
event at Cartmel in June: stays 19f: acts on soft and good to firm going: in cheekpieces last
4 starts: wears tongue tie: usually races close up. *Graeme McPherson*

SAM RED (FR) 6 b.g. Denham Red (FR) – Call Me Nana (FR) (Call Me Sam (FR)) **c107 p**
[2016/17 c17m^4 h21d h24.1s^2 h24d^4 h23.1g^2 h22.8g^6 Apr 15] lengthy gelding: useful **h135**
handicap hurdler: second at Bangor (½ length behind Duel At Dawn) in March: 6/5, fourth
in maiden at Killarney (12¾ lengths behind Gambling Girl) on chasing debut: left Alan
Fleming after first start: stays 3m: acts on good to firm and heavy going: tried in blinkers:
has worn tongue tie, including last 5 starts: should do better over fences. *Dan Skelton*

SAM'S A DIAMOND 5 b.g. What A Caper (IRE) – Barlin Bay (Karinga Bay) [2016/17 **h80**
b15.7s ab16g b15.8g^5 Apr 28] no form in bumpers: 66/1, fifth in maiden at Huntingdon **b–**
(24½ lengths behind Shining Romeo) on hurdling debut. *J. R. Jenkins*

SAM'S ADVENTURE 5 b.g. Black Sam Bellamy (IRE) – My Adventure (IRE) (Strong **b109**
Gale) [2016/17 b108: b16s^2 b16v* Jan 30] useful-looking gelding: useful form in bumpers:
won for third time in 4 starts at Ayr (by 3 lengths from Mcgowan's Pass) in January: will
be suited by further than 2m. *Brian Ellison*

SAM'S GUNNER 4 ch.g. Black Sam Bellamy (IRE) – Falcon's Gunner (Gunner B) **h93**
[2016/17 b13.7m b16s^4 h16d^4 Jan 24] second foal: dam (b85), third both starts in bumpers/ **b74**
well held only start over hurdles, half-sister to fairly useful hurdler/chaser (stays 3m)
Kilronan High: poor form in bumpers: 66/1, fourth in novice at Wetherby (22 lengths
behind Mr Big Shot) on hurdling debut: will be suited by at least 2½m. *Michael Easterby*

SAMSON 6 ch.g. Black Sam Bellamy (IRE) – Riverine (Risk Me (FR)) [2016/17 b86: **h92**
h16.7g h16.3g^4 h16g^6 h15.8m^6 h18.5m^5 h21.6s^2 h24d^3 Dec 15] angular gelding: bumper
winner: modest maiden hurdler: stays 2¾m: acts on soft and good to firm going: often in
hood: usually races nearer last than first. *Sophie Leech*

SAMSONITE (IRE) 5 ch.g. Pivotal – Silca's Sister (Inchinor) [2016/17 h15.5d h16.6s^{pu} **h–**
Mar 3] sturdy gelding: fair on Flat, stays 1¼m: no form over hurdles: in tongue tie second
start. *Claire Dyson*

SAMSON'S REACH 4 b.g. Phoenix Reach (IRE) – Court Wing (IRE) (Hawk Wing **b82**
(USA)) [2016/17 b15.8v b16.3s b16.7s* b15.8v^5 Mar 1] unfurnished gelding: first foal:
dam, showed little over hurdles, 1¾m winner on Flat, half-sister to useful hurdler (stayed
2½m) Benfleet Boy: modest form in bumpers: won at Bangor in February. *Richard Price*

SAM SPINNER 5 b.g. Black Sam Bellamy (IRE) – Dawn Spinner (Arctic Lord) [2016/17 **h139 p**
b104: h16.4d^4 h16.2s^2 h19.3d* h19.3s* Feb 3] bumper winner: useful form over hurdles:
won novices at Newcastle in November, and at Catterick in January (by 7 lengths from
Master of Irony) and February: stays 19f: races prominently, often travels strongly: remains
open to improvement. *Jedd O'Keeffe*

SAM'S TREASURE 5 ch.m. Black Sam Bellamy (IRE) – Poppy Day (Bal Harbour)   **b–**
[2016/17 b17g May 13] first foal: dam (c94) winning pointer: point winner: well beaten in bumper. *I. M. Mason*

SAMTHEMAN 12 b.g. Dancing Spree (USA) – Sisterly (Brotherly (USA)) [2016/17 c86,   **c– x**
h70: h21.6m c20g^{pu} Sep 20] good-topped gelding: modest hurdler/chaser at best, no form   **h–**
in 2016/17: stays 21f: acts on soft and good to firm going: has worn headgear: tried in tongue tie: often let down by jumping over fences. *Alan Phillips*

SAMTU (IRE) 6 b.g. Teofilo (IRE) – Samdaniya (Machiavellian (USA)) [2016/17 h110:   **h117**
h16.7g* h16.5d h16m^2 h16g Jul 12] fairly useful handicap hurdler: won at Bangor very early in season: second at Worcester in July: stays 2½m: acts on good to firm going: wears tongue tie: front runner/races prominently. *Dan Skelton*

SAMUEL MAEL DUIN 7 gr.g. Black Sam Bellamy (IRE) – Fad Amach (IRE)   **h–**
(Flemensfirth (USA)) [2016/17 h19.5g Dec 3] no form in bumpers/novice hurdle: tried in cheekpieces: dead. *Colin Tizzard*

SANAIJA 6 ch.m. Pivotal – Sanjida (IRE) (Polish Precedent (USA)) [2016/17 h87: h15.7g^5 **h103**
h17.9v h17.9d* h18.9s h17.4v^{pu} Jan 13] fair form over hurdles: won minor event at Argentan in November: left Nicky Henderson after first start, G. Cherel after third: stays 2¼m: acts on good to soft going: tried in cheekpieces. *Mme I. Pacault, France*

SAN BENEDETO (FR) 6 ch.g. Layman (USA) – Cinco Baidy (FR) (Lure (USA))   **c153**
[2016/17 h141: c19.3g* c20d* c21g^4 c18.8m^2 c19.9g^3 c20.8d^{ur} c20.5g^3 c15.8g*   **h–**
c16.4s* c16.9m* c15.8g* c15.5g^3 Apr 29]

With good Old Testament stoicism Paul Nicholls continues to tackle the uphill job of making bricks without straw. Like Moses in Egypt, Nicholls has found himself deprived of essential resources as the balance of power in jump racing has changed and his stable has struggled to find the raw material to turn into Grade 1 horses. It now seems a long time since the glory days of Kauto Star and Denman who had adjoining boxes at Manor Farm Stables, with plenty of other big names in the yard too. Silviniaco Conti wasn't in the same league as Kauto Star and Denman but he made a very good job of spearheading his stable's challenge for the big staying chases in the years that followed their retirement, although he has now gone. Some indication of the paucity of Grade 1 horses at Manor Farm Stables in the latest season is provided by the fact that the stable has won the Queen Mother Champion Chase five times but couldn't muster a runner, while its attempt on the Cheltenham Gold Cup and the Stayers' Hurdle, championship events it has won four times each, comprised 33/1-shot Saphir du Rheu and 25/1-shot Zarkandar, who managed fifth and seventh in them respectively. The stable didn't have a runner in the Champion Hurdle or the Ryanair Chase either, both races it has also won in the past. Pacha du Polder's victory in the Foxhunter at least stretched the stable's unbroken record of having a winner every year at the Festival to fifteen years, at the same time taking Paul Nicholls' Festival total to forty-one.

Cheltenham has, however, never been the be-all and end-all so far as Paul Nicholls is concerned. The ten-times champion trainer has always spread his net far and wide, to very good effect over the years, as he also did most successfully again in the latest season when he sent out the winners of one hundred and seventy-one races, a career record and more than any other stable in Britain in 2016/17, at a wins to runs ratio of one in four. The trainers' championship is decided on prize-money, though, and the stable's achievements were not enough to retain the trainers' championship, with the firepower of Nicky Henderson in the Grade 1 races proving decisive. For the second campaign running, Manor Farm Stables won only two Grade 1 races in Britain, those in the latest season being the 'Fighting Fifth' Hurdle at Newcastle with stable stalwart Irving (who was winning the race for the second time in three years) and the Maghull Novices' Chase at Aintree, the last-named victory coming from what must have looked a most unlikely source at one time, the Flat failure San Benedeto who had been turned into a useful hurdler in his first two seasons with Paul Nicholls, before being transformed into an even better chaser in the latest campaign.

San Benedeto won the Maghull on the eleventh of his twelve starts in a season that began with a successful debut over fences in a novice event at Sedgefield on May 10th 2016 and ended with a creditable third, beaten eight lengths and four and a half lengths behind Altior and the Queen Mother Champion Chase winner

Special Tiara in the Celebration Chase on Sandown's Finale card on April 29th 2017. San Benedeto followed up his Sedgefield win with a last-gasp victory over the useful Presenting Arms in what looked a stronger novice at Worcester in June, but he didn't attempt a third summer win under a double penalty and it was four months before he resumed his chasing career, trailing in last of four behind Virgilio in an intermediate chase at Newton Abbot. A better effort followed when, equipped with cheekpieces for the first time (he had often worn a hood previously), San Benedeto finished second to Master Dee in a small field for a novice handicap at Ascot. Two more placed efforts followed in handicap company, an open handicap at Newbury in November and a novice handicap at Kempton on Boxing Day, those sandwiched by his only non-completion of the campaign, when unseating his jockey at the tenth in the novice chase won by Whisper at Cheltenham's International meeting. A half-term report on San Benedeto would have been that the handicapper seemed to have him just where he wanted him, but San Benedeto may have surprised even his trainer with the extra that he found after the turn of the year when he won four races in a row, each of them progressively more valuable, before that creditable third on his final outing at Sandown.

The astute placing of its horses has always been one of the strengths of Manor Farm Stables and San Benedeto was found a good opportunity at Musselburgh in early-February in the grandly-titled totepool Scottish Champion Chase, a 0-140 handicap that attracted five runners, with San Benedeto, then on a BHA mark of 140, carrying joint second top weight. Musselburgh does its best to frame attractive programmes and its best cards regularly attract runners from the big southern stables (Seven Barrows also among them) but on-going concerns about the composition of the Joint Racing Committee which runs the course led the BHA to threaten to withdraw its licence to race unless it agreed to an independent review of its board structure. The Musselburgh Joint Racing Committee comprises four representatives of East Lothian Council and three racecourse representatives, the two groups frequently at loggerheads over priorities and development plans for the course which, nonetheless, has been one of the success stories of Scottish racing in recent times (the five Scottish racecourses generate more than £300m a year for Scotland's economy and provide 3,500 full-time jobs). Concerns about Musselburgh's governance were first raised by the BHA in December and matters came to a head in July 2017 when Musselburgh's licence lapsed and the BHA threatened to reallocate its allocated fixtures to other courses. In the end, the licence was reissued when the Joint Racing Committee agreed to the independent review, the result of which is still awaited at the time of going to press. The behind-the-scenes problems would have come as a surprise at the time to most racegoers who watched San Benedeto run out a wide-margin winner at his track, drawing clear from four out to beat Witness In Court by eight lengths, as the top weight and favourite Baltimore Rock, another southern raider, folded tamely. San Benedeto was sent North again the following month, not so far this time though, and he followed up, edging out the former Nicholls inmate Katgary off a 5 lb higher mark in the Betbright Handicap Chase at Doncaster, his first success in a class 2 event. Back in novice company, San Benedeto made it a hat-trick by winning another class 2, the valuable Ascot United FC Novices' Handicap at Ascot, a further 5 lb rise shrugged off as he beat the favourite Imperial Presence by seven lengths for a good prize that deserved a stronger field (San Benedeto was left in front when his stablemate Clic Work went wrong, suffering a serious tendon injury and being pulled up when still seeming a danger two out).

San Benedeto lined up in the Doom Bar Maghull Novices' Chase at Aintree just six days after his win at Ascot. His trainer labelled him 'first reserve' behind stablemate Politologue who, unlike San Benedeto, had gone to the Cheltenham

Mr P. J. Vogt's "San Benedeto"

Festival where he finished a creditable fourth in the Golden Miller. Charbel, who looked sure to be placed when coming down in the Arkle at Cheltenham, started favourite, ahead of the two Nicholls-trained challengers, but he ran well below his best, a mistake at the seventh seeming to unnerve him. Politologue was narrowly ahead of the Arkle fifth Forest Bihan, with under-pressure San Benedeto looking booked for third, when he unexpectedly stumbled and fell just a stride or two after jumping the last well. Left in front, Forest Bihan threw his own chance of victory away by idling badly and being passed near the finish by the rallying and more resolute San Benedeto who, by any reckoning, was a fortunate winner. 'God knows what I'll do with him now, he'll never get another chance to win a Grade 1 like that,' said his trainer afterwards, 'but he's been an amazing horse and sometimes fortune favours the brave'. It was hard to disagree with the assessment, but Paul Nicholls will certainly have his work cut out when planning San Benedeto's next campaign. Whatever happens from now on, however, no-one can argue that, in the latest season, the horse wasn't a tremendous credit both to himself and to his trainer.

		Sunday Silence (b or br 1986)	Halo
	Layman (USA) (ch 2002)		Wishing Well
San Benedeto (FR)		Laiyl (gr 1996)	Nureyev
(ch.g. 2011)			Alydaress
		Lure (b 1989)	Danzig
	Cinco Baidy (FR) (b 1998)		Endear
		Alchimia (br 1990)	Darshaan
			Balsamique

The tall, rather unfurnished San Benedeto was bred for the Flat, by the Sunday Silence stallion Layman (now in Sweden) out of Cinco Baidy, a winner over seven and a half furlongs as a three-year-old in France and a daughter of the American miler Lure, himself a son of Danzig. Speed is more evident in San Benedeto's pedigree than stamina, with his grandam Alchimia being a half-sister to Blue Note, the dam of Middle Park winner Zieten and Cheveley Park winner Blue Duster. Cinco Baidy's two previous winners, Ocean Baidy (by Ocean of Wisdom) and Cinco Boy (a brother to San Benedeto) gained their successes over middle distances in ordinary company on the Flat in France. San Benedeto raced six times on the Flat as a two-year-old, showing fairly useful form without winning and was switched to jumping at three when, after a promising second in a listed newcomers race, he found his way to Paul Nicholls for whom he won a novice at Wincanton in his first season. He progressed again the following season to win twice from nine starts, and also came third in the National Spirit Hurdle at Fontwell. San Benedeto, who wears a tongue tie and also cheekpieces nowadays, stays twenty-one furlongs and acts on good to firm and heavy going. He often travels strongly in his races and is usually ridden to come late. *Paul Nicholls*

SAND BLAST 6 b.g. Oasis Dream – New Orchid (USA) (Quest For Fame) [2016/17 b91: **h110** h20.3g⁵ h20d* h15.8d² h18.7g² h20.3g³ h18.7g⁵ h19m² Apr 20] fair hurdler: won novice at Worcester in June: stays 2½m: acts on good to firm and good to soft going: wears cheekpieces/tongue tie: front runner/races prominently. *Dan Skelton*

SANDGATE 5 ch.g. Compton Place – Jump Ship (Night Shift (USA)) [2016/17 h98: **h97** h16m h16d³ h16.8m² h16.3g³ h15.7g* h16g h15.7g⁵ h16g Apr 23] modest handicap hurdler: won at Southwell in August: left Neil Mulholland after seventh start: will prove best at 2m: acts on good to firm and good to soft going: has worn headgear/tongue tie: often races towards rear/travels strongly. *Kenny Johnson*

SANDHURST LAD (IRE) 6 b.g. Presenting – Off She Goes (IRE) (Sadler's Wells **h96** (USA)) [2016/17 b15.7d⁵ h21s h21.3s³ h23.1s⁵ h19.8s³ Mar 10] strong gelding: first foal: **b74** dam (h70) twice-raced sister to Cheltenham Gold Cup winner Synchronised: fifth in bumper: modest form over hurdles: will stay 3m: front runner/races prominently. *Warren Greatrex*

SAND STRIP 5 b.g. Crossharbour – Jannina (FR) (Useful (FR)) [2016/17 ab16g⁵ b16.3g **b84** Apr 1] half-brother to fairly useful hurdler/chaser Top Totti (19f-3m winner, by Sir Harry Lewis) and a winning pointer by Shaanmer: dam unraced half-sister to very smart staying chaser Antonin and to dam of top-class staying hurdler Mighty Man: modest form on first of 2 starts in bumpers. *Ben Case*

SANDY BEACH 7 b.g. Notnowcato – Picacho (IRE) (Sinndar (IRE)) [2016/17 c130, h96: c19.9g* c24d³ c24.2v^pu Feb 4] good-topped gelding: maiden hurdler: useful handicap chaser: won at Newbury (by 8 lengths from Ericht) in November: stays 23f: acts on heavy going: tried in tongue tie. *Colin Tizzard* **c135 h–**

SANDYMOUNT DUKE (IRE) 8 ch.g. Hernando (FR) – Joleah (IRE) (Ela-Mana-Mou) [2016/17 h140, b99: h24d³ c22.5m² c20.2m* c22.7g* c20s⁴ c24.5d⁵ Apr 29] strong, lengthy gelding: useful hurdler: useful form over fences: won maiden at Roscommon in June and novice at Killarney in July: stays 25f: acts on good to firm and good to soft going: front runner/races prominently. *Mrs J. Harrington, Ireland* **c136 h–**

SANDYMOUNT (IRE) 6 b.g. Yeats (IRE) – Flaiha (FR) (Esprit du Nord (USA)) [2016/17 b15.7s² b16.7g³ h20.3v* h19.7s⁴ h20.2g Apr 28] €43,000 3-y-o: half-brother to 3 winners, including useful French hurdler Magic Fabien (2¼m/19f winner, by Snurge) and fairly useful hurdler Grand Zouki (2½m-3m winner, by Garuda): dam French 2m hurdle winner: fair form in bumpers, placed all 3 starts: fair form over hurdles: won maiden at Southwell in December: will stay beyond 2½m. *Tom George* **h111 b94**

SANGRAM (IRE) 10 b.g. Blueprint (IRE) – Margeno's Fountain (IRE) (Royal Fountain) [2016/17 h58: h19.5d⁵ h15.3s⁵ h23.1s⁵ h16.8d⁵ h23.1g⁵ Apr 11] won once from 9 starts in points: poor middle-distance hurdler. *Jimmy Frost* **h56**

SANIBEL ISLAND (IRE) 5 b.g. Scorpion (IRE) – Topanberry (IRE) (Topanoora) [2016/17 b16.4m* h16s² h16g^F h16g* h16.5d² h16d⁶ h16s⁴ h16v⁴ h16v* h18.8g⁶ h16.5d⁵ Apr 25] fourth foal: half-brother to a winning pointer by Definite Article: dam (h106), 2½m hurdle winner, half-sister to useful hurdler/smart chaser (stays 3¼m) Mendip Express: fair form in bumpers: won maiden at Ballinrobe in May: useful hurdler: won maiden at Wexford in October and handicap at Navan in March: should stay beyond 2m: acts on heavy going: often races towards rear. *Gordon Elliott, Ireland* **h130 b92**

SANNDIYR (IRE) 9 b.g. Red Ransom (USA) – Sinndiya (IRE) (Pharly (FR)) [2016/17 h16g May 4] no form in bumpers/over hurdles: tried in cheekpieces: wears tongue tie. *Tracey Watkins* **h–**

SAN PIETRO (FR) 9 b.g. Poliglote – Sainte Berinne (FR) (Bering) [2016/17 c112, h100: c24.1g* h23.1d² c25.5d⁶ c24g^pu c21.1s^pu c26.3g² Mar 29] fair form over hurdles: fair chaser: won handicap at Bangor very early in season: stays 3¼m: acts on heavy going: often races prominently. *Richard Ford* **c108 h105**

SAN SATIRO (IRE) 6 b.g. Milan – Longueville Quest (IRE) (Witness Box (USA)) [2016/17 h21.6v⁴ h21.4m* h23.1m* h21.4f* Apr 23] £45,000 3-y-o: well-made gelding: will make a chaser: third foal: brother to fair chaser Milanesque (3m winner) and half-brother to fair hurdler/useful chaser Ronava (2m-2½m winner, by Blueprint): dam (c96/h94) maiden jumper (placed up to 2¾m): won both completed starts in points: fairly useful form over hurdles: won novice at Wincanton in April, and handicaps at Exeter (walked over) and Wincanton later in month. *Paul Nicholls* **h119**

SANTO DE LUNE (FR) 7 gr.g. Saint des Saints (FR) – Tikidoun (FR) (Kaldoun (FR)) [2016/17 h16.7s² Dec 22] twice-raced hurdler, off 3 years between starts: fairly useful form when 2¾ lengths second to Chalonnial in novice at Bangor in December, caught there back than ideal: open to further improvement. *Dan Skelton* **h119 p**

SAPHIR DE SOMOZA (FR) 7 b.g. Antarctique (IRE) – Planete d'O (FR) (Son of Silver) [2016/17 h19.5d h16g Dec 10] fair maiden hurdler at best (in France), no form in 2016/17: tried in blinkers. *Robert Walford* **h–**

SAPHIR DU RHEU (FR) 8 gr.g. Al Namix (FR) – Dona du Rheu (FR) (Dom Pasquini (FR)) [2016/17 c156, h138+: c23.8m³ c26g^F c20.8s² c23.4v* c26.3g⁵ c34.3d^F Apr 8] robust gelding: high-class hurdler at one time: still as good as that over fences: won minor event at Kelso (by 15 lengths from Firth of The Clyde) in February: second in Trophy Handicap Chase (length behind Foxtail Hill) at Cheltenham and fifth in Cheltenham Gold Cup: fell eleventh in Grand National final start: stays 3¼m: acts on heavy going: tried in blinkers. *Paul Nicholls* **c161 h–**

SAPPHIRE NOIRE (IRE) 4 b.f. Shantou (USA) – Cool Cool (FR) (Anabaa (USA)) [2016/17 b16.6d h19g h16.8s⁵ h16v Mar 23] £10,000 3-y-o: third foal: sister to useful 2m hurdle winner Shantou Rock: dam, ran once over hurdles (placed up to 11.5f on Flat in France), half-sister to Irish Grand National winner Butler's Cabin: tailed off in bumper: poor form over hurdles. *Nigel Hawke* **h84 b–**

SARAFINA 5 b.m. Mullionmileanhour (IRE) – Nala (USA) (Lion Heart (USA)) [2016/17 h63: h16.8s^ur h16.3m^ur h16.2d^pu Jun 4] lengthy mare: little form over hurdles: in cheekpieces last 2 starts. *David Thompson* **h–**

SARAH MARIE 7 b.m. Apple Tree (FR) – Not Now Nellie (Saddlers' Hall (IRE)) [2016/17 **h98** h83p: h23.3d⁴ May 5] sturdy mare: once-raced pointer: modest form over hurdles. *Philip Hobbs*

SARAZEN BRIDGE 6 b.g. Yeats (IRE) – Strictly Cool (USA) (Bering) [2016/17 h–: **h–** h23.3vᶠ h24sᵖᵘ May 18] dual point winner: no form over hurdles: tried in blinkers. *Jonjo O'Neill*

SAROQUE (IRE) 10 b.g. Revoque (IRE) – Sarakin (IRE) (Buckskin (FR)) [2016/17 c126, **c115** h–: c24.1v⁵ c26.2s c24.1d³ c26.7s³ c29.6s⁵ c25.7v² c22.9v² c24s³ Mar 30] workmanlike **h–** gelding: winning hurdler: fairly useful handicap chaser: stays 27f: acts on heavy going. *Venetia Williams*

SARPECH (IRE) 6 b.g. Sea The Stars (IRE) – Sadima (IRE) (Sadler's Wells (USA)) **h105** [2016/17 h99: h15.8g² h16g³ h15.8m* h15.8m h16.4g⁵ h15.8d h15.8g⁵ Apr 3] sturdy gelding: fair handicap hurdler: won at Huntingdon in October: raced around 2m: acts on good to firm going: front runner/races prominently. *Charlie Longsdon*

SARTORIAL ELEGANCE 6 b.g. Kayf Tara – Blue Ride (IRE) (King's Ride) [2016/17 **c126** h114, b95: c16m⁴ c21.1s³ c25.7d* c28.5sᵘʳ c25.1vᵖᵘ Mar 9] strong gelding: fair **h–** hurdler: fairly useful form over fences: won handicap at Plumpton in December: stays 3¼m: acts on heavy going: usually wears blinkers. *Colin Tizzard*

SARUNI (IRE) 6 b.g. September Storm (GER) – Bathsheba (Overbury (IRE)) [2016/17 **h–** b–: b13.6d⁶ b16.3g h20dᵖᵘ Jun 22] compact gelding: little sign of ability: tried in hood. **b60** *Jennifer Mason*

SASSY DIVA (IRE) 6 b.m. Kalanisi (IRE) – Regal Spirit (IRE) (Alflora (IRE)) [2016/17 **b97** b16d b16g³ b16d³ b16v² b17g Apr 6] rather unfurnished mare: second foal: dam unraced half-sister to smart hurdler/fairly useful chaser (stays 2¾m) Dressedtothenines: fairly useful bumper performer: placed in listed events at Gowran, Navan and Fairyhouse: in tongue tie last 4 starts: often travels strongly. *Shane Crawley, Ireland*

SATANIC BEAT (IRE) 8 br.g. Dark Angel (IRE) – Slow Jazz (USA) (Chief's Crown **c–** (USA)) [2016/17 h127: h15.9g⁶ h15.8g h20d h16.3g h15.7g² h19.1d³ h16g² h16.2g³ **h123** c17gᵖᵘ h16g² h15.5g⁴ h15.8d² h16.6g* Dec 10] neat gelding: fairly useful handicap hurdler: won at Doncaster in December: pulled up in novice handicap on chasing debut: unproven beyond 17f: acts on soft and good to firm going: wears headgear: tried in tongue tie. *Phil Middleton*

SATELLITE (IRE) 6 b.g. Danehill Dancer (IRE) – Perihelion (IRE) (Galileo (IRE)) **h94 +** [2016/17 h118p: h17.7g* h16.4g Oct 21] useful-looking gelding: fairly useful form over hurdles: won for second time in novice at Fontwell in August: went as if amiss final start. *Tim Vaughan*

SATURNAS (FR) 6 b.g. Davidoff (GER) – Sayuri (GER) (Acatenango (GER)) [2016/17 **h145** h16d* h16d² h16d* h18s Feb 12] brother to French 17f-19f hurdle/chase winner Kalilas and half-brother to French 19f chase winner Saquias (by Walk In The Park): 14.5f winner on Flat in France: smart form over hurdles: won maiden at Naas in November and Future Champions Novices' Hurdle at Leopardstown (by 2 lengths from Brelade) in December: second in Royal Bond Novices' Hurdle at Fairyhouse (6½ lengths behind Airlie Beach) in between: went as if amiss final start: should prove suited by further than 2m. *W. P. Mullins, Ireland*

SAUCYSIOUX 7 b.m. Tobougg (IRE) – Mohican Pass (Commanche Run) [2016/17 h94: **h–** h19.2g⁶ h25g⁶ h25mᵖᵘ Apr 17] modest hurdler at best, no form in 2016/17: has worn hood: usually races nearer last than first. *Michael Roberts*

SAUSALITO SUNRISE (IRE) 9 b.g. Gold Well – Villaflor (IRE) (Religiously (USA)) **c146** [2016/17 c161, h–: c27.3s c26g⁵ c24.1sᵘʳ c23.8s³ c30.2g Mar 15] well-made gelding: **h–** winning hurdler: very smart handicap chaser: largely below form in 2016/17: stays 29f: acts on heavy going: wears cheekpieces nowadays. *Philip Hobbs*

SAUVIGNON 6 b.m. Yeats (IRE) – Dalriath (Fraam) [2016/17 b16g h21.2d h16.2s h16.6d **h86** h20.3s² h20.3g⁶ Mar 28] second foal: dam (c97/h93), 2m-21f hurdle/chase winner, also 1m **b–** winner on Flat, half-sister to fairly useful hurdler Sharriba (2m winner): well beaten in mares bumper: modest form over hurdles: best effort at 2½m: acts on soft going: often races in rear. *Dan Skelton*

SAVELLO (IRE) 11 ch.g. Anshan – Fontaine Frances (IRE) (Lafontaine (USA)) [2016/17 **c69** c153, h134: h17.9s⁴ c15.9s c16.3dᶠ c16g³ c15.5s⁶ Jan 7] lengthy gelding: useful hurdler: **h115** smart chaser at best, lost his way in 2016/17: stays 2¼m: acts on heavy going: often wears hood: has worn tongue tie, including in 2016/17: often races in rear. *Dan Skelton*

SAVOY COURT (IRE) 6 b.g. Robin des Champs (FR) – North Star Poly (IRE) **h111** (Presenting) [2016/17 b110: h19.1s h21s^{pu} h20v^2 Mar 19] bumper winner: fair form over hurdles: best effort when second in maiden at Ffos Las in March: should stay beyond 2½m: front runner/races prominently. *Warren Greatrex*

SAYEDAATI SAADATI (IRE) 4 b.g. Montjeu (IRE) – Guessing (USA) (Kingmambo **h–** (USA)) [2016/17 h15.8d^{ur} h16.3g^6 h16.3g h15.8g Apr 17] disappointing maiden on Flat: no form over hurdles. *John Butler*

SAY MY NAME (IRE) 6 ch.g. Fleetwood (IRE) – River Reine (IRE) (Lahib (USA)) **c112** [2016/17 h121: h24d^{pu} h23.1s c23.6s^3 c30.7d c24.2s^4 h26s^4 Mar 30] sturdy gelding: **h112** fairly useful hurdler at best, step back in right direction final start: fair form over fences: stays 3¼m: acts on heavy going: wears headgear: front runner/races prominently, lazy. *Bob Buckler*

SBARAZZINA (FR) 6 b.m. Walk In The Park (IRE) – Sainte Parfaite (FR) (Septieme **h–** Ciel (USA)) [2016/17 b15.8d^6 b17.7d h20.5g^6 Oct 31] £17,000 4-y-o: fourth foal: sister to **b–** fair hurdler Andi'amu (2¼m-2½m winner) and half-sister to 2 winners on Flat: dam ran twice on Flat: no form in bumpers/novice hurdle: tried in tongue tie. *Neil Mulholland*

SCALES (IRE) 11 b.g. Bob Back (USA) – Mrs Avery (IRE) (Supreme Leader) [2016/17 **c–** c–, h114: h21.2v h20.5d^3 h19s^{ur} h21.4d^6 h21.9v^5 Mar 19] modest handicap hurdler: jumped **h92** poorly only outing over fences: stays 21f: acts on heavy going: has worn headgear: tried in tongue tie: often races towards rear. *Kerry Lee*

SCARLET FIRE (IRE) 10 b.g. Helissio (FR) – Ross Dana (IRE) (Topanoora) [2016/17 **c–** c109, h–: c24.2d c23.4g^{pu} Apr 8] good-topped gelding: multiple point winner: winning **h–** hurdler: fair chaser at best, no form in handicaps in 2016/17 after long absence: stays 3¼m: acts on soft going: usually wears tongue tie nowadays. *Nicky Richards*

SCARLET MINSTREL 5 b.g. Sir Percy – Sweet Mandolin (Soviet Star (USA)) **h107** [2016/17 h16g^3 h18.7m^2 h21.2m^F Apr 25] fairly useful on Flat, stays 2m: fair form over hurdles: best effort when second in maiden at Stratford: tried in visor. *Jonjo O'Neill*

SCARTARE (IRE) 6 br.g. Trans Island – La Speziana (IRE) (Perugino (USA)) [2016/17 **h72** h95: h15.7v^5 h15.7d h19.2v h24d^6 h20.3s^{pu} Mar 20] sturdy gelding: poor maiden hurdler: often in hood: usually races nearer last than first. *Rosemary Gasson*

SCEAU ROYAL (FR) 5 b.g. Doctor Dino (FR) – Sandside (FR) (Marchand de Sable **h151** (USA)) [2016/17 h135: h16.4g* h15.3m* h16.4s^4 h15.3d^3 h16.4g^6 h16g Apr 22] useful-looking gelding: smart hurdler: won minor event at Cheltenham (by 11 lengths from Leoncavallo) in October and Elite Hurdle at Wincanton (by 9 lengths from Rayvin Black) in November: third in Kingwell Hurdle at Wincanton (2¼ lengths behind Yanworth) in February: raced around 2m: acts on good to firm and heavy going: usually races towards rear, often travels strongly. *Alan King*

SCHAP 5 ch.m. Schiaparelli (GER) – Royal Keel (Long Leave) [2016/17 b13.7m^3 b15.7d^3 **b93** Dec 15] £1,000 3-y-o: half-sister to several winners, including useful hurdler/chaser Hidden Keel (2m-2½m winner, by Kirkwall) and fair hurdler/useful chaser Mystifiable (2¼m-2¾m winner, by Kayf Tara): dam unraced half-sister to high-class 2m hurdler Relkeel: fair form in bumpers: better effort when third in mares event at Towcester in December: left David Loder after first start. *Caroline Fryer*

SCHEU TIME (IRE) 4 br.g. Arakan (USA) – Time Limit (IRE) (Alzao (USA)) [2016/17 **b99** b13.2g^2 b16g^5 b16v^2 Feb 26] half-brother to 5f/6f winner Kateeva (by Statue of Liberty) and 7f winner Tiros (by Desert King): dam 1m winner: fairly useful form in bumpers: second in maiden at Naas final start. *James A. Nash, Ireland*

SCHIAPARANNIE 5 b.m. Schiaparelli (GER) – Annie's Answer (IRE) (Flemensfirth **b91 p** (USA)) [2016/17 b16s^3 b16.2g* Apr 25] third foal: dam (c110/h130), bumper and 2m/17f hurdle winner, also winning pointer: fair form in bumpers: in hood, won readily at Hexham in April: left Mark Walford after first start: will go on improving. *Malcolm Jefferson*

SCHINDLER'S PRINCE (IRE) 12 ch.g. Oscar Schindler (IRE) – Coppeen Storm **c105** (IRE) (Glacial Storm (USA)) [2016/17 c32.5g c23.8g^{pu} c24d* c24g* c24.1g* c24.1d^3 c25.5g^2 c25.5g c24.2m^2 c23.9g^3 Oct 15] workmanlike gelding: fair handicap chaser: won at Uttoxeter (twice, both novice events) and Bangor in July: left J. M. Ridley after first start: stays 3¼m: acts on good to firm and heavy going: wears cheekpieces/tongue tie. *Katy Price*

SCHLIPF 4 b.g. Supreme Sound – Zahara Joy (Cayman Kai (IRE)) [2016/17 b14d Oct 30] **b–** 14/1, seventh in junior bumper at Carlisle. *Iain Jardine*

SCHNABEL (IRE) 5 b.g. Ask – Velsatis (IRE) (Commanche Run) [2016/17 b15.7g³ **h100** b16d h19.5g⁶ h20.8d⁴ h16.6d⁵ h23.1d⁶ Mar 21] sixth foal: closely related to fair hurdler **b82** Oscar's Ballad (3m winner, by Oscar): dam (b68) ran twice in bumpers: fourth in Irish maiden point: modest form in bumpers: fair form over hurdles. *David Dennis*

SCHOOLBOY ERROR (IRE) 4 ch.g. Roderic O'Connor (IRE) – La Grande Zoa **h97** (IRE) (Fantastic Light (USA)) [2016/17 h16.3m² h16.8m³ Jul 17] fair on Flat, stays 1½m: modest form when placed both starts in juvenile hurdles. *Jamie Osborne*

SCHOOL FOR SCANDAL (IRE) 9 b.g. Pivotal – Sensation (Soviet Star (USA)) **c–** [2016/17 c–, h79: c16.3gᵖᵘ May 5] angular gelding: winning hurdler: no form over fences: **h–** tried in blinkers/tongue tie: often races towards rear. *Jimmy Frost*

SCOIR MEAR (IRE) 7 gr.g. Exit To Nowhere (USA) – Princess Rosie (IRE) (Roselier **h139** (FR)) [2016/17 h20v* h21.6s* h22.6d² h20s² h20v² h21.1g⁵ h20.5dᵖᵘ Apr 29] €2,500 4-y-o: lengthy gelding: eighth foal: half-brother to a winning pointer by Revoque: dam unraced half-sister to useful hurdler/chaser (17f-2½m winner) McGruders Cross: useful handicap hurdler: won at Tipperary in May and Galway in October: runner-up next 3 starts, including at Cork (½ length behind Moores Road) in January: stays 23f: acts on heavy going: often races towards rear/travels strongly. *Thomas Mullins, Ireland*

SCOOBY (IRE) 6 b.g. Dubai Destination (USA) – Maggie Howard (IRE) (Good Thyne **h106** (USA)) [2016/17 h100, b–: h20.7g³ h19.7s⁴ h23.1d³ h24v³ h23.9g* h24.2dᵖᵘ Mar 24] fair handicap hurdler: won novice event at Taunton in March: stays 3m: acts on soft going: in hood last 2 starts. *Graeme McPherson*

SCOOP THE POT (IRE) 7 b.g. Mahler – Miss Brecknell (IRE) (Supreme Leader) **h108** [2016/17 h118: h24.7g⁴ h23.1s⁵ Dec 9] good-topped gelding: fairly useful hurdler at best, step back in right direction completed start in 2016/17: should stay beyond 21f: acts on soft going: wears tongue tie. *Philip Hobbs*

SCOOTER BOY 8 b.g. Revoque (IRE) – Always Forgiving (Commanche Run) [2016/17 **c111** h110, b–: h19.9v³ h19.5d⁴ c21.4dᵖᵘ c19.2sᶠ c19.2s² c15.9d⁴ Apr 5] lengthy gelding: fair **h103** hurdler: similar form over fences: stays 2½m: best form on soft/heavy going: has worn hood, including in 2016/17. *Alex Hales*

SCOPPIO DEL CARRO 6 b.g. Medicean – Sadie Thompson (IRE) (King's Best **h–** (USA)) [2016/17 h104: h16g⁵ h15.8m h24dᵖᵘ Jul 10] fair hurdler at best, no form in 2016/17: tried in cheekpieces: wears tongue tie. *Charles Pogson*

SCORPION PRINCESS (IRE) 6 b.m. Scorpion (IRE) – Cailin's Princess (IRE) (Luso) **b–** [2016/17 b95: b17g Apr 6] lengthy mare: fairly useful at best in bumpers, stiff task sole outing in 2016/17. *Charlie Longsdon*

SCORPIONS STING (IRE) 8 b.g. Scorpion (IRE) – Strong Wishes (IRE) (Strong Gale) **c–** [2016/17 c99, h106: c16.4gᵖᵘ h16.2d² h16.2d² h16.2s⁴ Jul 10] modest handicap hurdler: **h97** maiden chaser: unproven beyond 17f: acts on heavy going: has worn headgear, including in 2016/17: tried in tongue tie: signs of temperament. *James Ewart*

SCORPIO QUEEN (IRE) 5 b.m. Scorpion (IRE) – Frankly Native (IRE) (Be My **h88 p** Native (USA)) [2016/17 b15.7g* h15.7d⁶ h20.7s⁶ h20.3g⁶ Mar 28] €30,000 3-y-o: half- **b87** sister to several winners, including fairly useful hurdler/very smart chaser Master of The Hall (2m-25f winner) and smart hurdler Featherbed Lane (2m-2½m winner) (both by Saddlers' Hall): dam unraced: won mares bumper at Southwell in May: modest form over hurdles: may yet do better in handicaps. *Nicky Henderson*

SCOTCHTOWN (IRE) 5 ch.g. Beneficial – Always Present (IRE) (Presenting) [2016/17 **h132** b16.8g⁴ h19.7g* h21.2v* h23.1s² h26s² h24.2d Feb 11] tall gelding: fifth foal: half-brother **b96** to 3 winning pointers: dam (c105/h77) 25f chase winner: third in Irish maiden point: fourth in bumper: useful form over hurdles: won novices at Wetherby in October and Ludlow (by 2¾ lengths from Another Venture) in November: second in handicap at Warwick (1½ lengths behind Tobefair) in January: stays 3¼m: acts on heavy going: front runner/races prominently. *Nigel Twiston-Davies*

SCOT DADDY (USA) 5 ch.g. Scat Daddy (USA) – Flor de Oro (USA) (Out of Place **h72** (USA)) [2016/17 h–: h16.8m h16m h15.9g h16dᶠ h15.8g h15.8g⁶ Jul 22] poor maiden hurdler: in hood last 2 starts: sometimes in tongue tie: often races freely, tends to find little. *David Dennis*

SCOTSBROOK NIGHT 4 b.f. Midnight Legend – Won More Night (Kayf Tara) **b70** [2016/17 b13.7g b12.6d b16.2v b16g⁵ Apr 17] angular filly: first foal: dam (c90/h92) 2m-19f hurdle/chase winner: little form in bumpers: tried in hood. *Shaun Lycett*

SCOTSMAN 9 b.g. And Beyond (IRE) – Kariba Dream (Hatim (USA)) [2016/17 c21.6d^{pu} **c–** May 4] poor maiden pointer: pulled up in novice hunter on chasing debut: wore tongue tie. *Stuart Coltherd*

SCOTSWELL 11 b.g. Endoli (USA) – Tofino Swell (Primitive Rising (USA)) [2016/17 **c119 §** c116§, h–§: c26.2d* c29.4m^3 c25.5d c26.2d^2 c32.4s^F c26.2s^5 c26.2s^3 c30g c26.2d* Apr 10] **h– §** plain, rather leggy gelding: winning hurdler: fairly useful handicap chaser: won at Kelso early and late in season: stays 4m: acts on good to firm and heavy going: usually leads: unreliable. *Harriet Graham*

SCOTTSDALE 4 b.g. Cape Cross (IRE) – High Praise (USA) (Quest For Fame) [2016/17 **b84** b13.7g^4 b13.7d^2 Nov 24] 15,000 3-y-o: half-brother to several winners on Flat, including smart 1¼m-1½m winner Eagles Peak (by Galileo): dam smart 7f-1½m winner: modest form in bumpers: second in junior event at Towcester in November. *Brian Ellison*

SCREAMING ROSE (IRE) 6 b.m. Darsi (FR) – Screaming Witness (IRE) (Shernazar) **h134** [2016/17 b94: h20g* h22d* h20v^3 h21d^2 h24g^2 h24s^4 h24d h24d^3 Apr 27] bumper winner: useful hurdler: won maiden at Killarney in July and novice there in August: third in handicap at Punchestown (6 lengths behind Minella Awards) final start: stays 3m: acts on good to soft going. *W. P. Mullins, Ireland*

SCRUMPY BOY 5 b.g. Apple Tree (FR) – Presuming (Mtoto) [2016/17 h21.4s^{pu} h15.3d **h80** h19.8v^4 h19g Mar 30] poor form over hurdles. *Richard Woollacott*

SCRUTINISE 5 b.g. Intense Focus (USA) – Tetravella (IRE) (Groom Dancer (USA)) **h102 p** [2016/17 h16v h15.8d h16.3g^5 Apr 1] useful-looking gelding: half-brother to smart hurdler/ useful chaser Grumeti (2m/17f winner, by Sakhee) and useful hurdler/fairly useful chaser Ellerslie Tom (2m-2¼m winner, by Octagonal): useful on Flat, stays 1¾m: fair form in novice/maiden hurdles: remains capable of better. *Tim Vaughan*

SCRUTINY 6 b.g. Aqlaam – Aunty Mary (Common Grounds) [2016/17 h–: h16.8d^{pu} **h–** h16.4g h16.8m Apr 19] no form over hurdles. *Barbara Butterworth*

SEA BEAT 7 ch.g. Beat Hollow – Maritima (Darshaan) [2016/17 h18.5g h20d h16.7d^{pu} **c–** Dec 26] fair hurdler at best, no form in 2016/17: lightly-raced maiden chaser: tried in visor. **h–** *Tim Vaughan*

SEACON BEG (IRE) 8 b.g. Generous (IRE) – Moon Storm (IRE) (Strong Gale) **c–** [2016/17 c–, h99: h16.8g^6 h19s^{pu} Feb 5] modest hurdler at best, little show in 2016/17: **h70** pulled up sole start over fences: stays 19f: acts on good to firm and good to soft going: usually wears tongue tie: usually races prominently. *Nikki Evans*

SEA LIGHT (IRE) 9 b.g. Brian Boru – Matinee Show (IRE) (Carroll House) [2016/17 **h128** h20d h24g^4 h21g^2 h24.2g^F h22d* h20g h25.3s^3 h24d* h24d Dec 28] fairly useful handicap hurdler: won at Killarney in August and Clonmel in November: stays 25f: acts on heavy going: often races towards rear. *Charles Byrnes, Ireland*

SEAMOOR SECRET 5 b.m. Sakhee's Secret – Labaqa (USA) (Rahy (USA)) [2016/17 **h–** h15.8d^R h16.3g Apr 1] poor maiden on Flat: no form over hurdles: wears tongue tie. *Alex Hales*

SEAMUS MOR (IRE) 9 b.g. Shantou (USA) – Kublai (IRE) (Presenting) [2016/17 c114, **c–** h99: h19g Dec 20] modest hurdler at best, well held only outing in 2016/17: maiden chaser: **h–** stays 3m: acts on heavy going: tried in cheekpieces: has worn tongue tie. *Fergal O'Brien*

SEAN AIRGEAD (IRE) 12 ch.g. Scribano – Ryleen Lady (IRE) (Lashkari) [2016/17 **c98 §** c114§, h103§: c24.2d^4 h20.5d c25.5d^5 c20.1s^3 c20.3d^6 c17.4v^2 c21.5d^{pu} c21.5g c20s^{pu} Dec **h– §** 26] winning hurdler: modest handicap chaser nowadays: stays 3m: acts on heavy going: wears headgear/tongue tie: temperamental. *Mark McNiff, Ireland*

SEAN BAN (IRE) 7 b.g. Flemensfirth (USA) – Galingale (IRE) (Galileo (IRE)) [2016/17 **c–** h111: c16.4s^{pu} Nov 22] runner-up in Irish maiden points: fair hurdler: pulled up in novice **h–** handicap on chasing debut: should stay beyond 17f: acts on heavy going: usually races close up. *Donald McCain*

SEARCHING FOR GOLD (IRE) 5 b.g. Gold Well – True Britannia (Lujain (USA)) **b95** [2016/17 b15.7d^4 b15.7m* Apr 13] £37,000 3-y-o, £88,000 4-y-o: first foal: dam (h106), 17f hurdle winner, also 7f-1¼m winner on Flat, half-sister to fairly useful hurdler (2m/17f winner) Break The Rules: off mark in Irish maiden points at second attempt: fairly useful form in bumpers: won maiden at Towcester in April: will stay further than 2m. *Charlie Longsdon*

SEARCHING (IRE) 5 ro.g. Mastercraftsman (IRE) – Miracolia (IRE) (Montjeu (IRE)) **h111** [2016/17 h109: h15.9g^2 h15.8g* May 30] sturdy gelding: fair form over hurdles: won maiden at Huntingdon in May: stays 2¼m: acts on heavy going: in cheekpieces last 2 starts: front runner/races prominently. *Gary Moore*

SEA

SEA REBELLE 8 b.m. Cockney Rebel (IRE) – Bianca Sforza (Anabaa (USA)) [2016/17 **h–**
h21s^pu h16.8m^pu Apr 15] little impact on Flat: no form over hurdles. *Mark Shears*

SEA SERPENT (FR) 5 b.g. Great Journey (JPN) – Serpolette (FR) (Dear Doctor (FR)) **h–**
[2016/17 h58: h19.1s^pu h16s^pu Dec 2] sturdy gelding: little form over hurdles: tried in visor/
tongue tie. *Gary Moore*

SEAS OF GREEN 10 ch.m. Karinga Bay – Emerald Project (IRE) (Project Manager) **h111**
[2016/17 h–: h16d h21s* h21.2d^4 h21.6s* h21v^3 h24g Apr 20] angular gelding: fair
handicap hurdler: won at Warwick in December and Fontwell in February: stays 2¾m: acts
on good to firm and heavy going: has worn hood: often races towards rear. *Paul Cowley*

SEA SOVEREIGN (IRE) 4 b.g. Sea The Stars (IRE) – Lidakiya (IRE) (Kahyasi) **b94**
[2016/17 b13.7d b14s^4 b16s^3 b16.6g^6 b17g Apr 7] 6,000 3-y-o: leggy, close-coupled
gelding: half-brother to several winners on Flat, including very smart 6f-1¼m winner
Linngari (by Indian Ridge): dam, useful 1¼m-1½m winner, half-sister to useful hurdler
(2m/17f winner) Cape Express: fair bumper performer. *Mark Pitman*

SEA THE FIRE (IRE) 10 b.g. Oscar (IRE) – Mariaetta (IRE) (Mandalus) [2016/17 **h–**
h15.8g^pu May 30] won only bumper start: pulled up in points/maiden hurdle: tried in hood.
Christopher Kellett

SEA THE SPRINGS (FR) 6 gr.g. Slickly (FR) – Cristal Springs (FR) (Loup Solitaire **h85**
(USA)) [2016/17 h95: h19g^pu h23.4g^3 h19.1d h17.7d^2 h19.1d h19v^5 h19.5v^2 Jan 31] good-
topped gelding: modest maiden hurdler: left Dan Skelton after second start: stays 2½m:
acts on heavy going: wears headgear: often races prominently. *Michael Roberts*

SEA WALL (FR) 9 b.g. Turgeon (USA) – Si Parfaite (FR) (Solon (GER)) [2016/17 c122, **c121**
h124: h15.7d h16g h16v^4 h16v^5 h15.9v* c16v* c15.9s* Mar 10] tall gelding: fairly useful **h116**
handicap hurdler: won at Plumpton in February: useful chaser: won handicaps at
Lingfield (conditional) and Leicester in March: unproven beyond 2m: best form on soft/
heavy going: wears headgear: often races prominently/travels strongly. *Chris Gordon*

SEBASTIAN BEACH (IRE) 6 b.g. Yeats (IRE) – Night Club (Mozart (IRE)) [2016/17 **h111**
h113: h21.6m^2 Apr 15] rather leggy gelding: fair handicap hurdler: stays 3m: acts on heavy
and good to firm going: has worn tongue tie. *Jonjo O'Neill*

SEBS SENSEI (IRE) 6 ch.g. Art Connoisseur (IRE) – Capetown Girl (Danzero (AUS)) **h–**
[2016/17 h102: h15.9g^pu h17.7m^5 Apr 17] maiden hurdler, no form in 2016/17: unproven
beyond 2m: acts on firm and good to soft going: tried in tongue tie. *Mark Hoad*

SECOND TIME AROUND 5 b.g. Midnight Legend – Silk Rope (IRE) (Presenting) **b85**
[2016/17 b15.7s^6 b15.8s^4 Mar 5] second foal: dam, lightly raced in bumpers, half-sister to
smart hurdler/very smart chaser (stayed 2½m) Defy Logic out of half-sister to top-class
chaser Strong Promise (stayed 3¼m): fair form in bumpers: better effort when fourth at
Huntingdon in March. *Alan King*

SECRET APPROACH (IRE) 6 b.g. Gamut (IRE) – No Time At All (IRE) (Saddlers' **h–**
Hall (IRE)) [2016/17 b16.2d^4 b17.8d h16g h16d h16d Nov 27] pulled up both starts in **b75**
points: modest form in bumpers: well held in maiden hurdles. *Neil McKnight, Ireland*

SECRET DOOR (IRE) 6 b.m. Stowaway – Cellar Door (IRE) (Saddlers' Hall (IRE)) **h118 p**
[2016/17 h111p, b85: h15.8s* h18.9g* Apr 15] good-topped mare: runner-up in Irish point
on debut: fairly useful form over hurdles: off 12 months, won mares handicaps at Ludlow
in March and Haydock in April: will stay at least 2½m: acts on heavy going: tried in
cheekpieces: open to further improvement. *Harry Fry*

SECRETE STREAM (IRE) 8 ch.g. Fruits of Love (USA) – Bonny River (IRE) (Exit **h128**
To Nowhere (USA)) [2016/17 h19.9v* h19.7d^4 Jan 14] close-coupled gelding: fairly useful
handicap hurdler: won at Uttoxeter in November: stays 2½m: acts on heavy going.
Malcolm Jefferson

SECRET INVESTOR 5 b.g. Kayf Tara – Silver Charmer (Charmer) [2016/17 h19.3d^2 **h122 p**
Nov 18] €38,000 3-y-o, £175,000 4-y-o: good-bodied gelding: third foal: brother to modest
hurdler Kayf Charmer (2m-2½m winner): dam (h129) 19f-21f hurdle winner: won Irish
maiden point on debut: 2/1, promising second in maiden at Ascot (7 lengths behind
Kimberlite Candy) on hurdling debut: will improve. *Paul Nicholls*

SECRET PASSENGER (IRE) 4 ch.g. Stowaway – Mtpockets (IRE) (Deploy) [2016/17 **b60**
b14.6s Dec 17] 4/1, seventh in junior bumper at Newcastle. *Brian Ellison*

SECRETSISTA 5 b.m. Presenting – Princess Rainbow (FR) (Raintrap) [2016/17 b–: **h–**
h15.6g^pu Nov 3] smallish mare: no form in bumpers/maiden hurdle. *Jennie Candlish*

SECRETS SAFE (IRE) 5 b.g. Arcano (IRE) – Keritana (FR) (One Cool Cat (USA)) **h93**
[2016/17 h98: h16m⁶ h16.5m h16g⁴ h20m⁴ h22.5g h24d h21.2gᵖᵘ h21d* h24s Jan 15]
modest handicap hurdler: won at Limerick in December: stays 21f: acts on good to firm and
good to soft going: usually wears headgear/tongue tie. *John Joseph Hanlon, Ireland*

SECRET STING (IRE) 7 b.g. Scorpion (IRE) – Roxtown (Bertolini (USA)) [2016/17 **c–**
h19.5g h19.1vᵖᵘ h19.1s h15.9g c25.7m⁴ Apr 16] no form: tried in cheekpieces. *Nick Gifford* **h–**

SECULAR SOCIETY 7 b.g. Royal Applause – Fantastic Santanyi (Fantastic Light **h79**
(USA)) [2016/17 h16g h16m h15.8g⁶ h16m h16g h15.9m⁴ h16.3m Oct 15] compact
gelding: fair on Flat, stays 11f: poor maiden hurdler: raced only at 2m: usually wears
tongue tie. *George Baker*

SEDGEMOOR TOP BID (IRE) 9 b.g. Marignan (USA) – Hazy Fiddler (IRE) **c–**
(Orchestra) [2016/17 c24.2mᵖᵘ May 3] multiple winning pointer: little form under Rules: **h–**
has worn headgear: tried in tongue tie. *J. Tickle*

SEE DOUBLE YOU (IRE) 14 b.g. Saddlers' Hall (IRE) – Mandy's Treasure (IRE) **c121**
(Mandalus) [2016/17 c–, h115: c20.3g² c24.1d⁴ h20.1d⁴ h24.3v h24.3sᵖᵘ h20.5vᵖᵘ h20.1vᵖᵘ **h106**
h23.1g Apr 22] angular gelding: fair handicap hurdler: lost form after fourth at Hexham in
June: fairly useful handicap chaser: stays 25f: acts on heavy going: has worn cheekpieces.
Ronan M. P. McNally, Ireland

SEEFOOD (IRE) 10 b.g. Kahyasi – Anne Theatre (Saddlers' Hall (IRE)) [2016/17 c138, **c135**
h–: c21.4g c25g⁵ c19.9g* c21.1d² h24.4s⁶ c21.1gᶠ Apr 7] lengthy, angular gelding: useful **h–**
hurdler at best: useful handicap chaser: won at Musselburgh in November: second in Grand
Sefton Chase at Aintree (5 lengths behind As de Mee) month later: stays 25f, effective at
shorter: acts on heavy going: wears headgear: often travels strongly. *Dr Richard Newland*

SEE IT IN 5 ch.m. Black Sam Bellamy (IRE) – Lucky Arrow (Indian Ridge) [2016/17 **b–**
b15.7d Dec 15] half-sister to several winners, including useful hurdler/chaser Tzora
(2m-19f winner, by Sakhee) and fair/unreliable hurdler Whispering Death (2m winner, by
Pivotal), stayed 2½m: dam ran once on Flat: tailed off in mares bumper. *Oliver Sherwood*

SEELATERALLIGATOR (IRE) 5 b.m. Getaway (IRE) – Charming Present (IRE) **b94**
(Presenting) [2016/17 b95: b16g b16d b16.7g* Mar 25] fair form in bumpers: won maiden
at Bangor in March. *Dan Skelton*

SEEMORELIGHTS (IRE) 5 b.g. Echo of Light – Star Lodge (Grand Lodge (USA)) **h121**
[2016/17 b17.1d⁶ h15.6g h16.2v* h23.8g³ h22v³ Feb 25] €5,000 3-y-o, £11,000 4-y-o: fifth **b75**
foal: half-brother to winners on Flat abroad by Whipper and Diamond Green: dam unraced:
twice-raced Irish pointer: modest form in bumpers: fairly useful form over hurdles: won
novice at Kelso in January: stays 3m: tried in hood. *Sandy Thomson*

SEE THE LEGEND 12 b.m. Midnight Legend – Amys Delight (Idiot's Delight) [2016/17 **h84**
h–: h20.2d h23.9s² h20.9d⁵ h24.3dᵇᵈ h24.3dᵖᵘ Nov 11] poor handicap hurdler: stays 3m: acts
on heavy going: in cheekpieces last 4 starts: often shapes as if amiss. *Sandy Forster*

SEE THE WORLD 7 b.g. Kayf Tara – My World (FR) (Lost World (IRE)) [2016/17 h92: **h101**
h21g⁴ Mar 18] tall gelding: bumper winner: fair form over hurdles. *Emma Lavelle*

SEE U AGAIN SON (IRE) 8 b.g. Acambaro (GER) – I'll See You Again (IRE) **c115**
(Presenting) [2016/17 c21.1d* May 12] £7,000 5-y-o, £2,000 6-y-o: third foal: half-brother
to fair/irresolute chaser Moscow Chancer (19f/2½m winner, by Moscow Society): dam
unraced: won 3 times in points, pulled up on return in February: 11/10, won maiden hunter
at Fontwell (by 19 lengths from Brice Canyon) on chasing debut: wore tongue tie. *D. C.
Gibbs*

SEEYOUALLINCOPPERS (IRE) 7 b.g. Saffron Walden (FR) – Millenium Love **c108 p**
(IRE) (Great Commotion (USA)) [2016/17 h120: h16d⁴ h20g* c19.5mᶠ h17s h22dᵖᵘ **h122**
h18.7g⁶ Sep 3] small gelding: fairly useful handicap hurdler: won at Cork in May: upsides
when fell heavily 2 out in maiden won by Xsquared at Limerick on chasing debut: stays
21f: acts on firm and soft going: has worn headgear, including final start: has worn tongue
tie. *Gordon Elliott, Ireland*

SEEYOUATMIDNIGHT 9 b.g. Midnight Legend – Morsky Baloo (Morpeth) [2016/17 **c159**
c153, h–: c20d* c24.1vᵖᵘ h25.8s² Mar 25] strong, rangy gelding: smart hurdler: very smart **h149**
chaser: won intermediate event at Carlisle (by 12 lengths from only rival Bristol de Mai) in
October: stays 4m: acts on heavy going: front runner/races prominently. *Sandy Thomson*

SEGO SUCCESS (IRE) 9 b.g. Beneficial – The West Road (IRE) (Mister Lord (USA)) **c139**
[2016/17 c143, h–: c24s⁶ c24.1v³ c24g⁴ c29.2sᵖᵘ c26s⁵ c24mᶠ Apr 18] good-topped **h–**
gelding: winning hurdler: useful handicap chaser: stays 25f: acts on good to firm and heavy
going: has worn headgear, including in 2016/17. *Alan King*

SELDOM HEARD 5 br.g. Bahri (USA) – Turtle Dove (Tobougg (IRE)) [2016/17 h15.7d h15.9d h19.7s^{pu} Jan 4] compact gelding: no form in varied events, including points: tried in tongue tie. *Harry Chisman*   **h–**

SELDOM INN 9 ch.g. Double Trigger (IRE) – Portland Row (IRE) (Zaffaran (USA)) [2016/17 c129, h125: c23.4d* c24.5g² c23.4s^F c23.4v* c26.2s² c31.8g^{pu} Apr 22] workmanlike gelding: fairly useful chaser: smart chaser: won novice at Kelso (by 21 lengths from Ballyboker Breeze) in October and listed event at same course (by 21 lengths from Tenor Nivernais) in March: reportedly bled final start: stays 3¼m: acts on heavy going: has worn cheekpieces, including last 3 starts. *Sandy Thomson*   **c145**   **h–**

SELFCONTROL (FR) 6 b.g. Al Namix (FR) – L'Ascension (FR) (River Sand (FR)) [2016/17 h17.7s^F Dec 26] 12/1, fell first in novice hurdle won by Bastien at Fontwell. *Paul Nicholls*   **h–**

SEMPRE MEDICI (FR) 7 b.g. Medicean – Sambala (IRE) (Danehill Dancer (IRE)) [2016/17 h153: h16s⁵ h16d² h16d⁴ h16d^{pu} Dec 4] close-coupled gelding: smart hurdler: below best in 2016/17, including when second in Grimes Hurdle at Tipperary (11 lengths behind Ivan Grozny) in July: stays 2½m: acts on heavy going: tried in tongue tie. *W. P. Mullins, Ireland*   **h139**

SENATUS (FR) 5 b.g. Early March – Winter Brook (FR) (Al Nasr (FR)) [2016/17 b15.8g² b15.6g* b15.7d b16.3g Mar 25] compact gelding: half-brother to 2 winners, including French hurdler/fairly useful chaser Will Tonic (17f-21f winner, by Lavirco): dam, French 15f/2m hurdle winner, also 6f winner on Flat: fair form in bumpers: won maiden at Musselburgh in November: tried in hood: mid-division in Flat maiden in April. *Karen McLintock*   **b94**

SENDIYM (FR) 10 b.g. Rainbow Quest (USA) – Seraya (FR) (Danehill (USA)) [2016/17 c89, h84: h21.2d* c16.4g³ h22.1g² h22.1m h22.1g⁵ h21.3d⁵ c15.6g Apr 25] modest handicap hurdler: won at Sedgefield very early in season: poor handicap chaser: stays 23f: acts on soft and good to firm going: has worn headgear, including final start: tried in tongue tie: often let down by jumping over fences. *Dianne Sayer*   **c76 x**   **h85**

SENIERGUES 5 ch.g. Midnight Legend – Lady Samantha (Fraam) [2016/17 b15.9g⁴ b16.7d⁶ h19.7s Nov 23] £50,000 3-y-o: second foal: dam (h76), 3m hurdle winner, half-sister to useful hurdler (stayed 25f) Lord Generous out of top-class 2½m-3m hurdle winner Lady Rebecca: fair form in bumpers: better effort when fourth at Ffos Las in May: well beaten in novice on hurdling debut. *Robert Stephens*   **h–**   **b87**

SENOR ALCO (FR) 11 gr.g. Dom Alco (FR) – Alconea (FR) (Brezzo (FR)) [2016/17 c84, h–: c24.2d^{pu} c20.9v⁴ c26.2d³ Apr 10] multiple point winner: maiden hurdler: poor maiden chaser: stays 3¼m: acts on good to firm and heavy going: often in headgear nowadays: tried in tongue tie. *Victor Thompson*   **c84**   **h–**

SENSE OF URGENCY (IRE) 5 ch.m. Captain Rio – Itsallaracket (IRE) (Rudimentary (USA)) [2016/17 b16g² b16d³ b17g⁵ Apr 15] first foal: dam (h122) bumper and 2m/2¼m hurdle winner: modest form in bumpers: best effort when third in mares maiden at Limerick in December: left M. P. Sunderland after: should prove suited by further than 2m. *Lucy Normile*   **b80**

SENSIBLE FRIEND (GR) 4 b.g. Reel Buddy (USA) – Senseansensibility (USA) (Capote (USA)) [2016/17 b13.7g³ ab16g b13.6g³ Mar 31] third foal: half-brother to 7f winner Saturn Way (by Bachelor Duke): dam, 1¼m winner, half-sister to fairly useful hurdler/useful chaser (stayed 3m) McMurrough: fair form in bumpers: best effort when third at Fontwell in March. *Amanda Perrett*   **b86**

SENSIBLE SIMPSON 6 b.g. Kayf Tara – Elaala (USA) (Aljabr (USA)) [2016/17 b15.8g h20d³ h19.9g² h20.6s^{pu} h20.3g^{pu} Mar 28] strong gelding: failed to complete both starts in maiden points: down the field in bumper: standout effort over hurdles when second in maiden at Uttoxeter: dead. *Sarah-Jayne Davies*   **h100**   **b–**

SENSULANO (IRE) 4 b.f. Milan – Espresso Lady (IRE) (Shantou (USA)) [2016/17 b15.8s⁴ Apr 1] €14,500 3-y-o: first foal: dam (h103), bumper winner, half-sister to useful hurdler/chaser (2m-2¼m winner) Saludos: 16/1, fourth in mares bumper at Uttoxeter (12¾ lengths behind Urca de Lima) on debut. *Noel Williams*   **b79**

SERENITY NOW (IRE) 9 b.g. Key of Luck (USA) – Imdina (IRE) (Soviet Star (USA)) [2016/17 h117: h15.8s^F Mar 2] fairly useful handicap hurdler: stays 2½m: acts on heavy going: tried in visor: often races towards rear/travels strongly. *Brian Ellison*   **h108**

SERGEANT BRODY 6 ch.g. Black Sam Bellamy (IRE) – Ardent Bride (Ardross) [2016/17 h20.5d⁴ Dec 28] €20,000 3-y-o: closely related to useful hurdler/smart chaser The Package (2m-3¼m winner) and fair hurdler Bound Hill (19f winner), both by Kayf Tara: dam lightly raced in bumpers/over hurdles: off mark in points at third attempt: 20/1, some encouragement when fourth in novice at Leicester (12¾ lengths behind Head To The Stars) on hurdling debut: likely to stay 3m: should do better. *Samuel Drinkwater* **h104 p**

SERGEANT MATTIE (IRE) 9 b.g. Naheez (USA) – Glyde Lady (IRE) (Shardari) [2016/17 h20d^pu c20s⁵ c20s⁴ Feb 8] useful hurdler at best/winning chaser, below form in 2016/17 after long absence: stays 21f: acts on soft going. *Charlie Longsdon* **c107 h—**

SERGEANT PINK (IRE) 11 b.g. Fasliyev (USA) – Ring Pink (USA) (Bering) [2016/17 c108, h—: c19.3d⁵ c21.1v^pu c21.3d Mar 21] good-topped gelding: winning hurdler: fair handicap chaser, out of form in 2016/17 after lengthy lay-off: stays 3m: acts on good to firm and heavy going: has worn headgear, including in 2016/17: tried in tongue tie. *Dianne Sayer* **c— h—**

SERGIO (IRE) 5 b.g. Flemensfirth (USA) – Aventia (IRE) (Bob Back (USA)) [2016/17 b15.6g⁴ h16v h15.3d h19.4s⁶ h21m Apr 4] sturdy gelding: fourth in maiden bumper at Musselburgh: no form over hurdles. *Tim Vaughan* **h— b74**

SERPICO (IRE) 6 br.g. Scorpion (IRE) – Call Her Again (IRE) (Old Vic) [2016/17 b16.7d² h16.7g^F h16d⁵ h15.8d h21s⁵ h19.1d² h23.4g⁵ Apr 17] €42,000 3-y-o: first foal: dam unraced sister to fair hurdler/useful chaser Whatwillwecallher (stays 21f) and half-sister to fairly useful hurdler/useful chaser Sizing Coal (stays 3¾m): second in bumper at Bangor: modest form over hurdles: should stay 3m: acts on good to soft going: in blinkers last 2 starts. *Oliver Sherwood* **h99 b93**

SERVEONTIME (IRE) 6 b.g. Echo of Light – Little Lovely (IRE) (Mizzen Mast (USA)) [2016/17 h16g⁵ h16g⁴ b17.5d h18.5g h17.7d h19.1s h16v^pu h16.5m⁴ Apr 20] first foal: dam lightly raced on Flat: tailed off in maiden bumper: modest maiden hurdler: left Miss Elizabeth Doyle after second start, Kevin McDonagh after third: in cheekpieces last 2 starts: tried in tongue tie. *Helen Nelmes* **h90 b—**

SESSION OR RESSION (IRE) 13 b.g. Shernazar – Chickabiddy (Henbit (USA)) [2016/17 c21.1d^pu May 12] multiple point winner: maiden hurdler: failed to complete both starts in hunter chases, running to fair level when unseating on first occasion in 2011/12: stays 2½m: best form on good going. *N. A. Pearce* **c— h—**

SET IN MY WAYS (IRE) 6 b.g. Presenting – Kerry's Girl (IRE) (Flemensfirth (USA)) [2016/17 h117, b94: h23.3s h20.3g h20.3d² c19.4g⁶ Jul 28] fair maiden hurdler: 9/11, well-held sixth in novice handicap at Stratford on chasing debut: stays 2½m: acts on heavy going: tried in cheekpieces: usually races towards rear: should do better over fences. *Jonjo O'Neill* **c75 p h112**

SET LIST (IRE) 8 b.g. Heron Island (IRE) – Copper Magic (IRE) (Zaffaran (USA)) [2016/17 c127, h111: c24g⁶ c25.5g³ c22.6m* c22.6g^F c25.6m⁴ c25.1m² c24m² Apr 18] sturdy gelding: maiden hurdler: useful handicap chaser: won at Stratford in July: stays 3¼m: acts on good to firm and good to soft going: wears headgear: front runner/races prominently: not straightforward. *Emma Lavelle* **c130 h—**

SETTIE HILL (USA) 4 b.g. Cape Blanco (IRE) – Claire Soleil (USA) (Syncline (USA)) [2016/17 b16.7d* Apr 27] fifth foal: half-brother to 3 winners on Flat, notably high-class 7f-9.5f winner Toast of New York (by Thewayyouare): dam ran 3 times in USA: 5/1, overcame difficulties when won bumper at Market Rasen (by neck from Peculiar Places) on debut. *Neville Bycroft* **b111**

SETTLEDOUTOFCOURT (IRE) 11 b.g. Court Cave (IRE) – Ardagh Princess (Proverb) [2016/17 c115, h—: c29.4m⁶ c26.2d c24.2d² c26g⁵ c26.9v² c23.8g² c31.9s* Mar 16] lengthy gelding: winning hurdler: fair handicap chaser: won at Hexham in March: stays 4m: acts on good to firm and heavy going: front runner/races prominently. *Lucinda Russell* **c102 h—**

SEVENBALLS OF FIRE (IRE) 8 b.g. Milan – Leadamurraydance (IRE) (Supreme Leader) [2016/17 h124: h25.8s² h23.4s^F h25s⁴ h24.3v⁵ c24.3v² c26.9v^F c31.9s³ c23.4s³ Apr 3] maiden Irish pointer: fairly useful handicap hurdler: fair form over fences: stays 4m: best form on soft/heavy going: in cheekpieces last 3 starts: hard ride and not one to rely on. *Iain Jardine* **c109 § h119 §**

SEVEN CLANS (IRE) 5 b.g. Cape Cross (IRE) – Cherokee Rose (IRE) (Dancing Brave (USA)) [2016/17 h16g⁶ h15.9g h15.9g⁵ Oct 31] fairly useful on Flat, stays 1¼m: well held in novice/maiden hurdles: wears tongue tie. *Neil Mulholland* **h61**

SEVEN DEVILS (IRE) 7 b.g. Definite Article – Top Lot (IRE) (Topanoora) [2016/17 **c107 x** c102p, h90, b81: c16m³ c17.1m* c16d⁶ c17.4g⁵ c21.6d³ c20.1s³ c15.5d⁵ Oct 24] maiden **h–** hurdler: fair handicap chaser: won novice event at Kelso in May: stays 2¾m: acts on soft and good to firm going: wears tongue tie: often races in rear: often let down by jumping. *Lucinda Russell*

SEVEN KINGDOMS (IRE) 5 b.g. Yeats (IRE) – Valrhona (IRE) (Spectrum (IRE)) **c101** [2016/17 h118: h16g⁶ᵖᵘ h16.6g⁶ h18.5s h24v⁴ h18.2g⁴ c19.2m* Apr 18] rather leggy **h87** gelding: fair hurdler, below form in handicaps in 2016/17: fair form over fences: won handicap at Exeter in April: stays 19f: acts on good to firm and heavy going: in cheekpieces last 4 starts: wears tongue tie. *David Dennis*

SEVEN NATION ARMY (IRE) 8 gr.g. Rock of Gibraltar (IRE) – Crepe Ginger (IRE) **c95** (Sadler's Wells (USA)) [2016/17 h16d h16.4m⁶ h16m² h16g² c19.9g h16g³ h16.5g³ h21.4s **h110** h16.5g⁴ h16.8s³ c15.9s³ c19.4d Apr 16] rather leggy gelding: fair maiden hurdler: modest form over fences: left Henry de Bromhead after fifth start: unproven beyond 2m: acts on soft and good to firm going: often wears headgear: wears tongue tie. *Alexandra Dunn*

SEVEN SUMMITS (IRE) 10 b.g. Danehill Dancer (IRE) – Mandavilla (IRE) (Sadler's **h93** Wells (USA)) [2016/17 h15.8g³ h20.5s³ h15.5v h15.7d⁵ h15.8v⁵ Mar 19] leggy gelding: modest handicap hurdler: stays 2½m: acts on soft going: tried in cheekpieces: has worn tongue tie: often races towards rear. *Sophie Leech*

SEVENTEEN BLACK (IRE) 9 b.g. Subtle Power (IRE) – Snowbaby (IRE) (Be My **c76** Native (USA)) [2016/17 c72, h76: c20.1d* c20.1g⁵ c20.1gᵇᵈ c21.2mᵖᵘ c20.1d Jun 29] **h–** winning hurdler: poor handicap chaser: won at Hexham very early in season: stays 2½m: acts on soft going: has worn headgear: usually races nearer last than first. *Stuart Coltherd*

SEVENTH SKY (GER) 10 b.g. King's Best (USA) – Sacarina (Old Vic) [2016/17 c144, **c141** h–: c24.1v² c21.1d⁴ c24.2sᶠ c24.1sᵖᵘ c24g c26sᵖᵘ Mar 4] good-topped gelding: winning **h–** hurdler: useful handicap chaser: second at Bangor (1¼ lengths behind Valadom) in November: stays 3m: acts on good to firm and heavy going: wears headgear/tongue tie. *Charlie Mann*

SEVERAL (USA) 5 b.g. Rock Hard Ten (USA) – Proud Fact (USA) (Known Fact (USA)) **h–** [2016/17 h15.8g May 30] disappointing maiden on Flat: tailed off in maiden on hurdling debut. *Kevin Frost*

SEVILLA 4 b.f. Duke of Marmalade (IRE) – Glittering Prize (UAE) (Cadeaux Genereux) **h–** [2016/17 h16.8sᶠ h16.7s h16.3dᵖᵘ Dec 14] rather leggy filly: fair maiden on Flat, stays 11.5f: no form over hurdles: in hood last 2 starts: tried in tongue tie. *Anabel K. Murphy*

SEW ON TARGET (IRE) 12 b.g. Needle Gun (IRE) – Ballykea (IRE) (Montelimar **c128 §** (USA)) [2016/17 c137, h–: c21g c16.3d c15.2d⁴ c15.2d² c16vˣ c16.4g⁶ Mar 25] lengthy **h–** gelding: maiden hurdler: fairly useful handicap chaser: won at Chepstow in February: stays 2½m: acts on any going: has worn tongue tie: front runner/races prominently: unreliable. *Colin Tizzard*

SEYMOUR ERIC 12 b.g. Bollin Eric – Seymour Chance (Seymour Hicks (FR)) [2016/17 **c–** c–, h95: h23sᵖᵘ May 11] sturdy, close-coupled gelding: useful hurdler at best, has **h–** deteriorated markedly: maiden chaser: stays 3¼m: acts on heavy going: wears headgear. *Martin Keighley*

SEYMOUR LEGEND 11 b.g. Midnight Legend – Rosehall (Ardross) [2016/17 c–, h80: **c–** h22mᵖᵘ c20.9s⁶ h22m h25d³ h23.9g h23.1g⁶ Apr 11] poor handicap hurdler: no form over **h73** fences: stays 25f: acts on good to soft going: wears headgear, including last 3 starts. *Jim Wilson*

SEYMOUR STAR 9 b.g. Alflora (IRE) – Seymour Chance (Seymour Hicks (FR)) **h126** [2016/17 h90: h21.2v⁶ h15.8d⁵ h21.2s* h21.2s* h21.7d* Mar 26] fairly useful hurdler: won maiden at Ludlow in January, and novice handicap at same course and novice at Hereford in March: will be suited by 3m: acts on soft going: front runner/races prominently. *Alastair Ralph*

S FOR ESTUARY (IRE) 8 b.g. Milan – Princess Supreme (IRE) (Supreme Leader) **c72** [2016/17 c71: c19.3s⁵ c19.3g⁵ c17.3m c20.1g⁵ c16.4gᵖᵘ Sep 27] off mark in points at eleventh attempt: poor form in chases: wore tongue tie: dead. *Victor Thompson*

SGROPPINO (IRE) 5 b.g. Getaway (GER) – Boadicea (Celtic Swing) [2016/17 b16.8g² **h98** b16.3v Mar 4] €26,000 3-y-o: useful-looking gelding: fifth foal: half-brother to 2 winners, including modest hurdler/winning pointer Gwyre (2½m winner, by Mull of Kintyre): dam French 8.5f winner: fairly useful form in bumpers: easily better effort when second at Newton Abbot in October. *Philip Hobbs*

SGT BULL BERRY 10 b.g. Alflora (IRE) – Cede Nullis (Primitive Rising (USA)) **c83**
[2016/17 c78, h72: h24g^{pu} h27g^{pu} c24d^{ur} c27.5g* Apr 23] winning hurdler: poor handicap **h–**
chaser: won at Stratford in April, only completed start in 2016/17: stays 3½m: acts on soft
going: tried in cheekpieces/tongue tie. *Peter Maddison*

SGT RECKLESS 10 b.g. Imperial Dancer – Lakaam (Danzero (AUS)) [2016/17 h–: h20g **c–**
Sep 12] tall, workmanlike gelding: useful hurdler at best, well held only outing (tongue **h–**
tied) in 2016/17: winning chaser: unproven beyond 2m: acts on good to firm and good to
soft going. *Simon Hodgson*

SHAAMA GRISE (FR) 5 gr.m. Montmartre (FR) – Shaama Rose (FR) (Verglas (IRE)) **h131**
[2016/17 h14.7s^3 h17.4s^2 h16s^2 h19.5s* h18.5d^2 Mar 10] once-raced on Flat:
useful handicap hurdler: won mares event at Chepstow in January: second at Sandown
(2¼ lengths behind Goodbye Dancer) in March: left G. Lassaussaye after second start:
stays 21f: acts on soft going: in hood last 4 starts. *David Pipe*

SHABACH (IRE) 10 b.g. Bach (IRE) – Jercost (IRE) (Shardari) [2016/17 c–, h–: c19.4g^3 **c71**
c22.6m^{pu} c21.2m c21.2m^2 c22.6m^5 c22.6g^5 Jul 28] close-coupled gelding: point winner: **h–**
once-raced hurdler: poor maiden chaser: left Andrew Nicholls after third start: stays 21f:
acts on good to firm going: has worn headgear, including in 2016/17: sometimes in tongue
tie. *Mike Sowersby*

SHADARPOUR (IRE) 8 b.g. Dr Fong (USA) – Shamadara (IRE) (Kahyasi) [2016/17 **h–**
h120: h26.5m h20g Sep 12] sturdy gelding: fairly useful hurdler at best, no form in
2016/17: stays 2¾m: acts on soft and good to firm going: often wears headgear.
Katie Stephens

SHADDAII (FR) 11 gr.g. April Night (FR) – Gypsie d'Artois (FR) (Mistigri) [2016/17 **h80**
h87: h21.6d^{ur} h21.4m^6 h19.5d^4 h19.8d^3 h19g^2 h19.1d^2 h16.5g^3 h20.5m^{ur} Apr 16] poor
handicap hurdler: stays 2½m: acts on soft going: wears tongue tie: front runner/races
prominently. *Robert Walford*

SHADES OF MIDNIGHT 7 b.g. Midnight Legend – Hannah Park (IRE) (Lycius **h132**
(USA)) [2016/17 h143: h20d^6 h24.2d^6 h25s^5 h19.9v^4 h20.5v^3 h25.8s^{pu} Mar 25] good-
topped gelding: useful handicap hurdler: stays 23f: acts on heavy going: wears tongue tie:
often races prominently. *Donald Whillans*

SHADOW BLUE (IRE) 8 br.g. Blueprint (IRE) – Rosie Belle (IRE) (Roselier (FR)) **h85**
[2016/17 h110: h19.1s^4 h16g h19g h16.5g h19.8v h16v^4 Mar 23] no form in points: modest
maiden hurdler: stays 19f: acts on heavy going: front runner/races prominently. *Steven
Dixon*

SHADOW CATCHER 9 ch.g. Haafhd – Unchain My Heart (Pursuit of Love) [2016/17 **c134**
c135, h–: h20g^5 c22.5g^6 c24v^{pu} c19.5d^5 c19.5g^5 c24d c24.5d^{ur} c21g^{pu} c25d^{pu} c18v^2 h18.8g^4 **h119**
c16d Apr 27] huntingly, angular gelding: useful hurdler at best: useful chaser: second in
minor event at Thurles (1½ lengths behind Westerner Point) in February: stays 23f,
effective at shorter: acts on good to firm and heavy going: wears headgear/tongue tie.
Gordon Elliott, Ireland

SHADOW RECRUIT (IRE) 5 ch.g. Primary (USA) – Balanchine Moon (Zilzal (USA)) **b–**
[2016/17 b17.1g Nov 7] tailed off in bumper: wore hood. *Stuart Crawford, Ireland*

SHADOWS LENGTHEN 11 b.g. Dansili – Bay Shade (USA) (Sharpen Up) [2016/17 **c125**
c129, h–: c19.4g^5 c20.1f^2 c19.4g^3 c19.4d^{ur} c19.1g^3 c19.9g^6 c24.2m^3 Apr 13] strong, **h–**
workmanlike gelding: winning hurdler: fairly useful handicap chaser: third at Wetherby in
October (listed event) and April: stays 3m: acts on good to firm and heavy going: usually
races towards rear. *Michael Easterby*

SHADY GLEN (IRE) 8 br.g. Dr Massini (IRE) – Poppins (IRE) (Invited (USA)) **c111**
[2016/17 c89, h79: h18.6g^{pu} c20d* c21.2m^4 c22.6m^2 c22.6g* c23m^2 c17.2m^3 Apr 17] **h–**
maiden hurdler: fair handicap chaser: won at Worcester in June and Stratford in July: stays
3m: acts on good to firm and good to soft going: wears headgear/tongue tie. *Graeme
McPherson*

SHADY SADIE (IRE) 10 b.m. Dushyantor (USA) – Beltane Queen (IRE) (Strong Gale) **c–**
[2016/17 c80, h–: c25.5m^{pu} c23.9g Aug 13] good-topped mare: maiden hurdler: poor **h–**
chaser at best, no form in 2016/17: stays 3m: acts on good to soft going: wears tongue tie:
usually races towards rear. *Rose Dobbin*

SHAH OF PERSIA 10 b.g. Fair Mix (IRE) – Queen Soraya (Persian Bold) [2016/17 **c–**
c117, h108: h20m^2 Jul 4] sturdy gelding: fair maiden hurdler: fairly useful chaser: stays **h112**
3m: acts on good to firm going: in headgear last 4 starts: wears tongue tie. *Warren Greatrex*

SHAIYZAR (IRE) 8 b.g. Azamour (IRE) – Shaiyzima (IRE) (Polish Precedent (USA))   **c89**
[2016/17 h96: c16.4s⁴ c24.2g² c24.2gᵖᵘ c25.5mᵖᵘ h23.3g h24g* h24g⁵ c23.8g³ c23.8dᵖᵘ   **h93**
h20.6m⁴ h23.9g Apr 26] modest handicap hurdler: won at Southwell in August: similar
form over fences: stays 3m: acts on soft going: wears headgear: has worn tongue tie: often
races towards rear. *David Thompson*

SHAKE DEVANEY (IRE) 7 b.g. Rakti – Ediyrna (IRE) (Doyoun) [2016/17 h83, b71:   **h–**
h20mᵖᵘ May 19] maiden hurdler, pulled up in handicap sole start (tongue tied) in 2016/17.
Fergal O'Brien

SHAKE IT UP (IRE) 8 br.g. Presenting – Miss Fresher (FR) (Pampabird) [2016/17   **c106**
c23g* c21.5d³ c22.7g c25g² c22.5d c25g⁵ c20v c26.3g⁴ Mar 29] dual point winner: maiden   **h–**
hurdler: fair chaser: won maiden hunter at Downpatrick in May: will stay beyond 3¼m:
acts on heavy going: tried in hood. *J. T. R. Dreaper, Ireland*

SHAKY GIFT (IRE) 8 b.m. Milan – Free Lift (Cadeaux Genereux) [2016/17 c–, h112:   **c90**
c23.6d⁴ c24.2sᵖᵘ Nov 15] winning Irish pointer: fair hurdler: maiden chaser: stayed 23f: **h–**
acted on soft going: dead. *Neil Mulholland*

SHALAMZAR (FR) 8 ch.g. Selkirk (USA) – Shamalana (IRE) (Sinndar (IRE)) [2016/17   **h70 §**
h–: h16.8s h16.8d⁶ h16d⁶ h15.7s⁵ Mar 8] close-coupled gelding: poor maiden hurdler:
unproven beyond 2m: acts on good to firm and good to soft going: in cheekpieces last 3
starts: races towards rear: moody. *Micky Hammond*

SHALIANZI (IRE) 7 b.g. Azamour (IRE) – Shalama (Kahyasi) [2016/17 h94:   **h86 §**
h17.7g h21.6g⁶ h19.1g² h19.1d⁵ h19.6m h20.5g⁴ h19.1s h19.1s⁶ h21.6vᵖᵘ Jan 29] tall,
lengthy gelding: modest handicap hurdler: left Gary Moore after sixth start: stays 19f: acts
on heavy going: wears headgear: temperamental. *Chris Gordon*

SHALUNA (IRE) 7 b.m. Shantou (USA) – Eluna (Unfuwain (USA)) [2016/17 h18.5s⁶   **h97**
h21v⁵ h20.7sᵖᵘ h15.7m* Apr 13] £15,000 6-y-o: sixth foal: closely related to fairly useful
hurdler/useful chaser Viva Steve (2m-3m winner, by Flemensfirth): dam (c83/h118) 2m
hurdle winner: won completed start in Irish points: modest form over hurdles: won mares
maiden at Towcester in April: has joined John Joseph Hanlon. *Kim Bailey*

SHAMAT (IRE) 7 b.g. Milan – Like A Dream (IRE) (Alzao (USA)) [2016/17 h16g⁶   **h91**
h16mᶠ h16m⁶ h20g h19s h17.3g³ h16.8g⁵ h16g Sep 30] second foal: half-brother to French
2¼m chase winner Dreamao (by Mull of Kintyre): dam (h112), 2m/2¼m hurdle winner,
also 7f-9.4f winner on Flat: lightly raced in bumpers/on Flat: modest maiden hurdler: best
effort at 17f: acts on good to firm going: sometimes wears headgear: front runner/races
prominently. *M. J. Tynan, Ireland*

SHAMBOUGG 6 b.g. Tobougg (IRE) – More Likely (Shambo) [2016/17 b90: h19.9sᵖᵘ   **h87**
h23.5g⁵ h19.9v⁶ h23.8dᶠ h25dᵖᵘ h23.1g³ Apr 11] runner-up in Irish maiden point: bumper
winner: modest form over hurdles: stays 23f: acts on heavy going: in blinkers last 3 starts.
Philip Hobbs

SHAMMICK BOY (IRE) 12 b.g. Craigsteel – Dulcet Music (IRE) (Topanoora)   **c–**
[2016/17 c–, h122: h21.6g⁵ May 5] lengthy gelding: useful hurdler at best, below that since   **h–**
2014/15: winning chaser: stays 21f: acts on heavy going: wears headgear: tried in tongue
tie: races prominently. *Victor Dartnall*

SHANANDOA 6 b.m. Shamardal (USA) – Divisa (GER) (Lomitas) [2016/17 h70, b86:   **h79**
h16m⁴ h15.7vᵖᵘ Jun 20] lengthy, angular mare: bumper winner: poor form over hurdles:
may prove best around 2m. *Brian Barr*

SHANANN STAR (IRE) 11 br.m. Anshan – Baile An Droichid (IRE) (King's Ride)   **c93**
[2016/17 c25.5s⁶ c25.1s³ c24.5vᵖᵘ c25.1d* c25.1v² c26.7d³ Mar 26] multiple point winner: **h–**
lightly-raced hurdler: modest handicap chaser: won at Wincanton in February: stays 3¼m:
acts on heavy going: wears headgear: often races towards rear. *Gordon Edwards*

SHANAWAY (IRE) 6 b.g. Stowaway – Shannagh Run (IRE) (Denel (FR)) [2016/17 h24g   **h92**
h20s³ h19.1s h15.9g² h19.9s Dec 6] €30,000 3-y-o: second foal: dam winning pointer:
pulled up in maiden point: well held in bumpers: modest form over hurdles: left Paul Nolan
after second start: stays 2½m: acts on soft going: sometimes in headgear: has worn tongue
tie: front runner/races prominently. *Neil King*

SHAN DUN NA NGALL (IRE) 6 b.g. Shantou (USA) – Omanah (USA) (Kayrawan   **h105**
(USA)) [2016/17 h16g* h16g² h20g h20gᵖᵘ h16.2d⁵ h16.3m* Oct 15] fair on Flat,
stays 16.5f: fair hurdler: won handicap at Down Royal in May and seller at Stratford in
October: unproven beyond 2m: acts on good to firm going: in headgear last 2 starts: tried
in tongue tie. *Gordon Elliott, Ireland*

Prix Les Grandes Gueules du Sport - Prix La Barka Hurdle, Auteuil—the prize goes to an Anglo-Irish raider for the sixth successive year as Shaneshill beats L'Ami Serge (right)

SHANESHILL (IRE) 8 b.g. King's Theatre (IRE) – Darabaka (IRE) (Doyoun) [2016/17 **c–** c150p, h158: h24d^F h24g^2 h20d^3 h20d^3 h24d^F h24d* h24g^{pu} h24d Apr 27] sturdy gelding: **h154** very smart hurdler: won John Mulhern Galmoy Hurdle at Gowran (by ¾ length from Snow Falcon) in January and Prix La Barka at Auteuil (by ¾ length from L'Ami Serge) shortly after end of British season: also placed in 2016/17 in Grade 1 at Percy Warner Park (neck behind Rawnaq), Lismullen Hurdle at Navan (4½ lengths behind Snow Falcon) and Hatton's Grace Hurdle at Fairyhouse (7 lengths behind Apple's Jade): smart chaser (second in 2016 RSA Chase when last seen over fences): stays 25f: acts on heavy going: front runner/races prominently. *W. P. Mullins, Ireland*

SHANGHAI SUNRISE 6 b.m. Royal Applause – Duchcov (Caerleon (USA)) [2016/17 **h83** h17.7d h18.5g^4 h19.5v^{pu} h19.8d^{pu} h15.9v^{pu} Jan 30] half-sister to useful hurdler/smart chaser Brick Red (2m/17f winner, by Dubawi): no form on Flat: poor form over hurdles. *Robert Walford*

SHANNON SILVER 8 b.g. Grape Tree Road – Pinch Me Silver (Silver Patriarch (IRE)) **c–** [2016/17 c–: c25.2s^6 Mar 8] multiple winning pointer: no form in hunter chases: tried in cheekpieces. *Mrs Anthea Morshead*

SHANPALLAS (IRE) 9 b.g. Golan (IRE) – Evnelu (IRE) (Old Vic) [2016/17 c142, **c–** h126+: h16d^5 h20m* h20g^4 h24s^4 c21v^5 Jan 1] workmanlike gelding: useful hurdler: won **h133** handicap at Ballinrobe (by ½ length from Cliff House) in May: smart chaser at best, well held in listed event final start in 2016/17: stays 3m: acts on soft and good to firm going. *Charles Byrnes, Ireland*

SHANROE IN MILAN (IRE) 5 b.g. Milan – Shanroe Scenario (IRE) (Presenting) **h111** [2016/17 h21.2g^2 h21.2d^4 h21.2s^2 h21.2s^3 h21.7s h23.1g^2 Apr 22] £30,000 4-y-o: first foal: dam unraced half-sister to dam of useful hurdler/high-class chaser (stayed 2¾m) Woolcombe Folly: runner-up in Irish maiden point: fair form over hurdles: likely to stay 3m: acts on soft going: front runner/races prominently. *Charlie Longsdon*

SHANROE SANTOS (IRE) 8 b.g. Definite Article – Jane Hall (IRE) (Saddlers' Hall **c129** (IRE)) [2016/17 c19.1g^5 c21.2g^F c24.2s^6 c23.6d^2 c24v* c24.2d* c24.1g Apr 15] lengthy **h–** gelding: winning hurdler: fairly useful handicap chaser: won at Warwick in February and Sandown in March: stays 3m: acts on heavy going: in cheekpieces last 4 starts. *Lucy Wadham*

SHANROE STREET (IRE) 7 b.g. Mustameet (USA) – Zaffran Lady (IRE) (Zaffaran **c105** (USA)) [2016/17 h105, b–: h23.3d c16.3s^5 c24.2d^5 c26.6g^2 c30.6g^5 Apr 28] Irish point **h–** winner: fair hurdle winner: similar form over fences: stays 31f: acts on heavy going. *Lucinda Russell*

SHANTOU BOB (IRE) 9 b.g. Shantou (USA) – Bobset Leader (IRE) (Bob Back (USA)) **h142** [2016/17 h–: h24.2d^2 h23.6s* h24s^5 Jan 28] sturdy gelding: has had breathing operation: winning pointer: useful handicap hurdler: won at Chepstow (by neck from Rolling Dylan) in December: stays 3m: acts on heavy going: tried in cheekpieces: wears tongue tie. *Warren Greatrex*

SHANTOU BREEZE (IRE) 10 b.m. Shantou (USA) – Homersmare (IRE) (Shardari) **c–** [2016/17 h24.5m^5 Apr 4] dual point winner: maiden hurdler: modest chaser at best: stays **h–** 21f: acts on firm and soft going: tried in visor: has worn tongue tie. *Michael Madgwick*

BetBright Best For Festival Betting Handicap Chase, Cheltenham—
the ex-Irish Shantou Flyer beats 2016 winner Village Vic (left) on his debut for new connections;
Top Gamble takes third for the second year running

SHANTOU FLYER (IRE) 7 b.g. Shantou (USA) – Carrigmorna Flyer (IRE) (Bob Back (USA)) [2016/17 c144, h125: c25d⁵ c20g² c22.5g c20.8s* c20.8s⁴ c21s² c34.3dᵖᵘ Apr 8] workmanlike gelding: fairly useful hurdler: very smart handicap chaser: won Grade 3 at Cheltenham (by 3 lengths from Village Vic) in January: second in Betfair Ascot Chase (15 lengths behind Cue Card) in February: left Colin Bowe after third start: stays 25f: acts on soft and good to firm going: wears tongue tie. *Rebecca Curtis*   **c155 h–**

SHANTOU MAGIC (IRE) 10 b.g. Shantou (USA) – Supreme Magical (Supreme Leader) [2016/17 c116, h–: c24gᶠ c24.2d⁵ Mar 10] sturdy gelding: winning pointer/hurdler: useful chaser at best, below that since 2014/15: left Charlie Longsdon after first start: stays 3m: acts on heavy going: tried in cheekpieces/tongue tie. *Captain W. B. Ramsay*   **c124 h–**

SHANTOU PRINCE (IRE) 8 b.g. Shantou (USA) – Princess Nina (IRE) (King's Theatre (IRE)) [2016/17 c24.2d² Mar 31] multiple point winner: 9/1, second in hunter at Wetherby (1½ lengths behind Ardea) on chasing debut. *Mrs G. B. Walford*   **c110**

SHANTOU ROCK (IRE) 5 b.g. Shantou (USA) – Cool Cool (FR) (Anabaa (USA)) [2016/17 h16d² h18.8d h16.3s² h15.8s* h15.7d² h15.8s* h15.8g* h16.8gᶠ Apr 11] €22,000 3-y-o, £30,000 4-y-o: angular gelding: second foal: dam, ran once over hurdles (placed up to 11.5f on Flat in France), half-sister to Irish Grand National winner Butler's Cabin: placed in Irish maiden points: useful hurdler: won maiden in February, novice (by 36 lengths from Comanche Chieftain) in March and handicap (by 21 lengths from Avispa) in April, all at Ludlow: unproven beyond 2m: acts on soft going: wears tongue tie: usually leads, strong traveller. *Dan Skelton*   **h140**

SHANTOU THEATRE (IRE) 7 ch.g. Shantou (USA) – As Lathair (IRE) (King's Theatre (IRE)) [2016/17 b71: h19.3m h22.1m May 28] little impact in bumpers/novice hurdles. *George Charlton*   **h–**

SHANTOU TIGER (IRE) 8 b.g. Shantou (USA) – Opus One (Slip Anchor) [2016/17 c119, h118: h25.4m h23.3d⁵ h26.4g⁵ h23.1g* h23.8g² h23.8g² l23.8g² h23.8g h26.4g⁴ Apr 15] close-coupled gelding: fair handicap hurdler: won at Bangor in October: maiden chaser: stays 3m: acts on soft and good to firm going: wears cheekpieces: usually leads. *Donald McCain*   **c– h111**

SHANTOU VILLAGE (IRE) 7 b.g. Shantou (USA) – Village Queen (IRE) (King's **c149 p** Theatre (IRE)) [2016/17 h143: c21.1g* c19.8g* c20.2m^F c21.1g* c20g* Apr 29] **h–** sturdy gelding: useful hurdler: smart form over fences: won novices at Fontwell in August, Cheltenham (by 4 lengths from Mick Thonic) in October and Fontwell again (easily by 12 lengths from Red Hanrahan) in April, and novice handicap at Sandown (by neck from Brother Tedd) later in April: should stay 3m: acts on good to firm and good going: usually leads, often travels strongly: remains open to improvement as a chaser. *Neil Mulholland*

SHANTY TOWN (IRE) 8 b.g. Zagreb (USA) – Rapsan (IRE) (Insan (USA)) [2016/17 **h112** h21.3s³ h20.5v⁴ h21v³ h23.1d⁵ Apr 27] tall gelding: runner-up sole start in Irish maiden points: fair form over hurdles: stays 21f: acts on soft going: has worn tongue tie. *David Dennis*

SHARIVARRY (FR) 11 ch.g. Ballingarry (IRE) – Sharsala (IRE) (Shahrastani (USA)) **c89** [2016/17 c–, h70: c24.2g* c24.2g* c20.1d³ c24.2d³ Jun 19] maiden hurdler: modest **h–** handicap chaser: won at Hexham in May and June: stays 3¼m: acts on soft and good to firm going: tried in cheekpieces/tongue tie: often races towards rear. *Victor Thompson*

SHARNEY SIKE 11 ch.g. And Beyond (IRE) – Squeeze Box (IRE) (Accordion) [2016/17 **c109** c26.2s⁶ c24.2s² c24.2d c23.4v³ Mar 18] tall, lengthy, angular gelding: maiden hurdler: fair **h–** handicap chaser: stays 3¼m: acts on heavy going. *Stuart Coltherd*

SHARP RESPONSE (IRE) 6 b.g. Oscar (IRE) – Lambourne Lace (IRE) (Un Desperado **h116** (FR)) [2016/17 b18v⁵ h19.7g* h19.7g³ h22.8v³ h18.9s⁵ h21.2s* h22v² h20.6m⁶ Apr 17] **b81** €28,000 3-y-o: closely related to 3 winners by Old Vic, including smart hurdler/winning pointer Ballyoptic (2½m-25f winner), and half-brother to fair hurdler/useful chaser Peoples Park (2m-2½m winner, by Presenting): dam well beaten: maiden pointer: fifth in maiden bumper at Tipperary: fairly useful hurdler: won novices at Wetherby in October and Sedgefield in February: left S. Curling after first start: may prove best at short of 2¾m: acts on heavy going: front runner/races prominently. *Sue Smith*

SHARP RISE (IRE) 10 b.g. Croco Rouge (IRE) – Missusan (IRE) (King's Ride) **c152** [2016/17 c131, h137: c16.5g* c16g* c17m² c20g* h21.6g^{ur} h16.3g* h21f³ Oct 15] smart **h154** handicap hurdler: won at Stratford (by 10 lengths from May Hay) in September: well below best when third in Grade 1 at Far Hills (18¼ lengths behind Rawnaq) final start: smart handicap chaser: won at Worcester (by 17 lengths from Miss Tenacious) and Uttoxeter (by ½ length from Roman Flight) in June, and at Uttoxeter again (by ½ length from One For The Boss) in July: effective at 2m to 2¾m: acted on soft and good to firm going: front runner/raced prominently: tail flasher: dead. *Charlie Longsdon*

SHATTERED LOVE (IRE) 6 b.m. Yeats (IRE) – Tracker (Bustino) [2016/17 b106: **h131** h16d* h16g² h18s² h16s* h18v* h21.1g h20d Apr 16] tall mare: point/bumper winner: useful hurdler: won mares maiden at Tipperary in October, listed mares novice at Thurles (by 37 lengths from Kalopsia) in December and Grade 3 mares novice at Fairyhouse (by 13 lengths from Forge Meadow) in February: should stay beyond 2¼m: acts on heavy going: wears tongue tie: usually races prominently, often travels strongly. *Gordon Elliott, Ireland*

SHAVAUGHN 5 b.m. Kheleyf (USA) – Shannon Falls (FR) (Turgeon (USA)) [2016/17 **h–** h19.1g^{pu} h20.3d^{pu} Jul 10] maiden on Flat: failed to complete both starts in points/over hurdles. *Alexandra Dunn*

SHEARLING 4 b.f. Rail Link – Casual (Nayef (USA)) [2016/17 b14s* b12.4d* b12.4d² **b99** b15.7s* b17g⁴ Apr 6] 25,000 3-y-o: well-made filly: third foal: half-sister to smart French 1½m winner Harlem (by Champs Elysees): dam, useful 7f-1½m winner, half-sister to fairly useful hurdler (stays 21f) Belize (by Rail Link) and dam (by Champs Elysees) of fairly useful bumper performer: won fillies junior race at Warwick in November, mares event at Wetherby in December and conditionals/amateur mares contest at Catterick in March: also second in mares event at Wetherby and fourth in Nickel Coin Mares' National Hunt Flat Race (6 lengths behind Dame Rose) at Aintree: travels strongly. *Brian Ellison*

SHEAR ROCK (IRE) 7 b.g. Spadoun (FR) – Sleeping Diva (FR) (Sleeping Car (FR)) **c123** [2016/17 h124: c19.4m² Oct 12] useful-looking gelding: fairly useful hurdler: 10/3, second **h–** in novice at Wetherby (neck behind Ballybolley) on chasing debut: stays 21f: best form on good/good to soft: wears hood: front runner. *Charlie Longsdon*

SHEELBEWHATSHEELBE (IRE) 7 b.m. Oscar (IRE) – Cheerymount (IRE) (Oscar **h83** Schindler (IRE)) [2016/17 h16.2s h16.5s⁶ h19g h16v³ Mar 22] poor form in bumpers/over **b67** hurdles: should be suited by 2½m+. *Richard Phillips*

SHEER POETRY (IRE) 6 b.m. Yeats (IRE) – Sassari (IRE) (Darshaan) [2016/17 h91:   **h103**
h21.6g* h21.4m* h23g³ h16.8d^F h18.5m^pu h22g Aug 11] sturdy mare: fair handicap
hurdler: won at Newton Abbot and Wincanton in May: stays 2¾m: acts on good to firm and
good to soft going: wears tongue tie nowadays: often races prominently. *Richard Woollacott*

SHEHADTORUN 7 b.m. Midnight Legend – La Marette (Karinga Bay) [2016/17   **b–**
b15.7g⁶ May 24] second foal: dam (h90) 2m-2¾m hurdle winner (stayed 25f): well beaten
in mares bumper (tongue tied): failed to complete all 5 starts in points. *Tom Gretton*

SHELFORD (IRE) 8 b.g. Galileo (IRE) – Lyrical (Shirley Heights) [2016/17 h139:   **c127**
h19.4s² h18.9v⁵ h24.4d h19.1s⁶ c24.5s* c25.2d² c23.6g² Apr 17] compact gelding: smart   **h145**
hurdler: fairly useful form over fences: won 3-runner maiden at Towcester in March: stays
3m: acts on heavy going: wears headgear nowadays. *Dan Skelton*

SHEMALZAN (FR) 8 b.g. Selkirk (USA) – Shemissa (IRE) (Fairy King (USA))   **h–**
[2016/17 h19.7s^F h21.2s^pu Jan 19] fairly useful 11f winner on Flat for Jean-Claude Rouget:
failed to complete both starts over hurdles. *Adrian Wintle*

SHEMAY 5 b.m. Shirocco (GER) – Shemanikha (FR) (Sendawar (IRE)) [2016/17 h16g   **h60**
h16g⁶ h16.2s Jul 10] modest maiden on Flat: poor form over hurdles: wears tongue tie.
Stuart Crawford, Ireland

SHENEEDEDTHERUN (IRE) 7 b.m. Kayf Tara – Lady Moon (FR) (Monsun (GER))   **h104**
[2016/17 h19.2v⁴ h20.3g⁴ h19.7g* Apr 23] £10,500 6-y-o: first foal: dam, French maiden
(placed up to 15f), half-sister to very smart hurdler/useful chaser (stayed 21f) Sky's The
Limit: off mark in Irish points at third attempt: fair form over hurdles: won mares maiden
at Wetherby in April. *Michael Scudamore*

SHEPHERD'S BIGHT (IRE) 5 b.g. Court Cave (IRE) – Orador Sur Glane (IRE)   **h89**
(Shernazar) [2016/17 b16.4d h17d³ Apr 5] €26,000 3-y-o: fourth foal: half-brother to fairly   **b–**
useful 2m hurdle winner King William (by Trans Island): dam winning pointer: tailed off
in maiden bumper: 80/1, showed more when third in novice at Carlisle (19¾ lengths
behind Mr Big Shot) on hurdling debut. *George Charlton*

SHE'S LATE 7 ch.g. Pivotal – Courting (Pursuit of Love) [2016/17 c–, h109: c19.9g²   **c102 §**
c23.9d³ c23g⁶ c21.2g⁴ c24.5m³ c20m* h21.2g⁵ c22.7f* h24v^pu Dec 11] close-coupled   **h80 §**
gelding: fair hurdler at best: fair handicap chaser: won at Ludlow (amateur) in October and
Leicester (novice event) in December: stays 3m: acts on firm and good to soft going: has
worn headgear: temperamental. *Jonjo O'Neill*

SHE'S REAL (IRE) 9 br.m. Definite Article – The Real Athlete (IRE) (Presenting)   **c82 +**
[2016/17 c25.3g⁴ Apr 27] €6,000 3-y-o, £15,500 5-y-o: fourth foal: half-sister to useful
hurdler/chaser Real Milan (2½m-25f winner, by Milan) and winning pointers by Milan and
Catcher In The Rye: dam, unraced, out of half-sister to Grand National winner Royal
Athlete: prolific winning pointer: 15/2, too free when fourth in mares hunter at Cheltenham
(30 lengths behind Popaway) on chasing debut. *Mrs H. Connors*

SHE TOLD YOU SO 7 b.m. Generous (IRE) – All Told (IRE) (Valanjou (FR)) [2016/17   **h–**
b16v h15.8d^pu h21s⁴ h20.7g^pu Apr 3] fourth foal: half-sister to fair hurdler/fairly useful   **b–**
chaser Explained (17f-2½m winner, by Exit To Nowhere): dam unraced: no form in
bumper/over hurdles: wears hood. *Mark Wall*

SHILLINGSWORTH (IRE) 4 b.g. Presenting – Miss Bobs Worth (IRE) (Bob Back   **b–**
(USA)) [2016/17 b15.3v Mar 9] well beaten in maiden bumper. *Colin Tizzard*

SHIMBA HILLS 6 b.g. Sixties Icon – Search Party (Rainbow Quest (USA)) [2016/17 h–:   **h103**
h17.7g² h16.8d h16g h16.3m⁵ h16m² h15.9g³ h15.9s* h15.9v* h15.9v³ h17.7g² Apr 21]
fair handicap hurdler: won at Plumpton in December and January: stays 2¼m: acts on good
to firm and heavy going: wears cheekpieces/tongue tie: usually races nearer last than first,
often travels strongly. *Lawney Hill*

SHIMLA DAWN (IRE) 9 b.g. Indian Danehill (IRE) – Tina Thyne (IRE) (Good Thyne   **c128**
(USA)) [2016/17 c130, h–: c19.9g^pu c21.6s² c24.2g³ Apr 23] rather leggy, lengthy gelding: **h–**
winning hurdler: useful handicap chaser: stays 2¾m: acts on heavy going: usually leads.
Mark Walford

SHINE A DIAMOND (IRE) 9 gr.g. St Jovite (USA) – Mossy Grey (IRE) (Step Together   **c79**
(USA)) [2016/17 c87, h76: h16.2g c15.6g c15.8g⁴ c19.9d⁴ c23.8g⁴ c23.8g⁵ c23.8g   **h68**
c23.8g⁴ h23.8g^bd c21.6d Apr 10] maiden hurdler: poor handicap chaser: stays 3m: acts on
soft and good to firm going: wears headgear/tongue tie: often races towards rear. *Lucinda
Russell*

SHINE AWAY (IRE) 7 b.m. Robin des Pres (FR) – Bramble Bree (IRE) (Rashar (USA)) c–
[2016/17 h107: h19.7g⁴ c20.3dᵖᵘ May 26] placed in Irish points: maiden hurdler, fair form h–
at best: pulled up in novice handicap on chasing debut: stays 19f: usually races prominently.
Sue Smith

SHINING ROMEO 5 b.g. Royal Applause – Silver Pivotal (IRE) (Pivotal) [2016/17 b83: h112 p
h15.8g* Apr 28] fair on Flat, stays 1½m: 20/1, won maiden at Huntingdon (by 7 lengths
from Tynecastle Park) on hurdling debut: open to improvement. *Denis Quinn*

SHININSTAR (IRE) 8 b.g. Westerner – Shiny Button (Bob's Return) [2016/17 h–
h95: h15.8s h16.7s h16.7d h15.7g Apr 21] no form in points: maiden hurdler, no form in
2016/17: tried in hood. *John Groucott*

SHINOOKI (IRE) 10 br.g. Blueprint (IRE) – Rapid Response (IRE) (Be My Native c–
(USA) [2016/17 c–, h111: h23.3s h23.4g² h23.4s* h25.5s h23.3s Apr 1] fair handicap h108
hurdler: won at Fakenham in January: winning chaser: stays 25f: acts on heavy going: has
worn headgear, including in 2016/17: often races prominently. *Alex Hales*

SHINTORI (FR) 5 b.g. Enrique – La Masai (FR) (Bernebeau (FR)) [2016/17 h104: c94
h16.8g c17.5g³ c15.7d² c16s⁵ c16s³ c17gꟳ Apr 15] lengthy, workmanlike gelding: maiden h62
hurdler: modest form over fences: raced around 2m: acts on soft going: in hood last 4 starts:
wears tongue tie: usually races close up, often travels strongly. *Richard Woollacott*

SHIROCCO CLOUD 5 br.m. Shirocco (GER) – Cloud Hill (Danehill (USA)) [2016/17 h–
h16.2dᵖᵘ h16.2m⁵ h20.1gᵖᵘ Oct 8] half-sister to modest hurdler Mista Rossa (3¼m winner,
by Red Ransom): no form on Flat/over hurdles: tried in tongue tie. *Andrew Hamilton*

SHIROCCODEE 4 b.f. Shirocco (GER) – La Marianne (Supreme Leader) [2016/17 b16v b–
b16.8g⁴ Apr 26] fourth foal: half-sister to fairly useful hurdler/useful chaser Ballykan
(2½m-3¼m winner, by Presenting) and a winning pointer by King's Theatre: dam (c103/
h108), bumper/21f hurdle winner (stayed 3m), half-sister to useful hurdler/chaser (stayed
3m) Banjaxed Girl and useful chaser (stays 25f) Gorsky Island: little show in bumpers.
Brian Barr

SHIVERMETIMBERS (IRE) 5 br.g. Black Sam Bellamy (IRE) – Kimouna (FR) b96
(Round Sovereign (FR)) [2016/17 b16v* Mar 12] £24,000 3-y-o: half-brother to useful
French hurdler Prospert Le Grand (2¼m winner, by Enrique) and fair hurdler The Banastoir
(2½m winner, by Presenting): dam, French 17f hurdle winner, half-sister to useful French
hurdler/chaser (17f-21f winner) Samson and to dam of useful hurdler/very smart chaser
(stayed 25f) Ma Filleule: 9/1, won bumper at Warwick (by 2¾ lengths from Another
Stowaway) on debut, responding well. *Venetia Williams*

SHOOFLY MILLY (IRE) 8 b.m. Milan – Jacksister (IRE) (Flemensfirth (USA)) h107
[2016/17 h100: h23.1s h25.5s⁴ h25.5v³ h23.1d² h23.1s* h26.4g⁴ Apr 23] fair handicap
hurdler: won at Exeter in March: stays 3¼m: acts on heavy going: wears headgear: often in
tongue tie nowadays: front runner: quirky. *Jeremy Scott*

SHOREACRES (IRE) 14 b.g. Turtle Island (IRE) – Call Me Dara (IRE) (Arapahos c–
(FR) [2016/17 c116, h–: c22.5dᵖᵘ May 5] lengthy, angular gelding: winning hurdler: h–
useful chaser at best: stays 3½m: acts on heavy going. *Mrs Gillian Jones*

SHORT FLIGHT (IRE) 5 b.g. Trans Island – Surricate (FR) (True Brave (USA)) h70
[2016/17 h16.6d h18.6s h21.4vᵖᵘ h16.4v³ Mar 18] third in Irish maiden point on debut:
poor form over hurdles: should stay at least 2½m. *Julia Brooke*

SHOTAVODKA (IRE) 11 ch.g. Alderbrook – Another Vodka (IRE) (Moscow Society c120
(USA) [2016/17 c137, h126: c29.2g⁵ c23.6g h19.9v³ c24.2s c26s³ c26g⁶ Mar 25] stocky h121
gelding: fairly useful handicap hurdler/chaser: stays 3¼m: acts on heavy going: wears
headgear: tried in tongue tie: usually races nearer last than first. *David Pipe*

SHOTGUN PADDY (IRE) 10 b.g. Brian Boru – Awesome Miracle (IRE) (Supreme c136 x
Leader) [2016/17 c146x, h–: c27.3s c29.2s³ c32.6s³ c31.8gᵖᵘ Apr 22] well-made gelding: h–
winning hurdler: useful handicap chaser: third in Classic Chase at Warwick (10½ lengths
behind One For Arthur) in January and Betfred Eider (Handicap Chase) at Newcastle (5½
lengths behind Mysteree) in February: stays 29f: acts on heavy going: tried in headgear:
often let down by jumping. *Emma Lavelle*

SHOTOFWINE 8 b.g. Grape Tree Road – Icy Gunner (Gunner B) [2016/17 h–: h16.2s⁶ h91
h23.1s* h23.8gꟳ h24g³ Apr 8] modest handicap hurdler: won at Market Rasen in December:
stays 3m: acts on soft going: in tongue tie last 3 starts: races prominently. *Nicky Richards*

SHOULD I STAY (FR) 9 b.g. Muhtathir – Dusky Royale (FR) (Double Bed (FR)) [2016/17 c–, h85: h23.1d h24.1s h19.3s⁶ c23.9spu c19.2sur Mar 8] good-topped gelding: fair hurdler at best, no form in 2016/17 after another lengthy absence: maiden chaser: stays 23f: acts on heavy going: has worn headgear, including in 2016/17. *Alan Brown* — **c–** **h–**

SHOUTING HILL (IRE) 7 br.g. Golan (IRE) – Brook Queen (IRE) (Lafontaine (USA)) [2016/17 h69: h23m h23m c24d⁴ c21gpu h23.3g h23.1g³ h20.5g³ Oct 31] winning Irish pointer: poor maiden hurdler: looked reluctant both starts in chases: stays 23f: usually in headgear: tried in tongue tie. *Johnny Farrelly* — **c62 §** **h74**

SHOW'S OVER (IRE) 6 b.g. Curtain Time (IRE) – Sailors Run (IRE) (Roselier (FR)) [2016/17 h82: h20.3vpu c23.8g⁴ c19.4m⁶ c22.6g* c23.4mF c19.7g² c16g* c18.9s⁴ Nov 23] maiden hurdler: modest handicap chaser: won novice events at Stratford in August and Ludlow in November: stays 23f: acts on good to soft going: in visor last 5 starts: wears tongue tie nowadays. *Tim Vaughan* — **c88** **h–**

SHREWD TACTICS (IRE) 6 ch.g. Broadway Flyer (USA) – Taking My Time (IRE) (High Roller (IRE)) [2016/17 b89p: h19.9s h18.8d h19.5s h15.7d⁴ c18.2g² Mar 30] rangy gelding: won Irish maiden hurdle on debut: poor form over hurdles: 9/2, second in novice handicap at Taunton (tongue tied, ¾ length behind Innocent Girl) on chasing debut: should stay beyond 2¼m: front runner/races prominently: open to more improvement as a chaser. *Evan Williams* — **c106 p** **h82**

SHRUBLAND 4 b.g. High Chaparral (IRE) – Ratukidul (FR) (Danehill (USA)) [2016/17 h16s⁴ h16.6g h15.8s³ h15.7s⁴ h19.1v⁶ h16dpu Mar 11] sturdy gelding: modest maiden on Flat, stays 2m: modest form over hurdles: wears headgear. *Alexandra Dunn* — **h96**

SHUIL ROYALE (IRE) 12 b.g. King's Theatre (IRE) – Shuil Na Lee (IRE) (Phardante (FR)) [2016/17 c135, h125: c25.8g* c26.1gpu c23m² c25g* c24.2spu c23.8m Apr 2] tall, useful-looking gelding: winning hurdler: smart handicap chaser: won at Newton Abbot (by 8 lengths from Indian Castle) in May and Aintree (veterans event, by 5 lengths from Your Busy) in October: stays 3¼m: acts on good to firm and heavy going: wears headgear/tongue tie: often races towards rear. *Harry Fry* — **c145** **h–**

SHUIL TEACHT ANIAR (IRE) 8 b.g. Allegoric (USA) – Shuil A Maidin (IRE) (Good Thyne (USA)) [2016/17 c20s c18d c25.4s c24spu c24.2s⁵ c21.3s⁵ c23.8g⁴ Apr 9] off mark in maiden points at fifth attempt: modest maiden chaser: tried in tongue tie: dead. *Maurice Phelan, Ireland* — **c85**

SHUTTHEFRONTDOOR (IRE) 10 b.g. Accordion – Hurricane Girl (IRE) (Strong Gale) [2016/17 c116, h141: h24.7d c26g c20.8spu c29d Apr 17] lengthy, useful-looking gelding: smart hurdler/chaser at best, well below that in 2016/17: stays 35f: acts on heavy going: has worn cheekpieces, including in 2016/17: wears tongue tie. *Jonjo O'Neill* — **c115** **h–**

SHWAIMAN (IRE) 7 br.g. Authorized (IRE) – Blue Lightning (Machiavellian (USA)) [2016/17 h124: h21g h21g Mar 18] sturdy gelding: fairly useful hurdler at best, mid-field in handicaps in 2016/17 after long absence: should stay beyond 2½m: acts on heavy going. *Michael Banks* — **h110**

SHY (CZE) 5 br.m. Tiger Cafe (JPN) – Solinka (CZE) (Monarch) [2016/17 b74: b16.2d⁴ h16.2m h16.2d h16.2s⁴ h16.2v⁶ h16.8d h19.4g⁶ c24.5s c21.3d³ c19.3d⁴ c17.4g⁵ Apr 24] poor form in bumpers: modest form over hurdles: poor form over fences: should stay beyond 2m: wears tongue tie. *George Charlton* — **c83** **h89** **b68**

SHY JOHN 11 b.g. Kier Park (IRE) – Shy Lizzie (Buzzards Bay) [2016/17 c114, h–: c24g⁵ c24.5v⁵ Feb 2] workmanlike gelding: once-raced hurdler: fair chaser at best, not same force nowadays: stays 3¼m: acts on heavy going, probably on good to firm. *Jennifer Mason* — **c64** **h–**

SI C'ETAIT VRAI (FR) 11 b.g. Robin des Champs (FR) – Bleu Perle (FR) (Pistolet Bleu (IRE)) [2016/17 c105, h–: c20.1dur c20d⁶ Nov 29] big, useful-looking gelding: winning hurdler: useful chaser at best, lightly raced and well below that since 2013/14: stays 21f: in cheekpieces last 3 starts: often in tongue tie nowadays. *Neil Mulholland* — **c–** **h–**

SIDBURY FAIR 6 br.m. Fair Mix (IRE) – Manque Pas d'Air (FR) (Kadalko (FR)) [2016/17 b66: h15.8s h21s Feb 10] poor form in bumpers/over hurdles. *Victor Dartnall* — **h67**

SIDBURY HILL 9 ch.g. Midnight Legend – Flora Macdonald (Alflora (IRE)) [2016/17 c109, h–: h21d² h18.5g May 25] workmanlike gelding: fair handicap hurdler: maiden chaser: stays 2½m: acts on heavy going: tried in cheekpieces. *Seamus Mullins* — **c–** **h107**

SIDE OF THE ROAD (IRE) 5 b.m. Beneficial – Roses And Wine (IRE) (Roselier (FR)) [2016/17 b15.6g b16v⁵ h16.2g Apr 28] €10,000 3-y-o: sixth foal: sister to fairly useful hurdler/winning pointer Monbeg Rose (2m winner), stays 2½m: dam winning pointer: down the field in bumpers/mares novice hurdle. *Donald Whillans* — **h–** **b–**

SIDEWAYS (IRE) 6 b.g. Gamut (IRE) – Daras Mayo (IRE) (Kasmayo) [2016/17 h20.6g⁴ h23.1v⁴ h24.3v² Jan 17] £45,000 5-y-o: first foal: dam, ran 3 times in points, half-sister to useful hurdlers/chasers Shoreacres (stays 3½m) and Call Me Vic (stays 3¼m): off mark in Irish maiden points at second attempt: modest form in novice/maiden hurdles. *David Dennis* — **h98**

SIDSTEEL (IRE) 6 b.g. Craigsteel – Clare Hogan (IRE) (Moscow Society (USA)) [2016/17 b–: b15.8d b14d h16.7d h15.8s h23.8s⁵ h19.6g⁴ Apr 22] well held in bumpers: poor form over hurdles. *John Groucott* — **h74** **b–**

SID'S TOPPER (FR) 7 b.g. Anabaa Blue – Last Sicyos (FR) (Sicyos (USA)) [2016/17 b16m h18.7mᵖᵘ Aug 24] no form in bumpers/maiden hurdle: tried in tongue tie. *Martin Keighley* — **h–** **b–**

SIENA BOUQUET (FR) 6 b.m. Saint des Saints (FR) – Sheyrinca (FR) (Sheyrann) [2016/17 b80p: h19d⁴ h16.7d² May 26] fourth in bumper: fair form over hurdles: better effort when second in mares maiden at Bangor: in tongue tie last 2 starts: has joined Johnny Farrelly. *Stuart Crawford, Ireland* — **h106**

SIERRA OSCAR (IRE) 5 b.g. Robin des Champs (FR) – John's Eliza (IRE) (Dr Massini (IRE)) [2016/17 b93: b15.8s⁴ h19.9s h15.8v h15.7d h20.7g* Apr 17] better effort in bumpers when third on debut in 2015/16: modest form over hurdles: won conditionals handicap at Huntingdon in April: open to further improvement. *Dan Skelton* — **h98 p** **b54**

SIGNED REQUEST (IRE) 10 b.g. Fantastic Quest (IRE) – Magic Sign (IRE) (The Parson) [2016/17 h–: c20d⁵ c20d⁶ c23.6g⁶ h19.9g⁴ c21.7d* Nov 24] workmanlike gelding: fair handicap hurdler: similar form over fences: won handicap at Towcester in November: stays 2¾m: acts on good to soft going: in tongue tie last 3 starts. *Henry Oliver* — **c106** **h97**

SIGURD (GER) 5 ch.g. Sholokhov (IRE) – Sky News (GER) (Highest Honor (FR)) [2016/17 h19.9g h16.5g⁴ h15.7g³ h16d h20.6m* Apr 9] brother to fairly useful French hurdler Skies In Blue (17f-2½m winner): modest maiden on Flat: fairly useful form over hurdles: won handicap at Market Rasen in April: stays 21f: acts on good to firm going. *Jonjo O'Neill* — **h115**

SILENT ACCOUNT (IRE) 6 b.g. Jimble (FR) – Mary Money (Vettori (IRE)) [2016/17 b15.8g h19.1g⁴ h15.7v⁶ h16.3mᵖᵘ h20vᵖᵘ Oct 17] third on completed start in Irish maiden points: no form in bumper/over hurdles. *Des Donovan, Ireland* — **h–** **b–**

SILENT DOCTOR (IRE) 7 br.g. Dr Massini (IRE) – Wild Noble (IRE) (Aristocracy) [2016/17 b–: h20gᵖᵘ h23g h18.7g Jul 28] runner-up completed start in points: no form in bumpers/maiden hurdles: tried in tongue tie. *Roy Brotherton* — **h–**

SILENT ENCORE (IRE) 5 ch.g. Curtain Time (IRE) – What Can I Say (IRE) (Mister Lord (USA)) [2016/17 b–: b13.7d h21sᵖᵘ h16.6d h16.6g⁵ h20.3g² h21.6g⁴ Apr 11] workmanlike gelding: no form in bumpers: fair form over hurdles: stays 2½m: in tongue tie last 5 starts: often races towards rear. *Ben Case* — **h104** **b–**

SILENT MAN (IRE) 7 br.g. Morozov (USA) – Outdoor Heather (IRE) (Presenting) [2016/17 h16.2g h20gᵖᵘ h16.2g⁶ h15.8v h16.6s h21.7sᵖᵘ h22g h15.8g⁶ Apr 28] good-topped gelding: third on completed start in Irish maiden points: poor maiden hurdler: should be suited by further than 2m. *Tom Weston* — **h72**

SILENT STEPS (IRE) 6 b.m. Milan – Taking Silk (IRE) (Mister Lord (USA)) [2016/17 h19.1d⁴ h20.7s⁵ h19.1s⁶ h24.5m² h24.3d² Apr 21] €16,000 3-y-o, £70,000 5-y-o: fourth foal: dam (h87) 2¾m hurdle winner: won completed start in Irish mares maiden points: fair form over hurdles: stays 3m: acts on good to firm and good to soft going. *Nicky Henderson* — **h105**

SILENT WARRIOR 5 br.g. Yeats (IRE) – Zariyka (IRE) (Kalanisi (IRE)) [2016/17 b–: h15.8s h16g⁴ h15.8d h21.3g h19.6g⁵ Apr 22] poor form over hurdles: tried in cheekpieces. *Charlie Longsdon* — **h75**

SILK HALL (UAE) 12 b.g. Halling (USA) – Velour (Mtoto) [2016/17 c113, h126: c15.9mᵖᵘ c17.4g³ c21.2m h20.1dᵖᵘ Jun 19] sturdy gelding: useful hurdler/fair maiden chaser at best, no form in 2016/17: stays 21f: acts on good to firm and heavy going: wears headgear: has worn tongue tie. *Dianne Sayer* — **c–** **h–**

SILK OR SCARLET (IRE) 5 ch.g. Mahler – Spirit of Clanagh (IRE) (Zagreb (USA)) [2016/17 b16.2g³ Apr 25] €25,000 3-y-o: first foal: dam unraced half-sister to useful hurdler/smart chaser (stays 35f) Double Seven: 7/1, third in bumper at Hexham (12 lengths behind Schiaparannie) on debut. *Tim Fitzgerald* — **b82**

bet365 Hurdle (West Yorkshire), Wetherby—a first win at graded level for Silsol,
who holds off Native River (noseband) and Lil Rockerfeller (right)

SILSOL (GER) 8 b.g. Soldier Hollow – Silveria (GER) (Groom Dancer (USA)) [2016/17 **c–** c140, h156: h25.4d h24.1g* Oct 29] sturdy gelding: very smart hurdler: won West **h156** Yorkshire Hurdle at Wetherby (by 2¾ lengths from Native River) in October (not seen out again): useful chaser: stays 3¼m: acts on heavy going: wears headgear/tongue tie. *Paul Nicholls*

SILVA SAMOURAI 8 gr.g. Proclamation (IRE) – Ladykirk (Slip Anchor) [2016/17 b–: **h–** h20.1g[pu] h15.6g[5] h16.4d h16.4s[pu] Dec 8] modest maiden on Flat, stays 1¼m: no form over hurdles: in hood last 4 starts. *Susan Corbett*

SILVER BULLION 6 br.g. Three Valleys (USA) – Silver Yen (USA) (Silver Hawk **b92** (USA)) [2016/17 b16s* b16v Jan 30] fourth foal: half-brother to 1½m-16.4f winner On Terms (by Aptitude): dam US 9f winner: fair form when won bumper at Ayr on debut in December: well beaten next time. *Pauline Robson*

SILVER COMMANDER 10 gr.g. Silver Patriarch (IRE) – New Dawn (Rakaposhi **c128 §** King) [2016/17 c24.2m c23g[2] Dec 30] rangy gelding: maiden hurdler: fairly useful **h–** handicap chaser: stays 25f: acts on good to soft going: tried in cheekpieces: wears tongue tie: weak finisher and not one to rely on. *Philip Hobbs*

SILVER DRAGON 9 gr.g. Silver Patriarch (IRE) – Gotogeton (Le Moss) [2016/17 c85§, **c– §** h92x: h27s* May 3] modest handicap hurdler: won at Sedgefield in May: maiden chaser: **h96 §** stays 4m: acts on heavy going: usually wears headgear: tried in tongue tie: temperamental. *Mike Sowersby*

SILVER EAGLE (IRE) 9 gr.g. Presenting – Lady Lincon (IRE) (Great Palm (USA)) **c– §** [2016/17 c101§, h–: c23.6g[F] h23.6m[4] h23.1s Nov 20] sturdy gelding: useful hurdler at **h95 §** best: maiden chaser: should stay further than 3m: acts on soft going: in headgear last 5 starts: usually wears tongue tie: has become thoroughly ungenuine. *Kim Bailey*

SILVER GENT (IRE) 9 gr.g. Milan – All's Rosey (IRE) (Roselier (FR)) [2016/17 c–, h–: **c–** c19.2d c20d[pu] h20.2s[3] Jul 27] winning pointer: fair hurdler: no form in chases: stays 2¾m: **h97** acts on soft going: tried in hood/tongue tie. *Donald McCain*

SILVERGROVE 9 b.g. Old Vic – Classic Gale (USA) (Classic Cliche (IRE)) [2016/17 **c97** c140, h–: c25g c25.5d c24d[6] Jan 14] workmanlike gelding: maiden hurdler: useful **h–** handicap chaser, well below best in 2016/17: stays 27f: acts on heavy going: wears tongue tie: usually leads. *Ben Pauling*

SILVER HOLLOW 5 gr.g. Beat Hollow – Onemix (Fair Mix (IRE)) [2016/17 b16.8d⁶ **b–**
Mar 21] well beaten in bumper. *Ben Pauling*

SILVERHOW (IRE) 6 br.g. Yeats (IRE) – Monte Solaro (IRE) (Key of Luck (USA)) **h121**
[2016/17 b99p: b16.3g³ h16s⁵ h21s h15.5d h16s* h19.9s² h16.8g* h19.8g⁶ Apr 29] good- **b99**
topped gelding: placed in bumpers: fairly useful handicap hurdler: won at Sandown
(amateur) in March and Cheltenham (conditionals/amateur) in April: stays 2½m: acts on
soft going: joined Colin Tizzard. *Nicky Henderson*

SILVER KAYF 5 gr.g. Kayf Tara – Silver Spinner (Silver Patriarch (IRE)) [2016/17 b93p: **b100**
b15.7d² b15.7d b16.3g³ Mar 25] well-made gelding: fairly useful form in bumpers: third in
Goffs UK Spring Sales Bumper at Newbury (4½ lengths behind Bullionaire) in March.
Kim Bailey

SILVER MAN 10 gr.g. Silver Patriarch (IRE) – Another Mans Cause (FR) (Highest Honor **c136**
(FR)) [2016/17 c136: h23d⁵ c20g⁴ h23g³ c25.5d² c25.5g³ c25g³ c33.4sᵖᵘ Mar 18] lengthy **h115**
gelding: fairly useful form over hurdles: useful handicap chaser: third at Warwick (length
behind Kilfinichen Bay) in September: stays 3¼m: acts on good to firm and good to soft
going: wears headgear: front runner/races prominently. *Jo Hughes*

SILVER SEA 4 b.g. Sholokhov (IRE) – Sword Roche (GER) (Laroche (GER)) [2016/17 **h–**
h16.2vᶠ h16.3sᶠ Mar 3] fairly useful on Flat, stays 1½m: well beaten when fell both starts
over hurdles. *Seamus Mullins*

SILVER SHUFFLE (IRE) 10 ch.g. Big Shuffle (USA) – Silvetta (Lando (GER)) **c– §**
[2016/17 c–§, h97§: h16g⁴ h22.1m² h24.7d* h25.4d⁶ h22.1d³ h19.9g⁶ h19.7d h24.1m Apr **h92 §**
13] modest handicap hurdler: won at Aintree (conditional) in June: maiden chaser: stays
25f: acts on good to firm and heavy going: has worn headgear: wears tongue tie: usually
races nearer last than first: unreliable. *Dianne Sayer*

SILVER STREAK (IRE) 4 gr.g. Dark Angel (IRE) – Happy Talk (IRE) (Hamas (IRE)) **h117**
[2016/17 h17.2d⁴ h16.2d³ h16g² h16.5g* h15.6g* h15.7mᵘ Apr 2] rather leggy gelding:
half-brother to fair hurdler Mica Mika (2m winner, by Needwood Blade): dam half-sister
to useful hurdler (stayed 3m) Sivota: fair maiden on Flat, stays 7.5f: fairly useful form over
hurdles: much improved when won handicaps at Taunton in December and Musselburgh in
March: left Ann Duffield after third start: raced around 2m: acts on good to soft going.
Evan Williams

SILVER TASSIE (IRE) 9 b.g. Shantou (USA) – Silver Castor (IRE) (Indian Ridge) **c130**
[2016/17 c135, h90: c24.3s⁵ c24g⁶ c24.2s⁶ c25.2sᵘʳ c24.3v* c26.2s³ c23.8gᵖᵘ Apr 26] **h–**
winning hurdler: useful handicap chaser: won at Ayr (by 6 lengths from Courtown Oscar)
in March: stays 25f: acts on good to firm and heavy going: tried in hood: often races
towards rear. *Micky Hammond*

SILVER TICKET (IRE) 6 gr.g. Tikkanen (USA) – Windmill View (IRE) (Glacial Storm **h69**
(USA)) [2016/17 h–, b–: h19.1d h19.1g³ h17.7v⁵ h20.7sᵖᵘ h17.7g Mar 31] sturdy gelding:
poor maiden hurdler on balance. *Laura Mongan*

SILVERTON 10 gr.m. Silver Patriarch (IRE) – Gretton (Terimon) [2016/17 c–, h–: h21.4s **c–**
c20.1s c21.5sᵖᵘ h20.6v⁴ c20.1vᵖᵘ Mar 28] maiden hurdler: fairly useful chaser at best, no **h–**
form in 2016/17: stays 23f: acts on heavy going: tried in cheekpieces. *Lucy Normile*

SILVER TRIX (IRE) 7 gr.m. Mahler – Sika Trix (IRE) (Try Prospect (USA)) [2016/17 **c–**
b–: h20.2m h16.2s⁶ h17.2g h19.9g⁶ h20.9d c16.4m⁵ Apr 19] no form in varied events: has **h–**
worn tongue tie. *George Bewley*

SILVINIACO CONTI (FR) 11 ch.g. Dom Alco (FR) – Gazelle Lulu (FR) (Altayan) **c160**
[2016/17 c169, h148: c24g² c24.1v⁴ c24g³ c25.3s⁴ c25g⁶ Apr 6] useful-looking gelding: **h–**
winning chaser: top-class chaser in his prime: won 7 Grade 1 events, including Bowl
Chase at Aintree, Betfair Chase at Haydock and King George VI Chase at Kempton, all on
2 occasions: third in King George VI Chase on third start but largely well below best in
2016/17: stayed 25f: acted on heavy going: wore headgear: in tongue tie last 2 starts: front
runner/raced prominently: has been retired. *Paul Nicholls*

SIMARTHUR 10 gr.g. Erhaab (USA) – Dusty Too (Terimon) [2016/17 c–x, h99§: h23.9d **c– x**
Jun 29] winning Irish pointer: fair hurdler at best, never a threat in handicap only outing in **h77 §**
2016/17: maiden chaser: stays 25f: acts on soft and good to firm going: wears headgear:
front runner/races prominently: often let down by temperament/jumping. *Lucinda Russell*

SIMENON (IRE) 10 b.g. Marju (IRE) – Epistoliere (IRE) (Alzao (USA)) [2016/17 h20g* **h144**
h24d* h24.4g⁴ h16d⁵ Nov 20] small gelding: useful hurdler: won minor events at Cork in
July (by 1¾ lengths from Mckinley) and August: stays 3m: acts on heavy going.
W. P. Mullins, Ireland

SIMMPLY SAM 10 b.m. Nomadic Way (USA) – Priceless Sam (Silly Prices) [2016/17 **c–** c–, h83: h21.2d² h16.4s³ h25.3d h19v* h19.9s h19.7d⁴ h20.5v⁶ Mar 10] poor handicap **h82** hurdler: won at Ayr in January: well beaten only outing over fences: stays 21f: acts on heavy going: in cheekpieces last 3 starts. *Marjorie Fife*

SIMONSIG 11 gr.g. Fair Mix (IRE) – Dusty Too (Terimon) [2016/17 c164, h151: c16d³ **c–** h21.4s c15.9sᶠ Nov 13] sturdy, lengthy gelding: high-class hurdler at best, won Neptune **h–** Investment Management Novices' Hurdle (Baring Bingham) at Cheltenham in 2011/12: also high-class chaser, last of 3 wins as novice in 2012/13 in Arkle Chase at Cheltenham: fell fatally there in November: stayed 21f: acted on heavy going. *Nicky Henderson*

SIMPLE AS THAT (IRE) 6 b.g. Stowaway – Suzy Q (IRE) (King's Ride) [2016/17 **h99** h16g⁴ h16.7s⁶ Nov 26] €85,000 3-y-o: seventh foal: dam, showed a little ability in bumpers, half-sister to useful hurdler/chaser (stayed 21f) The Railway Man: modest form over hurdles: better effort when fifth (promoted) in novice at Chepstow in October: wears tongue tie. *Jonjo O'Neill*

SIMPLY BLESSED (IRE) 6 ch.m. Flemensfirth (USA) – Simply Joyful (Idiot's **h70 §** Delight) [2016/17 b16d² b16m⁴ b16g⁴ b15.8m b20s b20d h21.9v h27s⁵ h25vᵖᵘ Feb 27] **b81** €10,000 3-y-o: dam: sister to bumper winner The Unsub and half-sister to fairly useful hurdler/chaser Hoopy (2½m-25f winner, by Presenting): dam, placed in points, half-sister to useful hurdler/chaser (stayed 3¾m) Papo Kharisma: modest form in bumpers: poor form over hurdles: in headgear last 2 starts: often races prominently: temperamental. *Peter Bowen*

SIMPLY NED (IRE) 10 ch.g. Fruits of Love (USA) – Bishops Lass (IRE) (Marju (IRE)) **c154** [2016/17 c157, h–: c17.1m² c15.9s² c17d³ c15.9g c15.5g Apr 22] tall, rather sparely-made **h–** gelding: winning hurdler: smart chaser: placed in handicap at Kelso (neck behind Theflyingportrait) in October, Shloer Chase at Cheltenham (9 lengths behind Fox Norton) in November and Paddy Power Cashcard Chase at Leopardstown (15 lengths behind Douvan) in December: unproven beyond 17f: acts on good to firm and heavy going. *Nicky Richards*

SIMPLY WINGS (IRE) 13 b.g. Winged Love (IRE) – Simply Deep (IRE) (Simply Great **c125** (FR)) [2016/17 c129, h–: c20.9v² c20.2s³ Mar 10] strong gelding: winning hurdler: fairly **h–** useful chaser: stays 3m: acts on heavy going: in cheekpieces last 3 starts: often races prominently/travels strongly. *Kerry Lee*

SINAKAR (IRE) 6 br.g. Manduro (GER) – Siniyya (IRE) (Grand Lodge (USA)) [2016/17 **h114** h105p: h19.9s* h23.3g² h23m⁵ Aug 17] fair form over hurdles: won conditionals seller at Uttoxeter in June, only outing for Conor Dore: stays 3m: in tongue tie last 2 starts. *Kerry Lee*

SINAMAS (IRE) 4 b.f. Dylan Thomas (IRE) – Sinamay (USA) (Saint Ballado (CAN)) **h–** [2016/17 h16.7vᵖᵘ Nov 9] sister to fairly useful hurdler Our Thomas and half-sister to useful hurdler Deepsand (by Footstepsinthesand), both 2m winners: no form in Flat maidens/juvenile hurdle. *Donald McCain*

SINBAD THE SAILOR 12 b.g. Cape Cross (IRE) – Sinead (USA) (Irish River (FR)) **h110** [2016/17 h107: h25g⁴ h24g⁴ h26g⁶ Sep 20] compact gelding: fair handicap hurdler: won at Huntingdon in May: stays 25f: acts on good to firm and good to soft going: has worn headgear: wears tongue tie: often races towards rear. *George Baker*

SINDARIN 4 b.g. Sulamani (USA) – Aunt Rita (IRE) (Grand Lodge (USA)) [2016/17 **b–** b16.4g Mar 24] tailed off in bumper. *Jim Goldie*

SINGAPORE SLING 4 b.g. Paco Boy (IRE) – Buena Notte (IRE) (Halling (USA)) **h–** [2016/17 h16sᵖᵘ Dec 8] compact gelding: fair form in 1m maidens on Flat: pulled up in juvenile on hurdling debut. *James Fanshawe*

SINGININTHEVALLEYS 8 b.m. Kayf Tara – Con's Nurse (IRE) (Crowning Honors **h78** (CAN)) [2016/17 h15.7d h20vᵖᵘ Dec 21] winning pointer: poor form over hurdles: in headgear last 3 starts. *James Evans*

SINGLEFARMPAYMENT 7 b.g. Milan – Crevamoy (IRE) (Shardari) [2016/17 h125: **c149** c23g³ c23.8d² c25.3g* c20.8sᵇᵈ c25g² Mar 14] good-topped gelding: fairly useful hurdler: **h–** smart form over fences: won novice at Cheltenham (by 2½ lengths from Arpege d'Alene) in December: second in Ultima Handicap Chase at same course (short head behind Un Temps Pour Tout) in March: stays 25f: acts on heavy going: usually wears hood: usually races nearer last than first. *Tom George*

Shawbrook Handicap Chase, Ascot—
a fine weight-carrying performance by Sire de Grugy; Quite By Chance (stripes) takes second

SINOUR (IRE) 7 b.g. Observatory (USA) – Siniyya (IRE) (Grand Lodge (USA)) [2016/17 h21.6m h16.8m[6] h16.3g[5] h19.1g[3] h15.8d[4] h19.9d[4] h16d[3] h15.5g[4] h20v Dec 12] maiden on Flat and in points: poor maiden hurdler: stays 19f: acts on good to soft going: wears hood/tongue tie. *Robert Stephens* **h79**

SIOUX CHIEFTAIN (IRE) 7 b.g. Mount Nelson – Lady Gin (USA) (Saint Ballado (CAN)) [2016/17 h116p: h16.3g[5] Apr 1] fairly useful winner on first of 2 starts over hurdles, well held in handicap on return year later. *Dr Richard Newland* **h–**

SIRABAD (FR) 7 b.g. Astarabad (USA) – Maille Sissi (FR) (Dernier Empereur (USA)) [2016/17 c128, h–: c15.7d* c16.4g[2] c16s[F] Mar 11] useful-looking gelding: winning hurdler: useful handicap chaser: won novice event at Wincanton (by 9 lengths from Red Devil Star) in November: best around 2m: acted on heavy going: often wore hood/tongue tie prior to 2016/17: dead. *Paul Nicholls* **c133 h–**

SIR ANTONY BROWNE 5 ch.g. Black Sam Bellamy (IRE) – Shayaza (Generous (IRE)) [2016/17 b106: h15.3v* h19.1s[2] h16.3g* h20.5d[3] Apr 21] good-topped gelding: bumper winner: useful form over hurdles: won novices at Wincanton in February and Newbury in March: best effort when third in similar event at Ayr (9½ lengths behind Give Me A Copper) final start: stays 2½m. *Alan King* **h134**

SIR DYLAN 8 b.g. Dylan Thomas (IRE) – Monteleone (IRE) (Montjeu (IRE)) [2016/17 h93: h15.3m* h15.3m* h18.7m* h17.7g* h15.8g h16.3m h16.3g[4] h16.3g[F] h19.1d[pu] Sep 4] fair handicap hurdler: won at Wincanton, Stratford and Fontwell, all in May: stays 2½m: acts on good to firm going: wears hood: often races towards rear: quirky. *Polly Gundry* **h104**

SIRE DE GRUGY (FR) 11 ch.g. My Risk (FR) – Hirlish (FR) (Passing Sale (FR)) [2016/17 c167, h–: c19.9g c16.9d* c15.5d[2] c16g[ur] Dec 27] rangy gelding: winning hurdler: still a top-class chaser: won Shawbrook Handicap Chase at Ascot (by 1½ lengths from Quite By Chance) in November: second in Tingle Creek Chase at Sandown (length behind Un de Sceaux) fortnight later: best around 2m: acts on good to firm and heavy going. *Gary Moore* **c165 h–**

SIRE DU BERLAIS (FR) 5 b.g. Poliglote – Royale Athenia (FR) (Garde Royale) [2016/17 h16.9s[3] h16.9s* h16s[3] h20.5d Apr 29] fourth foal: half-brother to fairly useful French hurdler Hermine du Berlais (17f winner, by Saint des Saints): dam (h145), French hurdler (2m-2½m winner), sister to smart hurdler/useful staying chaser Royal Rosa: useful form over hurdles: won 4-y-o event at Compiegne in May: third in listed novice at Punchestown (7¼ lengths behind Mick Jazz) in February: left N. Bertran de Balanda after second start: should stay further than 2m. *Gordon Elliott, Ireland* **h131**

SIR EGBERT 4 b.g. Kayf Tara – Little Miss Flora (Alflora (IRE)) [2016/17 b16s[3] b16.8s Feb 12] first foal: dam once-raced daughter of fairly useful chaser (stayed 3m) Mistletoe: fair form in bumpers: better effort when third in maiden at Warwick in January. *Tom Lacey* **b90**

SIR

SIR HUBERT 7 b.g. Multiplex – Lacounsel (FR) (Leading Counsel (USA)) [2016/17 h82: **h91**
h17.7d³ h19.1d h15.9s² h15.9v² h15.9v⁶ h15.9s⁴ h17.7m³ Apr 17] sturdy gelding: modest
maiden hurdler: should stay 2½m: acts on heavy going. *Richard Rowe*

SIRIUS STAR 8 b.g. Beat All (USA) – Miss Sirius (Royal Vulcan) [2016/17 h91: c21.4g* **c101**
c19.2g⁵ c23.9d² c21.4g c23.4m³ c24.2gᵖᵘ c19.3d c23.9d³ Apr 27] workmanlike gelding: **h–**
maiden hurdler: fair handicap chaser: won novice event at Market Rasen in May: stays 3m:
acts on soft and good to firm going: tried in hood: often races in rear. *Brian Rothwell*

SIR IVAN 7 b.g. Midnight Legend – Tisho (Sir Harry Lewis (USA)) [2016/17 h138: h20g **c136**
c20.2dᵖᵘ c22.4dᶠ c23d⁴ c23g³ c25.2dᶠ Mar 26] angular gelding: useful handicap hurdler: **h126**
similar form over fences: third in novice handicap at Taunton in March: stays 3m: acts on
heavy going: tried in hood: wears tongue tie: usually leads. *Harry Fry*

SIR LUKE ARNO 6 b.g. Lucarno (USA) – Never Lost (Golden Snake (USA)) [2016/17 **h–**
h15.8sᵖᵘ h15.7vᵖᵘ h17d Apr 5] good-topped gelding: no form in bumpers/over hurdles.
Christopher Kellett

SIR MANGAN (IRE) 9 b.g. Darsi (FR)   Lady Pep (IRE) (Cajetano (USA)) [2016/17 c–, **c–**
h134: h20d* Apr 16] sturdy gelding: useful handicap hurdler: won at Ffos Las (by neck **h132**
from Count Meribel) in April after 17-month absence: winning chaser: stays 27f: acts on
heavy going: has worn cheekpieces. *Dan Skelton*

SIR NORMAN 4 b.g. Kheleyf (USA) – Burza (Bold Edge) [2016/17 b13.7m Oct 2] well **b–**
beaten in junior bumper. *John Weymes*

SIR NOTE (FR) 7 gr.g. Victory Note (USA) – Niangara (FR) (Baby Turk) [2016/17 **c138**
c108p, h87: c17.2d* c15.8d³ c15.9m* c20.5g* c20.5g² c19.9g* Apr 17] rather leggy **h–**
gelding: winning hurdler: useful handicap chaser: won at Market Rasen in May, Leicester
in December, Kempton in February and Huntingdon (by 1½ lengths from Mercers Court)
in April: stays 2½m: acts on soft and good to firm going: has worn hood/tongue tie: sound-
jumping front runner. *James Eustace*

SIRO DEMUR (FR) 11 ch.g. Murmure (FR) – Jourenuit (FR) (Chamberlin (FR)) **c–**
[2016/17 c82, h–: c22.7sᵖᵘ Feb 28] sturdy gelding: maiden hurdler: fair chaser at best, **h–**
pulled up in hunter (tongue tied) only outing under Rules in 2016/17: stays 2½m: acts on
heavy going. *Philip Rowley*

SIR OLLAR (IRE) 8 ch.g. Publisher (USA) – Ollar Lady (IRE) (Avocat) [2016/17 **c92**
c25.3g⁶ c23gᵖᵘ May 27] won 3 times in points: modest form when sixth at Cheltenham on
completed start in hunter chases. *Martin Weston*

SIROP DE MENTHE (FR) 7 ch.g. Discover d'Auteuil (FR) – Jolie Menthe (FR) **h124**
(Bateau Rouge) [2016/17 h127: h21.9s* h23.4s⁵ h22.8s h19.8vᵖᵘ h16.3g⁶ h16.8g³ Apr 11]
angular gelding: fairly useful handicap hurdler: won at Ffos Las in November: lost form
after: stays 2¾m: acts on good to firm and heavy going: tried in headgear: often races
towards rear. *Susan Gardner*

SIRPERTAN 6 b.g. Sir Percy – Tanwir (Unfuwain (USA)) [2016/17 h98: h16g² h16.7g⁵ **h80**
h17.2gᵖᵘ Jun 1] maiden hurdler: raced around 2m: acted on good to firm and heavy going:
dead. *Marjorie Fife*

SIR PITT 10 b.g. Tiger Hill (IRE) – Rebecca Sharp (Machiavellian (USA)) [2016/17 **c– x**
c105x, h–: h19.9gᵖᵘ Jun 26] good-topped gelding: maiden hurdler/chaser: stays 2½m: **h–**
acts on heavy going: tried in cheekpieces/tongue tie: let down by jumping over fences.
Mark Brisbourne

SIR SCORPION (IRE) 8 b.g. Scorpion (IRE) – Lady Goldilocks (IRE) (Mister Lord **h134**
(USA)) [2016/17 h16d h16s² h20g* h16dᵇᵈ h16gᵖᵘ Jan 22] useful handicap hurdler: won at
Naas in November: stays 2½m: acts on heavy going. *Thomas Mullins, Ireland*

SIR TOBY (FR) 6 ch.g. Linngari (IRE) – Woodcut (SAF) (Fort Wood (USA)) [2016/17 **h117**
h16m² h16.7g* h17.7d² h16.7g⁶ Sep 24] fairly useful on Flat, stays 11.5f: fairly useful form
over hurdles: won novice at Market Rasen in July: tried in cheekpieces. *Dr Richard Newland*

SIR TOMMY 8 ch.g. Sir Harry Lewis (USA) – Rose of Overbury (Overbury (IRE)) **h–**
[2016/17 h16g Apr 23] poor form in bumpers: tailed off in novice on hurdling debut: wears
tongue tie. *Maurice Barnes*

SIRUH DU LAC (FR) 4 b.g. Turgeon (USA) – Margerie (FR) (Le Balafre (FR)) **h109**
[2016/17 h16.8s³ h16.3d² h16.8s⁴ Jan 28] tall gelding: has scope: fourth foal: half-brother
to fair French hurdler Txamantxoia (2m winner, by Sinndar): dam (c124/h114) French
hurdler/chaser (17f-2½m winner): fair form over hurdles: best effort when third in juvenile
at Exeter. *Nick Williams*

SIR VALENTINO (FR) 8 b.g. Early March – Valentine (FR) (Double Bed (FR)) **c159**
[2016/17 c141, h129: c19.2g* h20d⁴ c21.4g c17.5m* c15.5d⁵ c16g² c15.9g³ c16d⁶ Apr 25] **h130**
strong gelding: useful handicap hurdler: very smart chaser: won handicap at Market Rasen
(by 8 lengths from Turn Over Sivola) in May and Haldon Gold Cup at Exeter (by short
head from Garde La Victoire) in November: second in Desert Orchid Chase at Kempton
(½ length behind Special Tiara) in December and third in Queen Mother Champion Chase
at Cheltenham (6 lengths behind Special Tiara) in March: stays 2½m: acts on good to firm
and heavy going: wears tongue tie: often travels strongly. *Tom George*

SIR VINSKI (IRE) 8 ch.g. Vinnie Roe (IRE) – Mill Emerald (Old Vic) [2016/17 h121: **c–**
c20gᵖᵘ Nov 7] rather leggy gelding: fairly useful hurdler: pulled up in novice on chasing **h–**
debut: stayed 3m: best form on heavy going: tried in blinkers: often raced prominently:
dead. *Nicky Richards*

SIR WATTY (IRE) 13 b.g. Presenting – Bobby's Jet (IRE) (Bob's Return (IRE)) [2016/17 **c–**
c21.6dᵖᵘ May 4] won 3 times in points: pulled up both starts in hunter chases. *R. Gibson*

SIR WILL (IRE) 6 b.g. Yeats (IRE) – Tinopasa (FR) (No Pass No Sale) [2016/17 h89p, **h114**
b85: h15.8s³ h19.5d⁴ h25.5v⁴ h23.9s⁴ Feb 5] bumper winner: best form over hurdles: best
effort at 2m: acts on soft going: tried in cheekpieces/tongue tie. *Kerry Lee*

SISANIA (IRE) 4 gr.f. Mastercraftsman (IRE) – Avril Rose (IRE) (Xaar) [2016/17 **h89**
h17.7g* h15.8g³ h17.7d h15.9v Jan 2] fair maiden on Flat, stays 13f: modest form over
hurdles: won juvenile maiden at Fontwell in September. *Gary Moore*

SISSINGHURST (IRE) 7 b.g. Kalanisi (IRE) – Sissinghurst Storm (IRE) (Good Thyne **c–**
(USA)) [2016/17 b16d⁴ h16v³ h20.5d⁶ h23.9gᵖᵘ h16sᵖᵘ c19.9gᵖᵘ Apr 3] €37,000 3-y-o, **h95**
£12,000 6-y-o: workmanlike gelding: second foal: half-brother to a winning pointer by Old **b80**
Vic: dam (c85/h82) temperamental 3m/3¼m hurdle/chase winner: fell in maiden point on
debut: modest form in bumper/over hurdles: pulled up in novice handicap on chasing
debut: bred to be suited by 2½m+: acts on heavy going: tried in cheekpieces. *Nick Gifford*

SISTERBROOKE (IRE) 8 ch.m. Trans Island – Cool Merenda (IRE) (Glacial Storm **c–**
(USA)) [2016/17 c–, h–: c25.5d c22.5gᶠ May 14] sturdy, plain mare: no form in varied **h–**
events. *John Panvert*

SISTER SIBYL (IRE) 6 br.m. King's Theatre (IRE) – Rose of The Erne (IRE) (Presenting) **h111**
[2016/17 b94: h15.7d* h15.3s² h15.5g* h20.5g Mar 25] lengthy mare: bumper winner: fair
form over hurdles: won mares maiden at Towcester in November and mares novice at
Leicester in January. *Hughie Morrison*

SITTING BACK (IRE) 13 b.g. Flying Legend (USA) – Double Pearl (IRE) (Doubletour **c65**
(USA)) [2016/17 c56, h–: c21.1g⁶ c19.4m c20g c19.7gᵖᵘ c19.2dᵘʳ c21.1v⁵ c19.2g⁶ Mar 31] **h–**
maiden hurdler: poor handicap chaser nowadays: stays 2¾m: acts on heavy going: tried in
cheekpieces. *Diana Grissell*

SIX A SIDE (IRE) 9 b.g. St Jovite (USA) – Persian Leader (IRE) (Supreme Leader) **c102**
[2016/17 c21.6d* May 4] multiple winning pointer: 2/1, also won novice hunter at Kelso
(by 11 lengths from Danehills Well) on chasing debut. *Miss E. L. Todd*

SIXTEEN LETTERS (IRE) 5 b.g. Well Chosen – Back To Loughadera (IRE) (Bob **b67**
Back (USA)) [2016/17 h16.8d⁵ Mar 21] maiden pointer: 28/1, fifth in bumper at Exeter
(20½ lengths behind Just A Sting) in March. *Richard Woollacott*

SIXTIES IDOL 4 b.f. Sixties Icon – Fading Away (Fraam) [2016/17 h15.9g⁵ h15.9m³ Apr **h82**
17] half-sister to fair hurdler Brilliant Barca (2m winner, by Imperial Dancer): modest
maiden on Flat, stays 1½m: poor form over hurdles. *Sheena West*

SIXTY SOMETHING (FR) 11 gr.g. Dom Alco (FR) – Jaunas (FR) (Lute Antique (FR)) **c–**
[2016/17 c24.1sᵖᵘ c28.5sᶠ h26sᵖᵘ Jan 26] good-topped gelding: useful hurdler/chaser at **h–**
best, no form in 2016/17 after lengthy absence: stays 29f: wears headgear: tried in tongue
tie. *Paul Webber*

SIZING AT MIDNIGHT (IRE) 5 br.g. Midnight Legend – Issaquah (IRE) (Supreme **h75**
Leader) [2016/17 h24v h20s h19gᵖᵘ Mar 30] poor form over hurdles: left M. F. Morris after
second start. *Colin Tizzard*

SIZING BRISBANE 9 b.g. Nayef (USA) – Elaine Tully (IRE) (Persian Bold) [2016/17 **c109 p**
h16g h20g² c20d⁶ Oct 30] €65,000 3-y-o: half-brother to several winners, notably Grand **h108**
National winner Rule The World (by Sulamani) and bumper winner/smart hurdler
Venalmar (2½m winner, by Kayf Tara): dam (h117), 17f-2¾m hurdle winner, also won up
to 1¾m on Flat: fair form in bumpers/over hurdles: 6/1, sixth in novice at Carlisle
(11¾ lengths behind Gurkha Brave) on chasing debut: left Henry de Bromhead after
second start: tried in tongue tie: open to improvement over fences. *Colin Tizzard*

SIZING COAL (IRE) 9 b.g. Presenting – Hollygrove Cezanne (IRE) (King's Ride)   **c133**
[2016/17 c137, h117: c30d³ c24v* c25.5dᶠ c19.5vᵖᵘ c26s² Mar 17] maiden hurdler: useful   **h–**
chaser: won minor event at Sligo in September: stays 3¾m: acts on heavy going: has worn
cheekpieces. *J. T. R. Dreaper, Ireland*

SIZING CODELCO (IRE) 8 b.g. Flemensfirth (USA) – La Zingarella (IRE)   **c157**
(Phardante (FR)) [2016/17 c143, h133: c16d³ c15.9g c20.8sᵖᵘ c21d² c26.3s⁴ c20.8g   **h–**
c25g* c24.5d* Apr 29]

Sizing Codelco was among fifteen horses who arrived from Ireland at Colin
Tizzard's West Country yard at the end of August as the result of a parting of the
ways between owners Ann and Alan Potts and trainer Henry de Bromhead. A useful
hurdler in his younger days for de Bromhead, Sizing Codelco had shown himself
just as good sometimes over fences, though he had threatened more breakthroughs
than he had made, and was even put back over hurdles at the end of his first novice
chasing campaign (when he was also tried in cheekpieces and a tongue tie). Sizing
Codelco was raced only once for Henry de Bromhead at further than seventeen
furlongs—he contested the Grand Annual over two miles at the 2016 Cheltenham
Festival where he unseated his rider at the first—but he was stepped up in trip after
running poorly over two miles at Cheltenham in November on his first start for Colin
Tizzard (when sent off favourite). That was to prove the answer for Sizing Codelco
in the end, as it was for others among the new Potts intake including the
smart Viconte du Noyer who had been placed in the Red Rum Handicap over two
miles at Aintree the previous season but was stepped up to three miles three furlongs
on his first outing for Tizzard, landing the valuable Bet Victor Handicap Chase at
Cheltenham's November meeting. Sizing Codelco's transformation took longer
and, after he was pulled up in the Caspian Caviar Gold Cup back at Cheltenham
in December, after seeming to take little interest, there was even talk that his new
trainer had recommended sending him to the sales. A switch to forcing tactics in a
graduation chase run in the fog over two miles five furlongs at Ascot in December
produced a better effort (a good second to the novice Top Notch) and he again went
with plenty of zest when fourth to Tour des Champs, stepped up much further to
three miles two furlongs, in a handicap at Cheltenham on New Year's Day. Equipped
with blinkers and a tongue tie next time in the Plate at the Cheltenham Festival,
however, he turned in a poor effort, seeming to throw in the towel.

The Tizzard stable was in splendid form for most of the season but there
was a blip in the early spring when the yard had only a single winner from over
fifty runners (it had a disappointing Cheltenham Festival by and large). There was a
marked change of fortune at the Aintree and Punchestown spring festivals, though,

Betway Handicap Chase (Listed), Aintree—Sizing Codelco storms clear from the second last,
chased home by Rightdownthemiddle, Starchitect (striped sleeves) and Potters Legend (star on cap);
Value At Risk (cheekpieces) folds tamely; Sizing Codelco continues his improved form by
following up in another valuable handicap at Punchestown

Ann & Alan Potts's "Sizing Codelco"

and Sizing Codelco himself provided a resounding answer to those who had been inclined to write him off. Ridden at Aintree for the first time by Robbie Power, who had been appointed the new number-one rider for Ann and Alan Potts after winning the Cheltenham Gold Cup on Sizing John, Sizing Codelco (without headgear or tongue strap) turned the well-contested Betway Handicap into a rout. Power pressed on a long way out and Sizing Codelco responded to his urgings to storm clear from the second last, winning by thirteen lengths and eight from Rightdownthemiddle and Starchitect. That represented a clear career-best effort from Sizing Codelco but he bettered it when conceding weight all round at Punchestown three weeks later in the valuable Palmerstown House Pat Taaffe Handicap. Sizing Codelco chased the leaders before taking over from the second last and, responding well to pressure, got the better of Forever Gold and Heron Heights, who did themselves no favours when colliding at the last, by three and a half lengths and two and three quarters. On the evidence of those two performances at Aintree and Punchestown, there are more good races to be won with Sizing Codelco who looks a likely Grand National type if his connections decide to go down that route (he is currently 40/1 in some ante-post lists for the 2018 renewal).

Sizing Codelco (IRE) (b.g. 2009)	Flemensfirth (USA) (b 1992)	Alleged (b 1974)	Hoist The Flag
			Princess Pout
		Etheldreda (ch 1985)	Diesis
			Royal Bund
	La Zingarella (IRE) (b 1998)	Phardante (b 1982)	Pharly
			Pallante
		In Memoriam (b 1988)	Buckskin
			Superdora

The useful-looking Sizing Codelco is by Flemensfirth, a veteran now but still one of jumping's top sires who has had plenty of good horses who have stayed well. Sizing Codelco is a half-brother to the high-class L'Ami Serge (by King's

Theatre) who was also stepped up in trip to really good effect, winning the Grande Course de Haies (French Champion Hurdle) over three miles one and a half furlongs shortly after the end of the British season (he also has an essay in this Annual). Sizing Codelco's dam La Zingarella, who showed fairly useful form over hurdles and fences in France at up to two and a half miles, was also represented on the racecourse in the latest season by Market Rasen winner Viens Chercher (by Milan) who showed useful form over fences at up to three miles. La Zingarella is a half-sister to The Wicketkeeper, a useful chaser who was best at around two miles, and to another fairly useful two-mile chaser in Monastrell. This is the family of the 2000 Triumph Hurdle winner Snow Drop (who has gone to success as a broodmare, foaling the Prix Alain du Breil winner Lina Drop) and the smart hurdler/chaser Don't Touch It, also a winner in valuable handicap company at the latest Punchestown Festival. Snow Drop was out of a winning half-sister to Sizing Codelco's unraced grandam In Memoriam and Don't Touch It's dam is a granddaughter of Sizing Codelco's third dam Superdora who herself was out of a half-sister to Solfen who won the forerunners of the RSA Chase and the Stayers' Hurdle on successive days at Cheltenham in 1960 (Solfen also started second favourite for the 1962 Grand National). Sizing Codelco has been tried in various headgear and a tongue tie at different times in his career but his Aintree and Punchestown performances demonstrated that he is clearly better without. The key to him seems to be to have him in front or racing prominently. He should stay further than twenty-five furlongs and acts on heavy going, though the going at Aintree was good and at Punchestown no easier than good to soft. *Colin Tizzard*

SIZING GRANITE (IRE) 9 br.g. Milan – Hazel's Tisrara (IRE) (Mandalus) [2016/17 **c157** c151+, h–: c20.4s^{pu} h16.5g^5 c15.9g^{pu} h16.5g^5 c20d* Apr 26] tall, **h127** angular gelding: fairly useful form over hurdles: very smart handicap chaser: back to best when won Guinness Handicap Chase at Punchestown (easily by 5 lengths from Viconte du Noyer) in April: stays 2½m: acts on soft going: tried in cheekpieces: often in tongue tie in 2016/17. *Colin Tizzard*

Guinness Handicap Chase, Punchestown—a rejuvenated Sizing Granite leads home a 1,2 for connections (Viconte du Noyer came late for second); the other horse in the picture is fourth-placed Peoples Park

SIZING JOHN 7 b.g. Midnight Legend – La Perrotine (FR) (Northern Crystal)   **c170**
[2016/17 c154, h144: c16d³ c17d² c20d* c24.3s* c26.3g* c24.5d* Apr 26]   **h–**

Jodami and Imperial Call completed the Irish Gold Cup/Cheltenham Gold Cup double in the same season in the 'nineties; Kicking King and War of Attrition achieved the double in the Cheltenham Gold Cup and Punchestown Gold Cup earlier this century; and Sir des Champs and Carlingford Lough completed the Irish Gold Cup/Punchestown Gold Cup double in the same season even more recently. The opportunity to win Cheltenham's blue riband of steeplechasing and Ireland's two most prestigious weight-for-age steeplechases has existed since 1998/9 when the Punchestown Gold Cup was inaugurated (the Irish Gold Cup was first run in 1986/7). Until the latest season, Sir des Champs had come closest to completing the treble, finishing second at Cheltenham in 2012/13 when he won the other two, while Carlingford Lough also made the frame (a remote fourth) in the Cheltenham Gold Cup when he completed the Irish Gold Cup/Punchestown Gold Cup double in 2015/16. Imperial Call won all three races but not in the same season.

The relatively short history of the Irish Gold Cup and the Punchestown Gold Cup means that they are inevitably overshadowed by the Cheltenham showpiece. The Irish Gold Cup at Leopardstown in February still tends to be regarded as a stepping-stone to the Cheltenham race—it is ideally placed in the calendar to serve that purpose—but it shouldn't be. Like the Punchestown Gold Cup, a race whose importance as the season's finale for the top staying chasers is still growing, the Irish Gold Cup is first and foremost a good race in its own right, one that has been won by most of the big names among the top staying chasers in Ireland over the past thirty years. All of which makes Sizing John's Irish Gold Cup/Cheltenham Gold Cup/Punchestown Gold Cup treble in the latest season one of the finest achievements by an Irish-trained chaser in recent times and one that perhaps deserved to be celebrated more than it was at the time.

Sizing John had never run over a distance as far as three miles when he lined up for the Irish Gold Cup and, at the start of the season, few would have envisaged his forging such a successful new career for himself as a staying chaser. He had been a Grade 1 winner over two miles in his novice hurdling days—in the Future Champions Novices' Hurdle at Leopardstown—when he was also placed in the Supreme Novices' at Cheltenham and the Champion Novices' at Punchestown. Those last two races were won by Douvan who was also to become Sizing John's nemesis when the pair were sent chasing the next season. Sizing John showed smart form as a novice chaser when his biggest success came in the Grade 2 Craddockstown Novices' Chase over two miles at Punchestown. But he was again in the shadow of Douvan, runner-up to him in the Racing Post Novices' Chase at Leopardstown's Christmas meeting and in the Arkle at Cheltenham, and third to him in the Ryanair Novices' Chase at the Punchestown Festival. Sizing John didn't take on Douvan at Aintree, running instead in the Manifesto Novices', in which he was stepped up to two and a half miles for the first time. He was a beaten favourite when a below-form third to the ill-fated Arzal and L'Ami Serge that day, meeting with defeat, incidentally, for the only time so far over hurdles or fences in a race won by a horse other than Douvan. Douvan has beaten Sizing John no fewer than seven times over two miles.

Sizing John started the latest season with a new trainer, having been transferred to Jessica Harrington from Henry de Bromhead who had been the main trainer for a number of years for English owners Ann and Alan Potts whose notable successes had included many with horses carrying the prefix 'Sizing', a mining term describing the process of extracting minerals by crushing (Alan Potts made his fortune from the invention of a machine that sizes rock as it is mined). Sizing Europe, winner of the 2008 AIG Europe Champion Hurdle and seven further Grade 1 races over fences (including an Arkle and a Queen Mother Champion Chase), is the best horse owned by Ann and Alan Potts. But Sizing John, a fine jumper like Sizing Europe, isn't far behind him and is still only seven. As well as changing their trainer, Ann and Alan Potts also found themselves looking for a new jockey when Jonathan Burke, a former champion conditional in Ireland who had been a professional for only a few months when signed up as their retained rider in 2014/15, decided he was going to ride as a freelance. Twenty-year-old Burke cited the fact that more of the Potts-owned horses were being trained in Britain (fifteen were moved to Colin Tizzard) as having contributed to the break-up. The season didn't go well for Burke, however, when he spent four months on the sidelines with a shoulder injury and ended the campaign with just four wins (compared to fifty-five and forty-two in the two seasons he was retained by Ann and Alan Potts). Ironically, Burke will be riding more in Britain in the next season after being appointed stable jockey to Charlie Longsdon. Sizing John, who had given Burke his first Grade 1 win when successful in the Future Champions Novices' Hurdle, was ridden by Robbie Power for the first time when he made his reappearance in the latest season. He was one of four who lined up against 8/1-on Douvan in the open Grade 1 two-mile chase (run as the Paddy Power Cashcard Chase) at Leopardstown at Christmas. Sizing John chased home Douvan, sticking to his task admirably and finishing eight lengths behind in second, but there looked a very real chance that, kept to two miles, Sizing John could spend a third season in a row chasing Douvan in vain in the big races.

When Sizing John was seen next, it was over two and a half miles in the six-runner Ladbrokes Ireland Kinloch Brae Chase at Thurles in January, again ridden by Jessica Harrington's number-one Robbie Power who had suggested running Sizing John over further. Up against two other very smart second-season chasers in Sub Lieutenant (who had been runner-up to Sizing John in that 2014 Future Champions Novices' Hurdle) and Black Hercules, Sizing John started third favourite but he confirmed himself a high-class chaser at the trip by beating them both. Sizing John jumped well as usual and stayed on to lead in the final hundred yards, after the last fence was omitted due to a stricken jockey, wearing down Sub Lieutenant (trained by Henry de Bromhead) to win by two and a half lengths, with Black Hercules twelve lengths further back in third. Jessica Harrington announced after the race that 'we're stepping into the unknown a little bit but it could be the Irish Gold Cup next … and he'll be entered in everything at Cheltenham, though you'd imagine he'll go for the Ryanair at the Festival, but we'll see.' The Irish Gold Cup hadn't had a sponsor the previous year, following the decision by Hennessy, with whom the race became synonymous, to give up their long-standing support after the 2015 running, but Stan James took over in the latest season, entering the Irish sponsorship market after being prevented from sponsoring in Britain where the company did not have 'authorised betting partner' status (Coral was another regular sponsor in Britain to extend its sponsorship in Ireland after being caught up in the same dispute).

The Irish Gold Cup is already part of a card at Leopardstown that contains four Grade 1 races (the Spring Juvenile, the Flogas Novices' Chase and the Deloitte Novices' Hurdle are the others). That attractive programme, and the major races from Leopardstown's two other Sunday meetings in late-January and February, will combine to form, from the next season, a new two-day, weekend festival, mid-way between the Christmas programmes in Britain and Ireland and the Cheltenham Festival in mid-March. The Irish Champion Hurdle will be the feature event on the Saturday, with the Arkle Chase among the supporting races, and the Sunday programme will remain largely as it is, with the Irish Gold Cup the centre-piece. It is hoped that the revamped programme will attract more British challengers for Leopardstown's Grade 1s, though the new festival will still face competition from Cheltenham's Trials meeting at the end of January, with races like the Grade 1 Scilly Isles Novices' Chase at Sandown and the variety of races at Newbury's Betfair Hurdle meeting other counter attractions.

There were two British-trained challengers in the seven-strong field for the latest Irish Gold Cup, the Jonjo O'Neill-trained pair Minella Rocco and More of That. British-based trainers initially dominated the Irish Gold Cup, winning eight of the first nine renewals, but they have saddled only two winners in the twenty-two years since then, the most recent being Neptune Collonges in 2009 (Collier Bay is the last British winner of the Irish Champion Hurdle, back in 1996). Minella Rocco unseated his jockey as early as the fifth but, after the race had been run at a muddling gallop, More of That was among five still in with a chance on the approach to the final fence where the previous season's Cheltenham Gold Cup third Don Poli (runner-up in the Lexus at Christmas on his latest appearance) was in the lead

Stan James Irish Gold Cup, Leopardstown—a step up in trip reaps dividends for Sizing John (No.7) who defeats the Gigginstown pair Empire of Dirt and Don Poli (white face) in a falsely-run race, with 2015 and 2016 winner Carlingford Lough (hoops) in fourth

from Sizing John, and being pressed also by the Troytown Handicap Chase winner Empire of Dirt and Carlingford Lough, who was attempting a third win in the race and having his first outing over fences since winning the Punchestown Gold Cup in April. More of That had yet to be asked for everything when unseating his jockey after crumpling on landing at the last, leaving the four home-trained challengers to fight it out. The driven out Sizing John, who had jumped well except for a mistake at the sixth, asserted himself on the run-in to win by three quarters of a length and the same from Empire of Dirt and Don Poli, with Carlingford Lough eventually a further three and a half lengths away in fourth. Sizing John and Don Poli were now headed for the Gold Cup, it seemed, while Empire of Dirt's connections plumped for the Ryanair (Carlingford Lough didn't have a Gold Cup entry in the latest season). Sizing John was again ridden at Leopardstown by Robbie Power who had just returned to riding after being troubled with a back injury since a fall at Gowran in January (he had missed much of the first part of the season with an eye socket injury suffered in a fall at Galway in July which had left him with double vision at times and requires him to ride in specially-adapted goggles).

Although more was going to be required from him, Sizing John looked fully entitled to have a crack at the Gold Cup, especially as the Cheltenham race looked like turning into something of a substandard renewal, with the field nothing like the one envisaged by the ante-post betting in the autumn when Thistlecrack, Vautour, reigning champion Don Cossack and 2015 winner Coneygree were the first four in the betting. Vautour died in a freak accident at home and, although he went back into training, the outstanding Don Cossack never made it back to the racecourse and had to be retired with a recurrence of the injury that he had suffered at the end of 2015/16. Coneygree's training troubles also meant that he was on the sidelines when the Gold Cup came round and the exceptional novice Thistlecrack, who became a very firm ante-post favourite after winning the King George VI Chase at Kempton, also went wrong in the run up to Cheltenham. Valseur Lido, Don Poli (who had a setback in early-March) and the much-lamented Many Clouds, who collapsed and died after beating Thistlecrack in the Cotswold Chase at Cheltenham's Trials meeting, were others whose presence would have enhanced the Gold Cup field. Of those listed in

755

the top eight in the ante-post market at the start of November, only the veteran Cue Card, runner-up to stablemate Thistlecrack in the King George, and dual runner-up Djakadam made the line-up on the day, starting at 9/2 and 3/1 favourite respectively, split by another of Cue Card's stable-companions 7/2-shot Native River whose odds had shortened significantly after wins in the Hennessy Gold Cup and the Welsh Grand National. While Native River's stamina was proven, there were still a few question marks over 7/1-shot Sizing John's ability to see out the stiffer test of three and a quarter miles in a strongly-run Gold Cup. The only other runner in the thirteen-strong field to start at shorter than 14/1 was the Lexus Chase winner Outlander who had not been seen out since Christmas. More of That and Minella Rocco (who had won the National Hunt Chase from Native River twelve months earlier) both took their chance, while the stable of ten-times champion trainer Paul Nicholls could muster only 33/1-shot Saphir du Rheu, and that of Nicky Henderson didn't have a runner at all. Lizzie Kelly and her mount Tea For Two, who had finished fourth in the King George, provided some novelty value for the media.

Tea For Two and Kelly, the first female jockey to ride in the Gold Cup since Mrs Linda Sheedy on 500/1-shot Foxbury in 1984, were the first casualties, parting company after a bad mistake at the second fence. Sizing John travelled well throughout in a race run at a slightly muddling gallop. Just five lengths covered eleven of the runners three out and the final time was only seven seconds faster than the Foxhunter forty minutes later, and corresponded to a performance only 15 lb superior to that recorded by Pacha du Polder, the winner of that race. After Cue Card had fallen in the Gold Cup for the second year running at the third last (albeit not looking so dangerous this time), Sizing John responded well when asked for his effort, when the race really began in earnest, to take over at the second last. The leader Djakadam made a mistake there, which obviously didn't help him, and the fluent Sizing John kept on well after jumping the last to win by two and three quarters lengths from the strong-finishing Minella Rocco who took second from the always prominent Native River by a short head in the last strides. The first three were all seven-year-olds who had run well in novice chases at the meeting the year before (Minella Rocco just confirming the National Hunt Chase form with Native River) and, for Sizing John, it was the third year running he had finished in the first three in a Grade 1 at the Festival. Djakadam finished half a length behind Native River to make the frame in the Gold Cup for the third time, with Saphir du Rheu and More of That completing the first six.

Sizing John's trainer Jessica Harrington had already made history two days earlier when the success of Supasundae in the Coral Cup—also in the Potts's emerald green, yellow chevrons and sleeves, red cap and ridden by Robbie Power—had made her the most successful female trainer in Cheltenham Festival history.

Timico Cheltenham Gold Cup, Cheltenham—another relative test of speed sees Sizing John come out on top from strong-finishing Minella Rocco (second right, partly hidden) and Native River (noseband); 2015 and 2016 runner-up Djakadam (pale colours) has to settle for fourth this time

Coral Punchestown Gold Cup Chase, Punchestown—Sizing John completes a unique 'Gold Cup' treble but it is much closer this time as he has to dig deep to beat Djakadam (centre) and 2015 Cheltenham Gold Cup winner Coneygree (left) in a thriller

Mrs Harrington and Power went on to land a treble at the meeting when Rock The World won the closing Grand Annual Chase, that success taking Jessica Harrington to eleven Cheltenham Festival wins. Mrs Harrington had not had a runner in the Cheltenham Gold Cup before (a race won twice by Jenny Pitman and three times—with Best Mate—by Henrietta Knight) but she had won the Queen Mother Champion Chase twice with Moscow Flyer and the Champion Hurdle more recently with Jezki, and Sizing John's victory makes her only the sixth trainer, following Bob Turnell, Fred Winter, Fred Rimell, Nicky Henderson and Paul Nicholls, to have won the Gold Cup, the Champion Chase and the Champion Hurdle. Moscow Flyer, who also won the Arkle, died at the age of twenty-two in October after an attack of colic at the Irish National Stud where he spent his final years. The winner of thirteen Grade 1s, and trained throughout his career by Jessica Harrington, Moscow Flyer was a champion in a vintage period for two-mile chasers which also included Azertyuiop and Well Chief, from whom he won both the Tingle Creek Chase and the Queen Mother Champion Chase in the 2004/5 season, at the end of which the trio were rated 184+, 182 and 182 respectively. Moscow Flyer's tremendous career, by the way, included an unbeaten sequence of nineteen in races completed over fences, before he suffered a short-head defeat, after recovering from a monumental blunder two out, when 4/1-on for the Champion Chase at Punchestown at the end of that 2004/5 campaign. For Sizing John's jockey Robbie Power, the latest season put him firmly back in the public eye ten years after he won the Grand National on Silver Birch—'I was only twenty-five then and I thought I was going to win everything in racing. When you're thirty-five you appreciate it a bit more,' he said after the Gold Cup. Power was unveiled as first jockey to Ann and Alan Potts at the end of March and was in the limelight again at the Grand National meeting, where he was leading jockey (Finian's Oscar, Fox Norton and Pingshou gave him three more Grade 1 wins for his new employers).

The Coral Punchestown Gold Cup in the final week of the season attracted a field of six which featured two winners of the Cheltenham Gold Cup, with Coneygree returning to action five months after his last run in the Betfair Chase at Haydock, to take on the odds-on Sizing John. Djakadam was there again, after his creditable effort at Cheltenham, trying to go one better at Punchestown than in the two previous seasons when he had chased home first Don Cossack and then Carlingford Lough. Outlander, Champagne West and 100/1-shot Flemenstar, a shadow of his former self, were the three others in the line-up. The leading trio produced a thrilling spectacle as they fought it out over the last two fences where, possibly crucially, Sizing John was the only one to avoid a mistake at that point. Coneygree made the running, showing all his usual zest, but was headed by Djakadam when he clouted the second last, with

Sizing John right in contention too. Djakadam looked as though he might hold on until hitting the top of the final fence and landing awkwardly. He still led from Sizing John halfway up the run in but Sizing John found plenty under pressure to get up for a short-head victory in the shadow of the post, with Coneygree, who could find no extra in the last fifty yards, beaten a length and a half into third. The first three were miles clear of the others, Outlander having been pulled up when behind at the tenth. On his fifth outing since Christmas, Sizing John needed a gritty performance to get him home, after he also lost a front shoe during the race, with Robbie Power saying afterwards that he had never been completely happy at any stage. 'He felt a bit flat, but it's the end of a long season and he put his head down and battled,' he said. The Punchestown Gold Cup was the eighth Grade 1 of the season for Power (almost doubling his career total), with seven of the victories coming in the golden period he enjoyed from February onwards.

Sizing John (b.g. 2010)	Midnight Legend (b 1991)	Night Shift (b 1980)	Northern Dancer / Ciboulette
		Myth (b 1983)	Troy / Hay Reef
	La Perrotine (FR) (b 2000)	Northern Crystal (b 1988)	Crystal Glitters / North Cliff
		Haratiyna (b 1986)	Top Ville / Halwah

The useful-looking Sizing John is the second British-bred winner of the Cheltenham Gold Cup in three years, following Coneygree. British-breds Cue Card and Thistlecrack have won the last two editions of the King George VI Chase and with another British-bred, Special Tiara, winning the latest Queen Mother Champion Chase and yet another, Rule The World, winning the 2016 Grand National, British jumping-breds are enjoying a rare spell in the big-race limelight. With the exception of Cue Card, who is by King's Theatre, the horses mentioned above are not the product of sending the best British mares to Irish stallions either. Coneygree is by Karinga Bay, Thistlecrack and Special Tiara are both by Kayf Tara, the most successful British jumps stallion of the modern era, and Rule The World is by Sulamani. Sizing John's sire Midnight Legend, who died in 2016 at the age of twenty-five, was already at the veteran stage when Sizing John gave him his first Grade 1 winner (in the Future Champions Novices' Hurdle). Midnight Legend got to the top as a stallion by an unorthodox route, being a late starter at stud having been raced until he was eight, but he made his mark with the likes of Sparky May, Midnight Chase and Seeyouatmidnight before Sizing John came along. Midnight Legend raced for Mrs H. J. Clarke, the wife of Lord Gyllene's owner Stan Clarke who bought him privately for jumping after four seasons racing for Luca Cumani on the Flat, in which sphere he showed useful form, winning three times in listed company at up to a mile and three quarters (he also contested the St Leger). Midnight Legend won the Top Novices' Hurdle at Aintree and the Champion Novices' Hurdle at Punchestown in his first season with David Nicholson whose suggestion that Midnight Legend should be gelded had been turned down.

Stan (later Sir Stanley) Clarke had a long-term plan to stand Midnight Legend as a National Hunt stallion and, in fact, in his last two seasons with David Nicholson he combined stud duties with racing, serving twenty-five mares as a seven-year-old and twenty-four as an eight-year-old (he was reportedly covering a mare on the Sunday afternoon just twenty-four hours after running a fine race to finish third as an eight-year-old behind Istabraq and French Holly in the Aintree Hurdle on his only start beyond two miles). Midnight Legend was based at Conkwell Grange Stud at first but wasn't particularly popular with breeders and was eventually sold on to stand at Pitchall Farm in Warwickshire before some of his early runners began to show promise. Patronage improved steadily and he served a three-figure book the year that Sizing John's dam La Perrotine visited him. La Perrotine was a bumper/fair hurdle winner at up to twenty-one furlongs, her four wins—the bumper at Hexham and three novice hurdles at Sedgefield—all in races restricted to mares. La Perrotine was trained by Howard Johnson, through whom Sizing John's breeder Bryan Mayoh bought her privately 'in the bar at Doncaster Sales.' 'She had gone wrong on her tendons and, although I didn't know much about the sire [Northern Crystal was

Ann & Alan Potts Partnership's "Sizing John"

a Group 3-winning French miler], she stood 16.2 hands and was a good-looking mare, I'm glad it worked out,' says Mayoh. Sizing John is La Perrotine's third foal and a half-brother to the fairly useful but ill-fated Scholastica (by Old Vic) who was a dual winner in mares bumpers and won twice over hurdles in mares events, the second one a handicap at Ascot over two miles five and a half furlongs; she was also placed in a listed mares novice hurdle at Haydock. Sizing John's grandam Haratiyna, a winning miler, was an Aga Khan-bred half-sister to the Italian Derby winner Houmayoun and went on to breed winners on the Flat and over jumps, her winners in the latter sphere including the Irish twenty-one-furlong chase winner Harithabad and the fairly useful hurdler/chaser for Paul Nicholls, Harapour, who stayed two and three quarter miles. One of Haratiyna's daughters is the dam of the smart French hurdler Le Chateau, who came seventh in the Grande Course de Haies won by Un Temps Pour Tout, while another daughter is the dam of the useful Irish three-mile hurdler Acapulco, who had been a smart performer when trained on the Flat by Aidan O'Brien. The reliable Sizing John, who often travels strongly in his races, stays three and a quarter miles and acts on heavy going (though he doesn't need the mud). It bears repeating that his sound jumping is one of his major assets. Sizing John's connections, having seen him land one historic treble, reportedly have their sights on another—the 'Classic Triple Crown'—in the next season. The three races involved, the Betfair Chase, the King George VI Chase and the Cheltenham Gold Cup carry a million-pound bonus put up by Jockey Club Racecourses for any horse who wins all three (Kauto Star, in 2006/7, remains the only horse to have completed this treble). *Mrs J. Harrington, Ireland*

SIZING PLATINUM (IRE) 9 b.g. Definite Article – Quest of Passion (FR) (Saumarez) **c142**
[2016/17 c142, h120: c18g⁴ c22.5g c15.9g² c20.4s c16.3d⁴ c16dᶠ c16.3g c16d Apr 27] **h–**
workmanlike gelding: fairly useful hurdler: useful handicap chaser: second at Cheltenham
(11 lengths behind Fox Norton) in October: left Henry de Bromhead after second start:
stays 2¼m: acts on soft and good to firm going: tried in tongue tie: front runner/races
prominently. *Colin Tizzard*

SIZING SAHARA 9 gr.g. Shirocco (GER) – Aristocratique (Cadeaux Genereux) **c–**
[2016/17 c90, h–: c21.2gᵖᵘ c19.2dᵘʳ c20.2gᵖᵘ h19.2v⁴ h21.4d³ Feb 18] angular gelding: **h78**
poor handicap chaser nowadays: maiden chaser, no form in 2016/17: stays 19f: acts on
heavy going. *Paul Henderson*

SIZING SOLUTION (IRE) 9 b.g. King's Theatre (IRE) – Toulon Rouge (IRE) (Toulon) **c122**
[2016/17 c16m³ h16g c17g³ c21.5v³ c21.1gᵖᵘ c20g* Apr 17] angular gelding: fair handicap **h104**
hurdler: fairly useful chaser: won hunter at Cork in April: stays 21f: acts on soft and good
to firm going: has worn cheekpieces: wears tongue tie. *J. T. R. Dreaper, Ireland*

SIZING TENNESSEE (IRE) 9 ch.g. Robin des Champs (FR) – Jolivia (FR) (Dernier **c133**
Empereur (USA)) [2016/17 h138: c20.4g² c20.8d³ c20.5g⁴ c20.4gᵖᵘ Mar 14] strong **h–**
gelding: useful hurdler: useful form over fences: placed in novices at Cheltenham in
November and December (11½ lengths behind Whisper): stays 2½m: acts on heavy going:
tried in blinkers: usually races prominently. *Colin Tizzard*

SKADI 5 b.m. Kheleyf (USA) – Just Joey (Averti (IRE)) [2016/17 b16.7g May 14] first foal: **b–**
dam 5f winner: tailed off in mares bumper: modest form over 6f on Flat. *Brendan Powell*

SKEAPING 4 b.g. Excellent Art – Gale Green (Galileo (IRE)) [2016/17 h16g h16s h16d² **h99**
h16s Dec 26] fairly useful on Flat, stays 1½m: modest form over hurdles: tried in tongue
tie. *Gordon Elliott, Ireland*

SKELETON BOB (IRE) 5 b.g. Getaway (GER) – Bay Rebel (IRE) (Oscar (IRE)) **b82**
[2016/17 ab16g² b16v Dec 31] modest form in bumpers: dead. *Alan King*

SKEWIFF 5 b.m. Doyen (IRE) – Skew (Niniski (USA)) [2016/17 b15.8d* b17g Apr 6] **b82**
£15,000 3-y-o: lengthy, angular mare: sister to useful hurdler/smart chaser Valdez (2m-17f
winner) and closely related/half-sister to 3 winners on Flat: dam unraced: modest form in
bumpers: won mares event at Huntingdon in February. *Evan Williams*

SKIDDAW POPPY 6 b.m. Byron – Skiddaw Wolf (Wolfhound (USA)) [2016/17 b–: **h–**
h17.2gᵖᵘ Jul 18] no form in bumpers/maiden hurdle. *Maurice Barnes*

SKINT 11 b.g. King's Theatre (IRE) – No More Money (Alflora (IRE)) [2016/17 c88§, **c103 §**
h104§: h23.9g h20g h16.8m⁶ h15.9mᵖᵘ c21.7g* c18.2gᵖᵘ Apr 6] well-made gelding: fair **h87 §**
handicap hurdler, below best in 2016/17: fair handicap chaser: won at Taunton in March:
left Ali Stronge after fourth start: stays 2¾m: acts on soft and good to firm going: usually
wears headgear: has worn tongue tie: temperamental. *Michael Scudamore*

SKIP 4 ch.g. Peintre Celebre (USA) – Fluffy (Efisio) [2016/17 ab16g⁴ Mar 6] third foal: **b83**
closely related to 7f-1¼m winner Warfare (by Soviet Star): dam lightly raced on Flat: 9/4,
fourth in bumper at Lingfield (4¼ lengths behind The Big Bite) on debut. *Kevin Ryan*

SKIPTHECUDDLES (IRE) 6 b.g. Westerner – Autumn Sky (IRE) (Roselier (FR)) **h128**
[2016/17 b81: b15.8g* b16.4s⁴ h19.7s² h21.3s* h21.1g h24d Apr 27] good-topped gelding: **b86**
fair form in bumpers: won maiden at Towcester in May: fairly useful form over hurdles:
won novice at Wetherby in February: should stay 3m. *Graeme McPherson*

SKIPTHESCALES (IRE) 5 b.g. Winged Love (IRE) – Waterland Gale (IRE) (Fourstars **h92**
Allstar (USA)) [2016/17 h19.3d⁵ h17d² h19.3g³ Apr 15] €5,000 3-y-o: sixth foal: brother
to useful hurdler/chaser Universal Soldier (2½m-33f winner) and a winning pointer: dam
unraced: placed in Irish points: modest form when placed in novice hurdles at Carlisle: will
be suited by 3m. *Martin Todhunter*

SKYFIRE 10 ch.g. Storm Cat (USA) – Sunray Superstar (Nashwan (USA)) [2016/17 h75: **h–**
h16.8gᵖᵘ May 10] maiden hurdler: raced around 2m: tried in cheekpieces. *Nick Kent*

SKY FULL OF STARS (IRE) 7 b.g. Mahler – Gold Flo (IRE) (Fourstars Allstar (USA)) **c97**
[2016/17 h75: c17.1s³ c16.4sᵖᵘ c20.5sᶠ c15.5s² h16v⁶ c16.4s³ h16v* c15.7s* c16.3gᵘʳ **h99**
c17.1d⁴ c15.6g Apr 25] workmanlike gelding: modest handicap hurdler: won at Ayr in
February: modest handicap chaser: won novice event at Catterick in March: stays 3m: acts
on heavy going: wears headgear. *James Ewart*

SKY KHAN 8 b.g. Cape Cross (IRE) – Starlit Sky (Galileo (IRE)) [2016/17 h138: h20d⁵ **h127** h25.4m⁶ h21.3g⁶ h20.6s⁵ h19.9s⁵ h20g h20.2g² Apr 28] good-topped gelding: fairly useful handicap hurdler: stays 3m: acts on good to firm and heavy going: wears headgear: in tongue tie last 3 starts. *Lucinda Russell*

SKYLANDER (IRE) 8 b.g. Flemensfirth (USA) – Cat Burglar (IRE) (Robellino (USA)) **c111** [2016/17 c128, h115: c19.9g c20g⁶ h23g³ h23m* h27g² h23.3g⁶ c24.2g⁵ c24.2m⁵ h20.5d⁵ **h115** Nov 14] lengthy gelding: fairly useful handicap hurdler: won at Worcester in August: similar form over fences, below best in 2016/17: stays 27f: acts on good to firm and heavy going: wears headgear/tongue tie. *David Pipe*

SKYLARK LADY (IRE) 4 ch.f. Tamayuz – Allegrissimo (IRE) (Redback) [2016/17 **h92** h16.2d* h16.7d⁶ h16.7g³ h16.7d⁴ h15.8g⁵ h16g⁴ h16s² h15.3sᵖᵘ Mar 1] fair on Flat, stays 2m: won juvenile at Hexham in June: left Michael Wigham after seventh start: raced around 2m: acts on soft going: tried in headgear: front runner/races prominently. *Nikki Evans*

SKY LINO (FR) 5 b.g. Martaline – Sky Dance (FR) (Sky Lawyer (FR)) [2016/17 h103: **c89** h16.8g⁴ c20gᶠ Sep 6] fair maiden hurdler: chance of a place when fell 3 out in novice **h97** handicap won by Fact of The Matter at Worcester (in hood) on chasing debut: raced mainly around 2m: acted on heavy going: usually raced freely: dead. *Nick Williams*

SKY OF STARS (IRE) 4 b.g. Frozen Power (IRE) – So So Lucky (IRE) (Danehill **h–** (USA)) [2016/17 h16sᵖᵘ h15.8d h19g h15.8s³ Mar 23] rather leggy gelding: fair maiden on Flat, stays 1½m: no form over hurdles: has joined Olly Murphy. *Anabel K. Murphy*

SKYWARDS REWARD (IRE) 6 b.g. Dubawi (IRE) – Russian Society (Darshaan) **h88** [2016/17 b16.4s b16s⁶ h21.3s⁵ h19.3v³ h16d⁶ Mar 31] poor form in bumpers: modest form **b72** over hurdles: third in novice at Carlisle in March. *Micky Hammond*

SLANELOUGH (IRE) 5 b.g. Westerner – Tango Lady (IRE) (King's Theatre (IRE)) **h110 p** [2016/17 h16.2v h15.6g h16.2v² h19.4g² h18.1d² Apr 10] £45,000 4-y-o: third foal: half-brother to fairly useful hurdler/useful chaser Potters Point (2m winner, by Robin des Champs), stays 2½m: dam unraced sister to fairly useful 3m hurdle winner Tango Knight: runner-up in Irish maiden point on debut: fair form over hurdles: will stay at least 2¾m: acts on heavy going: in hood last 4 starts: usually races freely: remains with potential. *Rose Dobbin*

SLAYING THE DRAGON (IRE) 4 ch.g. Notnowcato – Empress Charlotte (Holy **b–** Roman Emperor (IRE)) [2016/17 b16s Feb 4] tailed off in bumper: modest form on Flat. *Nigel Tinkler*

SLEEP EASY 5 b.g. Rip Van Winkle (IRE) – Strictly Lambada (Red Ransom (USA)) **h130** [2016/17 h122p: h17.7d³ h16.6g³ h19g⁶ h21.4s* h21g⁶ Mar 18] compact gelding: useful form over hurdles: won handicap at Wincanton (by 5 lengths from Town Parks) in March: stays 21f: acts on soft going: in cheekpieces last 3 starts. *Neil Mulholland*

SLEEP IN FIRST (FR) 11 b.g. Sleeping Car (FR) – First Union (FR) (Shafoun (FR)) **c102** [2016/17 c109, h111: h17m h17.2g⁵ h16.2d* h17.2d³ c16gᵖᵘ c17.3d⁴ Aug 29] fair handicap **h105** hurdler: won at Hexham in June: fair handicap chaser: best form around 2m: acts on soft and good to firm going: has worn cheekpieces/tongue tie: usually races close up: signs of temperament. *James Ewart*

SLEEPING CITY (FR) 10 b.g. Sleeping Car (FR) – City Prospect (FR) (Diamond **h–** Prospect (USA)) [2016/17 h106: h16.8g May 4] good-topped gelding: fair handicap hurdler, well held only outing in 2016/17: raced around 2m: acts on good to soft and good to firm going: in cheekpieces last 4 starts: wears tongue tie nowadays: often races towards rear/travels strongly. *Victor Dartnall*

SLEEPY HAVEN (IRE) 7 b.g. Indian Haven – High Society Girl (IRE) (Key of Luck **c– x** (USA)) [2016/17 c119x, h120: h19.5g h15.7vᵘʳ h16d³ h15.5d* h16.2v² h19.6d h16.4v⁴ **h125** h16.3d⁴ h16.2s² h16.2g⁴ Apr 26] sturdy gelding: fairly useful handicap hurdler: won at Leicester in December: maiden chaser: unproven beyond 17f: acts on heavy going: tried in cheekpieces: has worn tongue tie: often let down by jumping over fences. *Jennie Candlish*

SLIDECHECK (IRE) 10 b.g. Dushyantor (USA) – Stormey Tune (IRE) (Glacial Storm **c96** (USA)) [2016/17 c99, h94: c20.3d⁴ c16.3s⁴ c16.3s³ c19.2d³ c21.1v* h19.9s Feb 6] winning **h–** hurdler: modest handicap chaser: won at Fontwell in January: stays 23f: acts on good to firm and heavy going: wears headgear/tongue tie. *Alexandra Dunn*

SLIDING DOORS (IRE) 4 b.g. Ask – Reseda (GER) (Lavirco (GER)) [2016/17 b15.6g² **b92** b17.7s³ b15.7m⁴ Apr 13] fifth foal: dam (c92/h100), 2m-19f hurdle winner, half-sister to dual Velka Pardubicka winner Registana: fair form when placed in bumpers. *Ian Williams*

SLIEVEARDAGH (IRE) 13 b.g. King's Theatre (IRE) – Gayephar (Phardante (FR)) **c86**
[2016/17 h21.6g⁶ c23.8dᵖᵘ h21.6m⁵ c22.6g² c21g⁶ c20.5g h20d h20gᵖᵘ Sep 6] sturdy **h74**
gelding: useful hurdler/chaser at one time, nothing like same force in 2016/17: left Sally
Randell after second start: stayed 23f: acted on good to firm and heavy going: wore tongue
tie: dead. *Fergal O'Brien*

SLIPPER SATIN (IRE) 7 b.m. Excellent Art – In The Ribbons (In The Wings) [2016/17 **h–**
h101: h22.1g⁶ Aug 27] fair hurdler at best, last in handicap sole start in 2016/17: stays
2¾m: acts on heavy going: tried in cheekpieces: wears tongue tie nowadays: front runner.
Simon West

SLOWFOOT (GER) 9 b.h. Hernando (FR) – Simply Red (GER) (Dashing Blade) **h–**
[2016/17 h17.7d Apr 29] useful form when won both starts over hurdles in 2014/15: most
disappointing since, mainly on Flat. *Jim Best*

SLOWMOTION (FR) 5 b.w. Soldier of Fortune (IRE) – Second Emotion (FR) **c138**
(Medaaly) [2016/17 h137: h18d⁵ h16d² c16sꟳ h20d² c16s* c16s* c22.5v² c20d* c21d² **h137**
Apr 28] useful hurdler: second in Fishery Lane Hurdle at Naas (4 lengths behind Missy
Tata) in November and EBF Mares' Hurdle at Leopardstown (17 lengths behind Let's
Dance) in December: similar form over fences: won mares maiden at Naas in January,
listed mares event there (by 4 lengths from Solita) in February and Grade 3 mares event at
Fairyhouse (by 2¾ lengths from Keppols Queen) in April: best effort when 1¼ lengths
second to Definite Ruby in mares handicap at Punchestown final start: stays 23f: acts on
heavy going: often races towards rear. *Joseph Patrick O'Brien, Ireland*

SMAD PLACE (FR) 10 gr.g. Smadoun (FR) – Bienna Star (FR) (Village Star (FR)) **c161**
[2016/17 c166, h–: c19.9g⁴ c26g c25.3s³ c26.3g c25g³ Apr 6] sturdy gelding: has had **h–**
breathing operation: winning hurdler: top-class chaser: respectable efforts at best in
2016/17, including on first 2 starts when fourth in Old Roan Chase at Aintree and seventh
in Hennessy Gold Cup at Newbury: stays 3¼m: acts on good to firm and heavy going: front
runner/races prominently. *Alan King*

SMADYNIUM (FR) 9 gr.g. Smadoun (FR) – Sea Music (FR) (Bering) [2016/17 c–§, **c130**
h111§: h16.2d* h17.2g h23.3d³ c20.3gᵘʳ h20.1s* c21s* c22d² c19.5s* c19.5v h20d c22dᵖᵘ **h98**
Apr 18] rather leggy gelding: modest hurdler: won sellers at Hexham very early in season
and in September: useful handicap chaser: won at Fairyhouse (lady riders event) in
November and Clonmel in December: left Julia Brooke after fifth start: stays 3m: acts on
heavy going: wears headgear: tried in tongue tie: front runner/races prominently. *John
Joseph Hanlon, Ireland*

SMAOINEAMH ALAINN (IRE) 5 b.m. Shantou (USA) – Dathuil (IRE) (Royal **h109 p**
Academy (USA)) [2016/17 b16g³ b16g⁵ b16g⁶ b16g⁴ b16d² h16v* Mar 23] half-sister to **b83**
fair 2½m hurdle winner Conclave (by Key of Luck) and several winners on Flat: dam
useful 1m winner: modest bumper performer: 3/1, won mares novice at Chepstow (in hood,
by 8 lengths from Multigifted with plenty in hand) on hurdling debut: left D. Buckley after
fifth start: should improve. *Robert Walford*

SMART BOY (IRE) 6 b.g. Mahler – Supreme Style (IRE) (Supreme Leader) [2016/17 **h76**
h89, b–: h20gꟳ h16s h22s³ h24.1s Dec 27] rather unfurnished gelding: poor maiden
hurdler: runner-up in point shortly after end of season: bred to be suited by 2¾m+.
Tim Easterby

SMART CATCH (IRE) 11 b.g. Pivotal – Zafaraniya (IRE) (Doyoun) [2016/17 c98x, **c86 x**
h101: h19.5dᵖᵘ h16.7d⁶ h20.5d² h16s⁶ c22.7s³ Mar 10] lengthy, angular gelding: modest **h94 §**
handicap hurdler/chaser nowadays: stays 25f: acts on soft going: in tongue tie last 3 starts:
usually races towards rear: has raced lazily, and often let down by jumping over fences.
Tony Carroll

SMART MONEY (IRE) 10 br.g. Spadoun (FR) – Victoria Day (Reference Point) **c–**
[2016/17 h16.7g Apr 29] rather leggy gelding: fair handicap hurdler at best, no show only **h–**
outing in 2016/17 after long absence/change of yard: maiden chaser: best around 2m: acts
on heavy going: tried in hood. *John Groucott*

SMART MOVER (IRE) 4 b.f. Fast Company (IRE) – Alltherightmoves (IRE) (Namid) **h–**
[2016/17 h15.8d Jan 25] fair but temperamental on Flat, stays 1m: never a danger in fillies
juvenile on hurdling debut. *Nikki Evans*

SMART RULER (IRE) 11 ch.g. Viking Ruler (AUS) – Celebrated Smile (IRE) **h109**
(Cadeaux Genereux) [2016/17 h112: h17.2g h17.2d⁶ h17.2d³ h17.2g⁵ h17.1d⁶ h19.4d*
h19.4g⁶ Jan 1] fair handicap hurdler: won at Musselburgh in November: stays 19f: acts on
good to firm and good to soft going: tried in eyeshields. *James Moffatt*

SMILEY (FR) 4 b.g. Blue Bresil (FR) – Loving Smile (FR) (Sillery (USA)) [2016/17 **b–**
b16g b15.7g⁴ Apr 21] compact gelding: no form in bumpers: tried in hood. *Seamus Mullins*

SMITHSTOWN (IRE) 5 b.g. Bushranger (IRE) – Pink Sovietstaia (FR) (Soviet Star **b–**
(USA)) [2016/17 b15.7d ab16g⁶ Nov 29] no form in bumpers: wears hood: in tongue tie
second start. *Laura Morgan*

SMOKING DIXIE (IRE) 6 ch.g. Beneficial – Jacksister (IRE) (Flemensfirth (USA)) **h91**
[2016/17 b80p: h20g h19.5s⁶ h20.5g⁴ h23.1s⁴ Mar .7] modest form over hurdles.
Ben Pauling

SMOKING JACKET (IRE) 7 b.g. Beneficial – Unalaska (IRE) (High Estate) [2016/17 **c114**
c98, h–: c17g* c15.7d³ c16.4dᶠ c16g⁵ Apr 27] sturdy gelding: maiden hurdler: fair form **h–**
over fences: won novice handicap at Stratford in October: unproven beyond 17f: acts on
good to soft going: often races towards rear. *Tom George*

SMOKY HILL (IRE) 8 gr.g. Galileo (IRE) – Danaskaya (IRE) (Danehill (USA)) [2016/17 **h–**
h–: h15.5vᵖᵘ Feb 1] modest on Flat nowadays, stays 15.5f: little form over hurdles: often in
headgear. *Tony Carroll*

SMOOTH STEPPER 8 b.g. Aflora (IRE) – Jazzy Refrain (IRE) (Jareer (USA)) [2016/17 **c131**
c129, h–: c24.1v c32.4s⁵ c23.4s* c32.6s⁶ c25gᵖᵘ Apr 8] workmanlike gelding: winning **h–**
hurdler: useful handicap chaser: won at Newcastle (by 7 lengths from Bigirononhiship) in
January: should stay beyond 3m: acts on heavy going. *Sue Smith*

SMUGGLER'S STASH (IRE) 7 ch.g. Stowaway – Sweetasanu (IRE) (Sri Pekan **c98 §**
(USA)) [2016/17 h94: c24.2s² c24.2v* c24.2s⁵ c24.5s⁴ c26.9vᵖᵘ c24.2s³ c24.2v³ c26.2g* **h–**
c30.6g Apr 28] maiden hurdler: modest handicap chaser: won at Hexham in December and
Carlisle in April: should stay beyond 3¼m: acts on heavy going: wears headgear:
temperamental. *Rose Dobbin*

SNAPPING TURTLE (IRE) 12 b.g. Turtle Island (IRE) – Rachael's Dawn (Rakaposhi **c– x**
King) [2016/17 c–x, h103: h27s⁶ h24d h25.3d* h25.3d⁴ h25.8v² h27vᵘʳ h25.3s⁶ h27g Mar **h88**
29] workmanlike gelding: modest handicap hurdler: won at Catterick in December: maiden
chaser (sketchy jumper): stays 27f: acts on heavy going. *Donald Whillans*

SNEAKING BUDGE 5 b.g. Nayef (USA) – Ikat (IRE) (Pivotal) [2016/17 h113: h19.9vᵖᵘ **h–**
Nov 12] sturdy gelding: fair hurdle winner as a juvenile, folded quickly in handicap only
outing in 2016/17. *Stuart Edmunds*

SNEAKY FEELING (IRE) 5 b.g. Oscar (IRE) – Shuil Aris (IRE) (Anshan) [2016/17 **h133 p**
b16.7s³ h18.8d* h20.3s h19.8s* Mar 10] lengthy, rather unfurnished gelding: first foal: **b91**
dam (c137/h124) 2m-2½m hurdle/chase winner (stayed 25f): fourth in Irish maiden point
on debut: third in bumper at Market Rasen: useful form over hurdles: won novices at
Newbury in December and Sandown (3-runner race by 22 lengths from Mr Clarkson) in
March: stays 2½m: remains open to improvement. *Philip Hobbs*

SNIPPETYDOODAH 9 b.m. King's Theatre (IRE) – Kimpour (FR) (Hawker's News **h92**
(IRE)) [2016/17 h88: h21.6d⁴ h20.5g² h23.4s² h20.5vᵖᵘ h20.5v* h21.6g² Apr 12] modest
handicap hurdler: won mares event at Plumpton in February: stays 23f: acts on heavy
going: wears hood/tongue tie: front runner. *Michael Roberts*

SNOWBALL (IRE) 10 gr.g. Alderbrook – Rosafi (IRE) (Roselier (FR)) [2016/17 h89: **c76**
h25d⁵ c20.9s⁵ c24d h25d⁵ c25.5s⁵ c24.5v* c25.1vᵖᵘ Mar 9] rather leggy gelding: modest **h75**
handicap hurdler, below best in 2016/17: poor form over fences: won handicap at Towcester
in February: stays 25f: acts on heavy going. *David Arbuthnot*

SNOW CASTLE (IRE) 5 b.g. Oscar (IRE) – Scartara (FR) (Linamix (FR)) [2016/17 **h95**
b16g⁵ b15.7s⁵ h15.7g³ Mar 28] €45,000 3-y-o: fifth foal: closely related to a winner on Flat **b79**
in France by King's Theatre and half-brother to fairly useful hurdler Pinnacle Panda
(2m-2½m winner, by Scorpion), stayed 3m, and modest hurdler Seven Acres (3m winner,
by Flemensfirth): dam French 11f winner: modest form in bumpers: 7/1, third in novice at
Southwell (5¾ lengths behind Fattsota) on hurdling debut, not looking keen. *Evan Williams*

SNOWED IN (IRE) 8 gr.g. Dark Angel (IRE) – Spinning Gold (Spinning World (USA)) **c–**
[2016/17 c–, h99: h17m³ h22.1g h16.2d⁴ h17.2g h20d⁶ h19s³ h15.7d* h15.7d² h15.7s⁶ **h94**
h16d⁵ h20.2g Apr 28] modest handicap hurdler: won at Catterick in January: didn't take to
chasing: left Barry Murtagh after second start: stays 21f: acts on good to firm and heavy
going: wears cheekpieces. *Barbara Butterworth*

Lismullen Hurdle, Navan—
Snow Falcon (left) knuckles down well to collar long-time leader De Plotting Shed

SNOW FALCON (IRE) 7 b.g. Presenting – Flocon de Neige (IRE) (Kahyasi) [2016/17   **h153**
h143: h24.4g* h20d* h24.2d^F h24d^3 h24d^2 h24g^5 h24.7g^3 h24d Apr 27] sturdy gelding:
smart hurdler: won minor event at Roscommon (by 5½ lengths from Sadler's Risk) in
August and Lismullen Hurdle at Navan (by 3¼ lengths from De Plotting Shed) in
November: placed after in Christmas Hurdle at Leopardstown (3¾ lengths behind Vroum
Vroum Mag), John Mulhern Galmoy Hurdle at Gowran (¾ length behind Shaneshill) and
Stayers' Liverpool Hurdle at Aintree (1¾ lengths behind Yanworth): stays 25f: acts on
heavy going: has worn headgear. *Noel Meade, Ireland*

SNOW LEOPARDESS 5 gr.m. Martaline – Queen Soraya (Persian Bold) [2016/17   **h129 p**
b95p: b16g* h16.3g^3 h19.4g* h20.8d^3 h20.5g* Mar 25] good-topped mare: fairly useful   **b103**
form in bumpers: won for second time in listed mares event at Gowran (by 3¼ lengths from
Takeittothelimits) in September: fairly useful form over hurdles: won mares novice at
Doncaster in November and Mares 'National Hunt' Novices' Hurdle Finale at Newbury
(by 4 lengths from Copper Kay) in March: will stay beyond 21f: open to further
improvement. *Charlie Longsdon*

SNOW RESCUE (IRE) 5 gr.g. Stowaway – Annilogs Palm (IRE) (Great Palm (USA))   **h67**
[2016/17 b17.7d^4 b14d h15.8s^6 h16.7g^5 h17.7g Apr 12] poor form in bumpers/over hurdles: **b58**
left Seamus Durack after first start. *Tom Gretton*

SNUKER 10 b.g. Snurge – Briar Rose (IRE) (Roselier (FR)) [2016/17 c–§, h85: c24.2d^{pu} **c76 §**
c24.2v^6 c24.3v^{pu} Jan 16] winning hurdler: modest handicap chaser at best, little form in   **h–**
2016/17 (including in points): stays 4m: acts on good to firm and heavy going: wears
headgear: has worn tongue tie: moody and can't be relied on. *James Ewart*

SOBER SAILOR (IRE) 10 b.g. Hawkeye (IRE) – Ronni Pancake (Mujadil (USA))   **h93**
[2016/17 h19.1s^4 h19.1s* h20.5v^2 Jan 2] placed both starts in Irish maiden points: modest
handicap hurdler: won at Fontwell (conditional) in December, only outing for Jamie
Poulton: stays 2½m: acts on heavy going. *Mark Hoad*

764

SO CELEBRE (GER) 4 ch.g. Peintre Celebre (USA) – Saldennahe (GER) (Next Desert (IRE)) [2016/17 h16m³ h16.4s³ h15.8d* h15.7m* h16.5g⁵ Apr 8] good-topped gelding: dam half-sister to very smart hurdler/useful chaser (stayed 2¼m) Salden Licht: fairly useful on Flat, stays 1¼m: fairly useful form over hurdles: won maiden at Huntingdon in March and juvenile handicap at Ascot in April: will prove best at 2m: acts on good to firm and good to soft going. *Ian Williams* **h125**

SOCIAL CLIMBER (IRE) 5 b.g. Strategic Prince – Ivy Queen (IRE) (Green Desert (USA)) [2016/17 h88: h16.8g h20g⁴ May 22] poor maiden hurdler: unproven beyond 2m: has worn blinkers: front runner/races prominently: temperamental. *Fergal O'Brien* **h69 §**

SOCKSY (IRE) 6 ch.m. Flemensfirth (USA) – Bachello (IRE) (Bach (IRE)) [2016/17 b16d h20d h21s⁴ h25.5v⁶ h19.2v* h24v³ h21s* Mar 16] €13,000 3-y-o: second foal: dam once-raced half-sister to useful hurdler (stayed 3m) Accordello out of high-class staying hurdler Marello: bumper winner: fairly useful hurdler: won mares novices at Towcester in February and March: left James Joseph Mangan after first start: stays 3m: best form on soft/heavy going: in tongue tie last 3 starts. *Fergal O'Brien* **h115**
b–

SOFFEL (FR) 5 br.g. Soldier of Fortune (IRE) – Elasili (FR) (Dansili) [2016/17 b15.7s⁶ b15.7d Feb 26] poor form in bumpers: in hood second start. *Laura Morgan* **b74**

SO FINE (IRE) 11 b.g. Definite Article – Not So Green (IRE) (Roselier (FR)) [2016/17 c117, h125: c25.8g h25.3spu c25.1dpu c25.5v³ Jan 8] good-topped gelding: fairly useful hurdler/chaser at best, largely let down by attitude in 2016/17: stays 27f: acts on soft and good to firm going: wears headgear: in tongue tie last 2 starts: front runner/races prominently: one to treat with caution. *Philip Hobbs* **c100 §**
h– §

SOIESAUVAGE (FR) 6 b.m. Lauro (GER) – Taffetas (FR) (Nikos) [2016/17 h16.3d⁶ h15.9d⁶ h16v⁴ h15.3s⁵ Mar 1] sturdy mare: second foal: half-sister to French 2¼m hurdle winner Sultan Silk (by Sulamani): dam, French 2¼m chase winner, half-sister to high-class hurdler (stays 25f) Yanworth: 15f winner on Flat in France: poor form over hurdles. *Gary Moore* **h81**

SOIXANTE SIX 9 gr.g. Fair Mix (IRE) – Pennant Princess (Alflora (IRE)) [2016/17 c16.3g h18.7m May 20] dual point winner: maiden hurdler: well held in hunter at Cheltenham (tongue tied) on chasing debut. *Tom Weston* **c–**
h–

SOLAR IMPULSE (FR) 7 b.g. Westerner – Moon Glow (FR) (Solar One (FR)) [2016/17 c146, h–: c16.9d c20.8s c20.8spu c15.8g³ c16.3g c21.1g Apr 7] good-topped gelding: has had breathing operation: winning hurdler: smart chaser at best, below that in 2016/17: best around 2m: has won on heavy going, best form under less testing conditions (acts on good to firm): has worn headgear/tongue tie, including in 2016/17. *Christopher Kellett* **c124**
h–

SOLATENTIF (FR) 7 b.g. Solon (GER) – Indian Mist (FR) (River Mist (USA)) [2016/17 h21.1s² h16.8g⁶ c17s² c19.9s⁴ h17.7d⁵ h16.8g⁵ Apr 19] sturdy gelding: bumper winner: fairly useful handicap hurdler: useful form over fences: better effort when second in novice at Plumpton (2½ lengths behind Baron Alco) in January: stays 21f: acts on soft and good to firm going. *Colin Tizzard* **c134**
h129

SOLDIER BOY (IRE) 5 b.g. Millenary – Oscar Mary (IRE) (Oscar (IRE)) [2016/17 b15.8g³ b15.8v Nov 12] modest form in bumpers: better effort when third at Uttoxeter in July: left Heather Dalton after that. *Barry Brennan* **b80**

SOLDIER IN ACTION (FR) 4 ch.g. Soldier of Fortune (IRE) – Ripley (GER) (Platini (GER)) [2016/17 h15.6g⁵ h16.6g* h16.8g Mar 17] sturdy gelding: smart on Flat, stays 1½m: useful form over hurdles: won juvenile at Doncaster (by 14 lengths from Apache Song) in February. *Nicky Henderson* **h131**

SOLIANA 5 ch.m. Dutch Art – Pink Stone (FR) (Bigstone (IRE)) [2016/17 h16.3mpu May 15] maiden on Flat: pulled up in mares novice seller on hurdling debut. *John O'Shea* **h–**

SOLIDAGO (IRE) 10 b.g. Vinnie Roe (IRE) – Native Belle (IRE) (Be My Native (USA)) [2016/17 h88: c22.5dpu May 5] modest hurdler: pulled up in novice handicap on chasing debut: stays 3m: acts on heavy going: usually wears headgear: tried in tongue tie. *Barry Leavy* **c–**
h–

SOLID STRIKE 9 b.g. Sir Harry Lewis (USA) – Solid Land (FR) (Solid Illusion (USA)) [2016/17 c26g⁴ Apr 27] multiple point winner: twice-raced in chases, fourth in hunter at Cheltenham very early in season. *Paul Collins* **c100**

SOLIGHOSTER (FR) 5 ch.g. Loup Solitaire (USA) – Miss Martine (FR) (Waki River **h126**
(FR)) [2016/17 b16.4d* b15.8d² h17.7v* h15.7v* h20.5s² h20.3g⁵ Apr 19] €33,000 3-y-o, **b101**
£55,000 4-y-o: half-brother to 2 winners in France by French Glory, including 2¼m hurdle
winner Frenchtine: dam unraced: won Irish maiden point on debut: fairly useful form in
bumpers: won maiden at Newcastle in November: fairly useful form over hurdles: won
novices at Fontwell in January and Towcester in February: stays 2½m: front runner/races
prominently, usually travels strongly. *Neil Mulholland*

SOLITA (IRE) 8 b.m. King's Theatre (IRE) – Wind Over Water (IRE) (Erins Isle) **c132**
[2016/17 c135, h127: c21s h16d² h16d h20d³ h16g c16s² c16.3gᵖᵘ Mar 17] useful hurdler/ **h130**
chaser: second in listed mares event over fences at Naas (4 lengths behind Slowmotion) in
February: stays 3m, at least as effective at much shorter: acts on heavy going: has worn
hood: wears tongue tie. *Paul Nolan, Ireland*

SOLOMN GRUNDY (IRE) 7 b.g. Westerner – Marika's King (IRE) (King's Ride) **h130**
[2016/17 h115p: h21.1s² h24.2d* h21.3s² h21g h24g⁵ Apr 20] lengthy gelding: third on
completed start in Irish points: useful handicap hurdler: won at Newbury in November:
stays 3m: acts on heavy going: often races in rear. *Neil Mulholland*

SOLOMON GREY (FR) 5 gr.g. Sulamani (IRE) – Sardagna (FR) (Medaaly) [2016/17 **b96**
b14d² b15.8d³ b16.3g² Apr 1] fifth foal: half-brother to 3 winners, including useful hurdler/
chaser Amore Alato (2m-3m winner, by Winged Love) and bumper winner/fairly useful
hurdler Only For Love (2m-2½m winner, by Kalanisi): dam (c120/h121) 2m-21f hurdle/
chase winner: fairly useful form in bumpers, placed all 3 starts. *Dan Skelton*

SOLONNG (IRE) 7 ch.g. Indian River (FR) – Cate's Oscar (IRE) (Oscar (IRE)) [2016/17 **h–**
h21d h21d h19.7sᵖᵘ Jan 4] no form in novice hurdles. *Venetia Williams*

SOLSTALLA 5 b.m. Halling (USA) – Solstice (Dubawi (IRE)) [2016/17 h89: h16g² **h107**
h17.7g² h16g* h16.8d* h17.7g³ h16m⁵ h15.3vᵖᵘ Mar 9] fair hurdler: won mares maiden at
Worcester and mares novice at Newton Abbot in September: stays 2¼m: acts on good to
soft going. *David Weston*

SOLSTICE DAWN 9 b.m. Lyphento (USA) – Ryders Hill (Zaffaran (USA)) [2016/17 h–: **c73 §**
h20.3v³ h19.9g c24vᵖᵘ c24d³ c24g⁵ h16.7g⁵ c23.4m² c24.2s⁵ h23.4s³ c23.6dᵘʳ Dec 4] poor **h73 §**
maiden hurdler: similar form over fences: stays 27f: acts on good to firm and heavy going:
has worn visor: unreliable. *Peter Winks*

SOLSTICE SON 8 b.g. Haafhd – Karasta (IRE) (Lake Coniston (IRE)) [2016/17 c127, **c113**
h–: c26.1g c24.5dᶠ Apr 29] sturdy gelding: winning hurdler: fairly useful handicap chaser: **h–**
stays 27f: acts on soft going: in blinkers last 4 starts: wears tongue tie. *Anthony Honeyball*

SOLSTICE STAR 7 b.g. Kayf Tara – Clover Green (IRE) (Presenting) [2016/17 h139: **c–**
c16d⁵ c21d⁵ c20v h16.8s h23.1s h23.6v⁴ h19.9s² h24g⁶ Apr 20] well-made gelding: useful **h131**
handicap hurdler: second at Uttoxeter (2¼ lengths behind Fortunate George) in March:
well held all starts over fences: best at short of 3m: acts on heavy going: has worn headgear,
including in 2016/17: wears tongue tie. *Martin Keighley*

SOLWAY BAY 15 b.g. Cloudings (IRE) – No Problem Jac (Safawan) [2016/17 c91§, **c– §**
h85§: c26.2dᵖᵘ c25.5g Jul 18] tall gelding: winning hurdler: fair chaser at best, no form in **h– §**
2016/17: stays 3¼m: acts on soft and good to firm going: has worn headgear: usually wears
tongue tie: not one to rely on. *Lisa Harrison*

SOLWAY DANDY 10 b.g. Danroad (AUS) – Solway Rose (Minster Son) [2016/17 h119: **h111 +**
h20.2g⁶ Apr 28] fairly useful handicap hurdler, encouraging return from 2-year absence at
Perth: stays 2½m: acts on heavy going. *Lisa Harrison*

SOLWAY DORNAL 12 b.g. Alflora (IRE) – Solway Donal (IRE) (Celio Rufo) [2016/17 **c76**
c–, h–: c23.9g⁶ c20.1gᵖᵘ Sep 5] winning hurdler: modest handicap chaser at best, very **h–**
lightly raced nowadays: stays 27f: acts on soft and good to firm going: usually wears
cheekpieces: has worn tongue tie. *Lisa Harrison*

SOLWAY LEGEND 10 ch.g. And Beyond (IRE) – Spicey Cut (Cut Above) [2016/17 **c99**
c100, h–: c23.8m³ c25.5m⁴ c20.1g* c23.8dᵖᵘ c24g c23.9g³ Aug 13] maiden hurdler: **h–**
modest handicap chaser: won at Hexham in June: stayed 3m: acted on soft going: dead.
Lisa Harrison

SOLWAY PRINCE 8 ch.g. Double Trigger (IRE) – Solway Rose (Minster Son) [2016/17 **h–**
h96: h16.2sᵖᵘ h23.8g Dec 14] modest hurdler at best, no form in 2016/17: stays 3m: acts on
soft and good to firm going: has worn cheekpieces. *Lisa Harrison*

SOLWAY SAM 14 b.g. Double Trigger (IRE) – Some Gale (Strong Gale) [2016/17 c79, **c74** h95: c23.8m³ h23.3g⁵ c24.2g³ c24.2d⁵ h23.3g c23.8s* c23.8gᵘʳ h23.3g h23.3s⁴ h24.3d³ **h71** h23.3s² h23.1s⁶ Dec 1] big gelding: poor handicap hurdler: poor handicap chaser: won at Perth in July: stays 25f: acts on soft and good to firm going: tried in cheekpieces: often races prominently. *Lisa Harrison*

SOLWAY STORM (IRE) 7 gr.g. Indian River (FR) – The Grey Lady (IRE) (Roselier **b–** (FR)) [2016/17 b89: b16.2g b16d Oct 24] regressive in bumpers, best effort when third on debut in 2015/16. *Lisa Harrison*

SOLWAY SUMMER 8 b.m. Double Trigger (IRE) – Solway Donal (IRE) (Celio Rufo) **h–** [2016/17 h23.9g Aug 20] no form in bumpers/over hurdles. *Lisa Harrison*

SOLWAY TRIGGER 8 b.g. Double Trigger (IRE) – Double Flight (Mtoto) [2016/17 **h59** h73: h19.9g⁶ h23.9gᵘʳ Sep 5] poor maiden hurdler: best effort at 3m. *Lisa Harrison*

SOMCHINE 9 b.g. Volochine (IRE) – Seem of Gold (Gold Dust) [2016/17 c120, h–: **c136** c21.1d³ c20.3s² c15.7v* c19.4v² c19.9s³ c15.7s* c19.4sᵖᵘ c15.7dᵘʳ c16s* c15.5g³ Apr 22] **h–** lengthy gelding: maiden hurdler: useful handicap chaser: won at Southwell in June, Wincanton in December and Hereford in March: has won over 21f, at least as effective at shorter: acts on heavy going: usually races towards rear. *Seamus Mullins*

SOME ARE LUCKY (IRE) 6 b.g. Gold Well – Foreign Estates (IRE) (Be My Native **c131** (USA)) [2016/17 h118, b95: h23.3d² h23.6m² c22.4d³ c22.7s³ c20s² h22.8g Apr 15] well- **h123** made gelding: fairly useful handicap hurdler: useful form over fences when third in novice handicap at Newbury (1¼ lengths behind Belami des Pictons) and second in similar event at Ludlow (2 lengths behind Kap Jazz): stays 3m: acts on soft and good to firm going: front runner/races prominently, often travels strongly. *Tom George*

SOME BUCKLE (IRE) 8 b.g. Milan – Miss Moppit (IRE) (Torus) [2016/17 c139p, **c143** h125: c19.9dᵖᵘ c16.9d c20.2s c22.6g* c19.9g³ Apr 15] useful-looking gelding: winning **h–** hurdler: useful handicap chaser: won at Stratford (by 14 lengths from Pull The Chord) in April: stays 2¾m: acts on soft going: wears tongue tie: waited with. *Tom George*

SOME CHAOS (IRE) 6 b.g. Brian Boru – Iruna Iris (IRE) (Golden Tornado (IRE)) **h88** [2016/17 b16d³ b16s h16.8v h19g h18.5d⁴ Feb 24] €40,000 3-y-o, £20,000 5-y-o: short- **b80** backed gelding: second foal: dam twice-raced sister to smart hurdler/chaser (2m-3m winner) Dancing Tornado: Irish maiden point winner: modest form in bumpers/over hurdles: will be suited by 2½m+: wears hood: often races towards rear. *Charles Whittaker*

SOMEDAY 5 b.g. Black Sam Bellamy (IRE) – Like Manner (Teenoso (USA)) [2016/17 **b106** b16d² b16s* b16d⁵ Apr 26] half-brother to bumper winner/smart hurdler Lifestyle (2m winner, by Karinga Bay) and fairly useful hurdler The Great Alfie (23f/3m winner, by Alflora): dam unraced half-sister to fairly useful hurdler/useful chaser Den of Iniquity and useful hurdler Overserved (both stayed 3m): useful form in bumpers: won maiden at Leopardstown (by ½ length from Voix des Tiep) in February. *Mrs J. Harrington, Ireland*

SOME FINISH (IRE) 8 b.g. Kayf Tara – Kylie Kaprice (GER) (Big Shuffle (USA)) **c94 §** [2016/17 c92, h54: c23.6gᵖᵘ c21.7d² c19.8d⁴ c20.2gᵖᵘ h19.2vᵖᵘ c19.2gᵖᵘ c24.5m* Apr 13] **h– §** maiden hurdler: modest handicap chaser: left alone second at Towcester in April: stays 2¾m: acts on heavy going: usually wears headgear: front runner/races prominently: temperamental. *Robin Dickin*

SOME INVITATION (IRE) 6 b.g. Presenting – Bolly (IRE) (Jolly Jake (NZ)) [2016/17 **h132 p** h19.7d* h21.7s h19.6g* h20.5d⁶ Apr 21] seventh foal: brother to fairly useful chaser Temple Grandin (3m winner) and half-brother to 2 winners, including fairly useful hurdler/ chaser Annie Other (2m-19f winner, by Bob Back): dam unraced half-sister to useful hurdler/top-class chaser (stayed 3¼m) Carlingford Lough: useful form over hurdles: won novices at Wetherby in November and Bangor (by 10 lengths from Walt) in March: should stay further than 2½m: in tongue tie last 2 starts: remains capable of better. *Dan Skelton*

SOME KINDA LAMA (IRE) 6 gr.g. Daylami (IRE) – Last Sunrise (IRE) (Shahanndeh) **h128** [2016/17 h109: h24.1g² h25.5g* h25.5g* h23.4s² h24.4g² Feb 22] rather unfurnished gelding: runner-up in Irish point on debut: fairly useful hurdler: won maiden and handicap at Hereford in October: best effort when second in handicap at Doncaster (tongue tied) final start: stays 3¼m: acts on heavy going: usually responds generously to pressure. *Charlie Mann*

SOME LAD (IRE) 12 b.g. Beneficial – Some News (IRE) (Be My Native (USA)) **c– §** [2016/17 c95§, h–§: c20.1mᵖᵘ c15.6d Jun 11] winning hurdler: modest chaser at best, no **h– §** form in 2016/17: stays 2¾m, but at least as effective at much shorter: acts on good to firm and heavy going: has worn headgear: unreliable. *Alison Hamilton*

Frank Ward Solicitors Arkle Novices' Chase, Leopardstown—jumping wins the day for sole finisher Some Plan as the hooded Royal Caviar becomes the last of his three rivals to depart

SOME PLAN (IRE) 9 b.g. Winged Love (IRE) – Lough Hyne (Classic Cliche (IRE)) [2016/17 h143: h15.7m c16g* c15.9sF c16s* c17g* c15.9g6 c20d6 Apr 16] good-topped gelding: useful hurdler: similar form over fences: won maiden at Punchestown in October, novice at Naas (by 5½ lengths from Road To Respect) in January and Frank Ward Solicitors Arkle Novices' Chase at Leopardstown (looked held when left alone last) in January: left Paul Nicholls after first start: unproven beyond 2m: acts on soft going: has worn hood: wears tongue tie: front runner/races prominently. *Henry de Bromhead, Ireland*   **c143 h—**

SOME REIGN (IRE) 6 b.g. Kayf Tara – Bridge Love (FR) (Astarabad (USA)) [2016/17 b16s* b16.2v2 b17g Apr 7] €27,000 3-y-o: third foal: closely related to a winning pointer by Milan: dam unraced half-sister to smart French hurdler/useful chaser (stayed 3¼m) Great Love: third in Irish maiden point on debut: fairly useful form in bumpers: won at Wetherby in January. *Rose Dobbin*   **b97**

SOMERSET JEM 8 b.g. Sir Harry Lewis (USA) – Monger Lane (Karinga Bay) [2016/17 h102: c20.9s4 c19.2v6 h21.4d h21.4m5 h23.1g Apr 22] modest handicap hurdler, below form in 2016/17: modest form over fences: better effort when fourth in novice handicap at Uttoxeter on return: stays 21f: best form on soft/heavy going. *Kevin Bishop*   **c92 h68**

SOMERSET LIAS (IRE) 9 b.g. Golan (IRE) – Presenting Gayle (IRE) (Presenting) [2016/17 c101, h–: c20.5mF h21.6m2 c23.8m5 h23.6d c23g* c26.3gpu c24.2s4 c23g2 c25.1vF c25.1m6 Apr 5] good-topped gelding: maiden hurdler: fair handicap chaser: won at Taunton in November: stays 27f: acts on good to firm and heavy going: has worn headgear, including in 2016/17: tried in tongue tie: front runner/races prominently: temperamental. *Bob Buckler*   **c104 § h97 §**

SOMEWHERE TO BE (IRE) 5 ch.g. Golan (IRE) – Somethinaboutmolly (IRE) (Choisir (AUS)) [2016/17 b15.8g5 b16g3 b16.4g4 h16.3d6 h21.6d h15.7s3 Jan 31] workmanlike gelding: first foal: dam unraced: fair form in bumpers/over hurdles: front runner/races prominently. *Martin Keighley*   **h108 b87**

SONAR DE SIVOLA (FR) 4 b.g. Noroit (GER) – Protege Moi (FR) (Green Tune (USA)) [2016/17 h16mpu Aug 30] pulled up in juvenile maiden hurdle on debut. *Nick Williams*   **h—**

SONG LIGHT 7 b.g. Echo of Light – Blue Lullaby (IRE) (Fasliyev (USA)) [2016/17 h129: h16.4s3 h16.3d4 h16.8g h15.9m2 Apr 16] leggy gelding: useful handicap hurdler: third in Greatwood Hurdle at Cheltenham (1¾ lengths behind North Hill Harvey) on return: raced around 2m: acts on soft and good to firm going: tried in cheekpieces: often travels strongly. *Seamus Mullins*   **h130**

SONG OF THE NIGHT (IRE) 6 b.g. Mahler – Pollys Attic (IRE) (Rashar (USA)) [2016/17 h75, b72: h23.3gpu h21mur h24g2 h23.9m2 h23.9g3 h24.1s6 h25m4 Apr 17] runner-up in Irish point on debut: modest maiden hurdler: stays 3m: acts on good to firm going: wears cheekpieces: tried in tongue tie: usually races prominently, often travels strongly. *Charlie Longsdon*   **h95**

SONG SAA 7 b.m. Midnight Legend – Mystere (IRE) (Montelimar (USA)) [2016/17 h108, b82: c20s³ c20.8g c23.5v^{pu} c19.9d* c22.7s* c20v³ c22.2g³ Apr 15] dual hurdle winner: fairly useful handicap chaser: won at Huntingdon and Leicester in February: stays 23f: acts on heavy going: in tongue tie last 4 starts: usually travels strongly. *Tom George* **c124 h–**

SONIC RAINBOW (GR) 5 ch.m. Harmonic Way – Rainbow Way (High Chaparral (IRE)) [2016/17 h18.2d^{ur} h16g h16g⁶ h16d h18.2d h19d⁶ h16g h19.9g^{pu} Aug 25] maiden on Flat: poor maiden hurdler: tried in cheekpieces: usually races towards rear. *Gordon Elliott, Ireland* **h67**

SONNEOFPRESENTING (IRE) 7 b.g. Presenting – Sonne Cinq (IRE) (Old Vic) [2016/17 h90p: h20.3g* c24v² c23.8s⁴ c20.3g² c21.4g* Sep 24] modest form over hurdles: won handicap chase at Southwell in June: fair form over fences: won handicap at Market Rasen in September: stays 3m: acts on heavy going: usually races close up. *Kim Bailey* **c112 h92**

SONNY B (IRE) 10 b.g. Spadoun (FR) – Miss Ell (IRE) (Houmayoun (FR)) [2016/17 c–, h136: h24d⁶ c25.3v² c22s³ c25.5d³ c24.5d c20v⁴ h22d Apr 17] useful handicap hurdler/ chaser: stays 25f: acts on heavy going: wears tongue tie. *John J. Walsh, Ireland* **c132 h–**

SONNY THE ONE 7 ch.g. Tobougg (IRE) – Annie Fleetwood (Anshan) [2016/17 c117, h–: c23.6d⁶ c20g^{ur} c25.5v² c20.2s⁴ c25.1d^f c24m Apr 4] workmanlike gelding: maiden hurdler: fair handicap chaser: stays 25f: acts on heavy going: wears headgear: tried in tongue tie: front runner/races prominently. *Robert Walford* **c109 h–**

SONOFAGUN (FR) 11 b.g. Turgeon (USA) – Detonante (FR) (Cardoun (FR)) [2016/17 c112x, h–: c20g⁴ c21.4g² c22.6s^{bd} c23d^{pu} Jun 29] angular gelding: winning hurdler: fair handicap chaser: stays 21f: acts on soft and good to firm going: has worn cheekpieces, including last 4 starts: tried in tongue tie: often let down by jumping over fences. *Ian Williams* **c108 x h–**

SON OF FEYAN (IRE) 6 ch.g. Nayef (USA) – Miss Penton (Primo Dominie) [2016/17 h–: h20.2d² h20.9d³ h24.3d h20.6s Dec 8] poor maiden hurdler: stays 21f: tried in tongue tie. *Lucy Normile* **h80**

SON OF MY HEART (USA) 12 b.g. Dynaformer (USA) – Sophie My Love (USA) (Danzig (USA)) [2016/17 c23.8d⁴ c20.5v² c25g² c23.8g² c23.8d⁵ Sep 21] winning hurdler: modest maiden chaser: pulled up all 3 starts in points in 2017: stays 3m: acts on soft going: has worn cheekpieces, including final start: usually wears tongue tie nowadays: often races towards rear. *Gordon Elliott, Ireland* **c96 h–**

SON OF SUZIE 9 gr.g. Midnight Legend – Suzie Cream Cheese (IRE) (Royal Charter (FR)) [2016/17 c111x, h–: c27.5g³ c26.1s* c25.5d⁵ c24v^f Feb 11] lengthy, useful-looking gelding: winning hurdler: fair handicap chaser: won at Uttoxeter in June: stays 3½m: acts on heavy going: usually in cheekpieces nowadays: front runner/races prominently: has been let down by jumping. *Fergal O'Brien* **c113 h–**

SONOFTHEKING (IRE) 9 b.g. King's Theatre (IRE) – Nikadora (FR) (Nikos) [2016/17 c97, h–: c24.2m* c21.1d^{pu} c23g² c25.1s* c22.7g⁴ c24v³ c25.2s^{pu} c24.2g⁵ Apr 11] useful-looking gelding: maiden hurdler: fair chaser: won hunter at Exeter in May and novice handicap at Wincanton in January: stays 25f: acts on good to firm and heavy going: tried in cheekpieces: wears tongue tie: often races prominently. *Nicky Martin* **c106 h–**

SOPHIE FATALE 5 b.m. Robin des Champs (FR) – Buffy (Classic Cliche (IRE)) [2016/17 b16s¹ b16s Feb 14] first foal: dam (h86) 2m hurdle winner: no form in bumpers. *Bruce Mactaggart* **b–**

SOPHIE OLIVIA (IRE) 5 gr.m. Ask – Gill's Honey (IRE) (Celio Rufo) [2016/17 b16.2m² b16s² b15.7g⁴ b17s⁶ h16.6g³ h19.4g² Mar 1] €7,500 3-y-o: fourth foal: half-sister to fair hurdler/winning pointer Ballinvegga (2½m winner, by Royal Anthem) and modest hurdler/fair chaser Gougane (2½m/21f winner, by Luso): dam bumper/fair 2¾m chase winner: modest form in bumpers: modest form over hurdles: better effort when third in mares novice at Musselburgh in January: should be suited by 2½m. *Martin Todhunter* **h97 b79**

SOPHISTICATED HEIR (IRE) 7 b.g. New Approach (IRE) – My Girl Sophie (USA) (Danzig (USA)) [2016/17 h15.7v^{pu} May 10] fairly useful on Flat, stays 1¼m: pulled up in maiden on hurdling debut. *David Loughnane* **h–**

SORROW (FR) 7 b.g. Early March – Cochinchine (IRE) (Namaqualand (USA)) [2016/17 b16.2s⁶ h16s h16m h20v Oct 17] last in bumper: no form over hurdles: in tongue tie last 2 starts. *Patrick Griffin, Ireland* **h– b–**

SO SATISFIED 6 b.g. Aqlaam – Pirouetting (Pivotal) [2016/17 h115: c15.6d⁴ c21.4g^{pu} c16s⁴ c20.1g⁴ c20.5d* c21.5s⁶ c23.8g² c26.2s c18v⁴ c21.1m⁶ Apr 19] fairly useful hurdler: fair handicap chaser: won novice event at Ayr in October: stays 3m: acts on soft and good to firm going: in cheekpieces last 3 starts: often races towards rear. *Iain Jardine* **c110 h–**

SO SHE SAYS (IRE) 5 b.m. Kalanisi (IRE) – Accordingtoherself (IRE) (Accordion) **b67**
[2016/17 b17.7s⁴ ab16g Nov 8] €9,000 3-y-o: first foal: dam unraced sister to high-class
hurdler/smart chaser (2m-2½m winner) Accordion Etoile: poor form in bumpers. *Suzy Smith*

SO STROPPY POPPY 5 ch.m. Phoenix Reach (IRE) – Toy Girl (IRE) (Cadeaux **h–**
Genereux) [2016/17 h16vᵖᵘ Mar 12] no form in Flat maidens/novice hurdle. *Shaun Harris*

SOULSAVER 5 ch.g. Recharge (IRE) – Lapina (IRE) (Fath (USA)) [2016/17 b71: h16d **h88**
h15.3d h16.5g h15.3s⁵ h15.9s² Mar 13] modest form over hurdles: should stay beyond 2m:
acts on soft going: tried in tongue tie: usually races towards rear. *Anthony Honeyball*

SOUNDS OF ITALY (IRE) 8 b.g. Milan – Sound Hill (FR) (Green Tune (USA)) **c–**
[2016/17 c26.2dᵖᵘ Apr 10] dual point winner: pulled up in maiden hunter on chasing debut.
Victor Thompson

SOUND THE BUGLE 7 b.g. Overbury (IRE) – Fusion of Tunes (Mr Confusion (IRE)) **h60**
[2016/17 b–: h20.8dᵖᵘ h15.8s h15.8v⁵ h20.7sᵖᵘ h15.8sᵖᵘ Apr 1] poor form over hurdles:
tried in hood. *Anthony Day*

SOUPY SOUPS (IRE) 6 ch.g. Stowaway – Near Dunleer (IRE) (Soviet Lad (USA)) **h123**
[2016/17 h99p, b87: h20.7g³ h21g h20g³ h19.8d* h23.4g* h23.8g² h23.6v h19.9m* Apr
19] off mark in Irish points at second attempt: bumper winner: fairly useful hurdler: won
handicaps at Wincanton (novice) and Fakenham in December, and novice at Sedgefield in
April: stays 3m: acts on good to firm and good to soft going: front runner/races prominently.
Neil Mulholland

SOURIYAN (FR) 6 b.g. Alhaarth (IRE) – Serasana (Red Ransom (USA)) [2016/17 c125, **c–**
h96: c24.2g⁶ h23.3d⁶ h24.4d⁴ h24.2s⁶ h20.5g⁵ Apr 22] rather leggy gelding: fairly useful **h102**
hurdler at best, below that in handicaps in 2016/17: maiden chaser: left Jamie Snowden
after second start: should stay beyond 2½m: acts on heavy going: has worn headgear,
including in 2016/17: often races prominently. *Peter Bowen*

SOUTHFIELD ROYALE 7 b.g. Presenting – Chamoss Royale (FR) (Garde Royale) **c122**
[2016/17 c142, h–: c25d c24d c26gᶠ c31.8g Apr 22] good sort: winning hurdler: smart **h–**
chaser as a novice, below form in handicaps when completing in 2016/17: stays 4m: acts
on heavy going: wears cheekpieces. *Neil Mulholland*

SOUTHFIELD THEATRE (IRE) 9 b.g. King's Theatre (IRE) – Chamoss Royale (FR) **c150**
(Garde Royale) [2016/17 c149, h–: c25.1mᶠ c26g Dec 9] good-topped gelding: winning **h–**
hurdler: smart handicap chaser: would have won Badger Ales Trophy at Wincanton on
return but for falling last: stays 25f: acts on soft and good to firm going: tried in tongue tie.
Paul Nicholls

SOUTHFIELD VIC (IRE) 8 ch.g. Old Vic – Chamoss Royale (FR) (Garde Royale) **c145**
[2016/17 c132, h140: h22.8m c23g* c23g* c23.6g c24.2m² c25.5g* Apr 21] lengthy **h132**
gelding: useful handicap hurdler: useful chaser: won novices at Worcester in May and
September, and at Fontwell in April: stays 25f: acts on soft and good to firm going: wears
headgear: usually races close up. *Paul Nicholls*

SOUTHPORT 5 b.g. Robin des Pres (FR) – First Katoune (FR) (Poliglote) [2016/17 h16.7g* **h114**
h15.8g² h20d² h21g h19.6d⁵ h25.5s h21.2g⁶ Apr 3] second foal: half-brother to a winning
pointer by Tobougg: dam, unraced, out of useful French hurdler/winning chaser around
2¼m Katoune: well held on completed start in Irish maiden points: fair hurdler: won maiden
at Market Rasen in October: stays 21f: acts on good to soft going. *Nigel Twiston-Davies*

SOVINNIE (IRE) 8 ch.g. Vinnie Roe (IRE) – Sohapara (Arapahos (FR)) [2016/17 h82: **h94 ?**
h23g h23m h23.1g⁶ h23g⁵ h25.6s h20g h23.9m Dec 8] maiden hurdler, poor on balance:
stays 23f: in cheekpieces last 3 starts: has worn tongue tie, including last 3 starts: front
runner/races prominently. *Jane Mathias*

SPACE CADET (IRE) 7 b.g. Flemensfirth (USA) – Shuil A Hocht (IRE) (Mohaajir **c132**
(USA)) [2016/17 c16.4v* c22.5d⁵ c25.5d² c21g c20v² c24s c24.5d Apr 29] maiden hurdler: **h–**
useful chaser: won maiden at Roscommon in October: second in handicap at Punchestown
(2¾ lengths behind Kansas City Chief) in December: barely stays 25f: acts on heavy
going: tried in cheekpieces. *Gordon Elliott, Ireland*

SPACE ODDITY (FR) 6 b.g. Al Namix (FR) – Schoune (FR) (Majorien) [2016/17 **h127**
h115p: h17.7s⁴ h18.5s⁴ h18.5s* h19g* h19.8vᵖᵘ h19g² Apr 6] fairly useful handicap
hurdler: won at Exeter and Taunton in January: stays 19f: acts on good to firm and heavy
going: wears hood: usually leads. *Harry Fry*

SPACE SHIP 7 ch.g. Galileo (IRE) – Angara (Alzao (USA)) [2016/17 h121: h16d h16g **h121**
h16g h18.2g⁴ h16d h20g h16d* Oct 29] fairly useful handicap hurdler: won at Ayr in
October: unproven beyond 2m: acts on heavy going: wears tongue tie: often races in rear:
has joined James Moffatt. *Robert Hennessy, Ireland*

SPE

SPADER (IRE) 4 b.g. Jeremy (USA) – Poulkovo (IRE) (Sadler's Wells (USA)) [2016/17   **h104 p**
h16s⁶ h16.5g⁶ h18.7d³ h16.3g³ Apr 15] compact gelding: fairly useful on Flat, stays 1¼m:
fair form over hurdles: tried in tongue tie: open to improvement. *Dan Skelton*

SPANISH FLEET 9 b.g. Cadeaux Genereux – Santisima Trinidad (IRE) (Definite   **c122**
Article) [2016/17 c–, h–: c20d³ c20g² c18s² c21.6v² c22.3v² c20.6v⁵ c26.2d Apr 10]   **h–**
winning hurdler: fairly useful maiden chaser: stays 2¾m: acts on heavy going: has worn
headgear, including in 2016/17: races lazily. *George Bewley*

SPANISH FORK (IRE) 8 br.g. Trans Island – Wings Awarded (Shareef Dancer (USA))   **h66 §**
[2016/17 h81§: h25gᵖᵘ h25mⁿ h25.6g⁵ Nov 4] leggy gelding: poor handicap hurdler: stays
27f: acts on firm and good to soft going: has worn headgear: tried in tongue tie: front
runner/races prominently: temperamental. *Sheena West*

SPANISH OPTIMIST (IRE) 11 b.g. Indian Danehill (IRE) – La Traviata (Spectrum   **c81 §**
(IRE)) [2016/17 c73§, h–: c21.1g⁴ c22.6mᵖᵘ c22.6mᵖᵘ c19.4gᵖᵘ Apr 9] winning hurdler/   **h–**
chaser, largely out of form over fences in 2016/17: stays 3m: acts on good to soft going:
tried in visor: has worn tongue tie: not one to rely on. *Sarah Robinson*

SPANISH QUEEN 5 b.f. Fantastic Spain (USA) – Smart Cassie (Allied Forces (USA))   **h68**
[2016/17 h16.8sᵘʳ h17.7d h16.8s h15.9s h16.8sᵖᵘ h16v h21.6mᵖᵘ Apr 15] well held in
maidens on Flat: little form over hurdles. *Mark Gillard*

SPANISH STARLING 5 b.g. Fantastic Spain (USA) – Clarice Starling (Saddlers' Hall   **b–**
(IRE)) [2016/17 b15.8m⁶ Apr 18] last in bumper. *Sarah-Jayne Davies*

SPARKLING DAWN 5 gr.m. Sulamani (IRE) – Clotted Cream (USA) (Eagle Eyed   **b92**
(USA)) [2016/17 b15.8d⁴ b15.8s³ Apr 1] sister to fair hurdler Revani (17f winner), stayed
21f, and half-sister to fairly useful hurdler Maska Pony (2m-2½m winner, by Celtic
Swing): dam, 6f winner, half-sister to high-class 2m hurdler Detroit City: fair form when
in frame in bumpers. *Johnny Farrelly*

SPARKLING ICE (IRE) 6 gr.m. Verglas (IRE) – Sand Crystal (IRE) (Singspiel (IRE))   **h74**
[2016/17 h76: h16.8s h19.9vᵖᵘ h16.5g⁶ h15.9s⁶ h16.8s⁴ h23.9g³ Mar 30] poor maiden
hurdler: stays 3m: tried in blinkers. *Laura Young*

SPARKLING RIVER (IRE) 7 gr.m. Indian River (FR) – Full Deck (IRE) (Roselier   **h114**
(FR)) [2016/17 h16g⁴ h15.7d⁵ h15.8s⁵ h19v* h19.7v² h23.8s⁴ h21v* Mar 22] €900 3-y-o,
£11,500 6-y-o: half-sister to fair/unreliable hurdler/winning pointer Turbulance (2¾m
winner, by Snurge) and modest hurdler Supreme Deck (2½m winner, by Supreme Leader):
dam unraced sister to useful chaser (stayed 25f) All The Aces: Irish maiden point winner:
fair handicap hurdler: won novice contest at Warwick in December and mares event there
in March: should stay 3m: acts on heavy going: usually leads: possibly unsuited by right-
handed tracks. *Henry Oliver*

SPARKY'S SECRET 4 b.g. Sakhee's Secret – Sparkling Montjeu (IRE) (Montjeu (IRE))   **h–**
[2016/17 b15.8v b16s h18.5m⁶ Apr 18] well held in bumpers/maiden hurdle: tried in   **b–**
cheekpieces. *George Baker*

SPARTILLA 8 b.g. Teofilo (IRE) – Wunders Dream (IRE) (Averti (IRE)) [2016/17 c83,   **c–**
h–: c22.5d c19.7dᵖᵘ c25.7sᵖᵘ Mar 13] maiden hurdler/chaser: tried in headgear/tongue tie: **h–**
dead. *Daniel O'Brien*

SPA'S DANCER (IRE) 10 b.g. Danehill Dancer (IRE) – Spa (Sadler's Wells (USA))   **h84**
[2016/17 h103: h16s h16g⁶ Dec 18] compact gelding: maiden hurdler: raced only at 2m:
acts on soft going: has worn hood: front runner/races prominently. *James Eustace*

SPECIAL CATCH (IRE) 10 b.g. Catcher In The Rye (IRE) – Top Quality (Simply Great   **c142**
(FR)) [2016/17 c133, h–: c17.1d² c15.5g* c19.1d⁴ c15.7sᵖᵘ c19.3s* c20.5s³ c20.1g²   **h–**
c20.1g² Apr 27] winning hurdler: useful handicap chaser: won at Ayr in October and
Sedgefield in January: second at Perth (2½ lengths behind Mystifiable) final start: left Keith
Reveley after fourth start: stays 2½m: acts on heavy going: usually races nearer last than
first, often travels strongly. *Malcolm Jefferson*

SPECIAL TIARA 10 b.g. Kayf Tara – Special Choice (IRE) (Bob Back (USA))   **c166**
[2016/17 c169, h–: c16d⁶ c15.9s³ c16g* c16.3s⁵ c15.9g* c15.5g² Apr 29]   **h–**
    The Queen Mother Champion Chase made headlines as much for the abject
display of 9/2-on Douvan as it did for the performance of the winner Special Tiara.
Douvan started the shortest-priced favourite for the race in over half a century,
and his unblemished record of nine impressive victories from as many starts over
fences had many celebrating his 'coronation' prematurely—before the deed was
actually accomplished. Douvan's eclipse, accounted for by a hairline fracture that
he suffered to his pelvis, illustrated once again that nothing can be taken for granted

in horse racing and that newsworthy performances cannot be produced to order. Unfortunately, the attention given to Douvan, and the analysis of his performance, meant that Special Tiara, a worthy winner among those who showed their form on the day, didn't get his just desserts at the time. It was his fourth appearance in the Queen Mother Champion Chase, a race in which he was third in both 2015 and 2016, and he produced a trademark performance, jumping with typical boldness in front and holding on gamely up Cheltenham's steep finishing climb to win by a head from Fox Norton.

Special Tiara gave his trainer Henry de Bromhead his second winner of the race, following Sizing Europe, who carried the colours of Ann and Alan Potts the owners of Fox Norton. The Potts-owned horses had been removed from de Bromhead before the start of the latest season (Fox Norton was a subsequent purchase), ending a long association with the trainer who credited them with helping to launch his career. Henry de Bromhead, a descendant of Lieutenant Gonville Bromhead who won a VC at Rorke's Drift in 1879 (he was played by Michael Caine in the 1964 film *Zulu*), took over his father's small string of fifteen horses at Knockeen in County Waterford on New Year's Day in 2000 when he had two runners, Fidalus and Wild Spice ('Fidalus was coming back from injury and wasn't fancied, but he won, and Wild Spice started 11/8 favourite and got beaten!'). It was de Bromhead's 'dream to have thirty horses' but it took a few years to build up the yard before the support of the likes of Ann and Alan Potts, Roger Brookhouse and Gigginstown House Stud (which increased its representation in the latest season) enabled the stable to expand to the extent that it now houses a string of well over a hundred and is established among Ireland's top training establishments. Henry de Bromhead enjoyed his best season so far in 2016/17, finishing third behind Willie Mullins and Gordon Elliott with sixty-eight wins and over €1.5m in total prize money.

Special Tiara is seen more often in Britain than in Ireland where he is trained, his connections believing he is at his best on good going or firmer, conditions less likely to occur in Ireland where testing going is the norm for much of the winter. All of Special Tiara's important victories have come in Britain including, before the latest season, Grade 1 successes in the 2013 Maghull Novices' Chase at Aintree and the 2015 Celebration Chase at Sandown. By contrast, Special Tiara's owner Sally Rowley-Williams now has all her horses trained in Ireland despite having enjoyed success with British yards in the past, her best horse before Special Tiara being the 2007 Champion Chase third River City. As a further complication, Mrs Rowley-Williams (also founder and honorary president of the Women In Racing organisation) returned to live in the States in August after thirty years in Britain, and she is clearly as good a traveller as her horse, making visits nowadays from her new home in Florida to see him race. One such 'flying' visit coincided with Special Tiara's second victory in the 32Red Desert Orchid Chase at Kempton in December when Mrs Rowley-Williams stood in the winner's enclosure greeting her winner just six hours after landing at Heathrow. Special Tiara had shaped as if needing the run on his reappearance, when third to Fox Norton in the Schloer Chase at Cheltenham

32Red Desert Orchid Chase, Kempton—
odds-on Special Tiara is pushed all the way by Sir Valentino before repeating his 2014 win

Betway Queen Mother Champion Chase, Cheltenham—hot favourite Douvan (right) is already well held as front runner Special Tiara holds off the late rally of Fox Norton (noseband)

(he had also been third in the 2013 renewal), and he started at odds on for the four-runner Desert Orchid Chase, for which the going was good. When second favourite Sire de Grugy blundered and unseated his rider at the second, the way looked open for front-running Special Tiara to go on to a straightforward victory. In the end, though, he had to work quite hard to hold off Haldon Gold Cup winner Sir Valentino, who was conceding him 6 lb, by half a length.

Special Tiara's victory in the Desert Orchid was his first since his win in the Celebration Chase twenty months earlier but he didn't have to wait so long to follow up. Having missed the British season's first open Grade 1 two-mile chase, the Tingle Creek at Sandown, in which he had finished an unlucky second in a controversial renewal twelve months earlier, Special Tiara contested the second, the Clarence House Chase, which was transferred to Cheltenham's Trials meeting at the end of January after the Ascot meeting at which it was due to be run was abandoned. Un de Sceaux added the Clarence House to his earlier success in the Tingle Creek but Special Tiara weakened after the third last and came last of the five finishers. The going at Cheltenham was soft and, although Special Tiara has won under such conditions (it was soft when he won his first Desert Orchid Chase), he was clearly below his best, for whatever reason.

Ground conditions were considerably less testing for the Betway Queen Mother Champion Chase at the Cheltenham Festival for which Special Tiara started 11/1 fourth favourite behind Douvan, God's Own (6/1) and Fox Norton (7/1). With the previous year's winner Sprinter Sacre retired and Un de Sceaux (runner-up to Sprinter Sacre) rerouted to the Ryanair Chase, Special Tiara and God's Own (fourth in 2016) were left to represent the 'old guard' among the leading two-mile chasers. At the age of ten, the joint oldest runner in the race, Special Tiara looked as if he had missed his chance to win a Champion Chase, notwithstanding the presence in the latest line-up of Douvan. Henry de Bromhead admitted as much, saying that 'the sunshine is great for him as the better the ground, the better his chance, but, realistically, we have come here for place money'. However, as the race itself showed, anything can happen in horse racing, and a repeat of the form he had shown twelve months earlier proved enough for Special Tiara to win the third Grade 1 of his career, fittingly in the most important championship of all for the two-mile chasers. Disputing the lead from the start and really pressing on from the fifth, the flamboyant Special Tiara continued to give an exhilarating display of bold and accurate jumping out in front and appeared set for a clear-cut victory when jumping the last fence two lengths ahead. However, he was strongly pressed on the run-in by Fox Norton who just failed to peg him back. The pair finished six lengths ahead of third-placed Sir Valentino, followed by Top Gamble and God's Own (who would have been third at worst but for bad mistakes four out and two out, doing well to recover from the first of them). Traffic Fluide completed the first six, while Douvan managed only

Mrs S. Rowley-Williams' "Special Tiara"

seventh. Special Tiara's jockey Noel Fehily, his regular partner nowadays, praised his mount afterwards—'He jumped better today than he has ever done with me and he got into a great rhythm.'

Special Tiara couldn't quite reproduce his Queen Mother Champion Chase form in the Celebration Chase at Sandown's Finale meeting against the outstanding novice Altior (who had beaten Fox Norton convincingly in the Game Spirit at Newbury before winning the Arkle at Cheltenham). Special Tiara jumped well, as usual, and made the running, but it was something of a mis-match and there was nothing he could do to resist the long odds-on winner who passed him between the last two fences and went on to beat him by eight lengths. Still, as Special Tiara's owner observed, 'I can always go home and look at the Queen Mother Champion Chase trophy to cheer myself up … it has pride of place in our sitting room.'

		Sadler's Wells	Northern Dancer
	Kayf Tara	(b 1981)	Fairy Bridge
	(b 1994)	Colorspin	High Top
Special Tiara		(b 1983)	Reprocolor
(b.g. 2007)		Bob Back	Roberto
	Special Choice (IRE)	(br 1981)	Toter Back
	(b 2002)	Mammy's Choice	Mandalus
		(br 1990)	Liffey's Choice

A big gelding, the exuberant Special Tiara wasn't bred to be a two-miler, his sire Kayf Tara usually being a strong influence for stamina and his unraced dam Special Choice being a daughter of Mammy's Choice, a fair handicap chaser who stayed three and a half miles. Stamina has always been the strong suit of most of the stock of Special Choice's sire Bob Back, as it has of the stock of Mandalus, the sire of Mammy's Choice. Mandalus had a remarkable career as a racehorse, showing useful form at six furlongs to two and three quarter miles (third in the Queen Alexandra Stakes) on the Flat. Mandalus was purchased as a five-year-old by Henry de Bromhead's father, who stood him in Ireland at an initial fee of £350, and he appears in the pedigrees of a number of the horses who have done well for the stable, also among them Sizing Europe and the 2015 Maghull Novices' Chase winner Sizing Granite, both of whom are out of dams sired by Mandalus. The aforementioned Fidalus, Henry de Bromhead's first winner, was by Mandalus. Special Tiara's great grandam the winning hurdler Liffey's Choice was by another thorough stayer Little Buskins. Special Tiara is the first foal out of Special Choice, and her second foal, Special Tiara's four-years-younger sister Special Diamond, was successful in a maiden hurdle at Cork for Henry de Bromhead early in the 2017/18 season. For all that he is bred to stay much further, Special Tiara is clearly best at two miles. A headstrong type (twice tried in a hood) who makes the running, it bears repeating that he is a bold and accurate jumper. He has been raced mainly on good to soft going or firmer in recent seasons, conditions which seem ideal for him nowadays (he has won on soft but was below form both times he encountered testing conditions in the latest season). *Henry de Bromhead, Ireland*

SPECIAL WELLS 8 ch.g. Alflora (IRE) – Oso Special (Teenoso (USA)) [2016/17 c113, h–: c20d³ c22.5v⁴ c24v⁴ c16v* c19.4d* c20.1s⁴ c20g⁴ Apr 15] big gelding: winning hurdler: fairly useful handicap chaser: won at Uttoxeter in December and Wetherby in January: stays 2½m: acts on heavy going. *Sue Smith*   **c120** **h–**

SPECTATOR 6 br.g. Passing Glance – Averami (Averti (IRE)) [2016/17 h18.7m h16.2m* h15.6g³ Nov 2] half-brother to very smart hurdler Taglietelle (2m-3m winner, by Tagula): fairly useful on Flat, stays 16.5f: fair form over hurdles: won maiden at Kelso in October: should stay 2½m. *Tim Vaughan*   **h105**

SPEEDALONG (IRE) 6 b.g. Vertical Speed (FR) – Emily's Bracelet (IRE) (Priolo (USA)) [2016/17 b–: h19.7s h19.8dᵖᵘ h19g⁴ h21g² Apr 24] sturdy gelding: fair form over hurdles: much improved when second in maiden at Warwick: stays 21f: in hood/tongue tie last 2 starts: usually races in rear. *Jeremy Scott*   **h102**

SPEED DEMON (IRE) 8 b.g. Beneficial – Brierfield Lady (IRE) (Montelimar (USA)) [2016/17 c112, h114: c20.5m³ c20.2gᵖᵘ c19.9dᵖᵘ Feb 9] lengthy gelding: won sole start in points: fair hurdler: maiden chaser, fair form at best: stays 25f: acts on good to firm and heavy going: has worn blinkers, including final start: signs of temperament. *Richard Phillips*   **c91** **h–**

SPEEDY RUNAWAY (IRE) 6 b.g. Presenting – Toasted Oats (IRE) (Be My Native (USA)) [2016/17 h15.5g h20.5d h21m Apr 18] well held in novice hurdles: tried in visor. *Paul Webber*   **h–**

SPELLBOUND 8 b.m. Doyen (IRE) – Kasamba (Salse (USA)) [2016/17 h21.6sᵖᵘ h26s⁵ h23.5s h21v² Mar 22] sturdy mare: fair handicap hurdler: stays 2¾m: acts on heavy going: tried in cheekpieces: has worn tongue tie. *Alan King*   **h102**

SPENCER LEA 9 b.g. Overbury (IRE) – Castanet (Pennekamp (USA)) [2016/17 h121: c21.4s³ Nov 17] angular gelding: fairly useful hurdler: 20/1, third in novice handicap at Market Rasen (5 lengths behind Cusheen Bridge) on chasing debut: stays 21f: best form on soft/heavy going. *Henry Oliver*   **c121** **h–**

SPENCER MOON (IRE) 9 b.g. Dr Massini (IRE) – Nana Moon (IRE) (Flemensfirth (USA)) [2016/17 c23.6m³ Apr 28] multiple point winner: maiden hurdler: fair form in chases: stays 3m: acts on good to firm and good to soft going: tried in cheekpieces. *Kieran Price*   **c106** **h–**

SPEREDEK (FR) 6 b.g. Kapgarde (FR) – Sendamagic (FR) (Sendawar (IRE)) [2016/17 h118: c25.2sᵖᵘ c20sᵖᵘ c18.2d* c15.5s* c16s* Mar 23] good-topped gelding: fairly useful hurdler: useful form over fences: won handicaps at Taunton (novice) and Sandown in February, and at Ludlow (by 11 lengths from Workbench) in March: has won over 23f, but at least as effective at much shorter: acts on heavy going: wears cheekpieces: has worn tongue tie: front runner, often travels strongly. *Nigel Hawke*   **c135** **h–**

SPERONIMO (FR) 5 b.g. Diamond Green (FR) – Spepita (FR) (Marathon (USA)) [2016/17 b–: h18.6sᶠ h15.8v h18.5s Feb 12] tall, rather unfurnished gelding: well held in completed starts in novice hurdles: has worn tongue tie. *Nigel Hawke*   **h–**

SPICE BOAT 5 ch.g. Shamardal (USA) – Frizzante (Efisio) [2016/17 h15.9mᵖᵘ Apr 16] maiden on Flat: pulled up in maiden on hurdling debut. *Paddy Butler*   **h–**

SPICE FAIR 10 ch.g. Trade Fair – Focosa (ITY) (In The Wings) [2016/17 h127: h19.8d⁵ h19.5g⁴ h24s³ h19s⁴ h21.4d⁴ h20.5v² h16d⁴ Mar 11] sturdy gelding: fairly useful handicap hurdler: stays 3m, as effective at much shorter: acts on heavy going. *Mark Usher*   **h124**

SPICE GIRL 4 ch.f. Black Sam Bellamy (IRE) – Karmest (Best of The Bests (IRE)) **b69**
[2016/17 b13.7g Nov 8] second foal: dam (h87), ran twice over hurdles, 6f-1½m winner on
Flat: 20/1, eighth in junior bumper at Huntingdon. *Martin Keighley*

SPICULAS (IRE) 8 ch.g. Beneficial – Alicia's Charm (IRE) (Executive Perk) [2016/17 **c120**
h16.8d² h16.8s⁴ h15.6g⁴ c15.9d² c16gᵖᵘ Apr 27] fairly useful handicap hurdler: similar **h115**
form when second in novice handicap at Carlisle on completed start over fences: stays
2½m: acts on heavy going: front runner/races prominently. *Malcolm Jefferson*

SPIDER'S BITE (IRE) 5 b.g. Scorpion (IRE) – Model Girl (Classic Cliche (IRE)) **b86**
[2016/17 b16gʳᵒ b16.3v b15.8m* Apr 25] rangy, useful-looking gelding: third foal: half-
brother to 2 winning pointers by Cloudings: dam (b75), ran once in bumper, half-sister to
smart hurdler/useful chaser (winner up to 25f) Silver Wedge: fair form in bumpers: won
4-runner event at Ludlow in April: will stay further than 2m. *Henry Daly*

SPIFER (IRE) 9 gr.g. Motivator – Zarawa (IRE) (Kahyasi) [2016/17 h87: h16.2mᵖᵘ **h63**
h16.2m⁶ May 29] useful at one time on Flat: lightly-raced maiden hurdler, modest form at
best. *Julia Brooke*

SPIKER THE BIKER (IRE) 13 b.g. New Frontier (IRE) – Hollies Promise (IRE) **c–**
(Good Thyne (USA)) [2016/17 c–, h86: h23.1gᵖᵘ c24.2gᵖᵘ Jun 4] winning pointer: maiden **h–**
hurdler/chaser: stays 27f: acts on good to firm and heavy going: wears headgear/tongue tie:
often races prominently. *Nigel Slevin, Ireland*

SPILLERS DREAM (IRE) 8 b.g. Shantou (USA) – Eibhlinarun (IRE) (Charnwood **c94 §**
Forest (IRE)) [2016/17 h20d⁴ h23g² c23g⁴ h23gᵖᵘ c24.2m³ c25gᵘʳ c25.2gᵖᵘ h23.9g h19.5vᵖᵘ **h94 §**
h15.8sᴿ Apr 1] modest maiden hurdler/chaser, has lost his way: left Philip Hobbs after third
start, Brian Barr after ninth: stays 23f: best form on good going: has worn headgear,
including last 5 starts: temperamental. *Hannah James*

SPINNING SCOOTER 7 b.g. Sleeping Indian – Spinning Coin (Mujahid (USA)) **h79**
[2016/17 b–: h16.7g⁵ h16.2g⁶ h19.9g h23.9s⁶ h19s Dec 5] poor form over hurdles: tried in
visor: wears tongue tie. *Maurice Barnes*

SPIN POINT (IRE) 5 b.g. Pivotal – Daneleta (IRE) (Danehill (USA)) [2016/17 h15.8v⁶ **h–**
h15.8d h16v Mar 12] fairly useful at best on Flat, stays 1½m: well held in maiden/novice
hurdles. *Ian Williams*

SPIRIT OF HALE 6 ch.g. Stowaway – Roseboreen (IRE) (Roselier (FR)) **h81**
[2016/17 b–: h15.8s h16.7s⁵ h16.7s h20.5v⁴ h21v h19.7d⁵ Mar 26] tall gelding: poor form
over hurdles. *Jennie Candlish*

SPIRIT OF KAYF 6 b.g. Kayf Tara – Over Sixty (Overbury (IRE)) [2016/17 b99: **h132 p**
h16.2s* h21.2gᶠ h22s* Nov 26] rather unfurnished gelding: bumper winner: useful form
over hurdles: won maiden at Hexham in September and novice at Newcastle (by 4½
lengths from Get On The Yager) in November: will probably stay 3m: usually races close
up: open to further improvement. *Sandy Thomson*

SPIRITOFTHEGAMES (IRE) 5 b.g. Darsi (FR) – Lucy Walters (IRE) (King's Ride) **h126 p**
[2016/17 h20.5d* h21.1g⁴ h21g² h19g* Mar 2] €20,000 3-y-o, £50,000 4-y-o: lengthy
gelding: half-brother to several winners, including bumper winner/useful hurdler Mackeys
Forge (2m winner, by Mr Combustible) and bumper winner/fairly useful hurdler Broughton
Green (25f winner, by Shernazar): dam (c91/h91), bumper winner, half-sister to fairly
useful hurdler/fair chaser (stayed 27f) Elzahann: won Irish maiden point on debut: fairly
useful form over hurdles: won maiden at Ayr in October and novice at Taunton in March:
will stay 3m: remains open to improvement. *Dan Skelton*

SPIRITUAL MAN (IRE) 5 b.g. Lawman (FR) – Vee Gita (IRE) (Vettori (IRE)) [2016/17 **h108**
h16g⁶ h15.3d⁴ h15.8s⁴ h15.8g² Apr 3] fair form on Flat/over hurdles. *Jonjo O'Neill*

SPLASH OF GINGE 9 b.g. Oscar (IRE) – Land of Honour (Supreme Leader) [2016/17 **c131 §**
c139, h–: c19.4g⁴ c19.9d⁴ c19.9g⁶ h22.8s* h22.8s² h23.6v⁵ h24g h24.7g Apr 8] lengthy **h134 §**
gelding: useful handicap hurdler: won at Haydock in December: useful handicap chaser:
stays 3m: acts on heavy going: has worn visor: usually races close up: temperamental.
Nigel Twiston-Davies

SPOCK (FR) 12 b.g. Lost World (IRE) – Quark Top (FR) (Perrault) [2016/17 c96, h–: **c89 §**
c19.4g⁵ c20.3g⁴ c23gᶠ c20dᵖᵘ c19.4mᵘʳ c20.3g⁵ c16.5m⁶ c16.5g³ c16g⁴ c20m² c19.7g* **h–**
c18.2g⁴ c16mᵘʳ Apr 18] winning hurdler: modest handicap chaser: won at Plumpton in
October: stays 21f: acts on good to firm going: wears headgear: tried in tongue tie: often
leads: unreliable. *Lady Susan Brooke*

SPOILS OF WAR (IRE) 8 b.g. Craigsteel – Mooreshill Lady (IRE) (King's Ride) [2016/17 **c93**
h–: h17.1d c16.9d⁵ c15.6v² c21.5s³ c24.3v⁵ c21.6v⁴ h19.3d⁶ Apr 5] maiden hurdler: modest **h73**
form over fences: stays 21f: acts on heavy going: in headgear last 2 starts. *Lucinda Russell*

SPOILT ROTTEN 8 b.g. Kayf Tara – Rosita Bay (Hernando (FR)) [2016/17 h–, b87: c16s^{pu} c15.9s^2 c19.9g^{pu} c15.7g^2 Apr 21] lightly raced over hurdles: fair form over fences: unproven beyond 2m: acts on soft going: in hood last 4 starts: often leads. *Mark Pitman* — **c111 h–**

SPOOKYDOOKY (IRE) 9 b.g. Winged Love (IRE) – Kiora Lady (IRE) (King's Ride) [2016/17 c137, h–: c24.1v^6 c23.6g c29.2s c30.7d^3 c33.4s c28.1g^{pu} Apr 19] workmanlike gelding: winning hurdler: fairly useful handicap chaser: stays 31f: acts on heavy going: tried in cheekpieces: wears tongue tie. *Jonjo O'Neill* — **c128 h–**

SPORTING MILAN (IRE) 6 b.g. Milan – Sports Leader (IRE) (Supreme Leader) [2016/17 h95, b77: h20g^4 h23d* h23g^2 Jul 21] runner-up in Irish point: modest form over hurdles: won novice handicap at Worcester in June: will be suited by 3m+: tried in cheekpieces. *Harry Whittington* — **h99**

SPORTS BARROW (IRE) 5 b.g. Windsor Knot (IRE) – Liberty Grace (IRE) (Statue of Liberty (USA)) [2016/17 h19.8m^{pu} h20d h16d h19.4g h16.2g^3 Apr 27] fair on Flat, stays 1¾m: fair handicap hurdler: left Ms Sandra Hughes after first start: best form around 2m on good going: often in cheekpieces: often races prominently. *Colin A. McBratney, Ireland* — **h100**

SPORTS DAY 5 b.m. Beat Hollow – Midsummer Magic (Muhtarram (USA)) [2016/17 b16.7g b15.8m^6 Oct 5] lengthy mare: second foal: half-sister to bumper winner/fair hurdler Summer Storm (2m/17f winner, by Lucarno): dam (h108), 2m hurdle winner (stayed 21f), half-sister to useful hurdler/chaser (stayed 2½m) Close Touch: well held in bumpers. *Charlie Longsdon* — **b–**

SPORTSREPORT (IRE) 9 b.g. Coroner (IRE) – Goforthetape (IRE) (Gothland (FR)) [2016/17 c109, h–: c17.4d^2 c17.2d c17.4g Jun 7] maiden hurdler: fair handicap chaser: unproven beyond 17f: acts on heavy going: wears headgear: tried in tongue tie: often races towards rear: not one to rely on (weak finisher). *Seamus Mullins* — **c109 § h–**

SPORTY YANKEE (USA) 4 gr.g. Paddy O'Prado (USA) – I Insist (USA) (Green Dancer (USA)) [2016/17 h15.8v* h15.9v^5 h16v^6 Feb 24] tall gelding: fairly useful on Flat, stays 1¾m: modest form over hurdles: won juvenile maiden at Ffos Las in December: tried in cheekpieces. *Martin Keighley* — **h96**

SPOSALIZIO (IRE) 10 ch.g. Dr Fong (USA) – Wedding Cake (IRE) (Groom Dancer (USA)) [2016/17 c22.6m^6 c19.9g^{pu} Mar 1] multiple winning pointer: maiden hurdler: fair chaser at best, no form in 2016/17: stays 21f: acts on good to firm going: tried in cheekpieces: wears tongue tie. *C. T. Dawson* — **c– h–**

SPREAD BOY (IRE) 10 b.g. Tagula (IRE) – Marinka (Pivotal) [2016/17 h16.2d h16.2d^4 h15.8g c16.4g^3 c15.6g^6 c17.4g^6 c16.4s* c16.4d^5 c16.4d^4 c15.7s c19.3v^6 c16.4d^{ur} Mar 14] poor maiden hurdler: poor handicap chaser: won at Sedgefield in November: raced mainly around 2m: acts on soft going: tried in hood/tongue tie. *Barry Murtagh* — **c73 h62**

SPRING HILL (IRE) 5 b.g. Stowaway – Miss The Post (Bustino) [2016/17 b–: b15.8g^4 May 9] modest form on second of 2 starts in bumpers. *Chris Bealby* — **b75**

SPRINGHILL LAD 10 b.g. Kayf Tara – Anouska (Interrex (CAN)) [2016/17 h103: c20.3g^{pu} Apr 29] maiden hurdler: pulled up in novice handicap on chasing debut: stays 3¼m: acts on heavy going. *Geoffrey Deacon* — **c– h–**

SPRING OVER (IRE) 11 ch.m. Samraan (USA) – Superswap (IRE) (Gone Fishin) [2016/17 c83, h–: h16v^2 h21.4v^2 h23.3s^{pu} c24.2v^F h23.9g^{pu} Apr 26] poor handicap hurdler: maiden chaser: stays 3m: acts on heavy going: wears tongue tie. *Ian Duncan* — **c– h79**

SPRING POOLS (IRE) 6 ch.m. Subtle Power (IRE) – Fey Macha (IRE) (Phardante (FR)) [2016/17 h21v^{pu} c20.3s^3 Feb 10] £4,000 5-y-o: sturdy mare: fifth foal: sister to a winning pointer: dam (h113) bumper/19f-3m hurdle winner: Irish maiden point winner: little show in mares novices over hurdles/fences. *Sam Thomas* — **c79 h–**

SPRING STEEL (IRE) 8 b.g. Dushyantor (USA) – Fieldtown (IRE) (Anshan) [2016/17 c108, h103§: c15.7g^{pu} c21.1g^{pu} c16.3g* c19.4g* c17.4g* h19.1g^3 h20.3m^2 h21m^2 Oct 5] close-coupled gelding: fair maiden hurdler: fair handicap chaser: won at Newton Abbot and Stratford in July, and at Fontwell in August: stays 21f: acts on good to firm and good to soft going: has worn hood: wears tongue tie: races prominently. *Alexandra Dunn* — **c102 h103**

SPRINGTOWN LAKE (IRE) 5 b.g. Gamut (IRE) – Sprightly Gal (IRE) (Old Vic) [2016/17 b16s h19.3m^2 Apr 2] €16,000 3-y-o, £95,000 4-y-o: good-topped gelding: fourth foal: dam ran once over hurdles: runner-up in Irish maiden point: well beaten in maiden bumper: 33/1, promise when second in maiden at Ascot (¾ length behind Tales of The Tweed) on hurdling debut: should improve. *Philip Hobbs* — **h118 p b–**

SPROGZILLA 8 gr.m. Fair Mix (IRE) – Gentle Approach (Rakaposhi King) [2016/17 h–, b–: h16.3m^{pu} h16.7g^5 h18.7g h15.7m^2 h16.5m Apr 20] pulled up in mares maiden point: modest form over hurdles: has worn hood: front runner/races prominently. *Hannah James* — **h89**

SPURNED GIRL 7 b.m. Passing Glance – Highlight Girl (Forzando) [2016/17 h65: h19g c–
h15.7g⁶ c17.4d⁴ Jun 1] little form over hurdles: tailed off in novice on chasing debut: h–
usually wears hood/tongue tie. *Robin Dickin*

SPYDER 9 b.g. Resplendent Glory (IRE) – Collect (Vettori (IRE)) [2016/17 h20.5g⁵ h–
h20.3s⁵ᵖᵘ h15.7d h15.7s h20.7g⁵ Apr 17] fairly useful hurdler at best, no form in 2016/17
after long absence: front runner/races prominently. *Tracey Leeson*

SPY IN THE SKY 8 b.m. Generous (IRE) – Lady Deploy (Deploy) [2016/17 h21vᵖᵘ h86
h15.5g h16.7s⁴ h19gᵖᵘ Feb 21] sturdy mare: modest form over hurdles: tried in tongue tie.
Fergal O'Brien

SQUABLIN 5 b.m. Revoque (IRE) – Smuglin (Sir Harry Lewis (USA)) [2016/17 b16.7d⁵ h–
b16.2d⁶ h16.2v h16s⁶ h16.7s⁵ h20.3v⁵ Mar 6] first foal: dam (c114/h111), 2½m-2¾m b–
hurdle/chase winner, half-sister to fairly useful hurdler/chaser (stayed 25f) Rattlin: well
held in bumpers/over hurdles: tried in hood. *Sue Smith*

SQUEAKY 6 br.m. Kayf Tara – Alta (Arctic Lord) [2016/17 b16m⁴ b16.2s⁶ h20.7s h19g h–
Feb 21] sixth foal: sister to 2 winning pointers and half-sister to modest hurdler She's b76
Noble (21f winner, by Karinga Bay): dam (c109/h123) bumper/17f hurdle winner (stayed
3m): modest form in bumpers: well held both starts over hurdles: should be suited by
further than 2m: wears tongue tie. *Nigel Twiston-Davies*

SQUEEZE ME 10 b.m. Grape Tree Road – Ask Me Not (IRE) (Shernazar) [2016/17 h–: h95
h23.3d² h19.9g⁶ h22.1g* h20.6s⁶ h20.3sᵖᵘ h17d⁶ h16.7g³ h19.9g⁵ h19.6g³ Apr 22] modest
handicap hurdler: won at Cartmel in June: stays 23f: acts on good to firm and good to soft
going: has worn cheekpieces: tried in tongue tie. *Gary Hanmer*

SQUIRREL ESQUIRE 9 b.g. Kayf Tara – Alta (Arctic Lord) [2016/17 c20.9sᵖᵘ Mar 13] c–
won 3 times in points: well held completed start in hunter chases. *Mrs A. Fox-Pitt*

SQUOUATEUR (FR) 6 gr.g. Martaline – Samansonnienne (FR) (Mansonnien (FR)) c132
[2016/17 h136: c17d⁵ c17d c16d c20vᵖᵘ c16s² c26gᵘʳ Mar 16] strong, lengthy gelding: h–
useful hurdler: similar form over fences: second in handicap at Naas (4¼ lengths behind
Westerns Son) in February: stays 2½m: acts on heavy going: wears tongue tie. *Gordon
Elliott, Ireland*

SR SWING 6 b.m. Passing Glance – Wigman Lady (IRE) (Tenby) [2016/17 h19.3g³ Nov h83
30] half-sister to fair hurdler Embsay Crag (2m-2½m winner, by Elmaamul): poor maiden
on Flat: 66/1, third of 5 in mares novice at Catterick (9 lengths behind Miss Maiden Over)
on hurdling debut. *Peter Niven*

STAFFORD JO 8 ch.g. Silver Patriarch (IRE) – Miss Roberto (IRE) (Don Roberto h–
(USA)) [2016/17 h103, b–: h15.8d May 5] lightly raced in bumpers/over hurdles: dead.
John O'Shea

STAFF SERGEANT 10 b.g. Dubawi (IRE) – Miss Particular (IRE) (Sadler's Wells h–
(USA)) [2016/17 h71: h15.9gᵖᵘ May 8] maiden hurdler: raced around 2m: acts on good to
soft going: tried in visor: usually races nearer last than first. *Mark Hoad*

STAGECOACH JASPER 11 b.g. Sir Harry Lewis (USA) – Flintwood (Gunner B) c– x
[2016/17 c23.6gᵖᵘ c25.2s⁵ Mar 8] big gelding: winning pointer: maiden hurdler/chaser: h–
stays 25f: acts on good going: in cheekpieces last 2 starts: often let down by jumping. *R. Tate*

STAGE ONE (IRE) 6 b.g. King's Theatre (IRE) – Tara Tara (IRE) (Fayruz) [2016/17 c100
h119p: h20g³ h15.8g³ h16.2s³ c17.2g³ c19.4d⁴ Apr 16] won second start in Irish points: fair h107
form over hurdles/fences: best effort at 2½m: acts on soft going: tried in cheekpieces: in
tongue tie last 5 starts. *Dan Skelton*

STAGS LEAP (IRE) 10 b.g. Refuse To Bend (IRE) – Swingsky (IRE) (Indian Ridge) h114
[2016/17 h103: h19.9g² Aug 25] fair handicap hurdler, lightly raced: stays 2¾m: acts on
good to firm and good to soft going: usually wears headgear. *Julia Brooke*

STAIGUE FORT 9 b.g. Kirkwall – Mulberry Wine (Benny The Dip (USA)) [2016/17 c–, c–
h–: h17sᵖᵘ h23.8g³ Mar 1] lengthy, good-bodied gelding: fairly useful hurdler at best, h104
lightly raced nowadays: too free only start over fences: stays 2¾m: acts on good to firm
going. *Susan Corbett*

STAMP YOUR FEET (IRE) 5 b.g. Galileo (IRE) – Nausicaa (USA) (Diesis) [2016/17 h118
b85: b13.6d* h16.3m² h16.7g³ h16.2s* h15.6g⁴ h15.8s³ h15.7g* h16.3d⁵ Apr 27] fairly b100
useful form in bumpers: won at Fontwell very early in season: fairly useful handicap
hurdler: won at Hereford in December and Haydock in April: will be suited by further than
2m: acts on soft going: in tongue tie last 2 starts: patiently ridden. *Tom George*

STAND BY ME (FR) 7 b.g. Dream Well (FR) – In Love New (FR) (Perrault) [2016/17 **b94** b85: b16.8g* May 25] fair form in bumpers: won at Newton Abbot in May after 12-month absence. *Alan Jones*

STANDING OVATION (IRE) 10 b.g. Presenting – Glittering Star (IRE) (Good Thyne **c122** (USA)) [2016/17 c133, h121: c26.1g c22.6m^{pu} c27.5g^2 Aug 18] well-made gelding: fairly **h–** useful hurdler/chaser: stays 3½m: acts on good to firm and heavy going: wears headgear/ tongue tie. *David Pipe*

STANDING STRONG (IRE) 9 b.g. Green Desert (USA) – Alexander Three D (IRE) **c–** (Pennekamp (USA)) [2016/17 c16s^{pu} h15.9g^{pu} May 8] no form over hurdles: pulled up in **h–** maiden on chasing debut: usually in headgear. *Zoe Davison*

ST ANDREWS (IRE) 4 ch.g. Rip Van Winkle (IRE) – Stellavera (FR) (Anabaa (USA)) **h66** [2016/17 h15.7d h16v^6 h16.3g^5 h18.7g^4 Apr 15] maiden on Flat: poor form over hurdles: tried in tongue tie. *Ian Williams*

STAND UP AND FIGHT (IRE) 5 b.g. Flemensfirth (USA) – Aylesbury Park (IRE) **h135 p** (Old Vic) [2016/17 h20g* h20d^3 h20s^4 h20s^2 Apr 2] first foal: dam lightly-raced sister to fairly useful hurdler (stayed 3m) Ask Vic and half-sister to useful hurdler/chaser (stayed 3m) The Hurl: useful form over hurdles: won maiden at Punchestown in October: third in Monksfield Novices' Hurdle at Navan (8¼ lengths behind Death Duty) in November and second in Grade 2 novice at Fairyhouse (4 lengths behind Al Boum Photo) in April: will be suited by further than 2½m: acts on heavy going: often travels strongly: even better to come. *Enda Bolger, Ireland*

STANLEY (GER) 6 bl.g. Pivotal – Sky Dancing (IRE) (Exit To Nowhere (USA)) **h–** [2016/17 h97: h16.7g^{pu} h16g^{pu} May 22] fairly useful on Flat, stays 1¼m: maiden hurdler, fair form at best: tried in tongue tie. *Jonjo O'Neill*

STANLOW 7 b.g. Invincible Spirit (IRE) – Ghazal (USA) (Gone West (USA)) [2016/17 **h–** h15.8d^R Oct 2] modest on Flat, stays 1¼m: refused third in maiden on hurdling debut. *Michael Mullineaux*

STANZA BOY (IRE) 5 b.g. Stowaway – Lisa Bleu (IRE) (Pistolet Bleu (IRE)) [2016/17 **b–** b16s b16v b15.8g Apr 9] no form in bumpers. *Deborah Faulkner*

STAR ASCENDING (IRE) 5 ch.g. Thousand Words – Sakaka (Tobougg (IRE)) [2016/17 **h–** h–: h17.2g^5 h19.9g h15.8d^6 Oct 13] fair on Flat, stays 1½m: limited impact over hurdles. *Jennie Candlish*

STAR BENEFIT (IRE) 7 b.g. Beneficial – Beautiful Night (FR) (Sleeping Car (FR)) **h63** [2016/17 h–: h19g h19.9g h19.9m^{pu} h23.3g^{pu} Jul 22] lengthy gelding: poor maiden hurdler. *Adrian Wintle*

STARCHITECT (IRE) 6 b.g. Sea The Stars (IRE) – Humilis (IRE) (Sadler's Wells (USA)) **c141 +** [2016/17 h142: h21.6g* c17.4s^3 c17s^3 c15.5v* c20.8g^5 c25g^3 c20.8g^5 Apr 19] compact **h147** gelding: smart handicap hurdler: won at Newton Abbot (by 5 lengths from Braavos) in May: useful form over fences: won novice at Ayr in January: stays 2¾m: acts on heavy going: has worn blinkers, including last 2 starts: wears tongue tie: often travels strongly. *David Pipe*

STARFALL 4 b.g. Misu Bond (IRE) – Davana (Primo Valentino (IRE)) [2016/17 b16.4v^5 **b–** b16d Mar 31] last in bumpers. *Christopher Wilson*

STAR FOOT (IRE) 6 b.g. Soviet Star (USA) – On The Backfoot (IRE) (Bob Back **h110** (USA)) [2016/17 h114, b91: h19d^6 h20.6g h16.3g^3 h15.7g^5 h19.9v^{pu} h16.5g^4 h16g^2 h16.3g^2 Apr 1] sturdy gelding: fair handicap hurdler: unproven beyond 17f: acts on soft going: has worn headgear: often in tongue tie: front runner/races prominently. *Jo Davis*

STARKIE 10 b.g. Putra Sandhurst (IRE) – Lysways (Gildoran) [2016/17 c119, h–: c16.4d^4 **c113** c16.4d^6 c16v^3 c19.2s^5 c16v^4 c18.2g^2 c17s* c15.7s^4 c17m^3 Apr 17] good-topped gelding: **h–** winning hurdler: fair handicap chaser: won at Plumpton in March: stays 2¼m: acts on heavy going: in headgear last 4 starts. *Chris Gordon*

STARLIGHT COURT (IRE) 6 b.g. Court Cave (IRE) – Marie The (FR) (Exit To **h106** Nowhere (USA)) [2016/17 h–p: h20g^4 h16.7v^4 h16.8g^5 h16.3g^2 Apr 23] fell in Irish maiden point: fair form over hurdles: unproven beyond 17f: acts on heavy going: has worn hood: tried in tongue tie. *Dan Skelton*

STARLIT NIGHT 5 b.m. Nayef (USA) – Perfect Night (Danzig Connection (USA)) **h61** [2016/17 h–: h21.6s^{pu} h16.8m^{pu} h16.3g h18.7m h16.8m h19.7g h16.5g^6 Apr 6] poor maiden hurdler: has worn hood: tried in tongue tie: usually races nearer last than first. *Chris Down*

STAR OF MASSINI (IRE) 10 b.g. Dr Massini (IRE) – Star of The Orient (IRE) **c–** (Moscow Society (USA)) [2016/17 c94, h–: c25.5d^{pu} May 12] prolific point winner: **h–** maiden hurdler/chaser: stays 2¾m: acts on heavy going. *N. W. Padfield*

STAR OF NAMIBIA (IRE) 7 b.g. Cape Cross (IRE) – Sparkle of Stones (FR) (Sadler's **h82** Wells (USA)) [2016/17 h16.7s^{pu} h16.6g^5 h16.6s^6 h15.8s^{pu} h15.8g Apr 28] fair maiden at best on Flat, stays 15f: poor form over hurdles: usually races prominently. *Michael Mullineaux*

STARPLEX 7 b.g. Multiplex – Turtle Bay (Dr Fong (USA)) [2016/17 h20.5s^5 h17s^4 **h103** h20.6g* h20.2g Apr 27] fair hurdler: won handicap at Newcastle in April: stays 21f: best form on good going. *Keith Dalgleish*

STAR PRESENTER (IRE) 9 b.g. Presenting – Star Councel (IRE) (Leading Counsel **c76** (USA)) [2016/17 c109, h–: c15.2g^3 Apr 23] maiden hurdler: fair handicap chaser: below **h–** form only outing in 2016/17: stays 2½m: acts on soft going: has worn headgear: often travels strongly. *Sam England*

STAR RIDER 5 gr.m. Cape Cross (IRE) – Starfala (Galileo (IRE)) [2016/17 h19.1d* **h102** h19.7s^3 h21.2d^6 Jan 25] useful on Flat, stays 21f: fair form over hurdles: won mares novice at Fontwell in December: should stay at least 2¾m: tried in cheekpieces. *Hughie Morrison*

STARS OVER THE SEA (USA) 6 b.g. Sea The Stars (IRE) – Exciting Times (FR) **h141** (Jeune Homme (USA)) [2016/17 h128: h16d^2 Apr 17] rather leggy gelding: smart on Flat, stays 1½m: useful hurdler: second in minor event at Fairyhouse (20 lengths behind Diakali) in April: raced around 2m: acts on good to soft going: usually wears hood/tongue tie: front runner/races prominently. *Henry de Bromhead, Ireland*

STAR TACKLE (IRE) 6 b.g. Milan – Grangebridge (IRE) (Strong Gale) [2016/17 **h101** h19.5d^5 h20d^5 h16s^3 Mar 13] £42,000 5-y-o: ninth foal: brother to a winning pointer: dam unraced half-sister to smart hurdler/fairly useful chaser (stayed 25f) Celtic Native out of half-sister to Grand National winner Red Marauder: off mark in Irish points at fifth attempt: fair form over hurdles: best effort when fifth in maiden at Ffos Las in November: likely to stay 3m. *Harry Whittington*

STAR TROUPER (IRE) 7 b.g. King's Theatre (IRE) – Wyndham Sweetmarie (IRE) **c–** (Mister Lord (USA)) [2016/17 h106: h18.5g^f h15.8g h16.3g h16g h15.7g^4 h21.3g^2 h19.5d^3 **h101** c20s^{ur} h16g h20.5g Apr 22] sturdy gelding: fair maiden hurdler: fell seventh on chasing debut: left Philip Hobbs after second start: stays 21f: acts on good to soft going: has worn hood: wears tongue tie: usually races in rear. *Sophie Leech*

STARVING MARVIN 9 b.g. Hawk Wing (USA) – Oleana (IRE) (Alzao (USA)) **c–** [2016/17 h113: h18.5g^5 c15.7d^{pu} Nov 17] lengthy gelding: fair hurdler: pulled up in novice **h105** handicap on chasing debut: unproven beyond 2m: best form on heavy going: usually made running: dead. *Rod Millman*

STATE SOVEREIGNTY 5 b.m. Authorized (IRE) – Sovereign's Honour (USA) **b89** (Kingmambo (USA)) [2016/17 b83: b16.2s^2 b16.2v^4 Feb 7] fair form in bumpers: best effort when second in mares event at Hereford in December. *Michael Scudamore*

STATE THE OBVIOUS (IRE) 5 ch.g. Presenting – New Vega (USA) (Blushing Flame **h72 p** (USA)) [2016/17 h19.9g^6 h16g h16.7g h16d h15.8v^{pu} Dec 16] £42,000 3-y-o: second foal: dam, pulled up both starts over fences in France, half-sister to high-class hurdler (stayed 3m) Quevega: poor form over hurdles: should still improve. *Jonjo O'Neill*

STATION CLOSED (IRE) 9 b.m. Kutub (IRE) – Laser Supreme (IRE) (Supreme **h83** Leader) [2016/17 h16g h16d^2 h16.4s^3 h16g h17.5d h16g h20.5v^4 h16s h16.2v Feb 16] poor maiden hurdler: left Adrian Brendan Joyce after sixth start: stays 2½m: acts on soft going: has worn blinkers, including in 2016/17: wears tongue tie. *Gordon Elliott, Ireland*

STATUS QUO (IRE) 4 b.g. Thewayyouare (USA) – Again Royale (IRE) (Royal **h89** Academy (USA)) [2016/17 h16.7s^{pu} h16.5g^4 h16m^6 h15.3f^3 Apr 23] lengthy gelding: fairly useful on Flat, stays 2m: modest form over hurdles: will be suited by 2½m+: in hood last 2 starts. *Harry Fry*

STAUNTON 6 b.m. Kayf Tara – Aranga (IRE) (Supreme Leader) [2016/17 h–, b–: h18.5g **h69** h23g^6 h23.8d^3 h21.4d^4 h25.5s^4 h20.5g^2 h26v^3 Feb 24] lengthy, rather unfurnished mare: poor maiden hurdler: stays 3m. *Susan Johnson*

STAY IN MY HEART (IRE) 8 ch.m. Medicean – Christmas Cracker (FR) (Alhaarth **h89 §** (IRE)) [2016/17 h90§: h21.2d^5 h23.3d^2 h23.3g* h23.3d^{rr} h23.9s^{pu} h23.8g^{rr} Nov 2] modest handicap hurdler: won at Hexham in May: stays 25f: acts on soft and good to firm going: has worn headgear: wears tongue tie: one to leave alone (refused to race/virtually did so last 3 starts). *Susan Corbett*

STAY OUT OF COURT (IRE) 6 b.g. Court Cave (IRE) – Lucky To Live (IRE) **h119**
(Salluceva) [2016/17 b16d³ h15.8v² h23.9g² h25v³ h21.3dᶠ Mar 31] €5,000 4-y-o, £42,000 **b79**
5-y-o: fourth foal: half-brother to fairly useful cross-country chaser Zest For Life (3m/25f
winner, by Lord Americo): dam ran twice in bumpers: runner-up both starts in Irish maiden
points: third in bumper: fairly useful form over hurdles: in cheekpieces last 2 starts: front
runner/races prominently. *David Pipe*

ST DOMINICK (IRE) 10 b.g. Oscar (IRE) – Kilcrea Breeze (IRE) (Fresh Breeze **c105**
(USA)) [2016/17 c128, h109: c23.8dᶠ c25.5d⁴ c24.2v⁴ c25.1vᴿ h23.1dᵖᵘ Mar 21] lengthy **h–**
gelding: maiden hurdler: fairly useful chaser at best, has gone wrong way: stays 3m: acts
on heavy going: tried in hood/tongue tie: usually races in rear. *Jackie du Plessis*

STEADY MAJOR (IRE) 5 b.g. Invincible Spirit (IRE) – Combust (USA) (Aptitude **h74**
(USA)) [2016/17 h16g h19.5g h16g h16.2s³ h16g h17.2g h16.8gᵖᵘ Sep 1] poor maiden
hurdler: in blinkers last 4 starts: wears tongue tie: often races towards rear. *Gordon Elliott,
Ireland*

STEALING MIX 7 b.g. Fair Mix (IRE) – Minimum (Terimon) [2016/17 b86: b16sᵖᵘ **h103**
h19g h19g⁶ h19g⁵ h23.9g⁶ h19.8f² h18.5g* Apr 26] good-topped gelding: Irish point **b–**
winner: best effort in bumpers when fourth at Wincanton in 2015/16: fair form over
hurdles: won maiden at Exeter in April: may prove best short of 3m: acts on firm going:
wears tongue tie. *Neil Mulholland*

STEAL MY THUNDER (IRE) 6 gr.g. Craigsteel – Party Woman (IRE) (Sexton Blake) **h–**
[2016/17 b82p: h20dᵖᵘ Oct 30] runner-up in Irish maiden point on debut: modest form in
bumper: pulled up in novice hurdle: dead. *Philip Hobbs*

STEAMBOAT BILL (IRE) 6 b.g. Kalanisi (IRE) – Freemantle Doctor (IRE) (Luso) **c90**
[2016/17 h20d h22.1m³ h24g² h24.8d* h24d⁴ c20s c20d⁶ c20s⁶ c20s⁵ c24s⁵ Jan 31] €5,000 **h126**
3-y-o: first foal: dam (c98/h95) bumper winner (stayed 2½m): fairly useful handicap
hurdler: won at Roscommon in July: modest form over fences: stays 25f: acts on heavy
going: often races towards rear. *Gordon Elliott, Ireland*

STEEL BOB (IRE) 5 b.g. Craigsteel – Lady Kamando (Hernando (FR)) [2016/17 **h– p**
b19.5g* h20.3sᵖᵘ Jan 1] fifth foal: half-brother to winning pointer by Definite Article: dam **b101**
(h68), maiden hurdler, closely related to useful hurdler (stayed 2½m) Doctor Goddard:
won point on debut: also won maiden bumper at Kilbeggan (by 12 lengths from Angelica
Yeats) in September: pulled up in listed novice on hurdling debut: left P. Crowley after first
start: will stay beyond 2½m: should do better. *Harry Fry*

STEEL CITY 9 gr.g. Act One – Serraval (FR) (Sanglamore (USA)) [2016/17 c–x, h114: **c– x**
h19.5v⁴ h16g³ h16v h20.3s h15.8s³ h18.5d⁵ h15.7g Apr 21] useful-looking gelding: **h99 x**
modest handicap hurdler: failed to complete both starts over fences: unproven beyond 17f:
acts on heavy going: wears headgear: races prominently: often let down by jumping.
Seamus Mullins

STEEL EXPRESS (IRE) 5 b.g. Craigsteel – Assidua (IRE) (Anshan) [2016/17 b91: **h97**
b16.8g h16m⁶ h15.3d⁶ h18.5s⁶ h18.5d h21.6g³ h16.8g⁶ Apr 26] fair form in bumpers: **b91**
modest form over hurdles: stays 2¾m: often races prominently. *Linda Blackford*

STEEL GOLD (IRE) 11 b.g. Craigsteel – It Time To Run (IRE) (Buckskin (FR)) [2016/17 **c– x**
c–x, h77: h23.3d h25gᵖᵘ May 30] poor hurdler at best: maiden chaser (sketchy jumper): **h–**
stays 3m: acts on good to firm going: often races prominently. *Tracey Leeson*

STEEL NATIVE (IRE) 6 b.g. Craigsteel – Princess Gloria (IRE) (Prince Rupert (FR)) **h98**
[2016/17 h20g⁵ h20g h20d h15.8v⁴ h19.6s⁶ h20s² h21.9vᶠ h21.9v² h21.9d⁴ Apr 16]
€3,500 3-y-o: brother to useful hurdler/winning pointer Prince of Steal (2m-2½m winner)
and half-brother to bumper winner/fair hurdler Cailin Vic Mo Cri (2½m winner, by
Old Vic): dam (h118) bumper and 2m/2¼m maiden winner: off mark in points at fifth
attempt: modest maiden hurdler: stays 2¾m: best form on soft/heavy going: has worn
hood: often races towards rear. *David Rees*

STEEL'S COTTON 8 b.m. Tikkanen (USA) – Last Spruce (USA) (Big Spruce (USA)) **h78**
[2016/17 h21.5g h22.5d⁵ h22.2g h19.7d⁶ h19.4g⁵ Mar 1] second foal: dam winning pointer:
maiden pointer: maiden hurdler, modest form at best: best effort at 21f: acts on good to soft
going: usually wears cheekpieces: in tongue tie last 2 starts: often leads. *Ian Ferguson,
Ireland*

STEELY ADDITION (IRE) 5 b.g. Craigsteel – Blond's Addition (IRE) (Lord Americo) **h110**
[2016/17 h15.3d³ h19g³ h16.7d⁴ Apr 27] €3,500 3-y-o, £45,000 4-y-o: fourth foal: dam
unraced: won maiden point on debut: fair form when third in novice hurdles at Wincanton
and Taunton: should prove suited by further than 2m. *Hugo Froud*

STELLAR NOTION (IRE) 9 b.g. Presenting – Green Star (FR) (Green Tune (USA)) **c143**
[2016/17 c–, h–: c19g* c17g c20s³ c24d² c24.5d⁴ c21g² c34.3dᵖᵘ c29dᵖᵘ Apr 17] well-made **h–**
gelding: winning hurdler: useful handicap chaser: won at Listowel in June: in frame 4
times after, including in Munster National at Limerick, Paddy Power Chase at Leopardstown
(7½ lengths behind Noble Endeavor) and Leopardstown Chase: stays 3m: acts on heavy
going: has worn tongue tie: front runner/races prominently, often travels strongly. *Henry de
Bromhead, Ireland*

STELLA'S FELLA 9 b.g. Septieme Ciel (USA) – Gaspaisie (FR) (Beyssac (FR)) **c– §**
[2016/17 c–, h–§: c20gᵖᵘ May 2] maiden hurdler: lightly-raced chaser, failed to complete **h– §**
last 2 starts: best effort at 2m: probably acts on good to soft going: tried in headgear:
temperamental. *Giles Smyly*

STEP BACK (IRE) 7 ch.g. Indian River (FR) – Stepitoutmary (IRE) (Roselier (FR)) **h107 +**
[2016/17 h23.8s* h24g Mar 17] €8,000 3-y-o, £47,000 6-y-o: sturdy gelding: half-brother
to 3 winners, including fairly useful chaser Prince of Leisure (3m/25f winner, by Hushang)
and fair hurdler Declan's Lad (2m winner, by Mister Mat), stayed 3m: dam unraced: won
3 times in Irish points: fair form over hurdles: won maiden at Ludlow in February:
100/1, ninth in Albert Bartlett Novices' Hurdle (Spa) at Cheltenham, possibly flattered.
Mark Bradstock

STEPHANIE FRANCES (IRE) 9 b.m. King's Theatre (IRE) – Brownlow Castle (IRE) **c135**
(Supreme Leader) [2016/17 c127p, h133: c15.7g* c16.5g* c16.5g² h16g* c17.4s* c16g³ **h129**
Dec 27] good-topped mare: fairly useful hurdler: won listed Mares' Hurdle at Wetherby (by
½ length from Midnight Jazz) in October: useful chaser: won novices at Southwell and
Worcester in August, and listed mares novice at Bangor (by 9 lengths from Presenting Lisa)
in November: unproven beyond 17f: acts on soft going: tried in tongue tie: often races
towards rear/travels strongly. *Dan Skelton*

STEPOVER 6 b.m. Midnight Legend – Ring Back (IRE) (Bob Back (USA)) [2016/17 **h98**
h96, b79: h20.3v⁴ h15.8g² h15.7d⁵ h15.9g⁴ h16g h16.6g* h16.6d⁴ h15.8d⁶ h15.7g* Apr 21]
workmanlike mare: modest handicap hurdler: won at Doncaster (twice) in January and
Southwell in April: stays 2½m: acts on good to soft going: has worn hood: wears tongue
tie: often races towards rear. *Alex Hales*

STEPS AND STAIRS (IRE) 7 b.g. Robin des Pres (FR) – Be Mine Tonight (IRE) **c103**
(Carroll House) [2016/17 h94: c24v* c24gᵖᵘ c23g³ c24gᵖᵘ c24.1s² Nov 26] winning **h–**
hurdler: fair form over fences: won novice handicap at Southwell in June: stays 3m: acts on
heavy going: usually wears cheekpieces. *Jonjo O'Neill*

STERNRUBIN (GER) 6 b.g. Authorized (IRE) – Sworn Mum (GER) (Samum (GER)) **h142**
[2016/17 h139: h15.7m* h16.4s⁵ h15.7d Dec 17] tall gelding: useful handicap hurdler: won
listed event at Ascot (by ½ length from Instant Karma) in October: raced around 2m: acts
on good to firm and heavy going: wears hood: usually leads. *Philip Hobbs*

STETCHWORTH (IRE) 6 ch.g. New Approach (IRE) – Hallowed Park (IRE) (Barathea **h68**
(IRE)) [2016/17 h15.6g⁵ h17s⁶ h19.3d Feb 20] fairly useful on Flat, stays 1¼m: poor form
over hurdles. *Russell Ross*

STEVE MEQUINE 4 ch.g. Native Ruler – Rabbit (Muhtarram (USA)) [2016/17 b16.7g **b–**
Apr 22] tailed off in bumper. *Sophie Leech*

ST GREGORY (IRE) 9 ch.m. Presenting – Ardrom (Ardross) [2016/17 h19.9sᵖᵘ h23.9s **c– §**
h23.9g² h23.3s* h24.3d* h24dᵖ h24.4g⁶ Dec 9] fair handicap hurdler: won at Hexham in **h101 §**
September, Ayr in October and Newcastle in November: winning chaser: stays 27f: acts on
soft going: has worn headgear, including last 5 starts: usually races prominently, often
lazily and not one to trust. *Nicky Richards*

William Hill Handicap Hurdle (Listed), Ascot—Sternrubin survives a mistake two out to make all

STHENIC (FR) 5 b.g. Fastnet Rock (AUS) – Ela's Giant (Giant's Causeway (USA)) [2016/17 h–: h21.2g h19.7d h20.6s^{pu} h19.7d h25.3s^{pu} Mar 8] big, strong gelding: no form over hurdles: in headgear last 3 starts: tried in tongue tie. *Micky Hammond* **h–**

STICKERS 10 b.g. Generous (IRE) – Dunsfold Duchess (IRE) (Bustino) [2016/17 c–, h–: h24s^{pu} May 18] runner-up in Irish maiden point: no form over hurdles/fences: dead. *Alan Jessop* **c– h–**

STICKING POINT 6 b.g. Needle Gun (IRE) – Blue Plaid (Clantime) [2016/17 h–: h15.8s Apr 30] well held both starts over hurdles: tried in hood: wears tongue tie. *Martin Keighley* **h–**

STICK TO THE PLAN (IRE) 5 b.g. Gold Well – Chloes Choice (IRE) (Presenting) [2016/17 h89, h106: h19.6d^6 h21v^4 h20.2g* Apr 27] first foal: dam unraced half-sister to fairly useful hurdler/high-class chaser (stayed 3m) Farmer Jack: fairly useful form over hurdles: won novice handicap at Perth in April: in tongue tie last 2 starts: open to further improvement. *Dan Skelton* **h122 p**

STIFF UPPER LIP (IRE) 7 b.g. Sakhee's Secret – Just In Love (FR) (Highest Honor (FR)) [2016/17 h96: h19.1v^4 h21.6v h21.6g^5 Mar 31] strong, compact gelding: modest handicap hurdler: stays 2½m: acts on heavy going: often in headgear. *Oliver Sherwood* **h99**

STILETTO BLADE 9 ch.m. Needwood Blade – Swing Along (Alhijaz) [2016/17 h19.9g^5 h15.7g^{pu} Aug 14] fourth foal: dam 7f/9.4f winner: no form, mainly in points. *Nicholas Pomfret* **h–**

STILL BELIEVING (IRE) 9 ch.m. Blueprint (IRE) – Im A Believer (IRE) (Erins Isle) [2016/17 c117, h110: c23g^2 c20.9g^3 c25.6g^3 c20.8g* c23.8d^2 h21.2s^3 h23.8s^3 h25.5d^4 c22.2g^2 Apr 15] angular mare: fair handicap hurdler: useful handicap chaser: won mares event at Cheltenham in December: career-best second in mares event at Haydock (neck behind Magic Money) in April: stays 3¼m: acts on good to firm and heavy going: often races towards rear. *Evan Williams* **c130 h102**

STILLETTO (IRE) 8 b.g. Westerner – Eastertide (IRE) (Alphabatim (USA)) [2016/17 c142, h126: c19.9g^F Nov 25] well-made gelding: fairly useful hurdle winner: useful chaser: stayed 2½m: acted on heavy going: usually wore hood: often raced towards rear: dead. *Johnny Farrelly* **c– h–**

STILL TOGETHER (IRE) 7 b.g. Alkaadhem – All-Together (Step Together (USA)) [2016/17 h89, b82: h19g^{pu} May 2] winning Irish pointer: maiden hurdler: bred to have been suited by 2½m+: acted on good to soft going: in headgear last 2 starts: tried in tongue tie: dead. *David Pipe* **h–**

STILL WILLIAM 5 b.g. Overbury (IRE) – Romany Dream (Nomadic Way (USA)) [2016/17 b15.8v b16.5g^5 Apr 6] £1,600 4-y-o: third foal: half-brother to poor hurdler Midnight Gypsy (2½m winner, by Midnight Legend): dam (c102/h80), unreliable bumper/2m-21f chase winner, half-sister to fairly useful hurdler/useful chaser (stayed 2½m) B The One: modest form on second of 2 starts in bumpers. *Jo Davis* **b81**

STILO BLUE NATIVE (IRE) 9 gr.g. Blueprint (IRE) – Reconciliation (IRE) (Be My Native (USA)) [2016/17 c105, h100: c16.4d^{pu} c23.4m^F h21.4s^6 h16.8s* h19.9d^6 h17s^4 h16.8v^4 h15.7s^2 h19.7m^5 Apr 13] quite good-topped gelding: modest handicap hurdler: won at Sedgefield in November: maiden chaser (often let down by jumping): left John Wade after second start: stays 21f: best form on soft/heavy going: tried in cheekpieces: usually races prominently. *Rebecca Menzies* **c– x h98**

STIPEND (IRE) 4 b.g. Beneficial – Erins Lass (IRE) (Erins Isle) [2016/17 b16g^5 Apr 24] well held in bumper. *Philip Hobbs* **b65**

STIPULATE 8 b.g. Dansili – Indication (Sadler's Wells (USA)) [2016/17 h15.6g^4 h15.6g^2 h15.6g^4 Feb 5] smart at one time on Flat, stays 14.5f: fair form over hurdles: better than result when second in maiden at Musselburgh in January, headed when blundering 3 out: in hood last 2 starts. *Brian Ellison* **h110**

STITCHED IN TIME (IRE) 10 b.g. Needle Gun (IRE) – Broken Pockets (IRE) (Broken Hearted) [2016/17 c–, h–: c24.2d^F c20g^5 c24d^{pu} c25.5g^{pu} Jul 18] point/hurdle winner: maiden chaser, no longer of any account: has worn cheekpieces, including last 4 starts: wears tongue tie: front runner/races prominently. *Sara Ender* **c– h–**

ST JOHN'S 4 b.g. Aqlaam – Diam Queen (GER) (Lando (GER)) [2016/17 b13.2g* b14s Jan 1] sturdy gelding: second foal: dam 7f/1m winner: fair form in bumpers: won junior event at Exeter in October. *Rod Millman* **b88**

ST JOHNS POINT (IRE) 9 b.g. Darsi (FR) – Dunsford Belle (IRE) (Insan (USA)) **c99 x**
[2016/17 c117, h–: c24g^{pu} c22.5v^{pu} c24.2d^5 c26.3g^F c23.8g^2 c23g^{bd} Jan 27] good-bodied **h–**
gelding: winning Irish pointer: winning hurdler: modest maiden chaser nowadays: stays
3m: acts on heavy going: wears headgear/tongue tie: often races prominently: often let
down by jumping over fences. *Charlie Longsdon*

ST LEWIS 7 b.g. Erhaab (USA) – Miss Lewis (Sir Harry Lewis (USA)) [2016/17 h68, b–: **h–**
h23.1g h20.3s^{ur} h15.8m Jun 9] little form over hurdles: tried in cheekpieces/tongue tie.
Jennie Candlish

ST MERRYN (IRE) 6 b.g. Oscar (IRE) – Kigali (IRE) (Torus) [2016/17 b16.7s^6 Dec 9] **b–**
third in maiden point on debut: tailed off in bumper. *Rebecca Curtis*

STOICAL PATIENT (IRE) 8 b.m. Shantou (USA) – Dust Gale (IRE) (Strong Gale) **c84**
[2016/17 h–, b–: c25.8g^{pu} c25.5d^{pu} h22m c17.4m* Sep 4] maiden hurdler: poor form over **h–**
fences: won handicap at Fontwell in September: left Mark Wall after second start, Harry
Fry after third: best effort at 17f: acts on good to firm going: sometimes in headgear.
Gary Moore

STOLEAWAY (IRE) 7 b.g. Stowaway – Karsulu (IRE) (Mukaddamah (USA)) [2016/17 **c106**
c24.1g* c27.5m^{pu} May 20] €16,000 3-y-o, £8,000 5-y-o: third foal: dam (h65) maiden
hurdler: dual winning pointer: fair form when winning novice hunter at Bangor with plenty
in hand very early in season: went as if amiss next time. *Philip Rowley*

STONEBRIGG LEGEND (IRE) 5 b.m. Midnight Legend – Forget The Ref (IRE) (Dr Massini **h69 p**
(IRE)) [2016/17 b16d^5 h16.8d^4 h19.9g^3 Apr 7] first foal: dam, winning pointer, sister to **b83**
fairly useful hurdler/chaser (winner up to 21f) Pocket Aces: modest form in bumpers: 11/2,
third in mares novice at Sedgefield (21½ lengths beating Louloumills) on hurdling debut:
will prove suited by 2½m+: open to improvement. *Sarah Humphrey*

STONEHAM 6 b.m. Sixties Icon – Cibenze (Owington) [2016/17 h110: h20.2m^2 h19.4g^4 **h118**
h19.4d^2 h19.4g^6 h19.4g h26.1g^3 h24.3d Apr 21] leggy mare: fairly useful handicap hurdler:
stays 3¼m: acts on good to firm and heavy going: wears hood: races well off pace.
Iain Jardine

STONE (IRE) 11 b.g. Lahib (USA) – Stone Beck (Lapierre) [2016/17 c25.3g^5 c20.9v^{pu} **c93**
Feb 1] multiple point winner: fair at best in hunter chases: should stay beyond 23f: left
Miss K. Adcock after first start: wears tongue tie. *Sam Jukes*

STONEMADFORSPEED (IRE) 9 b.g. Fruits of Love (USA) – Diamond Forever **h95 §**
(Teenoso (USA)) [2016/17 h54§: h21.4m^2 h21.6g^5 h20d^3 h23.1g^4 Jul 31] point winner:
modest handicap hurdler: stays 21f: acts on good to firm and good to soft going: tried in
headgear/tongue tie: usually races close up: has refused to race. *Roger Teal*

STONE QUERCUS (IRE) 4 b.g. Rock of Gibraltar (IRE) – Redglow (IRE) (Fasliyev **h101 §**
(USA)) [2016/17 h16.2d^3 h16.7d^3 h16.8m^6 h16.2g* h15.6g^2 h17.1g^5 h16.7s^4 h15.6g^2 Jan
3] fair maiden on Flat, stays 1¾m: fair hurdler: won 3-runner juvenile at Perth in
September: raced around 2m: acts on good to soft going: wears headgear: front runner/
races prominently: has looked reluctant and is one to be wary of. *Donald McCain*

STOP THE PRESS 8 b.g. Halling (USA) – Ryde On (Petoski) [2016/17 h110, b76: **c–**
h20.5g^{pu} c20.9s^{pu} Mar 11] off mark in maiden points at fifth attempt: fair hurdler at best: **h–**
pulled up in novice handicap on chasing debut: stays 19f: best form on soft/heavy going:
front runner/races prominently. *Mark Pitman*

STORM ALERT 10 ch.g. Karinga Bay – Rash-Gale (IRE) (Rashar (USA)) [2016/17 c–, **c–**
h88: c15.9s h25.5s^5 h26v^{ur} h23.6s^4 h23.1g Apr 11] good-topped gelding: fair hurdler at **h73**
best, on the downgrade: maiden chaser: stays 25f: acts on good to firm and heavy going:
has worn cheekpieces. *Susan Gardner*

STORMBAY BOMBER (IRE) 8 b.g. September Storm (GER) – Top Tottie (IRE) **c100**
(Alzao (USA)) [2016/17 c91, h100: c15.7g* c17.2g c16.4g^5 c15.7g^4 Apr 21] fair handicap: **h–**
fair handicap chaser: won at Southwell in May: unproven beyond 17f: acts on good to soft
going: tried in tongue tie: usually races close up. *Patrick Holmes*

STORM FORECAST (IRE) 6 b.g. September Storm (GER) – Katie Kelly (IRE) **h99**
(Deploy) [2016/17 h111, b89: h16.2v^2 h16.2g^{pu} Apr 25] bumper winner: fair form over
hurdles: tried in hood: dead. *Malcolm Jefferson*

STORMING STRUMPET 7 b.m. Kayf Tara – Rosita Bay (Hernando (FR)) [2016/17 **c116**
c103, h110: c20.2m^4 h19g^4 c20.2g^2 c15.9s^2 c20.8g^3 c19.4g* Apr 23] lengthy mare: **h89**
winning hurdler: fairly useful handicap chaser: won at Stratford in April: stays 21f: acts on
heavy going: wears tongue tie: often travels strongly. *Tom George*

STORM NELSON (IRE) 4 b.g. Gold Well – Dabiyra (IRE) (Linamix (FR)) [2016/17 **b76**
b16v^4 b15.7v Feb 15] modest form on first of 2 starts in bumpers. *Tom Lacey*

STORM OF SWORDS (IRE) 9 ch.g. Beneficial – Crossbar Lady (IRE) (Flemensfirth c–
(USA)) [2016/17 c–, h126: c16d^{pu} May 18] angular gelding: fairly useful hurdler: winning h–
chaser, pulled up only outing in 2016/17: stays 2¾m: acts on soft going: tried in
cheekpieces: usually leads. *Dan Skelton*

STORM PATROL 6 b.m. Shirocco (GER) – Material World (Karinga Bay) [2016/17 b91: b92
b15.7s^2 Feb 18] lengthy mare: fair form in bumpers: second in mares event at Ascot on sole
start in 2016/17: wears tongue tie. *Suzy Smith*

STORM WARNING (IRE) 5 b.g. September Storm (GER) – Ceo Draiochta (IRE) h–
(Erins Isle) [2016/17 b16.3s^4 b16.7s^6 h16.7m^5 Apr 9] good-topped gelding: brother to a b85
winning pointer and half-brother to useful hurdler/chaser Strongpoint (2m-3m winner, by
Bob Back): dam lightly raced on Flat: runner-up in point on debut: fair form in bumpers:
better effort when fourth at Newbury: tailed off in novice on hurdling debut. *Warren Greatrex*

STOWAWAY GOLD (IRE) 5 ch.m. Stowaway – Gold Flo (IRE) (Fourstars Allstar b62
(USA)) [2016/17 b15.7g^5 Aug 31] €3,000 3-y-o: fifth foal: half-sister to modest hurdler/
chaser Sky Full of Stars (2m winner, by Mahler): dam (h92), 2¾m hurdle winner (stayed
27f), half-sister to fair hurdler/useful chaser (2m/17f winner) Jigsaw Dancer and fairly
useful hurdler/chaser (stayed 21f) Ballyburke: 12/1, fifth in maiden bumper at Southwell.
Fergal O'Brien

STOWAWAY MAGIC (IRE) 6 b.g. Stowaway – Irish Mystics (IRE) (Ali-Royal (IRE)) h136
[2016/17 b98: h19d* h20.5d^2 h16.6d* h20d^5 h21m* h19.8g^2 Apr 29] won Irish maiden
point on debut: bumper winner: useful form over hurdles: won novices at Warwick in May
and Doncaster in January, and handicap at Kempton in April: stays 21f: acts on good to firm
and good to soft going: often races towards rear/travels strongly. *Nicky Henderson*

STOWAWAY ROSE (IRE) 5 b.m. Stowaway – Andromeda (IRE) (Barathea (IRE)) b–
[2016/17 b15.7d Dec 15] ninth foal: half-sister to a winning pointer by Bob Back: dam
lightly raced: well beaten in mares bumper: wore tongue tie. *Sam Thomas*

ST QUINTIN 7 b.g. Act One – Gloriana (Formidable (USA)) [2016/17 h100, b–: h23.1d^{pu} h–
h20.3g^{pu} h23m h19.9d^{pu} h18.7g^6 Apr 15] maiden hurdler, no form in 2016/17: left David
Brown after third start: tried in hood. *Matt Sheppard*

STRAIDNAHANNA (IRE) 8 gr.g. Medaaly – Sue's Song (Alflora (IRE)) [2016/17 c136
c132, h99: c24.1v^4 c24g c30g* c32.6s^{pu} c21.1g c31.8g^{pu} Apr 22] big, strong, close-coupled h–
gelding: maiden hurdler: useful handicap chaser: won at Catterick in January: stays 3¾m:
acts on heavy going. *Sue Smith*

STRAIT OF MAGELLAN (IRE) 5 ch.g. Captain Rio – Golden (FR) (Sanglamore h105
(USA)) [2016/17 h65p: h16.7g^2 h16d^2 h16.7d^4 h17d Feb 20] fair form over hurdles: raced
around 2m: acts on good to soft going. *Nicky Richards*

STRAIT RUN (IRE) 6 ch.g. Rock of Gibraltar (IRE) – Gentlemen's Guest (USA) h82
(Gentlemen (ARG)) [2016/17 h78: h16g h16.7g^{pu} h16.8g h16.4d^{pu} h16.8s^2 h16.8v^{pu} Feb
23] neat gelding: poor maiden hurdler: unproven beyond 17f: acts on soft/heavy
going: has worn headgear/tongue tie, including in 2016/17. *Micky Hammond*

STRAITS OF MESSINA (IRE) 8 b.g. Mountain High (IRE) – Scylla (Rock City) h97
[2016/17 h16.7s^2 h17.7v^3 h20.3s h18.5d Mar 21] modest handicap hurdler, off over 2 years
before return: stays 2¼m: acts on heavy going. *Tom Symonds*

STRANDS OF VELVET (IRE) 6 b.m. Oscar (IRE) – Saitenrolle (GER) (Tirol) h–
[2016/17 b15.7g^6 b16.4s b15.7s^5 h19.7g^{pu} Apr 23] strong mare: seventh foal: half-sister to b69
German 7.5f/9.5f winner Shadow Hill (by Tiger Hill): dam, German 7f winner, half-sister
to fairly useful hurdler (stayed 2¾m) Saitensohn: mid-division at best in bumpers: pulled
up in maiden on hurdling debut. *Iain Jardine*

STRANGSMILL (IRE) 8 b.m. Beneficial – Sweet Vale (IRE) (Supreme Leader) h96
[2016/17 h19.2v^{pu} h20v^4 h15.8g^2 h19.5g^3 Apr 17] first foal: dam placed in bumpers/point:
Irish maiden point winner: modest form in novice hurdles. *Sheila Lewis*

STRATEGIC ISLAND (IRE) 6 b.m. Strategic Prince – Island Music (IRE) (Mujahid h–
(USA)) [2016/17 h20.1g^{pu} h16.2d^{pu} Jun 19] point winner: little form over hurdles.
James Walton

STREAMS OF WHISKEY (IRE) 10 br.g. Spadoun (FR) – Cherry Tops (IRE) (Top of c110
The World) [2016/17 c23.9s* Feb 7] workmanlike gelding: winning hurdler: fairly useful h–
chaser at one time: won 3-runner hunter at Market Rasen in February after 2-year absence:
stays 25f: acts on heavy going. *Nicky Richards*

STREET ENTERTAINER (IRE) 10 br.g. Danehill Dancer (IRE) – Opera Ridge (FR) **c–**
(Indian Ridge) [2016/17 c119, h130: c22.7s⁴ c21.2gᵖᵘ Apr 17] sturdy gelding: useful **h–**
hurdler: maiden chaser, no form in hunters in 2016/17: stayed 25f: acted on soft going:
wore headgear/tongue tie: dead. *Mrs S. J. Stilgoe*

STREETS OF PROMISE (IRE) 8 b.m. Westerner – Miracle Lady (Bob's Return **c124**
(IRE)) [2016/17 c136, h124: c25.2v³ c32.6sᵖᵘ c27.9d³ Apr 16] sturdy mare: fairly useful **h–**
hurdler: useful handicap chaser: stays 3m: best form on soft/heavy going: wears
cheekpieces: usually leads. *Michael Scudamore*

STRICTLY ART (IRE) 4 b.g. Excellent Art – Sadinga (IRE) (Sadler's Wells (USA)) **h–**
[2016/17 h15.8sᵖᵘ Feb 8] modest on Flat, stays 10.5f: pulled up in juvenile on hurdling
debut. *Alan Bailey*

STRICTLY THE ONE (IRE) 7 b.g. Robin des Pres (FR) – Rita's Charm (IRE) (Arctic **h63**
Lord) [2016/17 h62: h21.2d⁴ h19.9g⁵ h24sᵖᵘ h19.9m h23.3g Jul 22] poor maiden hurdler:
should stay at least 2¾m: acts on good to firm going: has worn headgear/tongue tie.
Mike Sowersby

STRIKE FEAR (IRE) 5 b.g. Scorpion (IRE) – Skatey Kate (IRE) (Oscar (IRE)) [2016/17 **h–**
b15.6g⁵ b15.7g h19.3gʳᵒ Apr 15] little impact in bumpers: ran out on hurdling debut: tried **b–**
in hood. *Rebecca Menzies*

STRIKE WEST (IRE) 5 b.g. Westerner – Fuel Queen (IRE) (Flemensfirth (USA)) **h78**
[2016/17 b73: b16.8d h19.7d⁵ h19.9g³ Mar 29] poor form in bumpers/over hurdles. **b–**
Micky Hammond

STROBE 13 ch.g. Fantastic Light (USA) – Sadaka (USA) (Kingmambo (USA)) [2016/17 **c– §**
c92§, h–: c20.1mᵖᵘ c20.1d c23.8g⁵ c20.1g³ Sep 5] winning hurdler: fair chaser at best, **h–**
retains little ability: stays 3m: acts on good to firm and good to soft going: wears headgear:
front runner/races prominently: not one to trust. *Lucy Normile*

STROLLAWAYNOW (IRE) 10 b.g. Oscar (IRE) – Rose of Salome (IRE) (Roselier **c–**
(FR)) [2016/17 c106, h–: h24g⁵ c25.5gᵘʳ Aug 25] rangy gelding: fairly useful hurdler/ **h–**
chaser at best, well held completed start in 2016/17: stays 3m: best form on soft/heavy
going: usually wears headgear nowadays: has worn tongue tie, including last 4 starts:
usually races nearer last than first. *David Arbuthnot*

STRONG CONVICTION 7 ch.g. Piccolo – Keeping The Faith (IRE) (Ajraas (USA)) **h63**
[2016/17 h18.5d h22g⁴ Jul 28] angular gelding: maiden pointer: poor maiden hurdler:
unproven beyond 2m: acts on heavy going. *Susan Gardner*

STRONG ECONOMY (IRE) 5 ch.g. Sandmason – Odd Decision (IRE) (Little **h113**
Bighorn) [2016/17 b16d⁶ b16s h16s⁴ h20.5s² h21.4v* h20.5vᵘʳ h24.3d Apr 21] £5,800 **b65**
4-y-o: third foal: dam maiden pointer: unplaced in points: fair form over hurdles: won maiden
at Ayr in January: should stay 3m: acts on heavy going: front
runner/races prominently. *R. Mike Smith*

STRONGLY SUGGESTED 10 b.g. Kayf Tara – Branston Lily (Cadeaux Genereux) **c120 §**
[2016/17 c126, h–: c20g c20.3g* c16g c21g² c20g* c20d c19.4d⁶ c16.4d⁴ c19.4g² c21.3g* **h–**
Apr 23] compact gelding: winning chaser: fairly useful handicap chaser: won at Southwell
in June and Wetherby in April: stays 21f: acts on good to firm and heavy going: tried in
cheekpieces: has worn tongue tie: often races towards rear: unreliable. *Jonjo O'Neill*

STRONG PURSUIT (IRE) 7 ch.g. Flemensfirth (USA) – Loughaderra (IRE) (Strong **h130**
Gale) [2016/17 h21.6d⁶ h19.8d* h19.7s* h24.4dᵖᵘ h20.5d² Mar 24] €15,000 3-y-o, resold
£13,000 3-y-o, £90,000 5-y-o: rangy gelding: half-brother to 3 winners, including fair
hurdlers Look Who's Back (2½m winner, by Bob Back) and Loughaderra Dame (2¼m
winner, by King's Theatre): dam unraced sister to top-class chaser (stayed 3¼m) Strong
Promise: off mark in Irish maiden points at third attempt: useful form over hurdles: won
maiden at Wincanton in December and novice at Hereford (by 8 lengths from Town Parks)
in January: should stay further than 2½m: acts on soft going: usually leads. *Philip Hobbs*

STRONG TEAM (IRE) 4 b.g. Exceed And Excel (AUS) – Star Blossom (USA) (Good **b–**
Reward (USA)) [2016/17 b16.7m Apr 9] well held in bumper. *Chris Grant*

STRUMBLE HEAD (IRE) 12 b.g. Anshan – Milan Moss (Le Moss) [2016/17 c115, h–: **c113**
c24.1d⁵ c23.8d² c25.8m* c25.8m² c24.1g³ c25.8g⁶ c24m⁴ Oct 16] winning hurdler: fair **h–**
handicap chaser: won at Newton Abbot in July: stays 3¼m: acts on any going: wears
headgear: tried in tongue tie: usually leads. *Peter Bowen*

ST SAVIOUR 5 b.g. Danehill Dancer (IRE) – Titivation (Montjeu (IRE)) [2016/17 h127: **h126 x**
h17.7s h16.2s³ h15.3sᵘʳ h17.7v h19g⁶ h16.3g* h15.7g³ Apr 15] lengthy, sparely-made
gelding: fairly useful handicap hurdler: won at Stratford in April: likely to prove best at 2m:
acts on heavy going: wears headgear: often let down by jumping. *Philip Hobbs*

STUPID CUPID (IRE) 6 b.m. Beneficial – Supreme Arrow (IRE) (Supreme Leader) **b71**
[2016/17 b16.2v⁵ b15.8s b16g⁴ Apr 17] €8,000 3-y-o: third foal: dam (c110/h118), 2¾m/3m hurdle/chase winner, half-sister to useful/unreliable chaser (stayed 2½m) Swift Arrow: won Irish mares maiden point on debut: poor form in bumpers. *Sheila Lewis*

STYNES (IRE) 7 b.g. Aussie Rules (USA) – Magic Princess (Bahhare (USA)) [2016/17 **h115** h18.5m* h19.6g h16.3m⁴ h18.5m* h19.7g⁴ Oct 29] fairly useful handicap hurdler: won at Newton Abbot in July and Exeter in October: stays 2½m: acts on good to firm going: wears tongue tie: often travels strongly. *Graeme McPherson*

SUBCONTINENT (IRE) 5 b.g. Dubawi (IRE) – Saree (Barathea (IRE)) [2016/17 **h76 p** h19.7v⁵ Feb 1] half-brother to fair hurdler/fairly useful chaser Prince Khurram (2m-2½m winner, by Nayef): dam closely related to fairly useful hurdler (stayed 2½m) Washington Irving: useful on Flat, stays 10.5f: 6/1, fifth in maiden at Hereford (39¼ lengths behind Ice Cool Champs) on hurdling debut: should do better. *Venetia Williams*

SUB LIEUTENANT (IRE) 8 b.g. Brian Boru – Satellite Dancer (IRE) (Satco (FR)) **c167** [2016/17 c146, h141: c25d³ c19.5d* c19.5g* c20d³ c20d² c20.8g² c19.9g² Apr 7] **h–**
Sub Lieutenant's impressive hurdling debut win, in a large field of maidens at Fairyhouse on November 29th 2014, proved an emotionally-charged affair, being the first winner saddled by Sandra Hughes since she had taken over the training licence from her father Dessie, who had died just thirteen days earlier. For a while it was business as usual at Osborne Lodge, the Hughes' training establishment next to the Curragh racecourse. Big-race wins followed later that season thanks to a quickfire Grade 1 double by Lieutenant Colonel, while Thunder And Roses landed the Irish Grand National in the spring. However, a significant dip in results since then—Hughes notched up just thirteen wins in 2015/16 and eight in 2016/17 (compared to fifty-seven in her father's final full campaign)—prompted the trainer to hand in her licence in the spring of 2017. 'It was landed on top of me because Daddy died so suddenly. We took it on and gave it a go, but it's a numbers game—when you fall below a certain amount of numbers, it's tough and that's the problem,' remarked a philosophical Hughes in April (more on the difficulties currently facing some Irish jumps trainers can be found in Empire of Dirt's essay).
That 'numbers game' had been made especially tough for Hughes in May 2016, when Michael and Eddie O'Leary decided to remove the horses which run under the Gigginstown House Stud banner from the yard, and also from that of Tony Martin, after some disappointing results. In a separate move, they also split from champion trainer Willie Mullins four months later in a dispute over training fees. 'We're very much a results-based business,' explained Eddie O'Leary at the time of the Hughes/Martin reshuffle. Some viewed those particular decisions as quite harsh at the time, though it is worth noting that four in five of the switched horses (from both Hughes and Martin) won races for their new trainers in 2016/17. In addition, the huge scale of the Gigginstown operation (no fewer than one hundred and ninety-six individual horses ran in its maroon, white star and armlets in 2016/17) makes it dependent on good results. The O'Learys have never been associated with large gambles, so their only sizeable return is from prize money, which totalled €4m from their best-ever tally of one hundred and fifty-three wins on Irish soil in 2016/17.
Gigginstown's coffers were also bolstered by a significant prize money haul from another successful Cheltenham Festival meeting, where it enjoyed four wins (matching its previous best tally from 2011), taking the overall Festival total to nineteen—including Cheltenham Gold Cup wins with War of Attrition in 2006 and Don Cossack in 2016. One prize at Cheltenham which continues to elude Gigginstown, however, is the race Michael O'Leary has sponsored since 2006, the Ryanair Chase. To date there have been eight Gigginstown-owned runners in the Ryanair Chase, which have yielded four second places, two third places (including the unlucky Don Cossack in 2015) and a fourth. Sub Lieutenant followed in the footsteps of Mossbank (2008), First Lieutenant (2013) and Valseur Lido (2016) by filling the runner-up spot in the latest renewal, a reverse which was presumably all the more frustrating for the O'Learys given that victory went to the Mullins-trained Un de Sceaux. In truth, Sub Lieutenant never really looked like winning the latest Ryanair, with more patient tactics than usual adopted, though the manner in which he saw things out, after rather conceding first run, suggests he might have given

Gigginstown House Stud's "Sub Lieutenant"

the winner a real scare had he been asked for his effort sooner. It was a top-class performance by Sub Lieutenant, who had been disputing sixth before the home turn but was only a length and a half down by the line, pulling six lengths clear of third-placed Aso.

Some observers had felt that Sub Lieutenant was also the victim of a minor hard luck story on his previous start too, as the omission of the final fence (due to a stricken jockey) in the Kinloch Brae Chase at Thurles arguably counted against him, given how well he jumped under a front-running ride. Unlucky or not, there was clearly no shame for Sub Lieutenant (eventually beaten two and a half lengths) to be overhauled on that extended run-in by Sizing John, given what the winner went on to achieve subsequently. Another Ann and Alan Potts-owned horse got the better of Sub Lieutenant on his final start, when he was no match for the fast-improving Fox Norton in the Melling Chase at Aintree in April, though that latest second (beaten six lengths) still represented a creditable effort in what was an admirably consistent campaign for his new yard.

It was clear from the start that Sub Lieutenant was an improved performer in 2016/17, as he ran out an impressive wide-margin winner of a minor event at Limerick in October when making a winning debut for new trainer Henry de Bromhead. Even better was to come in the following month's Titanic Belfast Chase at Down Royal, a Grade 2 event for second-season chasers which has been monopolised in recent years by Paul Nicholls, who had won seven of the eight most recent renewals. Nicholls had to settle for third this time around, as his representative Ptit Zig was firmly put in his place by the Gigginstown pair Sub Lieutenant and

Outlander, the former putting in a superb round of jumping to win very easily, with three and a half lengths and a further seven and a half lengths back to the placed horses. Although he was unable to confirm his superiority over Outlander when third in the John Durkan Memorial Punchestown Chase in December, Sub Lieutenant still ran to form in finishing a close third (beaten two and a half lengths) to 2015 winner Djakadam, an uncharacteristic mistake at the last preventing him from pushing runner-up Outlander even closer. That run established Sub Lieutenant as a Grade 1 performer, and he went on to end the latest season with a Timeform rating 21 lb higher than in *Chasers & Hurdlers 2015/16*.

Sub Lieutenant (IRE) (b.g. 2009)	Brian Boru (b 2000)	Sadler's Wells (b 1981)	Northern Dancer / Fairy Bridge
		Eva Luna (b 1992)	Alleged / Media Luna
	Satellite Dancer (IRE) (b 1993)	Satco (br 1983)	Blakeney / Satwa
		Greek Empress (ch 1976)	Royal Buck / Greek Light

Although Sub Lieutenant rounded off his novice chasing campaign with a good third behind Zabana and Outlander in Grade 1 company at the 2016 Punchestown Festival (staged just after the start of Britain's 2016/17 season), a quick glance at his pedigree gives some clue as to why connections might have felt there was still some untapped potential. A son of 2003 St Leger winner Brian Boru, Sub Lieutenant is a close relative of the high-class staying chaser Lord Windermere (by Oscar, also a son of Sadler's Wells), winner of the 2013 RSA Chase and 2014 Cheltenham Gold Cup. He is the fifth foal out of thrice-raced Irish maiden hurdler Satellite Dancer, and one of five winners she has bred, a group which also includes his year-younger brother It Came To Pass, who was a very promising pointer/hunter chaser in 2015/16 but rather lost his way in handicap company during the latest season. Satellite Dancer has visited Lord Windermere's sire Oscar three more times in recent years, producing colts in 2012 and 2015, and a filly (named Windermere Sky) in 2014, all as yet unraced. Her most recent foal, a 2016 son of Shirocco, was sold for €25,000 in December. There were notable performers in this family tree before Lord Windermere and Sub Lieutenant came along, as Satellite Dancer was a half-sister to the dam of useful jumpers Start Me Up (who stayed well) and Stars Out Tonight (successful at two miles to twenty-five furlongs). Sub Lieutenant's grandam Greek Empress was an unraced half-sister to 1982 Queen Mother Champion Chase winner Rathgorman.

It is unlikely Sub Lieutenant will be asked to tackle two miles again, but equally it will be a surprise if he is kept just to trips of around two and a half miles from now on either, even though he has been campaigned exclusively at around that trip so far by de Bromhead. He made the frame several times in good company (over both hurdles and fences) at three miles earlier in his career, and the fact that he was a runner in the 2016 Irish Grand National (albeit pulled up late after seeming to find the trip too much) suggests that connections believe he has inherited plenty of the stamina found in his pedigree. A compact gelding, Sub Lieutenant has shown his form on ground ranging from good to heavy (yet to race on firmer than good) and is tongue tied nowadays. He was tried in a hood, cheekpieces and a visor for his previous yard, but ran without any headgear during the latest season and typically raced with plenty of zest towards the head of affairs. Sub Lieutenant is now firmly established as a top-class chaser—currently sidelined stable-companion Valseur Lido is the only Gigginstown-owned horse in training with a higher Timeform rating—and he should certainly continue to pay his way in 2017/18. *Henry de Bromhead, Ireland*

SUBLIME TALENT (IRE) 11 b.g. Sadler's Wells (USA) – Summer Trysting (USA) c– (Alleged (USA)) [2016/17 c110, h–: c16.3g^{pu} May 31] angular gelding: winning hurdler: h– fairly useful chaser at best, pulled up sole start in 2016/17: stays 2½m: acts on good to firm and heavy going: has worn headgear: wears tongue tie. *Evan Williams*

SUBOTAL (IRE) 4 ch.g. Pivotal – Suba (USA) (Seeking The Gold (USA)) [2016/17 b– b15.7d Feb 26] well held in bumper/Flat maiden. *Richard Guest*

SUBTLE GREY (IRE) 8 gr.g. Subtle Power (IRE) – Milltown Rose (IRE) (Roselier (FR)) [2016/17 c134, h–: c24.1s c23.4s^F Jan 23] good-topped gelding: winning hurdler: useful handicap chaser: running well when fatally injured in fall at Newcastle: stayed 3m: raced only on soft/heavy going. *Donald McCain* **c135 h–**

SUBTLE SOLDIER (IRE) 5 b.g. Subtle Power (IRE) – Killeen Queen (IRE) (Beneficial) [2016/17 b16.3s h16.7s⁵ h16vpu h16.3g Apr 1] rather leggy gelding: no form in bumper/novice hurdles: tried in tongue tie. *Evan Williams* **h– b–**

SUCH A LEGEND 9 ch.g. Midnight Legend – Mrs Fizziwig (Petoski) [2016/17 c123, h–: c19.2m² c20.3s⁴ c20.2g² c21.4g c19.4m* Apr 28] strong gelding: winning hurdler: fairly useful handicap chaser: won at Chepstow in April: stays 2½m: acts on soft and good to firm going: in tongue tie last 3 starts: front runner/races prominently. *Kim Bailey* **c124 h–**

SUDDEN WISH (IRE) 8 b.m. Jeremy (USA) – Fun Time (Fraam) [2016/17 h103: h17.7d h16g⁴ h19.1s⁵ h20.5gpu Jan 24] modest handicap hurdler: unproven beyond 2m: acts on good to firm and heavy going: usually in cheekpieces. *Gary Moore* **h86**

SUDSKI STAR (IRE) 9 br.g. Pilsudski (IRE) – Mogen's Star (IRE) (Be My Native (USA)) [2016/17 c96, h–: h16.2s³ c17.1spu h16.4s³ h16.4v⁵ h18.1d* Apr 10] fair handicap hurdler: won at Kelso (conditional) in April: fairly useful chaser at best, has lost his way over fences: stays 2½m: acts on heavy going: usually wears headgear/tongue tie: front runner/races prominently. *Harriet Graham* **c– h106**

SUE BE IT (IRE) 6 b.m. Presenting – Runaround Sue (IRE) (Among Men (USA)) [2016/17 b69: b16.7g⁵ b15.8m h16d⁴ h16.2s h15.5g³ h18.5m² Apr 15] poor in bumpers: modest form over hurdles: wears tongue tie. *Nikki Evans* **h99 b–**

SUE OSCAR (IRE) 7 b.m. Oscar (IRE) – Zaffaran Express (IRE) (Zaffaran (USA)) [2016/17 c20g² c25g h20.2d³ h22.5d⁴ c24g⁵ h23s h24s c23.8g h23.1s h27s h25dsu Feb 20] point winner: modest maiden hurdler: fair form over fences: left Gavin Patrick Cromwell after eighth start: stayed 3m: acted on good to soft going: often wore tongue tie: usually raced nearer last than first: dead. *Chris Grant* **c104 h93**

SUFFICE (IRE) 8 b.g. Iffraaj – Shallat (IRE) (Pennekamp (USA)) [2016/17 h–: h20g h16g* h15.7g⁶ h19.6m* Oct 2] poor handicap hurdler: won at Worcester in August and Huntingdon in October: stays 2½m: acts on good to firm and heavy going: has worn headgear. *Laura Young* **h81**

SUGAR BARON (IRE) 7 b.g. Presenting – Shuil Oilean (IRE) (Be My Native (USA)) [2016/17 h127: c25.1m* c20d^F c23.8d³ c26g⁶ c31.8gur c28.8g Apr 29] rangy gelding: fairly useful hurdler: useful form over fences: won novice at Wincanton in May: stays 29f: acts on good to firm and heavy going: in cheekpieces last 2 starts. *Nicky Henderson* **c136 h–**

SUGAR MIX 6 gr.g. Sagamix (FR) – Bruley (Weld) [2016/17 h–, b–: h15.8s h15.8s⁵ Mar 2] little form over hurdles: left Martin Keighley after first start: tried in cheekpieces. *Charlie Longsdon* **h57**

SUGAR STORM 6 b.m. Kayf Tara – Golden Buck (Golden Snake (USA)) [2016/17 b16.4s b16.7s h20.7g⁵ h21g⁵ Apr 24] well-made mare: first foal: dam unraced: well held in bumpers: poor form over hurdles: in tongue tie last 2 starts. *Fergal O'Brien* **h76 b–**

SUGGESTION 5 gr.g. Dansili – Jibboom (USA) (Mizzen Mast (USA)) [2016/17 b15.7g* b16.7g b16s⁵ h16.6d h19.7d⁶ h19.4s³ h16d* Mar 31] 7,000 3-y-o: third foal: half-brother to useful 7f/1m winner Flying Jib (by Oasis Dream): dam, US Grade 2 7f/1m winner, half-sister to useful/unreliable staying chaser Fortification: modest form in bumpers: won 2-runner maiden at Southwell in August: modest form over hurdles: much improved when won handicap at Wetherby in March: likely to prove best around 2m. *Philip Kirby* **h99 b77**

SUIT YOURSELF (IRE) 8 b.g. Flemensfirth (USA) – Corbetstown Queen (IRE) (Oscar (IRE)) [2016/17 h121p: c16.4gur c19.4g c16.3spu Jan 21] fairly useful hurdler: failed to complete all 3 starts in chases: stays 2¾m: wears tongue tie: often races towards rear. *Jonjo O'Neill* **c– h–**

SULAMANI THE LATE (FR) 5 b.g. Sulamani (IRE) – Delayed (FR) (Fijar Tango (FR)) [2016/17 b–: h15.7mpu h16.7s⁵ h16s h16.7d³ h19.9d² h15.8d³ Apr 16] modest form over hurdles: stays 2½m: acts on good to soft going: in cheekpieces last 2 starts: temperamental. *Dan Skelton* **h98 §**

SULTANA BELLE (IRE) 9 b.m. Black Sam Bellamy (IRE) – Sultana (GER) (Law Society (USA)) [2016/17 c–, h98: h16.8s⁶ h20.1g* c20.1d⁶ h20.2d h17.2d⁵ h20.2s h16.2d⁶ h23.3spu Nov 4] poor handicap hurdler: won mares event at Hexham in May: winning chaser: stays 21f: acts on soft and good to firm going: usually wore cheekpieces in 2016/17. *R. Mike Smith* **c– h82**

SULTANS PRIDE 5 b.g. Sulamani (IRE) – Pennys Pride (IRE) (Pips Pride) [2016/17 **b89** b16.4v² b16.7m⁵ Apr 17] brother to bumper winner/useful hurdler Crowning Jewel (2½m-2¾m winner) and half-brother to several winners, including fairly useful hurdler/ useful chaser Victor Hewgo (2½m-3m winner, by Old Vic): dam (b104), bumper winner (also 1¼m winner on Flat), half-sister to top-class chaser (stayed 2½m) Direct Route: fair form in bumpers: better effort when second in maiden at Newcastle in March. *Gillian Boanas*

SUMKINDOFKING (IRE) 6 br.g. King's Theatre (IRE) – Shannon Rose (IRE) **h123** (Topanoora) [2016/17 b16m* h15.7d* h16.8g h20.3s⁵ h21g⁵ h20g Apr 7] £70,000 5-y-o: **b104** well-made gelding: fifth foal: brother to useful hurdler/chaser Minella Foru (2m-3m winner) and closely related to bumper winner/fair hurdler Minella Hero (2m-25f winner, by Old Vic): dam (b85) bumper winner: winning Irish pointer: also won bumper at Chepstow (impressively by 12 lengths from Eaton Hill) in November: fairly useful form over hurdles: landed odds in maiden at Southwell later in November: stays 21f: acts on good to soft going: usually travels strongly. *Tom George*

SUMMER GETAWAY (IRE) 5 b.g. Getaway (GER) – Summer Crush (USA) (Summer **h105** Squall (USA)) [2016/17 b16.4g h15.3d h19.8d³ h21.4s Jan 7] €30,000 3-y-o: half-brother **b–** to several winners, including fair/temperamental hurdler/chaser Havetoavit (2m-2½m winner, by Theatrical): dam maiden on Flat: runner-up on last of 3 starts in Irish points: behind in bumper: fair form over hurdles: easily best effort when third in maiden at Wincanton in December. *Nick Mitchell*

SUMMER SOUNDS (IRE) 8 b.g. Definite Article – Marble Sound (IRE) (Be My **c90** Native (USA)) [2016/17 h93: h21.4d c19.1g⁴ c21.2g² c23.6gᵖᵘ Apr 3] maiden hurdler: **h–** modest form over fences: best effort when second in handicap at Fakenham in March: stays 21f: acts on good to soft going. *Tom Symonds*

SUMMER STORM 7 b.g. Lucarno (USA) – Midsummer Magic (Muhtarram (USA)) **c68** [2016/17 h98: h16.2d⁶ h17.2g* h19.5g h16g² h16d³ h16g* h18.4d³ h16g⁴ h16.2d⁴ **h104** c21vᶠ h16d⁵ c21s⁶ c16.2s⁵ Jan 31] fair handicap hurdler: won at Cartmel (conditionals/ amateur event) in August and Thurles in October: well held both completed starts over fences: left Rebecca Menzies after first start: stays 2¼m: acts on good to soft going: tried in cheekpieces: wears tongue tie. *John Joseph Hanlon, Ireland*

SUMMERY JUSTICE (IRE) 13 b.g. Witness Box (USA) – Kinsellas Rose (IRE) **c– §** (Roselier (FR)) [2016/17 c135§, h–: c24sᵖᵘ c22.3s c28sᵖᵘ c29.2vᵖᵘ Mar 12] sturdy gelding: **h–** winning hurdler: useful chaser at best, no form in 2016/17: stays 33f: wears headgear: usually races in rear: not one to trust. *Venetia Williams*

SUMOS NOVIOS (IRE) 9 b.g. Flemensfirth (USA) – Gaelic Million (IRE) (Strong **c139** Gale) [2016/17 c137: c20v* c25v⁴ c24s³ Mar 12] useful handicap chaser: won at Cork (by 7½ lengths from Mick The Jiver) in January: stays 3m: acts on heavy going: tried in tongue tie: usually races prominently. *W. J. Burke, Ireland*

SUN CLOUD (IRE) 10 b.g. Cloudings (IRE) – Miss Melrose (Bob Back (USA)) [2016/17 **c125** c135, h117: h23.9d⁴ h27g⁵ c28.4v⁵ c32.8gᵖᵘ c24.5d³ c26.3v² c24sᵖᵘ h26.6g* Apr 27] **h115** smallish, good-topped gelding: fair handicap hurdler: won at Perth (conditional) in April: fairly useful handicap chaser: stays 3¾m: acts on heavy going: in cheekpieces last 3 starts: tried in tongue tie. *Malcolm Jefferson*

SUNDANCE BOY 8 gr.g. Proclamation (IRE) – Just Beth (Carlingford Castle) [2016/17 **h–** b–: h15.7d h16.7sᵖᵘ Dec 22] no form in bumpers/over hurdles. *Giuseppe Fierro*

SUNDAY CENTRAL 6 ch.g. Central Park (IRE) – Sunday News'n'echo (USA) **h96** (Trempolino (USA)) [2016/17 b17.8d⁴ b16.2d² h15.8v⁵ h23.3v³ h15.5d h24.4g⁶ h19.8s⁶ **b99** h15.8s⁴ h21.7s⁴ h15.7s Mar 20] €30,000 3-y-o: sturdy gelding: half-brother to 3 winners, including fairly useful hurdler/chaser Evelith Echo (17f-2½m winner, by Overbury): dam (h107), 2m hurdle winner, also 1¼m-1½m winner on Flat: fairly useful form in bumpers: better effort when second at Perth in June: modest maiden hurdler: left Liam Lennon after second start: stays 23f: acts on heavy going: often races towards rear. *Tom Weston*

SUNDAY ROYAL (FR) 5 b.g. Sunday Break (JPN) – Princess d'Orange (FR) (Anabaa **h101** (USA)) [2016/17 h15.9dᵘʳ h15.5g³ h16.5g h16.3s⁶ Jan 18] neat gelding: fair maiden on Flat, stays 17f: fair form over hurdles: signs of temperament: has joined Mlle C. Cardenne. *Harry Whittington*

SUNGAI LONG 5 b.g. Lawman (FR) – Ammo (IRE) (Sadler's Wells (USA)) [2016/17 **h64** b89: b16d² h15.8d⁴ Jul 13] modest form in bumpers: 4/1, fourth in novice at Uttoxeter **b83** (33¼ lengths behind All For The Best) on hurdling debut: dead. *Michael Scudamore*

SUNNI MAY (IRE) 6 b.g. Presenting – Northwood May (Teenoso (USA)) [2016/17 b106: b16d³ h16v* h16d* h16d³ Dec 27] useful bumper performer: useful form over hurdles: won maiden at Cork in November and novice at Punchestown in December: third in Future Champions Novices' Hurdle at Leopardstown (6¼ lengths behind Saturnas, bad mistake 2 out) final start: likely to stay 2½m: tried in tongue tie. *Mrs J. Harrington, Ireland* **h137 b–**

SUNNY DESTINATION (IRE) 5 b.g. Dubai Destination (USA) – Railway House (IRE) (Ashkalani (IRE)) [2016/17 b16s² Dec 5] €9,000 3-y-o: first foal: dam, third in point, half-sister to useful hurdler/chaser (winner up to 2½m) Slieveardagh: 50/1, second in bumper at Ayr (1¼ lengths behind Silver Bullion) on debut: will be suited by further than 2m. *George Bewley* **b90**

SUNNY LEDGEND 12 b.g. Midnight Legend – Swordella (Broadsword (USA)) [2016/17 c118, h–: c24.5d² c24v⁴ c25.6dᵖᵘ c22.7s* c22.9vᶠ Mar 22] tall gelding: winning hurdler: fairly useful handicap chaser: won at Leicester in February: stays 3m: acts on good to firm and heavy going: has worn cheekpieces: tried in tongue tie: often travels strongly. *Andrew Martin* **c120 h–**

SUNNYTAHLIATEIGAN (IRE) 5 b.g. Robin des Pres (FR) – Wavering Bee (IRE) (Oscar (IRE)) [2016/17 b15.8g⁴ b16g⁴ h19.6m⁴ h19.3d⁶ h19.4g h19.1g* h20.3g* Apr 21] €7,000 3-y-o: useful-looking gelding: second foal: brother to a winning pointer: dam unraced half-sister to fair hurdler/fairly useful chaser (stayed 27f) Mister Friday: modest form in bumpers: fair form over hurdles: won handicaps at Fontwell (conditional) and Southwell (novice) in April: likely to stay further than 2½m: best form on good going: often races towards rear. *Ian Williams* **h108 b81**

SUN ODYSSEY 5 b.m. Mastercraftsman (IRE) – Penolva (IRE) (Galileo (IRE)) [2016/17 h16.2d⁵ h20.1g h20g h20s h22.1d⁵ h16.2s⁶ Mar 16] modest maiden on Flat, stays 11.5f: no form over hurdles. *Noel C. Kelly, Ireland* **h–**

SUN QUEST 13 b.g. Groom Dancer (USA) – Icaressa (Anabaa (USA)) [2016/17 h54§: h19.2g h17.7g h18.5d h21.4m h19.5vᵖᵘ Jan 10] compact gelding: fair hurdler at best, no form in 2016/17: has worn cheekpieces/tongue tie: usually races close up: untrustworthy. *Steven Dixon* **h– §**

SUNSET MARQUIS (IRE) 6 b.m. Kayf Tara – Miss Abrahnovic (IRE) (Deploy) [2016/17 b16s⁴ h16.2v⁴ h16.2sᶠ h18.1s⁶ Apr 3] first foal: dam (b84), placed in bumpers, out of half-sister to Scottish Grand National winner Baronet: placed in bumpers in 2015/16 for John Queally: modest form over hurdles: easily best effort when fourth in mares novice at Hexham: tried in cheekpieces: often races freely. *Alison Hamilton* **h97 b62**

SUNSHADE 4 b.f. Sulamani (IRE) – Spring Flight (Groom Dancer (USA)) [2016/17 b16g⁴ Apr 17] third foal: dam unraced half-sister to useful hurdler/chaser (stayed 2½m) Close Touch: 5/2, won mares maiden bumper at Fakenham (in hood, easily by 6 lengths from Rose Tree) on debut: seems sure to improve. *Nicky Henderson* **b95 p**

SUNSHINE CORNER (IRE) 6 b.m. King's Theatre (IRE) – Coolgreaney (IRE) (Bob Back (USA)) [2016/17 h128, b–: h22.8mᶠ May 7] good-topped mare: bumper winner: fairly useful hurdler: stayed 2¾m: acted on heavy going: usually raced prominently/travelled strongly: dead. *Lucy Wadham* **h–**

SUNSHINE MOUNTAIN (FR) 5 b.g. Librettist (USA) – Highest Price (FR) (Highest Honor (FR)) [2016/17 b13.7d b16.3v b17.7g Mar 27] tall gelding: no form in bumpers: tried in hood/tongue tie. *Chris Gordon* **b–**

Coral Cup Handicap Hurdle, Cheltenham—Supasundae comes out on top from Taquin du Seuil (right) in a typically competitive renewal

SUN SPIDER (IRE) 6 br.g. Scorpion (IRE) – Benedicta Rose (IRE) (Beneficial) [2016/17 **h–** h19.3d h22s Jan 23] placed both starts in Irish maiden points: well held in novice hurdles. *Brian Ellison*

SUN WILD LIFE (FR) 7 b.g. Antarctique (IRE) – Nidelia (FR) (Sleeping Car (FR)) **c99** [2016/17 c119, h–: c24.2m c25.1d⁶ Dec 13] good-topped gelding: maiden hurdler: fairly **h–** useful handicap chaser, below form in 2016/17: stays 3¼m: acts on heavy going: wears headgear: often races prominently. *Robert Walford*

SUPAKALANISTIC (IRE) 4 b.g. Kalanisi (IRE) – Keys Hope (IRE) (Luso) [2016/17 **b88** b16g⁴ Apr 24] €5,000 3-y-o: first foal: dam (b84), maiden, out of sister to smart hurdler (stayed 21f) In Contrast: 6/1, fourth in bumper at Warwick (5 lengths behind Not That Fuisse) on debut. *Nigel Twiston-Davies*

SUPAPOWERS (IRE) 11 ch.m. Subtle Power (IRE) – Hi Sheree (IRE) (Beau Sher) **c–** [2016/17 c103, h73: h26vᵖᵘ h23.6s⁴ Mar 13] angular mare: winning Irish pointer: modest **h86** maiden hurdler: fair form in chases: stays 27f: acts on good to firm and good to soft going: wears tongue tie. *Robert Stephens*

SUPASUNDAE 7 b.g. Galileo (IRE) – Distinctive Look (IRE) (Danehill (USA)) [2016/17 **h154** h143, b–: h20d⁴ h16d h20d* h16s² h21s⁴ h21.1g* h24.7g² Apr 8] big gelding: bumper winner: smart hurdler: won minor event at Punchestown (by 6½ lengths from Monksland) in December and Coral Cup at Cheltenham (by 2 lengths from Taquin du Seuil) in March: second in Stayers' Liverpool Hurdle at Aintree (length behind Yanworth) final start: left Henry de Bromhead after first start: stays 25f: acts on heavy going: often races prominently/ travels strongly. *Mrs J. Harrington, Ireland*

Ann & Alan Potts Partnership's "Supasundae"

SUPERB STORY (IRE) 6 b.g. Duke of Marmalade (IRE) – Yes My Love (FR) (Anabaa **h144**
(USA)) [2016/17 h145: h16.1g^{pu} h15.6g* Jan 1] close-coupled gelding: useful handicap
hurdler: won at Musselburgh (by ½ length from My Manekineko) in January after 5-month
absence: not seen out again: unproven beyond 17f: acts on good to soft going: usually
travels strongly. *Dan Skelton*

SUPER CHARGE 5 ch.g. Recharge (IRE) – Arctic Ring (Karinga Bay) [2016/17 b–: **h77**
h16.6g^6 h20.3^{pu} Apr 23] won maiden point on debut: poor form over hurdles:
should stay further than 2m. *Chris Fairhurst*

SUPERIOR COMMAND (IRE) 8 b.g. Lahib (USA) – Decent Dime (IRE) (Insan **c–**
(USA)) [2016/17 c115p, h95: c20g h19.9s^f h15.6g* h15.6g^2 h15.6g c17.1d^{pu} Apr 10] **h103**
fair handicap hurdler: won at Musselburgh in January: winning chaser, no form over
fences in 2016/17: stays 2¾m: acts on soft going: wears headgear: in tongue tie last 2 starts.
Lucinda Russell

SUPER LUNAR (IRE) 8 b.g. Super Celebre (FR) – Kapricia Speed (FR) (Vertical Speed **c65**
(FR)) [2016/17 h74: h23.9m^5 h24s^2 h24.7d^5 c24v^{pu} c25.5g^4 Jul 18] lengthy gelding: **h95**
runner-up in Irish point: modest maiden hurdler: little show in 2 chases: stays 3m: acts on
soft going: in cheekpieces last 3 starts: wears tongue tie. *Henry Hogarth*

SUPERMAN DE LA RUE (FR) 11 b.g. Akhdari (USA) – Impala de La Rue (FR) **c–**
(Brugnon (FR)) [2016/17 c–, h98: h19.9g c18.9s Nov 23] winning pointer: fairly useful **h–**
handicap hurdler at best, well held on return: maiden chaser: stays 19f: acts on soft and
good to firm going: has worn headgear. *Mary Evans*

SUPER MOON 5 b.g. Black Sam Bellamy (IRE) – Aussie Deal (IRE) (Flemensfirth **h–**
(USA)) [2016/17 h15.8m^6 h16.3m Jul 17] little show in Flat maiden/novice hurdles: tried
in hood. *Richard Phillips*

SUPER SAM 8 gr.g. Overbury (IRE) – Gaye Sophie (Environment Friend) [2016/17 **h114**
h19.7s* h20d* h18.9s^6 h26v^6 h25.5s^5 Mar 11] fair handicap hurdler: won at Hereford and
Ffos Las in November: stays 2½m: acts on soft going. *Venetia Williams*

SUPER SCORPION (IRE) 7 b.g. Scorpion (IRE) – Nolagh Supreme (IRE) (Supreme **c114**
Leader) [2016/17 h109: c19.4g^6 c19.4d^2 c19.4g^4 c20.3m^3 Sep 27] maiden hurdler: fair **h–**
form over fences: stays 19f: acts on good to soft going: tried in cheekpieces. *Debra Hamer*

SUPER SID (IRE) 5 b.g. Westerner – Super Sammy (Mesleh) [2016/17 b15.8g^3 Apr 9] **b77 p**
€18,000 3-y-o, £30,000 4-y-o: fifth foal: half-brother to fair chaser Theatre Princess (3m
winner, by King's Theatre): dam (c100/h97), 2m-21f hurdle/chaser, half-sister to
fairly useful/ungenuine hurdler/chaser (stayed 2½m) Super Nomad: runner-up in Irish
maiden point on debut: 8/1, third in bumper at Ffos Las (13¾ lengths behind Espoir de
Teillee) in April: likely to improve. *Tom Lacey*

SUPPLY AND DEMAND (IRE) 6 br.g. Scorpion (IRE) – Native Fashion (IRE) (Be **h94**
My Native (USA)) [2016/17 h–p: h18.5g^4 h15.8s h20.7d^{pu} Dec 26] modest form over
hurdles: should be suited by further than 2¼m. *Jonjo O'Neill*

SUPREME ASSET (IRE) 9 b.g. Beneficial – Hollygrove Supreme (IRE) (Supreme **c107**
Leader) [2016/17 c111, h–: c17.2d^3 c17.3d^3 c15.5g^2 c17.4s^3 c20.3s^3 c16.3s^5 Jan 23] good- **h–**
topped gelding: winning hurdler: fair handicap chaser: stayed 2½m: acted on heavy going:
often in headgear in 2016/17: inconsistent: dead. *Donald McCain*

SUPREME BOB (IRE) 11 b.g. Bob's Return (IRE) – Suprememories (IRE) (Supreme **c93**
Leader) [2016/17 c100, h–: c20s^3 c20.9d^{pu} c20v^{pu} c23.5v^{pu} Jan 31] winning hurdler: fair **h–**
handicap chaser at best, has lost his form: stays 21f: acts on heavy going: has worn
headgear, including last 2 starts: usually races nearer last than first. *Debra Hamer*

SUPREME DANEHILL (IRE) 9 b.g. Indian Danehill (IRE) – Monte Rosa (IRE) **c96**
(Supreme Leader) [2016/17 c–: c22.7s^{ur} c20.2s^3 Feb 28] multiple point winner: modest
maiden chaser: stays 23f: acts on soft and good to firm going: wears cheekpieces. *Alan Hill*

SUPREME GAEL 6 br.m. Supreme Sound – Italstar (IRE) (Galileo (IRE)) [2016/17 h–, **h–**
b76: h16.2m h16.2d^6 h20.6d h22.7s^{pu} h19.3d^{pu} Dec 13] placed in bumper: no form over
hurdles: in headgear last 3 starts. *Iain Jardine*

SUPREME PERFORMER 6 b.m. Multiplex – Follow My Leader (IRE) (Supreme **h–**
Leader) [2016/17 h16d h18.5s^{pu} Dec 15] poor form in bumpers: no show in novice hurdles:
tried in tongue tie. *Samuel Drinkwater*

SUPREME REGIME (IRE) 11 b.g. Old Vic – Shampooed (IRE) (Law Society (USA))   c–
[2016/17 c–: h24.3d^{pu} Oct 24] dual winning pointer: pulled up in handicap on hurdling   h–
debut: modest form when placed in hunter chases: in headgear last 2 starts. *Gemma Anderson*

SUPREME VINNIE (IRE) 8 b.g. Vinnie Roe (IRE) – Rapid Atlantic (IRE) (Supreme   h125
Leader) [2016/17 h16.5g^2 h16g^5 h16g* h19.5g* h16s h22.8g^2 h20g h24d* h25.3s h24d
Apr 18] bumper winner: fairly useful hurdler: won conditionals maiden at Kilbeggan in
June, and handicaps at same course later in month and Gowran in October: stays 3m: acts
on good to soft going: has worn headgear: wears tongue tie. *Miss D. M. O'Shea, Ireland*

SUPRISE VENDOR (IRE) 11 ch.g. Fath (USA) – Dispol Jazz (Alhijaz) [2016/17   c– §
c109x, h109: h17m^4 h16.2d h16.2s^{ur} h16.2s^5 h16.4s^5 h16v* h16.7s h16.4v^5 h16v* h18.1d   h103 §
Apr 10] close-coupled gelding: fair handicap hurdler: won at Ayr in January and March:
fair chaser: stays 2½m: acts on heavy going: front runner/races prominently: often let down
by attitude and isn't one to rely on. *Stuart Coltherd*

SURENESS (IRE) 7 ch.m. Hurricane Run (IRE) – Silk Dress (IRE) (Gulch (USA))   c–
[2016/17 c114, h–: h15.7m^3 h16.3m^3 Oct 15] workmanlike mare: fair handicap hurdler   h109
nowadays: maiden chaser: stays 2¼m: acts on good to firm and good to soft going: has
worn cheekpieces: wears tongue tie. *Charlie Mann*

SURE REEF (IRE) 8 ch.g. Choisir (AUS) – Cutting Reef (IRE) (Kris) [2016/17 h20d^3 h134
h16s^5 h20v^4 h21.1g h24d^6 Apr 27] big, workmanlike gelding: useful handicap hurdler:
barely stays 3m: acts on heavy going: usually races prominently. *W. P. Mullins, Ireland*

SURE THING (FR) 11 b.g. Ragmar (FR) – Harpe (FR) (Bayolidaan (FR)) [2016/17 c20g   c62
Jul 21] winning pointer/hurdler: maiden chaser, fair at best: stays 21f: acts on good to soft   h–
and good to firm going: has worn hood. *Karen McLintock*

SURF AND TURF (IRE) 11 ch.g. Beneficial – Clear Top Waltz (IRE) (Topanoora)   c125 x
[2016/17 c137, h–: c16m^{ur} c16g c19.4m^3 c20g^5 c18m^{ur} h19.7g Oct 29] workmanlike   h98
gelding: winning hurdler: fairly useful handicap chaser nowadays: left Kevin Frost after
second start: stays 2½m: acts on good to firm and good to soft going: has worn cheekpieces,
including final start: often let down by jumping. *Richard Hobson*

SURFING THE STARS (IRE) 6 b.g. Brian Boru – Golden Jorden (IRE) (Cadeaux   h–
Genereux) [2016/17 h–, b–: h19d^5 h19.9m h20d h15.8g h20.3m Sep 27] no form over
hurdles: has worn hood. *Laura Young*

SURPRISE US 10 b.g. Indian Ridge – Pingus (Polish Precedent (USA)) [2016/17 c–x, h–:   c– x
h16g^{pu} c16.3g^{pu} Jul 25] winning hurdler: little form over fences (often let down by   h–
jumping): usually wears headgear. *Mark Gillard*

SURTEE DU BERLAIS (IRE) 7 b.m. High Chaparral (IRE) – Marina du Berlais (FR)   h130
(Mister Sicy (FR)) [2016/17 h123: h24.5s* h24.4d h21v^3 h23.6v^3 Feb 25] good-bodied
mare: useful hurdler: won listed mares event at Kempton (by 3¼ lengths from Rons
Dream) in November: stays 3m: acts on heavy going: tried in cheekpieces. *Oliver Sherwood*

SUSIE SHEEP 7 ch.m. Robin des Champs (FR) – Haudello (FR) (Marignan (USA))   c119
[2016/17 c117, h103: c23.9s* Dec 1] maiden hurdler: fairly useful form over fences: won   h–
novice handicap at Market Rasen in December after 17-month absence: stays 3m: acts on
soft going: often in headgear: has worn tongue tie. *David Pipe*

SUSSEX ROAD (IRE) 7 b.g. Mahler – Rose Island (Jupiter Island) [2016/17 h81: h22g^{pu} c80 §
c21.2g c25.5m c25.5g^5 c25.5g^4 c24g^4 c25.5s^{pu} c24d^5 c25.6v^{pu} c18.9s^{pu} c15.9g^3 c20.9v^{pu} h– §
c16.1m^3 c16.1m^5 Apr 27] maiden hurdler/chaser: usually wears headgear: temperamental.
Aytach Sadik

SUTTER'S MILL (IRE) 6 b.g. Gold Well – Shamriyna (IRE) (Darshaan) [2016/17 h85:   h103
h16.2g^5 h21.2v^4 h20v^3 h23.1s^2 h23.4s^5 h21.6v^4 h20v^5 h23.6s* Mar 13] fair handicap hurdler:
won at Chepstow in March: will stay beyond 3m: acts on heavy going: in cheekpieces last
3 starts. *Evan Williams*

SUTTON MANOR (IRE) 6 b.g. Gold Well – Nighty Bless (IRE) (Executive Perk)   h140
[2016/17 h16g^2 h18s* h24v^3 h24g^4 h24s^2 h24v* h24g^5 h24d^3 h24d^5 Apr 27] €52,000 3-y-o,
£125,000 4-y-o: rangy gelding: chasing type: closely related to a winning pointer by Oscar
and half-brother to smart bumper winner Relic Rock (by Bienamado): dam unraced half-
sister to fairly useful hurdler (winner up to 2½m) Oscardeal: useful hurdler: won maiden at
Wexford in November and handicap at Thurles in February: stays 3m: acts on heavy going:
races prominently, often travels strongly. *Gordon Elliott, Ireland*

Ladbrokes Ireland Boyne Hurdle, Navan—Sutton Place (left) finds plenty to beat stable-companion De Plotting Shed and complete a five-timer

SUTTON PLACE (IRE) 6 b.g. Mahler – Glebe Beauty (IRE) (Good Thyne (USA)) [2016/17 h137p, b101: h16s* h21s* h24d^{pu} Apr 27] bumper winner: smart form over hurdles: stretched his winning run to five when successful in Limestone Lad Hurdle at Naas (by 7½ lengths from Supasundae) in January and Boyne Hurdle at Navan (by 3¾ lengths from De Plotting Shed) in February: went wrong final outing: stays 21f: acts on soft going: in tongue tie last 3 starts. *Gordon Elliott, Ireland*   **h160**

SUTTON SID 7 ch.g. Dutch Art – Drastic Measure (Pivotal) [2016/17 h–: h15.9g^{pu} May 8] maiden hurdler, lightly raced and no form since 2013/14: wears cheekpieces. *Michelle Bryant*   **h–**

SUZY'S MUSIC (IRE) 9 b.m. Gamut (IRE) – Vicky's Music (IRE) (Old Vic) [2016/17 c89p, h60: c20.1d⁶ c24.2d³ c24.2g⁵ c24.2s³ c25.2d² c24.2d⁴ c26.3g³ Mar 29] maiden hurdler: modest handicap chaser: stays 3¼m: acts on heavy going: in cheekpieces last 2 starts: usually races towards rear. *Stuart Crawford, Ireland*   **c93 h–**

SWALEDALE LAD (IRE) 10 b.g. Arakan (USA) – Tadjnama (USA) (Exceller (USA)) [2016/17 c124, h94: h16.7g⁶ h17.2m h20.3g h16.2s³ h16.8g³ h16.2d c19.3g² c17.4g⁵ h20.3d h16.7d* c15.7g Jan 12] tall, narrow gelding: modest handicap hurdler: won selling event at Market Rasen in December: fair handicap chaser: stays 19f: acts on good to firm and heavy going: has worn cheekpieces, including last 2 starts: weak finisher. *Richard Ford*   **c100 § h97 §**

SWALLOWS DELIGHT (IRE) 12 br.g. Tamayaz (CAN) – Windmill Star (IRE) (Orchestra) [2016/17 c103: c16.3g⁶ Apr 27] compact gelding: fair hunter chaser: stays 21f: acts on soft and good to firm going. *Mrs Julie Mansell*   **c88**

SWALLOWSHIDE 8 b.g. Hernando (FR) – Kentford Grebe (Teenoso (USA)) [2016/17 c21g⁵ c25.5d^{pu} May 12] dual winning pointer: winning hurdler: little impact in hunter chases: should stay 3m: acts on soft going: in hood last 2 starts. *J. H. Young*   **c81 h–**

SWAMP FOX (IRE) 5 br.g. Windsor Knot (IRE) – Brogella (IRE) (King's Theatre (IRE)) [2016/17 h16v* h16d³ h16d h16s³ h20.5d Apr 29] half-brother to fairly useful hurdler Rene's Girl (21f-3m winner, by Presenting): dam (h131) 2m-2¼m hurdle winner: useful on Flat, stays 17f: useful handicap hurdler: won at Listowel in September: should stay beyond 2m: acts on heavy going: has worn blinkers. *Joseph G. Murphy, Ireland*   **h133**

SWANSEA MILE (IRE) 7 b.g. Dylan Thomas (IRE) – Hurry Up Helen (IRE) (In The Wings) [2016/17 h131, b74. h15.7m h15.9g³ c20d³ c15 7d² Jul 10] sturdy gelding: useful hurdler at best: fairly useful form over fences: better effort when third in novice at Worcester in June: stays 2½m: acts on good to firm and good to soft going: often races towards rear/travels strongly. *Dan Skelton*   **c129 h123**

Mr John P. McManus' "Sutton Place"

SWATOW 5 b.m. Shantou (USA) – Sudden Beat (Beat All (USA)) [2016/17 b16.6d **h110** h20.3g² h19.5g² Apr 17] first foal: dam (b89), placed in bumpers, sister to fair hurdler/ **b–** useful chaser (stays 27f) Gentleman Jon: well beaten in mares bumper: fair form over hurdles: better effort when second in mares novice at Southwell in March. *Emma Lavelle*

SWEEPING BEAUTY 4 b.f. Authorized (IRE) – Brushing (Medicean) [2016/17 b13.7g² **b80** b12.4d³ b14s ab16g³ Jan 31] slightly-built filly: first foal: dam useful 6f-1½m winner: modest form in bumpers. *Mark H. Tompkins*

SWEEPING ROCK (IRE) 7 b.g. Rock of Gibraltar (IRE) – Sweeping Story (USA) **h94** (End Sweep (USA)) [2016/17 h95: h15.8m⁵ h15.7mᵖᵘ h16.8g² Apr 26] modest maiden hurdler: raced around 2m: acts on soft going: tried in cheekpieces/tongue tie. *John Spearing*

SWEET AS A NUT (IRE) 7 b.g. Vinnie Roe (IRE) – Sarahall (IRE) (Saddlers' Hall **c119 p** (IRE)) [2016/17 c22.5v* c26.3gᶠ Mar 17] third foal: half-brother to fairly useful 3m chase winner Wild Bill (by Westerner): dam (h77), winning pointer, half-sister to fairly useful hurdler/useful chaser (stays 25f) What A Warrior: won 3 times in points: fairly useful form when winning maiden hunter at Limerick in December on chasing debut with plenty in hand: let down by jumping in Foxhunter at Cheltenham: wears tongue tie: should still improve. *Michael Barry, Ireland*

SWEET BELLE 7 b.m. Black Sam Bellamy (IRE) – Phildante (IRE) (Phardante (FR)) **c90** [2016/17 h20.6d h16.4s h21.2d⁶ c19.2d⁵ c25.2s³ c16.3s⁴ c21.2g⁴ c26.3g² c26.3m* Apr 19] **h–** £8,500 6-y-o: half-sister to winning pointers by Classic Cliche and Overbury: dam winning pointer: off mark in points at fifth attempt: well held in maiden hurdles: modest form in chases: won handicap at Sedgefield in April: stays 3¼m: acts on good to firm and good to soft going: in cheekpieces last 2 starts: tried in tongue tie: often races towards rear. *David Thompson*

SWEET HOLLY 6 b.m. Kayf Tara – Presuming (Mtoto) [2016/17 h105, b–: h17.2g^pu h20.2f^3 h16.2s^3 h16.2s^4 h20.2g h18.1d^6 h16.2g^2 Apr 27] modest maiden hurdler: left Lucinda Russell after fifth start: unproven beyond 2m: acts on soft and good to firm going. *Malcolm Jefferson* **h97**

SWEETLITTLEKITTY (IRE) 7 b.m. Robin des Champs (FR) – Alcrea (IRE) (Commander Collins (IRE)) [2016/17 b84: b16.7g^6 h20d^5 h20d^F h23d* h20.5g^6 h23.1d h21.9d Apr 16] won Irish point on debut: modest at best in bumpers: modest form over hurdles: won novice at Worcester in June: will stay beyond 23f: acts on good to soft going: in cheekpieces/tongue tie last 5 starts: front runner/races prominently. *Rebecca Curtis* **h95 b–**

SWEETLITTLEMYSTERY 6 b.m. Black Sam Bellamy (IRE) – Eau de Vie (Terimon) [2016/17 b15.7d* b15.7s* b17g Apr 6] lengthy mare: fourth foal: closely related to fairly useful hurdler E Street Boy (2½m-2¾m winner, by Kayf Tara): dam, pulled up only start over hurdles, half-sister to fair hurdler/smart chaser (stayed 25f) Colonel Frank: fairly useful form in bumpers: won mares events at Towcester in December and Ascot in February: will stay further than 2m. *Brendan Powell* **b98**

SWEET MIDNIGHT 5 b.m. Mawatheeq (USA) – Sweet Reply (Opening Verse (USA)) [2016/17 h83: h16.8s Apr 28] lengthy mare: poor maiden hurdler: stays 19f: in cheekpieces last 2 starts. *John Holt* **h–**

SWEET'N'CHIC (IRE) 7 b.m. Midnight Legend – Sweetbitter (FR) (Turgeon (USA)) [2016/17 h75, b74: h21m^3 h21.6g^pu h21.6s^6 h25s^3 h20.5v^5 h23.9g h23v^pu Mar 6] poor maiden hurdler: stays 25f: acts on soft and good to firm going: front runner/races prominently. *Richard Rowe* **h80**

SWEETTOOTHTOMMY (IRE) 7 b.g. Definite Article – My Linda (IRE) (Bob Back (USA)) [2016/17 h-p: h19.5d h16d^3 h20.7d c26.3g^2 c25.7v^4 c23g^4 c24.5v^5 c19.2g^5 c23.6g^4 Apr 17] tall gelding: modest form over hurdles: fair form over fences: acts on good to soft going: wears headgear: often in tongue tie: temperamental. *David Pipe* **c100 § h97**

SWEET WORLD 13 b.g. Agnes World (USA) – Douce Maison (IRE) (Fools Holme (USA)) [2016/17 h93: h16.8g^4 h16.7g^4 h15.9d^6 Jun 16] small gelding: poor handicap hurdler nowadays: unproven beyond 17f: acts on any going. *Bernard Llewellyn* **h81**

SWIFT BLADE (IRE) 9 ch.g. Exceed And Excel (AUS) – Gold Strike (IRE) (Rainbow Quest (USA)) [2016/17 h16m^pu May 16] fairly useful at one time on Flat, stays 1½m: twice-raced over hurdles, pulled up in maiden in May. *Luke Dace* **h–**

SWIFT CRUSADOR 6 b.g. Kayf Tara – Goldenswift (IRE) (Meneval (USA)) [2016/17 h20v* Mar 1] €20,000 4-y-o, £30,000 6-y-o: half-brother to bumper winner/useful hurdler Golden Bay (21f/2¾m winner, by Karinga Bay) and bumper winner Keltic Cliche (by Classic Cliche): dam (c109/h107) 21f-3m hurdle/chase winner: off mark in Irish maiden points at fourth attempt: 3/1, fortunate when won novice at Ffos Las (by 30 lengths from We'll Be There) on hurdling debut, looking held when left clear run-in: open to improvement. *Evan Williams* **h111 p**

SWIFT DECISION 6 b.g. Araafa (IRE) – Saga River (FR) (Sagacity (FR)) [2016/17 b16.8m h21.6m^pu Jul 17] no show in varied events, including point. *Richard Woollacott* **h– b–**

SWINCOMBE SCORCHIO 7 b.g. Scorpion (IRE) – Lady Felix (Batshoof) [2016/17 c25.2s^5 c19.2s^4 c23.6v^2 c23.6s* c25.3g^4 Apr 20] fifth foal: half-brother to bumper winner/useful hurdler (2m-21f winner) Swincombe Flame and fairly useful chaser Lady Everywhere (19f winner), both by Exit To Nowhere: dam (c91/h114), 3m hurdle winner, also 2m winner on Flat: winning pointer: fairly useful form over fences: won on handicap debut at Chepstow in March: stays 3m: acts on heavy going: wears tongue tie: front runner/races prominently. *Polly Gundry* **c127**

SWINCOMBE TOBY 5 b.g. Tobougg (IRE) – Soloism (Sulaafah (USA)) [2016/17 h110: h16.8g^2 h16s h19.5s h23.9s^5 Feb 5] sturdy gelding: fair maiden hurdler: unproven beyond 17f: acts on heavy going: tried in blinkers. *Philip Hobbs* **h101**

SWING HARD (IRE) 9 br.g. Zagreb (USA) – Hurricane Jane (IRE) (Strong Gale) [2016/17 c111§, h–: c22.4v^pu c24.2s^5 c26.2s c24.2d^2 c26.3v^3 c21.3d* c21.3d^2 Mar 31] maiden hurdler: fair handicap chaser: won at Wetherby in March: stays 25f: acts on heavy going: front runner/races prominently. *Sue Smith* **c112 h–**

SWINGING CONCERTO 5 br.g. Rocamadour – Dizzy Frizzy (Loup Sauvage (USA)) [2016/17 b15.8s b15.7m^5 Apr 13] last in bumpers: tried in tongue tie. *Nigel Twiston-Davies* **b–**

SWINTON DIAMOND (IRE) 6 b.g. Dubai Destination (USA) – Absent Beauty (IRE) (Dancing Dissident (USA)) [2016/17 h85, b–: h16s^6 h20.8g^6 h19.7s^4 h21.2s h24.1m Apr 13] modest form over hurdles: left Ian Williams after third start: stays 2½m: acts on soft going: has worn hood: tail flasher. *Micky Hammond* **h88**

SWIZZLER (IRE) 8 b.g. Scorpion (IRE) – Arch Hall Lady (IRE) (Luso) [2016/17 c101, h–: c16.3g⁵ May 9] good-topped gelding: little show over hurdles: fair chaser, well held only outing in 2016/17: stays 2½m: acts on heavy going. *Ian Williams*   **c–**
h–

SWNYMOR (IRE) 8 b.g. Dylan Thomas (IRE) – Propaganda (IRE) (Sadler's Wells (USA)) [2016/17 h111: h20s⁴ May 11] well-made gelding: useful hurdler at best, has lost his way: stays 2½m: acts on heavy going: tried in cheekpieces: usually wears tongue tie. *Kevin Frost*   **h74**

SWOOP TO CONQUER (IRE) 5 br.g. Presenting – One Swoop (IRE) (Be My Native (USA)) [2016/17 b16.8m⁵ h21.6m² h15.8d⁶ h15.7d⁵ h24.4dᵖᵘ h21.3dᵖᵘ Mar 31] lengthy gelding: very green when fifth in bumper: fair form over hurdles: best effort at 2¾m: dead. *Nicky Henderson*   **h107**
b70

SWORD OF FATE (IRE) 4 b.g. Beneficial – Beann Ard (IRE) (Mandalus) [2016/17 b16.8g* Apr 26] €28,000 3-y-o: brother to bumper/point winner Benechenko and half-brother to 3 winners, including fair chaser Buckland Gold (2m-2½m winner, by Lord Americo): dam unraced: third on completed start in points: 5/1, won maiden bumper at Exeter (by 10 lengths from Koala Keel) in April: bred to be suited by 2½m+. *Tom Lacey*   **b98**

SWORD OF THE LORD 7 b.g. Kheleyf (USA) – Blue Echo (Kyllachy) [2016/17 h103: h15.8gᵘʳ h16.3d² h16m c19.4gᴿ c17g² c17d⁴ c16d* c20vᵖᵘ c16g⁶ h16.2s⁶ h19.9v⁴ Feb 11] fair maiden hurdler: fair form over fences: won novice handicap at Perth in September: unproven beyond 17f: acts on soft going: usually wears headgear: has worn tongue tie: usually races towards rear: temperamental. *Nigel Twiston-Davies*   **c110 §**
h102 §

SYBARITE (FR) 11 b.g. Dark Moondancer – Haida III (FR) (Video Rock (FR)) [2016/17 c–§, h117§: h26.4m⁶ c22.7s² Feb 16] rangy, well-made gelding: prolific point winner: useful hurdler/maiden chaser at one time: left Nigel Twiston-Davies after first start: stays 3½m: acts on heavy going: has worn headgear, including in 2016/17: has worn tongue tie: most temperamental (usually gets well behind). *Miss V. Collins*   **c115 §**
h– §

SYBIL GREY 8 gr.m. Fair Mix (IRE) – Gimme Shelter (IRE) (Glacial Storm (USA)) [2016/17 h–, b–: h19.3m⁴ h23.3gᵖᵘ h23.3sᵖᵘ Apr 28] modest form over hurdles: standout effort at 19f on good to firm going. *George Bewley*   **h86**

SYDNEY DE BAUNE (FR) 6 b.g. Califet (FR) – Perle de Baune (FR) (En Calcat (FR)) [2016/17 h–, b75: h19.5s h19.8v Mar 9] sturdy gelding: poor form over hurdles: may prove best around 2m: capable of better. *Robert Walford*   **h60 p**

SYKES (IRE) 8 b.g. Mountain High (IRE) – Our Trick (IRE) (Flemensfirth (USA)) [2016/17 h124: h24dꟳ h24.7m c24.2g² c23.6g* c23.6s⁶ c23dꟳ c23.4d⁴ c23.6g⁵ Apr 17] compact gelding: fairly useful hurdler: similar form over fences: won novice handicap at Chepstow in December: stays 25f: acts on heavy going. *Philip Hobbs*   **c127**
h–

SYLVAN LEGEND 9 b.g. Midnight Legend – Sylvan Warbler (USA) (Blushing Groom (FR)) [2016/17 c80, h54: c16.5s³ c15.7g² c17.4g² c20d⁵ c16.3g c17g Aug 11] winning hurdler: poor handicap chaser: stays 3m: acts on soft going: wears headgear/tongue tie: usually races close up, often freely. *Matt Sheppard*   **c76**
h–

SYLVATICA (IRE) 7 gr.m. Tikkanen (USA) – Dapples (IRE) (Accordion) [2016/17 h20.5g h16g⁶ Dec 18] little show in 2 Irish points in 2014: no form over hurdles: wore hood: dead. *Neil King*   **h–**

SYMPHONY OF ANGELS 5 b.g. Sulamani (IRE) – Flying Lion (Hunting Lion (IRE)) [2016/17 b16.3d b16.3v⁴ b15.8m³ Apr 18] fifth foal: half-brother to 1¼m-1½m winner Symphony of Kings (by Lucarno): dam 7f winner: fair form in bumpers: best effort when third at Ludlow in April: left Sarah-Jayne Davies after second start. *Graeme McPherson*   **b85**

SYRACUSE'S DREAM (FR) 6 gr.g. Lord du Sud (FR) – Laura's Dream (FR) (Bonnet Rouge (FR)) [2016/17 c23gᵘʳ Apr 6] winning pointer: pulled up only outing over hurdles: maiden chaser, raced mostly in French Provinces: has worn cheekpieces. *Mrs D. J. Treneer*   **c–**
h–

T

TABLE BLUFF (IRE) 8 ch.g. Indian Haven – Double Deal (Keen) [2016/17 c88, h–: c16.5g Sep 12] maiden hurdler: modest chaser at best, well held sole outing in 2016/17: unproven beyond 2m: acts on good to firm and good to soft going: tried in cheekpieces. *David Drinkwater*   **c–**
h–

TACENDA (IRE) 5 b.m. Flemensfirth (USA) – Tordasia (IRE) (Dr Devious (IRE)) [2016/17 b15.8s³ c17.5v³ Dec 15] €5,000 3-y-o, resold €13,000 3-y-o, €60,000 4-y-o: half-sister to 2 winners on Flat, including 1¼m winner Torina (by Golan): dam unraced half-sister to fairly useful hurdler/useful chaser (stayed 2½m) Dundrum: in front when unseated 2 out in Irish point: third in mares bumper at Ffos Las (4¼ lengths behind Just A Thought) in November: 20/1, also third in mares novice at Exeter (5¾ lengths behind Tagrita) on chasing debut: should improve. *Anthony Honeyball* **c108 p b93**

TACTICAL MANOEUVRE (IRE) 6 b.g. Marienbard (IRE) – Pride O'Fleet (IRE) (Bob's Return (IRE)) [2016/17 h86: c20.9spu c19.2dF h19v h23.1s h19g³ c21.7gpu h23.1g* h21.6gpu Apr 21] maiden pointer: modest handicap hurdler: won at Exeter in April: failed to complete on all 3 starts over fences: stays 23f: acts on heavy going: in tongue tie last 4 starts. *Alexandra Dunn* **c– h92**

TAGINE 6 b.m. Deltic (USA) – Panhandle (Riverwise (USA)) [2016/17 b15.3m May 10] fourth foal: dam winning pointer: tailed off in bumper. *Richard Mitchell* **b–**

TAGLIETELLE 8 b.g. Tagula (IRE) – Averami (Averti (IRE)) [2016/17 h155: c22.5g⁴ c20.5dF c18.2d⁸ c23g² h23.9g h20d⁶ c21.5dpu h24s³ h24s h21s⁶ h20.3g Mar 17] smallish, strong gelding: one-time smart hurdler, well below best in 2016/17: fairly useful form over fences: stays 3m: acts on good to firm and heavy going: wears headgear: has worn tongue tie, including in 2016/17. *Gordon Elliott, Ireland* **c121 h123**

TAGRITA (IRE) 9 b.m. King's Theatre (IRE) – Double Dream (IRE) (Double Eclipse (IRE)) [2016/17 h130: c19.9d* c17.5v* c22.7g³ Jan 24] rangy mare: winning hurdler: useful form over fences: won mares novices at Huntingdon (by 5 lengths from The Organist) in November and Exeter in December: stays 2¾m: acts on heavy going: wears tongue tie: usually races close up. *Paul Nicholls* **c130 h–**

TAHIRA (GER) 7 ch.m. Doyen (IRE) – Tennessee Queen (GER) (Big Shuffle (USA)) [2016/17 h97: h17m* h20d² h16.3m² h16g* h16.4g⁶ h16.3g⁴ h15.7v* h16.8g Mar 16] rather leggy mare: fairly useful hurdler: won novices at Aintree early in season, Warwick in September and Haydock (listed event, by 2¼ lengths from Capitaine) in November: left Kevin Frost after third start: stays 2½m: acts on good to firm and heavy going: tried in cheekpieces: in tongue tie last 2 starts. *Richard Hobson* **h126**

TAIGAN (FR) 10 b.g. Panoramic – Lazary (FR) (Bobinski) [2016/17 h–: h21.2mF h20d⁴ h23g⁴ c19.4g³ c24g³ Aug 23] rather leggy gelding: fair handicap hurdler nowadays: fair form over fences: stays 23f: acts on soft and good to firm going: in tongue tie last 4 starts. *Giles Smyly* **c107 h107**

TAJ BADALANDABAD (IRE) 7 ch.g. Shantou (USA) – Last Chance Lady (IRE) (Mister Lord (USA)) [2016/17 h136: h22.8m May 7] smallish, sparely-made gelding: runner-up in Irish maiden point: useful hurdler, well held sole outing in 2016/17: stays 25f: acts on heavy going: in headgear last 5 starts. *David Pipe* **h–**

TAJSEER (USA) 6 b.g. Medaglia d'Oro (USA) – Lear's Princess (USA) (Lear Fan (USA)) [2016/17 h16g b16g⁴ h16g² h16.2s² h20.2s² h16g⁴ h16.8g² h19.5g* h16s h16.3m² h19.3m h15.7g⁵ c23.4gpu Nov 26] workmanlike gelding: fair bumper performer: fair hurdler: won maiden at Kilbeggan in September: pulled up in Worcester Novices' Chase at Newbury on chasing debut: left Gordon Elliott after tenth start: stayed 2½m: acted on soft and good to firm going: usually wore tongue tie: dead. *Phil York* **c– h102 b86**

TAKASHIBA (IRE) 8 b.m. Flemensfirth (USA) – Capilano (IRE) (Executive Perk) [2016/17 h19.4gpu Dec 29] €14,500 4-y-o: third foal: dam unraced half-sister to useful hurdler/smart chaser (winner up to 2½m) Watson Lake: pulled up sole point start: in tongue tie, pulled up in novice on hurdling debut. *Mark Wall* **h–**

TAKE A BOW 8 b.g. Norse Dancer (IRE) – Madame Illusion (FR) (Solid Illusion (USA)) [2016/17 c119, h–: c24dpu h21.6g⁶ c25.7m* c25gpu c24.2s⁵ Dec 2] workmanlike gelding: fair hurdler at best: fairly useful chaser: won handicap at Plumpton in September: stayed 3¼m: acted on good to firm and good to soft going: usually wore cheekpieces: wore tongue tie: front runner/raced prominently: dead. *Lawney Hill* **c117 h–**

TAKE EM OUT (IRE) 5 b.g. Amadeus Wolf – Toorah Laura La (USA) (Black Minnaloushe (USA)) [2016/17 b16.5g² b16.8g⁵ Apr 26] €5,000 3-y-o: third foal: half-brother to 2 winners on Flat, including 13f winner Rocky Two (by Rock of Gibraltar): dam (c98/h110), French 17f hurdle winner, also 10.5f winner on Flat: runner-up both starts in Irish points: fairly useful form when second at Taunton on first of 2 starts in bumpers. *Tim Vaughan* **b95**

TAKEN BY FORCE (IRE) 4 b.g. Millenary – Along Came Polly (IRE) (Old Vic) **b–**
[2016/17 b15.8g Apr 3] placed both starts in points: well beaten in bumper. *Tom Weston*

TAKE THE CASH (IRE) 8 b.g. Cloudings (IRE) – Taking My Time (IRE) (High Roller **c111 p**
(IRE)) [2016/17 c110p, h–: c20d³ Feb 20] runner-up in maiden point: winning hurdler: fair **h–**
form over fences: shaped well when third in handicap at Carlisle on sole outing in 2016/17:
stays 2½m: acts on soft going: may yet do better as a chaser. *Donald McCain*

TAKE THE MICK 10 b.g. Ishiguru (USA) – Michaelmas Daizy (Michelozzo (USA)) **c85**
[2016/17 c115§, h–: c20s⁴ Feb 20] close-coupled gelding: point winner: maiden hurdler: **h–**
fairly useful chaser, below form sole outing in 2016/17: stays 3¼m: acts on heavy going:
wears headgear nowadays: not straightforward. *Ian Cobb*

TAKE TO HEART 5 b.g. Sakhee (USA) – Romantic Dream (Bustino) [2016/17 b15.7g² **h– p**
b16.6g³ ab16g² h19.3m Apr 2] useful-looking gelding: half-brother to 3 winners, including **b95**
useful hurdlers/chasers Close Touch (2m-2½m winner) and Open Hearted (17f-3m
winner), both by Generous: dam (b91), bumper winner on only start, sister to fairly useful
hurdler/chaser up to 3m First Love: fairly useful form in bumpers: best effort when second
at Lingfield in February: 10/1, promise when eighth in maiden at Ascot (21¼ lengths
behind Tales Of The Tweed) on hurdling debut: will improve. *Nicky Henderson*

TAKINGRISKS (IRE) 8 b.g. Golden Tornado (IRE) – Downtown Rosie (IRE) (Good **c129**
Thyne (USA)) [2016/17 h123: c20g³ c25.2dF c15.5v² c22.3v* c24.3v⁴ c25gᵖᵘ Apr 8] **h–**
winning hurdler: fairly useful form over fences: won novice handicap at Kelso in February:
stays 25f: acts on heavy going. *Nicky Richards*

TALENT TO AMUSE (IRE) 4 b.f. Manduro (GER) – Burn Baby Burn (IRE) (King's **h114 p**
Theatre (IRE)) [2016/17 h16.3g* h16m* Apr 18] half-sister to fairly useful hurdler/useful
chaser Baby King (2m winner, by Ivan Denisovich): fairly useful on Flat, stays 13.5f:
fair form over hurdles: won juvenile maiden at Stratford in March and mares novice at
Kempton in April: wears tongue tie: open to further improvement. *Emma Lavelle*

TALES OF MILAN (IRE) 10 b.g. Milan – The Millers Tale (IRE) (Rashar (USA)) **c103 §**
[2016/17 c99, h97: c26.1dᵖᵘ c24g* c23dᵖᵘ h24dⁿᵘ Jul 10] tall gelding: fairly useful hurdler **h– §**
at best, shaped as if amiss final outing in 2016/17: fair handicap chaser nowadays: won
at Southwell in June: stays 29f: acts on good to firm and heavy going: wears headgear:
usually wears tongue tie: usually leads: unreliable. *Phil Middleton*

TALES OF THE TWEED (IRE) 5 b.g. Robin des Champs (FR) – Dancer Privado **h119 p**
(IRE) (Alderbrook) [2016/17 b16.2d³ b15.7d³ h21.6d⁶ h19.3m* Apr 2] €75,000 3-y-o: **b91**
good-topped gelding: has reportedly had breathing operation: first foal: dam, unraced, out
of useful 2m hurdle winner Titled Dancer: fair form in bumpers: fairly useful form when
won maiden at Ascot on second of 2 starts over hurdles: should stay 2¾m: open to further
improvement. *Nicky Henderson*

TALKIN THOMAS (IRE) 11 b.g. Talkin Man (CAN) – Keerou Lady (IRE) (Be My **c–**
Native (USA)) [2016/17 c72, h92: c24.1g Apr 29] maiden pointer: winning hurdler: **h–**
maiden chaser, well beaten sole outing in 2016/17: stays 25f: acts on soft going: has worn
cheekpieces, including last 2 starts. *S. Croft*

TALKISCHEAP (IRE) 5 b.g. Getaway (GER) – Carrigmoorna Oak (IRE) (Milan) **b92**
[2016/17 b18v b16s² b16.3v³ b16.3g³ Apr 1] €10,500 3-y-o: sturdy gelding: third foal:
dam, unraced, out of sister to high-class hurdler/useful chaser (stayed 25f) Cockney Lad:
unbeaten in 3 points: fair form in bumpers: left Sean Thomas Doyle after first start.
Alan King

TALK OF THE SOUTH (IRE) 8 b.g. Milan – Smalltowntalk (IRE) (Carroll House) **c115**
[2016/17 h114: h25d² c19.2dᵖᵘ c22.5vᵖᵘ c24s² c25.7v^F c25.7v² c30.7d⁶ c29.2v² c26gᵖᵘ **h109**
Apr 20] sturdy gelding: Irish point winner: winning hurdler: fairly useful maiden chaser:
second in handicap at Warwick in March: stays 29f: acts on heavy going: often races in
rear. *Paul Henderson*

TALLOW FAIR (IRE) 12 b.g. Busy Flight – Carrigeen Wood (IRE) (Buckskin (FR)) **c108**
[2016/17 c24.2g³ Apr 25] multiple point winner: 66/1, third in hunter at Hexham (3¼
lengths behind Ardea) on chasing debut. *Miss L. V. Horner*

TAMARILLO GROVE (IRE) 10 b.g. Cape Cross (IRE) – Tamarillo (Daylami (IRE)) **h94**
[2016/17 h103: h20.3v h17.2m⁴ h16.8m⁶ h23.6d³ h21.2gᵖᵘ h23.8d⁶ Nov 28] smallish
gelding: modest handicap hurdler nowadays: stays 3m, at least when emphasis isn't much
on stamina: acts on soft and good to firm going: tried in cheekpieces: wears tongue tie.
Sophie Leech

TAMBOUR 4 b.g. Notnowcato – Tamso (USA) (Seeking The Gold (USA)) [2016/17 **b64** ab16g Dec 10] half-brother to 2 winners on Flat, including useful 1¼m-1½m winner High Church (by High Chaparral): dam unraced: 10/3, seventh in junior bumper at Lingfield: modest form in Flat maidens, mostly for Keith Dalgleish. *Roger Charlton*

TAMBOUR MAJOR (FR) 10 b.g. Myrakalu (FR) – Joaillere (FR) (Silver Rainbow) **c69** [2016/17 c95, h–: c16m c15.9s⁵ c20.1sᵖᵘ c19.9g⁶ c16.3g³ Apr 8] dual point winner: maiden **h–** hurdler: poor maiden chaser: unproven beyond 17f: acts on good to soft going: wears headgear: usually wears tongue tie. *Alison Hamilton*

TAMBOW (IRE) 5 ch.g. Sandmason – Adeeba (IRE) (Alhaarth (IRE)) [2016/17 b17.3g⁴ **b81** b16.2g Apr 28] fifth foal: dam lightly raced on Flat: pulled up in point: modest form in bumpers: better effort when fourth in maiden at Downpatrick in March. *Ian Ferguson, Ireland*

TAMBURA 7 b.m. Tamure (IRE) – Singing Cottage (Greensmith) [2016/17 h118: h23.3v³ **h115** h25g⁸ h24.5g⁶ h23.8s² h24v⁶ h23.8s⁵ h26sᵖᵘ Mar 30] strong, sturdy mare: fairly useful handicap hurdler: won mares event at Plumpton in November: stays 3¼m: acts on heavy going: usually races close up. *G. C. Maundrell*

TAM O'SHANTER (IRE) 4 b.g. Poet's Voice – River Mountain (Reset (AUS)) **h64 p** [2016/17 h16g⁶ h16m⁵ h16s Nov 23] some encouragement in maiden on Flat: poor form over hurdles: remains capable of better. *Jennie Candlish*

TANACANDO (FR) 5 b.g. Ballingarry (IRE) – Tamaziya (IRE) (Law Society (USA)) **b–** [2016/17 b16g Apr 24] well beaten in bumper. *Tim Vaughan*

TANARPINO 6 ch.g. Tobougg (IRE) – Got Tune (FR) (Green Tune (USA)) [2016/17 **c123** h120, b79: c20.9s³ c20v⁴ c19.9s⁴ c22.7s⁵ Feb 1] workmanlike gelding: winning Irish **h–** pointer: fairly useful hurdler: similar form over fences: stays 21f: acts on heavy going. *Jennie Candlish*

TANGLEY 5 b.m. Black Sam Bellamy (IRE) – All Rise (GER) (Goofalik (USA)) [2016/17 **h94 p** b15.8s ab16g h15.3s* Mar 1] £40,000 4-y-o: third foal: closely related to French 17f hurdle **b–** winner King Dancer (by King's Theatre): dam, lightly raced on Flat in Germany, half-sister to very smart hurdler/winning chaser (2m-2¾m winner) Auetaler: won mares maiden point on debut: well held in bumpers: 12/1, won mares novice at Wincanton (by ½ length from Kristal Hart) on hurdling debut: capable of better. *Harry Fry*

TANGO DE JUILLEY (FR) 9 b.g. Lesotho (USA) – Lasalsa de Juilley (FR) (Le Balafre **c–** (FR)) [2016/17 c152, h–: c20.8gᵖᵘ Mar 16] rangy gelding: winning hurdler: smart chaser at **h–** best, pulled up sole outing in 2016/17: stays 21f: acts on heavy going. *Venetia Williams*

TANGOLAN (IRE) 9 ch.g. Golan (IRE) – Classic Note (IRE) (Classic Secret (USA)) **c117** [2016/17 c121, h110: h20.6g⁵ h23.1g⁵ h23.9d* c23.8s⁴ c20.5d c20.1g² c23.8d⁴ c19.9m³ **h107** Oct 2] fair handicap hurdler: won at Perth in June: fairly useful handicap chaser: second at same course in September: stays 3m: acts on good to firm and good to soft going: has worn headgear, including last 3 starts: usually wears tongue tie: often races prominently. *Fergal O'Brien*

TANGO UNCHAINED (IRE) 8 b.g. Golan (IRE) – Crimson Bow (GER) (Night Shift **h–** (USA)) [2016/17 h104, b–: h21.6gᵖᵘ Jul 25] good-topped gelding: fair form on only completed start over hurdles, in 2015/16. *Mark Gillard*

TANIT RIVER (IRE) 7 br.g. Indian River (FR) – Tanit Lady (IRE) (Presenting) [2016/17 **c131** h116: c19.2s² c20d² c24.5g* h21.9s⁵ c23.6s* c19.9d⁶ c24sᵖᵘ Mar 18] fairly useful hurdler **h–** at best: useful form over fences: won novice handicaps at Towcester (by 21 lengths from Wait A Second) in November and Chepstow (by 17 lengths from Join The Clan) in January: stays 3m: acts on heavy going: has worn hood: wears tongue tie. *Tim Vaughan*

TANNER HILL (IRE) 9 b.g. Milan – Carlingford Leader (IRE) (Supreme Leader) **c– x** [2016/17 c90x, h66: h25dᵖᵘ h23.3s Jun 15] maiden hurdler, no form in 2016/17: winning **h–** chaser: stays 3m: acts on heavy going: wears headgear: not a fluent jumper of fences. *James Evans*

TANTAMOUNT 8 b.g. Observatory (USA) – Cantanta (Top Ville) [2016/17 h111: **h122** h20.2m³ h20.2d³ h23.9s* h24.2gᵇᵈ h23.3d³ h24.7g² h20.9s³ h20.5g* Apr 22] good-bodied gelding: fairly useful handicap hurdler: won at Perth in July and conditionals/amateur event at Ayr in April: stays 25f, effective at shorter: acts on soft going: tried in hood: wears tongue tie: often races towards rear/travels strongly. *Lucinda Russell*

TAPER TANTRUM (IRE) 5 b.g. Azamour (IRE) – Maramba (USA) (Hussonet (USA)) **h127**
[2016/17 h16.8g* h16.3g* h16m³ h16d Nov 12] fairly useful on Flat, stays 10.5f: fairly
useful form over hurdles: won maiden at Newton Abbot in August and novice at Stratford
in September. *Michael Bell*

TAP NIGHT (USA) 10 ch.g. Pleasant Tap (USA) – Day Mate (USA) (Dayjur (USA)) **c92**
[2016/17 c–, h120§: h19.4g⁶ h19.7s² h19.4g c20.5v⁴ h21.3d⁶ Mar 31] close-coupled **h110 §**
gelding: fair handicap hurdler nowadays: one-time useful handicap chaser, not at best sole
outing over fences in 2016/17: stays 21f: acts on heavy going: wears headgear: unreliable.
Lucinda Russell

TAQUIN DU SEUIL (FR) 10 b.g. Voix du Nord (FR) – Sweet Laly (FR) (Marchand **c158**
de Sable (USA)) [2016/17 c159, h–: h19.5g⁶ c20.4s* c24d⁵ c21s⁴ h21.1g² h24.7g⁴ **h152**
Apr 8]

'Coming now on to the racecourse, it's Devon Loch for the Queen Mother,
with E.S.B. in second place and then Eagle Lodge in third and Gentle Moya coming
very hard indeed for fourth place. Royal Tan moving up to have a battle. But Devon
Loch is holding off E.S.B. Now they're coming with 150 yards to go and Devon
Loch is about a length and a half ahead—he's stretching away! The hats are coming
off! He's three lengths clear. It's Devon Loch three lengths clear with a hundred
yards to go. Devon Loch … oh, he's gone down!!! Devon Loch has gone down!
I said he's gone down and been passed by E.S.B. with Gentle Moya in second place
and Eagle Lodge now coming up into third place, although he's just pipped on the
post by Royal Tan … well, Dick Francis is just holding his hand to his head—he can't
believe it!' That was how legendary BBC announcer and all-purpose commentator
Raymond Glendenning described the closing stages of the 1956 Grand National,
which featured the never-to-be-forgotten bellyflop by Royal runner Devon Loch
when victory seemed assured for him and jockey Dick Francis. Although the general
mood of the nation was one of despair at this heart-breaking defeat for the Queen
Mother—who was there at Aintree with the Queen and Princess Margaret—that
sentiment wasn't shared by one household in Fulham, where the inhabitants were
huddled round the radio getting very excited at what they were hearing. Sir Martin
Broughton, only nine at the time, was having his very first taste of horse racing
because of a rare bet placed by his father, Edward Samuel Broughton, who had
spotted that one of the fancied runners shared his initials. 'As a nine-year-old it
was difficult to understand quite what had happened, but I frankly didn't care—my
father's horse had won!' reflected Broughton, who explained that this experience
(coupled with a Christmas present of the Totopoly board game a few years later) was
the reason he became hooked on the sport.

Martin Broughton went on to become chairman of the then British Horseracing
Board from 2004 to 2007, which is just one high profile job he has held during a long
and varied career. A non-smoker, he worked his way up to chief executive during
a lengthy spell at British American Tobacco, and he has also served as chairman
of British Airways (from 2004 to 2013) and as president of the CBI. Broughton's
business mantra has been to never overstay his welcome in a role, and such expert
timing was perhaps never best displayed than during his brief tenure as chairman of
Liverpool Football Club—Broughton (a lifelong Chelsea fan) successfully oversaw
the sale of the club to its current American owners, the handover taking place just
twenty-four hours before the team lost 2-0 to Everton in the Merseyside Derby!
Despite all the great and the good that he must have encountered during these
various roles, it was Dick Francis, the chief victim of that 1956 Grand National
incident, who won Broughton's nomination when a guest on Radio 4's long-running
Great Lives series in 2012. 'A modest unassuming man who got right to the top of
two completely different professions,' was his glowing verdict on Francis, who was
a champion jumps jockey (in 1953/54) before becoming an international best-selling
author of racing-themed crime thrillers, selling over sixty million books.

The first of Cheltenham's big pre-Christmas handicaps, the BetVictor Gold
Cup Handicap Chase in November, provided the sort of thrilling climax Francis
would have been proud of. The Broughton-owned Taquin du Seuil got up in the
dying strides to catch long-time leader Village Vic, the pair of them among the top

BetVictor Gold Cup Handicap Chase, Cheltenham—a third win in the race for local trainer Jonjo O'Neill as Taquin du Seuil (centre) pounces late to beat the front-running Village Vic; Aso (left) fades into fourth after late mistakes

weights in what was a good-quality renewal of one of the oldest and most prestigious handicaps in the National Hunt calendar, Mackeson (1960 to 1995) and Paddy Power (2003 to 2015) being responsible for the longest-running titles during its history. Fresh from an eye-catching reappearance over hurdles, Taquin du Seuil was sent off an 8/1-shot at Cheltenham, fourth choice of seventeen in a market headed by his stable-companion More of That (who flopped badly and was pulled up). Things actually didn't go to plan for much of the way, as Taquin du Seuil didn't jump so fluently as usual under a fairly patient ride towards the inner and was still only disputing twelfth as the spring-heeled Village Vic blazed the trail over four out. After starting to make headway at the next, Taquin du Seuil found plenty on the run-in to overhaul Village Vic by a neck, with a further two lengths back to third-placed Buywise (runner-up in 2015), himself three lengths ahead of the fourth Aso (who would have finished closer but for late mistakes). It was a third win in the race for trainer Jonjo O'Neill (following Exotic Dancer in 2006 and Johns Spirit in 2013) but a first for Aidan Coleman, a success which cemented the jockey's new link-up with O'Neill in 2016/17 following the sudden change of role by his previous boss John Ferguson (who could yet return to the training ranks after quitting his job as chief executive of Godolphin in June).

Taquin du Seuil falls just below the very top chasers, as was again illustrated when he finished fifth in the Lexus Chase at Leopardstown and fourth in the Ascot Chase on his next two starts—he has now failed to reach a place on all five of his outings at Grade 1 level over fences since his novice season. His performances prompted a change to his Cheltenham Festival target, with connections opting to exploit his lower BHA hurdles mark in the Coral Cup rather than have a third tilt at the Ryanair Chase. The plan nearly worked too, as ten-year-old Taquin du Seuil (the joint oldest runner in the field) finished a fine two lengths second of twenty-five to Irish raider Supasundae, again finding plenty late on after travelling strongly in touch (2004 Coral Cup winner Monkerhostin had come closest previously to completing the unusual double, having also finished third when favourite in that year's Paddy Power Gold Cup). Taquin du Seuil was kept to the smaller obstacles for his final outing too, reproducing his Cheltenham form when a highly creditable three and a half lengths fourth to Yanworth in the Liverpool Hurdle at Aintree, though that performance also underlined that Taquin du Seuil is likely to find things similarly tough at Grade 1 level in this sphere too (the Stayers' Hurdle is said to be his Cheltenham Festival target in 2018).

Taquin du Seuil (FR) (b.g. 2007)	Voix du Nord (FR) (b 2001)	Valanour (b 1992)	Lomond
			Vearia
		Dame Edith (b 1995)	Top Ville
			Girl of France
	Sweet Laly (FR) (br 1999)	Marchand de Sable (b or br 1990)	Theatrical
			Mercantile
		Sweety (b 1984)	Le Nain Jaune
			Sweet Flying

A good sort, Taquin du Seuil is the first foal out of winning French hurdler (over nineteen furlongs) Sweet Laly, who was also a multiple Flat winner at trips ranging from eleven furlongs to a mile and three quarters. There are two further winners to report since this pedigree was discussed in *Chasers & Hurdlers 2013/14*, namely Taquin du Seuil's half-sisters Antilope du Seuil (by Alberto Giacometti), a fairly useful staying hurdler when with Gordon Elliott, and the winning French two-mile hurdler Cibellay du Seuil (by Martaline). Sweet Laly has also since produced the 2015 colt Fighter du Seuil (by Poliglote), as yet unraced. Meanwhile, Taquin du Seuil's late sire Voix du Nord continues to make his presence felt on British and Irish soil, with Defi du Seuil (from his penultimate crop) his signature performer in 2016/17, joining the likes of Vroum Vroum Mag, Vaniteux and Vibrato Valtat among his most notable progeny. Taquin du Seuil is fully effective at two and a half miles to twenty-five furlongs and is similarly versatile with regards to ground, having won five times on heavy but also posting several of his best efforts on good. As was alluded to earlier, he could prove harder to place from now on, which may prompt connections to consider an alternative option such as the Grand National. Broughton was out of luck with his runner in the latest Grand National—The Young Master (in whom he owns a share) crashed out at first Becher's—but he was part-owner of 2011 runner-up Oscar Time (also fourth in 2013) and the lure of the Aintree showpiece can be very strong. After all, when Dick Francis was asked in 2006 whether he would swap his stellar career as an author (complete with its great wealth) for winning the 1956 Grand National, he replied: 'Given the choice, I'd take winning the National every time ...' *Jonjo O'Neill*

TARA BRIDGE 9 b.g. Kayf Tara – Annie Greenlaw (Petoski) [2016/17 h115: c16g³ c16s⁶ c16v³ c17.4vF c17s* Mar 13] well-made gelding: maiden hurdler: fair form over fences: won novice handicap at Stratford in March: stays 2¾m, effective at much shorter: best form on soft/heavy going. *Chris Gordon* **c113 h–**

TARA DEE (IRE) 8 b.m. Golan (IRE) – Liberwoman (IRE) (Among Men (USA)) [2016/17 h15.8g⁵ Jun 26] well beaten in bumper/novice hurdle over 2 years apart. *Andrew Wilson* **h–**

TARA FLOW 7 b.m. Kayf Tara – Poppet (Terimon) [2016/17 h125: c19.9d⁴ h19.8s⁵ Jan 7] fairly useful hurdler at best, well held sole outing over hurdles in 2016/17: 11/4, fourth in mares novice at Huntingdon (21½ lengths behind Tagrita) on chasing debut: stays 2½m: acts on heavy going: should do better over fences. *Venetia Williams* **c107 p h–**

TARA MAC 8 b.m. Kayf Tara – Macklette (IRE) (Buckskin (FR)) [2016/17 h97: c22.5d⁵ c20.9g² h19.9s c22.6mᵖᵘ c16.5g c17gᵖᵘ c15.7g⁴ c16s* c21.2gF c20.9d⁵ Mar 26] angular mare: modest hurdler at best: modest handicap chaser: won at Lingfield in February: stays 3m, effective at much shorter: acts on soft going. *Tim Vaughan* **c96 h–**

TARA MIST 8 gr.m. Kayf Tara – Island Mist (Jupiter Island) [2016/17 h108: h21.2d* h18.5d⁴ h20.3g Apr 20] good-topped mare: fairly useful handicap hurdler: won mares event at Ludlow in January: stays 21f: acts on heavy going. *Henry Daly* **h115**

TARA RIVER (FR) 8 b.g. Stormy River (FR) – Tarabela (FR) (Johann Quatz (FR)) [2016/17 h17.9s² h21.4s h18.4sᵖᵘ h17.9s⁴ h16v⁵ Feb 25] smart on Flat for F. Rossi, stays 12.5f: fairly useful hurdler: second in minor event at Auteuil very early in season: well beaten in handicap on sole outing in Britain: left J-M. Baudrelle after fourth start: stays 21f: acts on soft going: tried in blinkers. *Brian Barr* **h128**

TARA ROAD 9 b.g. Kayf Tara – Sparkling Jewel (Bijou d'Inde) [2016/17 c115, h–: c20g c25.8m⁴ Jul 1] tall gelding: winning hurdler: fairly useful handicap chaser at best, largely below form since 2014/15: stays 21f: acts on heavy going: in cheekpieces last 4 starts: wears tongue tie: untrustworthy. *Rebecca Curtis* **c97 §** **h–**

TARA'S RAINBOW 7 b.m. Kayf Tara – Nile Cristale (FR) (Northern Crystal) [2016/17 h78: h21.4mᵖᵘ h19.6s⁴ h23.3s⁵ Mar 18] well-made mare: poor maiden hurdler: left Kim Bailey after first start: should prove suited by 3m: best form on good going: wears tongue tie. *Trevor Wall* **h71**

TARA TAVEY (IRE) 12 gr.m. Kayf Tara – Slieve League (IRE) (Roselier (FR)) [2016/17 c–, h112: h23.1m May 3] point winner: fair handicap hurdler: maiden chaser: stays 3m: acts on good to firm and heavy going: tried in cheekpieces: wears tongue tie: often races prominently/lazily. *Kevin Bishop* **c–** **h100**

TARA THE TIGER 6 b.m. Kayf Tara – El Tigress (GER) (Tiger Hill (IRE)) [2016/17 h98p: h19.9vᵖᵘ h20.6vᵖᵘ h19.9g Apr 7] modest hurdler at best, no form in 2016/17: in headgear last 3 starts: often races towards rear. *Tim Easterby* **h–**

TARA TIME 6 b.m. Kayf Tara – Prophets Honor (FR) (Highest Honor (FR)) [2016/17 b88: b15.7g⁵ b16.7g⁵ Oct 15] modest form in bumpers only when second on debut in 2015/16: dead. *Philip Kirby* **b57**

TARA VIEW 6 b.m. Kayf Tara – Temptation (FR) (Lando (GER)) [2016/17 b82: b16.7g* h15.8g* h21.2d* h21.2s* h20.5g⁴ Mar 25] angular mare: fairly useful form in bumpers: won mares event at Bangor early in season: fairly useful form over hurdles: won mares maiden in November, mares novice in December and mares handicap in February, all at Ludlow: fourth in Mares 'National Hunt' Novices' Hurdle Finale at Newbury in March: will stay beyond 21f. *Alan King* **h127** **b97**

TARA WELL (IRE) 7 b.m. Kayf Tara – Miss Baden (IRE) (Supreme Leader) [2016/17 h94, b78: h19.5gᵖᵘ Apr 8] off mark in Irish points at seventh attempt: maiden hurdler, pulled up sole outing in 2016/17: usually races close up. *Robin Dickin* **h–**

TAROUM (IRE) 10 b.g. Refuse To Bend (IRE) – Taraza (FR) (Darshaan) [2016/17 c–, h101: c19.7g² h20g⁵ c16d⁴ c20gᵖᵘ h19.5d³ c20m⁴ h20s* h20v h19.5v⁵ c17v⁴ c19.4g⁶ h19.5m⁵ Apr 28] dipped-backed gelding: modest handicap hurdler: won selling event at Fakenham in November: modest maiden chaser: stays 2½m: acts on soft and good to firm going: wears headgear/tongue tie: often races prominently: temperamental. *John Flint* **c90 §** **h90 §**

TARRONA 8 b.g. Kayf Tara – Lisrona (IRE) (Presenting) [2016/17 h20g⁶ h16d h19.7s h19.7v² h21.7s² h21.2gᶠ Apr 3] £2,000 4-y-o: second foal: dam well held in bumpers/over hurdles: fairly useful form over hurdles: second in handicap at Hereford in March: left Roy Brotherton after second start: stays 2¾m: best form on soft/heavy going: often races towards rear. *Alan Phillips* **h115**

TASHEBA 12 ch.g. Dubai Destination (USA) – Tatanka (IRE) (Lear Fan (USA)) [2016/17 c24.2d⁵ Mar 31] well-made gelding: dual point winner: winning hurdler: fairly useful chaser at best, well beaten in hunter in March: stays 3¼m: acts on good to firm and heavy going: has worn headgear: wears tongue tie. *Miss A. Collier* **c–** **h–**

TASTE THE WINE (IRE) 11 gr.g. Verglas (IRE) – Azia (IRE) (Desert Story (IRE)) [2016/17 h92: h18.5g h18.7m⁴ h16.8g⁴ h18.5d³ h16.8m⁴ h21.4m³ Oct 23] close-coupled gelding: poor handicap hurdler nowadays: stays 2½m: acts on good to firm and good to soft going: has worn cheekpieces/tongue tie, including in 2016/17. *Bernard Llewellyn* **h82**

TASTY GINGER (IRE) 4 ch.g. Tamayuz – Secret Fashion (King's Best (USA)) [2016/17 h15.8g⁴ h16m² h15.8m² h16.7v* h16.6g⁶ Dec 10] fair on Flat, stays 2m: fair form over hurdles: won juvenile maiden at Bangor in November: will stay further than 2m: acts on good to firm and heavy going. *J. R. Jenkins* **h100**

TAURIAN 6 b.m. Central Park (IRE) – Emma-Lyne (Emarati (USA)) [2016/17 h15.6g* h16g⁵ h16.8d³ h16.5g h16.5m² Apr 20] half-sister to modest hurdler Shropshirelass (2m-21f winner) and modest chaser Gold Carrot (2m winner), both by Beat All: fair on Flat, stays 1½m: modest form over hurdles: won mares maiden in November: raced around 2m: acts on good to firm going: tried in cheekpieces. *Ian Williams* **h88**

TAURITO (CZE) 6 br.g. Tiger Cafe (JPN) – Tempecorta (POL) (Don Corleone) [2016/17 h13.9g* h18.9d h18.5g⁵ c16.9d* c17.9d* h16.8g Dec 9] leggy gelding: winner up to 11.5f on Flat: fair form over hurdles: won minor event at Wroclaw very early in season: well beaten in handicap at Cheltenham in December: winning chaser, including in minor events at Wroclaw in September and October: stays 19f: acts on good to soft going. *Radim Bodlak, Czech Republic* **c?** **h101**

TAWAN 6 b.g. Tiger Hill (IRE) – Lady Netbetsports (IRE) (In The Wings) [2016/17 h62: **h57**
h16.8d[6] h16.8g[4] h23.9g h19.9g h18.1m[5] h20.1g[pu] Oct 8] poor maiden hurdler: tried in
cheekpieces. *Brian Rothwell*

TAWEYLA (IRE) 6 b.m. Teofilo (IRE) – Qasirah (IRE) (Machiavellian (USA)) [2016/17 **h114**
h117: h16d h16.6s[2] h16d[pu] Mar 21] fair handicap hurdler: unproven beyond 17f: acts on
soft going: often races prominently. *Pam Sly*

TAWS 6 b.m. Hernando (FR) – Reaf (In The Wings) [2016/17 h17.7v[4] h16.8s[2] h24.4s[3] **h111**
h21.2s[2] h19.9g[2] Apr 7] useful on Flat, stays 21.5f: fair form over hurdles: should prove
suited by at least 2½m: acts on soft going: tried in cheekpieces. *David Pipe*

TAYARAT (IRE) 12 b.g. Noverre (USA) – Sincere (IRE) (Bahhare (USA)) [2016/17 c–, **c– §**
h–§: h16.7g[pu] c23.9d[pu] c15.7v[pu] Jun 20] rather leggy gelding: fairly useful hurdler/fair **h– §**
chaser at best, no form in 2016/17: has worn headgear: has worn tongue tie, including in
2016/17: temperamental. *Michael Chapman*

TAYLOR (IRE) 8 b.m. Presenting – Britway Lady (IRE) (Norwich) [2016/17 h107: **c–**
h23.3d[5] h20.1g[4] h22.1g h19.9g[ur] h23.3d[6] c23.6d[pu] c23.8g[6] Dec 14] fair handicap hurdler, **h88**
below best in 2016/17: no form over fences: stays 2½m: acts on firm going: tried in
cheekpieces. *Micky Hammond*

TAYZAR 6 b.g. Kayf Tara – Matilda Too (IRE) (Definite Article) [2016/17 b16.6g[5] Feb 22] **b72**
signs of ability when fifth in bumper at Doncaster. *Malcolm Jefferson*

TEACHMETOBOUGGIE 7 ch.g. Tobougg (IRE) – Teachmetotango (Mister Baileys) **c–**
[2016/17 h87, b–: c16.4s[pu] h19.9g[pu] h23d[4] h23g[pu] h22m[pu] Aug 24] workmanlike gelding: **h62**
poor maiden hurdler: pulled up in novice handicap on chasing debut: unproven beyond 2m:
acts on heavy going: tried in visor. *Alexandra Dunn*

TEA FOR TWO 8 b.g. Kayf Tara – One For Me (Tragic Role (USA)) [2016/17 **c166**
c146p, h136: c23.8m[5] c19.9d[2] c24g[4] c24.2s* c26.3g[ur] c25g* Apr 6] **h–**
     When there's a new book to promote, nothing quite does the trick like
opening up a controversy. So it was with outspoken John McEnroe's assertion
that twenty-three-times Grand Slam tennis champion Serena Williams, whom he
described as 'the best female player ever', would be ranked around 700 if she played
on the men's circuit. The pregnant superstar (whose Grand Slam haul is thirty-nine
if doubles' titles are included) hit back immediately, as did her supporters, but
McEnroe stuck to his guns, suggesting that arguments about relative merits could
be solved by men and women playing on a joint tour and competing against each
other. When this issue came to a head in the 'seventies, the top-ranked female player
Billie-Jean King beat fellow American Bobby Riggs, a former world number-one
but then aged fifty-five, in an exhibition in Houston that was broadcast around the
world (Riggs had beaten Margaret Court, who won three Grand Slam titles that year,
6-2 6-1 in a similar exhibition four months earlier). A similar match took place in
1992 when forty-year-old Jimmy Connors, one of the 'greats' of the men's game in
his prime, beat women's champion Martina Navratilova (then thirty-five) 7-5, 6-2
(Connors was allowed only one serve per point and Navratilova was allowed to hit
into half the doubles court). Neither match proved a great deal and it really doesn't
matter anyway where Serena Williams would rank among the men, as men's and
women's tennis are two different games and all four Grand Slams offer equal prize
money nowadays (Williams is said to have earned over £66m).
     Horse racing, in common with other equestrian sports, is different, with men
and women competing against each other. With prejudices hard to shift, it is still
unusual to see female riders at the big meetings on the big days, so much so that
the lack of representation means that females with a big-race ride will often attract
attention because of the novelty value. When conditional Lizzie Kelly became the
first female ever to ride in the King George VI Chase and then the first to ride in the
Cheltenham Gold Cup for thirty-three years, she was in demand for interviews and
photo-calls, was signed up as a columnist for one of the major national newspapers
and found herself working again for the BBC at the Cheltenham Festival. Kelly
became the first woman jockey in Britain to record a Grade 1 victory over jumps
when winning the 2015 Kauto Star Novices' Chase on Tea For Two, who carries the
colours of her mother, and it was the same horse who gave Kelly her rides in the
King George and the Gold Cup in the latest season. Tea For Two's Kauto Star win

Betway Bowl Chase, Aintree—Tea For Two and Lizzie Kelly get the better of a sustained duel with 2016 winner Cue Card (noseband)

didn't result in Kelly losing what she calls the 'trainer's daughter stigma' and around three quarters of her rides have continued to come on horses trained by her stepfather Nick Williams. 'It is harder for girls,' says Kelly who, nonetheless, admits she feels uneasy about being cast as a breaker of the mould for members of her sex.

The introduction of a female allowance in France in March (2 kilos or 4.5 lb) caused quite a stir at the time, though it applies only in races below the top level. Interestingly, it has led to Flat jockey Hayley Turner, the first woman to ride a hundred winners in a year in Britain, coming out of retirement to ride in France. 'I've already done it without a claim,' says Turner, 'but if they're going to give it to me, I'll take it.' Nick Williams frequently has runners in France, and Kelly rode her first winner at Auteuil with the new allowance when Diamant Bleu was successful over hurdles there in May. There are no plans to introduce a female allowance into British racing (Tony McCoy's suggestion to that effect had received a mixed response) but such a concession would undoubtedly help Lizzie Kelly, who figures respectably on Timeform's jockey ratings, and others to secure more outside rides; she had only eleven wins (all for Williams) in 2016/17 at a strike rate of ten per cent and finished second to Bridget Andrews (sixteen wins) among the female jump jockeys in Britain. Both Andrews and Kelly are conditionals who can still claim, as can the next three female jump jockeys in the 2016/17 end-of-season table, amateurs Emma Todd and Page Fuller and professional Lucy Gardner. By contrast Lucy Alexander has found life tough without a claim since winning the conditionals' title in 2012/13 and had just eight wins (at a strike rate of 7%) in an injury hit 2016/17.

Tea For Two lined up for the King George VI Chase with two runs under his belt in the current season, a creditable fifth under top weight in the Sodexo Gold Cup Handicap at Ascot in October (when shaping as if just in need of the run) and a second to Josses Hill in the Peterborough Chase at Huntingdon. He went on to finish fourth at 25/1 (the outsider of five) to Thistlecrack in the King George, travelling very well for a long way in such exalted company and seeming to excel himself, beaten less than three and a half lengths by the winner and just a short head and a head by previous winners Cue Card and Silviniaco Conti, in the process reversing Huntingdon form with fifth-placed Josses Hill. Tea For Two was seen out once between the King George and the Cheltenham Gold Cup, coasting home by seventeen lengths from the only other finisher, after being left clear by the fall of his main rival Alary three out, in a graduation chase at Exeter in February. Probably the less said about Tea For Two's much publicised appearance in the Gold Cup the better. Starting at 40/1, he got only as far as the second fence where he made a bad mistake and parted company with Lizzie Kelly who described her return to the weighing room as 'the longest walk of my entire life, I wanted to crawl back.'

The fact that Tea For Two's participation in the Cheltenham Gold Cup ended so early might have had a beneficial influence on his subsequent performance in the Betway Bowl at Aintree three weeks later. He seemed none the worse after his experience at Cheltenham and, if his rider needed her confidence boosting, she had only to reflect on the fact that all three races for amateurs at the Cheltenham Festival, the National Hunt Chase, the Kim Muir and the Foxhunter, had been won by female jockeys, Lisa O'Neill, Gina Andrews and Bryony Frost—all riding without a weight allowance. In an open-looking renewal of the Bowl, the previous year's winner Cue Card, whose Gold Cup had ended at the third last, started favourite, ahead of the Irish Gold Cup runner-up Empire of Dirt, and the Gold Cup seventh Bristol de Mai and Silviniaco Conti, who had bypassed the Cheltenham Festival to wait for Aintree (he had twice won the Bowl). Tea For Two was a 10/1-shot in this company, even though only inches had separated him from runner-up Cue Card and Silviniaco Conti in the King George. As in all Tea For Two's races except on his reappearance, Lizzie Kelly could not claim her 5-lb allowance at Aintree because of the value and class of the race but, in the end, she didn't need it as the patiently-ridden Tea For Two got the better of a stirring battle from the second last with Cue Card, holding on gamely by a neck after leading approaching the last. Accurate jumping also helped Tea For Two to record a career best, winning his first Grade 1 in open company, as the first two pulled fifteen lengths clear of third-placed Smad Place. Bristol de Mai, Silviniaco Conti (whose retirement was announced after the race) and the pulled up Empire of Dirt were all well below their best on the day.

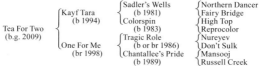

Tea For Two is a strong gelding who cost his present connections £24,000 at the Doncaster Spring Sales as an unbroken three-year-old. His sire Kayf Tara, a dual Gold Cup winner at Royal Ascot, has been a strong influence for stamina at stud and his dam One For Me was a fair hurdler who stayed two and three quarter miles. One For Me had had two winners by the time Tea For Two came up for sale, the modest miler Second To Nun (by Bishop of Cashel) and the useful handicap hurdler Katchmore (by Catcher In The Rye) who was successful at up to two and a half miles. She has since had a winning two-mile chaser in France, Act For Me (by Act One). This is not a particularly distinguished family on the dam's side, its most notable winner in recent generations being the game and consistent miler and mile and a quarter performer Jellaby, a half-brother to Two For Tea's fourth dam Silent Sail. Jellaby was a most unlucky loser in the 1978 Lockinge Stakes in which he lost his footing with the race in the bag and unseated his rider (there is a sequence of photographs of the incident in *Racehorses of 1978*). Tea For Two, who is usually held up, stays twenty-five furlongs and acts on good to firm and heavy going. He has been tried in a hood and wore ear plugs at Cheltenham to try to keep him calm in the preliminaries (his jockey described him as 'quite an angry chap who would get freaked out by the noise of the parade ring'). *Nick Williams*

TEA IN TRANSVAAL (IRE) 6 b.m. Teofilo (IRE) – Mpumalanga (Observatory (USA))   **h123**
[2016/17 h130: h16.2g⁴ h19.5g Oct 8] rather leggy mare: fairly useful handicap hurdler: unproven beyond 17f: acts on heavy going: front runner. *Evan Williams*

TEAK (IRE) 10 b.g. Barathea (IRE) – Szabo (IRE) (Anabaa (USA)) [2016/17 c–, h115: **c–** h21.2m^{pu} h25d^5 h23.9g^6 h24.2g^4 Nov 3] smallish gelding: fair handicap hurdler: lightly- **h103** raced chaser: stays 3¼m: acts on good to firm going: wears headgear: has worn tongue tie, including final start: often races towards rear. *Ian Williams*

TEALS LAD 8 b.g. Kayf Tara – Derry Ann (Derrylin) [2016/17 b74: h19.7g^{pu} Oct 12] **h–** little form in bumpers: pulled up in novice on hurdling debut. *Lee James*

TEARSOFCLEWBAY 6 b.m. Kayf Tara – Fenney Spring (Polish Precedent (USA)) **h112** [2016/17 h106: b16d h16g* h18.9s^5 h16v^2 h16s^3 h19d^6 Mar 30] useful-looking mare: **b83** bumper winner: fair form over hurdles: won mares novice at Worcester in October: left Philip Hobbs after fifth start: best effort at 2m: acts on heavy going: often travels strongly. *Gordon Elliott, Ireland*

TEA TIME FRED 8 b.g. Kayf Tara – Darjeeling (IRE) (Presenting) [2016/17 h106: **c–** h26.4m* h26.5m^2 c23m^F c25.7s^{pu} h23.9g Apr 9] lengthy gelding: fair handicap hurdler: **h110** won at Stratford early in season: failed to complete both starts over fences: stays 3¼m: acts on good to firm and heavy going. *Susan Gardner*

TEDDY TEE (IRE) 8 b.g. Mountain High (IRE) – Knocksouna Lady (IRE) (Oscar **c–** (IRE)) [2016/17 c125, h100: h25.8s^4 Apr 3] tall, lengthy gelding: fair handicap hurdler: **h100** fairly useful form when second in novice on only start over fences, in 2015/16: stays 3¼m: best form on soft/heavy going. *Nicky Richards*

TED'S LAD 7 b.g. Kayf Tara – Stravsea (Handsome Sailor) [2016/17 h104p, b79: h23d^6 **h57** Jun 29] fair form at best over hurdles: in tongue tie last 3 starts. *Alan King*

TED VEALE (IRE) 10 b.g. Revoque (IRE) – Rose Tanner (IRE) (Roselier (FR)) **c– x** [2016/17 c143x, h145: c20d^{ur} h16s^6 h16.1g Jul 28] medium-sized gelding: useful hurdler **h139 +** nowadays: winning chaser: unproven beyond 17f: acts on heavy going: has worn hood: prone to mistakes over fences. *A. J. Martin, Ireland*

TEE IT UP TOMMO (IRE) 8 gr.g. Clodovil (IRE) – Lamh Eile (IRE) (Lend A Hand) **h–** [2016/17 h–: h15.9g h15.9d Dec 12] fairly useful on Flat (stays 8.5f): no form over hurdles: tried in tongue tie. *Daniel Steele*

TEELIN STAR (IRE) 11 b.g. Beneficial – Glenarb Molly (IRE) (Phardante (FR)) **c–** [2016/17 h20.1d Jun 19] won both starts in points by a distance: bumper winner: well **h55** beaten in handicap on hurdling debut: maiden chaser for Patrick Hughes/Miss Elizabeth Doyle: stays 2½m: acts on heavy going: tried in tongue tie. *Nicky Richards*

TEENAGE DREAM (IRE) 9 b.g. Antonius Pius (USA) – Lucayan Star (IRE) (First **c89** Trump) [2016/17 c102, h–: c16.4d^5 c17.3m^F May 30] maiden hurdler: fairly useful **h–** handicap chaser, below form completed start in 2016/17: should stay 2½m: acts on good to firm and heavy going: has worn headgear, including last 2 starts: usually wears tongue tie. *Brian Ellison*

TEESCOMPONENTS LAD 4 b.g. Midnight Legend – Northern Native (IRE) (Be My **b90** Native (USA)) [2016/17 b14.6s^5 b15.7s^2 b16.2v^2 Mar 28] seventh foal: brother to bumper winner/fair 2½m hurdle winner Book At Bedtime and half-brother to bumper winners Delta Forty (by Alflora) and Dance of Time (by Presenting): dam (b99) bumper winner: fair form when second in conditional/amateur maiden at Catterick on second of 3 starts in bumpers. *Gillian Boanas*

TEESCOMPONENTS MAX 8 b.g. Grape Tree Road – Our Tees Component (IRE) **c81** (Saddlers' Hall (IRE)) [2016/17 h76: c16.4s^3 c15.7g^4 c15.6d^4 c16d Jun 30] maiden hurdler: **h–** poor form over fences: raced around 2m: acts on soft and good to firm going. *Keith Reveley*

TEETON POWER 6 ch.m. Black Sam Bellamy (IRE) – Teeton Priceless (Broadsword **b67** (USA)) [2016/17 b16.8g^3 Apr 26] third foal: dam winning pointer: 3/1, third in maiden bumper at Exeter (19 lengths behind Sword of Fate) in April: will be suited by 2½m+. *Tommy Morgan*

TEKAP (FR) 4 ch.g. Kapgarde (FR) – Textuelle (FR) (Roakarad) [2016/17 b16.3g Mar **b–** 25] tall gelding: 33/1, twelfth in Goffs UK Spring Sales Bumper at Newbury (24 lengths behind Bullionaire) in March. *Henry Daly*

TEKIBLUE DE L'ORME (FR) 4 b.g. Blue Bresil (FR) – Tekila de L'Orme (FR) **b–** (Ultimately Lucky (IRE)) [2016/17 b16.3g Mar 25] good-bodied gelding: tailed off in Goffs UK Spring Sales Bumper. *Paul Morgan*

TEKTHELOT (IRE) 11 b.g. Shantou (USA) – Bryna (IRE) (Ezzoud (IRE)) [2016/17 **h105** h107: h17.2m* May 28] fair handicap hurdler: won at Cartmel early in season: stays 3m: effective at much shorter: acts on soft and good to firm going: has worn headgear: often travels strongly. *Nicky Richards*

TELL THE TALE (IRE) 7 b.g. Craigsteel – Club Member (IRE) (Flemensfirth (USA))   **h103**
[2016/17 b16.2d³ b16.2s³ b16g² h17.7m² h19.7g⁴ h19.5d⁵ h15.3m² h15.7m⁴ Apr 13]   **b84**
€2,500 4-y-o: sturdy gelding: third foal: dam, unraced, out of half-sister to fairly useful
hurdler/useful chaser (stayed 3m) White Star Line: twice-raced pointer: modest form in
bumpers: fair form over hurdles: left Jason Cairns after second start: should prove suited
by further than 2½m: acts on good to soft going: usually races close up. *Neil Mulholland*

TELL US A TALE 7 b.g. Lucky Story (USA) – Alumisiyah (USA) (Danzig (USA))   **b–**
[2016/17 b15.7g b15.7d Dec 13] no form in 2 bumpers. *Sue Smith*

TELL US MORE (IRE) 8 b.g. Scorpion (IRE) – Zara's Victory (IRE) (Old Vic) [2016/17   **c146 x**
c142p, h–: c17d⁴ c16g* h16.8g Mar 17] sturdy gelding: useful hurdler at best, well held   **h– x**
final outing in 2016/17: smart form over fences: won Poplar Square Chase at Naas (by 4¼
lengths from The Game Changer) in November: stays 2½m: acts on heavy going: usually
travels strongly: often let down by jumping. *Gordon Elliott, Ireland*

TELMADELA (IRE) 7 b.g. Definite Article – Miss Pickering (IRE) (Accordion)   **h–**
[2016/17 b15.3s h19g Mar 30] off mark in points at fourth attempt: well beaten in bumper/   **b–**
maiden hurdle: in tongue tie first start. *Richenda Ford*

TEMPESTATEFLORESCO 9 b.g. Storming Home – Empress Dagmar (Selkirk   **c131**
(USA)) [2016/17 c25.8g* c24g⁶ c16.3g² c21.1g³ c24.4g⁶ c23.6g² c23.6s⁵ c23g³ c19.4m²
Apr 28] sixth foal: half-brother to winner on Flat in Italy by Robellino: dam unraced:
winning pointer: useful chaser: won novice at Newton Abbot in August: second in novice
handicaps at Chepstow in December (½ length behind Sykes) and April (length behind
Such A Legend): stays 3m: acts on good to firm going: wears tongue tie. *Colin Tizzard*

TEMPLATE (IRE) 6 ch.g. Iffraaj – Sagaing (Machiavellian (USA)) [2016/17 h117:   **h–**
h19.9spu Jun 15] sturdy gelding: fairly useful hurdler at best, pulled up sole outing in
2016/17: stays 19f: acts on soft going: in headgear last 2 starts: usually leads. *Harry Fry*

TEMPLEBRADEN (IRE) 10 b.g. Brian Boru – Baunfaun Run (IRE) (Roselier (FR))   **c102**
[2016/17 c25.3g⁴ Apr 27] multiple point winner: winning hurdler: fair maiden chaser: stays   **h–**
3m: acts on heavy going: tried in visor. *J. R. Bryan*

TEMPLE GRANDIN (IRE) 10 b.g. Presenting – Bolly (IRE) (Jolly Jake (NZ))   **c112 x**
[2016/17 c116x: c24s⁶ Jan 26] multiple winning pointer: fairly useful chaser: stays 3¼m:
acts on soft going: tried in tongue tie: often let down by jumping. *Philip Rowley*

TEMPLEHILLS (IRE) 6 b.g. Kalanisi (IRE) – Sissinghurst Storm (IRE) (Good Thyne   **c136 x**
(USA)) [2016/17 b–: h15.9g³ h19.9g* h21.2m* h20g c24d⁶ c21.2g* c22.7s⁶ c20v*   **h120**
c20vpu c20.4gpu Mar 14] tall gelding: fairly useful form over hurdles: won maiden at
Uttoxeter in September and novice at Ludlow in October: useful form over fences: won
handicaps at Fakenham in December and Warwick in February: stays 21f: acts on good to
firm and heavy going: wears hood: usually races close up: often let down by jumping. *Nigel
Twiston-Davies*

TEMPLE MAN 5 b.g. Sulamani (IRE) – Altogether Now (IRE) (Step Together (USA))   **b86**
[2016/17 b16.2d³ b16.7g² b15.7d⁴ Dec 13] half-brother to several winners, including fairly
useful hurdler/chaser Mac Aeda (2½m-25f winner, by Kayf Tara): dam, unraced, out of
half-sister to top-class staying chaser Marlborough: fair form in bumpers: best effort when
second at Market Rasen in October: will be suited by further than 17f. *Malcolm Jefferson*

TEMPLENABOE (IRE) 5 b.g. Milan – Pretty Impressive (IRE) (Presenting) [2016/17   **b68**
b16s⁶ Jan 2] Irish maiden point winner: 7/1, sixth in bumper at Ayr (20¼ lengths behind
Donna's Delight) in January. *Lucinda Russell*

TEMPLEROSS (IRE) 6 b.g. Presenting – Dame O'Neill (IRE) (Dr Massini (IRE))   **h129**
[2016/17 b102: h21.6d* h21.1g⁴ h23.9s* h24g h21d² h19.3s² Feb 18] well-made gelding:
fell in Irish maiden point: bumper winner: fairly useful form over hurdles: won novices at
Newton Abbot in September and Ffos Las in November: second in Lanzarote Hurdle
at Kempton in January: stays 3m: acts on soft going: usually races close up. *Nigel Twiston-
Davies*

TEMPLIER (IRE) 4 b.g. Mastercraftsman (IRE) – Tigertail (FR) (Priolo (USA))   **h118**
[2016/17 h15.9d⁴ h15.8s⁴ h16g h18.8g h15.9m⁵ Apr 16] well-made gelding: fair on Flat,
stays 1¾m: fairly useful form when won novice at Plumpton on hurdling debut in
December, went wrong way afterwards: best effort at 2m: acts on good to soft going: in
cheekpieces last 2 starts: usually leads. *Gary Moore*

TEMPO MAC (IRE) 7 b.g. Antonius Pius (USA) – Quecha (IRE) (Indian Ridge) [2016/17 h136: h16d* h17m h16g⁶ h16.1gᵖᵘ c16g* h19.5d³ c20.1s³ Sep 22] useful handicap hurdler: fairly useful form over fences: won maiden at Tramore in August: third in novice at Perth in September: unproven beyond 17f: acts on soft and good to firm going: has worn headgear. *Gordon Elliott, Ireland* — **c126 h136**

TEMPURAN 8 b.g. Unbridled's Song (USA) – Tenderly (IRE) (Danehill (USA)) [2016/17 c–, h–: h16.8m⁴ h16.7g⁴ h15.8m⁶ h19m⁶ Apr 27] sturdy gelding: fair handicap hurdler: won at Bangor in September: winning chaser: unproven beyond 17f: acts on good to firm going: has worn cheekpieces. *David Bridgwater* — **c– h106**

TENANT FARMER (IRE) 7 gr.g. Touch of Land (FR) – Miss McCormick (IRE) (Roselier (FR)) [2016/17 h21.6s³ h23.8v³ c21.2s³ c21.1v⁴ c20.2sᵖᵘ Mar 10] point winner: poor form over hurdles/in chases: stays 2¾m: raced only on soft/heavy going: in cheekpieces last 2 starts: often races towards rear. *Evan Williams* — **c69 h73**

TENGRI 5 b.g. Aqlaam – Jackie's Opera (FR) (Indian Ridge) [2016/17 b–: b16.3g* b16.8g Oct 7] fair form in bumpers: standout effort when winning at Stratford in September. *Alan King* — **b86**

TENNESSEE BIRD 9 b.g. Danbird (AUS) – Tennessee Star (Teenoso (USA)) [2016/17 h92§: h15.8gꟳ h19.9d⁶ h19.9g³ h19.9dᵛʳ h19.9vᵛʳ h23.1sᵖᵘ h19.3dꟳ h24.4d Jan 9] poor handicap hurdler: stays 23f: acts on soft going: tried in blinkers/tongue tie: temperamental. *Mike Sowersby* — **h81 §**

TENNIS CAP (FR) 10 b.g. Snow Cap (FR) – Jijie (FR) (Africanus (FR)) [2016/17 c144, h142: c20d⁴ c24.5d c21gᵖᵘ Jan 22] winning hurdler: useful handicap chaser: stays 2¾m, effective at shorter: acts on heavy going. *W. P. Mullins, Ireland* — **c132 h–**

TENOR NIVERNAIS (FR) 10 b.g. Shaanmer (IRE) – Hosanna II (FR) (Marasali) [2016/17 c149, h–: c23.8d³ c20.8s⁴ c20.8s³ c23.8s* c23.4v² c34.3d Apr 8] rangy, useful-looking gelding: winning hurdler: very smart handicap chaser: won listed event at Ascot (by 30 lengths from Go Conquer) in February: stays 3m: acts on heavy going: tried in cheekpieces: front runner/races prominently. *Venetia Williams* — **c156 h–**

TEN SIXTY (IRE) 7 br.g. Presenting – Senora Snoopy (IRE) (Un Desperado (FR)) [2016/17 h120: h20.5g* h24.4g³ c22.7g⁵ c22.7sᵖᵘ c22.4d* c25.3gꟳ Apr 20] well-made gelding: fairly useful handicap hurdler: won at Leicester in December: fairly useful form over fences: won handicap at Newbury in March: stays 3m: acts on soft going: in cheekpieces last 3 starts: usually races close up. *Philip Hobbs* — **c126 h124**

Keltbray Swinley Chase (Limited Handicap), Ascot—
Tenor Nivernais pulls clear again for a wide-margin win

TEN TREES 7 b.m. Millkom – Island Path (IRE) (Jupiter Island) [2016/17 h101, b88: h105 h25.4m⁴ h16.8d* h20.6s² Nov 17] bumper winner: fair handicap hurdler: won mares event at Sedgefield in November: stays 21f: acts on soft going. *Alan Swinbank*

TEO VIVO (FR) 10 gr.g. Great Pretender (IRE) – Ifranne (FR) (April Night (FR)) **c–** [2016/17 c–, h123: c19.3d h19.4g³ h16.2v* h16.4v* h16.2s³ Mar 25] useful handicap **h134** hurdler: won at Kelso in January and Newcastle (by 3 lengths from Nuts Well) in February: maiden chaser: stays 2½m: acts on heavy going: wears headgear: tried in tongue tie: races prominently, often travels strongly. *Pauline Robson*

TERRY THE FISH (IRE) 5 b.g. Milan – Have More (Haafhd) [2016/17 b16.7g⁶ h19.5d **h93** h21.3d h19.9v h25.6s³ Jan 31] €44,000 3-y-o: strong gelding: second foal: dam, lightly **b–** raced on Flat, half-sister to useful hurdler/very smart staying chaser Junior: green when sixth in bumper: modest form over hurdles: thorough stayer. *Jonjo O'Neill*

TESSIE B (IRE) 6 b.m. Kalanisi (IRE) – Christelle (Revoque (IRE)) [2016/17 **h–** b16.2m² b16g h16s h16g h16s Oct 31] third foal: half-sister to fairly useful hurdler/useful **b81** chaser Ivor's King (2m-2½m winner, by King's Theatre): dam maiden on Flat: modest form on first of 2 starts in bumpers: no form over hurdles. *Gavin Patrick Cromwell, Ireland*

TESTIFY (IRE) 6 b.g. Witness Box (USA) – Tanya Thyne (IRE) (Good Thyne (USA)) **h124** [2016/17 h17s* h19.5s² h23.1s* h22v² h24.7g Apr 7] strong gelding: seventh foal: brother to useful but ungenuine hurdler/chaser Wymott (2½m-25f winner) and half-brother to fair hurdler/fairly useful chaser Copsiano (2m-2½m winner, by Flemensfirth): dam unraced: runner-up in Irish maiden point: fairly useful form over hurdles: won novices at Carlisle in December and Bangor in February: should stay 3m: best form on soft/heavy going: front runner/races prominently. *Donald McCain*

TEST PILOT (IRE) 5 ch.g. Getaway (GER) – Chirouble (IRE) (High Roller (IRE)) **h91** [2016/17 b16.7g³ h15.8v⁶ h18.5s h19.3d⁶ Jan 25] €48,000 3-y-o: sixth foal: half-brother to **b86** fair hurdler/fairly useful chaser Red Rouble (21f-23f winner, by Moscow Society): dam, little form, half-sister to useful hurdlers Rouble (2m-2½m winner) and Kopeck (2m winner): better than result when well-beaten third in bumper: modest form over hurdles: in tongue tie last 3 starts. *Jonjo O'Neill*

TETRAITES STYLE (IRE) 5 b.g. Court Cave (IRE) – Kilmessan (IRE) (Flemensfirth **h66 p** (USA)) [2016/17 h16.4v⁴ Mar 18] €16,000 3-y-o: third foal: brother to 21f hurdle winner Courtinthemiddle: dam, unraced, closely related to fairly useful hurdler/useful chaser (winner up to 25f) Takagi and half-sister to fairly useful hurdler/chaser (stayed 31f) Victrix Gale: 16/1, shaped better than distance beaten suggests when fourth in novice hurdle at Newcastle (28½ lengths behind Reivers Lad) on debut: sure to improve. *Nicky Richards*

TEXAS FOREVER (IRE) 8 b.g. Heron Island (IRE) – Gravinis (FR) (Grape Tree Road) **c100** [2016/17 h79: c23.6gᶠ c21.7dᵖᵘ c16s² c15.7s² c15.9s³ h20.3s⁶ h19.6g² Apr 22] Irish **h97** maiden point winner: modest form over hurdles: fair form over fences: stays 2½m: acts on soft going: in headgear last 5 starts: usually races prominently. *Kim Bailey*

TEXAS JACK (IRE) 11 b.g. Curtain Time (IRE) – Sailors Run (IRE) (Roselier (FR)) **c132** [2016/17 c146d, h–: c25d c18gᵖᵘ c20d c19.5v c25v* c24vᵖᵘ c24sᵘʳ Mar 12] tall gelding: **h–** winning chaser: useful chaser nowadays: won minor event at Fairyhouse (by 6 lengths from Thunder And Roses) in February: stays 25f: acts on heavy going: has worn headgear, including last 4 starts. *Noel Meade, Ireland*

TG BOY 4 ch.g. Monsieur Bond (IRE) – Formidable Girl (USA) (Roman Ruler (USA)) **h–** [2016/17 b13.2g⁴ b13.7g⁵ b16.8v h18.5g Apr 11] first foal: dam maiden on Flat (stayed **b82** 8.6f): modest form in bumpers: best effort when fourth in junior event at Exeter in October: 50/1, seventh in novice seller at Exeter on hurdling debut. *George Baker*

THADY QUIL (IRE) 7 ch.g. Stowaway – Aunt Sue (IRE) (Shahanndeh) [2016/17 h108: **c83** h21.2m³ c25.8gᵖᵘ c23.6gᵖᵘ c24.5sᵖᵘ c19.9g³ Apr 28] runner-up both starts in Irish maiden **h103** points: fair maiden hurdler: poor form on completed start over fences: best effort at 21f: wears headgear: has worn tongue tie, including last 3 starts: front runner/races prominently. *Martin Keighley*

THAHAB IFRAJ (IRE) 4 ch.g. Frozen Power (IRE) – Penny Rouge (IRE) (Pennekamp **h62** (USA)) [2016/17 h15.3d⁵ Mar 26] fair maiden on Flat for Ismail Mohammed, stays 1½m: well beaten in novice on hurdling debut. *Alexandra Dunn*

THANKYOU VERY MUCH 7 b.m. Lucky Story (USA) – Maid of Perth (Mark of **c114** Esteem (IRE)) [2016/17 h96: h16.2s⁵ h16.7g³ h16.2g⁵ c15.7g³ c19.9g² c16.9d* c15.9f* **h94** c15.8g² c17.2m² Apr 9] modest handicap hurdler: fair form over fences: won handicaps at Musselburgh (novice event) in November and Leicester in December: stays 2½m: acts on firm and good to soft going: wears headgear/tongue tie: often travels strongly. *James Bethell*

THATCHERS GOLD (IRE) 9 b.g. Gold Well – Chesterfield Lady (IRE) (Taipan (IRE)) **c–** [2016/17 c70, h106: h19.9s⁶ h15.5d h19.2vᵖᵘ Feb 2] workmanlike gelding: won 2-finisher **h75** maiden point: fair handicap hurdler, below form in 2016/17: little form in chases: stays 2½m: acts on good to firm and heavy going: in cheekpieces on 3 of last 4 starts: front runner/races prominently. *Henry Oliver*

THAT MAN OF MINE (IRE) 5 ch.g. Thewayyouare (USA) – Do The Deal (IRE) **h80** (Halling (USA)) [2016/17 h83: h15.7vᶠ h19.9g h19.9g⁴ h19.9m⁴ h23.3gᵖᵘ h19.9g Aug 25] poor maiden hurdler: best effort at 2½m: acts on good to firm and good to soft going: often races in rear. *Mike Sowersby*

THAT'S A WRAP 6 b.g. Scorpion (IRE) – Full of Fruit (FR) (Apple Tree (FR)) [2016/17 **h133** h17.2sᵖᵘ h18.4d* h16d* h16d* h16g⁶ h20v² h19s Mar 12] seventh foal: half-brother to French hurdler/chaser La Cerisaie (17f/2¼m winner, by Old Vic): dam, lightly raced over hurdles/fences in France, half-sister to dam of Cheltenham Gold Cup winner Long Run: useful handicap hurdler: won at Galway in October, Navan in November and Leopardstown in December: second at Fairyhouse (3¼ lengths behind Presenting Percy) in February: stays 2½m: acts on heavy going: often travels strongly. *Thomas Mullins, Ireland*

THAT'S GONNA STING (IRE) 6 b.g. Scorpion (IRE) – Creme d'Arblay (IRE) **h95** (Singspiel (IRE)) [2016/17 h–, b79: h21.6d h19.9g⁴ h15.8g⁵ h15.8g⁵ h21.6g³ h21.6m⁴ h21.2g³ h23.8d* h23.9m⁵ h25.5s h26vᵖᵘ h23.1g Apr 11] modest handicap hurdler: won at Ludlow (conditional event) in November: stays 3m: acts on good to firm and good to soft going: wears tongue tie: usually races nearer last than first. *Jeremy Scott*

THATSHOWHEDIDIT (IRE) 8 ch.g. Kutub (IRE) – Last Hope (IRE) (Jurado (USA)) **c97** [2016/17 h109: h22.1mᵖᵘ c16.4m⁴ c20g⁶ c25d⁶ Aug 19] fair hurdler at best, pulled up on **h–** return in 2016/17: modest form on first of 3 starts over fences: stays 2¾m: acts on good to firm going: usually in headgear: wears tongue tie. *Mrs Gillian Callaghan, Ireland*

THAT'S THE DEAL (IRE) 13 b.g. Turtle Island (IRE) – Sister Swing (Arctic Lord) **c77 §** [2016/17 c77§, h–: c20.3g⁶ c24g² c24vᵖᵘ c23.9g c22.6g c16g⁴ c22.5d² c24d³ c16.5m³ **h–** c16.3s² c24dᵖᵘ c21.2s⁵ c20.2g⁵ c19.9d c20.3g⁶ c23.6g² Apr 28] well-made gelding: maiden hurdler: poor handicap chaser nowadays: stays 25f: acts on good to firm and heavy going: unreliable. *John Cornwall*

THATS YER MAN (IRE) 9 ch.g. Marignan (USA) – Glengarra Princess (Cardinal **c72** Flower) [2016/17 c64, h–: c20.9v² c20.9g⁴ c16.3g³ Jul 25] maiden hurdler: poor form over **h–** fences: stays 21f: acts on heavy going: tried in tongue tie. *Linda Blackford*

THAT WILL DO 7 ch.g. Desert King (IRE) – Dusty Shoes (Shareef Dancer (USA)) **h–** [2016/17 b–: h17.7g⁶ May 29] no form: dead. *Helen Nelmes*

THE ABSENT MARE 9 gr.m. Fair Mix (IRE) – Precious Lucy (FR) (Kadrou (FR)) **c–** [2016/17 c76§, h87§: h15.7v⁵ h15.8g c15.7g⁵ c15.7g Oct 3] modest hurdler at best: no **h–** form in 2016/17, including over fences (maiden chaser): tried in visor: usually wears tongue tie. *Sarah-Jayne Davies*

THE ARTFUL COBBLER 6 gr.g. Saint des Saints (FR) – Serhaaphim (Erhaab (USA)) **h97** [2016/17 h117, b–: h22.8v h26v h24v⁴ h23.1dᵘʳ h24s³ h24gᵖᵘ Apr 19] modest handicap hurdler: stays 3m: acts on heavy going: in cheekpieces last 4 starts: front runner/races prominently. *Henry Daly*

THEATRE ACT 6 ch.m. Act One – Theatre Belle (King's Theatre (IRE)) [2016/17 h100: **h103** h17m h25.4m h19.9g³ h20.9d⁶ h19.9g⁵ h20d* h17.1g* h20.6s⁵ h20.6s⁵ h21.2s* h17d³ h19.3d⁵ Apr 5] leggy, close-coupled mare: fair handicap hurdler: won at Carlisle in October and November (novice event), and Sedgefield in January: stays 21f: acts on soft going: often in cheekpieces: front runner/races prominently, often travels strongly. *Chris Grant*

THEATREBAR 9 b.g. King's Theatre (IRE) – Ardenbar (Ardross) [2016/17 h19.9d* **c–** h19.9v³ h21.2s* Feb 22] good-topped gelding: fairly useful handicap hurdler: won at **h124** Sedgefield in November and Ludlow in February: fairly useful form when second on both starts over fences in 2014/15 stays 3m: acts on heavy going: in tongue tie last 3 starts. *Dan Skelton*

Unicoin Group Handicap Chase, Cheltenham—the consistent pair Theatre Guide (left) and Perfect Candidate outstay Bally Longford (right) and fight out a close finish

THEATRE FLAME (IRE) 7 b.g. King's Theatre (IRE) – Bob's Flame (IRE) (Bob Back (USA)) [2016/17 h120, b–: c16.5g² c19.4g² c17.4g⁶ h16.4g h16d c16.4s⁴ c15.7vᶠ c15.9s³ c16.4s⁴ c16gᶠ Mar 18] good-bodied gelding: fairly useful hurdler at best, below form in 2016/17: fairly useful handicap chaser: won novice contest at Newbury in January: placed in similar events at Worcester in August, Stratford in September and Leicester in February: stays 19f: acts on soft going: tried in cheekpieces. *David Bridgwater* — **c126 h–**

THEATRE GOER 8 b.m. King's Theatre (IRE) – Clover Green (IRE) (Presenting) [2016/17 h113: h23.9d⁵ h23.3d² h23gᵖᵘ h25g² h24.4g⁴ h23.8s* h23.5s Feb 18] lengthy mare: point winner: fairly useful handicap hurdler: won mares event at Ludlow in January: stays 25f: acts on soft and good to firm going: tried in cheekpieces: front runner/races prominently. *Noel Williams* — **h118**

THEATRE GUIDE (IRE) 10 b.g. King's Theatre (IRE) – Erintante (IRE) (Denel (FR)) [2016/17 c151, h–: c19.4g² c26g c26g* c29.5s c24g³ c25g c28.8g³ Apr 29] tall gelding: winning hurdler: smart handicap chaser: won Grade 3 event at Cheltenham (by nose from Perfect Candidate) in December: third in BetBright Chase at Kempton (3 lengths behind Pilgrims Bay) in February and bet365 Gold Cup at Sandown (neck behind Henllan Harri) in April: stays 29f when conditions aren't testing: acts on soft going: usually in headgear: wears tongue tie. *Colin Tizzard* — **c153 h–**

THEATRE LEGEND 4 b.g. Midnight Legend – Theatre Belle (King's Theatre (IRE)) [2016/17 b17d Apr 5] well beaten in bumper. *Chris Grant* — **b–**

THEATRE MILL (IRE) 9 b.g. King's Theatre (IRE) – River Mill (IRE) (Supreme Leader) [2016/17 c122, h94: h16d⁵ c16d⁶ c17.4g⁴ c16g⁵ c20d² c19.2g⁴ c21g³ h26.5g c20.3m* c20.2m⁴ c20.2m² c16m² c20.3d⁵ h16.5m⁶ h16.8gᶠ Apr 26] workmanlike gelding: fairly useful handicap hurdler at best, below form in 2016/17: fairly useful handicap chaser: won at Southwell in September: second at Wincanton (conditional) in November: stays 21f: acts on soft and good to firm going: has worn hood: wears tongue tie: usually races nearer last than first. *Richenda Ford* — **c118 h96**

THEATRE ONE (IRE) 8 b.g. King's Theatre (IRE) – Jessica One (IRE) (Supreme Leader) [2016/17 h18.5dˢᵘ h20s h16.7g⁶ c20s⁵ c22.1gᵖᵘ Mar 26] point winner: poor form over hurdles: no form over fences: has worn hood: tried in tongue tie: usually leads, often races freely, tends to find little. *Mrs Caroline McCaldin, Ireland* — **c– h77**

THEATRE ROUGE (IRE) 5 b.m. King's Theatre (IRE) – Toulon Rouge (IRE) (Toulon) [2016/17 b91: b17g b15.7d⁶ h20.7s h21.4v⁴ h16.8s h21.6m* Apr 15] modest form in bumpers: fair form when won novice handicap at Newton Abbot on last of 4 starts over hurdles: wears hood: often races freely. *Philip Hobbs* — **h100 b78**

THEATRE ROYALE 5 ch.m. Sulamani (IRE) – Theatre Belle (King's Theatre (IRE)) [2016/17 ab16g h19gᵘʳ Feb 21] £600 4-y-o, resold £800 4-y-o: third foal: half-sister to fair hurdler Theatre Act (17f-21f winner, by Act One): dam (h129) 19f/2½m hurdle winner: well held in bumper: hampered and unseated third on hurdling debut: wears tongue tie. *Brian Barr* — **h– b–**

THEATRE STAGE (IRE) 5 b.g. Gamut (IRE) – Castletown Girl (Bob Back (USA)) [2016/17 h16.5s³ h16.8m² Apr 15] €26,000 3-y-o: third foal: half-brother to bumper winner Catching Shadows (by Catcher In The Rye): dam unraced half-sister to smart hurdler/high-class chaser (stayed 3m) Bellator: fair form over hurdles: better effort when second in novice at Newton Abbot in April: remains with potential. *Evan Williams* — **h101 p**

815

THEATRE TERRITORY (IRE) 7 b.m. King's Theatre (IRE) – Specifiedrisk (IRE) **h121**
(Turtle Island (IRE)) [2016/17 b97: h15.8s* h16.2g³ h20.5s^F h19.8s⁴ h20.5g⁶ h20.3g
Apr 20] useful-looking mare: Irish point winner: fairly useful form over hurdles: won
mares maiden at Uttoxeter in December: third in listed mares novice at Taunton (9½
lengths behind Coillte Lass) later in month: stays 21f: acts on soft going. *Nicky Henderson*

THEATRICAL STAR 11 b.g. King's Theatre (IRE) – Lucy Glitters (Ardross) [2016/17 **c130 x**
c135x, h–: h25.6g³ c23.6g⁴ c25g⁶ c26.2d h21.4s³ c24.2s² c24.2s⁵ c30.7d⁴ c23.8m Apr 2] **h117**
angular gelding: fairly useful handicap hurdler: useful handicap chaser: stays 31f: acts
on heavy going: has worn headgear/tongue tie, including in 2016/17: often let down by
jumping. *Colin Tizzard*

THEATRICAL STYLE (IRE) 8 b.g. Alhaarth (IRE) – Little Theatre (IRE) (Old Vic) **h81**
[2016/17 h108: h16.2d⁵ May 4] in frame both starts in Irish maiden points: fair handicap
hurdler, below form sole outing in 2016/17: should stay 2½m: best form on soft/heavy
going: in headgear last 4 starts: front runner/races prominently. *Donald McCain*

THE BACKUP PLAN (IRE) 8 ch.g. Presenting – Jay Lo (IRE) (Glacial Storm (USA)) **c97**
[2016/17 c106, h–: c20s^pu c25.5m³ c23g⁴ c20.3d² c21.1g³ c19.3g^pu Sep 27] maiden hurdler: **h–**
fair handicap chaser: stays 2½m: acts on good to firm and good to soft going: in blinkers
final start: usually leads. *Donald McCain*

THE BANASTOIR (IRE) 8 b.g. Presenting – Kimouna (FR) (Round Sovereign (FR)) **c95**
[2016/17 c–, h–: c15.9s⁴ c22.6g^bd Apr 23] little show in points: winning hurdler: **h–**
modest form on completed start in chases: stays 2½m: acts on soft and good to firm going.
Mrs Anthea Morshead

THE BARBURY QUEEN (IRE) 7 br.m. Milan – Royal Shares (IRE) (Royal Fountain) **h101**
[2016/17 h96, b79: h25d^ur h22m* May 15] fair form over hurdles: in cheekpieces, won
handicap at Stratford early in season: should stay 3m+: acts on good to firm and heavy
going. *Alan King*

THEBARROWMAN (IRE) 7 b.g. Mahler – Pixie Dust (IRE) (Desert King (IRE)) **h134**
[2016/17 h24d^pu h20v h22d⁵ h24d Apr 27] third foal: half-brother to fairly useful hurdler/
useful chaser Warrantor (2m-23f winner, by Turtle Island), stays 33f: dam (h97), bumper
winner, placed up to 2½m over hurdles: point/bumper winner: useful form over hurdles:
fifth in handicap at Fairyhouse (5½ lengths behind Showem Silver) in April: stays 2¾m:
acts on heavy going: tried in cheekpieces/tongue tie: front runner/races prominently.
A. P. Keatley, Ireland

THE BAY BANDIT 10 b.g. Highest Honor (FR) – Pescara (IRE) (Common Grounds) **c84**
[2016/17 c109, h94: h16.8g c17.4g⁴ Aug 18] fair hurdler/chaser at best, below form in **h–**
2016/17: raced around 2m: acts on good to firm and good to soft going: wears cheekpieces:
usually races towards rear. *Neil Mulholland*

THE BAY OAK (IRE) 8 b.g. Vinnie Roe (IRE) – Tournant Vic (IRE) (Old Vic) [2016/17 **c137**
h19.9d² h19.9s* h23.6g² h25.3d* h23.1s³ c25.2v² c25.2s² c27.9d* Apr 16] fairly useful **h118**
form over hurdles: won novices at Sedgefield (conditional) in November and Catterick
in January: useful form over fences: won maiden at Ffos Las in April: stays 3½m: acted
on heavy going: in cheekpieces last 2 starts: wore tongue tie: often raced prominently/
travelled strongly: dead. *Dan Skelton*

THE BIG BITE (IRE) 4 b.g. Scorpion (IRE) – Thanks Noel (IRE) (Tel Quel (FR)) **b89**
[2016/17 ab16g⁴ Mar 6] £30,000 3-y-o: fourth foal: dam unraced half-sister to smart
hurdler/very smart chaser (stayed 3¼m) Cooldine and useful hurdler/chaser (stayed 25f)
Fists of Fury: 14/1, won bumper at Lingfield (by 3½ lengths from Polly's Pursuit) in
March. *Tom Lacey*

THE BIG DIPPER 8 b.g. Alflora (IRE) – Pougatcheva (FR) (Epervier Bleu) [2016/17 **c95**
h103: h25d⁴ c23.9g⁴ c19.9g³ May 30] fair handicap hurdler, better than result on return in **h90**
2016/17: modest form over fences: stays 25f: acts on good to soft going: has worn tongue
tie, including last 3 starts. *David Dennis*

THE BISHOP (IRE) 9 b.g. Winged Love (IRE) – Charlie's Mary (IRE) (Daar Alzamaan **c82**
(IRE)) [2016/17 c90, h96: c23.8m^pu c24.2v⁴ c21.5s^pu c24.3v^pu h21.4v* h23.3s² c24.2v⁴ **h94 §**
Mar 28] modest hurdler: won handicap at Ayr in March: modest handicap chaser, below
form in 2016/17: stays 3m: acts on heavy going: has worn cheekpieces: temperamental.
N. W. Alexander

THE BLACK ROBIN (IRE) 7 br.g. Robin des Pres (FR) – Dihaila (FR) (Valanour **c–**
(IRE)) [2016/17 c19.5d⁶ c17m c17m c20.5m h18.5g c16d^pu c15.9s Dec 11] placed in **h–**
points: little impact over fences/sole outing over hurdles: left Denis Hogan after fourth
start. *Neil Mulholland*

THE BLUE BOMBER 5 b.g. Stimulation (IRE) – Mar Blue (FR) (Marju (IRE)) **h105**
[2016/17 b96: b13.6d² h16.2g² h16g² h15.8d h15.8s³ h17s⁴ h16.7mᶠ h15.8g⁶ Apr 17] **b87**
lengthy gelding: fair form in bumpers: fair maiden hurdler: raced around 2m: acts on soft
going: front runner/races prominently. *Mick Channon*

THEBOSS ON THEHILL (IRE) 9 ch.g. Bach (IRE) – Consproblem (IRE) (Mazaad) **h68**
[2016/17 h19.5gᵖᵘ h24.2s h20g⁵ h21.6m⁶ h25m h19.8dᵖᵘ Nov 17] modest maiden hurdler
for G. T. Lynch at best, below that level in 2016/17 after long absence: left Michael Winters
after first start, trained by Ross O'Sullivan second start only: tried in headgear. *Brian Barr*

THE BOTTOM BAR (IRE) 5 br.g. Stowaway – Serenade Leader (IRE) (Supreme **b–**
Leader) [2016/17 b13.7m⁶ Oct 15] 15/2, green when sixth in maiden bumper at Towcester.
Paul Webber

THE CALLER 6 b.g. Yeats (IRE) – Wyldello (Supreme Leader) [2016/17 b16.8g³ b16g* **h115**
h15.8d³ h16.3d h15.9v⁵ h15.9v* h19.5s³ h21.4f³ Apr 23] compact gelding: third foal: **b101**
closely related to fairly useful hurdler/useful chaser Cogry (19f-3¼m winner, by King's
Theatre), stays 33f: dam (h122), bumper and 2m/17f hurdle winner, sister to high-class
hurdler up to 25f Marello: fairly useful form in bumpers: won conditionals/amateur event
at Fakenham in October: fairly useful form over hurdles: won maiden at Plumpton in
January: third in handicap at Chepstow in March: stays 19f: best form on soft/heavy going:
often races lazily. *Warren Greatrex*

THECHAMPAGNESONICE 4 b.f. Compton Place – Extremely Rare (IRE) (Mark of **b–**
Esteem (IRE)) [2016/17 b13.2g ab16g Jan 31] fifth foal: sister to 5f winner Miss Complex
and half-sister to 2 winners on Flat, including 8.6f-1¼m winner Heezararity (by Librettist):
dam 5f/6f winner: no form in 2 bumpers. *David Weston*

THE CHARACTER 6 b.g. Bushranger (IRE) – Operissimo (Singspiel (IRE)) **h110**
[2016/17 h16.7d⁴ h16.7g* h15.6g* h16.8d³ h15.7s h16.8g* Apr 7] fairly useful at best on
Flat for Tom Dascombe, stays 12.5f: fair form over hurdles: won novices at Bangor in
September and Musselburgh in November, and handicap at Sedgefield in April: raced
around 2m: acts on good to soft going. *Donald McCain*

THE CHEESE GANG 5 b.g. Bahri (USA) – Aahgowangowan (IRE) (Tagula (IRE)) **b–**
[2016/17 b16.2d Jun 11] tailed off in bumper. *Susan Corbett*

THE CHILD (IRE) 8 b.g. Vertical Speed (FR) – Chancy Hall (IRE) (Saddlers' Hall **c–**
(IRE)) [2016/17 h–: c20vᵖᵘ h20.5vᵖᵘ Jan 16] compact gelding: well beaten on completed **h–**
start in Irish points: no form over hurdles: pulled up in novice handicap on chasing debut:
tried in tongue tie. *Anna Newton-Smith*

THE CHUCKMEISTER (IRE) 8 b.g. Germany (USA) – Lady Florian (Roselier (FR)) **c102**
[2016/17 c–, h–: h26gᵖᵘ c20v⁴ c25.5d* c25.5vᵖᵘ c24v³ c25.6dᵖᵘ Feb 26] maiden hurdler: **h–**
fair handicap chaser: won novice event at Fontwell in December: stayed 25f: acted on soft
going: in tongue tie last 5 starts: dead. *Chris Gordon*

THE CLOCK LEARY (IRE) 9 b.g. Helissio (FR) – Kiwi Babe (Karinga Bay) [2016/17 **c109**
c113§, h–: c21d⁵ c19.2g² c24.2g² Apr 23] sturdy gelding: winning hurdler: fair handicap **h–**
chaser nowadays: left Venetia Williams after first start: may prove best at shorter than 3m:
acts on heavy going: has worn headgear: front runner/races prominently, has found little.
Donald McCain

THE CLONLISK BUG (IRE) 7 b.g. Scorpion (IRE) – Apollo Lady (Alflora (IRE)) **h57 §**
[2016/17 h100, b84: h25d h23.4gᵖᵘ h25g⁶ May 30] modest maiden hurdler, well below
form in 2016/17: stays 2½m: best form on good going: tried in headgear: often races
prominently: ungenuine. *Kevin Frost*

THE CLYDA ROVER (IRE) 13 ch.g. Moonax (IRE) – Pampered Molly (IRE) **c– §**
(Roselier (FR)) [2016/17 h23.1s c25.5pᵖᵘ c30.7pᵖᵘ c24.5sᶠ Mar 16] stocky gelding: maiden **h–**
hurdler: fair chaser at best, no form since 2012/13 (lightly raced): wears headgear:
temperamental. *Helen Nelmes*

THE COBBLER SWAYNE (IRE) 8 b.g. Milan – Turtle Lamp (IRE) (Turtle Island **c113**
(IRE)) [2016/17 c122, h–: c19.4s⁶ c20d⁴ c21.3d⁴ Mar 21] sturdy gelding: maiden hurdler: **h–**
fair handicap chaser: stays 2¾m: acts on heavy going. *Lucinda Russell*

THE COFFEE HUNTER (FR) 5 gr.g. Doctor Dino (FR) – Mamamia (FR) (Linamix **c105**
(FR)) [2016/17 h105: h19d⁴ c17g² c15.7d⁶ c20.3d³ c16m⁴ Apr 25] rather unfurnished **h86**
gelding: modest maiden hurdler: fair form over fences: may prove best at 2m: acts on soft
going: often wears tongue tie. *Nick Williams*

817

THE COMPELLER (IRE) 5 b.g. Lawman (FR) – Mark Too (IRE) (Mark of Esteem (IRE)) [2016/17 h106: h16.2d⁶ h22.1mᵖᵘ May 30] fair maiden hurdler, below form in 2016/17: unproven beyond 2m: acts on good to soft going. *Lucinda Russell* **h75**

THECONNARTIST (IRE) 6 ch.g. Whitmore's Conn (USA) – Honeybrook (IRE) (Alderbrook) [2016/17 h23gᵖᵘ Sep 23] placed once from 6 starts in points: in cheekpieces, pulled up in seller on hurdling debut. *Denis Quinn* **h–**

THE CONN (IRE) 7 b.g. Milan – Grandy Invader (IRE) (Presenting) [2016/17 h–: h22.7dᵖᵘ Oct 22] maiden hurdler, pulled up sole outing in 2016/17: tried in headgear. *Sheena Walton* **h–**

THE CRAFTY BUTCHER (IRE) 10 b.g. Vinnie Roe (IRE) – Ivy Queen (IRE) (Green Desert (USA)) [2016/17 c–, h121: c24g h22.6d³ c24.5d² h24sᶠ c20s³ c24.5dᵖᵘ Apr 29] lengthy gelding: useful handicap hurdler: third at Navan (3¼ lengths behind Jury Duty) in November: useful handicap chaser: second in Paddy Power Chase at Leopardstown (3½ lengths behind Noble Endeavor) in December: left Gary Moore after first start: stays 3m: acts on heavy going: tried in blinkers: has worn tongue tie. *W. P. Mullins, Ireland* **c137 h134**

THE CRAZY CRAB (IRE) 11 b.g. Heron Island (IRE) – Smiths Lady (IRE) (Anshan) [2016/17 c20d⁶ Jun 22] winning pointer: no form in 2 chases, in hood second occasion. *Daniel O'Brien* **c–**

THE DELRAY MUNKY 5 b.m. Overbury (IRE) – Delray Beach (FR) (Saint Preuil (FR)) [2016/17 b16.2v⁴ h18.1s² Apr 3] first foal: dam (c112/h107) 17f-4m hurdle/chase winner: fourth in bumper at Kelso (4¼ lengths behind Better Getalong) in February: 6/1, second in maiden there (2 lengths behind Midnite Grace) on hurdling debut: will be suited by 2½m+. *Iain Jardine* **h96 b74**

THE DE THAIX (FR) 10 b.g. Polish Summer – Etoile de Thaix (FR) (Lute Antique (FR)) [2016/17 h23g c23gᵖᵘ Jul 21] point winner: no form under Rules: in cheekpieces last 2 starts. *Steve Flook* **c– h–**

THEDFACTOR (IRE) 8 b.g. Kalanisi (IRE) – Insan Magic (IRE) (Insan (USA)) [2016/17 c24.2d³ c20g⁶ Apr 15] maiden Irish pointer: no form over fences. *Jane Walton* **c–**

THE DOORMAN (IRE) 8 b.g. King's Theatre (IRE) – Amber Light (IRE) (Anshan) [2016/17 c20gᶠ c17gᵖᵘ h17.1d⁶ h19.4g h20.5s² h25.3g³ h21.2s² h22.7d Apr 10] fair maiden hurdler: fair handicap chaser: left M. F. Morris after second start: barely stays 25f: acts on soft going: wears tongue tie: races towards rear, often travels strongly: sketchy jumper of fences. *Ben Haslam* **c113 x h108**

THE DRACONIAN (IRE) 6 b.g. Kalanisi (IRE) – Lucky Hand (IRE) (Shernazar) [2016/17 b–: b16.8m³ May 3] modest form when third in bumper at Exeter on sole start in 2016/17 (wore cheekpieces). *David Pipe* **b81**

THEDRINKYMEISTER (IRE) 8 b.g. Heron Island (IRE) – Keel Row (Relkino) [2016/17 c118, h–: c22.4vᵖᵘ c21.1sᵖᵘ c24.2d* c23.6s⁴ Mar 13] rangy gelding: winning hurdler: fairly useful handicap chaser: won at Wetherby in February: stays 3m: acts on heavy going: in headgear last 5 starts: temperamental. *Kim Bailey* **c118 § h–**

THE DRUIDS NEPHEW (IRE) 10 b.g. King's Theatre (IRE) – Gifted (Shareef Dancer (USA)) [2016/17 c153, h–: c23.8d c25g c28.8g Apr 29] smallish gelding: winning hurdler: very smart handicap chaser, not at best in 2016/17: stays 29f: acts on heavy going: wears headgear: often races towards rear. *Neil Mulholland* **c142 + h–**

THE DUTCHMAN (IRE) 7 b.g. King's Theatre (IRE) – Shivermetimber (IRE) (Arctic Lord) [2016/17 h138: c15.2d* c23.4s³ c19.4s² c24.2sᶠ c16.3s² c19.9g² h21.4g Apr 22] sturdy gelding: useful hurdler: useful form over fences: won novice at Wetherby in November: stays 23f: acts on heavy going: tried in cheekpieces: front runner/races prominently. *Sandy Thomson* **c142 h129 +**

THE EAGLEHASLANDED (IRE) 7 b.g. Milan – Vallee Doree (FR) (Neverneyev (USA)) [2016/17 h136: h22.8m h24g⁶ Dec 9] useful-looking gelding: winning pointer: useful handicap hurdler: stays 25f: acts on heavy going: wears headgear/tongue tie: usually travels strongly. *Paul Nicholls* **h135**

THE FERBANE MAN (IRE) 13 b.g. Dr Massini (IRE) – Hi Up There (IRE) (Homo Sapien) [2016/17 c–, h–: c27.2d* May 12] multiple point winner: winning hurdler: fair chaser: won hunter at Fontwell early in season: stays 27f: acts on good to firm and heavy going: wears headgear: prone to mistakes. *Miss P. New* **c107 x h–**

THE FINGER POST (IRE) 10 b.g. Zagreb (USA) – Mystic Madam (IRE) (Lafontaine (USA)) [2016/17 h–: c19.2gᵖᵘ Nov 9] fell both starts in points: winning hurdler for A. J. Martin in 2013/14: in hood/tongue tie, pulled up in novice on chasing debut, jumping poorly. *Helen Nelmes* **c– x h–**

THE FLAME (IRE) 4 b.g. Flemensfirth (USA) – Molly Round (IRE) (Old Vic) [2016/17 **b96** b16s² Mar 13] first foal: dam (c106/h107), 19f-3m hurdle/chase winner, half-sister to useful hurdler (stayed 2½m) Our Bob: won maiden point on debut: 7/2, second in bumper at Chepstow (1½ lengths behind Amateur) in March. *Jonjo O'Neill*

THE FLOATING BEAR 6 br.g. Presenting – Queen's Leader (Supreme Leader) **b–** [2016/17 b16s Jan 14] in tongue tie, tailed off in maiden bumper. *Fergal O'Brien*

THE FLYING DOC (IRE) 9 b.m. Dr Massini (IRE) – Meadstown Miss (IRE) **c100** (Flemensfirth (USA)) [2016/17 c25.3g² Apr 27] multiple point winner: maiden hurdler for **h–** James Joseph Mangan: 5/2, second in mares hunter at Cheltenham (7 lengths behind Popaway) on chasing debut: stays 25f: acts on soft and good to firm going: has worn headgear/tongue tie. *E. Walker*

THEFLYINGPORTRAIT (IRE) 8 gr.g. Portrait Gallery (IRE) – Skule Hill Lass (IRE) **c129** (Close Conflict (USA)) [2016/17 c98, h87: c17.3g* h19.9m² c16d* h15.8g* c17.4g⁴ c16g* **h102** c17.1d* c17.1m* Oct 2] fair handicap hurdler: won at Uttoxeter in July: fairly useful handicap chaser: won at Cartmel in June, Perth in June/September and Kelso in September/ October: best around 2m: acts on good to firm and heavy going: tried in cheekpieces: wears tongue tie: front runner, usually travels strongly. *Jennie Candlish*

THE FRESH PRINCE (IRE) 7 b.g. Robin des Pres (FR) – Hayley Cometh (IRE) **c122** (Supreme Leader) [2016/17 h118, b86: c17g⁶ c19.9s⁴ c20v* c20.2d³ c20d² c20.1g² Apr 28] **h–** rangy gelding: winning hurdler: fairly useful form over fences: won handicap at Uttoxeter in January: second in novice handicap at Perth in April: stays 2½m: best form on soft/heavy going: front runner/races prominently. *Oliver Sherwood*

THEFRIENDLYGREMLIN 9 b.g. Vinnie Roe (IRE) – Queens Fantasy (Grand Lodge **c–** (USA)) [2016/17 h73: h19.5dᵖᵘ h20s⁶ h19.9vᵖᵘ c20.3sᶠ h19.2s Mar 16] poor hurdler at **h– §** best, no form in 2016/17: behind when fell fourth on chasing debut: often wears headgear: usually races close up: unreliable. *Tracey Leeson*

THE GAME CHANGER (IRE) 8 b.g. Arcadio (GER) – Gilt Ridden (IRE) (Heron **c150** Island (IRE)) [2016/17 c157, h–: c16d² c20.5m² c20s³ c20d⁴ h16g³ c16g² c16d⁴ c17sᵖᵘ **h144** c16.3g c17sᵖᵘ c29dᵖᵘ c16dᵖᵘ Apr 25] tall gelding: useful hurdler: third in minor event at Punchestown (7¾ lengths behind Hidden Cyclone) in October: very smart chaser: second in Grade 3 event at Killarney (2¼ lengths behind Clarcam) early in season and Poplar Square Chase at Naas (4¼ lengths behind Tell Us More) in November: stays 2½m: acts on soft and good to firm going: has worn headgear: wears tongue tie. *Gordon Elliott, Ireland*

THE GAME IS A FOOT (IRE) 10 b.g. Oscar (IRE) – Cooksgrove Rosie (IRE) **h95** (Mandalus) [2016/17 h98§: h20.5d⁴ h25s⁴ h15.9s* h19.7d h21.6g Mar 31] tall gelding: maiden pointer: modest handicap hurdler: won at Plumpton (conditional) in February: stays 2½m: acts on heavy going: tried in blinkers: often races towards rear. *Zoe Davison*

THE GEEGEEZ GEEGEE (IRE) 8 b.g. Beneficial – Shanann Lady (IRE) (Anshan) **c102** [2016/17 h113: c24s⁴ c20g⁵ c21.1d² c20.3m⁴ c17.4v* c21.1s⁵ c19.4g² Apr 8] winning **h–** hurdler: fair handicap chaser: won at Fontwell in February: stays 3m, effective at much shorter: best form on soft/heavy going: has worn headgear, including in 2016/17: usually wears tongue tie. *Anthony Honeyball*

THE GERMANY ONE (IRE) 6 b.g. Germany (USA) – Varna Princess (FR) (Varese **b–** (FR)) [2016/17 b16d Oct 24] tailed off in bumper. *Lady Jane Gillespie*

THE GIPPER (IRE) 7 b.g. King's Theatre (IRE) – Merrill Gaye (IRE) (Roselier (FR)) **h126** [2016/17 h125, b80: h17.7s⁵ h23.6gᶠ h16.2s² h19.9v⁵ h16v* Feb 25] sturdy gelding: fairly useful handicap hurdler: won at Chepstow in February: should stay further than 2m: best form on soft/heavy going: front runner/races prominently. *Evan Williams*

THEGIRLFROMMILAN (IRE) 7 b.m. Milan – Legendsofthefall (IRE) (Arctic Lord) **h101** [2016/17 b18v³ h21s⁶ h21.9v³ h20.5s⁴ h23.1dᵖᵘ h23.6v⁴ h24.5m³ Apr 4] good-topped **b83** mare: fourth foal: dam (c95/h86), 2½m hurdle winner, half-sister to fairly useful/ungenuine hurdler/chaser (stayed 23f) Craven: dual point winner: third in mares maiden bumper at Tipperary (11½ lengths behind Miss Eyecatcher) on sole start for Declan Queally: fair form over hurdles: stays 3m: best form on soft/heavy going: tried in cheekpieces. *Rebecca Curtis*

THE GOLDEN HOUR (IRE) 7 b.m. Gold Well – Kirktonmoor Katie (IRE) (Rich **h70** Charlie) [2016/17 b75: h15.9s h19.5v⁴ h19.5v⁶ Mar 6] runner-up in Irish mares maiden point: poor form over hurdles: often races towards rear. *Zoe Davison*

THE GREAT RAYMONDO 5 b.g. Passing Glance – Fantasy Parkes (Fantastic Light **b–** (USA)) [2016/17 b15.3vᵖᵘ Feb 2] pulled up in bumper. *Kevin Bishop*

THE GREEDY BOY 4 b.g. Atlantic Sport (USA) – Indian Girl (Erhaab (USA)) [2016/17 **h—**
h16v^{pu} Feb 24] modest maiden on Flat, stays 9.5f: pulled up in juvenile on hurdling debut.
Steve Flook

THEGREENDALEROCKET (IRE) 8 b.g. Oscar (IRE) – Classy Society (IRE) **c113**
(Moscow Society (USA)) [2016/17 c—, h104: c25.1m^3 c21g^2 c22.6s^F c23.6g^3 c26.2d* **h—**
c25.1d^{pu} c24.2v^{pu} c20s c20s^{pu} c23.6g^2 Apr 8] maiden hurdler: fair handicap chaser: won
novice event at Chepstow in October: left Jimmy Frost after seventh start: stays 3¼m: acts
on soft going: tried in cheekpieces/tongue tie. *Richard Woollacott*

THE GREENVET (IRE) 7 b.g. Acrobat (IRE) – Glacial Air (IRE) (Glacial Storm **c—**
(USA)) [2016/17 c20.9s^{ur} h21.6s h16.5s^5 h15.3d h23.9g^5 Mar 20] €2,500 4-y-o: sixth foal: **h91**
dam unraced: winning pointer: modest form on last of 4 starts over hurdles: unseated rider
ninth in novice at Hereford on chasing debut, struggling at time: stays 3m: in cheekpieces
last 3 starts. *Laura Young*

THE GREY TAYLOR (IRE) 8 gr.g. Royal Anthem (USA) – Penny Tan (IRE) (Roselier **c—**
(FR)) [2016/17 c135, h—: h16.8g^6 c19.4m c16.4s^5 h16.5g^{pu} c20.5d^6 Apr 21] tall, close- **h—**
coupled gelding: useful hurdler/chaser at best, no form in 2016/17: tried in tongue tie:
usually races close up. *Brian Ellison*

THE GRINDER (IRE) 5 b.g. Arcadio (GER) – Bincas Beauty (IRE) (Kayf Tara) **h106**
[2016/17 b17d h18.6s^{pu} h16.6g^2 h16.6g^3 h16d^6 h20.7g^3 Apr 17] €15,000 3-y-o, £6,500 **b—**
4-y-o: first foal: dam (h83), bumper winner, half-sister to fairly useful chaser (stayed 3¼m)
Definite Dawn: in frame completed start in Irish maiden points: last in bumper: fair form
over hurdles: stays 21f: best form on good going. *Nick Kent*

THE GROOVE 4 b.g. Azamour (IRE) – Dance East (Shamardal (USA)) [2016/17 **h76**
b13.2g^5 h19g h15.7d h18.7d^{pu} h16g^4 Apr 17] fifth in junior bumper at Exeter on sole outing **b—**
for David Loder: poor form over hurdles. *Fergal O'Brien*

THE GUNNER BRADY (IRE) 8 b.g. Heron Island (IRE) – Cooling Off (IRE) (Brief **c62**
Truce (USA)) [2016/17 c22.6m May 20] multiple point winner: maiden hurdler: modest **h—**
maiden chaser for Giles Smyly in 2014/15, well below that level on sole start in 2016/17:
stays 21f: acts on soft going: has worn tongue tie. *Tracey L. Bailey*

THE HAPPY CHAPPY (IRE) 6 b.g. Flemensfirth (USA) – Native Design (IRE) (Be **h105**
My Native (USA)) [2016/17 h25.5s^3 h23.8s^3 h26v^{pu} h25g^5 Apr 28] €130,000 3-y-o:
seventh foal: half-brother to 3 winners, including bumper winner/fairly useful chaser
Clouded Thoughts (19f winner, by Definite Article) and bumper winner/fairly useful
hurdler Carrigmoorna Storm (19f winner, by Glacial Storm): dam (h97) bumper winner:
won both starts in points: fair form over hurdles: left Paul Nicholls after first start: wears
tongue tie. *Sarah Humphrey*

THE HARD SHOULDER (IRE) 4 gr.g. Cloudings (IRE) – Our Witness (IRE) (Witness **b—**
Box (USA)) [2016/17 b14.6s Dec 17] tailed off in junior bumper. *Chris Grant*

THE HERDS GARDEN 8 b.g. Multiplex – Eternal Legacy (IRE) (Monashee Mountain **c120**
(USA)) [2016/17 c20g^2 c20g^2 c17.4m^F c19.5g^4 c19d^3 c15.9d^2 c17.1s c19.1g^F c16.3s^{ur} **h—**
h17s^6 c17.2g^{pu} c19.4g^3 Apr 23] fairly useful hurdler at best, won maiden at Fairyhouse in
2014/15: fairly useful maiden chaser: second in novice handicap at Carlisle in October: left
Noel Meade after fifth start: stays 2½m: acts on soft and good to firm going: has worn
headgear, including in 2016/17: has worn tongue tie. *Donald McCain*

THE HIGHLANDER (FR) 8 b.g. Caballo Raptor (CAN) – Chance Bleue (FR) **c89**
(Epervier Bleu) [2016/17 c24.2d^3 c20.2s^{pu} Feb 22] multiple winning pointer: maiden **h—**
hurdler for T. Trapenard: modest form on completed start over fences: barely stays 3m: acts
on soft going: tried in cheekpieces. *Mrs C. A. Coward*

THE HIKING VIKING 4 b.g. Beat Hollow – Swaythe (USA) (Swain (IRE)) [2016/17 **b—**
b16g Feb 25] tailed off in bumper. *Paul Webber*

THE HOLLOW GINGE (IRE) 4 b.g. Oscar (IRE) – Some Gem (IRE) (Flemensfirth **b92**
(USA)) [2016/17 b16.2v^3 b16.3g^5 Mar 25] £16,000 3-y-o: sturdy gelding: first foal: dam
(h91), 2½m hurdle winner, half-sister to very smart hurdler/winning chaser (stayed 3m)
Oscar Dan Dan (by Oscar): fair form in bumpers. *Nigel Twiston-Davies*

THE HOLYMAN 9 ch.g. Footstepsinthesand – Sunset (IRE) (Polish Precedent **h—**
(USA)) [2016/17 h18.7g^{pu} Aug 11] fairly useful at best for Jo Crowley, stays 1¼m:
in tongue tie, pulled up in novice on hurdling debut. *Mark Shears*

THEHOODLUM 10 b.g. Fraam – Trilby (In The Wings) [2016/17 h—: h23.9m^{pu} h23.9d^{pu} **h—**
Jun 30] no form: in blinkers final start. *Jean McGregor*

THE HORSECHESNUT (IRE) 9 ch.g. Definite Article – Ballinahowliss (IRE) c–
(Supreme Leader) [2016/17 c20s^F c23.8v^{pu} c24.1d⁵ c24.3v^{pu} Jan 30] winning pointer/ h–
hurdler: no form over fences: left David M. O'Brien after first start: often in cheekpieces:
wears tongue tie. *Jennie Candlish*

THEHOSSBEHIND (IRE) 6 ch.g. Mahler – Bayloughbess (IRE) (Lancastrian) h98
[2016/17 b78: h19.5d h15.8d h16.8g h16s⁶ h15.8s³ h21.2g* Apr 3] rather unfurnished
gelding: modest form when won handicap at Ludlow on last of 6 starts over hurdles: best
effort at 21f. *Ian Williams*

THE ICE FACTOR 9 b.g. Iceman – Kiruna (Northern Park (USA)) [2016/17 c–, h82: c74 §
h19.3m c20.1g⁶ h16.2d⁵ h17.2g c19.9g⁴ c17.1s^{pu} c19.9g⁵ Mar 1] maiden pointer: poor h55 §
handicap hurdler: poor maiden chaser: stays 2½m: acts on good to firm and good to soft
going: wears cheekpieces: has worn tongue tie: temperamental. *Alison Hamilton*

THE IMITATION GAME 4 b.f. Yeats (IRE) – Katmai (IRE) (Bob Back (USA)) b–
[2016/17 b16.8s b16.3s Mar 3] £15,000 3-y-o: third foal: dam (b99), bumper winner, half-
sister to triple Cheltenham Gold Cup winner Best Mate: no form in bumpers. *Susan Gardner*

THEINVAL (FR) 7 b.g. Smadoun (FR) – Kinevees (FR) (Hard Leaf (FR)) [2016/17 c128, c149
h141: c20d³ c20g* c21.4g³ c19.4g³ c20.4g⁴ c17d* c16.3g³ c15.8g² c20.5d² c20.5g² c20g h–
Apr 29] sturdy gelding: winning hurdler: smart chaser: won maiden at Uttoxeter (by
12 lengths from Jimmy The Jetplane) early in season and novice at Plumpton (by 2 lengths
from Theo's Charm) in December: second in Red Rum Handicap Chase at Aintree (length
behind Double W's), and listed handicap (3 lengths behind Two Taffs) and Future
Champions Novices' Chase (2 lengths behind Cloudy Dream) on successive days at Ayr,
all in April: stays 21f: acts on soft going: in cheekpieces last 5 starts: strong traveller.
Nicky Henderson

THE ISLANDER (IRE) 6 b.g. Fastnet Rock (AUS) – Blue Cloud (IRE) (Nashwan h–
(USA)) [2016/17 h16.2s^{pu} Jul 26] fairly useful at best on Flat (stays 7f), went wrong way:
in tongue tie, pulled up in novice on hurdling debut. *Patrick Griffin, Ireland*

THE ITALIAN YOB (IRE) 9 b.g. Milan – The Rebel Lady (IRE) (Mister Lord (USA)) c115 §
[2016/17 c124§, h–: c24.2s⁵ c21.1d c20.2m⁴ c20v⁴ c21.1s² c21.1g² c23m³ Apr 20] tall h–
gelding: winning hurdler: fairly useful handicap chaser: second at Fontwell in February:
stays 3m: acts on heavy going: wears blinkers: temperamental. *Nick Williams*

THE JAZZ SINGER 6 ch.g. Tobougg (IRE) – Ridgeway Jazz (Kalanisi (IRE)) [2016/17 h108
h103: h24m⁵ h20.2d⁴ h23.9s⁴ h20g⁴ h22s* h16g h23d* h23v⁵ h20.2g Apr 27]
maiden pointer: fair handicap hurdler: won at Navan in September and November: stays
23f: acts on heavy going: tried in tongue tie. *Colin A. McBratney, Ireland*

THE JOB IS RIGHT 9 gr.g. With Approval (CAN) – Common Request (USA) (Lear Fan c–
(USA)) [2016/17 c139, h137: c30d c24d^{pu} c24s^{pu} h24d c30.2d^{pu} Jan 28] sturdy gelding: h–
useful hurdler/chaser at best, no form in 2016/17: stays 4m: acts on good to firm and heavy
going: often in blinkers: usually races nearer last than first, often lazily. *M. Hourigan,
Ireland*

THE JUGOPOLIST (IRE) 10 b.g. Oscar (IRE) – Chance My Native (IRE) (Be My c88 §
Native (USA)) [2016/17 c–§, h–: c22.5g⁶ c16.3g³ c20m³ c24v³ c19.2g⁴ c22.6g^{ur} h–
c24g^{ur} c24g² c24g³ c20d⁵ c21.2g³ c19.9m³ c24.2s³ c23.6d* c25.6v⁴ c21.2s² c23.6s* c24v⁵
c23.6d⁶ c25.6d² c23.6g⁵ c23.6g⁶ Apr 17] lengthy, angular gelding: winning hurdler: modest
handicap chaser: won at Huntingdon in December (novice event) and January: stays 3¼m:
acts on heavy going: wears headgear: front runner/races prominently: temperamental.
John Cornwall

THE JUNIOR MAN (IRE) 6 b.g. Darsi (FR) – Pear Tart (IRE) (Rock Hopper) [2016/17 h–
b15.7v h22s⁴ h21.3s h21.3s Feb 4] third on completed start in Irish points: tailed off in b–
bumper: no form over hurdles. *John Norton*

THE KID 6 b.g. High Chaparral (IRE) – Shine Like A Star (Fantastic Light (USA)) h85
[2016/17 h15.7d^{pu} h16.5g h15.9s h19.7v h15.7v⁵ h15.9s³ h16v⁶ h21.9d⁵ Apr 26]
fair on Flat for John Quinn, stays 14.5f: modest maiden hurdler: left Tim Vaughan after
third start: best effort at 2m: acts on soft going: in cheekpieces last 5 starts: tried in tongue
tie. *Alexandra Dunn*

THE KINGS WRIT (IRE) 6 b.g. Brian Boru – Letterwoman (IRE) (Fourstars Allstar h100
(USA)) [2016/17 h23.1v^{pu} h19.7s h18.5s⁴ h18.5d Mar 21] £16,000 3-y-o: fourth foal: dam
unraced half-sister to useful chaser (stayed 4m) Out The Black: fair form on third of 4 starts
over hurdles: tried in tongue tie. *Richard Woollacott*

THE

THE KVILLEKEN 9 b.g. Fair Mix (IRE) – Wannaplantatree (Niniski (USA)) [2016/17   **c81 §**
c–, h95§: c16.5sᶠ h17.7g² h16d³ h18.7m² c16.5g⁴ h16.3g² c16g³ h19.6m² h16.3m³ h18.6g³   **h96 §**
h19ᵖ⁶ Nov 24] tall gelding: modest handicap hurdler: poor form over fences: stays 2¾m:
acts on good to firm and good to soft going: wears headgear: often races towards rear: not
straightforward (has found little). *Martin Keighley*

THE LAMPO GENIE 5 b.g. Champs Elysees – Samar Qand (Selkirk (USA)) [2016/17   **h99**
h101: h16.8g⁴ h15.7g³ h17.7g h23.1g³ h22g⁵ Aug 11] small gelding: modest maiden
hurdler: stays 23f: acts on good to soft going: in headgear last 3 starts. *Johnny Farrelly*

THE LAST BAR 7 b.m. Kayf Tara – Ardenbar (Ardross) [2016/17 h108: h16.8dᵖᵘ   **h–**
h20.6sᵖᵘ Dec 1] angular mare: fair maiden hurdler, pulled up both starts in 2016/17: stays
19f: acts on heavy going. *Dan Skelton*

THE LAST BRIDGE 10 b.g. Milan – Celtic Bridge (Celtic Cone) [2016/17 c80§, h73§:   **c82 §**
c24.1g³ c25.5g⁶ c24d³ h23.1sᵖᵘ c24.5v⁶ c29.2v* c23.8g³ c27.5g² Apr 23] modest hurdler at   **h– §**
best: poor handicap chaser nowadays: won at Warwick in March: stays 29f: acts on heavy
going: wears headgear/tongue tie: front runner/races prominently: unreliable, races lazily
more often than not. *Susan Johnson*

THE LAST BUT ONE (IRE) 5 b.g. Kutub (IRE) – Last Hope (IRE) (Jurado (USA))   **h99**
[2016/17 b16v² h19.8d⁶ h21.4s h18.5d h23.9g³ Apr 6] €24,000 3-y-o: fifth foal: brother to   **b89**
fair hurdler Thatshowhedidit (2¾m winner): dam (b82), lightly raced in bumpers, half-
sister to winning hurdler/fairly useful chaser (stayed 2½m) Sam Vaughan and fairly useful
2m hurdler Explain This: second in maiden bumper at Listowel (15 lengths behind Bargy
Lady) for Gordon Elliott: modest form over hurdles. *Paul Nicholls*

THE LAST DAY (IRE) 5 b.g. Oscar (IRE) – The Last Bank (IRE) (Phardante (FR))   **b92**
[2016/17 b15.8v b15.7s* b16.3g Mar 25] £26,000 3-y-o: seventh foal: half-brother to fairly
useful chaser On The Shannon (2½m-2¾m winner) and fair chaser I Am (17f-2½m
winner), both by Presenting: dam, ran once in bumper, sister to fair hurdler/fairly useful
chaser (2m-2½m winner) Dantes Bank and half-sister to useful hurdler (stayed 3m) Nancy
Myles: fair form in bumpers: won maiden at Southwell (dead-heated with Aye Aye Charlie)
in January. *Evan Williams*

THE LAST LEG (IRE) 8 b.g. Old Vic – Raphuca (IRE) (Be My Native (USA)) [2016/17   **h–**
h93: h19vᵖᵘ h24gᵖᵘ Apr 8] maiden hurdler, pulled up both starts in 2016/17: stays 23f: often
in visor. *Alison Hamilton*

THE LAST MELON 5 ch.g. Sir Percy – Step Fast (USA) (Giant's Causeway (USA))   **h–**
[2016/17 b–: h15.3m⁶ h15.8g⁴ h16.8g h16.8g⁵ Aug 20] poor form in bumpers: well beaten   **b74**
in novice on hurdling debut: in hood last 3 starts. *James Bennett*

THE LAST SAMURI (IRE) 9 ch.g. Flemensfirth (USA) – Howaboutthis (IRE) (Oscar   **c161**
(IRE)) [2016/17 c158, h–: c24g⁵ c25.5d³ c26s² c34.3d Apr 8] close-coupled gelding: **h–**
winning hurdler: high-class handicap chaser: third in Becher Chase at Aintree (length
behind Vieux Lion Rouge) in December: stays 4¼m: acts on good to firm and heavy going:
has worn hood: races prominently. *Kim Bailey*

THE LATE SHIFT 7 b.g. Midnight Legend – Ashnaya (FR) (Ashkalani (IRE)) [2016/17   **h76**
h79: h21.2dᵖᵘ h22.1mᵖᵘ h23.3g² Jul 22] poor maiden hurdler: stays 3m: acts on good to soft
going: in headgear last 4 starts: front runner/races prominently. *Barry Murtagh*

THELIGNY (FR) 6 gr.g. Martaline – Romilly (FR) (Subotica (FR)) [2016/17 h108p: **h128**
h20.9d* h19.6m* h19.5g* h16.3d² h20.5d* h22.8dᵖᵘ Feb 18] angular gelding: fairly useful
hurdler: won maiden at Kelso in September, novice at Huntingdon in October, and
handicaps at Lingfield in November and Newbury in December: stays 21f: acts on good to
firm and good to soft going: front runner/races prominently. *Tim Vaughan*

THE LINKSMAN (IRE) 5 b.g. Westerner – Lost Link (IRE) (Shernazar) [2016/17   **b97**
b66p: b16.8d⁶ b15.6gʳᵒ Jan 20] fairly useful form when won bumper at Sedgefield in
December: ran out next start. *Brian Ellison*

THE LION MAN (IRE) 7 b.g. Let The Lion Roar – Just Smart (IRE) (Anshan) [2016/17   **c–**
c–, h91: h21dᵖᵘ h19.9m⁴ h23d h15.8g h21mᵖᵘ h24g⁴ h24dᵖᵘ h23.9g⁶ h19.7d c15.7gᶠ Apr   **h74**
21] poor maiden hurdler: failed to complete both starts over fences: stays 3m: acts on soft
and good to firm going: wears headgear: front runner/races prominently. *Robin Dickin*

THELOBSTERCATCHER 13 gr.g. Silver Patriarch (IRE) – Everything's Rosy   **c101 §**
(Ardross) [2016/17 c29.4m⁵ c24sᵘʳ c29dᵖᵘ c22.5s⁵ c24vᵖᵘ c23v⁶ c25.5sᵘʳ Apr 7]   **h–**
workmanlike gelding: winning hurdler: fairly useful handicap chaser, below form in
2016/17: stays 29f: acts on good to firm and heavy going: wears headgear: often wears
tongue tie: unreliable. *P. A. Fahy, Ireland*

822

Paul & Clare Rooney's "The Last Samuri"

THE MAD WELL (IRE) 8 b.g. Milan – Silverfortprincess (IRE) (Mull of Kintyre (USA)) [2016/17 h104: h20v^F h20.5d* h20.5s* h21g h20.5v^3 h20.2g h20d^{pu} h16.2s h19.5s h21s h16.8s^3 Mar 7] pulled up sole start in points: fair handicap hurdler: won twice at Sligo early in season: left Denis Hogan after sixth start, Tim Vaughan after ninth: stays 21f: acts on heavy going: has worn cheekpieces/tongue tie, including in 2016/17: often races in rear. *Alexandra Dunn* **h112**

THEMANFROM MINELLA (IRE) 8 b.g. Shantou (USA) – Bobomy (IRE) (Bob Back (USA)) [2016/17 c117, h–: c23.5v^2 c29.6s^{pu} c25.1v^{ur} c24.2d^2 Mar 21] rangy gelding: winning hurdler: fairly useful handicap chaser: second at Lingfield in January and Exeter in March: stays 3m: acts on heavy going: wears cheekpieces/tongue tie: unreliable. *Ben Case* **c119 §** **h–**

THE MASTERS CHOICE (IRE) 5 b.g. High Chaparral (IRE) – Final Legacy (USA) (Boston Harbor (USA)) [2016/17 b–: b16.7g b16.7s^6 Nov 17] leggy gelding: no form in bumpers: tried in cheekpieces. *John Mackie* **b–**

THE MIGHTY ASH (IRE) 7 b.g. Arcadio (GER) – She's Got To Go (IRE) (Glacial Storm (USA)) [2016/17 b15.3s h16.8s^2 h19g^4 h17.7g^6 Apr 12] fifth foal: dam in frame in bumpers: maiden Irish pointer: well beaten in bumper: fair form over hurdles: best effort when second in maiden at Exeter in January. *Fiona Shaw* **h104** **b–**

THE MIGHTY DON (IRE) 5 ch.g. Shantou (USA) – Flying Answer (IRE) (Anshan) [2016/17 b85p: b17.7d* h19.5g^2 h17.7s^2 h20d* h19.8d Mar 11] rather unfurnished gelding: fairly useful form in bumpers: won at Plumpton in November: fairly useful form over hurdles: won novice at Fakenham in February: stays 2½m: tried in cheekpieces: often races prominently. *Nick Gifford* **h121** **b95**

THE MISSUS 6 b.m. Presenting – Violet Express (FR) (Cadoudal (FR)) [2016/17 h111, b84: h20m^2 May 13] leggy, angular mare: fair hurdler: enthusiastic sort, may prove best around 2m: acts on soft going: wears hood: often travels strongly. *Warren Greatrex* **h104**

stanjames.com International Hurdle, Cheltenham—The New One defeats old rival
My Tent Or Yours (right) to claim a third win in the race; 2015 winner Old Guard (centre)
is a remote third

THE MISTRESS (IRE) 6 b.m. Kalanisi (IRE) – Sonnerschien (IRE) (Be My Native (USA)) [2016/17 b15.8v³ b15.7v Feb 15] fifth foal: half-sister to fair hurdler Ivor's Queen (17f winner, by King's Theatre), stays 2½m: dam (h75), bumper winner, half-sister to useful hurdler/chaser (stayed 27f) Mumbles Head: modest form when third in mares maiden at Uttoxeter on first of 2 starts in bumpers: in tongue tie second start. *Dan Skelton* **b80**

THE MODEL COUNTY (IRE) 7 b.m. Robin des Champs (FR) – Ware It Vic (IRE) (Old Vic) [2016/17 h–, b84: h23.3v² h20.3d h24d² h23.3vᶠ h23.1s⁶ h26v* h23.6s h26v* Mar 22] sturdy mare: winning pointer: modest handicap hurdler: won at Warwick in February (conditionals/amateur event) and March: stays 3¼m: acts on heavy going: front runner/races prominently. *Alan Phillips* **h86**

THE MUMPER (IRE) 10 br.g. Craigsteel – Na Moilltear (IRE) (Miner's Lamp) [2016/17 c114, h–: c24s⁵ c27.6dᵖᵘ h23v c19.4g² Apr 9] fair hurdler, well held sole outing over hurdles in 2016/17: fair handicap chaser: stays 3m: acts on heavy going: in headgear last 2 starts: tried in tongue tie. *Neil King* **c114 h–**

THE MYTHOLOGIST (IRE) 9 ch.g. Motivator – Dilemma (Generous (IRE)) [2016/17 h77: h19.9mᵖᵘ c23g³ c23.9sᶠ c19.3d³ c25.1f* Apr 23] lengthy gelding: multiple point winner: maiden hurdler: modest form over fences: won handicap at Wincanton in April: stays 25f: acts on firm and soft going. *Tim Vaughan* **c94 h–**

THE NEW ONE (IRE) 9 b.g. King's Theatre (IRE) – Thuringe (FR) (Turgeon (USA)) [2016/17 h159x: h16.8s* h16g² h15.7s* h16.4g⁵ h20g³ h21.5g⁴ Apr 29] sturdy gelding: very smart hurdler: won International Hurdle at Cheltenham (by 3½ lengths from My Tent Or Yours) in December and Champion Hurdle Trial at Haydock (by length from Clyne) in January, both for third time: placed in Christmas Hurdle at Kempton (3¼ lengths behind Yanworth) in December and Aintree Hurdle (6½ lengths behind Buveur d'Air) in April: stays 21f: acts on heavy and good to firm going: usually leads: often let down by jumping. *Nigel Twiston-Davies* **h158 x**

THE NIPPER (IRE) 6 b.m. Scorpion (IRE) – Sharp Single (IRE) (Supreme Leader) [2016/17 b109§: b16dʳᵒ h19.7sᶠ h16v* h16.4v* h18.9v* h20g⁶ Apr 28] lengthy mare: useful bumper winner: fairly useful form over hurdles: won novices at Lingfield (mares event) in January, Newcastle (mares event) in February and Haydock in March: stays 19f: acts on heavy going: front runner/races prominently: has looked quirky (ran out once in bumper). *Warren Greatrex* **h127 b– §**

THEODORICO (IRE) 4 b.g. Teofilo (IRE) – Yes Oh Yes (USA) (Gone West (USA)) [2016/17 h16.6g h15.8g Apr 3] fairly useful on Flat, stays 1m: no form in 2 starts over hurdles. *David Loughnane* **h–**

THEO (IRE) 7 b.g. Westerner – Jemima Jay (IRE) (Supreme Leader) [2016/17 h94: **h102** h21.5g[3] h20v[2] h20g h20d h20g* h20d[4] h19.4g[4] h19.4g[4] h20s h19.5s[6] h22s[6] Mar 17] fair handicap hurdler: won at Fairyhouse in November: stays 21f: acts on heavy going: wears headgear: usually races towards rear. *Shane Donohoe, Ireland*

THE OMEN 11 b.g. Sir Harry Lewis (USA) – High Sturt (Petoski) [2016/17 c87, h–: **c75** c19.4s[4] c19.3v[2] c20.9v[4] Mar 19] maiden hurdler: poor handicap chaser nowadays: stays **h–** 21f: acts on heavy going: usually leads. *Tim Vaughan*

THE OPPIDAN (IRE) 7 b.g. Morozov (USA) – Pretty Flamingo (IRE) (Lycius (USA)) **h–** [2016/17 h24v[pu] Dec 11] runner-up in point: pulled up in novice on hurdling debut. *David Loder*

THE ORANGE ROGUE (IRE) 10 br.g. Alderbrook – Classic Enough (Classic Cliche **c113** (IRE)) [2016/17 c105, h–: c20.1s c24.3s[4] c20.5v* c21.6v* Mar 4] maiden hurdler: fair **h–** handicap chaser: won at Ayr in January and Kelso in March: stays 3m: raced only on soft/ heavy going: has worn headgear, including in 2016/17: in tongue tie last 2 starts: signs of temperament. *N. W. Alexander*

THE ORGANIST (IRE) 6 b.m. Alkaadhem – Go On Eileen (IRE) (Bob Back (USA)) **c125** [2016/17 h135p, b89: c19.9d[2] c20s[3] c22.7g[6] h19.9g h20.3g[4] Apr 20] compact mare: **h132** bumper winner: useful hurdler: fourth in listed mares handicap at Cheltenham in April: went wrong way over fences: stays 3m: acts on heavy going: often races in rear. *Oliver Sherwood*

THEO'S CHARM (IRE) 7 b.g. Presenting – Kates Charm (IRE) (Glacial Storm (USA)) **c133** [2016/17 h127: h22.8v[2] c17d[2] c19.2v[2] c20.8s h22.8d[3] h24g Mar 16] medium-sized **h133** gelding: useful handicap hurdler: third at Haydock (2 lengths behind Dadsintrouble) in February: useful form over fences: second in novice at Plumpton (2 lengths behind Theinval) in December and maiden at Exeter (5 lengths behind Robinsfirth) in January: should stay at least 3m: acts on heavy going: wears headgear. *Nick Gifford*

THE OTMOOR POET 4 b.g. Yeats (IRE) – Kristalette (IRE) (Leporello (IRE)) **h94** [2016/17 h16.7v[3] h16d[3] h15.7s[6] h16g[4] Apr 17] lengthy, rather sparely-made gelding: dam half-sister to top-class hurdler/very smart chaser (2m-19f winner) Overturn: fairly useful maiden on Flat, stays 1½m: modest form over hurdles: left Alan King after first start: should stay further than 2m. *Alex Hales*

THE OULD LAD (IRE) 9 b.g. Heron Island (IRE) – Badger Hammel (IRE) (Insan **c–** (USA)) [2016/17 c–, h–: c23.8s[3] c20g[pu] c25.5g[pu] Apr 24] tall, angular gelding: point **h–** winner: lightly-raced hurdler: fairly useful chaser at best, no form since 2014/15: in cheekpieces last 2 starts, tongue tied last 5: often races towards rear. *G. Slade-Jones*

stanjames.com Champion Hurdle Trial, Haydock—a third successive win in the race for The New One (left) as he concedes weight to the placed pair Clyne (centre) and L'Ami Serge

THE OUTLAW (IRE) 7 b.g. Presenting – Bonnie Parker (IRE) (Un Desperado (FR)) **h111 §**
[2016/17 h–: h19d² h16.3g³ h23g³ h20.3d* h20g⁵ h16.8g² h16.3g² h16.7g⁵ Sep 24] fair
hurdler: won novice seller at Southwell in July: left Paul Nicholls after fourth start: stays
23f: acts on good to soft going: has worn headgear, including final start: tried in tongue tie:
often travels strongly: irresolute. *Sophie Leech*

THE PAPARRAZI KID (IRE) 10 b.g. Milan – Banbury Cross (IRE) (Supreme Leader) **c142**
[2016/17 c143, h–: c21gᵘʳ c20s* c20vᵖᵘ c24g⁵ Apr 16] angular gelding: winning hurdler: **h–**
useful chaser: won veterans handicap at Wexford (by neck from Lisclogher Lad) in March:
stays 3m: acts on heavy going. *W. P. Mullins, Ireland*

THEPARTYSOVER 12 gr.g. Cloudings (IRE) – Just A Tipple (IRE) (Roselier (FR)) **c64**
[2016/17 c98, h103: h17.7g² h20d h21.6g⁴ h19.1s⁶ h17.7d h19.1sᵘʳ h20.5v⁴ h21.6v **h84**
h19.1v⁵ h19.8v⁶ h25g* c25.5g⁴ Apr 12] poor handicap hurdler nowadays: won at Plumpton
in March: maiden chaser: stays 25f: acts on heavy going: has worn headgear: wears tongue
tie: usually races towards rear. *Paul Henderson*

THE PERFECT CRIME (IRE) 8 b.g. Oscar (IRE) – Gimme Peace (IRE) (Aristocracy) **c–**
[2016/17 c–, h–: h22g May 21] rangy gelding: maiden hurdler/chaser, lightly raced and no **h–**
form since 2013/14: in headgear last 3 starts: tried in tongue tie. *Ian Williams*

THE PHANTOM (FR) 5 b.g. Apsis – Idee Recue (FR) (Sicyos (USA)) [2016/17 b89: **h101**
b16.7g h16.4d h16s h15.6g² Dec 14] runner-up on first of 2 starts in bumpers: fair form **b–**
when second in maiden at Musselburgh on last of 3 starts over hurdles: in hood last 3 starts.
Dianne Sayer

THE PHANTOM WINGER 8 gr.g. Double Trigger (IRE) – Arctic Chick (Henbit **h–**
(USA)) [2016/17 h22.1d⁵ h19.9g Sep 18] fair form in bumpers in 2014/15: no form over
hurdles: tried in headgear/tongue tie: temperament under suspicion. *Simon West*

THE PIERRE LARK (IRE) 7 b.g. Pierre – Kyle Lark (Miner's Lamp) [2016/17 h92, **h94**
b84: h20.6d h16.4v⁶ h15.8s⁵ Apr 1] winning Irish pointer: modest maiden hurdler:
should stay 2½m+: best form on soft/heavy going: in tongue tie last 3 starts. *Donald McCain*

THE POODLE FAKER 6 b.g. Pastoral Pursuits – Flirtatious (Generous (IRE)) [2016/17 **h97**
b87: h21dᵖᵘ h20.5v⁵ h20.5d⁴ h16m⁵ Apr 4] strong gelding: modest form over hurdles:
should stay 2½m: often races in rear. *Hughie Morrison*

THE POOLER (IRE) 5 b.g. Kalanisi (IRE) – Bakiya (USA) (Trempolino (USA)) **b–**
[2016/17 b16g⁶ Apr 8] placed in maiden point: well beaten in bumper. *Robert Walford*

THEPREMIERBROKER (IRE) 6 b.g. Sandmason – Neelia Nayr (IRE) (Boyne **h–**
Valley) [2016/17 h23d h21gᵖᵘ h15.8d⁶ h19.7g Oct 28] in frame both completed starts in
points: no form over hurdles: left Eric McNamara after second start. *Jennie Candlish*

THE QUEENS POSSE (IRE) 8 b.m. Cloudings (IRE) – Mum's Miracle (IRE) (Luso) **h–**
[2016/17 h19.3sᵖᵘ h16s Feb 14] €1,200 4-y-o, £900 7-y-o: sixth foal: closely related to
modest chaser Dushy Valley (3¼m winner, by Dushyantor) and half-sister to fair hurdler
Miracle House (2¾m winner, by Carroll House): dam unraced half-sister to useful chaser
(stayed 3m) Patricksnineteenth: maiden pointer: no form in 2 starts over hurdles. *Gemma
Anderson*

THE RAMBLIN KID 9 b.g. Westerner – Disallowed (IRE) (Distinctly North (USA)) **c–**
[2016/17 c116, h–: c20.1s⁵ c23.4vᵖᵘ Mar 18] lengthy, good-topped gelding: winning **h–**
hurdler: maiden chaser, no form in 2016/17: stays 23f: best form on soft/heavy going.
Micky Hammond

THEREDBALLOON 11 ch.g. Sulamani (IRE) – Sovana (FR) (Kadounor (FR)) [2016/17 **h98**
h97: h15.7g² Apr 21] modest handicap hurdler: stays 2½m: acts on soft going: has worn
hood. *Conrad Allen*

THEREYARSEE 8 b.g. Fair Mix (IRE) – Sea Laughter (IRE) (Presenting) [2016/17 **c–**
c25.1mᶠ Apr 5] multiple winning pointer: in tongue tie, fell ninth in hunter at Wincanton
on chasing debut. *Mrs S. Alner*

THE ROAD AHEAD 10 b.m. Grape Tree Road – Althrey Flame (IRE) (Torus) [2016/17 **h114**
h115: h20m h20d⁵ h19.6g h23.1g* Apr 22] fair handicap hurdler: won at Bangor in April:
stays 3m: acts on good to soft going: has worn headgear: often races towards rear.
Gary Hanmer

THE RODEO CLOWN (IRE) 12 b.g. Luso – Reuben Jane (IRE) (Toulon) [2016/17 **c–**
c22.6g⁶ Apr 23] multiple winning pointer: twice-raced hurdler: tailed off in hunter on **h–**
chasing debut. *G. E. Burton*

THE ROMFORD PELE (IRE) 10 b.g. Accordion – Back And Fore (IRE) (Bob Back   **c–** (USA)) [2016/17 c147, h143: h20d² h26.5g* h24.1g⁴ h24.2dᵖᵘ h24sᵖᵘ h21.1gᵖᵘ Mar 15] **h144** rather leggy gelding: useful hurdler: won handicap at Newton Abbot (by 2½ lengths from Young Dillon) in October: smart chaser (not seen over fences since unseating in 2016 Grand National): stays 3¼m: acts on good to firm and heavy going: wears headgear. *Rebecca Curtis*

THE SAINT JAMES (FR) 6 b.g. Saint des Saints (FR) – Aimela (FR) (Sagamix (FR))   **c137 x** [2016/17 c139x, h–: c16s² Apr 30] useful-looking gelding: winning hurdler: useful maiden   **h–** chaser: stayed 2½m: acted on heavy going: wore hood/tongue tie: often raced towards rear/ travelled strongly: tended to be let down by jumping over fences: dead. *Jonjo O'Neill*

THE SASKATOON 8 b.g. Desideratum – Skewsby Girl (Kayf Tara) [2016/17 h–:   **h–** h24.1g⁶ May 4] no form in novice hurdles. *Peter Maddison*

THE SCOURGE (IRE) 6 b.g. Whipper (USA) – House Rebel (IRE) (Spartacus (IRE))   **c–** [2016/17 c–, h101: c15.7g h16.3g Jul 28] fair hurdler at best, no form in 2016/17: twice-   **h–** raced chaser: unproven beyond 2m: acted on good to soft going: tried in headgear/tongue tie: dead. *Sarah Humphrey*

THE SNAPPY POET 8 ch.g. Byron – Runaway Star (Superlative) [2016/17 h20d*   **c78** h19.9g⁶ h21.6g² c20g⁵ c20gᵖᵘ h21.6g Oct 20] fair handicap hurdler: won at Worcester   **h107** (conditional) in June: poor form over fences: stays 2¾m: acts on good to soft going: wears headgear. *Jeremy Scott*

THE SOCIETY MAN (IRE) 10 ch.g. Moscow Society (USA) – Redruth (IRE) (Sri   **c95 §** Pekan (USA)) [2016/17 c101, h–: c21.4gᵖᵘ c20.3vᵖᵘ c16.5g⁴ c19.2d⁵ c21.2m c21.2g²   **h–** c19.2g⁴ c21.2g³ c23gᵖᵘ c15.9fᵘʳ c15.7gᵘʳ c17.2m⁵ c19.2d Apr 27] workmanlike gelding: winning hurdler: modest maiden chaser: stays 25f: acts on good to firm and heavy going: usually races nearer last than first: temperamental. *Michael Chapman*

THESPIS OF ICARIA (IRE) 11 b.g. Sadler's Wells (USA) – Hellenic (Darshaan)   **h–** [2016/17 h16g h23.1gᵖᵘ Oct 25] useful bumper winner: maiden hurdler, no form in 2016/17: stays 2½m: acts on good to firm going: tried in cheekpieces: in tongue tie last 5 starts. *Debra Hamer*

THE STORYTELLER (IRE) 6 ch.g. Shantou (USA) – Bally Bolshoi (IRE) (Bob Back   **h144 p** (USA)) [2016/17 b17.8g² b17.8d* b17.8d* b22.2gᶠ h22d² h19.7d* h22.7d* Jan 19] €67,000 3-y-o: **b99** third foal: brother to fair hurdler Boherna Lady (19f-23f winner) and half-brother to fairly useful hurdler/useful chaser Minella On Line (2½m-3¼m winner, by King's Theatre): dam (h105) 2m-19f hurdle winner: fairly useful form in bumpers: won at Downpatrick early in season: useful form over hurdles: won maiden at Down Royal in December and novice at Thurles (by 9 lengths from Battleford) in January: will stay 3m: acts on good to soft going: usually travels strongly: open to further improvement. *Gordon Elliott, Ireland*

THE SWEENEY (IRE) 5 b.g. Oscar (IRE) – Banningham Blaze (Averti (IRE)) [2016/17   **b95** b16v³ Dec 31] £62,000 3-y-o: fifth foal: closely related to fairly useful hurdler/chaser Knocklong (2m-25f winner, by Milan) and half-brother to 2 winners, including useful hurdler/chaser Presenting Arms (15f-19f winner, by Presenting): dam (h80), temperamental 19f hurdle winner, also 1½m-1¾m winner on Flat: 9/2, better than result when third in bumper at Warwick (4¾ lengths behind Marten) in December. *Emma Lavelle*

THE TAILGATER (IRE) 6 b.g. Oscar (IRE) – Zaffaran Express (IRE) (Zaffaran   **h117** (USA)) [2016/17 h85p, b86: h20.7g* h20.6g² h20.3g³ h19.3m⁶ h24.5s⁴ h19.4d² h24.4g⁶ h19gᶠ Apr 24] good-topped gelding: bumper winner: fairly useful hurdler: won maiden at Huntingdon early in season: stays 21f: acts on good to soft going: usually races towards rear. *Jonjo O'Neill*

THETALKINGHORSE (IRE) 9 b.g. Presenting – Praisethepreacher (IRE) (Sharifabad   **c113** (IRE)) [2016/17 c109: c24.2d³ Mar 31] multiple winning pointer: fair form in hunter chases: stays 3m. *G. T. H. Bailey*

THE TIN MINER (IRE) 6 br.g. Presenting – Sidalcea (IRE) (Oscar (IRE)) [2016/17   **h93** h20.5gᶠ h19.7sᵘʳ h21v⁶ h25.6g⁴ Apr 12] €40,000 3-y-o, £20,000 5-y-o: sixth foal: brother to bumper winner Forever Present and half-brother to fair hurdlers Wood Lily (2m winner, by Definite Article) and All The Best Mate (2½m winner, by Alflora): dam (b90), bumper winner, half-sister to triple Cheltenham Gold Cup winner Best Mate: running to a modest level when falling last in novice at Leicester, easily best effort over hurdles. *David Bridgwater*

THE TOURARD MAN (IRE) 11 b.g. Shantou (USA) – Small Iron (General Ironside) [2016/17 c124, h124: h23.1m* h25d* c23g* c24g* c25.2g⁵ h23.9g h24.7d⁵ h24g⁴ h24.7g h25g* Apr 24] compact gelding: useful handicap hurdler: won at Exeter and Warwick early in season and Warwick again (by 2¼ lengths from Thumb Stone Blues) in April: useful chaser: won novices at Worcester in June and Southwell (left well clear 2 out in 3-runner race) in August: stays 3¼m: acts on good to firm and heavy going. *Alan King* **c131 +** **h138**

THE TRIGGER (IRE) 8 ch.g. Beneficial – Ardrom (Ardross) [2016/17 h22dᵖᵘ h22.1d³ h23d h23.1g Jul 29] winning pointer: modest maiden hurdler: stays 2¾m: acts on good to soft going: tried in cheekpieces: in tongue tie last 4 starts. *Mrs Caroline McCaldin, Ireland* **h86**

THE TROLLIE DOLLY 4 gr.f. Hellvelyn – Highland Cascade (Tipsy Creek (USA)) [2016/17 b14s b12.6d Dec 14] neat filly: sixth foal: half-sister to French 7.5f-1¼m winner Shades of Light (by Echo of Light): dam 6f winner: no form in 2 bumpers. *Stuart Kittow* **b–**

THE TULLOW TANK (IRE) 9 b.g. Oscar (IRE) – Bobbing Back (IRE) (Bob Back (USA)) [2016/17 h16dᵈ c22.5g c20v³ Mar 19] rangy gelding: smart hurdler at best: useful chaser nowadays: third in Webster Cup Chase at Navan (10¼ lengths behind A Toi Phil) in March: should stay 3m: acts on heavy going: tried in cheekpieces: in tongue tie last 4 starts. *Alan Fleming, Ireland* **c137** **h119**

THE TWO AMIGOS 5 b.g. Midnight Legend – As Was (Epalo (GER)) [2016/17 b16.8g⁶ h16d⁵ h15.8d h19.4g⁴ h23.9g² h23.1d⁴ Mar 21] €22,000 3-y-o, €30,000 4-y-o: first foal: dam unraced half-sister to useful French hurdler/fairly useful chaser (17f-21f winner) Line Salsa: off mark in Irish maiden points at third attempt: well beaten in bumper: fair form over hurdles: stays 3m: best form on good going: in tongue tie since debut. *David Pipe* **h106** **b–**

THE UNIT (IRE) 6 b.g. Gold Well – Sovana (FR) (Kadounor (FR)) [2016/17 h113p, b88: h15.8s⁴ h16g³ h20.8g* h19g* h19g² h19g* h16.5g³ Apr 7] sturdy gelding: useful hurdler: won novices at Doncaster in November and Taunton in December, and handicap at latter course (by 8 lengths from Qualando) in March: third in Top Novices' Hurdle at Aintree (7 lengths behind Pingshou) in April: stays 21f: best form on good going: often races towards rear, usually travels strongly. *Alan King* **h138**

THEUNNAMEDSOLDIER 9 b.g. Revoque (IRE) – Miss Tango (Batshoof) [2016/17 c20.9vᶠ Dec 12] maiden hurdler: fatally injured when fell 3 out in novice handicap won by West Wizard at Ffos Las on chasing debut: stayed 2½m: acted on heavy going. *Nigel Hawke* **c–** **h–**

THE VOCALIST 5 b.m. Recharge (IRE) – Ivy Edith (Blakeney) [2016/17 b16.2s² b17g* Apr 15] €6,500 3-y-o: half-sister to 2 winners by Cloudings, including bumper winner Royal Stardust: dam (h119), bumper and 2m-2¼m hurdle winner, half-sister to top-class 2m hurdler Royal Derbi: fair form in bumpers: won mares event at Carlisle in April. *Stuart Crawford, Ireland* **b94**

THE WALLACE LINE (IRE) 6 b.g. Mastercraftsman (IRE) – Surval (IRE) (Sadler's Wells (USA)) [2016/17 h111: h23.6g⁶ h23.6s⁶ h26v² h23.3s⁶ h24g³ Apr 19] sturdy gelding: fairly useful handicap hurdler: third at Cheltenham in April: thorough stayer: acts on heavy going: tried in cheekpieces: often races towards rear. *Tim Vaughan* **h120**

THE WAY YOU DANCE (IRE) 5 b.g. Thewayyouare (USA) – Beautiful Dancer (IRE) (Danehill Dancer (IRE)) [2016/17 h16d⁶ h16m⁴ h19.9d⁴ h16.8g h16.8m* h16g* h15.8m⁴ h16.3g³ Apr 23] fair on Flat, stays 1½m: fair handicap hurdler: won at Newton Abbot (conditional event) in August and Worcester in September: unproven beyond 17f: acts on good to firm going: wears cheekpieces. *Neil Mulholland* **h108**

THE WEALERDEALER (IRE) 10 b.g. Vinnie Roe (IRE) – Lantern Liz (IRE) (Montelimar (USA)) [2016/17 c102, h–: h26.5d* h26.5g³ c24.2mᵘʳ h23.1g² Oct 18] lengthy gelding: fair handicap hurdler: won at Newton Abbot in June: fair form over fences: stays 3¼m: acts on good to firm and heavy going: has worn headgear. *Richard Woollacott* **c110** **h112**

THE WEE MIDGET 12 b.g. Mtoto – Fragrant Rose (Alflora (IRE)) [2016/17 c80§, h88§: h24gᵖᵘ c23gᵖᵘ h23.1g Sep 28] modest hurdler at best, no form in 2016/17: maiden chaser: usually wears headgear: front runner/races prominently: unreliable. *Arthur Whiting* **c– §** **h– §**

THE WELSH PADDIES (IRE) 5 b.g. Court Cave (IRE) – Masiana (IRE) (Daylami (IRE)) [2016/17 b15.8d* b16.3d b15.8s³ Mar 18] €27,000 3-y-o: rather unfurnished gelding: first foal: dam (b86) second in bumper: fairly useful form when won maiden at Ffos Las in November on first of 3 starts in bumpers. *Paul Morgan* **b95**

THE WEXFORDIAN (IRE) 8 b.g. Shantou (USA) – Going My Way (Henbit (USA)) **c101 §** [2016/17 c92, h–: c20s⁵ c22.7g⁶ h20.3s⁴ h15.7d² c15.7g² h18.5g² c17g³ Apr 23] well-made **h101 §** gelding: point winner: fair form over hurdles: fair maiden chaser: left Martin Keighley after sixth start: stays 2½m: acts on heavy going: often in headgear: temperamental. *Martin Hill*

THE WICKET CHICKEN (IRE) 5 b.m. Milan – Soniadoir (IRE) (Presenting) [2016/17 **b83** b15.7g³ b17s⁵ b16.8g³ Apr 20] £31,000 4-y-o: second foal: dam (h86) 2¼m hurdle winner: won Irish mares maiden point on debut: modest form in bumpers. *Neil Mulholland*

THE WINKLER (IRE) 8 gr.g. Medaaly – Osirixa (FR) (Linamix (FR)) [2016/17 **c134** c22.5m* c22.7gᵖᵘ Jul 12] lengthy gelding: fairly useful on Flat, stays 17f: winning hurdler: **h–** useful chaser: won novice at Killarney (by 1¾ lengths from Sandymount Duke) early in season: stays 3m: acts on good to firm and heavy going: has worn cheekpieces: often wears tongue tie nowadays. *Eoin Doyle, Ireland*

THE WISE ONE (IRE) 6 b.g. Tikkanen (USA) – Mary Mac Swiney (IRE) (Flemensfirth **h97** (USA)) [2016/17 h20.5s h16v³ h16.8v³ h19.4s³ h23.8g* h23.9g⁵ Apr 26] €10,000 3-y-o, £25,000 5-y-o: second foal: dam unraced half-sister to useful hurdler/fairly useful chaser (stayed 3m) Augherskea: Irish maiden point winner: modest form over hurdles: won handicap at Musselburgh in March: stays 3m: acts on heavy going: often races prominently. *James Ewart*

THE WORLDS END (IRE) 6 b.g. Stowaway – Bright Sprite (IRE) (Beneficial) **h146 p** [2016/17 h102: h20s³ h19.5s* h19.5s* h22.8d* h24gᶠ h24.7g* Apr 7]
    Trainer Tom George's tally of seventy-one wins in the latest season exceeded his previous best in twenty-four years with a licence by some way, while his Gloucestershire stable earned more than £1m for the first time in a single campaign. Whichever way you look at it, the latest season represented the best of George's training career to date, though one thing that was missing was that elusive second success at the Cheltenham Festival to add to the victory of the Polish-bred Galileo in the Baring Bingham Novices' Hurdle back in 2002. Singlefarmpayment came closest to ending his trainer's Cheltenham Festival drought since then, starting 5/1 favourite for the Ultima Handicap Chase and producing a polished performance for a novice, leading at the last and going down by just a short head to Un Temps Pour Tout. Sir Valentino, who had won the Haldon Gold Cup at Exeter in early-November, was another trained by George to acquit himself with credit at Cheltenham when six lengths third to Special Tiara in the Queen Mother Champion Chase, though stablemate God's Own might have bettered that but for costly late mistakes (he came fifth). God's Own went on to run as well as he ever has when a close third to Fox Norton in the Champion Chase at Punchestown in April, with Sir Valentino back in sixth. God's Own had won the same race twelve months earlier under Paddy Brennan, but was partnered on the most recent occasion, as on each of his six starts since then, by Adrian Heskin, who had been appointed as retained jockey at Down Farm in September. Heskin began his career in Ireland with Michael Hourigan, for whom he won the Cross Country Chase at Cheltenham and the bet365 Gold Cup at Sandown as an eighteen-year-old, claiming 7 lb, in 2010, before being appointed as number-one to leading owner Barry Connell in 2014. Heskin's biggest success in that role came when Martello Tower won the Spa Novices' Hurdle at the 2015 Cheltenham Festival, but Connell dispensed with his services less than thirteen months later, and, not long afterwards, Heskin linked up with George for the latest season.

Doom Bar Sefton Novices' Hurdle, Aintree—The Worlds End gains consolation for his Cheltenham spill as he holds on gamely from Beyond Conceit (No.2) and Debece (No.4)

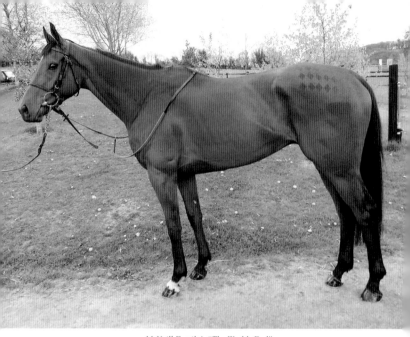

McNeill Family's "The Worlds End"

Heskin had fifty-four wins in his first full season in Britain (his best tally in Ireland was forty-four in 2014/15) and described the Grade 1 success of The Worlds End at Aintree as 'the icing on the cake'. The Worlds End had looked a potentially useful prospect when making a winning debut for Tom George in a bumper at Chepstow in April 2016 and his trainer seemed to have left plenty to work on when he failed to justify support when nine lengths third to Gayebury on his hurdling/seasonal debut over two and a half miles on testing ground at Ffos Las in November. The Worlds End improved plenty to get off the mark in an above average maiden at Chepstow the following month (when Brennan deputised for Heskin who rode Sir Valentino at Kempton the same afternoon). He then followed up in a novice event under a penalty over the same course and distance in January, not needing to improve but having more in hand than the three-length winning margin. The Worlds End stepped up to Grade 2 company for his next start, in the Prestige Novices' Hurdle at Haydock in February, and relished the opportunity to tackle the longest distance he had so far been faced with. He produced a smart effort to give 7 lb and a nine-length beating to the useful No Hassle Hoff, staying on very strongly. Up again in trip, trying three miles for the first time, The Worlds End was with the leaders and looked set to play a big part in the finish of the Spa Novices' Hurdle at the Cheltenham Festival when he crashed out at the second last.

The Worlds End found consolation three weeks later, in the Sefton Novices' Hurdle at Aintree, where he won gamely by half a length from Beyond Conceit without needing to better the form he had shown in the Prestige, but proving both his stamina and his ability to cope with a bigger field and a more competitive race. The Worlds End looks an exciting chaser for the future, but he remains open to more improvement as a staying hurdler first. That is likely to be the plan in the next season according to George, who also expressed his delight at how the first year of his partnership with Heskin had gone: 'We've had some very good winners this season and are high up in the table, but it's great to get that first Grade 1 together. Adrian is doing well. We understand each other. Paddy (Brennan) is still riding out and has won on this horse, but I knew the yard was getting stronger and we needed our own jockey.' Things might not have gone his way at the latest Cheltenham Festival, but The Worlds End is as short as 8/1 to win the Stayers' Hurdle in 2018 and end his trainer's long wait for another Festival success.

The Worlds End (IRE) (b.g. 2011)	Stowaway (b 1994)	Slip Anchor (b 1982)	Shirley Heights
			Sayonara
		On Credit (ch 1988)	No Pass No Sale
			Noble Tiara
	Bright Sprite (IRE) (b 2001)	Beneficial (b 1990)	Top Ville
			Youthful
		Last Sprite (ch 1984)	Tug of War
			Miss Sprite

The Worlds End, a good-topped gelding, is by Stowaway who stood at Whytemount Stud in Ireland until his death in 2015, and is perhaps best known as the sire of that grand servant Hidden Cyclone, a smart hurdler and very smart chaser, and of the top-class hurdler/very smart chaser Champagne Fever, the latest Lexus Chase winner Outlander and Champagne Classic who won at the latest Cheltenham and Punchestown spring festivals (the two last-named also have essays in this Annual). The Worlds End is the fifth foal out of the unraced Bright Sprite, but only the second to have raced after Egret (by Definite Article), who was runner-up in a bumper from five starts under Rules for Lucinda Russell. Bright Sprite is out of Last Sprite (by the stamina-packed Tug of War), a winner twice in bumpers and of a two and a quarter mile mares maiden hurdle at Fairyhouse and a half-sister to the fairly useful staying chaser Sergeant Sprite. The Worlds End was sold as a three-year-old for €20,000 at Goffs in June 2014, and made one start for trainer Sean Doyle in points, when falling at Ballinaboola in November 2015 when looking the likely winner. The Worlds End was withdrawn from the November Sale at Tattersalls five days later and bought privately by the McNeill family. The Worlds End, who remains open to improvement, is a strong traveller but he stays twenty-five furlongs. He acts on soft going (the going was good when he won the Sefton). *Tom George*

THE YANK 8 b.g. Trade Fair – Silver Gyre (IRE) (Silver Hawk (USA)) [2016/17 c106, h81: c15.7v⁶ c16g³ c17.2g^pu c17.4g^F c16g³ c16.3g* c15.7d^ur c16m* c17.2d⁴ Apr 27] compact gelding: maiden hurdler: fair handicap chaser: won at Newton Abbot in October and Ludlow in April: raced around 2m nowadays: acts on good to firm and good to soft going: usually wears headgear: has worn tongue tie, including in 2016/17. *David Bridgwater* — **c112 h–**

THEYDON PARK 4 b.g. Royal Applause – Velvet Waters (Unfuwain (USA)) [2016/17 b13.7m* h16s⁴ h16v³ h16s⁵ h16s⁴ Apr 2] half-brother to several winners, including modest/ungenuine hurdler Torran Sound (17f winner, by Tobougg), stayed 25f: dam 11.6f winner: won junior bumper at Huntingdon (dead-heated with Dentley de Mee) in October: fair form over hurdles: left Peter Charalambous after first start. *Joseph Patrick O'Brien, Ireland* — **h105 b80**

THE YOUNG MASTER 8 b.g. Echo of Light – Fine Frenzy (IRE) (Great Commotion (USA)) [2016/17 c152, h–: c25.5d^F h24s c25g⁶ c34.3d^F c28.8g Apr 29] workmanlike gelding: fairly useful hurdler, best excused sole run over hurdles in 2016/17: useful handicap chaser nowadays: sixth in Ultima Handicap Chase at Cheltenham (21¼ lengths behind Un Temps Pour Tout) in March: stays 29f: acts on heavy going: wears cheekpieces: tried in tongue tie. *Neil Mulholland* — **c138 h–**

THINGER LICHT (FR) 8 b.g. Clety (FR) – Family Saga (FR) (Caerwent) [2016/17 c114, h97: c22.6s³ c20d⁴ Jul 13] sturdy gelding: winning hurdler: fair handicap chaser: stays 3m: acts on good to firm and heavy going: wears headgear. *Dan Skelton* — **c105 h–**

THINK AHEAD 6 b.g. Shamardal (USA) – Moonshadow (Diesis) [2016/17 h16.4d^pu Nov 11] smart on Flat, stays 1¼m: pulled up as if amiss in novice on hurdling debut: should do better. *James Moffatt* — **h– p**

THINK OF ME (IRE) 8 b.m. Germany (USA) – Kate's Lass (IRE) (Montelimar (USA)) [2016/17 h88: c19.5d⁵ h20.5d³ h20g h20s³ h21d³ h16.7g h22m h21.3d h20s⁶ h20v^ᵛ h18.4d⁵ h16d h20s² h20v Feb 22] modest maiden hurdler: tailed off in mares event on chasing debut: stays 23f: acts on heavy going: tried in hood: usually races in rear. *Brian Francis Cawley, Ireland* — **c– h87**

THIRD ACT (IRE) 8 b.g. King's Theatre (IRE) – Starry Lady (IRE) (Marju (IRE)) [2016/17 c112§, h–§: h16m² h16.8s* h16d² c20.2s³ h21.6s⁶ h18.5m³ h16m² Apr 28] lengthy, useful-looking gelding: fair handicap hurdler: won at Exeter (conditional event) in November: fair maiden chaser: stays 2¾m: acts on soft and good to firm going: has worn headgear: often wears tongue tie: front runner/races prominently, often freely: one to be wary of. *Colin Tizzard*   **c102 §** **h113 §**

THIRD ESTATE (IRE) 5 b.g. Suleiman (IRE) – Fizanni (IRE) (Arzanni) [2016/17 b16g* b16.8g² h20g² Dec 18] first foal: dam (h81), winning pointer, half-sister to fairly useful chaser (stays 3¾m) Dystonia's Revenge: fair form in bumpers: won maiden at Down Royal in May: 5/1, some encouragement when second in maiden at Fakenham (15 lengths behind Argante) on hurdling debut: left Nigel Slevin after first start: tried in hood: open to improvement. *Neil King*   **h105 p** **b88**

THIRD INTENTION (IRE) 10 b.g. Azamour (IRE) – Third Dimension (FR) (Suave Dancer (USA)) [2016/17 c157§, h–: c19.9g* c21d⁶ c30.2m⁵ c24d h19.1s⁴ c30.2g c21.1gᶠ c22.7g⁴ Apr 29] tall gelding: has had breathing operation: smart hurdler at best, well beaten sole outing over hurdles in 2016/17: smart handicap chaser nowadays: won Old Roan Chase at Aintree (by 1¾ lengths from God's Own) in October: stays 25f: acts on heavy going: often wears headgear: wears tongue tie: temperamental. *Colin Tizzard*   **c148 §** **h–**

THIS IS IT (IRE) 5 b.g. Milan – Riviera Sands (IRE) (Mister Lord (USA)) [2016/17 b16s⁵ h21.6s³ h21.4s³ h23.1d² Mar 21] €30,000 3-y-o: sixth foal: brother to fairly useful hurdler/chaser Riviera Sun (2m-2½m winner) and half-brother to bumper winner Here's Jenny (by Presenting): dam unraced half-sister to useful hurdler/chaser (19f-3m winner) Here's Johnny: unplaced on completed start in points: fifth in bumper at Chepstow (7 lengths behind Cadeyrn): fair form over hurdles: best effort when second in novice handicap at Exeter in March: will be suited by 3m. *Nick Mitchell*   **h114** **b85**

THISONETIME (IRE) 6 b.g. Kalanisi (IRE) – Dizzy's Whisper (IRE) (Supreme Leader) [2016/17 b95: h19.9v⁵ h15.8v² h16.4v² h19.9m² h22g⁴ Apr 23] angular gelding: bumper winner: fair form over hurdles: may prove best around 2m: acts on heavy going: tried in cheekpieces: in tongue tie last 4 starts: front runner/races prominently. *Dan Skelton*   **h107**

THIS THYNE JUDE 9 gr.m. Silver Patriarch (IRE) – This Thyne (Good Thyne (USA)) [2016/17 h98: h20.2dᵘʳ h23.9s⁵ h23.9g³ h23.9g* h20.2gᶠ Apr 26] fair handicap hurdler: won novice event at Perth in September: will stay beyond 3m: best form on good going: usually races nearer last than first. *Lucy Normile*   **h102**

THISTLECRACK 9 b.g. Kayf Tara – Ardstown (Ardross) [2016/17 h174p: c23.6d* c24.4s* c23.4g* c24g* c25.3s² Jan 28]   **c174** **h–**

The extended entry on Native River includes a mention of Arkle's fourth appearance, fifty-one years ago, in the Hennessy Gold Cup at Newbury where he was beaten for the first time in nearly two years, failing by half a length to concede 35 lb to Stalbridge Colonist. Arkle was still only nine and it could scarcely be imagined at the time that, just over a month later, he would be running his last race. His next outing was not in the King George VI Chase at Kempton's Christmas meeting, as had been widely expected, but in the SGB Handicap Chase at Ascot just two and a half weeks after the Hennessy and only eleven days before Christmas. Out in front from the first fence under his customary 12-7, Arkle had his four opponents off the bit by halfway and went on to win by fifteen lengths. Normal service, it seemed, had been resumed. Thirteen days later, after making the journey back and forth once more to Tom Dreaper's Greenogue stables at Kilsallaghan, not far from Dublin airport, Arkle lined up for the King George VI Chase, a race he had won twelve months earlier by 'a distance'—the widest margin recorded for any of the twenty-seven wins during his career. The runner-up that day, Dormant, was in the line-up again, as was the third, and only other finisher, Arctic Ocean (he had finished a further distance behind), along with four others including the highly promising six-year-old Woodland Venture, the course and distance winner Maigret, and Foinavon, a former stablemate of Arkle now in different ownership, who was ridden in the King George by his trainer John Kempton. Mill House, twice runner-up to Arkle in the Cheltenham Gold Cup, was declared to run in the King George but pulled a muscle in his quarters on Christmas day. The death of the brilliant Dunkirk had marred the previous year's King George and the absence of both him and Mill House

Kempton racecourse stables, January 1967—Arkle starts on the long road to recovery; he received hundreds of get-well cards

led to Arkle being sent off at 9/2-on after Kempton's Boxing Day programme had been held over until the following day because of frost (with the second day's card abandoned).

The conditions of the King George in those days penalised winners according to the value of individual races they had won in recent times and, as the winner of a race value over £4,000, Arkle carried 21 lb extra, the maximum penalty. Mill House would have received 11 lb from Arkle had he been fit to run; Woodland Venture and Maigret received a stone, while Dormant received 21 lb. Dormant and Woodland Venture took on Arkle from the start but Arkle still made most of the running until surrendering the lead to Woodland Venture when making a bad mistake six from home and, though Arkle was back in front two fences later, Woodland Venture was challenging strongly when he came down at the second last. Left clear, Arkle jumped the final fence with a healthy lead over Dormant and it seemed impossible for him to be caught. But the 'impossible' happened and he was collared in the last fifty yards and went down by a length, to the general astonishment, bordering on disbelief, of the 16,000 or so who had packed the Kempton stands on a murky afternoon (the usual BBC TV audience had to make do with highlights of the race on *Grandstand* after a pioneering pay-per-view company had bought the rights to live coverage of the race). It was just the fourth defeat of Arkle's steeplechasing career, but one that was readily explained by the lameness in his off-fore after the race. Arkle was loaded into the horse ambulance for the short journey to the racecourse stables where an X-ray revealed a fractured pedal bone in his hoof.

The stables at Kempton were Arkle's home for the next two months until—with the world's media to see him off and meet him at the other end—he was able to be returned to Ireland where he began convalescence at his owner Anne, Duchess of Westminster's County Kildare estate. Get-well cards, letters and gifts—including the Guinness which had famously been part of his daily diet—had arrived regularly while Arkle was at Kempton, and the flow continued on his return home (many items addressed simply to 'Arkle, Ireland'). With time and rest, Arkle was able to return to light exercise at Greenogue ten months after the King George and the progess he made over that winter raised hopes that he might return to action at the Fairyhouse Easter meeting. However, Fairyhouse came and Arkle was absent, with a possible return now mooted for Christmas. In the meantime, Arkle's year-younger stablemate Fort Leney started favourite for the 1967 Cheltenham Gold Cup but managed only sixth behind Woodland Venture and Stalbridge Colonist. Foinavon won the 1967 Grand National at 100/1, escaping a melee at the twenty-third fence (Foinavon's Grand National-winning jockey John Buckingham, who became a jockeys' valet after quitting the saddle, died in December at the age of seventy-six). Fort Leney did go on to win the 1968 Gold Cup and, six months after that, it was finally announced that Arkle had been retired (he was completely sound but connections felt that a comeback at Leopardstown's Christmas meeting, a few days before his twelfth birthday, would be asking too much—'Not even Arkle, with his immense courage, could be expected to reproduce his old brilliance'). Arkle's retirement proved short-lived and he had to be humanely destroyed, aged only thirteen, after painful lesions developed in his hind legs which made him progressively more stiff and led to his frequently having to lie down.

Racing is a sport that values its history and its traditions and, although there is no permanent memorial to Arkle at Kempton, the two finest staying chasers since his day, Desert Orchid and Kauto Star, have both been commemorated with statues at the track (Desert Orchid's ashes are buried close to his statue). Both were Cheltenham Gold Cup winners but their reputations as great champions owed much to their outstanding records in the mid-season stayers' championship, the King George VI Chase, which the flamboyant grey Desert Orchid won four times and Kauto Star won five times. Kempton's flat, right-handed, fast-draining three-mile course is one of the fairest in the country—it has provided a very different test to the Cheltenham Gold Cup over the years—and both Desert Orchid and Kauto Star recorded their best performances there, Desert Orchid under 12-3 in the 1990 Racing Post Chase and Kauto Star when replicating Arkle's achievement by winning his fourth King George by 'a distance', the margin that used to be officially returned for any wins of over thirty lengths (Kauto Star's winning margin was retrospectively measured at thirty-six lengths). Kempton's historic jumps racecourse, superbly located close to the M25, is very much part of the sport's heritage, and is one of jumping's irreplaceable assets, all of which made it astonishing when Jockey Club Racecourses, which owns the course, announced plans in January for the track to be bulldozed in the next few years to make way for three thousand homes.

There had been talk in the early part of the century of doing away with Kempton's jumping course when priority was given to providing London with an all-weather track for Flat racing. In the end, jumping was switched to Kempton's Flat turf course when the all-weather track was eventually built and the fact that the Flat course was closer to the crowd than the original jumps track actually enhanced jumping at Kempton. The idea that the King George VI Chase should now be moved from Kempton, and run at sister course Sandown with its uphill finish and habitually more testing conditions (the Esher track has twice staged the King George, first in 1995 due to bad weather and then in 2005 because of that all-weather redevelopment), is as unacceptable as the idea of moving the Grand National from

Aintree or the Gold Cup from Cheltenham. Both Aintree and Cheltenham have come under threat of closure in the past and are now, like Kempton, part of the Jockey Club Racecourses portfolio, having been entrusted to an institution that most believed would be a steadfast custodian and protector of racing's heritage. Johnny Henderson, father of trainer Nicky, got together a group of investors to buy Cheltenham for £240,000 in 1963 when the course was threatened with being taken over by property developers; Henderson and his group set up Racecourse Holdings Trust and, a decade later, handed their shares to the Jockey Club for a nominal sum, on the understanding that future revenue would be ploughed back into racing. Johnny Henderson, rightly remembered at the Cheltenham Festival where his name is attached to the Grand Annual Chase, was also one of the unsung heroes of the campaign to save Aintree when it came close to oblivion in the late-'sixties and early-'seventies—with a number of renewals billed as 'the last Grand National'—before Ladbrokes negotiated a seven-year lease in 1975 with the Walton Group.

The Walton Group had bought Aintree from the Topham family in 1973 with a commitment to continuing to run the National, but had since run into difficulties (the public had voted with their feet when admission prices were put up steeply, leading to a National day crowd of only around 9,000 in 1975). The Walton Group gave the Levy Board an ultimatum in 1975, to either provide a £2m interest-free loan or purchase Aintree for £4m. With the situation approaching deadlock and the Jockey Club issuing an ultimatum that the 1976 National could be transferred to Doncaster, Ladbrokes stepped in and paid £1.6m for a lease on the course, and their custodianship provided valuable breathing space as well as rejuvenating the three-day Grand National meeting which became an all jumping festival. As Ladbrokes' tenure began to draw to a close, Racecourse Holdings Trust (of which Johnny Henderson was chairman) took the lead in trying to secure Aintree's future, suggesting that the money to buy the course should come equally from the Levy Board, the bookmakers and from the proceeds of a public appeal. Racecourse Holdings Trust ran the 1983 Grand National meeting under a one-year lease as the public appeal got under way. With Canadian distillers Seagram also lending their support and offering long-term sponsorship, enough money was raised to pay the Walton Group £3.4m for the

bet365 Novices' Chase (Worcester), Newbury—another smooth display as Thistlecrack maintains his 100% start over fences with a third win in novice company

32Red King George VI Chase, Kempton—a typical bumper Boxing Day crowd (near sell-out 21,164 attendance) at Kempton, with people still queuing to get in before the second race—yet just over a fortnight later came the shock news of plans to close the course

course and the rights to the Grand National, the deal signed shortly after the 1983 running of the race. The Government, which had missed numerous opportunities in on-going correspondence with the Topham family over the years, refused to help the Grand National appeal ('The Government is not in the business of making subsidies in this field'). In the end, public pressure and a well conducted press campaign were as influential as anything in securing Aintree's future and, although the public appeal itself raised a good deal less money than the £1m budgeted for, many organisations and individuals inside and outside racing made splendid contributions, with support coming from all sections of the nation, from the Royal Family to the man in the street, and also from abroad.

Neither Cheltenham nor Aintree has looked back since they were saved from the developers, and there is no reason why Kempton—which there is no pressing need to sell—should not thrive as a jumps course under dynamic management. Any 'Save Kempton' campaign launched within racing will be assured of support from local residents' groups opposed to the development of Kempton Park which lies in the green belt. A creature called the noctule bat is found in a special protection area near the racecourse and may yet have a part to play too, being 'a biodiversity action plan priority species' which is legally protected, as are all bats, with planning authorities legally obliged to consider whether they are likely to be affected by any proposed development, through pollution, for example.

Kempton's latest two-day King George meeting was part of a general success story in Christmas week for British racing which saw on-course crowds over the seven days totalling more than 200,000 for only the second time. Kempton attracted an official attendance of 21,164 on Boxing Day and 11,219 for the second day of the meeting, both increases on the previous year (Sandown's two biggest jump meetings of the season, Tingle Creek day and the Finale meeting, attracted 13,186 and 10,903 respectively). There was a line-up of just five—the joint smallest field (there were also five in 1996) since three went to post in 1984—for the 32Red King George VI Chase which was widely viewed as a match between stablemates Cue Card, winner of the previous year's renewal, and the exciting novice Thistlecrack, having his first serious examination after toying with the opposition in novice events at Chepstow in October and Cheltenham and Newbury in November. Thistlecrack had been a brilliant winner of the World Hurdle at the Cheltenham Festival in a dominant

836

campaign in 2015/16 and was installed as 6/1 ante-post favourite for the Cheltenham Gold Cup as soon as his connections confirmed at the start of October that he was being sent chasing. 'He's not an ordinary horse, is he? He's eight—and will be nine come March—and has never jumped a fence, and he's favourite for the Gold Cup, it's exciting times,' said his trainer Colin Tizzard. Foot-perfect at Chepstow, a little too bold for his own good at times at Cheltenham, and a sound-jumping, eight-length winner from Bigbadjohn of the Grade 2 Worcester Novices' Chase at Newbury—that was the summary of Thistlecrack's performances in those first three novice chases. There was clearly a lot more to come from him and, although it seemed to be generally assumed that the Kauto Star Novices' Chase on the King George undercard at Kempton would be next, his owners John and Heather Snook took the bold decision to pitch him in against Cue Card instead. Cue Card had won the Betfair Chase at Haydock for the third time and was the highest-rated chaser in Britain but, despite the fact that no novice had won the King George before, Thistlecrack shaded favouritism at Kempton, starting at 11/10 with Cue Card at 5/4. The three other runners were Josses Hill and the previous year's Kauto Star winner Tea For Two, first and second in the Peterborough Chase at Huntingdon, and Silviniaco Conti, winner of the King George in 2013 and 2014 but now largely looking a light of other days.

Boundless potential against proven form—could the King George live up to its billing? It turned out to be virtually no contest, with Thistlecrack winning his ninth successive race and producing a performance right out of the top drawer on only his fourth start over fences, a performance—the way Timeform interpreted the form in allowing extra for the manner and ease of his victory—that was superior even to that achieved by Coneygree (a possible for the King George until he was injured) when he won the 2015 Cheltenham Gold Cup as a novice, also on his fourth start over fences. Jumping exuberantly, particularly at the open ditches, Thistlecrack had the outcome settled well before the finish, stamping his class on his rivals with a decisive turn of foot after jumping the fourth last and being completely in command, out in front, all the way up the finishing straight. He won impressively by three and a quarter lengths, having gone six to eight lengths clear between the last two. Cue Card wasn't at his best and possibly paid for moving up alongside Thistlecrack in the back straight and trying to press him (ground conditions were probably a shade too firm for Cue Card too). Cue Card only just held off the third and fourth, Silviniaco Conti, who had looked well held turning for home after making some of the early running, and Tea For Two, who seemed to excel himself, the distances between the three being just a short head and a head. Thistlecrack's winning margin would have been much bigger had jockey Tom Scudamore, who never had to go for his whip, ridden him out, instead of standing up in his irons and holding his fist in the air as he eased him down over the last fifty yards. The winner's time of 5m 53.80sec was the fastest for a King George since One Man's record 5m 45.17sec in the 1996 running, though this reflects the drying conditions, with Might Bite in the process of posting a quicker time when he fell at the last, a long way clear, in the Kauto Star earlier on the card.

Two anouncements in January—of the enforced retirement of the 2016 Cheltenham Gold Cup winner Don Cossack and of the fact that Coneygree would not be in the Gold Cup line-up either—had Thistlecrack's trainer Colin Tizzard dreaming of 'doing a Michael Dickinson' with his five Gold Cup entries. Thistlecrack (at around evens), the Hennessy and Welsh National winner Native River, and Cue Card were the first three in the ante-post betting at the time and the Tizzard stable had taken delivery of a big-money Ann and Alan Potts purchase from France, Alary, who had been placed in the Grand Steeple-Chase de Paris and the Haye Jousselin. The smart handicapper Theatre Guide was the stable's fifth Gold Cup entrant (Coral offered 150/1 about the Tizzard stable saddling the first five and emulating Dickinson's achievement in the 1983 edition). In the event, Thistlecrack didn't make the Cheltenham Gold Cup line-up, and nor did Alary who, after failing to complete on his first two starts in Britain, ran in the Ryanair Chase (he was a well-

32Red King George VI Chase, Kempton—Thistlecrack comprehensively wins the battle of the two Tizzard stable stars, with 2015 winner Cue Card forced to settle for the runner-up spot in the race for the second year running

held sixth) at the Cheltenham Festival instead. Theatre Guide, in the same ownership as Cue Card, ran in the Ultima Handicap Chase at the Festival, leaving Native River (third) and Cue Card (fell at the third last) to represent the stable in the blue riband.

Thistlecrack himself completed his Gold Cup preparation as planned in the Cotswold Chase at Cheltenham's Trials meeting at the end of January but, sent off at 9/4-on, he was beaten a head by the ill-fated Many Clouds whose death out on the course straight afterwards was a sad aftermath to a fine battle from the second last. Thistlecrack headed Many Clouds briefly at the last but couldn't hold him off as he rallied on the run-in, the race developing into a late scrap under testing conditions. That played to the strengths of a battler like Many Clouds and, given how strongly Thistlecrack went through the race (as low as 1.02 on Betfair at one stage), connections must have pondered afterwards whether it might have been better if Scudamore had pressed on further from home, as he had at Kempton (Thistlecrack's jumping wasn't so fluent either under a more patient ride). Thistlecrack retained his position at the head of the ante-post betting on the Cheltenham Gold Cup after this first defeat over fences, but, towards the end of February, he suffered a small tendon tear which ruled him out for the rest of the season. He is expected to be back in racecourse action, if all goes well, around Christmas in time to perhaps try to repeat his win in the King George and then continue with his preparation for the 2018 Gold Cup. Provided he makes a full recovery, he will be a very strong contender at Cheltenham even at the age of ten.

The sturdy Thistlecrack and his stablemate Cue Card struck a blow for British National Hunt breeding with their one, two in the King George VI Chase. Yanworth's triumph in the Christmas Hurdle and Special Tiara's win in the Desert Orchid Chase were other important successes for British-breds at the two-day Kempton meeting where there would have been a clean sweep of the three Grade 1s if Might Bite had not fallen when in that unassailable lead in the Kauto Star Novices' Chase. Thistlecrack and Special Tiara are by the Overbury Stud stalwart Kayf Tara who is still going strongly at the age of twenty-three (his stud fee for the 2017 covering season was £10,000, the highest it has ever been). Kayf Tara was runner-up to perennial champion King's Theatre—like Kayf Tara a son of Sadler's Wells—in the *Racing Post* table of the leading jumping stallions in Britain and Ireland in 2016/17, but Kayf Tara wasn't far behind and might have ended up as champion himself had Thistlecrack not been ruled out of the major spring festivals. The late King's Theatre's final crop is now aged five and Kayf Tara has a number of crops bred from stellar books of mares still to reach the racecourse, so he certainly has every chance of becoming a rare British-based champion jumps sire in the modern era.

Thistlecrack (b.g. 2008)	Kayf Tara (b 1994)	Sadler's Wells (b 1981)	Northern Dancer / Fairy Bridge
		Colorspin (b 1983)	High Top / Reprocolor
	Ardstown (b 1991)	Ardross (b 1976)	Run The Gantlet / Le Melody
		Booterstown (ch 1971)	Master Owen / Vulgan's Rose

Thistlecrack's dam Ardstown, a daughter of Ardross who, like Kayf Tara, won two Gold Cups at Royal Ascot, was a fairly useful three-mile chaser. Ardstown was raced mainly in point-to-points and hunter chases (she won three of each) but point-to-pointing and hunter chasing was severely hit by the serious foot and mouth outbreak in 2001 and Ardstown was put into training with Venetia Williams, for whom she justified favouritism on her only start, in a handicap chase at Newbury (beating Plaid Maid, the dam of Coneygree). Ardstown's career at stud was fairly short-lived and she produced just six foals before she died in 2014, her first foal and first winner Kennel Bridge (by Classic Cliche) proving himself a fairly useful hurdler, successful at up to two and a half miles, before dying young. Ardstown's second foal Quick Approach (a brother to Thistlecrack) was owned by the Snooks but broke a leg before reaching the racecourse. The Snooks bought Thistlecrack for €43,000 as an unbroken three-year-old and he was very lightly raced in bumpers before finally making his debut over jumps as a seven-year-old when he went on to win the Sefton Novices' Hurdle at Aintree and finish an unlucky second in the Grade 1 novice hurdle over three miles at the Punchestown Festival. The Snooks also own Thistlecrack's smart half-brother West Approach (by Westerner), who is in training with Colin Tizzard and was third in the Cleeve Hurdle at Cheltenham in the latest season, and they paid £165,000 at the Cheltenham Festival Sales in 2016 for Ardstown's final foal, a sister to Thistlecrack, who went straight to stud to be covered by Shirocco. There is plenty of stamina on the distaff side of Thistlecrack's pedigree—Ardstown is a half-sister to the thorough stayer Celtic Town who won over both hurdles and fences—and it is little wonder that staying has proved to be Thistlecrack's game. Fairly unusually for one who stays so well, he is a strong traveller who, as a rule, either races close up or makes the running. He acts on heavy going but doesn't need the mud to show his best (ground conditions when he won the King George VI Chase favoured speed). *Colin Tizzard*

THOMAS BLOSSOM (IRE) 7 b.g. Dylan Thomas (IRE) – Woman Secret (IRE) **h100** (Sadler's Wells (USA)) [2016/17 h–: h16g h15.8g³ h16.8g* h16.4g h19g³ Dec 20] close-coupled gelding: fair handicap hurdler: won at Exeter (amateur event) in October: raced mainly around 2m: best form on good going: wears tongue tie: usually races towards rear. *Ali Stronge*

THOMAS BROWN 8 b.g. Sir Harry Lewis (USA) – Tentsmuir (Arctic Lord) [2016/17 **c138** c136, h–: c19.9d* c20.8s c20.8s c21.1g Apr 7] rangy gelding: winning hurdler: useful **h–** handicap chaser: won at Aintree (by length from On Tour) in November: stays 3m: acts on good to soft going: wears headgear. *Harry Fry*

THOMAS CAMPBELL 5 b.g. Yeats (IRE) – Hora (Hernando (FR)) [2016/17 b87p: **h138 p** b16.2d* h16.4g* h15.7d* h15.7d⁵ h20.3g⁵ h20g⁴ h19.8g Apr 29] good-topped gelding: **b108** useful form when won bumper at Kelso (by 14 lengths from Uncle Percy) early in season: similar form over hurdles: won maiden at Cheltenham in October and introductory event at Ascot in November: shaped well when fifth in Martin Pipe Conditional Jockeys' Handicap Hurdle at Cheltenham (4¼ lengths behind Champagne Classic) in March: will be suited by 3m: acts on good to soft going: remains open to improvement. *Nicky Henderson*

THOMAS CRAPPER 10 b.g. Tamure (IRE) – Mollycarrs Gambul (General Gambul)   **c138**
[2016/17 c136, h–: c18g⁶ c19.2g h19.5g c18.8m⁴ c20.4s⁶ c20.8s⁵ c20.8s c19.9s* c20.8g⁴   **h–**
c20.8gᵘʳ Apr 19] tall gelding: useful hurdler at best: useful handicap chaser: won Greatwood
Gold Cup at Newbury (by 20 lengths from Vic de Touzaine) in March: stays 21f: acts on
heavy going: usually in headgear nowadays: wears tongue tie. *Robin Dickin*

THOMAS DO (IRE) 6 b.g. Flemensfirth (USA) – Loughaderra (IRE) (Strong Gale)   **h91**
[2016/17 b16s h19.5v h19.3v² Mar 9] €22,000 3-y-o, £70,000 5-y-o: brother to useful 2½m   **b–**
hurdle winner/winning pointer Strong Pursuit and half-brother to 3 winners, including fair
hurdlers Look Who's Back (2½m winner, by Bob Back) and Loughaderra Dame (2¼m
winner, by King's Theatre): dam unraced sister to top-class chaser (stayed 3¼m) Strong
Promise: Irish maiden point winner: tailed off in bumper: modest form over hurdles: better
effort when second in novice at Carlisle: in tongue tie last 2 starts. *Donald McCain*

THOMAS HOBSON 7 b.g. Halling (USA) – La Spezia (IRE) (Danehill Dancer (IRE))   **h150**
[2016/17 h141: h20s³ h16g h21sᵖᵘ h21.1g h16d* h20.5d Apr 29] lengthy, angular gelding:
smart handicap hurdler: won at Fairyhouse (by 3 lengths from Veinard) in April: stays 21f:
acts on heavy going: front runner/races prominently: smart on Flat. *W. P. Mullins, Ireland*

THOMAS SHELBY (IRE) 6 b.g. Witness Box (USA) – Deemiss (IRE) (Buckskin   **h110**
(FR)) [2016/17 b89: h21d² h21d⁵ h21s⁴ h24.2s⁴ h24.3d Apr 21] fair form over hurdles:
should be suited by 3m: acts on soft going. *Alan King*

THOMAS TODD 7 b.g. Passing Glance – Miss Danbys (Charmer) [2016/17 b16.2d²   **h96**
b16.4g h20.6g⁴ h16g⁶ Apr 23] useful foal: half-brother to 2m chase winner Danby's Legend   **b81**
(by Midnight Legend): dam (h85) temperamental maiden hurdler: modest form in bumpers:
better effort when second in maiden at Kelso: seemingly modest form on first of 2 starts
over hurdles: in hood last 2 starts. *Laura Morgan*

THOMAS WILD 12 ch.g. Muhtarram (USA) – Bisque (Inchinor) [2016/17 c124x, h–:   **c128 x**
c29.1g c27.5g* c29.4m* May 30] medium-sized gelding: maiden hurdler: fairly useful   **h–**
handicap chaser: won at Stratford and Cartmel (veterans) early in season: stays 3¼m: acts
on good to firm and heavy going: tried in cheekpieces: often races prominently: prone to
mistakes. *Philip Hobbs*

THOMOND (IRE) 9 b.g. Definite Article – Hushaby (IRE) (Eurobus) [2016/17 c24s⁵   **c125**
c25d⁶ c22.5s⁶ c28g⁵ c25.5d c21d² c21g² c21.1g⁶ c22d³ Apr 18] strong gelding: winning   **h–**
hurdler: fairly useful handicap chaser: sixth in Topham Chase at Aintree in April: stays 29f:
acts on firm and soft going: wears tongue tie. *Noel Meade, Ireland*

THOONAVOLLA (IRE) 9 ch.g. Beneficial – Another Partner (Le Bavard (FR))   **c106**
[2016/17 c103, h–: c20s* h23g* h23g⁴ c22.6gᵖᵘ c20.3g² Apr 21] modest handicap   **h93**
hurdler: won at Worcester early in season: fair handicap chaser: won at same course 8 days
earlier: stays easy 3m: acts on soft and good to firm going: has worn cheekpieces: often
races prominently. *Tom Weston*

THORPE (IRE) 7 b.g. Danehill Dancer (IRE) – Minkova (IRE) (Sadler's Wells (USA))   **h101**
[2016/17 h105: h16.2d² h19.6g⁵ h24.3s h23.8g⁶ h19.4g Jan 1] sturdy gelding: fair handicap
hurdler: unproven beyond 2m: acts on soft going: tried in cheekpieces: in tongue tie last 5
starts. *Lucinda Russell*

THOUSAND STARS (FR) 13 gr.g. Grey Risk (FR) – Livaniana (FR) (Saint Estephe **h147**
(FR)) [2016/17 h153: h24d h21.4s h25.4d h16d⁶ Jul 9] small, sturdy gelding: one-time
high-class hurdler: won County Hurdle at Cheltenham in 2009/10, then fourth in Champion
Hurdle and Stayers' Hurdle there next 2 seasons, and also successful in Grande Course de
Haies d'Auteuil on 2 occasions: stayed 25f: acted on heavy going: wore headgear: tried in
tongue tie: has been retired. *W. P. Mullins, Ireland*

THREEBARMYMEN (IRE) 6 b.g. Winged Love (IRE) – Midnight Susie (IRE) **h98**
(Supreme Leader) [2016/17 h108: h21m³ h20.5g⁴ h20.7d h15.3s h21s^pu Feb 10]
modest maiden hurdler: would have stayed beyond 21f: acted on good to firm going: dead.
Jeremy Scott

THREE BLONDES (IRE) 6 b.m. Oscar (IRE) – Lady Belvedere (IRE) (Lord Americo) **b57**
[2016/17 b16.2d³ Jun 4] €1,600 3-y-o, £4,300 4-y-o: sixth foal: sister to fair 2½m hurdle
winner/winning pointer Midnight Walk and half-sister to a winning pointer by Beneficial:
dam unraced: 14/1, third in bumper at Hexham (23 lengths behind Mr Monochrome).
Nigel Tinkler

THREE COLOURS RED (IRE) 5 b.g. Camacho – Colour's Red (IRE) (Red Ransom **h103**
(USA)) [2016/17 h102: h16.7g h18.7g³ h16.7d² h16.3v³ h15.8m Apr 18] rather leggy
gelding: fair maiden hurdler: left Warren Greatrex after third start: stays 19f: acts on good
to soft going: often in headgear/tongue tie. *Robert Stephens*

THREE FACES WEST (IRE) 9 b.g. Dr Massini (IRE) – Ardnataggle (IRE) (Aristocracy) **c151**
[2016/17 c135p, h126: c24.5d^pu c24.1v* c23.4d* Dec 14] workmanlike gelding: winning **h–**
hurdler: smart form over fences: won handicap at Haydock (by 13 lengths from Firebird
Flyer) in November and graduation event at Newbury (by 13 lengths from Coologue) in
December: stays 3m: acts on heavy going: in cheekpieces last 2 starts. *Philip Hobbs*

THREE KINGDOMS (IRE) 8 ch.g. Street Cry (IRE) – Chan Tong (BRZ) (Hampstead **c138**
(URU)) [2016/17 c–, h129: c22.5g c18.2g⁵ c24v⁴ h19s Mar 12] lengthy gelding: useful **h–**
hurdler in 2013/14, below that level since: smart handicap chaser at best: better than result
when fifth at Galway (15 lengths behind Devils Bride) in July: stays 21f: acts on heavy
going: has worn headgear: often races in rear. *D. K. Weld, Ireland*

THREE MMM'S 6 b.m. Milk It Mick – Marinaite (Komaite (USA)) [2016/17 b15.7s^pu **b–**
b15.7d^pu Nov 15] third foal: half-sister to 2 winners on Flat, including 6f-1½m winner
Solarmaite (by Needwood Blade): dam 7f/1m winner: no form in 2 bumpers, in tongue tie
on second occasion. *Roy Bowring*

THREE MUSKETEERS (IRE) 7 b.g. Flemensfirth (USA) – Friendly Craic (IRE) **c152**
(Mister Lord (USA)) [2016/17 c147+, h–: c19.9g⁶ c19.9g^ur c21.4s* c24g⁶ h24.7g Apr 8] **h–**
strong, workmanlike gelding: useful hurdler at best, stiff task final outing in 2016/17: smart
chaser: won graduation event at Market Rasen (by 3 lengths from Kilcrea Vale) in January:
stays 2¾m: acts on heavy going: in cheekpieces last 3 starts. *Dan Skelton*

THREE OF A KIND (IRE) 8 b.g. Helissio (FR) – Monadore (IRE) (Oscar Schindler **c102 x**
(IRE)) [2016/17 h125: h23.1g c20.1s^pu c25.5m³ c23.8g⁴ h23.1s c25.6d^ur c20.2s^F Feb 28] **h–**
strong gelding: fairly useful hurdler at best, excuses in 2016/17: fair form on second of 2
completed starts over fences: barely stays 3m: acts on soft going: tried in cheekpieces:
usually wears tongue tie: usually races prominently: sketchy jumper of fences. *Fergal
O'Brien*

THREE STAR GENERAL 4 b.g. Montjeu (IRE) – Honorlina (FR) (Linamix (FR)) **h110**
[2016/17 h19.3m⁴ Apr 2] rather leggy gelding: fairly useful maiden on Flat, stays 1¾m:
22/1, fourth in maiden at Ascot (8 lengths behind Tales of The Tweed) on hurdling debut.
David Pipe

THREE STARS (IRE) 7 b.g. Westerner – Hapeney (IRE) (Saddlers' Hall (IRE)) **c141**
[2016/17 h137: c16g⁵ c17v* c18g* c15.9s³ c17d³ c17d⁵ c15.9g^pu c16.7d⁵ Apr 16] lengthy **h–**
gelding: winning hurdler: useful chaser: won maiden at Listowel in September and Buck
House Novices' Chase at Punchestown (by 2¼ lengths from Ball d'Arc) in October: third
in Grade 2 novice at Cheltenham (14 lengths behind Le Prezien) in November and Grade 3
novice at Navan (length behind Attribution) in December: stays 2¼m: acts on good to firm
and heavy going: usually races close up. *Henry de Bromhead, Ireland*

THREE SWALLOWSNICK (IRE) 6 b.m. Westerner – Sitges (IRE) (Bob Back (USA)) **h– p**
[2016/17 b16d* b16d* h20d^pu Dec 10] £110,000 5-y-o: first foal: dam unraced half-sister **b105**
to fairly useful hurdler/useful chaser (stayed 2½m) Rock Street: won both starts in points:
useful form in bumpers: won maiden at Wexford (by 3 lengths from Sweet Shirleen) in
October and listed event at Navan (by 3 lengths from Glens Harmony) in November: went
wrong in mares maiden on hurdling debut. *Gordon Elliott, Ireland*

THREE WAYS 6 b.g. Flemensfirth (USA) – Serenique (Good Thyne (USA)) [2016/17 **h130** h119, b95: h19.5g⁴ h23.9g⁵ h21.4s⁴ h24.4d* h23.1g Mar 25] sturdy gelding: bumper winner: useful handicap hurdler: won at Doncaster (by 1¼ lengths from Abbreviate) in February: stays 3m: acts on soft going: wears tongue tie: often races prominently. *Jamie Snowden*

THREE WISE MEN (IRE) 7 b.g. Presenting – Bilboa (FR) (Phantom Breeze) [2016/17 **c138** h16s³ h16.5g⁶ c20g³ c19d⁵ c17d² c17.7s³ c21d Apr 28] €34,000 3-y-o: seventh foal: half- **h128** brother to fairly useful chaser Doctor Pat (2½m-2¾m winner, by Definite Article) and bumper winner/fair hurdler Glorious Twelfth (21f winner, by Old Vic): dam (c138/h154), 2m-19f hurdle/chase winner, also 1½m winner on Flat: fairly useful form over hurdles: useful form over fences: third in handicap at Limerick in March: stays 2¼m: acts on soft going. *Henry de Bromhead, Ireland*

THROTHETHATCH (IRE) 8 b.g. Beneficial – Castletownroche (IRE) (Saddlers' Hall **c114** (IRE)) [2016/17 c114, h–: h20g* c20.5g⁴ Oct 29] fair form over hurdles: won handicap at **h110** Fakenham in October: fair handicap chaser: likely to stay beyond 2½m: acts on heavy going: in tongue tie last 2 starts: usually front runner. *Dan Skelton*

THRTYPOINTSTOTHREE (IRE) 6 b.g. Kodiac – Miss Taken (IRE) (Dubai **h–** Destination (USA)) [2016/17 h16.8gᵖᵘ h16.7gᵖᵘ Sep 28] poor maiden on Flat, stays 9.5f: no form in 2 starts over hurdles, in blinkers on second occasion. *Nikki Evans*

THUMB STONE BLUES (IRE) 7 b.g. High Chaparral (IRE) – Jade River (FR) (Indian **h129** River (FR)) [2016/17 b16d⁵ h21.2d* h19.9d² h19.4s* h21.4m² h25g² Apr 24] third foal: **b94** brother to fair 2½m hurdle winner Ride The Range and half-brother to bumper winner Blue Article (by Definite Article): dam (h92) French 17f hurdle winner: fair form in bumpers for J. R. Barry: fairly useful hurdler: won maiden at Sedgefield in December and novice at Doncaster in March: second in handicap at Warwick in April: stays 25f: acts on good to firm and heavy going: in tongue tie last 5 starts: usually races prominently. *Kim Bailey*

THUNDER AND ROSES (IRE) 9 b.g. Presenting – Glen Empress (IRE) (Lancastrian) **c147** [2016/17 c138, h117: c30d⁵ c28gᵖᵘ c24d c29d² c24.5d c25d c25v² c25v² c24s⁶ **h–** c34.3dʰʳ c29d⁴ Apr 17] sturdy gelding: winning hurdler: smart handicap chaser: second at Fairyhouse (4¼ lengths behind Forever Gold) in December and in Bobbyjo Chase there (½ length behind Pleasant Company) in February: fourth in Irish Grand National Chase at same course (15½ lengths behind Our Duke) in April: left Ms Sandra Hughes after first start: stays 3¾m: acts on heavy going: wears headgear/tongue tie. *M. F. Morris, Ireland*

THUNDERING HOME 10 gr.g. Storming Home – Citrine Spirit (IRE) (Soviet Star **h104** (USA)) [2016/17 h97: h15.3m* h15.3m² h18.5mᵖᵘ h21.4m⁶ h16.8s h19.1d h19g⁵ h17.7vᵖᵘ h19g⁴ h15.3s* h15.9s* h16g h16.8g* Apr 26] smallish gelding: fair handicap hurdler: won at Wincanton (conditional event) early in season, same course/Plumpton in March and Exeter in April: stays 19f: acts on good to firm and heavy going: wears headgear/tongue tie: usually races prominently. *Richard Mitchell*

THUNDER PASS (IRE) 6 b.g. High Chaparral (IRE) – Hadarama (IRE) (Sinndar (IRE)) **h86** [2016/17 h20d⁵ h16.8g⁴ h18.7m h16.7g⁴ h19.5d⁵ h21.6v h20.5d⁴ Jan 12] close-coupled gelding: fairly useful on Flat, stays 1¾m: modest maiden hurdler: stays 2½m: acts on good to soft going: often in headgear. *David Pipe*

THUNDER SHEIK (IRE) 9 b.g. Green Tune (USA) – Realy Queen (USA) (Thunder **c–** Gulch (USA)) [2016/17 c–, h127: h17.2m⁵ h16.7g⁴ h16.4sᵖᵘ h16g⁴ h15.8g⁵ Apr 3] compact **h108** gelding: fair handicap hurdler: twice-raced chaser: best around 2m: acts on soft and good to firm going: wears headgear: usually in tongue tie. *Nigel Twiston-Davies*

THYMEANDTHYMEAGAIN 8 b.m. Alflora (IRE) – Four Thyme (Idiot's Delight) **c–** [2016/17 c–, h–: c21.1dᵖᵘ May 12] no form, including in points. *P. J. Thomas* **h–**

THYNE FOR GOLD (IRE) 6 b.g. Robin des Pres (FR) – My Name's Not Bin (IRE) **c–** (Good Thyne (USA)) [2016/17 h90, b–: h19.3m⁴ h23.4g* h23.9g h19.9g h19.9d* h21.3g³ **h111** h19.3g* h19.4g⁵ h19.3d⁴ h19.3d² h22g³ c15.9d⁵ Apr 5] useful-looking gelding: runner-up in Irish maiden point: fair handicap hurdler: won at Fakenham (novice event) early in season, Uttoxeter in October and Catterick (conditional event) in November: well held in novice handicap at Carlisle on chasing debut: stays 23f: acts on good to firm and heavy going: tried in hood: usually races close up. *Donald McCain*

TIAR NA NOG (IRE) 5 b.m. Ask – Carmencita (Rock of Gibraltar (IRE)) [2016/17 **b76** b13.7m⁵ ab16g⁴ ab16g Jan 31] third foal: half-sister to 1¼m winners Steppe Daughter and Banreenahreenkah (both by Steppe Dancer): dam unraced: modest form in bumpers. *Denis Coakley*

TICKANRUN (IRE) 7 gr.g. Tikkanen (USA) – Dusty Lane (IRE) (Electric) [2016/17 **h93** h92, b63: h22.7d² May 4] modest maiden hurdler: stays 3m: acts on heavy going: in headgear last 5 starts: usually races prominently. *Chris Grant*

TICKENWOLF (IRE) 7 gr.g. Tikkanen (USA) – Emma's Choice (IRE) (Indian Danehill **c118** (IRE)) [2016/17 h107: h19.7g* h22.1m⁵ h23.3d² c20.1s* c26.3g² c23.8dᶠ c24.2mᵖᵘ **h116** Apr 13] big, lengthy gelding: fairly useful handicap hurdler: won at Wetherby early in season: second at Hexham (amateur event) in June: fairly useful form over fences: won novice handicap at Hexham in September: stays 3¼m: acts on soft going: often races towards rear. *Micky Hammond*

TICKERTY BOO (IRE) 5 gr.m. Tikkanen (USA) – La Fille d'Or (IRE) (Goldmark **b–** (USA)) [2016/17 b16.7m⁵ b16g Apr 23] £12,000 3-y-o: first foal: dam French 2¼m/19f hurdle/chase winner: no form in bumpers. *Brian Ellison*

TICKET TO RIDE (FR) 4 b.g. Al Namix (FR) – Eightdaysaweek (Montjeu (IRE)) **b– p** [2016/17 b16.8g Apr 26] third foal: dam, 11f winner, half-sister to fairly useful hurdler (stays 21f) Act Alone: off mark in maiden points at second attempt: shaped better than result when tailed off in maiden bumper: capable of better. *E. Walker*

TIDAL WAY (IRE) 8 gr.g. Red Clubs (IRE) – Taatof (IRE) (Lahib (USA)) [2016/17 c–, **c–** h–: h16d² h16.7gᶠ May 14] sturdy, close-coupled gelding: modest handicap hurdler: didn't **h90** take to chasing: unproven beyond 17f: acted on soft going: wore headgear: tried in tongue tie: dead. *Shaun Lycett*

TIDESTREAM 7 b.g. Galileo (IRE) – Sweet Stream (ITY) (Shantou (USA)) [2016/17 **c–** h103: h19.6m⁵ h21.4m² c20mᵖᵘ Nov 8] good-topped gelding: modest handicap hurdler: **h88** pulled up in novice handicap on chasing debut: probably stays 2½m: acts on soft going: tried in visor: wears tongue tie. *Tim Vaughan*

TIERRA VERDE 6 b.m. Josr Algarhoud (IRE) – La Corujera (Case Law) [2016/17 b16.7g⁴ **b86** b16g² Apr 23] £3,200 3-y-o: sixth foal: half-sister to 2 winners, including fair hurdler Peadar Miguel (2m/17f winner, by Danroad): dam maiden on Flat (stayed 7f): fair form in bumpers: better effort when second in mares event at Wetherby. *Harry Whittington*

TIGER MOUNTAIN (IRE) 6 b.g. Mountain High (IRE) – Our Trick (IRE) (Flemensfirth **h105** (USA)) [2016/17 b72p: b16.2d h22.7s⁴ h19.9s² h24.3s h21.2s⁵ Jan 29] poor form in **b–** bumpers: fair form on second of 4 starts over hurdles: should be suited by further than 2½m: often races lazily: temperament under suspicion. *Malcolm Jefferson*

TIGER ROLL (IRE) 7 b.g. Authorized (IRE) – Swiss Roll (IRE) (Entrepreneur) [2016/17 **c151 §** h108: h20dᵖᵘ c17m* c19.9g* c22.7g⁴ c18.2gᵘʳ c20.5g² c18.2d² c20s² c24d* c24.4g³ c23g³ **h–** c31.8g* c29dᵖᵘ Apr 17] lengthy, leggy gelding: winning hurdler: smart chaser: won maiden at Ballinrobe early in season, novice at Kilbeggan (by 3½ lengths from Valyssa Monterg) in June, Munster National Handicap Chase at Limerick (by 7 lengths from Stellar Notion)

JT McNamara National Hunt Challenge Cup Amateur Riders' Novices' Chase, Cheltenham—2014 Triumph Hurdle winner Tiger Roll (No.16) is very much on a going day as he completes a unique Festival double; Missed Approach (left) takes second after Edwulf (No.10) goes wrong late on

Gigginstown House Stud's "Tiger Roll"

in October and National Hunt Chase at Cheltenham (by 3 lengths from Missed Approach) in March: stays 4m: acts on good to firm and heavy going: wears headgear/tongue tie: unreliable. *Gordon Elliott, Ireland*

TIGERS EYE 5 b.g. Bach (IRE) – This Side (IRE) (Dr Massini (IRE)) [2016/17 b17.7d⁵ Nov 4] in hood, well beaten in bumper. *Robert Stephens* **b–**

TIGER TREK (IRE) 8 b.g. Tiger Hill (IRE) – Zayana (IRE) (Darshaan) [2016/17 h15.7gᵖᵘ h16d² h16.3v⁵ c16.5g² Jul 26] fair handicap hurdler: fairly useful form over fences: second in handicap at Worcester in July: stays 2½m: acts on good to soft going. *Dr Richard Newland* **c118 h114**

TIGER TWENTY TWO 6 b.g. Authorized (IRE) – Collette's Choice (Royal Applause) [2016/17 h104: h16.7g² h18.6g⁴ h20.6g⁵ h18.6g⁶ h20.6s⁶ Dec 1] modest maiden hurdler: stays 19f: acts on good to firm going: temperamental. *Brian Rothwell* **h95 §**

TIGRIS RIVER (IRE) 6 b.g. Montjeu (IRE) – Hula Angel (USA) (Woodman (USA)) [2016/17 h130: h17s⁴ h16.1g⁵ Jul 28] useful handicap hurdler: fifth in Galway Hurdle (3½ lengths behind Clondaw Warrior) in July: stays 2¼m: acts on heavy going: tried in cheekpieces: wears tongue tie. *Joseph Patrick O'Brien, Ireland* **h137**

TIKANITE (IRE) 6 b.g. Tikkanen (USA) – Scented Night (IRE) (Mandalus) [2016/17 b16.4g⁶ b16v⁶ Dec 31] €8,500 3-y-o, £8,000 4-y-o: seventh foal: half-brother to a winning pointer by Broadway Flyer: dam unraced sister to fairly useful hurdler/chaser (stayed 25f) Hilltopper: modest form in bumpers. *Shaun Lycett* **b83**

TIKKANBAR (IRE) 6 b.g. Tikkanen (USA)   Fields of Barley (IRE) (Zaffaran (USA)) [2016/17 b15.8v² b16.2v* b16.8v* b17g Apr 7] €5,000 4-y-o: fourth foal: half-brother to a winning pointer by Swift Gulliver: dam unraced: fairly useful form in bumpers: won at Hereford in February and Sedgefield in March. *Neil Mulholland* **b104**

TIKKANDEMICKEY (IRE) 11 gr.g. Tikkanen (USA) – Miss Vikki (IRE) (Needle **c111**
Gun (IRE)) [2016/17 c116, h99: c20d* c20g⁴ c20.1s⁴ c22.4vᵘʳ c20v² h20.1vᵖᵘ c20d³ c30.6g **h–**
Apr 28] fairly useful hurdler at best, pulled up sixth outing in 2016/17: fair handicap
chaser: won at Carlisle in October: stays 3m: acts on heavy going: has worn headgear,
including last 4 starts. *Raymond Shiels*

TIKKAPICK (IRE) 7 b.g. Tikkanen (USA) – Takeanotherpick (IRE) (Winged Love **c93 x**
(IRE)) [2016/17 c94x, h94: c25.8g² c21.1s³ c19.7dᶠ h15.3s³ c17.4v² c25.1vᵖᵘ c19.2g⁴ **h90**
Apr 11] workmanlike gelding: modest maiden hurdler/chaser: stays 3¼m: acts on soft
going: usually in headgear in 2016/17: front runner/races prominently: often let down by
jumping over fences. *Colin Tizzard*

TIKKETORIDE 9 gr.g. Tikkanen (USA) – Safe Arrival (USA) (Shadeed (USA)) [2016/17 **c– §**
h–§: c21.7gᵖᵘ May 31] maiden hurdler: pulled up in novice on chasing debut: has worn **h– §**
headgear, including last 5 starts: in tongue tie last 2 starts: ungenuine. *Peter Pritchard*

TIKKINTHEBOX (IRE) 5 b.g. Tikkanen (USA) – Surfing France (FR) (Art Francais **h102**
(USA)) [2016/17 b16.3g h19.5d h15.3d h19.7s h15.3s² h15.8sᵖᵘ h19g² Mar 30] €12,000 **b–**
3-y-o: half-brother to 3 winners, including bumper winner/useful hurdler Ifyouletmefinish
(17f winner, by Bonbon Rose): dam, French 17f-2¾m chase winner, also 7f winner on Flat:
seventh in maiden bumper: fair form over hurdles: will stay beyond 2½m: acts on soft
going: in hood/tongue tie last 3 starts. *Jeremy Scott*

TIME AND AGAIN (FR) 7 b.g. Sassanian (USA) – Petillante Royale (FR) (Vertical **c97 x**
Speed (FR)) [2016/17 h106: h16.8g c16.4gᵖᵘ c16.5g⁵ c20.9sᵖᵘ c16gᶠ c16s² c17g³ Apr 15] **h79**
sturdy gelding: fair maiden hurdler, probably needed run on return: modest form over
fences: stays 2¼m: acts on soft going: in hood last 3 starts: tried in tongue tie: often let
down by jumping. *Tim Vaughan*

TIME AND TIMES (IRE) 5 b.g. Yeats (IRE) – Shuil Bob (IRE) (Bob Back (USA)) **h96**
[2016/17 b18s³ b19.5d² b14d h16d h16s h20v h22sᶠ h20v* h20s Apr 2] fifth foal: dam **b90**
(b85), ran twice in bumpers, half-sister to fairly useful hurdler/winning chaser (stayed 3m)
King Ar Aghaidh out of Stayers' Hurdle winner Shuil Ar Aghaidh: fair form when second
in maiden at Kilbeggan on second of 3 starts in bumpers: modest form over hurdles: won
handicap at Cork in March: bred to stay 3m: acts on heavy going. *D. McNamara, Ireland*

TIME FOR CHAMPERS (IRE) 7 b.m. Robin des Champs (FR) – Someone Told Me **h62**
(IRE) (Saddlers' Hall (IRE)) [2016/17 h–: h20d⁵ h20vᵖᵘ h15.8vᵖᵘ h21.9d⁶ Apr 16] poor
maiden hurdler: best effort at 2m: wears hood: has worn tongue tie. *Nikki Evans*

TIMEFORFIRTH (IRE) 7 b.m. Flemensfirth (USA) – Don't Be Upset (IRE) (Exit To **h64**
Nowhere (USA)) [2016/17 h–: h15.8v h16.7d h20.5g⁶ Jan 24] runner-up in Irish mares
maiden point: poor form over hurdles: usually races towards rear. *Jennie Candlish*

TIME FOR MABEL (FR) 6 ch.g. Soldier of Fortune (IRE) – Athens Two O Four (USA) **h132**
(Distant View (USA)) [2016/17 h17m² h16g⁴ h16m* h17m* h16.1g h16g⁴ h16g h16d
Apr 18] fairly useful on Flat, stays 15f: useful hurdler: won maiden at Ballinrobe in
2015/16: also won minor event at Limerick and handicap at Killarney (by 1¼ lengths from
Cliff House) in July: raced around 2m: acts on soft and good to firm going: usually wears
cheekpieces: tried in tongue tie. *E. J. O'Grady, Ireland*

TIME FOR VINO (IRE) 9 b.g. Oscar (IRE) – Santavino (IRE) (Be My Native (USA)) **c76**
[2016/17 c26.2d⁵ Apr 10] off mark in maiden points at eleventh attempt: in cheekpieces,
33/1, fifth in maiden hunter at Kelso (22 lengths behind Havana Jack) on chasing debut.
Miss D. V. Carter

TIMEFORWEST (IRE) 5 b.m. Westerner – Shang A Lang (IRE) (Commander Collins **h118**
(IRE)) [2016/17 b17g h21s⁶ h21v h20.7s h20.6g* h23.9g* h24.5m* h24.3d⁶ Apr 21] **b–**
£20,000 4-y-o: sturdy mare: third foal: dam (b72), ran twice in bumpers, closely related to
fairly useful hurdler/smart chaser (stayed 2½m) Down In Neworleans and half-sister to
smart hurdler (stayed 21f) Chomba Womba: runner-up in maiden point: considerably
handled when seventh in mares bumper at Aintree: fairly useful handicap hurdler: won at
Market Rasen/Taunton (conditional event) in March and Kempton (mares event) in April:
stays 3m: acts on good to firm going: usually travels strongly. *Jonjo O'Neill*

TIME IS MONEY 8 b.m. Presenting – No More Money (Alflora (IRE)) [2016/17 h–, b89: **h99**
h18.5m⁵ h20.3g* h22m h20.3g³ Aug 23] bumper winner: modest form over hurdles: won
mares maiden at Southwell in June: stays 2½m: best form on good going. *Emma Lavelle*

TIME IS TICKIN 11 b.g. Alflora (IRE) – Miss Chinchilla (Perpendicular) [2016/17 c98, **c–**
h–: c25.5gᵘʳ c25.5g⁴ Jun 7] multiple winning pointer: twice-raced hurdler: maiden chaser, **h–**
no form in 2016/17 (wore blinkers/tongue tie): stays 3¼m: acts on heavy going: front
runner/races prominently. *Diana Grissell*

TIM

TIMELY GIFT (IRE) 4 b.g. Presenting – Give It Time (Kayf Tara) [2016/17 h16.3g⁴ **h64** h16g h15.8d⁵ Apr 16] poor form over hurdles. *Tim Vaughan*

TIME OF MY LIFE (GER) 6 ch.g. Nayef (USA) – Tamaja (GER) (Tiger Hill (IRE)) **h65 p** [2016/17 h17s⁶ h16s h15.7g Jan 12] fairly useful on Flat, stays 16.5f: poor form over hurdles: tried in cheekpieces: remains with potential. *Patrick Holmes*

TIMETOBENEFIT (IRE) 6 b.m. Beneficial – Shokalocka Baby (IRE) (Accordion) **h68** [2016/17 b16.6d h19g⁶ Feb 21] £20,000 5-y-o: first foal: dam, winning pointer, half-sister **b–** to fairly useful hurdler/fair chaser (stayed 3¼m) Mr Supreme (by Beneficial): off mark in Irish points at third attempt: tailed off in mares bumper: showed a bit when well beaten in mares novice on hurdling debut. *Richard Phillips*

TIME WISE 7 b.m. Kayf Tara – Ceoperk (IRE) (Executive Perk) [2016/17 b–: h21v **h–** h20.7s^pu h20.7g Apr 3] no form over hurdles. *Richard Phillips*

TIMON'S TARA 8 gr.m. Kayf Tara – Princess Timon (Terimon) [2016/17 h108: c20s^pu **c112** c20d^F c22.5v* h21.2s^pu c22.7s³ c20v⁴ c24v² Mar 22] well-made mare: fair hurdler at best: **h–** fair form over fences: won handicap at Uttoxeter in January: stays 3m: best form on heavy going: usually wears headgear: usually leads. *Robin Dickin*

TIMOTEO (FR) 4 b.g. Diamond Green (FR) – Goldnella (FR) (Goldneyev (USA)) **h120** [2016/17 h16.9m³ h16.9g² h16.6g⁵ h15.5d⁵ h16.7s² h16.6g⁴ h18.8g² Mar 25] sturdy gelding: dam French 17f hurdle winner: maiden on Flat: fairly useful maiden hurdler: second in juvenile at Bangor in January and juvenile handicap at Newbury in March: left H. de Lageneste after second start: stays 19f: acts on soft going: tried in hood: often races towards rear/travels strongly. *Alan King*

TIMS CRUSADER (IRE) 9 ch.g. Fruits of Love (USA) – Duiske Abbey (IRE) (Roselier **c–** (FR)) [2016/17 c16.5m May 19] dual winning pointer: maiden hurdler: well beaten in **h–** novice handicap on chasing debut. *Sarah-Jayne Davies*

TINCTORIA 7 b.m. Oratorio (IRE) – Blue Indigo (FR) (Pistolet Bleu (IRE)) [2016/17 h–: **h–** h15.8g h23.1g Sep 28] smallish, good-bodied mare: maiden hurdler, no form since 2013/14: wears headgear: often in tongue tie. *Adrian Wintle*

TINDARO (FR) 10 gr.g. Kingsalsa (USA) – Star's Mixa (FR) (Linamix (FR)) [2016/17 **c127** c134, h–: c19.2g³ c21.4g c19.4g* c19.4g c19.1g⁴ c23g^pu Jan 11] tall gelding: winning **h–** hurdler: useful handicap chaser: won at Stratford in August: stays 21f: acts on good to firm and good to soft going: has worn headgear, including last 4 starts: wears tongue tie. *Paul Webber*

TINELYRA (IRE) 11 b.g. Mr Combustible (IRE) – Ladyogan (IRE) (Torus) [2016/17 **c72 §** c89§, h–§: c24d³ c20d^F Jun 19] workmanlike gelding: maiden hurdler: modest handicap **h– §** chaser: stays 3m: acts on good to soft going: usually wears hood: wears tongue tie: unreliable. *Fergal O'Brien*

TINGO IN THE TALE (IRE) 8 b.g. Oratorio (IRE) – Sunlit Skies (Selkirk (USA)) **h83** [2016/17 h–: h15.8g⁵ h19.6g⁶ h16m⁶ h21.3d^pu Mar 21] poor maiden hurdler nowadays: left David Arbuthnot after third start: best around 2m: acts on soft going: tried in tongue tie. *Sophie Leech*

TINKERS HILL TOMMY (IRE) 6 b.g. King's Theatre (IRE) – Satco Street (IRE) **c108** (Satco (FR)) [2016/17 h72, b–: c23.6m² Apr 28] multiple winning pointer: once-raced **h–** hurdler: 16/1, second in novice hunter at Chepstow (5 lengths behind Repeat Business) on chasing debut. *Mrs Bridget Lewis*

TINKER TIME (IRE) 9 b.g. Turtle Island (IRE) – Gypsys Girl (IRE) (Husyan (USA)) **c128** [2016/17 c130, h–: c23.6g c23.8d² c18.2m³ c23g^pu c26g⁴ c28.4g² c24m⁴ Apr 18] **h–** workmanlike gelding: winning hurdler: useful handicap chaser: second at Ascot in November and Taunton in March: stays 3½m: acts on heavy going. *Bob Buckler*

TIN POT MAN (IRE) 11 br.g. Tillerman – White-Wash (Final Straw) [2016/17 c32.5g **c80** Apr 27] multiple winning pointer: winning hurdler: poor chaser nowadays: stays easy 3m: **h–** acts on any going: has worn headgear: wears tongue tie. *G. Hiscock*

TIN SOLDIER (FR) 6 b.g. Soldier of Fortune (IRE) – Everlast (FR) (Anabaa (USA)) **h143** [2016/17 h24.5s* h20.3v* h21.1g h24d³ Apr 26] sturdy gelding: lightly-raced maiden on Flat: smart hurdler: in frame several times for M. Seror in France: won maiden at Fairyhouse (by 1¼ lengths from Champagne Classic) in January and Michael Purcell Memorial Novices' Hurdle at Thurles (by length from Moulin A Vent) in February: third in Irish Daily Mirror Novices' Hurdle at Punchestown (2¾ lengths behind Champagne Classic) in April: stays 3m: acts on heavy going: tried in headgear. *W. P. Mullins, Ireland*

TINTED ROSE 5 ch.m. Black Sam Bellamy (IRE) – Miniature Rose (Anshan) [2016/17 **h104** b91: b17.7s* h20.6g³ h15.7d² h21.2d⁴ h18.6s³ h18.7gᵖᵘ Apr 15] fair form in bumpers: won **b87** maiden at Fontwell in October: fair form over hurdles: stays 21f: acts on soft going. *Charlie Longsdon*

TINTERN THEATRE (IRE) 6 b.g. King's Theatre (IRE) – Rith Ar Aghaidh (IRE) **h125** (Phardante (FR)) [2016/17 h20g³ h15.8v* h18.8d⁴ h19.9v² h19.3s⁵ h19.8d h21.2g* Apr 3] €35,000 5-y-o: sturdy gelding: half-brother to several winners, including fair hurdler/ chaser Rith Bob (2½m-2¾m winner, by Bob Back) and fair hurdler/winning pointer Fishing Bridge (2½m-3m winner, by Definite Article): dam, 2m hurdle winner, out of Stayers' Hurdle winner Shuil Ar Aghaidh: twice raced in Irish maiden points, runner-up second occasion: fairly useful hurdler: won maiden at Ludlow in November and novice there in April: second in handicap at Uttoxeter in January: will be suited by 3m: acts on heavy going: usually leads. *Nigel Twiston-Davies*

TINY DANCER (IRE) 9 b.g. Darsi (FR) – Taipans Girl (IRE) (Taipan (IRE)) [2016/17 **c–** c94, h85: c21.1sᵘʳ May 3] workmanlike gelding: maiden hurdler: fair chaser at best, failed **h–** to complete on sole outing in 2016/17: stays 25f: acts on heavy going: in visor last 4 starts. *Chris Grant*

TIPPERAIRY (IRE) 6 b.g. Flemensfirth (USA) – Bambootcha (IRE) (Saddlers' Hall **h–** (IRE)) [2016/17 h82, b75: h20.5vᵖᵘ Feb 1] rather unfurnished gelding: maiden hurdler, pulled up in handicap on sole outing in 2016/17: usually races towards rear. *Dan Skelton*

TIQUER (FR) 9 b.g. Equerry (USA) – Tirenna (FR) (Sleeping Car (FR)) [2016/17 c86, **c121** h–: c20v* c19.2v³ c19.1s* Mar 3] maiden hurdler: fairly useful handicap chaser: won at **h–** Uttoxeter in November and Doncaster in March: stays 2½m: acts on heavy going: tried in cheekpieces. *Alan Jones*

TIRADIA (FR) 10 b.g. Without Connexion (IRE) – Jimanji (FR) (Kadalko (FR)) [2016/17 **h91** h103: h16g h19.6g⁵ h16d⁴ h18.7m h16g⁵ h15.7g⁵ h19.6m³ h15.5g⁶ h15.8d* h17.7g h20g⁵ h15.8g Apr 28] sturdy gelding: modest handicap hurdler nowadays: won lady riders event at Huntingdon in March: stays 2½m: acts on soft and good to firm going: usually races towards rear. *J. R. Jenkins*

TIR DUBH (IRE) 8 br.m. Sandmason – Turbine Hill (IRE) (Hubbly Bubbly (USA)) **h94** [2016/17 h100: h25dᵖᵘ h23.3m h23g⁴ h21.2d⁴ h21.6d³ h26.5g Sep 16] modest hurdler: won maiden at Worcester in July: stays 3m: acts on good to soft going: in cheekpieces last 5 starts. *Robert Stephens*

TISFREETDREAM (IRE) 16 b.g. Oscar (IRE) – Gayley Gale (IRE) (Strong Gale) **c–** [2016/17 c–, h75§: h23.3d⁵ h20.3d³ h24v⁶ h25.5sᵖᵘ Jan 4] small gelding: poor handicap **h66 §** hurdler: winning chaser: stays 25f: acts on good to firm and heavy going: wears headgear: has worn tongue tie: ungenuine. *Peter Pritchard*

TISH HALL (IRE) 7 b.m. Desert King (IRE) – Sultana (GER) (Law Society (USA)) **h–** [2016/17 h–: h16.2g h16.2f⁶ h20.2d⁵ h16.2s h23g²d Aug 7] no form. *Stuart Crawford, Ireland*

TITANS APPROACH (IRE) 8 b.g. High Chaparral (IRE) – Armelles Approach (IRE) **c84** (Definite Article) [2016/17 c93, h92: c22.5d⁴ h22g³ h21.6g² h23d⁵ h23.3g Jul 22] **h95** modest maiden hurdler/chaser: stays 3m: acts on good to soft going: wears headgear. *Graeme McPherson*

TITCH STRIDER (IRE) 12 b.m. Milan – Just Little (Mtoto) [2016/17 h99: h21.6dˢᵘ **h78** h21.6d⁵ h21.4m⁴ h21.4m⁴ h25.6g⁶ h21.6s⁵ h23.9m⁶ h23.9g³ h23.9g h23.1s h23.1gᵖᵘ Apr 11] small, workmanlike mare: modest handicap hurdler, below best in 2016/17: stays 2¾m: acts on good to firm and good to soft going: often races in rear. *John Panvert*

TITIAN BOY (IRE) 8 ch.g. Spadoun (FR) – Leodotcom (IRE) (Safety Catch (USA)) **c101** [2016/17 h74: c20.5s* c20.5s* c15.5s³ c16.3v² Mar 18] maiden hurdler: fair form over **h–** fences: won handicaps at Ayr in November (novice event) and December: stays 2½m: raced only on soft/heavy going: in tongue tie last 2 starts: usually leads. *N. W. Alexander*

TITI DE MONTMARTRE (FR) 4 b.f. Montmartre (FR) – Royal Tiara (UAE) **h134** (Machiavellian (USA)) [2016/17 h15.9s² h14.9s⁵ h17.4s⁶ h17.4s* h17.9s⁴ h17.9s⁵ h17.9s* h17.4v* h16.8g h17.9s⁵ h19.4s⁴ Apr 29] smallish filly: half-sister to French 17f chase winner Tiara Man (by Muhtathir) and French 17f hurdle winner Air Force Royal (by Soldier of Fortune): once raced on Flat: useful hurdler: won fillies juvenile at Auteuil in June, and Prix Bournosienne at same course (by ½ length from Dabrovka) and Prix General de Saint-Didier at Enghien (by length from Desinvolte) in November: below form in Dawn Run Mares' Novices' Hurdle at Cheltenham in March: stays 2¼m: best form on soft/heavy going: in cheekpieces last 5 starts. *R. Collet, France*

TJONGEJONGE (FR) 6 b.g. Blue Bresil (FR) – Vavea (FR) (Saint des Saints (FR)) **c125** [2016/17 c–, h118: c23.9g* c22.4g c22.7s⁴ c22.4dᶠ h23.1m³ Apr 17] sturdy gelding: fairly **h93** useful hurdler at best: fairly useful handicap chaser: won at Market Rasen in November: stays 3m: acts on soft and good to firm going. *Charlie Longsdon*

TOARMANDOWITHLOVE (IRE) 9 ch.m. Choisir (AUS) – Deadly Buzz (IRE) **h80** (Darshaan) [2016/17 h86: h23.9m⁴ h20.1g² h20.2f⁴ h23.3s⁴ h22d³ h22.7s⁴ h25.3d⁵ h22s h20.6g³ Apr 8] poor maiden hurdler: stays 25f: acts on heavy going: has worn blinkers: wears tongue tie. *Susan Corbett*

TOAST AND JAM (IRE) 8 b.g. Clerkenwell (USA) – Summittotalkabout (IRE) (Lahib **c71 x** (USA)) [2016/17 c71x, h67: c22.5d² c20.3d⁶ c23g c23.9gᵖᵘ Aug 13] maiden hurdler: poor **h–** maiden chaser: stays 3m: acts on soft going: has worn hood: wears tongue tie: often let down by jumping. *Claire Dyson*

TOBACCO ROAD (IRE) 7 b.g. Westerner – Virginias Best (King's Best (USA)) **h100** [2016/17 h76p: h16.3g⁶ h16g h16.7g³ h15.7g² h19.7sᵘʳ h16.5g⁴ h16.8d Feb 24] fair maiden hurdler: best effort at 2m: best form on good going: wears hood: often races prominently/ freely. *David Pipe*

TOBEFAIR 7 b.g. Central Park (IRE) – Nan (Buckley) [2016/17 h110: h23.9g* h23.6g* **h137** h26s* h24.2d* h24g Mar 16] sturdy gelding: useful handicap hurdler: progressed plenty more in 2016/17, and won at Ffos Las in November, Chepstow in December, Warwick in January and Newbury (by 1½ lengths from Morello Royale) in February: stays 3¼m: acts on soft and good to firm going: has worn cheekpieces, including final start: often races towards rear. *Debra Hamer*

TO BEGIN 6 b.g. Tobougg (IRE) – Sagina (Shernazar) [2016/17 c99, h109: c21.3g⁶ **c86** c24.2gᵖᵘ c23mᵖᵘ Jul 4] dual point winner: fair hurdler: modest maiden chaser: stays 27f: **h–** acts on good to firm and good to soft going: wears tongue tie: often races towards rear: has bled. *Charlie Mann*

TOBERDOWNEY (IRE) 5 br.m. Stowaway – Velsheda (IRE) (Royal Vulcan) [2016/17 **h114** b16.2s* h16.3g⁵ h21s² h15.3s* h21.2d² h18.5d³ h18.9g⁶ Apr 15] €16,000 3-y-o: ninth foal: **b90** dam (h109), 17f-2½m hurdle winner (stayed 3m), half-sister to useful hurdler/chaser (2m-21f winner) Major Rumpus: won bumper at Perth (by 4 lengths from Tyrrell's Succes) in July for Stuart Crawford: fair form over hurdles: won mares novice at Wincanton in December: stays 21f: acts on soft going. *Oliver Sherwood*

TOBOGGAN'S GIFT 5 b.m. Major Cadeaux – Toboggan Lady (Tobougg (IRE)) **h88** [2016/17 h–: h17.2m² h19.6gᵘʳ Jul 29] lengthy mare: modest form on completed start over hurdles in 2016/17: likely to stay 2½m. *Ann Duffield*

TOBY LERONE (IRE) 10 b.g. Old Vic – Dawn's Double (IRE) (King's Ride) [2016/17 **c128** c130, h115: c20.9v* c22.7s² c24.5s* c25.1m³ Apr 5] rangy gelding: winning hurdler: **h–** useful chaser: won hunters at Hereford in February and Towcester in March: stays 3m: acts on heavy going: has worn headgear, including in 2016/17: front runner/races prominently. *Dan Skelton*

TOCORORO (IRE) 5 b.m. Teofilo (IRE) – Firecrest (IRE) (Darshaan) [2016/17 h16d⁴ **c130** h16.5g* h16g³ h16d³ c18.2g³ c22d* c18.2d* c16dᵖᵘ Oct 1] sister to fairly useful 2m hurdle **h123** winner Bantam and half-sister to 3 winning hurdlers, including useful winner around 2m All Set To Go (by Verglas): fair maiden on Flat, stays 11f: fairly useful hurdler: won minor event at Ballinrobe early in season: third in Grimes Hurdle at Tipperary (11½ lengths behind Ivan Grozny) in July: useful form over fences: won mares maiden at Tramore in August and Ballybrit Novices' Chase at Galway (by 16 lengths from Tiger Roll) in September: stays 2¾m: acts on heavy going: usually in hood: wears tongue tie. *Gordon Elliott, Ireland*

TODAY PLEASE (IRE) 7 b.g. Westerner – Casiana (GER) (Acatenango (GER)) **c114** [2016/17 h–p: h15.7g⁴ h16d⁴ h15.8m² h16g³ h16.5mᵖᵘ h16.6s* c16.1m* Apr 13] fair **h111** handicap hurdler: won at Worcester (novice event) in June and Doncaster in March: 11/8, also won novice handicap at Towcester (by 7 lengths from Fingers Crossed) on chasing debut: unproven beyond 17f: acts on soft and good to firm going: has worn tongue tie: often races prominently/travels strongly. *Henry Oliver*

TODD 7 b.g. Gentlewave (IRE) – Voice (Zamindar (USA)) [2016/17 h20g³ Oct 14] **h95** compact gelding: fair handicap hurdler, respectable effort on sole outing in 2016/17 (wore cheekpieces): stays 21f: acts on heavy going. *Anabel K. Murphy*

Betfair Cash Out Handicap Hurdle, Newbury—Tobefair (right) rallies strongly to beat Morello Royale and complete a remarkable seven-timer

TOE THE LINE (IRE) 8 b.m. Shantou (USA) – Bluebell Line (IRE) (Charnwood Forest (IRE)) [2016/17 h16s² h20d³ h16v⁴ h16g* h18s² h16.8gᶠ Mar 16] second foal: dam 1½m winner: useful on Flat, stayed 2m: fairly useful form over hurdles: won mares maiden at Leopardstown in January: second in mares handicap there in February: stayed 2½m: acted on soft going: dead. *John E. Kiely, Ireland* **h127**

TOE TO TOE (IRE) 9 br.g. Presenting – Tavildara (IRE) (Kahyasi) [2016/17 c78, h72: c20.9vᵖᵘ c20.9gᵖᵘ c16.5gᵖᵘ c17g⁶ c20m⁴ Oct 20] winning hurdler: poor maiden chaser: stays easy 2½m: acts on good to firm and good to soft going: has worn headgear, including last 2 starts: wears tongue tie: often races freely, tends to find little. *Kerry Lee* **c64 h–**

TOFFEE HOLLAND 6 b.g. Overbury (IRE) – Roslin (Roscoe Blake) [2016/17 b16.3dʳᵒ b16d⁴ b16.4s Nov 13] workmanlike gelding: poor form in bumpers: tried in hood. *Martin Keighley* **b72**

TOKARAMORE 5 b.m. Sulamani (IRE) – More Likely (Shambo) [2016/17 b16.2d* b16.2s* b16.4s Nov 12] small mare: second foal: half-sister to bumper winner Shambougg (by Tobougg): dam (c125/h97) 2m-25f hurdle/chase winner: fairly useful form in bumpers: won maiden at Kelso in September and mares event there in November: wears hood. *Iain Jardine* **b95**

TOKYO JAVILEX (FR) 10 b.g. Sleeping Car (FR) – Etoile du Lion (FR) (New Target) [2016/17 c–, h105: h23.1m h25.6gᵖᵘ h26.5d h23.3g h23g h27g⁵ h23.3g³ h25.6s⁴ Oct 1] sturdy gelding: modest handicap hurdler nowadays: winning chaser: stays 27f: acts on soft going: has worn headgear, including in 2016/17: wears tongue tie: often races towards rear: temperamental. *Nigel Hawke* **c– h90 §**

TOLEDO GOLD (IRE) 11 ch.g. Needwood Blade – Eman's Joy (Lion Cavern (USA)) [2016/17 c120, h–: c17.3m⁶ c17.3d⁵ h16.7g h15.7g⁴ h16.8gᵖᵘ c15.5d⁴ c15.5g⁴ Oct 29] medium-sized gelding: modest handicap hurdler/fairly useful handicap chaser at best, below form in 2016/17: unproven beyond 17f: acts on soft and good to firm going: has worn headgear, including in 2016/17: wears tongue tie: front runner. *Maurice Barnes* **c100 h73**

TOLETHORPE 6 ch.g. Halling (USA) – Tcherina (IRE) (Danehill Dancer (IRE)) [2016/17 b106p: h18.1d⁵ Apr 10] useful bumper winner: 18/1, some encouragement when fifth in novice at Kelso (11 lengths behind Blue Hussar) on hurdling debut: should improve. *Laura Morgan* **h99 p**

TOLKEINS TANGO (IRE) 9 ch.g. Beneficial – Aule (FR) (Vaguely Pleasant (FR)) **c111 §**
[2016/17 c117§, h–§: c19.2s³ c22.6d^{ur} c19.4g^{pu} Apr 8] well-made gelding: winning **h– §**
hurdler: fairly useful handicap chaser, below form in 2016/17: stays 21f: acts on heavy
going: wears tongue tie: untrustworthy. *Victor Dartnall*

TOMAHAWK WOOD 8 ch.g. Courteous – Meda's Song (Master Willie) [2016/17 h86: **c–**
c20.1s⁵ h20.5v* h20.5v⁵ h18.1d Apr 10] modest handicap hurdler: won at Ayr in January: **h93**
well beaten in novice handicap on chasing debut: stays 2¾m: best form on soft/heavy
going: tried in tongue tie. *Donald Whillans*

TOM BACH (IRE) 13 ch.g. Bach (IRE) – Fiovefontaine (IRE) (Lafontaine (USA)) **c–**
[2016/17 c64, h–: c25.5s^{ur} c25.3v^{pu} Dec 12] maiden hurdler: modest chaser at best, little **h–**
form since 2013/14: stays 25f: best form on heavy going: wears headgear. *Hywel Evans*

TOMBSTONE (IRE) 7 ch.g. Robin des Champs (FR) – Connaught Hall (IRE) (Un **h148**
Desperado (FR)) [2016/17 h145, b110: h16s³ h16v* h21.1g h20.6g Apr 28] strong
gelding: smart hurdler: won Red Mills Trial Hurdle at Gowran (by 4 lengths from Jezki) in
February: third in minor event at Navan (2¾ lengths behind Jezki) in January and Keelings
Irish Strawberry Hurdle at Fairyhouse (17½ lengths behind Renneti) in April: should stay
beyond 2¼m: acts on heavy going: tried in hood. *Gordon Elliott, Ireland*

TOMKEVI (FR) 6 b.g. Khalkevi (IRE) – Tamsna (FR) (Smadoun (FR)) [2016/17 c112, **c118**
h117: h17.1d h19.9d⁶ h19.9s h20.6s⁵ h19.3s² h19.9v* h20.5v^{pu} c20d² Apr 5] fair handicap **h111**
hurdler: won at Sedgefield in February: fairly useful handicap chaser: second at Carlisle in
April: stays 2½m: acts on heavy going: has worn headgear, including last 4 starts: in tongue
tie last 5 starts: often races towards rear. *Rebecca Menzies*

TOMMY O'DWYER (IRE) 8 b.g. Milan – Always Present (IRE) (Presenting) [2016/17 **c88**
c24d^{ur} h21.3s⁵ h19.7d c20.9d⁵ c26.2g Apr 15] multiple point winner: fairly useful form **h80**
over hurdles in 2014/15, well below that level in 2016/17: modest form on second of 3
starts over fences: left Micky Hammond after third start: stays 3m: acts on good to soft
going: sometimes in cheekpieces. *Patrick Holmes*

TOMMY RAPPER (IRE) 6 b.g. Milan – Supreme Evening (IRE) (Supreme Leader) **h137**
[2016/17 b107: h19.7s^{ur} h21s² h19.6d³ h24g Mar 17] useful-looking gelding: useful
bumper performer: useful form over hurdles: third in listed novice at Huntingdon (1¾
lengths behind Keeper Hill) in February: usually races towards rear, often travels strongly.
Dan Skelton

TOMMY SILVER (FR) 5 b.g. Silver Cross (FR) – Sainte Mante (FR) (Saint des Saints **h143**
(FR)) [2016/17 h136p: h15.8s⁵ h16.3d h16.5g* h20.3g h15.9m* h16g⁶ Apr 22] tall, good-
topped gelding: will make a chaser: useful handicap hurdler: won at Taunton in February
and Plumpton (by 9 lengths from Song Light) in April: should stay 2½m: acts on good to
firm and good to soft going: has worn tongue tie, including in 2016/17: often races
prominently. *Paul Nicholls*

TOMMY THE RASCAL 7 b.g. Multiplex – Tina Gee (Orchestra) [2016/17 h–: h23.3v⁶ **c83**
h24s^{pu} h25d* c21.2g² c21.2s^R c20.2g² c25.2s² c25.6d³ c24s² Mar 30] sturdy gelding: poor **h68**
handicap hurdler: won at Huntingdon in November: poor form over fences: stays 25f: acts
on soft going: wears cheekpieces: usually races close up: temperament under suspicion.
Jennie Candlish

TOM NEARY (IRE) 10 b.g. Atraf – La Fandango (IRE) (Taufan (USA)) [2016/17 c105, **c111**
h–: c25.1m^{ur} c24.2m³ c21.1d c24.2g³ Apr 11] lightly-raced hurdler: fair handicap chaser: **h–**
stays 3m: acts on good to firm going: wears tongue tie. *Robert Walford*

TOMSK (FR) 7 ch.g. Priolo (USA) – Kauto Relstar (FR) (Art Bleu) [2016/17 h–: h23.4g^{pu} **h–**
May 22] angular gelding: little form: tried in visor/tongue tie. *Tim Vaughan*

TOM WADE (IRE) 10 b.g. Rakti – Plutonia (Sadler's Wells (USA)) [2016/17 h16.7g^F **h77**
h16d h16.7g⁶ h15.8m⁵ h15.8g h15.8d⁵ h15.7g⁴ h15.8d^F h15.8d^{pu} Oct 13] compact gelding:
poor handicap hurdler nowadays: best around 2m: acts on soft and good to firm going: has
worn headgear, including last 4 starts: has worn tongue tie, including last 3 starts: tends to
find little. *Barry Leavy*

TONGANUI (IRE) 6 ch.g. Stowaway – Murrosie (IRE) (Anshan) [2016/17 b68: h15.8d⁶ **h94**
h18.5g³ h19.1s⁵ h19.8d h21.6g⁵ Apr 11] modest form over hurdles: stays 2¼m: tried in
cheekpieces. *Harry Fry*

TONTO'S SPIRIT 5 b.g. Authorized (IRE) – Desert Royalty (IRE) (Alhaarth (IRE)) **h123**
[2016/17 h–: h17.2m* h19.3d³ h16.8s* h17s* h15.7g Apr 15] fairly useful form over
hurdles: won novice at Cartmel early in season and handicaps at Sedgefield in January and
Carlisle in February: stays 19f: acts on soft and good to firm going: usually leads.
Kenneth Slack

TONY STAR (FR) 10 b.g. Lone Bid (FR) – Effet de Star (FR) (Grand Tresor (FR))   **c117**
[2016/17 c117, h–: c26.3g⁴ c24.5g* h23.9d* c26.1gᵖᵘ c21.4g c22.5g c25.1v⁴ c23.8s⁴   **h118**
c21.1g Apr 6] sturdy gelding: dual point winner: useful handicap hurdler at best: won at
Ffos Las in June: fairly useful chaser nowadays: won 2-runner hunter at Towcester early in
season: stays 3¼m: acts on heavy going: usually in cheekpieces in 2016/17: tried in tongue
tie. *Mickey Bowen*

TOO FAR GONE (IRE) 6 br.g. Jeremy (USA) – Rockahoolababy (IRE) (Kalanisi (IRE))   **h–**
[2016/17 h–, b–: h16m Jul 4] no form: dead. *Henry Oliver*

TOO HOT TO BOUGGIE 6 b.m. Tobougg (IRE) – Princess Hotpot (IRE) (King's   **b–**
Ride) [2016/17 b16g Feb 25] half-sister to several winners, including useful hurdler/chaser
Tarablaze (19f-25f winner, by Kayf Tara) and fair hurdler No Guarantees (2½m winner, by
Master Willie), stayed 3m: dam (c76/h102) 2m/19f hurdle/chase winner: tailed off in
bumper. *Derek Frankland*

TOOLA BOOLA 7 b.m. Tobougg (IRE) – Forsythia (Most Welcome) [2016/17 h74:   **h75**
h16.4s h16.4v² h16.8v⁴ h17g⁴ Apr 15] poor handicap hurdler: raced mainly around 2m:
acts on heavy going: tried in visor: temperament under suspicion. *Jedd O'Keeffe*

TOO MANY CHIEFS (IRE) 6 br.g. Indian River (FR) – Wahiba Hall (IRE) (Saddlers'   **c–**
Hall (IRE)) [2016/17 h106: h24.3s³ h24.4g h24.3s⁶ c21.6s⁶ c24.5sᵖᵘ h23.3s⁴ h22.7d*   **h101**
h20.1g Apr 25] maiden pointer: fair handicap hurdler: won at Kelso in April: little impact
in 2 starts over fences: stays 3m: acts on heavy going: tried in cheekpieces. *Sharon Watt*

TOO MANY DIAMONDS (IRE) 6 br.g. Diamond Green (FR) – Too Much Color   **h61**
(USA) (Spectrum (IRE)) [2016/17 h16.3dᵖᵘ h19.9g h15.8g h16.7dᶠ h16.5g Apr 6] modest
maiden on Flat, stays 8.5f: poor maiden hurdler: unproven beyond 2m: best form on good
going: in cheekpieces/tongue tie last 3 starts: has joined Dan Skelton. *Clare Ellam*

TOO MUCH TOO SOON (IRE) 8 b.g. Craigsteel – Zara Rose (IRE) (Zaffaran (USA))   **c–**
[2016/17 c–, h–: c21.4g⁶ c20.2gᵖᵘ Jan 12] sturdy gelding: maiden hurdler: maiden chaser,   **h–**
no form in 2016/17: unproven beyond 2m: acts on soft going: in cheekpieces last 3 starts:
wears tongue tie. *Paul Webber*

TOO SCOOPS (IRE) 10 ch.g. Alderbrook – Accordion To Bob (IRE) (Accordion)   **c63 §**
[2016/17 c116, h115: c20s⁴ May 11] fairly useful hurdler: fairly useful maiden chaser, well   **h– §**
beaten sole outing in 2016/17: stays 2½m: acts on heavy going: has worn headgear/tongue
tie, including in 2016/17: often leads: weak finisher. *Richard Woollacott*

TOOTSIE'S TRIUMPH 5 b.g. Cloudings (IRE) – Tootsie Too (Overbury (IRE))   **b–**
[2016/17 b15.8g b16g Oct 9] no form in 2 bumpers. *Mike Hammond*

TOPAMICHI 7 b.g. Beat Hollow – Topatori (IRE) (Topanoora) [2016/17 h–: h16.7gᶠ   **h–**
May 15] compact gelding: fairly useful on Flat, stays 10.5f: no form over hurdles. *Mark H.
Tompkins*

TOP AND DROP 6 b.m. Kayf Tara – Ismene (FR) (Bad Conduct (USA)) [2016/17 h90,   **c112 p**
b–: h16d² h20v² c21.3dᵘʳ h17.7s⁵ Mar 13] fair form over hurdles: upsides when unseated   **h100**
rider 3 out in novice handicap won by Money Maid at Wetherby on chasing debut: should
stay beyond 2½m: acts on heavy going: front runner/races prominently, often travels
strongly: remains with potential as a chaser. *Venetia Williams*

TOP BILLING 8 br.g. Monsun (GER) – La Gandilie (FR) (Highest Honor (FR)) [2016/17   **c–**
c122, h133: h23.9d h20d h23.1s h21.4s² h26sᵖᵘ h22.7v h24.3v⁵ h20.9sᵖᵘ Mar 25] leggy   **h108 §**
gelding: useful handicap hurdler, below form in 2016/17: maiden chaser: stays 3¼m: acts
on heavy going: has worn headgear: front runner/races prominently: temperamental.
Nicky Richards

TOP CAT DJ (IRE) 9 ch.g. St Jovite (USA) – Lady Coldunell (Deploy) [2016/17 c75, h–:   **c65 §**
c21.3gᵖᵘ c23.8m⁵ c20.1dᵖᵘ c20.1s⁶ c23.8g³ c23.8gᵖᵘ Feb 4] maiden hurdler: poor maiden   **h–**
chaser: stays 3m: acts on good to soft going: wears headgear: in tongue tie last 2 starts: best
treated with caution. *Chris Grant*

TOP CAT HENRY (IRE) 9 b.g. Dr Massini (IRE) – Bells Chance (IRE) (Needle Gun   **c125**
(IRE)) [2016/17 c128, h–: c21.1sᵇᵈ c20.9m³ c19.4g⁵ c26.6g⁵ c19.9g* c21.1g c23.8gᵖᵘ   **h–**
Apr 28] useful-looking gelding: winning hurdler: fairly useful chaser: won hunter at
Musselburgh in March: left Dr Richard Newland after third start: stays 21f: acts on good to
firm and heavy going: wears headgear/tongue tie. *N. W. Alexander*

TOP GAMBLE (IRE) 9 ch.g. Presenting – Zeferina (IRE) (Sadler's Wells (USA)) **c159**
[2016/17 c160, h–: c15.9s⁵ c20.8s³ c16.3s³ c15.9g⁴ c19.9g⁶ Apr 7] rangy gelding: winning **h–**
hurdler: high-class chaser: third in Grade 3 handicap (3½ lengths behind Shantou Flyer)
and Clarence House Chase (7¾ lengths behind Un de Sceaux) in January, both at
Cheltenham: stays 21f: acts on good to firm and heavy going: has worn tongue tie,
including last 4 starts. *Kerry Lee*

TOP GARRY (FR) 4 ch.g. Ballingarry (IRE) – Top Fleur (FR) (Mansonnien (FR)) **b–**
[2016/17 b15.8g⁶ Apr 3] well beaten in bumper. *Stuart Edmunds*

TOPHAM BAY (IRE) 5 b.m. Milan – Topham Gale (IRE) (Topanoora) [2016/17 b16.2s⁵ **h86**
b15.6g h16s⁶ h16.2s² h22.7sᶠ h16.2gᵖᵘ Apr 28] fourth foal: dam (b87), ran twice in **b–**
bumpers, out of half-sister to very smart hurdler/chaser up to 21f Feroda: no form in
bumpers: modest form over hurdles: should prove suited by further than 2m: tried in hood:
often races towards rear. *Lucinda Russell*

TOP MAN MARTY (IRE) 8 b.g. Westerner – Tribal Princess (IRE) (Namaqualand **h–**
(USA)) [2016/17 h–: h20sᵖᵘ Jan 1] bumper winner: maiden hurdler, pulled up sole outing
in 2016/17: stays 2½m: acts on soft going. *Sarah Humphrey*

TOP NOTCH (FR) 6 b.g. Poliglote – Topira (FR) (Pistolet Bleu (IRE)) [2016/17 **c157**
h158: c16d³ c16.2s* c17g* c21d* c20v* c19.9g² c19.9g³ Apr 6] **h–**

    Galaxy Sam was only a modest performer over jumps, winning just one of his
fifteen starts, but that victory in a conditional jockeys handicap hurdle at Fontwell
in January 2004 is likely to resonate more with leading owner Simon Munir than
many of his big-race successes. Galaxy Sam's thirteen-length victory was, after all,
a first over obstacles for the man who made his fortune in the finance industry and,
along with Isaac Souede, has made his presence felt at the very highest reaches of
National Hunt racing in recent years. Bloodstock agent Anthony Bromley is the
man responsible for finding most of the horses they own and, in an interview with
The Guardian in 2015, he provided some interesting background: 'They've been
friends for over 20 years, but it was only three years ago that they started to think
about doing this together. They're really enthusiastic, Simon goes racing a lot and
Isaac watches it all on computer screens around the world at all sorts of different
times of the day depending on which time zone he's in.' The two owners also have
a strong presence in France, as well as in Britain and Ireland, as recounted in the
essay on Top Notch's stable-companion L'Ami Serge. Soldatino gave Munir a first
Cheltenham Festival winner when landing the Triumph Hurdle in 2010, and it was
the same contest that gave the Munir/Souede partnership its first taste of glory at the
meeting in 2015, with Peace And Co leading home a one, two in the emerald green,
dark green sleeves. Peace And Co has had problems since—his workmanlike win at
5/1-on in a five-runner novice chase at Hexham shortly after the end of the British
season is his only success since and he has now been repatriated to France—but the
runner-up Top Notch has proved nothing if not consistent, and went on to establish
himself as a very smart performer in his second season over hurdles, something
which is often difficult for those stepping straight out of the juvenile ranks. That
said, Top Notch ended the campaign with a creditable nine and a half lengths fifth
to Annie Power in the Champion Hurdle at Cheltenham, a performance which, it
was fair to say, exposed his limitations at the top level over hurdles and led to the
decision to send him chasing in the latest season.

    Top Notch made his chasing debut in a red hot beginners chase for the time of
year at Uttoxeter in October, with all six of the runners boasting at least useful form
over hurdles. Though he could manage only third behind Charbel and Le Prezien,
Top Notch was beaten just a length and three quarters and left the impression he
would strip fitter for the outing, while also having benefited from the experience.
The form received a boost when Le Prezien won the November Novices' Chase
at Cheltenham (by four lengths from Hammersly Lake), and Top Notch didn't
need to improve to get off the mark over fences in a novice confined to four- and
five-year-olds at Warwick next time, travelling strongly and jumping well in the
main. He defied a penalty at Plumpton twelve days later, making all and keeping
on to win by six lengths from the 2016 Fred Winter runner-up Romain de Senam.
Top Notch stepped out of novice company and up in trip for a graduation chase at

Betfred TV Scilly Isles Novices' Chase, Sandown—a third successive win in the race for Daryl Jacob and owners Simon Munir and Isaac Souede as Top Notch proves too strong for Baron Alco (No.2) and Le Prezien

Ascot in December when the field was shrouded in fog for much of the way, though Top Notch improved again, on the face of it, completing his hat-trick when beating Sizing Codelco by a length and a quarter.

Stepped up to Grade 1 level in the Scilly Isles Novices' Chase at Sandown Park in February, Top Notch started second favourite behind Clan des Obeaux, who had produced a smart effort when half a length second to Whisper in the Dipper Novices' Chase at Cheltenham. Waited with in the early stages and jumping well in the main, Top Notch was still on the bridle when hitting the front before the last and quickened clear in impressive fashion on the run-in to win by five lengths from Baron Alco with his Uttoxeter rival Le Prezien a further length and a quarter back in third. The performance was well up to standard for the race and, in giving his owners a third consecutive Scilly Isles victory, following on from Gitane du Berlais and Bristol de Mai, Top Notch looked a leading contender for the Golden Miller Novices' Chase at Cheltenham, a race in which Munir and Souede had filled the minor placings in 2016 with Bristol de Mai (second) and L'Ami Serge (third). They again had to settle for minor honours, though Top Notch still took another significant step forward when chasing home Yorkhill and might even have given the winner more to think about but for a mistake two out, where Top Notch lost momentum before doing really well in the circumstances to be beaten just a length.

Top Notch's defeat added to a frustrating Festival for his owners and their retained jockey Daryl Jacob, with their six runners in the Grade 1 races at the meeting coming up short. Footpad, who was ridden by Ruby Walsh, and Sceau Royal managed fourth and sixth behind Buveur d'Air in the Champion Hurdle; the Challow Novices' Hurdle winner Messire des Obeaux finished a good three and three quarter lengths third to Willoughby Court in the Baring Bingham Novices' Hurdle; Wholestone was below his best when seven and a half lengths third in a muddling renewal of the Spa Novices' Hurdle; and Bristol de Mai finished a well-beaten seventh in the Gold Cup. In addition, L'Ami Serge finished an agonising second to Arctic Fire in the County Hurdle, failing by just a neck after a strong late rally. For Arsenal fan Simon Munir, who has a box at the Emirates, the reversals at Prestbury Park must have struck a chord with Arsenal's season in which they failed to make the top four in the Premier League for the first time in twenty-one years under manager Arsene Wenger. Top Notch had a busy campaign for a novice chaser and he himself failed to meet expectations when signing off with a five and a half lengths third to Flying Angel in the Manifesto Novices' Chase at Aintree, his effort at Cheltenham probably having taken its toll to some extent, though his performance maintained his record of finishing in the first three on each of his seven starts. The tough and reliable Top Notch has a BHA mark of 157, which is just 1 lb higher than that carried to victory by Taquin du Seuil in the BetVictor Gold Cup in the latest season, and that is the race which appeals as a suitable starting point in 2017/18, with the Ryanair Chase likely to provide Top Notch's best chance of success at the Cheltenham Festival.

Top Notch (FR) (b.g. 2011)	Poliglote (b 1992)	Sadler's Wells (b 1981)	Northern Dancer / Fairy Bridge
		Alexandrie (b 1980)	Val de L'Orne / Apachee
	Topira (FR) (b 1996)	Pistolet Bleu (b 1988)	Top Ville / Pampa Bella
		El Quahirah (b 1987)	Cadoudal / Belgaum

Top Notch, a compact gelding, is by the leading French-based jumps sire Poliglote, who covered a limited book of mares in 2017. 'Poliglote is still fertile and we're initially looking to book around twenty mares,' explained Franck Champion, commercial director at Haras d'Etreham in Normandy. 'After that we'll see. With age you have to manage these horses and there will be some selectivity in which mares he covers.' Poliglote's prowess as a stallion was well advertised at the latest Cheltenham Festival, with a winner (Let's Dance) and two seconds courtesy of Top Notch and Wonderful Charm (Foxhunter), while So French won the Grand Steeple-Chase de Paris, France's biggest jumps race, for the second consecutive year at Auteuil in May. Top Notch is out of the useful ten/twelve and a half furlong winner Topira, a half-sister to the smart miler Golani and to the winning hurdler/chaser Monte Cristo who was fairly useful over fences at up to two and a half miles. Elie Lellouche trained Golani and Topira and also the best progeny of Topira to have raced on the Flat to date, the smart Never Forget (by Westerner), who won the Prix de Malleret at Saint-Cloud in 2010. Top Notch is also a half-brother to three winners over hurdles, including the fairly useful Holy Virgin (by Saint des Saints), who won a fillies three-year-old hurdle at Auteuil in 2013. Top Notch passed through the ring unsold as a yearling and went on to win his first two starts over hurdles when trained by Guillaume Macaire, before being bought privately in October 2014. Top Notch, who often travels strongly in his races, stays twenty-one furlongs and acts on heavy ground. He is reportedly a firm favourite with the staff at Seven Barrows and it is easy to see why, as he is one of the most genuine and consistent performers in training. *Nicky Henderson*

TOPOFTHEGAME (IRE) 5 ch.g. Flemensfirth (USA) – Derry Vale (IRE) (Mister Lord (USA)) [2016/17 h21.6d* h20.3s⁴ h19.3s² Feb 18] €26,000 3-y-o, £120,000 4-y-o: tall, raw-boned gelding: will make a chaser: sixth foal: dam unraced half-sister to useful hurdler (probably stayed 3m) Artadoin Lad: won maiden point on debut: useful form over hurdles: won maiden at Ascot in December: best effort when second in novice there (neck behind Beyond Conceit) in February: remains with potential. *Paul Nicholls* — **h138 p**

TOP OF THE GLAS (IRE) 6 gr.g. Verglas (IRE) – Fury Dance (USA) (Cryptoclearance (USA)) [2016/17 h115: h16.2d* h19.9g* h16g⁴ h16.7s⁵ Feb 19] fairly useful hurdler: won maiden at Hexham and novice at Sedgefield in September: stays 2½m: acts on heavy going: has worn cheekpieces: usually races prominently. *Brian Ellison* — **h116**

TOP OF THE RANGE (IRE) 10 br.g. Presenting – Brenny's Pearl (IRE) (Good Thyne (USA)) [2016/17 c–, h–: c23dᵖᵘ Jun 29] deep-girthed gelding: useful hurdler: fairly useful chaser at best, pulled up both outings since 2013/14: stays 2¾m: acts on heavy going: tried in tongue tie. *Paul Morgan* — **c– h–**

TOP OF THE ROCKS (FR) 4 b.g. Rock of Gibraltar (IRE) – Runaway Top (Rainbow Quest (USA)) [2016/17 h16.3dᵖᵘ h16.8s h19g h16.5m Apr 20] sturdy gelding: modest on Flat, stays 2m: no form over hurdles: in cheekpieces/tongue tie last 3 starts. *Katie Stephens* — **h–**

TOP OF THE TOWN (IRE) 9 b.g. Craigsteel – Hil Rhapsody (Anshan) [2016/17 h21m h20d h23.6d* h24g* h23.9g⁴ Oct 22] fairly useful handicap hurdler: won maiden at Downpatrick in 2015/16: also won at Roscommon and Bellewstown in August: stays 25f: acts on good to soft going: has worn hood, including in 2016/17. *Charles Byrnes, Ireland* — **h125**

TOPOLSKI (IRE) 11 b.g. Peintre Celebre (USA) – Witching Hour (IRE) (Alzao (USA)) **h–**
[2016/17 h90: h17.7s Dec 26] smallish gelding: useful hurdler at best, lightly raced and
largely disappointing since 2011/12: stays 19f: acts on soft going: has worn tongue tie.
David Arbuthnot

TOP POCKET 5 b.g. Royal Applause – Movie Mogul (Sakhee (USA)) [2016/17 h17.7d **h–**
h15.9m⁶ Oct 31] modest maiden on Flat, stays 11f: well beaten both starts over hurdles.
Michael Madgwick

TOP PRIORITY (FR) 6 b.g. Solon (GER) – Firstote (FR) (Tot Ou Tard (IRE)) [2016/17 **h83**
h91, b91: h25d h24v⁴ h23.3g Jul 22] bumper winner: poor maiden hurdler: best effort at
17f: acts on good to soft going: tried in blinkers: in tongue tie last 3 starts. *Jonjo O'Neill*

TOP SET (IRE) 7 ch.g. Tamayuz – Pray (IRE) (Priolo (USA)) [2016/17 h76: h19g³ **h82**
h17.7g h19.9g Jul 5] poor maiden hurdler: best effort at 19f. *Richard Phillips*

TOP TUG (IRE) 6 ch.g. Halling (USA) – Top Romance (IRE) (Entrepreneur) [2016/17 **h126**
h16g* h15.8d³ h15.7g² h16.5g³ h21g Mar 18] strong gelding: half-brother to fair hurdler
Worth A King's (2½m/21f winner, by Red Ransom): useful on Flat, stays 1½m: fairly
useful form over hurdles: won novice at Kempton in November: second in novice at
Catterick in January: unproven beyond 2m: best form on good going. *Alan King*

TOP VILLE BEN (IRE) 5 b.g. Beneficial – Great Decision (IRE) (Simply Great (FR)) **h130**
[2016/17 b14d⁴ h15.5d⁴ h15.7v* h16.7s² h16g⁶ h16.2g⁴ Apr 27] €25,000 3-y-o, €70,000 **b101**
4-y-o: useful-looking gelding: third foal: dam, failed to complete in points, out of half-
sister to Champion Hurdle winner For Auction: won Irish maiden point on debut: also won
bumper at Ludlow (by 3½ lengths from Solomon Grey) in December: useful form over
hurdles: won novices at Leicester in January and Towcester in February: will stay further
than 2m: acts on heavy going: in hood last 2 starts: usually leads/races freely. *Nicky
Henderson*

TOP WOOD (FR) 10 ch.g. Kotky Bleu (FR) – Heure Bleu (FR) (Grand Tresor (FR)) **c127 §**
[2016/17 c144§, h–: c26.1g c15.5g⁵ c25gᵘʳ c22.9s c28.5s⁵ c24.5d⁴ c25.1v² Mar 9] lengthy **h–**
gelding: winning hurdler: useful handicap chaser, below form in 2016/17: stays 3½m: acts
on good to firm and heavy going: wears headgear/tongue tie: moody. *David Pipe*

TOQUICKLY 5 b.m. Tobougg (IRE) – Miss Quickly (Anshan) [2016/17 b75: **b57**
b16.2m⁵ May 29] poor form in bumpers. *Harriet Graham*

TOREADOR (FR) 10 b.g. Epalo (GER) – Etoile d'Or II (FR) (Lute Antique (FR)) **c62**
[2016/17 c20.1sᵖᵘ c23.8g⁶ c23.8g⁵ Jan 20] maiden point winner: little form under Rules: **h–**
has worn blinkers/tongue tie. *Andrew Hamilton*

TORERO 8 b.g. Hernando (FR) – After You (Pursuit of Love) [2016/17 h86: h16.8sᵖᵘ **h73 §**
h16.4s h22sᵖᵘ h19.7s⁶ h19.9s³ h16.3s⁶ h19.9d⁴ h21.3d⁴ Mar 21] sturdy gelding: poor
handicap hurdler: stays 2½m: acts on heavy going: wears headgear/tongue tie: usually
leads: temperamental. *Joanne Foster*

TORHOUSEMUIR 6 b.g. Sagamix (FR) – Royal Musical (Royal Abjar (USA)) [2016/17 **h99**
b71: h16.3m h15.8d⁵ h19.6dᶠ h19g h18.5d h15.7g⁴ Apr 21] little impact in bumpers: **b–**
modest form over hurdles: should stay 2¼m+: usually wears hood. *Sam Thomas*

TORNADO IN MILAN (IRE) 11 b.g. Milan – Julika (GER) (Nebos (GER)) [2016/17 **c134**
c127, h131: h19.6v² c16v* c19.4g² c19.4s⁴ h19.8v* c19.9s⁵ Mar 4] sturdy gelding: useful **h136**
handicap hurdler: won at Wincanton (by 15 lengths from Masters Hill) in February: useful
handicap chaser: won at Ludlow in November: stays 2½m: acts on heavy going: has worn
hood: front runner/races prominently. *Evan Williams*

TORNADO WATCH (IRE) 8 ch.g. Selkirk (USA) – Pattimech (USA) (Nureyev **h104**
(USA)) [2016/17 h18.5g* h16.2s* h18.2g* h19.3d⁶ h16s h20v h15.7s Mar 20] fair
handicap hurdler: won at Downpatrick in August and at Ballinrobe/Downpatrick again
in September: left Jonathan Fogarty after sixth start: stays 2¼m: acts on soft going: usually
races towards rear. *David Loughnane*

TORN ASUNDER (IRE) 10 b.g. Presenting – Shuil Mavourneen (IRE) (Welsh Term) **c–**
[2016/17 c102, h–: c16.3g Apr 27] point winner: winning hurdler: fair chaser: stayed 3m, **h–**
effective at much shorter: acted on good to firm and heavy going: tried in cheekpieces:
sometimes wore tongue tie: dead. *Gary Hanmer*

TORTUEUSE (IRE) 10 b.m. Indian Danehill (IRE) – Taffety (Last Tycoon) [2016/17 **h67**
h86: h16g h20s h15.9m⁵ h20s Dec 8] poor maiden hurdler: left Patrick Mooney after
second start: has worn headgear, including in 2016/17: tried in tongue tie. *David Peter
Dunne, Ireland*

TOSIE 5 b.m. Tikkanen (USA) – Azturk (FR) (Baby Turk) [2016/17 b16s Feb 14] fifth foal: **b–**
sister to fairly useful hurdler/chaser Ueueteotl (2½m-23f winner) and closely related to
bumper winner Huehuecoyotle (by Turgeon), both unreliable: dam, ran once over hurdles,
out of half-sister to outstanding 2m chaser Azertyuiop: well beaten in bumper. *James Ewart*

TOTAL ASSETS 9 b.m. Alflora (IRE) – Maid Equal (Pragmatic) [2016/17 c107, h–: **c110**
h23.3d[pu] c25.5m[pu] h22.7s[6] c26.3s[4] c26.2s* h24.1s[2] c25.2s[3] h25.8s* h25g* h26.6g[2] Apr 27] **h116**
rather leggy mare: fairly useful handicap hurdler: won at Kelso and Carlisle in April: fair
handicap chaser: won at Kelso in December: stays 27f: acts on good to firm and heavy
going: has worn cheekpieces: usually races prominently. *Simon Waugh*

TOTALIZE 8 b.g. Authorized (IRE) – You Too (Monsun (GER)) [2016/17 h131: h20.6g* **h142**
h22.8g[3] Jul 30] rather leggy gelding: useful handicap hurdler: won at Market Rasen in July:
third at Galway (¾ length behind Westerner Lady) later in month: stays 23f: acts on heavy
going: has worn hood. *Brian Ellison*

TOTALLY COMMITTED 4 b.g. Invincible Spirit (IRE) – Zanzibar (IRE) (In The **h–**
Wings) [2016/17 h16d[6] h16g[pu] Mar 18] medium-sized gelding: fairly useful on Flat, stays
1¼m: little impact in 2 starts over hurdles: wears hood. *Brendan Powell*

TOTAL REBELLION (IRE) 11 b.g. Craigsteel – Hil Rhapsody (Anshan) [2016/17 **c–**
c25.1m[4] c19.2g[pu] Apr 11] lengthy gelding: multiple winning pointer: fairly useful hurdler **h–**
in 2011/12: little impact in chases: stays 27f: acts on soft and good to firm going: has worn
headgear: usually wears tongue tie. *B. V. Lund*

TOTAL RECALL (IRE) 8 b.g. Westerner – Augest Weekend (IRE) (Dr Massini (IRE)) **c130**
[2016/17 h24d[bu] c22g[f] c17d[4] c18d[ur] c20s* c21g c20v[5] Feb 26] third foal: dam unraced **h–**
half-sister to high-class hurdler (stayed 2½m) Bimsey: winning hurdler: useful form over
fences: won novice at Navan in December: stays 2½m: acts on heavy going. *Ms Sandra
Hughes, Ireland*

TOTAL SUBMISSION 12 gr.g. Kayf Tara – Ardentinny (Ardross) [2016/17 c114, h80: **c89**
c21.1s[3] May 3] angular gelding: maiden pointer: winning hurdler: fairly useful chaser at **h–**
best, below form sole outing in 2016/17: stays 3m: acts on soft and good to firm going: has
worn cheekpieces/tongue tie. *John Groucott*

TOTHEMOONANDBACK (IRE) 9 gr.g. Dr Massini (IRE) – Mrs Jones (FR) (Saint **c111 §**
Preuil (FR)) [2016/17 c19.7d c25.7d[2] c28.5s[pu] Jan 2] good-topped gelding: maiden hurdler: **h–**
fairly useful handicap chaser: stays 3¼m: acts on heavy going: temperamental. *Gary Moore*

TOUCH KICK (IRE) 6 b.g. Presenting – Bay Pearl (FR) (Broadway Flyer (USA)) **h120**
[2016/17 b99p: b17d[4] h19.5g[4] h18.5s[4] h15.6g[2] h19.8d h19g* h20.5g[6] Apr 22] useful- **b88**
looking gelding: bumper winner: fairly useful form over hurdles: won maiden at Taunton
in March: stays 2½m: acts on soft going: wears hood/tongue tie. *Paul Nicholls*

TOUCH OF STEEL (IRE) 8 b.g. Craigsteel – Tourmaline Girl (IRE) (Toulon) [2016/17 **c– p**
h100: h25.4d[pu] h24g[pu] h20.9d[pu] c20.1g[6] h23.8g[5] h25.3d* h23.8g h27g Mar 29] modest **h88**
handicap hurdler: won at Catterick in January: tailed off in novice handicap on chasing
debut: stays 25f: acts on soft and good to firm going: usually wears headgear: usually races
nearer last than first: should do better as a chaser. *James Ewart*

TOUCH SCREEN (IRE) 7 b.g. Touch of Land (FR) – Capard Lady (IRE) (Supreme **c78**
Leader) [2016/17 b16.4g b21.6g[6] h19.8d h19g h19s[6] h16.8d[4] c16v[2] c24.2d[F] c21.1g[3] **h77**
Apr 12] maiden pointer: tailed off in bumper: poor form over hurdles/fences: unproven **b–**
beyond 17f: acts on heavy going. *Mark Gillard*

TOULOUSE THE PLOT 5 b.g. Tamure (IRE) – Red Reef (King's Best (USA)) **b–**
[2016/17 b16.8g Aug 10] tailed off in bumper. *Kim Bailey*

TOURBOY (IRE) 5 br.g. Whitmore's Conn (USA) – Annalecky (IRE) (Bob's Return **b–**
(IRE)) [2016/17 b16.3g b18g Apr 28] no form in 2 bumpers. *Mark Fahey, Ireland*

TOUR D'ARGENT (FR) 10 b.g. Martaline – Keep Well (FR) (Agent Bleu (FR)) **c– x**
[2016/17 c108x, h–: h20.2m h17d Jun 30] good-topped gelding: useful hurdler at best, no **h–**
form in 2016/17: maiden chaser: should stay beyond 2½m: acts on soft and good to firm
going: has worn headgear, including in 2016/17: often let down by jumping. *Gordon
Elliott, Ireland*

TOUR DES CHAMPS (FR) 10 b.g. Robin des Champs (FR) – Massada (FR) (Kashtan **c138**
(FR)) [2016/17 c136, h–: c26.3s* c28.4d[pu] Feb 18] well-made gelding: winning hurdler: **h–**
useful handicap chaser: won at Cheltenham (by short head from Doctor Harper) in January:
stays 3½m: acts on heavy going: has worn headgear: temperament under suspicion.
Samuel Drinkwater

TOUR DE VILLE (IRE) 7 b.g. Beneficial – Galant Tour (IRE) (Riberetto) [2016/17 **h101** h99p, b93: h16m⁴ h22.1m h20g⁶ h20m* h19.7s h19.4dᵖᵘ Jan 28] lengthy gelding: bumper winner: fair handicap hurdler: won novice event at Worcester in August: left Seamus Durack after fourth start: stayed 2½m: acted on good to firm going: often wore headgear/ tongue tie: raced well off pace: dead. *John Wainwright*

TOVIERE (IRE) 6 ch.g. Presenting – Aventia (IRE) (Bob Back (USA)) [2016/17 b90: **h115** h19d² h20.3g⁴ h22g² h24d³ h23.9g⁴ h19.3m³ Apr 2] rather unfurnished gelding: fairly useful form over hurdles: in frame on all 6 starts: stays 2¾m: acts on good to firm and good to soft going. *Oliver Sherwood*

TOWERBURN (IRE) 8 b.g. Cloudings (IRE) – Lady Newmill (IRE) (Taipan (IRE)) **h70** [2016/17 h93: h16.2d⁶ h22.1gᵖᵘ Jul 18] modest maiden hurdler, below form both starts in 2016/17: unproven beyond 2m: acts on good to soft going: tried in tongue tie. *Alison Hamilton*

TOWERING (IRE) 8 b.g. Catcher In The Rye (IRE) – Bobs Article (IRE) (Definite **c121 §** Article) [2016/17 h118: h25d³ h20.5g⁵ c24d² c23gᵖᵘ c24vᵖᵘ h24.3dᵖᵘ Apr 21] good-topped **h111 §** gelding: fair handicap hurdler: fairly useful form when second in novice handicap at Doncaster on completed start over fences: stays 3m: acts on good to firm and good to soft going: in headgear last 4 starts: temperamental. *Nicky Henderson*

TOWER OF ALLEN (IRE) 6 b.g. Beneficial – Baile An Droichid (IRE) (King's Ride) **h98** [2016/17 b–: h21mᵇᵈ h20.5g² h20d⁶ h20.5d h19g Mar 30] modest form over hurdles: stays 21f: acts on good to soft going. *Nicky Henderson*

TOWN HEAD 4 ch.g. Archipenko (USA) – Forever Loved (Deploy) [2016/17 b16d² **b95** Mar 21] sixth foal: half-brother to 3 winners on Flat, including useful 11f/1½m winner Indira (by Sleeping Indian): dam 1½m-15f winner: 7/1, promise when second in bumper at Wetherby (head behind Captain Woodie) in March. *Michael Easterby*

TOWN MOUSE 7 ch.g. Sakhee (USA) – Megdale (IRE) (Waajib) [2016/17 c121§, h–§: **c97 §** c20.3g⁴ h23.1g⁵ c17.4g⁵ c21.4g⁴ Sep 24] fairly useful handicap hurdler/chaser at best, well **h77** below form in 2016/17: stays 21f: acts on good to firm and good to soft going: often in headgear: front runner/races prominently: has carried head awkwardly/given trouble at start. *Neil King*

TOWN PARKS (IRE) 6 b.g. Morozov (USA) – Outdoor Heather (IRE) (Presenting) **h123** [2016/17 h21.2g⁴ h21s h19.7s² h21.2s* h21.4s² h21.2g² Apr 3] €28,000 3-y-o, £9,000 5-y-o: angular gelding: third foal: dam unraced: in frame both starts in Irish maiden points: fairly useful form over hurdles: won maiden at Ludlow in February: second in handicap at Wincanton in March: stays 21f: acts on soft going: often travels strongly. *Kerry Lee*

TOWNSHEND (GER) 6 b.g. Lord of England (GER) – Trikolore (GER) (Konigsstuhl **c146 p** (GER)) [2016/17 h132: c17s² c16s* c16dᶠ Apr 27] useful hurdler: smart form over fences: **h–** won maiden at Naas in March: stays 2½m: acts on heavy going: tried in hood: usually travels strongly: remains with potential as a chaser. *W. P. Mullins, Ireland*

TRACKMATE 11 b.g. Muhtarram (USA) – Cruz Santa (Lord Bud) [2016/17 h–: h22.1d **h–** h24.2d h19.1vᵖᵘ Jan 8] leggy gelding: useful hurdler at best, no form in 2016/17: tried in blinkers. *James Evans*

TRADEWINDS (FR) 9 b.g. Kapgarde (FR) – Royale Floriane (FR) (Cyborg (FR)) **c117** [2016/17 h122: c21.2g* c25.5dᶠ Jul 16] sturdy gelding: fairly useful hurdler: fairly useful **h–** form when won maiden at Cartmel in June on completed start over fences: stayed 3m: acted on soft going: tried in hood: dead. *Lucinda Russell*

TRADITIONAL DANCER (IRE) 5 b.g. Danehill Dancer (IRE) – Cote Quest (USA) **h129** (Green Desert (USA)) [2016/17 h20.2m* h18.1m² h23.9s³ h20.9m* h17.1d* h21.1sᵖᵘ h15.6g³ h15.6g³ h16g Apr 22] tall gelding: half-brother to French 19f chase winner Fitzgerald (by Barathea): lightly-raced maiden on Flat: fairly useful hurdler: won maiden at Perth early in season, and minor event at Kelso and handicap at Carlisle in October: stays 21f, effective at shorter: acts on good to firm and heavy going: tried in hood: front runner/ races prominently. *Iain Jardine*

TRAFALGAR (FR) 10 b.g. Laveron – Dzaoudzie (FR) (El Badr) [2016/17 c91, h–: **c82 §** c23.6gᶠ c23.6gᵖᵘ c26.2m² Apr 28] lengthy gelding: winning hurdler: poor handicap chaser **h–** nowadays: stays 3m: acts on soft going: has worn headgear, including last 4 starts: has worn tongue tie: temperamental. *Sarah-Jayne Davies*

TRAFALGAR ROCK 6 b.g. Mount Nelson – Helter Helter (USA) (Seeking The Gold (USA)) [2016/17 h19.9g* h20g* h19.9g⁴ h23g³ Sep 6] fairly useful on Flat, stays 2m: fairly useful form over hurdles: won maiden at Uttoxeter in June and novice at Worcester in July: stays 2½m. *Dr Richard Newland*   **h120**

TRAFFIC FLUIDE (FR) 7 b.g. Astarabad (USA) – Petale Rouge (FR) (Bonnet Rouge (FR)) [2016/17 c162p, h–: c16.4d⁴ c21s⁶ c15.9g⁶ c19.9g³ c22.7g² Apr 29] lengthy gelding: lightly-raced hurdler: very smart chaser: placed in Melling Chase at Aintree (17 lengths behind Fox Norton) and Oaksey Chase at Sandown (4½ lengths behind Menorah) in April: stays 23f: acts on soft going: tried in cheekpieces: usually races nearer last than first. *Gary Moore*   **c156 h–**

TRAFFICKER (IRE) 10 b.g. Flemensfirth (USA) – Sulawesi (IRE) (In The Wings) [2016/17 c103, h102: c23.9d⁴ c25.8m⁵ c23gᵖᵘ c23.9g c23.9g⁴ Aug 13] winning hurdler: fair handicap chaser, below form in 2016/17: stays 25f: acts on heavy going: usually in headgear. *Dr Richard Newland*   **c93 h–**

TRAKEUR (FR) 10 b.g. Myrakalu (FR) – Nataly (FR) (Ragmar (FR)) [2016/17 c56, h84: h21.4m³ h21.4m⁵ h16g⁴ h17.7g² c16.5g⁴ h21.6m h21.4m² h21.4mʳʳ Oct 23] maiden pointer: poor maiden hurdler/chaser: stays 2¾m: acts on good to firm going: wears headgear: refused to race final start. *Simon Hodgson*   **c– h73 §**

TRANS EXPRESS (IRE) 7 br.g. Trans Island – Hazel Fastrack (Shambo) [2016/17 h90, b80: h16d h16s² h18.5s⁴ h21.4s h19.8s⁵ h24.3d Apr 21] close-coupled gelding: fell in point: fair handicap hurdler: won at Exeter in December: stays 19f: acts on soft going. *Susan Gardner*   **h106**

TRANSIENT BAY (IRE) 7 b.g. Trans Island – Boarding Pass (IRE) (Accordion) [2016/17 h103: h19.9vᵖᵘ h24.3sᵖᵘ c20.5vᵖᵘ h19.9v* c20.5v⁴ Mar 10] fair handicap hurdler: won at Uttoxeter in February: shaped as if amiss both starts over fences: stays 23f: best form on heavy going: usually wears cheekpieces: tried in tongue tie: often races prominently. *Philip Kirby*   **c– h110**

TRANSLUSCENT (IRE) 7 b.g. Trans Island – Little Miss Diva (IRE) (Diktat) [2016/17 h16.2dᵖᵘ Jun 4] no form over hurdles: in tongue tie last 2 starts. *Maurice Barnes*   **h–**

TRAPPER PEAK (IRE) 8 b.g. Westerner – Banningham Blaze (Averti (IRE)) [2016/17 c106, h100: c16.3g⁴ c17.4g³ c15.7vᵖᵘ c16.3g⁴ h18.6g h18.7g² h23g⁵ h16g* h18.7g⁵ h15.5g* h15.5g² h16.7d⁴ h15.5d h15.5g² c15.7s⁵ h15.8s⁶ h15.8g⁴ Apr 28] sturdy gelding: fair hurdler: won conditionals selling handicap at Fakenham in October and seller at Leicester in November: fair handicap chaser: left Alexandra Dunn after twelfth start: stays 23f: acts on heavy going: wears headgear: usually wears tongue tie: temperamental. *Conor Dore*   **c103 § h105 §**

TRAP QUEEN (IRE) 4 b.f. Nayef (USA) – Quiritis (Galileo (IRE)) [2016/17 b12.4d Jan 14] sturdy filly: first foal: dam unraced sister to St Leger runner-up Mahler: well beaten in mares bumper. *K. R. Burke*   **b–**

TREACKLE TART (IRE) 5 b.m. Winged Love (USA) – Battle Over (FR) (Sillery (USA)) [2016/17 b15.7g⁴ b17g⁵ h21s h15.5g² h16.7s² h21.6g* h20.7g² Apr 28] €11,000 3-y-o: seventh foal: dam, French 2m-2¼m hurdle/chase winner, also 1¼m winner on Flat: modest form on first of 2 starts in bumpers: fair form over hurdles: won novice handicap at Exeter in April: stays 2¾m: acts on soft going. *Charlie Longsdon*   **h114 b77**

TREACY HOTELS BOY (IRE) 10 br.g. Overbury (IRE) – Bridgehotel Rose (IRE) (Synefos (USA)) [2016/17 c88, h81: c16.3gᵖᵘ c20.3gᵖᵘ c21.1g³ c21.1gᵖᵘ Aug 18] winning hurdler: poor maiden chaser nowadays: stays 21f: acts on heavy going: tried in cheekpieces. *Paul Henderson*   **c82 h–**

TREACYSWESTCOUNTY (IRE) 9 b.g. Urban Ocean (FR) – Bridge Hotel Lilly (IRE) (Roselier (FR)) [2016/17 c23.6g⁶ May 17] multiple winning pointer: twice-raced hurdler: in cheekpieces, 25/1, sixth in novice hunter at Huntingdon (21¼ lengths behind Hill of Gold) on chasing debut. *Miss L. Horsfall*   **c78 h–**

TREASURE THE RIDGE (IRE) 8 b.g. Galileo (IRE) – Treasure The Lady (IRE) (Indian Ridge) [2016/17 h19gᶠ h16.5g³ Mar 20] fairly useful on Flat, stays 2m: modest form when third in novice at Taunton on completed start over hurdles: wears headgear: tried in tongue tie. *Martin Hill*   **h99**

TREATY GIRL (IRE) 6 b.m. Milan – Back To Cloghoge (IRE) (Bob Back (USA)) [2016/17 h120: c19.9d³ c20.8g² c26d² c25.2sᵖᵘ Feb 3] sturdy mare: point winner: winning hurdler: fairly useful form over fences: second in handicap at Newbury in December: stays 3¼m: acts on soft going. *Ben Pauling*   **c126 h–**

TREAT YOURSELF (IRE) 10 b.g. Beat Hollow – Cartesian (Shirley Heights) [2016/17 **c111 §** c17d³ c17.1s c16.4d⁵ c18s c17.1s c16.3s⁴ c20.1v⁴ c19.9g² c21.3d⁴ c23.4g* c26.3m⁴ **h–** Apr 19] winning hurdler: fair handicap chaser nowadays: won at Newcastle in April: left A. L. T. Moore after first start: probably stays 3¼m: acts on heavy going: wears headgear: has worn tongue tie, including in 2016/17: often travels strongly: temperamental. *Micky Hammond*

TREBLE STRIKE (USA) 4 b.g. Hat Trick (JPN) – Lady Simpson (Yankee Victor **b79** (USA)) [2016/17 b13.7m⁴ b13.7g b13.7d ab16g⁴ Dec 10] fair maiden on Flat, stays 2m: modest form in bumpers. *Dean Ivory*

TREE OF LIBERTY (IRE) 5 ch.g. Stowaway – The Wrens Nest (IRE) (Shernazar) **h123** [2016/17 b16.7g³ h22.7s² h20.8d² h19.4g* h19.8gᵖᵘ Apr 29] €34,000 3-y-o, £54,000 4-y-o: **b95** fourth foal: dam (h101), 2m hurdle winner, sister to useful staying chaser Bewleys Berry: runner-up both starts in Irish maiden points: third in bumper at Market Rasen (4½ lengths behind Boreham Bill): fairly useful form over hurdles: won novice at Musselburgh in February: bred to stay 3m: usually races close up. *Charlie Longsdon*

TREGARO (FR) 11 b.g. Phantom Breeze – Touques (FR) (Tip Moss (FR)) [2016/17 **c93 §** c104§, h–: c21.4gᵖᵘ c19.9m² c20d⁵ c19.9dᵖᵘ Nov 19] rather sparely-made gelding: **h–** maiden hurdler: fair handicap chaser, below form in 2016/17: stayed 2½m: acted on good to firm and good to soft going: wore tongue tie: often raced in rear: weak finisher: dead. *Mike Sowersby*

TREHAN CROSS 8 b.m. Bandmaster (USA) – Halton Quay (Lir) [2016/17 c–, h–: c24.2g³ **c78** c26.3gᵘʳ c25.1s² c24.5vᵖᵘ c24.2g⁴ c27.5g⁶ Apr 23] angular mare: maiden hurdler: poor **h–** maiden chaser: stays 25f: acts on soft going: wears cheekpieces. *Jackie du Plessis*

TRENTMAN 5 ch.g. Denounce – Sharabosky (Shahrastani (USA)) [2016/17 b15.7d Feb **b–** 26] tailed off in bumper. *John Holt*

TRESHNISH (FR) 4 ch.g. Gold Away (IRE) – Didn't I Tell You (IRE) (Docksider **b76** (USA)) [2016/17 b14d⁶ b14.6s³ Dec 17] modest form on second of 2 starts in bumpers. *Sue Smith*

TRESOR DE LA VIE (FR) 10 gr.g. Epalo (GER) – Joie de La Vie (FR) (Quart de Vin **c–** (FR)) [2016/17 c–, h61: h21.4m h23gᵖᵘ Jul 12] winning pointer: maiden hurdler, no form **h–** in 2016/17: maiden chaser: stays 21f: acts on heavy going: usually wears headgear: wears tongue tie. *Victor Dartnall*

TRESPASSED (IRE) 4 b.g. Thewayyouare (USA) – Trespass (Entrepreneur) [2016/17 **h97** h16.3mᵖᵘ h16d² h16g³ h16g⁴ h16.2g³ h16.2d⁴ Sep 21] closely related to fair hurdler Roman Numeral (2m winner, by King's Best), stays 2¾m: fair maiden on Flat, stays 1½m: modest form over hurdles: raced only at 2m: acts on good to soft going: often in hood: wears tongue tie. *Gordon Elliott, Ireland*

TRESPASSERS WILL (IRE) 6 b.g. Scorpion (IRE) – Drum Majorette (Infantry) **c–** [2016/17 h101, b83: c21.4gᵖᵘ May 6] useful-looking gelding: fair maiden hurdler: pulled **h–** up in novice handicap on chasing debut: stayed 2½m: acted on soft going: tried in hood/ tongue tie: dead. *Fergal O'Brien*

TREVISANI (IRE) 5 b.g. Dubawi (IRE) – Geminiani (IRE) (King of Kings (IRE)) **h105 p** [2016/17 h16g h18.5m* Apr 18] good-topped gelding: dam half-sister to fairly useful hurdler (stayed 2½m) Motorway: fairly useful on Flat, stays 2m: fair form over hurdles: won maiden at Exeter in April, well on top finish: in blinkers first start: remains with potential. *Paul Nicholls*

TRIANGULAR (USA) 12 b.g. Diesis – Salchow (USA) (Nijinsky (CAN)) [2016/17 **c111 §** c23.4d* Mar 24] tall, angular gelding: dual winning pointer: maiden hurdler: fair chaser **h–** nowadays: very fortunate winner of hunter at Newbury in March: stays 3m: raced only on good going or softer (acts on heavy): wears headgear/tongue tie: ungenuine. *Mrs C. Fry*

TRIANGULATE 5 b.g. Zamindar (USA) – Heart of Hearts (Oasis Dream) [2016/17 **b–** b16.7g b16s Feb 4] fair form on Flat: no form in bumpers. *Micky Hammond*

TRIBAL DANCE (IRE) 11 br.g. Flemensfirth (USA) – Native Sparkle (IRE) (Be My **c62 §** Native (USA)) [2016/17 c84§, h–: h23.1d c25.8d⁵ c22.6g c25.5gᵖᵘ h23.1g⁵ c21.1s³ c20mᵖᵘ **h54 §** h20.5g⁶ Dec 1] smallish gelding: fair handicap hurdler/chaser at best, little form in 2016/17: stays 3¼m: acts on heavy going: usually wears headgear: tried in tongue tie: unreliable. *John O'Shea*

TRICKAWAY (IRE) 9 b.g. Stowaway – Rosie's Trix (IRE) (Luso) [2016/17 c–, h–: **c128** c20.3s* c21.6s* c22.9s c23.4s⁴ c24.2m Apr 13] rangy gelding: twice-raced hurdler: fairly **h–** useful handicap chaser: won at Southwell early in season and Kelso in November: left Philip Hobbs after first start: stays 2¾m: acts on soft going: front runner/races prominently. *Malcolm Jefferson*

TRICKY (IRE) 8 br.g. Indian Danehill (IRE) – Amelia Island (IRE) (Supreme Leader) **c83 p** [2016/17 h102: h16d² c16.5g⁴ Jul 12] fair form over hurdles: 3/1, fourth in novice handicap **h106** at Worcester (23 lengths behind Boss des Mottes) on chasing debut: unproven beyond 17f: acts on good to soft going: often races towards rear/travels strongly: open to improvement over fences. *Philip Hobbs*

TRICKY ISSUE (IRE) 5 b.m. Manduro (GER) – Tricky Situation (Mark of Esteem **h94** (IRE)) [2016/17 h15.3mᵘʳ h16.8dᵖᵘ h16g³ h15.3s⁴ h21.6g⁵ Apr 12] little form on Flat: modest form over hurdles: best effort at 2¾m: acts on soft going. *Seamus Mullins*

TRICKY SILENCE (IRE) 5 br.g. Whitmore's Conn (USA) – No Sound (FR) (Exit To **h66** Nowhere (USA)) [2016/17 h19.4s⁴ h20.3s h21m⁴ Apr 4] unplaced on completed start in points: poor form over hurdles. *Stuart Edmunds*

TRIGGER NICHOL (IRE) 5 b.g. Dubai Destination (USA) – Run For Cover (IRE) **b77** (Lafontaine (USA)) [2016/17 b16v⁵ b16.7g⁵ Apr 22] modest form on second of 2 starts in bumpers. *Nicky Richards*

TRIGGYWINKLE (FR) 8 b.m. Le Triton (USA) – Periwinkle (FR) (Perrault) [2016/17 **c91 §** c81: c16.3g* c16.5m c17.4gᵖᵘ c16.3sᵖᵘ c16.3g⁴ c20m³ c15.7d⁷ c18.9s⁶ c15.7d⁵ c23gᵖᵘ c16sᶠ c18.2g³ c21m⁵ c16.1mᵘʳ Apr 27] modest handicap chaser: won at Newton Abbot early in season and Wincanton in November: left Kevin Bishop after tenth start: stays 21f: acts on soft going: wears headgear/tongue tie: unreliable. *Laura Young*

TRILLERIN MINELLA (IRE) 9 b.g. King's Theatre (IRE) – Eva Fay (IRE) (Fayruz) **c94 §** [2016/17 c101§, h–: c24.1gᵖᵘ c27.5gᵖᵘ c20.9g² c20dᵖᵘ c20dᵖᵘ c23.9g* c21.2g c20.1d⁵ **h–** c23.8gᵖᵘ c24.2dᵖᵘ c15.6g Apr 25] lengthy gelding: maiden hurdler: modest handicap chaser nowadays: won at Market Rasen in July: left Graeme McPherson after sixth start: stays 3m: acts on soft going: usually a headgear: temperamental. *Kevin Hunter*

TRINITY HOUSE (IRE) 5 b.g. Shamardal (USA) – Love Style (USA) (Mr Prospector **b–** (USA)) [2016/17 b16.2d b16.8gᵖᵘ May 10] no form in 2 bumpers: in cheekpieces second start: wears tongue tie. *Michael Smith*

TRIOLO D'ALENE (FR) 10 ch.g. Epalo (GER) – Joliette d'Alene (FR) (Garde Royale) **c–** [2016/17 c155, h–: c26g c23.8d c24gᵖᵘ Feb 25] useful-looking gelding: lightly-raced **h–** hurdler: very smart chaser at best, no form in 2016/17. *Nicky Henderson*

TRIONA BEY 7 b.m. And Beyond (IRE) – Catriona (Bustino) [2016/17 b16.2g⁶ Aug 20] **b–** no form in bumpers. *Lisa Harrison*

TRIOPAS (IRE) 5 b.g. Stowaway – Aine Dubh (IRE) (Bob Back (USA)) [2016/17 b–: **h80** b17g h15.8dᵘʳ h19.4g h16.7d h15.8s h23.9g⁵ h23.9g h21.6gᵘʳ Apr 26] second in maiden **b72** point on debut: poor form in bumpers: poor maiden hurdler. *Tom Lacey*

TRIPLE CHIEF (IRE) 6 b.g. High Chaparral (IRE) – Trebles (IRE) (Kenmare (FR)) **c101** [2016/17 c97, h96: h15.8m⁴ c16g⁵ c15.7d³ c17v⁴ c15.9s³ c19.2s* c19.2g² Apr 11] **h87** workmanlike gelding: modest handicap hurdler: fair handicap chaser: won at Exeter in March: stays 19f: acts on heavy going: wears headgear: has worn tongue tie, including in 2016/17: often races towards rear. *Chris Down*

TRIPLE EIGHT (IRE) 9 b.g. Royal Applause – Hidden Charm (IRE) (Big Shuffle **h93** (USA)) [2016/17 h92: h16.7g² h17.2g⁵ h16.7g² h16d Nov 12] modest handicap hurdler: stays 19f: acts on good to firm and good to soft going: often wears headgear. *Philip Kirby*

TRIPTICO (FR) 11 gr.g. Turgeon (USA) – Al Kicks (FR) (Al Nasr (FR)) [2016/17 c20v⁴ **c90** c21.1v⁴ c20.9v⁵ c20.9v³ Mar 19] winning hurdler: modest handicap chaser nowadays: **h–** should stay 3m: acts on heavy going: tried in headgear/tongue tie. *Alexandra Dunn*

TRIUMPH DAVIS (IRE) 8 b.m. Flemensfirth (USA) – Bodhran Davis (FR) (Cadoudal **h– §** (FR)) [2016/17 h91: h27s h23.3g h25.4m⁵ h22.1d Jun 26] modest hurdler at best, no form in 2016/17: has worn headgear, including last 5 starts: usually races towards rear: untrustworthy. *Micky Hammond*

TROED Y MELIN (IRE) 5 b.g. Craigsteel – Kissangel (IRE) (Namaqualand (USA)) **b65** [2016/17 b16.8g⁴ Apr 26] runner-up on 3 of 4 starts in maiden points: well beaten in maiden bumper. *Chris Honour*

TROIKA STEPPES 9 b.g. Pasternak – Killerton Clover (High Season) [2016/17 c115, **c125** h–: c24d³ c25g* c25g² c21.1dᵖᵘ c23g⁴ c24.2sᵘʳ c24.2ᶠ c28.1gᵖᵘ Apr 19] big, strong **h–** gelding: lightly-raced hurdler: fairly useful handicap chaser: won at Cheltenham (amateur) in October: stays 25f: acts on heavy going: has worn tongue tie. *Fergal O'Brien*

TROJAN STAR (IRE) 7 b.g. Tikkanen (USA) – Mystical Queen (IRE) (Dr Devious **c105 §** (IRE)) [2016/17 c108, h102: c19.9g³ c16gᵘʳ c18m⁵ c19.9d* c16.5d³ c19.2d⁴ c19.9dᵖᵘ **h–** c24m³ c23.6g⁴ Apr 28] maiden hurdler: fair handicap chaser: won at Huntingdon in November: stays 3m: acts on good to firm and good to soft going: wears cheekpieces: usually wears tongue tie: moody. *Kim Bailey*

TRONGATE (IRE) 5 b.g. Dansant – Val Eile (IRE) (Aahsaylad) [2016/17 b16s³ b16s³ **h106** h20.5v² h16v² h24.3d Apr 21] first foal: dam, unraced, out of half-sister to Champion **b93** Hurdle winner Beech Road: pulled up in point: fair form in bumpers: better effort when third at Ayr in January: fair form over hurdles: best effort when second in maiden at same course. *R. Mike Smith*

TROPICAL SUNSHINE (IRE) 9 b.g. Bachelor Duke (USA) – Tropical Coral (IRE) **h83** (Pennekamp (USA)) [2016/17 h–: h16.7g² h16.7gᵖᵘ h15.8d h19.6g Apr 22] poor maiden hurdler: best effort at 17f. *Pippa Bickerton*

TROUBLED SOUL (IRE) 8 ch.m. Definite Article – Dorrha Lass (IRE) (Fourstars **c111** Allstar (USA)) [2016/17 h106, b77: h20g c19.5g³ h16g h19g c19.9m³ c20s² c20.8gᵖᵘ **h101** h20.7d³ Mar 15] sturdy mare: fair handicap hurdler: fair form over fences: left Denis Hogan after third start: stays 21f: acts on soft and good to firm going: tried in hood: usually wears tongue tie. *Fergal O'Brien*

TROUBLE IN PARIS (IRE) 10 ch.g. Great Palm (USA) – Ten Dollar Bill (IRE) **c69 §** (Accordion) [2016/17 c74§, h–: c20.1s² c20.5s³ c21.5s⁴ c24.3vᵖᵘ c20.1v⁴ c24.2g⁵ Apr 25] **h–** maiden hurdler: poor maiden chaser: stays 25f: acts on heavy going: has worn headgear, including final start: usually wears tongue tie: races towards rear: temperamental. *Barry Murtagh*

TROUFION (FR) 8 gr.g. Smadoun (FR) – La Troussardiere (FR) (Maresca Sorrento **c99** (FR)) [2016/17 c21.2s² c23.6g* c19.9g* Apr 28] winning pointer: maiden hurdler: modest **h–** form over fences: won handicaps at Huntingdon (twice) in April: stays 3m: acts on good to firm going: tried in tongue tie. *Caroline Bailey*

TRUCKERS GLORY (IRE) 7 ch.g. Mahler – Mary's Fun (IRE) (Glacial Storm (USA)) **c118** [2016/17 h21.2m² h23g³ h20d* h23.6m³ h23.9d⁴ c20.3d* c20.9vᶠ Feb 1] seventh foal: dam **h114** winning pointer: placed in Irish points: fair form over hurdles: won handicap at Ffos Las (conditional) in October: fairly useful form when winning novice handicap at Bangor in January on completed start over fences: should stay beyond 21f: acts on good to firm and good to soft going: in headgear last 4 starts: usually races close up. *Rebecca Curtis*

TRUCKERS HIGHWAY (IRE) 8 b.g. Rudimentary (USA) – Countessdee (IRE) **c116** (Arctic Lord) [2016/17 c118, h–: c20.3sᵖᵘ c17.4s⁴ c16d⁴ c20s c15.7dᵖᵘ Feb 26] maiden **h–** hurdler: fairly useful handicap chaser: won at Ludlow in January: stays 2½m: acts on heavy going: often in hood: has worn tongue tie: usually races prominently, tends to find little. *John Groucott*

TRUCKERS LODGE (IRE) 5 b.g. Westerner – Galeacord (IRE) (Accordion) [2016/17 **b105** b16g* Apr 8] third foal: dam, winning pointer, sister to useful/unreliable hurdler (stayed 3m) Cairdin: off mark in Irish maiden points at second attempt: 3/1, looked good prospect when won bumper at Chepstow by 9 lengths from Mont des Avaloirs: bred to stay 3m. *Tom George*

TRUE SELF (IRE) 4 b.f. Oscar (IRE) – Good Thought (IRE) (Mukaddamah (USA)) **b93 p** [2016/17 b14s² Nov 16] seventh foal: half-sister to 2 winners on Flat, including winner up to 1½m Sir Boss (by Tagula): dam unraced: 4/1, second in fillies junior bumper at Warwick (head behind Shearling): should progress. *Don Cantillon*

TRUSTAN TIMES (IRE) 11 b.g. Heron Island (IRE) – Ballytrustan Maid (IRE) **c95** (Orchestra) [2016/17 h24.4g⁴ h20.9s* c31.8g Apr 22] tall gelding: useful handicap hurdler: **h130** won at Kelso (by 2½ lengths from Rhymers Stone) in April: useful handicap chaser, well held in Scottish Grand National on final outing in 2016/17: stays 4m: acts on heavy going: tried in cheekpieces. *Mark Walford*

TRUST THOMAS 9 ch.g. Erhaab (USA) – Yota (FR) (Galetto (FR)) [2016/17 c116, h–: **c120** c15.6d* c17.3m³ c15.2m c15.5g² c15.2s⁵ c17.1s⁵ c15.7d⁵ c15.5s⁴ c15.5v³ c17.1dᵖᵘ Apr 10] **h–** good-bodied gelding: winning hurdler: fairly useful handicap chaser: won at Hexham (conditional) early in season: stays 2¾m, races around 2m nowadays: acts on heavy going: has worn headgear, including in 2016/17: tried in tongue tie. *Ann Hamilton*

TRY IT SOMETIME (IRE) 9 b.g. Milan – Lead'er Inn (IRE) (Supreme Leader) c76 §
[2016/17 c88, h79: c20.9g⁶ c19.4s⁵ c25.3v⁴ c25.2s⁵ c24.5v² h20s c25.2s⁵ c24.5s⁵ c23.8g⁶ **h–**
Apr 9] fair hurdler at best: poor handicap chaser nowadays: stays 25f: acts on heavy going:
wears headgear/tongue tie: temperamental. *Sheila Lewis*

TSAR ALEXANDRE (FR) 10 b.g. Robin des Champs (FR) – Bertrange (FR) (Torvay **c110**
(FR)) [2016/17 c–, h–: c23m² c23d² Jun 29] tall, useful-looking gelding: winning hurdler: **h–**
fair maiden chaser: stays 3m: acts on soft and good to firm going: wears tongue tie.
Warren Greatrex

TSUNDOKU (IRE) 6 ch.m. Medicean – Toberanthawn (IRE) (Danehill Dancer (IRE)) **h103**
[2016/17 h18.2g* h16.5g⁵ h16gᶠ h16.5g h21.4d h19.7s* h19.9vᶠ Feb 12] dam half-sister
to useful hurdler (stayed 19f) Hisaabaat: fair maiden on Flat, stays 1¼m: fair hurdler:
won maiden at Downpatrick early in season and handicap at Wetherby in January: left
Ms Margaret Mullins after third start: stays 2½m: acts on soft going. *Alexandra Dunn*

TUCKERS SPRING 6 b.m. Dr Massini (IRE) – Tuckers Bay (Karinga Bay) [2016/17 **b–**
b15.8d Jul 13] tailed off in maiden bumper: dead. *Barry Leavy*

TUDOR CITY (IRE) 5 b.g. Yeats (IRE) – She's Our Mare (IRE) (Commanche Run) **h127**
[2016/17 h104p: h16vᵖᵘ h16.4g² h16d² h16g² h16d* h16.5d Apr 25] fairly useful hurdler:
won maiden at Fairyhouse in April: second in Coral.ie Hurdle at Leopardstown in January:
raced only at 2m: acts on heavy going: tried in cheekpieces: wears tongue tie: often races
towards rear/travels strongly. *A. J. Martin, Ireland*

TUDORS TREASURE 6 b.g. Dr Massini (IRE) – Rude Health (Rudimentary (USA)) **h105**
[2016/17 h69, b66: h16.8m⁶ h19.9m² h21s³ h21.9v* h25g⁶ Apr 28] lengthy gelding: fair
handicap hurdler: won at Ffos Las in March: stays 2¾m: acts on good to firm and heavy
going: often races prominently. *Robert Stephens*

TUFFATTHETOP (IRE) 6 br.g. Kalanisi (IRE) – Anshabella (IRE) (Anshan) [2016/17 **h–**
h–: h23.9s⁶ h21.3d⁵ h24.1s h23.1gᵖᵘ Apr 11] rather lightly-built gelding: little form over
hurdles: dead. *Jonjo O'Neill*

TUFFSTUFF 9 b.g. Generous (IRE) – Life Line (Exit To Nowhere (USA)) [2016/17 h92: **h–**
h16mᵖᵘ h16d Jun 19] workmanlike gelding: maiden hurdler, no form in 2016/17: unproven
beyond 2m: acts on heavy going: often wears cheekpieces/tongue tie: front runner/races
prominently. *Brian Barr*

TUGBOAT (IRE) 9 b.g. Galileo (IRE) – Alleluia (Caerleon (USA)) [2016/17 c114, h–: **c–**
c23gᵖᵘ c24sᵖᵘ c23.8mᵖᵘ Apr 25] angular gelding: point winner: winning hurdler: fair chaser **h–**
at best, no form in 2016/17: often races in rear. *G. Slade-Jones*

TULLOW TONIC (IRE) 6 b.m. Beneficial – Annalecky (IRE) (Bob's Return (IRE)) **h100**
[2016/17 h92, b76: h19g⁶ h19.6g⁵ h20g⁴ h19.7g⁵ h21d* h20.5g* h19.8s* h24.4g h21.2d
Jan 25] rather unfurnished mare: fair handicap hurdler: won mares events at Towcester in
November and Leicester/Sandown in December: left Charlie Longsdon after third start:
stays 21f: acts on soft going: wears hood: often races in rear/travels strongly. *Tom Weston*

TULLY EAST (IRE) 7 b.g. Shantou (USA) – Ghillie's Bay (IRE) (King's Ride) [2016/17 **c147**
h137: c18d* c17d⁶ c17s² c20.4g* c16dᵖᵘ Apr 27] good-topped gelding: useful hurdler: **h–**
smart form over fences: won maiden at Thurles (by 5½ lengths from A Sizing Network) in
December and Close Brothers Novices' Handicap Chase at Cheltenham (by 1¼ lengths
from Ball Present) in March: second in Flyingbolt Novices' Chase at Navan (19 lengths
behind Ball d'Arc) in February: stays 2½m: acts on heavy going. *Alan Fleming, Ireland*

TULLYGLUSH (IRE) 5 b.m. Scorpion (IRE) – Ardsallagh's Lark (IRE) (Beneficial) **h95 p**
[2016/17 b16.2m* h22.1g* Jun 1] €8,000 3-y-o: sixth foal: half-sister to bumper winner **b84**
Itsalark (by Definite Article): dam (h105), bumper/2½m hurdle winner, sister to fairly
useful hurdler/useful chaser (stayed 2¾m) Washington Lad: modest form when won mares
bumper at Perth in May: 15/8, also won mares maiden at Cartmel (by short head from
Knocklayde Sno Cat) on hurdling debut: open to improvement. *Gordon Elliott, Ireland*

TULSA JACK (IRE) 8 b.g. Urban Ocean (FR) – Jessica's Pet (IRE) (King's Ride) **c135**
[2016/17 c30dᶠ c26m³ c24.6m⁵ c25s* h24.2g⁴ h24g⁶ c24dᵖᵘ c28.5g² c30d Apr 29] rather **h112**
leggy gelding: fairly useful handicap hurdler: useful handicap chaser: won Midlands
National Handicap Chase at Kilbeggan in July: second in Ulster National at Downpatrick
(head behind Anseanachai Cliste) in March: stays 29f: acts on soft and good to firm going:
wears blinkers. *Noel Meade, Ireland*

TUMSHIE 7 b.m. Rainbow High – Maryland (IRE) (Executive Perk) [2016/17 h19.9g^{pu} **h–**
May 29] third foal: dam (h87), bumper winner, half-sister to useful chaser (stays 29f)
Out Now: unplaced completed starts in points: pulled up in mares maiden on hurdling
debut. *Polly Gundry*

TURBAN (FR) 10 b.g. Dom Alco (FR) – Indianabelle (FR) (Useful (FR)) [2016/17 c145x, **c118 x**
h–: c20d h19.9v^{pu} c20.8s^{pu} c24d^4 c24.2v^5 c26s^{pu} c20d c25.7g* c24.2g^3 Apr 17] sturdy **h–**
gelding: useful hurdler at best, pulled up second outing in 2016/17: fairly useful handicap
chaser nowadays: won at Plumpton in March: left W. P. Mullins after first start: stays 3¼m:
acts on heavy going: tried in headgear: often let down by jumping. *Paul Henderson*

TURBO DU RANCH (FR) 10 gr.g. Useful (FR) – Zoumba du Ranch (FR) (Smadoun **c–**
(FR)) [2016/17 h15.9s h22g^{ur} h21.6g^F Apr 21] fairly useful hurdler at best, no form in **h–**
2016/17: winning chaser: usually wore headgear/tongue tie: dead. *Daniel O'Brien*

TURCAGUA (FR) 7 gr.g. Turgeon (USA) – Acancagua (FR) (Subotica (FR)) [2016/17 **h135**
b104: b16d^4 h22d^3 h20d* h20s^2 h24v^{pu} h24g^{pu} Mar 17] well-made gelding: bumper **b–**
winner: useful form over hurdles: won maiden at Punchestown (by 9½ lengths from
Champagne Classic) in December: second in Lawlor's Hotel Novices' Hurdle at Naas
(9 lengths behind Death Duty) in January: stays 2½m: acts on soft going: tried in hood.
W. P. Mullins, Ireland

TURKEY CREEK (IRE) 8 b.g. Scorpion (IRE) – Emesions Lady (IRE) (Bigstone **h–**
(IRE)) [2016/17 h19v^{pu} Dec 31] maiden hurdler, pulled up sole outing in 2016/17 (wore
tongue tie): should be suited by further than 17f. *Paul Webber*

TURNBURY 6 b.g. Azamour (IRE) – Scottish Heights (IRE) (Selkirk (USA)) [2016/17 **h61**
h16.3m h15.9g^{pu} h16d h15.9d h15.9v^6 Jan 2] fair on Flat, stays 1½m: poor form over
hurdles: raced only at 2m: tried in cheekpieces/tongue tie. *Nikki Evans*

TURN OVER SIVOLA (FR) 10 b.g. Assessor (IRE) – Notting Hill (FR) (Garde **c133 §**
Royale) [2016/17 c127§, h–: c18g^2 c19.2g^2 c19.4g^2 c16g c16.5g h16d c17d h16d c17s Jan **h–**
15] good-topped gelding: fairly useful hurdler at best, no form in 2016/17: useful handicap
chaser: second at Market Rasen (8 lengths behind Sir Valentino) early in season: left Alan
King after fifth start: stays 19f: acts on good to firm and heavy going: tried in cheekpieces:
often races towards rear: weak finisher. *Gordon Elliott, Ireland*

TURN TURK (IRE) 6 gr.m. Robin des Champs (FR) – Revelate (IRE) (Great Palm **b94**
(USA)) [2016/17 b16d* b16v^2 Feb 24] €10,000 3-y-o: third foal: dam unraced half-sister
to top-class chaser (2½m-3¼m winner) Celestial Gold and high-class hurdler (stayed 3m)
Fiveforthree: fair form in bumpers: won at Worcester in June: second in mares event at
Warwick in February. *Nicky Henderson*

*Close Brothers Novices' Handicap Chase (Listed), Cheltenham—well-backed Irish raider
Tully East (noseband) prevails from Gold Present (hoops), Two Taffs (cheekpieces) and
Powersbomb (No.12)*

TURTLE BOYS (IRE) 11 b.g. Turtle Island (IRE) – El Pina (Be My Guest (USA)) **c80** [2016/17 c32.5g Apr 27] multiple point winner: twice-raced hurdler: well beaten in 2 **h–** hunter chases: tried in cheekpieces/tongue tie. *G. Hiscock*

TURTLE CASK (IRE) 8 b.g. Turtle Island (IRE) – Sayce (IRE) (Supreme Leader) **c–** [2016/17 c–§, h99§: h24.6d⁴ h24.3s⁴ h23.3v⁴ h24.3s⁵ h21.2s h25.3s² h25.3s h21.3d³ Mar **h90** 31] strong gelding: modest handicap hurdler: pulled up both starts over fences: stays easy 25f: acts on heavy going: wears headgear: front runner/races prominently. *Dianne Sayer*

TURTLE TIM (IRE) 13 b.g. Turtle Island (IRE) – Acumen (IRE) (Phardante (FR)) **c–** [2016/17 c21gᵖᵘ May 5] multiple winning pointer: lightly-raced chaser, pulled up sole outing in 2016/17. *Miss S. L. Pidsley*

TURTLE WATCH 9 b.g. Where Or When (IRE) – Cita Verda (FR) (Take Risks (FR)) **c105** [2016/17 h121: h16d c16.3sᶠ c17.1s² c15.9s⁶ Feb 8] fairly useful handicap hurdler, **h81** considerably handled on return in 2016/17: below form when second in handicap at Kelso on second of 3 starts over fences: unproven beyond 17f: acts on soft going: tried in tongue tie: often races towards rear. *Rose Dobbin*

TUSCAN GOLD 10 ch.g. Medicean – Louella (USA) (El Gran Senor (USA)) [2016/17 **h101** h17.2d⁵ h25.4g⁴ h19.7g h24.1d³ h24.1d⁶ h25.3d² h25.3g* h27v⁵ Feb 12] well-made gelding: fair handicap hurdler: won at Catterick in January: stays 25f: acts on soft and good to firm going: has worn cheekpieces: often races prominently. *Micky Hammond*

TUTCHEC (FR) 10 gr.g. Turgeon (USA) – Pocahontas (FR) (Nikos) [2016/17 c67, h–: **c82** c23.4d c21.1sᵘʳ c21.7d⁶ c25.6v⁵ c25.2s³ Jan 11] maiden hurdler: poor handicap chaser **h–** nowadays: left Chris Grant after first start: stays 3¼m: acts on heavy going: has worn headgear, including in 2016/17. *Harry Whittington*

TWENTY EIGHT GUNS 7 b.m. Black Sam Bellamy (IRE) – Glory Be (Gunner B) **c127** [2016/17 h104: c20.1g⁴ c19.4s* c20.9d² c20.3s* c20.2s* c20d⁴ c22.2g h16.7d³ Apr 27] **h114** fair maiden hurdler: fairly useful handicap chaser: won at Ffos Las in November, Bangor in December and Wincanton (mares event) in January: stays 2¾m: acts on heavy going: wears cheekpieces: front runner/races prominently. *Michael Scudamore*

TWENTYPOUNDLUCK (IRE) 12 ch.g. Beneficial – Guitane Lady (IRE) (Commanche **c–** Run) [2016/17 c20.3vᵘʳ May 10] dual point winner: maiden hurdler: fairly useful chaser, **h–** unseated first sole outing in 2016/17: stays 2½m: acts on good to firm and heavy going: has worn headgear. *Paul Collins*

TWENTYTWO'S TAKEN (IRE) 9 b.m. King's Theatre (IRE) – Persian Desert (IRE) **c–** (Persian Mews) [2016/17 h127: h20dᶠ h23.3gᵖᵘ c20d h21.2s⁴ Feb 8] tall, rather sparely- **h95** made mare: fairly useful handicap hurdler, below form in novice handicap on chasing debut: tailed off in novice handicap on chasing debut: stays 21f: acts on heavy going: wears headgear: tried in tongue tie. *David Pipe*

TWIRLING MAGNET (IRE) 11 b.g. Imperial Ballet (IRE) – Molly Maguire (IRE) **c121 §** (Supreme Leader) [2016/17 c126, h–: c22.5d⁴ c22.6m³ c25.5g c25g⁵ c25gᵘʳ c24.2s⁴ c24vᵖᵘ **h–** c25.6dᶠ Jan 25] compact gelding: winning hurdler: fairly useful handicap chaser: third at Stratford in July: stays 25f: acts on soft and good to firm going: usually wears headgear/ tongue tie: often races towards rear/travels strongly: unreliable. *Jonjo O'Neill*

TWISTED PSYCHOLOGY (IRE) 11 b.g. Dushyantor (USA) – Friendly Concern **c–** (IRE) (Woods of Windsor (USA)) [2016/17 c23g c24d Oct 13] maiden point winner: little form in chases: in headgear last 2 starts: wears tongue tie. *Thomas Coyle, Ireland*

TWISTER MIX 6 gr.g. Fair Mix (IRE) – Reverse Swing (Charmer) [2016/17 b–: h23gᵖᵘ **c–** h20g⁵ h16.7g c25.8gᵖᵘ Aug 20] dual point winner: no form over hurdles: pulled up in **h–** novice handicap on chasing debut: in hood last 4 starts, tongue tied last 2. *Katy Price*

TWIST ON GINGE (IRE) 5 b.g. Craigsteel – Miss Top (IRE) (Tremblant) [2016/17 **h104 §** b92: b16g² b20s⁶ h23.3v² h23.6s³ h26v³ h24g⁴ h20.2gᵖᵘ Apr 27] tall, rather unfurnished **b90** gelding: fair form in bumpers: fair form over hurdles: stays 3¼m: best form on heavy going: tried in cheekpieces: often races prominently: not straightforward. *Nigel Twiston-Davies*

TWOFORTHEPRICE 5 b.m. Multiplex – Romping Home (IRE) (Rock Hopper) **b–** [2016/17 b15.8m b16.3m Jul 17] first foal: dam (c112/h109) 17f-21f hurdle/chase winner: no form in 2 bumpers. *Sarah-Jayne Davies*

TWO HOOTS (IRE) 6 gr.g. Tikkanen (USA) – Supreme Beneficial (IRE) (Beneficial) **h82 p**
[2016/17 b16d³ h17.7s⁵ h19.5v h16s⁵ h19g Mar 30] €4,200 3-y-o: second foal: dam **b61**
unraced half-sister to fair hurdler/useful chaser (stayed 4m) Kinburn: third in bumper at
Warwick: poor form over hurdles: will be suited by 3m: usually races towards rear: remains
capable of better. *Paul Nicholls*

TWOJAYSLAD 8 b.g. Kayf Tara – Fulwell Hill (Anshan) [2016/17 c111, h–: c20v* **c114**
c24dᵖᵘ c23.8gᵖᵘ c23.9d² Apr 27] maiden hurdler: fair form over fences: won handicap at **h–**
Warwick in December: stays 3m: acts on heavy going: tried in cheekpieces: often races
prominently. *Ian Williams*

TWO SMOKIN BARRELS 8 b.m. Kayf Tara – Coldabri (IRE) (Husyan (USA)) **c126**
[2016/17 h101p: h23.3g⁴ c24.2d* c24.2s* c23.4v* c25.2s⁴ c20.1v* c22.2g⁶ Apr 15] **h104**
workmanlike mare: fair form over hurdles: fairly useful form over fences: won novice
handicap and mares handicap at Wetherby in December, mares novice handicap at Kelso
in January and mares handicap at Newcastle in March: stays 3m: acts on heavy going.
Michael Scudamore

TWO STROKE (IRE) 11 b.g. Turtle Island (IRE) – Bannockburn (IRE) (Strong Gale) **c–**
[2016/17 c24.2dᵖᵘ c23.8mᵖᵘ c20.1gᵘʳ Jun 4] dual point winner: maiden chaser, failed to
complete all 3 starts in 2016/17. *Victor Thompson*

TWO SWALLOWS 7 b.m. Kayf Tara – One Gulp (Hernando (FR)) [2016/17 h24.4g* **h121**
h24.1s² h24v* h23.8s² h24g* Apr 20] fairly useful handicap hurdler: won at Doncaster
(mares event) in December, Towcester (mares event) in February and Cheltenham (by
½ length from Rolling Maul) in April: stays 3m: acts on heavy going. *Ben Pauling*

TWO TAFFS (IRE) 7 b.g. Flemensfirth (USA) – Richs Mermaid (IRE) (Saddlers' Hall **c147**
(IRE)) [2016/17 h135p: h20d* h22.8v c20.5g² c19.2d² c16.2v³ c20.4g³ c20.5d* Apr 21] **h116 +**
well-made gelding: useful hurdler: didn't need to be at best when won novice at Carlisle in
October: smart form over fences: won listed handicap at Ayr (by 3 lengths from Theinval)
in April: third in Close Brothers Novices' Handicap at Cheltenham (1½ lengths behind
Tully East) in March: stays 21f: acts on soft going: in cheekpieces/tongue tie last 2 starts:
often races towards rear, strong traveller. *Dan Skelton*

TWYCROSS WARRIOR 5 b.g. Cockney Rebel (IRE) – Gaelic Roulette (IRE) (Turtle **h91**
Island (IRE)) [2016/17 h97, b–: h16.3m⁶ h16.2g⁴ h21.2d Nov 28] modest maiden hurdler:
tried in tongue tie: often races towards rear. *Robin Dickin*

TWYFORD 10 b.g. Bach (IRE) – Commanche Token (IRE) (Commanche Run) [2016/17 **c– x**
c–, h–: h15.3m h15.3m c20.9gᵖᵘ Jul 2] winning pointer: maiden hurdler, no form in **h–**
2016/17: no form in chases (usually let down by jumping). *Laura Young*

TYCOON PRINCE (IRE) 7 b.g. Trans Island – Downtown Train (IRE) (Glacial Storm **h133**
(USA)) [2016/17 h133: h20d⁴ h18.1v⁵ Mar 5] strong gelding: reportedly had breathing
operation: useful form over hurdles: fourth in minor event at Punchestown (14 lengths
behind Supasundae) in December: stays 2½m: acts on heavy going: tried in hood: in tongue
tie last 4 starts. *Gordon Elliott, Ireland*

TYNECASTLE PARK 4 b.g. Sea The Stars (IRE) – So Silk (Rainbow Quest (USA)) **h104**
[2016/17 h15.8g³ h15.8g² Apr 28] maiden on Flat: fair form when placed on both starts
over hurdles. *Robert Eddery*

TYRE HILL (IRE) 8 b.g. Catcher In The Rye (IRE) – Stay At Home (IRE) (Blueprint **c–**
(IRE)) [2016/17 h62: h19.1d⁶ h21.6s c24.1sᵘʳ c26.3gᶠ Dec 20] poor maiden hurdler: failed **h62**
to complete both outings over fences: best effort at 19f: acts on good to soft going: tried in
cheekpieces: usually wears tongue tie. *David Dennis*

TYRELL (IRE) 4 b.g. Teofilo (IRE) – Sleeveless (USA) (Fusaichi Pegasus (USA)) **h117 p**
[2016/17 h16.8s⁴ h16s* Dec 8] fairly useful on Flat, stays 2m: fairly useful form over
hurdles: in blinkers, won juvenile at Warwick in December: will probably stay beyond 2m:
likely to progress further. *Alan King*

TYRRELL'S SUCCES (FR) 6 br.g. Forestier (FR) – Irish Succes (FR) (Turgeon **h107**
(USA)) [2016/17 h89: b16.2s² h16g h16d h16v h16d h20v⁵ h22s* h20.5g⁴ Apr 22] runner- **b96**
up both starts in maiden points: fairly useful form in bumpers: fair hurdler: won handicap
at Down Royal in March: stays 2¾m: acts on soft going. *Aaron Stronge, Ireland*

TZAR DE L'ELFE (FR) 7 b.g. Satri (IRE) – Rue Tournefort (FR) (Marchand de Sable **c–**
(USA)) [2016/17 h17.4s c22.4s⁵ c19.9g⁵ h25vᵖᵘ h25s h25s⁴ Mar 13] sturdy gelding: first **h88**
foal: dam lightly raced over hurdles/on Flat in France, half-sister to smart French hurdler/
useful chaser (17f-21f winner) Scout Master: modest maiden hurdler: maiden chaser: left
Mlle Louisa Carberry after third start: seems to stay 21f: has worn headgear, including in
2016/17: in tongue tie last 2 starts. *Richard Rowe*

TZORA 12 b.g. Sakhee (USA) – Lucky Arrow (Indian Ridge) [2016/17 h18.5g³ h21.6g⁶ Aug 20] sturdy gelding: fairly useful handicap hurdler: third at Newton Abbot in July: winning chaser: stays 2¾m: acts on soft and good to firm going: tried in tongue tie. *Martin Hill* — **c–ʰ120**

U

UBAK (FR) 9 b.g. Kapgarde (FR) – Gesse Parade (FR) (Dress Parade) [2016/17 c140, h149: h25.4d h20g⁵ h24.2d⁴ Nov 25] lengthy gelding: smart hurdler: fifth in handicap at Aintree (9¾ lengths behind Massini's Trap) in October: useful form over fences (jumped sketchily): stays 25f: acts on heavy going. *Gary Moore* — **c–ʰ145**

UBALTIQUE (FR) 9 b.g. Balko – Ode Antique (FR) (Subotica (FR)) [2016/17 c125§, h–§: c17.1d³ c15.2s³ c15.7s⁴ c16s² c16.3s* c15.5v⁵ c17.1sᵖᵘ Apr 3] good-topped gelding: winning hurdler: fairly useful handicap chaser: won at Haydock in January: stays 19f: acts on heavy going: wears blinkers/tongue tie: often races in rear: temperamental. *Donald McCain* — **c125 § h– §**

UBER ALLES (GER) 9 b.g. Doyen (IRE) – Ustina (GER) (Star Appeal) [2016/17 c24.2m h21.6m² h21.6g⁶ Jul 25] multiple winning pointer: fair form over hurdles: well beaten in hunter on chasing debut. *Mary Sanderson* — **c–ʰ100**

UCELLO CONTI (FR) 9 b.g. Martaline – Gazelle Lulu (FR) (Altayan) [2016/17 c151, h–: h20d c25.5d⁴ c24.5d c25d² c24s⁴ c34.3dᵘʳ Apr 8] sturdy gelding: winning hurdler: smart handicap chaser: fourth in Becher Chase at Aintree (2½ lengths behind Vieux Lion Rouge) in December: should stay beyond 3¼m: acts on good to firm and heavy going: wears tongue tie: often travels strongly. *Gordon Elliott, Ireland* — **c149 h–**

UEUETEOTL (FR) 9 gr.g. Tikkanen (USA) – Azturk (FR) (Baby Turk) [2016/17 c119, h–: h23.3d⁶ h23.3d* h22.1m c24.2d² h24.7g c25.2g³ Nov 30] big gelding: fairly useful handicap hurdler: won at Hexham (amateur) in June: fairly useful handicap chaser: second at same course in September: stays 25f: acts on soft going: wears headgear: front runner/races prominently: unreliable. *James Ewart* — **c118 § h115 §**

UGOLIN DE BEAUMONT (FR) 9 b.g. Alberto Giacometti (IRE) – Okarina de Beaumont (FR) (Ragmar (FR)) [2016/17 c19.2v⁴ c23.6sᵖᵘ c24.2d⁵ c24.2s² c28.1g² Apr 19] winning hurdler: fair form over fences: stays 3½m: acts on heavy going. *Bob Buckler* — **c113 h–**

UHLAN BUTE (FR) 9 ch.g. Brier Creek (USA) – Jonquiere (FR) (Trebrook (FR)) [2016/17 c121§, h–: c20.5sᵘʳ c20sᵖᵘ c20.5g⁴ c20.2s² c19.9g⁴ c20.1gᵘʳ Apr 27] workmanlike gelding: winning hurdler: fairly useful handicap chaser: stays 3m: acts on good to firm and heavy going: usually wears headgear: unreliable. *Venetia Williams* — **c125 § h–**

Randox Health Topham Handicap Chase, Aintree—
a valuable prize for champion conditional Harry Cobden as Ultragold (left) springs a surprise;
Grand Sefton winner As de Mee (noseband) fades into fifth this time

UJAGAR (IRE) 6 gr.g. Dalakhani (IRE) – No Secrets (USA) (El Corredor (USA)) **h76**
[2016/17 h–: h16.3s h15.8s[4] h16.5g* h16.5m[5] Apr 20] rather leggy gelding: poor form over
hurdles: won selling handicap at Taunton in April for Dai Burchell: likely to prove best
around 2m: acts on good to firm going: tried in tongue tie: often races towards rear.
Kevin Bishop

ULANDA (IRE) 5 b.m. Le Cadre Noir (IRE) – Hataana (USA) (Robellino (USA)) **h87**
[2016/17 h–: h16d[4] h16g[6] h16.4s h18.7m[6] h16v[5] h16.2s Sep 20] modest maiden hurdler:
unproven beyond 2m: acts on good to soft going: often in headgear: in tongue tie last 3
starts: usually races freely. *Paul John Gilligan, Ireland*

ULCK DU LIN (FR) 9 b.g. Sassanian (USA) – Miss Fast (FR) (Prince Fast (FR)) **c132 §**
[2016/17 c143, h–: c17g c16.9m c16.4g[5] c15.5s[pu] c19.9g c16g[5] Apr 17] quite good-topped **h–**
gelding: winning hurdler: useful handicap chaser: fifth at Newbury (5¼ lengths behind
Ultragold) in November: unproven beyond 17f: acts on any going: wears headgear/tongue
tie: travels strongly, but no battler. *Paul Nicholls*

ULIS DE VASSY (FR) 9 b.g. Voix du Nord (FR) – Helathou (FR) (Video Rock (FR)) **c126**
[2016/17 c129§, h–§: c17g[pu] c20d[5] c17.2g* c16g[3] c15.2m[6] h15.8m[5] c19.4d[5] c23.5g[pu] **h–**
c17.2d c21.4s[5] c20.2s[6] c19.2g[5] Mar 27] tall gelding: winning hurdler: fairly useful
handicap chaser: won at Market Rasen in July: left Dan Skelton after fourth start: stays
2¼m: acts on good to firm and heavy going: has worn headgear/tongue tie: often races in
rear. *Laura Morgan*

ULTIMATE DREAM (FR) 6 b.g. Ultimately Lucky (IRE) – Carazia (FR) (Labus (FR)) **h91**
[2016/17 h61: h23.1g[5] h24g[5] h23.8v[2] h24d* h23.3v h23.1g* Apr 11] modest handicap
hurdler: won at Towcester in December and Exeter in April: stays 3m: acts on good to soft
going: tried in blinkers: usually races prominently. *Jonjo O'Neill*

ULTIMATE HORSEMAN (IRE) 7 b.g. Kalanisi (IRE) – Dawn's Double (IRE) **h98 §**
(King's Ride) [2016/17 h19.9s[6] h25.3s[pu] h22g[4] h26.4g[5] Apr 15] €32,000 3-y-o: half-
brother to 3 winners, including fairly useful hurdler/useful chaser Toby Lerone (2½m-3m
winner, by Old Vic) and fairly useful hurdler/useful chaser Mr Warbucks (2m/2¼m winner,
by Norwich): dam (h107) bumper/2½m hurdle winner: bumper winner: fair maiden hurdler
for Gordon Elliott, below form in 2016/17: should stay beyond 3m: acts on good to soft
going: has worn headgear, including in 2016/17: often races towards rear: one to be wary
of. *Tim Vaughan*

ULTIMATUM DU ROY (FR) 9 b.g. Brier Creek (USA) – La Fleur du Roy (FR) **c117**
(Sleeping Car (FR)) [2016/17 c116, h–: c22.5v[5] c23.8g* c25.1d[2] c27.6d[pu] c25.6d* c23.8s[3] **h–**
c23.9d* Apr 27] good-bodied gelding: maiden hurdler: fairly useful handicap chaser: won
at Ludlow in November and January, and Market Rasen in April: stays 3¼m: acts on heavy
going: has worn cheekpieces: wears tongue tie. *Alex Hales*

ULTRAGOLD (FR) 9 b.g. Kapgarde (FR) – Hot d'Or (FR) (Shafoun (FR)) [2016/17 **c138 §**
c134, h–: c15.9g[6] c17.5m[5] c16.4g* c18.8d[bd] c19.4s[6] c15.5v c16.3g c21.1g* Apr 7] **h–**
sturdy gelding: maiden hurdler: useful handicap chaser: won at Newbury in November
and Topham Chase at Aintree (50/1, by length from Katnap) in April: best over shorter
than 3m: acts on soft going: wears tongue tie: usually races prominently: unreliable.
Colin Tizzard

ULUROO (FR) 5 b.g. Centennial (IRE) – Kica (FR) (Noir Et Or) [2016/17 b16.4v[4] **h87**
h16.2g[5] Apr 25] €57,000 3-y-o: half-brother to several winners, including useful hurdler/ **b–**
chaser Kaki de La Pree (23f-25f winner, by Kapgarde): dam winning French hurdler/chaser
up to 2¾m: tailed off in maiden bumper: 33/1, fifth in novice at Hexham (13½ lengths
behind Applaus) on hurdling debut. *Pauline Robson*

ULVA FERRY (IRE) 5 ch.g. Stowaway – Lisacul Queen (IRE) (Old Vic) [2016/17 h16s[6] **h84**
h20.5d Dec 28] first foal: dam unraced sister to fairly useful hurdler (2½m winner) Talbot
Road: poor form over hurdles. *Dan Skelton*

UMBERTO D'OLIVATE (FR) 9 b.g. Alberto Giacometti (IRE) – Komunion (FR) **c120 §**
(Luchiroverte (IRE)) [2016/17 c121§, h–: c24.2g* c24.5d c24.2v* c24v[ur] c24.2d c25.1d[4] **h–**
Mar 26] lengthy gelding: maiden hurdler: fairly useful handicap chaser: won at Exeter in
November and January: stays 31f: acts on heavy going: has worn headgear: front runner/
races prominently: temperamental. *Robert Walford*

U ME AND THEM (IRE) 8 ch.g. Vertical Speed (FR) – Bodies Pride (IRE) (John **c–**
French) [2016/17 c25.3g[pu] Apr 27] Irish maiden point winner: in cheekpieces, pulled up in
hunter on chasing debut. *Miss Hannah Taylor*

UN ACE (FR) 9 b.g. Voix du Nord (FR) – First Ball (FR) (Beyssac (FR)) [2016/17 c–,   **c129**
h138: c24s^{ur} c23.8m c27.3s c26g^6 c20.8g c19.9g^{pu} Apr 17] useful-looking gelding: useful   **h–**
hurdler: useful handicap chaser at best: stays 25f: acts on soft and good to firm going: in
headgear last 2 starts: wears tongue tie. *Kim Bailey*

UNANIMITE (FR) 6 ch.g. Kentucky Dynamite (USA) – Dame Blanche (USA)   **h129**
(Cherokee Run (USA)) [2016/17 h132: h21.6g h23.3d^4 h25g* h24.7d^6 Nov 5] sturdy
gelding: fairly useful handicap hurdler: won at Plumpton in October: stays 25f: acts on
good to soft going: usually wears headgear: tried in tongue tie: often races towards rear: has
joined P. Peltier, France. *David Pipe*

UN ANJOU (FR) 9 b.g. Panoramic – Idee d'Estruval (FR) (Port Etienne (FR)) [2016/17   **c106**
c117, h110: c17.4s^2 c17.2d^3 c19.2d^6 c16d^4 c17.4v^2 c17s^2 Mar 13] sturdy gelding: maiden   **h–**
hurdler: fair handicap chaser: stays 21f: acts on good to firm and heavy going: has worn
cheekpieces, including last 5 starts: tried in tongue tie. *David Dennis*

UN BEAU ROMAN (FR) 9 bl.g. Roman Saddle (IRE) – Koukie (FR) (Lute Antique   **c133 §**
(FR)) [2016/17 c138, h–: c18g^3 c17g^6 c21.4d^5 c17m c15.9g* c16.3d^2 c16.4d^6 c16.3g^{pu} **h–**
c20.8g^6 Apr 19] lengthy gelding: winning hurdler: useful handicap chaser: won at
Cheltenham in November: best up to 2¼m: acts on heavy going: wears hood: unreliable.
Paul Henderson

UNBLINKING 4 b.g. Cacique (IRE) – Deliberate (King's Best (USA)) [2016/17 h16s^3 **h95**
h16.5g h16s^6 Mar 13] angular gelding: fair maiden on Flat, best effort at 1½m: modest
form over hurdles. *Nigel Twiston-Davies*

UNBUCKLED (IRE) 7 b.m. Presenting – Una Kasala (GER) (Law Society (USA))   **h109**
[2016/17 h112, b104: h20m^4 May 13] sturdy mare: bumper winner: fair hurdler: stays 21f:
acts on good to soft going: often races prominently. *Neil King*

UNCLE ALASTAIR 5 b.g. Midnight Legend – Cyd Charisse (Kayf Tara) [2016/17   **b98**
b16s* b16s* Feb 14] €55,000 3-y-o: second foal: brother to 17f chase winner Movie
Legend: dam (h115), 2½m-2¾m hurdle winner, half-sister to fairly useful hurdler (stayed
19f) Emral Silk: fairly useful form in bumpers: won at Wetherby in January and Ayr in
February: will stay 2½m. *Nicky Richards*

UNCLE DANNY (IRE) 8 b.g. Catcher In The Rye (IRE) – Bobset Leader (IRE) (Bob   **c136**
Back (USA)) [2016/17 h20d c16m^5 c18d^5 c19d^f c20d^6 c16d^5 c20v* c20.8s^{bd} Jan 28] well-   **h–**
made gelding: half-brother to bumper winner/useful hurdler Shantou Bob (19f-3m winner,
by Shantou): dam unraced: winning pointer: fairly useful hurdler: useful chaser: won
maiden at Cork by 5 lengths from General Principle) in January: stays 2½m: best form on
soft/heavy going: has worn tongue tie, including last 3 starts. *John Queally, Ireland*

UNCLE JIMMY (IRE) 10 b.g. Alderbrook – Carrabawn (Buckskin (FR)) [2016/17   **c–**
h26.5g h24.2d^3 c25.2s^{pu} Dec 19] useful handicap hurdler: third at Newbury (2¼ lengths   **h137**
behind Solomn Grundy) in November: fairly useful form over fences: stays 25f: acts on
heavy going. *Philip Hobbs*

UNCLE MONTY (IRE) 8 b.g. Milan – She's A Gamble (IRE) (Teenoso (USA)) [2016/17   **c–**
c–, h90: c24.1g^5 c20.1d^5 c20g^{pu} h19.6d Aug 19] poor maiden hurdler: no form over fences: **h–**
best effort at 2½m: acts on heavy going: wears headgear: often races prominently: signs of
temperament. *Donald McCain*

UNCLE PERCY 5 b.g. Sir Percy – Forsythia (Most Welcome) [2016/17 b16.2d^2 b16d   **h84**
h15.8d h16.2v^6 h15.7s^4 Jan 31] fifth foal: half-brother to 3 winners, including fair hurdler/   **b87**
fairly useful chaser Pyracantha (2m-2½m winner, by Muhtarram) and fair hurdler Cowslip
(19f-2¾m winner, by Tobougg): dam, maiden on Flat, half-sister to useful hurdler/smart
chaser (stayed 25f) Eau de Cologne: fair form in bumpers: poor form over hurdles: left
Micky Hammond after first start: will be suited by 2½m+. *Ben Pauling*

UNCLE PETTIT (IRE) 9 b.g. Heron Island (IRE) – Special Ballot (IRE) (Perugino   **c76 x**
(USA)) [2016/17 c24d^{pu} c24d^{pu} c23g* c23.6g^{pu} c23.8g^{pu} Apr 9] workmanlike gelding: **h–**
maiden hurdler: poor handicap chaser: won at Taunton in December: stays 25f: acts on
heavy going: tried in cheekpieces: wears tongue tie: often let down by jumping. *Jonathan
Portman*

UNCLE TONE (IRE) 8 b.g. Pelder (IRE) – Daisy A Day (IRE) (Asir) [2016/17 h116:   **h105**
h24.7m^6 h23.1d^6 Apr 27] useful-looking gelding: fair handicap hurdler: left Tim Vaughan
after first start: stays 23f: acts on good to firm and heavy going. *Michael Appleby*

UNDERSTATEMENT 4 b.g. Authorized (IRE) – Usem (Bahamian Bounty) [2016/17   **b75**
b15.3v^5 b15.8g Apr 3] modest form in bumpers. *Warren Greatrex*

UNDER THE PHONE (IRE) 8 b.g. Heron Island (IRE) – Theo On The Bench (IRE) **c85**
(Mister Lord (USA)) [2016/17 c114, h–: c23.8m² May 8] winning hurdler: fair handicap **h–**
chaser: stays 3m, effective at shorter: acts on good to soft going: has worn headgear,
including last 3 starts: often races prominently. *Robin Dickin*

UNDER THE RED SKY (IRE) 10 ch.g. Insatiable (IRE) – Official Secret (Polish **c81 §**
Patriot (USA)) [2016/17 c75: c20.1d c24.2g³ c24.2s⁴ c20.1s⁶ c20.1s² c25.2dᵖᵘ c20.1v⁵
c20.9v² c20.1v² c24.2g³ Apr 25] poor maiden chaser: stays 3m: acts on heavy going: wears
cheekpieces: temperamental. *Kenny Johnson*

UN DE SCEAUX (FR) 9 b.g. Denham Red (FR) – Hotesse de Sceaux (FR) (April **c169**
Night (FR)) [2016/17 c174, h166+: h21.4s* h25.4d⁶ c15.5d* c16.3s* c20.8g* c16d² **h–**
Apr 25]

Four more top-class performances, three more Grade 1 wins from as many
starts in Britain, and a second Cheltenham Festival success. That was the admirable
record of the ever-reliable Un de Sceaux who was his stable's top earner in a testing
season for the yard which, for various reasons, was without the services of several
of its other star performers. Earlier in his career, Un de Sceaux had been kept out
of the limelight, campaigned away from the very best company in Ireland and
France, an approach which enabled him to remain unbeaten over hurdles but which
couldn't disguise his potential for bigger tests when the time came. A wealth of talent
elsewhere in Willie Mullins' yard was one reason for there being no rush to try Un
de Sceaux more highly. Another was his own immaturity, the rather highly-strung
Un de Sceaux's exuberant, trailblazing style leaving him little margin for error in
his jumping. A fall on his chasing debut was the only blot on his record when he
finally made his British debut in the 2015 Arkle at Cheltenham where his impressive
six-length victory over God's Own marked him down as a potential future two-
mile champion. However, twelve months later, and still unbeaten in completed
starts (he'd suffered another fall in Ireland in the meantime), Un de Sceaux finally
met his match when going down at odds on to a resurgent Sprinter Sacre in the
Queen Mother Champion Chase. A more emphatic defeat by the same rival, after a
bad mistake three out, in the Celebration Chase at Sandown, prompted a change of
direction for Un de Sceaux whose next two appearances—early in the latest British
season—came back over hurdles at Auteuil. He won the Prix La Barka in May over
twenty-one furlongs, the longest trip he had tackled thus far, but patently failed to
stay the extra half mile of the Grande Course de Haies d'Auteuil, finishing a weary
sixth, after having to compete for the lead with the top French hurdler Blue Dragon.

Sprinter Sacre's retirement in the autumn removed one major opponent
for Un de Sceaux on his return to chasing in the winter, though the emergence of
his stable's latest Arkle winner with Champion Chase aspirations, Douvan, hardly
made the two-mile chase division Un de Sceaux's for the taking. There was some
uncertainty about which of the pair would reappear in the Tingle Creek Chase in
December, but in the end it was Un de Sceaux who did duty at Sandown, starting
5/4 in a six-runner race sponsored again by Betfair. Un de Sceaux had been odds
on for the Tingle Creek the year before when withdrawn days beforehand after
failing to please in his work. The 2012 winner Sprinter Sacre paraded with the field
which included an old rival Sire de Grugy, seeking a third Tingle Creek to add to his
successes in 2013 and 2015. He had finished a long way behind Sprinter Sacre and
Un de Sceaux at Cheltenham and Sandown in the spring but had returned to form
when successfully conceding weight all round in a handicap at Ascot in November.
Sire de Grugy's stable-companion Ar Mad, winner of the Henry VIII Novices' Chase
in an excellent time on the same card twelve months earlier, and God's Own, who
had beaten Un de Sceaux's outstanding stable-companion Vautour in the Champion
Chase at Punchestown, were the other leading contenders, with the last two winners
of the Haldon Gold Cup, Sir Valentino and Vibrato Valtat (third in the Tingle Creek
when favourite the year before) the outsiders in the line-up. The more mature Un
de Sceaux is no longer quite the tearaway he once was, and instead it was Ar Mad,
having his first start for nearly ten months, who forced the pace in the Tingle Creek,
jumping boldly and going with zest until a mistake six from home, the first of the
three Railway fences, handed the lead to Un de Sceaux. The strong early pace set up

Betfair Tingle Creek Chase, Sandown—Un de Sceaux (left) survives a blunder at the second last to hold off 2013 and 2015 winner Sire de Grugy

a classic Sandown finish, with Un de Sceaux and Sire de Grugy battling it out up the hill from the home turn. A mistake from Un de Sceaux two out put Sire de Grugy right upsides and, when Un de Sceaux lost momentum by getting in close at the last, Sire de Grugy briefly showed ahead before Un de Sceaux's determined rally put him back in front to win by a length. God's Own stayed on well to finish just a neck behind Sire de Grugy in third, while Ar Mad was coming back at the leaders too in the closing stages, only another couple of lengths or so behind.

With Douvan kept in Ireland after recording facile wins at Cork and Leopardstown, Un de Sceaux was returned to Britain to attempt a second successive win in Ascot's Clarence House Chase, though he had a wasted journey first of all when the race fell victim to frost on its scheduled date. The Clarence House (and its predecessor the Victor Chandler) has often succumbed to the weather in its January slot, either leading to its abandonment or, more recently, to its transfer elsewhere. Cheltenham staged the 2013 Clarence House (won by Sprinter Sacre) when Ascot was snowed off, and it also staged the 2005 Victor Chandler, though that wasn't a weather-related switch, Ascot undergoing redevelopment that season (Warwick, Kempton and Sandown are other courses to have staged a rescheduled Victor Chandler Chase). The Spectra Cyber Security Solutions Clarence House Chase was therefore another addition to what became a nine-race card, starting at midday, on Cheltenham's Trials day, which had already accommodated an extra race, the cross-country chase having been postponed from the November meeting when the going on the cross-country course (which cannot be artificially watered) was deemed too firm. Having returned to Ireland since the previous Saturday, Un de Sceaux was one of four future Festival winners on the bumper card which, although it was marred by the death of the Cotswold Chase winner Many Clouds, was as star-studded as any outside the Festival itself. In the absence of Ar Mad, who had been declared in the original field at Ascot, none of Un de Sceaux's Tingle Creek victims re-opposed in the Clarence House and he was sent off at 2/1-on against six rivals, of whom only the previous season's Game Spirit winner Top Gamble and Special Tiara, recent winner of his second Desert Orchid Chase, were at single-figure odds. Un de Sceaux's most interesting opponent, though, was the 2015 Ryanair Chase winner Uxizandre who was making his first start since. After Special Tiara had made much of the running before dropping away to finish last of the five finishers, Un de Sceaux took over from the tenth to run out a convincing five-length winner from Uxizandre, with Top Gamble two and three quarter lengths back in third and the rest well beaten.

The Clarence House has been an excellent pointer to the Queen Mother Champion Chase in recent seasons, with Sprinter Sacre, Sire de Grugy and Dodging Bullets (fourth in the latest renewal) all winning both races before Un de Sceaux went down to Sprinter Sacre at the Festival in 2016. However, with Douvan firmly on course for the Champion Chase (after another exhibition round at Punchestown the week after the Clarence House), Un de Sceaux's Festival target was always likely to be the Ryanair instead. Running both horses in the Queen Mother was apparently never on the cards ('We'd rather have Ruby on both horses' explained Mullins), with Un de Sceaux only kept in the race in the event of something happening to Douvan beforehand. Of course, something did happen to Douvan, in the race itself, and Special Tiara's win, with Sir Valentino, Top Gamble and God's Own all close up, suggested Un de Sceaux might well have gone one better than the year before had he taken part.

Instead, then, Un de Sceaux went to post as the 7/4 favourite for the following day's Ryanair Chase in a field of eight, the joint smallest for the race along with the 2013 renewal won by Cue Card. Ill-fated stable-companion Vautour had won in a record fifteen-runner field the year before when becoming the first Irish-trained winner of the Ryanair, though, controversially, his participation had been much more of a surprise after a late switch from the Gold Cup, for which he had been one of the ante-post favourites (Vautour's expected appearance in the Gold Cup field almost certainly contributed to the sizeable turnout for the Ryanair). Visually, Un de Sceaux put up one of the latest Festival's most exhilarating performances, jumping better (his only mistake came at the first) than he had in the Champion Chase twelve months earlier, more in the style of his breathtaking Arkle victory. In ratings terms, Un de Sceaux's win has only been bettered by Cue Card and Vautour in the still relatively short history of the Ryanair. Un de Sceaux had a length and a half to spare at the post over the more patiently-ridden 8/1-shot Sub Lieutenant (runner-up to subsequent Gold Cup winner Sizing John in the Kinloch Brae Chase at Thurles on his previous start), though Un de Sceaux had been six clear jumping the last having gone clear before halfway, his advantage reduced only temporarily three out. To those in the stands, the result might have looked to vindicate Ruby Walsh's apparent decision to allow his mount to stride on from the fifth when others would have opted to restrain him (it was Un de Sceaux's first steeplechase at much beyond two miles), but judging from Walsh's post-race comments he apparently had little say in the matter. 'I kind of knew he'd run away with me at some stage but I thought if I can get through the first half mile with him on the bridle, and he then decides to run away, at least I'd gone far enough to get him home.' 'Ruby was only half in control at times' added Mullins, who says of Un de Sceaux 'My heart is in my mouth every morning watching him come up the gallops.'

Rank outsider Aso, who had had a rare off-day when well beaten in the Grade 3 handicap on Trials day in January, took third place in the Ryanair, beaten another six lengths, ahead of the 11/4 second favourite Empire of Dirt, owned, like the runner-up, by Michael O'Leary's Gigginstown House Stud. Uxizandre, next in the betting on 6/1, failed to progress from his promising return in the Clarence House and beat only one home after setting out to make all, as he had two years earlier. O'Leary is yet to win the race which he has backed with his own money under the Ryanair title

Spectra Cyber Security Solutions Clarence House Chase, Cheltenham—
a foot-perfect display from Un de Sceaux this time as he records a second successive win in the race,
which was transferred from Ascot's abandoned meeting

Ryanair Chase (Festival Trophy), Cheltenham—Un de Sceaux shows his versatility with regards to trip, pushed closest in the end by the sponsors' second string Sub Lieutenant (right)

ever since the race's second running in 2006, but Sub Lieutenant is just the latest of several who have gone close, with Mossbank, First Lieutenant and Valseur Lido all previously finishing runner-up. Valseur Lido, winner of the Champion Chase at Down Royal in November, was among the sixty horses O'Leary moved from Mullins at the end of September after a reported disagreement over training fees. Michael O'Leary didn't present the trophies after the latest Ryanair Chase, but that wasn't the snub to Un de Sceaux's trainer that some seemed to imply. Anita O'Leary did the honours—as she has done in previous years—'I am hoping one day I can snog my wife up there if and when I win it' joked her husband. Whether O'Leary and Mullins have kissed and made up is another question, though O'Leary warmly congratulated Mullins after the race (Mullins had done the same when Gigginstown's Apple's Jade, whom he used to train, had beaten Vroum Vroum Mag and Limini earlier in the week), while Michael O'Leary's brother and racing manager Eddie O'Leary suggested that Mullins could still train for Gigginstown again in future. Besides, as an organisation that, in Eddie O'Leary's own words is 'very much a results-based business' (speaking after Tony Martin and Sandra Hughes, the latter Sub Lieutenant's former trainer, were dropped from the Gigginstown roster in May 2016), a renewal of their association could clearly be beneficial to both parties.

Of the first five home in the Queen Mother Champion Chase, the narrowly beaten runner-up Fox Norton was the only one whom Un de Sceaux had not already met, and beaten, during the season. Their paths eventually crossed in the Boylesports Champion Chase at Punchestown by which time Fox Norton had confirmed himself a top-class and much improved performer when beating Sub Lieutenant by six lengths in the Melling Chase at Aintree. Un de Sceaux and Fox Norton dominated the betting, Un de Sceaux sent off a shade of odds on, but, after leading from the fourth, he was headed soon after the last and beaten a length and three quarters by Fox Norton, with God's Own half a length back in third. Fox Norton became only the second horse, after Sprinter Sacre, to beat Un de Sceaux when he has completed over fences, while Un de Sceaux's overall career record now stands at eighteen wins from twenty-two completed starts—he joined Willie Mullins after winning two bumpers in France. The top-class Un de Sceaux's incredible consistency is also worth stressing. On only a handful of occasions in the last three seasons has he not run up to, or close to, his Timeform rating.

Mr Edward O'Connell's "Un de Sceaux"

Un de Sceaux (FR) (b.g. 2008)	Denham Red (FR) (b 1992)	Pampabird (b 1979)	Pampapaul Wood Grouse
		Nativelee (b 1982)	Giboulee Native Berry
	Hotesse de Sceaux (FR) (ch 1995)	April Night (gr 1986)	Kaldoun My Destiny
		Olympe Occitane (ch 1980)	Diarifos Papakiteme

Un de Sceaux's pedigree does not need updating from previous Annuals, though it is worth pointing out that his little-used and now deceased sire Denham Red is also the sire of the dams of the high-class pair Ptit Zig and Petit Mouchoir, the latter another member of the Gigginstown batch which Mullins lost in the latest season. Ptit Zig's jumping rather let him down over fences and his return to hurdling was rewarded when he won the Grande Course de Haies in which Un de Sceaux underperformed. Un de Sceaux's own jumping—he's not the biggest for fences, being strong and compact—looked to be a potential chink in his armour in his clashes with Sprinter Sacre in the spring of the previous season, though he was generally better in that department in the latest season. Un de Sceaux, who can sometimes be ridden with a bit more restraint nowadays, stays twenty-one furlongs and acts on heavy ground. He would be one of the more interesting potential rivals for Altior when the latest Arkle winner graduates full time to open company. *W. P. Mullins, Ireland*

UNDISPUTED (IRE) 6 b.m. King's Theatre (IRE) – Gleanntan (IRE) (Lil's Boy (USA)) **h106 p**
[2016/17 b84: h20.6g² h20.3v³ Dec 11] fair form over hurdles, placed both starts in 2016/17: in hood last 2 starts: usually races nearer last than first: remains with potential. *Noel Williams*

UNEX PICASSO 9 b.g. Galileo (IRE) – Ruff Shod (USA) (Storm Boot (USA)) [2016/17   **c–**
c–, h–: h20.2g^{pu} Apr 28] good-topped gelding: modest hurdler at best, very lightly raced   **h–**
nowadays: pulled up on chasing debut: stays 3¼m: acts on good to firm and good to soft
going: has worn cheekpieces/tongue tie. *Barry Murtagh*

UN GUET APENS (FR) 9 b.g. Enrique – Belisama (FR) (Mansonnien (FR)) [2016/17   **c–**
h19.9d^{pu} h16v^2 h20.9s^2 Mar 25] fair handicap hurdler: winning chaser: stays 21f: acts on   **h107**
heavy going: has worn headgear, including in 2016/17. *James Ewart*

UNIDEXTER (IRE) 7 br.g. Footstepsinthesand – Run To Jane (IRE) (Doyoun) [2016/17   **h–**
h–: h15.8g^6 h19.6d h23.1g Sep 28] modest hurdler at best, no form since 2014/15: has worn
headgear: wears tongue tie. *Richard Ford*

UNIFY 7 b.m. Midnight Legend – Holy Smoke (Statoblest) [2016/17 h79: h21.6g^5 h23g^4 **c101**
h23.3s^4 h23g^5 c21.1g^3 c15.7m* c21.1s* c19.7g^3 c17.2g* c16g^3 c20.2f^2 c15.9f* c20.5g^3 **h78**
c20.2s^{ur} Jan 19] poor maiden hurdler: fair handicap chaser: won at Southwell in September,
Fontwell (conditional) in October, Market Rasen in November and Leicester (novice) in
December: left Grant Cann after third start: stays 3m: acts on firm and soft going: has worn
hood: wears tongue tie: races prominently. *Anthony Honeyball*

UNIONISTE (FR) 9 gr.g. Dom Alco (FR) – Gleep Will (FR) (Cadoudal (FR)) [2016/17   **c128**
c148, h–: c23.6g c27.3s c29.5s c26g Mar 16] tall, useful-looking gelding: winning hurdler: **h–**
smart chaser at best, out of sorts in 2016/17: should be suited by long distances: acts on
heavy going: has worn cheekpieces: tried in tongue tie. *Paul Nicholls*

UNION JACK D'YCY (FR) 9 b.g. Bonnet Rouge (FR) – Jacady (FR) (Fill My Hopes   **c– §**
(FR)) [2016/17 c125§, h–: h25.5v^5 Jan 11] modest form over hurdles: fairly useful chaser: **h92**
stays 29f: acts on heavy going: has worn cheekpieces: unreliable. *Deborah Faulkner*

UNION SAINT (FR) 9 b.g. Saint des Saints (FR) – Us Et Coutumes (FR) (Shining Steel)   **c–**
[2016/17 c130, h–: c19.2m^5 c24g^F May 14] winning hurdler: useful chaser, below form   **h–**
completed start in 2016/17: stays 27f, effective at much shorter: acts on good to firm and
heavy going: tried in tongue tie: often races towards rear. *Jimmy Frost*

UNISON (IRE) 7 b.g. Jeremy (USA) – Easter Song (USA) (Rubiano (USA)) [2016/17   **h128**
h112: h15.8m* h20d^5 h16.8g* h16.6g* h15.7d h15.3s^2 h15.3v* h15.7g Apr 15] sturdy
gelding: fairly useful handicap hurdler: won at Ludlow in May, Exeter and Doncaster
(intermediate) in November, and Wincanton in March: best around 2m: acts on good to
firm and heavy going: usually leads. *Jeremy Scott*

UNKNOWN LEGEND (IRE) 10 b.g. Heron Island (IRE) – Late Call (IRE) (Callernish)   **c–**
[2016/17 c107, h104: h24d^{pu} Jul 10] fair hurdler, pulled up sole start in 2016/17: fair   **h–**
chaser: stays 3m: acts on good to firm and heavy going: has worn hood: front runner.
Sarah Humphrey

UN NOBLE (FR) 7 gr.g. Near Honor (GER) – Noble Gary (FR) (Loup Solitaire (USA))   **c100**
[2016/17 c125, h–: c21.6s^{ur} c23.4s^{pu} c20.5s^{pu} c20.1g^4 Apr 8] winning hurdler: fairly useful   **h–**
handicap chaser, little form in 2016/17: should stay 3m: acts on heavy going. *Nicky Richards*

UNO VALOROSO (FR) 9 b.g. Voix du Nord (FR) – Danse d'Avril (FR) (Quart de Vin   **c107 §**
(FR)) [2016/17 c106, h–: c19.3d^4 c16.3s* c15.7d^{pu} c16.3v^{ur} c17.1s^{pu} Apr 3] close-coupled   **h–**
gelding: maiden hurdler: fair handicap chaser: won at Newcastle in January: stays 19f: acts
on heavy going: tried in cheekpieces: usually races close up: temperamental. *Mark Walford*

UNOWHATIMEANHARRY 9 b.g. Sir Harry Lewis (USA) – Red Nose Lady   **h165**
(Teenoso (USA)) [2016/17 h147p: h24.2d* h24.4d* h24s* h24g^3 h24d* Apr 27]

     Maybe it was asking too much, even for a lucky owner, to have bought the
future winners of the Champion Hurdle *and* the Stayers' Hurdle? Buveur d'Air and
Unowhatimeanharry were among the good jumpers who returned in new ownership
in the latest season carrying the emerald green, yellow hoops of J. P. McManus.
Both horses proved inspired purchases, though forty-eight hours after Buveur d'Air
won the Champion Hurdle, odds-on Unowhatimeanharry was beaten in the Stayers'
Hurdle, his only defeat in ten starts for his current stable. McManus completed the
notable Champion Hurdle/Stayers' Hurdle double in 2014 with Jezki and More of
That, Pat Muldoon being the only other owner to have won both races, with Sea
Pigeon (Champion Hurdle 1980 and 1981) and Town Ship (1977 Stayers'). Buveur
d'Air certainly wasn't bought as a potential Champion Hurdle winner—he spent
much of the season over fences after all—but Unowhatimeanharry, for all that he

JLT Long Walk Hurdle, Ascot—Unowhatimeanharry (hoops) already has the measure of the about-to-fall Ballyoptic, with Lil Rockerfeller (cheekpieces) inheriting second

had an off-day at Cheltenham, lived up to hopes that he would turn out to be a Stayers' Hurdle contender. In fact, in proving himself the top staying hurdler trained in Britain, there is a good chance he exceeded his new owner's hopes.

Unowhatimeanharry's progress since joining Harry Fry at the start of the previous season was well documented, but the big question at the start of the latest campaign was how much more might there be to come from a horse in his fourth season over hurdles and now approaching the age of nine? Having won a bumper on his debut, Unowhatimeanharry achieved ratings of 112 and 119 from those first two seasons over hurdles for Helen Nelmes when he was placed on seven occasions without getting his head in front. However, he won all five of his starts in the colours of the Harry Fry Racing Club in 2015/16, ending the season with a rating of 147p after winning the Spa Novices' Hurdle at Cheltenham. A lot more was needed for him to challenge the best staying hurdlers in open company, but, with another big step forward on his first start for his new owner, Unowhatimeanharry wasted no time in showing that he would be a danger to all in that division. Just like the previous season's outstanding staying hurdler Thistlecrack, Unowhatimeanharry made his breakthrough in the Long Distance Hurdle at Newbury's Hennessy meeting and, at least until the Festival, Unowhatimeanharry did a fine job of following in Thistlecrack's footsteps. Leading two out and clear when making a mistake at the last, Unowhatimeanharry ran out an impressive six-length winner of the bet365-sponsored contest from favourite Ballyoptic, the winner of the Sefton Novices' Hurdle at Aintree in the spring who would have gone close to winning both his starts in the new season had he not fallen at the last on the second of them in the West Yorkshire Hurdle at Wetherby. Irish challenger Snow Falcon also looked set to play a part in the finish at Newbury, falling three out when still to be asked for his effort.

The first two from the Long Distance Hurdle met again in the mid-season highlight for staying hurdlers, the JLT Long Walk Hurdle at Ascot, with Unowhatimeanharry sent off the 6/5 favourite despite facing ten rivals in a strong-looking renewal. His main threat according to the betting was Alex de Larredya, a 5/1-chance bidding to become another French-trained winner of the Long Walk after the Francois Doumen-trained Baracouda who won it four times (one of those renewals taking place at Windsor), the last three of them after he had been bought privately by J. P. McManus, for whom he also twice won the Stayers' Hurdle.

UNO

Alex de Larredya had finished runner-up to Ptit Zig in the Grande Course de Haies d'Auteuil in June, though he had Ptit Zig back in third more recently in the Grand Prix d'Automne. Ptit Zig and Ballyoptic came next in the betting on 8/1, along with Lil Rockerfeller who had run McManus' Champion Hurdle contender Yanworth close, conceding him weight, in the Ascot Hurdle. Those at longer odds included another former Grande Course de Haies winner Un Temps Pour Tout, back over hurdles after contesting the Hennessy, and eleven-year-old Reve de Sivola, winner of three Long Walks and runner-up to Thistlecrack the year before. While the going was not so testing as it can be at that time of year, a good pace made for a test of stamina in a race run in thick fog. The Thistlecrack colours, carried by his half-brother West Approach (a 40/1-shot), were to the fore as the television cameras picked up the leaders going to the second last, Ballyoptic disputing it with him, with Unowhatimeanharry moving well in pursuit of the first two. However, it was all change when the leaders re-emerged from the gloom in the closing stages, Unowhatimeanharry in front by then and going on to have four and a half lengths to spare at the line over Lil Rockerfeller. Un Temps Pour Tout was a further fourteen lengths back in third, ahead of Ptit Zig and Alex de Larredya, with the ill-fated Reve de Sivola sixth in what proved to be his final Long Walk—the 2017 race will be named in his honour following his death at Kelso in March. Ballyoptic and West Approach both departed at the final flight when looking set to be placed.

Graded contests outside the Festival can be lacking in competitiveness but that wasn't a criticism—at least in terms of numbers—that could be levelled at the season's top staying hurdles, as a bumper field turned out for Unowhatimeanharry's next step towards the Stayers' Hurdle in the galliardhomes.com Cleeve Hurdle at Cheltenham's Trials meeting. All fifteen entries stood their ground, though they bet 14/1 bar two with Ballyoptic (4/1) the only one backed against Unowhatimeanharry (11/10-on) who was conceding between 4 lb and 8 lb in the Grade 2 contest to most of his rivals who again included West Approach, Un Temps Pour Tout, Ptit Zig and Reve de Sivola. Thistlecrack had won the Cleeve by twelve lengths the year before, and while Unowhatimeanharry had less to spare—a length and three quarters over the 2015 World Hurdle winner Cole Harden (one of those receiving 8 lb)—with West Approach and Ballyoptic completing the frame, Unowhatimeanharry again

galliardhomes.com Cleeve Hurdle, Cheltenham—on an extended run-in because of the low sun, Unowhatimeanharry asserts from Cole Harden (cheekpieces) and the novice West Approach

Ladbrokes Champion Stayers' Hurdle, Punchestown—on a red letter day for trainer Harry Fry,
Unowhatimeanharry reverses Cheltenham form with Nichols Canyon (right) in a stirring finish

looked a class apart, going smoothly all the way and leading in the final furlong of the extended run-in, the final flight having been omitted on both circuits because of the low sun.

With his winning run now stretching to eight and, having beaten his chief British rivals at least once, Unowhatimeanharry returned to Cheltenham as many people's 'banker' in the Stayers' Hurdle. But, after holding every chance when brought to challenge the leader Lil Rockerfeller at the last, Unowhatimeanharry found less than he usually does and Nichols Canyon stayed on best up the hill, with Unowhatimeanharry finishing a one-paced third, just over four lengths behind the winner, clearly not in quite the same form as he had been earlier in the season, though still performing a good deal better than old rivals Ballyoptic and West Approach who were both pulled up. With Champion Hurdle disappointment Yanworth successfully stepping up to three miles in the Liverpool Hurdle for McManus, Unowhatimeanharry was given the chance to atone for his own reverse at Cheltenham in the Ladbrokes Champion Stayers' Hurdle at Punchestown. This was yet another really good renewal of one of the season's top staying hurdles, with each of the first three from the Stayers' Hurdle among those to re-oppose from Cheltenham. Nichols Canyon started at 7/4 to come out on top again, with Unowhatimeanharry next in the betting on 4/1, along with the same owner's progressive Sutton Place who had completed a five-timer in the Boyne Hurdle at Navan last time out. The latter went wrong, and Lil Rockerfeller finished well beaten after making most of the running, but Nichols Canyon and a back-to-form Unowhatimeanharry served up another of the Punchestown Festival's thrilling finishes, both giving their all as they pulled a long way clear of the rest. Unowhatimeanharry got first run on his rival off the home turn but was being hard driven on the run to the last, which both horses jumped well, Unowhatimeanharry then finding enough on the run-in as Nichols Canyon stayed on to be beaten just a head. Willie Mullins' second string Footpad finished eighteen lengths away in third, with the previous year's winner One Track Mind only fifth. Stressing how slow the gallop had been, winning rider Noel Fehily paid tribute to his mount's attitude in overcoming difficulties. 'Everything—plan A, plan B and plan C—went out the window because the last thing I wanted to be in front two out. I just felt that because we hacked early I had to go forward and luckily Unowhatimeanharry is such a tough little horse. I fired him at the last when he was very long for a little horse, but he has got the heart of a lion and doesn't give

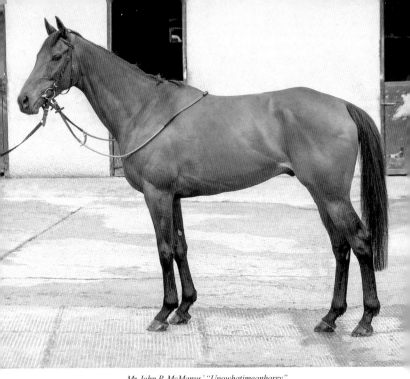

Mr John P. McManus' "Unowhatimeanharry"

up on you.' Fehily stood in for the injured Barry Geraghty on Unowhatimeanharry's last two starts, but he knew the horse well, having ridden him to four of his five wins in 2015/16.

Unowhatimeanharry (b.g. 2008)	Sir Harry Lewis (USA) (b 1984)	Alleged (b 1974)	Hoist The Flag
			Princess Pout
		Sue Babe (b 1978)	Mr Prospector
			Sleek Dancer
	Red Nose Lady (b 1997)	Teenoso (br 1980)	Youth
			Furioso
		Red Rambler (ch 1986)	Rymer
			Cytisus

The leggy Unowhatimeanharry was a second winner of the Long Walk for his sire, following the 2006 winner Mighty Man, while two other sons of Sir Harry Lewis, Diamond Harry and Restless Harry (twice), were placed in the race behind Big Buck's. Mighty Man was another good advertisement for his sire (who died in 2009), top class and most genuine and reliable, his other wins including two editions of the Liverpool Hurdle. A Stayers' Hurdle eluded Mighty Man too, though he started favourite when third to My Way de Solzen in 2006 and was three quarters of a length second to Inglis Drever a year later (he reversed the form with both when claiming those Aintree wins). He contested the Cheltenham race again in 2009 after nearly two years off with a serious tendon injury, finishing fifth to Big Buck's, and improved on that when second to the same rival at Aintree. Unowhatimeanharry's breeding was covered more fully in last year's Annual. His dam Red Nose Lady was a modest and ungenuine hurdler whose only other foal to reach the racecourse to date, Happy

Chance (a mare by Indian Danehill), finished tailed off in a couple of bumpers early in the latest season. Unowhatimeanharry stays three miles well and acts on heavy ground, though he doesn't need the mud. He wears a tongue tie nowadays and travels strongly in his races. It would be asking a lot for Unowhatimeanharry to improve still further, but he is a top-class hurdler now in any case, well up to winning more good staying contests. *Harry Fry*

UN PROPHETE (FR) 6 gr.g. Carlotamix (FR) – Pollita (FR) (Nombre Premier) [2016/17 c–, h99: h16s² h15.8d² h15.5d⁴ c16d* c15.7s* c15.9s² c17.1vᵖᵘ c16gᶠ Apr 3] big gelding: fair maiden hurdler: fairly useful form over fences: won handicaps at Ludlow (novice) and Southwell in January: unproven beyond 17f: acts on heavy going: often races in rear. *Venetia Williams*   **c128 h107**

UNSAFE CONDUCT 4 ch.g. Pasternak – Symbiosis (Bien Bien (USA)) [2016/17 b14s b16.3s h16gᶠ Apr 8] £13,000 3-y-o: rather unfurnished gelding: third foal: half-brother to fairly useful hurdler Kingfisher Creek (2m/17f winner, by Kayf Tara): dam (c106/h106) 2¼m-3m hurdle/chase winner: no form in bumpers: 66/1, third when fell last in novice won by Resolution Bay at Chepstow on hurdling debut. *Colin Tizzard*   **h90 b–**

UNSEEN (FR) 9 gr.g. Dom Alco (FR) – Cathou (FR) (Quart de Vin (FR)) [2016/17 h19dᵖᵘ h19.9g May 14] placed in maiden points: no form over hurdles. *Sam Thomas*   **h–**

UN TEMPS POUR TOUT (IRE) 8 b.g. Robin des Champs (FR) – Rougedespoir (FR) (Bonnet Rouge (FR)) [2016/17 c161, h–: h20d* c26g h24.4d³ h24s⁶ c25g* Mar 14]   **c162 h145 +**

David Pipe is approaching the halfway mark in his quest to match his father Martin's tally of thirty-four Cheltenham Festival wins, Un Temps Pour Tout bringing his tally to fifteen when scoring for the second year running in the Ultima Handicap Chase, the race run just before the Champion Hurdle on the opening day and traditionally known as the National Hunt Handicap Chase. Un Temps Pour Tout is the third horse to win the race in successive years, following Sentina in 1957 and 1958 and Scot Lane in 1982 and 1983. The Ultima isn't the only Festival race that David Pipe has won twice with the same horse, front-running Buena Vista having won the Pertemps Final two years in a row, in 2010 and 2011 (after being runner-up in 2009), when he became the first since Willie Wumpkins to win the Pertemps or its equivalent more than once. Festival regular (eight successive appearances) Buena Vista had begun his career with Martin Pipe, for whom he made his first two Cheltenham Festival appearances, sixth in the Champion Bumper (under twice Flat champion jockey Jamie Spencer) and third in the Supreme Novices'. Martin Pipe's Cheltenham Festival wins also included a winner of the Pertemps Final (when it was known as the Unicoin Homes Gold Card Final), Unsinkable Boxer, who started the shortest-priced favourite (5/2) in the history of the race and ran out one of its easiest winners. Tony McCoy recounts that, after he was legged up on Unsinkable Boxer in the paddock, Martin Pipe put his hand on his knee and said 'This is the biggest certainty you've ever sat on.' Pipe's assistant Chester Barnes bought a *Timeform Black Book* after Unsinkable Boxer's victory, principally to get the carrier bag that copies are sold in, so that he had somewhere to put his cash winnings on the horse!

The old adage 'horses for courses' applies to Cheltenham more than some other courses, but the Festival handicaps are among the most fiercely competitive in the calendar and course specialists Willie Wumpkins (also a Festival novice winner) and Buena Vista are the only horses to have won the same handicap hurdle at the Festival more than once. The chasers have a slightly better record with Chu-Teh (1967 and 1968) and Glyde Court (1985 and 1986) both dual winners of the Fulke Walwyn Kim Muir, a feat also achieved in the Grand Annual by Top Twenty (1958 and 1959) and Dulwich (1974 and 1976), while The Tsarevich (1985 and 1986) and Elfast (1992 and 1994) were dual winners of the Mildmay of Flete, now branded as the Brown Advisory & Merriebelle Plate. Garde Champetre (2008 and 2009) and Balthazar King (2012 and 2014) both won the Cross Country when it was a handicap. In addition, Political Pop won the 1981 Mildmay of Flete and the 1982 Kim Muir, while Flyer's Nap won the 1995 Kim Muir and the 1997 National Hunt

Ultima Handicap Chase, Cheltenham—Un Temps Pour Tout (blinkers) becomes just the third dual winner in this race's long history; Singlefarmpayment (second right), Noble Endeavor (left), Buywise (centre, partly hidden) and Go Conquer (No.20) chase him home

Handicap Chase. Blowing Wind (County and Plate), Idole First (Coral Cup/Plate), Alderwood (County and Grand Annual) and Holywell (Pertemps/National Hunt Handicap) all won Festival handicaps over hurdles and fences.

Un Temp Pour Tout's first win in the Ultima Handicap Chase was achieved while he was still a novice over fences and it was, in fact, the best performance by any staying novice chaser in the entire 2015/16 campaign. Better known as a hurdler, and winner of France's most important race over hurdles the Grande Course de Haies in 2015, Un Temps Pour Tout mixed hurdling and chasing in the latest season, running three times over hurdles and only once over fences (a below-form tenth in the Hennessy in November) before lining up again for the Ultima. He won a four-runner minor event at Aintree on his reappearance (though he was probably lucky that Zarkandar parted company with his rider at the last when looking the most likely winner) and then, after contesting the Hennessy, he was disappointing behind Unowhatimeanharry in both the Long Walk Hurdle at Ascot (eighteen and a half lengths third) and the Cleeve Hurdle at Cheltenham (sixth, never on terms). Carrying top weight of 11-12 in the Ultima Handicap Chase, off a BHA mark 7 lb higher than the previous year, Un Temps Pour Tout was one of three previous winners of the race in the line-up, along with the 2014 winner Holywell and the 2015 winner The Druids Nephew. Holywell and The Druids Nephew's stablemate The Young Master had filled the places behind Un Temps Pour Tout in 2016. Others with course form included the mercurial Buywise, Noble Endeavor (just touched off in the Martin Pipe in 2015 and travelling well when falling two out in the National Hunt Chase in 2016) and the novice Singlefarmpayment, who had won at the International meeting at the course in December. Singlefarmpayment, who started 5/1 favourite, has a record of sometimes being unruly before his races and, with the permission of the stewards, he was allowed to come late into the paddock. As in the previous year, Un Temps Pour Tout never put a foot wrong and, when it came to a battle, he showed considerable gameness to edge out Singlefarmpayment by a short head in a thrilling finish. Noble Endeavor was three and a half lengths further behind in third, with Buywise completing the frame; The Young Master and The Druids Nephew came sixth and seventh, while Holywell's fine run at the Festival (he also finished fourth in a Gold Cup) came to an end when he was pulled up. Un Temps Pour Tout wasn't seen out again after Cheltenham but will no doubt be primed to reach his peak for another Festival appearance in the next season, possibly in the Gold Cup (the form he showed in the Ultima is knocking on the door of Grade 1 form over fences).

Professor Caroline Tisdall & Bryan Drew's "Un Temps Pour Tout"

Un Temps Pour Tout (IRE) (b.g. 2009)	Robin des Champs (FR) (b 1997)	Garde Royale (br 1980)	Mill Reef
			Royal Way
		Relayeuse (b 1987)	Iron Duke
			Reliorneuse
	Rougedespoir (FR) (b 2003)	Bonnet Rouge (b 1997)	Pistolet Bleu
			French Free Star
		Annie d'Ecajeul (b 1993)	Jefferson
			Nuit d'Ecajeul

A strong gelding, Un Temps Pour Tout is Irish-bred but, as his name suggests, he has Gallic roots which have been documented in previous essays on him in *Chasers & Hurdlers* (this is the fourth time he has had an extended entry). His sire Robin des Champs was still standing in France when he covered Un Temps Pour Tout's French-raised dam Rougedespoir, who was pulled up on two starts over hurdles. When Rougedespoir's new Irish owner suddenly fell victim to the economic crash of 2008 and couldn't pay for her, an arrangement was made for Rougedespoir to visit Robin des Champs (by now in Ireland) again and for her and her foal born in Ireland (Un Temps Pour Tout) to be sent back to France the following spring. The best known relative of Un Temps Pour Tout in Britain is the 2007 Queen Mother Champion Chase winner Voy Por Ustedes, a half-brother to Un Temps Pour Tout's grandam Annie d'Ecajeul (who showed next to nothing in nine starts on the Flat) Un Temps Pour Tout stays twenty-five furlongs and acts on heavy going (though both his Festival wins have been on good ground). He is best in blinkers and wears a tongue tie and he usually races prominently. *David Pipe*

Sky Bet First Race Special Handicap Chase, Doncaster—
Upsilon Bleu holds off Double W's (white face) and Yorkist (left)

UNZING (FR) 9 b.g. Voix du Nord (FR) – Magik (FR) (Kadalko (FR)) [2016/17 c22.5v^{pu} **c119** c20.3d^3 c17.2d* c21.4s^3 c15.2d^f c15.7d^2 c15.7s^3 Mar 20] winning hurdler: fairly useful **h–** handicap chaser: won at Market Rasen in December: second at Southwell in February: stays 2¾m: acts on heavy going: in cheekpieces last 2 starts: often travels strongly. *Charles Pogson*

UP AND GO (FR) 9 ch.g. Martaline – Santoria (FR) (Limnos (JPN)) [2016/17 c–§, **c108 §** h110§: c21.2d^4 c21.6d^2 h20d^2 Oct 20] sturdy, medium-sized gelding: point winner: fair **h114 §** handicap hurdler/chaser: stays 2¾m: acts on heavy going: tried in headgear: in tongue tie last 3 starts. *Donald McCain*

UPBEAT COBBLER (FR) 9 gr.m. Brier Creek (USA) – Jade de Chalamont (FR) **c109** (Royal Charter (FR)) [2016/17 c99, h–: c24.5g* c23.6g* c23.8g^3 c24.2s^6 c22.2g Apr 15] **h–** good-topped mare: winning hurdler: fair handicap chaser: won at Towcester in May and Chepstow (conditional) in October: stays 3m: acts on heavy going: tried in cheekpieces: usually leads. *Henry Daly*

UP FOUR IT (IRE) 9 b.g. Luso – Newgate Beauty (IRE) (Beau Sher) [2016/17 h71: **h68** h25g^2 h17.7d^4 h15.9s^4 h19.5v* h19.5v h25m^3 Apr 17] plain gelding: poor handicap hurdler: won at Lingfield (amateur) in January on final start for Mark Hoad: left Jamie Poulton after second start: stays 19f: best form on soft/heavy going: wears hood: front runner. *Paddy Butler*

UPHAM RUNNING (IRE) 9 b.g. Definite Article – Tara Brooch (IRE) (Supreme **h–** Leader) [2016/17 h–: h15.9g^6 h21.6g^6 May 29] angular gelding: maiden pointer: modest hurdler at best, no form since 2014/15: best effort at 2½m: acts on heavy going: tried in blinkers. *Kate Buckett*

UP HELLY AA KING 6 ch.g. And Beyond (IRE) – Gretton (Terimon) [2016/17 b16v^3 **b85** b16.2v^{pu} Mar 28] seventh foal: half-brother to 3 winners by Silver Patriarch, including fairly useful 2½m chase winner Silverton (c67) and fair 3m hurdle winner Sunnyside (b67): dam ran twice in bumpers, half-sister to fairly useful hurdler/chaser (stayed 3m) Gulshan: fair form in bumpers: better effort when third at Ayr in March. *N. W. Alexander*

UPPERTOWN HAWK (IRE) 10 ch.g. Hawkeye (IRE) – Ileegan (IRE) (Nucleon (USA)) [2016/17 c23g⁴ May 27] multiple winning pointer: in tongue tie, tailed off in hunter on chasing debut. *Miss K. Adcock* — c54

UPSANDDOWNS (IRE) 9 b.g. Definite Article – Courtain (USA) (Diesis) [2016/17 c–, h–: c16.3g³ c16.5g³ c16.5g c16g³ c16.5g² c15.5s⁵ c16dᵖᵘ Jan 19] workmanlike gelding: winning hurdler: fair maiden chaser: stays 21f: best form on good going: tried in hood: wears tongue tie: often races prominently: often let down by jumping. *Evan Williams* — c113 x h–

UPSILON BLEU (FR) 9 b.g. Panoramic – Glycine Bleue (FR) (Le Nain Jaune (FR)) [2016/17 c144, h–: h20d c16.9d⁶ c19.9g² c16.4d* c16.3g Mar 17] strong gelding: useful hurdler at best: useful handicap chaser: won at Doncaster (by 1½ lengths from Double W's) in January: stays 23f, effective at much shorter: acts on heavy going: tried in hood: often travels strongly. *Pauline Robson* — c144 h–

UPSWING (IRE) 9 b.g. Beneficial – Native Country (IRE) (Be My Native (USA)) [2016/17 h139, h–: c23.6gᵖᵘ c27.3s⁵ c26gᵖᵘ c22.9sᵖᵘ c24s³ c24.2d³ c23.8g* c26g* Apr 20] strong gelding: winning hurdler: useful handicap chaser: won at Ffos Las and Cheltenham (by 2½ lengths from Belmount) in April: stays 27f: acts on heavy going: wears headgear: often races towards rear, sometimes idles: often let down by jumping. *Jonjo O'Neill* — c138 x h–

UP THE BEES 7 b.g. Kayf Tara – West River (USA) (Gone West (USA)) [2016/17 h–: h19.7gᵖᵘ h16s Nov 23] bumper winner: no form over hurdles. *Philip Kirby* — h–

UP THE JUNCTION 6 b.g. New Approach (IRE) – Hyabella (Shirley Heights) [2016/17 h–, b–: h19gᵖᵘ May 2] close-coupled gelding: no form over hurdles: tried in tongue tie: usually races towards rear. *Tim Vaughan* — h–

UPTHEMSTEPS (IRE) 12 br.g. Beneficial – Carrigloss (IRE) (Roselier (FR)) [2016/17 c–, h94: h23s⁵ May 11] winning hurdler/chaser, very lightly raced nowadays: stays 3m: acts on heavy going: usually wears headgear. *Ian Williams* — c– h80

UP THE NAVAN ROAD (IRE) 5 b.g. Stowaway – Tisiphone (IRE) (Exit To Nowhere (USA)) [2016/17 b17.8g² h15.9v h15.9v⁶ Jan 30] compact gelding: first foal: dam unraced: second in maiden bumper at Downpatrick (2 lengths behind Kagney) in September: poor form over hurdles: left Emmet Mullins after first start: in hood last 2 starts. *Michael Roberts* — h68 b89

UP TILL MIDNIGHT 8 ch.m. Midnight Legend – Uplift (Bustino) [2016/17 h68, b79: h21.6d h21.4dᵖᵘ Dec 13] no form over hurdles. *Lydia Richards* — h–

UP TO AL (IRE) 9 b.g. Heron Island (IRE) – Pretonic (Precocious) [2016/17 h89: h15.3m⁴ May 10] dual winning pointer: poor maiden hurdler: tried in cheekpieces. *Bob Buckler* — h68

UPTON WOOD 11 ch.g. Fleetwood (IRE) – Miss Counsel (Leading Counsel (USA)) [2016/17 c–§, h108§: h21g⁵ h19.9gᵖᵘ h19.9g Jun 26] workmanlike gelding: modest handicap hurdler: maiden chaser: stays 3m: acts on firm and good to soft going: wears headgear: front runner/races prominently: temperamental. *Chris Down* — c– § h88 §

UP YOUR GAME (IRE) 9 b.g. Milan – Katie Snurge (IRE) (Snurge) [2016/17 c–, h–: h23.3dᵖᵘ May 5] little form: in cheekpieces last 2 starts: wears tongue tie. *Roy Brotherton* — c– h–

URANOX (FR) 9 b.g. Special Kaldoun (FR) – Judelle (FR) (Agent Bleu (FR)) [2016/17 c–, h67: h25.6sᵖᵘ h20.5g⁴ c21.2gᵘʳ h15.9v Jan 16] poor form over hurdles: unseated rider first on chasing debut: stays 21f: acts on good to soft going: has worn headgear, including last 4 starts: has worn tongue tie, including final start. *Michael Roberts* — c– h66

URBAN GALE (IRE) 12 b.g. City Honours (USA) – Margale (IRE) (Strong Gale) [2016/17 c90x, h71: c26.3s² c25.5d⁴ c24.2d c24d c24.2s³ c25.2dᵖᵘ c24v² c26.3gᵖᵘ Mar 29] winning hurdler: modest handicap chaser: stays 27f: acts on heavy going: often wears headgear: tried in tongue tie: often let down by jumping. *Joanne Foster* — c85 x h–

URBAN HYMN (FR) 9 b.g. Robin des Champs (FR) – Betty Brune (FR) (Dark Stone (FR)) [2016/17 c–, h–: c24.2g⁴ c23.4d⁵ c21.4s⁶ c20.9s⁵ Dec 11] big, strong gelding: winning hurdler: fair maiden chaser: stayed 3m: acted on heavy going: tried in cheekpieces/tongue tie: front runner/raced prominently: dead. *Malcolm Jefferson* — c113 h–

URBAN KODE (IRE) 9 b.g. Kodiac – Urbanize (USA) (Chester House (USA)) [2016/17 h92: h20.2m* h20.2f⁵ h15.6g⁵ h16.4d h20.6s h19.4g² h19.4g⁴ h18.1d² h20.2g⁵ Apr 28] modest handicap hurdler: won at Perth (conditional) in May: stays 2½m: acts on good to firm and heavy going: wears headgear: often races prominently. *Lucinda Russell* — h92

URCA DE LIMA 4 b.f. Black Sam Bellamy (IRE) – Dame Fonteyn (Suave Dancer (USA)) [2016/17 b15.8s* Apr 1] seventh foal: closely related to fairly useful chaser The Cider Maker (3¼m winner, by Kayf Tara) and half-sister to 2 winners, including fair chaser Rateable Value (2¾m-25f winner, by Classic Cliche): dam (h84), maiden hurdler (stayed 2¾m), 1¾m winner on Flat, sister to fairly useful hurdler (stayed 3m) Dubai Seven Stars: 2/1, won mares bumper at Uttoxeter (by 1¼ lengths from Black Sam Bella) on debut. *Anthony Honeyball* **b98**

URGENT DE GREGAINE (FR) 9 b.g. Truth Or Dare – Hispanie (FR) (Bad Conduct (USA)) [2016/17 c21.4s² c17.9g* c21.9s⁴ c21.9s c20.9d³ c30.2d* Jan 28] lengthy gelding: modest form over hurdles: useful chaser: won claimer at Cluny in August and cross-country handicap at Cheltenham (tongue tied, by 3 lengths from Cantlow) in January: stays 3¾m: acts on good to soft going: in cheekpieces last 2 starts. *Emmanuel Clayeux, France* **c132 h88**

URIAH HEEP (FR) 8 b.g. Danehill Dancer (IRE) – Canasita (Zafonic (USA)) [2016/17 c109, h115: h20.2m⁵ h17.2m⁶ h16.2dᵖᵘ h16.2sᵖᵘ h20.2g Apr 28] sturdy gelding: modest handicap hurdler: winning chaser: unproven beyond 2m: acts on good to firm and good to soft going: often in cheekpieces. *R. Mike Smith* **c– h91**

URTHEONEIWANT (IRE) 7 b.m. Kayf Tara – Mascareigne (FR) (Subotica (FR)) [2016/17 h21g² h24g³ h20g² h18.5d⁴ h24.8d³ h22g h23g² h24g h21.5g⁶ h23.3d⁵ h20.3g⁴ h23d Nov 13] sixth foal: half-sister to bumper winner Nurse Ratched (by Presenting): dam, French 2m hurdle winner (also won at around 1½m on Flat), half-sister to Prix de l'Arc de Triomphe winner Trempolino: point winner: fairly useful handicap hurdler, placed on 5 occasions in 2016/17: maiden chaser: stays 25f: acts on good to soft going: usually wears hood. *Gordon Elliott, Ireland* **c– h115**

USUEL SMURFER (FR) 9 b.g. Loxias (FR) – Dyscovery (FR) (Mistigri) [2016/17 c139, h–: c24s² c30.2gᶠ Mar 15] angular gelding: winning chaser: second in cross-country event at Punchestown (1½ lengths behind Auvergnat) in February: stays 3m: acts on soft and good to firm going: tried in cheekpieces. *Alan Fleming, Ireland* **c136 h–**

UTILITY (GER) 6 b.g. Yeats (IRE) – Ungarin (GER) (Goofalik (USA)) [2016/17 b102: h15.7g⁴ h16d* h16s h21.2g Apr 3] useful-looking gelding: bumper winner: fair form over hurdles: won novice at Chepstow in November. *Jonjo O'Neill* **h109**

UT MAJEUR AULMES (FR) 9 ch.g. Northern Park (USA) – My Wish Aulmes (FR) (Lyphard's Wish (FR)) [2016/17 c134§, h–: c16.4g⁴ c15.7s² c16.2s⁵ c19.9g c16g³ Apr 27] rangy gelding: winning hurdler: useful handicap chaser: second at Haydock (6 lengths behind Gino Trail) in December: unproven beyond 2m: acts on heavy going: tried in cheekpieces: wears tongue tie. *Victor Dartnall* **c133 h–**

UTMOST ZEAL (IRE) 7 b.g. Big Bad Bob (IRE) – Dusseldorf (IRE) (Germany (USA)) [2016/17 h16m⁶ h17.2g⁵ h15.7g⁵ h18.5d c16.1mᶠ Oct 5] maiden hurdler, fair at best: modest form over fences: raced mainly at 2m: acted on good to firm and heavy going: often used to wear hood: in tongue tie last 3 starts: raced freely: dead. *Lawney Hill* **c– h90**

UXIZANDRE (FR) 9 ch.g. Fragrant Mix (IRE) – Jolisandre (FR) (Dear Doctor (FR)) [2016/17 c16.3s² c20.8g c19.9g Apr 7] tall gelding: winning hurdler: high-class chaser: second in Clarence House Chase at Cheltenham (5 lengths behind Un de Sceaux) in January after long absence: effective at 2m and has won over 25f: acts on good to firm and heavy going: usually wears headgear. *Alan King* **c160 h–**

V

VADO FORTE (FR) 4 b.g. Walk In The Park (IRE) – Gloire (FR) (Sillery (USA)) [2016/17 b16g Mar 18] €78,000 3-y-o: tall gelding: fourth foal: half-brother to French 6f winner Gloriskaya (by Take Risks): dam French 9f-10.5f winner: well beaten in maiden bumper: probably capable of better. *Tom Lacey* **b– p**

VAILLANT CREEK (FR) 8 b.g. Brier Creek (USA) – Ker Marie (FR) (Esprit du Nord (USA)) [2016/17 h115: h19.1d* h20.6g⁴ c22.5sᵖᵘ h20.3dᵖᵘ Jul 10] maiden pointer: fair hurdler: won maiden at Fontwell very early in season: pulled up in novice handicap on chasing debut: stays 21f: acts on heavy going: wears headgear: has worn tongue tie, including last 5 starts: usually leads. *Alex Hales* **c– h107**

VAILLANT NONANTAIS (FR) 6 b.g. My Risk (FR) – Sweet Life (FR) (Villez (USA)) **h116**
[2016/17 h93p, b90: h20.7g* May 30] fairly useful form over hurdles: won maiden at
Huntingdon in May: dead. *Nicky Henderson*

VALADOM (FR) 8 gr.g. Dadarissime (FR) – Laurana (FR) (Badolato (USA)) [2016/17 **c137**
c126, h–: c24g* h19.5g⁵ c24.1v* c21.1d^pu c24g h25.3d² c30.2d⁴ c30.2g Mar 15] **h115**
workmanlike gelding: fairly useful form over hurdles: better effort in 2016/17 when second
in novice at Catterick: useful handicap chaser: won at Uttoxeter (by 6 lengths from Indian
Stream) in May and Bangor in November: stays 25f: acts on good to firm and heavy going:
has worn cheekpieces: wears tongue tie: usually races close up. *Richard Hobson*

VALCO DE TOUZAINE (FR) 8 gr.g. Dom Alco (FR) – Narcisse de Touzaine (FR) **c129**
(Roi de Rome (USA)) [2016/17 c144, h126: h21.6g c23.8f³ c21.4g Jul 16] rather leggy **h–**
gelding: fairly useful hurdler: useful handicap chaser: won 3 Irish points in 2017: stays
2¾m: acts on good to firm and heavy going: wears hood/tongue tie: front runner/races
prominently. *Paul Nicholls*

VAL D'ARC (FR) 8 b.g. Le Balafre (FR) – Lextrienne (FR) (Neustrien (FR)) [2016/17 **c113**
c111, h–: c20s^pu c17.2g³ c16s* c19.3g^F Aug 25] maiden hurdler: fair handicap chaser: won **h–**
at Perth in July: left Richard Hobson after first start: stayed 2½m: acted on soft going: front
runner/raced prominently: dead. *Rebecca Menzies*

VALDAS PRINCESS 5 b.m. King's Theatre (IRE) – Valdas Queen (GER) (Platini **b74 p**
(GER)) [2016/17 b16g⁵ Apr 23] first foal: dam (b92), 1½m bumper winner, half-sister to
useful hurdler/chaser (stayed 3m) Victorias Groom: 7/1, fifth in mares bumper at Wetherby
(13¼ lengths behind Heartasia) in April: should improve. *Oliver Sherwood*

VAL DE FERBET (FR) 8 b.g. Voix du Nord (FR) – Intrigue Deferbet (FR) (Lights Out **c143**
(FR)) [2016/17 c–, h152: h20d² c22g⁴ h22.5g⁴ h24s² h20v* c20.4v² h24s c20v* c24g* **h138**
Apr 16] useful hurdler: won minor event at Limerick in December: second in similar event
at Clonmel (5½ lengths behind Clondaw Warrior) same month: useful chaser: won minor
event at latter course in March and Imperial Call Chase at Cork (by 12 lengths from A Toi
Phil) in April: stays 3m: acts on heavy going: often wears tongue tie: usually leads. *Andrew
McNamara, Ireland*

VAL DI COMINO (IRE) 6 br.m. Kalanisi (IRE) – Maxis Girl (IRE) (Mister Mat (FR)) **h–**
[2016/17 b16g h15.8s^pu Feb 8] sixth foal: sister to bumper winner/fairly useful hurdler **b–**
Maxanisi (2m winner), and half-sister to bumper winner/modest hurdler Jaya Bella (2¼m
winner, by Tikkanen) and a winning pointer by Alderbrook: dam unraced: tailed off in
mares bumper: pulled up in maiden on hurdling debut. *Sophie Leech*

VALENTINO'S CHOICE (IRE) 10 gr.g. Beneficial – Tenerife Pearl (IRE) (Bravefoot) **c93**
[2016/17 c23m³ c25.5g^pu c22g^pu c23.8g c23.8g^pu c25.2s^pu Feb 3] maiden hurdler: modest **h–**
maiden chaser: left Vincent Laurence Halley after third start: stays 3¼m: acts on good to
firm and good to soft going: has worn cheekpieces, including in 2016/17: tried in tongue
tie. *Gemma Anderson*

VALHALLA (IRE) 7 b.g. Scorpion (IRE) – Fox Theatre (IRE) (King's Theatre (IRE)) **c112 p**
[2016/17 h125: h26.5g³ h21.1g² h25.3s⁴ h24g³ c22.4d h23.4v^pu h16.5g* h15.7g⁶ h19.8g **h134**
Apr 29] good-topped gelding: won Irish maiden point on debut: useful handicap hurdler:
won at Taunton in March: second at Cheltenham (3¼ lengths behind Midnight Shot) in
October: 6/1, seventh in novice handicap at Newbury (25¾ lengths behind Belami des
Pictons) on chasing debut: stays 3¼m, effective at much shorter: acts on good to soft going:
wears tongue tie: should do better over fences. *Colin Tizzard*

VALID REASON 10 b.g. Observatory (USA) – Real Trust (USA) (Danzig (USA)) **h81 §**
[2016/17 h22d h24.3s h16v^pu h16.8m^pu Apr 19] useful-looking gelding: poor handicap
hurdler: stays 2¾m: acts on good to soft going: has worn headgear, including in 2016/17:
usually wears tongue tie: temperamental. *Noel C. Kelly, Ireland*

VALLEYOFMILAN (IRE) 10 b.g. Milan – Ikdam Valley (IRE) (Ikdam) [2016/17 **c116**
c123, h115: h27g c25.2g⁵ c24g^ur c23.8d⁴ c32.8g^F c23.8s^pu c28.4g⁵ Apr 15] fairly useful **h–**
hurdler: fairly useful handicap chaser: won at Ludlow (amateur) in January: stays 3¼m:
acts on soft and good to firm going: in cheekpieces last 5 starts: usually races close up.
Donald McCain

VALNAMIXE DU MEE (FR) 8 b.g. Al Namix (FR) – Kateline du Mee (FR) **c89**
(Panoramic) [2016/17 h–: h19.3m^F h20.1g⁶ h18.6g³ h22.1d⁴ c20g⁶ c23.8g² Sep 5] poor **h84**
maiden hurdler: modest form over fences: stays 3m: acts on good to soft going: in hood last
5 starts. *Kenny Johnson*

VALSEUR DU GRANVAL (FR) 8 b.g. Della Francesca (USA) – La Grande Vallee **c129**
(FR) (Chef de Clan (FR)) [2016/17 c104, h99: c16.3g* c18m⁴ c20.3g² c18m* c16m* **h–**
c16.4g⁴ c16.4g³ c16g⁴ Apr 27] tall, useful-looking gelding: maiden hurdler: fairly useful
handicap chaser: won at Towcester in May, Kempton in October and Chepstow in
November: stays 2½m: acts on soft and good to firm going: wears tongue tie. *Tom George*

VALSEUR LIDO (FR) 8 b.g. Anzillero (GER) – Libido Rock (FR) (Video Rock **c168**
(FR)) [2016/17 c167, h–: c24g* c24d⁴ Dec 28] **h–**

Horse racing in Britain and Ireland is interwoven, and horses, jockeys and
stable staff commute freely between the two countries every day. The countries share
a common stud book and, as far as possible, the racing is framed to provide a balanced
programme across the two jurisdictions. All of which has led to concerns about how
Britain's impending withdrawal from the European Union might affect the ease of
movement and open borders that the sport has become used to. A tripartite agreement
between the departments of agriculture, also involving France and pre-dating the
European Union, allows the free movement of racing and breeding thoroughbreds
between the three major European racing powers. Attempts are being made to keep
this in place after Brexit, while the British Government has also said that it will
not negotiate over the Common Travel Area, another long-standing UK-Ireland
agreement that allows free movement of British and Irish citizens between Ireland,
Northern Ireland and the rest of Britain. The 300-mile border between Ireland and
Northern Ireland virtually no longer exists, the change from road signs in miles to
those in kilometres just about the only evidence, on the motorway between Belfast
and Dublin, of the border being crossed. The imposition of tariffs on imports, and
of customs controls with travel documentation checks for horses and stable staff,
would be a severe inconvenience, leading inevitably to hold-ups which, in addition
to the extra red tape and form-filling, would certainly make the transporting of
racehorses a bigger undertaking, which might end up affecting the competitiveness
of European racing, as well as creating difficulties for the breeding industries in the
three countries (four-fifths of Ireland's thoroughbred exports are to Britain and bring
in nearly €200m for the Irish economy). The purchasing power of British owners
has already been hit, with the value of sterling falling by over ten per cent since the
decision to trigger Britain's exit from the EU. 'Unease because of the uncertainty'
describes the mood that prevails, and is likely to do so for some time, with clues
about the consequences of Brexit for racing in Britain and Ireland, and for Europe

*JNwine.com Champion Chase, Down Royal—the first Grade 1 of the campaign is won in fine style
by Valseur Lido on his first start for Henry de Bromhead*

more widely, not easy to find. Tentative indications are that the change is unlikely to be as seamless as many hope, though Britain and Ireland should at least be in a strong enough position to be able to negotiate some transitional arrangements that allow racing to prepare for and adapt to any new situation.

Two of Ireland's racecourses, Down Royal and Downpatrick, are in Northern Ireland—though they operate under the rules of the Irish Turf Club—and will technically be outside the European Union after Brexit. With ninety per cent of the runners at the two courses coming from stables in the Republic of Ireland, there is concern about the effect of restrictions on the free travel of racehorses (Dundalk is seven miles from the border and thirty per cent of its racegoers come from the North which gives that racecourse potentially a different problem). Down Royal's biggest day of the year is Champion Chase day in November, which usually features clashes between some of the best chasers in Britain and Ireland. The latest JNwine.com Champion Chase, the first Grade 1 of the season, attracted a field of seven, two from Britain (Silviniaco Conti, trained by Paul Nicholls who has won the race four times, and The Last Samuri) and five from the South. The southern raiders included two high-profile runners representing Gigginstown House Stud, Ireland's leading owners who had won four of the last five runnings. Both Valseur Lido and Don Poli had changed stables over the summer, leaving perennial champion trainer Willie Mullins for Henry de Bromhead and Gordon Elliott respectively, for whom they were making their first start. Their performances could hardly have been more different, with Valseur Lido running out an impressive winner—jumping well and cruising eleven lengths clear of runner-up Silviniaco Conti—while Don Poli was never travelling with any fluency and jumped ponderously before eventually being pulled up. With Gigginstown's then number-one jockey Bryan Cooper injured, Ruby Walsh had been given the choice between Valseur Lido (who started favourite) and Don Poli and had chosen Valseur Lido, on whom he would have been unbeaten in three races but for a last-fence exit when looking the most likely winner of the 2016 Irish Gold Cup. Walsh was also in the saddle when Valseur Lido won the Champion Novices' Chase at the 2015 Punchestown Festival (a race in which Don Poli, who had won the RSA Chase at Cheltenham, had another off-day). Valseur Lido had come second to his then-stablemate Vautour on two visits to the Cheltenham Festival, in the Golden Miller and twelve months after that in the Ryanair, but after his Champion Chase win at Down Royal there was talk that his third visit to the Cheltenham Festival might be to contest the Gold Cup (Henry de Bromhead, incidentally, landed a big-race double at Down Royal for Gigginstown when another recent addition to his string Sub Lieutenant landed the Grade 2 Titanic Belfast Chase). Unfortunately, Valseur Lido managed just one more appearance, when he headed a five-strong Gigginstown contingent for the Lexus Chase at Leopardstown's Christmas meeting, being the choice of a back-in-action Bryan Cooper and a well-backed 3/1 second favourite (behind the Mullins-trained Djakadam) in a field of thirteen. Heading to the last it looked as if Cooper had picked correctly, with Valseur Lido produced to hit the front at this stage having travelled smoothly under a patient ride. However, he couldn't deliver what he promised and was unable to even hang on for a place in the end, fading into fourth behind the Gigginstown pair Outlander and Don Poli, with Djakadam taking third. Whether Valseur Lido was more or less likely to contest the Gold Cup at Cheltenham, or have another shot at the Ryanair, became academic when he suffered a condylar fracture of a cannon bone on the gallops in January, only a few days after Gigginstown had decided to retire their outstanding 2016 Gold Cup winner Don Cossack after a recurrence of injury. It is hoped that Valseur Lido's injury will not be career-threatening (an operation to insert screws into the cannon bone was reported to have gone well).

Valseur Lido (FR) (b.g. 2009)	Anzillero (GER) (b 1997)	Law Society (br 1982)	Alleged / Bold Bikini
		Anzille (b 1986)	Plugged Nickle / Allegretta
	Libido Rock (FR) (b 1999)	Video Rock (b 1984)	No Lute / Pauvresse
		Vhiltida (b 1987)	Laostic / Hilda du Roy

The compact Valseur Lido is by the now-deceased German Group 1 winner Anzillero, whose dam was a half-sister to Urban Sea, the dam of Galileo and Sea The Stars. In contrast to that pair, Anzillero spent most of his time at stud covering AQPS (non-thoroughbred) mares in France like Valseur Lido's dam Libido Rock, who was placed at a mile and a half. Valseur Lido is Libido Rock's second winner, following the fairly useful Tango Lido (by Ungaro) whose biggest win came in a cross-country chase over three and a quarter miles at Lyon Parilly (where Valseur Lido won a bumper from two starts in France before joining the Mullins stable as a four-year-old). One of Libido Rock's half-sisters is the dam of the smart French chaser Rhialco who has finished second in a Prix La Haye Jousselin and third in a Grand Steeple-Chase de Paris, as well as winning in lesser pattern company over both hurdles and fences. Valseur Lido stays twenty-five furlongs but is fully effective at shorter and he acts on good to firm and heavy going. *Henry de Bromhead, Ireland*

VALUE AT RISK 8 b.g. Kayf Tara – Miss Orchestra (IRE) (Orchestra) [2016/17 c–, h145: c20d⁴ c20.3g* c25g c20.1g⁵ Apr 27] strong gelding: smart hurdler: useful form over fences: won novice at Bangor in October: stays 2½m: acts on heavy going: in cheekpieces last 2 starts: tried in tongue tie. *Dan Skelton*   **c133 h–**

VANCOUVER 5 ch.g. Generous (IRE) – All Told (IRE) (Valanjou (FR)) [2016/17 b15.7g² b17.7s⁶ b16.7g h16.6g⁴ h21.2d² h18.6s h20.6sᵖᵘ Feb 7] lengthy gelding: fifth foal: half-brother to fair hurdler/fairly useful chaser Explained (2m-2½m winner, by Exit To Nowhere): dam unraced: modest form in bumpers: fair form over hurdles. *Neil Mulholland*   **h106 b84**

VANILLA RUN (IRE) 6 b.m. Hurricane Run (IRE) – Vanilla Delight (IRE) (Orpen (USA)) [2016/17 b92: b16.2m* May 29] fairly useful form in bumpers: won mares event at Kelso in May: dead. *Chris Grant*   **b95**

VANITEUX (FR) 8 br.g. Voix du Nord (FR) – Expoville (FR) (Video Rock (FR)) [2016/17 c157, h149: c16.9d³ c16.3d³ c20.5d* c20.8g c15.5g* c15.5g⁴ Apr 29] well-made gelding: smart hurdler: very smart chaser: won listed event at Kempton by 2¼ lengths from Vibrato Valtat) in January and listed handicap at Ayr (by 5 lengths from Romain de Senam) in April: stays 2½m: acts on soft and good to firm going: in cheekpieces last 2 starts: has joined David Pipe. *Nicky Henderson*   **c159 h–**

VASCO DU MEE (FR) 8 b.g. Goldneyev (USA) – British Nellerie (FR) (Le Pontet (FR)) [2016/17 c119, h–: c32.5g* c27.5m⁵ c24.2d³ c23.6v* Mar 23] winning hurdler: fairly useful hunter chaser: won at Cheltenham very early in season and Chepstow in March: stays 33f: acts on heavy going: wears headgear/tongue tie. *Martin Weston*   **c129 h–**

VASCO D'YCY (FR) 8 b.g. Equerry (USA) – Ingrid des Mottes (FR) (Useful (FR)) [2016/17 c–, h–: h20.5s* h20.6v* h24.3d Apr 21] fair handicap hurdler: won at Ayr (conditional) in February and Newcastle in March: maiden chaser: stays 2¾m: acts on heavy going. *Julia Brooke*   **c– h110**

VAYLAND 8 ch.g. Generous (IRE) – Dotandadash (IRE) (Clerkenwell (USA)) [2016/17 c89, h112: c20m h15.5g h16.7sᵖᵘ h19g⁶ h15.8sᵖᵘ Apr 1] fair hurdler at best for David Pipe, no form in 2016/17: maiden chaser: left Micky Hammond after first start: tried in hood. *Barry Leavy*   **c– h–**

VBADGE TREAT (FR) 4 b.f. My Risk (FR) – Peutiot (FR) (Valanour (IRE)) [2016/17 b16.7g⁵ Mar 27] half-sister to several winners, including useful hurdler/chaser Calipto (2m-19f winner, by Califet) and useful French hurdler Seabreeze d'Ho (2¼m/19f winner, by Enrique): dam unraced: well beaten in mares maiden bumper: entitled to do better. *Harry Whittington*   **b– p**

VEAUCE DE SIVOLA (FR) 8 b.g. Assessor (IRE) – Eva de Chalamont (FR) (Iron Duke (FR)) [2016/17 c98§, h–: c25.7g⁴ c24vᵖᵘ h25.5s c23.5v⁵ c23.5v* c29.2v² Mar 22] lengthy gelding: winning hurdler: poor handicap chaser: won at Lingfield in March: stays 3m: acts on heavy going: tried in cheekpieces: wears tongue tie: often races prominently: unreliable. *Brian Barr*   **c83 § h–**

VEDANI (IRE) 8 b.g. Dalakhani (IRE) – Velandia (IRE) (Sadler's Wells (USA)) [2016/17 h–: h19.6d⁴ h19.8d² h21d h21.6d h26vⁿ Dec 31] close-coupled gelding: fair handicap hurdler: won at Bangor in May: best up to 2½m: acts on soft and good to firm going: has worn tongue tie. *Tony Carroll*   **h103**

VEINARD (FR) 8 ch.g. Shaanmer (IRE) – Ombline (FR) (Subotica (FR)) [2016/17 h108: **h128**
h20g h19.3d* h20d³ h16d² h16v² h16g h16.3d⁶ h16d² h16.5d⁶ Apr 25] good-bodied
gelding: fairly useful handicap hurdler: won at Clonmel in November: second at Fairyhouse
in April: stays 2½m: acts on heavy going: has worn hood: wears tongue tie: usually races
nearer last than first, often travels strongly. *Gordon Elliott, Ireland*

VELATOR 10 b.g. Old Vic – Jupiter's Message (Jupiter Island) [2016/17 c121§, h–: **c122**
c25.1m⁵ c24.1d² c23g² c25.8mᵖᵘ c27.5g³ c24g³ c25g³ c26g⁶ Dec 9] close-coupled gelding: **h–**
winning hurdler: fairly useful handicap chaser: third at Cheltenham (amateur) in October:
stayed 3½m: acted on soft going: wore headgear: tried in tongue tie: front runner/raced
prominently: dead. *Neil Mulholland*

VELOCITY BOY (IRE) 8 b.g. Westerner – Sambre (FR) (Turgeon (USA)) [2016/17 **c139**
h139: c17d⁶ c16d c20s² c16sᶠ c22s* c20v³ c24.5dᵘʳ Apr 25] useful hurdler: useful chaser: **h–**
won maiden at Punchestown in February: stays 2¾m: best form on soft/heavy going: tried
in hood/tongue tie: often leads. *W. P. Murphy, Ireland*

VELVET EDGE 8 b.m. Central Park (IRE) – Velvet Leaf (Rakaposhi King) [2016/17 h–: **h–**
h15.8g⁶ h15.8gᵖᵘ Jul 5] no form over hurdles: tried in tongue tie. *Anthony Day*

VELVET MAKER (FR) 8 b.g. Policy Maker (IRE) – Evasion de L'Orne (FR) (Beyssac **c–**
(FR)) [2016/17 c142, h–: h16s³ c16.3g Mar 17] angular gelding: useful hurdler: third in **h131**
handicap at Leopardstown (4 lengths behind Grand Partner) in February: useful chaser,
well held final start in 2016/17: stays 2¼m: acts on heavy going: has worn hood: front
runner/races prominently. *Alan Fleming, Ireland*

VELVET ROYALE (IRE) 9 b.m. Useful (FR) – Rebel Rebel (FR) (Pebble (FR)) **c58**
[2016/17 c22.6m May 20] sixth foal: half-sister to French chaser Ziggy Stardust (17f/21f
winner, by Roakarad): dam unraced half-sister to dam of very smart staying chaser Royal
Auclair: dual winning pointer: 40/1, seventh in novice hunter at Stratford on chasing debut.
Richard Pringuer

VENDOR (FR) 9 gr.g. Kendor (FR) – Village Rainbow (FR) (Village Star (FR)) [2016/17 **c133**
c–, h133: c16d⁶ c15.2d² Nov 12] leggy, useful-looking gelding: has reportedly had **h–**
breathing operation: useful hurdler: similar form over fences: second in novice at Wetherby
(neck behind The Dutchman) in November: stays easy 2½m: acts on heavy going: often
races prominently. *Sue Smith*

VENDREDI TROIS (FR) 8 b.g. Shaanmer (IRE) – Legende Sacree (FR) (Hawker's News **c–**
(IRE)) [2016/17 c107, h103: h23.3sᵘʳ h25.6g⁵ h18.7m² h19.5g Apr 17] modest maiden **h96**
hurdler: fair form over fences: has form at 3¼m, effective at much shorter: acts on soft and
good to firm going: often wears hood: front runner/races prominently. *Emma Lavelle*

VENEAUX DU COCHET (FR) 8 b.g. Saint des Saints (FR) – Al Imane (FR) (Alesso **c111**
(USA)) [2016/17 c16.9g* c16.9g³ h26.5m* Jul 1] fair form over hurdles: won handicap at **h114**
Newton Abbot in July: fair chaser: won claimer at Chatillon-Sur-Chalaronne in May: left
Emmanuel Clayeux after second start: effective from 19f to 3¼m: acts on good to firm and
heavy going. *Martin Hill*

VENETIAN LAD 12 ro.g. Midnight Legend – Henrietta Holmes (IRE) (Persian Bold) **c100 §**
[2016/17 c109, h–: c21.1dᵖᵘ c21.1d⁴ c21.1d⁶ c19.7d³ c17.4s⁴ c19.7s⁴ c17.4v⁴ c25.7s² **h–**
c25.5gᵖᵘ Apr 12] compact gelding: maiden hurdler: fair handicap chaser: stays 3¼m,
effective at shorter: acts on heavy going: tried in headgear: often races towards rear:
unreliable. *Lydia Richards*

VENGEUR DE GUYE (FR) 8 b.g. Dom Alco (FR) – Mascotte de Guye (FR) (Video **c122**
Rock (FR)) [2016/17 c125, h–: c20.1s⁵ c18.2g h16.2d⁶ h19.9v² h15.7s c16.3v² c15.5d² **h120**
c17.1s² Apr 3] good-topped gelding: fairly useful handicap hurdler: second at Uttoxeter in
November: fairly useful handicap chaser: second at Newcastle in February, Sandown in
March and Kelso in April: stays 2½m: acts on heavy going: has worn headgear: wears
tongue tie: often travels strongly. *Lucinda Russell*

VENITIEN DE MAI (FR) 8 b.g. Network (GER) – Meylba (FR) (Grand Tresor (FR)) **c134**
[2016/17 c137, h–: c19.5d⁴ c23g⁶ c24d⁵ c24.5dᶠ h24v⁶ c26gᶠ Mar 16] rather leggy **h102**
gelding: fair form over hurdles: useful handicap chaser: fifth in Troytown Handicap Chase
at Navan (14¼ lengths behind Empire of Dirt) in November: stays 3m: acts on heavy
going. *J. T. R. Dreaper, Ireland*

VENTERDON 6 b.g. Dr Massini (IRE) – Native's Return (IRE) (Presenting) [2016/17 **b–**
b16.8m May 3] well beaten in bumper. *Susan Gardner*

VENT NIVERNAIS (FR) 8 ch.g. Shaanmer (IRE) – Lobella (FR) (Hawker's News **c–**
(IRE)) [2016/17 c77, h80: h19.2sᵖᵘ c20.3sᵖᵘ h17.7vᵖᵘ Jan 8] strong gelding: poor hurdler/ **h–**
chaser: wears headgear. *James Evans*

VENTURA CASTLE 5 b.g. Paco Boy (IRE) – Bisaat (USA) (Bahri (USA)) [2016/17 h–: **h–** h18.5g h21.6g[pu] Jun 7] no form over hurdles: tried in headgear: in tongue tie last 4 starts. *Jamie Snowden*

VENTURE LAGERTHA (IRE) 8 ch.m. Fruits of Love (USA) – Millmounts Tara **h59** (IRE) (Kayf Tara) [2016/17 h61, b–: h16.3v h22g[6] Jul 28] poor maiden hurdler. *Brian Barr*

VENTUREPREDEMENTIA 6 b.g. Indian Danehill (IRE) – Sounds Familiar (IRE) **h–** (Orchestra) [2016/17 b–: b15.7g h19.4g[ur] Dec 29] little show in bumpers/novice hurdle. **b–** *Andrew Crook*

VENUE 7 b.g. Beat Hollow – Shirley Valentine (Shirley Heights) [2016/17 h112: h17.2m[3] **h124** h19.9g[6] h16.8g* h16.8g[2] h15.7m[2] h20g h15.6g* Nov 3] fairly useful handicap hurdler: won at Sedgefield in September and Musselburgh in November: unproven beyond 17f: acts on soft and good to firm going: tried in tongue tie. *Donald McCain*

VERCINGETORIX (IRE) 6 b.g. Dylan Thomas (IRE) – Great Artist (FR) (Desert **c–** Prince (IRE)) [2016/17 c113, h122: c17d[pu] c15.5g[6] c19.4d[pu] h15.5d h19.7m[2] Apr 13] **h96** lengthy gelding: fairly useful hurdler at best: fair form over fences, none in 2016/17: left Gordon Elliott after first start: stays 2½m: acts on good to firm and heavy going: often wears headgear: has worn tongue tie: has joined Iain Jardine. *Harriet Bethell*

VERDANA BLUE (IRE) 5 b.m. Getaway (GER) – Blue Gallery (IRE) (Bluebird **h133** (USA)) [2016/17 b16d b16g[2] b17g* b16g[4] h18.5s[ur] h16.2s* h19g* h16.8g[4] h20.3g[3] **b93** Apr 20] angular mare: seventh foal: half-sister to bumper winner/useful hurdler Wilde Blue Yonder (2m winner, by Oscar), stayed 2½m, and fair hurdler/useful chaser Blues And Twos (2¾m/23f winner, by Presenting): dam 6f winner: fair bumper performer: won at Killarney in July: useful form over hurdles: won mares novices at Hereford in January and Taunton in February: third in listed race at Cheltenham (2¼ lengths behind Brillare Momento) in April: left Edmond Kent after fourth start: likely to prove best up to 19f: acts on soft going: usually travels strongly. *Nicky Henderson*

VERDASCO (FR) 8 b.g. Sassanian (USA) – Babolna (FR) (Tropular) [2016/17 h20.3v[pu] **h–** May 10] maiden pointer: poor maiden hurdler: stays 2½m: acts on good to soft going: in headgear last 3 starts: tried in tongue tie. *Caroline Fryer*

VERING (FR) 11 b.g. Bering – Forcia (FR) (Homme de Loi (IRE)) [2016/17 c–§, h75§: **c– §** c20s[pu] c21.2g[pu] Apr 17] winning pointer: maiden hurdler/chaser, of no account nowadays: **h– §** often wears headgear/tongue tie: temperamental. *Mrs Linda Pile*

VERKO (FR) 8 br.g. Lavirco (GER) – Lady Vernizy (FR) (Video Rock (FR)) [2016/17 **c90** c108, h76: h21.4s c22.4v[4] c21.5v c21.1s[5] c20d[5] c21.6v[5] c20.1v[3] c24.2g[6] Apr 25] maiden **h–** hurdler: modest handicap chaser: stays 25f: best form on soft/heavy going: tried in cheekpieces: often races towards rear. *Micky Hammond*

VERNI (FR) 8 ch.g. Sabrehill (USA) – Nobless d'Aron (FR) (Ragmar (FR)) [2016/17 **h138** h113p: h16.8g* h15.7v[2] h19s* h20.3g[2] Mar 11] useful form over hurdles: won handicaps at Newton Abbot (novice) in October and Taunton in February: second in Martin Pipe Conditional Jockeys' Handicap Hurdle at Cheltenham (2¼ lengths behind Champagne Classic) in March: stays 2½m: acts on heavy going. *Philip Hobbs*

VEROCE (FR) 8 b.g. Assessor (IRE) – Pyvoine (FR) (Video Rock (FR)) [2016/17 c107, **c103** h–: c24.2d[2] Apr 30] maiden hurdler: fair handicap chaser: stays 3m: best form on soft/ **h–** heavy going. *Mark Walford*

VERONA OPERA (IRE) 6 b.m. King's Theatre (IRE) – Timissa (IRE) (Kahyasi) **h100** [2016/17 h96, b78: h17.8g[ur] h16.2g[4] h16d[2] h20.6d[5] h16d[6] h16d[4] h15.6g[2] h18s[5] h16v* h16.8g[3] h16.2g[2] Apr 28] bumper winner: fair hurdler: won novice at Ayr in February: unproven beyond 17f: acts on heavy going: has worn hood. *Stuart Crawford, Ireland*

VERSIFIER 5 b.m. Yeats (IRE) – Daprika (FR) (Epervier Bleu) [2016/17 b16.7g[4] b17.7d[3] **h93** h15.7d[pu] h17.7v h17.7v[2] h16.6s[4] Mar 3] £12,000 3-y-o: half-sister to bumper winner/fairly **b81** useful hurdler Fabrika (21f winner, by Presenting) and bumper winner Chasing Aces (by Definite Article): dam, French 17f chase winner (also 11f winner on Flat), half-sister to high-class hurdler/smart chaser (stayed 2½m) Geos: modest form in bumpers/over hurdles. *Oliver Sherwood*

VERTIGO (IRE) 5 b.g. Jeremy (USA) – Lady Coquette (SWE) (Mujadil (USA)) **h107** [2016/17 b16.2g* h16d[6] h20.5s[4] h16s h21.4v[2] h21.4v* h20.1v Mar 28] €6,000 3-y-o: fifth **b90** foal: half-brother to a winner on Flat in Italy by Motivator: dam maiden on Flat: placed on completed start in Irish points: won conditionals/amateur bumper at Hexham (by 2¼ lengths from Between The Waters) in October: fair form over hurdles: won maiden at Ayr in March: stays 21f: best form on soft/heavy going: often races towards rear. *Lucinda Russell*

VERY EXTRAVAGANT (IRE) 8 ch.m. Touch of Land (FR) – Raveleen Rose (IRE) **h118**
(Norwich) [2016/17 h101, b86: h23.3g* h25.6g* h23.3d* h25.3s^{pu} h25g^F h23.8m^4
Apr 25] sturdy mare: fairly useful handicap hurdler: won at Uttoxeter and Fontwell in
May, and again at Uttoxeter in October: stays 3¼m: acts on soft going: wears cheekpieces.
Neil Mulholland

VERY FIRST TIME 5 b.g. Champs Elysees – Like A Virgin (IRE) (Iron Mask (USA)) **h124**
[2016/17 h111, b95: h19.7g^6 h19.4g^4 h25s^2 h23.8g h22.8s h24.4g h25g^2 Apr 15] fairly
useful handicap hurdler: second at Carlisle in December: stays 25f: acts on heavy going.
Tim Easterby

VERYGOODVERYGOOD (FR) 6 b.g. Yeats (IRE) – Rose d'Or (IRE) (Polish **h121**
Precedent (USA)) [2016/17 h108, b91: h21.2m^5 h21.6g^3 h20g^3 h21.6g^2 h23.1g^3 h20g*
h19.5d* h21d^5 h21.3s h20.5v^3 h20v^2 h23.9g h23.8m^2 Apr 25] fairly useful handicap
hurdler: won at Ffos Las and Chepstow (conditionals novice event) in November: second
at Ffos Las in March and Ludlow in April: left Paul Morgan after fourth start: stays 3m:
acts on good to firm and heavy going: has worn headgear, including last 4 starts: has worn
tongue tie: often races lazily. *Nigel Twiston-Davies*

VERY LIVE (FR) 8 b.g. Secret Singer (FR) – Iona Will (FR) (Kadalko (FR)) [2016/17 **c93**
c101, h–: c16d^3 c16.4d^3 c17v^6 c20.2s^{ur} c19.9d^{ur} Mar 15] well-made gelding: maiden **h–**
hurdler: modest handicap chaser: unproven beyond 17f: best form on heavy going: wears
headgear. *Paul Webber*

VESPERAL DREAM (FR) 8 bl.g. Network (GER) – Pampanilla (FR) (April Night **c121**
(FR)) [2016/17 c130, h–: c19.2m^6 c20.1f^5 h26.5m^5 h18.5g^5 h20m^4 Aug 17] tall gelding: **h114**
fair handicap hurdler: fairly useful handicap chaser: stays 23f: acts on any going: wears
headgear/tongue tie: often races prominently: won point in February. *Paul Nicholls*

VESUVHILL (FR) 8 ch.g. Sabrehill (USA) – L'Orchidee (FR) (Gunboat Diplomacy **c79**
(FR)) [2016/17 c104p, h–: c20.3v c16.5d^2 Dec 26] sturdy gelding: winning hurdler: **h–**
maiden chaser: likely to prove best up to 2½m: acts on good to firm and heavy going: wears
hood: tried in tongue tie: has joined Gemma Anderson. *Ben Case*

VEXILLUM (IRE) 8 br.g. Mujadil (USA) – Common Cause (Polish Patriot (USA)) **c107**
[2016/17 c–, h97: c15.7m^3 c17.4g^4 c16.3s^{pu} c16g^6 c16.3g^5 c17.4g^2 c21.4g^2 c19.9m^5 **h–**
Oct 11] winning hurdler: fair handicap chaser: won at Fontwell in May: stays 21f: acts on
firm going: wears headgear: has worn tongue tie: often races towards rear. *Neil Mulholland*

VEZELAY (FR) 8 b.g. Dom Alco (FR) – Outre Mer (FR) (Sleeping Car (FR)) [2016/17 **c150**
c21.9s^4 c29.8s c21.9d h17.9s^4 h19.4s^2 c24.1v^3 c25.3s^F h21.4s^5 Mar 12] sturdy gelding: **h133**
useful hurdler: second in listed event at Auteuil (2 lengths behind Solway) in October:
smart chaser: fourth in Prix Ingre at Auteuil (7½ lengths behind As d'Estruval) very early
in season and third in Betfair Chase at Haydock (28 lengths behind Cue Card) in November:
fell last (would have finished fourth) in Cotswold Chase at Cheltenham in January: stays
27f: acts on soft going: has worn tongue tie. *Emmanuel Clayeux, France*

VIADUCT JACK (IRE) 8 b.g. King's Theatre (IRE) – Back Market Lass (IRE) (Bob **h84**
Back (USA)) [2016/17 h106: h23s^6 May 11] winning Irish pointer: fair form at best over
hurdles: best effort at 2½m: in cheekpieces last 2 starts. *Kim Bailey*

VIBRATO VALTAT (FR) 8 gr.g. Voix du Nord (FR) – La Tosca Valtat (FR) (Dom Alco **c154 §**
(FR)) [2016/17 c157, h–: c19.9g^3 c21d^5 c15.5d^6 c20.5d^2 c20v^2 c19.9s^{pu} c22.7g^5 Apr 29] **h–**
sturdy gelding: winning hurdler: smart chaser: second in listed event at Kempton (2¼
lengths behind Vaniteux) in January: stays 2½m: acts on good to firm and heavy going: in
headgear last 5 starts: wears tongue tie: temperamental. *Paul Nicholls*

VICANGELOME (FR) 8 b.g. Laveron – Medicis (FR) (Sicyos (USA)) [2016/17 **c110**
h19.9v^{pu} c21.2d^4 c15.5d^6 Mar 10] fairly useful hurdler/chaser, below form in 2016/17 after **h–**
change of yard: stays 2½m: best form on soft/heavy going: in tongue tie last 2 starts: often
travels strongly. *Ben Case*

VIC DE TOUZAINE (FR) 8 gr.g. Dom Alco (FR) – Diana de Vonnas (FR) (El Badr) **c136**
[2016/17 c129, h104: c20.2v^2 c19.9s^2 c25g^{ur} Mar 14] sturdy gelding: maiden hurdler: **h–**
useful handicap chaser: second at Wincanton in February: stays 2½m: best form on soft/
heavy going: often travels strongly. *Venetia Williams*

VICE ET VERTU (FR) 8 b.g. Network (GER) – Duchesse du Cochet (FR) (Native Guile **c111**
(USA)) [2016/17 c111, h–: c24s^5 c23.8v* c24v^5 c30.7d^5 c29.2v^{pu} c28.4g Apr 15] tall **h–**
gelding: winning hurdler: fair handicap chaser: won novice event at Ludlow in November:
stays 3m: best form on soft/heavy going: often wears headgear: tried in tongue tie.
Henry Daly

VICENTE (FR) 8 b.g. Dom Alco (FR) – Ireland (FR) (Kadalko (FR)) [2016/17   **c151** c152, h–: c26g^F c29.5s^6 c24d^6 c28.4d c34.3d^F c31.8g* Apr 22]   **h–**

Vicente may not have fulfilled the highest hopes for his new owner by delivering him another Grand National, but he did the next best thing when winning the Coral Scottish Grand National, which is the most valuable handicap chase in Britain after the Aintree showpiece. 'Mr Grand National' Trevor Hemmings purchased Vicente privately a few weeks before Aintree, adding him to his string after the death of Many Clouds who had shown himself to be right back to his best in the latest season after becoming the owner's third Grand National winner in 2015 (following Hedgehunter and Ballabriggs). Still only eight and already the winner of a Scottish National, Vicente looked 'an attractive proposition', according to Mr Hemmings' racing manager. 'The boss loves the Grand National and it was very unfortunate what happened to Many Clouds at Cheltenham, but we are delighted to be able to buy Vicente.' Vicente hadn't reached the frame on any of his starts since winning the 2016 Scottish National but his performances in races like the Hennessy (in which he eventually fell when looking held) and the Welsh Grand National had left the impression that he would probably bounce back in the spring. 'He does come right at this time of year,' his trainer Paul Nicholls said before Vicente's second appearance in the Scottish National. Vicente's Grand National challenge, on his debut over the National fences a fortnight earlier, had been short-lived. Starting at 16/1, he barely got into his stride before falling with Brian Hughes at the first. 'It's frustrating, but you'd rather it happened at the first than the twenty-first,' said his trainer. Vicente was none the worse for his Aintree mishap and, with stable jockey Sam Twiston-Davies back, was sent off 9/1 joint favourite with Southfield Royale in a maximum field of thirty at Ayr to become the first since Merigo, in 2010 and 2012 (second in 2011), to win two Scottish Grand Nationals, and the first to win successive editions since Androma in 1984 and 1985 (Barona also won successive editions in 1975 and 1976, on the second occasion just seven days after finishing fourth in the Grand National).

Coral Scottish Grand National Handicap Chase, Ayr—
Sam Twiston-Davies repeats his 2016 win aboard Vicente (noseband),
beating two horses trained by his father, Cogry (cheekpieces) and Benbens (star on cap)

Vicente carried 11-10 in the latest Scottish National but his BHA handicap mark had come down over the season to 146, the same mark he had defied as a novice in a stronger edition twelve months earlier. Top weight with 11-12 in the latest renewal was the novice Missed Approach (contesting his first handicap over fences) who had come second in the National Hunt Chase at Cheltenham, two places ahead of Arpege d'Alene who had 11-9 at Ayr. The Nicky Henderson-trained pair Premier Bond and Sugar Baron were other novices in the line-up, both having run well in the Kim Muir at the Cheltenham Festival. Novices have a good record in the Scottish National—three of the last six winners had run in the National Hunt Chase (including Vicente who had come fifth)—but that group didn't make an impact in the latest edition. The finish was dominated by horses who had shown up well in the race before, with Cogry (in fourth when falling four out in 2015) making much of the running with Missed Approach until collared in the final fifty yards by Vicente who was in touch the whole way and stayed on strongly under pressure. The pair were separated by a neck at the line, with the 2015 third Benbens again filling that berth, two lengths away, just ahead of Alvarado (twice fourth in the Aintree National) who had been runner-up at Ayr the year before to Vicente. The first four, incidentally, were all connected in some way to Grange Hill Farm at Naunton: winning jockey Sam Twiston-Davies is, of course, the son of Nigel the trainer of Cogry (whose claiming rider received a four-day ban for excessive use of the whip) and Benbens, while Alvarado is trained at the upper yard at Grange Hill Farm by Fergal O'Brien. The race was also something of a triumph for the winning owner too, whose two other runners Lessons In Milan and Vintage Clouds finished fifth and seventh. Missed Approach was eighth and Southfield Royale fifteenth (after helping to force the pace) of the seventeen finishers. Sugar Baron got no further than the first (which was dolled off on the second and third circuits while his rider Nico de Boinville was treated for an injury), Premier Bond was pulled up after never going well and Arpege d'Alene suffered fatal injuries on the flat before the eleventh fence. As at Aintree, the finishers in the Scottish National were dismounted on the course to be cooled down and the winning jockey made his way to the winner's circle without his mount.

			Dom Pasquini	Rheffic
	Dom Alco (FR)		(gr 1980)	Boursonne
	(gr 1987)	Alconaca	Nonoalco
Vicente (FR)			(ch 1978)	Vela
(b.g. 2009)			Kadalko	Cadoudal
	Ireland (FR)		(br 1988)	Koln
	(b 1996)	Beveland	Royal Charter
			(b 1989)	Queensland IV

The tall Vicente, a French AQPS (Autre Que Pur Sang, or other than thoroughbred), is by Dom Alco, the sire of those other AQPS stalwarts who have done so well for Vicente's trainer, Grand National winner Neptune Collonges and dual King George VI Chase winner Silviniaco Conti. Vicente's dam, the fairly useful French chaser Ireland, has bred several other winners, the best of them the smart French hurdler/chaser Porto Rico (by Video Rock) who stayed twenty-one furlongs. Vicente, who wears a hood, stays four miles well and acts on good to firm and heavy going. His connections are likely to fancy a second crack at the Grand National in 2018 and, although Vicente's jumping hasn't always been reliable—'he can miss one out'—he jumped well in the latest Scottish National and is worth another chance at Aintree. If he is returned to Ayr afterwards, he will be seeking to become the first horse to win the Scottish Grand National three times since the race was switched to Ayr in 1966—Queen's Taste (1953, 1954, 1956), Southern Hero (1934, 1936, 1939) and Couvrefeu II (1911, 1912, 1913) were triple winners at its former home Bogside. *Paul Nicholls*

VICENZO MIO (FR) 7 b.g. Corri Piano (FR) – Sweet Valrose (FR) (Cadoudal (FR))   **c121**
[2016/17 h125: h21g c22.3v^3 c20d^3 Mar 11] well-made gelding: fairly useful handicap   **h119**
hurdler: similar form over fences: better effort when third in novice handicap at Kelso in
February: likely to prove best short of 2¾m: acts on heavy going: wears tongue tie: has
joined Chris Gordon. *Paul Nicholls*

BetVictor Handicap Chase, Cheltenham—a marked step up in trip yields a valuable prize for the grey Viconte du Noyer on his debut for a new stable; Warrantor (second left) pushes him closest

VICONTE DU NOYER (FR) 8 gr.g. Martaline – Zouk Wood (USA) (Woodman (USA)) c150
[2016/17 c149, h126: c20.5m³ c27.3s* c25.5d c29.5sᵖᵘ c25gᵖᵘ c20d² Apr 26] lengthy, h–
rather sparely-made gelding: fairly useful hurdler: smart handicap chaser: won Grade 3 at
Cheltenham (by length from Warrantor) in November: second in Guinness Handicap Chase
at Punchestown (5 lengths behind Sizing Granite) in April: left Henry de Bromhead after
first start: stays 27f: acts on soft and good to firm going: tried in cheekpieces: has worn
tongue tie. *Colin Tizzard*

VIC'S LAST STAND (IRE) 7 b.m. Old Vic – Mislean (IRE) (Un Desperado (FR)) h110
[2016/17 h65p, b–: h17.2d⁵ h15.8d³ h15.8g² h19.9g* h16.8g* h19.9g* h20.6g² h19.9g²
h19.4g³ h24.4g⁵ h16.7g² h20.2g⁶ Apr 26] workmanlike mare: fair handicap hurdler:
completed hat-trick at Sedgefield (twice) and Uttoxeter in August/September: stays 21f:
acts on good to soft going: races prominently. *Gillian Boanas*

VICTARION (IRE) 5 b.g. Scorpion (IRE) – Gaye Preskina (IRE) (Presenting) [2016/17 b99
b15.3s⁴ b15.3v⁴ b15.8s² Mar 18] third foal: dam, unraced, half-sister to useful hurdler/
smart chaser (2¾m-3½m winner) Frantic Tan and fair hurdler/useful chaser (stayed 3¼m)
Irish Raptor: fairly useful form in bumpers: best effort when second at Uttoxeter in March.
Philip Hobbs

VICTOR HEWGO 12 b.g. Old Vic – Pennys Pride (IRE) (Pips Pride) [2016/17 c111, c–
h110: h23.3d h23.3d⁴ h23.3d² h23.3d⁴ Jul 13] good-topped gelding: fair handicap hurdler: h102
useful chaser at best: stays 3m: acts on soft and good to firm going: often in blinkers: often
races towards rear. *Keith Reveley*

VICTORIA SAYS (IRE) 5 b.m. Shantou (USA) – Ballestra (IRE) (Alflora (IRE)) h97
[2016/17 b16d b16s⁵ h16v⁴ h23.3g² Apr 25] first foal: dam (h78), second in bumper/lightly b–
raced over hurdles, half-sister to fairly useful hurdler/smart chaser (stays 25f) Wounded
Warrior (by Shantou): little impact in bumpers: modest form over hurdles: bred to stay at
least 2½m. *Stuart Crawford, Ireland*

VICTOR LEUDORUM (IRE) 10 b.g. Wareed (IRE) – Rock Garden (IRE) (Bigstone c116 §
(IRE)) [2016/17 c95§, h–§: h23.3gᵖᵘ h23g² h26.4g* c27.5g* c23gᵖᵘ Jan 11] big, strong h114 §
gelding: fair handicap hurdler: won at Stratford in August: fairly useful chaser: won
handicap there same month: left Charlie Mann after fourth start: stays 3½m: acts on good
to firm and heavy going: has worn cheekpieces: wears tongue tie: unreliable. *Steve Flook*

VIDE CAVE (FR) 8 b.g. Secret Singer (FR) – Kenna (FR) (Epervier Bleu) [2016/17 c66
c20.2mᶠ c17m c16gᵖᵘ Jul 5] winning hurdler: fairly useful at best over fences for Paul h–
Nicholls, poor form completed start in 2016/17: stays 2¼m: acts on good to firm going:
often wears tongue tie. *Ben Pauling*

VIENS CHERCHER (IRE) 6 b.g. Milan – La Zingarella (IRE) (Phardante (FR)) c134
[2016/17 c–, h127: c17.2g* c19.1g³ c19.9g⁴ c24g³ Jan 27] workmanlike gelding: fairly h–
useful hurdler: useful form over fences: won novice at Market Rasen in October: stays 3m:
acts on heavy and good to firm going: tried in cheekpieces: front runner/races prominently.
Brian Ellison

Betfred Becher Handicap Chase, Aintree—eventual winner Vieux Lion Rouge (No.9) clears Becher's Brook along with The Last Samuri (No.1) and Ucello Conti (noseband), who both made the frame

VIEUX LILLE (IRE) 7 b.g. Robin des Champs (FR) – Park Athlete (IRE) (Supreme **c131 x** Leader) [2016/17 h136, b103: c23.6g⁴ c24.2s³ c22.9s² c23.4d⁴ c26gᵖᵘ Mar 25] strong **h–** gelding: useful hurdler: similar form over fences: third in novice at Exeter (10¼ lengths behind American) in November and second in handicap at Haydock (8 lengths behind Yala Enki) in December: stays 3m: acts on heavy going: tried in cheekpieces: often races prominently: often let down by jumping. *Philip Hobbs*

VIEUX LION ROUGE (FR) 8 ch.g. Sabiango (GER) – Indecise (FR) (Cyborg (FR)) **c155** [2016/17 c144, h–: c25.5d* c28.4d* c34.3d⁶ Apr 8] lengthy gelding: winning hurdler: very **h–** smart handicap chaser: won Becher Chase at Aintree (by short head from Highland Lodge) in December and Grand National Trial at Haydock (by 3¼ lengths from Blaklion) in February: stays 3½m (not got home last 2 runnings of Grand National): acts on heavy going: has worn headgear, including last 5 starts: tried in tongue tie: strong traveller. *David Pipe*

VIF ARGENT (FR) 8 b.g. Dom Alco (FR) – Formosa (FR) (Royal Charter (FR)) [2016/17 **c–** c–, h106: h21gᵖᵘ h20m h20.6d Jun 17] rather leggy gelding: fairly useful hurdler at best for **h–** David Pipe, has lost his form: winning chaser: has worn blinkers/tongue tie. *Andrew Reid*

Betfred Grand National Trial Handicap Chase, Haydock—the perfect warm-up for Aintree as Vieux Lion Rouge (No.5) pulls well clear with fellow National hopeful Blaklion

VIKEKHAL (FR) 8 b.g. Khalkevi (IRE) – Gesse Parade (FR) (Dress Parade) [2016/17 c125, h–: c19m^5 c21.1d^5 c25.5m* c24.2s c24m^{pu} Apr 18] tall gelding: winning hurdler: fairly useful handicap chaser: won at Warwick (conditional) in November: stays 25f: acts on good to firm and heavy going: wears blinkers. *Gary Moore* — **c119 h–**

VIKING MISTRESS 9 b.m. Bollin Eric – Mistress Caramore (IRE) (Moscow Society (USA)) [2016/17 h–: h19.7g^3 c20v^F c16.5d^4 h20.6s^2 h23.8d^5 h23.9g^2 h22g^6 Apr 1] workmanlike mare: modest maiden hurdler: poor form over fences: stays 3m: acts on soft going: tried in cheekpieces: wears tongue tie. *Martin Keighley* — **c84 h93**

VIKING REBEL (IRE) 15 b.g. Taipan (IRE) – Clodagh's Dream (Whistling Deer) [2016/17 c88§, h–: c26.2d^{pu} May 4] rangy gelding: winning pointer: winning hurdler: useful chaser at best, pulled up in handicap sole start in 2016/17: stays 3¼m: acts on heavy going: wears cheekpieces: one to treat with caution. *Tim Reed* — **c– § h–**

VIKY DU REPONET (FR) 8 b.m. Voix du Nord (FR) – Opale du Moulin (FR) (Robin des Champs (FR)) [2016/17 h17.9s* c17.4d* c20.5g^{pu} Dec 29] second foal: half-sister to French hurdler/chaser Upalik du Reponnet (17f-19f winner, by Policy Maker): dam ran once over hurdles: useful hurdler: won minor event at Auteuil (by 5 lengths from Storm of Saintly) in September: useful chaser: won handicap at same course (by 3 lengths from Hawk The Talk) in October: left S. Foucher after second start: stays 19f: acts on heavy going: tried in hood/tongue tie: front runner: has rejoined former yard after sole start in Britain. *Paul Nicholls* — **c131 h137**

VILLAGE VIC (IRE) 10 b.g. Old Vic – Etoile Margot (FR) (Garde Royale) [2016/17 c155, h–: c20.4s^2 c20.8s^3 c20.8s^2 c20.8g c20.8g^{pu} Apr 19] rather sparely-made gelding: winning hurdler: very smart handicap chaser: placed in BetVictor Gold Cup in November, Caspian Caviar Gold Cup (1½ lengths behind Frodon) in December and Grade 3 (3 lengths behind Shantou Flyer) in January, all at Cheltenham: stays 21f: acts on heavy going: front runner/races prominently. *Philip Hobbs* — **c159 h–**

VINCENT (IRE) 7 b.g. Milan – Sand Eel (IRE) (Sandalay) [2016/17 h21.5g c17.4v^4 h22.7s^{pu} Dec 4] poor maiden hurdler: 16/1, fourth in maiden at Sligo (12¾ lengths behind Vinnie Luck) on chasing debut: tried in cheekpieces: wears tongue tie. *Mark McNiff, Ireland* — **c91 h–**

VINCENT ROW (IRE) 10 b.g. Vinnie Roe (IRE) – De Lissa (IRE) (Zaffaran (USA)) [2016/17 h24s h20d c25.2d^4 c20.1v^2 c23.8g^5 c24.2s^{pu} c24.2v^{pu} Mar 28] maiden hurdler: poor maiden chaser: left Ellmarie Holden after second start: stays 3¼m: acts on heavy going: has worn headgear/tongue tie: often let down by jumping. *Chris Grant* — **c82 x h–**

VINCENT'S FOREVER 4 b.g. Pour Moi (IRE) – Glen Rosie (IRE) (Mujtahid (USA)) [2016/17 h16.7s h16.5g^5 h16.5g^3 h16g^{pu} Apr 29] closely related to useful hurdler/winning chaser Kings Quay (2m/17f winner, by Montjeu) and useful/temperamental hurdler Calculated Risk (2m-2½m winner, by Motivator): fairly useful on Flat, stays 11f: modest form over hurdles: will prove suited by further than 2m: in hood/tongue tie last 3 starts. *David Pipe* — **h89**

VINCIAETTIS (FR) 6 b.g. Enrique – Over The Sea (FR) (Urban Ocean (FR)) [2016/17 h120, h117: h16.4v^{pu} Feb 25] smart bumper performer: fairly useful form over hurdles, pulled up sole start in 2016/17: front runner/races prominently. *Warren Greatrex* — **h–**

VINCITORE (FR) 11 b.g. Starborough – Viva Vodka (FR) (Crystal Glitters (USA)) [2016/17 c109, h–: c26.1s^{pu} c25.8g^5 c24.2m^{pu} c24.1d^5 c22.7s^4 c21.1g Apr 6] leggy gelding: dual winning pointer: winning hurdler: fair chaser: left Richard Phillips after third start: stays 3¼m: acts on soft and good to firm going: often wears headgear: in tongue tie last 3 starts. *Miss Sarah Rippon* — **c107 h–**

VINEGAR HILL 8 b.g. Kayf Tara – Broughton Melody (Alhijaz) [2016/17 h95: h23.3v^{pu} h20.3v* h20.3s* h24.5s* h23.1s^6 c20.3d^4 Jan 3] fair handicap hurdler: completed hat-trick at Southwell (twice) in May and Kempton in November: 7/1, fourth in novice handicap at Bangor (18¾ lengths behind Truckers Glory) on chasing debut: left Anna Brooks after third start: stays 3m: acts on heavy going: has worn visor: open to improvement over fences. *Stuart Edmunds* — **c101 p h112**

VINNIE LEWIS (IRE) 6 b.g. Vinnie Roe (IRE) – Ballyann Lewis (IRE) (Sir Harry Lewis (USA)) [2016/17 h18v^4 h20g h21d^3 h21.7s^4 h19.6s^2 Jan 13] first foal: dam (h103), winning pointer, half-sister to fairly useful chaser (stayed 23f) Marley Roca: winning pointer: modest form in bumpers: fair form over hurdles: left James Joseph Mangan after first start: will be suited by 3m+: may do better still. *Harry Whittington* — **h110 b84**

VINNIE RED (IRE) 8 ch.g. Vinnie Roe (IRE) – Conzara (IRE) (Mandalus) [2016/17 **c128** h15.8d³ c21.4d* c23.4d³ c23.4dᵖᵘ Mar 24] rangy gelding: fairly useful form over hurdles: **h119 +** third in handicap at Huntingdon in December: similar form over fences: won novice handicap at Market Rasen same month: should stay beyond 21f: acts on good to soft going: tried in tongue tie. *Fergal O'Brien*

VINNIESLITTLE LAMB (IRE) 9 b.m. Vinnie Roe (IRE) – Polar Lamb (IRE) (Brush **c87** Aside (USA)) [2016/17 c21.7d³ c20.9dᵖᵘ Mar 26] maiden hurdler: modest handicap chaser: **h–** stays 3m: acts on heavy going: has worn headgear. *Venetia Williams*

VINNIE TRENTA (IRE) 9 b.g. Vinnie Roe (IRE) – Proud Trenta (IRE) (King's Ride) **h79** [2016/17 h88: h17.7g h21.6mᵖᵘ Oct 6] maiden pointer: poor maiden hurdler: stays 21f: acts on heavy going: has worn tongue tie. *Arthur Whiting*

VINNIEWHITEFOOT 10 ch.g. Grape Tree Road – Mistress Return (Bob's Return (IRE)) **h62 §** [2016/17 h–: h15.8d⁵ May 5] winning pointer: poor form over hurdles: temperamental. *Gary Hanmer*

VINNY GAMBINI (IRE) 10 b.g. Vinnie Roe (IRE) – Red Velvet (So Factual (USA)) **c84** [2016/17 c105, h–: c21.5g⁵ c24.2d⁶ c26.3d⁴ c23.8gᶠ Jan 1] big gelding: winning hurdler: **h–** poor maiden chaser: stayed 21f: acted on heavy going: tried in headgear/tongue tie: dead. *Rose Dobbin*

VINTAGE CLOUDS (IRE) 7 gr.g. Cloudings (IRE) – Rare Vintage (IRE) (Germany **c132** (USA)) [2016/17 h132: c20g² c21.6v² c25.2d² c24.1sᶠ c28.4d³ c25gᶠ c31.8g Apr 22] useful **h–** hurdler: useful maiden chaser: second in novice at Haydock (10 lengths behind Politologue) in November: should stay long distances: best form on heavy going. *Sue Smith*

VINTAGE SALON (IRE) 6 b.m. King's Theatre (IRE) – Lounaos (FR) (Limnos (JPN)) **h97** [2016/17 b16d⁶ b17m b17.8d⁶ h16d* h20g⁴ h15.7g⁴ h16g h16d h16.8g Oct 18] second foal: **b60** dam (h142), 2m hurdle winner, also smart 1½m-2m winner on Flat: poor form in bumpers: modest form over hurdles: won mares maiden at Roscommon in July: unproven beyond 2m: acts on good to soft going: has worn headgear, including final start: tried in tongue tie: often races prominently. *James A. Nash, Ireland*

VINTAGE VINNIE (IRE) 8 b.g. Vinnie Roe (IRE) – Bobby's Jet (IRE) (Bob's Return **c135** (IRE)) [2016/17 c135, h–: h23g* c21.4g* c21g³ c20.4sᵖᵘ c21.1d c21.1g c20d⁵ Apr 26] tall, **h119** useful-looking gelding: fairly useful hurdler: won novice at Worcester in September: useful handicap chaser: won listed event at Market Rasen same month: stays 3m: acts on heavy going: has worn hood. *Rebecca Curtis*

VIOLETS BOY (IRE) 10 br.g. King's Theatre (IRE) – Sunshine Rays (Alflora (IRE)) **c119** [2016/17 c20.3m² c23.9gᵘʳ c22.4g c22.7f² Dec 7] useful-looking gelding: winning hurdler: **h–** fairly useful handicap chaser: second at Southwell in September: left Oliver Sherwood after second start: stays 23f: acts on good to firm and good to soft going: tried in cheekpieces: usually wears tongue tie. *Nick Mitchell*

VIOLETS GIRL 7 b.m. Black Sam Bellamy (IRE) – Sunshine Rays (Alflora (IRE)) **h95** [2016/17 h93: h15.9g⁵ h16.8d⁵ h16d h16.8g⁴ h15.3d⁵ h21.6v³ h25.5sᵖᵘ Jan 4] bumper winner: modest maiden hurdler: left Warren Greatrex after fourth start: stays 2¾m: acts on heavy going. *Nick Mitchell*

VIOLONISTE (FR) 8 b.g. Epalo (GER) – Parade (FR) (Robin des Champs (FR)) **h121** [2016/17 h88: h19.3m* h16.2d* h19.9g* h16s h15.6g² h16.4g³ Apr 8] placed in maiden points: fairly useful handicap hurdler: won at Carlisle (conditional) in May, and novice events at Perth in June and Uttoxeter in July: second at Musselburgh in March: left Sam England after first start: stays 2½m: acts on soft and good to firm going: tried in tongue tie: usually travels strongly. *Ronan M. P. McNally, Ireland*

VIRAK (FR) 8 b.g. Bernebeau (FR) – Nosika d'Airy (FR) (Oblat (FR)) [2016/17 c159, h–: **c142 d** c24.2g⁵ c23.4s⁶ c24.1s⁴ c23.8s⁵ c26g⁶ Apr 20] sturdy gelding: winning hurdler: very smart **h–** handicap chaser at best, largely out of sorts in 2016/17: should stay long distances: acts on heavy going: wears cheekpieces nowadays: tried in tongue tie. *Paul Nicholls*

VIRGIL EARP 10 b.g. Fasliyev (USA) – Karakorum (IRE) (Fairy King (USA)) [2016/17 **h86** h22m⁵ h21g⁵ h15.8gᶠ h20d⁵ h18.7m⁵ Jul 10] fairly useful hurdler at best for Noel Meade, well below that in 2016/17 after very long absence (likewise on Flat): stays 2¾m: acts on soft and good to firm going: has worn headgear, including last 5 starts: tends to find little. *Ian Williams*

VIRGILIO (FR) 8 b.g. Denham Red (FR) – Llesse de Marbeuf (FR) (Cyborg (FR)) **c144** [2016/17 c–, h139: c20d* c21g* c20.2mᵖᵘ c19.9g² c24g² c25g³ Apr 7] sturdy gelding: **h–** useful hurdler: useful chaser: won novice at Warwick in May and intermediate event at Newton Abbot in October: stays 25f: acts on heavy going: wears tongue tie. *Dan Skelton*

VIR

VIRGINIA CHICK (FR) 5 b.g. Nickname (FR) – Sweet Jaune (FR) (Le Nain Jaune **h–** (FR)) [2016/17 b16.8s⁵ h15.3v⁵ h15.3d h15.8d Apr 16] €28,000 3-y-o: half-brother to **b85** numerous winners, including useful hurdler/chaser Viking Blond (23f/3m winner, by Varese), stayed 29f, and useful but ungenuine hurdler Rosemauve (2¾m-3m winner, by Cyborg): dam unraced: fifth in bumper: no form over hurdles: bred to stay 3m: tried in blinkers: in tongue tie last 2 starts. *Evan Williams*

VIRGO THE FIRST (IRE) 7 b.g. Milan – Bridge of Tears (IRE) (Zaffaran (USA)) **c91 p** [2016/17 c23.6g³ May 17] second foal: dam (h78), maiden hurdler (stayed 2½m)/placed in points, half-sister to fairly useful hurdler (stays 2½m) Breaking Bits: point winner: 3/1, better than result when third in novice hunter at Huntingdon (5¼ lengths behind Hill of Gold) on chasing debut: open to improvement. *Martin Ward*

VIRNON 6 b.g. Virtual – Freedom Song (Singspiel (IRE)) [2016/17 h111: c16.4sᵘʳ c15.6v² **c117** c16s c18v² c15.7v² c17.2d* Apr 27] lengthy gelding: fair hurdler: fairly useful form **h–** over fences: won handicap at Market Rasen in April: stays 2¼m: acts on heavy going. *Alan Swinbank*

VIRTUALLY OURS (IRE) 5 ch.m. Virtual – Our Ethel (Be My Chief (USA)) [2016/17 **h–** b16.8g b16s b16.4s⁵ h16s Feb 14] no form in bumpers/maiden hurdle: dead. *Malcolm* **b–** *Jefferson*

VIRTUAL SONG 4 b.f. Virtual – Song of The Desert (Desert Sun) [2016/17 h15.8dᵖᵘ **h–** Oct 13] poor maiden on Flat: pulled up in juvenile maiden on hurdling debut. *Barry Leavy*

VIRTUEL D'OUDON (FR) 8 b.g. Network (GER) – La Belle Illusion (FR) (Turgeon **c–** (USA)) [2016/17 h23.1sᵖᵘ Feb 12] angular gelding: Irish maiden point winner: useful **h–** hurdler at best, pulled up sole start in 2016/17: fairly useful form over fences: stays 25f: acts on heavy going: usually in headgear. *David Pipe*

VIRTUOSE DU CHENET (FR) 8 b.g. Irish Wells (FR) – Lili Bleue (FR) (Epervier **c–** Bleu) [2016/17 c81, h–: c20.3vᵖᵘ c15.7g May 24] winning hurdler: poor maiden chaser: **h–** stays 19f: acts on soft going: has worn headgear/tongue tie, including final start: front runner/races prominently, tends to find little. *Venetia Williams*

VIRTUOSE DU GOUET (FR) 8 b.g. Voix du Nord (FR) – Newhaven (FR) (Subotica **c–** (FR)) [2016/17 h21sᵖᵘ h16.6sᵖᵘ h15.9s h25gʳʳ Apr 3] fair form over hurdles in France, **h– §** none in Britain in 2016/17: winning chaser: often wears headgear: one to treat with caution (refused to race final start). *Michael Wigham*

VISAGE BLANC 4 b.f. Champs Elysees – Russian Empress (IRE) (Trans Island) **h98** [2016/17 h16.7g⁶ h16g³ h16.8s⁵ Nov 20] fairly useful on Flat, stays 1½m: modest form over hurdles: tried in tongue tie. *Graeme McPherson*

VISANDI (FR) 5 b.g. Azamour (IRE) – Vadaza (FR) (Zafonic (USA)) [2016/17 h15.8d² **h104** h15.8g⁴ h19.7s⁴ h21.6gᵖᵘ Apr 11] fairly useful on Flat, stays 15f: fair form over hurdles: should be suited by 2¼m+: in tongue tie last 2 starts. *Jonjo O'Neill*

VISERION 5 ch.g. Tamayuz – Frivolity (Pivotal) [2016/17 h16.7s⁶ h15.5d³ h17s* h16.2v⁶ **h121** h16.8g² h16g* Apr 23] fairly useful form over hurdles: won novices at Carlisle in February and Wetherby in April: raced around 2m: acts on soft going: front runner/races prominently. *Donald McCain*

VISION D'AUTEUIL (FR) 5 b.g. Vision d'Etat (FR) – Pharistella (FR) (Double Bed (FR)) **b–** [2016/17 b16g Mar 18] sturdy gelding: in tongue tie, tailed off in maiden bumper. *Harry Fry*

VISION DE LA VIE (FR) 7 ch.g. Sin Kiang (FR) – Vidahermosa (FR) (Kahyasi) **c92** [2016/17 c94, h–: c26.3s⁵ c20.1g⁴ c23.8d* h23.9gᵖᵘ Aug 20] fair hurdler at best: modest **h–** handicap chaser: won at Perth in June: stays 3m: acts on soft going: wears blinkers: in tongue tie last 3 starts. *Pauline Robson*

VISION DES CHAMPS (FR) 8 b.g. Saint des Saints (FR) – Manita des Champs (FR) **c–** (Fabulous Dancer (USA)) [2016/17 c119, h–: c16.4sᵖᵘ c15.2m⁶ Apr 13] good-topped **h–** gelding: winning hurdler: fairly useful chaser for Gary Moore in 2015/16, no form in 2016/17: stays 2½m when emphasis is on speed: acts on good to firm and good to soft going: wears tongue tie: usually races close up. *Roy Brotherton*

VITAL EVIDENCE (USA) 7 b.g. Empire Maker (USA) – Promising Lead (Danehill **c104** (USA)) [2016/17 h–: h19.6g h15.9d² h15.7g³ c16.4g² c16.4dᶠ c16dᶠ Jan 19] quite good- **h102** topped gelding: fair maiden hurdler: fair form over fences: best effort when second in novice handicap at Sedgefield in October: unproven beyond 17f: acts on soft going: has worn headgear, including last 5 starts: sometimes in tongue tie: has joined Neil Mulholland. *Kim Bailey*

VITARRA 8 b.m. Kayf Tara – Vivante (IRE) (Toulon) [2016/17 b–: h19gᶠ h20.3gᵖᵘ **h–** Mar 28] chunky mare: no form over hurdles: tried in cheekpieces. *Jim Wilson*

VIVALDI COLLONGES (FR) 8 b.g. Dom Alco (FR) – Diane Collonges (FR) (El Badr)   **c90**
[2016/17 c150p, h–: c24.2d³ c29.2s^{pu} c26s^{pu} c31.8g^{pu} Apr 22] sturdy gelding: winning   **h–**
hurdler: smart chaser at best, out of sorts in 2016/17: stays 3¼m: acts on heavy going:
wears tongue tie. *Paul Nicholls*

VIVANT POEME (FR) 8 b.g. Early March – Hasta Manana (FR) (Useful (FR)) [2016/17   **h122**
h126: h21.6g⁴ Aug 20] winning pointer: fairly useful handicap hurdler: stays 2¾m: acts on
good to firm and heavy going: wears tongue tie: often races in rear, usually travels strongly.
Harry Fry

VIVA RAFA (IRE) 7 b.g. Scorpion (IRE) – Back To Stay (IRE) (Supreme Leader)   **h104**
[2016/17 h112, b92: h15.8g³ h20.3d⁴ h20.3d³ h19.1v^{pu} h23.9g Mar 2] fair maiden hurdler:
stays 2½m: acts on heavy going: has worn hood, including last 5 starts: in tongue tie last 3
starts. *Richard Phillips*

VIVAS (FR) 6 b.g. Davidoff (GER) – Lavircas (FR) (Lavirco (GER)) [2016/17 h112, b93:   **h112**
h21m⁴ h21g² h18.7m² h18.6g* h16s⁵ h18.6d⁶ h15.7g Apr 15] sturdy gelding: fair handicap
hurdler: won conditionals/amateur event at Market Rasen in November: stays 21f: best
form on good going: in tongue tie last 4 starts: usually races prominently. *Charlie Longsdon*

VIVA STEVE (IRE) 9 b.g. Flemensfirth (USA) – Eluna (Unfuwain (USA)) [2016/17   **c139**
c134, h–: c24.3s* c29.2s c24g Feb 25] lengthy gelding: winning hurdler: useful handicap   **h–**
chaser: won at Ayr (by 2¾ lengths from Ballyben) in November: best around 3m: acts on
heavy going: in tongue tie last 3 starts. *Fergal O'Brien*

VIVE LE ROI (IRE) 6 b.g. Robin des Pres (FR) – Cappard View (IRE) (Rudimentary   **h120**
(USA)) [2016/17 h116p, b100: h19.6g³ h21d³ Nov 24] useful-looking gelding: bumper
winner: fairly useful form over hurdles: front runner/races prominently. *Charlie Longsdon*

VIVE MA FILLE (GER) 5 b.m. Doyen (IRE) – Vive Madame (GER) (Big Shuffle   **h102**
(USA)) [2016/17 h15.3s³ h20.7s h16s⁴ Feb 4] useful on Flat, stays 16.5f: fair form over
hurdles. *Mick Channon*

VOCALISER (IRE) 5 b.g. Vocalised (USA) – Bring Back Matron (IRE) (Rock of Gibraltar   **h96**
(IRE)) [2016/17 h78: h15.7m⁴ h16s³ h15.8d h15.7s² h16.3v⁴ h15.7s³ h16g Apr 8] good-
topped gelding: modest maiden hurdler: raced only at 2m: acts on soft and good to firm
going: in cheekpieces/tongue tie last 2 starts: front runner/races prominently. *Robin Dickin*

VOCARIUM (IRE) 4 b.g. Poet's Voice – Vituisa (Bering) [2016/17 b16d* Apr 29]   **b105**
half-brother to several winners on Flat, including smart 1½m-2¼m winner Veracity (by
Lomitas): dam French 11.5f winner: 5/1, won maiden bumper at Punchestown (by 3
lengths from Lady Ischia) on debut. *Peter Fahey, Ireland*

VODKA ALL THE WAY (IRE) 5 b.g. Oscar (IRE) – Fully Focused (IRE) (Rudimentary   **b86**
(USA)) [2016/17 b16s⁵ b16.3s b16g³ Apr 8] €40,000 3-y-o: big, workmanlike gelding:
sixth foal: closely related to a winning pointer by Milan and half-brother to modest 17f
chase winner Instinctive (by Scorpion): dam unraced daughter of fairly useful hurdler/
chaser (stayed 3m) Flawless Finish: fair form in bumpers: will be suited by at least 2½m.
Philip Hobbs

VODKA RED (IRE) 9 b.g. Ivan Denisovich (IRE) – Begine (IRE) (Germany (USA))   **h71**
[2016/17 h91: h16.4v⁴ Mar 18] modest handicap hurdler: stays 21f: acts on good to firm
and heavy going: wears headgear: has worn tongue tie: often races in rear. *Kenny Johnson*

VODKA SOCIETY (IRE) 9 b.g. Moscow Society (USA) – Miss Chancey (IRE)   **c–**
(Warcraft (USA)) [2016/17 c23.6s^{ur} h20d Apr 18] tailed off in maiden on hurdling   **h–**
debut: unseated rider third in novice chase 6 weeks earlier. *David Peter Dunne, Ireland*

VODKA WELLS (FR) 7 b.g. Irish Wells (FR) – Kahipiroska (FR) (Mansonnien (FR))   **c122**
[2016/17 c128, h122: c15.6d² c17.3m⁵ c20.1s^{ur} c16.3g⁵ h17.2g⁶ h16.2d h16d³ h18.1s⁶   **h111**
h16.8s h16d c17.1d³ c15.2g^{pu} Apr 23] good-topped gelding: has reportedly had breathing
operation: fair handicap hurdler: fairly useful handicap chaser: second at Hexham
(conditional) in May: left Micky Hammond after sixth start: unproven beyond 17f: acts on
heavy going: has worn headgear, including last 2 starts. *Rebecca Menzies*

VOICE CONTROL (IRE) 5 gr.g. Dalakhani (IRE) – Scottish Stage (IRE) (Selkirk   **h115 p**
(USA)) [2016/17 h19.6m² Oct 30] half-brother to fairly useful hurdler Dumbarton (2m
winner, by Danehill Dancer), stays 2¾m, and fair hurdler Northern Meeting (2m winner,
by Dylan Thomas), both unreliable: fair on Flat, stays 2m: 12/1, second in novice at
Huntingdon (2 lengths behind Late Night Lily) on hurdling debut: entitled to progress.
Laura Mongan

VOICE FROM ABOVE (IRE) 8 b.m. Strategic Prince – Basin Street Blues (IRE)   **h58**
(Dolphin Street (FR)) [2016/17 h19.3g⁴ h15.6g Jan 3] poor maiden hurdler: should stay
beyond 2m: acts on good to soft going. *Patrick Holmes*

VOILA ERIC 5 b.g. Bollin Eric – Et Voila (Alflora (IRE)) [2016/17 b16v[6] Feb 25] runner-up in Irish maiden point on debut: tailed off in bumper. *Michael Scudamore* **b–**

VOIX D'EAU (FR) 7 b.g. Voix du Nord (FR) – Eau de Chesne (FR) (R B Chesne) [2016/17 c148, h–: c21.3m[3] c19.4g[3] c23.8m c24.2d[4] c20.8g c20.8g[pu] Apr 19] big, lengthy gelding: winning hurdler: smart handicap chaser: third at Haydock (9½ lengths behind Javert) in May: stays 21f: acts on good to firm and good to soft going: wears tongue tie: usually races towards rear. *Harry Fry* **c146 h–**

VOIX DES TIEP (FR) 5 b.g. Voix du Nord (FR) – Tiepataxe (FR) (Mad Tax (USA)) [2016/17 b16s[2] Feb 12] €40,000 3-y-o: fourth foal: dam French 17f chase winner: 7/4, promise when second in maiden bumper at Leopardstown (½ length behind Someday) on debut, clear of rest: sure to progress. *W. P. Mullins, Ireland* **b105 p**

VOLCANIC (FR) 8 br.g. Al Namix (FR) – Queen of Rock (FR) (Video Rock (FR)) [2016/17 c121, h119: h24.7m[3] h22.1m[2] h23d[4] h23g[3] h23g h27g[3] h25m[3] Sep 18] leggy gelding: fairly useful handicap hurdler: second at Cartmel in May and third at Sedgefield in September: fairly useful chaser: stays 27f: acts on good to firm and heavy going: tried in cheekpieces: wears tongue tie: front runner/races prominently. *Donald McCain* **c– h121**

VOLCANIC JACK (IRE) 9 b.g. Kodiac – Rosaria Panatta (IRE) (Mujtahid (USA)) [2016/17 c102§, h65§: c20.3v[5] c15.7g[6] c25.5m[ur] c21.2m* Jun 24] sturdy gelding: winning hurdler: poor handicap chaser: won at Cartmel in June: stays 2¾m: acts on soft and good to firm going: unreliable. *Michael Chapman* **c75 § h– §**

VOLNAY DE THAIX (FR) 8 ch.g. Secret Singer (FR) – Mange de Thaix (FR) (Mont Basile (FR)) [2016/17 c148, h147: c19.9d[5] c24d[pu] h21.5g[3] Apr 29] tall, useful-looking gelding: smart hurdler: third in Select Hurdle at Sandown (7½ lengths behind L'Ami Serge) in April: smart chaser, below best first 2 starts in 2016/17: stays 21f: acts on soft going. *Nicky Henderson* **c– h147**

VOLPONE JELOIS (FR) 4 gr.g. Vol de Nuit – Jenne Jelois (FR) (My Risk (FR)) [2016/17 h17.7d[2] h16.5g* h19g[3] h16.5s[2] h19g[3] h19m[2] Apr 27] half-brother to French hurdler/chaser Hilton Jelois (17f-19f winner, by Hannouma): fairly useful on Flat, stays 15f: fairly useful form over hurdles: won maiden at Taunton in December: stays 19f: acts on soft and good to firm going: tried in cheekpieces: front runner/races prominently. *Paul Nicholls* **h120**

VOLT FACE (FR) 8 ch.g. Kapgarde (FR) – Jourenuit (FR) (Chamberlin (FR)) [2016/17 h16.2s h19.6s[3] h23.9s[pu] c24.5s[2] c21.3d[5] c17.2m[2] Apr 17] tall gelding: fair handicap hurdler: fairly useful form over fences: best effort when second in handicap at Market Rasen in April: likely to prove best up to 2½m: acts on good to firm and heavy going: has worn hood: wears tongue tie. *Charlie Longsdon* **c118 h110**

VOLVALIEN (FR) 8 b.g. Network (GER) – Josvalie (FR) (Panoramic) [2016/17 h20.5d[4] c19.9g c16.5m[2] c16.4g* c20s[3] c16.3s[2] c16.4s* c21.1v[4] c17.2m[4] Apr 17] rather leggy gelding: bumper winner: modest form over hurdles: fairly useful handicap chaser: won novice events at Sedgefield in October and January: left Alan Fleming after second start: effective between 2m-2½m: acts on soft and good to firm going: has worn headgear, including last 3 starts: wears tongue tie: usually leads. *Brian Ellison* **c118 h99**

VOSNE ROMANEE 6 ch.g. Arakan (USA) – Vento Del Oreno (FR) (Lando (GER)) [2016/17 h124: h16.2m* h16.8g h16.5g h16g[4] Apr 22] smallish gelding: useful handicap hurdler: won at Perth in May: fourth in Scottish Champion Hurdle at Ayr (3½ lengths behind Chesterfield) in April: stays 2¼m: acts on good to firm and good to soft going: wears headgear/tongue tie: often travels strongly. *Dr Richard Newland* **h131**

VOTE OF CONFIDENCE (USA) 7 ch.g. Pleasantly Perfect (USA) – Sogna di Me (Danehill (USA)) [2016/17 h24m[3] h24g[2] h24g[pu] h23.6d h22g* h21.5g[4] h24d h19.6g* c20s[pu] c20.2m[2] Apr 5] fairly useful handicap hurdler: won at Down Royal in August and Bangor (conditional) in October: hasn't taken to chasing: left Gordon Elliott after eighth start: stays 3m: acts on good to firm and good to soft going: wears headgear: has worn tongue tie, including last 3 starts. *Laura Hurley* **c95 h120**

VOUVRAY (FR) 6 b.g. Califet (FR) – Cartzagrouas (FR) (Esprit du Nord (USA)) [2016/17 h21.4v[6] h25.3s[4] Feb 28] won Irish maiden point on debut: no form over hurdles. *Nicky Richards* **h–**

VOYAGE A NEW YORK (FR) 8 b.g. Kapgarde (FR) – Pennsylvanie (FR) (Dadarissime (FR)) [2016/17 c117, h–: c25d[3] c26.2d c28.4v c21.1d[F] Dec 3] tall gelding: winning hurdler: fairly useful handicap chaser: third at Aintree in June: best up to 3m: acts on heavy going: wears tongue tie: often races in rear. *Lucinda Russell* **c116 h–**

VROUM VROUM MAG (FR) 8 b.m. Voix du Nord (FR) – Naiade Mag (FR)   **c–**
(Kadalko (FR)) [2016/17 c151P, h155p: h16s* h20d² h24d* h16.6d* h19.9g² h16g   **h151**
Apr 28]

    After an unbeaten run of ten races, starting odds on every time, and culminating
in victories in the David Nicholson Mares' Hurdle at the Cheltenham Festival and
the Punchestown Champion Hurdle, Vroum Vroum merited the following summary
in *Chasers & Hurdlers 2015/16*: 'Vroum Vroum Mag's most progressive profile is
testament to the truth of the saying that you never really know how good a horse is
until it is beaten. She has looked value for plenty more as she has simply brushed
aside the opposition in nearly all her races so far and she still possesses untapped
potential.' Vroum Vroum Mag was kept over hurdles and duly won more good races
in the latest season, including when recording the third Grade 1 victory of her career
in the Christmas Hurdle at Leopardstown, but it can now be said with some certainty
that we know how good she is, following defeats at Fairyhouse and Cheltenham,
and an excusable one at Punchestown. She is a smart performer over hurdles, but no
better than that, and, if she still has untapped potential, it will not be revealed until
she goes back over fences. She is unbeaten in six starts in that sphere and still has
the scope to do much better. Interestingly, although Vroum Vroum Mag hasn't run
over fences since her win at Clonmel in November 2015, in a graded race for mares,
three of her six entries at the 2017 Cheltenham Festival included the Gold Cup, the
Queen Mother Champion Chase and the Ryanair.

    Vroum Vroum Mag's winning sequence since joining Willie Mullins came to
an end when she was beaten a short head by Apple's Jade on her seasonal debut in
the Hatton's Grace Hurdle at Fairyhouse in December (her win in the Punchestown
Champion Hurdle came shortly after the start of the 2016/17 British season). She
made smooth headway to edge ahead at the last and kept on under pressure before
being collared near the finish by a similarly smart and race-fit rival, the pair pulling
seven lengths clear of the remainder. Vroum Vroum Mag started at 15/8-on for the

Squared Financial Christmas Hurdle, Leopardstown—a third Grade 1 win for Vroum Vroum Mag,
whose stable companion Shaneshill falls heavily at the last

Christmas Hurdle at Leopardstown on her next start, ahead of Snow Falcon (5/1), Kotkikova (7/1) and Clondaw Warrior (8/1) and, in a line-up which didn't look particularly strong for a Grade 1, Vroum Vroum Mag was always going strongly and was still virtually on the bridle when leading at the last. She won by a length and a quarter from stablemate Clondaw Warrior (another stable-companion Shaneshill would also have been placed but for falling at the last). Snow Falcon finished another two and a half lengths back in third, though the steady pace resulted in there being little between seven of the runners entering the straight, and some of those behind the first three were flattered to finish so close.

The Christmas Hurdle was only the second time that Vroum Vroum Mag had run over three miles for the Mullins stable and she was dropped markedly in trip for her next start, in the Doncaster Mares' Hurdle in January, when she was nowhere near her best and made extremely hard work of what should have been a simple task (she was sent off at 5/1-on), just wearing down Midnight Jazz in the closing stages. There was plenty of talk through the winter about which race Vroum Vroum Mag should contest at the Cheltenham Festival, her three entries over hurdles being the Champion Hurdle, the Stayers' Hurdle and the David Nicholson Mares' Hurdle. Limini replaced her as ante-post favourite for the last-named after decisively defeating Apple's Jade in the Quevega Mares' Hurdle at Punchestown in February. After plenty of speculation that Vroum Vroum Mag might run in the Champion Hurdle (the last two winners Faugheen and Annie Power, both in the same ownership as Vroum Vroum Mag, were ruled out through injury), the decision was eventually made in Cheltenham week to run Vroum Vroum Mag and Limini against each other in the Mares' Hurdle.

Owner Rich Ricci explained the reasoning: 'The first question we had to ask ourselves was if they had travelled well from Ireland, and they have. Then we had to ask, from what we've seen Vroum Vroum Mag do this season, and the way she's been working, can we see her winning a Champion Hurdle and the collective response was no. Nothing she's done in her three starts this year suggests she could go into the Champion Hurdle with a live chance. It was the same with Limini [whom connections had considered supplementing], and that makes the mares race the right place to run the two of them.' Ruby Walsh chose to ride the 6/4 favourite Limini, with 11/4-shot Vroum Vroum Mag ridden by Paul Townend. Vroum Vroum Mag couldn't follow up her victory in the race twelve months earlier, faced with stronger competition this time around, but she showed more like her true form. In a muddling race, Vroum Vroum Mag finished a length and a half second to Apple's Jade (with Limini third), making up plenty of ground on the bridle widest of all and even edging ahead briefly after the last.

Vroum Vroum Mag must have come out of that race at Cheltenham in good order for she was all the rage on her final outing, in the latest renewal of the Punchestown Champion Hurdle, sent off 6/4 favourite in a ten-strong field that also featured the Champion Hurdle runner-up My Tent Or Yours, the County Hurdle winner Arctic Fire and the Supreme Novices' Hurdle winner Labaik. Vroum Vroum Mag's performance in trailing in seventh to Wicklow Brave can have a line put through it, however, as she reportedly finished lame. Now aged eight, it must be on the cards that Vroum Vroum Mag will be given another chance over fences in 2017/18, but her versatility is always likely to mean that she will be required to fit in around others belonging to her powerful connections, a pattern that will almost certainly continue in the next season.

		Voix du Nord (FR) (b 2001)	Valanour (b 1992)	Lomond
				Vearia
Vroum Vroum Mag (FR) (b.m. 2009)			Dame Edith (b 1995)	Top Ville
				Girl of France
		Naiade Mag (FR) (b 2001)	Kadalko (b 1988)	Cadoudal
				Koln
			Fortanea (b 1993)	Video Rock
				Alconea

Vroum Vroum Mag's pedigree has been discussed thoroughly in previous editions of *Chasers & Hurdlers*. To recap, she is the first foal of her dam, Naiade Mag, the winner of a chase over twenty-one furlongs at Moulins who was also placed over fences at Auteuil. Naiade Mag is a half-sister to the 2015 Grand National runner-up and 2017 third Saint Are, as both are out of Fortanea who won four AQPS races and another three times over hurdles and fences at up to around two and three quarter miles. Naiade Mag's fifth foal Dandy Mag (by Special Kaldoun) won one of his four starts for Willie Mullins in the latest season but finished well held in the Triumph Hurdle at Cheltenham behind Defi du Seuil, the leading juvenile hurdler who, like Vroum Vroum Mag, is by the now-deceased Voix du Nord, also sire of Taquin du Seuil, Vibrato Valtat and Vaniteux. Dandy Mag went on to win a minor event at Ballinrobe after the end of the 2016/17 season in Britain and Ireland, before showing much improved form when third in the Prix Alain du Breil at Auteuil in June where his year-older half-sister Cabriole Mag (by Gris de Gris) won a listed event over hurdles for fillies and mares the previous month. Vroum Vroum Mag, a sturdy mare who often travels strongly in her races, needs a good test at two miles and stays three miles. She acts on heavy going but doesn't need testing conditions (the going has been good on her two appearances at the Cheltenham Festival). A most versatile sort, it bears repeating that she remains with potential to do better over fences. *W. P. Mullins, Ireland*

VULGANS WATCH (IRE) 7 b.m. Presenting – Star Councel (IRE) (Leading Counsel (USA)) [2016/17 b16.3m⁶ b17.7d³ Sep 4] £22,000 6-y-o: fifth foal: sister to fair chasers Star Presenter (2m-2¼m winner) and Winston Churchill (19f/2½m winner): dam bumper winner/2½m-3m hurdle winner: off mark in Irish mares maiden points at fourth attempt: modest form in bumpers: will be suited by further than 2m. *David Loder* **b78**

VYTA DU ROC (FR) 8 gr.g. Lion Noir – Dolce Vyta (FR) (Grand Tresor (FR)) [2016/17 c144, h–: h20d³ c26g⁶ c26.3sᵖᵘ c24s⁵ c28.8g² Apr 29] good-topped gelding: smart hurdler at best: useful handicap chaser: head second to Henllan Harri in bet365 Gold Cup at Sandown in April: stays 4m: acts on heavy going: tried in tongue tie. *Nicky Henderson* **c140 h124 +**

W

WABANAKI (IRE) 7 b.g. Indian River (FR) – Treasure Island (Rainbow Quest (USA)) [2016/17 h100: h19.6d³ h15.9d⁴ c21.7vᶠ c16v⁵ c16s⁵ Mar 13] modest maiden hurdler: similar form over fences: unproven beyond 2m: tried in hood: usually races towards rear. *Evan Williams* **c91 h93**

WADE HARPER (IRE) 7 b.g. Westerner – Nosie Betty (IRE) (Alphabatim (USA)) [2016/17 h125, b–: c15.9d⁴ c19.9g⁵ c24.1sᵖᵘ c24d⁵ c18.2d² c16d⁵ c20s² c19.9g³ Apr 3] close-coupled gelding: bumper winner: fairly useful hurdler: fair maiden chaser: stays 2½m: acts on soft going: in cheekpieces last 3 starts: often wears tongue tie. *David Dennis* **c113 h–**

WADSWICK COURT (IRE) 9 b.g. Court Cave (IRE) – Tarasandy (IRE) (Arapahos (FR)) [2016/17 c125, h–: c21d² c20.1sᵘʳ c20.3g² c21.2d* c21.4g⁶ c24.2g⁵ c19.4v⁴ c23.6g³ Apr 17] useful-looking gelding: winning hurdler: fairly useful handicap chaser: won at Cartmel in August: stays 3m: acts on heavy going: usually wears cheekpieces: in tongue tie last 5 starts: races close up. *Peter Bowen* **c128 h–**

WAGNER KLASS (FR) 5 ch.g. Prince Kirk (FR) – Bartjack (FR) (Lost World (IRE)) [2016/17 b16.4s Dec 8] tailed off in bumper. *Kenny Johnson* **b–**

WAIKIKI WAVES (FR) 4 b.g. Alexandros – Lulabelle Spar (IRE) (Milan) [2016/17 b13.6g³ Apr 21] 7/2, third in bumper at Fontwell (13½ lengths behind White Valiant) in April. *Gary Moore* **b69**

WAIT A SECOND (IRE) 7 b.g. Scorpion (IRE) – Fast Time (IRE) (Be My Native (USA)) [2016/17 h110: c24g⁶ c20gᶠ c26.2d c24.5g² c23.6d³ c23.6sᶠ Jan 13] fair hurdler: similar form over fences: stayed easy 23f: acted on good to firm and heavy going: wore cheekpieces: often wore tongue tie: often travelled strongly: dead. *Jonjo O'Neill* **c106 h–**

WAIT FOR ME (FR) 7 b.g. Saint des Saints (FR) – Aulne River (FR) (River Mist (USA)) [2016/17 h137p: h15.7m h16g⁶ h16.8g h16.8g h19.8g* Apr 29] robust gelding: useful handicap hurdler: won at Sandown (by 6 lengths from Stowaway Magic) in April: stays 2½m: acts on heavy going: often wears hood: in tongue tie last 2 starts: usually travels strongly. *Philip Hobbs* **h138**

Star Sports Cheltenham Preview Evening Novices' Chase, Haydock—the progressive
Waiting Patiently maintains his 100% start over fences with a victory over the grey Politologue

WAITING PATIENTLY (IRE) 6 b.g. Flemensfirth (USA) – Rossavon (IRE) (Beneficial) [2016/17 h133p: c16.4s* c16.3s* c19.9s* Jan 21] useful hurdler: smart form over fences, completing hat-trick in novice handicap at Sedgefield (by 7 lengths from Burtons Well) in November, novice at Newcastle (by 2¼ lengths from Forest Bihan) in December and Grade 2 novice at Haydock (by 1¼ lengths from Politologue) in January: stays 2½m: acts on soft going: usually travels strongly: open to further improvement. *Malcolm Jefferson*   **c150 p**
h–

WAKANDA (IRE) 8 b.g. Westerner – Chanson Indienne (FR) (Indian River (FR)) [2016/17 c152, h–: c24.2g c23.4s⁵ c24.2s² c28.4dᵖᵘ c26s³ Mar 4] sturdy gelding: winning hurdler: smart handicap chaser: second in Rowland Meyrick Chase at Wetherby (7 lengths behind Definitly Red) in December: stays 3m: acts on good to firm and heavy going: usually races prominently. *Sue Smith*   **c150**
h–

WAKEA (USA) 6 b.g. Cape Cross (IRE) – Imiloa (USA) (Kingmambo (USA)) [2016/17 h16d² h16g⁴ h16.5g* h16g* h16d⁴ h16.8g h16.5gᶠ Apr 8] useful hurdler: first past post in maidens at Down Royal (disqualified after failing drugs test) in May and Clonmel in September, and handicap at Down Royal (9 lengths ahead of Ainslie) in November: raced around 2m: best form on good going: wears hood/tongue tie: front runner/races prominently. *Karl Thornton, Ireland*   **h141**

WAKE YOUR DREAMS (IRE) 9 b.g. Oscar (IRE) – Rose Karanja (Terimon) [2016/17 c–, h111: h25g² h26v h25.3s h23.8g⁴ h23.1g* h23.1m² Apr 17] sturdy gelding: fairly useful handicap hurdler: won at Market Rasen in March: second there in April: maiden chaser: stays 25f: acts on good to firm and heavy going: often wears headgear: tried in tongue tie: usually leads. *Jennie Candlish*   **c–**
h119

WALDEN PRINCE (IRE) 10 b.g. Saffron Walden (FR) – Kahyasi Princess (IRE) (Kahyasi) [2016/17 c122, h–: c15.8d² c19.4vᶠ c17m⁶ h17.7g⁶ c16.3g³ c18m⁴ c16v⁴ c16vᵖᵘ h20.5d³ h16.5gᶠ Jan 11] leggy gelding: fairly useful handicap chaser at best, little form in 2016/17: fairly useful handicap chaser: second at Aintree in June: left David Bridgwater after seventh start: best around 2m: acts on good to firm and heavy going: usually wears headgear: has worn tongue tie, including last 3 starts: often races towards rear: moody and not one to rely on. *Sophie Leech*   **c129 §**
h60 §

WALDORF SALAD 9 b.g. Millenary – Ismene (FR) (Bad Conduct (USA)) [2016/17 c131, h–: c24.1sᵖᵘ c25.2vᵖᵘ c23.8s c23.8v³ Mar 19] tall gelding: winning hurdler: useful handicap chaser, below best in 2016/17: stays 3m: best form on soft/heavy going: tried in headgear: front runner/races prominently. *Venetia Williams*   **c121**
h–

WALKAMI (FR) 6 b.g. Walk In The Park (IRE) – Ominncha (FR) (Exit To Nowhere (USA)) [2016/17 h109, b93: h21m² h19.9gᵖᵘ h25m h23.6d h19.6s c22.6gᵘʳ c26.2mᵘʳ Apr 28] good-topped gelding: fair maiden hurdler: no form over fences: stays 21f: acts on heavy going: has worn headgear, including in 2016/17. *Jonjo O'Neill*   **c–**
h102

WALKING IN THE AIR (IRE) 7 b.g. Flemensfirth (USA) – Rossavon (IRE) **c–**
(Beneficial) [2016/17 h128: h20d³ c21.4sᵖᵘ Nov 17] won Irish maiden point on debut: **h118**
fairly useful hurdler: fatally injured in novice handicap on chasing debut: stayed 21f: acted
on heavy going: front runner/raced prominently, often travelled strongly. *Dan Skelton*

WALK IN THE MILL (FR) 7 b.g. Walk In The Park (IRE) – Libre Amour (FR) (Lost **c137**
World (IRE)) [2016/17 c123: c17.5s* c20.2s* c20.8s c19.9g Mar 25] sturdy gelding: useful
handicap chaser: won at Exeter in November and Wincanton (by 22 lengths from Orbasa)
in January: stays 2½m: acts on soft going. *Robert Walford*

WALK OF GLEAMS 8 b.m. Gleaming (IRE) – Harlequin Walk (IRE) (Pennine Walk) **h74**
[2016/17 h80: h21.6d⁵ h21m⁵ May 16] poor maiden hurdler: stays 2¾m: acts on soft going:
often races prominently. *Anna Newton-Smith*

WALK ON AL (IRE) 9 b.g. Alflora (IRE) – Wave Back (IRE) (Bob Back (USA)) **c105 §**
[2016/17 c–, h93: h25dᵖᵘ c23.6d² c25.3v* c23.8vᶠ c23.6sᵖᵘ c28sᵖᵘ Feb 20] workmanlike **h–**
gelding: fairly useful hurdler at best, pulled up on return in 2016/17: fair handicap chaser:
won at Ffos Las in December: left Sally Randell after first start: stays 25f: acts on heavy
going: has worn cheekpieces, including last 5 starts: not one to trust. *Fergal O'Brien*

WALK WATERFORD 6 bl.g. Fair Mix (IRE) – Woore Lass (IRE) (Persian Bold) **h96**
[2016/17 b–: h16m³ Aug 30] last of 4 finishers in Irish maiden point: behind in bumper:
16/1, third in maiden at Worcester (3¾ lengths behind Barwick) on hurdling debut. *Jonjo
O'Neill*

WALSINGHAM GRANGE (USA) 4 b.g. Paddy O'Prado (USA) – Mambo Queen **h106**
(USA) (Kingmambo (USA)) [2016/17 h16.7v² h15.7g² h16s³ h15.7s* h15.8s² h16g⁵
h16.3g⁶ Apr 15] fairly useful on Flat, stays 10.5f: fair hurdler: won juvenile at Catterick in
February: raced around 2m: acts on soft going: in cheekpieces last 2 starts: front runner/
races prominently. *Pam Sly*

WALTER ONEEIGHTONE (IRE) 5 b.g. Morozov (USA) – Matinee Show (IRE) **h–**
(Carroll House) [2016/17 h20.3v h21.2s h20.5s h21v h19.6g⁶ Apr 22] no form over
hurdles. *Jonjo O'Neill*

WALTER WHITE (IRE) 7 b.g. Dark Angel (IRE) – Fun Time (Fraam) [2016/17 h94: **c95**
h16.8g³ c16.5g³ h16.8d* h18.5m⁵ c21.1dᶠ Sep 4] fair handicap hurdler: won lady amateur **h100**
event at Newton Abbot in June: modest form over fences: unproven beyond 17f: acted on
good to firm and good to soft going: wore tongue tie: dead. *Philip Hobbs*

WALT (IRE) 6 b.g. King's Theatre (IRE) – Allee Sarthoise (FR) (Pampabird) [2016/17 **h126**
b85: h20g³ h23.9s² h23.5d³ h19.1v* h21.4s³ h21.4d³ Mar 25] rather unfurnished
gelding: fairly useful handicap hurdler: won at Fontwell in January: left Nicky Henderson
after first start: stays 3m: acts on heavy going. *Neil Mulholland*

WALTZ DARLING (IRE) 9 b.g. Iffraaj – Aljafliyah (Halling (USA)) [2016/17 c122, **c–**
h–: h20.2d Jun 30] fairly useful hurdler/chaser, lightly raced nowadays: stays 3m: acts on **h–**
soft and good to firm going. *Keith Reveley*

WALTZ LEGEND (IRE) 11 b.m. Flying Legend (USA) – Vienna Waltz (IRE) **c87**
(Orchestra) [2016/17 c100, h–: c26.2m⁴ c18.5d⁴ c20g⁴ May 27] maiden hurdler: modest **h–**
maiden chaser: stays 3¼m: acts on good to firm and heavy going: usually wears blinkers:
has worn tongue tie. *Liam Lennon, Ireland*

WANDAOVER 5 b.m. Overbury (IRE) – Programme Girl (IRE) (Definite Article) **b–**
[2016/17 b16.2g Oct 8] £600 4-y-o: third foal: dam (h115) bumper and 2m/17f hurdle
winner: tailed off in bumper. *Neil Mechie*

WANNABE KING 11 b.g. King's Best (USA) – Wannabe Grand (IRE) (Danehill (USA)) **h–**
[2016/17 h–: h16.8dᵖᵘ h16.7g⁶ h16.2dᵖᵘ Jun 4] no form over hurdles: tried in tongue tie.
Ian Brown

WANT THE FAIRYTALE 4 b.f. Mount Nelson – Tattercoats (FR) (Whywhywhy **h99**
(USA)) [2016/17 h16.7s⁴ h19.6s³ h15.8g⁴ Apr 17] fair on Flat, stays 1½m: modest form
over hurdles. *Alan King*

WAR CREATION (IRE) 5 b.m. Scorpion (IRE) – Creation (IRE) (Definite Article) **h101**
[2016/17 b16.2s* h16.7d³ h15.8m* h16.2g⁴ Apr 28] €4,000 3-y-o: third foal: sister to **h98**
bumper winner/fairly useful hurdler Tamokey (2m winner): dam once-raced daughter of
fairly useful hurdler/useful chaser (stayed 3m) Palette: won bumper at Perth (by 3¼ lengths
from Woodfort) in September for Stuart Crawford: fair form over hurdles: won maiden at
Ludlow in April. *Nicky Henderson*

WARDEN HILL (IRE) 9 br.g. Presenting – Moon Storm (IRE) (Strong Gale) [2016/17 **c118** c128, h–: c24g^{ur} c24.2d^2 c26.3g Mar 17] workmanlike gelding: winning pointer: winning **h–** hurdler: fairly useful chaser: second in hunter at Fakenham in February: left Mick Channon after first start: stays 25f: acts on heavy going. *Mrs H. Connors*

WARDEN LAW (IRE) 6 b.g. Definite Article – Mrs Avery (IRE) (Supreme Leader) **h–** [2016/17 b16.2d b16.2d^5 h16.2d h15.6g h22d^6 Nov 14] no form in bumpers/over hurdles. **b–** *George Bewley*

WAR JOEY (IRE) 4 b.g. Primary (USA) – Wake Me Gently (IRE) (Be My Native (USA)) **b–** [2016/17 b14.6s Dec 17] tailed off in junior bumper: has joined Philip Kirby. *Ann Hamilton*

WARKSBURN BOY 7 b.g. Kayf Tara – Bonchester Bridge (Shambo) [2016/17 h89: **c65** h23.3d^{pu} h20.1g^{pu} h22.7s^{pu} h19.3d h20.5s^6 c24.2s^{pu} c15.6g^3 Apr 25] little form over hurdles/ **h–** fences: tried in cheekpieces: often in tongue tie: usually races prominently. *Sheena Walton*

WAR PATH (FR) 8 b.g. Walk In The Park (IRE) – Childermas (IRE) (Darshaan) [2016/17 **c–** c26g^{pu} c24s^{pu} c23.6m^{pu} Apr 28] multiple winning pointer: pulled up all starts under Rules: **h–** tried in cheekpieces. *Mrs Jane Price*

WARP FACTOR (IRE) 4 b.g. The Carbon Unit (USA) – Storminateacup (IRE) (Galileo **h125** (IRE)) [2016/17 h16g^{ur} h15.6g^2 h15.6g^2 h16s^5 h15.6g^2 Feb 4] fairly useful on Flat, stays 11f: similar standard over hurdles: runner-up 3 times in juveniles, including listed event at Musselburgh in February: raced at 2m: best form on good going. *John Patrick Shanahan, Ireland*

WARRANT OFFICER 7 gr.g. Misu Bond (IRE) – Kilmovee (Inchinor) [2016/17 h85: **h–** h15.9g May 8] poor hurdler: stays 19f: acts on soft going: front runner/races prominently, usually finds little. *Sheena West*

WARRANTOR (IRE) 8 b.g. Turtle Island (IRE) – Pixie Dust (IRE) (Desert King (IRE)) **c133** [2016/17 c133, h–: c27.3s^2 c26.3s^5 c28.4d c33.4s^3 c30d^5 Apr 29] stocky gelding: winning **h–** hurdler: useful handicap chaser: second in Grade 3 at Cheltenham (length behind Viconte du Noyer) in November: stays 33f: best form on soft/heavy going: usually wears tongue tie. *Warren Greatrex*

WARRIORS TALE 8 b.g. Midnight Legend – Samandara (FR) (Kris) [2016/17 c138, **c141** h136: c23.8m* c23.4d^3 c22.4g^2 c23.4d^5 c23d^3 c19.9s* c19.9g* c20.5d^5 Apr 21] **h–** workmanlike gelding: useful hurdler: useful chaser: won novice at Perth in May, and handicaps (2) at Newbury in March: stays 3¼m: acts on good to firm and heavy going: tried in hood: in tongue tie last 4 starts. *Paul Nicholls*

WARSAW PACT (IRE) 14 b.g. Polish Precedent (USA) – Always Friendly (High Line) **c–** [2016/17 c–, h81§: h21.4m h19.1d h24d^{pu} h23v h23.6s^6 h21.4d Mar 26] lengthy gelding: **h– §** fairly useful hurdler at best, no form in 2016/17: maiden chaser: has worn headgear, including last 2 starts: temperamental. *Steven Dixon*

WAR SINGER (USA) 10 b.g. War Chant (USA) – Sister Marilyn (USA) (Saint Ballado **c129** (CAN)) [2016/17 h124: c16.3g^2 c16.5g* c16.3d^3 c16.3m* c15.7g^5 c16.1g^F Jan 27] sturdy **h–** gelding: fairly useful hurdler: similar form over fences: won novices at Huntingdon in May and Newton Abbot in July: raced around 2m: acts on soft and good to firm going: wears headgear/tongue tie: usually races towards rear. *Johnny Farrelly*

WARTHOG (FR) 5 gr.g. Martaline – Shekira (FR) (Medaaly) [2016/17 b16v^2 b18g^6 Apr **b97** 28] €55,000 3-y-o: second foal: half-brother to French hurdler Sherman (17f/19f winner, by Muhtathir): dam (h142), French 17f-19f hurdle winner (including Prix Renaud du Vivier), also 12.5f/15f winner on Flat: off mark in Irish maiden points at second attempt: fairly useful form in bumpers: better effort when second at Chepstow in March: in tongue tie second start. *David Pipe*

WASHED ASHORE (IRE) 6 ch.g. Presenting – Give It Time (Kayf Tara) [2016/17 b91: **h111** b16.7d^4 h16g* h16g* h21.1g h16.4g h16g Dec 10] compact gelding: poor form in bumpers: **b71** fair form over hurdles: won maiden at Worcester in July and novice there in September: should be suited by at least 2½m: best form on good going. *Jonjo O'Neill*

WATAGUDDO 7 ch.m. Abzu – Whitegatesprincess (IRE) (Valiyar) [2016/17 h19.6s^6 **h–** h21s^{pu} Mar 16] sixth foal: dam (h65) 21f hurdle winner: no form over hurdles. *Claire Dyson*

WATCHMETAIL (IRE) 11 b.g. Amilynx (FR) – Ellie Anna (IRE) (Bravefoot) [2016/17 **h64** h60: h21.6g^3 h21.6g^3 h19.1g^4 h21.6m h19.1d^5 Oct 19] poor maiden handicap hurdler: stays 2¾m: acts on firm and soft going: has worn headgear: has worn tongue tie, including last 5 starts: races towards rear. *John Panvert*

WATCH THE BIRDIE (IRE) 9 b.m. Kodiac – Silk Point (IRE) (Barathea (IRE))   **c–**
[2016/17 c23.6m^{pu} Apr 28] prolific point winner: maiden hurdler: pulled up in novice   **h–**
hunter on chasing debut: best effort at 3m: acts on good to soft going: tried in tongue tie.
Miss C. Packwood

WATERCLOCK (IRE) 8 ch.g. Notnowcato – Waterfall One (Nashwan (USA)) [2016/17   **h–**
h119: h16d h21.3s h24.1s h25.3s^4 Feb 28] sturdy gelding: fair handicap hurdler, below
form in 2016/17: stays 2¾m: acts on good to firm and heavy going: usually wears headgear:
often races towards rear. *Micky Hammond*

WATER GARDEN (FR) 11 gr.g. Turgeon (USA) – Queenstown (FR) (Cadoudal (FR))   **c–**
[2016/17 c20.1d^{pu} Nov 11] good-topped gelding: winning hurdler: fairly useful chaser in   **h–**
2014/15, pulled up sole start since: stays 25f: acts on heavy going: has worn headgear,
including last 5 starts. *Rebecca Menzies*

WATERLOO WARRIOR (IRE) 5 b.g. Kalanisi (IRE) – Vindonissa (IRE) (Definite   **h113**
Article) [2016/17 b82: b16g2 h19.5m^2 h20.5d^6 h19.8d^5 h23.9g^{pu} h23.1s^2 Mar 7]   **b95**
good-topped gelding: fairly useful form in bumpers: second at Chepstow in October: fair
form over hurdles: stays 23f: acts on soft and good to firm going: in headgear last 4 starts.
Colin Tizzard

WATER RAIL 8 b.g. Manipulator (IRE) – Madame Mozaik (USA) (Sandpit (BRZ))   **h–**
[2016/17 h–: h21.4d^{pu} Dec 13] no form over hurdles. *Simon Earle*

WATER WAGTAIL 10 b.g. Kahyasi – Kentford Grebe (Teenoso (USA)) [2016/17 c23d   **c99 §**
c22.6g^5 c23g^3 c25.5s^3 c25.7g* c23g^3 c23.6s^{pu} c25.1d^3 c29.2v^F Mar 22] maiden hurdler: **h–**
modest handicap chaser: won at Plumpton in November: stays 3¼m: acts on heavy going:
wears cheekpieces: not straightforward. *Emma Lavelle*

WATER WILLOW 5 b.m. Tobougg (IRE) – Water Flower (Environment Friend)   **h70**
[2016/17 b80: h15.3m^3 h16.8d h16g h18.7m Aug 24] smallish mare: bumper winner: poor
form over hurdles: tried in tongue tie: has joined Bill Turner. *Harry Fry*

WAVE DANCER (IRE) 5 b.g. Montjeu (IRE) – Bonnie Byerly (USA) (Dayjur (USA))   **b64**
[2016/17 b16m^4 b16.8g^{pu} Oct 7] poor form in bumpers. *Brendan Powell*

WAXIES DARGLE 8 b.g. Sakhee (USA) – Cup of Love (USA) (Behrens (USA))   **h142**
[2016/17 h141: h20d h16d* h15.7d h24d h21.1g Mar 15] strong gelding: useful handicap
hurdler: won at Fairyhouse (by ¾ length from Morga) in December: stays 21f: acts on
heavy going: has worn tongue tie, including last 4 starts. *Noel Meade, Ireland*

WAY BACK THEN (IRE) 6 b.g. Robin des Champs (FR) – Ashwell Lady (IRE)   **b106**
(Presenting) [2016/17 b15.8d* Nov 28] second foal: dam once-raced half-sister to useful
hurdler/chaser (winner up to 21f) Ashwell Boy: runner-up in Irish maiden point on debut:
13/8, won bumper at Ludlow (by 2 lengths from Chez Castel Mail) in November: will be
suited by further than 2m. *Ben Pauling*

WAY BEFORE DAWN 10 ch.g. Nomadic Way (USA) – Isis Dawn (Rakaposhi King)   **c–**
[2016/17 c60: c24.2m^{pu} May 3] winning pointer: little form in hunter chases: in cheekpieces
last 2 starts. *Mrs Sarah Tickle*

WAY OF THE WORLD (IRE) 6 b.g. Flemensfirth (USA) – Night Heron (IRE) (St   **h99**
Jovite (USA)) [2016/17 b83: b15.8g^2 b15.9g h20g h20s h15.8v h15.8v h19.7v* h16.2v^2 **b83**
h20v^3 h25.5s Mar 11] in frame in point on debut: modest form in bumpers: modest
handicap hurdler: won conditionals novice event at Hereford in January: stays 2½m: best
form on heavy going: front runner/races prominently. *Sheila Lewis*

WAY UP HIGH 5 b.m. Getaway (GER) – High Life (Kayf Tara) [2016/17 b16.7g b14d   **b–**
Dec 21] third foal: dam (c95/h105), ungenuine 17f hurdle winner, half-sister to ungenuine
but smart bumper winner/useful hurdler (stayed 3m) Secret Ploy: poor maiden on Flat: no
form in bumpers: in tongue tie second start. *Steve Flook*

WAYUPINTHESKY (IRE) 10 gr.g. Cloudings (IRE) – Riancoir Alainn (Strong Gale)   **c101**
[2016/17 c100: c24.2g^4 c23.8g^3 Apr 28] multiple winning pointer: fair hunter chaser: stays
3¼m: acts on good to soft going. *Alison Hamilton*

WAYWARD SUN (IRE) 6 b.g. Double Eclipse (IRE) – Mahonrun (IRE) (King   **h–**
Charlemagne (USA)) [2016/17 h59: h19.3m^{pu} May 5] little sign of ability. *Micky Hammond*

WAY WILD WEST (IRE) 9 b.g. Westerner – Niamh's Leader (IRE) (Supreme Leader)   **h85**
[2016/17 h15.8s^4 Jun 15] modest maiden hurdler: should stay further than 17f: acts on
soft going: tried in cheekpieces: has worn tongue tie: won point shortly after end of season.
Sarah Hollinshead

WAZOWSKI 8 b.g. Overbury (IRE) – Malay (Karinga Bay) [2016/17 h100: h16.2d* **h103**
h20d⁶ h19.9g⁵ h20.1dᵘʳ h20d⁵ h19.9d h23.3vᵖᵘ h19.7v² h19.9v⁵ h17v³ h19.3d³ Apr 5]
fair hurdler: won novice at Hexham in June: stays 2½m: acts on heavy going: usually races
prominently. *Donald McCain*

WEALTH DES MOTTES (FR) 4 b.g. Silver Frost (IRE) – Wavy (FR) (Lavirco (GER)) **h120**
[2016/17 h16.9s* h16.4sᵖᵘ h16.6g⁶ h21m³ Apr 4] well-made gelding: second foal: dam,
French 1¼m/11.5f winner, half-sister to useful chaser (stayed 3¼m) Sulphur Springs: fairly
useful form over hurdles: won newcomers race at Clairefontaine in July on only start for
Francois Nicolle: disappointing in Britain: tried in tongue tie. *Paul Nicholls*

WEAPON OF CHOICE (IRE) 9 b.g. Iffraaj – Tullawadgeen (IRE) (Sinndar (IRE)) **h100**
[2016/17 h102: h16.2d⁴ h17.2g h16.2d² h16.2d h15.6g* h15.6g⁶ h15.7g h16.2g⁵ Apr 26]
fair handicap hurdler: won at Musselburgh in November: raced around 2m: acts on good to
soft going: usually wears headgear/tongue tie. *Dianne Sayer*

WEE BOGUS 4 b.g. Multiplex – Silver Gyre (IRE) (Silver Hawk (USA)) [2016/17 **b72**
b16.1g⁵ b16.7m Apr 17] poor form in bumpers. *Alistair Whillans*

WEE VENDETTA (IRE) 5 ch.g. Vinnie Roe (IRE) – Lady Velvet (IRE) (Golan (IRE)) **h–**
[2016/17 h16.2mᵖᵘ h16d Oct 29] little show over hurdles. *R. Mike Smith*

WELCOME BACH (IRE) 8 ch.g. Bach (IRE) – Massini's Daughter (IRE) (Dr Massini **h–**
(IRE)) [2016/17 h112: h21mᵖᵘ May 16] point winner: fair maiden hurdler, pulled up sole
start in 2016/17: stays 2¾m: easily best efforts on soft/heavy going. *Liam Corcoran*

WELCOME BEN (IRE) 8 b.g. High Roller (IRE) – Bramble Cottage (IRE) (Eurobus) **c92**
[2016/17 h106: h19.7g h20.2f⁶ h20.2s⁴ h21.4d c20.1sᵖᵘ c17.1s³ c16.3sᵖᵘ c17.1d* Apr 10] **h86**
maiden Irish pointer: fair handicap hurdler, below form in 2016/17: modest form over
fences: won handicap at Kelso in April: stays 21f: acts on soft and good to firm going: in
headgear/tongue tie last 3 starts: usually races close up. *Jackie Stephen*

WELCOMETOTHEJUNGLE 9 b.m. Lucky Story (USA) – Kasamba (Salse (USA)) **h–**
[2016/17 h112: h26.5mᵖᵘ Jul 17] lengthy mare: fair hurdler, pulled up sole start in 2016/17:
stays 2½m: acts on good to firm going: wears tongue tie. *Harry Fry*

WELD ARAB (IRE) 6 b.g. Shamardal (USA) – Itqaan (USA) (Danzig (USA)) [2016/17 **h97**
h–: h16.8g⁵ h16.3m h16m⁴ h16g² h16g⁵ h15.8sᵖᵘ Mar 18] modest maiden hurdler: raced
around 2m: best form on good going: usually races prominently. *Michael Blake*

WELL ABOVE PAR (IRE) 5 b.g. Gold Well – Glynn Glory (IRE) (Presenting) **h102**
[2016/17 b16v⁶ h16v² h16.2v³ Mar 28] €32,000 3-y-o: second foal: dam, no form, out of **b74**
sister to Welsh Grand National winner Supreme Glory: in frame completed starts in Irish
maiden points: poor form in bumper: fair form over hurdles. *Lucinda Russell*

WE'LL BE THERE 8 b.m. Kayf Tara – Teachmetotango (Mister Baileys) [2016/17 **h97**
h23.9gᵖᵘ h21.4v³ h20v² h19.5s² Mar 13] first foal: dam unraced half-sister to fairly useful
hurdler/useful chaser (stayed 19f) Green Tango: unplaced in point on debut: modest form
over hurdles: tried in tongue tie. *Stuart Kittow*

WELL END GIRL (IRE) 5 b.m. Yeats (IRE) – Ginandit (IRE) (Definite Article) **b–**
[2016/17 b15.3m⁴ Apr 5] fifth foal: half-sister to a winning pointer by Presenting: dam
(h82), maiden hurdler (stayed 2½m), half-sister to useful hurdlers (mainly around 2m)
Raise Your Heart, More Dash Thancash and Bolino Star: tailed off in maiden bumper.
John Butler

WELLFORTH (IRE) 13 b.g. New Frontier (IRE) – Faitch's Lady (IRE) (Dock Leaf) **c96 §**
[2016/17 c91, h75: c26.3s* c26.1sᵖᵘ c26.3s³ c24.2vᵖᵘ c29.6s² c25.2sᵖᵘ c29.6sᵖᵘ **h–**
Feb 10] smallish, close-coupled gelding: winning hurdler: modest handicap chaser: won at
Sedgefield in May: stays 3¾m: acts on heavy going: wears headgear: temperamental.
Clare Ellam

WELLINGTONBRIDGE 5 b.m. Scorpion (IRE) – Isabello (IRE) (Presenting) [2016/17 **b71**
b16.2s b16d⁶ b15.8s Apr 1] second foal: half-sister to bumper winner Odello (by King's
Theatre): dam unraced half-sister to useful hurdler/chaser (stayed 3m) Banjaxed Girl: poor
form in bumpers. *Warren Greatrex*

WELL JOEY (IRE) 6 b.g. Kayf Tara – Penny Queen (Nayef (USA)) [2016/17 b16g⁶ **h99**
b16.4d³ b16s⁴ h16s² h16vᵘʳ h20s h16g⁵ Apr 20] €19,000 3-y-o: first foal: dam (c92/ **b83**
h88) 2m chase winner: fifth in maiden on point debut: modest form in bumpers: similar
form over hurdles: left Stuart Crawford after third start: unproven beyond 2m: acts on soft
going: in tongue tie last 2 starts: often races prominently. *Mrs Prunella Dobbs, Ireland*

WELL METT (IRE) 10 b.g. Gold Well – Beit Millat (USA) (Alleged (USA)) [2016/17 **c96** c25.3g^F c23g^3 May 27] compact gelding: dual winner in points: winning hurdler: **h–** modest hunter chaser: stays 3½m: acts on firm and soft going: wears headgear/tongue tie. *Mrs C. Banks*

WELL PAINTED (IRE) 8 ch.g. Excellent Art – Aoife (IRE) (Thatching) [2016/17 **h–** h15.9g^{pu} Nov 28] modest on Flat, stays 11.5f: in tongue tie, pulled up in novice on hurdling debut. *Daniel Steele*

WELLS DE LUNE (FR) 6 b.g. Irish Wells (FR) – Pepite de Lune (FR) (Mansonnien **c129** (FR)) [2016/17 h124: c16s^4 c16g* c15.9d^3 c19.4d* c19.1g^6 c19.4s^5 Jan 24] good-topped **h–** gelding: fairly useful hurdler: similar form over fences: won handicaps at Warwick (novice) in September and Wetherby in November: stays 19f: acts on soft going: wears headgear: usually wears tongue tie: front runner, usually races freely. *Charlie Longsdon*

WELL SMITTEN (IRE) 5 b.g. Gold Well – The Dark One (IRE) (Mandalus) [2016/17 **b88** b16s b16.2v^2 b15.8v^6 Mar 1] €50,000 3-y-o: fifth foal: closely related to fair hurdler/chaser Near The Water (2m winner, by Oscar) and half-sister to a winning pointer by Flemensfirth: dam placed in point: fair form in bumpers: best effort when second at Hereford in February: will stay further than 2m. *Warren Greatrex*

WELLUPTOSCRATCH (FR) 6 b.g. Irish Wells (FR) – Aulne River (FR) (River Mist **h93** (USA)) [2016/17 h99p, b92: h16g^4 h16s^4 h19.8v^4 h16v^4 Feb 20] lengthy gelding: bumper winner: modest maiden hurdler: unproven beyond 2m: acts on soft going: in tongue tie last 3 starts. *David Arbuthnot*

WELSH DESIGNE 9 ch.g. Midnight Legend – Barton Dante (Phardante (FR)) [2016/17 **c76** h18.7m c20g^3 c23.8m^F c18.9s^3 h21.2m^6 Apr 25] winning pointer: no form over hurdles: **h–** poor form over fences: wears tongue tie. *Sirrell Griffiths*

WELSH SHADOW (IRE) 7 b.g. Robin des Champs (FR) – What A Mewsment (IRE) **c122 p** (Persian Mews) [2016/17 h141: h15.8s^2 c21.6v^3 c22.4d^6 Dec 31] lengthy gelding: useful **h142** handicap hurdler: second in Welsh Champion Hurdle (Limited Handicap) at Ffos Las (1¾ lengths behind Garde La Victoire) in October: fairly useful form over fences: stays 2½m: acts on heavy going: tried in tongue tie: should do better as a chaser. *Dan Skelton*

WELSH VIC 6 b.g. Mutamarkiz (IRE) – Swallow Breeze (Salse (USA)) [2016/17 b15.8g **b–** b16g b15.8s Oct 15] no form in bumpers: wears tongue tie. *Robert Stephens*

WEMYSS POINT 5 b.g. Champs Elysees – Wemyss Bay (Sadler's Wells (USA)) **b96** [2016/17 b15.6g^2 b15.6g^5 b16.4g^2 b16.7m^2 Apr 9] second foal: dam unraced: fairly useful form in bumpers: second at Market Rasen in April. *Philip Kirby*

WE NEVER GIVE UP (IRE) 11 b.m. Mull of Kintyre (USA) – Parker's Cove (USA) **c–** (Woodman (USA)) [2016/17 c–: c26g Apr 27] multiple point winner: no form in hunter chases: wears headgear. *Mrs Pauline Harkin*

WENYERREADYFREDDIE (IRE) 6 ch.g. Beneficial – Ware It Vic (IRE) (Old Vic) **h125 p** [2016/17 b98: h16.3d^3 h19.4g^2 h16.6s* Mar 3] strong gelding: fairly useful form over hurdles: won conditionals novice at Doncaster in March: will be suited by further than 2m: remains open to improvement. *Nicky Henderson*

WE SHALL RETURN 4 b.g. Sir Percy – Half Sister (IRE) (Oratorio (IRE)) [2016/17 **b–** b13.7m Oct 2] 3/1, ninth in junior bumper at Huntingdon. *Charles Hills*

WEST APPROACH 7 b.g. Westerner – Ardstown (Ardross) [2016/17 h126: h16.8g* **h143** h23.9g^2 h21.1g^3 h24s^5 h24.4d^{ur} h24s^3 h24g^{pu} h24.7g^{pu} Apr 7] workmanlike gelding: useful hurdler: won novice at Newton Abbot in May: third in Cleeve Hurdle at Cheltenham (3¼ lengths behind Unowhatimeanharry) in January: stays 3m: acts on heavy going: tried in tongue tie. *Colin Tizzard*

WESTBROOKE WARRIOR (IRE) 6 b.g. Robin des Champs (FR) – Tango Lady **h–** (IRE) (King's Theatre (IRE)) [2016/17 b–: h19.9g h23g^5 May 27] no form in bumpers/over hurdles: tried in cheekpieces: wears tongue tie. *David Pipe*

WEST CLASS (IRE) 6 b.g. Westerner – Catch The Class (Flemensfirth (USA)) **h78** [2016/17 b15.7g^5 h20.3v Dec 11] Irish maiden point winner: showed a bit in bumper/ **b78** maiden hurdle. *Peter Winks*

WEST COAST TIME (IRE) 5 b.g. Westerner – Refinement (IRE) (Oscar (IRE)) **b107** [2016/17 b16v* b19s^2 b16.4g Mar 15] rather unfurnished gelding: third foal: dam (h152) bumper winner/2m-3m hurdle winner: useful form in bumpers: won maiden at Cork (by 9½ lengths from Drumconnor Lad) in January: wears tongue tie. *Joseph Patrick O'Brien, Ireland*

WESTELLO (IRE) 6 b.m. Westerner – The Keane Edge (IRE) (Definite Article) h–
[2016/17 b16d b15.8g h22g^F Apr 23] second foal: dam unraced half-sister to fairly useful b–
hurdler/useful chaser (stayed 25f) Alright Now M'lad: little show in bumpers/novice
hurdle. *Graeme McPherson*

WEST END (IRE) 10 b.g. Westerner – Brown Bess (IRE) (Definite Article) [2016/17 c114 §
c113, h104: c23g* h23.9g^5 Sep 6] angular gelding: fair maiden hurdler: fair chaser: won h107 §
hunter at Worcester in May: stays 25f: acts on any going: wears headgear/tongue tie: often
races towards rear/travels strongly: unreliable. *Giles Smyly*

WESTENDORF (IRE) 6 b.g. Coroner (IRE) – Two of Each (IRE) (Shernazar) [2016/17 h124
b18v* h20.5g* h18.8d^3 h19.7s^4 h24.1s^{pu} h19.8d^5 h23.5m^6 h16.8g^F Apr 11] €12,000 b92
3-y-o: useful-looking gelding: second foal: dam (h74), winning pointer, half-sister to
useful hurdler (stayed 3m) Free To Dream: placed both starts in maiden points: won
maiden bumper at Tipperary (by 2¼ lengths from Naturally Blond) in May on only start for
J. D. Motherway: fairly useful hurdler: won novice at Leicester in November: stays 2½m:
acts on good to soft going: in tongue tie last 3 starts. *Jonjo O'Neill*

WESTEND PRINCE (IRE) 6 gr.g. King's Theatre (IRE) – Caltra Princess (IRE) h100
(Traditionally (USA)) [2016/17 h84: h21.6g^4 h21.4m^2 h21.6g* h16.8m h23g^6 Jul 26]
good-topped gelding: fair handicap hurdler: won at Fontwell in June: stays 2¾m: acts on
soft and good to firm going: in blinkers last 4 starts: wears tongue tie. *Colin Tizzard*

WESTEND STORY (IRE) 6 b.g. Westerner – Sarahall (IRE) (Saddlers' Hall (IRE)) h113
[2016/17 b115: h21s^3 h21.3s^2 h23.8s^{bd} Feb 22] lengthy gelding: fell both starts in Irish
points: smart bumper performer: fair form over hurdles: best effort when third in maiden at
Warwick in December: will prove suited by further than 2m. *Philip Hobbs*

WESTEND THEATRE (IRE) 8 b.g. Darsi (FR) – Ballyvelig Lady (IRE) (Project c67
Manager) [2016/17 c87, h–: c20.9v^6 Mar 9] maiden hurdler: modest maiden chaser: should h–
be suited by further than 2½m: best form on heavy going. *Jane Walton*

WESTERBEE (IRE) 6 b.m. Westerner – Pass The Honey (IRE) (Snurge) [2016/17 b88: h101
h16m^2 h21.7g^{pu} h16.3g^6 h16d* h17.7s^{ur} h16.5g^5 h16v^{pu} h15.8s^3 Feb 19] small, angular
mare: bumper winner: fair hurdler: won mares novice at Lingfield in November: unproven
beyond 2m: acts on good to soft going: tried in headgear: often leads. *Seamus Mullins*

WESTERLY BREEZE (IRE) 9 b.g. Westerner – Sup A Whiskey (IRE) (Commanche c–
Run) [2016/17 c–, h101: h23g^3 h21.6g^5 h26.4g^{pu} c23m^5 c23g^{pu} Sep 12] modest maiden h94
hurdler: hasn't taken to chasing: stays 27f: acts on good to firm and heavy going: wears
headgear: usually races prominently: has joined Sheila Lewis. *Edward Bevan*

WESTERN BOY (IRE) 8 b.g. Antonius Pius (USA) – Skala (IRE) (Hernando (FR)) c–
[2016/17 h16d^F h16.5d* Apr 25] small, rather leggy gelding: useful handicap hurdler: won h139
at Punchestown (by 1½ lengths from Light That) in April: didn't take to chasing: unproven
beyond 17f: acts on good to firm and heavy going: often races towards rear. *P. A. Fahy,
Ireland*

WESTERN BREEZE (IRE) 8 b.m. Westerner – Winsome Breeze (IRE) (Glacial Storm h64
(USA)) [2016/17 h110: h19.7g^{pu} h19.9d^{pu} h20.3s^{pu} h19.9g^6 Apr 7] fair hurdler at best,
out of form in 2016/17: stays 2½m: acts on heavy going: tried in cheekpieces: has joined
Dan Skelton. *Mark Walford*

WESTERN CAPE (IRE) 6 b.g. Westerner – Simons Girl (IRE) (Grand Plaisir (IRE)) h131
[2016/17 h118, b104: h23g^2 h22.8v^{pu} h21.4s^F Dec 26] sturdy gelding: second in Irish point
on debut: bumper winner: useful handicap hurdler: second at Worcester (neck behind
Herbert Park) in October: stayed 23f: acted on good to soft going: often raced in rear: dead.
Seamus Mullins

WESTERN CLIMATE (IRE) 8 b.g. Westerner – Jo Peeks (IRE) (Be My Native h116
(USA)) [2016/17 h21.2v^3 h21.7s^3 h19.7v* h20.5v h24g Apr 20] angular gelding: half-
brother to a winning pointer by Oscar: dam 2m hurdle winner: dual winning pointer: fairly
useful form over hurdles: won novice at Hereford in February: stays 2¾m: best form on
soft/heavy going: front runner/races prominently. *Tom Weston*

WESTERNER LADY (IRE) 7 b.m. Westerner – Cloghoge Lady (IRE) (Presenting) c137
[2016/17 h22g* h22.8g* c25d* c20s* c20s* c20g^2 c20d* c20d* c20d^F Apr 17] first foal: h142
dam (h93) 2¼m bumper winner: useful form over hurdles: won handicaps at Killarney
and Galway (by ½ length from Supreme Vinnie) in July: useful chaser: won maiden at
Kilbeggan in August, mares novice at Listowel in September, Grade 3 novice at Tipperary
(by 15 lengths from Deans Road) in October, Grade 3 mares event at Clonmel (by ½ length

from Thanks For Tea) in November and Grade 2 mares novice at Thurles (by 2½ lengths from Daisy's Gift) in January: stays 25f: acts on soft going: front runner/races prominently. *W. P. Mullins, Ireland*

WESTERNER POINT (IRE) 8 b.g. Westerner – Its Only Gossip (IRE) (Lear Fan (USA)) [2016/17 c17d c17v* c19.5v* h20d⁴ c18v* h24v* Mar 23] fairly useful handicap hurdler: won at Cork in March: useful chaser: won handicaps at Cork in November and Limerick (by ½ length from Montys Meadow) in December, and minor event at Thurles (by 1½ lengths from Shadow Catcher) in February: stays 3m: acts on heavy going: tried in hood: usually races close up. *Eoghan O'Grady, Ireland*   **c131 h115**

WESTERN HOME (IRE) 7 br.m. Kalanisi (IRE) – Western Road (GER) (King's Theatre (IRE)) [2016/17 c84p, h91, b74: h19.5g² c20.1d² c23.8sᶠ c21.2d* h23.9s⁴ h22.1g³ c23.8dᶠ Sep 21] point winner: fair form over hurdles: similar form over fences: won handicap at Cartmel in July: stays 3m: acts on soft going: often races towards rear, usually travels strongly. *Gordon Elliott, Ireland*   **c114 h107**

WESTERN JO (IRE) 9 b.g. Westerner – Jenny's Jewel (IRE) (Be My Native (USA)) [2016/17 c123p, h–: c23.9g² c21.4g⁴ c26.3g⁴ c23.9sᵖᵘ c23.9s⁴ c24.1dᵖᵘ Jan 3] sturdy gelding: winning hurdler: fair maiden chaser: stays 3m: acts on heavy going: has worn headgear, including last 2 starts: far from straightforward (has been reluctant to race). *Alan Brown*   **c114 § h–**

WESTERN LASS (IRE) 4 br.f. Westerner – Lady Roania (IRE) (Saddlers' Hall (IRE)) [2016/17 b16.2v³ b16.4g Mar 24] £10,000 3-y-o: second foal: half-sister to bumper winner Princess Roania (by Dubai Destination): dam (c83/h99), unreliable bumper/3m hurdle winner, half-sister to useful hurdler (stayed 2¾m) Some Article: poor form in bumpers: bred to be suited by 2½m+. *Katie Scott*   **b72**

WESTERN MILLER (IRE) 6 b.g. Westerner – Definite Miller (IRE) (Definite Article) [2016/17 h117, b99: h20.3g h21.6d⁴ Oct 19] fair handicap hurdler: stays 2¾m: acts on heavy going. *Charlie Longsdon*   **h100**

WESTERN RYDER (IRE) 5 b.g. Westerner – Seesea (IRE) (Dr Massini (IRE)) [2016/17 b15.9g* b16.7s² b15.7d* b16.3d² b16.4g⁵ b17g³ Apr 7] €40,000 3-y-o: well-made gelding: first foal: dam (b81), third in bumper, sister to fairly useful hurdler/chaser (stayed 21f) Glam Gerry: smart bumper performer: won at Ffos Las in May and listed event at Ascot (by 2 lengths from Imperial Eloquence) in December: placed in listed event at Newbury (3¼ lengths behind Daphne du Clos) in February and Grade 2 at Aintree (2½ lengths behind Lalor) in April: bred to stay further than 17f. *Warren Greatrex*   **b116**

WESTERN STORM (IRE) 5 b.g. Westerner – Torduff Storm (IRE) (Glacial Storm (USA)) [2016/17 b15.7g⁵ b16.6g⁶ h16.6d h21vᵖᵘ h21m⁴ Apr 18] €17,000 3-y-o, resold £20,000 3-y-o: fourth foal: half-brother to a winning pointer by Beneficial: dam unraced half-sister to useful staying chaser Torduff Express: modest form in bumpers/over hurdles: often in hood: often races towards rear. *Richard Phillips*   **h94 b75**

WESTERN SUNRISE (IRE) 8 b.m. Westerner – Presenting Gayle (IRE) (Presenting) [2016/17 h104, b87: h19.9g² h16.5g h20.5s⁶ h23.3s⁴ Apr 1] fair handicap hurdler: may prove best at short of 23f when conditions are testing: acts on soft and good to firm going. *Johnny Farrelly*   **h105**

WESTERN WAVE (FR) 5 b.g. Westerner – Kaprissima (FR) (Epervier Bleu) [2016/17 b89: h19.9g³ h21g⁴ h17.1d* h19.4g⁴ h19.5s Jan 8] fair form over hurdles: won novice handicap at Carlisle in October: unproven beyond 17f: acts on good to soft going: often races towards rear: has joined Tom George. *David Loder*   **h107**

WESTERN WAY (IRE) 8 b.g. Westerner – Faucon (Polar Falcon (USA)) [2016/17 h–: h24gᵖᵘ Jun 7] good-bodied gelding: fairly useful hurdler, pulled up on return: placed once from 6 starts on Flat later in 2016: stays 3¼m: best form on good going: wears headgear. *Don Cantillon*   **h–**

WESTFIELD KING (IRE) 8 b.g. King's Best (USA) – Ivorbella (IRE) (Daylami (IRE)) [2016/17 h24gᵖᵘ c17.4m c20d h25.6g⁵ h16.8g Apr 26] no form over hurdles: poor form over fences: left Ms Debbie Hartnett after third start: sometimes in tongue tie. *Tracey Barfoot-Saunt*   **c63 h–**

WEST HILL LEGEND 6 b.m. Midnight Legend – Bajan Blue (Lycius (USA)) [2016/17 h77, b–: h20sᵖᵘ May 11] poor form over hurdles. *Richard Woollacott*   **h–**

WESTINMARE (IRE) 6 b.m. Definite Article – Millanymare (IRE) (Old Vic) [2016/17 b17.8d* b16.2s³ b16.2g² h19.5g⁶ h19.5g h16v Apr 1] first foal: dam (c107/h110), 2¾m-3m hurdle/chase winner, sister to useful hurdler/chaser (winner up to 3m) Glasker Mill: fair form in bumpers: won maiden at Downpatrick in July: poor form over hurdles: will be suited by at least 2½m. *Gordon Elliott, Ireland*   **h67 b87**

WEST OF THE EDGE (IRE) 9 b.g. Westerner – Bermuda Bay (IRE) (Be My Native **c127** (USA)) [2016/17 c100, h103: c24.2d* c26.2s* h24.3s² c30.7d c29.2v* Mar 12] fair **h106** handicap hurdler: fairly useful handicap chaser: won at Wetherby in November, Carlisle in December and Warwick in March: stays 29f: acts on heavy going: has worn headgear: strong traveller. *Dr Richard Newland*

WESTREN WARRIOR (IRE) 8 b.g. Westerner – Charming Leader (IRE) (Supreme **c137** Leader) [2016/17 h133: h23.9g⁶ h22.8v⁵ c23.4s² c20dᶠ Dec 21] sturdy gelding: won **h129** completed start in Irish maiden points: useful handicap hurdler: similar form over fences: second of 5 to Aux Ptits Soins in novice at Kelso on completed start: stays 25f: acts on heavy going. *Dr Richard Newland*

WEST SHIP MASTER (IRE) 13 b.g. Oscar (IRE) – Lady of Aherlow (Le Bavard (FR)) **c79** [2016/17 c79, h–: c21.2m² c23g⁵ c20.1g³ c22g c24.2d Jun 19] winning hurdler: poor **h–** maiden chaser: stays 25f: acts on good to firm and heavy going: wears headgear: tried in tongue tie: usually leads. *Paul Stafford, Ireland*

WESTSTREET (IRE) 7 b.g. Westerner – Klipperstreet (IRE) (Supreme Leader) **c120** [2016/17 h123: c23.4d⁶ c25.2v² c23.6s² c25.5gᵖᵘ Apr 21] sturdy gelding: runner-up in Irish **h–** maiden point: fairly useful hurdler: similar form over fences: second in novice at Huntingdon in March: stays 25f: acts on heavy going: has worn headgear, including in 2016/17: often races in rear. *Oliver Sherwood*

WEST TO CROSSGALES (IRE) 6 b.g. Westerner – Mooreshill Bay (IRE) (Lord **h–** Americo) [2016/17 h18.6mᵖᵘ h21g⁶ Apr 24] Irish maiden point winner: too headstrong both starts over hurdles. *Charles Pogson*

WEST TORR (IRE) 6 br.g. Scorpion (IRE) – Native Craft (IRE) (Be My Native (USA)) **h112** [2016/17 b–: b15.3m² h20g² h20d* h20m⁵ h25.5g⁵ h19.9v³ h24.4d h15.8s³ h23.1d⁵ **b91** h18.5m² Apr 18] pulled up both starts in Irish maiden points: fair form in bumpers: fair hurdler: won novice at Ffos Las in June: stays 2½m: acts on good to firm and good to soft going: tried in cheekpieces. *Nigel Twiston-Davies*

WEST WIZARD (FR) 8 b.g. King's Theatre (IRE) – Queen's Diamond (GER) **c129** (Konigsstuhl (GER)) [2016/17 c109, h122: c23.8d² c20.9v* c19.4s⁶ c19.4v² c20.1g⁴ **h–** Apr 28] good sort: fairly useful hurdler: fairly useful handicap chaser: won novice event at Ffos Las in December: left Paul Morgan after fourth start: stays 3m: acts on heavy going: tried in cheekpieces/tongue tie. *Sophie Leech*

WEYBURN (IRE) 6 gr.g. September Storm (GER) – Saffron Pride (IRE) (Be My Native **c109** (USA)) [2016/17 h110, b90: c23dᵘʳ h23g h20g³ Jul 26] fair hurdler: every chance when **h109** unseated rider 2 out in novice handicap won by Horace Hazel at Worcester on chasing debut: stays 23f: acts on good to soft going: tried in hood/tongue tie. *Martin Keighley*

WHARANE (FR) 4 br.g. Diktat – Nova Lady (USA) (Mr Greeley (USA)) [2016/17 **h–** h16.7d Jun 17] modest maiden on Flat, stays 11.5f: well beaten in juvenile on hurdling debut: wore cheekpieces. *Ian Williams*

WHAT ABOUT CARLO (FR) 6 b.g. Creachadoir (IRE) – Boccatenera (GER) (Artan **h117 p** (IRE)) [2016/17 h16.4s⁶ h16.3d⁴ Dec 14] good-topped gelding: useful on Flat, stays 1¼m: fairly useful form over hurdles: better effort when fourth in maiden at Newbury in December: open to further improvement. *Eve Johnson Houghton*

WHAT ABOUT MOLLY (IRE) 7 ch.m. Stowaway – Great Legacy (IRE) (Great Palm **c–** (USA)) [2016/17 c–, h–: c24vᵖᵘ c23gᵖᵘ Jul 21] placed in points: no form over hurdles/ **h–** fences: tried in hood: wore tongue tie last 2 starts: dead. *Heather Dalton*

WHAT A DANDY (IRE) 6 b.g. Dandy Man (IRE) – Ibtihal (IRE) (Hamas (IRE)) **h61** [2016/17 h17.7d⁶ h15.8m⁶ Oct 2] modest on Flat, stays 1¼m: poor form over hurdles: in hood first start. *Jim Boyle*

WHAT A DIVA 6 b.m. Kayf Tara – Land of Glory (Supreme Leader) [2016/17 b79: h16g⁶ **h112** h15.8d² h19.5d h23.1s² h21s⁴ h20.6s* h24v* h24v⁵ h21.2g Apr 3] sturdy mare: fair handicap hurdler: won at Market Rasen (mares event) in January and Towcester in February: stays 3m: acts on heavy going: has worn tongue tie, including last 5 starts: front runner/races prominently. *Peter Bowen*

WHAT A DREAM 11 ch.g. Supreme Sound – Ben Roseler (IRE) (Beneficial) [2016/17 **c77** c91, h–: c20.1d⁵ c21.5s⁶ c20.1s⁴ c21.1v² c19.3v⁵ h20.5v⁴ c21.6d Apr 10] maiden hurdler: **h–** poor handicap chaser: stays 3m: acts on heavy going: wears headgear/tongue tie: races prominently. *Alison Hamilton*

WHAT A GAME (IRE) 6 ch.g. Milan – Moscow Mo Chuisle (IRE) (Moscow Society **c70** (USA)) [2016/17 h89: h24s⁴ h22.1m* h22.1d² h22g³ h27g³ h23.9g⁴ h23.4g⁴ c26.3d⁵ **h91** c26.3g⁶ c26.3m⁶ Apr 19] second on completed start in Irish maiden points: modest handicap hurdler: won novice event at Cartmel in May: poor form over fences: stays 27f: acts on soft and good to firm going: wears blinkers: tried in tongue tie: front runner/races prominently. *Tim Easterby*

WHAT A JOKE (IRE) 10 b.g. Vinnie Roe (IRE) – Shaping (Deep Run) [2016/17 h18.5g⁴ h21.6m⁵ h21.6m⁴ h23.9g⁶ h21m³ h23.1g⁶ c21.7d⁶ c25.2sᵘʳ c25.2dᵖᵘ c22.7sᵖᵘ Mar 10] Irish point winner: fair maiden hurdler: modest form over fences: left William Reed after third start: stays 3m: acts on good to firm and good to soft going: wears cheekpieces: has worn tongue tie, including last 2 starts: usually races prominently. *Oliver Greenall*   **c97** **h101**

WHATAKNIGHT 8 b.g. Midnight Legend – What A Mover (Jupiter Island) [2016/17 h132: h22.8m* c23.8d² c25.2g* h24s h24.4s² h24.7g⁶ Apr 8] good-topped gelding: useful handicap hurdler: won at Haydock (by 5 lengths from Minella Daddy) in May: useful form over fences: won maiden at Hereford (5/1-on, by 50 lengths from Sage Monkey) in October: stays 25f: acts on soft and good to firm going: wears tongue tie. *Harry Fry*   **c133 +** **h138**

WHAT A LAUGH 12 b.g. Kayf Tara – Just For A Laugh (Idiot's Delight) [2016/17 c124, h106: h20.3vᵖᵘ c21.4g⁴ c20.9m⁶ c23.8dᵖᵘ Dec 21] maiden hurdler: fair handicap chaser: stays 25f: acts on soft going: often races towards rear. *Gary Hanmer*   **c112** **h–**

WHAT A MOMENT (IRE) 7 b.g. Milan – Cuiloge Lady (IRE) (Beneficial) [2016/17 h115: h23.9s² c25g² c25g* c23.6g⁵ c24.2s⁵ c25.2vᵖᵘ c31.8gᵖᵘ Mar 14] workmanlike gelding: fair maiden hurdler: useful form over fences: won handicap at Cheltenham (amateur) in November: stays 25f: acts on soft going: has worn headgear, including last 2 starts: tried in tongue tie. *David Pipe*   **c132** **h103**

WHAT A SAGA 6 b.m. Sagamix (FR) – Born To Dream (IRE) (Supreme Leader) [2016/17 h18.5m⁴ h16.8d⁴ h19.9g⁵ h19.2g³ Nov 10] £2,200 3-y-o: fourth foal: half-sister to a winning pointer by Alflora: dam, winning pointer, half-sister to useful hurdler/smart chaser (stayed 23f) Chilling Place: placed twice in points: modest form over hurdles: tried in tongue tie. *Nick Williams*   **h90**

WHAT A SCORCHER 6 b.m. Authorized (IRE) – Street Fire (IRE) (Street Cry (IRE)) [2016/17 h97: h16.8g* h16.8m² h18.5m² h19g* h16.4g³ h16.2s⁴ h18.5s Dec 15] fair handicap hurdler: won at Newton Abbot (novice) in May and Warwick (mares event) in September: left Oliver Sherwood after first start: stays 19f: acts on good to firm and good to soft going. *Nikki Evans*   **h114**

WHAT A TEMPEST 7 b.m. Kayf Tara – What A Vintage (IRE) (Un Desperado (FR)) [2016/17 h69: h16dᶠ h21gᵖᵘ May 9] rangy mare: poor maiden hurdler: in hood last 3 starts: tried in tongue tie: usually races in rear, often freely. *Richard Phillips*   **h–**

WHAT A WARRIOR (IRE) 10 b.g. Westerner – Be Right (IRE) (Be My Native (USA)) [2016/17 c135, h–: c24s³ c26.1g c25.5d Jul 16] sturdy, good-bodied gelding: winning hurdler: useful handicap chaser: third at Uttoxeter (11½ lengths behind Katkeau) in April: stays 3¼m: acts on soft going: has worn cheekpieces, including final start: usually wears tongue tie: usually races close up. *Dan Skelton*   **c131** **h–**

WHATDOESTHEFOXSAY (IRE) 8 ch.m. Vinnie Roe (IRE) – She's The One (IRE) (Good Thyne (USA)) [2016/17 h98: h25.4m² h25.4d³ h25.4g* h27g³ Apr 7] point/bumper winner: fair handicap hurdler: won at Cartmel in July: stays 27f: acts on soft and good to firm going: front runner/races prominently. *Donald McCain*   **h105**

WHATDUHAVTOGET (IRE) 5 b.m. Presenting – Smooching (IRE) (Saddlers' Hall (IRE)) [2016/17 h15.8d* h16d² h16.8g h19g² h21.2s* h21.4g² Apr 22] good-topped mare: fourth foal: dam unraced half-sister to smart hurdler (stayed 3m) Moorish and to grandam of top-class hurdler/chaser around 2m Altior: won Irish maiden point on debut: fairly useful form over hurdles: won maiden at Uttoxeter in October and mares novice at Ludlow in March: stays 21f: acts on soft going. *Dan Skelton*   **h127**

WHAT ELSE (IRE) 6 b.g. Flemensfirth (USA) – Accordello (IRE) (Accordion) [2016/17 h16.8v h16d Jan 24] won completed start in Irish maiden points: well held both starts over hurdles. *Jonjo O'Neill*   **h74**

WHAT HAPPENS NOW (IRE) 8 b.g. Dr Massini (IRE) – Euro Burden (IRE) (Good Thyne (USA)) [2016/17 c100, h100, b77: c20m* c23.4m* c23g* c25gᵖᵘ Oct 23] winning pointer: fair form over hurdles: fairly useful form over fences: completed hat-trick in novice handicaps at Carlisle and Kelso in May, and Worcester in August: should stay 3m+: acts on good to firm and heavy going: has worn hood: usually leads. *Donald McCain*   **c119** **h–**

WHAT LARKS (IRE) 9 b.g. Pierre – Bint Rosie (Exit To Nowhere (USA)) [2016/17 c105, h–: c21gᵖᵘ c26.2d⁵ c25.3vᶠ h23.1d h23.6s⁵ Mar 13] sturdy good-topped gelding: poor maiden hurdler: fair handicap chaser: stays 3¼m: acts on heavy going: tried in cheekpieces: often races towards rear. *Hugo Froud*   **c101** **h61**

WHATMORE 5 b.g. Schiaparelli (GER) – Polymiss (FR) (Poliglote) [2016/17 b16.4g **h114** b16s⁴ h15.5d² h16.8sʳᵒ Feb 12] well-made gelding: chasing type: third foal: dam French **b83** hurdler/chaser (17f/2¼m winner): modest form in bumpers: fair form over hurdles: second in novice at Leicester on completed start: will be suited by 2¼m+. *Henry Daly*

WHATS HAPPENING (IRE) 10 b.g. Lahib (USA) – Rebeccas Star (IRE) (Camden **c134** Town) [2016/17 c137, h–: c24.2s² c26g c28.8g Apr 29] lengthy gelding: winning hurdler: **h–** useful handicap chaser: second in veterans event at Exeter (5 lengths behind Perfect Candidate) in February: stays 3½m: acts on good to firm and heavy going: tried in cheekpieces: wears tongue tie. *Tom George*

WHATS NOT TO LIKE (GER) 6 b.g. Saddex – Wild Girl (GER) (Platini (GER)) **b103** [2016/17 b16.3g² b16g³ Mar 18] €28,000 3-y-o: angular gelding: fourth foal: half-brother to 2 winners abroad, including Czech cross-country chaser Wavelight Laser (3¼m winner, by Silvano): dam German 6.5f-11f winner: fairly useful form in bumpers: better effort when second in maiden at Stratford in May. *Don Cantillon*

WHATSTHATALLABOUT (IRE) 6 b.m. Milan – Peinture Francaise (FR) (Pistolet **h115 p** Bleu (IRE)) [2016/17 h72, b70: h16g⁴ h16.7d² h20.3g³ h19.9g* h15.8g* h19.6g* Sep 28] lengthy, rather unfurnished mare: fairly useful hurdler: won at Uttoxeter (2) in July and Bangor in September: stays 2½m: best form on good going: often travels strongly: will go on improving. *Neil Mulholland*

WHAT'S THE SCOOP (IRE) 7 ch.g. Presenting – Dame d'Harvard (USA) (Quest **c–** For Fame) [2016/17 h117§: c16.4g c20d⁴ Mar 11] well-made gelding: fair form over **h– §** hurdles: little impact in novice handicap chases: best effort at 19f: acts on heavy going: one to be wary of. *Nicky Henderson*

WHATSTHESTORYMAN (IRE) 9 b.g. Alderbrook – Express Way Lady (IRE) **c88** (Camden Town) [2016/17 c88, h76: c20.1d³ c20.1m⁴ c20.1g* May 24] winning pointer: **h–** maiden hurdler: modest form over fences: won novice handicap at Hexham in May: will be suited by 3m: acts on good to firm and good to soft going: wears tongue tie. *Katie Scott*

WHAT'S UP RORY (IRE) 6 b.g. Craigsteel – Clifton Four (USA) (Forest Wildcat **c92** (USA)) [2016/17 c15.7s⁴ c16.2v⁴ c20.3s⁴ c16v² c16s* c16g³ Apr 9] first foal: dam (h86), **h–** maiden jumper (stayed 2¼m), half-sister to fair hurdler/fairly useful chaser (stayed 19f) Blacktoft: well held in bumper/maiden hurdle for P. J. Rothwell in early-2015/16: modest form over fences: won handicap at Chepstow in March: unproven beyond 2m: best form on soft/heavy going: sometimes in hood: in tongue tie last 3 starts: usually races towards rear. *Richard Price*

WHATS UP WOODY (IRE) 12 b.g. Beneficial – Lady Noellel (IRE) (Step Together **c120** (USA)) [2016/17 c106, h–: c26.2d² c26.2m³ c25dᵖᵘ c23.8g* c20.1s* c20.1s² c26.2d⁴ c20g⁵ **h–** Apr 15] good-topped gelding: winning hurdler: fairly useful handicap chaser: won at Perth (twice) in September: stays 31f, effective at much shorter: acts on good to firm and heavy going: tried in cheekpieces/tongue tie: front runner. *George Bewley*

WHATSWRONGWITHYOU (IRE) 6 ch.g. Bienamado (USA) – Greenfield Noora **b104** (IRE) (Topanoora) [2016/17 b16s b15.8s* b16.2g² Apr 28] £44,000 4-y-o: seventh foal: half-brother to a winning pointer by Presenting: dam unraced sister to fairly useful hurdler (stayed 21f) No Where To Hyde: off mark in Irish maiden points at second attempt: fairly useful form in bumpers: won at Ludlow in March: in hood last 2 starts. *Nicky Henderson*

WHATTHEBUTLERSAW (IRE) 8 br.g. Arcadio – Phar From Men (IRE) **h106** (Phardante (FR)) [2016/17 h98: h18.5m³ h19.1d* h20.7d² h21s⁶ h21.2m* Apr 25] lengthy gelding: fair handicap hurdler: won at Fontwell in December and Ludlow (novice) in April: stays 2¾m: acts on good to firm and heavy going: tried in tongue tie: often races towards rear. *Dominic Ffrench Davis*

WHATZDJAZZ (IRE) 5 b.m. Yeats (IRE) – What A Mewsment (IRE) (Persian Mews) **b92** [2016/17 b16d* b16d Mar 11] €15,000 3-y-o, £22,000 4-y-o: useful-looking mare: seventh foal: half-sister to 3 winners, including bumper winner/useful hurdler Welsh Shadow (2m-2½m winner, by Robin des Champs) and fairly useful hurdler/useful chaser Klepht (19f-2¾m winner, by Great Palm): dam, placed in point, sister to top-class chaser (2½m-3¼m winner) Celestial Gold and half-sister to high-class hurdler (stayed 3m) Fiveforthree: fair form in bumpers: won mares maiden at Fakenham in February. *Dan Skelton*

WHEN IN ROAM (IRE) 8 b.m. Flemensfirth (USA) – Roaming (IRE) (Be My Native **h98** (USA)) [2016/17 h89: h23.3v* h23.3g May 14] modest handicap hurdler: won novice event at Uttoxeter very early in season: stays 3m: best form on soft/heavy going: has worn headgear, including last 5 starts: usually races prominently. *John O'Shea*

WHERE'S CHERRY (IRE) 6 b.m. King's Theatre (IRE) – I'm Grand (IRE) (Raise A **h98 p**
Grand (IRE)) [2016/17 b–: h19.6g⁶ h15.7g² h21.6m² h20.6s³ Nov 17] sturdy mare: modest
form over hurdles: likely to stay 3m: tried in cheekpieces: remains open to improvement.
Fergal O'Brien

WHERE'S TIGER 6 b.g. Tiger Hill (IRE) – Where's Broughton (Cadeaux Genereux) **h101**
[2016/17 h107: h16.2d h16.2m⁴ May 12] fair handicap hurdler: unproven beyond 17f: acts
on good to firm and good to soft going: tried in tongue tie: front runner/races prominently.
Lucinda Russell

WHEREYABIN (IRE) 5 b.g. Ask – Silky Brook (IRE) (Alderbrook) [2016/17 b16.8g **b–**
Jul 25] tailed off in maiden bumper: has joined Mrs D. A. Love. *Brendan Powell*

WHICH ONE IS WHICH 6 b.m. King's Theatre (IRE) – Presenting Copper (IRE) **h111**
(Presenting) [2016/17 b98p: h21s h18.5s² h19.3s² h21vᵖᵘ Mar 12] tall mare: bumper
winner: fair form over hurdles: often races towards rear. *Jonjo O'Neill*

WHICHWAYTOBOUGIE 8 b.g. Tobougg (IRE) – Whichway Girl (Jupiter Island) **c93**
[2016/17 c20.3s⁵ c19.9g⁴ c20v⁴ Mar 12] workmanlike gelding: maiden pointer: winning **h–**
hurdler: modest form in hunter chases: stays 3m: acts on heavy going. *R. A. Owen*

WHILE YOU WAIT (IRE) 8 b.g. Whipper (USA) – Azra (IRE) (Danehill (USA)) **h96**
[2016/17 h104: h18.5m⁴ Apr 18] good-bodied gelding: modest handicap hurdler: stays 19f:
acts on soft and good to firm going: races towards rear. *Susan Gardner*

WHIMSICAL NOTION 7 b.g. Midnight Legend – Friendly Request (Environment **c72**
Friend) [2016/17 h74: c22.6m⁴ c25.8gᵖᵘ Oct 20] maiden hurdler: poor form over fences: **h–**
stays 23f: acts on good to firm going: tried in cheekpieces: in tongue tie last 4 starts: has
hinted at temperament. *Nigel Hawke*

WHIN PARK 5 b.g. Great Pretender (IRE) – Pocahontas (FR) (Nikos) [2016/17 b16s **h99**
h15.3d⁶ h16g h16.3g⁴ Mar 25] €52,000 3-y-o: rather unfurnished gelding: seventh foal: **b–**
half-brother to useful chaser Tutchec (2½m-3¼m winner, by Turgeon): dam, French
17f-21f hurdle/chase winner, also 13.5f winner on Flat, half-sister to outstanding 2m chaser
Azertyuiop: tailed off in bumper: modest form over hurdles. *Ben Pauling*

WHIPCORD (IRE) 6 gr.g. Tikkanen (USA) – Dapples (IRE) (Accordion) [2016/17 **h94**
h111p: h18.5g⁵ h15.3d⁴ h16.5g h22g⁶ Mar 25] Irish maiden point winner: modest maiden
hurdler: left Paul Nicholls after first start: best effort at 17f: acts on good to soft going:
wears tongue tie: front runner/races prominently. *Johnny Farrelly*

WHIPCRACKAWAY (IRE) 8 b.g. Whipper (USA) – Former Drama (USA) (Dynaformer **h68**
(USA)) [2016/17 h73: h15.3s h19.8v h16v² Mar 23] good-topped gelding: poor handicap
hurdler nowadays: stays 2¼m: best form on soft/heavy going: wears headgear: often races
towards rear. *Peter Hedger*

WHISKEY CHASER (IRE) 9 br.g. Flemensfirth (USA) – Cregane Lass (IRE) (Oscar **c109**
(IRE)) [2016/17 c114, h–: c22.4vᵖᵘ c24.3s² c24.1sᵖᵘ c24v² c23.4v² Mar 7] maiden hurdler: **h–**
fair handicap chaser: stays 3m: best form on soft/heavy going: in cheekpieces last 3 starts:
front runner/races prominently. *Donald McCain*

WHISKEY IN THE JAR (IRE) 5 b.g. Oscar (IRE) – Baie Barbara (IRE) (Heron Island **b107 p**
(IRE)) [2016/17 b16v² b16s* Mar 30] fifth foal: closely related to fairly useful hurdler
Harvey Logan (2m/19f winner, by Saffron Walden) and fair/unreliable 2m hurdle winner
Asockastar (by Milan), stays 23f: dam unraced half-sister to useful 2m hurdler Spirit
Leader, herself dam of high-class staying hurdler Prince of Scars: useful form in bumpers:
won maiden at Warwick (by 7 lengths from Samburu Shujaa) in March: left T. E. Hyde
after first start: bred to stay further than 2m: open to further improvement. *Dan Skelton*

WHISKEY JOHN 7 b.g. Westerner – Cherry Lane (Buckley) [2016/17 h80: h21.6g h22v³ **h69**
h20g³ Jul 21] poor maiden hurdler: likely to stay 3m: best form on heavy going: tried in
cheekpieces. *Laura Young*

WHISKEY MOON 5 b.g. Erhaab (USA) – Flaviola (IRE) (Moscow Society (USA)) **b–**
[2016/17 b16s b16.5g⁶ Apr 6] no form in bumpers. *Dominic Ffrench Davis*

WHISKY MARMALADE (IRE) 5 b.m. Duke of Marmalade (IRE) – Nashatara (USA) **h–**
(Nashwan (USA)) [2016/17 h100: h15.6g Jan 3] maiden hurdler, well held in handicap
only outing in 2016/17. *Ben Haslam*

WHISPER (FR) 9 b.g. Astarabad (USA) – Belle Yepa (FR) (Mansonnien (FR)) [2016/17 **c159**
c–, h–: c20.8d* c20.8s* c24.4g² c25g² Apr 7] tall, useful-looking gelding: very smart **h–**
hurdler: similar form over fences: won novice in December (by 2½ lengths from Baron
Alco) and Dipper Novices' Chase in January (by ½ length from Clan des Obeaux), both at

BetBright Dipper Novices' Chase, Cheltenham—
Whisper lowers the colours of odds-on Clan des Obeaux (right)

Cheltenham: second in RSA Chase at same course (nose behind Might Bite) in March and Mildmay Novices' Chase at Aintree (2 lengths behind same rival) in April: stays 25f: acts on good to firm and heavy going: has run well when sweating. *Nicky Henderson*

WHISPERING AFFAIR 6 b.m. Black Sam Bellamy (IRE) – City of Angels (Woodman (USA)) [2016/17 h20.2g⁴ Apr 26] half-sister to numerous winners, including useful hurdler/smart chaser I'm So Lucky (2m-2½m winner, by Zilzal) and useful hurdler Dream Esteem (2m winner, by Mark of Esteem): dam unraced: pulled up in maiden point: 33/1, fourth in maiden at Perth (24¾ lengths behind Royal Village) on hurdling debut. *Stuart Crawford, Ireland*   **h83**

WHISPERING HARRY 8 b.g. Sir Harry Lewis (USA) – Welsh Whisper (Overbury (IRE)) [2016/17 c123, h103: c18mᵖᵘ c16.4gᶠ h15.8s³ c15.7sᵖᵘ h15.8v⁶ c16vᵖᵘ Feb 11] sturdy gelding: fair handicap hurdler: fairly useful chaser, failed to complete in 2016/17: unproven beyond 17f: acts on heavy going: tried in tongue tie: front runner/races prominently: temperamental. *Henry Oliver*   **c– §** **h112 §**

WHISPERING NICK 7 b.g. Kayf Tara – Dalriath (Fraam) [2016/17 b15.7g⁵ b15.8d⁶ h18.8dᵖᵘ h15.8d h15.5d h15.8d Jan 25] €32,000 3-y-o, £20,000 6-y-o: good-topped gelding: first foal: dam (c97/h93), 2m-21f hurdle/chase winner, also 1m winner on Flat: modest form in bumpers: no form over hurdles: in cheekpieces/tongue tie last 3 starts: often races towards rear. *Robin Dickin*   **h–** **b81**

WHISPERING STORM (GER) 7 b.g. Samum (GER) – Wind In Her Hair (GER) (Turtle Island (IRE)) [2016/17 h109p, b83: h20.7dᵖᵘ h15.6g* h16gᵖᵘ h16.3g⁴ Apr 15] fair hurdler: won handicap at Musselburgh in February: raced mainly around 2m: usually wears hood: wears tongue tie: usually races close up, often travels strongly. *Neil Mulholland*   **h108**

WHITEABBEY (IRE) 12 b.g. Luso – Frantesa (Red Sunset) [2016/17 c71, h–: c24.2d⁵ Apr 30] prolific point winner: maiden hurdler: poor maiden hunter chaser: tried in blinkers. *Mrs R. Hewit*   **c55** **h–**

WHITE CHIEF (IRE) 6 b.g. Daylami (IRE) – Limbo Lady (USA) (Theatrical) [2016/17 b16m Jul 4] tailed off in bumper. *Laura Young*   **b–**

916

WHITEOAK STROLLER 4 b.f. Shirocco (GER) – Whiteoak (IRE) (Oscar (IRE)) **b63**
[2016/17 b15.7s⁴ b16g⁶ Apr 23] well-made filly: second foal: dam (h146) bumper/2m-3m
hurdle winner: poor form in bumpers. *Donald McCain*

WHITEOUT (GER) 6 b.m. Samum (GER) – Wassiliki (IRE) (Night Shift (USA)) **h137**
[2016/17 h141: h18d* h25.4dᵖᵘ h20d h24d⁴ h20vᶠ h20d⁴ h20d⁴ Apr 29] smallish mare:
useful hurdler: stays 3m: acts on heavy going: usually races close up. *W. P. Mullins, Ireland*

WHITE VALIANT (FR) 4 gr.g. Youmzain (IRE) – Minnie's Mystery (FR) (Highest **b97**
Honor (FR)) [2016/17 b13.7g* b14s b13.6g* Apr 21] small, close-coupled gelding: sixth
foal: half-brother to 3 winners on Flat, including useful 6f-1m winner Dream Walker (by
Gold Away): dam 7f-1½m winner in Jersey: fairly useful form in bumpers: won at
Huntingdon (junior) in November and Fontwell in April. *John Berry*

WHITLEY NEILL (IRE) 5 b.g. Shantou (USA) – Maidrin Rua (IRE) (Zaffaran (USA)) **b62**
[2016/17 b15.7v⁶ b16.8d Mar 21] poor form in bumpers: in hood first start. *David Pipe*

WHITSTABLE NATIVE 9 b.g. Bertolini (USA) – Break of Dawn (USA) (Mt **h79**
Livermore (USA)) [2016/17 h78: h17.2gᵘʳ h16.8m³ h15.9m⁶ h15.8m⁴ h15.8m⁵ h15.8d
Oct 28] close-coupled gelding: poor maiden hurdler: unproven beyond 17f: acts on soft and
good to firm going: wears tongue tie: usually races in rear. *Sophie Leech*

WHITSTABLE PEARL (IRE) 4 b.f. Kodiac – Amber's Bluff (Mind Games) [2016/17 **h–**
h16gᵖᵘ h15.8g Apr 3] modest on Flat, stays 1½m: no form over hurdles: has joined Neil
King. *Sophie Leech*

WHITSUNDAYS (IRE) 8 b.g. Kutub (IRE) – Urdite's Vic (IRE) (Old Vic) [2016/17 h101: **c105**
c21.4g³ c21.1v² c19.3d² c16.4g* c21.6d* Apr 10] winning pointer/hurdler: fair form over **h–**
fences: won handicaps at Sedgefield (novice) in March and Kelso in April: stays 2¾m: acts
on heavy going: in tongue tie last 5 starts: usually leads. *Donald McCain*

WHIZZ BANG 5 b.m. Schiaparelli (GER) – Whizz Back (IRE) (Bob Back (USA)) **h–**
[2016/17 b15.8g³ h15.8g Oct 28] £5,500 3-y-o, resold £12,000 3-y-o: third foal: dam (b84), **b75**
ran twice in bumpers, half-sister to fairly useful hurdler (stayed 3m) Beluckyagain out of
half-sister to smart hurdler/top-class chaser (stayed 25f) Tiutchev: third in bumper at
Huntingdon (5¾ lengths behind Monsieur Arkadin) in May: tailed off in mares maiden on
hurdling debut. *Robin Mathew*

WHIZZZEY RASCAL (IRE) 6 b.m. Robin des Pres (FR) – Thespian (IRE) (Tiraaz **h128**
(USA)) [2016/17 h16d h18.2d³ h21g h20g h20.5v⁴ h20.2g³ h19.5g* h24d⁶ h24g⁴ h20g **b–**
h16v⁴ h16v⁴ h16.7s* h21v⁵ Feb 11] fifth foal: half-sister to smart hurdler Clondaw Warrior
(2m-3m winner, by Overbury): dam unraced: bumper winner: fairly useful hurdler: won
mares maiden at Clonmel in September, and mares handicaps at Ayr and Bangor in
January: left Miss Elizabeth Doyle after tenth start: stays 3m: acts on heavy going: usually
wears tongue tie: often travels strongly. *Gordon Elliott, Ireland*

WHO AM I 11 b.g. Tamayaz (CAN) – Short Fuse (IRE) (Zaffaran (USA)) [2016/17 c96x, **c– x**
h–: h15.9d h20g⁴ h23g⁴ h23.1g⁵ h23m* h20d Oct 15] modest handicap hurdler: won at **h93**
Worcester in July (amateur) and August: modest maiden chaser: stays 23f: acts on soft and
good to firm going: wears headgear: often let down by jumping over fences. *Debra Hamer*

WHO DARES WINS (IRE) 5 b.g. Jeremy (USA) – Savignano (Polish Precedent **h147**
(USA)) [2016/17 h135: h19.5g⁴ h21.1sᵘʳ h16.3d* h15.7d h19.6d³ h21.1g³ Mar 15] compact
gelding: smart handicap hurdler: won listed event at Newbury (by 9 lengths from Theligny)
in November: third in Coral Cup at Cheltenham (4½ lengths behind Supasundae) in March:
should stay 2¾m: acts on heavy going. *Alan King*

WHOLESTONE (IRE) 6 br.g. Craigsteel – Last Theatre (IRE) (King's Theatre (IRE)) **h147**
[2016/17 h117p, b103: h21g* h23.9g* h21.1g² h24s* h20.3s* h24g³ Mar 17] sturdy
gelding: bumper winner: smart hurdler: won maiden at Warwick in September, and novices

*Neptune Investment Management Classic Novices' Hurdle, Cheltenham—the consistent Wholestone
pulls clear of William Henry on the extended run-in (due to low sun)*

at Cheltenham in October, December (Albert Bartlett Novices' Hurdle (Bristol), by length from Ami Desbois) and January (Classic Novices' Hurdle, by 3 lengths from William Henry): also second in Hyde Novices' Hurdle (length behind Peregrine Run) in November and third in Albert Bartlett Novices' Hurdle (Spa) (7½ lengths behind Penhill) in March, at same course: stays 3m: acts on soft going. *Nigel Twiston-Davies*

WHOS DE BABY (IRE) 9 gr.g. Bienamado (USA) – Beaus Rose (IRE) (Roselier (FR)) **c88** [2016/17 h96: c20.3g⁵ c20.3v⁴ c23.8gᵖᵘ c19.4m³ c19.4g² c22.6gᶠ c22.6m² c20g⁶ **h–** c20.9d² c22.6gᶠ c19.2d⁴ Apr 27] maiden hurdler: modest maiden chaser: stays 23f: acts on good to firm and heavy going: wears cheekpieces: front runner/races prominently. *Sarah-Jayne Davies*

WHO'S FOR TEA (IRE) 4 ch.f. Beat Hollow – Ring of Water (USA) (Northern Baby **b73 p** (CAN)) [2016/17 b16.8d⁵ Mar 14] closely related to 3 winners by King's Theatre, including fairly useful hurdler/useful chaser Minella Theatre (19f-3m winner), and half-sister to several winners, including smart hurdler/fairly useful chaser Minella Forfitness (2m-2½m winner, by Westerner): dam French 1¼m winner: 11/8, fifth in mares bumper at Sedgefield (11¾ lengths behind Cockley Beck) on debut: should do better. *John Joseph Hanlon, Ireland*

WHOSHOTWHO (IRE) 6 br.g. Beneficial – Inishbeg House (IRE) (Glacial Storm **b–** (USA)) [2016/17 b98: b16s Mar 30] fairly useful form on first of 2 starts in bumpers. *Nicky Henderson*

WHO'S MY JOCKEY (IRE) 4 b.g. Yeats (IRE) – Scandisk (IRE) (Kenmare (FR)) **b94** [2016/17 b16.7m* Apr 9] €60,000 3-y-o: closely related to top-class hurdler Hurricane Fly (2m-2½m winner, by Montjeu) and half-brother to 3 winners on Flat: dam Italian 7f winner: 13/8, won bumper at Market Rasen (by head from Wemyss Point) in April. *Philip Hobbs*

WHO YOU FOR (IRE) 7 b.g. Craigsteel – Knappogue Honey (IRE) (Anshan) [2016/17 **h95** h112, b99: h21g³ May 2] workmanlike gelding: Irish maiden point winner: bumper winner: maiden hurdler, fair at best: should prove suited by further than 21f: acts on good to firm going: usually races prominently. *Sarah Humphrey*

WICKED GAMES (IRE) 6 br.m. Flemensfirth (USA) – Tariana (IRE) (Revoque (IRE)) **c80 p** [2016/17 h93: h16.2g h22.7s h19s c24.2s⁴ Dec 26] Irish maiden point winner: modest **h–** maiden hurdler, little impact in 2016/17: 25/1, better than result when fourth in novice handicap at Wetherby (15¾ lengths behind Bankhall) on chasing debut: best effort at 19f: acts on heavy going: often races towards rear: should improve over fences. *Rose Dobbin*

WICKED SPICE (IRE) 8 b.g. Old Vic – Afdala (IRE) (Hernando (FR)) [2016/17 c79, **c112** h124: c24.2g⁵ c22.5s⁵ c23.8s* Jul 10] fairly useful hurdler: fair form over fences: won **h–** novice handicap at Perth in July: stays 3m: acts on soft going: in cheekpieces last 2 starts. *Nicky Richards*

WICKED WILLY (IRE) 6 br.g. Arcadio (GER) – How Provincial (IRE) (Be My Native **h118** (USA)) [2016/17 h115, b–: h19.9g³ h20g² h19.8d³ h19.6s* h23.1s* h19.8s² h23.1g³ h22.8g³ h26.6g³ Apr 27] fairly useful handicap hurdler: won at Huntingdon (conditional) and Market Rasen in January: third at Perth (conditional) in April: stays 27f: acts on soft going: often races in rear/travels strongly. *Nigel Twiston-Davies*

WICK GREEN 4 b.g. Sagamix (FR) – Jolly Dancer (Exit To Nowhere (USA)) [2016/17 **b82** b15.8d⁶ b16.7d Apr 27] second foal: dam winning pointer: modest form in bumpers: left Charlie Longsdon after first start. *Jennifer Mason*

WICKLOW BRAVE 8 b.g. Beat Hollow – Moraine (Rainbow Quest (USA)) **h161 §** [2016/17 h156: h16.4g h16g* Apr 28]

'Herding cats' might have been the phrase that came to mind when the field approached the tapes for the Betdaq Punchestown Champion Hurdle. The starter was no doubt keeping a close eye in particular on the Supreme Novices' winner Labaik who had given his latest display of reluctance (effectively refusing to race) at the start of the Herald Champion Novices' Hurdle just three days earlier. Another potential trouble-maker was Wicklow Brave whose very slow start on his previous outing in the Champion Hurdle at Cheltenham, in which he had finished eighth past the post, had earned him a Timeform 'squiggle', indicating he was one to treat with caution. That wasn't the first time that Wicklow Brave had shown reluctance at the tapes; he soon got behind when gambled on for the 2015 Imperial Cup, in which he was eventually pulled up, but that performance had quickly been followed by a reminder that Wicklow Brave has plenty of ability too when he ran away with the

County Hurdle at Cheltenham six days later. Ironically, neither Labaik nor Wicklow Brave proved the Punchestown starter's biggest headache; instead it was the latter's stable-companion Diakali who acted up the most, so much so that he had already been withdrawn by the time the ten other runners came under orders. Blinkered for the first time, Wicklow Brave needed some encouragement from the saddle from Mr Patrick Mullins, but did jump off (as did Labaik), albeit conceding several lengths to the rest of the field.

Wicklow Brave might not have been that keen to get going, but there was nothing wrong with his attitude once under way and by the entrance to the back straight he had pulled his way into the lead. Clear of the rest four out, he made the best of his way home under an enterprising ride though came under pressure on the run to the last with several rivals closing on him. Wicklow Brave had enough left on the run-in to hold on by a length and a half from the Champion Hurdle runner-up My Tent Or Yours with the latest County Hurdle winner Arctic Fire, representing the same connections as Wicklow Brave (and Diakali), a neck back in third. Labaik (who sustained a career-threatening injury) and Brain Power, a place behind Wicklow Brave in the Champion Hurdle at Cheltenham, completed the first five, both keeping on. In the absence of Diakali, Wicklow Brave was one of four runners for Willie Mullins in the Punchestown Champion Hurdle and, while the stable's 2016 winner Vroum Vroum Mag disappointed in seventh (finishing lame), Wicklow Brave's victory proved crucial in his trainer's late rally to retain his Irish title. Mullins has now won seven of the last eight runnings, with Hurricane Fly's four-timer (2010-2013) and Faugheen's success in 2015 preceding those of Vroum Vroum Mag and Wicklow Brave.

Wicklow Brave had begun his career in a bumper at the 2013 Punchestown Festival and went on to win three such races under Mr Patrick Mullins. His win at the latest Festival was his first over hurdles since his Cheltenham success two years earlier, though he had spent much of the intervening period running on the Flat, having finished third in the Morgiana (to stable-companions Nichols Canyon and Faugheen) and 'Fighting Fifth' Hurdles in the autumn of 2015. Indeed, in winning at Punchestown he joined a select group of horses to have won at the top level both on the Flat and over jumps, after another enterprising ride, this time from Frankie Dettori, had helped him upset Gold Cup winner Order of St George in the 2016

Betdaq Punchestown Champion Hurdle, Punchestown—
an enterprising ride by Mr Patrick Mullins aboard Wicklow Brave ...

... sees them hold off the better-fancied trio of My Tent Or Yours (hoops), Arctic Fire (right) and the grey Labaik

Irish St Leger. Wicklow Brave had been campaigned at some of the big meetings in Britain before that—second in the Ormonde Stakes at Chester, sixth in the Hardwicke at Royal Ascot, fourth in the Goodwood Cup and third in the Lonsdale Cup at York—and ended the year contesting the Melbourne Cup in which he beat only two home.

Whether or not the all-aged Irish St Leger can properly be considered a classic nowadays, Wicklow Brave's success at the highest level under both codes is nonetheless a rare achievement. The 1994 Doncaster winner Moonax was the last British classic winner to be tried over hurdles. Beaten a head in the Irish St Leger as a four-year-old, Moonax was also runner-up when favourite for the 1995 Gold Cup and collected further second places in France in the Prix du Cadran (twice) and Prix Royal-Oak, though he also won the latter contest after the St Leger at three. The quirky Moonax also earned himself a 'squiggle', losing his second Cadran when ducking away from the whip in a race in which he had tried to bite the winner in a tight finish the year before. Moonax entered the Champion Hurdle betting but a hurdling career was aborted after three runs in novice hurdles when he failed to build on a debut second at Huntingdon. Moonax's owner Sheikh Mohammed had more success over hurdles with Royal Gait, the 1992 Champion Hurdle winner having won both the Cadran and Royal-Oak earlier in his career for another owner, as well as being controversially demoted from first in the Gold Cup at Royal Ascot.

A St Leger winner who made more of a success of his jumping career than Moonax was the 1961 winner Aurelius. He earned a place at stud by enhancing his reputation at four, showing top-class form when second in the King George after winning the Hardwicke Stakes. Aurelius avoided a 'squiggle' 'although his temperament was not all it might have been' said *Racehorses*, permission having been obtained (in the days before starting stalls) for him to be held at the start.

But Aurelius failed at stud, was gelded and put back into training, winning a minor event on the Flat at Alexandra Park as an eight-year-old but being mainly campaigned over jumps. After winning a couple of novice hurdles, Aurelius finished second in a division of the Gloucestershire Hurdle at Cheltenham in 1966 and then won a handicap at the track's April meeting. The following season, he finished second past the post in the Champion Hurdle behind Saucy Kit but was disqualified after hanging left on the run-in. Aurelius went on to win a couple of races over fences as well, including the Scilly Isles at Sandown, though he refused on his last two appearances, his final start coming in the 1968 Hennessy Gold Cup.

Wicklow Brave (b.g. 2009)	Beat Hollow (b 1997)	Sadler's Wells (b 1981)	Northern Dancer / Fairy Bridge
		Wemyss Bight (b 1990)	Dancing Brave / Bahamian
	Moraine (br 2004)	Rainbow Quest (b 1981)	Blushing Groom / I Will Follow
		Cantilever (b 1995)	Sanglamore / Cantanta

The smallish, strong Wicklow Brave's pedigree has been dealt with before in his essays in *Chasers & Hurdlers 2014/15* and *Racehorses of 2016*. To recap, he comes from a successful Juddmonte family, though one that's yielded some good jumpers as well as Flat horses. His useful grandam Cantilever, winner of the Prix de Royaumont, was a half-sister to the 1998 Triumph Hurdle winner Upgrade and to Battle Group (by Wicklow Brave's sire Beat Hollow), smart winner of handicaps over both hurdles and fences at the 2013 Aintree Festival. Temperament is a family trait too, however, something Upgrade and Battle Group both shared, the latter making headlines for the wrong reasons back at Aintree a year later when refusing

Wicklow Bloodstock (Ireland) Ltd's "Wicklow Brave"

to start in the Grand National. Wicklow Brave has been raced only at around two miles over hurdles and he acts on heavy going, while he also has form on good to firm ground on the Flat. Punchestown was the first time he has worn headgear over hurdles, though he has been tried in a hood on the Flat. Wicklow Brave demonstrated his stable's strength in depth among its two-mile hurdlers, Mullins having to dig a little deeper into that squad in the latest season in the absence of former Champion Hurdle winners Annie Power and Faugheen. Wicklow Brave showed smart form again back on the Flat over the summer, though he also ruined his chance on one occasion by starting slowly. *W. P. Mullins, Ireland*

WICKLOW LAD 13 gr.g. Silver Patriarch (IRE) – Marina Bird (Julio Mariner) [2016/17 c113, h–: c23.4v³ c20.9v³ Mar 9] quite good-topped gelding: winning hurdler: fair hunter chaser: stays 25f: acts on heavy going: wears headgear. *N. W. Alexander* — **c110 h–**

WIDE AWAKE 8 b.m. And Beyond (IRE) – Quonarose (Feelings (FR)) [2016/17 h20.2s Jul 26] first foal: dam second in point: 100/1, seventh in maiden hurdle at Perth. *Sandy Thomson* — **h–**

WIDOW ON THE RUN (IRE) 6 b.m. Milan – O Mio My (IRE) (Roselier (FR)) [2016/17 b91: h15.3mᶠ May 5] placed in Irish maiden points/mares bumper: close up when fell 3 out in mares novice won by Lady Persephone at Wincanton on hurdling debut: dead. *Kim Bailey* — **h–**

WIESENTRAUM (GER) 11 ch.g. Next Desert (IRE) – Wiesenblute (GER) (Big Shuffle (USA)) [2016/17 c119, h–: c24.2g⁶ c29.2g c23.5g Dec 10] good-topped gelding: winning hurdler: useful chaser at best, no form in 2016/17: wears headgear: often races towards rear. *Lucy Wadham* — **c– h–**

WIFFY CHATSBY (IRE) 10 br.g. Presenting – Star Child (GER) (Neshad (USA)) [2016/17 c78, h–: c20.3vᵖᵘ c20d² c25.5m² c23g² h24g² h22m³ c25.8m⁴ Aug 31] rather leggy gelding: modest handicap hurdler: fair handicap chaser: left Dafydd Jones after first start: stays 3¼m: acts on soft and good to firm going: in headgear last 3 starts: wears tongue tie. *Peter Bowen* — **c106 h98**

WIG WAM WIGGLE (IRE) 5 b.g. Mahler – Last Sunrise (IRE) (Shahanndeh) [2016/17 b16.4v² b16.8v³ b16.2g⁴ Apr 25] €10,000 4-y-o: seventh foal: half-brother to 3 winners, including fairly useful hurdler Some Kinda Lama (25f winner, by Daylami) and fair hurdler Prince Garyantle (21f/25f winner, by Exit To Nowhere): dam unraced half-sister to useful hurdler/very smart chaser (stayed 27f) Therealbandit: fair form in bumpers: best effort when second in maiden at Newcastle in February. *Micky Hammond* — **b88**

WILBERDRAGON 7 b.g. Kayf Tara – Swaythe (USA) (Swain (IRE)) [2016/17 h122: h19.5g c20d³ c22.7g³ c20.2s³ c24.2m⁶ Apr 13] good-topped gelding: fairly useful hurdler: similar form over fences: third in novice handicap at Leicester in January: probably stays easy 23f: acts on heavy going: wears tongue tie: often races prominently. *Charlie Longsdon* — **c118 h–**

WILCOS MO CHARA (IRE) 9 b.g. Oscar (IRE) – She's A Venture (IRE) (Supreme Leader) [2016/17 h20.2g h16s* h16d² h19.9vᶠ h16s⁵ h20d Jan 26] smallish, strong gelding: fairly useful handicap hurdler: won at Navan in September: stays 2½m: acts on heavy going. *Anthony McCann, Ireland* — **h117**

WILD BILL (IRE) 8 b.g. Westerner – Sarahall (IRE) (Saddlers' Hall (IRE)) [2016/17 c122, h–: c24.2dᵖᵘ Feb 17] won all 3 completed starts in points: maiden hurdler: fairly useful chaser for Evan Williams in 2015/16, pulled up sole start in hunter in 2016/17: stays 3m: acts on heavy going. *Mrs A. Rucker* — **c– h–**

WILDEHEARTED WOMAN (IRE) 6 b.m. Oscar (IRE) – Burrator (Topanoora) [2016/17 b87: h16.2g³ h20.6g⁶ h21s h21.6sᵖᵘ h20.5gᶠ Jan 24] bumper winner: fair form over hurdles: best effort at 2½m: wears tongue tie. *Jamie Snowden* — **h103**

WILDEST DREAMS (IRE) 8 b.g. Flemensfirth (USA) – Suspicious Minds (Anabaa (USA)) [2016/17 c–, h–: c24.2dᵖᵘ c20.5sᵖᵘ c23.8g Jan 1] of little account: tried in cheekpieces: poor jumper. *Jane Walton* — **c– x h–**

WILD GINGER 6 ch.g. Presenting – Diamant Noir (Sir Harry Lewis (USA)) [2016/17 h72: h19.5mᶠ h21d⁶ Nov 24] poor form over hurdles: remains with potential. *Jonjo O'Neill* — **h76 p**

WILDMOOR BOY 6 b.g. Midnight Legend – Simple Glory (IRE) (Simply Great (FR)) [2016/17 h65: h22vᵖᵘ h18.7m h22g⁴ h18.7g* h16.3m² h16.4g* h15.5g⁶ h16s² h16vⱽ Feb 11] sturdy gelding: fair handicap hurdler: won at Stratford (novice) in August, Warwick in September and Cheltenham (novice) in November: stays 21f: acts on good to firm and heavy going: wears headgear/tongue tie: front runner. *Robin Dickin* — **h108**

WILD MURPHY (IRE) 6 b.g. Winged Love (IRE) – Yolande (IRE) (King Persian) **h–**
[2016/17 h20.6g[5] h19.7s[pu] Nov 23] winning pointer: no form over hurdles: in cheekpieces final start. *Noel Williams*

WILD ROVER (IRE) 8 b.g. Scorpion (IRE) – Pandalute (IRE) (Indian Danehill (IRE)) **c118**
[2016/17 c105, h117: c23.8m[d] May 8] rangy gelding: fair hurdler: fairly useful form **h–**
over fences: first past post in novice handicap at Ludlow (in cheekpieces) in May, but subsequently disqualified after failing drugs test: stayed 3m: acted on good to firm and heavy going: often raced prominently: dead. *Rebecca Curtis*

WILD WEST WIND (IRE) 8 b.g. Westerner – Mhuire Na Gale (IRE) (Norwich) **c138**
[2016/17 h120, b85: c20.2s* c25.2v* c24.2d[3] Feb 24] winning Irish pointer: fairly useful **h–**
hurdler: useful form over fences: won novice handicaps at Wincanton in January and Hereford (by ¾ length from The Bay Oak) in February: stays 3¼m: acts on heavy going: wears tongue tie: often races prominently, strong traveller. *Tom George*

WILLALDOO 6 b.m. Black Sam Bellamy (IRE) – Ella Falls (IRE) (Dancing Dissident **b77**
(USA)) [2016/17 b–: b16g[6] Aug 11] modest form in bumpers. *Henry Daly*

WILLEM (FR) 7 b.g. Turtle Bowl (IRE) – Zita Blues (IRE) (Zieten (USA)) [2016/17 **c123**
h122: h19.8m[3] c16.3g[2] c16.5g[4] c21d[pu] Jun 21] lengthy gelding: fairly useful handicap **h116**
hurdler: third at Wincanton in May: similar form over fences: best effort when second in novice handicap at Fakenham later in May: stays 21f: acts on soft and good to firm going: wears headgear: has worn tongue tie: won point shortly after end of season. *David Pipe*

WILLIAM H BONNEY 6 b.g. Midnight Legend – Calamintha (Mtoto) [2016/17 h129, **h130**
h96: h16g h16.8s* h16.3d h16d Mar 11] compact gelding: useful handicap hurdler: won at Cheltenham (by length from Man of Plenty) in January: raced around 2m: best form on soft/heavy going. *Alan King*

WILLIAM HENRY (IRE) 7 b.g. King's Theatre (IRE) – Cincuenta (IRE) (Bob Back **h143 p**
(USA)) [2016/17 h16.8g[2] h16.3d* h20.3s[2] h20.3g* Apr 19] good-topped gelding: useful form over hurdles: won introductory event at Newbury in December and novice at Cheltenham in April: second in Classic Novices' Hurdle at latter course (3 lengths behind Wholestone) in January: remains with potential. *Nicky Henderson*

WILLIAM MONEY (IRE) 10 b.g. Cloudings (IRE) – All of A Kind (IRE) (Orchestra) **c112**
[2016/17 c–, h–: c24.2d[6] h23.3g[4] c19.4s[2] c20.1v* c23.8s* h25.6d* h24g[2] c28.4m[2] Apr 27] **h98**
workmanlike, close-coupled gelding: modest form over hurdles: won handicap at Fontwell (conditional) in March: fair handicap chaser: won at Newcastle and Ludlow in February: left Chris Grant after second start: stays 3½m: acts on heavy going: has worn headgear: wears tongue tie: front runner. *Tim Vaughan*

WILLIAM OF ORANGE 6 b.g. Duke of Marmalade (IRE) – Critical Acclaim (Peintre **h110**
Celebre (USA)) [2016/17 h115: h16d[6] h16d[2] h16.6g h19.3g[5] h16d[4] h15.7g[4] Apr 15] strong gelding: fair handicap hurdler: stays 2½m: acts on heavy going: in headgear last 3 starts: has worn tongue tie, including in 2016/17. *Donald McCain*

WILLIAM WILD 9 b.g. Bollin Eric – Winnie Wild (Primitive Rising (USA)) [2016/17 **h–**
h23.3d[pu] h24s[pu] May 18] no form in bumpers/over hurdles. *Tina Jackson*

WILLIE BOY (IRE) 6 b.g. Tikkanen (USA) – Pandora's Moon (IRE) (Tamayaz (CAN)) **c129 p**
[2016/17 h20.1s[3] h16.7s[3] h20.5d[5] c20d[F] c20s* Mar 18] €19,000 3-y-o, £42,000 5-y-o: **h107 p**
good-topped gelding: first foal: dam, unraced, half-sister to fair hurdler/useful chaser (2m/17f winner) Jigsaw Dancer and fairly useful hurdler/chaser (stayed 21f) Ballyburke (by Tikkanen): won completed start in points: fair form over hurdles: fairly useful form over fences: won handicap at Uttoxeter in March: stays 2½m: acts on soft going: will go on improving. *Venetia Williams*

WILLIE HALL 13 b.g. Alflora (IRE) – G'ime A Buzz (Electric) [2016/17 c96§, h83§: **c– §**
c20.1m[4] h22.7s[pu] c15.5g[6] c16.4s[pu] c15.5s[pu] Dec 19] fair hurdler/chaser at best, no form in **h– §**
2016/17: has worn cheekpieces: often races towards rear: often finishes weakly and isn't one to rely on. *Lisa Harrison*

WILLIE THE WARRIOR (IRE) 8 ch.g. Medecis – Tordasia (IRE) (Dr Devious **h83 x**
(IRE)) [2016/17 h16.2d[F] h16d[4] h16g[F] h20g Oct 12] modest maiden on Flat, stays 1¼m: poor form over hurdles: tried in cheekpieces/tongue tie: often let down by jumping. *Peter Croke, Ireland*

WILL O'THE WEST (IRE) 6 b.g. Westerner – Simply Divine (IRE) (Be My Native **h126**
(USA)) [2016/17 h123, b80: h23.9g[3] h25.3s h21d h23.1g[F] Mar 25] good-topped gelding: fairly useful handicap hurdler: third at Cheltenham in October: stays 3m: acts on heavy going. *Henry Daly*

WILLOUGHBY COURT (IRE) 6 br.g. Court Cave (IRE) – Willoughby Sue (IRE) **h151 p**
(Dabali (IRE)) [2016/17 b113: h20.6g² h21s* h21s* h21.1g* Mar 15]

Willoughby Court's game head victory over Neon Wolf in the Baring
Bingham at Cheltenham provided a first Festival success for both his owners Paul
and Clare Rooney and his trainer Ben Pauling. The Rooneys' dark blue and yellow
quartered colours have become a familiar sight on racecourses in recent seasons,
particularly over jumps—they were carried into second place in the 2016 Grand
National by The Last Samuri—though the couple had a Royal Ascot success to
celebrate before registering their first win at the Festival when My Dream Boat won
the 2016 Prince of Wales's Stakes for Clive Cox. However, the majority of the
Rooneys' string of over a hundred horses, split between nearly thirty trainers, are
jumpers and, with only J. P. McManus having more runners and winners in Britain in
the latest season, the Rooneys finished third in the owners' prize-money table behind
McManus and the Simon Munir & Isaac Souede partnership.

The latest season, just his fourth with a licence after six years as assistant to
Nicky Henderson, was also the most successful yet for Willoughby Court's trainer
who had gained his first Grade 1 success with Barters Hill in the previous season's
Challow Novices' Hurdle. Barters Hill took an unbeaten record to the 2016 Festival
and started second favourite (drifting on the day after an eleventh hour injury scare)
for the Spa Novices' in which he finished a creditable fourth to Unowhatimeanharry.
Willoughby Court's claims in the Baring Bingham (branded nowadays as the
Neptune Investment Management Novices' Hurdle) were less strong—he started
fifth choice in the betting as a 14/1-shot behind 2/1 favourite Neon Wolf who was
unbeaten in a bumper and both of his starts over hurdles. On the other hand, it was
clear from Willoughby Court's first three starts over hurdles that he was improving
rapidly, though he had given the impression that the three-mile Spa might suit him
better at the Festival than the Baring Bingham over three furlongs shorter. Pauling
described Willoughby Court as being 'an impossible horse to train for two years
because he was so fractious and nervous', something which was evident in his
bumpers in which he nonetheless showed plenty of promise too. He ran green
when getting off the mark at the second attempt at Southwell on his reappearance
in 2015/16 and followed up under a penalty at Warwick in a race which Barters Hill
had won twelve months earlier. Barters Hill had gone on to complete a four-timer in

Neptune Investment Management Novices' Hurdle (Baring Bingham), Cheltenham—
Willoughby Court (right) provides his connections with their first Cheltenham Festival winner
as he gamely holds off favourite Neon Wolf; Messire des Obeaux (white face) takes third

the Grade 2 bumper at Aintree that season and Willoughby Court contested the same race after four months off, progressing again and shaping well in fifth behind rivals who had fought out the finish of the Champion Bumper at Cheltenham. The first three at Cheltenham—Ballyandy, Battleford and Bacardys—finished fourth, third and first at Aintree. All three of those proved at least useful novices in the latest season, as did Willoughby Court himself and the sixth horse at Aintree, Any Drama.

Willoughby Court came up against another useful type when beaten by Get On The Yager on his debut over hurdles at Market Rasen in November but went on to win his next two starts at Warwick before the Festival. Fitter for his reappearance, he accounted for a big field of maidens in December, making all and showing a good attitude to see off runner-up Tommy Rapper by three quarters of a length as the pair pulled clear. Get On The Yager was one of his rivals when Willoughby Court followed up, again making all, in the Grade 2 Leamington Novices' Hurdle (another race run under the Neptune Investment Management title) over the same course and distance in January. Pressing on in the back straight, Willoughby Court was clear on the home turn and found plenty as he pulled eight lengths clear of runner-up Gayebury, with Irish challenger Peregrine Run, who had completed a four-timer in a similar contest at Cheltenham on his latest start, just over a length further back in third. Get On The Yager was fourth with favourite Geordie des Champs last of the six.

David Bass, who had ridden Willoughby Court for both his wins at Warwick, was seen to particularly good effect making full use of his mount's stamina in the Baring Bingham. The jockey's only previous Festival win had come on the 33/1 outsider Darna in the Brown Advisory & Merriebelle Stable Plate two years earlier; like Pauling, he had begun his professional career with Nicky Henderson. 'My worry was that I hadn't ridden him on decent ground,' explained Bass afterwards. 'I feared his stamina might not come into play, so I rode him positively and he really got into a lovely rhythm.' Willoughby Court's jumping was key to his performance too and, having kicked on two out, he found extra when the ill-fated Neon Wolf, who pecked at the last when challenging, renewed his effort up the hill. Another of the leading contenders, Messire des Obeaux, kept on to take third three and three quarter lengths behind the first two, while second favourite Bacardys was eventually pulled up after losing all chance when badly hampered by the fatal fall of Consul de Thaix at the fifth.

Willoughby Court (IRE)
(br.g. 2011)

Court Cave (IRE)
(b 2001)

Willoughby Sue (IRE)
(br 2000)

Sadler's Wells
(b 1981)

Wemyss Bight
(b 1990)

Dabali
(b 1994)

Still Hoping
(b 1982)

Northern Dancer
Fairy Bridge
Dancing Brave
Bahamian
Doyoun
Dabiliya
Kambalda
Ganston Girl

Willoughby Court is a son of the well-bred but unraced Court Cave who is by Sadler's Wells out of the 1993 Irish Oaks winner Wemyss Bight. That makes Court Cave a brother to the Grand Prix de Paris and Arlington Million winner Beat Hollow, sire of Wicklow Brave among others in a stud career that began with Juddmonte but has since seen him moved to take up duties as a jumps stallion. The same family has produced top horses for Juddmonte such as Oasis Dream, Kingman and New Bay, but Wemyss Bight's half-sister Coraline is the dam of another couple of successful jumps stallions, the French-based pair Martaline and Coastal Path, the latter sire of Bacardys. Court Cave himself has already produced the high-class chaser Champion Court and the smart hurdler/chaser Court Minstrel. Willoughby Court should stay further than either of those two, as he is out of a half-sister to the very smart chaser Nil Desperandum. That horse might have gained his biggest win in the Drinmore Novices' Chase but there's no mention in the sales catalogues of the performances which sum him up best; he also won an Eider Chase and finished sixth and then fourth in two attempts at the Grand National (he was favourite for the 2007 National when suffering a fatal injury in front of the stands at Uttoxeter on his final preparatory run). Nil Desperandum and fair hurdler (winner up to three miles) Willoughby Joe were the two winners out of winning pointer Still Hoping, who also

Paul & Clare Rooney's "Willoughby Court"

produced Willoughby Court's dam Willoughby Sue. She finished well beaten in the two bumpers in which she completed. Willoughby Court is his dam's second foal after Markov (by another Sadler's Wells stallion Morozov) who made a winning debut for the Pauling stable in a Fontwell bumper in November before showing fairly useful form at up to three miles over hurdles. Willoughby Court changed hands twice as a yearling for just €3,800 and €6,000 before joining current connections after being bought for €48,000 as a three-year-old at the Goffs Land Rover National Hunt Sale. Pauling acquired his three-year-old brother for €34,000 at the same sale in 2016. A novice chasing campaign is being mapped out for the lengthy, rather unfurnished Willoughby Court in the next season, when he is likely to have a new jockey following the announcement in the summer that Daryl Jacob will ride for Pauling whenever not claimed by Simon Munir and Isaac Souede. The Rooneys, incidentally, have not employed a retained jockey since Jason Maguire (now their racing manager) was forced to retire through injury, a decision finally made in May, though he had not ridden competitively since February 2015. Hopefully, Willoughby Court's switch to the larger obstacles will have a happier outcome than the one pursued by Barters Hill who suffered a tendon injury early on his chasing debut at Cheltenham in November. A game front runner who will be well suited by three miles, Willoughby Court wore a tongue tie on his reappearance. *Ben Pauling*

WILLOUGHBY HEDGE 10 b.g. King's Theatre (IRE) – Mini Mandy (Petoski) [2016/17   **c136** c128, h–: c24.1s^{pu} c26d c24.2s* c24.2d^6 c24.1g* Apr 15] good-topped gelding: winning   **h–** hurdler: useful handicap chaser: won at Sandown in February and Haydock (by neck from Regal Flow) in April: stays 25f: acts on soft going: in headgear last 3 starts. *Alan King*

WILLOW BIRD 8 ch.m. Midnight Legend – Dubelle (Dubassoff (USA)) [2016/17 h18.5spu Dec 15] won both completed starts in points: pulled up in mares novice on hurdling debut: dead. *Anthony Honeyball* — **h–**

WILLOW ISLAND (IRE) 8 b.g. Dark Angel (IRE) – Cidaris (IRE) (Persian Bold) [2016/17 h61: h15.8d⁶ Oct 2] maiden hurdler: sometimes in tongue tie. *Sam England* — **h–**

WILLOW'S SAVIOUR 10 ch.g. Septieme Ciel (USA) – Willow Gale (Strong Gale) [2016/17 c140, h–: h15.7d h20.5d h19s² Mar 4] lengthy, useful-looking gelding: fairly useful handicap hurdler: second at Taunton in February: useful chaser: stays 21f: acts on heavy going: has worn cheekpieces: tried in tongue tie: often races towards rear. *Dan Skelton* — **c–** **h124**

WILLSHEBETRYING 6 b.m. Act One – Precedence (IRE) (Polish Precedent (USA)) [2016/17 h86: h19.1d⁵ h17.7v⁴ h19.5v⁵ h20.5v³ Feb 27] poor maiden hurdler: stays 21f: best form on heavy going: tried in visor. *Mark Hoad* — **h82**

WILLY BRENNAN (IRE) 6 br.g. Bushranger (IRE) – Miss Assertive (Zafonic (USA)) [2016/17 h97: h16.3g⁶ h18.7g⁴ Aug 11] lightly-raced hurdler, modest form at best: wore tongue tie: dead. *Jo Davis* — **h55**

WILLYEGOLASSIEGO 4 br.f. Kheleyf (USA) – Kryena (Kris) [2016/17 h16.8s h16s h15.9v h15.7vpu Mar 6] rather leggy filly: fair on Flat, stays 13f: no form over hurdles. *Neil Mulholland* — **h–**

WILTON MILAN (IRE) 9 b.g. Milan – Biondo (IRE) (College Chapel) [2016/17 c129, h–: c21.1s² c20d⁵ c19.4dpu c27.6d⁶ c23.6s⁵ c24.2d Mar 10] good-topped gelding: winning hurdler: fairly useful handicap chaser: second at Fontwell in October: left Dan Skelton after flat start: stays 3½m: acts on heavy going: has worn headgear: wears tongue tie: temperamental. *Miss L. Luxton* — **c117 §** **h–**

WINDING BAE (IRE) 5 b.m. Well Chosen – Despute (IRE) (Be My Native (USA)) [2016/17 b16g⁶ ab16g⁶ b16.7s Dec 22] sister to 2 winners, including fairly useful hurdler/ useful chaser Burtons Well (19f/2½m winner), and half-sister to useful hurdler/high-class chaser Burton Port (17f-25f winner, by Bob Back): dam unraced: poor form in bumpers. *Nicky Henderson* — **b72**

WIND OF HOPE (IRE) 8 b.g. September Storm (GER) – Ciara's Run (IRE) (Topanoora) [2016/17 c95, h109: c20.9v² c23.8gpu Apr 28] multiple point winner: fair hurdler: modest form in hunter chases: stays 23f: acts on heavy going: tried in cheekpieces: usually races nearer last than first. *Alan J. Brown* — **c99** **h–**

WIND PLACE AND SHO 5 br.g. Shirocco (GER) – Coh Sho No (Old Vic) [2016/17 h20.8g³ h20.8d⁶ h19.4g Jan 27] brother to fairly useful hurdler Iron Butterfly (2¼m-3m winner) and half-brother to fairly useful hurdler At The Money (2m-2¾m winner, by Robellino): dam (h108) 2½m/21f hurdle winner: useful on Flat, stays 21f: modest form over hurdles. *James Eustace* — **h99**

WINDSHEAR 6 b.g. Hurricane Run (IRE) – Portal (Hernando (FR)) [2016/17 h19.4g Mar 1] smart at one time on Flat, stays 14.5f: tailed off in maiden on hurdling debut. *Sophie Leech* — **h–**

WINDSPIEL (FR) 4 b.g. Sholokhov (IRE) – Wildlife (GER) (Waky Nao) [2016/17 ab16g h16m h21m Apr 18] well beaten in junior bumper/novice hurdles. *David Arbuthnot* — **h–** **b–**

WINDY WRITER (IRE) 7 b.g. Rudimentary (USA) – Hardabout (IRE) (Alderbrook) [2016/17 h98, b–: h16.7g h15.8d c19.9dF h15.7sF h15.7d⁶ h20.3v⁵ h15.7g⁶ Apr 21] modest maiden hurdler: fell heavily fourth on chasing debut: unproven beyond 2m: acts on good to soft going: often in cheekpieces. *Shaun Lycett* — **c–** **h98**

WINE WOMEN AN'SONG 6 b.m. Tiger Hill (IRE) – Kasamba (Salse (USA)) [2016/17 b17.7d² b13.6g⁶ Apr 21] fifth foal: half-sister to fairly useful hurdler Spellbound (19f winner, by Doyen) and fair hurdler Welcometothejungle (2½m winner, by Lucky Story): dam, 7f winner, half-sister to useful hurdlers/winning chasers (stayed 3m) Dancing Bay and Mister Dillon: modest form in bumpers. *Harry Fry* — **b79**

WINGED CRUSADER (IRE) 9 b.g. Winged Love (IRE) – Reine Berengere (FR) (Esprit du Nord (USA)) [2016/17 c114§, h–: c20.1sF c20.3s* c25.6d² c24vpu c23.6s³ Mar 13] useful-looking gelding: winning hurdler: fair handicap chaser: won at Bangor in December: stays 3¼m: acts on heavy going: usually wears visor: unreliable. *Nigel Twiston-Davies* — **c114 §** **h–**

WINGED EXPRESS (IRE) 8 b.g. Winged Love (IRE) – Zaffaran Express (IRE) (Zaffaran (USA)) [2016/17 c101, h100: c17.4g² h19.7sro c20v⁴ Dec 31] fair hurdler: modest chaser: stays 2½m: acts on good to firm and heavy going: wears headgear. *Alexandra Dunn* — **c98** **h–**

WINGS ATTRACT (IRE) 8 b.g. Winged Love (IRE) – Huncheon Siss (IRE) (Phardante (FR)) [2016/17 c127, h108: c21d⁶ c23.5g c24g² h24.4gᵖᵘ c24.2m⁵ Apr 13] strong gelding: fair hurdler: fairly useful handicap chaser: second at Doncaster in December: stays 3m: acts on good to soft going: often wears headgear: usually races close up, often lazily. *Olly Williams* **c124 h–**

WINGS OF SMOKE (IRE) 12 gr.g. King's Theatre (IRE) – Grey Mo (IRE) (Roselier (FR)) [2016/17 c136§, h–: c19.2m⁴ c23m⁶ c20g c19.9g² c20d² c15.7s⁴ c20v⁵ c22.6sᵖᵘ c21.1g Mar 31] winning hurdler: fairly useful handicap chaser: stays 2¾m: acts on good to firm and heavy going: has worn visor: wears tongue tie: often races in rear: untrustworthy (weak finisher). *Tim Vaughan* **c124 § h–**

WINIDO 5 b.g. Sulamani (IRE) – Princess Claudia (IRE) (Kahyasi) [2016/17 b16.7d⁴ b16.8m⁶ h15.8s h16.5s h20.5s⁶ h19.9sᵖᵘ Mar 18] little form in bumpers/over hurdles. *Tim Vaughan* **h– b65**

WINNER MASSAGOT (FR) 6 ch.g. Muhaymin (USA) – Winnor (FR) (Lesotho (USA)) [2016/17 h130: c16.4g c19.1g³ c19.1d² c17.4s⁴ c19.9gᵖᵘ Apr 17] tall, close-coupled gelding: fairly useful hurdler: similar form over fences: second in novice at Doncaster in January: stays 19f: acts on good to soft going: tried in cheekpieces: tends to find little. *Alan King* **c128 h–**

WINNI ALLFOURS 5 ch.m. Cockney Rebel (IRE) – Memo (Groom Dancer (USA)) [2016/17 ab16g Nov 22] seventh foal: half-sister to 2 winners on Flat, including useful 11f/1½m winner Tripitaka (by Sulamani): dam unraced: tailed off in bumper. *Zoe Davison* **b–**

WINNING SPARK (USA) 10 b.g. Theatrical – Spark Sept (FR) (Septieme Ciel (USA)) [2016/17 h117: h21.6g⁵ h19.8d² h19m* h19g⁴ h19s³ h20.5g⁶ Mar 27] good-topped gelding: fairly useful handicap hurdler: won at Taunton in December: second at Wincanton in November: stays 2½m: acts on good to firm and heavy going: has worn tongue tie. *Jackie du Plessis* **h121**

WINNING TICKET (IRE) 6 b.g. Kalanisi (IRE) – Saddlers' Venture (IRE) (Saddlers' Hall (IRE)) [2016/17 h103, b82b: h15.7v² h16.7g² h16.8g h16.8g⁵ h16m² c16.5dᵖᵘ h16.7d h16.4g h18.1dᵖᵘ Apr 10] fair maiden hurdler: pulled up in novice handicap on chasing debut: left Paul Morgan after fourth start, Nigel Twiston-Davies after seventh: unproven beyond 17f: acts on heavy going: in hood last 2 starts: has worn tongue tie, including in 2016/17. *Andrew Hamilton* **c– h103**

WINNINGTRY (IRE) 6 br.g. Flemensfirth (USA) – Jeruflo (IRE) (Glacial Storm (USA)) [2016/17 b93p: h20d³ h16.5g² h19.4g³ h19.8d* h24.3d* Apr 21] bumper winner: fairly useful form over hurdles: won maiden at Wincanton in March and novice handicap at Ayr in April: stays 3m: acts on good to soft going: front runner/races prominently. *Paul Nicholls* **h121**

WINSTON CHURCHILL (IRE) 11 b.g. Presenting – Star Councel (IRE) (Leading Counsel (USA)) [2016/17 c106, h–: c19.2s c24.5v³ c19.3v⁴ c16s⁶ Mar 13] maiden hurdler: modest handicap chaser: barely stays 25f: acts on good to firm and heavy going: in headgear last 2 starts: wears tongue tie. *Sophie Leech* **c95 h–**

WINTERED WELL (IRE) 9 b.g. Milan – Stratosphere (Selkirk (USA)) [2016/17 h116: h23.3s⁶ h23.1d⁵ May 25] lengthy gelding: fair handicap hurdler: stayed 25f: acted on heavy going: tried in cheekpieces: often raced towards rear: dead. *Jennie Candlish* **h102**

WINTER ESCAPE (IRE) 6 b.g. Robin des Pres (FR) – Saddleeruppat (IRE) (Saddlers' Hall (IRE)) [2016/17 h136P: h16.4s h16.8g⁵ h16g Apr 22] lengthy gelding: useful form over hurdles: fifth in County Hurdle at Cheltenham (2½ lengths behind Arctic Fire) in March: raced around 2m: acts on good to soft going: often travels strongly. *Alan King* **h138**

WINTER LION (IRE) 7 ch.g. Galileo (IRE) – Hill of Snow (Reference Point) [2016/17 h116: h17s* h17m h21.1g Oct 21] fairly useful handicap hurdler: won at Bellewstown in July: unproven beyond 17f: acts on soft going: wears tongue tie: usually leads. *Matthew J. Smith, Ireland* **h123**

WINTERLUDE (IRE) 7 b.g. Street Cry (IRE) – New Morning (IRE) (Sadler's Wells (USA)) [2016/17 h67p: h15.8g⁴ h16.7g* h17.2g Aug 27] fair form over hurdles: won novice at Bangor in July: will prove best around 2m. *Jennie Candlish* **h114**

WINTER WALK (IRE) 8 b.g. Blueprint (IRE) – Dubai Seven Stars (Suave Dancer (USA)) [2016/17 h23.3g⁶ h26.5g* Sep 16] winning pointer: fair form over hurdles: won handicap at Newton Abbot in September: stays 3¼m: acts on heavy going: open to further improvement. *Tim Vaughan* **h106 p**

WISECRACKER 4 br.g. Sageburg (IRE) – Folie Lointaine (FR) (Poliglote) [2016/17 ab16g h16.3s Mar 3] tailed off in junior bumper/juvenile hurdle: in hood final start. *Ben Case* **h– b–**

WISHFULL DREAMING 6 ch.g. Alflora (IRE) – Poussetiere Deux (FR) (Garde h133
Royale) [2016/17 h111p: h16g⁴ h16.4g⁵ h16s⁴ h16.5g⁵ h16.8g² Apr 11] lengthy gelding:
fairly useful handicap hurdler: won at Chepstow in October: will stay 2½m: best form on
good going: usually travels strongly. *Philip Hobbs*

WISHICOULD (IRE) 6 br.m. Asian Heights – Dark Wish (IRE) (Mister Lord (USA)) h117
[2016/17 h21v⁴ h20.5s³ h25s² h24.2s* h25.5d² Mar 26] €450 3-y-o, £18,000 5-y-o: plain
mare: second foal: dam unraced: off mark in Irish maiden points at second attempt: fairly
useful form over hurdles: won handicap at Newbury in March: stays 3¼m: acts on soft
going. *Charlie Mann*

WISH IN A WELL (IRE) 8 b.g. Gamut (IRE) – Lady Bellingham (IRE) (Montelimar c75
(USA)) [2016/17 c78, h–: c22.5d c16.1d c25.6vᵖᵘ c21.2s* c21.1v² c21.1v³ c21.2gᵘʳ c19.2g² h–
c19.2d³ Apr 27] maiden handicap chaser: poor handicap chaser: won at Fakenham (amateur) in
January: stays 21f: acts on heavy going: wears headgear: has worn tongue tie. *Ben Case*

WISHING AND HOPING (IRE) 7 b.g. Beneficial – Desperately Hoping (IRE) (Un c130
Desperado (FR)) [2016/17 h121: c20.3g² c19.7dF c20.2dF h21g³ Feb 25] useful-looking h126
gelding: fairly useful form over hurdles: third in handicap at Kempton in February: useful
form over fences: best effort when second in novice at Bangor (1¼ lengths behind Value At
Risk) in October: stays 21f: acts on good to soft going: often races in rear. *Alan King*

WISHING WELL 5 b.m. Bahri (USA) – Amourallis (IRE) (Dushyantor (USA)) [2016/17 h82 p
h–p: h16g⁵ Oct 29] strong mare: fairly useful on Flat, stays 2m: poor form over hurdles:
likely to progress further. *Micky Hammond*

WISHING WIND 7 b.m. Kayf Tara – Romantic Dream (Bustino) [2016/17 h87, b–: h–
h20.3gᵖᵘ Jun 7] well-made mare: fair form over hurdles, pulled up sole start in 2016/17.
Nicky Henderson

WISTARI ROCKS (IRE) 8 b.g. Heron Island (IRE) – Hi Honey (IRE) (Persian Mews) h96
[2016/17 h95: h15.8g* h15.8d⁴ h15.8d h16.8s⁴ Mar 7] modest handicap hurdler: won at
Uttoxeter in September (novice) and October: raced around 2m: acts on good to soft going.
Tim Vaughan

WISTY (IRE) 8 gr.g. Cloudings (IRE) – Alpine Message (Tirol) [2016/17 h20m h16g h125
h17.2d* h17.2d² h17.2g³ h16.2d* h16.7g³ h20g h16.2g⁶ Apr 26] fairly useful handicap
hurdler: won at Cartmel (amateur) in June and Kelso in September: left Edward Stanners
after second start: unproven beyond 17f: acts on good to firm and good to soft going: has
worn hood: usually leads. *Martin Todhunter*

WITCHESINTUNE 10 b.m. Beat Hollow – Music Park (IRE) (Common Grounds) c–
[2016/17 c20.9sᵖᵘ h26.5dᵖᵘ h19.2m³ Oct 5] sturdy mare: point winner: poor maiden h67
hurdler: pulled up both starts over fences: should stay at least 2½m: best form on soft/
heavy going. *Jimmy Frost*

WITCH'S HAT (IRE) 14 br.g. Hubbly Bubbly (USA) – Bold Shilling (IRE) (Meneval c–
(USA)) [2016/17 c–, h–: c21.1d⁵ May 12] sturdy gelding: winning pointer: maiden hurdler: h–
modest chaser at best: stays 3m: acts on heavy going: usually wears tongue tie. *A. Coveney*

WITHAM 4 b.f. Beat Hollow – Wistow (Sir Harry Lewis (USA)) [2016/17 b16d⁴ b15.7s⁴ b83
Mar 20] first foal: dam (c125/h121) 23f-25f hurdle/chase winner: modest form in bumpers.
Pam Sly

WITH HINDSIGHT (IRE) 9 b.g. Ad Valorem (USA) – Lady From Limerick (IRE) h104
(Rainbows For Life (CAN)) [2016/17 h16.2d³ h16.7g⁴ May 15] fair form over hurdles.
Steve Gollings

WITHOUT FRONTIER (IRE) 5 b.g. Stowaway – Hollygrove Samba (IRE) h92 §
(Accordion) [2016/17 b15.7g h16g h18.5g h15.8v h19.6sᵘʳ h19gʳᵒ h19.7d² h19.6g³ Apr 22] b–
seventh foal: half-brother to smart bumper/hurdle winner Captain Cutter (19f-21f winner,
by Westerner) and bumper winner/fair hurdler Yes Daddy (2m winner, by Golan), stays
2½m: dam unraced half-sister to top-class hurdler (stayed 3m) Mister Morose and to dam
of top-class chaser up to 3m Albertas Run: well beaten in maiden bumper: modest maiden
hurdler: likely to stay further than 2½m: acts on good to soft going: tried in cheekpieces: in
tongue tie last 4 starts: temperamental. *Tim Vaughan*

WITH PLEASURE 4 b.g. Poet's Voice – With Fascination (USA) (Dayjur (USA)) h98
[2016/17 h15.3v² h20g⁴ h16.5m² Apr 27] fair on Flat, stays 8.5f: modest form over hurdles:
best effort when second in maiden at Taunton in April: should stay beyond 2m. *John Flint*

WITHY MILLS 12 gr.m. Daryshnikov (AUS) – Gipsy Rose (Nicholas Bill) [2016/17 c §
c89§, h–§: c20sᵖᵘ h21gᵖᵘ c17.4g⁴ h21.6s h23.9m c17.4vᵖᵘ Jan 29] sturdy mare: poor h62 §
handicap hurdler/chaser, little form in 2016/17: stays 19f: acts on heavy going: wears
headgear/tongue tie: unreliable. *Kevin Bishop*

EMS Copiers Novices' Handicap Chase, Punchestown—the gambled-on Woodland Opera holds off Arbre de Vie (pale colours) and Balko des Flos (No.3)

WITNESS (FR) 8 b.g. Astarabad (USA) – Belle Yepa (FR) (Mansonnien (FR)) [2016/17 c16.4g^{pu} c15.2s^4 c15.2d^3 c15.7d^4 c19.2d^{pu} c15.2d^3 c20v^4 Mar 9] close-coupled gelding: winning hurdler: fair handicap chaser: stays 19f: acts on heavy going: has worn headgear, including last 4 starts: usually races towards rear. *Micky Hammond*   **c105 h–**

WITNESS IN COURT (IRE) 10 b.g. Witness Box (USA) – Inter Alia (IRE) (Dr Massini (IRE)) [2016/17 c140, h–: c19.2g^6 c23.8f^5 c19.4m* c17.1m^3 c15.9g c19.9d^6 c21.1d^{ur} c19.9g^5 c15.8g^2 c16.3g c15.8g Apr 6] tall, angular gelding: winning hurdler: useful handicap chaser: won at Stratford (by 1½ lengths from Roman Flight) in August: best efforts at shorter than 3m: acts on good to firm and heavy going: front runner/races prominently: unreliable. *Donald McCain*   **c138 § h–**

WITNESS TIME (IRE) 5 b.g. Witness Box (USA) – Emotional Melody (IRE) (Saddlers' Hall (IRE)) [2016/17 b16s^5 b16s^5 h16.4v^F h16.4v^5 h18.1d Apr 10] €22,000 3-y-o: first foal: dam (c104/h107), maiden jumper (stayed 3m), half-sister to smart hurdler/useful chaser (stayed 3m) Emotional Moment: modest form in bumpers: poor form over hurdles: will be suited by at least 2½m: in hood last 2 starts: should do better. *Rose Dobbin*   **h58 p b82**

WIXFORD (IRE) 6 b.g. Westerner – Chirouble (IRE) (High Roller (IRE)) [2016/17 b16d May 18] tailed off in bumper. *Johnny Farrelly*   **b–**

WIZARDS BRIDGE 8 b.g. Alflora (IRE) – Island Hopper (Be My Native (USA)) [2016/17 c130, h–: c25.1m^{pu} c24.2g^{pu} h23.6m* c24.2s h23.6g h21.4s^3 h23.5s^6 c21.1s* c25.5d^{pu} h19.5g^6 Apr 17] rangy gelding: fairly useful handicap hurdler: won at Chepstow in November: fairly useful handicap chaser: won at Fontwell in February: stays 3m: acts on good to firm and heavy going: has worn headgear: tried in tongue tie: temperamental. *Colin Tizzard*   **c115 § h117**

WIZARD'S SLIABH (IRE) 6 b.m. King's Theatre (IRE) – Darling Smile (IRE) (Darshaan) [2016/17 b15.8d^2 b16.2s* h20.6g* h21.2d^2 h21s^2 h20.5g Mar 25] €22,000 3-y-o: rather unfurnished mare: seventh foal: half-sister to 3 winners on Flat, including useful 7.5f-10.7f winner Acushladear (by Tagula): dam unraced: won bumper at Perth in July: fairly useful form over hurdles: won mares novice at Market Rasen in November: second in similar events at Ludlow in December and Warwick in January: tried in cheekpieces: in tongue tie last 5 starts. *Fergal O'Brien*   **h122 b81**

WOJCIECH 7 b.m. Lucarno (USA) – Pondimari (FR) (Marignan (USA)) [2016/17 h82:   **h– §**
h16.8g^{pu} h21.6s^{pu} h20g^{pu} h21.6g^{pu} Jul 25] lengthy mare: little form over hurdles: tried
in headgear: has worn tongue tie: often races towards rear: temperamental. *Martin Hill*

WOLFCATCHER (IRE) 5 b.g. King's Best (USA) – Miss Particular (IRE) (Sadler's   **h–**
Wells (USA)) [2016/17 h132: h19.3s h19.9s^{pu} Mar 18] compact gelding: fairly useful
hurdler at best, no form in 2016/17: unproven beyond 17f: best form on heavy going: tried
in cheekpieces/tongue tie. *Ian Williams*

WOLF OF WINDLESHAM (IRE) 5 ch.g. Mastercraftsman (IRE) – Al Amlah (USA)   **h113**
(Riverman (USA)) [2016/17 h136: h16.4g⁵ h16.4s^F h15.7d Dec 17] workmanlike gelding:
useful handicap hurdler, below best in 2016/17: raced around 2m: acts on good to soft
going: often races prominently. *Stuart Edmunds*

WOLF SHIELD (IRE) 10 b.g. King's Theatre (IRE) – Garlucy (IRE) (Un Desperado   **c– §**
(FR)) [2016/17 c114, h–: h22.1g³ h25.4d^{pu} Jun 26] strong gelding: modest handicap   **h96 §**
hurdler: fairly useful chaser: stays 25f: acts on good to firm and heavy going: has worn
cheekpieces, including last 2 starts: wears tongue tie: usually races prominently: unreliable.
Patrick Holmes

WOLF SWORD (IRE) 8 b.g. Flemensfirth (USA) – Dame O'Neill (IRE) (Dr Massini   **c127**
(IRE)) [2016/17 c115, h104: c20m² c16.4g⁵ c19.3d² c20v³ c20v⁴ c21.1s² c21.1v² c20.6v²   **h–**
c20g* Apr 15] strong gelding: fair hurdler: fairly useful chaser: won handicap at Uttoxeter
in December and novice at Carlisle in April: stays 21f: acts on good to firm and heavy
going: races prominently. *Sue Smith*

WOLFTRAP (IRE) 8 b.g. Mountain High (IRE) – Dear Money (IRE) (Buckskin (FR))   **h112**
[2016/17 h98: h16s⁴ h16.8g² h19.3m⁵ h21.2v⁴ h18.5s⁵ Dec 15] rather leggy gelding: fair
handicap hurdler: won at Worcester in May and Ludlow in November: stays 21f: acts on
heavy going: wears hood: tried in tongue tie: held up. *Philip Hobbs*

WONDERFUL CHARM (FR) 9 b.g. Poliglote – Victoria Royale (FR) (Garde Royale)   **c136**
[2016/17 c155, h–: c26.6g* c24.1d* c26.3g² c34.3d Apr 8] rangy gelding: has had   **h–**
breathing operation: winning hurdler: useful chaser nowadays: won hunters at Musselburgh
and Haydock in February: neck second to Pacha du Polder in Foxhunter at Cheltenham:
stays 27f: acts on soft going: wears headgear/tongue tie: usually races towards rear.
Paul Nicholls

WONGA SWINGER 7 b.g. Lucky Story (USA) – Chippewa (FR) (Cricket Ball (USA))   **h90**
[2016/17 h21d h21d h23.1s h19.6s⁵ h19.9s⁵ h15.8s^{pu} h17.7m* h16.8g* Apr 26] £4,500
4-y-o: seventh foal: dam (h108) 2m/17f hurdle winner: placed twice in points: modest
handicap hurdler: won novice events at Plumpton and Exeter in April: stays 2½m: acts on
soft and good to firm going: wears headgear: front runner/races prominently. *Sam Thomas*

WOODFORD COUNTY 10 b.g. Sonus (IRE) – Moylena (Bustomi) [2016/17 c124§,   **c88**
h–: c27.2s c28.8d^{pu} c28.5s c30.7d c31.9s⁵ Mar 16] sturdy gelding: winning hurdler: fairly   **h–**
useful chaser, well below best in 2016/17: stays 31f: acts on heavy going: wears headgear:
front runner/races prominently. *Philip Hobbs*

WOODFORT 5 gr.g. Dalakhani (IRE) – Akdara (IRE) (Sadler's Wells (USA)) [2016/17   **h111**
b16.2s² b15.8s* b16.4g⁴ b16.4s h15.8d h23.9g³ h20.8d² h23.8s^{ur} h20.5s³ h20v³ h21.9d⁴   **b98**
Apr 16] well-made gelding: brother to useful hurdler Aklan (2m winner), stayed 2½m, and
half-brother to several winners, including fairly useful hurdler/chaser Akarshan (2m/17f
winner, by Intikhab), stayed 21f: dam 1½m winner: fourth in Irish maiden point on debut:
fairly useful form in bumpers: won maiden at Ffos Las in October: fair maiden hurdler:
may prove best around 2½m: acts on good to soft going: front runner/races prominently.
Nigel Twiston-Davies

WOODLAND OPERA (IRE) 7 br.g. Robin des Champs (FR) – Opera Hat (IRE)   **c151**
(Strong Gale) [2016/17 h138: h20d* c20s⁵ c16d⁴ c17s³ c17s* c21d* Apr 28] useful   **h–**
hurdler: smart form over fences: won maiden at Fairyhouse (by 7 lengths from O Ceallaigh)
and novice handicap at Punchestown (by ¾ length from Arbre de Vie) in April: likely to
stay 3m: acts on soft going: in tongue tie last 4 starts. *Mrs J. Harrington, Ireland*

WOOD PIGEON (IRE) 8 b.g. Presenting – Come In Moscow (IRE) (Over The River   **c101**
(FR)) [2016/17 c19.5d³ h20.5g⁵ h23.9g Mar 2] maiden point winner: well held over   **h–**
hurdles: fair form over fences: left John Joseph Murphy after first start: stays 25f: acts on
heavy going: tried in cheekpieces. *Anabel K. Murphy*

WOODS WELL (IRE) 6 ch.g. Fleetwood (IRE) – Millbrook Marble (IRE) (Rudimentary (USA)) [2016/17 b16d* h16s² h20v* h24v³ h24s² h24dᵖᵘ h24d Apr 27] €7,000 3-y-o, £26,000 4-y-o: first foal: dam (h80) maiden in bumpers/over hurdles: runner-up on point debut: fairly useful form in bumpers: won maiden at Thurles in November: useful form over hurdles: won maiden at Fairyhouse in January: second in minor event at Thurles in March: stays 3m: acts on heavy going. *Gordon Elliott, Ireland* **h133 b101**

WOOD YER (IRE) 11 ch.g. Anshan – Glenasheen (IRE) (Presenting) [2016/17 c119, h–: c28.4v³ c23.5g⁶ c26.7s⁵ c29.6s³ c30.7sᶠ Mar 5] lengthy, angular gelding: maiden hurdler: fairly useful handicap chaser: third at Haydock in November: stays 3¾m: acts on heavy going: wears headgear/tongue tie. *Nigel Twiston-Davies* **c115 h–**

WOOLY BULLY 7 b.g. Sixties Icon – Baycliffe Rose (Karinga Bay) [2016/17 h17.7d Dec 6] fair hurdler for Alan King in 2013/14, well held sole outing since: should stay at least 2½m: acts on good to soft going. *Charlie Mann* **h–**

WORKBENCH (FR) 9 b.g. Network (GER) – Danhelis (FR) (Hellios (USA)) [2016/17 c138, h111: c21gᶠ c16.5g⁵ h19.1d² c17.4g* c24.2g⁴ c23.8m h16.5g c16.4s⁶ h16.3d c16s² c19.9g³ Apr 17] good-topped gelding: fair handicap hurdler: useful handicap chaser: won at Fontwell (by length from Purple 'N Gold) in September: stays 2½m: acts on heavy going: tried in cheekpieces: wears tongue tie: often races in rear. *Dan Skelton* **c131 h113**

WORK DU BRETEAU (FR) 7 ch.g. Network (GER) – Salinka (FR) (Green Tune (USA)) [2016/17 b18s h22m² h23.3d³ h22.1d⁴ h16.7g⁴ c19.4m³ h23.1g* Apr 22] €22,000 3-y-o: third foal: dam, French 1¼m-1½m winner, half-sister to fairly useful hurdler/chaser (stayed 2¾m) Sardagna: modest bumper performer: fair hurdler: won maiden at Bangor in April: 50/1, last of 3 finishers in novice at Wetherby (15¼ lengths behind Ballybolley) on chasing debut: left Thomas Mullins after second start: stays 23f: acts on good to firm and heavy going: has worn hood, including last 4 starts: tried in tongue tie. *Tim Reed* **c107 h112 b65**

WORKING TITLE (IRE) 15 b.g. Oscar (IRE) – Dantes Term (IRE) (Phardante (FR)) [2016/17 c16.4d* c16sᶠ c15.7s⁶ Jan 31] compact gelding: prolific winning pointer: winning hurdler: fair handicap chaser: won at Sedgefield in December: effective at 2m to 21f: acts on soft and good to firm going: has worn headgear: tried in tongue tie. *Samuel Drinkwater* **c100 h–**

WORK IN PROGRESS (IRE) 7 b.g. Westerner – Parsons Term (IRE) (The Parson) [2016/17 h134: h16d⁶ c19.2g² c25.2d⁴ h19.6d h16.5gᵖᵘ Feb 21] useful hurdler at best, well below that in 2016/17: fairly useful form over fences: better effort when second in maiden at Catterick in November: stays 21f: acts on soft going: often leads. *Dan Skelton* **c125 h–**

Guinness Kerry National Handicap Chase, Listowel—a first winner over fences for 7 lb-claiming amateur Lisa O'Neill as Wrath of Titans (noseband) asserts from Rightville Boy (right) two out, where stable-companion Lord Scoundrel departs

WORK (IRE) 4 b.f. Mastercraftsman (IRE) – Abbeyleix Lady (IRE) (Montjeu (IRE)) **h89**
[2016/17 h15.8v^{ur} h16.6g^4 h15.9v^3 h15.9s^5 Feb 13] rather leggy filly: fair on Flat, stays 2m: modest form over hurdles. *David Pipe*

WORLDOR (FR) 11 b.g. Lost World (IRE) – Karenzed (FR) (Synefos (USA)) [2016/17 **c–**
c–, h90: h16g May 2] compact gelding: modest hurdler, well held sole outing in 2016/17: **h–**
maiden chaser: unproven beyond 17f: acts on heavy going: wears hood/tongue tie: often races in rear. *Alexandra Dunn*

WORLD PREMIER (FR) 4 gr.g. Montmartre (FR) – Kelbelange (FR) (Ganges (USA)) **b101**
[2016/17 b16g* Apr 24] £25,000 3-y-o: half-brother to several winners, including useful French 17f chase winner Polistyle and fairly useful 2½m hurdle winner Pithivier (both by Poliglote): dam, French 1m-10.5f winner, half-sister to useful hurdler/smart chaser (stayed 2½m) Flat Out: 5/2, overcame greenness when won bumper at Warwick (by 8 lengths from Boughtbeforelunch) on debut. *Ben Pauling*

WOR ROM (IRE) 13 b.g. Subtle Power (IRE) – Snowbaby (IRE) (Be My Native (USA)) **c81 x**
[2016/17 c25.5d^4 May 12] winning pointer/hurdler: maiden chaser: thorough stayer: acts **h–**
on heavy going: usually wears headgear: often let down by jumping. *Miss Rose Grissell*

WOT A SHOT (IRE) 8 b.g. Refuse To Bend (IRE) – Ashdali (IRE) (Grand Lodge (USA)) **c101**
[2016/17 c81, h–: c16m* c17.1m^3 c16d^2 c16s^2 c16g^{pu} c16g^4 Apr 27] maiden hurdler: **h–**
fair handicap chaser: won novice event at Perth in May: stays 2¼m: acts on soft and good to firm going: has worn hood: tried in tongue tie: usually races nearer last than first. *Nicky Richards*

WOTZIZNAME (IRE) 7 b.g. Fruits of Love (USA) – Native Beau (IRE) (Be My Native **c132 p**
(USA)) [2016/17 h124p: h23.3d* c25d^2 h26.1g^4 Feb 5] point winner: useful form over **h136**
hurdles: won novice at Uttoxeter in May: 15/8, second of 3 in novice at Aintree (10 lengths behind Arpege d'Alene) on chasing debut: stays 3¼m: wears tongue tie: should do better over fences. *Harry Fry*

WOUNDED WARRIOR (IRE) 8 b.g. Shantou (USA) – Sparkling Sword (Broadsword **c139**
(USA)) [2016/17 c153, h–: c22d^4 c24d c25d^6 c25v^{pu} c34.3d^{pu} c29d^{pu} Apr 17] tall, lengthy **h–**
gelding: winning hurdler: smart chaser, below best in 2016/17: stays 25f: acts on heavy going: sometimes in headgear. *Noel Meade, Ireland*

WRATH OF TITANS (IRE) 8 b.g. Oscar (IRE) – Glen Empress (IRE) (Lancastrian) **c134**
[2016/17 c130, h111: c25d^4 h22.8g^6 h18.2g* c24v* c24d^6 c28g^{pu} Nov 6] fairly useful **h128**
hurdler: won minor event at Downpatrick in August: useful handicap chaser: won Kerry National Handicap Chase at Listowel (by 5 lengths from Rightville Boy) in September: left Ms Sandra Hughes after first start: stayed 3m: acted on heavy going: sometimes wore cheekpieces: dead. *Gordon Elliott, Ireland*

WRONG IMPRESSION 4 b.f. Schiaparelli (GER) – Princess Hotpot (IRE) (King's **b–**
Ride) [2016/17 ab16g Jan 31] £15,000 3-y-o: half-sister to several winners, including useful hurdler/chaser Tarablaze (19f-25f winner, by Kayf Tara): dam (c76/h102) 2m-19f hurdle/chase winner: well beaten in mares bumper. *Susan Gardner*

WUFF (IRE) 9 b.g. Beneficial – Dummy Run (IRE) (Glacial Storm (USA)) [2016/17 **c130**
c132, h–: c16.3s^6 c19.9d^5 c23.8v* c23.8g^5 Apr 9] strong gelding: winning hurdler: useful **h–**
handicap chaser: won at Ffos Las (by 1¼ lengths from Henllan Harri) in March: stays 3m: acts on heavy going: often in cheekpieces: wears tongue tie: often races prominently: temperament under suspicion. *Tom George*

WUN DESTINATION 8 b.m. Dubai Destination (USA) – Mourir d'Aimer (USA) **h–**
(Trempolino (USA)) [2016/17 h–, h–: h18.5m h18.5d^{pu} h16.8m h21.6g Aug 20] lengthy, plain mare: no form over hurdles: in cheekpieces/tongue tie last 2 starts. *John Panvert*

WYATT (IRE) 5 b.g. Lawman (FR) – Umlilo (Mtoto) [2016/17 b–: b15.8g^5 May 30] no **b–**
form in bumpers. *Philip Mitchell*

WYCHWOODS BROOK 11 b.g. Midnight Legend – Miss Millbrook (Meadowbrook) **c115**
[2016/17 c134, h–: c22.3s^5 c24.2s^{pu} c23.4s^{pu} c24.2s^{pu} Feb 12] plain, deep-girthed gelding: **h–**
winning hurdler: fairly useful handicap chaser, largely out of sorts in 2016/17: stays 25f: best form on heavy going. *Harry Whittington*

WYFIELD ROSE 8 b.m. Kayf Tara – Miniature Rose (Anshan) [2016/17 c–, h80: **c–**
h23.9m h23.3g* h22.1g h23.9d* h23.9g* h23.3d* h23.3g^2 h27g* h22s^{pu} h20.9s^{pu} h24.3d **h114**
Apr 21] smallish, workmanlike mare: fair handicap hurdler: won at Hexham (twice), Perth (2 novice events) and Sedgefield in first half of season: well held sole start over fences: stays 27f: acts on good to soft going: wears cheekpieces: tried in tongue tie: front runner/races prominently. *Alistair Whillans*

WYLDE MAGIC (IRE) 6 b.g. Oscar (IRE) – Voodoo Magic (GER) (Platini (GER)) **h115** [2016/17 b98: h20d⁴ h19.5g² h23.5d⁴ h21.2s³ h19.8d³ Mar 11] compact gelding: bumper winner: fairly useful form over hurdles: second in novice at Chepstow in December and third in EBF 'National Hunt' Novices' Handicap Hurdle Final at Sandown in March: stays 21f: acts on soft going: often races prominently. *Evan Williams*

WYMESWOLD 10 b.m. Alflora (IRE) – Dominie Breeze (Primo Dominie) [2016/17 h81: **h60** h23.1g⁴ h19.6g⁶ h22mᵖᵘ Jul 17] poor handicap hurdler: stays 2½m: acts on good to soft going. *Michael Mullineaux*

WYNDCREST (IRE) 10 b.g. Ridgewood Ben – Mollunde (IRE) (Un Desperado (FR)) **c82** [2016/17 c17.2g⁵ c17m³ c16.5gᶠ c21g² c21.1g² c17.4g⁵ c23g⁵ Sep 12] winning pointer: **h–** maiden hurdler: poor maiden chaser: stays 2¾m: best form on good going: wears headgear/ tongue tie: usually races towards rear. *Alexandra Dunn*

WYNFORD (IRE) 4 ch.g. Dylan Thomas (IRE) – Wishing Chair (USA) (Giant's **h83** Causeway (USA)) [2016/17 h15.7sᵖᵘ h16.2v h21.2gᵖᵘ h16m⁵ Apr 13] fairly useful on Flat, stays 2m: poor form over hurdles. *David Loughnane*

WY WORRY (IRE) 7 b.g. Millenary – Don't Fall (IRE) (Castle Keep) [2016/17 b–: **c–** c25.8mᵖᵘ Apr 15] point winner: pulled up in hunter on chasing debut (wore hood). *P. Ponting*

X

XAARCET (IRE) 10 b.g. Xaar – Anoukit (Green Desert (USA)) [2016/17 c118, h–: **c–** c19.3sᵖᵘ Apr 28] stocky gelding: winning hurdler: fairly useful chaser, pulled up sole outing **h–** in 2016/17: stays 3m: acts on heavy going: wears headgear/tongue tie. *T. H. Messenger*

XCLUSIVE 7 b.g. Pivotal – Dance A Daydream (Daylami (IRE)) [2016/17 h–: h16dᵖᵘ **h–** h16.8g h15.8dᵖᵘ Oct 28] maiden hurdler, no form in 2016/17. *Ronald Harris*

XHALE (FR) 5 b.g. Halling (USA) – Xanadu Bliss (FR) (Xaar) [2016/17 h16gᶠ h15.5g **h80** h19.6d h15.5v⁵ h16d³ h15.7s Mar 20] maiden on Flat for Francois Doumen: poor form over hurdles: likely to prove best at sharp 2m: acts on good to soft going. *Caroline Bailey*

XIN CHAO 4 b.f. Showcasing – Nelly's Glen (Efisio) [2016/17 b16.8d Mar 14] £3,800 **b–** 3-y-o: fifth foal: half-sister to 3 winners on Flat, including 6f-1m winner Justice First (by Zebedee): dam 7f winner: well beaten in mares bumper. *Brian Ellison*

XSQUARED (IRE) 9 b.g. Exceed And Excel (AUS) – Jemalina (USA) (Trempolino **c134 p** (USA)) [2016/17 c17d c17m³ c19.5m* c16g* c18.2g* Jul 28] winning hurdler: useful form **h–** over fences: won maiden at Limerick in June, minor event at Wexford in July and novice at Galway (by 6 lengths from Hurricane Ben) later in July: stays 2½m: acts on good to firm and good to soft going: wears headgear: open to further improvement over fences. *Peter Fahey, Ireland*

Y

YABADABADOO 9 b.g. Doyen (IRE) – Kabayil (Dancing Brave (USA)) [2016/17 **c– §** c110§, h–: c17.2dᵖᵘ May 25] lengthy gelding: maiden hurdler: fair chaser, run best excused **h–** sole outing in 2016/17: stays 21f: acts on good to firm and good to soft going: in tongue tie last 3 starts: usually races close up: temperamental. *Emma Lavelle*

YA HAFED 9 ch.g. Haafhd – Rule Britannia (Night Shift (USA)) [2016/17 c86, h–: **c–** c25.7gᵖᵘ c25.5g c25.5sᵖᵘ h25sᵖᵘ Dec 12] smallish, sturdy gelding: fair hurdler/chaser at **h–** best, no form in 2016/17: has worn headgear, including final start: tried in tongue tie: often races towards rear. *Sheena West*

YALA ENKI (FR) 7 b.g. Nickname (FR) – Cadiane (FR) (Cadoudal (FR)) [2016/17 c–, **c152** h140: h22.8v³ c22.9s* c24.2s⁴ c26s⁴ c26.2s* Mar 25] useful-looking gelding: useful **h134** handicap hurdler: third in Betfair Exchange "Fixed Brush" Handicap Hurdle at Haydock (8½ lengths behind Kruzhlinin) in November: smart handicap chaser: won at Haydock (by 8 lengths from Vieux Lille) in December and Kelso (by 7 lengths from Seldom Inn) in March: stays 3¼m: acts on heavy going: front runner. *Venetia Williams*

YALLA HABIBTI 4 b.f. Kayf Tara – Majeeda (IRE) (Jeremy (USA)) [2016/17 b14s **b–** Nov 16] first foal: dam unraced: 25/1, well held in fillies junior bumper at Warwick. *Lisa Williamson*

32Red.com Tommy Whittle Handicap Chase, Haydock—
Yala Enki makes most in a race run in thick fog

YALLTARI 6 gr.g. Kayf Tara – Lily Grey (FR) (Kadalko (FR)) [2016/17 h16s³ h19.7s³ **h100**
Mar 11] fourth foal: dam (b70) lightly raced in bumpers: fair form when third in novice at
Sandown on first of 2 starts over hurdles. *Venetia Williams*

YAMLLIK 5 b.g. King's Best (USA) – Anaamil (IRE) (Darshaan) [2016/17 h15.3dᵖᵘ Nov **h–**
17] fairly useful maiden at best on Flat, lost his way in 2016: in tongue tie,
pulled up in maiden on hurdling debut. *Brian Barr*

YANMARE (IRE) 7 b.g. Soapy Danger – Bell Walks Caroll (IRE) (Carroll House) **c105 x**
[2016/17 c–, h–: c23g⁶ c24d⁴ c25.5s* c24.5d* c26d⁴ c25.5s² c21.7v² c29.2v³ Mar 12] big, **h–**
workmanlike gelding: twice-raced hurdler: fair handicap chaser: won at Uttoxeter in
October, Warwick in November and Towcester in December: stays 29f: acts on heavy
going: tried in headgear: has worn tongue tie, including last 5 starts: often let down by
jumping. *Nigel Twiston-Davies*

YANWORTH 7 ch.g. Norse Dancer (IRE) – Yota (FR) (Galetto (FR)) [2016/17 **h164**
h158p: h19.3d* h16g* h15.3d* h16.4gᵈ h24.7g* Apr 8]
    For much of the season, Yanworth did a good impression of being a Champion
Hurdle horse. So much so that he started 2/1 at Cheltenham. However, in his only
defeat of the campaign, favourite backers soon knew their fate in the Champion
Hurdle as he was almost the first in trouble, seeming to down tools on meeting the
downhill stretch to three out, before running on again late after completely losing
his place. While his owner's two other runners, Buveur d'Air and My Tent Or Yours,
took the first two places, Yanworth was beaten nearly fourteen lengths behind them
in seventh. But given his first chance at three miles, Yanworth ended the season back
in the winner's enclosure, redeeming himself with his eighth win from ten starts over
hurdles in the Liverpool Hurdle. As one of the top novices the previous season, there
was no doubting Yanworth's ability to make his mark in the best open company. But
was he a stayer in the making, or a possible Champion Hurdle winner? He had
cruised through most of his novice hurdles, showing no lack of speed, but at the
same time had been impressive when stepped up to two and a half miles, on heavy
ground at that, at Cheltenham on his final start before the Festival. Over another
furlong in the Baring Bingham, he'd met with his first defeat over hurdles at the
hands of Yorkhill, but enjoyed a much less smooth passage than the winner and saw
the trip out well when pulling clear of the remainder. The ante-post markets gave
little clue in determining what Yanworth's 2017 Festival target might be, offering
him at 16/1 for both the Champion Hurdle and the Stayers'. Given the way he had
shaped in the Baring Bingham, Timeform thought the latter more likely.

*32Red.com Christmas Hurdle, Kempton—Yanworth (No.4) justifies favouritism as
The New One finishes runner-up in the race for a third time; 2013 winner My Tent Or Yours (No.2)
fades into fourth*

The choice of Yanworth's reappearance race didn't shed much light on the matter because that was over an intermediate trip, nineteen furlongs, in the Coral Hurdle at Ascot. Yanworth started a shade of odds on but, in what was to prove something of a theme for his season, in contrast to how smoothly he'd travelled in his novice races, he made hard work of things. There was the excuse of a muddling race, coupled with his first start for eight months, but after leading in the last hundred yards Yanworth prevailed only by three quarters of a length from the tenacious Lil Rockerfeller from whom he was receiving 4 lb. Yanworth's trainer Alan King described the race as 'five minutes of hell', relieved that Yanworth had managed to win despite not having worked on grass beforehand because of the dry autumn. King went on to nominate the Long Walk back at Ascot as Yanworth's possible next race, apparently setting him on a staying course. Faugheen had won the Ascot Hurdle in the same season as his Champion Hurdle, though the previous year's winner Annie Power had gone on to contest the World Hurdle instead. Dawn Run (1983/4) and Morley Street (1990/1) are the only Ascot Hurdle winners who had gone on to win the same season's Champion Hurdle before Faugheen. But six days after Yanworth's Ascot win, J. P. McManus' new acquisition Unowhatimeanharry made a winning reappearance in the Long Distance Hurdle at Newbury and it was he, not Yanworth, who ended up going for the Long Walk in which he beat Lil Rockerfeller with more authority than Yanworth had done.

Instead, Yanworth made his next appearance in the 32Red.com Christmas Hurdle at Kempton, though what the race gained with his presence it lost with the absence of both Faugheen (denied the opportunity of winning it for the third year running) and Vroum Vroum Mag who went for Leopardstown's Christmas Hurdle instead over three miles, which she won. Yanworth's Champion Hurdle credentials still looked likely to be tested at Kempton with My Tent Or Yours and The New One among his four rivals. My Tent Or Yours had beaten The New One half a length in the 2013 Christmas Hurdle, though in their most recent meeting The New One had conceded 8 lb to My Tent Or Yours when winning the International Hurdle at Cheltenham for the third time. Ch'tibello, who had My Tent Or Yours back in third in the Betfair Price Rush Hurdle at Haydock, and the hopelessly outclassed mare Gray Wolf River, a poor maiden, completed the field. Yanworth was sent off the 5/4 favourite, just ahead of The New One at 13/8 with My Tent Or Yours on 4/1. With his chief rivals becoming embroiled in a battle between themselves—My Tent Or Yours was asked to harry The New One for the lead from a long way out—Yanworth stayed on to lead approaching the last and ran out the winner by three and a quarter lengths. The New One held on for second with Ch'tibello, another two and a quarter lengths back, staying on to take third from My Tent Or Yours on the run-in, while Gray Wolf

River completed in her own time for fifth prize money. Although he won, Yanworth didn't entirely convince as a potential Champion Hurdle winner, largely due to some indifferent jumping; he made a mistake at the fifth and, in a less than fluent round overall, was also untidy at the last.

It was easier to be dismissive about Yanworth's Champion Hurdle chances all the time that Faugheen and Annie Power were still in the reckoning to regain or retain their crowns, but both of those had fallen by the wayside by the time Yanworth landed odds of 5/2-on in the Betway Kingwell Hurdle at Wincanton in February. He had been due to contest the Contenders Hurdle at Sandown earlier in the month, but missed that engagement after reportedly tweaking a muscle, his place taken instead by his owner's Buveur d'Air who made a surprise return to hurdling after winning both his novice chases. Buveur d'Air won easily at Sandown but Yanworth again made rather heavy weather of his task at Wincanton where he was fitted with cheekpieces for the first time. He did what was necessary, however, and, when shaken up, stayed on to beat Ch'tibello by a length with his stable-companion Sceau Royal another length and a quarter back in third, conceding 4 lb to both placed horses. Since the remeasuring of Britain's jumps courses, what was formerly Wincanton's 'two miles' is officially recognised nowadays as being actually nearer fifteen furlongs, making it one of the least exacting tests of stamina a jumper is likely to face. That wouldn't have been ideal for Yanworth and, with only one defeat to his name in eight starts over hurdles, he had put together a better record than most horses can boast going into a Champion Hurdle, even if he hadn't totally convinced in compiling it.

Even his own jockey was seemingly not entirely won over. Barry Geraghty had ridden Yanworth in all his races over hurdles, but was intent on leaving the decision about which of the McManus entries he would ride until as late as possible. In the end, it was a choice he didn't have to make. A fall on Triumph Hurdle contender Charli Parcs at Kempton in February left Geraghty with broken ribs and a punctured lung which ruled him out of the Festival. Yanworth, potentially, would have been just one among another very strong book of rides for Geraghty who had ridden at least one winner at every Festival since 2002. Geraghty's misfortune looked like being a good opportunity for McManus' Irish-based number-two Mark Walsh to ride a first Festival winner. But Yanworth's disappointing display in the Champion Hurdle (where he wore cheekpieces again) was followed by falls on Jer's Girl in the David Nicholson Mares' Hurdle and on Consul de Thaix in the following day's Baring Bingham, Walsh sustaining concussion and fracturing his left leg in the latter incident.

The Champion Hurdle proved a race to forget for Yanworth's trainer too as he was fined £2,000 in July after Yanworth's post-race drugs test returned a positive result, revealing traces of the anti-inflammatory triamcinolone acetonide or TCA, a substance which can be administered legitimately in training for therapeutic purposes. The penalty was above the entry-level figure as, in the opinion of the BHA's Disciplinary Panel, King's decision not to pursue elective testing was an unreasonable one in all the circumstances.' The trainer had relied instead on veterinary advice which suggested that there was no real risk of the substance still being in Yanworth's system on Champion Hurdle day, twenty days after the medication was last administered (Yanworth returned a negative test after the Kingwell, sixteen days after his first treatment with the medication Adcortyl which contains TCA). The Panel referred to several recent cases in which TCA had remained present in a horse's system well beyond the withdrawal period advised by vets, something which both the BHA itself and the National Trainers' Federation had emphasised, with the BHA guidance published as recently as February 2017: 'To be clear, there is NO published detection time for intra-articular corticosteroids and the mandatory fourteen day stand-down period should not be used as a detection time ... Trainers and their veterinary surgeons should take into account the above factors when deciding upon an adequate withdrawal period.'

Among the other recent cases of positive results for TCA which the Panel implied should have served as a warning was that of the Martin Keighley-trained Any Currency who became the first Cheltenham Festival winner to be disqualified

Ryanair Stayers' Liverpool Hurdle, Aintree—Barry Geraghty has to get serious as Yanworth holds off Irish raiders Supasundae (right) and Snow Falcon (left) over a longer trip

on technical grounds since 1980 when testing positive after his success in the 2016 Glenfarclas Chase, the cross-country event, almost six weeks after receiving an Adcortyl injection, something his trainer had described as a 'freakish' result. More embarrassingly for Yanworth's trainer, though, he had already experienced a similar case when Midnight Cataria was disqualified after finishing second at Kempton in October 2015. King had been fined £1,000 on that occasion after the positive test was traced to an injection of Adcortyl more than *seven weeks* (fifty-one days) beforehand. The Panel referred to the availability of elective testing, at a cost of £123.92 plus VAT, which allows connections to screen a horse prior to a race to make sure that any medication it has been receiving has cleared its system. Indeed, just such a test was conducted on McManus' 2011 Champion Hurdle favourite Binocular, the positive outcome (resulting from medication used to treat a skin allergy) forcing his withdrawal, though a lack of transparency and delays in communicating this information to the betting public led to criticism of how the situation was handled, both by the BHA and by Binocular's trainer Nicky Henderson. The Yanworth inquiry, incidentally, was the first to be conducted by the BHA's newly constituted Disciplinary Panel, about which there is more in the Introduction.

Geraghty was fit again for Yanworth's first try over three miles in the Ryanair Stayers' Liverpool Hurdle on Grand National day. None of the first three from the Stayers' Hurdle was in the line-up (they all ran later at Punchestown instead) and Yanworth was sent off the 9/4 favourite (albeit easy to back on the day) against ten rivals, among whom Cole Harden (fourth), Snow Falcon (fifth) and Ballyoptic (pulled up) had contested the Stayers' and were among Yanworth's main threats, along with the Coral Cup winner Supasundae. Yanworth had the cheekpieces left off and looked more at home over the longer trip, though Geraghty had to subject him to strong pressure on the run-in to prevail. Yanworth moved up two out to jump that flight in company with Snow Falcon, Ballyoptic and Supasundae, while, of that leading quartet, only Balloptic had dropped out of contention jumping the last. Geraghty's use of the whip was far from pretty, certainly fully deserving of the four-day ban he incurred as a result (for excessive force and exceeding the limit), as he drove out Yanworth to win by a length and three quarters of a length from Supasundae and Snow Falcon, with Coral Cup runner-up Taquin du Seuil not far behind in fourth. With those making the frame behind him no better than smart, Yanworth didn't need to reproduce the best form he had shown over shorter trips.

Yanworth (ch.g. 2010)	Norse Dancer (IRE) (b 2000)	Halling (ch 1991)	Diesis / Dance Machine
		River Patrol (b 1988)	Rousillon / Boathouse
	Yota (FR) (ch 1995)	Galetto (ch 1986)	Caro / Gold Bird
		Junta (b 1990)	Cariellor / Just Abroad

Yanworth's pedigree was covered in his essay in last year's Annual and, in truth, there's not much to be learned from it that we don't know already about him. He is the best horse to emerge from his immediate family on the distaff side, though his dam is a half-sister to Juntico and Azulejo who were useful winners at Auteuil, and he remains easily the best jumper sired by the high-class but temperamental middle-distance performer Norse Dancer. Yanworth also stays better than might have been gleaned from the records of his closest relatives; his dam's chase win in France came at around two and a quarter miles and none of her four other winners has been successful over as far as three miles. Yanworth is a compact gelding, and not an obvious chasing type, though he is reportedly to be sent over fences in the autumn, starting off over two and a half miles. He stays three miles and acts on heavy ground. *Alan King*

YASIR (USA) 9 b.g. Dynaformer (USA) – Khazayin (USA) (Bahri (USA)) [2016/17 h89§: h17.2g Jun 1] close-coupled gelding: fair hurdler at best, well held sole outing in 2016/17: stays 2¾m: acts on heavy going: has worn headgear: tried in tongue tie: often races in rear: moody. *Sophie Leech*   **h– §**

YASOOD (IRE) 4 b.g. Acclamation – Lucina (Machiavellian (USA)) [2016/17 h15.9m^{ur} h15.8g Oct 2] fair on Flat, stays 9.5f: well beaten on completed start over hurdles. *Phil McEntee*   **h–**

YEATCAMP LADY (IRE) 6 b.m. Yeats (IRE) – Lady Pennekamp (IRE) (Pennekamp (USA)) [2016/17 b15.8d⁴ b17.2g h20.2g⁵ h18d Dec 3] sixth foal: half-sister to a winning pointer by Indian Danehill: dam unraced: poor form in bumpers: no form over hurdles: tried in hood/tongue tie. *Paul Stafford, Ireland*   **h– b70**

YEATS BABY (IRE) 5 b.m. Yeats (IRE) – Cabo (FR) (Sagamix (FR)) [2016/17 h16g h16.3m h19.5d h15.7d h20.6d Dec 26] third foal: closely related to 1½m winner Secure Cloud (by High Chaparral): dam (h97), 2m hurdle winner, also 1¼m winner on Flat: fourth in Irish mares maiden point: no form over hurdles: in cheekpieces/tongue tie last 2 starts. *Ian Williams*   **h–**

YELLOW ADMIRAL (USA) 4 ch.g. Street Cry (IRE) – Painted Lady (USA) (Broad Brush (USA)) [2016/17 b16s Jan 6] 61/1, well held in bumper. *Philip Kirby*   **b–**

YELLOW KANGAROO (IRE) 5 b.g. Aussie Rules (USA) – Sue N Win (IRE) (Beneficial) [2016/17 b16.7d⁵ Jan 3] €16,000 3-y-o: fifth foal: brother to bumper winner/ fair hurdler Petuna (2m winner) and half-brother to useful hurdler/very smart chaser Rock The World (2m-2¼m winner, by Orpen): dam (h109) bumper/2m hurdle winner: 33/1, fifth in bumper at Bangor (11¼ lengths behind Just A Sting) on debut. *Evan Williams*   **b81**

YES DADDY (IRE) 9 b.g. Golan (IRE) – Hollygrove Samba (IRE) (Accordion) [2016/17 h111: h20g² h19.9g³ h19.9g⁴ c16m² Nov 2] lengthy, useful-looking gelding: fair handicap hurdler: fair form over fences: better effort when second in novice handicap at Chepstow: stays 2½m: acts on good to firm and good to soft going: has worn headgear, including final start. *Robert Stephens*   **c108 h108**

YES I DID (IRE) / b.m. Craigsteel – Younevertoldme (IRE) (Simply Great (FR)) [2016/17 h118, b97: h21.6d⁵ c21.1g* c20.8g⁶ c24.2s⁴ Dec 27] tall mare: fairly useful handicap hurdler: fair form over fences: won maiden at Fontwell in November: stays 25f: acts on soft going: tried in cheekpieces: front runner/races prominently. *Dan Skelton*   **c109 h109**

YES TOM (IRE) 12 gr.g. Tikkanen (USA) – Ammieanne (IRE) (Zaffaran (USA)) **c133**
[2016/17 c129, h128: c23m³ c20g c22.5g^pu Jul 27] lengthy gelding: winning hurdler: **h–**
useful handicap chaser: third at Ballinrobe (7½ lengths behind King Leon) in May: stays
3¼m: acts on good to firm and heavy going: wears headgear: tried in tongue tie: often races
towards rear. *Stuart Crawford, Ireland*

YEWLANDS (IRE) 6 b.g. Scorpion (IRE) – Calimesa (IRE) (Desert Prince (IRE)) **h79**
[2016/17 h85: h16.2g⁵ h20g⁶ Oct 23] sturdy gelding: poor form over hurdles: dead. *Jonjo*
O'Neill

YOOHOOF 5 b.m. Black Sam Bellamy (IRE) – Piece of Magic (Alflora (IRE)) [2016/17 **b–**
b15.8d May 5] first foal: dam (h68), maiden hurdler (stayed 23f), half-sister to fair hurdler/
fairly useful chaser (stayed 3¼m) Take A Bow: tailed off in mares bumper. *Michael Easterby*

YORGONNAHEARMEROAR (IRE) 6 b.g. Scorpion (IRE) – Etoile Margot (FR) **h115**
(Garde Royale) [2016/17 b88: b15.8g h15.8v⁴ h15.8d⁶ h16.6d⁴ h16.2v* h16v² h19.2m³ **b72**
Apr 13] poor form in bumpers: fairly useful form over hurdles: won novice handicap at
Hereford in February: should stay further than 2m: acts well on heavy ground: wears hood:
front runner/races prominently. *Henry Oliver*

YORKHILL (IRE) 7 ch.g. Presenting – Lightning Breeze (IRE) (Saddlers' Hall **c161 p**
(IRE)) [2016/17 h163p, b125p: h16d⁴ c16v* c19g* c19.9g* c20d² Apr 16] **h–**
  'He was a wild ride. He jumped left-handed, hung left-handed and was only
run on left-handed tracks. On his day he was a smashing horse but quite horrific
to ride.' So was the description of Charlie Potheen by Terry Biddlecombe, whose
successful spare ride on the tearaway front runner in the 1973 Great Yorkshire Chase
helped land him the plum role as stable jockey to Fulke Walwyn for his final season
in the saddle. Charlie Potheen had already gone through several jockeys by this
stage, and had given stand-in partner Richard Pitman a late scare when winning
the Hennessy Gold Cup at Newbury earlier that winter by nearly running out on
the run-in after hanging violently left. Biddlecombe was widely regarded as the
strongest jockey of his generation and went on to partner Charlie Potheen to a fine
third behind stable-companion The Dikler (under another strong man of that era
Ron Barry) in the 1973 Cheltenham Gold Cup, but even he endured 'an unholy
ride' aboard Charlie Potheen at Newbury later that year. 'Quite early on in the race
Charlie started to hang with me. I had to pull with all my might to stop him from
running out at the first in the straight. When he came to the last ditch, he was full of
running but he had cocked his jaw on me by this time, and I had to pull him right
off the runway at the side of the fence to get him in any sort of position to jump it,'
was Biddlecombe's version of the build-up to a bone-crunching fall which seemed
to leave its mark for the remainder of Charlie Potheen's career ('Charlie Potheen was
never the same horse afterwards'). Happily, The Dikler enjoyed a far longer career
at the top, but he shared many the same traits of Charlie Potheen during much of that
time. A giant, The Dikler was a headstrong sort who had developed a reputation for
running out during his Irish pointing days and could be hard to control on his way
to post, let alone in the race itself. He also often displayed a tendency to hang left.
Indeed, just three weeks before his finest hour in the 1973 Cheltenham Gold Cup,
The Dikler blotted his copybook by losing the Fairlawne Chase at Windsor in the
stewards' room—his then-jockey Barry Brogan had been powerless to prevent him
hanging so badly left that second-past-the-post Spanish Steps nearly ended up in the
River Thames!
  Fulke Walwyn is considered by many to be the finest trainer of chasers in
National Hunt history, so the fact that he (and leading jockeys of that era) struggled
to rein in the wayward tendencies of this headstrong pair is a perfect illustration of
the challenges involved in handling thoroughbreds. 'I'm 64 or 65 kilos and you're
sitting on 450 kilos—physically you cannot dominate that, it just doesn't add up.
If the horse wants to, he's going to win that argument every day of the week, so it
becomes a question of technique, knack and respect between the two of you. You
have to win the mental battle before you've any chance with the physical one,' is the
verdict of one of today's top jump jockeys Ruby Walsh, who mused last winter that
thoroughbreds were similar in temperament to children aged six to eight. 'If a child
of that age is grumpy, it usually just means they're hungry, tired or sick—it's the
same with horses. They share that innocence and willingness to please, there is no

JLT Novices' Chase (Golden Miller), Cheltenham—normal service resumes for the Mullins-Walsh team as Yorkhill opens day three of the Festival with a convincing victory over Top Notch (centre) and the grey Disko

nastiness in them.' As with children, however, some horses are less straightforward than others, hence the use of headgear and special bits or bridles to help to make them more tractable. Indeed, even Walsh conceded that some could test his patience at times—'Some are a bit like trying to do homework with a six-year-old whose mind keeps wandering off to the playground all the time …'

It is quite possible Walsh would have favoured meting out a month's detention to Yorkhill in the immediate aftermath of the Ryanair Gold Cup Novices' Chase at Fairyhouse in April, where the 7/4-on shot snatched defeat from victory's jaws in hugely frustrating fashion, losing his hundred per cent record over fences in the process. Refusing to settle in the early stages, Yorkhill pulled his way to the front with a circuit to go and then proceeded to give away ground at every fence thereafter by jumping markedly left, a trait which caused him to lose vital momentum (and the lead) when briefly shaping as if he might run out at the last. A strong late rally failed by just a neck against the fortunate winner Road To Respect, the fact that Yorkhill would have won on the bridle but for that last-fence incident some testament to his ability, given how much he had done wrong in the race before that. In truth, Yorkhill's quirks have been evident from the very start—he ran out with the race at his mercy in a four-year-old maiden point on his debut—and he has always shown a tendency to hang/jump left, though the latter trait hasn't prevented him recording five wins on right-handed tracks, including when an effortless wide-margin winner (8/1-on) of a two-mile beginners event at Fairyhouse on his chasing debut in December. In addition, one of his most errant displays before the Ryanair Gold Cup actually came on a left-handed track, when scraping home in the previous season's Mersey Novices' Hurdle at Aintree after giving Paul Townend (standing in for the injured Walsh) a torrid time of things, while he had jumped even more markedly left on occasions when suffering the only other defeat of his career (at 9/4-on) when fourth in the Champion Novices' Hurdle at Punchestown, technically his first start of the latest season, an experience that may explain his absence from the 2017 Punchestown Festival. The chances are that Yorkhill's appearances on the racecourse are always going to be something of a white-knuckle ride—for punters and jockeys alike!

That said, as *Chasers & Hurdlers 2015/16* stressed, the good points still far outweigh the bad ones so far as Yorkhill is concerned. He is clearly one of the best horses in training, while the fact that he figures so highly in the pecking order at Willie Mullins' all-powerful Closutton yard is also very revealing. After all, he is unbeaten in two appearances on the biggest stage of all, his victory in the Golden Miller Novices' Chase (branded nowadays as the JLT) at Cheltenham in March supplementing his victory over Yanworth in the Baring Bingham Novices' Hurdle at the Festival twelve months earlier. Yorkhill lined up against seven rivals in the Golden Miller, for which he was sent off the 6/4 favourite—those odds would probably have been shorter had Mullins and Walsh not drawn a rare blank on the opening two days of the meeting (a public schooling session by Yorkhill after racing at Leopardstown earlier in the month had been perceived as unconvincing and had also probably put some punters off). Yorkhill was the least experienced chaser in the Golden Miller field, his only outing over fences since that Fairyhouse stroll having come in a Grade 3 novice over nineteen furlongs at Leopardstown in January, where he had beaten Jett cosily by a length and a quarter. As it was, Yorkhill produced an accomplished round of jumping at Cheltenham, possibly helped by hugging the inner throughout and enjoying plenty of cover for most of the way—identical tactics, incidentally, to those Walsh had adopted on him for that Baring Bingham win. Having travelled strongly through the race under a patient ride (neatly sidestepping the fallen Balko des Flos four out), Yorkhill was produced by Walsh with a daring run up the inside of Top Notch (who lost momentum with a mistake) to take over at the second last. A smooth success seemed on the cards at this stage, but Yorkhill typically had other ideas and, not for the first time, idled briefly on the run-in. However, he found plenty once Walsh got serious with him and held off the rallying Top Notch by a length, with a further three lengths back to fellow Irish raider Disko in third—margins which rather underestimate Yorkhill's true superiority on the day. It was a third successive win in the race for Mullins and Walsh, following those of Vautour in 2015 and Black Hercules (for Yorkhill's owners Andrea and Graham Wylie) in 2015. It began a red letter day for the trainer-jockey combination as they also teamed up with Un de Sceaux, Nichols Canyon and Let's Dance to complete a memorable four-timer. Nichols Canyon, incidentally, was another winner for the Wylies and took their Cheltenham Festival tally to thirteen. Nearly half of those wins have been provided by Mullins, who is now the Wylies' sole trainer—they initially split their horses between Paul Nicholls and Mullins after their previous trainer Howard Johnson left the sport.

Yorkhill (IRE) (ch.g. 2010)	Presenting (br 1992)	Mtoto (b 1983)	Busted
			Amazer
		D'Azy (b 1984)	Persian Bold
			Belle Viking
	Lightning Breeze (IRE) (b 2004)	Saddlers' Hall (b 1988)	Sadler's Wells
			Sunny Valley
		Park Breeze (br 1988)	Strong Gale
			Park Delight

A rangy gelding, Yorkhill has raced only on good going or softer to date (acts on heavy), with both of his Cheltenham Festival wins coming on good. He has yet to tackle distances further than twenty-one furlongs under Rules but, despite his exuberant style of racing, he promises to stay a fair bit further if his breeding is anything to go by. Yorkhill's sire the 1995 Derby third Presenting was put down in August 2017 at the age of twenty-five due to the infirmities of old age. He was a first rate jumping sire and a grand servant over two decades to the County Cork stud Glenview, the National Hunt arm of Rathbarry Stud. Presenting started off at a fee of IR£850 and gradually rose to the top of the tree to become champion sire in the combined lists for Britain and Ireland in 2006/7, 2008/9, 2009/10 and 2010/11. He had the highest fee of any active jumping stallion in Britain and Ireland when he stood at €12,000 in 2011 and 2012 and proved a worthy successor to that other fine Rathbarry champion jumps stallion Strong Gale. Presenting sired two winners of the Cheltenham Gold Cup, War of Attrition (2006) and Denman (2008), and also sired the 2011 Grand National winner Ballabriggs (and three winners of the Irish Grand National). Yorkhill's pedigree on the distaff side was discussed in detail in *Chasers & Hurdlers 2015/16* and it bears repeating that he comes from an excellent jumping family, with Yorkhill's dam Lightning Breeze being a half-sister to the top-class staying chaser The Listener among others. There is little to add to what appeared then, other than to report that Vieux Lille (whose dam is a half-sister to Lightning Breeze) showed useful form at up to three miles over fences in the latest season, albeit without winning. The debate about what sort of trips Yorkhill will be campaigned over in 2017/18 will have to be put on the back burner until connections have actually decided what discipline he'll be tackling. Yorkhill's pronounced left-handed bias on that final start at Fairyhouse prompted Mullins to consider putting him back over the smaller obstacles. 'At home, he seems to jump straight enough! You think a horse will get better with age, but over fences it seems to bring it out more in him. He might be easier to ride over hurdles, it might be a lot easier on jockeys.'

Regardless of whether a campaign over hurdles or fences is chosen for him, it would be no surprise to see Yorkhill campaigned predominantly on left-handed courses from now on. Horses believed to favour right-handed tracks over left-handed tracks, or vice versa, is an overused (and usually bogus) theory that is too readily bandied about by punters and/or pundits but, in extreme cases, such as Yorkhill it is easy to see why it can be a big factor. The top-class chaser Captain Chris, for instance, is a recent example of a horse who was at least a stone better on right-handed tracks because of a tendency to hang and jump in that direction. In Mullins and Walsh (or his excellent understudy Townend), Yorkhill could hardly have a better team to harness his skills and, for all his waywardness, he remains with the potential to go to the very top, be it over hurdles or fences. It says plenty for him that Yorkhill is in the top four of the ante-post betting lists for both the 2018 Champion Hurdle (10/1) and 2018 Cheltenham Gold Cup (8/1) at the time of writing. *W. P. Mullins, Ireland*

YORKIST (IRE) 9 ch.g. Urban Ocean (FR) – Kilbarry Demon (IRE) (Bob's Return (IRE)) [2016/17 c130, h–: c16.9m⁶ c15.2s* c16.4d³ c15.8g⁴ c15.5g⁴ Apr 22] workmanlike gelding: winning hurdler: useful handicap chaser: won at Wetherby in December: third at Doncaster (3 lengths behind Upsilon Bleu) in January: stays 19f: acts on good to firm and heavy going: has worn headgear: wears tongue tie: usually races towards rear/travels strongly. *Dan Skelton* **c133 h–**

YORKSTERS PRINCE (IRE) 10 b.g. Beat Hollow – Odalisque (IRE) (Machiavellian (USA)) [2016/17 h16.2m⁵ h16.2m⁵ h16.2d⁶ h23.1gⁿᵘ Jul 31] well held in points: poor form over hurdles. *Jean McGregor* **h76**

YOU'LL DO 4 b.g. Approve (IRE) – Tentears (Cadeaux Genereux) [2016/17 h17d Apr 5] fair maiden on Flat, stays 9f: in tongue tie, tailed off in novice on hurdling debut. *Maurice Barnes* **h–**

YOUNEVERCALL (IRE) 6 b.g. Yeats (IRE) – Afarka (IRE) (Kahyasi) [2016/17 h126: h21g* h24d Apr 27] useful form over hurdles: won handicap at Kempton in November: stays 3m: acts on good to soft going. *Kim Bailey* **h141**

YOUNG CHEDDAR (IRE) 10 b.m. Croco Rouge (IRE) – Sin Ceist Eile (IRE) (Simply Great (FR)) [2016/17 c110, h–: c23.4dᵖᵘ Mar 24] smallish mare: maiden pointer: maiden hurdler: fair chaser, reportedly bled sole outing under Rules in 2016/17: stays 3¼m: acts on heavy going. *Ms G. Howell* **c– h–**

YOUNG DILLON (IRE) 8 b.g. Vinnie Roe (IRE) – Rongai (IRE) (Commanche Run) [2016/17 h126: h24.1g* h24g³ h25.4dᵖᵘ h25.6g* h26.5g² h23.9g⁴ h24.7d⁴ h23.1g h22.8g² Apr 15] useful hurdler: won novice at Wetherby (by 1¼ lengths from Some Kinda Lama) early in season and handicap at Fontwell in September: stays 3¼m: acts on soft going: wears headgear. *Dr Richard Newland* **h131**

YOUNG HURRICANE (IRE) 11 b.g. Oscar (IRE) – Georgia On My Mind (FR) (Belmez (USA)) [2016/17 c94, h–: c19.4gᵘʳ c24.2g² Apr 25] multiple winning pointer: winning hurdler: fair chaser: stays 25f: acts on heavy going: has worn blinkers/tongue tie. *G. C. Brewer* **c111 h–**

YOUNG LOU 8 b.m. Kadastrof (FR) – Wanna Shout (Missed Flight) [2016/17 h88: h23.1g² h23g h23.3v³ h24d² h25.5s³ h25.5s h25.6s⁴ h26v⁵ h26v² Mar 22] modest handicap hurdler: stays 3¼m: acts on heavy going: wears headgear: tried in tongue tie: often races prominently. *Robin Dickin* **h89**

YOUNG PALM (IRE) 10 gr.g. Great Palm (USA) – Young Amelie (FR) (Garde Royale) [2016/17 c100, h–: c17d h17d h16.2s Jul 10] maiden hurdler/chaser, no form in 2016/17: left Stuart Crawford after first start: has worn headgear, including in 2016/17: wears tongue tie. *Patrick Griffin, Ireland* **c– h–**

YOUR BUSY (IRE) 14 h g. Anshan – Springfort Society (IRE) (Moscow Society (USA)) [2016/17 c131, h124: h24d⁵ c26m² h24g² c26.1g h22g³ c25g⁶ c24v c23.6g³ c25g² c25gᵘʳ Nov 11] workmanlike gelding: fairly useful handicap hurdler/chaser: stays 3¼m: acts on good to firm and heavy going: tried in cheekpieces: wears tongue tie: front runner/races prominently. *James A. Nash, Ireland* **c128 h119**

YOU

YOU'RE A LADY 5 b.m. Midnight Legend – Pulling Strings (IRE) (Accordion) [2016/17 **b—**
b16g⁶ Apr 17] fourth foal: sister to fairly useful hurdler A Shade of Bay (2m-19f winner),
stayed 3m, and half-sister to fair hurdler Pulling Power (2m winner, by Erhaab): dam
unraced: well beaten in mares bumper. *Kim Bailey*

YOURHOLIDAYISOVER (IRE) 10 ch.g. Sulamani (IRE) – Whitehaven (Top Ville) **c87 §**
[2016/17 c–, h–: c15.7d⁴ c16.5g⁶ c15.7g² c17.4m⁴ c15.7m² c15.7g² h15.7d³ c16s² c16.4d³ **h70 §**
c16s³ c17v* c17v² Jan 30] rather leggy gelding: poor handicap chaser nowadays: modest
handicap chaser: won at Plumpton in January: stays 2½m: acts on heavy going: wears
headgear/tongue tie: usually travels strongly but finds little under pressure, and is one to be
wary of. *Tom Gretton*

YOUR PREFERENCE 8 b.g. Dolpour – Royal Reference (Royal Fountain) [2016/17 **h—**
h19.3gᵖᵘ Apr 15] well held completed start in points: in cheekpieces, pulled up in novice
on hurdling debut. *Lisa Harrison*

YOUR TURN (IRE) 6 b.m. Milan – Pop Princess (Compton Place) [2016/17 h16.2s² **h95**
h25.3sᶠ h18.9v² h17g⁵ Apr 15] £11,000 4-y-o: fifth foal: closely related to fair hurdler
Popboru (2½m winner) and fairly useful hurdler/winning pointer Boru Boy (3m winner),
both by Brian Boru: dam, ran twice on Flat, half-sister to useful hurdler around 2m Moving
On Up: third on completed start in Irish points: modest form over hurdles: tried in headgear.
Tom Gretton

YOU SAY WHAT (IRE) 7 b.g. Milan – Wave Back (IRE) (Bob Back (USA)) [2016/17 **c—**
h128, b86: c23.6g c24.2vᵖᵘ c25.7sᵖᵘ h23.9g Apr 9] workmanlike gelding: winning Irish **h109**
pointer: fair handicap hurdler: no form over fences: left Neil King after third start: stays
25f: acts on heavy going: tried in cheekpieces: races prominently. *David Pipe*

YOU TOO PET (IRE) 9 b.g. Norwich – Pollys Pet (IRE) (Little Bighorn) [2016/17 c101, **c88**
h–: c26g c23g² c25.2s² c25.7v⁴ c25.1v³ c24s³ h23.1g Apr 11] multiple point winner: twice- **h—**
raced hurdler: modest maiden chaser: stays 25f: acts on soft going: in cheekpieces last 3
starts: often races towards rear. *Jennifer Mason*

YPSILANTI (IRE) 8 ch.g. Beneficial – Glacialjoy (IRE) (Glacial Storm (USA)) [2016/17 **c110**
c25.3g c22.6m⁴ h15.5g h23.3v c19.1g* h19.2v⁶ c15.7s² c20.5m³ Apr 18] €9,000 3-y-o: **h75 p**
fourth foal: brother to a winning pointer: dam, pulled up in bumper only start, half-sister to
fairly useful chaser (winner up to 21f) Va Vavoom: winning pointer: poor form over
hurdles: fair form over fences: won novice handicap at Doncaster in January: stays 2½m:
acts on good to firm and heavy going: capable of better over hurdles. *Tom Weston*

YUKON DELTA (IRE) 10 ch.g. Old Vic – Red Fern (IRE) (Mister Lord (USA)) **c97 §**
[2016/17 h25.6d² h23.3s h25.6s³ h20.5g* h25.6g* c25.7g³ c23.6d⁵ h19.5v h25gᵘʳ h25m² **h96 §**
Apr 17] modest handicap hurdler: won at Plumpton in October and Fontwell in November:
modest form over fences: stays 3¼m: acts on soft and good to firm going: usually wears
headgear: temperamental. *Gary Moore*

YUL FINEGOLD (IRE) 7 b.g. Invincible Spirit (IRE) – Mascara (Mtoto) [2016/17 h–: **h83**
h15.8g⁴ h15.8g h19.6mᵖᵘ Oct 2] maiden hurdler, modest at best: best effort at 17f: acts on
heavy going. *Conor Dore*

YUR NEXT (IRE) 9 br.m. Definite Article – Listen Up (Good Thyne (USA)) [2016/17 **h103**
h86: h19.6m⁶ h21.6sᵖᵘ h19g³ h23.9m³ h23.9g* h23.9g² h23.9g* Jan 27] Irish point winner:
fair handicap hurdler: won at Taunton in December and January (novice event): stays 3m:
acts on good to firm going: in blinkers last 5 starts: wears tongue tie: usually races close up,
often travels strongly. *Johnny Farrelly*

Z

ZABANA (IRE) 8 ch.g. Halling (USA) – Gandia (IRE) (Danehill (USA)) [2016/17 c154p, **c161**
h–: c25d* c19.5g⁴ c20d* c24d Dec 28] well-made gelding: winning hurdler: high-class **h—**
chaser: won minor event at Gowran (by 1½ lengths from Kitten Rock, with Champagne
West third) in November: stays 25f: acts on good to firm and heavy going: front runner/
races prominently. *Andrew Lynch, Ireland*

ZABEEL STAR (IRE) 5 ch.g. Arcano (IRE) – Deep Winter (Pivotal) [2016/17 h75: **h—**
h15.7g Mar 28] lightly-raced maiden hurdler, well held sole outing in 2016/17. *Graeme
McPherson*

ZAINAT (IRE) 4 b.g. Masterofthehorse (IRE) – Think Fast (IRE) (Songandaprayer **h82**
(USA)) [2016/17 h16.2m⁴ h16g⁶ Oct 12] fair on Flat, stays 8.5f: poor form over hurdles.
K. R. Burke

ZAKETY ZAK 6 b.g. Overbury (IRE) – Jeanne d'Arc (Highest Honor (FR)) [2016/17 **h76** h59, b76: h16g h19.7g h21.3g* h24d⁴ h20.6s Dec 8] poor handicap hurdler: won conditionals novice event at Wetherby in October: will prove best up to 3m: acts on good to soft going: wears cheekpieces: has looked less than straightforward. *James Turner*

ZALGARRY (FR) 10 b.g. Ballingarry (IRE) – Spleen (FR) (Sillery (USA)) [2016/17 c–, **c–** h113: h19d h20d* h20d² Jun 29] fairly useful handicap hurdler: won at Ffos Las in June: **h116** fell on only outing over fences (in 2011/12): stays 3m: acts on good to firm and heavy going: tried in cheekpieces: usually races towards rear. *Arthur Whitehead*

ZALVADOS (FR) 4 ch.g. Soldier of Fortune (IRE) – Zariyana (IRE) (Desert Prince **h118** (IRE)) [2016/17 h16.3s² h17s² h15.7d² h16d³ h16.5g³ Apr 8] rather sparely-made gelding: fairly useful on Flat (stays 1¼m) for H-A. Pantall: fairly useful form over hurdles: placed all 5 starts, including in juvenile at Haydock in February and conditionals/amateur handicap at Aintree in April: raced around 2m: acts on soft going: tried in cheekpieces: in tongue tie last 3 starts: often travels strongly. *Oliver Greenall*

ZAMARKHAN (FR) 4 b.g. Great Journey (JPN) – Zannkiya (Sendawar (IRE)) [2016/17 **b73** b16.8g³ Apr 26] pulled up in point: 2/1, third in maiden bumper at Exeter (10¼ lengths behind Jaunty Flyer). *Tom Lacey*

ZAMA ZAMA 10 b.g. Sakhee (USA) – Insinuation (IRE) (Danehill (USA)) [2016/17 **c96** c106§, h–: c20s⁴ c19.9g c21.7g⁵ c16.1g⁵ Mar 20] good-topped gelding: winning hurdler: **h–** fair handicap chaser, below form in 2016/17: stays 25f, usually races at shorter: acts on good to firm and heavy going: usually in headgear. *Evan Williams*

ZAMDY MAN 8 b.g. Authorized (IRE) – Lauderdale (GER) (Nebos (GER)) [2016/17 **c143** c123p, h–: c16s* c20d² c16s* c16.3s* c20.4g Mar 14] strong, good-topped gelding: **h–** winning hurdler: useful chaser: won maiden at Uttoxeter early in season, and novices at Hereford in January and Newcastle (by 2 lengths from The Dutchman) in February: unproven beyond 2m: acts on heavy going. *Venetia Williams*

ZAMMIA (FR) 5 b.g. Kingsalsa (USA) – Aisyacall (FR) (Kahyasi) [2016/17 b–: b15.3m **b–** May 10] no form in bumpers. *David Dennis*

ZAMOYSKI 7 ch.g. Dutch Art – Speech (Red Ransom (USA)) [2016/17 h20.3g⁵ Mar 28] **h89** fair maiden hurdler, shaped better than result on sole outing in 2016/17: unproven beyond 2m: acts on soft going: usually in cheekpieces. *Steve Gollings*

ZAMPARELLI (IRE) 5 b.g. Mahler – Goulburn Bridge (IRE) (Rock Hopper) [2016/17 **h97** h24.5d⁶ h21s⁶ Feb 10] £30,000 4-y-o: workmanlike gelding: second foal: dam unraced: off mark in Irish points at third attempt: modest form over hurdles: wears tongue tie. *Dan Skelton*

ZANSTRA (IRE) 7 b.g. Morozov (USA) – Enistar (IRE) (Synefos (USA)) [2016/17 **c118** h120: c25g⁶ c20.3s² c19.4g c19.2v² c15.7v³ c23g⁶ Feb 21] lengthy gelding: fairly useful **h–** hurdler: similar form over fences: second in handicap at Exeter in January: should stay 3m: acts on heavy going: often races prominently. *Colin Tizzard*

ZANTE (FR) 5 ch.g. Zanzibari (USA) – Calling All Angels (FR) (Ange Gabriel (FR)) **h100** [2016/17 h100: h15.5g h15.8d² h19g⁶ h16m⁴ Apr 18] angular gelding: fair handicap hurdler: unproven beyond 2m: acts on good to soft going: tried in cheekpieces. *Gary Moore*

ZARA HOPE (IRE) 6 b.m. Stowaway – Agua Caliente (IRE) (Old Vic) [2016/17 h100, **h106** b84: h20.6g⁴ h20.6s⁶ h23.1g^pu Mar 27] fair handicap hurdler: won mares event at Market Rasen in October: should stay beyond 2½m: acts on soft going: front runner/races prominently. *Charlie Longsdon*

ZARAWI (IRE) 6 b.g. Marju (IRE) – Zarwala (IRE) (Polish Precedent (USA)) [2016/17 **c–** c103p, h100: h20.3g^pu h17.7g⁴ h15.9m Sep 18] fair handicap hurdler at best, well below **h70** form in 2016/17: second on only start over fences: left Charlie Longsdon after first start: stays 19f: acts on good to soft and good to firm going: usually wears cheekpieces: often races towards rear. *John Gallagher*

ZARIB (IRE) 6 b.g. Azamour (IRE) – Zariziyna (IRE) (Dalakhani (IRE)) [2016/17 h133: **c131** h22.8m h19.1s² h23.9g c16.1g³ c20.8d⁴ c20.2m* c20.8s^F h19g⁴ h16.3d⁵ h20.6m⁵ Apr 17] **h131** lengthy gelding: useful handicap hurdler: second at Fontwell (3¾ lengths behind Midnight Shot) in October: useful form over fences: won novice at Leicester (by ½ length from Master Dee) in December: stays 2½m: acts on good to firm and heavy going: has worn headgear/tongue tie, including in 2016/17. *Dan Skelton*

ZARKANDAR (IRE) 10 b.g. Azamour (IRE) – Zarkasha (IRE) (Kahyasi) [2016/17   **h147**
h20dur h19.3d5 h24.4d h22.8d* h24g h24.7g Apr 8] rather leggy gelding: has reportedly
had breathing operation: smart hurdler nowadays, off 17 months before return: won
Rendlesham Hurdle at Haydock (by 3¾ lengths from Aux Ptits Soins) in February: stays
25f: acts on heavy going: wears headgear/tongue tie. *Paul Nicholls*

ZARLIMAN (IRE) 7 ch.g. Zamindar (USA) – Zarlana (IRE) (Darshaan) [2016/17 h–:   **h78**
h16.8g h15.8g h15.9m2 h16.8m6 Oct 6] poor maiden hurdler: will prove best around 2m:
acts on good to firm going: in cheekpieces last 5 starts: has worn tongue tie. *Neil Mulholland*

ZAROCCO 4 b.f. Shirocco (GER) – Zariyka (IRE) (Kalanisi (IRE)) [2016/17 b17g3   **b71 p**
Apr 15] third foal: dam, unraced, closely related to useful hurdler (stayed 2½m) Zarinava:
strong 2/1, third in mares bumper at Carlisle (17 lengths behind The Vocalist) on debut:
likely to improve. *Iain Jardine*

ZARU (FR) 11 b.g. Laveron – Zianini (FR) (Dom Pasquini (FR)) [2016/17 h16.2d3   **c113**
c20.1d4 c16.3spu h22.7spu c24gpu h22.7v4 h16.4v Mar 18] strong gelding: fairly useful   **h90**
handicap hurdler/chaser, below form in 2016/17: stays 3m: acts on heavy going: wears
cheekpieces. *James Ewart*

ZARZAL (IRE) 9 b.g. Dr Fong (USA) – Zarwala (IRE) (Polish Precedent (USA))   **c–**
[2016/17 c135, h121: c16mur c16.5g5 h20.6gpu h18.5gpu h20v Mar 19] angular gelding: **h–**
fairly useful hurdler/useful chaser at best, no form in 2016/17: has worn headgear/tongue
tie, including in 2016/17: often races lazily. *Evan Williams*

ZAYFIRE ARAMIS 8 ch.g. Zafeen (FR) – Kaylifa Aramis (Kayf Tara) [2016/17 c97,   **c103**
h95: c20.9gpu c20d* c20gpu c23g Aug 11] lengthy, angular gelding: maiden hurdler: fair   **h–**
form over fences: won handicap at Worcester in June: stays 2½m: acts on heavy going:
races well off pace. *Michael Scudamore*

ZEBEDEE'S SON (IRE) 4 gr.g. Zebedee – Lady Ginevra (IRE) (Touch of The Blues   **h–**
(FR)) [2016/17 h17.7d6 Sep 4] poor on Flat, stays 9f: well beaten in juvenile on hurdling
debut. *Phil York*

ZEEHAN 4 gr.f. Aussie Rules (USA) – Cross Current (Sakhee (USA)) [2016/17 h18.7d4   **h89**
h15.8gpu Apr 3] fair on Flat, stays 13.5f: modest form when fourth in juvenile at Stratford
on completed start over hurdles. *Alan King*

ZENAFIRE 8 b.g. Firebreak – Zen Garden (Alzao (USA)) [2016/17 h16.7s h16.3s h15.7d3   **h112**
h15.8s2 h16g4 Apr 2] compact gelding: fair on Flat, stays 1¼m: fair form over hurdles:
likely to stay beyond 2m: acts on soft going. *Sarah Hollinshead*

ZEPHYR 6 ch.g. Shirocco (GER) – Pelagia (IRE) (Lycius (USA)) [2016/17 h100: h23spu   **h100**
h21.6gpu h22g4 h23.9m2 Apr 27] sturdy gelding: winning pointer: fair maiden hurdler:
stays 25f: acts on good to firm and heavy going: has worn headgear, including in 2016/17.
Nick Williams

ZEPHYROS BLEU (IRE) 7 b.g. Westerner – Quel Bleu (IRE) (Tel Quel (FR)) [2016/17   **c124**
h115: c20.9s6 c23.8v* c23.8v5 Mar 19] maiden hurdler: fairly useful form when won   **h–**
novice handicap at Ffos Las in December on second on 3 starts over fences: will stay
further than 3m: best form on heavy going: in cheekpieces last 4 starts. *Harry Whittington*

ZEPHYROS (GER) 6 br.g. Areion (GER) – Zandra (GER) (Lagunas) [2016/17 h15.9m3   **h103**
Apr 16] fair on Flat, stays 1¼m: 9/1, third in maiden at Plumpton (8½ lengths behind
Adrrastos) on hurdling debut. *David Bridgwater*

ZERACHIEL (IRE) 7 b.g. Winged Love (IRE) – At Dawn (IRE) (Lashkari) [2016/17   **c112**
h18.6s4 h16s6 h23.1d2 c23.6d5 c22.4s5 c24.2d* Mar 21] €19,000 3-y-o: sturdy gelding: **h108**
brother to useful hurdler/winning pointer Knight of Noir (19f/2½m winner), stays 3m, and
fairly useful hurdler/chaser Neil Harvey (2m-21f winner), and half-brother to fair 2¾m
hurdle winner Cannery Row (by Accordion): dam unraced daughter of National Hunt
Chase winner Hazy Dawn: winning pointer: fair form over hurdles: best effort when
second in maiden at Bangor in January: fair form over fences: won novice handicap at
Exeter in March: stays 3m: acts on good to soft going: in headgear last 4 starts. *Ian Williams*

ZEROESHADESOFGREY (IRE) 8 gr.g. Portrait Gallery (IRE) – Hazy Rose (IRE)   **c131**
(Roselier (FR)) [2016/17 c121p, h138: c24.2g* c24.2s2 h24s c22.7s2 c23.6s3 c23.8gpu   **h–**
Apr 9] big, workmanlike gelding: useful hurdler at best, below form third outing in
2016/17: useful form over fences: won novice at Wetherby (by 11 lengths from Royal
Vacation) in October: stays 3m: acts on heavy going: tried in cheekpieces: usually races
close up. *Neil King*

Sky Bet Handicap Chase (Listed), Doncaster—an enterprising ride from Tom Bellamy as the grey Ziga Boy becomes the first dual winner in the race's long history

ZERO GRAND (IRE) 6 b.g. Thousand Words – Ellistown Lady (IRE) (Red Sunset) [2016/17 h106p, b–: h19.9s⁴ h16s⁴ h20.5v⁴ h23.1d* h25.5s* Mar 11] fairly useful hurdler: won handicap at Exeter in February and novice at Hereford in March: stays 3¼m: acts on heavy going. *Johnny Farrelly* **h125**

ZERO VISIBILITY (IRE) 10 b.g. Classic Cliche (IRE) – Jessica's Pet (IRE) (King's Ride) [2016/17 c81, h84: c16.3d⁵ c19.4m⁴ c22.6gᵖᵘ c21gᵖᵘ c25.8g² c23g³ h18.5d Sep 26] winning Irish pointer: poor handicap hurdler: poor maiden chaser: barely stays 3¼m: acts on heavy going. *Katie Stephens* **c69 h65**

ZIGA BOY (FR) 8 gr.g. Califet (FR) – Our Ziga (FR) (Linamix (FR)) [2016/17 c137, h–: c24g⁶ c24.1v⁵ c25.5dᵘʳ c24g³ c24d* Jan 28] angular gelding: maiden hurdler: useful handicap chaser: won Sky Bet Chase at Doncaster (for second successive year, by 3½ lengths from Looking Well) in January: stays 25f: acts on heavy going: has worn cheekpieces, including at Doncaster: front runner/races prominently. *Alan King* **c141 h–**

ZIGGERSON HILL 10 ch.m. Kadastrof (FR) – Tregale (Chukaroo) [2016/17 h90: h21.6g⁴ h23.1s⁶ h21.4d Dec 13] dual winning pointer: modest form over hurdles: stays 21f: acts on soft going. *Jackie du Plessis* **h93**

ZIGGER ZAGGER (IRE) 8 b.g. Mountain High (IRE) – Main Suspect (IRE) (Be My Native (USA)) [2016/17 c98x, h102x: c18m⁵ c16.4s⁴ c19.9dᵖᵘ c20.5gᶠ c22.4dᵖᵘ c20.5m⁵ Apr 18] workmanlike gelding: fair maiden hurdler: modest maiden chaser: stays 2½m: acts on soft going: has worn hood: sketchy jumper. *Richard Rowe* **c92 x h– x**

ZIG ZAG (IRE) 4 b.g. Zoffany (IRE) – Le Montrachet (Nashwan (USA)) [2016/17 h16g⁵ h16g² h16.2s² h16d³ h16g² h16g* h16g⁶ h16s² h16.6g³ h16d⁴ h16.4g h16d Apr 16] compact gelding: fair on Flat, stays 11.5f: fairly useful hurdler: won juvenile maiden at Thurles in October: third in Summit Juvenile Hurdle at Doncaster (11¾ lengths behind Cliffs of Dover) in December: raced around 2m: acts on soft going: in tongue tie last 2 starts. *Joseph Patrick O'Brien, Ireland* **h118**

ZIPPLE BACK (IRE) 5 b.g. Sendawar (IRE) – With Conviction (IRE) (Barathea (IRE)) [2016/17 b91p: h16g² h16s³ h16.5g³ h20.8d³ Jan 9] fair form over hurdles: often races towards rear. *Alan King* **h114**

947

ZOLFO (IRE) 5 gr.g. Cloudings (IRE) – Hardy Lamb (IRE) (Witness Box (USA)) **h82**
[2016/17 h20d⁶ h18.9v h19.3s⁶ h19.4g Dec 29] €20,000 3-y-o, £40,000 4-y-o: sixth foal:
brother to a winning pointer: dam, ran twice in points, half-sister to useful chaser (stayed
3¼m) The Bushkeeper: runner-up in Irish maiden point: poor form over hurdles. *Jennie
Candlish*

ZORLU (IRE) 4 b.g. Invincible Spirit (IRE) – Special Assignment (USA) (Lemon Drop **h–**
Kid (USA)) [2016/17 h16s Dec 2] rather leggy gelding: maiden on Flat: tailed off in
juvenile on hurdling debut. *John O'Shea*

ZUBAYR (IRE) 5 b.g. Authorized (IRE) – Zaziyra (IRE) (Dalakhani (IRE)) [2016/17 **h138**
h140: h19.4s³ h15.3mᶠ h16s⁵ h16.3d h20g⁶ h16g² Apr 22] neat gelding: useful handicap
hurdler: runner-up in Scottish Champion Hurdle at Ayr (short head behind Chesterfield) in
April: stays 19f: acts on soft going. *Paul Nicholls*

ZULU OSCAR 8 b.g. Oscar (IRE) – Loxhill Lady (Supreme Leader) [2016/17 h136: **h129**
h21.6g* h19.8d h19.8vᵖᵘ h21.4d h16g* Apr 8] well-made gelding: fairly useful hurdler:
won seller at Newton Abbot early in season and handicap at Chepstow in April: left
Harry Fry after first start, George Baker after fourth: stays 2¾m: acts on soft going: tried in
blinkers: has worn tongue tie, including in 2016/17. *Jeremy Scott*

PROMISING HORSES

Selected British- and Irish-trained horses in *Chasers & Hurdlers* thought capable of noteworthy improvement are listed under the trainers for whom they last ran.

KIM BAILEY
Champion Chase (FR) 5 b.g h100p
Chateau Robin (IRE) 6 br.g h97p
Coco des Champs (IRE) 7 br.m h100 c86p
Laval Noir (FR) 6 b.g h105p
Rocky's Treasure (IRE) 6 b.g h126p

JACK R. BARBER
Ask The Weatherman 8 b.g c127p
Redmond (IRE) 7 b.g h84 c89p

ENDA BOLGER, IRELAND
Stand Up And Fight (IRE) 5 b.g h135p

ROSE DOBBIN
Coole Hall (IRE) 5 b.g h115p
Doktor Glaz (FR) 7 b.g h103 c103p
Minella Suite (IRE) 6 br.g h97 c100p
Slanelough (IRE) 5 b.g h110p
Wicked Games (IRE) 6 br.m c80p
Witness Time (IRE) 5 b.g h58p b82

GORDON ELLIOTT, IRELAND
Baby Twig (FR) 6 b.m b105p
Baltazar d'Allier (FR) 6 br.g h131p
Campeador (FR) 5 gr.g h153p
Cracking Smart (FR) 5 b. or br.g h123p b108
Hardline (IRE) 5 b.g h118p b105
Its All Guesswork (IRE) 5 b.g h110p b108
Mengli Khan (IRE) 4 b.g h136p
Mon Eldorado (FR) 5 b.g b90p
Monkshood (IRE) 5 br.g h115p b106
Potters Point (IRE) 7 b.g h118p c131p
Samcro (IRE) 5 ch.g b115p
Seeyouallincoppers (IRE) 7 b.g h122 c108p
The Storyteller (IRE) 6 ch.g h144p b99
Tullyglush (IRE) 5 b.m h95p b84

BRIAN ELLISON
Bordeaux Bill (IRE) 6 b.g h128p b90
Green Light 6 b.g h94p
Oscar Blue (IRE) 7 gr.g c104p
Our Kylie (IRE) 5 b.m h114p

PETER FAHEY, IRELAND
Xsquared (IRE) 9 b.g c134p

HARRY FRY
American (FR) 7 b.g c156p
An Siltean (IRE) 6 b.g h105p
Black Mischief 5 b.g h121p b93
Bullionaire (IRE) 4 b.g b105p
Hell's Kitchen 6 b.g c132P
Mountain Eagle (IRE) 8 b.g c111p
Neon Wolf (IRE) 6 b.g h152p b110p
Outofthisworld (IRE) 4 b. or br.f b97P
Queen Odessa (IRE) 6 b.m h102p
Secret Door (IRE) 6 b.m h118p
Tangley 5 b.m h94p
Wotzizname (IRE) 7 b.g h136 c132p

TOM GEORGE
Battle of Shiloh (IRE) 8 b.g h116p c139
Bigpipenotobacee (IRE) 6 b. or br.g h109p
Big Windmill (IRE) 6 b.g h97 c85p
Bomber Command (FR) 5 gr.g h98p b79
Boyhood (IRE) 6 b.g h123p
Broom Tip (IRE) 5 b.g h98p
Forgot To Ask (IRE) 5 b.g b100p
Just Before Dawn (IRE) 8 b.g h123p
Otter Moon 5 b.g h82p b86
The Worlds End (IRE) 6 b.g h146p

WARREN GREATREX
Cole Harden (IRE) 8 b.g h155 c123p
Don't Ask (IRE) 4 b.g b69p
Major Davis (FR) 5 b.g h100p b86
Penn Lane (IRE) 6 b.g h118p

MRS J. HARRINGTON, IRELAND
Our Duke (IRE) 7 b.g c167p

EDWARD HARTY, IRELAND
Coney Island (IRE) 6 b.g c159p

NICKY HENDERSON
Beyond Conceit (IRE) 8 b.g h145p
Brave Eagle (IRE) 5 b.g h123p
Burbank (IRE) 5 b.g h135p b98
Buveur d'Air (FR) 6 b.g h170 c155p
Call Me Lord (FR) 4 b.g h141p
Christmas In April (FR) 5 b.g h105p b87
Days of Heaven (FR) 7 b. or br.g h122+ c143p
Doux Pretender (FR) 4 b.g b95p
Jenkins (IRE) 5 b.g h142p
Kayf Grace 7 b.m h119P
Lough Derg Farmer (IRE) 5 b.g h122p
One For The Guv'nr (IRE) 8 b.g h113 c116p
Protek des Flos (FR) 5 b.g h129 c73p
Reigning Supreme (IRE) 6 b.g h128p
Scorpio Queen (IRE) 5 b.m h88p b87
Sunshade 4 b.f b95p
Tales of The Tweed (IRE) 5 b.g h119p b91
Thomas Campbell 5 b.g h138p b108
Wenyerreadyfreddie (IRE) 6 ch.g h125p
William Henry (IRE) 7 b.g h143p

PHILIP HOBBS
Action Replay (IRE) 6 b.g h115p
Book Direct (IRE) 6 b.g h117p
Bridge of Spies (IRE) 6 ch.g h85p
Casterly Rock (IRE) 5 b.g h106p
Daylami Days (IRE) 6 gr.g h81p
Defi du Seuil (FR) 4 b.g h151p
Earth Lady 5 b.m h98p b68
Ice Cool Champs (IRE) 6 ch.g h116p b99
Jerrysback (IRE) 5 b.g h122p
Longtown (IRE) 6 b.g h118p
Majestic Touch (IRE) 6 br.g h107p
Mance Rayder (IRE) 4 b.g b93p
New Millennium (IRE) 4 b.c h101p

Robbin'hannon (IRE) 6 ch.g h131p
Saddlers Encore (IRE) 8 br.g c109p
Sneaky Feeling (IRE) 5 b.g h133p b91
Springtown Lake (IRE) 5 b.g h118p
Tricky (IRE) 8 br.g h106 c83p

IAIN JARDINE
Daytripper 6 gr.m h103p
Rainy City (IRE) 7 b.g h133 c126p
River Icon 5 b.m h87p b81
Zarocco 4 b.f b71p

MALCOLM JEFFERSON
Cabin Boy (IRE) 4 b.g b62p
Kick On Dottie (IRE) 4 ch.f b62p
Mayo Star (IRE) 5 b.g h106p b91
Mountain Hawk (IRE) 5 b.g h92p
Mount Mews (IRE) 6 b.g h140p b115
Schiaparannie 5 b.m b91p
Waiting Patiently (IRE) 6 b.g c150p

MARTIN KEIGHLEY
Brillare Momento (IRE) 6 b.m h136p b95

ALAN KING
Beneagles (IRE) 5 b.g h123p
Chato (FR) 5 ch.g h88p b99
Cosmeapolitan 4 b.g h105P
David Cricket 5 b.g h88p b87
Holy Street (IRE) 5 b.g b64p
Inn The Bull (GER) 4 ch.g h100p
Lexington Law (IRE) 4 b.g h92p
Minella Charmer (IRE) 6 b.g c129p
My Khaleesi 6 b.m h120p b102

TOM LACEY
First du Charmil (FR) 5 ch.g h108p
Gabriel Oats 8 ch.g h88p
Isle of Ewe 6 b.m h117p b85
Super Sid (IRE) 5 b.g b77p

CHARLIE LONGSDON
Snow Leopardess 5 gr.m h129p b103

DONALD MCCAIN
Arctic Destination (IRE) 6 b.g h106p b92
Lastbutnotleast (IRE) 7 ch.m h127p
Our Dancing Dandy (IRE) 7 b.g h105p
Take The Cash (IRE) 8 b.g c111p

GRAEME MCPHERSON
Kayf Blanco 8 b.g h130 c129p
Ruby Wilde (IRE) 6 b.m h96p b80

GARY MOORE
Early du Lemo (FR) 4 gr.g h119p
Imari Kid (IRE) 4 b.g h113p
Kaveman 5 b.g b59p
Master of Speed (IRE) 5 ch.g h115p
Not Never 5 ch.g h108p

NEIL MULHOLLAND
Bellamy 6 ch.g h115p
Green Or Black (IRE) 5 gr.m h89p
Impulsive Star (IRE) 7 b.g h132p
Master Burbidge 6 b.g h111 c115p
My Story (IRE) 5 b.g b77p
Prettylittlething (IRE) 7 b.m h90p c99p

Shantou Village (IRE) 7 b.g c149p
Whatsthatallabout (IRE) 6 b.m h115p

W. P. MULLINS, IRELAND
American Tom (FR) 6 b.g c140p
Bacardys (FR) 6 b. or br.g h155p
Bachasson (FR) 6 gr.g c147p
Ballyward (IRE) 5 b.g b111p
Benie des Dieux (FR) 6 b.m c134P
Blazer (FR) 6 ch.g c136p
Caro des Flos (FR) 5 b.g h123p
Childrens List (IRE) 7 b.g h123 c138p
Come To Me (FR) 5 b.g h106p
Good Thyne Tara 7 b. or br.m h130p b104
Great Field (FR) 6 b.g c170p
Isleofhopendreams 10 b.g h126 c136p
Listen Dear (IRE) 7 b.m h130p c136p
Min (FR) 6 b.g c160P
Ria d'Etel (FR) 5 b.m h129p
Townshend (GER) 6 b.g c146p
True Self (IRE) 4 b.f b93p
Voix des Tiep (FR) 5 b. or br.g b105p
Yorkhill (IRE) 7 ch.g c161p

ADRIAN MURRAY, IRELAND
Killaro Boy (IRE) 8 ch.g h131p

PAUL NICHOLLS
Binge Drinker (IRE) 8 b.g c140p
Brelan d'As (FR) 6 b.g h139p
Brio Conti (FR) 6 gr.g h140p b97
Cliffs of Dover 4 b.g h139p
Copain de Classe (FR) 5 b.g h130p
Coup de Pinceau (FR) 5 b.g h114p b95
Give Me A Copper (IRE) 7 ch.g h136p
If You Say Run (IRE) 5 b.m b104p
Monsieur Co (FR) 4 b.g h128 c121p
Mont des Avaloirs (FR) 4 b.g b90p
Mr Mix (FR) 6 gr.g h138 c120p
Old Guard 6 b.g h149 c136p
Red Hanrahan (IRE) 6 b.g c114p
Ridgeway Flyer 6 b.g h124p
Secret Investor 5 b.g h122p
Topofthegame (IRE) 5 ch.g h138p
Trevisani (IRE) 5 b.g h105p
Two Hoots (IRE) 6 gr.g h82p b61

FERGAL O'BRIEN
Barney Dwan (IRE) 7 b.g h146 c138p
Benechenko (IRE) 5 b.g h86p b98
Colin's Sister 6 b.m h133p
Diamond Fort (IRE) 5 ch.g h116p b88
Dont Tell Val 5 b.m h73p b92
Out of Style (IRE) 6 b.g b88p
Where's Cherry (IRE) 6 b.m h98p

CONOR O'DWYER, IRELAND
Go Darsi Go (IRE) 8 b.g h127 c133p

JEDD O'KEEFFE
Sam Spinner 5 b.g h139p

JONJO O'NEILL
Allelu Alleluia (GER) 6 b.g h112p
As You Like (IRE) 6 b. or br.g h101p
Big Penny (IRE) 5 b.m h97p
Desert Cross 4 b.g h93p
Forza Milan (IRE) 5 b.g h124p b87

Lad of Luck (FR) 4 b.g h104p
Lithic (IRE) 6 b.g h122p
Manny Owens (IRE) 5 b. or br.g h86p
Miss Beatrice (IRE) 5 b. or br.m h96p b94
Noble Robin (IRE) 6 b.g h98p
Pleasure Dome 4 b.f h91p
Plus One (IRE) 5 b.g h114p
Pongo Twistleton 4 b.g h104p
Pop Rockstar (IRE) 5 b. or br.g h108p b78
Rosie McQueen (IRE) 5 b.m h112p
Set In My Ways (IRE) 6 b.g h112 c75p
State The Obvious (IRE) 5 ch.g h72p
Wild Ginger 6 ch.g h76p

BEN PAULING
Kildisart (IRE) 5 br.g b101p
Willoughby Court (IRE) 6 br.g h151p

DAVID PIPE
Baby Sherlock 8 ch.g h66p
Dauphine Ereine (FR) 5 b.m c109p
Juste Pour Nous 4 b.g h101p
Mount Haven (IRE) 7 b.g c105p
Mr Big Shot (IRE) 6 br.g h125p

NICKY RICHARDS
Baysbrown (IRE) 7 b.g h106 c81p
Booyakasha (IRE) 5 b.g b79p
Carry On Arcadio (IRE) 5 b.g b83p
Chapel Stile (IRE) 5 b.g h82p
Nando (GER) 5 b.g b79p
Tetraites Style (IRE) 5 b.g h66p

LUCINDA RUSSELL
Dr Hooves (IRE) 4 b.g h72p
Mr Grumpy 4 b.g h81p
One For Arthur (IRE) 8 b.g c157p

OLIVER SHERWOOD
Icing On The Cake (IRE) 7 b.g h113p c128
Piton Pete (IRE) 6 b.g h101p
Rayvin Black 8 b.g h143 c86p
Valdas Princess 5 b.m b74p

DAVID SIMCOCK
Captain Morley 6 b.g h95P

DAN SKELTON
Bedrock 4 b.g h134p
Blairs Cove 5 b.g h129p b93
Calling des Blins (FR) 5 b.m h73p
Captain Chaos (IRE) 6 ch.g c133p
Captain Forez (FR) 5 b.g h144p
Charming Zen (FR) 5 gr.g h136p
Cosmos des Obeaux (FR) 5 b.g h119p
Diese des Bieffes (FR) 4 gr.g b76p
Gibson Park 4 b.g h115p
Gortroe Joe (IRE) 5 b.g b85p
Hestina (FR) 4 b.f h116p
Honkytonktennessee (IRE) 8 b.g h109 c106p
Indirocco (GER) 4 ch.g h105p
Itsnonofurbusiness (IRE) 5 b.g b69p
L'Aigle Royal (GER) 6 b.g h115 c89p
Mohaayed 5 b.g h135p
One For Billy 5 b.g h93p b90
Oscar's Song (IRE) 6 b.m h86p b80
Ravens Hill (IRE) 4 ch.g h108p

Red Rising (IRE) 6 ch.g h125p
Return Flight 6 b.g h102 c129p
Robin Roe (IRE) 6 b.g h140p
Rock Chick Supremo (IRE) 6 b.m h86p
Roksana (IRE) 5 b.m h75p
Sam Red (FR) 6 b.g h135 c107p
Santo de Lune (FR) 7 gr.g h119p
Some Invitation (IRE) 6 b.g h132p
Spader (IRE) 4 b.g h104p
Spiritofthegames (IRE) 5 b.g h126p
Stick To The Plan (IRE) 5 b.g h122p
Welsh Shadow (IRE) 7 b.g h142 c122p
Whiskey In The Jar (IRE) 5 b.g b107p

SUE SMITH
Nomoreblackjack (IRE) 6 b.g h87p c130p

SANDY THOMSON
Spirit of Kayf 6 b.g h132p

COLIN TIZZARD
Machiato (IRE) 6 br.g b95p
Quiz Master (IRE) 5 b.g h84p b73
Robinsfirth (IRE) 8 b.g c144p
Sizing Brisbane 9 b.g h108 c109p
Valhalla (IRE) 7 b.g h134 c112p

NIGEL TWISTON-DAVIES
Kerisper (FR) 8 b.g c89p
One Forty Seven (IRE) 5 b.g h119p

ROBERT TYNER, IRELAND
Gurteen (IRE) 7 b.g h121 c140p

LUCY WADHAM
Potters Legend 7 b.g c141p

T. M. WALSH, IRELAND
Any Second Now (IRE) 5 b.g h138p

MARTIN WESTON
Arthur's Secret (FR) 7 b. or br.g c127p

HARRY WHITTINGTON
Dara's Present (IRE) 6 b.g h102p
Emerging Force (IRE) 7 b.g c140p
Jack Bear 6 b.g h90p

EVAN WILLIAMS
Monbeg Oscar (IRE) 5 b.g h111p b89
Morianour (FR) 6 b. or br.g h113p b82
Oxwich Bay (IRE) 5 b.g h116p b93
Radical Archie 6 ch.g h101p b90
Sainlouis des Pres (FR) 4 b.g b72p
Shrewd Tactics (IRE) 6 ch.g h82 c106p
Swift Crusador 6 b.g h111p
Theatre Stage (IRE) 5 b.g h101p

VENETIA WILLIAMS
Belami des Pictons (FR) 6 b.g c148p
Burtons Well (IRE) 8 b.g c134p
Cold As Ice (IRE) 5 gr.g h95p
Dark Force (FR) 4 gr.g b64p
Du Soleil (FR) 5 ch.g h111p
Lady Karina 6 b.m h109p
Luckime (IRE) 5 gr.g b90p
Subcontinent (IRE) 5 b.g h76p
Tara Flow 7 b.m c107p
Top And Drop 6 b.m h100 c112p
Willie Boy (IRE) 6 b.g h107p c129p

2016/17 IRISH STATISTICS

The following tables show the leading owners, trainers, jockeys, sires of winners and horses over jumps in Ireland during 2016/17 (May 1-April 29). The prize money statistics are in euros and have been compiled by *Timeform*. They relate to winning prize money only (prize money used to be converted to sterling at the prevailing rate at the time but that is no longer the case, though the prize money for individual races that appear in *'Selected Big Races'* has been converted to sterling).

OWNERS	Horses	Wnrs	Indiv'l Races Won	Runs	%	Stakes €
1 Gigginstown House Stud	196	95	153	877	17.4	2,633,543
2 Mr John P. McManus	258	84	121	891	13.6	1,664,588
3 Mrs S. Ricci	40	30	45	119	37.8	892,311
4 Cooper Family Syndicate	3	2	4	13	30.8	338,908
5 Ann & Alan Potts Partnership	31	8	10	87	11.5	315,436
6 Andrea Wylie/Graham Wylie	13	10	13	40	32.5	266,030
7 Mr R. S. Brookhouse	12	6	9	43	20.9	258,116
8 Ann & Alan Potts	7	3	3	7	42.9	241,900
9 Mr C. Jones	14	7	8	54	14.8	197,773
10 Act D Wagg Syndicate	1	1	2	5	40.0	188,070
11 Mr Anthony P. Butler	1	1	7	9	77.8	158,882
12 Luke McMahon	7	4	8	26	30.8	152,997

TRAINERS	Horses	Wnrs	Indiv'l Races Won	Runs	%	Stakes €
1 W. P. Mullins, Ireland	184	109	180	571	31.5	3,203,975
2 Gordon Elliott, Ireland	285	122	193	1,234	15.6	2,802,917
3 Mrs J. Harrington, Ireland	87	29	48	353	13.6	1,055,886
4 Henry de Bromhead, Ireland	118	47	68	427	15.9	1,038,193
5 Noel Meade, Ireland	92	38	57	367	15.5	789,497
6 Joseph Patrick O'Brien, Ireland	77	26	38	269	14.1	361,712
7 Colin Tizzard	7	3	3	7	42.9	241,900
8 John Patrick Ryan, Ireland	29	9	15	188	8.0	188,830
9 Harry Fry	5	2	2	5	40.0	182,900
10 Thomas Mullins, Ireland	27	10	16	118	13.6	167,501
11 John Joseph Hanlon, Ireland	44	14	20	185	10.8	164,346
12 Peter Fahey, Ireland	37	9	15	132	11.4	147,573

JOCKEYS (by winners)	1st	2nd	3rd	Unpl	Mts	%
1 R. Walsh	131	68	41	131	371	35.3
2 J. W. Kennedy	68	80	56	301	505	13.5
3 Davy Russell	60	50	49	215	374	16.0
4 M. P. Walsh	59	42	48	243	392	15.1
5 P. Townend	53	49	40	234	376	14.1
6 Sean Flanagan	46	50	51	380	527	8.7
7 D. E. Mullins	46	39	46	364	495	9.3
8 B. J. Cooper	45	43	37	146	271	16.6
9 Robbie Power	45	25	28	166	264	17.0
10 D. J. Mullins	44	44	45	236	369	11.9
11 Mr J. J. Codd	40	16	17	57	130	30.8
12 Mr P. W. Mullins	38	35	20	47	140	27.1

SIRES OF WINNERS	Horses	Indiv'l Wnrs	Races Won	Stakes €
1 Oscar (by Sadler's Wells)	131	33	48	852,604
2 Presenting (by Mtoto)	155	43	57	752,404
3 Flemensfirth (by Alleged)	132	44	57	683,121
4 Westerner (by Danehill)	105	29	46	627,177
5 Beneficial (by Top Ville)	171	37	56	486,982
6 Stowaway (by Slip Anchor)	80	25	38	479,273
7 King's Theatre (by Sadler's Wells)	105	31	52	474,630
8 Shantou (by Alleged)	60	19	33	412,446
9 Milan (by Sadler's Wells)	136	30	41	395,137
10 Midnight Legend (by Night Shift)	10	2	4	271,245
11 Yeats (by Sadler's Wells)	53	21	26	266,686
12 Robin des Champs (by Garde Royale)	41	13	22	265,119

LEADING HORSES	Won	Runs	€
1 Our Duke 7 b.g Oscar–Good Thyne Jenny	3	4	344,603
2 Sizing John 7 b.g Midnight Legend–La Perrotine	3	4	282,251
3 Clondaw Warrior 10 b.g Overbury–Thespian	2	5	208,271
4 Ball d'Arc 6 b.g Network–Pretty Moon	4	13	168,345
5 Westerner Lady 7 b.m Westerner–Cloghoge Lady	7	9	166,482
6 Lord Scoundrel 8 b.g Presenting–Noble Choice	1	5	150,000
7 Wicklow Brave 8 b.g Beat Hollow–Moraine	1	1	147,500
8 Unowhatimeanharry 9 b.g Sir Harry Lewis–Red Nose Lady	1	1	147,500
9 Fox Norton 7 b.g Lando–Natt Musik	1	1	147,500
10 Ballycasey 10 gr.g Presenting–Pink Mist	4	9	141,377
11 Airlie Beach 7 b.m Shantou–Screaming Witness	6	8	139,979
12 Petit Mouchoir 6 gr.g Al Namix–Arnette	2	3	137,100

<table>
<tr><th colspan="2">TIMEFORM TOP 20
IRISH CHASERS</th><th colspan="2">TIMEFORM TOP 20
IRISH HURDLERS</th></tr>
<tr><td>182</td><td>Douvan</td><td>165</td><td>Nichols Canyon</td></tr>
<tr><td>170p</td><td>Great Field</td><td>163</td><td>Arctic Fire</td></tr>
<tr><td>170</td><td>Sizing John</td><td>162</td><td>Petit Mouchoir</td></tr>
<tr><td>169</td><td>Djakadam</td><td>161§</td><td>Wicklow Brave</td></tr>
<tr><td>169</td><td>Un de Sceaux</td><td>160</td><td>Diakali</td></tr>
<tr><td>168</td><td>Valseur Lido</td><td>160</td><td>Sutton Place</td></tr>
<tr><td>167p</td><td>Our Duke</td><td>160§</td><td>Labaik</td></tr>
<tr><td>167</td><td>Sub Lieutenant</td><td>159</td><td>Footpad</td></tr>
<tr><td>166</td><td>Special Tiara</td><td>158</td><td>Apple's Jade (f)</td></tr>
<tr><td>165</td><td>Outlander</td><td>155p</td><td>Bacardys</td></tr>
<tr><td>163</td><td>Don Poli</td><td>155</td><td>Clondaw Warrior</td></tr>
<tr><td>163</td><td>Empire of Dirt</td><td>154</td><td>Ivan Grozny</td></tr>
<tr><td>162x</td><td>Champagne West</td><td>154</td><td>Shaneshill</td></tr>
<tr><td>161p</td><td>Yorkhill</td><td>154</td><td>Supasundae</td></tr>
<tr><td>161</td><td>Zabana</td><td>154§</td><td>Renneti</td></tr>
<tr><td>160P</td><td>Min</td><td>153p</td><td>Campeador</td></tr>
<tr><td>159p</td><td>Coney Island</td><td>153</td><td>Snow Falcon</td></tr>
<tr><td>159</td><td>Ballycasey</td><td>152</td><td>Ivanovich Gorbatov</td></tr>
<tr><td>159</td><td>Carlingford Lough</td><td>152</td><td>Penhill</td></tr>
<tr><td>158</td><td>Noble Endeavor</td><td>152</td><td>Presenting Percy</td></tr>
</table>

SELECTED BIG RACES 2016/17

Prize money for racing abroad has been converted to £ sterling at the exchange rate current at the time of the race. The figures are correct to the nearest £.

HAYDOCK Saturday, May 7 GOOD to FIRM

1 Pertemps Network Handicap Hurdle (Swinton) (Gr 3) (1) (4yo+) £34,170 1m7f144y (9)

GWAFA (IRE) *PaulWebber* 5-11-0[137] RichieMcLernon	6/1		1
ALL SET TO GO (IRE) *PaulNicholls* 5-10-13[136] (t) SeanBowen	9/1	1¼	2
CH'TIBELLO (FR) *DanSkelton* 5-11-4[141] HarrySkelton	9/2	1¾	3
John Constable (IRE) *EvanWilliams* 5-11-1[138] PaulMoloney	12/1	1½	4
All Yours (FR) *PaulNicholls* 5-11-8[145] (h+t) SamTwiston-Davies	12/1	2¼	5
Apterix (FR) *BrianEllison* 6-10-11[134] AidanColeman	16/1	2¼	6
Swansea Mile (IRE) *DanSkelton* 6-11-0[137] BridgetAndrews(5)	16/1	6	7
Wait For Me (FR) *PhilipHobbs* 6-11-2[139] (h) RichardJohnson	4/1f	¾	8
Manhattan Swing (IRE) *BrianEllison* 6-11-1[138] (b) TomScudamore	25/1	¾	9
Roman Flight (IRE) *DavidDennis* 8-11-5[142] (v) DarylJacob	40/1	1½	10
Regulation (IRE) *NeilKing* 7-10-9[132] (s) TrevorWhelan	33/1	1	11
Beltor *RobertStephens* 5-11-3[140] GavinSheehan	16/1	1½	12
Nuts Well *AnnHamilton* 5-10-13[136] CraigNichol	20/1	¾	13
Some Plan (IRE) *PaulNicholls* 8-11-8[145] (h+t) JackSherwood(5)	12/1	7	14
Astre de La Cour (FR) *RobertWalford* 5-11-3[140] JamieMoore	20/1	3	15
Cheltenian (FR) *PhilipHobbs* 10-11-12[149] (h) MichealNolan	25/1		pu

Saleh Al Homaizi & Imad Al Sagar 16ran 3m38.70

STRATFORD Friday, May 20 GOOD to FIRM

2 Pertemps Network Stratford Foxhunters Champion Hunters' Chase (2) (5yo+) £14,990 3m3f119y (18)

PAINT THE CLOUDS *WarrenGreatrex* 11-12-0 MrBarryO'Neill	2/1		1
MARITO (GER) *ColinA.McBratney,Ireland* 10-12-0 MrN.McParlan	7/4f	1¾	2
PACHA DU POLDER (FR) *PaulNicholls* 9-12-0 MrW.Biddick	5/1	nk	3
Mr Mercurial (IRE) *MrsSheilaCrow* 8-12-0 (t) MrP.Gerety	28/1	14	4
Vasco du Mee (FR) *MartinWeston* 7-12-0 (b+t) MissJosephineBanks	9/1	24	5
Foynes Island (IRE) *MissL.J.Cabble* 10-12-0 (s) MrD.Andrews	50/1	sh	6
On The Bridge (IRE) *JeremyScott* 11-12-0 (s+t) MissV.Wade	7/1		F

Peter Deal & Jill & Robin Eynon 7ran 6m49.80

UTTOXETER Sunday, Jun 26 GOOD

3 John Smith's Summer Cup (Handicap Chase) (L) (1) (5yo+) £45,016 3¼m13y (20)

DROP OUT JOE *CharlieLongsdon* 8-10-6[144] (s) GrahamWatters(3)	20/1		1
BALLYNAGOUR (IRE) *DavidPipe* 10-11-0[152] (h+t) DavidNoonan(3)	10/1	2	2
2 PACHA DU POLDER (FR) *PaulNicholls* 9-11-0[138] SamTwiston-Davies	8/1	5	3
Gas Line Boy (IRE) *IanWilliams* 10-10-0[138] (v) TomO'Brien	9/1	5	4
Menorah (IRE) *PhilipHobbs* 11-11-12[164] RichardJohnson	12/1	¾	5
Ballykan *NigelTwiston-Davies* 6-9-7[138] (t) JamieBargary(5)	16/1	6	6
Solstice Son *AnthonyHoneyball* 7-9-7[138] (b+t) HarryCobden(5)	12/1	16	7
Your Busy (IRE) *JamesA.Nash,Ireland* 13-9-11[138] (t) MsK.Walsh	25/1	5	8
Standing Ovation (IRE) *DavidPipe* 9-9-8[138] (b+t) MichaelHeard(5)	25/1	¾	9
Top Wood (FR) *DavidPipe* 9-10-6[144] (b+t) WayneHutchinson	16/1	15	10
What A Warrior (IRE) *DanSkelton* 9-9-13[138] (t) HarrySkelton	17/2	1	11
Al Co (FR) *PeterBowen* 11-10-1[139] (v) JamieMoore	11/2f		ur
Tony Star (FR) *PeterBowen* 9-8-13[138] (s) TrevorWhelan	40/1		pu
2 On The Bridge (IRE) *JeremyScott* 11-9-8[138] (s+t) NicodeBoinville	33/1		pu
Grandads Horse *CharlieLongsdon* 10-9-9[138] (s) JonathanMoore(5)	20/1		pu
Danimix (FR) *NeilMulholland* 11-9-12[138] (t) BrendanPowell	50/1		pu
Shuil Royale (IRE) *HarryFry* 11-10-1[139] (s+t) AidanColeman	9/1		pu
Saint Roque (FR) *PaulNicholls* 10-10-5[143] (s+t) ConorO'Farrell	25/1		pu
Katkeau (FR) *DavidPipe* 9-10-2[150] (h+t) TomScudamore	9/1		pu

The Jesters 19ran 6m22.60

GALWAY Wednesday, Jul 27 GOOD

4 thetote.com Galway Plate (Handicap Chase) (Gr A) (4yo+) £109,076 2¾m111y (14)

LORD SCOUNDREL (IRE) *GordonElliott* 7-10-7[145] DonaghMeyler(5)	10/1		1
ALELCHI INOIS (FR) *W.P.Mullins* 8-11-1[153] P.Townend	16/1	1¼	2
BALLYCASEY (IRE) *W.P.Mullins* 9-10-7[145] (s) R.Walsh	10/1	1¼	3
Devils Bride (IRE) *W.P.Mullins* 9-10-12[150] (t) D.J.Mullins	16/1	½	4
Clarcam (FR) *GordonElliott* 6-11-0[152] (s+t) J.W.Kennedy	10/1	1¼	5

954

Shadow Catcher *GordonElliott* 8-9-11[135] (s+t) D.E.Mullins 33/1   2¼   6
The Tullow Tank (IRE) *AlanFleming* 8-11-1[153] (t) DenisO'Regan 25/1   13   7
Bright New Dawn (IRE) *GordonElliott* 9-10-11[149] (t) K.C.Sexton 33/1   3   8
Shantou Flyer (IRE) *ColinBowe* 6-10-9[147] (t) A.P.Heskin 10/1   1½   9
Three Kingdoms (IRE) *D.K.Weld* 7-10-11[149] B.S.Hughes ....25/1   ½   10
Killer Crow (IRE) *GordonElliott* 7-9-10[134] (t) MissN.Carberry ....11/1   nk   11
Sizing Platinum (IRE) *HenrydeBromhead* 8-10-5[143] JonathanMoore(3) 25/1   1¾   12
Cantlow (IRE) *EndaBolger* 11-9-10[134] M.A.Enright 28/1   1¼   13
First Lieutenant (IRE) *M.F.Morris* 11-10-9[147] (b) SeanFlanagan 25/1   5   14
It's A Gimme (IRE) *JonjoO'Neill,GB* 9-9-13[137] (t) NiallMadden 33/1   8   15
Junction Fourteen (IRE) *EmmaLavelle,GB* 7-10-10[148] (t) AidanColeman 9/1   15   16
Ravished (IRE) *M.F.Morris* 8-9-11[135] (s) A.Ring(5) 33/1   3¼   17
The King of Brega (IRE) *HenrydeBromhead* 9-9-11[135] (s) A.E.Lynch 20/1   8   18
Home Farm (IRE) *HenrydeBromhead* 9-10-6[144] (s) L.P.Dempsey 20/1   55   19
Shanahan's Turn (IRE) *HenrydeBromhead* 8-10-13[151] (s) J.J.Burke ....16/1   ½   20
Yes Tom (IRE) *StuartCrawford* 11-9-10[134] (v+t) R.C.Colgan ....50/1   pu
Road To Riches (IRE) *NoelMeade* 9-11-10[162] B.J.Cooper ....9/4f   pu
Gigginstown House Stud 22ran 5m25.60

GALWAY Thursday, Jul 28   GOOD

5   **Guinness Galway Hurdle Handicap (Gr A) (4yo+)** £148,739   2m20y (9)
CLONDAW WARRIOR (IRE) *W.P.Mullins* 9-11-5[143] R.Walsh 9/2f   1
HIDDEN CYCLONE (IRE) *JohnJosephHanlon* 11-10-13[137] (s) D.E.Mullins .....25/1   ½   2
PRINCELY CONN (IRE) *ThomasMullins* 7-10-8[132] (s) RachaelBlackmore(5) ....16/1   ¾   3
Modem *Mrs.J.Harrington* 6-10-13[137] (b) M.J.Bolger 25/1   2   4
Tigris River (IRE) *JosephPatrickO'Brien* 5-10-11[135] (s+t) M.P.Walsh ....8/1   nk   5
Ancient Sands (IRE) *JohnE.Kiely* 8-10-11[135] B.Hayes 25/1   3   6
Pyromaniac (IRE) *A.J.Martin* 6-10-13[137] (s+t) DenisO'Regan ....7/1   ½   7
Quick Jack (IRE) *A.J.Martin* 7-11-10[148] DonaghMeyler(5) ....10/1   nk   8
Bentelimar (IRE) *J.R.Barry* 7-11-2[140] (h) BrianO'Connell 14/1   1   9
Ted Veale (IRE) *A.J.Martin* 9-11-7[145] ShaneShortall(3) ....20/1   nk   10
Moon Over Germany (IRE) *EdwardHarty* 5-10-11[135] DavyRussell ....10/1   ¾   11
Bamako Moriviere (FR) *W.P.Mullins* 5-11-10[148] (t) P.Townend 12/1   2½   12
Rashaan (IRE) *ColinThomasKidd* 4-10-3[133] SeanFlanagan ....33/1   ¾   13
Cliff House (IRE) *JohnJ.Walsh* 6-11-0[138] A.P.Heskin 25/1   1¼   14
Time For Mabel (FR) *E.J.O'Grady* 5-10-10[134] (s) A.E.Lynch 20/1   4½   15
Plinth (IRE) *JosephPatrickO'Brien* 6-11-1[139] (b+t) J.S.McGarvey 40/1   30   16
Rock The World (IRE) *Mrs.J.Harrington* 8-10-13[137] (s+t) D.J.Mullins 20/1   7   17
The Plan Man (IRE) *GordonElliott* 6-10-9[133] (t) J.W.Kennedy ....33/1   pu
Tempo Mac (IRE) *GordonElliott* 6-10-10[134] L.P.Dempsey ....33/1   pu
Superb Story (IRE) *DanSkelton,GB* 5-11-7[145] HarrySkelton ....5/1   pu
Act D Wagg Syndicate 20ran 3m38.00

LISTOWEL Wednesday, Sep 14   HEAVY

6   **Guinness Kerry National Handicap Chase (Gr A) (4yo+)** £87,500   3m (17)
   WRATH OF TITANS (IRE) *GordonElliott* 7-9-10[128] MsL.O'Neill(7) 7/1   1
   RIGHTVILLE BOY (IRE) *PatrickNeville* 8-10-0[128] R.P.Treacy(5) 16/1   5   2
3   GAS LINE BOY *IanWilliams,GB* 10-10-3[135] (v) TomScudamore 9/1   8   3
4   Three Kingdoms (IRE) *D.K.Weld* 7-11-1[147] DavyRussell 20/1   6½   4
4   Ballycasey (IRE) *W.P.Mullins* 9-11-9[155] R.Walsh 8/1   1½   5
   Aurora Bell (IRE) *ThomasCooper* 8-9-10[128] JonathanMoore(3) 16/1   3   6
4   First Lieutenant (IRE) *M.F.Morris* 11-10-11[143] (s) G.N.Fox 16/1   26   7
   Aranhill Chief (IRE) *S.J.Mahon* 9-9-12[132] (t) P.Townend 20/1   4½   8
3   Your Busy (IRE) *JamesA.Nash* 13-9-10[128] (s+t) MsK.Walsh 25/1   13   9
4   Clarcam (FR) *GordonElliott* 6-11-10[156] (s+t) C.M.Collins(7) 25/1   3½   10
   Phil's Magic (IRE) *MsSandraHughes* 6-9-10[128] (v) J.J.Burke ....20/1   F
   Realt Mor (IRE) *GordonElliott* 11-10-1[133] L.P.Dempsey ....25/1   F
4   Lord Scoundrel (IRE) *GordonElliott* 7-11-9[155] DonaghMeyler(5) ....10/1   F
4   Killer Crow (IRE) *GordonElliott* 7-10-0[132] (t) J.W.Kennedy ....7/1   bd
   Shesaportrait (IRE) *PatrickNeville* 8-9-12[130] (b) M.A.Enright ....14/1   pu
   Mad Brian (IRE) *MrsGillianCallaghan* 10-10-0[132] (h+t) R.C.Colgan ....14/1   pu
   Folsom Blue (IRE) *M.F.Morris* 9-10-1[133] (s) B.J.Cooper ....9/2f   pu
4   Shadow Catcher *GordonElliott* 8-10-6[138] (s+t) K.C.Sexton ....20/1   pu
Gigginstown House Stud 18ran 6m09.60

GOWRAN Saturday, Oct 1   GOOD to SOFT

7   **PWC Champion Chase (Gr 2) (5yo+)** £23,087   2½m (14)
6   BALLYCASEY (IRE) *W.P.Mullins* 9-11-3 R.Walsh 5/2   1
4   ROAD TO RICHES (IRE) *NoelMeade* 9-11-8 B.J.Cooper 6/4f   11   2
4   DEVILS BRIDE (IRE) *HenrydeBromhead* 9-11-6 (t) D.J.Mullins 5/1   1½   3

The Game Changer (IRE) *GordonElliott* 7-11-8 (t) DenisO'Regan ....11/1   hd 4
Pairofbrowneyes (IRE) *BarryJohnMurphy* 7-11-3 (s) M.P.Fogarty 25/1   11 5
Mr Fiftyone (IRE) *MrsJ.Harrington* 7-11-3 P.Townend 12/1   2 6
Rightdownthemiddle (IRE) *MichaelMulvany* 8-11-3 M.A.Enright ....50/1   ¾ 7
5   Rock The World (IRE) *MrsJ.Harrington* 8-11-6 (t) M.P.Walsh 10/1   6½ 8
Mrs S. Ricci 8ran 4m58.80

TIPPERARY Sunday, Oct 2   SOFT
8   **Istabraq Hurdle (Gr 2) (4yo+)** £31,001   2m (9)
IVAN GROZNY (FR) *W.P.Mullins* 6-11-7 (h) R.Walsh 2/5f   1
5   BENTELIMAR (IRE) *J.R.Barry* 7-11-4 D.E.Mullins 9/1   4¾ 2
HARGAM (FR) *NickyHenderson,GB* 5-11-4 M.P.Walsh 11/4   11 3
5   Plinth (IRE) *JosephPatrickO'Brien* 6-11-10 (b+t) J.S.McGarvey 25/1   20 4
Peppino (FR) *MrsS.A.Bramall* 6-11-4 A.Ring ....100/1   pu
Andrea Wylie/Graham Wylie 5ran 3m54.60

CHEPSTOW Saturday, Oct 8   GOOD
9   **Totepool Silver Trophy Handicap Hurdle (Gr 3) (1) (4yo+)** £28,475   2m3f100y (11)
BALLYOPTIC (IRE) *NigelTwiston-Davies* 6-11-3[148] RyanHatch(3) 9/2   1
CRIMSON ARK (IRE) *EmmaLavelle* 6-9-10[131] (h) TomScudamore 16/1   1¼ 2
FOREVER FIELD (IRE) *NickyHenderson* 6-10-2[133] NicodeBoinville ....14/1   ns 3
Who Dares Wins (IRE) *AlanKing* 4-10-8[139] WayneHutchinson ....6/1   ½ 4
Mr Mix (FR) *PaulNicholls* 5-10-7[138] HarryCobden(3) ....4/1f   nk 5
Taquin du Seuil (FR) *JonjoO'Neill* 9-11-3[148] AidanColeman 11/1   1 6
Debdebdeb *DanSkelton* 6-9-13[131] IanPopham 17/2   6 7
Caid du Berlais (FR) *PaulNicholls* 7-10-12[143] (t) SamTwiston-Davies 16/1   3½ 8
Wilberdragon *CharlieLongsdon* 6-9-10[131] (t) JonathanMoore(3) 16/1   7 9
Braavos *PhilipHobbs* 5-9-13[131] ThomasCheesman(5) 10/1   2¼ 10
Thomas Crapper *RobinDickin* 9-10-2[133] (s) CharliePoste 25/1   13 11
Tea In Transvaal (IRE) *EvanWilliams* 5-10-0[131] PaulMoloney ....9/1   ½ 12
Sleepy Haven (IRE) *JennieCandlish* 6-9-11[131] SeanQuinlan ....66/1   hd 13
Byron Flyer *IanWilliams* 5-9-12[131] JamieBargary(5) ....20/1   ½ 14
Mills & Mason Partnership 14ran 4m38.10

CHEPSTOW Sunday, Oct 9   GOOD
10   **Totepool Persian War Novices' Hurdle (Gr 2) (1) (4yo+)** £19,932   2m3f100y (11)
EL BANDIT (IRE) *PaulNicholls* 5-11-4 SeanBowen 13/2   1
COO STAR SIVOLA (FR) *NickWilliams* 4-11-0 LizzieKelly 9/2   1 2
MIRSAALE *KeithDalgleish* 6-11-4 BrianHarding 12/1   2 3
Three Ways *JamieSnowden* 5-11-4 (t) BrendanPowell 33/1   7 4
Valadom (FR) *RichardHobson* 7-11-0 (t) AlainCawley 20/1   28 5
Bagad Bihoue (FR) *PaulNicholls* 5-11-4 NickScholfield 6/1   37 6
No Comment *PhilipHobbs* 5-11-0 BarryGeraghty ....6/4f   ur
Birch Hill (IRE) *SophieLeech* 6-11-4 (t) TomScudamore ....50/1   pu
Canton Prince (IRE) *TimVaughan* 5-11-4 RichardJohnson ....9/1   pu
Colm Donlon, Barry Fulton & Richard Webb 9ran 4m41.00

LIMERICK Sunday, Oct 9   GOOD to SOFT
11   **JT McNamara Ladbrokes Munster National Handicap Chase (Gr A) (4yo+)**   3m (16)
£51,304
TIGER ROLL (IRE) *GordonElliott* 6-10-6[138] (b+t) DonaghMeyler(5) 20/1   1
STELLAR NOTION (IRE) *HenrydeBromhead* 8-10-3[135] D.J.Mullins 13/2   7 2
KYLECRUE (IRE) *JohnPatrickRyan* 9-10-2[134] (b) D.E.Mullins 12/1   3¼ 3
6   Rightville Boy (IRE) *PatrickNeville* 8-10-0[132] RachaelBlackmore 14/1   7½ 4
Dare To Endeavour *EricMcNamara* 9-10-0[134] R.Walsh 16/1   3 5
6   Wrath of Titans (IRE) *GordonElliott* 7-10-5[137] MsLisaO'Neill(7) 13/2   2¾ 6
6   Killer Crow (IRE) *GordonElliott* 7-10-0[132] (s+t) J.J.Burke 8/1   1 7
Rogue Angel (IRE) *M.F.Morris* 8-10-12[144] (b+t) G.N.Fox 25/1   3¼ 8
4   The King of Brega (IRE) *HenrydeBromhead* 9-10-1[133] (s) D.Robinson(7) 10/1   4¾ 9
On Fiddlers Green (IRE) *HenrydeBromhead* 6-9-13[131] M.A.Enright 7/2f   6 10
Federici *EndaBolger* 7-10-0[132] (s) R.C.Colgan ....9/1   pu
6   Folsom Blue (IRE) *M.F.Morris* 9-10-1[133] (s) A.Ring(5) ....14/1   pu
Elegant Statesman (IRE) *HenrydeBromhead* 9-10-1[133] (s+t) M.P.Walsh ....12/1   pu
Tulsa Jack (IRE) *NoelMeade* 7-10-2[134] (b) SeanFlanagan ....16/1   pu
The Job Is Right *M.Hourigan* 8-10-5[137] P.Townend ....12/1   pu
Gigginstown House Stud 15ran 6m02.70

CHELTENHAM Saturday, Oct 22   GOOD
12   **Randox Health Handicap Chase (2) (4yo+)** £31,280   1m7f199y (13)
FOX NORTON (FR) *NeilMulholland* 6-11-1[146] (h) NoelFehily 5/2f   1

4	SIZING PLATINUM (IRE) *ColinTizzard* 8-10-9[140] AidanColeman 10/1	11	2
	CASINO MARKETS (IRE) *EmmaLavelle* 8-10-1[132] TomScudamore 7/1	9	3
7	Mr Fiftyone (IRE) *MrsJ.Harrington,Ireland* 7-10-13[144] P.Townend 16/1	6	4
	Owen Na View (IRE) *FergalO'Brien* 8-9-13[131] (b) PaddyBrennan 25/1	2½	5
	UltragoId (IRE) *ColinTizzard* 8-10-6[137] (t) HarryCobden(3) 10/1	½	6
	Witness In Court (IRE) *DonaldMcCain* 9-10-13[144] WayneHutchinson 33/1	1½	7
	Always On The Run (IRE) *TomGeorge* 6-10-8[139] A.P.Heskin 12/1	14	8
7	Devils Bride (IRE) *HenrydeBromhead,Ireland* 9-11-12[157] (t) RachaelBlackmore(5) ..14/1	1¼	9
	Dunraven Storm (IRE) *PhilipHobbs* 11-11-5[150] RichardJohnson 25/1	2¾	10
7	Rock The World (IRE) *MrsJ.Harrington,Ireland* 8-11-4[149] (t) BarryGeraghty 8/1	1½	11
	Minella Definitely (IRE) *NeilMulholland* 9-9-9[131] (s) DavidNoonan(3) 100/1		F
	Croco Bay (IRE) *BenCase* 9-11-1[146] DarylJacob 33/1		ur
	Boondooma (IRE) *DrRichardNewland* 9-11-7[152] BrendanPowell 7/1		pu

Mr B. Dunn 14ran 3m50.80

AINTREE Sunday, Oct 23   GOOD

13 188Bet Monet's Garden Old Roan Handicap Chase (Gr 2) (1) (4yo+)   2m3f200y (16)
£36,576

	THIRD INTENTION (IRE) *ColinTizzard* 9-10-7[150] (t) AidanColeman 5/1		1
	GOD'S OWN (IRE) *TomGeorge* 8-11-9[166] A.P.Heskin 4/1	1¾	2
	VIBRATO VALTAT (FR) *PaulNicholls* 7-11-3[160] (t) NickScholfield 9/1	2½	3
	Smad Place (FR) *AlanKing* 9-11-10[167] WayneHutchinson 13/2	nk	4
	Royal Regatta (IRE) *PhilipHobbs* 8-10-7[150] (b+t) RichardJohnson 13/2	3½	5
	Three Musketeers (IRE) *DanSkelton* 6-10-9[152] HarrySkelton 7/4f	6	6
	Sire de Grugy (FR) *GaryMoore* 10-11-9[166] JamieMoore 20/1	5	7

Robert and Sarah Tizzard 7ran 4m51.50

WETHERBY Saturday, Oct 29   GOOD

14 Bet365 Hurdle (West Yorkshire) (Gr 2) (1) (4yo+) £22,780   3m26y (12)

	SILSOL (GER) *PaulNicholls* 7-11-1 (b+t) JackSherwood 13/2		1
	NATIVE RIVER (IRE) *ColinTizzard* 6-11-1 (s) RichardJohnson 5/2	2¾	2
	LIL ROCKERFELLER (USA) *NeilKing* 5-11-9 (s) TrevorWhelan 14/1	½	3
	The Romford Pele (IRE) *RebeccaCurtis* 9-11-1 (b) JonathanMoore 10/1	2¼	4
	If In Doubt (IRE) *PhilipHobbs* 8-11-1 BarryGeraghty 6/1	19	5
9	Ballyoptic (IRE) *NigelTwiston-Davies* 6-11-5 RyanHatch 6/4f		F

Michelle And Dan Macdonald 6ran 5m48.90

15 Bet365 Charlie Hall Chase (Gr 2) (1) (5yo+) £56,950   3m45y (19)

	IRISH CAVALIER (IRE) *RebeccaCurtis* 7-11-6 (s) JonathanMoore 16/1		1
3	MENORAH (IRE) *PhilipHobbs* 11-11-10 RichardJohnson 12/1	¾	2
	CUE CARD *ColinTizzard* 10-11-10 (t) PaddyBrennan 8/11f	2½	3
	Blaklion *NigelTwiston-Davies* 7-11-5 RyanHatch 7/2	5	4
	Virak (FR) *PaulNicholls* 7-11-0 (s) SeanBowen 10/1	4	5
	Dynaste (FR) *DavidPipe* 10-11-0 (b+t) TomScudamore 10/1	½	6
	Wakanda (IRE) *SueSmith* 7-11-6 DannyCook 33/1	38	7

Mr A. McIver 7ran 6m00.00

ASCOT Saturday, Oct 29   GOOD to FIRM

16 Byrne Group Handicap Chase (L) (1) (150) (4yo+) £34,170   2m192y (13)

	QUITE BY CHANCE *ColinTizzard* 7-11-1[135] TomO'Brien 8/1		1
	NOCHE DE REYES (FR) *TomGeorge* 7-10-8[128] A.P.Heskin 7/1	6	2
	FESTIVE AFFAIR (IRE) *JonjoO'Neill* 8-10-5[125] (s+t) JoshuaMoore 12/1	1	3
1	Roman Flight (IRE) *DavidDennis* 8-11-8[142] (v) NoelFehily 14/1	½	4
	All Together (IRE) *JohnnyFarrelly* 5-10-11[131] JamesBest 16/1	8	5
	Yorkist (IRE) *DanSkelton* 8-10-12[132] (t) HarrySkelton 5/2f	2¼	6
	Miss Tenacious *RonHodges* 9-11-0[134] HarryCobden(3) 16/1	3½	7
	Germany Calling (IRE) *CharlieLongsdon* 7-11-3[137] (s+t) AndrewTinkler ...13/2	7	8
12	Croco Bay (IRE) *BenCase* 9-11-12[146] DarylJacob 8/1	28	9
	Lord Ben (IRE) *DaiWilliams* 11-11-6[140] JamesBanks 40/1	1	10
	Ulck du Lin (FR) *PaulNicholls* 8-11-7[141] (b+t) NickScholfield 8/1	19	11

T Hamlin,J M Dare,J W Snook,J T Warner 11ran 3m55.60

17 William Hill Handicap Hurdle (L) (1) (4yo+) £34,170   1m7f152y (8)

	STERNRUBIN (GER) *PhilipHobbs* 5-11-10[142] (h) TomO'Brien 12/1		1
	INSTANT KARMA (IRE) *MichaelBell* 5-10-13[131] LeightonAspell 20/1	½	2
	MODUS *PaulNicholls* 6-11-7[139] (h) HarryCobden(3) 6/1	nk	3
	Fergall (IRE) *SeamusMullins* 9-11-3[135] KevinJohnson(5) 14/1	sh	4
1	Ch'tibello (FR) *DanSkelton* 5-11-12[144] HarrySkelton 6/1	¾	5
	My Manekineko *JamesA.Nash,Ireland* 7-10-9[127] (h) P.Townend 20/1	6	6
1	John Constable (IRE) *EvanWilliams* 5-11-7[139] DavyRussell 8/1	1¾	7

Colla Pier (IRE) *DavidPeterDunne,Ireland* 7-10-11[129] RobertDunne 25/1   4 8
Diego du Charmil (FR) *PaulNicholls* 4-11-9[141] (t) NickScholfield 3/1f   2 9
Minellaforleisure (IRE) *AlexHales* 8-11-5[137] HarryBannister(3) 33/1 1 10
Cloonacool (IRE) *StuartEdmunds* 7-11-3[135] JoshuaMoore 11/1 13 11
Hint of Mint *HarryFry* 7-10-12[130] NoelFehily 6/1 2¼ 12
Mr Terry Warner 12ran 3m34.90

18   **Sodexo Gold Cup Handicap Chase (Gr 3) (1) (4yo+)** £56,950   2m7f180y (20)
ANTONY (FR) *GaryMoore* 6-10-1[128] JamieMoore 11/1   1
  4 JUNCTION FOURTEEN (IRE) *EmmaLavelle* 7-11-6[147] (t) DarylJacob 16/1 4½ 2
SAPHIR DU RHEU (FR) *PaulNicholls* 7-11-11[152] NickScholfield ....9/4f sh 3
Fourth Act (IRE) *ColinTizzard* 7-10-10[137] (t) TomO'Brien 20/1   3 4
Tea For Two *NickWilliams* 7-11-12[153] LizzieKelly(5) 6/1   1 5
A Good Skin (IRE) *TomGeorge* 7-10-12[139] A.P.Heskin ....6/1 nk 6
Voix d'Eau (FR) *HarryFry* 6-11-8[149] (t) NoelFehily ....8/1 nk 7
Workbench (FR) *DanSkelton* 8-10-9[136] (t) HarrySkelton 33/1   6 8
Hadrian's Approach (IRE) *NickyHenderson* 9-11-0[141] PaulMoloney ....16/1 ½ 9
Buckhorn Timothy *ColinTizzard* 7-10-11[138] BrendanPowell ....10/1 ½ 10
Un Ace (FR) *KimBailey* 8-11-3[144] (t) DavidBass 14/1 13 11
Killala Quay *CharlieLongsdon* 9-10-11[138] (s) DavyRussell ....18/1 pu
The Winning Hand 12ran 5m50.10

CARLISLE Sunday, Oct 30   GOOD to SOFT
19   **Colin Parker Memorial Intermediate Chase (L) (1) (4yo+)** £15,661   2½m (16)
SEEYOUATMIDNIGHT *SandyThomson* 8-11-12 BrianHughes 15/8   1
BRISTOL DE MAI (FR) *NigelTwiston-Davies* 5-11-12 DarylJacob 2/5f 12 2
Mrs A. M. Thomson 2ran 5m05.00

DOWN ROYAL Friday, Nov 4   GOOD
20   **WKD Hurdle (Gr 2) (4yo+)** £27,928   2m (9)
  5 RASHAAN (IRE) *ColinThomasKidd* 4-11-2 SeanFlanagan 10/1   1
APPLE'S JADE (FR) *GordonElliott* 4-11-0 R.Walsh 1/2f 1½ 2
PETIT MOUCHOIR (FR) *HenrydeBromhead* 5-11-2 D.J.Mullins 9/4 1¾ 3
 17 My Manekineko *JamesA.Nash* 7-11-2 (h) P.Townend 33/1   5 4
Mrs T J Kidd & Mrs R Treacy 4ran 3m51.30

DOWN ROYAL Saturday, Nov 5   GOOD
21   **JNwine.com Champion Chase (Gr 1) (5yo+)** £75,675   3m (17)
VALSEUR LIDO (FR) *HenrydeBromhead* 7-11-10 R.Walsh 2/1f   1
SILVINIACO CONTI (FR) *PaulNicholls,GB* 10-11-10 (b) NoelFehily 11/4 11 2
  6 LORD SCOUNDREL (IRE) *GordonElliott* 7-11-10 KeithDonoghue 25/1 4½ 3
Sadler's Risk (IRE) *HenrydeBromhead* 8-11-10 D.J.Mullins 12/1 5½ 4
The Last Samuri (IRE) *KimBailey,GB* 8-11-10 DavidBass 10/1 5½ 5
Monksland (IRE) *NoelMeade* 9-11-10 (h) SeanFlanagan ....8/1   F
Don Poli (IRE) *GordonElliott* 7-11-10 (s) BarryGeraghty ....3/1 pu
Gigginstown House Stud 7ran 5m58.30

22   **Titanic Belfast Chase (Gr 2) (4yo+)** £26,577   2m3f120y (11)
The first fence was omitted on both circuits due to the low trajectory of the sun
SUB LIEUTENANT (IRE) *HenrydeBromhead* 7-11-8 (t) D.J.Mullins 6/4f   1
OUTLANDER (IRE) *GordonElliott* 8-11-12 R.Walsh 11/4 3½ 2
LE MERCUREY (FR) *PaulNicholls,GB* 6-11-10 (b+t) NoelFehily 3/1 7½ 3
Zabana (IRE) *AndrewLynch* 7-11-12 KeithDonoghue 6/1 3½ 4
  6 Shadow Catcher *GordonElliott* 8-11-5 (b+t) BarryGeraghty 25/1 2¾ 5
Net d'Ecosse (FR) *NoelMeade* 6-11-5 (v) P.Townend 20/1 30 6
Celtic Thunder (IRE) *R.K.Watson* 7-11-1 (s+t) I.J.McCarthy ....150/1 pu
Gigginstown House Stud 7ran 4m49.20

WINCANTON Saturday, Nov 5   GOOD to FIRM
23   **Stan James Elite Hurdle (Limited Handicap) (Gr 2) (1) (4yo+)** £31,892   1m7f65y (8)
SCEAU ROYAL (FR) *AlanKing* 4-11-10[149] DarylJacob 4/6f   1
RAYVIN BLACK *OliverSherwood* 7-11-5[144] (s) ThomasGarner(3) 7/1   9 2
ARISTO DU PLESSIS (FR) *JamesEwart* 6-11-10[149] (s) DaleIrving(5) 16/1 28 3
Zubayr (IRE) *PaulNicholls* 4-11-4[143] HarryCobden(3) ....2/1   F
Peckhamecho (IRE) *SophieLeech* 10-10-8[133] PatrickCowley(7) ....100/1 ur
Mr Simon Munir & Mr Isaac Souede 5ran 3m24.80

24   **Badger Ales Trophy Handicap Chase (L) (1) (150) (4yo+)** £34,170   3m1f30y (21)
GENTLEMAN JON *ColinTizzard* 8-10-6[130] (t) TomO'Brien 9/1   1
SET LIST (IRE) *EmmaLavelle* 7-10-5[129] (v) DarylJacob 10/1 25 2

958

FINGERONTHESWITCH (IRE) *NeilMulholland* 6-9-13[124] JamesBest 11/2   12 3
Bob Tucker (IRE) *CharlieLongsdon* 9-10-5[129] GrahamWatters(3) .... 20/1   ¾ 4
Roc d'Apsis (FR) *TomGeorge* 7-10-9[133] (s) PaddyBrennan 8/1   1¼ 5
Southfield Theatre (IRE) *PaulNicholls* 8-11-9[147] HarryCobden(3) .... 11/8f   F
Present Man (IRE) *PaulNicholls* 6-10-8[132] (t) JackSherwood(5) .... 7/2   ur

Mr J. P. Romans 7ran 6m21.50

AUTEUIL Sunday, Nov 6   SOFT

25   **Prix La Haye Jousselin Chase (Gr1) (5-y-o+)** £220,982   3m3f75y

MILORD THOMAS (FR) *D.Bressou,France* 7-10-10 JacquesRicou 16/10f   1
ALARY (FR) *Francois-MarieCottin,France* (s) 6-10-10 RegisSchmidlin .... 59/10   ½ 2
STORM OF SAINTLY (FR) *GuillaumeMacaire,France* 7-10-10 ThomasGueguen .36/10   2½ 3
So French (FR) *GuillaumeMacaire,France* 5-10-6 JamesReveley 3/1   15 4
Shannon Rock (FR) *J-P.Gallorini,France* 10-10-10 (b) StevenColas............... 21/1   4 5
Saint Palois (FR) *EmmanuelClayeux,France* 8-10-10 (b) FelixdeGiles 21/1   7 6
Djagble (FR) *J.BertrandeBalanda,France* 5-10-8 JonathanPlouganou .... 44/1   ds 7
Reglis Brunel (FR) *E.Lecoiffier,France* 11-10-10 ArnaudDuchene .... 39/1   pu
Tito Dela Barriere (FR) *E.Lecoiffier,France* 9-10-10 KevinNabet...................... 75/1   pu
Pindare (FR) *GuillaumeMacaire,France* 7-10-10 (b) NathalieDesoutter .... 32/1   pu

Mme Magalen Bryant 10ran 7m06.21

CHELTENHAM Friday, Nov 11   GOOD

26   **Neptune Investment Management Hyde Novices' Hurdle (Gr 2) (1) (4yo+)**   2m5f26y (10)
£17,085

PEREGRINE RUN (IRE) *PeterFahey,Ireland* 6-11-7 RogerLoughran 13/2   1
WHOLESTONE (IRE) *NigelTwiston-Davies* 5-11-7 DarylJacob 5/2f   1 2
WEST APPROACH *ColinTizzard* 6-11-7 AidanColeman 3/1   3½ 3
Spiritofthegames (IRE) *DanSkelton* 4-11-0 HarrySkelton 10/1   8 4
Baden (FR) *NickyHenderson* 5-11-0 AndrewTinkler 10/3   10 5
Leith Hill Lad *CharlieLongsdon* 6-11-4 RichardJohnson .... 33/1   ½ 6
Crosshue Boy (IRE) *SeanThomasDoyle,Ireland* 6-11-7 DavyRussell 33/1   3 7
Bally Gilbert (IRE) *BenPauling* 5-11-0 NicodeBoinville 16/1   18 8
Pilansberg *PaulNicholls* 4-11-4 (s) NickScholfield 20/1   16 9

Mr V. Byrne 9ran 5m05.80

CHELTENHAM Saturday, Nov 12   SOFT

27   **JCB Triumph Trial Juvenile Hurdle (Prestbury) (Gr 2) (1) (3yo)** £17,085   2m87y (8)

DEFI DU SEUIL (FR) *PhilipHobbs* 3-10-12 BarryGeraghty 5/4f   1
DIABLE DE SIVOLA (FR) *NickWilliams* 3-11-2 LizzieKelly 8/1   1¾ 2
LAMBEAU FIELD (USA) *CharlieLongsdon* 3-10-12 AidanColeman 33/1   58 3
Hazamar (IRE) *SophieLeech* 3-10-12 (t) P.Townend 66/1   1¾ 4
Red Hot Chilly (IRE) *DaiBurchell* 3-10-12 IanPopham 33/1   8 5
Dino Velvet (FR) *AlanKing* 3-10-12 WayneHutchinson .... 6/1   F
Nucky Thompson *RichardSpencer* 3-11-2 (h+t) NoelFehily .... 10/1   pu
East Indies *GaryMoore* 3-11-2 (h) JoshuaMoore .... 14/1   pu
Wealth des Mottes (FR) *PaulNicholls* 3-11-5 SeanBowen .... 7/2   pu

Mr John P. McManus 9ran 4m06.70

28   **BetVictor Handicap Chase (Gr 3) (1) (4yo+)** £28,475   3m3f71y (22)

VICONTE DU NOYER (FR) *ColinTizzard* 7-11-2[148] HarryCobden(3) 20/1   1
WARRANTOR (IRE) *WarrenGreatrex* 7-9-12[132] (t) GavinSheehan 14/1   1 2
MINELLA ROCCO (IRE) *JonjoO'Neill* 6-11-9[155] (t) BarryGeraghty .... 11/2f   hd 3
18 Fourth Act (IRE) *ColinTizzard* 7-10-5[137] (t) TomO'Brien 12/1   4½ 4
Upswing (IRE) *JonjoO'Neill* 8-10-5[137] (b) AidanColeman 11/1   1¾ 5
Alvarado (IRE) *FergalO'Brien* 11-10-4[136] PaulMoloney .... 14/1   nk 6
Shotgun Paddy (IRE) *EmmaLavelle* 9-10-8[140] DarylJacob .... 13/2   ½ 7
18 Un Ace (FR) *KimBailey* 8-10-10[142] (t) ConorShoemark 28/1   18 8
Doctor Harper (IRE) *DavidPipe* 8-10-6[138] TomScudamore 11/1   3 9
Unioniste (FR) *PaulNicholls* 8-11-2[148] NickScholfield .... 16/1   ½ 10
Sausalito Sunrise (IRE) *PhilipHobbs* 8-11-12[158] (s) RichardJohnson 8/1   9 11
Any Currency (IRE) *MartinKeighley* 13-10-7[139] (s) AndrewTinkler 25/1   6 12
Le Reve (IRE) *LucyWadham* 8-11-0[146] (b) NicodeBoinville .... 33/1   ur
Cogry *NigelTwiston-Davies* 7-10-2[134] (s) RyanHatch(3) .... 7/1   bd
Racing Pulse (IRE) *RebeccaCurtis* 7-10-4[136] JonathanMoore(3) .... 16/1   bd
Midnight Prayer *AlanKing* 11-10-7[139] WayneHutchinson .... 16/1   bd
Beg To Differ (IRE) *JonjoO'Neill* 6-10-11[143] (v) NoelFehily .... 16/1   pu

Ann & Alan Potts 17ran 7m27.00

29   **BetVictor Gold Cup Handicap Chase (Gr 3) (1) (4yo+)** £91,120   2½m78y (16)

9 TAQUIN DU SEUIL (FR) *JonjoO'Neill* 9-11-11[156] AidanColeman 8/1   1

VILLAGE VIC (IRE) *PhilipHobbs* 9-11-10[155] RichardJohnson ....20/1   nk   2
BUYWISE (IRE) *EvanWilliams* 9-11-5[150] PaulMoloney 12/1   2   3
Aso (FR) *VenetiaWilliams* 6-10-13[144] CharlieDeutsch(5) 14/1   3   4
Bouvreuil (FR) *PaulNicholls* 5-11-1[146] (h+t) GavinSheehan 12/1   1½   5
9 Thomas Crapper *RobinDickin* 9-10-3[134] (s+t) CharliePoste 33/1   8   6
Art Mauresque (FR) *PaulNicholls* 6-11-11[156] NickScholfield 25/1   1½   7
As de Mee (FR) *PaulNicholls* 6-10-8[139] (h) SeanBowen 7/1   2¾   8
12 Sizing Platinum (IRE) *ColinTizzard* 8-10-11[142] DarylJacob 20/1   9   9
Frodon (FR) *PaulNicholls* 4-10-11[151] HarryCobden(3) 6/1   7 10
Potters Cross *RebeccaCurtis* 9-9-10[131] P.Townend ....16/1   pu
Vintage Vinnie (IRE) *RebeccaCurtis* 7-10-7[138] JonathanMoore(3) ....16/1   pu
Double Shuffle (IRE) *TomGeorge* 6-11-0[145] A.P.Heskin ....10/1   pu
More of That (IRE) *JonjoO'Neill* 8-11-9[154] BarryGeraghty ....7/2f   pu
Sizing Granite (IRE) *ColinTizzard* 8-11-9[154] TomO'Brien ....20/1   pu
Annacotty (IRE) *AlanKing* 8-11-11[156] (s) IanPopham ....25/1   pu
3 Ballynagour (IRE) *DavidPipe* 10-11-12[157] (h+t) TomScudamore ....33/1   pu
Martin Broughton & Friends 1 17ran 5m16.30

CHELTENHAM Sunday, Nov 13 SOFT

30 Sky Bet Supreme Trial Novices' Hurdle (Sharp) (Gr 2) (1) (4yo+) £17,085   2m87y (8)
MOON RACER (IRE) *DavidPipe* 7-11-4 TomScudamore 9/4   1
10 MIRSAALE *KeithDalgleish* 6-11-4 BrianHarding 14/1   2¼   2
BALLYANDY *NigelTwiston-Davies* 5-11-0 RyanHatch ....5/4f   ½   3
Keep In Line (GER) *AlanKing* 4-11-4 WayneHutchinson ....5/1   ½   4
Movewiththetimes (IRE) *PaulNicholls* 5-11-4 BarryGeraghty ....8/1   ½   5
What About Carlo (FR) *EveJohnsonHoughton* 5-11-0 AidanColeman 33/1   21   6
Professor Caroline Tisdall & Bryan Drew 6ran 4m05.90

31 Racing Post Arkle Trophy Trial Novices' Chase (November) (Gr 2) (1)   1m7f199y (13)
(4yo+) £18,224
LE PREZIEN (FR) *PaulNicholls* 5-11-2 (t) BarryGeraghty 8/11f   1
HAMMERSLY LAKE (FR) *NickyHenderson* 8-11-2 PaulMoloney 12/1   4   2
THREE STARS (IRE) *HenrydeBromhead,Ireland* 6-11-8 RichardJohnson 11/2   10   3
Mick Thonic (FR) *ColinTizzard* 6-11-2 (t) AidanColeman ....8/1   F
1 Some Plan (IRE) *HenrydeBromhead,Ireland* 8-11-6 (t) D.J.Mullins ....9/2   F
Mr John P. McManus 5ran 4m02.50

32 Shloer Chase (Cheltenham) (Gr 2) (1) (4yo+) £42,712   1m7f199y (13)
12 FOX NORTON (FR) *ColinTizzard* 6-11-4 (h) AidanColeman 5/2   1
SIMPLY NED (IRE) *NickyRichards* 9-11-0 BrianHarding 16/1   9   2
SPECIAL TIARA *HenrydeBromhead,Ireland* 9-11-0 NoelFehily 2/1f   9   3
Module (FR) *TomGeorge* 9-11-0 A.P.Heskin 20/1   3¾   4
Top Gamble (IRE) *KerryLee* 8-11-10 RichardJohnson 8/1   3   5
Just Cameron *MickyHammond* 9-11-0 (t) BrianHughes 50/1   10   6
Savello (IRE) *DanSkelton* 10-11-6 (h+t) HarrySkelton 33/1   19   7
Simonsig *NickyHenderson* 10-11-0 BarryGeraghty ....3/1   F
Ann & Alan Potts 8ran 4m01.80

33 stanjames.com Greatwood Handicap Hurdle (Gr 3) (1) (4yo+) £56,950   2m87y (13)
NORTH HILL HARVEY *DanSkelton* 5-11-0[141] HarrySkelton 6/1   1
17 MODUS *PaulNicholls* 6-10-13[140] (h) HarryCobden(3) ....5/1   ½   2
SONG LIGHT *SeamusMullins* 6-10-3[130] KevinJones(5) 16/1   1¼   3
A Hare Breath (IRE) *BenPauling* 8-10-10[137] DavidBass ....14/1   ½   4
17 Sternrubin (GER) *PhilipHobbs* 5-11-4[145] (h) RichardJohnson 8/1   8   5
17 John Constable (IRE) *EvanWilliams* 5-10-10[137] ConorRing(3) 20/1   8   6
Leoncavallo (IRE) *BenPauling* 4-10-13[140] MrAlexFerguson(7) 9/1   1½   7
Brain Power (IRE) *NickyHenderson* 5-11-4[145] (s) PaulMoloney ....12/1   nk   8
Cyrus Moriviere (FR) *BenPauling* 6-10-8[135] (t) MauriceLinehan(3) 33/1   10   9
Jack The Wire (IRE) *DenisHogan,Ireland* 6-9-13[127] DenisHogan 16/1   4½ 10
Winter Escape (IRE) *AlanKing* 5-11-1[142] BarryGeraghty 3/1f   7 11
8 Hargam (FR) *NickyHenderson* 5-11-12[153] AndrewTinkler 25/1   26 12
Wolf of Windlesham (IRE) *StuartEdmunds* 4-10-10[137] JoshuaMoore ....20/1   F
Thunder Sheik (IRE) *NigelTwiston-Davies* 8-10-2[129] (s+t) RyanHatch(3) ....66/1   pu
Mad Jack Mytton (IRE) *JonjoO'Neill* 6-10-8[135] AidanColeman ....14/1   pu
Rossetti *NeilMulholland* 8-10-11[138] (h) NoelFehily ....33/1   pu
Mrs G. Widdowson & Mrs R. Kelvin-Hughes 16ran 3m56.40

NAVAN Sunday, Nov 13 GOOD to SOFT

34 For Auction Novices' Hurdle (Gr 3) (4yo+) £17,846   2m (10)
LABAIK (FR) *GordonElliott* 5-11-1 R.Walsh 11/4   1
MICK JAZZ (FR) *GordonElliott* 5-11-1 (h) KeithDonoghue 12/1   1¾   2

960

LE MARTALIN (FR) *NoelMeade* 5-11-1 (b+t) SeanFlanagan 6/5f   2¼   3
Wakea (USA) *KarlThornton* 5-11-1 (h+t) DonaghMeyler 5/2   23   4
Jaime Sommers (IRE) *MichaelJ.Bowe* 4-10-5 B.Hayes 33/1   2¼   5
Aidan J. O'Ryan 5ran 4m01.00

35   **Lismullen Hurdle (Gr 2) (4yo+)** £22,389   2½m (11)
      SNOW FALCON (IRE) *NoelMeade* 6-11-10 SeanFlanagan 5/1   1
      DE PLOTTING SHED (IRE) *GordonElliott* 6-11-5 KeithDonoghue 2/1   3¼   2
      SHANESHILL (IRE) *W.P.Mullins* 7-11-5 R.Walsh 11/10f   1¼   3
      Dedigout (IRE) *GordonElliott* 10-11-5 (t) M.A.Enright 10/1   6½   4
      Noble Endeavor (IRE) *GordonElliott* 7-11-5 (s) R.C.Colgan ....25/1   sh   5
      Taglietelle *GordonElliott* 7-11-5 (b) DenisO'Regan ....25/1   ½   6
      Ucello Conti (FR) *GordonElliott* 8-11-5 (t) K.C.Sexton 50/1   16   7
      Mrs Patricia Hunt 7ran 5m12.00

      CLONMEL Thursday, Nov 17   GOOD to SOFT
36   **Clonmel Oil Chase (Gr 2) (4yo+)** £25,431   2½m (12)
  4   ALELCHI INOIS (FR) *W.P.Mullins* 8-11-5 R.Walsh 2/1f   1
  6   CLARCAM (FR) *GordonElliott* 6-11-8 (s+t) J.W.Kennedy 12/1   5   2
  21   MONKSLAND (IRE) *NoelMeade* 9-11-1 (h) SeanFlanagan 5/2   5   3
      Dromnea (IRE) *M.F.Morris* 9-11-5 M.A.Enright ....25/1   ½   4
      Days Hotel (IRE) *HenrydeBromhead* 11-11-10 D.J.Mullins 16/1   1   5
      Draycott Place (IRE) *JohnPatrickRyan* 7-11-5 (t) D.E.Mullins 25/1   15   6
  22   Outlander (IRE) *GordonElliott* 8-11-8 B.J.Cooper ....9/4   F
      Luke McMahon/F. Murphy & Francis Mangan 7ran 4m56.20

      ASCOT Saturday, Nov 19   GOOD to SOFT
37   **Stella Artois 1965 Chase (Gr 2) (1) (4yo+)** £39,865   2m5f8y (17)
  13   ROYAL REGATTA (IRE) *PhilipHobbs* 8-11-7 (b+t) TomO'Brien 10/1   1
      KYLEMORE LOUGH *KerryLee* 7-11-7 JamieMoore ....13/2   hd   2
  13   GOD'S OWN (IRE) *TomGeorge* 8-11-11 A.P.Heskin 7/2   1¾   3
      Eduard (IRE) *NickyRichards* 8-11-1 CraigNichol ....7/1   ¾   4
  13   Vibrato Valtat (FR) *PaulNicholls* 7-11-7 (t) JamieMoore 7/1   3   5
  13   Third Intention (IRE) *ColinTizzard* 9-11-7 (t) DarylJacob 10/1   13   6
      Dodging Bullets *PaulNicholls* 8-11-1 (t) NickScholfield ....9/4f   pu
      Mrs Lesley Field & Mrs Eileen Murphy 7ran 5m14.00

38   **Coral Hurdle (Ascot) (Gr 2) (1) (4yo+)** £56,950   2m3f58y (10)
      YANWORTH *AlanKing* 6-11-4 BarryGeraghty 4/5f   1
  14   LIL ROCKERFELLER (USA) *NeilKing* 5-11-8 (s) TrevorWhelan .... 10/1   ¾   2
      GARDE LA VICTOIRE (FR) *PhilipHobbs* 7-11-0 TomO'Brien 4/1   10   3
      Court Minstrel (IRE) *EvanWilliams* 9-11-4 PaulMoloney ....25/1   ½   4
      Zarkandar (IRE) *PaulNicholls* 9-11-0 (b+t) SeanBowen 4/1   3¾   5
      Mr John P. McManus 5ran 4m37.90

      HAYDOCK Saturday, Nov 19   HEAVY
39   **Betfair Price Rush Hurdle (2) (4yo+)** £61,900   2m45y (9)
  17   CH'TIBELLO (FR) *DanSkelton* 5-11-1 HarrySkelton 5/1   1
      MELODIC RENDEZVOUS *JeremyScott* 10-11-3 (b) RichardJohnson 10/1   2¼   2
      MY TENT OR YOURS (IRE) *NickyHenderson* 9-11-3 (h) NoelFehily 10/11f   2   3
      Old Guard *PaulNicholls* 5-11-3 (s) HarryCobden 5/2   2¼   4
      The Can't Say No Partnership 4ran 4m11.40

40   **Betfair Exchange 'Fixed Brush' Handicap Hurdle (Gr 3) (1) (4yo+)** £45,560   2¾m177y (12)
      KRUZHLININ (GER) *PhilipHobbs* 9-10-13[136] (b) RichardJohnson 9/1   1
      THEO'S CHARM (IRE) *NickGifford* 6-10-7[130] (s) WayneHutchinson 15/2   2½   2
      YALA ENKI (FR) *VenetiaWilliams* 6-11-2[139] HarryCobden(3) 5/1f   6   3
      Donna's Diamond (IRE) *ChrisGrant* 7-10-10[133] RyanHatch(3) 50/1   2   4
      Westren Warrior (IRE) *DrRichardNewland* 7-10-13[136] BrianHughes 6/1   2¾   5
      Point The Way (IRE) *BrianEllison* 5-10-8[131] DannyCook 6/1   14   6
      Two Taffs (IRE) *DanSkelton* 6-11-1[138] HarrySkelton 7/1   9   7
      Rathpatrick (IRE) *EoinGriffin,Ireland* 8-10-12[135] JonathanMoore(3) ....20/1   ur
      Matorico (IRE) *JonjoO'Neill* 5-11-2[139] (s+t) AidanColeman ....20/1   ur
      Affaire d'Honneur (FR) *HarryWhittington* 5-10-5[128] (s) JoshuaMoore ....16/1   pu
      Western Cape (IRE) *SeamusMullins* 5-10-10[133] KevinJones(5) ....16/1   pu
      Ballybolley (IRE) *NigelTwiston-Davies* 7-10-11[134] JamieBargary(3) ....20/1   pu
  9   Caid du Berlais (FR) *PaulNicholls* 7-11-11[148] (t) StanSheppard(5) ....9/1   pu
      Paul & Clare Rooney 13ran 5m57.00

41   **Betfair Chase (Lancashire) (Gr 1) (1) (5yo+)** £117,604   3m24y (18)
  15   CUE CARD *ColinTizzard* 10-11-7 (t) PaddyBrennan 15/8f   1

CONEYGREE *MarkBradstock* 9-11-7 RichardJohnson 2/1   15 2
VEZELAY (FR) *EmmanuelClayeux,France* 7-11-7 (t) FelixdeGiles 50/1   13 3
21 Silviniaco Conti (FR) *PaulNicholls* 10-11-7 (b) NoelFehily 13/2   14 4
15 Irish Cavalier (IRE) *RebeccaCurtis* 7-11-7 (s) JonathanMoore ....14/1   pu
19 Seeyouatmidnight *SandyThomson* 8-11-7 BrianHughes ....4/1   pu
Mrs Jean R. Bishop 6ran 6m22.20

PUNCHESTOWN Sunday, Nov 20 GOOD to SOFT

42 **Ryans Cleaning Craddockstown Novices' Chase (Gr 2) (4yo+)** £23,017   2m (11)
IDENTITY THIEF (IRE) *HenrydeBromhead* 6-11-4 B.J.Cooper 2/5f   1
ORDINARY WORLD (IRE) *HenrydeBromhead* 6-11-4 DavyRussell 11/1   1 2
ATTRIBUTION *HenrydeBromhead* 6-11-4 D.J.Mullins 16/1   3 3
Ball d'Arc (FR) *GordonElliott* 5-11-4 R.Walsh 4/1   3½ 4
8 Bentelimar (IRE) *J.R.Barry* 7-11-4 D.E.Mullins 20/1   20 5
Gigginstown House Stud 5ran 4m06.00

43 **Florida Pearl Novices' Chase (Gr 2) (5yo+)** £21,617   2¾m110y (15)
A TOI PHIL (FR) *GordonElliott* 6-11-3 R.Walsh 3/1   1
JETSTREAM JACK (IRE) *GordonElliott* 6-11-3 J.W.Kennedy 6/1   7 2
DISKO (FR) *NoelMeade* 5-11-3 (h) B.J.Cooper 13/8f   5 3
Nambour (GER) *M.F.Morris* 6-11-3 (t) M.A.Enright ....7/2   nk 4
Space Cadet (IRE) *GordonElliott* 6-11-3 DavyRussell 8/1   27 5
Georges Conn (IRE) *JohnPatrickRyan* 8-11-3 D.E.Mullins 66/1   44 6
Gigginstown House Stud 6ran 5m58.80

44 **stanjames.com Morgiana Hurdle (Gr 1) (4yo+)** £43,966   2m (9)
NICHOLS CANYON *W.P.Mullins* 6-11-10 R.Walsh 8/13f   1
JER'S GIRL (IRE) *GavinPatrickCromwell* 4-11-0 BarryGeraghty 3/1   12 2
IVANOVICH GORBATOV (IRE) *JosephPatrickO'Brien* 4-11-7 (t) DavyRussell ..12/1   5 3
Sempre Medici (FR) *W.P.Mullins* 6-11-10 D.E.Mullins 7/1   2 4
Simenon (IRE) *W.P.Mullins* 9-11-10 D.J.Mullins 33/1   32 5
Andrea Wylie/Graham Wylie 5ran 3m52.40

NEWBURY Friday, Nov 25 Chase course: GOOD, Hurdles course: GOOD to SOFT

45 **Fuller's London Pride Novices' Chase (Berkshire) (Gr 2) (1) (4yo+)** £19,932   2m3f187y (16)
CLAN DES OBEAUX (FR) *PaulNicholls* 4-10-7 SeanBowen 5/2   1
VIRGILIO (FR) *DanSkelton* 7-11-8 (t) HarrySkelton 7/1   10 2
OUR KAEMPFER (IRE) *CharlieLongsdon* 7-11-1 (t) NoelFehily 10/1   4 3
Protek des Flos (FR) *NickyHenderson* 4-10-7 BarryGeraghty 10/3   41 4
One Track Mind (IRE) *WarrenGreatrex* 6-11-1 GavinSheehan 15/8f   37 5
G Mason,Sir A Ferguson,Mr&Mr P K Barber 5ran 4m51.20

46 **Bet365 Long Distance Hurdle (Gr 2) (1) (4yo+)** £28,475   3m52y (12)
UNOWHATIMEANHARRY *HarryFry* 8-11-4 (t) BarryGeraghty 7/2   1
14 BALLYOPTIC (IRE) *NigelTwiston-Davies* 6-11-4 RyanHatch 5/2f   6 2
15 MENORAH (IRE) *PhilipHobbs* 11-11-0 (s) RichardJohnson 7/1   6 3
Ubak (FR) *GaryMoore* 8-11-4 JoshuaMoore 9/1   1¼ 4
Reve de Sivola (FR) *NickWilliams* 11-11-8 DarylJacob 16/1   16 5
Shades of Midnight *DonaldWhillans* 6-11-0 (t) CallumWhillans 40/1   5 6
35 Snow Falcon (IRE) *NoelMeade,Ireland* 6-11-8 SeanFlanagan ....9/2   F
14 The Romford Pele (IRE) *RebeccaCurtis* 9-11-0 (b) JonathanMoore ....11/1   pu
Maximiser (FR) *SimonWest* 8-11-0 (t) AidanColeman ....25/1   pu
Mr John P. McManus 9ran 5m56.80

NEWBURY Saturday, Nov 26 Chase course: GOOD, Hurdles course: GOOD to SOFT

47 **Bet365 Novices' Chase (Worcester) (Gr 2) (4yo+)** £19,932   2m7f86y (18)
THISTLECRACK *ColinTizzard* 8-11-9 TomScudamore 1/8f   1
BIGBADJOHN (IRE) *RebeccaCurtis* 7-11-9 JonathanMoore 7/1   8 2
IBIS DU RHEU (FR) *PaulNicholls* 5-11-2 (h+t) NickScholfield 6/1   6 3
Pinnacle Panda (IRE) *TomLacey* 5-11-2 JamieMoore 25/1   99 4
Tajseer (USA) *PhilYork* 5-11-2 (t) MissK.Lyons ....100/1   pu
John and Heather Snook 5ran 5m45.00

48 **Bet365 Intermediate Hurdle (Limited Handicap) (Gerry Feilden) (L) (1) (155)** 2m69y (8)
  (4yo+) £25,628
9 WHO DARES WINS (IRE) *AlanKing* 4-11-10[140] WayneHutchinson 4/1   1
THELIGNY (FR) *TimVaughan* 5-10-11[127] AlanJohns(3) 17/2   9 2
MAKETHEDIFFERENCE (IRE) *TimVaughan* 8-9-13[120] (v) CharlieDeutsch(5) ..33/1   ½ 3
Ritual of Senses (IRE) *WarrenGreatrex* 6-11-0[130] HarryBannister(3) 14/1   6 4
Omessa Has (FR) *NickyHenderson* 4-11-5[135] JeremiahMcGrath 5/1   8 5
Holly Bush Henry (IRE) *GraemeMcPherson* 5-11-9[139] (t) KielanWoods 10/1   1 6

	Tommy Silver (FR) *PaulNicholls* 4-11-8[138] SeanBowen	3/1jf	6	7
	Ozzie The Oscar (IRE) *PhilipHobbs* 5-11-10[140] RichardJohnson	3/1jf		pu

HP Racing Who Dares Wins 8ran 3m52.30

49 Hennessy Gold Cup Chase (Handicap) (Gr 3) (1) (4yo+) £113,900 3m1f214y (20)

The fourth fence in the back straight was omitted on the final circuit due to being damaged

14	NATIVE RIVER (IRE) *ColinTizzard* 6-11-1[155] (s) RichardJohnson	7/2f		1
	CAROLE'S DESTRIER *NeilMulholland* 8-10-8[148] NoelFehily	25/1	½	2
	DOUBLE ROSS (IRE) *NigelTwiston-Davies* 10-10-9[149] JamieBargary(3)	50/1	5	3
18	Hadrian's Approach (IRE) *NickyHenderson* 9-9-13[140] (s) PaulMoloney	33/1	1¼	4
15	Blaklion *NigelTwiston-Davies* 7-11-0[154] RyanHatch	13/2	1	5
	Vyta du Roc (FR) *NickyHenderson* 7-10-3[143] TomO'Brien	8/1	1¼	6
13	Smad Place (FR) *AlanKing* 9-11-12[166] WayneHutchinson	11/1	¾	7
	Theatre Guide (IRE) *ColinTizzard* 9-10-9[149] (t) PaddyBrennan	14/1	7	8
	Aubusson (FR) *NickWilliams* 7-10-9[149] LizzieKelly(5)	25/1	¾	9
	Un Temps Pour Tout (IRE) *DavidPipe* 7-11-4[158] (b+t) TomScudamore	10/1	1¾	10
	Henri Parry Morgan *PeterBowen* 8-10-10[150] (s+t) SeanBowen	10/1	8	11
	Triolo d'Alene (FR) *NickyHenderson* 9-10-10[150] JeremiahMcGrath	25/1	sh	12
	Holywell (IRE) *JonjoO'Neill* 9-11-2[156] (b) RichieMcLernon	33/1	42	13
	Vicente (FR) *PaulNicholls* 7-10-11[151] (h) HarrySkelton	12/1		F
18	Saphir du Rheu (FR) *PaulNicholls* 7-10-13[153] NickScholfield	8/1		F
28	Upswing (IRE) *JonjoO'Neill* 8-9-11[140] (b) AidanColeman	25/1		pu
	Local Show (IRE) *BenPauling* 8-10-6[146] TomCannon	25/1		pu
	Regal Encore (IRE) *AnthonyHoneyball* 8-10-7[147] (t) BarryGeraghty	33/1		pu
	Coologue (IRE) *CharlieLongsdon* 7-10-8[148] A.P.Heskin	33/1		pu

Brocade Racing 19ran 6m25.00

NEWCASTLE Saturday, Nov 26 SOFT

50 stanjames.com 'Fighting Fifth' Hurdle (Gr 1) (1) (4yo+) £67,524 2m98y (9)

	IRVING *PaulNicholls* 8-11-7 HarryCobden	6/1		1
20	APPLE'S JADE (FR) *GordonElliott,Ireland* 4-11-0 JackKennedy	15/8f	ns	2
5	HIDDEN CYCLONE (IRE) *JohnJosephHanlon,Ireland* 11-11-7 (s) D.E.Mullins	12/1	2½	3
23	Sceau Royal (FR) *AlanKing* 4-11-7 DarylJacob	9/4	6	4
30	Mirsaale *KeithDalgleish* 6-11-7 BrianHughes	40/1	55	5
20	Petit Mouchoir (FR) *HenrydeBromhead,Ireland* 5-11-7 B.J.Cooper	4/1		F

Axom XLIX 6ran 3m56.60

51 At The Races Rehearsal Handicap Chase (L) (1) (4yo+) £45,560 2m7f91y (19)

	OTAGO TRAIL (IRE) *VenetiaWilliams* 8-11-3[146] LiamTreadwell	9/1		1
19	BRISTOL DE MAI (FR) *NigelTwiston-Davies* 5-11-11[154] DarylJacob	7/2	3¼	2
	DEFINITLY RED (IRE) *BrianEllison* 7-10-13[142] BrianHughes	5/4f	1¼	3
	Bishops Road (IRE) *KerryLee* 8-11-11[154] P.Townend	20/1	4½	4
15	Wakanda (IRE) *SueSmith* 7-11-9[152] DannyCook	10/1	14	5
15	Virak (FR) *PaulNicholls* 7-11-12[155] (s) HarryCobden(3)	7/1	17	6
	No Planning *SueSmith* 9-10-4[133] JackKennedy	12/1		F
3	Katkeau (FR) *DavidPipe* 9-11-6[149] (h+t) DavidNoonan(3)	20/1		F
	Clondaw Knight (IRE) *LucindaRussell* 8-10-3[132] (t) GrantCockburn(3)	28/1		pu

Mrs Marie Shone 9ran 6m02.20

NAVAN Sunday, Nov 27 GOOD to SOFT

52 Ladbrokes Troytown Handicap Chase (Gr B) (150) (4yo+) £50,427 3m (17)

	EMPIRE OF DIRT (IRE) *GordonElliott* 9-11-8[148] B.J.Cooper	12/1		1
	ABOLITIONIST (IRE) *EllmarieHolden* 8-10-5[131] RachaelBlackmore(5)	16/1	4	2
	BONNY KATE (IRE) *NoelMeade* 6-10-9[135] SeanFlanagan	12/1	1¼	3
35	Noble Endeavor (IRE) *GordonElliott* 7-11-1[141] (s) DavyRussell	7/2f	½	4
	Venitien de Mai (FR) *J.T.R.Dreaper* 7-10-9[135] M.A.Enright	20/1	8½	5
	Domesday Book (USA) *HenrydeBromhead* 6-10-12[138] (s) D.Robinson(7)	25/1	ns	6
	Raz de Maree (FR) *GavinPatrickCromwell* 11-10-10[136] G.N.Fox	16/1	½	7
	Bless The Wings (IRE) *GordonElliott* 11-11-0[140] (s+t) J.W.Kennedy	16/1	1¼	8
	Killer Miller (IRE) *NoelMeade* 7-10-11[137] BarryGeraghty	8/1	12	9
6	Realt Mor (IRE) *GordonElliott* 11-10-13[139] (h) KeithDonoghue	40/1	2¼	10
	Mountain King *GordonElliott* 7-10-9[135] (t) DenisO'Regan	25/1	½	11
11	Killer Crow (IRE) *GordonElliott* 7-10-5[131] (s+t) D.J.Mullins	16/1	3¼	12
43	Georges Conn (IRE) *JohnPatrickRyan* 8-9-13[125] D.E.Splaine	33/1	5	13
22	Shadow Catcher *GordonElliott* 8-10-12[138] (b+t) P.Townend	33/1	2¾	14
	Thunder And Roses (IRE) *M.F.Morris* 8-11-2[142] (s) R.A.Doyle(7)	40/1	nk	15
11	Folsom Blue (IRE) *M.F.Morris* 9-10-7[133] (b) A.Ring(5)	25/1	17	16
36	Draycott Place (IRE) *JohnPatrickRyan* 7-10-12[138] (t) D.E.Mullins	33/1	nk	17
6	Mad Brian (IRE) *MrsGillianCallaghan* 10-10-4[130] (t) R.C.Colgan	20/1	25	18
	Captain Von Trappe (IRE) *GordonElliott* 7-10-5[131] (s) DonaghMeyler(3)	25/1		F

Sambremont (FR) *W.P.Mullins* 6-10-11[137] R.Walsh ....8/1   bd
Hash Brown (IRE) *M.Hourigan* 7-10-2[128] M.P.Walsh ....10/1   pu
Down Under (IRE) *F.Flood* 9-10-4[130] J.J.Burke ....50/1   pu
Akorakor (FR) *GordonElliott* 7-10-5[131] (b+t) C.D.Timmons(5) ....33/1   pu
Woodford Island (IRE) *GordonElliott* 9-10-9[135] (t) RobbiePower ....20/1   pu
Cause of Causes (USA) *GordonElliott* 8-11-10[150] (s+t) L.P.Dempsey ....33/1   pu
Gigginstown House Stud 25ran 6m23.30

SANDOWN Friday, Dec 2 SOFT

53 **Neptune Investment Management Novices' Hurdle (Winter) (Gr 2) (1)**   2m3f173y (9)
(4yo+) £17,085
    MESSIRE DES OBEAUX (FR) *AlanKing* 4-11-7 DarylJacob 9/4   1
30 BALLYANDY *NigelTwiston-Davies* 5-11-0 SamTwiston-Davies ....11/10f   ½ 2
    CULTIVATOR *NickyHenderson* 5-11-7 (h) JeremiahMcGrath 12/1   2¼ 3
    Aintree My Dream (FR) *DanSkelton* 6-11-4 (t) HarrySkelton 15/2   9 4
    Coeur Blimey (IRE) *SusanGardner* 5-11-0 LucyGardner 20/1   15 5
    Kabanga Bay *PhilYork* 5-11-0 MissK.Lyons 150/1   1 6
    Apasionado (GER) *StuartEdmunds* 5-11-4 JoshuaMoore 10/1   1¼ 7
Mr Simon Munir & Mr Isaac Souede 7ran 4m59.90

SANDOWN Saturday, Dec 3 Chase course: GOOD to SOFT, Hurdles course: SOFT

54 **Racing Post Henry VIII Novices' Chase (Gr 1) (1) (4yo+) £25,628**   1m7f119y (13)
    ALTIOR (IRE) *NickyHenderson* 6-11-2 NoelFehily 2/7f   1
    CHARBEL (IRE) *KimBailey* 5-11-2 (t) DavidBass 11/2   6 2
    MAX WARD (IRE) *TomGeorge* 7-11-2 A.P.Heskin 20/1   14 3
    Marracudja (FR) *PaulNicholls* 5-11-2 (h+t) SamTwiston-Davies 10/1   1¾ 4
Mrs Patricia Pugh 4ran 3m54.50

55 **Jumeirah Hotels And Resorts December Handicap Hurdle (L) (1) (4yo+)**   1m7f216y (8)
£33,762
33 BRAIN POWER (IRE) *NickyHenderson* 5-11-10[142] (s) SamTwiston-Davies 9/2   1
    CONSUL DE THAIX (FR) *NickyHenderson* 4-11-0[132] JeremiahMcGrath ....13/2   ¾ 2
    KAYF BLANCO *GraemeMcPherson* 7-11-5[137] KielanWoods 14/1   4 3
    Wishfull Dreaming *PhilipHobbs* 5-10-12[130] TimO'Brien 9/2   1½ 4
23 Zubayr (IRE) *PaulNicholls* 4-11-12[144] NickScholfield 13/2   5 5
    Faithful Mount *IanWilliams* 7-10-8[126] (s) CharlieDeutsch(5) 10/1   4 6
    Graasten (GER) *GaryMoore* 4-10-4[122] JamieMoore 11/2   18 7
    Kingston (GER) *TonyCarroll* 7-10-2[120] LeeEdwards ....100/1   ¾ 8
    Indietir (FR) *DanSkelton* 4-11-9[141] NoelFehily 4/1f   19 9
    Bertimont (FR) *DanSkelton* 6-11-8[140] (t) JackSherwood(3) ....33/1   F
Mr Michael Buckley 10ran 3m58.60

56 **Betfair Tingle Creek Chase (Gr 1) (1) (4yo+) £84,405**   1m7f119y (15)
    UN DE SCEAUX (FR) *W.P.Mullins,Ireland* 8-11-7 R.Walsh 5/4f   1
13 SIRE DE GRUGY (FR) *GaryMoore* 10-11-7 JamieMoore 5/1   1 2
37 GOD'S OWN (IRE) *TomGeorge* 8-11-7 A.P.Heskin ....7/2   nk 3
    Ar Mad (FR) *GaryMoore* 6-11-7 JoshuaMoore 9/2   2¼ 4
    Sir Valentino (FR) *TomGeorge* 7-11-7 (t) NoelFehily 25/1   2 5
37 Vibrato Valtat (FR) *PaulNicholls* 7-11-7 (s+t) SamTwiston-Davies 16/1   15 6
E. O'Connell 6ran 3m51.60

57 **Betfair London National Handicap Chase (2) (150) (5yo+) £25,024**   3½m166y (24)
    ROCKY CREEK (IRE) *PaulNicholls* 10-11-12[144] JackSherwood(3) 10/1   1
    DOING FINE (IRE) *NeilMulholland* 8-10-8[126] (s+t) NoelFehily ....7/2f   nk 2
    MORNEY WING (IRE) *CharlieMann* 7-10-3[121] (s+t) JoshuaMoore 12/1   2½ 3
24 Bob Tucker (IRE) *CharlieLongsdon* 9-10-9[127] TomO'Brien 25/1   2½ 4
    Conas Taoi (IRE) *PaulMorgan* 7-10-3[121] CharlieDeutsch(5) ....4/1   ½ 5
    Belmount (IRE) *NigelTwiston-Davies* 7-11-0[132] SamTwiston-Davies 8/1   9 6
    Loose Chips *CharlieLongsdon* 10-11-7[139] (b) GrahamWatters(3) 12/1   23 7
    Court By Surprise (IRE) *EmmaLavelle* 11-10-12[130] NickScholfield ....12/1   hd 8
    Jimmy The Jetplane (IRE) *KimBailey* 8-11-7[139] (s) DavidBass 9/1   13 9
    Leg Iron (IRE) *SheenaWest* 11-10-2[120] (s) MarcGoldstein ....50/1   pu
    Woodford County *PhilipHobbs* 9-10-7[125] (s) CiaranGethings(5) ....25/1   pu
    Five In A Row (IRE) *BrianEllison* 8-11-4[136] A.P.Heskin ....5/1   pu
    Mountainous (IRE) *KerryLee* 11-11-8[140] (s) JamieMoore ....25/1   pu
The Johnson & Stewart Families 13ran 7m35.30

AINTREE Saturday, Dec 3 SOFT, National course (Becher & Sefton): GOOD to SOFT

58 **Betfred Becher Handicap Chase (Gr 3) (1) (6yo+) £78,582**   3m1f118y (21)
    VIEUX LION ROUGE (FR) *DavidPipe* 7-10-9[142] (s) TomScudamore 8/1f   1
    HIGHLAND LODGE (IRE) *JamesMoffatt* 10-10-4[137] (s) HenryBrooke ....20/1   sh 2

21	THE LAST SAMURI (IRE) *KimBailey* 8-11-12[159] BrianHughes	9/1	1	3
35	Ucello Conti (FR) *GordonElliott,Ireland* 8-11-11[148] (t) DarylJacob	11/1	1½	4
	One For Arthur (IRE) *LucindaRussell* 7-10-4[137] DerekFox	14/1	nk	5
	Portrait King (IRE) *PatrickGriffin,Ireland* 11-9-11[135] (s) ConorO'Farrell	25/1	13	6
	Bob Ford (IRE) *RebeccaCurtis* 9-10-2[135] JonathanMoore(3)	20/1	8	7
	Beeves (IRE) *JennieCandlish* 9-10-4[137] (v) SeanQuinlan	33/1	7	8
28	Midnight Prayer *AlanKing* 11-10-5[138] WayneHutchinson	25/1	16	9
11	Rogue Angel (IRE) *M.F.Morris,Ireland* 8-10-12[145] (b+t) G.N.Fox(3)	22/1	12	10
	Financial Climate (IRE) *OliverSherwood* 9-8-8[133] (s) ThomasGarner(3)	66/1	19	11
28	Viconte du Noyer (FR) *ColinTizzard* 7-11-7[154] AidanColeman	10/1	17	12
	Silvergrove *BenPauling* 8-10-5[138] (t) ConorShoemark	12/1	53	13
28	Alvarado (IRE) *FergalO'Brien* 11-10-2[135] PaulMoloney	10/1		F
	Sizing Coal (IRE) *J.T.R.Dreaper,Ireland* 8-10-3[136] MarkEnright	16/1		F
	Saint Are (FR) *TomGeorge* 10-11-0[147] (s+t) BrianHarding	14/1		F
	The Young Master *NeilMulholland* 7-11-3[150] (s) MrS.Waley-Cohen(3)	10/1		F
28	Cogry *NigelTwiston-Davies* 7-10-1[134] (s) RyanHatch	12/1		ur
	Milborough (IRE) *IanDuncan* 10-10-2[135] CraigNichol	33/1		ur
11	Dare To Endeavour *EricMcNamara,Ireland* 9-10-2[135] HarrySkelton	18/1		ur
	Ziga Boy (FR) *AlanKing* 7-10-4[137] TomBellamy	16/1		ur
	Aachen *VenetiaWilliams* 12-11-1[148] LiamTreadwell	33/1		pu

Prof Caroline Tisdall & Mr John Gent 22ran 6m51.20

59	**Betfred Lotto '£100K Cash Giveaway' Chase (L) (1) (4yo+) £22,780**		3m210y (19)	
	MANY CLOUDS (IRE) *OliverSherwood* 9-11-10 LeightonAspell	3/1		1
22	LE MERCUREY (FR) *PaulNicholls* 6-11-5 (b+t) SeanBowen	4/1	3½	2
41	IRISH CAVALIER (IRE) *RebeccaCurtis* 7-11-10 (s) JonathanMoore	4/1	43	3
	Cocktails At Dawn *NickyHenderson* 8-11-3 DarylJacob	11/1	31	4
28	Minella Rocco (IRE) *JonjoO'Neill* 6-11-5 (t) BarryGeraghty	7/4f		F

Mr Trevor Hemmings 5ran 6m42.90

60	**Betfred Grand Sefton Handicap Chase (2) (6yo+) £43,330**		2m5f19y (18)	
29	AS DE MEE (FR) *PaulNicholls* 6-11-0[137] SeanBowen	4/1f		1
	SEEFOOD (IRE) *DrRichardNewland* 9-10-11[134] (v) DarylJacob	8/1	5	2
	HENRYVILLE *HarryFry* 8-11-4[141] (t) NiallMadden	10/1	2	3
	Seventh Sky (GER) *CharlieMann* 9-11-12[149] (s+t) WayneHutchinson	12/1	17	4
	La Vaticane (FR) *DavidPipe* 7-11-1[138] (b+t) TomScudamore	9/1	8	5
11	Federici *DonaldMcCain* 6-10-13[136] BrianHughes	25/1	1	6
	The Italian Yob (IRE) *NickWilliams* 8-9-13[123] (b) AlanJohns(3)	25/1	3¼	7
29	Vintage Vinnie (IRE) *RebeccaCurtis* 7-11-1[138] JonathanMoore(3)	14/1	3¾	8
	Astracad (FR) *NigelTwiston-Davies* 10-10-11[134] JamieBargary(3)	12/1	¾	9
	Voyage A New York (FR) *LucindaRussell* 7-9-3[123] (t) HenryBrooke	33/1		F
	Howlongisafoot (IRE) *ChrisGordon* 7-10-6[129] (s) RyanHatch	33/1		F
	Rouge Et Blanc (FR) *OliverSherwood* 11-10-4[127] (s) LeightonAspell	25/1		ur
12	Witness In Court (IRE) *DonaldMcCain* 9-11-3[140] SeanQuinlan	40/1		ur
	Milgen Bay *OliverSherwood* 10-9-11[123] ThomasGarner(3)	33/1		pu
	Troika Steppes *FergalO'Brien* 8-10-5[128] (t) ConorShoemark	10/1		pu
10	Valadom (FR) *RichardHobson* 7-11-4[141] (t) ConorO'Farrell	8/1		pu
	Bennys Mist (IRE) *VenetiaWilliams* 10-11-8[145] (h) LiamTreadwell	10/1		pu

The Stewart Family & Judi Dench 17ran 5m38.70

FAIRYHOUSE Sunday, Dec 4   GOOD to SOFT

61	**Bar One Racing Royal Bond Novices' Hurdle (Gr 1) (4yo+) £43,220**		2m (9)	
	AIRLIE BEACH (IRE) *W.P.Mullins* 6-11-3 D.E.Mullins	4/1		1
	SATURNAS (FR) *W.P.Mullins* 5-11-10 P.Townend	7/1	6½	2
34	LE MARTALIN (FR) *NoelMeade* 5-11-10 (h+t) SeanFlanagan	14/1	2¾	3
	Penhill *W.P.Mullins* 5-11-10 R.Walsh	10/3	5½	4
	Forge Meadow (IRE) *MrsJ.Harrington* 4-11-0 RobbiePower	20/1	5½	5
	Peace News (GER) *HenrydeBromhead* 4-11-7 B.J.Cooper	7/4f		F
34	Labaik (IRE) *GordonElliott* 5-11-10 BarryGeraghty	7/1		rr

Supreme Horse Racing Club/K. Sharp 7ran 3m53.10

62	**Bar One Racing Hatton's Grace Hurdle (Gr 1) (4yo+) £50,000**		2½m (11)	
50	APPLE'S JADE (FR) *GordonElliott* 4-10-13 B.J.Cooper	4/1		1
	VROUM VROUM MAG (FR) *W.P.Mullins* 7-11-3 R.Walsh	4/7f	sh	2
35	SHANESHILL (IRE) *W.P.Mullins* 7-11-10 P.Townend	5/1	7	3
44	Ivanovich Gorbatov (IRE) *JosephPatrickO'Brien* 4-11-6 (t) BarryGeraghty	16/1	1¾	4
35	Dedigout (IRE) *GordonElliott* 10-11-10 J.W.Kennedy	40/1	13	5
36	Monksland (IRE) *NoelMeade* 9-11-10 (h) SeanFlanagan	25/1	nk	6
	Whiteout (GER) *W.P.Mullins* 5-11-3 D.E.Mullins	50/1	22	7

Gigginstown House Stud 7ran 4m58.50

63 Bar One Racing Handicap Hurdle (Gr A) (4yo+) £50,000   2m (9)

	WAXIES DARGLE *NoelMeade* 7-10-10[136] (t) SeanFlanagan	16/1	1
	MORGA (IRE) *DesmondMcDonogh* 6-10-4[130] B.R.Dalton(3)	16/1	¾ 2
34	MICK JAZZ (FR) *GordonElliott* 5-10-7[133] (h) J.W.Kennedy	5/1	4½ 3
	Voices of Spring (IRE) *A.J.Martin* 6-9-10[122] (h) DonaghMeyler(3)	16/1	1¼ 4
	Automated *GordonElliott* 5-10-1[128] (t) DenisO'Regan	14/1	½ 5
	Elusive Ivy (IRE) *GavinPatrickCromwell* 6-9-10[122] J.B.Kane(7)	33/1	5½ 6
	Solita (IRE) *PaulNolan* 7-10-4[130] (h+t) B.J.Cooper	14/1	2½ 7
	Gladiator King (IRE) *A.J.Martin* 7-9-10[122] (t) PhilipEnright	33/1	12 8
	St Stephens Green (IRE) *EmmetMullins* 5-9-12[124] D.E.Mullins	8/1	5 9
	Conright Boy (IRE) *MrsC.O'Leary* 7-9-10[122] (h+t) M.A.Enright	33/1	5½ 10
	Ainslie (IRE) *GordonElliott* 4-9-10[125] (t) MsL.O'Neill(7)	16/1	2½ 11
	Copy That (IRE) *EdwardHarty* 5-10-4[130] NiallMadden	8/1	9 12
	Macnicholson (IRE) *MrsJ.Harrington* 7-10-12[138] (b) RobbiePower	33/1	3¼ 13
	All The Answers *JosephPatrickO'Brien* 5-10-6[132] (h+t) J.J.Burke	14/1	F
	Campeador (FR) *GordonElliott* 4-10-13[142] BarryGeraghty	9/2f	F
	Sir Scorpion (IRE) *ThomasMullins* 7-10-4[130] M.P.Walsh	7/1	bd
44	Sempre Medici (FR) *W.P.Mullins* 6-11-10[150] R.Walsh	13/2	pu

Mr John P. McManus 17ran 3m55.70

64 Bar One Racing Drinmore Novices' Chase (Gr 1) (4yo+) £42,500   2½m (14)

	CONEY ISLAND (IRE) *EdwardHarty* 5-11-10 M.P.Walsh	8/1	1
	ANIBALE FLY (FR) *A.J.Martin* 6-11-10 (t) BarryGeraghty	7/2	2¼ 2
	ALPHA DES OBEAUX (FR) *M.F.Morris* 6-11-10 M.A.Enright	11/2	2¼ 3
	Road To Respect (IRE) *NoelMeade* 5-11-10 SeanFlanagan	10/1	3¾ 4
	Diamond King (IRE) *GordonElliott* 8-11-10 (t) DavyRussell	9/4f	3 5
43	A Toi Phil (FR) *GordonElliott* 6-11-10 B.J.Cooper	10/3	1¾ 6
	Lieutenant Colonel *GordonElliott* 7-11-10 (t) J.W.Kennedy	20/1	pu

Mr John P. McManus 7ran 5m03.90

HUNTINGDON Sunday, Dec 4 GOOD to SOFT

65 Betfred Peterborough Chase (Gr 2) (1) (4yo+) £37,018   2m3f189y (16)

	JOSSES HILL (IRE) *NickyHenderson* 8-11-6 NoelFehily	7/4f	1
18	TEA FOR TWO *NickWilliams* 7-11-5 LizzieKelly	6/1	6 2
29	MORE OF THAT (IRE) *JonjoO'Neill* 8-11-3 AidanColeman	3/1	3¾ 3
37	Dodging Bullets *PaulNicholls* 8-11-0 (t) SamTwiston-Davies	4/1	2¼ 4
	Volnay de Thaix (FR) *NickyHenderson* 7-11-0 AndrewTinkler	6/1	4½ 5

Mr A. D. Spence 5ran 4m50.10

CHELTENHAM Friday, Dec 9 GOOD

66 Unicoin Group Handicap Chase (Gr 3) (1) (4yo+) £25,628   3¼m (21)

49	THEATRE GUIDE (IRE) *ColinTizzard* 9-11-4[149] (b+t) PaddyBrennan	15/2	1
	PERFECT CANDIDATE (IRE) *FergalO'Brien* 9-11-2[147] (s) ConorShoemark	18/1	ns 2
	BALLY LONGFORD (IRE) *ColinTizzard* 8-10-5[136] (t) AidanColeman	12/1	3¾ 3
18	A Good Skin (IRE) *TomGeorge* 7-10-8[139] A.P.Heskin	5/1jf	6 4
28	Sausalito Sunrise (IRE) *PhilipHobbs* 8-11-12[157] (s) RichardJohnson	6/1	5 5
28	Un Ace (FR) *KimBailey* 8-10-9[140] (t) MikeyHamill(7)	22/1	hd 6
	Shutthefrontdoor (IRE) *JonjoO'Neill* 9-11-3[148] (s+t) BarryGeraghty	16/1	27 7
24	Southfield Theatre (IRE) *PaulNicholls* 8-11-9[154] SamTwiston-Davies	8/1	2½ 8
58	Cogry *NigelTwiston-Davies* 7-10-3[134] (s) RyanHatch	8/1	F
	Out Sam *WarrenGreatrex* 7-10-5[136] GavinSheehan	5/1jf	F
49	Regal Encore (IRE) *AnthonyHoneyball* 8-10-13[144] (t) MarkWalsh	16/1	pu
29	Ballynagour (IRE) *DavidPipe* 10-11-10[155] (h+t) TomScudamore	16/1	pu

Mrs Jean R. Bishop 12ran 6m40.80

CHELTENHAM Saturday, Dec 10 Race 67: GOOD to SOFT, Remainder: SOFT

67 Ryman Novices' Chase (2) (4yo+) £15,640   2½m166y (17)

	WHISPER (FR) *NickyHenderson* 8-11-0 DavyRussell	4/1	1
	BARON ALCO (FR) *GaryMoore* 5-11-5 JamieMoore	7/1	2½ 2
	SIZING TENNESSEE (IRE) *ColinTizzard* 8-11-0 AidanColeman	13/2	9 3
	Zarib (IRE) *DanSkelton* 5-11-0 (t) HarrySkelton	33/1	11 4
	Different Gravey (IRE) *NickyHenderson* 6-11-5 NoelFehily	8/11f	16 5
	San Benedeto (FR) *PaulNicholls* 5-11-8 (s+t) SamTwiston-Davies	25/1	ur

Walters Plant Hire Ltd 6ran 5m13.70

68 Caspian Caviar Gold Cup Handicap Chase (Gr 3) (1) (4yo+) £56,950   2½m166y (17)

29	FRODON (FR) *PaulNicholls* 4-10-10[149] SamTwiston-Davies	14/1	1
29	ASO (FR) *VenetiaWilliams* 6-10-12[144] CharlieDeutsch(5)	13/2	1½ 2
29	VILLAGE VIC (IRE) *PhilipHobbs* 9-11-12[158] RichardJohnson	6/1jf	hd 3
16	Quite By Chance *ColinTizzard* 7-11-1[147] TomO'Brien	20/1	½ 4

966

37 Kylemore Lough *KerryLee* 7-11-10^{156} JamieMoore 9/1 ½ 5
29 Bouvreuil (FR) *PaulNicholls* 5-11-0^{146} (h+t) BarryGeraghty 13/2 4½ 6
29 Buywise (IRE) *EvanWilliams* 9-11-5^{151} (v) PaulMoloney 10/1 11 7
Thomas Brown *HarryFry* 7-10-10^{142} (b) NoelFehily 6/1jf 11 8
Solar Impulse (FR) *ChristopherKellett* 6-10-13^{145} (b+t) SeanBowen 50/1 14 9
Full Shift (FR) *NickyHenderson* 7-9-12^{132} (s) JeremiahMcGrath 16/1 2 10
16 Roman Flight (IRE) *DavidDennis* 8-10-12^{144} (v) JamesDavies 33/1 16 11
Aloomomo (FR) *WarrenGreatrex* 6-10-8 GavinSheehan 10/1 F
King's Odyssey (IRE) *EvanWilliams* 7-11-1^{147} DarylJacob 11/1 F
Sizing Codelco (IRE) *ColinTizzard* 7-10-7^{139} (s) AidanColeman 25/1 pu
Turban (FR) *PaulHenderson* 9-10-11 NickScholfield 80/1 pu
32 Module (FR) *TomGeorge* 9-11-3^{149} A.P.Heskin 20/1 pu
Mr P J Vogt & Mr Ian Fogg 16ran 5m17.80

69 Albert Bartlett Novices' Hurdle (Bristol) (Gr 2) (1) (4yo+) £17,085 2m7f213y (12)
26 WHOLESTONE (IRE) *NigelTwiston-Davies* 5-11-5 DarylJacob 13/8f 1
AMI DESBOIS (FR) *GraemeMcPherson* 6-11-5 (t) KielanWoods 10/1 1 2
NO HASSLE HOFF (IRE) *DanSkelton* 4-10-12 HarrySkelton 13/2 3¼ 3
Impulsive Star (IRE) *NeilMulholland* 6-10-12 MrS.Waley-Cohen 7/1 3½ 4
26 West Approach *ColinTizzard* 6-11-5 AidanColeman 5/2 ns 5
Anchor Man (IRE) *PaulNicholls* 4-11-2 NickScholfield 12/1 3¼ 6
Mr Simon Munir & Mr Isaac Souede 6ran 6m06.70

70 stanjames.com International Hurdle (Gr 2) (1) (4yo+) £74,035 2m179y (8)
THE NEW ONE (IRE) *NigelTwiston-Davies* 8-11-8 RichardJohnson 13/8f 1
39 MY TENT OR YOURS (IRE) *NickyHenderson* 9-11-0 (h) BarryGeraghty 7/4 3½ 2
39 OLD GUARD *PaulNicholls* 5-11-8 SamTwiston-Davies 12/1 12 3
39 Melodic Rendezvous *JeremyScott* 10-11-0 (b) NickScholfield 16/1 9 4
38 Court Minstrel (IRE) *EvanWilliams* 9-11-4 PaulMoloney 33/1 12 5
Mister Miyagi (IRE) *DanSkelton* 7-11-2 HarrySkelton 9/2 31 6
S Such & CG Paletta 6ran 4m07.40

DONCASTER Saturday, Dec 10 GOOD
71 Bet365 December Novices' Chase (Gr 2) (1) (4yo+) £19,932 2m7f214y (18)
24 PRESENT MAN (IRE) *PaulNicholls* 6-11-8 (t) JackSherwood 5/1 1
POTTERS LEGEND *LucyWadham* 6-11-8 LeightonAspell 4/1 1¾ 2
O O SEVEN (IRE) *NickyHenderson* 6-11-8 AndrewTinkler 8/13f 1¾ 3
Bay of Freedom (IRE) *PeterFahey,Ireland* 7-11-8 BrianHughes 8/1 28 4
Woodhouse & Sutton 4ran 6m04.80

72 Bet365 Summit Juvenile Hurdle (Gr 2) (1) (3yo) £22,780 2m128y (8)
CLIFFS OF DOVER *PaulNicholls* 3-11-5 HarryCobden 1/3f 1
LORD JUSTICE (IRE) *JosephPatrickO'Brien,Ireland* 3-11-5 (t) JonathanMoore .8/1 2¾ 2
ZIG ZAG (IRE) *JosephPatrickO'Brien,Ireland* 3-11-5 J.J.Slevin 12/1 9 3
Bishop of Bling (IRE) *DrRichardNewland* 3-10-12 BrianHughes 18/1 13 4
Timoteo (FR) *AlanKing* 3-10-12 TomCannon 10/1 1 5
Tasty Ginger (IRE) *J.R.Jenkins* 3-11-2 JackQuinlan 33/1 ½ 6
Shrubland *AlexandraDunn* 3-10-12 (b) LeightonAspell 66/1 67 7
Mr and Mrs J. D. Cotton 7ran 3m55.30

CORK Sunday, Dec 11 SOFT
73 Kerry Group Hilly Way Chase (Gr 2) (5yo+) £26,050 2m1f (12)
DOUVAN (FR) *W.P.Mullins* 6-11-12 P.Townend 1/6f 1
36 DAYS HOTEL (IRE) *HenrydeBromhead* 11-11-10 PhilipEnright 16/1 22 2
FINE RIGHTLY (IRE) *StuartCrawford* 8-11-7 (h) MrB.G.Crawford 20/1 2½ 3
Ludo Et Emergo (IRE) *AndrewLee* 9-11-4 P.E.Corbett 100/1 39 4
Mozoltov *M.F.Morris* 10-11-4 (t) M.A.Enright 33/1 F
Gilgamboa (IRE) *EndaBolger* 8-11-4 BarryGeraghty 9/2 bd
7 The Game Changer (IRE) *GordonElliott* 7-11-10 (t) J.W.Kennedy 10/1 pu
Mrs S. Ricci 7ran 4m24.50

PUNCHESTOWN Sunday, Dec 11 GOOD to SOFT
74 John Durkan Memorial Punchestown Chase (Gr 1) (5yo+) £42,857 2½m (15)
DJAKADAM (FR) *W.P.Mullins* 7-11-10 R.Walsh 4/5f 1
36 OUTLANDER (IRE) *GordonElliott* 8-11-10 DavyRussell 9/1 1¼ 2
22 SUB LIEUTENANT (IRE) *HenrydeBromhead* 7-11-10 (t) B.J.Cooper 4/1 1¼ 3
36 Alelchi Inois (FR) *W.P.Mullins* 8-11-10 D.J.Mullins 25/1 20 4
Black Hercules (IRE) *W.P.Mullins* 7-11-10 D.E.Mullins 10/3 14 5
Mrs S. Ricci 5ran 5m16.30

75   Sky Bet Supreme Trial Kennel Gate Novices' Hurdle (Gr 2) (1) (4yo+)   1m7f152y (8)
£18,224

CAPITAINE (FR) *PaulNicholls* 4-11-7 (h) SamTwiston-Davies 9/1		1
CAPTAIN FOREZ (FR) *DanSkelton* 4-11-0 HarrySkelton 9/2	3½	2
30 KEEP IN LINE (GER) *AlanKing* 4-11-4 WayneHutchinson 7/2	1	3
Lough Derg Spirit (IRE) *NickyHenderson* 4-11-4 JeremiahMcGrath 11/4	3½	4
Thomas Campbell *NickyHenderson* 4-11-7 BarryGeraghty 5/2f	1¼	5
Blue Surf *AmandaPerrett* 7-11-0 LeightonAspell 20/1	7	6

Martin Broughton & Friends 2 6ran 3m46.40

76   Mitie Noel Novices' Chase (Gr 2) (1) (4yo+) £18,224   2m5f8y (17)

POLITOLOGUE (FR) *PaulNicholls* 5-11-6 SamTwiston-Davies 10/11f		1
ROCK THE KASBAH (IRE) *PhilipHobbs* 6-11-6 RichardJohnson 15/8	4	2
ROYAL VACATION (IRE) *ColinTizzard* 6-11-4 (s+t) AidanColeman 8/1	2¾	3
Captain Chaos (IRE) *DanSkelton* 5-11-0 HarrySkelton 10/1	4½	4

Mr J. Hales 4ran 5m21.70

77   JLT Long Walk Hurdle (Gr 1) (1) (4yo+) £56,950   3m97y (12)

46 UNOWHATIMEANHARRY *HarryFry* 8-11-7 (t) BarryGeraghty 6/5f		1
38 LIL ROCKERFELLER (USA) *NeilKing* 5-11-7 (s) NoelFehily 8/1	4½	2
49 UN TEMPS POUR TOUT (IRE) *DavidPipe* 7-11-7 (t) TomScudamore 16/1	14	3
Ptit Zig (FR) *PaulNicholls* 7-11-7 (b) SamTwiston-Davies 8/1	1¼	4
Alex de Larredya (FR) *FrancoisNicolle,France* 6-11-7 (t) DarylJacob 5/1	2	5
46 Reve de Sivola (FR) *NickWilliams* 11-11-7 D.J.Mullins 33/1	16	6
38 Zarkandar (IRE) *PaulNicholls* 9-11-7 (b+t) SeanBowen 20/1	½	7
Shelford (IRE) *DanSkelton* 7-11-7 (b) HarrySkelton 66/1	3	8
Surtee du Berlais (IRE) *OliverSherwood* 6-11-0 (s) LeightonAspell 66/1	21	9
46 Ballyoptic (IRE) *NigelTwiston-Davies* 6-11-7 RichardJohnson 8/1		F
69 West Approach *ColinTizzard* 6-11-7 TomO'Brien 40/1		ur

Mr John P. McManus 11ran 5m54.50

78   Lavazza Jolie Silver Cup Handicap Chase (L) (1) (4yo+) £56,950   2m7f180y (19)
The first fence on the final circuit was omitted due to a stricken jockey

66 REGAL ENCORE (IRE) *AnthonyHoneyball* 8-11-1[144] (t) BarryGeraghty 20/1		1
MINELLA DADDY (IRE) *PeterBowen* 6-10-13[142] (b) SeanBowen 9/2f	1¾	2
TENOR NIVERNAIS (FR) *VenetiaWilliams* 9-11-7[150] LiamTreadwell 33/1	½	3
Another Hero (IRE) *JonjoO'Neill* 7-10-5[134] RichieMcLernon 14/1	nk	4
59 Le Mercurey (FR) *PaulNicholls* 6-11-9[152] (b+t) SamTwiston-Davies 15/2	7	5
Irish Saint (FR) *PaulNicholls* 7-11-7[150] (t) NickScholfield 7/1	½	6
Fletchers Flyer (IRE) *HarryFry* 8-11-3[146] (t) NoelFehily 15/2	10	7
29 Annacotty (IRE) *AlanKing* 8-11-12[155] (s) IanPopham 40/1	19	8
The Druids Nephew (IRE) *NeilMulholland* 9-11-5[148] (s) TomScudamore 12/1	8	9
49 Triolo d'Alene (FR) *NickyHenderson* 9-11-5[148] JeremiahMcGrath 16/1	nk	10
Go Conquer (IRE) *JonjoO'Neill* 7-10-7[136] RichardJohnson 7/1		F
28 Fourth Act (IRE) *ColinTizzard* 7-10-8[137] (t) TomO'Brien 12/1		pu
37 Eduard (FR) *NickyRichards* 8-11-8[151] WayneHutchinson 11/2		pu
49 Holywell (IRE) *JonjoO'Neill* 9-11-11[154] (b) KillianMoore(3) 33/1		pu

Mr John P. McManus 14ran 6m04.40

79   Wessex Youth Trust Handicap Hurdle (Gr 3) (1) (4yo+) £85,425   1m7f152y (8)

55 BRAIN POWER (IRE) *NickyHenderson* 5-11-11[149] (s) D.J.Mullins 12/1		1
55 CONSUL DE THAIX (FR) *NickyHenderson* 4-10-11[135] JeremiahMcGrath 6/1	5	2
17 FERGALL (IRE) *SeamusMullins* 9-10-12[136] (s) KevinJones(5) 25/1	nk	3
Golden Spear *A.J.Martin,Ireland* 5-10-1[125] (t) DonaghMeyler(3) 4/1f	6	4
4 Quick Jack (IRE) *A.J.Martin,Ireland* 7-11-10[148] GrahamWatters(3) 14/1	nk	5
5 Pyromaniac (IRE) *A.J.Martin,Ireland* 6-11-1[139] (s+t) DenisO'Regan 25/1	¾	6
33 Modus *PaulNicholls* 6-11-7[145] BarryGeraghty 6/1	¾	7
Chesterfield (IRE) *SeamusMullins* 6-10-10[134] DanielSansom(10) 33/1	2¼	8
33 Wolf of Windlesham (IRE) *StuartEdmunds* 4-10-13[137] JoshuaMoore 20/1	4	9
63 Waxies Dargle *NoelMeade,Ireland* 7-11-10[148] (s) ConorBrassil(7) 25/1	7	10
33 Sternrubin (GER) *PhilipHobbs* 5-11-6[144] (h) TomO'Brien 12/1	1	11
17 Diego du Charmil (FR) *PaulNicholls* 4-11-3[141] (t) SamTwiston-Davies 16/1	7	12
Jolly's Cracked It (FR) *HarryFry* 7-11-9[147] NoelFehily 12/1	2¼	13
33 Hargam (FR) *NickyHenderson* 5-11-12[150] AndrewTinkler 50/1	3½	14
23 Rayvin Black *OliverSherwood* 7-11-6[144] ThomasGarner(3) 50/1	hd	15
Meet The Legend *DanSkelton* 5-11-0[138] (h+t) HarrySkelton 9/1	8	16
48 Who Dares Wins (IRE) *AlanKing* 4-11-11[149] WayneHutchinson 14/1	1	17
Unison (IRE) *JeremyScott* 6-10-8[132] MattGriffiths 50/1	32	18

Willow's Saviour *DanSkelton* 9-11-0[138] BridgetAndrews(3) 33/1   1½ 19
Mr Michael Buckley 19ran 3m40.00

NAVAN Sunday, Dec 18 SOFT

80 **Navan Novices' Hurdle (Gr 2) (4yo+) £21,429**   2½m (11)
      DEATH DUTY (IRE) *GordonElliott* 5-11-6 B.J.Cooper 6/4   1
      MONALEE (IRE) *HenrydeBromhead* 5-11-3 D.J.Mullins 7/1   3¾ 2
      INVITATION ONLY (IRE) *W.P.Mullins* 5-11-3 R.Walsh .... evsf   1½ 3
      Moulin A Vent *NoelMeade* 4-10-13 SeanFlanagan 14/1   3¾ 4
      Wishmoor (IRE) *M.F.Morris* 6-11-3 (t) DavyRussell 66/1   57 5
  61 Labaik (FR) *GordonElliott* 5-11-6 KeithDonoghue ....14/1   rr
      Gigginstown House Stud 6ran 5m16.60

KEMPTON Monday, Dec 26 GOOD

81 **32Red Kauto Star Novices' Chase (Gr 1) (1) (4yo+) £39,865**   3m (18)
  76 ROYAL VACATION (IRE) *ColinTizzard* 6-11-7 (b+t) PaddyBrennan 33/1   1
  45 VIRGILIO (FR) *DanSkelton* 7-11-7 (t) HarrySkelton 10/1   12 2
      AMORE ALATO *JohnnyFarrelly* 7-11-7 RichardJohnson 8/1   8 3
  71 Present Man (FR) *PaulNicholls* 6-11-7 (t) JackSherwood 10/1   24 4
  68 Frodon (FR) *PaulNicholls* 4-11-0 SamTwiston-Davies ....10/3   F
      Might Bite (IRE) *NickyHenderson* 7-11-7 DarylJacob ....11/2   F
      Churchtown Champ (IRE) *DanSkelton* 6-11-7 (t) TomScudamore ....20/1   F
      Caracci Apache (IRE) *NickyHenderson* 6-11-7 NoelFehily ....33/1   pu
  64 Anibale Fly (FR) *A.J.Martin,Ireland* 6-11-7 (t) BarryGeraghty ....3/1f   pu
  78 Minella Daddy (IRE) *PeterBowen* 6-11-7 (b) SeanBowen ....11/2   pu
      Mrs Jean R. Bishop 10ran 5m54.00

82 **32Red.com Christmas Hurdle (Gr 1) (1) (4yo+) £56,950**   2m (8)
  38 YANWORTH *AlanKing* 6-11-7 BarryGeraghty 5/4f   1
  70 THE NEW ONE (IRE) *NigelTwiston-Davies* 8-11-7 SamTwiston-Davies 13/8   3¼ 2
  39 CH'TIBELLO (FR) *DanSkelton* 5-11-7 HarrySkelton 14/1   2¼ 3
  70 My Tent Or Yours (IRE) *NickyHenderson* 9-11-7 (h) NoelFehily 4/1   2¼ 4
      Gray Wolf River *RichardHarper* 5-11-0 DanielHiskett 100/1   92 5
      Mr John P. McManus 5ran 3m45.00

83 **32Red King George VI Chase (Gr 1) (1) (4yo+) £119,025**   3m (18)
  47 THISTLECRACK *ColinTizzard* 8-11-10 TomScudamore 11/10f   1
  41 CUE CARD *ColinTizzard* 10-11-10 (t) PaddyBrennan 5/4   3¼ 2
  41 SILVINIACO CONTI (FR) *PaulNicholls* 10-11-10 (b) NoelFehily ....20/1   sh 3
  65 Tea For Two *NickWilliams* 7-11-10 LizzieKelly ....25/1   hd 4
  65 Josses Hill (IRE) *NickyHenderson* 8-11-10 DarylJacob 8/1   3½ 5
      John and Heather Snook 5ran 5m53.80

LEOPARDSTOWN Monday, Dec 26 GOOD to SOFT

84 **Knight Frank Juvenile Hurdle (Gr 2) (3yo) £22,692**   2m (8)
      BAPAUME (FR) *W.P.Mullins* 3-10-12 R.Walsh 13/8f   1
      LANDOFHOPEANDGLORY (IRE) *JosephPatrickO'Brien* 3-11-1 M.P.Walsh 9/4   1¾ 2
      MEGA FORTUNE (FR) *GordonElliott* 3-10-12 DavyRussell ....3/1   sh 3
  72 Zig Zag (IRE) *JosephPatrickO'Brien* 3-10-12 J.S.McGarvey 33/1   13 4
      Amaulino (FR) *ColinBowe* 3-10-12 M.P.Fogarty 50/1   9 5
      Champagne Pat (IRE) *JonathanSweeney* 3-10-12 (t) A.M.McCurtin 33/1   3 6
      Prospectus *GavinPatrickCromwell* 3-10-12 JonathanMoore 12/1   6½ 7
  72 Lord Justice (IRE) *JosephPatrickO'Brien* 3-10-12 (t) B.Hayes 16/1   17 8
      Soir de Chantenay (FR) *GavinPatrickCromwell* 3-11-1 M.A.Enright 66/1   4¾ 9
      Do No Complain (FR) *ThomasCooper* 3-10-12 (s) B.J.Cooper 66/1   31 10
      Mrs S. Ricci 10ran 3m54.40

85 **Racing Post Novices' Chase (Gr 1) (4yo+) £45,385**   2m1f (11)
      MIN (FR) *W.P.Mullins* 5-11-12 R.Walsh 4/5f   1
  42 ORDINARY WORLD (IRE) *HenrydeBromhead* 6-11-12 DavyRussell 25/1   9 2
  64 ROAD TO RESPECT (IRE) *NoelMeade* 5-11-12 SeanFlanagan ....20/1   ½ 3
      Baily Cloud (IRE) *M.F.Morris* 6-11-12 (s+t) M.A.Enright ....66/1   ¾ 4
  31 Three Stars (IRE) *HenrydeBromhead* 6-11-12 D.J.Mullins 25/1   8 5
      Tully East (IRE) *AlanFleming* 6-11-12 DenisO'Regan 16/1   1¾ 6
  42 Identity Thief (IRE) *HenrydeBromhead* 6-11-12 B.J.Cooper ....7/4   pu
      Mrs S. Ricci 7ran 4m08.10

LIMERICK Monday, Dec 26 HEAVY

86 **Shannon Airport Novices' Chase (Gr 2) (4yo+) £22,821**   2m3f120y (14)
      BELLSHILL (IRE) *W.P.Mullins* 6-11-4 P.Townend 4/9f   1

    HAYMOUNT (IRE) *W.P.Mullins* 7-11-4 MrP.W.Mullins 4/1   3¼ 2
42 ATTRIBUTION *HenrydeBromhead* 6-11-7 PhilipEnright 12/1   2 3
64 Diamond King (IRE) *GordonElliott* 8-11-4 (t) J.W.Kennedy 5/1   8½ 4
    Who's That (IRE) *LiamP.Cusack* 8-10-11 (s) S.G.McDermott 50/1   32 5
    Andrea Wylie/Graham Wylie 5ran 5m28.20

    WETHERBY Monday, Dec 26 SOFT

87 188Bet Rowland Meyrick Handicap Chase (Gr 3) (1) (4yo+) £22,780   3m45y (19)
51 DEFINITELY RED (IRE) *BrianEllison* 7-11-0[141] HenryBrooke 9/2   1
51 WAKANDA (IRE) *SueSmith* 7-11-8[149] DannyCook 12/1   7 2
49 BLAKLION *NigelTwiston-Davies* 7-11-12[153] JamieBargary(3) 2/1f   3½ 3
40 Yala Enki (FR) *VenetiaWilliams* 6-11-8[149] CharlieDeutsch(3) 7/2   18 4
    Ballyculla (IRE) *WarrenGreatrex* 9-10-9[136] (s) GavinSheehan 20/1   13 5
    Silver Tassie (IRE) *MickyHammond* 8-10-5[132] FinianO'Toole(5) 40/1   13 6
60 Seventh Sky (GER) *CharlieMann* 9-11-8[149] (s+t) JakeGreenall ....25/1   F
45 Our Kaempfer (IRE) *CharlieLongsdon* 7-10-11[138] (t) RichieMcLernon ....14/1   ur
49 Henri Parry Morgan *PeterBowen* 8-11-7[148] (s+t) DavidNoonan(3) ....7/1   ur
    Actinpieces *PamSly* 5-10-4[131] MissG.Andrews(3) ....12/1   pu
    Mr P. J. Martin 10ran 6m25.40

    CHEPSTOW Tuesday, Dec 27 SOFT

88 coral.co.uk Future Champions Finale Juvenile Hurdle (Gr 1) (1) (3yo) £28,475   2m11y (8)
27 DEFI DU SEUIL (FR) *PhilipHobbs* 3-11-0 RichardJohnson 4/5f   1
    EVENING HUSH (IRE) *EvanWilliams* 3-10-7 PaulMoloney 5/2   13 2
    DOLOS (FR) *PaulNicholls* 3-11-0 (t) SamTwiston-Davies 5/1   5 3
27 Dino Velvet (FR) *AlanKing* 3-11-0 WayneHutchinson 12/1   10 4
    Monday Club *DominicFfrenchDavis* 3-11-0 MarkGrant 50/1   10 5
    Mr John P. McManus 5ran 4m01.30

89 Coral Welsh Grand National Handicap Chase (Gr 3) (1) (4yo+) £85,425   3m5f110y (22)
49 NATIVE RIVER (IRE) *ColinTizzard* 6-11-12[155] (s) RichardJohnson 11/4f   1
52 RAZ DE MAREE (FR) *GavinPatrickCromwell,Ireland* 11-10-10[139] G.N.Fox(3) .33/1   1¾ 2
    HOUBLON DES OBEAUX (FR) *VenetiaWilliams* 9-11-10[153] (s) CDeutsch(3) ...33/1   15 3
28 Beg To Differ (IRE) *JonjoO'Neill* 6-10-13[142] (s) KillianMoore(5) 33/1   1½ 4
    Baie des Iles (FR) *RossO'Sullivan,Ireland* 5-11-0[143] (s) MsK.Walsh 25/1   5 5
49 Vicente (FR) *PaulNicholls* 7-11-8[151] (h) SamTwiston-Davies 12/1   3¼ 6
66 Theatre Guide (IRE) *ColinTizzard* 9-11-10[153] (b+t) PaddyBrennan 16/1   5 7
    Firebird Flyer (IRE) *EvanWilliams* 9-10-12[141] AdamWedge 10/1   8 8
49 Carole's Destrier *NeilMulholland* 8-11-5[148] LeightonAspell 6/1   5 9
51 Bishops Road (IRE) *KerryLee* 8-11-11[154] PaulMoloney 16/1   1¾ 10
    Royale Knight *DrRichardNewland* 10-10-11[140] (s) BrendanPowell ....33/1   ¾ 11
28 Unioniste (FR) *PaulNicholls* 8-11-2[145] NickScholfield 12/1   1¾ 12
    Emperor's Choice (IRE) *VenetiaWilliams* 9-10-10[139] JamieBargary(3) ......33/1   pu
    Goulanes (IRE) *NeilMulholland* 10-10-10[139] (b+t) WayneHutchinson ....33/1   pu
57 Mountainous (IRE) *KerryLee* 11-10-13[142] (s) GavinSheehan ....25/1   pu
    Milansbar (IRE) *NeilKing* 9-11-2[145] MarkGrant ....16/1   pu
    Onenightinvienna (IRE) *PhilipHobbs* 7-11-3[146] (s) TomO'Brien ....13/2   pu
51 Katkeau (FR) *DavidPipe* 9-11-6[149] (h+t) TomScudamore ....33/1   pu
    Harry Topper *KimBailey* 9-11-7[150] (s) DavidBass ....40/1   pu
58 Viconte du Noyer (FR) *ColinTizzard* 7-11-11[154] HarryCobden(3) ....20/1   pu
    Brocade Racing 20ran 7m50.70

    KEMPTON Tuesday, Dec 27 GOOD

90 32Red.com Wayward Lad Novices' Chase (Gr 2) (1) (4yo+) £22,780   2m (12)
54 ALTIOR (IRE) *NickyHenderson* 6-11-8 NoelFehily 1/9f   1
54 MARRACUDJA (FR) *PaulNicholls* 5-11-8 (h+t) SeanBowen 10/1   18 2
    STEPHANIE FRANCES (IRE) *DanSkelton* 8-11-1 BridgetAndrews 16/1   18 3
    Mrsrobin (IRE) *BarryBrennan* 6-10-9 (b) JamesBest ....100/1   ds 4
    Mrs Patricia Pugh 4ran 3m48.80

91 32Red Desert Orchid Chase (Gr 2) (1) (4yo+) £45,560   2m (12)
32 SPECIAL TIARA *HenrydeBromhead,Ireland* 9-11-0 NoelFehily 8/11f   1
56 SIR VALENTINO *TomGeorge* 7-11-6 (t) A.P.Heskin ....6/1   ½ 2
32 SAVELLO (IRE) *DanSkelton* 10-11-6 (h+t) BridgetAndrews 33/1   60 3
56 Sire de Grugy (FR) *GaryMoore* 10-11-10 JamieMoore ....2/1   ur
    Mrs S. Rowley-Williams 4ran 3m46.00

    LEOPARDSTOWN Tuesday, Dec 27 GOOD to SOFT

92 Paddy Power Cashcard Chase (Gr 1) (5yo+) £51,282   2m1f(11)
73 DOUVAN (FR) *W.P.Mullins* 6-11-12 R.Walsh 1/8f   1

	SIZING JOHN *MrsJ.Harrington* 6-11-12 RobbiePower	10/1	8	2
32	SIMPLY NED (IRE) *NickyRichards,GB* 9-11-12 BrianHarding	12/1	7	3
74	Black Hercules (IRE) *W.P.Mullins* 7-11-12 P.Townend	9/1	2	4
	Alisier d'Irlande (FR) *HenrydeBromhead* 6-11-12 (t) D.J.Mullins	33/1	2	5
	Mrs S. Ricci 5ran 4m03.00			

93 Paddy Power Future Champions Novice Hurdle (Gr 1) (4yo+) £42,863   2m (8)

61	SATURNAS (FR) *W.P.Mullins* 5-11-10 P.Townend	9/2		1
	BRELADE *GordonElliott* 4-11-7 J.W.Kennedy	8/1	2	2
	SUNNI MAY (IRE) *MrsJ.Harrington* 5-11-10 RobbiePower	7/2	4¼	3
	Riven Light (IRE) *W.P.Mullins* 4-11-7 R.Walsh	3/1	7½	4
61	Peace News (GER) *HenrydeBromhead* 4-11-7 B.J.Cooper	5/2f	½	5
61	Le Martalin (FR) *NoelMeade* 5-11-10 (h+t) SeanFlanagan	12/1	1¾	6
61	Lion In His Heart (IRE) *HenrydeBromhead* 5-11-10 DavyRussell	25/1	58	7
	Wicklow Bloodstock Ireland Ltd 7ran 3m55.60			

94 Paddy Power Chase (Extended Handicap) (Gr B) (150) (5yo+) £89,316   3m100y (17)

52	NOBLE ENDEAVOR (IRE) *GordonElliott* 7-11-3[143] DavyRussell	6/1		1
	THE CRAFTY BUTCHER (IRE) *W.P.Mullins* 9-10-1[127] R.Walsh	11/4f	3½	2
	OSCAR KNIGHT (IRE) *ThomasMullins* 7-10-4[130] L.P.Dempsey	14/1	1½	3
11	Stellar Notion (IRE) *HenrydeBromhead* 8-10-13[137] D.J.Mullins	25/1	2½	4
	Rogue Trader (IRE) *TomJ.Taaffe* 7-10-11[137] BarryGeraghty	6/1	4	5
	As de Pique (IRE) *GavinPatrickCromwell* 11-9-13[125] (s) J.B.Kane(7)	33/1	hd	6
58	Ucello Conti (FR) *GordonElliott* 8-11-4[144] (t) DarylJacob	10/1	4½	7
	Sonny B (IRE) *JohnJ.Walsh* 9-10-0[126] (t) C.D.Maxwell	33/1	1¾	8
58	Rogue Angel (IRE) *M.F.Morris* 8-11-3[143] (b+t) R.A.Doyle(7)	50/1	7	9
	Peoples Park (IRE) *TomJ.Taaffe* 7-10-5[131] SeanFlanagan	14/1	sh	10
52	Bless The Wings (IRE) *GordonElliott* 11-10-13[139] (s) J.W.Kennedy	33/1	4	11
36	Dromnea (IRE) *M.F.Morris* 9-10-8[134] M.A.Enright	18/1	5½	12
	Tennis Cap (FR) *W.P.Mullins* 9-11-5[145] N.M.Kelly(5)	50/1	4	13
52	Cause of Causes (USA) *GordonElliott* 8-11-9[149] (s+t) KeithDonoghue	50/1	¾	14
	Rolly Baby (FR) *W.P.Mullins* 11-10-9[135] MrR.Deegan(7)	33/1	1	15
	Kilford (IRE) *LeonardWhitmore* 10-10-2[128] B.R.Dalton	100/1	hd	16
	Gallant Oscar (IRE) *A.J.Martin* 10-11-8[148] RobbiePower	25/1	13	17
52	Captain Von Trappe (IRE) *GordonElliott* 7-10-5[131] (s) C.D.Timmons(5)	33/1	8½	18
	Colms Dream (IRE) *KarlThornton* 7-11-2[142] (h+t) DonaghMeyler(3)	16/1	2½	19
52	Folsom Blue (IRE) *M.F.Morris* 9-10-4[130] (s) B.J.Cooper	25/1	12	20
52	Thunder And Roses (IRE) *M.F.Morris* 8-11-3[143] (s+t) A.Ring(5)	33/1	13	21
	New Kid In Town (IRE) *W.P.Mullins* 7-9-11[123] JohnJ.Fitzpatrick(7)	33/1		F
52	Venition de Mai (FR) *J.T.R.Dreaper* 7-10-9[135] JonathanMoore	33/1		F
52	Killer Miller (IRE) *NoelMeade* 7-10-10[136] J.S.McGarvey	20/1		F
52	Shadow Catcher *GordonElliott* 8-10-11[137] (h+t) MsL.O'Neill(7)	66/1		ur
	It Came To Pass (IRE) *J.Culloty* 6-10-4[130] DenisO'Regan	16/1		pu
52	Sambremont (FR) *W.P.Mullins* 6-10-11[137] P.Townend	12/1		pu
51	Otago Trail (IRE) *VenetiaWilliams,GB* 8-11-10[150] RobertDunne	14/1		pu
	Mr C. Jones 28ran 6m07.30			

LEOPARDSTOWN Wednesday, Dec 28   GOOD to SOFT

95 Squared Financial Christmas Hurdle (Gr 1) (4yo+) £42,863   3m (10)

62	VROUM VROUM MAG (FR) *W.P.Mullins* 7-11-3 R.Walsh	8/15f		1
5	CLONDAW WARRIOR (IRE) *W.P.Mullins* 9-11-10 (h) MsK.Walsh	8/1	1¼	2
46	SNOW FALCON (IRE) *NoelMeade* 6-11-10 SeanFlanagan	5/1	2½	3
62	Whiteout (GER) *W.P.Mullins* 5-11-3 D.E.Mullins	66/1	3½	4
	Kotkikova (FR) *NickyHenderson,GB* 5-11-3 BarryGeraghty	7/1	2¼	5
35	De Plotting Shed (IRE) *GordonElliott* 6-11-10 J.W.Kennedy	14/1	nk	6
	Milsean (IRE) *M.F.Morris* 7-11-10 (t) B.J.Cooper	50/1	81	7
62	Shaneshill (IRE) *W.P.Mullins* 7-11-10 MrP.W.Mullins	10/1		F
	Mrs S. Ricci 8ran 6m07.70			

96 Lexus Chase (Gr 1) (5yo+) £75,642   3m (17)

74	OUTLANDER (IRE) *GordonElliott* 8-11-10 J.W.Kennedy	11/1		1
21	DON POLI (IRE) *GordonElliott* 7-11-10 D.J.Mullins	12/1	2¼	2
74	DJAKADAM (FR) *W.P.Mullins* 7-11-10 R.Walsh	5/4f	hd	3
21	Valseur Lido (FR) *HenrydeBromhead* 7-11-10 B.J.Cooper	3/1	4½	4
29	Taquin du Seuil (FR) *JonjoO'Neill,GB* 9-11-10 AidanColeman	20/1	4¼	5
65	More of That (IRE) *JonjoO'Neill,GB* 8-11-10 (s) BarryGeraghty	14/1	nk	6
22	Zabana (IRE) *AndrewLynch* 7-11-10 DavyRussell	8/1	4½	7
7	Road To Riches (IRE) *NoelMeade* 9-11-10 SeanFlanagan	16/1	1½	8
	Lord Windermere (IRE) *J.Culloty* 10-11-10 DenisO'Regan	25/1	22	9
	Arctic Skipper (IRE) *VincentLaurenceHalley* 7-11-10 RogerLoughran	100/1	1	10
73	Fine Rightly (IRE) *StuartCrawford* 8-11-10 (h+t) KeithDonoghue	50/1	20	11

Smashing (FR) *M.F.Morris* 7-11-10 M.A.Enright		66/1	26	12	
Wounded Warrior (IRE) *NoelMeade* 7-11-10 (s) JonathanMoore		66/1	2¼	13	

Gigginstown House Stud 13ran 6m02.40

97 **Willis Towers Watson European Breeders Fund Mares Hurdle (Gr 3) (4yo+)** 2½m (10)
£20,513

LET'S DANCE (FR) *W.P.Mullins* 4-10-12 R.Walsh	1/3f		1
SLOWMOTION (FR) *JosephPatrickO'Brien* 4-11-3 BarryGeraghty	9/2	17	2
63 SOLITA (IRE) *PaulNolan* 7-10-13 (t) RobbiePower	10/1	18	3
Daisy's Gift (IRE) *W.P.Mullins* 9-10-13 D.E.Mullins	9/1	13	4
Love On Top (IRE) *RaymondJohnMcCurtin* 8-10-13 F.A.McCurtin	66/1	57	5

Mrs S. Ricci 5ran 5m02.00

98 **Neville Hotels Novices' Chase (Fort Leney) (Gr 1) (4yo+)** £42,863 3m (17)

OUR DUKE (IRE) *Mrs.J.Harrington* 6-11-10 RobbiePower	4/1		1
64 CONEY ISLAND (IRE) *EdwardHarty* 5-11-10 BarryGeraghty	5/2f	½	2
43 DISKO (FR) *NoelMeade* 5-11-10 (h) JonathanMoore	20/1	½	3
Martello Tower (IRE) *MsMargaretMullins* 8-11-10 DenisO'Regan	7/1	21	4
64 A Toi Phil (FR) *GordonElliott* 6-11-10 KeithDonoghue	10/1	¾	5
Prince of Scars (IRE) *GordonElliott* 6-11-10 D.J.Mullins	11/1	2¾	6
43 Jetstream Jack (IRE) *GordonElliott* 6-11-10 DavyRussell	25/1	ns	7
Bellow Mome (FR) *W.P.Mullins* 5-11-10 D.E.Mullins	16/1	5½	8
Briar Hill (IRE) *W.P.Mullins* 8-11-10 R.Walsh	9/1		F
64 Alpha des Obeaux (FR) *M.F.Morris* 6-11-10 B.J.Cooper	9/2		pu

Cooper Family Syndicate 10ran 6m08.10

99 **Ryanair Hurdle (Festival) (Gr 1) (4yo+)** £51,282 2m (8)

50 PETIT MOUCHOIR (FR) *HenrydeBromhead* 5-11-10 B.J.Cooper	6/1		1
44 NICHOLS CANYON (FR) *W.P.Mullins* 6-11-10 R.Walsh	2/5f	7	2
62 IVANOVICH GORBATOV (IRE) *JosephPatrickO'Brien* 4-11-7 (t) DavyRussell	14/1	2¼	3
Footpad (FR) *W.P.Mullins* 4-11-7 DarylJacob	14/1	5	4
44 Jer's Girl (IRE) *GavinPatrickCromwell* 4-11-0 BarryGeraghty	5/1	2	5

Gigginstown House Stud 5ran 3m54.70

100 **Guinness Novices' Hurdle (Gr 2) (4yo+)** £22,821 3m (14)

61 PENHILL *W.P.Mullins* 5-11-6 P.Townend	3/1		1
CALL THE TAXIE (IRE) *EllmarieHolden* 5-11-3 RachaelBlackmore	9/1	7	2
LIVELOVELAUGH (IRE) *W.P.Mullins* 5-11-3 MrP.W.Mullins	9/4	13	3
Rathnure Rebel (IRE) *NoelMeade* 6-11-6 (h) SeanFlanagan	20/1	20	4
He Rock's (IRE) *S.J.Mahon* 7-11-3 (v+t) J.W.Kennedy	33/1	25	5

Mr Anthony Bloom 5ran 6m10.50

101 **Betfred Challow Novices' Hurdle (Gr 1) (1) (4yo+)** £22,780 2½m118y (10)

53 MESSIRE DES OBEAUX (FR) *AlanKing* 4-11-7 DarylJacob	10/3		1
BALTAZAR D'ALLIER (FR) *GordonElliott,Ireland* 5-11-7 BarryGeraghty	9/2	2	2
69 AMI DESBOIS (FR) *GraemeMcPherson* 6-11-7 (t) KielanWoods	14/1	4½	3
Elegant Escape (IRE) *ColinTizzard* 4-11-7 TomO'Brien	8/1	½	4
Major Mac *HughieMorrison* 4-11-7 A.P.Heskin	100/1	3¾	5
53 Cultivator *NickyHenderson* 5-11-7 NoelFehily	9/1	14	6
Peak To Peak (IRE) *PaulNicholls* 4-11-7 SamTwiston-Davies	20/1	24	7
Robin Roe (IRE) *DanSkelton* 5-11-7 HarrySkelton	7/4f		F

Mr Simon Munir & Mr Isaac Souede 8ran 4m58.10

102 **Betbright Dipper Novices' Chase (Gr 2) (1) (5yo+)** £18,224 2½m166y (17)

67 WHISPER (FR) *NickyHenderson* 9-11-7 DavyRussell	11/4		1
45 CLAN DES OBEAUX (FR) *PaulNicholls* 5-11-2 SamTwiston-Davies	10/11f	½	2
BRIERY BELLE *HenryDaly* 8-11-0 TomO'Brien	3/1	20	3
Never Equalled (IRE) *BernardLlewellyn* 8-11-0 RobertWilliams	33/1	40	4

Walters Plant Hire Ltd 4ran 5m28.70

103 **Betbright Best For Festival Betting Handicap Chase (Gr 3) (1) (5yo+)** 2½m166y (17)
£34,170

4 SHANTOU FLYER (IRE) *RebeccaCurtis* 7-11-2[149] (t) AidanColeman	20/1		1
68 VILLAGE VIC (IRE) *PhilipHobbs* 10-11-11[158] RichardJohnson	11/4f	3	2
32 TOP GAMBLE (IRE) *KerryLee* 9-11-12[159] (t) DavyRussell	8/1	½	3
78 Tenor Nivernais (FR) *VenetiaWilliams* 10-11-5[152] TomScudamore	7/1	5	4

29	Thomas Crapper *RobinDickin* 10-10-0[134] (s+t) CharliePoste	14/1	3¾	5
68	Quite By Chance *ColinTizzard* 8-11-0[147] TomO'Brien	6/1	6	6
68	Thomas Brown *HarryFry* 8-10-9[142] NiallMadden	8/1	7	7
87	Henri Parry Morgan *PeterBowen* 9-11-1[148] (v+t) RobertDunne	11/1		F
68	Solar Impulse (FR) *ChristopherKellett* 7-10-10[143] SamTwiston-Davies	50/1		pu
66	Shutthefrontdoor (IRE) *JonjoO'Neill* 10-10-12[145] (s+t) BarryGeraghty	18/1		pu
60	As de Mee (FR) *PaulNicholls* 7-10-12[145] SeanBowen	11/2		pu

Mr Carl Hinchy 11ran 5m31.30

104 Dornan Engineering Relkeel Hurdle (Gr 2) (1) (5yo+) £22,780   2½m56y (10)

	AGRAPART (FR) *NickWilliams* 6-11-4 LizzieKelly	16/1		1
	L'AMI SERGE (IRE) *NickyHenderson* 7-11-0 DarylJacob	2/1f	hd	2
77	COLE HARDEN (IRE) *WarrenGreatrex* 8-11-0 (s+t) RichardJohnson	7/1	7	3
	Lil Rockerfeller (USA) *NeilKing* 6-11-8 (s) TrevorWhelan	11/4	6	4
	Camping Ground (FR) *RobertWalford* 7-11-8 (t) AidanColeman	11/2	23	5
	Adrien du Pont (FR) *PaulNicholls* 5-11-4 (t) SamTwiston-Davies	6/1		ur

The Gascoigne Brookes Partnership III 6ran 5m10.30

SANDOWN Saturday, Jan 7   SOFT

105 32Red Tolworth Novices' Hurdle (Gr 1) (1) (4yo+) £25,628   1m7f216y (8)

	FINIAN'S OSCAR (IRE) *ColinTizzard* 5-11-7 TomO'Brien	11/10f		1
75	CAPITAINE (FR) *PaulNicholls* 5-11-7 (h) SamTwiston-Davies	2/1	5	2
	CHALONNIAL (FR) *HarryFry* 5-11-7 NoelFehily	8/1	3¾	3
	Global Stage *FergalO'Brien* 6-11-7 PaddyBrennan	25/1	1¼	4
	Charlemar (FR) *HarryWhittington* 5-11-7 AidanColeman	8/1	3½	5
	Celestial Path (IRE) *DavidPipe* 5-11-7 TomScudamore	33/1		pu

Ann & Alan Potts 6ran 4m08.10

NAAS Sunday, Jan 8   SOFT

106 Lawlor's Hotel Novices' Hurdle (Slaney) (Gr 1) (5yo+) £46,154   2½m (11)

80	DEATH DUTY (IRE) *GordonElliott* 6-11-10 J.W.Kennedy	5/6f		1
	TURCAGUA (FR) *W.P.Mullins* 7-11-10 P.Townend	7/1	9	2
	BLOOD CRAZED TIGER (IRE) *GordonElliott* 6-11-10 (h) D.J.Mullins	11/1	½	3
	Stand Up And Fight (IRE) *EndaBolger* 5-11-7 BarryGeraghty	16/1	7½	4
	Bel Ami de Sivola (FR) *NoelMeade* 6-11-10 SeanFlanagan	20/1	21	5
	Augusta Kate *W.P.Mullins* 6-11-3 R.Walsh	11/4		F

Gigginstown House Stud 6ran 5m09.20

WARWICK Saturday, Jan 14   SOFT

107 Neptune Investment Management Novices' Hurdle (Leamington) (Gr 2) (1)   2m5f (11)
(5yo+) £19,932

	WILLOUGHBY COURT (IRE) *BenPauling* 6-11-4 DavidBass	11/4		1
	GAYEBURY *EvanWilliams* 7-11-0 AdamWedge	9/2	8	2
26	PEREGRINE RUN (IRE) *PeterFahey,Ireland* 7-11-7 RogerLoughran	11/2	1¼	3
	Get On The Yager *DanSkelton* 7-11-0 DavidEngland	8/1	2¼	4
	Ballyhill (FR) *NigelTwiston-Davies* 6-11-7 WilliamTwiston-Davies	33/1	10	5
	Geordie des Champs (IRE) *RebeccaCurtis* 6-11-4 NoelFehily	7/4f	2	6

Paul & Clare Rooney 6ran 5m13.20

108 Betfred Classic Handicap Chase (Gr 3) (1) (5yo+) £34,170   3m5f54y (22)

58	ONE FOR ARTHUR (IRE) *LucindaRussell* 8-10-11[137] (t) DerekFox	14/1		1
	GOODTOKNOW *KerryLee* 9-10-10[136] (b) JakeGreenall	25/1	6	2
28	SHOTGUN PADDY (IRE) *EmmaLavelle* 10-10-13[139] DarylJacob	7/1f	4½	3
89	Houblon des Obeaux (FR) *VenetiaWilliams* 10-11-12[152] (s) CharlieDeutsch(3)	14/1	9	4
	Knockanrawley (IRE) *KimBailey* 9-10-10[136] (s) DavidBass	25/1	hd	5
	Rigadin de Beauchene (FR) *VenetiaWilliams* 12-10-3[129] (b) RobertDunne	16/1	hd	6
89	Mountainous (IRE) *KerryLee* 12-10-11[137] (s) JamieMoore	33/1	8	7
	Spookydooky (IRE) *JonjoO'Neill* 9-10-5[131] (t) LeightonAspell	12/1	9	8
	Russe Blanc (FR) *KerryLee* 10-10-8[134] (b) RichardPatrick(7)	20/1	hd	9
	Viva Steve (IRE) *FergalO'Brien* 9-10-13[139] (t) PaddyBrennan	8/1	½	10
	Kingswell Theatre *MichaelScudamore* 8-10-6[132] BenPoste(3)	33/1	12	11
	Kaki de La Pree (FR) *TomSymonds* 10-10-11[137] NoelFehily	15/2		F
58	Bob Ford (IRE) *RebeccaCurtis* 10-10-7[133] AdamWedge	25/1		pu
	Ballycross *NigelTwiston-Davies* 6-10-8[134] WilliamTwiston-Davies	12/1		pu
89	Emperor's Choice (IRE) *VenetiaWilliams* 10-10-9[135] NickScholfield	40/1		pu
58	Midnight Prayer *AlanKing* 12-10-13[139] TomBellamy	22/1		pu
	Sego Success (IRE) *AlanKing* 9-11-0[140] (b) WayneHutchinson	8/1		pu
89	Milansbar (IRE) *NeilKing* 10-11-3[143] TrevorWhelan	20/1		pu
28	Doctor Harper (IRE) *DavidPipe* 9-11-3[143] TomScudamore	10/1		pu

Vivaldi Collonges (FR) *PaulNicholls* 8-11-12[152] (t) SeanBowen ....25/1 pu
Two Golf Widows 20ran 7m47.50

KEMPTON Saturday, Jan 14 GOOD to SOFT

109 32Red Lanzarote Handicap Hurdle (L) (1) (4yo+) £22,780   2m5f (10)
79 MODUS *PaulNicholls* 7-11-4[145] (h) BarryGeraghty 7/1   1
      TEMPLEROSS (IRE) *NigelTwiston-Davies* 6-9-13[127] JamieBargary(3) 7/1   2¾ 2
      LORD OF THE ISLAND (IRE) *FergalO'Brien* 9-10-2[129] ConorShoemark 12/1   5 3
70 Old Guard *PaulNicholls* 6-11-12[153] SamTwiston-Davies 20/1   2 4
      Kalondra (IRE) *NeilMulholland* 6-10-8[135] (t) RichardJohnson ....12/1   sh 5
      Doesyourdogbite (IRE) *JonjoO'Neill* 5-10-11[138] AidanColeman 11/2f   1¾ 6
      Fountains Windfall *AnthonyHoneyball* 7-10-3[130] DavidNoonan(3) 12/1   1¼ 7
49 Local Show (IRE) *BenPauling* 9-10-12[139] A.P.Heskin ....20/1   ¾ 8
      Sam Red (FR) *DanSkelton* 6-10-6[133] (t) HarrySkelton 14/1   1½ 9
      Bennys King (IRE) *VenetiaWilliams* 6-10-1[128] LiamTreadwell ....15/2   nk 10
79 Chesterfield (IRE) *SeamusMullins* 7-10-6[133] KevinJones(5) ....10/1   hd 11
      Will O'The West (IRE) *HenryDaly* 6-10-3[130] TomO'Brien 12/1   30 12
      Jaleo (GER) *BenPauling* 5-10-10[137] MrAlexFerguson(7) ....8/1   F
Mr John P. McManus 13ran 5m12.90

FAIRYHOUSE Sunday, Jan 15 SOFT

110 Bar One Racing Dan Moore Memorial Handicap Chase (Gr A) (4yo+) £50,427 2m1f (12)
42 BALL D'ARC (FR) *GordonElliott* 6-10-9[133] J.W.Kennedy 3/1f   1
7   PAIROFBROWNEYES (IRE) *BarryJohnMurphy* 8-11-0[138] (s) M.P.Fogarty 6/1   9 2
52 DRAYCOTT PLACE (IRE) *JohnPatrickRyan* 8-10-13[137] (t) D.E.Mullins ....16/1   ¾ 3
      Caolaneoin (IRE) *ShaneNolan* 11-10-3[127] (t) R.C.Colgan 25/1   1¾ 4
94 Peoples Park (IRE) *TomJ.Taaffe* 8-10-7[131] BarryGeraghty 11/2   14 5
      Guitar Pete (IRE) *MsSandraHughes* 7-10-5[129] (v+t) RogerLoughran 20/1   3½ 6
      Leap Dearg (IRE) *JamesA.Nash* 9-10-4[128] P.Townend 20/1   3 7
      Dysios (IRE) *DenisW.Cullen* 9-10-5[129] (t) DenisO'Regan 16/1   11 8
      Turn Over Sivola (FR) *GordonElliott* 10-10-3[127] (s) SeanFlanagan 25/1   2½ 9
      Ttebbob (IRE) *Mrs.J.Harrington* 8-11-3[141] (h+t) RobbiePower 8/1   6 10
      Jarry d'Honneur (FR) *W.P.Mullins* 8-11-1[139] M.P.Walsh ....6/1   F
      Mister Hotelier (IRE) *MichaelJ.McDonagh* 10-10-3[127] (b) A.Ring(3) ....33/1   pu
      Baltimore Rock (IRE) *NeilMulholland,GB* 8-11-4[142] (s+t) R.Walsh ....7/1   pu
Gigginstown House Stud 13ran 4m27.70

THURLES Thursday, Jan 19 GOOD to SOFT

111 Ladbrokes Ireland Kinloch Brae Chase (Gr 3) (6yo+) £23,684   2½m (11)
      What should have been the final fence was omitted due to a stricken jockey
92 SIZING JOHN *Mrs.J.Harrington* 7-11-8 RobbiePower 3/1   1
74 SUB LIEUTENANT (IRE) *HenrydeBromhead* 8-11-8 (t) D.J.Mullins 11/10f   2½ 2
92 BLACK HERCULES (IRE) *W.P.Mullins* 8-11-10 R.Walsh 11/4   12 3
96 Smashing (FR) *M.F.Morris* 8-11-8 M.A.Enright 10/1   32 4
      Boxing Along (IRE) *VincentLaurenceHalley* 13-11-0 (h+t) SeanFlanagan 250/1   57 5
      Letter of Credit (IRE) *JamesJosephMangan* 12-11-0 (h) PhilipEnright ....80/1   F
Ann & Alan Potts Partnership 6ran 5m05.80

HAYDOCK Saturday, Jan 21 SOFT

112 Star Sports Cheltenham Preview Evening Novices' Chase (Gr 2) (1)   2m3f203y (15)
(5yo+) £18,224
      WAITING PATIENTLY (IRE) *MalcolmJefferson* 6-11-4 BrianHughes 11/4   1
76 POLITOLOGUE (FR) *PaulNicholls* 6-11-7 SamTwiston-Davies 6/4f   1¼ 2
      ITS'AFREEBEE (IRE) *DanSkelton* 7-11-4 (t) HarrySkelton 11/2   20 3
      Solatentif (FR) *ColinTizzard* 7-11-0 AidanColeman 12/1   57 4
46 Maximiser (IRE) *SimonWest* 9-11-0 JohnKington 14/1   5
      Bun Doran (IRE) *TomGeorge* 6-11-4 A.P.Heskin 6/1   6
Mr Richard Collins 6ran 5m15.10

113 Sky Bet Supreme Trial Rossington Main Novices' Hurdle (Gr 2) (1) (4yo+)   1m7f144y (8)
£17,085
      NEON WOLF (IRE) *HarryFry* 6-11-8 NoelFehily 4/5f   1
      ELGIN *AlanKing* 5-11-11 WayneHutchinson 3/1   9 2
      CRIEVEHILL (IRE) *NigelTwiston-Davies* 5-11-8 (h) SamTwiston-Davies 12/1   2 3
      Mohaayed *DanSkelton* 5-11-4 (t) HarrySkelton 12/1   4 4
      Craggaknock *MarkWalford* 6-11-8 (s) JakeGreenall 8/1   9 5
      Master of Finance (IRE) *MalcolmJefferson* 6-11-4 (s) BrianHughes 25/1   12 6
      Golden Town (IRE) *JamesMoffatt* 6-11-4 (s+t) HenryBrooke ....100/1   pu
Masterson Holdings Limited 7ran 3m54.90

114 stanjames.com Champion Hurdle Trial (Gr 2) (1) (4yo+) £42,712   1m7f144y (8)

82	THE NEW ONE (IRE) *NigelTwiston-Davies* 9-11-12 SamTwiston-Davies 6/1		1
	CLYNE *EvanWilliams* 7-11-4 AdamWedge 9/1	1	2
104	L'AMI SERGE (IRE) *NickyHenderson* 7-11-4 DarylJacob 13/8	3¾	3
	Cyrus Darius *MalcolmJefferson* 8-11-4 BrianHughes 16/1	21	4
50	Irving *PaulNicholls* 9-11-12 HarryCobden 6/1		F

S Such & CG Paletta 5ran 3m56.10

115 Peter Marsh Chase (Limited Handicap) (Gr 2) (1) (5yo+) £28,475   3m24y (18)

51	BRISTOL DE MAI (FR) *NigelTwiston-Davies* 6-11-2[154] DarylJacob 4/1jf		1
94	OTAGO TRAIL (IRE) *VenetiaWilliams* 9-10-13[151] CharlieDeutsch(3) 11/1	22	2
89	BISHOPS ROAD (IRE) *KerryLee* 9-10-11[149] JamieMoore 8/1	3½	3
51	Virak (FR) *PaulNicholls* 8-11-0[152] (s) HarryCobden(3) 16/1	10	4
	Berea Boru (IRE) *PeterBowen* 9-9-12[142] (s+t) SeanBowen 80/1	9	5
	Gevrey Chambertin (FR) *DavidPipe* 9-9-12[142] (b) DavidNoonan(3) 50/1	3½	6
	Vintage Clouds (IRE) *SueSmith* 7-9-12[142] DannyCook 9/1		F
87	Definitly Red (IRE) *BrianEllison* 8-10-11[149] HenryBrooke 5/1		ur
66	Sausalito Sunrise (IRE) *PhilipHobbs* 9-9-11-3[155] (s) RichardJohnson 12/1		ur
	Katenko (IRE) *VenetiaWilliams* 11-10-1[147] BrianHughes 25/1		pu
89	Firebird Flyer (IRE) *EvanWilliams* 10-10-2[142] AdamWedge 33/1		pu
	O Maonlai (IRE) *TomGeorge* 9-10-5[143] (t) A.P.Heskin 14/1		pu
87	Seventh Sky (GER) *CharlieMann* 10-10-11[149] (s+t) NoelFehily 40/1		pu
25	Alary (FR) *ColinTizzard* 7-11-10[162] (t) AidanColeman 4/1jf		pu

Mr Simon Munir & Mr Isaac Souede 14ran 6m22.10

LEOPARDSTOWN Sunday, Jan 22 GOOD

116 coral.ie Leopardstown Handicap Chase (Gr A) (5yo+) £51,754   2m5f (14)

98	A TOI PHIL (FR) *GordonElliott* 7-10-13[143] J.W.Kennedy 7/2f		1
94	STELLAR NOTION (IRE) *HenrydeBromhead* 9-10-9[139] D.J.Mullins 5/1	nk	2
94	ROLLY BABY (FR) *W.P.Mullins* 12-10-3[133] R.Walsh 10/1	1½	3
	Damut (IRE) *JosephDullea* 9-9-10[128] (h) SeanFlanagan 20/1	¾	4
52	Hash Brown (IRE) *M.Hourigan* 8-9-12[128] (t) N.McParlan 14/1	1	5
11	Kylecrue (IRE) *JohnPatrickRyan* 10-10-4[134] (b) D.E.Mullins 20/1	sh	6
7	Rightdownthemiddle (IRE) *GordonElliott* 9-10-3[133] DenisO'Regan 20/1	nk	7
	Lake Takapuna (IRE) *J.Culloty* 6-9-11[127] JonathanMoore 12/1	nk	8
36	Clarcam (FR) *GordonElliott* 7-11-10[154] (s+t) MsL.O'Neill(7) 16/1	2¼	9
52	Killer Crow (IRE) *GordonElliott* 8-9-10[128] (b+t) DonaghMeyler(3) 16/1	5½	10
	Total Recall (IRE) *MsSandraHughes* 8-10-0[130] RogerLoughran 12/1	½	11
43	Space Cadet (IRE) *GordonElliott* 7-10-3[133] J.J.Burke 7/1	29	12
94	New Kid In Town (IRE) *W.P.Mullins* 8-9-10[126] RachaelBlackmore(5) 20/1		F
42	Bentelimar (IRE) *J.R.Barry* 8-10-5[135] D.Robinson(5) 11/1		F
	The Paparrazi Kid (IRE) *W.P.Mullins* 10-10-11[141] M.P.Fogarty 33/1		ur
94	Shadow Catcher *GordonElliott* 9-10-7[137] (b+t) BarryGeraghty 33/1		pu
94	Tennis Cap (FR) *W.P.Mullins* 10-10-13[143] P.Townend 33/1		pu
94	Vukovar (IRE) *GordonElliott* 8-11-0[144] (t) DavyRussell 20/1		pu

Gigginstown House Stud 18ran 5m10.80

117 coral.ie Hurdle (Extended Handicap) (Gr B) (150) (4yo+) £51,754   2m (8)

	ICE COLD SOUL (IRE) *NoelMeade* 7-10-2[124] (t) SeanFlanagan 20/1		1
	TUDOR CITY (IRE) *A.J.Martin* 5-10-0[124] (t) R.C.Colgan 16/1	½	2
79	GOLDEN SPEAR (IRE) *A.J.Martin* 6-10-2[124] (t) DenisO'Regan 25/1	½	3
	Derulo (IRE) *MissElizabethDoyle* 6-10-3[125] (b) A.P.Heskin 25/1	¾	4
50	Hidden Cyclone (IRE) *JohnJosephHanlon* 12-11-10[146] (s) RachaelBlackmore(5) ..20/1	½	5
	That's A Wrap *ThomasMullins* 6-10-5[127] BarryGeraghty 8/1	nk	6
	Veinard (FR) *GordonElliott* 8-10-1[123] J.W.Kennedy 14/1	nk	7
	Heartbreak City (FR) *A.J.Martin* 7-10-3[125] (t) DonaghMeyler(3) 9/4f	1	8
	Thomas Hobson *W.P.Mullins* 7-11-7[143] P.Townend 12/1	sh	9
	After Rain (FR) *J.R.Barry* 7-10-5[127] (h) J.S.McGarvey 12/1	nk	10
	Cap d'Aubois (FR) *W.P.Mullins* 5-11-2[140] D.E.Mullins 25/1	2¼	11
97	Solita (IRE) *PaulNolan* 8-10-6[128] (t) D.Robinson(5) 33/1	3¼	12
	Top Othe Ra (IRE) *ThomasMullins* 9-9-10[118] A.W.Short(7) 25/1	½	13
	Light That (IRE) *MrsJ.Harrington* 5-10-3[127] RobbiePower 33/1	3¼	14
	Allblak des Places (FR) *W.P.Mullins* 5-11-4[142] (t) R.Walsh 12/1	4½	15
	Grand Partner (IRE) *ThomasMullins* 6-10-4[126] D.J.Mullins 40/1	¾	16
	Noble Inn (FR) *W.P.Mullins* 7 10 11[133] M.P.Fogarty 50/1	3	17
63	Gladiator King (IRE) *A.J.Martin* 8-10-1[123] (t) NiallMadden 25/1	5	18
	Head Turner (IRE) *P.A.Fahy* 6-9-12[120] J.J.Burke 50/1	3¾	19
63	Sir Scorpion (IRE) *ThomasMullins* 8-10-9[131] M.P.Walsh 16/1		pu

Gigginstown House Stud 20ran 3m43.20

GOWRAN Thursday, Jan 26   GOOD to SOFT

118   Goffs Thyestes Handicap Chase (Gr A) (5yo+) £50,682   3m1f (17)

	CHAMPAGNE WEST (IRE) *HenrydeBromhead* 9-11-7[154] D.J.Mullins 7/1		1
94	UCELLO CONTI (FR) *GordonElliott* 9-10-10[143] (t) DaryllJacob 7/1	7½	2
52	BONNY KATE (IRE) *NoelMeade* 7-10-5[138] SeanFlanagan 13/2cf	9½	3
	Pleasant Company (IRE) *W.P.Mullins* 9-11-1[148] (h) R.Walsh 10/1	¾	4
94	Rogue Angel (IRE) *M.F.Morris* 9-10-8[141] (b+t) RachaelBlackmore(5) 25/1	3	5
96	Wounded Warrior (IRE) *NoelMeade* 8-11-5[152] (s) G.N.Fox 25/1	1	6
94	Thunder And Roses (IRE) *M.F.Morris* 9-10-8[141] (s+t) BarryFoley(7) 33/1	1½	7
94	Bless The Wings (IRE) *GordonElliott* 12-10-5[138] (s) MsL.O'Neill(7) 25/1	nk	8
116	Clarcam (FR) *GordonElliott* 7-11-7[154] (s+t) KeithDonoghue 40/1	¾	9
	Roi des Francs (FR) *GordonElliott* 8-11-10[157] C.M.Collins(7) 22/1	9	10
	Montys Meadow (IRE) *JamesJosephMangan* 9-10-7[140] P.F.Mangan 10/1	13	11
98	Jetstream Jack (IRE) *GordonElliott* 7-10-7[140] DavyRussell 8/1		F
116	Shadow Catcher *GordonElliott* 9-10-4[137] (s+t) J.J.Burke 50/1		pu
94	Rogue Trader (IRE) *TomJ.Taaffe* 8-10-4[137] BarryGeraghty 13/2cf		pu
98	Prince of Scars (IRE) *GordonElliott* 7-10-7[140] J.W.Kennedy 13/2cf		pu
	Toon River (IRE) *MissM.L.Hallahan* 12-10-11[144] (t) DenisO'Regan 25/1		pu
	Measureofmydreams (IRE) *NoelMeade* 9-10-13[146] JonathanMoore 14/1		pu
	My Murphy (IRE) *W.J.Burke* 11-11-1[148] M.P.Walsh 16/1		pu

Mr R. S. Brookhouse 18ran 6m30.20

CHELTENHAM Saturday, Jan 28   SOFT

119   JCB Triumph Trial Juvenile Hurdle (Finesse) (Gr 2) (1) (4yo) £17,085   2m179y (8)

88	DEFI DU SEUIL (FR) *PhilipHobbs* 4-11-7 BarryGeraghty 1/5f		1
	RAINBOW DREAMER *AlanKing* 4-11-4 (v) WayneHutchinson 6/1	9	2
	EARLY DU LEMO (FR) *GaryMoore* 4-11-7 JamieMoore 25/1	16	3
	Siruh du Lac (FR) *NickWilliams* 4-11-0 LizzieKelly 25/1	69	4

Mr John P. McManus 4ran 4m16.50

120   Spectra Cyber Security Solutions Clarence House Chase (Gr 1) (1) (5yo+) £39,865   2m62y (14)

56	UN DE SCEAUX (FR) *W.P.Mullins,Ireland* 9-11-7 R.Walsh 1/2f		1
	UXIZANDRE (FR) *AlanKing* 9-11-7 BarryGeraghty 12/1	5	2
103	TOP GAMBLE (IRE) *KerryLee* 9-11-7 (t) DavyRussell 5/1	2¾	3
65	Dodging Bullets *PaulNicholls* 9-11-7 (t) NickScholfield 20/1	16	4
91	Special Tiara *HenrydeBromhead,Ireland* 10-11-7 NoelFehily 8/1	9	5
	Eastlake (IRE) *JonjoO'Neill* 11-11-7 (t) WayneHutchinson 50/1		pu
37	Royal Regatta (IRE) *PhilipHobbs* 9-11-7 (b+t) RichardJohnson 25/1		pu

E. O'Connell 7ran 4m11.90

121   Betbright Trial Cotswold Chase (Gr 2) (1) (5yo+) £56,950   3m1f56y (21)

59	MANY CLOUDS (IRE) *OliverSherwood* 10-11-10 LeightonAspell 8/1		1
83	THISTLECRACK *ColinTizzard* 9-11-10 TomScudamore 4/9f	hd	2
49	SMAD PLACE (FR) *AlanKing* 10-11-10 WayneHutchinson 7/1	17	3
83	Silviniaco Conti (FR) *PaulNicholls* 11-11-10 (b+t) NoelFehily 20/1	27	4
68	Kylemore Lough *KerryLee* 8-11-6 JamieMoore 8/1	3½	5
41	Vezelay (FR) *EmmanuelClayeux,France* 8-11-10 (t) FelixdeGiles 66/1		F
66	Perfect Candidate (IRE) *FergalO'Brien* 10-11-4 (s+t) PaddyBrennan 50/1		pu

Mr Trevor Hemmings 7ran 6m40.70

122   Neptune Investment Management Classic Novices' Hurdle (Gr 2) (1) (4yo+) £17,085   2½m56y (7)

Both flights in the home straight were omitted due to the low trajectory of the sun

69	WHOLESTONE (IRE) *NigelTwiston-Davies* 6-11-10 DaryllJacob 11/4f		1
	WILLIAM HENRY (IRE) *NickyHenderson* 7-11-7 DavyRussell 5/1	3	2
	POETIC RHYTHM (IRE) *FergalO'Brien* 6-11-3 PaddyBrennan 16/1	5	3
	Topofthegame (IRE) *PaulNicholls* 5-11-10 NoelFehily 11/2	2¾	4
101	Elegant Escape (IRE) *ColinTizzard* 5-11-10 TomScudamore 12/1	15	5
10	Coo Star Sivola (FR) *NickWilliams* 5-11-10 LizzieKelly 8/1	8	6
	Mr McGo (IRE) *DonaldMcCain* 6-11-7 WillKennedy 16/1	1½	7
	Sneaky Feeling (IRE) *PhilipHobbs* 5-11-7 RichardJohnson 12/1	46	8
75	Keep In Line (GER) *AlanKing* 5-11-7 WayneHutchinson 14/1	sh	9
	Kimberlite Candy (IRE) *TomLacey* 5-11-10 BarryGeraghty 7/1		pu

Mr Simon Munir & Mr Isaac Souede 10ran 5m02.80

123   galliardhomes.com Cleeve Hurdle (Gr 2) (1) (5yo+) £34,170   2m7f213y (10)

The flight in the home straight was omitted due to the low trajectory of the sun

77	UNOWHATIMEANHARRY *HarryFry* 9-11-8 (t) BarryGeraghty 10/11f		1
104	COLE HARDEN (IRE) *WarrenGreatrex* 8-11-0 (s+t) GavinSheehan 20/1	1¾	2

77	WEST APPROACH *ColinTizzard* 7-11-2 R.Walsh	14/1	1½	3
77	Ballyoptic (IRE) *NigelTwiston-Davies* 7-11-4 RichardJohnson	4/1	6	4
	Shantou Bob (IRE) *WarrenGreatrex* 9-11-0 (s+t) WayneHutchinson	22/1	4	5
77	Un Temps Pour Tout (IRE) *DavidPipe* 8-11-4 (b+t) TomScudamore	20/1	nk	6
109	Old Guard *PaulNicholls* 6-11-8 HarryCobden	33/1	5	7
77	Ptit Zig (FR) *PaulNicholls* 8-11-8 (b) NickScholfield	25/1	½	8
77	Reve de Sivola (FR) *NickWilliams* 12-11-8 LizzieKelly	66/1	34	9
	Whataknight *HarryFry* 8-11-0 (t) NoelFehily	33/1	¾	10
95	Kotkikova (FR) *NickyHenderson* 6-11-1 DarylJacob	14/1	½	11
	Knockara Beau (IRE) *GeorgeCharlton* 14-11-0 JanFaltejsek	100/1	2	12
103	Henri Parry Morgan *PeterBowen* 9-11-0 (t) JamieMoore	16/1	3½	13
58	The Young Master *NeilMulholland* 8-11-0 (s) MrS.Waley-Cohen	80/1	17	14
46	The Romford Pele (IRE) *RebeccaCurtis* 10-11-0 (b) DavyRussell	50/1	pu	

Mr John P. McManus 15ran 5m59.30

DONCASTER Saturday, Jan 28   GOOD to SOFT

124 Albert Bartlett River Don Novices' Hurdle (Gr 2) (1) (5yo+) £17,085   3m84y (11)

	CONSTANTINE BAY *NickyHenderson* 6-11-5 JeremiahMcGrath	4/1		1
69	NO HASSLE HOFF (IRE) *DanSkelton* 5-10-12 HarrySkelton	10/1	hd	2
	DUEL AT DAWN *AlexHales* 7-11-5 KielanWoods	50/1	13	3
	Happy Diva (IRE) *KerryLee* 6-10-9 (t) BrianHughes	5/1	1½	4
	Minella Aris (IRE) *TomGeorge* 6-11-2 (t) J.J.Burke	20/1	33	5
	Give Me A Copper (IRE) *PaulNicholls* 7-11-2 SamTwiston-Davies	5/4f	¾	6
	Dingo Dollar (IRE) *AlanKing* 5-11-2 TomCannon	25/1	7	7
101	Major Mac *HughieMorrison* 5-11-2 DavidBass	33/1	38	8
	Strong Pursuit (IRE) *PhilipHobbs* 7-11-2 TomO'Brien	7/1	pu	

Grech & Parkin 9ran 5m55.50

125 OLBG.com Doncaster Mares' Hurdle (Gr 2) (1) (4yo+) £28,475   2m128y (8)

95	VROUM VROUM MAG (FR) *W.P.Mullins,Ireland* 8-11-5 P.Townend	1/5f		1
	MIDNIGHT JAZZ *BenCase* 7-11-0 KielanWoods	17/2	hd	2
	COILLTE LASS (IRE) *PaulNicholls* 6-11-5 SamTwiston-Davies	6/1	7	3
	Intense Tango *K.R.Burke* 6-11-0 (t) BrianHughes	25/1	12	4
	Late Night Lily *DanSkelton* 6-11-0 HarrySkelton	20/1	11	5

Mrs S. Ricci 5ran 4m00.50

126 Sky Bet Handicap Chase (L) (1) (5yo+) £45,560   2m7f214y (18)

58	ZIGA BOY *AlanKing* 8-10-11[137] (s) TomBellamy	10/1		1
	LOOKING WELL (IRE) *NickyRichards* 8-10-6[132] RyanDay(5)	18/1	3½	2
78	ANOTHER HERO (IRE) *JonjoO'Neill* 8-10-10[136] AidanColeman	8/1	9	3
66	Out Sam *WarrenGreatrex* 8-10-10[136] (s) AndrewTinkler	8/1	2	4
40	Caid du Berlais (FR) *PaulNicholls* 8-11-6[146] (t) SamTwiston-Davies	12/1	10	5
89	Vicente (FR) *PaulNicholls* 8-11-9[149] (h) SeanBowen	11/1	7	6
	Ballyboker Breeze (IRE) *NickyRichards* 9-11-0[140] CraigNichol	12/1	½	7
49	Coologue (IRE) *CharlieLongsdon* 8-11-5[145] BrianHughes	12/1	1	8
37	Third Intention (IRE) *ColinTizzard* 8-10-12[152] (b+t) BrendanPowell	33/1	20	9
	Long Lunch *CharlieLongsdon* 8-10-6[135] (s+t) GrahamWatters(3)	22/1	5	10
78	Holywell (IRE) *JonjoO'Neill* 10-11-12[152] (b) KillianMoore(3)	25/1	15	11
	Southfield Royale *NeilMulholland* 7-11-7[147] (s) MrJamesKing(5)	6/1	25	12
47	Bigbadjohn (IRE) *RebeccaCurtis* 8-10-10[136] J.J.Burke	9/2f	F	
29	Potters Cross *RebeccaCurtis* 10-10-13[139] P.Townend	10/1	pu	

Axom LI 14ran 6m05.70

NAAS Saturday, Jan 28   SOFT

127 Limestone Lad Hurdle (Gr 3) (5yo+) £17,230   2m (8)

	SUTTON PLACE (IRE) *GordonElliott* 6-11-10 (t) M.P.Walsh	4/1		1
	SUPASUNDAE *MrsJ.Harrington* 7-11-5 D.E.Mullins	11/8f	7½	2
110	TTEBBOB (IRE) *MrsJ.Harrington* 8-11-1 (h+t) J.W.Kennedy	20/1	5½	3
	Minella Foru (IRE) *EdwardHarty* 8-11-1 M.A.Enright	20/1	8½	4
8	Ivan Grozny (FR) *W.P.Mullins* 7-11-10 (h+t) D.J.Mullins	6/4	9½	5
	Hunters Call (IRE) *JohnNeilan* 7-11-1 D.Robinson	33/1	11	6

Mr John P. McManus 6ran 3m57.00

LEOPARDSTOWN Sunday, Jan 29   GOOD

128 Nathaniel Lacy & Partners Solicitors '€50,000 Cheltenham Bonus For Stable Staff' Novices' Hurdle (Gr 2) (5yo+) £23,276   2½m (10)

97	LET'S DANCE (FR) *W.P.Mullins* 5-10-10 R.Walsh	8/11f		1
	KEMBOY (FR) *W.P.Mullins* 5-11-0 P.Townend	7/1	6	2
	JOEY SASA (IRE) *NoelMeade* 8-11-3 SeanFlanagan	6/1	11	3
93	Peace News (GER) *HenrydeBromhead* 5-11-0 (t) DavyRussell	6/1	5	4

Montalbano *W.P.Mullins* 5-11-0 (h) D.E.Mullins 14/1   13   5

106 Blood Crazed Tiger (IRE) *GordonElliott* 6-11-6 (h+t) J.W.Kennedy ....7/1   F

Mrs S. Ricci 6ran 4m41.60

129 Frank Ward Solicitors Arkle Novices' Chase (Gr 1) (5yo+) £72,930   2m1f (11)

  31 SOME PLAN (IRE) *HenrydeBromhead* 9-11-12 (t) DavyRussell 10/3   1

ROYAL CAVIAR (IRE) *W.P.Mullins* 9-11-12 (h) R.Walsh ....5/1   F

  85 IDENTITY THIEF (IRE) *HenrydeBromhead* 7-11-12 D.J.Mullins ....2/1   ur

Bleu Et Rouge (FR) *W.P.Mullins* 6-11-12 BarryGeraghty ....15/8f   ur

Mr R. S. Brookhouse 4ran 4m05.90

130 BHP Insurance Irish Champion Hurdle (Gr 1) (4yo+) £62,586   2m (8)

  99 PETIT MOUCHOIR (FR) *HenrydeBromhead* 6-11-10 D.J.Mullins 9/10f   1

  99 FOOTPAD (FR) *W.P.Mullins* 5-11-8 DarylJacob 12/1   1   2

  99 IVANOVICH GORBATOV (IRE) *JosephPatrickO'Brien* 5-11-8 (t) BGeraghty .13/2   37   3

  99 Nichols Canyon *W.P.Mullins* 7-11-10 R.Walsh ....7/4   F

Gigginstown House Stud 4ran 3m42.50

SANDOWN Saturday, Feb 4   HEAVY

131 Betfred TV Scilly Isles Novices' Chase (Gr 1) (1) (5yo+) £28,475   2½m10y (17)

TOP NOTCH (FR) *NickyHenderson* 6-11-3 DarylJacob 11/4   1

  67 BARON ALCO (FR) *GaryMoore* 6-11-3 JamieMoore 7/1   5   2

  31 LE PREZIEN (FR) *PaulNicholls* 6-11-3 (t) BarryGeraghty 3/1   1¼   3

  81 Amore Alato *JohnnyFarrelly* 8-11-3 (s) RichardJohnson 14/1   18   4

102 Clan des Obeaux (FR) *PaulNicholls* 5-11-0 (t) SeanBowen 13/8f   17   5

Mr Simon Munir & Mr Isaac Souede 5ran 5m19.80

WETHERBY Saturday, Feb 4   SOFT

132 Totepool Towton Novices' Chase (Gr 2) (1) (5yo+) £18,224   3m45y (19)

BAYWING (IRE) *NickyRichards* 8-11-0 RyanDay 33/1   1

CALETT MAD (FR) *NigelTwiston-Davies* 5-11-0 (t) JamieBargary 11/4   22   2

MISSED APPROACH (IRE) *WarrenGreatrex* 7-11-0 GavinSheehan 13/8f   7   3

Delusionofgrandeur (IRE) *SueSmith* 7-11-4 DannyCook 8/1   13   4

The Dutchman (IRE) *SandyThomson* 7-11-0 TomO'Brien ....11/2   F

  76 Captain Chaos (IRE) *DanSkelton* 6-11-0 HarrySkelton ....6/1   F

David & Nicky Robinson 6ran 6m42.20

PUNCHESTOWN Sunday, Feb 5   SOFT

133 Boylesports Tied Cottage Chase (Gr 2) (5yo+) £25,384   2m (11)

  92 DOUVAN (FR) *W.P.Mullins* 7-11-12 R.Walsh 1/14f   1

  52 REALT MOR (IRE) *GordonElliott* 12-11-4 J.W.Kennedy 33/1   6½   2

110 DRAYCOTT PLACE (IRE) *JohnPatrickRyan* 8-11-4 (t) D.E.Mullins 33/1   31   3

111 Smashing (FR) *M.F.Morris* 8-11-10 DavyRussell ....12/1   pu

Mrs S. Ricci 4ran 4m17.20

NEWBURY Saturday, Feb 11   GOOD to SOFT

134 Betfair Denman Chase (Gr 2) (1) (5yo+) £28,475   2m7f86y (18)

  89 NATIVE RIVER (IRE) *ColinTizzard* 7-11-6 (s) AidanColeman 11/10   1

  78 LE MERCUREY (FR) *PaulNicholls* 7-11-5 (b+t) SamTwiston-Davies 14/1   3¼   2

115 BRISTOL DE MAI (FR) *NigelTwiston-Davies* 6-11-6 DarylJacob 10/11f   6   3

Brocade Racing 3ran 6m05.70

135 Betfair Exchange Chase (Game Spirit) (Gr 2) (1) (5yo+) £28,475   2m92y (13)

  90 ALTIOR (IRE) *NickyHenderson* 7-11-5 NicodeBoinville 30/100f   1

  32 FOX NORTON (FR) *ColinTizzard* 7-11-10 (h) AidanColeman 5/1   13   2

120 DODGING BULLETS *PaulNicholls* 9-11-0 (s+t) SamTwiston-Davies 20/1   5   3

Traffic Fluide (FR) *GaryMoore* 7-11-0 JamieMoore 8/1   14   4

Mrs Patricia Pugh 4ran 4m04.90

136 Betfair Hurdle (Handicap) (Gr 3) (1) (4yo+) £88,272   2m69y (8)

  53 BALLYANDY *NigelTwiston-Davies* 6-11-1[135] SamTwiston-Davies 3/1f   1

  30 MOVEWITHTHETIMES (IRE) *PaulNicholls* 6-11-2[136] BarryGeraghty ....6/1   ¾   2

114 CLYNE *EvanWilliams* 7-11-9[143] AdamWedge 6/1   6   3

  33 Song Light *SeamusMullins* 7-10-13[133] KevinJones(5) 14/1   2   4

  55 Kayf Blanco *GraemeMcPherson* 8-11-2[136] KielanWoods 25/1   4½   5

117 Veinard (FR) *GordonElliott,Ireland* 8-10-6[126] (t) JackKennedy 16/1   1   6

  1 Beltor *RobertStephens* 6-11-1[135] TomO'Brien 20/1   4½   7

Boite (IRE) *WarrenGreatrex* 7-11-8[142] (s) ThomasGreatrex(7) ....16/1   hd   8

Eddiemaurice (IRE) *JohnFlint* 6-10-6[126] IanPopham 66/1   3¼   9

  1 Wait For Me (FR) *PhilipHobbs* 7-11-4[138] (h) PaddyBrennan 8/1   9   10

William H Bonney *AlanKing* 6-11-3[137] WayneHutchinson ....15/2   nk   11

978

De Name Escapes Me (IRE) *NoelMeade,Ireland* 7-11-5[139] AidanColeman 14/1 5 12
55 Zubayr (IRE) *PaulNicholls* 5-11-7[141] NickScholfield 20/1 2¼ 13
79 Hargam (FR) *NickyHenderson* 6-11-12[146] NicodeBoinville 40/1 5 14
107 Ballyhill (FR) *NigelTwiston-Davies* 6-11-2[136] TomHumphries(7) 28/1 1¼ 15
Gassin Golf *KerryLee* 8-10-13[133] (b+t) JamieMoore ....18/1 F
Options O Syndicate 16ran 3m56.70

WARWICK Saturday, Feb 11 HEAVY
137 Betway Kingmaker Novices' Chase (Gr 2) (1) (5yo+) £22,780 2m54y (12)
FLYING ANGEL (IRE) *NigelTwiston-Davies* 6-11-4 WilliamTwiston-Davies 7/2 1
GINO TRAIL (IRE) *KerryLee* 10-11-4 P.Townend 15/8f 4½ 2
40 TWO TAFFS (IRE) *DanSkelton* 7-11-0 TomScudamore 10/1 19 3
Chic Name (FR) *RichardHobson* 5-10-12 (v) ConorO'Farrell 40/1 11 4
Knockgraffon (IRE) *DanSkelton* 7-11-4 BridgetAndrews 6/1 9 5
Overtown Express (IRE) *HarryFry* 9-11-4 NoelFehily 5/2 4½ 6
Mr R. J. Rexton 6ran 4m11.00

LEOPARDSTOWN Sunday, Feb 12 SOFT
138 Spring Juvenile Hurdle (Gr 1) (4yo) £40,342 2m (8)
84 MEGA FORTUNE (FR) *GordonElliott* 4-11-0 (s) DavyRussell 9/2 1
84 BAPAUME (FR) *W.P.Mullins* 4-11-0 R.Walsh 7/4f 3½ 2
DINARIA DES OBEAUX (FR) *GordonElliott* 4-10-7 J.W.Kennedy 10/3 7 3
Meri Devie (FR) *W.P.Mullins* 4-10-7 P.Townend 4/1 2½ 4
Ex Patriot (IRE) *EllmarieHolden* 4-11-0 D.J.Mullins 22/1 1¾ 5
Bhutan (IRE) *JosephPatrickO'Brien* 4-11-0 (t) M.P.Walsh 25/1 26 6
Housesofparliament (IRE) *JosephPatrickO'Brien* 4-11-0 (t) BarryGeraghty 9/1 1¾ 7
Sword Fighter (IRE) *JosephPatrickO'Brien* 4-11-0 (t) J.S.McGarvey ....40/1 nk 8
Mr C. Jones 8ran 4m01.20

139 Deloitte Novices' Hurdle (Gr 1) (5yo+) £45,385 2¼m (9)
BACARDYS (FR) *W.P.Mullins* 6-11-10 MrP.W.Mullins 12/1 1
BUNK OFF EARLY (IRE) *W.P.Mullins* 5-11-9 P.Townend .... 11/2 ¾ 2
93 BRELADE *GordonElliott* 5-11-9 BarryGeraghty 8/1 2¼ 3
128 Blood Crazed Tiger (IRE) *GordonElliott* 6-11-10 (h+t) D.J.Mullins 12/1 3¾ 4
Barra (FR) *GordonElliott* 6-11-3 J.W.Kennedy 7/1 2 5
Chateau Conti (FR) *W.P.Mullins* 5-11-9 M.P.Fogarty 12/1 5½ 6
Bravissimo (FR) *W.P.Mullins* 6-11-10 MsK.Walsh 16/1 11 7
93 Riven Light (IRE) *W.P.Mullins* 5-11-9 D.E.Mullins 14/1 5 8
Gunnery Sergeant (IRE) *NoelMeade* 6-11-10 SeanFlanagan 28/1 36 9
93 Saturnas (FR) *W.P.Mullins* 6-11-10 R.Walsh 5/4f 5½ 10
Shanakiel Racing Syndicate 10ran 4m33.70

140 Flogas Novices' Chase (Dr P. J. Moriarty) (Gr 1) (5yo+) £43,589 2m5f60y (14)
98 DISKO (FR) *NoelMeade* 6-11-10 (h) SeanFlanagan 6/1 1
98 OUR DUKE (IRE) *MrsJ.Harrington* 7-11-10 RobbiePower 11/4 1¾ 2
BALKO DES FLOS (FR) *HenrydeBromhead* 6-11-10 D.J.Mullins 20/1 6 3
129 Bleu Et Rouge (FR) *W.P.Mullins* 6-11-10 BarryGeraghty 7/1 30 4
116 A Toi Phil (FR) *GordonElliott* 7-11-10 J.W.Kennedy 12/1 15 5
86 Bellshill (IRE) *W.P.Mullins* 7-11-10 R.Walsh .... 6/5f F
Gigginstown House Stud 6ran 5m28.60

141 Stan James Irish Gold Cup (Gr 1) (5yo+) £73,718 3m60y (17)
111 SIZING JOHN *MrsJ.Harrington* 7-11-10 RobbiePower 10/3 1
52 EMPIRE OF DIRT (IRE) *GordonElliott* 10-11-10 (t) J.W.Kennedy ....9/2 ¾ 2
96 DON POLI (IRE) *GordonElliott* 8-11-10 D.J.Mullins .... 9/4f ¾ 3
Carlingford Lough (IRE) *JohnE.Kiely* 11-11-10 BarryGeraghty 11/2 3½ 4
96 Road To Riches (IRE) *NoelMeade* 10-11-10 (s) SeanFlanagan 10/1 29 5
96 More of That (IRE) *JonjoO'Neill,GB* 9-11-10 (s) M.P.Walsh ....14/1 ur
59 Minella Rocco (IRE) *JonjoO'Neill,GB* 7-11-10 (t) AidanColeman ....7/1 ur
Ann & Alan Potts Partnership 7ran 6m24.60

HAYDOCK Saturday, Feb 18 GOOD to SOFT
142 Betfred Rendlesham Hurdle (Gr 2) (1) (4yo+) £22,780 2¾m177y (12)
77 ZARKANDAR (IRE) *PaulNicholls* 10-11-2 (b+t) HarryCobden 9/4 1
AUX PTITS SOINS (FR) *PaulNicholls* 7-11-2 SamTwiston-Davies 3/1 3¾ 2
104 AGRAPART (FR) *NickWilliams* 6-11-10 LizzieKelly ....11/8f nk 3
Desert Cry (IRE) *DonaldMcCain* 11-11-2 (b) WillKennedy 9/1 7 4
Anteros (IRE) *SophieLeech* 9-11-6 (s+t) TomScudamore 33/1 45 5
Sullivan Bloodstock Ltd & Chris Giles 5ran 5m35.00

143 Betfred Grand National Trial Handicap Chase (Gr 3) (1) (5yo+) £42,712   3½m97y (22)

58	VIEUX LION ROUGE (FR) *DavidPipe* 8-11-6[146] (s) TomScudamore 8/1		1
87	BLAKLION *NigelTwiston-Davies* 8-11-12[152] WilliamTwiston-Davies 7/2f	3¼	2
115	VINTAGE CLOUDS (IRE) *SueSmith* 7-10-10[136] BrianHughes 5/1	18	3
6	Gas Line Boy (IRE) *IanWilliams* 11-11-4[144] (v) A.P.Heskin 12/1	3½	4
	Cresswell Breeze *AnthonyHoneyball* 7-10-6[132] (t) DavidNoonan(3) 14/1	1¼	5
40	Kruzhlinin (GER) *PhilipHobbs* 10-11-6[146] (b) TomO'Brien 11/1	5	6
28	Warrantor (IRE) *WarrenGreatrex* 8-10-9[135] (t) GavinSheehan 16/1	6	7
108	Houblon des Obeaux (FR) *VenetiaWilliams* 10-11-9[149] (s) CharlieDeutsch(3) 14/1	8	8
126	Vicente (FR) *PaulNicholls* 8-11-7[147] (h) SamTwiston-Davies 10/1	2½	9
	Aqalim *TimVaughan* 7-10-11[137] (v) AlanJohns(3) 40/1		pu
	Tour des Champs (FR) *SamuelDrinkwater* 10-11-2[142] RobertDunne 25/1		pu
108	Goodtoknow *KerryLee* 9-11-2[142] (b) JakeGreenall 10/1		pu
87	Wakanda (IRE) *SueSmith* 8-11-10[150] DannyCook 9/1		pu

Prof Caroline Tisdall & Mr John Gent 13ran 7m25.20

144 Albert Bartlett Prestige Novices' Hurdle (Gr 2) (1) (5yo+) £16,938   2¾m177y (12)

	THE WORLDS END (IRE) *TomGeorge* 6-11-7 A.P.Heskin 11/4		1
124	NO HASSLE HOFF (IRE) *DanSkelton* 5-11-0 BridgetAndrews 9/4f	9	2
	BALLYARTHUR (IRE) *NigelTwiston-Davies* 7-11-4 (t) WilliamTwiston-Davies .8/1	16	3
	Progress Drive (IRE) *NickyRichards* 6-11-4 StephenMulqueen 20/1	20	4
	Report To Base (IRE) *EvanWilliams* 5-11-4 SamTwiston-Davies 4/1	4½	5
	Another Bill (IRE) *NickyRichards* 7-11-4 CraigNichol 25/1	42	6
48	Theligny (FR) *TimVaughan* 6-11-7 AlanJohns 13/2		pu

McNeill Family 7ran 5m37.10

ASCOT Saturday, Feb 18   SOFT

145 Sodexo Reynoldstown Novices' Chase (Gr 2) (1) (5yo+) £22,780   2m7f180y (20)

126	BIGBADJOHN (IRE) *RebeccaCurtis* 8-11-4 JonathanMoore 8/1		1
	FLINTHAM *MarkBradstock* 8-11-0 (s) NicodeBoinville 9/2	sh	2
78	FLETCHERS FLYER (IRE) *HarryFry* 9-11-7 (t) NoelFehily 7/2	2½	3
	Arpege d'Alene (FR) *PaulNicholls* 7-11-4 (b+t) SeanBowen 10/11f	4	4
	Laurium *NickyHenderson* 7-11-4 DavidBass 12/1	15	5

Mr Nigel Morris 5ran 6m11.60

146 Betfair Ascot Chase (Gr 1) (1) (5yo+) £85,425   2m5f8y (17)

83	CUE CARD *ColinTizzard* 11-11-7 (t) PaddyBrennan 4/9f		1
103	SHANTOU FLYER (IRE) *RebeccaCurtis* 7-11-7 (t) AdamWedge 22/1	15	2
120	ROYAL REGATTA (IRE) *PhilipHobbs* 9-11-7 (b+t) RichardJohnson 11/1	3¾	3
96	Taquin du Seuil (FR) *JonjoO'Neill* 10-11-7 AidanColeman 9/1	nk	4
59	Irish Cavalier (IRE) *RebeccaCurtis* 8-11-7 (s) JonathanMoore 14/1	5	5
135	Traffic Fluide (FR) *GaryMoore* 7-11-7 JamieMoore 20/1	24	6

Mrs Jean R. Bishop 6ran 5m25.60

WINCANTON Saturday, Feb 18   GOOD to SOFT

147 Betway Kingwell Hurdle (Gr 2) (1) (4yo+) £34,170   1m7f65y (7)

82	YANWORTH *AlanKing* 7-11-10 (s) BarryGeraghty 2/5f		1
82	CH'TIBELLO (FR) *DanSkelton* 6-11-6 HarrySkelton 8/1	1	2
50	SCEAU ROYAL (FR) *AlanKing* 5-11-6 DarylJacob 4/1	1¼	3
70	Melodic Rendezvous *JeremyScott* 11-11-2 (s) MattGriffiths 80/1	12	4
79	Rayvin Black *OliverSherwood* 8-11-10 (s) ThomasGarner 25/1	20	5
114	Irving *PaulNicholls* 9-11-10 NickScholfield 16/1	19	6

Mr John P. McManus 6ran 3m47.60

NAVAN Sunday, Feb 19   SOFT

148 Ladbrokes Ireland Boyne Hurdle (Gr 2) (5yo+) £22,692   2m5f (12)

127	SUTTON PLACE (IRE) *GordonElliott* 6-11-8 (t) BarryGeraghty 4/6f		1
95	DE PLOTTING SHED (IRE) *GordonElliott* 7-11-6 J.W.Kennedy 13/2	3¾	2
127	RENNETI (FR) *W.P.Mullins* 8-11-3 (b) R.Walsh 9/2	2½	3
127	Supasundae *MrsJ.Harrington* 7-11-3 RobbiePower 6/1	½	4
62	Dedigout (IRE) *GordonElliott* 11-11-3 (t) B.J.Cooper 25/1	4½	5
35	Taglietelle *GordonElliott* 8-11-3 (b) DenisO'Regan 66/1	23	6
127	Ttebbob (IRE) *MrsJ.Harrington* 8-11-3 (h+t) M.P.Walsh 33/1	3	7
95	Milsean (IRE) *M.F.Morris* 8-11-3 (s+t) M.A.Enright 66/1	19	8
117	Thomas Hobson *W.P.Mullins* 7-11-8 P.Townend 12/1		pu

Mr John P. McManus 9ran 5m34.20

149 Ten Up Novices' Chase (Gr 2) (5yo+) £21,432   3m (17)

	ACAPELLA BOURGEOIS (FR) *MsSandraHughes* 7-11-3 RogerLoughran 7/2		1
85	ROAD TO RESPECT (IRE) *NoelMeade* 6-11-3 B.J.Cooper 6/1	32	2

86 HAYMOUNT (IRE) *W.P.Mullins* 8-11-3 R.Walsh 8/1 11 3
81 Anibale Fly (FR) *A.J.Martin* 7-11-6 (t) BarryGeraghty 6/4f 5½ 4
118 Jetstream Jack (IRE) *GordonElliott* 7-11-3 (t) DavyRussell 12/1 9 5
98 Bellow Mome (FR) *W.P.Mullins* 6-11-3 P.Townend 16/1 2½ 6
Stone Hard (IRE) *GordonElliott* 7-11-3 J.W.Kennedy 20/1 7 7
Edwulf *JosephPatrickO'Brien* 8-11-3 (t) MrD.O'Connor 7/1 F
Slaneyville Syndicate 8ran 6m36.60

KEMPTON Saturday, Feb 25 GOOD

150 Betbright Genius Adonis Juvenile Hurdle (Gr 2) (1) (4yo) £17,085 2m (8)
MASTER BLUEYES (IRE) *AlanKing* 4-11-2 TomBellamy 13/2 1
88 EVENING HUSH (IRE) *EvanWilliams* 4-10-12 AdamWedge 6/1 11 2
FIDUX (FR) *AlanKing* 4-11-2 TomCannon 12/1 4 3
Flying Tiger (IRE) *NickWilliams* 4-11-5 LizzieKelly 16/1 3¼ 4
Bedrock *DanSkelton* 4-10-12 (t) HarrySkelton 25/1 4½ 5
Percy Street *NickyHenderson* 4-11-2 NicodeBoinville 16/1 ½ 6
Templier (IRE) *GaryMoore* 4-11-2 JamieMoore 66/1 5 7
27 East Indies *GaryMoore* 4-11-2 (h) JoshuaMoore 66/1 8 8
Ibleo (FR) *VenetiaWilliams* 4-11-5 CharlieDeutsch 25/1 17 9
Charli Parcs (FR) *NickyHenderson* 4-11-5 BarryGeraghty 8/15f F
The Barbury Lions 10ran 3m49.80

151 Betbright Best For Festival Betting Pendil Novices' Chase (Gr 2) (1) (5yo+) £18,224 2½m110y (16)
81 FRODON (FR) *PaulNicholls* 5-11-5 SamTwiston-Davies 8/11f 1
GOLD PRESENT (IRE) *NickyHenderson* 7-11-4 JeremiahMcGrath 13/2 2 2
CHARMIX (FR) *HarryFry* 7-11-0 (s) NoelFehily 7/4 29 3
Zigger Zagger (IRE) *RichardRowe* 8-11-0 AndrewGlassonbury 100/1 F
Mr P J Vogt & Mr Ian Fogg 4ran 5m02.20

152 Sky Bet Dovecote Novices' Hurdle (Gr 2) (1) (4yo+) £17,085 2m (8)
RIVER WYLDE (IRE) *NickyHenderson* 6-11-6 NicodeBoinville 11/4 1
113 ELGIN *AlanKing* 5-11-9 TomCannon 3/1 3½ 2
PETER THE MAYO MAN (IRE) *NeilMulholland* 7-11-9 NoelFehily 9/2 3 3
105 Capitaine (FR) *PaulNicholls* 5-11-9 (h) SamTwiston-Davies 7/4f 3¾ 4
Bazooka (IRE) *DavidFlood* 6-11-2 JamesBanks 80/1 17 5
Ronnie Baird *LauraYoung* 4-10-7 (h) RobertHawker 250/1 6 6
Mister Universum (GER) *DanSkelton* 5-11-2 HarrySkelton 33/1 12 7
Grech & Parkin 7ran 3m46.50

153 Betbright Handicap Chase (Gr 3) (1) (5yo+) £56,950 3m (18)
PILGRIMS BAY (IRE) *NeilMulholland* 7-10-2^{130} (s+h) JamesBest 25/1 1
29 DOUBLE SHUFFLE (IRE) *TomGeorge* 7-11-7^{149} (h) A.P.Heskin 11/2 ½ 2
89 THEATRE GUIDE (IRE) *ColinTizzard* 10-11-11^{153} (b+t) PaddyBrennan 11/1 2½ 3
68 Aso (FR) *VenetiaWilliams* 7-11-10^{152} CharlieDeutsch(3) 11/1 ½ 4
3 Ballykan *NigelTwiston-Davies* 7-10-12^{140} (s+t) WilliamTwiston-Davies 11/1 2¼ 5
13 Three Musketeers (IRE) *DanSkelton* 7-11-10^{152} (s) HarrySkelton 5/1 ½ 6
24 Fingerontheswitch (IRE) *NeilMulholland* 7-10-4^{132} (s+t) NiallMadden 12/1 7 7
78 Annacotty (IRE) *AlanKing* 9-11-12^{154} (s) IanPopham 33/1 3 8
78 Irish Saint (FR) *PaulNicholls* 8-11-4^{146} (t) SamTwiston-Davies 9/2f 1¾ 9
Opening Batsman (IRE) *HarryFry* 11-10-5^{133} (b+t) MrM.Legg(5) 14/1 18 10
108 Viva Steve (IRE) *FergalO'Brien* 9-10-11^{139} (t) TomBellamy 8/1 1½ 11
59 Cocktails At Dawn *NickyHenderson* 9-11-3^{145} NicodeBoinville 25/1 F
78 Triolo d'Alene (FR) *NickyHenderson* 10-11-2^{144} JeremiahMcGrath 16/1 pu
Clifford, Gosden & House 13ran 5m56.20

NEWCASTLE Saturday, Feb 25 SOFT

154 Betfred Eider Handicap Chase (2) (5yo+) £50,048 4m122y (25)
MYSTEREE (IRE) *MichaelScudamore* 9-11-0^{127} RobertDunne 10/1 1
108 KNOCKANRAWLEY (IRE) *KimBailey* 9-11-6^{133} (s) DavidBass 8/1 4 2
108 SHOTGUN PADDY (IRE) *EmmaLavelle* 10-11-10^{137} DarylJacob 6/1f 1½ 3
Harry The Viking *SandyThomson* 12-10-13^{126} (s) RachaelMcDonald(7) 20/1 4½ 4
108 Emperor's Choice (IRE) *VenetiaWilliams* 10-11-8^{135} (b) AidanColeman 20/1 6 5
Smooth Stepper *SueSmith* 8-11-7^{134} SeanQuinlan 14/1 6 6
108 Mountainous (IRE) *KerryLee* 12-11-6^{133} (s) RichardPatrick(7) 8/1 45 7
Alto des Mottes (FR) *HenryHogarth* 7-11-0^{127} (s) TonyKelly 14/1 F
115 Gevrey Chambertin (FR) *DavidPipe* 9-11-12^{139} (b) TomScudamore 16/1 ur
58 Portrait King (IRE) *PatrickGriffin,Ireland* 12-11-3^{130} (s) A.W.Short(7) 16/1 bd
57 Morney Wing (IRE) *CharlieMann* 8-11-0^{127} (s+t) GavinSheehan 33/1 pu
108 Russe Blanc (FR) *KerryLee* 10-11-3^{130} (b) BrianHughes 10/1 pu
115 Berea Boru (IRE) *PeterBowen* 9-11-6^{133} (v+t) SeanBowen 14/1 pu

58 Milborough (IRE) *IanDuncan* 11-11-6^{133} GrahamWatters(3) 14/1 pu
126 Out Sam *WarrenGreatrex* 8-11-8^{135} (s) AndrewTinkler 14/1 pu
Streets of Promise (IRE) *MichaelScudamore* 8-11-10^{137} (s) BenPoste(3) 20/1 pu
108 Milansbar (IRE) *NeilKing* 10-11-11^{138} TrevorWhelan 20/1 pu
Straidnahanna (IRE) *SueSmith* 8-11-12^{139} DannyCook 25/1 pu
Mrs Lynne Maclennan 18ran 9m12.60

FONTWELL Sunday, Feb 26 SOFT

155 Totepool National Spirit Hurdle (Gr 2) (1) (4yo+) £45,560 2m3f33y (10)

104 CAMPING GROUND (FR) *GaryMoore* 7-11-11 JoshuaMoore 9/1 1
LE ROCHER (FR) *NickWilliams* 7-11-3 TomScudamore 9/2 29 2
114 L'AMI SERGE (IRE) *NickyHenderson* 7-11-3 DarylJacob 2/1jf 22 3
126 Third Intention (IRE) *ColinTizzard* 10-11-3 (s+t) TomO'Brien 25/1 2 4
67 Different Gravey (IRE) *NickyHenderson* 7-11-3 NicodeBoinville 2/1jf 11 5
77 Shelford (IRE) *DanSkelton* 8-11-11 (b) NoelFehily 40/1 6 6
104 Adrien du Pont (FR) *PaulNicholls* 5-11-7 (t) SamTwiston-Davies 17/2 pu
Mr G. L. Porter 7ran 4m47.30

NEWBURY Saturday, Mar 4 SOFT

156 William Hill 'High 5' Supporting Greatwood Gold Cup Handicap Chase (Gr 3) (1) (5yo+) £28,475 2m3f187y (16)

103 THOMAS CRAPPER *RobinDickin* 10-10-2^{128} (s+t) CharliePoste 8/1 1
VIC DE TOUZAINE (FR) *VenetiaWilliams* 8-10-8^{134} TomScudamore 9/2 20 2
HOLLYWOODIEN (FR) *TomSymonds* 6-11-2^{142} JamesDavies 9/1 8 3
115 O Maonlai (IRE) *TomGeorge* 9-11-3^{143} (t) A.P.Heskin 13/2 20 4
Tornado In Milan (IRE) *EvanWilliams* 11-10-10^{136} AdamWedge 12/1 6 5
Dresden (IRE) *HenryOliver* 9-11-2^{142} RichardJohnson 9/1 3¾ 6
More Buck's (IRE) *PaulNicholls* 7-10-8^{134} (t) SeanBowen 8/1 pu
Oldgrangewood *DanSkelton* 6-11-3^{143} HarrySkelton 4/1f pu
56 Vibrato Valtat (FR) *PaulNicholls* 8-11-12^{152} (b+t) StanSheppard(5) 13/2 pu
Apis.uk.com 9ran 5m05.20

DONCASTER Saturday, Mar 4 SOFT

157 Betbright Grimthorpe Handicap Chase (2) (5yo+) £34,408 3¼m1y (19)

115 DEFINITLY RED (IRE) *BrianEllison* 8-11-0^{149} DannyCook 7/2 1
58 THE LAST SAMURI (IRE) *KimBailey* 9-11-12^{161} DavidBass 10/3f 14 2
143 WAKANDA (IRE) *SueSmith* 8-11-1^{150} SeanQuinlan 10/1 3½ 3
87 Yala Enki (FR) *VenetiaWilliams* 7-10-12^{147} CharlieDeutsch(3) 7/2 8 4
108 Sego Success (IRE) *AlanKing* 9-10-3^{138} (v) TomCannon 6/1 nk 5
126 Looking Well (IRE) *NickyRichards* 8-10-2^{137} RyanDay(5) 9/2 19 6
108 Vivaldi Collonges (FR) *PaulNicholls* 8-10-13^{148} (t) NickScholfield 14/1 pu
Mr P. J. Martin 7ran 6m39.50

KELSO Saturday, Mar 4 HEAVY

158 Totescoop6 Premier Kelso Novices' Hurdle (Gr 2) (1) (4yo+) £21,641 2¼m25y (10)

MOUNT MEWS (IRE) *MalcolmJefferson* 6-11-5 BrianHughes 11/8f 1
105 CHALONNIAL (FR) *HarryFry* 5-11-5 NoelFehily 4/1 49 2
FAIRLEE GREY *GeorgeCharlton* 8-11-5 JanFaltejsek 5/1 F
152 Capitaine (FR) *PaulNicholls* 5-11-8 (h) SamTwiston-Davies 9/4 pu
Mr Trevor Hemmings 4ran 4m52.40

SANDOWN Saturday, Mar 11 GOOD to SOFT

159 European Breeders' Fund Matchbook VIP 'National Hunt' Novices' Handicap Hurdle Final (Gr 3) (1) (4, 5, 6 and 7yo) £36,576 2m3f173y (9)

MINELLA AWARDS (IRE) *HarryFry* 6-11-8^{128} (t) NoelFehily 8/1 1
PRIME VENTURE (IRE) *EvanWilliams* 6-11-6^{126} TomO'Brien 14/1 1¼ 2
WYLDE MAGIC (IRE) *EvanWilliams* 6-10-10^{116} AdamWedge 10/1 2¼ 3
Crystal Lad (FR) *GaryMoore* 5-11-9^{129} JamieMoore 25/1 1¼ 4
Westendorf (IRE) *JonjoO'Neill* 6-11-6^{126} (t) MrJohnJ.O'Neill(7) 20/1 2¾ 5
Ramses de Teillee (FR) *DavidPipe* 5-10-13^{119} (t) TomScudamore 16/1 3 6
Touch Kick (IRE) *PaulNicholls* 6-11-3^{123} (h+t) NickScholfield 20/1 sh 7
Full Irish (IRE) *EmmaLavelle* 6-11-10^{130} DarylJacob 7/1 2¼ 8
The Mighty Don (IRE) *NickGifford* 5-11-10^{130} (s) LeightonAspell 14/1 nk 9
Another Venture (IRE) *KimBailey* 6-11-7^{127} DavidBass 11/1 2½ 10
Tintern Theatre (IRE) *NigelTwiston-Davies* 6-11-11^{131} WilliamTwiston-Davies 16/1 1½ 11
Cash Again (FR) *PaulNicholls* 5-11-1^{121} SamTwiston-Davies 12/1 7 12
Man From Mars *NickWilliams* 5-11-3^{123} LizzieKelly(3) 16/1 1 13
Lithic (IRE) *JonjoO'Neill* 6-10-11^{117} AidanColeman 6/1f 2¾ 14
Gaitway *NickyHenderson* 7-11-6^{126} NicodeBoinville 7/1 13 15

Phobiaphiliac (IRE) *NickyHenderson* 6-11-12[132] (h) JeremiahMcGrath ....20/1   pu
Masterson Holdings Limited 16ran 4m59.70

160 Matchbook Imperial Cup Handicap Hurdle (Gr 3) (1) (4yo+) £39,389   1m7f216y (8)

	LONDON PRIZE *IanWilliams* 6-11-2[128] TomO'Brien 10/1		1
	FIXE LE KAP (FR) *NickyHenderson* 5-11-12[138] DarylJacob 5/1f	1	2
	DAREBIN (GER) *GaryMoore* 5-10-11[123] (v) JoshuaMoore 25/1	3½	3
	Spice Fair *MarkUsher* 10-11-1[128] MrZ.Baker(7) 20/1	1¼	4
	Not Another Muddle *GaryMoore* 6-10-8[120] JamieMoore 6/1	½	5
	Bigmartre (FR) *HarryWhittington* 6-11-8[134] JeremiahMcGrath 16/1	¾	6
136	William H Bonney *AlanKing* 6-11-8[134] WayneHutchinson 11/2	3	7
136	Kayf Blanco *GraemeMcPherson* 8-11-9[135] (h+t) KielanWoods 7/1	1½	8
	Chieftain's Choice (IRE) *KevinFrost* 8-10-9[121] TomBellamy 10/1	1	9
136	Gassin Golf *KerryLee* 8-11-7[133] (s+t) RichardPatrick(7) 8/1	14	10
	Prairie Town (IRE) *TonyCarroll* 6-11-1[127] (s) LeeEdwards 40/1		F
	Disputed (IRE) *ChrisGordon* 7-10-13[125] (h) TomCannon 10/1		pu
	Max Do Brazil (FR) *DavidPipe* 5-11-2[128] (t) TomScudamore 14/1		pu

Mrs Margaret Forsyth 13ran 4m03.70

NAAS Sunday, Mar 12   SOFT

161 Download The Ladbrokes Exchange App Leinster National Handicap Chase (Gr A) (5yo+) £50,862   3m (16)

52	ABOLITIONIST (IRE) *EllmarieHolden* 9-11-1[137] RachaelBlackmore(3) 12/1		1
94	FOLSOM BLUE (IRE) *M.F.Morris* 10-10-10[132] (s) J.J.Slevin(5) 12/1	1¾	2
	SUMOS NOVIOS (IRE) *W.J.Burke* 9-11-3[139] (t) RobbiePower 12/1	10	3
118	Ucello Conti (FR) *GordonElliott* 9-11-10[146] (t) DarylJacob 7/1	3¾	4
52	Georges Conn (IRE) *JohnPatrickRyan* 9-10-0[122] D.E.Mullins 33/1	1	5
118	Thunder And Roses (IRE) *M.F.Morris* 9-10-10[146] (s+t) MsL.O'Neill(5) 16/1	2¾	6
116	Space Cadet (IRE) *GordonElliott* 7-10-11[133] DavyRussell 13/2	¾	7
	Archie Meade (IRE) *DanielJohnHoward* 12-9-13[121] (b+t) PhilipEnright 50/1	43	8
	Futuramic (IRE) *AndrewLynch* 10-9-13[121] R.C.Colgan 16/1	33	9
94	Kilford (IRE) *LeonardWhitmore* 11-10-3[125] L.P.Dempsey 25/1		ur
	Texas Jack (IRE) *NoelMeade* 11-11-3[139] (s) P.J.Reynolds(7) 28/1		ur
	After Aspen (IRE) *MissElizabethDoyle* 7-9-10[118] (s) A.Ring(3) 33/1		pu
	Fair Return *NoelMeade* 7-9-10[118] (t) M.A.Enright 12/1		pu
	Undressed (IRE) *NoelMeade* 9-10-4[126] (t) D.Robinson(5) 25/1		pu
	Vent de La Cote (FR) *MartinBrassil* 8-10-8[130] (t) M.P.Walsh 14/1		pu
116	Rightdownthemiddle (IRE) *GordonElliott* 9-10-11[133] J.W.Kennedy 10/1		pu
94	Sambremont (FR) *W.P.Mullins* 7-11-2[138] P.Townend 7/1		pu
118	Bonny Kate (IRE) *NoelMeade* 7-11-3[139] SeanFlanagan 6/1f		pu

Mrs Catherine Holden 18ran 7m03.10

CHELTENHAM Tuesday, Mar 14   GOOD

162 Sky Bet Supreme Novices' Hurdle (Gr 1) (1) (4yo+) £71,187   2m87y (8)

80	LABAIK (FR) *GordonElliott,Ireland* 6-11-7 JackKennedy 25/1		1
	MELON *W.P.Mullins,Ireland* 5-11-7 R.Walsh 3/1jf	2¼	2
152	RIVER WYLDE (IRE) *NickyHenderson* 6-11-7 NicodeBoinville 8/1	8	3
136	Ballyandy *NigelTwiston-Davies* 6-11-7 SamTwiston-Davies 3/1jf	1¼	4
	Cilaos Emery (FR) *W.P.Mullins,Ireland* 5-11-7 (h) D.J.Mullins 12/1	5	5
	Beyond Conceit (IRE) *NickyHenderson* 8-11-7 NoelFehily 16/1	hd	6
152	Flgin *AlanKing* 5-11-7 WayneHutchinson 14/1	6	7
	Capital Force (IRE) *HenrydeBromhead,Ireland* 6-11-7 DavyRussell 50/1	nk	8
	High Bridge *BenPauling* 6-11-7 MrAlexFerguson 20/1	3¼	9
	Pingshou (IRE) *ColinTizzard* 7-11-7 AidanColeman 25/1	8	10
	Magna Cartor *JohnJosephHanlon,Ireland* 7-11-7 RachaelBlackmore 200/1	2½	11
139	Bunk Off Early (IRE) *W.P.Mullins,Ireland* 5-11-7 P.Townend ....nk	nk	12
	Crack Mome (FR) *W.P.Mullins,Ireland* 5-11-7 D.E.Mullins 11/1	ns	13
	Glaring *AmandaPerrett* 6-11-7 LeightonAspell 40/1	56	14

Mr A. J. O'Ryan 14ran 3m52.80

163 Racing Post Arkle Challenge Trophy Novices' Chase (Gr 1) (1) (5yo+) £99,662   1m7f199y (13)

135	ALTIOR (IRE) *NickyHenderson* 7-11-4 NicodeBoinville 1/4f		1
	CLOUDY DREAM (IRE) *MalcolmJefferson* 7-11-4 BrianHughes 12/1	6	2
85	ORDINARY WORLD (IRE) *HenrydeBromhead,Ireland* 7-11-4 DavyRussell 25/1	9	3
129	Royal Caviar (IRE) *W.P.Mullins,Ireland* 9-11-4 (h) R.Walsh 6/1	7	4
	Forest Bihan *BrianEllison* 6-11-4 AidanColeman 12/1	1	5
129	Some Plan (IRE) *HenrydeBromhead,Ireland* 6-11-4 (t) D.J.Mullins 20/1	4	6
33	A Hare Breath (IRE) *BenPauling* 9-11-4 RichardJohnson 25/1	20	7
54	Charbel (IRE) *KimBailey* 6-11-4 (t) DavidBass 9/1		F

983

85 Three Stars (IRE) *HenrydeBromhead,Ireland* 7-11-4 RobbiePower ....66/1   pu
Mrs Patricia Pugh 9ran 3m54.10

164 Ultima Handicap Chase (Gr 3) (1) (5yo+) £59,797   3m1f (20)

123	UN TEMPS POUR TOUT (IRE) *DavidPipe* 8-11-12[155] (b+t) TomScudamore 9/1		1
	SINGLEFARMPAYMENT *TomGeorge* 7-10-13[142] (h) A.P.Heskin 5/1f	sh	2
94	NOBLE ENDEAVOR (IRE) *GordonElliott,Ireland* 8-11-11[154] DavyRussell 15/2	3½	3
68	Buywise (IRE) *EvanWilliams* 10-11-2[145] AdamWedge 33/1	7	4
78	Go Conquer (IRE) *JonjoO'Neill* 8-10-8[137] AidanColeman 20/1	¾	5
123	The Young Master *NeilMulholland* 8-11-7[150] (s) MrS.Waley-Cohen(3) 25/1	10	6
78	The Druids Nephew (IRE) *NeilMulholland* 10-11-3[146] (s) NoelFehily 10/1	8	7
153	Theatre Guide (IRE) *ColinTizzard* 10-11-10[153] (b+t) PaddyBrennan 33/1	2½	8
118	Clarcam (FR) *GordonElliott,Ireland* 7-11-10[153] (s+t) B.J.Cooper 50/1	¾	9
66	A Good Skin (IRE) *TomGeorge* 8-10-5[134] (s) RichardJohnson 14/1	1	10
	Label des Obeaux (FR) *AlanKing* 6-11-5[148] WayneHutchinson 16/1	13	11
153	Annacotty (IRE) *AlanKing* 9-11-8[151] (s) IanPopham 66/1	1¾	12
118	Measureofmydreams (IRE) *NoelMeade,Ireland* 9-11-3[146] SeanFlanagan 25/1	nk	13
153	Pilgrims Bay (IRE) *NeilMulholland* 7-10-9[138] (s+h) JamesBest 25/1	nk	14
123	Henri Parry Morgan *PeterBowen* 9-10-13[142] (s+t) SeanBowen 14/1	8	15
143	Vintage Clouds (IRE) *SueSmith* 7-10-5[134] SeanQuinlan 20/1		F
126	Caid du Berlais (FR) *PaulNicholls* 8-11-0[143] (t) StanSheppard(5) 20/1		F
156	Vic de Touzaine (FR) *VenetiaWilliams* 8-10-5[134] LiamTreadwell 25/1		ur
126	Coologue (IRE) *CharlieLongsdon* 8-11-1[144] BrianHughes 50/1		pu
47	Ibis du Rheu (FR) *PaulNicholls* 6-11-3[146] (h+t) SamTwiston-Davies 12/1		pu
126	Holywell (IRE) *JonjoO'Neill* 10-11-5[148] (b) RichieMcLernon 10/1		pu
18	Junction Fourteen (IRE) *EmmaLavelle* 8-11-5[148] (t) LeightonAspell 40/1		pu
89	Viconte du Noyer (FR) *ColinTizzard* 8-11-8[151] HarryCobden 33/1		pu

Professor Caroline Tisdall & Bryan Drew 23ran 6m20.90

165 Stan James Champion Hurdle Challenge Trophy (Gr 1) (1) (4yo+) £227,800   2m87y (8)

Order as they passed the post: Yanworth subsequently disqualified after testing positive for a prohibited substance

	BUVEUR D'AIR (FR) *NickyHenderson* 6-11-10 NoelFehily 5/1		1
82	MY TENT OR YOURS (IRE) *NickyHenderson* 10-11-10 (h) AidanColeman 16/1	4½	2
130	PETIT MOUCHOIR (FR) *HenrydeBromhead,Ireland* 6-11-10 B.J.Cooper 6/1	3	3
130	Footpad (FR) *W.P.Mullins,Ireland* 5-11-10 R.Walsh 14/1	3	4
114	The New One (IRE) *NigelTwiston-Davies* 9-11-10 SamTwiston-Davies 10/1	sh	5
147	Sceau Royal (FR) *AlanKing* 5-11-10 DarylJacob 25/1	2¾	6
147	Yanworth *AlanKing* 7-11-10 (s) MarkWalsh 2/1f	½	7
	Wicklow Brave *W.P.Mullins,Ireland* 8-11-10 P.Townend 22/1	¾	8
79	Brain Power (IRE) *NickyHenderson* 6-11-10 (s) D.J.Mullins 13/2	15	9
114	Cyrus Darius *MalcolmJefferson* 8-11-10 BrianHughes 50/1	14	10
30	Moon Racer (IRE) *DavidPipe* 8-11-10 TomScudamore 10/1		pu

Mr John P. McManus 11ran 3m51.00

166 OLBG Mares' Hurdle (David Nicholson) (Gr 1) (1) (4yo+) £61,897   2m3f200y (10)

62	APPLE'S JADE (FR) *GordonElliott,Ireland* 5-11-5 (t) B.J.Cooper 7/2		1
125	VROUM VROUM MAG (FR) *W.P.Mullins,Ireland* 8-11-5 P.Townend 11/4	1½	2
	LIMINI (IRE) *W.P.Mullins,Ireland* 6-11-5 R.Walsh 6/4f	ns	3
	Indian Stream *NeilMulholland* 8-11-5 (t) NoelFehily 33/1	3¾	4
	Briery Queen *NoelWilliams* 8-11-5 (h) RichardJohnson 33/1	½	5
	Midnight Tour *AlanKing* 7-11-5 TomCannon 66/1	4	6
	The Organist (IRE) *OliverSherwood* 6-11-5 LeightonAspell 100/1	5	7
	Rons Dream *PeterBowen* 7-11-5 SeanBowen 50/1	1¾	8
9	Debdebdeb *DanSkelton* 7-11-5 HarrySkelton 50/1	¾	9
125	Midnight Jazz *BenCase* 7-11-5 DarylJacob 50/1	2¾	10
	Lifeboat Mona *PaulNicholls* 7-11-5 (t) SamTwiston-Davies 16/1	4½	11
	Rock On The Moor (IRE) *Mrs.J.Harrington,Ireland* 9-11-5 RobbiePower 50/1	6	12
99	Jer's Girl (IRE) *GavinPatrickCromwell,Ireland* 5-11-5 MarkWalsh 14/1		F
	Hidden Identity (IRE) *TimVaughan* 11-11-5 (t) AlanJohns 200/1		bd
	Pass The Time *NeilMulholland* 8-11-5 (s) TomScudamore 100/1		bd
	Bon Chic (IRE) *JamesMoffatt* 8-11-5 HenryBrooke 250/1		pu
	Miss Crick *AlanKing* 6-11-5 WayneHutchinson 100/1		pu

Gigginstown House Stud 17ran 4m50.00

167 JT McNamara National Hunt Challenge Cup Amateur Riders' Novices' Chase (Gr 2) (1) (5yo+) £71,952   3m7f170y (25)

11	TIGER ROLL (IRE) *GordonElliott,Ireland* 7-11-6 (b+t) MsL.O'Neill 16/1		1
132	MISSED APPROACH (IRE) *WarrenGreatrex* 7-11-6 (s) MrN.McParlan 50/1	3	2
149	HAYMOUNT (IRE) *W.P.Mullins,Ireland* 8-11-6 MrP.W.Mullins 33/1	¾	3
145	Arpege d'Alene (FR) *PaulNicholls* 7-11-6 (b+t) MrW.Biddick 12/1	2½	4

984

A Genie In Abottle (IRE) *NoelMeade,Ireland* 6-11-6 MrJ.J.Codd 4/1f 17 5
Kerrow (IRE) *AlanKing* 7-11-6 MrJoshuaNewman 33/1 1½ 6
Beware The Bear (IRE) *NickyHenderson* 7-11-6 MrS.Waley-Cohen 9/2 2 7
Bells 'N' Banjos (IRE) *FergalO'Brien* 7-11-6 MissA.E.Stirling 80/1 4 8
132 Calett Mad (FR) *NigelTwiston-Davies* 5-11-4 (t) MrZ.Baker 33/1 2¾ 9
108 Ballycross *NigelTwiston-Davies* 7-11-6 MrH.F.Nugent 100/1 19 10
Arbre de Vie (FR) *W.P.Mullins,Ireland* 7-11-6 MsK.Walsh ....14/1 ur
98 Martello Tower (IRE) *MsMargaretMullins,Ireland* 9-11-6 (b) MrStevenClements 11/1 pu
145 Flintham *MarkBradstock* 8-11-6 (s) MrM.Legg ....33/1 pu
Dancing Shadow (IRE) *VictorDartnall* 8-11-6 (s) SeanHoulihan ....50/1 pu
149 Edwulf *JosephPatrickO'Brien,Ireland* 8-11-6 (t) MrDerekO'Connor ....5/1 pu
Champers On Ice (IRE) *DavidPipe* 7-11-6 (s+t) MrR.P.Quinlan ....7/1 pu
145 Bigbadjohn (IRE) *RebeccaCurtis* 8-11-6 MrBarryO'Neill ....14/1 pu
What A Moment (IRE) *DavidPipe* 7-11-6 (s) MrR.O.Harding ....100/1 pu
Gigginstown House Stud 18ran 8m21.80

168 Close Brothers Novices' Handicap Chase (L) (1) (140) (5yo+) £39,865   2½m78y (16)
85 TULLY EAST (IRE) *AlanFleming,Ireland* 7-11-8^{138} DenisO'Regan 8/1 1
151 GOLD PRESENT (IRE) *NickyHenderson* 7-11-7^{137} JeremiahMcGrath 14/1 1¼ 2
137 TWO TAFFS (IRE) *DanSkelton* 7-11-7^{137} (s+t) DavyRussell ....7/1 nk 3
Powersbomb (IRE) *BrianM.McMahon,Ireland* 7-11-8^{138} (h) MrJ.J.Codd 22/1 6 4
Last Goodbye (IRE) *MissElizabethDoyle,Ireland* 6-11-10^{140} SeanFlanagan ....22/1 ¾ 5
112 Bun Doran (IRE) *TomGeorge* 6-11-9^{139} A.P.Heskin 10/1 1 6
Relentless Dreamer (IRE) *RebeccaCurtis* 8-11-8^{138} (s+t) P.Townend 40/1 3 7
Deans Road (IRE) *HenrydeBromhead,Ireland* 8-11-8^{138} A.E.Lynch 33/1 4½ 8
Double W's (IRE) *MalcolmJefferson* 7-11-10^{140} BrianHughes 16/1 3¾ 9
Zamdy Man *VenetiaWilliams* 8-11-12^{142} AidanColeman 12/1 11 10
Burtons Well (IRE) *VenetiaWilliams* 8-11-7^{137} CharlieDeutsch(3) ....8/1 F
Killiney Court (IRE) *HenrydeBromhead,Ireland* 8-11-9^{139} (t) M.P.Fogarty ....33/1 F
Foxtail Hill (IRE) *NigelTwiston-Davies* 8-11-10^{140} WilliamTwiston-Davies .... 6/1f F
67 Sizing Tennessee (IRE) *ColinTizzard* 9-11-7^{137} (b) TomO'Brien ....14/1 pu
All Hell Let Loose (IRE) *HenrydeBromhead,Ireland* 8-11-7^{137} (t) B.J.Cooper .....14/1 pu
Captain Redbeard (IRE) *StuartColtherd* 8-11-9^{139} SamColtherd(5) ....22/1 pu
Templehills (IRE) *NigelTwiston-Davies* 6-11-9^{139} (h) DaveCrosse ....66/1 pu
112 Its'afreebee (IRE) *DanSkelton* 7-11-9^{139} (s+t) HarrySkelton ....11/1 pu
31 Hammersly Lake (FR) *NickyHenderson* 9-11-10^{140} D.J.Mullins ....16/1 pu
Mixboy (FR) *KeithDalgleish* 7-11-10^{140} BrianHarding ....16/1 pu
Mr Barry Connell 20ran 5m11.90

CHELTENHAM Wednesday, Mar 15 GOOD
169 Neptune Investment Management Novices' Hurdle (Baring Bingham)   2m5f26y (10)
(Gr 1) (1) (4yo+) £71,187
107 WILLOUGHBY COURT (IRE) *BenPauling* 6-11-7 DavidBass 14/1 1
113 NEON WOLF (IRE) *HarryFry* 6-11-7 NoelFehily .... 2/1f hd 2
101 MESSIRE DES OBEAUX (FR) *AlanKing* 5-11-7 DarylJacob 8/1 3¾ 3
Burbank (IRE) *NickyHenderson* 5-11-7 JeremiahMcGrath 50/1 4 4
128 Kemboy (FR) *W.P.Mullins,Ireland* 5-11-7 D.J.Mullins 16/1 1¼ 5
139 Brelade *GordonElliott,Ireland* 5-11-7 JackKennedy 18/1 1½ 6
Keeper Hill (IRE) *WarrenGreatrex* 6-11-7 GavinSheehan 25/1 2¾ 7
Skipthecuddles (IRE) *GraemeMcPherson* 6-11-7 KielanWoods ....66/1 ½ 8
De Dollar Man *EvanWilliams* 6-11-7 AdamWedge 50/1 7 9
100 Livelovelaugh (IRE) *W.P.Mullins,Ireland* 7-11-7 D.E.Mullins 16/1 1 10
122 Poetic Rhythm (IRE) *FergalO'Brien* 7-11-7 PaddyBrennan 66/1 28 11
Shattered Love (IRE) *GordonElliott,Ireland* 6-11-0 (t) B.J.Cooper 8/1 2¾ 12
79 Consul de Thaix (FR) *NickyHenderson* 6-11-7 MarkWalsh ....16/1 F
139 Bacardys (FR) *W.P.Mullins,Ireland* 6-11-7 R.Walsh ....4/1 pu
Bon Papa (FR) *W.P.Mullins,Ireland* 6-11-7 P.Townend ....18/1 pu
Paul & Clare Rooney 15ran 5m08.70

170 RSA Novices' Chase (Gr 1) (1) (5yo+) £99,662   3m80y (19)
81 MIGHT BITE (IRE) *NickyHenderson* 8-11-4 NicodeBoinville 7/2f 1
102 WHISPER (IRE) *NickyHenderson* 9-11-4 DavyRussell ....9/2 ns 2
140 BELLSHILL (IRE) *W.P.Mullins,Ireland* 7-11-4 R.Walsh 5/1 10 3
98 Alpha des Obeaux (FR) *M.F.Morris,Ireland* 7-11-4 B.J.Cooper 6/1 8 4
71 O O Seven (IRE) *NickyHenderson* 7-11-4 AidanColeman 25/1 30 5
149 Acapella Bourgeois (FR) *MsSandraHughes,Ireland* 7-11-4 RogerLoughran 5/1 13 6
Marinero (IRE) *HenrydeBromhead,Ireland* 8-11-4 D.J.Mullins ....25/1 ur
102 Briery Belle *HenryDaly* 8-10-11 TomO'Brien ....25/1 pu
87 Our Kaempfer (IRE) *CharlieLongsdon* 8-11-4 (t) SamTwiston-Davies ....20/1 pu
81 Royal Vacation (IRE) *ColinTizzard* 7-11-4 (b+t) PaddyBrennan ....12/1 pu

985

Heron Heights (IRE) *HenrydeBromhead,Ireland* 8-11-4 (t) PhilipEnright ....40/1   pu
Aurillac (FR) *RebeccaCurtis* 7-11-4 JonathanMoore ....100/1   pu
The Knot Again Partnership 12ran 6m08.60

171 Coral Cup Handicap Hurdle (Gr 3) (1) (4yo+) £54,102   2m5f26y (10)
148 SUPASUNDAE *MrsJ.Harrington,Ireland* 7-11-4[148] RobbiePower 16/1   1
146 TAQUIN DU SEUIL (FR) *JonjoO'Neill* 10-11-4[148] AidanColeman 12/1   2   2
79 WHO DARES WINS (IRE) *AlanKing* 5-11-2[146] WayneHutchinson 33/1   2½   3
62 Monksland (IRE) *NoelMeade,Ireland* 10-11-3[147] (h) DonaghMeyler(3) 66/1   1   4
Scoir Mear (IRE) *ThomasMullins,Ireland* 7-10-8[138] D.J.Mullins ....20/1   ½   5
109 Modus *PaulNicholls* 7-11-0[156] (h) StanSheppard(5) ....16/1   nk   6
123 Old Guard *PaulNicholls* 6-11-6[150] SamTwiston-Davies ....20/1   nk   7
Tin Soldier (FR) *W.P.Mullins,Ireland* 6-10-10[140] R.Walsh ....5/1   ns   8
River Frost *AlanKing* 5-10-13[143] TomCannon 25/1   1½   9
109 Kalondra (IRE) *NeilMulholland* 6-11-3[147] (t) NoelFehily 20/1   2   10
107 Peregrine Run (IRE) *PeterFahey,Ireland* 7-10-12[142] RogerLoughran ....7/1   nk   11
63 Automated *GordonElliott,Ireland* 6-10-12[142] JackKennedy 16/1   1¼   12
Hawk High (IRE) *TimEasterby* 7-10-10[140] (s) BrianHughes 25/1   4   13
70 Mister Miyagi (IRE) *DanSkelton* 8-11-5[149] HarrySkelton 16/1   1   14
Morello Royale (IRE) *ColinTizzard* 7-10-10[140] (t) DavidO'Brien 100/1   7   15
79 Waxies Dargle *NoelMeade,Ireland* 8-11-2[146] (t) SeanFlanagan 50/1   1   16
33 Leoncavallo (IRE) *BenPauling* 5-10-10[140] (s) MrAlexFerguson(7) 66/1   4½   17
148 Thomas Hobson (IRE) *W.P.Mullins,Ireland* 7-11-1[145] D.E.Mullins 50/1   1¼   18
136 Hargam (FR) *NickyHenderson* 6-10-10[140] (s) NicodeBoinville 14/1   6   19
Sure Reef (IRE) *W.P.Mullins,Ireland* 8-10-6[136] M.P.Fogarty ....40/1   ½   20
139 Bravissimo (FR) *W.P.Mullins,Ireland* 6-10-6[136] MsK.Walsh ....33/1   ¾   21
Tombstone (IRE) *GordonElliott,Ireland* 7-10-9[139] B.J.Cooper 7/2f   1¾   22
Robinshill (IRE) *NigelTwiston-Davies* 6-10-9[139] (t) JamieBargary(3) 100/1   44   23
117 Allblak des Places (FR) *W.P.Mullins,Ireland* 5-10-10[140] P.Townend ....40/1   pu
123 The Romford Pele (IRE) *RebeccaCurtis* 10-11-5[149] (b) JonathanMoore(3) ....66/1   pu
Ann & Alan Potts Partnership 25ran 5m04.60

172 Betway Queen Mother Champion Chase (Gr 1) (1) (5yo+) £208,300   1m7f199y (13)
120 SPECIAL TIARA *HenrydeBromhead,Ireland* 10-11-10 NoelFehily 11/1   1
135 FOX NORTON (FR) *ColinTizzard* 7-11-10 (h) AidanColeman ....7/1   hd   2
91 SIR VALENTINO (FR) *TomGeorge* 8-11-10 (t) PaddyBrennan 33/1   6   3
120 Top Gamble (IRE) *KerryLee* 9-11-10 (t) DavyRussell ....20/1   hd   4
56 God's Own (IRE) *TomGeorge* 9-11-10 A.P.Heskin 6/1   1   5
146 Traffic Fluide (FR) *GaryMoore* 7-11-10 JoshuaMoore ....50/1   nk   6
133 Douvan (FR) *W.P.Mullins,Ireland* 7-11-10 R.Walsh 2/9f   4   7
38 Garde La Victoire (FR) *PhilipHobbs* 8-11-10 RichardJohnson 14/1   17   8
92 Simply Ned (IRE) *NickyRichards* 10-11-10 BrianHarding 33/1   13   9
29 Sizing Granite (IRE) *ColinTizzard* 9-11-10 (t) TomO'Brien ....50/1   pu
Mrs S. Rowley-Williams 10ran 3m54.20

173 Glenfarclas Chase (Cross Country) (Gr 2) (5yo+) £40,235   3¾m37y (32)
94 CAUSE OF CAUSES (USA) *GordonElliott,Ireland* 9-11-4 (s+t) MrJ.J.Codd 4/1   1
118 BLESS THE WINGS (IRE) *GordonElliott,Ireland* 12-11-4 (s) DavyRussell 10/1   9   2
4 CANTLOW (IRE) *EndaBolger,Ireland* 12-11-4 A.P.Heskin 9/4f   1¼   3
Auvergnat (FR) *EndaBolger,Ireland* 7-11-4 RobbiePower 8/1   1¼   4
Amazing Comedy (FR) *PhillippeCottin,France* 7-11-4 (b+t) DavidCottin 50/1   4½   5
Ballyboker Bridge (IRE) *PeterMaher,Ireland* 10-11-4 (s) A.E.Lynch 25/1   1¼   6
Colour Squadron (IRE) *EndaBolger,Ireland* 11-11-4 MrDerekO'Connor ....33/1   ¾   7
155 Third Intention (IRE) *ColinTizzard* 10-11-4 (t) TomO'Brien 33/1   11   8
28 Any Currency (IRE) *MartinKeighley* 14-11-4 (t) AidanColeman 14/1   1½   9
108 Kingswell Theatre *MichaelScudamore* 8-11-4 (s) TomScudamore ....33/1   ½   10
60 Valadom (FR) *RichardHobson* 8-11-4 (t) JamieBargary ....100/1   ½   11
115 Sausalito Sunrise (IRE) *PhilipHobbs* 9-11-4 (s) RichardJohnson 8/1   46   12
Usuel Smurfer (FR) *AlanFleming,Ireland* 9-11-4 DenisO'Regan ....20/1   F
6 First Lieutenant (IRE) *M.F.Morris,Ireland* 12-11-4 (s) MarkEnright ....50/1   ur
Quantitativeeasing (IRE) *EndaBolger,Ireland* 12-11-4 NiallMadden ....25/1   pu
74 Alelchi Inois (FR) *W.P.Mullins,Ireland* 9-11-4 MrP.W.Mullins ....20/1   pu
Mr John P. McManus 16ran 8m12.90

174 Fred Winter Juvenile Handicap Hurdle (Gr 3) (1) (4yo) £45,560   2m87y (8)
150 FLYING TIGER (IRE) *NickWilliams* 4-11-5[134] RichardJohnson 33/1   1
DIVIN BERE (FR) *NickyHenderson* 4-11-10[139] NoelFehily ....9/2f   nk   2
NIETZSCHE *BrianEllison* 4-11-1[130] (h) DannyCook ....12/1   nk   3
Project Bluebook (FR) *JohnQuinn* 4-11-9[138] BrianHughes 14/1   5   4
27 Diable de Sivola (FR) *NickWilliams* 4-11-3[132] LizzieKelly(3) 33/1   1¼   5
150 Percy Street *NickyHenderson* 4-10-9[124] NicodeBoinville 16/1   1½   6

	Dakota Moirette (FR) *GordonElliott,Ireland* 4-11-2[131] B.J.Cooper	25/1	¾	7
88	Dino Velvet (FR) *AlanKing* 4-10-10[125] WayneHutchinson	11/1	hd	8
84	Zig Zag (IRE) *JosephPatrickO'Brien,Ireland* 4-10-12[127] (t) JodyMcGarvey(3)	66/1	3½	9
	Long Call *A.J.Martin,Ireland* 4-11-6[135] (t) DavyRussell	9/1	hd	10
	Domperignon du Lys (FR) *NickyHenderson* 4-11-4[133] DarylJacob	8/1	hd	11
119	Rainbow Dreamer *AlanKing* 4-11-3[132] (v) TomCannon	50/1	1¼	12
88	Dolos (FR) *PaulNicholls* 4-11-5[134] (t) SamTwiston-Davies	12/1	3¾	13
	Poker Play (FR) *DavidPipe* 4-11-4[133] (t) TomScudamore	16/1	1	14
	Dreamcatching (FR) *PaulNicholls* 4-11-2[131] StanSheppard(5)	12/1	2½	15
	Fadas (FR) *DanSkelton* 4-10-10[125] (s+t) HarrySkelton	40/1	7	16
	Dodgybingo (IRE) *NoelMeade,Ireland* 4-10-10[125] (b) SeanFlanagan	80/1	4½	17
	Candy Burg (FR) *VenetiaWilliams* 4-10-9[124] (t) LiamTreadwell	50/1	8	18
150	Fidux (FR) *AlanKing* 4-11-6[135] TomBellamy	50/1	4½	19
	Icario (FR) *GordonElliott,Ireland* 4-10-11[126] (h) JackKennedy	25/1		F
	Linger (IRE) *JohnJosephHanlon,Ireland* 4-11-3[132] RachaelBlackmore(3)	7/1		pu
84	Prospectus *GavinPatrickCromwell,Ireland* 4-11-4[133] R.Walsh	14/1		pu
	The Macaroni Beach Society 22ran 3m58.30			

175 Weatherbys Champion Bumper (Standard Open National Hunt Flat) (Gr 1) (1) (4, 5 and 6yo) £42,712 — 2m87y

	FAYONAGH (IRE) *GordonElliott,Ireland* 6-10-12 MrJ.J.Codd	7/1		1
	DEBUCHET (IRE) *MsMargaretMullins,Ireland* 4-10-11 D.E.Mullins	10/1	1¼	2
	CLAIMANTAKINFORGAN (FR) *NickyHenderson* 5-11-5 NicodeBoinville	22/1	1½	3
	Next Destination (IRE) *W.P.Mullins,Ireland* 5-11-5 R.Walsh	10/1	nk	4
	Western Ryder (IRE) *WarrenGreatrex* 5-11-5 GavinSheehan	7/1	nk	5
	Dans Le Vent (FR) *JamieSnowden* 4-10-11 AidanColeman	100/1	5	6
	And The New (IRE) *JohnnyFarrelly* 6-11-5 BrendanPowell	100/1	1½	7
	Mountain Rock (IRE) *A.P.Keatley,Ireland* 5-11-5 JackKennedy	66/1	½	8
	Cause Toujours (FR) *DanSkelton* 5-11-5 HarrySkelton	9/2f	½	9
	Nelson's Touch *DenisCoakley* 4-10-11 NickScholfield	100/1	¾	10
	Perfect Harmony (IRE) *AlanKing* 5-11-5 IanPopham	33/1	1½	11
	Better Getalong (IRE) *NickyRichards* 6-11-5 BrianHarding	50/1	1¼	12
	West Coast Time (IRE) *JosephPatrickO'Brien,Ireland* 5-11-5 (t) DavyRussell	16/1	¾	13
	Bakmaj (FR) *AlanFleming,Ireland* 5-11-5 DenisO'Regan	12/1	1½	14
	Carter McKay *W.P.Mullins,Ireland* 6-11-5 MrP.W.Mullins	11/2	2¾	15
	Robin The Raven (IRE) *KimBailey* 5-11-5 (s) DavidBass	33/1	3	16
	Quick Grabim (IRE) *R.P.McNamara,Ireland* 5-11-5 NoelFehily	25/1	8	17
	Imperial Eloquence (IRE) *FergalO'Brien* 5-11-5 PaddyBrennan	25/1	1	18
	My Mate Mark *MartinSmith* 4-10-11 TomCannon	50/1	24	19
	Irish Roe (IRE) *PeterAtkinson* 6-10-12 HenryBrooke	12/1	11	20
	Copernicus (IRE) *CharlieLongsdon* 5-11-5 (t) RichardJohnson	66/1	43	21
	Fisherman Frank *MichaelBlake* 6-11-5 TomScudamore	66/1		pu
	Mrs M. Gittins 22ran 3m51.20			

CHELTENHAM Thursday, Mar 16   GOOD

176 JLT Novices' Chase (Golden Miller) (Gr 1) (1) (5yo+) £89,275 — 2m3f198y (16)

	YORKHILL (IRE) *W.P.Mullins,Ireland* 7-11-4 R.Walsh	6/4f		1
131	TOP NOTCH (FR) *NickyHenderson* 6-11-4 DarylJacob	7/2	1	2
140	DISKO (FR) *NoelMeade,Ireland* 6-11-4 (h) B.J.Cooper	4/1	3	3
112	Politologue (FR) *PaulNicholls* 6-11-4 (h) SamTwiston-Davies	10/1	6	4
	Kilcrea Vale (IRE) *NickyHenderson* 7-11-4 JeremiahMcGrath	22/1	9	5
137	Flying Angel (IRE) *NigelTwiston-Davies* 6-11-4 NoelFehily	9/1	19	6
85	Baily Cloud *M.F.Morris,Ireland* 7-11-4 (s+t) MarkEnright	50/1		F
140	Balko des Flos (FR) *HenrydeBromhead,Ireland* 6-11-4 D.J.Mullins	16/1		F
	Andrea & Graham Wylie 8ran 4m59.30			

177 Pertemps Network Final Handicap Hurdle (L) (1) (5yo+) £54,102 — 2m7f213y (12)

	PRESENTING PERCY *PatrickG.Kelly,Ireland* 6-11-11[146] (t) DavyRussell	11/1		1
	BARNEY DWAN (IRE) *FergalO'Brien* 7-11-8[143] PaddyBrennan	16/1	3¾	2
	JURY DUTY (IRE) *GordonElliott,Ireland* 6-11-10[145] JackKennedy	9/1	2	3
	The Tourard Man (IRE) *AlanKing* 11-11-5[140] KevinDowling(10)	66/1	4½	4
	Sutton Manor (IRE) *GordonElliott,Ireland* 6-11-7[142] MsL.O'Neill(5)	16/1	2	5
	Electric Concorde (IRE) *J.Culloty,Ireland* 6-11-4[139] D.J.Mullins	20/1	nk	6
	Ballymalin (IRE) *NigelTwiston-Davies* 6-11-3[138] NoelFehily	12/1	1½	7
164	Caid du Berlais (FR) *PaulNicholls* 8-11-10[145] (t) StanSheppard(5)	25/1	nk	8
	For Good Measure (IRE) *PhilipHobbs* 6-11-3[138] RichardJohnson	10/1	1	9
10	El Bandit (IRE) *PaulNicholls* 6-11-8[143] SamTwiston-Davies	14/1	1	10
40	Theo's Charm *NickGifford* 7-11-3[138] (b) TomCannon	33/1	¾	11
	Golden Doyen (GER) *PhilipHobbs* 6-11-8[143] TomO'Brien	18/1	6	12
	Splash of Ginge *NigelTwiston-Davies* 9-11-6[141] JamieBargary(3)	33/1	nk	13

Isleofhopendreams *W.P.Mullins,Ireland* 10-11-4[139] R.Walsh ....14/1 nk 14
Rocklander (IRE) *TomGeorge* 8-11-5[140] A.P.Heskin ....12/1 hd 15
49 Aubusson (FR) *NickWilliams* 8-11-10[145] MrC.Williams(7) 66/1 8 16
Clondaw Cian (IRE) *SuzySmith* 7-11-2[137] (s) SeanBowen ....16/1 hd 17
107 Gayebury *EvanWilliams* 7-11-12[147] AdamWedge ....25/1 ½ 18
Alzammaar (USA) *SamEngland* 6-11-3[138] JonathanEngland ....25/1 nk 19
Arctic Gold (IRE) *NigelTwiston-Davies* 6-11-3[138] TomHumphries(7) 50/1 3¾ 20
69 Impulsive Star (IRE) *NeilMulholland* 7-11-5[140] MrS.Waley-Cohen(3) .... 8/1f ½ 21
Tobefair *DebraHamer* 7-11-8[143] (s) TrevorWhelan 10/1 15 22
Fingal Bay (IRE) *PhilipHobbs* 11-11-5[140] SeanHoulihan(7) 50/1 2½ 23
9 Mr Mix (FR) *PaulNicholls* 11-11-8[143] HarryCobden 50/1 10 24
Mr Philip J. Reynolds 24ran 5m49.30

178 Ryanair Chase (Festival Trophy) (Gr 1) (1) (5yo+) £170,850   2½m166y (17)
120 UN DE SCEAUX (FR) *W.P.Mullins,Ireland* 9-11-10 R.Walsh 7/4f 1
111 SUB LIEUTENANT (IRE) *HenrydeBromhead,Ireland* 8-11-10 (t) D.J.Mullins ...8/1 1½ 2
153 ASO (FR) *VenetiaWilliams* 7-11-10 (s) CharlieDeutsch 40/1 6 3
141 Empire of Dirt (IRE) *GordonElliott,Ireland* 10-11-10 (t) B.J.Cooper 11/4 1½ 4
83 Josses Hill (IRE) *NickyHenderson* 9-11-10 (s) NicodeBoinville 9/1 9 5
115 Alary (FR) *ColinTizzard* 7-11-10 (t) TomO'Brien 33/1 9 6
120 Uxizandre (FR) *AlanKing* 9-11-10 (s) WayneHutchinson 6/1 2½ 7
Vaniteux (FR) *NickyHenderson* 8-11-10 NoelFehily 14/1 2¼ 8
E. O'Connell 8ran 5m09.70

179 Sun Bets Stayers' Hurdle (Gr 1) (1) (4yo+) £170,850   2m7f213y (12)
130 NICHOLS CANYON *W.P.Mullins,Ireland* 7-11-10 R.Walsh 10/1 1
104 LIL ROCKERFELLER (USA) *NeilKing* 6-11-10 (s) TrevorWhelan ....33/1 ¾ 2
123 UNOWHATIMEANHARRY *HarryFry* 9-11-10 (t) NoelFehily 5/6f 3½ 3
123 Cole Harden (IRE) *WarrenGreatrex* 8-11-10 (s+t) GavinSheehan 9/1 3½ 4
95 Snow Falcon (IRE) *NoelMeade,Ireland* 7-11-10 SeanFlanagan 16/1 12 5
95 Clondaw Warrior (IRE) *W.P.Mullins,Ireland* 10-11-10 (h) MsK.Walsh 33/1 4 6
142 Zarkandar (IRE) *PaulNicholls* 10-11-10 (b+t) HarryCobden 25/1 3¾ 7
Jezki (IRE) *MrsJ.Harrington,Ireland* 9-11-10 (h) RobbiePower 15/2 3¾ 8
142 Agrapart (IRE) *NickWilliams* 6-11-10 LizzieKelly 66/1 2¼ 9
95 Shaneshill (IRE) *W.P.Mullins,Ireland* 8-11-10 P.Townend ....16/1 pu
123 West Approach *ColinTizzard* 7-11-10 TomScudamore ....28/1 pu
123 Ballyoptic (IRE) *NigelTwiston-Davies* 7-11-10 (t) SamTwiston-Davies ....14/1 pu
Andrea & Graham Wylie 12ran 5m49.80

180 Brown Advisory & Merriebelle Stable Plate Handicap Chase (Gr 3) (1)   2½m166y (17)
(5yo+) £59,797
149 ROAD TO RESPECT (IRE) *NoelMeade,Ireland* 6-10-13[145] B.J.Cooper 14/1 1
131 BARON ALCO (FR) *GaryMoore* 6-11-0[146] JamieMoore 10/1 6 2
68 BOUVREUIL (FR) *PaulNicholls* 6-10-13[145] (h+t) SamTwiston-Davies ..10/1 1¾ 3
156 Thomas Crapper *RobinDickin* 10-10-1[133] (s+t) CharliePoste 7/1 2¾ 4
Starchitect (IRE) *DavidPipe* 6-10-11[143] (t) TomScudamore 6/1 4 5
153 Ballykan *NigelTwiston-Davies* 7-10-8[140] (s+t) DarylJacob ....33/1 ½ 6
Rock Gone (IRE) *DrRichardNewland* 9-10-4[136] JoshuaMoore 25/1 6 7
29 Art Mauresque (IRE) *PaulNicholls* 7-11-9[155] NickScholfield 33/1 2¼ 8
60 Henryville *HarryFry* 9-10-9[141] (t) NoelFehily 12/1 1¼ 9
Katachenko (IRE) *DonaldMcCain* 8-10-1[133] (h) WillKennedy ....40/1 hd 10
103 Village Vic (IRE) *PhilipHobbs* 10-11-12[158] RichardJohnson 16/1 7 11
18 Voix d'Eau (FR) *HarryFry* 7-11-0[146] (t) MrM.Legg(5) 25/1 1¾ 12
66 Un Ace (FR) *KimBailey* 9-10-5[137] (s+t) DavidBass 25/1 1½ 13
68 King's Odyssey (IRE) *EvanWilliams* 8-10-13[145] AdamWedge 20/1 15 14
68 Sizing Codelco (IRE) *ColinTizzard* 8-10-8[140] (b+t) TomO'Brien 14/1 1½ 15
33 Mad Jack Mytton (IRE) *JonjoO'Neill* 7-10-3[135] RichieMcLernon ....28/1 F
16 Germany Calling (IRE) *CharlieLongsdon* 6-10-13[145] (s+t) KielanWoods ....100/1 F
16 All Together (FR) *JohnnyFarrelly* 6-10-1[133] BrendanPowell ....50/1 ur
Champagne At Tara *JonjoO'Neill* 8-10-4[136] AidanColeman ....25/1 pu
Pinkie Brown (FR) *NeilMulholland* 5-10-5[137] (h) A.P.Heskin ....66/1 pu
153 Cocktails At Dawn *NickyHenderson* 9-10-13[145] NicodeBoinville ....33/1 pu
Tango de Juilley (FR) *VenetiaWilliams* 9-11-4[150] CharlieDeutsch(3) ......20/1 pu
86 Diamond King (IRE) *GordonElliott,Ireland* 9-11-4[150] (t) DavyRussell ....5/1f pu
Cold March (FR) *VenetiaWilliams* 7-11-4[150] (b) LiamTreadwell ....50/1 pu
Gigginstown House Stud 24ran 5m09.50

181 Trull House Stud Mares' Novices' Hurdle (Dawn Run) (Gr 2) (1) (4yo+)   2m179y (8)
£45,560
128 LET'S DANCE (FR) *W.P.Mullins,Ireland* 5-11-7 R.Walsh 11/8f 1
139 BARRA (FR) *GordonElliott,Ireland* 6-11-2 (t) B.J.Cooper 12/1 2¾ 2

	DUSKY LEGEND *AlanKing* 7-11-5 WayneHutchinson	20/1	nk	3
	Verdana Blue (IRE) *NickyHenderson* 5-11-2 JeremiahMcGrath	25/1	nk	4
	Asthuria (FR) *W.P.Mullins,Ireland* 6-11-2 (h) D.E.Mullins	14/1	4½	5
	Awayinthewest (IRE) *P.A.Fahy,Ireland* 5-11-2 DavyRussell	100/1	¾	6
	La Bague Au Roi (FR) *WarrenGreatrex* 6-11-7 GavinSheehan	10/1	8	7
61	Forge Meadow (IRE) *MrsJ.Harrington,Ireland* 5-11-7 RobbiePower	12/1	1½	8
	Titi de Montmartre (FR) *R.Collet,France* 4-11-0 (s) LudovicPhilipperon	25/1	nk	9
	On Demand *ColinTizzard* 6-11-2 (t) TomO'Brien	100/1	½	10
125	Coillte Lass (IRE) *PaulNicholls* 6-11-7 SamTwiston-Davies	28/1	3½	11
	Tahira (GER) *RichardHobson* 7-11-7 (s+t) HarrySkelton	100/1	1¼	12
	Montana Belle (IRE) *HenrydeBromhead,Ireland* 7-11-2 (t) D.J.Mullins	100/1	2¼	13
61	Airlie Beach (IRE) *W.P.Mullins,Ireland* 7-11-7 P.Townend	4/1	4	14
	Groovejet *RichardSpencer* 6-11-2 SeanBowen	100/1	22	15
	Toe The Line (IRE) *JohnE.Kiely,Ireland* 8-11-2 DenisO'Regan	16/1		F

Mrs S. Ricci 16ran 4m01.90

182 Fulke Walwyn Kim Muir Challenge Cup Amateur Riders' Handicap Chase (2) (145) (5yo+) £41,972 — 3¼m (20)

What should have been the third last fence was omitted due to a stricken horse

52	DOMESDAY BOOK (USA) *StuartEdmunds* 7-11-4^{137} (b) MissG.Andrews	40/1		1
	PENDRA (IRE) *CharlieLongsdon* 9-11-12^{145} (b) MrDerekO'Connor	16/1	¾	2
	PREMIER BOND *NickyHenderson* 7-11-4^{137} (s) MrS.Waley-Cohen	9/1	¾	3
71	Potters Legend *LucyWadham* 7-11-6^{139} MrM.Legg	10/1	1	4
	Mall Dini (IRE) *PatrickG.Kelly,Ireland* 7-11-10^{143} (t) MsK.Walsh	11/2	½	5
	Sugar Baron (IRE) *NickyHenderson* 7-11-2^{135} MrJoshuaNewman(3)	25/1	4	6
108	Doctor Harper (IRE) *DavidPipe* 9-11-8^{141} (s+t) MsL.O'Neill	14/1	6	7
	Lessons In Milan (IRE) *NickyHenderson* 9-11-2^{135} (s) MrH.Hunt(5)	33/1	½	8
89	Unioniste (FR) *PaulNicholls* 9-11-8^{141} MrD.Maxwell(3)	33/1	3¾	9
	Forgotten Gold (IRE) *TomGeorge* 11-11-10^{143} (s) MrN.George(7)	50/1	½	10
	Whats Happening (IRE) *TomGeorge* 10-11-4^{137} (t) MrR.O.Harding	12/1	1¼	11
	Lamb Or Cod (IRE) *PhilipHobbs* 10-11-5^{138} (t) SeanHoulihan(7)	28/1	nk	12
126	Another Hero (IRE) *JonjoO'Neill* 8-11-3^{136} (t) MrJohnJ.O'Neill(5)	9/1	½	13
	Father Edward (IRE) *DavidPipe* 8-11-1^{134} (s) MrRexDingle(7)	66/1	9	14
	Kilfinichen Bay (IRE) *CharlieLongsdon* 9-11-2^{135} (t) MrJ.Nailor(7)	66/1	6	15
94	Venitien de Mai (FR) *J.T.R.Dreaper,Ireland* 8-11-2^{135} MrP.W.Mullins	25/1		F
49	Hadrian's Approach (IRE) *NickyHenderson* 10-11-7^{140} (s) MrW.Biddick	16/1		F
126	Southfield Royale *NeilMulholland* 7-11-8^{141} (s) MrJamesKing	7/1		F
	Squouateur (FR) *GordonElliott,Ireland* 6-11-2^{135} (t) MrJ.J.Codd	5/1f		ur
58	Alvarado (IRE) *FergalO'Brien* 12-11-0^{133} MrZ.Baker(3)	33/1		pu
	Balbir du Mathan (FR) *AlanFleming,Ireland* 8-11-1^{134} (t) MrStevenClements	50/1		pu
126	Potters Cross *RebeccaCurtis* 10-11-6^{139} MrBarryO'Neill	50/1		pu
109	Local Show (IRE) *SarahHumphrey* 9-11-8^{141} ThomasGreatrex(3)	50/1		pu
60	La Vaticane (FR) *DavidPipe* 8-11-10^{143} (b+t) MrD.Edwards	50/1		pu

Mr J. Humberstone 24ran 6m48.75

CHELTENHAM Friday, Mar 17 GOOD

183 JCB Triumph Hurdle (Gr 1) (1) (4yo) £71,187 — 2m179y (8)

119	DEFI DU SEUIL (FR) *PhilipHobbs* 4-11-0 RichardJohnson	5/2f		1
138	MEGA FORTUNE (FR) *GordonElliott,Ireland* 4-11-0 (s) DavyRussell	7/1	5	2
138	BAPAUME (FR) *W.P.Mullins,Ireland* 4-11-0 R.Walsh	10/1	sh	3
138	Ex Patriot (IRE) *EllmarieHolden,Ireland* 4-11-0 RachaelBlackmore	28/1	2	4
84	Landofhopeandglory (IRE) *JosephPatrickO'Brien,Ireland* 4-11-0 (t) RobbiePower	8/1	½	5
150	Charli Parcs (FR) *NickyHenderson* 4-11-0 NoelFehily	9/2	2½	6
	Coeur de Lion *AlanKing* 4-11-0 TomCannon	33/1	¾	7
	Landin (GER) *SeamusMullins* 4-11-0 JeremiahMcGrath	150/1	3¼	8
	Magie du Ma (FR) *DavidPipe* 4-10-7 (h) TomScudamore	40/1	½	9
150	Master Blueyes (IRE) *AlanKing* 4-11-0 WayneHutchinson	8/1	5	10
138	Dinaria des Obeaux (FR) *GordonElliott,Ireland* 4-10-7 B.J.Cooper	10/1	1¾	11
150	Evening Hush (IRE) *EvanWilliams* 4-10-7 AdamWedge	50/1	1	12
	Dandy Mag (FR) *W.P.Mullins,Ireland* 4-11-0 P.Townend	22/1	11	13
	I See You Well (FR) *SeamusMullins* 4-11-0 JamieMoore	200/1	16	14
	Soldier In Action (FR) *NickyHenderson* 4-11-0 NicodeBoinville	16/1	1	15

Mr John P. McManus 15ran 4m00.00

184 Randox Health County Handicap Hurdle (Gr 3) (1) (5yo+) £54,102 — 2m179y (8)

	ARCTIC FIRE (GER) *W.P.Mullins,Ireland* 8-11-12^{158} (h) P.Townend	20/1		1
155	L'AMI SERGE (IRE) *NickyHenderson* 7-11-6^{152} DarylJacob	25/1	nk	2
48	OZZIE THE OSCAR (IRE) *PhilipHobbs* 6-10-3^{135} TomO'Brien	50/1	nk	3
	Air Horse One *HarryFry* 6-10-8^{140} NoelFehily	10/1	2	4
33	Winter Escape (IRE) *AlanKing* 6-10-8^{140} WayneHutchinson	9/1	sh	5

130	Ivanovich Gorbatov (IRE) *JosephO'Brien,Ireland* 5-11-4^{150} (b+t) J.J.Slevin(5)	5/1f	nk	6
113	Mohaayed *DanSkelton* 5-10-2^{134} (t) IanPopham	16/1	½	7
148	Renneti (FR) *W.P.Mullins,Ireland* 8-11-3^{149} R.Walsh	11/1	¾	8
136	Wait For Me (FR) *PhilipHobbs* 7-10-3^{135} (h+t) RichardJohnson	10/1	nk	9
70	Court Minstrel (IRE) *EvanWilliams* 10-10-13^{145} AdamWedge	33/1	nk	10
34	Wakea (USA) *KarlThornton,Ireland* 6-10-10^{142} (h+t) DonaghMeyler(3)	33/1	nk	11
79	Diego du Charmil (FR) *PaulNicholls* 5-11-3^{149} (t) SamTwiston-Davies	12/1	7	12
113	Crievehill (IRE) *NigelTwiston-Davies* 5-10-5^{137} (h) JamieBargary(3)	33/1	1	13
110	Baltimore Rock (IRE) *NeilMulholland* 8-10-6^{138} (t) TomScudamore	66/1	¾	14
55	Bertimont (FR) *DanSkelton* 7-10-7^{139} (t) BridgetAndrews(3)	50/1	ns	15
33	North Hill Harvey *DanSkelton* 6-11-3^{149} HarrySkelton	8/1	1¼	16
	Kapstadt (FR) *IanWilliams* 7-10-3^{135} (t) WillKennedy	33/1	¾	17
136	Song Light *SeamusMullins* 7-10-3^{135} KevinJones(5)	20/1	4	18
136	Boite (IRE) *WarrenGreatrex* 7-10-8^{140} (s) GavinSheehan	50/1	13	19
128	Joey Sasa (IRE) *NoelMeade,Ireland* 8-10-8^{140} SeanFlanagan	20/1	¾	20
	Tell Us More (IRE) *GordonElliott,Ireland* 8-10-10^{142} B.J.Cooper	14/1	7	21
	Vosne Romanee *DrRichardNewland* 6-10-7^{139} (s+t) AidanColeman	18/1	3¾	22
	Dominada (IRE) *BrianEllison* 5-10-3^{135} BrianHughes	40/1	1¾	23
109	Jaleo (GER) *BenPauling* 5-10-3^{135} MrAlexFerguson(7)	40/1		F
136	De Name Escapes Me (IRE) *NoelMeade,Ireland* 7-10-4^{136} JonathanMoore(3)	28/1		pu

Wicklow Bloodstock (Ireland) Ltd 25ran 4m00.20

185 Albert Bartlett Novices' Hurdle (Spa) (Gr 1) (1) (4yo+) £71,187 — 2m7f213y (12)

100	PENHILL *W.P.Mullins,Ireland* 6-11-5 P.Townend	16/1		1
80	MONALEE (IRE) *HenrydeBromhead,Ireland* 6-11-5 D.J.Mullins	8/1	3½	2
122	WHOLESTONE (IRE) *NigelTwiston-Davies* 6-11-5 DarylJacob	13/2	4	3
124	Constantine Bay *NickyHenderson* 6-11-5 NicodeBoinville	12/1	8	4
101	Ami Desbois (FR) *GraemeMcPherson* 7-11-5 (t) KielanWoods	33/1	6	5
106	Augusta Kate *W.P.Mullins,Ireland* 6-10-12 R.Walsh	11/2	4	6
122	Elegant Escape (IRE) *ColinTizzard* 5-11-5 TomScudamore	100/1	½	7
	Tommy Rapper (IRE) *DanSkelton* 6-11-5 HarrySkelton	33/1	6	8
	Step Back (IRE) *MarkBradstock* 7-11-5 JamieMoore	100/1	½	9
	C'est Jersey (FR) *W.P.Mullins,Ireland* 5-11-5 (s) RobbiePower	100/1	6	10
26	Baden (FR) *NickyHenderson* 6-11-5 JeremiahMcGrath	100/1	21	11
144	The Worlds End (IRE) *TomGeorge* 6-11-5 A.P.Heskin	10/1		F
106	Death Duty (IRE) *GordonElliott,Ireland* 6-11-5 B.J.Cooper	13/8f		ur
106	Turcagua (FR) *W.P.Mullins,Ireland* 7-11-5 (h) D.E.Mullins	66/1		pu
	Any Drama (IRE) *HarryFry* 6-11-5 (s) NoelFehily	25/1		pu

Mr Tony Bloom 15ran 5m49.40

186 Timico Cheltenham Gold Cup Chase (Gr 1) (1) (5yo+) £327,462 — 3¼m70y (22)

141	SIZING JOHN *MrsJ.Harrington,Ireland* 7-11-10 RobbiePower	7/1		1
141	MINELLA ROCCO (IRE) *JonjoO'Neill* 7-11-10 (s+t) NoelFehily	18/1	2¾	2
134	NATIVE RIVER (IRE) *ColinTizzard* 7-11-10 (s) RichardJohnson	7/2	sh	3
96	Djakadam (FR) *W.P.Mullins,Ireland* 8-11-10 R.Walsh	3/1f	½	4
49	Saphir du Rheu (FR) *PaulNicholls* 8-11-10 SamTwiston-Davies	33/1	3	5
141	More of That (IRE) *JonjoO'Neill* 9-11-10 (s) AidanColeman	14/1	3½	6
134	Bristol de Mai (FR) *NigelTwiston-Davies* 6-11-10 DarylJacob	16/1	10	7
121	Smad Place (FR) *AlanKing* 10-11-10 WayneHutchinson	50/1	7	8
118	Champagne West (IRE) *HenrydeBromhead,Ireland* 9-11-10 D.J.Mullins	14/1	nk	9
96	Outlander (IRE) *GordonElliott,Ireland* 9-11-10 B.J.Cooper	10/1	24	10
146	Cue Card *ColinTizzard* 11-11-10 (t) PaddyBrennan	9/2		F
83	Tea For Two *NickWilliams* 8-11-10 LizzieKelly	40/1		ur
146	Irish Cavalier (IRE) *RebeccaCurtis* 8-11-10 (s) P.Townend	66/1		pu

Ann & Alan Potts Partnership 13ran 6m36.20

187 St. James's Place Foxhunter Challenge Cup Open Hunters' Chase (2) (5yo+) £26,982 — 3¼m70y (22)

3	PACHA DU POLDER (FR) *PaulNicholls* 10-12-0 BryonyFrost	16/1		1
	WONDERFUL CHARM (FR) *PaulNicholls* 9-12-0 (s+t) MsK.Walsh	7/2	nk	2
	BAREL OF LAUGHS (IRE) *PhilipRowley* 11-12-0 (s) MrAlexEdwards	100/1	nk	3
	On The Fringe (IRE) *EndaBolger,Ireland* 12-12-0 MrJ.J.Codd	11/8f	2	4
	Balnaslow (IRE) *GrahamMcKeever,Ireland* 10-12-0 MrDerekO'Connor	40/1	½	5
	Minella For Value (IRE) *DeclanQueally,Ireland* 11-12-0 MrD.Queally	100/1	½	6
	Ask The Weatherman *JackR.Barber* 8-12-0 (s) MrW.Biddick	13/2	2¼	7
2	Paint The Clouds *WarrenGreatrex* 12-12-0 MrBarryO'Neill	11/1	ns	8
	Mendip Express (IRE) *PhilipHobbs* 11-12-0 (t) MrD.Maxwell	66/1	16	9
	Salsify (IRE) *RodgerSweeney,Ireland* 12-12-0 MrStevenClements	50/1	13	10
	Pentiffic (NZ) *P.P.C.Turner* 14-12-0 MissL.M.Turner	150/1	ns	11
	Warden Hill (IRE) *MrsH.Connors* 9-12-0 MrT.Chatfeild-Roberts	100/1	3¾	12
	Aupcharlie (IRE) *J.T.R.Dreaper,Ireland* 11-12-0 MrM.J.O'Hare	33/1	1¼	13

Grand Vision (IRE) *ColinTizzard* 11-12-0 (s) MrM.Legg 50/1 7 14
Grand Jesture (IRE) *J.T.R.Dreaper,Ireland* 9-12-0 MrR.O.Harding 40/1 4 15
Current Event (FR) *MrsRoseLoxton* 10-12-0 MsL.O'Neill 66/1 2½ 16
Dolatulo (FR) *BenPauling* 10-12-0 (s) MrD.Gittins 66/1 33 17
Premier Portrait (IRE) *DrCharlesLevinson* 10-12-0 (s) MrG.Levinson 100/1 1 18
Sweet As A Nut (IRE) *MichaelBarry,Ireland* 7-12-0 (t) MrJ.C.Barry .... 14/1 F
Cottage Oak (IRE) *J.J.O'Shea* 14-12-0 MrH.Crow .... 150/1 pu
Lets Get Serious (IRE) *C.J.Miller* 11-12-0 MrC.J.Miller .... 200/1 pu
Black Thunder (FR) *WarrenGreatrex* 10-12-0 (s) MrS.Waley-Cohen .... 20/1 pu
Buckers Bridge (IRE) *M.F.Morris,Ireland* 11-12-0 (s) MrR.P.Quinlan .... 50/1 pu
The Stewart Family 23ran 6m42.00

188 Martin Pipe Conditional Jockeys' Handicap Hurdle (2) (145) (4yo+) £40,664 2½m56y (10)
CHAMPAGNE CLASSIC (IRE) *GordonElliott,Ireland* 6-11-3^{138} J.J.Slevin 12/1 1
VERNI (FR) *PhilipHobbs* 8-11-0^{135} ThomasCheesman 25/1 2¼ 2
RUNFORDAVE (IRE) *GordonElliott,Ireland* 5-11-5^{140} DonaghMeyler 9/1 1¼ 3
122 Coo Star Sivola (FR) *NickWilliams* 5-11-3^{138} LizzieKelly .... 13/2 ½ 4
75 Thomas Campbell *NickyHenderson* 5-11-2^{137} NedCurtis .... 20/1 nk 5
Born Survivor (IRE) *DanSkelton* 6-11-8^{143} BridgetAndrews 33/1 1¾ 6
10 No Comment *PhilipHobbs* 6-11-2^{137} (h) CiaranGethings 15/2 6 7
Battleford *W.P.Mullins,Ireland* 6-11-0^{135} A.W.Short(5) 9/2f 3 8
Dadsintrouble (IRE) *TimVaughan* 7-11-1^{136} HarryCobden 14/1 1¼ 9
Castello Sforza (IRE) *W.P.Mullins,Ireland* 6-11-3^{138} JonathanMoore .... 11/1 hd 10
48 Tommy Silver (FR) *PaulNicholls* 5-11-5^{140} StanSheppard 20/1 3½ 11
148 Taglietelle *GordonElliott,Ireland* 8-11-10^{145} (b) C.M.Collins(3) 20/1 6 12
109 Doesyourdogbite (IRE) *JonjoO'Neill* 5-11-2^{137} KillianMoore .... 33/1 ¾ 13
Massini's Trap (IRE) *JamesA.Nash,Ireland* 8-11-3^{138} (b) KieronEdgar .... 100/1 sh 14
Remiluc (FR) *ChrisGordon* 8-11-4^{139} (t) HarryReed(3) .... 50/1 ½ 15
Lac Fontana (FR) *PaulNicholls* 8-11-4^{139} JackSherwood 20/1 2¾ 16
Pain Au Chocolat (FR) *DanSkelton* 6-11-2^{137} (h+t) LewisGordon(5) .... 100/1 hd 17
Dell' Arca (IRE) *DavidPipe* 8-11-3^{138} (b) DavidNoonan 33/1 13 18
136 Ballyhill (FR) *NigelTwiston-Davies* 6-11-1^{136} JamieBargary .... 80/1 sh 19
Catamaran du Seuil (FR) *DrRichardNewland* 5-11-0^{135} (b) CharlieHammond(5) 33/1 48 20
Gibralfaro (IRE) *AlanKing* 5-11-8^{143} (s) TomBellamy .... 50/1 F
Rather Be (IRE) *NickyHenderson* 6-11-1^{136} CharlieDeutsch .... 10/1 ur
I Shot The Sheriff (IRE) *A.J.Martin,Ireland* 10-11-4^{139} (t) ShaneShortall .... 20/1 pu
Gigginstown House Stud 23ran 4m55.80

189 Johnny Henderson Grand Annual Challenge Cup Handicap Chase (Gr 3) (1) (5yo+) £59,797 2m62y (14)
12 ROCK THE WORLD (IRE) *MrsJ.Harrington,Ireland* 9-11-5^{147} (t) RobbiePower . 10/1 1
GARDEFORT (FR) *VenetiaWilliams* 8-11-0^{142} DarylJacob 20/1 1¾ 2
THEINVAL (FR) *NickyHenderson* 7-10-13^{141} (s) JeremiahMcGrath .... 9/1 nk 3
Dandridge *A.L.T.Moore,Ireland* 8-11-1^{143} (t) DavyRussell 13/2 2½ 4
16 Croco Bay (IRE) *BenCase* 10-10-13^{141} (s) KielanWoods 40/1 2 5
Calipto (FR) *VenetiaWilliams* 7-10-11^{139} (t) JamieBargary(3) .... 14/1 ½ 6
4 Bright New Dawn (IRE) *VenetiaWilliams* 10-11-3^{145} LiamTreadwell 50/1 3 7
131 Le Prezien (FR) *PaulNicholls* 6-11-4^{146} (t) SamTwiston-Davies 7/2f 2 8
12 Ultragold (FR) *ColinTizzard* 9-10-10^{138} (t) HarryCobden .... 100/1 sh 9
120 Eastlake (IRE) *JonjoO'Neill* 11-11-12^{154} (t) AidanColeman 28/1 1¼ 10
110 Pairofbrowneyes (IRE) *BarryJohnMurphy,Ireland* 8-10-12^{140} (s) M.P.Fogarty 18/1 1 11
Bold Henry *PhilipHobbs* 11-10-12^{140} RichardJohnson 33/1 1½ 12
103 Quite By Chance *ColinTizzard* 8-11-5^{147} TomScudamore 33/1 13 13
31 Mick Thonic (FR) *ColinTizzard* 7-10-7^{135} (t) PaddyBrennan 50/1 2 14
12 Mr Fiftyone (IRE) *MrsJ.Harrington,Ireland* 8-11-0^{142} D.E.Mullins .... 40/1 ¾ 15
103 Solar Impulse (FR) *ChristopherKellett* 7-10-9^{137} (b) BrianHughes .... 33/1 nk 16
Upsilon Bleu (FR) *PaulineRobson* 9-11-3^{145} HenryBrooke 33/1 4½ 17
60 Witness In Court (IRE) *DonaldMcCain* 10-10-7^{135} WillKennedy 40/1 3¼ 18
29 Sizing Platinum (IRE) *ColinTizzard* 9-10-13^{141} TomO'Brien 20/1 4½ 19
Velvet Maker (FR) *AlanFleming,Ireland* 8-11-2^{144} DenisO'Regan 16/1 2¼ 20
73 The Game Changer (IRE) *GordonElliott,Ireland* 8-11-8^{150} (t) B.J.Cooper 9/1 17 21
Un Beau Roman (FR) *PaulHenderson* 9-10-9^{137} (h) NickScholfield .... 66/1 pu
117 Solita (IRE) *PaulNolan,Ireland* 8-10-12^{140} (t) P.Townend .... 25/1 pu
135 Dodging Bullets *PaulNicholls* 9-11-9^{151} (s+t) NoelFehily .... 8/1 pu
Mr Michael Buckley 24ran 4m00.80

UTTOXETER Saturday, Mar 18 SOFT

190 Betfred Midlands Grand National (Open Handicap Chase) (L) (1) (5yo+) 4m1f92y (24) £70,337
CHASE THE SPUD *FergalO'Brien* 9-10-12^{130} PaddyBrennan 11/1 1

154	MYSTEREE (IRE) *MichaelScudamore* 9-11-1^{133} RobertDunne 8/1	1½	2
143	WARRANTOR (IRE) *WarrenGreatrex* 8-11-1^{133} (t) GavinSheehan 16/1	5	3
143	Houblon des Obeaux (FR) *VenetiaWilliams* 10-11-12^{144} (s) TomBellamy 20/1	2¾	4
	Blakemount (IRE) *SueSmith* 9-11-4^{136} DannyCook 20/1	hd	5
66	Cogry *NigelTwiston-Davies* 8-11-1^{133} JamieBargary(3) 12/1	2¾	6
108	Spookydooky (IRE) *JonjoO'Neill* 9-10-13^{131} (t) KillianMoore(3) 6/1f	¾	7
154	Portrait King (IRE) *PatrickGriffin,Ireland* 12-10-12^{130} (v) A.W.Short(7) 25/1	10	8
	Alfie Spinner (IRE) *KerryLee* 12-11-3^{135} (s+t) JamieMoore 25/1	nk	9
	Gonalston Cloud (IRE) *NickKent* 10-11-3^{135} (s) HenryBrooke 16/1	5	10
	Final Nudge (IRE) *DavidDennis* 8-11-8^{140} (s) TrevorWhelan 14/1		F
52	Mad Brian (IRE) *MrsGillianCallaghan,Ireland* 11-11-12^{129} (t) RichardJohnson ..13/2		pu
	Court Frontier (IRE) *PaulMorgan* 9-10-13^{131} DenisO'Regan 10/1		pu
154	Emperor's Choice (IRE) *VenetiaWilliams* 10-11-0^{132} (b) LiamTreadwell 33/1		pu
	Silver Man *JoHughes* 10-11-2^{134} (b) WillKennedy 40/1		pu
89	Goulanes (IRE) *NeilMulholland* 11-11-3^{135} (b+t) NoelFehily 14/1		pu
154	Out Sam *WarrenGreatrex* 8-11-3^{135} (s) AndrewTinkler 20/1		pu
115	Firebird Flyer (IRE) *EvanWilliams* 10-11-6^{138} (s) AdamWedge 33/1		pu
	Benbens (IRE) *NigelTwiston-Davies* 12-11-7^{139} MrZ.Baker(7) 50/1		pu
154	Gevrey Chambertin (IRE) *DavidPipe* 9-11-7^{139} (b) ConorO'Farrell 12/1		pu

Mrs C. Banks 20ran 9m12.50

NAVAN Sunday, Mar 19 HEAVY

191 Webster Cup Chase (Gr 2) (5yo+) £23,113   2½m (14)

140	A TOI PHIL (FR) *GordonElliott* 7-11-10 R.Walsh 6/5f		1
	NEARLY NAMA'D (IRE) *MsSandraHughes* 9-11-5 PhilipEnright 13/2	8	2
4	THE TULLOW TANK (IRE) *AlanFleming* 9-11-5 (t) DenisO'Regan 13/8	2¼	3
73	Mozoltov *M.F.Morris* 11-11-5 (t) SeanFlanagan 8/1	40	4
	Double Seven (IRE) *MartinBrassil* 11-11-5 (t) L.P.Dempsey 20/1		pu

Gigginstown House Stud 5ran 6m06.50

FAIRYHOUSE Sunday, Apr 2 SOFT

192 Normans Grove Chase (Gr 2) (5yo+) £21,804   2m1f (12)

7	BALLYCASEY (IRE) *W.P.Mullins* 10-11-10 R.Walsh 15/8		1
110	BALL D'ARC (FR) *GordonElliott* 6-11-10 B.J.Cooper 6/5f	½	2
	FLEMENSTAR (IRE) *AnthonyCurran* 12-11-12 B.M.Cash 20/1	26	3
133	Realt Mor (IRE) *GordonElliott* 12-11-4 DenisO'Regan 25/1	5½	4
12	Devils Bride (IRE) *HenrydeBromhead* 10-11-7 (t) D.J.Mullins 12/1	17	5
191	Nearly Nama'd (IRE) *MsSandraHughes* 9-11-4 RogerLoughran 10/1	15	6
189	The Game Changer (IRE) *GordonElliott* 8-11-10 (t) J.W.Kennedy 12/1		pu

Mrs S. Ricci 7ran 4m28.40

193 Rathbarry & Glenview Studs Novices' Hurdle (Gr 2) (4yo+) £23,087   2m (8)

	BLEU BERRY (IRE) *W.P.Mullins* 6-11-4 R.Walsh 2/1f		1
	OUTSPOKEN (IRE) *JosephPatrickO'Brien* 5-11-4 (t) BarryGeraghty 9/2	2¼	2
128	MONTALBANO *W.P.Mullins* 5-11-4 D.E.Mullins 25/1	2	3
139	Riven Light (IRE) *W.P.Mullins* 5-11-4 D.J.Mullins 16/1	½	4
	Chirico Vallis (FR) *GordonElliott* 5-11-4 (h) DavyRussell 16/1	14	5
	Avenir d'Une Vie (FR) *HenrydeBromhead* 5-11-4 B.J.Cooper 7/1	40	6
	Art of Security (IRE) *NoelMeade* 7-11-4 SeanFlanagan 50/1	9½	7
169	Brelade *GordonElliott* 5-11-4 J.W.Kennedy 7/2	39	8
139	Chateau Conti (FR) *W.P.Mullins* 5-11-4 P.Townend 11/2		pu

Luke McMahon 9ran 3m59.30

194 Easter Festival April 16th - 18th Novices' Hurdle (Gr 2) (4yo+) £21,804   2½m (10)

	AL BOUM PHOTO (FR) *W.P.Mullins* 5-11-5 P.Townend 10/1		1
106	STAND UP AND FIGHT (IRE) *EndaBolger* 5-11-5 J.S.McGarvey 25/1	4	2
188	RUNFORDAVE (IRE) *GordonElliott* 5-11-5 J.W.Kennedy 13/2	2¾	3
169	Livelovelaugh (IRE) *W.P.Mullins* 7-11-5 D.J.Mullins 7/1	¾	4
80	Wishmoor (IRE) *M.F.Morris* 7-11-5 (t) M.A.Enright 50/1	6½	5
80	Invitation Only (IRE) *W.P.Mullins* 6-11-5 R.Walsh 11/10f	1¼	6
	Minella Till Dawn (IRE) *GordonElliott* 5-11-5 DavyRussell 10/1		F
	Any Second Now (IRE) *T.M.Walsh* 5-11-10 BarryGeraghty 7/1		ur
93	Le Martalin (IRE) *NoelMeade* 6-11-5 (h+t) B.J.Cooper 16/1		pu

Mrs J. Donnelly 9ran 5m07.70

AINTREE Thursday, Apr 6 GOOD

195 Manifesto Novices' Chase (Gr 1) (1) (5yo+) £56,130   2m3f200y (16)

176	FLYING ANGEL (IRE) *NigelTwiston-Davies* 6-11-4 NoelFehily 5/1		1
163	CLOUDY DREAM (IRE) *MalcolmJefferson* 7-11-4 BrianHughes 4/1	1	2
176	TOP NOTCH (FR) *NickyHenderson* 6-11-4 DarylJacob 6/5f	4½	3

```
 54  Max Ward (IRE) TomGeorge 8-11-4 A.P.Heskin .................................12/1      4   4
151  Frodon (FR) PaulNicholls 5-11-4 SamTwiston-Davies ...........................5/1     36   5
 33  Cyrius Moriviere (FR) BenPauling 7-11-4 (t) DavidBass .......................40/1     35   6
     Mr R. J. Rexton 6ran 5m01.40
```

196 Doom Bar Anniversary 4-Y-O Juvenile Hurdle (Gr 1) (1) (4yo) £56,130   2m209y (9)

```
183  DEFI DU SEUIL (FR) PhilipHobbs 4-11-0 BarryGeraghty ...................4/11f      1
174  DIVIN BERE (FR) NickyHenderson 4-11-0 NoelFehily ...........................7/2     1¼   2
150  BEDROCK DanSkelton 4-11-0 (t) HarrySkelton .................................25/1     4½   3
174  Flying Tiger (IRE) NickWilliams 4-11-0 RichardJohnson ........................6/1    17   4
     Forth Bridge CharlieLongsdon 4-11-0 BrianHughes .............................7/1     nk   5
183  Landin (GER) SeamusMullins 4-11-0 JeremiahMcGrath .......................25/1      6   6
152  Ronnie Baird LauraYoung 4-11-0 (h) RobertHawker .........................100/1     52   7
 27  Nucky Thompson RichardSpencer 4-11-0 (h) A.P.Heskin ......................50/1           pu
     Mr John P. McManus 8ran 4m09.80
```

197 Betway Bowl Chase (Gr 1) (1) (5yo+) £84,195   3m210y (19)

```
186  TEA FOR TWO NickWilliams 8-11-7 LizzieKelly ..............................10/1      1
186  CUE CARD ColinTizzard 11-11-7 (t) PaddyBrennan ............................ 2/1f    nk   2
186  SMAD PLACE (FR) AlanKing 10-11-7 WayneHutchinson ......................10/1     15   3
178  Aso (FR) VenetiaWilliams 7-11-7 (s) CharlieDeutsch ..........................14/1      8   4
186  Bristol de Mai (FR) NigelTwiston-Davies 6-11-7 DarylJacob .....................9/2    1½   5
121  Silviniaco Conti (FR) PaulNicholls 11-11-7 (b+t) NoelFehily .....................7/1     8   6
178  Empire of Dirt (IRE) GordonElliott,Ireland 10-11-7 (t) B.J.Cooper ..........10/3          pu
     Mrs Jane Williams & Mr Len Jakeman 7ran 6m24.00
```

198 Betway Aintree Hurdle (Gr 1) (1) (4yo+) £112,260   2½m (11)

```
165  BUVEUR D'AIR (FR) NickyHenderson 6-11-7 BarryGeraghty .....................4/9f      1
165  MY TENT OR YOURS (IRE) NickyHenderson 10-11-7 (h) AidanColeman .........8/1     5   2
165  THE NEW ONE (IRE) NigelTwiston-Davies 9-11-7 SamTwiston-Davies ........11/2    1½   3
171  Old Guard PaulNicholls 6-11-7 HarryCobden ................................25/1     11   4
 20  Rashaan (IRE) ColinThomasKidd,Ireland 5-11-7 SeanFlanagan ................20/1      7   5
129  Identity Thief (IRE) HenrydeBromhead,Ireland 7-11-7 B.J.Cooper .............14/1      8   6
     Mr John P. McManus 6ran 4m55.60
```

199 Randox Health Foxhunters' Open Hunters' Chase (2) (6yo+) £23,720   2m5f19y (18)

```
     DINEUR (FR) MickeyBowen 11-12-0 (t) MrJamesKing .........................16/1      1
187  BALNASLOW (IRE) GrahamMcKeever,Ireland 10-12-0 MrDerekO'Connor ......7/1     1¾   2
     BIG FELLA THANKS TomGeorge 15-12-0 (t) MrN.George .....................40/1     1½   3
187  Pacha du Polder (FR) PaulNicholls 10-12-0 BryonyFrost .......................11/2     ¾   4
187  Mendip Express (IRE) PhilipHobbs 11-12-0 (t) MrD.Maxwell ...................25/1      1   5
     Darwins Fox (FR) DavidChristie,Ireland 11-12-0 (t) MrBarryO'Neill ..........40/1     hd   6
     Bear's Affair (IRE) PhilipRowley 11-12-0 MrAlexEdwards .....................12/1      3   7
  2  Mr Mercurial (IRE) MrsSheilaCrow 9-12-0 (t) MrW.Biddick ....................16/1     2½   8
     Rebel Rebellion (IRE) PaulNicholls 12-12-0 (b+t) MrMatthewHampton ......20/1      3   9
     Poole Master ChrisHonour 12-12-0 MrD.Edwards ...........................16/1     ¾  10
  3  Tony Star (FR) MickeyBowen 10-12-0 (t) MissJodieHughes ..................100/1     22  11
     Vincitore (FR) MissSarahRippon 11-12-0 (t) MrsClaireHardwick ..............150/1      2  12
     Damiens Dilemma (IRE) MrsL.A.Coltherd 9-12-0 MrN.Orpwood ...............150/1      ¾  13
     Loch Ba (IRE) FrancescaNimmo 11-12-0 MrJ.Jackson-Stops ...................33/1     2½  14
     Richmond (IRE) P.P.C.Turner 12-12-0 (s) MissL.M.Turner .....................200/1     4½  15
     Top Cat Henry (IRE) N.W.Alexander 9-12-0 (v+t) MrKitAlexander ............33/1     44  16
     Broken Eagle (USA) AlanHill 9-12-0 (t) MrJoeHill ..........................40/1           F
187  Black Thunder (FR) WarrenGreatrex 10-12-0 (s) MrsS.Waley-Cohen .........20/1           F
     Sam Cavallaro (IRE) MissH.Brookshaw 11-12-0 MrM.J.P.Kendrick ...........100/1           F
     Flash Garden (IRE) J.M.B.Cookson 9-12-0 MrT.Hamilton ....................50/1           F
     Distime (IRE) MrsA.J.Loder 11-12-0 MsK.Walsh ............................20/1           ur
     Never Complain (IRE) MrsF.Marshall 9-12-0 (s) MrCharlieMarshall ............100/1           ur
187  Premier Portrait (IRE) DrCharlesLevinson 10-12-0 (v) MrG.Levinson .............100/1           ur
187  On The Fringe (IRE) EndaBolger,Ireland 12-12-0 MrJ.J.Codd ................. 7/4f           pu
     Mr Moss (IRE) S.Rea 12-12-0 MrJ.Nailor .................................200/1           pu
     Fitz Volonte AndrewMartin 10-12-0 (t) MrJ.Martin .........................200/1           pu
     Sizing Solution (IRE) J.T.R.Dreaper,Ireland 9-12-0 (t) MrR.O.Harding ..........66/1           pu
     Decade Player (IRE) MissKellyMorgan 9-12-0 (t) MrD.Peters ................100/1           pu
     Mr Gwilym J. Morris 28ran 5m31.40
```

200 Betway Red Rum Handicap Chase (Gr 3) (1) (5yo+) £50,643   1m7f176y (12)

```
168  DOUBLE W'S (IRE) MalcolmJefferson 7-11-1¹³⁹ BrianHughes ..................8/1      1
189  THEINVAL (FR) NickyHenderson 7-11-6¹⁴⁴ (s) JeremiahMcGrath ..............15/2      1   2
168  BUN DORAN (IRE) TomGeorge 6-11-1¹³⁹ A.P.Heskin ..........................6/1f     3¾   3
 16  Yorkist (IRE) DanSkelton 9-10-10¹³⁴ (t) HarrySkelton ......................14/1      1   4
```

Romain de Senam (FR) *PaulNicholls* 5-10-10[134] (h+t) SamTwiston-Davies 10/1   1   5
137   Gino Trail (IRE) *KerryLee* 10-11-7[145] JamieMoore 14/1   5   6
92   Alisier d'Irlande (FR) *HenrydeBromhead,Ireland* 7-11-12[150] (t) D.J.Mullins ...11/1   6   7
189   Witness In Court (IRE) *DonaldMcCain* 10-10-9[133] WillKennedy 33/1   13   8
168   Foxtail Hill (IRE) *NigelTwiston-Davies* 8-11-5[143] JamieBargary(3) 10/1   15   9
189   Dandridge *A.L.T.Moore,Ireland* 8-11-5[143] (t) DavyRussell 7/1   4½ 10
   Doitforthevillage (IRE) *PaulHenderson* 8-10-5[129] (t) TomO'Brien ....11/1   F
   Rock On Rocky *MattSheppard* 9-10-4[128] (s+t) StanSheppard(5) ....20/1   pu
   Raven's Tower (USA) *BenPauling* 7-10-5[129] DavidBass ....12/1   pu
   Parsnip Pete *TomGeorge* 11-11-0[138] (t) PaddyBrennan ....14/1   pu
   Wharton & Wilson 14ran 3m58.70

201   Goffs Nickel Coin Mares' Standard Open National Hunt Flat (Gr 2) (1)   2m209y
(4, 5 and 6yo) £25,322
   DAME ROSE (FR) *RichardHobson* 4-10-8 AlainCawley 14/1   1
   OSCAR ROSE (IRE) *FergalO'Brien* 5-11-0 PaddyBrennan ....20/1   ½   2
   PETTICOAT TAILS *WarrenGreatrex* 5-11-0 (s) GavinSheehan 9/2f   3¾   3
   Shearling *BrianEllison* 4-10-8 RichardJohnson 5/1   1¾   4
   Redemption Song (IRE) *KevinFrost* 5-11-0 BrianHughes ....16/1   nk   5
   Martello Park (IRE) *MsMargaretMullins,Ireland* 5-11-0 (s) D.E.Mullins ....16/1   ½   6
175   Irish Roe (IRE) *PeterAtkinson* 6-11-0 HenryBrooke 10/1   3¼   7
   Monar Rose *BenCase* 5-11-0 (h+t) DarylJacob 100/1   3¼   8
   Polly's Pursuit (IRE) *NickyHenderson* 5-11-0 DavidBass 16/1   6   9
   Maria's Benefit (IRE) *StuartEdmunds* 5-11-0 CiaranGethings 14/1   2½ 10
   Skewiff *EvanWilliams* 5-11-0 TomO'Brien 28/1   4 11
   Donnachies Girl (IRE) *AlistairWhillans* 4-10-8 CraigNichol 100/1   4 12
   Sweetlittlemystery *BrendanPowell* 6-11-0 BrendanPowell 8/1   4½ 13
   Mountain Path *JonjoO'Neill* 4-10-8 AidanColeman 16/1   3 14
   Scorpion Princess (IRE) *CharlieLongsdon* 6-11-0 SamTwiston-Davies 33/1   8 15
   Sassy Diva (IRE) *ShaneCrawley,Ireland* 6-11-0 (t) DavyRussell 7/1   12 16
   Drops of Jupitor (IRE) *AnthonyHoneyball* 5-11-0 (h) NoelFehily 14/1   16 17
   Boogie Life *JimGoldie* 6-11-0 GrahamLee 50/1   86 18
   Mr Carl Hinchy 18ran 4m08.00

AINTREE Friday, Apr 7   GOOD
202   Alder Hey Children's Charity Handicap Hurdle (Gr 3) (1) (4yo+) £39,389   2½m (11)
188   RATHER BE (IRE) *NickyHenderson* 6-11-2[136] JeremiahMcGrath 10/1   1
   DREAM BERRY (FR) *JonjoO'Neill* 6-10-13[133] (t) BarryGeraghty ....8/1cf   ½   2
107   GEORDIE DES CHAMPS (IRE) *RebeccaCurtis* 6-11-1[135] JonathanMoore(3) ...12/1   ½   3
188   Thomas Campbell *NickyHenderson* 5-11-5[139] NicodeBoinville 8/1cf   9   4
9   Byron Flyer *IanWilliams* 6-11-0[134] TomO'Brien ....16/1   ¾   5
136   Zubayr (IRE) *PaulNicholls* 5-11-6[140] SamTwiston-Davies 16/1   1¾   6
   Clondaw Kaempfer (IRE) *DonaldMcCain* 9-10-11[131] (b+t) WillKennedy ...33/1   ns   7
171   Hawk High (IRE) *TimEasterby* 7-11-4[138] (b) BrianHughes 14/1   3¼   8
   Dashing Oscar (IRE) *HarryFry* 7-10-12[132] (t) NoelFehily 16/1   1   9
   Runswick Royal (IRE) *AnnHamilton* 8-11-8[142] RyanDay(3) ....16/1   ½ 10
184   North Hill Harvey *DanSkelton* 6-11-12[146] HarrySkelton ....9/1   ½ 11
   Sumkindofking (IRE) *TomGeorge* 6-10-10[130] A.P.Heskin ....8/1cf   nk 12
160   Bigmartre (FR) *HarryWhittington* 6-11-0[134] HarryBannister(3) ....33/1   nk 13
184   Crievehill (IRE) *NigelTwiston-Davies* 5-11-1[135] (h) JamieBargary(3) ....33/1   ½ 14
113   Craggaknock *MarkWalford* 6-10-11[131] (s) JakeGreenall 33/1   1¼ 15
180   Mad Jack Mytton (IRE) *JonjoO'Neill* 7-11-1[135] AidanColeman 33/1   5 16
117   Ice Cold Soul (IRE) *NoelMeade,Ireland* 7-11-0[134] (t) B.J.Cooper 12/1   1½ 17
   Sky Khan *LucindaRussell* 8-10-10[130] (s+t) DerekFox 16/1   1¼ 18
   Nautical Nitwit (IRE) *PhilipKirby* 8-11-0[134] AdamNicol ....100/1   ¾ 19
159   Crystal Lad (FR) *GaryMoore* 5-10-10[130] JamieMoore ....16/1   ¾ 20
163   A Hare Breath (IRE) *BenPauling* 9-11-8[142] DavidBass 40/1   9 21
   Allee Bleue (IRE) *PhilipHobbs* 7-11-1[135] RichardJohnson 40/1   12 22
   Matt & Lauren Morgan 22ran 4m54.90

203   Crabbie's Top Novices' Hurdle (Gr 1) (1) (4yo+) £56,130   2m103y (9)
162   PINGSHOU (IRE) *ColinTizzard* 7-11-4 RobbiePower 16/1   1
158   MOUNT MEWS (IRE) *MalcolmJefferson* 6-11-4 BrianHughes 9/4jf   4½   2
   THE UNIT (IRE) *AlanKing* 6-11-4 WayneHutchinson 7/1   2½   3
   High Secret (IRE) *PaulNicholls* 6-11-4 SamTwiston-Davies 12/1   1¼   4
162   River Wylde (IRE) *NickyHenderson* 6-11-4 NicodeBoinville 9/4jf   5   5
165   Moon Racer (IRE) *DavidPipe* 8-11-4 TomScudamore 4/1   3½   6
   American Gigolo *CharlieMann* 5-11-4 NoelFehily 50/1   1½   7
   Bulkov (FR) *MickyHammond* 5-11-4 JoeColliver 100/1   7   8

994

Chti Balko (FR) *DonaldMcCain* 5-11-4 WillKennedy 28/1   16 9
Ann & Alan Potts 9ran 4m03.00

204 Betway Mildmay Novices' Chase (Gr 1) (1) (5yo+) £56,130   3m210y (19)
170 MIGHT BITE (IRE) *NickyHenderson* 8-11-4 NicodeBoinville 8/13f   1
170 WHISPER (FR) *NickyHenderson* 9-11-4 DavyRussell 9/4   2 2
81 VIRGILIO (FR) *DanSkelton* 8-11-4 (t) HarrySkelton 14/1 18 3
170 Marinero (IRE) *HenrydeBromhead,Ireland* 8-11-4 B.J.Cooper 14/1 44 4
167 Calett Mad (FR) *NigelTwiston-Davies* 5-11-4 (t) DarylJacob 25/1 25 5
The Knot Again Partnership 5ran 6m20.40

205 JLT Melling Chase (Gr 1) (1) (5yo+) £112,260   2m3f200y (16)
172 FOX NORTON (FR) *ColinTizzard* 7-11-7 (h) RobbiePower 4/1   1
178 SUB LIEUTENANT (IRE) *HenrydeBromhead,Ireland* 8-11-7 (t) B.J.Cooper .. 10/3f 6 2
172 TRAFFIC FLUIDE (FR) *GaryMoore* 7-11-7 JoshuaMoore 14/1 11 3
121 Kylemore Lough *KerryLee* 8-11-7 JamieMoore ....16/1 ½ 4
172 God's Own (IRE) *TomGeorge* 9-11-7 A.P.Heskin 7/2 6 5
172 Top Gamble (IRE) *KerryLee* 9-11-7 (t) DavyRussell 10/1 1 6
178 Josses Hill (IRE) *NickyHenderson* 9-11-7 (s) NicodeBoinville 15/2 8 7
178 Uxizandre (FR) *AlanKing* 9-11-7 (v) BarryGeraghty 8/1 35 8
146 Royal Regatta (IRE) *PhilipHobbs* 9-11-7 (b+t) RichardJohnson ....25/1   pu
Ann & Alan Potts 9ran 4m57.80

206 Randox Health Topham Handicap Chase (Gr 3) (1) (5yo+) £67,356   2m5f19y (17)
What should have been the second last fence was omitted due to a stricken jockey
189 ULTRAGOLD (FR) *ColinTizzard* 9-10-5^{136} (t) HarryCobden 50/1   1
   KATNAP (FR) *JosephPatrickO'Brien,Ireland* 10-10-0^{131} (t) D.E.Mullins 22/1 1 2
190 PORTRAIT KING (IRE) *PatrickGriffin,Ireland* 12-9-7^{131} (v) ConorO'Farrell 66/1 6 3
170 O O Seven (IRE) *NickyHenderson* 7-11-7^{152} NicodeBoinville ....12/1 nk 4
103 As de Mee (FR) *PaulNicholls* 7-10-13^{144} SeanBowen ....8/1jf ½ 5
   Thomond (IRE) *NoelMeade,Ireland* 9-9-0^{131} (t) SeanFlanagan ....80/1 ½ 6
60 Vintage Vinnie (IRE) *RebeccaCurtis* 8-10-5^{136} JonathanMoore(3) 16/1 8 7
180 Henryville *HarryFry* 9-10-9^{140} (h+t) LeightonAspell ....11/1 nk 8
182 Father Edward (IRE) *DavidPipe* 8-9-13^{131} (s) DavidNoonan 100/1 8 9
180 Bouvreuil (FR) *PaulNicholls* 6-11-0^{145} (h+t) SamTwiston-Davies 9/1 4½ 10
186 Irish Cavalier (IRE) *RebeccaCurtis* 8-11-11^{156} P.Townend 33/1 1 11
189 Solar Impulse (FR) *ChristopherKellett* 7-10-2^{133} (b+t) DaveCrosse 100/1 3 12
154 Straidnahanna (IRE) *SueSmith* 8-10-8^{139} DannyCook 50/1 1¾ 13
103 Thomas Brown *HarryFry* 8-10-9^{140} (b) NiallMadden 20/1 1 14
   Mr Diablo (IRE) *J.P.Dempsey,Ireland* 8-10-11^{142} (t) LukeDempsey 16/1 1¾ 15
164 Clarcam (FR) *GordonElliott,Ireland* 7-11-7^{152} (s+t) B.J.Cooper 25/1 4 16
164 Go Conquer (IRE) *JonjoO'Neill* 8-10-4^{135} (t) AidanColeman 9/1 41 17
126 Long Lunch *CharlieLongsdon* 8-9-12^{131} (s+t) JamesDavies ....66/1   F
   Imjoeking (IRE) *LucindaRussell* 10-10-0^{131} (t) DerekFox ....33/1   F
60 Seefood (IRE) *DrRichardNewland* 10-10-4^{135} (v) RichardJohnson ....8/1jf   F
180 Ballykan *NigelTwiston-Davies* 7-10-9^{140} (s+t) DarylJacob ....16/1   F
168 Gold Present (IRE) *NickyHenderson* 7-10-11^{142} JeremiahMcGrath ......12/1   F
189 Bright New Dawn (IRE) *VenetiaWilliams* 10-10-12^{143} LiamTreadwell ......33/1   F
173 Third Intention (IRE) *ColinTizzard* 10-11-5^{150} (b+t) TomO'Brien ....20/1   F
   Gowanauthat (IRE) *CharlieMann* 9-9-13^{131} (s+t) HarryBannister(3) ....50/1   ur
180 Katachenko (IRE) *DonaldMcCain* 8-10-0^{131} WillKennedy ....25/1   ur
189 Quite By Chance *ColinTizzard* 8-11-0^{145} TomScudamore ....33/1   pu
189 Eastlake (IRE) *JonjoO'Neill* 11-11-7^{152} (s+t) BarryGeraghty ....14/1   pu
173 Alelchi Inois (FR) *W.P.Mullins,Ireland* 9-11-12^{157} R.Walsh ....25/1   pu
Brocade Racing J P Romans Terry Warner 29ran 5m28.20

207 Doom Bar Sefton Novices' Hurdle (Gr 1) (1) (4yo+) £56,130   3m149y (13)
185 THE WORLDS END (IRE) *TomGeorge* 6-11-4 A.P.Heskin 3/1   1
162 BEYOND CONCEIT (IRE) *NickyHenderson* 8-11-4 (h) BarryGeraghty .....9/1 ½ 2
   DEBECE *TimVaughan* 8-11-4 AlanJohns ....11/1 sh 3
185 Constantine Bay *NickyHenderson* 6-11-4 NicodeBoinville ....11/4f ¾ 4
177 Ballymalin (IRE) *NigelTwiston-Davies* 7-11-4 SamTwiston-Davies 16/1 9 5
169 Keeper Hill (IRE) *WarrenGreatrex* 6-11-4 GavinSheehan 9/1 8 6
185 Elegant Escape (IRE) *ColinTizzard* 5-11-4 TomO'Brien 25/1 13 7
107 Get On The Yager (IRE) *DanSkelton* 5-11-4 HarrySkelton 10/1 6 8
   Testify (IRE) *DonaldMcCain* 6-11-4 WillKennedy 33/1 44 9
179 West Approach *ColinTizzard* 7-11-4 (t) TomScudamore ....8/1   pu
   Monbeg Charmer (IRE) *CharlieLongsdon* 6-11-4 BrianHughes ....18/1   pu
McNeill Family 11ran 6m05.80

208 Weatherbys Private Bank Standard Open National Hunt Flat (Gr 2) (1) 2m209y
(4, 5 and 6yo) £25,322

	LALOR (GER) *RichardWoollacott* 5-11-4 RichardJohnson	33/1	1
	ENNISCOFFEY OSCAR (IRE) *EmmaLavelle* 5-11-4 AidanColeman	18/1	2½ 2
175	WESTERN RYDER (IRE) *WarrenGreatrex* 5-11-4 GavinSheehan	6/1	ns 3
	If The Cap Fits (IRE) *HarryFry* 5-11-4 NoelFehily	4/1	nk 4
175	Claimantakinforgan (FR) *NickyHenderson* 5-11-4 NicodeBoinville	6/1	¾ 5
175	And The New (IRE) *JohnnyFarrelly* 6-11-4 BrendanPowell	33/1	hd 6
	Point of Principle (IRE) *TimVaughan* 4-10-12 AlanJohns	66/1	1¾ 7
	Clondaw Castle (IRE) *TomGeorge* 5-11-4 PaddyBrennan	20/1	3¾ 8
	Black Op (IRE) *TomGeorge* 6-11-4 A.P.Heskin	10/3f	sh 9
	Tikkanbar (IRE) *NeilMulholland* 6-11-4 TomScudamore	22/1	¾ 10
	Amateur (IRE) *JohnFlint* 4-10-12 (s) RhysFlint	50/1	1¼ 11
	Run To Milan (IRE) *VictorDartnall* 5-11-4 NickScholfield	12/1	3½ 12
	Loud And Clear *IainJardine* 6-11-4 MartinDwyer	14/1	½ 13
	Carlos du Fruitier (FR) *BenPauling* 5-11-4 DavidBass	33/1	2¼ 14
	Sea Sovereign (IRE) *MarkPitman* 4-10-12 TimmyMurphy	100/1	4 15
	Some Reign (IRE) *RoseDobbin* 6-11-4 GrahamLee	66/1	¾ 16
	Bomber's Moon *NigelTwiston-Davies* 6-11-4 MarkGrant	50/1	22 17
	King of Realms (IRE) *IanWilliams* 5-11-4 TomO'Brien	25/1	11 18
	Larry *GaryMoore* 4-10-12 JamieMoore	25/1	6 19

Mr D. G. Staddon 19ran 4m04.50

AINTREE Saturday, Apr 8 GOOD

209 Gaskells Handicap Hurdle (Gr 3) (1) (4yo+) £39,389 3m149y (13)

109	FOUNTAINS WINDFALL *AnthonyHoneyball* 7-10-12[137] DavidNoonan	11/1	1
188	NO COMMENT *PhilipHobbs* 6-10-12[137] (h) BarryGeraghty	5/1	8 2
188	DADSINTROUBLE (IRE) *TimVaughan* 7-10-11[136] AlanJohns(3)	16/1	¾ 3
144	No Hassle Hoff (IRE) *DanSkelton* 5-10-9[134] HarrySkelton	4/1f	4 4
	Forthefunofit (IRE) *JonjoO'Neill* 8-10-10[135] (s) AidanColeman	25/1	9 5
123	Whataknight *HarryFry* 8-11-7[146] (t) NoelFehily	12/1	nk 6
177	Barney Dwan (IRE) *FergalO'Brien* 7-11-9[148] PaddyBrennan	9/1	¾ 7
177	The Tourard Man (IRE) *AlanKing* 11-11-1[140] KevinDowling(10)	25/1	ns 8
122	Mr McGo (IRE) *DonaldMcCain* 6-10-11[136] WillKennedy	50/1	2 9
166	Rons Dream *PeterBowen* 7-11-4[143] SeanBowen	33/1	3½ 10
	Duke Street (IRE) *DrRichardNewland* 5-10-10[135] SamTwiston-Davies	14/1	1¼ 11
	Joe Farrell (IRE) *RebeccaCurtis* 8-10-10[135] JonathanMoore(3)	20/1	7 12
142	Desert Cry (IRE) *DonaldMcCain* 11-11-11[150] (b) BrianHughes	50/1	1¼ 13
171	Morello Royale (IRE) *ColinTizzard* 7-11-0[139] (t) HarryCobden	33/1	2½ 14
177	Golden Doyen (GER) *PhilipHobbs* 6-11-4[143] TomO'Brien	33/1	1½ 15
171	Leoncavallo (IRE) *BenPauling* 5-10-11[136] (s) MrAlexFerguson(7)	50/1	½ 16
166	Briery Queen *NoelWilliams* 8-11-5[144] (h) LeightonAspell	16/1	9 17
177	For Good Measure (IRE) *PhilipHobbs* 6-10-13[138] RichardJohnson	16/1	2½ 18
188	Doesyourdogbite (IRE) *JonjoO'Neill* 5-10-10[135] RichieMcLernon	33/1	3½ 19
179	Zarkandar (IRE) *PaulNicholls* 10-11-12[151] (b+t) StanSheppard(5)	14/1	3¼ 20
177	Splash of Ginge *NigelTwiston-Davies* 9-11-1[140] JamieBargary(3)	25/1	13 21
164	Holywell (IRE) *JonjoO'Neill* 10-11-1[140] (s) MrJohnJ.O'Neill(7)	25/1	pu

The Fountains Partnership 22ran 6m03.00

210 Betway Mersey Novices' Hurdle (Gr 1) (1) (4yo+) £56,130 2½m (11)

105	FINIAN'S OSCAR (IRE) *ColinTizzard* 5-11-4 RobbiePower	3/1f	1
75	CAPTAIN FOREZ (FR) *DanSkelton* 5-11-4 HarrySkelton	14/1	3 2
169	MESSIRE DES OBEAUX (FR) *AlanKing* 5-11-4 DarylJacob	7/2	3¼ 3
	Benatar (FR) *GaryMoore* 5-11-4 JamieMoore	33/1	2 4
	Brio Conti (FR) *PaulNicholls* 6-11-4 SeanBowen	5/1	½ 5
181	La Bague Au Roi (FR) *WarrenGreatrex* 6-10-11 GavinSheehan	14/1	1¾ 6
	Chelsea Flyer (IRE) *EmmaLavelle* 6-11-4 AidanColeman	33/1	2½ 7
101	Cultivator *NickyHenderson* 6-11-4 BarryGeraghty	14/1	1½ 8
106	Bel Ami de Sivola (FR) *NoelMeade,Ireland* 6-11-4 B.J.Cooper	25/1	pu
	Reivers Lad *NickyRichards* 6-11-4 BrianHarding	40/1	pu
	Le Breuil (FR) *BenPauling* 5-11-4 DavidBass	11/1	pu
75	Lough Derg Spirit (IRE) *NickyHenderson* 6-11-4 NicodeBoinville	8/1	pu
	Bordeaux Bill (FR) *BrianEllison* 6-11-4 HenryBrooke	20/1	pu

Ann & Alan Potts 13ran 4m51.30

211 Doom Bar Maghull Novices' Chase (Gr 1) (1) (5yo+) £56,130 1m7f176y (12)

67	SAN BENEDETO (FR) *PaulNicholls* 6-11-4 (s+t) NickScholfield	4/1	1
163	FOREST BIHAN (FR) *BrianEllison* 6-11-4 BrianHughes	6/1	hd 2
163	CHARBEL (IRE) *KimBailey* 6-11-4 (t) DavidBass	6/5f	13 3
17	Colla Pier (IRE) *DavidPeterDunne,Ireland* 8-10-11 RobertDunne	33/1	18 4

176 Politologue (FR) *PaulNicholls* 6-11-4 (h) SamTwiston-Davies ....5/2   F
      Mr P. J. Vogt 5ran 3m56.50

212 Betway Handicap Chase (L) (1) (5yo+) £39,389   3m210y (19)
180 SIZING CODELCO (IRE) *ColinTizzard* 8-11-3[139] RobbiePower 10/1   1
161 RIGHTDOWNTHEMIDDLE (IRE) *GordonElliott,Ireland* 9-11-1[137] JackKennedy 16/1   13   2
180 STARCHITECT (IRE) *DavidPipe* 6-11-7[143] (b+t) TomScudamore 5/1   8   3
182 Potters Legend *LucyWadham* 7-11-4[140] (s) LeightonAspell 9/2f   5   4
      Emerging Force (IRE) *HarryWhittington* 7-11-6[142] DavidBass 8/1   5   5
164 Henri Parry Morgan *PeterBowen* 9-11-2[138] (s+t) SeanBowen 8/1   2¼   6
      Value At Risk *DanSkelton* 8-11-2[138] (s) HarrySkelton 8/1   10   7
      Takingrisks (IRE) *NickyRichards* 8-10-9[131] BrianHarding ....25/1   pu
154 Smooth Stepper *SueSmith* 8-10-12[134] HenryBrooke ....33/1   pu
      I Just Know (IRE) *SueSmith* 7-10-13[135] DannyCook ....7/1   pu
182 Lamb Or Cod (IRE) *PhilipHobbs* 10-11-0[136] (t) RichardJohnson ....14/1   pu
168 Relentless Dreamer (IRE) *RebeccaCurtis* 8-11-2[138] (s+t) JonathanMoore(3) ......20/1   pu
      Full Cry (IRE) *HenrydeBromhead,Ireland* 7-11-2[138] (t) A.E.Lynch ....20/1   pu
      Ruben Cotter (IRE) *MarkMcNiff,Ireland* 11-11-3[139] (s+t) DerekFox ....33/1   pu
      Knock House (IRE) *DonaldMcCain* 8-11-4[140] (t) WillKennedy ....16/1   pu
170 Our Kaempfer (IRE) *CharlieLongsdon* 8-11-12[148] (t) SamTwiston-Davies ....14/1   pu
      Ann & Alan Potts 16ran 6m23.10

213 Ryanair Stayers' Liverpool Hurdle (Gr 1) (1) (4yo+) £84,195   3m149y (13)
165 YANWORTH *AlanKing* 7-11-7 BarryGeraghty 9/4f   1
171 SUPASUNDAE *MrsJ.Harrington,Ireland* 7-11-7 RobbiePower 5/1   1   2
179 SNOW FALCON (IRE) *NoelMeade,Ireland* 7-11-7 SeanFlanagan ....9/1   ¾   3
171 Taquin du Seuil (FR) *JonjoO'Neill* 10-11-7 AidanColeman 20/1   1¾   4
179 Ballyoptic (IRE) *NigelTwiston-Davies* 7-11-7 RichardJohnson 7/1   3½   5
123 Ptit Zig (FR) *PaulNicholls* 8-11-7 (b) SamTwiston-Davies 14/1   18   6
153 Three Musketeers (IRE) *DanSkelton* 7-11-7 (s) HarrySkelton 25/1   12   7
142 Aux Ptits Soins (FR) *PaulNicholls* 7-11-7 SeanBowen 20/1   8   8
      Puffin Billy (IRE) *OliverSherwood* 9-11-7 LeightonAspell ....33/1   pu
179 Cole Harden (IRE) *WarrenGreatrex* 8-11-7 (v) GavinSheehan ....4/1   pu
155 Different Gravey (IRE) *NickyHenderson* 7-11-7 (s) NicodeBoinville ....16/1   pu
      Mr John P. McManus 11ran 6m03.30

214 Randox Health Grand National Handicap Chase (Gr 3) (1) (7yo+) £561,300   4¼m74y (30)
108 ONE FOR ARTHUR (IRE) *LucindaRussell* 8-10-11[148] (t) DerekFox 14/1   1
173 CAUSE OF CAUSES (USA) *GordonElliott,Ireland* 9-10-13[150] (s+t) MrJ.J.Codd . 16/1   4½   2
58   SAINT ARE (FR) *TomGeorge* 11-10-10[147] (b+t) DavyRussell 25/1   3¾   3
143 Blaklion *NigelTwiston-Davies* 8-11-1[152] NoelFehily .... 8/1f   ½   4
143 Gas Line Boy (IRE) *IanWilliams* 11-10-7[144] (v) RobertDunne 50/1   8   5
143 Vieux Lion Rouge (FR) *DavidPipe* 8-10-12[149] (s) TomScudamore 12/1   10   6
96   Lord Windermere (IRE) *J.Culloty,Ireland* 10-10-10[147] (t) LeightonAspell 33/1   1   7
78   Regal Encore (IRE) *AnthonyHoneyball* 9-10-13[150] (t) RobbiePower ....33/1   nk   8
118 Pleasant Company (IRE) *W.P.Mullins,Ireland* 9-10-12[149] (h) R.Walsh ....11/1   hd   9
190 Houblon des Obeaux (FR) *VenetiaWilliams* 10-10-12[149] (s) CharlieDeutsch 50/1   14 10
66   Ballynagour (IRE) *DavidPipe* 11-10-11[148] (h) DavidNoonan 66/1   2¾ 11
134 Le Mercurey (FR) *PaulNicholls* 7-11-0[151] (b+t) SeanBowen 50/1   1¼ 12
143 Goodtoknow *KerryLee* 9-10-7[144] (b) JakeGreenall 66/1   3½ 13
      Just A Par (IRE) *PaulNicholls* 10-10-9[146] (b) HarryCobden 33/1   3½ 14
182 La Vaticane (FR) *DavidPipe* 8-10-6[143] (b+t) RichieMcLernon 80/1   6 15
157 The Last Samuri (FR) *KimBailey* 9-11-10[161] DavidBass 16/1   7 16
103 Tenor Nivernais (FR) *VenetiaWilliams* 10-11-1[152] AidanColeman 40/1   6 17
118 Roi des Francs (FR) *GordonElliott,Ireland* 8-11-3[154] (b) JackKennedy 50/1   7 18
187 Wonderful Charm (FR) *PaulNicholls* 9-11-2[153] (s+t) MsK.Walsh 28/1   11 19
180 Cocktails At Dawn *NickyHenderson* 9-10-8[145] NicodeBoinville ....33/1   F
143 Vicente (FR) *PaulNicholls* 8-10-10[147] (h) BrianHughes ....16/1   F
164 The Young Master *NeilMulholland* 8-10-13[150] (s) Mrs.Waley-Cohen ....20/1   F
186 Saphir du Rheu (FR) *PaulNicholls* 8-11-5[156] SamTwiston-Davies ....16/1   F
161 Thunder And Roses (IRE) *M.F.Morris,Ireland* 9-10-7[144] (s+t) MarkEnright ....25/1   ur
89   Raz de Maree (FR) *GavinPatrickCromwell,Ireland* 12-10-9[146] G.N.Fox ....33/1   ur
164 Measureofmydreams (IRE) *NoelMeade,Ireland* 9-10-9[146] (s) DonaghMeyler ......40/1   ur
161 Ucello Conti (FR) *GordonElliott,Ireland* 9-10-12[149] (t) DarylJacob ....20/1   ur
182 Doctor Harper (IRE) *DavidPipe* 9-10-6[143] (b+t) ConorO'Farrell ....50/1   pu
118 Rogue Angel (IRE) *M.F.Morris,Ireland* 9-10-8[145] (b+t) B.J.Cooper ....20/1   pu
116 Stellar Notion (IRE) *HenrydeBromhead,Ireland* 9-10-9[146] D.J.Mullins ....50/1   pu
115 Bishops Road (IRE) *KerryLee* 9-10-10[147] JamieMoore ....66/1   pu
58   Highland Lodge (IRE) *JamesMoffatt* 11-10-11[148] (s) HenryBrooke ....25/1   pu
      O'Faolains Boy (IRE) *RebeccaCurtis* 10-10-11[148] P.Townend ....50/1   pu
157 Definitly Red (IRE) *BrianEllison* 8-10-12[149] DannyCook ....10/1   pu

997

153	Double Shuffle (IRE) *TomGeorge* 7-10-12[149] (h) A.P.Heskin 33/1	pu
3	Drop Out Joe *CharlieLongsdon* 9-11-1[152] (s) TomO'Brien 33/1	pu
118	Wounded Warrior (IRE) *NoelMeade,Ireland* 8-11-2[153] SeanFlanagan 33/1	pu
121	Perfect Candidate (IRE) *FergalO'Brien* 10-11-5[156] (s) PaddyBrennan 33/1	pu
146	Shantou Flyer (IRE) *RebeccaCurtis* 7-11-5[156] (t) JonathanMoore 50/1	pu
186	More of That (IRE) *JonjoO'Neill* 9-11-6[157] (s) BarryGeraghty 16/1	pu

Two Golf Widows 44ran 9m02.00

215 Pinsent Masons Handicap Hurdle (Conditional Jockeys' And Amateur Riders') 2m103y (9) **(2) (4yo+)** £30,950

109	CHESTERFIELD (IRE) *SeamusMullins* 7-11-1[132] DanielSansom(10) 8/1		1
160	CHIEFTAIN'S CHOICE (IRE) *KevinFrost* 8-10-3[120] HarryBannister(3) 16/1	5	2
	ZALVADOS (FR) *OliverGreenall* 4-9-12[123] (s+t) CharlieDeutsch(3) 16/1	¾	3
	Raise A Spark *DonaldMcCain* 7-10-10[127] (h) LorcanMurtagh(7) 50/1	6	4
	So Celebre (GER) *IanWilliams* 4-10-7[130] DavidNoonan 6/1f	nk	5
	Highland Fling (IRE) *GavinPatrickCromwell,Ireland* 5-10-6[123] (t) J.B.Kane(5) ..12/1	2½	6
184	Vosne Romanee *DrRichardNewland* 6-11-4[137] (s+t) CharlieHammond(7) 33/1	8	7
188	Remiluc (FR) *ChrisGordon* 8-11-7[138] (t) HarryReed(7) 33/1	¾	8
113	Master of Finance (IRE) *MalcolmJefferson* 6-10-8[125] (b) JamieHamilton(3) 12/1	1½	9
	Curious Carlos *PeterBowen* 8-11-2[133] (h) JamesBowen(7) 16/1	13	10
171	Robinshill (IRE) *NigelTwiston-Davies* 6-11-6[137] JamieBargary(3) 40/1	16	11
	Aminabad (FR) *PatrickGriffin,Ireland* 7-11-4[135] (t) A.W.Short(7) 50/1	5	12
188	Born Survivor (IRE) *DanSkelton* 6-11-12[143] BridgetAndrews(3) 13/2	16	13
160	Darebin (GER) *GaryMoore* 5-10-7[124] (v) JasonNuttall(10) 16/1	22	14
33	John Constable (IRE) *EvanWilliams* 6-10-12[129] (t) ConorRing(3) 7/1		F
184	Wakea (USA) *KarlThornton,Ireland* 6-11-11[142] (h+t) DonaghMeyler(3) 8/1		F
	The Grey Taylor (IRE) *BrianEllison* 8-10-9[126] MrJohnJ.O'Neill(7) 33/1		pu
	Cousin Oscar (IRE) *DonaldMcCain* 5-10-13[130] JamesCowley(5) 12/1		pu
	Jacks Last Hope *ChrisGrant* 8-11-2[133] (v) JonathanMoore(3) 16/1		pu

The Rumble Racing Club 19ran 3m57.50

FAIRYHOUSE Sunday, Apr 16 GOOD to SOFT

216 Irish Stallion Farms European Breeders Fund Mares Novices' Hurdle 2½m (10) **Championship Final (Gr 1) (4yo+)** £50,427

185	AUGUSTA KATE *W.P.Mullins* 6-11-7 D.J.Mullins 8/1		1
181	LET'S DANCE (FR) *W.P.Mullins* 5-11-7 R.Walsh 8/13f	½	2
181	BARRA (FR) *GordonElliott* 6-11-7 (t) DavyRussell 14/1	6½	3
	Good Thyne Tara *W.P.Mullins* 7-11-7 M.P.Fogarty 33/1	¾	4
	Colin's Sister *FergalO'Brien,GB* 6-11-7 PaddyBrennan 8/1	7	5
181	Airlie Beach (IRE) *W.P.Mullins* 7-11-7 P.Townend 8/1	¾	6
169	Shattered Love (IRE) *GordonElliott* 6-11-7 (t) B.J.Cooper 10/1	6	7

The Masters Syndicate 7ran 4m56.90

217 Ryanair Gold Cup Novices' Chase (Gr 1) (5yo+) £50,427 2½m (16)

180	ROAD TO RESPECT (IRE) *NoelMeade* 6-11-10 B.J.Cooper 7/2		1
176	YORKHILL (IRE) *W.P.Mullins* 7-11-10 R.Walsh 4/7f	nk	2
192	BALL D'ARC (FR) *GordonElliott* 6-11-10 DavyRussell 5/1	5	3
176	Baily Cloud (IRE) *M.F.Morris* 7-11-10 (s+t) P.Townend 66/1	½	4
86	Attribution *HenrydeBromhead* 7-11-10 D.J.Mullins 25/1	31	5
163	Some Plan (IRE) *HenrydeBromhead* 9-11-10 (t) A.E.Lynch 20/1	32	6

Gigginstown House Stud 6ran 5m04.60

FAIRYHOUSE Monday, Apr 17 GOOD to SOFT

218 Avoca Dunboyne Juvenile Hurdle (Gr 2) (4yo) £25,000 2m (9)

174	PROJECT BLUEBOOK (FR) *JohnQuinn,GB* 4-11-0 BarryGeraghty 9/2		1
183	DANDY MAG (FR) *W.P.Mullins* 4-11-0 P.Townend 8/1	½	2
183	EX PATRIOT (IRE) *EllmarieHolden* 4-11-0 RachaelBlackmore 13/8f	1	3
183	Dinaria des Obeaux (FR) *GordonElliott* 4-10-10 (t) B.J.Cooper 4/1	4½	4
	Orion d'Aubrelle (FR) *W.P.Mullins* 4-11-0 R.Walsh 5/1	17	5
	On The Go Again (IRE) *MichaelMulvany* 4-11-0 (t) A.E.Lynch 28/1	6	6
174	Long Call *A.J.Martin* 4-11-0 (t) RobbiePower 16/1	2¾	7

Mr John P. McManus 7ran 4m05.00

219 Keelings Irish Strawberry Hurdle (Gr 2) (5yo+) £35,593 2½m (11)

184	RENNETI (FR) *W.P.Mullins* 8-11-3 (b) R.Walsh 5/2		1
148	DE PLOTTING SHED (IRE) *GordonElliott* 7-11-3 DavyRussell 2/1f	9	2
171	TOMBSTONE (IRE) *GordonElliott* 7-11-6 B.J.Cooper 3/1	8½	3
95	Whiteout (GER) *W.P.Mullins* 6-10-10 P.Townend 7/1	4	4
64	Lieutenant Colonel *GordonElliott* 8-11-3 (t) J.W.Kennedy 10/1	5½	5

Mrs S. Ricci 5ran 5m10.90

998

220 **Boylesports Irish Grand National Chase (Extended Handicap) (Gr A) (5yo+)** 3m5f (24)
£228,814

140	OUR DUKE (IRE) *MrsJ.Harrington* 7-11-4[153] RobbiePower	9/2f	1
173	BLESS THE WINGS (IRE) *GordonElliott* 12-10-2[137] (s) J.W.Kennedy	12/1	14 2
161	ABOLITIONIST (IRE) *EllmarieHolden* 9-10-10[145] RachaelBlackmore(3)	14/1	¾ 3
214	Thunder And Roses (IRE) *M.F.Morris* 9-10-11[146] (s+t) J.J.Slevin(5)	25/1	¾ 4
	General Principle (IRE) *GordonElliott* 8-10-5[140] B.J.Cooper	16/1	1¾ 5
164	Noble Endeavor (IRE) *GordonElliott* 8-10-5[154] DavyRussell	14/1	1½ 6
167	Haymount (IRE) *W.P.Mullins* 8-10-7[142] R.Walsh	7/1	9½ 7
170	Alpha des Obeaux (FR) *M.F.Morris* 7-10-12[147] (h) D.J.Mullins	16/1	4 8
214	Measureofmydreams (IRE) *NoelMeade* 9-10-8[143] D.Robinson(5)	33/1	hd 9
206	Clarcam (FR) *GordonElliott* 7-11-4[153] (s+t) KatieO'Farrell(7)	66/1	11 10
173	First Lieutenant (IRE) *M.F.Morris* 12-10-3[138] (s) A.Ring(3)	50/1	12 11
103	Shutthefrontdoor (IRE) *JonjoO'Neill,GB* 10-10-9[144] (s+t) M.P.Walsh	28/1	13 12
21	Lord Scoundrel (IRE) *GordonElliott* 8-11-7[156] MsL.O'Neill(5)	33/1	1 13
127	Minella Foru (IRE) *EdwardHarty* 8-10-11[146] BarryGeraghty	14/1	F
94	Oscar Knight (IRE) *ThomasMullins* 8-10-1[136] M.A.Enright	12/1	ur
167	Arbre de Vie (FR) *W.P.Mullins* 7-10-5[140] (h) P.Townend	14/1	bd
161	Sambremont (FR) *W.P.Mullins* 7-10-3[138] D.E.Mullins	33/1	pu
161	Bonny Kate (IRE) *NoelMeade* 7-10-4[139] SeanFlanagan	20/1	pu
148	Dedigout (IRE) *GordonElliott* 11-10-5[140] (t) C.Brassil(5)	66/1	pu
214	Rogue Angel (IRE) *M.F.Morris* 9-10-6[141] (b+t) BarryFoley(7)	33/1	pu
214	Stellar Notion (IRE) *HenrydeBromhead* 9-10-7[142] A.E.Lynch	40/1	pu
214	Raz de Maree (FR) *GavinPatrickCromwell* 12-10-8[143] G.N.Fox	25/1	pu
145	Fletchers Flyer (IRE) *HarryFry,GB* 9-10-10[145] (t) NoelFehily	10/1	pu
214	Wounded Warrior (IRE) *NoelMeade* 8-10-12[147] JonathanMoore	50/1	pu
192	The Game Changer (IRE) *GordonElliott* 8-11-0[149] (t) M.P.Fogarty	66/1	pu
	Foxrock (IRE) *T.M.Walsh* 9-11-1[150] (b+t) DenisO'Regan	14/1	pu
214	Roi des Francs (FR) *GordonElliott* 8-11-1[150] BrianO'Connell	50/1	pu
167	Tiger Roll (IRE) *GordonElliott* 7-11-2[151] (b+t) DonaghMeyler(3)	16/1	pu

Cooper Family Syndicate 28ran 7m47.50

FAIRYHOUSE Tuesday, Apr 18 GOOD to SOFT

221 **Glascarn Handicap Hurdle (Gr A) (4yo+)** £50,000 2m (9)

171	THOMAS HOBSON *W.P.Mullins* 7-11-2[143] R.Walsh	7/1	1
136	VEINARD (FR) *GordonElliott* 8-9-10[123] (t) J.W.Kennedy	8/1	3 2
117	AFTER RAIN (FR) *J.R.Barry* 7-10-0[127] (h) RachaelBlackmore(3)	6/1	4¼ 3
5	Modem *MrsJ.Harrington* 7-10-13[140] (s) RobbiePower	25/1	3¼ 4
117	Golden Spear *A.J.Martin* 6-10-0[127] (t) DonaghMeyler(3)	6/1	2 5
	Chambord du Lys (FR) *W.P.Mullins* 5-10-0[127] P.Townend`	5/1f	1¼ 6
184	Joey Sasa (IRE) *NoelMeade* 8-10-12[139] SeanFlanagan	8/1	2 7
117	Grand Partner (IRE) *ThomasMullins* 9-10-6[133] A.W.Short(7)	12/1	6½ 8
20	My Manekineko *JamesA.Nash* 8-10-1[128] (h) M.A.Enright	20/1	1 9
202	Ice Cold Soul (IRE) *NoelMeade* 7-10-3[130] (t) B.J.Cooper	8/1	3¼ 10
63	St Stephens Green (IRE) *EmmetMullins* 6-9-10[123] D.E.Mullins	12/1	3¼ 11
	Joshua Lane (IRE) *EdwardHarty* 8-10-5[132] (b) M.P.Walsh	12/1	4½ 12
5	Time For Mabel (FR) *E.J.O'Grady* 6-10-5[132] (t) A.E.Lynch	33/1	15 13
	Calino d'Airy (FR) *HenrydeBromhead* 5-10-1[128] D.Robinson(5)	25/1	F

Mrs S. Ricci 14ran 3m58.00

CHELTENHAM Wednesday, Apr 19 GOOD

222 **Matt Hampson Foundation & NSIF Silver Trophy Chase (Limited Handicap)** 2½m166y (17)
(Gr 2) (1) (5yo+) £28,475

206	HENRYVILLE *HarryFry* 9-10-6[140] (h+t) NiallMadden	7/1	1
200	FOXTAIL HILL (IRE) *NigelTwiston-Davies* 8-10-6[140] SamTwiston-Davies	12/1	4 2
12	CASINO MARKETS (IRE) *EmmaLavelle* 9-9-10[138] AidanColeman	12/1	¾ 3
156	Dresden (IRE) *HenryOliver* 9-10-8[142] JamesDavies	25/1	8 4
212	Starchitect (IRE) *DavidPipe* 6-10-7[141] (b+t) TomScudamore	7/2f	hd 5
189	Un Beau Roman (FR) *PaulHenderson* 9-10-1[138] (t) TomO'Brien	50/1	15 6
180	Art Mauresque (FR) *PaulNicholls* 7-11-5[153] NickScholfield	8/1	8 7
180	Thomas Crapper (IRE) *RobinDickin* 10-10-3[138] (s+t) CharliePoste	11/2	ur
180	Voix d'Eau (FR) *HarryFry* 7-10-11[145] (t) NoelFehily	5/1	pu
180	Village Vic (IRE) *PhilipHobbs* 10-11-10[158] RichardJohnson	13/2	pu

R P B Michaelson & E M Thornton 10ran 5m09.20

AYR Saturday, Apr 22 GOOD

223 **Jordan Electrics Ltd Future Champion Novices' Chase (Gr 2) (1) (5yo+)** 2½m110y (18)
£25,978

195	CLOUDY DREAM (IRE) *MalcolmJefferson* 7-11-7 BrianHughes	11/4	1
200	THEINVAL (FR) *NickyHenderson* 7-11-4 (s) JeremiahMcGrath	8/1	2 2

999

156 OLDGRANGEWOOD *DanSkelton* 6-11-7 HarrySkelton 14/1   3¾ 3
131 Clan des Obeaux (FR) *PaulNicholls* 5-11-7 SamTwiston-Davies ....9/4   nk 4
195 Flying Angel (IRE) *NigelTwiston-Davies* 6-11-7 NoelFehily .... 7/4f   pu
    Mr Trevor Hemmings 5ran 5m01.70

224 QTS Scottish Champion Hurdle (Limited Handicap) (Gr 2) (1) (4yo+) £59,797   2m (9)
215 CHESTERFIELD (IRE) *SeamusMullins* 7-10-12¹⁴³ DanielSansom(7) 12/1   1
202 ZUBAYR (IRE) *PaulNicholls* 5-10-7¹³⁸ SamTwiston-Davies .... 12/1   sh 2
184 MOHAAYED *DanSkelton* 5-10-3¹³⁵ (t) HarrySkelton 5/1jf   2¼ 3
215 Vosne Romanee *DrRichardNewland* 6-10-4¹³⁵ (b+t) AidanColeman 40/1   1¼ 4
184 L'Ami Serge (IRE) *NickyHenderson* 7-11-10¹⁵⁵ DarylJacob ....8/1   ¾ 5
188 Tommy Silver (FR) *PaulNicholls* 5-10-11¹⁴² StanSheppard(3) ....7/1   sh 6
160 London Prize *IanWilliams* 6-10-3¹³⁵ TomO'Brien ....10/1   ns 7
202 Hawk High (IRE) *TimEasterby* 7-10-4¹³⁵ (b) BrianHughes ....20/1   ½ 8
165 Sceau Royal (FR) *AlanKing* 5-11-10¹⁵⁵ KevinDowling(10) ....8/1   ¾ 9
    Peace And Co (FR) *NickyHenderson* 6-10-13¹⁴⁴ (h) JeremiahMcGrath 12/1   1 10
184 Ozzie The Oscar (IRE) *PhilipHobbs* 6-10-7¹³⁸ RichardJohnson ....10/1   nk 11
184 Bertimont (FR) *DanSkelton* 7-10-5¹³⁶ (t) PaddyBrennan 18/1   2½ 12
125 Intense Tango *K.R.Burke* 6-10-2¹³⁵ (t) MrJohnJ.O'Neill(7) ....50/1   sh 13
184 Baltimore Rock (IRE) *NeilMulholland* 8-10-4¹³⁵ (t) A.P.Heskin 40/1   5 14
184 Winter Escape (IRE) *AlanKing* 6-10-10¹⁴¹ MarkWalsh 5/1jf   1½ 15
    Traditional Dancer (IRE) *IainJardine* 5-10-2¹³⁵ HenryBrooke 33/1   2½ 16
    The Rumble Racing Club 16ran 3m43.50

225 Coral Scottish Grand National Handicap Chase (Gr 3) (1) (5yo+) £122,442   3m7f176y (25)
What was the first fence was omitted on the second and third circuits because of a stricken jockey
214 VICENTE (FR) *PaulNicholls* 8-11-10¹⁴⁶ (h) SamTwiston-Davies 9/1jf   1
190 COGRY *NigelTwiston-Davies* 8-10-9¹³¹ (s) JamieBargary(3) ....18/1   nk 2
190 BENBENS (IRE) *NigelTwiston-Davies* 12-10-13¹³⁷ MrZ.Baker(7) 50/1   2 3
182 Alvarado (IRE) *FergalO'Brien* 12-10-7¹²⁹ BrianHughes ....16/1   nk 4
182 Lessons In Milan (IRE) *NickyHenderson* 9-10-13¹³⁵ (s) JeremiahMcGrath 40/1   3 5
190 Blakemount (IRE) *SueSmith* 9-10-12¹³⁴ HenryBrooke 25/1   3¼ 6
164 Vintage Clouds (IRE) *SueSmith* 7-10-12¹³⁴ DannyCook 14/1   5 7
167 Missed Approach (IRE) *WarrenGreatrex* 7-11-12¹⁴⁸ (s) LeightonAspell 20/1   5 8
212 Henri Parry Morgan *PeterBowen* 9-10-13¹³⁵ (s+t) RobertDunne ....16/1   nk 9
3 Al Co (FR) *PeterBowen* 12-10-13¹³⁵ (v) JamieMoore ....40/1   ns 10
182 Another Hero (IRE) *JonjoO'Neill* 8-10-13¹³⁵ (s) AidanColeman ....16/1   ¾ 11
167 Dancing Shadow (IRE) *VictorDartnall* 8-11-3¹³⁹ (s) NickScholfield ....33/1   hd 12
206 Portrait King (IRE) *PatrickGriffin,Ireland* 12-10-9¹³¹ (v) ConorO'Farrell 33/1   3¾ 13
    Battle of Shiloh (IRE) *TomGeorge* 8-11-6¹⁴² A.P.Heskin 25/1   3 14
182 Southfield Royale *NeilMulholland* 7-11-5¹⁴¹ (s) NoelFehily 9/1jf   3¼ 15
    Trustan Times (IRE) *MarkWalford* 11-10-10¹³² (s) JakeGreenall 16/1   23 16
96 Fine Rightly (IRE) *StuartCrawford,Ireland* 9-11-11¹⁴⁷ (h) A.E.Lynch 33/1   81 17
182 Sugar Baron (IRE) *NickyHenderson* 7-10-12¹³⁴ (s) NicodeBoinville ....10/1   ur
    Man With Van (IRE) *PatrickGriffin,Ireland* 11-10-5¹²⁷ (s) A.W.Short(7) ....66/1   ur
206 Father Edward (IRE) *DavidPipe* 8-10-6¹²⁸ (s) DavidNoonan ....66/1   pu
    Gone Too Far *DavidPipe* 9-10-7¹²⁹ (s) MichaelHeard(5) ....80/1   pu
190 Firebird Flyer (IRE) *EvanWilliams* 10-10-11¹³³ (s+t) TomO'Brien ....66/1   pu
    Dawson City (IRE) *PollyGundry* 8-10-11¹³³ WayneHutchinson ....25/1   pu
154 Shotgun Paddy (IRE) *EmmaLavelle* 10-11-1¹³⁷ (v) DarylJacob ....12/1   pu
206 Straidnahanna (IRE) *SueSmith* 8-11-2¹³⁸ SeanQuinlan ....50/1   pu
182 Premier Bond *NickyHenderson* 7-11-3¹³⁹ (s+t) DavidBass ....11/1   pu
    Seldom Inn *SandyThomson* 9-11-9¹⁴⁵ (s) DerekFox ....20/1   pu
167 Arpege d'Alene (FR) *PaulNicholls* 7-11-9¹⁴⁵ (b+t) SeanBowen ....10/1   pu
143 Kruzhlinin (GER) *PhilipHobbs* 10-11-10¹⁴⁶ (b) RichardJohnson ....25/1   pu
157 Vivaldi Collonges (FR) *PaulNicholls* 8-11-12¹⁴⁸ (t) HarryCobden ....33/1   pu
    Mr Trevor Hemmings 30ran 8m05.70

PUNCHESTOWN Tuesday, Apr 25   GOOD to SOFT
226 Herald Champion Novices' Hurdle (Gr 1) (5yo+) £49,580   2m100y (9)
162 CILAOS EMERY (FR) *W.P.Mullins* 5-11-12 (h) D.J.Mullins 8/1   1
162 MELON (IRE) *W.P.Mullins* 5-11-12 R.Walsh 5/4f   1 2
203 PINGSHOU (IRE) *ColinTizzard,GB* 7-11-12 DavyRussell 9/1   3¼ 3
181 Forge Meadow (IRE) *MrsJ.Harrington* 5-11-5 RobbiePower 9/1   13 4
162 Bunk Off Early (IRE) *W.P.Mullins* 5-11-12 P.Townend 9/1   11 5
152 Peter The Mayo Man (IRE) *NeilMulholland,GB* 7-11-12 NoelFehily 28/1   34 6
162 Labaik (FR) *GordonElliott* 6-11-12 J.W.Kennedy ....5/2   ds 7
    Luke McMahon 7ran 3m59.80

227 Boylesports Champion Chase (Drogheda) (Gr 1) (5yo+) £123,950 — 2m (11)

205	FOX NORTON (FR) *ColinTizzard,GB* 7-11-12 (h) RobbiePower	5/2		1
178	UN DE SCEAUX (FR) *W.P.Mullins* 9-11-12 R.Walsh	10/11f	1¾	2
205	GOD'S OWN (IRE) *TomGeorge,GB* 9-11-12 A.P.Heskin	7/1	½	3
189	Rock The World (IRE) *MrsJ.Harrington* 9-11-12 (t) D.J.Mullins	12/1	6½	4
192	Ballycasey (IRE) *W.P.Mullins* 10-11-12 P.Townend	16/1	3¼	5
172	Sir Valentino (FR) *TomGeorge,GB* 8-11-12 (t) PaddyBrennan	14/1	17	6
192	Realt Mor (IRE) *GordonElliott* 12-11-12 J.W.Kennedy	100/1		F
220	The Game Changer (IRE) *GordonElliott* 8-11-12 (t) B.J.Cooper	40/1		pu

Ann & Alan Potts 8ran 4m05.80

228 Goffs Land Rover Bumper (4 and 5yo) £49,580 — 2m

	VISION DES FLOS (FR) *RobertTyner* 4-11-4 MrD.O'Connor	12/1		1
	HOLLOWGRAPHIC (IRE) *W.P.Mullins* 4-11-4 MsK.Walsh	7/1	nk	2
	EARLY DOORS (FR) *JosephPatrickO'Brien* 4-11-4 MrP.W.Mullins	6/4f	1¾	3
	Gallant John Joe (IRE) *OliverMcKiernan* 4-11-4 MrR.Deegan(7)	50/1	1¼	4
	Rapid Escape (IRE) *GordonElliott* 4-11-4 MrJ.J.Codd	5/2	ns	5
	Boot Camp (IRE) *MrsJ.Harrington* 4-11-4 MissK.Harrington(3)	12/1	4¾	6
	Fortune Street (FR) *PaulNolan* 4-11-4 MrB.O'Neill	33/1	½	7
	Stacks Mountain *HenrydeBromhead* 4-11-4 MrD.Roche(3)	18/1	1¾	8
	Valdieu (FR) *GordonElliott* 4-11-4 MsL.O'Neill(5)	16/1	hd	9
	Spin A Yarn (IRE) *JosephPatrickO'Brien* 4-11-4 (t) MrT.Hamilton(5)	25/1	2	10
	Its Only A Dream (IRE) *CharlesO'Brien* 4-11-4 MrJohnJ.O'Neill(7)	33/1	2¼	11
	Cask Mate (IRE) *NoelMeade* 4-11-4 MrD.J.Benson(5)	25/1	¾	12
	Knockersally Lad (FR) *ThomasFoley* 4-11-4 MrP.T.Foley(7)	80/1	13	13
	Mujadel (FR) *NoelMeade* 4-11-4 MrP.Magee(7)	20/1	hd	14
	Dundeedy Lad (FR) *RobertTyner* 4-11-4 MrD.Skehan(5)	66/1	6½	15
	Stoical Sam (IRE) *JohnJosephHanlon* 4-11-4 MrR.O.Harding(3)	40/1	21	16

Mrs Grainne M. O'Connor 16ran 3m54.80

229 Growise Champion Novices' Chase (Ellier) (Gr 1) (5yo+) £49,580 — 3m120y (17)

176	DISKO (FR) *NoelMeade* 6-11-10 (h) B.J.Cooper	13/8f		1
149	ANIBALE FLY (FR) *A.J.Martin* 7-11-10 (t) M.P.Walsh	3/1	5	2
167	A GENIE IN ABOTTLE (IRE) *NoelMeade* 6-11-10 (s) SeanFlanagan	8/1	¾	3
191	A Toi Phil (FR) *GordonElliott* 7-11-10 J.W.Kennedy	12/1	5½	4
170	Acapella Bourgeois (FR) *MsSandraHughes* 7-11-10 (h+t) RogerLoughran	9/2	9	5
220	Alpha des Obeaux (FR) *M.F.Morris* 7-11-10 (h) D.J.Mullins	8/1	1¾	6
	Velocity Boy (IRE) *W.P.Murphy* 8-11-10 B.M.Cash	40/1		ur

Gigginstown House Stud 7ran 6m28.00

PUNCHESTOWN Wednesday, Apr 26 GOOD to SOFT

230 Irish Daily Mirror Novices' Hurdle (War of Attrition) (Gr 1) (4yo+) £49,580 — 3m (13)

188	CHAMPAGNE CLASSIC (IRE) *GordonElliott* 6-11-10 B.J.Cooper	14/1		1
185	PENHILL *W.P.Mullins* 6-11-10 R.Walsh	2/1f	2¼	2
171	TIN SOLDIER (FR) *W.P.Mullins* 6-11-10 (s) D.E.Mullins	8/1	½	3
185	Monalee (IRE) *HenrydeBromhead* 6-11-10 D.J.Mullins	4/1	9½	4
194	Al Boum Photo (FR) *W.P.Mullins* 5-11-9 P.Townend	8/1	1	5
177	Presenting Percy *PatrickG.Kelly* 6-11-10 (t) DavyRussell	5/2	½	6
80	Moulin A Vent *NoelMeade* 5-11-9 SeanFlanagan	20/1	12	7
169	Bon Papa (FR) *W.P.Mullins* 6-11-10 M.P.Walsh	25/1	54	8

Gigginstown House Stud 8ran 6m00.00

231 Coral Punchestown Gold Cup Chase (Gr 1) (5yo+) £126,050 — 3m120y (17)

186	SIZING JOHN *MrsJ.Harrington* 7-11-10 RobbiePower	9/10f		1
186	DJAKADAM (FR) *W.P.Mullins* 8-11-10 R.Walsh	5/2	sh	2
41	CONEYGREE *MarkBradstock,GB* 10-11-10 NicodeBoinville	6/1	1½	3
186	Champagne West (IRE) *HenrydeBromhead* 9-11-10 D.J.Mullins	14/1	42	4
192	Flemenstar (IRE) *AnthonyCurran* 12-11-10 A.E.Lynch	100/1	22	5
186	Outlander (IRE) *GordonElliott* 9-11-10 B.J.Cooper	8/1		pu

Ann & Alan Potts Partnership 6ran 6m23.60

232 Racing Post Champion I.N.H. Flat (Gr 1) (4, 5, 6 and 7yo) £49,580 — 2m

175	FAYONAGH (IRE) *GordonElliott* 6-11-7 MrJ.J.Codd	11/8f		1
	PALOMA BLUE (IRE) *HenrydeBromhead* 5-12-0 MrD.Roche	12/1	5½	2
	POLI ROI (FR) *GordonElliott* 5-12-0 MsK.Walsh	9/2	7	3
	Go Another One (IRE) *JohnMcConnell* 5-12-0 MrB.O'Neill	16/1	3¾	4
	Someday *MrsJ.Harrington* 5-12-0 MissK.Harrington	10/3	7	5
175	Carter McKay *W.P.Mullins* 6-12-0 MrP.W.Mullins	7/1	4	6
	Dell Oro (FR) *GaryMoore,GB* 4-11-4 MrS.Clements	25/1	1½	7

Mrs M. Gittins 7ran 3m50.50

233 Guinness Handicap Chase (Gr A) (5yo+) £49,580　　　　2½m (14)

172	SIZING GRANITE (IRE) *ColinTizzard,GB* 9-11-1[146] (t) RobbiePower	14/1	1
164	VICONTE DU NOYER (FR) *ColinTizzard,GB* 8-11-3[148] HarryCobden	25/1	5 2
206	IRISH CAVALIER (IRE) *RebeccaCurtis,GB* 8-11-10[155] (t) P.Townend	12/1	2¼ 3
110	Peoples Park (IRE) *TomJ.Taaffe* 8-9-10[127] RachaelBlackmore(3)	12/1	1¼ 4
206	Vintage Vinnie (IRE) *RebeccaCurtis,GB* 8-10-2[133] JonathanMoore	10/1	4½ 5
133	Draycott Place (IRE) *JohnPatrickRyan* 8-10-4[135] (t) D.E.Mullins	28/1	13 6
	Polidam (FR) *W.P.Mullins* 8-10-6[137] (h) R.Walsh	7/4f	3¾ 7
	Akito (IRE) *J.R.Barry* 7-10-0[131] SeanFlanagan	20/1	14 8
	Winter Magic (IRE) *JamesJosephMangan* 9-9-11[128] (b+t) PhilipEnright	25/1	41 9
212	Rightdownthemiddle (IRE) *GordonElliott* 9-10-1[132] J.W.Kennedy	6/1	F
149	Jetstream Jack (IRE) *GordonElliott* 7-10-9[140] (t) DavyRussell	7/1	F
192	Devils Bride (IRE) *HenrydeBromhead* 10-11-10[155] (s) D.Robinson(5)	25/1	F
206	Mr Diablo (IRE) *J.P.Dempsey* 8-10-8[139] (t) L.P.Dempsey	12/1	bd
161	Vent de La Cote (FR) *MartinBrassil* 8-9-12[129] (t) NiallMadden	14/1	pu

Ann & Alan Potts 14ran 5m14.40

234 Weatherbys General Stud Book European Stud Farms Fund Mares I.N.H. Flat (Liss A Paoraigh) (Gr 3) (4, 5, 6 and 7yo) £24,790　　　　2m

	MINUTESTOMIDNIGHT (IRE) *JonathanSweeney* 6-11-9 (t) MrJ.J.Codd	11/4f	1
	MYSTIC THEATRE (IRE) *W.P.Mullins* 6-11-9 MrP.W.Mullins	4/1	½ 2
	BLUEGRASS PRINCESS (IRE) *EamonO'Connell* 7-11-9 MrD.O'Connor	9/2	5 3
	Simone (IRE) *ShaneNolan* 5-11-9 MrS.Clements	25/1	sh 4
	Jelan (IRE) *MrsJ.Harrington* 5-11-9 MsK.Walsh	8/1	1¼ 5
	The Princetonian (IRE) *MrsJ.Harrington* 4-10-13 MrD.Roche	10/1	½ 6
	Half The Odds (IRE) *NoelMeade* 5-11-9 MrD.J.Benson	14/1	½ 7
	Dawn Shadow (IRE) *MrsD.A.Love* 5-11-9 MrA.Murphy	14/1	nk 8
	Frazel Express (IRE) *PeterFahey* 5-11-9 (t) MrB.O'Neill	20/1	4 9
	Vanellope (IRE) *PeterCroke* 5-11-9 MrH.D.Dunne	25/1	2 10
	Shimmer's Rock (IRE) *P.A.Fahy* 5-11-9 MrR.Deegan	10/1	nk 11
	Joy's Gift (IRE) *PeterMaher* 6-11-9 MrF.Maguire	40/1	30 12

Laurence Cornelius Murphy 12ran 3m57.40

PUNCHESTOWN Thursday, Apr 27   GOOD to SOFT

235 Ladbrokes Champion Stayers' Hurdle (Gr 1) (4yo+) £123,950　　　　3m (13)

179	UNOWHATIMEANHARRY *HarryFry,GB* 9-11-10 (t) NoelFehily	4/1	1
179	NICHOLS CANYON *W.P.Mullins* 7-11-10 R.Walsh	7/4f	hd 2
165	FOOTPAD (FR) *W.P.Mullins* 5-11-9 DarylJacob	9/1	18 3
219	De Plotting Shed (IRE) *GordonElliott* 7-11-10 DavyRussell	33/1	1½ 4
45	One Track Mind (IRE) *WarrenGreatrex,GB* 7-11-10 (s) G.Sheehan	33/1	ns 5
177	Jury Duty (IRE) *GordonElliott* 6-11-10 RobbiePower	25/1	ns 6
219	Lieutenant Colonel *GordonElliott* 8-11-10 (t) B.J.Cooper	100/1	½ 7
213	Snow Falcon (IRE) *NoelMeade* 7-11-10 SeanFlanagan	16/1	9 8
179	Clondaw Warrior (IRE) *W.P.Mullins* 10-11-10 (h) P.Townend	25/1	3¼ 9
179	Lil Rockerfeller (USA) *NeilKing,GB* 6-11-10 (s) RichardJohnson	8/1	½ 10
179	Shaneshill (IRE) *W.P.Mullins* 8-11-10 D.E.Mullins	14/1	4½ 11
148	Sutton Place (IRE) *GordonElliott* 6-11-10 (t) M.P.Walsh	4/1	pu

Mr John P. McManus 12ran 6m03.00

236 Ryanair Novices' Chase (Gr 1) (5yo+) £57,982　　　　2m (11)

	GREAT FIELD (FR) *W.P.Mullins* 6-11-10 J.S.McGarvey	9/10f	1
163	ORDINARY WORLD (IRE) *HenrydeBromhead* 7-11-10 DavyRussell	7/1	11 2
217	BALL D'ARC (FR) *GordonElliott* 6-11-10 B.J.Cooper	11/2	2¼ 3
	Listen Dear (IRE) *W.P.Mullins* 7-11-3 P.Townend	16/1	5½ 4
168	Powersbomb (IRE) *BrianM.McMahon* 7-11-10 (h) M.P.Fogarty	20/1	11 5
	Townshend (GER) *W.P.Mullins* 6-11-10 R.Walsh	8/1	F
	Ballyoisin (IRE) *EndaBolger* 6-11-10 M.P.Walsh	7/1	F
217	Baily Cloud (IRE) *M.F.Morris* 7-11-10 (s+t) D.J.Mullins	20/1	ur

Mr John P. McManus 8ran 4m06.70

PUNCHESTOWN Friday, Apr 28   Chase course: GOOD to SOFT, Hurdles course: GOOD

237 EMS Copiers Novices' Handicap Chase (Gr A) (5yo+) £49,580　　　　2m5f (15)

	WOODLAND OPERA (IRE) *MrsJ.Harrington* 7-11-6[142] (t) RobbiePower	11/4f	1
220	ARBRE DE VIE (FR) *W.P.Mullins* 7-11-4[140] R.Walsh	6/1	¾ 2
176	BALKO DES FLOS (IRE) *HenrydeBromhead* 6-11-7[143] B.J.Cooper	7/1	1¼ 3
	Kilcarry Bridge (IRE) *JohnPatrickRyan* 10+10-6[178] (t) DonaghMeyler(3)	25/1	2½ 4
	Champagne Harmony (IRE) *S.J.Mahon* 7-10-11[133] J.W.Kennedy	14/1	11 5
	Mystical Knight (IRE) *RebeccaCurtis,GB* 8-11-0[136] (t) J.S.McGarvey	33/1	4½ 6
168	Last Goodbye (IRE) *MissElizabethDoyle* 6-11-1[137] SeanFlanagan	8/1	¾ 7
212	Relentless Dreamer (IRE) *RebeccaCurtis,GB* 8-10-12[134] (s+t) D.J.Mullins	28/1	2¾ 8

1002

	11	On Fiddlers Green (IRE) *HenrydeBromhead* 7-10-8[130] A.E.Lynch	33/1	2½	9
		Three Wise Men (IRE) *HenrydeBromhead* 7-11-1[137] D.E.Mullins	12/1	7	10
		Dicosimo (FR) *W.P.Mullins* 6-10-13[135] (h) P.Townend	14/1	23	11
		Blackmail (IRE) *A.J.Martin* 9-11-5[141] (h+t) DenisO'Regan	33/1	1½	12
		Bright Tomorrow (IRE) *MrsJ.Harrington* 6-10-3[125] M.J.Bolger	25/1		F
189		Le Prezien (FR) *PaulNicholls,GB* 6-11-9[145] (t) M.P.Walsh	7/1		pu
180		Diamond King (IRE) *GordonElliott* 9-11-10[146] (t) DavyRussell	8/1		pu

Mrs T K Cooper/D Cooper/C A Waters 15ran 5m31.50

238 Hanlon Concrete European Breeders Fund Glencaraig Lady Mares Handicap Chase (Gr B) (4yo+) £37,186   2m5f (14)

What should have been the fourth last fence was omitted due to a stricken jockey

		DEFINITE RUBY (IRE) *GordonElliott* 9-10-13[126] (b) J.W.Kennedy	7/1		1
97		SLOWMOTION (FR) *JosephPatrickO'Brien* 5-11-7[134] M.P.Walsh	4/1f	1¾	2
63		ELUSIVE IVY (IRE) *GavinPatrickCromwell* 7-10-12[125] P.Townend	7/1	6	3
		Retour En France (IRE) *W.P.Mullins* 7-10-12[125] (s) R.Walsh	9/2	nk	4
166		Rock On The Moor (IRE) *MrsJ.Harrington* 9-11-10[137] D.E.Mullins	12/1	½	5
		Carole Rose (IRE) *LiamCasey* 7-9-12[111] M.A.Enright	16/1	1¼	6
		The Conker Club (IRE) *W.Harney* 11-10-2[115] (h) P.E.Corbett(3)	28/1	4½	7
		Presenting Mahler (IRE) *JohnPatrickRyan* 7-9-10[111] A.E.Lynch	66/1	¾	8
143		Cresswell Breeze *AnthonyHoneyball,GB* 7-11-3[130] (t) JonathanMoore	9/1	4¼	9
		Emcon (IRE) *W.J.Austin* 8-11-0[127] DavyRussell	14/1	11	10
		Girly Girl (IRE) *MrsJ.Harrington* 8-11-0[127] RobbiePower	9/1	1	11
		Ros Brin (IRE) *G.A.Kingston* 11-10-3[116] DonaghMeyler(3)	66/1	13	12
		Padraig's Joy (IRE) *DavidHarryKelly* 9-10-6[119] (s) SeanFlanagan	16/1	3¾	13
		Isabella Liberty (FR) *GordonElliott* 6-10-5[118] (s+t) DenisO'Regan	20/1		F
		Goulane Davina (IRE) *SeamusSpillane* 8-10-10[123] BarryFoley(7)	20/1		F
86		Who's That (IRE) *LiamP.Cusack* 9-10-12[125] (s) D.J.Mullins	25/1		F
		Keppols Queen (IRE) *MrsJ.Harrington* 9-11-5[132] (t) M.J.Bolger	12/1		ur

Mr James W. Power 17ran 5m37.40

239 Betdaq Punchestown Champion Hurdle (Gr 1) (4yo+) £123,950   2m (9)

165		WICKLOW BRAVE *W.P.Mullins* 8-11-12 (b) MrP.W.Mullins	12/1		1
198		MY TENT OR YOURS (IRE) *NickyHenderson,GB* 10-11-12 (h) AidanColeman	.8/1	1½	2
184		ARCTIC FIRE (GER) *W.P.Mullins* 8-11-12 (h) P.Townend	9/2	nk	3
226		Labaik (FR) *GordonElliott* 6-11-12 (v) DavyRussell	11/2	¾	4
165		Brain Power (IRE) *NickyHenderson,GB* 6-11-12 (s) D.J.Mullins	13/2	¾	5
127		Ivan Grozny (FR) *W.P.Mullins* 7-11-12 (h) MsK.Walsh	33/1	12	6
166		Vroum Vroum Mag (FR) *W.P.Mullins* 8-11-5 R.Walsh	6/4f	1	7
219		Tombstone (IRE) *GordonElliott* 7-11-12 J.W.Kennedy	25/1	3	8
198		Rashaan (IRE) *ColinThomasKidd* 5-11-12 SeanFlanagan	50/1	½	9
198		Identity Thief (IRE) *HenrydeBromhead* 7-11-12 B.J.Cooper	33/1	3	10

Wicklow Bloodstock (Ireland) Ltd 10ran 3m50.40

240 Tattersalls Ireland Champion Novices' Hurdle (Gr 1) (4yo+) £49,580   2½m (11)

169		BACARDYS (FR) *W.P.Mullins* 6-11-10 MrP.W.Mullins	10/1		1
210		FINIAN'S OSCAR (IRE) *ColinTizzard,GB* 5-11-10 RobbiePower	13/8f	sh	2
185		DEATH DUTY (IRE) *GordonElliott* 6-11-10 B.J.Cooper	9/2	7	3
216		Let's Dance (FR) *W.P.Mullins* 5-11-3 R.Walsh	3/1	nk	4
193		Bleu Berry (IRE) *W.P.Mullins* 6-11-10 P.Townend	8/1	11	5
		The Nipper (IRE) *WarrenGreatrex,GB* 6-11-3 G.Sheehan	25/1	2	6
169		Kemboy (FR) *W.P.Mullins* 5-11-10 D.J.Mullins	14/1	2½	7
194		Runfordave (IRE) *GordonElliott* 5-11-10 J.W.Kennedy	33/1		F
193		Outspoken (IRE) *JosephPatrickO'Brien* 5-11-10 (t) M.P.Walsh	14/1		pu

Shanakiel Racing Syndicate 9ran 4m53.80

PUNCHESTOWN Saturday, Apr 29   GOOD to SOFT

241 Irish Stallion Farms European Breeders Fund Mares Champion Hurdle (Gr 1) (4yo+) £49,580   2½m (11)

166		APPLE'S JADE (FR) *GordonElliott* 5-11-7 (t) B.J.Cooper	evsf		1
216		AIRLIE BEACH (IRE) *W.P.Mullins* 7-11-7 D.E.Mullins	16/1	14	2
		KARALEE (FR) *W.P.Mullins* 6-11-7 R.Walsh	11/4	1¾	3
219		Whiteout (GER) *W.P.Mullins* 6-11-7 D.J.Mullins	20/1	18	4
216		Augusta Kate *W.P.Mullins* 6-11-7 P.Townend	7/2	4	5
216		Barra (FR) *GordonElliott* 6-11-7 (t) J.W.Kennedy	20/1	13	6
		Lady Buttons *PhilipKirby,GB* 6-11-7 AdamNicol	50/1		pu

Gigginstown House Stud 7ran 4m54.00

242 AES Champion Four Year Old Hurdle (Gr 1) (4yo) £49,580   2m (9)

| 183 | | BAPAUME (FR) *W.P.Mullins* 4-11-0 R.Walsh | 2/1f | | 1 |
| 183 | | LANDOFHOPEANDGLORY (IRE) *JosephPatrickO'Brien* 4-11-0 (t) M.P.Walsh | 4/1 | 1¼ | 2 |

138	MERI DEVIE (FR) *W.P.Mullins* 4-10-7 D.J.Mullins	7/1	1	3
183	Mega Fortune (FR) *GordonElliott* 4-11-0 (s) DavyRussell	9/4	hd	4
218	Dinaria des Obeaux (FR) *GordonElliott* 4-10-7 (t) B.J.Cooper	14/1	7	5
218	Dandy Mag (FR) *W.P.Mullins* 4-11-0 P.Townend	8/1	4¼	6
218	On The Go Again (IRE) *MichaelMulvany* 4-11-0 (t) RachaelBlackmore	66/1	16	7

Mrs S. Ricci 7ran 3m55.30

243 Palmerstown House Pat Taaffe Handicap Chase (Gr B) (150) (5yo+) £29,580   3m120y (17)

212	SIZING CODELCO (IRE) *ColinTizzard,GB* 8-11-10[150] RobbiePower	4/1		1
	FOREVER GOLD (IRE) *EdwardCawley* 10-10-5[131] (b) C.D.Timmons(5)	12/1	3½	2
170	HERON HEIGHTS (IRE) *HenrydeBromhead* 8-10-11[137] (t) PhilipEnright	16/1	2¾	3
116	Hash Brown (IRE) *M.Hourigan* 8-10-3[129] (t) M.P.Walsh	12/1	3¼	4
	Sandymount Duke (IRE) *MrsJ.Harrington* 8-10-11[137] M.J.Bolger	7/1	nk	5
214	O'Faolains Boy (IRE) *RebeccaCurtis,GB* 10-10-12[138] P.Townend	10/1	3¾	6
161	Space Cadet (IRE) *GordonElliott* 7-10-7[133] J.W.Kennedy	14/1	½	7
	Fine Theatre (IRE) *PaulNolan* 7-10-9[135] M.P.Fogarty	12/1	25	8
148	Ttebbob (IRE) *MrsJ.Harrington* 8-10-12[138] (h+t) DavyRussell	12/1	5½	9
3	Solstice Son *AnthonyHoneyball,GB* 8-10-1[127] (t) JonathanMoore	25/1		F
94	The Crafty Butcher (IRE) *W.P.Mullins* 10-10-9[135] R.Walsh	10/3f		pu
118	Rogue Trader (IRE) *TomJ.Taaffe* 8-10-11[137] J.S.McGarvey	9/1		pu
204	Marinero (IRE) *HenrydeBromhead* 8-11-2[142] (s) B.J.Cooper	14/1		pu

Ann & Alan Potts 13ran 6m34.00

244 Ballymore Handicap Hurdle (Gr B) (4yo+) £49,580   2½m100y (21)

	OPEN EAGLE (IRE) *W.P.Mullins* 8-11-8[148] MrW.Mullins	20/1		1
202	DREAM BERRY (FR) *JonjoO'Neill,GB* 6-10-13[139] (t) L.P.Dempsey	20/1	½	2
194	LIVELOVELAUGH (IRE) *W.P.Mullins* 7-10-9[135] P.Townend	9/1	sh	3
221	After Rain (FR) *J.R.Barry* 7-10-1[127] (h) DonaghMeyler(3)	12/1	1¾	4
171	Automated *GordonElliott* 6-10-11[137] B.J.Cooper	16/1	1¼	5
219	Renneti (FR) *W.P.Mullins* 8-11-13[153] (b) D.E.Mullins	16/1	1¼	6
221	Thomas Hobson *W.P.Mullins* 7-11-10[150] MsK.Walsh	16/1	hd	7
210	Bel Ami de Sivola (FR) *NoelMeade* 6-10-2[128] SeanFlanagan	25/1	4¾	8
221	Modem *MrsJ.Harrington* 7-11-0[140] (s) P.D.Kennedy(3)	20/1	1¾	9
	Carrig Cathal *GordonElliott* 6-10-11[137] J.W.Kennedy	14/1	7	10
	Mine Now (IRE) *PeterFahey* 9-10-3[129] R.P.Treacy(5)	33/1	1¾	11
221	Grand Partner (IRE) *ThomasMullins* 9-10-7[133] (s) M.A.Enright	50/1	1	12
	Sire du Berlais (FR) *GordonElliott* 5-10-11[137] DavyRussell	9/1	1¼	13
117	Derulo (IRE) *MissElizabethDoyle* 6-10-7[133] (b) J.J.Slevin(5)	14/1	2¼	14
202	Geordie des Champs (IRE) *RebeccaCurtis,GB* 6-11-0[140] JonathanMoore	14/1	4¼	15
148	Milsean (IRE) *GordonElliott* 8-11-2[142] (t) C.Brassil(5)	33/1	2	16
45	Protek des Flos (FR) *NickyHenderson,GB* 5-10-8[134] J.S.McGarvey	25/1	33	17
171	Allblak des Places (FR) *W.P.Mullins* 5-10-12[138] D.J.Mullins	40/1	8½	18
184	Air Horse One *HarryFry,GB* 6-11-1[141] NiallMadden	8/1cf	1¾	19
	Oscar Sam (IRE) *MrsJ.Harrington* 8-11-1[141] RobbiePower	8/1cf	2	20
	Swamp Fox (IRE) *JosephG.Murphy* 5-10-8[134] BrianO'Connell	50/1	6½	21
	Pique Sous (FR) *W.P.Mullins* 10-10-7[133] (t) RachaelBlackmore(3)	20/1		F
	Bonbon Au Miel (FR) *W.P.Mullins* 6-10-11[137] R.Walsh	8/1cf		pu
171	Scoir Mear *ThomasMullins* 7-10-11[137] M.P.Walsh	8/1cf		pu

Supreme Horse Racing Club & Colin Gray 24ran 4m57.90

SANDOWN Saturday, Apr 29 GOOD

245 Bet365 Oaksey Chase (Gr 2) (1) (5yo+) £28,475   2¾m164y (21)

46	MENORAH (IRE) *PhilipHobbs* 12-11-10 RichardJohnson	9/4		1
205	TRAFFIC FLUIDE (FR) *GaryMoore* 7-11-0 (s) JoshuaMoore	15/8f	4½	2
205	JOSSES HILL (IRE) *NickyHenderson* 9-11-10 (s) NicodeBoinville	7/2	16	3
206	Third Intention (IRE) *ColinTizzard* 10-11-6 (b+t) AidanColeman	20/1	2	4
156	Vibrato Valtat (FR) *PaulNicholls* 8-11-6 (s+t) SamTwiston-Davies	12/1	16	5
222	Art Mauresque (FR) *PaulNicholls* 7-11-4 (s) NickScholfield	10/1		pu

Mrs Diana L. Whateley 6ran 5m41.10

246 Bet365 Celebration Chase (Gr 1) (1) (5yo+) £71,188   1m7f119y (13)

163	ALTIOR (IRE) *NickyHenderson* 7-11-7 NicodeBoinville	30/100f		1
172	SPECIAL TIARA *HenrydeBromhead,Ireland* 10-11-7 NoelFehily	4/1	8	2
211	SAN BENEDETO (FR) *PaulNicholls* 6-11-7 (s+t) SamTwiston-Davies	20/1	4½	3
178	Vaniteux (FR) *NickyHenderson* 8-11-7 (s) AidanColeman	12/1	1¾	4

Mrs Patricia Pugh 4ran 3m47.80

247 Bet365 Gold Cup Handicap Chase (Gr 3) (1) (5yo+) £84,405   3½m166y (24)

	HENLLAN HARRI (IRE) *PeterBowen* 9-9-10[126] (b) SeanBowen	40/1		1
49	VYTA DU ROC (FR) *NickyHenderson* 8-10-11[137] DarylJacob	6/1	hd	2
164	THEATRE GUIDE (IRE) *ColinTizzard* 10-11-12[152] (b+t) PaddyBrennan	20/1	nk	3

1004

225	Benbens (IRE) *NigelTwiston-Davies* 12-10-9[135] SamTwiston-Davies	14/1	nk	4
57	Doing Fine (IRE) *NeilMulholland* 9-10-3[129] (s+t) TomScudamore	9/2f	1¼	5
76	Rock The Kasbah (IRE) *PhilipHobbs* 7-11-2[142] RichardJohnson	8/1	nk	6
225	Sugar Baron (IRE) *NickyHenderson* 7-10-8[134] (s) NicodeBoinville	8/1	hd	7
164	The Druids Nephew (IRE) *NeilMulholland* 10-11-3[143] (v) NoelFehily	6/1	hd	8
214	The Young Master *NeilMulholland* 8-11-8[148] (s) MrS.Waley-Cohen(3)	8/1	7	9
182	Whats Happening (IRE) *TomGeorge* 10-10-10[136] (t) A.P.Heskin	14/1	10	10
214	Just A Par (IRE) *PaulNicholls* 10-11-9[149] HarryCobden	16/1	27	11
81	Present Man (IRE) *PaulNicholls* 7-11-2[142] (t) JackSherwood(3)	12/1		pu
28	Le Reve (IRE) *LucyWadham* 9-11-6[146] (b) LeightonAspell	33/1		pu
	Mr Einsley Harries 13ran 7m22.50			

248 Bet365 Select Hurdle (Gr 2) (1) (4yo+) £28,475　　　　2m5f110y (11)

224	L'AMI SERGE (IRE) *NickyHenderson* 7-11-0 DarylJacob	7/2		1
213	PTIT ZIG (FR) *PaulNicholls* 8-11-8 (b) NoelFehily	8/1	1½	2
65	VOLNAY DE THAIX (FR) *NickyHenderson* 8-11-0 NicodeBoinville	16/1	6	3
198	The New One (IRE) *NigelTwiston-Davies* 9-11-8 SamTwiston-Davies	5/2f	1½	4
171	Modus *PaulNicholls* 7-11-0 (h) HarryCobden	9/2	¾	5
	Beat That (IRE) *NickyHenderson* 9-11-0 AidanColeman	14/1	3¾	6
198	Old Guard *PaulNicholls* 6-11-8 NickScholfield	20/1	5	7
202	Rather Be (IRE) *NickyHenderson* 6-11-4 JeremiahMcGrath	5/1	8	8
	Mr Simon Munir & Mr Isaac Souede 8ran 5m20.70			

AUTEUIL Saturday, May 20　SOFT

249 Prix La Barka Hurdle (Gr 2) (5yo+) £66,737　　　　2m5f83y

235	SHANESHILL (IRE) *W.P.Mullins,Ireland* 8-10-6 R.Walsh	118/10		1
248	L'AMI SERGE (IRE) *NickyHenderson,GB* 7-10-10 DarylJacob	78/10	¾	2
	DEVICE (FR) *GuillaumeMacaire,France* 5-10-8 JamesReveley	9/10f	2	3
	Protekapril (FR) *G.Cherel,France* 7-10-9 (s) DavidCottin	111/10	2	4
77	Alex de Larredya (FR) *FrancoisNicolle,France* 7-11-0 GaetanMasure	78/10	4½	5
	Yoko (FR) *J-P.Gallorini,France* 6-10-6 MaximilienFarcinade	48/1	1	6
	Bosseur (FR) *G.Cherel,France* 6-10-8 KevinNabet	205/10	3½	7
	Capivari (FR) *Francois-MarieCottin,France* 5-10-6 RegisSchmidlin	161/10	1½	8
244	Open Eagle (IRE) *W P Mullins,Ireland* 8-10-8 P.Townend	77/10	2½	9
	Champ de Bataille (FR) *Francois-MarieCottin,France* 6-10-8 DamienMescam	26/1	30	10
	Andrea Wylie/Graham Wylie 10ran 5m20.45			

AUTEUIL Sunday, May 21　SOFT

250 Grand Steeple-Chase de Paris (Gr 1) (5yo+) £324,153　　　　3m5f182y

25	SO FRENCH (FR) *GuillaumeMacaire,France* 6-10-10 JamesReveley	12/10f		1
	PERFECT IMPULSE (FR) *A.Chaille-Chaille,France* 5-10-1 TristanLemagnen	68/10	6	2
	CARRIACOU (FR) *Mme I.Pacault,France* 5-10-6 StephanePaillard	206/10	4	3
	Sainte Turgeon (FR) *PatriceQuinton,France* 5-10-3 JordanDuchene	38/1	½	4
	Bipolaire (FR) *FrancoisNicolle,France* 6-10-10 ThomasGueguen	16/1	1	5
25	Shannon Rock (FR) *J-P.Gallorini,France* 11-10-10 (s) LudovicPhilipperon	148/10	7	6
	Saint Pistol (FR) *L.Viel,France* 9-10-10 ArnaudDuchene	145/10	1	7
	Winneyev (FR) *Mme I.Pacault,France* 6-10-10 ThomasBeaurain	161/10	¾	8
	Beguin d'Estruval (FR) *GuillaumeMacaire,France* 6-10-10 BertrandLestrade	32/1	20	9
	Vanilla Crush (FR) *J-P.Gallorini,France* 8-10-10 AnthonyLecordier	161/10		pu
	Valtor (FR) *E.Leray,France* 8-10-10 KevinNabet	44/1		pu
	Mon Nickson (FR) *J-P.Gallorini,France* 6-10-10 MrOliverD'Andigne	34/1		pu
	Mali Borgia (FR) *PhillippeCottin,France* 7-10-10 (b) DavidCottin	119/10		pu
	Paulougas (FR) *D.Bressou,France* 5-10-6 JacquesRicou	27/1		pu
	La Sulfureuse (FR) *Francois-MarieCottin,France* 6-10-6 RegisSchmidlin	31/1		rr
	Mme Magalen Bryant 15ran 7m27.83			

AUTEUIL Sunday, Jun 11　SOFT

251 Grande Course de Haies d'Auteuil Hurdle (Gr 1) (5yo+) £146,053　　　　3m1f77y

249	L'AMI SERGE (IRE) *NickyHenderson,GB* 7-10-10 (h) DarylJacob	58/10		1
249	ALEX DE LARREDYA (FR) *FrancoisNicolle,France* 7-10-10 (b) GaetanMasure	75/10	1½	2
249	SHANESHILL (IRE) *W.P.Mullins,Ireland* 8-10-10 R.Walsh	48/10	10	3
249	Bosseur (FR) *G.Cherel,France* 6-10-10 KevinNabet	45/1	hd	4
249	Capivari (FR) *Francois-MarieCottin,France* 6-10-10 RegisSchmidlin	48/1	2½	5
249	Yoko (FR) *J-P.Gallorini,France* 6-10-10 LudovicPhilipperon	58/1	5	6
	Tir Au But (FR) *G.Cherel,France* 10-10-10 (b) AlaindeChitray	30/1	1½	7
248	Ptit Zig (FR) *PaulNicholls,GB* 8-10-10 (b) SamTwiston-Davies	53/10	1¾	8
235	One Track Mind (IRE) *WarrenGreatrex,GB* 7-10-10 (s) GavinSheehan	17/1	ds	9
	Blue Dragon (FR) *G.Cherel,France* 6-10-10 DavidCottin	13/10f		pu
	Mr Simon Munir & Mr Isaac Souede 10ran 5m56.77			

252 Prix Alain du Breil Hurdle (Gr 1) (4yo) £106,579   2m3f85y

	PRINCE ALI (FR) *Guillaume Macaire,France* 4-10-8 Kevin Nabet 58/10	1
242	BAPAUME (FR) *W.P.Mullins,Ireland* 4-10-8 R.Walsh 43/10	½ 2
242	DANDY MAG (FR) *W.P.Mullins,Ireland* 4-10-8 P.Townend 32/1	4½ 3
181	Titi de Montmartre (FR) *R.Collet,France* 4-10-4 (s) Ludovic Philipperon 31/1	3 4
	D'vina (FR) *Richard Chotard,France* 4-10-4 Bertrand Lestrade 22/1	2 5
	Roxinela (FR) *Francois-Marie Cottin,France* 4-10-4 Regis Schmidlin 74/1	ds 6
	De Bon Coeur (FR) *Francois Nicolle,France* 4-10-4 James Reveley 3/10f	F

Mr Simon Munir & Mr Isaac Souede 7ran 4m39.18

INDEX TO SELECTED BIG RACES

Baron Alco (FR) 67^2, 131^2, 180^2
Barra (FR) 139^5, 181^2, 216^3, 241^6
Battleford 188
Battle of Shiloh (IRE) 225
Bay of Freedom (IRE) 71^4
Baywing (IRE) 132*
Bazooka (IRE) 152^5
Bear's Affair (IRE) 199
Beat That (IRE) 248^6
Bedrock 150^5, 196^3
Beeves (IRE) 58
Beg To Differ (IRE) 28^{pu}, 89^4
Beguin d'Estruval (FR) 250
Bel Ami de Sivola (FR) 106^5, 210^{pu}, 244
Bellow Mome (FR) 98, 149^6
Bells 'N' Banjos (IRE) 167
Bellshill (IRE) 86^4, 140^F, 170^3
Belmount (IRE) 57^6
Beltor 1, 136
Benatar (IRE) 210^4
Benbens (IRE) 190^{pu}, 225^3, 247^4
Bennys King (IRE) 109
Bennys Mist (IRE) 60^{pu}
Bentelimar (IRE) 5, 8^2, 42^5, 116^F
Berea Boru (IRE) 115^5, 154^{pu}
Bertimort (FR) 55^F, 184, 224
Better Getalong (IRE) 175
Beware The Bear (IRE) 167
Beyond Conceit (IRE) 162^6, 207^2
Bhutan (IRE) 138^6
Bigbadjohn (IRE) 47^2, 126^F, 145*, 167^{pu}
Big Fella Thanks 199^3
Bigmartre (FR) 160^6, 202
Bipolaire (FR) 250^5
Birch Hill (IRE) 10^{pu}
Bishop of Bling (IRE) 72^4
Bishops Road (IRE) 51^4, 89, 115^3, 214^{pu}
Black Hercules (IRE) 74^5, 92^4, 111^3
Blackmail (IRE) 237
Black Op (IRE) 208
Black Thunder (FR) 187^{pu}, 199^F
Blakemount (IRE) 190^5, 225^6
Blaklion 15^4, 49^5, 87^3, 143^2, 214^4
Bless The Wings (IRE) 52, 94, 118, 173^3, 220^2
Bleu Berry (FR) 193*, 240^5
Bleu Et Rouge (FR) 129^{ur}, 140^4
Blood Crazed Tiger (IRE) 106^3, 128^F, 139^4
Blue Dragon (FR) 251^{pu}
Bluegrass Princess (IRE) 234^3
Blue Surf 75^6
Bob Ford (IRE) 58, 108^{pu}
Bob Tucker (IRE) 24^4, 57^4
Boite (IRE) 136, 184
Bold Henry 189
Bomber's Moon 208
Bonbon Au Miel (FR) 244^{pu}
Bon Chic (IRE) 166^{pu}

Bonny Kate (IRE) 52^3, 118^3, 161^{pu}, 220^{pu}
Bon Papa (FR) 169^{pu}, 230
Boogie Life 201
Boondooma (IRE) 12^{pu}
Boot Camp (IRE) 228^6
Bordeaux Bill (IRE) 210^{pu}
Born Survivor (IRE) 188^6, 215
Bosseur (FR) 249, 251^4
Bouvreuil (FR) 29^5, 68^6, 180^3, 206
Boxing Along (IRE) 111^5
Braavos 9
Brain Power (IRE) 33, 55*, 79*, 165, 239^5
Brelade 93^2, 139^3, 169^6, 193
Briar Hill (IRE) 98^F
Briery Belle 102^3, 170^{pu}
Briery Queen 166^5, 209
Bright New Dawn (IRE) 4, 189, 206^F
Bright Tomorrow (IRE) 237^F
Brio Conti (FR) 210^5
Bristol de Mai (FR) 19^2, 51^2, 115*, 134^3, 186, 197^5
Broken Eagle (USA) 199^F
Buckers Bridge (IRE) 187^{pu}
Buckhorn Timothy 18
Bulkov (FR) 203
Bun Doran (IRE) 112^6, 168^6, 200^3
Bunk Off Early (IRE) 139^2, 162, 226^5
Burbank (IRE) 169^4
Burtons Well (IRE) 168^F
Buveur d'Air (FR) 165*, 198*
Buywise (IRE) 29^3, 68, 164^2
Byron Flyer 9, 202^5
C'est Jersey (FR) 185
Caid du Berlais (FR) 9, 40^{pu}, 126^5, 164^F, 177
Calett Mad (IRE) 132^2, 167, 204^5
Calino d'Airy (FR) 221^F
Calipto (FR) 189^6
Call The Taxie (IRE) 100^2
Campeador (FR) 63^F
Camping Ground (FR) 104^5, 155*
Candy Burg (FR) 174
Cantlow (IRE) 4, 173^3
Canton Prince (IRE) 10^{pu}
Caolaneoin (IRE) 110^4
Cap d'Aubois (FR) 117
Capitaine (FR) 75*, 105^2, 152^4, 158^{pu}
Capital Force (IRE) 162
Capivari (FR) 249, 251^5
Captain Chaos (IRE) 76^4, 132^F
Captain Forez (FR) 75^2, 210^2
Captain Redbeard (IRE) 168^{pu}
Captain Von Trappe (IRE) 52^F, 94
Caracci Apache (FR) 81^{pu}
Carlingford Lough (IRE) 141^4
Carlos du Fruitier (FR) 208
Carole's Destrier 49^2, 89
Carole Rose (IRE) 238^6
Carriacou (FR) 250^3

Carrig Cathal 244
Carter McKay 175, 232^6
Cash Again (FR) 159
Casino Markets (IRE) 12^3, 222^3
Cask Mate (IRE) 228
Castello Sforza (IRE) 188
Catamaran du Seuil (FR) 188
Cause of Causes (USA) 52^{pu}, 94, 173*, 214^2
Cause Toujours (FR) 175
Celestial Path (IRE) 105^{pu}
Celtic Thunder (IRE) 22^{pu}
Ch'tibello (IRE) 1^3, 17^5, 39*, 82^3, 147^2
Chalonnial (FR) 105^3, 158^2
Chambord du Lys (FR) 221^6
Champagne At Tara 180^{pu}
Champagne Classic (IRE) 188*, 230*
Champagne Harmony (IRE) 237^5
Champagne Pat (IRE) 84^6
Champagne West (IRE) 118*, 186, 231^4
Champ de Bataille (FR) 249
Champers On Ice (IRE) 167^{pu}
Charbel (IRE) 54^2, 163^F, 211^3
Charlemar (FR) 105^5
Charli Parcs (FR) 150^F, 183^6
Charmix (FR) 151^3
Chase The Spud 190*
Chateau Conti (FR) 139^6, 193^{pu}
Chelsea Flyer (IRE) 210
Cheltenian (FR) 1^{pu}
Chesterfield (FR) 79, 109, 215*, 224*
Chic Name (FR) 137^4
Chieftain's Choice (IRE) 160, 215^2
Chirico Vallis (FR) 193^5
Chti Balko (FR) 203
Churchtown Champ (IRE) 81^F
Cilaos Emery (FR) 162^5, 226*
Claimantakinforgan (FR) 175^3, 208^5
Clan des Obeaux (FR) 45*, 102^2, 131^5, 223^4
Clarcam (FR) 4^5, 6, 36^2, 116, 118, 164, 206, 220
Cliff House (IRE) 5
Cliffs of Dover 72*
Clondaw Castle (IRE) 208
Clondaw Cian (IRE) 177
Clondaw Kaempfer (IRE) 202
Clondaw Knight (IRE) 51^{pu}
Clondaw Warrior (IRE) 5*, 95^2, 179^6, 235
Cloonacool (IRE) 17
Cloudy Dream (IRE) 163^2, 195^2, 223*
Clyne 114^2, 136^3
Cocktails At Dawn 59^4, 153^F, 180^{pu}, 214^F
Coeur Blimey (IRE) 53^5
Coeur de Lion 183
Cogry 28^{bd}, 58^{pu}, 66^F, 190^6, 225^2
Coillte Lass (IRE) 125^3, 181
Cold March (FR) 180^{pu}

1009

ERRATA & ADDENDA

Chasers & Hurdlers 2015/16

Index To Photos   p1020 Weatherbys Private Bank Champion Standard Open National Hunt Flat, photo credit should be **Peter Mooney**

Chasers & Hurdlers 2009/10

Another Minx   dam Shady Minx was a **winning pointer** (not unraced)

Chasers & Hurdlers 2006/07

Nickname   was not gelded (he was returned to France as a stallion after his racing days and is the sire of Frodon who has an essay in this edition)

TIMEFORM 'TOP HORSES IN FRANCE'

Nearly ten years after first going to France for a working holiday with trainer Guillaume Macaire, James Reveley became the first foreign-born rider to win the French jump jockeys' title since the Cravache d'Or was first awarded in 1958. Reveley formerly split his riding commitments between the north of England, principally for his now-retired father Keith, and France, but basing himself permanently across the Channel in 2016 paid immediate dividends. He had been vying for the title with former champion David Cottin when the latter sustained a back injury in August which kept him out for the rest of the year. By the end of 2016 (the French jumps season covers the calendar year), Reveley too was sidelined after fracturing his left foot in a fall from Device in the Prix Renaud du Vivier in mid-November, though he had established a sufficient lead by then to take the title with 84 wins. After rehabilitation at Jack Berry House in Malton, Reveley resumed riding at Pau in February.

Support from Macaire (champion trainer again in 2016 with earnings of more than €8m) has been instrumental in deciding the destination of the jockeys' title in recent seasons and for the second year running it was the Macaire-trained **So French** who provided Reveley with his biggest win in the Grand Steeple-Chase de Paris. Taking up the running going out on the final circuit, like the year before, So French put in a superb jump at Auteuil's most formidable obstacle, the 'rail, ditch and fence' five from home, and then found plenty when challenged in the closing stages to win by six lengths. So French had been given a light build-up in the spring, winning a minor event over hurdles before beating his stable-companion, the 2014 Grand Steeple-Chase winner **Storm of Saintly**, in the Prix Murat. So French is only a six-year-old, and if he can avoid setbacks he would have good prospects of becoming the first horse to win three consecutive editions of the Grand Steeple-Chase since the seven-year-old Katko completed his hat-trick in 1990. Katko's trainer Bernard Secly holds the record for the most number of wins in the Grand Steeple-Chase but Macaire is only one behind him now with five victories. Since Katko, the Francois Doumen-trained Ucello II (1993/94) and the triple winner Mid Dancer, who won his first Grand Steeple-Chase aged six and was successful again aged ten and eleven

Grand Steeple-Chase de Paris, Auteuil—So French (left) and champion jockey James Reveley stay on best from the last to win France's top jumping prize for the second year running; the hooded Perfect Impulse fares best of the rest ahead of Carriacou (between first two), Sainte Turgeon and the light grey Bipolaire

Prix Heros XII, Auteuil—Magalen Bryant's pair So French (far side) and Milord Thomas (right) have won the last three editions of the Grand Steeple-Chase de Paris between them; the latter comes out narrowly on top in this Group 3 contest despite a hefty penalty, with eventual fourth Saint Pistol between them as they clear the water

in 2011/12, are the only others to have won in successive years. Katko's half-brother Kotkijet and Princesse d'Anjou, the last mare to be successful, are the other dual winners this century.

It was a mare, the five-year-old **Perfect Impulse**, hitherto unbeaten in completed starts over fences, who gave So French the most to do, making much of the running and regaining the lead from the home turn until finding him too strong after they'd touched down together over the final obstacle. Like So French the year before, she won the Prix Morgex in November on her final start against her own age-group, and had then won a couple of the top chases against older rivals in the spring, though in both the Prix Troytown and the Prix Ingre she was chased home by fellow five-year-olds, **Paulougas** in the Troytown and **Carriacou** in the Ingre. While Paulougas, winner of the Prix Orcada in the autumn, was pulled up in the Grand Steeple-Chase, Carriacou ran well to be beaten ten lengths in third. Carriacou had won the top four-year-old chase of the autumn, the Prix Maurice Gillois, from **Sainte Turgeon** and Paulougas. The mare Sainte Turgeon's only win over fences came on her chasing debut, but she belied long odds to complete the frame in the Grand Steeple-Chase in which five-year-olds therefore took the next three places behind the winner. **Bipolaire** finished a good fifth in the Grand Steeple-Chase after a narrow win in the listed Prix William Head beforehand, while **Mali Borgia** was among those pulled up after running up a hat-trick which included the Prix Robert de Clermont-Tonnerre (from Carriacou and Bipolaire) in March.

So French's American owner Magalen Bryant had her colours carried to victory in the 2015 Grand Steeple-Chase by **Milord Thomas**, only fourth in the 2016 edition, but he had returned to his best in the autumn to gain a third consecutive victory in the Prix La Haye Jousselin in which So French was a well-held fourth. Featuring three Grand Steeple-Chase de Paris winners (Storm of Saintly was third), this was the best chase at Auteuil in the period under review in which the first four home in the 2016 Grand Steeple Chase de Paris took the first four places, albeit in a different order. Injury meant that Milord Thomas wasn't seen out again, but he'd put up an even better performance earlier in the autumn when winning the Prix Heros XII for the second time, beating So French a head conceding him 10 lb. The form of those two wins makes Milord Thomas the top-rated French chaser for the third year running.

Prix La Haye Jousselin, Auteuil—Milord Thomas goes on to land the top chase of the autumn for the third year running, though Alary (blaze) pushes him close; the runner-up subsequently failed to live up to Gold Cup aspirations for new connections in Britain

The fourth member of this leading quartet of chasers was **Alary** who broke into the top flight with his third in the 2016 Grand Steeple-Chase. He ran creditably to be beaten less than two lengths into third in the Heros XII but proved better still when running Milord Thomas to half a length at level weights in the La Haye Jousselin, confirming himself an out-and-out stayer and a high-class one at that. Unusually for an already-established leading French chaser, Alary was then sold to race in Britain as a potential Gold Cup horse for owners Ann and Alan Potts but showed nothing like his French form in three starts for Colin Tizzard. A French-trained chaser who emerged with a bit more credit from two appearances in Britain for Emmanuel Clayeux was **Vezelay** who took a remote third behind Cue Card in the Betfair Chase and would have shown similar form, set to finish fourth, when falling at the last in the Cotswold Chase. There was, however, a shock French-trained winner on Cheltenham's Trials day when Vezelay's stable-companion **Urgent de Gregaine** was a 50/1 winner of the cross-country handicap from out of the weights. A number of French-trained chasers have contested Cheltenham's cross-country events over the years but none had previously been successful.

A possible runner in Britain in future is the Scottish-owned six-year-old **Bon Augure**, winner of the Prix des Drags in June in a close finish with **Saint Pistol** and **Shannon Rock** who had finished seventh and sixth respectively in the Grand Steeple-Chase. That took Bon Augure's record at Auteuil to eight wins from his last ten starts over hurdles and fences despite a lengthy absence prior to his return in March after making a miraculous recovery from being struck into and severing a tendon in the autumn of 2015. At the age of eleven, Shannon Rock was the senior runner in the Grand Steeple-Chase which he was contesting for the sixth time. Whilst unable to add to his unique record in that contest (runner-up four times), Shannon Rock retained plenty of ability, also finishing second in the Prix Georges Courtois (to the 2013 Grand Steeple-Chase winner **Bel La Vie**) and third in the Ingre as well as the Drags.

Away from Auteuil, Enghien specialist **Miss de Champdoux** ended an era when completing a double in the track's most important chase and hurdle, the Grand Steeple-Chase d'Enghien and the Prix Leopold d'Orsetti in the autumn, the latter for the second year running on her final career start before retiring to stud. Enghien, which served as the Paris region's number two jumps track, closed at the end of 2016 as a cost-cutting measure (it continues to stage trotting), with its major races transferred to Compiegne. **The Stomp**, successful in the Prix Romati, and **Jazz In Montreux**, in the Prix Hopper for four-year-olds, won the first two group races over fences at their new venue in the spring. Owned by top Flat trainer Jean-Claude Rouget, The Stomp is a smart and prolific winner over both hurdles and fences and made it five wins from six starts in the period under review when winning the listed Prix Dawn Run back over hurdles at Auteuil in June.

As well as owning two of the best chasers, Magalen Bryant also had her colours carried by a couple of the leading hurdlers, **Blue Dragon** and **Device**. However, both were struck by injury which prevented either of them from landing the Grande Course de Haies d'Auteuil. Device missed the race altogether following a setback, while Blue Dragon disappointed for the second year running, losing his lead after jumping errors on the final circuit and eventually being pulled up after suffering what proved to be a pelvic injury. It was also the final ride for Blue Dragon's usual partner David Cottin who announced his retirement afterwards to take up a training career. Cottin won the last of his three champion jockey titles in 2012—some of his first big wins at Auteuil as a teenager had come with future Gold Cup winner Long Run—though had been struggling with his weight more recently on top of his serious injury in 2016. Blue Dragon had mixed fortunes after finishing third in the 2016 Grande Course de Haies. He made a winning return on the Flat in the autumn only to disappoint badly when odds on for the Grand Prix d'Automne but then bounced back later in November to win the Prix Leon Olry-Roederer from stable-companions **Tir Au But** and **Bosseur**. Blue Dragon was still some way below top form when third in the Prix Juigne and Prix Hypothese in the spring, albeit trying to concede plenty of weight to Device both times, but looked back to something like his top-class best when running out a twelve-length winner of the Prix Leon Rambaud in April. Much more impressive than when successful in the same race in 2016, he led home another one, two, three for his trainer Guy Cherel, with **Solway**, the Grand Prix d'Automne and Prix Juigne runner-up, and Bosseur taking the places, the latter going on to finish a creditable fourth in the Grande Course de Haies.

As for Device, he made a smooth transition from being top four-year-old in the autumn to open company in the spring. Two more wins against his own age group in the autumn in the Prix de Maisons-Laffitte and Prix Pierre de Lassus preceded his heavy fall when holding every chance two out in the Renaud du Vivier, while he followed his wins in the Juigne and Hypothese with a promising staying-on third on less favourable terms in the Prix La Barka. As a full brother to So French, Device would have been an interesting runner stepped up in trip for the Grande Course de Haies but a bruised foot ruled him out. **Capivari** was the main beneficiary of Device's fall in the Renaud du Vivier (beating the Willie Mullins-trained Footpad a head) but struggled against older rivals in the spring, albeit not disgraced when fifth in the Grande Course de Haies.

French hurdlers have struggled to hold their own against British and Irish rivals in their top events in recent seasons and L'Ami Serge was the third consecutive British-trained winner of the Grande Course de Haies; the Nicky Henderson-trained gelding had

Prix Leon Rambaud, Auteuil—a repeat success in the race for Blue Dragon and former champion David Cottin who announced his retirement from the saddle after the top hurdler disappointed in the Grande Course de Haies again on his next start

Grand Prix d'Automne, Auteuil—Alex de Larredya keeps the top hurdling prize of the autumn at home for the first time since 2012, chased home by Solway

previously finished runner-up in the La Barka to Shaneshill, who was the sixth winner in a row of that contest for the visitors and a fourth for Willie Mullins. However, the big hurdle in the autumn, the Grand Prix d'Automne, was kept at home for the first time since 2012 by **Alex de Larredya**, runner-up to the Paul Nicholls-trained Ptit Zig in the 2016 Grande Course de Haies. He had that rival back in third in November. Alex de Larredya had no easy task under penalties in the spring, but followed a fifth in the Prix La Barka with a back-to-form second in the Grande Course de Haies for the second year running, completing a one, two for Simon Munir, joint owner of L'Ami Serge. Alex de Larredya also started second favourite for the Long Walk Hurdle at Ascot in December but ran well below his French form, finishing over twenty lengths behind the winner Unowhatimeanharry in fifth. However, it was on this one patently below-par performance that Alex de Larredya was given what amounted to a crass assessment in the latest Anglo Irish Jump Classifications. According to the published ratings, Alex de Larredya was a 12 lb inferior horse to Ptit Zig whom he'd beaten nine lengths at Auteuil the previous month! Alex de Larredya was only two lengths behind the same horse at Ascot, the same distance he was beaten in the Grande Course de Haies the previous June.

Few other hurdlers managed to make their mark in the top contests. Another smart hurdler in the Cherel yard was **Protekapril** who followed a win in a minor event at Compiegne on his return in April with a much improved effort to finish fourth in the La Barka. **Ultraji** was an improved performer in the autumn (after landing the Grande Course de Haies de Clairefontaine, a listed handicap, during the summer), finishing third to Alex de Larredya in the Prix de Compiegne and then turning the tables on him with a surprise win in the Prix Carmarthen, though he sadly broke a leg in a fall in the Grand Prix d'Automne.

Simon Munir and Isaac Souede held a strong hand in the four-year-old chase division. As well as owning **Edward d'Argent** who dominated for much of the season (six out of six over fences), they also won the Group 1 Prix Ferdinand Dufaure in May with **Srelighonn**, a race which Edward d'Argent had to miss through injury. Only beaten twice in ten starts all told, Edward d'Argent didn't win any of his chases by impressive margins but successfully conceded weight all round each time in reeling off the Prix Congress in November and then the Prix Duc d'Anjou, Prix Fleuret (in which only three took him on) and the Prix Jean Stern (giving 9 lb to Srelighonn, beating him a length) in the spring. In Edward d'Argent's absence, Srelighonn went on to gain a hard-fought head victory over his stable-companion, the filly **Dalia Grandchamp**, in the Ferdinand Dufaure, his first success over fences. Dalia Grandchamp had come up against Edward d'Argent three times herself, finishing third in both the Congress and the Jean Stern. **Dalko Moriviere** (who has since joined Willie Mullins) was another of Edward d'Argent's regular rivals, finishing placed behind him in five consecutive starts, notably when runner-up in the Congress and Duc d'Anjou. **Dica de Thaix** didn't switch to fences until May but made it two out of three over the larger obstacles when winning the Prix La Perichole (in which Dalko Moriviere fell when leading five out) from **Darling des Bordes** and **Burn Out** who had finished fourth and third respectively in the Ferdinand Dufaure.

The star four-year-old, though, was the filly **De Bon Coeur**, the clear leader of her generation over hurdles who should have been unbeaten in seven starts. Another of James Reveley's regular rides, she looked all set to end her campaign with a Group 1 success in the Prix Alain du Breil when, just like Device in the Renaud du Vivier, she took a crashing fall at the second last when holding a narrow lead, though happily horse and rider were none the worse. Starting at Enghien, De Bon Coeur won three times in the autumn, notably the Prix Cambaceres by nine lengths and the same from the Prix Georges de Talhouet-Roy winner **Invicter** (not seen out again) and the Paul Nicholls-trained Dolos. Returning in the spring, De Bon Coeur beat **D'vina** (the top-rated filly in the three-year-old ratings in *Chasers & Hurdlers 2015/16*) in both the Prix d'Indy and Prix de Pepinvast, by twelve lengths in the latter contest, before putting up her best effort when running out the easy nine-length winner of the Prix Amadou from another filly, **D'Entree de Jeu**. The other filly to make her mark was **Titi de Montmartre**, winner of the Prix Bournosienne against her own sex and also of the final running of the Prix General de Saint-Didier at Enghien before the turn of the year. She was never a threat against older mares in the Dawn Run Novices' Hurdle at Cheltenham, but ran at least respectably back at Auteuil, finishing fourth, one place ahead of D'vina, in the Alain du Breil.

The Alain du Breil was another good result for the Munir/Souede partnership with the Guillaume Macaire-trained **Prince Ali** being the main beneficiary of De Bon Coeur's fall. He had a spell over fences after being pulled up in the Cambaceres in the autumn but was an improved performer put back over hurdles in the spring, running up a hat-trick in a listed event, a well-contested Prix Questarabad (from stable-companion **Candide**, a former Group 3 winner on the Flat at two) and the Alain du Breil, in which he showed further improvement to hold off the Willie Mullins-trained Bapaume after being left in front. **Kalifko** had been one of the early leaders of his generation over hurdles and remained so without improving, reaching the frame on several occasions behind De Bon Coeur (including when third in the Amadou) and running creditably again when fifth in the Questarabad. **Izzo**, a useful Flat recruit from Germany, won his first three starts

Prix Amadou, Auteuil—
top four-year-old hurdler De Bon Coeur easily maintains her unbeaten record

Prix Alain du Breil, Auteuil—Prince Ali sees off the challenge of the Willie Mullins pair Bapaume and Dandy Mag, though the Group 1 contest would almost certainly have gone to De Bon Coeur had she not fallen when leading two out

over hurdles, including a listed contest at Compiegne, before a very good third in the Questarabad. **Pop Art du Berlais** started out in claiming company but was an improved performer when swapping cheekpieces for blinkers, winning two listed contests at Auteuil in June.

The early leader among the latest crop of three-year-old hurdlers was the Polish-bred colt **Tunis** who improved through all five of his starts for Guillaume Macaire. He was something of an outsider when beating stable-companion **Master Dino** in the listed Prix Stanley but was a short-priced favourite when beating much the same rivals a second time in the Prix Aguado in June. **Echiquier Royal** improved from fourth in the Stanley to second in the Aguado, relegating Master Dino to third. **Ajas** looks worth another chance to confirm early promise as he followed an easy debut success with a beating of Echiquier Royal, Tunis and Master Dino on his next start. However, he lost all chance after two bad mistakes before being pulled up when favourite for the Stanley. The top race so far for three-year-old fillies, the Prix Sagan, was fought out by **Gold Filly** and **Whetstone** (a half-sister to So French and Device) who pulled upwards of ten lengths clear of the remainder. However, **Ellen des Mottes** would have been involved too had she not fallen when leading two out.

Chasers (5yo+)

165	Milord Thomas 8	147	Miss de Champdoux (f) 8	142	Dos Santos 7
161?	*Alary 7	147	Vezelay 8	141	Prince Philippe 7
160	So French 6	146	Arry 7	141	Roi Mage 5
159	Storm of Saintly 8	146	Perfect Impulse (f) 5	140	Amazing Comedy 7
150p	The Stomp 7	145	Paulougas 5	140	Brut Imperial 6
150	Bel La Vie 11	144	Forthing 6	140	Djagble 6
150	Bipolaire 6	144	Lachlan Bridge 9	140	Triana du Berlais (f) 5
150?	Kelthomas 8	144	Sainte Turgeon (f) 5	140	Yoko 6
149	Bon Augure 6	144	Valtor 5	140?	Le But 7
148	Mali Borgia 7	144	Winneyev 6	139	Cobra de Larre 5
148	Saint Pistol 9	143	Jemy Baie 8	139	Tir Au But 10
148	Shannon Rock 11	143	Saint Palois 9	139	Vanilla Crush 8
147	Carriacou 5	143	Vizir d'Estruval 8	138	Golden Chop 9
		142	Beguin d'Estruval 6	138	Kada Rique (f) 6

138 Poly Grandchamp 5
138 Tzar's Dancer 9
137 Class Conti 5
137 Farlow des Mottes 9
137 Galop Marin 5
137 Punch Nantais 5
137 Vicomte d'Anjou 6
136+ Corscia (f) 6
136+ Pindare 8
136 Bob And Co 6
136 Pinson du Rheu 6
136 Vieux Morvan 8
136? La Sulfureuse (f) 6
135 Allen Voran 11
135 Chahuteur 5
135 Corazones 5
135 Diamant Catalan 6
135 Polipa 11
135 Rhialco 12
135 Viking de Balme 8
135 Virtus d'Estruval 8
135? Rasique 7
134 Amirande 7
134 Le Costaud 6
134 *Polidam 8
133 Capferret 5
133 Saint Poursain 5
132+ Terrific (FR) (f) 6
132 Adagio des Bordes 7
132 Bestarabad 6
132 Borice 6
132 Caresse d'Estruval (f) 5
132 Chiffre d'Affaires 8
132 Fiasco du Pecos 6
132 Flavin 6
132 Kyalco 7
132 Mon Nickson 7
132 Urgent de Gregaine 9
131+ *Viky du Reponet (f) 8
131 Tosca La Diva (f) 6
130 Karelcytic 6
130 Polygona (f) 7
130 Speed Fire 5
130 Urumqi 6
130 Via Dolorosa 5
129 Crack de Reve 5
129 Mallorca (f) 7
129 Poliboy 6
129 Quart de Rhum 8
129 Saint Xavier 5
129 Styline (f) 5
128 Baltico Prince 5
128 Bellaville (f) 5
128 Candaline (f) 5
128 Coastalina (f) 5
128 Concerto d'Allen (f) 5
128 Forest Forest 5
128 Gorvello 8
128 Mat Maker 7
128 Mister Bali 5
128 Ozamo 10
128 Scawork 8
128 Sundriver 7
128 Tito dela Barriere 10
128 Ultra Lucky 9
127+ Ubu Rochelais 9
127 Bagdad Cafe 6

127 Bar Yton 5
127 Boston Paris (f) 5
127 Caiman Land 5
127 Extreme Sud 9
127 Korfou de Maspie 8
127 Martinstar 5
127 Posilox 11
127 Saint Richard 5
127 Saying Again 11
127 Silver Chop 8
127 Taillenterre (f) 6
126 My Maj 8
126 Pythagore 12
126 *Ralianka (f) 5
126 Unzo du Bara 9
125 Argentier 7
125 Baby Boy 6
125 Baraka de Thaix 6
125 Bazille 6
125 Bialco 6
125 Calva du Rib 5
125 Comeken 7
125 L'Espiguette (f) 6
125 Miss Balkania (f) 5
125 Prince Sumitas 6
125 Titanesque 10
125 Vinga (f) 8

Hurdlers (5yo+)
167 Blue Dragon 6
160 Alex de Larredya 7
153 Device 5
152 Protekapril 7
152 Solway 6
150 Bosseur 6
149 Ultraji 9
148+ Terrific (FR) (f) 6
148 Capivari 6
147 The Stomp 7
147 Tir Au But 10
147? Perly de Clermont 11
145 Miss de Champdoux (f) 8
144 Saint Call 6
144 Yoko 6
143 Adagio des Bordes 7
143 Polygona (f) 7
142 Ballotin 6
142? Caresse d'Estruval (f) 5
142? Diamond Charm 8
141 Galop Marin 5
141 Rusquela 7
141 Saint Goustan Blue 5
141? Golden Chop 9
140+ Corscia (f) 6
140 Beyond Henry 5
140 Biloute de Houelle 9
140 Rock The Race 6
140? Le Chateau 8
139 Serienschock 9
138 Forest Forest 5
138 Prince Philippe 7
137 Azucardel 6
137 Champ de Bataille 6
137 Park Light 7
137 Silver Axe 7
137 Song And Whisper 7
137 *Viky du Reponet (f) 8

136 Curly Basc (f) 5
136 Paulougas 5
136 Plumeur 10
136 Ramdam 5
136 Taillenterre (f) 6
135 Hippomene 7
135 Isabe (f) 5
135 Vokalise (f) 5
134 Christmas Rose 5
134 Martalette (f) 7
134? Ami Sol 6
133 Achour 6
133 Fracafigura Has (f) 6
133 Lord Prestige 10
133 Politikar 5
133 Vezelay 8
133 Yosille (f) 5
132 Buck's Bank 9
132 Flight Zero 6
132 Perfect Impulse (f) 5
132 Poligroom 7
131 Brut Imperial 6
131 Dos Santos 7
131 Magneticjim 5
131 Mali Borgia 7
131 Storm of Saintly 8
130 Caiman Land 5
130 Corazones 5
130 Epicea 7
129 Amirande 7
129 Arry 7
129 Bon Augure 6
129 Cabriole Mag (f) 5
129 Cotton Bowl 5
129 Monsamou 8
129 My Maj 8
129 Roi Mage 5
129 Solonder 6
128+ Cobra de Larre 5
128+ Kobrouk 6
128+ Sainte Turgeon (f) 5
128 Capallyne 5
128 Carriacou 5
128 Irouficar Has 7
128 Kada Rique (f) 6
128 Panis Moon (f) 5
128 Sable Gris 5
127+ Forthing 6
127+ So French 6
127 Lachlan Bridge 9
127 Mocalacato Has 5
127 News Reel 7
127 Sierra Nevada (f) 7
126 Capharnaum 5
126 Farlow des Mottes 9
126 Friedrichspalast 5
126 Fyrmyin 6
126 Le Patriote 5
126 *Max do Brazil 5
126 Ponte Fortune (f) 5
126 Porlock Bay 6
126 Saint Poursain 5
126 Singapur 6
125+ Beguin d'Estruval 6
125+ Le But 7
125 Boston Paris (f) 5
125 Ci Blue 5

125	Compatriote *10*	143	Invicter	123	Daring Rose (f)
125	Coulmalinas *5*	142	D'vina (f)	123	Defit d'Estruval
125	Kasarca *5*	141	Kalifko	123	Ejo Pritchard (f)
125	Lauline (f) *5*	140	Izzo	123	Long Breeze
125	L'Espiguette (f) *6*	139	Candide	123	Lou Princess (f)
125	Pythagore *12*	139	D'Entree de Jeu (f)	123	Quiliano
125	Titi Loup *5*	138p	Miss Salsa Blue (f)	122	Beaute Promise (f)
125	Vlatan *5*	138	Pop Art du Berlais	122	Dad
125?	*Attalco *6*	137	Desinvolte	122	Danseur Jaguen
125?	Prince of Fields *5*	137	Got Away (f)	122	Grand Pretendant
125d	Happening *5*	137	Pyromane	122	Myboy
		136	Danse Avec Jersey	122	Olympic Torch
Chasers (4yo)		136	Jazz In Montreux	122	Pariano
145p	Edward d'Argent	134	Darling des Bordes	121	Delphi Collonges (f)
141	Srelighonn	134	Saint Calvados	121	Discret Et Royal
138p	Dalahast	134	Srelighonn	121	Djedda Conti (f)
138	Darling des Bordes	134	Titi de Montmartre (f)	121	Don Chaba
137	Dalia Grandchamp (f)	133p	Edward d'Argent	121	Epoustouflaunt (f)
136	Burn Out	133	Burn Out	121	Jubilatoire (f)
136	Dalko Moriviere	133	Hurkhan	121	*Monsieur Co
136	Dica de Thaix	133	Vision du Pont (f)	121	Nombe
133p	Castle du Berlais	132	Kakoline (f)	121	Un Comedien
133	Full Glass	132	Kingalola	120p	Duca de Thaix
132	Derby des Bruyeres	131	Burning Man	120	Doujani
130p	Jazz In Montreux	131	Dica de Thaix	120	Eclipse d'Ainay (f)
129	Malice des Epeires (f)	130	Salsaretta (f)	120	Hotmale Has
129	Tavera (f)	129	Dabrovka (f)	120	Nurmi
127	Polygame	128	A Mi Manera (f)	120	Pennymart
127	Square Marceau	128	Liberatore	120	Polygame
126p	Saint Rajh	128	Ludo Sol (f)	120	*Royal Hawk
126	Goldkhov	127p	Chameron	120	Tahanrun
126§	Ludo Sol (f)	127	Gold In Love (f)	120	*Wealth des Mottes
125	Danseur Jaguen	127	Grand Depart		
125	L'Estran	127	Le Mans	**Hurdlers (3yo)**	
124	Bergerac	127	Madiran	142	Tunis
123p	Daring Rose (f)	127	Mondieu	137	Gold Filly (f)
123	D'Accord d'Accord (f)	127	Saint Leo	136	Ajas
123	Dragon d'Estruval	127	Zapato	135	Echiquier Royal
123	Dream Roque	126p	Foreign Flower	135	Ellen des Mottes (f)
123	Kingalola	126	Daryasi	134	Master Dino
123	Middle	126	Destin d'Ajonc	134	Whetstone (f)
123	Okay Senam	126	*Poker Play	130p	Envoye Special
123	Prince Ali	126	Saint Pierrot	129	Malaya (f)
122+	Caruso Valtat	126	Spiderman	129	Santa Adelia (f)
122	Angel's Share (f)	126	Tavera (f)	127p	Mysterious Boy
122	Dont Stop Theparty	125p	Saint Rajh	127	My Way
122	Gold In Love (f)	125	Follow Me Soldier	125p	Opium
122	Ptiturf	125	Middle	125	Hell Boy
121p	Diva du Grand Val (f)	125	Roxinela (f)	124	Calotin
121p	*Monsieur Co	124	Felicie (f)	123	Elimay (f)
121	Discret Et Royal	124	Goddess Freja (f)	123	Spirit Sun
121	Kazarov	124	Kap Et Pas Cap	122	Brutus du Rheu
121	Topissime	124	Polimix	122	Rose Amelie Has (f)
121	West Kap	124	San Pedro de Senam	122	Shark du Berlais
120	Mainmise	124	Starkhov	121p	Ballywood
120	Pichelot	124	West Kap	121p	Demopolis
		123	Angel's Share (f)	121	Artemidor (f)
Hurdlers (4yo)		123	Castle du Berlais	121	World Amiral
158p	De Bon Coeur (f)	123	D'Accord d'Accord (f)	120	Equemauville
147	Prince Ali	123	Daddy Banbou	120	Moon Like Shadow (f)

NB Ratings relate to performances between July 2016 and June 2017. Horses marked with an * were trained in France for only part of the season; horses which were originally trained in France but subsequently showed much better form in Britain/Ireland are not included in the above lists.

INDEX TO PHOTOGRAPHS

PORTRAITS & SNAPSHOTS

Wicklow Brave............ 8 b.g. Beat Hollow – Moraine   *Caroline Norris*   921
Willoughby Court....... 6 br.g. Court Cave – Willoughby Sue   *Dinah Nicholson*   926

RACE PHOTOGRAPHS

coral.co.uk Best Price Guaranteed On Horse Racing Handicap Chase (Chepstow)	*Bill Selwyn*	82
Coral Cup Handicap Hurdle (Cheltenham)	*John Crofts*	792
coral.ie Hurdle (Extended Handicap) (Leopardstown)	*Caroline Norris*	397
coral.ie Leopardstown Handicap Chase (Leopardstown)	*Peter Mooney*	85
Coral Punchestown Gold Cup Chase (Punchestown)	*Bill Selwyn*	219
Coral Punchestown Gold Cup Chase (Punchestown)	*Peter Mooney*	757
Coral Scottish Grand National Handicap Chase (Ayr)	*John Grossick*	892
Coral Welsh Grand National Handicap Chase (Chepstow)	*Bill Selwyn*	564
Crabbie's Top Novices' Hurdle (Aintree)	*Bill Selwyn*	652
Deloitte Novices' Hurdle (Leopardstown)	*Caroline Norris*	91
Doom Bar Anniversary 4-Y-O Juvenile Hurdle (Aintree)	*Ed Byrne*	257
Doom Bar Maghull Novices' Chase (Aintree)	*George Selwyn*	722
Doom Bar Sefton Novices' Hurdle (Aintree)	*Ed Byrne*	829
Dornan Engineering Relkeel Hurdle (Cheltenham)	*George Selwyn*	40
EMS Copiers Novices' Handicap Chase (Punchestown)	*Caroline Norris*	930
European Breeders' Fund Matchbook VIP National Hunt Novices' Handicap Hurdle Final (Sandown)	*Ed Byrne*	521
Flogas Novices' Chase (Dr P. J. Moriarty) (Leopardstown)	*Healy Racing*	269
Florida Pearl Novices' Chase (Punchestown)	*Caroline Norris*	84
Frank Ward Solicitors Arkle Novices' Chase (Leopardstown)	*Caroline Norris*	768
Fred Winter Juvenile Handicap Hurdle (Cheltenham)	*Peter Mooney*	329
Fulke Walwyn Kim Muir Challenge Cup Amateur Riders' Handicap Chase (Cheltenham)	*Ed Byrne*	277
galliardhomes.com Cleeve Hurdle (Cheltenham)	*Ed Byrne*	876
Glenfarclas Chase (Cross Country) (Cheltenham)	*Ed Byrne*	180
Goffs Nickel Coin Mares' Standard Open National Hunt Flat Race (Aintree)	*John Grossick*	243
Grande Course de Haies d'Auteuil Hurdle (Auteuil)	*Bertrand*	454
Growise Champion Novices' Chase (Ellier) (Punchestown)	*Caroline Norris*	270
Guinness Galway Hurdle Handicap (Galway)	*Caroline Norris*	208
Guinness Handicap Chase (Punchestown)	*Bill Selwyn*	752
Guinness Kerry National Handicap Chase (Listowel)	*Caroline Norris*	932
Hennessy Gold Cup Chase (Handicap) (Newbury)	*Ed Byrne*	563
Herald Champion Novices' Hurdle (Punchestown)	*Bill Selwyn*	201
Herald Champion Novices' Hurdle (Punchestown)	*Healy Racing*	445
Irish Daily Mirror Novices' Hurdle (War of Attrition) (Punchestown)	*Caroline Norris*	188
Irish Stallion Farms European Breeders Fund Mares' Novices' Hurdle Championship Final (Fairyhouse)	*Caroline Norris*	86
JCB Triumph Hurdle (Cheltenham)	*Ed Byrne*	256
JLT Long Walk Hurdle (Ascot)	*George Selwyn*	875
JLT Melling Chase (Aintree)	*Ed Byrne*	337
JLT Novices' Chase (Golden Miller) (Cheltenham)	*John Crofts*	941
JNwine.com Champion Chase (Down Royal)	*Healy Racing*	886
John Durkan Memorial Punchestown Chase (Punchestown)	*Caroline Norris*	274
Johnny Henderson Grand Annual Challenge Cup Handicap Chase (Cheltenham)	*George Selwyn*	702
Jordan Electrics Ltd Future Champions Novices' Chase (Ayr)	*John Grossick*	211
JT McNamara National Hunt Challenge Cup Amateur Riders' Novices' Chase (Cheltenham)	*Ed Byrne*	843
Keltbray Swinley Chase (Limited Handicap) (Ascot)	*Ed Byrne*	812
Kempton racecourse stables, January 1967	*Central Press Photos*	833
Ladbrokes Champion Stayers' Hurdle (Punchestown)	*Caroline Norris*	877
Ladbrokes Ireland Boyne Hurdle (Navan)	*Caroline Norris*	796
Lavazza Jolie Silver Cup Handicap Chase (Listed) (Ascot)	*Ed Byrne*	687
Lawlor's Hotel Novices' Hurdle (Slaney) (Naas)	*Peter Mooney*	251
Lexus Chase (Leopardstown)	*Caroline Norris*	624
Lismullen Hurdle (Navan)	*Caroline Norris*	764
Manifesto Novices' Chase (Aintree)	*George Selwyn*	327
Martin Pipe Conditional Jockeys' Handicap Hurdle (Cheltenham)	*Martin Lynch*	187
Matchbook Imperial Cup Handicap Hurdle (Sandown)	*Ed Byrne*	475

ADDITIONAL PHOTOGRAPHS

The following photos appear in the Introduction:- Sizing John montage (portrait taken by Caroline Norris, racing shots by Peter Mooney and Bill Selwyn), Arkle at the Horse of the Year Show (Central Press), Altior wins the Arkle Challenge Trophy (John Crofts), Sprinter Sacre is retired (Bill Selwyn), Gordon Elliott leading trainer at Cheltenham (Caroline Norris), Michael and Anita O'Leary (Bill Selwyn), Sizing John and connections (Bill Selwyn), Nicky Henderson wins his fourth trainers' title (Bill Selwyn), Grand National weights launch at the Victoria & Albert Museum (George Selwyn), Brian Harding and Paul Moloney (both taken by George Selwyn).

Timeform Champions of 2016/17:- Altior (taken by Bill Selwyn)

Credits for the photographs in 'Top Horses In France' are as follows:-
Grand Steeple-Chase de Paris, Prix Heros XII, Prix La Haye Jousselin,
Prix Leon Rambaud, Grand Prix d'Automne, Prix Amadou,
Prix Alain du Breil (all taken by Bertrand)

HORSE OF THE YEAR

1975/76	Night Nurse	**178**
1976/77	Night Nurse	**182**
1977/78	Monksfield	**177**
1978/79	Monksfield	**180**
1979/80	Sea Pigeon	**175**
1980/81	Little Owl	**176**
1981/82	Silver Buck	**175**
1982/83	Badsworth Boy	**179**
1983/84	Dawn Run	**173**
1984/85	Burrough Hill Lad	**184**
1985/86	Dawn Run	**167**
1986/87	Desert Orchid	**177**
1987/88	Desert Orchid	**177**
1988/89	Desert Orchid	**182**
1989/90	Desert Orchid	**187**
1990/91	Morley Street	**174**
1991/92	Carvill's Hill	**182**
1992/93	Jodami	**174p**
1993/94	Danoli	**172p**
1994/95	Master Oats	**183**
1995/96	One Man	**179**
1996/97	Make A Stand	**165**
1997/98	Istabraq	**172+**
1998/99	Istabraq	**177+**
1999/00	Istabraq	**180**
2000/01	First Gold	**180**
2001/02	Baracouda	**169+**
2002/03	Best Mate	**182**
2003/04	Moscow Flyer	**183**
2004/05	Moscow Flyer	**184+**
2005/06	Brave Inca	**167**
2006/07	Kauto Star	**184+**
2007/08	Denman	**180p**
2008/09	Kauto Star	**184**
2009/10	Kauto Star	**191**
2010/11	Hurricane Fly	**172**
2011/12	Big Buck's	**176+**
2012/13	Sprinter Sacre	**192p**
2013/14	More of That	**173p**
2014/15	Don Cossack	**180**
2015/16	Don Cossack	**183**
2016/17	Altior	**175p**

Best Two-Mile Chaser

Year	Horse	Rating	Year	Horse	Rating
75/76	Lough Inagh	167	96/97	Martha's Son	177
76/77	Skymas	156	97/98	One Man	176
77/78	Tingle Creek	154	98/99	Direct Route	166
78/79	Siberian Sun	151	99/00	Flagship Uberalles	175
79/80	I'm A Driver	163	00/01	Flagship Uberalles	175
80/81	Anaglogs Daughter	171	01/02	Flagship Uberalles	170
81/82	Rathgorman	170	02/03	Moscow Flyer	170p
82/83	Badsworth Boy	179	03/04	Moscow Flyer	183
83/84	Badsworth Boy	177	04/05	Moscow Flyer	184+
84/85	Bobsline	164+	05/06	Kauto Star	166+
85/86	Dawn Run	167	06/07	Kauto Star	184+
86/87	Pearlyman	171	07/08	Master Minded	179
87/88	Pearlyman	174	08/09	Master Minded	179
88/89	Desert Orchid	182	09/10	Big Zeb	169
89/90	Desert Orchid	187	10/11	Big Zeb	172
90/91	Desert Orchid	178	11/12	Sprinter Sacre	175p
91/92	Remittance Man	173	12/13	Sprinter Sacre	192p
92/93	Katabatic	161?	13/14	Sire de Grugy	172
93/94	Viking Flagship	166	14/15	Un de Sceaux	169p
94/95	Viking Flagship	169	15/16	Douvan	180p
95/96	Klairon Davis	177	16/17	Douvan	182

Best Staying Chaser

Year	Horse	Rating	Year	Horse	Rating
75/76	Captain Christy	182	97/98	Cool Dawn	173
76/77	Bannow Rambler	163	98/99	Suny Bay	176
77/78	Midnight Court	164	99/00	See More Business	182
78/79	Gay Spartan	166	00/01	First Gold	180
79/80	Silver Buck	171	01/02	Best Mate	173
80/81	Little Owl	176		Florida Pearl	173
81/82	Silver Buck	175	02/03	Best Mate	182
82/83	Bregawn	177	03/04	Best Mate	176+
83/84	Burrough Hill Lad	175	04/05	Kicking King	182
	Wayward Lad	175	05/06	Beef Or Salmon	174x
84/85	Burrough Hill Lad	184	06/07	Kauto Star	184+
85/86	Burrough Hill Lad	183	07/08	Kauto Star	182
86/87	Desert Orchid	177	08/09	Kauto Star	184
87/88	Desert Orchid	177	09/10	Kauto Star	191
88/89	Desert Orchid	182	10/11	Long Run	184
89/90	Desert Orchid	187	11/12	Kauto Star	179
90/91	Desert Orchid	178	12/13	Bobs Worth	179
91/92	Carvill's Hill	182	13/14	Cue Card	180
92/93	Jodami	174p	14/15	Don Cossack	180
93/94	The Fellow	171	15/16	Don Cossack	183
94/95	Master Oats	183	16/17	Cue Card	174
95/96	One Man	179		Thistlecrack	174
96/97	One Man	176			

Best Novice Chaser

Year	Horse	Rating	Year	Horse	Rating
75/76	Bannow Rambler	152p	96/97	Strong Promise	171+
76/77	Tree Tangle	159§	97/98	Escartefigue	171p
77/78	The Dealer	145	98/99	Nick Dundee	164+
78/79	Silver Buck	151	99/00	Gloria Victis	172
79/80	Anaglogs Daughter	156	00/01	Bacchanal	161p
80/81	Clayside	145		Shotgun Willy	161
81/82	Brown Chamberlin	147p	01/02	Moscow Flyer	159p
82/83	Righthand Man	150	02/03	Beef Or Salmon	165p
83/84	Bobsline	161p	03/04	Strong Flow	156p
84/85	Drumadowney	159	04/05	Ashley Brook	154+
85/86	Pearlyman	150		Fundamentalist	154p
86/87	Kildimo	151p		Ollie Magern	154
87/88	Danish Flight	156p	05/06	Monet's Garden	156p
88/89	Carvill's Hill	169p	06/07	Denman	161p
89/90	Celtic Shot	152p	07/08	Tidal Bay	161+
90/91	Remittance Man	153p	08/09	Cooldine	158p
91/92	Miinnehoma	152p	09/10	Tataniano	158p
92/93	Sybillin	156	10/11	Wishfull Thinking	165
93/94	Monsieur Le Cure	156p	11/12	Sprinter Sacre	175p
94/95	Brief Gale	159	12/13	Simonsig	166p
95/96	Mr Mulligan	154			

13/14	Holywell	**158p**	15/16	Douvan	**180p**
	Balder Succes	**158**	16/17	Altior	**175p**
14/15	Vautour	**171p**			

Best Two-Mile Hurdler

75/76	Night Nurse	**178**	96/97	Make A Stand	**165**
76/77	Night Nurse	**182**	97/98	Istabraq	**172+**
77/78	Monksfield	**177**	98/99	Istabraq	**177+**
78/79	Monksfield	**180**	99/00	Istabraq	**180**
79/80	Sea Pigeon	**175**	00/01	Istabraq	**180**
80/81	Sea Pigeon	**175**	01/02	Limestone Lad	**167**
81/82	For Auction	**174**	02/03	Rooster Booster	**170**
82/83	Gaye Brief	**175**	03/04	Hardy Eustace	**167**
83/84	Dawn Run	**173**	04/05	Hardy Eustace	**165**
84/85	Browne's Gazette	**172**	05/06	Brave Inca	**167**
85/86	See You Then	**173**	06/07	Sublimity	**164**
86/87	See You Then	**173**	07/08	Sizing Europe	**165**
87/88	Celtic Shot	**170**	08/09	Binocular	**166**
88/89	Beech Road	**172**	09/10	Binocular	**168**
89/90	Kribensis	**169**	10/11	Hurricane Fly	**172**
90/91	Morley Street	**174**	11/12	Hurricane Fly	**173**
91/92	Granville Again	**165p**	12/13	Hurricane Fly	**173**
92/93	Mighty Mogul	**170**	13/14	Jezki	**171**
93/94	Danoli	**172p**	14/15	Faugheen	**171+**
94/95	Alderbrook	**174p**	15/16	Faugheen	**176**
95/96	Alderbrook	**174**	16/17	Buveur d'Air	**170**

Best Staying Hurdler

75/76	Comedy of Errors	**170**	97/98	Paddy's Return	**168**
76/77	Night Nurse	**182**	98/99	Deano's Beeno	**165**
77/78	Monksfield	**177**		Princeful	**165**
78/79	Monksfield	**180**	99/00	Limestone Lad	**177**
79/80	Pollardstown	**167**	00/01	Le Sauvignon	**178**
80/81	Daring Run	**171+**	01/02	Baracouda	**169+**
81/82	Daring Run	**171**	02/03	Baracouda	**175**
82/83	Gaye Brief	**175**	03/04	Iris's Gift	**172**
83/84	Dawn Run	**173**	04/05	Inglis Drever	**162**
84/85	Bajan Sunshine	**162**	05/06	Mighty Man	**166**
85/86	Gaye Brief	**167**	06/07	Mighty Man	**172**
86/87	Galmoy	**165**	07/08	Inglis Drever	**169**
87/88	Galmoy	**160**	08/09	Big Buck's	**174+**
88/89	Rustle	**169**	09/10	Big Buck's	**174+**
89/90	Trapper John	**159**	10/11	Big Buck's	**176+**
90/91	King's Curate	**164**	11/12	Big Buck's	**176+**
91/92	Nomadic Way	**162**	12/13	Big Buck's	**176+**
92/93	Sweet Duke	**161**	13/14	More of That	**173p**
93/94	Sweet Glow	**162**	14/15	Jezki	**168**
94/95	Dorans Pride	**167**	15/16	Thistlecrack	**174p**
95/96	Pleasure Shared	**163p**	16/17	Nichols Canyon	**165**
96/97	Paddy's Return	**164**		Unowhatimeanharry	**165**

Best Novice Hurdler

75/76	Grand Canyon	**159**	92/93	Montelado	**150p**
76/77	Outpoint	**154**	93/94	Danoli	**172p**
77/78	Golden Cygnet	**176**	94/95	Alderbrook	**174p**
78/79	Venture To Cognac	**162**	95/96	Pleasure Shared	**163p**
79/80	Slaney Idol	**143**	96/97	Make A Stand	**165**
80/81	Dunaree	**159**	97/98	French Holly	**151p**
81/82	Angelo Salvini	**149**	98/99	Barton	**153p**
82/83	Dawn Run	**168**	99/00	Monsignor	**158p**
83/84	Desert Orchid	**158**	00/01	Baracouda	**172**
84/85	Asir	**148p**	01/02	Intersky Falcon	**152p**
85/86	River Ceiriog	**158p**	02/03	Iris's Gift	**172**
86/87	The West Awake	**153p**	03/04	Inglis Drever	**152**
87/88	Carvill's Hill	**157p**	04/05	Ambobo	**149+**
88/89	Sondrio	**152p**	05/06	Black Jack Ketchum	**159p**
	Wishlon	**152+**	06/07	Wichita Lineman	**152p**
89/90	Regal Ambition	**151**	07/08	Binocular	**156p**
90/91	Ruling	**167**	08/09	Hurricane Fly	**157p**
91/92	Royal Gait	**164p**	09/10	Dunguib	**152**

10/11	Al Ferof	**158**	14/15	Douvan	**168p**
11/12	Simonsig	**162p**	15/16	Altior	**167p**
12/13	My Tent Or Yours	**167p**	16/17	Labaik	**160§**
13/14	Faugheen	**166p**			

Best Juvenile Hurdler

75/76	Valmony	**157**	97/98	Deep Water	**149p**
76/77	Meladon	**149**	98/99	Hors La Loi III	**162p**
77/78	Major Thompson	**144**	99/00	Grand Seigneur	**148p**
78/79	Pollardstown	**141**	00/01	Jair du Cochet	**163**
79/80	Hill of Slane	**144**	01/02	Scolardy	**147**
80/81	Broadsword	**144**	02/03	Nickname	**142**
81/82	Shiny Copper	**141**	03/04	Maia Eria	**143**
82/83	Sabin du Loir	**147p**	04/05	Faasel	**144p**
83/84	Northern Game	**142**		Penzance	**144p**
84/85	Out of The Gloom	**151**	05/06	Detroit City	**146p**
85/86	Dark Raven	**153p**	06/07	Katchit	**151**
86/87	Aldino	**154**	07/08	Binocular	**156p**
87/88	Kribensis	**143p**	08/09	Zaynar	**155p**
88/89	Royal Derbi	**144**	09/10	Soldatino	**147p**
89/90	Sybillin	**138**	10/11	Zarkandar	**155p**
90/91	Oh So Risky	**149p**	11/12	Grumeti	**148**
91/92	Staunch Friend	**151p**	12/13	Our Conor	**165p**
92/93	Shawiya	**141p**	13/14	Le Rocher	**152**
93/94	Mysilv	**144p**	14/15	Peace And Co	**161P**
94/95	Kissair	**143p**	15/16	Apple's Jade	**157p**
95/96	Escartefigue	**159**	16/17	Defi du Seuil	**151p**
96/97	Grimes	**138p**			

Best Bumper Performer

93/94	Aries Girl	**123**	06/07	Theatrical Moment	**124**
94/95	Dato Star	**120**	07/08	Cousin Vinny	**134**
95/96	Wither Or Which	**122**	08/09	Dunguib	**131**
96/97	Florida Pearl	**124**	09/10	Cue Card	**132**
97/98	Alexander Banquet	**126**	10/11	Cheltenian	**128**
98/99	Monsignor	**122**	11/12	Don Cossack	**128**
99/00	Quadco	**129**	12/13	Briar Hill	**130**
00/01	The Bajan Bandit	**128**	13/14	Shaneshill	**124**
01/02	Pizarro	**123**	14/15	Bellshill	**126**
	Rhinestone Cowboy	**123**	15/16	Ballyandy	**123**
02/03	Rhinestone Cowboy	**123**		Blow By Blow	**123**
03/04	Secret Ploy	**122**	16/17	Fayonagh	**118**
04/05	Karanja	**128**		Paloma Blue	**118**
05/06	Leading Run	**123**			

Best Hunter Chaser

75/76	Otter Way	**143**	96/97	Celtic Abbey	**136p**
76/77	Under Way	**124**		Fantus	**136**
77/78	Spartan Missile	**133**	97/98	Earthmover	**140p**
78/79	Spartan Missile	**133+**	98/99	Castle Mane	**148p**
79/80	Rolls Rambler	**132**	99/00	Cavalero	**142**
80/81	Spartan Missile	**169**	00/01	Sheltering	**136**
81/82	Compton Lad	**142**	01/02	Torduff Express	**130**
82/83	Eliogarty	**147**	02/03	Kingscliff	**137p**
83/84	Venture To Cognac	**149**	03/04	Earthmover	**133**
84/85	Further Thought	**141**	04/05	Sleeping Night	**148**
85/86	Ah Whisht	**148**	05/06	Katarino	**133+**
86/87	Observe	**146**	06/07	Drombeag	**131**
87/88	Certain Light	**147**	07/08	Christy Beamish	**137**
88/89	Call Collect	**142p**	08/09	Cappa Bleu	**139p**
89/90	Mystic Music	**143**	09/10	Baby Run	**135**
90/91	Mystic Music	**143?**	10/11	Baby Run	**139**
91/92	Rushing Wild	**127p**	11/12	Salsify	**139**
92/93	Double Silk	**122p**	12/13	Salsify	**140**
93/94	Double Silk	**130p**	13/14	Tammys Hill	**137**
	Elegant Lord	**130p**	14/15	Prince de Beauchene	**146**
94/95	Fantus	**139p**	15/16	On The Fringe	**138**
95/96	Elegant Lord	**138p**	16/17	Foxrock	**142**

BIG RACE WINNERS

The record, dating back to the 1992/3 season (earlier results can be found in *Chasers & Hurdlers 1991/92* and preceding editions), includes the Timeform Rating recorded by the winner in the race (not its Timeform Annual Rating), the weight carried (usually preceded by age), starting price, trainer, jockey and number of runners. Race conditions and sponsors' names in the race titles are for the 2016/17 runnings. An asterisk prior to a horse's name denotes that it was awarded the race.

Britain

BetVictor GOLD CUP HANDICAP CHASE (Gr 3) (Cheltenham 2½m110y)

Year	Rating	Horse	SP	Trainer	Jockey	Runners
1992	153	Tipping Tim 7-10-10: 11/2		N A Twiston-Davies	C Llewellyn	16
1993	160	Bradbury Star 8-11-8: 13/2		J T Gifford	D Murphy	15
1994	172	Bradbury Star 9-11-11: 5/1		J T Gifford	P Hide[3]	14
1995	164	Dublin Flyer 9-11-8: 4/1		T A Forster	B Powell	12
1996	154	Challenger du Luc 6-10-2: 7/1		M C Pipe	R Dunwoody	12
1997	159	Senor El Betrutti 8-10-0: 33/1		Mrs S Nock	J Osborne	9
1998	158	Cyfor Malta 5-11-3: 3/1		M C Pipe	A P McCoy	12
1999	152	The Outback Way 9-10-0: 9/1		Miss V Williams	N Williamson	14
2000	157	Lady Cricket 6-10-13: 5/1		M C Pipe	A P McCoy	15
2001	158	Shooting Light 8-11-3: 9/4		M C Pipe	A P McCoy	14
2002	166	Cyfor Malta 9-11-9: 16/1		M C Pipe	B J Geraghty	15
2003	161	Fondmort 7-10-3: 3/1		N J Henderson	M A Fitzgerald	9
2004	152	Celestial Gold 6-10-2: 12/1		M C Pipe	T J Murphy	14
2005	159	Our Vic 7-11-7: 9/2		M C Pipe	T J Murphy	18
2006	145	Exotic Dancer 6-11-2: 16/1		J O'Neill	A P McCoy	16
2007	149	L'Antartique 7-10-13: 13/2		F Murphy	G Lee	20
2008	153	Imperial Commander 7-10-7: 13/2		N A Twiston-Davies	P J Brennan	19
2009	155	Tranquil Sea 7-10-13: 11/2		E J O'Grady	A J McNamara	16
2010	153	Little Josh 8-10-5: 20/1		N A Twiston-Davies	S Twiston-Davies[3]	18
2011	160	Great Endeavour 7-10-3: 8/1		David Pipe	Timmy Murphy	20
2012	169	Al Ferof 7-11-8: 8/1		Paul Nicholls	R Walsh	18
2013	161	Johns Spirit 6-10-2: 7/1		Jonjo O'Neill	Richie McLernon	20
2014	147	Caid du Berlais 5-10-13: 10/1		Paul Nicholls	Sam Twiston-Davies	18
2015	149	Annacotty 7-11-0: 12/1		Alan King	Ian Popham	20
2016	158	Taquin du Seuil 9-11-11: 8/1		Jonjo O'Neill	Aidan Coleman	17

stanjames.com GREATWOOD HANDICAP HURDLE (Gr 3)
(Cheltenham 2m½f; listed prior to 2004)

Year	Rating	Horse	SP	Trainer	Jockey	Runners
1992	130	Valfinet 5-10-9: 7/2		M C Pipe	P Scudamore	9
1993	144	Leotard 6-12-0: 3/1		O Sherwood	J Osborne	7
1994	156	Atours 6-11-5: 3/1		D R C Elsworth	P Holley	10
1995	135	Lonesome Train 6-9-9: 33/1		C Weedon	B Fenton[5]	15
1996	146	Space Trucker 5-11-11: 7/1		Mrs J Harrington (Ir)	J Osborne	9
1997	139	Mr Percy 6-10-9: 14/1		J T Gifford	P Hide	17
1998	155	Grey Shot 6-11-5: 11/4		I A Balding	J Osborne	16
1999	132	Rodock 5-10-0: 11/4		M C Pipe	A P McCoy	13
2000	139	Hulysse Royal 5-10-0: 9/1		O Sherwood	J A McCarthy	12
2001	160	Westender 5-10-13: 11/8		M C Pipe	A P McCoy	13
2002	166	Rooster Booster 8-11-12: 7/1		P J Hobbs	S Durack	11
2003	161	Rigmarole 5-11-2: 33/1		P F Nicholls	R Walsh	10
2004	148	Accordion Etoile 5-10-6: 10/3		Paul Nolan (Ir)	J Cullen	9
2005	146	Lingo 6-10-6: 5/1		J O'Neill	A P McCoy	19
2006	160	Detroit City 4-11-12: 6/5		P J Hobbs	R Johnson	9
2007	145	Sizing Europe 5-11-6: 5/1		H de Bromhead (Ir)	T J Murphy	19
2008	129	Numide 5-10-3: 5/1		G L Moore	J Moore	12
2009	160	Khyber Kim 7-11-9: 9/1		N A Twiston-Davies	P J Brennan	15
2010	160	Menorah 5-11-12: 6/1		P J Hobbs	R Johnson	17
2011	158	Brampour 4-11-4: 12/1		Paul Nicholls	Harry Derham[7]	23
2012	138	Olofi 6-10-11: 8/1		Tom George	Paddy Brennan	18

2013	133	Dell' Arca 4-10-5: 12/1	David Pipe	Tom Scudamore	18
2014	151	Garde La Victoire 5-11-9: 10/1	Philip Hobbs	Richard Johnson	15
2015	154	Old Guard 4-11-3: 12/1	Paul Nicholls	Harry Cobden[7]	17
2016	144	North Hill Harvey 5-11-0: 6/1	Dan Skelton	Harry Skelton	16

BETFAIR CHASE (Lancashire) (Gr 1) (Haydock 3m1f, run over 3m previously)

2005	173	Kingscliff 8-11-8: 8/1	R H Alner	R Walford	7
2006	172	Kauto Star 6-11-8: 11/10	P F Nicholls	R Walsh	6
2007	172	Kauto Star 7-11-7: 4/5	P F Nicholls	S Thomas	7
2008	161	Snoopy Loopy 10-11-7: 33/1	P Bowen	S E Durack	6
2009	175	Kauto Star 9-11-7: 4/6	P F Nicholls	R Walsh	7
2010	161	Imperial Commander 9-11-7: 10/11	N A Twiston-Davies	P Brennan	7
2011	174	Kauto Star 11-11-7: 6/1	Paul Nicholls	R Walsh	6
2012	170	Silviniaco Conti 6-11-7: 7/4	Paul Nicholls	R Walsh	5
2013	176	Cue Card 7-11-7: 9/1	Colin Tizzard	Joe Tizzard	8
2014	171	Silviniaco Conti 8-11-7: 10/3	Paul Nicholls	Noel Fehily	9
2015	181	Cue Card 9-11-7: 7/4	Colin Tizzard	Paddy Brennan	5
2016	174	Cue Card 10-11-7: 15/8	Colin Tizzard	Paddy Brennan	6

HENNESSY GOLD CUP CHASE (HANDICAP) (Gr 3) (Newbury 3m2½f)

1992	150	Sibton Abbey 7-10-0: 40/1	F Murphy	A Maguire	13
1993	151	Cogent 9-10-1: 10/1	A Turnell	D Fortt[7]	9
1994	144	One Man 6-10-0: 4/1	G Richards	A Dobbin	16
1995	160	Couldnt Be Better 8-10-8: 15/2	C P E Brooks	D Gallagher	11
1996	147	Coome Hill 7-10-0: 11/2	W W Dennis	J Osborne	11
1997	170	Suny Bay 8-11-8: 9/4	C P E Brooks	G Bradley	14
1998	158	Teeton Mill 9-10-5: 5/1	Miss V Williams	N Williamson	16
1999	148	Ever Blessed 7-10-0: 9/2	M Pitman	T J Murphy	13
2000	158	King's Road 7-10-7: 7/1	N A Twiston-Davies	G Goldstein	17
2001	153	What's Up Boys 7-10-12: 14/1	P J Hobbs	P Flynn	14
2002	157	*Gingembre 8-10-9: 16/1	Mrs L C Taylor	A Thornton	25
2003	154	Strong Flow 6-11-0: 5/1	P F Nicholls	R Walsh	21
2004	150	Celestial Gold 6-10-5: 9/4	M C Pipe	T J Murphy	14
2005	161	Trabolgan 7-11-12: 13/2	N J Henderson	M A Fitzgerald	19
2006	157	State of Play 6-11-4: 10/1	E Williams	P Moloney	16
2007	176	Denman 7-11-12: 5/1	P F Nicholls	S Thomas	18
2008	160	Madison du Berlais 7-11-4: 25/1	D E Pipe	T Scudamore	15
2009	181	Denman 9-11-12: 11/4	P F Nicholls	R Walsh	19
2010	163	Diamond Harry 7-11-0: 6/1	Nick Williams	D Jacob	18
2011	149	Carruthers 8-10-4: 10/1	Mark Bradstock	Mattie Batchelor	18
2012	171	Bobs Worth 7-11-6: 4/1	Nicky Henderson	Barry Geraghty	19
2013	157	Triolo d'Alene 6-11-1: 20/1	Nicky Henderson	Barry Geraghty	21
2014	159	Many Clouds 7-11-6: 8/1	Oliver Sherwood	Leighton Aspell	19
2015	161	Smad Place 8-11-4: 7/1	Alan King	Wayne Hutchinson	15
2016	162	Native River 6-11-1: 7/2	Colin Tizzard	Richard Johnson	19

stanjames.com 'FIGHTING FIFTH' HURDLE (Gr 1)

(Newcastle 2m; Wetherby in 2008 and Newbury in 2010; Gr 2 prior to 2004; handicap prior to 1998)

1992	135	Halkopous 6-11-0: 7/4	M H Tompkins	S Smith Eccles	6
1993		Abandoned			
1994	142	Batabanoo 5-11-0: 6/4	Mrs M Reveley	P Niven	4
1995	151	Padre Mio 7-10-10: 5/1	C P E Brooks	R C Guest	7
1996	151	Space Trucker 5-10-4: 5/2	Mrs J Harrington (Ir)	J Shortt	8
1997	141	Star Rage 7-11-2: 6/1	M Johnston	D Gallagher	8
1998	170	Dato Star 7-11-8: 13/8	J M Jefferson	L Wyer	6
1999	155	Dato Star 8-11-8: 4/9	J M Jefferson	L Wyer	6
2000	155	Barton 7-11-0: 8/13	T D Easterby	A Dobbin	6
2001	147	Landing Light 6-11-8: 4/5	N J Henderson	J R Kavanagh	5
2002	153	Intersky Falcon 5-11-8: 11/10	J O'Neill	L Cooper	6
2003	146	The French Furze 9-11-0: 25/1	N G Richards	B Harding	8
2004	157	Harchibald 5-11-7: 9/4	N Meade (Ir)	P Carberry	8
2005	150	Arcalis 5-11-7: 9/4	J H Johnson	A Dobbin	9
2006	150	Straw Bear 5-11-7: 1/1	N J Gifford	A P McCoy	9
2007	158	Harchibald 8-11-7: 4/1	N Meade (Ir)	P Carberry	8
2008	165	Punjabi 5-11-7: 8/11	N J Henderson	B J Geraghty	6
2009	160	Go Native 6-11-7: 25/1	N Meade (Ir)	D J Condon	7
2010	157	Peddlers Cross 5-11-7: 9/4	D McCain	J Maguire	5
2011	165	Overturn 7-11-7: 7/4	Donald McCain	Jason Maguire	5

2012	156	Countrywide Flame 4-11-7: 11/4	John Quinn	*Denis O'Regan*	4
2013	151	My Tent Or Yours 6-11-7: 8/11	Nicky Henderson	*A P McCoy*	8
2014	152	Irving 6-11-7: 6/4	Paul Nicholls	*Nick Scholfield*	6
2015	157	Identity Thief 5-11-7: 6/1	Henry de Bromhead (Ir)	*B J Cooper*	7
2016	153	Irving 8-11-7: 6/1	Paul Nicholls	*Harry Cobden*	6

BETFAIR TINGLE CREEK CHASE (Gr 1) (Sandown 2m, Cheltenham 2m½f in 2000 & 2010)

1992	159	Waterloo Boy 9-12-0: 11/4	D Nicholson	*R Dunwoody*	5
1993	162	Sybillin 7-11-9: 6/1	J G FitzGerald	*P Niven*	7
1994	165	Viking Flagship 7-11-7: 9/2	D Nicholson	*A Maguire*	6
1995	159	Sound Man 7-11-7: 5/6	E J O'Grady (Ir)	*R Dunwoody*	5
1996	160	Sound Man 8-11-7: 10/11	E J O'Grady (Ir)	*R Dunwoody*	4
1997	168	Ask Tom 8-11-7: 6/1	T P Tate	*R Garritty*	7
1998	154	Direct Route 7-11-7: 7/1	J H Johnson	*N Williamson*	10
1999	167	Flagship Uberalles 5-11-7: 10/3	P F Nicholls	*J Tizzard*	6
2000	175	Flagship Uberalles 6-11-7: 3/1	N T Chance	*R Johnson*	7
2001	170	Flagship Uberalles 7-11-7: 7/2	P J Hobbs	*R Widger*	6
2002	163	Cenkos 8-11-7: 6/1	P F Nicholls	*R Walsh*	6
2003	174	Moscow Flyer 9-11-7: 6/4	Mrs J Harrington (Ir)	*B J Geraghty*	7
2004	184	Moscow Flyer 10-11-7: 2/1	Mrs J Harrington (Ir)	*B J Geraghty*	7
2005	164	Kauto Star 5-11-7: 5/2	P F Nicholls	*M A Fitzgerald*	7
2006	166	Kauto Star 6-11-7: 4/9	P F Nicholls	*R Walsh*	7
2007	157	Twist Magic 5-11-7: 5/1	P F Nicholls	*S Thomas*	8
2008	163	Master Minded 5-11-7: 4/7	P F Nicholls	*A P McCoy*	7
2009	168	Twist Magic 7-11-7: 9/4	P F Nicholls	*R Walsh*	5
2010	168	Master Minded 7-11-7: 10/11	P F Nicholls	*N Fehily*	9
2011	171	Sizing Europe 9-11-7: 11/8	H de Bromhead (Ir)	*A E Lynch*	7
2012	169	Sprinter Sacre 6-11-7: 4/11	Nicky Henderson	*Barry Geraghty*	7
2013	166	Sire de Grugy 7-11-7: 7/4	Gary Moore	*Jamie Moore*	9
2014	168	Dodging Bullets 6-11-7: 9/1	Paul Nicholls	*Sam Twiston-Davies*	10
2015	167	Sire de Grugy 9-11-7: 10/3	Gary Moore	*Jamie Moore*	7
2016	169	Un de Sceaux 8-11-7: 5/4	W P Mullins (Ir)	*R Walsh*	6

CASPIAN CAVIAR GOLD CUP (HANDICAP CHASE) (Gr 3) (Cheltenham 2m5f)

1992	151	Another Coral 9-11-4: 11/2	D Nicholson	*R Dunwoody*	10
1993	146	Fragrant Dawn 9-10-2: 14/1	M C Pipe	*D Murphy*	11
1994	145	Dublin Flyer 8-10-2: 10/3	T A Forster	*B Powell*	11
1995		Abandoned			
1996	156	Addington Boy 8-11-7: 7/4	G Richards	*A Dobbin*	10
1997	160	Senor El Betrutti 8-11-3: 9/1	Mrs S Nock	*G Bradley*	9
1998	141	Northern Starlight 7-10-1: 15/2	M C Pipe	*A P McCoy*	13
1999	162	Legal Right 6-10-13: 6/1	J O'Neill	*R Johnson*	9
2000	139	Go Roger Go 8-11-0: 7/1	E J O'Grady (Ir)	*N Williamson*	12
2001		Abandoned			
2002	151	Fondmort 6-10-5: 5/1	N J Henderson	*M A Fitzgerald*	9
2003	144	Iris Royal 7-10-13: 7/1	N J Henderson	*M A Fitzgerald*	17
2004	143	Monkerhostin 7-10-2: 4/1	P J Hobbs	*R Johnson*	13
2005	139	Sir OJ 8-10-0: 16/1	N Meade (Ir)	*P Carberry*	16
2006	151	Exotic Dancer 6-11-4: 8/1	J O'Neill	*A Dobbin*	12
2007	155	Tamarinbleu 7-11-8: 22/1	D E Pipe	*D O'Regan*	16
2008		Abandoned			
2009	160	Poquelin 6-11-8: 7/2	P F Nicholls	*R Walsh*	17
2010	164	Poquelin 7-11-7: 16/1	P F Nicholls	*I Popham*[5]	16
2011	156	Quantitativeeasing 6-10-7: 6/1	Nicky Henderson	*Barry Geraghty*	16
2012	145	Unioniste 4-9-9: 15/2	Paul Nicholls	*Harry Derham*[5]	14
2013	137	Double Ross 7-10-8: 7/1	Nigel Twiston-Davies	*Sam Twiston-Davies*	13
2014	148	Niceonefrankie 8-11-5: 16/1	Venetia Williams	*Aidan Coleman*	12
2015	144	Village Vic 8-10-0: 8/1	Philip Hobbs	*Richard Johnson*	14
2016	146	Frodon 4-10-10: 14/1	Paul Nicholls	*Sam Twiston-Davies*	16

stanjames.com INTERNATIONAL HURDLE (Gr 2)
(Cheltenham 2m1f, run at Newbury 2m½f in 2001 and at Ascot 2m in 2008)

1992	164	Halkopous 6-11-2: 8/1	M H Tompkins	*A Maguire*	6
1993	169	Staunch Friend 5-11-8: 6/1	M H Tompkins	*D Murphy*	7
1994	156	Large Action 6-11-4: 8/11	O Sherwood	*J Osborne*	8
1995		Abandoned			
1996	160	Large Action 8-11-8: 5/4	O Sherwood	*J Osborne*	7
1997	155	Relkeel 8-11-0: 8/1	D Nicholson	*R Johnson*	8

1998	163	Relkeel 9-11-8: 8/1	D Nicholson	*A Maguire*	5
1999	159	Relkeel 10-11-8: 13/2	A King	*R Johnson*	7
2000	160	Geos 5-11-4: 14/1	N J Henderson	*M A Fitzgerald*	8
2001	161	Valiramix 5-11-4: 1/2	M C Pipe	*A P McCoy*	4
2002	154	Rooster Booster 8-11-4: 11/8	P J Hobbs	*R Johnson*	9
2003	149	Rigmarole 5-11-4: 25/1	P F Nicholls	*R Thornton*	7
2004	161	Back In Front 7-11-8: 5/2	E J O'Grady (Ir)	*D N Russell*	7
2005	160	Harchibald 8-11-8: 10/11	N Meade (Ir)	*P Carberry*	9
2006	157	Detroit City 4-11-4: 4/6	P J Hobbs	*R Johnson*	4
2007	158	Osana 5-11-0: 7/1	D E Pipe	*P J Brennan*	8
2008	165	Binocular 4-11-4: 1/1	N J Henderson	*A P McCoy*	5
2009	161	Khyber Kim 7-11-4: 12/1	N A Twiston-Davies	*P J Brennan*	7
2010	157	Menorah 5-11-4: 7/4	P J Hobbs	*R Johnson*	9
2011	164	Grandouet 4-11-4: 5/2	Nicky Henderson	*Barry Geraghty*	8
2012	163	Zarkandar 5-11-4: 6/5	Paul Nicholls	*R Walsh*	7
2013	153	The New One 5-11-8: 2/5	Nigel Twiston-Davies	*Sam Twiston-Davies*	7
2014	159	The New One 6-11-8: 4/7	Nigel Twiston-Davies	*Sam Twiston-Davies*	8
2015	154	Old Guard 4-11-4: 7/1	Paul Nicholls	*Sam Twiston Davies*	6
2016	158	The New One 8-11-8: 13/8	Nigel Twiston-Davies	*Richard Johnson*	6

JLT LONG WALK HURDLE (Gr 1)
(Ascot 3m1f; Windsor in 2004, Chepstow in 2005 & Newbury in 2009 & 2010)

1992	156	Vagog 7-11-7: 15/2	M C Pipe	*M Foster*	9
1993	152	Sweet Duke 6-11-7: 7/2	N Twiston-Davies	*C Llewellyn*	9
1994	159	Hebridean 7-11-7: 10/3	D Nicholson	*A Maguire*	8
1995	153	Silver Wedge 4-11-7: 7/1	S Sherwood	*J Osborne*	11
1996	152	Ocean Hawk 4-11-7: 7/1	N A Twiston-Davies	*C Llewellyn*	6
1997	168	Paddy's Return 5-11-7: 8/1	F Murphy	*N Williamson*	7
1998	165	Princeful 7-11-7: 11/4	Mrs J Pitman	*R Dunwoody*	11
1999	164	Anzum 8-11-7: 4/1	A King	*R Johnson*	6
2000	172	Baracouda 5-11-7: 11/4	F Doumen (Fr)	*T Doumen*	9
2001	161	Baracouda 6-11-7: 2/5	F Doumen (Fr)	*T Doumen*	5
2002	167	Deano's Beeno 10-11-7: 14/1	M C Pipe	*A P McCoy*	5
2003	169	Baracouda 8-11-7: 2/7	F Doumen (Fr)	*T Doumen*	6
2004	156	Baracouda 9-11-7: 8/13	F Doumen (Fr)	*A P McCoy*	8
2005	157	My Way de Solzen 5-11-7: 12/1	A King	*R Thornton*	8
2006	141	Mighty Man 6-11-7: 8/11	H D Daly	*R Johnson*	9
2007	153	Lough Derg 7-11-7: 14/1	D E Pipe	*T Scudamore*	9
2008	161	Punchestowns 5-11-7: 3/1	N J Henderson	*B J Geraghty*	11
2009	165	Big Buck's 6-11-7: 1/2	P F Nicholls	*R Walsh*	8
2010	156	Big Buck's 7-11-7: 2/13	Paul Nichols	*A P McCoy*	6
2011	152	Big Buck's 8-11-7: 3/10	Paul Nicholls	*R Walsh*	7
2012	162	Reve de Sivola 7-11-7: 9/2	Nick Williams	*Richard Johnson*	7
2013	162	Reve de Sivola 8-11-7: 9/4	Nick Williams	*Richard Johnson*	5
2014	159	Reve de Sivola 9-11-7: 13/2	Nick Williams	*Daryl Jacob*	5
2015	168	Thistlecrack 7-11-7: 2/1	Colin Tizzard	*Tom Scudamore*	8
2016	155	Unowhatimeanharry 8-11-7: 6/5	Harry Fry	*Barry Geraghty*	11

WESSEX YOUTH TRUST HANDICAP HURDLE (Gr 3)
(Ascot 2m; Sandown in 2005 & 2006 (Jan), Listed until 2012)

2001	142	Marble Arch 5-10-11: 7/1	H Morrison	*N Williamson*	16
2002	139	Chauvinist 7-10-0: 15/2	N J Henderson	*N Williamson*	20
2003	138	Thesis 5-11-2: 33/1	Miss V Williams	*B J Crowley*	17
2004	141	Tamarinbleu 5-10-11: 14/1	M C Pipe	*A P McCoy*	23
2005	136	Desert Air 7-10-9: 25/1	M C Pipe	*T Scudamore*	20
2006	142	Acambo 5-11-9: 7/1	D E Pipe	*T J Murphy*	20
2007	133	Jack The Giant 5-11-0: 9/4	N J Henderson	*M A Fitzgerald*	17
2008	154	Sentry Duty 6-11-9: 12/1	N J Henderson	*B J Geraghty*	21
2009		Abandoned			
2010		Abandoned			
2011	135	Raya Star 5-10-1: 12/1	Alan King	*Wayne Hutchinson*	16
2012	150	Cause of Causes 4-10-13: 25/1	Gordon Elliott (Ir)	*Davy Condon*	21
2013	139	Willow's Saviour 6-10-5: 10/1	Dan Skelton	*Harry Skelton*	20
2014	150	Bayan 5-11-5: 14/1	Gordon Elliott (Ir)	*Davy Condon*	18
2015	145	Jolly's Cracked It 6-11-3: 7/1	Harry Fry	*Noel Fehily*	21
	138	Sternrubin 4-10-10: 9/1	Philip Hobbs	*Richard Johnson*	21
2016	158	Brain Power 5-11-11: 12/1	Nicky Henderson	*D J Mullins*	19

CORAL WELSH GRAND NATIONAL (HANDICAP CHASE) (Gr 3)

(Chepstow 3m5½f, Newbury in 1994)

1992	155	Run For Free 8-10-9: 11/4	M C Pipe	*M Perrett*	11
1993	126	Riverside Boy 10-10-0: 6/4	M C Pipe	*R Dunwoody*	8
1994	168	Master Oats 8-11-6: 5/2	K C Bailey	*N Williamson*	8
1995		Abandoned			
1996		Abandoned			
1997	146	Earth Summit 9-10-13: 25/1	N A Twiston-Davies	*T Jenks*	14
1998	139	Kendal Cavalier 8-10-0: 14/1	N J Hawke	*B Fenton*	14
1999	136	Edmond 7-10-0: 4/1	H D Daly	*R Johnson*	16
2000	149	Jocks Cross 9-10-4: 14/1	Miss V Williams	*B J Crowley*[1]	19
2001	140	Supreme Glory 8-10-0: 10/1	P G Murphy	*L Aspell*	13
2002	137	Mini Sensation 9-10-4: 8/1	J O'Neill	*A Dobbin*	16
2003	157	Bindaree 9-10-9: 10/1	N A Twiston-Davies	*C Llewellyn*	14
2004	135	Silver Birch 7-10-5: 10/3	P F Nicholls	*R Walsh*	17
2005	138	L'Aventure 6-10-4: 14/1	P F Nicholls	*L Aspell*	18
2006	159	Halcon Genelardais 6-11-3: 7/1	A King	*W Hutchinson*	18
2007	144	Miko de Beauchene 7-10-5: 13/2	R H Alner	*A Thornton*	18
2008	158	Notre Pere 7-11-0: 16/1	J Dreaper (Ir)	*A E Lynch*	20
2009	152	Dream Alliance 8-10-8: 20/1	P J Hobbs	*T J O'Brien*	18
2010	155	Synchronised 8-11-6: 5/1	Jonjo O'Neill	*A P McCoy*	18
2011	141	Le Beau Bai 8-10-1: 10/1	Richard Lee	*Charlie Poste*	20
2012	137	Monbeg Dude 8-10-1: 10/1	Michael Scudamore	*P Carberry*	17
2013	139	Mountainous 8-10-0: 20/1	Richard Lee	*Paul Moloney*	20
2014	136	Emperor's Choice 7-10-8: 9/1	Venetia Williams	*Aidan Coleman*	19
2016	139	Mountainous 11-10-6: 9/1	Kerry Lee	*Jamie Moore*	20
2017	162	Native River 6-11-12: 11/4	Colin Tizzard	*Richard Johnson*	20

32Red.com CHRISTMAS HURDLE (Gr 1) (Kempton 2m, Sandown 2005)

1992	170	Mighty Mogul 5-11-7: 3/1	D Nicholson	*R Dunwoody*	8
1993	155	Muse 6-11-7: 3/1	D R C Elsworth	*M Richards*	5
1994	158	Absalom's Lady 6-11-2: 9/2	D R C Elsworth	*P Holley*	6
1995		Abandoned			
1996		Abandoned			
1997	153	Kerawi 4-11-7: 4/1	N A Twiston-Davies	*C Llewellyn*	5
1998	165	French Holly 7-11-7: 5/2	F Murphy	*A Thornton*	5
1999	168	Dato Star 8-11-7: 11/8	J M Jefferson	*L Wyer*	4
2000	144	Geos 5-11-7: 9/4	N J Henderson	*M A Fitzgerald*	7
2001	153	Landing Light 6-11-7: 5/4	N J Henderson	*M A Fitzgerald*	5
2002	158	Intersky Falcon 5-11-7: 1/1	J O'Neill	*C F Swan*	6
2003	157	Intersky Falcon 6-11-7: 11/4	J O'Neill	*L Cooper*	6
2004	160	Harchibald 5-11-7: 8/11	N Meade (Ir)	*P Carberry*	7
2005	152	Feathard Lady 5-11-0: 6/4	C A Murphy (Ir)	*R Walsh*	7
2006	155	Jazz Messenger 6-11-7: 10/1	N Meade (Ir)	*N P Madden*	7
2007	153	Straw Bear 6-11-7: 9/2	N J Gifford	*A P McCoy*	6
2008	152	Harchibald 9-11-7: 7/1	N Meade (Ir)	*P Carberry*	7
2009	153	Go Native 6-11-7: 5/2	N Meade (Ir)	*D J Condon*	7
2010	163	Binocular 7-11-7: 13/8	Nicky Henderson	*A P McCoy*	6
2011	164	Binocular 7-11-7: 5/4	Nicky Henderson	*A P McCoy*	5
2012	158	Darlan 5-11-7: 3/1	Nicky Henderson	*A P McCoy*	7
2013	170	My Tent Or Yours 6-11-7: 11/8	Nicky Henderson	*A P McCoy*	6
2014	171	Faugheen 6-11-7: 4/11	W P Mullins (Ir)	*R Walsh*	6
2015	167	Faugheen 7-11-7: 1/4	W P Mullins (Ir)	*R Walsh*	5
2016	164	Yanworth 6-11-7: 5/4	Alan King	*Barry Geraghty*	5

32Red.com KING GEORGE VI CHASE (Gr 1) (Kempton 3m, Sandown 1996 (Jan) and 2005)

1992	161	The Fellow 7-11-10: 1/1	F Doumen (Fr)	*A Kondrat*	8
1993	167	Barton Bank 7-11-10: 9/2	D Nicholson	*A Maguire*	10
1994	158	Algan 6-11-10: 16/1	F Doumen (Fr)	*P Chevalier*	9
1996	179	One Man 8-11-10: 11/4	G Richards	*R Dunwoody*	11
1996	176	One Man 8-11-10: 8/13	G Richards	*R Dunwoody*	5
1997	167	See More Business 7-11-10: 10/1	P F Nicholls	*A Thornton*	8
1998	173	Teeton Mill 9-11-10: 7/2	Miss V Williams	*N Williamson*	9
1999	182	See More Business 9-11-10: 5/2	P F Nicholls	*M A Fitzgerald*	9
2000	180	First Gold 7-11-10: 5/2	F Doumen (Fr)	*T Doumen*	9
2001	172	Florida Pearl 9-11-10: 8/1	W P Mullins (Ir)	*A Maguire*	8
2002	170	Best Mate 7-11-10: 11/8	Miss H C Knight	*A P McCoy*	10

1037

2003	167	Edredon Bleu 11-11-10: 25/1	Miss H C Knight	*J Culloty*	12
2004	177	Kicking King 6-11-10: 3/1	T J Taaffe (Ir)	*B J Geraghty*	13
2005	167	Kicking King 7-11-10: 11/8	T J Taaffe (Ir)	*B J Geraghty*	9
2006	174	Kauto Star 6-11-10: 8/13	P F Nicholls	*R Walsh*	9
2007	176	Kauto Star 7-11-10: 4/6	P F Nicholls	*R Walsh*	7
2008	173	Kauto Star 8-11-10: 10/11	P F Nicholls	*R Walsh*	10
2009	188	Kauto Star 9-11-10: 8/13	P F Nicholls	*R Walsh*	13
2010	178	Long Run 6-11-10: 9/2	Nicky Henderson	*Mr S Waley-Cohen*	9
2011	179	Kauto Star 11-11-10: 3/1	Paul Nicholls	*R Walsh*	7
2012	166	Long Run 7-11-10: 15/8	Nicky Henderson	*Mr S Waley-Cohen*	9
2013	176	Silviniaco Conti 7-11-10: 7/2	Paul Nicholls	*Noel Fehily*	9
2014	172	Silviniaco Conti 8-11-10: 15/8	Paul Nicholls	*Noel Fehily*	10
2015	181	Cue Card 9-11-10: 9/2	Colin Tizzard	*Paddy Brennan*	9
2016	174	Thistlecrack 8-11-10: 11/10	Colin Tizzard	*Tom Scudamore*	5

SPECTRA CYBER SECURITY SOLUTIONS CLARENCE HOUSE CHASE (Gr 1)

(Ascot 2m1f, except Warwick in 1994, Kempton in 1997, 1999 and replacement race in 2003, Cheltenham in 2005, 2013 and 2017; Sandown in 2006 and 2007; Gr 2 Handicap prior to 2008)

1993	156	Sybillin 7-10-10: 9/2	J G FitzGerald	*M Dwyer*	11
1994	151	Viking Flagship 7-10-10: 3/1	D Nicholson	*R Dunwoody*	4
1995	160	Martha's Son 8-10-9: 3/1	T A Forster	*R Farrant*	8
1996	145	Big Matt 8-10-4: 8/1	N J Henderson	*M Fitzgerald*	11
1997	157	Ask Tom 8-10-10: 9/4	T P Tate	*R Garrity*	8
1998	155	Jeffell 8-10-11: 13/2	A L T Moore (Ir)	*C O'Dwyer*	9
1999	153	Call Equiname 9-11-3: 15/2	P F Nicholls	*R Thornton*	7
2000	151	Nordance Prince 9-10-0: 13/8	Miss V Williams	*A P McCoy*	10
2001	160	Function Dream 9-10-11: 2/1	Mrs M Reveley	*A Ross3*	10
2002	136	Turgeonev 7-10-4: 9/2	T D Easterby	*R McGrath*	8
2003	153	Young Devereaux 10-10-4: 9/2	P F Nicholls	*R Walsh*	9
2004	163	Isio 8-10-5: 4/1	N J Henderson	*M A Fitzgerald*	13
2005	179	Well Chief 6-11-10: 5/1	M C Pipe	*T J Murphy*	10
2006	145	Tysou 9-11-2: 10/1	N J Henderson	*M A Fitzgerald*	10
2007		Abandoned (replaced by substitute event of lower value)			
2008	161	Tamarinbleu 8-11-7: 12/1	D E Pipe	*T Scudamore*	6
2009	167	Master Minded 6-11-7: 1/4	P F Nicholls	*R Walsh*	5
2010	168	Twist Magic 8-11-7: 11/8	P F Nicholls	*R Walsh*	7
2011	168	Master Minded 8-11-7: 4/7	Paul Nicholls	*A P McCoy*	9
2012	165	Somersby 8-11-7: 9/2	Henrietta Knight	*Dominic Elsworth*	8
2013	171	Sprinter Sacre 7-11-7: 1/5	Nicky Henderson	*Barry Geraghty*	7
2014	172	Sire de Grugy 8-11-7: 5/4	Gary Moore	*Jamie Moore*	7
2015	167	Dodging Bullets 7-11-7: 7/2	Paul Nicholls	*Noel Fehily*	5
2016	174	Un de Sceaux 8-11-7: 1/2	W P Mullins (Ir)	*R Walsh*	5
2017	167	Un de Sceaux 9-11-7: 1/2	W P Mullins (Ir)	*R Walsh*	7

BETFAIR HURDLE (HANDICAP) (Gr 3) (Newbury 2m½f)

1993	147	King Credo 8-10-0: 10/1	S Woodman	*A Maguire*	16
1994	149	Large Action 6-10-8: 9/2	O Sherwood	*J Osborne*	11
1995	160	Mysilv 5-10-8: 9/4	C R Egerton	*J Osborne*	8
1996	148	Squire Silk 7-10-12: 13/2	A Turnell	*P Carberry*	18
1997	151	Make A Stand 6-11-7: 6/1	M C Pipe	*C Maude*	18
1998	145	Sharpical 6-11-1: 10/1	N J Henderson	*M A Fitzgerald*	14
1999	142	Decoupage 7-11-0: 6/1	C R Egerton	*J A McCarthy*	18
2000	155	Geos 5-11-3: 15/2	N J Henderson	*M A Fitzgerald*	17
2001	145	Landing Light 6-10-2: 4/1	N J Henderson	*M A Fitzgerald*	20
2002	157	Copeland 7-11-7: 13/2	M C Pipe	*A P McCoy*	16
2003	138	Spirit Leader 7-10-0: 14/1	Mrs J Harrington (Ir)	*N Williamson*	27
2004	149	Geos 9-10-9: 16/1	N J Henderson	*M Foley*	25
2005	152	Essex 5-11-6: 4/1	M J P O'Brien (Ir)	*B J Geraghty*	25
2006		Abandoned			
2007	132	Heathcote 5-10-6: 50/1	G L Moore	*J E Moore*	20
2008	131	Wingman 6-10-0: 14/1	G L Moore	*J E Moore*	24
2009		Abandoned			
2010	144	Get Me Out of Here 6-10-6: 6/1	J O'Neill	*A P McCoy*	23
2011	136	Recession Proof 5-10-8: 12/1	John Quinn	*Dougie Costello*	15
2012	159	Zarkandar 5-11-1: 11/4	Paul Nicholls	*R Walsh*	20
2013	162	My Tent Or Yours 6-11-2: 5/1	Nicky Henderson	*A P McCoy*	21
2014	142	Splash of Ginge 6-10-3: 33/1	Nigel Twiston-Davies	*Ryan Hatch[7]*	20

2015	139	Violet Dancer 5-10-9: 20/1	Gary Moore	*Joshua Moore*	23
2016	144	Agrapart 5-10-10: 16/1	Nick Williams	*Lizzie Kelly[5]*	22
2017	145	Ballyandy 6-11-1: 3/1	Nigel Twiston-Davies	*Sam Twiston-Davies*	16

BETFAIR ASCOT CHASE (Gr 1)
(Ascot 2m5½f, 2m3f in 2007, Lingfield 2m4½f in 2005 and 2006)

1995	158	Martha's Son 8-11-7: 1/1	T A Forster	*R Farrant*	6
1996	155	Sound Man 8-11-7: 1/2	E O'Grady (Ir)	*R Dunwoody*	5
1997	171	Strong Promise 6-11-7: 10/1	G A Hubbard	*N Williamson*	4
1998	176	One Man 10-11-7: 7/4	G Richards	*A Dobbin*	3
1999	156	Teeton Mill 10-11-7: 6/4	Miss V Williams	*N Williamson*	7
2000	155	Rockforce 8-11-7: 2/1	P F Nicholls	*J Tizzard*	5
2001	163	Tiutchev 8-11-7: 11/8	N J Henderson	*M A Fitzgerald*	4
2002	148	Tresor de Mai 8-11-7: 9/2	M C Pipe	*A P McCoy*	5
2003	162	Tiutchev 10-11-7: 15/8	M C Pipe	*A P McCoy*	7
2004	161	Hand Inn Hand 8-11-7: 15/2	H D Daly	*M Bradburne*	7
2005	154	It Takes Time 11-11-7: 14/1	M C Pipe	*J E Moore*	7
2006	156	Our Vic 8-11-7: 2/1	M C Pipe	*T J Murphy*	7
2007	166	Monet's Garden 9-11-7: 11/10	N G Richards	*A Dobbin*	7
2008	168	Kauto Star 8-11-7: 4/11	P F Nicholls	*R Walsh*	9
2009	166	Voy Por Ustedes 8-11-7: 6/5	A King	*R Thornton*	4
2010	153	Monet's Garden 12-11-7: 11/2	N G Richards	*B J Geraghty*	6
2011	167	Riverside Theatre 7-11-7: 11/10	Nicky Henderson	*Barry Geraghty*	7
2012	170	Riverside Theatre 8-11-7: 13/8	Nicky Henderson	*Barry Geraghty*	8
2013	167	Cue Card 7-11-7: 15/8	Colin Tizzard	*Joe Tizzard*	6
2014	175	Captain Chris 10-11-7: 8/11	Philip Hobbs	*Richard Johnson*	8
2015	166	Balder Succes 7-11-7: 4/1	Alan King	*Wayne Hutchinson*	5
2016	169	Silviniaco Conti 10-11-7: 2/1	Paul Nicholls	*Noel Fehily*	8
2017	174	Cue Card 11-11-7: 4/9	Colin Tizzard	*Paddy Brennan*	6

SKY BET SUPREME NOVICES' HURDLE (Gr 1) (Cheltenham 2m½f)

1993	150	Montelado 6-11-8: 5/1	P Flynn (Ir)	*C F Swan*	15
1994	144	Arctic Kinsman 6-11-8: 50/1	N A Twiston-Davies	*C Llewellyn*	18
1995	137	Tourist Attraction 6-11-3: 25/1	W P Mullins (Ir)	*M Dwyer*	20
1996	143	Indefence 5-11-8: 25/1	Mrs J Pitman	*W Marston*	27
1997	138	Shadow Leader 6-11-8: 5/1	C R Egerton	*J Osborne*	16
1998	144	French Ballerina 5-11-3: 10/1	P J Flynn (Ir)	*G Bradley*	30
1999	162	Hors La Loi III 4-11-0: 9/2	M C Pipe	*A P McCoy*	20
2000	143	Sausalito Bay 6-11-8: 14/1	N Meade (Ir)	*P Carberry*	15
2001		Abandoned			
2002	138	Like-A-Butterfly 8-11-3: 7/4	C Roche (Ir)	*C F Swan*	28
2003	151	Back In Front 6-11-8: 3/1	E J O'Grady (Ir)	*N Williamson*	19
2004	147	Brave Inca 6-11-7: 7/2	C A Murphy (Ir)	*B M Cash*	19
2005	144	Arcalis 5-11-7: 20/1	J H Johnson	*G Lee*	20
2006	142	Noland 5-11-7: 6/1	P F Nicholls	*R Walsh*	20
2007	145	Ebaziyan 6-11-7: 40/1	W P Mullins (Ir)	*D J Condon*	22
2008	149	Captain Cee Bee 7-11-7: 17/2	E P Harty (Ir)	*R Thornton*	22
2009	145	Go Native 6-11-7: 12/1	N Meade (Ir)	*P Carberry*	20
2010	145	Menorah 5-11-7: 12/1	P J Hobbs	*R Johnson*	18
2011	158	Al Ferof 6-11-7: 10/1	Paul Nicholls	*R Walsh*	15
2012	149	Cinders And Ashes 5-11-7: 10/1	Donald McCain	*Jason Maguire*	19
2013	165	Champagne Fever 6-11-7: 5/1	W P Mullins (Ir)	*R Walsh*	12
2014	154	Vautour 5-11-7: 7/2	W P Mullins (Ir)	*R Walsh*	18
2015	168	Douvan 5-11-7: 2/1	W P Mullins (Ir)	*R Walsh*	12
2016	164	Altior 6-11-7: 4/1	Nicky Henderson	*Nico de Boinville*	14
2017	153	Labaik 6-11-7: 25/1	Gordon Elliott (Ir)	*J W Kennedy*	14

RACING POST ARKLE CHALLENGE TROPHY CHASE (Gr 1) (Cheltenham 2m)

1993	158	Travado 7-11-8: 5/1	N J Henderson	*J Osborne*	8
1994	146	Nakir 6-11-8: 9/1	S Christian	*J Osborne*	10
1995	147	Klairon Davis 6-11-8: 7/2	A L T Moore (Ir)	*F Woods*	11
1996	153	Ventana Canyon 7-11-8: 7/1	E J O'Grady (Ir)	*R Dunwoody*	16
1997	146	Or Royal 6-11-8: 11/2	M C Pipe	*A P McCoy*	9
1998	137	Champleve 5-11-0: 13/2	M C Pipe	*A P McCoy*	16
1999	153	Flagship Uberalles 5-11-0: 11/1	P F Nicholls	*J Tizzard*	14
2000	152	Tiutchev 7-11-8: 8/1	N J Henderson	*M A Fitzgerald*	12
2001		Abandoned			
2002	159	Moscow Flyer 8-11-8: 11/2	Mrs J Harrington (Ir)	*B J Geraghty*	12

2003	158	Azertyuiop 6-11-8: 5/4	P F Nicholls	*R Walsh*	9
2004	146	Well Chief 5-11-3: 9/1	M C Pipe	*A P McCoy*	16
2005	150	Contraband 7-11-7: 7/1	M C Pipe	*T J Murphy*	19
2006	151	Voy Por Ustedes 5-11-2: 15/2	A King	*R Thornton*	14
2007	157	My Way de Solzen 7-11-7: 7/2	A King	*R Thornton*	13
2008	160	Tidal Bay 7-11-7: 6/1	J H Johnson	*D O'Regan*	14
2009	151	Forpadydeplasterer 7-11-7: 8/1	T Cooper (Ir)	*B J Geraghty*	17
2010	154	Sizing Europe 8-11-7: 6/1	H de Bromhead (Ir)	*A E Lynch*	12
2011	156	Captain Chris 7-11-7: 6/1	Philip Hobbs	*Richard Johnson*	10
2012	169	Sprinter Sacre 6-11-7: 8/11	Nicky Henderson	*Barry Geraghty*	6
2013	160	Simonsig 7-11-7: 8/15	Nicky Henderson	*Barry Geraghty*	7
2014	157	Western Warhorse 6-11-4: 33/1	David Pipe	*Tom Scudamore*	9
2015	169	Un de Sceaux 7-11-4: 4/6	W P Mullins (Ir)	*R Walsh*	11
2016	168	Douvan 6-11-4: 1/4	W P Mullins (Ir)	*R Walsh*	7
2017	161	Altior 7-11-4: 1/4	Nicky Henderson	*Nico de Boinville*	9

STAN JAMES CHAMPION HURDLE CHALLENGE TROPHY (Gr 1) (Cheltenham 2m½f)

1993	167	Granville Again 7-12-0: 13/2	M C Pipe	*P Scudamore*	18
1994	166	Flakey Dove 8-11-9: 9/1	R J Price	*M Dwyer*	15
1995	174	Alderbrook 6-12-0: 11/2	K C Bailey	*N Williamson*	14
1996	170	Collier Bay 6-12-0: 9/1	J A B Old	*G Bradley*	16
1997	165	Make A Stand 6-12-0: 7/1	M C Pipe	*A P McCoy*	17
1998	172	Istabraq 6-12-0: 3/1	A P O'Brien (Ir)	*C F Swan*	18
1999	164	Istabraq 7-12-0: 4/9	A P O'Brien (Ir)	*C F Swan*	14
2000	163	Istabraq 8-12-0: 8/15	A P O'Brien (Ir)	*C F Swan*	12
2001		Abandoned			
2002	161	Hors La Loi III 7-12-0: 10/1	J R Fanshawe	*D Gallagher*	15
2003	170	Rooster Booster 9-12-0: 9/2	P J Hobbs	*R Johnson*	17
2004	165	Hardy Eustace 7-11-10: 33/1	D T Hughes (Ir)	*C O'Dwyer*	14
2005	164	Hardy Eustace 8-11-10: 7/2	D T Hughes (Ir)	*C O'Dwyer*	14
2006	167	Brave Inca 8-11-10: 7/4	C A Murphy (Ir)	*A P McCoy*	18
2007	162	Sublimity 7-11-10: 16/1	J G Carr (Ir)	*P Carberry*	10
2008	163	Katchit 5-11-10: 10/1	A King	*R Thornton*	15
2009	164	Punjabi 6-11-10: 22/1	N J Henderson	*B J Geraghty*	23
2010	167	Binocular 6-11-10: 9/1	N J Henderson	*A P McCoy*	12
2011	168	Hurricane Fly 7-11-10: 11/4	W P Mullins (Ir)	*R Walsh*	11
2012	171	Rock On Ruby 7-11-10: 11/1	Paul Nicholls	*Noel Fehily*	10
2013	170	Hurricane Fly 9-11-10: 13/8	W P Mullins (Ir)	*R Walsh*	9
2014	170	Jezki 6-11-10: 9/1	Mrs John Harrington (Ir)	*Barry Geraghty*	9
2015	170	Faugheen 7-11-10: 4/5	W P Mullins (Ir)	*R Walsh*	8
2016	163	Annie Power 8-11-3: 5/2	W P Mullins (Ir)	*R Walsh*	12
2017	170	Buveur d'Air 6-11-10: 5/1	Nicky Henderson	*Noel Fehily*	11

OLBG.com MARES' HURDLE (David Nicholson) (Gr 1) (Cheltenham 2½m, Gr 2 prior to 2015)

2008	137	Whiteoak 5-11-0: 20/1	D McCain Jnr	*J Maguire*	13
2009	152	Quevega 5-11-3: 2/1	W P Mullins (Ir)	*R Walsh*	21
2010	148	Quevega 6-11-5: 6/4	W P Mullins (Ir)	*R Walsh*	17
2011	146	Quevega 7-11-5: 5/6	W P Mullins (Ir)	*R Walsh*	14
2012	137	Quevega 8-11-5: 4/7	W P Mullins (Ir)	*R Walsh*	19
2013	142	Quevega 9-11-5: 8/11	W P Mullins (Ir)	*R Walsh*	19
2014	139	Quevega 10-11-5: 8/11	W P Mullins (Ir)	*R Walsh*	16
2015	146	Glens Melody 7-11-5: 6/1	W P Mullins (Ir)	*P Townend*	15
2016	139	Vroum Vroum Mag 7-11-5: 4/6	W P Mullins (Ir)	*R Walsh*	19
2017	147	Apple's Jade 5-11-5: 7/2	Gordon Elliott (Ir)	*B J Cooper*	17

NEPTUNE INVESTMENT MANAGEMENT NOVICES' HURDLE (Baring Bingham) (Gr 1) (Cheltenham 2m5f)

1993	134	Gaelstrom 6-11-2: 16/1	N A Twiston-Davies	*C Llewellyn*	19
1994	138	Danoli 6-11-7: 7/4	T Foley (Ir)	*C F Swan*	23
1995	142	Putty Road 5-11-7: 7/1	D Nicholson	*N Williamson*	21
1996	142	Urubande 6-11-7: 8/1	A P O'Brien (Ir)	*C F Swan*	24
1997	144	Istabraq 6-11-7: 6/5	A P O'Brien (Ir)	*C F Swan*	17
1998	151	French Holly 7-11-7: 2/1	F Murphy	*A Thornton*	18
1999	153	Barton 6-11-7: 2/1	T D Easterby	*L Wyer*	18
2000	149	Monsignor 6-11-7: 5/4	M Pitman	*N Williamson*	14
2001		Abandoned			
2002	148	Galileo 6-11-7: 12/1	T R George	*J M Maguire*	27
2003	147	Hardy Eustace 6-11-7: 6/1	D T Hughes (Ir)	*K A Kelly*	19

2004	147	Fundamentalist 6-11-7: 12/1	N A Twiston-Davies	*C Llewellyn*	15
2005	147	No Refuge 5-11-7: 17/2	J H Johnson	*G Lee*	20
2006	146	Nicanor 5-11-7: 17/2	N Meade (Ir)	*P Carberry*	17
2007	147	Massini's Maguire 6-11-7: 20/1	P J Hobbs	*R Johnson*	15
2008	146	Fiveforthree 6-11-7: 7/1	W P Mullins (Ir)	*R Walsh*	15
2009	151	Mikael d'Haguenet 5-11-7: 5/2	W P Mullins (Ir)	*R Walsh*	14
2010	147	Peddlers Cross 5-11-7: 7/1	D McCain Jnr	*J Maguire*	17
2011	149	First Lieutenant 6-11-7: 7/1	M F Morris (Ir)	*Davy Russell*	12
2012	157	Simonsig 6-11-7: 2/1	Nicky Henderson	*Barry Geraghty*	17
2013	155	The New One 5-11-7: 7/2	Nigel Twiston-Davies	*Sam Twiston-Davies*	8
2014	155	Faugheen 6-11-7: 6/4	W P Mullins (Ir)	*R Walsh*	15
2015	154	Windsor Park 6-11-7: 9/2	D K Weld (Ir)	*D Russell*	10
2016	156	Yorkhill 6-11-7: 3/1	W P Mullins (Ir)	*R Walsh*	11
2017	151	Willoughby Court 6-11-7: 14/1	Ben Pauling	*David Bass*	15

RSA CHASE (Gr 1) (Cheltenham 3m½f)

1993	136	Young Hustler 6-11-4: 9/4	N A Twiston-Davies	*P Scudamore*	8
1994	148	Monsieur Le Cure 8-11-4: 15/2	J A C Edwards	*P Niven*	18
1995	159	Brief Gale 8-10-13: 13/2	J T Gifford	*P Hide*	13
1996	146	Nahthen Lad 7-11-4: 7/1	Mrs J Pitman	*W Marston*	12
1997	150	Hanakham 8-11-4: 13/2	R J Hodges	*R Dunwoody*	14
1998	169	Florida Pearl 6-11-4: 11/8	W P Mullins (Ir)	*R Dunwoody*	10
1999	161	Looks Like Trouble 7-11-4: 16/1	N T Chance	*P Carberry*	14
2000	152	Lord Noelie 7-11-4: 9/2	Miss H C Knight	*J Culloty*	9
2001		Abandoned			
2002	153	Hussard Collonges 7-11-4: 33/1	P Beaumont	*R Garritty*	19
2003	150	One Knight 7-11-4: 15/2	P J Hobbs	*R Johnson*	9
2004	149	Rule Supreme 8-11-4: 25/1	W P Mullins (Ir)	*D J Casey*	10
2005	150	Trabolgan 7-11-4: 5/1	N J Henderson	*M A Fitzgerald*	9
2006	145	Star de Mohaison 5-10-8: 14/1	P F Nicholls	*B J Geraghty*	15
2007	156	Denman 7-11-4: 6/5	P F Nicholls	*R Walsh*	17
2008	148	Albertas Run 7-11-4: 4/1	J O'Neill	*A P McCoy*	11
2009	158	Cooldine 7-11-4: 9/4	W P Mullins (Ir)	*R Walsh*	15
2010	152	Weapon's Amnesty 7-11-4: 10/1	C Byrnes (Ir)	*D N Russell*	9
2011	147	Bostons Angel 7-11-4: 16/1	Mrs J Harrington (Ir)	*Robbie Power*	12
2012	159	Bobs Worth 7-11-4: 9/2	Nicky Henderson	*Barry Geraghty*	9
2013	149	Lord Windermere 7-11-4: 8/1	J H Culloty (Ir)	*Davy Russell*	11
2014	152	O'Faolains Boy 7-11-4: 12/1	Rebecca Curtis	*Barry Geraghty*	15
2015	161	Don Poli 6-11-4: 13/8	W P Mullins (Ir)	*Bryan J Cooper*	8
2016	150	Blaklion 7-11-4: 8/1	Nigel Twiston-Davies	*Ryan Hatch*	8
2017	156	Might Bite 8-11-4: 7/2	Nicky Henderson	*Nico de Boinville*	12

BETWAY QUEEN MOTHER CHAMPION CHASE (Gr 1) (Cheltenham 2m)

1993	148	Deep Sensation 8-12-0: 11/1	J T Gifford	*D Murphy*	9
1994	166	Viking Flagship 7-12-0: 4/1	D Nicholson	*A Maguire*	8
1995	169	Viking Flagship 8-12-0: 5/2	D Nicholson	*C F Swan*	10
1996	172	Klairon Davis 7-12-0: 9/1	A L T Moore (Ir)	*F Woods*	7
1997	171	Martha's Son 10-12-0: 9/1	T A Forster	*R Farrant*	6
1998	163	One Man 10-12-0: 7/2	G Richards	*B Harding*	8
1999	164	Call Equiname 9-12-0: 7/2	P F Nicholls	*M A Fitzgerald*	13
2000	167	Edredon Bleu 8-12-0: 7/2	Miss H C Knight	*A P McCoy*	9
2001		Abandoned			
2002	166	Flagship Uberalles 8-12-0: 7/4	P J Hobbs	*R Johnson*	12
2003	167	Moscow Flyer 9-12-0: 7/4	Mrs J Harrington (Ir)	*B J Geraghty*	11
2004	172	Azertyuiop 7-11-10: 15/8	P F Nicholls	*R Walsh*	8
2005	181	Moscow Flyer 11-11-10: 6/4	Mrs J Harrington (Ir)	*B J Geraghty*	8
2006	165	Newmill 8-11-10: 16/1	J J Murphy (Ir)	*A J McNamara*	12
2007	160	Voy Por Ustedes 6-11-10: 5/1	A King	*R Thornton*	10
2008	179	Master Minded 5-11-10: 3/1	P F Nicholls	*R Walsh*	8
2009	164	Master Minded 6-11-10: 4/11	P F Nicholls	*R Walsh*	12
2010	169	Big Zeb 9-11-10: 10/1	C A Murphy (Ir)	*B J Geraghty*	9
2011	171	Sizing Europe 9-11-10: 10/1	H de Bromhead (Ir)	*A E Lynch*	11
2012	174	Finian's Rainbow 9-11-10: 4/1	Nicky Henderson	*Barry Geraghty*	8
2013	192	Sprinter Sacre 7-11-10: 1/4	Nicky Henderson	*Barry Geraghty*	7
2014	167	Sire de Grugy 8-11-10: 11/4	Gary Moore	*Jamie Moore*	11
2015	167	Dodging Bullets 7-11-10: 9/2	Paul Nicholls	*Sam Twiston-Davies*	9
2016	176	Sprinter Sacre 10-11-10: 5/1	Nicky Henderson	*Nico de Boinville*	10

2017 166   Special Tiara 10-11-10: 11/1   Henry de Bromhead (Ir) *Noel Fehily*   10

WEATHERBYS CHAMPION BUMPER (STANDARD OPEN NATIONAL HUNT FLAT) (Gr 1)
(Cheltenham 2m½f)

Year		Horse	Trainer	Jockey	Ran
1993	109	Rhythm Section 4-10-11: 16/1	H Scott (Ir)	*P Carberry*	24
1994	121	Mucklemeg 6-11-5: 7/2	E O'Grady (Ir)	*C F Swan*	25
1995	120	Dato Star 4-10-12: 7/2	J M Jefferson	*M Dwyer*	21
1996	122	Wither Or Which 5-11-6: 11/4	W P Mullins (Ir)	*W Mullins*	24
1997	124	Florida Pearl 5-11-6: 6/1	W P Mullins (Ir)	*R Dunwoody*	25
1998	126	Alexander Banquet 5-11-6: 9/1	W P Mullins (Ir)	*Mr R Walsh*	25
1999	122	Monsignor 5-11-6: 50/1	M Pitman	*B Powell*	25
2000	122	Joe Cullen 5-11-6: 14/1	W P Mullins (Ir)	*C F Swan*	17
2001		Abandoned			
2002	123	Pizarro 5-11-6: 14/1	E J O'Grady (Ir)	*J P Spencer*	23
2003	119	Liberman 5-11-6: 2/1	M C Pipe	*A P McCoy*	25
2004	118	Total Enjoyment 5-10-2: 7/1	T Cooper (Ir)	*J Culloty*	24
2005	123	Missed That 6-11-5: 7/2	W P Mullins (Ir)	*R Walsh*	24
2006	121	Hairy Molly 6-11-5: 33/1	J Crowley (Ir)	*P Carberry*	23
2007	122	Cork All Star 5-11-5: 11/2	Mrs J Harrington (Ir)	*B J Geraghty*	24
2008	122	Cousin Vinny 5-11-5: 12/1	W P Mullins (Ir)	*Mr P W Mullins*	23
2009	129	Dunguib 6-11-5: 9/2	P Fenton (Ir)	*Mr B T O'Connell*	24
2010	132	Cue Card 4-10-12: 40/1	C L Tizzard	*J Tizzard*	24
2011	128	Cheltenian 5-11-5: 14/1	Philip Hobbs	*Richard Johnson*	24
2012	127	Champagne Fever 5-11-5: 16/1	W P Mullins (Ir)	*Mr P W Mullins*	20
2013	130	Briar Hill 5-11-5: 25/1	W P Mullins (Ir)	*R Walsh*	23
2014	123	Silver Concorde 6-11-5: 16/1	D K Weld (Ir)	*Mr R P McNamara*	22
2015	122	Moon Racer 6-11-5: 9/2	David Pipe	*Tom Scudamore*	24
2016	123	Ballyandy 5-11-5: 5/1	Nigel Twiston-Davies	*Sam Twiston-Davies*	23
2017	115	Fayonagh 6-10-12: 7/1	Gordon Elliott (Ir)	*Mr J J Codd*	22

RYANAIR CHASE (Festival) (Gr 1) (Cheltenham 2m5f, Gr 2 before 2008)

Year		Horse	Trainer	Jockey	Ran
2005	160	Thisthatandtother 9-11-3: 9/2	P F Nicholls	*R Walsh*	12
2006	158	Fondmort 10-11-0: 10/3	N J Henderson	*M A Fitzgerald*	11
2007	157	Taranis 6-11-0: 9/2	P F Nicholls	*R Walsh*	9
2008	163	Our Vic 10-11-10: 4/1	D E Pipe	*T J Murphy*	9
2009	162	Imperial Commander 8-11-10: 6/1	N A Twiston-Davies	*P J Brennan*	10
2010	165	Albertas Run 9-11-10: 14/1	J O'Neill	*A P McCoy*	13
2011	165	Albertas Run 10-11-10: 6/1	Jonjo O'Neill	*A P McCoy*	11
2012	168	Riverside Theatre 8-11-10: 7/2	Nicky Henderson	*Barry Geraghty*	12
2013	163	Cue Card 7-11-10: 7/2	Colin Tizzard	*Joe Tizzard*	8
2014	163	Dynaste 8-11-10: 3/1	David Pipe	*Tom Scudamore*	11
2015	168	Uxizandre 7-11-10: 16/1	Alan King	*A P McCoy*	14
2016	180	Vautour 7-11-10: 1/1	W P Mullins (Ir)	*R Walsh*	15
2017	169	Un de Sceaux 9-11-10: 7/4	W P Mullins (Ir)	*R Walsh*	8

JLT NOVICES' CHASE (Golden Miller) (Gr 1, Gr 2 until 2013) (Cheltenham 2½m)

Year		Horse	Trainer	Jockey	Ran
2011	151	Noble Prince 7-11-4: 4/1	Paul Nolan (Ir)	*A P McCoy*	11
2012	160	Sir des Champs 6-11-4: 3/1	W P Mullins (Ir)	*Davy Russell*	10
2013	153	Benefficient 7-11-4: 20/1	A J Martin (Ir)	*Bryan Cooper*	13
2014	154	Taquin du Seuil 7-11-4: 7/1	Jonjo O'Neill	*A P McCoy*	12
2015	171	Vautour 6-11-4: 6/4	W P Mullins (Ir)	*R Walsh*	8
2016	154	Black Hercules 7-11-4: 4/1	W P Mullins (Ir)	*R Walsh*	9
2017	160	Yorkhill 7-11-4: 6/4	W P Mullins (Ir)	*R Walsh*	8

SUN BETS STAYERS' HURDLE (Gr 1) (Cheltenham 3m, 3m½f before 2002)

Year		Horse	Trainer	Jockey	Ran
1993	157	Shuil Ar Aghaidh 7-11-5: 20/1	P Kiely (Ir)	*C F Swan*	12
1994	157	*Balasani 8-11-10: 9/2	M C Pipe	*M Perrett*	14
1995	167	Dorans Pride 6-11-10: 11/4	M Hourigan (Ir)	*J P Broderick*	11
1996	158	Cyborgo 8-11-10: 8/1	M C Pipe	*D Bridgwater*	19
1997	154	Karshi 7-11-10: 20/1	Miss H C Knight	*J Osborne*	17
1998	161	Princeful 7-11-10: 16/1	Mrs J Pitman	*R Farrant*	9
1999	161	Anzum 8-11-10: 40/1	D Nicholson	*R Johnson*	12
2000	161	Bacchanal 6-11-10: 11/2	N J Henderson	*M A Fitzgerald*	10
2001		Abandoned			
2002	164	Baracouda 7-11-10: 13/8	F Doumen (Fr)	*T Doumen*	16
2003	173	Baracouda 8-11-10: 9/4	F Doumen (Fr)	*T Doumen*	11
2004	172	Iris's Gift 7-11-10: 9/2	J O'Neill	*B J Geraghty*	10
2005	162	Inglis Drever 6-11-10: 5/1	J H Johnson	*G Lee*	12

2006	163	My Way de Solzen 6-11-10: 8/1	A King	R Thornton	20
2007	164	Inglis Drever 8-11-10: 5/1	J H Johnson	P J Brennan	14
2008	169	Inglis Drever 9-11-10: 11/8	J H Johnson	D O'Regan	17
2009	172	Big Buck's 6-11-10: 6/1	P F Nicholls	R Walsh	14
2010	169	Big Buck's 7-11-10: 5/6	P F Nicholls	R Walsh	14
2011	162	Big Buck's 8-11-10: 10/11	Paul Nicholls	R Walsh	13
2012	168	Big Buck's 9-11-10: 5/6	Paul Nicholls	R Walsh	11
2013	162	Solwhit 9-11-10: 17/2	Charles Byrnes (Ir)	Paul Carberry	13
2014	167	More of That 6-11-10: 15/2	Jonjo O'Neill	Barry Geraghty	10
2015	164	Cole Harden 6-11-10: 14/1	Warren Greatrex	Gavin Sheehan	16
2016	169	Thistlecrack 8-11-10: 1/1	Colin Tizzard	Tom Scudamore	12
2017	163	Nichols Canyon 7-11-10: 10/1	W P Mullins (Ir)	R Walsh	12

JCB TRIUMPH HURDLE (4-y-o) (Gr 1) (Cheltenham 2m1f)

1993	133	Shawiya 10-9: 12/1	M O'Brien (Ir)	C F Swan	25
1994	133	Mysilv 10-9: 2/1	D Nicholson	A Maguire	28
1995	143	Kissair 11-0: 16/1	M C Pipe	J Lower	26
1996	144	Paddy's Return 11-0: 10/1	F Murphy	R Dunwoody	29
1997	130	Commanche Court 11-0: 9/1	T M Walsh (Ir)	N Williamson	28
1998	145	Upgrade 11-0: 14/1	N A Twiston-Davies	C Llewellyn	25
1999	151	Katarino 11-0: 11/4	N J Henderson	M A Fitzgerald	23
2000	135	Snow Drop 10-9: 7/1	F Doumen (Fr)	T Doumen	28
2001		Abandoned			
2002	147	Scolardy 11-0: 16/1	W P Mullins (Ir)	C F Swan	28
2003	134	Spectroscope 11-0: 20/1	J O'Neill	B J Geraghty	27
2004	134	Made In Japan 11-0: 20/1	P J Hobbs	R Johnson	23
2005	144	Penzance 11-0: 9/1	A King	R Thornton	23
2006	140	Detroit City 11-0: 7/2	P J Hobbs	R Johnson	17
2007	151	Katchit 11-0: 11/2	A King	R Thornton	23
2008	141	Celestial Halo 11-0: 5/1	P F Nicholls	R Walsh	14
2009	149	Zaynar 11-0: 11/2	N J Henderson	B J Geraghty	18
2010	145	Soldatino 11-0: 6/1	N J Henderson	B J Geraghty	17
2011	152	Zarkandar 11-0: 13/2	Paul Nicholls	Daryl Jacob	23
2012	147	Countrywide Flame 11-0: 33/1	John Quinn	Dougie Costello	20
2013	160	Our Conor 11-0: 4/1	D T Hughes (Ir)	Bryan Cooper	17
2014	150	Tiger Roll 11-0: 10/1	Gordon Elliott (Ir)	Davy Russell	15
2015	164	Peace And Co 11-0: 2/1	Nicky Henderson	Barry Geraghty	16
2016	156	Ivanovich Gorbatov 11-0: 9/2	Aidan O'Brien (Ir)	Barry Geraghty	15
2017	146	Defi du Seuil 11-0: 5/2	Philip Hobbs	Richard Johnson	15

ALBERT BARTLETT NOVICES' HURDLE (Spa) (Gr 1) (Cheltenham 3m, Gr 2 before 2008)

2005	139	Moulin Riche 5-11-7: 9/1	F Doumen (Fr)	R Thornton	18
2006	142	Black Jack Ketchum 7-11-7: 1/1	J O'Neill	A P McCoy	19
2007	147	Wichita Lineman 6-11-7: 11/8	J O'Neill	A P McCoy	20
2008	144	Nenuphar Collonges 7-11-7: 9/1	A King	R Thornton	18
2009	147	Weapon's Amnesty 6-11-7: 8/1	C Byrnes (Ir)	D N Russell	17
2010	145	Berties Dream 7-11-7: 33/1	P J Gilligan (Ir)	A E Lynch	19
2011	152	Bobs Worth 6-11-7: 15/8	Nicky Henderson	Barry Geraghty	18
2012	150	Brindisi Breeze 6-11-7: 7/1	Lucinda Russell	Campbell Gillies	20
2013	150	At Fishers Cross 6-11-7: 11/8	Rebecca Curtis	A P McCoy	13
2014	146	Very Wood 5-11-7: 33/1	Noel Meade (Ir)	P Carberry	18
2015	153	Martello Tower 7-11-7: 14/1	Mrs Margaret Mullins (Ir)	A P Heskin	19
2016	145	Unowhatimeanharry 8-11-5: 11/1	Harry Fry	Noel Fehily	19
2017	152	Penhill 6-11-5: 16/1	W P Mullins (Ir)	P Townend	15

TIMICO CHELTENHAM GOLD CUP CHASE (Gr 1) (Cheltenham 3m2½f)

1993	174	Jodami 8-12-0: 8/1	P Beaumont	M Dwyer	16
1994	171	The Fellow 9-12-0: 7/1	F Doumen (Fr)	A Kondrat	15
1995	183	Master Oats 9-12-0: 10/3	K C Bailey	N Williamson	15
1996	178	Imperial Call 7-12-0: 9/2	F Sutherland (Ir)	C O'Dwyer	10
1997	169	Mr Mulligan 9-12-0: 20/1	N T Chance	A P McCoy	14
1998	169	Cool Dawn 10-12-0: 25/1	R H Alner	A Thornton	17
1999	173	See More Business 9-12-0: 16/1	P F Nicholls	M A Fitzgerald	12
2000	176	Looks Like Trouble 8-12-0: 9/2	N T Chance	R Johnson	12
2001		Abandoned			
2002	173	Best Mate 7-12-0: 7/1	Miss H C Knight	J Culloty	18
2003	174	Best Mate 8-12-0: 13/8	Miss H C Knight	J Culloty	15
2004	169	Best Mate 9-11-10: 8/11	Miss H C Knight	J Culloty	10

2005	167	Kicking King 7-11-10: 4/1	T J Taaffe (Ir)	*B J Geraghty*	15
2006	169	War of Attrition 7-11-10: 15/2	M F Morris (Ir)	*C O'Dwyer*	22
2007	165	Kauto Star 7-11-10: 5/4	P F Nicholls	*R Walsh*	18
2008	176	Denman 8-11-10: 9/4	P F Nicholls	*S Thomas*	12
2009	184	Kauto Star 9-11-10: 7/4	P F Nicholls	*R Walsh*	16
2010	182	Imperial Commander 9-11-10: 7/1	N A Twiston-Davies	*P J Brennan*	11
2011	176	Long Run 6-11-10: 7/2	Nicky Henderson	*Mr S Waley-Cohen*	13
2012	167	Synchronised 9-11-10: 8/1	Jonjo O'Neill	*A P McCoy*	14
2013	179	Bobs Worth 8-11-10: 11/4	Nicky Henderson	*Barry Geraghty*	9
2014	161	Lord Windermere 8-11-10: 20/1	J H Culloty (Ir)	*Davy Russell*	13
2015	170	Coneygree 8-11-10: 7/1	Mark Bradstock	*Nico de Boinville*	16
2016	181	Don Cossack 9-11-10: 9/4	Gordon Elliott (Ir)	*B J Cooper*	9
2017	169	Sizing John 7-11-10: 7/1	Mrs J Harrington (Ir)	*Robbie Power*	13

MANIFESTO NOVICES' CHASE (Gr 1) (Aintree 2½m, Gr 2 prior to 2012)

2009	152	Tartak 6-11-4: 11/2	T R George	*P J Brennan*	8
2010	151	Mad Max 8-11-4: 4/1	N J Henderson	*B J Geraghty*	6
2011	155	Wishfull Thinking 8-11-4: 9/4	Philip Hobbs	*Richard Johnson*	7
2012	159	Menorah 7-11-4: 3/1	Philip Hobbs	*Richard Johnson*	5
2013	145	Captain Conan 6-11-4: 6/5	Nicky Henderson	*Barry Geraghty*	7
2014	153	Uxizandre 6-11-4: 11/4	Alan King	*A P McCoy*	4
2015	152	Clarcam 5-11-4: 5/1	Gordon Elliott (Ir)	*R Walsh*	6
2016	156	Arzal 6-11-4: 4/1	Harry Whittingham	*Gavin Sheehan*	8
2017	154	Flying Angel 6-11-4: 5/1	Nigel Twiston-Davies	*Noel Fehily*	6

RYANAIR STAYERS' LIVERPOOL HURDLE (Gr 1)
(Aintree 3m½f, Ascot 3m before 2004, Gr 2 prior to 2010)

1993	161	Sweet Duke 6-11-3: 5/1	N A Twiston-Davies	*C Llewellyn*	7
1994	162	Sweet Glow 7-11-7: 9/2	M C Pipe	*R Dunwoody*	12
1995	148	Cab On Target 9-11-7: 11/8	Mrs M Reveley	*P Niven*	6
1996	163	Pleasure Shared 8-11-10: 6/1	P J Hobbs	*W Marston*	7
1997	123	Trainglot 10-11-10: 1/2	J G FitzGerald	*R Dunwoody*	5
1998	160	Marello 7-11-5: 11/4	Mrs M Reveley	*P Niven*	7
1999	151	Galant Moss 5-11-3: 1/1	M C Pipe	*A P McCoy*	5
2000	160	Teaatral 6-11-7: 4/1	C R Egerton	*D Gallagher*	10
2001	147	Maid Equal 10-10-12: 14/1	M C Pipe	*Mr T Scudamore*	14
2002	149	Spendid 10-11-2: 2/1	A King	*W Marston*	7
2003	154	Deano's Beeno 11-11-10: 5/4	M C Pipe	*A P McCoy*	7
2004	153	Iris's Gift 7-11-10: 4/7	J O'Neill	*B J Geraghty*	8
2005	160	Monet's Garden 7-11-10: 11/2	N G Richards	*A Dobbin*	9
2006	166	Mighty Man 6-11-6: 11/4	H D Daly	*R Johnson*	12
2007	172	Mighty Man 7-11-10: 15/8	H D Daly	*R Johnson*	6
2008	157	Blazing Bailey 6-11-10: 5/1	A King	*R Thornton*	11
2009	173	Big Buck's 6-11-10: 5/6	P F Nicholls	*R Walsh*	10
2010	149	Big Buck's 7-11-7: 3/10	P F Nicholls	*R Walsh*	7
2011	166	Big Buck's 8-11-7: 4/6	Paul Nicholls	*R Walsh*	11
2012	159	Big Buck's 9-11-7: 2/9	Paul Nicholls	*R Walsh*	8
2013	158	Solwhit 9-11-7: 9/4	Charles Byrnes (Ir)	*Paul Carberry*	13
2014	158	Whisper 6-11-7: 4/1	Nicky Henderson	*Barry Geraghty*	7
2015	163	Whisper 7-11-7: 5/1	Nicky Henderson	*Nico de Boinville*	9
2016	162	Thistlecrack 8-11-7: 2/7	Colin Tizzard	*Tom Scudamore*	6
2017	155	Yanworth 7-11-7: 9/4	Alan King	*Barry Geraghty*	11

BETWAY BOWL CHASE (Gr 1) (Aintree 3m1f, Gr 2 prior to 2010)

1993	165	Docklands Express 11-11-5: 6/4	K C Bailey	*J Osborne*	4
1994	159	Docklands Express 12-11-5: 5/2	K C Bailey	*R Dunwoody*	4
1995	170	Merry Gale 7-11-9: 5/2	J T R Dreaper (Ir)	*G Bradley*	6
1996	161	Scotton Banks 7-11-9: 9/2	T D Easterby	*L Wyer*	6
1997	162	Barton Bank 11-11-5: 10/3	D Nicholson	*D Walsh*	5
1998	171	Escartefigue 6-11-13: 11/2	D Nicholson	*R Johnson*	8
1999	155	Macgeorge 9-11-5: 11/1	R Lee	*A Maguire*	5
2000	159	See More Business 10-12-0: 5/4	P F Nicholls	*M A Fitzgerald*	4
2001	173	First Gold 8-12-0: 7/4	F Doumen (Fr)	*T Doumen*	7
2002	168	Florida Pearl 10-11-12: 5/2	W P Mullins (Ir)	*B J Geraghty*	6
2003	171	First Gold 10-11-2: 14/1	F Doumen (Fr)	*T Doumen*	7
2004	168	Tiutchev 11-11-12: 11/2	M C Pipe	*A P McCoy*	8
2005	168	Grey Abbey 11-11-12: 7/2	J H Johnson	*G Lee*	8
2006	166	Celestial Gold 8-11-8: 8/1	M C Pipe	*T J Murphy*	9

2007	175	Exotic Dancer 7-11-12: 6/4	J O'Neill	A P McCoy	5
2008	170	Our Vic 10-11-10: 9/1	D E Pipe	T J Murphy	5
2009	170	Madison du Berlais 8-11-10: 12/1	D E Pipe	T Scudamore	10
2010	160	What A Friend 7-11-7: 5/2	P F Nicholls	R Walsh	5
2011	164	Nacarat 10-11-7: 7/2	Tom George	Paddy Brennan	6
2012	163	Follow The Plan 9-11-7: 50/1	Oliver McKiernan (Ir)	Tom Doyle	11
2013	170	First Lieutenant 8-11-7: 7/2	M F Morris (Ir)	Bryan Cooper	8
2014	165	Silviniaco Conti 8-11-7: 9/4	Paul Nicholls	Noel Fehily	6
2015	165	Silviniaco Conti 9-11-7: 7/4	Paul Nicholls	Noel Fehily	7
2016	181	Cue Card 10-11-7: 6/5	Colin Tizzard	Paddy Brennan	9
2017	166	Tea For Two 8-11-7: 10/1	Nick Williams	Lizzie Kelly	7

DOOM BAR ANNIVERSARY 4-Y-O JUVENILE HURDLE (Gr 1) (Aintree 2m1f)

1993	132	Titled Dancer 10-9: 9/2	J Coogan (Ir)	J Shortt	8
1994	135	Tropical Lake 10-9: 10/1	M Hourigan (Ir)	K O'Brien	12
1995	139	Stompin 11-0: 9/1	Miss H C Knight	J Osborne	18
1996	138	Zabadi 11-0: 8/1	D Nicholson	A P McCoy	11
1997	134	Quakers Field 11-0: 8/1	G L Moore	D Gallagher	12
1998	149	Deep Water 11-0: 8/1	M D Hammond	R Garritty	14
1999	147	Hors La Loi III 11-4: 8/15	M C Pipe	A P McCoy	6
2000	139	Lord Brex 11-0: 15/2	P J Hobbs	R Johnson	12
2001	154	Bilboa 10-13: 7/4	F Doumen (Fr)	T Doumen	14
2002	137	Quazar 11-4: 16/1	J O'Neill	A Dobbin	17
2003	133	Le Duc 11-0: 33/1	P F Nicholls	R Walsh	19
2004	131	Al Eile 11-0: 25/1	J Queally (Ir)	T J Murphy	18
2005	141	Faasel 11-0: 11/4	N G Richards	A Dobbin	12
2006	144	Detroit City 11-0: 3/1	P J Hobbs	R Johnson	13
2007	147	Katchit 11-0: 1/1	A King	R Thornton	12
2008	151	Binocular 11-0: 11/8	N J Henderson	A P McCoy	10
2009	154	Walkon 11-0: 2/1	A King	R Thornton	13
2010	136	Orsippus 11-0: 40/1	Michael Smith	D J Condon	11
2011	145	Zarkandar 11-0: 4/6	Paul Nicholls	R Walsh	9
2012	148	Grumeti 11-0: 11/4	Alan King	Robert Thornton	11
2013	139	L'Unique 10-7: 10/1	Alan King	Wayne Hutchinson	10
2014	144	Guitar Pete 11-0: 13/2	D T Hughes (Ir)	Paul Carberry	15
2015	145	All Yours 11-0: 16/1	Paul Nicholls	Sam Twiston-Davies	10
2016	157	Apple's Jade 10-7: 3/1	W P Mullins (Ir)	B J Cooper	9
2017	141	Defi du Seuil 11-0: 4/11	Philip Hobbs	Barry Geraghty	8

BETWAY MILDMAY NOVICES' CHASE (Gr 1) (Aintree 3m1f, Gr 2 prior to 2014)

1993	148	Cab On Target 7-11-3: 15/8	Mrs M Reveley	P Niven	5
1994	156	Monsieur Le Cure 8-11-9: 7/4	J A C Edwards	P Niven	6
1995	145	Banjo 5-11-0: 6/4	M C Pipe	R Dunwoody	4
1996	145	Addington Boy 8-11-10: 7/2	G Richards	B Harding	7
1997	143	Cyborgo 7-11-4: 13/8	M C Pipe	R Dunwoody	7
1998	148	Boss Doyle 6-11-7: 5/4	M F Morris (Ir)	A P McCoy	8
1999	140	Spendid 7-11-9: 10/3	D Nicholson	R Johnson	7
2000	147	High Game 6-11-4: 9/1	S E H Sherwood	N Williamson	8
2001	?	Whats Up Boys 7-11-4: 12/1	P J Hobbs	R Johnson	7
2002	154	Barton 9-11-9: 3/1	T D Easterby	A Dobbin	9
2003	142	Irish Hussar 7-11-2: 3/1	N J Henderson	M A Fitzgerald	9
2004	138	Simply Supreme 7-11-2: 13/2	Mrs S J Smith	R McGrath	11
2005	134	Like-A-Butterfly 11-11-2: 6/1	C Roche (Ir)	A P McCoy	10
2006	146	Star de Mohaison 5-11-0: 11/4	P F Nicholls	B J Geraghty	15
2007	149	Aces Four 8-11-5: 5/2	F Murphy	G Lee	10
2008	147	Big Buck's 5-11-3: 11/4	P F Nicholls	R Walsh	8
2009	146	Killyglen 7-11-3: 7/1	J H Johnson	D O'Regan	9
2010	139	Burton Port 6-11-4: 9/2	N J Henderson	B J Geraghty	10
2011	142	Quito de La Roque 7-11-4: 6/1	Colm Murphy (Ir)	Davy Russell	8
2012	158	Silviniaco Conti 6-11-4: 7/4	Paul Nicholls	R Walsh	5
2013	153	Dynaste 7-11-4: 9/4	David Pipe	Tom Scudamore	6
2014	158	Holywell 7-11-4: 7/2	Jonjo O'Neill	A P McCoy	6
2015	161	Saphir du Rheu 6-11-4: 13/8	Paul Nicholls	Sam Twiston-Davies	9
2016	152	Native River 6-11-4: 11/2	Colin Tizzard	Richard Johnson	8
2017	161	Might Bite 8-11-4: 8/13	Nicky Henderson	Nico de Boinville	5

DOOM BAR SEFTON NOVICES' HURDLE (Gr 1) (Aintree 3m½f)

| 1993 | 136 | Cardinal Red 6-11-4: 4/1 | Mrs F Walwyn | B de Haan | 6 |

1994	136	Corner Boy 7-11-4: 10/1	D Nicholson	*A Maguire*	11
1995	135	Morgans Harbour 9-11-4: 6/1	Mrs M Reveley	*P Niven*	15
1996	146	Pleasure Shared 8-11-6: 14/1	P J Hobbs	*P Carberry*	16
1997	140	Forest Ivory 6-11-4: 11/2	D Nicholson	*R Johnson*	12
1998	145	Unsinkable Boxer 9-11-4: 10/11	M C Pipe	*A P McCoy*	12
1999	141	King's Road 6-11-4: 3/1	N A Twiston-Davies	*C Llewellyn*	15
2000	148	Sackville 7-11-4: 12/1	Ms F M Crowley (Ir)	*B J Geraghty*	17
2001	140	Garruth 7-11-4: 16/1	T D Easterby	*R Garritty*	13
2002	139	Stromness 5-11-4: 8/1	A King	*R Thornton*	15
2003	159	Iris's Gift 6-11-4: 10/11	J O'Neill	*B J Geraghty*	9
2004	140	Accipiter 5-11-4: 14/1	G B Balding	*T Best*	13
2005	142	Asian Maze 6-10-11: 7/1	T Mullins (Ir)	*R Walsh*	17
2006	151	Black Jack Ketchum 7-11-4: 8/13	J O'Neill	*A P McCoy*	11
2007	150	Chief Dan George 7-11-4: 20/1	J Moffatt	*M A Fitzgerald*	10
2008	146	Pettifour 6-11-4: 16/1	N A Twiston-Davies	*P J Brennan*	13
2009	143	Ogee 6-11-4: 25/1	Mrs P Robeson	*J A McCarthy*	15
2010	144	Wayward Prince 6-11-4: 9/1	I Williams	*D Costello*	14
2011	139	Saint Are 5-11-4: 33/1	Tim Vaughan	*Richard Johnson*	19
2012	149	Lovcen 7-11-4: 8/1	Alan King	*Robert Thornton*	19
2013	147	At Fishers Cross 6-11-4: 11/8	Rebecca Curtis	*A P McCoy*	9
2014	153	Beat That 6-11-4: 6/1	Nicky Henderson	*Barry Geraghty*	18
2015	149	Thistlecrack 7-11-4: 25/1	Colin Tizzard	*Tom Scudamore*	16
2016	146	Ballyoptic 6-11-4: 9/1	Nigel Twiston-Davies	*Ryan Hatch*	15
2017	146	The Worlds End 6-11-4: 3/1	Tom George	*A P Heskin*	11

JLT MELLING CHASE (Gr 1) (Aintree 2½m)

1993	148	Deep Sensation 8-11-10: 7/4	J T Gifford	*D Murphy*	4
1994	161	Katabatic 11-11-10: 14/1	J T Gifford	*S McNeill*	5
1995	164	Viking Flagship 8-11-10: 5/2	D Nicholson	*A Maguire*	6
1996	172	Viking Flagship 9-11-10: 5/2	D Nicholson	*A P McCoy*	4
1997	177	Martha's Son 10-11-10: 5/2	T A Forster	*C Llewellyn*	4
1998	155	Opera Hat 10-11-5: 10/1	J R H Fowler (Ir)	*C O'Dwyer*	5
1999	166	Direct Route 8-11-10: 7/2	J H Johnson	*N Williamson*	6
2000	160	Direct Route 9-11-10: 11/8	J H Johnson	*N Williamson*	5
2001	167	Fadalko 8-11-10: 9/2	P F Nicholls	*R Walsh*	7
2002	158	Native Upmanship 9-11-10: 10/3	A L T Moore (Ir)	*C O'Dwyer*	8
2003	168	Native Upmanship 10-11-10: 5/4	A L T Moore (Ir)	*C O'Dwyer*	6
2004	170	Moscow Flyer 10-11-10: 1/1	Mrs J Harrington (Ir)	*B J Geraghty*	7
2005	176	Moscow Flyer 11-11-10: 4/9	Mrs J Harrington (Ir)	*B J Geraghty*	6
2006	156	Hi Cloy 9-11-10: 14/1	M Hourigan (Ir)	*A J McNamara*	11
2007	160	Monet's Garden 9-11-10: 4/1	N G Richards	*A Dobbin*	6
2008	170	Voy Por Ustedes 7-11-10: 5/1	A King	*R Thornton*	6
2009	163	Voy Por Ustedes 8-11-10: 11/8	A King	*R Thornton*	10
2010	165	Albertas Run 9-11-10: 8/1	J O'Neill	*A P McCoy*	11
2011	170	Master Minded 8-11-10: 11/2	Paul Nicholls	*R Walsh*	10
2012	170	Finian's Rainbow 9-11-10: 13/8	Nicky Henderson	*Barry Geraghty*	8
2013	183	Sprinter Sacre 7-11-10: 1/3	Nicky Henderson	*Barry Geraghty*	6
2014	159	Boston Bob 9-11-10: 5/1	W P Mullins (Ir)	*Paul Townend*	10
2015	180	Don Cossack 8-11-10: 3/1	Gordon Elliott (Ir)	*A P McCoy*	10
2016	160	God's Own 8-11-10: 10/1	Tom George	*Paddy Brennan*	6
2017	170	Fox Norton 7-11-7: 4/1	Colin Tizzard	*Robbie Power*	9

CRABBIE'S TOP NOVICES' HURDLE (Gr 1) (Aintree 2m½f)

1993	140	Roll A Dollar 7-11-6: 9/4	D R C Elsworth	*P Holley*	9
1994	141	Jazilah 6-11-6: 7/4	R Akehurst	*G McCourt*	8
1995	128	Sweet Mignonette 7-10-11: 4/1	Mrs M Reveley	*P Niven*	15
1996	132	Tragic Hero 4-10-8: 20/1	M C Pipe	*J Lower*	15
1997	131	Midnight Legend 6-11-0: 11/2	D Nicholson	*R Johnson*	9
1998	145	Fataliste 4-10-12: 7/2	M C Pipe	*A P McCoy*	10
1999	142	Joe Mac 5-11-8: 6/4	C Roche (Ir)	*C O'Dwyer*	9
2000	139	Phardante Flyer 6-11-10: 5/1	P J Hobbs	*R Johnson*	13
2001	133	Ilico II 5-11-5: 16/1	P J Hobbs	*A Maguire*	15
2002	144	In Contrast 6-11-5: 5/2	P J Hobbs	*R Johnson*	11
2003	150	Limerick Boy 5-11-0: 5/1	Miss V Williams	*A Dobbin*	12
2004	138	Royal Shakespeare 5-11-3: 25/1	S Gollings	*R Thornton*	12
2005	138	Mighty Man 5-11-0: 3/1	H D Daly	*R Johnson*	7
2006	147	Straw Bear 5-11-3: 2/1	N J Gifford	*A P McCoy*	16

2007	144	Blythe Knight 7-11-0: 14/1	J J Quinn	*A P McCoy*	8
2008	149	Pierrot Lunaire 4-10-8: 5/1	P F Nicholls	*R Walsh*	14
2009	140	El Dancer 5-11-0: 14/1	Mrs L Wadham	*D Elsworth*	11
2010	143	General Miller 5-11-4: 7/1	N J Henderson	*B J Geraghty*	9
2011	143	Topolski 5-11-4: 11/2	David Arbuthnot	*Daryl Jacob*	13
2012	146	Darlan 5-11-4: 7/4	Nicky Henderson	*A P McCoy*	12
2013	159	My Tent Or Yours 6-11-4: 4/11	Nicky Henderson	*A P McCoy*	4
2014	149	Josses Hill 6-11-4: 6/4	Nicky Henderson	*Barry Geraghty*	10
2015	159	Cyrus Darius 6-11-4: 8/1	Malcolm Jefferson	*Brian Hughes*	11
2016	151	Buveur d'Air 5-11-4: 11/4	Nicky Henderson	*Noel Fehily*	11
2017	140	Pingshou 7-11-4: 16/1	Colin Tizzard	*Robbie Power*	9

BETWAY AINTREE HURDLE (Gr 1) (Aintree 2½m)

1993	169	Morley Street 9-11-7: 6/1	G B Balding	*G Bradley*	6
1994	172	Danoli 6-11-7: 9/2	T Foley (Ir)	*C F Swan*	8
1995	167	Danoli 7-11-7: 2/1	T Foley (Ir)	*C F Swan*	6
1996	149	Urubande 6-11-7: 10/3	A P O'Brien (Ir)	*C F Swan*	8
1997	162	Bimsey 7-11-7: 14/1	R Akehurst	*M Fitzgerald*	7
1998	168	Pridwell 8-11-7: 6/1	M C Pipe	*A P McCoy*	6
1999	170	Istabraq 7-11-7: 1/2	A P O'Brien (Ir)	*C F Swan*	7
2000	159	Mister Morose 10-11-7: 16/1	N A Twiston-Davies	*C Llewellyn*	10
2001	157	Barton 8-11-7: 9/1	T D Easterby	*A Dobbin*	8
2002	156	Ilnamar 6-11-7: 9/1	M C Pipe	*R Walsh*	14
2003	159	Sacundai 6-11-7: 9/1	E J O'Grady (Ir)	*R Walsh*	11
2004	159	Rhinestone Cowboy 8-11-7: 5/2	J O'Neill	*Mr J P Magnier*	11
2005	159	Al Eile 5-11-7: 11/1	J Queally (Ir)	*T J Murphy*	9
2006	162	Asian Maze 7-11-0: 4/1	T Mullins (Ir)	*R Walsh*	9
2007	156	Al Eile 7-11-7: 12/1	J Queally (Ir)	*T J Murphy*	11
2008	159	Al Eile 8-11-7: 11/4	J Queally (Ir)	*T J Murphy*	9
2009	160	Solwhit 5-11-7: 6/1	C Byrnes (Ir)	*D N Russell*	16
2010	157	Khyber Kim 8-11-7: 7/2	N A Twiston-Davies	*P J Brennan*	7
2011	162	Oscar Whisky 6-11-7: 6/1	Nicky Henderson	*Barry Geraghty*	8
2012	163	Oscar Whisky 7-11-7: 9/4	Nicky Henderson	*Barry Geraghty*	5
2013	160	Zarkandar 6-11-7: 11/2	Paul Nicholls	*R Walsh*	9
2014	159	The New One 6-11-7: 4/9	Nigel Twiston-Davies	*Sam Twiston-Davies*	7
2015	167	Jezki 7-11-7: 3/1	Mrs J Harrington (Ir)	*A P McCoy*	6
2016	170	Annie Power 8-11-0: 4/9	W P Mullins (Ir)	*R Walsh*	6
2017	170	Buveur d'Air 6-11-7: 4/9	Nicky Henderson	*Barry Geraghty*	6

DOOM BAR MAGHULL NOVICES' CHASE (Gr 1) (Aintree 2m)

1993	135	Valiant Boy 7-11-10: 12/1	S Kettlewell	*R Garritty*	7
1994	136	Nakir 6-11-10: 6/5	S Christian	*J Osborne*	6
1995	144	Morceli 7-11-3: 11/4	J H Johnson	*N Williamson*	7
1996	135	Ask Tom 7-11-4: 10/1	T P Tate	*P Niven*	10
1997	145	Squire Silk 8-11-4: 2/1	A Turnell	*J Osborne*	6
1998	140	Direct Route 7-11-4: 9/2	J H Johnson	*P Carberry*	6
1999	141	Flagship Uberalles 5-10-11: 5/2	P F Nicholls	*J Tizzard*	7
2000	146	Cenkos 6-11-4: 7/2	O Sherwood	*D J Casey*	6
2001	139	Ballinclay King 7-11-4: 6/1	F Murphy	*A Maguire*	7
2002	144	Armaturk 5-11-1: 5/2	P F Nicholls	*T J Murphy*	5
2003	156	Le Roi Miguel 5-11-1: 9/4	P F Nicholls	*R Walsh*	5
2004	140	Well Chief 5-11-1: 15/8	M C Pipe	*A P McCoy*	10
2005	154	Ashley Brook 7-11-4: 3/1	K Bishop	*P J Brennan*	10
2006	155	Foreman 8-11-4: 4/1	T Doumen (Fr)	*A P McCoy*	7
2007	147	Twist Magic 5-11-1: 9/4	P F Nicholls	*R Walsh*	6
2008	151	Tidal Bay 7-11-4: 6/4	J H Johnson	*D O'Regan*	8
2009	152	Kalahari King 8-11-4: 9/4	F Murphy	*G Lee*	6
2010	153	Tataniano 6-11-4: 10/3	P F Nicholls	*R Walsh*	10
2011	150	Finian's Rainbow 8-11-4: 10/11	Nicky Henderson	*Barry Geraghty*	7
2012	160	Sprinter Sacre 6-11-4: 1/7	Nicky Henderson	*Barry Geraghty*	4
2013	152	Special Tiara 6-11-4: 28/1	H de Bromhead (Ir)	*Bryan Cooper*	6
2014	158	Balder Succes 6-11-4: 7/2	Alan King	*Wayne Hutchinson*	7
2015	155	Sizing Granite 7-11-4: 9/2	Henry de Bromhead (Ir)	*J J Burke*	6
2016	180	Douvan 6-11-4: 2/13	W P Mullins (Ir)	*P Townend*	5
2017	151	San Benedeto 6-11-4: 4/1	Paul Nicholls	*Nick Scholfield*	5

RANDOX HEALTH GRAND NATIONAL CHASE (HANDICAP) (Gr 3)

(Aintree 4¼m74y, 4m3½f 2013-15, 4½m before 2013)

Year		Horse	Trainer	Jockey	
1993		Void			
1994	159	Miinnehoma 11-10-8: 16/1	M C Pipe	R Dunwoody	36
1995	161	Royal Athlete 12-10-6: 40/1	Mrs J Pitman	J Titley	35
1996	157	Rough Quest 10-10-7: 7/1	T Casey	M Fitzgerald	27
1997	160	Lord Gyllene 9-10-0: 14/1	S A Brookshaw	A Dobbin	36
1998	156	Earth Summit 10-10-5: 7/1	N A Twiston-Davies	C Llewellyn	37
1999	152	Bobbyjo 9-10-0: 10/1	T Carberry (Ir)	P Carberry	32
2000	154	Papillon 9-10-12: 10/1	T M Walsh (Ir)	R Walsh	40
2001	?	Red Marauder 11-10-11: 33/1	N B Mason	Richard Guest	40
2002	146	Bindaree 8-10-4: 20/1	N A Twiston-Davies	J Culloty	40
2003	149	Monty's Pass 10-10-7: 16/1	J J Mangan (Ir)	B J Geraghty	40
2004	146	Amberleigh House 12-10-10: 16/1	D McCain	G Lee	39
2005	157	Hedgehunter 9-11-1: 7/1	W P Mullins (Ir)	R Walsh	40
2006	149	Numbersixvalverde 10-10-8: 11/1	M Brassil (Ir)	N P Madden	40
2007	147	Silver Birch 10-10-6: 33/1	G Elliott (Ir)	R M Power	40
2008	155	Comply Or Die 9 10 9: 7/1	D E Pipe	T J Murphy	40
2009	159	Mon Mome 9-11-0: 100/1	Miss V Williams	L Treadwell	40
2010	162	Don't Push It 10-11-5: 10/1	J O'Neill	A P McCoy	40
2011	159	Ballabriggs 10-11-0: 14/1	Donald McCain	Jason Maguire	40
2012	166	Neptune Collonges 11-11-6: 33/1	Paul Nicholls	Daryl Jacob	40
2013	145	Auroras Encore 11-10-3: 66/1	Sue Smith	Ryan Mania	40
2014	151	Pineau de Re 11-10-6: 25/1	Dr Richard Newland	Leighton Aspell	40
2015	168	Many Clouds 8-11-9: 25/1	Oliver Sherwood	Leighton Aspell	39
2016	156	Rule The World 9-10-7: 33/1	M F Morris (Ir)	David Mullins	39
2017	157	One For Arthur 8-10-11: 14/1	Lucinda Russell	Derek Fox	40

CORAL SCOTTISH GRAND NATIONAL HANDICAP CHASE (Gr 3)

(Ayr 4m½f, run over 4m1f until 2006)

Year		Horse	Trainer	Jockey	
1993	153	Run For Free 9-11-10: 6/1	M C Pipe	M Perrett	21
1994	134	Earth Summit 6-10-0: 16/1	N A Twiston-Davies	D Bridgwater	22
1995	144	Willsford 12-10-12: 16/1	Mrs J Pitman	R Farrant	22
1996	142	Moorcroft Boy 11-10-2: 20/1	D Nicholson	M Dwyer	20
1997	152	Belmont King 9-11-10: 16/1	P F Nicholls	A P McCoy	17
1998	137	Baronet 8-10-0: 7/1	D Nicholson	A Maguire	18
1999	153	Young Kenny 8-11-10: 5/2	P Beaumont	B Powell	15
2000	150	Paris Pike 8-11-0: 5/1	F Murphy	A Maguire	18
2001	150	Gingembre 7-11-2: 12/1	Mrs L C Taylor	A Thornton	30
2002	145	Take Control 8-10-6: 20/1	M C Pipe	R Walsh	18
2003	146	Ryalux 10-10-5: 15/2	A Crook	R McGrath	19
2004	159	Grey Abbey 10-11-12: 12/1	J H Johnson	G Lee	28
2005	138	Joes Edge 8-9-11: 20/1	F Murphy	K Mercer[3]	20
2006	141	Run For Paddy 10-10-2: 33/1	C Llewellyn	C Llewellyn	30
2007	138	Hot Weld 8-9-9: 14/1	F Murphy	P J McDonald[5]	23
2008	149	Iris de Balme 8-9-7: 66/1	S Curran	Mr C Huxley[7]	24
2009	141	Hello Bud 11-10-9: 12/1	N A Twiston-Davies	P J Brennan	17
2010	138	Merigo 9-10-0: 18/1	A Parker	T J Murphy	30
2011	149	Beshabar 9-10-4: 15/2	Tim Vaughan	Richard Johnson	28
2012	142	Merigo 11-10-2: 15/2	Andrew Parker	Timmy Murphy	24
2013	148	Godsmejudge 7-11-3: 12/1	Alan King	Wayne Hutchinson	24
2014	144	Al Co 9-10-0: 40/1	Peter Bowen	Jamie Moore	29
2015	142	Wayward Prince 11-10-1: 25/1	Hilary Parrott	Robert Dunne	29
2016	152	Vicente 7-11-3: 14/1	Paul Nicholls	Sam Twiston-Davies	28
2017	151	Vicente 8-11-10: 9/1	Paul Nicholls	Sam Twiston-Davies	30

bet365.com CELEBRATION CHASE (Gr 1) (Sandown 2m; Grade 2 until 2013)

Year		Horse	Trainer	Jockey	
2002	160	Cenkos 8-11-6: 8/1	P F Nicholls	B J Geraghty	5
2003	160	Seebald 8-11-6: 11/8	M C Pipe	A P McCoy	5
2004	163	Cenkos 10-11-10: 9/2	P F Nicholls	B J Geraghty	11
2005	164	Well Chief 6-11-10: 9/4	M C Pipe	T J Murphy	9
2006	153	River City 9-11-6: 9/1	N T Chance	T Doyle	4
2007	149	Dempsey 9-11-6: 5/4	C Llewellyn	T J Murphy	8
2008	157	Andreas 8-11-2: 9/2	P F Nicholls	R Walsh	11
2009	158	Twist Magic 7-11-6: 7/2	P F Nicholls	R Walsh	7
2010	151	I'm So Lucky 8-11-2: 9/1	D E Pipe	T Scudamore	8
2011	154	French Opera 8-11-2: 2/1	Nicky Henderson	A P McCoy	6

2012	169	Sanctuaire 6-11-2: 9/2	Paul Nicholls	*Daryl Jacob*	8
2013	166	Sire de Grugy 7-11-2: 6/1	Gary Moore	*Jamie Moore*	10
2014	158	Sire de Grugy 8-11-7: 2/7	Gary Moore	*Jamie Moore*	6
2015	167	Special Tiara 8-11-7: 3/1	Henry de Bromhead (Ir)	*Noel Fehily*	7
2016	179	Sprinter Sacre 10-11-7: 11/10	Nicky Henderson	*Nico de Boinville*	6
2017	175	Altior 7-11-7: 30/100	Nicky Henderson	*Nico de Boinville*	4

bet365 GOLD CUP CHASE (HANDICAP) (Gr 3) (Sandown 3m5½f)

1993	152	*Topsham Bay 10-10-1: 10/1	D H Barons	*R Dunwoody*	13
1994	148	Ushers Island 8-10-0: 25/1	J H Johnston	*C F Swan*	12
1995	145	Cache Fleur 9-10-1: 10/1	M C Pipe	*R Dunwoody*	14
1996	166	Life of A Lord 10-11-10: 12/1	A P O'Brien (Ir)	*C F Swan*	17
1997	139	Harwell Lad 8-10-0: 14/1	R H Alner	*Mr R Nuttall*	9
1998	155	Call It A Day 8-10-10: 8/1	D Nicholson	*A Maguire*	19
1999	144	Eulogy 9-10-0: 14/1	R Rowe	*B Fenton*	19
2000	168	Beau 7-10-9: 6/1	N A Twiston-Davies	*C Llewellyn*	20
2001	149	Ad Hoc 7-10-4: 14/1	P F Nicholls	*R Walsh*	25
2002	155	Bounce Back 6-10-9: 14/1	M C Pipe	*A P McCoy*	20
2003	156	Ad Hoc 9-10-10: 7/1	P F Nicholls	*R Walsh*	16
2004	147	Puntal 8-11-4: 25/1	M C Pipe	*D J Howard[1]*	18
2005	134	Jack High 10-10-0: 16/1	T M Walsh (Ir)	*G Cotter*	19
2006	159	Lacdoudal 7-11-5: 10/1	P J Hobbs	*R Johnson*	18
2007	141	Hot Weld 8-10-0: 6/1	F Murphy	*G Lee*	10
2008	154	Monkerhostin 11-10-13: 25/1	P J Hobbs	*R Johnson*	19
2009	137	Hennessy 8-10-7: 13/2	C Llewellyn	*A P McCoy[1]*	14
2010	149	Church Island 11-10-5: 20/1	M Hourigan (Ir)	*A P Heskin[1]*	19
2011	141	Poker de Sivola 8-10-12: 11/1	Ferdy Murphy	*Timmy Murphy*	18
2012	165	Tidal Bay 11-11-12: 9/1	Paul Nicholls	*Daryl Jacob*	19
2013	138	Quentin Collonges 9-10-12: 14/1	Henry Daly	*Andrew Tinkler*	19
2014	152	Hadrian's Approach 7-11-0: 10/1	Nicky Henderson	*Barry Geraghty*	19
2015	142	Just A Par 8-10-3: 14/1	Paul Nicholls	*Sean Bowen[1]*	20
2016	152	The Young Master 7-11-1: 8/1	Neil Mulholland	*Mr S Waley-Cohen[1]*	20
2017	127	Henllan Harri 9-10-0: 40/1	Peter Bowen	*Sean Bowen*	13

Ireland

thetote.com GALWAY PLATE (HANDICAP CHASE) (Galway 2¾m)

1993	153	General Idea 8-12-0: 9/2	D K Weld	*A Maguire*	21
1994	123	Feathered Gale 7-9-11: 8/1	A L T Moore	*F Woods*	22
1995	156	Life of A Lord 9-11-8: 12/1	A P O'Brien	*T Horgan*	21
1996	171	Life of A Lord 10-12-0: 9/2	A P O'Brien	*C F Swan*	17
1997	128	Stroll Home 7-9-12: 11/2	J J Mangan	*P Carberry*	22
1998	142	Amlah 6-9-13: 16/1	P J Hobbs (GB)	*B Powell*	22
1999	149	Moscow Express 7-11-4: 4/1	Miss F M Crowley	*R Walsh*	21
2000	118	Dovaly 7-9-13: 20/1	M J P O'Brien	*T P Rudd*	22
2001	132	Grimes 8-10-1: 4/1	C Roche	*C O'Dwyer*	14
2002	120	Rockholm Boy 9-10-5: 20/1	M Hourigan	*K Hadnett[1]*	22
2003	130	Nearly A Moose 7-10-1: 25/1	P Mullins	*R M Power[1]*	22
2004	130	Ansar 8-10-12: 10/1	D K Weld	*D J Casey*	22
2005	143	Ansar 9-11-11: 10/1	D K Weld	*D F O'Regan[1]*	22
2006	135	Far From Trouble 7-10-4: 8/1	C Roche	*R Loughran*	22
2007	136	Sir Frederick 7-9-10: 12/1	W J Burke	*K T Coleman[1]*	22
2008	153	Oslot 6-10-13: 11/4	P F Nicholls (GB)	*R Walsh*	22
2009	142	Ballyholland 8-10-9: 16/1	C A McBratney	*A J McNamara*	20
2010	143	Finger Onthe Pulse 9-10-12: 22/1	T J Taaffe	*A P McCoy*	22
2011	151	Blazing Tempo 7-10-4: 5/1	W P Mullins	*Paul Townend*	22
2012	145	Bob Lingo 10-10-13: 16/1	Thomas Mullins	*Mark Walsh*	20
2013	141	Carlingford Lough 7-10-7: 7/2	John E Kiely	*A P McCoy*	22
2014	161	Road To Riches 7-11-4: 14/1	Noel Meade	*Shane Shortall[1]*	22
2015	149	Shanahan's Turn 7-10-10: 16/1	Henry de Bromhead	*J J Burke*	22
2016	150	Lord Scoundrel 7-10-7: 10/1	Gordon Elliott	*Donagh Meyler[1]*	22

GUINNESS GALWAY HURDLE HANDICAP (Galway 2m)

| 1993 | ? | Camden Buzz 5-10-12: 4/1 | P Mullins | *C F Swan* | 22 |
| 1994 | 128 | Oh So Grumpy 6-10-9: 7/1 | Mrs J Harrington | *M Dwyer* | 27 |

1995	130	No Tag 7-10-11: 11/2	P G Kelly	*J Titley*	23
1996	127	Mystical City 6-10-1: 20/1	W P Mullins	*D Casey*	21
1997	150	Toast The Spreece 5-10-9: 12/1	A P O'Brien	*A P McCoy*	20
1998	130	Black Queen 7-10-2: 10/1	J E Kiely	*J Barry*	24
1999	152	Quinze 6-11-12: 11/1	P Hughes	*R Dunwoody*	25
2000	137	Perugino Diamond 4-9-8: 14/1	S O'Farrell	*J Culloty*	20
2001	136	Ansar 5-9-9: 6/1	D K Weld	*P Carberry*	20
2002	131	Say Again 6-10-7: 16/1	P Nolan	*J L Cullen*	24
2003	120	Sabadilla 9-9-7: 14/1	P M Verling	*P M Verling*	24
2004	129	Cloone River 8-10-7: 7/2	P Nolan	*J Cullen*	24
2005	128	More Rainbows 5-9-10: 33/1	N Meade	*N P Madden*	17
2006	132	Cuan Na Grai 5-10-9: 7/1	P Nolan	*P W Flood*	20
2007	143	Farmer Brown 6-10-11: 9/2	P Hughes	*D N Russell*	20
2008	131	Indian Pace 7-9-10: 7/1	J E Kiely	*P Townend[5]*	20
2009	152	Bahrain Storm 6-10-12: 20/1	P J Flynn	*S J Gray[5]*	20
2010	161	Overturn 6-11-6: 6/1	Donald McCain (GB)	*Graham Lee*	19
2011	146	Moon Dice 6-10-0: 20/1	Paul Flynn	*Tom Doyle*	20
2012	156	Rebel Fitz 7-11-5: 11/2	Michael Winters	*Davy Russell*	20
2013	145	Missunited 6-10-8: 7/1	Michael Winters	*Robbie Power*	20
2014	142	Thomas Edison 7-10-6: 7/2	A J Martin	*A P McCoy*	20
2015	143	Quick Jack 6-10-4: 9/2	A J Martin	*Denis O'Regan*	20
2016	145	Clondaw Warrior 9-11-5: 9/2	W P Mullins	*R Walsh*	20

JNwine.com CHAMPION CHASE (Gr 1) (Down Royal 3m, Gr 1 from 2002)

1999	164	Florida Pearl 7-11-10: 11/10	W P Mullins	*P Carberry*	6
2000	156	Looks Like Trouble 8-11-10: 5/4	N T Chance (GB)	*R Johnson*	5
2001	143	Foxchapel King 8-11-3: 4/1	M F Morris	*D J Casey*	7
2002	144	More Than A Stroll 10-11-10: 20/1	A L T Moore	*C O'Dwyer*	7
2003	143	Glenelly Gale 9-11-10: 7/1	A L T Moore	*C O'Dwyer*	4
2004	171	Beef Or Salmon 8-11-10: 1/1	M Hourigan	*T J Murphy*	8
2005		Abandoned			
2006	155	Beef Or Salmon 10-11-10: 11/4	M Hourigan	*A J McNamara*	7
2007	146	Taranis 6-11-10: 10/11	P F Nicholls (GB)	*R Walsh*	6
2008	149	Kauto Star 8-11-10: 2/5	P F Nicholls (GB)	*R Walsh*	5
2009	164	The Listener 10-11-10: 7/1	N Mitchell	*A J McNamara*	8
2010	162	Kauto Star 10-11-10: 4/7	Paul Nicholls (GB)	*R Walsh*	7
2011	161	Quito de La Roque 7-11-10: 11/4	Colm A Murphy	*Davy Russell*	7
2012	160	Kauto Stone 6-11-10: 4/1	Paul Nicholls (GB)	*Daryl Jacob*	8
2013	159	Roi du Mee 8-11-10: 12/1	Gordon Elliott	*Bryan Cooper*	6
2014	167	Road To Riches 7-11-10: 9/2	Noel Meade	*Paul Carberry*	8
2015	173	Don Cossack 8-11-10: 2/11	Gordon Elliott	*B J Cooper*	4
2016	168	Valseur Lido 7-11-10: 2/1	Henry de Bromhead	*R Walsh*	7

BAR ONE RACING HATTON'S GRACE HURDLE (Gr 1) (Fairyhouse 2½m)

1994	162	Danoli 6-12-0: 4/6	T Foley	*C F Swan*	7
1995	140	Dorans Pride 6-12-0: 1/5	M Hourigan	*J Broderick*	3
1996	160	Large Action 8-12-0: 9/4	O Sherwood (GB)	*J Osborne*	8
1997	136	Istabraq 5-12-0: 1/3	A P O'Brien	*C F Swan*	5
1998	151	Istabraq 6-12-0: 1/5	A P O'Brien	*C F Swan*	6
1999	177	Limestone Lad 7-11-9: 13/2	J Bowe	*S M McGovern*	5
2000	161	Youlneverwalkalone 6-11-12: 5/4	C Roche	*C O'Dwyer*	7
2001	167	Limestone Lad 9-11-12: 9/4	J Bowe	*P Carberry*	7
2002	152	Limestone Lad 10-11-12: 8/15	J Bowe	*B J Geraghty*	5
2003	138	Solerina 6-11-7: 7/4	J Bowe	*G T Hutchinson*	10
2004	157	Solerina 7-11-7: 4/5	J Bowe	*G T Hutchinson*	5
2005	158	Solerina 8-11-7: 6/4	J Bowe	*G T Hutchinson*	5
2006	153	Brave Inca 8-11-12: 10/3	C A Murphy	*A P McCoy*	5
2007	152	Aitmatov 6-11-10: 2/1	N Meade	*P Carberry*	8
2008	156	Catch Me 6-11-10: 7/4	E J O'Grady	*A J McNamara*	8
2009	140	Oscar Dan Dan 7-11-10: 11/2	T Mullins	*D N Russell*	7
2010	155	Hurricane Fly 6-11-10: 11/4	W P Mullins	*Paul Townend*	11
2011	149	Voler La Vedette 7-11-3: 7/4	Colm A Murphy	*A E Lynch*	4
2012	158	Zaidpour 6-11-10: 7/4	W P Mullins	*R Walsh*	5
2013	160	Jezki 5-11-10: 4/6	Mrs John Harrington	*A P McCoy*	5
2014	148	Lieutenant Colonel 5-11-10: 7/2	Ms Sandra Hughes	*Bryan J Cooper*	5
2015	155	Arctic Fire 6-11-10: 4/5	W P Mullins	*R Walsh*	7
2016	148	Apple's Jade 4-10-13: 4/1	Gordon Elliott	*B J Cooper*	7

JOHN DURKAN MEMORIAL PUNCHESTOWN CHASE (Gr 1)

(Punchestown 2½m, run at Fairyhouse in 1997 and 2010)

1992	143	Gold Options 10-11-4: 10/1	P McCreery	M Dwyer	9
1993	141	Cahervillahow 9-11-4: 3/1	M F Morris	N Williamson	11
1994	166	Merry Gale 6-12-0: 9/4	J Dreaper	K O'Brien	5
1995	161	Merry Gale 7-12-0: 6/4	J Dreaper	R Dunwoody	7
1996	152	Royal Mountbrowne 8-11-8: 7/1	A P O'Brien	C F Swan	6
1997	171	Dorans Pride 8-12-0: 2/5	M Hourigan	R Dunwoody	5
1998	153	Imperial Call 9-12-0: 13/8	R Hurley	P Carberry	8
1999	152	Buck Rogers 10-11-8: 16/1	V Bowens	K Whelan	8
2000	157	Native Upmanship 7-11-12: 9/10	A L T Moore	C O'Dwyer	4
2001	163	Florida Pearl 9-11-12: 5/1	W P Mullins	P Carberry	4
2002	168	Native Upmanship 9-11-12: 5/4	A L T Moore	C O'Dwyer	5
2003	167	Beef Or Salmon 7-11-12: 4/5	M Hourigan	T J Murphy	7
2004	165	Kicking King 6-11-12: 2/1	T J Taaffe	B J Geraghty	6
2005	163	Hi Cloy 8-11-12: 7/1	M Hourigan	A J McNamara	8
2006	149	In Compliance 6-11-12: 5/1	M J P O'Brien	B J Geraghty	8
2007	166	The Listener 8-11-10: 1/1	R H Alner (GB)	D A Jacob	10
2008	165	Noland 7-11-10: 9/4	P F Nicholls (GB)	S Thomas	8
2009	154	Joncol 6-11-10: 9/4	P Nolan	A P Cawley	5
2010	157	Tranquil Sea 8-11-10: 5/2	E J O'Grady	Andrew J McNamara	8
2011	162	Rubi Light 6-11-10: 5/2	Robert Hennessy	A E Lynch	7
2012	174	Flemenstar 7-11-10: 1/1	Peter Casey	A E Lynch	3
2013	162	Arvika Ligeonniere 8-11-10: 4/7	W P Mullins	R Walsh	3
2014	160	Don Cossack 7-11-10: 13/8	Gordon Elliott	Brian O'Connell	6
2015	175	Djakadam 6-11-10: 7/4	W P Mullins	R Walsh	7
2016	169	Djakadam 7-11-10: 4/5	W P Mullins	R Walsh	5

PADDY POWER CASHCARD CHASE (Gr 1)

(Leopardstown 2m1f, 2¼m 1996-1997, handicap prior to 1999, Grade 1 from 2004)

1992	117	Saraemma 6-10-2: 5/1	J H Scott	C F Swan	9
1993	?	Lasata 8-10-12: 6/1	M F Morris	C O'Dwyer	9
1994	139	Brockley Court 7-11-2: 7/2	Mrs J Harrington	C F Swan	9
1995		Abandoned			
1996	155	Merry Gale 8-10-13: 5/4	J T R Dreaper	R Dunwoody	5
1997	108	MacAllister 7-9-13: 7/1	V Bowens	B Bowens³	4
1998	143	Papillon 7-10-11: 11/4	T M Walsh	R Walsh	4
1999	139	Merry Gale 11-11-5: 8/1	J T R Dreaper	P Moloney	10
2000	142	Papillon 9-12-0: 8/1	T M Walsh	R Walsh	4
2001	146	Knife Edge 6-12-0: 1/1	M J P O'Brien	T P Rudd	8
2002	151	Moscow Flyer 8-11-12: 4/9	Mrs J Harrington	B J Geraghty	6
2003	151	Moscow Flyer 9-11-12: 2/7	Mrs J Harrington	B J Geraghty	6
2004	153	Central House 7-11-12: 9/2	D T Hughes	P Carberry	4
2005	155	Hi Cloy 8-11-12: 8/1	M Hourigan	A J McNamara	5
2006	154	Nickname 7-11-12: 5/2	M Brassil	N P Madden	6
2007	153	Mansony 8-11-12: 2/1	A L T Moore	D N Russell	6
2008	155	Big Zeb 7-11-12: 5/1	C A Murphy	M M O'Connor	7
2009	160	Golden Silver 7-11-12: 5/2	W P Mullins	P Townend	7
2010	158	Big Zeb 9-11-12: 1/1	Colm A Murphy	Barry Geraghty	4
2011	159	Big Zeb 10-11-12: 7/10	Colm A Murphy	Robbie Power	5
2012	164	Sizing Europe 10-11-12: 1/3	H de Bromhead	A E Lynch	5
2013	162	Benefficient 7-11-12: 9/1	A J Martin	Bryan Cooper	7
2014	161	Twinlight 7-11-12: 16/1	W P Mullins	R Walsh	9
2015	160	Flemenstar 10-11-12: 16/1	Anthony Curran	A E Lynch	6
2016	182	Douvan 6-11-12: 1/8	W P Mullins	R Walsh	5

PADDY POWER CHASE (EXTENDED HANDICAP) (Leopardstown 3m½f)

1996	137	New Co 8-10-6: 11/4	M F Morris	C O'Dwyer	17
1997	140	Time For A Run 10-11-1: 12/1	E J O'Grady	Mr P Fenton	21
1998	142	Calling Wild 8-11-3: 8/1	P F Nicholls (GB)	J Tizzard	26
1999	135	Inis Cara 7-10-8: 11/1	M Hourigan	R P McNally⁵	20
2000	116	Call Me Dara 7-9-4: 33/1	R Tyner	N P Mulholland⁸	23
2001	112	I Can Imagine 6-9-2: 12/1	R Tyner	J P Elliott⁵	23
2002	115	Coq Hardi Diamond 8-9-11· 14/1	N Meade	G T Hutchinson³	21
2003	122	World Wide Web 7-10-1: 8/1	J O'Neill (GB)	L Cooper	28
2004	129	Keepatem 8-10-8: 7/2	M F Morris	C O'Dwyer	30
2005	123	Black Apalachi 6-10-5: 25/1	P J Rothwell	J L Cullen	26

2006	147	Cane Brake 7-11-3: 14/1	T J Taaffe	A B Joyce[7]	28
2007	125	Newbay Prop 8-9-10: 14/1	A J Martin	R Geraghty	29
2008	141	Wheresben 9-10-7: 33/1	S Fahey	Mr J A Fahey[7]	28
2009	138	Oscar Time 8-10-3: 10/1	M M Lynch	R M Power	28
2010	153	Majestic Concorde 7-11-9: 33/1	D K Weld	Mr R P McNamara	28
2011	132	Cross Appeal 5-10-4: 7/1	Noel Meade	Paul Carberry	26
2012	144	Colbert Station 8-10-11: 5/1	T M Walsh	A P McCoy	28
2013	130	Rockyaboya 9-10-3: 7/1	W P Mullins	R Walsh	28
2014	141	Living Next Door 8-10-9: 20/1	A J Martin	Denis O'Regan	26
2015	142	Minella Foru 6-10-8: 7/1	Edward Harty	Barry Geraghty	28
2016	158	Noble Endeavor 7-11-3: 6/1	Gordon Elliott	Davy Russell	28

LEXUS CHASE (Gr 1) (Leopardstown 3m, Gr 2 prior to 2002)

1992	153	General Idea 7-11-11: 9/4	D K Weld	B Sheridan	10
1993	150	Deep Bramble 6-11-11: 4/1	M Hourigan	P Niven	9
1994	151	Commercial Artist 8-12-0: 9/1	V Bowens	G Bradley	5
1995		Abandoned			
1996	149	Johnny Setaside 7-12-0: 2/1	N Meade	R Dunwoody	7
1997	170	Imperial Call 8-12-0: 4/7	F Sutherland	C O'Dwyer	4
1998	?	Dorans Pride 9-12-0: 4/1	M Hourigan	P Carberry	6
1999	157	Rince Ri 6-12-0: 9/2	T M Walsh	C O'Dwyer	6
2000	162	Rince Ri 7-12-0: 5/1	T M Walsh	R Walsh	7
2001	164	Foxchapel King 8-12-0: 9/2	M F Morris	D J Casey	8
2002	156	Beef Or Salmon 6-11-9: 5/1	M Hourigan	T J Murphy	7
2003	171	Best Mate 8-11-12: 8/11	Miss H C Knight	J Culloty	8
2004	171	Beef Or Salmon 8-11-12: 9/4	M Hourigan	P Carberry	6
2005	169	Beef Or Salmon 9-11-12: 9/10	M Hourigan	P Carberry	5
2006	164	The Listener 7-11-10: 7/1	R H Alner	D Jacob	6
2007	162	Denman 7-11-10: 4/9	P F Nicholls (GB)	R Walsh	6
2008	168	Exotic Dancer 8-11-10: 4/1	J O'Neill (GB)	A P McCoy	9
2009	158	What A Friend 6-11-10: 11/2	P F Nicholls (GB)	S Thomas	11
2010	164	Pandorama 7-11-10: 7/2	Noel Meade	Paul Carberry	12
2011	165	Synchronised 8-11-10: 8/1	Jonjo O'Neill (GB)	A P McCoy	9
2012	170	Tidal Bay 11-11-10: 9/2	Paul Nicholls (GB)	R Walsh	9
2013	163	Bobs Worth 8-11-10: 11/4	Nicky Henderson (GB)	Barry Geraghty	9
2014	161	Road To Riches 7-11-10: 4/1	Noel Meade	Bryan J Cooper	9
2015	160	Don Poli 6-11-10: 4/6	W P Mullins	B J Cooper	6
2016	165	Outlander 8-11-10: 11/1	Gordon Elliott	J W Kennedy	13

RYANAIR HURDLE (Gr 1) (Leopardstown 2m, Grade 1 in 1993 and from 2002)

1992	140	Novello Allegro 4-11-2: 6/1	N Meade	C F Swan	7
1993	150	Fortune And Fame 6-12-0: 2/1	D K Weld	B Sheridan	7
1994	145	Boro Eight 8-11-7: 11/10	P Mullins	T P Treacy	4
1995	140	Kharasar 5-11-7: 10/1	A Mullins	M Dwyer	10
1996	144	Theatreworld 4-11-2: 2/1	A P O'Brien	C F Swan	6
1997	136	Istabraq 5-12-0: 1/6	A P O'Brien	C F Swan	5
1998	150	Istabraq 6-12-0: 1/10	A P O'Brien	C F Swan	3
1999	161	Istabraq 7-12-0: 1/8	A P O'Brien	C F Swan	6
2000	161	Moscow Flyer 6-12-0: 5/1	Mrs J Harrington	B J Geraghty	7
2001	157	Istabraq 9-11-12: 4/11	A P O'Brien	C F Swan	6
2002	158	Liss A Paoraigh 7-11-7: 11/10	J E Kiely	B J Geraghty	5
2003	146	Golden Cross 4-11-7: 66/1	M Halford	A P Lane	7
2004	163	Macs Joy 5-11-12: 7/1	Mrs J Harrington	B J Geraghty	6
2005	163	Brave Inca 7-11-12: 9/4	C A Murphy	A P McCoy	5
2006	160	Brave Inca 8-11-12: 6/4	C A Murphy	R Walsh	4
2007	157	Al Eile 7-11-10: 9/2	J Queally	T J Murphy	6
2008	158	Sublimity 8-11-10: 3/1	R A Hennessy	P A Carberry	9
2009	159	Solwhit 5-11-10: 8/11	C Byrnes	D N Russell	6
2010	159	Hurricane Fly 6-11-10: 8/11	W P Mullins	Paul Townend	5
2011	153	Unaccompanied 4-11-0: 10/3	D K Weld	Paul Townend	7
2012	169	Hurricane Fly 8-11-10: 1/5	W P Mullins	R Walsh	5
2013	168	Hurricane Fly 9-11-10: 11/10	W P Mullins	R Walsh	5
2014	157	Hurricane Fly 10-11-10: 5/6	W P Mullins	R Walsh	7
2015	159	Nicholas Canyon 5-11-10: 2/5	W P Mullins	R Walsh	4
2016	162	Petit Mouchoir 5-11-10: 6/1	Henry de Bromhead	B J Cooper	5

BHP INSURANCE IRISH CHAMPION HURDLE (Gr 1)
(Leopardstown 2m, run at Fairyhouse 1995)

Year		Horse	Jockey/Trainer 1	Trainer 2	Field
1993	144	Royal Derbi 8-11-10: 14/1	N A Callaghan (GB)	*D Murphy*	11
1994	166	Fortune And Fame 7-11-10: 4/5	D K Weld	*A Maguire*	7
1995	144	Fortune And Fame 8-11-10: 1/2	D K Weld	*M Dwyer*	5
1996	160	Collier Bay 6-11-10: 5/1	J A B Old (GB)	*J Osborne*	11
1997	150	Cockney Lad 8-11-10: 10/1	N Meade	*R Hughes*	7
1998	150	Istabraq 6-11-10: 4/11	A P O'Brien	*C F Swan*	7
1999	165	Istabraq 7-11-10: 8/15	A P O'Brien	*C F Swan*	6
2000	160	Istabraq 8-11-10: 2/9	A P O'Brien	*C F Swan*	6
2001	160	Istabraq 9-11-10: 4/11	A P O'Brien	*C F Swan*	7
2002	143	Ned Kelly 6-11-10: 11/8	E J O'Grady	*N Williamson*	8
2003	152	Like-A-Butterfly 9-11-5: 6/4	C Roche	*C F Swan*	5
2004	151	Foreman 6-11-10: 8/1	T Doumen (Fr)	*T Doumen*	8
2005	160	Macs Joy 6-11-10: 11/8	Mrs J Harrington	*B J Geraghty*	6
2006	164	Brave Inca 8-11-10: 6/5	C A Murphy	*A P McCoy*	7
2007	161	Hardy Eustace 10-11-10: 9/1	D T Hughes	*C O'Dwyer*	8
2008	160	Sizing Europe 6-11-10: 10/3	H de Bromhead	*A J McNamara*	6
2009	155	Brave Inca 11-11-10: 11/4	C A Murphy	*R Walsh*	9
2010	162	Solwhit 6-11-10: 5/6	C Byrnes	*D N Russell*	7
2011	169	Hurricane Fly 7-11-10: 4/9	W P Mullins	*Paul Townend*	5
2012	168	Hurricane Fly 8-11-10: 4/5	W P Mullins	*R Walsh*	5
2013	169	Hurricane Fly 9-11-10: 1/6	W P Mullins	*R Walsh*	5
2014	163	Hurricane Fly 10-11-10: 4/7	W P Mullins	*R Walsh*	4
2015	167	Hurricane Fly 11-11-10: 11/10	W P Mullins	*R Walsh*	6
2016	176	Faugheen 8-11-10: 3/10	W P Mullins	*R Walsh*	5
2017	162	Petit Mouchoir 6-11-10: 9/10	Henry de Bromhead	*D J Mullins*	4

STAN JAMES IRISH GOLD CUP (Gr 1) (Leopardstown 3m)

Year		Horse	Jockey/Trainer 1	Trainer 2	Field
1993	161	Jodami 8-12-0: 11/8	P Beaumont (GB)	*M Dwyer*	7
1994	160	Jodami 9-12-0: 5/4	P Beaumont (GB)	*M Dwyer*	6
1995	162	Jodami 10-12-0: 13/8	P Beaumont (GB)	*M Dwyer*	6
1996	176	Imperial Call 7-12-0: 4/1	F Sutherland	*C O'Dwyer*	8
1997	168	Danoli 9-12-0: 6/1	T Foley	*T Treacy*	8
1998	165	Dorans Pride 9-12-0: 6/4	M Hourigan	*R Dunwoody*	8
1999	166	Florida Pearl 7-12-0: 8/15	W P Mullins	*R Dunwoody*	7
2000	170	Florida Pearl 8-12-0: 8/11	W P Mullins	*P Carberry*	7
2001	169	Florida Pearl 9-12-0: 5/4	W P Mullins	*R Johnson*	7
2002	167	Alexander Banquet 9-12-0: 3/1	W P Mullins	*B J Geraghty*	5
2003	159	Beef Or Salmon 7-12-0: 1/1	M Hourigan	*T J Murphy*	5
2004	166	Florida Pearl 12-11-12: 5/1	W P Mullins	*R Johnson*	7
2005	167	Rule Supreme 9-11-12: 11/2	W P Mullins	*D J Casey*	7
2006	160	Beef Or Salmon 10-11-12: 2/5	M Hourigan	*P Carberry*	7
2007	167	Beef Or Salmon 11-11-12: 11/4	M Hourigan	*A J McNamara*	5
2008	157	The Listener 9-11-10: 2/1	R H Alner (GB)	*D A Jacob*	8
2009	168	Neptune Collonges 8-11-10: 8/13	P F Nicholls (GB)	*R Walsh*	6
2010	159	Joncol 7-11-10: 9/4	P Nolan	*A P Cawley*	7
2011	159	Kempes 8-11-10: 5/1	W P Mullins	*D J Casey*	9
2012	156	Quel Esprit 8-11-10: 5/4	W P Mullins	*R Walsh*	7
2013	167	Sir des Champs 7-11-10: 11/8	W P Mullins	*Davy Russell*	4
2014	161	Last Instalment 9-11-10: 8/1	Philip Fenton	*Brian O'Connell*	7
2015	161	Carlingford Lough 9-11-10: 4/1	John E Kiely	*A P McCoy*	8
2016	167	Carlingford Lough 10-11-10: 20/1	John E Kiely	*Barry Geraghty*	10
2017	164	Sizing John 7-11-10: 100/30	Mrs J Harrington	*Robbie Power*	7

BOYLESPORTS IRISH GRAND NATIONAL CHASE (EXTENDED HANDICAP)
(Fairyhouse 3m5f)

Year		Horse	Jockey/Trainer 1	Trainer 2	Field
1993	142	Ebony Jane 8-10-7: 6/1	F Flood	*C F Swan*	27
1994	148	Son of War 7-10-10: 12/1	P McCreery	*F Woods*	18
1995	169	Flashing Steel 10-12-0: 9/1	J Mulhern	*J Osborne*	18
1996	145	Feathered Gale 9-10-0: 8/1	A L T Moore	*F Woods*	17
1997	142	Mudahim 11-10-3: 13/2	Mrs J Pitman (GB)	*J Titley*	20
1998	143	Bobbyjo 8-11-3: 8/1	T Carberry	*P Carberry*	22
1999	138	Glebe Lad 7-10-0: 8/1	M J P O'Brien	*T P Rudd*	18
2000	150	Commanche Court 7-11-4: 14/1	T M Walsh	*R Walsh*	24
2001	140	Davids Lad 7-10-0: 10/1	A J Martin	*T J Murphy*	19
2002	138	The Bunny Boiler 8-9-9: 12/1	N Meade	*R Geraghty[5]*	17

1053

2003	137	Timbera 9-10-12: 11/1	D T Hughes	*J Culloty*	21
2004	129	Granit d'Estruval 10-10-0: 33/1	F Murphy (GB)	*B Harding*	28
2005	129	Numbersixvalverde 9-10-1: 9/1	M Brassil	*R Walsh*	26
2006	134	Point Barrow 8-10-8: 20/1	P Hughes	*P A Carberry*	26
2007	140	Butler's Cabin 7-10-4: 14/1	J O'Neill (GB)	*A P McCoy*	29
2008	140	Hear The Echo 7-10-0: 33/1	M F Morris	*P W Flood*	23
2009	147	Niche Market 8-10-5: 33/1	R H Buckler (GB)	*H Skelton[3]*	28
2010	142	Bluesea Cracker 8-10-4: 25/1	J Motherway	*A J McNamara*	26
2011	139	Organisedconfusion 6-9-13: 12/1	A L T Moore	*Miss N Carberry*	25
2012	147	Lion Na Bearnai 10-10-8: 33/1	Thomas Gibney	*A P Thornton[3]*	29
2013	135	Liberty Counsel 10-9-5: 50/1	Mrs D A Love	*Ben Dalton[5]*	28
2014	148	Shutthefrontdoor 7-10-13: 8/1	Jonjo O'Neill (GB)	*Barry Geraghty*	26
2015	143	Thunder And Roses 7-10-6: 20/1	Ms Sandra Hughes	*Ms K Walsh*	28
2016	145	Rogue Angel 8-10-9: 16/1	M F Morris	*G N Fox[3]*	27
2017	167	Our Duke 7-11-4: 9/2	Mrs J Harrington	*Robbie Power*	28

BOYLESPORTS CHAMPION CHASE (Drogheda) (Gr 1)
(Punchestown 2m, handicap before 1999, run at Fairyhouse, 2m100y in 2001)

1993	144	Viking Flagship 6-10-7: 5/4	D Nicholson (GB)	*R Dunwoody*	8
1994	138	Saraemma 8-10-12: 16/1	J H Scott	*K F O'Brien*	9
1995	148	Strong Platinum 7-11-1: 3/1	P Burke	*C O'Dwyer*	9
1996	177	Klairon Davis 7-12-0: 5/2	A L T Moore	*F Woods*	8
1997	171	Klairon Davis 8-12-0: 11/10	A L T Moore	*F Woods*	7
1998	162	Big Matt 10-10-11: 16/1	N Henderson (GB)	*M A Fitzgerald*	8
1999	154	Celibate 8-11-9: 7/1	C J Mann (GB)	*R Dunwoody*	6
2000	157	Get Real 9-11-6: 3/1	N J Henderson (GB)	*M A Fitzgerald*	7
2001	162	Micko's Dream 9-12-0: 5/1	W P Mullins	*R Walsh*	9
2002	140	Strong Run 9-12-0: 4/1	N Meade	*P Carberry*	7
2003	148	Flagship Uberalles 9-12-0: 8/1	P J Hobbs (GB)	*R Johnson*	7
2004	153	Moscow Flyer 10-11-12: 4/11	Mrs J Harrington	*B J Geraghty*	7
2005	155	Rathgar Beau 9-11-12: 8/1	E Sheehy	*J R Barry*	7
2006	159	Newmill 8-11-12: 5/4	J J Murphy	*A J McNamara*	6
2007	149	Mansony 8-11-12: 13/2	A L T Moore	*D N Russell*	7
2008	151	Twist Magic 6-11-12: 6/4	P F Nicholls (GB)	*R Walsh*	9
2009	162	Master Minded 6-11-12: 3/10	P F Nicholls (GB)	*R Walsh*	6
2010	161	Golden Silver 8-11-12: 12/1	W P Mullins	*P Townend*	11
2011	172	Big Zeb 10-11-12: 9/4	Colm A Murphy	*Barry Geraghty*	6
2012	167	Sizing Europe 10-11-12: 8/13	H De Bromhead	*A E Lynch*	6
2013	178	Sprinter Sacre 7-11-12: 1/9	Nicky Henderson (GB)	*Barry Geraghty*	5
2014	160	Sizing Europe 12-11-12: 7/1	Henry de Bromhead	*A E Lynch*	8
2015	157	Felix Yonger 9-11-12: 5/1	W P Mullins	*D E Mullins*	9
2016	168	God's Own 8-11-12: 9/1	Tom George (GB)	*Paddy Brennan*	7
2017	168	Fox Norton 7-11-12: 5/2	Mrs J Harrington	*Robbie Power*	8

CORAL PUNCHESTOWN GOLD CUP (Gr 1) (Punchestown 3m1f, run at Fairyhouse in 2001)

1999	175	Imperial Call 10-11-9: 8/1	R Hurley	*R Walsh*	5
2000	157	Commanche Court 7-11-9: 10/3	T M Walsh	*R Walsh*	11
2001	158	Moscow Express 9-12-0: 14/1	Ms F M Crowley	*B J Geraghty*	6
2002	173	Florida Pearl 10-12-0: 13/8	W P Mullins	*B J Geraghty*	6
2003	170	First Gold 10-12-0: 7/4	F Doumen (Fr)	*T Doumen*	7
2004	170	Beef Or Salmon 8-11-12: 5/4	M Hourigan	*T J Murphy*	6
2005	169	Kicking King 7-11-12: 8/11	T J Taaffe	*B J Geraghty*	6
2006	160	War of Attrition 7-11-12: 4/5	M F Morris	*C O'Dwyer*	6
2007	161	Neptune Collonges 6-11-12: 8/1	P F Nicholls (GB)	*R Walsh*	10
2008	166	Neptune Collonges 7-11-10: 9/10	P F Nicholls (GB)	*R Walsh*	9
2009	167	Notre Pere 8-11-10: 15/8	J T R Dreaper	*A E Lynch*	12
2010	159	Planet of Sound 8-11-10: 14/1	P J Hobbs	*R Johnson*	11
2011	151	Follow The Plan 8-11-10: 20/1	Oliver McKiernan	*T J Doyle*	8
2012	164	China Rock 9-11-10: 20/1	M F Morris	*Barry Geraghty*	8
2013	171	Sir Des Champs 7-11-10: 2/1	W P Mullins	*Davy Russell*	8
2014	165	Boston Bob 9-11-10: 5/2	W P Mullins	*R Walsh*	9
2015	180	Don Cossack 8-11-10: 5/2	Gordon Elliott	*Paul Carberry*	8
2016	167	Carlingford Lough 10-11-10: 12/1	John E Kiely	*Barry Geraghty*	6
2017	168	Sizing John 7-11-10: 9/10	Mrs J Harrington	*Robbie Power*	6

LADBROKES CHAMPION STAYERS HURDLE (Gr 1)
(Punchestown 3m, run at Fairyhouse in 2001)

1995	146	Derrymoyle 6-11-11: 8/1	M Cunningham	*M Dwyer*	8
1996	154	Derrymoyle 7-12-0: 10/3	M Cunningham	*M Dwyer*	10
1997	164	Paddy's Return 5-11-12: 10/3	F Murphy (GB)	*N Williamson*	8
1998	157	Derrymoyle 9-12-0: 10/1	M Cunningham	*A P McCoy*	8
1999	164	Anzum 8-12-0: 7/1	D Nicholson (GB)	*R Johnson*	6
2000	159	Rubhahunish 9-11-11: 5/1	N A Twiston-Davies (GB)	*C Llewellyn*	9
2001	141	Bannow Bay 6-11-12: 11/8	C Roche	*C F Swan*	9
2002	144	Limestone Lad 10-11-12: 4/6	J Bowe	*P Carberry*	9
2003	144	Holy Orders 6-11-12: 6/1	W P Mullins	*J R Barry*	6
2004	163	Rhinestone Cowboy 8-11-12: 5/2	J O'Neill (GB)	*Mr J P Magnier*	8
2005	137	Carlys Quest 11-11-12: 25/1	F Murphy (GB)	*K J Mercer*	9
2006	151	Asian Maze 7-11-7: 8/13	T Mullins	*R Walsh*	12
2007	150	Refinement 8-11-7: 16/1	J O'Neill (GB)	*A P McCoy*	9
2008	163	Blazing Bailey 6-11-10: 10/3	A King (GB)	*R Thornton*	12
2009	163	Fiveforthree 7-11-10: 5/4	W P Mullins	*R Walsh*	10
2010	152	Quevega 6-11-5: 5/2	W P Mullins	*P Townend*	13
2011	154	Quevega 7-11-5: 8/11	W P Mullins	*R Walsh*	10
2012	157	Quevega 8-11-3: 11/10	W P Mullins	*R Walsh*	7
2013	159	Quevega 9-11-3: 6/4	W P Mullins	*R Walsh*	6
2014	149	Jetson 9-11-10: 20/1	Mrs John Harrington	*Davy Russell*	9
2015	158	Jezki 7-11-10: 5/2	Mrs John Harrington	*M P Walsh*	11
2016	160	One Track Mind 6-11-10: 10/1	Warren Greatrex (GB)	*Gavin Sheehan*	9
2017	163	Unowhatimeanharry 9-11-10: 4/1	Harry Fry (GB)	*Noel Fehily*	12

BETDAQ PUNCHESTOWN CHAMPION HURDLE (Gr 1)
(Punchestown 2m, run at Leopardstown in 2001)

1999	177	Istabraq 7-12-0: 1/4	A P O'Brien	*C F Swan*	7
2000	161	Grimes 7-11-9: 6/1	C Roche	*C F Swan*	9
2001	168	Moscow Flyer 7-12-0: 6/1	Mrs J Harrington	*B J Gerraghty*	7
2002	145	Davenport Milenium 6-12-0: 11/2	W P Mullins	*R Walsh*	6
2003	151	Quazar 5-11-13: 7/2	J O'Neill (GB)	*A Dobbin*	6
2004	149	Hardy Eustace 7-11-12: 3/1	D T Hughes	*C O'Dwyer*	9
2005	163	Brave Inca 7-11-12: 2/1	C A Murphy	*A P McCoy*	5
2006	166	Macs Joy 7-11-12: 11/4	Mrs J Harrington	*B J Geraghty*	4
2007	156	Silent Oscar 8-11-12: 20/1	H Rogers	*R M Power*	8
2008	161	Punjabi 5-11-12: 2/1	N J Henderson (GB)	*B J Geraghty*	6
2009	164	Solwhit 5-11-12: 2/1	C Byrnes	*D N Russell*	9
2010	161	Hurricane Fly 6-11-12: 3/1	W P Mullins	*P Townend*	11
2011	168	Hurricane Fly 7-11-12: 1/2	W P Mullins	*R Walsh*	6
2012	163	Hurricane Fly 8-11-12: 4/11	W P Mullins	*R Walsh*	4
2013	160	Hurricane Fly 9-11-12: 1/4	W P Mullins	*R Walsh*	6
2014	162	Jezki 6-11-12: 4/5	Mrs John Harrington	*A P McCoy*	3
2015	160	Faugheen 7-11-12: 1/6	W P Mullins	*R Walsh*	4
2016	151	Vroum Vroum Mag 7-11-5: 4/6	W P Mullins	*R Walsh*	6
2017	161	Wicklow Brave 8-11-12: 12/1	W P Mullins	*Mr P W Mullins*	10

International

GRAND STEEPLE-CHASE DE PARIS (Gr 1) (Auteuil 3m6f, 3m5f prior to 2014)

1993	163	Ucello II 7-10-1	F Doumen	*C Aubert*	9
1994	164	Ucello II 8-10-1	F Doumen	*C Aubert*	9
1995	169	Ubu III 9-10-1	F Doumen	*P Chevalier*	13
1996	164	Arenice 8-10-1	G Macaire	*P Sourzac*	7
1997	173	Al Capone II 9-10-1	B Secly	*J-Y Beaurain*	6
1998	161	First Gold 5-9-11	F Doumen	*Mr T Doumen*	11
1999	168	Mandarino 6-10-1	M Rolland	*P Chevalier*	11
2000	165	Vieux Beaufai 7-10-3	F Danloux	*P Bigot*	12
2001	169	Kotkijet 6-10-5	J-P Gallorini	*T Majorcryk*	11
2002	153	*El Paso III 10-10-8	B Secly	*L Metuis*	14
2003	155	Line Marine 6-10-3	C Aubert	*C Pieux*	11
2004	145	Kotkijet 9-10-8	J-P Gallorini	*T Majorcryk*	16
2005	144	Sleeping Jack 6-10-8	J Ortet	*C Pieux*	18

1055

2006	139	Princesse d'Anjou 5-9-13	F M Cottin	*P Carberry*	16
2007	151	Mid Dancer 6-10-8	A Chaille-Chaille	*C Gombeau*	12
2008	147	Princesse d'Anjou 7-10-4	F M Cottin	*P Carberry*	16
2009	161	Remember Rose 6-10-8	J-P Gallorini	*C Pieux*	13
2010	162	Polar Rochelais 7-10-8	P Quinton	*J Zuliani*	13
2011	162	Mid Dancer 10-10-8	C Aubert	*Sylvain Dehez*	14
2012	160	Mid Dancer 11-10-10	C Aubert	*Sylvain Dehez*	19
2013	159	Bel La Vie 7-10-10	G Macaire	*Bertrand Lestrade*	16
2014	155	Storm of Saintly 5-10-6	G Macaire	*Vincent Cheminaud*	15
2015	160	Milord Thomas 6-10-10	D Bressou	*Jacques Ricou*	14
2016	158	So French 5-10-6	G Macaire	*James Reveley*	13
2017	160	So French 6-10-10	G Macaire	*James Reveley*	15

GRANDE COURSE DE HAIES D'AUTEUIL (Gr 1) (Auteuil 3m1½f)

1993	?	Ubu III 7-10-5	F Doumen	*A Kondrat*	14
1994	?	Le Roi Thibault 5-10-1	G Doleuze	*Y Fouin*	8
1995	?	Matchou 6-10-5	J Lesbordes	*D Mescam*	12
1996	155	Earl Grant 7-10-5	B Secly	*J Y Beaurain*	10
1997	163	Bog Frog 8-10-5	B Secly	*J Y Beaurain*	15
1998	161	Mantovo 6-10-5	M Rolland	*F Benech*	8
1999	168	Vaporetto 6-10-5	J P Gallorini	*T Majorcryk*	10
2000	164	Le Sauvignon 6-10-5	J Bertran de Balanda	*D Bressou*	7
2001	178	Le Sauvignon 7-10-5	J Bertran de Balanda	*D Bressou*	9
2002	161	Laveron 7-10-8	F Doumen	*T Doumen*	10
2003	140	Nobody Told Me 5-9-13	W P Mullins (Ir)	*D J Casey*	8
2004	149	Rule Supreme 8-10-8	W P Mullins (Ir)	*D J Casey*	7
2005	147	Lycaon de Vauzelle 6-10-8	J Bertran de Balanda	*B Chameraud*	8
2006	154	Mid Dancer 5-10-3	A Chaille-Chaille	*C Pieux*	9
2007	152	Zaiyad 6-10-8	A Chaille-Chaille	*J Ricou*	14
2008	160	Oeil du Maitre 6-10-8	J P Gallorini	*S Colas*	13
2009	151	Questarabad 5-10-3	M Rolland	*R Schmidlin*	7
2010	162	Mandali 6-10-8	J-P Gallorini	*C Soumillon*	8
2011	162	Thousand Stars 7-10-8	W P Mullins (Ir)	*R Walsh*	10
2012	163	Thousand Stars 8-10-10	W P Mullins (Ir)	*R Walsh*	12
2013	165	Gemix 5-10-6	N Bertran de Balanda	*David Cottin*	14
2014	170	Gemix 6-10-10	N Bertran de Balanda	*David Cottin*	13
2015	162	Un Temps Pour Tout 6-10-10	David Pipe (GB)	*James Reveley*	15
2016	162	Ptit Zig 7-10-10	Paul Nicholls (GB)	*Sam Twiston-Davies*	12
2017	161	L'Ami Serge 7-10-10	Nicky Henderson (GB)	*Daryl Jacob*	10

SAVE £135 A YEAR!

Race Passes are the ultimate form guide, featuring ratings, all the Timeform Flags, In-Play Hints and symbols, live Betfair prices – plus unlimited use of a 12-year archive and Horse Searches. Subscriptions give you open access to Timeform data, starting from just £10 for 24 hours, to £75 for 28 days.

Why not sign-up by Direct Debit. You'll save £5 every month and get 29 free days per year. That's worth £135.

Race Passes

Ratings. Flags. Form. In-Play.
Search any horse, any race, any time.

**Find out more at timeform.com
and view Race Passes on the App**